Construction
Materials
Reference Book

Construction Materials Reference Book

Edited by
David K. Doran
BSc(Eng), DIC, FCGI, CEng, FICE, FIStructE

With specialist contributors

Butterworth-Heinemann Ltd
Linacre House, Jordan Hill, Oxford OX2 8DP

 PART OF REED INTERNATIONAL BOOKS

OXFORD   LONDON   BOSTON
MUNICH   NEW DELHI   SINGAPORE   SYDNEY
TOKYO   TORONTO   WELLINGTON

First published 1992

British Library Cataloguing in Publication Data
Construction materials reference book.
  I. Doran, D.K.
  691.029

ISBN 0 7506 1004 2

Library of Congress Cataloguing in Publication Data
Construction materials reference book / edited by
  David K. Doran with specialist contributors.
    p.   cm.
    Includes bibliographical references and index.
    ISBN 0 7506 1004 2
    1. Building materials – Handbooks, manuals, etc.
    I. Doran, David K.
    TA403.4.C66   1990
    624.1'8 – dc20   90–44115
                                              CIP

Typeset by P & R Typesetters Ltd, Salisbury, England
Printed and bound by Bath Press Limited

Contents

Preface   ix

Notation   x

List of Contributors   xi

Overview · Models for Materials

1 Materials, Models, Idealizations and Reality
Introduction · Development of a material or
process · Exploring materials: the role of experiment ·
Stress-strain relations—classes of material behaviour ·
Generalization of data · Rheological models · Concluding
discussion

Part One · Metals and their Alloys

2 Aluminium
Introduction · Sources · Manufacturing process · Alloy types ·
Chemical composition and mechanical properties · Physical
properties · Special properties · Durability and protection ·
Materials selection · Fabrication and construction · Standard
products and availability of materials · Standards

3 Cast Iron
Introduction · Historic (mainly 19th century) cast iron ·
Modern grey cast iron · Ductile or nodular (spheroidal
graphite) cast iron · Appendices

4 Wrought Iron
Introduction · Types of wrought iron · Metallurgy and texture ·
Strength of wrought iron · Conclusions · Appendix

5 Steel
General description · Manufacturing processes ·
Microstructures of steel · Weldable structural steels · Welding
of steels · Other steels · Fast fracture · Fatigue performance ·
Corrosion and corrosion protection · British Standards

6 Steel Reinforcement for Reinforced Concrete
Introduction · Bars · Wire and fabric · Prestressing steels

7 Other Metals
Introduction · Copper · Copper alloys · Gold · Lead · Nickel ·
Silver · Tin · Zinc

Part Two · Non-Metals

8 Adhesives
Introduction · Surface treatments · Performance testing of
adhesives · Applications of resin adhesives · Appendix

9 Asbestos
Introduction · Mining and processing methods · World
production of asbestos · Practical applications of asbestos in
construction and industry · Legislation · Health effects of
exposure to asbestos · Asbestos control and maintenance

10 Bituminous Materials for use in Road Construction
Introduction · Asphalts · Coated macadams · Manufacturing
processes · Storage hoppers or silos · Pre-laying preparation
work · Laying bituminous materials by hand · Laying
bituminous materials by machine · Control of laying
tolerances · Precoated chippings · Laying in adverse weather
conditions · Compaction · Sampling and testing · Appendices

Ceramics

11 Brick and Brickwork
Introduction · Types of brick · Manufacture of bricks ·
Properties of bricks · Brickwork

12 Vitrified Clay Pipes for Drainage and Sewerage
The past, the present and the future · Stages of manufacture ·
Inspection · Jointing · Trenchless construction · Standards ·
Performance of flexible joints · Packaging, stacking and
mechanical handling · Availability · Heat resistance ·
Abrasion resistance · Strength · Research · Chemical
resistance · Summary

13 Ceramics—Tiles and Tiling
Introduction · Scope · Terminology · General · Clay roof
tiles · Ceramic wall tiles and tiling · Ceramic floor tiles
and tiling · Maintenance

Concrete

14 Concrete, An Overview
Introduction · Hydraulic cements · Cement quality ·
Ground-granulated blast-furnace slag, flyash and silica
fume · Cements for special purposes · Handling and
storage of cement · Cement admixtures · Aggregates · Ready
mixed concrete · Steel reinforcement · The use of fibres in
concrete · The use of polymers in concrete · Mix
designs · Mortars, screeds and renders · Grouts · Concrete
properties · Durability · Concrete practice · Striking of

formwork · Curing · Exposed aggregate finishes to concrete surfaces · Precast concrete · Testing methods, quality and compliance · Future opportunities · Health and safety

15 Admixtures and Polymers
Introduction · Air-entraining agents for concrete and mortar · Water-reducing agents/plasticizers for concrete · Superplasticizers · Retarders · Accelerators · Corrosion inhibitors · Permeability reducers

16 Concrete Aggregates
Introduction · Sources · Processes of production · Types of aggregates for concrete · Common impurities · Physical properties of aggregates · Standards · Lightweight aggregates

17 Concrete Blocks and Blockwork
Introduction · Types of block · Manufacture · Curing systems · Packaging · Properties of blocks · Properties of blockwork

18 Cements
Introduction · Portland cement · Other cementitious materials blended with Portland cement · The supply of quality-controlled cementitious materials · Some of the variables specified in British Standards for cements and cementitious materials · The chemistry of pozzolanic reactions · Factors affecting the performance of cements in concrete · The durability of concrete · Aluminous cements

19 Curing Membranes
Introduction · Curing-membrane types · Benefits of curing membranes · Standard specification for curing membranes

20 Glass-Fibre Reinforced Cement
Introduction · Raw materials · Principles of glass-fibre reinforcement · Mechanical properties · Physical and chemical properties · Design principles · Applications · Production · Process and quality control · Standards and product approvals · TheGlass-fibre Reinforced Cement Association

21 Mortars, Renders and Screeds
Introduction · Mortar · Rendering · Screeds

22 Mould Oils and Release Agents
Introduction · Mechanism of oils and chemical release agents · Chemical types of release agents · Site problems with release agents

23 Silica Fume
General description · Sources and production · Types and chemical composition · Physical properties · Reactivity of silica fume · Chemical reactions and reaction products · Microstructure of Portland cement–silica fume pastes and mortars · Properties of fresh concrete containing silica fume · Mechanical properties and shrinkage of hardened concrete containing silica fume · Durability of silica fume concrete · Applications · Standards · Storage and transportation

24 Sprayed and Sprayed Fibre Concrete
Introduction · Materials · Production and installation · Physical properties · Specification · Quality control · Design considerations

25 Concrete Tiles and Slates
Introduction · Concrete tiles · Lightweight-aggregate tiles · Slates · Wind loading and fixings · Costs

26 Cork
Introduction · Manufacture · Types · Applications · Standards · Site precautions

27 Fabrics
Sources · Manufacture · Environmental properties of fabrics · Structural properties of fabrics · Applications

28 Geotextile Properties Related to Structure and Design
Introduction · Geotextile structure · Serviceability · Separation · Filtration · Drainage · Reinforcement · Economics · Conclusions

29 Glass
Introduction · Manufacture of basic flat glass · Types of glass · Processed glasses · Structural glazing · Cutting of glass · Specification of glass · Standards

30 Mineral-Fibre Products
Introduction · Sources · Manufacturing process · Types · Roll products · Batt and slab products · Miscellaneous products · Chemical composition and properties · Physical properties (general) · Thermal properties · Acoustic properties · Fire properties · Standards and approvals · Usage and abusage · Proprietary brand examples

Paint and Preservatives

31 Paint: Non-absorbent Surfaces
Introduction · The corrosion of steel · Surface preparation · Paint types · Zinc in corrosion control · Specifications · Heavy-duty coatings

32 Preserving and Coating Timber
Introduction · Hazards to timber · Timber preservation · Coatings for timber

33 Paint: Absorbent Surfaces other than Timber
Introduction · Weathering of buildings · Cleaning buildings · Substrate preparation · Paint application · Paints and coatings for mineral surfaces · Transport of gases and water vapour through paints · Water-borne paints · Oil-based paints · Solvent-thinned paints · Two-pack systems · Moisture-curing polyurethane paints · Coating systems applied hot · Clear finishes, stains and sealers · Impregnants

34 Paint: Intumescent Coatings for Structural Fire Protection and Other Building Applications
Description · Use of intumescent coatings as fire protection · Chemistry and process · Selection of commercial products · Performance under fire and fire-test conditions · Environmental stability · Manufacture · Raw materials · Forms and uses · Application · Current consumption and market levels · Design of formulations · Certification

35 Plaster and Plasterboards
Introduction · Plaster range · Plastering · Plastering treated backgrounds · Mixing · Problems and remedies · Plasterboard dry linings · Composition · Performance · Design and planning considerations · Site organization · Site work

Polymers

36 Polymers in Construction: An Overview
Introduction · Natural polymers–harnessed by man.
Synthetic polymers–thermosets · Synthetic polymers–
thermoplastics · Coatings, castings and laminates · Resin
mortars · Polymer emulsions · Seals and sealants ·
Inorganic polymers · Reactive polymers ·
Rubbers · Engineeringproperties · The future

37 Natural and Synthetic Rubbers
Introduction · Production of base elastomers · Available
forms · Vulcanization and 'compounding' · Moulding of
thermoplastic elastomers · Properties of elastomers ·
Example applications · Elastomers–appropriate and
inappropriate use · Standards and specifications ·
Conclusions · Research and Trade Associations

38 Acrylic and Polycarbonate Plastics
Introduction · Acrylic plastics · Polycarbonates · Structural
properties · Weather resistance · Temperature effects · Fire
safety

39 Polymer Dispersions
Introduction · Manufacture and design
variables · Explanation of the binding ability of polymer
dispersions · Selection of dispersion type · Properties and
applications of mortars containing dispersions · Site-usage
notes

40 Polyethylene (Polyethene)
Structure, manufacture and properties · Fabrication and
usage · Uses in building and construction · European
standardization

41 Polystyrene
History · Manufacture · Physical properties · Fire
properties · Chemical properties · Wall insulation · Roof
insulation · Floor insulation · Civil engineering

42 Polytetrafluoroethylene
Material properties · Manufacture · Fabrication ·
Applications · Bearings · Slides · Friction with PTFE
surfaces

43 Vinyl Materials
Introduction · General description · Production of PVC ·
Compounding of PVC · Processing of PVC compositions ·
Properties and applications of rigid PVC (PVC-U) · Flexible
PVC products · PVC/metal sheet laminates · Future
developments of PVC in the building industry

44 Aramid Fibres for Civil-Engineering Applications
Introduction · Development · Current production
processes · Properties of aramid yarns · Applications ·
Conclusion · Appendix

45 Glass Reinforced Plastics
Introduction · What are GRP materials? · GRP constituent
materials · Methods of manufacture of GRP construction
products · GRP as a structural material · Using and
specifying GRP for construction

46 Thermosetting Resins
General description · Application · The production and
curing reactions of thermosetting resins · Modification of
thermosetting resins · Properties · Responsibilities of the
formulator and the end-user

47 Silanes and Siloxanes
Waterproof agents for concrete · Basic structure and the
reaction mechanism for impregnating waterproof agents
made of silanes and siloxanes · Features of impregnating
waterproof agents made of silanes and siloxanes ·
Prevention of deterioration of concrete with impregnating
waterproof agents made of silanes and siloxanes ·
Usefulness of silanes and siloxanes

48 Slurries and Grouts
Introduction · Overview of
applications · Materials · Mixing ·
Grout and slurry composition · Excavation slurries ·
Bentonite–cement self-hardening slurries · Structural
grouts · Geotechnical grouts · Chemical grouts · Sampling
slurries and grouts · Testing grouts and slurries · Testing
hardened properties · Specifications · Conclusions

49 Stone
Introduction · Types of building stone · The use of stone ·
Maintenance

50 Timber
Introduction · Moisture content · Sources of timber ·
Timbers—their properties and their uses · The structural use
of timber · Wood-based panel products · Uses of wood-based
panel products in building construction and allied applications ·
Timber fasteners · Structural uses of timber · Trussed rafters ·
Joinery timber · Possible future requirements

51 Vermiculite
Introduction · Technical data · Exfoliated vermiculite · Health
and safety aspects · Applications of vermiculite in the building
industry

INDEX

Preface

There are probably several hundred different materials used in construction. Some of these, for example metals, are used in elemental form, while many others combine chemically and/or structurally to produce materials of great strength, stiffness and durability. In this work of reference the most widely used materials have been selected for inclusion, with chapters from over fifty expert contributors.

It was neither desirable nor practical to supply specialist authors with a strait-jacket of guidelines from which to develop their themes. Although not all items are applicable to all materials, the following list was made available to each contributor as a broad framework within which to work.

- General description
- Sources
- Manufacture process
- Chemical composition and properties
- Physical properties
- Dimensional stability
- Durability
- Use and abuse
- Standards (ISO, EURO and BSI)
- Proprietary brand examples
- Bibliography and References

The book is arranged in two main sections dealing with *metals* and *non-metals*. For each material the book offers a comprehensive chapter together with selected references for those who need a deeper understanding. In the case of concrete (where many materials combine) and polymers (where levels of understanding may be less than elsewhere) an overview has been provided in Chapters 14 and 36.

The perceived audience for this book is twofold.

(a) Professionals (architects, engineers, surveyors, builders) who are contemplating using a material for the first time, or who require to update knowledge of one they are using after a time lapse.

(b) Students or laymen seeking an introduction to construction materials.

Environmentalists, safety experts and others ask penetrating questions about our materials. Our authors have borne these in mind in drafting their work and have tried to strike a balance between known facts and some, as yet, unsubstantiated speculation on the degree of hazard presented by the use of some materials.

Some of our naturally occurring materials remain plentiful; others are near extinction unless new deposits are discovered. Even some 'renewable' materials are in danger; it is well known that European hardwoods are virtually extinct. Acid rain, if unchecked, will continue to damage forests in the UK and elsewhere; rain forests need to be preserved. Increasing energy costs will make it imperative to optimize mineral extraction methods (it is necessary to excavate 2 tonnes of South African rock to produce about 30 grams of gold). Recycling of materials is partly an answer to some of these difficulties but there are pitfalls. Firstly, the energy balance must be struck to see if it is worthwhile. Secondly, there may be problems with the quality of recycled material. For example Dr J. R. Moon (Chapter 5) points out that significant concentrations of impurities (tramp metal) are found in recycled steel. A high level of quality control will be required to produce satisfactory standards.

Such a book could not have been achieved without support and encouragement. I have had both in abundance. I would like to acknowledge Dr John Dougill (who also wrote a chapter) who first suggested that I undertook the task, Dr Susan Hemmings the original Commissioning Editor and her successor Paddy Baker, Pippa McLeish who administered the work with tact, humour and firmness. Perhaps most of all I should thank the specialist authors who have not only contributed of their expertise but have patiently absorbed my cajoling. There will be many others who remain unnamed but not forgotten.

Finally I would like to thank my wife Maureen for her help and encouragement and my daughter, Dr Susan Doran (Ove Arup) for freely contributing the views of the younger professional on a number of issues.

David Doran
Wanstead, London, 1991

Notation

Units of measurement in this book are given using the system of negative indices favoured in the SI system, rather than oblique strokes. Under this system, a unit of measurement which would appear *after* an oblique stroke (or in the *denominator* of a fraction) is given a negative index.

For example:

- newtons per square millimetre is written $N\,mm^{-2}$ (rather than N/mm^2)
- watts per square metre per degree Celsius is written $W\,m^{-2}\,°C^{-1}$ (rather than $W/m^2/°C$ or $W/m^2\,°C$)

Note that this only applies to a unit which is being *divided into* another (metres, square millimetres, square metres or degrees Celsius in the previous examples). Negative indices are not used in the following examples:

- *Torque* has dimensions of force × distance, and so can be measured in newtons × metres, or newton metres (N m)
- *Electrical energy* has dimensions of power × time, and so can be measured in kilowatts × hours, or kilowatt hours (kW h).

For further information, the reader is referred to *Quantities, Units and Symbols*, published by The Symbols Committee of The Royal Society, The Royal Society, London, 1975.

List of Contributors

W J Allwood BSc
BP Chemicals

R H Andrews
Pemtech Associates Ltd

G H Arnold BSc, CEng, MIChemE
European Vinyls Corporation (UK) Ltd

D C Aslin BA
Prometheus Developments Ltd

S Austin BSc, PhD, CEng, MICE
Loughborough University of Technology

R C Baker BSc, MICE
Grove Consultants Ltd

M J Bayley MSc(Eng)
Technical Support Manager, Alcan Offshore

C Bodsworth MMet, PhD, CEng, FIM
Brunel, The University of West London

R G Bristow BSc(Eng), MICE, MIStructE
G Maunsell and Partners

C E G Bland FIWEM, FRSH
Clay Pipe Development Association Ltd

P S Bulson CBE, DSc, FEng
Chairman, British Standards Committee on the Structural Use
of Aluminium

C J Burgoyne PhD
Engineering Department, Cambridge University

R N Butlin PhD
Building Research Establishment

F G Buttler PhD, MRSC, CChem
Consultant Chemist

N C Clark
Mandoval Ltd

V A Coveney PhD
Bristol Polytechnic

J Crisfield HND(BLDG)
Vencel Resil Ltd

J V Crookes MSc, CChem, MRSC
Cuprinol Ltd

D A Cross BSc(Hons), DMS
Vencel Resil Ltd

S H Cross CPhys, MInstP, AMI, CorrST
The Glassfibre Reinforced Cement Association

D E J Cunningham MICorrST
Herbert Industrial Coatings

R Dennis CChem, MRSC
Doverstrand Ltd

J Dodd AIoR
The Marley Roof Tile Co Ltd

J W Dougill MSc(Eng), DIC, PhD, FEng, FICE, FIStructE,
FASCE
Institution of Structural Engineers

J J Farrington MICE
Staffordshire County Council

M G Grantham BA, MRSC, MIQA, MIHT, CChem
Technotrade Ltd

R Harris BSc
Wimpey Environmental Ltd

B A Haseltine BSc(Eng), FCGI, DIC, FEng, FICE, FIStructE,
FICeram, MConsE
Jenkins & Potter Consulting Engineers

L Hodgkinson
Cormix Construction Chemicals
Chairman, Technical Committee, Cement Admixtures
Association

S A Hurley BSc, PhD
Taywood Engineering Ltd

M L Humpage BTech, CChem, MRSC
Fosroc Technology

T S Ingold BSc, MSc, PhD, DIC, EurIng, CEng, MConsE,
FICE, FIHT, FGS, FASCE, MSocIS(France)
Consulting Geotechnical Engineer

G K Jackson
Pilkington Glass Consultants

S A Jefferis MA, PhD, CEng, MICE, FGS
W J Engineering Resources Ltd

M Kawamura Dr Eng
Kanazawa University, Japan

R I Lancaster FICE, FIStructE, FCIArb, FACI
Consulting Engineer

C D Lawrence
British Cement Association

M Malinowsky
Consulting Engineer

J R Moon PhD
University of Nottingham

K Nakano Dr Eng
Osaka Cement Co. Ltd, Japan

P Olley
C Olley & Sons Ltd

D O'Sullivan
Formerly of British Gypsum plc

J Pitts PhD, BSc, DipEng, CEng, MIMM, MIGeol, MIQA, FGS
Geotechnical and Environmental Consultants Ltd

C D Pomeroy DSc, CPhys, FInstP, FACI, FSS
Formerly of the British Cement Association

B Ralph MA, PhD, ScD, CEng, CPhys, FIM, FInstP, Hon.FRMS, Eur.Ing
Brunel, The University of West London

P J Ridd BSc(Eng), DMS
Cemfil International Ltd

P Robins BSc, PhD, CEng, MICE
Loughborough University of Technology

K D Ross
Building Research Establishment

J D N Shaw
SBD Ltd

P M Smith
Eurosil: UK Mineral Wool Association

J G Sunley MSc, FIStructE
Kewstoke Ltd

J Sutherland FEng, BA, FICE, FIStructE
Consultant to Harris & Sutherland

R A Sykes BSc
Wimpey Environmental Ltd

L J Tabor FPRI
Fosroc CCD Ltd

D J Thompsett MA(Cantab)
Vencel Resil Ltd

A K Tovey CEng, FIStructE, ACIArb, MSFSE
Building and Structures Department, British Cement Association

Overview

Models for
Materials

Materials: Models, Idealizations and Reality

J W Dougill MSc(Eng), DIC, PhD, F Eng, FICE,
FIStructE, FASCE
Director of Engineering,
Institution of Structural Engineers

Contents

1.1 Introduction 1/3

1.2 Development of a material or process 1/3

1.3 Exploring materials: the role of experiment 1/4

1.4 Stress–strain relations—classes of material behaviour 1/4

1.5 Generalization of data 1/4

1.6 Rheological models 1/5
    1.6.1 Plasticity: one-dimensional loading 1/6
    1.6.2 Plasticity: first view of combined stresses and the yield surface 1/7
    1.6.3 Results from a two-dimensional rheological model 1/7

1.7 Concluding discussion 1/10

Acknowledgements 1/11

1.1 Introduction

Everyone involved with construction is concerned, either directly or indirectly, with materials. Also, each person will have a different view of a material depending on their own role in the construction process.

The designer must take an abstract predictive view of material performance. He bases his ideas on estimates for properties that have still to be realized in practice and on models that help to quantify performance. The materials manufacturer and supplier deals with specific physical materials and the requirements for performance provided by specifications and control tests. The constructor is concerned with the technology for putting the material in place and acceptance criteria for these operations. The eventual user of the construction requires the materials to perform as desired with an emphasis on serviceability, durability and compatibility between components. The viewpoints are different but need to be reconciled if design and construction are to lead to a successful structure.

The common element in all these situations is the material itself. The communication link between the different types of users of a material is the description used for the material. Again, these descriptions are determined by the user and the viewpoint being adopted. The descriptions may be based on mathematical idealizations or models—elastic, plastic, etc.— involving recogizable properties amenable to experimental determination—Young's modulus, thermal conductivity, permeability for instance. Alternatively, the descriptions may be based on standard specifications or trade descriptions for particular products—Parafil cable, Permaline, Cemfil, etc. Not everyone uses all these descriptions and many of the problems of selection and use of materials are associated with attempts to match the description or requirements arising from different viewpoints.

A designer is concerned with providing the descriptions and instructions to enable his concept to be translated into reality. The link between concept and physical performance is a key area for engineering judgment leading to a realistic appraisal of performance and the development of appropriate specifications. It is evident that engineering judgment is just as central to the appreciation of materials behaviour as it is to the design of structures in general.

1.2 Development of a material or process

Before considering the need to model materials, it is helpful to reflect on how materials are developed and come into use. Some of the interactions are shown in *Figure 1.1*.

The period of initial use is preceded by invention of a new material or recogniton of the capability of an existing one. Use here is small scale and experimental which, if successful, is followed by a period of development needing significant resources and industry involvement. Because of the real or imagined commercial benefits, the development stage will be kept secret and may lead to the acquisition of patents before the stage of speculative use.

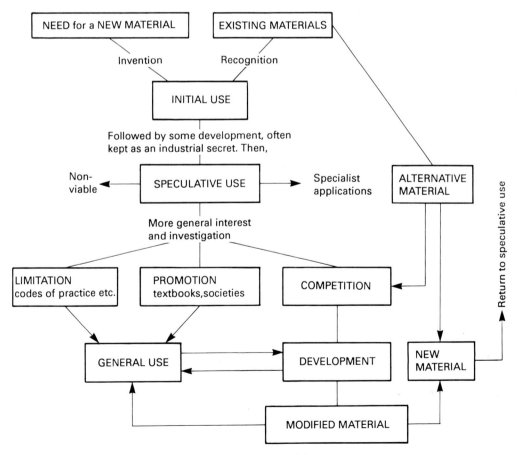

Figure 1.1 Possible pattern for the development of an idealized material or process

The stages prior to speculative use and involving the acquisition of patents mark the end of the birth of a new material. This occurred for reinforced concrete in the period from the mid-1800s to the turn of the century when a variety of concrete systems were being used in France and E. Coignet and F. Hennebique had patented systems for the use of reinforcement in concrete which would be recognizable today.

The period between the start of speculative use and general use is one of growth for the material. However, not all materials or processes emerge beyond the period of speculative use. The material may not be viable—chemical prestressing for instance—or be suitable for only limited specialist applications—preload systems for prestressing tanks, bentonite slurries for diaphragm walls or cut-offs. Alternatively, the material or process is useful and too attractive commercially to be retained exclusively by the originators. Patents are then circumvented and the use becomes more widespread.

More widespread use inevitably brings competition. The introduction of reinforced concrete into Great Britain was almost coincident with the first uses of structural steel for framed buildings. Competition leads to an emphasis on promotion, the formation of specialist technical societies and the preparation of guides and text books. With the pressures of competition and promotion comes the need for moderation and limitation through Building Regulations and Codes of Practice.

The period of general use is one of maturity and small scale development driven by competition and the challenge of alternative new materials. This is the stage of reinforced concrete at the present time.

The pattern suggested by *Figure 1.1* provides a model for the development of a material or process. It is unlikely to be universally applicable but even in those circumstances provides some insights into the stages of development and the conflicting interests which are involved.

1.3 Exploring materials: the role of experiment

Confronted with any new engineering material, the first question is whether it is useful and the second is whether it provides advantages in properties, cost, supply or convenience over materials already being used. A view of its properties and performance has to be established and this is most convincingly done by physical tests on the real material.

During the stages of initial and speculative use, testing may take the form of a demonstration showing how the whole system works incorporating the material. Similar tests are also undertaken at the promotion stage, for example the use of fire tests on complete houses to promote confidence in the early use of reinforced concrete.

A second more detailed role of testing is to establish the physical properties of the material. Often the aim is to place the material into a class of materials whose general pattern of behaviour is known and can be described by a limited number of index properties. For instance, if the material can be shown to be time-independent, linear, elastic and isotropic, measurements are needed of only two elastic parameters (Young's modulus and Poisson's ratio) in describing the response to applied load. Alternatively, the experiments may reveal novel phenomena that need to be described in new terms before they can be exploited or accommodated in engineering design. Again, the experiments should indicate the uniformity or reproducibility of the material and the reliance that can be put on the results of experiment.

In many cases the experiment itself is based on an idealized situation. The means of making a test specimen or the techniques used for materials sampling can introduce extraneous influences due to size, boundary conditions and materials disturbance.

Inevitably also, the tests themselves cannot cover all the variety of situations that the materials might experience in use. Judgment is needed in using materials beyond the range for which they can be tested or even in interpolating behaviour between the results of different tests. One aid to judgment is the use of mathematical models to provide a formal generalization of behaviour for different classes of ideal material. An appropriate model suggests key properties that can be measured experimentally by tests on the real material and provides the means to use these properties in situations more general than those covered by the experiments.

The idea of classes of materials and the form of model that can be adopted is now taken up in terms of a material's response to stress. This is a limited view but the concepts of exploration, generalization and finally mathematical formulation would be common to a more general model building process. The discussion has the advantage also that the mathematical description of a materials response to stress, the constitutive equation, is an area that has been studied in depth and the ideas are familiar.

1.4 Stress–strain relations—classes of material behaviour

Stress–strain relations essentially represent the behaviour of ideal materials that do not necessarily exist in the same idealized simplified form in the physical world. A broad classification indicating the three main types of ideal material (elastic, plastic, and viscous) is shown in *Figure 1.2*. It will be noted that the classification is not based on the phenomena involved nor on any particular material description based on composition. The key to the choice of stress–strain relation is the range of phenomena to be described. Different equations may be appropriate for different situations involving the same physical material.

Experiments may show that the material being investigated exhibits each of the three ideal characteristics in one form or another. The development of an appropriate mathematical description then involves equations representing combinations of behaviour and the interactions between them. Concrete is such a material. Under low loads or short duration, the material may be considered elastic and almost linear. For sustained loads, creep becomes important and a visco-elastic description is needed, possibly with some allowance for ageing. At higher loads, cracking occurs within the structure of the material causing dissipation of energy and irreversible strains which can be described in terms of plasticity. Each element of idealized behaviour has its role in describing the phenomena observed in the physical material.

1.5 Generalization of data

Tests on materials provide only a limited range of data. The results need to be generalized if they are to form the basis for a theoretical model for a particular class of material. In doing this, three approaches appear to be used depending on the style and inclination of the investigator.

The classical analyst's approach to generalization is to define an ideal material, at the outset, in terms of a set of characteristics that lead to a mathematical description but at the same time restrict the range of the resulting stress–strain relations. For example, the definition of elasticity as time independent, deformation path-independent behaviour is sufficient to develop a theory for non-linear elasticity involving the concept of the potential energy function. Further restrictions to linearity and isotropy reduce the theory to the familiar one in which only

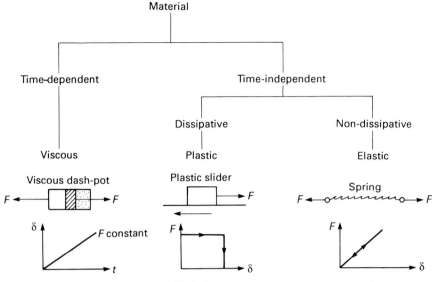

Figure 1.2 Classification of ideal material behaviour

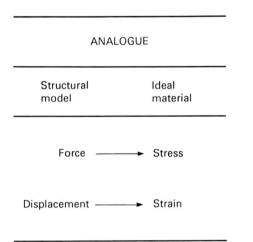

Figure 1.3 Relationships underlying use of rheological models

two parameters are needed for the material's description. Ideally, if the postulated characteristics of path-independence, linearity and isotropy can be recognized in a physical material, it has no choice but to behave according to the theory.

Matching postulated characteristics with real behaviour may not always be straightforward. Drucker's definition of plasticity involves a requirement on energy dissipation that implies that the slope of the stress–strain curve is positive but also requires the relation between increments of stress and strain to be linear. The first condition can be observed in tests relatively easily whereas it would be difficult to confirm directly the second order assumption on increments of stress and strain. The theory is still valid but more difficult to relate to a particular physical material.

A second method of generalization is by extending the range of application of existing theories. For instance, attempts have been made to describe non-linear behaviour by making the elastic moduli in the theory of elasticity dependent on stress or some combination of stress. This is an attractive route for the experimentalist, as the form of experiment and descriptive parameters is determined by the underlying theory. The approach has the advantage that the results will be easily assimilated and may possibly be applied using techniques based on the simpler underlying theory. There are disadvantages also and some restrictions may need to be adopted on the way the theory is stretched if it is to remain generally applicable.

A third route to generalization is by model building using rheological models to provide combinations of the ideal material's behaviour shown in *Figure 1.2*. This is a less direct approach but enables both exploration and generalization of conceptual models to be attempted and also leads to a consistent mathematical formulation of overall behaviour.

1.6 Rheological models

The idea underlying the use of rheological models is that a structure can be used to produce the behaviour observed in an element of material. The force–displacement relations obtained for the structure are taken to be analogous to the stress–strain relations in the material being modelled as indicated in *Figure 1.3*.

The elements used in the structure—a viscous dash-pot, friction slider and spring, are shown in *Figure 1.2* and match the three basic classes of ideal behaviour. A structure comprising a combination of these elements exhibits behaviour having features from the three main types.

Most often, rheological models have been used to study unidirectional behaviour with the load–extension relation for the model being taken to represent the uni-axial stress–strain relationships for the material. The approach has the advantages that:

(1) the behaviour from the model is in accordance with the laws of thermo-dynamics provided the postulated structure is properly analysed;

(2) the logic required to distinguish different types of behaviour accompanying loading, unloading and reloading is easily established and can be incorporated into numerical schemes; and

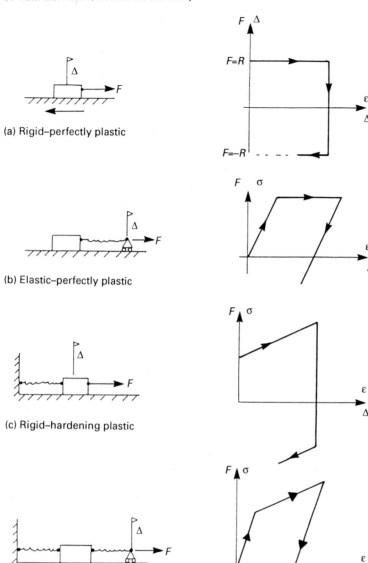

(a) Rigid–perfectly plastic

(b) Elastic–perfectly plastic

(c) Rigid–hardening plastic

(d) Elastic–hardening

Figure 1.4 Elasto-plastic behaviour from rheological models

(3) the structural model can be relatively easily extended to more than one dimension so enabling behaviour under combined stresses to be explored and described.

In passing, it is helpful to note that rheological models need have no physical correspondence with the material being described. Any correspondence of the individual structural components with phases of physical material will be accidental. This is in contrast to the use of micro-mechanical models where the intention is to model the actual structure of a material, albeit in a simplified way, and so derive the behaviour of the gross material.

The following sections illustrate the use of rheological models in the context of developing an understanding of plasticity and developing stress–strain relations.

1.6.1 Plasticity: one-dimensional loading

Figure 1.4 shows a range of different combinations of elastic and plastic behaviour produced by spring and friction block

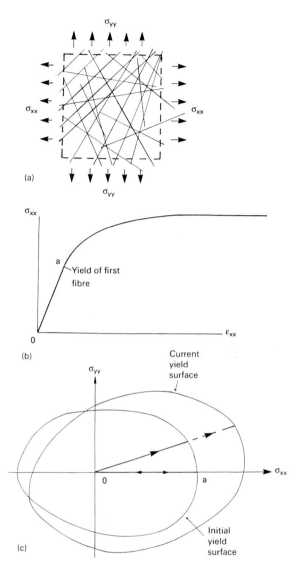

(a)

(b)

(c)

Figure 1.5 Qualitative view of behaviour of a fibrous material with perfectly plastic elements

models. The friction block introduces a discontinuity into the system corresponding to the initiation of slip in the model or the commencement of *yield* in a material. In the model, the discontinuity occurs because the block remains stationary until the net force acting on the block equals the sliding resistance R, which always acts in a direction to oppose motion.

The classical model for plasticity is that shown in *Figure 1.4(b)* corresponding to an *elastic-perfectly plastic material*. Before the discontinuity—or yield—occurs, behaviour is linear-elastic. Following yield, the block slips at constant force, so that there is no hardening. Other models modify this ideal behaviour by introducing *hardening* or by making the elastic strains negligible in the *rigid-plastic* models. Note that hardening builds a memory into the material in that the force to cause the block to slip, or the stress required to produce further plastic deformation, is affected by the earlier history of loading.

Before going to a formal generalization of one of these models it is interesting to use the basic idea of a rheological model to explore some of the implications of plasticity for behaviour under combinations of stress.

1.6.2 Plasticity: first view of combined stresses and the yield surface

Imagine a sheet of material formed of a network of fibres of a linear elastic-perfectly plastic material of the sort shown in *Figure 1.4(b)*. The fibres are randomly distributed and orientated in any given sample of material and either the cross-section or the yield stress varies from fibre to fibre. Imagine also the sheet can be subject to stresses σ_{xx} and σ_{yy} as shown in *Figure 1.5(a)* all other stresses being zero.

Consider the effects of uniaxial loading with σ_{xx} given and $\sigma_{yy}=0$. At first, behaviour is linear-elastic. Then, one fibre yields followed by a succession of yielding fibres leading to a stress-strain response of the kind shown in *Figure 1.5(b)*.

If we consider combined loading, there will be combinations of σ_{xx} and σ_{yy} which can be applied for which the material will remain elastic and no fibre will yield. These combinations of stress define a region in stress space $(\sigma_{xx}, \sigma_{yy})$ bounded by a surface (the *initial yield surface*) which corresponds to the condition for yield of a single fibre. If loading continues so as to move the point representing the current state of stress outside this surface, more fibres yield and plastic deformation occurs. However, at each stage, a region in $(\sigma_{xx}, \sigma_{yy})$ stress space can be defined which encloses states of stress which can be applied *without causing additional plastic deformation*, i.e. without causing additional fibres to yield. The boundary of this region is the *current yield surface* for the material shown in *Figure 1.5(c)*.

The idea of a yield surface plays a central role in classical plasticity theory. It is used to distinguish between behaviour which is purely elastic and that in which elastic strains are accompanied by plastic deformation. Different constitutive laws are necessary for these regions of behaviour. Again, study of a suitable rheological model gives an indication of the type of law required to describe behaviour consequent on plastic deformation.

1.6.3 Results from a two-dimensional rheological model

We now attempt to obtain a view of plasticity under more general stress conditions from a two-dimensional model based on the rigid-strain hardening solid. A plan view of the model is shown in *Figure 1.6*. This comprises a block on a rough surface and two anchoring springs in the x and y directions. Forces X and Y are applied to the blocks and these are restricted by the forces in the springs and the frictional resistance R which acts in a direction opposite to that of the movement of the block. Inertia effects are ignored.

In using the model, the forces X and Y are to be interpreted as stresses σ_{xx} and σ_{yy} in an element of material. Slip of the block corresponds to yield in the material and, as the behaviour is rigid-plastic with all the deformation irrecoverable, the block displacements (u, v) represent the plastic strain components $(\varepsilon_{xx}, \varepsilon_{yy})$.

Consider the forces acting on the block. For motion to occur at an angle θ to the x direction

$$(X - ku)\cos\theta + (Y - kv)\sin\theta = R \tag{1.1}$$

$$(X - ku)\sin\theta - (Y - kv)\cos\theta = 0 \tag{1.2}$$

From these equations and *Figure 1.6*

$$\tan\theta = (Y - kv)/(X - ku) = \delta v/\delta u \tag{1.3}$$

and

$$(X - ku)^2 + (Y - kv)^2 = R^2 \tag{1.4}$$

This last equation (1.4) corresponds to the *yield surface* for the material and the equation must be satisfied at all times when the block is moving, i.e. when the material is at yield and there is a change in plastic deformation. The nature of this yield

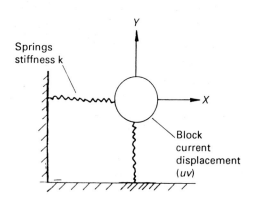

Springs stiffness k

Block current displacement (uv)

Figure 1.6 Two-dimensional rheological models for a rigid hardening plastic material

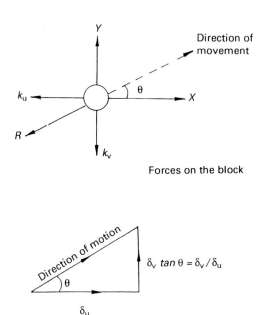

Direction of movement

Forces on the block

$\delta_v \ tan \ \theta = \delta_v / \delta_u$

Direction of motion

δ_u

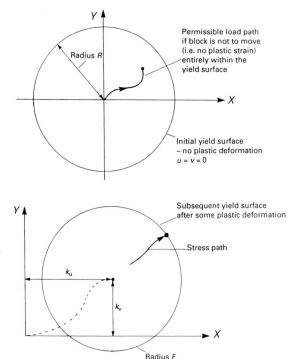

Permissible load path if block is not to move (i.e. no plastic strain) entirely within the yield surface

Radius R

Initial yield surface – no plastic deformation u = v = 0

Subsequent yield surface after some plastic deformation

Stress path

Radius F

Figure 1.7 Initial and subsequent yield surface from the analogue

surface is made clearer in *Figure 1.7* as a graph in X, Y (load) space or $(\sigma_{xx}, \sigma_{yy})$ stress space. We note how the current position of the yield surface provides the condition for distinguishing between behaviour that is 'rigid' and that which involves yield and 'plastic deformation'. With a marginally different model, a similar surface would provide criteria for distinguishing between load paths accompanied by elastic behaviour or combined elastic and plastic deformation.

The relation between increments of stress and increments of plastic deformation is termed the *flow rule*. Later, we will find an explicit form for the flow rule for the model material. Before doing this, we look in more detail at the yield surface and note how this changes its position in (X, Y) space as the block is moved. In doing this, we set ourselves the problem of deducing the displacement history caused by some prescribed history of loading. In what follows, it is convenient to use the variables

$$X' = X/k, \ Y' = Y/k \ and \ R' = R/k \tag{1.5}$$

to describe the loads. The yield criterion (1.4) then becomes

$$(X' - u)^2 + (Y' - v)^2 = R'^2 \tag{1.6}$$

so that, when this is plotted in (X', Y') space, the centre of the circle (now radius R') occurs at the point (u, v). In this way, as the circle moves, its centre traces out the displacement path (u, v). It is evident, also, that the direction of the plastic strain increment vector $(\delta u, \delta v)$ is known from equation (1.3) which now takes the form

$$tan \ \theta = (Y' - v)/(X' - u) = \delta v/\delta u \tag{1.7}$$

This solution is illustrated in *Figure 1.8*. The plastic strain increment vector is directed along the line connecting the point (u, v) with the load (X', Y'). In terms of the material rather than the structural model, the plastic strain increment vector is in a direction at right angles to the yield surface at the point representing the current state of stress. This property is known as *normality* when adopted in general theories of plasticity.

The way in which the direction of the plastic strain increment vector is fixed by the current state of stress and the form of the yield surface leads to a graphical construction for the plastic strain increment. This is illustrated in *Figure 1.9*. In applications, the prescribed load path is divided into segments representing successive increments of loading from which the displacement increment can be found. An example of such a development is shown in *Figure 1.10*. Note the tendency for the displacement path to tuck in behind the load path. This suggests that the material has a gradually fading memory of the earlier details of the plastic deformation history. We note that the graphical construction leads to a unique solution for the displacement path for any given history of loading. On the other hand, it is

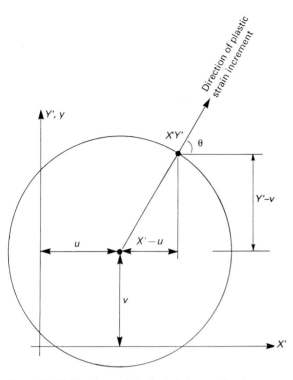

Figure 1.8 Yield surface and plastic strain increment vector

clear from *Figure 1.11* that the inverse statement is not true and that a given displacement path can be achieved by a variety of (X, Y) paths. Accordingly, we would expect the formal expression for the relation between $(\delta u, \delta v)$ and $(\delta X, \delta Y)$ to be singular.

To obtain the flow rule, we return to equation (1.4) and note that this must continue to be satisfied for loads $(X + \delta X, Y + \delta Y)$ and displacements $(u + \delta u, v + \delta v)$. This implies that the function

$$F = (X - ku)^2 + (Y - ku)^2 = R^2 \qquad (1.8)$$

does not change during slip, so that

$$dF = (\partial F/\partial X)\delta X + (\partial F/\partial Y)\delta Y + (\partial F/\partial u)\delta u + (\partial F/\partial v)\delta v = 0 \quad (1.9)$$

Use of the results in equation (1.9) with the kinematic constraint in equation (1.3) then leads to the following expression for the *flow rule*

$$\begin{bmatrix} \delta u \\ \delta v \end{bmatrix} = \frac{1}{kR^2} \left[\begin{array}{c|c} (X-ku)^2 & (X-ku)(Y-kv) \\ (X-ku)(Y-kv) & (Y-kv)^2 \end{array} \right] \begin{bmatrix} \delta X \\ \delta Y \end{bmatrix}$$
$$(1.10)$$

1.6.3.1 Direct extension of the model results

An obvious generalization from the model is to adopt a loading function of the form

$$F = (\sigma_{ij} - k\varepsilon_{ij})(\sigma_{ij} - k\varepsilon_{ij}) - R^2 \qquad (1.11)$$

to give a yield surface $F = 0$ in stress space. *Figure 1.8* suggests that the plastic strain increment may be written

$$\dot{\varepsilon}_{ij} = \psi(\sigma_{ij} - k\varepsilon_{ij}) \qquad (1.12)$$

where ψ is a scalar and the superior dot indicates an increment.

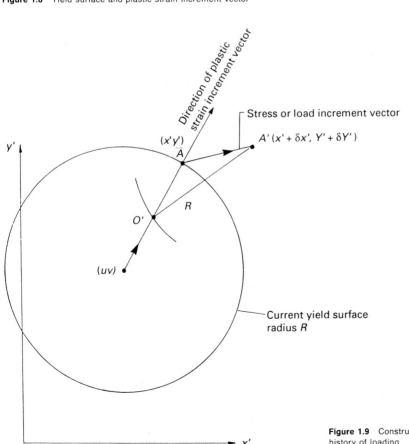

Figure 1.9 Construction of the deformation path from a given history of loading

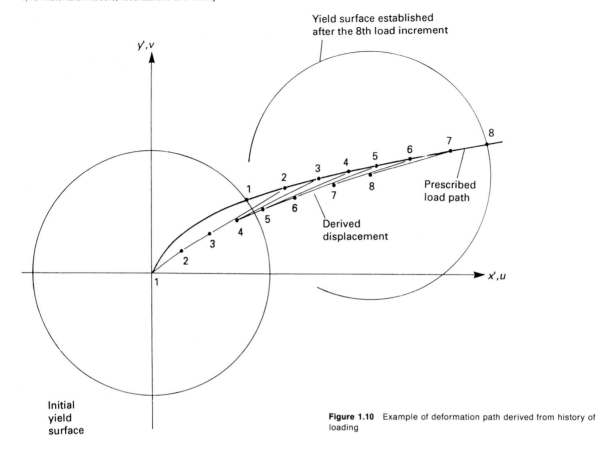

Figure 1.10 Example of deformation path derived from history of loading

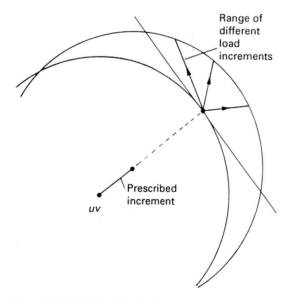

Figure 1.11 Ambiguity of the load increment for a prescribed increment of displacement

The condition that the stress point stays on the yield surface during plastic deformation requires that

$$\dot{F} = 2(\sigma_{ij} - k\varepsilon_{ij})(\dot{\sigma}_{ij} - k\dot{\varepsilon}_{ij}) = 0 \tag{1.13}$$

Equations (1.12) and (1.13) provide the value ψ and so lead to the flow rule

$$\dot{\varepsilon}_{ij} = (1/kR^2)(\sigma_{ij} - k\varepsilon_{ij})(\sigma_{km} - k\varepsilon_{km})\dot{\sigma}_{km} \tag{1.14}$$

connecting the increments of stress and strain.

The approach used in extending the results of the two-dimensional model is limited as the form of the loading function has been inferred from the model. Experiment suggests that the yield surface for most real materials cannot be represented by a hypersphere in stress space so that equation (1.14) will not be generally applicable. The results of the model can, however, be used to infer the elements necessary in a general theory.

1.7 Concluding discussion

A variety of views of materials and modelling materials have been presented. It is evident that there is no single viewpoint and that the development and use of materials is subject to historical and commercial factors in addition to technical aspects.

Materials exist in a physical form and are manufactured,

tested, used in construction and lived with in completed buildings or products. Materials also exist on paper as abstract descriptions that enable them to be bought and sold or alternatively enable calculations to be undertaken to predict performance relevant to a particular design.

A designer deals in ideas and uses models to bridge the gap between his own concepts and the realities of construction. Models for materials' behaviour have a similar role in providing the engineering designer with a tool for describing and assessing his own concepts. Inevitably there is a mismatch between the model and reality leading to the need for judgment in design and understanding in use.

The techniques described have focused on stress–strain behaviour of engineering materials. However, no great imagination is required to suggest how temperature effects, ageing or internal breakdown could be included in the models provided the description continues to be relevant to a representative region or point within the material.

In the past, engineers appear to have been primarily concerned with failure defined as collapse or structural breakdown. The emphasis has been on strength and behaviour under load. Recently, more attention has been given to serviceability and durability of structures, with time and the environmental conditions being the main controlling influences. This change in emphasis does not remove the need for models and adequate descriptions of materials' behaviour. It merely points the way to the need for a broader class of model to assist the engineering designer.

Acknowledgements

A chapter such as this should have an extensive bibliography or no references at all. In choosing the latter course, I feel that I should acknowledge the considerable influence on my knowledge of materials provided by the works of R. E. Gibson, D. C. Drucker and Z. P. Bazant.

Part One

Metals and their Alloys

2

Aluminium

M J Bayley MSc(Eng)
Technical Support Manager, Alcan Offshore

P S Bulson CBE, DSc, FEng
Chairman, British Standards Committee on
the Structural Use of Aluminium

Contents

2.1 Introduction 2/3

2.2 Sources 2/3

2.3 Manufacturing process 2/3
    2.3.1 Bayer process 2/3
    2.3.2 Electrolytic reduction 2/4
    2.3.3 Fabrication processes 2/4

2.4 Alloy types 2/7
    2.4.1 Introduction 2/7
    2.4.2 Classification of alloys 2/8
    2.4.3 Temper designations 2/9

2.5 Chemical composition and mechanical properties 2/10
    2.5.1 Chemical composition 2/10
    2.5.2 Mechanical properties 2/10
    2.5.3 Non-specification mechanical properties 2/16

2.6 Physical properties 2/17
    2.6.1 Density 2/17
    2.6.2 Modulus of elasticity 2/17
    2.6.3 Coefficient of thermal expansion 2/17
    2.6.4 Thermal conductivity 2/17
    2.6.5 Electrical resistivity and conductivity 2/17
    2.6.6 Melting point 2/18
    2.6.7 Ductility 2/18
    2.6.8 Non-magnetic properties 2/18
    2.6.9 Dielectric properties 2/18
    2.6.10 Reflectivity 2/18
    2.6.11 Affinity for oxygen 2/18
    2.6.12 Resistance to food and chemicals 2/18

2.7 Special properties 2/18
    2.7.1 Creep 2/18
    2.7.2 Fatigue strength 2/18
    2.7.3 Properties at elevated temperatures 2/18
    2.7.4 Low-temperature properties 2/18
    2.7.5 Fire 2/18
    2.7.6 Thermite sparking 2/18

2.8 Durability and protection 2/18
    2.8.1 Inherent corrosion resistance 2/18
    2.8.2 Durability of alloys 2/19
    2.8.3 Protection 2/19

2.9 Materials selection 2/21
    2.9.1 Heat-treatable alloys 2/21
    2.9.2 Non-heat-treatable alloys 2/22

2.10 Fabrication and construction 2/23
    2.10.1 Cutting 2/23
    2.10.2 Drilling punching and blanking 2/23
    2.10.3 Bending and forming 2/23
    2.10.4 Welding 2/23
    2.10.5 Bolting and riveting 2/25
    2.10.6 Finishes 2/25

2.11 Standard products and availability of materials 2/26
    2.11.1 General 2/26
    2.11.2 Standard products 2/26
    2.11.3 Availability of materials 2/26

2.12 Standards 2/27
    2.12.1 British Standards Institution standards 2/27
    2.12.2 International Organization for Standardization
    (ISO) standards 2/29

Bibliography 2/29

2.1 Introduction

Over the last century, aluminum, together with its alloys, has grown from a newly produced metal, first going into commercial production in 1886, to the second most used metal in constructional engineering. Aluminium alloys, each in a range of available forms, tempers and properties, have been developed to meet the needs of all forms of construction. The metal is light with good to excellent corrosion resistance and can be produced economically in a wide range of forms. The ease of extrusion of many of its alloys enables their use in complex extruded sections in many applications throughout the construction industry. Successful use of the correct aluminium or aluminium alloy in all applications is founded on a sound understanding of the properties and other aspects of the material.

2.2 Sources

Aluminium, by reason of its chemical reactivity, is not found in its pure state, but in combination with other elements. Aluminium is the most common metallic element in the earth's crust which contains approximately 15% of Al_2O_3 (8% aluminium). In most occurrences the aluminium content is too small for economic extraction, but the principal ore of commercial value, and that most frequently used in the production of aluminium, is a group termed 'bauxites'. This contains mainly hydrated alumina together with oxides of iron, silicone and titanium. The bauxites are regarded as the end-products of the slow weathering of aluminium bearing rocks, often igneous but not necessarily so, over millions of years in regions of heavy rainfall common in tropical or subtropical areas. Some bauxites occur as sedimentary or alluvial deposits from water which has carried them away from the weathering rocks. In either case the products are mainly surface deposits and are extracted by open-cast quarrying. The bauxite is then washed and screened to remove extraneous dirt. The locations of the world's principal bauxite deposits are shown in *Figure 2.1.*

2.3 Manufacturing process

2.3.1 Bayer process

The most commonly used process of refining bauxite to alumina is the Bayer process. This may take place close to the mine but in many instances the bauxite is transported to more distant locations for processing.

In the initial stage of the Bayer process, bauxite, mainly impure alumina trihydrate ($Al_2O_3 \cdot 3H_2O$), is crushed into a fine powder and mixed in a hot solution of caustic soda (NaOH). This caustic soda dissolves the trihydrate in pressure digestors, to form sodium aluminate ($Na_2O \cdot Al_2O_3$), leaving the impurities undissolved:

$$2NaOH + Al_2O_3 \cdot 3H_2O \rightarrow Na_2O \cdot Al_2O_3 + 4H_2O + impurities\downarrow$$

The impurities, mainly the oxides of iron, silicon and titanium, are contained in a residue which is removed by filter presses and discarded. The red colour of the residue has earned it the name 'red mud' and to date no way has been found of reclaiming the oxides from this residue.

The clear sodium aluminate solution is pumped into a large tank called a precipitator. Here very fine and pure alumina trihydrate is added as 'seed', and under agitation with compressed air and with gradual cooling, the sodium aluminate solution decomposes into pure alumina trihydrate and caustic soda:

$$Na_2O \cdot Al_2O_3 + 4H_2O \xrightarrow{seed} Al_2O_3 \cdot 3H_2O\downarrow + 2NaOH$$

The alumina trihydrate precipitates onto the seed causing it to grow to a slightly coarser size. This trihydrate is allowed to separate from the caustic soda solution by settling, after which it is passed through rotary kilns at a temperature of approximately 1100°C to drive off the chemically combined water.

$$Al_2O_3 \cdot H_3O \xrightarrow{1000\ C} Al_2O_3 + 3H_2O\uparrow$$

Figure 2.1 Location of the world's principal bauxite deposits

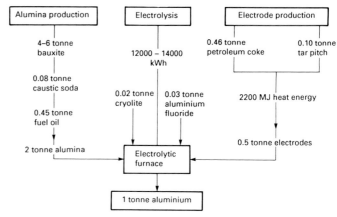

Figure 2.2 Raw materials and energy requirements for the production of aluminium

The resulting product is alumina oxide (Al_2O_3), a white powder which is known as calcined alumina. The caustic soda solution left behind in the precipitator is returned to the start of the process to be used again with fresh bauxite. The raw materials and energy requirements in the Bayer process are shown in part of *Figure 2.2*.

2.3.2 Electrolytic reduction

Aluminium metal is obtained from the calcined alumina at smelters by an electrolytic reduction process in cells known as 'pots'. This operation requires large quantities of power so that the smelters are always located close to sources of electricity, commonly hydroelectric. A pot consists of two main parts, the first, a block of carbon which has been formed by baking a mixture of petroleum coke and pitch. This block serves as an anode, or positive electrode, through which electric current enters the pot. Under the anode is a large rectangular steel box lined with carbon made by baking a mixture of metallurgic coke and pitch. This lining is the cathode, or negative electrode, through which the current leaves the pot.

The cavity between the anode and cathode is filled with a molten liquid electrolyte consisting of cryolite (Na_3AlF_6) obtained either in its natural form from Greenland or made synthetically, and aluminium fluoride (AlF_3) which is made from alumina trihydrate, fluorspar and sulphuric acid. The calcined alumina is added to the electrolyte in which it dissolves. The energy from the electric power passes from the anode through the electrolyte to the cathode causing the alumina in solution to break down into molten aluminium, which settles to the bottom of the pot.

The molten aluminium is syphoned or 'tapped' from the bottom of the pot in crucibles and transferred to holding furnaces where blending of the alloy takes place. After the quality of the metal has been checked by analysis, it is cast into ingots. *Figure 2.2* shows the materials and energy requirements to produce one tonne of aluminium. Ingots may vary in size and form depending on the type of process in which they are to be used later. The ingots range from 2 to 20 000 kg depending on their eventual use and the type of equipment used to process them. The large ingots are produced by semicontinuous direct casting.

2.3.3 Fabrication processes

The cast metal produced from the smelter is fabricated by various processes into forms of the aluminium alloys suitable for the manufacture of the finished product. The broad classifications of fabricating include rolling, drawing, extrusion, forging and casting, with additional special processes such as roll forming and superplastic forming. The starting point for fabrication is usually a rectangular or round ingot. These ingots may be obtained ready made from the smelter to the exact shape and composition required, or made at the fabricating plant by the remelting of new ingot and recovered scrap, and recasting to the desired shape after the addition of the various alloying elements. *Figure 2.3* outlines the various fabricating routes which are described briefly below.

2.3.3.1 Casting

Aluminium alloy castings are normally produced by one of three methods depending on alloy, quality, finish required and the intended production run. Raw castings from the casting process are fettled to remove the risers, feeders and unwanted material, machined if necessary and, where appropriate, heat treated. The three principal methods of casting are sand casting, gravity die casting and pressure die casting.

(*i*) *Sand casting* Sand casting into sand moulds contained in metal boxes, incorporating sand cores for hollow parts, is applied to castings of all sizes and degrees of complexity, but thin castings are more difficult. This method is the least costly when relatively few castings are required and wooden patterns are generally used, being quick to produce.

(*ii*) *Gravity die casting* Gravity die, or permanent mould, casting employs molten metal poured under gravity into metal moulds. Small grain growth is promoted by the high cooling rate in the metallic die and enables high mechanical properties to be obtained. The high cost of the die is partly offset by greater production rates, but runs of 1000–5000 are normally required to justify the cost. The finish is normally better than with a sand casting.

(*iii*) *Pressure die casting* Pressure die or die castings are made by forcing liquid metal under pressure into steel moulds. This process enables smooth, thin, dimensionally accurate castings with high mechanical properties to be produced. The very high cost of tooling and equipment usually only justifies this method for very large production runs.

(*iv*) *Other casting methods* Other casting methods such as low pressure die casting, suction casting, investment casting and shell moulding may be used to obtain particular results or to take advantage of the individual characteristics of some alloys.

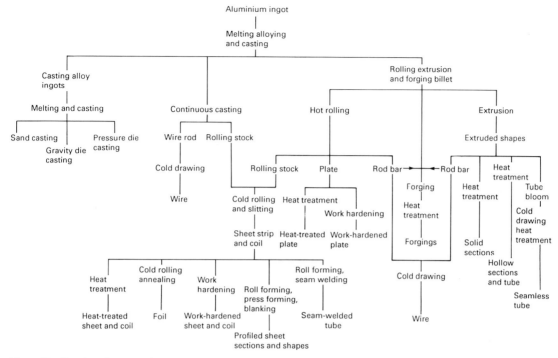

Figure 2.3 Manufacturing routes for semifabricated aluminium and aluminium alloy products

2.3.3.2 Rolling

One of the major ways of converting cast primary aluminium to a usable form is by rolling, where it is possible to reduce an ingot down to plate material having a maximum thickness of about 250 mm, through thinner plate to sheet and down to foil as thin as 0.01 mm and less. Rolling the cast metal replaces the brittle coarse cast structure by a stronger and more ductile material. The degree of ductility and strength achieved are functions of the amount of rolling, the rolling temperature and the alloy composition. These properties are defined by the term temper which specifies the characteristic structural and mechanical properties produced in an alloy by the transformation processes such as the mechanical working or heat treatment.

Plate and re-roll stock are produced by hot rolling of ingots made by semicontinuous direct chill casting to the required alloy and size. Ingots up to $650 \times 2100 \times 5000$ mm in size can be produced. Most plate is finished rolled on the hot line and, where it is required in a temper other than soft or heat treated, the work hardened temper is obtained by control of the temperature and the degree of reduction in the final pass. Plates up to 3000-mm wide by 15 000-mm long and with thicknesses from 6.5 to 155 mm are produced in certain alloys.

Cold rolling is performed on re-roll coil stock or, in the case of heavy gauge material, on hot mill slabs cut into lengths, on four-high mills either on single stand or multistand tandem mills. Plate and sheet can also be produced by rolling continuously cast strip. For work-hardened alloys re-roll stock is normally soft enough for cold rolling without the need for preliminary annealing, but heat-treatable alloys may require annealing. The reduction in thickness during cold rolling depends on the gauge of the starting stock, final thickness, required temper, grain size and other metallurgical property requirements. Reductions up to 60% can be achieved but the more highly alloyed materials which work harden more rapidly require smaller reductions per

mass with annealing between the passes. Intermediate tempers are achieved by at least one annealing in the rolling schedule.

Both plate and sheet are finished by flattening, stretching and trimming to size and, where necessary, heat treatment. Tension levelling is also employed. Special finishes to plate and sheet can be incorporated into the rolling process to provide tread plate, stucco embossed and patterned sheet. Sheet and strip can be roll formed through progressive stands of rolls to form many shapes, such as those for cladding products, structural sections and building-system components. Prepainted sheet is frequently used.

2.3.3.3 Extrusion process

The extrusion process is simplistically compared to squeezing toothpaste from a tube. Cylindrically shaped billets of the required aluminium alloy are first heated to a temperature of around 550°C. They are then placed in a steel container and forced, while still in a hot plastic state, through a steel die at one end of the cylinder by a hydraulic ram. The ram pressure depends on the size of the section and billet, but presses up to 10 000-tonne capacity are available giving pressures at the die face of around 680 N mm^{-2}. The die is supported by a series of back dies and bolsters so that the main press load is transferred to the front platen of the press.

The shape of the extruded section is controlled by the die and the press forces involved, and both solid and hollow extrusions can be made. A fully enclosed void or hollow section requires a plug or mandrel in the die supported by a bridge, where the extruded stream of metal is split at the bridge and reunited at the mandrel before emerging from the die. A semihollow shape requires a strong tongue in the die.

The emerging extrusion is rapidly cooled by water or air quenching, as part of the heat-treatment process, guided along a moving run-out table and cut into production lengths of up to 40 m. The lengths are given a controlled stretch to straighten them and are then cut into the finished order lengths. A final heat treatment is given to heat-treatable alloys to obtain the optimum physical properties to complete the general production process.

The design and manufacture of the dies, so that the metal flows uniformly through the die, is the most critical stage in the extrusion process and it sometimes takes one or two trial extrusions before the die is perfected and ready for production. The size of the section is limited to the size of the ingot container in the extrusion press. Container sizes depend on the press capacity and range from 150 mm up to 600 mm in special cases. Some extrusion presses have large rectangular containers allowing sections up to 800 × 100 mm maximum to be extruded.

Three principal categories of extruded shape are available: solid, hollow and semihollow.

(1) *Solid-shaped sections* are those which have no areas either wholly or partly enclosed (see *Figure 2.4*). These may be simple sections or complex sections with many special features.

Figure 2.4 Simple solid section

(2) *Hollow-shaped sections* have one or more wholly enclosed areas (see *Figure 2.5*). These again may be simple hollow sections, such as round or rectangular tube or more complex sections involving additional features or multihollows.

Figure 2.5 Simple hollow section

(3) *Semihollow-shaped sections* are those which have partly enclosed features, having a substantial closed area in relation to the width of the gap (see *Figure 2.6*).

Figure 2.6 Semihollow section

Figure 2.7 shows a wide range of extruded sections suitable for many applications.

2.3.3.4 Tube

Aluminium and aluminium alloy tube can be manufactured by one of a number of methods; the final requirements and alloy may dictate which method is used.

(*i*) *Seam welded tube* Seam welded tube is produced by a continuous process from strip, which is roll formed to a tube shape and tungsten inert gas (TIG) welded to form the complete tube. The weld flash can be removed both internally and externally to achieve a smooth finish. Subsequent rolling can convert the cross-section to rectangular or to other shapes and the use of perforated strip enables perforated tube to be produced. This method is normally confined to one alloy, and tube with a high diameter-to-thickness ratio is produced.

(*ii*) *Extruded tube* Tube can be extruded in a range of alloys either through a bridge or porthole die or over a piercing mandrel. Where the bridge die method is used the quality of seams or rewelds cannot be guaranteed, so that pressure or highly stressed applications of this form of tube are not recommended. The integrity of the welds can be inspected by drift testing into the ends of samples cut from the tube. The piercing method uses a hollow billet, either cast hollow, predrilled or pierced from a solid billet, and is extruded using a circular die and piercing mandrel. This produces seamless tube which is suitable for high stressed applications. Tube obtained by the bridge method normally falls in the size range 10–100 mm diameter with a thickness of 1.0 mm upward. Tube produced by the piercing method ranges from 30 to 200 mm in diameter with a thickness of 2.5 mm upward.

(*iii*) *Drawn tube* Seamless tube is manufactured by piercing a billet of the appropriate alloy with a mandrel and extruding a circular hollow tubular section of uniform thickness, known as tube bloom, over the tip of the mandrel. A circular steel die determines the outside shape. This tube bloom is subsequently drawn, to achieve the required shape, size, tolerances and mechanical strength, on drawbenches using steel dies and plugs to control the outer and inner dimensions of the tube. This method enables high quality tube both in heat-treatable and non-heat-treatable alloys to be made with close tolerance, thin walls, improved bore surface finish and predictable performance under internal pressure. The manufacturing size available depends to an extent on the alloy and ranges in outside diameter from 5 to 550 mm with wall thicknesses from 0.5 to 19 mm.

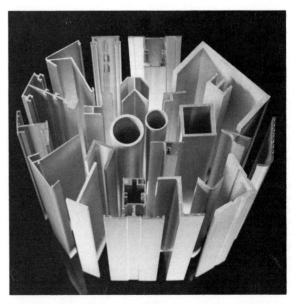

Figure 2.7 Typical extruded sections

2.3.3.5 Forging

Aluminium alloys may be formed to a desired shape by hot forging. Forgings gain substantial increase in toughness and reliability through improvement in the grain structure in the worked metal. By taking advantage of the metal flow, maximum mechanical properties can be obtained at critically stressed sections. Both heat-treatable and non-heat-treatable alloys can be forged. Two principal methods of forging are applied to aluminium.

(*i*) *Die forgings* Die forgings, which are most common, are made in closed dies with impressions that are finished accurately to the desired shape. In general, die forgings only require machining for holes and recesses which cannot easily be included in the dies. Larger and more complex shapes may be forged by a series of progressive forging operations in a series of dies. The high cost of the dies requires moderate to large quantities to warrant die forging.

(*ii*) *Hand forgings* Hand forgings are produced by working a bar or billet between flat dies or other simple tools. The pieces are shaped roughly to the required geometry and contour with little or no lateral containment and require machining to produce the finished component.

2.3.3.6 Superplastic forming

Certain aluminium alloys may be formed superplastically. These alloys will stretch to over 10 times their normal length at high temperatures and this allows complex parts to be formed from sheet in a single press cycle by forcing the heated sheet with compressed air into a female cavity or over a male former. The single surface tooling saves on tool cost over matched die methods and only aluminium or mild steel tools are required. Whilst the cycle time for forming is high as compared with that for die forming, the low cost of the tooling gives optimum production levels of around 50 to 10000 parts. Alloys are available for forming building panels where sizes in excess of 2 m × 1 m have been produced.

2.4 Alloy types

2.4.1 Introduction

Aluminium is rarely used in construction in its pure form but is alloyed with small proportions of alloying elements. The term aluminium is frequently used to include aluminium alloys as the proportions of the alloying elements which they contain is very small. The wide range of alloys that have been developed and formulated are defined in various national and international standards using different methods of alloy nomenclature. Although the International Organization for Standardization (ISO) has attempted to unify the nomenclature of aluminium alloys within the world, it still differs in many countries including the UK in British Standards. In addition, many trade names are still used to identify aluminium alloys.

Aluminium alloys are usually classified with respect to the fabrication process, the chemical composition and to their ability to respond to either heat treatment or work hardening. The classification is shown in *Figure 2.8*. The fabrication process divides aluminium alloys into the two broad categories of casting alloys and wrought alloys. The latter are semifabricated by rolling, extrusion, forging and drawing, etc. Within the category of cast and wrought alloy there are two major classes: heat-treatable and non-heat-treatable alloys.

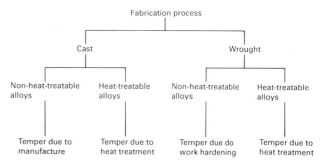

Figure 2.8 Alloy classification

2.4.1.1 Heat-treatable alloys

The heat-treatable alloys are those which derive strength by one or more thermal treatments and in which copper, magnesium, zinc and silicon are the important alloying elements. After working these alloys to produce the desired shape such as plate, extrusions, forgings, etc., or by casting, they are then subjected to thermal treatment at elevated temperatures to take the constituent alloying elements into solid solution. The metal is quenched from the solution heat-treatment temperature, too quickly for the dissolved elements to be precipitated; the solution remains supersaturated and the metal is temporarily soft.

This condition is unstable and precipitation gradually takes place in the form of fine particles within the grains and on the grain boundaries. The final particle size enhances the tensile strength of the metal, which is then said to have age-hardened or aged. Depending on the alloy composition and on the intended use, the material in the quenched condition may be subjected to flattening or straightening operations before the natural ageing can take place, and in certain circumstances the precipitation can be delayed by refrigeration. The final desired level of mechanical properties may be developed by allowing the alloy to age naturally at ambient temperature for a period of a few days. Alternatively, the alloy may be subjected to a precipitation or artificial ageing treatment by holding it at a temperature usually within the range 120–200°C for a number of hours. Certain alloys respond better to artificial ageing and produce a greater degree of precipitation and hardening than by natural ageing. Excessive precipitation treatment, either in temperature or in time, causes undesirable growth of the precipitated particles, reducing their effectiveness in strengthening the metal. The beneficial effects of heat treatment will be lost if the material is reheated to between 200 and 350°C.

These heat-treatable alloys make it possible to use aluminium where work hardening alloys are not suitable, and where the temporary softness of the alloy gives an opportunity for severe forming.

2.4.1.2 Non-heat-treatable alloys

The second of the two major classes of alloys are the non-heat-treatable alloys, also described as work hardening alloys. These are alloys which depend upon forming by rolling, wire drawing, tube drawing, etc., or by casting for the development of the metal structure and properties for the application. The non-heat-treatable alloys are those which are commercially pure and those in which manganese and magnesium are the important alloying elements.

The desired degree of strength, hardness and ductility is achieved through controlling the amount of working during fabrication; during mechanical shaping, distortion of the grain structure of the metal is caused along the slip planes. The balance between strength and ductility can be controlled by fully or partly softening the material at any stage during the fabrication through full or partial annealing at a temperature in the range 350–450°C. Annealing allows some relief of the internal stresses and rearrangement of the deformed structure at that temperature. As the temperature of annealing rises the distorted original grains disappear and new grains grow to form a stress-free system. This recrystallization brings the metal back to its softest state.

2.4.2 Classification of alloys

Different systems of nomenclature are employed to classify alloys both in the wrought and cast product forms, each related to their chemical composition by alloying elements, whilst separate nomenclature systems define the condition or temper in which the material is supplied. Some classification methods allow alloys to be grouped in different families with similar mechanical or other properties or through the form of product.

Aluminium alloys are classified in one of two ways: to a numerical designation or to an alphanumerical designation. The main numerical system originates from North America whilst the alphanumeric system comes from Europe. Either designation system of identifying the chemical composition is usually followed by a symbol or symbols which identify the semimanufacturing process and temper.

2.4.2.1 Numerical designation

(i) *Casting alloys* British Standard BS 1490 adopts a numerical designation system for casting alloys in which the alloys are defined by numbers in sequence of development and are preceded by the letters LM (light metal). The numbers have no significance to the alloy content; e.g. LM6, LM25.

The Aluminum Association in North America utilizes a four-digit numerical designation system for aluminium alloy casting and ingots. The first digit indicates the alloy group as given in *Table 2.1*. The second two digits identify the aluminium alloy or indicate the purity. The final digit, which is separated from the others by a decimal point, indicates the product form, i.e. 0 indicates castings and 1 indicates ingot.

Table 2.1 Major alloying elements in the four-digit classification system for cast alloys

First digit	Major alloying element
1**.*	Pure aluminium (greater than 99%)
2**.*	Copper
3**.*	Silicon plus copper and/or magnesium
4**.*	Silicon
5**.*	Magnesium
6**.*	Unused series
7**.*	Zinc
8**.*	Tin
9**.*	Other elements

(ii) *Wrought alloys* The numerical designation system is recommended for an international designation system for wrought aluminium and wrought aluminium alloys and is adopted in the USA by the Aluminum Association. This system is now employed in the British Standards covering aluminium alloys for general engineering purposes: BS 1470 to BS 1475 and the supplementary series BS 4300. The system is also currently used as an alternative within Europe, but in standardization work now commenced for CEN standards the

four-digit system will be used predominantly with the current ISO alphanumerical system in second position.

The four-digit system for wrought aluminium alloys consists of a four-digit number. The first of the four digits in the designation indicates the alloy group according to the major alloying elements as given in *Table 2.2*.

Table 2.2 Major alloying elements in the four-digit classification system for wrought alloys

First digit	Major alloying element
1***	Aluminium of 99.0% minimum purity or higher
2***	Copper
3***	Manganese
4***	Silicon
5***	Magnesium
6***	Magnesium and silicon
7***	Zinc
8***	Other elements
9***	Unused series

In the first group (1***), the third and fourth figures indicate the percentage of aluminium above 99%, i.e. 1080 indicates aluminium with a minimum purity of 99.80%. The second digit indicates modifications in impurity limits or the addition of alloying elements. If the second digit is zero the metal is unalloyed and contains only natural impurities within the specified limits.

In the groups 2*** to 8***, the last two digits have no special significance but serve only to identify the different alloys in the group. The second digit indicates alloy modifications and, if zero, indicates the original alloy. Where national variations of existing alloys are registered, they are identified by a letter after the numerical designation. These letters are assigned in alphabetical sequence, starting from A but omitting I, O and Q.

Examples of the four-digit numerical system for wrought alloys are compared with the alphanumerical system in *Table 2.3*.

Table 2.3 Examples of the four-digit numerical alloy nomenclature system

Four-digit numerical system	Alphanumerical system	Major alloying elements
3103	Al Mn1	Manganese
5083	Al Mg4.5 Mn	Magnesium
6082	Al Si1 Mg Mn	Magnesium and silicon

2.4.2.2 Alphanumerical designation

(i) *Casting alloys and wrought alloys* The alphanumeric designation system is most common in Europe and is employed in ISO 3522 for casting alloys and in ISO R 209 for wrought alloys, and is used or adapted in various European national standards. In this system each alloy is identified by a group of letters and figures. The first set identifies the base metal, i.e. aluminium, which is referred to as Al. The second group represents the alloying elements where the chemical symbol for the element is used. These may be followed by numbers indicating the percentage of that element in the alloy. When

Table 2.4 Examples of the alphanumerical alloy designation system

Alphanumerical system	Four-digit numerical system		Major alloying elements
Al Mg5	514.1	LM5	Magnesium
Al Si12	A413.2	LM6	Silicon
Al Si7 Mg	356.1	LM25	Silicon and magnesium
Al Mn1	3103		Manganese
Al Mg4.5 Mn	5083		Magnesium and manganese
Al Si1 Mg Mn	6082		Silicon, magnesium and manganese

several alloying elements are deemed to be required in the designation they are arranged in order of decreasing nominal content. Examples of the alphanumerical ISO system are given in *Table 2.4*.

2.4.3 Temper designations

2.4.3.1 General

Temper designation systems are used for all wrought and cast aluminium and aluminium alloys except ingots and they follow the alloy designation and are often separated by a hyphen. The designation is based on the sequence of basic treatments employed in semifabrication and used to achieve the various tempers in the products. One of the principal methods employed originates from the US Aluminum Association and is used in ISO 2107 as an alternative system. ISO 2107 carries as its main temper designation system a variation of the AA system. National standards employ the ISO system or variations on that system. Some of the British Standards for aluminium alloys for general engineering purposes adopt the ISO 2107 alternative system, whilst others not recently revised still use an old British Standard method of nomenclature similar to that in ISO 2107.

Within both the ISO 2107 and Aluminum Association systems, the basic temper designation consists of letters. Subdivisions of these basic tempers, where required, are indicated by one or more digits or digits and letters, following the basic designation letter. These recognize the specific sequences of treatments applied during manufacture of the product which significantly influence the characteristics of the finished product. Should some other variation of the same sequence of basic operation be applied to the same alloy, resulting in different characteristics, then additional digits or letters are added to the designation.

2.4.3.2 Basic temper designations

The following letters indicate the basic temper designations, which apply to all systems and forms.

(1) *M: as manufactured.* The as-manufactured temper designation applies to those products which acquire some temper from a hot shaping process such as extrusion or casting and for which some mechanical property limits apply.
(2) *F: as fabricated.* The as-fabricated temper designation applies to the products of those shaping processes in which no special control over thermal or strain hardening is employed. For wrought products, there are frequently no specific requirements for mechanical properties levels. Where British Standards have not yet been revised in line with ISO 2107 this basic temper is defined by the letter M.
(3) *O: annealed.* The annealed temper designation applies to those wrought products which are annealed to obtain the lowest possible strength condition, and to cast products which are annealed to improve their ductility and dimensional stability.
(4) *H: strain hardened.* The strain-hardened or work-hardened temper designation applies only to those wrought products subjected to the application of some form of cold work after annealing (or hot forming). It may also apply to a combination of cold work and partial annealing or stabilizing, in order to achieve the specified mechanical properties. The letter H is always followed by further digits or letters, indicating the degree of strain hardening finally achieved.
(5) *T: thermally treated,* to produce stable tempers other than F, O or H. The thermally treated or heat-treated temper designation applies to those products which receive some thermal treatment, with or without supplementary strain hardening, to produce stable tempers. The letter T is always followed by one or more digits or letters, indicating the specific sequence of heat treatments applied.

2.4.3.3 Subdivisions of basic temper designations

Subdivisions of the basic tempers other than M, F and O are indicated by the addition of further digit or letter combinations which relate to the specific sequence of fundamental treatments which significantly influence the final characteristics of the product. The nomenclature system used in the subdivision of the basic temper designation systems differs in some degree from system to system.

(i) Subdivisions of H temper For wrought products the subdivisions of the strain-hardened H temper are made according to the final degree of strain hardening achieved. The digit which comes first after the H indicates the particular combination of basic operations as follows. In those British Standards which have not been recently revised this first digit is omitted.

(1) *H1: strain hardened only.* This designation applies to those products which are strain hardened or work hardened usually by roll reduction to achieve the desired strength without any supplementary thermal treatment such as partial annealing. The number or letter following this designation indicates the degree of the strain hardening.
(2) *H2: strain hardened and partially annealed.* This designation applies to those products which are strain hardened to a higher degree than the desired final amount and are then reduced in strength to the required level by partial annealing. The number or letter following this designation indicates the degree of strain hardening that remains after the product has been partially annealed.
(3) *H3: strain hardened and stabilized.* This designation applies to those products which are strain hardened and whose properties are then stabilized by low temperature heat treatment resulting in a slightly lower tensile strength and with improved ductility. This designation applies only to those alloys which would gradually age-soften at room temperatures unless stabilized. The number or letter following this designation indicates the degree of strain hardening achieved before the stabilizing treatment.

The final degree of strain hardening achieved is indicated by the digit or letter which follows H1, H2 or H3. In the following, the asterisk represents the first digit (1, 2 or 3) if used, as appropriate.

(1) *H*2 or H*B.* A tensile strength which is approximately midway between that of the O annealed temper and that of the H*4 or H*D temper.

(2) *H*4 or H*D*. A tensile strength which is approximately midway between that of the O annealed temper and that of the H*8 or H*H temper.

(3) *H*6 or H*F*. A tensile strength which is approximately midway between that of the H*4 or H*D temper and that of the H*8 or H*H temper.

(4) *H*8 or H*H*. A fully hard temper.

(5) *H*9 or H*J*. A temper with a tensile strength which is in excess of the H*8 or H*H.

The fully hard temper H*8 or H*H has been assigned to indicate tempers having a final degree of strain hardening equivalent to that resulting from approximately 75% reduction in area. In ISO 2107 the tensile strength in the H*8 and H*H tempers is based on the minimum tensile strength in the annealed (O) temper, and the standard defines the addition in tensile strength to be achieved.

(*ii*) *Subdivisions of T temper* Subdivisions of the T temper for wrought and cast products are defined according to the particular heat-treatment process applied. The most common subdivisions applied being T4 and T6. The digit or digits that follows the T indicates the specific combination of basic heat treatments as follows.

(1) *T1 or TA*. Indicates where a product has been cooled from an elevated-temperature shaping process and naturally aged to a substantially stable condition. This temper designation applies to products which are not cold worked after cooling from this elevated temperature process, or in which the effect of cold work in flattening or straightening may not be recognized in the mechanical-property limits.

(2) *T2 or TC*. Indicates where a product has been cooled from an elevated-temperature shaping process, cold worked, and subsequently naturally aged to a substantially stable condition. This temper designation applies to those products which are cold worked to improve strength after cooling from an elevated-temperature process, or in which the effect of cold work in flattening or straightening is recognized in the mechanical-property limits.

(3) *T3 or TD*. Indicates where a product has been solution heat treated, cold worked, and subsequently naturally aged to a substantially stable condition. This temper designation applies to those products which are cold worked by a controlled amount to improve their strength after solution heat treatment, or in which the effect of cold work in flattening or straightening is recognized in the mechanical-property limits.

(4) *T4 or TB*. Indicates where a production has been solution heat treated and naturally aged to a substantially stable condition. This temper designation applies to those products which are not cold worked after solution heat treatment, or in which the effect of any cold work in flattening or straightening may not be recognized in the mechanical-property limits.

(5) *T5 or TE*. Indicates where a product has been cooled from an elevated-temperature shaping process and then subsequently artificially aged. This temper designation applies to those products which are not cold worked after cooling from an elevated-temperature shaping process, or in which the effect of cold work in flattening or straightening may not be recognized in the mechanical-property limits.

(6) *T6 or TF*. Indicates where a product has been solution heat treated and then artificially aged. This temper designation applies to those products which are not cold worked after solution heat treatment, or in which the effect of cold work in flattening or straightening may not be recognized in the mechanical-property limits.

(7) *T7 or TM*. Indicates where a product has been solution heat treated and stabilized. This temper designation applies to those products which are stabilized after solution heat treatment to carry them beyond the point of maximum strength to provide some special characteristic.

(8) *T8 or TH*. Indicates where a product has been solution heat treated, cold worked and then artificially aged. This temper designation applies to those products which are cold worked to improve strength, or in which the effect of cold work in flattening or straightening is recognized in the mechanical property limits.

(9) *T9 or TL*. Indicates where a product has been solution heat treated, artificially aged, and then cold worked. This temper designation applies to products which are cold worked to improve strength.

(10) *T10 or TG*. Indicates where a product has been cooled from an elevated-temperature shaping process, cold worked, and then finally artificially aged. This temper designation applies to those products which are cold worked to improve strength, or in which the effects of cold work in flattening or straightening is recognized in the mechanical-property limits.

Additional digits to the T tempers have been assigned for stress-relieved wrought products as follows.

(1) *T*51*. Stress relieved by controlled stretching. This applies to wrought products which have been stretched after solution treatment to give a permanent set of approximately 1.5–3.0%.

(2) *T*52*. Stress relieved by compression.

(3) *T*54*. Stress relieved by combined stretching and compressing.

2.5 Chemical composition and mechanical properties

2.5.1 Chemical composition

The nominal composition of all alloys is defined by the British Standard or other national standards covering the wrought or cast forms and products. The compositions are also defined in the original registration of the alloy in the Aluminum Association register of alloys. In all specifications the presence of the major alloying elements is covered by a percentage range, whilst the presence of the more minor elements is usually restricted to a maximum percentage. Many alloy specifications employ a wide compositional range for the presence of some elements. In some instances two or more alloys may have overlapping compositional ranges, so that identification of the actual alloy by chemical analysis is not clear. Normally, within any specification a manufacturer works to his own in-house composition, which lies within the standard range of composition. The composition of the major aluminium alloys used in construction together with those of the nominally pure aluminium materials is given in *Table 2.5*.

2.5.2 Mechanical properties

2.5.2.1 General

Material and product specifications normally define minimal values, and in some cases maximum values for three principal mechanical tensile properties, ultimate strength, 0.2% proof stress and elongation of the material. These properties will be dependent on the product form, thickness and temper or heat treatment condition of supply. These minimum mechanical properties are given in *Table 2.6* for plate, sheet and strip materials, in *Table 2.7* for extruded bar round tube and sections, in *Table 2.8* for drawn and seam welded tube, in *Table 2.9* for

Table 2.5 Chemical composition (%) of wrought and cast aluminium alloys[a]

Material designation	Silicon	Iron	Copper	Manganese	Magnesium	Chromium	Zinc	Other restrictions	Titanium	Others Each	Others Total	Aluminium
1080A	0.15	0.15	0.03	0.02	0.02	—	0.06	(Ga 0.03)	0.02	0.02	—	99.80 min
1050A	0.25	0.40	0.05	0.05	0.05	—	0.07	—	0.05	0.03	—	99.50 min
1200	1.0 Si + Fe		0.05	0.05	—	—	0.10	—	0.05	0.05	0.15	99.00 min
1350	0.10	0.40	0.05	0.01	—	0.01	0.05	(Ga 0.03, B 0.05, V + Ti 0.02)	—	0.03	0.10	99.50 min
3103	0.50	0.7	0.10	0.9–1.5	0.30	0.10	0.20	(Zr + Ti 0.10)	—	0.05	0.15	Rem
3105	0.6	0.7	0.30	0.30–0.8	0.20–0.8	0.20	0.40		0.10	0.05	0.15	Rem
5083	0.40	0.40	0.10	0.40–1.0	4.0–4.9	0.05–0.25	0.25		0.15	0.05	0.15	Rem
5154A	0.50	0.50	0.10	0.50	3.1–3.9	0.25	0.20	(Mn + Cr 0.10–0.50)	0.20	0.05	0.15	Rem
5251	0.40	0.50	0.15	0.10–0.50	1.7–2.4	0.15	0.15		0.15	0.05	0.15	Rem
5454	0.25	0.40	0.10	0.50–1.0	2.4–3.0	0.05–0.20	0.25		0.20	0.05	0.15	Rem
6061	0.40–0.8	0.7	0.15–0.40	0.15	0.8–1.2	0.04–0.35	0.25		0.15	0.05	0.15	Rem
6063	0.2–0.6	0.35	0.10	0.10	0.45–0.9	0.10	0.10		0.10	0.05	0.15	Rem
6063A	0.30–0.6	0.15–0.35	0.10	0.15	0.6–0.9	0.05	0.15		0.10	0.05	0.15	Rem
6082	0.7–1.3	0.50	0.10	0.40–1.0	0.6–1.2	0.25	0.20		0.10	0.05	0.15	Rem
7020	0.35	0.40	0.20	0.05–0.50	1.0–1.4	0.10–0.35	4.0–5.0	(Zr 0.08–0.20; Zr + Ti 0.08–0.25)	—	0.05	0.15	Rem
LM2	9.0–11.5	1.0	0.7–2.5	0.5	0.30	—	2.0	(Ni 0.5; Pb 0.3; Sn 0.2)	0.2	—	0.05	Rem
LM4	4.0–6.0	0.8	2.0–4.0	0.2–0.6	0.20	—	0.5	(Ni 0.3; Pb 0.1; Sn 0.1)	0.2	0.05	0.15	Rem
LM5	0.3	0.6	0.1	0.3–0.7	3.0–6.0	—	0.1	(Ni 0.1; Pb 0.05; Sn 0.05)	0.2	0.05	0.15	Rem
LM6	10.0–13.0	0.6	0.1	0.5	0.10	—	0.1	(Ni 0.1; Pb 0.1; Sn 0.05)	0.2	0.05	0.15	Rem
LM25	6.5–7.5	0.5	0.20	0.3	0.20–0.6	—	0.1	(Ni 0.1; Pb 0.1; Sn 0.05)	0.2	0.05	0.15	Rem

[a] Compositions are maximum values unless shown as a range or a minimum. Rem. remainder. Table compiled from BS 1470, BS 1474, BS 4300/17, BS 1490 and BS 2897.

Table 2.6 Mechanical properties of aluminium and aluminium alloy plate, sheet and strip materials[a]

Alloy designation British Standard	Alloy designation ISO standards	Product forms	Temper designation	Thickness (mm) Over	Thickness (mm) Up to and including	Minimum 0.2% proof stress (N mm^{-2})	Minimum tensile strength (N mm^{-2})	Elongation (%) $5.65\sqrt{S_0}$	Elongation (%) 50 mm	Durability rating	Related British Standard
1080A	Al 99.80	Plate, sheet, strip	F	3.0	25.0	—	—	—	—	A	BS 1470
			O	0.2	6.0	—	—	—	29–35		
			H14	0.2	12.5	—	90	—	5–8		
			H18	0.2	3.0	—	125	—	3–5		
1050A	Al 99.50	Plate, sheet, strip	F	3.0	25.0	—	—	—	—	A	BS 1470
			O	0.2	6.0	—	55	—	22–32		
			H12	0.2	6.0	—	80	—	4–9		
			H14	0.2	12.5	—	100	—	4–8		
			H18	0.2	3.0	—	135	—	3–4		
1200	Al 99.0	Plate, sheet, strip	F	3.0	25.0	—	—	—	—	A	BS 1470
			O	0.2	6.0	—	70	—	20–30		
			H12	0.2	6.0	—	90	—	4–9		
			H14	0.2	12.5	—	105	—	3–6		
			H16	0.2	6.0	—	125	—	2–4		
			H18	0.2	3.0	—	140	—	2–4		
1350	Al 99.50	Sheet, strip	O	—	—	—	—	—	25	A	BS 2897
			H4	—	—	—	95	—	8		
			H8	—	—	—	145	—	3		
3103	Al Mn1	Plate, sheet, strip	F	0.2	25.0	—	—	—	—	A	BS 1470
			O	0.2	6.0	—	90	—	20–25		
			H12	0.2	6.0	—	120	—	5–9		
			H14	0.2	12.5	—	140	—	3–7		
			H16	0.2	6.0	—	160	—	2–4		
			H18	0.2	3.0	—	175	—	2–4		

Designation		Form	Condition	Thickness over (mm)	Thickness up to (mm)	0.2% proof stress (N/mm²)	Tensile strength (N/mm²)	Elongation on 5.65√So (%)	Elongation on 50 mm (%)	Standard	Note
3105	Al Mn Mg	Sheet, strip	O	0.2	3.0	—	110	—	16–20	BS 1470	A
			H12	0.2	3.0	115	130	—	2–5		
			H14	0.2	3.0	145	160	—	2–4		
			H16	0.2	3.0	170	185	—	1–3		
			H18	0.2	3.0	190	215	—	1–2		
5083	Al Mg4.5 Mn	Plate, sheet, strip	F	2.0	25.0	—	—	14	12–16	BS 1470	A
			O	0.2	80.0	125	275	—	5–8		
			H22	0.2	6.0	235	310	—	4–8		
			H24	0.2	6.0	270	345	—			
5154A	Al Mg3.5	Sheet, strip	O	0.2	6.0	85	215	—	12–18	BS 1470	A
			H22	0.2	6.0	165	245	—	5–8		
			H24	0.2	6.0	225	275	—	4–6		
5251	Al Mg2	Plate, sheet, strip	F	3.0	25.0	—	—	—	—	BS 1470	A
			O	0.2	6.0	60	160	—	18–20		
			H22	0.2	6.0	130	200	—	4–8		
			H24	0.2	6.0	175	225	—	3–5		
			H28	0.2	3.0	215	255	—	2–4		
5454	Al Mg3 Mn	Plate, sheet, strip	F	3.0	25.0	—	—	—	—	BS 1470	A
			O	0.2	6.0	80	215	—	12–18		
			H22	0.2	3.0	180	250	—	4–8		
			H24	0.2	3.0	200	270	—	3–6		
6082	Al Si1 Mg Mn	Plate, sheet, strip	O	0.2	3.0	—	—	—	15–16	BS 1470	B
			T4	0.2	3.0	120	200	—	15		
				3.0	25.0	115	200	12	—		
			T6	0.2	3.0	255	295	—	8		
				3.0	25.0	240	295	—	8		
		Plate	T451	6.0	90.0	115	200	15	—		
		Plate	T561	6.0	90.0	240	295	8	—		
				90.0	115.0	230	285	7	—		
				115.0	150.0	220	275	6	—		
7020	Al Zn4.5 Mg1	Plate, sheet, strip	TB	0.2	25.0	170	280	10	12	BS 4300/14	C
			TF	0.2	25.0	270	320	8	10		

ª Table compiled from BS 1470, BS 2897 and BS 4300/14.

Table 2.7 Mechanical properties of aluminium and aluminium alloy extruded bar, round tube and sections[a]

Alloy designation British Standard	Alloy designation ISO standards	Product forms	Temper designation	Thickness or diameter (mm) Over	Thickness or diameter (mm) Up to and including	Minimum 0.2% proof stress (N mm^{-2})	Minimum tensile strength (N mm^{-2})	Elongation (%) 5.65$\sqrt{S_0}$	Elongation (%) 50 mm	Durability rating	Related British Standard
1050A	Al 99.50	All	F	—	—	—	60[b]	25[b]	23[b]	A	BS 1474
1200	Al 99.0	All	F	—	—	—	65[b]	20[b]	18[b]	A	BS 1474
1350	Al 99.50	All	M	—	—	—	60	25	23	A	BS 2898
			H2	—	—	—	85	15	13		
5083	Al Mg4.5 Mn	All	O	—	150	125	275	14	13	A	BS 1474
			F	—	150	130[b]	280[b]	12[b]	11[b]		
5154A	Al Mg3.5	All	O	—	150	85	215	18	16	A	BS 1474
			F	—	150	100[b]	215[b]	16[b]	14[b]		
5251	Al Mg2	All	F	—	150	60[b]	170[b]	16[b]	14[b]	A	BS 1474
6061	Al Mg1 Si Cu	All	T4	—	150	115	190	16	14	B	BS 1474
			T6	—	150	240	280	8	7		
6063	Al Mg0.7 Si	All	O	—	200	—	140[c]	15	13	B	BS 1474
			F	—	200	—	100[b]	13[b]	12[b]		
			T4	—	150	70	130	16	14		
				150	200	70	120	13	—		
			T5	—	25	110	150	8	7		
			T6	—	150	160	195	8	7		
				150	200	130	150	6	—		
6063A	Al Mg0.7 SiA	All	T4	—	25	90	150	14	12	B	BS 1474
			T5	—	25	160	200	8	7		
			T6	—	25	190	230	8	7		
6082	Al Si1 Mg Mn	All	O	—	200	—	170[c]	16	14	B	BS 1474
			F	—	200	120	110[b]	13[b]	12[b]		
			T4	—	150	100	190	16	14		
				150	200		170	13	—		
			T5	—	6	230	270	—	—		
			T6	—	20	255	295	8	8		
			T6510	20	150	270	310	8	7		
				150	200	240	280	5	—		
7020	Al Zn4.5 Mg1	All	TB	—	25	190	300	12	10	C	BS 4300/14
			TF	—	25	280	340	10	8		

[a] Table compiled from BS 1474, BS 2898 and BS 4300/15. [b] Typical properties. [c] Maximum permitted value.

Table 2.8 Mechanical properties of aluminium and aluminium alloy drawn tube and seam-welded tube[a]

Alloy designation British Standard	Alloy designation ISO standards	Product forms	Temper designation	Wall thickness (mm) Over	Wall thickness (mm) Up to and including	Minimum 0.2% proof stress (N mm^{-2})	Minimum tensile strength (N mm^{-2})	Elongation (%) $5.65\sqrt{S_0}$	Elongation (%) 50 mm	Durability rating	Related British Standard
1050A	Al 99.50	Drawn tube	O	—	12	—	95[b]	—	—	A	BS 1471
			H4	—	12	—	100	—	—		
			H8	—	12	—	135	—	—		
1200	Al 99.0	Drawn tube	O	—	12	—	105[b]	—	—	A	BS 1471
			H4	—	12	—	110	—	—		
			H8	—	12	—	140	—	—		
5083	Al Mg4.5 Mn	Drawn tube	O	—	10	125	275	12	—	A	BS 1471
			H2	—	10	235	310	5	—		
5154A	Al Mg3.5	Drawn tube	O	—	10	85	215	16	—	A	BS 1471
			H4	—	10	200	245	4	—		
5251	Al Mg2	Drawn tube	O	—	10	60	160	18	—	A	BS 1471
			H	—	10	175	225	5	—		
		Seam-welded tube	M	0.8	1.0	220	245	—	3	A	BS 4300/1
				1.2	2.0	220	245	—	5		
6061	Al Mg1 Si Cu	Drawn tube	TB	—	6	115	215	—	12	B	BS 1471
				6	10	115	215	—	14		
			TF	—	6	240	295	—	7		
				6	10	225	295	—	9		
6063	Al Mg0.7 Si	Drawn tube	O	—	10	—	155[b]	—	—	B	BS 1471
			TB	—	10	100	155	—	15		
			TF	—	10	180	200	—	8		
6082	Al Si1 Mg Mn	Drawn tube	TB	—	6	115	215	—	12	B	BS 1471
				6	10	115	215	—	14		
			TF	—	6	255	310	—	7		
				6	10	240	310	—	9		

[a] Table compiled from BS 1471 and BS 4300/1. [b] Maximum permitted value.

Table 2.9 Mechanical properties of aluminium and aluminium alloy ingots and castings[a]

Alloy designation British Standard	Alloy designation ISO standards	Product forms	Temper designation	Minimum tensile strength ($N\,mm^{-2}$)	Elongation[c] on $5.65\sqrt{S_0}$ (%)	Durability rating	Related British Standard
LM2	Al Si10 Cu2	Gravity die cast	M	150	1–3	C	BS 1490
		Pressure die cast	M	150	—		
LM4	Al Si5 Cu3	Sand cast	M	140	2	C	BS 1490
		Gravity die cast	M	160	2		
		Sand cast	TF	230	—		
		Gravity die cast	TF	280	—		
LM5	Al Mg5 Si1	Sand cast	M	140	3	A	BS 1490
		Gravity die cast	M	170	5		
LM6	Al Si12	Sand cast	M	160	5	B	BS 1490
		Gravity die cast	M	190	7		
LM25	Al Si7 Mg0.5	Sand cast	M	130	2		
		Gravity die cast	M	160	3		
		Sand cast	TE	150	1		
		Gravity die cast	TE	190	2		
		Sand cast	TB7	160	2.5		
		Gravity die cast	TB7	230	5		
		Sand cast	TF	230	—		
		Gravity die cast	TF	280	2		

[a] Table compiled from BS 1490.

forging and forging stock and in *Table 2.10* for ingots and castings.

2.5.2.2 Tensile strength

The tensile strength of aluminium and aluminium alloys, as for other metals is defined by the stress required to break in a tensile testing machine a test piece of standard dimensions as defined in BS 18. The values of tensile strength increase with work hardening or heat treatment for any alloy and, in addition, vary with thickness and for various product forms. Nominally pure aluminium in the annealed condition has the lowest tensile strength, whilst the more alloyed materials in the fully heat-treated condition offer the highest strength. Alloys such as 2014A used in special applications such as aerospace and defence are available with properties considerably in excess of any alloy given in *Tables 2.5* to *2.10*. Compressive strength is rarely specified for aluminium alloys normally used in construction and is generally taken as the same as the tensile strength.

2.5.2.3 Proof strength

Aluminium and aluminium alloys do not show a sharply defined yield point during test. In order to define the shape of the stress–strain curve, BS 18 defines the proof stress as that stress which produces, whilst the load is still applied, a non-proportional extension equal to the specified percentage of the extension gauge length. In general, this extension is specified as 0.2% for aluminium.

Figure 2.9 shows the form of the stress–strain curves for some aluminium alloys, including 2014A a very high strength aerospace alloy. The relationship between 0.2% proof stress and ultimate stress depends not only on the alloy but on the temper or degree of heat treatment.

2.5.2.4 Elongation

Elongation is a useful guide to the ductility of a material and

is determined as a percentage of a stated gauge length inscribed in the tensile specimen. The gauge length is determined by the form of the test piece. The choice of the test piece depends on the size and form of the product but is normally either a proportionally round test piece when the gauge length is $5.65\sqrt{S_0}$, where S_0 is the cross-sectional area of the test piece, or a rectangular test piece when a 50 mm gauge length is used.

2.5.3 Non-specification mechanical properties

2.5.3.1 Shear strength

Shear strengths of aluminium alloys vary widely with alloy and temper from below $60\,N\,mm^{-2}$ for annealed commercially pure material to over $200\,N\,mm^{-2}$ for fully heat treated 6082 material.

2.5.3.2 Bearing strength

Bearing yield strength varies between 1.5 and 1.8 times the tensile 0.2% proof stress depending on alloy and temper.

2.5.3.3 Hardness

Hardness is not normally specified as there is no simple relationship between tensile strength and hardness, but it is sometimes used as a coarse indication of tensile strength during inspection. Typical Vickers hardness values range from 20 for commercially pure annealed material to in excess of 100 for fully heat treated alloys and fully tempered non-heat-treatable materials.

2.5.3.4 Impact strength

Impact testing generally has no real significance to aluminium alloys as there is no transition temperature below which brittle fracture occurs. In fact the mechanical properties improve as the temperature decreases.

Table 2.10 Mechanical properties of aluminium and aluminium alloy forging stock and forgings[a]

Alloy designation British Standard	Alloy designation ISO standards	Product forms	Temper designation[b]	Thickness (mm) Over	Thickness (mm) Up to and including	Minimum 0.2% proof stress (N mm^{-2})	Minimum tensile strength (N mm^{-2})	Minimum elongation on $5.65\sqrt{S_0}$ (%)	Durability rating	Related British Standard
1050A	Al 99.50	Forged	M	—	150	—	60	22	A	BS 1472
5083	Al Mg4.5 Mn	Forged, extruded	M	—	150	130	280	12	A	BS 1472
5154A	Al Mg3.5	Forged, extruded	M	—	150	100	215	16	A	BS 1472
5251	Al Mg2	Forged, extruded	M	—	150	60	170	16	A	BS 1472
6063	Al Mg0.7 Si	Forged, extruded	TB	—	150	85	140	16	B	BS 1472
				150	200	85	125	13		
			TF	—	150	160	185	10		
				150	200	130	150	6		
6082	Al Si1 Mg Mn	Forged	TB	—	150	120	185	16	B	BS 1472
		Extruded	TB	—	150	120	190	16		
				150	200	100	170	13		
		Forged	TF	—	150	255	295	8		
		Extruded	TF	—	20	255	295	8		
				20	150	270	310	8		
				150	200	240	280	5		

[a] Table compiled from BS 1472. [b] Properties in M condition for information only.

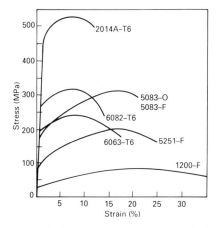

Figure 2.9 Stress–strain curves for some aluminium alloys

Most alloys used in general construction are not subject to unstable crack growth in the elastic stress field and their fracture toughness is high. Tests to determine fracture toughness are normally applied to the high-strength alloys, particularly aerospace materials.

2.6 Physical properties

The physical properties of aluminium and aluminium alloys vary by a usually small degree from alloy to alloy as well as with form, size, shape, temper and heat-treatment condition. The mechanical properties of the alloys in various tempers and degrees of heat treatment are limited by official specifications, but many physical properties are not.

2.6.1 Density

The density of aluminium is approximately one-third that of steel and copper. Pure aluminium has a density of 2.6898 g cm^{-3}. Small amounts of alloying element produce both cast and wrought alloys with a density range of 2.66–2.80 g cm^{-3}.

2.6.2 Modulus of elasticity

The Young's modulus of aluminium is about one-third that of steel and for pure aluminium has a value of 68.3 GPa. The modulus varies in value for the alloys up to 74 GPa for the high strength copper bearing alloys.

2.6.3 Coefficient of thermal expansion

Pure aluminium has a coefficient of thermal expansion approximately twice that of steel at 23.5×10^{-6}°C^{-1} over the range 10–100°C. Alloying elements have a small effect, producing a range of $20–25 \times 10^{-6}$°C^{-1} for casting alloys and $22–24 \times 10^{-6}$°C^{-1} for wrought alloys.

2.6.4 Thermal conductivity

Aluminium is a good conductor of heat with a conductivity of pure aluminium of 244 W m^{-1} °C^{-1}, about 4.5 times greater than that for steel. The thermal conductivity reduces with increased alloying to 109 W m^{-1} °C^{-1} for wrought alloys and to below 100 W m^{-1} °C^{-1} for some casting alloys.

2.6.5 Electrical resistivity and conductivity

Pure aluminium has a high electrical conductivity at 63% of the International Annealed Copper Standard (IACS) and an electrical resistivity of 2.69 $\mu\Omega$ cm at 20°C. These values increase with alloying to a resistance of over 6 $\mu\Omega$ cm at 20°C for some alloys and a conductivity down to below 28% IACS.

2.6.6 Melting point

Pure aluminium melts at 660°C but the presence of alloying elements reduces the melting point by up to 130°C depending on the alloy.

2.6.7 Ductility

Whilst elongation is a useful measure of the ductility, where a material is to be formed, further tests such as a bend test are further indication of the workability of the alloy. Where deep drawing is to be performed, a cupping test is used where a punch is forced into a clamped portion of sheet. The depth of penetration at fracture indicates the ability of the material to be deep drawn. Such methods show up coarse-grain structure and variations in directional properties which can prevent successful forming.

2.6.8 Non-magnetic properties

Aluminium and aluminium alloys are regarded as non-magnetic with a magnetic susceptibility or ratio of their magnetization to the magnetizing force at 18°C of 0.63×10^{-6}.

2.6.9 Dielectric properties

The natural oxide film has dielectric properties which can be enhanced by electrolytic anodizing.

2.6.10 Reflectivity

A clean bright surface of commercially pure aluminium reflects 80–85% of visible incident radiation, and about 90% of heat radiation. Special electrical and chemical treatments are required to develop and maintain the full reflecting power of aluminium. Emissivity varies with wavelength, but is typically 0.30 for a wavelength of 0.65 μm.

2.6.11 Affinity for oxygen

Aluminium has a natural affinity for oxygen, forming a protective layer of aluminium oxide on exposure to air.

2.6.12 Resistance to food and chemicals

Aluminium is an inert non-toxic metal which can safely be used in contact with most foodstuffs, but protection is required against the acid action of some products. The metal is resistant to many chemical substances including ammonia, sulphuretted hydrogen nitric and acetic acids, but is adversely affected by most alkalis, sulphuric and hydrochloric acids, chlorides and carbonates and fluorides.

2.7 Special properties

2.7.1 Creep

Only commercially pure aluminium shows any significant creep at room temperature. If, however, the working temperature is raised to around 200–250°C for prolonged periods, the creep characteristics of some alloys need to be considered.

2.7.2 Fatigue strength

Aluminium alloys with the exception of some of the aluminium magnesium alloys, do not exhibit endurance or S–N curves which flatten out at high cycle values. As the alloys do not show this 'fatigue limit', a maximum stress is normally quoted for a given life. Typical values of fatigue strength at 50×10^6 cycles range from 20 MPa for annealed commercially pure material to 124 MPa for 6082-T6 material. 5083 and 5154A alloys with high manganese content exhibit higher values. Where welding details or other forms of joint are involved, the fatigue life can be seriously affected. Certain welded-joint details can greatly reduce the fatigue strength.

2.7.3 Properties at elevated temperatures

In general, aluminium and aluminium alloys show a reduction in strength at temperatures much above 100°C. At 200°C the strength is approximately half that at room temperature and above 350°C most alloys have lost almost all their strength. Aluminium alloys melt in the range 550–650°C depending on the alloy. On cooling from elevated temperatures, the original strength is not restored as the effects of work hardening or heat treatment are, to some extent, removed by heating and the structure is permanently changed. The more prolonged the period of exposure to elevated temperature the more significant the permanent loss of strength.

2.7.4 Low-temperature properties

Aluminium and aluminium alloys generally exhibit higher tensile strengths and elongations at sub-zero temperatures than at room temperature. No alloys suffer from brittleness at low temperature and there is no point below which brittle fracture occurs.

2.7.5 Fire

If aluminium or aluminium alloys are exposed to a fire sufficient to raise the temperature of the metal to between 550 and 650°C then, depending on the alloy, the metal will melt. In the normal forms of plate, sheet, extrusion, forgings and castings, wire and foil the metal will not burn. As with other metals, aluminium and aluminium alloys in the form of finely divided powder or flakes can be made to burn. Aluminium is rated as non-combustible as defined by BS 476: Part 4 and provides a class-1 surface for spread of flame when tested in accordance with BS 476: Part 5. Because the metal melts, advantage can be taken of the fire venting that occurs with aluminium cladding in localizing the fire, preventing the spread of heat and smoke and reducing any consequent damage. Where fire resistance is required, the metal must be insulated to prevent the temperature rising above a specific temperature (usually 200°C) during the required time period.

2.7.6 Thermite sparking

Thermite sparking occurs when a glancing blow by a steel or aluminium striker initiates a transfer of oxygen between intimately mixed aluminium and rust particles. The mechanism requires a single impact on a smear of aluminium on rusty steel. Actual ignitions of inflammable gas mixture by thermite sparks are exceedingly rare as they require exacting preconditions for their occurrence. The preconditions include the gas/air mixture, the quality of the smear, the impact angle, the rigidity of the impacted body, the alloying elements of the metal and the newness of the smear.

2.8 Durability and protection

2.8.1 Inherent corrosion resistance

Aluminium has a high resistance to corrosion due to a film of aluminium oxide which begins to form as soon as the metal is exposed to air. This film slowly increases in thickness, with the rate of increase falling off after a number of days. Then no further oxidation takes place unless the film is ruptured. The film is hard and strongly adherent and forms more rapidly and to a greater thickness at high temperatures and at high humidity. This invisible oxide layer protects the underlying surface of the metal indefinitely, but prolonged exposure to a moist atmosphere causes slight corrosion, with a visible film which is white to grey depending on the alloying elements present. This corrosion film can easily be rubbed off leaving the original permanent protective film behind. In many instances the aluminium alloys listed in *Table 2.5* can be used in the mill finish condition without the need for added protection. Chlorides and sulphates in the atmosphere increase the rate of attack and produce a rougher surface under which superficial pitting is formed. As the atmosphere becomes more aggressive, the roughening will be worse and the oxide film may become soluble. The metal then ceases to be fully protected and added protection may be necessary.

In coastal and marine environments the surface of unprotected metal will roughen and acquire a grey, stone-like appearance and some alloys require protection. Where aluminium is immersed in freshwater or seawater, special precautions may be necessary. Where corrosion of the surface does occur the rate normally follows a negative exponential form and, after an initial fairly rapid weathering during the first few months, there is very little further change over extensive periods of 20–30 or even up to 80 years.

2.8.2 Durability of alloys

The alloys listed in *Tables 2.6–2.10* are categorized into three ratings (A, B and C) in descending order of durability. These ratings may be used to guide the user on the need and degree of protection required. In constructions employing more than one alloy, including filler wires in welded construction, the protection should be chosen in accordance with the lowest durability ratings.

2.8.3 Protection

2.8.3.1 Overall protection

The need to provide overall protection to aluminium and aluminium alloy components constructed from the alloys or combination of alloys listed in *Tables 2.6–2.10*, when exposed to different environments, is given in *Table 2.11*. When selecting the appropriate column for an atmospheric environment in *Table 2.11*, it should be remembered that there may be localities within a region that have microclimates vastly different from the environmental characteristics of the region as a whole. A rural region may, for example, have a local environment more closely resembling an industrial atmosphere at sites close to and downwind of factories. Similarly, a site near the sea but close to shore-based industrial installations may, with the appropriate prevailing winds, have the characteristics of an industrial, rather than marine, atmosphere. The environment may not necessarily be the same for a component inside a building as it is for one outside.

Because of these factors, localized conditions of greater severity may result and the precise conditions prevailing at the actual location should be studied before deciding on the appropriate environment column of *Table 2.11*.

(i) Methods of overall protection Where aluminium or aluminium alloys require added protection, the protection system applied to parts, or all, of the construction should be chosen carefully by the designer. Where there is a direct aesthetic content, the aluminium surface may be given decorative finishes such as by painting, anodizing or certain chemical conversion processes described in Section 2.10. These processes will also impart varying degrees of protection to the aluminium.

Where painting is required this should be preceded by appropriate pretreatment, and the subsequent operations should be carried out in sequence without intermediate delays. Surfaces should be thoroughly dry, and the coatings applied preferably when the ambient temperature is above 4°C. Painting of contact surfaces should also be included.

The surface should be cleaned, dried and thoroughly degreased using an appropriate organic solvent, and treated to ensure paint adhesion. This may involve mechanical roughening with abrasive paper or abrasive-impregnated nylon pads or by abrasive blasting, provided that, in each case, the abrasive is either alumina or other non-metallic and copper free grit. Other materials may contaminate the surface of the aluminium. Mechanical roughening may be done with corrosion-resistant steel-wire brushes. Alternatively, paint adhesion may be promoted by the use of a chromate conversion coating, etch primer or wash primer, provided that the metal surface is clean and free from thick or irregular oxide coatings.

The pretreated or metal-sprayed surfaces should first receive a priming coat with an inhibiting pigment containing zinc chromate or other approved chromate, in a suitable water-resistant vehicle. The priming coat and all subsequent coats should not contain any copper, mercury or tin compounds, graphite or carbonaceous materials and, preferably, no lead compounds as these would be detrimental to the aluminium.

The primed surface is then painted with one or more coats of paint chosen to suit the environment. This paint must be

Table 2.11 General protection of aluminium structures

Alloy durability rating	Material thickness (mm)	Requirement according to environment[a]							
		Atmospheric						Immersed	
		Rural	Industrial/urban		Marine			Freshwater	Seawater
			Moderate	Severe	Non-industrial Moderate	Moderate	Severe		
A	All	None	None	P	None	None	P	None	None
B	<3	None	P	P	P	P	P	P	P
	≥3	None	None	P	None	None	P	P	P
C	All	None	P[b]	P	P	P	P	P[c]	NR

[a] P, protection; NR, not recommended. [b] Requires only local protection to weld and heat-affected zones in urban non-industrial environments. [c] Not recommended if of welded construction.

Table 2.12 Additional protection at metal-to-metal contacts to combat crevice and galvanic effects

Metal joined to aluminium	Bolt or rivet metal	Procedure according to environment								
		Atmospheric				Marine			Immersed	
		Rural		Industrial/urban		Non-industrial	Industrial		Freshwater	Seawater
		Dry un-polluted	Mild	Moderate	Severe		Moderate	Severe		
Aluminium	Aluminium	0	0	0	2	2	0	2	0	2
	Steel, aluminized or galvanized steel, stainless steel	1	1	3	4	4	3	4	5	5
Zinc or zinc coated steel	Aluminium	0	0	2	2	2	2	2	2	5
	Steel, aluminized or galvanized steel, stainless steel	1	1	3	4	4	3	4	5	5
Steel, stainless steel, cast iron, lead	Aluminium	0	0	3	3	3	3	3	5	5
	Steel, aluminized or galvanized steel, stainless steel	1	1	4	4	4	4	4	5	5
Copper[a]	Aluminium	0	NR	NR	NR	NR	NR	NR	NR	NR
	Copper, copper alloy	0	3	5	5	5	5	5	5	5

[a] Contact surfaces and joints of aluminium to copper or copper alloys should be avoided if possible. If they are used, the aluminium should be of durability rating A or B, and the bolts and nuts should be of copper or copper alloy. NR, not recommended.

compatible with both the priming coat and any subsequent coats. An aluminium paint system can be used consisting of a non-leafing undercoat and leafing finishing coat. Bituminous paint conforming to BS 3416 is also recommended for normal use, with dip-applied hot bitumen as an alternative. The materials should be applied direct to a roughened surface.

Aluminium materials may be supplied ready painted, using either a liquid-solvent based or a dry-powder coating process as described in Section 2.10. These finishes can be applied prior to fabrication, to partly fabricated material, or following fabrication.

2.8.3.2 Metal-to-metal contacts including joints

Additional consideration should be given to the protection of contacting surfaces in crevices and the contact between aluminium and certain other metals or washings from these metals which can cause electrochemical attack of aluminium. Such conditions can occur within a component or structures. Contact surfaces and joints of aluminium to aluminium or to other metals, and contact surfaces in bolted, riveted and welded constructions, may need additional protection. *Table 2.12* indicates by a number a degree of protection that may be necessary to provide a durable system in the proposed environment. The numbers in *Table 2.12* indicate varying degrees from 0 to 5 of added protection which are necessary to provide a totally durable system. Full details are contained in CP 118, but are generally as follows.

(*i*) *Protection procedure 0* No additional treatment shall be applied.

(*ii*) *Protection procedure 1* The heads of steel bolts and rivets may, for appearance, be overpainted with a priming coat,

followed by a coat of aluminium paint; protection is otherwise not required.

(*iii*) *Protection procedure 2* Both contact surfaces, including bolt and rivet holes, should be cleaned and pretreated before assembly, and receive one priming coat of paint extending beyond the contact area. The surfaces should be brought together while the priming coat is still wet. Subsequently, the heads of steel bolts and rivets, and the surrounding areas, should be overpainted with at least one priming coat, care being taken to seal all crevices and edges. Where stainless-steel fasteners are used there is generally no need to overpaint the heads of these fasteners for protective purposes.

(*iv*) *Protection procedure 3* Procedure 2 should be followed, but additional protection should be given by a robust impervious tape insulant applied onto and extending beyond the contact surfaces. This should be applied before assembly, but after the priming coat on the contacting surfaces is dry. A neoprene gasket or washer may be used instead of tape where suitable. Additional protection may also be provided on assembly by using a two-pack polysulphide elastomeric jointing compound.

(*v*) *Protection procedure 4* Procedure 3 should be followed, but the heads of steel bolts, rivets and the surrounding areas around any junctions with steel or cast iron, that are not already metal sprayed or galvanized, should be metal sprayed with aluminium. The spraying can be done either before or, preferably, after assembly and then overpainted with at least one priming coat of paint. A lesser degree of protection is afforded by a chlorinated rubber or zinc rich paint system, instead of metal spraying.

(*vi*) *Protection procedure 5* Procedure 4 should be followed, but in addition full electrical insulation between the two metals should be ensured by insertion of non-absorbent non-conducting gaskets and washers to prevent metallic and electrical contact between the different metals of the joint.

2.8.3.3 Contact with other non-metallic materials

(i) Contact with concrete, masonry or plaster Aluminium in contact with dense compact concrete, masonry or plaster in a dry unpolluted or mild environment can suffer from corrosion. To prevent attack, the contacting surface should be coated with at least one coat of bituminous paint. In an industrial or marine environment at least two coats of heavy-duty bituminous paint should be used with the surface of the contacting material similarly painted. Submerged contact between aluminium and these materials is not recommended, but if unavoidable the use of a suitable mastic or a heavy duty damp course separation layer is recommended. Lightweight and similar concrete products can require additional consideration when water or damp can extract a steady supply of aggressive alkali from the cement.

(ii) Embedment in concrete Where aluminium is embedded in concrete it should first be protected with at least two coats of bituminous paint or hot bitumen, the coats extending at least 75 mm above the concrete surface after embedment. Where the concrete contains chlorides, at least two coats of plasticized coal-tar pitch are recommended, and the finished assembly should be overpainted locally to seal the surface with the same material, after the concrete has fully set. Care should also be taken to avoid metallic contact in the concrete between the embedded aluminium parts and any steel reinforcement.

(iii) Contact with timber Timber in contact with aluminium should be primed and painted in accordance with good practice for industrial, damp or marine environments.

Some wood preservatives are harmful to aluminium. As a general guide the following preservatives are considered safe for use with aluminium without special precautions: coal-tar creosote; coal-tar oil; chlorinated naphthalenes; zinc napthanates; pentachlorophenol; organo-tin oxides; *o*-phenylphenol; fluorochrome arsenate dinitrophenol.

Preservatives containing copper naphthenate, copper–chrome, copper–chrome–arsenate or borax–boric acid should not be used unless special precautions are taken to seal the surface of contact. Preservatives containing zinc chloride, mercury salts or copper sulphate should not be used in association with aluminium. Where there are through fastenings in oak, chestnut and western red cedar, these should be avoided as they are likely to be harmful to aluminium unless the timber is well seasoned.

(iv) Contact with soils Where aluminium is buried in soil the surface should be protected with at least two coats of bituminous paint, hot bitumen, or plasticized coal-tar pitch. Additional wrapping tapes may be used to prevent mechanical damage to the coating.

(v) Immersion in water Where aluminium parts are immersed in freshwater or seawater, aluminium alloys of durability rating A should be used. *Table 2.12* gives the protection requirements for freshwater and seawater immersion.

(vi) Contact with chemicals used in the building industry Fungicides and mould repellents may contain metal compounds based on copper, mercury, tin and lead which, under wet or damp conditions, could cause corrosion of the aluminium. These effects may be countered by protecting the contacting surfaces. Some

cleaning materials can also affect the surface of the aluminium, and care should be taken to ensure that the effects will not be detrimental to the aluminium. Quick and adequate water rinsing will often be adequate, but temporary measures may be necessary to protect the aluminium from contact with the cleaners.

(vii) Contact with insulating materials used in the construction industry Products such as glass fibre, polyurethane and various rigid products may contain corrosive agents which can be extracted under moist conditions and may damage the aluminium. Insulating materials should be tested for compatibility with aluminium under damp and saline conditions. Where problems are likely to occur, a sealant should be applied to the aluminium surfaces.

2.9 Materials selection

The choice of a suitable material for any application of aluminium to construction is determined by a combination of factors—strength, durability, physical properties, weldability, formability and availability—both in the alloy and particular form required. The alloys listed in *Table 2.5* are described below subdivided into heat-treatable and non-heat-treatable alloys. The alloys are also given a durability rating which is used in Section 2.8.

2.9.1 Heat-treatable alloys

2.9.1.1 General

Alloys in the series 2***, 6*** and 7*** are described as heat treatable, and the following are those heat-treatable aluminium alloys considered applicable to general construction.

2.9.1.2 Alloy 6082

The commonest of the heat-treatable alloys and the principal structural alloy used in the UK is the medium-strength alloy, 6082 (Al Si1 Mg Mn). It is available in most forms; solid and hollow extrusions, plate, sheet, tube and forging, and of durability rating B. It is usually used in the fully heat-treated condition (i.e. 6082-T6), and in welded and non-welded structures. The choice of this alloy is based on its combination of properties of formability, weldability, moderate corrosion resistance and medium strength after heat treatment. Care must be taken to account for the loss of strength in welded joints in the heat-affected zone (HAZ). This is a commonly used alloy for shapes from stock.

2.9.1.3 Alloy 6061

Alloy 6061 (Al Mg1 Si Cu) is an alternative alloy to 6082 and is the principal structural alloy used in North America. It is normally available in extrusion and tube, but can be produced in sheet on special request. The alloy has a durability rating B and has very similar properties to 6082 with a slight improvement in formability and surface finish. However, it has a slightly lower strength and is more difficult to extrude.

2.9.1.4 Alloy 6063

Alloy 6063 (Al Mg0.7 Si) is used in applications where strength is not of paramount importance and must be compromised with appearance. It is available in extrusions, tube and forging and is particularly suitable for thin-walled and intricate extruded sections. The alloy is of durability rating B and is preferred to

6082, because it combines moderate strength with good durability and surface finish and the ability to be extruded into intricate shapes. It is particularly responsive to anodizing and similar patented finishing processes. The strength properties of 6063 are less than 6082 and, like the latter, there is a loss of strength in welded joints in the heat-affected zone. It is the most commonly used alloy for shapes from stock. It is used mainly for architectural applications such as curtain walling and window frames.

2.9.1.5 Alloy 6063A

Alloy 6063A (Al Mg0.7 Si A) is available in extruded forms only. Of durability rating A, it offers an increased strength over 6063 in the fully heat-treated condition whilst still retaining most of the benefits of 6063. It is used extensively in architectural applications where strengths in excess of those obtained from 6063 are required.

2.9.1.6 Alloy 7020

Alloy 7020 (Al Zn4.5 Mg1) is available in simple extruded shapes and in sheet and plate. It is of the lower durability rating C, but has a better post-weld strength than the 6*** series alloys. This is due to its natural ageing properties, although it is not only restricted to welded structures. The material is, however, sensitive to environmental conditions and for satisfactory performance the correct methods of manufacture and fabrication must be followed together with a control of composition and mechanical properties. If cold worked in the fully heat-treated condition the alloy is susceptible to stress corrosion cracking and close collaboration between the designer, user, manufacturer and fabricator is essential.

2.9.1.7 Alloy LM4

Alloy LM4 (Al Si5 Cu3) is a casting alloy of durability rating C which can be heat treated to moderate levels of mechanical properties to sustain relatively high static loading. It is the most used and versatile of casting alloys but is seldom pressure die cast. Its foundry characteristics permit its use for fairly thin or thick sections and where pressure tightness is required. Other applications include handles and casings.

2.9.1.8 Alloy LM25

Alloy LM25 (Al Si7 Mg0.5) is a general-purpose casting alloy with excellent foundry characteristics, high resistance to corrosion and good mechanical properties suitable for many applications. It has a durability rating B. It is available in four conditions of heat treatment in both sand and gravity die castings, where hardness, strength and impact resistance can be increased to high levels and is mainly used for architectural and food-manufacturing installations.

2.9.2 Non-heat-treatable alloys

2.9.2.1 General

Alloys in the series 1***, 3*** and 5*** are described as non-heat-treatable, and the following are those non-heat-treatable aluminium alloys considered applicable to general construction.

2.9.2.2 Alloy 1080A

Alloy 1080A (Al99.80) is principally available in sheet form but can be made in simple extruded sections. It is commercially pure, with a durability rating A, and is highly resistant to chemical attack and weathering. It is easily worked and welded but is one of the lowest strength aluminium alloy. It is used where its very high purity is important and where ductility is critical, such as with worked flashings.

2.9.2.3 Alloy 1050A

Alloy 1050A (Al99.50) is generally available in sheet and plate, but also in simple extrusions, drawn tube and forgings. It is commercially pure, with a durability rating A, and is highly resistant to chemical attack and weathering. It is easily worked and welded but is one of the lowest strength aluminium alloy. It is used where high purity is important and where ductility is critical, such as with worked flashings and formed trim.

2.9.2.4 Alloy 1200

Alloy 1200 (Al99.0) is generally available in plate and sheet forms only, but can also be used in simple extruded sections and drawn tube. It is of durability rating A. It is a commercially pure aluminium with high ductility, and is highly resistant to chemical attack and weathering. It has a very good general corrosion resistance. Although it is available in tempered forms, it is used for architectural work where components are not highly stressed and for chemical-process equipment.

2.9.2.5 Alloy 1350

Alloy 1350 (Al99.50) is normally available in simple extrusions and tube but can be rolled into sheet for special requirements. It has a durability rating A and with conductivity of 61.5 of the International Annealed Copper Standard IACS. It is used principally for electrical bus-bar, lightning conductor and other applications where its low resistivity is critical.

2.9.2.6 Alloy 3103

Alloy 3103 (Al Mn1) is of durability rating A and is available in sheet and plate forms only. It is stronger and harder than 'commercially pure' aluminium but has the same high ductility, weldability and very good corrosion resistance. It is used extensively for building sheet and for storage tanks, chemical equipment and cryogenic used. For the latter, where higher strengths are required, consideration should be given to the use of alloy 5251.

2.9.2.7 Alloy 3105

Alloy 3105 (Al Mn Mg) is available in sheet form only, in a range of tempers, and has a durability rating A. The use of this alloy is becoming more prevalent in general engineering and for profiled building sheet because of its superior properties over 3103 in hardness and strength. It retains good ductility.

2.9.2.8 Alloy 5083

Alloy 5083 (Al Mg4.5 Mn) is available in plate, sheet, drawn tube and forging and is limited to simple extruded sections as it is hard to extrude, particularly in hollows. Of durability rating A, 5083 is used for welded structures, plating and tank work, as it can be welded readily without significant loss of strength when in the annealed condition and has high ductility. The tensile strength of 5083 in the O and F conditions is lower than 6082-T6, but is significantly higher if the latter is welded. It is ductile in the soft condition but work hardens rapidly, becoming extremely tough. Alloy 5083 is restricted to applications where the temperature is below 65°C because long exposure at above this temperature can result in grain boundary precipitation of magnesium/aluminium intermetallic compounds. These compounds corrode preferentially in some adverse environments. This effect is aggravated if the alloy is subjected to subsequent cold-working operations. Apart from its easy welding and good formability properties, alloy 5083 also exhibits very good durability, especially in marine environments.

2.9.2.9 *Alloys 5251, 5154A and 5454*

Alloys 5251 (Al Mg2), 5154A (Al Mg3.5 A) and 5454 (Al Mg3 Mn) are available in sheet, plate and simple extrusions and all are of durability rating A. Alloys 5154A and 5251 are also available as drawn tube and forgings. These three alloys are ductile in the soft condition, but work harden rapidly. They have good weldability and very good resistance to corrosive attack, especially in a marine atmosphere, and for this reason are used in panelling and structures exposed to marine atmospheres. Alloys 5154A and 5454 are stronger than 5251. The strongest 5000 series alloy offering immunity to stress corrosion when exposed to elevated temperatures is 5454. The 5000 series alloys with a magnesium content greater than 3% may be susceptible to stress corrosion when exposed to elevated temperatures.

2.9.2.10 *Alloy 5251 in seam-welded tube*

Seam-welded tubes are produced from 5251 strip (Al Mg2) giving a durability rating B to the tube, which is further strengthened by work hardening through forming and finishing rolls. The main uses of this alloy are in general engineering such as garden furniture, handrails and ladders.

2.9.2.11 *Alloy LM2*

Alloy LM2 (Al Si10 Cu2) is a medium-strength casting alloy with good resistance to atmospheric corrosion and a durability rating C. It is good for thin intricate sections and is used for any die-cast components unless high resistance to corrosion is required, such as in marine environments. Anodizing produces a dark grey finish. Typical applications include cast rainwater goods.

2.9.2.12 *Alloy LM5*

Alloy LM5 (Al Mg5 Si1) is a medium-strength casting alloy designed to give high resistance to corrosion. It therefore has a durability rating A. It possesses excellent finishing properties where it maintains a surface of high polish and is used where high quality anodizing is required. It is only suitable for relatively simple shapes, formed mainly by sand casting, but can be gravity die cast. Typical uses include castings for architectural and decorative purposes, including door furniture, and in marine applications.

2.9.2.13 *Alloy LM6*

Alloy LM6 (Al Si12) is another medium-strength casting alloy which has excellent foundry characteristics, high ductility and impact strength, together with good corrosion resistance giving it a durability rating B. These characteristics permit the production of thin-walled intricate-shaped castings without the danger of hot tearing or cracking. It is suitable for both sand and chill castings and for a wide range of uses in general, marine and electrical applications. It is also suitable for castings of above average complexity and size such as large building cladding panels. Its uses extend to welded applications and its ductility allows shape correction to improve fit-up.

2.10 Fabrication and construction

Aluminium and aluminium alloys in wrought forms such as sheet, plate and extrusions as well as in cast forms, can be fabricated in much the same way as other metals and, in general, similar equipment and tools can be used.

2.10.1 Cutting

Aluminium sheet and plate can be cut by machining, shearing or arc-cutting depending on the alloy and its thickness. Plate as well as extruded sections can be cut by band saw, circular saw or by machining, but saws should have a tooth form and pitch to suit the thickness and alloy. Flame cutting should not be used because the temperature can change the mechanical properties of the material.

2.10.2 Drilling punching and blanking

Holes in thin materials or large holes in thicker materials can be produced by punching, whilst holes in thicker materials are drilled using high speeds. Blanking of aluminium sheet is generally performed in punch presses, giving high production rates and enabling close tolerances to be maintained, especially with the harder temper materials.

2.10.3 Bending and forming

Pure aluminium is easily bent and formed and if work hardening occurs can be annealed to allow further forming. In general, the non-heat-treated materials can be formed, drawn or spun easily, although the more alloyed work materials such as 5083 work harden rapidly and may need interstage annealing. Heat-treatable alloys can be bent in the heat-treated condition provided generous bend radii are employed, but if bending to acute angles is required forming in the annealed condition or immediately after solution treatment is recommended. In the softer tempers non-heat-treatable sheet materials can be bent flat, but stronger materials need more generous bend radii to avoid cracking. Minimum bend radii for different alloys and thicknesses are obtainable from the manufacturers.

Simple extruded sections are readily bent on normal tooling, but more complex sections require special tooling to maintain the shape of the section around the bend. Wrap or stretch forming methods are used. Surface finish on forming tools is important as the surface of the aluminium is easily marked and a highly polished surface to the tooling is essential.

2.10.4 Welding

Aluminium alloys are, in general, welded by using one of three main processes: fusion, resistance and solid-phase bonding. For general engineering fabrication the normal process used is fusion welding by the tungsten inert gas (TIG) or metal inert gas (MIG) process.

2.10.4.1 *TIG process*

The tungsten inert gas (TIG) process is the most widely used and most suitable for alloy thicknesses of 1.2–9.5 mm. In the TIG process, an a.c. arc is struck between a non-consumable tungsten electrode and the work piece, with the filler rod, if required, being fed independently. Fluxes are not required, but to prevent reoxidation, the weld pool is enveloped by a shield of inert argon gas. Control of the heat input and wire feed enables the welder to have fine control over penetration and neat and intricate welds can be achieved.

Table 2.13 Selection of weld filler metal for parent metal combinations

First part	Al–Si castings LM2 LM4 LM6 LM25	Al–Mg castings LM5	3*** alloys 3103 3105	1*** alloys 1050A 1080A 1200 1350	7020	6*** alloys 6061 6063 6063A 6082	5*** alloys 5154A 5251 5454	5083
5083	NR[b]	Type 5	Type 5	Type 5	5556A	Type 5	Type 5	5556A
		Type 5	Type 5	Type 5	Type 5	Type 5	Type 5	Type 5
		Type 5	Type 5	Type 5	5556A	Type 5	Type 5	Type 5
5*** alloys 5154A 5251 5454	NR[b]	Type 5	Type 5	Type 5	Type 5	Type 5	Type 5	
		Type 5	Type 5	Type 5	Type 5	Type 5	—[c]	
		Type 5	Type 5	Type 5	Type 5	Type 5	Type 5	
6*** alloys 6061 6063 6063A 6082	Type 4	Type 5	Type 4	Type 4	Type 5	Type 4/5		
	Type 4	Type 5	Type 4	Type 4	Type 5	Type 4		
	Type 4	Type 5	Type 4	Type 4	Type 5	Type 4		
7020	NR[b]	Type 5	Type 5	Type 5	5556A			
		Type 5	Type 5	Type 5	Type 5			
		Type 5	Type 5	Type 5	Type 5			
1*** alloys 1050A 1080A 1200 1350	Type 4	Type 5	Type 4	Type 1[d]				
	Type 4	Type 5	Type 3/4	Type 1[e]				
	Type 4	Type 5	Type 4	Type 1[d]				
3*** alloys 3103 3105	Type 4	Type 5	Type 3[d]					
	Type 4	Type 5	Type 3					
			Type 3[d]					
Al–Mg castings LM5	NR[b]	Type 5						
		Type 5						
		Type 5						
Al–Si castings LM2 LM4 LM6 LM25	Type 4							
	Type 4							
	Type 4							

Filler metal groups				Durability
Type 1	1080A	1050A		A
Type 3	3103			A
Type 4	4043A	4047A		B
Type 5	5056A	5356	5556A 5183	A

[a] Filler metals for parent combination to be welded are shown in one group, which is located at the intersection of the relevant parent metal row and column. In each group, the filler metal for maximum strength is shown in the top line: in the case of 6*** and 7020 alloys, this will be below the fully heat-treated parent metal strength. The filler metal for maximum resistance to corrosion is shown in the middle line. The filler metal for freedom from persistent weld cracking is shown in the bottom line. [b] NR, not recommended. The welding of alloys containing approximately 2% or more of Mg with Al–Si (5–12% Si) filler metal (and vice versa) is not recommended because sufficient Mg_2Si precipitate is formed at the fusion boundary to embrittle the joint. [c] The corrosion behaviour of weld metal is likely to be better if its alloy content is close to that of the parent metal and not markedly higher. Thus for service in potentially corrosive environments it is preferable to weld 5154A with 5154A filler metal or 5454 with 5554 filler metal. However, in some cases this may only be possible at the expense of weld soundness, so that a compromise will be necessary. [d] If higher strength and/or better crack resistance is essential, type-4 filler metal can be used. [e] For welding 1080A to itself, 1080A filler metal should be used.

2.10.4.2 MIG process

In the metal inert gas (MIG) process, a d.c. arc of reverse polarity is struck between the workpiece and a continuously fed aluminium wire which acts both as filler and electrode. The arc itself cleans the electrode and weld pool and reoxidization is prevented by a shield of inert gas, usually argon, which envelops the area; fluxes are unnecessary. The filler wire is fed semiautomatically; wire is fed mechanically from the gun into the weld pool at a speed balanced with the rate of burn-off, which is in turn determined by the current setting required for the weld. Conditions can normally be set to give spray transfer, enabling position welding to be done at high speed. Penetration cannot be controlled as closely as in the TIG process, and so joints must be backed or welded from both sides. The MIG process is suitable for any thickness of aluminium from 1.6 mm upwards.

Both processes can achieve high-quality welds, but preparation of the workpieces to produce the correct edge preparation, clean, dry and oxide free surfaces is of great importance. The oxide film is normally removed by scratch brushing and the parts welded within 8 h, before the oxide film reforms. The environment for the welding of aluminium and aluminium alloys should always simulate shop conditions.

The majority of alloy combinations can be welded successfully by both processes. The careful selection of filler wires is necessary to achieve compatibility, strength, freedom from cracking, corrosion resistance and colour matching. The welds on certain alloys do not respond well to anodizing. *Table 2.13*, reproduced from BS 3019, shows the selection of filler wires for alloy combinations.

The effect of heat during welding produces a softer heat affected zone (HAZ) adjacent to the weld, which in the case of tempered or heat-treated materials, reduces the strength in this zone which extends approximately 25 mm from the centre of the weld. In addition, the greater thermal expansion of the aluminium alloys makes weld distortion a greater problem than with steel.

2.10.5 Bolting and riveting

Normal bolting and riveting methods are applied to aluminium using aluminium, steel and stainless-steel fasteners. Selection of the fastener materials is dictated by both strength and the compatibility to offer the required durability to the assembly. Propriety fasteners and self-tapping screws are frequently used.

2.10.6 Finishes

2.10.6.1 General

Pure aluminium and many aluminium alloys may be used in various applications and environments without the need for added protection to the surface. When exposed to the oxygen in the atmosphere the surface rapidly acquires a hard and strongly adherent oxide film, which protects the metal. A protective finish is not required. If this film is broken by scratching or abrasion it rapidly reforms as a protective surface.

The natural finish on aluminium and aluminium alloys produced by the normal manufacturing process is known as 'mill finish'. The surface of the metal may be treated to produce a number of finishes which can be to preserve the original appearance of the aluminium, provide protection against the environment, to provide colour or decoration, or to alter the surface texture of the metal.

2.10.6.2 Mechanical finishes

The most frequently used methods of mechanically finishing aluminium are impressing or embossing, polishing or linishing. Patterns in the form of indented or raised dots, lozenges, chequered effects together with stucco and hammer embossing are all produced by passing the sheet material through patterned rolls under pressure. Mechanical finishes including wire brushing, grit blasting, burnishing, linishing and polishing are frequently applied to the surface prior to anodizing or lacquering in order to preserve the finish. The response to these processes varies with the alloy. Very high polish is readily obtainable on pure aluminium and suitable alloys by chemical and electrolytic means as well as by mechanical means.

2.10.6.3 Electrochemical finishes

The natural oxide film on aluminium may be thickened electrolytically to increase the protection and provide decoration by the process called anodizing. After cleaning and etching, the metal is immersed in an acid bath and subjected to an electrolytic process that artificially thickens the oxide film to such an extent that subsequent exposure to the atmosphere does not change the appearance of the surface. When first formed, the film is absorbent and can be dyed or pigmented to give one of a range of decorative colours.

The thickness of the anodic film is controlled by the current density and immersion time and ranges from 5 μm up to 120 μm depending on application. Most architectural aluminium for use in exposed environments is given a coating of 25 μm. Since most anodic films are transparent, the surface of the aluminium should be treated before anodizing to provide a uniform texture or surface appearance and to reduce rolling or extrusion marks. The final appearance depends more on the preanodizing treatment than on the process itself.

Care is required when colour-matching different alloys as

colour variations occur. Hard anodized coatings are used to provide abrasion resistance to components and to reduce surface friction in sliding applications.

2.10.6.4 Conversion coatings

The conversion coating process is essentially a pretreatment carried out on aluminium materials prior to painting. The process imparts colour to the metal and advantage is taken of its effect as a decorative finish and to reduce glare. The colour achieved depends on the process and on the alloy and can be grey, grey/black, green to blue or yellow to orange. The process involves etch cleaning of the material followed by dipping the material into chromate or phosphate solutions, followed by rinsing operations.

2.10.6.5 Painting

Painting or coating of aluminium and aluminium alloys can be performed by using many processes and with many types of materials. The principal methods employed are described below.

(i) *Protective and decorative air-drying coatings* Most paints in common use, with the exception of lead based paints, are suitable for use with aluminium. The quality of the paint system very much depends on the adhesion of the coating to the substrate, and the natural oxide film does not provide a good key for paints. To provide a good key for any paint system it is necessary to remove the oxide film by mechanical or chemical means, and to provide an additional surface layer which will provide the bond between the aluminium and the paint.

Preparation is by cleaning with solvent, and removal of the oxide film by wire brushing, or etching. This is followed by a conversion coating and/or the application of an etch primer or chromate metal primer, usually zinc chromate. The air-drying undercoats and finishing coat are then applied.

Where painting is to provide for protection, the paint is required to provide a barrier between the aluminium and the reactive agents. The selection of the paint barrier is dependent upon the degree of protection required, but can include bituminous paints, epoxy bitumen paints, chlorinated rubber and epoxy paints.

(ii) *Thermosetting stoved liquid paints* The use of stoving or heat curing of paints enables better paint-film properties to be achieved. Liquid paints formed from resins, including alkyds, acrylics, polyesters, epoxies, polyvinylidene fluoride (PVF2) and organasols, may be factory applied to the prepared aluminium substrate. Application can be by spray or electrostatic spraying or on coil by reverse roller coating. The paint is then cured by heat. Such systems provide very durable coatings which are harder and more abrasion resistant than air-dried films.

(iii) *Electropainting* Electropainting involves paint application by electrophoresis. The prepared metal is dipped into a bath of water-based acrylic or polyurethane paint in suspension. By the application of a voltage, charged particles of paint are attracted to the aluminium and adhere uniformly over the surface, enabling corners to be evenly coated. The film is dried and stoved. Such systems enable paint films of approximately 25 μm thickness to be applied and are used to prepaint lengths of aluminium extrusions for windows and architectural systems.

(iv) *Powder coating* Powder coating has now become an important process, particularly in painting aluminium extrusions. In a similar way to electrostatic spray painting, the liquid is replaced by solid dry acrylic, polyester or polyurethane

Table 2.14 The general availability of product forms[a]

Alloy	Plate	Sheet and strip	Extruded sections				Drawn tube	Longitudinally welded tube	Forgings	Castings
			Solid bar and simple sections	Complex sections	Round and rectangular tube	Hollow section				
1050A	A	A	A	—	—	—	A	—	A	—
1080A	A	A	A	—	—	—	—	—	—	—
1200	MS	MS	A	—	—	—	A	—	—	—
1350	—	A	A	—	A	—	—	—	—	—
3103	MS	MS	—	—	—	—	—	—	—	—
3105	—	M	—	—	—	—	—	—	—	—
5083	MS	MS	A	—	—	—	A	—	M	—
5154A	M	M	A	—	—	—	A	—	M	—
5251	M	MS	A	—	—	—	A	MS	M	—
5454	M	M	A	—	—	—	—	—	—	—
6061	A	A	M	M	M	M	M	—	M	—
6063	—	—	MSX	MS	MS	M	M	—	M	—
6063A	—	—	M	M	M	M	—	—	—	—
6082	MS	MS	MSX	M	MS	M	M	—	M	—
7020	A	A	A	—	—	—	—	—	—	—
LM2	—	—	—	—	—	—	—	—	—	M
LM4	—	—	—	—	—	—	—	—	—	M
LM5	—	—	—	—	—	—	—	—	—	M
LM6	—	—	—	—	—	—	—	—	—	M
LM25	—	—	—	—	—	—	—	—	—	M

[a] MS, standard product manufactured to order with a limited range available from stock; M, standard product manufactured to order; A, special product manufactured by special arrangement; X, includes sections from BS 1161.

powder particles. Even build-up of the film is possible and stoved coatings of 50–120 μm are possible. These coatings provide hard abrasion-resistant surfaces, but thinning occurs at sharp edges. Minimum bend radii or corner radii on extruded sections or formed components are, therefore, recommended.

2.11 Standard products and availability of materials

2.11.1 General

The range of aluminium and aluminium alloys given in *Table 2.5* is not produced in all wrought and cast forms. This may be seen by examination of *Tables 2.6–2.10*. In addition, alloys in some forms are only produced by special arrangement. The general availability of the various product forms for each alloy is indicated in *Table 2.14*.

2.11.2 Standard products

Whilst all product forms are the subject of British Standard materials specifications (see Section 2.12.1.2), in the majority of cases these specifications do not lay down standard products. British Standards do, however, cover some specific aluminium products such as structural sections to BS 1161, profiled building sheet to BS 4896 and scaffold tube to BS 1139. Many application standards cover the design, construction and use of products and systems made from aluminium components produced to the relevant materials specification (see Section 2.12.1.7). Such products include: window systems, door systems, secondary glazing, patent glazing, ladders, trestles, access staging, scaffolding, expanded metal, hand railing, parapet systems, flooring, planking, cast rainwater goods, cast domestic radiators, piping systems, profiled building sheet and flat roofing sheet.

Table 2.15 BS 1161 standard extruded sections—range of sizes

Section type	Size range (mm)
Equal angles	30×30–120×120
Unequal angles	50×38–140×105
Channels	60×30–240×100
T-sections	50×38–120×90
I-sections	60×30–160×80
Equal bulb angles	50×50–120×120
Unequal bulb angles	50×37.5–140×105
Lipped channels	80×40–140×70
Bulb T-sections	90×75–180×150

2.11.3 Availability of materials

Rolled and extruded aluminium and aluminium alloy products are obtainable either through a network of stockists or direct from the mills. This choice of supplier depends on the product requirements, the quantity needed and availability offered.

2.11.3.1 Structural sections

Most extruders offer a wide range of standard structural sections which include those to BS 1161 listed in *Table 2.15*. A limited range of these sections are available from stock in 6082-T6 or 6063-T6 alloys. The majority of extrusions are, however, made to order either from existing dies or following the production of new purpose-designed dies. The low cost of these dies encourages flexibility in design, but the minimum production quantities necessary in all cases should not be overlooked. When designing a new section the designer should consult the manufacturer at an early stage to confirm the feasibility of the new section. Some sections or products are made by drawing, forming or roll forming, and these operations may require special tooling.

2.11.3.2 Tube

A small range of tube sizes and types are available from stock in 6082 and 6063 alloys, but in the majority of cases tube will be made to order (see *Table 2.14*). These may be produced by extrusion, by drawing or seam welding.

2.11.3.3 Sheet and plate

Sheet and plate is stocked in a limited range of alloys in sheet sizes and thicknesses frequently suitable for many applications (see *Table 2.14*). Large quantities or special sizes are rolled to order, but minimum quantities will apply. Material is available from stock as patterned sheet and as treadplate for walkway surfaces. There is a wide range of standard rolled roofing and cladding products, some of which are available in moderate quantities from stock in both mill finish and painted, but which are, in general, produced to order.

2.11.3.4 Forgings

Forgings are supplied to order as hand forgings or die forgings, the former normally requiring all-over machining to achieve the finished dimensions, whilst the latter are produced to the finished dimensions.

2.11.3.5 Castings

Castings are always designed and supplied to order. For small-quantity production or where dimensional tolerances and surface finish is of lesser concern sand castings are commonly used, produced from patterns made at moderate cost. Where larger quantities and greater dimensional accuracy are required together with a high surface finish, chill castings are generally used. The cost of the metal tooling necessary may be high, especially where pressure die castings are used.

2.12 Standards

2.12.1 British Standards Institution standards

British Standards cover the following aspects of aluminium and aluminium alloys (published by BSI, Milton Keynes).

2.12.1.1 General

BS 3660 *Glossary of terms used in the wrought aluminium industry.*

2.12.1.2 Materials

BS 1470 *Specification for wrought aluminium and aluminium alloys for general engineering purposes: plate sheet and strip.*
BS 1471 *Specification for wrought aluminium and aluminium alloys for general engineering purposes: drawn tube.*
BS 1472 *Specification for wrought aluminium and aluminium alloys for general engineering purposes: forging stock and forgings.*
BS 1473 *Specification for wrought aluminium and aluminium alloys for general engineering purposes: rivet, bolt and screw stock.*
BS 1474 *Specification for wrought aluminium and aluminium alloys for general engineering purposes: bars, extruded round tube and sections.*
BS 1475 *Specification for wrought aluminium and aluminium alloys for general engineering purposes: wire.*
BS 1490 *Specifications for aluminium and aluminium alloy ingots and castings.*

BS 4300 *Specification for wrought aluminium and aluminium alloys for general engineering purposes (supplementary series):*
BS 4300/1 *aluminium alloy longitudinally welded tube;*
BS 4300/10 *5454 drawn tube;*
BS 4300/11 *5454 forging stock and forgings;*
BS 4300/12 *5454 bars, extruded round tube and sections;*
BS 4300/13 *5554 welding wire;*
BS 4300/14 *7020 plate sheet and strip; and*
BS 4300/15 *7020 bar, extruded round tube and sections.*
BS 1845 *Filler metals for brazing.*
BS 2901: Part 4 *Specification for filler rods and wires for gas-shielded arc welding: aluminium and aluminium alloys and magnesium alloys.*

2.12.1.3 Structural sections and fixings

BS 1161 *Specification for aluminium alloy sections for structural purposes.*
BS 1202: Part 3 *Specification for nails: aluminium nails.*
BS 4620 *Specification for rivets for general engineering purposes.*

2.12.1.4 Testing

BS 18 *Methods of tensile testing of metals (including aerospace materials).*
BS 4315: Parts 1 and 2 *Methods of test for resistance to air and water penetration (windows and walling).*
BS 6161: Parts 1–15 *Methods of test for anodic oxide coatings on aluminium and its alloys.*
BS 6682 *Method for the determination of bimetallic corrosion in outdoor exposure corrosion tests.*

2.12.1.5 Welding and welding-procedure approval

BS 3019: Part 1 *Specification for TIG welding of aluminium magnesium and their alloys.*
BS 3451 *Methods of testing fusion welds in aluminium and aluminium alloys.*
BS 3571: Part 1 *Specification for MIG welding of aluminium magnesium and their alloys.*
BS 4870: Part 2 *Specification for approval testing of welding procedures: TIG or MIG welding of aluminium and its alloys.*
BS 4871: Part 2 *Specification for approval testing of welders working to approved welding procedures: TIG or MIG welding of aluminium and its alloys.*
BS 4872: Part 2 *Specification for approval testing of welders when welding procedure approval is not required: TIG or MIG welding of aluminium and its alloys.*

2.12.1.6 Painting, coating and finishing and corrosion protection

BS 1615 *Methods for specifying anodic oxidation coatings on aluminium and its alloys.*
BS 3987 *Specification for anodic oxide coatings on wrought aluminium for external architectural applications.*
BS 4842 *Specification for liquid organic coatings for application to aluminium alloy extrusions, sheet and preformed sections for external architectural purposes, and for the finish on aluminium alloy extrusions, sheet and preformed sections coated with liquid applied organic coatings.*
BS 5599 *Specification for hard anodic coatings on aluminium for engineering purposes.*
BS 6150 *Code of practice for the painting of buildings.*
BS 6496 *Specification for powder organic coatings for application and stoving to aluminium alloy extrusions, sheet and preformed sections for external architectural purposes, and for*

the finish on aluminium alloy extrusions, sheet and preformed sections coated with powder organic coatings.

PD 6484   Commentary on corrosion at bimetallic contacts and its alleviation.

2.12.1.7 Standards covering the design, manufacture or application of aluminium products

BS CP 118   The structural use of aluminium.

BS CP 143: Part 1   Sheet roof and wall coverings: aluminium, corrugated and troughed.

BS CP 153: Parts 1 and 2   Windows and rooflights.

(BS 8118: Parts 1 and 2   The structural use of aluminium, Draft only.)

BS 2037   Specification for portable aluminium ladders, steps, trestles and lightweight staging.

BS 2997   Specification for aluminium rainwater goods.

BS 3049   Pedestrian guardrails (metal).

BS 3495   Specification for aluminium refuse storage containers.

BS 3989   Specification for aluminium street lighting columns.

BS 4868   Specification for profiled aluminium sheet for building.

BS 4873   Specification for aluminium alloy windows.

BS 5222: Parts 1 and 2   Specification for aluminium piping systems.

BS 5286   Specification for aluminium framed sliding glass doors.

BS 5395: Parts 1–3   Stairs, ladders and walkways.

BS CP 5516   Patent glazing.

BS 5649: Parts 1–8   Lighting columns.

BS CP 5974   Temporarily installed suspended scaffolds and access equipment.

BS CP 6180   Protective barriers in and around buildings.

BS 6375: Parts 1 and 2   Performance of windows.

BS 6651   Protection of structures against lightning.

BS 6779: Part 1   Specification for parapets of metal construction.

DD 72   Design requirements for access and working scaffolds.

DD 82   Specification of requirements for suitability of materials for use in contact with water for human consumption with regard to the effect on the quality of the water.

2.12.1.8 Electrical applications

BS 215: Parts 1 and 2   Specification for aluminium conductors and aluminium conductors, steel-reinforced for overhead power transmission.

BS 2627   Specification for wrought aluminium for electrical purposes: wire.

BS 2897   Specification for wrought aluminium for electrical purposes: strip with drawn or rolled edges.

BS 2898   Specification for wrought aluminium and aluminium alloys for electrical purposes: bars, extruded round tube and sections.

BS 3242   Specification for aluminium alloy stranded conductors for overhead power transmission.

BS 3988   Specification for wrought aluminium for electrical purposes: solid conductors for insulated cables.

BS 4579: Part 3   Specification for performance of mechanical and compression joints in electric cable and wire connectors: mechanical and compression joints in aluminium conductors.

BS 5593   Specification for impregnated paper-insulated cables with aluminium sheath/neutral conductor and three shaped solid aluminium phase conductors (CONSAC), 600/1000 V for electricity supply.

Table 2.16   ISO standards for aluminium and aluminium alloy materials and products

Type and content of standard	Castings	Forgings	Wire rod	Drawn wire	Drawn products: rods, bars and tubes	Extruded products: rods, bars, tubes, profiles	Rolled products: sheet, strip and plates
Terminology	ISO 3134-1 ISO 3134-4	ISO 3134-1 ISO 3134-3	ISO 3134-1 ISO 3134-3	ISO 3134-1 ISO 3134-3	ISO 3134-1 ISO 3134-3	ISO 3134-1 ISO 3134-3	ISO 3134-1 ISO 3134-3
Designation of alloys	ISO 2092	ISO 2092	ISO 2092	ISO 2092	ISO 2092	ISO 2092	ISO 2092
Form of product	—	—	—	ISO 209-2	ISO 209-2	ISO 209-2	ISO 209-2
Composition	ISO 3522	—	—	ISO 209-1	ISO 209-1	ISO 209-1	ISO 209-1
Temper designation	ISO 2107	ISO 2107	ISO 2107	ISO 2107	ISO 2107	ISO 2107	ISO 2107
Technical delivery conditions	ISO 7722	—	—	ISO 6365-1	ISO 6363-1	ISO 6362-1	ISO 6361-1
Mechanical and physical properties	ISO 3522	—	—	—	—	ISO 6362-2	ISO 6361-2
Dimensions and tolerances	—	—	—	—	Round bars ISO 5193 and ISO 7274	Profiles ISO 6362-4	Strips ISO 6361-3 Sheets and plates ISO 6361-4

—, No ISO standard.

2.12.2 International Organization for Standardization (ISO) standards

ISO standards covering terminology, designation of aluminium and aluminium alloys, forms of product, composition, temper designation, technical delivery conditions, mechanical and physical properties, dimensions and tolerances are covered by those standards listed in *Table 2.16*.

Bibliography

In addition to the standards listed in Section 2.12 the following provide additional information on aluminium and aluminium alloys.

Materials and properties

ALUMINIUM FEDERATION, *The Properties of Aluminium and its Alloys*, 8th edn (1983)
ALUMINIUM STOCKHOLDERS ASSOCIATION, *About Aluminium* (1981)
KING, F., *Aluminium and its Alloys*, Ellis Horwood Ltd, Chichester (1987)
MAZZOLANI, F. M., *Aluminium Alloy Structures*, Pitman Advanced Publishing Program, London (1985)

THE ASSOCIATION OF LIGHT ALLOY REFINERS, *The Properties and Characteristics of Aluminium Casting Alloys* (1980)

Production method and forming

ALUMINIUM EXTRUDERS ASSOCIATION, 'Shaping up with aluminium extrusions', *Engineering* (Nov. 1977)
ALUMINIUM FEDERATION, *Designer's Guide to Rolled Aluminium*, Parts 1–8 (1986–1988)
ALUMINIUM FEDERATION, *Bending Aluminium* (1987)

Welding

ALUMINIUM FEDERATION, *Can You Weld It—Aluminium* (1986)
BLEWETT, R. V. 'Modern Techniques for Welding Aluminium and Its Alloys': Part 1, *Aluminium Industry*, **2**, No. 2 (May 1983); Part 2, *Aluminium Industry*, **2**, No. 3 (July 1983); Part 3, *Aluminium Industry*, **2**, No. 4 (Sep. 1983)

Finishing

HENLEY, V. F., *Anodic Oxidation of Aluminium and its Alloys*, Pergamon Press, Oxford (1982)
KING, R. G., *Surface Treatment and Finishing of Aluminium*, Pergamon Press, Oxford (1988)

3

Cast Iron

J Sutherland FEng, BA, FICE, FIStructE
Consultant to Harris & Sutherland

Contents

3.1 Introduction 3/3

3.2 Historic (mainly 19th century) cast iron 3/3
    3.2.1 Types of cast iron 3/3
    3.2.2 Grey cast iron 3/3

3.3 Modern grey cast iron 3/10
    3.3.1 General 3/10
    3.3.2 British Standard for grey cast iron 3/10
    3.3.3 Grey cast iron in construction today 3/11

3.4 Ductile or nodular (spheroidal graphite) cast iron 3/11
    3.4.1 History and method of manufacture 3/11
    3.4.2 British Standard for ductile cast iron 3/11
    3.4.3 Structural use of ductile cast iron 3/11

Appendix 3.1 History of the manufacture and use of grey
               cast iron in construction 3/12
Appendix 3.2 Tensile strength of 19th century grey cast iron 3/13
Appendix 3.3 Development of the understanding of the bending
               strength of grey cast iron 3/13

Acknowledgements 3/14

References 3/15

Bibliography 3/15

3.1 Introduction

The most fundamental difference between cast iron and either wrought iron or steel lies in the higher carbon content of the former. The broad range of values for this proportion are given in *Table 3.1*.

Cast iron used in the construction industry may be divided into three main categories:

(1) 'Historic' cast iron, that is mainly grey cast iron, as widely used in structures between about 1780 and 1880 but also including some malleable cast iron, made by the heat treatment of white iron castings.
(2) Modern grey cast iron, which is virtually the same as the historic grey iron but is generally of a higher quality and is covered by British Standards. It is mainly used in mechanical engineering rather than in structures.
(3) Ductile cast iron, or spheroidal graphite cast iron, which again is little used in construction today but which is covered by British Standards and could have a major future as a structural material. It is a relatively modern material dating from after 1946.

In discussing the properties and uses of cast iron it is convenient to adhere to these categories, although there must be some overlapping between the three.

Category (1), historic iron, is only really of interest to civil and structural engineers in connection with the appraisal, repair and adaptation of existing structures. The most notable characteristics of this type of iron are its much greater strength in compression than in tension and its non-linear behaviour under tensile load. These features present problems of analysis which are not shared by the other metals normally used for structures.

Although the main outlet for category (2), modern grey cast iron, is in mechanical equipment it is still used extensively on the municipal side of civil engineering for pipes, pipe fittings, bollards, manhole covers, gratings and other applications where simple robustness is needed rather than a calculable structural performance. Nevertheless, in all these fields it is liable to be superseded to a large extent by category (3), ductile cast iron.

The most important features of ductile cast iron are that it is comparably strong in tension and in compression and that its strength and stiffness are similar to those of rolled steel, yet it can be moulded into complex shapes with the same freedom as grey cast iron.

The basic properties of these three categories of cast iron are discussed in Sections 3.2 to 3.4 below, while the history and methods of manufacture and more detailed information on strength are covered in outline in the Appendices given at the end of the chapter.

3.2 Historic (mainly 19th century) cast iron

3.2.1 Types of cast iron

The carbon in historic cast iron occurs either in the form of free graphite flakes or in the combined form of iron carbide. The main characteristics of the three types of cast iron available in the 19th century (grey, white or malleable) are summarized in *Table 3.2*.

Virtually all the cast iron used in major construction was grey cast iron with nearly all the carbon in the form of free graphite.

White cast iron was only useful in construction as a step towards the manufacture of small components of malleable cast iron produced by the prolonged heat treatment of white iron castings. This process was quite widely used for step irons, hinges, locks, catches and for some decorative ironwork of a delicate character which would be subject to accidental damage. These components are outside the main subject of this chapter, but will be referred to again briefly in Section 3.4 in relation to ductile or spheroidal graphite cast iron which has inherent properties very similar to those achieved in malleable castings.

3.2.2 Grey cast iron

3.2.2.1 Metallurgy[1]

The microstructure of a typical grey cast iron with its flakes of graphite is shown in *Figure 3.1*, while the range of the carbon content and the effect of this on the melting temperature is shown in *Figure 3.2*. Elements other than carbon are present in small quantities in all commercial cast irons, notably silicon (Si) and phosphorus (P), which with the carbon content affect the properties of the material. It is thus the equivalent carbon content which matters rather than the total carbon content when considering grey cast irons. This equivalent is defined as:

$$\text{Equivalent carbon content (\%)} = \text{Total carbon content (\%)} + \frac{\text{Si}(\%) + \text{P}(\%)}{3}$$

Basically, high percentages of phosphorus make for brittle iron and the lower the equivalent carbon content the greater the tensile strength. However, with historic iron, over which there can no longer be any control, a knowledge of the metallurgy of any casting can only be of use as one of several indications of quality which can help in appraisal.

3.2.2.2 Strength in tension and compression

Historic grey cast iron was roughly one-fifth or one-sixth as strong in tension as in compression, although today the ratio for even low strength grey irons is nearer to 4 than to 5 or 6. *Figure 3.3* shows typical stress/strain relationships in both tension and compression for the same iron. It can be seen that not only is the iron much weaker in tension but it is also less stiff and, what is more, the stress/strain curve is non-linear in tension almost from the start.

This fact can well be explained by looking at the microstructure shown in *Figure 3.1*. The flakes of graphite have little or no tensile strength but they are thin. Thus in compression they have almost no effect on the behaviour of the iron matrix. However, when the material is subjected to tension the graphite contributes virtually nothing and, as a result, the cross-sectional area of material able to resist the pull is much less. In addition, as the tension load increases, the matrix opens out and becomes progressively more distorted as failure approaches.

On top of this explainable, but not so easily quantifiable, behaviour there is the question of size of casting. As castings become larger they cool more slowly and this results in a coarser arrangement of graphite flakes and thus a weaker structure. A guide to this is given in BS 1452: 1977 in relation to modern castings (see Section 3.3), but clearly the same principle applies to historic cast iron.

Because of this variation due to size, 'repeatability' of apparent tensile strengths depend on casting the same standard size and shape of test specimen and also on machining this to a standard form. In the case of existing iron structures, tensile specimens

Table 3.1 Carbon contents of cast iron, steel and wrought iron

Material	Carbon content (%)
Cast iron	2.0–4.5 (generally 2.5–4.0)
Steel	0.2–1.0
Wrought iron	0.02–0.05

Table 3.2 Types of historic (mainly 19th century) cast iron

Type of cast iron	Microstructure	Physical properties	Uses	Notes
Grey	Graphite in flake form in an iron matrix. Flakes form discontinuities	Strong in compression. Relatively weak in tension. Good resistance to corrosion. Easily machined and cut. Very large castings practicable. Limited ductility	Main form of cast iron used in construction, for columns, beams, decorative panels, etc., as well as machinery	Historic cast iron nearly all grey iron. Little used in construction today except for pipes, pipe fittings, manhole covers, etc.
White	No free graphite. Carbon combined with iron as hard carbides. Low equivalent carbon. Low silicon content	Very hard and very brittle. Machined by grinding only	Surfaces needing high resistance to abrasion	Virtually irrelevant to construction industry
Malleable	Made by prolonged heat treatment of white iron castings. Carbides transformed into graphite in nodular form with few discontinuities in iron matrix	Very strong in tension as well as compression, with good ductility	Hinges, catches, step irons and similar castings of limited size. Decorative panels of fragile design	Likely to be superseded by ductile iron which has similar properties and can be cast in a wide range of section thicknesses (see Section 3.4)

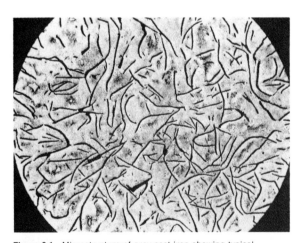

Figure 3.1 Microstructure of grey cast iron showing typical distribution of flake graphite. (From Angus,[1] by permission)

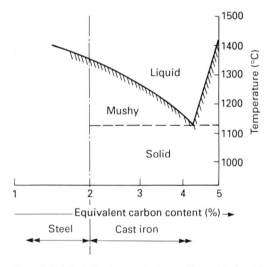

Figure 3.2 Effect of carbon content on melting point of cast iron

cut from large castings may show lower values than those from standard (relatively small) test specimens cast from a similar mix.

A large number of tensile tests have been carried out on grey cast iron over the last 150 years or more. The results of some of these are summarized in Appendix 3.2. It can be seen that, although tensile strengths vary quite widely, they seldom fall below 100 N mm^{-2} (6.5 ton in.$^{-2}$) and are likely to be higher, but perhaps seldom above 150 N mm^{-2} (10 ton in.$^{-2}$) in the period up to 1850 and seldom above about 225 N mm^{-2} (15 ton in.$^{-2}$) until towards the end of the century.

The elongation of grey cast iron at failure is low, generally less than 0.75%, which may be compared with, say, 10–30% for wrought iron. This low overall elongation to failure is responsible for grey cast iron's reputation as being a brittle material. However, if brittle materials are defined strictly as those which fall at or near the end of their linear elastic range with little or no non-elastic yielding, then grey cast iron is not brittle. In tension its non-elastic strain at failure is typically four times the elastic strain, but the total strain is still very small.

In view of the very high compressive strength of almost all grey cast iron, simple compression has rarely been found to be a problem. Tests made in the 19th century showed strengths of the order of 775–1100 N mm^{-2} (50–70 ton in.$^{-2}$). This range is similar to that given BS 1452: 1977 for modern grey cast iron (see *Table 3.5*); these values are for direct compression on stocky specimens. With columns, buckling must of course be considered as well as eccentricity of loading.

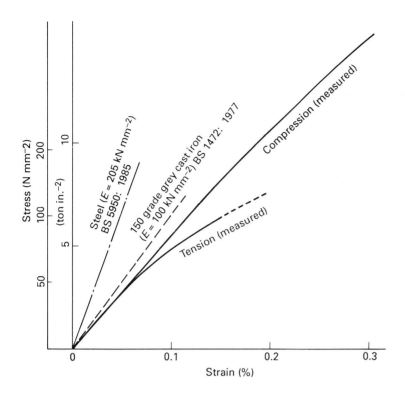

Figure 3.3 Typical stress/strain relationship of grey cast iron in tension and compression. (From Clark[20])

3.2.2.3 Strength in bending

With the wide difference in strength in compression and tension, together with variations due to mix and to size of casting and the non-linear behaviour under tensile loads, the bending strength of cast iron has been a source of confusion ever since the early 19th century.

Simple modulus-of-rupture tests on large grey cast iron beams show much wider variations in apparent strength with size of section than can be explained as variations in tensile strength. *Table 3.3* gives these variations as demonstrated by a number of actual tests on cast iron beams and bars made in the 19th century and tests made on 19th-century beams in the present century. It can be seen that on an elastic (modulus-of-rupture) basis a bar of grey iron of dimensions 25 mm × 25 mm is likely to be much stronger in bending than a major I-beam of similar material and could well be 2.5–3 times as strong. Furthermore, it has been shown in three separate sets of tests that 25-mm² bars cut from large beams and tested to failure have a modulus of rupture between about 1.9 and 2.7 times that proved for the beams from which they were cut.

It is significant that some tests on large I-beams have shown the modulus of rupture to be almost equal to the lowest end of the range of tensile strengths shown in Appendix 3.2, whereas with small bars it has frequently been shown to be between 1.5 and 2 times as great. It is also notable that the modulus of rupture of small I-beams and inverted-T-beams appears generally to be higher than that of large I-beams. These anomalous test results and the changing thinking on cast iron beams in the 19th century are discussed in greater detail in Appendix 3.3.

The shift of the neutral axis, as put forward by Eaton Hodgkinson in the 1830s, goes some way towards explaining this apparent effect of scale, while the coarser graphite structure in large castings also contributes to this. However, to date, a fully satisfactory explanation of all these test results has not yet come to light.

Although in grey cast iron beams the stress distribution is known to depart increasingly from the elastic form as failure approaches, there is not enough consistent evidence at present from which to formulate a general method of calculating bending strength from the actual stress/strain relationship in tension and compression.

In this admittedly frustrating situation, the nearest one may get to *a general likely lower limit* for the *ultimate bending strength* of beams in grey cast iron, short of making individual load tests, is simply to calculate the modulus of rupture using a tensile strength of about $100–110 \text{ N mm}^{-2}$ (6.5–7.0 ton in.$^{-2}$) which is about the lowest level of modulus of rupture found in tests on sound beams, as can be seen from *Table 3.3*.

In many cases this level of apparent ultimate strength is likely to be too conservative, especially with beams of small to moderate section which may be 1.5 times, or even twice, as strong.

3.2.2.4 Strength in shear

Because of the necessarily thick webs of beams in grey iron, shear is not likely to be a problem. It is not even mentioned in most early publications on cast iron. BS 1452: 1977 gives 173 N mm^{-2} as the shear strength for the lowest grade of modern grey cast iron and elsewhere it is given as a varying ratio of shear strength to tensile strength. Today this ratio is considered to be between 1.1 and 1.2.

3.2.2.5 Impact resistance and fatigue

It is not practicable to state a test for the impact resistance of historic grey cast iron by which its performance can be compared with that of, say, structural steel. Few would claim that the resistance of grey cast iron to major impacts is very good. Furthermore, the resistance reduces gradually with falling

Table 3.3 Results of flexural tests on different sizes of grey cast iron beam and on small specimens cut from beams tested

Test set (Ref.)	Date of test	Shape of beams	Depth of section (mm)	Results of flexural tests on beams or bars				Results of flexural tests on 25 mm × 25 mm specimens from beams tested				X/Y
				No. of specimens	Modulus of rupture (N mm^{-2})			No. of specimens	Modulus of rupture (N mm^{-2})			
					High	Low	Mean, X		High	Low	Mean, Y	
A* (12+13)	Various, 19th century mainly	Square	25	Many	400	280	340 approx.	—	—	—	—	—
		Rect. 25 wide	75	1 (?)			258					
		Rect. 50 wide	75	1 (?)	—	—	250					
		square	75	1 (?)			200					
B (12+13)	Various 19th century	Small I or inverted T	100 ↓ 175	7	203	143	175	—	—	—	—	—
C (14)	1984	Inverted T	333	2	210	156	183	—	—	—	—	—
D* (15)	1934	I	298	6	190	138	156	12	464	394	427	2.7
E* (16)	1987	I	360	1	—	—	122	5	250	218	237	1.9
F* (17)	1944	I	298 ↓ 634	12	135	116	122	9	390	252	332	2.7
G1† (18)	1968	I	460 & 675	2 } 4 }	118	101	108	—	—	—	—	—
G2† (18)	1968	I	460	2	159	158	158.5	—	—	—	—	—

* D–F: 358 N mm^{-2} mean for wt 25 mm × 25 mm specimens, close to results for set A.
† Beams in set G2 noted as superior to those in set G1.

temperature and with increasing phosphorus content. On the credit side it can be said that cast iron has a low sensitivity to fatigue (see Section 3.2.2.9) and considerable damping qualities.[1]

3.2.2.6 Deflection

With a notably curved stress/strain relationship in tension, any value given for the elastic modulus of grey cast iron needs to be qualified. For the lower end of its strength range BS 1452: 1977 gives a constant figure of 100 kN mm^{-2} both for tension and compression which is roughly half the figure for steel. This is within the limits of about 80–150 kN mm^{-2} quoted in many early publications and should be accurate enough for deflection calculations on structural cast iron within the range of working stresses most likely to be encountered in historic cast iron structures. This can be seen in *Figure 3.3*

3.2.2.7 Effects of heat and fire resistance

The coefficients of linear expansion for temperatures between 0 and 200°C is approximately 10–12 × 10^{-6} per °C. Above 400°C the loss of strength becomes very marked. Nevertheless, in actual fires cast iron columns have frequently survived while the wrought iron or steel structures which they supported have collapsed. Also there are indications that when cast iron has cracked in fires this has often been due to the movement of other parts of the structure in the fire rather than the direct effect of fire on the cast iron. An interesting and helpful study of the effect of fire on cast iron in structures has been published.[2]

3.2.2.8 Forms of cast iron used in construction

Before considering the practical appraisal of grey cast iron as used in the construction industry it is worth looking at some examples to get an idea of the varying forms and sizes of the castings and their functions. Apart from bollards, manhole covers, pipes and similar minor items, grey cast iron was used structurally on a very large scale in major bridge arches and in columns, beams and trusses, particularly between 1775 and 1875. In many of these applications it was combined with wrought iron using hidden rivets and ingenious arrangements of socketed joints which are not easy to analyse without demolition. *Figure 3.5* shows one of the earliest examples of interlocking cast iron bridge sections, treated almost as if made of timber (1779), while *Figure 3.6* gives some idea of the climax reached in the refinement of cast iron arch bridges by 1823–1826.

Single iron castings of up to 1 m or more in structural depth and about 20 m long were used for bridge beams or for the 'standards' of major industrial structures (*Figure 3.7*). All cast iron structures with columns, main and secondary beams in the material (*Figure 3.8*) were quite common around 1830–1850.

Figure 3.9 shows a typical combination of cast iron column, decorative cast iron bracing brackets and wrought iron roof structure, while *Figure 3.10* shows part of a multistorey frame with the junction of a cast iron column and main beams of riveted wrought iron and secondary ones of cast iron. Care is needed in analysing such structures to make sure that the joining of the materials and the nature of each is fully understood.

Flaws can occur in historic structures which are not discernible until shown up by fracture. *Figure 3.11* shows a beam tested to failure. It can be seen that not only is the section of the beam

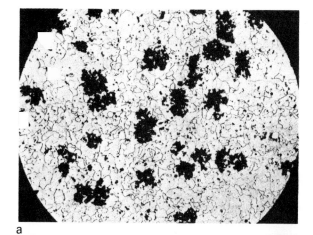

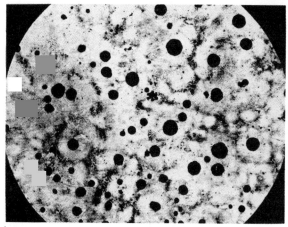

Figure 3.4 (a) Microstructure of malleable cast iron (white iron casting after prolonged heat treatment): available since mid-19th century. (b) Microstructure of ductile (spheroidal graphite) cast iron showing similar form to that of malleable iron but produced in 'as-cast' condition by chemical additions: available since 1949 only. (From Angus,[1] by permission)

uneven but there is also a major fault in the casting which caused it to break at this point rather than at the point of maximum bending moment.

Columns of cast iron generally present fewer problems in appraisal than do beams, but where columns are circular and hollow it is advisable to check the wall thickness by drilling say at three points round the circumference before calculating the load-bearing capacity; cores may well have been displaced during casting and a single drilled hole could be misleading.

3.2.2.9 Practical appraisal of the strength of grey cast iron

Following on from the uncertainties of assessing the real strength of cast iron, in bending in particular, there is the question of choosing an approach to appraisal that can be used in practical circumstances. Here the easiest answer is to start with a document with an official status, even if it ignores many of the theoretical uncertainties.

The most immediately useful advice, with real status, on the appraisal of cast iron structures is that given in the Department Standard BD21/84 *The Assessment of Highway Bridges and Structures*. This standard was published by the Department of Transport in 1984, but was prepared by a working party drawn

from a total of eight government departments or national authorities.[3] Unlike its limit state treatment of wrought iron and steel, this standard gives permissible stresses for cast iron which vary with the proportion of live to dead load according to published graphs. The maximum permissible stresses are given in *Table 3.4* but it should be noted that the highest levels of these only apply to dead loads or favourable combinations of dead and live load. Anyone wishing to use this standard should read the whole of the relevant sections of the standard in order to be sure of understanding all the qualifications stated and the basis for the requirements laid down.

In using these permissible stresses (see *Table 3.4*) BD21/84 assumes an elastic basis for analysis with no allowance for fatigue in cast iron 'because the level of stress permitted in this standard provides a reasonable assurance against fatigue failure'. For highway bridges, BD21/84 also gives advice on how the section modulus of beams may be 'increased' to allow for composite action with fill. The permissible compressive stresses in cast iron are mainly relevant to struts and columns and here BD21/84 gives advice based on the Rankine–Gordon formula.

Although intended for bridges and other highway structures it is hard to see any reason why the advice in BD21/84 should not be applied to cast iron in buildings and other structures. In buildings the effects of live loads and, in particular, dynamic ones are likely to be less than with highway bridges.

An alternative 'official' guidance on the strength of historic cast iron is that given in the London Building Regulations.

Figure 3.5 Early structural cast iron with interlocking joints like timber (Ironbridge 1779)

Figure 3.6 Climax of elegant cast iron bridge construction; all interlocking castings; a minimum of wrought iron tie rods and bolts (Mythe Bridge Tewkesbury 1823–1826)

Figure 3.7 Large I-section cast iron column supporting mixed cast and wrought iron roof structure (No. 8 Machinery Shop in Chatham Maritime)

Figure 3.8 Part of building structure with columns, main beams and secondary beams all in cast iron but external walls of masonry

These regulations were first published in the London County Council General Power Act of 1909 and limit the permissible tensile stress in cast iron (including tensile bending stress) to 23 N mm^{-2} (1.5 ton in.$^{-2}$) and compressive stress to 124 N mm^{-2} (8 ton in.$^{-2}$); this guidance was most recently discussed in 1976 in GLC Bulletin No. 91.[4] This tensile figure, which building-control officers frequently refer to, is appreciably

Figure 3.9 Combination of hollow cast iron column, decorative cast iron bracing brackets and wrought iron roof structure (Retford Station)

Figure 3.10 Structural joints in multistorey frame between sections of cast iron column, riveted wrought iron main beams and cast iron secondary beams (Boat Store Sheerness 1858–1860)

more restrictive than the varying scale in BD21/84 especially in cases where the proportion of permanent load is high.

In many existing structures elastic analyses of cast iron beams are likely to show tensile stresses in excess of the GLC figure of 23 N mm^{-2} and even beyond the limits in BD21/84, yet these structures have been giving good service for many decades. In such cases appraising engineers would do well to use their

judgement, applying their own factor of safety to likely minimum strengths (see Sections 3.2.2.2 to 3.2.2.4).

With its low elongation to failure in tension, its poor resistance to impact and the possibility of hidden flaws (as shown in *Figure 3.11*) the behaviour of grey cast iron in beams tends to be 'brittle' (in the conventional meaning of the word) and failure can be sudden. This needs to be remembered when choosing a factor of safety. On the more encouraging side, end fixity of beams, composite action and load sharing may be very helpful factors and are all worth considering when simplistic stress analysis proves inadequate. Previous good performance, type of loading

Figure 3.11 Cross-section of cast iron beam after failure in bending test, showing irregular shape and major flaw in tensile flange which caused premature failure (Paul Cooper)

Table 3.4 Limits of permissible stresses for cast iron in BD21/84

	All permanent loads or most favourable combinations of permanent and live load	*All live load*
Compression	154 N mm^{-2} (10 ton in.$^{-2}$)	80 N mm^{-2} (5.2 ton in.$^{-2}$)
Tension	46 N mm^{-2} (3 ton in.$^{-2}$)	24.5 N mm^{-2} (1.6 ton in.$^{-2}$)
Shear	46 N mm^{-2} (3 ton m^{-2})	See explanation in BD21/84

and seriousness of failure are all relevant to the final judgement made. The report on 'Appraisal of Existing Structures' by the Institution of Structural Engineers gives some useful advice on approaches to appraisal.[5]

It is also worth remembering that the practice of proof-loading cast iron beams was prevalent in the 19th century. Records may even exist of required proof loads, especially for important buildings. Actual loads applied may also have been recorded. Such records are worth searching for as one of the most useful guides to appraisal.

Finally, on the question of appraisal it should be remembered that cast iron has good damping qualities and needs little maintenance. For these reasons appraising engineers may not be doing their clients a good turn by replacing cast iron beams by steel for the sake of greater certainty. That greater certainty may be accompanied by more vibration and a much higher maintenance bill in the future. When in doubt, appraising engineers could well resort to some form of testing rather than immediately insisting on replacement or strengthening.

Welding is often perfectly practicable for repairs to grey cast iron but needs to be carried out with care. It it best confined to castings of limited size which can be removed, taken to a works experienced in such repairs, preheated and welded using the most appropriate electrodes. If in doubt advice should be sought from the Welding Institute[6] or the British Cast Iron Research Association.[7]

Where repairs to grey cast iron structures need to be carried out *in situ*, a cold repair method like the proprietary Metalock process is probably best. This 'stitches' the crack, provides a substantial and controllable tensile strength and when completed is virtually invisible.

There is a long tradition of repairs to cast iron structures by simple plating with wrought iron or steel plates or angles bolted across cracks. Although such repairs must be considered second rate and are liable to severe corrosion in exposed positions there may be a good case for leaving existing ones alone if they have been in place for some time, are well protected and are not offensively noticeable.

3.3 Modern grey cast iron

3.3.1 General

The properties of grey cast iron made today are fundamentally the same as those of historic iron. The carbon is in the same flake graphite form and there is a similar difference in strength and stiffness in tension and compression.

While in the 19th century engineers specified their cast iron by its origin (e.g. Low Moore No. 1, Butterley No. 2, or,

frequently, some mix of different irons) today users can ask for actual strength properties within a range covered by a British Standard specification knowing that there are foundries capable of meeting this standard. Of course it is always possible to demand properties which are higher or in some other way different from those in the British Standard, but for the most part it is best to adjust the design of a component to comply with one in the British Standard range with which the industry will be familiar.

As with all products, but with cast iron in particular, specification is not enough to achieve quality. Users of castings need to satisfy themselves that the foundries they approach are familiar with and capable of working to a standard quality. In addition, a system of quality control and testing needs to be set up if tensile strength or some other property is important.

Modern foundries are capable of producing castings in quantity to a high standard by industrialized methods. However, there are also small foundries working on more of a craft level, but capable of doing very satisfactory work. For decorative cast iron or the replacement of castings which are not critical structurally such small firms may give better value and be more adaptable than the bigger organizations.

Engineers and other users not familiar with the cast iron industry would do well to consult the British Foundries Association[8] for advice on the selection of foundries for a particular type of casting. This association will also give advice on the general properties of cast iron, while for more specific technical advice and testing the British Cast Iron Research Association[7] may be a more appropriate source of information.

3.3.2 British Standard for grey cast iron

The appropriate British Standard for grey cast iron in BS 1452: 1977. This standard specifically excludes any requirements on methods of manufacture and chemical composition but lays down physical properties for seven grades of cast iron, the distinction between these being tensile strength as measured on test bars machined from standard tensile test specimens. The main properties of these grades are given in *Table 3.5.* but it is emphasized that properties other than tensile strength are given for guidance and do not form part of the British Standard to be used for acceptance or rejection. Other properties of grey cast iron, such as density, coefficient of thermal expansion, notched tensile strength and fatigue limit, are also quoted in BS 1452: 1977 for guidance only.

Comparing the tensile strengths of the various grades of grey cast iron in BS 1452: 1977 with the low likely strengths of historic grey cast iron, the large increase is very noticeable. Today most

Table 3.5 Main structural properties of grey cast iron (from BS 1452: 1977)

	Basis of acceptance	*For guidance only (quoted in BS 1452: 1977 based on BCIRA data)*				
Grade No.	Tensile strength ($N\,mm^{-2}$)	0.1% Proof stress tension ($N\,mm^{-2}$)	Compressive strength ($N\,mm^{-2}$)	0.1% Proof stress compression ($N\,mm^{-2}$)	Shear strength ($N\,mm^{-2}$)	Elastic modulus* ($N\,mm^{-2}$)
150	150	98	600	195	173	100×10^3
180	180	117	672	234	207	109×10^3
220	220	143	768	286	253	120×10^3
260	260	169	864	338	299	128×10^3
300	300	195	960	390	345	135×10^3
350	350	228	1080	455	403	140×10^3
400	400	260	1200	520	460	145×10^3

* See Section 3.2.2.7 on elastic modulus.

engineering castings are in the strength range 180–260 N mm^{-2}, but their tensile strength may exceed that of wrought iron and even approach the strength of steel. However, it is well to remember that grey cast iron still has a very low elongation to failure and in that sense is essentially a 'brittle' material, admittedly with good damping qualities but a low or at best uncertain resistance to impact. Furthermore, in real castings as opposed to test sections the tensile strength decreases with increasing thickness of the material and depends on the shape and proportions of the casting.

BS 1452: 1977 includes, for the five lowest-strength grades, a set of curves relating the likely tensile strength of the material in different thicknesses of casting to that of a standard test piece of 30-mm diameter. This relationship is stated to be only approximate but indicates that with, say, 150-grade iron its strength in a casting 70-mm thick or more may well be below 100 N mm^{-2}.

Note: Since this section was written BS 1452: 1977 has been superseded by BS 1452: 1990 and much of the general guidance on the properties of cast iron referred to here has been omitted.

3.3.3 Grey cast iron in construction today

After 70–100 years of oblivion, interest in structural grey cast iron has revived, mainly for its appearance and flexibility of form rather than its real physical qualities. Grey cast iron is certainly suitable for columns in areas protected from accidental damage and where fire regulations are not paramount. It is also now used for brackets, bracing members and, to a limited extent, for beams. In such situations, if tensile and bending strengths are important in relation to design stresses, proof-loading of individual elements would be desirable, just as it was in the 19th century.

One of the greatest virtues of grey cast iron is its durability. In most situations it will last for decades or possibly even centuries with nothing more serious happening than the formation of a surface coating of rust. However, this cannot wholly be relied upon; for instance, quite severe corrosion was found recently in hidden parts of the Palm House at Kew, although admittedly after some 140 years. Paint or other surface coatings are often found desirable for visual reasons and such treatments not only protect the surface but act as an indicator of corrosion when they start to break down. Even if not entirely free from the effects of corrosion there seems to be no doubt that the durability of grey cast iron when exposed to the weather is considerably greater than that of wrought iron which, in turn, is better than that of steel.

The performance of cast iron and, in particular, the avoidance of cracks during cooling depend very much on the design of the casting. For instance, sharp internal angles should be avoided and the transitions from one thickness to another should be gradual or avoided to the greatest extent that is compatible with the use of the casting. The reason of course is to minimize different rates of cooling within the casting. What is more, smooth transitions and curved junctions ease the flow of the metal during pouring and thus reduce the danger of hidden blow holes. The design of castings is a skilled operation and engineers and architects should, wherever possible, discuss the details of the casting with an experienced iron-founder, preferably the one who will be responsible for the actual casting, before finally fixing the shape and section thicknesses.

While wholly suitable for many purposes where flexibility of form and general robustness are the main requirements, it is questionable whether grey cast iron is the best material to specify today for structures. A more recent and in almost every respect superior structural cast iron is now available. This is ductile or spheroidal graphite iron the properties of which are discussed in the following section.

3.4 Ductile or nodular (spheroidal graphite) cast iron

3.4.1 History and method of manufacture

Malleable iron, already mentioned in Section 3.2.1, is manufactured by the prolonged heat treatment of completed castings of white cast iron. This treatment produces a material with the carbon concentrated in small clusters in a strong matrix (*Figure 3.4(a)*) instead of being spread widely in the form of flake graphite as in the case of grey cast iron. Without the flake graphite to break up the structure these malleable castings have greater tensile strength and much greater resistance to impact. In fact malleable castings behave more like steel than grey cast iron.

Malleable cast iron was used extensively in the second half of the 19th century, but because of the need to heat completed castings it was found more suitable for small components than beams and columns. Naturally, it was also appreciably more expensive than grey cast iron.

Although malleable castings are still made today and are covered by a current British Standard, BS 6681: 1986, the material is being superseded to an increasing extent in the construction industry by ductile, or spheroidal graphite, cast iron. This material has only been in existence since 1946 when H. Morrogh of the British Cast Iron Research Association discovered that a similar microstructure to that of malleable iron after transformation could be produced by chemical additions to the mix before casting, the additions being magnesium and cerium. A typical microstructure of ductile iron produced in this way is shown in *Figure 3.4(b)*.

With a tensile strength in its 'as-cast' state almost as high as that of steel and a high resistance to impact, ductile iron has technical advantages over virtually all other types of cast iron which the construction industry has been surprisingly slow to recognize. However, ductile iron is now being used on an increasing scale both in mechanical engineering and in the construction industry. Pipes, tunnel-lining segments, heavy-duty covers and street furniture are increasingly being made of ductile iron in place of grey cast iron.

3.4.2 British Standard for ductile cast iron

The appropriate British Standard for ductile cast iron is BS 2789: 1985. This lists grades whose main properties are immediately identifiable from their reference numbers. Thus 600/3 has a tensile strength of 600 N mm^{-2} and a minimum elongation of 3%, while 400/18 has a tensile strength of 400 N mm^{-2} and a minimum elongation of 18%.

For most structural uses a strength of 400 N mm^{-2} in tension is very reasonable, especially if combined with a high minimum level of elongation. Furthermore, the ductile irons at the lower end of the strength table (400/18 and below) have a defined level of resistance to impact, a feature wholly lacking in grey cast iron. Thus it is now possible to combine the strength and ductility of wrought iron and structural steel with the freedom of form which has always been a special feature of grey cast iron.

As with BS 1452 for grey iron castings, BS 2789: 1985 gives a performance specification based on tensile strength rather than defining the chemical composition.

3.4.3 Structural use of ductile cast iron

It is indeed curious that ductile (spheroidal graphite) iron has not been used more in structures. The joints in the Nodus space frame system are an exception, while there have been a number of 'one-off' structural applications, for example at the Renault Centre, Swindon, although on a very small scale, and for actual roof trusses at the Menil Gallery in Houston (*Figure 3.12*); even there the actual castings of which the trusses are made are only

Figure 3.12 Roof trusses in ductile cast iron for Menil Gallery Houston, USA (Courtesy of Ove Arup & Partners)

about 1 m long. Its main rival is cast steel with which even higher tensile strengths are possible. It is worth considering some of the characteristics of these two materials in parallel.

Ductile iron is perhaps 25% more expensive than grey cast iron, but is almost half the price of cast steel. Of course these differences can vary quite widely although the order of the costs is unlikely to change.

Ductile iron has better fluidity and is dimensionally more stable in the transition from the liquid to the solid state than is cast steel. It is thus easier to achieve finer detailing and more accurate castings with ductile iron.

The tensile strength of ductile iron is less than that of most cast steels but it can readily be made more than adequate for most structural uses. As far as elongation to failure and impact resistance are concerned ductile iron is generally comparable with the lower grades of cast steel and, of course, is greatly superior in these respects to grey cast iron.

One advantage of cast steel over ductile iron is that it can be welded more easily and with greater certainty. Opinions differ on the advisability of welding ductile cast iron. Some say never weld it and others that this is perfectly feasible if carried out correctly. Undoubtedly the heat alters the structure of the iron and there is a danger that some ductility may be lost locally. However, in spite of problems, even highly stressed castings have been welded successfully, especially in mechanical engineering where repetition makes research into techniques more worthwhile than is usual with structures. Heat treatment after welding may be advisable but this is much simpler with small components than with major structural sections. Welding of ductile cast iron should not be undertaken lightly and expert advice should be sought before embarking on any design which depends on it.

Although welding could be a problem there are many situations, as with columns or arch voussoirs for instance, in which its economy relative to cast steel, its freedom of form and its robustness could be used to great advantage without any need for welding.

It is notable that grey cast iron continued to be used for columns for almost 50 years after it was superseded by wrought iron and steel for beams and trusses. With ductile iron this use could be revived but this time the columns would have a resistance to impact or to unintended bending moments which the grey iron ones lack. Jointing could be by socketing and bolting as in the 19th century, and the scope for slenderness and elegance of form would be large. With structural members used essentially in compression even some positional welding could be tolerated without worry.

There are many other structural situations where ductile iron could have a place. In the minds of the average engineer all cast iron is brittle and a material to be avoided. This is a prejudice which needs to be surmounted.

Assuming that there is a rebirth of structural cast iron in the form of ductile iron, there will be a need for a new level of quality assurance and quality control, not just of the iron as a material but of the finished casting. Such a need arises with any 'new' material. It arose with precast concrete, which in general is being produced to a far higher level of quality today than that of 30 or 40 years ago when the material first came into vogue.

Appendix 3.1: History of the manufacture and use of grey cast iron in construction

The change from the inefficient extraction of iron in a semimolten state in a primitive Catalan furnace to the achievement of molten iron is often attributed to the invention of the blast furnace as if this was a single brilliant idea. This was not the case. The blast furnace evolved through a succession of improvements to the design of furnaces in several countries over quite a long period. The date when molten (or cast) iron could be produced consistently and in usefully large quantities is uncertain, but it is generally accepted that in Europe this took place around 1500 AD, about 2000 years later than in China.

The extraction of iron from iron ore (in Britain mostly ferric oxide or haematite), is a process of chemical reduction, the carbon in the fuel combining with the oxygen in the ore to give iron plus carbon monoxide. In the blast furnace this reaction took place, and still does, by burning a fuel mixed with ore in a tall furnace, the combustion being assisted by a 'blast' of air injected at the bottom.

Initially, the fuel was charcoal which had two disadvantages. First, its use was leading to a level of deforestation so great that this had to be controlled. Secondly the size of furnace was limited by the tendency for the charcoal to crush under the total load, or charge, in the furnace, thus blocking the air flow on which combustion depends. It was not until the technique of smelting with coke was mastered that the way was open for large furnaces to be set up and the production of cast iron on a big enough scale to be attractive to the construction industry.

In spite of other claims, Abraham Darby I is generally thought to have been the first to use coke successfully for smelting. This was around 1709, but it was not until towards the end of the 18th century and, after other contributions to the technique, that large-scale casting of structural elements started. The addition of limestone to help absorb impurities which could be drawn off separately as molten slag was a later development.

The celebrated Ironbridge at Coalbrookdale completed in 1779 (*Figure 3.5*) was one of the earliest examples of structural cast iron in Britain, soon to be followed by other cast iron arch bridges and some church and domestic architecture and then the textile mills of Bage, Strutt and others in the 1790s and early 1800s. In addition, there were cast iron pipes, increasing quantities of cast iron in machinery and in items like railings, quite apart from cannons and cannon balls. After 1800 and particularly after 1820, the structural use of cast iron grew out of all proportion reaching a climax in the early 1840s.

Even though weaker in tension than in compression, the tensile strength and stiffness of grey cast iron exceeded those of timber and thus the spanning capacity of beams was immediately increased. In addition, the incombustibility of the material led to extensive use of 'fireproof' construction first in the textile mills and later in public buildings of all types.

By 1850 cast iron was being eclipsed by riveted wrought iron (see Chapter 4), especially for beams, and, although cast iron columns and brackets continued into the present century, by the 1920s the use of the material in structures had all but ceased. One or two well-publicized failures of cast iron beams, such as that at Radcliffe's Mill in Oldham in 1844 and the Dee Bridge in 1847, did much to destroy faith in cast iron as a spanning material. Nevertheless, in other fields the use of grey cast iron has continued in the construction industry where robustness combined with good resistance to corrosion are more important than structural capacity; manhole covers, gratings and bollards are typical.

There has been a limited revival of the structural use of grey cast iron in the 1980s mainly in connection with 'heritage' projects.

Appendix 3.2: Tensile strength of 19th century grey cast iron

Table A3.2.1 shows a comparison made by Professor W. C. Unwin[9] of the results of a number of tensile tests on grey cast iron published between 1815 and 1887. Up to 1850 published strengths averaged about 110 N mm^{-2} (7 ton in.$^{-2}$) with a maximum of just over 150 N mm^{-2} (10 ton in.$^{-2}$). Hodgkinson who was responsible for most of the tests took great care to ensure that he was testing purely in tension, although his specimens were not of the form used today. Other test results of the same period show similar strengths.

After 1850 tensile strengths seemed to increase quite markedly, but it is possible that by that time testing was most common with high-grade iron such as that used for cannons. One of the biggest problems with early tests on all materials is to know how often the same test results have been reported by more than the original authors. This makes the calculation of a characteristic value from such reports of uncertain value.

Present tests, using modern techniques, of the tensile strength of specimens cut from mid-19th-century structures are not easy to find. Quite frequently bending tests have been carried out without related ones being made on tension. However, the results of tensile tests on 20 specimens mainly from quite large

beams carried out in four separate appraisals from 1934 to 1987 are as follows:

Lowest	104 N mm^{-2}	(6.7 ton in.$^{-2}$)
Highest	243 N mm^{-2}	(15.7 ton m^{-2})
Mean	187 N mm^{-2}	(12.2 ton m^{-2})

There are not enough samples here from which to draw broad conclusions; one dominant set of high results may be giving a too optimistic mean value.

Taking all these results together it would seem unwise to rely on today's minimum strength of 150 N mm^{-2} as given in BS 1452: 1977 when considering large 19th-century castings, even when assessments based on hardness tests point to this. BS 1452: 1977 specifically warns that the relationship of hardness to tensile strength is uncertain.

Appendix 3.3: Development of the understanding of the bending strength of grey cast iron

To understand the present state of knowledge on the bending strength of grey cast iron it may be helpful to see how certain misconceptions arose and how these were partially corrected later, yet still leaving uncertainties which remain today. The first misconception—in some ways an understandable one—was Thomas Tredgold's. It was published in 1822 and persisted for more than 20 years.

Tredgold[10] reported tests on bars 25 mm × 25 mm square in bending with a span of 405–914 mm and a central point load. From these tests he derived a formula for the 'safe' load capacity of cast iron beams based on what he saw as the limit of elastic behaviour. When dissected this 'all-in-one' formula can be seen to be based on the modulus of rupture and a straightforward bending moment. He provided constants to adjust his formula for different types of loading and beam sections. The modulus of rupture as found varied between 280 and 400 N mm^{-2}

Table A3.2.1 Tensile strength of grey cast iron (from Unwin[9])

Experimenter	No. of tests	Cross-section (in.^{2})	Tenacity (ton in.$^{-2}$)			Probable No. of fusion	Condition of test bars	Reference
			Highest	Lowest	Mean			
Minard and Desormes	13	0.23–0.5	9.08	5.09	7.19	—	Rough	Love, *Résistance de la Fonte* (1815)
Hodgkinson and Fairbairn	—	1–4	9.76	6.00	7.37	2nd	Rough	*Brit. Assoc. Rep. VI*, (1837)
	81	3–4.5	10.5	4.9	6.83	2nd	Rough	*Report on App. Iron* (1849)
Woolwich	53	—	15.3	4.2	10.4	2nd and 3rd	?	*Report of 1858* (1856)
	6	—	—	—	13.7§	—	—	*Report on Metal for Cannon* (1856)
Wade	4	—	—	—	9.1†	—	—	*Report on Metal for Cannon* (1856)
Turner‡	—	1.0	15.7	4.75	—	2nd	Rough	*J. Chem. Soc.* (1885)
Rosebank foundry	23	—	18.2	6.5	15.3*	—	—	*Industries* (April 1887)
Uwin	6	0.75	—	—	13.7	2nd	Turned	—
	3	1.0	17.3	14.9	15.7	2nd	Turned	—
Wade	—	—	20.5‖	—	—	—	—	—

* Selected as good iron.
† Selected as bad iron.
‡ Special series of experimental test bars, with varying proportion of silicon.
§ Mean of ten best specimens.
‖ Highest result obtained.

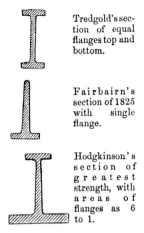

Tredgold's section of equal flanges top and bottom.

Fairbairn's section of 1825 with single flange.

Hodgkinson's section of greatest strength, with areas of flanges as 6 to 1.

Figure A3.3.1 Evolution in the cross-section of cast iron beams between 1820 and 1840. (From Fairbairn[19])

(18–26 ton in.$^{-2}$) with an apparent elastic limit of 106 N mm^{-2} (6.83 ton in.$^{-2}$). Effectively he was advocating a design method for grey cast iron based on a safe tensile stress strength of 106 N mm^{-2} thinking he had a factor of safety of between 2.6 and 3.8, whereas for larger beams this stress was dangerously near the upper limit. He also extracted from his formula and advised the direct use of this same 'safe' stress of 106 N mm^{-2} in tension and compression. Given the engineering knowledge of the time, much of Tredgold's reasoning was sound; he had no reason to doubt the validity of extrapolation from small bending tests. What was less sound was his dismissal of ultimate tensile strengths of 112 N mm^{-2}, which he knew had been found earlier by Captain Sam Brown, and of 130–135 N mm^{-2} as found by J. Rennie, in favour of the unexplained figure of 438 N mm^{-2} given by Musschenbroeck.

Basing his thinking on an assumed elastic behaviour with equal strength in tension and compression, Tredgold advocated cast iron I-beams with equal top and bottom flanges as the most economical section. Such beams were widely used in bridges and major buildings at least as late as the 1840s. In many cases, perhaps almost universally in major structures, each beam was proof-loaded, the proof-loads together with full dimensions quite frequently surviving on drawings of the period. Not surprisingly, some of these proof-loads were very high.

The man who partly corrected Tredgold's misconception was Eaton Hodgkinson who carried out an extensive series of tests on cast iron which were first published in 1831.[11] Hodgkinson not only showed by test that grey cast iron was much stronger in compression than in tension, but he also deduced that in beams the neutral axis must rise towards the compression face, due to the non-linear behaviour in tension, so that the amount of material in tension increased with a corresponding increase in load-bearing capacity.

Hodgkinson 'observed' that this rise of the neutral axis of a beam could bring the axis as close to the compression face as 1/5 or 1/6 of the overall depth. This observation was based on the form of fracture of inverted-T beams or those with very small top flanges. If Hodgkinson's interpretation of what he saw had been wholly correct it would have gone almost all the way towards an explanation of the difference between Tredgold's ultimate tensile strength of 280–400 N mm^{-2} derived from the modulus of rupture and Hodgkinson's own tensile strengths of 110–115 N mm^{-2} based on a direct pull with careful precautions against eccentricity. Regretably, more recent tests do not support the concept of so large a shift in the neutral axis.

Having shown that the grey cast iron of his time was about six times as strong in compression as in tension and that the ultimate tensile strength of that iron was about 100–115 N mm^{-2}, Eaton Hodgkinson evolved his 'ideal section' of beam *with a bottom flange of up to six times the area of the top flange*. In practice this proportion was generally found to be impractical, and in most 'Hodgkinson' beams the proportion is nearer to 3:1 or 4:1. *Figure A3.3.1* shows the cross-sections of cast iron beams as advocated by Tredgold, Fairbairn and Hodgkinson.

'Hodgkinson' beams were widely used from the 1830s onwards, mainly in industrial and engineering structures, but Tredgold's thinking seemed to persist in civic and domestic building until at least 1850.

For practical design Hodgkinson also put forward a very simple formula for the ultimate bending strength of cast iron beams. This is shown in *Figure A3.3.2*. It was clearly based on the concept of a very large shift of the neutral axis and was extensively used throughout the 19th century and even quoted in handbooks after 1900. Comparing the strengths of beams actually tested with equivalent strengths calculated from Hodgkinson's formula, it can be shown that this formula tends to bracket the real strengths although it over-estimates the strength of some of the larger beams by 40% or more.

By the middle of the 19th century it was probably thought that the analysis of cast iron beams had been mastered. The reason why little or no more work was done on the structural performance of cast iron between Hodgkinson's very original achievements around the early 1830s and the present century was not just that the problems appeared to be solved. By the 1850s not only was cast iron beginning to get a bad name as an unreliable material but it was being overtaken as the fashionable 'advanced' material by wrought iron.

Today we are much less certain[12,13] that we understand how best to design or analyse cast iron beams, yet old structures are increasingly being found in need of appraisal, either for increased traffic loads in the case of bridges or renovation and adaptation in the case of buildings. Several studies and well-monitored tests made during the last 50 years have raised new uncertainties. The main ones are:

(a) The shift of the neutral axis cannot be used on its own to explain the very large difference between the modulus of rupture of small bars and their tensile strength. Tests on beams with strain gauges show that the shift of the axis is quite small, say 5% of the overall depth of section or a little more but much less than Hodgkinson believed.

(b) The large difference between the modulus of rupture of big beams and of small bars cannot wholly be explained as a combination of shifting neutral axis and of grain size due to the different rate of cooling between large castings and small ones. Small bars cut from large castings have been shown to have as high a modulus of rupture as small bars cast as such.

Table 3.3 shows the significant results of these tests. It is unfortunate that each test did not include strain gauges, tensile tests and bending tests on small specimens cut from the beams. However, there are enough corroborations to rule out experimental error as the source of the anomalies.

Acknowledgements

The British Cast Iron Research Association, the British Foundry Association, Glynwed Foundries and Ballantine Boness Iron Co. Ltd. provided information used in parts of this chapter as did John Thornton and Paul Craddock of Ove Arup & Partners and J. A. Allen. G. N. J. Gilbert has been especially helpful.

(A) GENERAL CASE (no reference to stress)

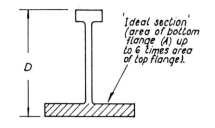

'Ideal section'
(area of bottom
flange (A) up
to 6 times area
of top flange).

$$Breaking\ load = W_{ULT} \frac{C.A.D.}{L}$$

(Where L = span & C is a constant)

(B) PARTICULAR CASE (test basis and results)

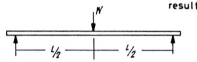

$$W_{ULT} = \frac{26\ A.D.}{L} \quad or \quad \frac{24\ A.D.}{L}$$
$$\qquad\quad cast\ erect \qquad\quad cast\ on\ side$$

(Where L, A, D in inches & W in tons.)

(C) EQUIVALENT TO (B) IN TERMS OF STRESS

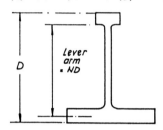

lever
arm
= ND

$$W_{ULT} = \frac{4t.\ A.N.D.}{L}$$

(Where t = ultimate tensile strength
of cast iron)

Figure A3.3.2 Hodgkinson's empirical formula for the strength of cast iron beams (shown in relation to his 'ideal' beam section but more broadly applied)

References

1 ANGUS, G. T., *Cast Iron: Physical Engineering Properties*, Butterworth, London (1976)
2 BARNFIELD, J. R. and PORTER, A. M., *The Structural Engineer*, **62A** (12), (1984)
3 DEPARTMENT OF TRANSPORT, The Assessment of Highway Bridges and Structures, *Departmental Standard BD 21/84*. Issued by the Department of Transport 1984 and prepared by a working party with representatives from: Department of Transport; Scottish Development Department; Department of the Environment for Northern Ireland; Association of County Councils; Association of Metropolitan Authorities; British Railways Board; London Transport; British Waterways Board
4 GLC, Cast Iron Columns and Beams, *GLC Bulletin No. 91* (2nd series), (Jan. 1976)
5 ISE, *The Appraisal of Existing Structures*, report issued by the Institution of Structural Engineers, 11 Upper Belgrave Street, London SW1X 8BH
6 THE WELDING INSTITUTE, 11 Pall Mall, London SW1
7 THE BRITISH CAST IRON RESEARCH ASSOCIATION, Alvechurch, Birmingham B48 7QB
8 THE BRITISH FOUNDRIES ASSOCIATION, Bridge House, Smallbrook, Queensway, Birmingham B5 4JP
9 UNWIN, W. C., *The Testing of Materials of Construction*, Longmans, London (1910)
10 TREDGOLD, T., *A Practical Essay on the Strength of Cast Iron*, J. Taylor, London (1822)
11 HODGKINSON, E., *Manchester Literary and Philosophical Society. Memoirs*, 2nd Series. Vol. 5, pp. 407–554 (1831)
12 SUTHERLAND, R. J. M., Thomas Tredgold. Part 3: Cast Iron, *Trans. Newcomen Society*, **51**, (1979–80)
13 SUTHERLAND, R. J. M., Recognition and Appraisal of Ferrous Metals, *Symposium on Building Appraisal, Maintenance and Preservation*, Bath University (July 1985)
14 BRE, *Loading Tests on Cast Iron Beams*, Building Research Establishment private report (1984)
15 GOUGH, H. J., Tests on Cast Iron Girders Removed from the British Museum, *I.C.E. Selected Engineering Papers No. 161* (1934)
16 COOPER, P. E., The Behaviour of Cast Iron Beams in Bending, M.Eng. Thesis, Leeds University (1986–87)
17 CHETTOE, C. S., DAVEY, N. and MITCHELL G. R., The strength of cast iron girder bridges, *Proc. ICE*, Paper No. 5418 (1944)
18 BRE, *Static Strength of Cast Iron Girders*, Building Research Station Private Report (1968)
19 FAIRBAIRN, W., *On the Application of Cast and Wrought Iron to Building Purposes* (1864)
20 CLARKE, E., *The Britannia and Conway Tubular Bridges*, Day and Son, London (1850)

Bibliography

Compared with other materials little has been written since 1900 on the properties of cast iron as used in the construction industry. Cast iron receives passing mention in many books on the properties of materials and specialist papers have been written on its properties mainly in relation to mechanical rather than civil or structural engineering. As well as the specific references in this chapter the following two books may prove useful.

ANGUS, H. T., *Cast Iron: Physical and Engineering Properties*, Butterworth, London (1976)
GLOAG, J. and BRIDGEWATER, D., *A History of Cast Iron in Architecture*, Allen & Unwin, London (1948)

The first of these books covers the engineering properties of cast iron and the second gives one of the best introductions to its use in the past.

4

Wrought Iron

J Sutherland FEng, BA, FICE, FIStructE
Consultant to Harris & Sutherland

Contents

4.1 Introduction 4/3

4.2 Types of wrought iron 4/3

4.3 Metallurgy and texture 4/3

4.4 Strength of wrought iron 4/3
    4.4.1 General 4/3
    4.4.2 Ultimate tensile strength of hot-worked
        sections 4/4
    4.4.3 Tensile strength of wrought iron plates parallel
        and perpendicular to the grain or direction of
        rolling 4/4
    4.4.4 Relative strength in tension and compression 4/6
    4.4.5 Variation of strength of wrought iron with size of
        sections 4/6
    4.4.6 Modulus of elasticity, elastic limit and elongation
        at failure 4/6
    4.4.7 Effect of cold working 4/6
    4.4.8 Strength in shear 4/7
    4.4.9 Impact resistance, 'crystallization' and
        fatigue 4/7
    4.4.10 Effect of temperature 4/8
    4.4.11 Practical appraisal of the strength of wrought
        iron 4/8
    4.4.12 Durability of wrought iron 4/9
    4.4.13 Repairs to wrought iron 4/9

4.5 Conclusions 4/9

References 4/9

Appendix 4.1 History of the manufacture and use of wrought
        iron 4/10

4.1 Introduction

Compared with cast iron, wrought iron is a simple material. Its structural properties are effectively the same in tension, compression and bending and far more certain than those of cast iron. It is a ductile material free from the 'brittleness' of grey cast iron and compared with historic grey cast iron about two to three times as strong in tension.

Between the mid-1840s and the early 1850s wrought iron gradually took over from cast iron as the high-performance structural material and was recognized as such until towards the end of the 19th century when, in turn, it was superseded by mild steel, a material of greater all-round strength capable of being formed industrially into much larger structural sections.

Today there is no wrought iron industry at all in Britain, although attempts are being made to reintroduce it on a museum level. Even though in most respects today's steel is a superior material there are some properties of wrought iron which are better than those of steel, notably its greater resistance to corrosion and the ease with which it can be shaped or 'wrought' into complex shapes of varying section.

In the sections which follow most of the references to tests and many of the opinions quoted date from the 19th or early 20th centuries. The reason for this is that virtually no research has been carried out on wrought iron in the last 75–100 years and very little has been written on the subject except of the most general nature. Appraising engineers should bear this time-scale in mind, especially when making comparisons with more recent experience with steel. When in doubt they may feel the need to carry out their own confirmatory tests, but before deciding to do so they could well consider the discussion of attitudes to practical appraisal given in Section 4.4.11.

4.2 Types of wrought iron

It is convenient to divide wrought iron into two types, although basically they are both the same material. These types are:

(a) *Blacksmith's wrought iron.* Virtually all iron before the introduction of the blast furnace (around 1500 in Europe) was of this type, extracted in a pasty, never molten, state and formed into the required shape by hammering. This was essentially a small-scale craft process which was gradually superseded by wrought iron produced from cast iron in a finery or a puddling furnace.

(b) *Industrialized wrought iron.* Henry Cort's patent of 1783 for the puddling furnace is broadly accepted as the start of wrought iron on an industrial scale, although this was only the climax of a number of developments. The important point with the puddling process was that it lifted the production of wrought iron from a craft level to what was to become one of the great industries of the 19th century.

Some further information on the production of wrought iron and on the development and waning of the processes is given in the Appendix to this chapter.

4.3 Metallurgy and texture

Basically, wrought iron has a simple metallurgy, being virtually pure iron with only 0.02–0.05% of carbon (compared with 0.2–1.0% for steel and 2.0–5.0% for cast iron). It has mainly been formed either by hammering or rolling and, in the case of structural sections (plates, bars, flats, angles, T-sections, channels and joints), rolling became virtually universal. Unlike the granular nature of cast iron, wrought iron has a fibrous texture, similar to timber, but this texture is only noticeable

(a)

(b)

Figure 4.1 (a) Fibrous texture of wrought iron as disclosed by partial cutting through and then tearing a wrought iron bar. (b) Granular structure of cast iron fracture shown for comparison with fracture of wrought iron

when the material is torn or when it is seriously corroded. The forms of fracture of wrought and cast iron are compared in *Figure 4.1.*

In rolled or cut forms it is very difficult to distinguish wrought iron from steel, but, when fractured, steel has essentially a much finer and less fibrous texture. One feature of wrought iron which shows up when it is polished and etched is the presence of fine lines of slag strung out in the direction of rolling. This slag is the inevitable residue of the hand puddling process with which it would be impossible to remove all impurities. The slag veins have little, if any, effect on the strength of the wrought iron in the direction of rolling but can reduce the strength perpendicular to the grain (see Section 4.4.3) and make welding more difficult (see Section 4.4.12).

4.4 Strength of wrought iron

4.4.1 General

There is no current British Standard for wrought iron as a material and no British Standard Code dealing with its structural use. As a result, practical assessments of the strength of wrought iron applied by engineers today often bear little relationship to the way we consider other materials like steel or concrete. Some think we should use the design criteria current when the structure or component was built or manufactured. As a result decisions often err on the side of excessive conservatism, but this is not necessarily the case.

Today the most helpful 'official' advice on the structural properties of wrought iron is given in the standard BD21/84, *The Assessment of Highway Bridges and Structures*, issued in 1984 by the Department of Transport together with a number in other national authorities.[1] This document is virtually unique in considering wrought iron in limit-state terms and in providing authoritative and up-to-date advice on its use in structures. However, it was written for the assessment of a particular range of structures, essentially bridges, and deals with all materials used in this range. Thus its treatment of wrought iron is far from comprehensive.

The broader relevance of this document and its limitations are considered in Section 4.4.11, but before discussing these it is worth looking at what we know of the actual properties of wrought iron and at some doubts—even myths—which have grown up over the years.

4.4.2 Ultimate tensile strength of hot-worked sections

A very large number of tensile tests have been made on wrought iron over a period of about 200 years. In many cases only the ultimate strength was recorded without reference to final elongation, elastic limit or elastic modulus. Inadequate recording (and the repetition of results without giving full credits) makes it difficult either to compare these tests or to analyse them statistically. However, a representative record of actual test results is given in *Tables 4.1* and *4.2*. These test results may usefully be compared with some generalized values for strength put forward at different times and shown in *Table 4.3*.

The strength of wrought iron might be expected to have increased as techniques improved during the 19th century. This does not appear to be the case. Some of the earliest test results show high tensile strengths for wrought iron—almost as high as those one would expect for mild steel today. Part of the high strength may be due to work hardening, but in general these figures all appear to be for hot-rolled sections of roughly 25–35 mm side or diameter.

It can be seen from *Tables 4.1* and *4.2* that the tensile strength of wrought iron may apparently vary between 258 N mm^{-2} (17 ton in.$^{-2}$) and 557 N mm^{-2} (36 ton in.$^{-2}$). However, the upper limit here seems unlikely to be repeated very often and the range given in the withdrawn British Standard, BS 51: 1939 (*Table 4.3*), is probably more representative of what one is likely to find.

Individual tests in relation to any structure, or even on the iron in the same member in that structure, could be confusing unless repeated many times. The strength of wrought iron can vary almost as much within the length of a member as between different members or even different manufacturers. This is discussed further in Section 4.4.11.

4.4.3 Tensile strength of wrought iron plates parallel and perpendicular to the grain or direction of rolling

Wrought iron plate has been stated as being as little as two-thirds as strong perpendicular to the grain (or direction of rolling) as parallel to it. While there appears to be quite strong evidence for the existence of such a difference there is much less certainty about the extent of this or whether in practice it is significant.

Test figures quoted by Humber[2] show that for some 16 different sources of plate the amount by which the strength across the grain is reduced below that along the grain varies

Table 4.1   Recorded results of tests on strength and ductility of wrought iron bars, flats, angles, etc. (see *Table 4.3* for wrought iron plate)

Author and date of publication	No. of tests	Ultimate tensile strength		Yield stress		Elongation at failure	Notes
		Range (N mm^{-2})	Mean (N mm^{-2})	Range (N mm^{-2})	Mean (N mm^{-2})	(%)	
Barlow,[15] 1837	9 (yield 6)	420–491	448	221–329	272	—	Telford/Brunton test
	7	407–482	453	—	—	0.5–12.1 (mean 5.1)	S. Brown tests
	10	387–526	464	278–417	340	—	M. Brunel tests (best iron)
	10	464–557	495	340–433	371	—	M. Brunel tests (best best iron)
	6	417–510	479	—	—	—	M. Brunel (best iron)
	3	—	—	155–186	170	—	P. Barlow (not to destruction)
Hodgkinson,[16] 1849	1	368	368	195	195	3.5	Fixing ⎫ Taken from plots
	1	—	—	200	200	—	failed ⎬ of stress/strain early ⎭ curves
Humber,[2] 1870	6	285–386	346	—	—	—	Ship straps, angles, etc.
	4	283–303	291	166–185	171	—	Very soft Swedish iron
	188	308–476	397	—	—	—	Bars ⎫ Kirkaldy
	72	261–440	378	—	—	—	Angle irons ⎭ tests
Unwin,[6] 1910	12	348–475	387	170–216	196	—	Steel Committee tests
Cullimore,[10] 1967	10	278–352	322	195–258	223	—	Flat tie bars from Chepstow railway bridge
Sandberg (private comm.), 1986	4	327–340	336	227–252	239	—	All from the same flat tie member
Overall mean			396		260		

Table 4.2 Typical recorded results of tests on strength and ductility of wrought iron plate compared with test results for bars, flats, angles, etc.

Author and date of publication	No. of tests	Direction of loading in relation to grain	Ultimate tensile strength		Yield stress		Elongation at failure	Notes
			Range (N mm^{-2})	Mean (N mm^{-2})	Range (N mm^{-2})	Mean (N mm^{-2})	(%)	
Fairbairn,[3] 1850	11	Along	312–407	348	—	—	—	Plate 6–7 mm thick
	8	Across	286–425	356	—	—	—	Strength very similar in both directions
Clark,[8] 1850	12	Along	278–340	303	—	—	0.6–12.5	Plate 12–17 mm thick
	2	Along	304–312	308	—	—	—	Strengths on average
	2	Across	258–262	260	—	—	—	14% lower across grain than along it
Humber,[2] 1870	16	Along	299–404	355	—	—	—	Strength on average 8.2%
	16	Across	285–380	326	—	—	—	Lower across gain than along it
Unwin,[6] 1910	51	Along	336–443	377	185–281	240	6.4–30.9	Tests from Bohme, Berlin, 1884
	13	Across	307–360	325	200–237	215	1.7–16.9	UTS* averages 14% less across grain and yield 10% less than along it
Warren,[9] 1894	1	Along	338	338				
	1	Along	324	324	165	165		
	1	Across	280	280				

Overall mean along grain   358

% Reduction on strength of bars, etc. (*Table 4.1*)   9.6   ⎱ Taken together strength across gain as disclosed by these tests

Overall mean across grain   327   ⎰ averages 8.7% less than that along the grain

% Reduction on strength of bars, etc. (*Table 4.1*)   17.4

* UTS, ultimate tensile strength.

Table 4.3 Typical figures for the strength and ductility of wrought iron as published (or required) at different dates but not necessarily related directly to any tests (see also *Tables 4.1* and *4.2*)

Author and date	Ultimate tensile strength (N mm^{-2})		Yield stress (N mm^{-2})	Elongation at failure (%)	Notes
Clark,[8] 1850	Bars, etc.	371	185	—	Records 'useful' strength in tension and compression as 185 N mm^{-2} and cites bar sinking in compression at 232 N mm^{-2}
	Plate along grain	309			
Matheson,[17] 1873	Bars, etc.	309–371	'Permanent set' likely	—	
	Plate	278–340	at 155–170		
Humber,[2] 1870	Bars 387 (325 compression)		—	—	See Section 4.4.4
	Plates 340 (278 compression)				
Warren,[9] 1894		309–371	185	—	
British Standard SI-1939 (withdrawn)	Bars, angles, etc. (varies slightly with size)	309–387	—	14–33 depending on grade	
	Plates with grain	309–371		6–14 depending on grade and thickness	
	Plates across grain	263–375		3–5 depending on grade and thickness	
BD21/84: D.o.T.* basis for assessment of bridges, 1984	—		220 characteristic yield strength given for use in assessment		

* D.o.T., Department of Transport.

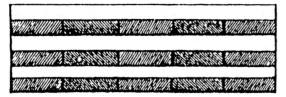

Figure 4.2 Method of laying up wrought iron flats (Lowmoor-iron plates) in layers at right angles to each other prior to rolling into plate iron. (From Fairbairn[3])

from less than 2% to almost 18%, with an average reduction of between 8 and 9%. Humber dismisses this variation as 'mattering little' in most cases.

Fairbairn[3] also gives some test results showing similar differences, but he also gives others that show no change or even greater strength perpendicular to the grain. He states that there is no material difference in the two directions and gives a diagram (*Figure 4.2*) showing how plate is made by piling strips of iron laid in opposing directions, as is the case for plywood, and then rolling the assembly.

BS 51: 1939 (withdrawn) recognizes a difference by requiring strengths for wrought iron plate as:

With the grain   309–371 N mm^{-2} (20–24 ton in.$^{-2}$)
Across the grain   263–325 N mm^{-2} (17–21 ton in.$^{-2}$)

These figures indicate a reduction of between 12 and 15% in strength across the grain compared with that along the grain.

The Department of Transport standard BD21/84[1], *The Assessment of Highway Bridges and Structures*, makes no mention of a possible difference in strength with direction of grain, while the Institution of Structural Engineers report,[13] *The Appraisal of Existing Structures*, 1980, warns that the tensile strength across the grain could be as little as three-quarters or even two-thirds of that along it.

There seems to be general agreement that all wrought iron plate is slightly weaker than bars, rods or other 'longitudinal' wrought sections of the same basic iron (see *Table 4.2*). The variation with the direction of loading in relation to the grain probably depends very much on the way in which the plates were made up which cannot readily be checked today. However, the bulk of the actual tests reported point to the strength across the grain averaging about 8% less than along the grain and at worst not more than 10–15% less.

In most structural uses (apart from boilers and other pressure vessels) the tensile strength of rolled wrought iron plate is probably less significant than that of, say, angles, flats or tie rods and thus a small variation in strength with the direction of grain may not matter. Nevertheless, it is important that appraising engineers be aware of this possible difference and, in this connection, look out for signs of lamination or splitting.

4.4.4 Relative strength in tension and compression

Lower ultimate strengths in compression than tension are stated as fact in some early writings and repeated without refutation, or with only partial refutation, in later handbooks. For instance, the ultimate strength has been quoted[4] from 1879 as: tension 325 N mm^{-2} and compression 247 N mm^{-2}. This anomaly was largely but not wholly dispelled by the research for the Britannia and Conway tubular bridges in the 1840s which isolated the problem of plate buckling. Today, as with steel, it is generally agreed that for practical purposes the two strengths are the same. The last British Standard for wrought iron (BS 51: 1939) specified tensile strength alone, with no mention of compression.

Tests referred to in Section 4.4.6 show effectively identical stresses of yield in tension and compression.

4.4.5 Variation of strength of wrought iron with size of sections

Most wrought iron structures are composed of flats, plate, angles, T-sections, channels and joists all of modest thickness (up to 25 mm and generally less). In this range the variation of strength with thickness appears to be small. Wrought iron tie rods are seldom more than 50–60 mm in diameter and again with these the tensile strength of the actual material seems to be sensibly constant. However, in the case of some large forgings the tensile strength has been shown to be appreciably reduced, even down to about 100 N mm^{-2} as pointed out in a paper by Malet in 1859[5] and discussed by Unwin.[6] Appraising engineers would do well to look particularly closely both at real strength and stress levels in the comparatively rare situations where large forgings are used in structures.

4.4.6 Modulus of elasticity, elastic limit and elongation at failure

In the 19th century a large proportion of the tests on wrought iron were confined to ultimate tensile strength, the aim being simply to ensure an adequate factor of safety for design according to elastic theory using a 'safe' stress of 62–93 N mm^{-2} (4–6 ton in.$^{-2}$). The result of this emphasis on ultimate strength is that there are comparatively few figures for the limit of elasticity, or yield, on which most present-day structural analysis is based.

Table 4.1 shows some figures for yield strength given in different publications which indicate an almost absolute minimum stress at yield of 170 N mm^{-2} and enough actual test results well over 200 N mm^{-2} to make the characteristic figure for yield in BD21/84 look reasonable.

Figures quoted for the elastic modulus range from just over 170 kN mm^{-2} to nearly 220 kN mm^{-2}, with a mean of, say, 195 kN mm^{-2}.

As in the case of the elastic limit, there are few published figures for elongation at failure and even fewer plots of stress against strain. Nevertheless, from the figures given in BS 51: 1939 (withdrawn) as summarized in *Table 4.3*, it can be seen that an elongation at failure of between 15 and 30% might be expected for linear sections like rods, angles, channels, etc., but possibly only about 6–14% for plate along the grain and even half those figures across the grain. Comparing these figures with an ultimate elongation of 0.75% or less for cast iron, one can see how welcome the ductility of wrought iron was to engineers when the material came into general use for bridges in the late 1840s.

One set of 'autographic curves' for wrought iron in tension, as published by Unwin,[6] is shown in *Figure 4.3*. These curves mostly show a distinct flattening at yield and then an increase in slope, as one expects for steel, but more plots are needed to make sure of this feature.

The effect of cold working on the ultimate tensile strength, elastic limit and elongation is discussed in Section 4.4.7.

4.4.7 Effect of cold working

As one might expect, cold working, whether cold rolling, cold hammering or wire drawing, has quite a marked effect on the properties of wrought iron.[6] *Table 4.4* shows two examples of the effect of cold rolling. More test results are needed to establish the changes quantitatively but the trend is clear. Cold working increases the ultimate tensile strength and the elastic limit but reduces the elongation to failure and effectively makes the material more brittle.

Cutting by shearing and forming holes by punching has the same effect locally as cold rolling or hammering, i.e. the iron around the hole tends to be made more brittle.[6] For this reason

Table 4.4 Effect of cold working on the properties of wrought iron

Form of iron	Type of cold working	Ultimate tensile strength (N mm^{-2})	Elastic limit (N mm^{-2})	Elongation to failure (%)	Source
Bar	Hot rolled to 32 mm diameter	402	—	20.3	Unwin[6] quoting from Fairbairn
	Subsequently cold rolled down to 25 mm diameter	594	—	8.0	
Plate	Hot rolled to 8 mm thick	367	224	15.0	Unwin[6] quoting from Considere
	Subsequently cold rolled down to 7.1 mm thickness	460	408	7.0	
Wire	Hot rolled	449 max. 283 min. 366 mean (approx.)	—	—	Rankine[7]
	Subsequently	787 max. 490 min. 635 mean (approx.)	—	—	

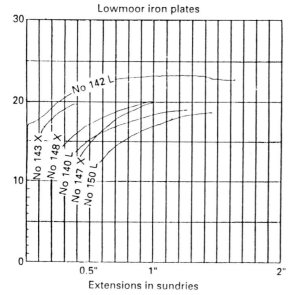

Figure 4.3 Typical stress/strain curves for wrought iron plate. (From Unwin[6])

some engineers have insisted on drilled holes rather than punched ones. Others have maintained that the effect is too local to be significant.

Wire drawing has a particularly marked effect on the strength of wrought iron as can be seen from Rankine's range of ultimate tensile strengths[7] given in *Table 4.4*. The wire may be more than 70% stronger with apparently the same basic material.

The effect of work hardening can of course be nullified by subsequent annealing.

4.4.8 Strength in shear

Shear strength has been given little attention in writings on wrought iron, or at least little attention compared with tensile strength.

For rivets, Clark[8] quoted results of experiments made in the 1840s showing an average shear strength of 370 N mm^{-2} in single shear and 340 N mm^{-2} in double shear for rivet iron with

a tensile strength of 340 N mm^{-2}. He concluded that the shear strength and the tensile strength are the same.

Later writers such as Warren[9] and Unwin[6] gave shear strengths of between 67 and 77% of the tensile strength for different irons, but did not give details of how these were tested.

Unwin also quoted shear tests made by Bauschinger (1874) mainly on wrought iron plate. These tests were made in six different directions in relation to the direction of rolling and showed that for 10 different irons a shear force in the two directions causing delamination within the thickness of the material was only about half the shearing force that the plates would resist in the other four directions. Regrettably these results are not related to the tensile strength of the material and it is not clear how significant they are in relation to practical construction.

4.4.9 Impact resistance 'crystallization' and fatigue

It appears to be generally agreed that the impact resistance of wrought iron is good—certainly vastly better than that of grey cast iron—and that it is not notch sensitive. However, there are too few precise test results with which to quantify these properties with confidence.

One sometimes hears it said that the wrought iron in a structure had 'gone crystalline' and thus 'become brittle'. There were a number of papers about this published in the mid-19th century, especially in relation to brittle failures of railway axles. On investigation some of these apparently showed a coarse crystalline structure (possibly as shown in *Figure 4.4*) rather than the traditional fibrous one (as shown in *Figure 4.1*), but others did not.

Today, expert opinion is inclined to the view that such obvious crystallinity existed unseen from the time of manufacture and that in normal conditions of temperature and use the phenomenon of 'going crystalline' does not exist. If investigated today the failures would probably be attributed to fatigue. Places where there had always been a coarsely crystalline and thus less resilient structure could be more sensitive to repeated loading than adjacent ones where the structure was normally fibrous. Rankine,[7] in the 19th century, went a long way towards dismissing the theory of progressive crystallization.

The classic work on fatigue was carried out by Wohler (1871) and by Bauschinger, both on wrought iron and steel. More recent investigations have been mainly limited to steel, but in the last 20 years two interesting investigations have been carried out by Cullimore, one on iron from Brunel's dismantled

Figure 4.4 Wrought iron with partially crystalline structure as disclosed after fracture

Chepstow rail bridge[10] and the other on Clifton Bridge at Bristol.[11,12] All three are generally reassuring in relation to the conditions to which these structures were subjected, but it could be misleading to try to generalize from these cases within the length of this chapter. Readers with a particular interest should refer to the published papers.

The likelihood of fatigue being a serious factor with wrought iron structures is discussed briefly in Section 4.4.11.

4.4.10 Effect of temperature

The coefficient of linear expansion of wrought iron is of the same order as that of cast iron and steel being generally between 10×10^{-6} and 12×10^{-6} per °C at normal working temperatures. As with cast iron and steel, the strength of wrought iron starts to drop off sharply above about 400°C. For this reason its behaviour in fire is likely to be very similar to that of structural steel.

4.4.11 Practical appraisal of the strength of wrought iron

The first problem with the appraisal of wrought iron structures is to establish without doubt whether one is dealing with true wrought iron or with steel (see Section 4.3). Once having done this, one can start to consider the material's quality and strength.

Much surviving wrought iron was probably sized by eye with no calculation of its strength in relation to its function. Its quality was not defined by tensile strength but largely by the amount of work put into its refining. (See the Appendix to this chapter.) When the strength of the wrought iron was calculated, a working stress of 4–6 ton in.$^{-2}$ (62–93 N mm^{-2}) was usually adopted, this figure giving a factor of safety of between 4 and 5 or at worst 3 in relation to the ultimate strength of the material. For railway bridges a safe or working stress of 5 ton in.$^{-2}$ (77 N mm^{-2}) was laid down by the Board of Trade in 1859 and this figure became almost standard in the 19th century in most fields.

Proof loading of important components was also quite common in the early or mid-19th century. In 1821, Telford was proving the links for the Menai Suspension Bridge to a stress of 10.75 ton in.$^{-2}$, based on an ultimate strength of 27 ton in.$^{-2}$. This proof stress was comfortably below the yield found by Telford, but more than double his working stress of 5 ton in.$^{-2}$.

Proof testing seemed to decline after the 1850s as confidence in calculation grew.

Many engineers consider that 19th century iron structures should be appraised on the basis used at the time of their design, that is with a working stress of 77 N mm^{-2} (5 ton in.$^{-2}$). However, such an appraisal ignores any advances made in our understanding in the last 100 years and is neither compatible with our approach to materials like steel and reinforced concrete today nor with recent thinking on appraisal as outlined in the Institution of Structural Engineers' (ISE) report[13] nor with the Department of Transport's Standard BD21/84.[1]

BD21/84 starts with a characteristic yield stress of 220 N mm^{-2} for wrought iron and a partial factor of safety for the material of 1.2.

Applying the partial factors of safety for loading of 1.4 for dead and 1.6 for live load used in design today and taking the mean of these, the *equivalent working stress* becomes

$$\frac{220}{1.2 \times 1.5} = 122 \text{ N mm}^{-2} \ (7.9 \text{ ton in.}^{-2})$$

This is nearly 60% higher than the 19th century safe stress of 77 N mm^{-2} and is still based on quite conservative partial factors of safety. The partial factors of safety for dead and live load in BD21/84 are generally less than the factors of 1.4 and 1.6 used in this comparison which indicates that a higher equivalent working stress could be justified for appraisals. The ISE report on appraisal[12] also advocates reduced partial factors of safety where conditions are known. It is interesting to note that the permissible working stress for wrought iron given in the Department of Transport's earlier assessment code BE4: 1967 was 8.4 ton in.$^{-2}$ or 130 N mm^{-2}.

The great advantage of applying a limit-state approach to appraisal with a characteristic strength of 220 N mm^{-2} for wrought iron is that some loss of section due to corrosion and some historic overloading may often be justifiable where this would have been a matter of concern using 19th century working stresses. The vital questions are whether BD21/84, intended primarily for bridges and other transport structures, can be applied to wrought iron in buildings and elsewhere and whether the characteristic strength of 220 N mm^{-2} is more broadly relevant than to just bridges. It would be difficult to argue that the criteria for safety in road or rail bridges, with large and varying live loads, are not adequate for most buildings. On the question of the adequacy of the characteristic strength of 220 N mm^{-2} it is worth looking at the basis of this.

The figure of 220 N mm^{-2} was based on over 500 tests analysed by British Railways Board. Most of these test results were collected by the Swiss from a large number of European Countries. The results of the analysis were:

Mean yield stress	263 N mm^{-2}
Standard deviation	24 N mm^{-2}
Characteristic yield stress (95% confidence)	221 N mm^{-2}
Lowest individual result	184 N mm^{-2}

Comparing these figures with the limited number of yield figures given in *Tables 4.1* and *4.2* shows a good measure of agreement.

It is notable that BD21/84 makes no distinction between wrought iron plate and 'linear' sections and no distinction as to loading along and across the grain. Also it makes no mention of any separate treatment of shear.

BD21/84 plays down the value of testing material in individual normal structures in favour of 220 N mm^{-2}, stating:

It must be appreciated that the yield stress of wrought iron determined from samples varies over a wide range, typically from 180 to 340 N mm^{-2}, and this range is not necessarily much narrower when samples are taken from the same structure. It is, therefore, unlikely that a few test results will provide any more reliable information about the strength of the material in the structure as a whole than the value given which is based on a large number of tests.

Nevertheless, BD21/84 does warn that the iron should be examined carefully for laminations, inclusions and deformities. If the iron does not appear to be sound it suggests testing and gives guidance on this.

Clearly it must be up to individual appraising engineers to establish the exact criteria to use. However, for wrought iron, BD21/84 provides a good starting point and has the advantage of a highly authoritative group of 'official' sponsors, which are listed in BD21/84.[1]

Where wrought iron plate in the webs of beams or in pressure vessels is highly stressed it may be appropriate to consider reduced stresses in tension (see Section 4.4.3). Also, for shear, especially in rivets, it would be prudent, short of further information, to work to a characteristic stress lower than 220 N mm^{-2} (see Section 4.4.8). BD21/84 gives no positive guidance on fatigue in wrought iron because of the problem of assessing past stress history. It refers to 'Part 10 of BS 5400 as implemented by Departmental Standard BD9/81 when fatigue endurance calculations are considered necessary.'

In nearly all buildings the problem of fatigue simply does not arise. Fluctuating load stresses are usually very low. Even with road bridges the variations in stress due to vehicles will probably be insignificant in most cases in relation to the fatigue life of the wrought iron, but appraising engineers would do well to check the possible levels of repeated change of stress as a matter of routine and consider these in relation to Dr Cullimore's three papers[10-12] and the Department of Transport's standards.

4.4.12 Durability of wrought iron

There appears to be no dissent today from the belief that wrought iron is more durable than steel when subjected to wet or corrosive conditions, but less durable than cast iron. It is quite common to find that steel in repairs made to 19th century wrought iron, say in the 1930s, has rusted more 40–50 years later than the original metal. There is a good case on grounds of durability for keeping steel out of wrought structures wherever this is practicable.

4.4.13 Repairs to wrought iron

The traditional methods of jointing wrought iron in the construction industry were: (a) forge welding, and (b) riveting. Forge welding was mainly confined to the forming of eye bars on flat ties and the upset ends to tie bars of square or circular section. The standard method of joining rolled wrought iron sections was originally by riveting, with a limited number of bolted connections to suit the conditions on a particular site; adjustable wedged ends to tie rods were also common.

Today, forge welding and riveting are as much dead techniques as the manufacture of wrought iron. With steel the standard methods of joining are by bolting or electric-arc welding. The most secure way of joining wrought iron today, or of making new fixings to wrought iron structures, is by bolting. However, this is not always practicable and may well involve the addition of cleats and brackets which, unless well designed, not only look unsightly but may give an impression of engineering incompetence.

In the past, electric-arc welding has been used with varying success on wrought iron, but many experts are confident that it is perfectly feasible to use this technique with this material given appropriately skilled operatives and the correct electrodes. The two special problems with the welding of wrought iron, as opposed to steel, are the greater possibility of lamination and the effect of the threads of slag on quality of the metal in the

weld. Butt welds between the ends of members perpendicular to the grain should present the least difficulty because, given adequate preparation, the weld should act uniformly across the whole cross-section. However, when welding to the sides of plates it may be appropriate to cut a groove to ensure that the weld 'bites' well into the plate, otherwise the joint may only be to the immediate skin and a failure due to lamination could follow. It would be prudent to consult the Welding Institute[14] for advice before carrying out any welding on wrought iron.

4.5 Conclusions

Wrought iron is, to a large extent, a maligned material. Its strength is not much below that of mild steel; the characteristic yield stress of 220 N mm^{-2} for wrought iron given in BD21/84 is only just less than the figure of 230 N mm^{-2} for pre-1955 steel given in the same standard. Furthermore, the resistance of wrought iron to rusting is certainly better than that of steel and wrought iron is more readily formed into complex shapes of varying section. Making joints (especially by welding) is a problem but is a far from impossible one to solve.

Availability of wrought iron is certainly a problem and one which is almost certain to become progressively worse as stocks of the material suitable for re-use are gradually used up.

References

1 DEPARTMENT OF TRANSPORT, The Assessment of Highway Bridges and Structures, *Departmental Standard BD21/84* (1984; with Amendment No. 1, 1989)
Issued by the Department of Transport and prepared by a working party with representatives from: Department of Transport; Scottish Development Department; Department of the Environment for Northern Ireland; Association of County Councils; Association of Metropolitan Authorities; British Railways Board; London Transport; British Waterways Board

2 HUMBER, W., *Cast and Wrought Iron Bridge Construction*, Lockwood, London (1870)

3 FAIRBAIRN, W., *Iron: Its History, Properties and Processes of Manufacture*, A & C Black, Edinburgh (1869). More detailed test results are given in Fairbairn's paper *An Experimental Inquiry into the Strength of Wrought Iron Plates and their Riveted Joints* read to the Royal Society (13 June 1850)

4 BATES, W., *Historical Structural Steelwork Handbook*, BCSA, London (1984)

5 MALET, R., On the coefficients T_e and T_r of elasticity and of rupture of wrought iron, *Proc. ICE*, **XVIII** (1858–59)

6 UNWIN, W. C., *The Testing of Materials of Construction*, Longmans, London (1910)

7 RANKINE, W. J. M., *A Manual of Civil Engineering*, C. Griffin, London (1872)

8 CLARK, E., *The Britannia and Conway Tubular Bridges*, Day and Son, London (1850)

9 WARREN, W. H., *Engineering Construction in Iron, Steel and Timber*, Longman, London (1894)

10 CULLIMORE, M. S. G., Fatigue strength of wrought iron after weathering in service, *The Structural Engineer*, **45** (5), (May 1967)

11 CULLIMORE, M. S. G., The Clifton Suspension Bridge—preservation for utilisation, *IABSE Proceedings*, p. 100/86 (1986)

12 CULLIMORE, M. S. G., Fatigue and fracture investigation carried out on the Clifton Suspension Bridge, *Proc. ICE, Part 1*, **84** (April 1988)

13 ISE, *The Appraisal of Existing Structures*, Institution of Structural Engineers, 11 Upper Belgrave Street, London SW1X 8BH

14 THE WELDING INSTITUTE (TWI), Abington Hall, Abington, Cambridge CB1 6AL

15 BARLOW, P., *A Treatise on the Strength of Timber, Cast Iron, Malleable Iron and Other Materials*, John Weale, London (1837)

16 Evidence to the Royal Commission on the application of iron to railway structures (1849)

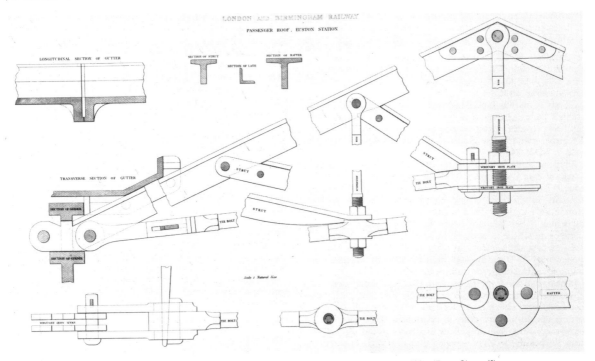

Figure A4.1.1 All wrought iron roof truss designed by Charles Fox for Euston Station in the mid-1830s. (From Simms[18])

17 MATHESON, E., *Works in Iron: Bridge and Roof Structures*, E. & F. N. Spon, London (1873)
18 SIMMS, F. W., *Public Works of Great Britain*, John Weale, London (1838)

Bibliography

Several of the publications referred to in the references to this chapter are worth consulting on a broad basis for an idea of the status of wrought iron in the 19th century, notably references 2, 3, 6–8, 16 and 17. In addition, the following may be found helpful.

SCHUBERT, H. R., Extraction and production of metals: iron and steel, in: *A History of Technology*, Vol. IV, Chap. 4 (ed. Singer *et al.*), Oxford University Press, Oxford (1958)
GALE, W. K. V., The rolling of iron, *Trans. Newcomen Soc.*, **XXXVII** (1964–65)
GALE, W. K. V., Wrought iron: a valediction, *Trans. Newcomen Soc.*, **XXXVI** (1963–64)
HEMPSTEAD, C. A. (Ed.), *Cleveland Iron and Steel: Background and 19th Century History*, British Steel Corporation, London (1979)
SUTHERLAND, R. J. M., The introduction of structural wrought iron, *Trans. Newcomen Soc.*, **XXXVI** (1963–64)
ASHTON, T. S., *Iron and Steel in the Industrial Revolution*, Manchester University Press, Manchester (1924) (mainly economic history)
GALE, W. K. V., *The Black Country Iron Industry*, The Iron and Steel Institute, London (1966)

Appendix 4.1: History of the manufacture and use of wrought iron

The earliest iron in the western world, from about 1000 BC, was all wrought iron produced from iron ore by a process of chemical reduction, generally in a Catalan furnace. It was never liquid

Figure A4.1.2 Britannia Bridge: four span (140 m max.) continuous tubular beams in wrought iron deep enough for trains to pass through. The bridge was destroyed by fire in 1970

Figure A4.1.3 Britannia Bridge: riveting the wrought iron plate. (From Clark[8])

Figure A4.1.4 Britannia Bridge: splitting of the wrought iron plate along the rivet lines due to contraction following the fire of 1970

(or if so only as a freak), but after extraction was purified and shaped by blacksmiths who worked, or wrought, it by hammering when in a semi-solid state. In Britain the organization of the 'industry' in the Middle Ages became quite sophisticated, but the actual process remained essentially a craft one.

The first step towards industrialization came with the introduction of the blast furnace around 1500 AD and the resulting possibility of melting and casting iron. This is described briefly in Appendix 3.1 to Chapter 3. However, even after the use of cast iron became practicable (and increasingly economical), the demand for wrought iron continued because of its much greater ductility and tensile strength.

The demand for wrought iron was met partly by continued production directly from iron ore and partly by the refining of cast iron in a 'finery', a furnace in which the greater part of the carbon was oxidized by a blast of air. The finary was only really effective for this purpose with very pure cast iron and it was not

until Henry Cort's twin inventions of the puddling furnace and grooved rollers in the early 1780s that the way was open to produce wrought iron on a truly industrial scale. Strictly speaking these inventions were both parts of a continuing development of techniques by Cort and several others, but they stand out as particularly important milestones.

The puddling furnace not only made it possible to produce good wrought iron from poor cast pig iron, by largely eliminating harmful ingredients like phosphorous and sulphur, but it also enabled the production of wrought iron to be carried out on a much larger scale.

Henry Cort's concurrent invention of grooved rollers harnessed to increasing availability of steam power was the perfect complement to the puddling process. It enabled the iron from the puddling furnace to be processed into useful forms such as flats, angles, T-sections and rods, at a rate compatible with the increased production of the actual material. Large-scale manufacture of rolled plate went almost in parallel and was followed by bulb angles, channels and joists.

It may seem curious that what was made possible by Cort and others in the 1780s did not have much impact on the construction industry until the late 1830s or, possibly, the 1840s. One reason for this delay was almost certainly the great success of cast iron between about 1780 and 1850. In this period and in particular between 1780 and the late 1830s there was little incentive to use a more expensive material to replace a cheap one which was apparently performing well.

It was the unprecedented loadings of the railways and the increasingly bad press of cast iron, following some notable collapses of cast iron structures in the mid to late 1840s, which did most for the wrought iron industry in Britain.

Wrought iron was used for the chains of suspension bridges and in roof trusses in the early 19th century, the latter reaching a high degree of sophistication in the roof of Euston Station (1836–37) (*Figure A4.1.1*), but the real breakthrough came after the very successful completion of the Conway and Britannia Tubular bridges in 1848 and 1850 (*Figures A4.1.2–A4.1.4*). Although these were not quite the first wrought iron girder

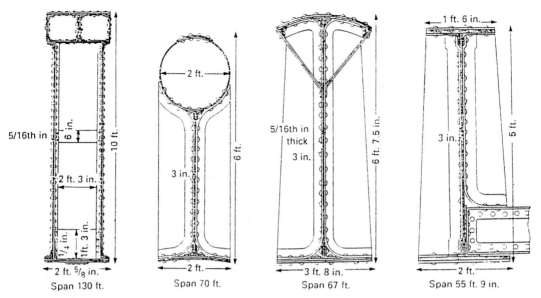

Figure A4.1.5 Typical forms of riveted bridge girders in wrought iron of the period between the Britannia Bridge and the establishment of the simple plate girder which dominated the late 19th century and much of the 20th century. (From Humber[2])

bridges to be built, it was the development work done for them by Stephenson, Fairbairn and Hodgkinson between 1845 and 1847 which, more than anything else, established the use of wrought iron in construction. From 1850 until towards the end of the 19th century, riveted wrought iron remained the 'advanced' structural material gradually superseding cast iron except for columns, brackets and other components where tensile stresses were very low or did not exist. *Figure A4.1.5* shows typical sections of riveted wrought iron bridge girder of the period immediately following the Britannia Bridge.

For the greater part of the 19th century wrought iron was not specified in relation to tensile strength or metallurgical purity but according to place of origin and the number of reheatings and rerollings to which it had been subjected. Hence the rather curious classifications as 'best', 'best–best' and 'best–best–best'

denoting the number of times the iron has been reworked and thus its degree of refinement. Tests reported by Fairbairn indicated that there was a limit to the number of reworkings which was beneficial.[3]

Steel gradually replaced the use of wrought iron in construction, but it was not until the completion of the Forth Bridge in 1890 that it became really established as a material for bridge building and other major structural work. Today no wrought iron is produced in Britain except experimentally at Ironbridge Gorge Museum. It is doubtful whether the extreme rigour of the work of puddling would be acceptable today, but, if reliable molten steel had not become available, it is possible that the late 19th century experiments with the mechanized puddling of wrought iron would have been carried to a successful conclusion.

5

Steel

J R Moon PhD
Department of Materials
Engineering and Materials Design,
University of Nottingham

Contents

5.1   General description 5/3

5.2   Manufacturing processes 5/3
   5.2.1   General 5/3
   5.2.2   Raw materials 5/3
   5.2.3   Primary steelmaking 5/3
   5.2.4   Secondary steelmaking: treatment in ladle 5/4
   5.2.5   Casting 5/5
   5.2.6   Mechanical forming processes 5/5
   5.2.7   Finishing processes 5/7
   5.2.8   Potential defects in products: quality assessment 5/7

5.3   Microstructures of steels 5/8
   5.3.1   General 5/8
   5.3.2   Inclusions 5/8
   5.3.3   Microstructural nomenclature and principles 5/9
   5.3.4   Ferrite–pearlite steels 5/9
   5.3.5   Microstructure control 5/12

5.4   Weldable structural steels 5/13
   5.4.1   General 5/13
   5.4.2   Grading system 5/13
   5.4.3   Equivalent standards 5/13
   5.4.4   Relative costs 5/13
   5.4.5   Steelmaking requirements 5/13
   5.4.6   Weldability requirements 5/14
   5.4.7   Steel compositions 5/14
   5.4.8   Properties 5/14
   5.4.9   Weathering grades 5/14

5.5   Welding of steels 5/14
   5.5.1   General 5/14
   5.5.2   Shapes and sizes of welds 5/14
   5.5.3   Choice of material 5/14
   5.5.4   Methods and consumables 5/15
   5.5.5   Welding defects 5/15
   5.5.6   Joint configurations and constraints 5/20
   5.5.7   Static strengths of welds 5/20

5.6   Other steels 5/21
   5.6.1   Steel plate, sheet and strip 5/21
   5.6.2   Structural steels 5/21
   5.6.3   Stainless steels 5/21
   5.6.4   Hollow sections 5/22
   5.6.5   Steels for fasteners 5/23
   5.6.6   Ropes and roping steels 5/23

5.6.7   Steel castings 5/23

5.7   Fast fracture 5/24
   5.7.1   Failure possibilities 5/24
   5.7.2   Methods for measuring K_{IC} 5/24
   5.7.3   Crack tip-opening displacement 5/25
   5.7.4   Uses of K_{IC} and δ_c 5/26

5.8   Fatigue performance 5/26
   5.8.1   General 5/26
   5.8.2   Methods of characterizing material properties 5/26
   5.8.3   Crack-growth data 5/27
   5.8.4   Applications in design of welded structures 5/28

5.9   Fire resistance 5/28

5.10 Corrosion and corrosion protection 5/29
   5.10.1   General 5/29
   5.10.2   Uniform corrosion 5/29
   5.10.3   Galvanic corrosion 5/30
   5.10.4   Crevice corrosion 5/31
   5.10.5   Splash zones 5/31
   5.10.6   Corrosion protection 5/31
   5.10.7   Cathodic protection 5/34
   5.10.8   Weathering and stainless steels 5/34
   5.10.9   Stress corrosion 5/35
   5.10.10 Corrosion fatigue 5/36
   5.10.11 Availability and use of data for stress corrosion and corrosion fatigue 5/36

5.11 British Standards 5/36
   5.11.1   General 5/36
   5.11.2   General steels 5/36
   5.11.3   Structural steels 5/36
   5.11.4   Steel castings 5/37
   5.11.5   Materials quality 5/37
   5.11.6   Welding 5/37
   5.11.7   Connections and fasteners 5/37
   5.11.8   Ropes 5/37
   5.11.9   Steels for concrete reinforcement and prestressing 5/37
   5.11.10 Corrosion and protection 5/37
   5.11.11 Testing 5/38
   5.11.12 Uses 5/38

References 5/38

Bibliography 5/38

5.1 General description

The term 'steels' encompasses a multitude of materials. Smithell's *Metals Reference Book*[1] contains some 62 pages devoted to steels—approximately 600 combinations of composition and treatment are listed.

Constructional steels are a subset whose limits are defined by:

(1) availability in large quantity at acceptable cost;
(2) ability to be fashioned into suitable sectional shapes;
(3) acceptable strength;
(4) acceptable toughness; and
(5) ability to be welded without the need for stringent precautions.

The main group of materials that meet these requirements are alloys of iron with carbon and various other alloying elements, principally manganese. Manganese is always present in amounts between 0.5 and 1.5%. It serves at least two useful purposes simultaneously (see Section 5.2.4). Weldability requirements place an upper limit on the carbon content at about 0.25%; high-strength fasteners may contain more. Other alloying elements may be introduced deliberately or be irremovable impurities. Each may act alone in determining the properties of the steel. More frequently, the metallurgy is dominated by interactions between the constituents of the steel.

The quality control of steels produced in the first half of this century was by control of composition and avoidance of obvious manufacturing defects. The introduction of all welded structures in the 1940s gave rise to a series of problems caused by fast brittle fractures. These were overcome by tighter control of composition and of metallurgical features such as grain size. More recent developments of high-strength low-alloy (HSLA), or microalloyed, steels demand much more stringent controls over both composition and structure. Tightly controlled rolling schedules are necessary for this purpose. Current research is aimed at producing the same quality of steel with less demanding control over rolling.

5.2 Manufacturing processes

5.2.1 General

The overall production route for steels is summarized in *Figure 5.1*. Most steel now made in the UK is derived from two raw materials: liquid pig iron and scrap. In 1984, 15.12 million tonne of steel was made in the UK, using 7.86 million tonne of scrap.

The refining methods which convert these materials into steel have changed considerably since Bessemer's invention (announced in 1856) and the development of the open-hearth method (introduced in 1865). Since about 1970, most Bessemer and open-hearth furnaces have been discarded in favour of the basic oxygen process and related processes and the electric arc furnace.

Much steel made by the older methods is still in use and so these methods are dealt with here as well as the more modern ones.

5.2.2 Raw materials

5.2.2.1 Liquid pig iron

The iron-making blast furnace produces liquid pig iron from iron ore, coke, limestone and air. The Redcar furnace at British Steel, Teeside, produces 70 000 tonne of pig iron each week—20 such furnaces produce the equivalent to the entire world output in the mid-1920s.

Typically, the pig iron contains (by weight) 3–4% carbon, 0.3–1% silicon and various other impurities, depending on the purity of the original ingredients. In much European practice,

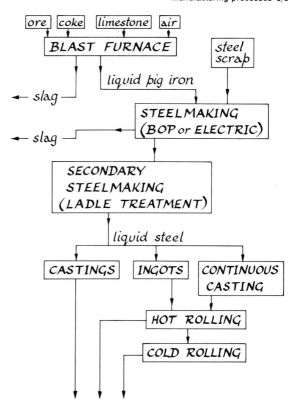

Figure 5.1 Scheme to show the routes of production for steels (BOP, basic oxygen process)

the other impurities of consequence are 2–2.5% phosphorus and about 0.05% sulphur. The use of imported ores in the UK usually gives rather lower phosphorus and sulphur contents.

5.2.2.2 Scrap

Roughly half the scrap used for new steelmaking arises in the steelworks itself; this is readily characterized and is usually recycled completely. Other sources are divided between 'prompt industrial scrap' and 'obsolete scrap'. The former is the discard from industrial manufacturing and, again, is characterized with ease. Obsolete scrap is the stuff of scrapyards which can contain unpredictable and sometimes severe contamination with copper, tin and other 'tramp elements'.

Continued recycling of materials is causing a slow drift upward of tramp-metal concentrations in the final steel. Although not yet a serious problem, the trend needs to be watched carefully and its potential consequences thoroughly researched.

5.2.3 Primary steelmaking

Primary steelmaking refers to the refining processes used to produce liquid steel. The aim is to produce a melt of the required composition. Typical ranges required for structural steels are:

carbon	0.15–0.25%
manganese	0.5–1.5%
sulphur and phosphorus	<0.05%

In addition the temperature of the melt must be raised. The high concentrations of impurities in pig iron allow it to be molten at about 1200°C, the approximate temperature of delivery from a blast furnace. As the impurities are removed, the temperatures required to keep the material molten climb towards the melting temperature of pure iron (about 1535°C).

5.2.3.1 The Bessemer/Thomas process

This process has not been used for large-scale production since about 1970. Indeed, BS 4360: 1986 (weldable structural steels) forbids its use. The Bessemer/Thomas converter was a cylindrical vessel which might contain between 20 and 150 tonne of molten metal. The bottom was perforated to allow air to be blown through the liquid charge to burn out the impurities. Enough heat was generated to cause the necessary temperature rise. Sometimes too much heat was generated and the melt was cooled by the addition of cold scrap. A complete production cycle would take about 30 min.

Acid and basic processes Bessemer's original furnaces were lined with refractories composed mainly of silica. Silicon and carbon were readily removed, but phosphorus and sulphur were not. This was particularly unfortunate in most of Western Europe where the most readily available ores were rich in phosphorus.

To remove phosphorus, it was necessary to dissolve it in slags based on the use of lime. These are chemically basic and would react aggressively with silica based furnace linings, which are chemically acidic. To resist lime slags, chemically basic linings are needed. These were developed in the late 1870s by Sidney Gilchrist Thomas and his cousin Percy Gilchrist. The linings are based on the use of burnt dolomite or magnesite. In many parts of the world, basic lined converters are known as Thomas converters. Thus, we have

Bessemer or *acid* steel: high phosphorus content (unless low phosphorus ores are used, as in the USA).
Thomas or *basic* steel: low phosphorus content.

5.2.3.2 The open-hearth (Siemens) process

This process was introduced for large-scale production in the last quarter of the nineteenth century. It is now obsolete in the UK, but is still in use in some parts of the world.

A large shallow bath of molten metal was purified relatively slowly by the use of appropriate slags. Furnaces containing, say, 200 tonne of metal were tapped at intervals of about 8–10 h. Overall production rates of 35 tonne h^{-1} were regarded as good.

Temperature was controlled by independent means and did not rely on exothermal burning of impurities, as in the Bessemer/Thomas process. This allowed much larger proportions of scrap to be used in the furnace charge; amounts varied between 40% and over 80%, averaging 45%.

Furnaces were lined with acid or basic refractories, depending on the quality of the pig-iron used.

One of the major advantages of open-earth steel was its low nitrogen content (0.004–0.006%) compared with 0.01–0.02% in Bessemer steel; nitrogen is an embrittling element.

5.2.3.3 The basic oxygen process

This is the main process in current use. Like the Bessemer/Thomas method, it relies on exothermic oxidation of impurities to raise the melt temperature. In this case, pure oxygen is used instead of air, and is usually introduced through a lance from the top of the furnace. Charges of up to 350 tonne are common, with cycle times of about 40 min giving production rates of about 500 tonne h^{-1} (14–15 times that of open-earth furnaces in the 1950s).

There are a number of variations on this basic idea. Sometimes the oxygen is diluted with argon to allow bottom blowing.

The use of oxygen instead of air has several advantages. No heat is wasted in heating nitrogen and no nitrogen is available to be dissolved in the metal.

To produce 1 tonne of steel in this way requires, typically:

0.8 tonne hot metal at about 1300°C,
0.3 tonne cold scrap steel,
0.07 tonne slag-making materials,
0.1–0.5 tonne pure oxygen, delivered at c. 10 atmos pressure and at a rate of c. 0.02 tonne min^{-1}.

5.2.3.4 Electric arc steelmaking

This process can be used for either liquid or totally solid furnace charges. Again, acid or basic furnace linings may be used depending on the phosphorus content of the charge. The process is used mainly for high quality alloy steels; refining and alloying can be carried out in a well-controlled way.

The process is also used as the source of material for 'mini-mills'. These are based on the use of scrap which can be readily remelted in arc furnaces. Quality control is mainly through control of the input scrap. Much of the product is in the form of reinforcing bar for concrete (see Chapter 6).

5.2.4 Secondary steelmaking: treatment in ladle

Whatever process is used, the liquid steel is not finished when it is tapped from the furnace. If it were cast without further treatment, the gases evolved as it solidified would cause the melt to foam and give a very porous product. Furthermore, the small amount of sulphur remaining in the steel must be tied up into an acceptable form. If this is not done, the sulphur would react with iron to form thin films of iron sulphide between the iron crystals, with a consequent host of processing problems and deleterious effects on properties. Several things need to be done.

It is necessary to deoxidize the melt. This may be done by addition of manganese and silicon, which react with dissolved oxygen to form insoluble particles of oxides. The oxygen can no longer react with dissolved carbon to produce gas bubbles of carbon monoxide and carbon dioxide. The deoxidizing additions are usually made in the form of ferro-alloys which also contain carbon. This limits the amount of deoxidizer which can be added without changing the carbon content unacceptably. In such circumstances, further deoxidation may be achieved by adding aluminium or other elements having a high affinity for oxygen. The alumina particles generated are tiny and can help control grain size during hot rolling. In some practice, aluminium is added specifically for this purpose.

The sulphur problem is also dealt with by the addition of manganese. Manganese sulphide is formed in preference to iron sulphide and forms into globular particles which are separated from one another in the solid product. The embrittling effect of iron sulphide is thereby removed.

It may be necessary to adjust the carbon and manganese contents to give the grade of steel required. Between them, these two elements have a great influence on the properties of structural steels. These will be dealt with in more detail later, but for the moment it is sufficient to say that carbon improves strength and manganese gives low-temperature toughness (see Section 5.3.4).

In both primary and secondary steelmaking, many inclusion particles or liquid droplets arise in the melt. The removal of such inclusions is a matter of some importance and may be achieved in a number of ways. The simplest method is to let the particles float to the top of the ladle and draw the steel to be used from the bottom (see Section 5.3.2).

Vacuum degassing is a practice now being brought into widespread use. In this process the melt is held under reduced pressure to remove residual gases. Sometimes, argon is bubbled through the melt to help the process by sweeping out the unwanted oxygen, nitrogen and hydrogen. Less deoxidizing addition is needed and fewer harmful inclusions are found in the product (see Section 5.3.2.1).

5.2.5 Casting

Like that for steelmaking, the technology for casting has changed significantly in the last 20 years or so. Previously, all steel products were made either directly into shaped castings, or were cast into ingots for subsequent processing. In the advanced industrialized countries, the ingot route for bulk steel production is disappearing in favour of continuous casting. In 1989, about 80% of all steel produced by British Steel was continuously cast.

5.2.5.1 Ingot casting

Ingots are usually of simple geometry (matchbox shapes or cylinders) which can weigh up to 20 tonne. They are made by pouring molten steel into cast-iron moulds. Top pouring gives rise to splashing and poor surface quality; bottom pouring gives a quieter melt and better surface quality.

Rimming steel ingots If the melt has not been deoxized, the dissolved oxygen reacts with dissolved carbon as the melt cools and begins to solidify. A volume increase caused by generation of bubbles of carbon monoxide counteracts the volume shrinkage of the steel as it solidifies. The result is a flat top to the ingot. Subsequent hot rolling collapses the pores and welds their surfaces together.

The main advantages of rimming steels are to the steelmaker. They are not suitable for structural use. Recent standards such as BS 5400: 1980 and BS 4360: 1986 expressly forbid the use of rimming steels, except for the lowest grades.

Killed and semi-killed steel ingots The term 'killed' comes from the use of a deoxidized steel, i.e. where the foaming action of a rimming steel has been killed. This may be done by any of the methods referred to in Section 5.2.4.

The relatively quiet conditions in the absence of bubble evolution gives the ingot a structure of the form shown in *Figure 5.2*.

Before subsequent processing, the top part of the ingot containing the shrinkage pipe must be cut away. Bands of inclusions are caused by interactions between the solidifying material and convection currents in the melt. These are retained throughout all further solid-state processing.

The deoxidation is often only partly completed. A small number of bubbles are allowed to form as a balance against the solidification shrinkage. Such steels are known as 'semi-killed' or 'balanced'. Some 85% or so of steels produced by the ingot route are in this category.

5.2.5.2 Steel castings

Most steel compositions can be cast directly into complex shaped components. Examples include stern frames for ships and nodal regions for large structures (oil rigs, etc.).

Solidification shrinkage is large, but good process design can avoid porosity and other defects in the finished casting. The castings are usually heat treated to relieve any residual stresses caused by uneven cooling and to refine the grain structure of the material.

In general, acceptable yield strengths and tensile strengths are obtained, although toughness is often poor when compared with wrought counterparts.

British Standards for general engineering purposes are listed in BS 3100: 1991.

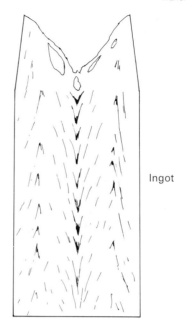

Ingot

Slab rolled from ingot

Figure 5.2 The structure of an ingot of killed steel

5.2.5.3 Continuous casting

Most structural steel now made in the UK is produced by continuous casting. The process cannot be used for rimming steels and is most suitable for fully killed steels. It gives billets which are nearer to the final section size than are ingots: the heaviest rolling mills used for the initial stages of ingot rolling are no longer needed. Associated refinements such as electromagnetic stirring in the mould cup give more uniform structures than for ingots. The fast cooling also gives a finer grain structure.

5.2.6 Mechanical forming processes

Mechanical forming processes are used to convert ingot or continuously cast materials into the shapes and sizes required. An equally important purpose of such processes is to modify and control the microstructure and properties of the products.

5.2.6.1 Rolling

Rolling is the most widely used process; it can be done hot or cold. A wide range of cross-sectional shapes can be produced. A flow chart leading to the principal products is shown in *Figure 5.3. Figure 5.4* clarifies some of the jargon used to describe semi-finished and finished products.

Hot-rolling All constructional steels are hot rolled to begin with; for many products, especially those with large metal thicknesses, this is the only stage. Ingots or continuously cast slabs are preheated to 1200–1300°C to make them soft enough to deform and shape. The temperature falls as processing is continued and preheating to lower temperatures is often necessary at intermediate stages. The total amount of work done by rolling and the finishing temperatures are important in the metallurgical control of quality. For example, BS 11: 1985 for railway rails requires at least 8:1 reduction in cross-sectional

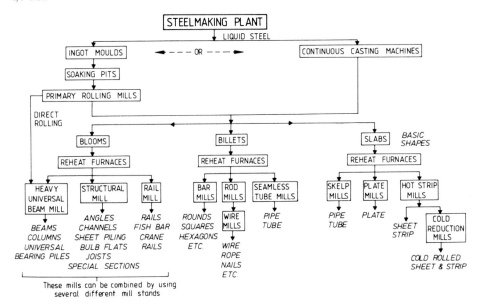

Figure 5.3 Principal product routes. (Reproduced by kind permission of the Director, The Steel Construction Institute)

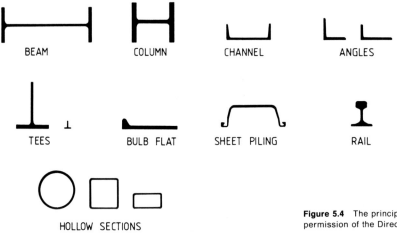

Figure 5.4 The principal structural sections. (Reproduced by kind permission of the Director, The Steel Construction Institute)

linear dimensions by hot rolling. In general low finishing temperatures (*c.* 900°C) are required. To give very fine grain sizes, which means a good combination of strength and toughness, *controlled rolling* may be used. This entails close control over finishing temperatures, which are usually close to 850°C, but may be as low as 650–750°C.

Cold rolling Cold rolling cannot be used to the same degree as hot working for shaping purposes, because of the increased strength of the cold workpiece. Modest reductions can be achieved by rolling to give better size tolerances and surface qualities. It is used mainly for lightweight sections. Work hardening during the process gives increases in yield strength at the expense of ductility and toughness. Profiling by bending, folding, etc., into corrugated or other shapes may be used to add section stiffness to thin strip or sheet products (*Figure 5.5*).

5.2.6.2 Other hot-working processes

Forging Hot forging is used to make shaped, usually blocky, artifacts which need to have properties better than those of castings. Presses or various forms of stamps, hammers, etc., are used to shape hot steel and to modify coarse as-cast structures into more homogeneous and finer grained wrought structures.

Seamless tube forming Seamless tubing is produced by hot deformation of initially cylindrical billets. Rolls which generate a spinning motion about the billet axis as well as motion along the billet axis are used to force the billet around a mandrel which defines the internal diameter of the tube.

5.2.6.3 Wire drawing

In wire drawing, a feedstock is pulled through a die by the

(a)

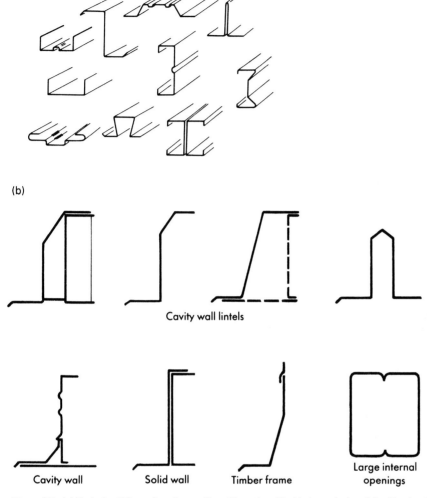

(b)

Cavity wall lintels

Cavity wall   Solid wall   Timber frame   Large internal openings

Figure 5.5 (a) Typical cold-formed section profiles. (Reproduced by kind permission of the Director, The Steel Construction Institute.) (b) Sections of some of the steel lintels used in domestic housing. (Reproduced from *Metals and Materials*, the journal of the Institute of Metals, Vol. 4, No. 6, 1988, p. 357)

product. If the material did not work harden, the process would not work. Successive reductions through many dies can be used to impart very high strengths by work hardening. The price paid is reduction in ductility and toughness.

5.2.6.4 Hollow sections

Seamless tube making is described above. Other hollow sections are made by folding and welding along the length of the part. Some tube is made by coiling strip in a helical fashion and welding along the helical seam.

5.2.7 Finishing processes

Finishing processes include heat treatment, straightening and other adjustments to tolerance, surface preparation for painting by shot blasting, etc., painting, galvanizing, plastic coating, etc.

5.2.8 Potential defects in products: quality assessment

5.2.8.1 Chemical composition

Methods of sampling are given in BS 1837: 1970, and methods for analysis are given in *BS Handbook No. 19.*

5.2.8.2 Size and shape tolerances

Size and shape tolerances are given in BS 4360: 1986, BS 4848: 1975, 1980, 1986 and BS 4: 1980.

5.2.8.3 Surface condition

Surfaces may contain defects arising from the casting and rolling processes. Usually, these are rolled-in oxides or scale or surface cracks. Strip and wide flats are dealt with in BS 6512: 1984.

Various methods of repair may be practiced, either with or without permission. Minor defects may be removed by local grinding, provided that the thickness is not reduced too much (more than 4% or 3 mm, whichever is less; hollow sections can lose up 12.5% or 3 mm, whichever is less).

Surfaces may also be repaired by welding. Defects are first ground out and filler metal deposited by welding can be used to restore section size. Not more than 20% of metal thickness may be removed and restored. Steels to grades 50 and 55 of BS 4360: 1986 may not be repaired in this way.

Methods and controls on the use of welding for this purpose are subject to the same standards as for joining by welding. These are dealt with in Section 5.5.

5.2.8.4 Internal defects

Internal defects may include holes, cracks, excessive quantities of inclusions or agglomerations of inclusions in particular regions of cross-sections. Of particular concern are potential agglomerations of anisotropically shaped inclusions. These are best removed by appropriate secondary steelmaking processes and/or inclusion shape control (see Section 5.3.2). If such agglomerates exist, they can seriously weaken the material in the through-thickness direction. Lamination failures can occur if the material is subjected to tension in that direction, either directly (usually as a result of welding) or as a consequence of buckling under longitudinal compression.

Quality assessment is done ultrasonically; the relevant standard giving details of methods and grades is BS 5996: 1980. Usually, a soundness grade of LC1 or better is required. This demands that the total area of defects discovered should not exceed 3.5% of the area examined and that the largest individual discontinuity should be smaller than 9700 mm^2.

5.2.8.5 Mechanical property requirements

It should be remembered that mechanical properties may be different in different directions. Details of appropriate testing procedures should be agreed. Section 3 in BS 4360: 1986 specifies sampling and testing methods.

5.3 Microstructures of steels

5.3.1 General

Some mechanical properties of steels are independent of their microstructures. The elastic moduli of all *plain carbon* structural steels are constant, irrespective of their composition or metallurgical condition (*Tables 5.1* and *5.2*).

All the strength and toughness properties are governed by the steel compositions and their microstructures. Much of the improvement in the available combinations of properties made during the last 20 years or so has been by control of

microstructures. The aim is to produce a very low inclusion content and a fine ferrite grain size.

5.3.2 Inclusions

Inclusions are particles of foreign materials in the steel, which arise from three main sources:

(1) small particles of furnace or ladle linings, etc., which have been washed into the molten metal—these are usually up to several millimetres in size, small in number and readily avoided by good steelmaking practice;
(2) entrained slag which is usually of large particles and readily avoided by good steelmaking; and
(3) products of chemical reactions in secondary steelmaking designed to convert impurities into a less harmful form.

Inclusions large enough to be observed optically are mostly entrained slag or manganese sulphide. At hot-rolling temperatures, these are plastic and are elongated along with the metal in the direction of rolling (see *Figure 5.6*). Highly anisotropic properties result, ductilities and toughness in the 'through thickness' direction being substantially worse than those in the rolling direction.

Some inclusions are too small to be seen readily using optical microscope and they must be detected by more expensive methods. They are mainly equi-axed in shape. Among this group are oxides and nitrides of aluminium or some other deoxidizing additions. Their effects are indirect, usually not harmful and sometimes beneficial, since their presence is helpful to the production of fine ferrite grain-sizes (see Section 5.3.4.1).

Table 5.2 The elastic moduli of steels*

	E (GPa)	G (GPa)	K (GPa)	v
Mild	205–210	80–85	160–170	0.27–0.30
0.75%C	210	80	170	0.29
1.0%C, 1.0%Mn 0.65%Cr, 1.0%W (hardened)	200–205	75–80	165	0.29–0.30
Stainless				
Austenitic	190–205	75–85	130–170	0.25–0.30
Ferritic	200–215	80–85	145–180	0.27–0.30
Martensitic	215	85	165	0.28

$$* G = \frac{E}{2(1+v)}; \qquad K = \frac{E}{3(1-2v)}.$$

These data (taken from a number of sources) are subject to measurement errors of, mostly, about ±5%.

Table 5.1 Physical properties

	Density at 20°C (kg m^{-3})	Coefficient of thermal expansion (10^{-6} K^{-1})	Thermal conductivity (0–100°C) (W m^{-1} K^{-1})	Specific heat (0–100°C) (J kg^{-1} K^{-1})
Pure iron	7870	12.1	78	455
Wrought low carbon steel	7860	12.2	65	480
Cast low carbon steel		12.2	49	
Medium carbon steel	7860	12.2	51	485
High carbon steel	7850	11.1	48	490

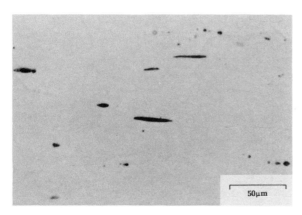

Figure 5.6 Inclusions in steel, elongated in the direction of rolling. This is a particularly dirty steel chosen to illustrate inclusions. Most structural steels are much better than this. (Reproduced by kind permission of the Director, The Steel Construction Institute)

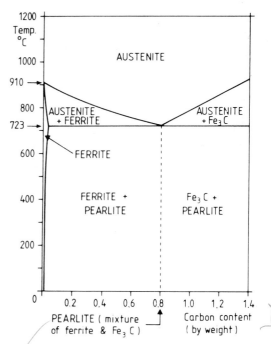

Figure 5.7 Part of the iron–carbon constitutional diagram. For further details see text. (Reproduced by kind permission of the Director, The Steel Construction Institute)

5.3.2.1 Clean steels

The secondary steelmaking methods described in Section 5.2.4 are aimed at reducing inclusions content. Sulphur contents of 0.01% or less can be produced; sulphur contents as low as 0.0006% have been obtained.

In addition to reducing the content of large inclusions, *inclusion shape control* is also part of modern practice. Calcium, cerium or other rear-earth elements combine with sulphur in preference to manganese. The resulting inclusions are less deformable than manganese sulphide and remain as equi-axed particles in the rolled products.

Such steels have much better ductilities and toughnesses than their more ancient equivalents. In particular, the through-thickness properties are greatly improved. These steels are especially valuable for applications which require fairly thick sections to be fabricated by welding, e.g. pressure vessels, oil and gas pipelines, and offshore structures.

5.3.3 Microstructural nomenclature and principles

Figure 5.7 is a part of the iron–carbon equilibrium diagram. This relates the stability of different structures to the combination of carbon content and temperature.

Ferrite: virtually pure iron, with the body-centred-cubic crystal structure. It is stable at all temperatures below 720–910°C depending on the carbon content of the steel.

Pearlite: a fine lamellar mixture of roughly 90% ferrite and 10% cementite containing 0.8% carbon by weight. It is stable at all temperatures below c. 720°C.

Cementite: iron carbide (Fe_3C), a compound containing 6.67% carbon by weight.

Bainite and martensite: products found in steels cooled rapidly from temperatures in the range of austenite stability, or in more slowly cooled alloy steels.

Austenite: the form of steel stable at temperatures above 720–910°C, depending on carbon content; it has a face-centred-cubic crystal structure and dissolves up to 2% carbon.

5.3.4 Ferrite–pearlite steels

A low carbon steel, slowly cooled from a temperature in the austenite range, consists of many polyhedral grains of ferrite and a few patches of pearlite (*Figure 5.8*).

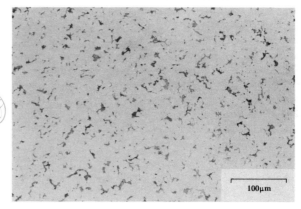

Figure 5.8 A ferrite–pearlite steel: in this case the steel contains 0.12% carbon and has been normalized. The ferrite grain size is about 10 μm

5.3.4.1 Ferrite grain size

The grain size of the ferrite is crucially important in several respects. Methods to control grain size will be dealt with later. Here we consider the effect of the grain size on the properties of steels.

Yield strength   The yield strength of a ferritic steel is determined by its grain size according to the Petch equation:

$$\sigma_y = \sigma_0 + kd^{-1/2}$$

where σ_y is the yield strength of the polycrystalline metal, σ_0 is the yield strength of a very large single crystal of the same metal (for ferrite in carbon steels $\sigma_0 \simeq 5$ MPa), k is a material constant

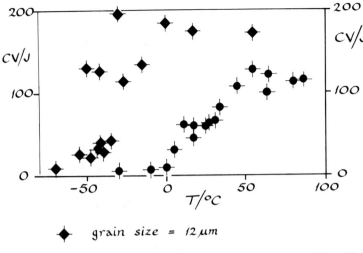

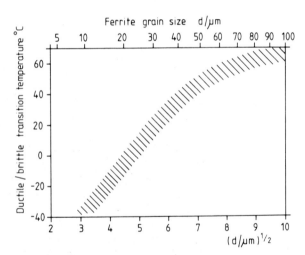

$\blacklozenge$ grain size = 12 μm

$\bullet$ grain size = 24 μm

Figure 5.9 The toughness of mild steel samples as a function of temperature

Figure 5.10 The effect of ferrite grain size on the ductile–brittle transition temperature of mild steel. (Reproduced by kind permission of the Director, The Steel Construction Institute)

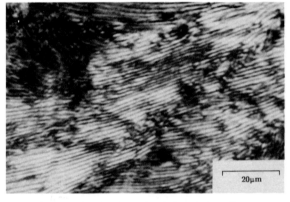

Figure 5.11 Pearlite: laminations of ferrite and cementite. (Reproduced by kind permission of the Director, The Steel Construction Institute)

(in this case 1.26 MPa m$^{1/2}$) and d is the grain size of the ferrite crystals (in metre). Thus, if $d \simeq 25$ μm, the $\sigma_y \simeq 255$ MPa and if $d \simeq 5$ μm then $\sigma_y \simeq 570$ MPa.

Ultimate tensile strength This is increased by a reduction in grain size, but the effect is not characterized as easily as for yield strength.

Toughness Significant improvements in toughness, especially at low temperatures, accompanies reduction in grain size.

Toughness as a function of temperature is shown for the same steel at two different grain sizes in *Figure 5.9*. The ductile–brittle transition temperature is reduced when the grain size is small (see *Figure 5.10*).

5.3.4.2 Pearlite

This is a finely divided laminated mixture of roughly 90% ferrite and 10% cementite (iron carbide, Fe_3C) (*Figure 5.11*). The scale of subdivision is close to the wavelength of visible light (c. 0.5 μm).

Cementite is hard and strong, but brittle; it transmits these qualities to the pearlite of which it is part. The properties of pearlite also depend on the spacing of the lamellae. The finer the spacing, the stronger is the pearlite.

In general, finer pearlite spacings arise from more rapid cooling of the steel from temperatures in the range of austenite stability.

5.3.4.3 Tensile properties of ferrite–pearlite steels

The properties of ferrite–pearlite mixtures are roughly the average of those of the constituents, weighted according to their volume fractions in the microstructure. Grossly simplifying, the pearlite content changes, roughly linearly, from zero at 0.01%

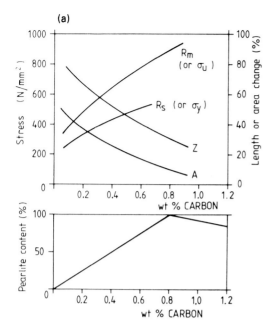

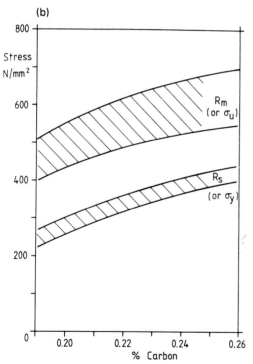

5.3.4.4 Notch-toughness of ferrite–pearlite steels

The impact toughness of steels containing ferrite decreases catastrophically as the ambient temperature is lowered, as depicted in *Figure 5.9*.

A large number of factors influence this so-called ductile–brittle transition:

(1) the carbon/pearlite content;
(2) the manganese content;
(3) the inclusion content and type; and
(4) the ferrite grain size.

The effects of the carbon/pearlite and manganese contents are shown in *Figures 5.13* and *5.14*, respectively, which are self-explanatory.

With regard to inclusion and type, *Figure 5.15* shows the effects of elongated inclusions on test-pieces cut with notches in different directions. This demonstrates the 'through thickness' problems of older steels. Clean steels which also incorporate inclusion shape control are considerably better in this respect.

With regard to ferrite grain-size, the ductile–brittle transition temperature (DBTT) is reduced when the grain size is reduced (see *Figures 5.9* and *5.10*), i.e.

$$\text{DBTT} \propto \sqrt{\text{grain-size}}$$

Both the tensile strength and the toughness at low temperatures are improved by reductions in grain size. This is the

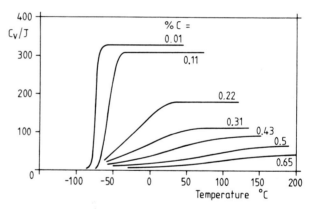

Figure 5.13 The effect of carbon content on the ductile–brittle transition of normalized steels. (Reproduced by kind permission of the Director, The Steel Construction Institute)

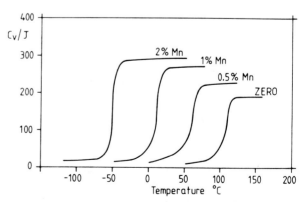

Figure 5.14 The effect of manganese content on the ductile–brittle transition of furnace-cooled 0.05% carbon steels. (Reproduced by kind permission of the Director, The Steel Construction Institute)

Figure 5.12 (a) The effects of carbon content on the pearlite content and tensile test properties of normalized steels. (b) The strengths and carbon contents of normalized steels specified in BS 4360: 1986. (Reproduced by kind permission of the Director, The Steel Construction Institute)

carbon to 100% at 0.8% carbon. The general effects of this content on properties are shown in *Figure 5.12*. Increasing carbon content increases strength at the expense of ductility and toughness.

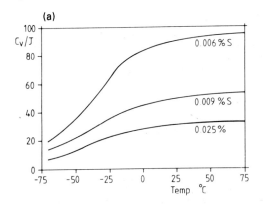

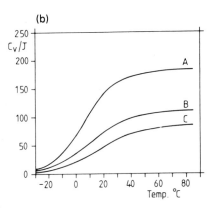

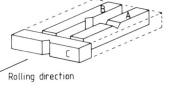

Rolling direction

Figure 5.15 (a) The effect of sulphur content on the toughness of high-strength low-alloy (HSLA) steel (minimum yield stress $R_s = 450 \text{ N mm}^{-22}$). (b) The effect of the orientation on notch toughness of as-rolled low-carbon steel plate. (Reproduced by kind permission of the Director, The Steel Construction Institute)

incentive for microstructural control in steel production. Much 'historical steel' has grain sizes in the range 10–50 μm. Modern grain-controlled steels have grain sizes of about 5 μm or less. This may not seem much of a change, but the property changes which this has brought about are profound.

5.3.5 Microstructural control

5.3.5.1 Normalizing

Normalizing is a heat-treatment process which plays a number of roles simultaneously. The steel is heated to a temperature of about 850°C and allowed to cool naturally in still air. The main purposes are to relieve any residual stresses caused by rolling, etc., and to control the ferrite grain size.

At the high temperatures applied, the steel structure consists of grains of austenite. On cooling, ferrite grains grow from the austenite grain boundaries and, finally, pearlite is formed.

The ferrite grain size and the interplanar spacing in the pearlite are both smaller if formed from fine-grained austenite. In ordinary steels, prolonged heating or too high a temperature causes austenite to coarsen and rolling schedules are usually organized to prevent this.

Steels containing small amounts of aluminium or, better, titanium or niobium form small particles by reaction with oxygen or carbon. These inhibit austenite grain growth and give fine-grained ferrite as a result. The 'D', 'E' and 'F' grades of steels in BS 4360: 1986 are examples of steels which use this method of grain-size control (they are normally used in the normalized condition).

5.3.5.2 Hot-rolling and controlled rolling

Structural steel sections are produced by rolling ingots or continuously cast material into the required forms. The early stages of rolling are carried out at temperatures easily deformed. The deformation breaks down the microstructure but the poly-crystalline structure of the austenite is continuously reformed by a process known as recrystallization. The amount and rate of deformation and the rolling temperatures affect the grain size; heavy deformations at low temperatures give small grains.

Grain-refining elements such as aluminium, titanium or niobium inhibit the growth of austenite grains and give finer

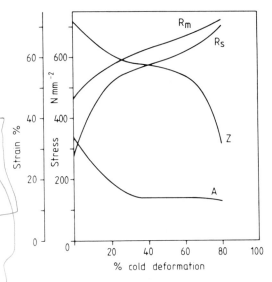

Figure 5.16 The effects of cold work on the tensile properties of steel (0.13–0.18%C, 0.6–0.9%Mn). (Reproduced by kind permission of the Director, The Steel Construction Institute)

grained ferrite and pearlite when the steel is finally cooled. In many cases there is little or no difference between a hot-rolled steel and a normalized steel.

5.3.5.3 Cold-deformation

Low carbon steels in thin section sizes may be rolled at ambient temperatures. This breaks up the ferrite–pearlite structures and causes work hardening: recrystallization cannot occur at these temperatures. The properties change with deformation as shown in *Figure 5.16*.

Other methods of cold working, such as wire drawing, can impart larger deformations. With suitable metallurgical adjustment, high carbon steels can be rendered ductile enough to allow extensive deformation. Very large amounts of work hardening can give very high-strength wires for ropes, etc.

Table 5.3 Coding systems for steels according to BS 4360: 1990 and BS EN 10 025: 1990*

BS 4360

The code consists of a number representing the ultimate tensile strength of the steel in hectobars (1 hectobar = 10 MPa = 10 N mm^{-2}). This is followed by a letter representing the impact performance of the steel (see below)

Grade	Ultimate tensile strength (MPa)	
	1979 edition	1986 and 1990 editions
40	400–480	340–500
43	430–540	430–580
50	490–620	490–640
55	550–700	550–700

BS EN 10 025: 1990

The code consists of the symbol for iron (Fe) followed by a number which represents the minimum ultimate tensile strength of the steel in megapascals. This is followed by a letter representing the impact performance of the steel (see below). This procedure is identical with that used in the equivalent International Standard (ISO 630: 1980).

Further letter groupings may be added in the following order (these are used only when required).
(a) De-oxidation code: FU, rimming steel; FN, rimming steel NOT allowed; FF, fully killed steel with further requirements.
(b) Application code: KQ, cold flanging; KP, cold roll forming; KZ, cold drawing.
(c) The letter 'N', indicating that the steel has been normalised (this is implied for grades D1 and DD1).

Letter	Impact performance of steel
A	No test (abolished in 1990 standards)
B	27 J at 20°C
C	27 J at 0°C
D	27 J at −20°C (1979 and 1986 only)
DD	27 J at −30°C (1979 and 1986 only)
DD1	40 J at −20°C (1990 only)
DD2	40 J at −20°C (1990 only)
E	27 J at −40°C (1979 and 1986 only)
EE	27 J at −50°C
F	27 J at −60°C

* Based on BS 4360: 1979, 1986 and 1990 Weldable structural steels and BS EN 10 025: 1990 Hot rolled products of non-alloy structural steels and their technical delivery conditions; courtesy of British Standards Institution.

5.4 Weldable structural steels

5.4.1 General

BS 4360: 1986 was until recently the cornerstone in Britain defining structural steels which may readily be welded. In 1990, this was replaced by two new standards: BS EN 10 025: 1990 Hot rolled products of non-alloy structural steels and their technical delivery conditions, and BS 4360: 1990 Weldable structural steels (it is intended that this too will be replaced by a series of four new European standards).

The appearance of these standards and the earlier versions of BS 4360 (1979 and 1986) has made redundant a number of earlier standards, namely:

A grades—BS 15: Earlier mild-steels for general structural purposes

B grades—BS 968: High yield stress (welding quality) structural steel; and

C, D and E grades—BS 2762: Notch ductile steel for bridges and general building purposes.

5.4.2 Grading systems

The grading systems of the two 1990 standards differ. These are given in *Table 5.3*. The systems give information about the minimum required ultimate tensile strengths and the impact performance of the steels at low temperatures.

5.4.3 Equivalent standards

Equivalences between the 1986 version of BS 4360 and the two replacements of 1990 are given in *Table 5.4*.

5.4.4 Relative costs

The higher grade steels demand better control over steelmaking practice, inspection and certification. This is reflected in the costs of the materials which, obviously, will depend on the form and quantity of the product required (see *Table 5.5*).

5.4.5 Steelmaking requirements

The Bessemer process is forbidden. Any other processes may be used; the most likely is the basic oxygen process. Rimming steel is forbidden. The higher strength grades (50 and 55) usually contain grain-refining additions.

Material may be supplied in various conditions:

(1) as-rolled—hot rolled with no specified controls on rolling temperature;
(2) normalized (see Section 5.3.5.1);
(3) temperature controlled rolled (TCR)—hot rolled with tem-

Table 5.4 Equivalences between the two standards published in 1990 and the 1986 version of BS 4360

BS 4360: 1986	BS EN 10 025: 1990
40B	Fe 360 B
40C	Fe 360 C
40D	Fe 360 D1, Fe 360 D2
43B	Fe 430 B
43C	Fe 430 C
43D	Fe 430 D1, Fe 430 D2
50B	Fe 510 B
50C	Fe 510 C
50D	Fe 510 D1, Fe 510 D2
50DD	Fe 510 DD1, Fe 510 DD2

BS 4360	
1986	1990*
40E	40EE
43E	43EE
50E	50EE
50F	50F
55C	55C
55E	55EE
55F	55F

* Nomenclature is unchanged but grades E have been upgraded to EE.

Table 5.5 Rough guide to the costs of different grade steels

Grade	43A	50B	55C
Relative cost*	100	110	125

* 100, cheapest; 125, most expensive.

Table 5.6 The maximum permissible carbon equivalent (CE) value for different steel grades

Grade	Maximum CE (%)
40	0.39–0.41
43	0.39–0.41
50	0.43–0.47
55	0.41–0.53

perature in the austenite range; the material is equivalent to normalized steel; or

(4) thermomechanical controlled rolled (TMCR)—hot rolled with significant deformation at temperatures low in the austenite range or lower; this gives refined grain sizes and beneficial properties; subsequent normalizing or other heat treatment will cause grain growth and deterioration of properties.

5.4.6 Weldability requirements

Weldability is limited by the carbon equivalent value (CE) of the steel. This quantity is calculated as described in Section 5.5.3. Maximum permissible CEs vary according to product form, thickness and steel grade (see *Table 5.6.*).

5.4.7 Steel compositions

Steels contain 0.16–0.25% carbon, 1.5–1.6% manganese and, 0.1–0.5 silicon. The higher strength grades (50 and 55) have grain-refining additions of aluminium, niobium and vanadium in small quantities and achieve their properties through grain-size control; this may be aided by normalizing or by thermo-mechanically controlled rolling.

Low-temperature grades demand more stringent control over phosphorus and sulphur contents, i.e. of inclusions.

5.4.8 Properties

Tensile and impact properties vary a little with product form and thickness. In general, the more mechanical deformation that can be imparted during rolling, the better are the properties. Full details are given in BS 4360: 1986. Examples of data for flat products are given in *Table 5.7*.

5.4.9 Weathering grades

Weathering grade equivalents are available for grades 50A, 50B and 50C. These are designated WR50A, etc., and have extra additions of chromium, copper and, in 50A, nickel, which confer the weathering quality (see Section 5.10.8). The mechanical properties of these steels differ little from those of the equivalent non-weathering grades. For the corrosion aspects of these steels see Section 5.10.5.

5.5 Welding of steels

5.5.1 General

Welding is a complex operation which involves not only the formation of a joint but also thermal cycling and chemical reactions in the locality. Molten weld metal must be protected from adverse reactions with the environment. Differential expansions and contractions can cause distortions and/or residual stresses and the local heat treatment of the steels can cause microstructural and property changes.

Table 5.7 Properties of structural steels according to BS 4360: 1986 (plates and wide flats)

Grade	Tensile strength ($N\ mm^{-2}$)	Minimum yield strength at 16 mm ($N\ mm^{-2}$)	Charp V-notch impacts 27 J at (°C)
40A	340/500	235	—
40B	340/500	235	20†
40C	340/500	235	0
40D	340/500	235	−20
40EE	340/500	260	−50
43A	430/580	275	—
43B	430/580	275	20†
43C	430/580	275	0
43D	430/580	275	−20
43EE	430/580	275	−50
50A	490/640	355	—
50B	490/640	355	20†
50C	490/640	355	0
50D	490/640	355	−20
50DD	490/640	355	−30
50EE	490/640	355	−50
50F	490/640	390	−60
55C	550/700	450	0
55EE	550/700	450	−50
55F	550/700	450	−60

* Reproduced from BS 4360: 1986; courtesy British Standards Institution.
† The specified impact values are verified by test only at the request of the purchaser.

Structural steels, as defined by BS 4360: 1986, are chosen for their weldability, i.e. so that property changes brought about by welding produce a joint which is acceptable for the service envisaged.

When the weld zone is raised to the melting temperature of the steel, the solid metal immediately adjacent to it is heated to temperatures well within the austenite range. On removal of the heat source, the whole reaction cools at rates determined by the conduction of heat into the surrounding cold metal. These rates of cooling can be very rapid, sometimes exceeding $1000°C\ s^{-1}$.

Depending on the steel composition and the rate of cooling, the local microstructure might revert to ferrite and pearlite or might form martensite or bainite. The properties of these products are shown in *Figure 5.17*. To avoid problems such as quench cracking, hydrogen embrittlement and the formation of locally brittle regions, a maximum hardness of about $HV = 350\ kg\ mm^{-2}$ is taken as an acceptable rule of thumb (tensile test data corresponding to this hardness are given in *Figure 5.17*).

Ways in which suitable weld properties may be obtained are:

(1) by choosing appropriate material to be welded;
(2) by choosing a suitable welding method (energy input) and consumables; and
(3) by preheating the weld zone and surrounding metal.

5.5.2 Shapes and sizes of welds

The terms used to describe the shapes and sizes of butt and fillet welds are given in *Figure 5.18*.

5.5.3 Choice of material

The tendency to form the undesirable products martensite or bainite at a given cooling rate depends on the steel composition.

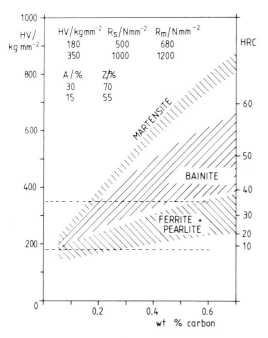

Figure 5.17 The effect of carbon content on the hardness of various steel microstructures. (Reproduced by kind permission of the Director, The Steel Construction Institute)

Even if such products form, they would be acceptable, provided the hardness generated does not exceed a Vickers hardness (HV) of 350 kg mm^{-2}.

The criteria used to aid material choice are:

(1) the carbon content of the steel;
(2) the carbon equivalent (CE) of the steel which takes account of the influences of other alloying elements

$$CE = C + \frac{Mn}{6} + \frac{Cr + Mo + V}{5} + \frac{Ni + Cu}{15}$$

where the chemical symbols represent the percentage by weight of that element in the steel.

Weldable steels, i.e. steels which may be readily welded with few precautions, are normally required to have CE < 0.4–0.5% (BS 5135: 1984 specifies CE < 0.54%) and C < 0.25–0.3%. For example, BS 4360: 1986 defines structural steels suitable for welding. Two examples are:

	C (%)	Mn (%)	CE (%)
Grade 43A	0.25	1.6	0.52
Grade 50D	0.18	1.5	0.43

Note that, although grade 50D contains only three-quarters as much carbon as grade 43A, it has a yield strength of 355 MPa compared with 275 MPa for grade 43A. This difference is achieved by control of grain size.

5.5.4 Methods and consumables

Steels may be welded by most of the available methods. Oxyacetylene welding can be used for thin sections but cannot deliver enough power to cope with thick sections. Most welding of sections thicker than about 2 mm is done by arc methods. These include manual-metal-arc, submerged-arc and gas-shielded-arc methods. Relevant standards for methods, plant, consumables, operators and inspection are listed in Section 5.11.6.

Guidance on the scope of inspection, acceptance criteria and correction is available in *BCSA Publication No. 1/89*.[2]

5.5.5 Welding defects

Some typical weld defects are shown in *Figure 5.19*.

5.5.5.1 Poor weld shape, incomplete penetration and side-wall fusion

A skilled welder should be able to avoid these defects by good practice. The defects arise from using a badly chosen welding current, incorrect diameter of electrode, poor electrode manipulation and the presence of mill-scale on the work.

5.5.5.2 Slag inclusions

Defects due to slag inclusions arise from inadequate practice. Most often defects are due to incomplete removal of slag in multi-run welds and at the roots of incompletely penetrating welds.

5.5.5.3 Porosity

Porosity arises from gas evolution as the weld pool solidifies and from shrinkage on solidification. Most often the cause is moisture on unclean surfaces and improperly dried electrodes. Rust is a notorious harbourer of moisture.

Unstable arc conditions associated with too long an arc and with starting up an arc can also give rise to porosity. The unreplenished weld pool left at the end of a run can also be a site of potential porosity.

None of the types of defect described so far seriously impair properties of welds if they are isolated and small. They do, however, give warning of poor practice and of potentially more serious defects.

5.5.5.4 Solidification cracking

This usually manifests itself as a centreline crack often, but not always, breaking the surface of the weld. The cracks can be deep.

The cause is usually that the weld metal contains too high an impurity content. Electrodes are usually chosen to have carbon, sulphur and phosphorus contents lower than those of the base metal. Dilution of the weld metal can occur, i.e. melting of base metal and its mixing with the metal originating from electrodes. High dilution, i.e. a large proportion of base metal, increases the impurity content and accentuates the potential for solidification cracking. High dilution processes include submerged-arc and root-runs in manual-metal-arc welding. Suitable choices of consumables and process should normally avert the problem. Situations of high constraint (see later) can aggravate the problem.

5.5.5.5 Hydrogen cracking

Hydrogen can be absorbed into molten and solid hot metal during welding. It can give rise to cracking of a very characteristic appearance which can appear some time after the weld has been completed. The time to the appearance of cracks may be days or months. Because of this, the terms 'delayed cracking' or 'hydrogen induced delayed cracking' are used.

Three factors influence the probability of cracking:

(1) the amount of hydrogen picked up during welding;
(2) the residual stresses developed; and
(3) the toughness of the material where the crack appears (this is often in the heat-affected zone, just below the weld).

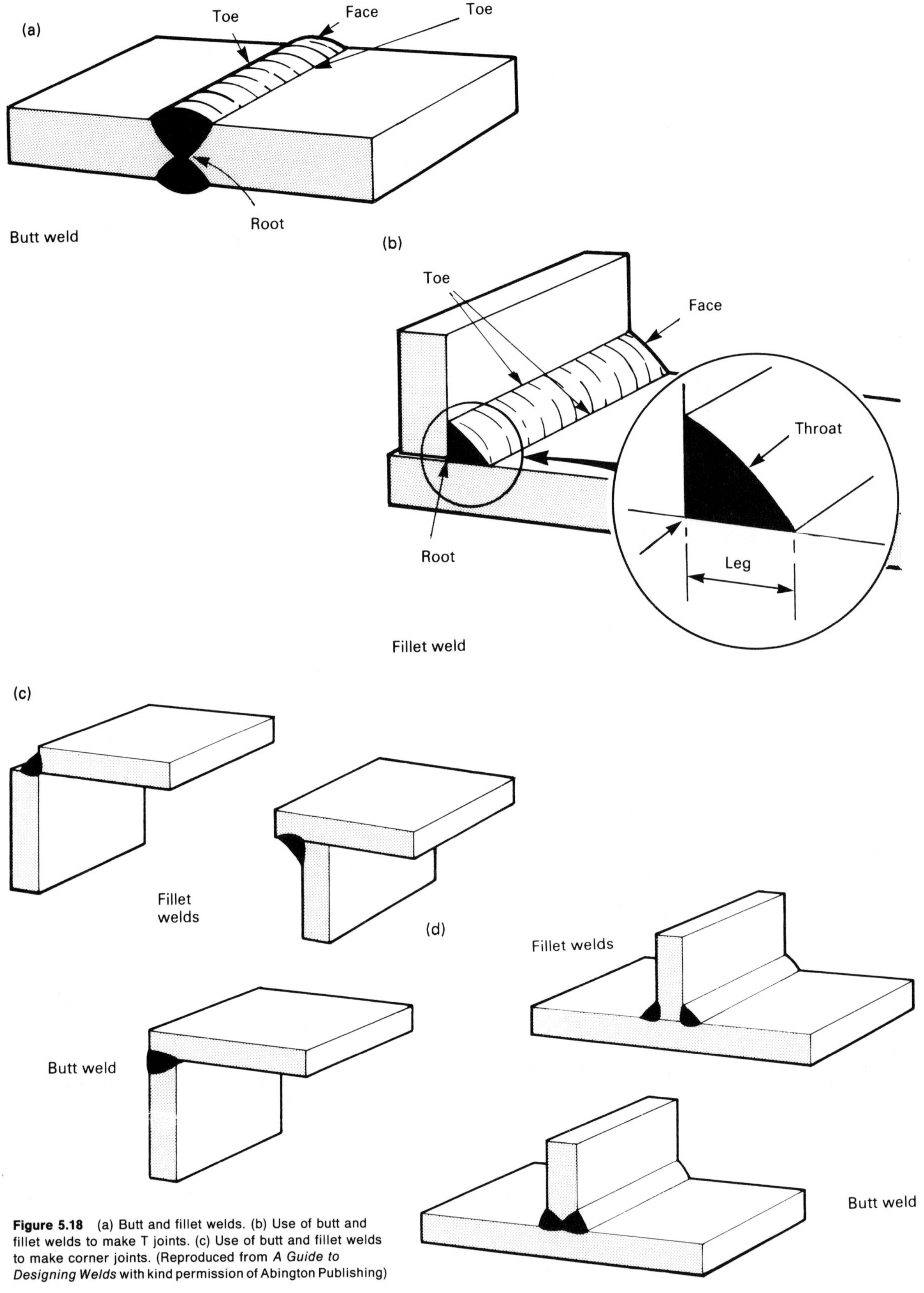

(a)

Toe

Face

Toe

Root

Butt weld

(b)

Toe

Face

Throat

Root

Leg

Fillet weld

(c)

Fillet
welds

(d)

Fillet welds

Butt weld

Butt weld

Figure 5.18 (a) Butt and fillet welds. (b) Use of butt and
fillet welds to make T joints. (c) Use of butt and fillet welds
to make corner joints. (Reproduced from *A Guide to
Designing Welds* with kind permission of Abington Publishing)

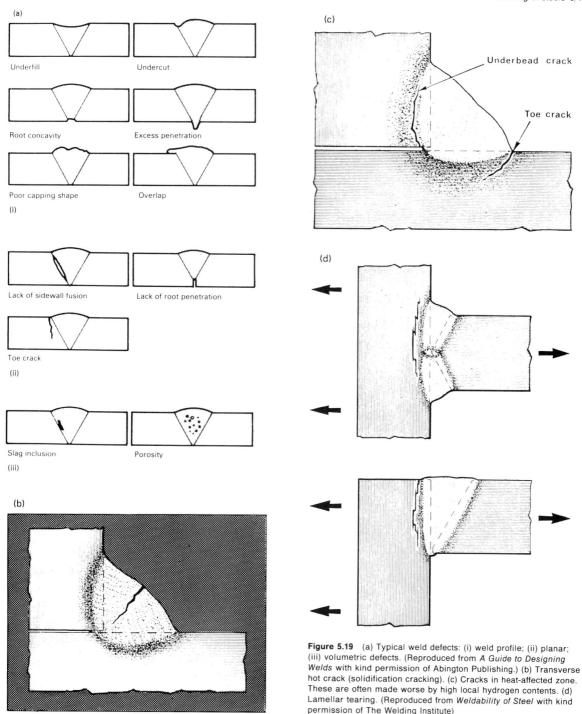

Figure 5.19 (a) Typical weld defects: (i) weld profile; (ii) planar; (iii) volumetric defects. (Reproduced from *A Guide to Designing Welds* with kind permission of Abington Publishing.) (b) Transverse hot crack (solidification cracking). (c) Cracks in heat-affected zone. These are often made worse by high local hydrogen contents. (d) Lamellar tearing. (Reproduced from *Weldability of Steel* with kind permission of The Welding Institute)

Reduction of hydrogen content is a matter of choosing suitable electrodes, keeping them and the base metal clean and dry and good welding practice. Hydrogen scales (A to D) exist to provide a framework for the specification of consumables (*Table 5.8*).

Residual stresses and metallurgical changes are influenced by cooling rates after welding. High heat input gives slower cooling rates, whilst large metal thickness increases cooling rates. Preheating of the work before welding can also be used to slow down the rate of cooling. Diagrams such as *Figure 5.20(a)* are available in BS 5135: 1984 to guide the choice of the preheating

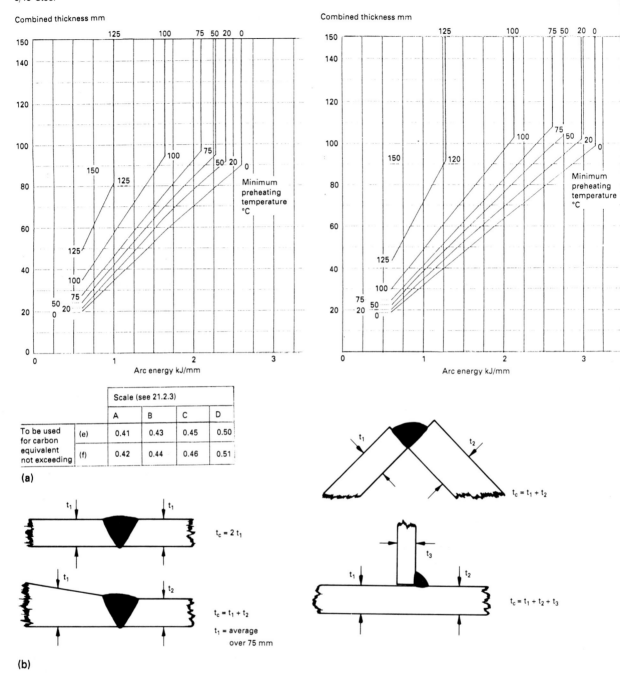

Figure 5.20 (a) Welding preheat diagrams. (Reproduced from BS 5135: 1984; courtesy of British Standards Institution.) (b) Definitions of the combined thickness of a welding joint

temperature. In this standard the arc energy (in joule per millimetre) is defined by:

$$\text{Energy} = VI/w$$

where V is the arc voltage, I is the arc current and w is the welding speed (in millimetre per second).

The same expression holds for MAG and MIG welding; for submerged-arc-welding the energy is increased by a factor of 1.25 and for TIG welding it is reduced by a factor of 1.2.

The combined thickness is defined in *Figure 5.20(b)*; it represents the total thickness of metal through which heat may be conducted from the weld zone. For example, a steel with CE < 0.44 may be welded with consumables in hydrogen scale B using the following alternative conditions: a combined thickness of 30 mm and either an arc energy of 0.75 kJ mm^{-1} and preheating to 75°C or an arc energy of > 1 kJ mm^{-1} and no preheating.

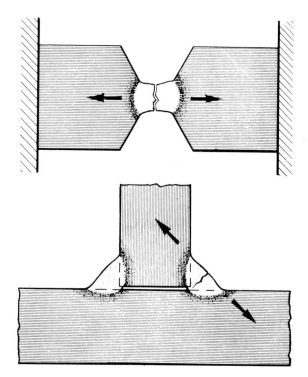

Figure 5.21 Examples of constraints. (Reproduced from *Weldability of Steel* with kind permission of The Welding Institute)

Table 5.8 Hydrogen scales

Scale	Diffusible hydrogen content (ml/100 g deposited metal)
A	> 15
B	> 10, ⩽ 15
C	> 5, ⩽ 10
D	⩽ 5

* Reproduced from BS 5135: 1984; courtesy of British Standards Institution.

5.5.5.6 Lamellar tearing

For lamellar tearing to occur, welding stresses must be tensile in the through-thickness direction of the base metal; fillet welds often give rise to such stresses. The base material must also be susceptible to cracking under the action of these stresses.

Susceptibility is a function of inclusion content, shapes and

Table 5.9 Static load capacities of full penetration butt welds*

Throat thickness (mm)	Shear load capacity (kN mm^{-1})		Tension or compression load capacity (kN mm^{-1})	
	Grade 43	Grade 50	Grade 43	Grade 50
5	0.83	1.06	1.38	1.78
10	1.65	2.13	2.75	3.55
20	3.18	4.08	5.3	6.8
40	6.36	8.16	10.6	13.6

* Data taken from 'Steelwork Design: Guide to BS 5950, Part 1, 1985, volume 1, Section Properties and Member Capacities', second edition (1987), Steel Construction Institute.

(a)

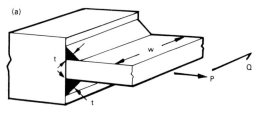

Weld throat area = t × w
Weld stress for tension load P = P/2tw
Weld stress for shear load Q = Q/2tw

(b)

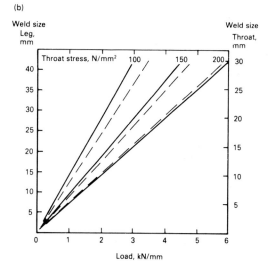

Figure 5.22 (a) Calculation of the stress on a fillet weld. (b) Fillet weld design chart showing the strength of fillet welds in terms of load/mm. (Reproduced from *A Guide to Designing Welds* with kind permission of Abington Publishing)

distributions. Inclusions elongated in rolling directions in plates are transverse to the through-thickness stresses. Sufficient local concentrations of inclusions allow cracks to form and to link up to form an extended defect (see *Figure 5.19(d)*).

The usual measure of susceptibility is the reduction in area observed in a tensile test using samples taken with their axes parallel to the thickness direction of the plate. A short-transverse reduction in area (STRA) of better than 20% is taken to indicate that the material is not susceptible to lamellar tearing. Steels

Table 5.10 Static load capacities of fillet welds between plates at right angles*

Leg length† (mm)	Load capacity (kN mm^{-1})	
	Grade 43 electrode E43 weld $\sigma_y = 215\ N\,mm^{-2}$	Grade 50 electrode E51 weld $\sigma_y = 255\ N\,mm^{-2}$
5	0.753	0.893
10	1.51	1.79
15	2.26	2.68
20	3.01	3.57

* Data taken from 'Steelwork Design: Guide to BS 5950, Part 1, 1985, volume 1, Section Properties and Member Capacities', second edition (1987), Steel Construction Institute.
† Throat thickness = 0.7 × leg length.
‡ Electrodes to BS 639: 1986.

that satisfy this requirement are usually of low sulphur content and sometimes incorporate inclusion shape control.

The pressure of hydrogen can aggravate the potential for lamellar tearing. Low hydrogen electrodes are advised when the joint shape and material are suspect. Note that old steels and repairs may not be as well characterized as new work.

5.5.6 Joint configurations and constraints

Thermal contraction of solid weld metal and heat-affected zones after welding gives rise to tensile stresses acting across the weld. These can be relieved by plastic deformation of the hot metal by cracking. Which occurs depends on the constraint of the weld; high constraint encourages cracking.

Situations of high constraint are those involving small thicknesses of hot metal in contact with large volumes of structure which can deform only elastically. Examples include root pass welds in thick plates and narrow, deeply penetrating welds (see *Figure 5.21*).

Where high constraint is likely to be a problem, some alleviation can be obtained by use of low carbon, sulphur and phosphorus consumables and methods which involve low dilution. Alternatively the weld should be redesigned to give less constraint. Advice on these matters is given in Appendix G of BS 5135: 1984.

The fatigue codes in BS 5400: Part 3: 1982 include considerations arising from the constraint of various types of weld (see Section 5.8.4).

5.5.7 Static strengths of welds

5.5.7.1 Butt welds

In the design codes of BS 5400: 1980 and BS 5950: 1982–1987 it is assumed that a full penetration butt weld has the same static strength as the base metal. An incompletely penetrating butt weld is assumed to have a throat thickness 3 mm less than the actual penetration depth. Thus, the maximum tensile or compressive load bearing capacity is calculated using the specified yield strength of the weakest member in the joint. Maximum strength in shear is taken as 0.6 of that in tension.

Some examples of load capacities are given in *Table 5.9*. These values make no allowance for additional stresses which would arise from bending of eccentric welds under normally uniaxial loads.

5.5.7.2 Fillet welds

The stress distribution in fillet welds is complex, depending on the overall geometry of the joint and of the weld metal and the manner of loading (*Figure 5.22*). The simplest approach is to take the maximum load as that which develops the yield stress of the weld metal at the weld throat. The throat depth for a simple T-joint is 0.7 of the leg length; this value was used to calculate the load capacities listed in *Table 5.10*.

More complex estimates of stresses are required for other geometries of weld and modes of loading. These differ between BS 5400: 1980 (bridges) and BS 5950: 1982–1987 (buildings). The methods are based in part on analytical stress models and in part on experimental data. Further details can be found in the relevant standards.

5.5.7.3 The strength of the weld metal

BS 639: 1986 contains information about the mechanical properties of weld metals used to join base steels with an ultimate tensile strength of < 650 MPa, i.e. structural steels. BS 639: 1986 is the British enactment of ISO 2560. The approach specified is to produce volume of weld metal large enough to carry out tensile tests and Charpy V-notch impact tests. Electrodes identical to those used to produce the weld metal are then classified according to the results.

A typical coding for an electrode might be E 51 5 4 BB (160 3 0 H). The first part of the code gives information about strength, toughness and electrode coating (STC code). The second part (in brackets) deals with operational matters, electrode efficiency, welding positions, power requirements and the hydrogen content of weld metal.

The STC code The first item is the letter E, which indicates a flux covered electrode. This is followed by four digits: the first two give information about minimum mechanical properties and the third and fourth digits indicate the temperatures at which the Charpy V-notch energies are 28 and 47 J, respectively. The final item in the STC code is a letter code identifying the nature of the flux coating.

Thus, the STC code of the example reads as follows:

(1) the electrode is flux covered;
(2) the weld metal minimum yield stress is 360 MPa;
(3) the weld metal Charpy V-notch energy is 28 J at −40°C and 47 J at −30°C; and
(4) the flux coating is a basic, high-efficiency type.

The additional code The additional code consists of a further five digits followed, when appropriate, by the letter H. The first triad of digits represents the electrode efficiency, i.e. the percentage to the nearest 10% of (mass of weld metal/mass of metal core in electrode). Note that the welding efficiency may be more than 100% because iron powder may be included in the flux covering. The fourth and fifth digits give information about suitable welding positions and power supplies. Details are given in the standard. The final letter (H) indicates that the deposit will contain less than 15 ml of diffusable hydrogen per 100 g of weld metal.

Thus, the additional code in the example is to be read as follows:

(1) the electrode efficiency is 160%;
(2) it can be used for flat welds and in the horizontal or vertical position;
(3) the electrode may be used only in d.c. according to the manufacturer's instructions; and
(4) the electrode is hydrogen controlled.

For full details of the codes and their meanings, refer to BS 639: 1986.

5.6 Other steels

5.6.1 Steel plate, sheet and strip

BS 1449: Part 1: 1983 is a wide ranging standard which deals with general engineering steels as well as those for structural use. Where appropriate, approximate equivalence to BS 4360: 1986 is noted.

5.6.2 Structural steels

5.6.2.1 Steel designation

For carbon and carbon–manganese steels, the grade designation gives information about processing and surface finish as well as chemical composition and properties. For example: B HS 30 P means a balanced steel (B), hot-rolled using a narrow mill (HS), grade 30, and a surface with a pickled finish (P); and K CR 34/20 means a killed steel (K), cold-rolled using a wide mill (CR), of grade 34/20.

The lettering system giving conditions is more or less self-explanatory, HR and HS represent hot-rolled material, CR and CS represent cold-rolled material. Cold-rolled materials are taken as those produced such that the final 25% reduction in thickness is by cold rolling. The number system giving the composition depends on the type of steel under consideration. Structural carbon–manganese steels and microalloyed steels are designated by two numbers representing their ultimate tensile strength and yield strength (in kilobar). Thus for grade 34/20 the yield stress is 20 kbar (200 MPa) and the ultimate tensile strength is 34 kbar (340 MPa).

Steels for manufacturing by cold forming are designated by a single number (1, 2, 3, 4, 14 or 15) which can be interpreted only by reference to the standard.

Steels for heat treatment and general engineering purposes are designated by numbers representing their carbon content; thus grade 30 has a range of allowable carbon content from 0.25% to 0.35%.

5.6.2.2 Mechanical properties

A simplified abstract of properties of steels for structural use is given in *Table 5.11*. Where appropriate, equivalences to BS 4360: 1986 are included.

5.6.3 Stainless steels

The quality of stainlessness is imparted to steels by the presence of at least 12% of chromium in the steel. Oxidation and/or corrosion produces a dense adherent oxide film which acts as a barrier to further corrosion. Further aspects of corrosion behaviour are dealt with in Section 5.10.8.

5.6.3.1 Metallurgy of stainless steels

The presence of large amounts of chromium in the steel has profound effects on its metallurgy. This is further compounded by the presence of further alloying elements.

Broadly, there are three types of stainless steel: martensitic, ferritic, and austenitic.

5.6.3.2 Martensitic stainless steels

Typically, these steels contain c. 13% chromium and more than 0.1% carbon. They may be heat treated by quenching and tempering to give martensitic microstructures which are hard and strong but of poor toughness. Typical applications are as cutlery and razorblades. They are not much used for structural purposes.

5.6.3.3 Ferritic stainless steels

These are steels containing very little carbon (<0.08%) with chromium contents ranging from 13% to 17%. Metallurgically, these steels do not undergo phase changes like those of plain carbon and carbon–manganese steels. At all temperatures below melting only the ferrite phase (body-centred-cubic crystal structure) is stable. Metallurgical control is confined to control of composition and of grain size through processing schedules.

5.6.3.4 Austenitic stainless steels

These steels generally have higher strengths and ductilities than ferritic steels. They are more costly since they contain a minimum of 8% nickel in addition to the chromium. Carbon contents must be maintained as low as practicable, typically below 0.1%.

The nickel in the steels stabilizes the austenite (face-centred cubic) crystal structure at all temperatures below melting. Like

Table 5.11 Mechanical properties of carbon–manganese and microalloyed steels*

Processing	Grade	σ_y (MPa)	UTS (MPa)	Minimum percentage elongation		Mandrel diameter for 180° bend†	BS 4360: 1986 equivalent‡
				50 mm	80 mm		
Carbon–manganese steels							
H or C	34/20	200	340	29	27	2a	
H or C	37/23	230	370	28	26	2a	40B
H only	43/25	250	430	25	23	3a	43A
H only	50/35	350	500	20	18	3a	50B
Microalloyed steels§							
H or C	40/30	300	400	26	24	2a	
H or C	43/35	350	430	23	21	2a	
H or C	46/40	400	460	20	18	3a	
H or C	50/45	450	500	20	18	3a	
H or C	60/55	550	600	17	15	3.5a	55C

* Based on BS 1449: 1983; courtesy of British Standard Institution. For qualifying remarks, refer to the standard.
† a = sheet thickness.
‡ Equivalences to BS 4360: 1986 are not exact.
§ Microalloyed grades are also available with improved formability; the percentage elongation is c. 2% more, the mandrel diameter in the bend test c. 2a less, whilst the strengths are the same; these grades are designated 40F30, etc.

Table 5.12 Compositions and properties of stainless steels (all in softened condition)*

Grade	Typical composition (%)				0.2% proof stress (MPa)	Ultimate strength (MPa)	Elongation (%)	Sensitization time† (min)
	C	Cr	Ni	Other				
Ferritic								
403 S17	0.08	13			245	420	20	
430 S17	0.08	17			245	430	20	
Austenitic								
304 S15	0.05	18	9		195	500	40	15
309 S24	0.12	23	14		205	510	40	0
310 S24	0.12	24	20		205	510	40	0
316 S11	0.03	17	12	2.25 Mo	190	490	40	30
317 S12	0.03	18	15	3.5 Mo	195	490	40	30
320 S31	0.08	17	12	2.25 Mo Ti = 5C	210	510	40	30

* Based on BS 1449: Part 2: 1983; courtesy of British Standards Institution.
† Time quoted is the time for which a sample is held at 650°C to bring about sensitivity to stress corrosion cracking: this is assessed according to BS 5903 (see Sections 5.10.8 and 5.10.9).

ferritic steels, metallurgical control is through composition and grain size.

Problems can arise in this type of steel from preferential corrosive attack at grain boundaries (see Section 5.10.6). Steels which suffer from this phenomenon are said to be 'sensitized'. Attack can be avoided by proper control of processing or by composition control. To avoid sensitization, carbon contents should be as low as possible (i.e. <0.05%) and/or additions of titanium or niobium can be made to tie-up the carbon as fine particles of titanium or niobium carbide. Steels containing titanium or niobium are said to be 'stabilized'.

5.6.3.5 Specifications for stainless steels

The relevant British Standard is BS 1449: Part 2: 1983. This gives information about mechanical properties and susceptibility to stress corrosion cracking. Examples of mechanical properties for each group of steels are given in *Table 5.12*. For further information on stress corrosion cracking, see Sections 5.10.8 and 5.10.9.

5.6.4 Hollow sections

5.6.4.1 Tubes

Tubes are available in the full range of carbon, carbon–manganese and stainless steels. They may be made by seamless tube making methods or by methods which involve a welded seam. Finishing operations may be carried out hot or cold and the finished tubes may or may not be heat treated.

BS 6323: 1982 deals with a range of tubes for general engineering purposes. Steels are defined by a code consisting of three parts.

(1) a triad or tetrad of letters indicating the manufacturing method (*Table 5.13a*);
(2) a number, defining the steel type (some examples of a few which fall within a range broadly comparable to BS 4360: 1986 are given in *Table 5.13(b)*; this table also gives information for a few stainless steels); and
(3) a final group of letters indicating the condition of the tube.

Properties are controlled by the general principles outlined earlier. For details, refer to the standard.

Table 5.13 Steel tubes*
(a)

Method of manufacture	Designation
Hot finished, welded	HFW
Hot finished, seamless	HFS
Cold finished, seamless	CFS
Electric resistance welded (including induction welded)	ERW
Cold finished electric resistance welded (including induction welded)	CEW
Submerged arc welded	SAW
Longitudinally welded stainless	LW
Cold finished longitudinally welded stainless	LWCF

(b)

Type and grade of steel	Minimum UTS (MPa)	Grade
Carbon and carbon–manganese		
0.2 C max.	360	3
0.25 C max.	410	4
0.2–0.3 C, 1.2–1.5 Mn	650	7
Austenitic stainless		
304 S15	510	21
316 S13	480	22
321 S31	510	24

* Based on BS 6323: 1982; courtesy of British Standards Institution.

5.6.4.2 Welded, cold-formed sections

These sections are produced mainly by longitudinal welding of cold-rolled and shaped steels, with steel thicknesses in the range 1.5–7 mm. Details of materials, tolerances, etc., are given in BS 6363: 1983.

5.6.5 Steels for fasteners

5.6.5.1 Black bolts and nuts

Black bolts and nuts are usually fashioned by finish machining of hot- or cold-forged steel. The composition of the steel is left to the discretion of the manufacturer except for controls on nitrogen, sulphur and phosphorus contents. For nuts, the requirements are less exacting than for bolts.

The relevant standard is BS 4190: 1967, which grades bolts and nuts by their mechanical properties. It follows from ISO recommendations.

The grading system for bolts uses a two-number code, e.g. 4.8. The first number is the minimum UTS/10, where the ultimate tensile strength (UTS) is in kilogram force per square millimetre (kgf mm^{-2}). The second number is $10 \times$ (yield stress/UTS).

The details of properties and grades are given in *Table 5.14*.

For nuts, only the first number is used.

5.6.5.2 High strength friction grip bolts

These are manufactured by forging, after which the steel is hardened by quenching and tempering. No specifications are laid down for composition, except for maximum limits on nitrogen, sulphur and phosphorus contents. The bolts are specified according to their load-carrying ability. The material properties taken for this purpose are listed in *Table 5.15*.

The relevant standard for the bolts is BS 4395: 1969.

5.6.6 Ropes and roping steels

Steel wires for ropes are required to have high tensile strength. They contain between 0.5 and 1.0% carbon and are cold drawn. A process known as 'patenting', involving working and annealing at temperatures which do not produce austenite, imparts

Table 5.14 Properties of steels for black bolts and nuts*

Property	Grade		
	4.6 hot forged	4.8 cold forged	6.9 cold forged
Yield stress (MPa)	235	314	530
UTS (MPa)	392	392	588
Yield stress/UTS	0.6	0.8	0.9
Elongation to fracture (%)	25	14	12
Hardness, HV (30)	110–170	110–170	170–245

* Based on BS 4190: 1967; courtesy British Standards Institution.

Table 5.15 Properties of steels for high strength friction grip bolts*†

Range of thread diameter (mm)	Yield or 0.2% proof stress (MPa)	UTS (MPa)	HV 30 (kg mm^{-2})
General range			
12–24	635	827	260–330
27–36	558	725	225–292
Higher grade bolts			
16–33	882	981	280–380

* Based on BS 4395: 1969; courtesy British Standards Institution.
† Further tests are mandatory for full compliance with the standard. These include measuring the load required to cause the bolt length to extend by 12.5 μm and tests for strength under conditions which simulate a wedge under the bolt head.

Table 5.16 Strength and fracture requirements for general-purpose and high-duty rope wire*

Strength grade (MPa)	Minimum No. of twists to failure for a wire length of 100 diameters		Minimum No. of reverse bends through a radius of 3.75 mm (general-purpose and high-duty wire)
	General-purpose wire	High-duty wire	
1370	31	NA	14
1570	30	34	14
1770	27	31	13
1860	25	28	—
1960	23	25	12
2050	22	NA	10
2150	20	NA	10

NA, not available.
*Data are for bright drawn wire, 1.0–1.3 mm diameter. For other finishes and diameters, data will be different. For details refer to BS 2763: 1982.

Table 5.17 Letter codes for steel castings*

First letter (steel type)	
A	Carbon or carbon–manganese steels
B	Low alloy steels
Second letter (use)	
None	General-purpose use
L	Low-temperature toughness
W	Wear resistance
T	High tensile strength
M	Magnetic properties

* Reproduced from BS 3100: 1991; courtesy of British Standards Institution.

sufficiently ductility. The resulting microstructures contain very small spherical particles of cementite in a work-hardened ferrite matrix.

Strength grades are defined in BS 2763: 1982 (which incorporates recommendations given in ISO 2232: 1973 and ISO 3154: 1976). A twisting ductility and a resistance to reversals of bending are also required. Examples are given in *Table 5.16*.

The wires are available with a bright, drawn finish or in several zinc coated versions. Variations exist in the size ranges and finishes which can match an individual strength.

Details are given in the standard. Relevant standards for the assembled ropes are listed in Section 5.11.8.

5.6.7 Steel castings

A wide variety of complex shapes may be made in the form of steel castings. In the as-cast condition, the microstructures are variable from surfaces to bulk, there may be more porosity and residual stresses. Heat-treatment gives more uniform structures and anneals out residual stresses. Porosity is usually not affected by heat treatment but, as long as its amount is not too large, and it is not in critical regions of the casting, it may be acceptable. Inspection by testing for pressure tightness and by radiography and ultrasonic methods may be advisable, depending on the proposed use.

The relevant standard for general engineering castings is BS 3100: 1991; castings for containing pressure are specified in BS 1504: 1976. The 1976 version of BS 3100 uses a coding system which replaces a variety of earlier standards. The code consists of one or two letters followed by a number (*Table 5.17*). The number is arbitrary. There are different rules for stainless steels.

5.6.7.1 Compositions

The compositions and mechanical properties of some selected steels are given in *Table 5.18*. Data for stainless steels are not given here; for details see BS 3100: 1991.

5.7 Fast fracture

Fast fracture is often referred to as brittle fracture. A prerequisite is that a crack-like defect exists in the material. If both the crack and the applied stress are small, the crack is likely to be stable. If the crack size or the stress or both are increased, a critical condition will ultimately be reached at which the crack becomes unstable and extends. As a crack extends, energy is absorbed by the creation of new areas of fracture surface and by plastic deformation of metal ahead of the advancing crack. The rate of energy in relation to the release of elastic strain energy as the material unfolds determines whether the crack will extend or not. Once it becomes unstable, the crack can propagate at rates of up to several kilometre per second.

5.7.1 Failure possibilities

A plate containing a centre crack will respond to a tensile load perpendicular to the crack according to the relative magnitudes of four stresses (*Figure 5.23*):

σ_y the yield stress of the material, as measured in a tensile test;
σ_0 the applied stress measured at the site of the crack, assuming the crack does not exist;
σ_n the net stress on the material across the plane containing the crack; and
σ_c the local, concentrated, stress acting at the crack tip.

There are four possible conditions:

(1) $\sigma_c > \sigma_n > \sigma_0 > \sigma_y$: all stresses are greater than the material yield stress; failure is by general yield and any crack propagation will be by ductile tearing; this absorbs a large amount of energy.
(2) $\sigma_c > \sigma_n > \sigma_y > \sigma_0$: yielding occurs at and near the plane containing the crack; this is gross yielding; usually crack growth is stable unless massive strain energies are released.
(3) $\sigma_c > \sigma_y > \sigma_n > \sigma_0$: local yielding occurs, but the plastic zone does not reach the boundaries of the plate; elastic–plastic conditions are said to prevail and crack growth may be stable or unstable.
(4) $\sigma_y > \sigma_c > \sigma_n > \sigma_0$: no plastic yielding occurs anywhere; if σ_c is large enough, brittle fracture can occur.

These possibilities assume that the plate is thick enough for plane strain conditions to prevail, i.e. for there to be no component of strain acting along the line of the crack edge.

Conditions (3) and (4) give unstable crack growth when the applied stress and the crack size combine to exceed a critical value of stress intensity, K_{IC}:

$$K_{IC} = Y\sigma\sqrt{\pi a}$$

where $\sigma = \sigma_0$ which is the stress acting in the region of the crack tip in a direction perpendicular to the plane of the crack—this ignores any stress concentration effects due to the crack itself, but should include residual stresses; a is the depth of a surface crack or half the length of an embedded crack; Y is a numerical factor containing information about the geometry of the crack and the place where it is found; and K_{IC} is the critical value of stress intensity, also known as the *plane-strain fracture toughness parameter*.

5.7.2 Methods for measuring K_{IC}

In principle, K_{IC} is measured simply by observing the fracture stress of a test piece containing an artificially introduced crack of known size. For such measurements to be valid, plane strain conditions must hold. Test piece sizes and shapes have been

Table 5.18 Carbon and carbon–manganese steel castings*

Constituent	Grade						
	A1	*A2*	*A3*	*A4*	*A5*	*A6*	*AL1*
Carbon (%)	0.25	0.35	0.45	0.25	0.33	0.33	0.20
Silicon (%)	0.60	0.60	0.60	0.60	0.60	0.60	0.60
Manganese (%)	0.90	1.0	1.0	1.60	1.60	1.60	1.10
Phosphorus (%)	0.05	0.05	0.05	0.05	0.05	0.05	0.04
Sulphur (%)	0.05	0.05	0.05	0.05	0.05	0.05	0.04
Residuals (%)	—†	—	—	—	—	—	—
Heat treatment‡	At manufacturer's discretion			N N+T H+T	N N+T H+T	H+T	At manufacturer's discretion
Max. section (mm)	—	—	—	—	100	63	—
Lower yield stress (MPa)	230	260	295	320	370	495	230
UTS (MPa)	430	490	540	540	620	690	430
Elongation on 5.65 $A_0^{1/2}$ (%)	22	18	14	16	13	13	22
Charpy V-notch test							
T (°C)	20	20	20	20	20	20	−40
Energy (J)	27	20	18	30	25	25	20

* Reproduced from BS 3100: 1991; courtesy British Standards Institution.
† Cr <0.25%, Mo <0.15%, Ni <0.4%, Cu <0.3%, total <0.8%.
‡ N, normalized; H, heat-treated by quenching into oil or water; T, tempered.

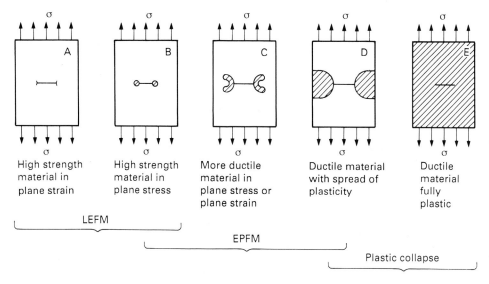

Figure 5.23 Response of a plate containing a centre crack to a tensile load applied perpendicular to the crack. LEFM, linear elastic fracture mechanics; EPFM, elastic–plastic fracture mechanics. (Reproduced from *Fracture Mechanics*[4] by permission of Edward Arnold (Publishers) Ltd)

standardized and must obey certain rules. Full details are given in BS 5447: 1977.

The size restrictions are instructive. For a beam test piece like that shown in *Figure 5.24*, neither the crack depth (a) nor the beam thickness (b) must be less than

$2.5(K_{IC}/\sigma_y)^2$

where σ_y is the yield or 0.2% proof stress for the material. The crack depth must also be between 0.45 and 0.6 of the beam depth.

For structural steel, K_{IC} at 20°C is typically about 150 MPa m$^{1/2}$ and σ_y is between 230 and 450 MPa depending on the grade. For valid testing, cracks must be between 280 mm and 1 m deep, with rather large test pieces to contain them! Consequently, such tests are rarely done.

An alternative approach is provided by the measurement of the crack tip opening displacement (CTOD).

5.7.3 Crack tip-opening displacement

The problems of validity of the K_{IC} approach arise because the stress system can cause plastic deformation in the region of the crack tip, before the crack can extend. In *Figure 5.25* a crack is shown opening as a wedge of plastically deformed material develops at its tip. Crack propagation is delayed until a critical value of the opening displacement is reached at the crack tip, δ_c. Provided that the applied stress, σ, is less than about two-thirds of the material yield, σ_y,

$$\delta_c = \frac{\pi}{E\sigma_y} \sigma^2 a$$

$$\delta_c = \frac{K_{IC}^2}{YE\sigma_y}$$

The method of testing uses test pieces similar to those used for K_{IC} testing. Clip gauges mounted at the open end of the crack are used to monitor the crack-opening displacement.

Several critical conditions are possible, giving different values of δ_c. Usually, it is the initiation of unstable growth, whether arrested or not which defines the critical displacement, δ_c. Full details of how data are translated into values of δ_c are given in BS 5762: 1979. Typically δ_c is between 0.1 and 0.2 mm.

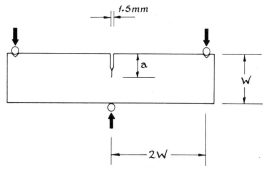

Figure 5.24 Dimensions for bend test pieces; for more complete details see BS 5447: 1977. $a/w = 0.45$ to 0.55; thickness $\simeq 0.5w$

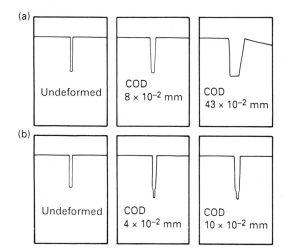

Figure 5.25 Crack tip opening displacement (COD): (a) at tip of machined notch; (b) at tip of fatigue crack. Neither crack shows any extension as faces move apart. (Reproduced from *Weldability of Steel* with kind permission of The Welding Institute)

Table 5.19 Fracture data for two steels*

Material	K_{IC} (MPa m$^{1/2}$)	σ_y (MPa)	$\left(\dfrac{K_{IC}}{\sigma_y}\right)^2$ † (mm)	C_v (J)
Mild steel	75	275	75	7
Low-alloy steel	120	515	55	24

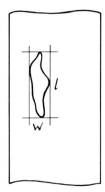

* Reproduced from *Brittle Fracture of Welded Structures* by kind permission of The Welding Institute.
† $(K_{IC}/\sigma_y)^2$ is used to calculate the critical crack size for a tensile stress equal to the material yield stress; it is an indicator of the defect tolerance of the material.

5.7.4 Uses of K_{IC} and δ_c

The concepts and tests to measure K_{IC} and δ_c were developed mainly for high strength alloy steels where test pieces of sensible sizes are valid. Structural steels require large test pieces and other practical problems are encountered in the testing of weld-metal and heat-affected zones.

The approach is most useful for assessing the tolerance of materials to crack-like defects. This can aid in the choice of materials in the first place or in decision-making when defects are found in existing structures.

Table 5.19 gives some data for two steels. The low-alloy steel has better toughness than the mild steel, as measured by K_{IC} and by impact testing, C_v. But, if the low-alloy steel is used in a manner to exploit its higher yield strength, the parameter $(K_{IC}/\sigma_y)^2$ must be considered. This is an indicator of the material tolerance to defects and shows that mild steel is better in this regard than the low-alloy steel. Of course, the low-alloy steel could be under-used at stresses suitable for mild-steel, but at extra cost.

In assessing existing defects, the total tensile stress acting across the plane of the crack must be used. These include

(1) average membrane stresses;
(2) tensile stresses arising from bending;
(3) secondary stresses which include all those stresses necessary to maintain continuity of the structure and include thermal stresses and residual stresses; for welded structures the residual stress is taken as the yield stress of the local material containing the crack; and
(4) stress concentrations, i.e. stresses in the system which do not cause noticeable distortion.

Defect sizes to be used also need some thought. *Figure 5.26* illustrates the concept of containing rectangles in situations where adjacent defects interfere with one another. Checks need to be made to assess whether the remaining ligaments will or will not collapse plastically before proceeding with fracture-toughness calculations. Recommendations for all these procedures are available in PD 6493: 1980.

To carry out assessments, values for K_{IC} are required, but these are often difficult to find. Measurements of K_{IC} or δ_c of the material to be used would be the ideal course of action, but this is often not possible. In such cases, some guidance is available from the results of impact testing using standard Charpy V-notch test pieces. The procedures are detailed in PD 6493: 1980, but must be carried out with care. Firstly, there are the usual experimental errors to be taken into account. Secondly, these procedures apply only to restricted ranges of steels. Thirdly, cracks in the Charpy test pieces must propagate in the plane and direction relative to the steel stucture which is the subject of the K_{IC} analysis.

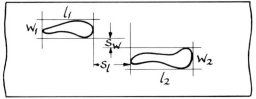

to interact,
$$S_w \leqslant \frac{W_1 + W_2}{2}$$
$$S_l \leqslant \frac{l_1 + l_2}{2}$$

if interact, then,
$$W = W_1 + W_2 + S_w$$
$$l = l_1 + l_2 + S_l$$

Figure 5.26 Defect dimensions and interaction criteria

5.8 Fatigue performance

5.8.1 General

Fatigue failure occurs as a result of repeated applications of stresses less than those needed to bring about failure by a single application. It occurs by the generation and gradual growth of cracks; the growth rate is increased by increasing the amplitude of the stress variation experienced and accelerates as the crack grows.

5.8.2 Methods of characterizing material properties

5.8.2.1 σ_r–N (or S–N) relationships

The simplest method of characterizing a material's properties is to establish the σ_r–N curve for the material. This plots (on logarithmic scales) the stress range experienced (σ_r in BS 5400: 1980, S in PD 6493: 1980) against the number of stress cycles (N) that the material will survive before it fails. The curve has a characteristic shape, as shown in *Figure 5.27*. Test data are usually badly scattered and a statistical approach must be used. When the maximum stress is below the material yield stress, the relationship is

$$N\sigma_r^m = K_0 \times \Delta^d$$

This is the Basquin law, in which K_0 is a material constant, Δ is 10^{-s}, where s is the standard deviation observed for log N at

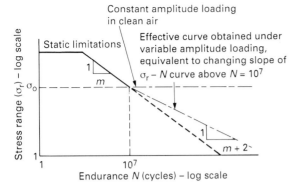

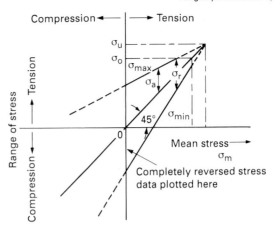

Figure 5.27 A typical σ_r–N relationship. Note that only the portion of the figure shown as a full line is based on experimental evidence. (Reproduced from BS 5400: 1980; courtesy of British Standards Institution)

constant σ_r, and d is the number of standard deviations below the mean line through the log σ_r/log N plot. The line usually taken for design purposes is two standard deviations below the mean (representing a failure probability of 2.3%).

If the stress variation is of constant range, there is, for steels, an endurance limit (σ_0), i.e. a stress range below which no further crack growth occurs. This usually occurs at a stress range of 1/3 to 1/2 the yield stress of the steel and for lives greater than 10^7 cycles.

However, if the stress range is variable, with occasional excursions above σ_0, these excursions will cause a crack to continue growing. The overall effect is to apparently reduce σ_0 and to give the line of slope $-1/(m+2)$ in *Figure 5.27*.

5.8.2.2 Influence of mean stress (Goodman)

Fatigue endurance depends not only on the stress range experienced but also on the mean value of the stress. Various descriptions are used to describe the stress history.

(1) mean stress, $\bar{\sigma}$, and stress range, $\Delta\sigma$;
(2) maximum stress, σ_{max}, and stress ratio, R,

$$R = \frac{\text{minimum stress}}{\text{maximum stress}}$$

The usual method of expressing the data is by use of a Goodman diagram. Two versions are shown in *Figure 5.28*. The approach is conservative, experimental data generally lying above the design lines.

Note that, in some design codes, fatigue data make assumptions about the values of mean stress. For example, in BS 5400: 1980 it is assumed that residual stresses equal to the yield strength of the material exist in welds. The stress range is taken to operate downward from the yield stress.

5.8.2.3 Effects of variable loading (Miner's law)

More often than not, the stress history experienced is not simple, but consists of a number of different stress ranges about differing mean stresses, repeated different numbers of times. In this case, there are n_1 repetitions of the stress range σ_1. A simple repetition of σ_1 only would cause failure in N_{f1} cycles.

Thus, for the n_1 repetitions at σ_1, the fraction of the life of the material used up is n_1/N_{f1}. As the material is not a cat it has only one life, but it does have a full one. Formally,

$$\sum_i \left(\frac{n}{N_f}\right)_i = \frac{n_1}{N_{f1}} + \frac{n_2}{N_{f2}} + \cdots = 1$$

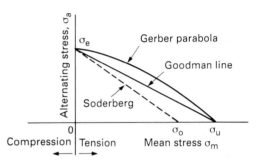

Figure 5.28 Two versions of the Goodman diagram. (Reproduced from G. E. Dieter, *Mechanical Metallurgy*, 1976 with permission of McGraw-Hill, Inc.)

5.8.3 Crack-growth data

Much of the life measured from σ_r–N curves is spent initiating cracks. Once formed, these grow at rates which depend on the local stress intensity at the crack tip. The stress intensity is defined as

$$K = \sigma\sqrt{\pi a}\, C$$

where C is a geometrical constant, σ is the stress acting in the region (calculated neglecting any effects caused by the crack), and a is a measure of the crack size (usually its depth into the material from the free surface). The geometrical constant takes into account the local stress concentration caused by the geometry of the region. Variations in σ at constant crack size, a, give variations in K, i.e. $\Delta\sigma \to \Delta K$. The crack growth rate per cycle (da/dN) varies with ΔK as shown in *Figure 5.29*. In this figure ΔK_{th} is a threshold value, below which no measurable crack growth occurs. Typical values are often as low as 10 MPa m$^{1/2}$ or less. In region 2, the Paris equation holds:

$$\frac{da}{dN} = A(\Delta K)^m$$

where m is typically between 2 and 4.

Figure 5.30 shows how a crack increases in size with exposure to repeating cycles of constant stress range. For most of its life the crack is too small to be detected easily;

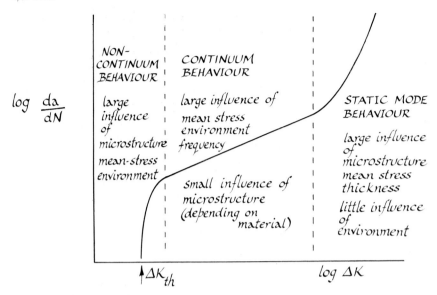

Figure 5.29 The variation of the crack growth rate per cycle (da/dN) with ΔK. ΔK_{th} is the threshold value below which no measureable crack growth occurs

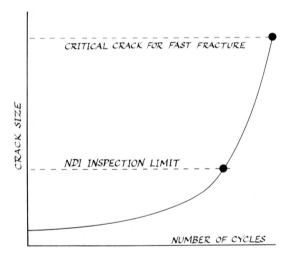

Figure 5.30 The increase in crack size with exposure to repeated cycles of constant stress range. NDI, non-destructive inspection

about 80% of the size increase occurs in the last 10% of life.

In applying this approach, specific data relevant to the material through which the crack is advancing should be used. In the (likely) absence of specific data, there is some general information that may be used for guidance.

For butt welds in steels with yield stresses of less than 600 MPa, and a 99.5% probability of survival, in clean air at room temperature.

$m = 4$

$A = 1.7 \times 10^{-15}$ when da/dN is in mm/cycle and ΔK is in N mm$^{3/2}$

$A = 1.7 \times 10^{-6}$ when da/dN is in m/cycle and ΔK is in MPa m$^{1/2}$

These data refer to crack growth by cleavage or by microvoid coalescence. When growth is by striation formation

$m = 3$

$A = 3 \times 10^{-13}$ (for mm/cycle and N mm$^{-3/2}$)
$A = 3 \times 10^{-4}$ (m/cycle and MPa m$^{-1/2}$)

5.8.4 Applications in design of welded structures

Simply shaped, wrought, parts of structures subject to fatigue spend a large part of their total life waiting to initiate a crack. But welds usually have metallurgical or surface defects associated with them which help to initiate cracks quickly. Fatigue failure of welded structures nearly always occurs at the welds or in their heat-affected zones. Awkwardly shaped welds with large stress concentrations aggravate this condition.

Factors which determine the life of a welded detail include the geometry of the detail and the properties of the weld metal. Detail geometry is important for two reasons: it determines the stress concentrations when loaded, and it affects the workmanship that can be expected and the likely quality of the weld. For ordinary structural steels these effects outweigh the effects of small variations in inherent properties of parent and weld metals. Special steels for offshore and other critical uses are exceptions to this generalization.

The approach taken in BS 5400: 1980 is to classify welded details according to the severity of their influence on fatigue life. Design data in the form of σ_r–N relationships are presented for each class. These data correspond to two standard deviations below the mean. They assume that applied stress ranges operate downward from the yield stress in tension, in order to take the possibility of residual stresses into account.

For details of the approach, refer to BS 5400: Part 10: 1980.

5.9 Fire resistance

The Building Regulations (Part E) demand that the load-bearing members of a structure should not fail before a preselected time has elapsed. Test details are given in BS 476: Part 8: 1972. For simply supported beams with distributed load, failure is defined

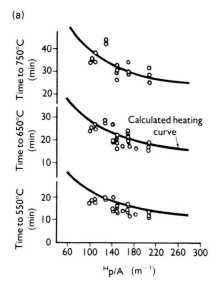

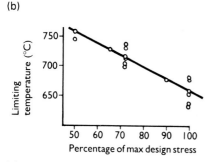

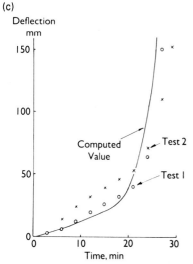

as a vertical deflection at centre span of $L/30$, where L is the span. Loaded beams are heated at a standard rate until failure occurs and the time to failure is measured. Fire resistance times of 0.5, 1, 1.5, 2, 3 or 4 h are required depending on the nature, use and contents of the building.

To test large beams is costly and only a small number of full-scale tests have been done. Not unexpectedly, these tests show that to reach the specified failure deflection the lower flange must reach temperatures which reduce as the design stress is increased. The rate of temperature rise is a function of the sectional shape, specifically of its perimeter/area ratio (*Figure 5.31*).

These observations form the basis of a computerized model which is being developed at the Swinden Laboratories of British Steel. The model has been applied to three floor designs incorporating steel beams and concrete slabs, with encouraging agreement with experimental data.[3]

5.10 Corrosion and corrosion protection

5.10.1 General

Inevitably, steel will rust when in the presence of moisture and oxygen. About 1 tonne of steel is lost in the UK every 90 s. The rate of attack varies substantially, depending on the environmental conditions and the methods used to protect the metal. Careful design can do much to reduce corrosion rates.

5.10.2 Uniform corrosion

The rate of uniform attack is a function of the environment and the material (*Table 5.20*). In clean rural environments, a relative humidity of about 60% or more is required to cause noticeable rusting (*Figure 5.32*). The rust forms a layered structure on the

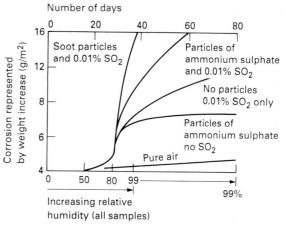

Figure 5.32 The influence of relative humidity and pollution on the corrosion of iron. (Reproduced from *Controlling Corrosion. 1. Methods*, with permission of HMSO)

Figure 5.31 (a) Composition of observed and predicted data on the effect of the section factor on the time taken for the lower flange to reach various temperatures in a BS 476: Part 8: 1972 test. (b) Effects of stress on the limiting temperature for a deflection of $L/30$ in a BS 476: Part 8: 1972 fire test. (c) Comparison of observed and predicted deflection vs. time curves for an unprotected, fully loaded 356 mm × 171 mm, 67 kg m^{-1} steel beam in a BS 476: Part 8: 1972 fire test. (Reproduced from *Metals and Materials*, the journal of the Institute of Metals, Vol. 2, No. 1, 1986, p. 25, and Vol. 2, No. 5, 1986, p. 274)

Table 5.20 Examples of metal loss rates (μm year^{-1})

	Environment		
	Rural	*Maritime*	*Industrial*
Mild-steel to BS 4360: 1986	5	6.5	15–75
Weathering steel to BS 4360: 1986	1.3	4	2.5

surface, consisting of various iron oxides and hydroxides. They are generally impure and can retain moisture and water-soluble salts, which can accelerate further corrosion. (In atmospheres containing chlorides or sulphur oxides,) the rust can concentrate these materials, generating pits which can be both dangerous to performance and difficult to remove.

Weathering grades of steel are designed to produce oxide layers of different character. Chromium and copper in the steel help to produce a dense and adherent oxide film which acts as a barrier to the environment. Corrosive substances can still pass through the film but at a rate whch reduces as the film thickens. As a result, corrosion rates decrease parabolically with time (*Figure 5.33*). The film is protective only if it remains intact. (Mechanical or chemical disruption allows corrosion to continue.) It follows that when using weathering steels care must be taken to avoid such disruption.

5.10.3 Galvanic corrosion

This is the most common type of corrosion. Electrochemical cells are set up on the surface by contact with other metals or by local variations in the metal itself or in the environment.

A simple electrochemical corrosion cell is shown in *Figure 5.34*. Two different metals are immersed in an electrolyte. These metals acquire different electrode potentials and when connected through an external circuit a current flows. The anodic electrode corrodes and the cathodic electrode is protected as a consequence of ionic drifts in the electrolyte to close the circuit.

Anodes and cathodes arise in many ways. On a plain metal surface, some grains are anodes and others cathodes; grain boundaries are often anodic to the grains either side of them. Regions which have been cold worked are anodic to regions which have not been; nail heads are anodic to nail shanks. Rust and mill scale is cathodic to bare steel; this is why it is important to apply paint over clean and dry surfaces.

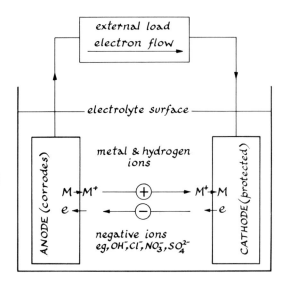

Figure 5.34 A galvanic corrosion cell. Internally, the cathode receives electrons from the external circuit. Externally the cathode receives electrons from the corrosion cell. To stop corrosion one of the following must be done: (i) stop the anode reactions; (ii) stop the cathode reactions; and/or (iii) stop the electron flow in the external circuit

Table 5.21 The electrochemical series

Base	Magnesium
	Zinc
	Aluminium (commercially pure)
	Cadmium
	Duralumin
	Mild-steel
	Cast-iron
	Stainless steels (active)
	Lead
	Tin
	Nickel
	Copper alloys
	Stainless steel (passive)
	Silver
	Graphite
	Gold
Noble	Platinum

Bimetallic corrosion can be particularly severe and often arises at design details where different materials are used. Metals can be arranged in an electrochemical series (*Table 5.21*). The metals at the base end will be anodes when in contact with metals from the noble end. The further apart are the metals in the series, the greater is the difference in electrode potentials and the more aggressive is the attack on the anode. Thus, when iron is in contact with copper, the iron corrodes at an accelerated rate and the copper is protected. When iron and zinc are in contact, the iron is cathodic and protected whilst the zinc is anodic and corrodes. This is the principle behind the use of galvanizing.

Note that stainless steels are listed twice in *Table 5.23*. When covered with an intact oxide film, they are passive, but when in conditions which disrupt the oxide film they are exposed to the environment and can corrode, i.e. they are active.

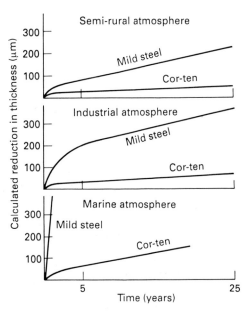

Figure 5.33 The effects of small alloying additions on the resistance of steel to atmospheric corrosion. Cor-Ten contains 2.3% alloying elements, particularly copper, chromium and phosphorus. (Reproduced from *Controlling Corrosion. 1. Methods*, with permission of HMSO)

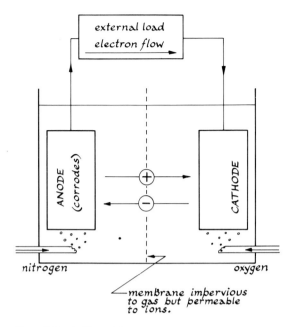

Figure 5.35 A differential aeration cell

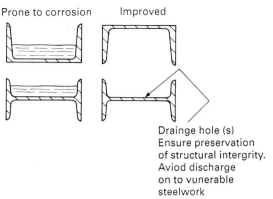

(a) Retention of dirt and water

Drainge hole (s)
Ensure preservation
of structural intergrity.
Aviod discharge
on to vunerable
steelwork

5.10.4 Crevice corrosion

Crevices arise in many ways, through bad design details or by the generation of pits. The significant thing about crevices is that they are sites starved of oxygen and in which aggressive substances from the environment can be concentrated. Even without the impurities, oxygen starvation can accelerate corrosion in the crevice if the rest of the structure is in contact with a good oxygen supply.

Figure 5.35 shows an electrochemical cell composed of two pieces of the same steel immersed in electrolytes which are in contact with one another and which differ only in their oxygen content. One electrolyte is enriched in oxygen and the other is starved of oxygen. A potential difference arises, the oxygen starved electrode being the corroding anode.

Crevice corrosion is particularly insidious because the attack is hidden from view in the crevice. Examples of common crevices are shown in *Figure 5.36*. The best way to avoid crevice corrosion is to design away the crevices (see Section 5.10.5.1).

Differential aeration can arise in ways other than at crevices. For example, should a pipeline pass through regions of sandy soil and clay, ready oxygen access in the sandy regions makes the pipe cathodic and corrosion is encouraged in the oxygen impoverished clay. Another example is given in *Figure 5.37* which shows the same principles operating under a single drop of water.

5.10.5 Splash-zones

Parts of structures which are immersed in water but are in the zone which alternately dries and is re-wetted are particularly susceptible to corrosion. The main reason for this is that during the drying phase the remaining water droplets become more concentrated in aggressive salts. The corrosion rate as a function of height in relation to water levels is shown in *Figure 5.38*.

5.10.6 Corrosion protection

5.10.6.1 Design aspects

For corrosion to occur, there must be liquid water in contact

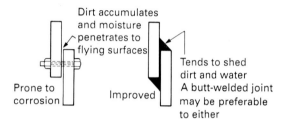

(b) Comparison of bolted and welded lap joints

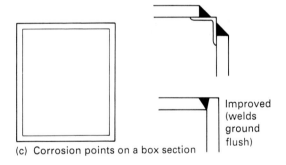

(c) Corrosion points on a box section

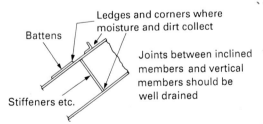

(d) Corrosion points on inclined members

Figure 5.36 Corrosion points. (Reproduced from BS 5493: 1977; courtesy of British Standards Institution)

with the metal. Designs which shed water rather than trap it are clearly desirable. It should also be remembered that accumulations of dirt and other debris can hold water for surprisingly long times. Simple changes which introduce drainage holes and which avoid introducing narrow gaps, ledges, etc.,

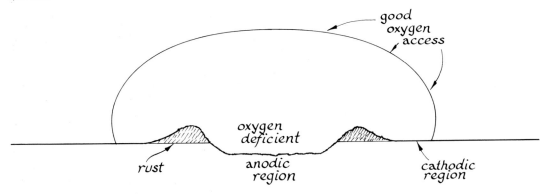

Figure 5.37 Differential aeration due to a single drop of water

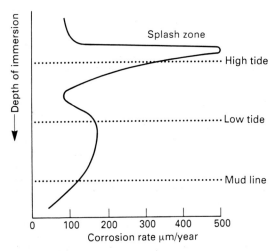

Figure 5.38 Corrosion rates at different positions for a steel structure partly immersed in sea water. (Reproduced from *Corrosion Control in Engineering Design* with permission of the DOI)

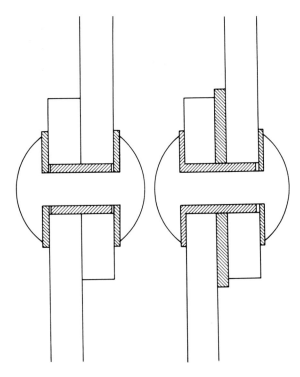

Figure 5.39 Insulated joints for use when plates and fasteners are electrochemically different

can do much to reduce corrosion. Free access for cleaning and painting is also desirable. Extensive recommendations can be found in BS 5493. 1977.

The avoidance of galvanic corrosion also begins with good design and choice of materials. Steel fasteners are often used in aluminium structures because aluminium fasteners are not strong enough. To avoid galvanic corrosion, it is necessary to open the galvanic circuit; if no current flows, there is no corrosion. This can be achieved using electrically insulating sleeves and gaskets (*Figure 5.39*). Alternatively, thought might be given to replacing a fastened joint by a welded one.

Welded joints can be sites of local corrosion. This might arise from small differences in electrode potentials between the base metal and weld metal, but is more likely to do with the position and surface finish of the weld. Rough weld surfaces and welds in corners are more likely to trap moisture and dirt than are smooth welds away from corners.

5.10.6.2 Surface treatment

Coatings on steel fall broadly into those which provide active protection through electrochemical action and those which are inert barriers to the environment. Whichever type of coating

is used, it is important that it be applied to a properly prepared surface.

Hot-rolled steel is often covered by a bluish layer of mill-scale. This is cathodic to the steel and for long-lasting treatments must be removed, as must any deposits of rust or dirt. Hand methods may be used but the quality of preparation is not usually good and is very dependent on the operator. Flame cleaning uses short, hot flames to flake dirt and adherent oxide from surfaces, but again is operator dependent. For high-quality preparation, pickling or blast cleaning is required.

Pickling gives a clean surface by immersion or swabbing with various acids. Dilute (<5%) hydrochloric acid is effective, as is warm sulphuric acid (c. 10%). In both cases, thorough washing is needed after treatment. Phosphoric acid is more expensive but leaves a thin phosphate coating which passivates the steel and provides a good base for painting.

Blast cleaning can be done dry or wet using almost any suitable abrasive. Steel or cast-iron shot or grit (angular particles) and corundum are the most widely used abrasives.

If steel has been allowed to rust for a long time it is likely to be pitted and cleaning methods must get to the bottoms of the pits. This may involve long blast times and high qualities may not be economically practical. Early treatment is desirable.

5.10.6.3 Active coatings

Zinc coating on steel provides protection galvanically. The zinc is anodic to the steel, which is cathodically protected. The zinc is usually applied by the steelmaker to pickled surfaces, although it may be sprayed into place on site. The zinc may be sprayed on, applied by hot dipping or electroplating or by heating the surface in contact with zinc powder (sheradizing).

Alternatives to zinc are aluminium or cadmium which act in the same way. (Note that cadmium plated bolts, etc., should be treated with caution because of the high toxicity of cadmium.) The protection afforded by a zinc coating is a function of the coating thickness. The galvanic action slowly uses up the zinc and, ultimately, its protection will be lost (see *Figure 5.40*).

5.10.6.4 Barrier coatings

Inorganic Barrier coatings include such things as enamels and cement, although the term is usually taken to mean thin barriers produced either by surface modification or by painting, etc.

Galvanized coating, specified minimum weight, g/m²

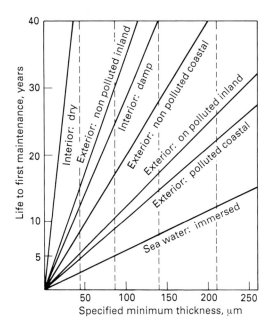

Figure 5.40 Typical lives of zinc coatings in selected environments. (Reproduced from BS 5493: 1977; courtesy of British Standards Institution)

Conversion coatings are produced by phosphating or, less frequently, by chromating. These produce thin layers of phosphate or chromate which provide limited protection but form a good base for paint.

Organic Thick coatings of substances such as pitch, tar and bitumen are useful for steel structures to be buried in earth, usually in association with cathodic protection (see Section 5.10.7).

Paint is a complex medium. It can give good long-term protection if applied to well cleaned and prepared surfaces. It may be applied by brushing, spraying or, in factory environments, by processes such as electrophoresis. Whichever paint is used and however it is applied, the underlying surface must be well prepared (Section 5.10.6.1). Paint applied over rust will not prevent further rusting at the site and will blister in a short time. Advice on preparation and painting is in BS 5493: 1977.

Three paint layers are typically used. A priming layer, typically 30–40 μm thick, in contact with the steel is designed to adhere well to the metal and contains particles of zinc, zinc chromate, zinc phosphate or red lead which are active corrosion inhibitors. An undercoat layer on top of the primer is the main provider of thickness. Typically, this layer is about 60 μm thick. A finish layer to provide the required texture and colour is about 25 μm thick. Each layer may be composed of more than one coat, although economic considerations keep the number of coats to a minimum.

All paints are permeable to air and water vapour to some degree and the protection afforded is directly proportional to the thickness of the paint. A minimum thickness of about 75 μm is adequate for many purposes. High-build paints, usually epoxy resins, can give up to 400 μm thickness in a single coat.

Paints may be classified in any number of ways, according to purpose, method of application, mechanism of hardening, pigment or vehicle. *Table 5.27* lists the main types of paint according to the vehicle.

(a) *Bitumen* is not a good medium and is difficult to apply. However, it is cheap and can be used in thicknesses up to several millimetres. It is impermeable to water and very suitable for structures to be immersed in water or below ground. The disadvantages of bitumen paints is that they are attacked by oils.

(b) *Drying oils* include traditional paints based on linseed and similar oils and those which use alkyd resins as the medium. They are of low cost, give gloss surfaces and are suitable for non-aggressive environments.

(c) *Chlorinated rubbers* are expensive but give good protection in aggressive environment. Ship paints and paints for use in the chemical industry are often of this type.

(d) *Vinyl paints* are based on polyvinyl chloride (PVC) or polyvinyl acetate (PVA), usually giving thick, somewhat rubbery coatings.

(e) *Epoxy resins* are strong, and can be used as thick layers (up to 400 μm). They can be degraded and go chalky due to the action of strong sunlight. Suitable pigments which absorb the ultraviolet wavelengths in sunlight can help in this respect. Mixtures of epoxy resins and tar give improved resistance to water penetration and are used widely where contact with water is expected to be lengthy. The gates of the Thames flood barrier are protected by 750 μm of this type of paint.

(f) *Polyurethane paints* have most of the attributes of epoxy paints, but are less degradable and more expensive.

Table 5.22 Main generic types of paint and their properties*

Paint type	Cost	Tolerance of poor surface preparation†	Chemical resistance	Solvent resistance‡	'Over-coatability' after ageing§	Comments
Bituminous	Low	Good	Moderate	Poor	Good—with coating of same type	Limited to black and dark colours. Thermoplastic
Oil based	Low	Good	Poor	Poor	Good	
Alkyd, epoxy ester, etc.	Low/medium	Moderate	Poor	Poor/moderate	Good	Good decorative properties
Chlorinated rubber	Medium	Poor	Good	Poor	Good	High-build films remain soft and are susceptible to 'sticking' during transport
Vinyl	High	Poor	Good	Poor	Good	
Epoxy	Medium/high	Very poor	Very good	Good	Poor	Susceptible to 'chalking' in ultraviolet light
Urethane	High	Very poor	Very good	Good	Poor	Better decorative properties than epoxies
Inorganic silicate	High	Very poor	Moderate	Good	Moderate	May require special surface preparation

* Reproduced by kind permission of the Director, The Steel Construction Institute.
† Types rated poor or very poor should only be used on blast-cleaned surfaces.
‡ Types rated poor or very poor should not generally be overcoated with any other type.
§ Types rated poor or very poor require suitable preparation of the aged surface if they are to be overcoated after an extended period.

Plastic coatings Steel, especially in sheet form, can be coated with protective and decorative plastics. Thin ($<100\ \mu m$) layers differ little from the epoxy or polyurethane paints. Thicker coatings (up to $250\ \mu m$) of PVC, polyesters and some fluorocarbons provide better protection. The coatings are adherent and can withstand mechanical shaping methods such as folding and even deep drawing. They are widely used for cladding and roofing.

A summary of some types of coating for use on steel cladding is given in *Table 5.23*.

5.10.7 Cathodic protection

In the electrochemical cells referred to in Sections 5.10.3 and 5.10.4, the cathodic partner is protected by the corrosion of an anode. An equivalent means of protection is afforded to a structure by imposing a current, so that the area to be protected is made sufficiently cathodic.

Figure 5.41 shows two methods of application. A necessary condition is that a current path exists between the anode and the protected structure, i.e. the structure must be fully immersed in water or in the earth. Anodes may be inert and the current imposed by an external d.c. power source. Alternatively, the anode may be a substance from the more basic end of the electrochemical series (usually magnesium or zinc). In this case, the anode is sacrificial and the current arises from the electrochemical difference between the anode and cathode.

In most practical circumstances, the current required to protect uncoated structures is too large to be economical. Coatings reduce the current necessary. A typical protection system for a buried pipeline would consist of a coating of reinforced coal-tar or bitumen together with cathodic protection.

5.10.8 Weathering and stainless steels

Weathering steels are plain carbon or low-alloy steels containing up to about 2% total of copper, chromium, nickel and phosphorus. As a result of atmospheric attack these steels build up a dense, adherent layer of protective oxides. The layer thickens over a period of years and gradually affords more protection (*Figure 5.33*).

The coating develops an attractive appearance and needs no further protection. In use, allowance must be made for the steel loss and the surfaces must not allow water to stand on any areas; the film forms only under conditions of wetting and drying.

Circumstances which would disrupt the film should be avoided, e.g. mechanical disruption by scuffing, etc., and chemical disruption by use in inappropriate environments. Chlorides and industrial pollutants disrupt the film and use in marine or industrial environments is not advised.

Stainless steels take these principles further. At least 12% of chromium is required in the steel to give it its stainless quality. This is frequently combined with other alloying elements to give three groups of stainless steel; ferritic, martensitic and austenitic. For the mechanical aspects of these steels see Section 5.6.2.

The corrosion resistance is imparted by a very thin, dense and adherent oxide film which forms in microseconds. Like weathering steels, stainless steels may be used unprotected but are subject to possible disruption of the film. The film is much more resistant to mechanical damage than those that form on weathering steels.

Chemical disruption can arise either from the environment or from the underlying metal. Chlorides are particularly aggressive environments in this respect. Resistance to pitting in marine and other environments is improved by the presence in the steel of up to c. 5% molybdenum. The effects exerted by the underlying metal are more subtle. Steels of the austenitic

Table 5.23 Summary of properties of weathering and top coats used on organic coated steel systems for building cladding*

	Advantages	Limitations
Plastisol	A thick tough leather grain embossed coating. Excellent range of properties. Withstands site handling	Some limitations on use outside UK
Pvf$_2$	Good colour retention and durability. Excellent resistance to fats and oils, both animal and vegetable, and to petroleum oils and aliphatic hydrocarbons	Coating more easily scratched than Plastisol. Poor mar resistance
Architectural polyester	Good exterior durability, flexibility and temperature stability	Medium-life product. Exhibits slight chalking and colour changes in high ultraviolet environments outside UK
Silicone polyester	Good exterior durability. Hard stain-resistant coating. Good temperature stability	Low flexibility

* Reproduced from *Metals and Materials*, the journal of the Institute of Metals, Vol. 4, No. 6, 1988, p. 359.

(a)

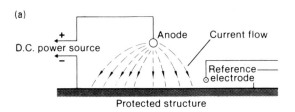

(b)

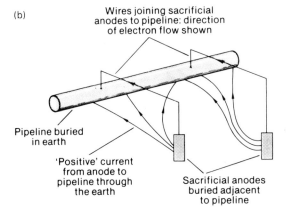

Figure 5.41 Cathodic protection by means of (a) an impressed current and (b) sacrificial anodes. (Reproduced from *Controlling Corrosion. 1. Methods* with permission of HMSO)

type can suffer from grain-boundary attack and from a phenomenon known as weld decay. The steels are meant to contain almost no carbon. Any residual carbon can react with chromium in the metal to form particles of chromium carbide. The important corollary is that chromium is tied up in this way and cannot contribute its full effect to the formation of the oxide film. These phenomena are brought about by inappropriate thermomechanical histories and tend to occur at the grain boundaries of the steel. Local attack of these grain boundaries and intergranular failure is a possibility. The steels can be tested for this by heating under prescribed conditions and then subjecting them to an accelerated corrosion test (*Table 5.13*).

Steels susceptible to these forms of attack are said to be sensitized. The problem may be avoided by correct thermo-mechanical treatment or, better, by attention to steel composition. Carbon contents must be as low as possible ($\ll 0.1\%$) in order to avoid tying up the chromium. Alternatively, niobium or titanium may be added to the steel to tie up the carbon and release the chromium to do its corrosion-resisting job. Steels of this type are stabilized. For welding, stabilized steels will avoid problems in heat-affected zones.

5.10.9 Stress-corrosion

When a material containing a crack is loaded mechanically in a clean dry atmosphere, the crack behaves as described in Section 5.7. The crack either propagates or not according to the value of the stress intensity at the crack tip, $K_{IC} = \sigma\sqrt{\pi a}\, C$.

If a non-propagating crack subject to a steady load is placed in another environment, the crack might or might not grow. If it does grow it will ultimately reach a critical size and fracture will occur. This is the phenomenon of *stress corrosion*. Necessary conditions for this to occur are that there be a crack, that it be subject to a load and that it be in an environment which causes the crack to grow. *Figure 5.42* shows what happens during stress corrosion. If the stress intensity at the crack tip is less than K_{ISCC} the crack is stable and will not grow. If K is between K_{ISCC} and K_{IC}, the crack grows at a rate determined by K. Values of K_{ISCC} and the nature of the growth law in the crack-growth regime depend on the material and on specific details of the environment. Usually, those environments which cause rapid uniform attack do not give rise to stress-corrosion cracking. It is more usual in environments which cause pitting or in those which disrupt protective films.

For design purposes, it is necessary to establish values of K_{ISCC} and the growth law. The growth law is usually of the form

$$\frac{da}{dt} = A(K)^m$$

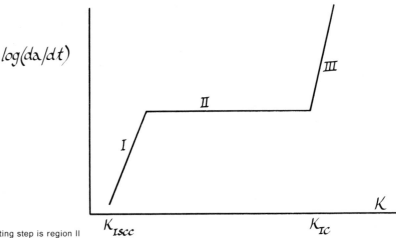

Figure 5.42 Stress corrosion. The rate-limiting step is region II

Table 5.24 Susceptibility to stress-corrosion cracking*

Material	Environment promoting stress-corrosion cracking
Carbon steels	Nitrates, carbonates, hydroxides, ammoniacal water
Austenitic stainless steel	Chlorides, sulphuric acid
High-strength steels	Moist air, water, chlorides, sulphates, sulphides

* This table notes only a few of the most common environments which promote stress-corrosion cracking. Absence of a particular environment from this list should not be taken to imply that it causes no problems. Specific details should be checked.

where m is between 1 and 3. Few data are generally available, although steel suppliers should be able to help. If necessary, tests may be carried out using test pieces of the form used for determining K_{IC} in the appropriate environment. Specimen sizes can be smaller as K_{ISCC} is often much lower than K_{IC} and $(K_{ISCC}/\sigma_y)^2$ is often only a few millimetres.

The susceptibility of different steels to stress-corrosion cracking is given in *Table 5.24*.

5.10.10 Corrosion fatigue

Fatigue behaviour is also sensitive to environment. Simple loss of material clearly raises stresses, but more profound effects are reductions in endurance limit and threshold stress intensities for crack propagation and increases in steady-state crack-growth rates. Like stress-corrosion cracking, the effects of corrosion fatigue are specifically dependent on details of the environment. The most profound influences are exerted by those media which also accelerate stress-corrosion cracking. If such effects are suspected, experiments to establish data may be necessary.

5.10.11 Availability and use of data for stress corrosion and corrosion fatigue

One of the problems with these phenomena is their specific nature. Many test data are available and steel suppliers should be able to help. It must be recognized clearly that the data may change with small changes in environmental conditions (e.g. the salinity and temperature of seawater). It is wise to check that

the data are valid for the conditions actually prevailing, and if they are not the necessary tests should be done.

5.11 British Standards

All British Standards are published by the British Standards Institution, Milton Keynes.

Equivalent International (ISO) and European (Euronorm) standards are given in parentheses where appropriate.

5.11.1 General

BS 6562: 1986 Terms used in the iron and steel industry (Euronorm 79)

5.11.2 General steels

BS 29: 1987 Carbon steel forgings above 150 mm ruling section

BS 970 Wrought steels in the form of blooms, billets, bars and forgings
Part 1: 1983 Carbon, carbon–manganese, alloy and stainless steels (ISO 683; Euronorms 31, 61, 83, 84, 85, 86, 87, 88, 95)

BS 1449 Steel plate, sheet and strip
Part 1: 1983 Carbon and carbon–manganese plate, sheet and strip (ISO 3574, 3576, 5001, 5951; Euronorms 48, 51, 111, 112, 130, 131, 139, 140, 149)

BS 6323: 1982 Tubes for general engineering purposes (ISO 3304).

5.11.3 Structural steels

BS 4: 1980 Hot-rolled sections

BS 2994: 1987 Cold-rolled steel sections

BS 4360: 1986 Weldable structural steels (equivalents are given in Section 5.4.3)

BS 4848 Hot-rolled structural steel sections
Part 2: 1975 Hollow sections (ISO R657/14)
Part 4: 1986 Equal and unequal angles (ISO 657; Euronorms 56, 57)
Part 5: 1980 Bulb flats (Euronorm 67)

BS 6363: 1983 Welded cold formed steel structural hollow sections (ISO 4019)

5.11.4 Steel castings

BS 1504: 1976 Steel castings for pressure purposes

BS 3100: 1991 Steel castings for general engineering purposes

5.11.5 Materials quality

BS 3683: Parts 1–5: 1984–1989 Glossary of terms used in non-destructive testing (ISO 5576)

BS 5710: 1986 Methods for macroscopic assessment of the content of non-metallic inclusions in wrought steels (ISO 3763)

BS 5996: 1980 Methods for ultrasonic testing and specifying quality grades of ferritic steel plate (Euronorm 160)

BS 6512: 1984 Limits and repair of surface discontinuities of hot-rolled steel plates and wide flats (ISO 7788; Euronorm 163)

BS 6780: 1986 Through thickness reduction in area of steel plates and wide flats (measurement) (ISO 7778; Euronorm 164)

5.11.6 Welding

BS 499: several parts: 1980–1989 Welding terms and symbols (ISO 4063, 2553)

BS 638: Parts 1–8: 1979–1988 Arc welding plant equipment and accessories (ISO 700; IEC 245, 246, 974)

BS 639: 1986 Covered electrodes for the manual metal arc welding of carbon and carbon–manganese steels (ISO 544, 547, 2401, 2560)

BS 709: 1983 Destructive testing of fusion welded joints and weld metal in steel (ISO 4136)

BS 1453: 1987 Filler materials for gas welding (ISO 546)

BS 2600 Radiographic examination of fusion welded butt joints in steels (ISO 1106, 2504)
Part 1: 1983 Thickness between 2 and 50 mm.
Part 2: 1973 Thickness between 50 and 200 mm

BS 2901: 1983 Filler rods and wires for gas-shielded arc welding (ISO 864; Euronorm 144)

BS 2910: 1986 Radiographic examination of fusion welded circumferential butt joints in steel pipes

BS 3923 Methods for ultrasonic examination of welds
Part 1: 1986 Manual
Part 2: 1972 Automatic

BS 4165: 1984 Electrode wires and fluxes for submerged arc welding of carbon steel and medium tensile steel

BS 4515: 1984 Welding of steel pipelines on land and offshore

BS 4570: 1985 Fusion welding of steel castings

BS 4870: Parts 1–4: 1981–1988 Approval testing of welding procedures
Part 1: 1981 Fusion welding of steel

BS 4871 Approval testing of welders working to approved welding procedures
Part 1: 1982 Fusion welding of steel

BS 4872 Approval testing of welders when procedure approval is not required
Part 1: 1982 Fusion welding of steel

BS 5135: 1984 Metal-arc welding of carbon and carbon–manganese steels

BS 5289: 1983 Code of practice. Visual inspection of fusion-welded joints

BS 6072: 1986 Method for magnetic particle flaw detection (commentary in PD 6513: 1985)

BS 6443: 1984 Method for penetrant flaw detection

PD 6493: 1980 Guidance on some methods for the derivation of acceptance levels for defects in fusion welded joints

BS 7084: 1989 Carbon and carbon–manganese steel tubular cored welding electrodes

5.11.7 Connections and fasteners

BS 3643: 1981 ISO metric screwthreads (ISO 68, 261, 262, 724, 965)

BS 3692: 1967 ISO metric precision hexagon bolts, screws and nuts (ISO 272, 4759)

BS 4190: 1967 ISO metric black hexagon screws and nuts (ISO 272, 885, 888, 4759)

BS 4320: 1968 Black metal washers (ISO R887)

BS 4395: 1969 High strength friction grip bolts and associated nuts and washers for structural engineering (ISO 225, 272, 885, 888, 4759, R887)

BS 4604: Parts 1–3: 1970–1973 The use of high strength friction grip bolts in structural steelwork

BS 6105: 1981 Stainless steel for fasteners (ISO 3506)

5.11.8 Ropes

BS 302: 1987 Stranded steel wire ropes (ISO 2408)

BS 2763: 1982 Round carbon steel wire for ropes (ISO 2232, 3154)

BS 6570: 1986 Selection care and maintenance of steel wire ropes (ISO 3578)

5.11.9 Steels for concrete reinforcement and pressure

See Chapter 6.

5.11.10 Corrosion and protection

BS 476 Fire tests on building materials and structures
Part 8: 1972 Test methods and criteria for the fire resistance of elements of building construction

BS 729: 1986 Hot dip galvanized coatings on iron and steel articles (ISO 1459, 1460, 1461)

BS 2569: 1988 Sprayed metal protective coatings (ISO 2063)

BS 2989: 1982 Hot dip zinc and iron-zinc flat sheets (ISO 3575; Euronorms 142, 143, 147, 148)

BS 3083: 1988 Hot dip zinc and aluminium–zinc corrugated sheets

BS 4921: 1988 Sheradized coatings on iron or steel

BS 5493: 1977 Code of practice for protective coating of iron and steel structures against corrosion

BS 6536: 1985 Carbon steel sheet and strip, hot-dip Al–Si coated (ISO 5000; Euronorm 154)

BS 6781: 1986 Continuously organic coated flat products (Euronorm 169)

BS 7079: 1989 Preparation of steel substrates before application of paints and related products (ISO 8501, 8503)

DD 24: 1973 Recommendations for methods of protection against corrosion of light section steel used in building

PD 6484: 1984 Commentary on corrosion at bimetallic contacts and its alleviation

5.11.11 Testing

BS 18: 1987 Methods for tensile testing of metals (ISO 6892)

BS 131: Parts 1–5: 1972–1989 Methods for notched bar tests (ISO R148, R83, R442; Euronorm 7)

BS 240: 1986 Method for Brinell hardness test (ISO 156, 6506; Euronorms 3, 125, 128)

BS 427: 1981 Method for Vickers hardness test (ISO 6507, R146; Euronorms 5, 124, 127)

BS 891: 1989 Method for Rockwell hardness test (ISO 6508, 716)

BS 1639: 1989 Methods for bend testing of metals (ISO 7438, 8491; Euronorms 6, 12, 13)

BS 5447: 1977 Methods of test for plane-strain fracture toughness (K_{IC}) of metallic materials

BS 5762: 1979 Methods for crack opening displacement (COD) testing

5.11.12 Uses

BS 11: 1985 Railway rails

BS 449: 1969 Use of structural steel in building

BS 2573: Rules for design of cranes (ISO 4301)
Part 1: 1985 Classification, stress calculations and design criteria for structures
Part 2: 1980 Classification, stress calculations and design of mechanisms

BS 5400 Steel, concrete and composite bridges (ISO 2394)
Part 6: 1980 Materials and workmanship: steel
Part 10: 1980 Code of practice for fatigue

BS 5950 Structural use of steelwork in building
Part 1: 1985 Code of practice for design in simple and continuous construction: hot rolled sections
Part 2: 1985 Materials, fabrication and erection: hot-rolled sections
Part 4: 1982 Code of practice for design of floors with profiled steel sheeting
Part 5: 1987 Code of practice for design of cold formed sections

References

1 BRANDES, E. A. (Ed.), *Smithells Metals Reference Book*, Butterworths, London (1983)
2 BRITISH CONSTRUCTIONAL STEELWORK ASSOCIATION
3 *Metals and Materials*, **2**, 25, 26, 274–276 (1986)
4 EWALDS, H. L. and WANHILL, R. J. H. *Fracture mechanics*, Fig. 6.1, Edward Arnold, Sevenoaks (1985)

Bibliography

General

AMERICAN SOCIETY FOR METALS, *Metals handbook*
JACKSON, N. (Ed.), *Civil engineering materials*, 3rd edn, McMillan, London (1983)
BRANDES, E. A. (Ed.), *Smithells Metals Reference Book*, Butterworths, London (1983)
ROSS, R. B. *Metallic materials specification handbook*. 3rd edn, E & F.N. Spon, London (1980)

Specifications

BRITISH CONSTRUCTIONAL STEELWORK ASSOCIATION (BCSA), 'National structural steelwork specification for building construction', *BCSA Publication No. 1/89*, BCSA, London (1989)
BRITISH STEEL CORPORATION (BSC), *Iron and steel specifications*, BSC, Sheffield (1979)
UNTERWEISER, P. M. and PENZENIK, M. *Worldwide guide to equivalent irons and steels*, American Society for Metals, Ohio (1979) (This lists equivalent standards published by ISO, in Europe (AECMA and Euronorm), in the Americas (COPANT) and in Australia, Belgium, Canada, Denmark, Finland, France, Germany, India, Italy, Japan, Mexico, Norway, South Africa, Sweden, Switzerland, Turkey, the UK and the USA.)

General metallurgy

PICKERING, F. B., *Physical metallurgy and the design of steels*, Applied Science, New York (1978)

Welding

EASTERLING, K., *Introduction to the physical metallurgy of welding*, Butterworths, London (1983)
LANCASTER, J. F., *Metallurgy of welding*, Allen & Unwin, London (1987)
PRATT, J. L., *Introduction to the welding of structural steelwork*, Constrado (now BCSA), London (1979)

Corrosion and protection

COMMISSION OF EUROPEAN COMMUNITIES DIRECTORATE GENERAL, *Durability of steel structures*, CECDG, Information market and innovation, Luxembourg (available from British Constructional Steelwork Association, London)
DEPARTMENT OF INDUSTRY, *Controlling corrosion*, a series of booklets, HMSO, London (1979)

Advisory bodies

British Constructional Steelwork Association Ltd, 35 Old Queen Street, London SW1H 9HZ, UK
The Welding Institute, Abington Hall, Abington, Cambridge CB1 6AL, UK
National Corrosion Service, National Physical Laboratory, Teddington, Middlesex TW11 0LW, UK
British Steel
    General Steels Group—BSC Sections, Structural Advisory Services, Steel House, Redcar, Cleveland TS10 5QL, UK
    Tubes Division, Technical Sales, Corby, Northamptonshire NN17 1UA, UK

6

Steel Reinforcement for Reinforced Concrete

R I Lancaster FICE, FIStructE, FCIArb, FACI
Consulting Engineer

Contents

6.1 Introduction 6/3

6.2 Bars 6/3
    6.2.1 Terminology 6/3
    6.2.2 Methods of manufacture 6/3
    6.2.3 Types 6/4
    6.2.4 Sizes and lengths 6/4
    6.2.5 Tolerances 6/4
    6.2.6 Chemical composition 6/4
    6.2.7 Tensile properties 6/4
    6.2.8 Test bending 6/5
    6.2.9 Practical bending 6/5
    6.2.10 Joining bars 6/5
    6.2.11 Product testing and certification 6/5

6.3 Wire and fabric 6/5
    6.3.1 Terminology 6/5
    6.3.2 Process of steel manufacture 6/5
    6.3.3 Process of wire or bar manufacture 6/5
    6.3.4 Process of fabric manufacture 6/5
    6.3.5 Sizes of wire and bar 6/5
    6.3.6 Standard fabric types 6/5
    6.3.7 Tolerances 6/5
    6.3.8 Bond classification of wire and fabric 6/6
    6.3.9 Chemical composition 6/6
    6.3.10 Tensile properties 6/6
    6.3.11 Rebend test 6/6
    6.3.12 Practical bending 6/7
    6.3.13 Product testing and verification 6/7

6.4 Prestressing steels 6/7
    6.4.1 Terminology 6/7
    6.4.2 Methods of manufacture 6/7
    6.4.3 Sizes and properties 6/7
    6.4.4 Mechanical properties 6/8
    6.4.5 Quality assurance 6/8
    6.4.6 Site precautions 6/8

Acknowledgements 6/9

References 6/9

6.1 Introduction

This chapter is based on the current versions of the British Standards and is divided into three main sections.

(1) Carbon steel bars for the reinforcement of concrete (BS 4449: 1988).
(2) Cold reduced wire (BS 4482: 1985) and welded steel fabric for the reinforcement of concrete (BS 4483: 1985).
(3) Pre-stressing steel wire and strand (BS 5896: 1980) and bars (BS 4486: 1988) for the reinforcement of concrete.

The more important technical contents are reproduced by permission of the British Standards Institution (BSI) and the complete standards are available from them at Linford Wood, Milton Keynes MK14 6LE.

In referring to the contents of this chapter, it should be borne in mind that standards are subject to revision from time to time and when a revised version is published it supersedes the previous version. European standards are in preparation and will supersede all the standards quoted by 1992 at the latest.

The term 'steel reinforcement' is used here to embrace bars, wire fabric and prestressing steels, although the term is not universally accepted as including prestressing steels.

The publications referred to are listed in the References section.

6.2 Bars

6.2.1 Terminology

Steel bars for use in reinforced-concrete construction are termed reinforcing bars, sometimes shortened to rebars. The wider term 'reinforcement' also includes bars. The smaller sizes, up to 16 mm, are commonly manufactured in coiled form or 'coils' which after straightening are cut into standard lengths; the lengths are known as 'bars'.

Grade 250 plain round steel bars (formerly known as 'mild steel' bars) are manufactured in the smaller sizes and grade 460 deformed high-yield steel bars are manufactured in the full size range. The term 'hot-rolled' has been misused to mean high yield; this is incorrect because all bars are hot rolled initially even though some are subsequently cold worked.

The word 'deformed' together with the suffix 'type 1' or 'type 2' is used to distinguish between two levels of bond performance in concrete. However, now that type 1 (the former square twisted or chamfered square twisted bars) is no longer available, only type 2 is used. This will lead to a reversion to the more descriptive term 'ribbed'.

Figure 6.1 shows a typical use of bars fixed in position and *Figure 6.2* shows a beam cage prefabricated in a factory.

6.2.2 Methods of manufacture

BS 4449 specifies that the steel-making process shall be by refining molten iron in a top blown basic oxygen converter or by melting in a basic lined electric arc furnace.

In the UK and most commonly in the rest of Europe, the scrap–electric arc furnace–continuous billet casting process is used. The billets are reduced to bar sizes by a further hot-rolling process. Straight lengths are produced in a bar mill and coils in a rod mill. Thus all bars are hot rolled initially. High-yield (grade 460) bars obtain their physical characteristics in three

Figure 6.1 Bars fixed in position prior to concreting. (Courtesy of Rom Ltd)

Figure 6.2 A beam cage prefabricated in a factory. (Courtesy of Rom Ltd)

basic ways:

(1) By a quenching and tempering process in the last hot-rolling stage.
(2) By adding small quantities of key elements to the molten steel. This is the microalloying process.
(3) By taking a lower strength product from the steel mill and enhancing its properties by subsequent cold working.

Bars produced by any of the above methods perform similarly in concrete and are interchangeable.

6.2.3 Types

The basic types of bar available in the UK and complying with BS 4449 are:

(1) Grade 250 bars in plain round form (smaller sizes only).
(2) Grade 460 bars in a ribbed profile complying with the bond classification type 2 (defined in BS 4449 by projected rib area or by a pull-out test).

Stainless-steel bars are also available to BS 6744: 1986 standard—'Austenitic stainless steel bars for the reinforcement of concrete'—with properties similar to bars suitable to BS 4449: 1988. A British Standard is also in preparation covering fusion bonded epoxy coated reinforcement.

6.2.4 Sizes and lengths

It should be noted that the word 'size' is used in preference to 'diameter'. 'Size' implies 'nominal size', that is the diameter of a circle with an area equal to the effective cross-sectional area of the bar. With a ribbed bar it is not possible to measure a cross-dimension which equals the size of the bar because the circle circumscribing the ribs will have a diameter greater than the nominal size.

The cross-sectional area derived from the mass per metre run using an assumed density of 0.00785 kg mm^{-2} per metre run is given in *Table 6.1*. Grade 250 plain round bars are available in sizes 8, 10, 12 and 16 mm. Grade 460 bars are commonly available and stocked in sizes 8, 10, 12, 16, 20, 25, 32 and 40 mm. Sizes 6 and 50 mm may be obtained by special arrangement, but they are rolled to order and their use can result in delay.

The standard length of bars cut at the steel mill and available

from suppliers is 12 m. However, sizes 6, 8 and 10 mm are sometimes stocked in 6, 9 or 10 m lengths. The maximum length of bar obtainable by special arrangement and with adequate notice is 18 m. Longer lengths can be produced by the use of bar couplers.

6.2.5 Tolerances

The tolerance applicable to cross-sectional area, expressed as the tolerance on mass per metre length is $\pm 9\%$ for 6 mm, $\pm 6.5\%$ for 8 and 10 mm, and $\pm 4.5\%$ for $\geqslant 12$ mm.

The permitted tolerance on length is ± 25 mm.

BS 4466: 1989 specifies the tolerance on bent bars. For a bending dimension up to and including 1000 mm, a tolerance of ± 5 mm is permitted. For bending dimensions over 1000 mm and up to and including 2000 mm, discrepancies of $+5$ mm and -10 mm are acceptable. Over 2000 mm the limits are $+5$ mm and -25 mm.

6.2.6 Chemical composition

Based on cast analysis the following maxima are specified in BS 4449: 1988; carbon 0.25%; nitrogen 0.012%; sulphur and phosphorus are limited to 0.060% for grade 250 and 0.050% for grade 460.

A maximum carbon equivalent is also specified as 0.42 for grade 250 and 0.51 for grade 460. The carbon equivalent value (CEV) is calculated from the sum of the following percentage values

$$C + \frac{Mn}{6} + \frac{Cr + Mo + V}{5} + \frac{Ni + Cu}{15}$$

A deviation is permitted between cast analysis and product analysis of 0.02% for carbon, 0.005% for sulphur and phosphorus, 0.001% for total nitrogen and 0.03% for CEV.

BS 4449: 1988 states the full criteria for product analysis.

6.2.7 Tensile properties

The specified characteristic strengths for the grades 250 and 460 are, as the grade description implies, 250 and 460 N mm^{-2} and the elongation at fracture on a gauge length of five times the size of the bar must be at least 22% or 12%, respectively. The yield stress is measured at 0.33% and 0.43% strain for the two grades and the results are evaluated as specified in BS 4449.

The tensile strength of a bar must exceed the yield stress by 10% or a value between 5% and 10% according to a scale

Table 6.1 The cross-sectional area[a] of various bar sizes

Size (mm)	Cross-sectional area (mm^2)	Mass per metre (kg)
6[b]	28.3	0.222
8	50.3	0.395
10	78.5	0.616
12	113.1	0.888
16	201.1	1.579
20	314.2	2.466
25	490.9	3.854
32	804.2	6.313
40	1256.6	9.864
50[b]	1963.5	15.413

[a] Derived from the mass per metre run using an assumed density of 0.00785 kg mm^{-2} per metre run. [b] Non-preferred size.

Table 6.2 The minimum radii of former specified in BS 4466: 1989 for practical use

Size (mm)	Radius (mm)	
	Grade 250	Grade 460
6	—	18
8	16	24
10	20	30
12	24	36
16	32	48
20	—	60
25	—	100
32	—	128
40	—	160
50	—	200

which slides with the ratio of the actual (measured) yield stress and tensile strength.

The author finds the use of the terms 'strength' and 'stress' in BS 4449 somewhat confusing since

$$stress = \frac{value\ measured}{cross\text{-}sectional\ area}$$

and

strength = stress × cross-sectional area

However, in this case 'strength' or 'tensile strength' means tensile stress at maximum load and 'specified characteristic strength' means 'specified characteristic yield stress' (250 or 460).

6.2.8 Test bending

BS 4449 specifies both a test bend and a rebend test. The diameter of former (or mandrel) around which a bar must be bent without any transverse rupture of the metal is twice the bar size for grade 250 and three times the bar size for grade 460.

6.2.9 Practical bending

BS 4466: 1989 covers the bending dimensions and scheduling of steel reinforcement for concrete. Because all designers, detailers or fabricators need to be familiar with the whole of BS 4466: 1989, it is not reproduced here. However, the minimum radii of former specified for practical use are given in *Table 6.2*.

An important limitation for the transport of bent bars is that the shape must be contained within an imaginary rectangle with the shorter sides not exceeding 2750 mm.

6.2.10 Joining bars

All bars complying with BS 4449: 1988 are defined as weldable. A complete guide to the welding of reinforcement is contained in a new British Standard, BS 7123: 1989. Various forms of proprietary coupling devices are also available. These are outlined in CIRIA Report Number 92.

6.2.11 Product testing and certification

The 1988 version of BS 4449 gives recommendations for third-party certification of product conformity and also batch-acceptance testing where third-party certification does not exist.

6.3 Wire and fabric

6.3.1 Terminology

Starting from a plain round wire in coil form a cold-drawing or cold-reducing process is used to produce a high-yield wire in coil form. This coil is then straightened for use as ordinary reinforcement or for welding into sheets of fabric. The high-yield wire may be plain round, ribbed or indented in various patterns.

Welded fabric or 'fabric' (not 'mesh') is the correct term for wires or bars welded into sheet form (*Figure 6.3*). Fabric comprises a mesh of wires or bars welded into sheets. Material complying with BS 4482: 1985 or BS 4449: 1988 can be used, but the welded product must comply with BS 4483: 1985.

6.3.2 Process of steel manufacture

For cold-reduced steel wire complying with BS 4482, the current (1985) standard requires that the steel shall be made by any process except the air or mixed air/oxygen bottom blown basic converter process. In the case of the oxygen processes, the free nitrogen content as determined in the cast analysis must not exceed 0.008%.

Where bars complying with BS 4449 are used the provisions of that standard apply.

6.3.3 Process of wire or bar manufacture

Wire complying with BS 4482: 1985 can be cold reduced by drawing through a die or by a cold-rolling process. A bar to BS 4449: 1988 can be manufactured by microalloying by quenching and tempering or by cold working in a number of ways.

Both wire and bar with a specified characteristic strength of $460\ N\ mm^{-2}$ satisfy the basic requirements for use as reinforcement, either on their own or as fabric after welding into sheets.

6.3.4 Process of fabric manufacture

Fabric produced to BS 4483: 1985 comprises a square or rectangular mesh of wires or bars that are welded together at some or all of the cross-over points in a shear-resistant manner. In practice, electric-resistance welding machines are used and for the standard ranges of fabric every intersection is welded. *Figure 6.3* shows a modern welding machine producing standard sheets of fabric to BS 4483.

6.3.5 Sizes of wire and bar

The most commonly produced sizes of wire are 5, 6, 7, 8, 9, 10, 12 and 16 mm. Bars are most commonly 6, 8, 10, 12 and 16 mm. However, fabric can be made with other intermediate sizes to suit different requirements.

6.3.6 Standard fabric types

The standard fabric types available from stock are listed in *Table 6.3*. Other types of fabric are manufactured to specification as defined in BS 4483.

6.3.7 Tolerances

The tolerance on mass per metre run for wire is ±6% under 12 mm and ±4.5% for 12 mm and over. The allowable tolerance on the mass per square metre of fabric to BS 4483 is ±6%.

The tolerance on sheet size is ±25 mm or ±0.5%, whichever is greater.

The tolerance on pitch (centres) of adjacent wires is ±15 mm or 7.5% of the nominal pitch, whichever is greater.

Figure 6.3 A welded fabric being manufactured

6.3.8 Bond classification of wire and fabric

Wire can be plain round, indented or ribbed. In the case of fabric made with plain round wire the bond performance allowed depends on the number of shear-resistant welded intersections.

Indented wire and indented wire fabric is classified as having a deformed type-1 bond performance as defined in the relevant design code. Ribbed wire or bar and fabric made from these materials are generally deformed type-2 reinforcement with a bond performance defined in the relevant design code. The geometric criteria or, alternatively, the performance criteria for type-1 and type-2 deformations are defined in BS 4482: 1985 together with the relevant test method.

6.3.9 Chemical composition

For wire made to BS 4482: 1985, the CEV (see bar section for definition) must not exceed 0.42%. The cast analysis must not exceed 0.25% for carbon and 0.060% for sulphur and phosphorous. Bars must comply with the requirements of BS 4449.

6.3.10 Tensile properties

The tensile properties of bar are covered by BS 4449. For wire the specified characteristic yield strength is 460 N mm^{-2} and the minimum tensile strength is 510 N mm^{-2}. In addition, either the actual tensile strength must exceed the actual yield strength by at least 5% or the elongation at fracture across a gauge length of five times the size of wire must be 12% or more.

For welded fabric the tensile test must meet the requirements of BS 4482: 1985 or BS 4449: 1988 according to whether bar or wire has been used. In addition, in a shear test on a welded intersection, a load of 0.25 times the nominal cross-sectional area of the smaller wire (or bar) times 460 must not produce failure of the weld.

6.3.11 Rebend test

Bars used for fabric must pass the BS 4449: 1988 tests for bending and rebending. Wire must pass the rebend test defined in BS 4482: 1985 using a former diameter equal to five times the size of the wire. After welding the wire (or bar) between welds must pass the rebend test specified in BS 4482: 1985 (4449).

Table 6.3 Standard fabric types available from stock

Fabric reference	Longitudinal wires			Cross wires			
	Nominal wire size (mm)	Pitch (mm)	Area (mm^2 m^{-1})	Nominal wire size (mm)	Pitch (mm)	Area (mm^2 m^{-1})	Mass (kg m^{-2})
Square mesh							
A393	10	200	393	10	200	393	6.16
A252	8	200	252	8	200	252	3.95
A193	7	200	193	7	200	193	3.02
A142	6	200	142	6	200	142	2.22
A98	5	200	98	5	200	98	1.54
Structural mesh							
B1131	12	100	1131	8	200	252	10.9
B785	10	100	785	8	200	252	8.14
B503	8	100	503	8	200	252	5.93
B385	7	100	385	7	200	193	4.53
B283	6	100	283	7	200	193	3.73
B196	5	100	196	7	200	193	3.05
Long mesh							
C785	10	100	785	6	400	70.8	6.72
C636	9	100	636	6	400	70.8	5.55
C503	8	100	503	5	400	49	4.34
C385	7	100	385	5	400	49	3.41
C283	6	100	283	5	400	49	2.61
Wrapping mesh							
D98	5	200	98	5	200	98	1.54
D49	2.5	100	49	2.5	100	49	0.77
Stock sheet size	Length 4.8 m			Width 2.4 m			Area 11.52 m^2

6.3.12 Practical bending

As defined in BS 4466, for practical bending of fabric the radius of former used must be at least 15, 18, 21, 24 and 27 mm for wire sizes 6, 8, 10, 12 and 16 mm, respectively.

6.3.13 Product testing and verification

The producer of wire or fabric is required to carry out tests at the frequency specified in BS 4482: 1985 and BS 4483: 1985 and make these available for inspection at the request of the purchaser for up to 6 years after delivery.

6.4 Prestressing steels

6.4.1 Terminology

Prestressing steels (or tendons) are produced in the form of wire and strand to BS 5896: 1980 or of bar to BS 4486: 1988.

6.4.2 Methods of manufacture

Steel for prestressing materials may be made by any process except the air and mixed air/oxygen bottom blown processes. The cast analysis must not show more than 0.040% sulphur or 0.040% phosphorus.

Wire made to BS 5896: 1980 is made by cold drawing a high carbon content steel rod through a series of reducing dies. The wire may be crimped mechanically or have the surface indented to improve bond when used in short units.

To enhance the mechanical properties further, the drawn wire is run through a mechanical straightening process followed by a stress-relieving low-temperature heat treatment or through a controlled tension and low-temperature heat-treatment process ('hot stretch'). The latter process gives low relaxation properties. The wire is then rewound into large diameter coils (usually in 200–500 kg weights) from which it pays out straight. In this form it is suitable for making parallel bundles for post-tensioned applications.

Seven-wire strand made to BS 5896: 1980 is made by spinning six cold drawn wires in helical form round a slightly larger straight central wire. The strand is then stress-relieved or 'hot stretched', the latter imparting low relaxation behaviour (see *Figure 6.4*).

Die-drawn strand is made by drawing a seven-wire strand through a die under controlled tension and temperature for low relaxation. The drawing process also compacts the wires giving a larger steel area in the same circumscribing circle as the normal strand. Coils of strand are usually supplied in weights of 2–3 tonnes, for ease of handling on site.

Prestressing bars to BS 4486: 1988 are made by hot rolling microalloyed steels under controlled conditions and then stretching them in a controlled manner at about 90% of their characteristic strength. Bars may be plain or deformed with a maximum length of 18 m. The prepared ends are threaded by cold rolling and bars can be joined end to end by couplers (see *Figure 6.5*).

6.4.3 Sizes and properties

The most commonly used sizes of wire, strand and bar are shown in *Table 6.4*. Other less used sizes of wire and strand are included in BS 5896.

Figure 6.4 A coil of seven-wire strand. (Courtesy of Bridon Ropes Ltd)

Figure 6.5 A prestressed bar with threaded end and locking nut. (Courtesy of McCalls Special Products)

6.4.4 Mechanical properties

For prestressing steels it is customary for the manufacturer to supply a test certificate defining the size, breaking load, relaxation type and load-extension properties (the latter covering at least elongation at fracture), 0.1% proof load or load at 1% extension and modulus of elasticity. These and other characteristics are illustrated in *Figure 6.6*.

The requirements for relaxation and typical examples are given in *Tables 6.5* and *6.6*.

6.4.5 Quality assurance

UK suppliers of prestressing steels operate the BSI Kitemark third-party QA scheme in addition to high levels of inspection and testing.

6.4.6 Site precautions

Prestressing steels require careful handling and storage and surface contamination and mechanical or heat damage must be avoided at all stages. The steel should be unloaded under cover and stored in clean, dry buildings free from the effects of wind-blown or soil-contaminated deleterious matter. Otherwise, storage should be off the ground by the use of impervious supports and the material should be covered with waterproof sheeting with air circulation access below the underside of the steel. For long-term storage sealed polythene bags or tight wrapping should be used. A bag of silica gel or vapour-phase inhibitor should be included inside the bag or wrapping. Steel in ungrouted ducts also requires protection.

Table 6.4 The most commonly[a] used sizes of wire, strand and bar

Type	Nominal diameter (mm)	Specified characteristic breaking load (kN)	Nominal area (mm^2)	Approximate length (m kg^{-1})
Wire	7.0	60.4	38.5	3.31
Strand				
'Standard'	12.5	164	93	1.37
	15.2	232	139	0.92
'Super'	12.9	186	100	1.27
	15.7	265	150	0.85
'Drawn'	12.7	209	112	1.12
	15.2	300	165	0.77
	18.0	380	223	0.57
Bar type/strength				
Smooth or deformed	26.5	568	552	0.230
1030 N mm^{-2}	32	830	804	0.158
	36	1048	1018	0.125
	40	1300	1257	0.101

[a] Products outside British Standard specifications often used are: strand 15.4 mm/250 kN and 15.5 mm/261 kN. Refer to manufacturers' publications.

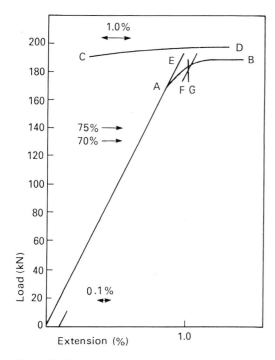

Figure 6.6 Representative load–extension diagram for a 12.9-mm strand. OA, elastic range; A, limit of proportionality; C, continuation of B at lower extension magnification; D, elongation at fracture (maximum load); OE, modulus line or line of proportionality; F, 0.1% offset from OE; G, 1.0% total extension; 70% and 75%, indication of prestressing load range

Table 6.5 Maximum 1000-h relaxation[a] at 20°C

	Initial load/breaking load (%)		
	60	70	80
Bar	3.5	6.0	
Strand and straight wire			
Relaxation class 1	4.5	8.0	12.0
Relaxation class 2	1.0	2.5	4.5

[a] From BS 5896: 1980 and BS 4486: 1988.

Table 6.6 Typical 1000-h relaxation at 20°C for strand

Initial load/breaking load (%)	Relaxation 1 (%)	Relaxation 2 (%)
60	3.4	1.00
65	4.4	1.04
70	5.6	1.10
75	7.6	1.60

Prestressing steels should be unloaded carefully avoiding shock loading and distortion of coils. Local damage should be avoided at all times and kinking of wire and strand in coil avoided. Bar threads should be protected.

Cutting should only be done by mechanical cutters on wire and abrasive discs on strand. Flame cutting should only be used with the greatest care and supervision and stray heating of adjacent tendons must be avoided.

Acknowledgements

The author acknowledges that the information in Section 6.4 was provided by Mr K. W. Longbottom, the Chairman of the committees for BS 5896: 1980 and BS 4486: 1988.

References

BRITISH STANDARDS INSTITUTION, *BS 4449 Carbon steel bars for the reinforcement of concrete*, Milton Keynes (1988)
BRITISH STANDARDS INSTITUTION, *BS 4466 Specification for scheduling dimensions for bending and cutting of steel reinforcement for concrete*, Milton Keynes (1989)
BRITISH STANDARDS INSTITUTION, *BS 4482 Cold reduced wire for the reinforcement of concrete*, Milton Keynes (1985)
BRITISH STANDARDS INSTITUTION, *BS 4483 Steel fabric for the reinforcement of concrete*, Milton Keynes (1985)
BRITISH STANDARDS INSTITUTION, *BS 4486 (Amended) Hot rolled and hot rolled and processed high tensile alloy steel bars for the prestressing of concrete*, Milton Keynes (1988)
BRITISH STANDARDS INSTITUTION, *BS 5896 High tensile steel wire and strand for the prestressing of concrete*, Milton Keynes (1980)
BRITISH STANDARDS INSTITUTION, *BS 6744 Austenitic stainless steel bars for the reinforcement of concrete*, Milton Keynes (1988)
BRITISH STANDARDS INSTITUTION, *BS 7123 Metal arc welding of steel for concrete reinforcement*, Milton Keynes (1989)
BRITISH STANDARDS INSTITUTION, *BS 8110, Part 1 Structural use of concrete*, Milton Keynes (1988)
CONSTRUCTION INDUSTRY RESEARCH AND INFORMATION ASSOCIATION, 'Reinforcement Connector and Anchorage Methods', *CIRIA Report 92*, London (1981)
LANCASTER, R. L, 'Steel reinforcement—production and practice', *Concrete Society Current Practice Sheet No. 64* (1984)
LONGBOTTOM, K. W., 'Steel for pre-stressed concrete', *Concrete Society Digest No. 4* (1984)

7

Other Metals

C Bodsworth MMet, PhD, CEng, FIM
Brunel, The University of West London

B Ralph MA, PhD, ScD, CEng, CPhys, FIM, FInstP, Hon.FRMS, Eur.Ing
Brunel, The University of West London

Contents

7.1 Introduction 7/3
    7.1.1 Cost of pure metal 7/3
    7.1.2 Minerals and extraction 7/4
    7.1.3 General physical and mechanical properties 7/4
    7.1.4 Colour of metals and glass thermal-barrier coatings 7/6

7.2 Copper 7/7
    7.2.1 Characteristics 7/7
    7.2.2 Corrosion principles 7/7
    7.2.3 Sources and production 7/9
    7.2.4 Unalloyed copper grades 7/9
    7.2.5 Joining 7/11
    7.2.6 Other applications 7/11

7.3 Copper alloys 7/12
    7.3.1 Introduction 7/12
    7.3.2 Brass 7/12
    7.3.3 Tin bronze 7/14
    7.3.4 Aluminium bronze 7/16
    7.3.5 Beryllium bronze 7/17
    7.3.6 Memory alloys 7/17

7.4 Gold 7/18
    7.4.1 Overview 7/18
    7.4.2 Sources and production 7/19
    7.4.3 Gold and gold alloys 7/20
    7.4.4 Gold coatings 7/22
    7.4.5 Gold in joining 7/22

7.5 Lead 7/22
    7.5.1 Overview 7/22
    7.5.2 Sources and production 7/23
    7.5.3 Metallic lead 7/23
    7.5.4 Lead sheet 7/23
    7.5.5 Lead pipe 7/24
    7.5.6 Fusible alloys 7/25
    7.5.7 Other uses of lead 7/25

7.6 Nickel 7/26
    7.6.1 Characteristics 7/26
    7.6.2 Sources and production 7/26
    7.6.3 Nickel and nickel alloys 7/26
    7.6.4 Nickel coatings 7/28

7.7 Silver 7/29
    7.7.1 Overview 7/29
    7.7.2 Sources and production 7/29
    7.7.3 Silver and silver alloys 7/29

7.8 Tin 7/30
    7.8.1 Summary of applications 7/30
    7.8.2 Sources and production 7/30
    7.8.3 Pure tin 7/30
    7.8.4 Tin coatings 7/31
    7.8.5 Solders 7/31
    7.8.6 Bearings 7/32
    7.8.7 Pewter 7/32

7.9 Zinc 7/32
    7.9.1 Characteristics 7/32
    7.9.2 Sources and production 7/33
    7.9.3 Zinc coatings 7/33
    7.9.4 Die castings 7/34
    7.9.5 Wrought zinc 7/35
    7.9.6 Other uses 7/36

References 7/36

Bibliography 7/36

7.1 Introduction

The metals reviewed in this chapter are gold, silver, copper, nickel, lead, tin and zinc. The first three can be classed as noble metals in the sense that they lie above hydrogen in the electrochemical classification of metals (i.e. they cannot release hydrogen from solution) and hence exhibit good resistance to corrosion by acids. Nickel, also, is passive in neutral and alkaline solutions. With the exception of zinc, however, all these metals exhibit a corrosion resistance that is far superior to that of unalloyed iron or aluminium, and numerous archaeological artefacts testify to the outstanding durability of these metals. The last three, lead, tin and zinc, together with cadmium, are usually referred to as 'white metals' since they are the main constituents of the soft, metallic bearings which have a whitish colouration.

It should be appreciated that none of these metallic elements find tonnage application in the main structures of buildings. However, in each case they have important combinations of properties which are exploited in the construction industry. In discussing these elements it is the intention of this chapter to explain some of the background to the business of materials selection (see, for instance, Crane and Charles[1] or Ashby and Jones[2] for a much deeper treatment).

In the remaining subsections of this chapter, an outline is given of the relevant principles governing the production and properties of the metals under discussion. In particular, we outline the underlying chemistry of the extraction of these metals in order that their relative costs may be appreciated, before considering the origin of some of their critical properties. The subsequent sections deal with these metals and their alloys one at a time, but with considerable cross-referencing. Thus in Section 7.2.2 we give an overview of the subject of corrosion which, whilst directed to copper, is of more general relevance since in the majority of civil-engineering applications the primary justification for the use of these expensive metals and alloys is their resistance to corrosive environments.

7.1.1 Cost of pure metal

Gold and silver are instinctively recognized as expensive precious metals, but pure copper, nickel and tin also cost several thousand pounds per tonne. Compared with these metals, lead and zinc are relatively inexpensive. The reasons for the relative costs are fairly complex. Gold and silver do not form stable oxides in contact with air. Zinc oxide (ZnO) is more stable than ferrous oxide below about 1600°C, but the other metals form oxides which are less stable at all temperatures than ferrous oxide. With the exception of zinc, therefore, the oxides can be reduced more easily than iron oxide to the metallic form and so, on this account, it might be expected that they could be less expensive.

Table 7.1 lists some data[3] for the production and the reserves of the metals considered here. Data on aluminium and iron are given for comparison. Column 1 lists the average concentration of the metals in the earth's crust, smaller concentrations are also present in seawater. On the basis of these data, one might expect gold to be expensive; but, on the same basis, one would expect lead to be more expensive than copper while zinc should be priced similarly to nickel. The limited data on the scarcity value, indicated by the estimated static lifetime of the known workable deposits, also bears no relation to the cost of the metal. The last column of *Table 7.1* shows the level of concentration of the metal, relative to the average concentration, which is required to produce a workable ore body. Whereas many quite large ore bodies possess the degree of enrichment required for workable deposits of iron and aluminium, relatively few, small and widely distributed deposits exhibit the enrichment required for the extraction of these expensive metals. Multiplication of the data in the first and last columns of *Table 7.1* for each metal also reveals the metallic contents of the ore which are considered workable. Thus aluminium and iron bearing deposits are considered worthy of treatment with about 25% and 30%, respectively, of the metallic element, but there are numerous deposits which supply present demand containing much higher concentrations of these metals. In contrast, the cut-off grades for the other metals contain about 4% metal for lead and zinc, 0.5% for copper and 0.0001% for gold.[3] This means that large amounts of rock have to be extracted from the ground, crushed to a fine size to release the metal-bearing mineral and then separated by gravity, flotation, etc., to produce 1 tonne of the metallic mineral. Few rich deposits containing significantly more than the minimum workable grade remain in the earth and the cost of extraction increases as the metal content of the ore body decreases.

Many of the metals occur together in mixed ore bodies and the cost of extraction of lead, for example, is lowered by the value of the silver which is extracted at the same time. About half the zinc produced is obtained from mixed zinc–lead ores and the two metals can be reduced from their ores simultaneously and separated by gravity difference in the molten state. Again, costs may be reduced by recovery of small amounts of silver and gold which are often associated with the zinc–lead ore. Likewise, copper and nickel are often associated in the same ore body and an important copper–nickel alloy, called Monel, can be produced by the simultaneous reduction of these two metals.

Several of the metals show extensive solid solubility in each other and, when they are associated together in the same ore body, expensive separation treatments such as electrolysis and vacuum distillation may be required to produce the pure metals. Other elements may also be present in small amounts in the metal and may have significant effects on the properties of the metal. Inevitably, the cost increases rapidly as the purity of the

Table 7.1 Metal resources in the earth's continental crust[3]

Metal	Average concentration (g t^{-1})	Mine production 1986 (Mt)	Recoverable reserves (Mt)	Static lifetime (years)	Workable concentration / Average concentration
Copper	55	8.11	1000	120	73
Gold	0.004				250
Lead	13	3.4	170	50	3000
Nickel	75	0.73	1200	1650	
Tin	2	0.17	25	150	2500
Zinc	70				570
Aluminium	82 300				4
Iron	56 300				4

metal is increased from a commercial grade of, say, 99.5% to a premium grade of $\geqslant 99.9\%$ purity.

7.1.2 Minerals and extraction

The extraction of metals from their ores is a complex topic but the first principles may be understood in terms of the thermodynamic stability of metallic compounds as a function of temperature. *Figure 7.1* gives examples of such diagrams for oxides and sulphides (others are available for nitrides, chlorides, etc.). In general, this diagram shows that oxides of gold will be unstable to decomposition at all temperatures, whilst silver oxide will be expected to decompose thermally above *c.* 200°C. To extract other metals will require the use of reducing agents, such as carbon, carbon monoxide or electrons (electrolytic reduction).

The stability of an oxide or sulphide increases with increasing negative value of its free energy of formation. Thus, under equilibrium conditions, metallic aluminium will react with any of the metal compounds lying above it on, say, the oxide diagram, resulting in the formation of aluminium oxide (alumina) and the reduction of the other oxides to the metal. For most metals the stability of the oxide is greater than the stability of the sulphide form. Tin and zinc conform to this general rule, but the other metals considered in this chapter behave differently. The sulphides of copper, lead, nickel and silver are much more stable than the oxides. This has some important consequences:

whereas the ores of aluminium, iron and tin occur naturally in oxide form, copper, lead, nickel, silver and zinc occur more commonly as sulphides, which increases the complexity of metal extraction and results in the release of large volumes of polluting, sulphur-bearing gas. Furthermore, when the metal is exposed in service to atmospheres containing sulphur dioxide and other sulphur compounds, the normally protective oxide surface coat will be reduced. In some cases this may be replaced by a sulphide coating as in the tarnishing of silver. More commonly, a water-soluble sulphate film is formed which is readily dissolved in rainwater and results in accelerated corrosion of the metal. Whilst Ellingham diagrams may be used to classify the thermodynamic driving force necessary to extract metals, these clearly do not take into account kinetic factors (see for instance Gilchrist[4]).

7.1.3 General physical and mechanical properties

Table 7.2 lists data, taken mainly from the ASTM *Metals Handbook*,[5] of typical values for the physical and mechanical properties of the pure metals. These data should be used with caution, since properties often change quite markedly when small amounts of impurities or deliberate trace additions are present in otherwise 'pure' metals. To take an extreme example, the electrical resistivity of copper at 99.90% purity is markedly higher than at 99.99% purity if certain elements are present. In

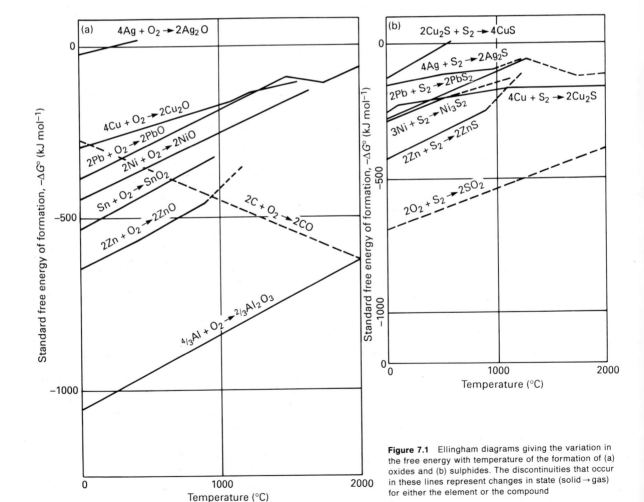

Figure 7.1 Ellingham diagrams giving the variation in the free energy with temperature of the formation of (a) oxides and (b) sulphides. The discontinuities that occur in these lines represent changes in state (solid → gas) for either the element or the compound

Table 7.2 Physical and mechanical properties of the pure metals

Property	Metal						
	Copper	Gold	Nickel	Silver	Lead	Tin	Zinc
Atomic number	29	79	28	47	82	50	30
Atomic weight	63.54	196.97	58.71	107.89	207.21	118.69	65.38
Atomic radius (nm)[5]	12.75	14.41	12.45	14.44	17.49	15.1	13.3
Crystal structure	f.c.c.	f.c.c.	f.c.c.	f.c.c.	f.c.c.	b.c.t.	c.p.h.
Melting point (°C)[5]	1083	1063	1453	960.8	327.4	231.9	419.5
Boiling point (°C)[5]	2595	2970	2730	2210	1725	2270	906
Density (g cm^{-3})[5]	8.96	19.32	8.9	10.49	11.34	7.30	7.14
Specific heat at 20°C (J g^{-1})[5]	0.380	0.131	0.440	0.234	0.129	0.230	0.383
Thermal conductivity 0–100°C (J cm cm^{-2} s^{-1} C^{-1})	3.93	2.97	0.92	4.19	0.347	0.377	1.13
Coefficient of linear thermal expansion[2] 0–100°C (cm cm C^{-1}) × 10^6	16.5	14.2	13.3	19.68	29.3	23	39.7
Electrical resistivity at 20°C ($\mu\Omega$ cm^{-1})[5]	1.673	2.35	6.84	1.59	20.65	13	5.92
Temperature coefficient of electrical resistance (°C^{-1})	0.0039	0.004		0.0041	0.0042	0.00447	0.00419
Yield or 0.2% proof stress (N mm^{-2})							
Annealed	60	0	103	55	8	14	
Hard	325	205	620				
Ultimate tensile stress (N mm^{-2})							
Annealed	220	130	410	130	16	16	140
Hard	385	220	700				160
Elongation (%)							
Annealed	55	45	45	54	40	90	60
Hard	4	4	15	48			45
Hardness (DPN)							
Annealed	45	25	70	25	4	5	35
Hard	115	58	230	5			

almost all cases, the effect of the impurities or trace additions on the properties is more serious if they are held in solid solution in the metal than if they are present as precipitates. The physical properties also vary with temperature. The values listed for thermal conductivity and thermal expansion are average values, applicable over the range 0–100°C. The electrical resistivity values are for 20°C and the temperature coefficients for resistivity show that the resistance of copper changes by about 25% between 0 and 100°C. The mechanical properties are sensitive to temperature variations around ambient also, particularly for the low-melting-point metals.

The atomic weights show that gold and lead are heavy metals, whereas the atomic weight of nickel is similar to, and copper and zinc are only slightly heavier than, iron. Silver and tin have similar atomic weights, lying in between these two groups. Pure copper, gold, lead, nickel and silver form face-centred-cubic crystal structures (*Figure 7.2*) at all temperatures up to their melting points and their atomic sizes are not too dissimilar. They all exhibit monovalency. According to the Hume-Rothery rules,[6] these are ideal candidates for extensive intersolubility. In fact, gold and copper, and copper and nickel are miscible in all proportions in the solid state (i.e. form a complete range of solid solutions). Gold–copper and gold–nickel alloys are completely miscible also at high temperatures in the solid state but decompose into a mixture of two phases at lower temperatures. The atomic size of lead is very much larger and, correspondingly, lead is only sparingly soluble in the other metals. At room temperature tin forms a body-centred-tetragonal structure, but the stable form below 13.2°C is a diamond cubic structure which shows non-metallic properties. Fortunately, the transformation to the low-temperature structure is very sluggish.* Tin is partially soluble in copper, forming the tin bronzes. Zinc forms

a close-packed-hexagonal structure but the *c/a* ratio (see *Figure 7.2*) is much greater than ideal (1.8 *vs.* 1.63). The resultant poor atomic packing accounts for the low value of the density, relative to the atomic weight. Again, zinc is soluble in copper but has only very limited solid solubility in the other metals of this group.

The melting points of copper, gold, nickel and silver are all high, but lead, tin and zinc all have low melting points. This has important consequences. Whereas the first four metals are relatively stable at room temperature, the last three tend to recrystallize when deformed at room temperature and suffer from extensive deformation by creep; that is, continued extension with time under a low load. Copper, silver and gold have high values of thermal conductivity and very low values of electrical resistivity, relative to the other metals considered. These properties, together with their good oxidation and corrosion resistance, account for their extensive use in electronics and electric-power distribution.

Nickel and gold have relatively low coefficients of thermal expansion. In solid solution in iron, nickel lowers still further the coefficient for iron, producing the 'Invar' alloys with a zero expansion coefficient.

Only nickel and copper, in the pure metal form, exhibit sufficient strength for engineering applications and both metals are work hardened significantly by mechanical working below the recrystallization temperature. In marked contrast, lead, tin and zinc are characteristically soft materials which do not work

* However, there are claims that Napoleon's defeat at Moscow may in part be atttributed to this. It is said that his soldiers during this very long cold campaign wore trousers which had buttons made of tin which crumbled after transforming to the low temperature, brittle form of this element.

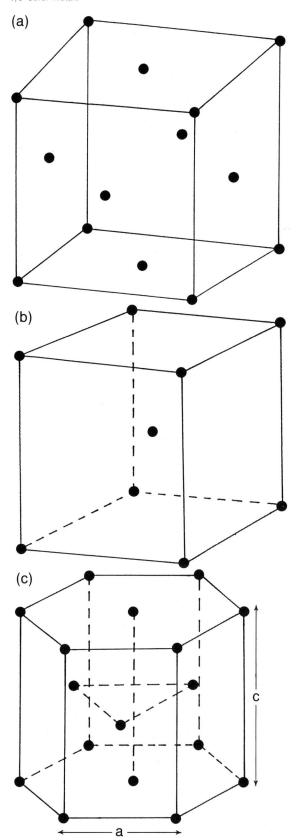

(a)

(b)

(c)

harden significantly, if at all, in the pure metal form and are not suitable for structural applications.

Partially because of cost, but also because of the poor mechanical properties, most of the applications of the latter three metals are as additions to alloys or as coatings to impart specific physical and/or chemical properties on the surface of a stronger substrate. It is often the case that the required combination of properties, such as strength, toughness, fatigue, wear, corrosion and oxidation resistance, required for a particular application cannot be achieved, or can be achieved only at high cost from a single metal or alloy. A satisfactory solution may be obtained by using one metal to meet the bulk mechanical requirements and coating the surface with another metal to enhance specific attributes, such as corrosion resistance, which are deficient in the first metal. In other cases, a coating such as gold leaf or silver plate is applied to produce the required decorative surface appearance on a cheap metal substrate at a very small fraction of the cost of a solid gold or silver artefact.

7.1.4 Colour of metals and glass thermal-barrier coatings

Very thin layers of some metals and metallic compounds are transparent to the shorter wavelengths of visible light, but are opaque to the longer wavelengths which transfer most of the thermal energy. This phenomenon is utilized in thermal-barrier layers on glazing units to prevent condensation on the glass and reduce heat loss from within the building.

The phenomenon is more readily understood from a consideration of the colour and reflectivity of metals. When visible light strikes the surface of a metal, the light photons are absorbed and transfer their energy to the valence electrons, which are excited into higher energy levels. The light is re-emitted from the surface as these electrons decay back to their normal energy levels. The high reflectivity of the monovalent metals, silver, gold and, to a lesser extent, copper is due to the very loose binding of their single valence electrons, resulting in very rapid rates of decay and almost 100% re-emission. Other metals with stronger electron binding (and hence lower electrical and thermal conductivity) suffer from a less rapid decay and reflect only part of the incident light, resulting in a more matt appearance. With very thin layers, only a few atoms thick, the light photons may be emitted from the rear surface of the layer and the metal appears to be transparent. With greater thickness, the photons are emitted only from the side exposed to the incident light and the metal is opaque.

Most metals absorb and reflect equally all wavelengths in the visible spectrum and hence have a white appearance. Certain metals, however, notably gold, copper and their alloys, reflect only the infra-red and longer wavelengths of visible light. Light photons from lower wavelength light interact also with electrons in the filled band underlying the valence electron band and are absorbed, resulting in the yellow to red colouration. A thin layer of these metals will transmit the shorter, absorbed radiations whilst the longer wavelengths associated with thermal transfer are reflected back from the surface. The transmitted waves are regenerated as white light by absorption and reflection from walls, etc., behind the metal film, so the film may appear to have a similar colour on both the front and the rear surfaces. The actual colour of the film is determined by the composition of the metal, the thickness of the film and the reflectivity of the walls which regenerate the white light. The intensity of the light transmitted can be intensified by sandwiching the film between two layers of a transparent dielectric material. The dielectric layers can also modify the colour of the film.

Figure 7.2 Illustrations of the common structures of metals: (a) face-centred cubic; (b) hexagonal close packed; (c) body-centred cubic

A very thin layer of copper between layers of tin oxide (SnO_2) produces a champagne colouration on glass. If the copper is replaced by silver, the film is colourless or pale blue, depending on the film thickness. Although tin oxide is harder than the copper or tin layer, these films are easily damaged, so they are usually applied to the outer surface of the inner glass sheet of sealed double-glazing units. More durable coatings, which can be applied to single sheets of glass, but which transmit less light, can be obtained with very thin layers of titanium nitride (which has a golden colour in bulk form) or combinations of stainless steel and titanium nitride. These films are normally produced by sputtering or by vacuum deposition (see Section 7.4.4).

In the following sections all compositions of alloys are expressed in terms of weight percent (wt%) of the elements.

7.2 Copper

7.2.1 Characteristics

It is not known whether copper or gold was the first metal used by mankind, but copper was certainly the first metal used for the production of tools and utensils. Copper artefacts have been dated to over 9000 years old. The earliest use was most probably nodules of metallic or 'native' copper, found on or near the surface of the earth, but it is known that copper was being smelted by the sixth century B.C. The Copper Age continued until, fortuitously, ore deposits were used which contained both copper and arsenic. The arsenical bronze alloy produced could be worked into cutting tools with a longer life of the cutting edge, presumably at the expense of the life of the smelters! Other ores, containing copper and tin, produced a tougher tin bronze. Eventually, early man was able to smelt both copper and tin and then alloy them to produce tin bronzes remarkably similar in composition to those used day. The Bronze Age continued until man had learned not only how to smelt iron but also how to harden it to produce tools and weapons which, in their turn, were superior to bronze.

Copper is a very ductile metal, with comparatively good strength and toughness. This combination of ductility (that is a large plastic extension before failure which makes it readily formable) strength and toughness (really its ability to avoid brittle failure) is characteristic of elements with the face-centred-cubic structure. These properties vary little over a very wide temperature range, from cryogenic temperature to near the melting point. By contrast, metals with the other common structures, body centred cubic and hexagonal close packed, show extensive temperature sensitivity of their mechanical properties. Copper is non-magnetic and has a higher electrical and thermal conductivity than any of the common metals other than silver. It is readily machined, soldered, brazed and welded. The pure metal has an attractive colour, but a wide range of colours can be produced by alloying, or the surface appearance can be changed by plating with other metals, by applying organic coatings or by chemical treatments. The workability is markedly dependent on the concentrations of impurity elements present. In particular, these impurities may melt at relatively low temperatures and form grain boundary films which markedly lower the hot workability. Copper and its alloys are also readily cast into shapes.

Pure copper has a higher resistance to oxidation than iron, aluminium or any of the other common engineering metals. When oxidized, it forms a black outer scale of cupric oxide (CuO). Between this and the metal surface a thin reddish layer of cuprous oxide (Cu_2O) is formed, which adheres firmly to the metal surface and restricts the passage of oxygen to continue the oxidation reaction. This high resistance to oxidation was the reason for the use of copper plate to fabricate the fire boxes of steam locomotives.

7.2.2 Corrosion principles

Copper is usually classed as a noble metal, with high resistance to corrosion. It is inert in potable water and has good resistance both to seawater and deaerated, non-oxidizing acids. It is less resistant to alkalis (which may be leached out of concrete), to ammonia and to sulphur compounds.

When any two metals are in contact, an electrical potential is developed, which causes a flow of electrons from one metal to the other. But this transfer can continue only if a liquid is in contact which can simultaneously transfer positive ions of one metal to the other. When this happens, the metal with the most negative electropotential is dissolved, whilst the less electro-negative (or electropositive) metal is not attacked. The liquid itself does not have to be corrosive, for the reaction can occur at a low rate even in distilled water. This process is called galvanic corrosion. The metal which is attacked is called the anode and the one which is protected is called the cathode.

The chemical reaction involved is most readily considered as two separate, but simultaneous reactions. At the anode surface, metal atoms are dissolved as positive ions in the solution, with the release of electrons:

$$M \rightleftharpoons M^{n+} + ne^-$$

where n is equal to the valence of the ion. The electrons are consumed at the cathode surface by one or more of three principal mechanisms:

$$2H^+ + 2e^- = 2H = H_2 \text{ (gas)}$$

$$4H^+ + O_2 + 4e^- = 2H_2O$$

$$2H_2O + O_2 + 4e^- = 4OH^-$$

The concentration of hydrogen ions is sufficient in strong acid solutions for the release of hydrogen gas. This is the gas which is released during charging of a lead–acid accumulator which is actually an electrically induced corrosion process. But the concentration of hydrogen ions decreases rapidly with decreasing acidity of the solution (i.e. increasing pH) and is so low in neutral and alkaline solutions that this reaction can be ignored. The cathodic reaction then depends upon the availability of oxygen in the solution to facilitate electron discharge by the second and third reactions. Indeed, variation from place to place in the oxygen content of the solution in contact with a metal may be sufficient to set up corrosion cells in the absence of bimetallic coupling, the regions of high oxygen content being cathodic with respect to the regions of low oxygen content. It follows that to minimize corrosion, wherever possible, solutions in contact with metals should be neutral and with low oxygen content.

The corrosion reaction generates an electrical potential between the anodic and the cathodic areas. This electrochemical potential per unit area of interface increases with increasing ease of dissolution of the metal. Thus metals may be classified in order of the potential developed. The sequence is sensitive to the composition of the conducting liquids, and metals close to each other in the list may interchange places as the acidity or alkalinity of the liquid is changed. The following list shows the position of copper and its alloys, relative to other common metals and alloys, when in contact with seawater:

Anodic
Magnesium and magnesium alloys
Zinc and zinc alloys
Galvanized steel
Aluminium
Duralumin (aluminium, 4.5% copper)
Mild steel
Cast iron
Tin–lead solder

Austenitic stainless steel (active)
Lead
Tin
Muntz metal (60% copper, 40% zinc)
Nickel (active)
Brass (70% copper, 30% zinc)
Copper
Aluminium bronze
Silicon bronze
Monel (67% nickel, 33% copper)
Silver solder (70% silver, 30% copper)
Nickel (passive)
Inconel (76% nickel, 16% chromium, 8% iron)
Austenitic stainless steel (passive)
Silver
Gold
Cathodic

Metal	Standard electrode potential (V)
Gold	+1.50
Silver	+0.80
Nickel (passive)	
Copper	+0.34
Chromium (passive)	
Lead	−0.13
Tin	−0.14
Nickel (active)	−0.25
Iron	−0.44
Chromium (active)	−0.74
Zinc	−0.76
Aluminium	−1.66
Magnesium	−2.37

Figure 7.3 Compatible metal couples: (○) The most cathodic member of a series; (●) an anodic member (from Ashby and Jones[2])

Extreme examples of the way that metals respond to changes in the environment in contact with their surfaces are shown by the two positions listed for nickel and for austenitic stainless steel. The corrosion resistance of the latter relies upon the formation of a chromic oxide layer on the surface to prevent contact of the corrodant with the metal and render it passive. But, under strongly reducing conditions the oxide film cannot form, corrosion continues unhindered and the metal is said to be active.

The list shows that when copper and iron are in metallic contact with each other and with a conducting liquid, then iron will be dissolved (and any copper in the solution will be precipitated out of solution). The rate of attack on the iron depends markedly on the relative areas of the anodic and cathodic couple. For example, an iron rivet, with a relatively small surface area, would corrode very rapidly if inserted into a copper plate. But, when the situation is reversed, a small copper rivet inserted into a steel plate causes only slow corrosion of the steel because the attack is spread over a much larger area from a small area of cathode. Similarly, copper tubes which have been bright annealed (i.e. heat treated in a reducing atmosphere) may have a thin layer of carbon covering the surface. If the tubes are subsequently cold drawn to size, the carbon film on the bore of the tube may be scored by the mandril. Since carbon is passive to most corrodants, the small areas of copper exposed at the score marks can corrode rapidly if the carbon film is not removed from the rest of the surface before service use.

In general, the risk of galvanic corrosion increases with increasing difference in the electromotive potential of the two materials forming the corrosion couple. *Figure 7.3* illustrates the corrosion compatibility of different pairs of materials where compatibility is defined as a difference of not greater than 0.25 V in the electrode potentials of the metals or alloys.

Bimetallic galvanic corrosion can be prevented by electrically insulating the metals from each other with a non-conducting layer of plastic or similar material. The rate of attack may also slow considerably if a coating of a relatively impermeable substance is formed deliberately or fortuitously over the metal surfaces. Copper and iron pipes coupled together in a domestic water or central-heating system may give a long life in a hard-water district, where an impermeable calcareous deposit forms over the inner bore of the tubes, but fail rapidly in a soft-water system.

Galvanic corrosion can occur when only one metal is present. For example, water invariably contains a small amount of dissolved oxygen and carbon dioxide. Differences in the concentrations of these substances in the water at the metal surface can set up local electrolytic cells on the metal. The oxygen in the water may be depleted under patches of scale, accumulation of dirt or at the bottom of crevices in the metal surface. The metal in contact with the oxygen depleted water then becomes anodic to the rest of the metal surface and is corroded preferentially, resulting in pitting. Similarly, a pipe partially submerged in water may suffer from water-line attack just below the water surface, where the oxygen content of the water is lower than at the air–water interface. Thus it is important to ensure that when copper (and other metals) are in prolonged contact with water which is stationary or circulating at a low rate (as in central-heating systems during the summer period) the water is treated to remove the dissolved oxygen and carbon dioxide.

The corrosion resistance of a metal is affected by the presence of other elements which may be present in the solid metal. If the other elements are present as precipitates or as phases of different composition, the corrosion resistance is changed to a greater extent than when those elements are dissolved completely in the host metal (i.e. do not form a separate phase, but remain in solid solution). For example, copper can hold over 30% zinc in solid solution. The corrosion resistance of zinc is very inferior to copper but the above list shows that brass containing 70% copper and 30% zinc is only slightly inferior to pure copper in seawater. If the zinc content is increased to 40%, however, the solid solubility limit is exceeded and a second phase is precipitated. The list shows, correspondingly, that Muntz metal is more anodic than 70/30 brass.

Some metals form an adherent, continuous layer of oxide or of a compound such as a carbonate or sulphate when exposed to certain corrosive fluids. This layer acts as a barrier, restricting egress of the corrodant to the metal surface and reduces the corrosion rate. The different positions for nickel and for austenitic stainless steels for the active and passive conditions in the above list are really dependent on whether or not the corrosive conditions allow the formation of a barrier layer. Copper forms a protective oxide film and also forms a complex carbonate–hydroxide–sulphate layer, giving rise to the green patina on copper sheet exposed to atmospheres containing traces of sulphur dioxide. But these films do not enhance significantly the resistance of copper to corrosive liquids. Aluminium is strongly anodic to copper but, when held in solid solution in copper, it increases the resistance to corrosion by forming a strongly adherent layer of alumina on the surface. The corrosion resistance of aluminium bronze is, correspondingly, higher in seawater than pure copper. If the passive film is breached, the nobility of the copper protects the metal, giving the film a chance to reform. Pure aluminium is also protected by an alumina film, but the metal is so anodic that corrision continues at a rapid rate if the film is breached, giving little chance for it to reform.

These principles are illustrated with other examples in the following review of particular metals.

7.2.3 Sources and production

Copper is found mainly as sulphide minerals, often associated with iron sulphides and small amounts of silver, gold and other metals, as enriched zones where it has condensed from gases released from molten magmas which have penetrated the surrounding rock. Near to the surface, the enriched zones are often oxidized to form copper oxide. In other regions, notably in Africa, the copper has been leached from the rock by percolating waters and redeposited in sedimentary rocks.

Copper ores are mined in many countries. The major source is the west coast of North and South America. Significant quantities are still produced in Europe, albeit from small and widely scattered deposits, but the total production from European mines exceeds the output from the African copper belt. Most of the high-grade ores have been worked-out and few deposits which are now being exploited contain more than about 1% copper.

Reference was made in Section 7.1 to the high cost of the non-ferrous metals considered in this chapter. The complex, multi-stage extraction and refining processes required to produce the pure metal are well illustrated by consideration of the production of copper. The resultant output, measured in tonnes of refined metal per man-hour is very low when compared, for example, with the production of steel via the blast furnace and LD converter route, with consequent escalation in cost.

The low-grade sulphide ores are first crushed to a fine size and the copper is then concentrated by a flotation process, in which the mineral is suspended in water to which flotation reagents are added which adhere preferentially to any exposed copper sulphide surfaces. These reagents make the ore particles water repellant. When a stream of air bubbles are blown upwards through the water, the ore particles become attached to the bubbles and rise to the surface, where they accumulate in a froth, leaving the copper-free rock particles to sink to the bottom. The dried copper concentrate, now containing about 25% copper, may be refined via several different routes, but the most common is 'flash smelting' in which the exothermic reaction between part of the sulphur in a column of falling ore particles and oxygen in an ascending gas stream generates sufficient heat to melt the ore. Copper sulphide is more stable than iron sulphide and part of the iron is oxidized to form a slag which floats on the sulphide melt. The latter is called a matte. Almost all the remaining iron is then oxidized out of the matte in a rotary, horizontal converter, producing metallic *blister copper* containing up to 98.5% copper with a little sulphur and up to 0.8% oxygen. In a second furnace, the remaining sulphur and traces of other impurities such as lead and zinc are oxidized out and the oxygen content is reduced (fire refining). Originally this was achieved by stirring the molten metal with green wood poles (giving rise to the term, poling) but, today, hydrocarbon gases are bubbled through the bath to produce a reducing atmosphere. Hydrogen in the gas reacts with the dissolved oxygen to form steam, which escapes from the molten metal. If the oxygen content is reduced to about 0.05% the metal does not form a shrinkage pipe on casting, but solidifies with a flat top, due to reaction between the oxygen and hydrogen rejected from solid solution to form blowholes during solidification. This is termed *tough-pitch copper*. Alternatively, the metal may be treated with a deoxidizing agent to remove the remaining oxygen before solidification. Almost any metal can be used to deoxidize copper, but the most common and cheapest addition is phosphorus. A small excess of phosphorus is left in the metal and this is referred to as *phosphorus deoxidized copper*. Alternatively, the tough-pitch copper is cast into slabs for electrolytic refining. Here, the application of an electrical potential between an anode and a cathode causes the copper to dissolve and form positive ions in a solution, releasing electrons at the impure anode, whilst the positive ions combine with electrons and precipitate from the solution as a pure, oxygen-free metal on the cathode. This is the basis of both electrorefining and electroplating. Any precious metals such as silver, gold and the platinum group elements are not plated out from the solution, but are recovered as a sludge from the base of the electrolyte tank for subsequent refining.

Copper oxide ores follow a different route. The copper is usually leached out of the crushed ore with sulphuric acid forming a weak solution of copper sulphate. The copper concentration is increased by treatment with a chelating reagent to form an organic compound which is separated and reacted with strong sulphuric acid to produce a concentrated solution of copper sulphate containing few impurities which is suitable for electrorefining.

About one-third of the copper produced annually is used as copper metal or copper containing small amounts of other elements. Most of the remainder is used in the production of copper base alloys (see Section 7.3) or as alloying conditions in, for instance, aluminium base alloys (such as Duralumin) and in corrosion-resistant 'Corten' steels. In the latter case, the principles of corrosion referred to above are exploited by adding around 2% of copper to the steel which initially increases the rate of 'rusting' of the steel. The result is that a much more extensive iron oxide film (brown in colour) is formed which is protective against further corrosion, provided the atmosphere is moderately polluted. This has found favour as a cladding and structural material in many buildings.

7.2.4 Unalloyed copper grades

The various types of unalloyed copper, referred to above, are readily deformed into sheet, strip, bar, rod, etc. They can withstand heavy reductions in size at room temperature, but the strength increases and the ductility decreases progressively with increasing percentage deformation. An annealing (softening) treatment at temperatures up to 600°C may be required when extensive deformation is required and the material may be annealed again after deformation to restore ductility. These annealing processes are relatively complex and their control has much to do with controlling properties. As the temperature of a deformed piece of metal is increased, one may identify three processes: recovery, recrystallization and grain growth. In the recovery process the pattern of deformed grains is retained whilst the population of other defects is reduced and rearranged, leading to substantial changes in electrical resistivity. The recrystallization process replaces the deformed grain structure with a completely new set of grains by a nucleation process. This causes major changes to the mechanical properties, and control of the recrystallization process permits a control of the overall grain size and hence resultant properties.

Grain size is a key parameter in controlling particularly strength and toughness following equations of the Hall–Petch type: $\sigma_y = \sigma_i + k_y d^{-1/2}$ (see *Figure 7.4*) where σ_y is the yield stress, σ_i a friction stress related to the fundamental material, k_y a constant and d the grain size. Essentially, for lower temperature applications a fine (refined) grain size gives advantages of improved strength and toughness. However, for application at higher temperature, under what are termed creep conditions, in general, a large grain size is to be preferred—mainly to avoid failure by grain boundary sliding. At higher temperatures still, grain growth occurs with the larger grains growing at the expense of the smaller ones. By varying the percentage reduction at room temperature, the annealing temperature and the time at temperature, the metal can be produced in the annealed, quarter-hard, half-hard, hard, etc., condition, according to the intended use. Since the metal does not undergo a change between phases during heating (unlike low carbon steel) care has to be exercised during annealing to avoid excessive grain growth, resulting in loss of toughness and increased risk of grain boundary corrosion.

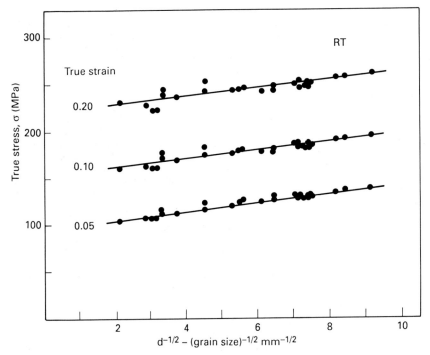

Figure 7.4 A plot of the room-temperature flow stress of copper at selected strains as a function of grain size. Good agreement with a Hall–Petch relationship is seen (from Hansen and Ralph [7])

Small additions of cadmium or (residual) silver raise the temperature at which the metal recrystallizes and softens, reducing the risk of excessive grain growth and improving the strength at elevated temperatures.

Seamless copper tubing for potable water and central-heating systems, etc., is produced either by extrusion or by rotary piercing at temperatures above the recrystallization temperature. In extrusion, a hollow billet is forced through a die and over a mandrel which determines the size of the bore. The Mannessmann rotary piercer uses three work rolls mounted at an angle to the axis of a copper cylinder. Rotation between the work rolls creates tensile stresses at the centre of the cylinder, causing a hole to open up. Simultaneously, the rolls drive the cylinder forward over a conical plug which is located where the central hole begins to form. The plug extends the hole to the required inner diameter and smooths the surface of the hole. Smaller diameter tubes and wall sections thinner than can be produced by these methods are manufactured by cold reducing the tube between eccentric grooved rolls over a tapered mandrel or by drawing the tube through a die fixed to a draw bench. Similar techniques are used for fabricating tubes from copper alloys, particularly in the single-phase process (e.g. 70/30) brass.

Wrought copper and copper alloys are usually specified according to BS 2870–2875, and the last number relating to the form required: i.e. sheet, strip and foil; tubes; forgings; wire; rods and sections; and plate. Other British Standard specifications relate to copper for electrical applications.

The mechanical properties of wrought unalloyed copper are not sensitive to the presence of most impurities in the range 0–0.15%. Typical values at room temperature are given in *Table 7.3*. Strength decreases and ductility increases as the temperature is raised above ambient, the range of change becoming rapid above about 200°C. The shear strength decreases from about three-quarters of the tensile strength in the annealed condition to about half in the hard condition. Copper does not have a clearly defined fatigue limit and fatigue damage can accumulate

Table 7.3 Typical mechanical properties at room temperature of unalloyed copper

Copper type	0.2% Proof stress (N mm^{-2})*	Ultimate tensile strength (N mm^{-2})	Elongation (%)	Hardness (HV)
Annealed	60	220	55	45
Hard	325	385	4	115

* 1 N mm^{-2} ≈ 1 MPa.

at stresses above about 10 N mm^{-2}. Creep can occur at only slightly elevated temperatures and the creep rate becomes significant above about 200°C. A small silver content is beneficial in retarding softening and reducing the creep rate.

In contrast to the mechanical properties, the electrical resistivity of copper is sensitive to the amount and the composition of the impurities which are present in solid solution. Silver causes a small increase. Cadmium and zinc have a slightly greater effect. Most other solutes have a larger effect, increasing in severity in the order nickel < tin < aluminium < berrylium < arsenic < iron < silicon < phosphorus. Hence, elements other than phosphorus are used as deoxidizers when electrical conductivity is of paramount importance. Elements which are virtually insoluble in copper, such as lead, sellenium and tellurium which are added to improve machinability, have very little effect.

In descending order of purity (and hence cost) the common grades of unalloyed copper, with British Standard designation in brackets, are as follows.

Oxygen free high-conductivity copper (C 103) 99.95% copper (minimum) is produced most commonly in wire form by remelting electrolytically refined copper under a protective, non-oxidizing atmosphere, casting, rolling to rod and drawing to wire. The electrical conductivity is 58 m Ω^{-1} mm^{-1} at 20°C. Up to 0.01% of silver is often included to increase the creep resistance.

Electrolytic tough-pitch high-conductivity copper (C 101) 99.90% copper (minimum) is again produced by remelting electrolytically refined copper, but under more oxidizing conditions to produce a residual oxygen content of about 0.05%. The oxygen is present as a precipitate, Cu_2O, which does not affect the electrical properties but, if the metal is exposed to high temperatures in a reducing atmosphere for bright annealing, welding, brazing, etc., the oxide reacts with any hydrogen present in the atmosphere. Since hydrogen can diffuse fairly rapidly through solid metal at elevated temperatures, the reaction occurs at the site of the cuprous oxide particles within the solid metal. The product of the reaction is steam, which cannot diffuse through the metal and builds up a pressure at the reaction site which may be sufficient to cause cracking of the metal, and/or the formation of blisters on the metal surface from reaction sites just below the surface. This damage can occur with any grade of copper containing oxygen as cuprous oxide and increases progressively with increase in the oxygen content. Up to 0.1% silver may be added to improve creep resistance and resistance to softening after cold work.

Fire-refined tough-pitch high-conductivity copper (C 102) is similar in composition and properties to C 101, but is produced without electrolytic refining.

Fire-refined tough-pitch copper (C 104) with 99.85% copper contains similar or slightly higher oxygen contents to C 101, but impurities other than silver may be as high as 0.5% with a corresponding fall in electrical conductivity to about 50 m Ω^{-1} mm^{-2} at 20°C.

Phosphorus deoxidized copper (C 106) is fire-refined copper which has been deoxidized with phosphorus, leaving a residual content of 0.013–0.05% phosphorus in the metal. Since the phosphorus is present in solid solution, the electrical conductivity is decreased further to about 42 m Ω^{-1} mm^{-2}. Arsenic in the range 0.3–0.5% may be added to fire-refined tough-pitch copper (C 105) and phosphorus deoxidized copper (C 107) as a cheaper, but less effective, way of improving creep resistance and elevated-temperature properties than by adding silver. It enhances also the oxidation and corrosion resistance.

Copper–cadmium (C 108) contains cadmium in the range 0.7–1.3% which enhances both room- and elevated-temperature properties with improved fatigue and wear resistance, whilst retaining good electrical conductivity. This grade is often used for overhead cables for electric traction.

Free machining grades normally contain between 0.3 and 0.7% of lead, tellurium (C 109) or sulphur (C 111). All three elements have very low solubility in copper and are present as small precipitates disseminated throughout the copper matrix. These precipitates affect the workability. For example, copper and lead form a eutectic system which begins to melt when the temperature exceeds 326°C. The molten phase produced reduces the ductility during hot working. Conversely, tellurium forms an intermetallic compound with copper which is ductile at elevated temperatures but brittle during cold working. The free-machining additive is selected accordingly to suit the temperature range to be used for mechanical working.

British Standard grades C 101, C 102 and C 103 are normally selected where electrical conductivity or purity of product are of paramount importance. The less-expensive tough-pitch grades, with or without arsenic, are normally chosen for domestic water

and heating systems, and architectural applications such as roofing and cladding, etc. The deoxidized grades are used whenever there is a risk of exposure to reducing atmospheres and the arsenical grades are usually preferred for elevated-temperature use such as in steam pipes, stills, heat exchangers and condensers.

7.2.5 Joining

Since copper does not form an oxide coat spontaneously on exposure to air, it is relatively easy to clean the surface and join together by soldering or brazing before an oxide has reformed. Copper surfaces are readily coated with molten tin, requiring only a flux such as ammonium chloride or zinc chloride to prevent reoxidation. The fluxes are corrosive to copper, however, and must be washed or wiped off the surface after treatment. The tin component of lead–tin solders is soluble in copper and produces a strong bond, but the ductility is reduced if the soldering temperature is too high, allowing excessive reaction and the formation of larger amounts of copper–tin intermetallic compounds. Tin–silver solders are now used for soldering joints in potable water systems, but tin–lead solders are less expensive and are used for other applications (see Section 7.8.5).

Copper artefacts can be brazed with a copper alloy containing up to 50% zinc to lower the melting point. Copper–zinc alloys have slightly inferior corrosion resistance, compared with pure copper, which may result in corrosion at the joint in arduous service conditions and some zinc may be lost by volatilization if the brazing temperature is to high. Silver may be added to the brazing alloy to depress the melting point further, without adverse effect on the corrosion resistance. Tough-pitch coppers are usually brazed in a furnace in a reducing atmosphere to avoid the risk of hydrogen embrittlement.

The very high thermal conductivity of copper creates problems in fusion welding: preheating of the joint region and high rates of heat input are required to obtain satisfactory welds. Flame welding is best avoided with the undeoxidized, tough-pitch grades because of the risk of reaction between hydrogen and the copper oxide.

Copper-rich materials are used extensively as filler rods in the welding of other high-melting-point metals. Phosphorus deoxidized tough-pitch copper, sometimes with up to 3% silicon and/or manganese, is popular, or with up to 3% zinc for autogenous welding.

7.2.6 Other applications

Dispersion-hardened, unalloyed copper is produced by incorporating finely divided particles of refractory oxides, such as alumina, silica, thoria, titania or zirconia, via a powder metallurgy route. The powder mixture is pressed to shape and sintered at elevated temperature to eliminate voids and approach the theoretical density. These materials retain high strengths up to about 600°C.

Molten copper readily wets many materials, so it is readily strengthened by fibre reinforcement by either continuous or discontinuous fibres of carbon, molybdenum, tungsten, tantalum, etc. Fibre-reinforced copper provides higher room- and elevated-temperature strength.

A range of inorganic and organic compounds based on copper are used in animal feeds, fertilizers, biocides and fungicides.

Copper oxide is a major ingredient of the yttrium–barium–copper–oxygen type of superconductors which have zero electrical resistivity at temperatures below about 100 K. To date, superconductors have found only specialist applications (e.g. in body scanners and in magnetic detectors). However, the new high-critical-temperature ceramic superconductors such as $YBa_2Cu_3O_{7-\delta}$ have attracted enormous interest and the next few decades should see these materials finding very much wider application.

7.3 Copper alloys

7.3.1 Introduction

Copper forms a complete range of solid solutions with gold and with nickel. Alloys comprising these elements are described in Sections 7.4.3 and 7.6.3, respectively. Copper also forms fairly extensive ranges of solid solutions with aluminium, silicon, tin and zinc. The first three elements are the principal constituents of the Bronzes, whilst the brasses are based on copper–zinc alloys. The phase diagrams for copper with each of these elements are complex, but each shows a range of (α) solid solution extending from room temperature up to the solidus temperature, with a face-centred-cubic crystal structure, similar to pure copper. An ordered intermetallic (β) compound is formed at higher concentrations. The α and β phases are separated by a two-phase ($\alpha + \beta$) region. In general, the α phase is soft and ductile, whereas the β phase is hard and brittle. Other compounds are formed at still higher concentrations of the alloy elements, but the metal is then so brittle that it is unsuitable for general use.

7.3.2 Brass

The copper rich portion of the copper–zinc binary phase diagram is shown in *Figure 7.5*. The equilibrium solubility of zinc in copper is 35% at room temperature. The solubility increases to 39% at 454°C and then decreases to 32.5% at 798°C. Alloys containing between 32.5 and 37% zinc solidify as a phase* mixture of $\alpha + \beta$. If equilibrium is maintained during cooling, the β phase will disappear as the temperature decreases to 454°C. But this solid-state reaction is sluggish and requires very slow cooling rates to reach completion. With further decrease in temperature, the β phase should reappear, but this is even more sluggish and, to all intents and purposes, can be ignored at low temperature (hence the dotted extension of the solid solubility limit). To ensure that the alloys remain single phase during processing, and allowing for the effects of impurities on the phase boundaries, the commercial single-phase (α) alloys contain a maximum of 37% zinc.

Alloys containing more than 32.5% zinc start to solidify as a mixture of the face-centred-cubic α phase and the body-centred-cubic β phase. The proportion of β phase increases with increasing zinc content until, with 37% zinc, the alloy solidifies completely as the β phase. During cooling to room temperature, the β phase partially transforms to α. The dotted line, starting at 454°C in the $\alpha + \beta$ phase is the boundary for an 'order–disorder' type of transformation. Above this temperature the copper and zinc atoms are distributed randomly over the atomic sites in the crystal structure. Below this temperature the atoms become ordered, each zinc atom being surrounded by copper atoms as nearest neighbours and vice versa. The ordered structure is stronger, but markedly less ductile, than the higher temperature random or disordered atomic arrangement. There are other significant changes in properties, such as electrical conduction, which accompany transformation from the disordered to ordered states. The intermetallic γ phase begins to appear when the zinc content exceeds 50%. This phase is brittle and alloys containing more than 50% zinc are of no commercial significance.

The variation in the room-temperature mechanical properties with composition for simple copper–zinc alloys (i.e. with no other alloy elements added) is also shown in *Figure 7.5*. Both strength and ductility increase initially with increasing zinc

content with tensile stress increasing more rapidly than proof stress. The ductility peaks at 30% zinc and falls thereafter with increasing amounts of the β phase. Proof stress and tensile stress continue to increase with zinc content in the annealed condition, but show little change in the cold-worked (hard) state. The strength is retained at sub-zero temperatures and at elevated temperatures up to about 300°C.

The workability of brass varies with composition in a similar manner. Single-phase brasses can be deformed extensively at room temperature and are readily fabricated into sheet, tube or wire. The 70/30 composition is more readily shaped by deep drawing, stretch forming and spinning than any other commercial non-ferrous metal or alloy. Cold workability is decreased severely by the presence of the brittle, ordered β phase, as evidenced by the more limited increase in strength which can be obtained by cold working the $\alpha + \beta$ (e.g. 40% zinc) alloys. However, these alloys are more readily deformed at elevated temperatures and they are used mainly as hot-rolled sheet or bar, extruded material with complex cross-section and hot-forged (or hot-stamped) artefacts such as taps, water fittings and fasteners.

Cold-worked material can be softened by a recrystallization anneal at temperatures between 500 and 600°C. Care must be exercised to avoid excessive grain growth during annealing of single-phase materials. This is particularly important with sheet material which is subsequently cold formed to shape. When a coarse-grain sheet is deformed over a radius, the individual grains remain essentially planar, with the majority of the deformation concentrated in the vicinity of the grain boundaries, resulting in the aptly named 'orange peel' appearance of the surface in reflected light. Single-phase brasses are fairly readily machined, but the machinability is markedly improved by addition of up to 4% lead. The brittle β constituent results in a marked increase in machinability of two-phase and β brasses, which is increased further by a small addition of lead. Lead dissolves in the β phase at high temperatures, avoiding the formation of molten grain boundary films which cause problems in the hot working of copper and single-phase alloys. Most of the brass compositions are also available as sand, investment, gravity and die castings.

The brasses have good resistance to atmospheric corrosion, forming a thin adherent oxide or tarnish layer in a dry atmosphere and the green patina in moist atmosphere. They are resistant to alkalis and organic acids, but in some potable waters and in seawater, brass may suffer from a form of attack known as *dezincification*. The attack is most severe in stagnant water containing high concentrations of oxygen and carbon dioxide. The surface of the alloy dissolves in the solution and copper is redeposited on the surface in a sponge-like form, whilst bulky zinc corrosion products accumulate in the liquid. Dezincification is not usually a problem with zinc contents up to about 20% but becomes progressively worse as the zinc content is increased beyond this level. Alloys containing the β phase are particularly prone to this form of attack, since the β phase is attacked preferentially. Attack can be prevented in single-phase α alloys by the addition of up to 0.1% arsenic, and arsenical brass should be specified for all aqueous applications. However, two-phase and β brasses are not protected by arsenic additions and these alloys should not be used in contact with water where dezincification may occur.

Brasses are also susceptible to another form of attack described as *stress corrosion cracking* or *season cracking* over a range of composition susceptibility similar to that for dezincification†. This is, simply, a form of corrosion attack, most

---

* The concept of a phase is quite complex, but for the purposes of understanding this text it can be taken as a thermodynamic entity. It is perhaps best defined through the Gibbs phase rule and this can be simplified by saying that a phase may exist over a range of temperature and composition but always with the same crystal structure (in the solid state this will often mean face centred cubic, etc. (see *Figure 7.2*)). Our interest in phase diagrams arises because they allow us to predict how heat treatment may be used to control microstructures and hence properties.

† One (in)famous case occurred during the seige of Mafeking. Here brass-cased shells, which had not been stress-relief annealed, were stored in some stables. The ammonia-containing atmosphere led to considerable problems.

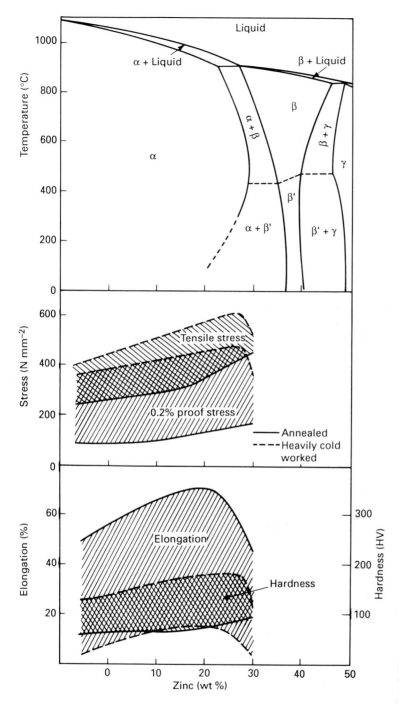

Figure 7.5 Part of the copper–zinc phase diagram and the variation in mechanical properties with composition for wrought brass

commonly along grain boundaries which emerge at the surface, due to the simultaneous application of a stress and the presence of a specific corrodant. With brass, moist ammonia is the corrodant mainly responsible and mercury and moist chlorine gas can also cause attack (but low chlorine concentrations in solution for water purification are benign). The severity of the attack increases with increase in stress and/or concentration of the corrodant, but does not occur if either stress or corrodant is removed. There is no cure, other than plating the surface to form a corrosion barrier, if the component is stressed in service.

But failure can occur, in the absence of an applied service stress, due to residual stresses in a cold-worked material. This can be avoided by a stress-relieving heat treatment after completion of the cold work. The alloy is heated to between 250 and 300°C, the temperature increasing within this range with increasing zinc content, to relax the residual stresses but without detriment to the strength increment produced by the cold deformation. It is important to ensure that the material is not strained subsequently by forced fitting, etc., during installation for service.

There are over 40 British Standard Compositions for brass.

These are given in BS 2870–2875 and 1400, referred to previously for copper specifications. Wrought brass alloys are designated by the letters CZ. The more common compositions are as follows:

7.3.2.1 α Brass alloys

Gilding metals (CZ 101, 102, 103) containing 10–20% zinc are used for architectural applications such as ornamental grills and shopfronts, condenser tubes, marine hardware, etc. The name arises from the attractive golden colour.

Cartridge brass (CZ 106) with 30% zinc is used extensively for articles formed by deep drawing and stretch forming including the production of cartridge cases, whence the name. It is used also for grillwork and building furniture such as hinges, locks and plumbing fittings.

Common or basis brass (CZ 108) at the limit of the α-phase field, with 37% zinc, is markedly less ductile and is used only for simple forming operations. Other elements may be added to enhance specific properties. Manganese and silicon increase the strength, arsenic increases corrosion resistance, whilst aluminium, nickel and tin enhance both strength and corrosion resistance. All these elements form solid solutions with brass and the zinc content must be reduced if the alloy is to remain single phase. The Guillet factors express the zinc equivalent of the addition elements. Thus, the Gillet factor for silicon is 10, which means that 1% of silicon is equivalent to the effect of 10% of zinc in relation to the solid solubility limit. Other factors are 6 for aluminium, 2 for tin, 0.8 for nickel and 0.5 for manganese.

Admiralty brass (CZ 111), containing 28% zinc, 1% tin and about 0.05% arsenic, is often specified for salt-water applications, particularly for mixtures of fresh and salt water.

Aluminium brass (CZ 110) (22% zinc, 2% aluminium and about 0.5% arsenic) has excellent resistance to clean seawater, due to the formation of a protective alumina film on the surface which provides improved resistance also to impingement by high-velocity water. The strength is markedly enhanced, both in the annealed and the cold worked condition, at the expense of the ductility. The alumina film creates problems with the casting or soldering of this alloy.

7.3.2.2 Two-phase (duplex) alloys

Muntz metal (CZ 109), named after the inventor, is the generic name for two-phase alloys containing 38–43% zinc. These alloys, usually with lead added for enhanced machinability, are very popular for the production by hot stamping of plumbers fittings, etc., the high plasticity facilitating the reproduction of fine surface detail. They are used architecturally as panel sheets and also as structural members, such as end-plates for condensers, but the presence of the β phase results in severely limited cold workability. The ratio of α to β phases depends on composition and the rate of cooling. The microstructure can be modified also by hot working as the α phase separates. These factors can cause significant variations in the mechanical properties.

Manganese brass (CZ 136) is sometimes still incorrectly called manganese bronze. The manganese is added to increase the strength, but usually other elements such as iron, aluminium and silicon are added to enhance further the strength. Tensile strengths approaching 600 N mm^{-2} can be obtained with these alloys and they are usually referred to as high-tensile brasses. The high strength is utilized in, for example, the production of window frames such as the window in the west wall of Coventry Cathedral.

Naval brass (CZ 112) contains 37% zinc with the addition of 1% tin to enhance the corrosion resistance. As the name suggests, the alloys was first developed for marine applications. It is used for tubeplates for condensers and heat exchangers and for hardware submerged in seawater.

The lower copper content of the two-phase brasses increases the plasticity immediately after solidification. These compositions are often preferred for the manufacture of die castings, since the increased plasticity reduces the risk of hot tearing in the mould.

7.3.2.3 β Alloys

The ordered β phase has very low ductility and pure β alloys are not used even for the production of cast artefacts. The melting point is lowered progressively, however, as the zinc content is increased and an alloy containing about 50% zinc is used for welding and brazing copper and α-phase alloys. Some zinc is lost by volatilization from the filler metal during joining, resulting in more ductile joints than might be expected with this composition. But the presence of the β phase in the join increases the risk of localized corrosion, relative to the single-phase materials.

Brass alloys exhibit a range of colours, from the golden yellow of the gilding metal, through the yellow colour characteristic of the dual-phase alloys, to the brownish hue of manganese bronze. Additionally, the alloys are readily electroplated for surface appearance with chromium or silver. An electroplate coating is sometimes also applied to prevent the development of localized corrosion cells between the α and β phases.

7.3.3 Tin bronze

Although tin bronze was the first alloy used by mankind, its use today is limited by the high cost of tin. When held in solid solution in copper, tin increases the strength and the preferential oxidation of the tin produces a thin surface layer of tin oxide which imparts enhanced corrosion protection. However, these improvements can be achieved more effectively and at lower cost by the addition of aluminium to copper, so the use of tin bronzes tends to be limited to specific applications such as coinage, piping for fuel systems, springs and bearings where the colour, wear resistance, low coefficient of friction and/or other specific properties justify the higher cost.

The solid solubility of tin in copper is restricted, compared with zinc. It increases with decreasing temperature from 13.5% at 798°C to a maximum of 15.8% at 585°C but then decreases to about 1% at room temperature (*Figure 7.6*). This decrease in solubility is accompanied by the precipitation of hard and brittle δ and ε intermetallic phases. Fortunately, the precipitation is very sluggish and only occurs after prolonged exposure to low temperatures. However, the temperature range over which the copper rich alloys solidify is very wide. This results in the non-attainment of equilibrium with normal commercial freezing rates and alloys containing more than about 8% tin solidify with some of the hard, brittle β phase present. The β phase is stable only over a limited temperature range and decomposes on cooling to form the even more brittle intermetallic phases.

Tin oxidizes more readily than copper and tin oxide has a higher density than the metallic alloy, so any tin oxide formed whilst the metal is molten remains entrapped within the metal after it has solidified, markedly reducing the ducility. Either zinc or phosphorus can be added to deoxidize the melt, but phosphorus is the more effective. Wrought copper–tin alloys containing about 0.03% residual phosphorus are called phosphor bronzes (British Standard designation PB 101–104). These contain a maximum of 8.5% tin to produce a single-phase (α) alloy but, with the higher tin contents in this range, it may be

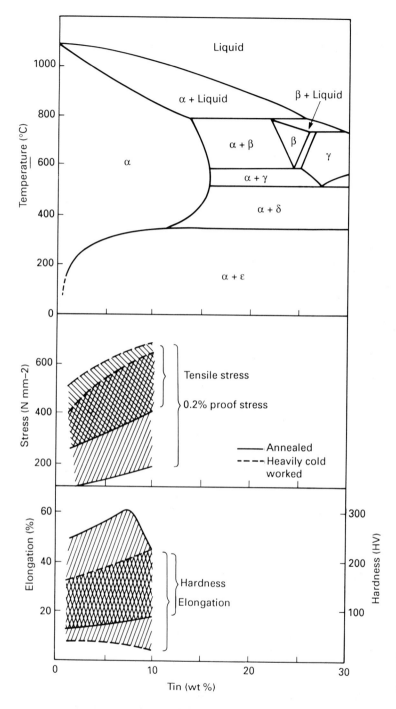

Figure 7.6 Part of the copper–tin phase diagram and the variation in mechanical properties with composition for wrought tin bronzes

necessary to anneal the as-cast alloy in order to homogenize the microstructure and remove any traces of β phase prior to cold working. The single-phase alloys are readily fabricated into sheet, bar, rod, etc., by either hot or cold working, but the usual restrictions with copper alloys on impurities such as lead, which produce low-melting-point phases, apply if the alloy is to be hot worked. Lead additions to improve machinability are only tolerated in alloys which are shaped by cold working.

Alloys containing more than 8.5% tin can be hot worked, but are not commonly used in the wrought condition because

of the brittleness of the intermetallic phases. These compositions are more commonly used in the cast form.

Gunmetal, originally used for casting bronze cannon, is the generic name for a series of alloys which contain 3–10% tin and up to 2% nickel to improve the strength and hardness. These alloys contain zinc to act both as a deoxidizer, as an alloy element to replace part of the more expensive tin and copper and to improve the casting properties. The zinc content ranges from 2 to 9% and increases as the tin content is decreased. Up to 5% lead may be added to increase machinability. These compositions are used for the production of bronze statues and also for pumps and valves. Bronze bearings are normally cast with about 20% tin and up to 2% each of nickel and zinc. The lead content ranges from 0 to 20%, depending upon the plasticity required for bedding-in the bearing. Bells are often cast in a 20% tin bronze and higher tin contents, up to 40%, have a long history of application for mirror surfaces.

Porous bronze for self-lubricating bearings is produced by the powder metallurgy route.

7.3.4 Aluminium bronze

Aluminium bronze is the most versatile of all the copper alloys, providing a wide range of properties by variation of the composition and processing. Some of the alloys have comparable strength to mild steel and corrosion resistance superior even to stainless steel in certain environments. They have an attractive golden colour and have good resistance to tarnish, due to the formation of a transparent alumina surface layer which also confers good wear resistance. On outdoor exposure the green patina, which is characteristic of copper and copper alloys, develops only slowly. In general, the alloys retain their strength well at elevated temperatures, oxidize at a low rate and have good creep and high-temperature-fatigue properties. Aluminium bronzes have much higher damping capacity than steel. One of the attributes of copper alloys is their non-sparking behaviour, which makes them suitable for use in potentially combustible and explosive environments. The high hardness attainable with aluminium bronzes facilitates their use in place of steel for applications in these conditions.

Probably the most important attribute of the aluminium bronzes is their outstanding corrosion resistance to a wide range of environments including strong, non-oxidizing acids, organic acids, chlorides and sulphur dioxide. They have very high resistance to conditions which in most other metals would give rise to pitting or crevice corrosion, but should not be used in contact with strong alkalis which can dissolve the alumina surface film. These alloys are not immune to stress corrosion cracking, but are very much less susceptible than the brasses to this type of damage.

Aluminium bronzes show very good resistance to high-velocity erosion (impingement attack) and to cavitation. The former occurs when high-velocity fluids, often containing suspended solids, impinge on the metal surface. If the protective surface film is removed in this zone, the underlying metal can corrode rapidly. But the alumina surface film is hard and firmly adherent, so it is not easily removed. If the film is damaged, the protective layer is rapidly reformed. Cavitation is more the result of mechanical damage than corrosion. In highly turbulent water, vapour bubbles may form at the metal surface where the fluid flow produces low-pressure pockets. These bubbles then collapse on the metal surface where the fluid pressure is higher, producing shock waves (hammering) which can detach the protective film and fragments of the underlying metal by the propagation of fatigue cracks. The high strength of some of the alloys and the tenacity of the surface film makes them strongly resistant to this form of damage. For the same reasons, these alloys have high resistance to corrosion fatigue.

The phase diagram for mixtures of copper and aluminium is complex, showing the formation of a number of intermetallic compounds which limit the useful compositions to relatively low aluminium contents, similar to the copper–tin alloys. Copper can hold 7.5% aluminium in solid solution when the alloys have just solidified (*Figure 7.7*). The solubility increases with decreasing temperature to 9.4% at 565°C and remains constant at lower temperatures. In contrast to copper–tin alloys, the freezing range of aluminium bronzes is very narrow and alloys containing up to 7% aluminium solidify as single (α)

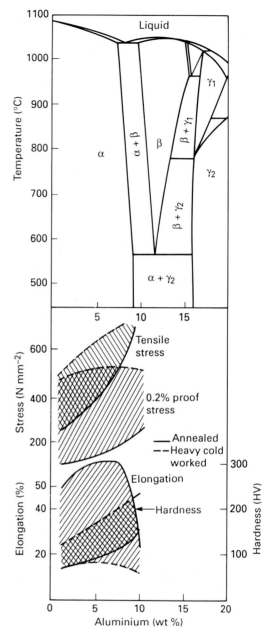

Figure 7.7 Part of the copper–aluminium phase diagram and the variation in mechanical properties with composition for wrought aluminium bronzes

phase. When the solid solubility limit is exceeded, the β phase is, again, the first intermetallic compound which forms. This phase decomposes at 565°C by a eutectoid reaction, similar to that which occurs in plain carbon and low-alloy steels, to produce a Widmanstätten* type structure of α and a second intermetallic compound, γ_2. Alloys in the range 7.5–9.5% aluminium solidify as a mixture of the α and β phases, but the

---

* Widmanstätten refers to a particular plate-like morphology of one solid phase precipitated from another; usually nucleated at the grain boundaries. The morphology arises from kinetic constraints which have to do with atomic matching across the interfacial plane and the form of diffusion field.

β phase transforms more or less completely to α on very slow cooling. In the range 9.5–11.8% aluminium the alloys solidify as β phase, from which some α separates on slow cooling, and the remaining β is transformed by the eutectoid reaction at 565°C. However, if the alloys are cooled rapidly (i.e. water quenched) from the pure β-phase condition, these changes can be suppressed and replaced by a martensitic (diffusionless) type of transformation which is again similar to the behaviour of plain carbon and low-alloy steels, although the hardness increment is less because there is no interstitial (e.g. carbon) solute to distort the lattice. As with steels, the properties can be modified by a low-temperature heat treatment (tempering) after quenching to room temperature.

Wrought alloys are designated CA in BS 2870–2874.[9]

7.3.4.1 α Alloys

The most common wrought alloy contains 6–7.5% aluminium, to which a total of 1–2.5% of iron, manganese and nickel may be added to refine the grain size, increase the strength and stabilize the α phase (CA 102 and CA 106). When cold worked, these alloys work harden very rapidly and are difficult to deform, so they are usually supplied in the hot-worked condition as plate, sheet, strip, seamless tube, bar, forgings, etc., which are given only moderate cold deformation to form the required shapes. They are not normally formed by extrusion because the abrasive oxide coating covering a relatively strong substrate results in fairly rapid wear of the extrusion dies.

7.3.4.2 Two-phase alloys

Two-phase wrought alloys contain 8–11% aluminium with 4.0–5.5% each of the iron and nickel (CA 4) or combinations of iron, nickel and manganese (CA 6). The β phase has only slightly inferior corrosion resistance to the α one but, if the alloys are slowly cooled, the decomposition of the β phase produces some γ_2 phase which has a higher aluminium content and, correspondingly, a poorer corrosion resistance than the α phase. In contact with some solutions, there is a probability of preferential loss of aluminium similar to, but on a lesser scale than, the phenomenon of dezincification of the brasses. This only occurs if the γ_2 phase is present in the microstructure. Water quenching which suppresses β decomposition results, therefore, in improved corrosion resistance. If the hard β phase is retained by quenching, the two-phase alloys exhibit better resistance to impingement attack than the α alloys. However, the nickel and iron additions in most two-phase alloys result in the formation of a κ phase and not a γ_2 one when the β phase decomposes on slow cooling. This κ phase is rich in nickel and has a higher resistance to corrosion, preventing also the preferential loss of aluminium and so obviating the need for water quenching solely to preserve the corrosion resistance.

Castings in aluminium bronze usually have a two-phase composition. The narrow freezing range and the high ductility, just after freezing is completed, facilitate the production by sand, gravity and (particularly) by die casting of strong castings free from microporosity, hot tears and similar casting defects.

Aluminium bronzes are widely used for pump casings and impellers, valves, etc., in fresh and saline water systems, particularly where high-velocity fluid flows are encountered, and for piping and condensers for high-pressure steam. Reinforcing bars and clamps for the repair of old buildings are now frequently made from aluminium bronze instead of iron, to avoid the swelling which occurs from the formation of rust. Cast and wrought forms are used for load-bearing plates and expansion joints in bridges and buildings. Architectural uses include cladding, where the golden yellow colour is sometimes selected as a cheaper alternative to gold alloy coatings.

The alumina surface coating on the aluminium bronzes creates problems in joining, similar to those encountered in joining of pure aluminium and its alloys, but compounded by the higher thermal conductivity of the copper based alloys. The most successful joining method, producing high-strength joints compatible with the strength of the alloys, is fusion welding by gas shielded arc processes, using an inert gas (usually argon or helium) to prevent oxidation of the aluminium in the molten pool of weld metal.

7.3.5 Beryllium bronze

Beryllium has a low solid solubility in copper just below the melting point and the solubility decreases very rapidly with decrease in temperature. Alloys within this solid solution range can be age hardened, similar to the Duralumin-type of aluminium–copper alloys. The most common alloy contains 1.6–1.9% beryllium, together with a total of up to 0.6% of cobalt, iron and nickel to act as grain refiners (BS designation CB 101). When quenched from 750–800°C, the alloy elements are held in solid solution and the metal is readily shaped by cold working. On ageing at 300–350°C, a copper–beryllium compound forms as a very fine precipitate. In the aged condition the ultimate tensile strength is in the range 1100–1300 N mm^{-2} and the hardness approaches 400 HV. The electrical conductivity is lowered markedly by the elements remaining in solid solution, but no other alloy matches the conductivity at this strength level. The aged alloy also has a high elastic limit and fatigue resistance, as a result of which it is used for springs, pressure gauges diaphragms and non-sparking tools.

7.3.6 Memory alloys

In the description of the aluminium bronzes, reference was made to the production of a martensite-type phase when alloys containing only the β constituent are quenched. Most of the brasses and bronzes which form a β phase can also form a martensitic-type structure when quenched to ambient or sub-zero temperatures from temperatures where the β phase is the only one present. Some of these martensites exhibit a phenomenon which is described as pseudo-elastic behaviour. In alloys which show the more usual type of martensitic transformation, the microstructure is changed if the alloys are quenched to form martensite and then heated to retransform the martensite. With pseudo-elastic behaviour, however, the martensite reverts on reheating to form a microstructure more or less identical to that which existed prior to the quench. If these alloys are deformed in the martensitic condition, the original dimensions are recovered when they are heated to restore the original β microstructure. This is the basis of an important group of materials which are marketed as memory alloys. In a typical application, the alloy is formed into a coiled spring, which is extended at a temperature below the martensite transformation temperature range. On reheating through the critical temperature, the spring reverts to its original length. Such devices can be used for fire sprinklers, thermally activated window openers, fire catches on hatch covers (as at York Minster), etc.* Ferrules which shrink on heating are used in solder-free 'do-it-yourself' plumbing repairs for joining pipes together.

In most of the simple brass and bronze alloys, the martensite does not start to form until the alloys have been cooled at least to room temperature. In β brass, for example, the martensite does not start to form until the alloy has been quenched to about −40°C. This means that the alloys have to be deformed at sub-zero temperatures and refrigerated until the heat-recovery

---

* A major application of this technology in Japan is for wiring within anatomical support wear—apparently the annual sale of brassières applying this system is currently 12 million.

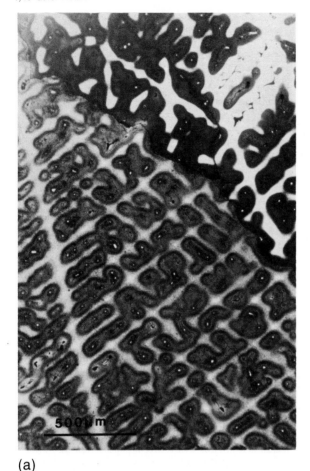

(a)

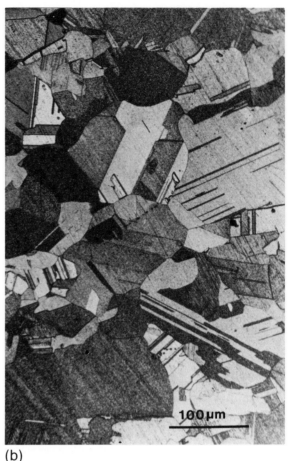

(b)

Figure 7.8 Typical photomicrographs, using a light microscope, of examples of copper based alloys. (a) As-cast 70/30 α brass: despite appearances this microstructure is single-phase α, but the solidification process leads to variations in composition in the dendritic structure which are revealed by etching. (b) Annealed 70/30 α brass: this is a recrystallized structure achieved by cold working and annealing. Copious annealing twins are revealed and are characteristic of this treatment. Here the composition is uniform (cf. (a)) and the variation in contrast from the etching process is due to orientation differences between the grains. (c) Sandcast 60/40 αβ brass: the lighter etching α phase is revealed in a background of β. The α has formed in a Widmanstätten morphology as a part of a peritectic/solid-state precipitation reaction. (d) Leaded 60/40 α/β brass formed by extrusion: this high-temperature working process elongates the lead phase (seen here in dark contrast). (e) Chill-cast microstructure of a 10% aluminium bronze. (f) Chill-cast microstructure of a phosphor bronze (10% tin, 0.5% phosphorus). (g) As-cast microstructure of a leaded gun metal (12% tin, 1.5% zinc, 0.5% lead).

strain is required. By suitable combination of alloy elements, the reversion temperature of the martensite can be increased to several hundred degrees Celsius. Typical alloys, with reversion temperatures in excess of 100°C and giving heat-recoverable strains of much greater magnitude than are obtainable from bimetallic strip, are based on β brass with additions of aluminium, silicon or tin and on β aluminium bronze with nickel and/or manganese additions. Certain alloys of nickel and aluminium also display this effect (see Section 7.6.3). In each group, the actual temperature range within which the strain is recovered is determined by the alloy composition and pretreatment.

Postscript Within this section and elsewhere in this chapter, extensive reference has been made to the microstructures achieved by combinations of alloying and thermomechanical processing. One of the standard procedures in developing an acceptable 'basket of properties' is to choose, 'engineer' and stabilize a suitable microstructure. Much of physical metallurgy/

materials technology is based around this concept. *Figure 7.8* gives some typical microstructures in copper alloys as revealed by light microscopy together with an explanation of some of the overall features. Light microscopy with a resolution of a fraction of a micrometre, remains central to such studies, but it should be appreciated that a wide range of other microscopic techniques with resolutions down to the atomic level are now employed extensively in studies of the microstructure/property inter-relationships of materials.

7.4 Gold

7.4.1 Overview

Gold is usually described as the most ductile metal, for it is fairly readily reduced to foil of only 0.1 μm thickness. It has a relatively high density which, combined with the high cost per unit weight, results in usage limited to very specialized applications. It has higher electrical resistivity, but higher thermal

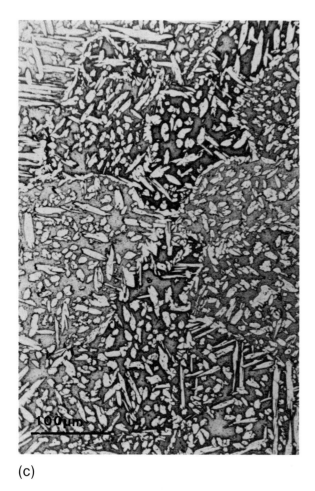

(c)

(d)

conductivity and lower hardness than silver. Its major advantage over other common metals, however, is that it does not form an oxide at room or elevated temperatures, and does not rely upon the formation of an oxide surface film for oxidation and corrosion protection. Pure gold does not even tarnish in fairly benign atmospheres.

Whereas most metals readily form sulphide, silicate, carbonate, oxide, etc., compounds during solidification and weathering of molten magma injected into the earth's crust, gold does not form compounds, other than with the relatively rare element tellurium, and is found in the metallic or 'native' form. This accounts for its use in antiquity, when gold nuggets must have been fairly readily collected from the surface of the earth and were readily fabricated without need for any pretreatment into items for jewellery and decoration. Indeed, about 5000 years ago, silver was priced at the same level as gold and, when first produced in metallic form, iron was valued more highly than gold.* The value of gold only appreciated when the readily available surface deposits had been exhausted.

Pure gold is strongly resistant to both dilute oxidizing and strong reducing acids (the standard test for distinguishing between gold and gold-coloured copper alloys is to check the reaction with a drop of dilute nitric acid) and dissolves only in aqua regia acid. It reacts only slowly with oxidizing halide salts such as ferric chloride, but more rapidly with nascent chlorine.

* At Napoleon's court, aluminium was chosen for the platters for the most important members whilst the lesser dignitaries had to make do with gold.

The addition of ammonia to gold chloride causes the precipitation of a highly explosive fulminate compound. This compound dissolves readily in alkaline cyanides, to form a gold cyanide (e.g. $KAu(CN)_2$) which proves useful both in the extraction and electroplating of gold, and in mercury to form an amalgam.

Silver and gold are almost completely miscible in the solid state. The solid solubility of gold with copper and gold with nickel is quite high at room temperature. The solubility increases rapidly with increase in temperature and the alloys become completely miscible before they begin to melt (i.e. below the solidus temperature). Gold is only sparingly soluble in the other common metals, but is usually slightly more soluble in the metal sulphides.

7.4.2 Sources and production

The 'gold rushes' of relatively recent times and the Spanish treasure fleets of the sixteenth century testify to the widespread distribution of small concentrations of gold in most areas of the world, but South Africa and the USSR are the two major present-day sources of the metal. Annual production of metallic gold averages only about 1200 tonnes. It is rare today to find an ore body containing more than about 20 g tonne^{-1} of gold. In metallic form, gold is invariably associated with up to 10% silver.

The very high density of gold facilitates separation by gravity after the finely divided gold particles have been released from

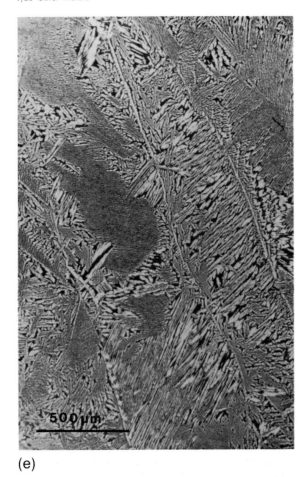

(e)

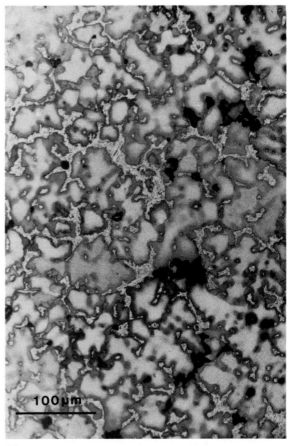

(f)

the bed rock by crushing and grinding. The historical reference to Jason's golden fleece is most probably an allusion to the ancient practice of lining the base of a sluice with sheepskin in which the gold was trapped whilst the lighter rock fragments were washed away in the water stream.* In more recent times, gold was recovered by coating copper plates with mercury to form a copper amalgam and gold particles coming into contact with the plate formed a gold amalgam. The dried amalgam was then heated in retorts to distill off the mercury for re-use, leaving a deposit of gold containing some copper.

In modern practice, the ore pulp is leached with an alkaline cyanide solution, which is filtered before treatment with a zinc–lead alloy powder to precipitate the gold from solution. The metal is melted to oxidize the residual zinc and silver is separated by bubbling chlorine through the melt to form a silver chloride slag. Other impurities are removed simultaneously as volatile chlorides. A significant proportion of the annual gold production, however, is recovered from the anode slimes during the electrolytic refining of other non-ferrous metals which contain small amounts of gold associated with their ores.

7.4.3 Gold and gold alloys

Proof gold, refined to the highest standards of purity, contains less than 0.01% impurity, but normal commercial pure gold is usually in the range 99.95–99.98%. The high lustre, oxidation and corrosion resistance of the pure metal is of little use,

* For a recent account, see Severin,[10] p. 223.

however, because the very low hardness and lack of protection by a hard oxide film results in fairly rapid wear even under conditions of very light loading. Usage tends to be limited to applications such as thin films on glass, thermal limit switches, and dental and medical applications. For general use, the metal is alloyed usually with silver, copper, zinc and sometimes nickel, to improve the durability. Instead of expressing the gold content of these alloys in percentage terms, the purity, particularly in the jewellery and decorative-wear trades, is conventionally expressed in 'carats' (1/24 parts) or 'fineness' which is the weight fraction of gold in the alloy in thousandths. Thus pure gold is 24 carat with a fineness of one thousand. Eighteen-carat gold contains 18/24 parts equal to 75% gold and has a fineness of 750.

Alloying gold with these metals can either preserve a colour very similar to pure gold or produce a range of other colours, simply by varying the ratio of the metals added. A wide range of alloy compositions is available, but the list given in *Table 7.4* is indicative of the alloy types and colours.[11] The nickel is usually present to prevent grain coarsening during annealing. Larger additions of nickel, in the range 10–17% produces a white colour, but these alloys are not readily worked and have lost favour in preference to pure palladium.

The 14- and 18-carat gold alloys in *Table 7.4* are single phase when first solidified, but may decompose into a mixture of two phases or undergo an ordering reaction on slow cooling. At low temperatures the stable forms of Au_3Cu, $AuCu$ and $AuCu_3$ are all ordered with regular arrangements of one atomic species around the other. Raising the temperature in each case leads to

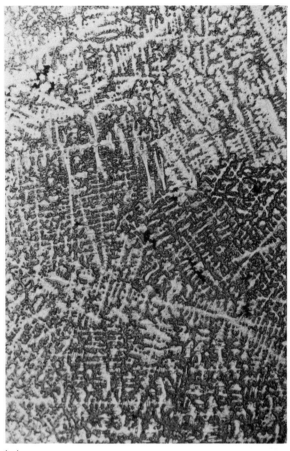

(g)

diagram when gold is added. The 9-carat gold alloys exhibit this eutectic reaction and hence their ductility cannot be improved by quenching.

As might be expected, the increased hardness and wear resistance obtained by alloying is gained at the expense of oxidation and corrosion resistance. The 18-carat alloys show good tarnish resistance and attack by acids is only marginally greater than that for pure gold if the alloy is single phase. Hardness increases with the degree of mechanical working, reaching about 220 VDH after 60% deformation. Annealing to soften the alloy is necessary if much greater deformation is required, but very rapid grain growth can occur if the alloy is annealed after only small amounts of cold work. The 14-carat alloys tarnish slowly in air if single phase, but tarnish more rapidly if phase separation is allowed to occur by ageing or slow cooling. The copper and silver content reduces the workability and zinc is added both to improve the workability and to serve as a deoxidant. These alloys may suffer from stress corrosion cracking (i.e. accelerated failure under the conjoint effects of an imposed stress in a corrosive environment) in the presence of mercury, oxidizing salts such as ferric chloride or moderately strong solutions of nitric acid. The 9-carat alloys provide the highest strength, hardness and wear resistance, but also the lowest ductility and corrosion resistance. The zinc present in the alloy reduces the susceptibility to stress corrosion cracking. The eutectic reaction also results in low solidus temperatures, which can give rise to problems in soldering and brazing.

Gold and gold alloys are readily worked or cast to produce a wide variety of shapes although, as indicated above, cold working becomes increasingly more restricted, with the need for intermediate softening (annealing) treatments, as the alloy content increases. The high malleability of pure gold is best exemplified by gold leaf, which can be produced by rolling and/or hammering to the thickness required without the application of heat. However, one of the attributes of gold, which is normally considered as highly desirable, proves to be detrimental in the production and application of gold foil. Most engineering metals and alloys form an oxide coating even at room temperature. This prevents the bonding together of two pieces of metal by the application of pressure (i.e. pressure welding) until the oxide coating is removed or disrupted. But gold does not form an oxide film and if two surfaces of the foil come in contact, for example by accidental folding, they are readily welded together by moderate pressure. 22-Carat golds are normally used for the production of leaf, the ratio of silver to copper in the alloy being used to adjust the colour. These alloys are almost as malleable as pure gold, but offer slightly better resistance to pressure welding.

When applied as a decorative finish to base-metal sculptures and decorative work, the oxide coat on the base metal prevents

a disordered structure where the atomic species are randomized in their arrangements. Subtle changes in properties accompany such order–disorder transformations which may be exploited. Hence, for optimum cold workability, it is necessary to quench the 18-carat gold from about 400°C and the 14-carat alloy from 650°C. The alloys and then readily workable, but not as easily as pure gold, and can be age hardened by heating to about 300°C to cause phase separation or ordering to occur after shaping is completed. Silver–copper alloys form a eutectic system and the eutectic reaction extends part way into the ternary phase

Table 7.4 Some gold alloy compositions and their colours[11]

| Carat | Composition (wt%) | | | | | Colour |
	Gold	Silver	Copper	Zinc	Nickel	
22	91.7	—	8.3	—	—	Reddish
	91.7	6.2	2.1	—	—	Yellow
	91.7	1.2	7.1	—	—	Deep yellow
18	75.0	9.0	16.0	—	—	Rich yellow
	75.0	20.0	5.0	—	—	Yellow
14	58.3	4.0	31.2	6.4	—	Reddish yellow
	58.3	7.5	26.6	6.6	1.0	Orange yellow
9	37.5	12.5	46.5	3.5	—	Reddish yellow
	37.5	5.5	53.5	3.5	—	Yellowish red

pressure welding of the gold leaf to the substrate. Mechanical interlocking with a rough surface on the substrate is limited, since the surface roughness is perpetuated on the outer surface of the gold leaf, so it is usual to fix the leaf with an adhesive. A practical way of reducing the risk of pressure welding of the gold leaf to itself is to sputter the gold (see below) on to a polymer film to form a gold layer of the requisite thickness. The gold is bonded to the required substrate with an adhesive and the polymer backing is removed when the adhesive has set.

7.4.4 Gold coatings

Gold and gold alloys are readily electroplated on to a wide variety of metal substrates, including copper, brass, mild steel and zinc alloys (e.g. zinc die castings; see Section 7.9.4). A nickel plating is often applied first. The gold is normally at quite low concentration in the plating solution to reduce loss by 'drag out' when the plated artefacts are removed from the bath and is usually present as cyanide ions in a cyanide solution. Various chemicals are added to increase the rate and uniformity of deposition and to form a bright deposit which does not require subsequent burnishing or buffing. The relevant British Standard for gold electroplated coatings is BS 4292.[12]

The colour of the deposit can be varied by co-deposition of alloying elements to vary the composition of the coatings, in the same way that the colour of wrought or cast gold can be varied. Other elements such as antimony may also be deposited in amounts greater than can be held in solid solution in wrought alloys (i.e. in supersaturated solid solution) to increase the hardness and wear resistance of the coating. The composition of the plating solution has to be controlled carefully to ensure that the alloy elements are deposited in solid solution in the gold and not as separate elements with consequent deterioration in corrosion resistance. Coatings can be produced over a wide range of thicknesses from 2–3 μm upwards, but the upper limit is usually about 25 μm because of the cost.

Gold (and other metal) layers can also be formed by vacuum coating techniques (often referred to as physical vapour deposition, PVD). In essence, the substrate to be plated and a source of the plating metal are placed in an evacuated chamber, the source is activated to release atoms and these are transported across the intervening space to condense on the substrate. Two techniques are commonly used.

For vacuum evaporation, the chamber is evacuated to a pressure below 10^{-5} torr (1.3 μPa) and the source is heated by resistance heating, arc discharge, laser or electron beam, etc., to a temperature at which the vapour pressure of the source material is at least 10^{-3} torr (0.13 mPa). The metal vapour released condenses on the cold metal substrates (but also on any other cold surfaces with which it comes into contact). Gold has a high boiling point and the required vapour pressure is only obtained if the gold is heated almost to its melting temperature.

Sputtering is achieved in an inert-gas atmosphere (usually argon) at higher pressures, usually in the range 10^{-1}–10^{-3} torr (13.3–0.13 mPa). A potential difference of 500–5000 V is applied between the source and the target substrate. Atoms are released from the source by ion bombardment and attracted by the potential difference to the target, thus preventing deposition on other surfaces. Under normal operating conditions, only silver can be sputtered at a more rapid rate than gold. Copper is deposited at about the same rate, but all other metals are more difficult to use for coating by this means. This technique is usually preferred to vacuum evaporation for gold coating.

As discussed in Section 7.1, very thin deposits can be formed by PVD and one common application is gold coating of glass to reduce heat transmission, where deposits not greater than about 20 nm in thickness are required to ensure that sufficient light is transmitted. A gold surface reflects almost all incident light in the infra-red and longer wavelengths of visible light. But the reflectivity diminishes rapidly with decreasing wavelength below 650 nm and becomes almost constant at a very low level below 500-nm wavelength. This accounts for the gold–yellow colour of the pure metal. Thin films of gold are optically semi-transparent to transparent and the colour of the light transmitted in the −650 nm range varies from green through yellow to red or violet, depending on the thickness of the film and its mode of formation. The amount of light transmitted can be increased by sandwiching the gold between two dielectric layers. These thin coatings are very easily damaged and it is customary to apply the coating to the inner surface of a double-glazing unit. Cheaper coatings, giving comparable light transmission and heat-barrier effects are now being produced using copper and titanium nitride in place of gold.

7.4.5 Gold in joining

Gold surfaces are readily joined to each other by pressure welding, due to the absence of an oxide film, as described above. This attribute facilitates fusion welding and also diffusion bonding under pressure at about 1000°C, where atoms exchange positions across the joining line and eliminate the interface. Gold-plated surfaces are frequently joined by soldering. Particularly for electronic applications, it is common practice to gold plate terminals, etc., in order to prevent surface oxidation, prior to soldering, which would result in weak or dry joints. Lead–tin solders containing about 65% tin are commonly used, but gold dissolves very rapidly in the molten solder to form embrittling gold–tin compounds. For this reason, the thickness of the gold coating is kept as thin as possible to ensure high dilution of gold in the solder. It follows that lead–tin solders are unsuitable for use with bulk gold articles.

Gold brazing alloys are used for joining gold surfaces and for joining other metals together where a high-melting-point braze is required. Colour match with the joined surfaces can be achieved by using gold–silver–copper alloys and varying the silver-to-copper ratio. Melting points above 800°C, narrow freezing ranges and good fluidity are obtained with 80% gold and 20% copper, with 60% gold, 20% silver and 20% copper and with 82% gold plus 18% nickel. A gold–5% iridium alloy gives lower melting temperatures and a wide freezing range.

7.5 Lead

7.5.1 Overview

Lead is the least expensive of the metals reviewed in this chapter, the cost per tonne being roughly one-third of the next most expensive metal, zinc, and about one-twentieth of the cost of tin or nickel. Pure lead metal has a face-centred-cubic structure and is therefore very ductile and easily worked. Its low melting point results in flow under low loads at room temperature (i.e. creep deformation). Lead has poor fatigue strength, but excellent damping capacity, partly as a result of its high density. It has good lubricity and a relatively high coefficient of thermal expansion.

Pure lead has good corrosion resistance to sulphuric, chromic and phosphoric acids, forming insoluble salts on the metal surface which prevent further attack. In acid solutions, it is cathodic to iron and the iron is attacked preferentially. In alkaline solutions the polarity is reversed; lead is then anodic to iron and protects the iron from attack. Lead has good corrosion resistance in hard water, where the calcium and magnesium salts form compact, insoluble carbonate films on the surface as evidenced by the lead sheeting in the Roman baths at Bath, which is still in good condition nearly 2000 years after its installation. In soft water these salts are not present so no protective film is formed and the lead slowly corrodes. The rate of corrosion then increases in proportion to the amounts of oxygen and carbon dioxide dissolved in the water. Comparison of the service life of lead water pipes in soft- and hard-water districts, or the fairly rapid penetration of lead pipes when a water softener is installed in a system which has operated satisfactorily for years on untreated water, provide confirmation of this behaviour. Lead has reasonably good resistance to seawater, rural, industrial and marine atmospheres.

Care is required, however, to ensure that potential corrosive conditions are recognized and appropriate measures are taken to prevent attack from bimetallic couples, crevice corrosion, differential aeration, etc. (see Section 7.2.2). Buried lead pipes can be attacked by a combination of incompletely cured cement and penetration of road de-icing salts. Calcium hydroxide in the cement can react with sodium chloride from the salt to release sodium hydroxide, creating an alkaline solution which attacks lead rapidly. Even timber can produce corrosive conditions, because tannic and acetic acids, which attack lead, can be released from damp wood.

The most common uses of lead are as sheet and pipe for corrosion protection and as battery grids for storage batteries. It is also an essential constituent of the alloys used to produce printing type (type metals). In alloy form, it is a constituent of the common solders and some of the soft Babbitt bearing metals. (These last two applications are dealt with in Section 7.8.) Lead has only low solubility in most metals and in the majority of applications only 1–2% of other metals are added to the lead. The low solubility of lead in other metals is used to advantage in the production of free machining alloys. Lead has a high surface tension and very low solubility in copper and steel, for example, so lead additions to these metals exist as small globules disseminated through the solid metal. During machining, the turnings break off into small segments whenever the cutting tool encounters one of these soft lead particles.

Chemical compounds of lead have been widely used as paint additives and as anti-knock additives to petrol, but their use is diminishing as the environmental consequences are more fully recognized. Lead is a health hazard. It is readily absorbed by living tissues and precautions should be taken to avoid inhalation of lead dust and fumes.

7.5.2 Sources and production

Lead is most commonly extracted from the earth as the sulphide (PbS), usually in associated with zinc sulphide (ZnS) but lead carbonate and lead sulphate are also recovered. The major suppliers are the USA, Mexico, Australia, Canada and the USSR. The sulphide ores are concentrated by crushing and flotation and then sintered to agglomerate and remove sulphur. The oxidized sinter cake is usually reduced in the lead blast furnace, in which the zinc is removed by volatilization. The molten lead is cooled to just above its melting point to separate the less soluble impurities which are skimmed off the surface. The metal is then reheated to about 750°C to oxidize-out impurities such as arsenic, antimony and tin. Many lead ores have valuable silver and gold contents and zinc is added at this stage to precipitate Au_2Zn_3 and Ag_2Zn_3 which form a crust on the top of the lead as the temperature is lowered. Any remaining zinc is removed by vacuum distillation or by blowing chlorine gas through the melt to form zinc chloride ($ZnCl_2$). Alternatively, the metal may be refined electrolytically and this treatment is often necessary to remove harmful bismuth impurities.

7.5.3 Metallic lead

Pure lead is very soft and creeps readily under very small loads at ambient temperature. Consequently, the pure metal is only used where corrosion resistance or specific properties are required. The purest form is called 'chemical lead' with a purity of at least 99.98% lead (BS 334[13]). Addition of up to 0.1% tellurium refines the grain size and increases the flow resistance. Up to 0.3% arsenic is added to increase the strength for applications such as cable sheathing and battery grid plates (BS 801[14]), although for the latter application up to 0.1% calcium and 1–3% tin are now added to reduce gassing in the sealed batteries which do not require topping up. Small additions of copper (<0.1%) improve the corrosion resistance and 0.25% cadmium together with 2–3% tin improve the fatigue strength. Hard lead contains antimony, usually in the range 4–9%. All these grades are readily deformed by rolling, extrusion, etc., at or just above ambient temperature to produce sheet and pipe. The purer grades can be rolled to lead foil (often with an outer layer of tin) as thin as 0.02 mm for use as moisture protection in the building industry.

7.5.4 Lead sheet

Lead sheet for roof and wall coverings is covered by BS 6915.[15] The sheet is very soft and can creep under its own weight at room temperature. The creep rate is very sensitive to the grain size of the metal. Whereas the strength of lead sheet increases with decreasing grain size, the resistance to creep increases as the grain size is increased (*Figure 7.9*). Strength and creep resistance are improved by addition of antimony and with 6% antimony the tensile strength is approximately doubled. *Figure 7.10* shows the relationship between the applied load and temperature to give a total elongation of 1% after a constant time under load for pure lead and various lead–antimony alloys.

Lead containing up to 7% antimony is used for roofing, where the protective corrosion films give good resistance to rural, industrial and marine environments with relatively low initial and maintenance costs and with a long service life. Thermal expansion is relatively high, however, so it is customary to limit the area of the sheets and to provide only loose interlocking in order to minimize distortion caused by ambient heating (e.g.

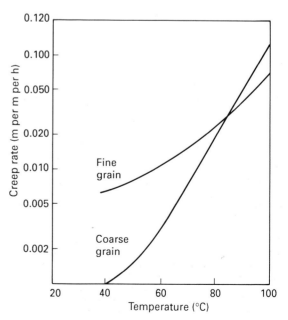

Figure 7.9 Creep rate of commercial lead under an applied load of 0.49 N mm^{-2} in relation to temperature and grain size. (Redrawn from Hoffman[16])

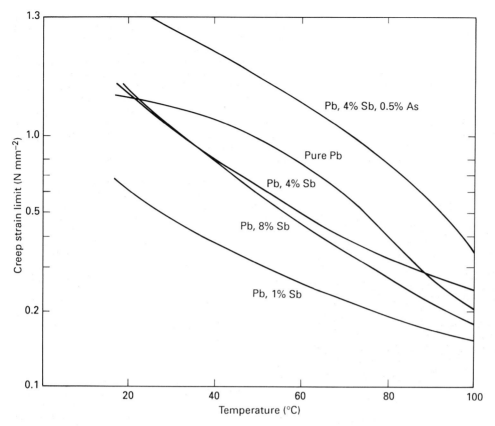

Figure 7.10 Creep strain limits for wrought pure lead and various lead–antimony alloys producing 1% elongation after 5×10^4 h (5.7 years) under load

Figure 7.11). Lead sheet is used also for flashing, but should be protected by a layer of bitumen when it is in contact with fresh concrete to minimize corrosive attack. Other applications include shower pans, sink tops and linings for bins storing containers of strong acids, where, again, the corrosion-resistance properties are an advantage.

Perhaps the major drawback to the use of lead for roofing, etc., is the weight. A 1-mm thick sheet of lead weighs approximately 12.5 kg m^{-2}, requiring stronger structural support than with lighter weight cladding materials. The high density of lead, however, is an advantage for shielding against X-rays and γ-rays. A few millimetres thickness of lead sheet provides better protection than a thick concrete wall. The high internal damping capacity, coupled with the high density and low stiffness also makes lead sheet an excellent material for use as a sound barrier.

Lead sheet is widely used to isolate moving machinery and prevent transmission of mechanical vibrations to the floor. Very noisy equipment may be entirely encased in a lead lined cubicle. Thicker lead sheet is used under foundations to insulate buildings from extraneous vibrations. One interesting development, currently being explored in Japan, is the use of lead as an earthquake damper. Instead of lead sheet, the building slab is isolated from the ground by a rubber pad which supports the entire weight of the building. Movements in the rubber pad due to terrestrial displacements are damped by columns of lead fixed between the base of the building and the earth.

A higher strength sheet can be produced by dipping a low carbon steel sheet in a bath of molten lead with a chloride flux, held at a temperature of about 350°C, to produce a coating thickness normally in the range 5–20 μm. The appropriate standard for these hot-dip coatings is BS 6582.[17] Lead does not readily wet and adhere to steel, so tin is usually added to the bath to form a lead–tin layer on the surface of the steel, to which the coating adheres more firmly. The tin content can range from 2 to 25% but, for Terne coatings (*terne* meaning dull, from the French) the tin content is usually in the range 3–15%. The lead coating serves as a lubricant in bending and forming operations and the coated sheet is readily joined by soldering or spot welding. The thickness of the lead coating can be controlled by variation of the bath temperature, time of immersion of the sheet in the bath and by rolling or vibrating the sheet as it emerges from the bath. The coated sheet can be substituted for lead sheet in any of the normal roofing and gutter applications, but it is used mainly for fire doors, lining tanks in contact with petroleum products and for housings for electrical switch gear, fuse boxes, etc., in sulphur rich environments.

7.5.5 Lead pipe

Lead is readily welded at comparatively low temperatures, so pipe has been made since the Roman era by forming lead sheet into a tube over a mandrel and welding the seams together. This method has been superseded today by seamless tube produced by extrusion. This high ductility of lead facilitates the production by this method of tube with almost unlimited variation in bore and wall thickness. The tube is readily joined with the lead–tin solders (see Section 7.8.5) and the low melting point facilitates fusion welding with a simple flame torch. Up to 6% antimony may be added to the lead to increase the

a simple 60% Bi, 40% Cd alloy melts at 144°C. Some compositions (eutectic alloys) melt and freeze at a constant temperature, whilst others melt over a temperature range.

Whereas most metals contract during solidification and cooling to room temperature, bismuth shows an expansion. Depending on composition, therefore, these alloys can show a net contraction, zero volume change, or a net expansion on cooling. Iridium and tin confer 'wettability' on other metals. These alloys are widely used for fire alarms and automatic fire sprinkler systems, safety plugs in boilers, electrical fuses, etc. The wide range of alloys available allows selection of melting points over fairly small temperature intervals up to 250°C. The alloys are used also to prevent collapse and distortion of soft-metal tubes during bending. The molten alloy is poured into the tube to fill completely the cross-section where the bend is required and the bismuth compensates for thermal contraction. After bending, the alloy is melted out and can be re-used. The alloys do not oxidize readily or volatilize at temperatures up to about 100°C above their melting points, so there is no problem from drossing or major change in composition (and, therefore, in melting point) after repeated use. The first two compositions in *Table 7.5* are particularly useful for cold bending, since they melt readily in hot water and a hot-water flush through the tube after remelting serves to remove any remaining traces of the fusible alloy, thereby minimizing the risk of creating corrosion cells. Other uses include radiation shielding, fusible cores for injection moulding and for encapsulation of engineering artefacts to facilitate machining.

7.5.7 Other uses of lead

The low melting point, high ductility, high corrosion resistance and durability of lead are attributes which have led to a wide range of applications of the metal, from lead shot for shotgun ammunition to leaded windows. Engineering artefacts such as bolts, nuts, washers, plates and brackets may be lead coated for enhanced corrosion resistance. The lead may be applied by hot dipping or by spraying. Where clearances are restrictive, as on the threads of high-strength nuts and bolts, the coating may be electrodeposited. Electrodeposits on steel may be pure lead or lead–tin alloys.

Lead has a good resistance to seawater, forming a compact adherent corrosion film which makes the alloy ideal for the cathodic protection of steel structures in seawater. Lead blocks, or alloys of lead with silver, tin or antimony, are connected by a conductor to the steel and an impressed DC current is applied to reverse the normal corrosion polarity so that the lead behaves anodically to the steel.

Type metal, used in printing, is lead containing small amounts of antimony to harden the metal and increase wear resistance and tin additions to increase fluidity and reduce brittleness. Reusable type (i.e. not remelted each time) may contain up to

Figure 7.11 Lead sheet cladding on the Department of Materials Science and Metallurgy, Cambridge University (*c.* 1970, Ove Arup and Partners). Some creeping of the sheet is apparent. (Courtesy D. Barber and D. Starnell)

strength and improve the creep resistance, but supports are still required to prevent sagging and expansion loops are necessary if the pipes are exposed to widely fluctuating temperatures. Large-diameter pipes are sometimes fabricated from lead lined steel or cast iron pipes to minimize these problems.

A lead sheathing is frequently extruded around electricity and telecommunication cables, which are to be installed underground, by essentially the same technique used to produce copper pipe. A polythene or neoprene outer coating is sometimes applied for additional protection against severe corrosive conditions.

Care should be taken during installation of pipe and lead covered cable to insulate the lead from other metals which are either electropositive or electronegative to lead when the assembly is immersed in water or water is conveyed through the pipe. Galvanic corrosion is more serious with soft water and with oxygen starvation. Lead and brass are not too widely separated in the electrochemical series, but a galvanic couple with copper or brass results eventually in perforation of the lead, whereas iron is perforated if coupled to the lead. In addition, care should be taken to protect the lead from uncured concrete.

7.5.6 Fusible alloys

Mixtures of lead and bismuth form a series of low-melting-point (eutectic type) alloys and the melting point can be depressed further by addition of other elements with low melting points. These alloys are usually called *fusible alloys*; typical compositions and melting points are given in *Table 7.5*. Many other compositions are produced. Not all contain lead. For example,

Table 7.5 Typical compositions and melting points lead–bismuth (fusible) alloys

Melting point (°C)	*Composition* (wt%)					
	Pb	*Bi*	*Sn*	*Cd*	*In*	*Sb*
46.8	22.6	44.7	8.3	5.3	19.1	—
70	27.3	49.5	13.1	10.1	—	—
				(Quaternary eutectic)		
96	32	52.5	15.5	—	—	—
				(Ternary eutectic)		
113	25	50	25	—	—	—
247	87	—	—	—	—	13

20% of each of these elements. Reference was made earlier to applications of lead in batteries and bearings.

The use of lead in the form of chemical compounds is diminishing rapidly since the public has become more health-conscious. There is still limited use of red lead (Pb_3O_4), but the use of carbonate, phosphite and silicate as paint pigments has virtually ceased and lead-free petrol is reducing the demand for tetraethyl and tetramethyl lead anti-knock additives.

7.6 Nickel

7.6.1 Characteristics

Nickel is a hard, tough, malleable metal which exhibits relatively high thermal and electrical conductivities. Its mechanical properties are similar to those for low carbon steel and it is ferromagnetic. The pure metal has a silvery white appearance. The very large values of magnetostriction find outlets in applications such as non-destructive testing, ultrasonic cleaning and echo sounding.

Under favourable conditions, a strongly adherent passivating coating is formed over the surface and nickel then shows corrosion resistance similar to austenitic stainless steels and only slightly inferior to silver. In the passive condition, it does not readily discharge hydrogen from non-oxidizing acids and provides good corrosion resistance against hydrochloric, sulphuric, phosphoric and organic acids. It has good resistance also to caustic alkalis, salt solutions and ammonia. Under conditions where the passive film is removed, however, as in contact with strong solutions of oxidizing acids, its corrosion resistance is inferior to α brass. Copper and molybdenum additions enhance the resistance to impingement and pitting attack. Nickel and nickel alloys are not generally susceptible to stress-corrosion attack, but they are unsuitable for use in sulphur bearing atmospheres.

The metal is expensive (the cost is similar to tin) and this limits the applications of the metal and its alloys to applications where the corrosion resistance and/or elevated temperature mechanical properties cannot be equalled by less-expensive materials; these include components for pumps, valves, autoclaves, etc., in the chemical, food and pharmaceutical industries.

The major use of nickel is as an alloying element to confer enhanced corrosion resistance, strength and toughness on other engineering materials such as steels, cast iron, copper and aluminium. The next most important use is for corrosion and wear-resistance coatings on other materials. Only a relatively small proportion is processed into nickel rich alloys, but key technologies, such as aerospace, depend on these materials.

7.6.2 Sources and production

Although nickel deposits are found in many parts of the world, there are few large workable deposits and this accounts partly for the high cost. Until comparatively recent times, the only major source was the Sudbury mine in the Canadian province of Ontario, but other sources in the Far East are now of comparable importance.

Pentlandite, a nickel–iron sulphide, is the major ore which is mined. It is usually associated with copper sulphide. The ore, containing 1–3% nickel, is crushed, concentrated by flotation, roasted and then smelted to form a nickel–iron–copper sulphide matte. The iron is oxidized out and the matte is cooled slowly, allowing separation of the nickel and copper sulphides which are then separated mechanically. Pure nickel is normally produced by electrolytic refining, but in oxide form it can be refined also by the formation and dissociation of nickel carbonyl ($Ni(CO)_4$). Less-pure ores are sometimes treated by ammonia leaching to produce a solution which, after concentration, can be passed direct to the electrolytic cell.

When remelted for alloying, nickel readily absorbs carbon, oxygen and sulphur. Carbon is usually limited in specifications to a maximum of 0.05% to avoid the risk of graphitization when the metal is exposed to temperatures above about 300°C, resulting in loss of ductility. Magnesium, titanium and/or magnanese are normally added to deoxidize the melt and increase the ductility. Sulphur, which forms intercrystalline films in the metal, should be held to very low levels.

7.6.3 Nickel and nickel alloys

The relevant British Standards for wrought nickel are BS 3072[18] (sheet and plate), BS 3073[19] (strip), BS 3074[20] (seamless tube) and BS 3076[21] (bar). Pure nickel is rarely used in wrought form, because of the high cost of the metal, but there are a number of important nickel rich alloys, which are usually referred to by proprietary names. These fall into two groups: those designed to give good resistance to oxidation and corrosion up to moderately elevated temperatures; and the nickel base super-alloys, e.g. 'Nimonic'-type alloys for high-temperature applications in gas turbine engines, etc.

Pure nickel is produced in two grades. Grade 201 has a lower carbon content than Grade 200 and is less susceptible to graphitization. Both grades possess reasonable strength, ductility and hardness and have very good resistance to alkaline solutions up to about 250°C.

Nickel and copper form a very useful range of alloys. In the copper rich, cupro–nickel alloys, the nickel confers moderate strengthening with negligible loss of ductility (*Figure 7.12*) and with reduced risk of stress-corrosion cracking. Corrosion resistance to seawater is enhanced and the strength is retained at moderately elevated temperatures.

Monel is perhaps the best known of the family of nickel–copper alloys. The two most popular grades are Monel 400 and Monel K 500. Monel 400 contains approximately 67% nickel and 31% copper with about 1% residual iron and 0.15% carbon. The latter alloy contains up to 3% aluminium, substituted for part of the copper, and 0.6% titanium. Nickel and copper are completely miscible in the solid state and the 400 alloy is a simple solid solution, so there is no risk of galvanic attack between phases. The nickel content is sufficiently high to suppress the risk of stress-corrosion cracking, particularly in contact with chlorides, and this is the alloy commonly used for the manufacture of chloride cylinders and valves. Titanium and aluminium can form precipitates with nickel and the addition of these elements to Monel K 500 confers the ability to increase the hardness and strength by age hardening. Typical mechanical properties of nickel alloys are given in *Table 7.6*.

Nickel alloys exhibit high toughness and ductility over a wide temperature range, from sub-zero up to about 400°C and the mechanical properties of the age-hardening alloy are comparable with some low-alloy steels. Otner Monels contain up to 4% silicon to confer increased strength by precipitation of the compound Ni_2Si, but brittle silicides form at higher silicon contents.

'Monel' alloys show negligible corrosion in contact with potable and distilled water and provide better resistance to sulphuric and hydrofluoric acids than either copper or nickel. Hence they find use in stills and distillation columns and for gate valves on reservoirs. They are used widely in the chemical and petrochemical industries. Monel alloys also show good resistance to salt water and are widely used for marine fittings, including seawater valves, pumps and shafts. They are rather less suitable for applications in stagnant seawater, where biofouling by marine organisms may promote corrosion by the formation of differential aeration areas. Like all single-phase alloys, Monel alloys are difficult to machine and the machinability is improved in the cold-worked condition.

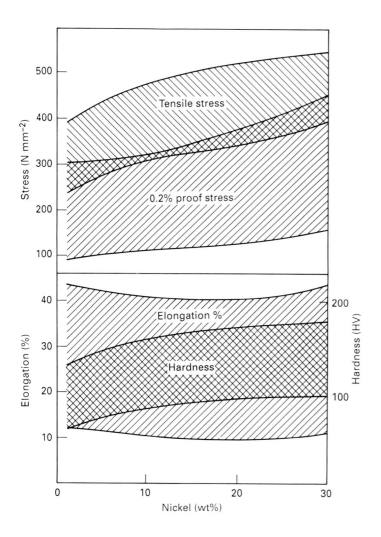

Figure 7.12 Typical mechanical properties for wrought cupro–nickel alloys: (——) annealed condition; (– – –) heavily cold-worked condition

Table 7.6 Typical mechanical properties of nickel alloys

	0.2% Proof stress (N mm^{-2})	UTS (N mm^{-2})	Elongation (%)	Hardness (VDN)
Monel 400 annealed	250	520	45	140
Monel K 500 annealed	500	650	35	270
Annealed and aged	700	1000	20	300

Inconel alloys contain chromium and iron, the concentrations of these elements ranging, for example, from 16% chromium, 7% iron in Inconel 600 to 21% chromium, 46% iron in Inconel 800. These alloys also show good resistance to industrial and marine atmospheres and they are resistant to stress-corrosion

cracking. The 800 alloy is often used in preference to austenitic stainless steel in chloride environments for this reason. The higher chromium content alloys also provide reasonable corrosion resistance with oxidizing acids. They are used mainly for elevated-temperature applications, where their high strength, oxidation and corrosion resistance are most beneficial. The 600 alloy is used for applications as diverse as sheathing for electric-cooker elements, sheathing of steam-heated drier rolls, steam tubes in pressurized water reactors, in papermaking and in processing vessels for food manufacture and monomer and polymer production. Inconel has good resistance to hot caustic alkalis. The 800 alloy is used extensively for furnace equipment and for reformers in the petrochemical industry.

Alloys of these elements are also used extensively for electrical-resistance heating. *Nichrome*, containing 80% nickel and 20% chromium is widely used for resistance elements for household appliances and for industrial furnaces up to 1150°C, particularly where the element is subjected to frequent heating and cooling. The nickel oxide is firmly adherent and resists spalling due to thermal stresses, but small amounts of other metals are sometimes included to enhance the spalling resistance. The alloy is particularly useful under reducing conditions and in sulphur bearing atmospheres. Less-expensive compositions, for example, 60% nickel, 16% chromium, 24% iron, are used for lower temperature and less-corrosive applications such as hot-water heaters and heating elements for electric irons and toasters.

Nickel based super alloys such as the *Nimonic* alloys are a complex variant of nickel–chromium alloys which are used primarily for high-temperature applications such as the blades, etc., in the combustion zones of gas turbine engines. The chromium content is usually in the range 14–20% with two or more other elements at concentrations of up to 22% cobalt, 10% molybdenum, 20% iron, 3% titanium and 6% aluminium. Nickel–titanium–aluminium precipitates are responsible for the high strength and creep resistance of these alloys, using similar principles to the age-hardening Monel alloys.

Nickel–iron alloys provide useful combinations of magnetic and thermal expansion properties. When nickel is added to iron, the coefficient of thermal expansion decreases slowly and then more rapidly as the nickel content increases, reaching a minimum value at approximately 36% nickel. The coefficient increases rapidly again with further addition of nickel. The minimum value is displaced to lower nickel contents by the addition of carbon or cobalt and to higher nickel contents by chromium and manganese. The 36% nickel alloy, known as *Invar*, has a mean coefficient of linear expansion of 1.54 $\mu m\ mK^{-1}$ over the temperature range 20–210°C, approximately one-eighth of the expansion coefficient for low carbon steel. The coefficient is higher both at sub-zero temperatures and above 210°C. An even lower value of the coefficient is obtained by replacing part of the nickel with 4–5% cobalt.

Invar rods and tapes are used as standards for surveying work, for compensating pendulums and hairsprings, and as one of the two materials comprising bimetallic strip. Invar has a very low elastic modulus and a positive temperature coefficient of this modulus, the opposite sign to that shown by most metals. Deformation at room temperature causes a further lowering of the coefficient of thermal expansion, but the value increases again, very slowly, after the deformation is completed. A stable value is obtained by heating to about 100°C, holding at temperature for a few hours and cooling extremely slowly back to ambient temperature. The alloy is ferromagnetic at room temperature, but the magnetic properties are lost progressively with increase in temperature above about 150°C.

Small variations in the nickel content above or below 36% are used to produce alloys with expansion coefficients to match those of other materials; for example, to match the expansion of glass for glass-to-metal seals.

The magnetic permeability of nickel–iron alloys decreases also with increasing nickel content, reaching a minimum with about 30% nickel and then increases again with further increase in nickel content. Between approximately 28 and 30% nickel, depending on the minor concentrations of other elements present, the alloys are non-magnetic at room temperature, whereas *Permalloy* which contains 78% nickel has a high initial permeability and a very low magnetostriction (i.e. small dimensional change on magnetization). These high nickel content alloys are used as 'soft' magnets where a narrow magnetic hysteresis loop is required with low field strengths.

Nickel–titanium alloys containing 50% titanium exhibit the shape-memory effect whereby an alloy strip or wire which has been formed into a shape above a certain critical temperature which is then deformed below that temperature, reverts spontaneously to the original shape when heated above the critical temperature (see Section 7.3.6). In contrast with the copper based alloys which show this effect, the nickel–titanium alloys do not suffer from stress corrosion. The alloys do not age harden and can be thermally cycled through the martensitic transformation without any significant loss of properties. By variation of the composition, the alloys can be made to actuate over a range of temperature from about −10 to +100°C. They are most frequently used in the form of a coil spring, which reverts to its original dimensions when the control temperature is reached. Typical applications include automatic opening hatches in the event of fire, to give access to the roof of York Minster, compression fittings on hydraulic pipes and a coffee percolator in which the water is only allowed to contact the coffee when the water temperature reaches 70°C and activates the alloy.

Nickel silver is actually a copper-rich alloy, usually containing a higher concentration of zinc than of nickel, so it is really a nickel bearing brass. The alloys are single phase and nominally contain 65% copper. Nickel contents range from 10 to 18% and zinc from 15 to 25%. In general, the zinc content decreases as the nickel content increases. Nickel–silver alloys provide higher resistance to atmospheric corrosion than copper and other copper alloys. These alloys are frequently used as a substrate which is finished by electroplating to give a decorative finish (hence the EPNS range of tableware, etc.). They provide moderately high wear resistance and thus find application also, for example, as contact springs in telecommunications.

The proprietary alloys are usually available in wrought form as plate, sheet, strip, bar, rod, wire, etc. Pure nickel and many of the alloys are produced also as castings with compositions similar to the wrought form. In some cases, higher concentrations of the alloy elements are added, producing compositions which cannot be worked mechanically, to enhance the corrosion resistance and/or the mechanical properties, particularly at elevated temperatures.

7.6.4 Nickel coatings

Nickel coating has been traditionally applied to steel, copper, brass, plastics and other surfaces to enhance the wear and corrosion resistance. It is rarely applied as a finishing layer for decorative purposes, because pure nickel tarnishes in air, gradually developing a yellowish hue. The precious metals do, of course, provide an attractive electroplated finish, but a less-expensive chromium electroplate is frequently selected when a highly reflective finish is required. Chromium coatings give good wear resistance and the transparent surface layer of chromium oxide (Cr_2O_3) provides oxidation and corrosion protection, whilst preserving the bright appearance. Despite marked improvements in the production of chromium plate, however, it is very difficult to produce layers completely free of cracks and porosity. Any such defects which penetrate through the coating allow access of corrosive substances to the substrate material. Corrosion can then occur locally within the substrate or at the interface with the chromium coating, leading to surface stains and ultimately to detachment of areas of coating. Nickel coatings do not suffer so severely from porosity and cracking, so a layer of nickel is conventionally applied to the surface, prior to the deposition of the chromium layer. Hard nickel deposits may also be electroplated to build up the surface of worn components. Electroplated nickel coatings are covered by BS 4758.[22]

Electroplating suffers from the inherent disadvantage that the coating thickness is not uniform, the thickness at any point on the surface of the plated article depending partially on the distance between that point and the anode surface. Expensive jigging in the plating bath and subsequent machining is required to obtain adequate coverage of complete surfaces with precise dimensional control. It is virtually impossible to obtain uniform coating of blind holes. Deposition rates are also relatively low. These problems apply to the plating of any metal, including nickel.

During the last decade, a new process, called 'electroless nickel coating', has been developed commercially, which can be used to deposit nickel coatings of uniform thickness at a much more rapid rate than with electroplating. In electroplating, nickel ions in solution combine with electrons provided by the external electricity supply at the cathode surface to deposit nickel atoms on the surface. The electrons are supplied by a strong reducing agent in electroless nickel plating. The surface of the substrate serves initially as a catalyst for the combination of the electrons with the positive ions and the deposited atoms then act as the catalyst, giving an autocatalytic reaction. When plating on to polymers and other non-conducting surfaces in this way, it is necessary first to activate the surface by adsorption of a reducing agent and precoating with a conductor such as palladium. The reducing agent is usually sodium hypophosphate, which is a more expensive source of electrons than mains electricity. Using this reducing agent, the coating deposited comprises both nickel and phosphorus atoms, the phosphorus content increasing with increasing acidity and decreasing activity of the nickel ions (controlled by complexing agents) in the plating solution. The usual range is from 7 to 12% phosphorus; the coatings tend to be porous at lower phosphorus contents and too brittle at higher concentrations. Coating thicknesses in excess of 100 μm are readily produced.

As-deposited electroless nickel coatings are amorphous if the phosphorus content exceeds 7%. They are tough and provide good corrosion resistance. The microhardness is about 600 VDH, compared with 300 VDH for electroplated nickel and about 120 VDH for bulk nickel. If the coating is heat treated, however, the hardness increases with increasing temperature, reaching a peak of 1100 VDH after 1 h at 400°C, accompanied by a fall in strength and ductility. This hardness is comparable with the hardness of chromium plating. Whereas the hardness of the latter decreases rapidly when the temperature is raised above about 200°C, the nickel coating only begins to soften above 400°C. The increase in hardness at 400°C is due to crystallization of the coating and deposition of hard particles of nickel phosphide (Ni_3P) in a eutectic structure with almost pure nickel. The softening at higher temperatures results from progressive coarsening of the phosphide particles.

Electroless nickel gives good wear-resistant surfaces under favourable conditions, but it must be stressed that wear resistance is not solely a function of the hardness of the surface. For example,[23] the as-deposited coating suffers from severe wear when sliding against a plain carbon steel surface; the low interfacial energy and the high surface free energies result in adhesion at the interface (i.e. a form of pressure welding) resulting in detachment of fragments of the nickel deposit. Heat treatment to precipitate nickel phosphide prevents adherence and the wear resistance is markedly improved. Improved wear resistance is obtained if the mating surface is chromium plated or if both surfaces are coated with electroless nickel. Where gouging occurs, however, the wear resistance is better in the non-heat-treated condition.

Composite coatings can be produced by either electroplating or by the electroless process. Hard particles such as silicon carbide or diamond can be co-deposited to increase the wear resistance, or soft lubricant particles of PTFE or graphite can be incorporated to lower the coefficient of friction and reduce the risk of galling.

7.7 Silver

7.7.1 Overview

Silver has the highest reflectivity of all metals, reflecting about 95% of all but ultraviolet light in the visible spectrum. Although it has lower resistance to oxygen than gold, it does not normally oxidize at ambient temperatures. Probably because of these properties, it was one of the first metals used by man. There is evidence that it was being smelted at least 6000 years ago and silver objects about 4000 years old can be seen in museums. This metal was obviously valued, because the first silver coins were minted in the sixth century B.C., although it was being used as a basis for trade at a much earlier date. In the eighth century A.D., British 'sterling' silver coins were produced, with 240 sterlings equal to one pound weight (the penny unit of our pre-decimal currency). Hallmarking of silver goods by an official assayer, to certify the purity of the metal, was introduced in 1238 A.D.

Today, silver is little used for coinage, limited mainly to special commemorative issues. The major use is as light-sensitive chloride and bromide compounds in photographic emulsions. Silver has the highest electrical conductivity of all metals and a high thermal conductivity; hence its second largest market is in electronics applications. It is only a little less malleable and ductile than gold and the pure metal will recrystallize at a little above room temperature after severe cold deformation, properties which have facilitated its use for solid silver jewellery and tableware. Less pure silver must be heated to above 300°C to soften it. It is also readily electroplated on a wide variety of metal substrates. The pure metal has a high resistance to attack by foods, organic acids and halogens. It has high resistance to wet chlorine gas and hence finds use in water-purification systems. But silver dissolves in alkaline cyanides, nitric acid, hot hydrochloric acids and reducing acids if oxidizing agents are present. It is not resistant to sulphur or compounds of sulphur. The surface discolouration or tarnish which forms so readily on silver decorative wear is not an oxide but silver sulphide, formed by reaction of the metal with traces of sulphur dioxide in the atmosphere. This tarnishing can be prevented by plating it with a very thin layer of rhodium. Silver is attacked also by low-melting-point metals such as bismuth, indium, lead, tin, mercury, sodium and potassium.

7.7.2 Sources and production

Silver occurs naturally mainly as sulphide minerals and occasionally as chloride or oxide compounds. The major supplies come from North and South America, with Australia third in importance. Few, if any, small remaining deposits are worth mining for silver alone, but most silver is recovered during the extraction of other metals. Roughly half of the annual production is recovered from copper ores and about one-quarter from ores mined for lead and zinc. Most of the remainder comes from silver recycled from photographic emulsions and residues and from remelted silver artefacts. A few deposits contain up to 100 g of silver per tonne of ore, but 1–20 g tonne^{-1} is more typical. The silver chloride crust obtained from the refining of lead and zinc is heated in a retort to distil off the remaining zinc and then heated in an oxidizing atmosphere to remove the lead, leaving a mass of molten silver. Ores containing silver and gold are treated as for gold extraction, with the silver and gold dissolved in a cyanide solution and precipitated out by the addition of zinc dust. The silver–gold mixtures remaining are melted and cast into anodes for electrorefining, during which the silver is plated out on to the cathode, retaining the gold at the anode.

7.7.3 Silver and silver alloys

Pure silver is soft and ductile, which limits its usefulness. More commonly it is alloyed with small amounts of copper to increase the strength and hardness. *Sterling silver* contains not less than 92.5% silver with copper as the principal alloy element. Silver and copper form a eutectic system, with the eutectic point at

28.5% copper being 779°C. The solubility of copper in silver is a maximum of 8.8% at the eutectic temperature, but decreases rapidly as the temperature is lowered, so most of the copper is precipitated out during slow cooling. Since copper has good corrosion resistance, this does not detract significantly from the service life at low temperatures, but the copper may oxidize selectively if the alloys are exposed to high temperatures before the copper reverts back to the solid solution.

Pure silver and sterling silver are used in the food, chemical and pharmaceutical industries for heating coils, stills and condensers where absence of metallic contamination is critical, for electrical contacts, for catalysts and in silver treated carbon filters for water purification.

Molten silver has a low surface tension and readily wets most clean, solid metal surfaces, hence its wide use for brazing. The silver–copper eutectic composition (28.1% copper) is generally used, but small amounts of tin, zinc and/or cadmium are sometimes added for lower temperature applications. These brazes form strong seals and are often selected for use where thermal cycling, for example in refrigeration units or water-sprinkler systems, impose severe strains on the metal joints.

For somewhat lower temperature applications, silver solders containing up to 50% copper and 30% zinc are used. Again, small amounts of tin or cadmium may be added to lower the working temperature range. Solders with moderate to high silver contents can produce strong joints with good elevated temperature stress resistance. Tin–silver solder, containing about 3.5% silver, is used for plumbing joints in potable-water systems where tin–lead solders are prohibited.

Silver is readily electroplated, usually from cyanide solutions. Relevant British Standards for electroplated coatings are BS 2816[24] and BS 3382.[25] For decorative and tableware, silver is commonly applied to a 'nickel–silver' alloy of copper and nickel (see Section 7.6.3), but it can be applied also to other metal substrates, often over an underlay of nickel. For decorative finishes, the coating thickness is usually in the range 10–40 μm, the life-expectancy increasing with increasing thickness. Thicker layers, up to about 1 mm, are plated on to steel shells for bearings subjected to high speeds, fatigue and corrosive conditions and on to electrical contacts. Thin films can be prepared by vacuum deposition and by sputtering in a similar way to the production of gold films (Section 7.4.4).

Silver finds limited use also in compound form. Silver oxide is used in silver batteries which have markedly higher electrical storage capacity than lead–acid batteries. The oxide is use in dry cells for hearing aids, etc. Silver halide has photochromic properties; when coated on glass it darkens progressively in bright light and reverts when the light source is obscured.

7.8 Tin

7.8.1 Summary of applications

Tin is usually described as a soft metal. The pure metal is white with a bluish tinge and has a high lustre, but if it is heated in air above about 170°C a thin layer of a hard, yellow oxide forms on the surface. This oxide is non-porous and adheres firmly to the metal, preventing further oxidation.

The major application of tin (40–45% of total consumption) is in the production of tin plate for food and beverage containers, lining surfaces in contact with high-purity water in distillation plants, etc. The pure metal is also used as a molten bath over which molten glass is floated in the manufacture of sheet glass. In metallic form, the other major applications involve the manufacture of alloys. About 25% of total consumption is as low-melting-point solders and a further 10% is used in the production of white-metal bearings. As noted previously, tin is also the major alloy addition in the tin bronzes and is a minor

addition in some other alloys. Tin is also widely used in the form of chemical compounds. Tributyltin compounds are used as wood preservatives. Other uses are as antifouling treatments for marine applications (although mollusc poisoning has limited use in esturine waters) and as pesticides. Tin compounds such as zinc hydroxystannate are being developed as fire retardants for plastics with the additional benefit of reducing the emissions of toxic gases during combustion. Stannous oxide (SnO_2) is widely used as a very thin, optically invisible film on glass to impart scratch resistance. Thin films can also produce attractive, decorative irridescent effects, whilst thicker films can make the glass electrically conductive.

7.8.2 Sources and production

The most common naturally occurring form of tin is as the oxide mineral, cassiterite. This is usually found as small particles disseminated in hard-rock formations, similar to those which have been exploited at various times in Cornwall. Weathering and erosion of exposed outcrops of rock have resulted in natural concentrations (alluvial or placer deposits) of tin in river beds. Such deposits were worked, certainly as early as the Iron Age in Cornwall, and still constitute one of the major sources of the ore in the Far East (i.e. Malaysia, Indonesia, Burma and Thailand). Placer deposits with tin contents as low as 0.01 wt% are currently being processed. Underground mining in countries such as Bolivia, Nigeria, the USSR, China and Australia, involves the additional cost of extracting the ore from the earth and crushing to suitable size. Consequently, the cut-off grade for mining usually contains at least 0.8 wt% tin.

Whatever the source, the ore is crushed to release the cassiterite and treated to produce a concentrate containing at least 70% tin oxide. The concentrate is smelted in a reverberatory furnace and then remelted and refined by blowing air or steam through the bath followed by filtration to remove solid oxides. Alternatively, it is electrolytically refined. Vacuum distillation may be used to remove volatile impurities such as lead, bismuth and antimony.

7.8.3 Pure tin

The commonest grade of pure tin, known variously as 'commercial tin grade A', 'straights tin' or 'electrolytic tin', contains at least 99.8% tin and conforms to BS 3252.[26]

Above 13.2°C, the stable form of tin is the body-centred-tetragonal β structure. Body-centred-cubic metals exhibit extensive temperature dependence of their fracture toughness, being brittle at low temperatures and ductile at higher temperatures. This behaviour is attributed to the temperature dependence of the slip systems in these materials. At low temperatures some part of the deformation may be taken up by deformation twinning. The twinning is accompanied by an audible clicking sound, giving rise to the phenomenon known as 'tin cry' when a bar or rod of pure tin is bent. This does not affect the ductility of the metal. Since tin and its dilute alloys readily recrystallize during deformation at room temperature, they can be rolled into thin foil without the need for intermediate softening (annealing) treatments. Indeed, an alloy containing about 8% zinc was at one time widely used as tin foil, but due to cost, it has now been replaced by aluminium.

In the chemical sense, the β form of tin exhibits only weak metallic properties. The diamond-cubic α form, which is stable below 13.2°C exhibits distinctly non-metallic properties. The density of the α form is only 5.75 g cm^{-3}, whereas the β phase has a density of 7.30 g cm^{-3}. Consequently, the β to α transformation is accompanied by a large volume expansion and the solid metal is converted into a coarse powder (tin paste). Fortunately, the transformation is very sluggish and rarely occurs above about $-50°C$, but it is more readily nucleated at higher temperatures if particles of α tin come into contact with the β tin. Small amounts of impurities, notably lead, bismuth and arsenic, further stabilize the high temperature form. The classic example of the resistance to transformation is the tin coated cans lost by the Perry expedition to the Arctic. These tins were buried in the ice in 1824 and were found to be still in good condition when they were recovered and examined in 1938. Tin shows good corrosion resistance in normal and marine atmospheres and in neutral or weakly alkaline solutions, but is rapidly attacked by strong acids, strong alkalis and halide gases.

7.8.4 Tin coatings

As noted above, the major use of tin is as tin plate, which is a very thin layer of tin applied electrolytically to the surfaces of unalloyed, low carbon steel sheet and strip. In the electrochemical series, tin is more noble than iron, so when the two metals are in contact iron would be expected to be anodic and corrode in preference to tin. However, tin forms a very thin, optically invisible and strongly adherent corrosion product on the surface which provides a relatively strong resistance to neutral and weakly alkaline solutions. If the tin completely covers the surface of the steel, it acts as an impermeable barrier to the solutions and provides protection of the steel. Electrolytic coatings do tend to be porous and, if the pores extend to the surface of the steel, then the steel will corrode rapidly at these sites. Until comparatively recent times, this corrosion was avoided by applying a relatively thick coating of tin and then flash melting (flow brightening) of the surface of the tin to cause it to melt and fill the pores. The escalating price of tin, competition from aluminium and plastic containers and the introduction of chromized steel sheet with good anti-corrosion properties stimulated the tin plate manufacturers to greater efforts and, today, very thin layers of tin down to 0.5 μm thick are applied which do not require flow brightening. The good lubricity of tin, which facilitates the forming of shaped articles by deep drawing, and the ease with which decorative patterns, etc., can be printed on the surface of tin, have led to a resurgence in the use of the ubiquitous tin container.

Terneplate is the name given to hot-dip coating of steel, in which thicker coatings are applied by dipping the steel sheet into a bath of molten lead–tin alloy. The coated metal is used for roofing and weather sealing. It is used also for applications as diverse as cable sheathing and chassis for electronic components. Electroplated, equi-atomic tin–nickel coatings also give a lustrous finish combined with very good tarnish resistance and resistance to wear. Less-expensive protection can be provided by coating steel with alloys of tin and zinc. Coatings containing 75% tin and 25% zinc give the best non-sacrificial corrosion protection of this group of alloys; they provide superior corrosion resistance to the more toxic cadmium coatings. At the opposite end of the range, coatings containing 15–30% tin and 70–85% zinc markedly increase the time before rust appears on steel panels.

One potential use for tin coating of steel which is being considered is the protection of reinforcing bars. The tin coating will deform readily with the bar and not rupture on forming to shape, but it must be remembered that, under normal conditions, the coating is non-sacrificial and any steel surfaces exposed by mishandling would have to be coated on-site before being embedded in concrete. Attention must be drawn to the statement of 'normal conditions' above. Under certain conditions, the polarity of tin and iron can be reversed. For example, under the anaerobic conditions which exist within a sealed tin food can, tin becomes electronegative to iron and then provides sacrificial protection.

Tin coatings are sometimes applied to copper and copper alloys for decorative purposes. Copper and tin bronze can be coated by hot dipping, but the brasses are best coated electrolytically. Aluminium bronzes are not suitable for tin coating because of the tenacious alumina surface film. BS 1872[27] relates to tin electroplated coatings and BS 3384[28] refers specifically to tin coatings on copper and copper alloys.

7.8.5 Solders

The second major use of tin is in the form of solder. Molten tin has a very low surface tension with most of the common metals and readily wets the surface of those metals at temperatures well below their melting points. It also adheres firmly to the metal surfaces, providing a relatively strong bond.

Most common solders are alloys of tin and lead (BS 219[29]). Small amounts of antimony may be added to improve the creep resistance and inhibit the β–α transformation. The tin–lead phase diagram shown in *Figure 7.13* is the eutectic type, with the melting points of both tin and lead being depressed with addition of the second metal. Alloys containing 61.9% tin melt and freeze at a constant temperature of 183°C. All other compositions freeze over a range of temperatures, as indicated on the diagram, but, for all compositions between approximately 20 and 97% tin, the last liquid disappears under equilibrium conditions on cooling past 183°C.

Compositions around 50% tin, 50% lead have relatively low melting points and are popular for general-purpose work. For plumbing purposes a higher lead content is usually preferred, giving a wider freezing range and allowing the joint to be wiped whilst the solder is still in the pasty stage. The time taken for the solder to solidify completely increases, however, as the lead content is increased up to 80% and requires increasing care to avoid movement of the components which are being joined whilst the solder is solidifying. For plumbing applications, therefore, the most popular solders contain about 65% lead. Similar compositions are used for soldering heat exchangers and

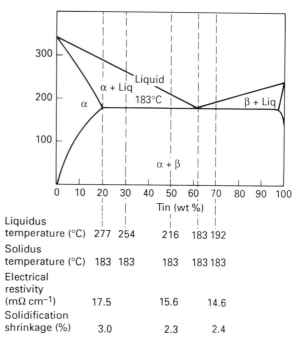

Liquidus temperature (°C)	277	254	216	183 192
Solidus temperature (°C)	183	183	183	183 183
Electrical restivity (mΩ cm⁻¹)		17.5	15.6	14.6
Solidification shrinkage (%)		3.0	2.3	2.4

Figure 7.13 The tin–lead phase diagram and some properties of common solders

for joining cables. For soldering tin plate, the lead content has to be kept low to obtain a reasonable colour match and corrosion resistance to the tin plate. Tinmans solder accordingly contains about 65% tin. Similar compositions are also used for soldering electrical and electronic connections, where electrical resistivity of the joint is important. Lead–tin alloys with low tin content are also used for filling dents and crevices at welds and seams to improve the appearance and remove corrosion pockets. Lead–tin alloys are also used for the manufacture of organ pipes.

Two lead free tin solders containing about 0.6% copper or 3.5% silver (BS 864[30]) are used where a low electrical resistivity is important. The resistivity of the tin–silver solder is about 1.05 $\mu\Omega$ mm^{-1}. This composition is now being used for soldering of potable-water systems, where lead containing solders have been banned. Tests at the International Tin Research Institute have shown that the capillary rise of the silver solder between copper junctions is as good as with the traditional plumber's solders. The silver solder has a liquidus temperature of 245°C and solidus temperature of 221°C, so the freezing range is significantly less than with plumber's solder. Both solders confer better creep resistance on the joint than the traditional, lower freezing point solders.

Tin–antimony solders containing about 5% antimony are used for joining stainless steel where lead has to be avoided. A tin–zinc alloy is used for joining aluminium components, producing joints with good resistance to galvanic corrosion.

7.8.6 Bearings

Tin is an essential constituent of white-metal bearings, mainly because tin has a low coefficient of friction with most engineering metals. However, the metal is too soft for use in the pure form so it is alloyed to increase strength. The tin rich *Babbitt* bearings contain 82–90% tin, 4–8% antimony and 3–8% copper. Bismuth and lead are held to very low levels to avoid the formation of low-melting-point phases. The load on the bearing is supported by the formation of a hard β phase (SbSn) which appears as cuboids in the microstructure. The density of the cuboids is lower than that of the tin rich solid solution in which they are embedded and, during casting, the cuboids tend to segregate towards the top surface. In addition to its effect in increasing the hardness, strength and fatigue resistance, the copper addition helps to prevent this segregation by precipitating a γ phase (Cu$_6$Sn$_5$). This phase precipitates as fine interlocking needles which prevent flotating of the cuboids and ensures a uniform distribution. There is also a series of lead based Babbitt bearing compositions with, typically 75–85% lead, 8–15% antimony and 5–10% tin. These compositions are less expensive than the tin rich alloys, but their maximum loading is lower. Arsenic is regarded as a detrimental constituent of the tin rich compositions, but up to 1% is sometimes added to the lead rich alloys to increase the maximum load which can be supported.

7.8.7 Pewter

Pewter has been used for utensils and decorative wear since the time of the Roman Empire. Originally, pewter was manufactured from simple lead–tin alloys, but this was discontinued because of the toxicity of lead in contact with food and drink. Modern pewter is similar in composition and microstructure to the tin rich Babbitts. The composition of the popular Britannia metal, specified in BS 5140,[31] is 91% tin, 7% antimony and 2% copper.

7.9 Zinc

7.9.1 Characteristics

In terms of the tonnage used, zinc is the fourth most important metal. Only iron, aluminium and copper exceed the annual production of about 5 million tonnes of zinc. This may seem surprising until it is realized that almost half the production is used for coatings of other metals and a significant quantity is processed into zinc chemicals. Zinc is used as an alloying element in aluminium, copper and magnesium alloys. Zinc and zinc rich alloys are used mainly for the production of die castings and only a very small proportion is used in wrought form. The melting point of zinc is higher than that of lead and tin, but it boils at 911°C and has a significant vapour pressure at much lower temperatures. As a result of the low melting point, the pure metal suffers from creep at room temperature and it has no clearly defined Young's modulus. Its crystal structure is described as close packed hexagonal, but it is not really close packed; each atom has six near neighbours and six others at a slightly greater distance, with partially homopolar bonding resulting in a tendency towards non-metallic properties. This crystal structure results in a lack of slip systems and marked directionality of the properties within the grain. Zinc tends to crystallize with a coarse grain size. Hence, in spite of the low melting point, the metal is not readily deformed at room temperature and it must be heated at temperatures up to 150°C for extrusion. Since frictional heat, particularly during extrusion, can further raise the temperature of the metal, low working rates must be used to avoid insipient melting and the development of hot shortness.

In the electrochemical series, only magnesium has a more negative electromotive force than zinc, so, in a galvanic couple, zinc corrodes in preference to all the common engineering and precious metals and alloys. Hence there is a high probability of attack if zinc is in metallic contact with any of the common engineering metals in a moist or wet environment. For corrosion protection zinc must either be electrically insulated from the other metals, to prevent electron transfer, or encased from the more noble metals (e.g. coatings) to prevent egress of corrosive solutions to the interface. Zinc is sometimes described as being amphoteric, exhibiting corrosion resistance only in neutral and weakly alkaline solutions. It is readily attacked in acidic or strongly alkaline solutions. When exposed to the atmosphere zinc forms a voluminous, white coating of zinc oxide or hydroxide, which is porous, poorly adherent and does not retard further corrosion. If carbon dioxide is present in the atmosphere, however, this coating is replaced by a thin, compact, crystalline and adherent film of zinc carbonate which is optically almost transparent and acts as a barrier to further attack, resulting in a lower rate of corrosion than with exposed iron or steel. In general, zinc provides better protection against marine than against industrial atmospheres. Chlorine in marine atmospheres produces a film of zinc oxychloride (ZnOZnCl$_2$) which is protective except against salt-water splashes and high salt contents in the atmosphere. Industrial atmospheres, on the other hand, often contain sulphur dioxide which attacks and dissolves the protective carbonate layer, producing a soluble salt, i.e.

$$ZnCO_3 + SO_2 \rightleftharpoons ZnSO_3 + CO_2$$

Removal of the carbonate coat allows direct attack on the underlying zinc metal to produce more zinc sulphite and continued dissolution of the metal.

Condensation of moisture from industrial atmospheres can produce quite strongly acidic films on the metal surface and this is the major cause of attack. Crevices in the metal surface and dust accumulations which absorb the acidic condensate prolong the period of contact and exacerbate the problem. Rain, however, contains less sulphur dixoide and is beneficial as a means of washing away the acidic deposits and accumulations of dust.

For exposure to industrial atmospheres, therefore, it is

important that zinc and zinc coatings should be protected as far as possible from the risk of condensation. For example, zinc in roofs should be installed with adequate slope to encourage drainage of condensates. A free flow of atmospheric air should be allowed on the underside since temperature differences are more likely to cause condensation on the underside of the sheet. Zinc should not be placed directly in contact with cement, mortar or other moisture-retaining materials and, where thermal insulation is applied to the roof, a ventilated space should be left between the insulation and the roof sheeting. A chromate passivating film is sometimes applied to protect against corrosion from restricted air circulation during storage.

A protective carbonate film is also formed in neutral and slightly alkaline solutions. In water this coating behaves similarly to that of lead in that the rate of attack increases with increasing purity of the water and with increasing concentrations of dissolved oxygen and carbon dioxide. Zinc coatings may fail through pitting in stagnant water with low oxygen content. In closed water systems, it is common practice to add an inhibitor such as sodium dichromate or sodium silicate to protect the zinc. Zinc and zinc alloys are attacked more rapidly than lead by tannic and acetic acid released from moist timber. Hence, pine, poplar, spruce and Scots pine are the only timbers which should be used in contact with zinc. Excessive amounts of lead and aluminium as residual impurities in the zinc can give rise to intergranular corrosion problems in moist atmospheres, because these impurities form films at the grain boundaries.

7.9.2 Sources and production

Zinc is extracted from the earth mainly as zinc sulphide (ZnS) or as an iron zinc sulphide, usually mixed with lead sulphide. The main deposits are located in North and South America, the USSR and Australia, but it is also mined in Europe, Africa and Japan. After crushing, concentration and roasting and following the procedure described for lead, zinc can be smelted in a blast furnace. The zinc oxide is reduced in the furnace stack and zinc is volatilized. The zinc in the furnace off-gas is condensed in a lead splash condenser and 2.5% zinc can dissolve in the lead at 550°C. The lead flows from the condenser to a cooler. The solubility of the zinc decreases with decreasing temperature and metallic zinc floats on top of the lead. Liquation and fractional distillation are applied to increase the purity of the zinc after separation from the lead. Alternatively, the zinc metal may be produced by electrolytic deposition from a purified solution obtained by sulphuric acid leaching of the roasted ore concentrate. Commercial grades of zinc may contain several residual impurity elements including up to 0.1% lead, and 0.01% iron and cadmium. These elements do not appear to affect the corrosion resistance, but do affect adversely the ductility and toughness of the metal. Purer grades of zinc, containing lower concentrations of impurity elements, are produced by electrolysis of the refined metal.

7.9.3 Zinc coatings

Since zinc is electronegative to the common engineering metals, it provides true galvanic protection to these metals and does not act solely as a corrosion barrier as is the case, for example, with tin and lead coatings on steel. A continuous film of zinc on steel does serve as a corrosion barrier, but it will also protect the steel if the film is not continuous. Small pores in the film are rapidly filled with zinc corrosion products, but cut edges and relatively large areas of steel may also remain free from corrosion, depending on the exposure conditions. Note, however, that the relative positions of iron and zinc in the galvanic series may be changed at elevated temperatures. For example, zinc may become cathodic to iron (i.e. iron is attacked preferentially) in some potable waters at temperatures as low as 60°C, so

galvanized steel is not suitable for domestic hot-water-storage tanks.

The most common form of zinc coating is hot-dip galvanizing of unalloyed, low carbon steel. The relevant British Standard is BS 729.[32] Small artefacts are treated by a batch process. Sheet-steel coating is usually on a continuous line, the annealed steel passing through a degreasing tank before immersion in a bath of molten zinc held at 420–460°C. Excess zinc is removed by rollers or air wipers as the coated sheet emerges from the bath. The coating thickness usually varies between 5 and 25 μm,* the thickness being controlled by the air wipers and by varying the temperature of the bath and/or the time of residence in the bath. The 'spangled' surface appearance, revealing the individual grains of zinc, is a characteristic of hot-dip coatings. The spangle or grain size can be decreased to some extent by increasing the rate of cooling of the sheet as it emerges from the bath. A flatter spangle surface, more suitable for painting, can be obtained by adding a small amount of antimony to the bath. 'Galvanized iron' wire (which is actually galvanized, low carbon steel) is coated by a similar process.

Although the molten zinc is in contact with the steel for only a short period of time, it is long enough for some iron to dissolve in the zinc. The iron–zinc binary phase diagram shows that the two metals are completely soluble in each other when molten, but in equilibrium are only sparingly soluble in each other and form a series of iron–zinc compounds in the solid state. The zinc remains molten for insufficient time for equilibrium to be attained; otherwise the coating would consist entirely of these iron–zinc compounds. Instead, there is a zinc concentration gradient, varying from iron rich adjacent to the steel surface to pure zinc at the outer surface. This pure zinc layer is usually about half the thickness of the coating. In general, the thickness of the pure zinc layer increases with increasing total thickness of the coating, but it depends also on the bath temperature and the length of time for which the zinc remains molten. Corrosion removes first the pure zinc layer and exposes layers progressively richer in iron resulting in a gradual change of colour, the surface becoming progressively darker as the more iron rich layers are exposed. This is not detrimental from the corrosion perspective, but the colour change serves as a useful indication that the sacrificial protection is nearing exhaustion and signals the need for the application of paint, etc., to maintain the life of the structure. The interdiffusion of iron and zinc results in a strong bonding between the coating and the substrate, giving a very high peel resistance.

The service life of hot-dip coatings does not seem to be affected by small amounts of impurities in the zinc, so the less pure (and hence less expensive) grades of zinc are used for this purpose. When exposed to the atmosphere externally in roofing sheets, etc., the useful life increases as the concentration of pollutants in the air, such as sulphur dioxide, is decreased. Typical lifetimes in relation to the coating thickness are listed in *Table 7.7*, whereas for internal applications where condensation is avoided a coating thickness of about 5 μm should give a useful life of about 20 years.

Table 7.7 Typical lifetimes (years) in relation to thickness of hot-dip zinc coatings[5]

Coating thickness (μm)	Atmosphere		
	Rural	Marine	Severe industrial
5	3	1	0.5
25	14	7	3
50	30	13	6

* Zinc coatings are often specified by weight: $100 \text{ g mm}^{-2} \equiv 0.3 \text{ oz ft}^{-2} \equiv 14.1 \text{ μm}$.

The iron–zinc alloy layers reduce the ductility of the coating, relative to pure zinc, and somewhat decrease the formability of the coated metal. With rimmed and aluminium killed steels this is the only detrimental effect. With silicon killed steels, however, if the residual silicon content in the steel is high, the alloy layers tend to crack during bending and shaping. The strong adherence of the coating to the steel facilitates extension of the surface-layer cracks into the substrate with detrimental effects to the fatigue life of the steel.

Electrogalvanizing, in which the zinc is deposited on the surface of the sheet or wire from a zinc chloride or sulphate solution, avoids the formation of the alloy layers. Since the zinc is not molten, the formation of zinc grains on the surface is avoided and the deposit has a smooth matt grey appearance of pure zinc, which is preferable for painting. The cost is, naturally, higher than with the hot-dip process and increases with increasing thickness of the coat. This process is, therefore, usually limited to thicknesses of about 5 μm, suitable for indoor applications or as a surface preparation for structures which are to be protected by painting. One inherent advantage of electrogalvanizing is the ability to apply controlled differential coating thicknesses on the two sides of steel sheet, thus economizing on the quantity of zinc used. Electrogalvanizing is also used to produce zinc coatings containing 10–12% nickel which offer enhanced protection against salt spray for use in motor-car chassis construction plant, etc. These coatings, which are more readily welded and painted than pure zinc coatings, are being substituted for cadmium coatings. Paintability can be enhanced further by over-plating with an iron rich layer. Electroplated zinc coatings are covered in BS 1706.[33]

Hot-dip galvanizing baths often contain small amounts of aluminium to modify and control the iron–zinc alloy layers, improving the ductility. In the early 1980s, a new hot-dip zinc coating containing about 5% aluminium plus a small amount of mischmetal was marketed under the trade name of *Galfan*. The corrosion resistance proved to be two to three times better than a simple zinc coating and the coated steel has excellent formability. Aluminium and zinc form a binary eutectic system with the eutectic point at 5% aluminium melting at 382°C. Thus the bath can be operated at a lower temperature than for pure zinc and, as the aluminium readily melts in the eutectic alloy, it is possible to supply the aluminium in the form of suitable grades of scrap metal, avoiding the cost of first melting and casting the aluminium. The growth in production of this alloy coating has been spectacular and the world production in 1988 approached 0.5 million tonnes.

British Steel is the major producer of zinc coated sheet in the UK, and markets hot-dip galvanized, electro-galvanized, electrogalvanized zinc–nickel and zinc–aluminium coatings under the trade names Galvatite, Zintec, Nizec and Zalutite, respectively.

Recent developments in the production of multilayer electrogalvanized steel for use by car manufacturers may ultimately find specialized architectural applications. These developments are designed to enhance both corrosion resistance and the appearance of painted surfaces. Typical coatings of this type comprise a thin layer of metallic zinc, followed by a layer of zinc oxide plus chromic oxide and a zinc rich epoxy top coat, or a zinc–nickel coat covered with a thin chromate layer and finished with a very thin organic silicate outer layer.

Zinc coatings are applied also by other methods for specialist applications. Engineering artefacts such as nuts, bolts, washers and fasteners can be mechanically plated. The artefacts are tumbled in an aqueous solution containing powdered zinc and glass beads. Depending on the time of contact and the concentration of the solution, uniform coating thicknesses of up to about 5 μm can be developed. The coatings have a matt-grey appearance. Thicker and more strongly adherent coatings can be built up by *sherardizing* (a high-temperature form of mechanical plating), where the artefacts are tumbled in zinc dust at temperatures close to the melting point of pure zinc. Atomized zinc particles can be sprayed on to steel work after erection, provided that the surface is clean and free of rust (e.g. after shot blasting). Thinner sprayed deposits tend to be porous (although the pores are rapidly blocked by zinc corrosion products), but thick layers of zinc can be applied by this method. In some cases sufficient protection can be provided by application of a paint containing finely divided zinc, a volatile solvent and chemicals formulated to increase adherence of the zinc to the surface of the substrate.

All zinc coatings suffer from the formation of bulky corrosion products until exposed to atmospheres containing CO_2. This can be a problem, particularly in storage when the sheets are stacked closely together, allowing very limited circulation of air over the surfaces. The problem is avoided by dipping the sheets in a solution of chromic acid or alkaline dichromate to form a thin chromate film over the surface. Alternatively, as in Colourcoat which is widely used in buildings, a polymer coat is applied on top of the zinc layer.

7.9.4 Die castings

The second major use of zinc is for the production of die castings. This is, truly, a near-net-shape forming process for the production of small artefacts such as building hardware, padlocks and components for typewriters, motor cars, camera bodies and vending machines. Fine detail, very thin wall sections (less than 1-mm thick) and intricate shapes can be produced to close dimensional limits in small castings weighing up to about 200 g. Low-melting-point alloys of other metals are produced as die castings, but only copper and aluminium alloys produce components with higher strength and with better room-temperature impact properties than can be obtained with zinc alloys. Consequently, the majority of die castings produced for use at temperatures below about 100°C are cast in zinc.

In pressure die casting, a measured quantity of molten metal is injected under pressure into a heated, permanent, split metal mould. The two halves of the mould are clamped together, or closed under hydraulic pressure during injection and ports provide for the insertion of removable cores. The small cross-sectional areas of the castings produced result in very rapid solidification so the two halves of the die can be opened almost immediately after the metal injection is completed and the casting is then released by activating ejector pins. Fine slits at the die parting line allow escape of entrapped air from within the die cavity, with minimal metal flash formation, as the metal is injected. But the very rapid filling of the die and solidification of the metal may result in porosity of thicker cross-sections, particularly where alternating thick and thin sections make feeding difficult. Zinc die castings are very easily machined, but the castings replicate the surface finish of the moulds and the only treatment usually required is the removal of the feeder sprue and any flash formed at the die parting line. The dimensional accuracy is also high, so no machining to final size is required, but the die parting line should intersect the surfaces where the lowest accuracy can be tolerated since some slight separation of the two die halves may occur when the metal is injected. The process is usually automated for mass production, thus producing castings at low cost.

Very pure grades of zinc (usually 99.99% zinc) must be used for the production of die castings. Small quantities of some impurities give rise to embrittlement. In particular, the concentrations of lead and cadmium should be 0.003% maximum and the tin content should be kept below 0.001%. Otherwise, the castings are susceptible to intercrystalline corrosion, forming bulky corrosion products which cause the castings to swell. Several alloy compositions are in common use, but the *Mazak* alloys are very popular, conforming to BS 1004 (see *Table 7.8*).

Table 7.8 Composition of the Mazak alloys

Alloy	Standard	Composition (%)		
		Al	*Cu*	*Mg*
Mazak 3	BS 1004A	3.9–4.3	0.001 max.	0.03–0.06
Mazak 5	BS 1004B	3.9–4.3	0.75–1.25	0.03–0.06

The first of the compositions in *Table 7.8* is an approximately binary eutectic composition, whilst the second corresponds to the ternary eutectic. Thus the melting point is depressed by the aluminium addition and is further depressed by the copper and both elements increase the strength with respect to pure zinc. Optimum mechanical properties in these alloys are only developed by rapid solidification. Hence the die casting process is ideal. Typical minimum values for ultimate tensile strength at room temperature are 280 N mm^{-2} for *Mazak 3* and 330 N mm^{-2} for *Mazak 5*. Both alloys give elongation to failure of about 6% and Izod impact values of over 50 J at ambient temperature; these values apply to freshly cast material. Over a period of time, which may extend to years at room temperature, the alloys age, resulting in a decrease in strength and an increase in ductility. This is accompanied by a small contraction during the first month or so, followed by a very slight expansion. These changes can be accelerated and the properties and dimensions stabilized by elevated-temperature ageing at about 100°C for 3–6 h. The zinc–aluminium alloys have poor creep resistance. New alloys containing titanium and copper (ILZRO 14 and 16) behave much better in this respect, but the dies must be kept cool in order to minimize attack by the alloy.

As with zinc coatings, die castings are susceptible to the formation of corrosion films. A tarnish film will slowly develop even in a relatively low-humidity indoor atmosphere. Hence it is customary to provide some form of surface treatment to preserve the appearance. For less-demanding applications, a simple chromate, phosphate or lacquer dip may suffice. Electroless nickel gives a black colouration with enhanced wear resistance. Almost any metal can be electrodeposited on the surface, but copper, brass, nickel and chromium are most commonly applied. Thin chromium platings tend to be porous and the zinc corrosion products formed at the pores soon cause surface deterioration. It is common to plate successive thin layers of different metals, such as copper followed by nickel followed by chromium, in preference to a single thicker layer of chromium.

7.9.5 Wrought zinc

Zinc is also produced in the form of sheet, strip and foil (as thin as 0.02 mm), rod, wire and extruded sections. The purer grades will recrystallize and soften during rolling at room temperature, but harder grades require inter-annealing or, preferably, are rolled at a little above 100°C.

Wrought zinc sheet is used for roofing and cladding of buildings (BS 6561[34]), for roll capping and covering standing seams on zinc coated constructions and for gutters and downpipes. The major limitations of these applications, apart from cost, are the inherently low creep resistance at room temperature and the high value of the thermal expansion coefficient (*Table 7.2*). A relatively recent development is the production of zinc sheet containing at least 0.05% titanium to increase the creep resistance and at least 0.10% copper to improve the mechanical strength. High purity (electrolytic) grades of zinc, containing low concentrations of impurity elements, must be used for the manufacture of this alloy to retain sufficient ductility and toughness, but mechanical working by rolling to produce the required sheet gauge or hammering to produce profiles for roof fittings, etc., must be performed with metal temperatures above about 100°C. Attempts are being made to produce finer grain sizes and change the deformation mode from twinning to slip, which would facilitate lower temperature deformation. Corrosion resistance is at least as good as commercial zinc. The surface gradually weathers to produce a patina which has a more greyish colouration than commercial zinc. A phosphate pretreatment produces a durable darker gray patina.

The zinc–copper–titanium sheet exhibits directional properties in a manner similar to pure zinc. That is, the close-packed-hexagonal grains tend to rotate to produce common alignments during rolling, with the result that the sheet shows lower strength and higher ductility in the rolling direction than in the transverse direction. Typical properties (BS 6561A[34]) are given in *Table 7.9*. The creep rate at room temperature under a load of 70 N mm^{-2} is not greater than 5×10^{-3} in the rolling direction, compared with a value of 1% for commercial grade zinc. The coefficient of thermal expansion is also lowered to about 23×10^{-6} cm cm^{-1} °C^{-1}. The density (7.18 g cm^{-3}) is significantly lower than for galvanized mild steel (7.85 g cm^{-3}) and hence requires less support. Thus, a sheet measuring 2000 mm × 1000 mm × 1 mm (thick) weighs 14.36 kg in zinc–copper–titanium and 15.7 kg in galvanized steel. This grade of sheeting is not, at present, manufactured in the UK but it has been used, for example, for roofing at Brighton railway station, Salisbury Playhouse, the Rusty Pelican Restaurant at Queens Dock, Glasgow, and for reroofing several school buildings. It is widely used in Canada, where the alloy was first developed, and in Europe.

Deep drawing grades used, for example, for the production of the outer cans for dry batteries, may contain up to 0.08% lead and 0.3% cadmium to increase the strength. For nameplates and weather seals the metal may contain up to 1.0% copper. In sheet form, the close-packed-hexagonal crystal structure of zinc results in properties which are directionally orientated, as noted above. Typical values for the ultimate tensile strength and elongation to failure for zinc–lead–cadmium sheet are 150 N mm^{-2} and 40%, parallel to the rolling direction and 200 N mm^{-2} and 32% normal to the rolling direction.

Zinc alloy sheet was one of the first metallic alloys exploited commercially for superplastic forming. This is a process in which the material is formed at very slow strain rate at temperatures above half the melting point in degrees Kelvin, either by blow forming a clamped sheet on to a female die or advancing a male forming die into the clamped sheet. Uniform, controlled flow of the metal is obtained only if it is deformed by Newtonian flow and not by conventional slip and twinning processes. This can be achieved if the material is processed to produce an extremely fine-grain structure, which remains stable throughout the forming operation, which may take several minutes at the elevated temperature. The formability is characterized by values of the strain-rate-sensitivity exponent (*m*) greater than 0.5, compared with values of 0.01–0.02 for deformation by slip or twinning, where *m* is defined as

$$\sigma_y = k\dot{\varepsilon}^m$$

where σ_y is the yield stress, k is a constant and $\dot{\varepsilon}$ is the true strain rate. Although the forming process is very slow, it is

Table 7.9 Typical properties of zinc–copper–titanium sheet[34]

	Rolling direction	*Transverse direction*
Minimum UTS (N mm^{-2})	150	200
Minimum elongation (%)	30	15

economically viable because quite complex shapes can be produced with large surface area and thin cross-section in one forming operation. The production of similar shapes by conventional techniques frequently requires the production and joining of several smaller components.

The aluminium–zinc phase diagram shows a solid-state, eutectoid reaction at 275°C (similar to the transformation which occurs at 723°C in alloys of iron and carbon, i.e. plain carbon steels), the eutectoid point being located at 22% aluminium. This is the composition chosen for superplastic zinc sheet. A very fine, microduplex eutectoid structure can be formed, which is stabilized by fine precipitates formed by small copper and magnesium additions. The sheet is shaped at about 250°C. During subsequent service, the formed sheet must not be heated above about 100°C to avoid a return to the superplastic state and it must not be subjected to sustained heavy loads even at room temperature unless it is first heat treated to coarsen the grain size.

7.9.6 Other uses

Zinc anodes, connected by a conductor to metallic structures, are widely used for cathodic protection of steelwork in salt water and for pipes, conduits, etc., buried in the soil. In the latter case, care has to be taken to prevent the formation of a protective corrosion coating on the zinc, thereby impeding the electrolytic reaction.

Zinc oxide, sulphide and chromate are used extensively in paints and this accounts for about 10% of the weight of zinc produced annually. Zinc sulphide is also used in phosphors for fluorescent lights and cathode ray tubes.

References

1 CRANE, F. A. A. and CHARLES, J. A., *Selection and Use of Engineering Materials*, Butterworths, London (1989)
2 ASHBY, M. F. and JONES, D. R. H., *Engineering Materials*, Pergamon, Oxford (1980)
3 SØRENSEN, H., *Materials in Modern Society*, 10th Risø International Symposium on Metallurgy and Materials Science, p. 53 (1989)
4 GILCHRIST, J. D., *Extraction Metallurgy*, Pergamon, Oxford (1967)
5 ASTM, *Metals Handbook*, 9th edition, Vol. 2 (1979), and Desk Edition (1985) American Society for Metals, Ohio
6 HUME-ROTHERY, W., *The Structure of Metals and Alloys*, 2nd edition, The Institute of Metals, p. 60 (1944)
7 HANSEN, N. and RALPH, B., *Acta Met.*, **30**, 411–417 (1982)
8 BRITISH STANDARDS INSTITUTION, *BS 2870 Rolled copper and copper alloys* (1980); *2871 Tubes* (1971); *2873 Wire* (1969); *2874 Rods* (1986), Milton Keynes
9 BRITISH STANDARDS INSTITUTION, *BS 2870 Rolled copper and copper alloys, sheet, strip and foil* (1980); *2874 Rods and sections* (1986), Milton Keynes
10 SEVERIN, T., *The Jason Voyage*, Simon and Schuster, New York (1985)
11 RAPSON, W. S. and GREENEWALD, T., *Gold Usage*, Academic Press, London (1978)
12 BRITISH STANDARDS INSTITUTION, *BS 4292 Gold and gold alloys for engineering purposes*, Part 1, Milton Keynes (1989)
13 BRITISH STANDARDS INSTITUTION, *BS 334 Compositional limits of chemical lead*, Milton Keynes (1982 (1989))
14 BRITISH STANDARDS INSTITUTION, *BS 801 Lead and lead alloy sheaths for electric cables*, Milton Keynes (1984)
15 BRITISH STANDARDS INSTITUTION, *BS 6915 Design and construction of fully supported lead sheet roof and wall coverings*, Milton Keynes (1988)
16 HOFFMAN, W., *Lead and Lead Alloys*, Springer-Verlag, Berlin, p. 215 (1970)
17 BRITISH STANDARDS INSTITUTION, *BS 6582 Continuously hot-dip lead alloy coated cold reduced carbon steel flat rolled products*, Milton Keynes (1985)
18 BRITISH STANDARDS INSTITUTION, *BS 3072 Nickel and nickel alloys: sheet and plate*, Milton Keynes (1983)
19 BRITISH STANDARDS INSTITUTION, *BS 3073 Nickel and nickel alloys: strip*, Milton Keynes (1977 (1989))
20 BRITISH STANDARDS INSTITUTION, *BS 3074 Nickel and nickel alloys: seamless tube*, Milton Keynes (1983)
21 BRITISH STANDARDS INSTITUTION, *BS 3076 Nickel and nickel alloys: bar* (1976 (1983))
22 BRITISH STANDARDS INSTITUTION, *BS 4758 Electroplated coatings of nickel for engineering purposes*, Milton Keynes (1986)
23 GAWNE, D. T. and MA, U., 'Engineering properties of chromium plated and electroless and electroplated nickel', *Surface Engineering*, **4**, 239 (1988)
24 BRITISH STANDARDS INSTITUTION, *BS 2816 Electroplated coatings of silver and silver alloys for engineering*, Milton Keynes (1989)
25 BRITISH STANDARDS INSTITUTION, *BS 3382 Electroplated coatings on threaded components*: Parts 1 and 2 (1961) *Cadmium or zinc steel*; Parts 3 and 4 (1965) *Nickel/chromium on steel, copper*; Parts 5 and 6 (1967) *Tin/silver on copper/brass*; Part 7 (1966) *Thicker platings*, Milton Keynes
26 BRITISH STANDARDS INSTITUTION, *BS 3252 Ingot tin*, Milton Keynes (1986)
27 BRITISH STANDARDS INSTITUTION, *BS 1872 Electroplated coatings of tin*, Milton Keynes (1984)
28 BRITISH STANDARDS INSTITUTION, *BS 3384 Dental gold solders*, Milton Keynes (1984 (1989))
29 BRITISH STANDARDS INSTITUTION, *BS 219 Soft solders*, Milton Keynes (1977 (1989))
30 BRITISH STANDARDS INSTITUTION, *BS 864 Capillary and compression tube fittings of copper: tubes*, Milton Keynes, Part 2 (1983)
31 BRITISH STANDARDS INSTITUTION, *BS 5140 Pewter* Milton Keynes (1974 (1988))
32 BRITISH STANDARDS INSTITUTION, *BS 729 Hot dip galvanized coatings on iron and steel*, Milton Keynes (1971 (1986))
33 BRITISH STANDARDS INSTITUTION, *BS 1706 Electroplated coatings of cadmium and zinc on iron and steel*, Milton Keynes (1960)
34 BRITISH STANDARDS INSTITUTION, *BS 6561 Zinc alloy sheet and strip for building*, Milton Keynes (1985)

Bibliography

A number of Research Institutes and Trade Associations deal specifically with the metals covered in this chapter. Many of these produce publications listing compositions, mechanical and physical properties and usage of the metals, alloys, chemical compounds, etc., with which they are concerned. Some offer advice on materials selection and possible suppliers. The following list provides the addresses of some of these organizations.

COPPER DEVELOPMENT ASSOCIATION, Orchard House, Mutton Lane, Potters Bar, Herts
GALVANISERS ASSOCIATION (see Zinc Development Association)
INCO (ALLOY PRODUCT RESEARCH LABORATORIES (NICKEL)), Wiggin Street, Birmingham
INTERNATIONAL TIN RESEARCH INSTITUTE, Kingston Lane, Uxbridge, Middlesex
LEAD DEVELOPMENT ASSOCIATION, 42 Weymouth Street, London W1
ZINC DEVELOPMENT ASSOCIATION and ZINC ALLOY DIECASTERS ASSOCIATION, 34 Berkeley Square, London

Part Two

Non-Metals

8

Adhesives

J D N Shaw
SBD Ltd

Contents

8.1 Introduction 8/3

8.2 Surface treatment 8/4
    8.2.1 Concrete 8/4
    8.2.2 Steel 8/4
    8.2.3 Brick 8/4
    8.2.4 Wood 8/4
    8.2.5 Glass 8/4
    8.2.6 Rubber 8/4
    8.2.7 Glass reinforced plastics 8/4

8.3 Performance testing of adhesives 8/5

8.4 Applications of resin adhesives 8/5
    8.4.1 Adhesives for segmental precast prestressed
        concrete structures 8/5
    8.4.2 Strengthening of reinforced concrete structures
        by external bonding of steel plates 8/6
    8.4.3 Structural repair of cracked concrete structures
        by resin injection 8/9
    8.4.4 Resin bonded skid resistant road surfaces 8/11

References 8/11

Appendix 8/12

8.1 Introduction

A wide range of adhesives have been used for many decades in the construction industry. Historically, many of the adhesives used were based on natural products from many parts of the world and were highly effective as adhesives in essentially non-structural applications.

As a result of World War II, in the early 1940s many of the natural product raw materials for adhesive manufacture were unobtainable and, consequently, effective adhesives had to be developed based on raw materials which were available or could be synthesized from crude oil or, more especially, coal. One of the most notable of the early wartime adhesives was the continued development of phenol/formaldehyde resorcinol/formaldehyde and urea/formaldehyde adhesives for wood, in particular for the construction of the Mosquito fighter aircraft. Over the past 40 years, reactive adhesives, based on formaldehyde, have continued to be used in the off-site manufacture of many timber based building materials including plywood, chipboard and resin bonded structural beams.[1,2]

There are now a range of British Standards covering the technical performance of these adhesives in tests which cover their long-term performance under diverse application and service conditions.[1,3-5]

In the 1940s, the first synthetic polymer dispersions were produced and began to be widely used in the manufacture of the first emulsion paints. These were then based almost entirely upon polyvinyl acetate (PVAC) and this still continues to be the basis of many emulsion paints today, although other polymer dispersions such as acrylics and PVAC copolymers are also used. It was realized in the 1950s that PVAC dispersions were also a basis for the formulation of adhesives for a wide range of building materials from adhesives for floor screeds to timber adhesives—in fact, adhesives to bond any slightly porous building materials. By the mid-1960s, adhesives based on PVAC had become the almost universal adhesives in the construction industry.[6,7] Once an adhesive becomes so widely used in the construction industry, where the control of the use of adhesives may be rather limited compared to adhesives used under controlled factory conditions, problems inevitably occur and, as a result, PVAC adhesives have been used in a number of applications where good long-term performance of the adhesive under severe service conditions was required.[8,9] These applications included their use as a bonding agent for external renderings, adhesives for bonding external brick slips and floor screeds in wet service conditions, and repairs to damaged precast concrete units.[8,10]

Relatively short-term tests had been carried out to demonstrate the excellent performance of PVAC based adhesives in wet service conditions and at that time it was considered that, by careful formulation, PVAC adhesives did have sufficient stability to wet alkaline service conditions not to break down when used as external adhesives for bonding to concrete. It is now accepted that PVAC homopolymer adhesives, however carefully formulated, are not adequately resistant to wet alkaline service conditions because, in time, the polymer breaks down by saponification. Depending upon the precise formulation of the PVAC adhesive used and the service conditions, these adhesives break down in approximately 5–10 years and evidence as to whether the adhesive was used during construction may disappear as the break-down products are water soluble. It is important to note that PVAC homopolymer adhesives are still considered excellent adhesives for bonding many building materials for service in dry internal applications.[7,8,11]

Similar adhesives suitable for service in external or wet service conditions based on other polymer dispersions such as styrene butadiene rubbers, acrylic polymers and copolymers of vinyl acetate with other monomers such as ethylene or vinyl 'Versatate', which are not prone to alkaline saponification, are now widely available.

In recent years, the repair of concrete structures has become a significant part of the construction industry. Many of the repairs are necessary because the steel reinforcement within the concrete has corroded and expanded causing the concrete cover to crack and, eventually, fall off if remedial action is not taken. In many cases, the inadequate concrete cover is removed and replaced by conventional concrete or, often, by a polymer based repair mortar. In a repair situation, the bond between the parent concrete and the repair material is most important. Fully hydrated ordinary Portland cement is itself an excellent adhesive, providing that the prepared surface of the parent concrete can be maintained adequately wet to ensure proper hydration of the cement matrix at this interface. This in practice is often difficult to achieve and an epoxy resin or polymer latex bonding aid is often used to ensure a reliable bond between the repair material and the parent concrete. With an epoxy resin bonding system specifically formulated for bonding green uncured concrete to cured concrete, a bond is achieved which is significantly stronger than the shear strength of good quality concrete or mortar.[9,12]

Polymer latex bonding aids, which are applied to the prepared concrete either as neat coats of latex or as slurries with cement, are widely used. They are more simple to use and cheaper than epoxy resin bonding aids and give a good tough bond which, however, is 'less structural' than that achieved using the correct epoxy bonding aid. However, under severe drying conditions, the 'open time' for polymer latex bonding coats can be too short to be a practical method of ensuring a good bond between the repair mortar and the parent concrete.[9,12]

As an alternative to polymer latex slurry bond coats, there are now available factory blended, polymer-modified cementitious bonding aids based on special spray dried copolymer powders blended with cement, fine sand and other special additives which are simply gauged with water on site and applied to the prepared parent concrete to give a 'stipple' finish. Even when allowed to set overnight, this type of bonding aid gives a good 'key' for the repair mortar and prevents rapid loss of water from the repair mortar, which may result in inadequate hydration at the interface and thus poor bond to the parent concrete. However, application of the repair mortar whilst this key coat is still tacky is recommended wherever practicable. In some instances an epoxy bonding aid is required to function as an impermeable barrier between the repair mortar and the parent concrete. In these cases, two coats of the bonding aid are applied and, whilst still tacky, are dressed with clean sharp sand.[9] This ensures an excellent mechanical key between the two coats and the repair mortar.

In the construction industry, adhesives with high bond strength and high compressive strength are often required and two-component adhesives based on epoxy resins and, to a lesser extent, upon polyester, acrylic or polyurethane resins, are used in a very diverse range of applications. It is important to note that the general term 'epoxy resin' covers a range of ambient temperature curing materials which vary from flexible semi-elastic coatings and sealants to epoxy resin based concretes with compressive properties higher than good quality concrete. Virtually all epoxy resins used in the construction industry are based on Bisphenol A or F resins with an epoxy equivalent weight of approximately 200 and a wide range of hardeners or curing agents based on polyamides, polyamidoamines, aliphatic polyamines, cycloaliphatic amines or aromatic amines modified to give both the curing characteristics at site temperatures and ultimate cured properties required. Other ingredients such as reactive or non-reactive diluents, graded fillers and other additives conferring special properties are often also incorporated by the manufacturer to give specific properties either in the cured or uncured state.

The 'formulation'—the putting together of the complete recipe—of an epoxy adhesive to meet an engineer's requirements is a complex matter and engineers cannot be expected to understand completely the complex chemistry involved. Epoxy resin adhesives used in the construction industry are often derived from formulations originally developed for 'high-tech' applications in the aircraft industry where adhesives can be applied under very controlled application conditions to very carefully prepared substrates. Application of adhesives in the construction industry is inevitably far less controlled and 'formulations' have to be developed so that they are as 'user-friendly' as possible. This may involve colouring the resin and hardener components so that the properly mixed adhesive has a distinctly different hue from either of the components. Ensuring the mixed adhesive will stick to damp concrete over a wide range of substrate temperatures (3–30°C) may be a further requirement and in winter can involve the provision of heating.

One limitation of site applied resin based adhesive which has certainly restricted their use in the UK, significantly more than in some other countries, is that they gradually lose their mechanical properties at temperatures above approximately 60–70°C and become increasingly subject to creep under load as the temperature rises.[13] It is important to note that the thermal conductivity of resin based materials tends to be significantly lower than for conventional cementitious building materials. Nevertheless, this loss of strength restricts their use in structural applications to structures where the risk of fire is minimal or where the structure is designed so that loss of structural integrity does not take place due to loss of strength of the resin material within the time period permitted by the fire regulations. Often resin based adhesives are used in conjunction with some other form of mechanical fixing which is satisfactory for short-term loads under fire conditions, but under repeated dynamic loading in service may break down rapidly. In fact, a 'belt and braces' design philosophy is often used when employing resin based adhesives in the construction industry.[14] A combination of mechanical or chemical anchors with resin based adhesives is often desirable to prevent any possibility of adhesive failure due to peel which tends to be a weak point for rigid adhesive systems, although the strength of the concrete substrate is always the limiting factor.

8.2 Surface treatment

In all cases of bonding, careful preparation of the bonding surfaces to a clean (especially free from oils or greases), sound condition is imperative. Although epoxy resin adhesives which bond well to damp substrates or even under water are now available, for optimum adhesive performance bonding to dry surfaces should be undertaken wherever possible. It is important to note that, in the vast majority of the applications of adhesives in the construction industry, one or both materials to be bonded are concrete or other cementitious material. It is well known that concrete generally has compressive strengths of 20–50 N mm^{-2}, but has much lower tensile and shear strengths. In most adhesive applications the bond strength achieved will depend upon the surface strength of the prepared concrete because the adhesive will generally be much stronger than concrete.

Typical surface preparation procedures for various substrates are described below.

8.2.1 Concrete

The surface of concrete and other cementitious surfaces should be carefully prepared, preferably by mechanical means, to give a clean lightly profiled sound surface. Typical methods include scabbling, needle gunning, grit blasting and high pressure water jetting. Acid etching, generally with 10% hydrochloric acid, can also be used but care must be taken to ensure that all traces of the acid, etc., are removed. In general, the surface strength of the prepared concrete should be greater than 1 N mm^{-2} in tension.

8.2.2 Steel

All steel surfaces should be degreased and abraded to a bright metal finish, ideally by grit blasting to SA 2.5, immediately before bonding. If immediate bonding is not possible, a solvent based epoxy resin holding primer should be applied. Excellent bond strengths are achieved to well prepared conventional mild steels. However, the bond strengths to some grades of stainless steel are less good and special complex chemical surface treatments may be needed to achieve optimum bond performance, although in most applications the bond is more than adequate if the surface is abraded well.

8.2.3 Brick

Brick surfaces should be clean and free from all friable material. In general, scrubbing with a hard bristle brush is adequate. Some bricks have very weak surfaces and should never be bonded with high strength resin adhesives, particularly in external applications.

The bonding of brick slips on to reinforced concrete as an architectural feature is often specified. The use of some form of mechanical support in conjunction with an adhesive is to be recommended. Soft joints at appropriate intervals to accommodate the differential movement between the bonded/pointed slips and the concrete substrate must be incorporated.

8.2.4 Wood

Most woods simply require abrading with a medium abrasive. However, some woods may exude oily substances and require careful degreasing before bonding.

8.2.5 Glass

Glass should be carefully cleaned with a warm detergent solution and dried carefully. The durability of the bond to glass can be markedly improved by pretreating the glass with a solution of a suitable silane coupling agent.

8.2.6 Rubber

Different rubbers may require complex surface treatments to achieve optimum bond performance. Natural rubber, which is commonly used in the fabrication of rubber bridge bearing systems, often contains processing waxes which markedly affect the bond strengths. To ensure high bond strengths the surface should be carefully treated with an appropriate solvent to remove all traces of wax or grease and then carefully treated with concentrated sulphuric acid followed by washing with water and drying. The acid causes the surface of the rubber to harden and form microcracks which provide an excellent key for the adhesive.

8.2.7 Glass reinforced plastics

Glass reinforced plastics simply require careful degreasing with an appropriate solvent and abrading to give a lightly profiled surface.

8.3 Performance testing of adhesives

There are at present very few fully accepted performance tests for resin based adhesives. Consequently, different specifiers often specify adhesives to be tested by different test methods. In the UK, BS 6319: Part 7[15] and BS 6319: Part 4[16] are used, but many other critical properties are tested by many different test methods, some of which are extremely complex and expensive to carry out. At present CEN TC 104 WG8[17] has the task of producing a specification for structural adhesives by the end of 1992 which, it is hoped, will clarify the situation.

8.4 Applications of resin adhesives

The applications for resin based adhesives in the construction industry are very diverse and include:

(1) bonding concrete to concrete—both mature to mature or fresh green concrete to mature concrete to form basically a monolithic concrete between the two layers without the extensive use of mechanical connections; and
(2) bonding brick, masonry, steel, glass, ceramics, wood, glass reinforced plastics, concrete, plastics, rubber, etc., to itself or other materials, but most commonly to mature concrete.[11,14,18,19]

Four interesting applications for sophisticated construction adhesives are described in detail below. These are:

(1) segmental construction of bridges, etc., using stress distributing adhesives;
(2) stengthening of reinforced concrete structures by external bonding of steel plates;
(3) resin injection to repair cracked concrete structures; and
(4) the development of an adhesive for skid resistant road surfaces.

8.4.1 Adhesives for segmental precast, prestressed concrete structures

Much of the development of interesting novel structural uses for resin based adhesives occurred in the early 1960s and their use as stress distributing weatherproof joints for post-tensioned reinforced concrete structures built from precast units is a notable example.

The first reported structures where precast units were bonded together with resin adhesives are the Coventry Cathedral constructed in 1960–1962[20] and Choisy-le-Roi Bridge over the River Seine near Paris constructed in 1962.[21]

Bridge construction, in particular spectacular long-span bridges, is probably the largest tonnage use of structural resin adhesive in civil engineering worldwide. The construction concept using resin adhesives is to cast precast reinforced concrete units using a matched moulding technique so that the matching end of one unit treated with a thin easily removed release film is used as the form for the next unit. This technique ensures that units when installed on site match very well and the resin adhesive joint is very thin (generally 1–2 mm).[11,18,22] Three main factors influence the choice of resin adhesive joints:

(1) *Speed of construction*—in comparison with conventional ordinary Portland cement (OPC) concrete, resin based adhesives develop mechanical strength within much shorter times allowing much more rapid assembly of cast structures. In the famous Sydney Opera House, constructed in 1963–67, construction time savings of approximately 25 weeks were achieved.[22,23] The whole shell roof structure was made up from curved hollow concrete ribs to form a series of continuous spherical surfaces united from precast segments

cast with matching faces and made longitudinally continuous by post-tensioning across transverse epoxy joints.
(2) *To enable a precision design to be accurately set out in the casting yard*—in addition to the speed of construction, the use of a resin adhesive in the construction of Sydney Opera House enabled the critical 'orange segment' geometry of the curved roof to be carefully checked before assembly up in the air.[23]
(3) *Appearance*—architects often require very thin joints so that they are as inconspicuous as possible and do not detract from the continuous flow lines of their designs. Sir Basil Spence was very aware of this benefit when he used resin bonding for the slender cruxiform columns of Coventry Cathedral.

In segmental construction, resin adhesives act as a stress distributing layer ensuring a uniform stress distribution across the joints and, most importantly, because of their dimensional stability and excellent bonding characteristics also ensure a weatherproof joint in long-term service.[24,25]

The stress distributing resin adhesive joint is subject to a relatively low compressive load, generally not more than 10 N mm^{-2}. The ultimate compressive strength of the resin adhesives used is in excess of 75 N mm^{-2} when tested according to BS 6319: Part 2.[26] Experience has shown that creep of resin systems, often of considerable concern to civil engineers, is rarely a problem if the service stress is less than 20–25% of the ultimate strength of the resin. In the case of segmental construction, the aspect ratio of the stress distributing adhesive layer is such that, even at higher stresses, creep should not be a problem. In fact, the first bridge to be constructed using resin bonded joints in the UK, the Rawcliffe Bridge, built in 1966 used an epoxy resin adhesive formulation which is now known to be much more prone to creep than the epoxy resin adhesive formulations used today. Rawcliffe Bridge with its resin bonded joints is reported to be in excellent condition today.[24] Since then, a number of bridges have been constructed in the UK using resin bonded segmental construction, including: the Byker Viaduct, Tyne & Wear, 1979;[25] Trent River Bridge, 1980; East Moors Viaduct, Cardiff, 1984; and Stanstead Abbotts By-pass, 1987 (see *Figures 8.1 to 8.6*).

For this critical application engineers need to be able to specify a suitable adhesive with regards to both practical application characteristics and long-term performance. At present there are no fully established national standards; however, in 1978 FIP produced FIP/9/2,[27] which has been widely adopted although some of the test methods proposed are certainly not commonly used for other structural adhesives.

FIP/9/2[27] comprehensively covers all aspects of adhesive performance. The test methods and acceptance limits listed include the following.

(1) Useable life in 'pot' for a pack of the mixed adhesive in bulk at material temperature on site. Normally a minimum of 30 min is required.
(2) Open time of the adhesive 2–3 mm thick applied on to concrete over the range of site air and substrate temperatures predicted during construction. The adhesive must remain in a fluid state for sufficient time after application to enable the segments to be brought together and the excess adhesive to be squeezed out to ensure full bonding of the matching surfaces.
(3) The rheology of the adhesive is important to ensure that the adhesive can be readily applied uniformly over the surfaces to be bonded and will remain in place without sagging until the bonding is commenced.
(4) The bond strength 24 h after application under typical site temperature and humidity conditions: failure in concrete is generally required.

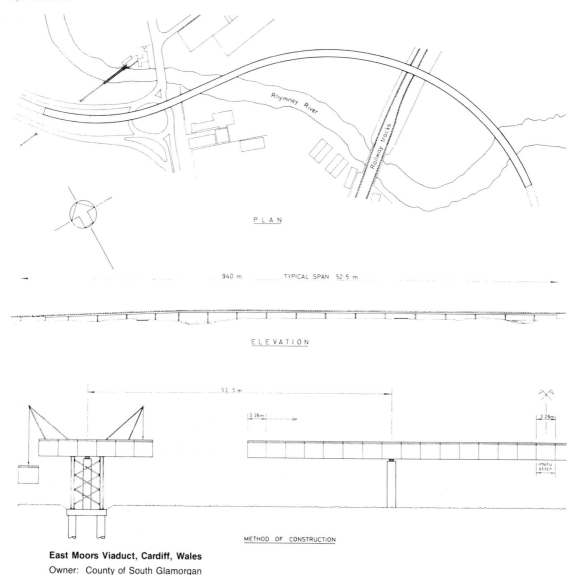

P L A N

940 m   TYPICAL SPAN 52.5 m

E L E V A T I O N

52.5 m

3.28m

3.28m

insitu
stitch

METHOD OF CONSTRUCTION

East Moors Viaduct, Cardiff, Wales
Owner: County of South Glamorgan
Client: Shephard, Hill Ltd.
Value: £7m.

Figure 8.1

(5) Compressive strength: both the rate of development of strength at application temperature and the ultimate strength. The resin adhesive should develop a higher strength than the concrete being bonded within 24–72 h of application.

(6) Shrinkage: the shrinkage of suitable epoxy resin adhesives is generally negligible.

(7) Creep: because the stress levels are low and the aspect ratio high, creep should not be a problem with an adhesive with a compressive strength of at least 75 N mm^{-1}.

(8) Shear strength at maximum service temperature: in the UK adequate strength at 50°C is generally required, otherwise creep could become a problem.

(9) Water absorption: some adhesives can absorb significant quantities of water which will reduce their strength and long-term durability. A maximum water absorption of 0.5% weight after 14 days immersion is generally required.

8.4.2 Strengthening of reinforced concrete structures by external bonding of steel plates

The strengthening of load bearing reinforced concrete structures by bonding on steel plate reinforcement externally is another notable example of the application of construction adhesives. From the published literature, it would appear that the concept was developed almost simultaneously in South Africa and France in about 1965.[28,29] In South Africa, resin bonded reinforcement was used for the rapid emergency repair of a road overbridge damaged by the impact of a mobile crane which ruptured some of the steel reinforcement in several beams.[29]

Since 1965, extensive testing has been carried out in South Africa, France, Switzerland, Japan, Belgium and the UK.[14,28,29–31] This has demonstrated that resin bonding of flat steel plates to the external surfaces of structural concrete beams,

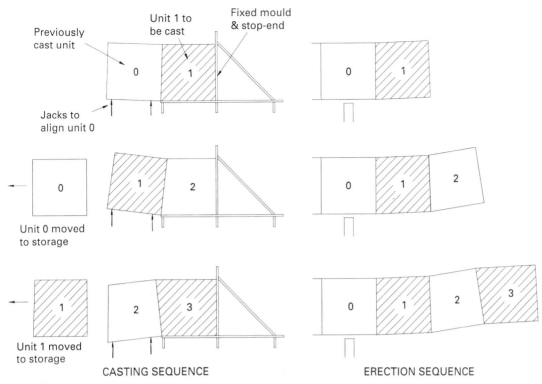

Figure 8.2

Figure 8.3 Reproduced by courtesy of R. Benaim & Partners

East Moors Viaduct, Cardiff, U.K.

Figure 8.4 Reproduced by courtesy of R. Benaim & Partners

columns, etc., can be a practicable and economic way of strengthening highway bridges and buildings.

Because of gradual loss of strength of ambient cured resin adhesives at temperatures above about 60°C (discussed above), the use of resin bond steel reinforcement has been restricted in the UK to the strengthening of highway bridges or other structures where the risk of fire is minimal or to strengthening buildings where the inherent strength of the structure prior to strengthening is considered adequate in the short-term under fire conditions.[13] This technique has been used much more widely in other countries, notably Belgium and Japan, than in the UK.[30]

The first structure in the UK to be strengthened using resin bonded steel plates was an eight-storey building in Harlow, Essex in 1966. Due to a revision of building regulations regarding performance under very high winds, the vertical columns and lift shaft required strengthening which was achieved by bonding steel plates with an epoxy resin adhesive.[11,18]

Several bridges including the M5 Quinton Bridges, 1974,[11,32–34] the M20/M25 Swanley Interchange Bridges, 1977,[9] the M1 Brimsworth Road Bridge, 1983,[35] the A10 Brandon Creek Bridge, 1986, and an overbridge at the M2 Farthing Corner Service Station, 1987,[34] have been strengthened by the use of steel plate bonded on externally using epoxy resin based adhesives.

The strengthening of the Quinton Bridges was undertaken whilst adjacent lanes of the bridge were in service, which meant that, inevitably, the adhesive would be subject to some minor load cycling during curing. Laboratory tests were therefore undertaken to investigate the effect of strain cycling on epoxy resin bonded steel to steel lap shear test specimens during cure of the adhesive. It was found that the shear strength was reduced by approximately 30%. However, the shear strengths achieved were still significantly higher than the shear strength of good

quality concrete, which is the limiting factor in strengthening concrete structures by steel plate bonding.[11,34]

One aspect which short-term and accelerated testing could not fully prove was whether external bonded plates would prove durable in service over many years. It is now 16 years since the Quinton Bridges were strengthened and, apart from some very small areas of corrosion, the externally bonded reinforcement is still performing well. The adhesives used are no longer available because of the potential handling hazards of some of the constituents of the adhesive formulations. However, safer formulations of very similar composition with equivalent performance are available.

In many instances adhesives which have proved satisfactory for use in segmental construction techniques have also been used in steel plate bonding, but properties other than those listed by FIP/9/2[27] need to be considered. These include the following.

(1) A flexural modulus (BS 6319: 1990[36]) of 2–10 kN mm^{-2} is required. If the modulus is outside these limits it may be either too prone to creep or too rigid to withstand possible local stress concentrations in service.
(2) The bond and durability of the bond to steel is important, although the strength of the concrete is generally the most critical factor.

Mays and Hutchinson[33] have suggested two tests for durability based on test methods for adhesives used in aircraft and automobile construction:

(1) a test derived from DIN E 54451: 1977 to measure the shear bond strength; and
(2) a test derived from the Boeing Wedge Test to measure the durability of the resin adhesive/steel bond under stress. Bonded test specimens under stress generated by the wedge can be stored under severe temperature/humidity cycles and

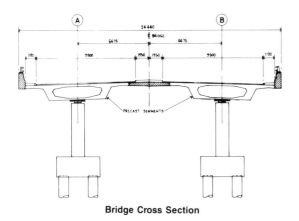

Bridge Cross Section

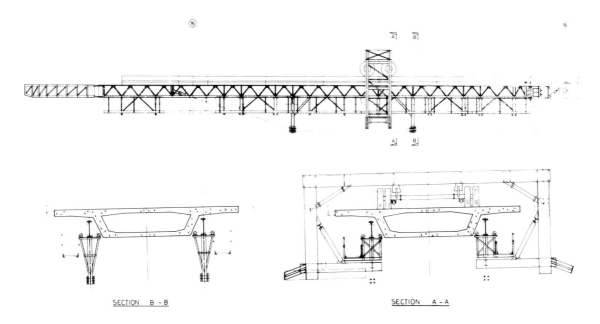

SECTION B ~ B

SECTION A ~ A

Erection Gantry

Stanstead Abbotts by-pass, River Lea and New River Viaducts

Client: Shephard, Hill/Fitzpatrick JV
Owner: Hertfordshire County Council
Value of Contract: £8m.

Figure 8.5 Reproduced by courtesy of R. Benaim & Partners

their performance compared with the performance of proven adhesives systems under the same conditions.[37]

An outline practical specification for the strengthening of structures by the bonding of steel plates is given in Appendix 1.

8.4.3 Structural repair of cracked concrete structures by resin injection

Reinforced concrete structures are designed such that the inevitable cracking of the concrete is restricted so that no cracks at the surface should exceed approximately 200–300 μm thickness. For many reasons, cracking in excess of the design acceptance limits occurs rather too often either during con-struction or during the service life of the structure. If such cracks are not sealed or structurally bonded, further deterioration may occur.

Before deciding on the most appropriate methods/materials for repairing/sealing cracks, it is imperative to establish the cause of the cracking and, where a permanent structural bonding of the crack is required, to carry out any other strengthening which may be necessary. It is possible to restore the structure to the original tensile/shear strength of the uncracked concrete by injection with low viscosity epoxy resins specifically developed for repairing cracks, provided that the bonding surfaces of the concrete at the crack interface are clean and sound. Cracking is caused by tensile stresses and, if these stresses recur after crack repair, the concrete may crack again. If it is not possible to

Figure 8.6 Reproduced by courtesy of R. Benaim & Partners

establish and rectify the cause of the original cracking, it is recommended to cut out along the surface of the crack and treat it as a normal movement joint or, alternatively, to cut out a normal straight movement joint adjacent to the crack and then repair the crack by resin injection.[11,38] In the main, epoxy resin injection systems are used for structural crack repair using gravity, pressure and vacuum injection techniques. Low viscosity polyester and acrylic resins are also used, but their bonding characteristics to slightly damp or even wet concrete, a common occurrence when repairing cracked concrete in the UK, are generally inferior to epoxy resin systems specifically formulated for bonding to wet surfaces.

In cases where it is required to fill/bond a network of cracks with 'dead ends', voids behind tiles or honeycombed concrete a combination of vacuum, to remove the majority of air in the cracks, etc., and pressure injection has proved most effective in some instances.[39,40]

The concept of using epoxy resin injection systems as a means of repairing cracked concrete so that, when repaired, the concrete again acts monolithically has been established for over 20 years and during that time some notable 'rescues' have been carried out.[41]

An interesting example where resin injection proved very effective was in rebonding a 'cold joint' crack which occurred during the construction of a reinforced concrete motorway bridge due to movement of the supporting formwork whilst the concrete was green. Initially, it was thought that this movement had purely caused this 'cold joint', of approximately 0.5 mm width, and sufficient resin was injected to more than fill the 'crack'. Subsequently, it was realized that the movement had also produced voids underneath the reinforcement and further extensive injection of resin was undertaken to fill all the voids and the crack completely. To demonstrate to the engineers that

the resin had restored bond across this 'cold joint' crack, a 100 mm diameter core was drilled at an angle of 30° to the line of the joint. This was a practical site use of the slant shear test developed by Kreigh at the University of Phoenix, Arizona.[42] A modification of this test is now incorporated in BS 6319: Part 4.[16]

The cores taken from the bridge were cut into cylinders and subjected to compressive testing. Compressive strengths of a similar strength to the adjacent monolithic concrete with failure away from the bond line were achieved to the relief of the contractors and engineers concerned. It is reported that, after more than 10 years in service, the repaired concrete continues to perform as if it was monolithic concrete.

In 1975, another most interesting crack repair was carried out which involved the glueing together of a massive crack at the midpoint of a 50 m span of a four-lane carriageway viaduct being constructed across a river valley caused by falsework settlement during construction. This was a massive concrete balanced cantilever, 3 m deep over the central support and reinforced with a mat of four layers of 50 mm bars which occupied the top 250 mm. The 100 mm square grid thus formed effectively prevented access for men to compact the concrete into the main part of the structure below. It was decided to place the concrete up to underside of the reinforcement mat which could then be installed on a convenient horizontal construction joint: concreting could then be completed in a second, much smaller pour.[41]

The bottom pour was carried out as planned and all appeared to be well. A very fine vertical crack that occurred over the central support column was attributed to thermal effects and was not considered important. However, this crack continued to open steadily and it was realized that the mass of unreinforced concrete had divided over the piled support and that the two halves were slowly rotating in opposite directions. Evidently, the scaffold cage support was sinking into the weak alluvial ground upon which it was founded.

After much anxious consideration, it was decided that, if and when this rotation could be halted, then the crack would need completely filling/rebonding with a suitable resin material. It was realized that resin injection before the 'crack' had been stabilized by carrying out the top pour would not be effective. It was, therefore, decided to complete the construction as originally planned but with additional shear connections between the mass concrete and the top layer of reinforced concrete and to then fill the crack with resin. By this time, the crack measured about 2.5 m in height spanning the complete four-carriageway width of the viaduct approximately 23 m and wedge shaped from zero at the bottom to over 100 mm at the top. In order to gain good access to the crack, a 100 mm core was drilled at the centre of the viaduct following the crack down to the bottom. A piece of plastic pipe was bonded into the core which would project above the surface of the top pour. Injection tubes were also fixed down both the side walls of the structure. Within 24 h after placing the top reinforced concrete, the rotation stopped, stabilizing the crack completely.

Resin 'injection' of the stabilized crack was carried out by filling the core with clean dry 5 mm aggregate and then pouring in a long pot life epoxy resin system to fill completely both the 45% voids in the aggregate and the crack. The resin was pressured into the complete depth and width of the crack by using a nitrogen gas cylinder. The complete injection operation took approximately 2 h, the resin being carefully mixed in 4-l batches and a total of approximately 230 l of resin were used. After an appropriate cure period, in this case approximately 3 weeks, a very slow curing resin was used and the concrete temperature was below 7°C. Cores were taken across the crack. These cores demonstrated total filling even at narrow crack widths and excellent bonding across the crack. Thirteen years later, the injection resin is still holding the viaduct together under very heavy traffic loads.

8.4.4 Resin bonded skid resistant road surfaces

In the 1950s, the UK Transport and Road Research Laboratory carried out some research on improving the skin resistance of urban roads. This work indicated that refactory grade calcined bauxite aggregates were much more resistant to polishing under traffic than conventional natural road stones and, not unexpectedly, in tests simulating traffic conditions over a period of 5 years also maintained a much higher level of skid resistance.[29,33]

In the mid-1960s, the Greater London Council (GLC), together with the Traffic Department of the Metropolitan Police, realized a great number of accidents in London involved skidding and took place within approximately 20 m of road junctions, pedestrian crossings and the approaches to roundabouts.[43] The total cost of these accidents to the community, damage to vehicles, ambulance and hospital costs, loss of earnings due to personal injury or death was found to be remarkably high and the GLC sought to come up with a cost-effective method of bonding calcined bauxite chippings on to perfect sound, primarily bituminous, road surfaces which had lost their skid resistance in the vicinity of road junctions, etc. It was accepted that conventional surface-dressing techniques would not be able to hold the calcined bauxite in place under braking forces experienced at road junctions for a sufficiently long time for their use to be economic. The GLC invited resin manufacturers to carry out trials using high performance resin based adhesives to bond calcined bauxite on to the road surface. In the summer of 1966, approximately 10 different resin binders, the majority based on tar or bitumen extended epoxy resin systems, were applied in 1 m wide strips across the A23 close

to Lambeth Parish Church on a sharp corner, approaching a pedestrian crossing. Half the width of the road was treated one Sunday morning and the other the following Sunday.[10] Some of the binder systems had lost the bauxite chippings within 2–3 days of application and it was thought that this was due to the unsuitable rheology of the binder resulting in 'wicking' of the resin up between the chippings, leaving insufficient binder in contact with the road surface to hold the calcined bauxite. Modifications to the rheology were made to these binders by the incorporation of fillers before the second half of the road was treated. This overcame the rapid loss of chippings from these trial strips.

The initial results of these small trials were so promising that, early in 1967, the GLC decided to go ahead with full-scale trials on six major road junctions where a large number of accidents involving skidding had been recorded. These trials rapidly demonstrated the effectiveness and, in the first year, there was a reduction of over 50% in accidents involving injury. It was appreciated that the road areas requiring treating with resin bonded non-skid-surface dressings were all at very busy junctions and it was, therefore, essential that the treatment could be carried out at night and permit reopening the roads fully for the morning rush hour. Special lorry mounted two-component metering and mixing equipment, connected directly to a special sprayer was developed. This proved very effective and the machines developed 20 years ago are still in use today. It has been reported that between 1967 and 1983 some 2000 sites were treated in Greater London which it is estimated has prevented some 30 000 accidents involving injury occurring.[44] In the UK, bitumen extended epoxy resin skid resistant surface dressings have made a significant contribution to road safety by reducing accidents at busy road junctions, roundabouts, etc., and it is now estimated that approximately 500 000–750 000 m² of road surfacing are being treated annually. In most situations, the improvements in skid resistance that can be achieved are durable for in excess of 10 years. There are, therefore, probably in excess of 7 million m² of treated roads in the UK today.

References

1 BUILDING RESEARCH ESTABLISHMENT, *BRE Digest 340 Choosing wood adhesives*, Garston (January 1989)
2 BRITISH STANDARDS INSTITUTION, *BS 4169 Specification for glue laminated timber structural members*, Milton Keynes (1970)
3 BUILDING RESEARCH ESTABLISHMENT, *BRE Digest 314 Gluing wood successfully*, Garston
4 BRITISH STANDARDS INSTITUTION, *BS 3544 Methods of test for polyvinyl acetate adhesives for wood*, Milton Keynes (1962)
5 BRITISH STANDARDS INSTITUTION, *BS 1203 Specification for synthetic resin adhesives for plywood*, Milton Keynes (1979)
6 TIMBER RESEARCH AND DEVELOPMENT ASSOCIATION, *Introduction to the specification of glue laminated members* (1979)
7 BRITISH STANDARDS INSTITUTION, *BS 5270 Specification for polyvinyl acetate (PVAC) emulsion bonding agents for internal use with gypsum building plasters*, Milton Keynes (1976 (1988))
8 COAD, J. R. and ROSAMAN, D., 'Failure with site applied adhesives', *Building Technical File No. 7*, BRE Building Research Advisory Service, Garston (October 1984)
9 SHAW, J. D. N., Materials for concrete repair. *Proc. 1st Int. Conf. on Deterioration and Repair of Reinforced Concrete in the Arabian Gulf*, Bahrain (October 1985)
10 SHAW, J. D. N., 'Adhesives in the construction industry', *Construction & Building Materials*, **4** (June 1990)
11 HEWLETT, P. C. and SHAW, J. D. N., Structural adhesives in civil engineering. In *Developments in Adhesives*, Vol. 1 (ed. W. C. Wake), pp. 25–75, Applied Science Publishers, New York (1977)
12 TABOR, L. J., 'Twixt old and new'. Presented at *Structural Faults and Repair 85'*, ICE Conference, London (April 1985)
13 UK STANDING COMMITTEE ON STRUCTURAL SAFETY,

Fifth Report of the Committee for the Two Years Ending 30th June 1982

14 TABOR, L. J., 'Effective use of epoxy and polyester resins in civil engineering structures[9], *Report No. 69*, Construction Industry Research and Information Association (1978)

15 BRITISH STANDARDS INSTITUTION, *BS 6319 Part 7 Tensile strength using bonded 'dog bone' specimens*, Milton Keynes (1985)

16 BRITISH STANDARDS INSTITUTION, *BS 6319 Part 4 Slant shear strength*, Milton Keynes (1984)

17 *CEN TC 104 WG8 Protection and repair of concrete structures*

18 SHAW, J. D. N., 'A review of resins used in construction', *International Journal of Adhesion and Adhesives*, **2**, 77–83 (1982)

19 MAYS, G. C., 'Structural applications of adhesives in civil engineering', *Materials Science and Technology*, **1** (November 1985)

20 O'BRIEN, T., *Jointing Structural Precast Concrete Units with Resin Adhesives*, RILEM, Paris (1967)

21 *Ann. Inst. Technique Batimen Trav. Publics.*, Suppl. 204 (1964)

22 O'BRIEN, T., 'Resins in construction—20 years experience in many different structures'. Presented at *FeRFA Seminar 'Resins in Construction—20 years experience'*, London (October 1984)

23 ARUP, O. M. and ZUNC, C. J., 'Sydney Opera House', *Structural Engineering*, **47** (March 1969)

24 SIMS, F. A., 'Applications of resins in bridge and structural engineering'. Presented at *FeRFA Seminar 'Resins in Construction—20 years experience'*, London (October 1984)

25 SMYTH, W. J. R., BENAIM, R. and HANCOCK, C. J., 'Tyne and Wear Metro: Byker Viaduct', *Proceedings of the Institution of Civil Engineers, Part 1*, **68**, 701–718 (1980)

26 BRITISH STANDARDS INSTITUTION, *BS 6319 Part 2*, Milton Keynes

27 FIP, *FIP/9/2 A proposal for a standard for acceptance tests and verification of epoxy bonding agents for segmental construction* (1978)

28 HUGENSCHMIDT, F., 'Epoxy adhesives for concrete and steel'. Presented at *First International Congress on Polymer Concretes*, London (May 1975)

29 FLEMING, C. J. and KING, G. E. M., *The Development of Structural Adhesives*, RILEM, Paris (1967)

30 MAYS, G. C. and RAITHBY, K. D., 'Bonded external reinforcement for strengthening concrete bridges', *Contractors Report DGR 474/229* to Transport and Road Research Laboratory, Crowthorne (1984)

31 VAN GEMERT, D. and MAESSCHALK, R., 'Structural repair of a reinforced concrete by epoxy bonded steel reinforcement', *The International Journal of Cement Composites and Lightweight Concrete*, **5**, 247–255 (1983)

32 MANDER, R. F., 'Bonded external reinforcement—a method of strengthening structures'. Presented at *Symposium on Adhesives and Sealants in Building*, Plastics and Rubber Institute, London (1977)

33 MAYS, G. C. and HUTCHINSON, A. R., 'Engineering property requirement for structural adhesives', Paper 9327. *Proceedings of the Institution of Civil Engineers, Part 2*, 485–501 (September 1985)

34 GILL, J. D. and TILLY, G. P., 'Use of resin bonded plates for strengthening reinforced concrete', Institution of Civil Engineering, Structural Engineering Group Informal Discussion, London (7 October 1987)

35 JONES, R., SWAMY, R. N. and HOBBS, B., 'Bridge strengthening using epoxy bonded steel plates', *Highways—Concrete 90* (July 1990)

36 BRITISH STANDARDS INSTITUTION, *BS 6319 Part 3*, Milton Keynes (1990)

37 MARCEAU, J. A., MOJI, Y. and McMILLAN, J. C., *Adhesives Age*, 28–34 (October 1977)

38 SHAW, J. D. N., 'The use of resin injection techniques in construction and repair'. Presented at *Symposium on Adhesives and Sealants in Building*, Plastics and Rubber Institute, London (1977)

39 ANON., 'Vacuum—new accessory for repair', *Concrete Construction*, **24**, 315–319 (May 1979)

40 HEAYES, N., 'Balvac speeds up repair jobs', *Contract Journal* (8 March 1979)

41 SHAW, J. D. N., 'The use of epoxy resins in structural repairs: some interesting case histories'. Presented at *International Conference on Structural Failure ICSF 87*, Singapore Concrete Institute (March 1987)

42 AMERICAN CONCRETE INSTITUTE, 'Causes, evaluation and repair of cracks in concrete structures', *Committee Report No. 2241.R-84, ACI Journal* (May–June 1984)

43 LAMB, D. R., 'Some UK developments in skin resistant road surfacings'. Presented at the *Second International Skid Prevention Conference*, Columbus, Ohio (May 1977)

44 STOTT, P., 'Institution of Civil Engineers, President's Inaugral Address, London 7 November 1989', *New Civil Engineer*, 50–51 (9 November 1989)

45 BRITISH STANDARDS INSTITUTION, *BS 1204: Parts 1 & 2 Synthetic resins (phenolic and aminoplastic) for wood*, Milton Keynes (1979)

46 BRITISH STANDARDS INSTITUTION, *BS 6446 Specification for manufacture of glued structural components of timber and wood based panel products*, Milton Keynes (1984)

47 SIMS, F. A., 'The application of epoxy resins in bridge construction with particular reference to Rawcliffe Bridge'. Presented at *Resins and Concrete Symposium*, University of Newcastle-upon-Tyne (April 1973)

48 SHAW, J. D. N., 'Epoxy resin compositions—materials for the engineer'. Presented at symposium *Liquid Polymers*, University of Surrey, Guildford (1972)

49 GAUL, R. W. and SMITH, E. D., 'Effective and practical structural repair of cracked concrete', *Special Publication No. 21, Epoxies with concrete*, American Concrete Institute (1963)

50 SHAW, J. D. N., 'The use of epoxy resin for the restoration of strength of deteriorated concrete structures'. *Symposium on Advances in Concrete*, Concrete Society, Birmingham (1971)

51 KREIGH, J. D., 'Arizona Slant Shear Test', *Journal of American Concrete Institute*, **73**, 373–377 (1976)

52 GILES, G. C., 'The skidding resistance of roads and the requirements of modern traffic', *Proceedings of the Institution of Civil Engineers*, **6**, 216–249 (February 1957)

53 JAMES, J. G., *Report LR 84, Calcined bauxite and other artificial, polish-resistant roadstones'*, Transport and Road Research Laboratory, Crowthorne (1967)

54 HATHERLY, L. W., MAHAFFY, J. H. and TWEDDLE, A., 'The skid resistance of city streets and road safety', *Journal of the Institution of Highway Engineers*, **16**, 3–12 (1969)

Appendix 1: Specification for steel plate bonding

A typical practical specification for the site bonding of steelwork to concrete structures is as follows.

A.1 Epoxy resin adhesive

The adhesive shall conform with the performance requirements of the specification. The material shall be stored, mixed and applied strictly in accordance with the manufacturer's instructions.

A.2 Site conditions

The work shall be carried out in a protected environment, at a temperature between 5°C and 25°C or other temperatures in accordance with the manufacturer's instructions. The location of the concrete beams, position of anchors, etc., relative to the steelwork to be bonded should be checked. (Note: anchors installed into the concrete are required both to assist installation and to ensure that there is no possibility of adhesive failure occurring at the plate ends due to peel.)

A.3 Application

The bonding shall be carried out by an approved specialist subcontractor under the supervision of an operative experienced in this type of work, in accordance with the manufacturer's instructions.

A.3.1 Preparation of concrete

The bonding surfaces of the concrete shall be grit blasted to ensure all concrete laitance and other contaminants are removed and to produce a clean roughened surface with a maximum profile of approximately 2 mm.

Any local irregularities protruded by more than approximately 2 mm shall be carefully removed by appropriate means to be agreed with the engineer.

Where the level of concrete surface is out of place by more than 2 mm the surface shall be grit blasted as above and the surface levelled to the tolerances required by the application of an epoxy resin mortar as approved by the engineer, in accordance with the manufacturer's instructions.

The bonding of the steel plate on to surfaces trowelled with an epoxy resin mortar shall take place within 16 h. If this is not possible the mortar surface shall be grit blasted to expose the surface of the aggregate particles in the mortar.

A.3.2 Installation of anchors

The location of the reinforcement within the concrete shall be established using an approved cover meter. Drill holes in the concrete and install the anchors according to the engineer's instructions. Stop drilling *immediately* if reinforcement is encountered and obtain further instructions from the engineer. Under no circumstances should the reinforcement be damaged by drilling. Install the anchors according to the engineer's instructions.

A.3.3 Fabrication of steelwork

Check the trowelled surface regularity, etc., of the concrete and the location of the anchors relative to the new steelwork to be bonded in place.

The steelwork shall be fabricated according to the instructions from the engineer. Care shall be taken to ensure that holes drilled in the steelwork are correctly aligned with the holes drilled in the concrete to take the anchors.

A.3.4 Surface preparation of the steel surfaces

All steel bonding surfaces shall be cleaned to remove all grease or other contamination and the surface grit blasted to Swedish Standard Quality SA 2.5 with a profile not exceeding 100 μm using a chilled cast iron grit to G 24 BS 2451. Immediately after blasting a two-pack epoxy bonding primer, as recommended by the manufacturer of the adhesive, shall be applied to give a dry film thickness of 15–20 μm. When the primer has cured (approximately 24 h) carefully wrap the fabrication in polythene sheet (or similar) to ensure bonding surfaces do not become contaminated or suffer mechanical damage before erection.

The primed surfaces shall be flash grit blasted immediately prior to bonding into place. Any small areas of damaged surface shall again be grit blasted to SA 2.5 immediately prior to applying the adhesive.

A.3.5 Bonding steelwork into place

The mixing and application of the adhesive shall be carried out using a mechanical mixer in accordance with the manufacturer's instructions under the supervision of an operative experienced in this type of work.

The adhesive shall be spread on to the bonding surfaces of the steelwork at a rate of approximately 5–8 kg m^{-2}. The adhesion shall be applied to form a longitudinal ridge along the centre line of the plate.

The steel shall be offered up to the prepared concrete and bolted into position without delay. The bolts and wedges (where appropriate) shall be tightened to ensure that the adhesive is squeezed out all along the sides of the steel and complete contact of the adhesive and steel over the whole bonding area is assured. The excess adhesive shall be carefully cleaned off before it sets.

A.3.6 Protection of the steelwork

Once the adhesive is fully cured the exposed surfaces of the steelwork shall be carefully coated with an approved anti-corrosion coating system in accordance with the manufacturer's instructions.

9

Asbestos

R Harris BSc
Wimpey Environmental Ltd

Contents

9.1 Introduction 9/3
    9.1.1 Structure and physical properties 9/3
    9.1.2 Historical origins and uses of asbestos 9/4

9.2 Mining and processing methods 9/4
    9.2.1 Extraction methods 9/4
    9.2.2 Milling 9/4

9.3 World production of asbestos 9/5

9.4 Practical applications of asbestos in construction and industry 9/5
    9.4.1 Asbestos textile products 9/6
    9.4.2 Asbestos cement products 9/7
    9.4.3 Asbestos insulating board 9/9
    9.4.4 Asbestos insulation materials (thermal) 9/10
    9.4.5 Asbestos insulation materials (acoustic) 9/11
    9.4.6 Sprayed coatings 9/11
    9.4.7 Felts, plastics, textured paints and other asbestos containing materials 9/12

9.5 Legislation 9/13
    9.5.1 Historical development 9/13
    9.5.2 Modern legislation 9/13

9.6 Health effects of exposure to asbestos 9/14
    9.6.1 Asbestosis 9/14
    9.6.2 Lung cancer 9/15
    9.6.3 Mesothelioma 9/15
    9.6.4 Other asbestos related illnesses 9/15

9.7 Asbestos control and maintenance 9/16
    9.7.1 Planned maintenance 9/16
    9.7.2 Encapsulation of asbestos 9/16
    9.7.3 Removal of asbestos 9/16

Bibliography 9/17

9.1 Introduction

Over the centuries, since the first recorded use of asbestos, the mineral has become progressively more popular as its many physical and chemical properties became known. In fact for many reasons asbestos has become a household name. The range of products in common use which contain asbestos is very large. The common perception of asbestos as the corrugated sheeting on garage and factory roofs is merely the tip of the iceberg. The layman would probably be surprised to learn that asbestos may be found in many domestic installations from the brake pads on his car to the textured paint on his ceilings and possibly in the dental amalgam used in his fillings. The applications of asbestos in the construction industry are no less diverse.

9.1.1 Structure and physical properties

Asbestos is the general term used to describe a number of naturally occurring crystalline metal silicates which, because of the array of physical and chemical properties they possess, such as their resistance to chemical attack, immense thermal stability and good tensile strength, have become extremely useful materials for use in many industrial and construction applications. The minerals, when crystallized, form narrow parallel rods in tight groups or bundles. These minerals, if physically stressed will break not only into shorter lengths, but will split into progressively finer fibrils. It is this particular facet which is the major reason for the mineral's array of physical properties.

There are six main types of asbestos which have been used over the years, namely chrysotile (commonly known as white asbestos), amosite (known as brown asbestos), crocidolite (blue asbestos), anthophyllite, actinolite and tremolite. Several other minerals are classed as asbestos but have not been commercially used for various reasons. Asbestos can be classified into two groups, the serpentines and the amphiboles, labels which refer primarily to aspects of their crystalline structure (see *Table 9.1*).

Chrysotile is the only popularly used serpentine mineral, though other non-fibrous asbestos types, lizardite and antigorite, are also serpentines. The serpentine group is distinct from the amphibole group in that their crystalline structures are formed in layer lattices. Chrysotile appears white to the naked eye, hence its popular name of white asbestos.

Amphiboles, which include the remainder of the asbestos types mentioned, are chain silicates which means that, in contrast to the layered crystalline formation of the serpentines, they form preferentially along the lengthwise direction of the fibres, giving them a strong lengthwise tensile strength. Crocidolite and amosite are the only amphibole minerals to have been mined in significant quantities. Visually, crocidolite appears deep blue to turquoise in colour and amosite a distinctive grey brown.

Chrysotile, because of its crystalline structure, has a very soft nature when broken in fibre tufts, thus making the material ideal for weaving. Amphiboles, and in particular amosite, are very rigid and hence unsuitable for weaving, but have excellent

Table 9.1 Asbestos types, chemical formulae and physical properties

Asbestos type	Approx. chemical formula	Asbestos group	Colour	Physical properties
Chrysotile	$3MgO, 2SiO_2, 2H_2O$	Serpentine	White/pale green	Alkaline resistance: good Acid resistance: poor Heat resistant to: 650°C Average density: 2.5×10^3 kg m^{-3} Tensile strength: very good
Amosite	$5.5FeO, 1.5MgO, 8SiO_2, H_2O$	Amphibole	Pale brown	Alkaline resistance: good Acid resistance: fair Heat resistant to: 800°C Average density: 3.3×10^3 kg m^{-3} Tensile strength: good
Crocidolite	$Na_2O, Fe_2O_3, 3FeO, 8SiO_2, H_2O$	Amphibole	Blue/turquoise	Alkaline resistance: good Acid resistance: good Heat resistant to: 650°C Average density: 3.3×10^3 kg m^{-3} Tensile strength: excellent
Anthophyllite	$7MgO, 8SiO_2, H_2O$	Amphibole	White/pale brown	Alkaline resistance: good Acid resistance: excellent Heat resistant to: 800°C Average density: 3.0×10^3 kg m^{-3} Tensile strength: poor
Actinolite	$2CaO, 4MgO, FeO, 8SiO_2, H_2O$	Amphibole	Pale green	Alkaline resistance: fair Acid resistance: fair Heat resistant to: 900°C Average density: 3.1×10^3 kg m^{-3} Tensile strength: poor
Tremolite	$2CaO, 5MgO, 8SiO_2, H_2O$	Amphibole	White	Alkaline resistance: good Acid resistance: excellent Heat resistant to: 1000°C Average density: 3.0×10^3 kg m^{-3} Tensile strength: poor

thermal properties which have been utilized in a variety of insulation materials.

9.1.2 Historical origins and uses of asbestos

Asbestos is an extremely versatile and abundant naturally occurring material which has been used by man for over 4000 years, though commercial exploitation of the material is somewhat more recent. The earliest known instance of its use was as a binding and reinforcing additive to pottery, examples of which, reinforced with asbestos, have been found in archaeological sites in Finland and have been estimated as dating back to before 2000 BC.

Reference has been made to the use of asbestos in ancient Egypt, China and Greece. In fact the ancient Greeks were so impressed by the material's amazing fire resistance and its hard-wearing nature that they gave it the name by which we know it today, derived from the Greek for indestructable—asbestos. The Romans are known to have used asbestos as lamp wicks and, when woven, as heat-resistant cloth. Applications such as these, though, were very rare and the material was treated as something of a novelty. There is very little evidence of asbestos being used in the Middle Ages outside the occasional instances as lamp wicks in parts of Europe and Asia.

Asbestos was not fully exploited as a major commercial commodity until the 19th century. At this time the mineral caught the imagination of the textile industry in Europe where textile manufacturing had boomed, primarily in France and the north of Britain. Mill owners were quick to spot the market-place potential of a material whose fibres could be woven like wool or cotton to produce a virtually indestructible fire-resistant fabric.

Chrysotile (white) asbestos was the most amenable to milling and manufacture, whilst the amosite and crocidolite varieties were too rigid and brittle to be woven. As a result, in 1877, the first large-scale commercial mining operations commenced in Canada. Two mines were sunk in Thetford and Coleraine, but could not keep pace with demand. Further mining operations started in other parts of Canada to be followed shortly in Russia and many other parts of the world. From these small beginnings, production grew from 10 000 tonne year^{-1} in 1880 to 95 000 tonne year^{-1} in 1925.

In the 1920s amosite and crocidolite began to be mined in significant quantities. Amosite and crocidolite exhibit excellent thermal-insulation properties and tensile strength and became popular for use in a variety of products, though their main use was as a constituent in insulation materials. Asbestos-board products were manufactured on a large scale for the first time. Asbestos cement and later asbestos insulation boarding were produced in vast quantities in purpose-built factories which further fuelled the need for more and more asbestos to be mined.

In the 1930s the first serious doubts about the health effects of working with, or being exposed to, asbestos were confirmed and legislation, the first of a series of progressively more stringent codes of practice for work with asbestos, was issued. This had no effect whatsoever on the demand for the material and production continued to rise at ever faster rates.

The advent of the Second World War, rather than slowing the production of asbestos, actually increased production to record levels. The virtual destruction of European cities led to an even greater need for asbestos—large numbers of families were homeless and to provide immediate shelter large numbers of estates of prefabricated dwellings were constructed all over Europe, these dwellings being almost entirely clad with asbestos cement sheeting.

Asbestos production soared up to the 1970s when the stringent controls on asbestos were introduced. Eventually, in 1985, the importation of amosite and crocidolite was banned along with the installation of any product containing them. In the minds of the public and Government, asbestos was too dangerous to be considered for future use. The installation of asbestos is now practically at an end. Its safe removal and disposal is the huge task which remains.

9.2 Mining and processing methods

9.2.1 Extraction methods

Asbestos is a mineral and, despite the basic formation processes being the same, from the mining and extraction point of view the different varieties of asbestos present a series of different problems. Two factors which affect the cost-effectiveness of a potential mining operation include the type of asbestos involved and the effects of geological movement on fibre orientation.

9.2.1.1 Effect of asbestos type

In general, serpentine and amphibole minerals crystallize out in the bedrock in different ways; chrysotile, for example, is typical for serpentine mineral formation. Seams of chrysotile are very narrow, generally between 10 and 50 mm in thickness, but are usually found in several close-packed layers. The thickness of the seams and their proximity to adjacent seams is an important factor in deciding whether a seam formation is worth mining as this usually decides the amount of non-asbestos material which has to be extracted at the same time and hence the percentage yield. Amphiboles, however, are usually formed in thicker seams varying between 10 and 250 mm.

9.2.1.2 Effect of geological movement on fibre orientation

Under ideal conditions when a mineral seam is formed, asbestos crystallizes at right angles to the surrounding rock faces, a condition sometimes called 'cross-fibre formation'. From an extraction point of view this condition maximizes the exposed portion of fibrous asbestos, minimizes the potential interface with the adjoining rock and, consequently, increases the potential yield of the ore. In cases where geological action has effected this situation and transverse movement occurs within the surrounding bedrock, the fibre direction is seen to be roughly parallel to the surrounding rock and the seam is condensed. The relative interface with the surrounding rock is increased and the amount of fibrous mineral which can be extracted is reduced. The worst case would be if the seam were grossly distorted. This would mean that the fibrous mineral is practically enmeshed in loops of surrounding bedrock and hence the proportion of bedrock which needs to be mined to release a significant proportion of asbestos would increase so much as to become prohibitive.

The yield of asbestos from the parent rock in a good seam would be approximately 25%. For economical mining, 10% asbestos content by weight is more usual.

The most common extraction method is by open-cast mining, though occasionally asbestos is mined from deep pits. If the surrounding bedrock is of a hard formulation it is not uncommon for drilling or dynamiting to be used in order to expose the asbestos. The mining operation is normally quite indiscriminate and extracts a high percentage of non-asbestos material enmeshed with the mineral which has to be extracted. The next distinct phase in the operation to produce pure fibrous asbestos is called milling.

9.2.2 Milling

The initial refining process is the separation of bedrock from the fibrous material. The asbestos ore is then ready to be refined to eliminate the remaining rock and to leave it in the form of separated asbestos fibre clumps.

In modern methodology the first stage is the mechanical crushing of the ore to expose and free the fibrous asbestos. At this stage the mineral is hydrated and separation of the distinct fibres in this state is difficult. In most modern mills the surface moisture is extracted by passing the crushed ore through a high-temperature kiln, usually maintained at 160°C. This is sometimes combined with a vibratory system to keep the ore constantly agitated to help in the separation process.

The dried mineral ore is then ready for grading, although additional crushing stages are sometimes necessary. The grading process is carried out sequentially, sieving over vibrating trays which are usually inclined with the crushed ore being poured over them. As it falls, the heavier pieces of ore, usually including pieces of the parent rock, fall to the base quickly whilst the remaining fibrous material segregates along the trays according to size and weight.

There are a series of vacuum extraction hoods at intervals along the tray system which pull out the partially graded asbestos fibres. Depending upon the need for accuracy in the grading of the ore this process may be repeated one or more times. It is possible to grade to fibre length if required at this stage which is important for chrysotile intended for textile manufacturing.

The final graded material is generally stored in hoppers before being bagged in preparation for transportation to the manufacturing process. There are three grades of milled fibres, crude fibres, which are generally the longer fibres for use in textile production, mill fibres and shorts, the lowest grade. In the production of chrysotile, approximately 8% of total fibre output can be used for textile manufacture.

In the early days the milling process was quite different. Ore was mechanically crushed but grading was done using open sieving trays. The quality of the final product was very poor by modern standards. Often the fibres were opened by hand, a process known as 'hand cobbing' where the excess rock was hacked off with hammers to expose the asbestos. This practice was quite common, especially in areas where labour was cheap.

The shipment of the fibrous mineral is now carried out under relatively stringent conditions. The raw material is usually sealed inside industrial-grade polythene bags, rather than the earlier hessian sacks, which are then transported inside sealed containers.

Usually, further stages of milling are required before the mineral can be used in particular manufacturing processes. Textile production usually requires complete separation of chrysotile fibres before weaving can commence.

The crude opened chrysotile fibres are normally fed into a carding machine where they undergo a highly mechanized process designed to turn the raw material into a series of asbestos strands for future weaving. The carding machine comprises a series of large, very quickly rotating cylinders whose surfaces are covered with tiny metal spikes. Chrysotile fibre is fed onto the rotating cylinders and the rotating spikes have the effect of 'combing' the fibres, getting them into a fairly parallel orientation and then feeding them into a spinner which produces a single sliver or rope. The carding process was extremely dusty. Early attempts at wetting the carding process failed as it led to premature rusting of key components inside the carding machines.

9.3 World production of asbestos

Compared with the tonnage of asbestos which is mined today, the production total up to the end of the 19th century is negligible. No commercial usage could be seen for the material although its physical properties were well known and documented. Serious commercial production commenced in 1876 in Canada where the large chrysotile deposits were mined, primarily for export to Europe for use in the production of fire-resistant textiles. The first chrysotile mines were at Thetford and Coleraine and were shortly followed by a series of mines across Quebec province. Chrysotile mining commenced in Russia in approximately 1880 and, as demand increased, mining operations began in places such as Australia, Zimbabwe, Swaziland, the USA, Turkey and Italy, but Canada remained the main production centre for asbestos, producing approximately 75% of world tonnage.

By 1890 world production of chrysotile had just reached $10\,000$ tonne year^{-1}, and this figure rose to $25\,000$ tonne year^{-1} by the turn of the century. At this point the commercial extraction of crocidolite was commencing and was followed shortly by the large-scale mining of amosite. Crocidolite was found mainly in South Africa, though deposits were also exploited in Australia and South America.

However, amosite was only found in workable quantities in the north-east Transvaal area of South Africa and full-scale mining of the mineral started in approximately 1910. The demand for amosite and crocidolite increased steadily with their use in boarding products and as thermal insulation, but they still only comprised a very small fraction of the overall world production of asbestos which was dominated by chrysotile. By the end of the 1920s the annual production of chrysotile had reached $120\,000$ tonne year^{-1}.

By 1945 the annual production of chrysotile had reached nearly $600\,000$ tonne, with crocidolite being mined at $11\,000$ tonne year^{-1} and amosite at $12\,000$ tonne year^{-1}.

Despite growing concern about the health effects of exposure to asbestos, the material continued to be used in even greater quantities in the post-war construction boom. The national priority was to build large numbers of modern well-constructed homes for an increasing population, many of whom were still living in Victorian slum accommodation or bomb-damaged housing.

Large numbers of estates and high-rise developments were constructed in the 1950s and 1960s and asbestos featured frequently in their construction, both for insulation purposes and, more importantly, as a fire precaution. By the 1960s chrysotile production had reached 3 million tonne year^{-1} with crocidolite and amosite production rising to $60\,000$ tonne year^{-1}.

It was in the 1970s that the extent of the health problems associated with even minor exposure to asbestos was realized. Public awareness of the issue grew and pressure increased for action against the use of asbestos.

The installation of asbestos materials was discouraged in Britain and most other developed countries in the west, culminating in 1985 with the banning of the importation and use of crocidolite and amosite or any products containing them. This has led to the slowing down in the rate of production of all types of asbestos (see *Figure 9.1*).

Today, production levels for all types of asbestos stands at around 5 million tonne year^{-1}. However, with the increasing worldwide ban on the use of asbestos and increasing availability of non-asbestos replacements, the future production levels seem likely to fall, although usage in the third world is likely to persist for the foreseeable future.

9.4 Practical applications of asbestos in construction and industry

Asbestos has been incorporated in a vast array of products which have been used by the construction industries, from the earliest

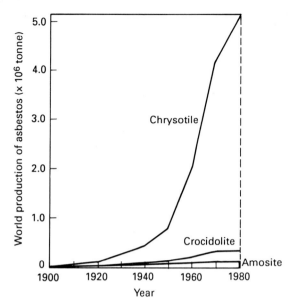

Figure 9.1 Growth in world production of asbestos to 1980 with production levels for chrysotile, amosite and crocidolite

chrysolite rope used as fire-proof gasketting to boilers and fires, through to asbestos cement sheeting as a roofing material and as thermal insulation to hot-water services.

The different varieties of asbestos were found to have different physical and chemical properties which have been used in a range of products which take best advantage of these abilities. A summary of approximate asbestos content and types of asbestos used in popular construction materials is shown in *Table 9.2*.

Asbestos was not really used as a construction material until 1910 with the advent of asbestos cement sheeting and the use of asbestos on a large scale for thermal insulation. After that date the variety of uses increased dramatically until it became arguably one of the most versatile construction materials in use.

The British Standards for asbestos products are listed in *Table 9.3*.

9.4.1 Asbestos textile products

As mentioned in the Introduction, asbestos, even in its early usage was found to have very good fire-resistant properties. Chrysotile, when crudely broken up to expose its fibres, shows fibres of sufficient length and flexibility to be woven into fabric. This ability was fully exploited in the 1870s and led to the major commercial usage of the material that we know today.

Crocidolite, in some isolated cases, has been woven into fabric, but generally the amphibole minerals are too rigid and liable to lateral breakage to be used in textile products. Chrysotile has been used almost exclusively for this purpose.

The method of manufacture of asbestos fabric is similar to that for ordinary textiles. Following initial milling of the chrysotile ore the raw material is sorted into longer fibres which undergo several refining stages whereby the fibres are opened and cleared of contaminants before being passed on for spinning into thread. The thread can be prepared in several thicknesses and in several degrees of refinement depending upon the final product in which it is to be used. Extremely coarse thread is used in the manufacture of chrysotile rope for gasketting and padding purposes, whereas finer threads of higher quality are

sent to the weaving mills for use in the production of textiles such as fire blankets and electrical-wire covering.

In appearance, chrysotile thread is a white silky material, similar to white canvas in the woven form, but relatively heavy. The material is hardwearing, difficult to cut and, because of its general use as a fire-retardant material, the weave is to an extremely close specification so as not to allow fire or thermal penetration.

Textiles are woven in a range of thicknesses and styles. Asbestos tapes are typically 3–10 cm in thickness. Asbestos rope is available in thicknesses up to and, occasionally in excess of, 10 cm. The woven fabric has been produced in thicknesses of 1800–3600 mm and is simply stitched together where larger coverage is required.

Asbestos fabric has been used in a number of products over the years, such as fire blankets, which are commonly used in plant rooms, kitchens and laboratories, fire-proof asbestos suits, gloves and helmets used in a variety of industrial applications, including foundry work, and the fire services. Asbestos rope has been used extensively as a sealing material and as gasketting to boilers, flues and around fireplaces. It has also been used occasionally as thermal insulation. Asbestos tape is used in gasketting and seals, for thermal and electrical insulation in fuses and as fire curtaining in theatres. It was used extensively before, and just after, the Second World War as an outer insulation wrapping to high-tension electric cables.

Being manufactured out of virtually pure chrysotile, asbestos fabric, if excessively abraded, is likely to shed large numbers of asbestos fibres into the air and it is consequently treated as a significant potential hazard. Because of this and the ever more stringent legislative controls on the use of asbestos, fire blankets and other heat-resistant products are rapidly being removed from service and replaced with non-asbestos alternatives.

Glass fibre and some other man-made mineral fibres are the most popular replacement materials and are almost as efficient as chrysotile. They have been used to manufacture virtually all of the products previously made with chrysotile but are, of course, much more expensive to produce. A minor problem with man-made mineral fibre is the tendency for the fibres to break and fray when the material is damaged or creased; hence the working life of non-asbestos products is generally shorter than their asbestos counterparts.

Table 9.2 Typical asbestos content and types used in common asbestos products and materials

Asbestos material	Probable asbestos content (%)	Main asbestos types used*	Other asbestos types used*
Textured paint	2–12	Ch	A
Bituminous felt	3–20	Ch	
Thermoplastics	5–20	Ch	A
Asbestos cement	10–20	Ch	C
Insulation board	15–40	A	Ch, C
Asbestos millboard	30–65	A	Ch
Gasket material	30–60	Ch	An, A
Brake linings	30–60	Ch	
Thermal insulation	20–75	Ch, C, A	
Sectional insulation	30–80	Ch, A	C
Spray coatings	60–90	A, C	Ch
Asbestos textiles	60–100	Ch	C

* Ch, chrysotile; C, crocidolite; A, amosite; An, anthophyllite.

Table 9.3 British Standards and associated documentation for asbestos products

Product	Standard
Asbestos cement	
Boards impregnated for electrical purposes	BS 3497: 1979 (1986)
Building products—test methods	BS 4624: 1981
Corrugated sheet roof and wall covering	BS 5247: Part 14 (1975)
Flue pipes and fittings (light quality)	BS 567: 1973 (1989)
Flue pipes and fittings (heavy quality)	BS 835: 1973 (1989)
Pipes and fittings for sewerage and drainage	BS 3656: 1981
Pressure pipes and joints	BS 486: 1981
Rainwater goods	BS 569: 1973 (1987)
Slates and sheets for building	BS 690: Parts 1–4 (1973–1981)
Cisterns	BS 2177 (withdrawn)
Asbestos cement decking	BS 3717 (1972) (withdrawn)
Soil, waste and ventilating pipes and fittings	BS 582: 1965
Asbestos cement pipelines	
Field pressure testing	BS 5886: 1980
Guide for laying	BS 5927: 1980
In land	CP 2010: Part 4, 1972
Asbestos insulating board	
Asbestos insulating boards and asbestos wallboards	BS 3536 (withdrawn)
Sprayed asbestos	
Sprayed asbestos insulation	BS 3590 (withdrawn)
Others	
PVC (vinyl) asbestos floor tiles	BS 3260: 1969
Bitumen sheet roof coverings	CP 143 (16)
Asbestos packed sheet conduit	BS 731: Part 1, 1952 (1980)
Untreated asbestos paper (for electrical purposes)	BS 3057: 1958
Woven tape for electrical insulation	BS 1944: 1973 (1984)
Compressed asbestos fibre jointing	BS 2815: 1973
Compressed asbestos fibre jointing (oil resistant)	BS 1832: 1972
Compressed asbestos fibre jointing (rubber bonded for aircraft)	Aero FD5

9.4.2 Asbestos cement products

Asbestos cement products are by far the most common asbestos-containing materials in use and it is estimated that approximately 70% of world asbestos production is used in its manufacture. The range of products made with asbestos cement is diverse. Its origins lie in the late 19th century when crude cement products were first made, but it was realized that, despite its obvious potential, hand-made cement products were not a commercial proposition.

The mechanized production processes required were vigorously researched but were not realized until 1910 when the standard production method, which is basically the same as that used today, commenced operation.

Asbestos cement is manufactured using chrysotile asbestos (occasionally crocidolite is used in addition to the chrysotile) mixed with Portland cement. The process involves mixing finely graded tufts of chrysotile with Portland cement and water, usually with chrysotile comprising 10% of the overall bulk although this is liable to change slightly from time to time and with different brands. These raw materials are thoroughly mixed to form a paste which is then poured into flat trays.

Suspended in the slurry in the trays are a rotating array of cylinders whose surfaces are meshed so as to sieve the slurry, picking up the cement-covered asbestos fibres on its surface. As the cylinders rotate, they come into contact with a moving conveyor belt, the speed of rotation of the cylinder matches that of the conveyor belt and, as the two moving surfaces come close to contact, strong suction pressure is applied through the conveyor belt, effectively sucking the slurry off the rotating cylinder and onto the belt.

The thin layer of chrysotile and Portland cement is then carried along on the conveyor belt to the next phase of the manufacturing process. At the far end of the conveyor belt the material is cut into selected lengths which are transferred onto another series of rotating cylinders. This process continues with more and more layers being added onto the roller until the coating has reached the required thickness.

The material is quite malleable, but retains its form when cut and stripped from the cylinder. In this state it can be cut and formed. This process provides the raw material used for a variety of asbestos cement products.

When dried and formed, asbestos cement is an extremely hard formulation material (approximate density $1600 \, \text{kg m}^{-3}$), grey in appearance and very difficult to break. If cracked, the exposed edges are usually fairly straight with obvious clumps of chrysotile fibres sticking out. The material is very hard wearing and is designed for external use, its effective life is usually 30–40 years, although weathering and the effects of algae and mosses may reduce the time before the material saturates and the cementitious bonding collapses.

The material is extremely hard wearing but does undergo slight changes when first installed in an open environment. The surface will initially be effected by rainfall which, because of general air pollution, is slightly acidic. This reacts with the Portland-cement bonding to dissolve the cement preferentially, exposing the asbestos tufts, but this effect is slight and quickly stabilizes. The boarding tends to compress with age and this

Figure 9.2 Corrugated asbestos cement sheeting and asbestos cement rainwater goods

has the effect of increasing the material's hardness, but at the expense of increasing the board's tendency to cracking when impacted. In the first few months of use all sheeting products warp slightly which can result in cracking problems if the board has been too tightly fixed.

Generally, because of the hardness of cement products and the relatively small amount of asbestos present, it is very difficult to liberate fibres from the material. Normal handling of asbestos cement will not create a significant hazard, but elevated airborne fibre levels will be created if the material is machined.

9.4.2.1 Sheeting (corrugated and flat)

Asbestos cement sheeting is manufactured in a variety of forms, shapes and sizes (*Figure 9.2*). Boards are shaped by pressing the still-wet chrysotile cement sheet between two flat formers to produce flat asbestos cement panels, or onto corrugated formers to produce the very popular corrugated asbestos cement sheeting. These panels have been manufactured with a variety of profile designs. The main use for these sheets is as roofing panels and exterior cladding to buildings. Indeed, after the Second World War asbestos cement sheeting was used in vast quantities to build prefabricated dwellings. The durability of the material is further demonstrated by the fact that estates of these asbestos cement 'prefabs' are still standing and being used today.

The material is generally produced in 2400 mm × 1200 mm sheets, but the different types of corrugated and shaped boards will obviously vary in size.

The roofing sheets are fixed in a variety of ways, usually by retaining bolts or screw nails. However, due to the hard nature of the board, it is likely to crack under excess pressure. Hence asbestos cement panels are usually fixed with rubber or moulded metal washers to prevent damage during installation. Due to the long serviceable life of asbestos cement boarding, it is often the fixings which decay first and hence it is common to find the retaining bolts covered with a rubber or plastic seal to provide weather protection. The retaining bolts are usually 6 or 8 mm in diameter depending on the size and the shape of the board they hold. The holes through which the retaining bolts are placed should be 2 mm larger in diameter than the retaining bolts to allow a degree of movement of the board. If too tightly fixed, the board would be liable to crack as it warped with time.

One problem associated with asbestos cement sheeting is the way it behaves in fires. At high temperatures the differential stressing inside the board increases to such an extent that the material shatters in an explosive manner. Although this process is described as a problem, in some cases it may be an advantage since it would form holes which could ventilate any possible fire.

Today there are many non-asbestos replacements available. Their physical characteristics are similar to asbestos cement and they are becoming more popular in use. They contain cellulose, calcium silicate and glass fibres instead of chrysotile and are manufactured in much the same way as asbestos cement.

9.4.2.2 Rainwater goods

Asbestos cement has been used to make a range of roofing accessories and rainwater goods including ridging tiles, guttering and drainpipes (*Figure 9.3*). The products are manufactured in the same way as asbestos cement sheeting, the only difference being in the final moulding operation. Guttering and specially-shaped tiles are formed by allowing the still-malleable asbestos cement to fall into preshaped moulds. Similarly, the piping products, including rainwater pipes and larger diameter drain products, are formed by wrapping the cement material around a cylindrical former. This technique has been widely used in the manufacture of asbestos cement water tanks and cisterns which were installed in large numbers in post-war housing stock.

Non-asbestos replacements for these products are available but, again, are expensive in comparison to the original asbestos cement products. Typical replacement materials include plastics, aluminium and steel.

9.4.2.3 Slates

Asbestos cement slate-like roofing tiles have been used extensively for many years. They have proven to be a cheap, attractive alternative to other forms of roofing tiles; they are relatively light and hence require a reduced level of roofing support.

The tiles are usually 6-mm thick, are of very hard formulation and are manufactured with various colouring additives or coatings to give the distinctive slate-grey appearance. The tiles usually contain between 10% and 30% chrysotile asbestos.

Asbestos cement slates differ from natural slate in several ways: they do not display the laminar splitting of real slate; they are all identical in size, shape and thickness; the external surface is very smooth; and the obverse face has a characteristic, stippled effect.

In the 1980s several asbestos-free imitation slates came on the market and sold well, probably due to widespread bans being placed by local authorities on the installation of asbestos products in housing. Some asbestos-free slates are virtually identical to their asbestos counterparts and can only be told apart under microscopic examination.

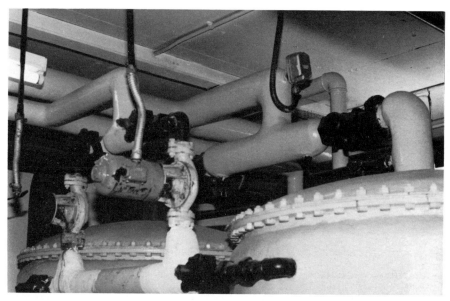

Figure 9.3 Asbestos insulation to pipework

9.4.2.4 Decking, decorative goods and high-temperature flues

The vast majority of asbestos cement production is taken up by the manufacture of asbestos cement sheeting and rainwater goods. A small proportion has been used for various diverse applications.

Certain asbestos cement products are coloured and textured to provide highly decorative, hard-wearing products. One popular brand is 'Eternit' boarding which can have a high-gloss black surface finish and which contains approximately 30% chrysotile. Eternit has mainly been used to make roof tiles, but has also been used as window ledging, for worktops and as battening to window surrounds. The material was produced in a range of shades and was popular in schools where it was sometimes used as a chemical-resistant worktop for laboratories.

Flue piping, though generally constructed with chrysotile, was occasionally made with amosite asbestos. This was used for flues where high temperatures were likely and for which amosite, with its excellent thermal qualities and high tensile strength proved invaluable.

Asbestos cement was popularly used in the manufacture of walkway and decking tiles. Walkway tiles were a common phenomenon on flat asphalt roofs. The tiles are normally 12 in. square and 0.5 in. thick and are held in place with bitumen adhesive to form hard-wearing pathways across the flat asphalt. The material was installed predominantly in the 1950s and 1960s and is mainly found in large high-rise blocks.

9.4.3 Asbestos insulating board

Asbestos insulating board products are generally softer and less dense than their asbestos cement counterparts, having a density of approximately $500 \, \mathrm{kg \, m^{-3}}$ and have a greater percentage content of asbestos. Chrysotile, amosite and crocidolite have all been used in the manufacture of insulating boards, but by far the most commonly used constituent is amosite.

The percentage content of asbestos varies, typically being 20–40%, but greater proportions of asbestos are not uncommon, especially in the millboard varieties.

The method of manufacture of the boards is intrinsically the same as for asbestos cement sheeting. However, there is one main difference which lies in the constituent materials used. In products such as Cape Board's 'Asbestolux', lime is used instead of cement and is mixed with the silica and cured with high-pressure steam to form a strong cementing compound.

Asbestos insulation boarding is usually manufactured in 2400 mm × 1200 mm sheets and in a range of thicknesses, typically 6, 9 and 12 mm, although some boards were manufactured up to 50 mm in thickness. Other standard products have also been made, including ordinary and drilled acoustic ceiling tiles.

Insulation boarding is usually grey/white in appearance and is relatively soft in comparison to asbestos cement. However, it is liable to breakage and abrasion if excessively stressed. If the boarding is broken it will expose a jagged fibrous edge with clusters of fibres (usually amosite) being clearly visible.

Insulation boarding is normally used internally or in semi-sheltered locations. It has excellent resistance to humidity and damp but is liable to degenerate if saturated. This material exhibits good thermal insulation and offers fire resistance up to approximately 1100°C, hence it is understandable that its main practical application is as a fire-retardant barrier.

Typical installations of asbestos insulation boarding include fire-retardant panels to heater cupboards, ducts, doors and ceilings, partition-wall panels, internal thermal insulation to curtain walling, acoustic and general-purpose ceiling tiles and soffit boarding to stairs and eaves. Insulation boarding will be found, predominantly, in post-war buildings. Its installation reached a peak in the 1960s and early 1970s when its use was so popular that large buildings constructed without insulation boarding are the exception rather than the rule.

The production of asbestos insulation boarding ceased in the UK in 1980 and the import of amosite, the main fibrous additive to the boarding, was banned in 1985. It is possible that insulation boards manufactured before 1980 may have been installed some considerable time after this date and it is therefore dangerous to assume, purely because of the date of installation of a board, that the same board cannot contain asbestos.

Non-asbestos insulating boards have been available for many years and are being used to replace their asbestos counterparts as they are removed for maintenance or health-and-safety reasons. These boards are produced in a similar manner to asbestos boards, but contain a mixture of man-made or vegetable fibre generally mixed with mica. The boards are mostly softer than their asbestos counterparts and, although they are similar in appearance, can sometimes be told apart by the glittering effect of mica being present on the board's surface. A typical example of non-asbestos insulation board is 'Supalux' which is produced by Cape Boards.

Examples of proprietary brand asbestos insulating boards which were commonly used are Asbestolux, Marinite and Turnasbestos.

Asbestos insulation board, if disturbed, is likely to liberate significant levels of airborne asbestos and, if drilled or machined, may give off enough fibres to exceed the current control limits. As with all asbestos products, work involving its disturbance or removal is subject to notice being given to the appropriate enforcing authority and should be carried out by licensed contractors.

9.4.4 Asbestos insulation materials (thermal)

One of the major physical properties of asbestos is its excellent thermal resistance and, after asbestos boarding products, asbestos insulation is the next most popular application of the material. All types of asbestos have been used in thermal insulation, but although amosite and crocidolite exhibit the best thermal characteristics (due in part to their bulk when opened) and have proved to be the most cost-effective to use, chrysotile is the most frequently used component in insulating products.

The main application of asbestos in this role is as insulation to hot-water and steam pipes (*Figure 9.3*) and cladding to boilers and calorifiers, though occasionally the raw material has been used in a variety of roles such as loft and cavity-wall insulation. The material has also been sprayed onto surfaces to form insulating layers; this is discussed in more detail in Section 9.4.6.

The insulation properties of asbestos have been known for many centuries, but it was not until the early 20th century that it was thus used in any significant quantity. In its most common form the material was applied by hand as a thick paste to pipes, boilers and other hot surfaces where heat retention was required. This thermal insulation material, for use on pipes and boilers, was made with three main constituents: a bonding mortar, a filling material, and a fibrous binding agent.

The fibrous binding agent was usually one or more varieties of asbestos and could well have been mixed with some other non-asbestos fibre such as glass fibre or vegetable fibre. The bonding agent would normally be a lime or mortar compound, and the mixture was usually filled with diatomaceous earths, silica and a variety of other ingredients which were at hand when the batch was mixed. There were virtually no specified or proprietary brand mixtures for insulation materials and hence the make-up of the material was very haphazard.

The insulation was mixed on site by the lagging contractors, usually in a large drum. The ingredients, in ever-varying proportions, were mixed with water into a very thick, clay-like consistency, and handfuls of the material were then applied to the appropriate surface or pipe. The surface was normally pre-prepared by the addition of a chicken-wire wrapping to provide a bond, but this was not always the case. If the material was to be sealed into a duct and had little prospect of disturbance or being seen, then it is unlikely that any decorative surface coating would have been applied, but if it was in open view a thin outer layer of a plaster-like matter (itself often containing asbestos) may have been applied. In most cases the surface was finished off by use of a wet cloth being rubbed over the surface of the insulation which provided a smooth finish and prepared the insulation for painting if required. A distinctive feature of asbestos insulation to pipework was the rounded effect at the end of each length of insulation.

This basic method by which asbestos insulation was applied has changed little over the years and asbestos-free insulation materials are applied in this manner even today.

Asbestos insulation was installed until the early 1970s, and the thermal qualities of these materials were excellent, but varied dramatically due to the differing mixtures used. The installation method, however, was also very slow, labour intensive, and, consequently, expensive. Therefore it was not surprising that eventually a manufacturing process was created to make preformed sections of asbestos pipe and boiler insulation.

This material was usually manufactured using chrysotile or amosite and was formed by compressing the material into shapes suitable for direct application onto pipes and boilers. The preformed sections were available in a full range of sizes to fit all commonly used pipes and in various thicknesses designed to provide a range of thermal conductivities. The material usually contained a very high percentage of asbestos and would be held in place with a muslin or canvas outer covering with metal retaining clips set at regular intervals. Insulation blocks for use on boilers and other hot surfaces were either held in place with chicken wire and an outer plaster coating or wire pinned to the boiler casing and then covered. The material is quite soft and could be cut easily with a knife to fit any discontinuities in the insulated surface.

Since there have been so many variations of pipe insulation, it is extremely difficult to predict if a given piece of insulation contains asbestos or not. Some other insulation methods which include asbestos as an additional, though not obvious, ingredient include preformed sectional glass fibre or paper pipe insulation where all bends, corners and discontinuities in the pipes are covered with asbestos, and when asbestos has been used as an inner insulating layer and covered by an outer glass fibre sectional layer. If it is suspected that the material contains asbestos it is wise to have the material tested by a competent analytical laboratory, with samples being taken to the core of the insulation in several representative locations.

Due to the high percentage content of asbestos in insulating materials and the relative ease with which they can be damaged, there is a high potential risk of large numbers of asbestos fibres being released into the air. In the past insulation has been very badly damaged during maintenance. Unfortunately it has been installed on pipes and boilers where mechanical failures occur regularly and, due in part to ignorance of the dangers involved and the need to repair any faults quickly, in many cases the insulation has simply been hacked off for ease of access, creating a serious environmental hazard.

Damaged areas should be noted and remedial action carried out as soon as is practicable. It is important to remember that under current legislation all work involving this material should be carried out by licensed specialist contractors and that 28-days notice of intention to work on the material should be given by the specialist contractor to the appropriate enforcing authority.

Asbestos insulation materials have been installed primarily in large buildings such as schools, hospitals, factories and also on ships, all of which make use of large boiler-fired heating and hot-liquid systems. In large buildings the distances that the heated water is required to travel could be very great indeed and hence the need for good thermal insulation is paramount.

Since the Second World War there have been many non-asbestos insulation products on the market, mainly manufactured with man-made mineral fibres such as glass fibre or rockwool. These are usually in preformed sections for ease of installation. However, their thermal properties are generally not as pronounced as for asbestos insulation and the material, if unprotected, is liable to deteriorate rapidly, especially in areas of regular maintenance.

9.4.5 Asbestos insulation materials (acoustic)

Asbestos as an acoustic insulation material is a relatively modern phenomenon dating back to the years just before the Second World War for its first significant use. There are several product types which have been applied in an acoustic-insulation role, namely sprayed asbestos, asbestos boarding, loose raw asbestos and composite materials containing asbestos.

Sprayed asbestos is one of the most popular noise-reducing agents in use. This popularity is due in part to its joint advantages of combining noise attenuation with thermal insulation and fire resistance. The application and make-up of the sprayed material is described in Section 9.4.6, but the property which gives sprayed asbestos its noise-attenuating properties is the way in which the fibre tufts are blown onto the surface, leaving tiny gaps and air passages honeycombing the surface layers. Basically, a large proportion of the incident noise landing on the surface will be diverted along these passages and dissipated.

The most popular locations where sprayed asbestos is used as acoustic insulation are in theatres, where the material is applied to walls and ceilings, the ceilings of plant and boiler rooms and basement car-parks where there is occupied accommodation above. Asbestos-free sprayed coatings are now commonly available utilizing mica instead of the usual amosite or crocidolite.

Asbestos insulation board is very popular in offices and public areas where general noise reduction is required. The material itself is not particularly noise reductive, the noise-attenuating ability coming primarily from the shaping and marking of board surfaces.

Two main types of acoustic-insulation board are in common use: (1) drilled board which has holes (approximately 5 mm in diameter) drilled at regular intervals across the board; and (2) the more modern textured boards which have a sculptured surface with many air gaps which act as deflective acoustic traps. Both types of insulation board are normally found as tiling to suspended ceilings and are designed to cut down reflected noise rather than transmitted noise as in the case of sprayed asbestos. Hence, these ceiling tiles are normally used in offices to soak up general office noise in their textures and holes.

The material was installed on a large scale in post-war Britain, but gave rise to certain maintenance problems. As mentioned earlier, the tiles were mainly attached to suspended ceilings above which many electrical and water services often run. This meant that the tiles were regularly being removed to facilitate maintenance. The tiles were normally screwed onto the suspended ceiling frame which meant that inconsiderate maintenance removal led to regular breaking of the boarding due to its soft nature.

Modern acoustic tiling is manufactured with textured surfacing using either glass fibre or other man-made fibrous material. These tiles have the advantage of being light and are usually unfixed, just resting on the suspended ceiling frame, giving quick uncomplicated access to the ceiling void.

Other acoustic insulation uses of asbestos have included the raw asbestos mineral in its loose fibrous form being used as acoustic padding to ceilings and walls. However, this type of installation is rare and is not thought to have been a standard use.

Asbestos has been used in many instances in partnership with other materials to provide acoustic insulation. Its most common form is as insulation boarding with slabs of man-made mineral fibre, usually in a sandwich construction, added to walls and ceilings to reduce noise transmission and to increase thermal insulation. This is typically found in converted buildings where the structure use has changed and where more stringent controls on noise and fire/thermal insulation are required such as converted houses in multiple occupation.

Figure 9.4 Sprayed amosite to structural steelwork

Chrysotile mixed with coarse felt has occasionally been used to provide an acoustic matting for use in auditoria. This was mainly installed in theatres and cinemas from 1920 onwards and was stuck to the walls with heavy adhesive and covered with canvas.

All acoustic uses of asbestos rely on the soft and open nature of the material to provide the acoustic attenuation. It is this softness which also makes the materials potentially very hazardous as they will readily liberate large numbers of asbestos fibres if disturbed or broken. For this reason, great care should be taken when dealing with possible asbestos acoustic materials.

9.4.6 Sprayed coatings

The spray coating of surfaces with asbestos is a relatively modern process and is designed to apply a coating quickly and efficiently either for acoustic, thermal or fire insulation to surfaces and structural steelwork (*Figure 9.4*).

The method uses raw finely crushed and opened asbestos fibre, a cementitious binding compound and water. The asbestos, usually crocidolite or amosite, is fed into a hopper and is mixed with the binding agent and water in a high-pressure compressed-air stream. This material impacts on the surface at very high velocity where it adheres. In many cases the sprayed surface is primed with an adhesive agent first. Application continues until the specified thickness of coating has been achieved. The relatively small amount of moisture would eventually evaporate and the material would dry into a semi-rigid but easily damaged coating.

Typical uses of sprayed asbestos include sprayed coatings to ceilings of boiler rooms, schools, basement car-parks, etc., where a combination of fire resistance and acoustic or thermal insulation is required and, more frequently, applied to the structural steel framework of buildings as a fire-resistant barrier. It has proved especially useful in the latter application. Being a sprayed coating it can penetrate awkward gaps in steelwork and give a quick efficient all-over fire-proof coating. Most steel-framed buildings are sprayed with a sufficiently thick coating to provide 1-h fire resistance which roughly corresponds to a coating thickness of approximately 15–20 mm. However, with time the material has been known to lose adhesion and fall away exposing sections of steel.

The application of sprayed asbestos to steelwork was generally not used until after the Second World War. The first documented evidence on the use of this method in the UK was in 1935 when it was used as sprayed fire and thermal insulation to railway carriages.

Other instances of the material's use include acoustic insulation to auditoria, and fire proofing and thermal and acoustic insulation to ships bulkheads.

Since this material comprises large amounts of loosely bonded, raw asbestos fibre it is considered to be potentially the most hazardous form of asbestos currently in use. The coatings are soft and very easily damaged. It has been used in plant rooms and other high-activity areas which are liable to regular disturbance and, hence, to the possibility of damage. *In schools, where the material is frequently used, it is often disturbed and played with by children.*

Very large numbers of asbestos fibres are easily released into the air with only slight disturbance of the coating and, because of this, the material is being removed by specialist contractors and replaced with modern asbestos-free sprayed coatings which use mica or vermiculite.

Serious asbestos-related diseases are frequently being diagnosed amongst operatives who have carried out asbestos spraying in the past and, because of this, the spraying of asbestos is now banned in many countries, including the UK.

9.4.7 Felts, plastics, textured paints and other asbestos containing materials

Asbestos, primarily chrysotile, has been included in a great many relatively minor applications over the years. Some of the other diverse uses which have found application in construction are included below.

9.4.7.1 Thermoplastics and reinforced plastics

Asbestos has been used in conjunction with plastics to produce a series of products. The best known use is as thermoplastic floor tiling commonly found in kitchens and bathrooms. Thermoplastic floor tiles were made with a small proportion (typically 5–10%) of chrysotile asbestos which was finely opened before mixing with the thermoplastic resins and colouring additives. This means that the material is very well bonded and it is virtually impossible to extract or find the asbestos in the material. Therefore, from a health point of view the tiling presents a relatively minor hazard in normal usage.

There were several variants of this material including linoleum products which contained chrysotile. This linoleum was relatively heavy duty and is more likely to be found in public buildings, offices and factories. Modern thermoplastic floor tiles do not contain asbestos.

9.4.7.2 Textured paints

Many textured paints contained a small proportion of chrysotile asbestos as a binding and texturing agent. The usual percentage content was less than 5% and was often less than 1% in later brands. The paints were intended for both internal and external applications and gave a long-lasting decorative finish.

The paints were sold in powdered form to which water was to be added, or ready made up. The material did give some cause for concern in its powdered form as it could liberate asbestos fibres during mixing. It may also pose a hazard during removal as the material bonds well to correctly prepared surfaces and is difficult to dislodge. If power tools are used to abrade the paint off a surface then it is likely that elevated levels of airborne asbestos will arise.

9.4.7.3 Jointing materials and gaskets

Chrysotile has typically been used in the manufacture of gasketting and jointing products for many years. It has been used in the pure woven form (see Section 9.4.1) in boiler and heavy plant applications, but also in conjunction with other materials.

Chrysotile cloth has been used with a rubberized coating for liquid gasketting purposes and has been used extensively in engine gasketting. This particular form of gasketting is made of resinous material mixed with finely graded chrysotile, usually as much as 60%, which is evenly distributed throughout the matrix. In applications such as cylinder head gasketting in automobiles, the gasketting compound is usually sandwiched in a metal casing. However, as ordinary gasketting, it is used on its own.

9.4.7.4 Asbestos paper

Asbestos paper products have been made for many years and are used in several applications. The manufacturing process for asbestos paper is much the same as for ordinary paper. Finely opened asbestos fibres are suspended in water to form a slurry, which is evenly sieved and spread onto a fine mesh felt forming surface, compressed to expel the majority of the water, and heated to dry the material which is then rolled and available for use. Amosite is the most widely used type of asbestos in the manufacture of asbestos paper, though chrysotile and crocidolite have been used.

The paper, in this basic form, is used for fire-retardant purposes in locations such as linings to electrical fuse boxes, though its other main use is in a thermal insulation role. In this case the paper is made in various thicknesses and formed into a corrugated 'cardboard' effect sheeting. This is often used as insulation to the outer casings of boilers and flue pipes (*Figure 9.5*) and was used to manufacture preformed sectional pipe lagging in the years after the Second World War.

In appearance, the material is light grey and looks like ordinary paper. It is easily abraded and can generate significant levels of asbestos fibres if damaged.

9.4.7.5 Bituminous felts

Felts produced with bituminous backing were frequently manufactured with a small chrysotile content to increase the

Figure 9.5 Asbestos paper (corrugated) as thermal insulation to a hot water cylinder

material's bonding strength and to prevent cracking due to temperature fluctuations. The main usage of the material has been as a roof covering, but it has also been used as damp proof coursing and as flashing. The practical lifetime of roofing felts varies as it is prone to damage, but is at least 10–15 years.

The finely opened chrysotile asbestos is immersed in the bituminous material and is very difficult to extract, hence the material presents a minor health risk with normal handling.

Other minor uses of asbestos include its addition to sealants and mastics where a very small proportion of chrysotile has been added to provide bonding and to prevent slumping.

9.5 Legislation

9.5.1 Historical development

Since the large-scale commercial use of asbestos began in the UK in the late 19th century, a series of chronic illnesses began to occur with alarming regularity among workers in the asbestos industry. At first the correlation between the disease and exposure to asbestos was not really noticed, but by 1910 a series of papers had been published following years of research which linked cases of what we now call 'asbestosis' to people who had worked in the asbestos industry. The disease was of the lungs and was obviously related to inhaled airborne asbestos dust. In the 1920s many more cases of asbestosis were diagnosed among asbestos workers and it eventually became so obvious a health risk that the government was forced to act.

In 1931 the Asbestos Industry Regulations were drafted which eventually came into force in 1933. These regulations were aimed solely at the asbestos manufacturing industry and were designed to improve the working conditions of asbestos workers. Great emphasis was placed on lowering dust levels at the workplace. This meant the increasing introduction of air-extraction systems to industrial processes alongside tighter requirements on the standards of shopfloor cleanliness, plus the compulsory medical surveillance of all asbestos workers.

In the 1920s the asbestos industry had expanded rapidly and into many new areas. Asbestos work was no longer confined just to the factories and, although chrysotile was by far the most popular form of asbestos used, amosite and crocidolite were being installed in significant quantities. The installation of asbestos as insulation in particular caused many people to be exposed to very high levels of asbestos fibres. Gradually, as the long-term effects of asbestos exposure of laggers and other associated workers began to appear with even greater frequency, it became clear that the Asbestos Industry Regulations were inadequate. They were not diverse enough to cover all types of asbestos-related works. To compound the problem, new types of asbestos-related disease were being diagnosed, including lung cancer and mesothelioma, incidences of which appeared to be associated with exposure to crocidolite. Mounting pressure eventually resulted in the introduction of The Asbestos Regulations (1969). These regulations applied to all factories including construction sites and anywhere else where asbestos works are undertaken. The only asbestos works exempt from these regulations are those which do not give off asbestos dust.

The regulations again placed great emphasis on the ventilation of work processes, good house keeping and the safeguarding of personnel by personal respiratory protection and protective clothing.

Strict codes of practice for all work involving asbestos were introduced, including the regular servicing of equipment and the requirement to notify Her Majesty's Inspectorate of Factories at least 28 days before works, including removal, on any asbestos material which contained crocidolite.

However, the one area not covered by legislation was the non-occupational exposure to asbestos. This shortcoming was eventually to be covered by the implementation of the Health and Safety at Work, etc., Act (1974).

9.5.2 Modern legislation

The Asbestos Regulations (1969) and the Health and Safety at Work, etc., Act (1974) were the hub of modern-day legislation on work with asbestos products. The Health and Safety at Work Act placed a great deal of responsibility not only on employers, but also on employees to safeguard the health and well-being of all other persons involved with asbestos works.

The act required employers to provide training and supervision of staff to ensure health and safety, the preparation of a specific safety policy and the requirement that any asbestos-related works which were carried out did not expose anybody to risk. Employees were similarly charged with maintaining their own health and safety and that of anybody else who is likely to be affected by their actions.

The Asbestos Regulations and the Health and Safety at Work Act, although giving a series of legislative requirements, did not give any detailed advice on the practical implementation of its requirements in what was becoming an increasingly specialized and technical field. To answer many technical questions raised by the legislation a series of guidance notes and codes of practice were issued by the Health and Safety Executive (see *Table 9.4*). These give guidance on such matters as the likely levels of airborne asbestos to be expected during typical asbestos processes, recommended protective equipment, and procedures for working with various asbestos products and installations.

9.5.2.1 The asbestos (Licensing) Regulations (1984)

In the early 1980s, in line with ever more stringent legislation governing the handling of asbestos, the Health and Safety Executive began considering methods of controlling and monitoring persons to be allowed to carry out works on the more hazardous types of asbestos products. To implement this a licensing system was considered. The draft document was put forward in 1983 and was fully introduced in August 1984 as the Asbestos Licensing Regulations (1984).

Table 9.4 Summary of current legislation, Codes of Practice and Guidance Notes for work with asbestos

---

Legislation
The Control of Asbestos at Work Regulations (1987)
The Asbestos (Licensing) Regulations (1983)
The Asbestos (Prohibition) Regulations (1985)
The Health and Safety at Work, etc., Act (1974)

Codes of Practice
Approved Code of Practice—The Control of Asbestos at Work
Approved Code of Practice—Work with Asbestos Insulation, Asbestos Coating and Asbestos Insulating Board

Guidance notes—Environmental Hygiene Series
EH 10   Asbestos: Exposure Limits and Measurement of Airborne Dust Concentrations
EH 35   Asbestos Dust Concentrations at Construction Processes
EH 36   Work with Asbestos Cement
EH 37   Work with Asbestos Insulating Board
EH 41   Respiratory Protective Equipment for Use Against Asbestos
EH 47   The Provision, Use and Maintenance of Hygiene Facilities for Work with Asbestos Insulation and Coatings

These regulations stated that a person cannot carry out work on asbestos insulation materials or asbestos coatings unless they possess a licence issued by the Health and Safety Executive. This was primarily an attempt to improve the standards of asbestos-removal contractors whose performance was not controllable. Indeed anybody could have set themselves up as an asbestos-removal contractor, no proof of professional competence having hitherto been needed. Under the new regulations, significant departures from, or contravention of, the asbestos regulations could result in a large fine and possible withdrawal of their license, which resulted in a ban on carrying out further asbestos removal operations. The regulations also insisted on regular medical examinations for all operatives involved in asbestos works and for the introduction of formal training on health-and-safety aspects of asbestos-removal works.

9.5.2.2 *Asbestos* (*Prohibitions*) *Regulations* (*1985*)

In the early 1980s serious action was being considered in the UK and in Europe to stop the use of asbestos insulation and spraying and to discourage the import of what were considered to be the more hazardous amphibole varieties of asbestos for use in the asbestos industry.

Draft proposals for the Asbestos (Prohibitions) Regulations were prepared in 1983 for consideration, but were not adopted or enforced until 1985. The main effects of the document were that amosite and crocidolite were banned from being imported, as was their use in the manufacturing processes. The sale of products which contained amosite or crocidolite was also banned. The use of asbestos products containing chrysotile in any form of insulation role was also banned as was the use of asbestos-spraying techniques. Other uses of asbestos were exempt, including asbestos cement and other low dust products with a minor asbestos content.

9.5.2.3 *Control limits*

With the introduction of The Asbestos Regulations (1969) there had been no real quantified level of airborne asbestos dust which was set as the hygiene standard to be achieved. This was due, in no small part, to the fact that there was no practical method of measuring the airborne dust levels. However, guidance in this area was needed, and eventually arrived in the 1970s when recommended airborne asbestos levels were set at two fibres per millilitre of air (fibre ml^{-1}) for chrysotile and amosite and 0.2 fibre ml^{-1} for crocidolite since it was thought to be the most hazardous type of asbestos.

Employers, for a given asbestos process, were required to attempt to reduce the airborne asbestos fibre levels to the minimum practicable level. If this level was above these control limits then respiratory protection should be worn by workers. If below this level respiratory protection was deemed to be unnecessary. These figures were adopted in the issue of formal guidance notes in 1976, but this was still for guidance only and was not, as yet, a legal requirement. In 1983 the latest draft of Guidance Note EH10 was issued and the control limits were decreased to 1 fibre ml^{-1} for chrysotile, 0.5 fibre ml^{-1} for amosite and 0.2 fibre ml^{-1} for crocidolite. These limits were changed again in 1984 to 0.5 fibre ml^{-1} for chrysotile and 0.2 fibre ml^{-1} for crocidolite and amosite.

9.5.2.4 *The Control of Asbestos at Work Regulations* (*1987*)

In 1987 new regulations were drafted to replace the ageing Asbestos Regulations (1969). The Control of Asbestos at Work Regulations (1987) were designed to take account of new developments in the asbestos field, to extend the range of cover

of the regulations and to include the control limits, making them legally enforceable for the first time.

The new regulations, implemented on 1 March 1988, had several main features. Now, most work involving the disturbance of asbestos must be formally assessed by employers and the likely levels of exposure to asbestos predicted. Once this has been carried out the employer is obliged to take action to either prevent or reduce it. This is to work alongside the now regulatory control limits, which are the airborne asbestos fibre levels above which respiratory protection must be worn.

Action levels have now been introduced which are levels of asbestos exposure over a 12-week period above which the Health and Safety Executive must be informed and which require the creation and labelling of 'asbestos areas'. All workers in these areas will be required to have regular medical examinations and detailed records of these have to be kept by employers.

Codes of Practice and Guidance Notes. To accompany the regulatory documents a series of codes of practice and guidance notes have been issued to give detailed advice on many facets of working with asbestos products. Details of the guidance notes and codes of practice available are shown in *Table 9.3*.

9.6 Health effects of exposure to asbestos

Since the first years of the large-scale commercial exploitation of asbestos minerals there has been a growing awareness that people involved in working with the material were developing a series of disabling and occasionally fatal illnesses. The first signs of the effects of asbestos were noted very early, but were put down to various unassociated ailments. The early years of the 20th century saw the first serious investigations into lung disorders in asbestos workers and noted several instances of pleural fibrosis. In the 1920s the number of cases of fibrosis of the lung in asbestos workers was rising and a cause–effect relationship became undeniable. The condition became known as 'asbestosis' and its discovery, largely as a result of epidemiological evidence, hastened the introduction of legislation to reduce the level of exposure of people working in the asbestos industry.

As the uses and applications of asbestos grew, the incidence of asbestos-related illness grew also. Asbestos was being used on a large scale as an insulation material and, in addition to the use of chrysotile, new types of asbestos, amosite and crocidolite, were being installed. Cases of asbestosis outside the asbestos-manufacturing industry were on the increase as well.

After the Second World War, more research was carried out into the links between asbestos and a range of illnesses. Epidemiological evidence was emerging which showed a high incidence of lung cancer in persons occupationally exposed to asbestos. This was compounded in the 1950s by further evidence of asbestos workers and laggers having a greater incidence of a rare malignant tumour called mesothelioma, which invariably proved fatal.

Since then, mounting evidence of causal relationships of asbestos to these and other diseases has led to the virtual ban on the use of this material in the UK and extremely strict restrictions on the disturbance of installed asbestos.

9.6.1 Asbestosis

Asbestosis is the fibrosis of the lung as a result of exposure to asbestos dust. It is sometimes, but not always, accompanied by the presence of pleural plagues or localized thickenings of the parietal pleura, normally along the line of the ribs. The condition is undoubtedly a result of occupational exposure to asbestos in one of the high-exposure areas such as textile manufacture, lagging or spraying. It is extremely unlikely to occur with a minor exposure to asbestos.

Epidemiological data correlating exposure to asbestos dust and the incidence of the disease show evidence that there is a dose–response relationship, i.e. that a greater exposure to asbestos is likely to result in a higher risk of contracting the disease, though this is a general trend and some results contradict this.

The exact mechanism by which the disease progresses is as follows. Initially, the presence of asbestos in the lung causes an irritation to the surrounding tissue. The body's protective systems react to this and try to remove the foreign matter by despatching macrophages which cover and attempt to remove the obstruction. If they cannot do this, the ongoing irritation might eventually cause a progressive scarring resulting in the area developing a localized fibrosis. This is confined to a very small area at first but eventually spreads internally and along the periphery of the lung. There are usually many of these localized areas of fibrosis which appear like a cobweb if seen under X-ray analysis and which eventually merges as they grow creating diffuse interstitial fibrosis. With time the fibrosis spreads to cover the whole lung.

Symptoms of the disease usually take several years to show up following initial exposure to asbestos. They include difficulty in breathing following exertion, which becomes progressively more acute as the disease advances, frequent occurrence of an unproductive cough and slight chest pains are also common, usually under the sternum, scapula or between the shoulder blades, and the condition has associated basal crepitations which are very fine crackling noises given out as the lungs move, generally these are only audible using a stethoscope, but are considered to be the first reliable signs of the disease. Lung function is rapidly impaired with asbestosis, and occasionally, arthritic clubbing of the fingers has been an associated symptom of the disease.

Once diagnosed, there is little practical treatment for asbestosis, though the disease, if uncomplicated by lung cancer, is not always fatal.

In early cases, when exposure was far greater, asbestosis may have taken up to 5–6 years to develop, with subsequent death in 10–12 years, but, as standards of air cleanliness increased along with standards of medical care, the story today is quite different. Often the disease does not develop for 15–20 years and can sometimes be contained.

9.6.2 Lung cancer

Instances of lung cancer (carcinoma of the bronchus due to exposure to asbestos dust) had been known for many years before the tentative link was established between it and exposure to asbestos dust. It was just after the Second World War that a high incidence of people, suffering from asbestosis, were found to have died from associated lung cancers. A great deal of epidemiological research was quickly carried out in the following years which backed up the apparent connection between lung cancer and occupational exposure to asbestos dust.

The exact causal mechanism of the cancer is not completely clear, but the disease starts in the lining membrane of the bronchus where a cellular change takes place in the lining membrane. This may or may not lead to the formation of cancerous cells, but, if it does, the cancerous transformation grows and becomes a discernible tumour. This usually has the effect of blocking the bronchus and impairing breathing. The cancerous cells gradually spread throughout the body and eventually result in death.

The disease can sometimes be treated successfully but only if caught at an early stage. The treatment usually involves the surgical removal of the cancer and additional radiological and chemotherapy treatments.

The likelihood of incidence of lung cancer was found to be many times greater when the people involved were smokers; smoking has been found to be a contributory factor in cases of asbestosis also.

9.6.3 Mesothelioma

Mesothelioma is an uncommon highly malignant tumour of the serosal surfaces which may occur in the pleura and peritoneum. The existence of mesothelioma had been known for some considerable time, but was not acknowledged as being related to asbestos exposure until a study was carried out among crocidolite miners in South Africa in 1959 when a high mortality rate due to this disease was detected. Other evidence soon backed up the results of this study. An alarming aspect of the epidemiological data concerning mesothelioma was that its incidence was not confined to asbestos workers. People with peripheral exposure to asbestos also contracted the disease, such as women who have contracted mesothelioma whose only recorded exposure to asbestos had been the washing of their husbands overalls which had been covered with asbestos dust. However, its incidence in asbestos workers was much greater, pointing to a dose–response relationship. Smoking does not appear to effect the occurrence of mesothelioma.

The disease was noted to be more common amongst people working with crocidolite rather than any other asbestos minerals, and very few cases were noted amongst people working with chrysotile. This effect had not gone unheeded and was a major factor in deciding the occupational control limits for asbestos (see Section 9.7) which were much stricter for crocidolite.

Mesothelioma does not usually manifest itself for some considerable time and can take up to 40–50 years from the incidence of exposure before symptoms of the tumour begin to appear.

There appears to be no way of combatting the disease at present, and from the initial point of detection of the tumour death usually occurs within 12 months.

9.6.4 Other asbestos-related illnesses

Several diseases have been linked with exposure to asbestos over the years. Some links have been proven and commonly accepted, whilst others remain relatively doubtful.

Skin complaints are common with the regular handling of asbestos, primarily in the textile manufacturing industry. Asbestos impregnation of the skin leads to the formation of corns, warts and other hardened-skin complaints. Dermatitis has also been recorded amongst workers who regularly handle other asbestos products.

Cancer of the digestive tract associated with the taking in of asbestos fibres in water and food or in mucus secreted from the lungs have not been positively linked. In any case these cancers occur frequently in the non-exposed population and epidemiology does not give any clear indications of asbestos being the cause.

Cancer of the larynx is another disease linked with exposure to asbestos but, again, it has not been conclusively proven due to the high incidence of this disease among the general population and proven links with smoking.

Cancer of the ovaries has been linked with exposure to asbestos, but firm proof from epidemiological research has not yet been obtained.

9.7 Asbestos control and maintenance

Asbestos had been in common use in the UK for nearly 30 years before the first ideas of the health problems associated with exposure to it came to light. No significant controls on the use of asbestos were enforced until the Asbestos Industry Regulations were drafted in 1931. These regulations placed an emphasis on the need to control exposure to the substance and introduced the requirement for ventilation extract systems in areas where asbestos work was being carried out. Strict standards of cleanliness were introduced, but they remained confined to the asbestos-manufacturing industry.

Until the 1970s the use of asbestos had expanded and with the final awareness of the health implications came the realization that the safe management of thousands of asbestos installations was going to be an immense problem. Asbestos was not only used in industry and construction but was also present in homes and was being disturbed on a daily basis during maintenance, delagging, demolition and domestic decoration. The problem of maintaining existing asbestos installations is a large one and is generally tackled in three phases: (1) surveying for asbestos and compiling a list of its locations; (2) encapsulation of existing asbestos to prevent damage; and (3) asbestos removal.

9.7.1 Planned maintenance

Many companies and managing authorities operate an asbestos register of all asbestos products used in their buildings. This is usually compiled following a full survey carried out by specialist consultants, with samples being taken of any suspect materials and analysed under cross polar microscopy and using dispersion staining techniques to confirm the presence of asbestos.

The possible disturbance of asbestos installations is generally avoided in two ways: firstly by referring all maintenance operations through the register to check if asbestos is near the area where the work is to take place, and secondly by the distinctive marking of asbestos materials, usually with the 'a' mark.

During the survey stage it is likely that a number of damaged or potentially hazardous asbestos installations will crop up. The specialist consultant would normally make recommendations in his survey report as to the best way to deal with the material. This would generally involve either encapsulation, which is the sealing of the material *in situ* to prevent further damage, or complete removal under controlled conditions.

9.7.2 Encapsulation of asbestos

Often asbestos products and installations are liable to accidental damage and, depending on the degree of damage caused, a decision must be taken as to whether the damage can be repaired or if the damage is so great that repair is impossible and complete removal must be carried out. The decision must primarily be made on health-and-safety grounds, and specialist advice should normally be sought, including whether or not the work should be carried out by a licensed contractor. Financial considerations will also play a part, it is often more cost effective to remove asbestos, although it may be more expensive in the short term, as there will be savings in the long term on maintenance and the cost of eventual removal at some point in the future. Encapsulation techniques vary for different types of asbestos installations.

9.7.2.1 Asbestos boarding products

Asbestos cement sheets and asbestos insulating boards are encapsulated in varying ways depending on their location. Asbestos cement is sometimes covered externally by a layer of bitumen-backed canvas to provide external weather proofing, but internally with a paint seal. Asbestos insulation board is usually located internally or in sheltered locations and should also normally be paint sealed.

It is wise to consider the use of fire-resistant paints for the encapsulation of asbestos board products as this will augment the boards fire-resistant ability and usually affords a thicker protective coating to prevent mechanical damage. In instances where there is no fire-retardant role any water-based paint will provide a durable surface seal. In cases where regular and heavy impact may occur a stronger rigid barrier is required and the material should be effectively boxed in.

9.7.2.2 Asbestos insulation

Asbestos insulation is a prime area where encapsulation works are regularly carried out. The material is easily damaged and is often broken during regular maintenance to pipework, boilers and calorifiers. The incentive to encapsulate is often very great since removal is not only expensive, but usually involves shutting down the boilers, an action which cannot be seriously considered in schools and hospitals.

Encapsulation techniques include the shrouding of pipe, boiler and calorifier insulation with an outer layer. This layer can be plastic, stainless steel, aluminium hammer cladding, a calico and canvas covering, or a solid plaster outer casing.

9.7.2.3 Sprayed asbestos coating

Bearing in mind the extremely friable nature of sprayed asbestos coatings, if damage occurs the work involved in repairing the damage is likely to create an even greater potential hazard. It is more probable in the case of damage that sprayed materials are removed and replaced. If, however, the material is to be sealed, the encapsulation of the coating is fraught with problems. The usual method is to spray the asbestos with a very thick coating of a fire retardant elastomeric sealant. This operation, if carried out at too high a pressure, is likely to blow asbestos fibres free of the surface and even dislodge loosened sections. The optimum encapsulation method is to apply a light, low pressure spray coating initially, to seal the surface, and then to apply a thick secondary coating, gradually building up the overall thickness of the seal. Rigid coverings to sprayed asbestos are rare, unless installed immediately after spraying, attachment of a solid covering cannot normally be fixed without disturbing the asbestos in some way.

All work involving asbestos insulation and sprayed coatings is notifiable to the Health and Safety Executive and advice should be sought as to whether licensed asbestos-removal contractors should carry out the work.

9.7.3 Removal of asbestos

With the advent of the Asbestos Regulations (1969) and subsequent legislation and guidance, strict procedures and guidelines were laid down for the treatment and removal of asbestos-containing materials. Until 1969 asbestos removal had not been subject to controls and had been removed by ordinary labourers as part of their general construction or demolition duties.

The removal of asbestos is a process which can give rise to extremely high levels of airborne fibres and create a significant health hazard. The modern asbestos-removal contractor can control the levels of asbestos fibres given off during removal in several ways, but the main method is by enclosure and negative pressure.

Virtually every instance of asbestos removal must be carried out by a licensed removal contractor (see Asbestos (Licensing)

Figure 9.6 Asbestos removal in progress

Regulations (1983)) and this contractor is legally obliged to give 28-days notice of his intention to carry out asbestos works to the local enforcing authority which is usually the Health and Safety Executive. The Health and Safety Executive factory inspector may require a written method statement from the contractor before he will allow work to start and may visit the site during the work to ensure that the work method is being adhered to.

In cases of emergency, or where asbestos works need to be carried out within 28 days, the factory inspector or local enforcing authority has the power to issue a waiver of the 28-day notice, but this is only done in exceptional circumstances.

Areas in which asbestos-removal work is to be carried out are normally isolated by the construction of an asbestos working enclosure (*Figure 9.6*). This is usually built around a timber frame using heavy-duty (typically 1000 gauge) polythene and sealed with heavy-duty adhesive tape to form an airtight enclosure. All non-cleanable materials are removed from the work area; if this is not possible they are covered using heavy-duty polythene which is sealed in place with adhesive tape. To test the enclosure for leaks, an electric smoke generator or smoke bombs can be used to fill the enclosure with thick dark smoke. If traces leak from the enclosure then it is obvious there is a gap in the sheeting which requires repair before asbestos removal operations can begin.

Entry to and egress from the enclosure is via a series of decontamination airlocks, which are a series of compartments where dirty clothing is taken off, the operatives shower and clean their respirators and, finally, change into clean clothing.

The enclosure is normally placed under negative pressure which is achieved by placing a very large, high-efficiency, air vacuum machine facing onto the working enclosure. These units, which can each pull up to 2500 ft³ air per minute and have a 99.997% efficient filtration system, suck contaminated air from the enclosure setting up a negative pressure inside. This means that any airflow at the boundary of the enclosure, through any possible gaps, is always *into* the work area and contaminated air inside *cannot* escape except through the high-efficiency filter.

Asbestos removal inside the enclosure on small operations is usually carried out under dry conditions. However, the Health and Safety Executive's guidance recommends that wet stripping be carried out where possible (i.e. the damping down and soaking of the asbestos installation before removal) since this cuts down the amount of airborne asbestos generated at source.

Asbestos waste products from the removal operation should then be placed inside a double layer of polythene asbestos waste bags. These bags are heavy duty and labelled as containing asbestos and carrying the name of the asbestos-removal contractor using them. The sealed sacks are then cleaned and removed to a sealed, lockable skip to await transportation to a site licensed for the disposal of asbestos waste.

Once an enclosure has been stripped of its asbestos the entire area has to undergo a very fine clean so that all residual dust and debris is removed. A visual inspection is carried out, usually by a specialist analytical agency, before the enclosure can be air tested to determine whether it is fit for reoccupation. The specialist analytical agency is required to carry out air testing inside the enclosure after the area is found to be visually clear of asbestos to prove that asbestos fibre levels are low enough to remove the sheeting. Air sampling pumps are placed inside the enclosure and, while they are in operation, the analyst should actively disturb the enclosure to simulate conditions of normal occupancy.

The acceptable clearance level is 0.01 fibre ml⁻¹ or less which is as low as can be detected with modern optical microscopic analytical techniques. Analytical techniques are laid down in guidance notes EH 10 and MDHS 39/2. If this level is attained, a certificate of air clearance is issued and the area can be returned to normal use with the enclosure being dismantled and disposed of as asbestos waste.

Other minor variations of asbestos-removal methodology exist and, in general, the above method would only apply to high-fibre-level operations such as the removal of insulation materials and insulation boarding in an internal environment. Asbestos cement products removed externally would not normally warrant such strict precautions.

Bibliography

ADVISORY COMMITTEE ON ASBESTOS, *Asbestos: Final Report*, Vols I and II, HMSO, London (1979)
BERRY, C., GILSON, J. C., HOLMES, S., LEWINSON, H. C. and ROACH, S. A., Asbestosis; a study of dose response relationships in an asbestos textile factory, *British Journal of Industrial Medicine*, 98–112 (May 1979)
CURWELL, S. R. and MARCH, C. G., *Hazardous Building Materials*, E & F Spon, London (1986)
DOLL, R., Mortality from lung cancer in asbestos workers, *British Journal of Industrial Medicine*, **12** (2), 81–86 (1955)
MEREWETHER, E. R. A., *Asbestosis and Carcinoma of the Lung*, Annual report of the Chief Inspector of Factories 1947, HMSO, London (1947)
MICHAELS, L. and CHISWICK, S. S., *Asbestos Properties, Applications and Hazards*, Vol. 1, Wiley, New York (1979)
PYE, A. M., A review of asbestos substitute materials in industrial applications, *Journal of Hazardous Materials* (Sep. 1979)
WAGNER, J., STEGGS, C. and MARCHAND, P., Diffuse pleural mesothelioma and asbestos exposure in the north west Cape Province, *British Journal of Industrial Medicine*, 260–271 (Oct. 1960)

10

Bituminous Materials for use in Road Construction

J J Farrington MICE
Staffordshire County Council

Contents

10.1 Introduction 10/3

10.2 Asphalts 10/3
    10.2.1 Wearing courses 10/3
    10.2.2 The mix design process 10/4
    10.2.3 Asphalt base courses 10/8
    10.2.4 Asphalt road and airfield bases 10/8
    10.2.5 Asphalt regulating courses 10/9
    10.2.6 Medium-temperature asphalts for use in
            wearing courses 10/9
    10.2.7 Mastic asphalt in wearing courses 10/9

10.3 Coated macadams 10/10
    10.3.1 Road-base macadams 10/11
    10.3.2 Base-course macadams 10/11
    10.3.3 Wearing-course macadams 10/12

10.4 Manufacturing processes 10/14
    10.4.1 Recycled materials 10/16

10.5 Storage hoppers or silos 10/16

10.6 Pre-laying preparation work 10/17

10.7 Laying bituminous materials by hand 10/17

10.8 Laying bituminous materials by machine 10/18

10.9 Control of laying tolerances 10/21

10.10 Precoated chippings 10/22

10.11 Laying in adverse weather conditions 10/23
    10.11.1 Cold weather 10/23
    10.11.2 Rain 10/24

10.12 Compaction 10/25

10.13 Sampling and testing 10/26

References 10/27

Appendix 10.1 Aggregates 10/27

Appendix 10.2 Binders 10/29

Appendix 10.3 Mix-design examples 10/30

Appendix 10.4 Medium-temperature asphalt
              specification 10/31

Appendix 10.5 Paver operation monitoring form 10/32

Appendix 10.6 Extracts from H16/76 10/33

10.1 Introduction

To the layman in the UK, all black road construction materials are simply 'tarmac'. However, the materials are produced either as asphalts or coated macadams, and are significantly different in terms of composition, application and cost and each material type has its own British Standard. Many engineers have little or no familiarity with either bitumens or those aggregate properties which are significant in road-building materials. Appendix 1 therefore gives a brief description of the terms found in specifications and an extensive list of references.

Figure 10.1 shows typical compositions of two products in each type of bituminous material, a hot-rolled asphalt wearing course, a mastic asphalt, which is now used primarily for its waterproofing properties, a dense bituminous macadam and an open-textured macadam. The differing bitumen contents indicate the relative costs of the materials since bitumen is very substantially more expensive than the other constituent materials. The properties and uses of each material type are discussed in the following sections.

10.2 Asphalts

In ths USA and many other parts of the world, any bituminous material is described as an asphalt. In the UK, asphalts have specifically been gap-graded materials with relatively high bitumen contents. They derive a significant part of their strength from the bitumen and are produced for use in wearing courses, base courses or road bases. The combination of high bitumen content and the stiff bitumen used in their manufacture results in their generally only being laid successfully at relatively high temperatures by paving machines. The relevant British Standard, BS 594: 1985,[1] has two parts, the first covering the specification for constituent materials and asphalt mixtures and the second dealing with the transport, laying and compaction of rolled asphalts.

10.2.1 Wearing courses

It is important to realize that the most commonly used type of rolled asphalt wearing course typically contains approximately 55% sand, passing a 2.36-mm sieve, and 30% coarse aggregate, usually having a nominal particle size of 14 mm. The physical characteristics of the sand in terms of grading, and particularly particle shape, have a most significant affect both on the ease with which the material may be laid, and on its performance in the road or pavement. In general, rolled asphalt wearing courses are dense, virtually impermeable and very durable. Mixes may contain up to 55% coarse aggregate, but those with less than this very highest stone content derive their skid resistance from the application and rolling-in to the top of the mat of precoated chippings with high polished stone values. Chipped rolled asphalts are specified for the wearing courses on all motorways and trunk roads constructed in accordance with the pavement design standards issued by the Department of Transport (DTp).[2] Most other highway authorities adopt these standards and, as a result, the majority of heavily trafficked roads in both urban and rural areas are surfaced with this material. Properly laid and compacted, an asphalt wearing course should have a life of 10–15 years, depending on how sensibly it was specified, how well it was laid, the strength of the road base and the weight of traffic it carries. Most material is specified by engineers who are familiar with its characteristics, but anyone with little or no experience in its use should be aware of the problems associated with its specification, manufacture and use.

Until the late 1970s all wearing course asphalts were produced as 'recipe mixes' and these are still widely used, particularly in urban areas. Most wearing courses are laid with a design thickness of 40 mm and, in addition to the sand and coarse aggregate, a recipe mix will typically contain about 10% filler, that is aggregate passing a 75-μm sieve, and 7.8% bitumen which is 50 penetration (pen) grade if the sand is natural sand but may be 70 pen or even 100 pen if the sand is coarse or either wholly or partially composed of crushed rock fines. For recipe mixes the natural sand ideally has an almost spherical particle shape and this gives the material very good workability at laying stage. *Figure 10.2* shows a microphotograph of a natural sand which would produce a highly workable, easily laid recipe mix which, if laid in a normal urban situation with no significant texture and no channelized heavy vehicle flows, could be expected to give 15 or more years of good service. All wearing course asphalts used in the UK used to be produced as recipe mixes but the periods of unusually fine weather in the summers of 1976 and 1977 resulted in the surfaces of road pavements reaching temperatures in excess of 50°C and on the more heavily trafficked roads, many recipe-type wearing courses rutted excessively in the wheel tracks of lanes used by heavy goods vehicles, or deformed badly on roundabouts after giving years

Figure 10.1 Four bituminous materials: (a) hot-rolled asphalt; (b) dense bitumen macadam; (c) open-textured macadam; (d) mastic asphalt

Figure 10.2 Asphalt sand seen through a microscope. This would make a very workable mix which would not readily resist deformation unless produced with a very stiff or modified binder

Figure 10.3 Hot-rolled asphalt showing deep wheel-track rutting which occurred during one hot summer after 14 years of satisfactory service

of satisfactory performance. *Figure 10.3* illustrates a typical example of severe rutting in a 14-year-old wearing course asphalt. Similar failures occurred in wearing courses throughout Europe and national highway authorities reacted by quickly altering their specifications to produce more stable wearing courses, usually by reducing their bitumen content. In the UK, the DTp began to specify design-type wearing course asphalts in which the bitumen content was 'designed' or determined by the compressive testing of several cylindrical samples made from the proposed aggregates, but at differing bitumen contents.

These so-called 'Marshall mixes' or 'high-stability asphalts' have strengths which had been shown[3] to give superior resistance to wheel-track rutting at high ambient temperatures and their use has brought two significant changes to the production of asphalt wearing courses. The first is the move away from using the well-rounded natural sands shown in *Figure 10.2* to either more coarsely graded natural sands with better intergranular interlock, or to sands produced by crushing rock, the so-called 'crushed-rock fines'. A typical sample of crushed-rock fines is illustrated in the microphotograph in *Figure 10.4*. Comparison with *Figure 10.2* shows that, whereas the natural sand resembles miniature stone spheres, the crushed-rock fines are composed totally of very angular particles. Anyone familiar with concrete can easily understand the effect on the handling characteristics of a concrete made with such differing aggregate shapes and the effects are exactly the same in rolled asphalts, even at high laying temperatures.

Figure 10.4 Crushed-rock fines. These make a very harsh mix but are often blended with sands in the production of high-stability asphalts

In the north, where well-rounded asphalt sands have never been plentiful, recipe mixes have been produced using coarser natural sandfines which are combined with a much higher binder content than they strictly need to perform adequately at ambient temperatures since the bitumen is needed to lubricate the particles when it is hot and overcome the internal friction of the mix if it is to be handled successfully at laying and compaction stages. However, this excess 'workability aid' bitumen tends to make these mixes both less resistant to wheel-track rutting at high ambient temperatures and more expensive, since the bitumen is the costliest component in the asphalt. The second consequence of the adoption of design-type mixes has been to reduce the binder content relative to those which are traditionally used in recipe mixes, whatever the type of fine aggregate now being used. Compared with recipe mixes, therefore, these designed mixes are relatively dry and may be harsh, with lower workabilities, and they may require significantly greater compaction and care at the laying stage. The successful use of these mixes depends on their being laid and compacted whilst the material is at high temperatures by competent laying gangs.

Unfortunately, this move to design-type mixes was made at about the same time that the DTp introduced the requirement for a texture depth of 1.5 mm to increase the skidding resistance of roads on which at least 85% of traffic travels at speeds in excess of 55 miles per hour. The Transport and Road Research Laboratory (TRRL) Research Report SR340[4] describes the background to this requirement, and texture depth is more fully described in the DTp Specification for Highway Works.[5] However, the initial reaction on sites was to ensure that the pre-coated high polished-stone-value (PSV) chips were no longer fully rolled-in virtually flush with the surface of the asphalt, but that compaction was controlled to ensure that part of the chips remained standing proud of the surface. This in turn resulted in some wearing courses receiving less rolling than they might have otherwise and this, coupled with the lower binder contents, which makes them more difficult to compact fully in any event, resulted in many design mix wearing courses having poor durability often lasting less than 6 or 7 years.

In 1985, a revised edition of BS 594[1] was published and this contains four categories of wearing-course mix:

(1) those produced using primarily natural sand fines with binder contents determined from Marshall tests for particular ranges of stability, and designated 'design type F';
(2) other design mixes based on crushed-rock fines, or coarse sands called 'design type C';
(3) 'type F' recipe mixes; and
(4) 'type C' recipe mixes.

The last two categories are virtually the same recipe mixes used since the early 1970s when crushed-rock fines were first permitted, and the type F recipe mixes are little changed from those used since before World War I, except that they have lower binder contents.

10.2.2 The mix design process

It is important for engineers involved in the specification and use of hot-rolled asphalts to understand the design process which determines the bitumen-content/mix-stability relationship, so that they are better able to understand the significance of test results. The full method is described in detail in BS 598: Part 3,[6] but essentially consists of manufacturing in the laboratory six sets of three, well compacted, cylindrical specimens of the asphalt using the fine and coarse aggregates and filler combined to comply with the grading specifications contained in BS 594: Part 1, Tables 3 and 4 reproduced here as *Tables 10.1* and *10.2*. The specimens are each 101.6 mm in diameter and 63.5 mm long

Table 10.1 BS 594: Part 1: 1986: Section 3: Table 3. Composition of design type F wearing-course mixtures

Column number	7	8	9	10	11	12
Designation*	0/3†	30/10	30/14	40/14	40/20	55/20
Nominal thickness of layer (mm)	25	35	40	50	50	50
Percentage by mass of total aggregate passing BS test sieve						
28 mm	—	—	—	—	100	100
20 mm	—	—	100	100	95–100	90–100
14 mm	—	100	85–100	90–100	50–85	35–80
10 mm	—	85–100	60–90	50–85	—	—
6.3 mm	100	60–90	—	—	—	—
2.36 mm	95–100	60–72	60–72	50–62	50–62	35–47
600 μm	80–100	45–72	45–72	35–62	35–62	25–47
212 μm	25–70	15–50	15–50	10–40	10–40	5–30
75 μm	13.0–17.0	8.0–12.0	8.0–12.0	6.0–10.0	6.0–10.0	4.0–8.0
Maximum percentage of aggregate passing 2.36 mm and retained on 600 μm BS test sieves	22	14	14	12	12	9
Minimum target binder content % by mass of total mixture‡	9.0	7.0	6.5	6.3	6.3	5.3

* The mixture designation numbers (e.g. 0/3 in column 7) refer to the nominal coarse aggregate content of the mixture/nominal size of the aggregate in the mixture, respectively.
† Suitable for regulating course.
‡ In areas of the country where prevailing conditions are characteristically colder and wetter than the national average the addition of a further 0.5% of binder may be beneficial to the durability of the wearing courses.

Table 10.2 BS 594: Part 1: 1985: Section 3: Table 4. Composition of design type C wearing-course mixtures

Column number	13	14	15	16	17
Designation*	0/3	30/10	30/14	40/14	40/20
Nominal thickness of layer (mm)	25	35	40	50	50
Percentage by mass of total aggregate passing BS test sieve					
28 mm	—	—	—	—	100
20 mm	—	—	100	100	95–100
14 mm	—	100	85–100	90–100	50–85
10 mm	—	85–100	60–90	50–85	—
6.3 mm	100	60–90	—	—	—
2.36 mm	90–100	60–72	60–72	50–62	50–62
600 μm	30–65	25–45	25–45	20–40	20–40
212 μm	15–40	15–30	15–30	10–25	10–25
75 μm	13.0–17.0	8.0–12.0	8.0–12.0	6.0–10.0	6.0–10.0
Minimum target binder content % by mass of total mixture†	9.0	7.0	6.5	6.3	6.3

* The mixture designation numbers (e.g. 0/3 in column 13) refer to the nominal coarse aggregate content of the mixture/nominal size of the aggregate in the mixture, respectively.
† In areas of the country where prevailing conditions are characteristically colder and wetter than the national average the addition of a further 0.5% of binder may be beneficial to the durability of the wearing courses.

and are produced in preheated steel moulds. It should be noted that these grading specifications are exactly the same as for the types F and C recipe mixes listed above. However, whereas the recipe mixes each have two levels of fixed bitumen content, for use with either crushed rock or steel slag, and gravel or blast-furnace slag coarse aggregates, each set of three of these design-mix samples is made with a different binder content, increasing in 0.5% increments. Each end of each sample is compacted mechanically with 50 blows of a 4.5-kg weight sliding vertically through a distance of 457 mm. The sample is removed from the steel mould and weighed in both air and water to determine its density. The sample is then stored in a water bath maintained at a constant temperature of 60°C. Eventually the samples attain this temperature and each is then inserted into the split cylindrical test head of a Marshall apparatus, an example of which is shown in *Figure 10.5*. A constant rate of compression of 50 mm min^{-1} is then applied to the sample, and the maximum load it carries is recorded as its compressive strength, or 'Marshall stability'. The maximum deformation, or 'flow', is also recorded, and except for use in the most heavily loaded UK pavement wearing courses, this is limited to 5 mm. The results derived from testing each set of three samples at a given binder content are then averaged and graphs plotted of binder content vs. stability, compacted aggregate density, and mix density. The optimum binder contents derived from the three graphs are averaged to give the design binder content, and then for 30% coarse aggregate mixes, at least 0.7% added to give the target binder content since experience has shown this to be necessary to achieve the required degree of workability on site. Footnotes to Tables 3 and 4 of BS 594: Part 1 (see *Tables 10.1* and *10.2*) state that in areas of the UK where prevailing conditions are characteristically colder and wetter than the national average, the addition of a further 0.5% of binder may be beneficial to the durability of the wearing course.

Figure 10.5 Test head of Marshall apparatus used to determine stability and flow of test specimen

This applies to all wearing-course materials, regardless of the coarse aggregate content. BS 594: Part 1, Tables 3 and 4 also state the minimum target binder contents as percentages by mass of total mixture, but it must be realized that these values are based on the durability known to have been achieved by the use of particular natural sands. It cannot be too strongly stressed that wearing-course materials produced using other sands at these lower binder contents may not be sufficiently workable to be laid or, if they are laid, be durable in any event.

The design process is thus no more than a method of selecting the binder content for a recipe mix of aggregate, and ensuring that the laboratory-produced asphalt achieves the specified stability. The Marshall test itself has a tolerance of ± 2 kN because of its relatively poor repeatability and the values listed in Table 11 in BS 594: Part 1, reproduced here as *Table 10.3*, which gives the criteria for the stability of laboratory-designed asphalts, reflect this tolerance. The apparent anomaly between the stabilities required for traffic flows of less than 1500 commercial vehicles per lane per day and (cvpd) and 1500–6000 cvpd reflect the difficulties experienced in achieving low stabilities when using the coarser fines available. A recent paper by Choyce[7] describes these difficulties and also those of working to binder contents even as high as those minima stated in Table 4 of BS 594. An asphalt producer will normally have 'off-the-shelf' designs to cater for the categories of stability in Table 11 of BS 594[1] and these will frequently be checked by the test's being repeated in a laboratory commissioned by the customer

Table 10.3 BS 594: Part 1: 1986: Appendix B.2: Table 11. Criteria for the stability of laboratory design asphalt

Traffic (cvpd)	Marshall stability of complete mix (kN)
<1500	2 to 8*
1500–6000	4 to 8
>6000	6 to 10

* It may be necessary to restrict the upper limit where difficulties in the compaction of materials might occur.
Note 1. For stabilities up to 8.0 kN the maximum flow value should be 5 mm. For stabilities in excess of 8.0 kN a maximum flow of 7 mm is permissible.
Note 2. The stability values referred to should be obtained on laboratory mixes.

using samples of the constituent materials supplied by the producer. Any differences between the two sets of results have to be resolved before the designed asphalt is produced for use on site. The actual graphs of binder content vs. stability, compacted aggregate density and mix density for a real-life mix are reproduced in *Figure 10.6* and the stability curve with two peaks is seen to be anything but the simple asymptotic shape normally seen in text books. Nevertheless, there is little difficulty in selecting the relevant peak value of binder content to be used in the averaging equation to determine the design binder content. The mix design calculations for this particular asphalt are reproduced in Appendix 10.3, and give a target binder content of 7.2%.

BS 594 allows a 0.6% tolerance on the nominal target binder content and the effect of this on the stability of the material

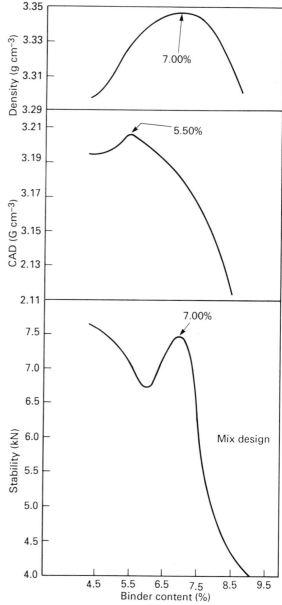

Figure 10.6 Typical Marshall test results

used in the laboratory tests should be determined. It can be seen from the binder/stability curve in *Figure 10.6* that the stability at the target binder content is 7.4 kN; at target -0.6% it is 7.2 kN and at target $+0.6\%$ it is 5.4 kN. In this instance, since the asphalt was required to have a stability sufficient to resist wheel-track rutting in a wearing course carrying 1500–6000 cvpd, of between 4 and 8 kN, the stabilities at the limits of the binder tolerances were acceptable.

However, some fine aggregates exhibit extremely rapid changes in stability within the limits of specified binder content, and at these limits the stability values might even be outside the specified ranges. In these instances, the customer's representative, normally the engineer on a civil-engineering site, will either reject the proposed mix as unacceptable, or ask the supplier if he is prepared to limit his binder tolerances to less than 0.6%, which is possible on a microprocessor-controlled plant, but can lead to difficulties in interpreting test results, since the reproducibility limit for the analysis of coated macadams to determine binder content is 0.5%.

The durability of an asphalt, or any other bituminous mix, is related to its air-void content after compaction, and this in turn is determined by both the physical characteristics of the aggregate, the binder content and the degree of effective compaction the material receives on site. Whilst the concrete industry has the slump test and the compacting-factor test, both used to determine the workability and ease of placing of concrete mixes, there is no equivalent test in the bituminous materials industry. In consequence, the anticipated workability of a mix remains a matter of judgement on the part of both the contractor's and the client's laboratory technicians and only the use of the material on site gives any reliable guidance on any fine-tuning necessary to optimize the mix. There is a growing realization that many of the mixes designed in the late 1970s and early 1980s are lasting only half as long as some of those recipe mixes which survived the extremely hot summers of 1976 and 1977 without becoming rutted in the wheel-track zones, due to what is now realized was a totally fortuitous use of sands with good mechanical interlock. This lack of durability is the result of the oxidation of the binder which, in turn, results from both incomplete compaction and an excess of voids in the aggregate structure of the mixes being filled with air rather than bitumen. Since additional bitumen would have both made the mixes more workable and filled some of the air voids, the mix failures are indirectly due to low binder contents. In short, the move to designed mixes and away from recipe mixes has eliminated the wheel-track-rutting problem, but in some cases has resulted in a lack of durability. In consequence, many engineers have tended to revert to the use of recipe mixes. In the south-east of England in particular, many engineers observed no wheel-tracking in the 1976 and 1977 summers and thus never moved away from recipe mixes. In these instances, since most of the research on asphalts had been conducted using Thames Valley sands, their recipe mixes were the very materials around which the bulk of the national standards had been written and hence what were recipe mixes to them were effectively previously well-researched design mixes. Whilst the presence of an excess of voids unfilled with bitumen is clearly seen to cause problems, it should be equally recognized that when all the voids are filled with bitumen, the particle-to-particle contact of aggregate in the material is destroyed and the mix becomes highly unstable. This can be seen not only from the manner in which the stability of a design asphalt decreases with increasing binder content, but probably also in the severe rutting of some of the 1970s recipe mixes which, in addition to being produced with spherically shaped sands, with inadequate mechanical interlock, also possibly had excessively high binder contents. It is also likely that at least some of those engineers still using recipe mixes will experience wheel-track-rutting problems with them, particularly as the volume and weight of traffic continues to increase.

However, there is a further aspect to mix design, which has hardly been addressed by either BS 594 or BS 598 and that is resistance to fatigue. If resistance to wheel-track rutting is considered as being at one end of the design see-saw, resistance to fatigue is at the other, and herein lies a further problem. There is no recognized design method for achieving a specific resistance to fatigue cracking or for producing material with a predetermined elastic stiffness or load-spreading ability. The latter properties are particularly relevant in terms of macadams and will be discussed later. In asphalts, and particularly in rolled-asphalt wearing courses, the trend towards specifying design mixes with higher stabilities, i.e. greater stiffnesses, than recipe mixes with the same aggregate grading has virtually eliminated wheel-track rutting and, so long as the binder content has not been reduced to such an extent that the mix has an excessive voids content, these materials can successfully carry extremely high vehicular flows on the most heavy-traffic categories of road, i.e. trunk roads and motorways. However, these are the very road pavements which have been built from new, or have been substantially rebuilt, in the last three decades with well-designed, stiff road bases. In consequence, the strains in the wearing course are generally quite low, and certainly within the capacity of the materials, at least until their binders have oxidized excessively. Unfortunately, the major part of the highway system in the UK was initially constructed well before the introduction of pavement-design standards in the 1960 edition of Road Note 29,[8] and their lack of flexural stiffness results in them deflecting excessively under heavy axle loadings. The use of an unsuitably stiff design-mix rolled-asphalt wearing course on one of these relatively flexible road bases results in the premature cracking of the wearing course due to its fatigue strength being exceeded. Therefore, some highway engineers specify mixes with relatively low stabilities and also introduce a further variable, the Marshall quotient (Q), into their specifications:

$$Q = \frac{\text{Mix stability } (S)}{\text{Flow } (F)}$$

For lightly trafficked, very flexible rural roads, a quotient of 0.6–0.9 is sometimes stated and the technician in the supplier's laboratory knows that he will need to produce an asphalt with a low stability and a high flow in order to satisfy this requirement. It is not recommended that this quotient should be used in specifications since the precision of both stability and flow tests are relatively poor. Often a 50 pen or even a 70 pen grade bitumen will be too stiff for use on lightly trafficked roads and instead a 100 pen binder may be used. This increasing use of 100 pen bitumen was recognized in the 1985 revision of BS 594 which included the softer bitumen in the national asphalt specification for the first time.

Thus, whilst there is no BS 598 test for fatigue, engineers have intuitively moved to relatively high binder contents with softer bitumens to achieve the necessary fatigue strength, even at the risk of wheel-track rutting, since on a weak road base carrying relatively little heavy traffic the risk of the impermeable wearing course cracking and allowing water to penetrate the road base materials and eventually cause weakening of the carriageway subgrade is seen as a potentially greater problem than wheel-track rutting, and one to be avoided at all costs.

It can be seen, therefore, that the highway engineer bases maintenance decisions on his experience in the use of locally produced materials tempered with his understanding of the basic properties of them and the manner in which the mix variables relate to one another, which he derives from reading the published results of research. He would appreciate being able to use a more numerate approach in his selection and specification of pavement materials, but until standards have been established for measuring such mix properties as elastic stiffness, fatigue resistance and durability, he must continue to rely on his own experience.

10.2.3 Asphalt base courses

Hot-rolled asphalt base courses are always manufactured as recipe mixes using 50 pen grade bitumen and a variety of gap-graded natural aggregates. (Outside the UK, base courses are often called binder courses.) Although the binder content of a typical base course is significantly lower than that of the wearing course with which it will be overlaid, it is nevertheless almost 50% greater than in a dense macadam base course. This, coupled with the much higher fines content of the asphalt makes it a very dense, impermeable mixture with high fatigue strength and the combination of both hot-rolled asphalt base course and wearing course considerably enhances the strength of any road pavement. This is clearly illustrated in *Figure 10.7* which shows the superior performance of these materials relative to the admittedly very much weaker macadams then in use, which were manufactured with softer bitumens than is now normal, i.e. 300 pen. These results were observed on full scale road pavement experiments conducted by the TRRL.

An additional benefit of rolled-asphalt base course is that its relatively high degree of impermeability enables it to be used as a very temporary running surface for low-speed roads whilst at the same time sealing the lower layers of the road pavement and the subsoil from the ingress of water. To ensure that safety standards are not temporarily diminished, the PSV of the coarse aggregate in the base course needs to be at least 50, which effectively bars the use of most limestones in its production. However, base-course asphalt has also been used successfully in temporary wearing courses replacing oxidized, weak bituminous macadams on the hard-shoulders of motorways which are to carry the initial contraflow traffic whilst their second carriageways are to be strengthed or reconstructed. In these situations the binder contents specified in BS 594 have been increased by 0.5% and the skidding resistance enhanced by the application of precoated chippings at 7–9 kg m^{-2} at laying temperatures of 140°C or thereabouts.

Base-course materials are usually machine laid and the hand laying of even small quantities, in patching for instance, frequently results in the segregation of the larger stone fractions.

10.2.4 Asphalt road and airfield bases

Current DTp practice is to require the same thickness of road-base construction in flexible pavements, whether built using hot-rolled asphalt road base or dense bitumen macadam road base. This is a relatively recent practice and, until 1985, the higher binder content of the rolled asphalt, coupled with its stiffer bitumen and higher fines content was always acknowledged as producing the stiffer of the two materials. Hence, although the rolled-asphalt road base was more expensive, a lesser thickness was required. For example, the most recent edition Road Note 29,[8] valid until 1985, required a 120-mm thickness of dense bitumen macadam but only a 100-mm thickness of rolled-asphalt roadbase to carry 4 million standard axles. Contractors are now given the option of using the same thicknesses of either material and, not surprisingly, opt for the cheaper macadam. In new works, therefore, very little rolled-asphalt road base is used, unless the pavement is designed to carry an initial daily flow of more than 3000 commercial vehicles in one direction. (This is a very heavy flow and usually associated only with motorway pavements.) Linear elastic pavement-design theory is based on the supposition that a prime mode of failure is by fatigue cracks forming at the bottom of the bituminous road base and spreading upwards to the wearing course. Since both 40-mm and 28-mm nominal coarse-aggregate-size rolled-asphalt road bases contain at least 50% more bitumen than the equivalent macadam, they have a greater fatigue strength and current DTp pavement-design standards therefore require the use of a 125-mm thickness of this bitumen-rich material in the bottom layer of roadbase in these very heavily trafficked pavements.

Furthermore, highway engineers rebuilding road pavements are occasionally faced with the dilemma of trying to construct the new pavement on a subgrade which has been substantially damaged by public-utility undertakers in laying or repairing their own mains and cables. Extensive precontract site investigation may have failed to reveal this problem and the removal of the poor ground might require considerable additional expense in excavating around the utility equipment or even its temporary or permanent diversion. However, attempts to lay dense bitumen macadams on areas of existing sub-bases in these situations which may have a CBR of less than 5% are often

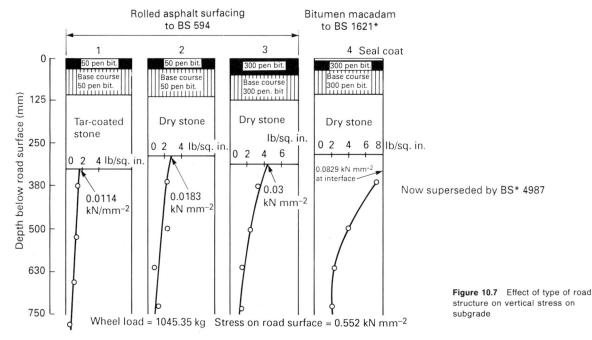

Figure 10.7 Effect of type of road structure on vertical stress on subgrade

quite unsuccessful because of the difficulty in achieving aggregate interlock. Instead the macadam moves continually beneath the roller over the poor ground and fails to develop its potential flexural strength. In these situations, the engineer may attempt to use hot-rolled asphalt in the road base, and capitalize on its higher binder content which, if the material is actually laid at relatively high temperature, say in excess of 150°C, gives it very high workability and enables it to be compacted with ease. Since its strength is derived substantially from its strong binder and not from aggregate interlock, once it has cooled to ambient temperature it will often perform successfully in these marginal situations and form a good construction platform for the laying and compaction of further layers of roadbase using dense bitumen macadam, or, if there is still doubt, using further asphalt roadbase layers.

So much for bituminous mixtures for road pavement but how do they differ from those used on airfield runways and taxi-ways? It is necessary to understand that airfields differ from roads in two vital respects. The first is that any tendency for pavement material to degrade could result in loose aggregate being sucked into gas turbines with totally destructive consequences. The second is that the day-time closure of a civil airfield runway can cause either severe, or even total loss of aircraft handling capacity, with very adverse revenue effects for the airfield operator. Thus almost all paving operations on civil airfields are night-time jobs. On military airfields, operations are transferred to another air-base, but the effects of loose material being ingested, i.e. foreign-object damage or FOD, are potentially more serious with military aircraft than with civil planes.

Whereas the hot rolled asphalt or bitumen macadam wearing courses of public highways in the UK are trafficked across their entire width to some extent, and in consequence, in the first hot summer after laying receive a degree of secondary compaction, most of the width of the average runway rarely if ever carries an aircraft tyre, so the opportunity for any secondary compaction never occurs. This results in the airfield engineer specifying a very dense asphaltic concrete, produced with high quality aggregates and binders and compacted to pre-determined densities. All aggregates have a maximum of 2% absorption, which is not a specified requirement for road mixtures. Surface texture is necessary to avoid aqua-planing of aircraft as they land at relatively high ground speeds on wet runways. The operator's requirement of a 1 mm sand patch texture depth cannot be satisfied by the asphaltic concrete wearing course but needs to be provided using either pervious macadams or friction courses, ('drainage asphalts' as they are described in continental Europe) as overlays to the structural runway materials, or by saw-cutting grooves 4 mm × 4 mm at 25 mm centres in the newly laid dense asphaltic concrete wearing courses.

The extremely serious consequences of the deterioration or deformation of runway surfaces resulted in the mixtures being designed using the Marshall method as specified in the PSA Specification for Military Airfields and the BAA Specification for civil airfields several decades before mix design became usual for highway wearing courses. The contractor's mix design process is monitored by the client's engineers and trial mixtures are laid on non-critical areas of the airfield to ensure that the mixtures, plant and laying crews are all combining to produce the required quality of finished work or are adjusted or changed until they do. Compaction involves the use of pneumatic tyred rollers in conjunction with the 8–10 steel tyred rollers seen on roadworks, and is monitored by coring to assess compliance with the specified 98% of Marshall density of the job standard mix, or 96% across joints. Joints are potential areas of weakness as in roadworks but generally receive more attention on airfield contracts because of these compacted density requirements.

Surfaces are laid to very shallow end and crossfalls and contractors have to comply with the extremely severe require-ment of laying to maximum tolerances of 3 mm under a 3 metre straight edge, wherever it is placed.

It is quite impossible to complete any but the smallest job in a single night so the contractor has to plan his works on the basis that the runway cannot be closed to operational use until late at night and must be capable of safely accepting aircraft landings in the relatively early morning, say by 6.30 or 7.00 am. Frequently the first aircraft scheduled to land will have become air-borne before he starts work and failure to open a safe landing surface the next day is totally unacceptable and reflected in contractual penalty sums.

Major items of plant are therefore at least duplicated, and depending on the nightly planned tonnage of materials to be laid, he will install either one on-site mixing plant with substantial hot-bin storage, or two on-site plants. The work areas are illuminated by mobile lighting sets and every effort is made to minimize the time interval between laying and rolling to avoid cooling winds adversely affecting the quality of the new mat. Airfields, by definition are unobstructed and there are no natural windbreaks.

Ramps at the end of a night's work are formed at gradients of between 1 in 100 and 1 in 200 depending on the maximum ramp thickness. Then, before flying operations restart, the works area is swept as necessary and checked to ensure that no loose tools, equipment or other potential hazards have been left in the operational areas.

Airfield jobs are thus seen to be generally more demanding than roadworks and anyone moving into airfield pavement works should read some recent excellent* papers on the subject.

10.2.5 Asphalt regulating courses

Whilst the laid thicknesses of bituminous pavement layers can be varied within limits as they are laid, it is often necessary to reshape them either as part of remedial works or in marrying-in new works to existing road pavements. The reshaping or 'regulating' is carried out using either a 'sand carpet' or thin base-course material. Sand carpet is merely hot-rolled asphalt wearing course without its course aggregate, and this can be laid down to a feather-edge. For thicknesses in excess of 30 mm it is usual to use a base-course asphalt with a maximum aggregate size of 10 mm. Older bituminous surfaces need to be 'tack-coated' using a cold-applied K-1-40 bituminous emulsion to assist the bonding of the regulating course, which may then be overlaid as soon as it has cooled to ambient temperature.

10.2.6 Medium-temperature asphalts for use in wearing courses

Medium temperature asphalts (MTAs) are those materials produced using 100 pen grade bitumens. These were originally produced by major bituminous-material suppliers under various trade names as cheaper alternatives to hot-rolled asphalt, but with substantially greater durability than bituminous macadams. The materials were laid in relatively thin layers (25–30 mm) with a nominal application of chippings on housing estates in many large cities, carrying very few, if any, vehicles larger than a double-decker bus, and gave extremely good service with lives of up to 20 years before they needed any maintenance. Their use was extended by some county highway authorities onto lightly trafficked rural roads, with stone contents up to 55%, and with no precoated chippings. With a maximum aggregate size of 20 mm these had about the same texture as

---

* Additional information on airfield pavements can be obtained from *ICE Proceedings*, June 1991 Part 1, papers 537, 547, 563 and 575 by Parrish, Davies, Broadhead and Austin respectively.

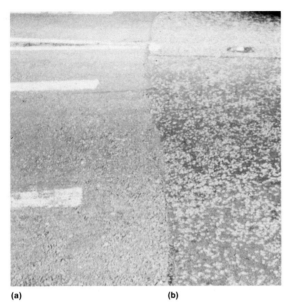

(a)   **(b)**

Figure 10.8 (a) 'Trimasco 65%' stone content asphalt (manufactured by Tarmac Quarry Products Ltd). (b) Normal 30% stone content hot-rolled wearing course asphalt

the lightly chipped housing-estate roads and provided good skid resistance at traffic speeds of less than 50 miles h^{-1}. More recently, and particularly because of the difficulty in supplying precoated chippings to the chip-spreading machine on heavily trafficked urban roads, high-stone-content MTAs are being increasingly used in some areas of England. The 20 mm maximum aggregate size materials designated 55/20 in Tables 3 and 5 of BS 594[1] are less favoured than non-BS 594 materials with 14 mm maximum aggregate size, for which a typical grading is given in Appendix 10.1. A secondary advantage is the economy resulting from not using precoated chippings, which saves about 10% of the cost of the hot-rolled asphalt wearing course. It is normal to specify an absolute minimum PSV of 55 for the MTA coarse aggregate and in high-risk areas, defined in Appendix 2 of DPt Technical Memo H16/76,[9] a minimum PSV of 60 is specified. SFC values of 70–80 are not uncommon on unchipped MTAs, compared with values of 0.6–0.65 on a chipped HRA but with the chips well rolled in, in the traditional manner, giving texture depths of approximately 0.7–1.0 mm rather than the 1.5 mm always specified for high-speed roads.

Once more, the coated-stone industry has produced its own patented variants, such as Trinasco 65 and 55 from Tarmac Quarry Products, and these form very stable, durable wearing courses suitable for any urban use and many rural uses.

Figure 10.8 shows the differences in texture between a Trinasco 65 and a conventional hot-rolled asphalt wearing course. In West Yorkshire, highway engineers developed MTAs using crushed blast-furnace-slag aggregates and these have been very successful in reducing the incidence of skidding accidents at what were formerly high-risk sites.

Lower-stone-content hot rolled asphalt materials are for use in footway wearing courses.

10.2.7 Mastic asphalt in wearing courses

Mastic asphalt is an extremely expensive material by virtue of its very high binder content. It is now rarely, if ever, used in carriageways or footways, except in high prestige areas and in reinstating existing surfaces which tend to be extremely durable

due to the lack of oxidation of the binders. Mastic asphalt is produced by mixing approximately equal volumes of coarse aggregate, filler and hard bitumen in stirred, heated tanks, from which the material is removed as a molten liquid, in buckets. It is then discharged onto the surface to be overlaid and the material spread by highly skilled operatives working on their hands and well-padded knees, using wooden floats and finish it to the correct tolerances. Footway surfaces are finished with a crimping pattern roller. Carriageways are finished with an application of hand-spread precoated chippings which are lightly rolled-in.

The relevant standards are BS 1446,[10] for natural rock asphalt fine aggregate, and BS 1447[11] for mastic asphalt produced using limestone aggregate.

The work is highly specialized and should only be entrusted to experienced mastic asphalt contractors.

10.3 Coated macadams

The concept of stone-to-stone contact and interlock which is fundamental to all macadams, is attributed to McAdam, a Scottish civil engineer who was a contemporary of Thomas Telford, and he is understood to have adopted this principle in rebuilding existing roads which had been formed from much larger pieces of stone, but nevertheless failed. McAdam realized that these failures were due to both a lack of aggregate interlock between the large pieces of stone and a weakening of the subsoil due to water penetrating the road pavement. In addition to using much smaller maximum aggregate sizes than was then customary, McAdam required all stones to be small enough to fit into a man's mouth, he also formed the upper surface to a camber capable of draining rainwater to the edge of the road and sealed the upper crust with smaller stone sizes down to dust. Road pavements built with an excessive camber simply resulted in vehicles running on the crown of the road with resultant rutting and premature failure, and McAdam ensured that his unbound macadam roads were built with just sufficient camber to be self-draining, and no more.

The earliest coated macadams were produced by hand mixing crushed stone with tar from gasworks, much as concrete is still mixed in small quantities, but on heated metal plates. Later, they were also mixed in mechanically driven concrete mixers, but no doubt in the same manner in which clients even today are reluctant to pay a little more for better-quality materials, these tarmacadams were not widely used until the advent of the rubber-tyred bicycle and motor car at the end of the nineteenth century. Then the tar-coated stone was seen primarily as a smooth running surface which was dust free, in contrast to the uncoated macadams which needed watering in summer to control the dust nuisance, and easily pot-holed due to rain or snow and frost action. The soft gas tars were processed to make them less temperature susceptible and the use of tarmacadam spread rapidly in the 1920s with gas–tar binders being supplemented by the bitumens then becoming available. Large arrays of materials were produced but most were relatively open textured with up to 20% voids after laying and rolling. In the late 1950s dense tar surfacing and dense bitumen macadam wearing courses were developed within the industry and a dense bitumen macadam base course specification was produced by the Road Research Laboratory after intensive testing. All these materials relied for their superior performance on denser gradings of aggregate with additional fines in particular, and higher contents of stiffer binders. The tar and bitumen-bound materials each had their respective lobbies and national standards, but the advent of North Sea gas in the 1960s resulted in tar very rapidly becoming virtually unobtainable except from plants which produced smokeless fuels for domestic use. There is, therefore, now only one national standard for coated macadams, BS 4987: 1988,[12] which covers macadams produced with either penetration-grade or cut-back bitumen and tar. Tar is still more temperature susceptible than its bitumen equivalent but does have the significant advantage that it is totally resistant to spillages of such oil-based products as petrol, diesel, kerosene and lubricating oil. It is therefore sometimes specified for use in car parks, refuelling areas and lay-bys but there is an increasing trend to use a tar-based surface dressing binder as a surface sealant to a bituminous wearing course rather than to produce the latter with a tar binder. In this section, therefore, it is assumed that the binders used in macadams will be penetration-grade or cut-back bitumens.

Today coated macadams are perceived as having the fundamental aggregate interlock, which gives them their resistance to deformation and load-spreading ability, but also some tensile strength derived from the binder which gives them resistance to fatigue and, for the denser macadams at least, a degree of impermeability to water which assists in protecting the subgrade soils. One of the prime functions of the binder is to act as a lubricant at laying stage, and assist in breaking down the intergranular friction, which in turn further enhances the aggregate interlock.

BS 4987[12] contains the grading and binder requirements for no less than 16 coated macadam mixtures including two roadbase materials, five base-course mixtures and no less than nine wearing courses. Given that each material can be produced, in theory at least, with two grades of either tar or bitumen, the individual highway engineer should have no difficulty in selecting a material which is virtually ideal for his site, within the limits of a macadam. In addition, the DTp has recently published specifications[5] for a further two road-base macadams, developed in a joint exercise with the TRRL, the British Aggregate Construction Materials Industries' Asphalt and Coated Macadam Product Group (BACMI/ACMA) and the Refined Bitumen Association (RBA). These four materials were deemed to be still in the experimental stage and were, therefore, not included in the latest edition of BS 4987 until included by a recent amendment.[12] However, this large array of materials is rarely, if ever, totally used by the average engineer, who instead usually uses only specific materials with which he is familiar. Perhaps with some justification, the bituminous-material producers frequently enquire whether the standard does not contain too many materials, and the engineer who has little or no experience in the use of macadams needs some help in making his selection. If he was working on a military airfield using the Property Services Agency's Specification,[13] he would specify his macadam in terms of its Marshall stability, optimum binder content range, maximum flow, air voids in the laboratory-produced samples and voids in the aggregate filled with binder. This latter requirements would ensure that the mix was not so overfilled with binder that the fundamental aggregate interlock was impaired, the stability would ensure the load-spreading ability of his macadam, and the minimum binder content range would ensure its durability. He would also expect the producer to exercise particular care in producing the large tonnages of each material used in an airfield pavement and the producer, in turn, given long production runs would be working to the specified binder-content tolerances of $\pm 0.3\%$ rather than $\pm 0.6\%$ as specified in the British Standards for asphalts and macadams.

However, an engineer is not usually working on airfield pavements and, despite considerable research into macadams and numerous pieces of laboratory equipment to measure behaviour under simulated traffic loadings, creep characteristics and tensile strength of macadams as well as asphalts, the lack of any agreed standards has resulted in the British Standard for macadams containing no mix design method but instead being based on good working practices with empirically-derived recipe-mix materials.

With all recipe-mix macadams, the basic need to achieve full aggregate interlock is not achieved if the constituent sizes are not combined in the form of a relatively smooth grading curve. Unfortunately, a minority of less reputable material producers have sometimes been tempted to reduce the proportions of certain aggregate sizes in their mixes, particularly the 10 mm and 6 mm stone sizes, since these have enhanced value as surface-dressing chippings. The fact that a macadam complies with the overall requirements of BS 4987[12] when it is sampled will not therefore necessarily ensure its quality of performance in the pavement. Likewise, aggregates may contain a certain element of oversized material. However, when macadams are produced with a maximum percentage of oversized material, and particularly if the binder content is near the lower specified tolerance level, they frequently show signs of distress when compacted, and do not develop the usual degree of characteristic interlock. Such macadams should be regarded as unsatisfactory for use in permanent works, whether or not they meet the requirements of the specification, since they merely illustrate the difficulties of working at the limits established by writing empirically based national specifications around all materials known to perform well, somewhere in the UK.

10.3.1 Roadbase macadams

The load-carrying capacity of any bituminous road pavement and its ability to relieve the natural subgrade of critical values of vertical strain depends primarily on the stiffness or elastic modulus of the roadbase. A roadbase material which deforms in the wheel-tracked zones has too low a modulus; however, the *in situ* performance of the material depends not only on the written specification but also on the manufacturer producing it to specification, and its being transported, laid and compacted on a stable construction platform, sufficient to achieve 95% of the percentage refusal density (PRD). A summary of this test for compaction, and the conditions to be achieved in the transport, laying and compaction stages are given later. However, assuming all these requirements are achieved, the engineer may elect to use either 40 mm dense bitumen macadam (DBM) in his road base or DBM with a maximum aggregate size of 28 mm.

In general terms, a 40-mm DBM will tend to segregate more readily than a 28-mm material, particularly if it is produced in a hard-stone quarry. Unfortunately, in the process of eliminating many of the macadams which existed in BS 4987 prior to the 1973 revision, 28-mm DBM was excluded and many engineers have consequently had no experience in using this material. Many others witnessed laying gangs struggling to control the segregation of some 40-mm DBMs when laid by machine, particularly at the edges of the laid mats, and began to specify dense bitumen macadam to a 28-mm base course grading but with a reduced binder content. The question of what binder content to use was resolved by the need to minimize the extra cost of the 28-mm material, and with a bitumen content of 3.5% in the 40-mm road-base DBM, and 4.7% in the 28-mm base-course mix, most specified a nominal binder content of 4.0%.

In the 1988 revision of BS 4987,[12] note was taken of these improvised requirements and the 28-mm DBM roadbase which was observed to perform at least as well as the 40-mm material, but with significantly less segregation, was reintroduced into the British Standard.

The 28-mm DBMs made with crushed limestones are easily compacted and even this 0.5% additional binder can result in materials which are too lively under the roller, particularly when the roadbase layer is very well compacted. Some engineers therefore require 28-mm DBM road base produced from crushed limestone to contain no more than 3.5% bitumen, particularly if it is to be laid on a well-supervised site. BS 4987: Part 1: 4.5.1, Notes 1 and 2 give further guidance on this aspect of macadams.

Whichever British Standard dense roadbase macadam is selected, it is important to note that whereas they may be produced using either 100 or 200 pen grade bitumen, for equal load-spreading ability a road base constructed with the softer bitumen needs to be approximately 30% greater in total thickness than one built with 100 pen DBM. Current DoT pavement-design standards[2] were initially based entirely on the use of 100 pen grade bitumen in dense road base macadam but two new macadams were introduced in a recent revision to the Department's own specification.[5] These are 'heavy-duty macadam' and 'DBM 50', both of which can be produced as either 40 or 28 mm maximum aggregate size macadams but they are manufactured using 50 pen bitumen rather than 100 pen and the heavy-duty macadam also includes an additional quantity of filler, 7% to 11% rather than the 2% to 8% present in both conventional dense macadam and DBM 50. The latest revision to the DTp's pavement-design standard HD/14/87, contains graphs of pavement loading vs. road pavement thickness which take account of the greater strength of these two new materials and it is interesting to note that DTp policy is to use the materials to reduce pavement thickness rather than to extend pavement life. Many highway authorities have adopted the new dense macadams but have opted to build extra life into their road pavements since experience has shown that traffic growth has been consistently underestimated since the oil crisis of the early 1970s. Indeed, since the DTp published HD/14/87[2] they have increased their traffic forecasts which indicates that these other authorities may have adopted the wiser philosophy. The additional cost of manufacturing these materials on an asphalt plant already provided with both tank capacity for the storage of 50 pen grade bitumen and the ability to add filler to a mix is relatively small. Nevertheless, the price paid by the customer will probably depend to a greater degree on the distance these macadams have to be hauled from mixing plants capable of producing them compared with the distance a conventional macadam made with 100 pen bitumen has to be hauled. The latter will possibly have no filler added to that produced in the aggregate-crushing processes and carried by the aggregate, so-called 'gratuitous filler'. Commercial considerations also enter into the pricing process and it is therefore impossible to give any specific guidance on the question of the prices of these improved dense macadams relative to conventional DBM.

10.3.2 Base-course macadams

There are now six base-course macadams, one open graded and three dense graded specified in BS 4987: 1988[12] and the two improved base-course macadams originally specified in the DTp specification, but now included in BS 4987 by amendment.

10.3.2.1 Open-graded base course macadam

This material has a low fines content, less than 25% when produced from crushed rock or 20% when made from crushed gravel, and this together with the fact that the fines are mixed with either a cut-back 100 bitumen or a penetration grade bitumen (but never harder than 200 pen), means that it can be hauled long distances without significant cooling or loss of workability. The material is only suitable for use in road pavements carrying traffic densities of less than 250 cvpd and its highly permeable nature allows rainwater easy access to the road base and eventually the subgrade. Its open texture also implies that it should not be left uncovered by wearing course since dirt will readily fill the surface voids and prejudice the bond with the wearing course. Open-textured base course should normally only be used as a carriageway base course on an

unbound road-base material such as wet-mix macadam. With binders of 300 pen and the softer cut-backs open graded base course is very popular for footways where it is laid directly onto the sub-base. Its open texture in this non-critical loading situation is a distinct advantage as when combined with an open-textured wearing course it gives a virtually puddle-free footway for pedestrians, at least in its early life.

The open grading results in relatively rapid binder oxidation and this material needs to be produced with very soft bitumens to achieve its characteristically good durability under light traffic loadings.

10.3.2.2 Dense base course macadam

Apart from the DTp's materials produced with 50 pen grade binders, there are three dense base course materials specified in BS 4987: 1988:[12] 40 mm maximum aggregate size, 28 mm material, and a 20 mm mix. These materials are very strong and are laid on dense roadbase macadams on roads carrying the heaviest traffic. Using the well-known rule-of-thumb that a material may be laid up to five times as thick as its maximum aggregate size, but should never be laid thinner than, at the very least, 1.5 times and preferably this size, the 40 mm material is capable of being laid up to 200 mm thick, but could only be laid to a base-course thickness of 60 mm with extreme difficulty. The only justifiable reason for producing this material is that it utilizes aggregate sizes required for 40 mm dense roadbase macadam. It will segregate readily if made from hard stone and there is no good reason to specify it.

Both the 28-mm and the 20-mm materials perform basically the same function, but for base courses with thicknesses of 50–60 mm the smaller material will be more readily laid to the required tolerances, particularly if any part of the roadbase exists with high spots which can be 15 mm above the specified level and still comply with the DTp specification. From the viewpoint of both the client and the laying gang, therefore, there appears to be no justification for any material other than the 20-mm dense-graded base-course macadam.

The dense base courses will provide a safe, temporary running surface on low-speed roads, but if this use is envisaged the material should be produced using crushed rock with a suitable minimum PSV, commonly 45, to eliminate softer limestones, which could polish.

A major factor in the selection of base-course binder is the specification for the wearing course with which it is to be overlaid. If this is to be a hot-rolled asphalt, it may be laid at temperatures anywhere in the range of 100–180°C, although compaction at the lower temperature could be difficult. A typical laying temperature could easily be as high as 160°C, and at this temperature any 200 pen grade bitumen in a dense base course would rapidly soften. This could result in excessive movement of the base course under the weight of the roller on the wearing course. This is a relatively common problem and often results in the hot-rolled-asphalt wearing-course level tolerances being outside the specification limits. For a base course beneath a hot-rolled-asphalt wearing course, therefore, the engineer should always specify the 100 pen grade bitumen.

If the superimposed wearing course is not a hot-rolled asphalt, the engineer should, nevertheless, consider the following factors before deciding to use the softer, 200 pen bitumen. The dense base courses are produced with either 100 pen or 200 pen bitumen and dense material should only be specified if it is to be machine laid. The 100 pen material will be 30% stronger than the 200 pen one and, whilst it is a hotter material, and will cool more readily in winter, problems caused by cold material are more often due to poor site organization than mixing and delivery temperatures. Therefore, such problems are as likely to occur with the cooler 200 pen material as they are with the 100 pen macadam. Until the most recent revision of BS 4987: 1988,[12] macadams were commonly produced with a lower binder content if 200 pen bitumen was specified instead of 100 pen and, as a result, they were marginally cheaper. The users were clearly unaware of the greater structural strength of the harder binder material or, as has been stated elsewhere, were not prepared to pay even marginally extra for a better material. The 1988 edition of BS 4987: 1988[12] requires the same binder content whether 100 pen or 200 pen is specified. There appears, therefore, to be no single logical reason for specifying 200 pen material, and the engineer who wants a good strong machine-laid base-course of between 40 and 100 mm thickness, and this is a very thick base course, should specify 20 mm dense base course with 100 pen bitumen.

10.3.2.3 Single-course macadam

In a recent typical 6-month period, one national bituminous material producer reported that 40 mm single-course macadam comprised 0.2% of his total production tonnage. The only materials produced in lesser quantities were two which were omitted from BS 4987: 1973! The concept of using a single course of relatively weak, easily segregated hand-laid 40-mm open-textured material instead of a base course and a wearing course is difficult to justify for any reason other than the surfacing of farm roads, the speed of construction in areas too small for paver operation, or, simply, economy. Since commercial vehicles of any reasonable weight will tend to displace the single-course macadam when they turn, its use should ideally be confined to office car parks and drives to private houses and farms, but even these works can be built to a higher standard with other more durable hand-laid materials. There certainly appears to be no good reason to use 40 mm single-course material on public roads and, unless the engineer is required to overlay a farm drive, using a 100-mm thickness 40 mm open-textured macadam which is then sealed with grit, he should avoid the material altogether.

10.3.2.4 DTp Specification base-course macadams

The DTp's own dense base courses were until recently only included as amendments to the 1985 Specification for Highway Works.[14] 'Heavy duty macadam' and 'DBM 50', both use 50 pen grade bitumen, and are intended for machine laying on heavily trafficked road pavements. Either will form a good base course and, since the ready availability of either or both will depend on the location of the site in relation to mixing plants and whether the plants can add additional filler to the aggregate, and since the price is dictated as much by the supplier's commercial consideration as by production and haulage costs plus profit, the engineer might be best advised to specify that the contractor may elect to use either the 20 mm dense graded base course to BS 4987: 1988[12] with 100 pen bitumen, or either of these two materials now included in BS 4987 and price his tender accordingly.

Three further points concerning dense base-course materials produced to any specification are that the DTp's permitted alternative materials listed in Appendix B to HD/14/87[2] include base courses made with crushed rock or slag coarse aggregates only, thus excluding gravels for all classes of road pavement initially carrying more than 100 commercial/vehicles per day. In addition, where the binder is tar, a most unlikely situation, the fine aggregate also must be crushed rock or slag fines.

Finally, where the materials are subject to a high degree of compaction, as on well supervised sites with a percentage refusal density specification, recipe-mix dense macadams may become so well compacted that their voids become over-filled with binder. This in turn reduces them to an unstable, easily rutted state and, for this very reason, BS 4987: 1988: Part 1, 4.5.1

Footnote 3, permits the binder content to be reduced by 0.5% by agreement between the supplier and purchaser.

10.3.3 Wearing-course macadams

BS 4987: 1988[12] contains specifications for two open-graded wearing-course materials, and one medium-graded, one fine-graded, one dense-graded, two close-graded and two pervious macadams. Fortunately, the DTp have not found it necessary to add to this seemingly bewildering array.

Appendix B to BS 4987: 1988 stresses the need to ensure that the coarse aggregates in any macadam wearing course used on carriageways are resistant to polishing, particularly on high-speed roads and at junctions and on roundabouts. This advice is particularly relevant in view of the DTp's recent emphasis on providing better skidding resistance on trunk roads, and the DTp publications HA/36/87[15] and HD/15/87[16] should be on any highway engineer's reading list. It also draws attention to the rate at which aggregates are abraded by heavy traffic in particular and refers to guidance published in DPt Technical Memorandum H16/76.[9] For convenience, Appendices 1 and 2 to this document are reproduced in Appendix 10.6 to assist the engineer in specifying his PSV and aggregate-abrasion value (AAV) requirements. Only fine-grade wearing courses are likely to be finished with an application of precoated chippings. (This memo is soon to be superseded.)

10.3.3.1 Open-graded wearing-course macadams

BS 4987: 1988[12] specifies both 14 mm and 10 mm open-graded macadams. Both are very permeable materials and will therefore need to be surface dressed after a few years to arrest the oxidation of the binder and hence enhance their durability. It is recommended that bituminous grit, 'sealing grit', should be brushed into a newly laid open-textured wearing course before it is trafficked. Whilst they are initially the cheapest type of wearing-course material, they are the weakest by virtue of their open gradings and soft binders and their need for surface dressing increases their true long-term costs.

The open-graded material is suitable for use on footways as well as carriageways and car parks and its open texture and free draining ability results in it being 'puddle' free for at least the duration of the normal 12-month maintenance period. However, 10-mm aggregate is a valuable surface-dressing material and many suppliers would prefer users to specify the 14-mm macadam.

Some open-graded materials are produced with specially fluxed bitumens which make them very workable for up to a week or more. These are called 'deferred-set' materials and are intended for use in temporary trench reinstatement work and emergency patching only since they are not durable.

However, there is an increasing tendency for deferred-set macadams to be used in permanent public works. This may result in the laying gangs earning substantial bonuses but there are no advantages to either the taxpayer or ratepayer. That this practice exists at all is simply due to a combination of poor management control in some highway authorities and ignorance which results from a lack of training. There is no British Standard for either deferred-set materials or their binders. Hand-laid macadams in permanent works should instead be specified to be produced with either a 300 pen bitumen or a 200 pen bitumen fluxed with a volatile fluxing agent which evaporates in about 6–8 h, and the materials used and compacted whilst relatively hot.

10.3.3.2 Close-graded wearing-course macadams

'Close graded' is a new term introduced in the 1988 revision of BS 4987: 1988[12] and is intended to draw attention to the fact that such materials, which were previously described as 'dense', are not impermeable. There are two sizes, 14 mm and 10 mm, both of which are suitable for use in carriageways which have no surface-texture-depth requirement so long as they are produced with suitable binder and good quality aggregates. Machine-laid materials should be produced with 100 pen binder for the reasons previously stated, but if they are to be hand laid, and particularly on footways, 300 pen grade bitumen or an even softer cut-back bitumen is advisable. Adequate compaction is essential to achieve a minimum of interconnected voids in the macadams and so delay their disintegration due to the affects of water and oxygen. Neither is as durable as the medium-temperature asphalts with high stone contents and no precoated chippings (described earlier). Both close-graded materials are used in considerable quantities.

10.3.3.3 Dense wearing-course macadam

The 6 mm macadam has been included in BS 4987: 1988[12] because of its increasingly widespread use by highway authorities. It has been well used on less heavily trafficked roads but there is little experience of its use under heavy traffic. Its use should therefore be restricted to roads carrying less than 250 cvpd. Its dense grading coupled with adequate compaction should enable it to form a durable wearing course, assuming it is produced with suitable binder and aggregates. It is not normally used in footway work and should, wherever possible, be machine laid.

10.3.3.4 Medium-graded wearing-course macadam

Medium-graded wearing course is produced in one nominal size only, 6 mm, and is intended specifically for use under light (i.e. car) traffic, footways, playgrounds and the like. It can be machine laid or hand laid, often in the latter case as a cold-laid material, but note that BS 4987: 1988[12] suggests the percentage of fine aggregate should be reduced either to enhance its workability for hand laying, or to increase its permeability and thus prevent the formation of rainwater puddles at low spots.

The specifier can also increase the binder content by up to 10% as a further aid to workability, particularly if it is to be hand laid cold in areas which will not be trafficked. In some areas the material is produced with limestone aggregate which is particularly specified for use in school playgrounds since this softer rock causes less skin abrasion when children fall down.

10.3.3.5 Fine-graded wearing-course macadam

BS 4987: 1988[12] specifies 3 mm fine-graded wearing-course only. This used to be described as fine cold asphalt, although it is not strictly an asphalt within the UK meaning of the word. It provides a suitable wearing course for use on low-speed roads, and is usually finished with a light application of precoated chippings. Its small maximum aggregate size makes it suitable for laying in thin layers, never more than 25 mm thick. The binder is either a cut-back bitumen or a 300 pen grade bitumen which enables it to be either machine laid or hand laid with ease.

10.3.3.6 Pervious wearing-course macadams

The 20 mm and 10 mm pervious macadam wearing courses were included in BS 4987 for the first time in 1988.[12] A pervious macadam has an aggregate grading which is designed to give it a void content after rolling to refusal of 15–20% when first trafficked, and it is laid on an impermeable base course. This very open texture enables rainwater to drain through the wearing course rather than across it, thus producing driving conditions in which there is virtually a complete absence of spray produced from vehicle wheels, but intimate road-to-tyre contact and, as a

result, good skin resistance. Research indicates that a three-point reduction in the PSV of a pervious macadam aggregate, relative to the PSV of precoated chippings in hot-rolled asphalt, will give no reduction in the skidding resistance of the road surface.

One immediate result of this large void content is that the binder is subjected to accelerated oxidation and any tendency for an aggregate to be stripped of its binder will be similarly accelerated. To minimize the oxidation problem, the binder-film thickness needs to be maximized and one way of achieving this is to add to the mix a low-mass, high-volume filler such as rock wool or cellulose fibre. These materials can be considered to act in the same manner as a mass of feathers in that the particles are fastened to the aggregate by the normal binder content in the mix, but then themselves become coated with further binder. In this way, the ability of the aggregate to carry binder, which is otherwise limited, is considerably enhanced. The drawback is that each additional 1% of binder in the mix reduces the void content by approximately 2.5%, but the macadam is nevertheless still extremely effective in reducing road spray. Efforts to increase the binder content without using these low-density fillers usually results in binder drainage from the aggregate either from uppermost materials to lowermost within the delivery lorries, or, in extreme cases, even off the rear of the lorries. Daines[17] has developed a laboratory test for determining the optimum binder content for a particular aggregate, but this gives results which the author considers need to be increased by at least 0.5%.

Binder stripping has been minimized by the use of hydrated lime filler. Gritstone aggregates appear to produce durable materials. One series of TRRL-supervised trials have been conducted since 1984 to determine which grade of bitumen, or what form of modified binder, is most durable and, to date, it appears that a 200 pen grade unmodified binder or a 100 pen grade enhanced with natural rubber both give good results as do 100 pen binders with low-density fillers. The tests are reported in TRRL Report RR57.[17]

Pervious macadams are becoming increasingly used in Holland for their secondary benefit, the reduction of road/tyre noise. The reduction in noise is immediately apparent when driving from a hot rolled asphalt onto a pervious macadam and is at least 3 dbA.

A good pervious macadam should last for at least 10 years. The materials specified in BS 4987: 1988[12] have binder contents of 3.7%, with a tolerance of ±0.3%, to avoid binder drainage. However, it is considered that these are too low to produce the most durable materials and on balance, a binder content of 4.2–4.5% gives a thicker binder film without significant binder drainage problems.

The drainage of the edge of the base course needs to be carefully considered at design stage and may be direct off the edge of the base course into a french drain on rural, unkerbed carriageways. On kerbed carriageways, drainage is to a 150 mm wide pervious macadam free channel at kerb face, exposing the top of the base course, discharging into conventional road gullies, or into 'Beany-blocks' or safti-curbs laid below the top of the base course level.

However, it is absolutely paramount to realize that the material must be compacted to total refusal in order to achieve full mechanical interlock of the aggregate and to minimize wheel-track rutting in service. Joints between mats are best avoided since they retard the flow of water within mats and engineers considering the use of pervious macadams could do worse than read a recent paper on practical aspects of its use.[18]

10.4 Manufacturing processes

Asphalts are produced at higher temperatures than most macadams because of their more viscous binders and they are

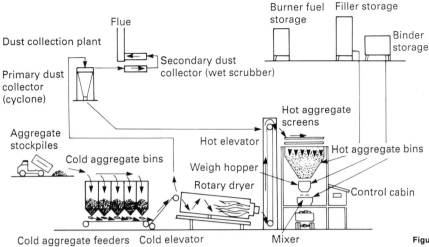

Figure 10.9 Typical asphalt mixing plant

usually manufactured in so-called 'asphalt plants', which may be either the static type located in a quarry or at a railhead near to a substantial marketing area, or mobile, located on or very close to a site. The prime feature of both types is that the coarse aggregate and the sand are dried and heated in cylindrical rotary driers and then screened prior to storage in high level, insulated aggregate bins. The drivers are 3 m or more in diameter and up to 12 m long, usually fired with oil. The filler is brought to each plant in road tankers which are coupled to the filler silo before discharging their loads under pressure, or recovered from the filtered exhaust gases from the plant, or produced as a combination of both. The bitumen is produced in a high-temperature process at an oil refinery and is maintained at relatively high temperatures in order to facilitate pumping and handling. It is delivered to the plant in insulated tankers which are discharged into well-insulated, clearly labelled, heated bitumen storage tanks. This clear labelling is important to ensure that the wrong penetration grade of bitumen is not inadvertently discharged into a tank.

To produce an asphalt, the plant operator introduces predetermined and carefully controlled weights of each required size of hot aggregate and cold filler into the pug-mill or paddle mixer prior to the introduction of the hot bitumen. The mixing process continues until all the aggregate is coated with bitumen and the constituents are combined into a homogeneous mixture at the correct temperature, when the completed batch is usually discharged into a skip mounted on steeply inclined rails. This lifts the batch to the top of the insulated storage hopper into which it is discharged whilst the mixer is recharged with materials and commences to mix the next batch. Delivery lorries are usually loaded direct from this hot bin, which acts as a surge hopper and, if properly sealed and insulated, can hold mixed material for at least 12 h without detriment. A typical asphalt plant is shown in *Figure 10.9*, although there are many variations on the form of layout and type of individual components.

Environmental concern has resulted in considerable reductions in dust and smoke discharged into the atmosphere from plants. This is achieved by blowing air through the length of the drum of the rotary drier, then ducting it to a filter house whence the dust is recovered and frequently re-used as filler. Increasing concern is now causing mixer manufacturers to collect even the hydrocarbon fumes arising from the mixer and to duct these into the drier where they can be burned.

In older plants, the correct proportioning of the various constituents by weight depends entirely on both the skill of the plant operator in weighing the correct batch sizes for each constituent, and that of the plant technician in gauging what weight of moisture and filler will be lost from the batch in the mixer. Production tolerances, particularly for binder contents, are relatively large to allow for some degree of human error and the imperfections in the plant's weighing and aggregate feed mechanisms. However, the asphalt industry has benefitted since 1980 from the attention of electronics engineers and all new plants and many older ones are now equipped with micro-processor-control mechanisms which give better control of aggregate gradings, and weigh the dried stone batched for a mix to determine its weight very quickly and accurately and thereby ensure that the correct amount of the very expensive bitumen is discharged into the mixer.

The specific gravity of bitumen varies with its temperature but the microprocessor can nevertheless calculate the correct amount so rapidly that no excess bitumen is used, and the bitumen savings alone can justify the expense of these electronic controls. Other advantages include the fact that the plant can be operated by one man, who can be relatively unskilled, that full details of all mixes produced and materials used are automatically logged to give better plant-management data and that there is better fault logging. Particular mix combinations are stored in electronic memories to which only authorized personnel have access and this feature prevents many quality-control problems from arising. The industry has not been renowned for its willingness to invest capital, but the fact that virtually 70% of all UK plants are already microprocessor controlled itself indicates the cost-effectiveness of the investment.

When problems do occur they are usually the result of either mechanical failures in the plant machinery or human error in activities such as stockpiling the incorrect materials in one or more of the storage hoppers. The microprocessor available so far is unable to detect that the wrong sieve size of aggregate is contained in any particular hopper, and whilst it ensures that the weigh-batcher correctly weighs the predetermined quantity of material from a hopper, the resultant mixed batch may nevertheless fail to meet the specification if that hopper held the wrong aggregate size.

Occasionally, the wrong grade of bitumen will be added to the mixer, normally due to error at the delivery stage and in asphalts this usually results in a softer than specified binder being used which is only detected on site when an item of contractor's plant stands overnight on a newly laid mat and forms indentations in a material which would not normally deform. The use of the incorrect binder can usually be determined by removing a sample of the material from the completed mat and sending it to a laboratory for the recovery of the bitumen and its subsequent testing to determine its penetration. All binders harden in the mixing and laying process and it is usual to find that the recovered bitumen is one grade harder than it was in the quarry storage tank. Thus a specified 50 pen grade binder, which complies with the bitumen specification if it has any penetration between 40 and 60 but will be assumed to be mid-range at 50 pen, will be at about 35 pen on recovery from the newly laid road pavement, but could be down to 25 pen if it was delivered to the quarry at the minimum specified pen value of 40. If the recovered pen is 70 or thereabouts, the mix was obviously not made with the 50 pen binder.

A further problem is the use of damp aggregates, or even saturated aggregates after a recent period of inclement weather. The coarser sizes drain rapidly but sands do not and, in extreme cases, the difficulty experienced in driving off the excess moisture in the rotary drier can reduce the throughput of the plant by up to 30% or more. This creates difficulties in maintaining deliveries of materials to sites and occasionally less-reputable producers will resort either to drying the sand incompletely or heating it excessively. In the former case, the material can arrive on site in an unusually highly workable condition and the paving gang then experience difficulty in working within the specified level tolerances. Overheated material can be monitored by the judicious use of asphalt thermometers in the loads of material being delivered to site, since material is now rarely overheated to the extent where it is obviously brown and burned rather than black when discharged from the delivery lorries. A haze of blue smoke over a load when the insulating tarpaulin covers are removed from the back of the lorry should alert site staff to check the delivery temperature, even if this is not part of their routine, which it should be. Materials which have 'slumped' excessively in the delivery lorries can be detected without even removing the tarpaulin covers and these should be checked initially for excessively high temperature. If the temperature is satisfactory, samples may be removed for laboratory determination of both bitumen and water content.

All these problems are clearly recognized within the companies making bitumen materials and the better-run companies have introduced quality-assurance schemes to reduce or eliminate their occurrence. It is significant that even on microprocessor-controlled production plants, the operator still visually inspects the batches discharged from the mixer as a double check, and technical staff still check the temperature of material in dispatch lorries and take samples on a regular basis for laboratory analyses.

Whilst the asphalt plant uses preheated aggregates stored in hot bins, a batch heater plant will use pre-dried aggregates fed into cold storage bins and then assembled in the correct proportions to form a 2–4 tonne batch, depending on the size of mixer. This specific batch of aggregate is then flame heated to the correct temperature and discharged into the mixer where the filler and hot binder are added. After the requisite mixing time, the completely mixed batch is discharged to either a delivery lorry or a hot storage bin. Once more there are numerous variations on this basic format, but the prime advantage of the batch mixer is its high versatility in producing numerous diverse mixes in any random order.

Macadams are produced at lower temperatures than asphalts and, since crushed rock frequently carries sufficient filler to satisfy specifications, some plants, such as those in limestone quarries, will have no filler silos. This and their lower operating temperatures make these plants unsuitable for producing asphalts. However, asphalt plants will produce macadams, given adequate supplies of suitable aggregates.

A relatively recent innovation is the introduction of continuous drum mixers into one end of which the cold and frequently damp virgin aggregate is fed. The aggregate passes through a high-temperature zone where it is heated and dried by the oil or gas flames. Once clear of the flame zone, the hot dry aggregate is sprayed with hot bitumen and mixed inside the rotating drum, being continuously lifted by the internal flights, then dropped, then lifted as it progresses towards the lower discharge end of the drum. From here it is usually lifted by an enclosed bucket elevator into one of several well-insulated hot storage silos or bins. Whereas the conventional asphalt plant shown in *Figure 10.9* has an output of up to 150 tonne h^{-1}, a large drum mixer will produce as much as 600 tonne h^{-1}, but these large outputs and the ensuing economies of scale are only derived from long production runs. As a result, plants equipped with large drum mixers usually also have a conventional batch mixer plant for producing small quantities for their low-volume customers who pay high prices for material and are a very profitable market sector.

The problems occasionally experienced with asphalt plants and batch heaters can also occur with drum mixers and some engineers regret the acceptance into national specifications of moisture contents of up to 1% in materials produced in drum mixers.

10.4.1 Recycled materials

The oil crisis of the early 1970s and consequent rapid escalation in the cost of bitumen focussed attention on the possibility of recycling bituminous materials, usually cold planings removed from road pavements in maintenance operations. A hot recycling operation must be used for asphalts and dense macadams, but cold recycling can be used for lower grade materials being either planed asphalts or macadams.

In the hot process, the recycled aggregates, which already contain a substantial mass of bitumen suitable for reuse, cannot be heated by passing them through a direct flame-heated high-temperature zone into the drier since this would simply burn and destroy the binder. Instead, therefore, they are fed into a 'drum mixer' beyond the burner, and heated by direct contact with the virgin aggregate which has already been flame heated. Therefore, the process is as for virgin materials except that less new bitumen is added to the mix, which makes it more economical than material produced without recycled materials. Where the binder on the recycled aggregates is unsuitable for re-use, these may simply be added to virgin aggregate in a batch mixer and then coated with new binder. The DTp and the Department of Energy are concerned to encourage the use of recycled materials as this not only reduces the consumption of valuable natural resources (bitumen and aggregate), but also requires less energy in the total production process. The DTp is, however, insistent in requiring that mixtures which incorporate recycled materials to achieve the same specification compliance as products made with 100% virgin raw materials.

The usually considerable volume of water contained in the recycled feedstock materials makes it essential to check-weigh the batched material before final adjustments are made to the total amount of added binder and this in turn virtually dictates that the plant is controlled by a microprocessor.

A further variation on recycling is to process existing carriageway wearing courses and base courses in which the bitumen has oxidized to failure by pulverizing *in situ* to reduce them to almost to their original aggregate components. Bituminous emulsion is then mixed *in situ* with the aggregate. Any new aggregates required to achieve the specified grading will have been previously spread over the pavement prior to the pulverising stage. The newly mixed loose material is graded to the correct levels before being compacted to refusal.

The surface of the recycled material is surface dressed before reopening the road to traffic and this process, known as 'retreading' provides a cost-effective method of maintaining lightly trafficked roads.

Deeper *in situ* pulverization of road-base materials, followed by *in situ* addition of cement and bitumen emulsion provides a cost-effective method of substantially strengthening a failing road base in pavements and road pavements carrying light to medium traffic loadings, particularly if this recycled material is then overlaid using hot-rolled asphalt base course and wearing course.

The 'Repave' process heats an existing wearing course asphalt sufficiently to reflux the bitumen and then loosens it by raking the hot material before overlaying it using a conventional paver laying new hot-rolled asphalt 20–25 mm thick rather than the normal 40 mm thickness of new material. If the job is carried out properly the new asphalt boards completely with the reheated older material and provides a cost-effective way of up-grading the wearing course on roads which are structurally sound. However, like surface dressing, the Repave process will not remedy structural defects in carriageway pavements. The repaved surface is finished with precoated chippings as for conventional material. Repave is more fully described and specified in HA/14/82[19] which particularly draws attention to the need to ensure that the existing bitumen is not too oxidized.

Recycling, whether by removal to plants off-site or carried out *in situ*, makes use of the enormous reserves of quarried aggregate which already exist in all highway authorities' road pavements and highway engineers involved in maintenance management will doubtless make increasing use of these techniques as their confidence in them increases.

10.5 Storage hoppers or silos

High-output mixers can only operate efficiently if they can both mix large tonnages of the same materials and discharge the mixed materials into sealed and insulated storage containers. However, the question of how long materials can be stored without affecting their quality is frequently raised and it is important to understand both the problems associated with hot-bin storage and, equally, how to overcome them. Both hoppers and silos may be associated with the segregation of mixed products and the oxidation, and hence reduction in long-term durability, of the bitumen.

The extent to which a material segregates will depend to some degree on its maximum aggregate size and grading but, whatever the material, segregation is best minimized by dumping complete batches of mixed product into the storage vessel and not by feeding it in as a trickle. The distance the material ideally falls inside the hopper or silo is also important, and the silo needs to be reasonably full at all times (unless near the end of the working day) in order to minimize this free-fall distance, rather than empty it then refill completely in cycles throughout the day.

Oxidation varies with both the temperature of the stored material and its type. An open-textured material will be more permeable and hence be more easily oxidized than a dense one and a higher storage temperature will enhance the rate of oxidation. A basic knowledge of chemistry indicates that a product stored at 180°C could oxidize six times faster than the same product stored at 130°C. But this is not generally realized. Oxidation is minimized by reducing the time in which a material is exposed to oxygen and efforts have been made to fill the void at the top of hot bins with superheated steam or inert gas to displace atmospheric oxygen. However, any oxygen present combines with the hydrocarbon vapours from the bitumen to form carbon dioxide which, frequently, effectively solves this problem. Both the top doors for filling the bins and the bottom doors for discharging mixed materials into transport need to be properly sealed to prevent heat leaking out and oxygen leaking in. Storage temperatures must be maintained by insulation and not by heating the storage container, except for the base cone which is kept warm to assist bottom discharge.

To work effectively, all hoppers and silos must be emptied each day to avoid material adhering in lumps to the walls, and eventually causing the stored products to accumulate and cause a feed blockage, or even be discharged as cold lumps which can at the very least cause the need for remedial work in the laid mat and at worst can damage the customer's paver. Personnel should never enter either a hopper or silo to free blockages until all traces of hydrocarbon fumes have been cleared by venting at both top and bottom. The effectiveness of a hot bin's wall insulation and doors in keeping the stored materials hot can best be checked by means of thermographic imagery. If the container is well designed and well maintained it should be capable of storing problem materials for at least 24 h without oxidation.

10.6 Pre-laying preparation work

Before new material is laid it is important to ensure that the surfaces to be overlaid are clean and tack-coated if necessary with a K1-40 bituminous emulsion sprayed evenly over all bituminous surfaces and any new or old concrete surfaces which are to be overlaid. It is very poor workmanship to simply wave the emulsion lance around and spray narrow strips of tack coat in some random pattern.

Previously unpaved areas should be considered for spraying with a total weed-killer and the sub-base should always be checked for soft areas in the final stages of its compaction. New drains beneath any area to be paved should be checked and any remedial work should be completed well before wearing-course stage. Soiled paved surfaces which are to be overlaid can be thoroughly cleaned using mobile water tankers with high-pressure water jets. Brushing wet mud with a hand or mechanical brush is not effective nor is tack-coating dried mud which lies on top of a lower bituminous layer.

All surface ironwork should be fixed to final levels and painted with bitumen before any wearing-course material is laid. Irregular surfaces should be checked and regulated using suitable materials and all plant checked mechanically and fuel and water tanks topped-up. The layout of the mats to be laid by hand or machine need to be planned to ensure that, for instance, that delivery lorries do not stand on, turn on or even cross newly laid paved areas.

Last, but not least, the safety of both the travelling public and of the workforce actually on site needs to be considered and this requires adequate pre-planning of the traffic control to be used on the job and liaison with both the Police and representatives of the highway authority if the job is anticipated to cause any degree of traffic congestion. Bus services and even fire engines and ambulances could be delayed, particularly in urban areas. Traffic control should be carried out to the standards laid down by the DTp in Chapter 8 of the Traffic Signs Manual.

10.7 Laying bituminous materials by hand

Hand laying to fine tolerances is skilled work and all hand laying is hard work. To make the job as easy as possible all hot material should be well sheeted on delivery to retain its heat. This simple operation maintains the material's workability and facilitates laying and compaction. When loads of new material are delivered, they should ideally be tipped into a series of small heaps on clean, hard surfaces along the job to minimize the sheer effort of wheel-barrowing materials any further than necessary. Large heaps also tend to pre-compact the material at the bottom and result in lumps and tolerance problems in the finished layer.

Once work has started on a particular heap and it has been

unsheeted, it should be spread and rolled as soon as possible. The most skilled members of the hand-lay gang are the rakers who can place material within small level tolerances by deft raking. Excessive raking will segregate denser materials which should be laid by machine whenever possible. Ideal hand-lay materials are open-graded macadams with cut-back or soft straight-run binders, maximum penetration 300 pen, or cold-laid materials coated with bitumen emulsions. When very tight level control must be achieved, the materials need to be laid in strips bounded by pre-levelled wooden battens which are removed as the next strip is laid.

There is unfortunately an increasing tendency for deferred-set macadams to be used for all classes of hand-lay, simply because they are relatively so much easier to lay. The laying gangs, therefore, lay larger areas and their earnings are greater than they would be using conventional BS 4987:1988[12] macadams. This tendency should be vigorously discouraged since deferred-set materials are only intended for use in temporary patching works and, unless they are produced with modified binders, which add to their cost, they have poor durability. Durable deferred-set binders are available but clients will not pay for their marginal extra costs so quarries, not surprisingly, do not commonly stock them.

Joints are a weakness in any material and, when hand-laying up to an existing mat it is common for coarser aggregate to be be raked to the edge of the new material, which sometimes results in an extremely open, segregated, mat edge and, consequently, in a very poor joint. To avoid this, the new material should be raked up and onto the first mat and the coarser aggregate then quickly pulled off it in a flicking action of the rake which projects these larger factions into the middle of the new mat. This may leave a slight excess of fines at the new joint edge but, as long as these are well compacted, this is a lesser problem than an excess of coarse aggregate. The degree of surcharge to be used when placing material will depend on the characteristics of the material itself, but is normally 25–30%. Hand-lay gangs frequently work with either a bucket of diesel oil or a hot brazier close to hand, and spare tools are stood in them. The hand tools used gradually accumulate a coating of thick binder and fine aggregate and these are exchanged with cleaned tools before being stood in the diesel or fire to clean them. The hand tools also include hand rammers to compact material in between valve boxes, near walls and wherever else it is difficult to compact the new material with a roller.

Compaction is carried out as soon as possible after laying, using small rollers, either dead-weight machines with a minimum weight of 2.5 tonne, or well-maintained vibrating machines with a minimum mass of 700 kg. Small vibrating-plate compactors are usually quite ineffective substitutes for rollers and should only be used in trench reinstatement work.

Figure 10.10 Typical asphalt paving machine

In reinstatement works using materials such as hot-rolled asphalt wearing course, it is vital to spread the materials to the correct surcharge and to compact them whilst the temperature is sufficiently high and such material should ideally be manufactured with softer binders than those used in machine-laid material.

Levels should be checked after initial application of the roller so that additional material may be added and rolled into low areas, or high spots raked-off before compaction is completed.

Material is usually paid for on an area and thickness basis and some less reliable gangs may spread as thinly as possible and then allow them to cool so that the eventual compaction reduces the layer thicknesses by minimal amounts. These layers will tend to be less durable as not only will they lack aggregate interlock, but also they will be more prone to oxidation and binder stripping. This problem is not confined to hand-laid materials and specifiers who neglect to include compaction requirements in their contacts are as responsible as the laying gang for the poor durability.

10.8 Laying bituminous materials by machine

A typical paving machine used to lay bituminous materials is shown on *Figure 10.10*. The first bituminous paver, which ran on rails at the edges of the mat, was built in the USA in 1931 and by 1936 the concept had been developed by Barber Green to include virtually all the features of present-day pavers except that their machines ran on crawler tracks. In 1954, Blaw Knox in the USA produced a rubber-tyred machine and for some years there was controversy in the industry about which type of machine was better for which job. However, for some years both companies have built both types of machine in a variety of sizes and similar machines are now produced by companies all over the world. Nevertheless, most pavers are now rubber-tyred rather than crawler-tack mounted.

A typical paver can be considered as having three main elements:

(1) the hopper unit at the front of the paver, carried on its own solid tyres, in the case of the rubber-tyred machine, into which the material to be laid is unloaded directly from the delivery vehicle;

(2) the tractor unit, carried on the driving wheels, with the power unit, drive controls and fuel tanks, and through which the bituminous material is moved from the hopper on twin conveyors, manufactured from articulated steel components, to the rear of the unit. Here the discharged material is spread laterally by power-driven augers, or 'screws', across the full width of the mat which is to be laid; and

(3) the floating screed, which is the 'magic' element in the paver and which enables it to lay material to very fine tolerances despite the paver's wheels running on a relatively uneven surface.

The main parts of the hopper are shown in *Figure 10.11*. The free-running, non-driven push rollers mounted on the front face of the hopper unit come into contact with the rear wheels of the delivery vehicle, which is pushed along by the paver as it unloads. The actual operation of reversing the delivery vehicle virtually up to the paver's rollers is a fine art and if the lorry driver bumps into the paver he will create a transverse ripple across the width of the freshly laid mat which is almost impossible to eradicate by subsequent rolling. Having reversed carefully to within inches of the paver, the delivery driver, who has previously unfastened the ropes securing the tarpaulin which protects and insulates his load, carefully elevates the lorry's tipping body so that the new material feeds by gravity at a

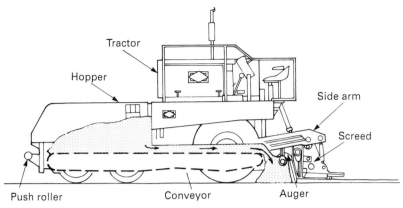

Tractor
Hopper
Side arm
Screed
Push roller
Conveyor
Auger

Figure 10.11 Material flow path (side view)

Figure 10.12 Timber insulation to sides of paver hopper

steady rate into the hopper. In the meantime the paver has moved forward to contact the lorry and both vehicles move forward together. If the delivery driver discharges his load much too quickly, then the front of the paver may simply be buried in material; a little too quickly and the hopper becomes overfilled. This results in material falling off the front of the hopper and passing beneath the paver, and its wheels in some instances, so that it becomes part of the laid mat without having been compacted by the paver's tamping mechanism. A further problem with hoppers is that the pavers are built to either USA or continental European designs and, in both these areas, winters are so severe that all paving stops. Consequently, the problems of hot-delivered material being cooled by contact with the non-insulated sheet-steel sides and bottom to the hopper have not been addressed. In the UK, the public sector financial systems often result in extra funds being made available for paving work in the middle of winter, when the problems of materials cooling in contact with the sheet-steel hopper sides are considerably enhanced. Client's engineers have drawn the attention of paver builders to this problem and it has resulted in a belated effort on their part to offer merely insulated hopper sides on new pavers, but only as an optional extra. *Figure 10.12* shows a paver hopper which has been insulated by a contractor following discussions with a resident engineer, using 50-mm hardwood bolted onto the inside of the hopper and this immediately results in material cooling less rapidly in the hopper and, in turn, less remedial work for the laying contractor.

A typical paving gang works to one over-riding principle which is that they will lay any material which will actually pass through the paver. The result is that material which becomes cooled on the hopper sides, the so-called 'wings' because they can be mechanically elevated, is discharged into the hopper bottom, and thence onto the rear feeding conveyors, immediately prior to delivery of a new load of hot material. The gang works on the principle that the colder material will be mixed with the hot new material, and eventually either become partially reheated or become part of the central 'oil-lane' area of the new mat and thus lie outside the more heavily stressed wheel-tracked zones of the road pavement. Constant supervision by a clerk of works should solve this problem, but rarely does, and engineers should not hesitate to include a clause in their specifications requiring that the hopper of any paver should be insulated either by the manufacturer or by the system referred to above.

The tractor unit's main points of interest to the civil engineer are the auger units or 'screws' and the way in which the delivery of material to them is either automatically regulated, or not. The layout of the two feed conveyors and augers and the material flow path are shown clearly in *Figure 10.13*. Any material which contains aggregate larger than 20 mm will have a tendency to segregate, and the segregated aggregate tends to be carried by the augers to the edges of the mat. For this reason alone, many engineers specify that their dense roadbase macadams should have a maximum aggregate size of 28 mm rather than 40 mm which was the only roadbase material specified in the 1973 edition of BS 4987. If, for any reason, the newly delivered material has cooled and formed into lumps, these will be broken down to some extent in the process of being distributed by the augers. However, any lumps still remaining will be pushed to the edges of the new mat width and, in some cases, they will block the egress of material from the augers to beneath the front edge of the paver's screed. This is extremely serious, as will be seen later.

The augers should maintain a constant pressure head of new material in front of the following screed, and this is achieved by ensuring that the auger's flights are always at least half covered, and ideally two-thirds covered. The paver driver controls the depth of material about the augers by switching on and off the twin conveyors from the hopper. Alternatively, the paver can be fitted, at extra cost, with an automatic feed control, which is able to sense either mechanically or by infra-red beam, the depth of material surrounding the augers. These are preferred to driver control by many engineers, since any lack of attention to the feed rate by the paver driver can result in the augers being totally submerged in new material and then becoming completely uncovered. This will be referred to later when the action of the screed is examined. The width of mat laid by the paver can be increased and some manufacturers have designed auger

Push rollers Conveyors Augers Crown adjusters

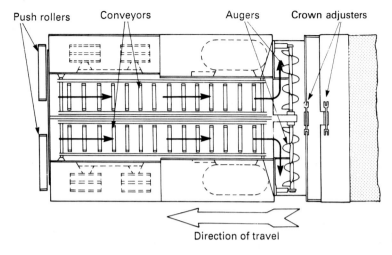

Direction of travel

Figure 10.13 Material flow path (plan view)

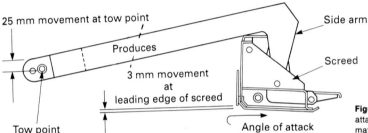

25 mm movement at tow point

Produces

3 mm movement at leading edge of screed

Tow point

Side arm

Screed

Angle of attack

Figure 10.14 Levelling action, the angle of attack is increased to increase thickness of laid material and vice versa

systems which can be rapidly lengthened by the paver gang rather than by a fitter. When a fitter is required, the paver will sometimes operate without the benefit of the extended augers, material simply being allowed to be pushed to the outer limits of the screed's extended length by the combined action of the non-extended augers and the forward motion of the machine itself. This tends to increase any segregation problems which might already exist with larger materials.

The screed is that element of the paver which most directly affects the quality of the laid mat, and in over-simple terms can be considered as a rigid L-shaped plate carried on a pair of strong steel box section side arms, as shown diagrammatically in *Figure 10.14*. When the paver is travelling between site or has finished laying on a site and is travelling to the parking area, the screed is supported on two lifting rams as well as at the tow points. At the commencement of laying, the lifting rams lower the screed onto hard packing pieces which have the same height as the uncompacted thickness of the material which is about to be laid. The screed is heated to the temperature of the new material by propane gas burners or electric elements to ensure that the material passes easily beneath it and does not stick to it. These screed heaters are not a means of heating either the material being laid or the layer being overlaid.

When laying starts the paver is driven forward and the weight of the screed is almost entirely carried by the material which is being fed to it by the augers and which it is shaping, ironing and compacting. The leading end of each side arm has a hinged fixing to the 'tow points' on the tractor unit and carries little weight, but transmits the traction forces to the screed. The geometry of the screed and its hinged fixing to each 'tow point' is such that any movement at the 'tow point', due for instance to the tractor's tyres moving over an undulation in the road pavement layer on which it is travelling, is reduced by about 85% at the screed.

The upright part of the L-shaped plate carries a compacting plate, the tamper, which moves vertically up and down so that its lower edge actually tamps and compacts the new material which is about to pass under the screed. The tamper speed can be varied within limits to alter the degree of compaction.

In continental Europe, highway authorities have specified compacted as-laid densities for bituminous materials for some years and their machines now include 'super-pavers' the screeds of which not only tamp and vibrate the new material, as do the 'combination screeds', which are available but so rarely used in the UK, but also which have such heavy screeds that the laid mat needs virtually no subsequent roller compaction.

The width of the screeds may be increased by either bolting-on extension pieces of variable width, the so-called 'boxes', or by using hydraulically extending screeds in which the extension pieces are carried by rigidly fixed horizontal hydraulically powered rams as shown in *Figure 10.15*. The latter type of machine is very versatile, particularly when laying in urban areas where, for instance, the extended screed can be retracted briefly to pass by a gully in a road channel. However, despite claims by manufacturers, the hydraulically extended screeds are not as rigid as the older fashioned bolt-on extension 'boxes' and gangs laying mats which are near the maximum laying width capability of their paver cannot be expected to achieve wearing-course tolerances without extreme difficulty, even if all the other variables which affect laying tolerances are held constant.

Perhaps the most important characteristic of the screed is its ability to change the thickness of the material being laid, whilst the paver continues to move forward pushing the delivery vehicle. The thickness change is achieved by altering the 'angle of attack' of the screed, that is the angle between the underside of the screed and a plane parallel to the surface of the layer being overlaid. The angle of attack is shown in *Figure 10.14*. Increasing the angle of attack produces a thicker mat, and

Figure 10.15 Hydraulic rams used to vary width of screed

decreasing it results in a thinner mat. The angle of attack is altered by adjusting the screed depth cranks situated at each end of the screed, which tilt it relative to the side arms, or by increasing or decreasing the height of the tow points relative to the surface being overlaid. Note, however, that whilst there is an immediate affect on the mat thickness, and that 85% of the change is achieved after two lengths of the side arms, the full change is not made for a further three lengths. Those 'screwmen' who are seen to be constantly altering the angle of attack are rarely giving the paver time to react to their adjustments.

Since the screed is pulled forward by the tractor with virtually its full weight on the newly laid material, it follows automatically that any halt in the paver's forward travel results in the screed starting to settle into the new mat, thus altering its level and even forcing it to be below the specified lower tolerance level. Pavers are designed to travel forward constantly whilst laying and the paving operation should not start until there are two or three lorry loads of material on site, ready to be unloaded, with other loads in transit. In addition, when the paver stops, the material beneath it or immediately behind it cannot be compacted, and if the machine remains stationary for any length of time, the supervisor may need to instruct that a transverse joint should be cut at the limit of that material which was compacted and the cooling, unrolled areas be removed before paving recommences. This is a particular problem if the new material is hot-rolled asphalt which is to be finished with precoated chippings, since the unrolled area then may extend from beneath the machine to the rear of the chip spreader.

Cold lumps of material passing through the paver have been referred to earlier, but it is when they reach the leading edge of the screed that the problem becomes serious since they form wedges at the extremities of the screed and block the movement of that material from the augers to the underside of the screed, which should be forming the edges of the new mat. Therefore, instead of the paver leaving a newly laid, full-width, smoothly ironed, 85% compacted mat in its trail, it leaves a less than full width mat with very jagged edges. Members of the gang then hurry to shovel material from the augers and make good the edges of the mat by hand. Unfortunately, this hand-placed material is not laid with any surcharge and has obviously received no compaction from the paver. When the first roller

reaches it, it is merely rolled down to the level of the adjacent machine-laid material, and the hand-laid edges subsequently develop less than their full potential load-carrying strength. If a wearing course mat is being laid when the problem occurs, the hand-placed material may be chipped before rolling, but the inevitable result, whether asphalt or macadam is being used, is that the edges of the mat disintegrate whilst the mat is still quite young, but more often than not, when it is old enough for the contractual maintenance period to have expired. A classic illustration of this form of problem is shown in *Figure 10.16*. The laying gang often relies on the fact that sooner or later the lumps will simply disintegrate under the combined action of the tamper on the screed and their being dragged along by the machine on the underlying material so that the problem will solve itself. Once more, the problem should not occur on a well-supervised job and supervisory staff should be particularly aware of the possibility of this type of problem occurring if, when the load arrives, the lifted tail-boards reveal a solidified face as shown in *Figure 10.17*. Note, however, that if material has been carried in the specially built insulated lorries required for hauling hot bituminous mixtures, there may still be a tendency for materials to cool to less than adequate temperatures

Figure 10.16 Edge of asphalt mat showing affect of very poor compaction, probably due to lumps of cold material blocking flow of hot material to edges of paver screed

Figure 10.17 Material which has cooled and solidifed despite the use of an insulated delivery lorry

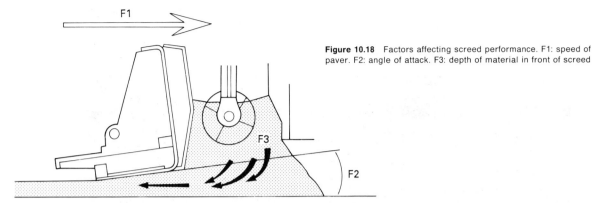

Figure 10.18 Factors affecting screed performance. F1: speed of paver. F2: angle of attack. F3: depth of material in front of screed

Figure 10.19 Mat-levels follower to control thickness of new material laid adjacent to an existing mat

Figure 10.20 Averaging beam used to control levels of new mat

for laying if the paving gang's progress on site has been disrupted for any reason and the lorry has stood on site for some hours. Sometimes the cool crust can be broken away and set aside and the remainder of the load used quite satisfactorily.

10.9 Control of laying tolerances

Laying the required thicknesses of materials is only part of the problem. The other part is to lay it within the specified tolerances. Even then, the material may be laid to tolerance, but rolled to become out of tolerance. Tolerances are checked using a standard alloy 3-m long straight edge and a graduated alloy wedge and the work is extremely tedious. To speed up the work, the moving straight edge may be used. This is known on many sites as 'the yellow submarine' due to its colour and its obviously submarine-like shape. However, the majority of tolerance checking is carried out from dipping lines, 50 lb breaking strain fishing line, stretched between steel pins driven in at each side of an unpaved road, or supported on blocks which stand on the tops of kerbs, where kerbs exist. In either case, the dipping team measures down from the line, which is pulled tight at a predetermined height above the finished wearing-course levels to the top of the layer being checked. These distances are immediately translated into the thickness required in the next layer, which has yet to be laid, to produce an upper surface which will be exactly as specified and knowing the relevant layer-thickness tolerances, it is very easy to

determine if the layer being checked has been correctly laid or if it is too high or too low, in which case some remedial works will be required.

In the paving gang, the driver operates the tractor and controls the forward speed of the paver, the rate at which material is fed to the augers and the path followed by the machine. The control of the finished mat levels is the responsibility of the 'screwman' who alters the angle of attack of the screed as required by the dips he has noted on the underlying mat.

The screwman's job is highly skilled and an unskilled man will often be altering his angle of attack too frequently for one change to have occurred before he starts another. It is important that the speed of the paver should be matched to the rate at which materials are delivered, to ensure as far as possible that the paver only stops as delivery lorries are changed, or else the screed sinks into the mat. Likewise, the paver should be refuelled before laying starts to ensure it does not run out of fuel part way through a mat.

Factors which affect the ability of the machine to lay material within tolerance include:

(1) the forward speed of the paver—the faster it moves, the thinner mat it lays, even if the angle of attack is unaltered;
(2) the skill of the screwman in adjusting the angle of attack to the changing requirements of the underlying layer; and
(3) the skill of the driver, or the attachment of an automatic feed control to ensure that the augers work under a relatively constant head of new material.

These three prime factors are illustrated in *Figure 10.18*.

Figure 10.21 A chip-spreading machine following a paver. Note that the bucket loader is approaching with another charge of precoated chippings and note the man lifting the board needed to produce a chip-free margin at the right-hand side of the new mat. Note also the two men hand chipping odd areas

In addition, a factor outside the gang's control is the general level of maintenance of the machine which is sometimes a problem in the UK but never in the USA where machines are stripped and rebuilt each winter to ensure they work properly in their intensive laying season, in which 400 million tonne of blacktop are laid compared with 30 million tonne in the UK.

Other factors are the non-regularity of the layer being overlaid, the moisture content of the material, particularly in the case of hot-rolled asphalt, the consistency in terms of temperature and binder content of material delivered from one source, and the total lack of consistency and required surcharge if, for instance, vehicles from different quarries bring a very large tonnage of different road-base macadams to the paver in random order. If large tonnages are required, their deliveries should be arranged so that the gang lays all the material from one source and then the material from another source, and so on.

Towards the end of the day, the fatigue of the gang itself is a prominent factor and any gang required to lay more than a 1 km length of new mat in a day, of any material, will not be able to do so for more than a few days running without severe fatigue. This level of output is related to a closed carriageway; on roads that are still carrying public traffic much smaller outputs will severely tire the gang and result in tolerance problems.

To assist gangs to achieve consistently good level control on closed sites, the paver can be equipped with a mat follower, such as that shown in *Figure 10.19* which relieves the screwman of level control, or an averaging beam as illustrated in *Figure 10.20* or even be equipped with a sensor to follow a control wire, set up at the correct levels at the edge of the road pavement or steel pins. The third method is commonly regarded as a little too esoteric in the UK and is thus rarely seen. However, on a closed site, engineers should not hesitate to specify an averaging beam, which can also be used successfully on surfaces left when a wearing course has been removed using a cold planer. Although the delivery driver is not regarded as a member of the laying gang, his bumping the lorry into the paver or leaving his lorry brakes applied can also cause tolerance problems at laying stage.

10.10 Precoated chippings

The UK has the safest roads in Europe, primarily due to the use of hot rolled asphalt wearing-course material finished with precoated chippings which have a relatively high resistance to polishing, or high PSV. The chippings are usually gritstone and are coated with $1.5 \pm 0.5\%$ of 50 pen bitumen. Occasionally, the bitumen is carbonized in the production process, and if this is suspected, the chippings should be sampled and sent to a laboratory for a hot-sand-tray test. In any event, it is desirable to check the PSV of the chippings and their compliance with shape requirements and to do this a sample of 25 kg is required which should be placed in a strong clean bag and clearly labelled before dispatch to the testing laboratory.

It is not uncommon for chippings to become coated with dust when stored on or close to the site and, since this prevents them from bonding to the asphalt, it is essential that they should be hosed down to clean them prior to laying. Chippings should be entirely coated and specifications make no provision for any to be uncoated. Stockpiles with uncoated or partially coated chippings should not be accepted.

Chippings are spread by the conventional chipping machine, an example of which is shown in *Figure 10.21* and which was designed by the then Road Research Laboratory. This machine has remained virtually unimproved since. The chippings are laid cold basically because nobody has addressed the question of preheating them, however advantageous this might be from time to time. To adhere to a wearing-course asphalt, the chip has to be heated sufficiently to flux the bitumen with which it is coated. This bitumen is then able to combine with the hot bitumen in the matrix of the asphalt and fix the chip which has been virtually entirely rolled into the body of the mat, even if 1.5 mm texture depth is specified.

It is the temperature of the top 10 mm or so of wearing-course asphalt which is critical to this exercise, since if this is too cool there is insufficient heat flowing from it to heat the chip and flux its coating of bitumen. Unfortunately, the chip may be well rolled-in and appear fixed until the newly laid mat is opened to traffic and serious chip loss can then occur. Note that with the relatively heavy rate of spread of chippings needed to achieve texture depth, at least $12.5\text{--}13.5 \text{ kg m}^{-2}$, the DTp advise that a chip loss of 5% is not critical. However, serious chip loss from any particular area of a mat, and especially at the ends of loads where materials from the uninsulated paver hopper have been discharged, will inevitably result in a gradual attrition of the wearing-course material due to the combined affects of oxidation, rain, freeze/thaw cycles, and traffic.

To ensure that adequate heat reserves exist in the mat, and

particularly if using relatively high-stability materials, some engineers may usefully specify a minimum mid-depth of mat temperature of 140°C behind the chip spreader, where the chips lie on top of the mat, but have yet to be rolled-in. Even this temperature will not suffice if there is a cold wind blowing across the mat since the crust will still cool too readily to heat the precoated chippings and the only remedy in these situations will be either to suspend the laying operations or to reheat the chippings and the crust of the new wearing course carefully with a lorry-borne infra-red heater and then re-roll the mat.

Occasionally, the chipper will discharge the chippings onto a mat into orderly rows with little scatter. This is unacceptable and is usually due to problems in the drive mechanism of the chipping machine causing it to move forward in a series of jerks. The mat needs to be taken up and the chipper replaced immediately with one which is working properly. Another occasional problem concerns the quality of the chippings themselves. Good stone is uniform in colour but a weathered stone tends to be brown. Chipped areas may show some brown stone since the quarry manager cannot economically remove all weathered surfaces from the production area, but, since this is very poor, its use in excess of 1% should be strongly discouraged.

Occasionally, the chip spreader will lay the chippings with a noticeable unchipped strip down the middle of the mat. This problem can be overcome quite easily be securing a strip of conveyer-belt rubber or similar material to the rear of the chipper so that it drags on the new mat and redistributes the chippings.

Feeding the chipper is an enormous problem in urban areas, because the loading shovel is frequently in conflict with traffic running past the job, and, almost as a direct result, many engineers now specify unchipped, high-stone-content asphalt, the so-called 'medium-temperature asphalt', to eliminate the traffic congestion caused by feeding the chipper. This is a 55% stone content asphalt frequently produced with a 100 pen grade bitumen rather than the stiffer 50 pen material.

10.11 Laying in adverse weather conditions

Adverse weather conditions are those which are less than ideal, and ideal may be summarized as warm and dry with no wind or even stiff breeze. Note that hot sunny weather can to some extent be adverse since a wearing course may may remain too hot and either be too easily deformed by traffic for the job to be opened to traffic and progress at normal speed, or chippings may be rolled too easily into the hot mat to achieve the specified texture depth.

10.11.1 Cold weather

Material loses its heat and workability very quickly as a result of exposure to cooling winds, or even to breezes blowing across the newly laid mat, or even into the rear of unsheeted but yet to be unloaded delivery lorries. Specifications usually require laying to cease as the temperature falls to 0°C. However, ambient temperature alone is rarely critical, and a recent paper by Daines and Hunter[20–21] describes the wind-chill cooling problem in detail. Conventional materials used in roadbases and base courses are relatively unaffected by either cooling wind or ambient temperature, so long as their initial temperatures on discharge into the paver hopper of a warm machine are sufficiently high, because the mat thicknesses in these layers are such as to contain large reserves of heat. Note the emphasis on a warm machine, because in winter a load of roadbase may easily lose 20°C in passing through a paver. It is advisable for the first load laid to be the hottest available, normally the last to arrive, rather than the first to arrive, which

by custom and practice is the first to be used and return to the quarry for a second money-earning delivery. Site staff involved in supervision may, therefore, anticipate some reaction to their request that the load which has just arrived should immediately jump the queue, but it is certainly in their client's interest that the hottest load should be used to try to warm-up the paver as quickly as possible.

Material laid in thin wearing courses cools faster than any other and it is important to note that there is an envelope of not much than 10 min in which lorries have to be unsheeted, the material unloaded and laid, any precoated chippings applied and compaction completed if a wearing course laid in less than ideal conditions is to be durable and give the client value for money. If the criteria described by Daines[20] cannot be achieved, the quality of the finished work is likely to be poor. Laying a 50-mm thick wearing course rather than a 40-mm thick layer considerably enhances the durability of wearing courses laid in winter. The DTp give contractors the option of using 45 mm or 50 mm thick wearing course asphalt, with reduced base course thickness, to counter the effects of windchill, rather than customary 40 mm mat.

The contractor includes in his overheads the costs of losing some time each year as a result of adverse weather, whether due to extremes of cold or rain, and site staff should grasp the basic understanding of the materials being laid to realize that there is no magic in the minimum temperature of 8°C frequently written into specifications for laying stiffer wearing courses.

Equally, they should realize that over-laying very cold surfaces is to be avoided since it literally drains heat from the bottom of the new mat which impairs full-depth compaction and, in wearing-course materials, can actually result in the formation of shear planes near mid-depth. The bottom of the new mat has stiffened and its crust has cooled due to both the coolness of the roller drum and the water sprinkled on it to stop bitumen adhering to it, and the chilling affect of any breeze or wind. The middle of the mat is still plastic and continued rolling can actually displace the top of the mat relative to the bottom in these situations. The shear planes have usually knitted together at the end of the maintenance period and it is not known to what extent they affect a mat's durability, but to be on the safe side they are better avoided.

It is better to ensure, therefore, that if very cold materials are to be overlaid, and particularly if the new material is a wearing course, that the contractor has the opportunity to heat the top of the lower layer carefully using a bank of mobile gas heaters. The question of cost will be solved by either writing this requirement into the contract if the client's needs are such that the materials need to be laid in wintery conditions, thus giving the contractor a fair opportunity to price for it, or requiring him to pay for it if the need is due to delays which he has caused. *Figures 10.22* and *10.23* illustrate wearing-course asphalt and macadam, respectively, which have been laid too cold. The hot-rolled asphalt in *Figure 21.22* was knowingly laid in less than ideal conditions to meet a political requirement that a road should be opened on a specific date, and oxidized rapidly due to poor compaction resulting in turn from too low rolling temperatures, within 3 years. The macadam reached the condition shown in *Figure 10.23* in less than 3 years, despite its material composition being identical to the material in the adjacent mat.

10.11.2 Rain

If all paving operations were suspended every time it rained in the UK the cost of material laid on the dry days would be a great deal more expensive than it is. The effect of rain depends on its intensity and on what material is currently being laid. Hence, the laying of a hot-rolled-asphalt roadbase material with

on the wearing course is as if it was being laid on a rubber mat rather than a good, sound construction platform. *Figure 10.24* shows a wearing-course asphalt which has been destroyed at laying stage by being laid on too wet a base course. Sometimes base courses become soiled, for a variety of reasons, and are cleaned using high-pressure water jets. Any excess of water left on the base course can be substantially removed using compressed-air hoses or a mechanical sweeper, not to produce a dry base course, but one which has no measurable depth of standing water on it.

Site staffs supervising paving works should be aware of the specified requirements for mat thicknesses, delivery and rolling temperatures and of the problems associated with laying materials. The laying summary chart shown in Appendix 10.5 is a useful record sheet for use in adverse weather, or at the start of the job, since it enables the resident engineer to identify immediately whether the gang and the delivery drivers are working in unison, or whether drivers are too slow in unsheeting and marshalling their lorries to and from the paver.

10.12 Compaction

For some years it has been realized that the durability and load-spreading ability of a bituminous mixture depends on the compaction it receives at laying stage whilst the material is still workable. *Figure 10.25* shows the virtually 100% increase in flexural strength of a dense-road-base macadam which results merely from its being compacted to reduce the air voids from 12% to 6%, at virtually no extra cost. Compaction has enhanced the aggregate interlock of the macadam and reduced its permeability both to water and, equally importantly, to atmospheric oxygen. Thus it is less likely to suffer binder stripping problems and premature oxidation and embrittlement of the bitumen. Furthermore, rainwater is less likely to permeate the road pavement and cause deterioration of the subgrade. Wearing-course macadams can be particularly permeable and, when poorly compacted, have very short lives as shown in *Figure 10.23*.

Aggregate is blasted, excavated, crushed, graded, batched, heated, coated, loaded, hauled and laid, but even if these operations are carried out faultlessly, the client will not get value

Figure 10.22 Wearing-course asphalt (less than 3-years old) rolled when too cold to be properly compacted

Figure 10.23 Dense bitumen macadam wearing course (less than 3-years old). Left-hand mat rolled when too cold to be properly compacted; the material in the right-hand mat has the same composition

a compacted thickness of 125 mm and a laying temperature of perhaps 160°C will be unaffected by anything less than a torrential downpour. However, wearing-course asphalt should ideally not be laid in any rain which is sufficiently intense to warrant the wearing of a raincoat since, quite apart from the effect of the rain on the temperature of the surface of the mat, UK practice is to run pavers uphill. Any rain on the base course therefore tends to run downhill to the new wearing-course material being spread by the paver's augers and the screed and rollers are then compacting asphalt which, at material temperatures well in excess of 100°C, immediately converts the rain water on the base course into steam. Similarly, on the level, in or after heavy rain, the same occurs and the base course is effectively covered with an elastic compressible layer. The effect

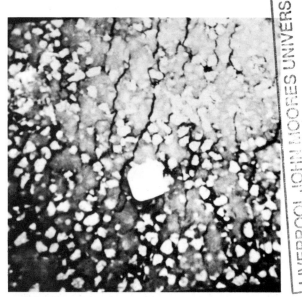

Figure 10.24 Wearing-course asphalt laid on a very wet base course

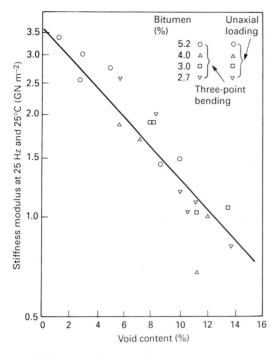

Figure 10.25 Effect of compaction on dynamic stiffness. (From TRRL Supplementary Report SR 717[29])

for money from the pavement material unless the roller drivers compact it adequately. The term 'adequately' is defined in the specification for the works and, at worst, this may merely require the material to be rolled until there are no roller marks left on its surface. An easy method of achieving this is to lay material at the cooler end of the laying temperature range and this will certainly ensure that a tonne of material covers the greatest possible area. Since contractors are rarely paid for bituminous material on a tonnage basis, but instead on an area and thickness basis, such specifications give them little incentive to compact a material to refusal.

Before examining an improved compaction specification, it is worth recognizing the many factors which affect compaction. Those factors controlled by the supplier include the aggregate type, grading and shape, particularly its flakiness, the binder content and viscosity, the moisture content of the material after drying and the mixing temperature. The haulier is responsible for ensuring there is as little difference between the latter and the delivery temperature which itself will dictate the maximum temperature at discharge to the paver.

Once delivered, factors influencing compaction include the heat lost awaiting discharge, the maintenance and operation of the paver and the heat losses in the paving operation as described in the previous section. These heat losses may be excessive if the rollers are not ready to roll the newly laid mat, with full water tanks for sprinkling and full fuel tanks.

The industry standard for rollers is the ubiquitous 8 tonne deadweight, non-vibrating roller which can be ballasted to increase its compacting ability. Smaller contractors sometimes try to use rollers which are too small, because they have traded-in their dead-weight rollers for smaller vibrating machines. These rollers are excellent machines on the correct job, but it is futile to expect them properly to compact a 3.7-m wide machine-laid mat at normal laying rates. Even the 8 tonne machines may be inadequate on a very stiff or rapidly cooling mat, particularly

if they are un-ballasted or mechanically defective, and specifications usually require two rollers to be working on a mat.

Vibrating rollers with variable amplitude and frequency need to operate at frequencies of 30–50 Hz and amplitudes of 0.4–0.8 mm for bituminous materials, using the lower amplitudes for thin layers and the higher ones for thick layers. The manufacturers of smaller vibrating rollers offer optional accessories for driver comfort, such as cabs, but these are rarely purchased and drivers sometimes tend, therefore, to operate them without vibration simply to improve their own comfort, particularly if unsupervised. In the non-vibrating mode, these rollers are relatively ineffective. The large rollers are equipped with driver comforts and there is therefore less tendency for drivers to opt for non-vibrating operation, but this should not be taken for granted.

Pneumatic-tyred rollers are commonly used on the macadams laid in airfield pavements, but are rarely used on roadworks. If they are, supervising staff should ensure that they are familiar with the manufacturer's tyre-pressure recommendations.

The most effective way to improve compaction is to ensure that the specification has an end product, i.e. 'as placed', requirement. This is commonly a percentage of the Marshall density which was established in the testing laboratory, especially for those macadams which are designed to achieve stability requirements on overseas sites and on UK airfields. More commonly, for road jobs, a percentage refusal density (PRD) requirement is specified. This latter test, described fully in the Specification for Highway Works, essentially involves the removal of six 150-mm diameter cores from the macadam layer in question, and their weighing in air and then water to establish their density, and by implication, the *in situ* density of the original mat. Each of the cores is placed in its own purpose-made cylindrical steel mould and heated for several hours in an oven. The cores are then removed and, whilst the binder is still fluid, compacted to total refusal using a part-worn Kango hammer inserted into each end of the steel cylinder in turn for 2 min. Specification trials have proved that all macadams reach refusal density less than 2 min after the necessary reheating and have also established the heating capacity of suitable ovens. The refusal density of each core is determined by weighing in air and water as before and the original density then expressed as a percentage of the refusal density. The macadam is deemed to satisfy the average density specification if all six cores are 95 PRD, as long as no individual core has a value of less than 93 PRD, otherwise it needs to be removed. The test is described fully in BS 598:Part 104.[6]

The test is totally foolproof, requiring no agreement between the parties to the contract on such commonly disputed matters as specific gravity or composition of samples and its only drawback is the time needed to complete it (2.5–3 days). As a means of resolving contractual disputes it is excellent, but as a site control test it leaves room for improvement.

In the meantime, therefore, some client's engineers continue to use nuclear density meters to monitor the compaction of finished mats, and cores are only removed from suspect areas. The samples are then taken to the laboratory and the air-void content checked against that value which represents 93 PRD and which has been determined as the commencement of laying blacktop on that site. The air-void test takes about 1 day since it is difficult to core a mat which has been cooling for less than 6–8 h after laying.

The contractor will often express a preference to work with air-void control on site and only use the PRD test for resolving disputes, because of the time saving. Frequently, the larger blacktop contractors will assign a technician to the site with a nuclear gauge so that he can monitor the results being achieved by the rollers whilst the material is still hot and, if necessary, call the rollers back to re-roll marginal areas before the mat has cooled.

The nuclear gauges used most frequently in the UK are manufactured in the USA and were designed primarily for monitoring of earthworks compaction. They were first used on UK sites in 1978, but are now widespread and the speed with which macadams are now laid and then checked to determine compliance with the specification before being overlaid, particularly on the very fast-moving motorway-strengthening or rebuilding sites, would be impossible to achieve without nuclear gauges. Their use and safe storage are fully described in the makers' instructions, but it is important to realize that their use of even low-level radioactive sources brings them under the control of the Nuclear Radiation Protection Board. They are thus subject to relatively arduous conditions of use, storage and the monitoring of exposure to radiation of staff involved with the gauges. Nevertheless, the ability to monitor the compacted density of a freshly rolled mat in less than 5 min to within 2% of core density, and with an experienced operator frequently to within 1%, makes them a very effective item of site control equipment.

The French have developed an entire family of nuclear gauges specifically for use in bituminous-pavement construction and no doubt these will appear on UK sites as greater cross-channel movement of personnel occurs. Attempts by roller manufacturers to incorporate gauges into or as bolt-on accessories on rollers have been abandoned after much research, although several contractors have improvised various means of fastening conventional hand-held gauges to rollers, with the microprocessor forming part of the gauge being duplicated in the driver's cab.

It is not possible to use the PRD test on asphalts because, at the Kango hammer compaction stage, the additional binder used in asphalts becomes readily displaced from the heated cores and the splashing hot bitumen becomes unacceptable in both safety and environmental terms.

Efforts to control the compacted densities of hot-rolled asphalts in wearing-course, base-course and road-base layers using specified air-void contents are not always successful and no national specification makes provision for monitoring compaction on asphalts for this reason. It is also argued that, in the case of HRA wearing courses, any significant lack of compaction usually manifests itself within the maintenance period and so can be remedied in any case, and road-base and base-course asphalts contain so much binder that compaction should never be a problem.

To summarize, compaction is vital to ensure both the development of the full structural load-carrying potential of any bituminous layer and its durability. Compaction should not be difficult to achieve with any material so long as it is rolled whilst the binder viscosity is still sufficiently low for aggregate interlock to be developed and enhanced, and this depends entirely on the temperature at which rolling started and having sufficient suitable rollers on site to do the job.

10.13 Sampling and testing

Sampling should always be carried out in accordance with BS 598: Part 100[6] by staff who have been properly trained, even if they are not experienced. The Institute of Asphalt Technology market an excellent video showing the finer points of sampling and this is available to non-members (price in 1991 £30).

Testing is a highly specialized job and should only be carried out by experienced personnel in a properly equipped laboratory. The DPt's policy is to ensure that any laboratory engaged in quality control on one of its sites should be NAMAS accredited by 1991.

Engineers wishing to establish the quality of materials delivered to one of their sites but who lack the necessary experience are advised to contact the nearest Highway Authority materials laboratory who will either carry out the work for them on a rechargeable basis or, alternatively, give them details of one of the well-established, nationally renowned privately owned companies who offer sampling and testing services.

References

1   BRITISH STANDARDS INSTITUTION, *BS 594 Hot rolled asphalt for roads and other paved areas*, Milton Keynes (1985)
2   DEPARTMENT OF TRANSPORT, *HD/14/87, Structural design of new road pavement*, London (1987)
3   SZATSKOWSKI, W. S., 'Rolled asphalt wearing courses with high resistance to deformation', in *Conference Proceedings, The Performance of Rolled Asphalt Road Surfacing*, Institute of Civil Engineers, London (1980)
4   SALT, G. F., 'Research on skid resistance at the Transport and Road Research Laboratory (1927–1977), *TRRL Report S 340* (1977)
5   DEPARTMENT OF TRANSPORT, *Specification for highway work*, London (1986)
6   BRITISH STANDARDS INSTITUTION, *BS 598 Parts 2, 3, 100, 101, 102, 104, Sampling and examination of bituminous mixtures for roads and other paved areas, Parts 1–3*, Milton Keynes (1974–89)
7   CHOYCE, P. W., 'HRA wearing course containing crushed rock fine aggregate', *Highways* (January 1979)
8   TRANSPORT AND ROAD RESEARCH LABORATORY, *Road Note 29, A guide to the structural design of new road pavements* (1960)
9   DEPARTMENT OF TRANSPORT, *H16/76 Specification requirements for aggregate properties and texture depth for bituminous surfacing to new roads*, London (1976)
10 BRITISH STANDARDS INSTITUTION, *BS 1446*, Milton Keynes (1973)
11 BRITISH STANDARDS INSTITUTION, *BS 1447*, Milton Keynes (1988)
12 BRITISH STANDARDS INSTITUTION, *BS 4987 Coated macadam for road and other paved areas*, Milton Keynes (1988)
13 PROPERTY SERVICES AGENCY, *PSA specification for airfield pavement works. Part 4 Bituminous surfacing*
14 DEPARTMENT OF TRANSPORT, *Specification for highway works*, London (1985)
15 DEPARTMENT OF TRANSPORT, *HA/36/87 Skidding resistance of in-service trunk roads*, London (1987)
16 DEPARTMENT OF TRANSPORT, *HD/15/87 Skidding resistance of in-service trunk roads*, London (1987)
17 DAINES, M. E., 'Pervious macadam: trials on trunk road A38 Burton bypass', *TRRL Report RR57*, London
18 FARRINGTON, J. J. and ROBERTS, K., 'Practical aspects of pervious macadam', *IHT Seminar*, Keele University (1985)
19 DEPARTMENT OF TRANSPORT, *HA/14/82, In situ recycling: the re-pave process*, London (1982)
20 DAINES, M. E., 'Cooling of bituminous layers and time available for their compaction', *TRRL Report RR4*, London
21 HUNTER, R., 'Cooling of bituminous layers', *IHTT* (1986)
22 BRITISH STANDARDS INSTITUTION, *BS 882 Aggregates from natural sources for concrete*, Milton Keynes (1983)
23 BRITISH STANDARDS INSTITUTION, *BS 1047 Air-cooled blast furnace slag aggregate for use in construction*, Milton Keynes
24 BRITISH STANDARDS INSTITUTION, *BS 812 Methods for sampling and testing of mineral aggregates sands and filters*, several parts, Milton Keynes (1975–1991)
25 BRITISH STANDARDS INSTITUTION, *BS 3690 Bitumens for building and civil engineering, Parts 1–3*, Milton Keynes (1982–89)
26 BRITISH STANDARDS INSTITUTION, *BS 76 Specification for tars for road purposes*, Milton Keynes (1976)
27 BRITISH STANDARDS INSTITUTION, *BS 434 Bitumen road emulsions, Parts 1–2*, Milton Keynes (1984)
28 TRANSPORT AND ROAD RESEARCH LABORATORY, *Road Note 39*
29 TRANSPORT AND ROAD RESEARCH LABORATORY, *Supplementary Report SR 717*

Appendix 10.1 Aggregates

General requirements

These are covered by BS 882[22] and BS 1047.[23] Testing aggregate is covered by BS 812.[24]

Clay on aggregate has the effect of preventing the binder coating the stone. In analysis it simply appears as filler. If visiting a mixing plant, keep a watch for clay on aggregates, amongst other matters.

Natural aggregates are either igneous, metamorphic or sedimentary. Respective examples are granite, quartzite and limestone. Crushed rocks fragment to exploit any natural planes of weakness, but the crushing mechanism itself will dictate to some extent the shape of the crushed aggregate. Ideally, these should be near cubic to give good mechanical interlock, although workability suffers. Jaw crushers and cone crushers both tend to produce flakier materials than impact crushers which are becoming increasingly common despite higher maintenance costs. Damaged screens at crushing plants allow the passage of oversized stone, although some oversized material is permitted. Problems are also caused by over-loaded screens when plants are running at or above peak capacity.

It is important to have evidence of the satisfactory previous use of a slag source in macadam, or else to have the necessary sampling and testing completed before a source is given any form of even provisional approval.

Uncrushed gravel is either excavated wet or dry. Wet won materials are frequently washed to remove the clay or silt but dry won gravels may be dirty and inadequately washed. Bitumen does not adhere easily to the smooth surface of gravel and BS 4987[12] requires 2% of cement or hydrated lime to be added to the mix to minimize the binder-stripping problem.

Aggregate testing

The qualities which are of most importance in a road-making aggregate are:

(1) resistance to polishing (polished stone value, PSV) (trafficked surfaces only);
(2) resistance to abrasion (aggregate abrasion value, AAV);
(3) resistance to crushing (aggregate crushing value, ACV);
(4) resistance to crushing (aggregate 10% fines value);
(5) resistance to impact (aggregate impact value, AIV);
(6) particle shape, flakiness and elongation;
(7) particle grading;
(8) cleanliness—dust and clay content;
(9) relative density; and
(10) water absorption.

The above qualities are not listed in order of priority.

Polished Stone Value (PSV) (BS 812: Part 114: 1989[24])

Used to test for skid resistance. Pads are made up from uncoated chippings (passing 20 mm, retained 14 mm) set in an epoxy resin mortar, are mounted on the circumference of a 400 mm diameter wheel. The pads are subjected to polishing by a rubber tyre (200 mm diameter) with water and corn emery and emery flour fed into it. The polishing process continued for 6 h after which the polished pads are removed and tested for skid resistance using a portable pendulum skid tester. Values: 80, extremely skid resistant; 30, very easily polished—useless.

Aggregate abrasion value (AAV) (BS 812: Part 113: 1990[24])

Used to assess wear under traffic. Sample pads consisting of a minimum of 24 chippings (passing 20 mm, retained 14 mm) set in epoxy resin are made up and carefully weighed. The pads are then placed under load against a revolving metal tray and sand is fed onto the tray at a given rate. When the tray has completed 500 revolutions the pads are removed and weighed again.

$$AAV = \frac{3\,(\text{Original mass} - \text{Final mass of pad})}{\text{Relative density of chipping on saturated surface dry basis}}$$

Values: <1 for some flints to >15 which is too soft for coated stone.

Aggregate crushing value (ACV) (BS 812: Part 110: 1990[24])

The ACV is a relative measure of the resistance of the aggregate to a gradually applied compressive load. A sample of chippings (passing 14 mm, retained 10 mm) is placed in a 150 mm diameter steel mould and compressed under a load of 400 kN. The percentage of fines (passing 2.36 mm) formed during the test is termed the ACV. Values: 10, exceptionally strong; 35, too weak for wearing courses. For aggregates with values greater than 30 it is advisable to use the 10% fines test.

Particle density and water absorption (BS 812: Part 107: 1991[24])

The method to be used is varied with the size and type of material. The three main methods are as follows:

(1) a wire basket, i.e. weight in air and water, for aggregates larger than 10 mm nominal size;
(2) the gas-jar method for aggregates between 40 and 5 mm;
(3) a pycnometer may be used for aggregates smaller than 10 mm nominal size.

Specific gravity (SG)

Sample soaked in distilled water for 24 h then surface dried and weighed in air. Then oven dried at 105°C for 24 h and weighed again in air. Poor precision.

$$SG = \frac{\text{Weight of oven-dried sample in air}}{\text{Loss of weight of saturated sample in water}}$$

Values: 2.5–3.0; average 2.68. Mainly used to determine air voids.

Water absorption

Determined in similar manner to RD.

$$\text{Water absorption} = \frac{\text{Saturated oven dried weights}}{\text{Oven dried weight}}$$

Values: 0.1–2% for wearing courses.

Bulk density (BS 812: Part 2: 1975)

Principally for blast-furnace slag to assess binder content, the lower the value, the higher the binder demand.

Bulk density in toluene (BS 812: Part 2: 1975)

Used for fillers, the finer the filler the lower the bulk density and the greater the stiffening action on the binder.

10% Fines test (BS 812: Part 111: 1990[24])

Used when ACV >30. Similar to ACV test but the load is only applied until 10% fines are formed. The weight used is called the '10% fines value'. Values: 400 KN, very good; 10 KN, weak (e.g. chalk, broken brick). Test gives some idea of risk of aggregate crushing under roller.

Aggregate impact test (AIV) (BS 812: Part 112: 1990[24])

A measured mass of chippings, passing 14 mm, retained 10 mm contained in a 100 mm diameter steel mould, are given 15 blows from British Standard 14-kg hammer falling through 380 ± 5 mm. The percentage subsequently found to pass the 2.36 mm sieve is known as the 'aggregate impact value'. Values are similar to ACV.

Particle shape (elongation) (BS 812: Section 105.2: 1990[24])

Particles of aggregate are classified as elongated when they have a length of more than 1.8 of their nominal size. The sample should be graded and the particles from each sieve size checked individually against the appropriate setting on the elongation gauge. The particles which will not pass through the gauge are elongated and are combined and weighed. The elongation index is the mass of elongated particles expressed as a percentage of the sample tested.

Particle shape (flakiness) (BS 812: Section 105.1: 1989[24])

Particles of aggregate are termed flaky when they have a thickness of less than 0.6 of their nominal size. The sample should be graded and each nominal size range checked against the appropriate gauge setting. Particles which pass through the gauge are termed flaky. The 'flakiness index' is the mass of the flaky particles expressed as a percentage of the mass tested. The results may be reported for each individual size or combined for the sample as a whole.

Particle-size distribution (BS 812: Part 103.1: 1985[24])

The preferred method of testing for a sample containing clay or other fines is to wash the sample over a fine sieve before dry sieving the remainder. Dry sieving of a sample is less accurate and more laborious unless the sample is free from clay, etc. The minimum mass of a sample to be tested is given in BS 812: Part 103.1.[24] After washing and drying the sample is passed over a nest of sieves and the mass retained on each sieve is recorded and expressed as a percentage of this original mass before washing; the material lost during washing is determined by difference. The results are calculated as a cumulative percentage passing each sieve and may be in either tabular or graphical form.

Appendix 10.2 Binders

Petroleum–bitumen binders are manufactured in a wide range of grades to BS 3690: Part 1: 1989,[25] the consistency varying from soft and fluid to hard and brittle. The type of binder chosen must suit the prevailing weather, traffic and construction. It should also satisfy the following criteria:

(1) be capable of being made sufficiently fluid, either by heat or by being cut-back, to be sprayed or mixed with and adequately coat the mineral aggregate;
(2) become hard enough at normal temperatures to resist deformation under traffic; and
(3) retain a degree of flexibility at low temperatures such that it will not suffer brittle failure.

Once the flow properties of binders are established they are normally controlled by checking the viscosity at specified temperature. These less viscous binders are easier to use in hand-laid work and it is important to realize that the fluxing agent evaporates over time. With fluxed binders, the viscosity is so low that it is measured using a standard tar viscometer and expressed as the time in seconds taken for a 50-ml sample at 40°C to flow through a 10-mm diameter hole in the apparatus.

Cut-back bitumens are produced from 100 to 300 pen bitumens by fluxing them with either creosote or kerosene to comply with BS 3690: Part 1: 1984.

Bitumen is a by-product of the refining of crude oil which has been heated in a continuous evaporation and distilling process to produce petrol, paraffin, fuel oil, lubricating oil and bitumen. It is produced in differing grades of hardness or viscosity and its basic parameters are measured by two tests: (1) that for softening point, measured using a standard 'ring and ball' apparatus; and (2) the penetration test which determines the distance in 1/10 of a millimetre which a standard needle penetrates into a bitumen sample in 5 s at 25°C. Thus a 100 pen grade bitumen is harder and more viscous than a 200 pen grade bitumen. (Grades vary from 15 pen to 450 pen but the most commonly used are 50 in rolled asphalt, and 50, 100 and 200 in macadams).

Road tar to BS 76: 1974[26] is produced from the fractional distillation of coal and, when UK gas was produced from coal, tar was widely used. Now, however, it is sedom used except in circumstances where a road surface is designed to resist oil and petrol spillage damage. Tar is more readily affected by ambient temperatures than bitumen, being soft in summer heat and brittle in winter cold. Its viscosity is measured in the standard tar viscometer and the temperature at which a 500-ml sample flows out of the container in 50 s is called the equi-viscous temperature (EVT). Tars for use in coated macadams are prefixed C, so a C30 tar is less stiff than a C58 grade tar. Tar is denser than bitumen so that a given volume needs a larger mass and dense tar surfacing is relatively difficult to lay even by machine, except on the most straightforward site.

Bitumen emulsions to BS 434: Part 1: 1984[27] are produced in colloid mills in which the bitumen is suspended in a finely divided condition in water with the aid of emulsifying agents. There are two types of emulsions: anionic and cationic. Anionic emulsion is a solution in which the aqueous phase is normally alkaline and cationic emulsion is usually in acidic solution. It is important to note that the two types of emulsion should never be mixed as the bitumen will coagulate and drop out of suspension. Emulsions are produced using bitumen selected from the range 70–300 pen.

The standard tests are for viscosity, particle charge and water content. The viscosity is measured in seconds using either Redwood No. II or Engler viscometers at 20°C and the water content checked using a Dean and Stark condenser. Particle charge is determined by passing a current through the emulsion between two electrodes and noting which electrode attracts the bitumen.

Emulsions are used extensively for surface dressing, (see TRRL Road Note 39[28]) and for tackcoat, sealing, and cold *in situ* mixes. For roadworks those most commonly used are K-1-40, a fast-breaking cationic emulsion with 40% bitumen, which is a cold applied tack-coat and K-1-70, a hot-applied surface-dressing binder with 70% bitumen.

Appendix 10.3 Mix-design examples

Design asphalt (BS 598: Part 107): Blankshire County Council

Date of test: xxxx
Laboratory: Roadmac, Brinton
Coarse aggregate: 14 mm 30% basalt
Fine aggregate: Sand 60%; fine sand 40%

Design category: 4–8 kN
Quarry: Humpkins

Grading		Total passing (wt%)			BS 594: 1985: Table 3, Column 9
		Coarse	Fine	Filler	Combined
20 mm	BS sieve	100			100
14 mm	BS sieve	87			96.0
10 mm	BS sieve	34			79.5
6.3 mm	BS sieve	3	100		69.9
2.36 mm	BS sieve		95		66.0
600 μm	BS sieve		79		56.4
212 μm	BS sieve		26	100	24.6
75 μm	BS sieve		3	91.5	10.0

Filler: limestone
Binder: 50 pen bitumen. Penetration 54. Softening point 52.0°C

Design criteria:

Binder content for optimum stability	7.0%
Binder content for optimum density	7.0%
Binder content for optimum dry density	5.5%
Design binder content	6.5%
Addition factor	0.7%
Proposed target binder content	7.2%

Marshall characteristics at the proposed target binder content:

Stability	7.4 kN
Flow	3.5 mm
Stiffness	2.11 kN mm^{-1}
Voids	2.9 vol% (Not a BS598 Part 107 requirement, but useful)

Table A10.3.1 Illustration of test results (complete set not shown)

Constituents	Mix proportions of aggregate (%)		Mass (g)
Coarse aggregate: 14 mm	20 mm: nil	RD:	
Fine aggregate 60/40	14 mm: 31.0	RD: 2.86	
Filler: limestone	10 mm:	RD:	
Binder: 50 pen	Sand: 60.0	RD: 2.64	
	Filler: 9.0	RD: 2.72	
	Binder: 50 pen	RD: 1.030	

Binder (%)		Wt. in air (g)	Wt. in water (g)	Volume (cm^3)	Density (g cm^{-3})	Mean	Voids (vol%)	Mean	Stability (kN)	Corr. stability (kN)	Mean	Flow (mm)	Mean	CAD (g cm^{-3})	Mean
4.5	A	1180.3	668.5	511.8	0.306		8.7		7.90	7.98		0.3		0.202	
	B	1179.5	665.4	514.1	0.094	2.298	9.2	9.0	7.78	7.78	7.62	1.9	0.1	0.191	0.195
	C	1179.2	665.1	514.1	0.094		9.2		7.10	7.10		0.2		0.191	
5.0	A	1187.4	675.1	510.3	0.318		7.5		7.70	7.78		0.4		2.202	
	B	1187.1	674.5	510.6	0.316	0.314	7.6	7.7	7.02	7.09	7.46	0.2	0.4	0.200	0.198
	C	1185.1	671.6	513.5	0.308		7.9		7.52	7.52		0.5		0.193	
5.5	A	1188.4	679.5	508.9	0.335		6.1		7.15	7.29		0.7		0.207	
	B	1188.8	679.1	509.7	0.332	0.333	6.2	6.2	7.05	7.12	7.16	0.4	0.5	0.204	0.005
	C	1189.9	679.8	510.1	0.333		6.2		7.00	7.07		0.4		0.204	
6.0	A	1194.0	684.5	509.5	0.344		5.0		6.40	6.46		0.5		0.203	
	B	1191.7	681.4	510.3	0.335	0.338	5.3	5.2	6.32	6.38	6.72	0.7	0.6	0.195	0.198
	C	1194.9	683.2	511.7	0.335		5.3		7.25	7.32		0.7		0.195	
6.5	A	1195.4	686.2	509.2	0.348		4.0		6.58	6.65		0.7		0.195	
	B	1196.6	686.1	510.5	0.344	0.346	4.2	4.1	7.28	7.35	7.16	0.8	0.8	0.192	0.194
	C	1196.6	686.5	510.1	0.346		4.1		7.40	7.47		0.9		0.194	

Appendix 10.4 Medium-temperature asphalt specification

Table A10.4.1 Example of layout of Appendix 7/1 with inserted data for a rural principal road

Permitted Pavement Option—Flexible Construction

(1) Location:

(2) Grid for checking surface levels of pavement courses (Clause 702.4)
      Longitudinal dimension: 10 m
      Transverse dimension: 2 m

(3) Surface regularity (Clause 702.7): category of road A

(4) Percentage refusal density required: roadbase and basecourse

(5) Coarse aggregate
      Nominal size: 20 mm
      Minimum PSV: 60
      Maximum AAV: 10 (depends on traffic; see H16/75)

(6) Surface texture requirements: sand patch method (clause 921)

	Clause	Material	Grade of binder	Thickness (mm)	Special requirements BS 594 Part 1 Table 3, Column 9
Surfacing Wearing course	911	Rolled asphalt (design)	50 pen	50	Marshall stability target: 6 kN Tolerance: ± 2 kN Flow: 5 mm Minimum air temperature for laying wearing course 0°C
Basecourse		Dense bitumen macadam	100 pen	50	

Appendix 10.5 Paver operation monitoring form*

Distance (m)	Time (min)	Machine stopped	Machine moving	Wings up	Wings down	Lorry in	Lorry out	Tonnage
Ch. 6853	09.26 h							
0	0		×		×	×		16.00
30	13						×	
37	14			×				
38	15				×			
39	15	×						
42	$15\frac{1}{2}$					×		15.92
42	16		×					
82	$24\frac{1}{2}$						×	
82	$24\frac{1}{2}$	×						
82	25		×					
83	$25\frac{1}{4}$			×				
83	27	×						
87	$27\frac{1}{4}$					×		15.75
88	29		×					
121	39						×	
121	$39\frac{1}{4}$			×				
121	$39\frac{1}{2}$	×						
121	40		×					
131	$42\frac{3}{4}$				×			
132	43	×				×		15.71
132	$43\frac{1}{2}$		×					
169	$54\frac{1}{2}$	×†						
169	$61\frac{1}{4}$		×					
175	63						×	
176	63	×						
176	$63\frac{1}{4}$		×	×				
179	$64\frac{1}{2}$	×						
179	65				×	×		16.56
179	$67\frac{1}{4}$		×					
212	75	×						
212	$77\frac{1}{2}$		×					
212	79						×	
222	$79\frac{1}{4}$			×				
227	80	×			×			
227	81					×		19.55
227	84		×					
276	94	×					×	
276	$101\frac{3}{4}$		×	×				
286	$104\frac{1}{4}$				×	×		16.65
286	105	×						
286	$105\frac{1}{2}$		×					
335	114			×			×	
336	$114\frac{1}{2}$	×						
336	$114\frac{3}{4}$		×		×			
337	115	×				×		16.65
337	$116\frac{3}{4}$		×					
379	$124\frac{1}{2}$						×	
380	$124\frac{3}{4}$		×					
383	$125\frac{1}{2}$				×			
384	126	×				×		19.80
384	$127\frac{1}{2}$		×					
436	$137\frac{1}{2}$	×					×	
436	138			×				
436	139		×					
452	$142\frac{1}{2}$	× End of mat						

* This is a real example. The paver and chipper speeds should have been more closely coordinated. The mat which stood unchipped at Ch. 169 became a remedial work patch. The form's use is recommended whenever poor laying practice or slow delivery lorry turn-around is observed.
† To allow chipper to catch with paver.

Appendix 10.6 Extracts from H16/76[9] *

Table A10.6.1 Appendix 1 to H16/76[9]

Site	Approximate percentage of all roads in England	Definition	Minimum PSV		Remarks
A1 (difficult)	<0.1	Approaches to traffic signals on roads with 85 PT speed of traffic greater than 40 miles h^{-1} (64 km h^{-1}) Approaches to traffic signals, pedestrian crossings and similar hazards on main urban roads	<250 cvlpd 250–1000 cvlpd 1000–1750 cvlpd >1750 cvlpd	60 65 70 75	Risk rating 6 Values include +5 units for braking/turning
A2 (difficult)	<4	Approaches to and across major priority junctions on roads carrying more than 250 cvlpd† Roundabouts and their approaches Bends with radius less than 150 m on roads with an 85 PT speed of traffic greater than 40 miles h^{-1} (64 km h^{-1}) Gradients of 5% or steeper, longer than 100 m	<1750 cvlpd 1750–2500 cvlpd 2500–3250 cvlpd >3250 cvlpd	60 65 70 75	Risk rating 4 Values include +5 units for braking/turning
B (average)	<15	Generally straight sections of and large radius curves on: motors; trunk and principal roads; other roads carrying more than 250 cvlpd	<1750 cvlpd 1750–4000 cvlpd >4000 cvlpd	55 60 65	Risk rating 2
C (easy)	<81	Generally straight sections of lightly trafficked roads, i.e. <250 cvlpd Other roads where wet skidding accidents are unlikely to be a problem	45		No risk rating applied Many local aggregates have a PSV well above 45 and normally these should be used

PT, percentile. cvlpd, Commercial vehicles per lane per day.
* Understood to be in the course of revision.
† The 250 cvlpd applies to each approach.

Table 10.6.2 H16/76 Appendix 2: Traffic loadings and maximum aggregate abrasion values for flexible surfacings

	Traffic (cvlpd)					
	<250†	≤1000	≤1750	≤2500	≤3250	>3250
Maximum AAV for chippings	14	12	12	10	10	10
Maximum AAV for aggregate in coated macadam wearing courses	16	16	14	14	12	12

* Understood to be in the course of revision.
† For lightly trafficked roads carrying less than 250 cvlpd aggregate of higher AAV may be used where experience has shown that satisfactory performance is achieved by aggregate from a particular source.

11

Bricks and Brickwork

B A Haseltine BSc(Eng), FCGI, DIC, FEng, FICE, FIStructE, FICeram, MConsE
Jenkins & Potter Consulting Engineers

Contents

11.1 Introduction 11/3

11.2 Types of brick 11/3
    11.2.1 Common bricks 11/3
    11.2.2 Facing bricks 11/3
    11.2.3 Engineering bricks 11/4
    11.2.4 Damp-proof-course bricks 11/4
    11.2.5 Terms that describe bricks by the manufacturing process 11/5

11.3 Manufacture of bricks 11/6
    11.3.1 Clay and shale bricks 11/6
    11.3.2 Clay preparation 11/7
    11.3.3 Shaping the bricks 11/7
    11.3.4 Calcium silicate bricks 11/8
    11.3.5 Concrete bricks 11/8

11.4 Properties of bricks 11/8
    11.4.1 Size 11/8
    11.4.2 Water absorption 11/9
    11.4.3 Compressive strength 11/9
    11.4.4 Soluble-salt content 11/9
    11.4.5 Frost resistance 11/9
    11.4.6 Efflorescence 11/9
    11.4.7 Thermal movement 11/9
    11.4.8 Moisture movement 11/9

11.5 Brickwork 11/10
    11.5.1 Cavity walls 11/10
    11.5.2 Mortar for brickwork 11/10
    11.5.3 Properties of brickwork 11/11

Acknowledgements 11/13

Bibliography 11/13

11.1 Introduction

Bricks are probably the oldest industrialized building material known to man. Surviving examples of brickwork from *ca.* 1300 BC still maintain an attractive appearance as can be seen from the photograph of Choga Zanbu Zigorat (*Figure 11.1*). The earliest bricks were made from clay, taken from close to the surface of the ground, or from river banks, moulded into shape by hand and dried in the sun. 'Adobes' as they are known have been found in the remains of Jericho dating back to about 8000 BC. The Bronze Age Mycenaeans had learnt how to 'fire' the sun-dried bricks to give them greater permanence. By the time of the Roman occupation of Britain, the technique of burning the moulded bricks to give them durability was well-known and practiced. Many examples of Roman bricks exist to this day as testimony to the sound techniques that the Romans had in producing their burnt clay products.

Clay bricks over the centuries were traditionally made locally and not transported very far, so that they had widely differing characteristics depending on the material available and the way in which the bricks were treated by the maker; it was quite usual for the bricks to be made on the building site, so that they did not need to be transported at all—assuming that there were suitable supplies of soft mouldable clay available (*Figure 11.2*). Much of the attraction of brickwork, both historic and modern, lies in the textures, colours and variations that arise from the use of materials made from various clays and manufacturing processes.

In the 19th century a process was developed for making bricks from sand and lime by subjecting them to high-pressure steam (autoclaving) to bind the materials together by the formation of calcium silicate. Additionally, bricks are now made from concrete, and there are even plastic imitations.

In Britain, a brick has traditionally been of such a size that it can be picked up in one hand, to be laid on a bed of mortar. Modern processes permit clay to be formed into much larger units and, whilst this is done in other countries, it is not practiced in the UK. Again in other countries, large calcium silicate units are manufactured and used but they are not made in the UK.

In addition to being used in walls, either for their attractive facing appearance, or as part of the structural support system, bricks are used as features in landscaping work and as hard paving, both inside and outside buildings. Features and pavings are not covered in the rest of this chapter.

Modern clay brick-making plants make use of deeply quarried shales and marls as well as soft clays and brick earths; such materials exist naturally over a great deal of the UK (*Figure 11.3*). Other materials may be added to the clay in the manufacturing process to improve the properties, for instance sand, chalk or chemical admixtures.

Calcium silicate brick production requires a supply of suitable sand and this is not so readily available in the UK as it is in some continental countries. Some calcium silicate bricks use a coarse aggregate as well as sand, and these are usually known as flint–lime bricks, as opposed to sand–lime. Apart from sand, aggregate and lime, other admixtures may be used in the process, particularly colouring agents; the final process is autoclaving (*Figure 11.4*). Concrete bricks are made using the normal materials associated with concrete, i.e. sand, fine aggregate and cement, to which, additionally, colouring agents are added.

11.2 Types of brick

Bricks are classified both by their quality as it would affect their use, and the manufacturing process as it affects their appearance. BS 6100: Section 5.3: 1984: Glossary of Terms, gives extensive definitions of the relevant words, but a distinction needs to be drawn between the following usage categories.

11.2.1 Common bricks

Common bricks are those that are used where they will not normally be exposed to view and where there is no claim as to their appearance. They are suitable for general use in construction, given that they possess adequate strength and durability for the location. The term relates to appearance only and has no significance in the classification of bricks in BS 3921: 1985.

11.2.2 Facing bricks

Facing bricks have a suitable appearance for use where they will be exposed to view so that they give an attractive and pleasing effect. Very many types of facing brick are available and the choice can be made either from catalogues and display panels or from examples of work carried out in the particular brick. A wide range of facing bricks is shown in *Figure 11.5*.

Common terms to describe appearance are:

Sandfaced. Sand is incorporated on the surfaces during manufacture so that it affects both colour and texture.
Rustic. Bricks which have a texture imposed mechanically; a variety of patterns is available.
Multi-coloured. This implies a variation in colour which may occur as a difference from brick to brick or across the faces of individual bricks.
Blue, yellow, red, etc. A direct description of colour which is

Figure 11.1 Part of Choga Zanbu Zigorat built *ca.* 1300 BC

Figure 11.2   Engraving showing brickmaking on site

Figure 11.3   Clay being won from a deep quarry

often added to some other description, e.g. multi-red facings, etc.

Smooth. No surface texture.

The designation of a brick as facing does not imply that it will be durable in all locations. (See Section 11.5.)

11.2.3 Engineering bricks

The term 'engineering bricks' is used almost only in Great Britain. These bricks may be facing bricks, but are not defined with facing qualities in mind. Engineering bricks are required to conform to defined upper limits for water absorption and lower limits for compressive strength as specified in BS 3921: 1985. The bricks are used where high strength and/or resistance to aggressive environments is required.

11.2.4 Damp-proof-course bricks

Damp-proof bricks are ones with defined upper limits to water absorption, similar to engineering bricks, but without the

Figure 11.4 Calcium silicate brick manufacture—an autoclave

Figure 11.5 A selection of facing bricks

strength requirements of engineering. Two courses of such bricks are permitted to fulfil the function of a damp-proof course according to BS 743: 1970 and are particularly useful at the base of free-standing and retaining walls, where the continuity of the brickwork is maintained without the plane of weakness that a sheet damp-proof course introduces.

11.2.5 Terms that describe bricks by the manufacturing process

11.2.5.1 Extruded wire cut

About one-third of all bricks in the UK are made by extruding a column of stiff clay, which is then cut by wires. The header and stretcher surfaces may be left smooth from the steel die or a texture can be applied immediately. Such bricks are usually perforated to facilitate the extruding, drying and firing processes. An extrusion production line is shown in *Figure 11.6.*

11.2.5.2 Pressed bricks

Pressed bricks and, more particularly, the type made by the semi-dry pressed method, Flettons, account for most common bricks. Many facing bricks are made in this way but have a texture applied.

11.2.5.3 Soft-mud bricks

Soft-mud bricks are usually machine moulded from soft clays which often have a high water content. Such bricks have long been associated, though no longer exclusively, with those commonly made in the south and east of England. A special version of this process produces simulated hand-made bricks by using a machine that gives the hand-throwing action.

11.2.5.4 Stock bricks

This term is used somewhat loosely and was originally applied to hand-made bricks from the south of England, as they were

Figure 11.6 A modern extrusion plant for making clay bricks

Figure 11.7 A stock brick being made in a mould

made on a 'stock'—a piece of wood positioning the mould (*Figure 11.7*). Now the term 'stock' is often used to describe bricks made by the soft-mud process.

11.2.5.5 Hand-made bricks

These are formed by hand-throwing a clot of soft clay into a mould. Sometimes the preparation of the clot may be assisted by mechanical means.

Hand-made, stock and soft-mud bricks are often sought after for their attractice unevenness of colour, texture and shape resulting from the raw materials and the methods of shaping and firing used. They tend to have lower compressive strengths and higher water absorptions than other types of brick but are often frost-resistant.

11.2.5.6 Special bricks

Standard bricks are shaped as rectangular prisms, but a variety of other shaped bricks is commonly made. These include bricks with splayed or rounded edges (*Figure 11.8*). Forms in regular production are described in BS 4729: 1971. Those shapes which are commonly made are known as 'standard specials' to distinguish them from other forms which might be made especially for a particular application.

11.3 Manufacture of bricks

11.3.1 Clay and shale bricks

There are four main stages in the manufacture of clay and shale bricks:

    (1) obtaining and preparing the material;
    (2) shaping;
    (3) drying; and
    (4) firing.

When a plastic clay with high moisture content is used in the

Figure 11.8 A range of standard special bricks

process there is usually an intermediate stage of drying between the shaping and firing processes. For facing bricks the finished appearance may depend upon additional work at the shaping stage, usually either by the application of coloured sand to the surface of the wet clay or by mechanical texturing of the surface (see Section 11.2). In some processes other materials are added to the clay, either to improve appearance or to incorporate combustible materials to assist firing.

11.3.2 Clay preparation

After the clay has been extracted it is prepared by crushing, grinding and mixing in a variety of ways, depending upon the type of raw material and particular requirements of the subsequent shaping process. Water content is controlled so that the material going on to the shaping process may vary from very wet to relatively dry clay dust.

11.3.3 Shaping the bricks

There are five systems; one is an extrusion process, while the others all involve material being forced into moulds by pressure.

In the extrusion method holes of a variety of shapes may be formed through the bricks; these are known as perforations. In the moulding processes indentations such as frogs and hollows may be formed.

The shaping method used depends upon the type of raw material and, in particular, upon water content and type of brick required. The five shaping methods are described briefly below.

11.3.3.1 Hand-made bricks

Hand-making is the traditional method in which a lump of high quality very plastic clay is rolled in moulding sand and hand thrown into a mould. Although more expensive than machine making, the method gives a particularly attractive surface finish that is difficult to reproduce mechanically.

Because the material is very plastic and has a high water content, considerable shrinkage occurs during drying and firing, with the result that bricks may vary in size and shape. Within limits, these variations are welcomed for the character they provide in facing work, but there are design implications. Thin mortar joints are rarely suitable and, even with fairly wide joints, building to closely controlled dimensions may be difficult on short lengths of brickwork where there are insufficient joints over which to average out the dimensional variation of the bricks. Hand-made bricks usually have one frog.

11.3.3.2 Soft-mud bricks

Soft-mud bricks are made from high-moisture-content clay which is machine formed by mechanically forcing the clay into sanded moulds. A wide variety of bricks is made in this way, especially in the south-east of England. Many have very similar properties to hand-made types, although they may not have quite the same character of surface finish.

The well-known yellow London stock brick is a rather special type of this general class, chalk or lime and breeze or other combustible material being added to the clay at the mixing stage. Soft-mud bricks often have one frog.

11.3.3.3 Semi-dry bricks

This is the process used in the making of Fletton bricks. Preparation results in a fine clay dust which is delivered to machines where it is pressed to shape in moulds. Usually the pressing process is repeated; for example, most Fletton bricks receive four pressings in one cycle of the process. Because the material is relatively dry the shaped bricks go direct to the kilns for firing, without intermediate drying.

Bricks made by this process are fairly regular in shape and size, but the commons are unattractive in appearance. When intended for facing work they may be either sand faced or machine textured after the pressing process. These surface finishes are often noticeably different in colour from the body of the brick and care is needed in delivery and site handling to avoid unsightly damage.

Pressed bricks may have one or two frogs or may have a variety of other shaped holes pressed in to produce the class of brick described as 'cellular'.

11.3.3.4 Stiff-plastic bricks

This is a similar process to the semi-dry one, but, because the clays and shales used have an inherently low plasticity, some water is added to the clay dust before the material is delivered to an extrusion pug which forces roughly brick-sized clots into moulds. A press die gives the final shape and compaction to each brick. The water content is low enough for the bricks to go direct from pressing to kiln.

11.3.3.5 Wire-cut bricks

Most clays, except those that have a high indigenous water content, are used in this method. After preparation the clay is extruded through dies, with or without forming perforations through the full thickness of the bricks. The extruded column of clay is of the correct length and width of the finished bricks and is cut with wires to the required brick thickness. The wire-cut process also provides flexibility in producing varying sizes and shapes of brick and is an economical method for mass production.

The wire cutting often leaves drag marks across the bed faces of the bricks and occasionally some distortion to the arris may occur. Facing and engineering bricks are sometimes pressed after being wire cut, to provide smoother faces and sharper arrisses.

Wire-cut bricks do not have frogs. Holes formed during the extrusion process vary considerably in number and size and, according to BS 3921: 1985, the resultant bricks are called 'perforated' if the total volume of holes is less than 25% of the volume of the brick.

Until the 1970s, perforated bricks were more widely used abroad than in the UK, but now a large part of the UK production is of perforated bricks. Advantages of perforated bricks include reduction in process times, reduction in weight and some increase in thermal insulation value. The perforations do not appear to affect rain penetration through walls after completion, but, because the holes go right through the bricks, vertically as laid, they are vulnerable to saturation from rain during construction. Saturation will increase drying-out time, may inhibit early decoration and will increase risk of efflorescence and possibly of frost damage. Good protection against excessive wetting during construction, important for all brickwork, is especially necessary with perforated bricks.

11.3.3.6 Drying

Drying is necessary in all cases where the brick, after forming, is soft and unable to withstand the weight of other bricks when stacked for firing. This is the case with all hand-made and soft-mud types and also with wire-cut bricks where the moisture content of the extruded column is relatively high. Drying is carried out in a series of chambers or tunnels in which the bricks are arranged so that a flow of heated air can pass over them and the temperature and humidity of the air is regulated to control the shrinkage which takes place during drying.

11.3.3.7 Firing

Firing produces a number of complicated chemical and physical changes in clay and the degree of control obtained is important. Ultimate firing temperature and type of atmosphere affect colour. Soluble-salt content in the finished bricks is partially dependent upon firing conditions. There are four firing methods as described below.

Clamp A centuries-old method, still sometimes used for stocks and hand-made bricks. Green bricks are closely stacked on a layer of fuel while the bricks themselves also contain combustible material. The clamp is set on fire and usually allowed to burn itself out. Control is dependent on the amount of fuel added, with the result that bricks may vary considerably in quality. The bricks are sorted into grades before sale.

Intermittent kilns Except for clamps, intermittent kilns were the only method of firing until 1858, when the Hoffman continuous kiln was introduced. Intermittent kilns are now principally used for the manufacture of special types of bricks.

Continuous kilns A continuous kiln consists of a number of chambers connected in such a way that the fire can be led from one to another, so that the stationary bricks are heated, fired and cooled. The system combines economy and a good degree of control.

Tunnel kilns Tunnel kilns are a more recent innovation and their use has increased considerably in recent years. In tunnel kilns the fire remains stationary while bricks, carried on kiln cars, pass along a tunnel through preheating, firing and cooling zones. The ability to vary temperatures and track speeds provides optimum conditions for quality control.

11.3.3.8 Quality control

Quality is an ever more important aspect of brick manufacture; many works are now 'quality assured' under approved schemes. Testing of individual batches of bricks may be carried out and methods and standards for size, compressive strength, water absorption, soluble-salt content and liability to efflorescence are defined in BS 3921: 1985. While check testing by the user is always an option available to him, the expense of testing may often be avoided by obtaining from the manufacturer data from control charts from their continuous checking.

There is no standard for colour control and, because colour variation is dependent upon raw material and processing,

variations may occur between batches in addition to those within a single batch. Where a large quantity of bricks is required to be consistent in colour it is important to discuss the requirement with the manufacturer to see if this is feasible.

Dimensional control for clay bricks, as defined in BS 3921: 1985, is sometimes not very satisfactory for users. It depends upon the overall measurement of 24 bricks falling within prescribed limits; this does not exclude the possibility of some bricks being considerably different from the 'standard' size, with an upper limit (see Section 11.4).

11.3.4 Calcium silicate bricks

The raw materials used for calcium silicate bricks are lime, silica sand and water. Crushed or uncrushed siliceous gravel or crushed siliceous rock are sometimes used instead of, or in combination with, sand.

The raw materials are mixed in carefully controlled proportions, with colouring materials added as required. The material is shaped by pressing and the bricks are then loaded onto bogies and passed into autoclaves where they are steamed under pressure. By varying autoclaving time and steam pressure the performance characteristics of the bricks can be adjusted.

Colour and quality are determined by the mix and the autoclaving process. Calcium silicate bricks are a uniform product of fairly regular size and shape, with sharp arrises and little colour variation.

Arrises are susceptible to damage which, because of the inherent regularity of the bricks, may be very noticeable. Care in handling facing bricks is important.

11.3.5 Concrete bricks

Concrete bricks are made from a carefully controlled mixture of cement, sand and aggregate together with additives such as colouring agents. The mixture is pressed and/or vibrated into brick-sized moulds in much the same way as calcium silicate bricks are made. The moulded bricks are then cured, either in steam chambers or in the air. The product is regular in size and colour.

11.4 Properties of bricks

11.4.1 Size

The size of a brick is defined in the relevant British Standard. The actual size of a brick is referred to as the work size and the space that it occupies, with its mortar joint, is called the co-ordinating size.

The work size of clay, calcium silicate and concrete bricks is 215 mm × 102.5 mm × 65 mm and the co-ordinating size is 225 mm × 112.5 mm × 75 mm. Other sizes are made, e.g. thinner bricks and some of the old Northern 3-in. bricks (83 mm with joint) are still used. Attempts have been made to interest the market in larger bricks, but, apart from one type (170 mm wide) for load-bearing use, there has been little progress.

Bricks vary in size depending on the manufacturing process; clay, when dried and fired, shrinks variably, and so clay bricks tend to have greater variation between one another than do calcium silicate or concrete bricks. The maximum and minimum overall measurements for a random sample of 24 clay bricks are given in BS 3921: 1985 (*Table 11.1*). Maximum and minimum work sizes for a sample of 10 calcium silicate bricks are given in BS 187: 1978 (*Table 11.2*). Concrete brick tolerances are given in BS 6073: Part 1: 1981 (*Table 11.3*).

Table 11.1 Limits of size for clay bricks

Specified dimension (mm)	Overall measurement of 24 bricks (mm)	
	Max.	Min.
65	1605	1515
102.5	2505	2415
215	5235	5085

Table 11.2 Limits on manufacturing size of calcium silicate bricks

	Length	Width	Height
Max. limit of size (mm)	217	105	67
Min. limit of size (mm)	212	101	63

Table 11.3 Dimensional deviations of concrete bricks

	Maximum dimensional deviation (mm)	
Length	+4	−2
Height	+2	−2
Thickness	+2	−2

11.4.2 Water absorption

The water absorption of a clay brick is the percentage of the increase in weight of a dry brick when it has been saturated. It is one of the parameters for the definition of engineering bricks and damp-proof-course bricks. The water absorption of the bricks used in a wall affects the mode of rain penetration through the outer leaf of a cavity wall and is used to define the flexural strength used in lateral load design.

11.4.3 Compressive strength

The compressive strength of a brick is the mean of 10 crushing tests, when the failing load is divided by the gross area of the brick. This quantity is used in engineering calculations. Bricks with frogs must have the frogs filled in order to reach their design strength as that is the way they are tested. The compressive strength of perforated bricks relates to the gross area of the brick bed and no allowance needs be made for the perforations which do not need to be filled in bricklaying. Different types of clay bricks have compressive strengths ranging from about 7 to well over 100 N mm^{-2} and calcium silicate and concrete from about 21 to nearly 60 N mm^{-2}.

11.4.4 Soluble-salt content

Most clays used in brick-making contain soluble salts that may be retained in the fired bricks. If brickwork becomes saturated for long periods, soluble sulphates may be released. These may cause mortars that have been incorrectly specified or batched and have a low cement content to deteriorate under sulphate attack. Of course sulphates from the ground or other sources may be equally destructive. Some clay bricks meet limits placed on the level of certain soluble salts in BS 3921: 1985 and these

are designated 'L', signifying low soluble-salt content. Those that do not meet the limits are designated 'N' for normal soluble-salt content.

11.4.5 Frost resistance

The British Standard for clay bricks (BS 3921: 1985) contains no mandatory test method for classifying frost resistance, and manufacturers are required to state the frost resistance of their clay bricks by classifying them from experience in use as:

F   which means frost resistant, even when used in exposed positions where the bricks will be liable to freezing while saturated. In practice, saturation of brickwork is likely not only in copings, cappings and sills but also in walls immediately below flush cappings and sills as they offer little protection. Protection from saturation is particularly advisable for brickwork immediately below large areas of glass or impervious cladding.

M   which means moderately frost resistant and suitable for general use in walling that is protected from saturation. This means the use of features and details such as overhanging verges, eaves, copings and projecting sills that have protective drips.

O   which means not frost resistant. Such bricks are seldom made deliberately. They are only suitable for internal use but must be protected when exposed on site and are liable to saturation and freezing.

The frost resistance of calcium silicate bricks is generally higher for the higher strength classes. However, calcium silicate bricks should not be used where they may be subject to salt spray, e.g. on sea fronts, or to de-icing salts.

11.4.6 Efflorescence

Efflorescence is a crystalline deposit left on the surface of clay brickwork after the evaporation of water carrying dissolved soluble salts. Manufacturers have to state the category to which the bricks being offered correspond when subjected to the efflorescence test described in BS 3921: 1985, namely the categories nil, slight or moderate. Specifiers should be aware that these categories do not relate to the degree of efflorescence to which brickwork may be liable under certain site conditions. The risk of efflorescence, which is harmless and usually temporary, can best be minimized by protecting both the bricks in the stacks as well as newly built brickwork from rain (see BS 5628: Part 3: Clause 3.5: 1985).

11.4.7 Thermal movement

Bricks expand on being warmed, and shrink when cooled. In practice it is the expansion and contraction of the brickwork, rather than of the individual units, that is of interest to the user. Some reversible movement will occur in brickwork exposed to temperature variation. The type of brick will not make any significant difference and the coefficient of thermal expansion in a horizontal direction will be about 5.6×10^{-6} for a 1°C temperature change. For a 10-m length of wall, variation in length between summer and winter might be about 2 mm. Vertical expansion may be up to 1.5 times the horizontal value. *BRE Digest 228* lists thermal movements for many materials.

11.4.8 Moisture movement

Clay bricks expand on cooling from the kiln, as some of the molecules of water reattach themselves after being driven off by the heat of the kiln. This expansion is effectively non-reversible, unless the bricks are refired. The magnitude of this movement

Figure 11.9 A fin-walled sports hall

varies according to the type of brick. Fortunately, a considerable portion of the expansion takes place quite quickly, probably at least half of it occurring within a few days. The remainder may take place slowly over a considerable period (see *BRE Digest No. 228*).

In addition, there is a small reversible movement due to wetting and drying of clay bricks. Calcium silicate bricks tend to shrink as they dry out after manufacture, and then expand again if wetted. The drying shrinkage may range from less than 0.01% to about 0.04%. Limits for drying shrinkage are no longer specified in BS 187: 1978.

Concrete bricks behave like other concrete products, e.g. blocks, in that they shrink on drying and expand on wetting. BS 6073: Part 1: 1981 gives a limit on the drying shrinkage that can be permitted of 0.04%.

As with thermal movement, it is the movement of the brickwork itself that is of interest to the user. Moisture movement in bricks may occur in the form of an irreversible movement which continues throughout the life of the building. Very occasionally, there can be a third type of movement, occurring as a continuing expansion in which bricks expand on drying and expand again if wetted. The amount of information on this type of movement is limited but it is clear that bricks should not be delivered straight from the kilns and used immediately.

11.5 Brickwork

There would be little point in manufacturing bricks if they were not to be used in brickwork, and it is the varied and attractive appearance of brickwork, together with its long-lasting characteristics, that have made it such a popular material for thousands of years. There are many examples of ancient brickwork that illustrate this point. In addition to an attractive

and durable appearance, brickwork can give weather resistance, support loads, in-fill other structural elements, and provide thermal, sound and fire resistance. Historically, brickwork might have been the only element of masonry, meaning brickwork, stonework or blockwork, in a building, but in modern times there has been an increasing amalgamation of brickwork and concrete blockwork to combine the strengths and overcome the weaknesses of each material, so that most brickwork now is a facing material used in combination with concrete brickwork. The most common combination of brickwork and blockwork arises in the cavity wall. This is not to say that brickwork does not still have important structural uses, but it is no longer commonplace for the entire load of a building to be carried on the brickwork. Brickwork is still used structurally for its great strength, in combination with its appearance, when these are required, and new forms of building have been developed to take advantage of this. *Figure 11.9* shows a 'fin'-walled sports hall.

Bricks may be arranged in various patterns called 'bond', and this can affect the strength of a wall, its appearance or its cost. Walls that are as thick as the thickness of the brick are usually laid in stretcher band—the familiar half overlap, showing only the 'stretcher' face of the brick. However, one-third overlap is sometimes used. In walls thicker than the thickness of the brick, English or Flemish bond are the most common, with the variants English garden wall and Flemish garden wall. For special purposes, e.g. to incorporate reinforcement in small pockets, bonds such as Quetta (named after the Indian town where it was first used) have been developed. Detailed guidance on bonding patterns is given in textbooks on building construction, and in BS 5628: Part 3: 1985.

11.5.1 Cavity walls

After initial use in the late 19th century, cavity walls became really popular between the two World Wars and are now the universal application of masonry to the external envelope of buildings. It is only since the late 1950s that the brick inner skin of a cavity wall has been replaced with one in concrete blockwork. Initially, when the required U value of an external wall was capable of being provided by a brick inner and outer skin, with a 50-mm cavity, blockwork was used as a cheaper material, perhaps faster to lay. As required U values have fallen, the inner leaf has been built in various forms of insulating concrete block, and there has been a need with some blocks to incorporate further insulation in the cavity itself. In 1989, requirements for minimum U values were lowered again, and it will either be necessary to use thicker insulating block inner skins of cavity walls, or to revert to dense materials, even brick, for the inner leaf skin and to use adequate insulating material in the cavity.

The detailing of cavity walls is well covered in text books of building construction and BS 5628: Part 3: 1985. A commonly neglected aspect of cavity walls is the provision, and method of fixing, of the ties that link one skin to the other. Wind forces and small movements are resisted by the wall ties, so their type, spacing and embedment are very important. Pushing wall ties into semihardened mortar, or bending them up or down in position, lead to understandable problems of strength and durability.

11.5.2 Mortar for brickwork

Brickwork is the combination of the individual bricks with mortar to form a strong assembly. Variation in the colour or treatment of the mortar joint can have a profound effect on the appearance of the finished work; variation in the strength of the mortar can influence significantly the strength of the brickwork

Table 11.4 Mortar mixes

		Mortar designation	Type of mortar† (proportions by volume)		
			Cement:lime:sand‡§	Air-entrained mixes‖	
				Masonry cement:sand‡	Cement:sand with plasticizer‡
↑ Increasing strength and improving durability	Increasing ability to accommodate movements due to temperature and moisture changes ↓	(i) (ii) (iii) (iv) (v)	1:0 to $\frac{1}{4}$:3 1:$\frac{1}{2}$:4 to $4\frac{1}{2}$ 1:1:5 to 6 1:2:8 to 9 1:3:10 to 12	1:$2\frac{1}{2}$ to $3\frac{1}{4}$ 1:4 to 5 1:$5\frac{1}{2}$ to $6\frac{1}{2}$ 1:$6\frac{1}{2}$ to 7	1:3 to 4 1:5 to 6 1:7 to 8 1:8

Increasing resistance to frost attack during construction ⟶
⟶ Improvement in adhesion and consequent resistance to rain penetration

* Where mortar of a given compressive strength is required by the designer, the mix proportions should be determined from tests following the recommendations of Appendix A of BS 5628: Part 1: 1978.
† The different types of mortar that comprise any one designation are approximately equivalent in compressive strength and do not generally differ greatly in their other properties. Some general differences between types of mortar are indicated by the arrows at the bottom of the table, but these differences can be reduced.
‡ The range of sand contents is to allow for the effects of the differences in grading upon the properties of the mortar. In general, the lower proportion of sand applied to grade G of BS 1200, whilst the higher proportion applies to grade S of BS 1200.
§ The proportions are based on dry hydrated lime. The proportion of lime by volume may be increased by up to 50% (v/v) in order to obtain workability.
‖ At the discretion of the designer, air-entraining admixtures may be added to lime:sand mixes to improve their early frost resistance. (Ready-mixed lime:sand mixes may contain such admixtures.)

both in compression and flexure. The type of mortar and the joint finish can make a large difference to the rain resistance of the finished wall.

Traditional mortars were made with lime and sand, sometimes with a cement of whatever sort was available. Such lime–sand or weak-cement–lime–sand mortars were very flexible and accommodated the movement that occurred in the brickwork, whether arising from the properties of the bricks or the movement of the building as a whole. It is often said, now as a left-over from times when these mortars were used, that the mortar should be as weak as possible in order to allow differential movement to be accommodated; the mortar must not be stronger than the brick, etc. However, in modern terms, this is really no longer true. The weakest mortar practicable is a 1:2:9, which is very strong in comparison with lime mortar; it sticks to the bricks and holds them together in much the same way as do the stronger 1:1:6 or even 1:$\frac{1}{4}$:3 mortars. None of the modern cement–lime–sand mortars, or their equivalents, allow any real 'flexing' of the brickwork to accommodate expansion or settlement. Furthermore, it is unlikely that the mortar *will* be stronger than the bricks; a 1:$\frac{1}{4}$:3 mortar is unlikely to be stronger than 15–20 N mm^{-2}, whereas almost all bricks, except for some stock or soft-mud types, are stronger than this.

Mortar mixes as defined in BS 5628: Part 3: 1985 and an indication of the trends that their properties have in affecting strength, rain resistance, etc., are given in *Table 11.4*.

Mortars are available in many colours to match or contrast with the bricks. Coloured mortar is most easily made with premixed coloured lime:sand delivered to site and mixed there with the appropriate amount of cement.

11.5.3 Properties of brickwork

11.5.3.1 Appearance

The appearance of brickwork, apart from the obvious effect of choice of brick texture, colour and pattern of arranging the bricks, is affected to a surprising extent by the colour of the mortar. *Figure 11.10* shows a panel of brickwork, laid in the same brick, but with different coloured mortar joints. Similarly, appearance is affected by the type of pointing used, so that a

Figure 11.10 Panel brickwork with different coloured mortar joints, same brick

far greater texture is seen if the joint is raked out than if it is flush pointed (but see Section 11.5.3.2).

The pattern of laying the bricks, i.e. the bond, affects the appearance, and there is some beautiful brickwork where more than one colour of brick has been used in a regular pattern. Nowadays, so many walls are 'half brick', i.e. the thickness of the width of the brick, that the bond is nearly always 'stretching'.

It is rarely satisfactory to assess the likely appearance of brickwork from a sample of the bricks themselves; at least a sample panel, built in the mortar to be used, and with the chosen type of pointing, needs to be seen. Ideally, examples of other finished work in the brick should be inspected.

Appearance can be adversely affected by batch variations in brick colour; some manufacturers mix their production to even out this effect, but it is usually essential for the contractor to mix bricks from a number of packs as the work is carried out.

11.5.3.2 Rain resistance

In detailing, the outer leaf of cavity brickwork should never be considered waterproof but it should be specified and built such that its rain resistance is maximized. All joints must be filled (except weepholes). This means avoiding deep furrowing of bed joints and, in particular, ensuring that all cross-joints are solidly filled and that the mortar is not just applied to front and rear vertical edges. It is generally considered that the use of lime in mortars enhances the bond between bricks and mortars and hence the rain resistance of the brickwork.

Tooled flush joints, for example bucket handle and struck weathered joints, are the most rain resistant. A special tool or the edge of the trowel is used not only to shape the joint but also to press the mortar into intimate contact with the bricks and consolidate the surface of the mortar.

Flush joints are a little less rain resistant. The surplus mortar is cut off using the edge of a trowel in an upward slicing motion. The joint is not subsequently tooled and the surface, therefore, tends to be torn rather than consolidated.

Recessed joints, especially if not 'tooled', considerably increase the amount of rain penetrating the outer leaf and they should never be used with clay bricks having perforations near to the surface or with clay bricks whose frost resistance is not adequate.

It should not need stating, but it does, that mortar allowed to bridge the cavity of an external wall can allow water to cross the cavity and negate the rain-resisting function of the wall. Ensuring clean lines of ties and damp-proofing trays is vital.

11.5.3.3 Structural properties

Brickwork has extremely good load-bearing capacity and many successful high-rise structures have been built relying only on the brickwork to carry the load to the ground. The detailed design of such walls is beyond the scope of this book, but BS 5628: Part 1: 1978 gives detailed information, and is supplemented by the *Handbook to BS 5628: Part 1*, published by BDA.

However, it is not only the vertical-load-bearing capacity of brickwork that is important; much brickwork is external to a building, and as such, is exposed to wind. This puts the brickwork into bending, so that it can span as a beam or slab to the supporting framework (see *Figure 11.11*). The flexural

strength of brickwork, as it is known, is affected by the type of brick and, if clay bricks are used, by its water absorption. The mortar used also influences the flexural strength, as does the condition of the bricks being laid, e.g. bone dry or damp. More detail is given in BS 5628: Parts 1 and 3 and in the handbook referred to above.

Brickwork is also used in conjunction with reinforcement or prestressing tendons to act as a strong and economic structural material. More detail can be found in BS 5628: Part 2: 1985.

11.5.3.4 Movement of brickwork

Allowance needs to be made for the movements that occur in brickwork from wetting and drying, long-term irreversible moisture expansion of clay bricks, and thermal expansion or contraction. This is done by breaking the brickwork down into defined lengths, or heights, by a complete break—a movement joint. In clay brickwork, such joints are primarily expansion joints, but in calcium silicate and concrete brickwork they are mostly for shrinkage purposes. Guidance on the spacing and detailing of movement joints is given in BS 5628: Part 3. For clay brickwork it is suggested that an allowance of 1 mm per 1 m expansion is made, so that for joints at 12-m centres 12 mm of expansion must be catered for. Since most fillers (they must be easily compressible and not, for example, cane fibre) can only accept movement of 50% of their width, this can mean rather wide joints which need to be sealed effectively. When clay brickwork is built into a framed structure (particularly, but not exclusively, reinforced concrete) joints are needed to prevent the shortening of the frame and expansion of the brickwork from causing a build up of compressive stress in the wall. Failure to appreciate this soon enough has led to many failures of 1960s and early 1970s brickwork in reinforced concrete structures.

11.5.3.5 Thermal resistance

Brickwork, in itself, is rarely called upon to provide a thermal barrier against heat loss in modern buildings. Requirements for energy conservation make mandatory *U* values far lower than can be achieved with a solid wall alone. Most brickwork in external walls is, therefore, part of a composite system; this may be, and usually is, a cavity wall, but is is also possible to use brickwork alone lined with high-quality polystyrene insulation. British Ceramic Research Ltd have given details of such a method, called SLIM (single-leaf-insulated masonry). To achieve the low *U* values required in a cavity wall, either lightweight concrete blocks are used as the inner leaf of the cavity wall, or dense aggregate blocks with insulation in the cavity are used. It is sometimes necessary to use brick, cavity insulation and lightweight block to achieve the desired insulation level.

11.5.3.6 Sound insulation

Brick walls are excellent barriers to sound transmission; the effectiveness of a sound barrier is the amount by which it reduces noise level expressed as decibels (dB). For solid walls, average insulation over the normal frequency range is largely dependent upon the weight per unit area of the wall. Each doubling of weight adds about 6 dB to the insulation value. It follows that a change from half-brick to full-brick thickness provides about a 6-dB improvement, but that to obtain a further 6-dB improvement would mean doubling the thickness to a two-brick wall. For the same reason it follows that differences in the weight of differing types of brick are of little practical importance. A change from the lightest to heaviest might just be noticeable in a half-brick wall. Average insulation values for ordinary brick walling are given in *Table 11.5*.

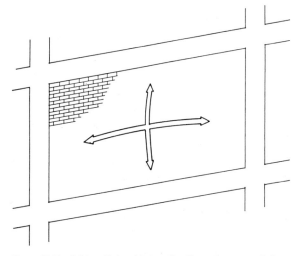

Figure 11.11 Brick walls bend in two directions when supported on their edges and subjected to wind loads

Table 11.5 Average sound insulation value of brick walls

Construction	Average sound reduction (dB)
Half-brick wall, unplastered	42
Half-brick wall, plastered both sides	45
One brick wall, plastered both sides	50
Cavity wall of two half-brick skins with butterfly wall ties not more than one per m²; wall plastered both sides	50
One-and-a-half-brick wall	52/3

11.5.3.7 Fire resistance

As for sound resistance, brick walls give good resistance to the passage of fire. The periods of resistance are given for various thicknesses, plaster type and loading condition in BS 5628: Part 3: 1985.

11.5.3.8 Durability

Brick walls built for internal use only require frost and soluble-salt resistance for the period in which they will be exposed to the weather during construction. Most bricks have sufficient durability for this purpose and good building practice will reduce vulnerability to a minimum.

For walls that may be exposed to the weather during their lifetime, the soluble-salt content of the bricks is important. However, a distinction must be drawn between efflorescence, which is unsightly but rarely harmful, and sulphate attack which can cause serious damage.

The crystallization of soluble salts on the exterior of brick buildings causes efflorescence, usually in the form of white patches. For efflorescence to occur there must be soluble salts and enough water drying out to carry the salts in solution to the surface. Given a sufficient supply of salts and water, efflorescence can persist, but it is generally seen in the early life of a building during the initial drying period. To avoid efflorescence, saturation of walls during construction should be avoided and detailing should prevent excessive subsequent wetting. It is noticeable, for example, that efflorescence quite often occurs only in positions such as exposed parapet walls.

Salts may be present in bricks or be introduced from other materials such as mortar or from soil. Calcium silicate and concrete bricks do not contain harmful salts. Sulphate action occurs when water carries sulphates from clay bricks or from contamination into mortar which contains tricalcium aluminate. The resulting expansion of mortar may be serious, causing cracking or spalling of mortar joints, and occasionally resulting in spalling of facing bricks. Because fairly persistent wetting of the brickwork is one of the factors, the trouble is most often seen in situations such as chimneys, parapets or free-standing walls exposed on both sides, and in earth-retaining walls, but it may occur anywhere where walls are not protected from excessive dampness, if there are sufficient salts to affect the mortar.

The best precaution against sulphate attack is to keep walls dry, but for many positions this is not feasible. In such situations, therefore, a reasonable combination of brick and mortar must be used. The sulphate resistance of mortars can be increased by specifying fairly cement-rich mixes such as $1:\frac{1}{4}:3$ or $1:\frac{1}{2}:4\frac{1}{2}$ or, more effectively, by using a sulphate-resisting cement instead of ordinary Portland cement.

As explained earlier, clay bricks are classified as L or N depending on whether they have low or normal quantities of soluble sulphates. For susceptible positions a class-L brick should be used.

The frost resistance of clay bricks is defined in BS 3921: 1985 as F, M or O (see above). Calcium silicate and concrete bricks generally have good frost resistance, especially with the higher strength classes. The choice of a brick for durability in a particular building can be made from BS 5628: Part 3: 1985: Table 3 Durability of Masonry in Finished Construction; the table covers brickwork and blockwork. Frost resistance of the mortar is also necessary; if $1:1:6$ or $1:\frac{1}{4}:3$ mortars are used, this will normally be achieved. Table 3 of BS 5628: Part 3: 1985 also gives recommended mixes.

A comprehensive range of situations is covered as follows:

(1) work below or near external ground level;
(2) damp-proof-course;
(3) unrendered external walls (other than chimneys, cappings, copings, parapets or sills);
(4) rendered external walls;
(5) internal walls and inner leaves of cavity walls;
(6) unrendered parapets;
(7) rendered parapets;
(8) chimneys;
(9) cappings, copings and sills;
(10) freestanding boundary and screen walls;
(11) earth-retaining walls; and
(12) drainage and sewerage.

Care is needed in the choice of brick and mortar for given situations, but when care is given it is repaid in durable brickwork that will last the lifetime of the building of which it forms a part.

Acknowledgements

Grateful thanks are given to the Brick Development Association for their help in providing background material and photographs. Helpful advice on the choice of clay and calcium silicate bricks can be obtained from them. Advice on concrete bricks is given by CBMA at 60 Charles Street, Leicester LE1 1FB, UK.

Bibliography

British Standards Institution

BS 187: 1978, Specification for calcium silicate (sandlime and flintlime) bricks
BS 743: 1970, Specification for materials for damp proof courses
BS 1243: 1978, Specification for metal ties for cavity wall construction
BS 3921: 1985, Specification for clay bricks
BS 4729: 1971, Specification for shapes and dimensions of special bricks
BS 5628: Code of practice for use of masonry
BS 5628: Part 1: 1978, Structural use of unreinforced masonry
BS 5628: Part 2: 1985, Structural use of reinforced and prestressed masonry
BS 5628: Part 3: 1985, Materials and components, design and workmanship
BS 6073: Precast concrete masonry units
BS 6073: Part 1: 1981, Specification for precast concrete masonry units
BS 6073: Part 2: 1981, Method for specifying precast concrete masonry units
BS 6100: Glossary of building and civil engineering terms
BS 6100: Part 5: 1985, Masonry

Building Research Establishment Digests

BRE Digest 157: 1981, Calcium silicate brickwork

BRE Digest 160: 1973, Mortars for bricklaying
BRE Digest 164 Parts 1 & 2: 1974, Clay brickwork
BRE Digest 165 Parts 1 & 2: 1974, Clay brickwork

Useful books

HANDYSIDE and HASELTINE, *Bricks and Brickwork*, Brick Development Association, Windsor
HASELTINE and MOORE, *Handbook to BS 5628: Part 1: 1978*, Brick Development Association, Windsor

Trade associations concerned with bricks, brickwork and concrete blockwork

ACBA — Aggregate Concrete Block Association, 60 Charles Street, Leicester LE1 1FB

AACPA — Autoclaved Aerated Concrete Products Association Ltd, Thermalite House, Station Road, Coleshill, Birmingham B46 1HP

BDA — Brick Development Association, Woodside House, Winkfield, Windsor, Berks SL4 2DX

CSBA — Calcium Silicate Brick Association, 24 Fearnley Road, Welwyn Garden City, Herts AL8 0HW

BCA — British Cement Association, Wexham Springs, Slough, Berks SL3 6PL

CBA — Concrete Brick Association, P.O. Box 449, Cardiff CF1 1QA

12

Vitrified Clay Pipes for Drainage and Sewerage

C E G Bland FIWEM, FRSH
Clay Pipe Development Association

Contents

12.1 The past, the present and the future 12/3

12.2 Stages of manufacture 12/3
　12.2.1 Clay extraction 12/3
　12.2.2 Clay preparation 12/3
　12.2.3 Pipe formation 12/3
　12.2.4 Fitting formation 12/3
　12.2.5 Drying 12/3
　12.2.6 Firing 12/3
　12.2.7 Cooling 12/4
　12.2.8 Energy analysis 12/4
　12.2.9 Appearance 12/5

12.3 Inspection 12/5

12.4 Joints 12/5
　12.4.1 Manufacture 12/5

12.5 Jointing 12/5
　12.5.1 On site 12/5
　12.5.2 Repair and adaptor couplings 12/5
　12.5.3 Cutting pipes to length 12/6

12.6 Trenchless construction 12/6

12.7 Standards 12/6

12.8 Performance of flexible joints 12/6
　12.8.1 Specification 12/6
　12.8.2 Speed of laying 12/7
　12.8.3 Pipeline testing 12/7

12.9 Packaging, stacking and mechanical handling 12/7

12.10 Availability 12/7

12.11 Heat resistance 12/7

12.12 Abrasion resistance 12/7

12.13 Strength 12/7
　12.13.1 General 12/7
　12.13.2 Crushing strength 12/7
　12.13.3 Design 12/7
　12.13.4 Bending moment resistance 12/7
　12.13.5 Bedding 12/8

12.14 Research 12/8
　12.14.1 Structural research 12/8
　12.14.2 Hydraulics 12/9

12.15 Chemical resistance 12/10

12.16 Summary 12/11

References 12/11

12.1 The past, the present and the future

Many thousands of years ago, man learnt that clay is easy to shape and mould, and that when soft clay pots are burnt in a fire, they are irreversibly and permanently changed into strong, rigid, impermeable vessels.

Clay minerals are found in abundance over the face of the earth and early clay water vessels have been excavated in many parts of the world.

Clays were formed from igneous silicate rocks through the continuous processes of physical and chemical breakdown over enormous periods of geological time. They were moved from the site of their formation by rain and underwent considerable sorting and contamination as they gradually made their way from the higher grounds of the earth's crust to the lower parts of the land surface. Rivers carried them to their estuaries and then into the sea, and sometimes extensive deposits were raised above sea level by subsequent earth movements.

Clays have been used as a material for making pipes for drainage purposes since the beginning of civilization. Over 3500 years ago, clay pipes were used for the drainage of the Royal Palace of Knossos in Crete—and these are still in good condition today.

In Roman times, engineers used clay pipes not only for drainage purposes but also for carrying drinking water. When the Romans invaded Britian they brought their knowledge with them and clay pipes were used in the villas and fortifications built during their occupation.

When the legions withdrew, Britain entered the dark ages and public-health engineering stood still for more than a 1000 years. In towns and cities, open drains ran down the centre of the streets. As late as the 1850s Members of Parliament were sometimes unable to use the terraces of the House of Commons because of the stench coming from the river. Disraeli described the conditions of the towns of industrial England as 'gutters of abomination whose exhalations were sufficient to taint the atmosphere of the whole Kingdom, and fill the country with fever and pestilence'.

In 1839, Edwin Chadwick, the great public health reformer, became interested in the possibilities of drainage by the use of clay pipes. He gradually convinced people that this was the best method of drainage and soon the newly formed Boards of Health were advocating their use everywhere. These early pipes were either turned on a potter's wheel or moulded from thick sheets of clay.

The first machines to extrude pipes came from Switzerland. These were used in a factory built by Henry Doulton on the Thames embankment at Lambeth in 1846. Gradually more clay pipe works were constructed near suitable clay deposits all over the country. By the 1930s vitrified clay drainage goods were manufactured at over 75 works in various parts of the UK and Ireland.

The industry has been rationalized into a smaller number of large production units, with factories now incorporating modern manufacturing and processing techniques (*Figure 12.2*). This technological advance has only been possible through the expenditure of large amounts of capital and effort on research and product development. Individual manufacturers carry out extensive research programmes. In addition, sponsored research is conducted for the Clay Pipe Development Association (CPDA) at various research centres. Research will continue on production techniques and product development. The aim is to produce high-quality pipes, fittings and joints to meet all drainage requirements. Success in this research will continue the advances already made, thus enabling vitrified clay pipes to be laid more economically.

12.2 Stages of manufacture

12.2.1 Clay extraction

There are many types of clay but only a few are suitable for the manufacture of pipes. The clays deposited at different periods of geological time are sometimes interspaced between other minerals, each clay stratum having its own chemical and physical characteristics.

Before being used in pipe manufacture, samples of clays, or mixtures of various clays, are tested so that their performance characteristics can be predicted. The clays are extracted from the ground by various mechanical methods of quarrying and each selected stratum of clay is separately removed and stored.

12.2.2 Clay preparation

Clays from the various strata may be blended together in predetermined proportions. The blended clay is then broken down by a crusher and is ground to fine particle size in a grinding mill.

The ground clay is then passed over screens which reject any oversized material. At this point in the manufacturing process a small proportion of finely ground prefired material known as 'grog' is added to some clays to assist in the drying and firing processes. The clay and grog then pass through a mixer where water is added so that the mixture becomes just sufficiently plastic to be extruded. Prior to extrusion, air trapped in the clay is removed by shredding the clay in a vacuum chamber to achieve a uniform body which is free of voids.

12.2.3 Pipe formation

Socketed pipes are formed either horizontally or vertically by very high pressure extrusion, the sockets being formed first. Plain-end pipes are extruded continuously. Pipes are cut and trimmed so that, after drying and firing, they have accurate dimensions.

12.2.4 Fitting formation

Clay pipe fittings are made either by automatic extrusion, sticking extruded shapes together or hand moulding. At this stage of manufacture the pipes and fittings are soft and dark grey in colour.

12.2.5 Drying

The natural water content of the clay together with the water added to aid the formation of the pipes and fittings is removed by drying. Methods of drying include:

(1) *chamber or shed drying*—the pipes are positioned either vertically on boards or horizontally in cradles and hot air is passed through and around them;
(2) *roller drying*—the pipes are continuously rotated by rollers, as they pass through the dryer enclosure; and
(3) *tunnel drying*—the pipes are set vertically on kiln cars, which are moved through a tunnel dryer.

Fuel economies are made through the utilization of waste heat from the kiln flue gases in the drying process.

When the pipes are dry they become 'white hard', and they are then ready to be fired in a kiln.

12.2.6 Firing

After drying, the pipes are fired, either in continuous tunnel or roller kilns or in intermittent kilns. In tunnel kilns, firing is continuous, and operating temperatures are maintained for very

Figure 12.1 A modern, highly insulated 'top-hat' intermittent kiln. This is moved over a preset batch of pipes or fittings, allowing setting and drawing of one batch while another is fired

long periods of time, during which cars laden with pipes are pushed through the temperature zones. Straight pipes are set vertically on kiln cars, normally one high, perhaps with fittings on top or at the sides.

In roller kilns, pipes are processed individually as they are moved through the various stages of the firing cycle.

Intermittent kilns are heated and cooled under controlled conditions as successive batches of dried pipes are placed in them. In the down-draught type of intermittent kiln, pipes are frequently set vertically two high, with fittings placed on top. The 'top-hat' principle allows a highly insulated mobile kiln to be placed over the preset pipes and fittings. This allows setting and drawing of batches while another batch is fired (*Figure 12.1*).

In all types of kiln, the temperature of the pipes is raised progressively, and at 200°C any remaining water which has been mechanically combined with the clay during the manufacturing process is removed. Beyond this point, the chemically combined water in the clay particles is driven off and a period of oxidation follows at temperatures between 550 and 750°C, during which carbon and other combustible products are converted to gaseous form.

As the temperature reaches approximately 900°C 'vitrification' begins to take place. This is the physio-chemical process whereby the aluminosilicate clay particles sinter together under the action of the fluxes which occur naturally in the clay body. This fluxing action, which continues as the pipes are fired to a finishing temperature of about 1100°C, ensures that, upon cooling, a high-density, strong, impervious clay body is produced.

12.2.7 Cooling

After the pipes have been held at the top temperature for the required time, cooling begins. The temperature is first lowered fairly rapidly to approximately 650°C. Then, to allow for changes which take place in the crystalline structure of the clay, cooling to about 450°C is undertaken more slowly. After this temperature has been reached, the rate of cooling is again increased until the pipes finally reach a temperature at which they can be handled. During drying and firing, pipes contract by about 10% from their extruded size.

12.2.8 Energy analysis

The clay pipe industry commissioned a comprehensive analysis of the energy required to support the total production process for vitrified clay pipes. Boustead and Hancock[1] showed that clay pipes used the least amount of total energy.

Figure 12.2 A kiln control centre, illustrating the extensive use of remote and computer control and monitoring systems

12.2.9 Appearance

Products made in modern factories do not need to be glazed because vitrification takes place throughout the wall thickness. A dense vitrified body is achieved by careful selection and blending of the clays, high extrusion pressures and precise temperature control throughout the firing process.

The colour of the fired product is dependent upon the chemical composition of the blended clays. The colours of vitrified clay pipes range from light buff to deep reddish brown.

12.3 Inspection

To ensure that vitrified clay pipes are produced to very high standards, quality control is carried out during manufacture by plant and laboratory tests and with the aid of automatic testing devices. Normal flexibly-jointed vitrified clay pipes and fittings are produced to the requirements of the European Standard BS EN 295[2]. Unjointed normal and extra chemically resistant pipes and fittings, surface water pipes and fittings and their flexible joints, perforated pipes and fittings and ducts are covered by BS 65[3].

Visual or mechanical inspection and dimensional testing is carried out as the pipes are removed from the kilns, followed by testing for impermeability, chemical resistance and strength.

Manufacturers operate Quality Management Schemes to the requirements of either EN 29002[4] or BS 5750 Part 2[5], as appropriate to the standard. The management of the systems and product quality are assessed by BSI Quality Assurance, under the Kitemark scheme, to provide independent assurance of the quality of vitrified clay, pipes and fittings manufactured and supplied to both European and British standards. Under the scheme all aspects of manufacturing and testing are inspected independently several times each year and a continuous record of all in-house testing is maintained for inspection by the Quality Control Officer at each manufacturer's works.

12.4 Joints

12.4.1 Manufacture

There are two types of mechanical push-fit joint applied to vitrified clay pipes in the UK: the sleeve joint and the O-ring joint. The sleeve joint is used with plain-end pipes, and the O-ring joint is used with socketed pipes. Both types of joint are made to comply with the requirements of the appropriate Standards.

For O-ring jointing, the pipes have polyester fairings cast around the outside of the spigot and the inside of the socket at the factory. Metal moulds are placed in the socket and around the spigot of the pipes. The polyester is poured into the annular space between the mould and the pipes, after passing through accurately controlled metering pumps. Temperatures are closely controlled to maintain accurate finished dimensions to the fairings.

The coupling for the sleeve joint is made from polypropylene with two rubber gaskets incorporated into the sleeve to give the sealing action between the pipe and the sleeve. In the O-ring joint the sealing action is achieved by a rubber O-ring located in the groove in the spigot moulding which is compressed between the spigot and socket fairings. Again, close attention is paid to quality control throughout the manufacture of the joints.

The combination of vitrified clay pipes and push-fit flexible joints has proved to be the leading form of underground drainage used in Britain.

12.5 Jointing

12.5.1 On site

With both types of flexible joint it is essential that the mating surfaces are clean and that the lubricant supplied by the manufacturer is used. Any other type of lubricant could have a detrimental effect on the long-term performance of the joints.

With the O-ring-type joint, the O-ring is placed into the groove on the spigot moulding and the socket of the previously laid pipe is lubricated.

The spigot is then placed up to the socket of the mating pipe and pushed in with a slight side-to-side action. The rubber O-ring is thereby compressed to make a flexible watertight seal.

For sleeve jointing, a coupling is fitted onto one end, before lowering the pipe into the trench.

The pipe is placed on a clean, firm base; lubricant is applied to the chamfered pipe end and the coupling is pressed onto the lubricated end.

For jointing in the trench the plain end of the pipe is lubricated and located in the coupling of the previously laid pipe and pushed in firmly by hand.

When a traditional mortar joint is used, tarred gaskin or a proprietory gasket is placed around the spigot before it is placed into the mating socket. After the pipe has been trued for line and level, the cement mortar joint is made. The mix should be one part cement to three parts of sharp sand. The moisture content should be sufficient to allow the joint to be made without the mortar falling from the underside of the joint. A 45° fillet is then made between spigot and socket. Any mortar which has reached the inside of the pipe is then cleaned away.

12.5.2 Repair and adaptor couplings

Flexible couplings are available for a wide range of replacement and repair operations. They may be used for the placing of new

Figure 12.3 O-ring jointed socketed clay pipes laid on a flat bed of granular material for a surface water drainage scheme

pipes into a drain or sewer to replace damaged or failed pipes, for the insertion of junctions into existing pipelines or for the connection of different sizes or types of pipes.

A full range of adaptors and connectors is available for jointing above-ground rainwater and waste pipes and other underground pipe materials directly to clay drainage systems.

12.5.3 Cutting pipes to length

A chain-cutter may be employed on site when it is necessary to cut a pipe to a specific length. In the case of the sleeve joint, the broken edge of the cut pipe is trimmed with a light hammer or special trimming tool. Jointing lubricant can then be applied to this end which is pushed into a sleeve coupling.

To minimize the need for cutting, special make-up lengths of pipe are made for use with the O-ring joint. If a pipe has to be cut, the shortened length should be the pipe which enters the inspection chamber or manhole. A cement mortar joint is then applied between the pipe and the channel pipe. This short length should not extend more than 150 mm from the external face of the structure.

A flexible joint should be positioned as close to the external face of the structure as possible in order to alleviate differential movement which is likely to occur between the pipeline and the structure. If this movement is likely to be large, the first pipe next to the structure should be a short length with flexible joints to increase the flexibility of the pipeline.

12.6 Trenchless construction

There are many advantages in laying pipes by trenchless techniques in some situations, such as in busy streets, under inaccessible areas or in bad ground conditions.

A range of clay pipes from DN100 upwards can be installed as drains, sewers or conduits by various jacking techniques.

In pipe bursting, the clay pipe is jacked into the space enlarged by a pipe-bursting mole, which breaks out the existing pipeline and travels ahead of the new pipeline which is jacked in behind it. Given suitable ground conditions it is possible not only to replace the pipeline 'size-for-size', but also to increase the pipeline diameter by up to two size increments.

For microtunnelling, the clay pipe is jacked into the native soil behind either a steerable auger boring or a 'slurry shield' microtunnelling machine.

The pipes used for these applications are normally 1.0–1.5 m in length to permit minimal access pit excavation sizes and fit the jacking frames. They have been used satisfactorily with leading Japanese, German and UK microtunnelling-machine operators.

12.7 Standards

BS EN 295[2] is the European Standard for 'normal' flexibly jointed clay pipes and fittings. Part 1 of the standard specifies the product requirements, BS EN 295-1. Part 2 specifies Sampling and Quality Control, BS EN 295-2. Part 3 specifies Test Methods, BS EN 295-3. BS 65[3] covers unjointed normal and extra chemically resistant pipes and fittings, surface water pipes and fittings and their flexible joints, perforated pipes and fittings and ducts.

CPDA publishes a booklet 'New Standards for Vitrified Clay Pipes and Fittings' which fully describes the contents of the two standards.

Rubber seals used in jointing vitrified clay pipes are supplied to either ISO/DIS 4633[6] or BS 2494[7] (Type D) as appropriate to the standard.

Providing that pipes manufactured to BS EN 295 or BS 65 as appropriate are correctly laid and jointed, they will easily meet the test requirements of the Codes of Practice BS 8301[8] and BS 8005: Part 1[9].

12.8 Performance of flexible joints

12.8.1 Specification

It is important not only that sewage or other effluents should be unable to exfiltrate pipelines, but also that ground water should be unable to enter. Contamination of water supplies can be caused by exfiltration. Excessive infiltration can cause high costs in pumping and sewage treatment. Flexibly jointed vitrified clay pipes to BS EN 295-1[2] are capable of withstanding an internal hydraulic pressure of 50 kPa (0.5 bar) for 15 minutes without leakage. Pipe joint assemblies are capable of withstanding specified angular deflection and shear resistance tests under both internal and external pressures of 5 kPa (0.05 bar) and 50 kPa (0.5 bar) for 5 minutes without visible leakage. Surface water pipes and surface water pipe joint assemblies to BS 65[3] are capable of withstanding an internal pressure of 30 kPa (0.3 bar) for 5 minutes.

12.8.1.1 Straight draw

In the straight-draw test the pipes are drawn 10 mm apart.

12.8.1.2 Deflection

In the deflection test one pipe is deflected relative to the other by the value given in *Table 12.1*.

12.8.1.3 Shear resistance

A pipe joint assembly specified to BS EN 295 is required to withstand a shear load of 25 N/mm of nominal size applied to the spigot and of one pipe while the socket of the other pipe is held firmly in a test rig. Joints which allow more than 6 mm line displacement are supported so that this displacement is not exceeded.

The angular-deflection capabilities of the joints are important where pipes are laid in areas where movement can occur, particularly in made-up ground or an area of mining subsidence. The shear capabilities allow some differential movement between one pipe and another.

All these tests ensure that joints for vitrified clay pipes will accommodate any normal ground movement without risk of leakage.

Orchard[7] has explained the mechanism of mining subsidence and described appropriate means of laying clay pipes.

Table 12.1 Deflections of some vitrified clay pipe sizes

Nominal size (mm)	Deflection per metre of deflected pipe length (mm)	Approximate equivalent angular deflection (°)
100–200	50	3
225–500	30	1.75
600–1000	20	1.25

12.8.2 Speed of laying

The use of mechanical push-fit joints allows pipe laying to keep up with trench excavation, and also allows testing to be carried out immediately after laying. A full range of jointed fittings is available for vitrified clay pipes. These joints allow pipes to be laid all the year round, even in the most adverse weather conditions.

12.8.3 Pipeline testing

Pipes and joints may be tested as pipelines once they have been laid. The testing of drains and sewers is governed by the requirements of BS 8301:1985,[8] the Code of Practice for building drainage and BS 8005:1987,[9] the British Standard for sewerage. Similar requirements appear in the Water Authorities' Association (WAA) 'Civil engineering specification for the water industry'[10] and 'Guide for developers—sewers for adoption',[11] the Department of Transport Specification for Highway Works 1986[12] and in Approved Document H to the Building Regulations 1985.[13]

Cooperation between the authors of these different documents has led to the adoption of compatible requirements for both water and air testing of drains and sewers, with the exception that water test heads for sewers are slightly different to those for drains. All the requirements are easily met when clay-pipe systems are correctly laid.

A booklet on testing has been produced by the CPDA[14] which covers the procedures to be adopted when carrying out tests to all the above specifications.

12.9 Packaging, stacking and mechanical handling

Vitrified clay pipes can be delivered to site in prepacked form and can be off-loaded quickly from the delivery vehicle either by the customer's own plant such as fork-lift truck or crane or by unloading equipment attached to the delivery vehicle. When a fork-lift truck is attached to the prime mover of an articulated delivery vehicle, the prime mover may be detached from the loaded trailer on site and be employed as a fork-lift truck to unload the packs of pipes.

Fittings in crates, steel cages or shrink-wrapped packs can be off-loaded in a similar manner to pipes.

O-rings, sleeves and lubricant should be stored in their containers in cool, dark conditions until they are required for use, because they tend to deteriorate if subject to ultraviolet light for long periods of time. Pipes which are not delivered in a pack should be stacked in a pyramid form with the joints on the spigot ends projecting so that no damage occurs to the fairings.

12.10 Availability

Factories producing clay pipes are well situated to give an efficient service throughout the UK and for export. Comprehensive stocks of pipes and fittings are maintained at manufacturers' works and depots, as well as by all leading builders' merchants.

The range of inexpensive drainage fittings in vitrified clay is very comprehensive, enabling flexible and economical drainage layouts to be achieved.

12.11 Heat resistance

Drains and sewers often have to carry effluents at elevated temperatures. For example, the temperature of discharges from laundries and domestic washing machines can approach 100°C. Clay pipes have a low coefficient of thermal expansion and, therefore, there is very little longitudinal movement in the pipeline when the temperature is raised. Any such movement can be accommodated in the joints. Hot effluents do not soften clay pipes.

12.12 Abrasion resistance

When surface water enters a sewer it often carries road grit. This grit can erode pipe materials, but vitrified clay pipes are very resistant to this type of abrasive attack.

Experiments were carried out at Manchester University and at the British Ceramic Research Association to compare the erosion resistance of various drainage materials. The particles used were even more abrasive than road grit. The results showed that vitrified clay pipes were pre-eminently suitable for surface-water sewers. In practice, roughening and loss of strength from erosion may be ignored in the design of a vitrified clay sewer.

12.13 Strength

12.13.1 General

The loads on buried pipes are caused by the backfill above the pipes with additional wheel loads or distributed surcharge loads.

The amount of total structural load that a pipeline can carry is dependent upon the combination of the strength of the pipe (see *Figure 12.4*) and the bedding on which it is laid (see *Figure 12.5*), so that high strength beddings can be used with low strength pipes, or low strength beddings can be used with high strength pipes.

Modern methods of manufacture and control have enabled manufacturers to guarantee their pipes to be of high minimum-load-bearing strength.

BS EN 295-1 gives a range of minimum crushing strengths in 3 groups for 100 and 150 mm diameter pipes and in a range of classes for larger sizes. Higher crushing strengths than those given in the standard may be declared providing that they conform to the requirements of the next higher class when calculated according to a formula given, or are in step of 6 kN m^{-1} for 100 and 150 mm diameter pipes.

BS 65[3] states the crushing strength values in three categories: standard strength, extra strength and super strength. Higher crushing strength values may be claimed by the manufacturer in conjunction with appropriate high bending-moment-resistance values.

12.13.2 Crushing strength

The crushing strengths for a range of nominal sizes of vitrified clay pipe given in BS EN 295-1 are listed in *Table 12.2* for flexibly jointed pipes.

12.13.3 Design

The strengths used in design together with new bedding factors for clay pipes for classes F and B bedding recommended by the Water Authorities' Association[13] are listed in *Table 12.2*; these give the limits of cover set out in *Table 12.3*, using wide trench design criteria.

12.13.4 Bending moment resistance

Both BS EN 295-1 and BS 65[3] also give values of bending moment resistance which the smaller diameter pipes must have.

Figure 12.4 Crushing test on a large diameter clay pipe

Table 12.2(a) Crushing strength (FN) in kN m⁻¹ DN100 and 150

Nominal size (DN)	Crushing strength (FN)		
100	22	28	34
150	22	28	34

Table 12.2(b) Crushing strength (FN) in kN m⁻¹ ≥DN200

Nominal size (DN)	Class L*	Class Number		
		95	120	160	200
200			24	32	40
225			28	36	45
250			30	40	50
300			36	48	60
350			42	56	70
400		38	48	64	
450		43	54	72	
500		48	60	80	
600	48	57	72		
700	60	67	84		
800	60	76	96		
1000	60	95			
1200	60				

* Lower strength pipes

These values are related to the crushing strengths. When correctly bedded, pipes will not fracture in beam before their design crushing loads are exceeded. Higher values of bending moment resistance may be claimed in conjunction with higher crushing strengths. The bending moment resistance values of some sizes of vitrified clay pipe are listed in *Table 12.4*.

12.13.5 Bedding

There are two main types of bedding: flexible and rigid. For flexible bedding, the pipe is laid either directly on the trimmed bottom of the trench or on an imported material used as a bed, or bed and haunch, or total surround. Rigid beddings employ concrete, which can be used either as a bed, or bed and haunch, or arch, or total surround. The latter beddings are only used in extreme conditions. The crushing strengths in the standards have been calculated to allow flexible beddings to be used in all normal conditions.

12.14 Research

12.14.1 Structural research

Research is continuously carried out for the Clay Pipe Development Association on methods of bedding clay pipes. Work was carried out on test rigs and in trenches in the pipe testing facilities of British Ceramic Research Limited and the Water Research Centre to simulate site conditions. The pipes and the trenches were fully instrumented to give the optimum amount of data from each test. This research showed that, after any necessary socket holes had been cut, clay pipes could be laid directly on many types of trench formation trimmed only by a spade to line and level. It also showed that where the trench formation was unsuitable, all sizes of pipes could be laid on beds of imported granular material.

The original work on minimum beddings was accepted in the report of the Department of the Environment's Working Party on Sewers and Water Mains[16] published in 1975. Since then, minimum beddings have been included in all subsequent major specifications and design guides. The most important of these are currently: 'A guide to design loadings for buried rigid pipes',[17] 'Civil engineering specification for the water industry',[10] 'Sewers for adoption',[11] BS 8301,[8] BS 8005: Part 1[9] and 'The Building Regulations 1985, Approved Document H, Drainage and waste disposal'.[13]

The culmination of the structural design research programme was reached with the recommendation of increased bedding

Table 12.3 Limits of cover between which vitrified clay pipes can be laid in any width of trench

Nominal bore (mm)	Bedding construction	Crushing strength (kN m⁻¹)	Main traffic roads (m)	Other roads (m)	Fields and gardens (m)
100	Class D or N	22	0.6–4.2	0.6–4.6	0.4–4.7
		28	0.4–5.7	0.5–6.0	0.4–6.0
		34	0.4–7.1	0.4–7.3	0.4–7.3
		40	0.4–8.5	0.4–8.6	0.4–8.6
	Class F	22	0.4–8.0	0.4–8.2	0.4–8.2
		28	0.4–10.0+	0.4–10.0+	0.4–10.0+
		34	0.4–10.0+	0.4–10.0+	0.4–10.0+
		40	0.4–10.0+	0.4–10.0+	0.4–10.0+
	Class B	22	0.4–10.0+	0.4–10.0+	0.4–10.0+
		28	0.4–10.0+	0.4–10.0+	0.4–10.0+
		34	0.4–10.0+	0.4–10.0+	0.4–10.0+
		40	0.4–10.0+	0.4–10.0+	0.4–10.0+
150	Class D or N	22	1.1–2.0	0.9–2.9	0.6–3.1
		28	0.7–3.4	0.7–3.9	0.6–4.0
		34	0.6–4.5	0.6–4.9	0.6–4.9
		40	0.6–5.5	0.6–5.8	0.6–5.8
	Class F	22	0.6–5.2	0.6–5.5	0.6–5.6
		28	0.6–6.9	0.6–7.1	0.6–7.1
		34	0.6–8.5	0.6–8.6	0.6–8.7
		40	0.6–10.0+	0.6–10.0+	0.6–10.0+
	Class B	22	0.6–7.2	0.6–7.3	0.6–7.4
		28	0.6–9.3	0.6–9.4	0.6–9.4
		34	0.6–10.0+	0.6–10.0+	0.6–10.0+
		40	0.6–10.0+	0.6–10.0+	0.6–10.0+
225	Class D or N	28	—	1.1–2.3	0.6–2.6
		36	0.9–2.6	0.8–3.3	0.6–3.5
		45	0.6–3.9	0.6–4.3	0.6–4.4
	Class F	28	0.6–4.3	0.6–4.7	0.6–4.8
		36	0.6–5.9	0.6–6.2	0.6–6.2
		45	0.6–7.6	0.6–7.7	0.6–7.8
	Class B	28	0.6–6.1	0.6–6.3	0.6–6.3
		36	0.6–8.0	0.6–8.2	0.6–8.2
		45	0.6–10.0+	0.6–10.0+	0.6–10.0+
300	Class D or N	36	—	1.2–2.1	0.6–2.5
		48	0.8–2.7	0.8–3.4	0.6–3.5
		60	0.6–4.0	0.6–4.4	0.6–4.5
	Class F	36	0.6–4.2	0.6–4.6	0.6–4.6
		48	0.6–6.0	0.6–6.2	0.6–6.2
		60	0.6–7.7	0.6–7.8	0.6–7.8
	Class B	36	0.6–5.9	0.6–6.1	0.6–6.2
		48	0.6–8.1	0.6–8.2	0.6–8.3
		60	0.6–10.0+	0.6–10.0+	0.6–10.0+
375	Class D or N	36	—	—	0.9–1.9
		45	—	1.1–2.4	0.6–2.7
		60	0.8–3.0	0.8–3.6	0.6–3.7
	Class F	36	0.7–3.2	0.7–3.8	0.6–3.9
		45	0.6–4.5	0.6–4.9	0.6–5.0
		60	0.6–6.4	0.6–6.6	0.6–6.7
	Class B	36	0.6–4.8	0.6–5.2	0.6–5.2
		45	0.6–6.3	0.6–6.5	0.6–6.6
		60	0.6–8.7	0.6–8.8	0.6–8.8

continued

Table 12.3 *continued*

Nominal bore (mm)	Bedding construction	Crushing strength (kN m^{-1})	Main traffic roads (m)	Other roads (m)	Fields and gardens (m)
400	Class D or N	38	—	—	0.9–1.8
		48	—	1.2–2.3	0.6–2.6
		64	0.8–2.9	0.8–3.6	0.6–3.7
	Class F	38	0.8–3.0	0.7–3.7	0.6–3.8
		48	0.6–4.4	0.6–4.8	0.6–4.9
		64	0.6–6.3	0.6–6.5	0.6–6.5
	Class B	38	0.6–4.6	0.6–5.0	0.6–5.1
		48	0.6–6.2	0.6–6.4	0.6–6.5
		64	0.6–8.5	0.6–8.6	0.6–8.6
450	Class D or N	43	—	—	0.8–1.9
		54	—	1.1–2.4	0.6–2.7
		72	0.8–3.0	0.7–3.7	0.6–3.8
	Class F	43	0.7–3.2	0.7–3.8	0.6–3.9
		54	0.6–4.5	0.6–4.9	0.6–5.0
		72	0.6–6.4	0.6–6.7	0.6–6.7
	Class B	43	0.6–4.8	0.6–5.2	0.6–5.2
		54	0.6–6.3	0.6–6.6	0.6–6.6
		72	0.6–8.7	0.6–8.8	0.6–8.9
500	Class D or N	48	—	—	0.8–1.9
		60	—	1.1–2.4	0.6–2.7
		80	0.8–3.0	0.7–3.6	0.6–3.7
	Class F	48	0.7–3.2	0.7–3.8	0.6–3.9
		60	0.6–4.5	0.6–4.9	0.6–4.9
		80	0.6–6.4	0.6–6.6	0.6–6.7
	Class B	48	0.6–4.8	0.6–5.2	0.6–5.2
		60	0.6–6.3	0.6–6.5	0.6–6.6
		80	0.6–8.6	0.6–8.8	0.6–8.8
600	Class D or N	48	—	—	—
		57	—	—	0.8–1.9
		72	—	1.0–2.4	0.6–2.7
	Class F	48	1.0–2.1	0.8–3.1	0.6–3.2
		57	0.7–3.2	0.7–3.8	0.6–3.9
		72	0.6–4.6	0.6–4.9	0.6–5.0
	Class B	48	0.6–3.8	0.6–4.3	0.6–4.4
		57	0.6–4.8	0.6–5.2	0.6–5.2
		72	0.6–6.4	0.6–6.6	0.6–6.6

Table 12.4 Bending moment resistance (BMR) in kN m^{-1} for crushing strength values (FN) in kN m^{-1}

Nominal size (DN)	FN	BMR	FN	BMR	FN	BMR
100	22	1,0	28	1,3	34	1,7
150	22	2,8	28	3,4	34	4,0
200	24	5,2	32	6,2	40	7,4
225	28	6,5	36	7,4	45	9,0

factors for clay pipes by the Water Authorities' Association.[13] It is recommended that bedding factors of 1.9, 2.5 and 2.5 are used with clay pipes to class F, B and S bedding respectively. This means that clay pipes on these beddings can be laid deeper than before, with consequent savings in the cost of imported granular bedding material.

In some conditions previously requiring strengthening with concrete, the design strength can now be achieved with pipes laid on beddings of single-size granular material either taken up to half-pipe height, or used as a total surround. Only in rare cases of abnormally high loadings do clay pipes up to 1000 mm nominal diameter need concrete bedding for strength purposes.

The author has written two booklets[18,19] to aid designers in the specification of beddings for buried pipelines.

12.14.2 Hydraulics

The original research carried out by the Hydraulics Research Association on the hydraulic roughness of mature sewers showed that when a pipeline was used to carry sewage, the hydraulic

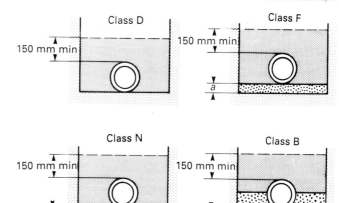

Note: When placing sidefills, the crown of the pipe should remain in view to avoid damage by tamping. The first layer placed above the pipe should be thick enough to protect the crown.

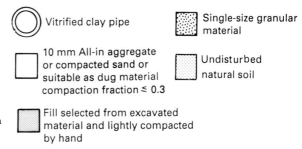

Vitrified clay pipe

Single-size granular material

10 mm All-in aggregate or compacted sand or suitable as dug material compaction fraction ≤ 0.3

Undisturbed natural soil

Fill selected from excavated material and lightly compacted by hand

Figure 12.5 In machine-dug uniform soils: *a* is, for sleeve jointed pipes, a minimum of 50 mm, for socketted pipes a minimum of 100 mm under barrels but not less than 50 mm under sockets. In rock or mixed soils containing rock bands, boulders, large flints or stones or other irregular hard spots: *a* is, for sleeve jointed pipes, a minimum of 150 mm, for socketted pipes a minimum of 200 mm under barrels and 150 mm minimum under sockets

roughness of that pipeline was greater than that of a new clean pipeline with clean water flowing through it. Hence its hydraulic capacity is less.

As little work was carried out on the hydraulic characteristics of small-bore pipes with sewage passing through, the Clay Pipe Development Association sponsored research at the Water Research Centre (Stevenage Laboratory)—formerly the Water Pollution Research Laboratory—to determine the amount of microbiological slime adhering to the interior of pipes of certain materials. The first series of experiments was carried out with four different types of drainage material: clay, asbestos cement, pitch fibre and uPVC. These tests were carried out with sewage flowing continuously at various constant velocities in a half-full pipeline. The results showed that in a 6-week period, the growth and weight of slime was statistically independent of the pipe material, but dependent upon the velocity of sewage. The determination of the hydraulic roughness of clay and uPVC pipelines were the next tests to be carried out. A constant flow of sewage was maintained for many days with the pipeline flowing full. The results showed no significant differences in hydraulic roughness between clay and uPVC for 100-mm bore pipes, although the hydraulic roughness varied continuously with the growth and sloughing off of slime from the walls of the pipes.

Further work by the Hydraulics Research Station (HRS) on concrete, asbestos cement, uPVC and clay pipes in a rig using 225 mm nominal diameter pipes has shown that when the pipes are flowing partially full at varying depths of flow, clay and uPVC pipes have a lower hydraulic resistance than pipes made of cement bonded materials.

Table 12.5 Design values of hydraulic roughness in used sewers for typical peak DWF velocities[18]

Velocity (m s⁻¹)	k_s (mm)
>1.5	0.3
>1.0	0.6
0.76–1.0	1.5

Subsequent research and analysis carried out by the Water Research Centre (WRc) on the HRS work and on live sewers led to the determination of the design values of hydraulic roughness in used sewers, for typical peak DWF velocities set out in *Table 12.5*. These values have been published in the WRc 'Sewer rehabilitation manual'[20] and also BS 8005: Part 1.[9]

Sometimes pipes carry liquids such as chemical wastes which will not deposit material on the walls of the pipeline. To determine the hydraulic roughness of clay pipes for these cases, tests were carried out at Wimpey Laboratories.

Design values of 0.03 should be used for pipes up to 150 mm diameter, and 0.06 for larger pipes.

The author has provided a booklet[18] to assist the designer of foul and surface water drainage and sewerage schemes to size pipelines hydraulically by the use of the Colebrook and White uniform flow equation. The information is given in tabular form and the range of nominal bores covered is 100–1000 mm. The recommended k_s values for both foul and surface water flow design are used to calculate the data for both full and partially full pipes.

12.15 Chemical resistance

Although the effluents normally accepted into pipe sewers are not very aggressive in themselves, they can produce chemicals which attack pipe and jointing materials which contain Portland cement. This is particularly true where gradients are slack and flows low or an infrequently discharged pumping main empties into a sewer. Micro-organisms in sewage and industrial waste produce hydrogen sulphide gas which, when it condenses on the walls of a sewer, will be oxidized by the micro-organism *Thiobaccillus thiooxidans* to form sulphuric acid. This acid attacks Portland cement and pipelines which contain Portland cement can have their strength diminished and porosity increased. Total collapse of the sewer can even take place.

The calcium in Portland cement can also be attacked by sulphates in ground waters.

Sulphides and sulphates do not attack vitrified clay pipes. Many industries produce aggressive effluents which vitrified clay pipes carry successfully. Vitrified clay pipes have excellent chemical resistance.

Pipes used in house drainage must withstand chemicals used in the home such as detergents, bleaches and other aggressive cleaning agents. Vitrified clay pipes are especially suitable for carrying these effluents.

12.16 Summary

Drains and sewers must remain in service for very many years. The cost of repairing or replacing a pipeline which has failed is extremely high. Vitrified clay pipes have been made durable and impermeable by the manufacturing processes in which changes in the physical and chemical structure of the clay take place. A vitrified clay pipeline is a permanent structure and the inherent structural strength of the pipes allows them, in many instances, to be laid directly in the trench bottom or with only very little additional bedding material being brought on to the site. The hard vitrified surface of the pipes gives them hydraulic smoothness and high abrasion resistance. Resistance to high and low temperatures is obtained through the low coefficient of thermal expansion of vitrified clay pipes. Chemical and biological resistance is achieved through the inert chemical structure of the vitrified clay body of the pipe. Together, a unique combination of benefits that has kept clay pipes supreme in their

field for over 3500 years—a supremacy which looks as if it will remain unchallenged in the foreseeable future.

References

1 BOUSTEAD, I. and HANCOCK, G. F., 'Energy requirements of a vitrified clay pipe drainage system', in *Resources and Conservation*, Vol. 6 (1981)
2 BRITISH STANDARDS INSTITUTION, *BS EN 295, Vitrified clay pipes and fittings and pipe joints for drains and sewers*, Milton Keynes (1991)
3 BRITISH STANDARDS INSTITUTION, *BS 65 Vitrified clay pipes, fittings, joints and ducts*, Milton Keynes (1988)
4 BRITISH STANDARDS INSTITUTION, *EN 29002, European Standard equivalent to BS 5750 Quality systems*, Milton Keynes (1987)
5 BRITISH STANDARDS INSTITUTION, *BS 5750*
6 INTERNATIONAL ORGANIZATION FOR STANDARDIZATION *ISO/DIS 4633 Rubber seals – joint rings for water supply, drainage and sewerage pipe lines – specification for materials*, (1986)
7 BRITISH STANDARDS INSTITUTION, *BS 2924 Elastomeric joint rings for pipework and pipelines*, Milton Keynes (19??)
8 BRITISH STANDARDS INSTITUTION, *BS 8301 Building drainage*, Milton Keynes (1985)
9 BRITISH STANDARDS INSTITUTION, *BS 8005: Part 1 Guide to new sewerage construction*, Milton Keynes (1987)
10 WATER AUTHORITIES' ASSOCIATION, *Civil engineering specification for the water industry*, 2nd edn.
11 WATER AUTHORITIES' ASSOCIATION, *Guide for developers—sewers for adoption*, 2nd edn.
12 DEPARTMENT OF TRANSPORT, *Specification for highway works 1986*, London (1986)
13 BUILDING RESEARCH ESTABLISHMENT, *The Building Regulations 1985, Approved Document H, Drainage and Waste Disposal*, HMSO, London (1985)
14 CLAY PIPE DEVELOPMENT ASSOCIATION, *Testing of drains and sewers—water and air tests*
15 WATER AUTHORITIES' ASSOCIATION, *Information and guidance note No. 4-11-02*
16 DEPARTMENT OF THE ENVIRONMENT, London
17 TRANSPORT AND ROAD RESEARCH LABORATORY, *A guide to design loadings for buried rigid pipes*
18 BLAND, C. E. G., *Design tables for determining the bedding construction of vitrified clay pipelines*, Clay Pipe Development Association
19 BLAND, C. E. G., *Simplified tables for determining the bedding construction of vitrified pipelines*, Clay Pipe Development Association
20 WATER RESEARCH CENTRE, *Sewer rehabilitation manual*

13

Ceramics—Tiles and Tiling

R C Baker BSc, MICE
Grove Consultants Ltd

Contents

13.1 Introduction 13/3

13.2 Scope 13/3

13.3 Terminology 13/3

13.4 General 13/3
    13.4.1 Brief history 13/3
    13.4.2 Manufacture of ceramic tiles 13/3
    13.4.3 Durability 13/4
    13.4.4 Accommodation of movement 13/4
    13.4.5 Substrates for wall and floor tiling 13/4
    13.4.6 Joints and jointing 13/6
    13.4.7 Tolerances 13/7
    13.4.8 Principal mechanical and physical properties 13/7
    13.4.9 Fixing ceramic tiles 13/7

13.4 Clay roof tiles 13/8
    13.5.1 Types and sizes 13/8
    13.5.2 Availability 13/8
    13.5.3 Fixing clay tiles for roofing 13/8
    13.5.4 Plain clay tiles—applications other than roofing 13/9

13.6 Ceramic wall tiles and tiling 13/12
    13.6.1 Types and sizes 13/12
    13.6.2 Availability 13/12
    13.6.3 Fixing ceramic wall tiles 13/12
    13.6.4 Mosaics 13/13

13.7 Ceramic floor tiles and tiling 13/14
    13.7.1 General 13/14
    13.7.2 Fixing ceramic floor tiles 13/14

13.8 Maintenance 13/15

Bibliography 13/15

13.1 Introduction

Tiles are widely used in building as a cladding, covering, or finish to roofs, walls and floors, as they have proved to provide adequately the combined functions of weather protection, resistance to wear and decoration. A number of materials may be used to form tiles, the main requirement being that the material can be formed or worked into regular thin shapes having the required properties of low permeability and attractive finished appearance. Such materials include fibre composites, thermoplastics, marble, terrazo, glass, slate, stainless steel and copper. One commonly used material is natural clay which, after processing and shaping, is baked to provide ceramic tile products.

13.2 Scope

In this chapter ceramic tiles for roof cladding, interior and exterior wall cladding and floor finishes are considered. Standards for the manufacture of ceramic wall and floor tiles, together with the necessary skills and details for the successful application of tiling, are fully documented in British Standards and other manuals produced by major manufacturers of tiles. Additional information in the form of research papers and advisory documents is also available from relevant research organizations and trade associations. It is not the intention of this work to reproduce the above information. However, the author appreciates difficulties that can be encountered concerning the availability, collation and interpretation of relevant information when work is to be carried out, or problems are either presented or anticipated.

The aims and objectives of this chapter are to discuss and establish criteria which are fundamental to the satisfactory long-term performance of tiling, to provide guidance for the occasional user, and to act as a source of reference for all users. Major users can draw upon the excellent service and technical information offered by leading tile manufacturers.

13.3 Terminology

There are many terms used to describe baked-clay products and their application, depending upon their use, manufacturing process and finish. The most notable of these terms are listed below.

(1) *Ceramic:* product of burnt clay. Porcelain, brick, tile, fireclay, stoneware, faience, pottery, earthenware.
(2) *Earthenware:* low-grade porous ceramic product made from ordinary brick-earths. Used for pottery and, when glazed, for building drainage and some tiles.
(3) *Faience:* large glazed terracotta tiles, either single or double fired.
(4) *Fireclay:* clay which is rich in silica and alumina. Used for grate backs and flue liners. Can be subjected to high temperatures without becoming glassy.
(5) *Porcelain:* highest grade ceramic of high strength, with low water absorption and hard glaze. Used for some wall tiles, sanitary ware, electrical insulators and capacitors.
(6) *Stoneware:* salt-glazed high-strength ceramic resistant to corrosive effluent. Used in laboratories and several industries.
(7) *Terracotta:* high quality unglazed earthenware used for building blocks and decorative items.
(8) *Tile:* a thin flat or profiled sheet of burnt clay, either glazed or unglazed, for floor or roof coverings.

13.4 General

13.4.1 Brief history

The term 'ceramics' is used to describe the plastic arts of the potter and other workers in clay, and is derived from the Greek 'keramos' meaning 'potters clay'. It is also interesting to note that the Latin word for tile is 'tegula' from the verb 'tego' meaning to cover. The art of producing ceramics from indigenous materials, especially earthenware, has roots in ancient civilizations sited around the Mediterranean, as demonstrated by archaeological discoveries of pottery, and other clay products used as decoration, utensils and building materials.

Wall tiles were used in Babylon and ancient Egypt, and later in Persia and Rome. The Greeks made use of a 'Spanish' type of tile for roofing, and similar to the Romans, used ceramic wall and floor tiling consisting mainly of tesselated, or mosaic work. The larger square or rectangular tile did not make an appearance until about 1600 AD with the characteristic blue Delft tile, many of which depicted a scene or figure.

Roman pavements were decorated with mosaics executed with inlaid cubes of various stones, and 12th century European pictorial mosaic frescoes include metals and glass, amongst the most notable surviving examples being those belonging to St Marks, Venice, and some chapels of Westminster Abbey.

In medieval Britain, around the year 1200, a large number of small works were producing clay tiles to replace roofs of wood shingles or thatch. This activity was most prevalent in the southern part of the country, where there is an abundance of clay deposits. Manifest examples are the Oast Houses in Sussex, and the use of plain tiles as wall cladding in other southern counties. Tiles, along with bricks, were manufactured close to the site of the intended buildings, and at this time were all hand made, flat, incorporated two holes for fixing with oak pegs, and of a size similar to the wooden shingles in use at the time.

In the early 19th century tile-making machines began to appear as precursors of modern machines, but mainly to produce profiled rather than plain tiles, which continued to be hand made for some time.

13.4.2 Manufacture of ceramic tiles

A ceramic product is the result of baking or firing minerals, usually in the form of a locally available clay, at high temperature in an oven or kiln. Raw clays made in the UK are generally based upon the mineral kaolinite, with crystalline aluminium oxide and traces of quartz, mica and iron oxide. The proportions of quartz, silica and other constituents may be adjusted during processing of the clay to suit the manufacturing process. The end-product is brittle, hard and lacks ductility.

Both the period and temperature of firing determine the amount of minerals converted to a glass, which acts as a binder. Most of the desirable properties such as density, strength, hardness, chemical and frost resistance, and dimensional stability improve with increased glass content. Undesirable attributes are increased brittleness and cost. Products such as porcelain have a high glass content and are sometimes described as fully vitrified, whilst earthenware products have a low glass content.

It is the combination of clay processing with conditions of firing that determines the properties and appearance of the finished product, which will be unique to the works concerned.

13.4.2.1 Roof tiles

The manufacture of hand-made roof tiles follows closely that for bricks, the stages being, obtaining the clay or 'clay-getting', tempering, shaping, drying and baking in an oven at a temperature of about 1100°C. Hand-made tiles, although more expensive than the machine-made product, have a more uniform consistency, and are consequently superior in terms of strength, resulting in fewer breakages during handling and maintenance, texture and less susceptible to frost damage by lamination. They are much in demand for refurbishment work and special effects.

Machine-made roof tiles are formed by extruding a uniform strip of processed clay for cutting into tile-size bats which are then shaped, dried and fired. All clay roof tiles adopt the basic colour of the burnt clay, and whilst the surface of hand-made tiles can be produced to a variety of finishes, machine-made clay tiles are normally smooth or sand faced.

13.4.2.2 Wall tiles

In most cases slight variations in size and colour between roof tiles adds to the appeal of the finished roof, and is not necessarily detrimental to their performance. Wall tiles, however, can often be inspected at close quarters, are generally thinner than roof tiles, and are expected to conform to a regular pattern of jointing whilst presenting an overall uniform appearance of colour, pattern and texture. Variations in thickness between tiles which cannot be accommodated in the bedding will inhibit cleaning and lead to grimy areas unacceptable for areas where hygiene is important such as hospitals and kitchens. Great care is therefore required during all stages of manufacture to ensure a uniform product with close dimensional tolerance. In order consistently to achieve the close tolerances required, all ceramic wall tiles are machine made, either by extrusion or dust pressing.

Double-fired wall tiles are formed by pressing a mixture of flint and clay dust into steel dies under high pressure, and firing at about 1100°C to give a slip or biscuit, usually white, buff or brown in colour. Biscuits are then treated with a glazing solution and matured at a temperature of about 1025°C for up to 10 days. Single-fired tiles are the result of treating the pressed processed clay with glazing solution before firing in order to give the finished product from a single baking.

An alternative method is to form tiles by extruding a column of clay which is then cut into predetermined lengths. Tiles may be extruded as single tiles, or as double tiles which are split after firing to form separate tiles. Split tiles may be recognized by a series of parallel ribs on the back face.

13.4.2.3 Floor tiles

Ceramic tiles for flooring are divided into quarries and clay tiles. Clay used for quarries is less refined than that used for clay floor tiles which are manufactured to closer tolerances. Quarries and floor tiles may be glazed or unglazed, and of various textures and patterns to inhibit slip. They are manufactured using similar methods to those described for wall tiles, but are considerably thicker and are of the natural clay colours of red, brown, blue and buff.

13.4.3 Durability

Ceramic tiles are amongst the most durable of building materials. They are resistant to attack by most acids and alkalis, and can be frost resistant. Tiling, if properly carried out, is impervious to fluids such as oils, grease and cleaning materials, and is also resistant to the weather. Clay tiles and tiling are not resistant to hydrofluoric acid or strong caustic solutions.

The body or slip of a tile, however, is pervious and will absorb moisture to a degree irrespective of whether the face is glazed, or is in the form of a dense hardened skin resulting from the method of manufacture.

It is essential for the satisfactory performance of tiling in service to prevent moisture or any other liquid penetrating or bypassing the surface glaze or hardened skin to the body of the tile, or beyond, to the bedding or background materials. Such penetration may result in frost damage, expose bedding and background materials to attack by dissolved chemicals, and cause dimensional changes due to variations in moisture content. The value of grout between tiles, and the filling and sealing of other joints, in this respect should never be underestimated.

The impact resistance of clay tiles is not high as damage to glaze or face hardened skin can easily occur, and any tile that is not solidly bedded may shatter if subjected to mechanical force. Attention should therefore be given to protecting surfaces, edges and corners which are subject to impact damage, the avoidance of lipping between adjacent tiles and solid bedding for floors accepting wheeled traffic, and the effective filling and sealing of all joints.

13.4.4 Accommodation of movement

Elements and components of buildings, including their cladding, are subject to cyclic, and sometimes progressive, dimensional change. Unless provision is made to accommodate movement brought about by dimensional change, distortion of the building will occur and, if of sufficient magnitude, cause disruption at structural supports, bowing of wall panels, curling of screeds and floor slabs, and subsequent failure of claddings and finishes. Movement is the nett result of dimensional changes arising from creep, drying shrinkage, change of temperature, change of moisture content, frost and chemical action. Any combination of these effects may occur, the separate movements not necessarily being in the same direction. Other contributory factors are foundation behaviour, vibration and, externally, the effects of wind.

Tiling is no exception to the above and, whereas there is normally sufficient 'elbow room' for roof tiles to move freely, due to the method of fixing, tolerances and open joints, tiling to walls and floors cannot in itself accommodate movement if all joints are grouted and large areas are constrained by changes in direction at wall/wall and floor/wall junctions, together with direction changes provided by openings for doors, windows and service items.

Wall and floor tiling acts as cladding to a construction made up from a number of layers of material of differing thickness and properties (*Figures 13.1–13.3*). Each layer will be subject to dimensional change depending upon its material properties and the environmental conditions imposed. In some cases adjacent layers may be straining in opposite directions leading to separation at their boundary.

In the absence of correctly designed and constructed joints to limit accumulated movement, tiling is likely to fail by delamination, arching or crushing.

13.4.5 Substrates for wall and floor tiling

Traditional methods and standards of workmanship for masonry and concrete construction will rarely provide a surface which can be tiled upon directly. Although work can be expected to be within acceptable structural dimensional tolerances, there will often be sufficient misalignment, lipping of precast units, bowing, out of plumb, out of level, shutter marks and other local defects which would be mirrored in the face of directly applied tiling and fail to provide an acceptable perceived finish. In the majority of cases it will be necessary to create a true surface by 'dubbing-out' the as-built work with render or levelling screed and, thereby, provide a smooth, plane, correctly aligned surface, with uniform suction, to accept tiling (see also Section 13.4.7).

If through using special techniques close building tolerances are achieved with a true surface, consideration may be given to tiling directly upon an as-built surface by accommodating

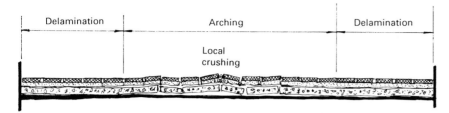

Figure 13.1 The effect of movement on wall and floor tiling. There may be more than one zone of arching within a confined panel

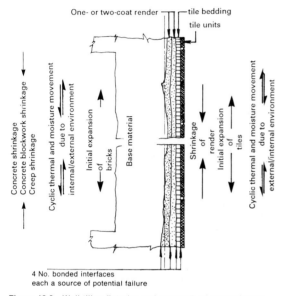

Figure 13.2 Wall tiling (interior and external) as cladding to a construction made up of a number of layers of differing thickness and properties. Base material: *in situ* or precast concrete, concrete blockwork, or brickwork

tile bedding. This method is not generally recommended, however, as uniform adhesion over the whole area is unlikely and there is still the possibility that minor deviations and local defects will unduly influence the finished appearance of the tiling.

Renders to walls, and screeds to floors must be rigid, stable, firmly attached to and compatible with the background or base material. They must also have sufficient strength in themselves to support the tiling, resist all applied loading, including wind suction where appropriate, and provide an effective uniform key for subsequent coats and tile adhesion.

For many years the construction industry has made extensive use of system building, especially timber-frame and steel-frame dwellings. These consist essentially of site-assembled factory-produced elements with close dimensional tolerance, allowing internal dry wall lining to be used without the necessity of dubbing out with wet plaster. Experience over many years and thousands of dwellings has shown that in these circumstances ceramic tiles may be applied directly to the surface of plasterboard lining. Where tiling is to be applied direct to the face of plasterboard, it is recommended that in order to reduce the weight to a minimum, only thin (4 mm) tiles are used applied to the plasterboard face intended for decoration with a thin-bed organic adhesive. Attention should be given to the adhesive manufacturer's instructions regarding the preparation or priming of the plasterboard surface.

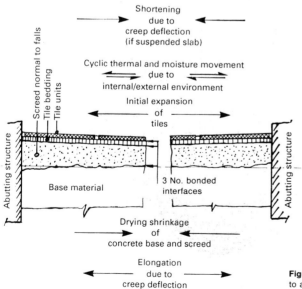

Figure 13.3 Floor tiling ('on the ground' or suspended) as cladding to a construction made up of a number of layers of differing thicknesses and properties. Base material: usually dense concrete

13.4.5.1 Substrate requirements for ceramic wall tiling

The stability of substrates is paramount for successful tiling, and special attention should be given to the maturity of the background or base material, and, eventually, to the substrate itself.

Cement–sand renders intended to support ceramic wall tiling should not be applied to brickwork, concrete blockwork or *in situ* concrete until a high proportion of movement due to drying shrinkage, creep and expansion of clay units is judged to have occurred. The initial expansion of clay bricks and ceramic tiles takes place within a few weeks. In contrast, the drying period for *in situ* concrete extends over many years, the minimum recommended period before application of render being 4–6 months, or longer if the drying period has been cold or humid. When estimating an acceptable drying period for concrete blockwork, consideration should be given to the type of block, the moisture content at time of use and the effectiveness of weather protection during construction. If in doubt, the same criteria as for *in situ* concrete should be used.

In high-rise buildings, if compatible with the overall programme, consideration may be given to carrying out the tiling work from the top of the building downwards to allow maximum time for shortening due to creep to take place.

The attachment of a substrate render to the base material is a combination of mechanical key and adhesion. To provide an effective mechanical key, it is recommended that joints to brickwork and blockwork are raked out to a depth of 15 mm and in the case of dense concrete either the surface be scabbled to a depth of 3 mm to expose the coarse aggregate partially, or dovetailed slots or other keying shapes be cast into the work. As an aid towards achieving adequate adhesion it may be appropriate to use a proprietory bonding agent, applied in accordance with the manufacturer's instructions.

Surface preparation consists of removing dust and loose particles and, except where instructions for the use of a bonding agent state otherwise, wetting the surface of masonry or concrete with clean water to avoid high initial suction. No 'free' water is to be present on the surface immediately before application of render.

When selecting materials and mix proportions for the render, it is important to consider both the likelihood of shrinkage cracking, and its compatibility with the base material. Cement-rich mixes should be avoided, and the adopted mix no stronger than 1:3, preferably 1:4, ordinary Portland cement:sharp sand; a one-quarter part of hydrated lime may be added to improve workability. The incidence of shrinkage may be reduced further by incorporating 'coarse' aggregate (maximum size 6–8 mm) to give a fine concrete (1:1.5:3). Renders to materials containing sulphates, such as fletton bricks, which are likely to become damp or wet in service require the use of sulphate resisting cement.

Before applying render the locations of all the joints in the background and structure, separating membranes, damp-proof courses and boundaries between dissimilar materials should be noted so that their bridging can be avoided. At all these locations a movement joint should be formed through the total thickness of render acting as substrate (but see Section 13.4.6 regarding the use of mechanically fixed reinforcing mesh for the latter condition).

The applied thickness of render should generally be 10–12 mm, with local areas up to 18 mm thick due to deviations in the base material. Where an appreciable area requires dubbing-out to a thickness exceeding 18 mm, two coats, each of maximum thickness 10 mm, should be applied. The undercoat must be allowed to cure adequately and dry out before applying the top coat. The drying time required can be up to 1 week in cold wet weather, and about 3 days in warm, dry periods. Note that longer drying times are required before the application of tiling (see Section 13.6.3.1(i)). Working-up the surface of a render coat to produce a cement-rich skin, as so easily happens with the use of a steel trowel, should be avoided because this may lead to failure of the tiling due to the combined action of shrinkage and lamination. The surface from a wooden float, together with scratching or scraping, will normally provide an adequate key for either subsequent coats of render or tiling.

Freshly applied render must be protected from frost, and effectively cured to prevent premature drying out due to hot weather or wind.

13.4.5.2 Substrate requirements for ceramic floor tiles (levelling screeds)

The substrate requirements for ceramic floor tiles are similar to those for wall tiling, but with special attention being given to strength and level. To accommodate falls for drainage, levelling screeds are generally of greater average thickness than rendering to walls and may be laid in a single operation. Floor tiling, however, may either be bounded or non-bounded as discussed in Section 13.7.2.

13.4.6 Joints and jointing

With the exception of vertical tile hanging using plain clay tiles nailed to timber battens, it is essential that ceramic wall and floor tiling be provided with sufficient and effective joints such that the cumulative effect of irreversible and cyclic movements are adequately limited and accommodated. The necessary provision is normally provided in two ways: narrow joints between individual tiles, and wider (movement) joints circumscribing and dividing large areas of tiling. Each type of joint contributes in its own way toward the satisfactory performance of the tiling. The function of narrow joints between tiles is two-fold. First, they perform as a sealant in preventing liquids from bypassing the glazed surface and soaking the tile body, bedding and substrate, which could lead to failure brought about by dimensional change and possible frost or chemical attack. Second, they accommodate dimensional variations between tiles. Furthermore, if the grout material is chosen with care, a proportion of the movement from adjacent tiles can be absorbed, limiting the maximum accumulated strain at various interfaces and reducing the accumulated movement to be accommodated at wide joint locations. The width of narrow joints will vary upwards from a 'normal' 3–10 mm for the largest size tiles.

Material used for bedding tiles is rarely suitable for grouting between tiles, and should not be allowed to remain squeezed up between tiles. This is especially true where a sand/cement bedding has been used, and this should be removed as tiling progresses by raking out to at least the tile thickness.

Over large areas of tiling, wide movement joints are normally constructed at between 3 and 4.5 m centres in each principal direction, in addition to those constructed at the following locations.

(1) The underside of beams and sides of columns.
(2) Around columns, walls, machine bases, stair seatings, etc.
(3) Subject to the spacings given above, at changes in direction (internal and external corners, wall/floor and wall/ceiling junctions) which normally implies the total perimeter of tiled areas.
(4) At positions of movement and other separating joints in the structure and substrate.
(5) Where the area to be tiled passes across the interface between dissimilar materials, along the line of that interface, such as the abutment of masonry to dense concrete.

Movement joints should be 10–12 mm wide and penetrate the full thickness of the tiling including bedding and substrate. Joints

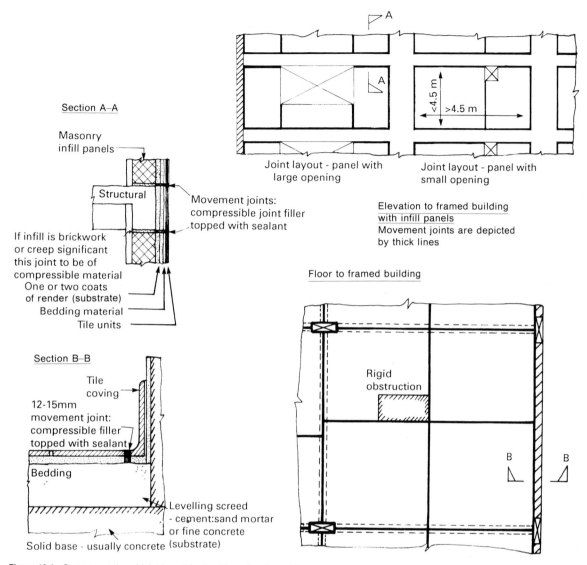

Figure 13.4 Some examples of joint layout for the tiling of walls and floors

should be filled with cellular polythene, cellular rubber, fibre board or other suitable compressible material and capped with an elastomeric sealant.

In the design of some elevations, where the above guidelines are rigorously applied, movement joints can fall at relatively close centres. Subject to the designer's approval and detail, this condition may be overcome with the use of galvanized or stainless-steel reinforcing mesh mechanically fixed to the background. Some examples of joint layout for tiling on walls and floors are illustrated in *Figure 13.4*.

13.4.7 Tolerances

British Standards for wall and floor tiles specify permissible deviations as plus or minus a percentage of tile dimension in accordance with certain sampling procedures. The values given vary according to the size of tile and the degree of moisture absorption. For guidance, typical values of permissible deviation associated with the manufacture of tiles, based upon a work size

of $150 \times 150 \times 5$ mm thick (10 mm thick for floor tiles), and the satisfactory application of tiling are given in *Table 13.1*. Specific information should be obtained from the relevant tile manufacturer.

13.4.8 Principal mechanical and physical properties

Typical values for various types and categories of tile are given in *Table 13.2*.

13.4.9 Fixing ceramic tiles

Depending upon the type and end use, there are only two methods of fixing ceramic tiles: by nailing and clipping, and by adhesion.

Nailing and clipping is used for tiling to pitched roofs and for vertical tile hanging. The nails and clips should be corrosion resistant, i.e. aluminium alloy, copper, stainless steel or silicon bronze. Galvanized steel nails are not recommended. Tradition-

Table 13.1 Typical values of permissible deviation (mm) associated with the manufacture[a] and satisfactory application of tiles

Parameter	Wall tiles, dust pressed, $E \leqslant 3\%$	Floor tiles, extruded, $E \leqslant 3\%$		Roof tiles, plain clay
		Split	Quarries	
Length and width of face	± 1.12	± 1.87	± 3.00	Hand made NA Machine made ± 3
Thickness	± 0.50	± 1.00	± 1.00	NA
Straightness of sides	± 0.90	± 0.75	± 0.90	NA
Rectangularity	± 0.90	± 2.25	± 1.50	NA
Curvature				
Centre	± 1.06	± 1.06	± 3.18	NA
Edge	± 0.75	± 0.75	± 2.25	NA
Warpage	± 1.06	± 1.70	± 3.18	NA
Substrate	As specified for tiling work. Typically local deviation of ± 3 mm in 3 m	Specified falls ± 15 mm. Typically local deviation of ± 3 mm in 3 m		BS 5606

[a] Based on a work size of $150 \times 150 \times 5$ mm thick, or 10 mm thick floor tiles. E is the percentage water absorption by mass. NA, not applicable.

Table 13.2 Typical values of the principal mechanical and physical properties of tiles

Property	Wall tiles, dust pressed	Floor tiles, extruded		Roof tiles, plain clay
		Split	Quarries	
Modulus of rupture (N mm^{-2})	27	20	20	15
Coefficient of thermal expansion ($\times 10^{-6}$ K^{-1})	9	4–8	5–13	8
Moisture movement[a]		0.6 mm m^{-1} for tiles where $6\% < E \leqslant 10\%$		

[a] See footnote to *Table 13.1*.

ally, nailing is combined with sand:cement bedding at ridge, hip and verge. However, several major tile manufacturers have recently developed dry-fix roofing systems which avoid entirely the use of wet bedding.

Adhesion is used for tiling to walls and floors and some areas of roofing. The tiles are bedded in a medium which has good adhesion to both the substrate and back face of the tile. The bedding may be a cement:sand mix not stronger than 1:3 which is used as traditional 'tiling-on', a modified cement:sand mortar, or a proprietory adhesive used in accordance with manufacturer's instructions.

13.5 Clay roof tiles

13.5.1 Types and sizes

The two categories of tiles are:

(1) *interlocking tiles* which have a single lap in the longitudinal direction; and
(2) *plain tiles* which have a double lap in the lateral direction.

The origin of each category is historical, and it is easy to understand how many of the current tile profiles have been derived from the 'classical' sections illustrated in *Table 13.3*.

13.5.2 Availability

Plain clay roof tiles and their accessories are available throughout most of the UK. Single-lap interlocking tiles, however, are currently produced by large UK manufacturers only as a concrete product, but the clay version is available from some medium to small producers, and more readily on the

European market. The availability of clay tiles for roofing is likely to improve with the advent of the single European market in 1992.

13.5.3 Fixing clay tiles for roofing

This section deals only with the fixing of tiles. Reference should be made to the appropriate Building Regulations and manufacturer's information to ensure compliance with statutory requirements relating to structural stability, ventilation and energy conservation. As mentioned previously, the basic method of fixing roof tiles is by nailing and clipping to timber battens which are, in turn, adequately connected to the roof structure. For the size and spacing of battens the reader is referred to the appropriate manufacturer's details relating to type and size of tile. The battens must at least be capable of supporting the weight of one man, between rafters, during construction.

Each tile is initially supported on the batten by one or more nibs at the head of the tile, and this support is supplemented by nailing at the head of the tile, and/or clipping, to resist the action of wind suction. Records show that areas of tiling are regularly stripped off roofs during winter gales; the great storm of October 1987 exposed many old roofs where the original nail fixings had rotted away.

The action of wind on roofs often results in suction which is concentrated at ridge, verge and eaves. Under certain conditions, suction can occur over an entire roof slope area, and if nailing or clipping is inadequate the roof slope can be stripped, starting with peeling from verges, and sometimes from eaves and ridges. Roofs of shallow pitch are particularly susceptible to wind suction (see *Figure 13.5*). It therefore follows that, in general, the minimum amount of fixings to any tiled roof is that for a

Table 13.3 Classical roof tiles sections

Description of tiling	Typical sections	Typical dimensions (mm)	Roof pitch (degrees to horizontal)	
			Min.	Max.
Spanish	Over tiles 185–145 / 100–75 / Under tiles / Over tiles taper towards head, under tiles taper towards tail / 185–225	Length 376	35	40–50
Italian	Over tiles 150 / 75 / Under tiles / 235	Length 375	35	40–50
Single Roman	Over and under tiles taper towards head and tail esp. / 75 / 250	250 × 340	35	40–50
Double Roman	75 / 345	340 × 420	35	40–50
Pantiling	60 / 250	250 × 335	30	47.5
Plain	Nibs / Nibs / Cross-section / Long-section	165 × 265	40	Vertical

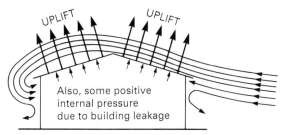

Also, some positive internal pressure due to building leakage

Figure 13.5 Generation of uplift on shallow pitch roofs

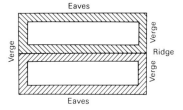

Figure 13.6 Plan of typical roof showing ridge, verge and eaves bands for minimum fixings. Width of bands is approximately three tiles

band around the roof slope perimeter within which each tile is fixed with two nails or is clipped, the width of the band depending upon roof geometry and wind speed (see *Figure 13.6*). It should be noted that interlocking tiles suited to roofs of shallow pitch, down to 17.5°, are not provided with holes for nailing at the head, and should be fixed only with clips. This is due to the risk of water penetration at pitches less than 30° from wind-driven rain.

The information given in *Table 13.4* is provided only for the purpose of illustrating how the fixing pattern, for duo-pitched roofs to two-storey houses, varies with roof pitch and wind

speed. The information given in these charts should not be implemented without first checking with the designer and/or tile manufacturer. Nailing patterns may be formulated for other wind speeds.

13.5.4 Plain clay tiles—applications other than roofing

Due to their handy size and shape combined with moisture-resistant properties, builders have found plain clay tiles to be a versatile product, being successfully employed over many years for a number of applications other than roofing, some of which

Table 13.4 Example of how the fixing pattern for duo-pitched roofs varies with roof pitch and wind speed: two-storey house, height to ridge of structure H = 6.6 to 9.2 m single lap interlocking tiles only

Basic wind speed V = 38 m s^{-1}				Basic wind speed V = 50 m s^{-1}			
Pitch (°)	*Ground roughness category*				*Ground roughness category*		
	1	*2*	*3*	*4*	*1*	*2*	*3*	*4*
17.5–22								
22.5–29.5								
30–44.5								
≥45								

	Key	Wind uplift ($kN\ m^{-2}$)	Suggested mechanical fixings
(i)		0–0.7	No fixing required for uplift, but advisable to use **BS 5534: Part 1: 1978, CL 34.4** minimum (i.e. every perimeter tile should be mechanically fixed).
(ii)		0–0.7	No fixing required for uplift, but in every tile one or two nails at head (to reduce chatter and shear on pitches of 45–55°, over 55° use (xi)).
(iii)		>1.0	Use verge clips at verge perimeter, or preferably dry or cloaked verges.
(iv)		0.7–1.2	Every tile one nail at head (most convenient hole).
(v)		1.2–1.5	Every tile two nails at head (if risk of cracking tile use next fixing key).
(vi)		0.7–1.2	Alternative tiles in each row (chequer pattern) clipped at toe plus every perimeter tile clipped. Note that nail holes are not practical, because of risk of water penetration, at pitches of less than 30°.
(vii)		1.2–1.5	
(viii)		1.5–2.0	Alternative tiles in each row (chequer pattern) clipped at toe plus every perimeter tile clipped.
(ix)		1.5–2.0	Combination of (viii) and (iv) (to reduce chatter and shear on pitches over 45–55°, over 55° use (xi)).
(x)		2.0–2.5	Every tile one clip at toe.
(xi)		2.5–3.1	Every tile one clip at toe and one nail at head.
(xii)		2.5–3.1	Every tile one clip at toe. Note nail holes are not practical, because of water penetration, at pitches of less than 30°.

N.B. Fixing each tile in alternate rows is *not* recommended, being much less effective than alternate tiles in each row (chequer pattern).

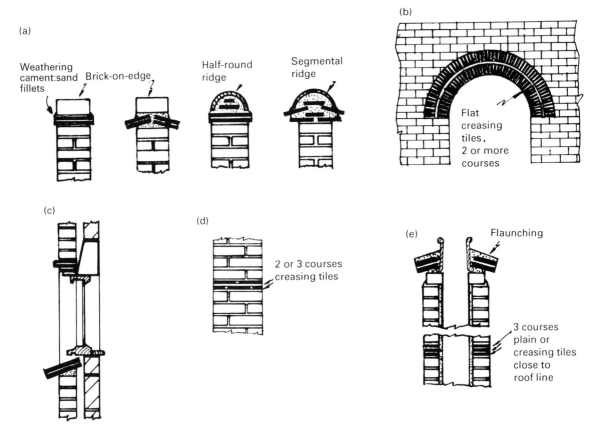

Figure 13.7 Some examples of the uses of plain clay roofing and creasing tiles. (a) Copings to parapets and walls; (b) structural and decorative arches, various profiles; (c) window heads and cills; (d) DPC free-standing walls; (e) chimneys. For compliance with resistance to moisture, thermal performance and structural stability refer to the appropriate national building regulations

are illustrated in *Figure 13.7*. To further their use, some manufacturers make special creasing tiles which are of similar face dimensions to roofing tiles, but are 12 mm thick and without camber, nibs or holes.

13.6 Ceramic wall tiles and tiling

13.6.1 Types and sizes

Although clay based, wall tiles are typically referred to as ceramic tiles, unlike roof tiles which retain their clay designation. Wall tiles for internal and external use may be glazed or unglazed, plain or decorated. The surface of a tile may be smooth, textured or profiled, according to its function or intended finished appearance. All tiles are manufactured with a body flat and true to close tolerances. Tiles for external use must be frost resistant, and this property, for any tile to be used as such, should be verified with the manufacturer.

Although other shapes are available, tiles manufactured for internal use are normally either square or rectangular, with face dimensions ranging from 300 mm to 100 mm, with thickness from 8.5 mm to 5.5 mm. In addition, for external use, larger sizes are available, up to 600 × 300 × 30 mm. Tiles for external use are often used internally to create a desired effect

13.6.2 Availability

There is an extremely wide range of tile sizes, shapes, colours

and finish combinations available, designers and stockists being able to draw upon many manufacturers in the UK, Europe and American markets. Some factories will accept orders for special tiles where murals and other special effects are specified, but a reasonably large area of tiling needs be involved to make the exercise cost effective.

13.6.3 Fixing ceramic wall tiles

Ceramic wall tiles are fixed by combining the adhesion characteristics of substrate surface and tile with a suitable bedding compound. Tiles should only be fixed to a true surface and on no account should the bedding be varied solely to compensate for overall deviations in the substrate. It is highly desirable that adhesion of the substrate surface is uniform in order to avoid differential internal strains which may lead to failure of the tiling. If there is any doubt, the surface should be prepared, either by priming or by the application of render.

13.6.3.1 Bedding tiles

One of three types of bedding material may be used for bedding wall tiles.

(1) Cement:sand mortar.
(2) Modified cement:sand mortar in which synthetic resin emulsions such as styrene butadiene, are used to enhance the adhesive properties of the mortar.

(3) Resin mortars, usually either an epoxy or polyester resin blended with a filler of finely ground aggregate to give a smooth material suitable for trowelling.

(*i*) *Cement:sand mortar* This is the traditional method of fixing wall tiles in either an internal or external situation. Preliminary work includes an assessment of the maturity of the substrate, preparation of the surface to be tiled, noting existing joints in the work, and marking the locations where additional joints are to be provided through the tiling.

Shrinkage-related failures can be minimized if a high proportion of movement due to curing and drying of the substrate is allowed to occur before commencement of tiling. As a guide, 3–6 months may be necessary for substrates of *in situ* concrete, and at least 2 weeks (4 weeks in cold wet periods) should be allowed for cement:sand substrates.

The surface of a substrate to which tiling is to be applied should be free of dust and other contaminants, and also provide an adequate key to enhance adhesion of the bedding mortar. For render, a scratched or scraped surface is normally adequate, but where tiles are to be applied directly to a true dense concrete surface it may be necessary to achieve an adequate key by scabbling the concrete, or by other designed means such as the mechanical attachment of plastic or stainless-steel mesh.

Locations of joints through the structure and substrate should be noted for continuation through the tiling. The lines of perimeter and other intermediate joints to be provided through the tiling should be set out and marked for reference, with due consideration given to reducing the amount of tile cutting to a minimum. Ideally this aspect should be considered at an early planning stage.

To control suction, the surface of the substrate should be wetted according to its condition, and the tiles soaked in water for about 0.5 h before draining. There must be no free water on either surface immediately before bedding.

The mortar used for bedding is ordinary Portland cement:clean sharp sand not stronger than 1:3 nor weaker than 1:3.5 by volume, with no additives or admixtures. The process of bedding tiles should be devoted to achieving solid bedding. This is especially important for external tiling, wet areas such as kitchens and bathrooms, and where tiling may be subject to mechanical damage. Solid bedding implies not more than 5% voids. Tiles may be bedded by fully buttering the back of each tile and applying directly to a clear substrate, or by a combination of buttering and applying to a substrate upon which a layer of bedding material has been freshly floated. The bedding material should be applied when it has stiffened slightly to a plastic consistency. The recommended minimum thickness of bedding material is about 6 mm increasing to a maximum of about 10 mm to compensate for local deviations in substrate and dimensional tolerances in tiles. On no account should the thickness of bedding be gradually increased solely to produce a true finished surface. The substrate should be made true before tiling is commenced.

Where the bedding material is unsuitable for forming grouted joints between tiles, it should be raked out to the depth of the tile and, in some cases, the thickness of bedding also, in order to allow subsequent grouting to meet the specification for water resistance, movement and colour.

(*ii*) *Modified cement:sand mortar* This mortar is normally available as proprietory products which may be referred to as adhesives. The precautions to be taken in respect to adequate key, drying times and joints are similar to those described for cement:sand above. When using modified mortars it is essential to comply strictly with the manufacturer's instructions for mixing and application.

There are two basic methods of application the one being used depending on the thickness of bedding, i.e. either thin bed or thick bed. Whichever method is adopted the tiles and substrate surface must be dry, and attention should be given to the 'open time' or workable life of the bedding after which the spread material dries or skims over, preventing tile adhesion. Never spread a greater area than can be covered within the open time; start by covering about 1 m^2 and subsequently adjust to the rate of tiling.

The thin-bed method is intended for use where the substrate surface is true to 1.5 mm in 3 m and the backs of tiles are not deeply keyed. The mixed adhesive is spread on the substrate using a comb or notched trowel to give a uniform thickness of about 3 mm. The back face of the tile is buttered to fill any depressions and help achieve solid bedding. The tile is then pressed firmly onto the coated substrate, and tamped and aligned with the aid of a 2 m straight edge. The joints are then raked out as for cement:sand bedding.

The thick-bed method makes use of adhesives which can accommodate local deviations of up to 13 mm in the substrate surface. Apart from the thickness of bedding, the procedure is similar to that given for the thin-bed method.

It should be noted that adhesives intended for thin bedding are not necessarily suited to thick bedding, and vice versa.

(*iii*) *Resin mortars* Resin mortars are normally available as proprietory products. The notes and procedure given for the modified cement:sand mortar should be followed as applicable. The mixing and application of a resin mortar must be done strictly in accordance with the manufacturer's instructions, with particular attention being paid to shelf life and open time. It is important to remember that resin mortars, especially two-part materials, require a greater degree of application expertise than do cement:sand mortars, and the manufacturer's technical claims may not be realized on site if there are application difficulties, or operators are inexperienced.

13.6.3.2 *Grouting tiling*

Specified grout material should completely fill all joints other than designed movement joints, have low shrinkage, be impermeable and achieve the desired finished appearance.

Grouting should be done up to 12 h after bedding. The grout is rubbed and/or brushed into the joints until they are flush filled and the face of the tiling is cleaned before the grout hardens.

13.6.4 Mosaics

Mosaics consist of coloured marble or ceramic prisms, from 6 mm^2 to 25 mm^2 square or hexagonal shapes on plan and 6 mm to 25 mm thick. The tesserae are glued to a piece of paper on which a pattern or picture is often drawn, and then reversed for fixing. Sometimes nylon net or strips are glued to the back face with the intention of enhancing adhesion with the bedding mortar or adhesive.

Mosaics are supplied in square or rectangular sheets suited to handling, which restricts the maximum dimension to about 600 mm. They are used for either internal or external cladding to walls, and as an alternative to conventional tiling for lining swimming pools. In the latter case, the use of an epoxide mortar for bedding and grouting is recommended in order to provide long-term durability for permanent immersion in aggressive conditions. The guidelines given previously for ceramic tiles in respect of substrate drying times, adequate key and joints, apply equally to mosaics.

Proprietory mosaics are available with either a paper face or a nylon or similar backing. Sheets of paper-faced mosaics are pregrouted with a 1:1.5 cement:sand mix to fill the joints between tesserae. Cement:sand bedding is prepared and applied as for wall tiling, and allowed to stiffen slightly. Pregrouted sheets are then placed in position and well tamped into the bed using a 2 m straight-edge to align with the other sheets. After about 4 h the paper face is moistened and removed and grouting complete using the same mix as for pregrouting the backs of the sheets.

Mosaics with nylon backing may be bedded in either cement:sand or fixed with an adhesive. As they do not have a paper face they are face grouted after fixing to full depth of tesserae.

Mosaics have several advantages over conventional tiles in that they adapt to gently curving surfaces, and are more readily cut to cover areas of varying size and shape.

13.7 Ceramic floor tiles and tiling

13.7.1 General

Whilst the fundamental requirements for wall tiling also apply to floor tiling, the disposition of floor tiling introduces conditions whereby some of those requirements may be relaxed, and others need to be applied more stringently. These aspects are discussed in general terms below.

The surface of floor tiling will be subjected to the rigours of traffic, either pedestrian alone or that combined with hard- or soft-wheeled vehicles. It is essential in such circumstances that tiles are solidly bedded and carefully chosen according to their ability to resist impact, abrasion and scuffing. The edges of movement joints should be protected against damage by wheel loads.

Although most tiled floors will be laid to a fall, a film of water or other fluids, from cleaning or the weather, is likely to lie on the surface for some time, particularly in local depressions, leading to possible staining and penetration of the substrate. Internal floors are then at risk of failure due to moisture movement of the substrate and chemical attack, whilst in an external situation there is the added risk of frost damage. In addition to those properties identified above, selected tiles and grout material should have high impermeability, and be frost resistant when used externally. Depending upon usage and maintenance, the resistance of grout to chemical attack should also be considered.

Provided the flooring acts as a series of fully supported, heavy flat rigid plates between joints, then according to the magnitude and nature of traffic, it is not essential that the tiling is firmly attached to its substrate as in the case of wall tiling. In fact loose attachment can be a distinct advantage as greater freedom of interface movement is then allowed. The 'semidry' method of bedding floor tiles, described later, relaxes the requirements for the provision and spacing of movement joints.

The shortening of vertical structural members due to creep, and its effect upon wall tiling has been discussed. Where concrete floors are suspended, there will be creep deflection bringing about a change in length between the tiling and its supporting layers due to curvature, adding to stress at the various interfaces and leading to possible delamination. The comments made previously for wall tiles in respect of type, size and availability, apply equally to quarries and clay floor tiles. Tiles for flooring however, are generally thicker than wall tiles for a given size.

13.7.2 Fixing ceramic floor tiles

There are two distinct systems for fixing floor tiles:

(1) Fully bonded where the tile bedding is intended to adhere to the substrate.
(2) That using methods whereby bonding between the substrate and the tile bedding is either prevented or severely curtailed.

13.7.2.1 Fully bonded systems

(i) *Cement:sand mortar bedding* This is the traditional method of fixing ceramic floor tiles using solid bedding where there is to be heavy traffic. Due attention should be given to cleanliness, mechanical key, adhesion, control of suction and provision of joints, as discussed previously for wall tiling, with the added provision of joints where a floor is continuous over supports.

A bedding mix of one part ordinary Portland cement to between three and four parts of clean sharp by volume is spread over the substrate to the required thickness and allowed to develop to a stiff plastic consistency. Adhesion between tiles and bedding may be improved by applying a coat of slurry or cement-based adhesive to the backs of tiles which are then rubbed into the bedding and tamped to line and levels using a 2 m straight-edge.

The thickness of bedding used is related to tile thickness as indicated below:

Thickness of tile (mm)	Bedding thickness (mm)	
	Min.	Max.
≤10	10	15
>10	15	20

On no account is the thickness of bedding to be adjusted solely to achieve specified falls.

The grouting of the joints between tiles is usually done about 12 h after laying, to ensure bond with substrate and tiles without displacement. In the absence of a grout specification, a stiff mix of 1:1 cement:fine sand should be rammed or worked into joints until they are flush filled. The surplus grout must be removed before it hardens.

(ii) *Cement-based adhesive bedding—thin bed* Cement-based adhesives are usually available as proprietory products, and as such should be mixed and applied strictly in accordance with the manufacturer's instructions. Due to the recommended maximum thickness of about 5 mm, this method is only suited to substrates which are laid to close tolerances. A uniform thickness of adhesive is spread on the dry substrate, and the back of each dry tile buttered with adhesive to fill any depressions or ribbing. Buttered tiles are rubbed into the bedding and tamped to level with a 2 m straight-edge. Eventually, joints in the floor tiling are raked out, and grouted as described in (i) above, except that extra care must be taken to ensure compatibility between grout and bedding materials.

13.7.2.2 Separating systems

(i) *Fully separated* In this method the tile bedding is prevented from bonding to the substrate by providing a separating layer of sheet material such as polythene, bituminous felt or building paper, with 100 mm lapped joints (see *Figure 13.8*). The recommended precautions and procedure are otherwise essentially the same as those for cement:sand bedding given under Section 13.7.2.1(i), except that the minimum and maximum thicknesses of bedding are 15 mm and 25 mm, respectively.

(ii) *Partial separation by the semidry mix method—thick bed* The effective bond with the substrate can be reduced, and strains thereby dissipated, by using a mix of 1:4 cement:sharp sand, or 1:1.5:3 fine concrete, with 'earth-dry' consistency. The minimum and maximum thicknesses of bedding are 40 mm and 70 mm, respectively. The advantages of this method are that there is a reduced tendency to delaminate, the thickness of bedding may be adjusted to correct for minor discrepancies in level, no perimeter joints are required under 6 m, and the spacing of intermediate movement joints is relaxed to 9-m centres. The

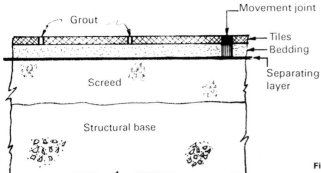

Figure 13.8 Illustration of the fully separated method of bedding ceramic floor tiles

bedding mix is spread generously over an area of substrate and thoroughly compacted by tamping to the required levels and falls. The mix should not be spread over a greater area than can be covered by tiling in a single operation whilst the bedding is still plastic. Bonding of tiles is achieved with a 1:1 slurry of cement:fine sand which has been allowed to stand for about 15 min before reworking to a creamy consistency. The reworked slurry is trowelled evenly over recently compacted bedding to a thickness of 3 mm, and dry tiles buttered with slurry are placed in position on the slurried bedding. The tiles are then beaten to the correct line and level with wooden or rubber beaters as work progresses. Finally, the joints between tiles are grouted as described in Section 13.7.2.1(i) but within 4 h of laying to ensure that the grout marries with the bedding.

13.8 Maintenance

Although tiling is a far from low-cost finish, its virtue lies in permanence with low maintenance cost. Wall tiling and plain tiling to roofs require virtually no maintenance. However, tiling with a north-facing aspect may need cleaning with a fungicide from time to time to remove algae and moss growth.

Tiled floors should be frequently and regularly swept to avoid material being ground into the surface by foot traffic, thereby damaging joint realants. They should be periodically washed with warm water containing a sulphate free soapless detergent or approved cleaning agent. As little water as possible should be used and an area should never be flooded as this increases the risk of damage by water penetration and the formation of efflorescence. Immediately after cleaning, as much water as possible should be removed from the surface with the aid of a squeegee. Where marks on floors persist, these may be removed with the aid of white spirit, scouring powder or bleach applied locally by hand. A tiled floor should never be polished as this destroys any non-slip property of the tiles and gives rise to a dangerous situation for pedestrians.

Bibliography

BRITISH STANDARDS INSTITUTION, *BS 402 Clay roofing tiles and fittings; Part 1: Specification for plain tiles and fittings*, Milton Keynes (1990)
BRITISH STANDARDS INSTITUTION, *BS 4131 Specification for terrazo tiles*, Milton Keynes (1973)
BRITISH STANDARDS INSTITUTION, *BS 5385 Wall and floor tiling, Part 1 (1976): Code of practice for internal ceramic wall tiling and mosaics in normal conditions; Part 2 (1978): Code of practice for external ceramic tiling and mosaics; Part 4: Code of practice for ceramic tiling and mosaics in specified conditions*, Milton Keynes
BRITISH STANDARDS INSTITUTION, *BS 5534 Slating and tiling, Part 1 (1978): Design; Part 2 (1986): Design charts for fixing roof slating and tiling against wind uplift; Part 3 (1989): Code of practice for ceramic tiling and mosaics in specified conditions; Part 4 (1986)*, Milton Keynes
BRITISH STANDARDS INSTITUTION, *BS 5606 Accuracy in building*, Milton Keynes (1978)
BRITISH STANDARDS INSTITUTION, *BS 5980 Specifications for adhesives for use with ceramic tiles and mosaics*, Milton Keynes (1980)
BRITISH STANDARDS INSTITUTION, *BS 6431 Ceramic floor and wall tiles, Parts 1–9: Specifications for extruded and dust-pressed tiles, including classification and marking; Parts 10–23: Test method for physical and mechanical properties and chemical resistance*, Milton Keynes (1983–1986)
BRITISH STANDARDS INSTITUTION, *CP 3: Part 2 Wind loads*, Chap. V, Milton Keynes (1972)
BRITISH STANDARDS INSTITUTION, *CP 202 Code of practice for tile flooring and slab flooring*, Milton Keynes (1972)
BUILDING RESEARCH ESTABLISHMENT, 'Clay tile flooring', *BRE Digest 79* (revised 1976)
BUILDING RESEARCH ESTABLISHMENT, 'Floor screeds', *BRE Digest 104* (1973)
BUILDING RESEARCH ESTABLISHMENT, 'Floors: cement-based screeds—specification', *BRE Defect Action Sheet 51* (May 1984)
BUILDING RESEARCH ESTABLISHMENT, 'Floors: cement-based screeds—mixing and laying', *BRE Defect Action Sheet 52* (May 1984)
BUILDING RESEARCH ESTABLISHMENT, 'Internal walls: ceramic wall tiles—loss of adhesion', *BRE Defect Action Sheet 137* (November 1989)

British Cement Association (formerly Cement & Concrete Association)

BARNBROOK, G., *Construction Guide: Laying Floor Screeds*
MONKS, W., *Appearance Matters 2: External Rendering*

Research and other organizations

BRITISH CERAMIC RESEARCH LIMITED, Queens Road, Penkhull, Stoke-on-Trent ST4 7LQ
HARRISON, R. and DINSDALE, A., *Internal wall tile fixing*
ENGLISH HERITAGE, *Practical building conservation technical handbook, Vol. 2, Brick, terracotta and earth*, J. Ashurst and N. Ashurst (eds)

Trade associations

BRITISH CERAMIC TILE COUNCIL, Federation House, Station Road, Stoke-on-Trent ST4 2RU
BRITISH CERAMIC MANUFACTURERS' FEDERATION, Federation House, Station Road, Stoke-on-Trent ST4 2SA

14

Concrete, An Overview

C D Pomeroy DSc, CPhys, FInstP, FACI, FSS
Formerly of the British Cement Association

Contents

14.1　Introduction 14/3

14.2　Hydraulic cements 14/3

14.3　Cement quality 14/4

14.4　Ground-granulated blast-furnace slag, flyash and silica fume 14/4

14.5　Cements for special purposes 14/5

14.6　Handling and storage of cement 14/6

14.7　Cement admixtures 14/6

14.8　Aggregates 14/6
　　　14.8.1 Aggregate gradings 14/6

14.9　Ready-mixed concrete 14/7

14.10 Steel reinforcement 14/7

14.11 The use of fibres in concrete 14/7

14.12 The use of polymers in concrete 14/8

14.13 Mix designs 14/8

14.14 Mortars, screeds and renders 14/9

14.15 Grouts 14/10

14.16 Concrete properties 14/10
　　　14.16.1 Workability 14/10
　　　14.16.2 Setting time 14/10
　　　14.16.3 Early-age behaviour 14/10
　　　14.16.4 Strength 14/11
　　　14.16.5 Permeability and porosity 14/11
　　　14.16.6 Elastic modulus 14/11
　　　14.16.7 Shrinkage 14/11
　　　14.16.8 Creep 14/12
　　　14.16.9 Thermal expansion 14/12

14.17 Durability 14/12
　　　14.17.1 Acid and sulphate attack 14/13
　　　14.17.2 Alkali–aggregate reaction 14/13
　　　14.17.3 Freeze–thaw damage 14/14

14.18 Concrete practice 14/14

14.19 Striking of formwork 14/14

14.20 Curing 14/14

14.21 Exposed aggregate fnishes to concrete surfaces 14/15

14.22 Precast concrete 14/15

14.23 Testing methods, quality and compliance 14/16

14.24 Future opportunities 14/17

14.25 Health and safety 14/17

References 14/17

14.1 Introduction

According to the *Oxford English Dictionary*, concrete is 'formed by the cohesion of particles into a mass. It is a composition of stone chippings, sand, gravel, pebbles etc. formed into a mass with cement (or lime)'. This definition offers the scope for many variations in composition, and today these variations are exploited by the producers of concrete to make materials of different strength and elastic modulus, of different densities or porosities, of different texture or colour and for resistance to different environments. Because of the large number of options available to the concrete producer and user, the whole subject of concrete technology has moved from one of relative simplicity to one where specialist skills may be required if the best selection or choice of constituents is to be made. There will always be uses for concrete where basic skills are all that are required but economical production of concrete of the highest quality requires a deep understanding of the subject.

Concrete is not a new material and a little background history helps to place modern concrete technology in perspective. More concrete has been produced during the past two decades than in the rest of human existence, but it is not a modern invention. The earliest known concrete, which dates from about 5600 BC, formed the floor of a hut in Yugoslavia. The 'cement' was red lime, which probably came from 200 miles upstream, and this was mixed with sand, gravel and water before being compacted to form the hut floor. The first written proof of the ancient use of mortars is found in Egyptian hieroglyphics on a wall in Thebes dated about 1950 BC. This shows all the operations of concrete construction from metering the water and materials, to the use in the structure.[1] Recently, it has even been claimed that the pyramids themselves were made from cast concrete blocks and not from cut stone.[2]

There are also existing examples of concrete made by the Romans in many of the countries occupied by them and *Figure 14.1* shows a sample of concrete that encased a clay pipe in Lincolnshire. This concrete is interesting, since the aggregate is largely pieces of broken fired clay and carbon waste. The mortar is crushed lime and the specimen had a cube strength of about 40 MPa. It could be argued that the builders were good environmentalists who used up the broken pot, but the Romans learned that pot could be pozzolanic and add to the strength of the concrete as it reacted with the lime.

Another example of 'modern' thinking is found in the dome of the Pantheon in Rome, built in 27 BC. The dome, made of lightweight concrete, using volcanic pumice as the aggregate, spans almost 50 m. It has stood for over 2000 years and is clearly durable. It was unreinforced, so that steel corrosion or rusting was not a problem to be contended with.

Concrete is thus not a new material, the name itself coming from '*concretus*', a Latin word for bringing together to form a composite. Even admixtures, such as blood or milk were used to improve workability and appearance and it is very humbling to relate modern sophistication to the practical evidence of the past. However, after the fall of the Roman Empire, the skills needed to make effective limes, mortars and concretes, seem to have been lost and it was only some 200 years ago that the modern concrete industry came into existence with the development and evolution of the hydraulic cements used today.

14.2 Hydraulic cements

Although Joseph Aspdin is usually credited as the father of the modern Portland cement industry, it is likely that he developed his ideas from the earlier works of John Smeaton and the Reverend James Parker of Northfleet. Smeaton was charged in 1756 with the rebuilding of the Eddystone Lighthouse off the

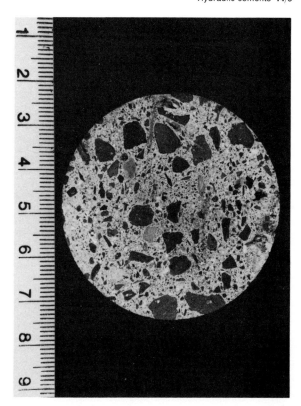

Figure 14.1 Roman concrete, containing broken shards and carbon as aggregate

south-west coast of England and he demonstrated that he could make a durable mortar that could be used to bind interlocking stone segments together. The mortar contained burnt Aberthaw blue lias, a limestone and some natural pozzolanas from Italy. The lighthouse withstood the ravages of the Atlantic storms for over 100 years before it was replaced by the present structure. The original lighthouse was dismantled block by block and re-erected on land in Plymouth, but the original foundations were left and they still exist over 200 years after being built.

The contribution to the development of cement by Parker is attributed to his observation that when a stone, picked up on a beach near his home, was thrown on a fire, it became calcined and, when pulverized and mixed with water, it hardened to form a cement. Parker thought he had rediscovered the ancient 'Roman' cements and hence gave his invention this name.

These cements had little potential for wide commercial development and it was the patented inventions of Aspdin that led to the modern cement industry, although very substantial improvements have taken place since his original work near Wakefield. It was only when in 1845 a bottle kiln was built near Swanscombe in Kent that the firing temperature of the mixture of chalk and clay was high enough to cause the chemical reactions that are fundamental to the production of modern cements.

Since that time, the blends of raw materials that are fired in the kilns have been refined and the manufacturing process has changed from one of batch production, in the bottle kilns, to continuous production in the modern rotary kilns, a single one of which can produce 1 000 000 tonne year^{-1}. As the raw materials pass through the kiln, their temperature is gradually increased to a peak in excess of 1400°C when the calcium carbonate from the limestone or chalk is dissociated into calcium oxide and carbon dioxide and the oxides of calcium, silicon, aluminium and iron are transformed into the active ingredients of Portland cement. The resulting product is a clinker that leaves the kiln at a temperature of about 1000°C and is then cooled to about 60°C, the rate of cooling having a significant effect on the crystallographic form of the clinker constituents.

Portland cement clinkers are generally composed of four principal components:

(1) tricalcium silicate, $3CaO.SiO_2$;
(2) dicalcium silicate, $2CaO.SiO_2$;
(3) tricalcium aluminate, $3CaO.Al_2O_3$;
(4) tetracalcium aluminoferrite, $4CaO.Al_2O_3.Fe_2O_3$.

These proportions can be varied by the selection of different raw materials and by the kiln temperature profiles. The constituents of Portland cement clinker are not pure compounds but contain minor impurities within the crystal structures and these can have a significant effect on the performance of the cements. There are also other impurities such as magnesia (MgO) and free lime (CaO) which the cement chemist must ensure are kept within acceptable limits if the cement is to be consistently sound. There will also be small amounts of alkali (KOH and NaOH) present.

The clinkers are ground to a fine powder with the addition of a small proportion of gypsum (calcium sulphate) which is added to control the rate of hardening that will take place when the Portland cement is mixed with water. The fineness of the powder is one of the parameters that can be used to control the strength-generating characteristics of the cement.

Within Europe, attempts are being made to describe a family of cements that cover the main products currently in use. The differences between the constituents and properties of cements in different countries have introduced difficulties, but it is probable that a Comité Européen de Normalisation (CEN) Standard (EN(V) 197) will shortly be available. Cements of different strength potential and with different constituent formulations will be defined. The kinds of difference that have existed in Europe are the combinations with ordinary Portland cement of natural pozzolanas in Italy, the use of inert fillers such as limestone at different replacement levels, the inclusion, particularly in France, of more than one addition to ordinary Portland cement to make a composite cement and, in the UK, the limitation of additions to an ordinary Portland cement to gypsum (BS 12: 1978[3]). These differences are not purely academic, because it is important to be able to specify and produce durable concrete and as this relies on cement contents and water, cement ratios, it is essential to know that the cement selected does not have any unsatisfactory or unsuspected attributes. This is discussed further under Section 14.13.

In the UK, revisions have already been made to the suite of British Standards for Portland cements in anticipation of a European Standard (ENV 197 cement: composition, specification and conformity criteria). This voluntary standard may be used optionally instead of national standards (e.g. BS 12:1978[3]) for a period of 3–5 years. At the end of this time a voluntary standard must be replaced by a full European Standard (an EN) or be withdrawn.

The revisions to the British Standards for Portland cements permit the inclusion of up to 5% of minor additional constituents. These are likely to be selected from finely ground limestone, blast-furnace slag or pulverized-fuel ash. The revisions also accept a change from the use of 100 mm concrete cubes to determine the strength potential of the cement to a mortar prism test and the definitions of strength bands within which cements of specified classes must lie.

14.3 Cement quality

Portland cements react chemically with water to form calcium or aluminium silicate hydrates (CSH or ASH) and these reactions can occur over a long period of time. The hydration mechanism is complex and still not fully understood. Each of the main cement constituents react exothermally at a different rate. As the reactions take place, the originally water-filled spaces between the cement grains become progressively filled by calcium silicate hydrate gel to form a strong hardened cement paste. The strength of this paste is controlled largely by its residual porosity: the lower the porosity the higher its strength.

The quality of a cement is frequently related to the strength that it will generate at 28 days when a standard mortar or concrete is made, using well-characterized aggregates and a given ratio of water to cement. However, strength is only one aspect of quality and cements can be designed to have other special properties as well.

During the past 30 years, the strengths of UK ordinary Portland cements have increased (*Table 14.1*).

Ordinary Portland cement, although the most widely used cement in the world, is not the only available type. It is often combined with blast-furnace slag or flyash to make a composite cement.

14.4 Ground-granulated blast-furnace slag, flyash and silica fume

Blast-furnace slag is a waste material or by-product produced during the manufacture of iron in a blast-furnace. These slags are composed predominantly of the oxides similar to those found in Portland cement, calcium, magnesium, silicon and aluminium, although the proportions are different and depend on the particular raw materials used to make the iron and on the blast-furnace operation. When the slag leaves the blast-furnace, it must be cooled and the rate of cooling has a large effect on the suitability of the slag as a hydraulic cement, the faster the rate of cooling the better. The slags, often produced as glassy pellets, are ground into a powder to form the basis of a cement. Although ground-granulated blast-furnace slag is cementitious and reacts with water, the rate of reaction is slow and it is necessary to blend the powdered slag with Portland cement to produce a cement that is suitable in practice. The extent of use of blast-furnace slags has varied from one country to another and depends largely upon economic factors. Its use in the UK has been modest, even though the first British Standard for Portland blast-furnace slag was issued in 1923 (BS 146: Part 2: 1973[4]).

More recently, powdered slags have become available for inclusion in concrete mixes in combination with Portland cement, and in 1986 the first British Standard for ground-granulated blast-furnace slag was issued (BS 6699: 1986[5]).

Table 14.1 Strength development of concrete: total water:cement ratio = 0.6; cement content 300 kg m^{-3}

	Compressive stength (MPa)		
	3 day	*7 day*	*28 day*
Pre-1950	13	20	32
1950–54	14	22	34
1960	16	24	35
1975–79	20	30	41
1980	24	33	44

Portland blast-furnace slag, used either as a component in a composite cement or in combination with ordinary Portland cement in the correct proportions in a concrete mix, can make perfectly satisfactory concrete which will differ in performance in certain respects from that made with an ordinary Portland cement. As already mentioned, blast-furnace slag tends to develop strength more slowly, although to some extent this can be compensated for by grinding the cement more finely. The user must, therefore, understand the cement and make the relevant changes to his concreting practice. This will usually imply a longer curing time and possibly an extension of the time before formwork is stripped.

Concretes, properly compacted and cured, made from Portland blast-furnace slag will generally have good resistance to chloride penetration and chemical attack.

Pulverized-fuel ash, known also as flyash or PFA, is another waste product, formed in electricity-generating stations by burning pulverized coal that is fed into the furnaces. The pulverized-fuel ash is electrostatically precipitated from the furnace flue gases. It consists primarily of alumino-silicate glass spheres, together with other minerals such as quartz, iron oxides and mullite. Flyash is a pozzolanic and not a hydraulic material, i.e. it reacts with lime to form hydrates that are similar to the hydrates formed when Portland cement reacts with water. A combination of Portland cement and flyash can thus provide the essential ingredients for a composite cement in which the Portland cement reacts initially to form calcium silicate hydrates and lime (Portlandite) and, in turn, the lime will react with the flyash to supplement the hydration products. The pozzolanicity of flyashes varies, the reactivities being dependent on the original coal used in the furnace, the efficiency of the burning and the fineness of the powder. Some flyashes contain high levels of lime naturally, but these are available only in a few places in the world (e.g. the USA and Greece) and derive from the use of lignite or sub-bituminous coals. In the UK there are standards both for pulverized-fuel ashes for use in concrete,[6,7] and for composite cements made from a Portland cement and PFA combination.[8,9] These relate solely to low-lime flyashes. In the USA, the American Society for Testing Materials ASTM C 618 standard[10] defines both types of flyash.

As with ground-granulated blast-furnace slags, flyash or pulverized-fuel ash can be used satisfactorily as a component in concrete, but it must be used properly. Its performance will depend on the selected Portland cement, the fineness of the combined powders and on the proportion of flyash relative to the cement. Curing will normally have to be increased to ensure performance comparable with an ordinary Portland cement and the effects of change at ambient temperature may be important. It is usually necessary to increase the total cementitious content in a concrete mix to attain the same 28-day strength. However, the use of flyash does offer benefits, particularly with regard to the workability and cohesion (reduced bleeding) of mixes, but the concretes must be sufficiently cured to achieve equal performance to an ordinary Portland cement concrete.

Another waste product that has been used in recent years is silica fume, known sometimes as microsilica or condensed silica fume. It comprises very fine spherical particles of almost pure non-crystalline silica that are by-products of the ferrosilicon industries. Reduction of quartz to silicon in electric-arc furnaces produces SiO vapours that oxidize and then condense into the microsilica powders. As with flyash, these powders are highly pozzolanic and react with lime to form silicate hydrates. The powders are one order of magnitude finer than Portland cements and, hence, a proportion can pack between the cement grains and thereby provide the basis for a dense and low permeability hardened cement paste. Silica fume is not available in vast tonnages, but it has many applications in specialist areas. It can be difficult to handle as a powder and is often introduced into concrete as an aqueous slurry.

All three industrial by-products, blast-furnace slag, flyash and silica fume, have beneficial attributes, but it is essential to use these materials correctly if problems are to be avoided.

14.5 Cements for special purposes

The term 'Portland cement' does not describe a unique prouct. In the USA, for example, there are four types of Portland cement described in the ASTM C 150 (Standard Specification for Portland cement).[11] The four types of cement are compared in *Table 14.2*.

In the UK, the primary standard for Portland cement (BS 12: 1991[3]) does not differentiate so distinctly between the classes of cement, but there are a set of standards for hydraulic cements. These include:

(1) BS 12: 1991[3]—Portland cement.
(2) BS 146: 1991[4]—Portland blast-furnace slag cement.
(3) BS 4027: 1991[12]—sulphate resistant Portland cement.
(4) BS 6588: 1991[8]—Portland pulverized-fuel ash cement.

There are also standards for low-heat, alumina and super-sulphated cements.

In addition, there are available in some countries a variety of hydraulic cements for special purposes. In particular, there is a family of expansive cements which can be used to offset cracking due to drying shrinkage or even to prestress reinforcing steels.[13] There are oil-well cements that must be usable at the high temperatures prevalent and there are ultrarapid hardening cements that are very finely ground and in which the constituents are selected to react early with water.

The specifier of cement thus has a wide number of options and needs to know both what is required to ensure the satisfactory construction of the structure and what is available. Sometimes it is even possible to make special cements to satisfy special manufacturing requirements. Typically, coarse-ground cements are often made to facilitate the production of concrete pipes using a spinning method and other precast products.

Table 14.2 USA cement classifications

ASTM type	Typical use	Typical compound composition[a]			
		C_2S	C_3S	C_3A	C_4AF
I	General	45–55	20–30	8–12	6–10
II	General, with some resistance to sulphate attack	40–50	25–35	5–7	6–10
III	High early strength	50–65	15–25	8–14	6–10
IV	Sulphate resistance	40–50	25–35	0–4	10–20

[a] C, CaO; S, SiO_2; A, Al_2O_3; F, Fe_2O_3.

14.6 Handling and storage of cement

Cement may be delivered in bulk or in bags or sacks. Bulk deliveries are stored in silos which should be weatherproof to minimize the risk of air-setting. Where different types of cement are being used, precautions must be taken to avoid confusion and the inadvertent combination of dissimilar cements when successive deliveries are made. Bags should be stored on pallets or a raised floor, be kept dry and be used in the sequence of delivery, because cements tend to lose 'strength' during prolonged storage.

14.7 Cement admixtures

Although it is believed that the Romans added blood and milk to mortars to improve their properties, the more controlled use of chemical admixtures is comparatively recent. The principal developments in this field have occurred since the Second World War, although the first uses were probably made during the 1930s. What are admixtures and why should they be used? Hewlett[14] defines admixtures as 'materials that are added to concrete at some stage in its making to give to the concrete new properties either when fluid or plastic and/or in the set or cured condition'. Admixtures are quite distinct from any additions made to the cement during its manufacture and from flyash, ground-granulated blast-furnace slag or silica fume which may be added to a concrete mix.

The purposes of using an admixture is to change the properties of the concrete, either in the fresh state or in the hardened form, thereby making it more suitable for its purpose. The main changes that can be made are:

(1) To improve the workability of the concrete without increasing water content, thus making it easier to place without the penalty of reduced strength.
(2) To reduce the water content while keeping the workability constant, thus increasing the strength.
(3) To accelerate or to retard the setting of the concrete, in order to facilitate the construction schedule.
(4) To entrain bubbles of air, thereby improving the resistance of concrete to cycles of freezing and thawing.
(5) To improve water-proofness (reduce permeability).
(6) To improve pumpability.
(7) To add colours (pigments) to concrete.

More recently, the range of admixtures has increased to include corrosion inhibitors, fungicides and gas formers, the latter being used to make low-density and high-air-content materials.

Careful consideration has to be given to the suitabilities of the admixtures for their particular purpose, and also about any deleterious side-effects or the effects of overdosing. For example, air entrainment will greatly improve the resistance of concrete to frost attack, but it will also reduce the strength of the concrete. There is therefore the need for the correct use of admixtures and, in the UK, the Cement Admixtures Association,[15] formed in the 1960s, has given excellent guidance on their use, and their effects on the performance of the concrete.

There is no doubt that admixtures are a widely used component of concrete and, in the future, different types of admixtures will be developed to impart special properties.

14.8 Aggregates

The essential components of concrete are a hydraulic cement, aggregates and water, the aggregates generally filling the greater proportion of the mix. Aggregates come from many sources and can be selected to make concretes with different properties and performance characteristics. The aggregate for normal concrete will comprise a range of different sized particles, the gradings being chosen to ensure good packing when mixed with cement and suitable rheological properties that allow the concrete to be cast and compacted easily and well.

In the UK, gravels and sands, both from land-based quarries and from marine beds, have provided the main sources of aggregate, although crushed rocks are becoming more widely used as the reserves of gravel become depleted or as environmental pressures preclude their extraction. Crushed rocks may be used with natural sands or with rock fines to give a suitable aggregate grading. The choice of aggregates will depend largely on local availability because they are an expensive commodity to transport. Fortunately, there are many types of rock that can be used safely in concrete, although it is necessary to avoid some and to take precautions when using others. In some parts of the world, it is difficult to obtain the good aggregate gradings that are vital to the production of a good workable concrete.

Concrete can be made without a component of sand or fines, (no-fines concrete), or with very dense aggregates to satisfy special needs (e.g. radiation shielding). There are also lightweight aggregates, often man-made, that can be used to make low density concretes. These aggregates include 'Lytag' made by pelletizing and sintering pulverized-fuel ash, expanded clays and shales and naturally occurring volcanic rocks such as pumice. Light-weight aggregates may be used with light-weight fines or with normal sands to produce a range of concretes with different densities and strengths.

Care must be taken to keep the chloride levels in concrete low when it is to be used in reinforced concrete and in prestressed concrete and stringent levels are set in codes for structural concrete.[16] In some parts of the world, particularly the Middle East, the land-based aggregates are heavily contaminated with salts and these can be particularly harmful when used in reinforced concrete.

Other aggregate characteristics that require care are their shrinkability and freeze–thaw resistance, the presence of high levels of fine particles of clay and the inclusion of constituents that can react deleteriously with the alkalis in cement. Small proportions of reactive silica, silicates or certain carbonates can react with alkalis. A small amount of reaction can be tolerated and might even be beneficial (i.e. add to the cementing or binding potential), but if there is too much reaction, the concrete may crack. For cracking to occur, not only must critical quantities of the reactive component be present, but there must also be sufficient alkalis and water. In particular, with an alkali–silica reaction, the gel formed will only expand and then possibly cause cracking if plenty of water is available.

14.8.1 Aggregate gradings

The proportions of the different sizes of particle in an aggregate sample to be used to make concrete are found by sieving, using sieves of approved mesh sizes. In the UK, the sieves should conform with BS 410: 1986[17] and the tests carried out in accordance with BS 812.[18] Although various aggregate gradings may be used to obtain special effects and surface finishes, it is normal to select an aggregate for use in concrete that satisfies the grading limits described in BS 882. At the concrete mixer, the aggregate may be added as a graded or 'all-in' aggregate or, more usually, in higher quality work it is formed from a combination of fractions of single sizes of aggregate. It is customary to consider the fines separately from the coarser fractions of the aggregate and BS 882: 1983[19] defines three classes of fines: C, coarse; M, medium; and F, fine.

These standard classifications of aggregates, together with information on particle shape, water absorption and density are used to design concrete mixes that will meet strength and performance goals. It is important to have a consistent supply of aggregates and to store them without risk of contamination if a consistent quality of concrete is to be produced.

14.9 Ready-mixed concrete

Although it was possible to buy ready-mixed concrete from a few plants in the UK before World War Two, it was not until the 1950s that the industry grew rapidly, and now there are about 1000 plants operating in Britain. This change had significant effects upon the use of concrete in construction. Perhaps the largest effect has been the disappearance from construction sites of an operative who knows how to make concrete, the right combination of aggregates and cement to use and the way to control the consistency of the fresh mix. Instead, the specialists, who can design concrete mixes to meet the specified requirements are more likely to be found at the ready-mixed concrete plant. This can result in the provision of more consistent and economical mixes, but it does not ensure that the concrete is necessarily right for the job and of the right consistency. It is important to provide complete, sound and unambiguous specifications for the required concrete and all too frequently disputes arise because inadequate or incomplete specifications are provided.

Today, many ready-mixed concrete suppliers have sophisticated computer-controlled plants and it can be possible to provide customers with accurate records of the constituents of the concrete supplied. However, if only strength is specified, the supplier has the freedom to use his expertise and select a mix design at the lowest cost. This may mean using a lower cement content, perhaps with a small addition of a plasticizer to make the concrete workable. While this may satisfy the specification, it will not necessarily guarantee an adequate performance. Thus, ready-mixed concrete is a valuable construction material that can be supplied very conveniently at a time to suit the customer; however, it can also be inadequate if not properly specified.

In the UK, the Quality Scheme for Ready-mixed Concrete[21] has done much to improve the standards of the industry and the requirements of the European Common Market are likely to strengthen these controls even further to ensure a fair balance of risk between concrete supplier and purchaser. This is, in fact, in full agreement with the recommendation of Vitruvius,[22] who in 27 BC said 'When writing the specification careful regard is to be paid both to the employer and the contractor'. The problems of today are not new.

An important amendment has been made to the British Standard on methods for specifying concrete (BS 5328:1990[20]). A family of mixes has been described for specific or 'designated' uses. The UK producers of ready-mixed concrete who satisfy the stringent requirements of the Quality Scheme for Ready-mixed Concrete have undertaken to supply concretes that conform fully with the given designated mix proportions. These mixes were selected to satisfy the relevant requirements of the prevailing product and structural British Standards. This system should make the specification of the right concrete for a given use much easier.

14.10 Steel reinforcement

Because concrete is weak in tension, it will normally be reinforced with steel. In most reinforced structures, a reinforcement pattern is chosen to provide the greatest contribution to the tensile zones, but not exclusively so. The design of concrete structures is well covered by BS 8110: 1985[23] and by the ACI 318, building code requirements for reinforced concrete.

A European Code for Structural Concrete has been approved for publication by CEN as an ENV, or voluntary standard, which may be used instead of existing national standards such as BS 8110:1985[23] in the UK. The European Code relies on the CEN ENV 206 (Concrete—performance, production, placing and compliance criteria) for the specification of suitable concretes for different purposes. These voluntary standards can operate alongside national standards for a period of 3–5 years, by which time either they will have been revised sufficiently for adoption as a full and mandatory European Standard (an EN) or they must be withdrawn.

During this century, the strengths of steel for reinforcement have risen, the permissible values of stress for design rising from about $100 \, \text{N mm}^{-2}$ in the 1920s to over $400 \, \text{N mm}^{-2}$ now. These changes, coupled with the higher strength concretes which are now readily available, enable lighter structures with longer spans to be built.

There are two main grades of steel used for reinforcement: mild steel and high-yield steel (sometimes known as high-tensile steel). Plain, smooth, round bars are made by hot rolling mild steel. High-yield steel is made either by hot rolling a low-alloy steel or by cold working (twisting and stretching) a mild-steel bar. Stainless-steel bars can also be obtained at a cost premium.

Reinforcement is well specified by national standards that cover not only the steel grade and dimensions of the bars, but also the cutting and bending schedules. The most common way to order steel is 'cut and bent'. This is delivered to site in bundles that have been cut and bent ready for assembly into cages or directly into the work. Alternatively, straight bars, usually in 12-m lengths, are obtained directly from stockists or a steel mill. Cutting and bending is then carried out on site; this will normally be undertaken only on large jobs.

Reinforcement for pavements or slabs is usually provided as a welded mesh which will be supported on plastic or steel chairs to ensure that it is laid flat with the correct depth of cover. Unfortunately, steel rusts when exposed to a moist environment and many of the concrete structures that have shown signs of deterioration have suffered in this way. The alkaline level in concrete is normally sufficiently high to passivate the steel, i.e. to stop it rusting, but this protection will be lost if carbon dioxide (CO_2) from the atmosphere permeates through the concrete to the steel, carbonating the calcium hydroxide and calcium silicate hydrates as it does so. This process can take many years, particularly in a continually moist environment or if the concrete is of low permeability. Chlorides, either from de-icing salts or from sea spray, can also permeate the concrete and provide an environment in which corrosion will start.

One way to reduce the risk of corrosion is to ensure there is sufficient concrete cover to the steel and that this is of good quality and is well cured. In addition, special steels (stainless) can be used in critical zones, and more recently epoxy-coated bars, have been introduced, although these have not yet been fully proven to be corrosion resistant.

14.11 The use of fibres in concrete

In biblical times straw was used in clay bricks and it was obviously an essential component since the Pharaoh, to punish Moses and Aaron, cut off the supplies of straw and made the people collect their own. Why should this be? Clay bricks, like concrete, are brittle and weak in tension and it is necessary to provide something that will limit the effects of cracking. Conventional steel reinforcement carries the tensile loads in a concrete element, but the use of reinforcement imposes limitations to the geometrical size of the unit. The steel must normally be embedded with sufficient cover for protection from the environment.

The only way to allow the fabrication of thin, yet tough, mortar or concrete products is to use thin fibres to control the cracking. Asbestos fibres have been most widely used, particularly for corrugated sheeting and for cladding panels. Certain types of the very fine asbestos fibres have been found to cause a crippling lung disease, asbestosis, and mesothelioma, a cancer of the lining of the chest. Ingestion of food containing asbestos dust can also cause cancer of the stomach. It is, therefore, imperative to use only white asbestos (chrysotile) in a properly controlled manner.[24]

Other fibres, that do not have the same health hazards, used in cement-based products include glass, steel, polymer, cellulose, carbon and a variety of natural materials such as coconut. Each type of fibre imparts different characteristics to the concrete and also some limitations.

Briefly, although not exclusively, the principal virtues of using fibres in concrete are:

(1) To increase the cohesivity of a fresh mortar or concrete mix, enabling special manufacturing methods to be used and, in particular, the manufacture of thin sheets.
(2) To limit the growth of cracks and help to carry the tensile forces on the element.
(3) To prevent brittle failure and to provide ductility.
(4) To absorb energy and thereby provide impact resistance.

Normal glass is chemically attacked by the alkalis in cement and although an alkali-resistant fibre CEMfil, based on zirconium oxides, is available, there is still a measurable deterioration in performance of a cement composite with time, and it is important to allow for this in design. However, further fibre developments are taking place such as the use of glass-fibre coatings.

Steel fibres of various shapes (crimped, hooked or straight) and of different formulation, have been widely used, but close to the surface of concrete they can cause rust staining unless stainless. Because of their flexural stiffness, they are not so easily mixed as glass or polymer, but they nevertheless have many successful applications.

Polymer fibres have the disadvantage of a low elastic modulus so that polymer–cement composites may crack at low loads, but this is not always a disadvantage and in fresh concrete their presence may limit the opening or the propagation of cracks at early ages. Some polymer fibres have been produced with higher moduli (such as Kevlar, a polyamide), but these tend to be more expensive and so have limited, although useful, applications.

Carbon fibres have also been used, and although these have both high strength and high modulus and are very durable, the cost has proved prohibitive. However, modern technology could lead to cheaper and, hence, more promising opportunities for carbon fibres.

Fibre applications, apart from thin and corrugated sheet and pipe manufacture, tend to be selective and be used where the benefits they impart are particularly useful. Architects find that the properties of the freshly mixed composite can enable novel constructions to be made. Repair specialists can produce coatings that have greater coherence and a lower risk of cracking. Permanent formwork can be made which has low permeability, is compatible with the concrete to be placed and has an attractive appearance. Thus, there are many uses for fibre concretes, but the choice of fibre will depend on the particular application.

14.12 The use of polymers in concrete

Organic polymers are used in concrete for a variety of reasons. One such reason is to change the rheological behaviour of fresh concrete in order to make it flow more easily or to allow lower water contents to be used. Such applications are considered in Section 14.7. Polymers are also used to alter the behaviour of

hardened concrete and, in particular, to make concretes that are more resistant to chemical attack, which have a higher tensile and compressive strength than conventional Portland cement concretes, or which are more able to accommodate strains without cracking.

Polymer concretes can be made in which the aggregates are embedded totally within the polymer matrix. Such concretes have been used to make architectural panels, floors, work-bench surfaces and even machine-tool beds. However, this kind of concrete does not fall within the scope of this chapter.

Polymers can be added to conventional concrete in a number of ways. The most common is to form an aqueous polymer emulsion which is added to the Portland cement and aggregate during mixing. The polymers include natural rubbers, styrene butadiene, acrylic and epoxy emulsions. The concrete mixes will normally contain at least 275 kg m^{-3} ordinary Portland cement. Care must be taken during mixing to avoid the entrapment of excess amounts of air. Often an antifoaming agent will be required. These concretes harden normally and will generally have a lower permeability than conventional concretes, a better durability against aggressive environments and an increased failure strain. Such concretes have been used in repairs and here, the bond between the old and new concretes is generally high. These concretes can be used on overlays on factory floors, in garages and as patching repairs. They are usually known as polymer–Portland-cement concretes or PPCC.

This designation separates the above from a second kind of polymer application, polymer-impregnated concrete (PIC). Here, an organic monomer is introduced into the dried surface of hardened concrete and then polymerized, usually by a thermally activated catalytic process. This process forms a very strong and impermeable surface to the concrete. The polymers used include methylmethacrylate, styrene butadiene and esters. PIC has been used to repair damaged concretes, particularly frost-damaged bridge decks in the USA and to make concretes more resistant to highly aggressive chemicals, such as acids. Very high strength concretes can be produced using the PIC system and compressive strengths over 250 N mm^{-2} have been reported.

Polymers can add useful properties to concrete, but they are expensive as compared with the price of Portland cements. Thus, they will only be used in selected applications where their special attributes can be beneficial.

As with all special concretes, their economic use requires a proper appraisal of the requirements. As an example, if a higher strength but higher cost product allows weight and size reductions, there can be savings that offset the material costs. With tunnel linings, thinner sections mean smaller excavations and easier segment handling and PIC has been used in such applications.

14.13 Mix designs

The first serious attempt to understand the factors that govern the strength potential of concrete was made in the early years of the 20th century by Duff Abrams[25] who showed experimentally that the strength of fully compacted concrete was inversely related to the water:cement ratio. This principle is still relevant today, but must be used with circumspection because of the wide variety of hydraulic cements available and because combinations of hydraulic and pozzolanic cements are used. However, the basic tenet still dominates the rules that must be applied if good quality, dense and strong concrete is to be produced, namely that for any given cement or cementitious combination, the lower the water:cement ratio, the higher will be the strength and the lower the permeability of the concrete. There are practical limits to the reduction in water content in a concrete because the mix must be sufficiently workable to be placed and compacted fully to displace virtually all the entrapped air in the mix.

In practice, the highest possible strength concretes will seldom be required so that the task of the concrete producer is to select a concrete mix that economically fulfils all specified requirements. These requirements will include:

(1) The workability of the fresh concrete.
(2) The strength (usually, but not exclusively, at 28 days).
(3) The durability.
(4) Possibly the density, the air-entrainment and the choice of aggregates.

The variables that the mix designer must consider are the choice of aggregate and the grading of the particles, the sand, the cement, the water:cement ratio and the possible inclusion of admixtures. The proportions of each component can be based on volumes or on weight, and while the former has some attractions, most mixing plants rely on weight batching. It is now general practice to refer to the weights of the different concrete constituents that, in combination, will produce a unit volume of concrete. For example, the cement content might be given as 300 kg m^{-3}, the aggregate content as 1900 kg m^{-3} and the water content as 180 kg m^{-3}.

In the UK, one of the earliest mix-design publications was *Road Note No. 4, Design of Concrete Mixes*, prepared at the Road Research Laboratories.[26] This was superseded in 1975 by the Department of the Environment (DOE) publication *Design of Normal Concrete Mixes*. These publications were concerned solely with the use of Portland cements in combination with different aggregates and gradings. Recently, the latter publication has been revised (in 1988) to include advice on the use of pulverized-fuel ashes as partial cement replacements and, to a lesser extent, the use of ground-granulated blast-furnace slag.[27] In the USA, both the ACI and the Portland Cement Association have published recommended procedures for mix design and these broadly parallel those used in the UK.

Variations in the batching of the components in a concrete mix, in the way it is mixed and in its placing, compaction and curing, result in a variable product. It is essential to allow for such practical effects when selecting a concrete for a defined purpose. The better the control of the total system of manufacture and use, the smaller need be the margins between the specified concrete mix and the target levels chosen by the supplier. Sophisticated statistical procedures must be adopted, with careful monitoring of the concrete produced, to ensure that the concrete supplied is both economical and fit for its purpose. The mix design process should be carried out in a logical way. There are variations in the sequence of the steps followed but basically they are:

(1) The selection of a water:cement ratio that is likely to give the required strength. This will be the free water:cement ratio after allowing for the proportion of water that is absorbed by the aggregates.
(2) The selection of a water content that will give the desired workability of the mix.
(3) Calculation of a cement content per cubic metre from the water:cement ratio and the water content.
(4) Calculation of the total aggregate content, from knowledge of the cement and water contents.
(5) Selection of the aggregate grading, taking account of the specified top sizes and the aggregate shape and type. This will include both the coarse and fine fractions.

The selected values are obtained from graphical and tabular presentations in the mix design publications. It will normally be necessary to carry out trial mixes and, where necessary, to make adjustments to ensure that all specified requirements are met. Frequently, a maximum water:cement ratio and a minimum cement content will be specified. It may be found that, because of durability requirements, when these requirements are met the strength will exceed that specified; this should be seen as a bonus and not a justification to reduce the cement contents or to add more water to the mix.

When pulverized-fuel ash is used, it has been suggested[27] that only a proportion can be equated directly to the Portland cement that it replaces and a cementing efficiency factor, k, of 0.3 is adopted using

$$\frac{W}{C+kF}=\frac{W_1}{C_1}$$

where W, C and F are the free water, the cement and the flyash contents (by weight), respectively, and W_1 and C_1 are the free water and ordinary Portland cement contents of a concrete of similar workability and 28-day strength.

The performance of ground-granulated blast-furnace slags is variable and depends, on the ordinary Portland cement used in combination; the use of such a consistent method as that used for flyash has not been found possible and values of k between 0 and 1 have been found to apply. It is necessary to determine the relevant factor for each selected ordnary Portland cement/slag combination. This factor can then be used to design other concrete mixes using the same ordinary Portland cement/slag combination.

It is important to note that no account has been taken of admixtures, although the DOE *Design of Normal Concrete Mixes*[27] does include consideration of air-entrained concrete mixes for ordinary Portland cement concretes.

Specifications for concrete are frequently ambiguous. They should be as simple as possible to avoid difficulties. If a minimum cement content and maximum water:cement ratio are essential for the assurance of durability, this should be made abundantly clear. If strength is all that matters, the cement content can often be reduced, thereby cutting the cost of the concrete, but this should only be done when it is safe to do so. If a particular type of cement is required, such as a sulphate resistant Portland cement, this too should be stated clearly.

Mix design, for all but the most simple jobs, requires sensible care by someone who is aware of the options. In particular, when composite cements are chosen or flyash or slag are added to the mix, it must not be assumed that the performance of the concrete, the workability, the strength gain or the sensitivity to curing will be unaffected. The choice will finally be one of economics, so that savings in material costs will have to be weighed against any extra costs that result from slower strength gain, delays in stripping formwork or the need for longer curing.

14.14 Mortars, screeds and renders

Mortars are used principally in the construction of masonry walls. The type of mortar mix used will depend on the type of brick or block used and the degree of exposure to which it is subjected. Blocks are normally laid on weaker mortars in order to confine cracks to the joints and not within the blocks. A mortar must remain easily workable for a reasonable length of time, but also develop strength quickly enough to allow construction to continue uninterrupted. It should bond well with the blocks or bricks, be durable and, where necessary, be resistant to attack from the sulphates that can occur in some clay bricks.

Mortars usually comprise:

(1) cement, lime and sand (1:1:5 to 6);
(2) cement, mortar plasticizer and sand (1:5 to 6);
(3) masonry cement, sand (1:4 to 5).

Stronger mixes will be required when dense masonry is used. BS 4887: 1987[28] describes some of the admixtures that can be used to entrain air, and thereby reduce the risk of danger from freezing and thawing, and to retard set.

Mortar plasticizers are used to reduce the amount of water required in the mix and this will significantly reduce the shrinkage and improves the bond with masonry. For small jobs it is convenient to use premixed bags of mortar.

Screeds are used to provide a level surface on a concrete raft or slab. They are not wearing surfaces but provide a surface on which tiles, flexible coverings (plastic or rubber), or carpeting can be laid. Screeds must be laid onto a clean and wetted surface to obtain a good bond. A typical mix is one part of cement to three parts of sand by weight and the water:cement ratio should be kept below 0.45. As with all good concreting, the screed must be cured by keeping it damp for several days. Screeds are usually less than 75-mm thick and may be laid on waterproof membranes (plastic sheets) that separate the screed from the concrete base. Thin screeds are liable to curl if allowed to dry out too quickly.

Renders are mortars that are normally applied to vertical walls to produce various visual finishes. BS 5262[29] describes a family of mortar mixes that can be used for a diverse range of applications. Renders will usually be built up in two or three layers, depending upon the nature of the substrate. Monks[30] has described the different sequences in detail. Frequently, a stipple coat is applied that is cement rich (water:cement = 1:1.5 or 2) to improve bond or reduce suction. This coat will be covered with a thicker undercoat that might be a 1:1:6 cement:lime:sand mix on top of which a weaker finishing coat will be applied (1:2:9, say). These proportions are only typical examples because there are many factors that must be considered.

14.15 Grouts

Grouts are cement-based fluid mixtures used to fill voids. In particular, they are pumped into ducts in structural elements through which prestressing or post-tensioning reinforcement passes. The grout has two functions: it prevents corrosion of the steel tendons and provides an efficient bond between the tendon and the structural member.

Grouts are also used to fill voids between structural members, such as tunnel-lining segments and the surrounding rock. Another example is the filling of the gap between steel sleeves used to repair the legs of steel drilling platforms in the North Sea. Grouts are usually made from ordinary Portland cement or Portlant blast-furnace cement, sand and water. Admixtures are freqently used to aid workability and to minimize segregation of the constituents as the grout is forced into place. Grouts are normally pumped into place from a low position in the void or duct to be filled. Bleed holes are employed to help the upward flow and to ensure that void filling is effective. High-speed mixers are frequently used. These may 'shear' the cement grains which helps to create a stable and effective grout.

The greatest problem is to ensure that the voids or ducts are completely filled and that filtration of the solids from the water does not occur as the grout is forced into narrow ducts or through areas of reinforcement congestion. It is also essential to fill a series of ducts sytematically. On some occasions unfilled ducts have been found with the consequence that the steel reinforcement is more prone to early corrosion.

14.16 Concrete properties

Mention has already been made of concrete workability and strength but there is more to concrete than this. The important properties of concrete are discussed below.

14.16.1 Workability

The need to be able to place concretes within forms or moulds is obvious, but there is more to this statement than may be inferred. The concrete must be sufficiently fluid to flow within the moulds and within and around the steel reinforcement cages without significant segregation of the aggregate from the cement-paste matrix. Once in place, the concrete needs to be fully compacted in order to remove unnecessary air and this is particularly important below the steel and between the steel and the formwork. If the mix is too stiff it will hang-up and leave air pockets which are aesthetically unacceptable on the surface and which do not provide adequate protection to the reinforcement. If the concrete has too high a water content segregation can occur, and where the concrete flows over horizontal bars plastic settlement cracks may form. The workability required will depend upon the chosen compaction methods. Where highly fluid concrete is needed, for pumping to a high level say, it is important that the mix design be suitable and selected to minimize bleeding effects. In such cases, it is helpful to rework (revibrate) the concrete surface before the concrete finally hardens.

The methods used to check workability are mentioned later. The one chosen must be relevant to the need. Where high workability is needed, the slump test is not suitable and flow-table tests should be used.

Another important factor is the duration for which the concrete stays workable. As hydration occurs, or as moisture is lost, the concrete will stiffen and become more difficult to place in the forms and around the steel. Frequently, the concrete will be brought back to a workable state by the addition of water, although this practice is strongly deprecated if it effectively increases the water:cement ratio. However, concrete badly compacted because of its stiffness can be more unsatisfactory than concrete to which small water additions have been made. A preferred alternative is the addition of a plasticizer or workability aid that restores mobility without adjusting the water content.

14.16.2 Setting time

After hydration of Portland cement has started, there is a dormant period when nothing appears to be happening. This is fortunate because it provides a period during which concrete can be transported to the site and be placed. After a period of about 2–4 h, the concrete will begin to set, reaching final set about 2 h later. These times depend significantly on the prevailing climate and on the selected cements. Special cements such as high alumina cement and ultrarapid hardening Portland cement react much more quickly and can harden very quickly after the addition of water.

14.16.3 Early-age behaviour

As soon as water is added to concrete, the cement starts to react exothermally and the temperature will rise. The rate of temperature rise will depend primarily upon the temperature when the concrete is cast, the type and amount of cement and the size of the pour. Once the concrete hardens, thermal-stress gradients will be set up and at early stages where the concrete is restrained these will be predominantly compressive. Later the concrete will cool and tensile strains will be induced that can be large enough to cause cracking. Where this risk is high, it is possible to specify the use of a low-heat cement, but coupled with the low heat will be a low rate of strength gain which may not be acceptable. An alternative method for reducing the risk of cracking is to lay thermally insulating mats on the surface of the concrete and, while this may mean an even higher temperature increase in the concrete as hydration proceeds, it can also ensure that thermal-strain gradients are kept sufficiently low and thereby minimize the risk of cracks occurring.

There are thus different ways to overcome thermal problems deriving from the heat of hydration. Using a low-heat cement is not always the best solution because the lower strengths achieved during the early ages of the concrete can mean that smaller strain gradients (lower thermal gradients) result in cracking than for the faster reacting types.

Flyash and slag cements are often used to reduce the temperature rises in concrete. The heat evolution of both these additions is affected by the temperatures at which they are used and temperature rises may be greater than expected.

14.16.4 Strength

When a structure is built, the concrete is required to reach a certain strength before the forms are struck or additional structural loads are applied. For these reasons, concrete is frequently specified by strength, usually compressive strength. The compressive strength of concrete is usually measured using either cast concrete cubes of 100 or 150 mm side or cylinders of 300×150 mm diameter (or 200×100 mm). Strengths measured on cylinders are about 80% of those of cubes made from the same concrete. For design purposes, the characteristic strength is used. This is the value below which 5% of the measured strengths may lie, due to the variability of the concretes and of the testing itself.

The compressive strength can also be determined from cores cut from hardened concrete in a pavement or structure. The results will depend upon the casting direction and can also vary with the height of the casting (e.g. the top of a wall or column will often be weaker than the area close to the foot).

The tensile strength of concrete is about one-tenth of the compressive strength. This strength is seldom specified but can be measured in a flexural test or by splitting a cylinder by a diametral compressive load. All these tests are described in detail in BS 1881.[31]

The rate of gain in strength depends not only on the selected concrete mix and the chosen cement, but also on the ambient temperature and on the curing regime. *Figure 14.2* shows some of these effects for ordinary Portland cement. At low temperatures, the early strengths will be low, but if a sufficiently long curing time is allowed, the concrete may finally exceed the

strength of concrete cured at higher temperatures and thereby develop strength early.

14.16.5 Permeability and porosity

Another property of importance is the permeability of concrete. Powers[32] suggested that the pore structure of concretes largely controls both its strength and durability and that it is essential to keep the water:cement ratio low if the porous structure is to become discontinuous with no channels through which fluids or gases could permeate. For water:cement ratios of about 0.7, Powers showed that there was insufficient potential hydration to provide a discontinuous or segmented matrix. At the other extreme, for water:cement ratios of 0.4, the matrix could become a closed-pore system after about 3 days hydration. Modern cements, both ordinary Portland and the composite varieties, do not satisfy the exact pattern described by Powers, but the general principle still applies, namely that at high water:cement ratios it is not possible to make very impermeable concrete. With composite cements, because hydration may be slower than that of an ordinary Portland cement, it is usually necessary to extend the hydration period (the duration of wet curing) to establish the same result. However, if prolonged curing occurs, in a marine environment for example, concretes made from composite cements will often have lower permeabilities.

14.16.6 Elastic modulus

The elastic modulus of concrete is closely related to the strength of normal concrete and to the modulus of the aggregate used and its volume concentration. In general, the elastic modulus $E_c = f(E_a, E_p, V)$, where E_a is the modulus of the aggregate, E_p is the modulus of the hardened cement paste and V is the volume proportion of aggregate. In practice, it is seldom necessary to be too precise and BS 8110: 1985[23] for example, lists typical values as indicated in *Table 14.3*. Additional information is provided for more demanding situations. Light-weight aggregate concretes have lower moduli and the relevant manufacturer's data sheets should be consulted.

14.16.7 Shrinkage

As concrete dries it shrinks, the rate and extent of shrinkage depending on the size of the structural member and the ambient environment.[33] *Figure 14.3* provides a representation of these interactive effects and enables shrinkage strains to be estimated at 6 months and virtually at completion of movement (30 years) for normal dense aggregate concretes. Aggregates that have a high moisture movement, such as Scottish dolerites, have a higher shrinkage at early ages.

Table 14.3 Normal ranges of elastic moduli of concretes related to concrete strengths[a]

Characteristic cube strength at 28 days ($N \, mm^{-2}$)	Elastic modulus (28 days) ($kN \, mm^{-2}$)	
	Mean	*Range*
20	24	18–30
25	25	19–31
30	26	20–32
40	28	22–34
50	30	24–36
60	32	26–38

[a] From ref. 23.

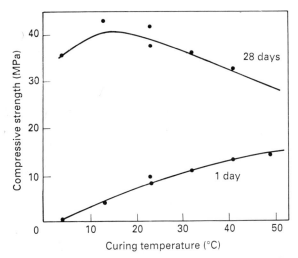

Figure 14.2 The effect of ambient temperature on the compressive strength at 1 and 28 days of an ordinary Portland cement concrete kept wet

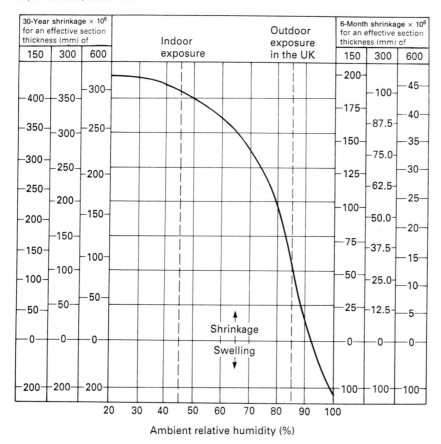

Figure 14.3 Shrinkage strains likely to be reached by concretes of different section thickness exposed to different environments: values are given for 6-month and 30-year exposures

In practice, the temperature and humidity around the concrete will change periodically and if rain falls onto the concrete the rate of shrinkage will be greatly reduced. In some instances dry concrete will expand if it is suddenly soaked. Shrinkage can also be caused by the carbonation of the concrete by the carbon dioxide in the atmosphere.

14.16.8 Creep

Concrete subjected to stress will deform with time, the deformation being known as creep. The creep strains are very dependent upon the environment, as well as on the applied stress, the concrete mix, aggregate and aggregate concentrations. If the concrete is always saturated with water, the creep, known as basic creep, will be much smaller than that when drying occurs concurrently, the total movement then being greater than the basic creep and shrinkage strains combined. Because environmental effects are very dependent upon the size of the structural elements, the estimation of the creep of concrete is not always very precise and where annual cycles of weather occur, there can be large variations in structural movement.[34]

Various methods have been proposed to help the concrete structural designer. Parrott[33] chose a graphical method (*Figure 14.4*), subsequently adopted in BS 8110, that makes allowance for most of the controlling parameters. As an alternative, mathematical models can be used in computer programs. None of the methods are likely to give results that are more accurate than about 15–20%, but even this is adequate for most design

needs, because design allowances must be made for structural movements.

14.16.9 Thermal expansion

Allowance may also have to be made for thermal expansion. A value of $8–12 \times 10^{-6}°C$ is usually adequate. Where concrete is painted black or other dark colours, there can be a significant fluctuation in temperature when it is exposed to intermittent sunlight. In such circumstances, particularly with thin section sizes, movements may be larger than expected with a consequent risk of cracking.

14.17 Durability

Like all materials, concrete is affected by the environment in which it is used and, in particular, corrosion of the reinforcing steel can reduce the serviceability of a structure. Many volumes have been written on this subject alone, so that only brief mention of some important considerations will be given here.

The causes of deterioration in concrete include the ingress into the concrete of chlorides from marine spray or from deicing salts or carbon dioxide from the atmosphere followed by the onset and development of corrosion of the reinforcement. These are probably the two most serious causes. The effects are

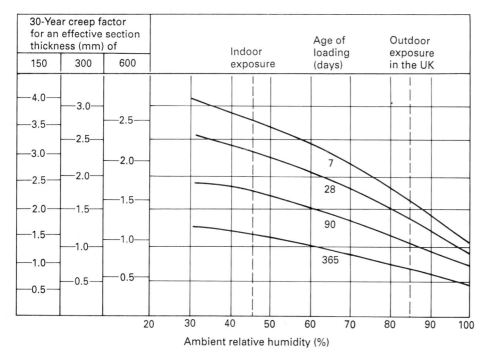

Figure 14.4 Creep factors for concretes subject to a sustained stress, σ_u, for 30 years in different environments. The creep strain at 30 years is given by $\varepsilon = (\sigma_u/E) \times$ creep factor, where E is the elastic modulus of the concrete at the time of loading

Table 14.4 Recommended cements for use in sulphate exposure

Sulphate class	Sulphate in soil (%)	Suitable cement and additions[a]	Minimum cement content (kg m^{-3})	Water:cement
1	<0.2	OPC, SRPC, PFA, slag	—	—
2	0.2–0.5	As above	330	0.50
		OPC + PFA[b] or slag[c]	310	0.55
		SRPC	280	0.55
3	0.5–1.0	OPC + PFA[b] or slag[c]	380	0.45
		SRPC	330	0.50
4	1.0–2.0	SRPC	370	0.45
5	>2	SRPC plus protective coating	370	0.45

[a] OPC, ordinary Portland cement; SRPC, sulphate resistant Portland cement; PFA, pulverized-fuel ash. [b] BS 3892: Part 1: 1982[6], pulverized-fuel ash in range 25–40%. [c] BS 6699: 1986[5] ground-granulated blast-furnace slag in range 70–90%.

minimized by choosing a good-quality, low-permeability concrete, using an appropriate cement and aggregate, and ensuring there is an adequate depth of cover to the steel, including any secondary stirrups or ties, and that this cover concrete is properly compacted and, in particular, is adequately cured. Failure of any one of these requirements will reduce the quality of the concrete. Frequently, the first signs of spalling caused by steel corrosion occur at locations where the specified cover to the concrete has not been satisfied. Such a failure is not a criticism of the materials but of the workmanship on site or in the factory and of the supervision.

Chlorides can also come from the concrete constituents, from the cement, from the aggregates or from any admixtures used. Limitations are imposed, depending on the use of the concrete.

14.17.1 Acid and sulphate attack

Concrete can be damaged by acid waters and by the sulphates present in groundwaters. If acids, or even neutral flowing water, are to be handled, it is essential to take suitable precautions. Sulphate resistance can be provided by the use of sulphate resistant Portland cement with a $3CaO.Al_2O_3$ level below 3.5%. Ordinary Portland cements containing a sufficiently high level of pulverized-fuel ash or ground-granulated blast-furnace slag also provide a measure of protection as indicated below. More extensive information is provided in BS 8110: Part 1: 1985.[16]

Harrison[35] has provided detailed guidance on the way in which the concrete grades given in *Table 14.4* can be used to provide protection against the acid waters in the ground or flowing in concrete pipes and culverts. It can be seen from *Table 14.4* that the quality of the concrete as indicated by cement content and water:cement ratio is as important as the choice of cement.

14.17.2 Alkali–aggregate reaction

The reaction between the alkalis present in the pore fluid of damp concrete and certain aggregate constituents may generate stresses within concrete that are large enough to cause cracking. The Building Research Establishment (BRE) Digest 330[36] provides guidance on the precautions that can be taken to minimize the risk of this reaction occurring when the reactive component is siliceous. Hobbs[37] has recently published an authoritative monograph on the subject. The Institution of Structural Engineers has also provided guidance on the structural effects of alkali–silica reaction.[38]

The risk of cracking due to alkali–silica reaction is minimal if any of the following apply:

(1) The source of aggregate has been used satisfactorily over a long period of time.
(2) The quantity of alkali (Na_2O(eq)) in the concrete mix is below 3.0 kg m^{-3}.
(3) A low alkali cement, below 0.6% alkali, is used.
(4) The concrete is consistently exposed to a dry environment.

Even when there is evidence of the alkali–silica reaction in concrete, usually obtained by the petrographic examination of thin sections cut from concrete cores, the likelihood of serious cracking will remain low because small quantities of the reaction product, a gel, will fill pores or may even exude from the concrete without causing damage. However, even when significant cracking has been observed, structural load tests generally show the effects to appear more serious than they are.[37]

Alkali–silica reaction will continue until either the alkalis in the concrete or the reactive constituent in the aggregate has been depleted by the reaction. The implication is that, in most cases, there is a finite limit to the amount of damage or cracking that can occur. Once this stage is reached, normal remedial work can be carried out, provided that no extra alkalis are made available to react with any residual reactive aggregate. Again, it must be emphasized that water is needed to cause the reaction product, the gel, to expand and it is possible that an unexpected soaking of dry concrete, in which alkali–silica reaction has occurred, could result in cracking, but this will be very rare.

14.17.3 Freeze–thaw damage

A more common cause of damage occurs when wet concrete is subjected to freezing and thawing cycles. The normal way of avoiding this form of damage is to entrain air into the concrete. A chemical admixture is used that introduces a stable family of small air bubbles into the concrete. This entrainment of air will lower the strength of the concrete so that some additional cement may be required to meet strength requirements. The inclusion of about 5% air will provide good frost resistance, but will also reduce the strength of the concrete by about one-quarter. It is normally possible to reduce the water content of air-entrained concrete and thereby regain some of the strength loss.

The air bubbles should be small, about 0.5 mm, and evenly dispersed in the paste. The bubbles tend to add cohesivity to the mix and increase the workability. Air-entrained concrete is recommended for all forms of exposed paving where freezing cycles are likely to occur. Air entrainment generally increases the durability of concrete, and reduces the likelihood of plastic settlement and the formation of plastic settlement cracks. The amount of air-entraining agent required will depend on the cement used; in particular the dosage will be higher when flyash is included in the mix. Over vibration should be avoided as this can reduce the air content of the concrete.

14.18 Concrete practice

Mention has already been made of the use of highly workable concretes that can be made using organic plasticizers. This is but one change in the concrete industry that has altered site practice. Most concrete used on medium and large sites is delivered from a ready-mixed concrete plant and it will be transported to the place of work by skips, trucks or, frequently, by pump. Because several different mixes may be used on a site, it is vital to install a good acceptance and control procedure to ensure that the correct concrete is used on all occasions. The concrete will normally be vibrated into place and this must be done thoroughly and consistently if all voids and honeycombed areas are to be avoided.

Before compaction, a 75-mm slump concrete may contain 5% entrapped air (which is distinct from deliberately entrained air), while for one of 25-mm slump this could be as high as 20%. For each 1% of air, the strength of the concrete falls by about 5% so that the need for compaction is clearly apparent. Compaction also reduces the permeability of the concrete and improves the bond between the concrete and the steel reinforcement. Concrete should be placed in layers less than 0.5 m thick and each layer vibrated in turn before further concrete is added. Before any concrete is placed, the forms should be closely examined to ensure they are clean, that no water is lying at the bottom and that the reinforcement is properly fixed. Spacers should be used to provide the required cover to the steel.

For most concrete placed in forms, poker vibrators are used. These must be moved systematically to ensure that all parts of the casting are uniformly compacted. Care must be taken to remove the poker slowly in order to avoid weak zones being left near the surface. For slabs, it is preferable to use beam vibrators to obtain a satisfactory flat surface. In addition, poker vibrations should be used close to the edges of slabs to ensure proper compaction.

If plastic settlement occurs around the reinforcement, the concrete should be revibrated while it is still workable. Reworking the surface of concrete in this way is usually beneficial.

14.19 Striking of formwork

The period which should elapse before formwork is struck will vary from job to job and according to the prevailing temperature. As already mentioned, the types of cement used have a large influence on the early-strength development and it is prudent to find out these effects if the cast concrete is to be strong enough to be self-supporting and able to carry imposed loads. CIRIA[39] have published tables of striking times for normal dense-aggregate concretes. In winter it can be helpful to insulate the moulds both to avoid freezing and to reduce the stripping times. In winter, the removal of an insulated or timber form can subject the concrete to a thermal shock (a sudden drop in temperature) that could result in cracking. This can be avoided by releasing and not removing forms or by the use of insulating mats.

14.20 Curing

It is fairly common to hear people talking about concrete drying out. If this is allowed to occur at early ages, the quality of the concrete will be poor. Concrete gains strength by hydration, which is a chemical reaction between cement and water and as soon as the forms have been removed, or with slabs, immediately after finishing the concrete, it is essential to start a curing routine. That is, precautions must be taken to avoid the premature drying of the concrete and to replenish any losses that occur. The quality of the surface layer is particularly important since this protects the steel reinforcement from the effects of carbon dioxide from the air or from the chloride ions that come from de-icing salts or marine spray. The rate of moisture loss is highly dependent on the local weather, being particularly severe on a hot and windy day.

There are two main methods of curing:

(1) Water or moisture is kept in close contact with the surface by ponding, applying water with a sprinkler, covering with damp sand or with damp hessian.
(2) Evaporation is prevented by covering with plastic sheeting or by the application of a chemical curing membrane.

The choice of method will depend upon the structural element used. With a slab or pavement, spraying can be used, but this is not possible for the soffit of an *in situ* cast beam. Again, it is emphasized that curing must start as early as possible, because once concrete has dried out some permanent changes occur that are likely to leave the concrete more porous and, therefore, prone to the ingress of carbon dioxide or chlorides. BS 8110: Part 1: 1985[16] includes a table of minimum curing times (*Table 14.5*), which take into account the differences between cements and the prevailing ambient conditions.

The application of curing is relatively complex, particularly if the appearance of the concrete is to be uniform and free of blemishes. Furthermore, if screeds are to be applied to a horizontal slab, the use of curing membranes on the substrate can cause poor bond. Thus, it is important to choose the correct method of curing, but whatever method is selected it must be applied consistently because failure to do so is the cause of many of the problems that occur in concrete practice: the shrinkage cracking, the poor quality of 'cover-crete' and the variations in colour that are unsightly.

14.21 Exposed aggregate finishes to concrete surfaces

There are many ways in which the surface of concrete can be finished to provide an attractive visual appearance. Plastic moulds have been used to form surfaces that resemble the contours of rocks, heavily grained timber forms are used to produce 'board-marked' finishes and ribs have been cast in. The possibilities are endless and include the class of exposed aggregate finishes obtained by the removal of the surface mortar without significant damage to the body of the concrete.

There are two common methods:

(1) Exposure of the aggregate by washing and brushing. Normally a retarder will be painted onto the formwork to keep the surface soft while the bulk of the concrete hardens.
(2) Abrasive blasting of the surface.

The choice of size and type of aggregate is obviously important in order to provide the required effects. In some instances, large pieces of aggregate will be laid on the base of horizontal formwork and concrete will be cast onto this. The mortar surface will be removed soon after the forms are struck by wet brushing. When any of these special surface effects are used, the depth of cover to the steel reinforcement must be measured from the deepest indentation or deformations into the surface.

14.22 Precast concrete

Many concrete products are factory made. These range from concrete bricks and blocks to large precast concrete beams or segments of tunnel linings. An advantage of factory production is the greater degree of uniformity and control that can be achieved. This is particularly true when special cladding panels are designed and manufactured to add a quality visual appearance to a structure. As already discussed, special finishes can be given to exposed concrete panels and these are best made in a controlled environment.

The concrete mixes used for precasting differ from those that are suitable on site. Drier mixes can be hydraulically rammed into moulds, vacuum dewatering is possible and spinning techniques can be used in the manufacture of pipes. Because fabrication methods are so different from conventional concreting practice, it is often more convenient to undertake product testing instead of the material tests that are used to measure the quality and consistency of concrete used on site or delivered from a ready-mixed plant.

Table 14.5 Minimum periods (days) of curing and protection

Type of cement[a]	Ambient conditions after casting[b]	Average surface temperature of concrete		
		5–10°C	Above 10°C	t (any temperature between 5°C and 25°C)
OPC, RHPC, SRPC	Average	4	3	$\dfrac{60}{t+10}$
	Poor	6	4	$\dfrac{80}{t+10}$
All except RHPC, OPC and SRPC and all with GGBS or PFA	Average	6	4	$\dfrac{80}{t+10}$
	Poor	10	7	$\dfrac{140}{t+10}$
All	Good	No special requirements		

[a] OPC, Ordinary Portland cement (see BS 12); RHPC, rapid-hardening Portland cement (see BS 12); SRPC, sulphate-resisting Portland cement (see BS 4027); ggbs, ground-granulated blast-furnace slag; PFA, pulverized-fuel ash.
[b] Good: damp and protected (relative humidity greater than 80%; protected from sun and wind). Average: intermediate between good and poor. Poor: dry or unprotected (relative humidity less than 50%; not protected from sun and wind).

A major difference in the factory is the use of warmth to speed up the hydration of the cement and, therefore, speed up the throughput of the products. There are too many variations in procedure for discussion here, but they include steam curing and autoclaving, as well as the use of more mild heating regimes. A large market has been developed for aerated autoclaved concrete blocks that are of very low density and are used to provide good thermal insulation in buildings.

14.23 Testing methods, quality and compliance

All products should be tested and checked for compliance. Unfortunately, a concrete structure cannot be tested in its entirety, so that it is necessary to make checks on the various elements that go into the construction. These checks start with the materials. It is normally accepted that the steel delivered to a site will comply with specification and it is unusual to sample and test it. In the UK, a quality-assurance scheme known as CARES[40] provides protection to the consumer.

With concrete, the situation is more confusing because not only must the material delivered to a site be able to generate the desired long-term properties such as strength, stiffness and durability, but it must also be in a state in which it can be delivered to the job, by truck, skip or pump, be placed in the forms and be compacted into place. It may also be necessary to check the air content of the mix. There are a host of site tests to check these early-age properties and for the UK these are described in BS 1881.[31] A similar range of tests is covered in other countries, many of the tests now being International Standards. The most common site tests are the slump test for workability and the test for the air content. Concrete is commonly pumped to the place of use. A special mix must be chosen that does not segregate or bleed under the action of the pumping pressure. The mix must also be adequately fluid. These characteristics are controlled primarily by the grading and proportions of sand in the mix. Normal workability tests do not characterize a pumpable concrete nor are there, at present, any widely accepted tests. It is necessary to observe the pumping operation and to adjust the sand component and to use plasticizers to achieve a satisfactory mix. Visual monitoring of the operation is currently the most effective way to ensure consistency and absence of segregation. Because cement content is critical to the manufacture of good and durable concrete, tests have been developed that can unscramble a sample from a mix delivered to site to ensure that it complies with the specification. One such test, known as rapid-analysis machine (RAM) test (*Figure 14.5*), enables a check of cement content, proportion of flyash or slag and the water:cement ratio to be determined on site and very rapidly. Tests on site are often too late to provide the best control of production and third-party quality-assurance schemes are now being used to monitor the quality of concrete produced from ready-mixed plants. In the UK, following several years of development, the Quality Scheme for Ready-mixed Concrete (QSRMC) has done much to raise the consistency of supply of concrete to jobs, both large and small, so that gradually the need to test concrete on site is waning.

Site conditions and the prevailing weather will have a large effect on strength development. Another family of tests is available to help monitor this stage of concrete development. The tests include measuring the maturity of concrete (by integrating time and temperature in the concrete), by matching the strength gain of a companion concrete specimen subjected to the temperature profile within the structural member to the *in situ* strength and also by measuring the actual strength of a structure by pull-out tests.

Another important check is that of cover to the steel. Once concrete has been cast, it is really too late to realign the steel.

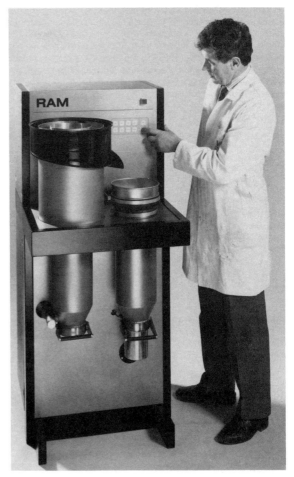

Figure 14.5 The rapid-analysis machine (RAM) for the analysis of constituents of fresh concrete

However, the steel can be displaced during casting and some checks are sensible. Electromagnetic devices are available to masure the cover to the steel and these too are described in BS 1881[31] and other National Standards. The use of such a device on site will often have the effect of raising site standards, thereby ensuring satisfactory construction.

Most structural design is based on the 28-day strength of concrete so that the most common test of concrete is that of the compressive strength of a cube or cylinder of concrete. A badly made and unrepresentative sample of concrete can be misleading and in extreme cases can result in concrete being wrongly rejected with the consequent expensive removal and replacement of completed work. Good sampling and testing practice is described fully in BS 1881[31] and this should be followed closely.

When disputes do occur, it is normal to carry out further tests on the structural concrete using non-destructive tests or surface-strength tests such as indentation or pull-out tests. Ultrasonic pulses can be transmitted through concrete to show up large flaws or gross variations in concrete quality throughout the element or structure. Frequently, cores are cut and these can be used to measure strength in compression or tension by diametral compressive loading. They can also be sliced to study the gradations in quality, such as permeability or strength.

Any faults found late in the construction process will be expensive to remedy; it is much better and cheaper to 'get it right' first time. This requires adequate training of the staff involved and sufficient checks to ensure that the main requirements of good practice are being supplied. These can briefly be summarized by the 'Cs': i.e. the *constituents* in the mix, the *cover* to the steel, the *compaction* of the concrete and, finally, the *curing*. The quality-assurance schemes should provide a guarantee that the constituents *specified* are delivered, but some checks, such as the RAM test, can be made. It is essential, therefore, to specify what is required for the particular job and it is sensible to discuss this with the concrete supplier to ensure that he knows all the facts. The advent of 'designated mixes' for defined applications may make life less complicated in the future.[41]

The steel must be correctly fixed and held in the forms so that it does not displace during casting of the concrete. The concrete must be able to flow round the steel without segregation and must be uniformly compacted throughout the mix, particularly in areas close to the corners of moulds. Where air entrainment is required, special care is needed to ensure good compaction without excess loss of air. Finally, the benefits of all these stages will be nullified if the concrete is not properly cured.

All of these stages add up to good site practice. The test methods and quality-assurance systems are there to help the contractor to check that the job is well done. This will ensure a good and durable concrete structure.

14.24 Future opportunities

The expectations of our society are always changing or being affected by events in the world. Fear of an oil shortage in the 1970s ensured a lasting interest in energy conservation and this, in turn, made concrete-block manufacturers seek ways to manufacture thermally insulating materials. The current aerated concrete technology may not be able to meet future demands for insulation in the UK and either it may have to develop further or other ways will have to be found in which to meet specifications. This is one example of the pressures on established industries to change.

Some of the ways in which concretes with widely different properties can be made have already been described. In Denmark,[42] a very strong cement has been made using Portland cement, silica fume and a plasticizer or water reducer. This cement, called DENSIT, has a strength that is more than double that of conventional cements and the hydrate matrix is extremely dense and virtually impermeable. Unfortunately, concretes made with this cement tend to be brittle and so cannot withstand impact or shock loads safely. To overcome this, Bache[43] incorporated steel fibres to provide some ductility. In this way, concrete can be tailored for special purposes. Such changes in formulation will be expensive, so that economic judgements will have to be made about the value of these new products in the future.

Designers will have to think afresh about the best ways to exploit the possibilities concrete technology has made available. Solutions completely different from those traditionally used will be necessary, but such opportunities will only result if there is a wider perception and knowledge of what can be done. Architects, structural designers and materials specialists will have to work in close harmony if society is to gain from the possibilities on offer.

Concrete, as we currently know it, can be used better and in more aesthetically acceptable ways. More emphasis must be paid to the provision of long service life, with proper allowance for maintenance and repair. Some of the basic principles have been discussed and these should be followed meticulously.

14.25 Health and safety

Portland and other hydraulic cements are harmless in normal use. However, alkalis are released when water is added and direct contact of freshly mixed concrete with the skin should therefore be avoided. The abrasive nature of the aggregate can aggravate the effects of alkalis on the skin. Any concrete or mortar on the skin should be removed with soap and water. If cement enters the eye, it should be washed out with plenty of clean water and medical treament sought without delay.

Protective clothing should be worn and care taken to avoid getting concrete into wellington boots. Clothes contaminated with cement should be thoroughly cleaned before reuse. The use of waterproof gloves is strongly advised.

References

1   STANLEY, C. C., *Highlights in the History of Concrete*, Cement & Concrete Association, Slough, **44** (1979)
2   MORRIS, M., 'Archaeology and technology', *J. Am. Conc. Inst.*, **9**, 28–35 (1987)
3   BRITISH STANDARDS INSTITUTION, *BS 12 Specification for Portland cement*, Milton Keynes (1991)
4   BRITISH STANDARDS INSTITUTION, *BS 146 Specification for Portland blast-furnace cement*, Milton Keynes (1991)
5   BRITISH STANDARDS INSTITUTION, *BS 6699 Ground-granulated blast-furnace slag for use with Portland cement*, Milton Keynes (1986)
6   BRITISH STANDARDS INSTITUTION, *BS 3892 Pulverised-fuel ash: Part 1 Specification for pulverised-fuel ash for use as a cementitious component in structural concrete*, Milton Keynes (1982)
7   BRITISH STANDARDS INSTITUTION, *BS 3892 Pulverized-fuel ash: Part 2 Specification for pulverised-fuel ash for use in grouts and for miscellaneous uses in concrete*, Milton Keynes (1984)
8   BRITISH STANDARDS INSTITUTION, *BS 6588 Specification for Portland pulverised-fuel ash cement*, Milton Keynes (1991)
9   BRITISH STANDARDS INSTITUTION, *BS 6110 Specification for pozzolanic cement with pulverised-fuel ash as pozzolana*, Milton Keynes (1985)
10 AMERICAN SOCIETY FOR TESTING MATERIALS, *Standard specification for flyash and raw or calcined natural pozzolana for use as a mineral admixture to Portland cement concrete, ASTM C618-89*, Philadelphia
11 *AMERICAN SOCIETY FOR TESTING MATERIALS, Standard specification for Portland cement, ASTM C150-89,* Philadelphia
12 BRITISH STANDARDS INSTITUTION, *BS 4027 Specification for sulphate-resisting Portland cement*, Milton Keynes (1991)
13 MEHTA, P. K., *Concrete: Structure, Properties and Materials*, Prentice Hall, NJ, p. 206 (1986)
14 HEWLETT, P. J. (Ed.), *Cement Admixtures: Use and Applications*, Longman Scientific and Technical, Harlow, p. 166 (1988)
15 CEMENT ADMIXTURES ASSOCIATION, *Admixture Data Sheet*, 8th edn, Cement Admixtures Association Ltd, Southampton, p. 1 (1989)
16 BRITISH STANDARDS INSTITUTION 8110: Part 1, *Structural Use of Concrete. Code of Practice for Design and Construction*, Milton Keynes (1985)
17 BRITISH STANDARDS INSTITUTION, *BS 410 Specification for test sieves*, Milton Keynes (1986)
18 BRITISH STANDARDS INSTITUTION, *BS 812 Testing aggregates.* Separately dated parts: *Part 1 Methods for determination of particle size and shape* (1975); *Part 2 Methods for determination of physical properties* (1975); *Part 100 General requirements for apparatus and calibrations* (1990); *Part 101 Guide to sampling and testing aggregates* (1984); *Part 102 Methods for sampling* (1989); *Part 103 Methods for determination of particle size distribution, Part 103.1 Sieve tests* (1985); *Part 103.2 Sedimentation test* (1989); *Part 105 Methods for determination of particle shape, Part 105.1 Flakiness index* (1989); *Part 105.2*

Elongation index of coarse aggregate (1990); *Part 106 Method of determination of shell content in coarse aggregate* (1985); *Part 109 Methods for determination of moisture content* (1990); *Part 110 Methods for determination of aggregate crushing value (ACV)* (1990); *Part 111 Methods for determination of ten percent fines value (TFV)* (1990); *Part 112 Methods for determination of aggregate impact value (AIV)* (1990); *Part 113 Methods for determination of aggregate abrasion value (AAV)* (1990); *Part 114 Method for determination of polished-stone value* (1989); *Part 117 Method for determination of water-soluble chloride salts* (1988); *Part 118 Methods for determination of sulphate content* (1988); *Part 119 Method for determination of acid-soluble material in fine aggregate* (1985); *Part 120 Methods for testing and clarifying drying shrinkage of aggregates in concrete* (1989); *Part 121 Method for determination of soundness* (1989); *Part 124 Method for determination of frost heave* (1989); Milton Keynes

19 BRITISH STANDARDS INSTITUTION, *BS 882 Specification for aggregates from natural sources for concrete*, Milton Keynes (1983)

20 BRITISH STANDARDS INSTITUTION, *BS 5328 Methods for specifying concrete, including ready-mixed concrete*, Milton Keynes (1990)

21 QUALITY SCHEME FOR READY-MIXED CONCRETE, *Regulations*, QSRMC, London, p. 14 (1984)

22 VITRUVIUS, *De Architectura (27 BC)*, Granger, F. (Translator), Harvard University Press, Harvard (1931)

23 BRITISH STANDARDS INSTITUTION, *BS 8110 Structural use of concrete, Part 1 Code of practice for design and construction; Part 2 Code of practice for special circumstances*, Milton Keynes (1985)

24 DEPARTMENT OF THE ENVIRONMENT, 'Asbestos: Health precautions in industry', *Health and Safety Executive, Report No. 44*, HMSO, London (1975)

25 ABRAMS, D. A., 'Design of concrete mixtures', *Bulletin 1*, Structural Materials Research Laboratory, Lewis Institute, Chicago (1918)

26 *Design of Concrete Mixes, Road Note No. 4*, 2nd edn, HMSO, London (1950)

27 DEPARTMENT OF THE ENVIRONMENT, *Design of Normal Concrete Mixes*, 2nd edn, Building Research Establishment, Garston, p. 42 (1988)

28 BRITISH STANDARDS INSTITUTION, *BS 1887 Mortar admixtures*, Milton Keynes (1987)

29 BRITISH STANDARDS INSTITUTION, *BS 5262 Code of practice for external rendered finishes*, Milton Keynes (1978)

30 MONKS, W., 'External rendering', *Publication No. 47.102*, British Cement Association, Slough, pp. 32 (1988)

31 BRITISH STANDARDS INSTITUTION, *BS 1881 Testing concrete*. Separately dated parts: *Part 5 Methods of testing hardened concrete for other than strength* (1970); *Part 101 Methods of testing fresh concrete on site* (1983); *Part 102 Method for determination of slump* (1983); *Part 103 Method for determination of compacting factor* (1983); *Part 104 Method for determination of Vebe time* (1983); *Part 105 Method for determination of flow* (1984); *Part 106 Methods for determination of air content of fresh concrete* (1983); *Part 107 Method for determination of density of compacted fresh concrete* (1983); *Part 108 Method for making test cubes from fresh concrete* (1983); *Part 109 Method for making test beams from fresh concrete* (1983); *Part 110 Method for making test cylinders from fresh concrete* (1983); *Part 111 Method for normal curing of test specimens (20°C method)* (1983); *Part 112 Method of accelerated curing of test cubes* (1983); *Part 113 Method for*

making and curing no-fines test cubes (1983); *Part 114 Methods for determination of density of hardened concrete* (1983); *Part 115 Specification for compression testing machines for concrete* (1986); *Part 116 Method for determination of compressive strength of concrete cubes* (1983); *Part 117 Method for determination of tensile splitting strength* (1983); *Part 118 Method for determination of flexural strength* (1983); *Part 119 Method for determination of compressive strength using portions of beams broken in flexure (equivalent cube method)* (1983); *Part 120 Method for determination of the compressive strength of concrete cores* (1983); *Part 121 Method for determination of the static modulus of elasticity in compression* (1983); *Part 122 Method for determination of water absorption* (1983); *Part 124 Methods for analysis of hardened concrete* (1988); *Part 125 Methods for mixing and sampling fresh concrete in the laboratory* (1986); *Part 127 Method of verifying the performance of a concrete cube compression machine using the comparative cube test* (1990); *Part 201 Guide to the use of non-destructive methods of test for hardened concrete* (1986); *Part 202 Recommendations for surface hardness testing by rebound hammer* (1986); *Part 203 Recommendations for measurement of velocity of ultrasonic pulses in concrete* (1986); *Part 204 Recommendations on the use of electromagnetic covermeters* (19889; *Part 205 Recommendations for radiography of concrete* (1986); *Part 206 Recommendations for determination of strain in concrete* (1986); *Part 209 Recommendations for the measurement of dynamic modulus of elasticity* (1990); Milton Keynes

32 POWERS, T. C., 'The non-evaporable water content of hardened Portland cement pastes', *ASTM Bull.*, **158**, 68 (1949)

33 PARROTT, L. J., 'Simplified methods of predicting the deformation of structural concrete', *Development Report 3*, Cement and Concrete Association, Slough, pp. 11 (1979)

34 PARROTT, L. J., 'A study of some long-term strains measured in two concrete structures', *RILEM International Symposium on Testing of in-situ Structures*, Vol. 2, Budapest, p. 140 (1977)

35 HARRISON, W. H., 'Durability of concrete in acidic soils and waters', *Concrete*, **21**, 18–24 (1987)

36 BUILDING RESEARCH ESTABLISHMENT, 'Alkali–aggregate reaction in concrete', *Digest 330*, Building Research Establishment, Garston (1988)

37 HOBBS, D. W., *Alkali–silica Reaction in Concrete*, Thomas Telford, London, pp. 184 (1988)

38 INSTITUTION OF STRUCTURAL ENGINEERS (ISE), *Structural Effects of Alkali–Silica Reaction*, ISE, London, pp. 32 (1988)

39 HARRISON, T. A., 'Tables of minimum striking times for soffit and vertical formwork', *CIRIA Report No. 67*, CIRIA, London, pp. 24 (1977)

40 UK CERTIFICATION AUTHORITY FOR REINFORCING STEELS (CARES), *CARES Manual*, CARES, Sevenoaks, Kent (1987)

41 HARRISON, T. A. and DEWAR, J. D., 'Designated mixes—a new concept for the specification and compliance of concrete', *Construction News*, **6091**, pp. 31 (1988)

42 HJORTH, L., 'Development and application of high-density cement-based materials', *Phil. Trans. Roy. Soc., London*, **A310**, 167 (1983)

43 BACHE, H. H., 'The new strong cements: their use in structures', *Physics in Technology*, **19**, 43 (1988)

44 BRITISH STANDARDS INSTITUTION, *BS 5075 Concrete admixtures: Part 1 Accelerating admixtures (1982); Part 2 Determination of resistance to loadings in shear (1986); Part 3 Superplasticity admixtures (1985)*, Milton Keynes

15

Admixtures and Polymers

L Hodgkinson
Cormix Construction Chemicals
Chairman, Technical Committee, Cement Admixtures
Association

Contents

15.1 Preface 15/3

15.2 Air-entraining agents for concrete and mortar 15/3
    15.2.1 History of air entrainment 15/3
    15.2.2 Benefits of air entrainment 15/3
    15.2.3 Mechanism of freeze–thaw attack 15/4
    15.2.4 Mechanism of frost protection 15/4
    15.2.5 Spacing factor and its significance 15/4
    15.2.6 Mechanism of air entrainment 15/5
    15.2.7 Types of air-entraining agents 15/6
    15.2.8 Use of air-entraining agents 15/6
    15.2.9 Effect of cement substitutes 15/7
    15.2.10 Other effects 15/8
    15.2.11 Measurement of air 15/8
    15.2.12 Standard specifications 15/8
    15.2.13 Mortar plasticizers (mortar air entrainers) 15/9

15.3 Water-reducing agents/plasticizers for concrete 15/9
    15.3.1 History of usage 15/9
    15.3.2 Mechanism of concrete plasticizers 15/9
    15.3.3 Chemical types of plasticizer 15/9
    15.3.4 Benefits of plasticizers and water-reducing agents 15/12
    15.3.5 Water-reducing agents with different cements 15/13
    15.3.6 Water-reducing agents with ground-granulated blast-furnace slag 15/13
    15.3.7 Water-reducing agents with pulverized-fuel ash 15/13
    15.3.8 Water-reducing agents with silica fume 15/14
    15.3.9 Standard specifications for water-reducing agents 15/14

15.4 Superplasticizers 15/14
    15.4.1 History of usage 15/14
    15.4.2 Mechanism of superplasticizers 15/14
    15.4.3 Chemical types of superplasticizers 15/15
    15.4.4 Advantages of superplasticizers 15/17
    15.4.5 Standard specification for superplasticizers 15/17

15.5 Retarders 15/18
    15.5.1 Mechanism of retardation 15/18
    15.5.2 Benefits of retardation 15/20
    15.5.3 Chemical types of retarder 15/20
    15.5.4 Standard specification for retarders 15/20

15.6 Accelerators 15/21
    15.6.1 History of accelerators 15/21
    15.6.2 Mechanism of acceleration 15/21
    15.6.3 Benefits of accelerators 15/23
    15.6.4 Chemical types of accelerator 15/23
    15.6.5 Standard specifications for accelerators 15/23
    15.6.6 Sprayed concrete accelerators 15/23
    15.6.7 Mechanism of shotcrete accelerators 15/23

15.7 Corrosion inhibitors 15/24
    15.7.1 Chemical types of corrosion inhibitors 15/24
    15.7.2 Mechanism of corrosion and corrosion inhibitors 15/24
    15.7.3 Benefits of corrosion inhibitors 15/24

15.8 Permeability reducers 15/24
    15.8.1 The nature of the permeability of concrete 15/24
    15.8.2 The theory of permeability reducers 15/26
    15.8.3 Benefits of permeability reducers 15/26
    15.8.4 Standard specification for permeability reducers 15/27

References 15/27

Bibliography 15/28

15.1 Preface

Admixtures and polymers have been incorporated into concretes and mortars, knowingly or unknowingly since ancient times. The most widely documented evidence of this is possibly the practice of Roman engineers to add ox blood to building mortars in order to improve the physical properties of such mortars.

Since those times, the use of admixtures has become universal, particularly in modern societies where the centralized production of large volumes of concrete has enabled both quality and cost to be optimized. In the USA, Japan, West Germany, Australia and Russia, the acceptance is so wide, that virtually all concretes contain an admixture.

The United Kingdom is not typical of modern western Europe, and admixture usage has been slow to gain the degree of acceptance that would have been expected. There are a number of reasons for this, mainly historical in origin. The early admixture industry built up a poor image, based upon products of variable quality, for which exaggerated technical claims were made. The problems of corrosion associated with the uncontrolled use of calcium chloride based admixtures further damaged the reputation of the admixture industry. Finally, the failure of many structures utilizing high alumina cement based concretes caused many engineers to be very wary of any untried materials and the construction industry in the UK became deeply conservative.

It was the emergence of larger and more professional admixture companies, who were able to offer higher quality products, and a higher level of service that enabled the admixture industry to overcome its poor, past performance. Largely through the initiative of such a new and professional industry, national standards were introduced for concrete admixtures during the 1970s which did much to redress the past, and overcome the conservatism which had arisen out of those technical shortcomings.

The formation of the Cement Admixtures Association (CAA) has provided further impetus to creating an improved image of the admixture industry. To this end, the introduction of the CAA Quality Scheme has enabled the UK industry to achieve a deserved credibility.

The growth in the use of admixtures has not resulted solely from the effects of the admixture industry itself. An increased awareness of the technical properties of concrete, combined with an appreciation of the commercial opportunities and the practical limitations of the material, have led to a greater understanding and confidence within the construction industry. Cement replacement materials such as ground granulated blast-furnace slag, pulverized fuel ash and silica fume have all gained acceptance, and the use of admixtures in conjunction with such materials is now widely accepted.

It is the intention of this chapter to summarize the main groups of admixture, describe the individual chemical structures of the more commonly available types, and to attempt to relate these structures to their effects on both plastic and hardened concrete. The main types of admixture covered are air-entraining agents and mortar plasticizers, water-reducing agents and concrete plasticizers, superplasticizers, accelerators, corrosion inhibitors, retarders and permeability reducers. Where applicable, reference is made to the relevant national standard, and a brief interpretation of the requirement of such standards is given.

15.2 Air-entraining agents for concrete and mortar

Air entrainment is the deliberate inclusion of a small quantity of air, in the form of very small individual bubbles, into concrete or mortar. It should not be confused with air entrapment, which normally occurs by accident, when concrete is poorly compacted or when small quantities of air are unable to be vibrated out of a plain concrete.

The prime function and purpose of the deliberate inclusion of air into concrete is to increase the durability of concretes and, in particular, to improve the freeze–thaw durability.

15.2.1 History of air entrainment

The use of air-entraining agents, in modern times, resulted from the accidental inclusion of a material into a cement which was subsequently used for the production of concrete used in a road in the north-east of America in the 1930s. It was observed that some sections of the concrete carriageway exhibited enhanced durability as compared with other sections. An investigation into the phenomenon concluded that small volumes of air had been entrained into the concrete which had shown enhanced durability.[1] These observations led to a controlled study, culminating in the production of the first deliberately air-entrained concrete carriageway in 1939, by the New York Department of Public Works.

15.2.2 Benefits of air entrainment

The ability of small volumes of air, in the form of deliberately entrained microscopic spherical bubbles, to enhance the resistance of concrete to freeze–thaw damage is very obvious (*Figure 15.1*).[2] The effects are so beneficial, and so cost-effective, that most concrete roads, aircraft runways or exposed concrete slabs which are likely to be subjected to freezing and thawing cycles use mixes that include an air-entraining agent specified in their designs.

In addition to the durability benefits, air entrainment has a considerable influence on the rheology of fresh concrete. The minute bubbles of air behave like lubricating spheres, imparting additional cohesion to a concrete. Their size is such that they also improve the overall grading of a concrete and prevent

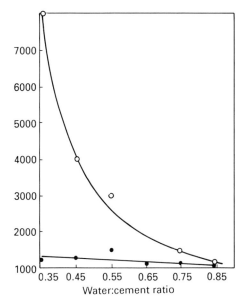

Figure 15.1 The role of air entrainment in reducing frost damage in concrete. Water:cement ratio of concrete moist cured for 14 days versus number of cycles needed to cause 25% loss in weight. O, Air entrained; ●, control, no air

segregation and bleeding. Air-entraining agents, therefore, show considerable benefits when used to improve the quality of concrete produced with poorly graded aggregate, particularly those which are deficient in fine-fines, such as those obtained by sea-dredging. Similarly, air entrainment will prevent the segregation of poorly graded concretes. Air entrainment will thus help to prevent sand runs, bleeding and segregation of concretes.

15.2.3 Mechanism of freeze–thaw attack

Concrete is susceptible to freeze–thaw damage when it is either immature or saturated and is particularly susceptible when both conditions arise. Many failures of slabs can be attributed to early freeze–thaw damage of the immature concrete which manifests itself at a later age.

The mechanism of freeze–thaw attack is very complicated and probably more than one mechanism operates depending on the severity of the frost, the degree of saturation of the concrete and whether deicing salts are used on the concrete. The most easily understood mechanism is probably responsible for most surface-related problems. Surfacewater freezes in the neck of saturated capillaries, causing an increase in volume of about 9%. This causes a very high localized pressure to form in the upper, surface levels of the concrete leading to surface spalling when the stresses cannot be restrained by the concrete.

When deicing salts are used, a different mechanism operates. The action of a deicing chemical has a more damaging effect than frost alone. Freeze–thaw damage does not derive from the formation of ice at all, but from the osmotic pressure which develops as water diffuses and migrates through the gel pores under an induced temperature gradient. The greater the rate and extent of the temperature drop, the greater the moisture movement and induced osmotic pressure within the concrete, and hence the greater the potential for stress-induced failure.

15.2.4 Mechanism of frost protection

The benefit of using an air-entraining agent results from its ability to entrain, within the matrix of a concrete, millions of air voids which can relieve the stress induced by freezing. These air voids are typically 0.05–1.25 mm in diameter.

The air voids deliberately entrained are much larger than any of the capillary pores and tend to block the pores, as well as to increase the paste volume. The air voids remain full of air, even in a saturated concrete. This is achieved by a combination of two effects. First, air voids deliberately entrained by certain neutralized wood resins and soaps tend to have a hydrophobic outer layer (see Section 15.2.6). This hydrophobic layer prevents water ingress except under pressure. Secondly, surface-tension effects also tend to prevent the air voids from becoming saturated with water.

When concrete is subjected to freeze–thaw cycling, rapid moisture movement is accommodated by the large number of micro-air-voids. Water columns present in capillaries are able to discharge into the voids, thereby preventing any stress build up by rapid moisture movements caused by thermal gradients.

15.2.5 Spacing factor and its significance

The effectiveness of entrained air in preventing frost damage depends on both the quantity and distribution of air voids within the concrete paste, because each air void can have only a localized effect. The maximum distance of any point in the cement paste from the periphery of an air void is called the spacing factor. The effects of this bubble-spacing factor upon the durability of entrained air indicate, not surprisingly, that the spacing factor required to achieve a satisfactory durability

is very much dependent upon the freezing rate to which the concrete is subjected.[3] The relationship between the frost durability and air-void-spacing factor at two rates of freezing is shown in *Figure 15.2*. A spacing factor of less than 0.25 mm (250 μm) is generally regarded as desirable for conferring acceptable freeze–thaw protection. However, it has been demonstrated that a spacing factor of 250 μm is only necessary when the freezing rate exceeds 11°C h^{-1}. For temperature drops of 6°C h^{-1}, the critical spacing factor is 450 μm, and is probably about 300 μm for temperature drops of 8°C h^{-1}. In view of these values, a requirement for 250 μm is probably far too stringent a requirement for concrete in a climate such as that of the UK. The spacing factor is difficult to measure and the accuracy of its measurement, and the effects that site practice have on its variability may make its adoption as a specifiable requirement for concrete somewhat dubious in value.

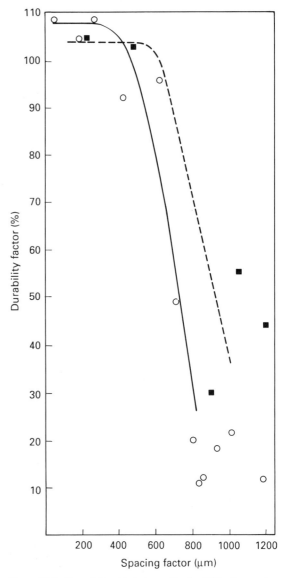

Figure 15.2 The relationship between the durability of concrete, the spacing factor and the rate of freezing: ■, 4°C h^{-1}; ○, 6°C h^{-1}

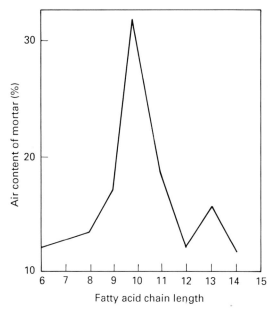

Figure 15.3 The relationship between the chain length of linear fatty acid soaps and their ability to entrain air

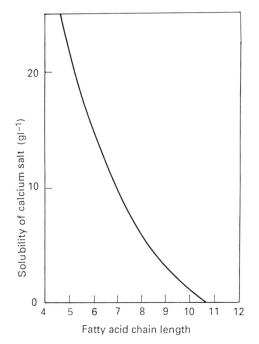

Figure 15.4 The relationship between the chain length of linear fatty acid soaps and the solubility (at 20°C) of their calcium salts

15.2.6 Mechanism of air entrainment

There are numerous types of air-entraining agent and, depending on which type is used, the mechanism will vary according to the molecular structure. The mechanism of air entrainment of fatty acid soaps is well understood and is probably typical of anionic air-entraining agents. *Figures 15.3* and *15.4* show how the air-entraining ability of a fatty acid soap is related to the limited solubility of its calcium salt.[4] When an air-entraining

agent is added to concrete it is immediately converted to its calcium salt. Because the molecules are surface active, having a hydrophobic (water hating) backbone and hydrophylic (water loving) head they align themselves at the air–water interphase as shown in *Figure 15.5*. This arrangement dramatically reduces the surface tension and, when mixing occurs, air entrainment results from the mechanical action. The bubbles formed are then stabilized by a second layer of molecules derived from insoluble calcium salts which have been distributed throughout the water phase.

It is reasoned that short-chain fatty acids of chain length C_8 and less do not exhibit sufficient surface activity, and the calcium soaps of long-chain fatty acids are too insoluble. Only sodium decanoate has both surface activity and a calcium salt with limited solubility. Calcium abietate (formed by neutralized wood-resin type air-entraining agent when contacted with cement or lime) has an identical limited solubility to calcium decanoate and the mechanism is probably similar to that of the linear fatty acids.

The insoluble skin is quite important in stabilizing the system, and may well contribute to the ability to prevent freeze–thaw damage to concrete. There is some evidence to suggest that particular air-entraining agents do not give the expected

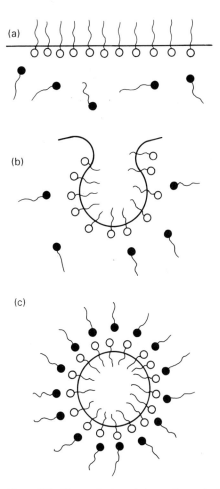

Figure 15.5 The mechanism of air entrainment by fatty acid soaps. (a) Water-soluble surfactant molecules lower surface tension; (b) mechanical agitation causes bubble formation; (c) bubbles stabilize by skin of insoluble calcium salt

durability benefits, and it has been suggested that the air voids have no hydrophobic protection.[5] In concrete, air bubbles may well be stabilized by interaction with cement grains and also with aggregate surfaces (*Figure 15.6*).[6]

15.2.7 Types of air-entraining agents

The most widely used air-entraining agent is derived from the alkali salt of wood resin. Chemically the material is sodium abietate (*Figure 15.7*). These resins are extracted from pinewood and neutralized. They are characterized by their very dark yellow colour and smell of pine. The best-known example is Vinsol resin which has a long history of usage.

Sodium abietate is an anionic surfactant, characterized by a negative charge on the hydrophylic part of the molecule. Anionic surfactants are very commonly used, and there are numerous types sold commercially. Typical of anionic types are sodium dodecyl benzene sulphonate (*Figure 8*) and sodium decanoate (*Figure 15.9*).

Cationic surfactants are not commonly used, but may have specialist applications. Cationic surfactants are commonly used to stabilize bithumen emulsions and could be used in bithumen cementitious composites such as Hardicrete. An example is cetyl trimethyl ammonium bromide (CTAB) (*Figure 15.10*); note the positive charge on the hydrophylic head of this compound.

Non-ionic surfactants have no charge at all and entrain air by a unique mechanism. They are usually derived from organic alcohols or phenols condensed with ethylene oxide units. A typical example is nonylphenol 6E0 (*Figure 15.11*). These materials are able to reduce the surface tension of water by attracting water molecules at each ether linkage in the polyether chain. This chain is hydrophylic whilst the nonylphenol is hydrophobic.

15.2.8 Use of air-entraining agents

To achieve the optimum benefits of freeze–thaw durability, it is necessary to entrain the correct level of air into the cement paste. As the maximum aggregate size of a concrete increases, then its paste volume decreases. It is for this reason that the level of air entrainment required varies depending on the size of the aggregates. The recommended air contents for UK and USA requirements are summarized in *Table 15.1*.

In theory, for a given mix design, it should be possible to conduct a trial mix to determine the dosage level of an air-entraining agent required to give the correct level of air, and then, provided no change was made, the level of air would always be correct. Unfortunately, air entrainment responds to any variability in the composition of a concrete mix, or to any variability in its production or delivery. Many variables have been identified and the magnitude of these variations have been studied.[9] As a guide, the major likely causes of the change in air content are summarized in *Table 15.2*.[10]

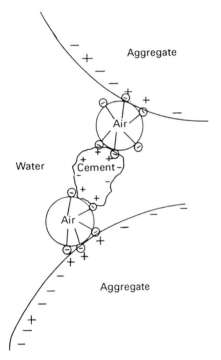

Figure 15.6 Mechanism for the stabilization of air bubbles in concrete

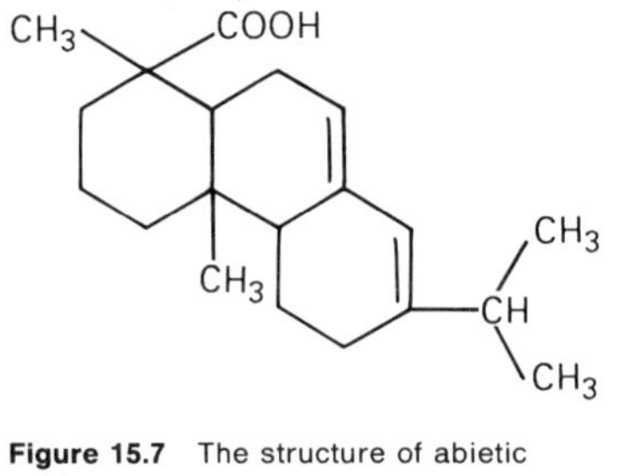

Figure 15.7 The structure of abietic acid

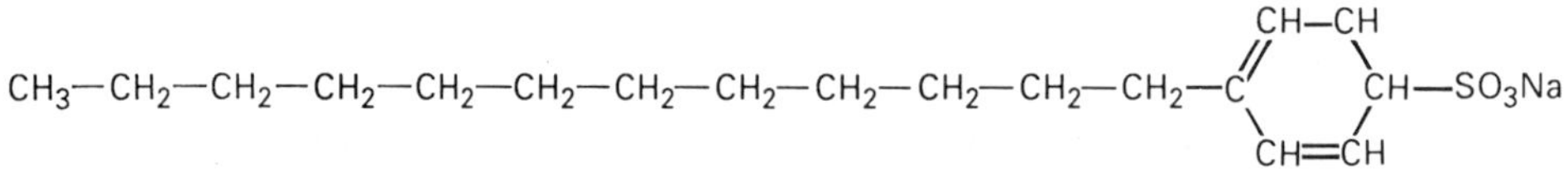

Figure 15.8 The structure of sodium dodecyl benzene sulphonate

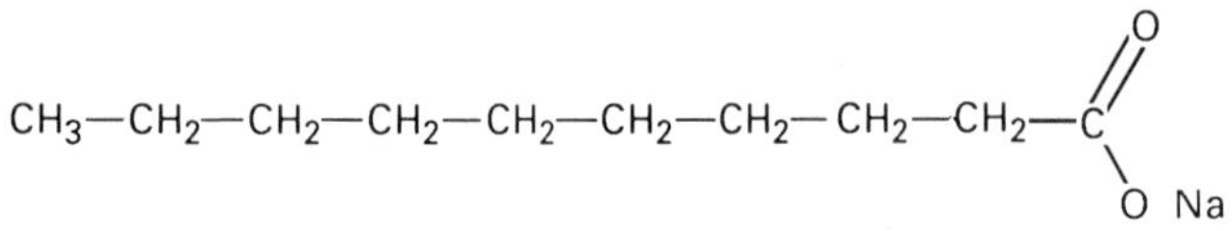

Figure 15.9 The structure of sodium decanoate

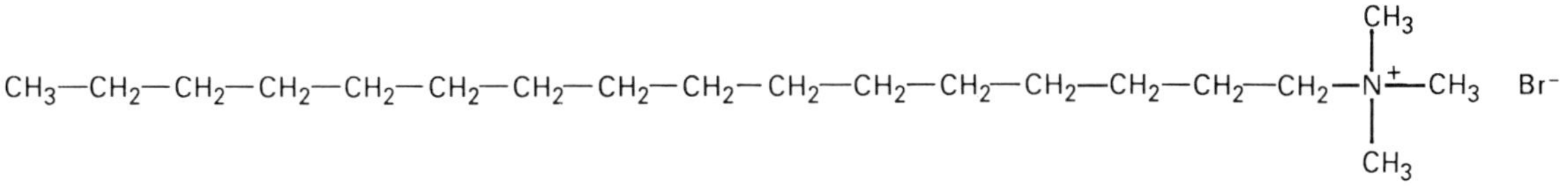

$$CH_3-CH_2-CH_2-CH_2-CH_2-CH_2-CH_2-CH_2-CH_2-CH_2-CH_2-CH_2-CH_2-CH_2-CH_2-CH_2-\overset{\overset{\displaystyle CH_3}{|}}{\underset{\underset{\displaystyle CH_3}{|}}{N^{\pm}}}-CH_3 \quad Br^-$$

Figure 15.10 The structure of cetyl trimethyl ammonium bromide

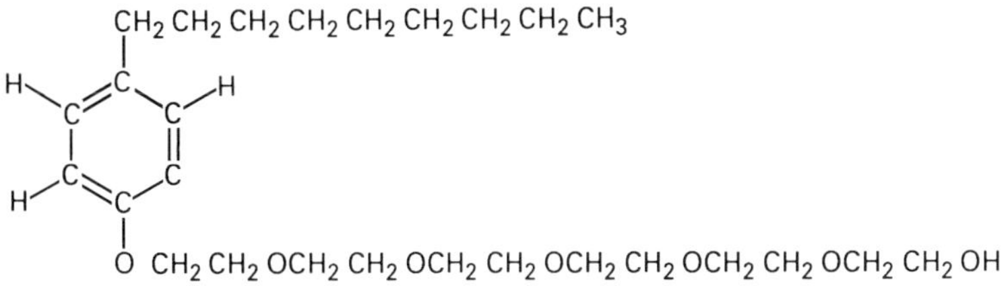

Figure 15.11 The structure of nonylphenol 6EO

15.2.9 Effect of cement substitutes

15.2.9.1 Ground-granulated blast-furnace slag

In normal circumstances, ground-granulated slag has a minimal effect on the level of air entrained, provided the fineness of the slag is controlled. There have been occasions where the activity of a slag has been adjusted by finer grinding and, in these

circumstances, the fine slag has caused an increase in air content. When pumped into silos, slag can dramatically increase in temperature due to friction and this effect has been known to cause excessive air entrainment. This is an odd effect, as in normal circumstances, high concrete temperatures would be expected to lead to a reduction in air content.

15.2.9.2 Pulverized fuel ash

The use of air-entraining agents in the presence of UK-produced pulverized fuel ashes, invariably requires the use of higher levels of air-entraining agent than expected. It is now widely accepted that the major significant factor involved in air-entraining pulverized fuel ash concretes is related to the loss on ignition of the pulverized fuel ash.[11]

Two major effects are related to the loss on ignition of the ash. First, the level of the carbon has a major effect on the dosage of air-entraining agent required. In general, a starting

Table 15.1 USA[8] and UK[7] recommended levels of air entrainment

Nominal maximum aggregate size (mm)	Average air content (%)	
	UK	*USA*
40	4.0	5.5
20	5.0	6.0
10	7.0	7.5

Table 15.2 Factors that influence the air content of concrete[a]

Increasing air content	Decreasing air content	Example change	Estimated effect (target 5% air content)
Lower temperature	Higher temperature	10–20°C	Reduction 1–1.25%
Higher slump	Lower slump	50–100 mm	Increase of 1%
Sand grading coarser	Sand grading finer	Fine to medium, or medium to coarse	Increase of <0.5%
Sand content increased	Sand content decreased	35–45%	Increase 1–1.5%
Decrease in sand fraction passing 150 μm	Increase in sand fraction passing 150 μm	+50 kg m^{-3}	Reduction of 0.5%
Decrease in cement content inclusive of sand-content adjustment	Increase in cement content inclusive of sand-content adjustment	+50 kg m^{-3}	Reduction of 0.5%
—	Inclusion of organic impurities	Inclusion	Positive and negative effects reported
—	Inclusion of PFA	Inclusion	Significant reduction linked to carbon in ash
—	Increase in hardness of water	Increased hardness	Reduction
Increase in mixing efficiency	Decrease in mixing efficiency	Better mixing efficiency	Increase linked to dispersion of admixture
Positive dispensing tolerance	Negative dispensing tolerance	±5%	±0.25%
—	Prolonged agitation	1 h	Reduction of 0–0.25%
		2 h	Reduction of 1%

[a] The values given are indicative only. The effects should not be treated cumulatively since they are not necessarily independent.

dosage is about twice that of a plain ordinary Portland cement concrete. If the loss on ignition changes dramatically, then the level of air will also change. Thus, if the loss on ignition of an ash cannot be controlled, then it is difficult to control an air-entrained concrete produced from it. Secondly the loss on ignition also has a destabilizing effect on the air. The correct level of air is obtained immediately when the concrete is produced, so by the time the concrete is delivered to site, the level of air may have reduced dramatically. It appears that wood-resin type air-entraining agents are particularly susceptible to this problem. On-site batching or dosing would undoubtedly remove much of the problem of air loss. This could explain why some contractors have managed quite nicely, whilst others have had seemingly unsurmountable problems.

Fortunately, there are now appearing novel air-entraining agents which have been designed specifically to combat these problems.[12] These materials have polar compounds deliberately incorporated into their formulations which are preferentially adsorbed onto the active sites of the carbon in the pulverized fuel ash. The polar compounds satisfy the demands of the carbon, leaving the surfactant to function as normal.

It should be noted that pulverized fuel ashes produced in countries other than the UK are derived from different coals and may have quite different effects. Ashes in the USA, for example, may be derived from brown coal or lignite, and the loss of ignition of these ashes may actually assist in air entrainment.

15.2.9.3 Condensed silica fume

Because of the very fine nature of silica fume, the dosage rate of air-entraining agents invariably has to be increased when using this material.

15.2.10 Other effects

As mentioned previously, air entrainment improves the cohesion of poorly graded concrete. However, unless changes are made, normal concretes can be made too cohesive, can become sticky and surface blemishes in the form of 'blow holes' or 'pin holes' may result. It is normal practice to reduce the fines content of air-entrained concrete by 5%. For rich mixes containing large quantities of total fines (including cement), larger reductions in fines need to be made.

The presence of air normally causes a loss in strength. As a rough approximation, every 1% of air included causes a corresponding loss in strength of 5%.[13] It should be noted, that most of the quoted data relating to the strength of concretes assumes full and complete compaction. Incomplete compaction and hence the presence of voids will reduce strength. This explains why the strength of low workability, poorly graded mixes is actually improved by air entrainment. The air content increases but the voids content is dramatically reduced. Air entrainment is the deliberate inclusion of microscopic voids and normally causes strength loss as compaction is normally assumed to be close to the theoretical value. When studied in more detail, the effects are complicated (*Table 15.3*).[14] In

Table 15.3 The effect of air entrainment on concrete strengths

Cement content (kg m^{-3})	Change in flexural strength (%)	Change in compressive strength (%)
225	+2	+5
310	−13	−19
390	−11	−21

general, where harsh or poorly graded aggregates are used, or when low cement contents are used, then the strength losses are minimal. On the other hand, where the cement content is high and the anticipated strength is high, then the strength losses are significant, and may pose problems if not anticipated.

15.2.11 Measurement of air

There are three basic methods for measuring the air content of concrete: the pressure method, the volumetric method and the gravimetric method.

15.2.11.1 Pressure method

The pressure method is described in BS 1881: Part 106: 1983,[15] and ASTM C231-82.[16] Both forms of the method rely on the principle of Boyle's law by measuring the drop in water level over a specified sample of air-entrained concrete when it is compressed to a specified pressure.

15.2.11.2 Volumetric method

The volumetric method is described in ASTM C173-78[17] and consists of measuring the drop in the water level when air is detrained from a small sample of concrete.

15.2.11.3 Gravimetric method

The gravimetric method is described in ASTM C138-81[18] and consists of comparing an accurately determined plastic density of a concrete with its theoretical density and calculating the air content. This method is often used in the laboratory as the information is already available for the calculation of the yield of a concrete mix.

15.2.12 Standard specifications

BS 5075: Part 2: 1982[19] is the British Standard specification for air-entraining agents. The standard covers three basic areas of compliance. First, it covers admixture uniformity which relates to the physical properties of the admixture with respect to solids content, pH, colour, etc. Secondly, it covers the ability of the air-entraining agent to entrain air reproducibly in concrete, and examines side-effects such as delay of set, air stability, strength loss and density reduction. Thirdly, it specifies a freezing–thawing cycle based on a 50-cycle test conducted in a domestic chest freezer. Typical results are illustrated in *Figure 15.12*. Dilations in excess of 0.005% after 50 cycles are deemed to indicate that the air entrained does not confer sufficient freeze–thaw durability. When such a test is completed using good quality granite aggregates, plain concrete containing no air-entraining agent disintegrates well before the test has been completed.

In the USA, ASTM C260-77[20] standard specification for air-entraining admixtures for concrete includes uniformity tests, but the performance tests are made relative to a reference air-entraining admixture derived from neutralized Vinsol resin. The performance tests include bleeding and flexural strength in addition to those in the British Standard. The freezing and thawing durability tests are more severe and far more expensive to carry out than those in the UK test.

ASTM C666-80[21] includes descriptions of two test methods. One procedure specifies a rapid freezing and thawing cycle in water; the alternative method specifies freezing in air and thawing in water. The test duration is 300 cycles or until the relative dynamic modulus of elasticity drops to 60% of the initial value.

Neither the British nor the American standard specify a spacing factor as a criterion for acceptance. It is likely, however,

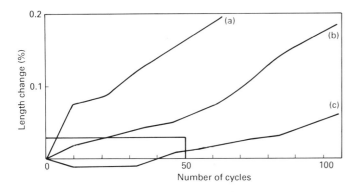

Figure 15.12 The response of concretes to BS 5075: Part 2[19] freeze–thaw cycling (24-h cycle): (a) no air entrainment; (b) poor air entrainment; (c) good air entrainment

that a spacing factor will be incorporated into any future European Standard.

In addition to the national standard, there is a surface freeze–thaw test developed by RILEM committee 4-C DC.[22] This can be carried out with or without the use of a deicing chemical. In the test, which uses deicing solution, the surface of the specimen is subjected to freezing and thawing whilst ponded with a 3% solution of a deicing chemical. The effects are assessed by measurement of surface weight loss, or more usually by the percentage area spalled. This is a very severe test and the results are very much related to the permeability and density of the test specimen. For this reason, results from the RILEM test do not correlate well with either the BS 5075: Part 2 or ASTM C666-80 results.

15.2.13 Mortar plasticizers (mortar air entrainers)

Mortar plasticizers, unlike concrete plasticizers, are air-entraining agents. They are of the same generic type as described for use in concrete, except that they are used at a higher dosage in order to entrain higher levels of air into mortar. Their prime function is to improve the plasticity and rheology of building mortars. These are the oldest admixtures; mortar plasticizer in the form of ox blood was used by the ancient Romans. In addition to the benefits conferred on the plastic mortar there is also the benefit of enhanced freeze–thaw durability and enhanced durability in the presence of sulphate ions.

Traditional mortar plasticizers are based on dilute solutions of neutralized wood resin, but with the increase in the use of ready-to-use retarded mortars, a greater emphasis has been placed on the air stability of mortar plasticizers for use in retarded mortars and specialist products have emerged with enhanced air retention.

The performance of mortar plasticizers is encompassed by BS 4887: Part 1: 1986.[23] This standard was revised mainly because of the development of the retarded mortar admixtures, and mortar retarders are now covered specifically in BS 4887: Part 2: 1986.[24]

The air content of mortars is measured either by density or by the pressure method. Small mortar air meters are now commercially available which can measure air contents of up to 30%. Because the air content of mortar is relatively high as compared with concrete, the density method is quite accurate provided that the composition of the mortar is known.

15.3 Water-reducing agents/plasticizers for concrete

Concrete plasticizers are a group of materials which, when added to concrete in small dosages, are able to impart significant increases in workability. Alternatively, the same compounds can be added to concrete, and, in order to maintain a constant workability, a water reduction can be made. Concrete plasticizers should not be confused with mortar plasticizers which are chemically dissimilar and are covered in a separate section.

15.3.1 History of usage

The earliest mention of the use of small quantities of organic materials to increase the fluidity of cementitious systems was in the USA in the early 1930s.[25] During the 1930s and 1940s, numerous references were made to the use of lignosulphate type materials.[26,27] During the 1950s, the use of hydroxy compounds became common as these materials became commercially available. At the present time, numerous chemicals are now used to give specific properties to concrete and these are discussed below.

15.3.2 Mechanism of concrete plasticizers

When cement clinker is ground to a fine powder, steel balls are used to physically smash the large clinker particles into smaller broken fragments. Cement grains, therefore, are extremely angular and not of a shape conducive to good contact with water. In addition, when cement grains make contact with water they have a tendency to attract one another to form flocs or agglomerates. These agglomerates are badly shaped and water has great difficulty in uniformly contacting the cement and imparting sufficient workability to produce a plastic system. The addition of a concrete plasticizer has a significant, beneficial effect on the rheology of such a cement paste containing agglomerates. Concrete plasticizers have varying structures, but all have in common the same functional chemical groups which chemically adsorb onto the cement.

Water-reducing agents chemically bond to surface calcium or aluminium ions of the cement grains. They achieve this by bonding through their carboxyl, sulphonate or hydroxy functional groups which are attached to the backbone of the organic compound. Once bonded to the surface, the presence of free polar functional groups elsewhere on the organic molecule attracts water molecules and the agent becomes solvated, with the formation of a sheath of associated water molecules. Some typical likely mechanisms are illustrated in *Figure 15.13*. The net result is a breaking up of the agglomerates into a dispersion (*Figure 15.14*) which is accompanied by a large increase in workability of the system (*Figure 15.15*).

15.3.3 Chemical types of plasticizer

As previously mentioned, all plasticizers have certain functional groups in common, and their modes of action are identical.

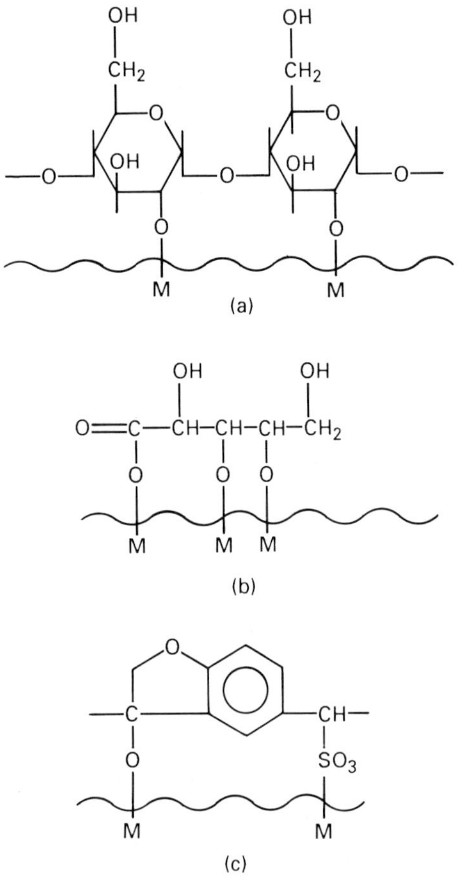

OH   OH
|
CH₂   CH₂

(a)

OH   OH
|
O=C—CH–CH–CH–CH₂

(b)

(c)

Figure 15.13 The adsorption of plasticizer molecules onto a cement surface. (a) Hydroxylated polymer; (b) hydroxy carboxylic acid; (c) lignosulphonate

However, the properties of each plasticizer are highly dependent upon the chemical structure and relative number and type of each functional group present. The major categories of such materials are discussed individually below.

15.3.3.1 Lignosulphonate

All lignosulphonates are derived from naturally occurring lignin. Lignin is a complex material which combines with cellulose fibres to form wood. To manufacture paper, it is necessary to extract the cellulose fibres, and to do this the lignin must be digested. Sodium sulphite or metabisulphite is used to dissolve out the lignin which is sulphonated to form soluble lignosulphonate. The dark solution is neutralized, fermented to remove hexose sugars and evaporated to form a concentrated solution commonly called sulphite lye. The end-product will vary depending on the original wood type, the pulping process, the neutralizing alkali, and the degree of fermentation.[28]

The structure of the lignosulphonate molecules is extremely complicated and in solution it forms a spherical macromolecular structure, with active carboxyl, sulphonate and phenolic hydroxyl groups at its surface. The simplest repeating unit is a substituted phenyl propane unit[29] which is illustrated in *Table 15.16*. During the fermentation process, hexose sugars are destroyed, but the pentose sugars remain. Thus most lignosulphonates contain residual sugars which cause retardation of set. Sodium and calcium lignosulphonate plasticizers are still

the most widely used products and their use can be traced back to the 1940s.

15.3.3.2 Hydroxylated polymers

The hydroxylated polymers are derived from naturally occurring chemicals. They are normally produced by partial hydrolysis of corn or potato starch to form lower molecular weight polyglycosides.[30] The chemical structure of these polymers is illustrated in *Figure 15.17*. These materials contain only aliphatic hydroxyl groups and are very efficient water-reducing agents. They do cause some retardation and for this reason they are normally used in combination with other raw materials.

15.3.3.3 Hydroxy carboxylic acids

Hydroxy carboxylic acids materials contain carboxylic acid groups and aliphatic hydroxyl groups. In general, they are normally much smaller molecules than either lignosulphonate or hydroxylated polymers, and are usually derived from simple sugars called monosaccharides. These materials are used mainly as the raw materials for retarding plasticizers.

The most commonly used compounds for incorporation into plasticizer formulations are salts of gluconic acid or heptonic acid. The structures of these two compounds are illustrated in *Figure 15.18*. Gluconic acid is manufactured either from cellulose by hydrolysis, or, more commonly, from glucose. Sodium gluconate can be obtained in a very refined form which makes it a very easily controlled and very predictable retarding plasticizer. Sodium heptonate is also derived from glucose, but its carbon backbone is longer by one carbon atom. Sodium heptonate is also a widely used material.

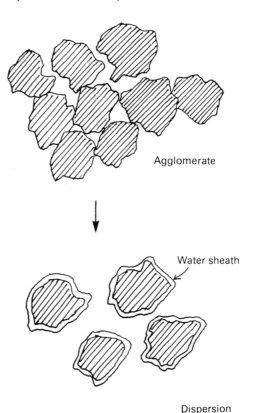

Agglomerate

Water sheath

Dispersion

Figure 15.14 Deflocculation of cement grains

15.3.3.4 Acrylic acid/acrylic ester copolymers

These custom built copolymers were a major development of the early 1980s.[31] Water-soluble polymers have been produced using optimum molar proportions of acrylic acid and hydroxypropylmethacrylic acid (*Figure 15.19*). Because they are synthetically produced, the properties of these compounds can be very precisely controlled. The main advantage of these materials is related to extended workability, but they can cause retardation, and for this reason are normally used in conjunction with other raw materials.

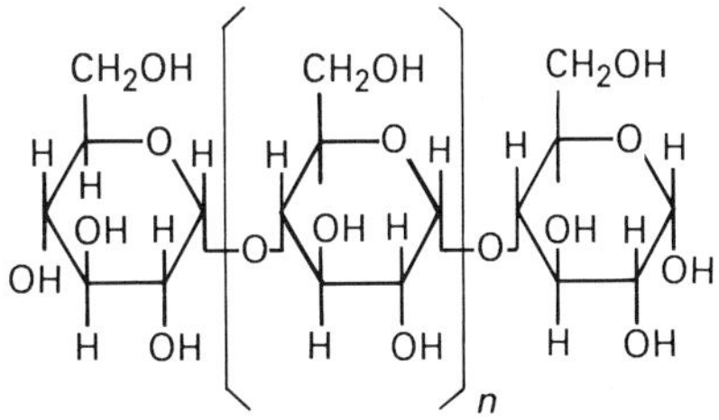

Figure 15.17 The simplified structure of polyglycoside based plasticizer

(a)

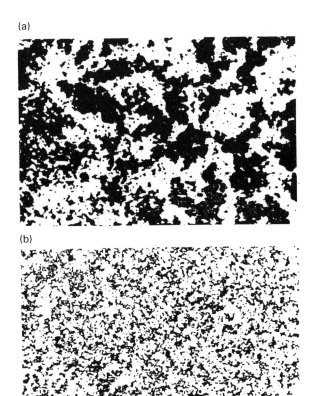

(b)

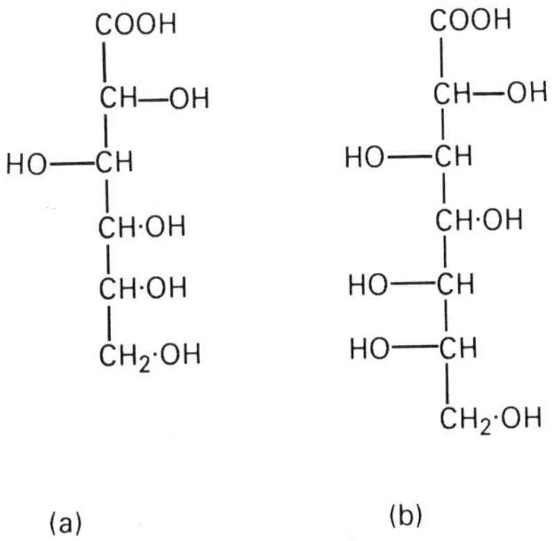

Figure 15.18 The structure of hydroxy carboxylic acid based plasticizers. (a) Gluconic acid; (b) heptonic acid

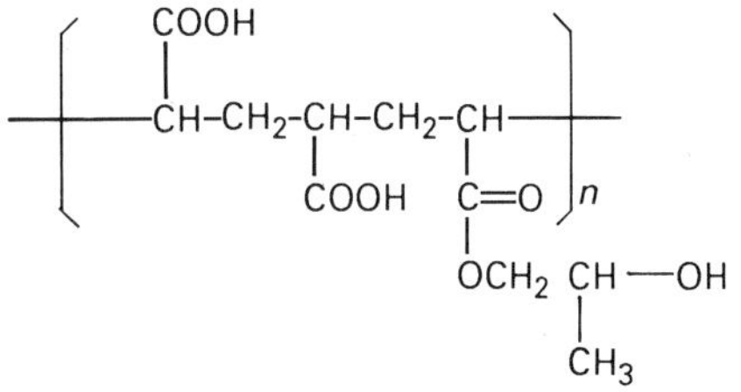

Figure 15.15 Cement paste before (a) and after (b) the addition of plasticizer. (a) Agglomerated cement grains; (b) dispersed cement grains

Figure 5.19 The simplified structure of hydroxylpropylmethacrylate/acrylic acid copolymer

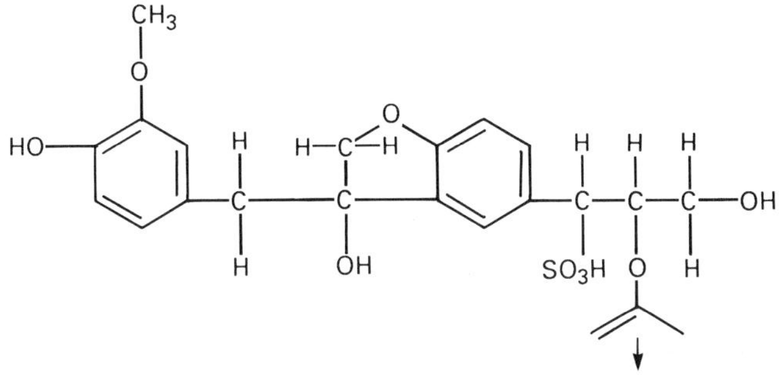

Figure 15.16 The simplified structure of the lignosulphonate molecule

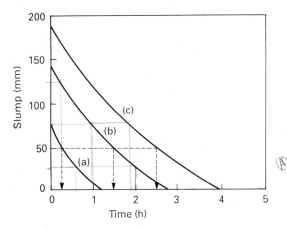

Figure 15.20 The principle of workability extension using a concrete plasticizer. (a) Control concrete, no admixture; (b) single dose of lignosulphonate plasticizer; (c) double dose of lignosulphonate plasticizer

15.3.4 Benefits of plasticizers and water-reducing agents

15.3.4.1 Workability increase

The addition of a plasticizer to a concrete mix will result in a large increase in workability. Most concretes are designed for strength and normally have rigid constraints on water:cement ratio, and additional water cannot, therefore, be used to increase the workability. More water would reduce strength, permeability and, consequently, durability. The use of a plasticizer results in a higher workability, but without any change in the water:cement ratio and thus the strength and durability of the concrete are preserved.

15.3.4.2 Workability extension

Concrete is a dynamic material, and from the moment it is batched, it begins to lose workability by hydration processes. Unfortunately, only a small amount of hydration is required to produce a large loss of workability. The most successful way of achieving a reasonable working concrete for a considerable period of time after batching, is to batch the initial concrete to a high initial workability using a concrete plasticizer. This principal is illustrated in *Figure 15.20*.

If the concrete in the quoted example has a specified workability of 50 mm slump, then it can be handled only for 15 min. With the addition of a concrete plasticizer, the same concrete can be delivered/handled for 90 min. A double dosage of plasticizer would enable the life of the concrete to be extended by 2.5 h.

15.3.4.3 Strength increase

If a plasticizer/water reducer is used in a concrete mix and the water content is reduced to retain the original workability, then the concrete mix attains a lower water:cement ratio. This mix, having a similar cement content to a control mix which contains no admixture, will develop greater strength than the control mix (*Figure 15.21*).

For example, mix (a) in *Figure 15.21* with a water:cement ratio of 0.55 and a workability of 75 mm slump, will achieve a strength of about 35 N mm^{-2} after 14 days. The same concrete, but containing a water-reducing agent, again batched at a workability of 75 mm slump, will now have a lower water:cement ratio of 0.50 and will achieve a strength of about

40 N mm^{-2} at 14 days. The use of a retarding plasticizer will delay the initial strength gain, but the strength will eventually exceed that of the other concretes and reach about 42 N mm^{-2} at 14 days. Provided that retarded concretes are correctly cured, they will normally produce higher ultimate strengths than normal concretes. The reason for this phenomenon is that, with retarded concretes, the hydration process is far more ordered, than with non-retarded concretes.

15.3.4.4 Cement reduction

For a given set of aggregates, cement type and at a constant workability, there is a relationship between strength and cement content. Most ready-mixed concrete producers use such a relationship to supply strength-designed mixes. If a plasticizer is incorporated into the same set of mixes and the workability maintained, then a similar relationship can be derived (*Figure 15.22*). It can be seen from *Figure 15.22* that when using a plasticizer a lower cement content can be used to achieve a given grade of concrete. Note that the curve for the control concrete tends to flatten at the higher cement content end of the graph. This is because cement becomes less efficient and less able to fully hydrate as the cement content exceeds 450 kg m^{-3}. Note that the curve for the plasticized mix is steeper at the high cement content end. This is particularly true of hydroxy carboxylic acid type plasticizers which are very efficient and can be used to great advantage when producing high strength concretes. This same effect can be very useful when constraints on cement content caused by total alkali considerations preclude the use of high cement contents to achieve a high target strength.

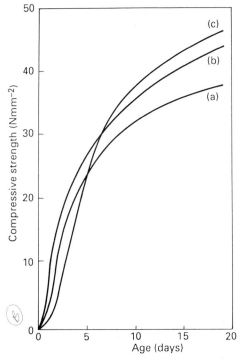

Figure 15.21 Compressive strength gain (at constant workability) using water-reducing agents. (a) Control concrete, water:cement = 0.55; (b) plasticized/water-reduced concrete, water:cement = 0.50; (c) water-reduced/retarded concrete, water:cement = 0.50

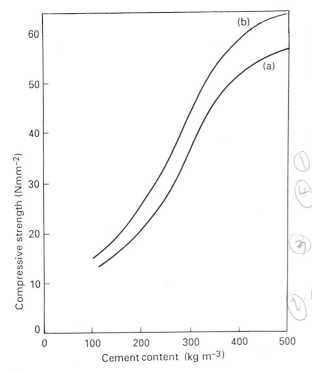

Figure 15.22 Cement content related to the compressive strength for plain and plasticized mixes. (a) Control concrete, no admixture; (b) water-reduced concrete

15.3.4.5 Retardation of set

Retarding plasticizers are very often used to delay the set of concretes, particularly where large pours are involved. This subject will be dealt with in more detail in Section 15.5.

15.3.5 Water-reducing agents with different cements

With cement hydrates, the tricalcium aluminate phase (C_3A) must be controlled by the addition of gypsum. When an admixture is used, the admixture is also preferentially adsorbed onto the tricalcium aluminate phase. Thus the level of C_3A in a cement is a very important factor in its interaction with admixtures. For this reason, sulphate resistant cements, which have a deliberately low $(CaO)_3Al_2O_3$ (C_3A) content, are plasticized to a greater degree than are ordinary Portland cements. For the same reason, sulphate resistant cements tend to be retarded to a greater degree, as more of the admixture is then adsorbed onto the strength developing phase (i.e. the tricalcium silicate).

A study of the variation of admixture performance with a large range of cements available in the UK showed a reassuring uniformity of response to admixture.[32]

15.3.6 Water-reducing agents with ground-granulated blast-furnace slag

Ground-granulated blast-furnace slag is hard and angular and physically quite similar to ordinary Portland cement. For these reasons, it deflocculates well in the presence of water-reducing agents. Evaluation of admixture combination in the presence of UK-derived ground-granulated blast-furnace slags indicates a favourable response to water-reducing admixture.[33,34] This effect is illustrated in *Figure 15.23*.

However, caution must be taken when using admixtures in concretes containing large proportions of slag. The admixture dosage may well have to be retarded, as the early strength of slag concretes is lower than that of an equivalent grade using only ordinary Portland cement. This is particularly important in cold weather as long delays in set often leads to bleeding of slag concretes, with the possibility of plastic settlement cracking or unseen water lenses forming under reinforcement, leading to bond loss.

15.3.7 Water-reducing agents with pulverized-fuel ash

Unlike ordinary Portland cement and ground-granulated blast-furnace slag, pulverized-fuel ashes are perfectly spherical in form and are thus ideally shaped for inclusion into concretes. It is for this reason that pulverized-fuel ash always improves the cohesion of a concrete and will normally reduce bleeding of concretes.

Pulverized-fuel ash cannot replace cement on a one-to-one weight-to-weight basis because its cementitious activity is not as great as ordinary Portland cement. Water-reducing admixtures are often used to boost both the early strength and the characteristic strength of pulverized-fuel ash concretes. Pulverized-fuel ash does not contribute chemically to early strength, because all its activity is latent pozzolanic in nature and derives from the later reaction with the lime released by the tricalcium silicate reaction. Water-reducing admixtures are useful in compensating for this lower early strength. The evaluation of admixtures in the presence of UK-derived

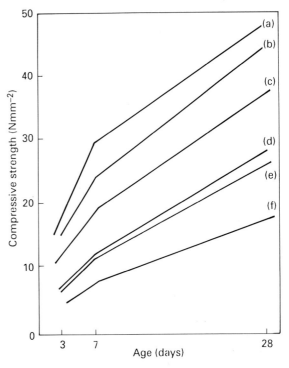

Figure 15.23 The strength gain of mixes containing 40% ground-granulated blast-furnace slag, 60% ordinary Portland cement, and plasticizing admixtures: (a) 300 grade, hydroxy carboxylic acid; (b) 300 grade, lignosulphonate; (c) 300 grade, control; (d) 200 grade, hydroxy carboxylic acid; (e) 200 grade, lignosulphonate; (f) 200 grade, control

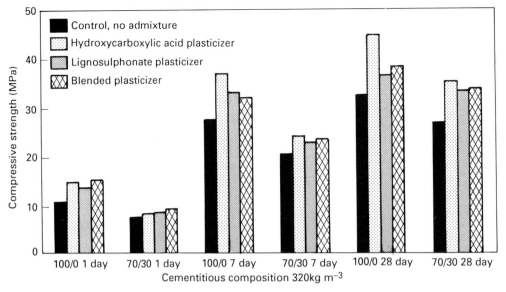

Figure 15.24 The strength gain of mixes containing pulverized fuel ash with plasticizing admixtures: all concretes to 50-mm slump

pulverized-fuel ashes complying with the requirements of BS 3892: Part 1: 1982[35] has shown a favourable response (see *Figure 15.24*).[36]

15.3.8 Water-reducing agents with silica fume

Silica fume is composed of extremely small glassy, spherical particles of silicon dioxide (SiO_2), each having a size several orders of magnitude smaller than cement particles. For this reason, the water demand of silica fume can be excessive, but its cementing properties are estimated as being between four and five times that of cement. Silica fume is normally supplied in a slurry form, and superplasticizing admixtures are normally used to stabilize such slurries. It is inadvisable to use retarding water-reducing admixtures in concretes containing fume which itself contains an admixture. Advice should be sought from suppliers regarding the nature of silica fume slurry. In most cases, a superplasticizer is used to reduce greatly the water demand of silica fume concretes. In this manner, the strength gain from silica fume concretes can be quite dramatic.

15.3.9 Standard specifications for water-reducing agents

BS 5075: Part 1: 1982[37] is the British Standard specification for accelerating admixtures, retarding admixtures and water-reducing admixtures. The standard covers three basic areas of compliance. First, it covers admixture uniformity which relates to the physical properties of the admixtures. The performance criteria first assess the ability of the admixture to increase the workability of a test mix. Plasticizing admixtures must demonstrate the ability to increase the workability, by at least 0.03, as measured by the compacting factor. Secondly, the performance criteria assess the ability of the admixture to reduce the water content, at a fixed workability and demonstrate an increase in strength. A mandatory 8% water reduction is specified in the standard, so as to comply with the hardened strength tests which take 28 days to complete. The requirements of BS 5075: Part 1: 1982 are summarized in *Table 15.4*.

The American standard ASTM C494[38] is similar to the British Standard in many ways. The test mix is similar, but the standard only requires a minimum 5% water reduction. There is no test mix described specifically for measuring workability increase. ASTM C494 covers all plasticizers under categories A, B, C, D and E, and also covers superplasticizers under types F and G; these are discussed in Section 15.4.

15.4 Superplasticizers

Superplasticizers are very similar to normal plasticizers in many respects, but differ mainly in that they may be added at a relatively high dosage without causing adverse side-effects. This effect is illustrated diagrammatically, in *Figures 15.25–15.27*, where a superplasticizing admixture is compared with a lignosulphonate type plasticizer. It should be noted that at low dosage levels conventional plasticizers are, in fact, more efficient than superplasticizers. It is the ability to produce dramatic effects at a relatively high dosage level which distinguishes them from normal water-reducing admixtures.

15.4.1 History of usage

Some of the first recorded additions of organic materials to concrete used similar raw materials to those used in modern superplasticizers. However, raw materials have improved and it was not until the 1960s that the use of superplasticized concrete appeared in Japan. In Europe, Germany has taken the lead in the use of superplasticized concrete. In the UK, its use has grown slowly, and although superplasticizers are now widely used, it is usually only for specialist applications.

15.4.2 Mechanism of superplasticizers

The mechanism by which superplasticizers produce their effect is very similar to normal plasticizers. In general, all superplasticizers are large polymeric molecules. Most have rigid skeletons, chemically substituted exclusively with sulphonate groups, which adsorb onto surface aluminium or calcium on the cement grains. Sulphonate functional groups are exclusively present in true superplasticizers, as sulphonate is not as strongly

Table 15.4 The performance requirements and tests stated in BS 5075: Part 1: 1982[37]

Property	Type of admixture				
	Accelerating	Retarding	Normal water-reducing	Accelerating water-reducing	Retarding water-reducing
Test-mix concrete A					
Compacting factor relative to control-mix concrete	Not more than 0.02 below	Not more than 0.02 below	At least 0.03 above	At least 0.03 above	At least 0.03 above
Stiffening times					
for 0.5 N mm^{-2}	More than 1 h	At least 1 h longer than control mix	—	—	—
for 3.5 N mm^{-2}	At least 1 h less than control mix	—	—	—	—
Minimum compressive strength as % of control-mix concrete					
at 24 h	125	—	—	125	—
at 7 days	—	90	90	—	90
at 28 days	95	95	90	90	90
Test-mix concrete B					
Compacting factor relative to control-mix concrete	—	—	Not more than 0.02 below	Not more than 0.02 below	Not more than 0.02 below
Stiffening time					
for 0.5 N mm^{-2}	—	—	Within 1 h of control mix	More than 1 h	At least 1 h longer than control mix
for 3.5 N mm^{-2}	—	—	Within 1 h of control mix	At least 1 h less than control mix	—
Minimum compressive strength as % of control-mix concrete					
at 24 h	—	—	—	125	—
at 7 days	—	—	110	—	110
at 28 days	—	—	110	110	110

absorbed as either carboxyl or hydroxy groups. It is for this reason that superplasticizers do not significantly retard the set of concrete. Sulphonate, in molecular terms, is a very bulky functional group, and is very easily sterically hindered, i.e. due to their size other parts of the molecule interfere with it. It is for this reason that the most successful superplasticizers have the sulphonate groups substituted onto aromatic rings which are rigid and probably assist in keeping the sulphonate groups orientated outwards. Superplasticizers do not have a significant effect on the surface tension of water, and for this reason there is little tendency for them to entrain air, even at relatively high dosage rates.

15.4.3 Chemical types of superplasticizer

In 1976 a joint Cement Admixtures Association and Cement and Concrete Association working party defined the various types of superplasticizers and divided them into categories.[39] The same designation will be used here.

15.4.3.1 Category A: sulphonated melamine–formaldehyde condensates

The structure of these materials is shown in *Figure 28*. Usually the number of repeating units (*n*) is about 60, giving a molecular weight of 20 000. Note that the sulphonate group is attached to the flat rigid melamine ring leaving it free from the axis of the main polymer chain. Category-A superplasticizers are the

nearest to ideal as they have very little effect on set, even at high dosage and do not have any tendency to entrain air.

15.4.3.2 Category B: sulphonated naphthalene–formaldehyde condensates

The structure of these materials is shown in *Figure 15.29*. The value of *n* is usually 5–10 giving a molecular weight of about 2000. Although these materials have been available for about 30 years, until the early 1970s the only materials available were in the form of the dimer (*n* = 2). These materials had a significant effect on the surface tension and had to be used with defoaming materials. Modern polymers would probably be improved if the chain length was longer, but viscosity considerations probably limit the value of *n*. Category-B superplasticizers give more workability extension than do type A ones, tend to be more efficient in terms of dosage, but do give some extension of set.

15.4.3.3 Category C: modified lignosulphonates

As described in the previous section, lignosulphonates are naturally occurring macromolecules with a very complicated structure. Unrefined lignosulphonates have a distribution of molecular size covering quite a large range of molecular weight (*Figure 15.30*). Medium molecular weight lignosulphonates have a tendency to entrain air at higher than normal dosage. Lower molecular weight lignosulphonates tend to retard the set of concrete, as do the residual pentose sugars which cannot be fermented. The high molecular weight lignosulphonates, however, possess very useful properties. They are quite efficient plasticizers at low dosage. Lignosulphonates which are refined by techniques such as ultrafiltration thus make very efficient superplasticizers (*Figure 15.31*). They retard far more than either category-A or category-B superplasticizers, but nevertheless provide a very useful raw material.

15.4.3.4 Category D

This category was included in the 1970s to allow for the inclusion of certain formulated products based on hydroxylated polymers. The development of superplasticizers based on acrylic acid/hydroxypropylmethacrylic acid copolymer has given more importance to this category.[31] Superplasticizers based on these copolymers are widely used in piling, when good workability retention is of paramount importance.

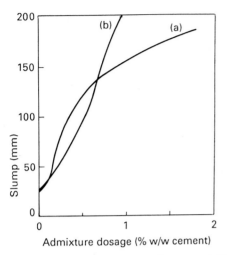

Figure 15.25 A comparison of the effects on workability of the addition of: (a) a normal lignosulphonate plasticizer, and (b) a superplasticizer

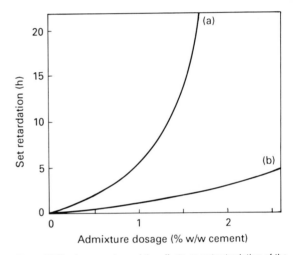

Figure 15.27 A comparison of the effects on set retardation of the addition of: (a) a normal lignosulphonate plasticizer, and (b) a superplasticizer

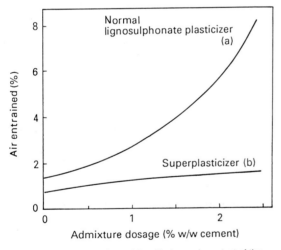

Figure 15.26 A comparison of the effects on air content of the addition ot: (a) a normal lignosulphonate plasticizer, and (b) a superplasticizer

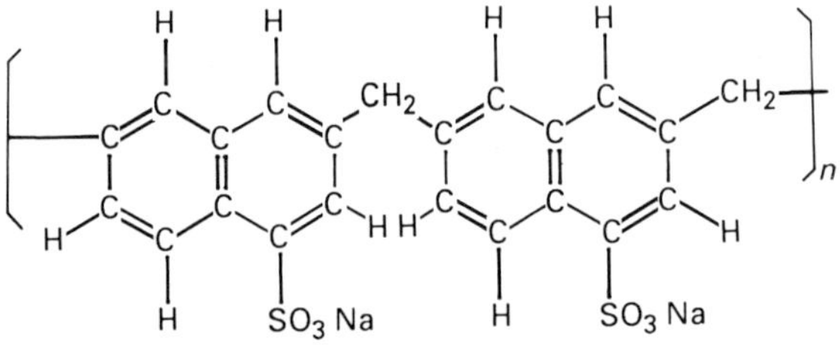

Figure 15.29 The structure of sodium naphthalene sulphonate type superplasticizers

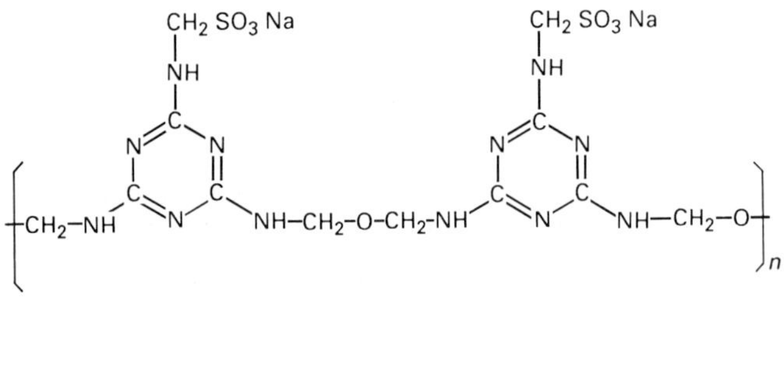

Figure 15.28 The structure of sulphonated melamine–formaldehyde type superplasticizers

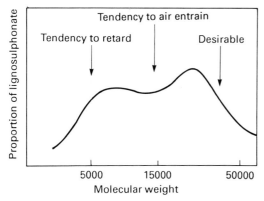

Figure 15.30 The molecular-weight distribution of unrefined lignosulphonate

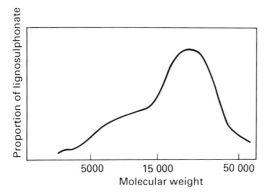

Figure 15.31 The molecular-weight distribution of lignosulphonate refined by ultrafiltration

15.4.4 Advantages of superplasticizers

Just as conventional plasticizers are used to increase workability or reduce water content, then superplasticizers are used to greatly increase workability to produce flowing concrete or greatly reduce water to give high early strength concretes.

15.4.4.1 Flowing concrete

Flowing concrete is concrete which is made virtually self-levelling by the addition of a superplasticizer. The concrete may be placed very easily and after a predictable period it should revert to, and behave like, a normal concrete. It should set normally and be able to accept a power float in normal practice. The relative typical dosage levels required to produce flowing concrete are summarized in *Figure 15.32* and the typical behaviour and workability loss of that concrete is illustrated in *Figure 15.33*. Flowing concrete should be carefully designed with suitable aggregate to make sure that it does not segregate.[40]

15.4.4.2 High-strength water-reduced concrete

Superplasticizers can be used to reduce the water content of a mix by up to 25% in order to achieve a special effect. The effect has to be special, as the dosage of superplasticizer required to achieve this effect needs to be relatively high (1.5–2.5% v/w cement) and the expense can be prohibitive. The most common

requirement is to achieve a very high target strength or to achieve a very high early strength. A typical example is illustrated in *Figure 15.34*. In the example, the use of the superplasticizer could only be justified if a requirement existed for a strength of 30 N mm^{-2} at an age of 1 day.

15.4.5 Standard specification for superplasticizers

15.4.5.1 BS 5075: Part 3: 1985

BS 5075: Part 3: 1985[41] is the British Standard specification for superplasticizers. The standard has performance criteria related to the major applications of these products. Test-mix A assesses the ability of the superplasticizer to produce flowing concrete, and measures the loss of workability of that concrete to class the material as either a superplasticizer or a retarding superplasticizer. Test-mix B assesses the ability of the superplasticizer to reduce the water content of a test mix by a mandatory 16%. Minimum-strength increases must be exceeded at 1, 7 and 28 days. The requirements of BS 5075: Part 3: 1985 are summarized in *Table 15.5*.

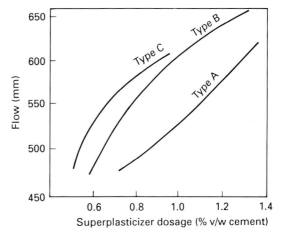

Figure 15.32 The relative dosages of various categories of superplasticizer needed to produce flowing concretes

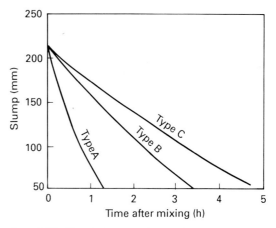

Figure 15.33 The relative rates of workability loss with various categories of superplasticizer

15.4.5.2 ASTM C494

As stated previously, ASTM C494[38] covers all plasticizers. It includes two categories of superplasticizer as types F and G. No tests are made to assess the ability to produce flowing concrete. All tests relate to the performance of the superplasticizer, evaluated at a dosage sufficient to give a minimum mandatory 12% water reduction. The requirements of ASTM C494 are summarized in *Table 15.6*.

15.5 Retarders

Retarders are admixtures which are added to concrete to delay its set.

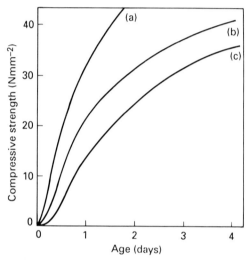

Figure 15.34 The relative rate of strength gain of water-reduced concretes: (a) superplasticizer; (b) normal water reducer; (c) control

15.5.1 Mechanism of retardation

Studies of the hydration of pure cement compounds have shown that retardation of cement depends primarily on retardation of alite $((CaO)_3SiO_2; C_3S)$. A retarder may retard or accelerate the hydration of $(CaO)_3Al_2O_3$ (C_3A), thus leading to the practical problem of premature set, or excessive slump loss.[42] There is no single theory that will explain all the phenomena associated with set retardation.

Retardation can be caused by absorption of organic compounds onto the surface of cement compounds, thereby preventing attack by water. It would appear that chelation (i.e. the formation of chemical complexes) may be the most important mechanism of absorption. Calcium, aluminium, iron or silicon ions are all potentially capable of chelating organic compounds. The best chelating unit is typified by the β-hydroxycarboxylate grouping (*Figure 15.35*). Tartaric acid which contains this grouping is a very powerful retarder, whilst succinic which does not have the β-hydroxyl group is not. Similarly, maleic acid, which is capable of chelation, retards, but its structural isomer fumaric acid, which cannot chelate, does not (*Figure 15.36*).

It is unlikely that organic molecules retard by chelation to the anhydrous cement surface. It is more probable that chelation occurs at active sites on the first hydration products and that these chelates prevent further access of water. The initial hydration products obviously bury some retarder which was probably absorbed on the anhydrous surface of the cement, because it is well known that delayed additions of retarder produce a greater retardation effect.

Retarders probably affect the morphology of the osmotic membrane formed during initial hydration. Just as accelerators seem to produce a coarser, more permeable membrane, then retarders produce a finer, more tightly packed, less permeable membrane. The modification of the membrane is responsible for the observed effect on the available lime in solution (*Figure 15.37*).

Complexes are formed between aluminate and sugars, and similar complexes are predicted for hydroxy acids. With tartaric acid, the concentration of calcium and alumina increase sharply, and this phenomenon could well be explained by the formation

Table 15.5 The performance requirements of BS 5075: Part 3: 1985

Property	Test method	Superplasticizing	Retarding superplasticizing
Test-mix A[a]			
Flow	Flow table to BS 1881: Part 105	510–620 mm	510–620 mm
Workability loss on standing, back to that of initial control slump	Slump to BS 1881: Part 102	At 45 min: not less than initial control	At 4 h: not less than initial control
		At 4 h: not more than initial control	
% compressive strength on control	BS 1881: Part 116		
at 7 days		Not less than 90%	Not less than 90%
at 28 days		Not less than 90%	Not less than 90%
Test-mix B[b]			
Slump relative to control	BS 1881: Part 102	Not more than 15 mm less	Not more than 15 mm less
Stiffening time relative to control			
for 0.5 N mm^{-2}	BS 4551	Within 1 h	1–4 h longer
for 3.5 N mm^{-2}	5075 test method	Within 1 h	
% compressive strength on control	BS 1881: Part 116		
at 1 day		Not less than 140%	—
at 7 days		Not less than 125%	Not less than 125%
at 28 days		Not less than 115%	Not less than 115%

[a] Contains plasticizer and has the same water content as the control, giving a high workability flowing concrete.
[b] Contains superplasticizer and has the water content reduced to give equal workability to the control mix.

Table 15.6 The performance requirements of ASTM C494[38]

	Type A, water reducing	Type B, retarding	Type C, accelerating	Type D, water reducing and retarding	Type E, water reducing and accelerating	Type F, water reducing, high range	Type G, water reducing, high range and retarding
Water content (max. % of control)	95	—	—	95	95	88	88
Time of setting, allowable deviation from control (h:min)							
Initial: at least	—	1:00 later	1:00 earlier	1:00 later	1:00 earlier	—	1:00 later
not more than	1:00 earlier, nor 1:30 later	3:30 later	3:30 earlier	3:30 later	3:30 later	1:00 earlier, nor 1:30 later	3:30 later
Final: at least	—	—	1:00 earlier	—	1:00 earlier	—	—
not more than	1:00 earlier, nor 1:30 later	3:30 later	—	3:30 later	—	1:00 earlier, nor 1:30 later	3:30 later
Compressive strength (min. % of control)							
1 day	—	—	—	—	—	140	125
3 days	110	90	125	110	125	125	125
7 days	110	90	100	110	110	115	115
28 days	110	90	100	110	110	110	110
6 months	100	90	90	100	100	100	100
1 year	100	90	90	100	100	100	100
Flexural strength (min. % control)							
3 days	100	90	110	100	110	110	110
7 days	100	90	100	100	100	100	100
28 days	100	90	90	100	100	100	100
Length change, max. shrinkage (alternative requirements)							
Percentage of control	135	135	135	135	135	135	135
Increase over control	0.010	0.010	0.010	0.010	0.010	0.010	0.010
Relative durability factor (min)	80	80	80	80	80	80	80

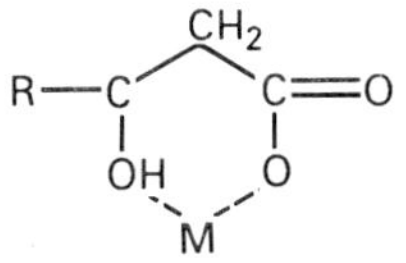

Figure 15.35 The structure of the β-hydrocarboxylate group

(a)   (b)

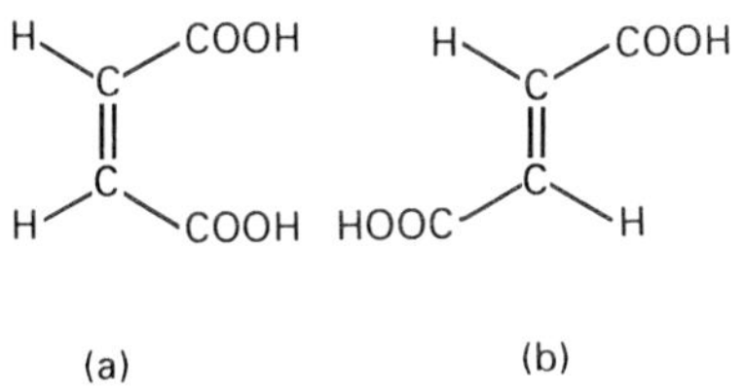

Figure 15.36 The structures of the stereoisomers: (a) maleic acid and (b) fumaric acid

of a very stable chelate with alumina. The effects of retarders on the amount of lime in solution at relatively early ages is illustrated in *Figure 15.38*.

It is interesting to compare *Figure 15.37* and *15.38* as it can be seen that retarders increase the amount of lime in solutions at early age (up to 1 h), but delay the amount of lime in solution during the period 1–10 h.

In summary, a likely mechanism of retardation has been proposed by Young.[42] The organic admixture may be first concentrated at the surface of aluminate hydrates by preferential adsorption. Rather than slowing down the initial rate of attack by water, an increased activity is observed due to complexing between organic molecules and the aluminate ions. Residual retarder is probably chelated on the CSH gel formed initially, and this coating inhibits the migration of both water molecules in and calcium ions out. When precipitation of calcium hydroxide occurs, the crystal growth is poisoned and the process slowed. Subsequent to the period of initial reactivity, the retardation of C_3S, and the length of the dormant period is determined by the amount of chelation at the CSH boundary and on the nucleation of calcium hydroxide.

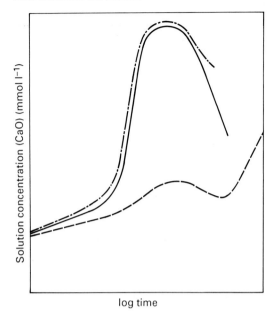

Figure 15.37 The effects of tartaric acid and succinic acid on the concentration of lime in solution. (———) control; (–·–·–) succinic acid; (————) tartaric acid

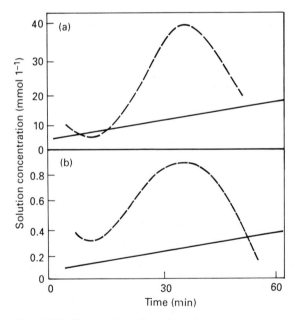

Figure 15.38 The short-time effects of retarder upon solution concentration: (———) control; (–·–·–) tartaric acid. (a) CaO; (b) Al_2O_3

15.5.2 Benefits of retardation

Retarders are used exclusively to delay the set of concretes, mortars, cements, grouts and many types of cementitious formulations. They are not particularly successful when used in concrete to retain workability. They are far more successful when used in combination with a plasticizer and the workability of the system raised. Similarly, when used in retarded-mortar

systems, maintaining workability by incorporating air is almost as important as delaying the set with a retarder. When used to delay the set, they are very predictable. They find universal use in delaying the set of large pours to enable a large working front to be maintained. They also find wide application in slipforming where prediction and control of set is vital. It should be noted that in these two applications it is not vital to retain high workability, because mechanical vibration is normally available.

15.5.3 Chemical types of retarder

There are numerous commercially available retarders, but most find specific application on an arbitrary basis. Citric acid (*Figure 15.39*) and tartaric acid (*Figure 15.40*) find wide application in dry cementitious compositions, probably because they are pure, hard crystalline materials which are thermally stable, non-hygroscopic and do not significantly affect the workability. Sodium gluconate and sodium heptonate are widely used in concrete and mortars as they are also effective plasticizers. Sucrose (*Figure 15.41*) is also a very strong retarder. The effects of a large number of organic compounds are summarized and classified according to their retarding power in *Table 15.7*.

15.5.4 Standard specification for retarders

As for concrete plasticizers and retarding plasticizers, retarders are covered in BS 5075: Part 1: 1982[37] and in the ASTM C494,[38] the contents of which are summarized in *Tables 15.4* and *15.6*, respectively.

The growth in the use of ready-to-use retarded mortars in Europe and in the UK has justified the issuing of a British Standard specific to mortar retarders: BS 4887: Part 2: 1987.[24] The performance test requirements given in this standard are summarized in *Table 15.8*. These test requirements apply to two types of retarded mortars: one containing hydrated lime and a second test mortar containing just sand and cement. The standard gives precise compositions for the two test mortars and for the sand used in the tests.

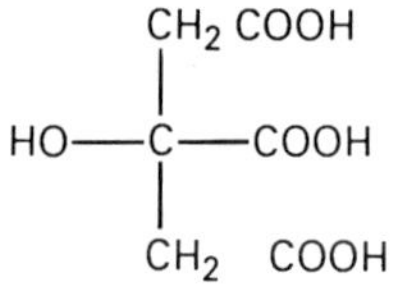

Figure 15.39 The structure of citric acid

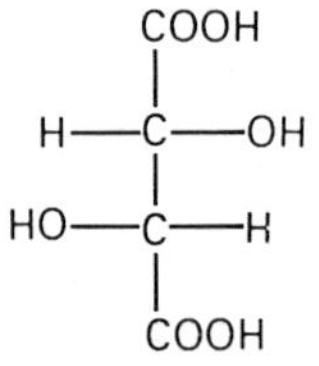

Figure 15.40 The structure of tartaric acid

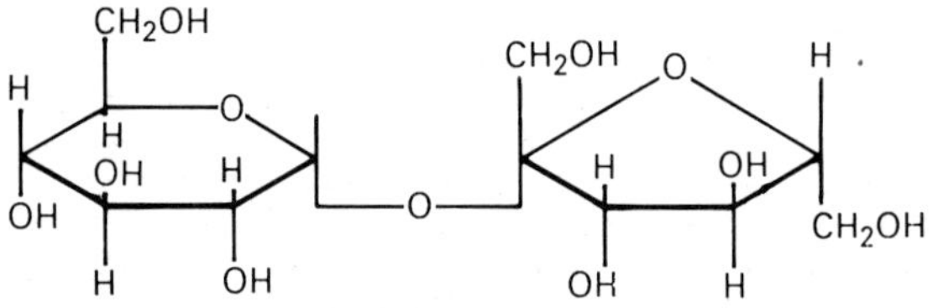

Figure 15.41 The structure of sucrose

Table 15.7 Classification of retarders according to retarding power[a]

Group	Slight or negligible retarding effect	Feeble retarding effect	Powerful retarding effect
A	Methanol, sodium formate, formaldehyde, diethoxymethane		
B	Ethanol, calcium acetate, acetaldehyde, glycol, glyoxal, oxalic acid, dioxane		Glycolaldehyde, glycolic acid
C	Propyl alcohol, i-propyl alcohol, 1,3-propanediol, 1,2-propanediol, alkyl alcohol, propanol, acetone, propionic acid, acrylic acid, 2-chloropropionic acid, malonic acid, 2-hydroxypropionic acid, 1-hydroxypropionic acid (lactic acid)	Glycerin, tartronic acid, butyl acetate, glyceric acid	Acetal, pyruvic acid, glycerolaldehyde, dihydroxy acetone, ketomalonic acid
D	Fumaric acid, aldol Succinic acid anhydride	Maleic acid, erythritol Succinic acid, acetoin	Malic acid, maleic acid anhydride Tartaric acid, dihydroxy tartaric acid, ethyl acetoacetate
E	Chloral hydrate, glycine, EDTA Urea, adipic acid, 4-hydroxypentan-2-one Cupferron (ammonium salt of N-nitrosophenyl hydroxylamine)	Diacetone alcohol, acetyl acetone, phoron 8-Hydroxyquinoline	α-Ketoglutaric acid, β-ketoglutaric acid, gluconic acid Citric acid, 3% EDTA, sucrose, glucose, fructose, sorbitol, pentaerythritol
F	Anthraquinone, phenol	Hydroquinone, salicylaldehyde, phloroglucinol, resorcinol, 1,4-napthoquinone chromotropic acid	Quinone, catechol, pyrogallol, bile acid, 1,2-napthoquinone, sulphonic acid
G	Zinc oxide (in 3,6-N NaOH solution), beryllium oxide (in 3,6-N NaOH solution), arsenic trioxide, antimony pentoxide Red lead, chromium chloride, potassium dichromate, cuprous oxide, cupric oxide, mercury nitrate, murcury chloride, stannous chloride, sodium hypophosphite, potassium pyrophosphate	Lead sulphate, lead nitrate, orthoboric acid, antimony trioxide, cadmium oxide, vanadium pentoxide Cupric nitrate, sodium bisulphite, potassium tetrathionate, sodium tetrathionate, sodium hexametaphosphate, concentrated ammonia	Zinc oxide Zinc chloride Zinc carbonate, zinc oxide in ammoniacal solution, beryllium sulphate, lead oxide, boron oxide, arsenic pentoxide, sodium pyrovanadate, metaphosphoric acid Borax

[a] Unless otherwise stated, all substances were used in an amount of 1% of the cement.

15.6 Accelerators

Accelerators are materials which are used to accelerate either the setting process of a mortar or concrete or to accelerate its hardening process.

15.6.1 History of accelerators

The history of the use of accelerators is dominated by the use of calcium chloride. Calcium chloride has been used as an admixture for a longer period than most other admixtures, and its first use can be traced to a patent issued in 1875.[43] There is considerable confusion and misunderstanding regarding the effects of chloride, particularly as the material is banned from use in structural concretes in such countries as the UK, but allowed in Canada and the USA, provided precautions are taken. There is no doubting its technical effectiveness as an accelerator, but no doubt either as to its effects of promoting corrosion of reinforcement if its concentration reaches critical levels.

15.6.2 Mechanism of acceleration

Most inorganic electrolytes accelerate the hydration of $(CaO)_3SiO_2$ (C_3S), with soluble calcium salts being the most effective. Despite the long and extensive use of calcium chloride as a commercial accelerator, very little is known about the mechanism of its influence on C_3S hydration. Many investigators have compared the behaviour of different metal chlorides and have attempted to correlate the effectiveness of the cations.

The influence of various anions on the accelerating process has also been studied. An examination of calorimeter curves would seem to indicate that many inorganic ions are potentially better accelerators than chloride (*Figure 15.42*). However, in practice, no other material has ever matched calcium chloride in effectiveness, and because of the low cost of waste calcium chloride as a by product of the Solvay process for the production of sodium carbonate, no other accelerator comes close to out-performing calcium chloride on economic grounds. Research workers have tried to correlate the behaviour of accelerators with their ionic mobility (*Figure 15.43*). Again, it

Table 15.8 Performance requirements of BS 4887: Part 2: 1987[24]

Characteristic	Test reference	Requirement (mean of two batches)
Consistence after		
standard mixing	C.2	Mean dropping ball penetration of 10 ± 0.5 mm
28-h standing	C.5	Not more than 4.0 mm less than the value after standard mixing
Air content after		
standard mixing	C.3	14.0–20.0%
28-h standing	C.7	Not less than 70% of the value after standard mixing
Resistance to penetration after 52-h standing	C.6	Not less than 5 N mm^{-2}
28-day compressive strength on cubes made after		
standard mixing	C.4	Not less than that of the control mix
28-h standing	C.8	Not less than that of the control mix

anion such as chloride can penetrate the initial protective layer to the underlying C_3S, enabling a continuation of diffusion. In fact, it could be argued that chloride functions by interfering with the natural self-retardation of C_3S hydration. Ironically, it is this very mobility of chloride ion which, at present, is causing so much concern when considering corrosion. Chloride ion is able to migrate and concentrate under the influence of small electric potentials which can be set up by corroding metals.

Different calcium salts do not produce the same type of acceleration (*Figure 15.44*). Calcium nitrate, for example, is a good set accelerator, but does not produce significant strength increase. This is probably type A in Young's classification.

Thiocyanates, however, do not have any effect on set, but do enhance strength quite significantly; this could be type C. Calcium chloride affects both set and strength and can be considered as type B.

The acceleration of C_3S hydration may also affect the hydration of $(CaO)_3Al_2O_3$ (C_3A). Calcium chloride can accelerate the formation of ettringite in the presence of gypsum. Many salts can form complex hexagonal calcium aluminate

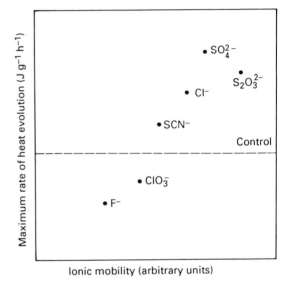

Figure 15.43 Acceleration related to ionic mobility

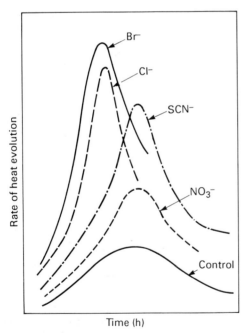

Figure 15.42 The acceleration produced by some anions

is apparent that calcium chloride is not unique in accelerating cement.

Young[42] and other workers[44] have tried to explain the mechanism of soluble salts by considering each stage of C_3S both separately and sequentially. The importance of the liquid phase, particularly with respect to calcium hydroxide super-saturation, is supported by many researchers. A highly mobile

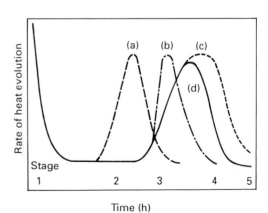

Figure 15.44 Types of acceleration: (a) shortened induction; (b) faster rate of reaction during stage 3; (c) increased heat during stages 3 and 4; (d) control

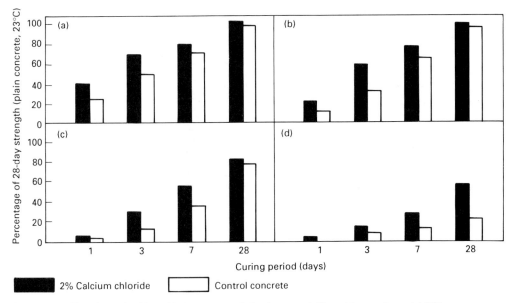

Figure 15.45 The effects of calcium chloride on strength development at different temperatures: (a) 23°C; (b) 13°C; (c) 5°C; (d) −5°C

hydration of the type C_3A, $CaX_2 \cdot nH_2O$. Thus, if C_3A forms hexagonal hydrates in the early stage of hydration then the possibility exists for complex formation with the admixture.

Triethanolamine (TEA) is a very interesting material, which in practice is used as an accelerator, although most organic compounds retard the hydration of cements. TEA does in fact retard C_3S and most of its accelerating characteristics are attributed to its effect on C_3A. A comparison of the effects of TEA in white Portland cement would seem to indicate that the ferrite phase is also affected by TEA. The mechanism of action of TEA is probably by chelation to metal ions, particularly on the surface of tricalcium aluminate.

15.6.3 Benefits of accelerators

The main benefits of accelerators are to be observed at low temperature. When used at temperatures above 20°C, even calcium chloride, which is probably the most technically effective concrete accelerator, produces very little benefit to early and later-age compressive strength. However, when used at low temperatures, particularly below 10°C, accelerators have a profound beneficial effect on the set and subsequent strength development of concrete. The effects of accelerators are summarized in *Figure 15.45*.

Because of the problem associated with the corrosion of chloride based concrete accelerators, chloride free accelerators are now available. In general, these are technically less effective than chloride based accelerators and are more expensive. Their only advantage is that they do not cause corrosion of embedded ferrous metal in concrete.

15.6.4 Chemical types of accelerator

Calcium chloride is still the most widely used concrete accelerator. Where the concrete contains no embedded ferrous metal, then chloride is ideally suited and is extremely cost effective in cold weather. Sodium chloride is also an effective concrete accelerator, and seawater has been used to cast unreinforced marine structures quite successfully, although efflorescence may be a problem. There are now a number of chloride free accelerators commercially available, none of which are as effective as calcium chloride.

Calcium nitrite $(Ca(NO_2)_2)$ is probably the most effective of the commercial alternatives to chloride. Nitrites do not cause corrosion, and indeed there is evidence to support the view that they inhibit corrosion. Sodium nitrite $(NaNO_2)$ is also effective and is widely used in the UK. Calcium thiocyanate $(Ca(SCN)_2)$ is theoretically good, but is not commercially available in large quantities. The sodium salt, sodium thiocyanate $(NaSCN)$, is used extensively in the UK. Sodium thiosulphate $(Na_2S_2O_3)$ is also used as a proprietary chloride free accelerator.

Calcium nitrate, $Ca(NO_3)_2$ does have accelerating properties, particularly as a set accelerator. There is evidence, however, that this material causes stress corrosion, and for this reason it is banned for use with prestressing tendons. Calcium formate $(Ca(OOCH)_2)$ may also enhance pitting corrosion, although to nowhere near the same degree as does chloride. When formates are used in combination with nitrites it is likely that no risk of corrosion exists.

15.6.5 Standard specifications for accelerators

As for other categories of admixtures, accelerators and accelerating plasticizers are covered in the UK by BS 5075: Part 1: 1982[37] and in the USA by ASTM C494.[38] For performance requirements see *Tables 15.4* and *15.6*, respectively.

15.6.6 Sprayed concrete accelerators

Accelerators used for sprayed concrete or gunite are different from normal wet concrete accelerators. Sprayed concrete accelerators are normally based on aluminates or silicates and sometimes sodium hydroxide. All are highly alkaline and classed as corrosive. They should never be used without full eye and body protection, as alkali burns can be serious, particularly to the eyes.

15.6.7 Mechanism of shotcrete accelerators

Shotcrete accelerators function by a precipitation reaction. For example, sodium aluminate in contact with calcium ions derived from the cement reaction forms calcium aluminate. Calcium aluminate is metastable and disproportionates into lime and aluminium hydrate which, being insoluble, precipitate and cause a rapid workability loss. Similarly, sodium silicate reacts with calcium ion to form insoluble calcium silicate, which precipitates causing rapid workability loss.

The use of such accelerators greatly enhances very early strength, but any such gain is always made at the expense of later strengths. When shotcrete accelerators are used, it is common to sacrifice as much as half the later-age strength.

There is no standard specification which covers shotcrete accelerators, and they will not comply with the requirements of BS 5075: Part 1: 1982[37] or ASTM C494.[38]

15.7 Corrosion inhibitors

A corrosion inhibitor is an admixture added to a concrete, and is primarily designed to reduce the corrosion of embedded steel. Corrosion inhibiting admixtures are not widely used in the UK, but are very commonly used in the USA and Canada. This disparity probably reflects the harsher winters encountered in those countries with continental climates, as compared with those countries with temperate climates. Chloride is still used in structural concretes in Canada, and the use of deicing salts is more prolonged there than in the UK.

15.7.1 Chemical types of corrosion inhibitors

The effectiveness of numerous chemicals as corrosion inhibitors has been investigated, including chromates, phosphates, hypophosphites, fluorides and nitrites.[46,47] Organic inhibitors include sodium benzoate, ethyl aniline and mercaptobenzothiazole. Some chemicals have been shown to have undesirable side-effects on the physical properties of concrete and, in particular, on the compressive strength of concrete. Calcium nitrite, which is widely used as a chloride free accelerator, has been extensively tested as a corrosion inhibitor,[48] and this chemical is marketed commercially as such. Other nitrites, particularly sodium nitrite, are probably equally effective as corrosion inhibitors, but efflorescence or alkali aggregate reactivity need to be considered.[49]

15.7.2 Mechanism of corrosion and corrosion inhibitors

The corrosion of reinforcement in concrete is an electrochemical process and is very complicated in origin, because under normal circumstances concrete provides a protective environment for steel.[50] Problems only occur with corrosion of reinforcement when some external agent is able to disturb the protective, passive oxide layer present around the steel in concrete. It is a common misconception, that most corrosion is caused by an external chemical such as chloride derived from deicing salts. This type of corrosion is common in such structures as bridge decks in countries with a harsh climate. It normally occurs in conjunction with poor design, construction or detailing.

Much corrosion in the UK probably originates from microcracking, which provides water and air with a direct route to unprotected steel. Lack of cover caused by poor alignment of reinforcement is a second major cause of corrosion. This is normally associated with surface carbonation which reduces the pH of the surface layers of the concrete and enables water and oxygen to deactivate the protective passive layer.[51] The rate of carbonation is very dependent upon the saturation of the concrete, but it is also fundamentally related to its permeability, and good quality concrete is the best protection against this process occurring. A low water:cement ratio will slow the diffusion of carbon dioxide, oxygen and chloride.

The mechanism of corrosion inhibition with an admixture is not well understood and probably varies with chemical type. It is interesting to note that most of the chemicals used as corrosion inhibitors react with free radicals. A free radical is a molecular fragment having one or more unpaired electrons. It is well known that many chemical oxidation processes are initiated by free radicals, and the corrosion of steel may well be such a process. It is also well known that complex oxides of iron form free radicals and some transfer mechanisms of corrosion may well involve free radicals. Nitrites could possibly quench free-radical reactions, thereby inhibiting the corrosion process.

15.7.3 Benefits of corrosion inhibitors

Corrosion inhibitors and, in particular, those based on calcium nitrite are widely used in the USA to provide added protection to concretes which are in a highly corrosive environment. Concrete bridge decks are particularly prone to risk from chloride permeation and the use of corrosion inhibitors is just one of many ways in which the performance of concrete is being extended. For example, calcium nitrite has been used in the presence of microsilica,[52] where the microsilica has primarily been used to reduce the permeability of the concrete.

15.8 Permeability reducers

15.8.1 The nature of the permeability of concrete

Concrete, by virtue of its very nature, is a permeable, porous material. This fundamental permeability arises from the presence of pores, as shown by the simplified model in *Figure 15.46*. Powers[53] suggested that there are two types of pores: gel pores and capillary pores. In general, gel pores are extremely small and are of molecular dimensions. Capillary pores are variable in size and are mainly responsible for the practical permeability exhibited by normal concretes.

Powers elegantly explained why all practical concretes have pores (see *Figure 15.47*). For example, consider the hydration of a cement paste with a water:cement ratio of 0.475 by weight. At zero time, 40% by volume of the paste will be unhydrated cement and 60% by volume will be water. This is because cement is denser than water and water:cement ratios are always stated as a weight ratio. In this example we are primarily interested in the volume changes. After 50% hydration, approximately 10 days at 20°C, then half the cement will have reacted, leaving 20% volume of unhydrated species. The hydrated species, reacted cement, then occupies 42% of the space. Of the remaining space, 34% by volume is capillary water and 4% is empty pores. Given a drying environment, then the 34% of capillary water will gradually evaporate leaving a total of 38% of capillaries. Thus, a typical concrete with a similar water:cement ratio and of reasonable maturity is about one-third full of holes. Even after 100% hydration, a condition which never happens in practice, the concrete is about 15% porous in drying conditions.

The size and frequency of capillary pores varies with the age of the concrete and with its water:cement ratio. Thus, concrete with high water:cement ratios, low cement contents and at early ages, has a larger number and larger volume of pores than do concretes with low water:cement ratios, high cement contents and at mature ages. For example, the void system of a cement paste with a water:cement ratio of 0.23 at day 1 is somewhat similar to the expected void system of a cement paste with a water:cement ratio of 0.70 at day 14. Maturity and water:cement ratio are, therefore, of paramount importance in determining the porosity and permeability of a concrete; this relationship is shown quite clearly in *Figure 15.48*. It is significant that concretes with a water:cement ratio of greater than 0.70 will, even when

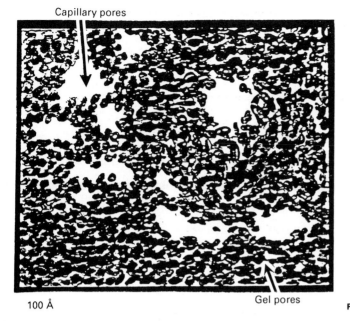

Capillary pores

100 Å

Gel pores

Figure 15.46 A simplified model of cement paste

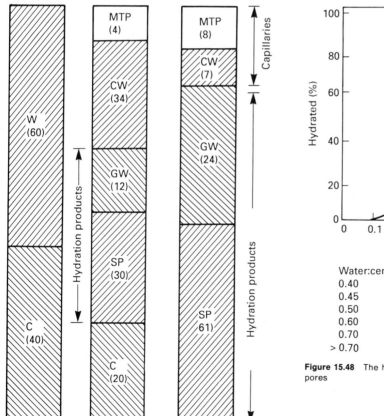

Figure 15.47 The hydration of a cement paste with a water:cement ratio of 0.473. C, cement; SP, solid product; GW, gel water; CW, capillary water; MTP, empty pores

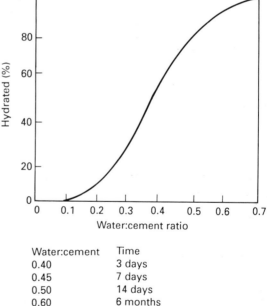

Water:cement	Time
0.40	3 days
0.45	7 days
0.50	14 days
0.60	6 months
0.70	1 year
> 0.70	Never

Figure 15.48 The hydration required to achieve discontinuous pores

hydrated to 100%, never create a discontinuous pore system. Even good quality concrete with water:cement ratios in the range 0.55–0.60 require a high degree of maturity before producing a discontinuous pore system.

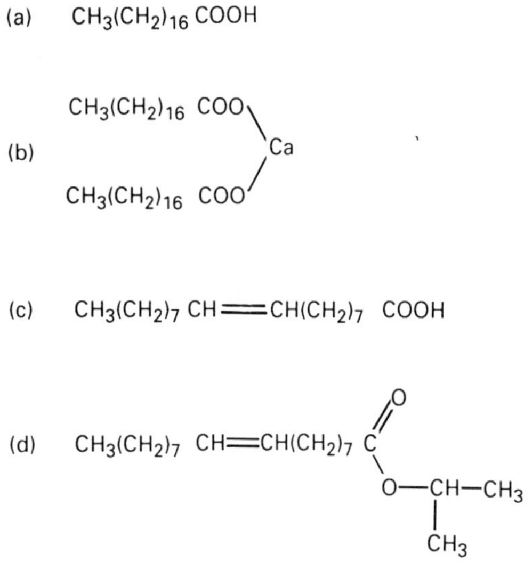

(a) $CH_3(CH_2)_{16} COOH$

(b)

$$CH_3(CH_2)_{16} COO$$
$$\diagdown$$
$$Ca$$
$$\diagup$$
$$CH_3(CH_2)_{16} COO$$

(c) $CH_3(CH_2)_7 CH \!=\!\!=\! CH(CH_2)_7 COOH$

(d) $CH_3(CH_2)_7 CH \!=\!\!=\! CH(CH_2)_7 C$
with ester group:
$$\overset{O}{\underset{O-CH-CH_3}{\overset{\|}{C}}}$$
$$\underset{CH_3}{|}$$

Figure 15.49 The chemical structure of some typical permeability reducers: (a) stearic acid; (b) calcium stearate; (c) oleic acid; (d) isopropyloleate

15.8.2 The theory of permeability reducers

In theory, the pressure (P) required for water to enter a capillary in the surface of concrete is given by the general equation

$$P = -\frac{2\gamma \cos \theta}{r}$$

where θ is the contact angle between the water and the surface, r is the radius of the capillary, and γ is a constant.

Thus, if the capillaries are small, then the pressure required is large. Conversely, if the capillaries are large, then the pressure required is small. Similarly, if the contact angle (θ) is small, then the value of $\cos \theta$ is large, and the value of P becomes large and negative. Thus, water is spontaneously sucked into the substrate. A spot placed on a block of plain concrete will demonstrate this. If the contact angle θ can be altered to a value greater than $90°$, then $\cos \theta$ becomes negative, making P positive. Thus, a significant pressure is required to push water into the capillaries.

Waterproofers should, therefore, really be designated as permeability reducers. Some products are actually accelerators which really rely on their ability to speed up the rate of maturing of a concrete. Other products are essentially plasticizers, which reduce permeability by relying on their ability to reduce the water:cement ratio of a concrete. Of particular interest are those products which function by their ability to increase the contact angle of water at the cement–air interphase, thereby increasing the pressure required for water to permeate through the concrete. The structure of some typical 'waterproofers' are shown in *Figure 15.49*. In general, these compounds are all based on long-chain fatty acids, their salts or their esters. All these materials have a common molecular structure, having a long hydrophobic, paraffinic backbone, but with a hydrophylic head. These molecules align themselves so that the hydrophylic (water liking) head adheres to the concrete surface. The hydrophobic (water hating) tail tends to be pushed away from the surface, thereby preventing any incoming water from entering by forming a wax-like surface. Just as water rolls back on a wax surface, so water will roll back on a concrete which has been treated with a permeability reducer.

15.8.3 Benefits of permeability reducers

To assess the benefits of permeability reduced concrete, there are a number of simple tests which can be used to quantify the results of permeability reduction. These tests are described below.

15.8.3.1 Total water absorption

A specific method for the determination of the water absorption of concrete specimens cored from a structure or precast component is cited in BS 1881: Part 122: 1983.[54] A general method, applicable to precast concrete products is given below.

Dry a sample of the concrete at 110°C for 2 days. Cool in a dry environment. Weigh dry (W_D), immerse sample in water and weight at 10-min intervals (W_t) to measure water uptake. This test gives information related to the permeability of the matrix. The percentage absorption (A) at time t is then given by

$$A = \frac{W_t - W_D}{W_D} \times 100\%$$

15.8.3.2 Initial surface absorption test (ISAT)

This test is very good for assessing the permeability of the actual surface of the concrete, as opposed to the permeability of the matrix. The full details of the test are described in BS 1217.[55] There is no British or American Standard method that involves the use of capillary rise. Capillary rise is a method cited in the national standards of a number of European countries and a new version based on these tests is currently being considered by CEN Technical Committee TC104 WG3, for inclusion in the European Standard Performance Tests for Permeability Reducing Admixtures.

15.8.3.3 Capillary rise

The capillary rise test gives more information related to the matrix, and is normally used for tall, thin specimens. The sample is dried at 100°C for 2 days and then immersed edge- or end-on in a shallow tray containing about 1 in. depth of water. After a given time the moisture front can be seen advancing up the concrete. The rate of advance of the front gives a good guide to the permeability of the concrete matrix. It is interesting to look at the theory behind capillary rise, as the results from this simple test can be related to the pore-size distribution of a test concrete (*Figure 15.50*).[56] The concrete can be photographed or the height of the moisture front can be plotted versus time.

15.8.3.4 Water spot test

The water spot test is not a standard test. This is an extremely simple test, but one which gives information on the surface and matrix permeability. Water (1 ml) is pipetted or carefully fed from a dropper onto the surface of the concrete. A stop-watch is used to time the point at which all the water has been drawn into the concrete.

In addition to the above tests, it is advisable to test treated concrete for air content and compressive strength. Such permeability reducers, such as oleic acid, are extremely effective, but do entrain air into wet concretes. For this reason, certain materials are ideal for use in strength concretes; others are ideal in mortars or renders where air is quite desirable; and other materials are good in dry concretes where air cannot be entrained at all.

Medium strength, wet concretes as commonly used for wet precast operations, respond very well to the addition of a permeability reducer (*Figure 15.51*). Similarly, block paving (*Figure 15.52*) also appears to benefit when using the criteria of

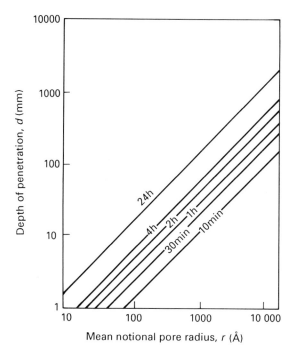

Figure 15.50 The relationship of pore radius to capillary rise. The depth of penetration (d), or capillary rise, is calculated from $d = \sqrt{(r^2 p_0 t)/4\mu}$, where p_0 is the atmospheric pressure, μ is the viscosity and t is time

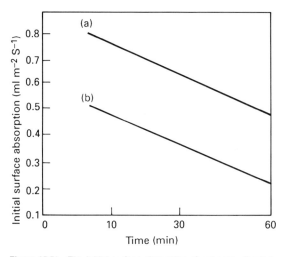

Figure 15.51 The initial surface absorption of wet cast, vibrated paving flags: (a) control; (b) 1% permeability reducer

the ISA test. Pressed flags have a very low permeability when tested by the ISA test; so low that the addition of the permeability reducer appears of little benefit.

Wet cast concretes, when tested by capillary rise, appear to benefit significantly when a permeability reducer is added, as do pressed bricks.

In general, the four tests complement one another, but this is not always true. In some cases, dramatic changes occur with the water spot test. These changes are probably related to those in the surface finish and often occur when air is entrained.

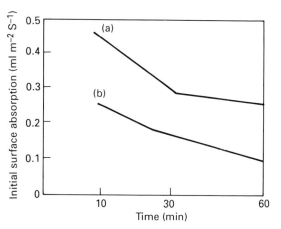

Figure 15.52 The initial surface absorption of block paving: (a) control; (b) 1% permeability reducer

Permeability reducers based solely on polar fatty compounds to reduce permeability have no effect at high water pressure. This is because the water pressure overcomes the resistance and enters the concrete pores. Some proprietary formulations have fine particulate material incorporated into them, such as bentonite. Such fine material successfully blocks capillary pores, even under pressure. In theory, silica fume should be ideal for this purpose.

Reduced permeability and reduced water absorption leads to a more durable product. Numerous precast objects are produced for their pleasing aesthetic appearance, which is ruined by soiling, discoloration or staining. Many precasters have built test panels or test walls and concluded that permeability reducers improve colour retention. Possibly they may have observed that the ingress of water has prevented soiling and algal growth and, by deduction, this has apparently improved colour retention. Efflorescence is a difficult problem and there is evidence that permeability reducers assist in reducing its incidence. The blocking or reduction in the size of capillaries helps possibly to reduce the migration of soluble salts under conditions of differential humidity.

15.8.4 Standard specification for permeability reducers

There are no British or American standards related to permeability reducers. A proposed European standard will have a section dealing with permeability reducers. A section in the European code will deal with permeability reducers.

References

1 JACKSON, F. H., *ACI Journal*, **14**, 509 (1944)
2 US BUREAU OF RECLAMATION, 'Investigation into the effect of water cement ratio on the freezing–thawing resistance of non-air- and air-entrained concrete', *Concrete Laboratory Report No. C-810*, Denver, Colorado (1955)
3 PIGEON, M., PREVOST, J. and SIMARD, J. M., 'Freeze thaw durability versus freezing rate', *ACI Journal*, 684–692 (Sep.–Oct. 1985)
4 RIXOM, M. R., *Proceedings of the Workshop on the Use of Chemical Admixtures in Concrete*, University of New South Wales, pp. 149–176 (1975)
5 KREIJGER, P. C., *Proceedings of the International Symposium on Admixtures for Mortar and Concrete*, Brussels, pp. 237–244 (1967)
6 HEWLETT, P. C., 'Physico-chemical mechanisms of admixtures', C & CA Training Course—Admixtures for Concrete (June 1982)

7 BRITISH STANDARDS INSTITUTION, *BS 8110 Structural use of concrete*, Milton Keynes, Part 1 (1985)

8 AMERICAN CONCRETE INSTITUTE, *Manual of Concrete Practice, ACI 211*

9 CORNELIUS, D. F., 'Air entrained concretes: a survey of factors affecting air content and a study of concrete workability', *RRL Report LR363*, Road Research Laboratory, Ministry of Transport (1970)

10 BROWN, B. V., 'Air entrainment—Part 2', Concrete Society Current Practice Sheet, *Concrete Magazine* (Jan. 1983)

11 WADDICOR, M. J. and HODGKINSON, L., 'A study of some variables within pulverised fuel ashes which affect the air entraining ability of admixtures in concrete', *ERMCO Conference*, London (22–26 May 1983)

12 CORMIX LTD, Warrington, British Patent Application (1988)

13 WRIGHT, P. J. F., 'Entrained air in concrete', *Proceedings of the Institute of Civil Engineers, Part 1*, **2**, 337–358 (1953)

14 KLIEGER, P., 'Effect of entrained air on strength and durability of concrete made with various sizes of aggregate', *Highway Research Board Proceedings*, **31**, 177–201 (1952)

15 BRITISH STANDARDS INSTITUTION, *BS 1881 Testing concrete*, Milton Keynes, Part 1 (1983)

16 AMERICAN SOCIETY FOR TESTING MATERIALS, *ASTM C231-82 Test method for air content of freshly mixed concrete by the pressure method*

17 AMERICAN SOCIETY FOR TESTING MATERIALS, *ASTM C173-78 Test method for air content of freshly mixed concrete by the volumetric method*

18 AMERICAN SOCIETY FOR TESTING MATERIALS, *ASTM C138-81 Test method for unit weight, yield and air content (gravimetric) of concrete*

19 BRITISH STANDARDS INSTITUTION, *BS 5075 Concrete admixtures*, Milton Keynes, Part 2 (1982)

20 AMERICAN SOCIETY FOR TESTING MATERIALS, *ASTM C260-86 Specification for air entraining admixtures for concrete*

21 AMERICAN SOCIETY FOR TESTING MATERIALS, *ASTM C666-84 Test method for resistance of concrete to rapid freezing and thawing*

22 RILEM 4-C DC

23 BRITISH STANDARDS INSTITUTION, *BS 4887 Mortar admixtures*, Milton Keynes, Part 1 (1986)

24 BRITISH STANDARDS INSTITUTION, *BS 4887 Mortar admixtures*, Milton Keynes, *Part 2 Specification for retarding admixtures* (1986)

25 US Patent 643 740 (1932)

26 US Patent 2 081 642 (1937)

27 US Patent 2 229 311 (1941)

28 COOK, H. K., *Proceedings of the International Symposium on Admixtures for Mortar and Concrete*, Brussels, pp. 135–136 (1967)

29 JOISEL, A., *Physico Chemistry of Admixtures for Cement and Concrete*, p. 40 (1973)

30 British Patent 1 068 886 (1967)

31 BRADLEY, G. and HOWARTH, I. M., 'Water soluble polymers: the relationship between structure, dispersing action, and rate of cement hydration', *Cement, Concrete and Aggregates CCAGDP*, **8**, 68–75 (1986)

32 MOSS, E. L., 'A study of varying sources of ordinary Portland cements with Cormix plasticisers and air entraining agents', *Cormix Technical Note No. 48*, Cormix, Warrington (1988)

33 CORMIX, 'A study of the effects of Cormix plasticisers and air entraining agents in Cemsave-cement concretes', *Cormix Technical Note No. 23*, Cormix, Warrington

34 CORMIX, 'The evaluation of Cormix plasticisers and air entraining agents in mix designs containing Clyde ground blast-furnace slag GX5', *Cormix Technical Service Report CD 87 116*, Cormix, Warrington (May 1988)

35 BRITISH STANDARDS INSTITUTION, *BS 3892 Specification for pulverized fuel ash for use as a cementitious component in structural concrete*, Milton Keynes, Part 1 (1982)

36 CORMIX, 'The influence of Cormix plasticisers on concretes containing a 70/30 CAA reference ordinary Portland cement pulverised fuel ash (Pozzolan) combination, *Cormix Technical Note No. 24*, Cormix, Warrington

37 BRITISH STANDARDS INSTITUTION, *BS 5075 Concrete admixtures*, Milton Keynes, *Part 1 Specification for accelerating admixtures* (1982)

38 AMERICAN SOCIETY FOR TESTING MATERIALS, *ASTM C494*

39 CEMENT AND CONCRETE ASSOCIATION/CEMENT ADMIXTURES ASSOCIATION, *Superplasticising Admixtures in Concrete, Joint Working Party Report 45.030* (Jan. 1976) (reprinted June 1978)

40 CORMIX, 'Fine aggregates and flowing concrete', *Cormix Technical Note No. 4*, Cormix, Warrington

41 BRITISH STANDARDS INSTITUTION, *BS 5075 Concrete admixtures*, Milton Keynes, *Part 3 Specification for superplasticizing admixtures* (1986)

42 YOUNG, J. F., *Cement and Concrete Research*, **2**, 415–433 (1972)

43 MILLAR, W. and NICHOLS, C. F., 'Improvements in means of accelerating the setting and hardening of concretes', *Patent 2886*, London (4 Mar. 1885)

44 SKALNY, J. and YOUNG, J. F., *Mechanisms of Portland Cement Hydration*, Sub Theme World Cement Technology Coupers (1974)

45 RAMACHANDRAN, V. S. and FELDMAN, R. F., 'Time-dependent and intrinsic characteristics of Portland cement hydration in the presence of calcium chloride', *Il Cemento*, **75**, 311–322 (1978)

46 VERBECK, G. J., 'Mechanisms of corrosion of steel in concrete', *Corrosion of Metals in Concrete*, SP-49, ACI, Detroit, pp. 21–38 (1975)

47 GRIFFIN, D. F., 'Corrosion inhibitors for reinforced concrete', *Corrosion of Metals in Concrete*, SP-49, ACI, Detroit, pp. 95–102 (1975)

48 ROSENBERG, A. M., GAIDIS, J. M., KOSSIVAS, T. G. and PREVITE, R. W., 'A corrosion inhibitor formulated with calcium nitrite for use in reinforced concrete', *Chloride Corrosion of Steel in Concrete*, STP-629, ASTM, Philadelphia, pp. 89–99 (1977)

49 CRAIG, R. J. and WOOD, L. E., 'Effectiveness of corrosion inhibitors and their influence on the physical properties of Portland cement mortars', *Highway Research Record No. 328*, Highway Research Board, pp. 77–78 (1970)

50 ACI, 'Corrosion of metals in concrete, ACI Committee 222 Report', *ACI Journal* (Jan.–Feb. 1985)

51 HAMADA, M., 'Neutralisation (carbonation) of concrete and corrosion of reinforcing steel', *Proceedings of 5th International Symposium on the Chemistry of Cement*, Tokyo, 1968, Cement Association of Japan, Tokyo, **3**, 343–360 (1969)

52 BERKE, N. S., PFEIFER, D. W. and WEIL, T. C., 'Protection against chloride-induced corrosion', *Concrete International* (Dec. 1988)

53 POWERS, T. C., 'The physical structure and engineering properties of concrete', *Bulletin 90*, Portland Cement Association Research Department, p. 39, Chicago (1958)

54 BRITISH STANDARDS INSTITUTION, *BS 1881 Testing concrete*, Milton Keynes, Part 122 (1983)

55 BRITISH STANDARDS INSTITUTION, *BS 1217 Specification for cast stone*, Milton Keynes (1986)

56 CONCRETE SOCIETY, 'Permeability testing of site concrete—a review of methods and experience', *Technical Report of a Concrete Society Working Party* (Nov. 1985)

Bibliography

ACI, *ACI Manual of Concrete Practice, Part 1: Materials and General Properties of Concrete*, ACI (1987)

BLAKE, L. S., *Recommendations for the Production of High Quality Concrete Surfaces*, Cement and Concrete Association (1967)

HEWLETT, P. C., *Cement Admixtures, Uses and Applications*, 2nd edn, Longman Scientific and Technical, London (1988)

NEVILLE, A. M., *Properties of Concrete*, Pitman, London (1978)

RAMACHANDRAN, V. S., *Chemical Admixtures Handbook, Properties, Science and Technology*, Noyes (1984)

RIXOM, M. R., *Chemical Admixture for Concrete*, Spon (1978)

16

Concrete Aggregates

J Pitts PhD, BSc, DipEng, CEng, MIMM, MIGeol, MIQA, FGS
Geotechnical and Environmental Consultants Ltd

Contents

16.1 Introduction 16/3

16.2 Sources 16/3
    16.2.1 General 16/3
    16.2.2 Dredged 16/3
    16.2.3 Arid zones 16/3

16.3 Processes of production 16/4
    16.3.1 General 16/4
    16.3.2 Crushing 16/5
    16.3.3 Sizing 16/6
    16.3.4 Scrubbing 16/6
    16.3.5 Dewatering 16/6

16.4 Types of aggregates for concrete 16/8

16.5 Common impurities 16/8
    16.5.1 General 16/8
    16.5.2 Chalk 16/8
    16.5.3 Organics 16/8
    16.5.4 Sulphide minerals 16/8
    16.5.5 Micas 16/9
    16.5.6 Clay, silt and dust 16/10
    16.5.7 Shell content 16/10
    16.5.8 Chloride and sulphate content 16/11

16.6 Physical properties of aggregates 16/12
    16.6.1 General 16/12
    16.6.2 Grading 16/12
    16.6.3 Particle shape and surface texture 16/14
    16.6.4 Bulk and relative density 16/14
    16.6.5 Water absorption and surface moisture 16/14
    16.6.6 Mechanical properties 16/14
    16.6.7 Durability 16/14
    16.6.8 Frost resistance 16/15
    16.6.9 Salt weathering 16/15
    16.6.10 Alkali–aggregate reactivity 16/15

16.7 Standards 16/17

16.8 Lightweight aggregates 16/19
    16.8.1 General 16/19
    16.8.2 Origins and early developments 16/19
    16.8.3 20th Century developments 16/19
    16.8.4 Manufacture and products 16/19
    16.8.5 Properties 16/20

References 16/21

16.1 Introduction

Most of the volume of concrete consists of coarse and fine aggregate. The properties of the aggregate have a marked influence on the density, strength, durability, shrinkage, creep and thermal properties of the concrete. Some definitions of concrete aggregates are given in *Table 16.1*. Properties of aggregates have been reviewed by several authors.[1-4]

Aggregates must fulfil two basic requirements:

(1) be stable within the concrete in a particular environment and for a designed time period; and
(2) not adversely affect the properties or cost of either the fresh or hardened concrete.

Therefore, aggregates should be of a type and purity which will not adversely influence the setting of the cement or the durability of the concrete. Furthermore, they should also be of a grading, shape and surface texture which will produce a workable mix and a strong concrete.

Three types of information are required in order to describe an aggregate fully:

(1) basic data describing the aggregate generally understandable by all members of the industry;
(2) specialist data concerning physical, mechanical and chemical characteristics; and
(3) specialist petrological/petrographic data.

16.2 Sources

16.2.1 General

High-quality aggregate suitable for concrete must contain an assemblage of minerals and possess a texture which fulfil the two basic requirements stated above. As a result, the range of geological materials utilized is limited: well-compacted or recrystallized sedimentary rocks, especially limestones and sandstones; some conglomerates and breccias; some metamorphic rocks, particularly high-grade, quartz-feldspar-rich, mica-poor types; and fresh igneous rocks. However, a further major source comprises sand and gravel deposits, essentially unconsolidated, and mainly originating as either alluvial or fluvio-glacial deposits. These sediments have undergone a complex set of processes of 'stabilization' by the gradual preferential removal of less-stable components. These processes, weathering, erosion, transportation and deposition, result in accumulations of sand and gravel consisting predominantly of silica-rich minerals, predominantly quartz, but also flint, chert and quartz-rich rock fragments.

These same processes when taken individually may have less beneficial influences on properties of rock masses with respect to their usefulness for use as concrete aggregates. Over most of the UK, northern Europe, and northern North America, glacial action scraped off much of the decomposed or partially decomposed rock materials which would otherwise need to have been removed prior to quarrying and rock crushing for aggregates. In non-glaciated areas, particularly with humid climates, significant decomposition of rocks can be present to depths of many tens of metres.

Guidance on aggregate use in relation to weathering state[3] compared with a well-known classification of rock weathering for engineering purposes[5] is shown in *Table 16.2*.

16.2.2 Dredged

Approximately one-sixth of concrete aggregates used in England and Wales are from sea-dredged sources, and this rises to one-quarter in the south-east of England. The areas exploited around the British coast are controlled by the issue of licences by the Crown Estate Commissioners. Some beach sands are also won as aggregates, although implications for erosion are considerable and are carefully evaluated prior to the issue of a licence.

Most British marine-dredged aggregates have origins similar to land-based sources, namely fluvial or glacial, and have subsequently been flooded by the post-glacial rise in sea level. Many of these aggregates have subsequently been reworked and are now beach sands. Therefore, they tend to be mineralogically mature with an abundance of siliceous particles and fragments of resistant igneous rocks. However, the shell and chloride contents are regarded as potentially deleterious components.

16.2.3 Arid zones

In arid areas, rocks and superficial deposits are influenced by weathering processes which frequently result in the accumulation of aggressive salts requiring removal prior to use in concrete. Furthermore, transportation by wind and gravity are dominant processes which result in poorly graded deposits of widely different particle sizes, either coarse angular screes or aolian dunes consisting predominantly of fine sand and silt. Limestones are a major rock type in the Middle East. They weather by solution which, in conjunction with the limited movement of surface water, restricts the supply of alluvium. As a result, clear, well-graded, alluvial sands and gravels are generally absent.

The following three factors acting either alone or in combination represent the main forms of reactivity and unsoundness in the Middle East[6] which impose effective working limits:

(1) contamination by evaporite minerals, most notably chlorides and sulphates;
(2) reactive minerals within available materials, with the potential for alkali–silica, alkali–silicate and alkali–carbonate reactivity; and
(3) materials which are unsound as opposed to reactive or whose physical breakdown may encourage reactivity.

Although each has been identified in the Middle East, rapid chloride-promoted rusting of reinforcement in concrete has tended to mask these longer-term processes of deterioration.

Active wadis within the mountains and a limited portion of the alluvial fans formed where they emerge onto the desert plain are sources of relatively clean, well-graded sands and gravels. Their torrent-bedded, poorly sorted structure makes them potentially good sources of 'all-in' material. The active periodic flooding ensures that groundwater movement is potentially downwards and that sulphates and chlorides do not accumulate to significant levels.

Upward movement of groundwater is, however, the dominant process and gives rise to a hard, well cemented surface layer called a 'duricrust', composed of precipitates from pore fluids. This layer most commonly comprises calcium and

Table 16.1 Definitions of concrete aggregate in major standards

Standard	Definition
BS 882: 1983	A granular material obtained by processing natural materials
ASTM C125-88	Granular materials, such as sand, gravel, crushed stone or iron blast-furnace slag
DIN 4226: Part 1	A mixture (in bulk) of uncrushed and/or crushed natural and/or artificial mineral particles. It consists of dense particles either of approximately the same, or of different, size

Table 16.2 Weathering and alteration grades[3]

Term	Grade	Description	Characteristics
Fresh	IA	No visible sign of rock material weathering	Aggregate properties not influenced by weathering. Mineral constituents of rock are fresh and sound
Faintly weathered	IB	Discolouration on major discontinuity (e.g. joint) surfaces	Aggregate properties not significantly influenced by weathering. Mineral constituents sound
Slightly weathered (this grade is capable of further subdivision)	II	Discolouration indicates weathering of rock material and discontinuity surfaces. All the rock material may be discoloured by weathering and may be somewhat weaker than its fresh condition	Aggregate properties may be significantly influenced by weathering. Strength and abrasion characteristics show some weakening. Some alteration of mineral constituents with micro-cracking
Moderately weathered	III	Less than half of the rock material is decomposed and/or disintegrated to a soil. Fresh or discoloured rock is present either as a continuous framework or as corestones	Aggregate properties will be significantly influenced by weathering. Soundness characteristics markedly affected. Alteration of mineral constituents common with much micro-cracking
Highly weathered	IV	More than half of the rock material is decomposed and/or disintegrated to a soil. Fresh or discoloured rock is present either as a discontinuous framework or as corestones	Not generally suitable for aggregate but may be suitable for lower parts of road, pavement and hardcore
Completely weathered	V	All rock material is decomposed and/or disintegrated to soil. The original mass structure is still largely intact	Not suitable for aggregate, or pavement but may be suitable for select fill
Residual soil	VI	All rock material is converted to soil. The mass structure and material fabric are destroyed. There is a large change in volume, but the soil still has not been significantly transported	May be suitable for random fill

calcium–magnesium carbonates (calcrete and dolocrete), calcium sulphate (gypcrete if strong, gypcrust if weak), and sodium chloride (salcrust). When the soluble materials are inert, the improvement in material properties may enable them to be used as aggregate sources. This is most commonly the case where weak limestones develop a calcrete capping. The accumulation of sulphates and chlorides more commonly render this an adverse process, although calcrete has no definite base and passes gradually into unhardened limestone below. The depth of working must be carefully controlled in order to maintain quality. However, calcretes generally cannot be considered as particularly good materials on physical and mechanical grounds, apart from possible chemical problems.

Silica sands are rare in the Persian Gulf region where carbonate sands predominate. Also, the heavy dependence on beach and coastal sands as sources of fine aggregate in the Middle East reflects the poor gradings of inland deposits.

Contamination of stockpiles of aggregate in the Middle East must be prevented by placement on a layer of dense concrete or asphalt laid to a fall and provided with effective drainage. Windbreaks may also be required to prevent wind-blown dust or salts contaminating stockpiles.

16.3 Processes of production

16.3.1 General

The raw materials for concrete aggregates are, broadly speaking, either essentially unconsolidated sands and gravels dug (*Figure 16.1*) from pits, or hard rocks blasted from quarries. The processing requires that size reduction and particle sizing are then carried out to produce a material complying with an end-user specification. The main processes involved are

Figure 16.1 Bucket-wheel excavator operating in a large sand and gravel working in Singapore

therefore:

(1) crushing; and
(2) sizing.

In addition, and depending very much on the detailed make-up of the original material, some kind of selection or screening process, or washing and dewatering process may be required.

The types of plant employed and its disposition depends on the characteristics of the raw material, the water available, the size of operation required, and the market to be supplied. Such a complex array of factors results in a very wide variety in the organization of quarries and pits. That organization is usually

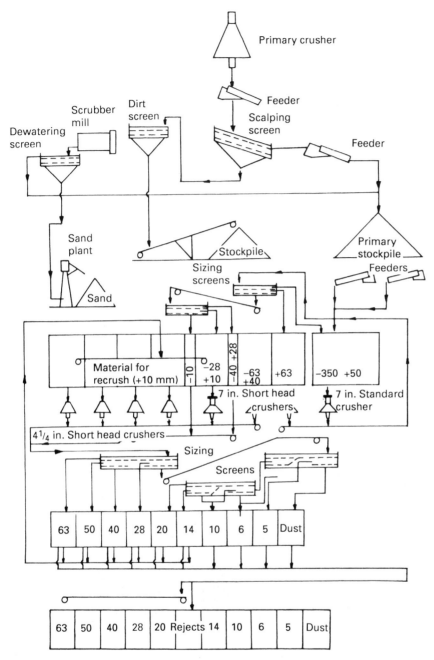

Figure 16.2 Flowsheet for a large hard rock quarry in the UK

shown as a flowsheet, but because of the variation of operations in detail, standard flowsheets cannot be formulated despite the relatively small range of plant type utilized. Indeed, unless the flowsheet reflects specific needs, the operation is likely to be fraught with commercial and technical problems.

Some examples of flowsheets for hardrock quarries and pits in both temperate and arid areas are given in *Figures 16.2* to *16.5*.

16.3.2 Crushing

The main aim of crushing is to reduce a material to a range of relevant sizes with a minimum production of fines. Adjustments

can be made to machines in order to achieve this, whilst also maintaining desirable shape characteristics. It is common for more than one stage of crushing to take place.

The nature of the aggregate source will tend to determine precisely what method of crushing plant is installed. Impact machines are most commonly used in limestone quarries or for 'correcting' the shape of materials prone to producing flaky or elongated particles by conventional crushing. However, if the quartz content of such materials is high, then abrasion is frequently a problem. The more conventional crushing plant utilizes double- or single-toggle jaw crushers depending on rock strength. In large, continuous operations, gyratory crushers are

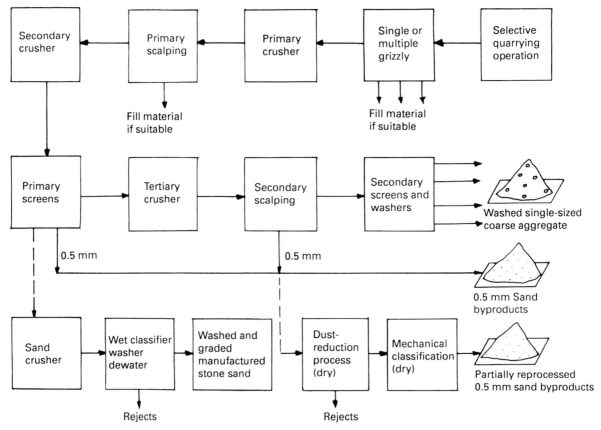

Figure 16.3 Flowsheet showing suggested scheme for production of crushed-rock aggregate in hot arid environments[23]

used. Core crushers are the most suitable type of secondary crushers as there is a uniform maximum-size material entering. However, cone crushers may further aggravate any problems of particle shape, and it may be necessary to adjust the reduction ratio to correct any problems. This results in extra stages of screening and recycling of the coarse fraction and must be balanced commercially against the production of unusable materials.

16.3.3 Sizing

Screening is the most common operation carried out in order to size material. The process involves grading particles by allowing undersize material to fall through a wire mesh, holes in a plate or spaces between parallel bars. Screening is also a useful method of effecting the rejection of unsuitable material, for example in mixtures of relatively strong and weak rocks where, after crushing, the latter is likely to be concentrated in the fine fraction. Repeated crushing and screening should result in a usable product largely devoid of the weaker constituents. Screening can also be used to reduce proportions of flaky and elongate particles, although this should be achieved by making adjustments to crushers at an early stage of production.

16.3.4 Scrubbing

The clay and fines content of some sand and gravel deposits may be so great that they cannot be screened or classified until they have undergone initial cleansing by scrubbing. This is normally done in a deep bath of slurry containing a long rotating cylinder fitted with lifter bars. The large amounts of water and the self-abrading action of the particles reduces any fines to a slurry which can be simply removed through screens.

In some desert areas, the gypsum content of sand is decreased by scrubbing and desliming. The process results in the disintegration of the soft gypsum enabling removal to take place as fines in suspension.

However, wet materials, particularly clayey materials, may cause blocking of screens. Unless a combination of further crushing to provide additional dry surfaces, and the tolerance of the equipment, can accommodate the moisture, then much more expensive wet processing may be required.

16.3.5 Dewatering

Large amounts of water are involved in wet screening, classifying and scrubbing. Recycling of the water and minimizing handling prior to sale necessitates that as much water as possible is removed from the aggregate. Where coarse aggregates are concerned, the classifiers allow dewatering to occur by the introduction of a delay immediately prior to removal of the product. Screens also permit simple dewatering, and with the application of high-frequency vibration can effectively dewater even some fine aggregates.

Dewatering screens work on the principle of generating maximum packing of particles by producing minimum pore space and hence water-retention capacity. They are made of low-friction/high-abrasion-resistance plastic or rubber and have

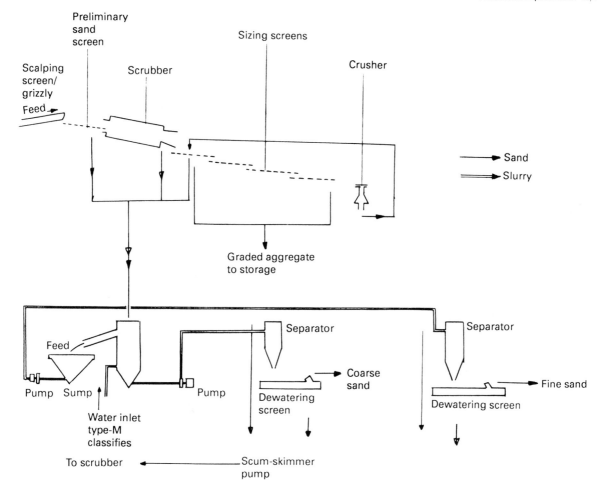

Figure 16.4 Flowsheet for production of natural sand and gravel aggregate in the UK

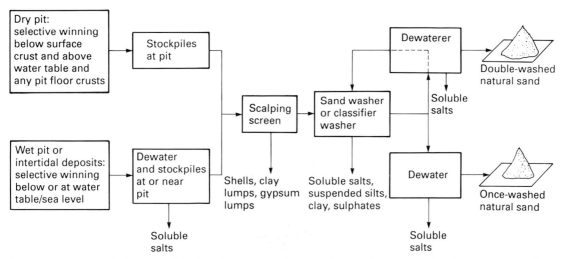

Figure 16.5 Flowsheet showing suggested scheme for production of processed natural-sand aggregate in hot arid environments[2,3]

a series of slots orientated perpendicular to the flow of sand. They have a shallow reverse slope and are driven by linear vibration. A thick 'cake' of sand moves across the screen which is densified by the vibration reducing the water content to perhaps 15% or even less.

Dewatering of waste fines is usually the most difficult process to operate efficiently. The mixture of silt and clay usually has to settle out in ponds or lagoons over a considerable period of time. Some chemical flocculants are available that accelerate the rate of setting; these are, however, expensive. Such setting ponds occupy large areas with problems of sterilization of resources, and production of a waste material eventually requiring either disposal or beneficiation before it can be used. In general, the silt and clay content of a potential resource is, therefore, an important consideration as to whether or not it will be exploited.

Table 16.3 Components of aggregate considered non-alkali silica reactive[10]

Air-cooled	Expanded	Microgranite
blast-furnace	clay/shale slate	Quartz*†
slag	Feldspar*	Schist
Andesite	Gabbro	Sintered pulverized-fuel ash
Basalt	Gneiss	Slate
Diorite	Granite	Syenite
Dolerite	Limestone	Trachyte
Dolomite	Marble	Tuff

* Feldspar and quartz are not rock types but are discrete mineral grains principally in fine aggregate.
† No highly strained quartz and not quartzite.

16.4 Types of aggregates for concrete

The classification of natural aggregates is as lightweight or dense according to their bulk density or particle density. In the BS1 system, a fine aggregate is one in which particles mainly pass a 5.0 mm BS 410: 1983 test sieve and does not contain more coarse material than permitted for the grading specified.[7] A coarse aggregate is one in which most particles are retained on a 5.0 mm BS 410: 1983 test sieve with no finer material than permitted for the various sizes specified.

In the ASTM system,[8] 4.75 mm (No. 4 sieve) is the nominal dividing size of coarse and fine aggregate. The system under the DIN scheme[9] relates mainly to all-in aggregate, the grading characteristics being specified according to the maximum size of aggregate particles.

Coarse aggregate can be:

(1) Gravel: (i) uncrushed gravel which results from the natural disintegration of rock; (ii) crushed gravel; or (iii) partially crushed gravel.
(2) Crushed rock.
(3) Blended coarse aggregate produced by the controlled blending of gravel and crushed rock.

Fine aggregate can be:

(1) Sand: (i) uncrushed sand; or (ii) partially crushed sand.
(2) Crushed gravel fines.
(3) Crushed rock fines.
(4) Blended fine aggregate.

In addition, 'all-in aggregate' may be produced which is a mixture of both coarse and fine fractions.

Specification and definitions of the geological characteristics of aggregate are given by BSI, ASTM and DIN as well as other authorities. However, the recent increase in interest generated by alkali–aggregate reactivity has led to the specification of more detailed petrological and mineralogical characteristics.[10]

Major specifications, e.g. Specification for Highway Works,[11] have adopted the recommendations, and detailed petrographic examination is now commonplace. A British Standard (which will be designated BS 812: Part 104) to cover petrographic examination of aggregates is to be issued shortly. In addition to the textural characteristics suitable for sound aggregate, details of the mineralogy are also considered (see *Tables 16.3* and *16.4*). An alternative method of providing geological information has been proposed[1] and is called the CADAM (classification and description of aggregate materials) system.

16.5 Common impurities

16.5.1 General

Undesirable constituents, for example shells, chalk, coal, particles of organic origins, pyrite, lead and zinc minerals, and micas, need to be identified and quantified before a source is used.

16.5.2 Chalk

Chalk is a soft limestone which is often frost susceptible and can cause 'pop-outs'. Limits on content are often arbitrary in that a maximum calcium carbonate content is specified. As a result, limits can be onerous. Although chalk is difficult to distinguish in analysis,[12] it is usually sufficiently distinctive to a geomaterials engineer for it to be quantified accurately.

16.5.3 Organics

Coal represents a range of mineral particles of organic origin from hard, chemically inert anthracite to soft, reactive brown coal or lignite. The problems vary from an increase in frost susceptibility (softer coals) to surface staining on decorative concrete surfaces. An example of the latter was experienced on the floor of a new shopping centre at Warrington. The fine aggregate used in the concrete came from part of the Wrexham delta terrace, an important source of sand and gravel of glacial origin in north Wales. Discrete beds containing particles of coal eroded from nearby carboniferous rocks are contained within the outwash (*Figure 16.6*) and it is these particles which were incorporated within the aggregate. The alkaline cleansing solutions applied to the floor of the shopping centre very quickly caused 'bleeding' from the coal particles and discolouration of the concrete.

Other organic debris tends to be much less stable even than coal, and contains humic acids and lignins which have a retarding effect on the setting and hardening of concrete. Less than 0.1% of such chemicals may significantly retard the rate of gain in strength of the concrete.[12] A test described in BS 812: 1988 will readily indicate the presence of such materials.

16.5.4 Sulphide minerals

Pyrite is an iron sulphide mineral commonly found in rocks which have suffered hydrothermal alteration, and in slates. It is most likely to be found in aggregates from crushed igneous rocks. It is a brass-yellow, cubic mineral and is normally not very reactive. However, far more reactive is another iron sulphide mineral, marcasite, which is found in flint gravels and

Table 16.4 Some guidance for the assessment of rock types not included in *Table 16.3*[10]

Rock type	Definition	Potentially alkali-reactive components that may sometimes be present
Arkose	Detrital sedimentary rock containing more than 25% feldspar	See sandstone
Breccia	Coarse detrital rock containing angular fragments	See sandstone
Chert	Micro- or crypto-crystalline silica	See flint
Conglomerate	Coarse detrital rock containing rounded fragments	See sandstone
Flint	Strictly, chert occurring in cretaceous chalk	Chalcedonic silica and micro- or crypto-crystalline quartz. Some varieties may contain opaline silica
Granulite	Metamorphic rock	Highly-strained quartz
Greywacke	Detrital sedimentary rock containing poorly sorted rock fragments and mineral grains	May be alkali–silicate reactive.* See sandstone
Gritstone	Sandstone with coarse, angular grains	See sandstone
Hornfels	Fine-grained, thermally metamorphosed rock	Glass† or devitrified glass. Highly-strained‡ and/or microcrystalline quartz. Phyllosilicates*
Quartz	Discrete mineral grains very common in fine aggregates	Highly-strained‡ quartz
Quartzite	(i) Sedimentary or *ortho*-quartzite (ii) Metamorphic or *meta*-quartzite	See sandstone. Highly-strained‡ quartz and/or high-energy quartzite grain boundaries
Rhyolite	Fine-grained to glassy acid volcanic rock	Glass† or devitrified glass. Tridymite. Cristobalite. Opaline or chalcedonic veination or vugh-fillings
Sandstone	Detrital sedimentary rock. The grains are most commonly quartz, but fragments or grains of almost any type of rock or mineral are possible	Highly-strained quartz. Some types of rock cement, notably opaline silica, chalcedonic silica, and micro-crystalline or crypto-crystalline quartz. Phyllosilicates

* Phyllosilicates are sheet silicate minerals, including the chlorite, vermiculite, mica and clay mineral groups. Within the UK a few cases of possible alkali–silicate reaction have been reported in coarse aggregates containing greywacke and related rocks. The matrix in such rocks is very finely divided and consists of phyllosilicates, quartz and other minerals.
† Rocks containing more than 5% (by volume) glass, partially devitrified glass or devitrified glass should be classified as potentially alkali reactive.
‡ If the average undulatory extinction angle obtained from at least 20 separate quartz grains (measured in thin section under a petrological microscope) is more than 25° the quartz should be classified as 'highly strained'. Rocks containing more than 30% highly-strained quartz should be classified as potentially alkali reactive.

Figure 16.6 Detrital coal in glacial outwash deposits worked as an aggregate source at Rossett, North Wales

which has usually originated from certain organic material in the chalk. Marcasite is normally revealed readily if suspect particles are placed in saturated limewater, where, if reactive, they will quickly cause the liquid to turn green due to the presence of ferrous sulphate.

16.5.5 Micas

Micas are most commonly found in certain regional metamorphic rocks and igneous rocks with acidic (silica rich) affinities. They are commonly found, therefore, either in crushed-rock sources or in natural sands derived from mica-bearing rocks, usually close to the source rock. The main problems with micas accrue from their softness, weakness and platy structure, the last of these relating to the perfect cleavage of the mineral which causes poor bonding with the cement paste. The most common micas are biotite, and muscovite, the former a dark-brown or black mica, the latter, silver-coloured. Muscovite is generally more harmful than biotite in a concrete aggregate. However, biotite mica within concrete made with a crushed granite aggregate in Hong Kong, commonly displayed shrinkage when present as discrete particles (*Figure 16.7*).

Micas also have implications for water:cement ratios. From tests on muscovite,[13] it has been found that a 1% increase in the mica content in the total aggregate requires an increase of about 0.02 in water:cement ratio in order to maintain constant workability. This, in turn, is accompanied by a loss in

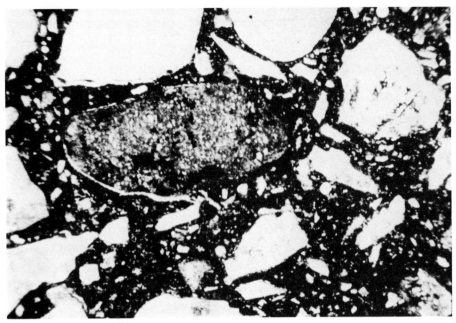

Figure 16.7 Aggregate shrinkage around a biotite grain in fine aggregate of concrete from Hong Kong (photomicrograph; magnification × 50)

compressive strength of as much as 5% for a 1% increase in mica content, whereas at a constant water:cement ratio the loss in strength is about 3% for a 1% increase in mica content. Difficulties also exist in describing the effects on a strictly quantitative basis.[13] Mica tends to have a large and variable specific surface and, so, weight for weight, different samples might be expected to have significantly different effects on concrete. Therefore, in practice, it is preferable to perform tests on concrete with a specific mica-bearing aggregate in order to determine specific detrimental effects.

Results of tests on muscovite mica in concrete[14] show that a maximum limit of 1% mica by weight of fine aggregate should be applied unless laboratory trials can be undertaken. Phyllite, a low-grade metamorphic mica-rich rock is contained in the so-called 'mica trap' of the Channel Islands. This has been found to cause disintegration of concrete as a result of expansion.

16.5.6 Clay, silt and dust

Surface coatings of clay on aggregates reduce the effectiveness of the bond between the aggregate and paste adversely affecting the strength and durability properties of the concrete. A similar result may accrue from dusty aggregate, usually in the form of silt-sized, non-reactive coatings resulting from either natural processes, e.g. weathering, or processing (e.g. crushing). Shrinkage or increased water demand are also very important, the latter relating to the large surface area of silt and dust.

The widespread pluvial trains and sheets found in the Middle East are being exploited increasingly as wadi deposits become worked out. However, the common gypsum or carbonate cement, and content of friable clay or weathered particles makes many such sources very dusty on crushing. The serpentines of the Middle East have abundant microcracks infilled with magnesium or calcium carbonates, and these too produce dusty aggregate.

Fines content of aggregate is normally determined by a method of wash grading or sedimentation. However, determination of clay content by methylene blue absorption is specified

in the draft Euro-code, and the procedure for determining methylene blue absorption is described in detail in an experimental French standard.[15] The principle of the test is based on the colour change of a methylene blue solution which is the result of preferential absorption of the blue onto clay particles.

16.5.7 Shell content

Within the catalogue of impurities likely to influence the quality of concrete from marine-dredged aggregates are sea shells. Sea shells are composed mainly of calcium carbonate which, if present as a minor component of an aggregate will not lead to problems in concrete.[16] Indeed, neither the British[7] nor American[8] Standard specifications cite limits for shell content in fine aggregate, and only the British Standard gives limits for coarse aggregates (20% for 10–5 mm; 8% for 10 mm).

Sea shells have particular implications for the permeability of concrete, although it has been claimed[16] that most shells fill with paste and, therefore, do not present such a problem (*Figures 16.8* and *16.9*). Flat shells and most broken shells are flaky and result in problems of workability associated with flaky aggregate in general. However, marine aggregates are generally better rounded than most land-based sources and the flaky nature of shells is offset by this.

The carbonate sands of the Gulf are composed of worn debris of marine organisms which produce good workability, but which are also absorptive, have poor gradings and trap air, chlorides and sulphates in the porous and sometimes hollow particles. These sands can be blown inland to contribute to aolian dunes of the interior, although the effect diminishes with distance from the coast.

The carbonate mineral is often aragonite which has a low long-term stability. A high aragonite content and high porosity can lead to unexpected relationships between absorption and specific gravity, resulting in a water demand higher than generally expected for silica sand. The expansion accompanying the conversion of aragonite to calcite is not thought to be

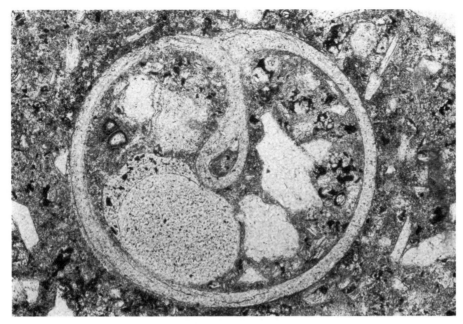

Figure 16.8 Photomicrograph of shell showing body cavity largely infilled with paste (magnification × 50)

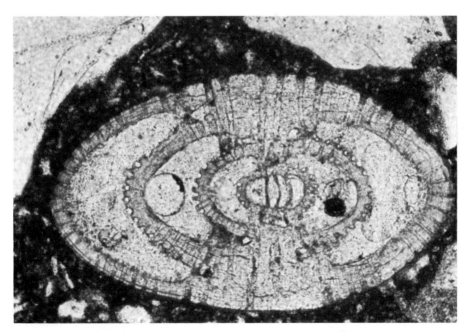

Figure 16.9 Photomicrograph of shell showing body cavity devoid of paste (magnification × 50)

important in the engineering time-scale. It is often specified that the proportion of hollow shells retained on the 2.36-mm sieve should not exceed 3% by weight of the entire aggregate sample.

16.5.8 Chloride and sulphate content

Chlorides can be of particular concern in both marine-dredged and arid-land sources of concrete aggregate.

Marine-dredged aggregates contain a small quantity of natural chlorides which have little influence on plain concrete made with cement complying with the British[17] or American[18] Standard specifications except, according to BACMI,[19] to slightly increase the rate of hardening. However, sulphate-resisting cement and super-sulphated cement characteristically contain lower levels of tricalcium aluminate (C_3A) and a lower proportion of the free chloride ions are combined with the organic complexes. Furthermore, durability of concrete exposed to ingress of chlorides, e.g. in marine environments, is lower if

Table 16.5 Chloride content of concretes from marine aggregates[20]

Concrete grade	C30	C35	C40	C45	C50
Minimum cement content (kg m^{-3}) BS 8110: 1985 (*Table 16.4*)	275	300	325	350	400
Assumed maximum aggregate:cement ratio	6.9	6.3	5.7	5.3	4.5

Chloride ion in combined aggregate (wt%)					
Maximum	0.06	0.46	0.43	0.39	0.37	0.32
chloride ion	0.05	0.40	0.37	0.34	0.32	0.28
in concrete	0.04	0.33	0.30	0.28	0.26	0.23
(wt% cement)*	0.03	0.26	0.24	0.22	0.21	0.19
	0.02	0.19	0.18	0.17	0.16	0.14
	0.01		0.11	0.11	0.10	0.10

* Derived from aggregate + cement. (The chloride content of cement is assumed to be at the maximum of the typical range[21] of 0.01–0.05% for ordinary Portland cement.)

Table 16.6 Suggested working limits for chloride and sulphate contamination in concrete aggregates in the Middle East[23]

Total chlorides (as Cl)	In fine aggregate not more than 0.06% Cl by weight of fine aggregate. In coarse aggregate not more than 0.03% Cl by weight of coarse aggregate. Overriding requirement: in concrete not more than 0.3% Cl by weight of cement
Total sulphates (as SO$_3$)	In fine aggregate not more than 0.4% of fine aggregate. In coarse aggregate not more than 0.4% of coarse aggregate. Overriding requirement: in concrete not more than 4.0% by weight of cement

made with sulphate-resisting cement than with ordinary Portland cement.

Concretes containing embedded metals are of much greater concern.[20] *Table 16.5* lists the chloride contents of different grades of concrete based on a cement chloride content of 0.05%.[21]

For a maximum chloride content[7] of 0.06%, based on mix proportions for reinforced concrete, the 0.4% specified as a chloride limit in BS 8110: 1985 is exceeded if the cement content is low. For well-washed aggregates, the chloride limits attained should be rather less than 0.06%, and the result of a Building Research Establishment (UK) project[20] indicated typical chloride contents of 0.035% for combined coarse and fine marine aggregates.

In arid environments where chlorides often occur in conjunction with sulphates, complex interactions may result which, for example, result in an up to three-fold increase in the solubility of calcium sulphate (gypsum), leading to much more rapid reactions. The working limits shown in *Table 16.6* should be applied with caution when both occur together in concentrations close to those limits.[23]

The chemical trends in coastal regions of deserts are well established. On storm beaches, chlorides generally do not exceed 0.006% near the surface because of downward leaching by rainfall. The chloride levels increase to about 0.05% at about 1.0 m above the water table, increasing rapidly both downwards and inland towards the sabkha to an average of 0.3%. Sulphates display no similar increase with respect to depth, the main variation being lateral towards the margin of the beach complex where it meets the sabkha. Sulphates and chlorides may, however, be blown from sabkhas and salinas and become incorporated in aolian dunes. Indeed, some dunes at the leeward edge of sabkhas may be composed largely of gypsum.

Testing for chlorides is generally performed by classical volumetric analysis, but quicker methods are required in Middle East conditions where such determinations acquire greater significance. The nephelometer method in which the density of a barium sulphate precipitate in suspension is measured saves valuable preparation time. Titration strips give a rapid assessment of chloride content by colorimetry. However, because significant quantities of chlorides may be held in pores of aggregates, grinding is desirable, otherwise further time is required for diffusion. Even the British Standard method specifies only 24-h immersion with occasional shaking, and doubts have been expressed[23] as to whether this is sufficient.

Sulphate testing is normally carried out using methods developed for soils or lightweight aggregate. However, total acid-soluble rather than water-soluble sulphates should be determined, and the British Standard tests[24,25] both require that the sample be ground to finer than 420 μm in order to liberate the sulphate. The recent British Standard for sulphate testing of concrete aggregates (BS 812: Part 118: 1988) utilizes a procedure very similar to that of the BS 1377: 1975 method for soils.

16.6 Physical properties of aggregates

16.6.1 General

The determination of the properties of aggregates can, depending upon the end-use of the concrete, lead to an extensive programme of testing. Some of the tests and the standards followed in carrying them out are shown in *Table 16.7*.

16.6.2 Grading

This is probably the most important characteristic providing a combination of coarse and fine aggregate producing:

(1) the lowest possible surface area per unit volume; and
(2) the lowest void content per unit volume; resulting in
(3) the lowest possible water content; and
(4) the lowest cement content,

in order to achieve the levels of workability and strength required.

Good correlation of BS and ASTM sieve sizes exists.[4] However, in the International Standard of sieve sizes for aggregates[26] there is lack of unanimity, with sizes from one series not overlapping with the BS and ASTM sizes.[4]

Grading limits for aggregates[7,8] are very wide enabling a wide variety of materials to be used. It is therefore also important to consider the overall grading characteristics of the combined coarse and fine aggregates in the proportions to be employed in a particular mix.[3]

Four grading zones for fine aggregates are specified in BS 882: 1983 characterized by the <600 μm content. The high numbered zone has the higher proportion of fines. Fine aggregate from any one of the zones will produce concrete of a given workability and strength by reducing the proportion of fine aggregate from higher zones, thus creating an equivalent overall grading of the combined aggregates.[3] Concrete made with aggregate outside the grading limits of BS 882: 1983 can be evaluated by producing trial mixes.

Table 16.7 Aggregate tests by standard and specification

Test	Standard			
	BS	*ASTM*	*DIN*	*Other (ref. no.)*
Definitions and descriptions	BS 6100: 1984, Section 5.2	C294-86, C638-84	4226: Part 1	
Grading, dry method	BS 812: 1985, Part 103	C136-84a	4226: Part 3, 3.1	
Grading, wet method	BS 812: 1985, Part 103	C117-87	4226: Part 3, 3.1	
Clay, silt, dust content	BS 812: 1975, Part 1	C117-87, C142-78	4226: Part 3, 3.6.1	15
Relative density and water absorption	BS 812: 1975, Part 2, Clause 5	C127-84	4226: Part 3, 3.4	
Moisture content		C128-84		
Surface moisture		C556-84		
Particle shape	BS 812: 1985, Section 105.1 BS 812: 1975, Part 1, Clause 7.4	D3398-81	4226: Part 3, 3.2	
Bulk density of aggregates including voids and bulking	BS 812: 1975, Part 2, Clause 6.0	C29-87	4226: Part 3, 3.3	
Lightweight pieces		C123-83		
10% Fines value	BS 812: 1975, Part 3, Clause 8			
Aggregate impact value	BS 812: 1975, Part 3, Clause 6			
Aggregate crushing value	BS 812: 1975, Part 3, Clause 7			
Aggregate abrasion value	BS 812: 1975, Part 3, Clause 9			
Polished stone value	BS 812: 1975, Part 3, Clause 10			
Los Angeles abrasion value		C131-81, C535-81		
Petrography	BS 812: Part 104 (draft)	C295-85	52, 100	
Soundness/frost resistance		C88-83, C33-81, C682-87	4226: Part 3, 3.5	
Potential alkali–aggregate reactivity			4226: Part 3, 4.2	
Mortar bar		C227-87		
Chemical methods		C289-87	38	
In presence of admixtures		C441-81		
Rock cylinder method		C586-81		
Osmotic cell test				39
Mortar prism test				40–43
Concrete prism test				44–46
Gel pat test				47
Drying shrinkage				*BRE Digest 35* (1968)
Organic content		C40-84	4226: Part 3, 3.6.2	
Sulphate content	BS 812: 1988, Part 118		4226: Part 3, 3.6.4	
Chloride content	BS 812: 1988, Part 117		4226: Part 3, 3.6.5	
Impurities affecting hardening			4226: Part 3, 3.6.3	

Additional care is required when producing concrete containing very fine or very coarse sands. The major consideration is that the grading of a sand is suitable for the aggregate blend in a particular concrete. Furthermore, grading characteristics for a particular supply should not vary beyond one in ten consecutive samples falling outside the specified grading limits of the specification.[1]

Very coarse sands can lead to harsh mixes resulting in bleeding, particularly at low cement contents. The use of very fine sands demands that a balance be achieved between adequate cohesiveness of the mix and keeping water demand to a minimum in response to the large surface area. The problems arising from the use of coarse and fine sands can be alleviated by the judicious use of air entrainment and water-reducing admixtures, respectively.

Special concretes may require specially graded aggregates, and it has been recommended that single-sized coarse aggregate be used, being separately batched to provide the precise grading characteristics required. The requirement may be for very high strength or particular aesthetic or uniformity characteristics.

In situations where resistance to scour or high mechanical stability immediately after compaction is required, then gap graded aggregate may be required. These types of concrete also need greater applications of design, production, handling and placing skills.[1] Advantages accruing from utilizing very coarse (75–150 mm maximum) aggregate in bulk pours may be realized by reducing cement content and heat generation. However, risks of segregation are greater. The main requirement is that the coarsest fraction is not of lesser quality than the $\leqslant 40$ mm sizes, a problem most commonly related to particle shape. Many crushed sources achieve improvements in particle shape following secondary and tertiary crushing.

Although practice in the UK has shown that grading *per se* is not a common source of problems in domestic aggregate sources, this is not necessarily the case elsewhere. Specifiers should ensure that impracticable and uneconomic requirements are not imposed.[1] Coastal sands from the Gulf are well sorted and commonly have narrower and often finer gradings than generally preferred for concrete. A survey of beach sands from Qatar indicated that, of 365 gradings, 46% did not conform completely to any of the BS 882: 1983 grading zones. A similar survey in Dubai showed 62% in zone 5 of BS 882: 1983 with 26% finer than zone 4.

Aolian sands are mainly in the 50–600 μm size range with a content of about 10%. It is occasionally possible to select parts of dunes with better grading or to mix the dune sand with e.g. crushed rock fines, assuming that contaminants are within acceptable limits.

The most important effects of the narrow grading and fine particle size of aolian sands are the increased water demand and tendency to bleed. However, the smoothness and roundness tend to limit the water demand for a given degree of workability. The effects of poor grading or high water demand can be partially compensated for in the mix design, and concrete of 25–30 N mm^{-2} is possible made with selected dune sands, possibly with additives to reduce water demand.

16.6.3 Particle shape and surface texture

The shape and textural characteristics of aggregates tend to influence the properties of fresh, wet concrete more than those of hardened concrete. The workability of a mix is influenced by rough, flat or elongate particles, requiring more water (and cement to maintain the water:cement ratio) in order to produce workable concrete. The shape and texture of aggregate particles are most important for the bonding generated with the cement paste, and particularly the implications this has for the flexural strength of hardened concrete. For high-strength concretes, the full compressive strength may not be attainable because of an insufficiently strong bond. It has been shown[27] that an increase in the angularity number (BS 812: 1975) from 1 to 10 caused a 10% reduction in the compaction factor.

An approximate cubic shape for aggregate particles with a minimum of flat or elongate grains is desirable. Elongate particles should be limited to 10–20% by weight of the total aggregate.[3] This requirement is also relevant to crushed sources where flat and elongate particles tend to become more numerous in smaller sized fractions. This will depend very much on the original nature of the material and also the method of processing, the former generally assuming greater importance.

16.6.4 Bulk and relative density

The bulk density or unit weight of an aggregate is a reflection of its grading characteristics, producing a particular void content for a degree of compaction. Its major importance is in converting mixes specified by volume into proportions by mass.

The relative density is particularly important to the properties of the final mix, and especially so where a minimum density of concrete is required. In general, higher values of relative density tend to indicate a high susceptibility to segregation during handling and compaction, 'bleeding' and plastic settlement.

16.6.5 Water absorption and surface moisture

Estimates of several characteristics of aggregate particles can be made from water-absorption characteristics, including strength, shrinkage, soundness, and general durability. As a general guideline, aggregates with a low capacity for absorption (less than 1%) tend to be preferable. The British Standard recommends that aggregate absorption should not 'generally' exceed 3%, with 2.5% often being specified for overseas work.[1]

The various test procedures relevant to aggregates usually specify a particular moisture condition, each having implications for batch weights of aggregates, bulking characteristics and mix proportions, i.e.

(1) Oven-dry—in a fully absorbant state.
(2) Air-dry—contains some internal moisture and partially absorbent.
(3) Saturated surface dry—neither contributing water to nor taking water from a mix.
(4) Damp or wet—possessing excess water at the surface.

16.6.6 Mechanical properties

The mechanical properties of coarse aggregates should indicate adequate resistance to breakdown during handling, transportation, mixing and compaction. Furthermore, they should be such that the compressive strength and performance of the hardened concrete are not impaired. However, the contribution to the strength of the concrete probably relates also to the absorption and bonding characteristics with the cement paste. The elastic modulus of aggregate influences the amount of creep and shrinkage which can be accommodated by the concrete, and because of point loads at contacts, aggregates should have a crushing strength several times that of concrete. The strength and elastic properties of aggregates accrue mainly from their mineralogical composition, texture and structure. Therefore, the presence merely of strong minerals will not guarantee a strong aggregate if the grains are not bonded together strongly. Weathering, even in its very early stages, is an extremely important process causing disruption of intercrystalline as well as cemented bonds. In natural sands and gravels, processes of weathering, erosion, transportation and deposition have already contributed much to the maturing of a potential aggregate supply by the preferential removal of weak components. Crushed rock sources have not similarly benefitted and depend upon their primary properties for suitability as aggregates. However, certain minerals which are highly resistant to natural processes of denudation may be reactive in concretes (see Section 16.6.10).

Abrasion properties of aggregates are important in certain special circumstances, notably pavement-quality concretes, heavy-duty floors, marine defences and river-training walls. Again, mineralogy and texture are particularly important, with fresh igneous and non-foliated metamorphic rocks producing the best results.

Testing methods utilized for determining strength characteristics normally depend upon applying a load to a graded aggregate and recording the reduction in weight or size of the original fraction. Unfortunately, correlations between the various strength and abrasion values are not well established, and each is very susceptible to the precise state of weathering of the original sample.

16.6.7 Durability

The durability of an aggregate has been defined as:

'The ability of individual particles to retain their integrity and not to suffer any mechanical or chemical changes, to extents which could adversely affect the properties or performance of concrete in either engineering or aesthetic respects'.[1]

The durability of an aggregate depends on the environment in which it is to be used, and several different types of aggregate may need to be employed within any one project depending on the local environmental conditions to which concretes are exposed.

Once again, the petrology of the materials forming the aggregate are of particular significance in determining durability characteristics. However, and particularly for new, untried sources, apparent stability of the natural environment needs to be checked against the new environmental conditions which will be encountered by the aggregate in a concrete structure. Of particular note are zones of regular wetting and drying, exposure to salt, permanently shaded areas, exposure to aggressive chemicals or effluents, and high or low temperatures.

One particular aspect of durability which is considered particularly important is aggregate 'soundness'. This has been described as:

'the ability of aggregate to resist excessive changes in volume as a result of changes in physical conditions'.[3]

The most common processes leading to significant volume changes in aggregates are freeze–thaw, shrinkage, thermal, salt crystallization, and moisture ingress. Unsound aggregate may be grouped, according to the form of their volume change, into:

(1) particles which expand disruptively, for example argillaceous limestones, porous rocks and minerals notably certain cherts and slates;
(2) particles which shrink, notably certain altered dolerites and basalts containing chlorites, greywackes, argillaceous rocks and mica schists. Some correlations have been established between shrinkage and water absorption,[28] and content of secondary minerals;[29] and
(3) particles which disintegrate, such as friable rocks and clay lumps, leading to pitting of the surface of concrete.

Weathered or hydrothermally altered igneous particles may fall into either group depending upon the extent of the alteration[5] and the nature of the alteration products. Weak porous limestones not completely altered to calcite, clay inclusions in calcrete and fragments of carbonate or gypsum duricrusts are common types of unsound inclusions in aggregates from desert areas.

16.6.8 Frost resistance

In the UK, soundness requirements are rarely specified in detail other than that the aggregate should be 'sound'. However, the Property Services Agency (PSA) is an important exception when specifying pavement quality concrete for airfield runways. Their requirements for frost resistance of aggregates were based on a soundness test similar to the one used in American practice, although having small but potentially significant variations in the test method. A major concern of the PSA was disintegration of aggregate particles and ingestion into jet engines. Some breakdown of flint aggregates containing a porous coating or 'cortex' has been experienced with pop-outs developing on pavement surfaces. The cortex is a dull white exterior 'crust' to flint particles which has been ascribed to weathering.[30] The cortex is coarsely porous and contrasts markedly with the glossy dense interior of unaltered flint. The frost susceptibility of the cortex is related to absorption and micro-porosity characteristics, and there is a greater tendency for pop-outs to occur when 'white' flints were used than when 'black' or 'brown' flints were.[30] The 'white' flints were those possessing a significant cortex.

Subsequent work by Harry Stanger Ltd on flint gravels from Kent, and on *in situ* flints in frost-shattered chalk cliffs at Pays de Caux, France[31] has shown that a cortex develops fairly uniformly in all colours of flint. However, the critical cortex volume and the presence or absence of cracks determines the tolerance of the flint aggregate to freeze–thaw processes. Research on flint gravels from Kent has indicated that the detailed geomorphological setting and geological history of the flints are particularly important factors. The sources investigated were from second and third river terraces, a storm beach, and an offshore source. Some details of the particle mineralogy and patina thicknesses are shown in *Figure 16.10*. The reworking of the gravel deposits ranged from slight (second terrace) to very high (storm beach) and resulted in considerable variation in the preservation of the cortex. Field evaluation of sources therefore provides a good initial assessment of the likely frost susceptibility of sources.

As a result of the pop-out problem and certain other factors, the PSA now specify a standard crushed limestone coarse aggregate for pavement-quality concrete. However, on smaller projects, economy demands that local materials, which may include flint gravels, are used.

16.6.9 Salt weathering

The construction boom in the hot, arid countries of the Middle East during the 1970s highlighted the significance of salt crystallization processes on aggregate durability and concretes in general. The salts are mainly derived from groundwater or from within the ground, although salts on inadequately washed aggregates also occur. This method of rock decay is particularly prevalent in the coastal sabkhas and the salinas of desert interiors where evaporation from exposed surfaces can be constantly replenished by capillary movement. The salts are predominantly sulphates and chlorides which crystallize within pores and cracks in aggregate particles. Expansion pressures result in cracking of the walls of pores and, ultimately, in disintegration.

A similar process occurs with the cyclical dehydration/rehydration of salts in pores and the volume changes associated with it. The most common change has been identified as that between gypsum and anhydrite resulting from dew-fall at night and subsequent drying out during the day.[3]

The sodium or magnesium sulphate soundness test (ASTM C88) provides a better indicator of susceptibility to these processes than to freeze–thaw. Water-absorption characteristics also show a fairly good correlation. Nevertheless, anomalies occur in the results from both types of testing, and more work is required on the subject.

The more porous materials included in, for example, a load from a quarry in the Middle East, may present problems with respect to both physical and chemical characteristics. Some significant improvement can be made simply by loading rock from a face onto grizzly screens and rejecting material below a certain size, say 50 or 70 mm, prior to transferring the oversize material for primary crushing. Additional scalping will then further improve the product. However, an expensive alternative, hand selection at a blown face prior to primary crushing, may be justified. Improvements with respect to chloride and sulphate contamination by selective screening at a limestone plant[23] is shown in *Figure 16.11*.

16.6.10 Alkali–aggregate reactivity

It is now over 50 years since the first papers on alkali–aggregate reactivity (AAR) were published in the USA. The body of research information and case studies has increased greatly during the last decade and tests for assessing the potential reactivity of aggregate sources are now specified generally (e.g. Department of Transport[11]).

The processes, irrespective of detailed mineralogy, involve the reaction of certain types of aggregate with the alkali hydroxides in cement, potentially causing the formation of an expansive gel and cracking of the concrete (*Figure 16.12*).

There are three types of reactivity generally recognized, although the precise identification and categorization is not always straightforward. The three types are:

(1) Alkali–silica reaction (ASR) in which alkalis react with amorphous, very finely crystalline or disordered forms of silica. In addition to the minerals opal, chalcedony, chert, etc., some very fine grained or glassy rocks, particularly of a volcanic origin, are susceptible, and these can be of basic as well as acidic (geological sense, referring to silica content) composition.
(2) Alkali–silicate reaction is potentially more common than originally defined[32] and is based mainly on aggregates produced from phyllo-silicate-rich rocks such as phyllites. In the case of certain basic volcanic glasses, in which free silica minerals are unlikely to exist, there is a point of overlap with alkali–silica reaction.
(3) Alkali–carbonate reaction (ACR) is most commonly

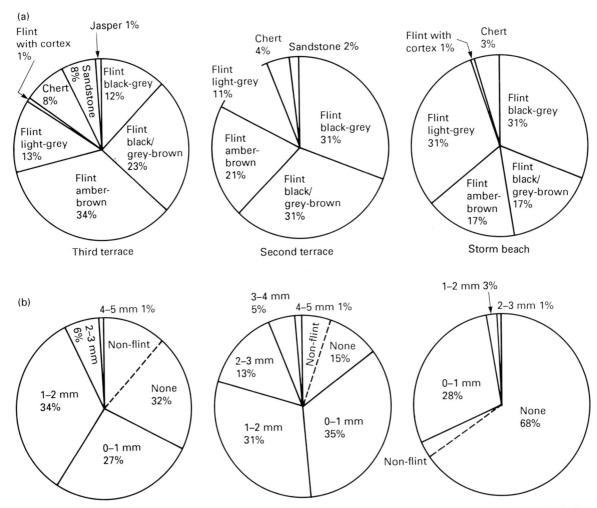

Figure 16.10 (a) Particle mineralogy and (b) patina thickness of flint gravel aggregates from three different sources in south-east England

associated with dolomite-rich and argillaceous limestones. The process of dedolomitization is the best documented.[33] Reactions involving clay minerals in limestones are more likely to be forms of alkali-silicate reaction. In addition, silica minerals frequently of organic origin, contained within limestones also occasionally display ASR.

Petrographic analysis is employed in order to identify the presence of potentially reactive minerals and many such techniques have been described.[34] However, the proportion of the minerals as well as chemical and environmental characteristics relating to the availability of alkalis and moisture are probably even more important in assessing whether reactivity is likely to be disruptive.[1,35] Petrographic methods will tend to indicate the most appropriate suite of tests to be performed subsequently, although several of these are long-term and thus highlight the necessity of adopting a medium- to long-term view of properties of aggregates in any planning decisions.

Guidance on specifying aggregates in order to minimize the risk of damage to concrete has been provided[10] and the findings are widely utilized. Nevertheless, certain anomalies still exist. Of particular significance for particularly fine aggregates used in the UK is the question of quartzite. The breakdown of

quartzites produces discrete quartz grains, albeit usually strained, which represent a common and probably ubiquitous component of sands. Quartzite grains which consist of assemblages of strained quartz are also similarly found in virtually all sources of natural sands. The guidance in the Hawkins Report is that highly strained quartz above a certain concentration and quartzite should not be present. The secondary microcrystalline quartz present at the individual crystal margins in a quartzite is considered a more reactive component than the disordered (strained) quartz, and it is therefore necessary to distinguish between the two materials.

Both expansive and non-expansive ASR and ACR have been reported from Middle East aggregates. Some of the alkalis may have resulted from contamination from sodium chloride rather than just the cement and it has been shown[36] that the addition of various alkali salts, including chlorides, results in increased expansion of test mortar bars.

The widely utilized Palaeocene limestones of the Gulf contain both dolomite and clay, the joint presence of which renders them sources of potential ACR. The Mesozoic limestones of the Oman Range, notably from Ras-al-Khaimah, contain a red calcareous clay in solution cavities which must be removed to produce a better-quality aggregate. Shaly horizons are also present which

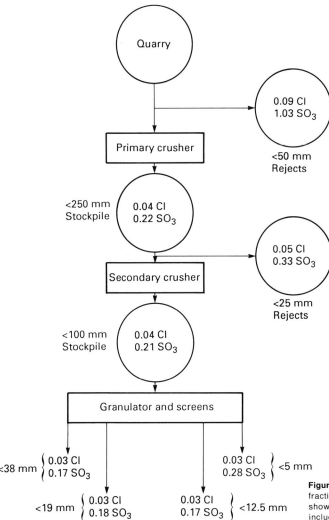

Figure 16.11 Chloride and sulphate contents of various size fractions from an operating quarry in calcrete in the Middle East, showing concentrations of salts in rejected undersized fractions, including the <5 mm fraction[23]

give 40% losses in soundness tests (ASTM C88). Both the red clay and shale produce pop-outs if incorporated into concrete. Aggregates from volcanic sources have been identified as a source of reactivity, possibly alkali–silicate, although the cherts, a common constituent of some gravels, are believed to be unreactive.

Routine petrographic analysis of aggregate sources is now common and most aggregate producers are aware of the advisability of carrying out repeat analyses as a matter of course in order to take into account natural variability. It is similarly advisable to perform routine petrographic analysis on crushed sources and also to note macro-features within quarries and their implications for aggregates. Crushed sources may contain evenly disseminated deleterious substances, but are more likely to contain them as the composition of the rock mass in the quarry varies or in variable proportions determined by processing.

Effects of both ASR and ACR may be evaluated from mortar bar tests (ASTM C277 and ASTM C342). A rock prism test has also been developed for assessing ACR (ASTM C586) in which the samples are placed in a caustic soda solution. However, the test is considered insufficiently sensitive for many carbonate rocks from the Middle East and ordinary mortar-bar tests are often preferred.[23]

The results from these tests are available only after several months. Quicker tests for assessing ASR exist. The quick chemical test (ASTM C289) can produce unreliable results in the presence of magnesium carbonates and silicates, both of which are common constituents of Middle East dolomites and serpentinites. The gel-pat test should be tested at 20°C as recommended, but also at 35°C to simulate local conditions. Reacting particles can be observed and identified. However, in both tests, reactivity rather than the expansion resulting from reactivity are tested for. A range of procedures for testing aggregates for reactivity has recently been reviewed.[37] As well as the relatively familiar tests, some less-common methods are covered including the dissolution test,[38] osmotic cell test,[39] mortar prism tests[40–43] and concrete prism tests.[44–46]

16.7 Standards

The major standards in use for aggregate testing and evaluation are British, American and German. Virtually all aspects of

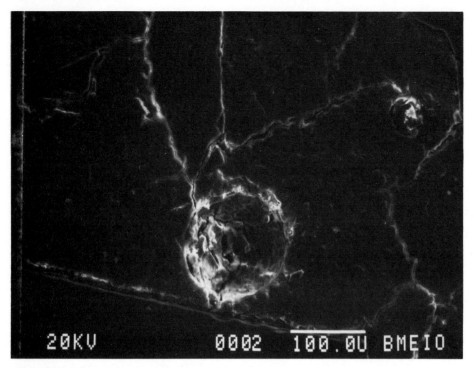

Figure 16.12 Electron photomicrograph of expansive gel in cracked concrete (Scale bar = 0.1 mm)

Table 16.8 Suggested schedule of tests on Middle East aggregates for use in concrete under exposed conditions[23]

Scope	Test	Authority	Suggested limits	Remarks
Physical properties and classification	Grading	BS 812: Part 103	BS 882	
	Elongation index	BS 812: Part 103	Not exceeding 25%	
	Flakiness index	BS 812: Parts 1 & 105.1	Not exceeding 25%	
	Specific gravity	BS 812: Part 2	—	Limits dependent on rock type. Five cycles using magnesium sulphate solution
	Water absorption	BS 812: Part 2	Not exceeding 20%	
	Soundness	ASTM C-88	Loss not exceeding 16%	
	Aggregate shrinkage	BRE Digest No. 35	Not exceeding 0.05%	
	Petrography	ASTM C-295		
Contamination and reactivity	Silt, clay and dust	BS 812: Part 1	BS 882	
	Clay lumps	ASTM C-142	Not exceeding 2.0%	
	Organic impurities	ASTM C-40	Advice given in ASTM C-40	
	Sulphate content	BS 1377: Test 9	Not exceeding 0.4% (w/w)	Subject to overall limits on total mix
	Chloride content	BS 812: Part 117	Not exceeding 0.06% (w/w)	
	Potential alkali reactivity	ASTM C-227 or C-289	Advice given in ASTM C-227 and ASTM C-289	
Mechanical properties	10% fines value	BS 812: Part 3	Not less than 8 ton	
	Aggregate crushing value	BS 812: Part 3	Under 25%	Officially superseded by 10% fines test but still widely used
	Aggregate impact value	BS 812: Part 3	Not exceeding 22%	
	Los Angeles abrasion	ASTM C-131 or C-535	Not exceeding 40%	Relevant to wearing surfaces only

testing are covered by one of the major national standards. The main tests utilized in concrete aggregate evaluations and the standards governing test procedures are listed in *Table 16.7*.

For Middle East conditions, the inherent variability in many of the materials means that their properties can only be expressed on a probability basis.[23] Particular emphasis needs to be placed on tests for fines, unsoundness, aggregate reactivity, and chloride and sulphate contents. The tests listed in *Table 16.8* are required as routine for aggregates in a Middle East setting, particularly when new sources are being investigated.

16.8 Lightweight aggregates

16.8.1 General

Lightweight aggregates are specialized materials having an apparent specific gravity significantly less than that of normal fine and coarse mineral aggregates. They range from extremely lightweight types used in insulating and non-structural concrete, to expanded shales, clays and slates used in structural concrete. The apparent specific gravity depends on the quantity of air contained, the highest air contents enhancing insulation but producing lower strengths. British Standards define lightweight aggregate as having a density of less than 960 kg m^{-3} for coarse aggregate or 1200 kg m^{-3} for fine aggregate:[48] alternatively,[22] having a particle density of not more than 2000 kg m^{-3}. The ASTM definition is of 'aggregate of low density used to produce lightweight concrete, including: pumice, scoria, volcanic cinders, tuff, and diatomite; expanded or sintered clay, slate, diatomaceous shale, perlite, vermiculite, or slag; and end products of coal or coke combustion'.[49]

16.8.2 Origins and early developments

Pumice from Italy and Greece was used in the days of the Roman Empire as lightweight aggregate in concrete, for example in the construction of the Colosseum and the Pantheon. Although extremely durable, the pumice produced concrete much weaker than is the norm today. However, despite the strength developments in cementitious binders, cements remained relatively weak, both light and heavy aggregate were stronger than the cementing agent, and both types of aggregate performed comparably.

The development of Portland cement by Joseph Aspdin in the early 19th century led to a cementing medium which resulted in concrete far in excess of the strength of natural lightweight aggregates. Heavy natural mineral aggregates provided the hardness and resistance to crushing and shear under compression which lightweight aggregate could not. The differences in performance became even more pronounced with further improvements in both the cement and its manufacture. Although several new sources of lightweight aggregate were tried (among them other types of pumice, scoriaceous and vesicular lavas, diatomite, formed from minute marine fossils), none could match the strength of concrete made with 'conventional' aggregates.

16.8.3 20th Century developments

Major developments in the use of concrete made with lightweight aggregates have taken place throughout this century. In the USA, the early developments occurred during the last years of the First World War, particularly in the development of concrete ships, the need arising from a shortage of good quality steel plate. Development work undertaken in the early years of this century on expanded shale, clay and slate were developed further most particularly by S. J. Hayde, a brickmaker who had faced the long-standing problem of excessive expansion of some bricks during firing. Although useless as bricks, this material represented a potentially useful source of lightweight aggregate, consisting of non-connected air voids generated by expanding gases within the original clays and shales when heated. The material was glass-hard and impermeable, but also much lower in density than natural mineral aggregates. Although similar in appearance to the natural sources of lightweight aggregate used centuries before, the burned shales, clays and slates produced a material that was much more uniform in quality and characteristics.

The lightweight aggregate used in the USA in the shipbuilding industry during and shortly after the First World War consisted of fine aggregate with an average density of 705 kg m^{-3}.

When applied to buildings, some obvious benefits quickly accrued. Although more expensive than conventional aggregate by a factor of 2.4, the economies achieved in one project where foundation conditions were difficult more than compensated for the extra costs arising from reducing deadweight with concrete made with expanded shale aggregate. In another example, an original 14-storey building had its foundations strengthened in order to take additional floors. The number of additional floors was to have been eight, but this was increased to 14 by employing structural lightweight concrete which achieved a 28-day strength of more than 24 N mm^{-2}. In the UK, concrete using a clinker aggregate was used in the construction of the British Museum.

The main applications of lightweight concrete in the UK have been in the form of block masonry. However, some structural applications, notably on prestressed lightweight concrete in grandstands, have been employed. Lightweight aggregate concrete is dealt with for structural uses in both BS 8110: 1985 and the Code of Practice for Design of Concrete Bridges. However, its use may be restricted by imposed reductions in the design stresses in shear and torsion, the permissible span:depth ratios, the modulus of elasticity, and also by increases in anchorage lengths. The lower stresses from self-weight do, however, partially offset these effects.

A recent study made by the Concrete Society on the economics of the use of lightweight aggregate concrete for bridges considered structures with a span of about 25 m where lightweight aggregate concrete had been used for precast beams and the *in situ* deck, but not for columns or abutments. Typically, five beams rather than six could be used because of the weight saving, although the decks were thicker because of higher transverse bending movements resulting from wider beam spacing.

Small cost savings accrued overall from using lightweight concrete in such circumstances, with further savings arising from reduced foundation sizes, reduced column sizes and formwork requirements, generally lighter formwork and falsework and lower erection loads. Savings were quantified as 4% for 60-m spans and 8% for 200-m spans.

Lightweight aggregates can, in the most general sense, be classified as either suitable or unsuitable for use in structural concretes. However, an alternative view is that all concretes of a particular strength should be considered in the same way, irrespective of the aggregate used. Recent research on shear strength of lightweight aggregate tends to support the latter view.

16.8.4 Manufacture and products

In addition to the natural sources of lightweight aggregate mentioned briefly above, the following represent the more commonly available manufactured types.

16.8.4.1 Expanded clays and shales and slates

Production of lightweight aggregate from shale and slate involves their controlled heating by the rotary kiln or the sintering method. Siliceous clays, shales and slates will expand (bloat) on heating as a result of the liberation of gases at the temperature of incipient fusion, that is, when the raw materials soften, but before they are totally molten. This is usually in the range 1000–1200°C, and leaves a honeycomb of small cells separated by walls of vitrified material. The material is crushed and graded after it has cooled.

Three particular products of these processes are used in the UK, namely 'Aglite', 'Leca' and 'Sintag'. These are manufactured from clay and shale, the use of slate having ceased in the UK for environmental reasons.

16.8.4.2 Expanded slag

Expanded slag uses molten slag from pig iron blast furnaces as a raw material. If a controlled amount of water or steam with compressed air is applied to the molten slag, a porous material resembling pumice and known as 'foamed slag' is produced.

If the molten slag is bloated with water in a rotating drum, rounded 'pelletized expanded slag', commercially available as 'Pellite' or 'Lycrete', is produced. Expanded slag is dealt with in BS 877: 1977.[50] Air-cooled blast-furnace slag complying with BS 1047: 1983 is also suitable, but steel slag is not covered by this standard and is not suitable as a concrete aggregate.[51]

16.8.4.3 Furnace clinker, ash and slag

Furnace clinker has been used for many years in the UK as a concrete aggregate, but has declined as oil, gas and pulverized fuels have been used to fire furnaces. Clinker, and the closely associated furnace bottom ash, are dealt with in BS 1165: 1977.[52]

However, the increases in oil prices have resulted in increased consumption of coal in many regions and the utilization of the waste from coal burning, including furnace slag as aggregate. The main problem has been volume changes which occur when moisture is present, in some cases resulting in the complete destruction of concrete containing furnace slag aggregate. This does not occur with pulverized-fuel ash, another waste product of burning coal. Cycles of drying and saturation of concrete prisms containing furnace slag aggregate have proved successful as an accelerated durability test,[53] and have shown that durability and the extent of volume change in the slag depend mainly on the content of unburned coal. The greater the degree of coking of the unburnt coal residue, the less volume change is likely to occur, although the extent of expansion also depends on the amount of moisture available.

16.8.4.4 Sintered pulverized-fuel ash

Pulverized-fuel ash is the ash from flue gases created by modern thermal power stations. The extremely fine material is damped, mixed with coal slurry, pelletized, and sintered at 1200°C to cause fusion, but not melting, of the pellets. This results in the lightweight aggregate known as 'Lytag'.

16.8.4.5 Exfoliated vermiculite

Vermiculites form a group of layer-lattice or sheet silicates generally related to chlorites, micas, and clay minerals. They expand greatly when heated (to about 1000°C), the steam generated forcing the layers apart. As well as its use as a lightweight aggregate, this light, cellular material is widely used for thermal insulation and packaging.

16.8.4.6 Expanded perlite

Perlite is a glassy volcanic rock of rhyolitic (acid) composition which has a 'perlitic' texture. This consists of curved to spherical cracks produced by contraction during cooling. When heated to about 1800°C, the water contained in the perlite is dissociated causing expansion of the lava into a cellular material of low density.[48]

16.8.4.7 Plastic

Plastic beads of, e.g. expanded polystyrene, often with a resin-cement coating have been utilized as aggregates. The plastic is softened and an expanding agent dissolved causing an approximately four-fold increase in diameter.

16.8.5 Properties

A summary of standards covering the use of lightweight aggregates is given in *Table 16.9*. Some of the basic properties include typical ranges of density of the common types of lightweight aggregate (*Table 16.10*), and the typically available gradings used in lightweight concrete (*Table 16.11*).

Clinker aggregate has the best properties if it is obtained from high-temperature furnaces in which combustibles have been minimized. Unburnt or partially burnt coal produces unsound

Table 16.10 Air-dry densities (loose) of lightweight aggregates[54]

Type	Density (kg m^{-3})
Sintered pulverized-fuel ash	770–1040
Expanded slag	700–970
Expanded clays and shales	320–960
Pumice	480–880
Diatomite	450–800
Expanded perlite	50–240
Exfoliated vermiculite	60–160
Plastic	10–20

Table 16.9 Lightweight aggregate tests (in addition to *Table 16.7*) by standard

Material	Test	Standard		
		BS	ASTM	DIN
Clinker and furnace bottom ash	All physical and chemical	BS 1165: 1985 BS 3681: Part 2: 1983		
Lightweight aggregates	All physical and chemical	BS 3681: 1983, Part 2	C330-87, C331-87 C332-87	4226, Part 2 4226, Parts 3, 6 and 7
	Organic impurities		C40-84	
	Staining		C641-82	
	Loss on ignition		C114-85	
Blast-furnace slag	Description			4226, Part 3, 5.1
	Lime unsoundness			4226, Part 3, 5.2.1
	Iron unsoundness	BS 1047: 1983		4226, Part 3, 5.2.2
	Dicalcium silicate unsoundness (falling)	BS 1047: 1983		

Table 16.11 Typical gradings for use in lightweight concrete[54]

Type	Typically available gradings (mm)
Sintered pulverized fuel-ash	12-8, 8-5, 5 down (crushed)
Expanded slag	
Foamed	14-3, 3 down
Pelletized	12-3, 3 down
Expanded clays and shales	
Aglite	15-10, 10-5, 5 down
Leca	20-10, 10-3, 3 down
Sintag	14-5, 5 down
Expanded perlite	6 mm max. (Zone L1 of BS 3797)
Exfoliated vermiculite	7-6, 6-5
Plastic	4 (max.)

aggregate prone to shrinkage, and a limit of 10% on the amount of combustible material for general concreting work has been recommended,[52] although higher percentages can be tolerated for interior work (20%) and precast concrete blocks (25%). However, the sulphur content of clinker precludes its use in reinforced concrete. Air-cooled blast-furnace slag aggregate has good fire-protection properties.[55]

High strength structural concrete can be made using lightweight aggregate, and further improvements in strength, workability and cohesion have been reported[56] using a combination of Pellite and Trent Valley sand. Cube strengths of $67 \, \text{N} \, \text{mm}^{-2}$ were achieved with a ratio of splitting to compressive strength of 0.06 for a compressive strength of $60 \, \text{N} \, \text{mm}^{-2}$.

References

1 COLLIS, L. and FOX, R. A., Aggregates: sand, gravel and crushed rock aggregates for construction purposes, *Engineering Geology Special Publication No. 1*, Geological Society (1985)

2 MURDOCK. L. J. and BROOK, K. M., *Concrete Materials and Practice*, 5th edn, Edward Arnold, London (1979)

3 FOOKES, P. G., An introduction to the influence of natural aggregates on the performance and durability of concrete, *Quarterly Journal of Engineering Geology*, 13, 207–229 (1980)

4 NEVILLE, A. M., *Properties of Concrete*, 3rd edn, Pitman, London (1981)

5 ANON., The description of rock masses for engineering purposes, *Quarterly Journal of Engineering Geology*, 10, 355–388 (1977)

6 FOOKES, P. G. and HIGGINBOTTOM, I. E., Some problems of construction aggregates in desert areas, with particular reference to the Arabian peninsular. 1. Occurrence and special characteristics, *Proceedings of the Institution of Civil Engineers, Part 1*, 68, 39–67 (1980)

7 BRITISH STANDARDS INSTITUTION, *BS 882: Specification for aggregates from natural sources of concrete*, Milton Keynes (1983)

8 AMERICAN SOCIETY FOR TESTING MATERIALS, *ASTM C33-86: Standard specification for concrete aggregates*, Philadelphia (1986)

9 DIN, *DIN 1045: Concrete and reinforced concrete structures design and construction*, Köln (1972). Translated and published by BSI, Hemel Hempstead (1973)

10 HAWKINS, M. R., Alkali silica reaction: guidance notes and model specification clauses, *Concrete Society Technical Report No. 30*, The Concrete Society, London (1987)

11 DEPARTMENT OF TRANSPORT, *Specification for Highway Works. Part 5*, HMSO, London, pp. 19–20 (1986)

12 KEEN, R. A., Impurities in aggregates for concrete, *Advisory Note No. 18*, Cement and Concrete Association, Wexham Springs, Slough (1970)

13 DEWAR, J. D., Effect of mica in the fine aggregate on the water requirement and strength of concrete, *Technical Report TRA/370*, Cement and Concrete Association, Wexham Springs, Slough (1963)

14 FOOKES, P. G. and REVIE, W. A., Mica in concrete—a case history from eastern Nepal, *Concrete*, 16, (1982)

15 AFNOR, Granulats—essai au bleu de methylène, *Experimental Standard p18-592*, AFNOR, Paris (1980)

16 CHAPMAN, G. P. and ROEDER, A. R., The effect of sea shells in concrete aggregates, *Concrete*, 4, 71–79 (1970)

17 BRITISH STANDARDS INSTITUTION, *BS 12: Specification for Portland cement*, Milton Keynes (1989)

18 AMERICAN SOCIETY FOR TESTING MATERIALS, *ASTM C150-86: Standard specification for Portland cement*, Philadelphia (1986)

19 BACMI, Marine dredged aggregates—a technical appraisal, British Aggregate Construction Materials Industries, London (1987)

20 GUTT, W. and COLLINS, R. J., Sea-dredged aggregate in concrete, *Building Research Establishment Information Paper IP7/87*, HMSO, London (1987)

21 LEES, T. P. and SYM, R., The precision of the method for determining the chloride content of cement recently proposed for BS 4550, *World Cement*, 17, 204–210 (1986)

22 BRITISH STANDARDS INSTITUTION, *BS 8110: Part 1 Code of Practice for design and construction*, Milton Keynes (1985)

23 FOOKES, P. G. and HIGGINBOTTOM, I. E., Some problems of construction aggregates in desert areas, with particular reference to the Arabian peninsular. 2: Investigation, production and quality control, *Proceedings of the Institution of Civil Engineers, Part 1*, 68, 69–90 (1980)

24 BRITISH STANDARDS INSTITUTION, *BS 1377: Methods of test for soils for civil engineering purposes, Test 9*, Milton Keynes, pp. 48–50 (1975)

25 BRITISH STANDARDS INSTITUTION, *BS 3681: Part 2 Methods for the sampling and testing of lightweight aggregates for concrete*, Milton Keynes (1973)

26 ISO, *ISO/DIS 6274: International Standard of sieve sizes for aggregates* (1980)

27 KAPLAN, M. F., Flexural and compressive strength of concrete as affected by the properties of coarse aggregates, *Journal of American Concrete Institute*, 55, 1193–1208 (1959)

28 SNOWDEN, L. C. and EDWARDS, A. G., The moisture content of natural aggregate and its effect on concrete, *Magazine on Concrete Research*, 14, (1962)

29 WEIMERT, H. J., Engineering petrology for roads in South Africa, *Engineering Geology*, 2, 359–362 (1968)

30 ROEDER, A. R., Some properties of flint particles and their behaviour in concrete, *Magazine of Concrete Research*, 29, 92–99 (1977)

31 LAUTRIDOU, J. P., LETAVERNIER, G., LINDE, K., ETLICHER, B. and OZOUF, J. C., Porosity and frost susceptibility of flints and chalk: laboratory experiments, comparison of 'glacial' and 'periglacial' surface texture of flint materials, and field investigations, *Proceedings of the 4th International Flint Symposium*, Brighton, pp. 269–282 (1983)

32 GILLOTT, J. E., DUNCAN, M. A. G. and SWENSON, E. G., Alkali–aggregate reaction in Nova Scotia. Part IV, Character of the reaction, *Cement and Concrete Research*, 3, 521–535 (1973)

33 SIMS, I. and SOTIROPOULOS, P., Standard alkali-reactivity testing of carbonate rocks from the Middle East and North Africa, *Proceedings of the 6th International Conference, Alkalis on Concrete, Research and Practice*, Copenhagen (1983)

34 DOLAR-MANTUANI, L., *Handbook of Concrete Aggregates. A Petrographic and Technological Evaluation*, Noyes, New Jersey (1983)

35 FRENCH, W. J., A review of some reactive aggregates from the United Kingdom with reference to the mechanism of reaction and deterioration, *Proceedings of the 7th International Conference on Alkali–Silica Reactions in Concrete*, Ottawa, pp. 226–230 (1986)

36 MEHTA, P. K., Effect of chemical additions on the alkali–silica expansion, *Proceedings of the 4th International Conference on Effects of Alkalis in Cement and Concrete*, Purdue, pp. 229–235 (1978)

37 HOBBS, D. W., *Alkali–Silica Reaction in Concrete*, Thomas Telford, London (1988)

38 GERMAN COMMITTEE FOR REINFORCED CONCRETE, *Guidelines for Alkali–Aggregate Reactions in Concrete*, German Building Standards Committee of DIN eV, subject speciality VII (1986)

39 STARK, D., Osmotic cell test to identify potential for

alkali–aggregate reactivity, *Proceedings of the 6th International Conference on Alkalis in Concrete*, Copenhagen, pp. 351–357 (1983)

40 CHATTERJI, S., An accelerated method for the detection of alkali–aggregate reactivities of aggregates, *Cement and Concrete Research*, **8**, 647–650 (1978)

41 OBERHOLSTER, R. and DAVIES, G., An accelerated method for testing the potential reactivity of siliceous aggregates, *Cement and Concrete Research*, **16**, 181–189 (1986)

42 MING-SHU, T., A rapid method for identification of alkali-reactivity of aggregate, *Cement and Concrete Research*, **13**, 417–422 (1983)

43 TAMURA, H., An experiment on rapid identification of alkali-reactivity of aggregate, *Review of the 38th General Meeting of the Cement Association of Japan*, Tokyo, pp. 100–103 (1984)

44 CANADIAN STANDARDS AUTHORITY, *CSA A23.2–14A: Alkali–aggregate reaction (concrete prism test)*. Methods of Test for Concrete, Ottawa, pp. 183–185 (1977)

45 BRITISH STANDARDS INSTITUTION, *BS 812: Part 123 Draft, Concrete prism method. Testing aggregates. Methods for the assessment of alkali–aggregate reactivity potential*, Milton Keynes (1988)

46 HOBBS, D. W., Testing for alkali–silica reactivity, *Cement and Concrete Association Test Methods*, Cement and Concrete Association, Wexham Springs, Slough (1985)

47 JONES, F. E. and TARLETON, R. D., Recommended test procedures. Part VI: Alkali–aggregate interaction. Experience with some forms of rapid and accelerated tests for alkali–aggregate reactivity, *National Building Studies Research Paper 25*, HMSO, London (1958)

48 BRITISH STANDARDS INSTITUTION, *BS 3797: Part 2 Specification for lightweight aggregate for concrete*, Milton Keynes (1976)

49 AMERICAN SOCIETY FOR TESTING MATERIALS, *ASTM C125-88: Standard terminology relating to concrete and concrete aggregates*, Philadelphia (1988)

50 BRITISH STANDARDS INSTITUTION, *BS 877: Part 2 Foamed or expanded blast furnace slag lightweight aggregate for concrete*, Milton Keynes (1977)

51 BRITISH STANDARDS INSTITUTION, *BS 1047: Air-cooled blast furnace slag aggregate for use in construction*, Milton Keynes (1983)

52 BRITISH STANDARDS INSTITUTION, *BS 1165: Clinker aggregate for concrete*, Milton Keynes (1977)

53 ROSZAK, W., Durability of furnace slag as a concrete aggregate, *Proceedings of the 3rd International Conference on the Durability of Building Materials and Components*, Espoo, Finland, Vol. 3, pp. 135–144 (1984)

54 SPRATT, B. H., *An Introduction to Lightweight Concrete*, 6th edn, Cement and Concrete Association, Wexham Springs, Slough (1980)

55 BUILDING RESEARCH ESTABLISHMENT, Concrete. Part 1: Materials, *BRE Digest 325*, Garston, Watford (1987)

56 MAYFIELD, B. and LOUATI, M., Can Pellite be used in structural concrete?, *Concrete*, **22**, 27–28 (1988)

17 Concrete Blocks and Blockwork

A K Tovey CEng, FIStructE, ACIArb, MSFSE
Building and Structures,
British Cement Association

Contents

17.1 Introduction 17/3

17.2 Types of block 17/3
    17.2.1 Solid block 17/3
    17.2.2 Cellular block 17/3
    17.2.3 Hollow block 17/3
    17.2.4 Common block 17/3
    17.2.5 Facing block 17/4
    17.2.6 Architectural masonry block 17/4
    17.2.7 Insulating block 17/4
    17.2.8 Coursing unit 17/4

17.3 Manufacture 17/4
    17.3.1 Aggregate concrete blocks 17/4
    17.3.2 Autoclaved aerated concrete blocks 17/5

17.4 Curing systems 17/5
    17.4.1 Normal air curing 17/5
    17.4.2 Steam curing at atmospheric pressure 17/5
    17.4.3 Autoclaving 17/6

17.5 Packaging 17/6

17.6 Properties of blocks 17/6
    17.6.1 Size 17/6
    17.6.2 Weight 17/7
    17.6.3 Compressive strength 17/7
    17.6.4 Frost resistance 17/7
    17.6.5 Thermal movement 17/7
    17.6.6 Moisture movement 17/7
    17.6.7 Blockwalling 17/7
    17.6.8 Mortars 17/8

17.7 Properties of blockwork 17/9
    17.7.1 Appearance 17/9
    17.7.2 Rain resistance 17/9
    17.7.3 Structural properties 17/10
    17.7.4 Movements 17/10
    17.7.5 Thermal insulation 17/10
    17.7.6 Sound insulation 17/10
    17.7.7 Fire resistance 17/11
    17.7.8 Durability 17/11

Acknowledgements 17/11

References 17/11

17.1 Introduction

Examples of the use of concrete date as far back as 5600 BC, but the concrete block, as we know it today, based on the use of Portland cement, was not introduced into the UK. until around 1850. Joseph Gibb patented a process to manufacture a product to imitate the dressed stone of that period. The blocks so produced were generally hollow with moulded faces.

It was not until the early 1900s, coinciding with the significant growth in the production of Portland cement, that the concrete-block industry became established. The first noticeable growth between 1918 and 1939 came about as a result of the house-building programme following World War I. These were mainly clinker blocks and used for partition walls in houses. However, the most significant period of development and growth did not occur until the building programme following World War II. Since that time, the growth of concrete blocks has, indeed, been notable and has increased from around 4 million m^2 in 1955 to around 110 million m^2 in 1988, as shown in *Figure 17.1*.

The main reasons for this growth were due to the promotion of cavity walls, and the steady improvements in thermal-insulation requirements for dwellings resulting in the development of lightweight aggregate blocks, and autoclaved aerated concrete blocks. That, coupled with their low cost, lighter weight and ease of handling, provided economy in terms of time and cost of construction.[1] Further developments have taken place[2,3] which demonstrate means of improving the efficiency of masonry construction without sacrificing either the important aspect of freedom of design or the potential for achieving very high standards of quality and performance.

Developments have taken place with the product and, in addition to the common and insulating blocks, a wide range of high-quality facing units have emerged. Realization of their structural potential has resulted in the development of the strength range. The increase in the use of concrete blocks and concrete bricks is such that concrete masonry is currently the major masonry material used in the UK (*Figure 17.1*).

17.2 Types of block

The general specification of concrete masonry units is covered by BS 6073.[4] This standard is separated into two parts; both concrete blocks and concrete bricks are dealt with. A 'block' is defined as a walling unit of length, width, or height greater than that specified for a brick, subject to its height when laid in its normal aspect not exceeding either its length or six times its thickness. There is also a limitation in that no dimension shall exceed 650 mm in order to avoid confusion with other precast slabs or panels.

17.2.1 Solid block

These are units which basically contain no formed holes or cavities other than those inherent in the material. (Autoclaved aerated blocks are thus, by definition, 'solid'.) The standard, however, allows for the incorporation of small transverse slots, to facilitate cutting with a bolster, and are often incorporated into aggregate concrete blocks.

17.2.2 Cellular block

These units have one or more formed holes or cavities which do not wholly pass through the block. The voids are generally used to lighten or improve the thermal insulation of the unit. They are laid with the closed end uppermost in order to proide a continuous surface to spread the mortar.

17.2.3 Hollow block

Hollow blocks quite simply have one or more cavities which pass through the block. Typically within the UK, these units tend to have two large voids and may be employed for reinforced work. Large multiple-voided units, as manufactured in certain European countries, could come into this category.

BS 6073[4] does not currently define other units, but the following outlines those which are commonly referred to, although the description may vary between manufacturers.

17.2.4 Common block

This term is used to describe those units which are used for general construction work where appearance is not of paramount importance, e.g. below ground level or where not normally exposed to view.

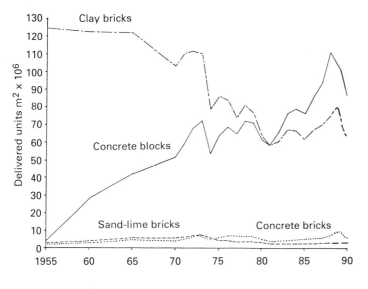

Figure 17.1 Deliveries of bricks and blocks in the UK since 1955

17.2.5 Facing block

These units are specifically made or selected to have a consistent shape and texture. Close-textured blocks suitable for painting usually come into this category.

17.2.6 Architectural masonry block

This is a term often used to describe a higher specification for facing blocks. The normal facing- or paint-quality units are manufactured to achieve acceptable shape and texture but require no particular control on colour. Units specifically manufactured to have consistent shape, texture and colour tend to be referred to as 'architectural masonry blocks'. Such blocks are produced in a range of finishes from fine smooth-textured surfaces through to rustic split-faced and exposed aggregate units.

17.2.7 Insulating block

All concrete blocks provide some degree of thermal insulation but the term 'insulating block' tends to be applied to those manufactured from lightweight aggregate or autoclaved aerated concrete and having inherent thermal insulating properties provided by the block material. Some blocks may have thermal-insulation material incorporated within the block, applied externally or have a combination of both. These are often referred to as *composite insulated blocks* and extend the range of dense and lightweight aggregate materials.

17.2.8 Coursing unit

These are masonry units made of similar materials to the parent block and used to aid coursing and bonding in block masonry.

17.3 Manufacture

In general, the manufacture of concrete blocks may be separated into two distinctly separate processes

(1) that used for the production of aggregate concrete blocks; and

(2) that used for the production of autoclaved aerated concrete blocks.

17.3.1 Aggregate concrete blocks

The process of manufacture of aggregate concrete blocks has evolved over the years but principally still involves the production of units from multi-use steel moulds. The concrete-block industry in fact developed using the simple single-pallet machine. In this process, an earth-dry concrete mix was manually compacted into a rigid mould box containing a simple replaceable bottom pallet. The unit, upon compaction, was ejected upwards by means of a foot-operated lever and moved away on its pallet to be cured. The process is no longer used for mass produced units, but similar machines are still used today to produce hand-made very high-quality architectural masonry blocks.

17.3.1.1 Egg-lay process

By the 1950s, manufacturers had started to mechanize block making on multiple mould machines, mainly of the mobile or egg-lay type. Many of these plants were commissioned during and after World War II using old airfields where runways provided an ideal base for the production of blocks. The typical 'egg-lay' production plant is shown in *Figure 17.2*.

The mix is transferred by concrete feed truck to the block machine. The concrete mix is placed into a holding hopper situated in the top of the block machine. From the holding hopper the mix falls into a feed tray above the mould box, the feed tray moves back and forwards depositing concrete evenly into the mould box. The mould box is profiled to suit the size and type of block and can accommodate from 4 to 44 100-mm thick blocks depending on the type of machine.

Once the mould box has been filled, a profiled steel head is lowered into the top of the mould box. The head is controlled to ensure that the block is to the correct height and the top surface has a good finish. High-frequency vibrators fixed to the mould box enable the concrete to be compacted. The blocks are ejected immediately from the mould onto the ground. The block machine moves to the next position and repeats the cycle. The blocks remain on the ground (pad) until they are

Figure 17.2 Block manufacture—egg-lay process

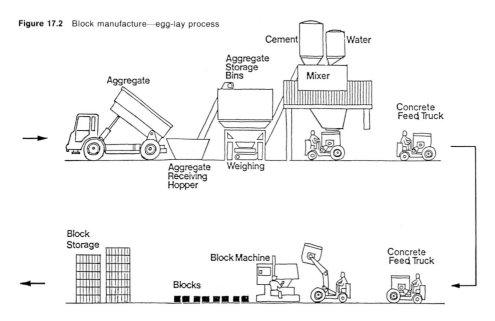

cured sufficiently for handling. This period is dependent on weather conditions and can vary between 2 and 4 days. The blocks are removed from the pad and put into the stock yard and allowed to cure fully; they are then ready for delivery.

The egg-lay operation is a low-capital system; one of its drawbacks is that the production output and the product quality can be affected by weather. To overcome this problem, some manufacturers have small areas which are covered by a frame shelter for at least 1 days make. The process is, however, still largely dependent on weather conditions, but typically can produce around 15 000 blocks (100 mm) per day.

17.3.1.2 Static process

In the last 20 years or so, the industry has developed into a highly mechanized and efficient industry and has progressively moved towards the use of static operations using automatic pallet type machines producing a high-quality product.

The batching plant and block machine operations are similar to those discussed for the egg-lay system. The typical production plant is shown in *Figure 17.3*. The difference between the two operations is that, in the static process, the block machine is fixed in position and the blocks are made onto steel or wooden pallets and are ejected from the block machine and placed into a stacker. The blocks are then transported to curing chambers where they remain until adequately cured for handling. The main manufacturing operation thus takes place under cover in controlled conditions. On leaving the curing chambers the blocks are cubed and placed in the stock yard ready for delivery.

The major advantage of the static operation is that production can take place throughout the year in all weather conditions, thus limiting the amount of lost production. A very high standard of block can be produced with a high degree of consistency. This controlled manufacturing process can produce in excess of 25 000 units (100 mm) per day.

17.3.2 Autoclaved aerated concrete blocks

The manufacture of aerated blocks is a completely different operation than that for aggregate concrete blocks or bricks (*Figure 17.4*). There are various combinations of raw materials used depending on the patented process employed, but typically consist of either: (a) Portland cement, lime and silica sand; or (b) Portland cement, lime and pulverized-fuel ash (PFA).

The aggregate (sand or PFA) is mixed with water and placed into a slurry tank. The slurry is heated and fed to a high-speed mixer where it is mixed with cement and lime, and a small quantity of aluminium powder in suspension. The mixture is then poured into large steel moulds; the aluminium powder reacts with the free lime in the cement to give off hydrogen which is naturally replaced by air and which provides the aeration and expansion resulting in a light microcellular structure.

The mould sides are removed and the partially set material, 'the cake', is transported on rails to the cutting area where vertical and longitudinal wires slice it into appropriate block sizes. The formed blocks are then transported to high-pressure-steam autoclaves where they are cured.

17.4 Curing systems

Adequate curing of blocks is essential to ensure that the cement hydrates sufficiently for the blocks to be handled without being damaged. Methods of curing vary but typically include the following.

17.4.1 Normal air curing

With air curing, no capital investment is required but the process is slow, requiring 3–7 days depending upon atmospheric conditions and, in addition, plant operation may have to cease at temperatures approaching freezing point. The blocks must be kept moist while being cured and must be protected from wind and sun. After this initial curing period, the blocks should be protected from rain so that they are as dry as possible before delivery. Because of the slow speed and difficulty of controlling conditions, air curing is seldom used in the larger plants.

17.4.2 Steam curing at atmospheric pressure

In this process, pallets of blocks are placed into large chambers and, once filled, steam is injected at normal atmospheric pressure to accelerate curing. This method (used by most of the larger block-making plants) can give high early strength and maturity. There is no appreciable difference in the shrinkage characteristics of such blocks when compared with normal-air-cured blocks, unless the blocks are cooled so that they dry quickly and are kept dry.

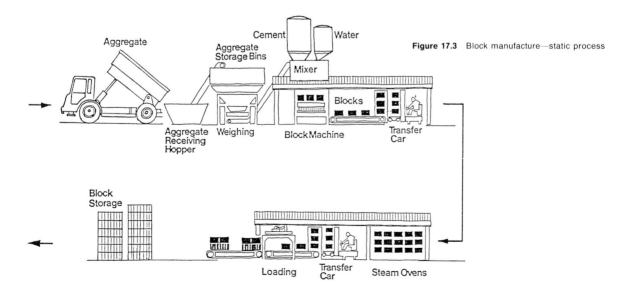

Figure 17.3 Block manufacture—static process

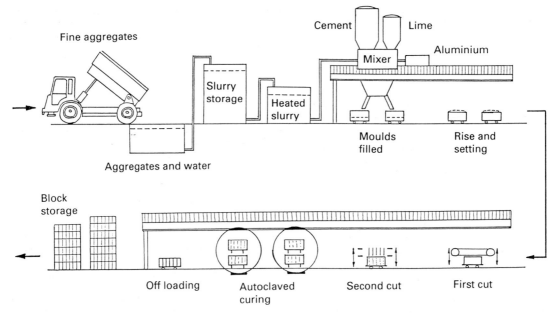

Figure 17.4 Block manufacture—autoclaved aerated concrete

17.4.3 Autoclaving

In this process, the blocks are cured in autoclaves with steam at high pressure. This requires special equipment which is expensive to install and operate. Autoclaving is an essential operation in the manufacture of aerated concrete blocks but is also used in the manufacture of other types of blocks. The advantages of this process are:

(1) it reduces irreversible moisture movements;
(2) autoclaved blocks tend to be more uniform in colour; and
(3) dry blocks can be delivered within 24 h, thus reducing storage.

In addition, autoclaving can allow a reduction in cement content of blocks or provide increased strength and hence offset some of the equipment operating costs.

17.5 Packaging

For many years, blocks were delivered to site by tipper truck and tipped on the site with little regard for the amount of damage caused and the additional costs because of extra handling.

Today, the customer normally insists on packaging methods which will reduce waste and handling costs. The most common form of packaging is banded cubes either on pallets, with formed holes within the cube for fork lifting or in cubes for crane off-load.

The weight of the packs is dependent on their size and weight of the product. As a guide, the approximate weight of a $900 \times 900 \times 900$ cube is: dense concrete blocks 1.4–1.5 tonne; lightweight blocks 0.65–0.86 tonne; and aerated blocks 0.35–0.52 tonne.

Many of the up-to-date plants have shrink-wrapping machines which help to protect the blocks on site. This service is especially important for architectural masonry.

17.6 Properties of blocks

17.6.1 Size

Concrete blocks are available in a wide range of sizes, as shown in *Table 17.1*. However, the sizes shown represent a general survey and the full range is unlikely to be available from all manufacturers. The dimensions given in *Table 17.1* are work sizes (10 mm less than the co-ordinating space to allow for nominal mortar joints) which are to be controlled within the

Table 17.1 Work sizes of blocks

Length (mm)	Height (mm)	60	75	90	100	115	125	140	150	175	190	200	215	220	225	250
390	190	*	*	*	*	*		*	*		*	*				
440	140	*	*	*	*			*	*		*	*			*	
440	190	*	*	*	*			*	*		*		*	*		
440	215	*	*	*	*	*	*	*	*	*	*	*	*	*	*	*
440	290	*	*	*	*			*	*		*	*	*			
590	140		*	*	*			*	*		*	*	*			
590	190		*	*	*			*	*		*	*	*			
590	215		*	*	*		*	*	*	*	*		*		*	*

Table 17.2 Dimensional deviations of blocks

Dimension	Maximum deviation (mm)
Length	$+3-5$
Height	$+3-5$
Thickness	$+2-2$ average
	$+4-4$ at any individual point

deviations given in *Table 17.2*. It should be noted that other sizes are available and in use, although no single manufacturer necessarily produces the complete range of work sizes shown.

17.6.2 Weight

The density of concrete used for the manufacture of concrete blocks ranges from about 475 kg m^{-3} for the lightest autoclaved aerated concrete blocks to around 2000 kg m^{-3} for dense aggregate units. Blocks may, therefore, vary in weight from slightly less than 3 kg for thin units to over 40 kg for large solid units. Blocks in the upper weight range are difficult to handle and may well require mechanical handling as is commonly employed with stone masonry. A better alternative where 215 mm dense aggregate block walls are required would be to use 215 × 100 mm units laid flat.

17.6.3 Compressive strength

It should be noted that in BS 6073[4] only blocks equal to or greater than 75 mm are tested for compressive strength. Blocks less than 75 mm are only tested for transverse strength and are intended for non-load-bearing partitions. The test is, in essence, to ensure adequate handlability.

For the purpose of compliance, the compressive strength is determined from the mean of a set of 10 tests. In addition, a control involving the standard deviation of the sample is imposed.

The compressive strength of blocks ranges from 2.8 to 35.0 N mm^{-2}, as shown in *Table 17.3*. Typical compressive strengths for autoclaved aerated concrete blocks will range between 2.8 and 7.0 N mm^{-2}, for lightweight aggregate blocks from 3.5 to 10.5 N mm^{-2}, and for dense aggregate blocks from 7 to 21 N mm^{-2}.

17.6.4 Frost resistance

Concrete blocks are inherently durable and, as a result, there are no specific requirements for frost resistance laid down in the block standard.[4] Full recommendations for minimum quality of units and mortar are given in BS 5628: Part 3.[5]

17.6.5 Thermal movement

The linear movement due to temperature changes in blocks is generally considered to be reversible in that the material expands on heating and contracts on cooling back to its original dimension. However, the movement that actually occurs within a wall after construction depends not only on the range of temperature but also on the initial temperature of the material and on the degree of restraint. Care needs to be exercised, therefore, when trying to determine thermal movements in

Table 17.3 Compressive strength of blocks corresponding to BS 5628[5] strength categories

Block strength	2.8	3.5	5.0	7.0	10.0	15.0	20.0	35.0

Table 17.4 Maximum permitted shrinkage of concrete masonry units

Material	Shrinkage (%)
Concrete bricks and dense and lightweight aggregate block	0.06
Autoclaved aerated concrete blocks	0.09

practice.[5] The free linear movement will vary, dependent on the block material, but will typically be within the range $7-14 \times 10^{-6}$ per °C. (See also Section 17.6.7.)

17.6.6 Moisture movement

Concrete blocks undergo dimensional changes as a result of moisture variation. The units will expand on wetting and shrink as a result of drying. Since the units contain more water than is necessary to hydrate the cement, the overall effect is to produce long-term shrinkage as the units dry to equilibrium. This is normally greater than subsequent moisture wetting and, as a result, an irreversible shrinkage occurs. The exception is where units are in a permanently wet environment, e.g. below ground where little shrinkage occurs. The values shown in *Table 17.4* represent the maximum permitted shrinkage laid down in BS 6073[4] for concrete units.

The British Standard test, which is currently being reviewed, determines the shrinkage between saturation and oven-dry conditions (relative humidity 17%). In practice, a wall is seldom totally saturated at the time of construction and typically will fall to an equilibrium condition of between 50 and 85% relative humidity (RH). As a result, the drying shrinkage may well be less than that determined by the British Standard test. In addition, the British Standard values represent the upper limits, and many units, particularly those that have undergone autoclaved curing, may have appreciably lower test results. Care therefore needs to be taken when determining expected movement by use of the tabulated limits in BS 6073[4] (*Table 17.4*), particularly as the actual movement will, in addition, depend on the initial moisture content of the units as placed.[5] (See also Section 17.6.7.)

17.6.7 Blockwalling

Concrete blockwork is, by definition, a combination of units and mortar. The resulting combination may fulfil a variety of functions such as providing elements for housing, commercial and industrial building. Concrete units may often be used in conjunction with clay brickwork as for example in a cavity wall or bonded junction. In such circumstances, account should be taken of the possible differential movement between the two dissimilar materials. (Note the thermal/moisture movements given in this chapter as compared with those for clay brickwork given in Chapter 11.) The concrete masonry diaphragm wall offers substantial strength benefits from a small increase in materials (eight times more lateral strength for an 8% increase in material quantities).[6]

Blockwork can also provide attractive facing work, give weather resistance and provide the necessary thermal, sound and fire resistance required for a variety of structures (*Figures 17.5* to *17.8*). It is also highly cost-effective compared with other forms of construction. It should also be noted that concrete blockwork is commonly combined with clay brickwork and, in such cases, particular attention should be given to the effects of differential movements.

Masonry is traditionally good in compression but weak in tension. The latter, however, may be overcome by the inclusion of either reinforcement or prestressing steel.

Figure 17.5 North Hill Close, Brixham, Devon. The local architecture is reflected in the use of a white rendering over insulating block walls

Figure 17.6 Houses in Buxton, Derbyshire, showing the use of chisel-dressed concrete masonry

17.6.8 Mortars

Many of the current problems occurring with mortars are due to inadequate specification and lack of supervision on site. There is often a lack of appreciation of the necessity for long-term durability and too much emphasis is placed on those properties of the fresh mortar leading to ease of use.

Mortar should be precisely specified taking into account available materials and future exposure conditions and should be produced and used under supervision. It should have good working properties to facilitate use, including a water or consistence retentivity appropriate to the suction of the material on which it is being applied. For very high suction materials, the use of admixtures to achieve this may be required but, in

general, attention to the sand properties and mix proportioning is sufficient. Concrete units should not be wetted prior to use.

Two principal forms of mortar specification are used. 'Prescription' mixes, formulated by the designer in accordance with th materials to be used, are satisfactory for traditional brick and block work. 'Performance' specifications may be preferable for bedding mortars to be used for calculated load-bearing brick or block work.

Bearing in mind that the mason is probably interested only in those qualities of the fresh mortar which promote easy working and handling, the specification should be more concerned with ensuring durability and fitness for purpose of the hardened mortar.

Traditionally, lime mortars were employed for masonry construction, typical lime:sand proportions being 1:3. Although lime mortars offer excellent workability characteristics, they rely on the loss of water and carbonation to gain strength slowly

Figure 17.7 Flats built of concrete masonry at Buxton, Derbyshire

Figure 17.8 Concrete facing blocks provide a smart internal finish to this office at Welsh Back, Bristol

Table 17.5 Mortar mixes and properties*

		Mortar designation	Cement:lime:sand	Masonry cement:sand	Cement:sand with plasticizer
▲ Increasing	Increasing ability	i	$1:0-\frac{1}{4}:3$		
strength	to accommodate	ii	$1:\frac{1}{2}:4-4\frac{1}{2}$	$1:2\frac{1}{2}-3\frac{1}{2}$	$1:3-4$
and	movements due	iii	$1:1:5-6$	$1:4-5$	$1:5-6$
improving	to temperature	iv	$1:2:8-9$	$1:5\frac{1}{2}-6\frac{1}{2}$	$1:7-8$
durability	and moisture	v	$1:3:10-12$	$1:6\frac{1}{2}-7$	$1:8$
	changes ▼				

Increasing resistance to frost attack during construction ⟶
⟵ Improvement in adhesion and consequent resistance to rain penetration

* Direction of change in properties is shown by the arrows.

Table 17.6 Strength requirements for mortar

Mortar designation	Mean compressive strength at 28 days (N mm^{-2})	
	Preliminary laboratory tests	Site tests
i	16.0	11.0
ii	6.5	4.5
iii	3.6	2.5
iv	1.5	1.0

and this constraint on the rate of construction has led to the widespread use of cement mortars.

A comparison of the properties of different types of mortar (proportions by volume) and their approximate equivalence is shown in *Table 17.5*. For further details, including the accompanying notes, reference should be made to BS 5628: Part 3.[5] For most general-purpose concrete-masonry construction, the lowest grade of mortar practicable should be employed. For most general-purpose concrete-masonry construction a 1:1:6 cement:lime:sand mortar is suitable. High-strength load-bearing masonry and reinforced masonry generally require a 1:$\frac{1}{4}$:3 or 1:1$\frac{1}{2}$:4$\frac{1}{2}$ cement:line:sand mortar.

Table 17.6 indicates the order of strength that may need to be obtained.[4] The bond strength of the mortar to the units is often far more important than the compressive strength which is not a prime requirement. Given a reasonable sand grading, the bond strength achieved will depend on the workmanship of the masonry and the type and condition of the units at the time of laying, together with the subsequent curing regime.

17.7 Properties of blockwork

17.7.1 Appearance

The range of concrete blocks available in the UK as regards to colour and texture is now very wide. The appearance of walls is extended further by using different bonding patterns and a variety of coloured mortars, either matching or contrasting with the blocks. Although the appearance of blockwork is affected by the colour of the mortar (either matching or contrasting), it does not have the same detailed effect as can occur with brickwork because of the wider spacing of mortar joints. The colour of mortar is selected to enhance the appearance of the units and care needs to be taken to minimize colour variations due to batching and mixing.

There are a number of tools for finishing joints and various types of joint profile that may be employed. Tooled joints are to be preferred as they assist in preventing water ingress and, consequently, help to ensure long-term durability.

Clearly, building a fair-faced wall requires attention to detail over and above that required for common blockwork. Because of the unit size, careful planning is required at design stage to obviate unnecessary cutting of blocks and breaking of the bond pattern. Special blocks for use at corners and reveals are available together with units for producing masonry lintels over openings. The units and materials should be handled carefully and stored on site. Precautions should also be taken to prevent finished work from becoming stained as a result of site activities.

Manufacturers operate quality-control procedures to minimize colour and texture variations. However, variation resulting from different manufacturing batches may occur and can lead to 'banding' or 'patches' in the finished work. This, apart from mortar variation, is the most common cause of colour variation in masonry, particularly that seeking total uniformity of colour. Masonry units having individual colour variation, either naturally occurring or introduced during manufacture, tend to overcome banding and patch effects and produce random and acceptable colour variation in the finished work. Units of more general uniform colour may require pallets to be opened and the units mixed to ensure an even dispersion of colour variation.

17.7.2 Rain resistance

A number of tests using a BS 4315[7] test rig have been carried out on concrete masonry walls to show their performance, but unfortunately it is not possible to relate standard block parameters, such as strength, density, porosity and permeability to the subsequent behaviour of a wall built from the units. However, concrete blockwork can provide effective resistance to the passage of rain and recommended wall constructions are given in BS 5628: Part 3.[5]

There are two general mechanisms by which walls resist rain penetration. Firstly, the action of a wall built with high absorption units is analogous to that of an overcoat which absorbs and retains water and subsequently dries without penetration. In persistent rain, the absorptive wall eventually becomes saturated throughout. Hence, successful performance depends upon cyclic rain conditions, which are the most common in the UK. The thickness of the wall is obviously important with absorptive units since this governs the effectiveness as a barrier against rain penetration. Alternatively, a wall built with impermeable units set in full joints of strong cement:lime:sand mortar acts like a plastic raincoat in keeping water out. However, because there is a greater quantity of 'run off' water, this type of wall is particularly susceptible to workmanship defects where water, aided by wind pressure may penetrate badly filled joints.

Irrespective of the type of unit used to construct the wall, the forming of the joint and its profile are important factors in rain resistance. Perpend joints should be well filled. Tooled joints are more resistant to the ingress of water. Recessed joints reduce the effective thickness of the wall and may aggravate frost attack on the units. Where hollow units are used, BS 5628: Part 3[5] suggests that shell bedding may enhance rain resistance.

The advantage of a cavity wall is its superior rain resistance to a single-leaf wall; however, it is not a total barrier to water and there are a number of ways in which water can bridge the cavity. To avoid water crossing to the inner leaf, it is essential to keep cavities clean, i.e. free from debris and mortar droppings. Wall ties should be correctly located with water drips downwards. Ties should not slope from outer to inner leaf, therefore the coursing of units requires attention.

The inclusion of cavity insulation to improve thermal performance can lead to problems if detailing and workmanship are not to a high standard. Filling the cavity of a cavity wall with thermal insulating material (either injected or built-in) can affect its resistance to driving rain.[8] Partially filled cavities, in which a 50-mm cavity is retained, are usually satisfactory provided the insulation material is fixed firmly to the inner leaf, but with fully filled cavities extra care is required.

Cleanliness is essential to prevent mortar dropping onto the top of full-fill insulation bats already installed in the cavity when continuing the lift, and laths may be used to advantage. It is sensible to build the outer leaf first when employing full-fill insulation since this enables excess mortar on the inner face to be removed, thus avoiding mortar projections from outer to inner leaf.

17.7.3 Structural properties

The range of structural applications for concrete blockwork is extremely wide and may range from housing through to high-rise buildings, industrial and other structures. It may also be used for retaining walls, bridge abutments and other civil engineering work. Recommendations for the design of unreinforced walls are given in BS 5628: Part 1,[9] and for reinforced and prestressed masonry in BS 5628: Part 2.[10]

Masonry is weak in tension and for economic design it is essential to exploit its compressive strength and to design to minimize tensile stress. Excessive tensile stresses can be catered for by the use of steel reinforcement in reinforced masonry, or by overcoming the tensile stresses by prestressing the masonry.[11]

The wide range of block strengths available enables concrete blocks to be used economically for both low- and high-rise structures. In addition, hollow blocks can easily be reinforced to improve stability and provide strong points within a structure as may be required, for example in buildings over five storeys high.

When comparing blocks and bricks of a given compressive strength, it is important to take into account the differing unit/aspect ratio. As an example, a similar wall strength can be achieved by using a 215 mm high by 100 mm thick solid block of strength 7 N mm^{-2} as would be achieved by using a typical brick of strength 15–20 N mm^{-2}.

17.7.4 Movements

Movements to which concrete masonry walls are subjected during the life of a structure can, if not adequately allowed for, be great enough to cause considerable cracking. The materials used for masonry (blocks, bricks and mortar) undergo dimensional changes due to wetting and drying, to carbonation and to changes in temperature. These are the principal sources of movement.

Tensile strength of masonry is usually insufficient to prevent cracking if these movements are restrained. To minimize the risk, movement joints should be provided to reduce stresses due to shrinkage and thermal effects. Usually when cracking occurs it is found that the physical properties of units and other common materials are not understood and that precautions to cater for possible movements have not, therefore, been taken.

Where the lengths of walling are quite short, e.g. internal walls in house construction, movement joints are not usually provided. In some locations, however, internal walls may be subjected to both shrinkage and thermal stresses and movement joints should then be provided. Movement joints are likely to be necessary in fair-faced walls whether external or internal, but in the latter the joints may often be spaced further apart. The correct location and spacing of movement joints is an important factor affecting the risk of cracking. Individual projects require individual attention and manufacturers will often be able to offer advice.

Recommendations for the control of movement may be found in BS 5628: Part 3[5] and Tovey.[12]

17.7.5 Thermal insulation

There are various concrete blocks with good thermal-insulation properties, such as autoclaved aerated blocks, lightweight aggregate blocks, multi-slotted lightweight aggregate blocks, foam-filled blocks of lightweight or dense aggregate and blocks with insulation applied to the face.

The thermal conductivity of a given concrete is often determined from the density of the material.[13] However, some materials differ considerably from the standard relationship and have better thermal conductivity values than predicted by density.

The resistance of a solid block is determined readily from its thermal conductivity, but special consideration is needed for multi-slotted blocks.[13] However, both of these are best obtained from the manufacturer.

The level of thermal insulation for dwellings and other buildings is controlled by the Building Regulations 1985.[14] In general terms, the requirements for external walls of dwellings and most other buildings will be satisfied by the provison of a U value of 0.6 W m^{-2} which is to be reduced to 0.45 W m^{-2} K^{-1} as from April 1990.[15] This has led some manufacturers to develop lower-density materials and composite insulated blocks in order to comply with the insulation requirements within an acceptable wall thickness.

In addition to the variety of units, a range of wall constructions may be employed.[12]

17.7.6 Sound insulation

Generally, the greater the mass built into the wall the greater its ability to resist air-borne sound. Concrete masonry walls, including those comprising two leaves of the lighter thermal-insulating blocks, can provide adequate levels of sound insulation between adjoining properties. Blocks may also be used for internal walls to provide good levels of sound insulation between adjoining rooms.

Examples of walls able to satisfy the sound-insulation requirements for separating walls are given in Approved Document E[16] to the Building Regulations.[14] The value of mass required should be taken as the total mass of the wall including the weight of mortar and plaster. Some manufacturers, however, are able to offer constructions which are lighter than those indicated while still complying with the regulations.

There is a relationship between the mass of a wall and its sound insulation. However, there are several factors which affect the sound insulation of an element, such as stiffness, permeability, and absorption characteristics so that two walls being of the same mass but of different dimensions may well perform differently. However, the mass of a solid wall is often used to assess its likely sound insulation. A wall built from hollow blocks is likely to perform in a similar way to that of an impervious solid wall of the same mass.[17]

With cavity walls, the sound insulation is related not only to the surface mass but also to the width of the cavity and the rigidity and spacing of the wall ties. A cavity wall with a 50 mm nominal cavity with leaves connected by wire ties may be expected to have a resistance to sound transmission similar to that of a solid masonry wall of the same surface mass.[14] An improvement in the resistance to sound transmission may be achieved by lowering the coupling effect between the leaves, i.e. by widening the cavity or by omitting the ties. In both cases, structural stability must be maintained.

17.7.7 Fire resistance

It is of paramount important that a building should not collapse during fire and the occupants should be protected from fire and smoke until they can be evacuated. Concrete blocks have good fire resistance and are capable of providing a degree of fire resistance far in excess of the notional required period for dwellings. Typically, a 100 mm solid block wall will provide a notional fire resistance period of 2 h. The fire resistance of different types of unit depends upon the class of aggregate employed (dense, lightweight or aerated) and whether they are hollow or solid.[5]

17.7.8 Durability

The durability of masonry will vary according to the nature of the units, the composition of the mortar and the degree of exposure to the weather, atmospheric pollution and aggressive conditions. Concrete blocks are durable materials suitable for most normal applications. Full recommendations for the minimum quality of units and mortar are given in BS 5628: Part 3.[5]

The main factors which influence the frost resistance of hardened concrete are the degree of saturation and the pore structure of the concrete. In general, concrete masonry has good resistance to frost attack but additional consideration should be given to masonry subjected to extreme conditions if it is likely to remain saturated for long periods of time. Care is necessary in the choice of units where these are liable to be splashed by road de-icing salts, since such salts have a detrimental effect on the frost resistance of concrete.

Aqueous solutions of sulphates can attack the hardened cement in concrete; the chemical reactions occurring depend upon the nature of the sulphate present and the type of the cement. When concrete is subjected to sulphate attack, compounds occupy a greater volume than the compounds they replace, causing expansion and subsequent disintegration of the concrete. Where such sulphate is anticipated (i.e. from soil or atmosphere), careful consideration must be given to the selection of the concrete masonry units. Some manufacturers have authoritative evidence (i.e. agrement certificates) to confirm the suitability of products in sulphate conditions. Alternatively, measures to protect concrete masonry (i.e. by tanking) may be necessary.[5]

Steel components are often incorporated in masonry construction, these include various forms of tie and also reinforcing steel. Many of the components rely, wholly or in part, on the surrounding masonry and infill concrete to provide protection against corrosion. Concrete is eminently suited to this purpose since it provides an alkaline environment which promotes the formation of a passive film at the steel–concrete interface. Thus, steel in concrete is normally completely protected against corrosion. It should be noted, however, that mortar readily carbonates and it may be necessary to use stainless steel or similarly durable reinforcement except in internal situations.[5,10]

Acknowledgements

The author would express his thanks to the British Cement Association for permission to reproduce the photograph used in this chapter.

References

1 KINNIBURGH, W., 'Comparison of building times required to building walls', *Building* (Oct. 1968)
2 ANDERSON, W. E. and ROBERTS, J. J., 'Efficient masonry house design', *Reprint 3/84*, Cement and Concrete Association, Wexham Springs (1984)
3 ANDERSON, W. E., ROBERTS, J. J. and WATT, P., 'Efficient masonry housebuilding—design approach', *Publication 48.055*, Cement and Concrete Association, Wexham Springs (1985)
4 BRITISH STANDARDS INSTITUTION, *BS 6073 Precast concrete masonry units. Part 1: Specification for precast masonry units, Part 2: Method of specifying precast masonry units*, Milton Keynes (1981)
5 BRITISH STANDARDS INSTITUTION, *BS 5628 Code of Practice for use of masonry. Part 3: Materials and components, design and workmanship*, Milton Keynes (1985)
6 PHIPPS, M. E. and MONTAGUE, T. I., *The Design of Concrete Blockwork Diaphragm Walls*, Aggregate Concrete Block Association, Leicester
7 BRITISH STANDARDS INSTITUTION, *BS 4315: Part 2 Permeable walling constructions (water penetration)*, Milton Keynes (1970 (1983))
8 BUILDING RESEARCH ESTABLISHMENT, 'Cavity insulation', *BRE Digest 236*, HMSO, London (1980)
9 BRITISH STANDARDS INSTITUTION, *BS 5628 Code of Practice for structural masonry. Part 1: Unreinforced masonry*, Milton Keynes (1978)
10 BRITISH STANDARDS INSTITUTION, *BS 5628 Code of Practice for structural masonry. Part 2 Reinforced and prestressed masonry*, Milton Keynes (1985)
11 PHIPPS, M. E. and MONTAGUE, T. I., *The Design of Prestressed Concrete Blockwork Diaphragm Walls*, Aggregate Concrete Block Association, Leicester (n.d.)
12 TOVEY, A. K., 'Concrete masonry for the designer', *Publication 48.049*, Cement and Concrete Association, Wexham Springs (1981)
13 CHARTERED INSTITUTE OF BUILDING SERVICES, *CIBS Guide, Section A3: Thermal properties of building materials*, London (1980)
14 *The Building Regulations 1985*, HMSO, London (1985)
15 *The Building Regulations 1989. Approved Document L*, HMSO, London (1989)
16 *The Building Regulations 1985. Approved Document E*, HMSO, London (1985)
17 BRITISH STANDARDS INSTITUTION, *BS 8223 Code of Practice for sound insulation and noise reduction for buildings*, Milton Keynes (1987)

18

Cements

F G Buttler PhD, MRSC, CChem
Consultant Chemist

Contents

18.1 Introduction 18/3

18.2 Portland cement 18/3

18.3 Other cementitious materials blended with
Portland cement 18/4
18.3.1 Pulverized-fuel ash 18/4
18.3.2 Ground-granulated blast-furnace slag 18/4
18.3.3 Silica fume 18/4
18.3.4 Chemical compositions of pulverized-fuel ash,
ground-granulated blast-furnace slag and
silica fume 18/4
18.3.5 Physical characteristics of pulverized-fuel ash,
ground-granulated blast-furnace slag and
silica fume 18/5

18.4 The supply of quality-controlled cementitious
materials 18/5
18.4.1 Portland cement 18/5
18.4.2 Pulverized-fuel ash 18/5
18.4.3 Ground-granulated blast-furnace slag 18/6

18.5 Some of the variables specified in British Standards
for cements and cementitious materials 18/7
18.5.1 Fineness 18/7
18.5.2 Setting time 18/7
18.5.3 Soundness 18/7
18.5.4 Magnesia 18/7
18.5.5 Heat of hydration 18/7

18.6 The chemistry of pozzolanic reactions 18/8

18.7 Factors affecting the performance of cements
in concrete 18/8
18.7.1 Compressive strength 18/8
18.7.2 Rate of strength development 18/8
18.7.3 Temperature rise in concrete 18/9
18.7.4 The effect of temperature on reaction rate 18/9

18.8 The durability of concrete 18/9
18.8.1 Resistance to attack by sulphate 18/9
18.8.2 The protection of steel reinforcement 18/9
18.8.3 The alkali–silica reaction 18/10
18.8.4 Freeze–thaw resistance of hardened concrete 18/11

18.9 Aluminious cements 18/11
18.9.1 Manufacture and composition 18/11
18.9.2 Hydration of aluminious cements 18/11
18.9.3 Properties of aluminious cement concrete 18/11

References 18/12

Bibliography 18/12

18.1 Introduction

In the present context a cement can be defined as a material which hardens from a plastic state and which can be used to bind together aggregate particles. In the construction industry the most important of these materials is Portland cement. When mixed with water this forms a plastic paste which sets and then steadily increases in compressive strength. As well as being used as a cementitious material on its own, Portland cement is frequently blended with pulverized-fuel ash (also called flyash) and with ground-granulated blast-furnace slag. Neither pulverized-fuel ash nor ground-granulated blast-furnace slag are normally used as cementitious materials on their own, but produce additional amounts of binding materials by reacting with the calcium hydroxide formed on hydration of the Portland cement. Because of this it is appropriate to consider the production, reactions and use of Portland cement before examining its use in combination with either pulverized-fuel ash or ground-granulated blast-furnace slag.

18.2 Portland cement

Portland cement is produced by igniting a mixture of two materials; one rich in lime, such as limestone or chalk, and the other rich in silica, such as clay or shale. In the most commonly used manufacturing process, the finely ground raw materials are dry blended. On heating, water is lost from the clay or shale and the limestone or chalk is decomposed to give lime and carbon dioxide. At the high temperatures used the lime combines with the dehydrated clay or shale to form Portland-cement clinker. The clinker is cooled and finely ground: at this stage a small amount of gypsum (calcium sulphate) is often added to prevent the cement from setting too rapidly when it is subsequently mixed with water.

The compositions of Portland cements are carefully controlled and usually lie within the ranges shown in *Table 18.1*. It is customary to give the chemical compositions in terms of oxides because the compounds present have empirical formulae which can be expressed in terms of the sums of the oxides of the individual elements. In addition, as shown in *Table 18.1*, cement chemists frequently use single letters to denote the oxide formulae. The chemical analysis of a cement is useful for quantitative calculations but does not give a direct representation of the proportions of the compounds present. The most abundant compounds are listed below together with the various methods of expressing their empirical formulae:

(1) tricalcium silicate, Ca_3SiO_5, $(CaO)_3SiO_2$, C_3S;
(2) dicalcium silicate, Ca_2SiO_4, $(CaO)_2SiO_2$, C_2S;
(3) tricalcium aluminate, $Ca_3Al_2O_6$, $(CaO)_3Al_2O_3$, C_3A; and
(4) calcium aluminoferrite, $Ca_4Al_2Fe_2O_{10}$, $(CaO)_4Al_2O_3Fe_2O_3$, C_4AF.

In the present context, C_3S and C_2S are the most important of the compounds present and together they constitute about 75% of the mass of the Portland cement; their proportions vary but there is generally at least twice as much C_3S as C_2S.

When Portland cement is mixed with water a number of complex reactions occur and hydrated products of low solubility are formed. Of most relevance are the reactions of C_3S and C_2S, both of which form a mixture of hydrated calcium silicates and aluminosilicates (often referred to as CSH gel) and calcium hydroxide, but in different proportions. The CSH gel is highly cementitious and constitutes about 65% of the products of the fully hydrated Portland cement, whilst the calcium hydroxide, $Ca(OH)_2$, constitutes about 20%. The proportions of the two compounds vary and depend on the composition of the unhydrated cement. The $Ca(OH)_2$ is not cementitious but can be converted into additional quantities of CSH gel by using blends of Portland cement and pozzolanas such as pulverized-fuel ash and ground-granulated blast-furnace slag. The reaction with water of the other compounds present in the Portland cement are of less importance but, in a simplified form, all are summarized below.

$$C_3S \quad +xH_2O \rightarrow \quad C_ySH_z \quad + \quad (3-y)CH$$

tricalcium   water   hydrated calcium   calcium
silicate   silicates   hydroxide
                       (CSH gel)   (Portlandite)

After longer times, the above reaction can be represented by

$$C_3S \quad +xH_2O \rightarrow \quad C_{1.5}SH_y \quad + \quad 1.5CH$$

$$C_2S \quad +xH_2O \rightarrow \quad C_ySH_z \quad + \quad (2-y)CH$$

dicalcium   water   hydrated calcium   calcium
silicate   silicates   hydroxide
                       (CSH gel)   (Portlandite)

Similarly, after longer times, this can be represented by

$$C_2S + xH_2O \rightarrow C1.5SH_y + 0.5CH$$

$$C_3A \quad + \quad C_4AF \quad + xC\bar{S}H_2 + water \rightarrow$$

tricalcium   calcium   gypsum
aluminate   aluminoferrite

$$yC_6A\bar{S}_3H_z + \quad\quad\quad (A,F)H_3$$

ettringite   amorphous hydrous
               aluminium and iron oxides

The setting time and the rate of strength development is affected by the proportions of the compounds present in the Portland cement. The proportion of C_3A is normally comparatively small but, because its reaction with water is very rapid, it can, unless controlled, lead to an immediate stiffening of the cement paste (flash set). In order to prevent this happening a controlled amount of gypsum ($CaSO_4 \cdot 2H_2O$) is added to the ground clinker. Gypsum and C_3A react in the presence of water to form insoluble calcium sulphoaluminates with little hydraulic properties. Gypsum also reacts with C_4AF.

The main reactions responsible for strength development are those associated with the hydration of C_3S and C_2S. The former reacts more rapidly than the latter so that, for cement particles of comparable fineness and surface area, there will be an increase in the rate of strength development as the ratio $C_3S:C_2S$ increases in the Portland cement. It follows, therefore, that the early age strength per unit weight of cement used can be enhanced. However, the fineness of a cement is a major factor

Table 18.1 Typical chemical compositions of Portland cement

Oxide formula	Cement chemist's nomenclature for oxide formula	Content (%)
SiO_2	S	17–25
CaO	C	60–67
Al_2O_3	A	3–8
Fe_2O_3	F	1.5–4.5
MgO	M	0.5–4.0
K_2O	K	0.1–1.5
Na_2O	N	0.1–1.0
SO_3	$\bar{S}$	2.0–3.0
LOI[a]		1.5–2.5
Free lime		0.5–1.5
Insoluble residue		0.3–1.5

[a] LOI, loss on ignition.

influencing its rate of hydration and hence of its strength development, because the reactions occur at the interface of the cement particles with water. Ordinary Portland cement is usually ground so that its surface area is in the range 300–350 $m^2 kg^{-1}$ (BS 12:1978[1] specifies a minimum of 225 $m^2 kg^{-1}$), whereas rapid-hardening Portland cement normally has a surface area in the range 400–450 $m^2 kg^{-1}$ (specified minimum 325 $m^2 kg^{-1}$). It follows, therefore, that an ordinary Portland cement with a high C_3S content from one works may show a similar early-age strength development to a more finely ground rapid-hardening Portland cement with a lower C_3S content from another works. These two types of Portland cement have similar setting times and, with equivalent cement, water and aggregate contents, there will probably be little difference in the long-term strengths of the concretes produced.

18.3 Other cementitious materials blended with Portland cement

As stated earlier, Portland cement is often blended with pulverized-fuel ash, ground-granulated blast-furnace slag, or silica fume (see Chapter 23). Although ground-granulated blast-furnace slag has some latent hydraulic qualities, its use in concrete relies largely on its reaction with some of the calcium hydroxide produced by the hydration of Portland cement. In this sense it can be grouped with pulverized-fuel ash and silica fume, both of which rely on their pozzolanic reactions with lime to produce hydrated cementitious products.

The term 'pozzolana' is derived from the volcanic tuff which occurs at Pozzuoli near Naples in Italy. This volcanic tuff in a finely ground form has been used as a building material since ancient times. The terms 'pozzolan' and 'pozzolanic' are now used more widely and can be defined as 'any siliceous or siliceous and aluminous material which shows little or no cementitious property on its own but will, in the presence of moisture, react with calcium hydroxide at ordinary temperatures to form compounds possessing cementitious properties'. In order to react as a pozzolan, a material needs to be present as small particles with a large surface area and to be in a non-crystalline form.

18.3.1 Pulverized-fuel ash

In the UK, the fine ashes which are precipitated from the exhaust gases produced by the combustion of pulverized bituminous coal used for electricity generation are known as pulverized-fuel ash. The coal consists of a mixture of carbonaceous matter and various minerals, e.g. clays, shales, sulphides and carbonates. At the high temperatures in the boiler furnace, the minerals undergo physical and chemical changes which are dependant not only on the temperature but also on the source of the coal and the length of time for which it is maintained at a high temperature. All the minerals are converted into oxides and many of them are fused into tiny glass spheres of complex silicates. The method of extraction of pulverized-fuel ash from the flue gases varies with the design of the plant. In some cases cyclones are used to remove most of the coarser particles before electrostatic precipitation of the finer material. In other systems only the latter type of precipitation is used. Normally the quantity of ash extracted decreases as the flue gases pass through the various extraction stages; at the same time the fineness of the ash increases.

Although, from a particular coal source, the overall chemical composition and the glass content of the ash is likely to remain fairly constant with time, there can be, because of changes in power station operating conditions, changes in fineness and carbon content even for ashes taken from one part of the extraction system. These parameters are of particular importance in relation to the use of pulverized-fuel ash in concrete. It is therefore necessary that selection, classification and blending procedures are used in order that material complying with British Standards can be supplied on a regular basis.

18.3.2 Ground-granulated blast-furnace slag

Blast-furnace slag is formed as a byproduct of the manufacture of iron in the blast furnace. The slag results from the fusion of the lime arising from the limestone added to the furnace with the siliceous and aluminous residues from the iron ore and from the coke used for its reduction.

The quality of the iron produced in the blast-furnace is related to the chemistry of the fluxing materials and the slag. In order to manufacture iron of consistent quality, the composition of the slag is monitored by frequent chemical analyses so that suitable modifications can be made to the composition of the raw materials and to the operating conditions in the blast-furnace. It follows that the slag processor starts with a material of known chemical composition which, for slag from any one source, shows little variation with time .

In order to produce ground-granulated blast-furnace slag, the molten slag from the blast-furnace is rapidly quenched with water so that a high proportion of the slag solidifies as a glassy granulated product with a consistent degree of vitrification and chemical composition. The rapidly cooled product is dewatered and dried; it is then ground in conventional cement clinker grinding mills to cement fineness. No additional materials are added and the uniformity of the product is monitored by measuring, using microscopy, the proportion of glassy particles which are present.

18.3.3 Silica fume

Silica fume is a byproduct of the manufacture of silicon and ferro-silicon using processes which involve the high-temperature reduction of quartz (silicon dioxide). During the manufacturing process, some silicon monoxide vapour leaves the high-temperature reducing parts of the furnace where it was formed; in the upper cooler parts of the furnace, the silicon monoxide is converted into microspheres of amorphous silica. After removing the coarser particles using a cyclone, the finely divided silica microspheres (silica fume) are collected on baghouse filters. A more detailed discussion of silica fume is given in Chapter 23; mention is made of it here so that its properties can be compared with those of the other materials used in combination with Portland cement.

18.3.4 Chemical compositions of pulverized-fuel ash, ground-granulated blast-furnace slag and silica fume

Because of the varying proportions of inorganic oxides which are produced on combustion of coal, the chemical composition of pulverized-fuel ash is variable. However, from a fixed coal source the chemical composition of pulverized-fuel ash is reasonably constant. According to ASTM C618[2] ashes can be divided into two categories. Ashes in the first of these, class F, are formed by burning anthracite or bituminous coals. They normally contain less than 5% CaO (the total analyses being expressed in terms of oxides) and are, therefore, sometimes called 'low calcium flyashes'. To belong to this class the sum of the silica, alumina and iron oxide contents must exceed 70%. These ashes have pozzolanic qualities but have no cementitious properties on their own. Ashes of this type form the bulk of production worldwide and represent those from British coals. The second of the categories, class C, are normally produced by burning lignite or sub-bituminous coals. They contain more

Table 18.2 Typical chemical compositions (wt%) of cementitious materials

Oxide	Portland cement	Ground-granulated blast-furnace slag	Pulverized-fuel ash	Silica fume
SiO_2	20	37	48	92
CaO	65	40	3	0.2
Al_2O_3	5	11	26	0.7
Fe_2O_3	3	0.3	10	1.2
MgO	1.1	7	2	0.2
Na_2O	0.2	0.4	1.0	1.2
K_2O	0.9	0.7	3.0	1.9
SO_3	2.4	0.3	0.7	—
S^{2-}	—	1.0		
Other oxides	1.4	2.3	1.3	2.6
LOI[a]	1	—	5	—

[a] LOI, loss on ignition.

CaO than the class-F ashes and are sometimes called 'high calcium flyashes'. The sum of the silica, alumina and iron oxide contents must exceed 50%. In addition to their pozzolanic behaviour, class-C ashes may also have some cementitious properties in their own right.

Typical chemical compositions (expressed as oxides) of pulverized-fuel ashes produced in the UK and of ground-granulated blast-furnace slag and silica fume are given in *Table 18.2*. A typical analysis of Portland cement is included in the table for the purpose of comparison. *Table 18.2* shows, particularly with respect to the proportions of CaO and SiO_2 present, the dissimilarity between the materials. Although pulverized-fuel ash, ground-granulated blast-furnace slag and silica fume, when blended with Portland cement, behave as cementitious materials and give rise to hydrated calcium silicates and aluminates, their reactions are somewhat different. Pulverized-fuel ash and silica fume contain very little CaO and form hydrated cementitious products by undergoing a pozzolanic reaction with the calcium hydroxide liberated by the Portland cement. On the other hand, ground-granulated blast-furnace slag can contribute a considerable amount of CaO to the reaction processes.

The percentage of SiO_2 in all three materials is greater than that in the Portland cement with which they are blended. It therefore follows, for all of these materials, that the hydrated calcium silicates formed after reaction have lower $CaO:SiO_2$ molar ratios than those formed from Portland cement alone.

All the cementitious materials contain alkali-metal ions. Unlike Portland cement, where a large proportion of the alkali metal ions are present as water-soluble sulphates, the alkali-metal ions in pulverized-fuel ash, ground-granulated blast-furnace slag and silica fume are concentrated in the glassy structure of their particles and their water-soluble alkali-metal ion contents are low. As the glass particles react they liberate alkali metal ions, but these do not affect the alkalinity of the concrete in the same way as those derived from Portland cement. Because of the lower $CaO:SiO_2$ molar ratio in the hydrated calcium silicates, a greater proportion of alkali-metal ions are removed from solution.

Pulverized-fuel ash contains some unburnt carbonaceous matter, normally taken as equivalent to its loss on ignition (LOI). It is important that the loss on ignition is maintained at a low level (British Standards recommend a maximum of 7.0%) both for aesthetic and technical reasons. High carbon ashes may not show satisfactory water reduction when used in concrete

and, because they absorb admixtures, they may reduce the effectiveness of air-entraining agents.

18.3.5 Physical characteristics of pulverized-fuel ash, ground-granulated blast-furnace slag and silica fume

Typical values of the fineness, bulk density and density of pulverized-fuel ash, ground-granulated blast-furnace slag and silica fume are given in *Table 18.3*. The following points should be noted.

(1) Portland cement, pulverized-fuel ash and ground-granulated blast-furnace slag (suitable for use in concrete) have similar finenesses. However, the spherical particles in silica fume are very much finer.
(2) The relative densities show that when pulverized-fuel ash, ground-granulated blast-furnace slag and silica fume are blended with Portland cement there is, on a mass basis, an increase in the volume of cementitious powder as compared with that of the same total mass of Portland cement. This is particularly significant with Portland cement/pulverized-fuel ash blends where 70:30 proportions by mass are common. The difference in the relative densities has important implications on the concrete workability.

18.4 The supply of quality-controlled cementitious materials

18.4.1 Portland cement

A number of different types of Portland cement are manufactured. BS 12: 1978[1] gives the requiremements of both ordinary Portland cement and rapid-hardening Portland cement. The main difference between these cements is the fineness to which the clinker is ground; this is reflected in the rate of strength development which is needed for compliance. BS 1370: 1979[3] is the specification for low-heat Portland cement which is sometimes used to reduce the temperature rise in concrete. BS 4027: 1980[4] is the specification for sulphate resisting Portland cement. This can be used to reduce sulphate attack on concrete. Details of the requirements of the standards for these Portland cements are given in *Table 18.4*.

18.4.2 Pulverized-fuel ash

In order that pulverized-fuel ash will give satisfactory performance when used in concrete a number of parameters must be carefully controlled. Detailed requirements are included in several British Standards and in the corresponding standards from other countries. The British Standards covering the supply of pulverized-fuel ash for blending with Portland cement at the mixer are BS 3892: Parts 1 and 2: 1982.[6,7] The standards dealing

Table 18.3 Typical physical characteristics of cementitious materials

	Portland cement	Ground-granulated blast-furnace slag	Pulverized-fuel ash	Silica fume
Fineness ($m^2\,kg^{-1}$)	340	350	380	15 000
Bulk density ($kg\,m^{-3}$)	1400	1200	900	240
Density ($g\,cm^{-3}$)	3.1	2.9	2.3	2.2

Table 18.4 British Standard requirements for Portland cements[a]

Property	BS 12: 1978[1]		BS 1370: 1979[3]	BS 4027: 1980[4]
	OPC	RHPC	LHPC	SRPC
Fineness ($m^2 kg^{-1}$)	225	325	275	250
Insoluble residue (%)	1.5	1.5	1.5	1.5
Magnesia, MgO (%)	4.0	4.0	4.0	4.0
Sulphur as SO_3 (%)	3.0	3.0	2.5[b]	2.5
			3.0[c]	
Loss on ignition (%)				
temperate climates	3.0	3.0	3.0	3.0
tropical climates	4.0	4.0	4.0	4.0
Compressive strength of concrete[d] ($N mm^{-2}$)				
at 3 days	13	18	5	10
at 28 days	29	33	19	27
Setting time[d]				
initial (min)	45	45	60	45
final (h)	10	10	10	10
Soundness[d] (mm)	10	10	10	10
Heat of hydration[d] ($kJ kg^{-1}$)				
7 days			250	
28 days			290	

[a] OPC, ordinary Portland cement; RHPC, rapid-hardening Portland cement; LHPC, low-heat Portland cement; SRPC, sulphate resisting Portland cement.
[b] When C_3A is 5% or less.
[c] When C_3A is more than 5%.
[d] Tested as described in BS 4550: Part 3: 1978.[5]

Table 18.5 British Standard requirements[a] for the use of pulverized-fuel ash in concrete

Property	Requirement in BS 3892: Part 1: 1982[6]	Typical values of material supplied to BS 3892: Part 1: 1982[b]	Requirement in BS 3892: Part 2: 1982[7]	
			Grade A	Grade B
Loss on ignition (%)	7.0 (max.)	3.5	7.0 (max.)	12.0 (max.)
Fineness[b] (%)	12.5	6.0	12.5–30	30–60
Relative density ($kg m^{-3}$)	NS	2300	NS	NS
Sulphuric anhydride, SO_3 (%)	2.5 (max.)	0.7	2.5 (max.)	2.5 (max.)
Magnesia, MgO (%)	4.0 (max.)	1.2	4.0 (max.)	4.0 (max.)
Moisture content (%)	0.5 (max.)	0.1	0.5 (max.)	0.5 (max.)
Water requirement	Not exceeding 95% of ordinary Portland cement	92%	NS	NS
Pozzolanic activity	85% (min.) (recommendation only)	—	NS	NS

[a] NS, not specified. [b] Percentage retained by a 45-μm sieve.

with factory-made blends (composite cements) are BS 6588: 1985 and BS 6610: 1985.[8,9]

(1) *BS 3892: Part 1: 1982*.[6] Pulverized-fuel ash complying with this standard must have good pozzolanic qualities, be of low variability and be suitable for use in structural concrete made in accordance with BS 8110: 1985.[10]

(2) *BS 3892: Part 2: 1982*.[7] This standard is for grades of ash which are suitable, for example, in concrete applications where water reductions are of less importance than in structural concrete or where they can be achieved in other ways such as by hydraulic pressing of precast products. Two grades of ash are specified in this standard. Both grades A and B are coarser than that required by BS 3892: Part 1: 1982[6] and in grade B a higher loss in ignition is allowed.

The details of the requirements of BS 3892: Parts 1 and 2: 1982[6,7] are listed in *Table 18.5*.

(3) *BS 6588: 1985*.[8] This standard covers a factory-made blend of Portland cement and pulverized-fuel ash in which the proportion of the latter lies between 15 and 35% by mass. If both the constituents are interground then the pulverized-fuel ash must comply with all the requirements of BS 3892: Part 1: 1982[6] except for 'fineness'. If the constituents are dry blended after the Portland-cement clinker has been ground, then the pulverized-fuel ash must comply with all the requirements of BS 3892: Part 1: 1982.[6]

(4) *BS 6610: 1985*.[9] This standard is similar to BS 6588: 1985[8] except that the proportion of pulverized-fuel ash lies between 35 and 50% by mass.

18.4.3 Ground-granulated blast-furnace slag

As a cementitious material, ground-granulated blast-furnace slag should comply with BS 6699: 1986,[11] the detailed requirements of which are given in *Table 18.6*. In order to ensure that the ground-granulated blast-furnace slag should have good cementitious properties the standard requires that it contains a minimum of 40% 'pure glass' and 85% of 'glassy particles', both

Table 18.6 British Standard requirements for the use of ground-granulated blast-furnace slag with Portland cement

Property	BS 6699: 1986[11]
Fineness ($m^2 kg^{-1}$)	275 (min.)
Glass content (%)	
pure glass	40 (min.)
glassy particles	85 (min.)
Insoluble residue (%)	1.5 (max.)
Magnesia, MgO (%)	14.0 (max.)
Sulphide, S^{2-} (%)	2.0 (max.)
Loss on ignition (%)	
temperate climates	3.0 (max.)
tropical climates	4.0 (max.)
Chemical modulus	> 1.0
$(CaO + MgO + Al_2O_3)/SiO_2$	
$CaO:SiO_2$ ratio	< 1.4
Moisture content (%)	1.0 (max.)

Table 18.7 British Standard requirements for Portland blast-furnace cements

Property	BS 146: Part 2: 1973[12]	BS 4246: Part 2: 1974[13]
Slag content (%)	≤ 65	50–90
Fineness[a] ($m^2 kg^{-1}$)	225 (min.)	275 (min.)
Compressive strength of concrete[a] ($N mm^{-2}$)		
at 3 days	8	3
at 7 days	14	7
at 28 days	22	14
Setting times[a]		
initial (min)	45	60
final (h)	10	15
Soundness[a] (mm)	10	10
Insoluble residue (%)	1.5	1.5
Magnesia, MgO (%)	7.0	9.0
Sulphur, S^{2-} (%)	1.5	2.0
Sulphur, as SO_3 (%)	3.0	3.0
Heat of hydration[a] ($kJ kg^{-1}$)		
at 7 days	NA	250
at 28 days	NA	290

[a] Tested as described in BS 4550: Part 3: 1978.[5] NA, not applicable.

of which are more cementitious than crystalline particles. To achieve this, the molten slag must have been rapidly cooled to prevent the formation of crystalline material. In addition, the chemical modulus $(CaO + MgO + Al_2O_3)/SiO_2$ must be greater than unity. This ensures that the ground-granulated blast-furnace slag is chemically reactive. There is also a maximum limit of 1.4 to the $CaO:SiO_2$ molar ratio in order to ensure soundness (q.v.).

BS 6699: 1986[11] is the specification for ground-granulated blast-furnace slag as a material. There are two important British Standards relating to cements in which ground-granulated blast-furnace slag is combined with Portland cement. BS 146: Part 2: 1973,[12] describes the combination of Portland cement and ground-granulated blast-furnace slag with up to 65% of the latter. The other standard, BS 4246: Part 2: 1974,[13] is similar but it covers blends containing between 50 and 90% ground-granulated blast-furnace slag. Although blends containing between 50 and 65% of this material are common to both standards, there are significant differences in their com-

pliance clauses, particularly with respect to strength development and maximum heat of hydration. Details of the requirements of the standards are given in *Table 18.7*.

18.5 Some of the variables specified in British Standards for cements and cementitious materials

18.5.1 Fineness

The fineness of cements and cementitious materials has a major influence on the rate of strength development and heat evolution in concrete. It is usual for all Portland cements, ground-granulated blast-furnace slag and blends between the two to be ground to much greater fineness then specified in the British Standards. The fineness of pulverized-fuel ash is specified in terms of the percentage by mass of the material retained on a 45-μm sieve rather than in terms of its surface area. As with the other cementitious materials used in concrete, the pulverized-fuel ash supplied for use in structural concrete is much finer than required for compliance with BS 3892: Part 1: 1982.[6]

18.5.2 Setting time

Tests for setting times are normally carried out on a cement paste. Setting is caused by the selective hydration of the compounds present in the Portland cement. The first two constituents to react are C_3A and C_3S; the flash setting properties of the former are delayed by the addition of gypsum to the ground clinker so that it is the C_3S which sets first. The rate of reaction of C_2S is less than that of C_3S.

18.5.3 Soundness

It is essential that a cement paste does not show a large change in volume once it has set. Any appreciable expansion could, under the conditions of restraint in concrete, result in the disruption of the hardened cement paste. Expansion can arise due to the slow or delayed hydration of the compounds present in the Portland cement. In addition, the reactions of free lime, magnesia (periclase) and calcium sulphate in the hardened cement paste can also cause expansion.

Because unsoundness in a cement is not likely to become apparent until some time after it has been used in concrete, it is usual to specify that the cement should be tested in an accelerated manner. This is frequently done by measuring the expansion of a cylinder of cement paste of standard consistency when cured under controlled conditions. The expansion of Portland cements is limited to 10 mm, this being the amplified expansion of the cylinder determined by the separation of the pointers in an apparatus designed by Le Chatelier.

18.5.4 Magnesia

Magnesium oxide (magnesia, MgO) is formed from magnesium carbonate which may be present in the materials used for the manufacture of Portland-cement clinker. Only about 1.5% MgO can be taken into solid solution and quantities in excess of this can occur as free magnesium oxide in a well-crystallized form known as periclase. This form hydrates slowly and, if present in sufficient quantity, can give rise to problems of delayed expansion. Magnesia is rarely present in large quantities in the raw materials used for cement manufacture in the UK but, even so, the British Standards specify a maximum of 4.0% MgO.

18.5.5 Heat of hydration

The hydration of cement is an exothermic reaction and the

amount of heat generated per unit mass of cement at any specified stage of hydration is known as the heat of hydration of the cement. In thin sections of structural concrete the heat generated is quickly lost to the environment so that the temperature rise in the concrete is usually not large enough to cause significant stress when the concrete returns to ambient temperatures. However, in large sections where the temperature rise may be as great as 50°C, problems can arise due to thermal cracking. The observed temperature rise depends on a number of factors such as cement content and type, the ambient temperature and the kind of formwork used. BS 1370: 1979[3] and BS 4246: Part 2: 1974[13] both give the limits for the heat of hydration of cement.

18.6 The chemistry of pozzolanic reactions

As stated earlier, a pozzolan is a material which will react with calcium hydroxide in the presence of moisture to give products which have cementitious properties. Both naturally occurring pozzolans, e.g. those of volcanic origin, and 'manufactured' pozzolans, e.g. pulverized-fuel ash, ground-granulated blast-furnace slag and silica fume, all contain a high proportion of silica often present as silicates and aluminosilicates. Before the advent of Portland cement, mixtures of lime with finely ground volcanic ashes or calcined clays were widely used as hydraulic cements for making mortars and concretes. However, it is generally now more convenient to use Portland cement in conjunction with pulverized-fuel ash, ground-granulated blast-furnace slag and silica fume and to rely on their reactions with the lime liberated on hydration of the Portland cement to enable the pozzolanic reaction to proceed.

The pozzolanic reaction produces hydrated calcium silicates of similar composition, but of lower $CaO:SiO_2$ molar ratio, to those formed by the hydration of the C_3S and C_2S provided by the Portland cement. It therefore follows that:

(1) the hydrated calcium silicate:calcium hydroxide ratios in the reaction products increase as the pozzolanic reaction takes place; and
(2) the overall $CaO:SiO_2$ molar ratio in the hydrated calcium silicates decreases with time.

In an unreacted Portland cement, the $CaO:SiO_2$ molar ratio is in the region of 3.5. This is considerably greater than the corresponding molar ratio of the hydrated calcium silicates formed after hydration of the Portland cement where the value is approximately 1.5. In effect, therefore, although some of the CaO from the Portland cement is required to form products such as ettringite, the use of a blend containing a pozzolan with a highly reactive silica content enables a greater quantity of cementitious material to be formed per unit weight of Portland cement than can be achieved by the use of Portland cement alone.

Of particular importance when using blended cements are the relative rates of hydration of the Portland cement and the pozzolanic reactions of pulverized-fuel ash, ground-granulated blast-furnace slag and silica fume. Because of its extreme fineness, silica fume reacts very rapidly with lime but, normally, only comparatively small quantities of silica fume are blended with Portland cement. On the other hand, when pulverized-fuel ash or ground-granulated blast-furnace slag are blended with Portland cement considerable quantities of the former materials are used (frequently in the regions of 30% and 50% by mass for pulverized-fuel ash and ground-granulated blast-furnace slag, respectively). For these mixtures the Portland cement hydration reactions are more rapid than the pozzolanic reactions and generally the concrete will have set before the pulverized-fuel ash or ground-granulated blast-furnace slag give any significant contribution to early-age strength. The Portland cement continues to hydrate after the concrete has set but the effect of the pozzolanic reaction largely becomes apparent at later ages. Because of this, as discussed below, not only is the rate of strength development altered, but the long-term durability of the concrete can be improved.

Although the discussion above largely related to the formation of hydrated calcium silicates from the siliceous materials present in the pozzolans, the alumina contents are also involved in the formation of cementitious products. In addition, the amounts of sodium and potassium ions present in the Portland cement and pozzolans have an important bearing on the reactivity of the constituents and on the behaviour of the concrete produced. These aspects are dealt with later.

18.7 Factors affecting the performance of cements in concrete

It is inappropriate in the present context to discuss in detail all the factors which affect the performance of cements in concrete. However, some discussion is useful as a vehicle for explaining the practical implications of using different types of cement.

18.7.1 Compressive strength

The compressive strength of hardened concrete is one of its most important properties. It is easily measured and is frequently specified. The proportion of water in the cement paste has a major effect on the strength of concrete. As stated by Abrams,[14] at a given age and for the same materials and conditions of test, the strength of a fully compacted concrete depends only on the water:cement ratio used in the mix and rises as this ratio falls. Apart from the water:cement ratio, there are other factors which influence the observed compressive strength of the concrete. These include the efficiency of curing, the temperature during the curing period and the degree of compaction.

It is therefore desirable in order to optimize the final compressive strength of the concrete that the water content of the original mix should be reduced whilst maintaining the fresh concrete in a workable condition that allows for satisfactory compaction.

Pulverised-fuel ash is frequently used to reduce the water demand of concrete. This is reflected in the requirement of BS 3892: Part 1: 1982[7] that a mix of pulverized-fuel ash and Portland cement should have a water demand not exceeding 95% of that of a comparable mix made with Portland cement as the only cementitious material. Similar requirements are not included in the standards dealing with ground-granulated blast-furnace slag where reduction in the water demand is more difficult. When Portland cement is replaced by pulverized-fuel ash on a weight-for-weight basis there is a considerable increase in the fine-powder volume because pulverized-fuel ash will normally have a lower relative density than the Portland cement (approximately 2.3 and 3.1 g cm^{-3}, respectively).

Since, typically, the size of most of the pulverized-fuel ash particles is in the range 1–10 μm, they supplement the effect of the fine Portland cement particles in reducing voids between aggregate particles so that less water is required to produce a concrete of given consistency. The use of less water improves both the ultimate compressive strength of the concrete and its durability.

18.7.2 Rate of strength development

Because of the differences in the rates of hydration of Portland cement and the rates of the pozzolanic reactions between calcium hydroxide and pulverized-fuel ash or ground-granulated blast-furnace slag there are differences in the rates of gain in compressive strength made either with Portland cement alone or with blended cements. At early ages the rate of strength development is less with blends if the comparison is made on the basis of equal cementitious content by weight (i.e. some of the Portland cement being replaced on a weight-for-weight basis by pulverized-fuel ash or ground-granulated blast-furnace slag). The reduction in the water content associated, in particular, with the use of pulverized-fuel ash is not sufficient in the short term to compensate for the differences in the rates of formation of the hydrated cementitious material by the various processes. In the long term, even with equal cementitious contents, greater strengths may be attained by using a blend, although the actual performance depends on the proportions of the materials in the blend and on the quality of the materials.

However, particularly when pulverized-fuel ash is used, it is usual to change the mix design of the concrete so that similar 28-day compressive strengths are obtained. There are a number of ways of doing this but many involve an increase in the proportion of pulverized-fuel ash above that required by weight-for-weight replacement of the Portland cement. The adoption of methods giving equivalent 28-day compressive strengths not only improves performance at early ages but is likely to give the greatest enhancement in the long-term strength and to lead to a greater durability of the concrete.

18.7.3 Temperature rise in concrete

The use of blends is beneficial in reducing the temperature rise and the consequent stresses which are imposed on the concrete as it cools down. Both the quantity of energy liberated and the rate at which it is produced are reduced due to the differences in the energies associated with the hydration of the Portland cement and the pozzolanic reactions and to the differences in the rates of these reactions. The use of blends should result in less microcracking due to thermal stress. In addition, the use of blends helps to heal any cracks that are formed. Although the rate of the pozzolanic reaction increases with rising temperature, it still does not occur to any large extent until after the concrete has set. The products of the pozzolanic reaction are formed in a set system and, therefore, have the ability to heal microcracks in the concrete and to reduce the pore-size distribution in the hydrated cement paste giving improvements to both the strength and durability of the concrete.

18.7.4 The effect of temperature on reaction rate

The rates of hydration of Portland cement and the pozzolanic reactions of pulverized-fuel ash and ground-granulated blast-furnace slag are temperature dependent. As explained above, the slower rates of the latter can be beneficial in reducing the temperature rise in concrete. On the other hand, particularly with respect to the use of pulverized-fuel ash, the rate of the pozzolanic reaction is very slow at low temperatures. It follows therefore that, although care should be exercised when placing all forms of concrete under such conditions, special attention should be paid to the use of blends of Portland cement with pulverized-fuel ash. Particularly in thin sections some increases may be observed in formwork striking times.

18.8 The durability of concrete

The durability of concrete is its resistance to attack associated with the penetration by liquids and gases carrying aggressive ions and molecules. Durability is related to the permeability, porosity and pore-size distribution of the concrete. These properties are determined by the cement content, the water:cement ratio and by the type of cementitious material present in the mix. These factors affect the quantity and distribution of the hydrated cementitious material present in the final concrete. The degree to which the concrete is compacted and cured also has an influence on its durability.

The permeability of concrete is due to the presence of voids within it and the degree of permeability depends on the volume, diameter and continuity of such voids. The use of blends of Portland cement with pulverized-fuel ash and ground-granulated blast-furnace slag can reduce the permeability in a number of ways. Thus, by using suitable mix designs, reductions can be made in the voidage due to excessive bleeding and settlement, poor compaction and thermal cracking. However, of most importance is the alteration in the pore-size distribution of the concrete caused by the pozzolanic reaction. This has the effect, as fresh hydrated material is formed within the voids of the set concrete, of converting large pores into fine ones and of reducing the continuity between them.

18.8.1 Resistance to attack by sulphates

The two main reactions which are responsible for the deterioration of concrete on exposure to sulphates are the conversion of (i) calcium hydroxide into calcium sulphate (gypsum) and (ii) hydrated calcium aluminates into hydrated calcium sulphoaluminates (e.g. ettringite). For both these reactions the products occupy a greater volume than do the starting materials and, in consequence, their formation causes expansion and disintegration of the concrete. The beneficial effect of using blends of Portland cement with pulverized-fuel ash and ground-granulated blast-furnace slag on the sulphate resistance of concrete is well established and the use of blends is recommended. The requirements for concrete exposed to sulphates are subdivided according to the severity of the attack and are expressed in terms of the concentrations of the sulphate present. The suggestions made in BRE Digest 250: 1981[15] are summarized in *Table 18.8*. If blends are used the pulverized-fuel ash should comply with BS 3892: Part 1: 1982[6] and the ground-granulated blast-furnace slag to BS 6699: 1986.[11]

There are a number of possible reasons for the increased sulphate resistance of concretes containing pulverized-fuel ash and ground-granulated blast-furnace slag above that afforded to comparable concretes by ordinary Portland cement. The lower permeability of the concrete produced from the blend makes it more difficult for the sulphate to penetrate into the surface layers and, in addition, some of the calcium hydroxide produced by the hydration of the Portland cement will have been removed by the pozzolanic reactions. It is also possible that the lower concentration of tricalcium aluminate in the blend compared with that present in many ordinary Portland cements plays a part in the increased sulphate resistance of the concrete. It should be noted, as indicated in *Table 18.8*, that for high sulphate resistance the use of sulphate resisting Portland cement which has a low C_3A content is recommended.

18.8.2 The protection of steel reinforcement

The corrosion of the steel reinforcement which is used in concrete is caused by electrochemical reactions. During corrosion a part of the steel surface becomes anodic and metal ions go into solution, whilst at a cathodic region oxygen gas which has diffused to the metal surface is converted into hydroxyl ions.

$$2Fe \rightarrow 2Fe^{2+} + 4e \qquad \text{anodic region} \qquad (18.1)$$

$$O_2 + 2H_2O \rightarrow 4OH^- - 4e \quad \text{cathodic region} \qquad (18.2)$$

Adding equations (18.1) and (18.2)

$$2Fe + O_2 + 2H_2O \rightarrow 2Fe^{2+} + 4OH^-$$

Table 18.8 Cement types recommended for use in concrete exposed to sulphate attack in near-neutral groundwaters

Class	Total sulphate, SO_3, in soil (%)	Sulphate, SO_3, in 2:1 water:soil extract (g l^{-1})	Sulphate, SO_3, in groundwater (g l^{-1})	Type of cement[a]	Minimum cement content (kg m^{-3})	Maximum free water:cement ratio
1	0.2	1.0	0.3	OPC or RHPC or combinations of either with GGBS or PFA. Or PBFC	250[b] 300[c]	0.70[b] 0.60[c]
2	0.2–0.5	1.0–1.9	0.3–1.2	OPC or RHPC or combinations of either with GGBS or PFA. Or PBFC	330	0.50
				OPC or RHPC combined with 70–90% GGBS OPC or RHPC combined with 25–40% PFA	310	0.55
				SRPC	290	0.55
3	0.5–1.0	1.9–3.1	1.2–2.5	OPC or RHPC combined with 70–90% GGBS OPC or RHPC combined with 25–40% PFA	380	0.45
				SRPC	330	0.50
4	1.0–2.0	3.1–5.6	2.5–5.0	SRPC	370	0.45
5	>2	>5.6	>5.0	SRPC + protective coating	370	0.45

[a] OPC, ordinary Portland cement; RHPC, rapid-hardening Portland cement; PBFC, Portland blast-furnace cement; SRPC, sulphate resisting Portland cement; GGBS, ground-granulated blast-furnace slag complying with BS 6699: 1986;[11] PFA, pulverized-fuel ash complying with BS 3892: Part 1: 1982.[6] The cement contents and water:cement ratios refer to dense fully compacted concrete.
[b] Plain concrete.
[c] Reinforced concrete.

The products of these reactions then combine to form iron(II) hydroxide

$$2Fe^{2+} + 4OH^- \rightarrow 2Fe(OH)_2$$

Further oxidation occurs which converts the iron(II) hydroxide to rust.

Corrosion of the reinforcement will not occur if the pore solutions of the concrete in which the steel is embedded remain sufficiently alkaline. Under these conditions the formation of a passive film on the metal surface prevents corrosion. However, the carbonation of concrete lowers its alkalinity to a point where the steel becomes depassivated and, therefore, if sufficient carbonation occurs and the carbonation front reaches the steel surface the metal will be destroyed. In good-quality concrete of low permeability the rate of movement of the carbonation front is very slow and, provided sufficient cement has been used and sufficient cover has been given to the steel, its integrity will remain indefinitely. The protection of steel reinforcement is, therefore, dependent on the prevention of the diffusion of carbon dioxide through the concrete and, in certain environments, on the prevention of the ingress of chloride ions which make it easier for the steel to be corroded by oxygen.

At first sight it might appear that to replace Portland cement by pulverized-fuel ash and ground-granulated blast-furnace slag could, by removing calcium hydroxide from the concrete, lower the alkalinity to a point below which the passivity of the steel would be removed. However, because of the incompleteness of the pozzolanic reactions a large proportion of the calcium hydroxide produced from the Portland cement remains in the concrete as a buffer against carbonation. In addition, the sodium and potassium hydroxides in the pore solutions help to keep the alkalinity at a level at which passivity is maintained. It is also sometimes assumed that it is only the calcium hydroxide present which reacts with carbon dioxide. This is not the case and reaction also occurs with the hydrated calcium silicates and aluminates to give calcium carbonate and hydrous silica and alumina.

It is generally found that if comparison is made between concretes with and without pulverized-fuel ash but having the same cementitious content and the same water:cement ratio, those concretes containing pulverized-fuel ash carbonate more rapidly at early ages. However, if the results from concretes of equivalent 28-day compressive strength are compared it is found that there is no significant difference in the rates of carbonation, irrespective of whether or not the concretes contain pulverized-fuel ash. This is true for concretes in which the pulverized-fuel ash content lies between 25 and 30% of the total cementitious content and applies even when those concretes are poorly cured. The reason for this is probably due to the fact that, despite some of the calcium hydroxide having been removed, concretes of similar permeabilities are produced and, therefore, the rate of movement of the carbonation fronts are similar.

18.8.3 The alkali–silica reaction

The alkali–silica reaction occurs when the hydroxyl ions present in the pore solutions of a concrete react with certain forms of silica in the aggregate. If the product of that reaction absorbs water and swells, the resulting pressures can crack the concrete. It is believed that damage arising from this reaction can occur in any concrete where there is a combination of:

(1) a critical amount of reactive silica in the aggregate;
(2) a sufficiently high alkalinity in the pore solutions; and
(3) sufficient moisture to enable the reaction to proceed.

If one of these factors is removed the risk of damage to the concrete alkali–silica expansion is minimized.

It has been shown that the alkalinity of the pore solutions in cement pastes, mortars and concretes is above pH 13 and is largely due to the presence of sodium and potassium hydroxides in solution. The alkali-metal ions in Portland cement are present both as sulphates and in solid solution. The former, which generally constitute more than 50% of the total alkali-metal ions present and for high alkali Portland cements can be considerably greater than this, dissolve rapidly in the mixing water. By reaction with some of the calcium hydroxide produced by the hydration of the cement these sulphates have an immediate effect on the alkalinity of the pore solutions. The alkali-metal ions in solid solution are liberated more slowly as the cement hydrates.

The alkali-metal ions in pulverized-fuel ash and ground-granulated blast-furnace slag are not present in the same form as in Portland cement. Although, particularly for pulverized-fuel ash, the total concentration of alkali-metal ions may be greater than in Portland cement, only a small proportion of those present in pulverized-fuel ash are water soluble and most are located in the glass particles. As the pozzolanic reaction takes place and these particles are consumed the alkali-metal ions are liberated but, as is the case with those from Portland cement, not all of them contribute to the alkalinity of the pore solutions.

When minimizing the risk of the occurrence of alkali–silica reaction in concrete it is generally found, in practice, that it is difficult to ensure that reactive particles are absent from the aggregate. Most attention has, therefore, been paid to limiting the alkalinity of the concrete via the control of the alkali contents of the cementitious materials used. The recommendations suggested for achieving this include either the use of a Portland cement with a reactive alkali content with a maximum of 0.6% Na_2O_{eq} or the use of blends of Portland cement with either pulverized-fuel ash or ground-granulated blast-furnace slag. Blends containing silica fume are also sometimes recommended. If blends containing either pulverized-fuel ash or less than 50% ground-granulated blast-furnace slag are used, it is recommended that the reactive alkali content of the concrete should be calculated and should be less than 3.0 kg Na_2O_{eq} m^{-3}. With respect to pulverized-fuel ash and ground-granulated blast-furnace slag this can be achieved by using either

(1) a blend containing at least 25% by mass of pulverized-fuel ash complying with BS 3892: Part 1: 1982[6] (site blending); or
(2) a blend containing at least 25% by mass of ground-granulated blast-furnace slag complying with BS 6699: 1986[1] (site blending); or
(3) an equivalent factory-made blend (BS 6588: 1985[8] and BS 146: Part 2: 1973[12]).

The use of a blend containing more than 50% ground-granulated blast-furnace slag complying with BS 6699: 1986[11] is deemed satisfactory without it being necessary to calculate the reactive alkali content of the concrete.

18.8.4 Freeze–thaw resistance of hardened concrete

As the temperature of hardened concrete is lowered the water in the capillary pores of the cement paste can freeze and expand. Repeated cycles of freezing and thawing have a cumulative effect and damage to the concrete can occur.

The risk of frost damage is reduced by the use of concrete mixes which have a low water:cement ratio so that the resulting cement paste contains only small capillaries. In other words the concrete should have a low permeability so that water is not imbibed. It is important that, whatever the mix design, sufficient hydration of the cement has taken place before the concrete is exposed to frost attack. The greater the degree of hydration the greater is the reduction in the amount of freezable water in the cement paste. It is also important that the concrete has been subjected to good compaction.

The resistance of concrete to frost attack can also be improved by air entrainment. Properly entrained air produces discrete cavities in the cement paste so that the permeability of the concrete is not increased. On freezing, these cavities become filled with water from the cement paste and, therefore, relieve the hydraulic pressures developed. When the temperature rises again the water from the cavities returns to the cement paste so that a permanent resistance to freezing and thawing is given to the concrete. The use of air-entraining agents in combination with low water:cement ratios is, therefore, desirable if high

resistance to frost attack is required. Satisfactory freeze–thaw resistance can be obtained when both blends of Portland cement with ground-granulated blast-furnace slag and Portland cement with pulverized-fuel ash are used. However, the suppliers of ground-granulated blast-furnace slag and pulverized-fuel ash should be consulted. As mentioned earlier, the use of pulverized-fuel ash can increase the dosage of air-entraining agent required because of absorption by the carbon present.

18.9 Aluminous cements

Aluminous cements are not Portland cements and are thus dealt with separately. Moreover, because they do not produce calcium hydroxide when mixed with water they are not normally used in combination with ground-granulated blast-furnace slag and pulverized-fuel ash.

18.9.1 Manufacture and composition

Aluminous cements are made by fusing a mixture of aluminous and calcareous materials, generally bauxite and limestone. At the high temperatures used the limestone decomposes to carbon dioxide (CO_2) and calcium oxide (CaO), the latter then combining with the aluminium oxide (Al_2O_3) from the bauxite to give a clinker consisting of a mixture of calcium aluminates. The clinker is then ground to the fineness required for its use as a cement. The aluminous cements most frequently used contain approximately 40% Al_2O_3 and are often called cement Fondu. However, particularly for refractory applications, compositions containing up to 80% Al_2O_3 are manufactured and these are known as high aluminous cements.

The principal hydraulic constituents of aluminous cements are calcium aluminates. Smaller proportions of compounds containing silica and iron oxides are also present. The main compounds present are monocalcium aluminate, CA, and $C_{12}A_7$; the reactivity of calcium aluminates increases as the CaO:Al_2O_3 ratio increases. However, because of the high proportion of CA its reaction with water makes it, in practice, the most important hydraulic constituent present.

18.9.2 Hydration of aluminous cements

At normal temperatures the hydration of aluminous cements results in the formation of hydrated calcium monoaluminate (CAH_{10}) as the main reaction product. Smaller amounts of C_2AH_8 and hydrous alumina are also formed. However, these hydrated calcium aluminates are metastable and can, at higher temperatures and in the presence of moisture, change to give the stable hydrated calcium aluminate C_3AH_6 and further quantities of hydrous alumina. These changes are accompanied by a loss of water and a reduction in the volume of the hydrated cement paste. The phenomenon is known as 'conversion' and the amount of change occurring as the 'degree of conversion'.

At normal temperatures conversion may take many years, but at temperatures in the region of 40°C a considerable amount of change can occur within a few months. Irrespective of whether the conversion occurs early or late in the life of the concrete the process results in a loss of strength, increased porosity and reduced resistance to chemical attack. Because of the danger of conversion care needs to be taken when this cement is used for normal building purposes.

18.9.3 Properties of aluminous cement concrete

An outstanding feature of aluminous cement is its very high rate of strength development. Up to 80% of the final strength of the concrete is achieved at the age of 24 h and, depending on the mix design, the concrete can be strong enough for formwork to be struck after about 8 h.

Aluminous cements were first developed to resist sulphate attack on concrete and are extremely satisfactory for this purpose. The high resistance to sulphates is due both to the absence of calcium hydroxide in the hydrated cement paste and to the low permeability of the concrete. Aluminous cement concrete shows good resistance to attack by seawater.

However, because of the danger of conversion of the hydrated calcium aluminates formed initially into C_3AH_6 and hydrous alumina, the use of high aluminous cements as a structural material is no longer acceptable in many instances. Not only does conversion cause a loss in strength but there is also an increase in the porosity of the paste and the permeability of the concrete. Such changes can decrease the resistance to sulphate attack and to freezing and thawing.

Dehydrated aluminous cement concrete retains considerable strength and, at high temperatures, the hydraulic bond is replaced by a good ceramic bond. Because of this aluminous cements are important refractory materials. Concretes made with aluminous cement and crushed firebrick are stable to about 1300°C. For applications at temperatures up to 1600°C it is necessary to use fused alumina or carborundum as aggregate. For use to even higher temperatures, e.g. 1800°C, it is necessary to use high aluminous cements in the preparation of the original concrete. These cements contain up to 80% Al_2O_3 and very little silica and iron oxides. In contrast, concrete made with Portland cement cannot withstand exposure to high temperatures. Refractory high aluminous cement concretes also show good resistance to acid attack from oxides of sulphur in the flue gases produced on combustion of both oil and coal.

References

1 BRITISH STANDARDS INSTITUTION, *BS 12 Ordinary and rapid-hardening cement*, Milton Keynes (1978)
2 AMERICAN SOCIETY FOR TESTING MATERIALS, ASTM C618, *Fly ash and raw or calcined natural pozzolan for use as a mineral admixture in Portland cement concrete*, Chicago (1980)
3 BRITISH STANDARDS INSTITUTION, *BS 1370 Low heat Portland cement*, Milton Keynes (1979)
4 BRITISH STANDARDS INSTITUTION, *BS 4027 Sulphate-resisting Portland cement*, Milton Keynes (1980)
5 BRITISH STANDARDS INSTITUTION, *BS 4550: Part 3 Working limits on tolerances and dimensions*, Milton Keynes (1978)
6 BRITISH STANDARDS INSTITUTION, 'Specification for pulverized-fuel ash for use as a cementitious component in structural concrete', *BS 3892: Part 1*, Milton Keynes (1982)
7 BRITISH STANDARDS INSTITUTION, 'Specification for pulverized-fuel ash for use in non-structural concrete and grout', *BS 3892: Part 2*, Milton Keynes (1982)
8 BRITISH STANDARDS INSTITUTION, 'Specification for Portland pulverized-fuel ash cement', *BS 6588*, Milton Keynes (1985)
9 BRITISH STANDARDS INSTITUTION, 'Specification for pozzolanic cement with pulverized-fuel ash as a pozzolana', *BS 6610*, Milton Keynes (1985)
10 BRITISH STANDARDS INSTITUTION, 'The structural use of concrete', *BS 8110*, Milton Keynes (1985)
11 BRITISH STANDARDS INSTITUTION, 'Specification for ground-granulated blast-furnace slag for use with Portland cements', *BS 6699*, Milton Keynes (1986)
12 BRITISH STANDARDS INSTITUTION, 'Portland blast-furnace cement', *BS 146: Part 2*, Milton Keynes (1973)
13 BRITISH STANDARDS INSTITUTION, 'Low heat Portland blast-furnace cement', *BS 4246: Part 2*, Milton Keynes (1974)
14 ABRAMS, D. A., 'Design of concrete mixtures', *Bulletin No. 1*, Structural Materials Research Laboratory, Lewis Institute, Chicago (1918)
15 BUILDING RESEARCH ESTABLISHMENT, 'Concrete in sulphate bearing soils and groundwaters', *BRE Digest 250* (1981)

Bibliography

LEA, F. M., *The Chemistry of Cement and Concrete*, Edward Arnold, London (1970)
BYE, G. C., *Portland Cement, Composition, Production and Properties*, Pergamon Press, Oxford (1983)
NEVILLE, A. M., *Properties of Concrete*, Pitman Publishing Ltd., London (1981)
BOGUE, R. H., *The Chemistry of Portland Cement*, Reinhold, New York (1955)

19

Curing Membranes

L Hodgkinson
Cormix Construction Chemicals
Chairman, Technical Committee, Cement Admixtures
Association

Contents

19.1 Introduction 19/3

19.2 Curing-membrane types 19/3
    19.2.1 Resin in solvent solutions 19/4
    19.2.2 Wax emulsions 19/4
    19.2.3 Solutions of metallic silicates 19/4

19.3 Benefits of curing membranes 19/4

19.4 Standard specification for curing membranes 19/4

References 19/4

19.1 Introduction

Concrete develops its strength through a process of hydration, and this hydration is a continuous process if water is made available to carry it on. Hydration stops once a concrete has dried out and strength development will not follow the normally expected path (*Figure 19.1*). If the concrete is rewetted, then hydration will recommence, but, theoretically, it will never achieve the same strength as the water-cured concrete.

Not all concretes can be cured under water as laboratory specimens are. Ponding is the nearest to ideal method, but vertical surfaces are difficult to cure on site.[1] Polythene, in theory, is a good curing agent, as is wet hessian draped over concrete, but keeping hessian wet and in position is extremely difficult and tedious. Curing membranes are solutions which, when sprayed onto a concrete surface, assist in the prevention of moisture loss and improve the curing of the concrete.

Curing membranes, applied as soon as is practicable, are a convenient, efficient and cost-effective way of curing on site. Curing of concrete paving should be commenced as soon as the concrete is laid, as any moisture loss can lead to plastic shrinkage cracking. This type of cracking is likely to occur at any time up to the initial set of the concrete, and its likelihood is very much related to wind speed, relative humidity and air temperature (*Figures 19.2* and *19.3*).[2] Concrete paving and concrete runways in the UK are now required to be cured with an approved aluminized curing membrane.[3]

BS 8110: Part 1: 1985[4] contains guidelines for the duration of curing of concrete and lists the use of a curing membrane as one of five alternative procedures to be used.

19.2 Curing-membrane types

There are numerous types of curing membrane, but generally they fall into three categories: resin in solvent solutions; wax emulsions; and solutions of metallic silicates.

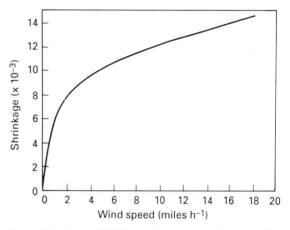

Figure 19.2 The early shrinkage of concrete as a function of wind speed at its surface: shrinkage at 8 h

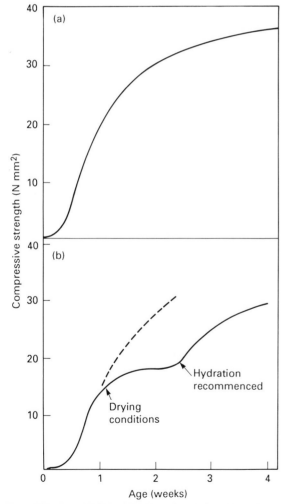

Figure 19.1 A comparison of the strength gain of water-cured concrete and a typical site-cured concrete. (a) Water-cured concrete; (b) site-cured concrete

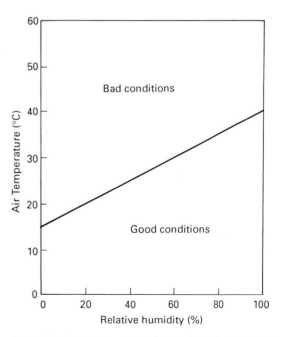

Figure 19.3 The influence of climate upon the curing condition of concrete.

19.2.1 Resin in solvent solutions

These are resins dissolved in a light, volatile, flammable solvent. The resins are normally reactive and are designed to break down slowly under the influence of ultraviolet radiation. The two principal types of reactive resin are:

1. polycyclopentadiene resins;
2. coumarin–indene resins.

Saturated hydrocarbon resins are sufficiently good in terms of their ability to reduce moisture loss, but they do not degrade. They can be used if the membrane can be left permanently on the concrete.

Where a surface coating is likely to be applied, subsequent to the curing compound, then it is inadvisable to use a degrading-type membrane as its complete removal cannot be guaranteed. In these situations, curing membranes based on styrene–acrylic type resins are commonly used. These materials can act as primers for subsequent coatings. Their efficiency as curing membranes, however, is not good, and more than one coat may need to be applied if a specified efficiency of curing is required.

19.2.2 Wax emulsions

Wax emulsions are white, oil-in-water emulsions. They have been widely used in the Middle East for about 20 years, mainly because of their good response to the ASTM test procedures. They are non-toxic, non-flammable, water miscible and quite efficient and, because of their ease of handling, they are gaining popularity in the UK. However, they are non-degradable and have to be removed if subsequent coating of the concrete is required.

19.2.3 Solutions of metallic silicates

Unmodified solutions of metallic silicates do not film-form and are very poor at reducing the moisture loss of concrete surfaces. Their action is so poor, that normal metallic silicates should not be marketed for this application. There are developments underway to improve the performance of silicates and to improve their ability to film-form. Only when they can film-form will silicates become useful as curing membranes.

19.3 Benefits of curing membranes

To achieve the full potential of any concrete mix, good curing is essential. This is particularly true of concrete which contains significant proportions of ground-granulated blast-furnace slag, pulverized-fuel ash or silica fume. The full benefits of cement-replacement materials are not realized unless good curing is adopted. Because the initial set of concrete-containing blended cements can be significantly longer than for ordinary Portland cement concretes, then they are particularly vulnerable to plastic shrinkage cracking at early ages.

19.4 Standard specification for curing membranes

There is no British Standard test method for the evaluation of curing membranes. A Draft for Development DD 147: 1987 is currently under evaluation, and this method is identical to that quoted in the Department of Transport Specification for Roads and Bridge Works: 1986.[3] This method is likely to be adopted as a British Standard (Test method for assessing curing membranes). These methods quantify the performance of curing membranes by measuring an efficiency index.

The American specification is ASTM C309.[6] This standard does not quantify the efficiency, but quotes a maximum permitted moisture loss of $0.55 \, kg \, m^{-2}$ during a 72-h test.

Correlation between the UK and USA tests is not good. Because the British test procedures require the test membrane to be applied immediately, these tests favour solvent-based systems. The American tests specify a period of conditioning prior to the application of the test membrane, and for this reason water-based systems perform very well.

References

1 BIRT, J. C., 'Curing concrete—an appraisal of attitudes, practices and knowledge', *CIRIA Report 43* (Feb. 1973)
2 MILLS, R. H. and MALINOWSKY, R., 'Strength–maturity relationship of concrete which is allowed to dry', *Proceedings of the RILEM Symposium, Haifa (July 1960)*
3 DEPARTMENT OF TRANSPORT, *Specification for Road and Bridge Works, HMSO, London (1986)*
4 BRITISH STANDARDS INSTITUTION, *BS 8110: Part 1 Code of practice for design and construction*, Milton Keynes (1985)
5 BRITISH STANDARDS INSTITUTION, *DD 147: Method of test for curing compounds for concrete*, Milton Keynes (1987)
6 AMERICAN SOCIETY FOR TESTING MATERIALS, *ASTM C309-81 Specification for liquid membrane-forming compounds for curing concrete*, Philadelphia

20

Glass-Fibre Reinforced Cement

S H Cross CPhys, MInstP, AMI, CorrST
The Glassfibre Reinforced Cement Association

P J Ridd BSc(Eng), DMS
Cemfil International Ltd

Contents

20.1 Introduction 20/3
    20.1.1 General description 20/3
    20.1.2 Geographic profile 20/3

20.2 Raw materials 20/3
    20.2.1 Cements 20/0320.2.2 Fillers 20/4
    20.2.3 Admixtures 20/4
    20.2.4 Polymers 20/4
    20.2.5 Pigments 20/5
    20.2.6 Alkali-resistant glass fibres 20/5
    20.2.7 Health aspects of glass fibres 20/5

20.3 Principles of glass-fibre reinforcement 20/5
    20.3.1 The effect of glass fibres on the strength of the
        mortar matrix 20/5
    20.3.2 Tensile stress–strain curves 20/5
    20.3.3 Compressive stress–strain curves 20/6
    20.3.4 Bending stress–strain curves 20/7
    20.3.5 Strain to failure 20/7
    20.3.6 The effects of orientation of glass fibres 20/7
    20.3.7 Shear strength 20/8
    20.3.8 Impact resistance 20/8
    20.3.9 Elastic modulus and Poisson's ratio 20/8
    20.3.10 Effect of ageing 20/8

20.4 Mechanical properties 20/8
    20.4.1 Typical initial property values 20/8
    20.4.2 Effect of age on initial property values 20/9
    20.4.3 Creep and stress-rupture behaviour 20/10
    20.4.4 Fatigue performance 20/10

20.5 Physical and chemical properties 20/10
    20.5.1 Shrinkage 20/10
    20.5.2 Thermal expansion 20/11
    20.5.3 Chemical resistance 20/11
    20.5.4 Sulphate resistance 20/11
    20.5.5 Acids and alkalis 20/11
    20.5.6 Marine environments 20/12
    20.5.7 Freeze–thaw behaviour 20/12
    20.5.8 Thermal conductivity 20/12
    20.5.9 Sound 20/12
    20.5.10 Permeability 20/12
    20.5.11 Abrasion resistance 20/12
    20.5.12 Density 20/12
    20.5.13 Water absorption and apparent porosity 20/12
    20.5.14 Potable-water approval 20/12
    20.5.15 Ultraviolet light 20/13

20.6 Design principles 20/13
    20.6.1 Mechanical design 20/13
    20.6.2 Physical design 20/14
    20.6.3 Installation considerations 20/15
    20.6.4 Design problems 20/15

20.7 Applications 20/16
    20.7.1 Agricultural products 20/16
    20.7.2 Architectural features 20/16
    20.7.3 Building systems 20/17
    20.7.4 Cable ducting 20/17
    20.7.5 Cladding 20/17
    20.7.6 Fire protection and insulation 20/18
    20.7.7 Flooring and roofing 20/19
    20.7.8 Formwork 20/20
    20.7.9 Irrigation and drainage 20/22
    20.7.10 Marine applications 20/22
    20.7.11 Renders 20/22
    20.7.12 Sewer, tunnel and shaft liners 20/22

20.8 Production 20/23
    20.8.1 Sprayed glass-fibre reinforced cement 20/23
    20.8.2 Premixed glass-fibre reinforced cement 20/23
    20.8.3 Other processes 20/23

20.9 Process and quality control 20/24
    20.9.1 Process control 20/24
    20.9.2 Quality control 20/24

20.10 Standards and product approvals 20/24
    20.10.1 Alkali-resistant glass fibre 20/25
    20.10.2 Materials 20/25
    20.10.3 Test methods 20/26
    20.10.4 Product standards 20/26
    20.10.5 Product approvals 20/26
    20.10.6 Standards in preparation 20/26
    20.10.7 Overseas standards and product approvals 20/26

20.11 The Glassfibre Reinforced Cement Association
    (GRCA) 20/26

20.11 The Glassfibre Reinforced Cement Association
    (GRCA) 20/26

Acknowledgements 20/26

References 20/26

Bibliography 20/27

20.1 Introduction

20.1.1 General description

Glass-fibre reinforced cement (GRC) is a combination of specially developed alkali-resistant glass fibres and a cement/sand mortar. The resultant composite is a concrete-like material combining the compressive properties of cement mortars with the valuable flexural and tensile strength of the glass fibres.

Early attempts to use commercially available silicate glass fibres to reinforce Portland cement failed because of the vulnerability of the fine glass fibres to the highly alkaline environment of the cement matrix. Cemfil alkali-resistant glass fibre was developed by Pilkington following a fundamental breakthrough by the UK Building Research Establishment. Pilkington took up the commercial development of this innovation under licence from the National Research Development Corporation and the present generation of GRC products and applications is the result of many years of collaborative development by Pilkington, the BRE and the NRDC, together with the innovative ideas of GRC specifiers and users.

During the rapid expansion of the GRC industry worldwide, the Glass-fibre Reinforced Cement Association (GRCA) was formed in 1975 and has been instrumental in the further development of procedures, codes of practice and standards for GRC materials and products. GRC has wide-ranging applications in the architectural, building, civil and general engineering industries. In typical section thicknesses of 6–20 mm, GRC is widely used as an alternative material to precast concrete, sheet metal, cast iron, timber, plastics and asbestos cement, where the inherent advantages and manufacturing flexibility of GRC, combined with its light weight, non-combustibility, fire resistance and general toughness, make it an appropriate and economical material for use in a range of product forms.

GRC does not consist of a single material composition but can be composed of different formulations according to the properties required of the finished product. Mostly, however, GRC has a fibre content of 3.5% or 5% by weight (2.9% or 4.1% by volume) combined with a cement/sand mortar (which often contains equal proportions of cement and sand). Normal concrete admixtures are commonly used, particularly plasticizers and superplasticizers which allow a reduction in the water content. The inclusion of acrylic polymer dispersions in GRC formulations is becoming increasingly popular as it assists curing and further improves the toughness and durability of GRC components. Other additives and admixtures have been used in GRC where there is a need to exploit other properties (e.g. the use of PFA 'cenospheres', perlite or air-entraining agents to obtain a reduction in density or improved fire resistance).

Methods of manufacture vary and include vibration casting, extrusion, injection moulding, spraying and rendering. Each technique imparts different characteristics to the end product.

Clearly then, GRC is not one material with fixed properties, but is a composite with a wide range of possible formulations and resulting properties.

20.1.2 Geographic profile

Alkali-resistant glass fibre is manufactured both in the UK and Japan, and is distributed worldwide through a network of agents. GRC products have been used in over 60 countries worldwide. Many of these countries have their own glass-fibre reinforced cement (GRC) manufacturers producing a wide variety of products ranging from sheep dips to architectural cladding panels.

The product profile varies considerably in different regions of the world. In the USA, the cladding of buildings far outweighs any other application and it is there that the steel-stud-frame GRC cladding panel evolved. This system gained rapid acceptance due to the rapid closure of the building envelope and an overall cost saving and is now widely accepted in many countries. European examples can be seen in Dublin and Belfast. (For further details see Section 20.7.5).

A wide range of products is made in Europe and includes most of those listed in Section 20.7. There is also a significant export trade, both in product and licensing. The Middle East and many of the Far Eastern countries find considerable application for sun screens as well as cladding, and in Japan and South East Asia the versatility of GRC in reproducing the various forms of traditional architecture is widely utilized.

Novel forms of building components which provide thermal insulation not possible with other materials are used with conventional construction techniques to meet stringent building requirements in Scandinavia and Switzerland. South Africa has some very prestigious GRC cladding projects as well as low-cost housing, whilst modular housing has been developed in Romania. China has recently started producing a variety of products, but there is limited information as to the volume or type of product, although it is believed that most of the output is to the construction industry.

20.2 Raw materials

The main constituents of glass-fibre reinforced cement (GRC) are cement, sand and alkali-resistant glass fibre. Ordinary and rapid-hardening Portland are the most commonly used cements, although others, including sulphate resisting, pozzolanic and high alumina cement, may also be used. The aggregate will usually be a fine sand with a particle size of 150 μm to 1.2 mm, and will be used at aggregate:cement ratios of 0.5–1. Other fine inorganic aggregates and fillers can also be incorporated where particular properties or surface finishes are required.

The water:cement ratio is typically within the range 0.3–0.4. It is often kept to a minimum by the use of water-reducing admixtures. Standard concrete admixtures or those especially formulated for GRC may be used, as appropriate. In some cases, acrylic polymers are used to enhance certain properties.

The glass fibre is supplied either as a continuous roving (which is cut during the GRC manufacturing process into strands of 12–38 mm length) or as precut chopped strands 3–25 mm in length. It is included in the GRC mix at a nominal content of 5% (by weight) for sprayed GRC (see Section 20.8.1) and at 3.5% (by weight) for pre-mixed GRC (see Section 20.8.2).

20.2.1 Cements

The most widely used cements in glass-fibre reinforced cement (GRC) manufacture are ordinary Portland cement (OPC) and rapid-hardening Portland cement (RHPC) and should be to British Standard Specification BS 12[1] or equivalent.

RHPC is chemically very similar to OPC but is more finely ground and, because of this, develops strength more rapidly at early ages. This permits more rapid demoulding of products than with conventional cements and is often preferred for GRC for this reason. It should be noted that the term 'rapid-hardening' has a different meaning to the term 'quick-setting'. GRC made with rapid-hardening cement stiffens and initially hardens at a similar rate to that of OPC; it is after the initial hardening that the strength gains more rapidly. RHPC should be stored and used in the same way as OPC. RHPC is slightly more expensive than OPC.

White Portland cement is made from raw materials containing only a very small quantity of iron compounds. It is used in GRC either alone or with pigments where a white or light-coloured finish is required. Because of this, and the fact that white cement costs more than OPC, extra care must be taken in handling the cement to avoid contamination, and in the batching, mixing, and transportation and to ensure that all equipment is kept clean. It is equally important to make sure that the finished GRC is protected against discoloration. The setting and strength-development properties are similar to those of grey OPC and, apart from the extra care necessary, there is no difference in the methods of using it or in storage.

Other types of cement, such as high alumina, sulphate resistant, rapid setting and pozzolanic cements may be used where the application demands it and should be to the relevant British Standard or equivalent. Alternative cements will be chosen on the same basis as for their use in conventional concrete, such as the use of sulphate resisting cement where the product is exposed to ground conditions where sulphate attack might be expected. Care should be taken that the choice of cement is relevant and complies with statutory regulations.

It is important that cement is correctly stored. Cement must be kept dry, and it should be noted that damp air can be as harmful as direct moisture. Cement stored in impermeable containers will keep indefinitely. Cement stored in bulk in a well-protected silo will be satisfactory up to about 3 months. Cement in normal three-ply paper bags stored under good conditions can lose about 20% of its strength after 4–6 weeks.

20.2.2 Fillers

20.2.2.1 Sand

Sand is incorporated in glass-fibre reinforced cement composites, largely in order to reduce the normal drying shrinkage and reversible moisture movement of the cement paste. In general, ordinary building sands are not recommended as they are of variable moisture content (making mix control difficult) and may contain oversize particles which cause blockages in spray equipment, or clay minerals which result in excessive water uptake. For this reason, the use of graded, washed and dried silica sand is strongly recommended. Silica sands to the following requirements are readily available in most countries.

All sand should be washed and dried. It will then contain less soluble matter and fine particles and allow accurate control of the water:cement ratio.

The particle shape and surface texture should conform to BS 812. The preferred shape is round or irregular. Flaky and/or elongated particle shapes should be avoided. Similarly, smooth surface texture is preferred and honeycombed particles should be avoided.

Sands of the following chemical composition have been used in the UK and found to be satisfactory.

1. Silica: >96%.
2. Moisture: <2%.
3. Soluble salts (i.e. alkalis): <1%.
4. Loss on ignition: <0.5%.
5. Organic matter: must not affect the setting of the cement.
   SO_3, <0.4% (4000 ppm);
   Cl, <0.06% (600 ppm).

The recommended grading is for a particle size not greater than 1.2 mm (i.e. 100% passing a BSS 14 or ASTM 16 sieve) for sprayed GRC and not greater than 2.4 mm (i.e. 100% passing a BSS 7 sieve) for premixed GRC. The fine fraction should not be more than 10% passing 150 μm (BSS 100 or ASTM 100 sieve).

The silica content of the sand need not necessarily be as high as 96%. There are good quality sands with much lower silica content which are suitable for GRC manufacture.

A value for loss on ignition of up to 3% can be accepted provided that the material is hard, non-crushable, non-reactive and of similar shape and grading to that described above.

20.2.2.2 Pulverized-fuel ash

Pulverized-fuel ash is a pozzolanic material obtained from the flue discharges of boilers fired by pulverized coal. The use of pulverized-fuel ash as a replacement for between 25 and 35% of the cement can be used to produce glass-fibre reinforced concrete (GRC) with improved long-term durability in damp/wet environments. Where pulverized-fuel ash is used as a partial cement replacement, there is also a slight reduction in shrinkage. However, the use of pulverized-fuel ash usually reduces the early strength of the composite and, therefore, greater care may be required in demoulding products.

20.2.2.3 Crushed aggregates

Many varieties of aggregate used in concrete may be crushed to a suitable grading for use in glass-fibre reinforced cement (GRC). These include marble, limestone, dolomite and granite. For calcium carbonate based aggregates the loss-on-ignition test will not be relevant.

20.2.2.4 Lightweight aggregates

Lightweight aggregates such as perlite and PFA cenospheres may be used where there is a requirement to produce a low-density formulation (e.g. for ceiling tiles, partitions, fire protective coatings for steel and for fire barriers). The use of such materials usually improves the fire performance of glass-fibre reinforced cement (GRC) composites, but is generally associated with a reduction in mechanical properties.

20.2.3 Admixtures

Standard concrete admixtures or those specially formulated for glass-fibre reinforced cement (GRC) manufacture may be used as appropriate to the particular process and to obtain the required properties of GRC. Admixtures are generally added to produce the following effects.

In the manufacture of GRC:
1. increasing the workability without increasing the water/cement ratio;
2. improving the cohesion;
3. reducing segregation;
4. reducing bleeding;
5. retarding the setting (stiffening) process;
6. accelerating the setting (stiffening) process.

On the properties of hardened GRC:
1. increasing the rate of early strength development;
2. increasing the strength;
3. decreasing the permeability;
4. improving fire resistance.

Admixtures are added to mixes in small amounts and care must be exercised to ensure that only the correct dose as specified by the manufacturer is added. Calcium chloride is normally acceptable as an admixture except when metal fixings are used or GRC is used in juxtaposition with conventional concrete reinforcement.

20.2.4 Polymers

Many glass-fibre reinforced cement (GRC) manufacturers find some advantage in using acrylic polymers in their mixes. The main reasons are to allow 'air' or 'dry-curing' of GRC products and to improve the mechanical properties of the material. The influence of acrylic polymers in modifying GRC can be explained by the mechanism of film formation.

When processing a polymer-modified GRC matrix, very fine polymer particles will disperse throughout the entire matrix

Figure 20.1 Alkali-resistant glass fibre rovings and chopped strands

between the cement and sand particles, and penetrate the gaps between the glass fibres. Whilst curing, when the mortar has lost sufficient water through evaporation, the polymer particles will coalesce with each other above a critical minimum temperature known as the 'film forming temperature'. This results in a cohesive polymer film, which is spread uniformly throughout the matrix. The film of coalesced polymer acts as a barrier to further evaporation. Under appropriate conditions it effectively seals the GRC products to retain sufficient water for hydration. This process can eliminate the need for a wet cure.

Benefits to the properties of polymer GRC include a reduction in initial drying shrinkage and the subsequent moisture movement caused by wetting and drying, reduced permeability and water absorption and, under appropriate circumstances, improvement to toughness and strength and better long-term durability. Possible disadvantages of using a polymer in GRC include the failure of the standard combustibility tests if the polymer is added at sufficiently high levels, the possibility of 'false setting' in hot climates and a reduction in the Young's modulus of the matrix, thereby increasing deflections.

20.2.5 Pigments

Pigments to British Standard BS 1014[3] or equivalent may be used to colour the glass-fibre reinforced cement (GRC), although special care is required to achieve uniformity of colour in certain applications.

20.2.6 Alkali-resistant glass fibre

The fibre is supplied in various forms (*Figure 20.1*) all of which originate from continuous filaments drawn from an alkali-resistant glass composition occurring in the $Na_2O–CaO–ZrO_2–SiO_2$ phase system. Simultaneously drawn fibres are combined into strands, which are used either for producing 'chopped strands', available in various lengths for use in glass-fibre reinforced cement (GRC) premix, or combined as multiple strands to form a continuous 'roving' which is then used in the

factory with appropriate equipment to chop it to the required short lengths during the GRC manufacturing process. Chopped strands are supplied in lengths of 3–25 mm, with lengths of 12–25 mm being the most common. Rovings are supplied in wound bundles of approximately 20 kg.

20.2.7 Health aspects of glass fibres

The drawing process gives accurate thickness control of the alkali-resistant glass fibres which are constant at 13 and 20 μm diameter and substantially above the range of respirable particles. Evidence to date has shown that these fibres cause no long-term health hazard, although in some cases temporary skin irritation may be experienced.

20.3 Principles of glass-fibre reinforcement

20.3.1 The effect of glass fibres on the strength of the mortar matrix

Fibrous materials have been used for many thousands of years to stabilize matrices which are inherently unreliable. Straw in mud bricks and horse-hair plaster are two examples. The role of the fibrous material is to include small regions of high-strength material which control the propagation of cracks from voids in the matrix and thereby give a reliable tensile strength to an otherwise brittle and unreliable material.

Alkali-resistant glass fibres perform this role in cement/mortar matrices, which are inherently brittle and have unreliable tensile strength. The full strength of the mortar can thus be utilized because of the presence of glass fibre, and it can be shown[4,5] that the presence of sufficient glass fibres may increase the mortar strength above the expected levels.

20.3.2 Tensile stress–strain curves

When glass-fibre reinforced cement (GRC) is tested in tension, the load-extension curve produced takes one of two forms, which

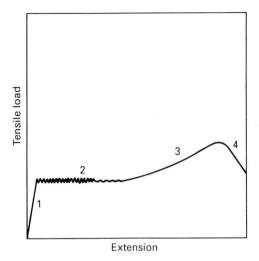

Figure 20.2 Representative tensile load-extension diagram for GRC: curve type A

are shown schematically in *Figures 20.2* and *20.3*. Curve type A (*Figure 20.2*) is representative of freshly made sprayed and cured GRC and curve type B (*Figure 20.3*) is representative of vibration cast (premix) GRC or of aged sprayed GRC. In both these diagrams, the initial linear portion of the curve (region 1) is determined by the fibres and matrix acting together as an elastic composite, the stiffness and stress being given by the appropriate version of the 'law of mixtures'. Thus, for example:

$$E_c = k_1 k_2 k_3 E_f V_f + E_m V_m \qquad (20.1)$$

and

$$\sigma_c = E_c \varepsilon_c = (k_1 k_2 k_3 E_f V_f + E_m V_m)\varepsilon_c \qquad (20.2)$$

i.e.

$$\sigma_c = k_1 k_2 k_3 \sigma_f V_f + \sigma_m V_m \qquad (20.3)$$

where E is Young's modulus, V is the volume fraction, ε is the strain and σ is the stress. The subscripts c, f and m denote

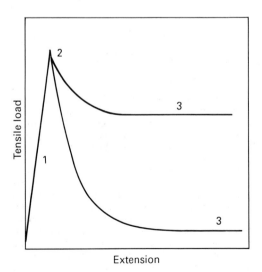

Figure 20.3 Representative tensile load-extension diagram for GRC: curve type B

composite, fibre and matrix, respectively. The fibre-property terms in these equations are modified by the 'efficiency factors' k_1, k_2 and k_3, which may not be identical in all equations but are usually similar in value. These factors take account of the effects of the use of fibres in finite lengths (k_1), in bundles or strands (k_2) and orientated in different directions (k_3).

At about the mortar-failure stress, cracks propagate around the glass fibres and the subsequent behaviour depends upon whether the fibres are sufficient to carry the load (type A) or not (type B). This transitional point of the curve is designated the bend-over point.

In GRC designated type A, the glass fibres act as reinforcing agents. Moving away from the crack face, load is transferred back from fibre to matrix by shear forces at the fibre–matrix interface and in the matrix, until the stress and strain in the matrix has again risen to the failure level and a new crack is formed. This continues until the material is traversed by an array of very fine cracks—often difficult to see—at a spacing governed by the matrix strength, bond strength and fibre concentration (region 2). On further loading the fibres extend and the existing cracks widen (region 3). In these ways regions of considerable extension, and high energy absorption are introduced.

The ultimate tensile strength arises when the bridging fibres across one particular crack are either broken or pulled out of the matrix, although the failure is gradual rather than abrupt (region 4).

The criterion for fibres breaking or pulling out of the matrix depends upon the depth of embedment of the fibres. There is a critical length of strand above which the strand will always break if the fracture plane is at the midpoint of the strand, but if the strand is shorter than half this critical length on either side of the fracture plane, the strand will always pull out. The critical length is proportional to the strength of the fibres and inversely proportional to the physical shear bond between the fibre and the matrix. It also depends upon the strand geometry.

In GRC designated type B, the ultimate tensile strength occurs slightly above the level of the bend-over point, after which the load drops (region 2) to a level which the fibres can sustain (region 3), the fibres subsequently being broken or pulled out of the matrix. The values for load in region 3 will depend on the amount, orientation, length and strength of the fibre.

Practical tests[6,7] have been used to demonstrate the features of GRC types A and B up to the maximum loads, although the transition between regions 2 and 3 for type A is often difficult to detect. Type A GRC is characterized by visible multiple cracking of the sample, whereas type B material often has only one visible crack. Many testing machines are unable to detect the regions in which the ultimate tensile strength has been reached, but these can be demonstrated[8] by using special test equipment.

20.3.3 Compressive stress–strain curves

The stress–strain curve of glass-fibre reinforced cement (GRC) when tested in compression is linear up to high stresses and is similar to the curve which would be obtained from testing the matrix without any fibre (*Figure 20.4*). The presence of the fibre does, however, confer a more controlled manner of failure.

The effect of fibre depends on the orientation of the fibre relative to the direction of the compressive stress; fibres running parallel to the direction of compression create fracture planes which can reduce the compressive strength to about 70% of values obtained in testing across the plane of fibres.[9] The compressive strength of GRC is typically 6–8 times the tensile strength.

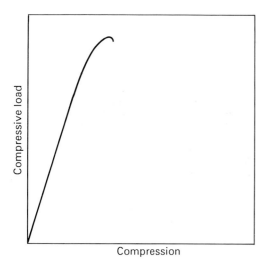

Figure 20.4 Representative load–compression diagram for GRC

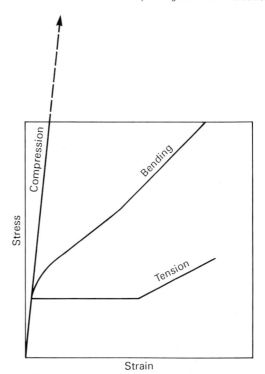

Figure 20.5 Schematic stress–strain curves for GRC

20.3.4 Bending stress–strain curves

Considering a rectangular glass-fibre reinforced cement (GRC) beam subject to bending and assuming a linear strain distribution through the beam up to failure, as in simple bending, the loaded surface of the beam will be in compression and the free surface in tension. For a given strain, the stresses in the GRC must follow the tensile and compressive stress–strain curves.

Up to the tensile bend-over-point strain, the resulting stress distribution remains linear. Above the bend-over-point strain the distribution of stress on the tensile side of the neutral axis changes, and to satisfy equilibrium (total tensile force = total compressive force) the neutral axis moves towards the compressive side, which again causes a redistribution of stress through the thickness.

If apparent stress and strain are calculated from a simple bending theory, the resulting bending stress–strain curve lies between the compressive and tensile curves. It contains two points of interest, the elastic limit, commonly termed the limit of proportionality, and the highest calculated stress, termed the modulus of rupture.

If the tensile and compressive stress–strain curves for any particular specimen of GRC are known, the bending curve can be estimated (*Figure 20.5*).[8,10] (The reverse operation can also be performed, but with more difficulty.) Such an estimate of the bending curve suggests that the limit of proportionality is similar to the bend-over point, but practical tests show the limit of proportionality to be about 1.7 times the bend-over point. However, brittle materials often show higher strength in bending than in tension,[11] so this is not surprising.

The modulus of rupture is found to be about 2.5 times the ultimate tensile strength for most variations of GRC composition and this has been justified theoretically.[10]

20.3.5 Strain to failure

The strain to failure of glass-fibre reinforced cement (GRC) is usually associated with tensile or bending tests of GRC and is the strain at which the ultimate tensile strength or modulus of rupture is achieved.

20.3.6 The effects of orientation of glass fibres

The fibre is only able to provide strength and stiffness in the direction of the fibre. Fibres which are not aligned with the direction of stress act in a less efficient manner than those that are. Hence, a composite with the fibres all aligned in one direction will provide maximum resistance to stress in that direction. However, in most products, it is not practical to make use of this orientation property to its maximum effect.

In thin section products, the major stresses are normally in the plane of the section and advantage can be taken by using sprayed glass-fibre reinforced cement (GRC) which lays down the fibre in a random two-dimensional array in the plane of the material. In this way the efficiency factor k_3 (Section 20.3.2) is about twice as high as for vibration cast premix GRC where the fibres are randomly orientated in three dimensions and form GRC which is virtually isotropic.

A further effect of orientation is on the quantity of fibre that can be incorporated into the matrix. This packing density of the glass fibre strands is higher if there is some degree of alignment and this shows in the manufacture of GRC, where 5% by weight (4.1% by volume) is commonly used in sprayed GRC, but only 3.5% by weight (2.9% by volume) is used in vibration cast premix GRC.

The effect of orientation also needs to be considered in a negative sense. If the fibres are assumed to be randomly orientated (in either two or three dimensions), then unintentional alignment of the fibres may give rise to planes of weakness. This can arise in the manufacture of premix GRC if the mix is badly placed. Machine-sprayed GRC, and occasionally hand-sprayed GRC, can be subject to preferential alignment of the fibres, and for this reason test specifications usually require that properties are measured in two directions.[12] The most obvious effect of orientation arises in the different shear properties of sprayed GRC.

20.3.7 Shear strength

If the shear stresses are confined to the plane of the glass-fibre reinforced cement (GRC), the measured in-plane shear strength is similar to the ultimate tensile strength (UTS). This follows logically if the material is assumed orthotropic or isotropic, because the shear stress (SS) should equal

$$SS = UTS/(1 + \gamma) \tag{20.4}$$

where γ is Poisson's ratio.

However, if there is a shear stress out of the plane of sprayed GRC, there will be a complementary interlaminar shear stress which is not resisted by any contribution from the fibres. It can be postulated that the interlaminar shear strength of sprayed GRC will be similar to the matrix shear strength (MSS) or to

$$MSS = BOP/(1 + \gamma) \tag{20.5}$$

where BOP is the bend-over point.

Practical tests support this contention.[9]

20.3.8 Impact resistance

Impact loads on glass-fibre reinforced cement (GRC) normally inflict damage over a localized area. The presence of the fibres in GRC restricts the propagation of cracks outside the zone of stressed material. This damage can often be repaired with no detriment to the GRC product.

The impact strength of GRC is normally measured using a modified Izod test machine, on samples 25–50 mm wide and 6–12 mm thick. The values obtained in such a test are of little use except for the purpose of comparison with other samples of GRC and other materials which have been subjected to the same test. Such comparisons show the impact strength of GRC to be higher than that of many other fibre-cement materials.

The impact strength of GRC is high when many long fibres fail by being pulled out of the matrix, this process absorbing a great deal more energy than fibre breakage. However, this implies relatively low values for the factors k_1 and k_2 in equations (20.1) and (20.2) (Section 20.3.2), indicating that the fibres are used somewhat less efficiently in terms of other GRC strength properties. The impact strength of GRC is lower when few fibres are pulled out of the GRC. If the fibres have a very short critical length (see Section 20.3.2) the GRC may exhibit brittle characteristics under impact loads.

20.3.9 Elastic modulus and Poisson's ratio

The modulus of glass-fibre reinforced cement (GRC) usually quoted is the gradient of the initial linear part of the tensile stress–strain curve. While it should be possible to obtain values from bending tests, most commercial testing machines are too 'soft' to give an accurate value without using some correction factor.

Although the 'law of mixtures' (Section 20.3.2) applies, it can be shown by the insertion of any reasonable values in equation (20.1) that the composite modulus is not significantly different from the modulus of the matrix. Measured values are not in disagreement with this.

The same reasoning applies to the value of Poisson's ratio which is also similar to that of the mortar matrix.

20.3.10 Effect of ageing

The glass fibres used to make glass-fibre reinforced cement (GRC) are resistant to alkaline conditions, but are not proof against them. If the GRC composite remains moist, alkalis from the cement can attack the glass fibre. The attack takes the form of layers of reaction products building up on the surface of the fibre, accompanied by etching of the fibre surface. The presence of flaws and stress-raisers at the surface results in a reduction in the strength of the glass fibre, even though with alkali-resistant fibres there is no significant reduction in the fibre diameter. The rate of attack is dependent upon temperature and use is made of this in accelerated tests to determine the long-term behaviour[13] and to assess acceptable levels of strength retention of alkali-resistant fibres.[14]

This loss of strength influences those properties of the GRC composite which are most dependent upon the fibre strength. If the composite is used in dry conditions (less than about 50% relative humidity) the alkaline attack is very much reduced and has a limited effect upon the fibre strength. For alkali-resistant fibre the microcrack control mechanism as described in Section 20.3.2 is relatively unaffected by this strength loss, because the fibre is always many times stronger than the matrix. Matrix-based properties change little with age, although conditions in service can affect properties such as the modulus and the limit of proportionality which are lower in dry conditions than in wet conditions.

The general effect of the loss of strength in the fibre can be assessed by considering the tensile stress–strain curve. GRC which initially follows a type-A curve (Section 20.3.2, *Figure 20.2*) will have the ultimate tensile strength and strain to failure gradually reduced until it eventually follows a type B curve (Section 20.3.2, *Figure 20.3*), the level of glass strength, length and orientation affecting the value of the stress for the tail portion of the curve. GRC which initially follows a type-B curve suffers only a change in the value of stress for the tail portion of the curve.

The fall in glass strength also increases the number of fibres which fail by breaking rather than pulling out of the matrix. This has a marked effect upon the impact strength of GRC which is sensitive to this phenomenon (Section 20.3.8). This is seen in practical tests where the broken ends of GRC samples have smaller quantities of shorter fibres protruding when old than when freshly made.

The general effects of ageing on the various properties of GRC composites are given in *Table 20.1*. Further implications of the magnitude of the effects and rates of change for specific formulations are given in Section 20.4.

Ageing effects are not a problem provided that proper design practice is adhered to. This ensures that the strength of a product is always adequate to meet its service demands during its lifetime. As with any other product, research continues on continuous improvements and the glass-fibre manufacturers have improved the ageing resistance of alkali-resistant fibres over the years. In addition, a considerable amount of work is being carried out to develop matrix formulations of lower alkalinity. These improved matrix formulations use materials such as pulverized fuel ash, silica fume, ground granulated blast furnace slag and *meta*-kaolinite to improve significantly the long term durability.

20.4 Mechanical properties

The mechanical properties of glass-fibre reinforced cement (GRC) depend upon the mix formulation and the processing method used.

20.4.1 Typical initial property values

Typical initial properties that might be expected from standard glass-fibre reinforced cement (GRC) formulations are summarized in *Table 20.2*. Achievement of these properties in practice requires adequate care, quality control, compaction and curing during manufacture. Changes to the water:cement ratio, sand:cement ratio, glass content, strand length and cement type can alter the material properties.

Table 20.1 The general effects of ageing on the various properties of GRC composites

Property	Initial stress–strain curve[a]	
	Type A	*Type B*
Bend-over point	Little change	Little change
Ultimate tensile strength	Decreases to a stable level	Little change
Compressive strength	Little change	Little change
Limit of proportionality	Little change	Little change
Modulus of rupture	Decreases to a stable level	Little change
Strain to failure	Decreases substantially	Little change
In-plane shear strength	Little change	Little change
Interlaminar shear strength	Decreases to a stable level	Little change
Impact strength	Decreases substantially	Decreases
Modulus	Little change	Little change
Poisson's ratio	Little change	Little change

[a] Standard GRC aged in wet conditions.

Table 20.2 Typical initial mean property values of GRC

Property	Sprayed GRC	Vibration cast (premix) GRC
Dry density (t m^{-3})	1.9–2.1	1.9–2.0
Compressive strength (MPa)	50–80	40–60
Young's modulus (GPa)	10–20	13–18
Impact strength (kJ m^{-2})	10–25	8–14
Poisson's ratio	0.24	0.24
Bending		
Limit of proportionality (MPa)	7–11	5–8
Modulus of rupture (MPa)	19–31	10–14
Direct tension		
Bend-over point (MPa)	5–7	4–6
Ultimate tensile strength (MPa)	8–11	4–7
Strain to failure (%)	0.6–1.2	0.1–0.2
Shear		
In-plane (MPa)	8–11	4–7
Interlaminar (MPa)	3–5	NA[a]

[a] NA, not applicable.

20.4.2 Effect of age on initial property values

The mechanical properties of glass-fibre reinforced cement (GRC) can be split into two simple categories: those which are strongly linked to the quality of the matrix, and those which are linked to the glass-fibre content.

20.4.2.1 Matrix-dependent properties

For the two formulations of sprayed material, those properties which are more dependent upon the matrix are compressive strength, modulus, Poisson's ratio, limit of proportionality, bend-over point, and the interlaminar shear strength. All the properties of vibration cast (premix) glass-fibre reinforced cement (GRC), except impact strength, are dependent on the matrix. These properties vary little with the age of the GRC, but may increase marginally in humid environments as the cement in the matrix continues to hydrate.

20.4.2.2 Glass-fibre dependent properties

Those properties which are more dependent upon the glass fibre are the impact strength of all types of glass-fibre reinforced

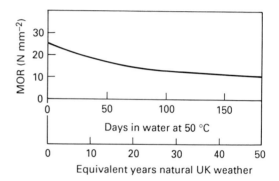

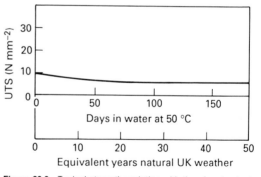

Figure 20.6 Typical strength variation with time for standard hand-sprayed GRC containing 5% alkali-resistant fibre. Sand:cement ratio 0.5; water:cement ratio 0.3. UTS, ultimate tensile strength; MOR, modulus of rupture

cement (GRC) and the modulus of rupture, ultimate tensile strength, strain to failure and in-plane shear strength of sprayed GRC. *Figure 20.6* shows two curves that depict the effect of ageing in hot water which accelerates the alkali attack upon the fibre.[15] These curves are shown for standard hand sprayed GRC (*Table 20.2*) and are scaled according to the time spent in hot water and the equivalent age in UK weather. The method of accelerating the ageing of GRC has been developed from research over a period of 15 years and is applicable only to glass fibres in a standard sand/cement matrix. It has been assessed by continuing correlation with real-time data from GRC exposed in many climates around the world for periods of up to 15 years.

The relationship between 'days in hot water' and natural

Table 20.3 Estimated long-term stable property values for standard GRC

Property	Sprayed GRC	Vibration cast (premix) GRC
Compressive strength (MPa)	75	50
Modulus (GPa)	25	20
Impact strength (kJ m^{-2})	4	3
Poisson's ratio	0.24	0.24
Limit of proportionality (MPa)	10	8
Modulus of rupture (MPa)	13	10
Bend-over point (MPa)	5.5	4.5
Ultimate tensile strength (MPa)	5.5	4.5
Strain-to-failure (%)	0.04	0.03
In-plane shear strength (MPa)	5.5	4.5
Interlaminar shear strength (MPa)	4	NA

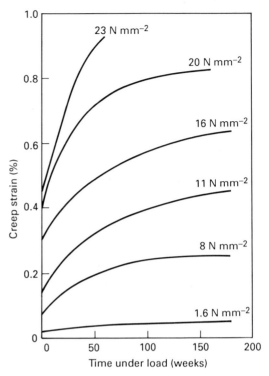

Figure 20.7 Results of tests to measure the flexural creep of dry stored, spray-dewatered GRC samples containing 5% by weight of alkali-resistant fibre. Sand:cement ratio 0.5; water:cement ratio 0.3

weathering depends upon the mean annual temperature and humidity of the exposure conditions. Warmer, damper environments will produce more rapid reductions in properties, leading to the same long-term, stable values. It should be noted that the recommended design stresses should be well within the ultimate strength of the material, and for most applications should also be within the elastic range of the material.

The curves in *Figure 20.6* show the properties depicted decreasing with time to a stable long-term, limiting value. It is obviously important in terms of design and confidence in GRC that the long-term properties are known and this has been the subject of much investigation and discussion.[15-18] Impact strength, strain to failure and in-plane shear strength also show decreasing property levels over similar time periods, achieving stable values after about 150 days in water at 50°C. An estimate of the long-term stable property values of the standard GRC formulations from *Table 20.2* is shown in *Table 20.3*. The rate of alkali attack upon the fibre is considerably reduced in dry environments (less than about 50% relative humidity).[16]

20.4.3 Creep and stress-rupture behaviour

Glass-fibre reinforced cement (GRC) is quite capable of bearing load over prolonged periods. In common with other cement and concrete materials, the initial (elastic) deformation is followed by a further slow creep deformation when the load is maintained.

The creep behaviour of GRC is very similar in general form to that of cement paste and sand/cement mortars. In direct tension, creep strains are smaller than expansion–contraction strains due to humidity changes; in bending the creep rate decreases with time.

At bending stresses below the limit of proportionality (the normal working range of the material), the creep behaviour of spray-dewatered GRC is identical to that of the matrix material. Creep strain is proportional to the initial strain and under long-term loading will exceed the initial strain by a factor of 2–4. This means, for example, that a panel installed horizontally which exhibits some deflection under self weight would be expected to show a deflection with time of approximately three times the initial amount.

No stress rupture failures have been observed at up to twice the normal recommended working-stress level, in experiments in which samples have been kept under a constant bending load in dry air, under water at 18/20°C, or in natural UK weather conditions for periods of about 8 years (*Figure 20.7*).

20.4.4 Fatigue performance

Repeated load fatigue tests have been carried out in bending and direct tension on samples of sprayed glass-fibre reinforced cement (GRC). Bending tests gave fatigue lives greater than 10^5 cycles at the limit-of-proportionality stress level and greater than 10^7 cycles at the normal flexural working-stress levels (*Figure 20.8*). Direct-tension-test results indicate lives in excess of 10^4 cycles at the bend-over point and over 10^7 cycles at the normal tensile working-stress levels (*Figure 20.9*).

20.5 Physical and chemical properties

20.5.1 Shrinkage

All cement-based materials are susceptible to dimensional changes as they are wetted and dried. After manufacture and cure, subsequent drying results in shrinkage from the original state. Rewetting results in expansion but not to the extent of restoring it to its original size. There is, therefore, an initial irreversible shrinkage, followed in subsequent service conditions by a reversible dimensional movement during changes in moisture content.

The ultimate shrinkage of cementitious materials is highest when the matrix is based on pure cement. Shrinkage is reduced by the addition of aggregates not susceptible to moisture movement. This is standard practice for mortars and concretes and is well documented. Typically, a silica sand would be used in glass-fibre reinforced cement (GRC) manufacture at sand:cement ratios of 0.5 or 1. Such composites would typically display ultimate shrinkages of 2000 and 1600 microstrain, respectively, of which between two-thirds to three-quarters will be reversible.

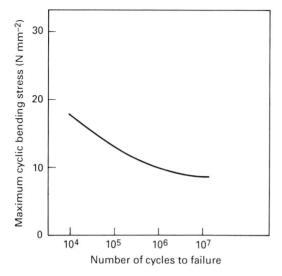

Figure 20.8 Flexural fatigue of hand-sprayed GRC containing 5% by weight of alkali-resistant fibre. Sand:cement ratio 0.5; water:cement ratio 0.33

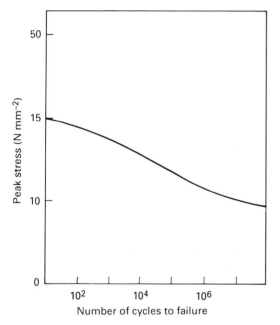

Figure 20.9 Tensile fatigue of hand-sprayed GRC containing 5% by weight of alkali-resistant fibre. Sand:cement ratio 0.5; water:cement ratio 0.33

It should be noted that the amplitude of reversible movement quoted is between fully dried and fully saturated conditions. In practice, these extremes may not be experienced in normal weathering conditions and, therefore, the amount of movement to be accommodated in practice may well be less.

Both the initial irreversible shrinkage and the reversible moisture movement can be reduced by the inclusion of acrylic polymers in the mix. An addition of 5% acrylic polymer solids to cement by weight has been shown to reduce the reversible shrinkage by approximately 40%. This reduction is higher at higher polymer addition levels.

Since GRC is a relatively impermeable material, changes in external humidity can take a considerable period of time to affect the moisture content of the GRC. A 10-mm thick sprayed GRC will take about 20 days to approach equilibrium with changes in external humidity, and thicker sections take even longer. This clearly has implications for the design and installation of components in that shrinkage and moisture movement will need to be unrestrained in order to avoid undesirable stresses in the GRC.

20.5.2 Thermal expansion

The coefficient of thermal expansion is in the range 10–$20 \times 10^{-6} °C^{-1}$ which is within the range of values for other cementitious materials. Glass-fibre reinforced cement (GRC), in common with cement paste and, to a less noticeable extent, mortars and concretes, exhibits an anomalous behaviour in that the thermal-expansion coefficient varies with the moisture content of the material. The coefficient has a value at the lower end of the range when the material is fully dry or fully saturated. At intermediate levels of moisture content (50–80% relative humidity) the upper value applies. The reason for this behaviour is that the thermal-expansion coefficient is made up of two movements: the normal kinetic thermal coefficient and a swelling pressure, a complex effect caused by moisture transfer within the system.

20.5.3 Chemical resistance

The rate of chemical attack on cementitious materials depends largely upon the extent to which reactive elements in the cement are exposed to aggressive agents and this is a function of permeability. The permeability of glass-fibre reinforced cement (GRC) is lower than that of normal concretes and, consequently, GRC shows good resistance to chemical attack.

GRC also benefits from having a high cement content, which is another factor that determines the chemical resistance of concretes. Improved performance against chemical attack may be expected from the use of special cements, e.g. high alumina cement or supersulphate cement.

20.5.4 Sulphate resistance

In the presence of moisture and sulphates a reaction takes place causing degradation of the cement, although glass-fibre reinforced cement (GRC) is less sensitive than most concretes. Resistance to sulphate attack is increased by the use of sulphate-resisting cement and it is usual practice to use this type of cement for the manufacture of GRC which may be in contact with sulphate solutions. Typical of such applications are silage tanks, drainage components, sewer linings and junction boxes which may be used in contact with sulphate-bearing soils.

20.5.5 Acids and alkalis

Portland cement releases calcium hydroxide during hydration and is highly alkaline (pH 12.5). Consequently, alkaline solutions present no particular hazard to glass-fibre reinforced cement (GRC). Cemfil glass is relatively unaffected by acidic environments, although ordinary Portland cement may be degraded after long-term exposure to acids. Such conditions may arise due to the action of sour silage and in sewers under certain conditions where bacterial action has produced sulphuric acid, and in certain types of soil, but can be countered by the use of sulphate-resisting cement or high alumina cement.

20.5.6 Marine environments

Seawater and sea-spray exposure of glass-fibre reinforced cement (GRC) gives mechanical-property changes similar to those in freshwater exposure and natural weather at equivalent temperature. Some surface carbonation can occur which may detract from the appearance of the GRC, but which is not detrimental to its mechanical properties, unlike reinforced concrete where both the salts and carbonation result in increased attack on the reinforcement.

20.5.7 Freeze–thaw behaviour

In certain climates, glass-fibre reinforced cement (GRC) may be subjected to long periods at sub-zero temperatures and to freeze–thaw conditions. Laboratory tests based on BS 4624: 1970[19] and DIN 274: 1986[20] have been carried out on sprayed GRC containing 5% fibre and various sand contents. There was no visible change in the appearance of the samples after the tests and the mechanical property values of the modulus of rupture, the limit of proportionality, Young's modulus and the impact strength were unchanged. The general freeze–thaw behaviour of GRC is, therefore, very good.

A more severe test based on ASTM C666-73[21] has also been performed on GRC and on fully compressed asbestos cement sheet as a comparison. This test involves freezing and thawing in water, a process which is unlikely to be encountered in actual use. After 300 cycles between $-20°C$ and $+20°C$, GRC showed relatively little change in properties, the limit of proportionality increased by up to 20%, while the modulus of rupture, Young's modulus and the impact strength decreased by up to 20%. The mechanical properties of asbestos cement were much more seriously affected.

20.5.8 Thermal conductivity

The thermal conductivity of glass-fibre reinforced cement (GRC) depends on the density of the material and the moisture content. For normal-density GRC, dependent on the moisture content, the conductivity will be between 0.5 and 1.0 W m^{-1} °C^{-1}. This range will be significantly lower for low-density material, a figure of 0.2 W m^{-1} °C^{-1} at a density of 1 t m^{-3} being typical.

20.5.9 Sound

The sound insulation of a homogeneous material depends on three physical properties:

1. surface mass (weight per unit area);
2. stiffness (dependent upon panel shape);
3. damping.

Of these properties, the surface mass is the most important in determining the sound insulation at the lower frequencies. A typical 10-mm thickness of glass-fibre reinforced cement (GRC) which has a surface mass of 20 kg m^{-2} will have an average sound reduction of about 30 dB.

20.5.10 Permeability

20.5.10.1 Water-vapour permeability

Measurements of water-vapour permeability have been made according to BS 3177[22] for tropical conditions (38°C, 90% relative humidity). Values obtained on freshly made material range from 1×10^{-4} to 11×10^{-4} g s^{-1} MN^{-1} and depend to a certain extent on the degree of compaction of the GRC. Highly compacted GRC tends to have a lower permeability than less well-compacted GRC.

Exposure of GRC over a period of 1–2 years in most natural weathering conditions leads to a reduction in the permeability by a factor of about 2. For 10-mm GRC, the above results indicate that the water-vapour permeance will be less than 1.3 metric perms (a measure of permeance; see Section 20.5.10.2).

20.5.10.2 Water permeance

Permeance is defined as the quantitative measure of a permeating substance through a barrier of specified thickness. Measurements made according to BS 473.550[23] on freshly made 8-mm thick glass-fibre reinforced cement (GRC) have shown results in the range 0.02–0.40 ml m^{-2} min^{-1}. As with water-vapour permeability, the water permeance tends to decrease after about 1–2 years natural weathering to the lower end (0.1 ml m^{-2} min^{-1}) of the range.

20.5.10.3 Air permeance

The air permeance for 10-mm thick glass-fibre reinforced cement (GRC) will be about 2 metric perms.

20.5.11 Abrasion resistance

Since there has been interest in the resistance of glass-fibre reinforced cement (GRC) to wind-blown sand, GRC has been tested according to a modified form of ASTM C418-68[24] which involves directing a jet of air-driven sand at the sample. Under this test, the GRC samples performed well in comparison with concrete and asbestos cement, showing a volume loss of 0.27–0.3 cm^3 against 0.32 cm^3 for a concrete paving slab and 0.37 cm^3 for semicompressed asbestos cement to 0.52 cm^3 for fully compressed asbestos cement.

20.5.12 Density

The density of standard glass-fibre reinforced cement (GRC) materials is commonly around 2.0 t m^{-3}. GRC forms lightweight components by virtue of thin section, rather than by lightness of the material, although low-density versions of the material are possible.

The significance of density, however, goes beyond the simple concept of weight. Density is a good indicator of material quality, a high density indicating a well-compacted, well-made material of correct water:cement ratio. The more useful figure is the dry density, and normal values for a good quality material are 1.9–2.1 t m^{-3} for hand-sprayed material and 1.9–2.0 t m^{-3} for vibration cast material.

20.5.13 Water absorption and apparent porosity

Water absorption and apparent porosity of glass-fibre reinforced cement (GRC) are determined as part of the routine quality-control measurement of wet and dry bulk density. Typical values for hand-sprayed GRC with a sand:cement ratio of 0.5 are: water absorption 12%, and apparent porosity 24%. It should be noted that these figures are higher than those for typical concretes, which would normally exhibit a water absorption of less than 10%. This is a direct result of the higher cement content in GRC. The permeability of GRC, as discussed earlier is, however, significantly lower than that of concrete.

20.5.14 Potable-water approval

Tests by the National Water Council indicate that drinking water may be passed through or stored in glass-fibre reinforced cement (GRC) without harmful effect, although official approval is only given for specific formulations.

20.5.15 Ultraviolet light

Glass-fibre reinforced cement (GRC) is not susceptible to degradation arising from exposure to ultraviolet light.

20.6 Design principles

As with any material, there are applications which are appropriate for glass-fibre reinforced cement (GRC) and some which are not, and this judgement in a particular circumstance must be based on the characteristics of the material. Generally, GRC components can be used in situations where the stresses can be evaluated at realistic safe levels, where the resulting component is economic, and where the consequences of failure are limited in extent.

Because of the uniformity of reinforcement in a two-dimensional plane, GRC used as a flat sheet can be treated as a homogeneous isotropic material and the techniques used for the analysis of GRC stresses, strains and deflections are identical to those used with isotropic materials such as metals, provided that the stresses are within the elastic limit of the material.

20.6.1 Mechanical design

The design of any product must satisfy many requirements, many of which may be peculiar to the individual product. Adequate strength against specified loads is an obvious requirement and, therefore, mechanical design will commonly be performed to ensure satisfactory performance under the most severe loading condition. The loads to which a product may be subjected during demoulding, when it has not developed its full strength, and the subsequent handling in factory or on site prior to exposure to normal service should not be ignored.

20.6.1.1 The approach to mechanical design

As with other materials, it is normal practice to design glass-fibre reinforced cement (GRC) at stresses below the elastic limit. The elastic limits of GRC in compression, bending (limit of proportionality), tension (bend-over point) and shear do not change significantly in most environments, so that the initial property values can be used as a reference (*Figure 20.10*).

Design stresses are also selected with respect to long-term strength values. In conditions where there is a reduction of ultimate strength, accelerated ageing tests[4] indicate that the strength stabilizes. Design stresses should be based on this stable value, allowing a suitable factor of safety. In terms of the bending strength of a good-quality hand-sprayed GRC, a typical design stress is 6 MPa, which covers both these requirements.

The high initial ultimate properties of the material are beneficial in the early life of the product, allowing the use of higher design stresses for structures such as permanent formwork, which may require high strength only in the early life of the product.

20.6.1.2 Choice of design stress levels

Since glass-fibre reinforced cement (GRC) is not one material, but a family of closely related materials, the design stresses to be used will depend on the choice of formulation and manufacturing process. In addition, each individual material will have several design stress levels because the material characteristics result in different strengths depending upon the type of loading and the section being loaded.

The design stress chosen must also be related to the quality of manufacture, because the manufacturer is not just using the material to make GRC components, but also creating the material from its basic constituents.

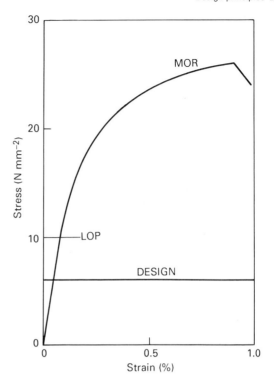

Figure 20.10 Relationship between limit of proportionality (LOP), modulus of rupture (MOR) and a selected design stress

(*i*) *Design stresses* The normal test data available from a GRC manufacturer relates to bending tests on small coupons of GRC. The results can be analysed statistically to give characteristic values of the initial limit of proportionality and modulus of rupture. Typical design stresses for the GRC formulations indicated in *Table 20.2* (Section 20.4.1), provided that the characteristic strength values are not less than as stated, are given in *Table 20.4*.

GRC is often used in constructions where the stress is neither

Table 20.4 Typical design stresses[a] for the GRC formulations indicated in *Table 20.2*

Stress type	Loading example	Design stress (MPa)	
		5% spray GRC	*3.5% premix GRC*
Compressive	Compressive	12	12
Bending	Bending solid beams or plates	6	4
Tensile	Cylindrical hoop stresses	3	2
Tensile	Bending sandwich panels	3	2
Web shear	In-plane shear of webs in box sections	2	1
Bearing shear	Shear loading at bearing positions	1	1

[a] These design stresses were obtained by applying a reduction factor of approximately 1.8 to the long-term cracking strength (e.g. limit of proportionality and bend-over point) of the GRC. The values apply to cases where the characteristic strength values are not less than: modulus of rupture—sprayed GRC 19 MPa, premix GRC 8 MPa; limit of proportionality—sprayed GRC 6.5 MPa, premix GRC 5 MPa.

pure bending nor pure tension. Bending of box sections (often used to strengthen GRC products) is an example. In this case the design stress will be between the values for bending and tension. Taking 4 MPa for sprayed GRC and 2.5 MPa for premix GRC might be appropriate. However, if in doubt it is advisable to use the lower values for tensile design stress and to perform load tests to check the product behaviour.

The values of design stress may be increased where loads are of limited duration and occur early in the life of the material (e.g. permanent formwork). Conversely, reduced values (e.g. one-third of the normal values) may be desirable when considering the stresses imposed by demoulding a product at an early stage in the curing cycle when the limit of proportionality of the material may be low.

Consideration may be given to reducing the design stresses if a permanent load is to be applied to the GRC in order to take account of the effects of creep.

20.6.1.3 Minimum thickness

For normal applications of glass-fibre reinforced cement (GRC) the following minimum design thicknesses have been found satisfactory for handling and processing:

1. Premix (vibration cast or spraymix) 10 mm;
2. Machine spray 6 mm;
3. Hand spray 8 mm;
4. Render 3 mm.

20.6.1.4 Analysis

Glass-fibre reinforced cement (GRC) products can usually be subdivided into interacting parts, each of which can be tested individually as a beam or plate element and analysed accordingly using formulae available in standard texts.[25]

The formula for deflection gives an estimate of the short-term deflection. For sustained loads or dead weight, the creep of the GRC should be considered. A simple method is to multiply the deflection due to sustained loads by a factor of 3 to obtain the long-term deflection.

20.6.2 Physical design

20.6.2.1 Thermal movement

Cladding panels on a building may experience surface temperatures varying from $-10°C$ to $60°C$ (light colours) or $80°C$ (dark colours) over the period of 1 year in the UK and, therefore, substantial expansion or contraction may take place. The coefficient of thermal expansion is generally taken as 20×10^{-6} °C^{-1}. A 2-m panel exposed to temperature variations of $90°C$ may, therefore, move by up to 3.6 mm.

20.6.2.2 Moisture movement

The amount of shrinkage or moisture movement which may realistically be seen in service is up to 0.15% or 1.5 mm m^{-1} length. Such an amount of movement requires design consideration in many ways, such as allowance for movement at fixing positions and selection of suitable joint widths.

20.6.2.3 Stresses and deflections due to moisture and thermal movement

Moisture and temperature gradients within glass-fibre reinforced cement (GRC) products will induce stresses and/or deflections in the product. Since GRC is normally made in relatively thin sections the possibility of significant differences in temperature through the thickness of the material is small, but moisture

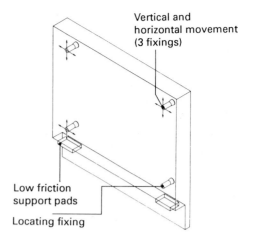

Figure 20.11 Panel fixings should allow freedom of movement

differentials can occur and the product will tend to bow out of the plane of the material. For example, if a damp flat GRC sheet is placed upon a flat surface, the upper surface of the GRC will start to dry by evaporation while the lower surface will not. The resulting bow is usually a temporary state because the effect is often reversible. If different areas of a product are subject to different conditions of temperature and moisture the product will tend to change shape to accommodate the induced movement.

If movement is prevented either by fixing restraint or integral stiffness caused by the panel shape, significant stresses can be developed, particularly in panels of sandwich construction. Good design of GRC products would include a minimal number of fixings, making sure that these accommodate the movement of the GRC (*Figure 20.11*), and would also restrict the number of changes of section, ensuring that those which are necessary are as gradual as possible.

20.6.2.4 Thermal insulation

The thermal conductivity of glass-fibre reinforced cement (GRC) having a density of 1900–2100 kg m^{-3} will usually be in the range 0.5–1.0 W m^{-1} °C^{-1}, depending upon the moisture content.

20.6.2.5 Fire performance

Glass-fibre reinforced cement (GRC) has been subjected to extensive fire testing to demonstrate the performance of different mix designs and forms of construction. GRC is generally classed as non-combustible in accordance with BS 476: Part 4,[26] providing that organic matter is not present at levels above 1%.

Most mixes will also satisfy Class 0 for fire propagation (BS 476: Part 6[27]) and Class 1, zero spread, for surface spread of flame (BS 476: Part 7[28]).

Fire resistance performance to BS 476: Part 8[29] varies greatly with mix design and GRC panel construction. A single skin of GRC will not satisfy the insulation criterion and the standard cement/sand mix cannot be relied on to maintain integrity. To guarantee integrity in single-skin form, it is necessary to use a cement/PFA/air entrainment mix, a low-density perlite/cement mix or other similar mix with reduced density and increased porosity.

Specially developed low-density GRC mixes are used to manufacture products offering fire protection, such as fire-protection board, window surrounds and formwork. Such products not only remain intact and provide insulation from fire, in the case of permanent formwork it helps to prevent the concrete from spalling, thereby giving improved protection to the reinforcing steel.

Fire doors and barriers based on a proprietary cladding of low-density GRC (900–1000 kg m^{-3}) have successfully exceeded 1-h stability, integrity and insulation when tested to BS 476: Part 8: 1972[29] and also when using the considerably more severe furnace temperatures conforming to the CEGB Specification E/TSS/EX5/7080 Issue 5.[30]

The cement/PFA/air-entrainment mix is only used for internal applications at present. A single skin of GRC can provide a 1-h fire resistance to all three criteria if a suitable thickness of a fire-resistant insulant, such as vermiculite/cement or gypsum, is applied to the GRC.

Sandwich panels containing a lightweight poly(styrene) bead aggregate concrete core perform well in the fire-resistance test: all three criteria are readily achieved with ratings of up to 4 h.

20.6.2.6 Sound reduction

The amount of sound reduction obtained with glass-fibre reinforced cement (GRC) is proportional to the surface mass (weight per unit area). This will apply to both single-skin and sandwich construction. If reductions larger than 20–40 dBA are required it is generally uneconomic to increase the surface mass and specialized sound-absorbing systems should be used.

20.6.3 Installation considerations

20.6.3.1 Fixing systems

Many types of fixing commonly used with concrete, stone, asbestos cement, glass-fibre reinforced plastic (GRP) or steel can be used directly or adapted to glass-fibre reinforced cement (GRC), giving a wide range of possible arrangements.

In respect of the materials used for fixing components, GRC is no different to concrete and the choice of material is likely to be influenced by the local statutory authority. Austenitic stainless steel and non-ferrous inserts are preferable. Galvanized mild steel may be used and the coating weight of zinc will be dictated by the durability required. Unprotected mild steel must not be used under any circumstances for cast-in fixings. Where dissimilar metals are in contact with one another, there is a possibility of galvanic corrosion occurring. This can be avoided by the use of isolation materials such as neoprene and synthetic resin-bonded fibres.

In all cases the fixing system should be designed such that the force transmitted through the fixing is transferred to a sufficiently large area of GRC. For example, the fixing should be encapsulated in a block of GRC, or oversize washers or plates should be used to spread the load.

The fixing system should make allowance for site and manufacturing tolerances, for thermal and moisture movement of the GRC, and for movement of the structure. For example, one fixing can be used to locate a component, whilst all other fixings allow movement relative to it. Because of the occurrence of bowing with sandwich construction products, fixing systems for these should not restrict small rotational movements and should not be placed in positions which restrict the bowing of the product.

When used to carry high loads, the fixing should be encapsulated in a block of good-quality GRC with a minimum width of 100 mm and a minimum dimension of 50 mm between the fixing and the edge of the component. The detail of the fixing area should be such that it is easily accessible during manufacture.

The results of pull-out tests on encapsulated fixings in GRC show results similar to those of the same fixings used in concrete.

20.6.3.2 Jointing and sealing

The techniques used to 'seal' joints between glass-fibre reinforced cement (GRC) components are similar to those used for natural stone, precast concrete or asbestos cement. The degree of 'sealing' can vary from simple overlap joints designed to resist rain penetration, to compression joints, designed to resist liquids under hydrostatic pressure.

20.6.3.3 Handling

Some provision will be required for the lifting, storage and transportation of the glass-fibre reinforced cement (GRC). This should be considered at the design stage and the GRC component should be designed to resist handling forces. This is particularly important during demoulding, when the GRC is incompletely cured and has not developed its full strength. An appropriate design-stress value at demoulding stage would be 1 MPa which would cover most eventualities.

The incorporation of strategically positioned lifting points, the use of frames, both in handling and transportation, and the manufacture of properly designed storage racks may assist in reducing problems encountered during the handling of GRC, particularly large components. The consideration of this at the design stage will simplify problems which might otherwise cause unnecessary difficulties.

20.6.4 Design problems

Problems in the use of glass-fibre reinforced cement (GRC), other than faults attributable to poor workmanship, supervision, or handling, have generally been related to building cladding panels of double-skin construction and of a particular configuration. Double-skin panels can be of a variety of forms and the crucial design aspect relates to the possible relative movement, restraints and consequential stresses in the laminar structure.

The basic elements in a double-skin panel are the two facing panels and the core material between them. If these three elements are free to move independently of each other, then dimensional changes in the skin on one side of the panel in relation to the skin on the other side, such as may occur with temperature differentials or differences in moisture content, are able to take place without stress. Similarly, if the core material, although bonded to the skins, is of a low-modulus material, then relative movements will be accommodated by strain in the core material without undue stress or panel deformation. This method is used successfully for large panels of high insulation value (*Figures 20.13* and *20.23*).

However, if the core material is rigid, such as polystyrene bead concrete, or if there is some other form of rigid connection between the two skins such as the formation of closed box sections, then differential movement between panel skins can only be accommodated by a change in the geometry of the panel, which will attempt to assume a degree of sphericity. If this consequential movement is permitted by limiting the number of fixings (maximum of four) and by ensuring that the fixings have an appropriate degree of translational and rotational freedom, then there will be no stress problems induced by movement constraint.

Problems will appear, however, if such a panel is unduly restrained. This can occur with very large panels where wind loading may demand more than four fixings. If the intermediate fixings are not designed to allow sufficient freedom of movement to avoid constraint-induced stresses, then cracking of the panel can occur. Similarly, constraint-induced stresses will occur in panels of any configuration if the fixings provide undue rigidity, whether due to inappropriate design or insufficient care in installation.

Figure 20.12   GRC wall and cornice units replicating original masonry at Hays Wharf, London

Figure 20.13   Insulated GRC cladding panels on electronics research laboratory, Isle of Wight

It should also be borne in mind that the introduction of major compound curvatures and other geometric features in double-skinned panels can create integral restraints which are not readily apparent. Such limitations are not found with single-skin panels.

By attention to these basic principles many thousands of square metres of GRC cladding have been and are being successfully used. The adoption of the steel-stud-frame system (*Figure 20.14*) in recent years virtually ensures that constraint-induced stresses are avoided and that fixing constraints during erection are eliminated.

20.7 Applications

Two decades after its inception, glass-fibre reinforced cement (GRC) can be found in a wide range of applications. The civil engineering, architectural and agricultural sectors all use the inherent properties of GRC to their advantage. In this section some of the main applications are highlighted.

20.7.1 Agricultural products

The impact resistance, durability and light weight of articles made from sprayed glass-fibre reinforced cement (GRC) has led to the manufacture of a number of standard products for use in agricultural applications. Cattle drinking troughs (*Figure 20.15*), fish-farming tanks and sheep dips (*Figure 20.16*) are amongst the products which all benefit from being lightweight and easy for the farmer to install. Glass-fibre reinforced renders are used for agricultural buildings (see Section 20.7.11).

20.7.2 Architectural features

The mouldability of vibration cast (premix) glass-fibre reinforced cement (GRC) lends itself to the production of intricate mouldings for architectural applications. It allows the fine reproduction of detail required for refurbishment work such as cornices (*Figure 20.17*), column capitals and balustrades. It provides the strength required for slender Islamic sunscreens, which are made in a variety of sizes up to 10 m^2 in area (*Figure 20.18*).

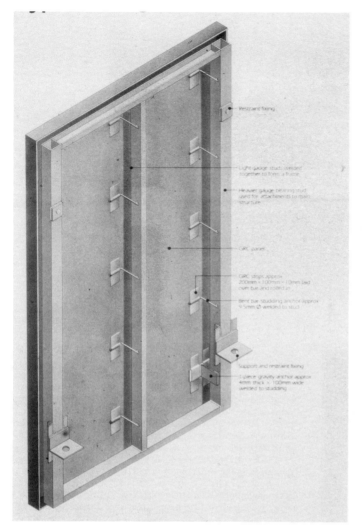

Figure 20.14 General form of GRC steel stud-frame cladding panel

20.7.3 Building systems

Glass-fibre reinforced cement (GRC) building systems have been developed for low-cost housing in underdeveloped countries, luxury accommodation in the Middle East, and factory and office systems in Western Europe (see *Figure 20.19*). The sprayed GRC panels can be designed to contain a high level of insulation, and can incorporate fine surface finishes. The light weight of sprayed GRC panels makes their handling and installation quick and simple without the need for heavy lifting gear, and allows buildings to be dismantled and moved if necessary.

20.7.4 Cable ducting

Glass-fibre reinforced cement (GRC) cable ducts are used for road and rail side cable ducting, and also as housings for underground cable systems. The main advantages of the material are its light weight, slim cross-section and high impact strength. These allow the cable ducts to be handled easily with fewer breakages and fewer obstructions.

The impact resistance of GRC and its accompanying weight reduction has led to its use as duct covers, both for precast concrete and for GRC cable ducts. It has also been used for making walkway covers over service trenches in motorway tunnels.

20.7.5 Cladding

As a construction material, glass-fibre reinforced cement (GRC) allows relatively thin cross-section products to be used, resulting in low component weights, usually one-third to one-fifth that of an equivalent concrete element. This gives substantial savings in transport, on-site storage, handling and erection costs. Manufacturing techniques enable the material to be formed in a wide range of shapes or profiles. As well as traditional architectural styles, complex surface designs can also be incorporated either as relief or intaglio.

GRC offers the architect a design freedom which can be exploited to full advantage without sacrificing any performance or environmental demands which may be required. Being non-combustible, GRC presents no limitations in terms of

Figure 20.15 Cattle drinking trough

Figure 20.16 Sheep dip

imposing a fire load on buildings, and its light weight gives opportunities for reducing foundation and structural requirements of a building in addition to the savings in on-site handling costs.

Examples of the use of GRC cladding are shown in *Figures 20.20* and *20.21*.

Cladding-panel designs in GRC range from simple flat or ribbed single skin sheets to more complex composite elements offering high thermal insulation and good fire resistance. Furthermore, the ability of GRC to resist weathering, water penetration and chemical corrosion, together with good acoustic and impact properties, make it an attractive material for industrial building construction. The light weight of GRC panels, especially in conjunction with the steel-stud-frame system (see *Figure 20.14*), makes them ideally suitable for cladding buildings in seismic areas (see *Figure 20.22*).

GRC cladding panels can be designed in a number of configurations, depending upon the required panel size and performance criteria. The most simple form of construction is the single-skin flat sheet, which can be strengthened by forming either flanges or stiffening ribs around the perimeter. By encapsulating a suitable core material such as polystyrene in skins of GRC a strong sandwich construction is formed. Such panels provide good insulation and fire resistance, but the construction is limited to flat panels to avoid any inbuilt restraint of thermal and moisture movement.

A well-established form of building construction, first developed in the Netherlands, uses GRC panels produced on a continuous production line as the outer skins of a sandwich, enclosing a polyisocyanurate foam core. This composite panel, which can be up to 12 m long, is used in a construction system of very high performance. The system is widely used for buildings where the internal environment has to be carefully controlled, such as cold stores and electronics factories (*Figures 20.13* and *20.23*).

A rapidly growing development in building construction is the use of GRC panels in conjunction with lightweight steel stud frames, made from rolled steel sections which may be corrosion protected by galvanizing or other type of coating, or made from stainless steel. The frame carries a single-skin GRC panel which is connected to the stud frame by flexible steel anchors during manufacture. These anchors are typically arranged at 600 mm centres and are designed to permit thermal and moisture movement of the GRC face without the creation of undue stress. The GRC panels can reproduce a variety of architectural variations of contour, texture and surface finish, and the stud-frame configuration lends itself to the easy application of insulation and linings (see *Figure 20.14*).

20.7.6 Fire protection and insulation

Proprietary, low-density glass-fibre reinforced cement (GRC) formulations are used both for fire doors, fire barriers and cable penetration units to stringent specifications (see Section 20.6.2.5). Fire doors for marine and off-shore applications have been certified by the Department of Transport and Lloyds Register of Shipping for both A60 and B15 ratings (*Figure 20.24*).

Figure 20.17 GRC restoration in Oxford Street, London

Figure 20.18 Sunscreens on the Ministry of Communications Building, Oman

Figure 20.19 'Executive' modular building

Figure 20.20 GRC cladding on the Bank of N T Butterfield, Bermuda

GRC insulation applications include external building insulation systems which involve the application of render over insulation boards which are fixed to the original building structure. In Sweden, where the insulation of buildings is taken very seriously, polystyrene blocks encapsulated in sprayed GRC are used to insulate the floor slabs and foundations of buildings.

20.7.7 Flooring and roofing

Alkali-resistant glass fibre can be used to reinforce slab toppings and screeds, offering improved impact resistance and allowing reductions in thickness. Fibre can also be used in concrete slabs to reduce the risk of shrinkage cracking.

Glass-fibre reinforced cement (GRC) free-access flooring systems have been developed in Europe, the USA and Japan.

Figure 20.21   GRC cladding on the Credit Lyonnais Bank, London

Figure 20.22   GRC cladding on the Madison Hotel, Seattle

Figure 20.23   Proprietary method of securing insulated GRC panels

They offer improved fire resistance over many existing systems and the rolling load resistance is claimed to be better.

For roofing applications, corrugated GRC sheet is finding uses in place of its asbestos-containing competitors by offering greater toughness and no health risk. GRC simulated slates (*Figure 20.25*) are often used in place of the natural product because of its cost savings, durability and ease of installation.

GRC promenade tiles produced on automatic equipment are used on flat roofs to provide pedestrian access for fire exits or maintenance purposes. The additional load imposed is far less than with conventional paving blocks and installation is easier.

20.7.8 Formwork

The immediate advantage of glass-fibre reinforced cement (GRC) as permanent formwork is that it is easy to fabricate flat

Figure 20.24 GRC fire door being tested to BS 476: Part 8[29] (60-min insulation, stability and integrity)

Figure 20.25 GRC simulated slates

or moulded shapes of high quality, with or without factory applied finishes. Moreover, the completed appearance can be inspected on site before concrete is cast into the formwork. GRC is a crack-resistant material compatible with concrete, having good fire resistance and low permeability, which assists in guaranteeing adequate cover to the steel reinforcement in the structural concrete contained by the formwork. If the concrete is cast in immediate contact with the GRC, excellent bonding is achieved.

20.7.8.1 Architectural formwork

In building construction, the versatility of glass-fibre reinforced cement (GRC) has led to its use in major architectural design features, externally for walls and internally for ceilings. Permanent formwork provides a means of designing for and realizing shape, profile and textured surfaces on the concrete substrate structure. Subsequently, the GRC surface offers benefits in terms of durability and fire resistance. Applications

Figure 20.26 GRC flat sheet being used as permanent formwork on a bypass bridge over a canal

include bridge abutments and coffer ceiling pans with integral ducting.

20.7.8.2 Civil-engineering formwork

Glass-fibre reinforced cement (GRC) permanent formwork can have important practical and economic benefits in areas of restricted access or difficult working conditions where it may be impractical to fabricate, install and strike conventional formwork. It has also been shown that GRC permanent formwork offers effective protection to the reinforced concrete by providing the structure with a durable skin which is less permeable to the passage of chlorides, and has a far lower rate of carbonation than good-quality concrete. These benefits are particularly important in the applications of bridge decks, parapets and columns which can be subject to aggressive environments.

GRC permanent formwork has been used extensively for many years, particularly in the UK and Norway. Flat-sheet GRC (*Figure 20.26*) provides an economic solution for bridging short spans where closely placed 'U' or inverted 'T' beams are used. For greater spans a variety of corrugated or channel configurations are used.

20.7.9 Irrigation and drainage

Spun-concrete pipes reinforced with alkali-resistant glass fibre are produced in many countries for surfacewater drainage and sewer liners. Their design, with a simple in-line jointing system, enables a narrower trench to be excavated and simplifies handling and installation.

Glass-fibre reinforced cement (GRC) is used as a component for both field-drainage and water-irrigation systems. In addition to drainage pipes, other applications include ditch liners, headwall units, inspection chambers and junction boxes for drainage systems and channel or bank linings, canalets and junction or distribution boxes for irrigation water courses and distributory canals (*Figure 20.27*). GRC troughs have also been used as condensation and spray collection channels in motorway tunnels.

The principal advantages of GRC in this particular application include good resistance to erosion and chemical attack and high resistance to wear penetration, together with very good hydraulic flow characteristics. The relatively light weight of the GRC components and their toughness makes them simple to handle, transport and install with fewer breakages, particularly in areas of poor accessibility.

20.7.10 Marine applications

Glass-fibre reinforced cement (GRC) has been used around the world to form flotation units for pontoons. The sprayed GRC forms a protective coating over a low density core material (e.g. polystyrene) to form a strong, buoyant float. GRC has also been used as permanent formwork to protect reinforced concrete from the chlorides in seawater and sea-spray.

20.7.11 Renders

Renders containing alkali-resistant glass fibre are widely used in the agricultural industry in the construction of farm buildings. The strength of glass-fibre reinforced cement (GRC) renders allows walls to be built by stacking concrete blocks (*Figure 20.28*) without mortar, and applying a 5-mm thick skin to each face of the wall. The result is stronger than a conventionally mortar-jointed wall, and can be built more quickly.

The benefits of the high impact resistance of GRC are now extensively utilized in wall renders in security applications and for squash-court walls. The crack-suppressing properties of the glass fibre make it suitable for the reinstatement of weathered and deteriorated masonry.

20.7.12 Sewer, tunnel and shaft liners

Specially shaped glass-fibre reinforced cement (GRC) sections are made, both for the full relining and the invert lining, of old man-entry sewers and as a secondary lining or formwork for new sewers (*Figure 20.29*). The sprayed GRC linings have a good resistance to chemical attack and abrasion whilst offering very good flow characteristics.

In tunnelling, GRC is used both as permanent tunnel formwork, and for rock stabilization by site spraying directly onto the tunnel walls.

GRC sections are used as permanent formwork shaft liners and liners for spiral bunkers in coal mines. Its performance is enhanced by its good abrasion resistance, and the light weight of GRC sections makes them easy to handle underground.

20.8 Production

Glass-fibre reinforced cement (GRC) can be produced by several different techniques, ranging from simple manual processes to sophisticated mechanical systems. All systems first require the

Figure 20.27 GRC channels being used for irrigation in an Egyptian settlement project

Figure 20.28 'Three-man loading' of concrete blocks with no mortar joints and 3 mm skin of GRC on the top and the bottom

Figure 20.29 GRC sewer linings

Figure 20.30 Sector of 10-m diameter dome for export to the Middle East

production of a slurry of the matrix components. The fibre is then added, either at a further mixing stage or by simultaneous spraying on or into moulds. Moulds may be made of steel, timber, glass-fibre reinforced plastic (GRP), rubber, polystyrene or other similar materials which will give the required finish and allow demoulding with the use of a mould-release agent.

Once in the mould the product is compacted and, after being left to harden for a suitable time (typically overnight), the product is demoulded and taken to be cured. Care must be taken during the demoulding and early handling of products as they will not have attained their full strength.

As a guide to practical curing regimes, GRC products will achieve a substantial proportion of their ultimate strength when the main cure is carried out for 7 days, at >95% relative humidity, and at a minimum temperature of 15°C. A suitable post-curing regime will allow the remainder of the strength to be realized. The cure may be accelerated by the use of steam curing. By adding an acrylic polymer to the mix it is possible to cure GRC materials under ambient conditions because, providing the minimum film forming temperature (typically 10–15°C) is attained, the polymer forms a film around the mix particles, thereby retaining moisture.

The two principal processes used for the manufacture of GRC components are the 'spray' process and the 'premix' process.

20.8.1 Sprayed glass-fibre reinforced cement

In the manufacture of glass-fibre reinforced cement (GRC) by the 'spray' process, simultaneous sprays of cement and sand/mortar slurry and chopped alkali-resistant glass fibre are deposited simultaneously from a spray head into or onto a suitable mould. The spray head may be hand held or mounted on a machine. The mortar slurry is prepared in a high-dispersion mixer and is fed to the spray gun from a metering pump unit and is broken into droplets by compressed air. Alkali-resistant glass fibre roving is fed to a glass-fibre chopper–feeder mounted on the spray head, which chops the fibre to predetermined lengths (typically 25–40 mm) and injects the chopped strands into the mortar spray so that a uniform layer of fibre and mortar is deposited on the mould. The slurry typically has a sand:cement ratio of up to 1:1 and a water:cement ratio of 0.33. The water:cement ratio should be kept as low as possible, consistent with satisfactory spray and incorporation characteristics, because increasing the water:cement ratio leads to a reduction in the strength of the product. Admixtures may be used to achieve the required workability with minimum water

content. The proportion of fibre to slurry is adjusted so that the resulting composite contains, typically, 5% by weight of glass fibre.

Developments in mechanized spray equipment include a computer-controlled machine capable of spraying profiles such as channels at high output rates.

An example of the use of sprayed GRC is shown in *Figure 20.30*.

20.8.2 Premixed glass-fibre reinforced cement

The 'premix' process for producing glass-fibre reinforced cement (GRC) is more closely allied to precast concrete manufacture. The mixing process consists of two stages. The first is designed to produce a high-quality slurry and the second incorporates the alkali-resistant glass fibre into the mix.

The actual mix formulation used depends upon the type of product being made, but a typical mix has a sand:cement ratio of up to 1:1 and a water:cement ratio not exceeding 0.39. Up to 4% by weight of alkali-resistant glass-fibre chopped strands can be incorporated into the mix, although a more typical content is 3.5%. The fibre length may be in the range 3–25 mm, with 12 mm being the most common.

Premixed GRC can be used for vibration casting, injection moulding, pressing or extruding products.

20.8.3 Other processes

Formulations containing between 0.5% and 2.5% by weight of alkali-resistant fibre have been developed for rendering, applied either by spraying or trowelling to a thickness of 3–10 mm. The product is supplied as a dry, preblended, bagged mix, requiring only the addition of water. The finished render has superior resistance to impact and shrinkage cracking and is less permeable to water than normal sand/cement render. Fibre-reinforced renders are also used in dry-block wall construction and external insulation systems.

Other formulations containing similar quantities of fibre have been developed for screeds. The impact and crack resistance of the fibre-reinforced screeds enables them to be laid more thinly than conventional screeds (6–10 mm).

Alkali-resistant glass fibre added at a rate of approximately 1% by weight of total mix can also be used in normal sprayed concrete mixes to give improved cracking- and impact-resistance performance.

20.9 Process and quality control

Process- and quality-control procedures in glass-fibre reinforced cement (GRC) production are of vital importance to the producer. The control of raw material usage and quality of the GRC produced enables the producer to ensure that production is efficient and within budget. Records and data taken during manufacture provide the information necessary to give both producer and customer confidence that the products conform to the specification defined in the contract.

20.9.1 Process control

In order to control the production operation to ensure that raw-material losses can be kept to a minimum and the consistency and accuracy of mixes is maintained, there are certain tests which should be performed during production.

20.9.1.1 Raw-material testing

The factory testing of raw materials should only occasionally be necessary, provided that the relevant certification is provided by the suppliers. Such test certificates should be kept for reference in case any problems arise with a particular days production.

20.9.1.2 Slump test

The slump test is a simple test which ensures that the slurry workability is consistent. It will help to highlight any inaccuracies in the mix before the product is manufactured.

20.9.1.3 Fibre-content test

When spray equipment is being set up it is necessary to ensure that the correct proportions of slurry and glass fibre are being sprayed so that the required fibre content is achieved. This involves spraying the slurry and glass fibre separately for a set period of time and weighing the materials. The spray parameters can then be adjusted until the correct balance between glass fibre and slurry is achieved. This process check should be performed on each machine before starting production each day and after each shutdown for cleaning.

20.9.1.4 Thickness control

The thickness of cast glass-fibre reinforced cement (GRC) products is governed by the mould design. However, with sprayed GRC the thickness is more operator dependent. The panel thickness specified is the minimum for all points on the panel, and should be checked with a simple pin-gauge at a large number of points over the panel surface during spraying.

20.9.1.5 Glass-fibre 'wash-out' test

As well as the fibre-content test which is performed before spraying commences, it is recommended that the fibre content of the sprayed material is also tested. This is done by cutting samples from newly sprayed test boards, weighing them in a mesh basket, washing away the slurry to leave just the glass fibre, drying the fibre and reweighing. This allows accurate calculation of the fibre content of the mix.

20.9.2 Quality control

20.9.2.1 Test samples

Once the equipment has been set up and manufacture has commenced, at some time during that production run a glass-fibre reinforced cement (GRC) test board will be produced.

The dimensions of test board are typically $1000 \times 1000 \times 10$ mm thickness (and should be produced during each production run). After demoulding, the boards should be conditioned in the same environment as the products which they represent. Once cured, accurate test specimens (or coupons) should be accurately cut from the GRC board. The specimens for flexural testing should be 50 ± 1 mm in width and approximately 300 mm in length. The specimens should be cut from a region of board which is of uniform thickness and of smooth surface. In addition, 50×50 mm samples should also be taken from the board for the calculation of the density, apparent porosity and water absorption. In general, six of the larger test specimens are required to give an adequate average value of the flexural strengths (limit of proportionality and modulus of rupture). Specimens cut at different orientations will enable any directional characteristics of the board to be detected[18].

20.9.2.2 Mechanical testing of samples

The mechanical properties of glass-fibre reinforced cement may be determined from flexural tests.[12,31] The important parameters needed to assess the quality of material made are the limit of proportionality and the modulus of rupture. Test samples would normally be subjected to a four-point bend test in which the minor span distance must always be one-third of the major span distance, since this assumption is made in the calculation of the above two parameters. It is important to ensure that the ratio major-span:sample-thickness is not less than 16:1 and, ideally, is 20:1. The outer rollers of the test jig are, therefore, positioned correctly to achieve this ratio. This is done by measuring the thickness of the individual sample and moving the rollers accordingly to the correct position. The speed at which the test is performed will also affect the results. It is recommended that the crosshead speed should be approximately 2 mm min^{-1}. (See *Figures 20.31* and *20.32*.)

20.9.2.3 Product testing

With new products and new designs it will often be necessary to perform load tests on prototypes in order to determine the suitability of the design to meet expected loads. This is particularly important when, because of the complexity of the product, certain assumptions and simplifications must be made in the design. If products are being tested to failure the actual strength of the material will need to be determined by sample testing and the ratio of ultimate stress (e.g. modulus of rupture) to design stress should be less than the ratio of ultimate load to design load. This should keep the actual stress at design load within the design stress.

20.9.2.4 Recording test data

If the process- and quality-control tests are to be of any value, they will need to be accurately recorded. If there are any defects it should be possible to bring together raw-material test data and process- and quality-control test results related to the relevant production. The data should also be readily available in case it is needed by the engineer. In many cases the recording of test data will be a contractual requirement, or needed in order to conform with quality-assurance schemes.

20.10 Standards and product approvals

The need to establish standards for glass-fibre reinforced cement products in the industry has been recognized from the outset. Indeed, the original policy of releasing the technology to users through a development licence agreement, adopted by

Figure 20.31 Flexural testing with electronically controlled test machine

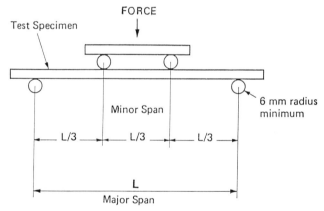

Figure 20.32 Typical test specimen

Pilkingtons when first making alkali-resistant glass fibre available commercially, was an endeavour to establish reliable standards of manufacture and to control applications within the boundaries of the understanding of the then new material. Subsequently, responsibility for industry standards was adopted by the Glassfibre Reinforced Cement Association (GRCA) and, more recently, national standards have been produced for various individual products.

The nature of the material is not, however, conducive to the preparation of simple standards. Unlike many materials which have closely defined composition and performance, GRC materials can have a wide range of compositions and different modes of production, resulting in a range of properties and durability characteristics. It is, therefore, necessary for materials standards to include both prescriptive clauses and performance criteria in order to ensure fitness for purpose. Similarly, standards for some GRC products must define material composition as well as performance.

20.10.1 Alkali-resistant glass fibre

There is, as yet, no British Standard governing alkali-resistant glass fibre, but GRCA Specification S 0105[32] defines rovings and chopped strands for reinforcement of cement and concrete, whilst GRCA specification S 0104[33] specifies the standard procedure for determining the strength retention of alkali-resistant glass fibre in cements and mortars.

20.10.2 Materials

GRCA Specification S 0108[31] defines the composition, quality and performance of Grade 21 glass-fibre reinforced cement (GRC), a general-purpose material normally produced by spray processing for use in applications such as cladding panels where reliable uniform in-plane strength and good durability are required to ensure satisfactory product design.

20.10.3 Test methods

GRCA Specification S 0103[34] describes standard test procedures for glass-fibre reinforced cement (GRC) materials, as does BS 6432: 1984.[12]

20.10.4 Product standards

Standard specifications for individual glass-fibre reinforced cement (GRC) products include the following.

1. BS 3445: 1981, Fixed agricultural water troughs and water fittings.
2. BS 6171: 1982, Prefabricated solid-fuel storage bunkers.
3. DD 76: 1981, Precast concrete pipes strengthened by continuous alkali-resistant glass-fibre rovings.
4. GRCA S 0106, Guide to specification for glass-fibre reinforced cement cladding.

20.10.5 Product approvals

1. British Board of Agrément Certificate No. 82/1016, Fibrocem blockmix glass-fibre reinforced rendering.
2. British Board of Agrément Certificate No. 81/833, Alkali-resistant cement Slimline glass-fibre reinforced cement pipes.
3. British Board of Agrément Certificate No. 85/1458, Tunnel glass-fibre reinforced cement slates.

20.10.6 Standards in preparation

Specifications for the following product groups, which include glass-fibre reinforced cement (GRC) products, are currently under preparation by ISO and CEN Technical Committees and will eventually form the basis of British Standards.

1. Fibre-reinforced cement slates.
2. Fibre-reinforced cement corrugated sheets.
3. Fibre-reinforced cement flat sheets.
4. Sprayed non-polymer GRC cladding.
5. Method for determing the strength retention of glass fibre in cement and mortar.

20.10.7 Overseas standards and product approvals

Many product specifications have been published by approval authorities in overseas countries, including those listed below.

20.10.7.1 American Society for Testing Materials

1. ASTM C947-81, Standard test method for flexural properties of thin-section glass-fibre reinforced cement.
2. ASTM C948-81, Standard test method for dry and wet bulk density, water absorption and apparent porosity of thin-section glass-fibre reinforced cement.
3. ASTM C887-79a, Standard specification for packaged dry combined materials for surface bonding mortar.

20.10.7.2 Prestressed Concrete Institute (PCI), USA

1. Recommended practice for glass-fiber reinforced cement panels, *Journal of PCI*, **26** (1981).
2. Guide specification for glass-fiber reinforced cement panels.

20.10.7.3 CSTB, France

1. GS1: Préfabrication lourde (Groupe Specialisé No. 1).
   Avis Technique préalable, mure des façade Girec 5 (16 Nov. 1987).
   Avis Technique d'usine, Betsinor No. 1/87-594.
2. GS7: Etanchéité et isolation de parois verticales.
   Avis Technique Cridotherm Colle, Ste Appli 5 No.

7/87-592 (modificatif au No. 7/85-401).
Avis Technique Cridotherm fixé mécaniquement, Ste Appli 5 No. 7/87-552.
Avis Technique Ste Creabat Véture PBF 450, No. 7/87-524.
3. GS16: Produits et procédés spéciaux pour la maçonnerie.
   Avis Technique préalable Brugeaud BHE (29 Oct. 1987).
   Avis Technique d'usine Brugeaud BHE No. 16/87-170.
   Avis Technique préalable Manuboie Ste Saret (9 Jun. 1987).
   Avis Technique d'usine Ste Saret No. 16/87-175.

20.10.7.4 South African Bureau of Standards

SABS (1969): Concrete non-pressure pipes (Amendment No. 4, 1979).

20.11 The Glassfibre Reinforced Cement Association (GRCA)

Formed in 1975, the GRCA has a worldwide membership of companies engaged in the glass-fibre reinforced cement industry. Associate membership is also available for professionals, other associations and those not engaged in the industry.

The Association publishes a variety of specifications and literature and organizes a major series of biennial international congresses. A Register of Members and Product Index is also available on request from the Administration Office.

The Glassfibre Reinforced Cement Association
107 Standishgate
Wigan
WN1 1XL

Tel. (0942) 825371
Fax. (0942) 495469

Acknowledgements

Acknowledgements are made to all those members of the Glass-fibre Reinforced Cement Association who have freely provided information, photographs and illustrations for use in this article, particularly to Cem-Flh International Ltd and the Glass-fibre Reinforced Cement Association itself, who allowed extensive use of their various technical reports and publications in preparing this article.

References

1 BRITISH STANDARDS INSTITUTION, *BS 12 Ordinary and rapid-hardening Portland cement*, Milton Keynes (1978)
2 BRITISH STANDARDS INSTITUTION, *BS 812: Parts 1, 2, 3 Testing aggregates*, Milton Keynes (1975)
3 BRITISH STANDARDS INSTITUTION, *BS 1014 Pigments for Portland cement*, Milton Keynes 1975 (1986)
4 AVESTON, J., COOPER, G. A. and KELLY, A., 'Single and multiple fracture', *The Properties of Fibre Composites*, IPC Science and Technology Press, pp. 15–26, Guildford (1971)
5 NAIR, N. G., 'Mechanics of glass fibre reinforced cement', *RILEM Symposium, Fibre Reinforced Cement and Concrete*, The Construction Press Ltd, pp. 81–93 (1975)
6 OAKLEY, D. R. and PROCTOR, B. A., 'Tensile stress–strain behaviour of glass fibre reinforced cement composites', *RILEM Symposium, Fibre Reinforced Cement and Concrete*, The Construction Press Ltd, pp. 347–359 (1975)

7 PROCTOR, B. A., OAKLEY, D. R. and WIECHERS, W., 'Tensile stress/strain characteristics of glass fibre reinforced cement', *Composites—Standards Testing and Design*, IPC Science and Technology Press, pp. 106–107, Guildford (1974)

8 LAWS, V. and WALTON, P. L., 'The tensile–bending relationship for fibre reinforced brittle matrices', *RILEM Symposium Testing and Test Methods of Fibre Cement Composites*, The Construction Press Ltd, pp. 429–438 (1978)

9 OAKLEY, D. R., *2nd International Symposium: The Mechanical Properties of Glass Reinforced Cement Composites*, Weitgespannte Flachentragwerke, SFB 64, pp. 160–167 (1979)

10 LAWS, V., 'The relationship between tensile and bending properties of non-linear composite materials', *Journal of Materials Science*, **17**, 2919–2924 (1982)

11 ROARK, R. J., *Formulas for Stress and Strain*, 5th edn, McGraw-Hill, New York, pp. 198–199 (1975)

12 BRITISH STANDARDS INSTITUTION, *BS 6432 Methods for determining properties of glass-fibre reinforced cement material*, Milton Keynes (1984)

13 LITHERLAND, K. L., OAKLEY, D. R. and PROCTOR, B. A., 'The use of accelerated ageing procedures to predict the long-term strength of GRC composites', *Cement and Concrete Research*, Vol. 11, Pergamon Press, Oxford, pp. 455–466 (1981)

14 GLASSFIBRE REINFORCED CEMENT ASSOCIATION (GRCA), 'GRCA method of test for strength retention of glass fibre in cements and mortars', *GRCA S 0104/0184*, The Glassfibre Reinforced Cement Association, Newport (Jan. 1984)

15 LITHERLAND, K. L., OAKLEY, D. R. and PROCTOR, B. A., 'The use of accelerated ageing procedures to predict the long term strength of GRC composites', *Cement and Concrete Research*, **11**, 455–466 (1981)

16 BUILDING RESEARCH ESTABLISHMENT, *Information Paper IP 36/79*, Garston (1979)

17 PROCTOR, B. A., 'Past development and future prospect for GRC materials', *Proceedings of 3rd International Congress on Glass Fibre Reinforced Cement, Paris, 1981*, Glass Reinforced Cement Association, pp. 50–67 (1981)

18 PROCTOR, B. A., OAKLEY, D. R. and LITHERLAND, K. L., 'Developments in the assessment and performance of GRC over 10 years', *Composites*, 173–179 (Apr. 1982)

19 BRITISH STANDARDS INSTITUTION, *BS 4624 Asbestos and asbestos building products*, Milton Keynes (1970)

20 DIN, *DIN 274 Asbestos cement sheets, asbestos cement boards* (1936)

21 AMERICAN SOCIETY FOR TESTING MATERIALS, *ASTM C666-73 Procedure A—resistance of concrete to rapid freezing and thawing*, Philadelphia

22 BRITISH STANDARDS INSTITUTION, *BS 3177 Method for determining the permeability to water vapour of flexible sheet materials used for packaging*, Milton Keynes (1959)

23 BRITISH STANDARDS INSTITUTION, *BS 473.550 Specification for concrete roofing tiles and fittings*, Milton Keynes (1980)

24 AMERICAN SOCIETY FOR TESTING MATERIALS, *ASTM C418-68*, Philadelphia

25 ROARK, R. J. and YOUNG, W. C., *Formulas for Stress and Strain*, 5th edn, McGraw-Hill, New York (1975)

26 BRITISH STANDARDS INSTITUTION, *BS 476: Part 4 Non-combustibility test for materials*, Milton Keynes (1984)

27 BRITISH STANDARDS INSTITUTION, *BS 476: Part 6 Method of test for fire propagation for products*, Milton Keynes (1981)

28 BRITISH STANDARDS INSTITUTION, *BS 476: Part 7 Method of classification of the surface spread of flame of products*, Milton Keynes (1987)

29 BRITISH STANDARDS INSTITUTION, *BS 476: Part 8 Test methods and criteria for the fire resistance of elements of building construction*, Milton Keynes (1972)

30 CENTRAL ELECTRICITY GENERATING BOARD (CEGB), *Specification E/TSS/EX5/7080 Issue 5*

31 GLASSFIBRE REINFORCED CEMENT ASSOCIATION, 'Specification for glass fibre reinforced cement (GRC) material: grade 21', *GRCA S 0108/0187*, Glassfibre Reinforced Cement Association, Newport (Jan. 1987)

32 GLASSFIBRE REINFORCED CEMENT ASSOCIATION, 'Specification for alkali-resistant glass fibre rovings and chopped strands for reinforcement of cements and concretes', *GRCA S 0105/0286*, The Glassfibre Reinforced Cement Association, Newport (Feb. 1986)

33 GLASSFIBRE REINFORCED CEMENT ASSOCIATION, 'GRCA method of test for strength retention of glass fibre in cements and mortars', *GRCA S 0104/0184*, The Glassfibre Reinforced Cement Association, Newport (Jan. 1984)

34 GLASSFIBRE REINFORCED CEMENT ASSOCIATION, 'GRCA methods of testing glass-fibre reinforced cement (GRC) material', *GRCA S 0103/0481*, The Glassfibre Reinforced Cement Association, Newport (Jun. 1981)

Bibliography

TRUE, G. F., *GRC Production and Uses*, Associated Book Publishers (1986)

PRESTRESSED CONCRETE INSTITUTE, *Recommended Practice for Glass Fiber Reinforced Concrete Panels*, Prestressed Concrete Institute, USA

GLASSFIBRE REINFORCED CEMENT ASSOCIATION (GRCA), *Full Proceedings of GRCA Biennial Congresses* (seven publications, covering seven congresses, available separately), The Glassfibre Reinforced Cement Association, Newport

21

Mortars, Renders and Screeds

R A Sykes BSc
Wimpey Environmental Ltd

Contents

21.1 Introduction 21/3

21.2 Mortar 21/3
    21.2.1 Purpose of mortar 21/3
    21.2.2 Mortar materials 21/3
    21.2.3 Types and properties of masonry mortars 21/3
    21.2.4 Site batching and mixing of masonry mortars 21/3
    21.2.5 Ready-to-use mortars 21/4
    21.2.6 Assessment of physical properties of mortars 21/4
    21.2.7 Analysis of mortars 21/4
    21.2.8 Winter working with mortars 21/5
    21.2.9 Problems with masonry mortars 21/5

21.3 Rendering 21/5
    21.3.1 Purpose of rendering mortars 21/5
    21.3.2 Rendering materials 21/5
    21.3.3 Types and properties of renders 21/5
    21.3.4 Application of rendering materials 21/6
    21.3.5 Application of rendering to external insulation materials 21/6
    21.3.6 Problems with rendering 21/7

21.4 Screeds 21/7
    21.4.1 Purpose of screeds 21/7
    21.4.2 Screed materials 21/7
    21.4.3 Types and properties of screed 21/7
    21.4.4 Mixing of screed materials 21/8
    21.4.5 Laying and curing of screed 21/8
    21.4.6 Problems with screeds 21/8

References 21/8

Bibliography 21/9

21.1 Introduction

This chapter deals with masonry mortars, rendering and floor screeds produced with mixes based on cement, lime and sand. The characteristics of different specifications are described, and guidance on factors that can affect the performance of the materials is given. Finishes for renders and screeds which are of other than cementitious materials are not included in this section.

21.2 Mortar

21.2.1 Purpose of mortar

The purpose of mortar is to bond masonry units to produce a continuous load-bearing element which will provide protection from wind and rain. In order to perform for an adequate period, generally the order of decades, the mortar must be formed of durable materials and be compatible with the units to which it is bound. Although made up of simple materials, the requirements of a mortar can be complex in that it has to satisfy one range of parameters when plastic and a further set of parameters when hardened. In the plastic state, mortar must be workable in order to enable the bricklayer to spread the material easily and of a consistency for it to adhere but not stiffen too rapidly. In the hardened state, mortar must provide a degree of resistance to rain penetration, be frost resistant and contribute to the strength of the masonry.

21.2.2 Mortar materials

Mortars are made up of sand in conjunction with one or more of the following materials: ordinary Portland cement, blast-furnace cement, sulphate-resisting cement, masonry cement, lime, plasticizers, air-entraining agents or other admixtures including pigments and water. A relatively recent development is the modification of mortars with organic resins.

Sands for masonry mortars should comply with BS 1200.[1] This standard relates to crushed-gravel sands or crushed-stone sands in addition to naturally occurring ones. Sand should be hard, clean and free from deleterious materials. The specification limits make allowance for fine sands which have evidence of satisfactory performance in use. Fine materials make the mortar easy to work in the plastic state but may lead to lower ultimate strength and, if fine and silty, also shrink on drying out. Conversely, a relatively coarse sand with low fines content can produce a mortar with poor workability as water is not retained and bleeding out can occur.

Cements should comply with: BS 12[2] (ordinary and rapid-hardening Portland cement), or BS 146[3] (Portand blast furnace cement), or BS 4027[4] (sulphate-resisting cement), or BS 5244[5] (masonry cement) which contains a proportion of non-cementitious material.

Lime for masonry mortar is usually non-hydraulic. It can be mixed on site from dry hydrated lime or is available already mixed, proportioned with sand, and known as 'coarse stuff'.

21.2.3 Types and properties of masonry mortars

British Standards, brick manufacturers and block manufacturers recommend a range of cement and sand volume proportions for mortars for use in different situations. Mortar properties should be related to the strength and drying shrinkage, moisture and thermal movement characteristics of the masonry units. The mortar strength should be the lowest possible, taking into account structural requirements and durability. In addition to cement providing strength to a mortar, it also exhibits drying shrinkage and reduces the capability to accommodate movement. The risk of cracking of masonry built with units of high drying shrinkage characteristics, such as calcium silicate bricks or low-density concrete blocks, is reduced by using a low-strength mortar. These low-strength mortars accommodate movement by developing many fine cracks. Similarly, cracking due to thermal movement in very long walls, such as those enclosing large estates, used to be avoided by using weak lime mortars. In specific brickwork detailing such as parapets and copings, high cement content and hence high-strength mortars are necessary for durability. Methods for achieving a compromise between these various properties are given in *Table 21.1*.

21.2.4 Site batching and mixing of masonry mortars

The performance of a mortar is closely related to the proportion of binder and, in particular, cement content and, therefore, weighing the materials provides the most accurate batching. Traditionally, mix proportions are described by volume which necessitates gauging boxes. This demands a double handling operation with transfer of materials to the boxes and then to the mixer. The water content of both sand and lime influences their bulk and this must be allowed for in volume proportioning. Damp sand can occupy 35% greater volume than a similar

Table 21.1 Mortar mixes[a]

		Mortar designation	Type of mortar		
			Cement:lime:sand (by volume)	Air-entrained mixes	
				Masonry cement:sand (by volume)	Cement:sand with plasticizer (by volume)
Increasing strength and improving durability	Increasing ability to accommodate movements due to temperature and moisture changes	i	1:0 to 0.25:3		
		ii	1:0.25:4 to 4.5	1:2.5 to 3.5	1:3 to 4
		iii	1:1:5 to 6	1:4 to 5	1:5 to 6
		iv	1:2:8 to 9	1:5.5 to 6.5	1:7 to 8
		v	1:3:10 to 12	1:6.5 to 7	1:8

Increasing resistance to frost attack during construction ⟶
Improvement in adhesion and consequent resistance to rain penetration ⟵

[a] Courtesy of British Standards Institution. Direction of change in properties is shown by the arrows.

weight of dry sand. In practical terms, bucket and shovel batching is used for the sand which introduces a persistent inaccuracy, and cement addition to standard, small, rotating-drum mixers is basically as a full bag or as half a bag. The number of mortar specifications should, therefore, be kept to a minimum.

The sand and lime materials should be placed in the mixer prior to the addition of cement. Only sufficient water to provide adequate workability should then be added. Any additive should be proportioned in accordance with the manufacturer's instructions. Mortar should be thoroughly mixed, but over-mixing, particularly of air-entrained mortars, must be avoided. Continuous mixing, with partial discharging of the mixer contents, followed by make-up replenishment materials fed to the mixer can lead to very variable mortar proportions.

21.2.5 Ready-to-use mortars

Ready-to-use retarded-cement mortars reduce the problems associated with site-mixing operations, particularly inaccurate batching and colour variation. Material is readily available for the bricklayer when he is on site. Raw-material ordering and storage is reduced as is the mixing plant and associated batching control. This all takes place under controlled conditions at purpose-built batching plants with more efficient mixing and weighing control apparatus.

Designers must be aware of practical considerations associated with these mortars. Unlike a retarded floor-screed mix which is placed over a concrete base as an additional layer potentially requiring only compatibility with the substrate, retarded mortars are required to be compatible with a range of substrates varying from dense aggregate to aerated concrete blocks and fletton to Staffordshire Blue bricks, all of which have varying absorption properties. The mortars are generally best suited to bricks and blocks of high to medium suction which removes water relatively rapidly from the green mortar and permits initial stiffening of the mortar. The practice recommended by brick manufacturers for controlling suction by prewetting bricks must be considered, in conjunction with recommendations for weather protection of bricks on site prior to use. Where the mortar is used with low-suction bricks or blocks, the mortar producers should be advised as stiffening times can become increased to the extent that severe limits are placed on the number of courses that can be laid without slipping occurring. In addition to retarding admixtures, these mortars generally incorporate an air-entraining agent, either complementing or supplementing lime, to provide workability and durability in terms of frost resistance. Ready-to-use mortars complying with BS 4721[6] can generally be used for two working days. Rapid changes in weather conditions can influence the stiffening times. These mortars in particular must not be tempered with water once they have stiffened.

The factory production of ready-to-use mortars, often with blending of sands to achieve the appropriate grading requirements of BS 1200,[1] consistently leads to the production of higher strength mortars than for site-produced mortars.

Preparation of cubes for compressive-strength testing with retarded mortars under site conditions can lead to more than 7 days within steel moulds being needed prior to demoulding without collapse of the cubes. The lack of suction of the moulds and with the minimum designed stiffening times of BS 4721[6] mortars of 36 h can lead to actual stiffening times in excess of 60 or 70 h, followed by curing times in excess of 36 h to enable the cubes to be strong enough to demould satisfactorily.

21.2.6 Assessment of physical properties of mortars

BS 4551[7] for methods of testing mortar screeds and plasters provides methods for testing mortars comparatively, based on a standard consistence measurement. Consistence is not strictly comparable to the workability required by a bricklayer. It is a basic characteristic which permits direct comparison of the strength, flow and stiffening time of different mortars. Testing carried out on mortars used by the bricklayer, for compressive strength, should only be applied as a means of controlling batch quality, i.e. cement content. If mortars are specified by volume to BS 5628: Part 3,[8] no guidance on mortar strengths is given. The actual strength obtainable must be established for the sands being used.

A useful guide for practical purposes is that given in *Table 21.2* which gives a range of mortar strengths that have been used by one major building contractor for over 30 years as a method of controlling batch quality. The guidance provided in BS 5628: Part 1[9] should be treated with caution and specifiers should be certain that the requirements are fully understood before mortars are specified by strength rather than by volume batching. The mortar strengths given are for mortars of special category of construction control only. To achieve these mortar-strength limits it is not uncommon to find that local building sands require changes in nominal volume proportions with higher cement contents being required. BS 5628: Part 1[9] gives only the minimum strength and it is not uncommon for the lower limits to be greatly exceeded where attempts are made to ensure that no mortar-test results fall below the minimum. This is not only uneconomic in terms of cement usage but may, in some circumstances, be technically unacceptable.

21.2.7 Analysis of mortars

Once in place and hardened, establishing the strength of brickwork mortar is impractical. Where assessment is required, mix proportions of set mortars can be determined. In order to assess the material placed between bricks and blocks, chemical analysis in accordance with BS 4551[7] can be used to determine

Table 21.2 Expected strength range of ordinary Portland cement mortars

Masonry and rendering mortars BS designation	Volume mix proportions		Compressive strength at 7 days (N mm^{-2})				
	Cement:sand	Cement:lime: sand	Category A	Category B		Category C	
			Satisfactory	High	Low	High	Low
iii	1:6	1:1:6	0.7–3.0	3.0–7.0	—	>7.0	<0.7
ii	—	2:1:9	1.7–4.8	4.8–7.0	0.7–1.7	>7.0	<0.7
ii	1:4.5	—	1.9–6.0	6.0–8.6	0.9–1.9	>8.6	<0.9
i	1:3	1:0.25:3	4.5–10.4	10.4–12.0	3.0–4.5	>12.0	<3.0

[a] Category A, satisfactory batching control; category B, batching should be checked; category C, likely to cause failure.

the constituents of mortars. The accuracy with which mix proportions of hardened mortars can be determined depends on the particular constituents of the mortar and also, to some extent, on the skill and experience of the analyst. Physical examination of the samples is an important part of the assessment. The determination depends on the measurement of the content of calcium compounds and soluble silica in the mix. Sands which contain limestone, sea shells or other sources of calcium compounds or which contain soluble silica materially affect the accuracy of the test. For this reason it is necessary either to provide samples of the original materials or the equivalent information. For example, in cases where a cement:lime:sand mortar is made with calcareous aggregate there is little chance of obtaining a result of meaningful accuracy. It should also be noted that, although this method of chemical analysis is used by engineers to assess the composition and, hence, characteristic strength of mortar of Victorian or early 20th century buildings, the results may be unreliable. The determination is for analyses of modern hydrated lime and ordinary Portland cement. The hydraulic limes and cements available in the Victorian era are likely to have differing chemical and physical properties.

21.2.8 Winter working with mortars

Winter working with mortars must be restricted to temperatures above 3°C. Attempts to use steam in place of mixing water, or to provide heating for the aggregates, and ensuring that hot cements are used in the mortar mix, will not ensure adequate temperature conditions. Over 80% of the bulk of any masonry construction is in the bricks or blocks. For practical purposes these cannot be kept heated in low ambient-temperature conditions. This results in mortars attaining low temperatures in the completed work. For sub-zero temperatures, antifreeze should not be used in the mortar mix as the masonry units will also be below freezing.

21.2.9 Problems with masonry mortars

Failures associated with mortars in service can be both physical and chemical.

The durability of a mortar to weathering is dependent upon the binder content. The higher the cement content, the more durable the mortar.

Cracking of mortar may be either associated with structural movement or incompatibility between moisture or thermal movement of the masonry units to which it is bound. The addition of lime to mortar can, however, reduce the effects of cracking as it can produce autogenous healing of hairline cracks.

Mortars can be chemically attacked by sulphates from groundwater, some fired-clay products, atmospheric pollution or byproducts from industrial processes or solid-fuel-burning fires. In construction using bricks of known high soluble sulphates contents, in conditions where they are likely to remain wet for considerable periods, the mortar for bonding the units should be made using sulphate-resisting cement. In ground conditions with potential high sulphate bearing waters, sulphate-resisting cement should also be used. The use of sulphate-resisting cement minimizes problems of chemical attack, but does not prevent them occurring.

With fresh mortars applied in low-temperature conditions, frost attack can occur. The water present in the mortar which has developed limited strength expands on freezing to disrupt the mortar material. Air entrainment considerably increases the resistance of fresh mortar to frost attack. Calcium chloride is not an appropriate accelerator/antifreeze because it can result in the mortar being continually damp due to its hydroscopic

nature and, in addition, it can promote corrosion of metal components such as wall ties.

21.3 Rendering

21.3.1 Purpose of rendering mortars

Cement-based coatings can be applied, generally to masonry backgrounds, either as internal plastering or external rendering to produce a uniform surface to which finishes may be applied. External renders also perform the function of improving the weather resistance of the masonry. Like brickwork mortars, renders are basically made up of sand and cement with lime or other additives to provide the required performance.

21.3.2 Rendering materials

Sands for rendering should be of the appropriate grading, preferably complying with BS 1199,[1] clean and free from deleterious material. The sharpest sand that can be satisfactorily handled should be used for undercoats, and final coats where the finish texture can be achieved. Coarse particles may have to be removed where the final coat is finished by being tooled. Cements recommended for brickwork mortars are suitable for rendering.

Additives can be used in rendering to retain water and assist workability. For specialist applications, polymers and glass fibre can be introduced to reduce shrinkage.

Any pigments used should be to BS 1014.[10] Depending upon the sand used, with some dark colours some lime bloom may be seen.

21.3.3 Types and properties of renders

The specification of a rendering mix is determined by its required performance and type of finish.

BS 5262[11] for external rendering states a range of volume proportions of cement, lime and sand for rendering mixes for differing situations of exposure conditions and background substrates.

BS 5492[12] for internal plastering provides specifications for a range of backgrounds with various finish requirements and includes cementitious renders in addition to gypsum plasters.

To avoid risks of cracking, the render must be compatible with the background. The undercoat or backing coat must be the strongest coat, to be followed by successively weaker coats. The appropriate mixes suitable for rendering and the recommended mixes for background and exposure are given in *Tables 21.3* and *21.4* for external applications. The more severe the exposure the greater the need for a stronger final coat.

Cementitious renders for internal plasters are generally of similar composition for both undercoats and final coats. Mix types I, III or IV are suitable for dense and moderately strong backgrounds depending on whether very strong to weak final surfaces are required. A type-III or type-IV mix is recommended where gypsum/lime or weak lime finishes are to be used. On metal lathing, type-III or type-IV mixes are recommended for internal plasters.

The satisfactory performance of rendering depends upon the design specification in addition to the appropriate specification for the mix determined by background properties and exposure conditions. External rendering must be adequately protected at all edges from the ingress of water. Detailing must ensure that there is an overhang, or flashing, at the top and edges of the render and care must be taken around openings—particularly at sills—to prevent water ingress. Rendering should preferably not be applied below damp-proof course, and should be designed to throw off water away from the wall. At parapets, render

Table 21.3 Mixes suitable for rendering[a]

| Mix type | Cement:lime:sand | Cement:ready-mixed lime:sand | | Cement:sand (using plasticizer) | Masonry cement:sand |
		Ready-mixed lime:sand	Cement:ready-mixed material		
I	1:0.25:3	1:12	1:3	—	—
II	1:0.5:4 to 4.5	1:8 to 9	1:4 to 4.5	1:3 to 4	1:2.5 to 3.5
III	1:1:5 to 6	1:6	1:5 to 6	1:5 to 6	1:4 to 5
IV	1:2:8 to 9	1:4.5	1:8 to 9	1:7 to 8	1:5.5 to 6.5

[a] Courtesy of British Standards Institution.

Table 21.4 Recommended mixes for external renderings in relation to background materials, exposure conditions and finish required[a]

| Background material | Type of finish | First and subsequent undercoats | | | Final cost | | |
		Severe	Moderate	Sheltered	Severe	Moderate	Sheltered
Dense, strong, smooth	Wood float	II or III	II or III	II or III	III	III or IV	III or IV
	Scraped or textured	II or III	II or III	II or III	III	III or IV	III or IV
	Roughcast	I or II	I or II	I or II	II	II	II
	Dry dash	I or II	I or II	I or II	II	II	II
Moderately strong, porous	Wood float	II or III	III or IV	III or IV	III	III or IV	III or IV
	Scraped or textured	III	III or IV	III or IV	III	III or IV	III or IV
	Roughcast	II	II	II	As undercoats		
	Dry dash	II	II	II			
Moderately weak, porous	Wood float	III	III or IV	III or IV			
	Scraped or textured	III	III or IV	III or IV			
	Dry dash	III	III	III	As undercoats		
Metal lathing	Wood float	I, II or III	I, II or III	I, II or III	II or III	II or III	II or III
	Scraped or textured	I, II or III	I, II or III	I, II or III	III	III	III
	Roughcast	I or II	I or II	I or II	II	II	II
	Dry dash	I or II	I or II	I or II	II	II	II

[a] Courtesy of British Standards Institution.

should not be applied to both faces as evaporation of water will be restricted.

Movement joints should not be rendered over. The geometry of rendering should be kept as near to square as possible, with the proportion of height to length being no greater than 1:1.5. Panels of rendering should be no more than 25 m².

21.3.4 Application of rendering materials

The successful application of rendering depends upon the correct preparation of the substrate for the backing coat. The preparation can range from cleaning down and damping, to raking out of joints or requiring the fixing of expanded metal lathing.

For external rendering the prepared background is first given a backing coat which should be applied and allowed to shrink and dry out for as long as possible before the second coat is applied. The backing coat should be as uniform in thickness as possible, being between 8 and 16 mm thick. The surface should be scratched when stiffened to provide a key for the following coat. On three-coat work, the second coat should be applied 8–13 mm thick and scratched to receive the finish coat. Three-coat applications are generally used on metal lathing, woodwool slabs and in high-exposure conditions.

The finish coats to external rendering can be wet dash, dry dash, textured finish or plain finish. The wet dash or rough cast mix is thrown directly onto the undercoat. For dry dashing a

final 10 mm render coat is applied. Aggregate which has been wetted sufficiently to dampen the aggregate surface is thrown into the final render coat. For textured finishes, a final coat of between 10 and 13 mm is applied. For plain coats, a wood-float finish is applied to a 6–10 mm finish coat.

For internal work, two-coat work should be of the order of 10–13 mm, and three-coat work of the order of 19 mm total thickness. A reasonably smooth and flat surface can be achieved with two coats, but three-coat work may be required to achieve plumb.

Where the top coat is also the final finish, a wood-float finish should be applied.

21.3.5 Application of rendering to external insulation materials

Where rendering is applied over external insulation, the specification and control of mixes becomes critical. Any insulation, whether polymer, inorganic rigid foam board, or inorganic fibre batt, is a relatively weak or friable background on which to apply rendering and a reinforcement mesh or lathing is necessary to support the backing coat. As with rendering to lathing, a second undercoat and finish coat is applied. The rendering on external insulation is subjected to exposure conditions more severe than on a masonry background in the same location in terms of both thermal and moisture movement. There is no heat sink provided by the background insulation as would be the case with masonry. This causes the render to be subjected to a wider temperature range. With the low permeability of the insulant, the render has a higher moisture content in relative terms as there can be no absorption by the masonry background. The likelihood of cracking is, therefore, greater. Raw-material specification and control, by means of maintaining appropriate sand grading, reducing variability between mix batches and, in application, controlling variations in rendering thickness, will contribute to reducing the risks of cracking of the rendering. Many proprietary external insulation systems with cementitious rendering have prebagged aggregates or render mixes which may include polymer or fibre additives to assist in reducing the risks of cracking. These reduce the variability of the raw materials for use in the rendering. The risks of failure due to thermal movement can also be reduced by the use of light-coloured renders. In addition detailing requires more close attention especially for movement at joints and around openings.

21.3.6 Problems with rendering

Failures of rendering can be attributed to problems in design, materials or application. By design, all external rendering must be protected from ingress of water at its perimeter in order to prevent cracking or loss of bond. Rendering can limit the ingress of water to a substrate but it is not, in itself, totally waterproof.

The substrate to which rendering is applied also limits the durability properties of the rendering that can be applied. As the density of concrete blocks used for the background is reduced below about $1500 \, \text{kg m}^{-3}$, generally to improve thermal performance properties of the building, the tendency for cracking to occur within string rendering will increase because of differential thermal and moisture movements. The likelihood of cracking can be reduced in this situation or where the substrate is friable, by using expanded metal lathing. The lathing must be rigidly secured, especially in situations where there is timber or insulation material between the reinforcement and the substrate. The first coat of rendering applied to the lathing should be scratched to provide a key for subsequent coats and must be allowed to dry out for a sufficient period to allow for shrinkage.

Cracking of rendering as a result of sulphate attack may occur with bricks of high sulphate content being used as the background in conditions of high risk of exposure to water. Expansion of the cement in the brickwork mortar or in the render backing coat can lead to disruption of the rendering. Where bricks of high soluble sulphate content have to be used as a background for rendering, sulphate-resisting cement should be used in the brickwork mortar and the render backing coat. The sulphate-resisting cement only reduces the risks of sulphate attack. Detailing to maintain the bricks in as protected conditions as possible is equally important.

Complete isolation of the rendering from the background can be achieved with metal lathing over a separating membrane.

Crazing of the surface coat is generally indicative of a too rapid drying of the surface coat either in conjunction with a relatively high cement content, or with the use of a too fine sand in the render coat. Crazing is also commonly caused by the use of a steel float to provide the finish which brings a cement-rich layer of laitence to the surface.

For a smooth, plain surface finish, a wood float should be used and the surface must not be too rigorously worked over.

Cracking and hollowness in renders can be the result of a low pressure of application of the render, in that no key is formed between coats, or where high relative shrinkage between layers can take place. Within a typical render with two interfaces there are four surfaces, each of which can be an area of potential failure. The use of a weak first-coat mix followed by a strong

second coat will produce shear between the two bonding surfaces that may result in failure of the weaker coat or shrinkage cracking of the strong coat.

21.4 Screeds

21.4.1 Purpose of screeds

The purpose of a screed is to provide, by means of a layer of mortar, a level surface in flooring applications and to provide falls in flat concrete roofs. Screeds are designed for application over a concrete sub-base to receive surface finishes which may range from thin flexible sheeting to ceramic tiling. A screed is not intended to be the final wearing surface.

21.4.2 Screed materials

Screed mortars generally comprise sand and cement, both of which can be modified by additives or partially, or wholly substituted by other materials such as polymers in order to provides specific performance requirements. For thick screed layers it is not unusual to add a proportion of 10-mm aggregate.

For producing satisfactory screeds, the specification for the sand in a sand/cement screed mortar should be a fine aggregate complying with BS 882: 1983[13] grading limit M of Table 5, but with not more than 10% of the sand passing sieve size 150 μm. In addition, the aggregates must not contain deleterious material such as coal or iron particles which may affect the finished surface of the screed. The cements for screeds should be of the same specification as for brickwork mortars.

Admixtures for sand and cement screeds can assist workability or alter rates of setting and hardening. The admixtures should comply with the appropriate part of BS 5075.[14] A number of polymer-based additives are available to improve adhesion and strength for thin or feathering screeds. These are based on polyvinyl acetate (PVA) styrene butadiene rubber (SBR) or acrylic polymers.

Ready-to-use cement and sand screeds are available which should comply with the screed materials requirements and BS 4721.[6]

To enable floor finishes to be completed more rapidly, the need for screeds with rapid drying times can be made with proprietary screeds that should be mixed and applied in accordance with the manufacturer's instructions.

21.4.3 Types and properties of screed

Screeds can be designed to be applied in one of four ways.

1. Monolithic with the concrete base. This requires the screed to be applied within 3 h of placing the concrete base.
2. Bonded to the concrete base. The screed is laid onto a concrete base which has hardened and subsequently been prepared on the surface to receive the screed. The minimum thickness of the screed at any point should be 25 mm. Thickness of a bonded screed above 40 mm should be avoided to reduce risks of curling and cracking.
3. As an unbonded screed. The screed is laid on a separating layer, which may be a damp-proof course. This form of screed construction gives the shortest drying time prior to application of the finish layer, as drying-out periods will depend only on screed thickness and not those of the combined concrete base and screed. The minimum thickness of the screed at any point should be 50 mm.
4. As a floating screed. The screed is laid on an insulating material. The minimum thickness of the screed at any point should be 65 mm.

21.4.4 Mixing of screed materials

The cement and sand screed mix should have the minimum amount of water added to give sufficient workability and allow the material to be thoroughly compacted. Pan-type mixers should be used to ensure efficient mixing of materials. The cement:aggregate ratio should be between 1:3 and 1:4.5 by weight.

21.4.5 Laying and curing of screed

Screed should be laid either between carefully levelled and trued battens or between strips of screed laid and compacted to finished level.

For a bonded screed where a high degree of bond is required the surface laitence of the concrete base should be mechanically removed to expose the coarse aggregate. A thin layer of neat cement grout should be applied to the prewetted or dampened concrete and the screed applied and compacted while the grout is wet.

The screed should be fully compacted by heavy hand or mechanical tamping. To ensure adequate compaction in screeds above 50 mm the screed should be laid in two approximately equal layers.

The screed should be kept protected by waterproof sheeting for at least 7 days after laying to enable the screed to gain strength prior to drying out. After 7 days the screed should be allowed to dry out slowly.

Where sheet and non-ceramic tiling finishes are to be applied, a hygrometer measuring the relative humidity of air in a sealed enclosure above the screed should indicate 75% relative humidity, or less, before the flooring is laid. For tile and stone flooring covered by CP 202: 1972,[15] and BS 5385: Part 3: 1989[16] at least 2 weeks air drying of the screed after curing should be allowed prior to application of the finish.

A soundness, or impact, test for assessing the suitability of completed screeds has been devised by the Building Research Establishment and is described in BS 8203.[17] The degree of indentation after hammer blows on the surface indicates likely serviceability.

21.4.6 Problems with screeds

The most common problems associated with screeds relate to breaking up of screed surfaces, curling and hollowness.

Breaking up of the screed is generally a result of one or more factors in combination: poor compaction, particularly at joints or the perimeter of the screed, and poor mixing and distribution of cement within the screed. With inadequate compaction a well-trowelled surface may be on a crust only a few millimetres thick, with the main body of the screed a weak open-textured material. Joints and perimeters are particularly difficult to compact adequately. The use of a roller or plate vibrator on screeds of large area is considered essential as the effect of hand tamping will be variable. The use of tilting-drum mixers for producing the screed mixes leads to problems of poor distribution of cement in the screed and the tendency for cement to ball up is greater than in a paddle mixer which is more suitable for these drier mixes.

Assessment of failed floor screeds by chemical analysis of the constituents is often misleading. Weak screeds are more generally a result of poor cement distribution, with balled cement, rather than an overall lack of cement. The specification of an impact, or soundness, test to assess newly laid screeds or screeds which have failed in service can provide a more satisfactory guide to performance.

Curling of screeds is associated with inadequate curing and drying out. Adequate curing of the screed is essential to promote hydration of the low-water-content cement and sand mix with the appropriate development of strength within the screed. Protection of the screed surface is, therefore, critical. The use of a surface-applied curing agent is not advisable as these products may affect the bond of the flooring finish. Only after curing should drying out of the screed be allowed to commence. This drying out process should be applied slowly so that unequal stresses due to differential drying shrinkage occurring within the screed thickness does not occur. Estimated drying times for a 50-mm screed are approximately 1 day per millimetre of screed. Curling of a screed becomes unacceptable when it is visible, as cracking may occur under load.

The likelihood of curling is reduced by laying screeds in as large an area as possible in one operation. Although some cracking is likely to occur, the cracks and associated curling will generally be less than at the joints of small bays. On bonded screeds above 40-mm thick, there is an increasing risk of loss of adhesion from the base of concrete. Curling at joints can lead to adjacent cracking of the screed on being loaded.

On unbonded screeds there is the possibility of reversible moisture movement which can result in rippling of thin-sheet finishes at joints as the screed curls and subsequently reverts to a flatter profile.

Hollowness of bonded screeds is a result of debonding from the sub-base. This is generally associated with shrinkage cracks and joints, with some curling. The loss of adhesion can be a function of preparation of the concrete surface or curing. Inadequate curing and drying lead to differential drying shrinkage and cracking. The use of a bonding agent in the screed system to promote bond between sub-base and screed will increase the preparation requirements. The use of a bonding agent is not a substitute for adequate preparation of the concrete surface.

References

1 BRITISH STANDARDS INSTITUTION, *BS 1199 and BS 1200 Specifications for building sands from natural sources*, Milton Keynes (1976)
2 BRITISH STANDARDS INSTITUTION, *BS 12 Portland cement (ordinary and rapid hardening)*, Milton Keynes (1989)
3 BRITISH STANDARDS INSTITUTION, *BS 146 Portland blast-furnace cement*, Milton Keynes (1973)
4 BRITISH STANDARDS INSTITUTION, *BS 4027 Sulphate resisting cement*, Milton Keynes (1980)
5 BRITISH STANDARDS INSTITUTION, *BS 5224 Specification for masonry cement*, Milton Keynes (1976)
6 BRITISH STANDARDS INSTITUTION, *BS 4721 Ready-mixed building mortars*, Milton Keynes (1986)
7 BRITISH STANDARDS INSTITUTION, *BS 4551 Methods of testing mortars, screeds and plasters*, Milton Keynes (1980)
8 BRITISH STANDARDS INSTITUTION, *BS 5628: Part 3 Code of practice for masonry, Part 3: Materials and components design and workmanship*, Milton Keynes (1985)
9 BRITISH STANDARDS INSTITUTION, *BS 5628: Part 1 Code of practice for masonry, Part 1: Unreinforced masonry*, Milton Keynes (1978)
10 BRITISH STANDARDS INSTITUTION, *BS 1014 Pigments for cement, magnesium oxychloride and concrete*, Milton Keynes (1986)
11 BRITISH STANDARDS INSTITUTION, *BS 5262 External rendered finishes*, Milton Keynes (1978)
12 BRITISH STANDARDS INSTITUTION, *BS 5492 Code of practice for internal plastering*, Milton Keynes (1977)
13 BRITISH STANDARDS INSTITUTION, *BS 882 Specifications for aggregates from natural sources for concrete*, Milton Keynes (1983)
14 BRITISH STANDARDS INSTITUTION, *BS 5075: Parts 1 (1982) Specification for accelerating admixtures; 2 (1986) Determination of resistance to loading in shear; 3 (1985) Specification for superplasticizing admixtures*, Milton Keynes
15 BRITISH STANDARDS INSTITUTION, *CP 202 Tile flooring and slab flooring*, Milton Keynes (1972)

16 BRITISH STANDARDS INSTITUTION, *BS 5385 Wall and floor tiling, Part 3: Code of practice for the design and installation of ceramic floor tiles and mosaics*, Milton Keynes (1989)
17 BRITISH STANDARDS INSTITUTION, *BS 8203 Installation of sheet and tile flooring*, Milton Keynes (1987)

Bibliography

BRITISH STANDARDS INSTITUTION, *BS 890 Building lime*, Milton Keynes (1972)
BRITISH STANDARDS INSTITUTION, *BS 4049 Glossary of terms applicable to internal plastering, external rendering and floor screeding*, Milton Keynes (1966)
BRITISH STANDARDS INSTITUTION, *BS 4887 Mortar admixtures*, Milton Keynes, Part 1 (1986), Part 2 (1987)
BRITISH STANDARDS INSTITUTION, *BS 5385 Wall and floor tiling, Part 1: Code of practice for the design and installation of internal ceramic wall tiling and mosaics in normal conditions*, Milton Keynes (1990)
BRITISH STANDARDS INSTITUTION, *BS 8000 Workmanship on building sites, Part 3 (1989): Code of practice for masonry, Part 9 (1989): Code of practice for cement/sand floor screeds and concrete floor toppings, Part 10 (1989): Code of practice for plastering and rendering*, Milton Keynes
BRITISH STANDARDS INSTITUTION, *BS 8204 In situ floorings, Part 1: CP for concrete bases and screeds; Part 2: CP for concrete wearing surfaces*, Milton Keynes (1987)
BUILDING RESEARCH ESTABLISHMENT, 'Floor screeds', *BRE Digest 104*
BUILDING RESEARCH ESTABLISHMENT, 'Mortars for bricklaying', *BRE Digest 160*
BUILDING RESEARCH ESTABLISHMENT, 'External rendered finishes', *BRE Digest 196*
BUILDING RESEARCH ESTABLISHMENT, 'Choosing specifications for plastering', *BRE Digest 213*
CEMENT AND CONCRETE ASSOCIATION, *Appearance Matters: External Rendering*, 8th edn

22

Mould Oils and Release Agents

L Hodgkinson

Cormix Construction Chemicals
Chairman, Technical Committee, Cement Admixtures
Association

Contents

22.1 Introduction 22/3

22.2 Mechanism of oils and chemical release agents 22/3

22.3 Chemical types of release agents 22/4

22.4 Site problems with release agents 22/4
    22.4.1 Absorbent shuttering 22/5
    22.4.2 Overapplication of release agent 22/5

Bibliography 22/5

22.1 Introduction

Concrete is such a versatile material because it can be produced in a plastic state and then cast into infinitely variable shapes by the use of a mould. The range of materials used to produce moulds in which to cast concrete is nominally quite small. Wood is the most common on site, whilst steel is the most common in precast factories. Glass-reinforced plastic is also commonly used. It is this apparent simplicity which has led to a lack of appreciation of the technology associated with the correct use of release agents.

The basic function of a release agent is to prevent the concrete from bonding to the mould in which it is formed. The failure to perform this task results in 'plucking', where pieces of immature concrete are ripped from the concrete unit and left adhered to the mould surface. On wooden moulds, the opposite effect can be seen where stronger concretes rip wood from the mould, leaving wooden fragments adhering to the concrete. The most disastrous failures occur, however, when mature concretes bond irreversibly to a strong-steel formwork leading to the loss of both the formwork and the concrete units.

22.2 Mechanism of oils and chemical release agents

In terms of mechanism, there are basically two types of release agent. The first type, typified by mould oils, rely on the formation of a physical barrier between the mould and the concrete. Because the barrier is only physical in nature, it must be relatively thick. When concrete is poured into the mould, the oil prevents any contact with the mould. On demoulding, the physical barrier of the oil splits in two: half stays on the mould; half stays on the concrete unit (*Figure 22.1*).

Materials of this type have three basic disadvantages: (i) the initial application rate must be high; (ii) the wastage of the oil is high; and (iii) the concrete units produced are contaminated with oil which may lead to problems with subsequent surface treatments. Problems may also occur with oil being deposited on operatives, leading to industrial skin complaints. This is a particular problem with unrefined heavy oils, which may contain a significant level of polynuclear aromatic compounds which are carcinogenic and have been shown to be a cause of skin cancer. Mould oils do have the advantage in that the mould, after removal of the unit, is left with a small amount of oil and is ready to receive an additional application of mould oil for the next casting cycle. Refined oils are now available which have had the dangerous polynuclear aromatics refined down to an acceptable level. These are more expensive, but provided that certain basic precautions are taken in their safe handling, their use will greatly reduce the incidence of skin disease.

The second type of release agent, typified by chemical release agents, relies on a chemical reaction between the release agent and the concrete in the mould. Because the action is chemical in nature, these materials need only be applied very sparingly, typically through a fog or mist spray. When concrete is placed in the mould, the chemical release agent deactivates a microscopic layer of the concrete surface adjacent to the mould. When the unit is demoulded, the concrete surface breaks apart, leaving this microscopic layer on the mould (*Figure 22.2*). This layer is not obvious to the naked eye, but can be detected as a fine waxy, dusty layer when a mould is wiped with the hand. The concrete unit produced is perfectly clean and uncontaminated with any oil. This is particularly important if the concrete unit is to receive any subsequent surface application or needs to be joined to other fresh concrete.

Materials of this type have the advantage that they are far more economical and are generally safer because the lighter carrier oils contain very low levels of polynuclear aromatics and because the concrete units have no oil contamination. The disadvantage of this type of agent is related to the deactivated dust left on the mould after stripping. This dust must be brushed off to prevent build-up which will, after numerous casts, lead to plucking.

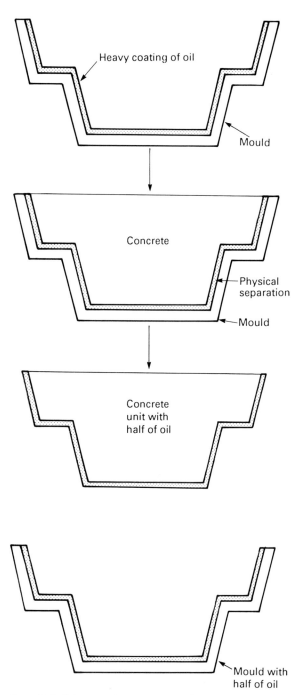

Figure 22.1 Scheme to show the mechanism of mould oils

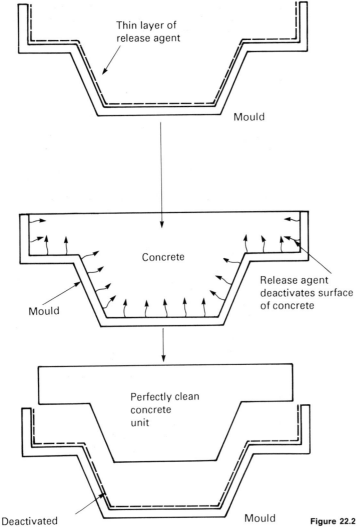

Figure 22.2 Scheme to show the mechanism of chemical release agents

22.3 Chemical types of release agents

The simplest types of release agents are based on heavy oils. These are heavy petroleum fractions and should not be used as concrete release agents unless they have been solvent refined to reduce the level of polynuclear aromatics down to a level of about 4%.

Chemical release agents are normally based on lighter petroleum fractions and contain an active ingredient, normally a soap oil. Soap oil is a term used to describe any oily fatty acid which will act as a release agent by conversion to its calcium salt or soap and thus deactivate a cement surface. The most common 'soap oils' are tall oil fatty acid, oleic acid or blends of these. Tall oil is a by-product of wood-pulp processing and contains a significant proportion of oleic acid and some linoleic acid.

The use of oils and release agents is often made more economical by emulsification with water, or by blending with emulsifiers to enable them to be emulsified. Two types of emulsion are produced: oil-in-water emulsions and water-in-oil emulsions.

Oil-in-water emulsions (*Figure 22.3*) tend to be white or pale cream, with low viscosity and, most importantly, can be diluted with water. The latter property is due to the fact that water is the continuous phase. Milk for example, is an oil-in-water emulsion. Many blends of oil and emulsifier are supplied so that water may be added on site to produce oil-in-water emulsions.

Water-in-oil emulsions (*Figure 22.3*) tend to be characterized by their higher viscosity and, most significantly, they are immiscible with water. This is because oil is the continuous phase and it is this phase that determines the miscibility. Most mould creams are water-in-oil emulsions. Water-in-oil emulsions are generally factory produced and are not modified on site.

22.4 Site problems with release agents

Release agents are very simple to manufacture and it is very rare for a finish problem to be caused by an inherent fault in

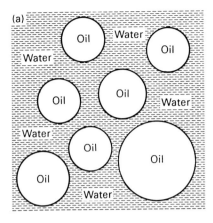

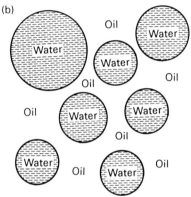

Figure 22.3 Scheme to show the structure of emulsions: (a) oil-in-water emulsion; (b) water-in-oil emulsion

the product. A finish problem is far more commonly caused by the interaction with another problem or by misuse of the release agent. The most common problems associated with the use of release agents are absorbent shuttering and overapplication of agent.

22.4.1 Absorbent shuttering

For a first-class fair-faced finish it is necessary to apply a thin layer of chemical release agent to a sealed surface. To seal ply it is recommended that a good-quality polyurethane varnish is applied prior to any casting. If the ply surface is unsealed, a number of problems may occur. The most common problem is that of migration of wood sugars. These are absorbed into the concrete surface causing a combination of dark staining, variable colour, variable dusting or generally heavy dusting. Heavy dusting is particularly prevalent in the soffits of large concrete pours as the concrete pressure forces the release agent into the form, extracting the sugars.

22.4.2 Overapplication of release agent

Chemical release agents should be applied very sparingly because when overapplied two problems may occur. Where excess release agent collects in the corners of moulds, heavy dusting can occur. Where there is excess agent on large flat horizontal surfaces, then the concrete pressure causes the excess release agent to collect into droplets which form imperfections quite like 'blow holes', but with more rounded edges. These holes normally occur together with staining which gives a clue as to their true origin.

Bibliography

BLAKE, L. S., *Recommendations for the Production of High Quality Concrete Surfaces*, Cement and Concrete Association, Wexham Springs (1967)

23

Silica Fume

M Kawamura Dr Eng
Kanazawa University, Japan

Contents

23.1 General description 23/3

23.2 Sources and production 23/3

23.3 Types and chemical composition 23/3

23.4 Physical properties 23/3
      23.4.1 Colour 23/3
      23.4.2 Specific gravity 23/3
      23.4.3 Bulk density 23/4
      23.4.4 Shape of silica-fume particles 23/4
      23.4.5 Particle-size distribution 23/4
      23.4.6 Specific surface area 23/4
      23.4.7 Structure 23/4

23.5 Reactivity of silica fume 23/4

23.6 Chemical reactions and reaction products 23/5
      23.6.1 Accelerating effect on the hydration of
             cement 23/5
      23.6.2 Effects of silica fume on pore-solution
             composition 23/5
      23.6.3 Characteristics of reaction products 23/5
      23.6.4 A model for the reaction mechanism of silica
             fume in cement paste 23/6

23.7 Microstructure of Portland cement–silica fume pastes
      and mortars 23/6
      23.7.1 Microstructure of Portland cement–silica fume
             pastes 23/6
      23.7.2 Effect of silica fume on the microstructure of the
             interfacial zone in mortars 23/6
      23.7.3 Effect of silica fume on pore structure 23/6

23.8 Properties of fresh concrete containing silica
      fume 23/7
      23.8.1 Water demand 23/7
      23.8.2 Cohesiveness 23/7
      23.8.3 Air entrainment 23/7
      23.8.4 Bleeding 23/7
      23.8.5 Plastic shrinkage 23/7
      23.8.6 Setting time 23/8

23.9 Mechanical properties and shrinkage of hardened
      concrete containing silica fume 23/8
      23.9.1 Compressive strength 23/8
      23.9.2 Tensile and flexural strength 23/9
      23.9.3 Young's modulus 23/9
      23.9.4 Bond strength 23/9
      23.9.5 Creep 23/9
      23.9.6 Abrasion resistance 23/9
      23.9.7 Drying shrinkage 23/9

23.10 Durability of silica-fume concrete 23/10
      23.10.1 Permeability 23/10
      23.10.2 Freezing and thawing resistance 23/10
      23.10.3 Chemical attack 23/11
      23.10.4 Inhibition of alkali–silica reaction 23/12
      23.10.5 Corrosion of steel reinforcement 23/12

23.11 Applications 23/12
      23.11.1 Reduction in cement content in concrete 23/12
      23.11.2 Ultra-high-strength concrete 23/12
      23.11.3 High-strength lightweight concrete 23/13
      23.11.4 Fibre-reinforced concrete 23/13
      23.11.5 Silica-fume grouts 23/13
      23.11.6 Miscellaneous 23/13

23.12 Standards 23/13

23.13 Storage and transportation 23/13

References 23/13

23.1 General description

Silica fume is a by-product in the manufacturing process of silicon metal and ferrosilicon alloys. Other names used are microsilica, silica dust and condensed silica fume. Investigations of silica fume as a mineral admixture for concrete have been made since the early 1950s. The addition of silica fume significantly influences the rheological behaviour of fresh concrete, leading to an increased water demand in the production of concrete. The availability of superplasticizers gave an impetus to the use of silica fume as a part of the cementitious material in concrete to produce very high-strength concrete. Furthermore, since the early 1970s, this new pozzolanic material has attracted a great deal of attention from the viewpoint of environmental regulations and energy conservation in the cement and concrete industry as well as the encouragement of the use of pozzolans for improving the durability of concrete. Extensive research and development have been conducted since that time in order to use silica fume: (i) as a substitute for cement to reduce the costs of concrete products; (ii) as an admixture to improve the quality of concrete; and (iii) as a concrete-making material to produce concrete products and structures with high performance. As a result of this research, silica fume is found to be a highly efficient pozzolanic material with a considerable potential for use in concrete. In fact, diverse applications of silica fume have been developed and a number of projects have been undertaken in Scandinavian countries, especially in Norway and Denmark. However, judicious use of the material has been recommended to solve specific problems and to produce high-performance concrete, because of the relatively limited supplies of the material.[1]

23.2 Sources and production

Silicon and ferrosilicon are produced in a submerged-arc electric furnace in which the electrodes are deeply driven into the raw materials (*Figure 23.1*).[2] The raw materials comprise quartz and coal with wood chips. Iron is added to the raw materials in the production of ferrosilicon. The metallurgical reactions occur below the electrodes at high temperatures of around 2000°C. Silica-fume particles are produced by the oxidation and condensation of the gaseous silicon suboxide (SiO) which is formed in the reaction zone via complex chemical reactions. The gaseous SiO or other combustion gases entrain particles with varied composition, size and density. These particles are mainly fines from various raw materials, vaporized impurities (Mg, Na,

K, etc.), metals (Si, Mn, etc.) and very fine SiO_2 particles produced by the condensation and oxidation of the SiO vapour.

Two types of submerged-arc electric furnace with and without heat-recovery systems are used in the production of silicon and ferrosilicon. The different furnaces lead to different silica fumes in terms of their carbon content and colour. The amount of silica fume generated from a silicon alloy furnace varies with the type of alloy. About 600 kg and 300 kg of silica fume are generated by the production of each ton of silicon and ferrosilicon alloys, respectively.

23.3 Types and chemical composition

The main alloys produced in the submerged-arc electric furnace are silicon and ferrosilicon, calcium–silicon, ferrochromium silicon, calcium–manganese–silicon, silicomanganese and magnesium ferrosilicon. Different types of silica fume are generated corresponding to the different types of silicon alloys produced in the submerged-arc electric furnace. The chemical composition of the silica fume generated from furnaces depends on the type of furnace, the nature of the loading of the furnace, the chemical composition of the raw materials (quartz, coal and metallic compounds) and the design of the furnace (i.e. with or without a heat-recovery system); see *Table 23.1*.[3]

In general, silica fume is characterized by its high silica content, except for the silica fume produced in the production of the calcium–silicon and manganese silicon. The silica fumes from alloy with high calcium or manganese contents should be treated as different materials on which little research has been carried out as a concrete-making material.[4] The silica content varies widely in the same manner as the silicon content varies in the alloy produced. The silica fume contains other minor constituents such as alumina, lime, magnesia and alkali. However, the magnesia content in the ferrochromium silicon, the potassium oxide content in the manganese silicon, and the lime content in the calcium–silicon silica fume are relatively high. The carbon content and the loss on ignition can vary from 0.6 to 3.7% and from 1.1 to 7.9%, respectively. The silica fume usually used in the production of concrete comes from ferrosilicon alloys. It should be noted that some silica fumes, e.g. those supplied as a mixture of FeSi 75% and FeSi 50% or a mixture of FeSi 75% and CaSi, cannot be used in cement or concrete.[5,6] Blended materials from different sources for concrete can be supplied to produce a consistent silica fume with silica contents varying by ±2%.[4]

23.4 Physical properties

23.4.1 Colour

The colour of silica fume mainly depends on the carbon content. The iron content also affects its colour to a lesser extent. The colour of silica fume varies from a very dark grey to a whitish colour. When the furnace has a heat-recovery system, the silica fume is whitish. The open electric-arc furnace without a heat-recovery system produces a very dark silica fume. The colour of silica fume is not important in the production of concrete. However, the surface of concrete products containing a silica fume rich in carbon takes on a bluish shade with time.[3] Concrete incorporating silica fume becomes dark compared to conventional concrete. Concrete incorporating silica fume with a high percentage of carbon may be particularly dark.

23.4.2 Specific gravity

The specific gravity of silica fume is above that of amorphous silica of 2.20, depending on its chemical composition. The specific gravity of Si silica-fume particles is 2.23.[3]

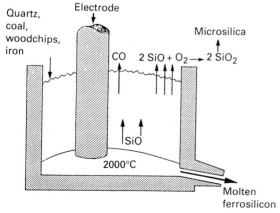

Figure 23.1 Schematic diagram of silica-fume formation in an electric-arc furnace[2]

(figure labels: Quartz, coal, woodchips, iron; Electrode; Microsilica; CO; $2SiO + O_2 \rightarrow 2SiO_2$; SiO; 2000°C; Molten ferrosilicon)

Table 23.1 Chemical composition of condensed silica fumes[3]

Component	Content of fume (wt%)						
	Si	*FeSi 75%*	*FeSi 75% (heat recovery)*	*FeSi 50%*	*FeCrSi*	*CaSi*	*SiMn*
SiO_2	94	89	90	83	83	53.7	25
Fe_2O_3	0.03	0.6	2.9	2.5	1.0	0.7	1.8
Al_2O_3	0.06	0.4	1.0	2.5	2.5	0.9	2.5
CaO	0.5	0.2	0.1	0.8	0.8	23.2	4.0
MgO	1.1	1.7	0.2	3.0	7.0	3.3	2.7
Na_2O	0.04	0.2	0.9	0.3	1.0	0.6	2.0
K_2O	0.05	1.2	1.3	2.0	1.8	2.4	8.5
C	1.0	1.4	0.6	1.8	1.6	3.4	2.5
S	0.2		0.1				2.5
MnO		0.06		0.2	0.2		36.0
LOI	2.5	2.7		3.6	2.2	7.9	10.0

23.4.3 Bulk density

The bulk density of silica fume is an important characteristic in handling the material in the cement and concrete industry. The loose bulk density of various types of silica fume measured in the loose state ranges from 230 (FeSi 75%) to 535 kg m^{-3} (SiMn). The compacted density measured after a loose silica fume has been compacted by vibration varies from 300 (FeSi 75%) to 705 kg m^{-3} (SiMn).[3]

23.4.4 Shape of silica-fume particles

Silica-fume particles observed by using a scanning electron microscope appear round (*Figure 23.2*). Their spherical shape originates from the condensation of SiO vapour in the process of their formation.

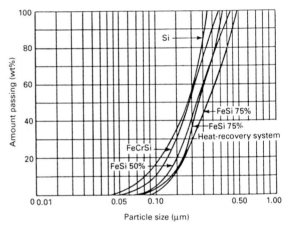

Figure 23.3 Particle-size distribution of silica fume[3]

23.4.6 Specific surface area

The specific surface area obtained by theoretical calculation and the Brunauer–Emmett–Teller (BET) method[7] varies from 13 000 to 23 000 m^2 kg^{-1}.[8] The specific surface area of silica fume is much higher than that of Portland cement and other pozzolans usually used in cement and concrete (1000–1500 m^2 kg^{-1}).

23.4.7 Structure

All types of silica fume are found to be amorphous from their powder X-ray diffraction patterns. The amorphous nature of the internal structure of silica fumes is attributable to their formation through the oxidation and rapid condensation of SiO vapours.

23.5 Reactivity of silica fume

Silica fume is a pozzolanic material. Pozzolanic activity is defined as the amount of material that reacts with lime in the presence of water. The amount of lime which reacts with pozzolanic materials depends on their physical and chemical characteristics. The pozzolanic activity of silica fume in cement paste has been reported to be low,[9] medium[10] and high.[11–13]

The pozzolanic activity of silica fume can vary with its fineness

Figure 23.2 Scanning electron micrograph of silica-fume particles (scale = 1 μm)

23.4.5 Particle-size distribution

The size-distribution curves of various silica fumes in weight are given as percentage weight in *Figure 23.3*.[3] The size distribution of the spheres of a given silica fume is measured using a scanning electron microscope. The typical diameter of the various types of silica fume ranges from 0.18 to 0.26 μm (see *Figure 23.3*).

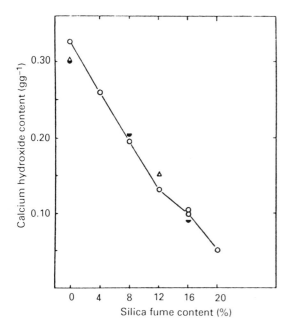

Figure 23.4 Calcium hydroxide content of mature cement pastes with different silica-fume contents.[12] Age: △, 52 days; ▼, 110 days; ○, 65 days. Water:cement ratio = 0.60

and composition. Regourd[11] found that silica fume was the most reactive of the four types of pozzolanic materials of natural volcanic rock and silica, flyash and silica fume. Chatterji *et al.*[9] reported that the pozzolanic activity of silica fume was not as high as that of Aerosil-200. Sellvold *et al.*[12] reported a high pozzolanic activity of a silica fume. The calcium hydroxide content as determined by thermogravimetric analysis for mature pastes are plotted against silica-fume content in *Figure 23.4*. The calcium hydroxide content decreases linearly with increasing silica-fume content. Extrapolation of the straight line in *Figure 23.4* to zero calcium hydroxide content indicates that all the calcium hydroxide produced during the hydration of cement is consumed at a silica-fume content of about 24%.

A comparison of the pozzolanic activity of three different silica fumes showed that the three silica fumes differed in the amounts of calcium hydroxide consumed by a pozzolanic reaction in the silica fume–cement paste mixtures.[14] Usually, the amount of calcium hydroxide which reacts with a pozzolanic material is determined by X-ray diffraction, differential thermal analysis and chemical analysis. The hydration of cement almost stops or slows down in cement pastes with silica fume at a low water:cement ratio.[9] It should be noted, therefore, that the amount of calcium hydroxide in silica-fume bearing cement pastes determined in the way as described above does not necessarily represent the true pozzolanic activity of the material in some cases.

23.6 Chemical reactions and reaction products

Silica fume acts as an active reactant in the hydration of cement pastes containing silica fume. Silica fume affects the hydration of cement chemically as well as physically.

23.6.1 Accelerating effect on the hydration of cement

Silica fume accelerates the hydration of cement by acting as nuclei for the hydration products; this effect is due to the small

size of silica-fume particles. It has been elucidated that the amount of chemically combined water increases with increasing silica fume content during the early hydration in silica-fume bearing cement pastes.[12] It has also been confirmed that this accelerating effect is not chemical in nature, but can only be explained in terms of the small particles acting as nuclei for the formation of hydration products.[12] A calorimetric study by Wu and Young[15] also indicated that the early reaction is accelerated strongly by silica fume. Furthermore, these workers demonstrated the rapid reaction between the silica fume and the calcium hydroxide released from the alite.[15] Nelson and Young[16] reported that silica fumes reduce the calcium hydroxide content of cement pastes as early as 1 day.

23.6.2 Effects of silica fume on pore-solution composition

Analyses of pore solutions expressed from cement pastes containing silica fume show that the addition of silica fume greatly affects the chemistry of the pore solution.[17–19] Diamond[17] revealed that silica fume in Portland-cement pastes increases the alkali content of the pore solution over the first day as compared with that expected if the silica fume had acted as an inert diluent. However, the subsequent removal of alkalis and OH^- ions from the pore solution results in low alkali levels and pH values at later ages. As shown in *Figure 23.5*,[18] the OH^- ion concentration in pore solutions extracted from cement paste with silica fume decreases with time at a greater rate for a higher replacement level. The pH value of the pore solution in pastes without silica fume (13.9) was reduced to 11.9 during the 84-day hydration of cement pastes with 30% silica fume.[18]

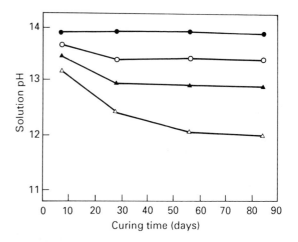

Figure 23.5 Influence of silica fume on the pH value of pore solutions in cement pastes at different stages of curing.[18] Silica-fume content (% cement replacement): ●, 0%; ○, 10%; ▲, 20%; △, 30%

23.6.3 Characteristics of reaction products

From the study on the hydration of C_3S in the presence of silica fume, Wu and Young[15] derived the conclusion that silica fume probably reacts preferentially with calcium hydroxide, and that it subsequently reacts with the C–S–H already formed. They postulated that three kinds of C–S–H are formed in C_3S–silica fume systems: (i) that directly from C_3S; (ii) that from the reaction between calcium hydroxide and silica fume with a slightly low C:S ratio; and (iii) that formed from the reaction between silica fume and C–S–H with a high degree of polymerization and a very low C:S ratio.[15] The C:S ratio in the actual cement–silica-fume mixtures range from 0.9 to 1.3.[10,12] Regourd[11] measured the C:S ratio of C–S–H in cement pastes cured for 28 days at 20°C and in 200-day-old field concretes after a cold winter by electron-probe X-ray microanalysis. It was found from these measurements that the higher the amount of silica fume added, the lower the C:S ratio of the C–S–H produced in the mixtures. The reduction of the C:S ratio in C–S–H increases the capacity of the C–S–H to incorporate alkalis.[19] Elimination of alkalis from pore solutions in cement–silica-fume systems[14,17,18] is responsible for the retention of alkalis by the C–S–H with a low C:S ratio.

23.6.4 A model for the reaction mechanism of silica fume in cement paste

A model for explaining the behaviour of silica fume in cement pastes has been proposed from the examination of the pozzolanic behaviour of silica fume in Ca(OH)$_2$ solutions.[20] According to this model, silica-fume particles in cement pastes tend to form a gel-like coating which leads to interparticle coagulation and agglomeration shortly after the constituents are mixed with water. These early agglomerations are a silica-rich-'gel' coating with only very small traces of calcium. The gel soon reacts with the Ca(OH)$_2$ liberated from the cement hydration to form additional C–S–H. The gel formation can take up water and stiffen the mixture.

23.7 Microstructure of Portland cement–silica fume pastes and mortars

23.7.1 Microstructure of Portland cement–silica fume pastes

The C–S–H in the silica-fume–cement mortars is very dense and amorphous in appearance, in contrast to the fibrous or reticulated C–S–H of other flyash or natural silica cement mortars.[11] The C–S–H gel particles in silica-fume concrete cannot be visualized as individual particles, but rather as a massive, dense structure.[21] Calcium hydroxide appears as small local crystals rather than a large mass. Electron-probe X-ray microanalysis has indicated that substantial amounts of silicon, aluminium, sulphur and potassium are present in a number of calcium hydroxide grains in concrete specimens containing silica fume.[22] Sarkar and Aitcin[22] reported that these impure calcium hydroxide grains were in the process of transformation to C–S–H. In particular, in a new material of DSP densified systems of ultra-fine particles of silica homogeneously arranged (DSP),[23,24] silica fume plays a role as a filler as well as a pozzolanic material. Scanning-electron photomicrographs show that clinker grains in DSP are more visible than in those Portland-cement pastes without silica fume made with a low water:cement ratio.[25] The intergranular rupture predominates in a concrete without silica. Conversely, transgranular fracture through aggregate grains is seen on fracture surfaces of DSP concrete.[25]

23.7.2 Effect of silica fume on the microstructure of the interfacial zone in mortars

Silica fume significantly modifies the microstructure of the interfacial zone between aggregate and cement-paste matrix. The microstructure of the interfacial zone in mortars containing silica fume is dense and homogeneous. Calcium hydroxide layers or gaps are not found in the interfacial zone.[25,26] Densification of the interfacial zone is attributable to the suppression of bleeding in the fresh mortar and the filling of the space in the vicinity of

the sand-grain surface with silica fume particles.[26] The reduction in the amounts of calcium hydroxide formed in the interfacial zone also leads to the inhibition of the formation of ettringite.[22] These changes arising from the incorporation of silica fume increase the bond strength between the aggregate and the cement paste. Furthermore, a very strong bond between the cement paste and the aggregate in DSP concretes arises from the characteristics of the microstructure of the interfacial zone, i.e. no oriented crystal of calcium hydroxide, no visible 'auréole de transition' and no Hadley grains.[27]

23.7.3 Effect of silica fume on pore structure

23.7.3.1 Cement paste

The subdivision of spaces between cement grains by very fine particles of silica fume and the precipitation of reaction products around the fine silica-fume particles during the hydration of the constituents results in a refinement of the pore system. From measurements of water adsorption, Sellevold et al.[12] drew the conclusion that the total volume of pores in the cement pastes is not influenced by the amount of silica fume added, but that the volume of gel pores increases linearly with increasing silica-fume content. This refinement is also clearly reflected in the pore-size-distribution curves shown in Figure 23.6. The pore-size-distribution curves were obtained by using the mercury-intrusion technique. It can be seen from Figure 23.6 that the increase in silica-fume content leads to finer pore structures and to smaller total volumes of mercury intruded. Comparison of the curves for the 12% silica fume (4) and the inert filler of calcium carbonate bearing paste (2) shows that the refinement of pore structure in silica-fume cement pastes can be mostly attributed to the pozzolanic reaction of silica fume.

Another characteristic of the pore structure in cement paste containing silica fume is pore discontinuity.[28–30] Hysteresis formed between the pore-size-distribution curves obtained by the first and the second mercury intrusion indicates pore discontinuity which means the rupture of a portion of pores caused by the first mercury intrusion.[28] The hysteresis increases

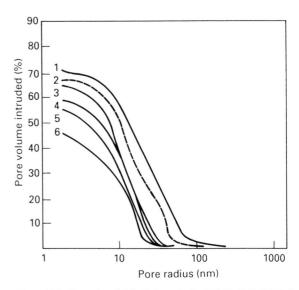

Figure 23.6 Pore-size-distribution curves for mature cement pastes containing various amounts of silica fume (as measured by mercury intrusion).[12] Water:cement ratio = 0.60; age = 65 days. Silica-fume cement paste: 1, Silica-fume free; 2, inert filler of CaCO$_3$. Silica-fume cement paste: 3, 8%; 4, 12%; 5, 16%; 6, 20%

with increasing silica-fume content. Relatively numerous discontinuous pores are formed in cement paste containing silica fume.

23.7.3.2 *Cement mortars*

The pore volume in the size range 97 000–875 nm increases considerably with the addition of silica fume in mortars with a sand:cement ratio of 2.25.[29] These coarse pores are considered to be formed at the interface between the sand grains and the paste matrix. Some of the calcium hydroxide crystallized around the sand grains may redissolve to react with the silica away from the interface.[30] Feldman[31] reported that the coarse pores in silica-fume mortars may be produced by the dissolution of these calcium hydroxide crystals. The assumption that the existence of the relatively coarse pores in silica-fume–cement mortars are responsible for the removal of the calcium hydroxide crystals through their reaction with silica has been proven by Buil and Delage.[33]

23.8 Properties of fresh concrete containing silica fume

Silica fume affects the hydration of cement during the initial stages. Silica-fume particles appear to form a gel-like coating leading to interparticle coagulation shortly after they are mixed with water.[20] Small particles of silica fume also act as a filler for the spaces among cement grains. As a result of the chemical reactions and filler effect of silica fume, the addition of silica fume to cement considerably affects the rheological characteristics of fresh cement–water systems, i.e. it increases the yield value and plastic viscosity. The addition of silica fume to concrete, therefore, influences its water demand, stability, bleeding, segregation of constituents, air entrainment, plastic shrinkage and setting time.

23.8.1 Water demand

The water demand to maintain a given slump increases almost linearly with increasing silica-fume content when no water-reducing agents are used[34,35] (*Figure 23.7*). Water-reducing agents are more effective in reducing water requirement in silica fume concrete than in normal concrete.[34] However, in lean concrete, the water requirement to maintain a slump does not change[8] or decrease[36] as silica fume is added. Another case in which the addition of silica fume does not affect the water demand is the decrease in water required to fluidize a mortar by replacing parts of cement by silica fume in cement-based DSP (see Section 23.11.2) using a large amount of super-plasticizer.[23]

The results obtained by Sellevold and Radjy[34] show that the amount of water-reducing agent to be added should be in proportion to the amount of silica fume in the concrete. However, Markestad[36] reported that the water reduction due to the addition of a water-reducing agent increases proportionally with the concentration of admixture in the mixing water in silica-fume concretes.

The workability of silica-fume concretes is influenced by the time at which superplasticizers are added, in the same way as in concretes without silica fume. The changes of slump with time in silica-fume concrete are similar to those of concretes without silica fume only when the addition of a superplasticizer is delayed.[37] However, the loss of slump with time in silica-fume concrete is greater than that in concretes without silica fume when a superplasticizer is added at the time of mixing.[37]

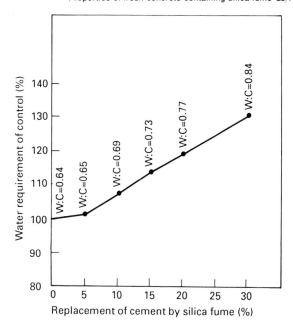

Figure 23.7 Influence of silica fume on the water demand of concrete.[35] The slump of the mixes was kept constant by increasing the water content with increasing amounts of silica fume. Water:cementitious material (w:c) ratio of control mix = 0.64; no superplasticizers used

23.8.2 Cohesiveness

The rheological properties of silica-fume concretes in the static state appear to be different from those in the dynamic state. Thus, the workability of silica-fume concretes when vibrated cannot be predicted from the measurements of slump values.[34] The slump value of silica-fume concretes for a given workability is 30–50 mm higher than that of normal concretes.

Fresh concretes containing silica fume require greater energy input for a given flow in dynamic workability tests such as the Thaulow Stroke (Norway) at a given slump value.[38] This requirement of greater energy input to silica-fume concretes is responsible for the cohesiveness of the concretes.

23.8.3 Air entrainment

The incorporation of silica fume requires a higher dosage of an air-entraining agent for a given volume of entrained air in concrete. Carette and Malhotra[35] reported an increase of dosage from 170 ml m^{-3} for the control to 1090 ml m^{-3} for the silica-fume concrete at a replacement level of 30% silica fume. The increase in the dosage of an air-entraining agent with increasing amounts of silica fume can be attributed to its very high surface area and the presence of carbon in itself. The air entrainment in silica-fume concrete varies, according to the type of silica fume used, from 5 to 6.5% in usual concretes.

23.8.4 Bleeding

Bleeding of concrete rapidly decreases with increasing amounts of silica fume. Little bleeding was found to occur in concretes with 10% silica-fume replacement.

23.8.5 Plastic shrinkage

Special care should be taken against cracking due to plastic shrinkage in concretes containing silica fume. The fact that silica-fume concretes are vulnerable to plastic-shrinkage cracking can be explained by their great reduction in bleeding. However, this problem can be overcome by appropriate curing measures which should be taken immediately after placing the concretes.

23.8.6 Setting time

According to the thermal calorimetry measurements of Meland,[40] the substitution of cement by 10% silica fume accelerates the rate of heat evolution. However, penetration measurements on mortars have indicated that incorporation of less than 10% silica fume in cement pastes without super-plasticizer did not affect the setting time, but that a replacement level of 15% in the cement pastes with superplasticizer increased the setting time markedly.[6] The retardation of setting in the latter cements may be partly due to the superplasticizer added. However, there is an indication that the retardation in setting brought about by the addition of lignosulphate is eased by the use of silica fume in pastes.[38]

23.9 Mechanical properties and shrinkage of hardened concrete containing silica fume

The addition of silica fume to concretes improves their various mechanical properties through its filler and pozzolanic effects. On the other hand, the use of silica fume increases water demand in the production of workable concretes. Since there are other numerous parameters which influence the reactivity of silica fume in concrete, there exists an optimum amount of silica fume that leads to the most effective results.

23.9.1 Compressive strength

23.9.1.1 Water:cement ratio law in silica fume concrete

The relationship between compressive strength and water:cement ratio in 28-day-old concretes with and without silica fume is shown in *Figure 23.8*.[34] As shown in the figure, the water:cement ratio law holds for silica-fume concrete. The replacement of cement by silica fume shifts the strength versus water:cement ratio curve upwards. *Figure 23.8* includes data for concretes with and without a superplasticizer and an ordinary water-reducing admixture.

23.9.1.2 Efficiency factor

The efficiency factor was introduced to convert the efficiency of silica fume in developing the strength of concrete to an equivalent amount of cement.[38] The efficiency factor is calculated on the basis of the comparison between concrete strength and the water:cement ratio and between concrete strength and the water:(cement + silica fume) ratio. The value of this factor ranges from 2 to 5.[41] The efficiency factor of silica fume varies with: (i) silica-fume content; (ii) curing conditions; (iii) age; (iv) cement content; (v) type and dosage of superplasticizers; and (vi) type of cement.[41]

23.9.1.3 Compressive strength at a constant slump

The water demand of silica-fume concretes without super-plasticizers is linearly proportional to the amount of silica fume. In such cases, the strength of silica-fume concrete exceeds that of the control only at low water:cement ratios or at long ages.[36] However, the drawback of a lower strength development at early ages in silica-fume concrete brought about by its greater water demand can be overcome by the use of a superplasticizer. According to the report by Sellevold and Radjy,[34] the water

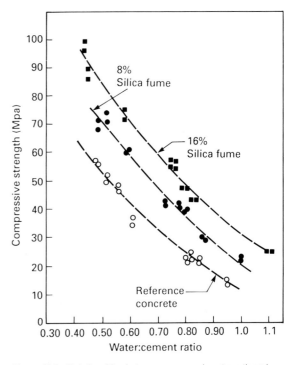

Figure 23.8 Relationships between compressive strength and water:cement ratio in 28-day-old concretes (standard Portland cement) with and without silica fume.[34] ×, 16% silica fume; ●, 8% silica fume; ○, reference concrete

demand for a given silica-fume content can be controlled by adjusting the dosage of superplasticizer.

23.9.1.4 Strength development

The strength development of silica-fume concrete depends on the curing temperature. The contribution of silica fume to strength development at a curing temperature of 20°C is most active between 3 and 28 days. Almost the same compressive strengths were obtained up to the age of 7 days in concretes containing 0–20% silica fume.[42] This result indicates the accelerating effect of silica fume on the hydration of cement. The strength development of silica-fume concrete due to the pozzolanic reaction appears after 7 days of curing. The compressive strength of non-superplasticized concrete containing silica fume up to a replacement level of 20% was increased by about 43 and 55% at the age of 28 and 90 days, respectively.[42] It should be noted that the relationship between the strength at early and long ages in ordinary concretes does not hold in silica-fume concretes. However, the compressive strengths at early ages (up to 28 days) of silica-fume concretes containing an aqueous lignosulphonate based plasticizer are low as compared with those of concretes without silica fume.[43]

The time dependence of the strength development of concrete is different for different water:cementitious material ratios. For example, while there is little change in compressive strength between 1 and 3 days at a high water:cementitious material ratio of 0.6 in silica-fume concretes with a superplasticizer, a marked increase in strength at 3 days was confirmed at a low water:cementitious material ratio of 0.4.[44]

23.9.1.5 Effects of drying

The comparison of the strength at age 90 days between 100 mm³ cubic concrete specimens cured in water and exposed to air in the laboratory indicates that, in concretes with and without silica fume, strengths of concretes cured in air are 10–20% lower than those cured in water.[34] However, there is little difference in strength loss due to drying between concretes with and without silica fume.

23.9.2 Tensile and flexural strength

The relative tensile and flexural strength of non-superplasticized concrete with and without silica fume is greatly different from the relative compressive strength of the two types of concrete.[1] The flexural and splitting tensile strength of 28-day-old concretes containing silica fume is greater than that of the corresponding silica-fume-free concretes which are made to keep the slump of the mixes constant at replacement levels of less than 15%. The relationship between the ratios of flexural or tensile strength to compressive strength and the replacement of silica fume actually varies widely with various factors.[41] However, in general, the ratio of flexural or tensile strength to compressive strength of silica-fume concretes decreases with increasing amounts of silica fume.

The efficiency factors of flexural and tensile strength (see Section 23.9.1.2) are in the ranges 4–16 and 3–8 under a wet curing condition, respectively, but those of both strengths obtained in a dry curing condition range from 0 to 3. Thus, the flexural and tensile strength of silica-fume concretes are very sensitive to curing conditions. Furthermore, more serious reductions in flexural or tensile strength occur in concretes without superplasticizers than in superplasticized concretes. This may be explained by the facts described above, i.e. that the dispersion of silica fume particles in concrete is important in the development of flexural or tensile strength in silica-fume concrete.

23.9.3 Young's modulus

The linear part of stress–strain curves in low stress ranges for concretes containing silica fume extends to greater strains than in silica-fume-free concretes.[45] The descending part after the maximum stress in stress–strain curves for silica-fume concretes is steeper than that in curves for concretes without silica fume.[38] This brittle nature seen in concretes containing silica fume is a general tendency in high strength concretes.

Malhotra and Carette[46] have presented data on the Young's modulus of silica-fume concretes. They found no significant difference between the Young's modulus for concretes with silica fume and that of the control. The incorporation of silica fume at a replacement level of 20% appeared to reduce slightly the Young's modulus at a water:cementitious material ratio of 0.4, 0.5 and 0.65, although the compressive strengths increased with increasing amounts of silica fume. A small reduction in Young's modulus in silica-fume concretes has also been reported by Takagi and Akashi.[45] However, there is an indication that the static Young's modulus of silica-fume concretes increases with increasing compressive strength.[47]

23.9.4 Bond strength

23.9.4.1 Concrete-to-concrete bond

Silica fume is very effective in improving the bond at joints or between layers formed in the placement of concrete.[38]

23.9.4.2 Bond between aggregate and cement paste

The alteration of the microstructure of the interfacial zone between aggregate and cement paste by the incorporation of silica fume[25,26,48] seems to improve the bond strength between the two phases.[11]

23.9.4.3 Bond between concrete and steel reinforcement

The bond strength between steel bars and lightweight concretes containing silica fume increases almost linearly with increasing amounts of silica fume. There is evidence that the bond strength between steel bars and concrete is trebled by the addition of 40% silica fume.[49] The linear increase in the bond strength with increasing amounts of silica fume was confirmed in pull-out tests for steel bars embedded in natural aggregate concretes. Incorporation of silica fume at a replacement of 20% in lightweight aggregate concrete resulted in a 5% increase in bond strength.[50] The improvements in the ultimate bond strength of steel bars with silica-fume concrete are mostly associated with increased compressive strength. However, the high bond strength between round steel bars and silica-fume concretes may result from increased friction between the two.

23.9.4.4 Bond between fibres and concrete

The addition of silica fume is very effective in increasing the compressive strength of steel-fibre-reinforced concretes with low cement contents.[52] The toughness of fibre-reinforced concretes is greatly increased by the addition of silica fume.[52,53] The usefulness of silica fume as an ingredient in steel-fibre-reinforced shotcrete was confirmed in Scandinavia.[38] Silica fume greatly improves the strength, deformability, impact resistance and drying shrinkage of carbon-fibre-reinforced cement.[54] The improvement in these properties is attributed to the increased bond strength between the carbon fibres and the matrix due to the addition of silica fume. The reinforcing performance of polypropylene fibres can be improved substantially by the use of superplasticized silica fume cement paste matrix.[55]

The bond strength between steel fibres and the new material of DSP (see Section 23.7.1) is extremely high. Pull-out tests conducted on 6-mm steel bars embedded in DSP mortars showed a pull-out force of about 9 kN, as compared with about 2 kN in ordinary mortars.

23.9.5 Creep

From creep tests on $\phi 16 \times 100$ cm cylinders under 10 MPa at $20°$C and 50% relative humidity, Buil and Acker[56] obtained results which show that the creep deformation of silica-fume concrete is smaller than that of the reference in a unsealed condition, but there was no significant difference in creep between them in tests conducted with sealed specimens. Wolsiefer[47] also reported the occurrence of smaller creep deformations (by 19%) at 12 months in high-strength concretes with silica fume than in ordinary high-strength concretes. However, the results of creep tests carried out in water and air at $20°$C[57] indicate that the creep of silica-fume concretes is higher than that of concretes without silica fume at the same level of compressive strength.

23.9.6 Abrasion resistance

Silica-fume concrete has high abrasion resistance. According to the data obtained from an underwater abrasion test method,[58,59] the resistance of silica-fume concretes to abrasion erosion is about three times as high as that of conventional concrete.

23.9.7 Drying shrinkage

23.9.7.1 Cement paste

Shrinkage of cement pastes cured for 28 days increased with

increasing amounts of silica fume in shrinkage tests performed at a relative humidity of below 50%.[38] Feldman and Hwang[29] confirmed the increase in drying shrinkage on addition of 30% silica fume, by measuring the shrinkage at the relative humidities of 58, 42, 11 and 0% for cement pastes cured for 90 days. They related the increased shrinkage in silica-fume-cement pastes to the elimination of calcium hydroxide which acts to restrain the shrinkage of cement paste, and to the increased amounts of C–S–H in the material.

23.9.7.2 Concrete

The shrinkage of concrete is controlled both by the shrinkage characteristics of the cement-paste phase and by the volume fraction and rigidity of the aggregate. Thus, the higher shrinkage potential of silica-fume-bearing cement paste at a given water:cementitious material ratio (see Section 23.9.7.1) is not necessarily reflected in the shrinkage of concrete. Furthermore, curing and environmental conditions, and the shape and size of specimens also affect the test results. Not all the test results which have been obtained are comparable.

Carette and Malhotra[35] carried out two series of shrinkage tests: one with a constant slump maintained by increasing the water content with increasing amounts of silica fume, and the other with a constant water:cementitious material ratio maintained by adding a superplasticizer for a given slump. The data from both series of tests indicate less shrinkage for the concretes containing silica fume at 84 days, with the exception that concrete containing 30% silica fume showed slightly higher shrinkage values in the former series. However, in the series in which a superplasticizer was used, concretes with a silica-fume replacement of 30% had slightly lower shrinkage than did the others at 420 days.[6] Wolsiefer,[47] Løland and Hustad,[60] and Buil and Acker[56] have also reported lower shrinkage in concrete containing silica fume than in controls, while some data obtained by Pistilli *et al.*[61] and Johansen[62] indicate higher shrinkage in silica-fume concretes than in ordinary concretes. There are other data indicating that there are only marginal differences between slag cement concretes containing silica fume and ordinary concretes.[46]

It should be noted that the addition of superplasticizers has conflicting effects on the shrinkage of concrete, i.e. the reduction in the volume fraction of the cement-paste phase and its high shrinkage potential due to the superplasticizer.

23.10 Durability of silica-fume concrete

23.10.1 Permeability

23.10.1.1 Drying rate

The relative diffusion rates of water vapour in cement pastes have been calculated from data obtained by drying tests at 11% relative humidity.[12] The addition of 20% silica fume was found to reduce the relative diffusion coefficient of the pastes to about 20% of that of concrete without silica fume.

23.10.1.2 Water permeability

The permeability coefficient of cement pastes prepared at a water:cementitious material ratio of 0.25 with 20% silica fume at the age of 180 days was 1×10^{-13} m s^{-1}.[6]

Gjørv[63] reported that the addition of 10% silica fume in concrete with 100 kg m^{-3} cement reduced its permeability coefficient from 1.6×10^{-7} to 4.0×10^{-10} m s^{-1}. The same author also reported that the permeability coefficient of a concrete containing 20% silica fume and 100 kg m^{-3} cement was the same as that of a concrete containing 250 kg m^{-3} of cement but no silica fume.

23.10.1.3 Air permeability

The coefficient of air permeability of a concrete containing silica fume decreases with increasing amounts of silica fume.[64]

23.10.1.4 Chloride permeability

Gautefall[65] measured the effective diffusion coefficient of cement pastes containing 5–15% silica fume using circular disks with a thickness of 3 mm fitted into diffusion cells. He found that the diffusion coefficient of cement pastes decreases with increasing replacement level of cement by silica fume. A 15% silica-fume-bearing cement paste made at a water:cementitious ratio of 0.5 has an effective diffusion coefficient which is about one-seventh of that without silica fume. Roy and co-workers[66,67] indicated that the effective diffusion coefficients of Cl$^-$ and Cs$^+$ across water saturated cement paste disks containing silica fume were about one-seventh to one-thirtieth of those for cement pastes without silica fume. They also reported that there was an increase in the diffusion coefficient for Cl$^-$ and Cs$^+$ at later ages (viz. at least 100 days) in silica-fume-bearing cement pastes, as occurs in ordinary cement pastes.

The chloride ion penetration characteristics have been studied on 10 cm^3 concrete cubes made from concretes containing silica fume and the control.[68] The concrete containing 10% silica fume was found to be the most promising to prevent steel reinforcement from corroding in concretes exposed to chloride solution. Some data obtained from rapid chloride permeability tests indicate that the replacement of cement by 10% silica fume reduces the chloride permeability of concretes to about one-sixth that of concretes without silica fume.[69]

23.10.2 Freezing and thawing resistance

23.10.2.1 Silica-fume cement pastes

The extent of ice formation in a virgin water-saturated and in resaturated samples with and without silica fume was investigated using low-temperature calorimetry.[12] Ice formation occurred at a few degrees below 0°C in cement pastes without silica fume, while cement pastes containing 8 and 16% silica fume showed the first freezing peak at around −20°C. These results suggest that cement pastes containing silica fume can resist frost action without the use of an air-entraining agent.

23.10.2.2 Silica-fume mortars

The improved frost resistance of mortars containing silica fume has been shown by several workers.[70–72] Hwang and Feldman[70] carried out freezing and thawing tests for mortars with water:cementitious material ratios of 0.45 and 0.60, containing 0, 10 and 30% silica fume. They found that the addition of 10% silica fume at the lower water:cementitious material ratio of 0.45 improved the frost resistance of mortars without the addition of air-entraining admixtures, but that the replacement of 30% cement by silica fume provided poor frost resistance to mortars. The improvement of frost resistance in mortars containing 10% silica fume was attributed to the creation of relatively inaccessible pores in the range 20 000–350 nm at the interfacial zone around the sand grains due to the reactions of the silica fume with Ca(OH)$_2$ (see Section 23.7.3.2).[70,71] The poor frost resistance of the mortar with 30% silica fume was attributed to its low permeability, and to the high silica fume content leading to a relatively large amount of evaporable water in the pores due to incomplete hydration.[70]

23.10.2.3 Silica-fume concretes

Some Norwegian researchers have shown satisfactory performance of concretes containing silica fume under repeated cycles

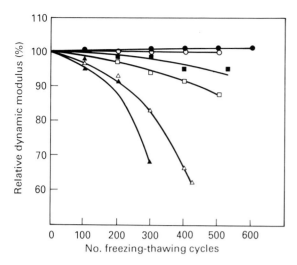

Figure 23.9 The relative dynamic modulus versus the number of freezing–thawing cycles.[35] Water:cementitious material ratio = 0.40; a superplasticizer was used. ●, Control; ○, 5% silica fume; ■, 15% silica fume; □, 10% silica fume; △, 20% fume; ▲, 30% silica fume

of freezing and thawing.[63] However, the regimes of freezing and thawing tests and the number of cycles to be applied to the test specimens affect the test results. As shown in *Figure 23.9*, concretes incorporating 5, 10 and 15% silica fume and the control performed satisfactorily in freezing and thawing tests carried out according to ASTM C 666, Procedure A.[35] However, concretes with 20 and 30% silica fume began to show some damage and considerable expansions after 250 cycles.[35] Yamoto *et al.*[72] also obtained similar data. They reported that concretes with a water:cementitious material ratio of 0.25 showed very high freezing and thawing resistance even in non-air-entrained concretes. These results are inconsistent with the finding that non-air-entrained concretes containing 10 and 20% silica fume showed very low durability factors[73] even at the water:cementitious material ratio of 0.25.[74] Very high strength concretes incorporating 10 and 20% silica fume were also found to perform poorly in freezing and thawing tests even in air-entrained concretes, although air-entrained concretes without silica fume performs satisfactory at water:cementitious material ratios of 0.30 and 35.[74] The poor durability of very-high-strength silica-fume concrete may be responsible for a very dense cement matrix which, in turn, adversely affects the movement of water within concrete.[35]

Incorporation of silica fume in concretes with the water:cementitious material ratio of about 0.5 at a moderate replacement level affects their frost resistance differently from very-high-strength concrete. The improvement of the freezing and thawing resistance of the field concretes due to the addition of silica fume has been attributed to a refinement of the pore structure of the concrete (see Section 23.7.5). However, the relation between microstructure and freeze–thaw durability appears complicated. The use of silica fume significantly decreases the value of the critical air-void spacing factor obtained by ASTM C 666 tests.[76] This means that silica-fume concrete is more susceptible to internal cracking caused by freeze–thaw cycles.[76] However, the length changes of silica-fume concretes with high spacing factors in the freezing and thawing tests were smaller than those of the ordinary concretes with similar spacing factors. Furthermore, scaling was reduced by the use of silica fume. The smaller length changes of the silica fume concretes as well as the reduced scaling in the freezing and thawing testing may be explained by the

lower permeability of silica-fume–cement-paste matrix (see Section 23.10.1.2). The response of silica-fume–cement-paste systems to drying and rewetting is much slower as compared with ordinary concretes. Test specimens should, therefore, be subjected to more cycles of freezing and thawing than normally prescribed.[38]

23.10.3 Chemical attack

The resistance of concrete to attack by aggressive agents is improved by the incorporation of silica fume. The improvement of the durability of concrete results from: (i) the reduction in mobility of harmful ions in concrete; (ii) the increase in the amount of aluminium incorporated in the C–S–H products, resulting in the reduction of the amount of alumina available for reaction with sulphates to produce ettingite; and (iii) the lower content of calcium hydroxide due to its reaction with silica fume in concrete. A Norwegian report states that concretes containing 15% silica fume showed the same performance as those with a sulphate-resisting cement after 26 years of exposure.

23.10.3.1 Sulphate resistance

Corrosion of concrete due to $(NH_4)_2SO_4$ is more severe than that due to H_2SO_4 and NH_4NO_3.[77,78] The presence of silica fume increases the durability of mortar in a 10% $(NH_4)_2SO_4$ solution.[77] Silica fume prevents sulphate corrosion which is predominant in $(NH_4)_2SO_4$ solution. However, it was found from another experiment[78,79] that a 5% $(NH_4)_2SO_4$ solution destroyed samples with silica fume to the same degree as those without silica fume. The severe deterioration of silica-fume concretes was attributed to the decomposition of C–S–H due to $(NH_4)_2SO_4$ solution.[78,79] None of the mortars containing 5, 10, 20 and 30% silica fume immersed in a 10% Na_2SO_4 solution all showed any expansion or weight loss over 16 months.[80] However, in the same mortar prisms ($25 \times 25 \times 285$ mm) immersed in 10% $MgSO_4$ solution, deep longitudinal cracks occurred along their corners at the high replacement levels of 20 and 30%, while at the low replacement levels of 5 and 10% no deterioration was observed.[80] It should be noted that the volume of pores larger than 0.1 μm in diameter as well as the total pore volume in mortars with the high replacement levels of 20 and 30% increased remarkably after immersion in 10% $MgSO_4$ solution for 1 year.

23.10.3.2 Resistance against chloride solutions

Cylinders, $\phi75 \times 160$ mm, made from mortars containing 10 and 30% silica fume were exposed to a chloride solution composed of 27.5% $CaCl_2$, 3.9% $MgCl_2$ and 1.2% NaCl. The addition of silica fume at a high water:cementitious material ratio decreases the resistance of mortars against salt solution attack. At a low water:cementitious material ratio, however, the silica fume is efficient in improving the resistance of mortars against salt solution attack. In particular, the 30% silica-fume-bearing mortars with a water:cementitious material ratio of 0.45 and cured for long periods showed the greatest resistance to chloride solution attack.[81]

23.10.3.3 Resistance against other solutions

Silica fume addition greatly increases the resistibility of mortars against the 10% NH_4NO_3 solution.[77] The superiority of silica-fume concretes or mortars in resistance to the 1% HCl and 2% H_2SO_4 solution was confirmed.[78,80] However, the dosage of silica fume at the high replacement level of 20 or 30% aggravated the resistance of mortars against the attack by the 2% H_2SO_4 solution compared with the control.[80]

23.10.4 Inhibition of alkali–silica reaction

The alkali–silica reaction results from the presence of concentrated alkali hydroxide solutions in the pores of the concrete. The ability of silica fume to remove alkalis and OH^- ions from the pore solution (see Section 23.6.2)[17] suggests that silica fume can inhibit the alkali–silica reaction in concretes containing alkali reactive aggregates. Icelandic experiences[83,84] has shown that the replacement of an Icelandic cement by 5–7.5% silica fume could resolve alkali problems in that country. The level of cement replacement by silica fume required to inhibit expansion due to alkali–silica reaction varies widely with the type of reactive aggregates. The replacement of 10% cement by silica fume is required in mortars containing a South African reactive aggregate,[85] while the addition of 34% silica fume by weight of cement could reduce expansions of mortars containing an opal aggregate to under 20% that of mortars without admixtures.[86] Different silica fumes differently affect the expansive behaviour of mortars containing the Beltane opal aggregate.[87] Small additions of silica fume, e.g. replacement levels of 5%[88] and 10%[87] in the use of some silica fumes, caused increased expansion in mortars containing a highly reactive aggregate of opal. The use of superplasticizers also influences the magnitude of expansion.[88] Silica fume in Portland-cement pastes increases the alkali content of the pore solution over the first day of hydration.[17] Thus, the use of silica fume can promote the alkali–silica reaction while the concrete is in a fresh state.[89] There is another indication that the enhanced expansion with a small amount of silica fume was related to delayed transformation of gel to sol.[90] However, a field case study on concretes prepared with silica-fume substitutions from 10 to 40% indicates that the alkali–silica reaction can be inhibited in concretes containing the coarse aggregate with very reactive fine vitreous silica particles.[91]

23.10.5 Corrosion of steel reinforcement

The influence of silica fume on protection of steel reinforcement against corrosion seems complicated, because there are numerous factors to be taken into consideration in the corrosion of steel reinforcement in concrete. Factors affecting the corrosion of steel reinforcement in concrete are: (i) hydroxyl ion and/or free chloride ion concentration in pore solution; (ii) carbonation rate in concrete; (iii) mobility of chloride ions; (iv) oxygen diffusion rate; and (v) electrical resistivity. Effects of silica fume on factors (i) and (iii) have been partly described previously (see Sections 23.6.2 and 23.10.1.4).

23.10.5.1 Binding capacity of chloride

The capacity of cement to bind chloride ions declines as increasing proportions from 10 to 30% of the cement are substituted by silica fume.[18] Page and Vennesland[28] attributed the effect of silica fume on the chloride binding capacity of cement to increased solubility of Friedel's salt at the reduced pH (see Section 23.6.2). However, Byfors et al.[92] obtained the result that the chloride binding capacity of cement pastes incorporating 10% silica fume was greater than that of the original Swedish ordinary Portland cement paste. The reasons for this difference remain ambiguous.

23.10.5.2 Carbonation

Exposure of concrete prisms for 14.5 months showed that carbonation depths decreased greatly in silica-fume concretes with a superplasticizer, but that the addition of silica fume without plasticizers had a minor effect on the carbonation depth.[93] Calcium hydroxide content, curing conditions and CO_2 diffusion rates influence the rate of carbonation in silica-fume

concrete. In particular, carbonation in silica-fume concrete is sensitive to early curing conditions as compared with that in ordinary concrete. Silica fume had no effect on the rate of carbonation in well-cured test specimens, but increased the rate of carbonation after a long period of exposure in test specimens poorly cured in early ages.[63] According to a field case study,[38,94] there was no great difference between the mean values of carbonation depths from 40- to 80-month-old concretes with and without silica fume. Silica-fume concrete, however, showed greater variation in carbonation depth than did the control.

23.10.5.3 Electrical resistibility

The addition of silica fume increases substantially the electrical resistivity of concrete. The ohmic resistance of concrete containing 10 or 20% silica fume at the unit cementitious material content of 250 kg m^{-3} was 2.1 and 6.2 times as high as that of silica-fume-free concretes, respectively.[63]

23.10.5.4 Oxygen diffusion

It is assumed that the oxygen diffusion rate decreases with increasing amounts of silica fume.[63]

23.10.5.5 Corrosion rate

The highly dense silica-fume mortars provide a high degree of corrosion protection to steel reinforcement embedded in the mortar.[95] This high degree of corrosion protection was explained by the lack of water penetration and the high electrical resistivity.[95] The incorporation of silica fume in cement pastes greatly increases the ratio of free chloride ion concentration to hydroxyl ion concentration in their pore solution.[96] However, electrochemical monitoring of corrosion of steel electrodes embedded in silica-fume-bearing cement pastes indicated that the ratio of free chloride ion concentration to hydroxyl ion concentration in the pore solution was not a reliable index for comparing the corrosiveness of hardened cement pastes with varying silica-fume content.[96] The dense microstructure of silica-fume-cement pastes appears to restore the passivity of steel electrodes after some initial corrosion has occurred.[96] However, a scanning electron microscopic study on the interfacial zone between steel and calcium chloride bearing cement pastes with silica fume showed that steel electrodes embedded in silica-fume-cement pastes were more sensitive to chloride induced corrosion.[97] It may be certain that replacement of cement by up to 30% silica fume does not adversely affect the passivity of mild steel in cement pastes in the absence of chloride contamination.[96]

23.11 Applications

23.11.1 Reduction of cement content in concrete

Silica fume can be used to reduce the materials costs for making concrete. From economic aspects, the possible reduction in unit cement contents ranges from 50 to 150 kg m^{-3} for concretes with strengths of 15–40 MPa.[98] Although the efficiency factors in silica-fume concretes range from 2 to 5 (see Section 23.9.1.2), a possible substitution level of cement by silica fume from an economic point of view depends on the availability of silica fume and other pozzolanic materials, and on relative cement costs.

23.11.2 Ultra-high-strength concrete

A combination of silica fume, Portland cement and super-plasticizers can produce ultra-high-strength concretes. The new materials from which the ultra-high-strength concretes are made, are termed DSP (densified systems containing homogeneously arranged, ultrafine particles).[23] Extraordinary strong and durable DSP materials with the characteristics of a very dense arrangement of fine particles are produced by using heavy mechanical compaction to overcome the locking surface forces acting among small particles.[23] Applications of DSP materials cover the production of underwater concrete, injection in cable ducts and ducts for poststressed concrete, matrices for various reinforced materials, and gravity- and winded-load structures.

23.11.3 High-strength lightweight concrete

Binding materials with silica fume increase the strength of light-weight aggregate concretes.[39] Strengths of up to 100 N mm^{-2} have already been achieved with the additions of up to 10–15% silica fume.[99] Such concretes can be applied successfully to high structures and marine oil structures worldwide. It is possible to make lightweight concretes with an air content of up to 40% of the concrete volume by using expanded clay as the lightweight aggregate and an air-entraining agent.

23.11.4 Fibre-reinforced concrete

The addition of silica fume improves the anchorage of fibres in steel-fibre-reinforced concretes (see Chapter 24). It was confirmed that addition of silica fume increases the toughness index of steel-fibre-reinforced concretes.[52] The replacement of 20% of the cement by silica fume is the optimum cement and water content to improve the performance of steel-fibre-reinforced concrete.

Glass-fibre-reinforced cements lose their tensile strength and toughness even when alkali-resistant glass fibres are used. Replacing about 45% of the cement by silica fume reduces the pH of the pore solution to such low levels that the toughness of glass-fibre-reinforced cements is retained.[100] Direct addition of silica fume in glass-fibre strands prior to incorporation of the strands in cement-paste matrices was found to be effective for improving the durability of the composites.[101,102]

The addition of silica fume is very effective for the dispersion of carbon fibres in carbon-fibre-reinforced cement composites.[54] The strength, deformability, impact strength, waterproofness and drying shrinkage of carbon-fibre-reinforced cement are improved by the incorporation of silica fume.[54]

23.11.5 Silica-fume grouts

Silica-fume grouts, mortars and repair materials can be used to replace polymer concrete in certain applications.[99] Silica-fume–cement grouts are more thixotropic and more stable than plain cement grouts.[103] Ordinary Portland cement grout containing both flyash and silica fume can achieve high strength and expansivity with the use of calcium sulphate hemihydrate.[104] The advantages of the grouts containing silica fume are a longer pot-life, thixotropic properties and little segregation. Silica-fume mortars have been applied up to 100 mm thick in one pass on vertical surfaces in a repair contract.[99]

23.11.6 Miscellaneous

Rebound losses in shotcrete with silica fume were virtually eliminated.[99]

Approximately 20% of crusher fines are generated in demolition of old concrete. Calcium hydroxide from hydration of unhydrated cement grains in such fines can react with siliceous particles to give calcium silicate products. The addition of 5–10% silica fume greatly improved the compressive strength of such products.[105]

23.12 Standards

There is no comprehensive specification for silica fume at present. The new edition of Canadian Standard A23.5: 1987[106] includes the physical and chemical requirements for silica fume in its use in concrete. Norwegian standards also exist.[107] Although the ASTM Designation C 618 does not cover the specification for silica fume, ASTM is preparing to issue a revised C 618 designation including clauses for the use of silica fume as a mineral admixture in concrete.

No standards exist for ordinary prescribed mixes which allow the use of silica fume in concrete at present. However, in the UK, silica-fume concretes can be used in accordance with special requirements for silica-fume concrete in BS 5328: 1981.[108]

23.13 Storage and transportation

A separate silo and a batching and conveying system should be installed to prevent air pollution due to the extreme fineness and the mobility of silica fume during batching operations in a concrete mixing plant.[98]

The transportation of silica fume is another problem to be solved for its use in making concrete, because the volume of loose silica fume is 4–5 times greater than that of bulk cement having the same weight (see Section 23.4.3). Silica fume has been handled in three different states (pellets, slurry and powder) in its transportation. Transportation of this material in the raw powder state requires a relatively high investment.[98] The storage and transportation of silica fume as slurry is the cheapest method, but generally requires occasional agitation, regardless of the dosage of admixtures. The pH of this slurry is adjusted to be between 4.5 and 5.5 in order to stabilize its homogeneity. Various chemical admixtures are used to make slurry. However, normal concrete can be produced with silica fume slurry that contains no admixture.[109]

References

1 MALHOTRA, V. M. and CARETTE, G. G., 'Silica fume concrete—properties, applications and limitations', *Concrete International*, **5**, 40 (1983)
2 HJORTH, L., 'Microsilica in concrete', *Nordic Concrete Research, Publication No. 1, Paper 9*, Nordic Concrete Federation, Oslo (1982)
3 AITCIN, P.-C., PINSONNEALT, P. and ROY, D. M., 'Physical and chemical characterization of condensed silica fumes', *American Ceramic Bulletin*, **63**, 1487 (1984)
4 PARKER, D. G., 'Microsilica concrete. Part 1: the material', *Concrete*, **19**, 21 (1985)
5 KILLIN, A. M., 'Progress report: air pollution control study of the ferroalloy industry', *Electric Furnace, Proc.*, **31**, 66 (1973)
6 MALHOTRA, V. M., RAMACHENDRON, V. S., FELDMAN, R. F. and AITCIN, P.-C., *Condensed Silica Fume in Concrete*, CRC Press, Inc., Boca Raton, FL, p. 221 (1987)
7 LOWELL, S. and SHIELDS, J. E., 'Powder surface area and porosity', *Powder Technology Series*, Chapman and Hall, London, p. 30 (1984)
8 AITCIN, P.-C., 'Physico-chemical characteristics of condensed silica fume'. In *Condensed Silica Fume* (ed. Aitcin, P.-C.), Les Editions de l'Université de Sherbrooke, Quebec, p. 16 (1983)
9 CHATTERJI, S., THAULOW, N. and CHRISTENSEN, P., 'Pozzolanic activity of byproduct silica fume from ferro-silicon production', *Cement and Concrete Research*, **12**, 781 (1982)
10 TRAETTEBERG, A., 'Silica fume as a pozzolanic material', *Il Cimento*, **75**, 369 (1978)
11 REGOURD, M., 'Pozzolanic reactivity of condensed silica fume'. In *Condensed Silica Fume* (ed. Aitcin, P.-C.), Les Editions de l'Université de Sherbrooke, Quebec, p. 20 (1983)
12 SELLEVOLD, E. J., BAGER, D. H., KLITGAARD, JENSEN, K. and KNUDSEN, T., 'Silica fume–cement pastes:

hydration and pore structure', *Report BML 82.610*, The Norwegian Institute of Technology, Trondheim, Norway, p. 19 (1982)

13 CHENG-YI HWANG and FELDMAN, R. F., 'Hydration reactions in Portland cement–silica fume blends', *Cement and Concrete Research*, **15**, 585 (1985)

14 KAWAMURA, M., TAKEMOTO, K. and HASABA, S., 'Effectiveness of various silica fumes in preventing alkali–silica expansion', *Proceedings of Katharine and Bryant Mather International Conference, Concrete Durability*, Vol. 2 (ed. Scanlon, J. M.), p. 1809 (1987)

15 ZHAO-QI WU and YOUNG, J. F., 'The hydration of tricalcium silicate in the presence of colloidal silica', *Journal of Material Science*, **19**, 3477 (1984)

16 NELSEN, J. A. and YOUNG, J. F., 'Addition of colloidal silicas and silicates to Portland cement pastes', *Cement and Concrete Research*, **7**, 277 (1977)

17 DIAMOND, S., 'Effects of microsilica (silica fume) on pore solution chemistry of cement pastes', *Journal of American Ceramic Society*, **66**, C-82 (1983)

18 PAGE, C. L. and VEUNESLAND, Ø., 'Pore solution composition and chloride binding capacity of silica-fume cement pastes', *Matériaux et Constructions*, **16**, 19 (1983)

19 RAYMENT, P. L., 'The effect of pulverised-fuel ash on the C/S molar ratio and alkali content of calcium silicate hydrates in cement', *Cement and Concrete Research*, **12**, 133 (1982)

20 GRUTZECK, M. W., ATKINSON, S. and ROY, D. M., 'Mechanism of hydration of condensed silica fume in calcium hydroxide solutions'. In *ACI Special Publication SP-79* (ed. Malhotra, V. M.), American Concrete Institute, Detroit, p. 643 (1983)

21 DIAMOND, S., 'Scientific basis for the use of microsilica in concrete', *First Seminar—Elkem Microsilica Technology*, Elkem Chemicals, San Paulo (Sep. 1984)

22 SARKAR, S. L. and AITCIN, P.-C., 'Comparative study of the microstructures of normal and very-high-strength concretes', *Cement, Concrete and Aggregate*, **9**, 57 (1987)

23 BACHE, H. H., 'Densified cement/ultrafine particle-based materials', *Second International Conference on Superplasticizers in Concrete, CBL Report No. 40*, CBL, Ottawa, p. 35 (Jun. 1981)

24 HJORTH, L., 'Development and application of high-density cement-based materials', *Technology in the 1990s: Developments in Hydraulic Cements*, The Royal Society, London, p. 167 (1983)

25 REGOURD, M., 'Microstructure of high strength cement paste systems', *Proceedings of the Symposium of the Material Research Society*, **42**, 3 (1985)

26 BENTUR, A. and COHEN, M. D., 'Effect of condensed silica fume on the microstructure of the interfacial zone in Portland cement materials', *Journal of American Ceramic Society*, **70**, 738 (1987)

27 HADLEY, D. N., 'The nature of the paste–aggregate interface', Ph.D. Thesis, School of Civil Engineering, Purdue University (1972)

28 FELDMAN, R. F., 'Pore structure damage in blended cements caused by mercury intrusion', *Journal of American Ceramic Society*, **62**, 30 (1984)

29 FELDMAN, R. F. and CHENG-YI HWANG, 'Properties of Portland cement–silica fume pastes. I: porosity and surface properties', *Cement and Concrete Research*, **15**, 765 (1985)

30 CHENG-YI HWANG and FELDMAN, R. F., 'Dependence of frost resistance on the pore structure of mortar containing silica fume', *Journal of American Concrete Institute*, **82**, 740 (1985)

31 FELDMAN, R. F., 'The effect of sand/cement ratio and silica fume on the microstructure of mortars', *Cement and Concrete Research*, **16**, 31 (1986)

32 CHENG-YI HWANG and FELDMAN, R. F., 'Influence of silica fume on the microstructural development in cement mortars', *Cement and Concrete Research*, **15**, 285 (1985)

33 BUIL, M. and DELAGE, P., 'Some further evidence on a specific effect of silica fume on the pore structure of Portland cement mortars', *Cement and Concrete Research*, **17**, 65 (1987)

34 SELLEVOLD, E. J. and RADJY, F. F., 'Condensed silica fume in concrete'. In *ACI Special Publication SP-79* (ed. Malhotra, V. M.), American Concrete Institute, Detroit, p. 677 (1983)

35 CARETTE, G. G. and MALHOTRA, V. M., 'Mechanical properties, durability and drying shrinkage of Portland cement concrete incorporating silica fume', *Cement, Concrete and Aggregate*, **5**, 3 (1983)

36 MARKESTAD, S. A., 'A study of the combined influence of silica fume and water reducing admixture on water demand and strength of concrete', *Matériaux et Constructions*, **19**, 39 (1986)

37 MANGIALARDI, T. and PAOLINI, A. E., 'Workability of superplasticized microsilica–Portland cement concretes', *Cement and Concrete Research*, **18**, 351 (1988)

38 SELLEVOLD, E. J. and NILSON, T., 'Condensed silica fume in concrete: a world review'. In *Supplementary Cementing Materials for Concrete* (ed. Malhotra, V. M.), CANMET SP86-8E, Canada, Chap. 3, p. 428 (1987)

39 BÜRGE, T. A., 'High strength lightweight concrete with condensed silica fume'. In *ACI Special Publication SP-79* (ed. Malhotra, V. M.), American Concrete Institute, Detroit, p. 643 (1983)

40 MELAND, I., 'Influence of condensed silica fume and fly ash on the heat evolution in cement pastes'. In *ACI Special Publication SP-79* (ed. Malhotra, V. M.), American Concrete Institute, Detroit, p. 643 (1983)

41 JAREN, P., 'Use of silica fume in concrete'. In *ACI Special Publication SP-79* (ed. Malhotra, V. M.), American Concrete Institute, Detroit, p. 625 (1983)

42 SANDUIK, M. and GJØRV, O. E., 'Effect of condensed silica fume on the strength development of concrete'. In *ACI Special Publication SP-91* (ed. Malhotra, V. M.), American Concrete Institute, Detroit, Vol. 2, p. 893 (1986)

43 MAAGE, M., 'Strength and heat development in concrete: influence of fly ash and condensed silica fume'. In *ACI Special Publication SP-91* (ed. Malhotra, V. M.), American Concrete Institute, Detroit, Vol. 2, p. 923 (1986)

44 MALHOTRA, V. M., 'Mechanical properties, and freezing and thawing resistance of non air-entrained and air-entrained condensed silica fume concrete using ASTM Test C666, Procedures A and B', *Mineral Sciences Laboratories, Division Report MRP/MSL 84-153 (OP&J)*, Minerals Research Program, CANMET, Ottawa (1984)

45 TAKAGI, N. and AKASHI, T., 'Properties of concrete containing silica fume', *Transactions of the Japan Concrete Institute*, **6**, 47 (1984)

46 MALHOTRA, V. M. and CARETTE, G. G., 'Mechanical properties of concrete incorporating both fly ash and condensed silica fume', *Proceedings of RILEM-ACI Symposium on Technology of Concrete When Pozzolans, Slags and Chemical Admixtures Are Used*, Monterey, Mexico, p. 395 (1985)

47 WOLSIEFER, J., 'Ultra-high-strength field placeable concrete with silica fume admixture', *ACI Concrete International*, **6**, 25 (1984)

48 CARLES-GIBERGUES, A., GRANDET, J. and OLLIVIER, J. P., 'Contact zone between cement paste and aggregate'. In *Proceedings of the International Conference on Bond in Concrete* (ed. Bartos, P.), Applied Science Publishers, Barking, p. 24 (1982)

49 BÜRGE, T. A., 'High strength lightweight concrete with condensed silica fume'. In *ACI Special Publication SP-79* (ed. Malhotra, V. M.), American Concrete Institute, Detroit, p. 731 (1983)

50 ROBINS, P. J. and AUSTIN, S. A., 'Bond of lightweight aggregate concrete incorporating condensed silica fume'. In *ACI Special Publication SP-91* (ed. Malhotra, V. M.), American Concrete Institute, Detroit, p. 944 (1986)

51 BÜRGE, T. A., 'Densified cement matrix improves bond with reinforcing steel'. In *Proceedings of the International Conference on Bond in Concrete* (ed. Batos, P.), Applied Science Publishers, Barking, p. 273 (1982)

52 RAMAKRISHNAN, V. and SRINIVASAN, V., 'Performance characteristics of fiber reinforced condensed silica fume concretes'. In *ACI Special Publication SP-79* (ed. Malhotra, V. M.), American Concrete Institute, Detroit, Vol. 2, p. 797 (1983)

53 RAMAKRISHNAN, V., COYLE, W. V., KULANDEISAUY, and SCHRADER, E. K., 'Performance characteristics of fiber reinforced concretes with low fiber contents', *Journal of American Concrete Institute*, **78**, 388 (1981)

54 OHAMA, Y., AMANO, M. and ENDO, M., 'Properties of carbon fiber reinforced cement with silica fume', *Concrete International: Design and Construction*, **7**, 58 (1985)

55 KENCHEL, H. and SHAH, S., 'Applications of polypropylene

fibers in Scandinavia', *Concrete International: Design and Construction*, **2**, 32 (1985)

56 BUIL, M. and ACKER, P., 'Creep of silica fume concrete', *Cement and Concrete Research*, **15**, 463 (1985)

57 TAZAWA, E. and YONEKURA, A., 'Drying shrinkage and creep of concrete with condensed silica fume'. In *ACI Special Publication SP-91* (ed. Malhotra, V. M.), American Concrete Institute, Detroit, Vol. 2, p. 903 (1986)

58 LIU, T. C., 'Abrasion resistance of concrete', *Journal of American Concrete Institute*, **78**, 341 (1981)

59 HOLLAND, T. C. *et al.*, 'Use of silica-fume concrete to repair abrasion erosion damage in the Kinzua Dam Stilling Basin'. In *ACI Special Publication SP-91* (ed. Malhotra, V. M.), American Concrete Institute, Detroit, p. 84 (1986)

60 LØLAND, K. E. and HUSTAD, T., 'Report 2: mechanical properties', *Report No. STF65 A81031, FCB/SINTEF*, The Norwegian Institute of Technology, Trondheim (1981)

61 PISTILLI, M. F., RAU, G. and CECHNER, R., 'The variability of condensed silica fume from a Canadian source and its influence on the properties of Portland cement concrete', *Cement, Concrete and Aggregate*, **6**, 33 (1984)

62 JOHANSEN, R., 'Report 6: long-term effects', *Report No. STF65A 81031*, Cement and Concrete Research Institute, The Norwegian Institute of Technology, Trondheim (1983)

63 GJØRV, O. E., 'Durability of concrete containing condensed silica fume'. In *ACI Special Publication SP-79* (ed. Malhotra, V. M.), American Concrete Institute, Detroit, p. 695 (1983)

64 NAGATAKI, S. and UJIKE, I., 'Air permeability of concretes mixed with fly ashes and condensed silica fume'. In *ACI Special Publication SP-91* (ed. Malhotra, V. M.), American Concrete Institute, Detroit, p. 1049 (1986)

65 GAUTEFALL, O., 'Effect of condensed silica fume on the diffusion of chlorides through hardened cement paste'. In *ACI Special Publication SP-91* (ed. Malhotra, V. M.), American Concrete Institute, Detroit, p. 991 (1986)

66 KUMAR, A. and ROY, D. M., 'Pore structure and ionic diffusion in admixture blended Portland cement systems', *Proceedings of the 8th International Congress on the Chemistry of Cement*, FINEP, Rio de Janeiro, Vol. V, p. 73 (1986)

67 LI, S. and ROY, D. M., 'Investigation of relations between porosity, pore structure, and Cl⁻ diffusion of fly ash and blended cement paste', *Cement and Concrete Research*, **16**, 749 (1986)

68 MARUSIN, S. L., 'Chloride ion penetration in conventional concrete and concrete containing condensed silica fume'. In *ACI Special Publication SP-91* (ed. Malhotra, V. M.), American Concrete Institute, Detroit, p. 1119 (1986)

69 KAWAMURA, M. and TORII, K., 'A study on chloride permeability of concrete', *Extended Abstracts of the 44th Annual Meeting of CAJ*, pp. 584–589 (1990)

70 CHENG-YI HWANG and FELDMAN, R. F., 'Dependence of frost resistance on the pore structure of mortar containing silica fume', *Journal of American Concrete Institute*, **5**, 740 (1985)

71 LITUAN, G. G., 'Air entrainment in the presence of superplasticizers', *Journal of American Concrete Institute*, **80**, 326 (1983)

72 YAMATO, T., EMOTO, Y. and SOEDA, M., 'Strength and freezing and thawing resistance of concrete incorporating condensed silica fume'. In *ACI Special Publication SP-91* (ed. Malhotra, V. M.), American Concrete Institute, Detroit, p. 1095 (1986)

73 AMERICAN SOCIETY FOR TESTING AND MATERIALS, 'ASTM G666-84 Resistance of concrete to rapid freezing and thawing', *Annual Book of ASTM Standards*, **04.02**, p. 403. American Society for Testing and Materials, 1916, Race Street, Philadelphia, PA 19103 (1985)

74 MALHOTRA, V. M., PAINTER, K. A. and BILODEAU, A., 'Mechanical properties and freezing and thawing resistance of high-strength concrete incorporating silica fume', *Cement, Concrete and Aggregate*, **9**, 65 (1987)

75 AITCIN, P.-C. and VEJINE, D., 'Resistance to freezing and thawing of silica fume concrete', *Cement, Concrete and Aggregate*, **1**, 38 (1984)

76 PIGEON, M., PLEAU, R. and AITCIN, P.-C., 'Freeze–thaw durability of concrete with and without silica fume in ASTM C666 (Procedure A) test method: internal cracking and scaling', *Cement, Concrete and Aggregate*, **8**, 76 (1986)

77 POPOVIC, K., UKRAINCIK, V. and DJUREKOVIC, A., 'Improvement of mortar and concrete durability by the use of condensed silica fume', *Durability of Building Materials*, **2**, 171 (1984)

78 MEHTA, P. K., 'Durability of low water–cement ratio concretes containing latex or silica fume as admixtures', *Proceedings of RILEM-ACI Symposium on Technology of Concrete When Pozzolans, Slags, and Chemical Admixtures Are Used*, Autonomous University of Nuevo Leon, Monterey, Mexico, p. 325 (1985)

79 MEHTA, P. K., 'Studies of chemical resistance of low water/cement ratio concretes', *Cement and Concrete Research*, **15**, 909 (1985)

80 TORII, K. and KAWAMURA, M., 'Effect of fly ash and silica fume on the resistance of mortars against sulphate attack', *Review of the 42nd General Meeting of Cement Association of Japan*, Tokyo, May, 1988, Cement Association of Japan, Tokyo (1988)

81 FELDMAN, R. F. and CHENG-YI HWANG, 'Resistance of mortars containing silica fume to attack by a solution containing chlorides', *Cement and Concrete Research*, **15**, 411 (1985)

82 AMERICAN CONCRETE INSTITUTE, 'ACI Committee Report: guide to selection and use of hydraulic cements', *Journal of American Concrete Institute*, **82**, 901 (1985)

83 ASGEIRSSON, H. and GUDMUNDSSON, G., 'Pozzolanic activity of silica dust', *Cement and Concrete Research*, **9**, 249 (1979)

84 GUDMUNDSSON, G. and ASGEIRSSON, H., 'Parameters affecting alkali expansion in Icelandic concretes', *Proceedings of the 6th International Conference on Alkalis in Concrete*, Danish Concrete Association, Copenhagen, Denmark, p. 217 (1983)

85 OBERHOLSTER, R. E. and WEBSTRA, W. B., 'The effectiveness of mineral admixtures in reducing expansion due to the alkali–aggregate reaction with Melmesbury Group aggregates', *Proceedings of the 5th International Conference on Alkali–Aggregate Reaction in Concrete*, National Building Research Institute of the Council for Scientific and Industrial Research, Cape Town, (s 252/31) (1981)

86 SPRUNG, S. and ADADIAN, M., 'The effect of admixtures on alkali–aggregate reaction in concrete', *Proceedings of the Symposium on Effect of Alkalis on the Properties of Concrete*, Cement and Concrete Association, London, p. 125 (1976)

87 KAWAMURA, M., TAKEMOTO, K. and HASABA, S., 'Effectiveness of various silica fumes in preventing alkali–silica expansion'. In *ACI Special Publication SP-100* (ed. Scanlon, J. M.), American Concrete Institute, Detroit, p. 1809 (1987)

88 PERRY, C. and GILLOT, J. E., 'The feasibility of using silica fume to control expansion due to alkali–aggregate reactions', *Durability of Building Materials*, **3**, 133 (1985)

89 HOBBS, D. W., *Alkali–Silica Reaction in Concrete*, Thomas Telford Ltd, London, p. 123 (1988)

90 KAWAMURA, M., TAKEMOTO, K. and HASABA, S., 'Effect of silica fume on alkali–silica expansion in mortars'. In *ACI Special Publication SP-91* (ed. Malhotra, V. M.), American Concrete Institute, Detroit, p. 999 (1986)

91 AITCIN, P.-C. and REGOURD, M., 'The use of condensed silica fume to control alkali–silica reaction—a field case study', *Cement and Concrete Research*, **15**, 711 (1985)

92 BYFORS, K., HANSSON, C. M. and TRITTHART, J., 'Pore solution expression as a method to determine the influence of mineral admixtures on chloride binding', *Cement and Concrete Research*, **16**, 760 (1986)

93 VENNESLAND, Ø. and GJØRV, O. E., 'Silica concrete protection against corrosion of embedded steel'. In *ACI Special Publication SP-79* (ed. Malhotra, V. M.), American Concrete Institute, Detroit, p. 719 (1983)

94 SKJOLSVOLD, O., 'Carbonation depth of concrete with and without condensed silica fume'. In *ACI Special Publication SP-91* (ed. Malhotra, V. M.), American Concrete Institute, Detroit, p. 1031 (1983)

95 PREECE, C. M., ARUP, H. and FRØLUND, T., 'Electrochemical behavior of steel in dense silica cement mortar'. In *ACI Special Publication SP-79* (ed. Malhotra, V. M.), American Concrete Institute, Detroit, p. 785 (1983)

96 PAGE, C. L. and HAVDAHL, J., 'Electrochemical monitoring of corrosion of steel in microsilica cement paste', *Matériaux et Constructions*, **18**, 41 (1985)

97 MONTERIO, P. J. M., GJØRV, O. E. and MEHTA, P. K.,
    'Microstructure of the steel–cement paste interface in the
    presence of chloride', *Cement and Concrete Research*, **15**, 781
    (1985)
98 SKRASTINS, J. I. and ZOLDUERS, N. G., 'Ready-mixed
    concrete incorporating condensed silica fume'. In *ACI Special
    Publication SP-79* (ed. Malhotra, V. M.), American Concrete
    Institute, Detroit, p. 813 (1983)
99 PARKER, D. G., 'Microsilica concrete. Part 2: in use', *Concrete*,
    20, 19 (1986)
100 BERGSTRÖM, S. G. and GRAM, H.-E., 'Durability of
    alkali-sensitive fibers in concrete', *The International Journal of
    Cement Composites and Lightweight Concrete*, **6**, 75 (1984)
101 BENTUR, A. and DIAMOND, S., 'Direct incorporation of
    silica fume into glass fibre strands as a means for developing
    GFRC composites of improved durability', *The International
    Journal of Cement Composites and Lightweight Concrete*, **9**, 127
    (1987)
102 BENTUR, A., 'Treatment of glass fibre strands in polymer and
    silica fume dispersions to improve the aging performance of glass
    fibre reinforced concretes', *Advances in Cement Research*, **1**, 147
    (1988)

103 DOMONE, P. L. and TANK, S. B., 'Use of condensed silica
    fume in Portland cement grouts'. In *ACI Special Publication
    SP-91* (ed. Malhotra, V. M.), American Concrete Institute,
    Detroit, p. 1231 (1986)
104 WAKELIY, L. D. and BUCK, A. D., 'Effects of different fly ash
    and silica fume on selected properties of an expansive grout'. In
    ACI Special Publication SP-91 (ed. Malhotra, V. M.), American
    Concrete Institute, Detroit, p. 1261 (1986)
105 HANSEN, T. C. and NARUD, H., 'Recycled concrete and silica
    fume make calcium silicate bricks', *Cement and Concrete
    Research*, **13**, 626 (1983)
106 CANADIAN STANDARDS ASSOCIATION, *CSA A23.5
    Supplementary cementing materials and guidelines for their use in
    concrete*, Rexdale, Ontario (1987)
107 NORWEGIAN NATIONAL STANDARDS, *NS 3420* and
    NS 3474 (1978)
108 BRITISH STANDARDS INSTITUTION, *BS 5328 Methods for
    specifying concrete, including ready mixed concrete*, Milton
    Keynes (1981)
109 PARKER, D. G., 'Microsilica concrete. Part 1: the material',
    Concrete, **19**, 21 (1985)

24

Sprayed and Sprayed Fibre Concrete

P Robins BSc, PhD, CEng, MICE
Loughborough University of Technology

S Austin BSc, PhD, CEng, MICE
Loughborough University of Technology

Contents

24.1 Introduction 24/3
    24.1.1 Scope 24/3
    24.1.2 Definitions 24/3
    24.1.3 Comparison of dry and wet processes 24/3
    24.1.4 Comparison of fibre- and mesh-reinforced
        sprayed concrete 24/3

24.2 Materials 24/4
    24.2.1 General 24/4
    24.2.2 Cement 24/4
    24.2.3 Aggregates 24/4
    24.2.4 Additives 24/4
    24.2.5 Silica fume 24/4
    24.2.6 Fibres 24/4
    24.2.7 Mix proportions 24/5
    24.2.8 Mesh and bar reinforcement 24/5

24.3 Production and installation 24/5
    24.3.1 The dry-mix production process 24/5
    24.3.2 Dry process spraying and rebound 24/6
    24.3.3 The wet-mix production process 24/7
    24.3.4 Wet process spraying and rebound 24/7

24.4 Physical properties 24/8
    24.4.1 Introduction 24/8
    24.4.2 Compressive strength 24/8
    24.4.3 Flexural strength 24/8
    24.4.4 Flexural toughness 24/9
    24.4.5 Impact resistance 24/9
    24.4.6 Bond to substrate 24/10
    24.4.7 Shrinkage 24/10
    24.4.8 Water absorption 24/10
    24.4.9 Permeability 24/10
    24.4.10 Freeze–thaw resistance 24/10
    24.4.11 Reinforcement corrosion 24/11

24.5 Specification 24/11
    24.5.1 Current documentation relating to sprayed
    concrete 24/11
    24.5.2 Specification of sprayed fibre concrete 24/11

24.6 Quality control 24/12
    24.6.1 Introduction 24/12
    24.6.2 Preconstruction testing 24/12
    24.6.3 Panels for routine quality-control testing 24/12
    24.6.4 Fibre-content determination 24/12
    24.6.5 Strength testing 24/12
    24.6.6 Testing for properties other than strength 24/13

24.7 Design considerations 24/13
    24.7.1 Suitable applications 24/13
    24.7.2 Construction method 24/14
    24.7.3 Reinforcement 24/14
    24.7.4 Fibres 24/14
    24.7.5 Mix design 24/15
    24.7.6 Moment capacity 24/15

References 24/16

24.1 Introduction

24.1.1 Scope

This chapter is concerned with two specialist materials used in the construction industry: sprayed concrete and fibre-reinforced concrete. Sprayed concrete can be produced using either the dry-mix or wet-mix process. The emphasis here is placed upon the dry process because this accounts for the vast majority of applications in the UK and many other countries. Recently, however, the wet process has been increasingly used in Scandinavia, parts of Europe and North America.

Sprayed concrete may be plain, mesh reinforced, fibre reinforced or heavily reinforced for primary structural applications (where a significant moment capacity is required). Plain, mesh- and bar-reinforced sprayed concretes differ only from their cast-concrete equivalents in the method of construction and the relatively minor changes in concrete material properties that result. In contrast, fibre-reinforced sprayed concrete is a different type of composite, being reinforced on a micro rather than a macro scale. The use of fibre reinforcement significantly alters material behaviour by providing post-crack ductility and this in turn dictates the type of application to which it is best suited. The engineer is thus likely to need more information on the newer and less familiar fibre-reinforced option, and this is reflected in the balance of this chapter.

24.1.2 Definitions

Sprayed concrete can be defined as mortar or concrete conveyed through a hose and pneumatically projected at high velocity from a nozzle into place. Sprayed concrete is also sometimes referred to as *gunite* or *shotcrete*, terms which the Concrete Society[1] have defined as sprayed concrete with a maximum aggregate size of <10 mm and $\geqslant 10$ mm, respectively. This terminology does not distinguish between the two processes of producing sprayed concrete, namely dry and wet.

In the *dry (mix) process* cement, dry or moist aggregate and any other dry additives are batched and mixed together before being fed into a purpose-made machine or gun. The mixture is pressurized, metered into a compressed-air stream and conveyed through a delivery hose to a nozzle where water is introduced under pressure as a spray to wet the mix before it is projected into place. The dry materials may be prebagged, site batched or truck mixed. This is the original sprayed-concrete process, developed in 1911 by the Cement Gun Company of Allentown, Pennsylvania who called the material 'gunite'.

In the *wet (mix) process* the cement, aggregate, admixtures and water are batched and mixed together on site or in transit mixers before being fed into the delivery equipment or pump. The mix is metered into a delivery hose and conveyed by compressed air or peristaltic action to the nozzle where compressed air is injected to project the material into place.

Losses may result from material not reaching, failing to adhere to or bouncing off the target surface. These losses are collectively referred to as *rebound*.

24.1.3 Comparison of dry and wet processes

The dry and wet processes are compared in *Table 24.1*. The main advantages of the dry process are: (a) straightforward mix design; (b) good stop/start flexibility because there is no hydrating material in the machinery or hoses; and (c) good *in situ* properties, particularly compaction and strength. The main advantages of the wet process are: (a) lower material losses; (b) better control of water content and mixing; and (c) a cleaner, relatively dust-free, spraying environment.

24.1.4 Comparison of fibre- and mesh-reinforced sprayed concrete

The inclusion of fibres in concrete improves its post-crack ductility, toughness, impact resistance, fatigue resistance and flexural strength. The type and amount of improvement is dependent upon the fibre's tensile properties (strength and stiffness), its bond strength (governed by shape and surface texture) and the amount of fibres. The main fibre types in use are steel (produced from wire, sheet and melt extraction), glass and polypropylene. The size and quantity of fibre reinforcement is usually limited by practical considerations concerned with the mixing process. Fibres vary considerably in cost but none can be considered cheap. Their use is, therefore, limited to forms of construction which will benefit substantially from the energy-absorbing characteristics of fibre concrete. Certain applications of sprayed concrete fall into this category.

In many circumstances sprayed concrete is not required to carry large loads in flexure and is conveniently reinforced with light mesh. The purpose of the mesh is mainly to hold the concrete together in the event of cracking. The alternative of a sprayed fibre concrete lining has the following possible advantages:

(1) considerably greater post-crack resistance or toughness;
(2) much higher impact resistance;
(3) improved flexural strength;
(4) saving in cost of fixing mesh reinforcement;
(5) faster construction;
(6) reduced design thickness; and
(7) reduced volume of material required to cover uneven surfaces.

These must be balanced against the possible disadvantages of fibre reinforcement:

(1) cost of fibres;
(2) fibre rebound may be higher than material rebound (i.e. cement and aggregate);
(3) discomfort (particularly with steel fibres);
(4) occasional difficulty in mixing and spraying; and
(5) durability of fibres.

Table 24.1 Comparison of wet and dry processes

Characteristic	Dry process	Wet process
Water content	Variable, controlled by nozzleman	Constant, controlled during batching
Use of admixtures	Accelerator occasionally used	Plasticizers and accelerators common
Stop/start flexibility	Good	Poor, concrete can set in hoses
Material rebound	High, 15–35% on vertical surface	Low, 10–15% on vertical surface
Homogeneity of concrete	Fluctuating water:cement ratio causes variation	Pumping can cause segregation
In situ properties	Good compaction and strength	Less remarkable but less variable
Spraying environment	Usually dusty	Relatively clean

Of these the main concern is cost and durability. Stainless steel and polypropylene fibres are durable, but carbon steel fibres may corrode and glass fibres, even the alkali-resistant type, deteriorate with age in a cement matrix.

24.2 Materials

24.2.1 General

The materials used in sprayed concrete are basically the same as those used in ordinary cast structural concrete. Most sprayed concrete placed to date in the UK has used the dry process with a sand:cement ratio of around 3.0:1 by weight. *In situ* proportions can be significantly different from those of the dry mix due to the differential rebound of the individual constituents. Typical data is quoted by Ward and Hills.[2]

In Norway most sprayed concrete produced today is by the wet process and in Sweden and Finland this method is now competing with the dry process.[3] The materials typically used in these countries for wet process sprayed concrete are aggregate, cement, microsilica, plasticizers, accelerators and fibres. Plasticizers and even superplasticizers are used to give a suitable pumping consistency at low water:cement ratios, and accelerators are added to achieve a quick set and allow application of thicker layers.

24.2.2 Cement

Ordinary Portland cement is the most commonly used binder, although other cements such as sulphate resisting and rapid hardening can be used if conditions require them. High alumina cement finds limited application in civil engineering but is the norm in the refractory industry.

24.2.3 Aggregates

24.2.3.1 Dry mix

The grading of aggregates is critical in sprayed concrete due to the lack of external vibration and the changes in mix proportions as a result of rebound. Heavier particles rebound more than the lighter sand grains and cement, resulting in a more finely graded material *in situ* with a higher cement content. Gradings should therefore be kept coarse to ensure a balanced *in situ* material. Aggregates should conform with BS 882: 1983[4] or equivalent national standard.

In the UK a zone-2 sand with 6 mm maximum aggregate size is most common. Other recommended gradings are given by Kobler,[5] gradation curve no. 1 of ASTM C33,[6] ACI Committee 504[7] and equipment manufacturers. Aggregates used are usually of marine or river origin since irregular, angular or flaky aggregate is more abrasive and can cause blockages.

24.2.3.2 Wet mix

Of crucial importance is the need to achieve a balance between the concrete characteristics required to produce a pumpable mix and those characteristics required to project it into place with minimum losses and segregation. Correct aggregate grading is more critical than in the dry process and dependent upon the pumping distance and equipment. Engineers should be guided by the equipment manufacturers recommendations, but pumping gradings are discussed by Kempster.[8,9] The amount of large aggregate particles should be kept low (because of high rebound) and the sand content high (to ensure adequate consistency). The sand should have a high fines content, one equipment manufacturer's recommending approximately 500 kg m^{-3} of material smaller than 0.25 mm, including cement.

24.2.4 Additives

A variety of additives and admixtures are added to sprayed concrete, particularly with the wet process, to improve strength, adhesiveness, cohesiveness, freezing–thawing and abrasion-resistance characteristics, and to reduce rebound. Increased material costs can be offset by savings in the amount of sprayed concrete and labour.

Accelerators are common in the dry process to increase early strength and reduce dust. In the wet process an accelerator (often sodium silicate) is sometimes added at the nozzle to ensure rapid set.[10] Jones[11] gives a discussion on suitable admixtures. Wallace[12] recently reported that a potassium aluminate based accelerator produced rapid set without early strength loss in the wet process; he also claims that it reduced dust and rebound in the dry process.

Water-reducers (commonly lignosulphonic acids or hydroxylated carboxylic acids) and superplaticizers are also employed in the wet process to improve workability and cohesiveness; Krantz[13] describes the use of both types of admixture.

Air-entrainment in the dry process has generally proved unsuccessful, but can be used in the wet process, although it is difficult to obtain *in situ* air contents above 5%.[14] There is some evidence that sprayed concrete requires a lower air content (2–3%) for freeze–thaw resistance than conventionally placed concrete.[14]

Polymer latex additives (such as styrene-butadiene) have been utilized in the dry process to try and improve adhesion, resistance to chlorides and freeze–thaw attack, and to reduce permeability.[13–15] Schorn[16] has investigated an epoxy resin (polyvinylacetate) in the dry process, added as an emulsion through a special water ring in the nozzle, to try to minimize the effect of differential shrinkage between the sprayed layer and its substrate.

24.2.5 Silica fume

Silica fume is being increasingly used in the sprayed concrete industry, particularly in Scandinavia and North America. It is added in both the dry and wet processes, usually at between 5 and 15% by weight replacement of cement. There are many advantages claimed for this pozzolanic material including a reduction in rebound, easier application of thicker layers, lower dust in the dry process, better adhesion to both dry and wet surfaces, improved resistance to wash-out by water, and improved strength and durability.

Morgan[17] has reported on the extensive application in western Canada of dry process silica fume sprayed concrete reinforced with steel fibres for repair of marine structures, rock-slope stabilization, tunnel linings and aqueducts. Skatun[10] and Opsahl[3] have reported that nearly all sprayed concrete work carried out in Norway is now done by the wet process, with silica fume a common additive at around 10% by weight of cement. In the wet process a water reducer or superplasticizer is invariably required to maintain workability.

24.2.6 Fibres

24.2.6.1 General

Fibres for sprayed concrete are manufactured from one of three materials: steel, polypropylene or glass. Of the three, steel fibres account for by far the largest usage, having applications in mine and tunnel linings, rock-slope stabilization, thin-shell dome construction, refractory linings, dam construction, repair of surfaces, and fire-protection coatings. Glass-fibre reinforcement of sprayed concrete is less common, principally because of concern over long-term durability (due to alkali attack of the glass); one reported application is the repair of a navigation lock in Washington State.[18] Uses of dry process sprayed concrete with polypropylene fibres have only recently begun to be reported,[19] but include applications such as tunnel linings, shell domes, repair and as a component in stucco-type overlay systems.[20]

24.2.6.2 Steel

Steel fibres for sprayed concrete are available in a wide variety of shapes, sizes and metal types. Cross-sections may be round, rectangular, semicircular or crescent shaped, and fibre lengths can vary from about 12 mm up to as much as 75 mm. However, most successful sprayed-concrete applications have used fibres with lengths in the range 18–30 mm, with 20–25 mm being the most common. Typically, aspect ratios (length:diameter) are in the range 40–75, values above this being very difficult to spray.

The three most common fibre types used for sprayed concrete are:

(1) hooked wire—a cold drawn carbon steel fibre with hooked ends for improved bond;
(2) slit sheet—a short slit-sheet carbon steel fibre with a rectangular cross-section and enlarged ends; and
(3) melt extract—a melt-extracted high carbon or stainless steel fibre with crescent-shaped cross-section and rough surface texture.

The stainless steel (AISI 430, 446 or 304) melt extract fibre has the obvious advantage of being corrosion resistant. Stainless-steel wire and slit-sheet fibres, though available, are prohibitively expensive for civil applications and are only used in high temperature refractory concrete. Corrosion of carbon steel fibres in civil applications has been reported to be minimal with little effect on properties of steel-fibre reinforced concrete; fibre corrosion has been observed to be confined to fibres exposed on a surface, with internal fibres showing no corrosion.[20]

24.2.6.3 Polypropylene

Polypropylene fibres have been used since the early 1970s in the UK to reinforce concrete pile caps.[21] This older type of 'chopped string' fibre was not popular for sprayed concrete. More recently, new types of fibrillated fibre have become available with reported higher elastic modulus (up to 18 GPa), higher tensile strength (up to 700 MPa) and improved bond due to fibrillation. Fibres are available in lengths of around 5–50 mm with a cross-section of the order of $120 \times 20 \ \mu m$.

24.2.7 Mix proportions

In the dry process, fluctuations in water content and differential rebound of materials make mix design difficult. Dry-mix proportions are, therefore, based on experience, typical sand:cement ratios being in the range 3:1 to 4:1 by weight (resulting in *in situ* ratios in the range 1.8:1 to 3.2:1, depending on the amount of rebound) with a water:cement ratio between 0.35 and 0.45. These rich low water content mixes can achieve compressive strengths of 40–70 MPa. Fibres, if included, are typically 18–35 mm long, with 25 mm often being preferred from the standpoint of in-place sprayed concrete strength and ease of mixing and placing. Shorter fibres are easier to mix and shoot and rebound less, but the hardened concrete strength properties, particularly toughness and post-crack resistance, are lower. The amount of steel fibres included has ranged from about 1.5 to 6% by weight of dry mix material, with around 4% being most common. Examples of mix designs are given elsewhere.[20,22–28]

In contrast, wet process sprayed concrete can be designed for strength and workability in a similar way to conventionally pumped concrete. The mix design is affected by the pumping distance, hose diameter and required output rate. Aggregates are commonly 10 mm, with 20 mm sometimes being used for large-volume applications. Water:cement ratios are typically 0.4–0.55. Mixes often contain additives, the most common being a water reducer or superplasticizer, silica fume, and an accelerator (added at the nozzle). The latter allows higher slump mixes to be sprayed. Fibre sizes and contents are similar to those used in the dry process. Examples of wet process mix designs are given elsewhere.[3,10,23,24,27,29,30]

24.2.8 Mesh and bar reinforcement

Light meshes are common as reinforcement in sprayed concrete where major strengthening is not required; the mesh is intended to hold the sprayed concrete layer together in the event of cracking or debonding from the substrate. The mesh is often located near the centre of the layer where it makes little contribution to moment resistance. Typically, meshes are 75×75 mm or 100×100 mm with a wire diameter around 2.5–4.0 mm, giving a steel area of 90–130 mm² m⁻¹. Lighter meshes are easier to handle and fix but should be rigid enough to prevent vibration during placement of the sprayed concrete. Waller[31] examined four different meshes (50–175 mm² m⁻¹) for use at the Dinorwig pumped storage scheme, and found that all performed satisfactorily in terms of rebound and bond between the sprayed concrete and slate substrate.

In fully structural situations, conventional mild steel or high yield reinforcement will be required. Care must be taken, however, to provide adequate spacing to prevent inclusion of rebound behind or between bars. A fuller discussion of good practice relating to reinforcement is given elsewhere.[26,32]

24.3 Production and installation

24.3.1 The dry-mix production process

Detailed descriptions of plant, equipment and spraying techniques are reported elsewhere.[20,26,32] Guns are usually of the rotating-barrel type and require a large compressor (typically 17 m³ min⁻¹ capacity). Dry materials are often auger fed into the gun via a predampener, which reduces dust and improves hydration at the nozzle. Sledge- or truck-mounted automated systems together with robot spraying arms are used for large-volume applications, such as tunnelling.

The dry-mix materials may be volume batched (using gauging boxes) but are usually weight batched. Materials can be mixed on site, in a transit mixer, or preblended and bagged off site. A bag size of 25 kg is most common, but large bags containing from 0.5 tonne up to 1.5 tonne[33] can be used.

If the mix contains fibres, the main requirement in the production process is to ensure an uninterrupted flow of material to the nozzle with a reasonably uniform distribution of fibres at the specified fibre content. A suitable technique for dispensing fibres into the mix and getting the mix through the gun is essential. Production methods usually involve either manual site batching, automated site batching, or prebagging.[34] Manual site batching is the cheapest and most commonly used method in the UK, with an output rate of 1–1.5 m³ h⁻¹ being readily achieved. The use of a conveyor, with or without predampening, enhances the process. The main disadvantage of manual site batching is the difficulty in controlling fibre content and fibre dispersion.

Automated site batching involves conveying the cement–aggregate mix from a batching plant to the spraying site by a transit mixer. Fibre reinforcement can be added at the batching plant, directly into the transit mixer (not recommended), or at the conveyor to the gun (possibly using a fibre dispenser). With

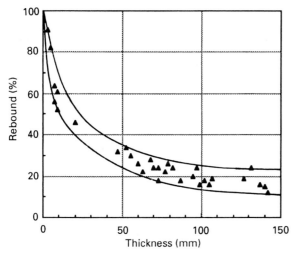

Figure 24.1 Effect of layer thickness on material rebound (Parker et al.[37])

automated site batching, the output rate will usually be limited by the gun's capacity or the amount the nozzleman can handle (up to $10 \, \text{m}^3 \, \text{h}^{-1}$ may be possible).

24.3.2 Dry-process spraying and rebound

24.3.2.1 Construction technique

Spraying technique and the set up of the gun are principally concerned with achieving a balance between good compaction and hence good *in situ* properties on the one hand (high gunning pressure, low water content) and low rebound of material on the other (low gunning pressure, high water content). Discussions of good spraying practice and associated construction techniques are given by Ryan,[26] the American Concrete Institute[32,35] and the Concrete Society.[36]

24.3.2.2 Material rebound

Material rebound is influenced by many factors, including direction of spraying, spraying distance, aggregate grading, aggregate moisture content, water pressure, water-ring and nozzle design, additives and admixtures, layer thickness and surface conditions.

Detailed studies by Parker et al.[37,38] and Ward and Hills[2] have shown that typical particle velocities are in the range $20–50 \, \text{m s}^{-1}$. Material rebound decreases as a layer is built up (*Figure 24.1*), the softer and more plastic surface retaining more particles. Rebound has been measured to be in the range 15–25% when spraying a 100-mm thick vertical layer,[37–43] but 20–30% might realistically be expected under site conditions. Rebound increases as the nozzle inclination is raised from the horizontal; overhead values of 20–40% have been reported.[20–42] Material rebound is also dependent on the nozzle-to-target-surface distance, a distance of around 1.0 m usually being optimum.

Material rebound has a marked effect upon the grading and proportions of the materials *in situ*. Ward and Hills[2] sprayed 50-mm thick vertical panels and measured the grading and composition of the *in situ* material and rebound, and compared these with that of the dry mix (*Figure 24.2*). It is important that engineers design and specify concrete mixes taking likely *in situ* proportions into consideration.

24.3.2.3 Fibre rebound

Researchers are almost unanimous in finding that steel fibres rebound more than material, values in the range 15–60% being reported. Fibre rebound, like material rebound, is influenced by layer thickness. The *in situ* fibre content, which clearly governs the material performance, will usually be substantially less than the dry fibre content. *In situ* fibre content and fibre rebound can be determined from a simple fresh-concrete analysis (washing a weighed sample through a 150-μm sieve) using the following formulae.[34] The *in situ* fibre content, FC_i, expressed as a percentage by weight of the dry materials is given by:

$$FC_i = WFC_i \frac{(1 + WCR + ACR_i)}{(1 + ACR_i)} \% \qquad (24.1)$$

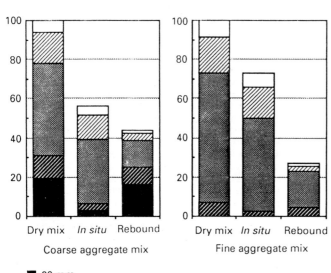

20 mm
10 mm
5–0 mm
Ordinary Portland cement
Water

Figure 24.2 Typical relative dry mix, *in situ* and rebound proportions (Ward and Hills[2])

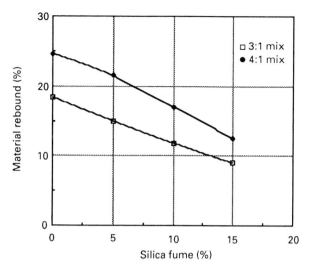

Figure 24.3 Effect of silica fume on material rebound

where WFC_i is the *in situ* fibre content (% of wet material), WCR is the water:cement ratio and ACR_i is the *in situ* aggregate:cement ratio. The fibre rebound, R_f, is given by

$$R_f = 100 - \frac{WFC_i(1 + WCR + ACR_i)}{FCR}\% \qquad (24.2)$$

where FCR is the dry-mix fibre:cement ratio (all ratios are by weight).

The authors' experience is that steel-fibre rebound under site conditions is likely to be 40–50% when spraying a 100-mm thick layer.

There is very little data available on the rebound of polypropylene fibres. However, on a recent repair contract involving the use of high-modulus fibrillated fibres to reinforce a 35-mm thick mortar coating, a fibre rebound in the range 35–40% (which was of similar order to the material rebound) was recorded.[44]

24.3.2.4 Silica fume

It has been reported that the inclusion of silica fume can significantly reduce material rebound. Morgan[17,45] has described its extensive use in Canada. When spraying a 50-mm layer overhead, incorporating silica fume in the mix was found to reduce rebound from 40% to 25%. Morgan attributed this reduction to the greater cohesion and adhesion of silica fume concrete and also pointed out that the material is very resistant to wash-out by water, making it particularly suitable for applying in running water or tidal conditions. Morgan[45] has reported details of 16 projects where dry-process silica-fume sprayed concrete has been recently used.

The authors have conducted trials in the UK and found that additions of silica fume in the range 5–15% by weight replacement of cement reduced material rebound by up to 50% in both a 3:1 mix and a 4:1 mix. The data given in *Figure 24.3* are based on some 37 different mixes both with and without fibre reinforcement. The inclusion of silica fume also significantly reduces fibre rebound. The use of 10% by weight cement replacement reduced fibre rebound from 56% to 40% in a 3:1 mix and from 65% to 50% in a 4:1 mix.

24.3.3 The wet-mix production process

Significant developments in wet-process spraying technology during the last 10 years have enabled the process to compete with its dry counterpart in certain applications, particularly tunnelling. Descriptions of plant, equipment and spraying technique have been given elsewhere.[20,26,32] The most common types of pump used in concrete spraying are worm pumps, piston pumps, peristaltic pumps and pressurized cylinder pumps.

For low-output applications, materials are usually volume or weight batched on site, sometimes in a mixer forming part of the pump; fibres, if included, are simply batched with the other ingredients. Output rates of up to 3–5 m³ h⁻¹ are achievable. For medium- and large-output applications, materials will be premixed in a batching plant/transit mixer and fed directly into the pump. Retarders and/or accelerators may well be required, the latter being metered into the delivery hose or directly at the nozzle. Output rates for a single machine of 7–9 m³ h⁻¹ can be obtained, although automated systems with robot spraying arms and a mobile pump can achieve up to 20 m³ h⁻¹.

Steel-fibre reinforcement has been successfully used on a large scale in Scandinavia.[3,10,30] Fibre contents of up to 5% by weight (1.5% by volume) are reported, the fibres being batched with other dry materials. Littlejohn[46] has reported that fibres can be added through a dispenser into the plastic mix with the Challange–Cook system. In the Besab wet system, steel fibres are added at a specially designed nozzle, allowing high-aspect-ratio fibres to be sprayed at 5% by weight.[47] Descriptions in publications of fibre addition are generally vague with little discussion on appropriate fibre sizes and contents. Opsahl and Buhre[3] reported that 18-mm long fibres are most common in Norway but that lengths up to 35 mm are possible. Ostfjord[48] discussed the applications in Sweden of straight fibres up to 60 mm long and 0.5–0.6 mm in diameter.

24.3.4 Wet process spraying and rebound

24.3.4.1 Construction process

As with the dry process, the construction method is required to produce both satisfactory *in situ* concrete properties and acceptable levels of wastage. The wet process, unlike the dry process, results in relatively low rebound and, consequently, the emphasis in development has been on mix design. The latter is principally controlled by the need to balance the conflicting concrete characteristics required for pumpable and sprayable mixes.

One approach is to produce a high-workability mix (120–200 mm slump) that can be easily pumped, and then to add an accelerator at or near the nozzle so that the concrete adheres better when sprayed. This method is commonly used on tunnelling projects where high output rates, overhead spraying and minimum disruptions due to blockages are required. Sodium silicate, at 10–20% by weight of cement, is the most commonly used accelerator to date, but with the penalty of significant strength loss at all ages. More recently, potassium aluminate based accelerators have been developed, which give no early strength loss and only a 10–20% reduction in 28-day strength.[12] Other advantages claimed for this liquid admixture are greater layer thicknesses and lower rebound.

An alternative approach, favoured in the limited amount of UK wet-process production, is to produce a medium-workability concrete (50–75 mm slump) incorporating a water reducer which is sprayed without an accelerator. This method was used on the canoe slalom course at Holme Pierrepont and at Riyadh zoological gardens.[49] These were contracts where overhead spraying and high early strength were not required and the output rate was moderate.

Discussions of good spraying practice are given by Ryan,[26]

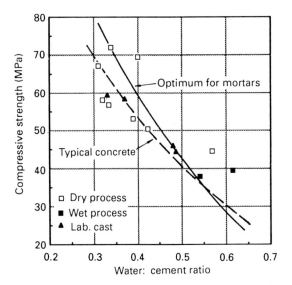

Figure 24.4 Relationship between 28-day compressive strength and water:cement ratio (Hills[51])

the American Concrete Institute[32,35] and the Concrete Society.[36]

24.3.4.2 Rebound

Material rebound with the wet process is low, typically 5–10% being reported for vertical surfaces.[3,49] Little detailed information is available due to the lack of concern over such relatively small losses. The dosage of accelerator admixture may, however, be adjusted to take account of the orientation and hardness of the surface to be sprayed.[50]

24.4 Physical properties

24.4.1 Introduction

The majority of data on properties reported here are associated with the dry process, reflecting the larger amount of published information available for this method. Properties of unreinforced sprayed concrete are given together with information on the effect of fibre reinforcement. Most of the sprayed fibre concrete data relate to steel-fibre reinforcement, there being few reported studies on sprayed concrete containing polypropylene or other fibres.

The inclusion of fibres in sprayed concrete can enhance many of the properties of the basic material. The toughness, impact resistance, shear strength, flexural strength, durability and fatigue-endurance limit may all be improved. The mode of failure is altered, large deformations occurring before rupture with the material carrying significant load after cracking. A large increase in strain-to-failure provides post-crack resistance which can be particularly advantageous in repair situations and in tunnel and mine linings where there may be relatively large deformations.

Physical properties are dependent upon the *in situ* proportions of the concrete mix, which may be significantly different to the batched quantities. The emphasis in quality control should therefore be on *in situ* testing. Most specifications on sprayed concrete address factors such as material proportions and grading and strengths, but other equally important parameters such as bond to substrate, permeability and freeze–thaw resistance are often ignored because of lack of information. The problem is further complicated by the difficulty of measuring or

quantifying acceptable limits for these properties and of determining if such limits have been exceeded.

As with conventionally cast concrete, strength and durability are dependent upon good workmanship as well as correct design and specification. Spraying concrete is a skilled and sometimes quite technical process and, as a consequence, it would be difficult to overestimate the importance of giving full consideration to the construction stage during design.

24.4.2 Compressive strength

The compressive strengths of dry-process sprayed concrete reported in literature are in the range 30–60 MPa at 28 days, obtained with aggregate:cement ratios of between 4:1 and 2.5:1 and unspecified water:cement ratios.

Reported values for conventional ordinary Portland cement wet-process sprayed concrete are generally in the range 20–45 MPa for water:cement ratios of 0.7–0.45. The addition of silica fume and a water reducer can produce strengths up to 60 MPa.

In a comparison of sprayed and cast site-produced concretes Hills[51] demonstrated that the compressive strength of both dry- and wet-process sprayed concrete broadly follows the relationship with water:cement ratio for cast concretes and mortars (*Figure 24.4*). He obtained strengths between 37 and 72 MPa with water:cement ratios of between 0.61 and 0.31.

The compressive strength of sprayed concrete is only marginally affected by the inclusion of fibres and depends on the orientation of the roughly two-dimensional fibre plane relative to the direction of compressive loading. *Figure 24.5* shows the effect of *in situ* fibre content of melt extract (25 mm long), hooked end drawn wire (25 mm), and enlarged end-slit sheet fibres (18 mm) on the core compressive strength of dry-process sprayed concrete, obtained by the authors.[52]

24.4.3 Flexural strength

Sprayed concrete is often subjected to flexural loading in service. Plain-matrix strengths will be similar to cast-concrete strengths and typically in the range 2.5–5 MPa, depending on mix proportions and layer thickness. Light mesh is commonly used to reinforce sprayed concrete; however, it is often located near

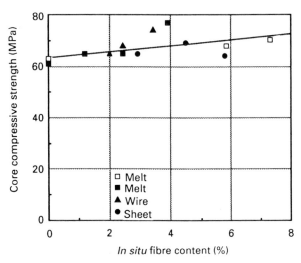

Figure 24.5 Effect of fibre content on compressive strength (dry process)

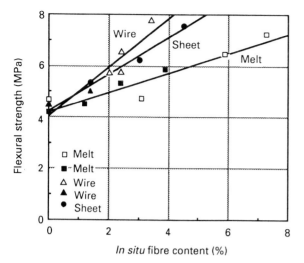

Figure 24.6 Effect of fibre content on ultimate flexural strength (dry process)

the mid-depth of the section where it provides little or no flexural strengthening. More heavily reinforced sections will have significantly higher moment capacity, which can be calculated using reinforced concrete theory (see Section 24.7.6).

Improved flexural strength is a widely perceived reason for using sprayed fibre concrete. A significant difference between the performance of plain and fibre-reinforced sprayed concrete is evident from the strengths and load–deflection curves produced from a standard beam flexural test.

Two values of flexural strength are significant: the limit of proportionality strength, and the ultimate flexural strength (or modulus of rupture). The former is only marginally influenced by fibres, but the latter increases significantly with fibre volume as the fibre reinforcement delays formation of the first major flexural crack. This usually coincides with peak load; however, above a critical fibre volume (where there are sufficient fibres to sustain the tensile load carried by the concrete prior to cracking), the composite is theoretically capable of carrying even more load and will sustain multiple cracking. Sprayed concrete *in situ* fibre contents will rarely reach the critical fibre volume.

Flexural strength can be increased by an order of up to 100%, depending on the fibre type, size and content. Values reported for the dry process are in the range 5–10 MPa.[20,53–57] *Figure 24.6* gives typical results for the three steel-fibre types investigated by the authors.[52] The superiority of hooked-end wire fibres for flexural strengthening is clearly evident.

Information on flexural strengths for wet-process sprayed fibre concrete is more sparse, through Vanderwalle[30] and Opsahl and Buhre[3] quote strengths of around 10 MPa for fibre contents of around 4.5–6% by weight of drawn-wire or slit-sheet fibres.

Very little information is available on the properties of polypropylene-fibre-reinforced sprayed concrete. The authors[44] have measured limits of proportionality and ultimate flexural strengths of 3.9–4.7 MPa and 5.2–6.6 MPa for 40 mm thick specimens containing 0.25–0.7% by weight *in situ* of high-yield fibrillated polypropylene fibres, with lengths of 6 and 12 mm, respectively.

Flexural fatigue properties have not been reported for sprayed fibre concrete, though fatigue-performance information is available for cast steel-fibre concrete.[56] The addition of steel fibres has been found to increase fatigue life considerably and decrease crack widths under fatigue loading. Generally, the fibres seem to increase fatigue strength relatively more than they do the static flexural strength.

24.4.4 Flexural toughness

Toughness of sprayed concrete is increased considerably by the addition of fibres. Fibres impart significant post-crack ductility as evidenced by fibre concrete beam load/deflection curves.

There have been several alternative methods proposed for determining a toughness index from the load/deflection curve. All involve determining a total area under the curve up to some chosen cut-off point and dividing this by an area thought to represent that which would be obtained without fibres; this has either been taken as the area under a plain beam's curve up to failure or, more conveniently, the area under the fibre-reinforced beam up to the limit of proportionality. ASTM C1018: 1985[58] specifies cut-offs which are multiples of the limit of proportionality deflection to determine toughness indices termed I_5, I_{10} and I_{30}, corresponding to cut-offs of 3, 5.5 and 15.5 times the limit of proportionality deflection. The subscripts 5, 10 and 30 correspond to the indices that would be obtained with a fundamentally significant and readily understandable form of material behaviour, namely perfect elastic–plastic behaviour.

The I_{30} toughness index obtained from a series of dry-process trials[52] using three steel-fibre types is given in *Figure 24.7*. The hooked-wire and melt-extract fibres achieved I_{10} values of around 10 at *in situ* fibre contents of approximately 2.5% and 4% by weight, respectively; the enlarged end-slit-sheet fibre achieved an I_{10} of only 6 at 4.5% by weight.

The I_{10} toughness index values for 12-mm long polypropylene-fibre-reinforced dry-process sprayed concrete measured by the authors[44] were 8, 10 and 15 for *in situ* fibre contents of 0.25%, 0.48% and 1.2% by weight. The corresponding I_{30} values were 16, 22 and 43, respectively.

24.4.5 Impact resistance

Impact resistance, or toughness under dynamic loading, is also significantly increased by the presence of fibres. The ACI Committee 544 has published a test procedure[59] for measuring impact resistance in which the number of blows to crack and separate a disc specimen is recorded. ACI Committee 506[20] reported that plain sprayed concrete specimens normally fail at from 10 to 40 blows, whereas the number of blows required to crack and separate fibrous specimens at 28 days ranges from about 100 to 500 or more depending upon the fibre content, fibre length and type.

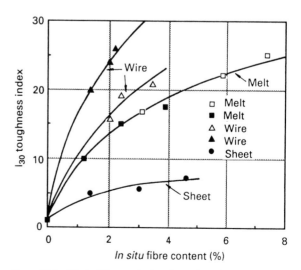

Figure 24.7 Effect of fibre content on flexural toughness (dry process)

24.4.6 Bond to substrate

The bond strength of sprayed concrete to its substrate is clearly of importance to the engineer. However, little bond data is available and the test methods employed vary considerably.

ACI Committee 506[20] reported bond strengths to a rough surfaced granitic gneiss of 3.7 MPa *in situ*, but only 0.9 MPa in the laboratory, obtained by pulling off a 610 × 610 mm embedded steel plate. Core pull-off tests on the same material gave strengths of 1.5–2.6 MPa and 0.9 MPa for plain and fibre-reinforced materials, respectively. Bond strengths of about 1.0 MPa are also reported for steel-fibre-reinforced sprayed concrete applied to granite using the wet process.

Opsahl[60] quotes bond strengths for mesh- and fibre-reinforced wet process sprayed concrete of 0–1.0 MPa and 0.8–2.5 MPa, respectively, measured from 60-mm diameter core pull-off tests. It might be expected that the presence of mesh can reduce the bond of sprayed concrete to a substrate by obstructing the jet of material being shot at the surface and also by allowing the formation of sand pockets behind the bars.

ACI Committee 506[32] also give bond strengths, obtained from a shear test on 150-mm cores, of 2.8–6.0 MPa for dry-process sprayed concrete and 0.9–2.3 MPa for wet-process sprayed concrete.

Ryan[40] has described an adhesion test in which a 600 × 600 mm sprayed-concrete slab is pulled off its substrate, and concludes that the bond strength so measured should exceed 1.0 MPa if the adhesion is to be relied upon in design.

24.4.7 Shrinkage

A knowledge of shrinkage strains is important, particularly when sprayed concrete is used in repair work, though reported information on shrinkage is sparse. Although dry-process sprayed concrete has a relatively low water:cement ratio, it can shrink significantly. Shrinkage is proportional to both water content and cement content, so that the relatively high *in situ* cement contents of dry-process sprayed concretes can produce high values of drying shrinkage.

Schrader and Kaden[14] quoted typical shrinkage values of 900×10^{-6} for dry process sprayed concrete (water:cement = 0.37 and cement content 505 kg m^{-3}) and 600×10^{-6} for wet-mix (water:cement = 0.42 and cement content 415 kg m^{-3}).

Hills[51] concluded that shrinkage values for sprayed concretes lie broadly within the expected range for cast concretes. For the site-produced sprayed concrete mixes investigated by Hills,[51] drying shrinkage at 6 months lay in the range $400–1000 \times 10^{-6}$; wet-process sprayed concrete, with its higher water:cement ratio, showed generally the greatest shrinkage; wetting expansion was in the range $0–100 \times 10^{-6}$.

Shrinkage values for sprayed fibre concrete have rarely been reported, but Ramakrishnan[54] found that shrinkage was reduced by about 30% on inclusion of 1.0% by volume (in the dry mix) of 30-mm long hooked-end-wire fibres.

24.4.8 Water absorption

Properly applied dry-process sprayed concrete is a relatively dense well-compacted material and, consequently, its water absorption is quite low. Hills[51] recorded 30-min water absorptions (to BS 1881: 1983[61]) in the range 2.3–3.6% with the dry process and 3.5–4.7% for the wet process, the latter reflecting the higher water content of these mixes. These results were within the range 2.6–4.0% for equivalent cast concretes. The authors[52] have found that the inclusion of steel fibres in the mix produces small increases in absorption values (*Figure 24.8*).

Little[62] also found that the presence of drawn-wire fibres increased the boiled absorption from 7.0% for plain sprayed

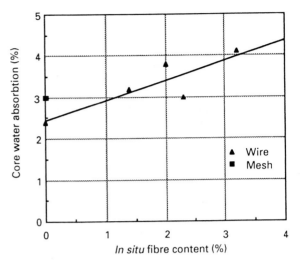

Figure 24.8 Effect of fibre content on water absorption (dry process)

concrete to 8.1% with fibres. Jones[23] quotes boiled absorptions in the range 4–8% for steel fibre sprayed concrete containing silica fume.

24.4.9 Permeability

Though permeability is one of the prime factors governing the durability of concrete, there is relatively little published information relating to sprayed concrete. Whilst a low-permeability concrete matrix is generally desirable, it should be appreciated that a mix with higher permeability that has not cracked can be more watertight than a low-permeability mix which develops substantial microcracks due to drying shrinkage.

Values obtained from the initial surface absorption test[61] for dry- and wet-process sprayed concrete have been found to be in the range for conventionally cast concretes,[51] namely 0.14–0.35 ml m^{-2} s^{-1} for dry mix and 0.35–0.41 ml m^{-2} s^{-1} for wet mix after 30 min. The Concrete Society[63] suggest a range of 0.17–0.35 ml m^{-2} s^{-1} for 'average'-quality concrete.

Schrader and Kaden[14] quote permeabilities for dry-process sprayed concrete in the range 3×10^{-10} to 3×10^{-13} m s^{-1} for moderately low to very high strength concrete. Opsahl and Buhre[3] determined permeabilities of drilled cores of wet-process silica-fume modified sprayed concrete containing 1% by volume of slit-sheet fibres. Values quoted were between 2×10^{-14} and 1×10^{-13} m s^{-1} for a 45 MPa compressive strength mix and $< 10^{-15}$ m s^{-1} for a 75 MPa mix. They also stated that concrete may be considered watertight when the coefficient of permeability is less than 10^{-12} m s^{-1}.

24.4.10 Freeze–thaw resistance

Dry-process sprayed concrete (with high strength and low water:cement ratio) is generally reported as being resistant to freeze–thaw conditions encountered in service. Schrader and Kaden[14] discuss the subject in some depth, pointing out that the resistance of sprayed concrete to freeze–thaw damage is no different from an equivalent cast concrete, the entrained-air content being the principal factor governing performance. Using the ASTM C666: 1980[64] test procedure, sprayed concrete samples without significant air contents will deteriorate progressively, although very high strength material (above 70 MPa) may resist freeze–thaw damage without air entrainment. Johnston[56] concluded from ASTM tests that a proper entrained-air void system is just as necessary for steel-fibre concrete as for plain concrete.

Air entrainment of sprayed concrete using the dry process has generally been found to be unsuccessful. Up to 5% air has been found to remain in sprayed concrete applied by the wet process, although less than half of the voids were of a sufficiently small size to be effective in providing durability.[14]

Opsahl and Buhre[3] carried out ASTM C666: 1980 freeze–thaw tests on specimens of wet-process silica-fume sprayed concrete containing steel fibres, and concluded that good air-void characteristics were achieved without the use of air-entraining agents, durability factors in the range 60–80 being obtained for sprayed concrete of 60–70 MPa compressive strength.

24.4.11 Reinforcement corrosion

The corrosion of steel mesh within sprayed concrete is governed by the usual factors, principally the permeability of the matrix and the severity of the environment. Reference should be made to standard reinforced-concrete practice (for example, BS 8110: 1985[65]) where durability is controlled by the amount of cover and limitations on the mix proportions. Top-cover and back-spacer requirements (the latter to allow satisfactory bond and reinforcement encasement) effectively limit the thickness of mesh-reinforced sprayed concrete to a minimum of 50 mm.

Fibre-reinforced sprayed concrete does not generally suffer from these restrictions and can therefore be applied in thinner layers. Polypropylene and stainless-steel fibres are naturally durable reinforcement materials. Carbon steel fibres will not corrode whilst protected by the alkaline environment of the concrete. Even when the exposure conditions cause reduced alkalinity, only the outer few millimetres of a good quality impermeable concrete are affected and, provided the matrix remains uncracked, most of the fibres within remain protected.[66] If cracking occurs, the continued effectiveness of the fibre reinforcement will depend on the crack width, the severity of the corrosive environment, and the diameter of the fibres. Some studies[67] have shown that if crack widths remain in the range 0.03–0.08 mm, carbon steel fibres will not oxidize even after several years of exposure. Other work[66] has shown that, although corrosion took place in a moist marine environment when crack widths were in the range 0.1–0.3 mm, much of the composite strength was retained because the steel fibres were not initially stressed to anywhere near their ultimate strength, and could therefore tolerate a considerable reduction in diameter by corrosion before failing and allowing the crack to open further.

Schupack,[68] reporting on a series of investigations on the durability of steel-fibre concrete exposed to severe environments, concluded that the corrosion of carbon steel fibres in concrete beams, after 10-years exposure in a marine environment, seemed to be limited to the depth of carbonation (maximum around 3 mm). Even with chloride ion penetration, the fibre corrosion was limited to the concrete surface.

Carbon steel fibres located at or near an exposed surface can be expected to corrode with time; however, a thin flash coating of plain sprayed concrete will prevent surface rusting.

24.5 Specification

24.5.1 Current documentation relating to sprayed concrete

The first UK specification was produced in 1976 by the Association of Gunite Contractors.[69] This was rewritten in 1986 by the renamed Sprayed Concrete Association.[70] The current document contains general information together with guidance on design and specification for both dry and wet processes.

In 1979 the Concrete Society[71] published a report relating to the repair of fire-damaged structures with sprayed concrete, which included advice on specification. The Construction and Formwork Committee of the Concrete Society subsequently produced a specification for sprayed concrete[1] in 1979, which is an end-product or performance specification intended for application to both new construction, including tunnels, and to repair and strengthening work. The following year a code of practice[36] followed by guidance notes on the measurement of sprayed concrete[72] were published, the latter including the format for a schedule.

The American Concrete Institute standard specification was first published in 1977, and became part of their manual of concrete practice[7] in 1982. The most recent guidance on sprayed concrete in the USA is the ACI Committee 506 recommended practice for shotcreting[35] adopted as a standard of the American Concrete Institute in 1966 and revised in 1983. This publication gives recommendations on the applicability of sprayed concrete to different types of construction, on material requirements, and on application procedures. Equipment requirements are given for both dry and wet processes, and the need for a well-qualified application crew is stressed.

24.5.2 Specification of sprayed fibre concrete

There are no formal specifications or codes of practice available for sprayed fibre concrete, although passing reference to fibres occurs in some of the documentation relating to sprayed concrete. The engineer should, therefore, make reference to standards relating to cast fibre concrete, in conjunction with standard specifications for conventional sprayed concrete, before drawing up a specification for sprayed fibre concrete. Modifying a specification for conventional sprayed concrete so that it can be used to specify sprayed fibre concrete should not be a difficult task, provided the specifier has a clear idea of the purpose for which the fibres are being used, and makes sure that adequate provisions are made to ensure that the finished product complies with what he has actually specified.

In the USA, ACI Committee 544 has published a guide for specifying, mixing, placing and finishing steel-fibre-reinforced concrete.[73] The report describes the current technology with regard to all these operations, the emphasis being on the differences between conventional concrete and steel-fibre concrete and on how to deal with them. Guidance is provided on mixing techniques to achieve uniform mixtures, placement techniques to ensure adequate compaction, and finishing techniques to assure satisfactory surface textures.

The Concrete Committee of the Japan Society of Civil Engineers has published recommendations for the design and construction of steel-fibre-reinforced concrete.[74] This publication covers similar ground to that covered by the ACI Committee 544 report.[73]

A specification for steel fibres has recently been produced by the American Society for Testing and Materials,[75] though there is still no standard specification for fibres in the UK. The Japanese Society of Civil Engineers (JSCE) Concrete Committee have also published a specification for steel fibres for concrete[76] and seven standard test methods relating to the testing of steel-fibre-reinforced concrete;[77] the specification covers fibres for cast and sprayed concrete applications, the only difference being that longer firbres (of 40 mm length) are not permitted for sprayed applications. These two specifications cover drawn-wire, slit-sheet, melt-extract and milled-steel fibres, and define materials for fibres, fibre shape and size, and minimum tensile strength.

The only formal published guidance on the use of steel fibre sprayed concrete is from the JSCE in the form of a guideline for construction of steel-fibre-reinforced shotcrete.[78] This document gives advice on the quality of steel-fibre shotcrete, on materials and mix proportions, on equipment, on placing, and on quality control and inspection. Both dry and wet processes are covered, and particular emphasis is given to the importance of regulating the water in the dry process to keep to the specified water:cement ratio. The material performance is specified in terms of strength (compressive and flexural) and toughness. The difference between the discharged mix and the adhered mix is emphasized, and the importance of allowing for the effect of rebound in the design of the discharged mix is underlined. Quality-control tests required either during production or upon completion include fibre-content determination, strength tests, toughness tests, and determination of the layer thickness of the sprayed fibre concrete.

24.6 Quality control

24.6.1 Introduction

Quality control of sprayed concrete is more difficult than that for conventional cast concrete because the mix proportions *in situ* may differ substantially from the batched proportions and the concrete quality is more operative dependent. The latter is illustrated by one sprayed-concrete job where the compressive strength was increased from 10 to 40 MPa merely by changing from an inexperienced to an experienced crew.[79]

The most reliable determination of the quality of sprayed concrete in place is obtained by performing tests on samples extracted from a typical gunned section. However, this is a costly procedure and it may sometimes be impracticable to obtain specimens in this way for regular control tests. The next best solution, though even this has its shortcomings, is to extract cores from test panels gunned under field conditions. Test panels are also of use before the commencement of a job to check that the gunning crew can produce the required quality of sprayed concrete using the equipment, materials and mix proportions proposed for the job.

Both the American Concrete Institute[35] and the Concrete Society[36] give guidance on the preparation and testing of test panels for conventional sprayed concrete. However, there is no equivalent guidance for sprayed fibre concrete aside from that given by the JSCE, whose guideline[78] has a section relating to testing and inspection.

The inclusion of fibres in sprayed concrete has two important, and quite separate, implications for quality-control testing: firstly, measurements need to be made of *in situ* fibre contents actually achieved; and secondly, since the prime reason for using fibres will not be the enhancement of compressive strength, a routine quality control strength test (other than a core compressive test) is desirable.

24.6.2 Preconstruction testing

ACI Committee 506[35] describe at some length investigations that may be carried out prior to the start of the field work to verify that the specified quality of sprayed concrete can actually be expected in the structure. Test panels (minimum 750 mm square) should be sprayed from each position required by the work (downhand, vertical or overhead) and for each mix design being considered. In addition to visual examination (for soundness and uniformity of material) and strength tests, tests for absorption, shrinkage, resistance to freezing–thawing and other properties are also suggested.

In a large sprayed steel-fibre-concrete tunnel project[80] in British Columbia a quality-assurance programme included at the preconstruction stage: seminars to train inspectors in proper inspection and testing procedures; evaluation of the contractor's spraying crew; equipment and materials; evaluation of the proposed mix design; and establishment of a sprayed-concrete testing laboratory at the site.

24.6.3 Panels for routine quality-control testing

Most specifications for sprayed-concrete projects call for the making of test panels during construction, from which test specimens are cut or sawn. Whilst test panels are more convenient than *in situ* sampling, an obvious disadvantage is that the operator is aware that a test specimen is being produced and, consequently, the sample may not necessarily be a representative one. The edge effect of the panel and the backing material may also affect the measured concrete properties.

24.6.4 Fibre-content determination

The engineer must choose between specifying a batched or *in situ* fibre content and then ensure that the appropriate material is regularly sampled during construction. The specification of an *in situ* fibre content is clearly preferable (particularly with the dry process), but the testing technique is slightly more complicated.

The authors have successfully carried out simple wash-out tests[43] at numerous sprayed fibre concrete trials to determine *in situ* fibre contents. The wash-out test is suitable for small or medium sized jobs, but for large contracts a quicker and more sophisticated technique, such as an electromagnetic method[81] might be preferable. An additional advantage of the wash-out test is that the removed material can also be used to determine cement contents, water:cement and aggregate:cement ratios, and rebound figures. The method is similar to that of the Rapid Analysis Machine (RAM), developed by the Cement and Concrete Association (now the British Cement Association), but is performed by hand. The *in situ* fibre content and fibre rebound can be calculated using equations (24.1) and (24.2).

24.6.5 Strength testing

24.6.5.1 Core compression

Compressive strength is the principal measure of quality control of plain sprayed concrete and, whilst being relatively unaffected by the presence of fibres, still gives a reliable indication of the matrix quality of sprayed fibre concrete. Cores also allow visual inspection of sprayed concrete quality.

In situ coring is clearly superior to coring a test panel from the point of view of obtaining representative test specimens and it is also the only effective method which can be used to investigate specific areas for bond, compaction and other properties. However, both the Concrete Society[36] and the American Concrete Institute[35] allow compressive testing of cores extracted from test panels for routine quality control. If this is done it is prudent to take test cores periodically from the completed work to ensure that the control tests reflect the quality of material in the structure.

24.6.5.2 Beam flexure

A beam flexural test is clearly a potential candidate as a quality-control test for sprayed fibre concrete since it yields information on the limit of proportionality and the ultimate flexural strengths as well as toughness;[59] these are all important properties of fibre concrete and are all affected by *in situ* fibre content. However, beam samples can only be obtained from test panels and the test method is more complicated than an axial test.

The most likely application of flexural testing is as part of a preconstruction testing programme to check compliance with specified minimum strengths and toughnesses, and to determine the necessary associated *in situ* fibre contents.

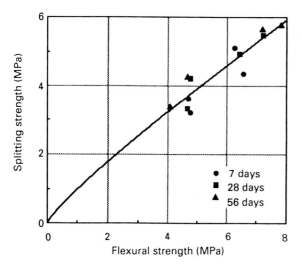

Figure 24.9 Relationship between core splitting and flexural strengths

24.6.5.3 Core splitting

Concrete cores are really the only feasible test specimens that can be extracted from the hardened *in situ* sprayed concrete. Because the core compressive test yields no useful information on the effects of fibres, the authors have investigated two indirect tensile tests on cores as potential quality-control tests for sprayed fibre concrete: a core cylinder splitting test[82] and a core point-load test.[82–84] The splitting test investigated was similar to the standard cylinder splitting test for plain concrete described in BS 1881: 1983,[61] but was carried out on 100-mm diameter cores. In the point-load test a core is placed between two conical loading platens and the compressive load required to split the specimen is recorded. An index of strength is calculated from this failure load.

The relationships between beam flexural strengths and core splitting and point-load strengths are shown in *Figures 24.9* and *24.10*. It can be seen that both core splitting and point-load strengths are sensitive to changes in fibre content and vary approximately linearly with flexural strength over the practical range of sprayed-concrete strengths. The curve shown in *Figure 24.10* was obtained from a regression analysis of cast fibre concrete point-load index data.

24.6.5.4 Other strength tests

The preparation of test panels and coring are time consuming and quite costly procedures. Simple *in situ* tests which can be carried out frequently and relatively cheaply would clearly be an attractive alternative, if any such tests could be shown to yield reliable and useful information on the strength properties of sprayed concrete.

Some success has been claimed[46] for the Windsor Probe system, a test method in which the penetration into the concrete of a hardened alloy steel bolt, fired from a gun, is measured. On the Dinorwig pumped storage scheme[31] the use of a pull-out shot bolt test was found to give quite a good correlation with core strength for concrete up to 25 MPa, beyond which the standard error increased.

The Lok and Capo pull-out tests have been investigated for measurement of *in situ* compressive strength of sprayed steel fibre concrete,[62] although the methods were found to be unsuitable for routine quality-control testing.

One important property that is rarely evaluated is the bond strength between sprayed concrete and its substrate. A potential quality-control test method is the core pull-off test[85] in which a cored specimen is pulled from its substrate *in situ*, though the method has yet to be evaluated for sprayed concrete.

24.6.6 Testing for properties other than strength

The Concrete Society[1,36] refer to the use of hammer tests, γ radiography, rebound hammer and covermeter devices, and measure of ultrasonic-pulse velocity. Hammers or short steel bars are often used on site to sound the concrete to locate hollow areas, poor compaction, cracking, lack of bond, and similar problems.

In addition to strength testing, cores of *in situ* sprayed concrete can be inspected for voids, sanding and lack of bond to the substrate, and allow verification of the thickness of the sprayed concrete layer. Cores may also be used for density and water-absorption determinations, the latter being of particular relevance for water-retaining linings. Alternatively, in these situations an *in situ* permeability test such as the ISAT[61] or Figg test[86] may be carried out.

24.7 Design considerations

24.7.1 Suitable applications

Concrete can be sprayed as opposed to cast in many instances, the choice being based on convenience, speed and cost of construction. Sprayed concrete is particularly suitable where thin or variable-thickness layers are required or where the technique reduces or eliminates the need for formwork. Sprayed concrete may be appropriate where access is difficult or where normal casting techniques cannot be employed. The good bond to a substrate may also be an important design consideration.

Applications fall into two broad categories: new structures (such as roofs, thin shells, walls, swimming pools, tanks, tunnel linings, reservoirs, sewers, and protective coatings, including fire protection of steelwork) and strengthening or repair of existing structures (including walls, bridges, aqueducts, sewers, sea walls, chimneys, slope stabilization, and deteriorated brick, masonry and steel structures generally). Some applications are structural, whilst in others the sprayed concrete is required to carry little or no load.

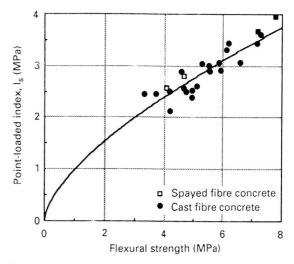

Figure 24.10 Relationship between point-load index and flexural strength

Applications of sprayed fibre concrete include slope stabilization, underground support in tunnels and mines, and repair of a wide variety of structures (e.g. reinforced-concrete bridges, brick and masonry arches, road, rail and canal tunnels; locks, quays and sea defences; sewers and aqueducts; and high-security walls). In addition, cast fibre concrete has been used to repair hydraulic structures, such as aqueducts, spillways, sluiceways, stilling basins, low-pressure tunnels and tailraces. One of the main reasons for choosing fibre reinforcement in these applications is that it substantially improves certain material properties that are particularly beneficial in many repair situations; these are nearly all associated with energy absorption (increased tensile strain to failure, toughness, impact resistance and fatigue endurance), though some improvements in strength (particularly flexural and shear strength) also occur. In sprayed fibre concrete applications there may also be advantages arising from the method of construction.

24.7.2 Construction method

The first task is to identify that spraying is a more appropriate method of construction than casting. The engineer should then consider whether a particular production process (dry or wet) is to be specified or whether the decision can be left to the contractor. This choice can significantly influence the drawing up of the specification and associated quality-control procedures.

At this early stage the designer must also decide if the sprayed concrete is to be reinforced and, if so, whether to use bar reinforcement, fibres or mesh. In certain situations the designer might choose to specify fibre reinforcement principally on the basis of a potentially faster construction time. Alternatively, it may be left to the contractor to decide whether to take advantage of this and other possible benefits such as reduced volume of material and avoidance of steel fixing.

24.7.3 Reinforcement

If substantial flexural-load-carrying capacity is required then continuous steel mesh or bars will be needed, located near the tensile face of the section. In this case fibre reinforcement of the full section will not normally be justified, but a thin surface layer may still be used to provide impact and wear resistance.

If major flexural strengthening is not required then the choice of reinforcement is between fibres and a light mesh, both of which may give a modest improvement in flexural strength. Although potentially greater, the moment of resistance of a mesh-reinforced section will usually be less than that of a steel-fibre-reinforced section because the mesh is invariably located near the centre of the sprayed concrete layer. In virtually all other respects the properties of a fibre reinforced matrix will be equal or superior to those of a plain matrix containing steel mesh.

A discussion of the relative merits of fibre and mesh reinforcement which may help in choosing the most appropriate reinforcement type is given in Section 24.1.4.

24.7.4 Fibres

In choosing the most appropriate fibre, there are three decisions to be made: one concerning the material (steel or polypropylene), the second concerning the fibre type (manufacturing process), and the third concerning the fibre geometry.

24.7.4.1 Fibre material

The vast majority of applications to date have been with steel fibres. This has been due to the uncertain durability of glass fibres and the relatively modest improvements brought about by using the older type of polypropylene fibres. In addition, neither of these two types of fibre were particularly suited to the dry-spraying process.

More recently, a high yield, fibrillated polypropylene fibre has come on to the market which is claimed to have improved stiffness and bond. Although applications of this fibre type are very limited it may well have potential in repair situations (particularly in the wet process) where thin durable coatings are required to provide protection rather than strengthening.

Steel fibres will probably continue for the present to be the first choice in most applications because of their wide usage and the amount of information available on properties and performance. In addition, where flexural strengthening is required from the fibre concrete, steel fibres are the obvious choice.

24.7.4.2 Steel fibres

There is a wide variety of steel fibres available. The straight round wire, straight deformed round wire and straight slit-sheet fibres are older, first generation steel fibres which are less likely to be specified in sprayed concrete today. The second generation steel fibres were designed to give improved performance, especially better bond and mixing characteristics. The enlarged end-slit-sheet fibre, popular in Scandinavia and Australia, is not currently available in the UK. Although it is easy to spray, the toughness of the composite material has been found to be significantly lower than that of equivalent melt extract and hooked-end drawn-wire fibre mixes. In the UK the choice at present is between melt extract and hooked-end wire fibres.

In terms of the composite's mechanical performance, particularly toughness, the hooked-end wire fibre is superior to the melt-extract fibre (for the same fibre length and fibre content), because it is a strong, hard drawn wire with a very efficient end anchorage. In terms of fibre durability, stainless-steel melt-extract fibre is undoubtedly superior to any carbon steel fibre. Although wire and slit-sheet fibres are available in stainless steel, their cost is prohibitive for civil applications. It is still a matter of debate, however, where stainless-steel fibres are necessary to ensure the composite's durability.

Although a wide range of fibre lengths is available from manufacturers (typically 12–75 mm), the usual length for sprayed concrete work is between 18 and 30 mm, with 25 mm being the most common. Above this range steel fibres become increasingly difficult to spray and below it the efficiency of the fibre decreases.

There is also a selection of fibre diameters available with drawn-wire fibres (typically 0.25–0.80 mm), but for sprayed concrete it is necessary to restrict the aspect ratio (length : diameter) to around 65 or less if production problems are to be avoided. Thus a common choice is a 25 mm × 0.5 mm fibre. Melt-extract fibres can also be made in a variety of cross-sectional sizes, but in practice manufacturers offer as standard a single size which should have an equivalent aspect ratio for sprayed work.

24.7.4.3 Polypropylene fibres

There is very little information available on appropriate polypropylene fibre types and geometry for use in sprayed concrete. The older type of 'chopped string' fibre has been generally superseded by more modern fibrillated types because of their somewhat higher modulus (up from about 2 to 4 GPa), improved bond and better dispersion in the matrix.

Some fibre types are marketed principally for shrinkage crack control in cast concrete. They are available typically in lengths of 12, 19 and 50 mm and have a denier of less than 125. Their modulus is approximately 3.5 GPa. These fibres are claimed to be effective in reducing shrinkage cracking at very low fibre

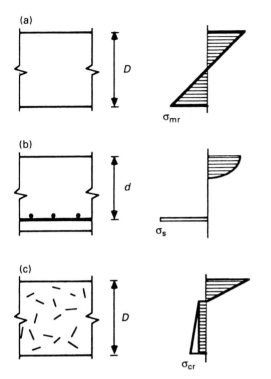

Figure 24.11 Typical stress blocks for design. (a) Unreinforced; (b) bar reinforced; (c) fibre reinforced

contents of around 1 kg m^{-3} (0.04% by weight), and have been used at this dosage on at least one UK sprayed-concrete project.

High modulus fibrillated polypropylene fibres have been used recently in sprayed concrete at significantly higher fibre contents (0.25–0.75%). They are available in lengths of 6 to 48 mm with a denier of between 15 and 80 (width 100–300 μm and thickness 20–40 μm). Their modulus is quoted as up to 18 GPa.

24.7.5 Mix design

The mix design will be influenced by whether the engineer wishes to specify or encourage the use of one particular process. With the wet process, a minimum cement content, a maximum water:cement ratio, and an air content can be specified, together with strength, and these can all be easily checked for compliance. However, a more sophisticated mix design, possibly including an accelerator, may be necessary to achieve medium to high strengths.

With the dry process, it is more difficult to specify limits on mix proportions because of the difficulties of checking compliance *in situ* (the *in situ* mix proportions being considerably different to those of the dry mix). The engineer should specify a compressive strength, but could as an alternative specify a prescribed mix which it is felt will give the desired performance when placed.

For certain applications the mix design may not be controlled by compressive strength but by other physical properties such as freeze–thaw resistance or water permeability. In the latter case a higher strength mix may be specified along with *in situ* permeability or core water-absorption quality-control tests.

24.7.6 Moment capacity

There are a number of approaches that may be used to determine the moment capacity of a sprayed-concrete section, some of

which are outlined below. The methods are described for the case of the sprayed section acting alone, though in some applications the engineer may wish to consider the concrete to be acting compositely with its substrate.

24.7.6.1 Unreinforced

An elastic stress block (*Figure 24.11(a)*) can be assumed and a moment capacity calculated based on published flexural strength (modulus of rupture) data. The designer should be aware that measured moduli of rupture decrease with increasing specimen thickness. The ultimate moment of resistance, M_u, is given by:

$$M_u = \frac{\sigma_{mr}}{\gamma_m} b \frac{D^2}{6} \tag{24.3}$$

where σ_{mr} is the modulus of rupture of the matrix, b is with width of section, D is the overall depth of section, and γ_m is a material partial safety factor.

24.7.6.2 Mesh reinforced

The ultimate moment of resistance may be calculated from conventional reinforced-concrete theory using a stress block similar to that shown in *Figure 24.11(b)* or a simplified version. Assuming a maximum lever arm of 0.95d (as recommended by BS 8110: 1985[65]), then:

$$M_u = A_s \frac{\sigma_s}{\gamma_m} 0.95d \tag{24.4}$$

where d is the effective depth, A_s is the area of the steel and σ_s is the strength of the steel.

It should be noted that for a single layer of light mesh (around 100 mm^2 m^{-1}) the ultimate moment capacity may often be that of the matrix alone before cracking (and hence given by equation (24.3)).

24.7.6.3 Bar reinforced

A conventional reinforced-concrete design approach will apply (*Figure 24.11(b)*). Using BS 8110: 1985[65] the ultimate moment capacity of a singly reinforced section will be the lesser of

$$M_u = A_s \frac{\sigma_s}{\gamma_m} z \tag{24.5}$$

and

$$M_u = 0.234 \frac{\sigma_{mc}}{\gamma_m} bd^2 \tag{24.6}$$

where z is the lever arm and σ_{mc} is the compressive strength of the matrix.

24.7.6.4 Fibre reinforced

Whilst many theories of fibre-reinforced behaviour have been proposed, none have been widely accepted as a basis for design. Three possible methods are outlined below.

The most basic approach is to use published flexural strength data (such as that given in *Figure 24.6*), obtained assuming an elastic stress block, to calculate a moment capacity. Equation (24.3) will apply, with the apparent modulus of rupture of the composite, σ_{cr}, replacing the modulus of rupture of the plain matrix, σ_{mr}.

A second approach is to predict a modulus of rupture for a particular fibre concrete using an equation based on a regression analysis of fibre-concrete data. The equation proposed by Swamy and Mangat[87] and recommended by ACI Committee

544: 1988[88] gives

$$\sigma_{cr} = 0.97\sigma_{mr}(1 - v_f) + 3.41 v_f \left(\frac{l}{d}\right)_f \qquad (24.7)$$

where v_f is the volume fraction of the fibres and $(l/d)_f$ is the fibre aspect ratio.

The third, and perhaps most correct, design method is to assume a more realistic stress block such as that shown in *Figure 24.11(c)*. Such an approach recognizes that the increase in flexural strength obtained with fibre reinforcement is associated with a shift in the neutral axis and is not due to a substantial increase in the composite's tensile strength. It is generally held that the concrete is still behaving elastically in compression, though various shapes have been suggested for the stress distribution in the tensile region.

Hannant[89] has proposed a rectangular tensile stress block and a neutral axis depth of $D/4$. His approach, however, assumes that the composite is capable of carrying more load after the formation of the first flexural crack. In reality most sprayed fibre concrete has a fibre content below the critical fibre volume required for this to happen, though the composite will continue to carry load after cracking, albeit at a reduced level.

Mangat and Gurusamy[90] consider the case where peak load coincides with the formation of the first flexural crack and, consequently, the matrix in tension contributes to the ultimate moment capacity. These authors derived an expression for the moment capacity assuming a trapezoidal tensile stress block. However, their approach, as well as Hannant's, requires a knowledge of the interfacial bond stress between fibre and matrix, and information on this property is not readily available for steel or polypropylene fibres. Mangat and Gurusamy[90] overcame this difficulty by equating the moment capacity of their stress block to that of an elastic triangular stress block, and obtained an expression for the apparent modulus of rupture of the composite, σ_{cr}, which is almost identical to equation (24.7). However, it would be misleading to assume from this type of expression that moment capacity is independent of fibre type; some steel-fibre types are more efficient than others and will, therefore, sustain a higher fibre/matrix bond stress.

References

1   CONCRETE SOCIETY CONSTRUCTION & FORMWORK COMMITTEE, *Specification for Sprayed Concrete*, Concrete Society, London, 4 (1979)
2   WARD, W. H. and HILLS, D. L., Sprayed concrete—tunnel support requirements and the dry mix process, *Shotcrete for Ground Support* (SP-54), American Concrete Institute, Detroit, 475–532 (1977)
3   OPSAHL, O. A. and BUHRE, K. E., Why wet process steel fibre reinforced shotcrete?, *Proceedings of US–Sweden Joint Seminar on Steel Fibre Concrete*, Stockholm, 51–65 (1985)
4   BRITISH STANDARDS INSTITUTION, *BS 882 Specification for aggregates from natural sources for concrete*, Milton Keynes, 8 (1983)
5   KOBLER, H. G., Dry-mix coarse aggregate shotcrete as underground support, *Shotcrete* (SP-14), American Concrete Institute, Detroit, 33–58 (1966)
6   AMERICAN SOCIETY FOR TESTING MATERIALS, *ASTM C33-81 Standard specification for concrete aggregates*, Philadelphia, 8 (1981)
7   ACI COMMITTEE 506, Standard specification for materials, proportioning and application of shotcrete, *ACI Manual of Concrete Practice*, Part 5, American Concrete Institute, Detroit (1982)
8   KEMPSTER, E., Pumpability of mortars, *Contract Journal*, **217**, 28–30 (1967)
9   KEMPSTER, E., Pumpable concrete, *Contract Journal*, **229**, 605–607, 740–741 (1969)
10 SKATUN, O., Applications of wet process steel fibre reinforced shotcrete in Scandinavia, *Proceedings of the 3rd International Symposium on Developments in Fibre Reinforced Cement and Concrete*, Sheffield, July, Paper 9.6 (1986)
11 JONES, M., Why add to shotcrete?, *Tunnels and Tunnelling*, **17**(7), 53–58 (1985)
12 WALLACE, M., Wet shotcreting just got better, *Concrete Construction*, **32**(11), 965–967 (1987)
13 KRANTZ, G. W., Selected pneumatic gunites for use in undergound mining: a comparative engineering analysis, *US Bureau of Mines Information Circular 8984*, 64 (1984)
14 SCHRADER, E. K. and KADEN, R. A., Durability of shotcrete, *Concrete Durability* (SP-100), American Concrete Institute, Detroit, 1071–1101 (1987)
15 RAMAKRISHNAN, V., Steel fibre reinforced shotcrete—a state of the art report, *Proceedings of US–Sweden Joint Seminar on Steel Fibre Concrete*, Stockholm, 7–24 (1985)
16 SCHORN, H., Epoxy modified shotcrete, *Polymers in Concrete* (SP-89), American Concrete Institute, Detroit, 249–260 (1983)
17 MORGAN, D. R., Dry mix silica fume shotcrete in western Canada, supplementary paper at *2nd International Conference on Use of Fly Ash, Silica Fume, Slag and Natural Pozzolans in Concrete* (ACI/CANMET), Madrid, April (1986)
18 SCHRADER, E. *et al.*, Deterioration and repairs of navigation lock concrete, *Performance of Concrete in a Marine Environment* (SP-65), American Concrete Institute, Detroit, 557–576 (1980)
19 BOYES, R. G. H., Assimilating concrete progress, *Civil Engineering*, 43–53 (Aug. 1986)
20 ACI COMMITTEE 506, State-of-the-art report on fibre reinforced shotcrete, *Concrete International*, **6**(12), 15–27 (1984)
21 FAIRWEATHER, A. D., Use of polypropylene film fibres to increase impact resistance of concrete, *Proceedings of International Building Exhibition Conference*, London, 41–44 (Nov. 1971)
22 SUTCLIFFE, H. and McCLURE, C. R., Large aggregate shotcrete challenges steel ribs as tunnel support, *Civil Engineering, ASCE*, **39**(11), 51–55 (1969)
23 JONES, M. B., Testing sprayed concrete's fibre, *Tunnels and Tunnelling*, **19**(7), 45–48 (1987)
24 HAACK, A., Single-shell *in-situ* concrete tunnel lining: experience in the Federal Republic of Germany, *Tunnelling and Underground Space Technology*, **3**(1), 56–66 (1988)
25 HOCHMUTH, W., KRISCHKE, A. and WEBER, J., Subway construction in Munich, developments in tunnelling with shotcrete support, *Rock Mechanics and Rock Engineering*, **20**(1), 1–38 (1987)
26 RYAN, T. F., *Gunite: A Handbook for Engineers*, Eyre and Spottiswoode, Leatherhead, 63 (1973)
27 AMERICAN CONCRETE INSTITUTE, *Shotcrete for Ground Support* (SP-54), American Concrete Institute, Detroit, 533 (1976)
28 ANON., New tunnel faces may cut delay at Carsington, *New Civil Engineer*, 4 (28 Apr. 1983)
29 NISHIOKA, K. *et al.*, Present status on applications of steel fibre concrete in Japan, **2**(4), 205–232 (1980)
30 VANDEWALLE, M., Steel fibre reinforced shotcrete, *Proceedings of the 3rd International Symposium on Developments in Fibre Reinforced Cement and Concrete* (RILEM), Sheffield, Paper 3.11 (July 1986)
31 WALLER, E., Dinorwig tunnels and caverns, *Proceedings of Symposium on Sprayed Concrete* (CI 80), Concrete Society, London, 36–51 (Apr. 1980)
32 ACI COMMITTEE 506, *Guide to Shotcrete*, American Concrete Institute, Detroit, 41 (1985)
33 WALLACE, M., For reinforcing Canadians prefer steel fibres, *Concrete Construction*, **32**(9), 775–776 (1987)
34 ROBINS, P. J. and AUSTIN, S. A., Sprayed steel fibre concrete, Part 1—production and installation, *Concrete*, **19**(3), 17–19 (1985)
35 ACI COMMITTEE 506, Recommended practice for shotcreting, *ACI Standard 506-66*, American Concrete Institute, Detroit, 15 (1983)
36 CONCRETE SOCIETY CONSTRUCTION & FORMWORK COMMITTEE, *Code of Practice for Sprayed Concrete*, Concrete Society, London, 16 (1980)
37 PARKER, H. W., FERNANDEZ-DELGADO, G. and LORIG, L. J., A practical new approach to rebound losses, *Shotcrete for Ground Support* (SP-54), American Concrete Institute, Detroit, 149–187 (1977)
38 PARKER, H. W., Current field research programme on shotcrete,

Use of Shotcrete for Underground Structural Support (SP-45), American Concrete Institute, Detroit, 330–350 (1974)

39 AUSTIN, S. A. and ROBINS, P. J., *Dramix Supaspray sprayed concrete trials*, Department of Civil Engineering, Loughborough University of Technology, 38 (1987)

40 RYAN, T. F., Steel fibres in gunite: an appraisal, *Tunnels and Tunnelling*, **7**(7), 74–75 (1975)

41 GULLAN, G. T., Shotcrete for tunnel lining, *Tunnels and Tunnelling*, **7**(9), 37–47 (1975)

42 KOBLER, H. G., Dry-mix coarse-aggregate shotcrete as underground support, *Shotcreting (SP-14)*, American Concrete Institute, Detroit, 33–58 (1966)

43 ROBINS, P. J., AUSTIN, S. A. and PEASTON, C. H., Rebound of sprayed fibre concrete, presented at *5th International Conference on Composite Structures*, Paisley (24–26 July 1989)

44 ROBINS, P. J. and AUSTIN, S. A., *Sprayed Fibre Concrete Repair of Budbrooke Water Tower*, Department of Civil Engineering, Loughborough University of Technology, 22 (1988)

45 MORGAN, D. R., Dry-mix silica fume shotcrete in Western Canada, *Concrete International*, **10**(1), 24–32 (1988)

46 LITTLEJOHN, G. S., Wet process shotcrete, *Proceedings of Symposium on Sprayed Concrete (CI 80)*, Concrete Society, London, 18–32 (Apr. 1980)

47 SANDELL, N. and WESTERDAHL, B., System Besab for high strength steel fibre reinforced shotcrete, *Proceedings of US–Sweden Joint Seminar on Steel Fibre Concrete*, Stockholm, 25–40 (June 1985)

48 OSTFJORD, S., Lack of practical standards and test methods restrict the development of steel fibre shotcrete, *Proceedings of US–Sweden Joint Seminar on Steel Fibre Concrete*, Stockholm, 41–50 (June 1985)

49 SHATTUCK, D. W., The new zoological gardens, Riyadh, *Civil Engineering*, 2021 (Nov./Dec. 1985)

50 MULLER, D., Concrete spraying—wet or dry?, *Strassen und Tiefbau*, **38**(4) (1984)

51 HILLS, D. L., Site-produced sprayed concrete, *Concrete*, **16**(12), 44–50 (1982)

52 ROBINS, P. J. and AUSTIN, S. A., Repair using sprayed fibre concrete, *Proceedings of the International Conference on Case Histories in Structural Failures*, Singapore, K67–79 (20–22 March 1989)

53 HENAGER, C. H., Steel fibrous shotcrete: a summary of the state-of-the-art, *Concrete International*, **3**(1), 50–58 (1981)

54 RAMAKRISHNAN, V., Steel fibre reinforced concrete—a state of the art report, *Proceedings of US–Sweden Joint Seminar on Steel Fibre Concrete*, Stockholm, 7–24 (June 1985)

55 RAMAKRISHNAN, V. *et al.*, Comparative evaluation of fibre shotcretes, *Concrete International*, **3**(1), 56–69 (1981)

56 JOHNSTON, C. D., Steel fibre-reinforced concrete—present and future in engineering construction, *Composites*, **13**(2), 113–121 (1982)

57 MORGAN, D. R., Steel fibre shotcrete—a laboratory study, *Concrete International*, **3**(1), 70–74 (1981)

58 AMERICAN SOCIETY FOR TESTING MATERIALS, *ASTM C1018-85 Standard method of test for flexural toughness and first-crack strength of fibre-reinforced concrete*, Philadelphia, 8 (1985)

59 ACI COMMITTEE 544, Measurement of properties of fibre reinforced concrete, *ACI Manual of Concrete Practice, Part 5*, American Concrete Institute, Detroit (1982)

60 OPSAHL, O. A., Steel fibre reinforced shotcrete for rock support, Report for Royal Norwegian Council for Scientific and Industrial Research, *NTNF Project 1053.09511*, 33 (1982)

61 BRITISH STANDARDS INSTITUTION, *BS 1881 Testing concrete*, Milton Keynes (1983)

62 LITTLE, T. E., An evaluation of steel fibre reinforced shotcrete for underground support, *Canadian Geotechnical Journal*, **22**(4), 501–507 (1985)

63 CONCRETE SOCIETY WORKING PARTY ON PERMEABILITY TESTING, Permeability testing of site concrete, *Proceedings of Conference on Permeability of Concrete and Its Control*, London, 1–68 (Dec. 1985)

64 AMERICAN SOCIETY FOR TESTING MATERIALS, *ASTM C666-80 Standard test method for resistance of concrete to rapid freezing and thawing*, Philadelphia, 7 (1980)

65 BRITISH STANDARDS INSTITUTION, *BS 110 Structural use of concrete, Part 1: Code of practice for design and construction*, Milton Keynes (1985)

66 HANNANT, D. J. and EDGINGTON, J., Durability of steel fibre concrete, *Symposium on Fibre Reinforced Cement and Concrete (RILEM)*, Construction Press Ltd, 159–169 (1975)

67 SCHRADER, E. K. and MUNCH, A. V., Dock slab repair by fibrous concrete overlay, *Journal of the Construction Division, ASCE*, **102**(CO-1), 179–196 (1976)

68 SCHUPACK, M., Durability of SFRC exposed to severe environments, *Proceedings of US–Sweden Joint Seminar on Steel Fibre Concrete*, Stockholm, 479–496 (June 1985)

69 ASSOCIATION OF GUNITE CONTRACTORS, *Code of Practice for the Spraying of Concrete by the Dry Process Otherwise Known as Gunite or Shotcrete*, London, 4 (1976)

70 SPRAYED CONCRETE ASSOCIATION, *Code of Practice for Wet Process and Dry Process Sprayed Concrete*, London, 16 (1986)

71 CONCRETE SOCIETY WORKING PARTY ON FIRE DAMAGED STRUCTURES, Assessment of fire-damaged concrete structures and repair by gunite, *Technical Report No. 15*, London, 28 (1978)

72 CONCRETE SOCIETY CONSTRUCTION & FORMWORK COMMITTEE, *Code of Practice for Sprayed Concrete*, London, 16 (1980)

73 CONCRETE SOCIETY CONSTRUCTION & FORMWORK COMMITTEE, *Guidance on the Measurement of Sprayed Concrete*, London, 2 (1981)

74 ACI COMMITTEE 544, Guide for specifying, mixing, placing, and finishing steel fibre reinforced concrete, *ACI Journal*, **81**(2), 140–147 (1984)

75 JAPAN SOCIETY OF CIVIL ENGINEERS, Recommendations for the design and construction of steel fibre reinforced concrete, *Concrete Library of JSCE*, **3**, 4–29 (June 1984)

76 JAPAN SOCIETY OF CIVIL ENGINEERS, Specification of steel fibres for concrete, *Concrete Library of JSCE*, **3**, 41–44 (June 1984)

77 JAPAN SOCIETY OF CIVIL ENGINEERS, Method of tests for steel fibre reinforced concrete, *Concrete Library of JSCE*, **3**, 45–74 (June 1984)

78 JAPAN SOCIETY OF CIVIL ENGINEERS, Guideline for construction of steel fibre reinforced shotcrete, *Concrete Library of JSCE*, **3**, 31–39 (June 1984)

79 READING, T. J., Shotcrete as a construction material, *Shotcreting (SP-14)*, American Concrete Institute, Detroit, 1–14 (1966)

80 MORGAN, D. R. and McASKILL, N., Rocky Mountain tunnels lined with steel fibre reinforced shotcrete, *Concrete International*, **6**(12), 33–38 (1984)

81 UOMOTO, T. and KOBAYASHI, K., *In situ* test to determine fibre content of steel fibre reinforced concrete by an electro-magnetic method, *In Situ/Nondestructive Testing of Concrete (SP-82)*, American Concrete Institute, Detroit, 673–688 (1984)

82 ROBINS, P. J. and AUSTIN, S. A., Melt extract fibre reinforced sprayed concrete, *Composite Structures 3: Proceedings of the 3rd International Conference on Composite Structures*, Elsevier Applied Science, London, 242–253 (1985)

83 ROBINS, P. J., Point-load test for tensile strength estimation of plain and fibrous concretes, *In Situ/Nondestructive Testing of Concrete (SP-82)*, American Concrete Institute, Detroit, 309–325 (1984)

84 ROBINS, P. J. and AUSTIN, S. A., Core point-load test for steel fibre reinforced concrete, *Magazine of Concrete Research*, **37**(133), 238–242 (1985)

85 LONG, A. E. and MURRAY, A. McC., The pull-off partially destructive test for concrete, *In Situ/Nondestructive Testing of Concrete (SP-82)*, American Concrete Institute, Detroit, 327–350 (1984)

86 FIGG, J. W., Methods of measuring the air water permeability of concrete, *Magazine of Concrete Research*, **25**(85), 213–219 (1973)

87 SWAMY, R. N. and MANGAT, P. S., Influence of fibre geometry on the properties of steel fibre reinforced concrete, *Cement and Concrete Research*, **4**, 451–465 (1974)

88 ACI COMMITTEE 544, Design considerations for steel fibre reinforced concrete, *ACI Journal*, **85**(5), 563–580 (1988)

89 HANNANT, D. J., *Fibre Cements and Fibre Concretes*, Wiley, Chichester, 219 (1978)

90 MANGAT, P. S. and GURUSAMY, K., Flexural strength of steel fibre reinforced cement composites, *Journal of Materials Science*, **22**, 3103–3110 (1987)

25

Concrete Tiles and Slates

J Dodd AIoR
The Marley Roof Tile Co Ltd

Contents

25.1 Introduction 25/3

25.2 Concrete tiles 25/4
    25.2.1 Description and historical development 25/4
    25.2.2 Sources and availability 25/5
    25.2.3 Authority 25/5
    25.2.4 Manufacture 25/5
    25.2.5 Types 25/6
    25.2.6 Appearance 25/10
    25.2.7 Roof-surface effects 25/10
    25.2.8 Performance criteria 25/11
    25.2.9 Sitework and installation 25/12
    25.2.10 Thermal insulation 25/17
    25.2.11 Condensation 25/17
    25.2.12 Sound insulation 25/17
    25.2.13 Fire resistance 25/17

25.3 Lightweight-aggregate tiles 25/17
    25.3.1 Manufacture 25/18
    25.3.2 Installation 25/18

25.4 Slates 25/18
    25.4.1 Concrete reconstructed stone slates 25/18
    25.4.2 Fibre-cement slates 25/20
    25.4.3 Resin- and polymer-bonded slates 25/21
    25.4.4 Polymer-modified-cement slates 25/22
    25.4.5 Sitework and supply 25/22

25.5 Wind loading and fixings 25/23
    25.5.1 Calculation of wind loads 25/26

25.6 Costs 25/26

Bibliography 25/27

25.1 Introduction

The increased specification and refurbishment of pitched roofs has meant a demand for roofing products capable of meeting the needs of modern technological design.

In this chapter, man-made concrete tiles, slates and 'dry-fix' accessories are described, and reflect their contribution in providing durable, aesthetic, and cost-effective alternatives to natural roofing materials.

As well as the previous factors, planning authorities have strict policies with regard to the choice and colour of roofing materials for use within conservation areas or on listed buildings. Re-roofing with heavier materials can also involve requirements to comply with Building Regulations in respect of structural stability.

Modern concrete tiles have been gradually changing their utilitarian and functional image to one of style, variety and liveliness. Since their inception in Britain over 60 years ago, concrete tiles have been backed up by guarantees of durability. The material is ideally suited to high-speed, computer-controlled production, enabling it to be made widely available in high quality and at low cost. This versatility allows the product to be produced in a wide range of profiles and colours.

Improved manufacturing methods have answered the criticism concerning the loss of colour pigmentation and surface textures in some early concrete tiles. Recently, the industry has concentrated on imitating the appearance of natural 'weathered' tiles, which, although criticized by the idealists, has the advantages of improved performance, quality assurance and cost savings. It is now possible to reproduce the shape, colour and texture of natural roofing materials (*Figure 25.2*). Future developments are likely to improve the colours, sizes and shapes

of available tiles, eventually making them indistinguishable from natural products.

Evidence of the technical superiority of the concrete tile can be seen in the development of lightweight tiles. The growing demand for the refurbishment of older roofs presents a recurring problem. Until now, it has been difficult to replace old slates and clay tiles with standard concrete tiles, without the expense and inconvenience of roof strengthening. By incorporating all the benefits of existing tile technology with respect to performance and complete flexibility in installation, it is now possible to reproduce traditional tile designs for a specific technical application.

Man-made slates are available in a large variety of forms, but basically give the appearance of the standard-size natural product. Manufacturers have recently substituted asbestos fibres in their material with fibre cement or resin-based compounds which closely copy the surface texture of riven slate (*Figure 25.3*). The advantages of these tiles are their lighter weight and the more extensive colour range. Specific areas like the Cotswolds, Derbyshire and parts of Yorkshire require products closely resembling the local stone and in variable sizes for local installation techniques (*Figure 25.4*).

Perhaps the most important development has been the introduction of the interlocking slate (*Figure 25.5*). The ease of installation and improved performance characteristics will mean that, in some areas, cost savings can be made in installation and in the supporting structure. The use of new materials technology has enabled a thinner and stronger product to be made.

The growing interest in refurbishment has also seen a revival in roof decoration finials, crested ridge and chimney pots. Special fittings are also often required as roofs become more complex in design.

Only a few manufacturers are producing authentic copies of old tile designs and fittings. The ability of manufacturers to supply specialized products is often an important factor to architects wishing to specify sensitively designed products for conservation projects.

Dry-fix systems (*Figure 25.7*) are becoming more popular because they allow roofs to be completed in all weathers and

Figure 25.1 Concrete plain tiles with pitched roof dormer

Figure 25.2 Deep profiled concrete interlocking tiles with variegated colours

Figure 25.3 Man-made fibre–cement slates

Figure 25.4 Reconstructed stone slates

Figure 25.5 Concrete interlocking slates

eliminate the need for traditional mortar at ridges and verges. Dry-fix systems have been developed by the leading concrete-tile manufacturers to suit most product ranges and incorporate ventilation apertures allowing an unrestricted air flow to overcome condensation in insulated roof spaces. Apart from the ease of installation, dry-fix systems mean that frost and wind damage are negligible and the roof becomes virtually maintenance free.

Research into new materials technology will, in the future, play a far greater role in the development of roofing products. However, for as long as today's modern buildings continue to be built using traditional methods and materials, the roof-coverings market will remain dominated by slates and tiles.

25.2 Concrete tiles

25.2.1 Description and historical development

Over 2000 years ago the Greeks and Romans knew about concrete as a building material, but it was not until the middle of the 19th century that it was first used for making roof tiles. The invention of concrete roof tiles is accredited to an Austrian builder and farmer Adolph Kroher. In the small mountain village of Staudach, in the Chiemgau, he utilized a local deposit of quick-setting, natural cement in conjunction with sand from a nearby quarry to produce a 'diamond'- pattern design tile. These early tiles were handmade with primitive cast iron pallets,

Figure 25.6 Plain tiles as vertical cladding to gable wall

Figure 25.7 Dry-fix roof components for verge and ridge

and at the 1879 Arnhem Exhibition, examples, about 35 years old, were shown to be free from signs of weathering or porosity. This was the first demonstration of the durability of concrete as a tile-making material.

The expansion of the concrete-roof-tile industry in Germany never materialized, and naturally, attention was focused elsewhere. By 1895, German and Danish hand machines were imported into England and many of these 'diamond'-pattern tiles are still in existence giving satisfactory maintenance-free service.

The development of concrete-tile production in England began after the First World War when the unavailability of traditional roofing materials, slates and clay tiles, led to the development of tile machinery on a commercial basis.

The simple 'Winget' hand press produced the traditional 'Broseley' pattern plain tile (size 10 in. × 6 in.) and the larger 'Marseilles' interlocking tile profiles were also available. The concrete roof tile was not widely accepted until the late 1920s, when the General Strike disrupted the production of clay tiles and prevented the supply of foreign imports. In the 1930s automated factories were established and improved colouring techniques were developed to overcome early criticisms regarding durability of colour coatings and textured finishes. Concrete roof tiles were seen to offer the specifier a real choice of profile and colour, and by 1939 accounted for 22% of the market (cf. slate 32% and clay 46%). After the Second World War expansion continued due to the post-war housing 'boom' and the concrete tile, due to its speed of production and installation, enabled builders to roof houses and buildings at the required output rate. Today, concrete tiles account for about 75% of the UK pitched-roof market with a total of six manufacturers located close to the major conurbations throughout the country.

25.2.2 Sources and availability

Most manufacturers produce similar tile designs and these are widely available at stockists of building and roofing materials. Mechanized packaging and delivery systems enable rapid availability of material direct from stock and for delivery to site. Tiles are usually priced per 1000 with fittings priced per 100 or individually, depending on their size and complexity.

25.2.3 Authority

Concrete roof tiles should comply with the requirements of BS 473.550: 1990. There is also a Code of Practice for the installation of tiles (BS 5534: Part 1: 1990 and Part 2: 1986) which also gives guidance on calculation of the fixing requirements to resist wind uplift.

25.2.4 Manufacture

The production of durable concrete roof tiles requires both the use of good quality raw materials and careful quality control at the production stage. Modern concrete tiles are made on highly automated plant based on a high-pressure extrusion and compaction operation.

25.2.4.1 Materials

Concrete tiles are manufactured from four traditional raw materials:

(1) *Sand.* Clean siliceous sand, graded and free of all deleterious materials, is used to ensure ease of manufacture and minimum voids on compaction. Petrographical examination of sand is carried out to determine the mineralogical composition. This can show the possible existence of deleterious materials, including reactive siliceous compounds which could give rise to alkali–aggregate reaction.

(2) *Cement.* A good quality Portland cement is required complying with the requirements of BS 12: 1978. This cement provides good strength development and a renowned durability.

(3) *Pigments.* Inert inorganic oxide pigments which are resistant to normal weathering and atmospheric conditions are used to colour the concrete. The pigments must also be resistant to alkali attack, degradation by ultra-violet light, be weather fast, colour stable and should not adversely affect the setting or hardening of the concrete mix.

(4) *Water.* Clean water free of all deleterious salts is used.

The above materials are weighed by proportion into a suitable batch mixer, which is automatically controlled to ensure consistency between batches.

25.2.4.2 Compaction and extrusion

The wet concrete mix is fed to a fully automated production line and compacted and continuously extruded at high speed onto profiled moulds which pass through the tile machine where pressures in excess of $500 \, \text{N m}^{-2}$ are applied. This process ensures a high-density product, essential for high strength and low permeability. Recent technology involving colour injector machines has been developed to provide random-coloured concrete mixes.

As the freshly extruded tiles are supported by their moulds they are accurately cut to length. Tiles which are to receive a sanded or granulated finish have a cementitious pigmented slurry applied to the surface over which the sand or granules are spread. The granules are produced from graded silica sands pigmented to a range of colours and stabilized using rotary kilns.

25.2.4.3 Curing

The tiles, still on pallets, are fed into either batch type curing chambers or continuous chambers in which racks of tiles pass through an inlet, travel through the cabinet and exit 8–24 h later. The chambers are kept in an accurately controlled environment with temperatures of around 40°C and high humidity, which accelerates the hydration of cement with maximum strength development and low permeability. The tiles are then de-moulded and treated to remove efflorescent salts. Most manufacturers apply a coloured polymer emulsion to the surface at this stage to help suppress efflorescence which can occur when the tiles are installed. Acrylic paints are also applied to provide colour and to help seal sanded and textured surface finishes. The cured tiles are assembled and packaged automatically and stored outside to mature for a further one to two weeks prior to delivery.

25.2.4.4 Packaging

Most modern concrete tiles are strap banded in packs of approximately 32 (interlocking tiles) and 10 (plain tiles). Some manufacturers shrink-wrap these packs onto timber pallets with heavy-duty polythene to protect them during transit and on site. Lorries with mechanized off-load facilities can deliver to site or contractors' yards and stack tiles within a minimum space requirement up to three pallets high.

25.2.5 Types

Concrete roof tiles are available in two formats: (1) double-lap plain tiles; and (2) single-lap interlocking tiles. The types of concrete tiles available are listed together with their physical properties in *Table 25.1*.

25.2.5.1 Double-lap plain tiles

By nature of its design the plain tile (*Figure 25.8*) is an extremely versatile product and is best suited for use in complex roof shapes were dormers, valleys and hips require a small-scale roofing module. Plain tiles are also an effective cladding material and are often used on the upper storeys of buildings to reduce the weight of the structure or to provide an attractive contrast in shape and texture. Ornamental shapes are available and can be used to create interesting patterns.

The batten gauge is equal to

$$\frac{(\text{length of tile}) - (\text{length of lap})}{2}$$

and, since the length of the product is at the practicable minimum, the lap should not exceed approximately 90 mm (88 mm gauge).

As shown in *Figure 25.9(a)*, double lap means that the top of any tile is covered by two tiles and at any section over the battens there are three thicknesses of tile. Lap is measured from the tail of the top tile to the back edge of the lower tile, thus disregardring the centre tile in the sandwich. It is also worth noting that the effective pitch of a double-lap plain tile is about 7° less than the rafter pitch (see *Figure 25.9(b)*).

The size and format of the concrete plain tile owes much to its clay counterpart. Tiles are manufactured to a size of 267 mm × 165 mm and have a curvature or 'camber' over both length and width. The camber is a purely functional feature as it is intended to reduce the capillary action of rainwater which can be drawn both upwards and sideways. It also creates a

Table 25.1 Types of concrete roofing tile

Type of tile	Size (mm)	Max. gauge (mm)	No. of tiles per m^2	Metre run of battens per m^2	Weight (75 mm lap) (kg m^{-3})	Min. pitch (°) Smooth surface finish	Min. pitch (°) Granuled finish
Plain	267 × 165	100	60	10	78	35	35
Interlocking							
Bold roll	420 × 330	345	9.7	2.9	48	17.5	30
Double pantile	420 × 330	345	9.8	2.9	47	22.5	25
Double Roman	420 × 330	345	9.7	2.9	45	22.5	25
Concrete slate	420 × 330	345	10.0	3.0	52	17.5	—
Single pantile	387 × 230	312	15.9	3.2	48	25	30
Interlocking trough	387 × 230	312	16.0	3.2	49	25	30

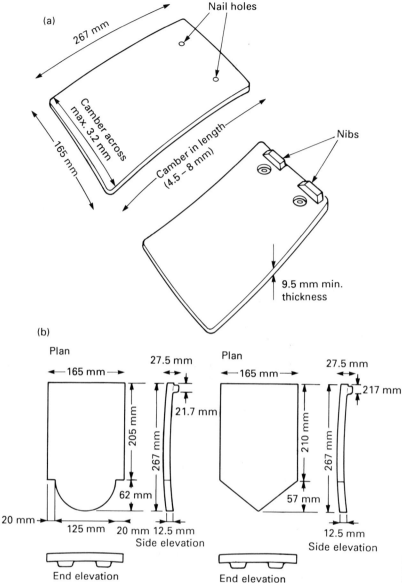

Figure 25.8 (a) Standard concrete double-lap plain tile–top and underside. (b) Plain feature tiles

pleasant contrast of light and shade when viewed from ground level.

Like the plain clay tile, the concrete version should be laid with a minimum headlap of 65 mm in situations of moderate exposure. In areas of high risk from bad weather laps should be increased to 75–90 mm.

As headlap increases, the angle of the face of the tile decreases and, as a general rule, the lap should not exceed about one-third of the length of the product. The rafter pitch must also be sufficient to ensure that the effective pitch of the tiles is not too low. For concrete plain tiles the minimum rafter pitch is 35°.

25.2.5.2 Single-lap tiles

Interlocking tiles have long been used to reduce the number of tiles required to cover a given roof area and, thereby, cut the cost of the finished roof. Concrete interlocking single-lap tiles are designed with a side lap and an interlocking ridge which engages in a channel of the adjacent tile. At the overlap of one tile above another, interlocking tiles have anticapillary grooves on the underside of the tail and sometimes ribs on the surface near the head of the tile. A variety of concrete interlocking tile designs is shown in *Figure 25.10*.

The number, position and size of these anticapillary grooves and ribs can greatly improve the resistance to driving rain of the tile by providing small cavities which capture wind-driven rain. The tile side-lock is normally designed with a minimum of gaps, but allowing some lateral adjustment of approximately 3 mm with maximum flexibility for optimum water-carrying capacity and resistance to driving rain (see *Figure 25.11*).

Concrete interlocking single-lap tiles are available in a wide range of profiles and surface finishes and many designs copy traditional designs e.g. pantiles and double Roman. The design

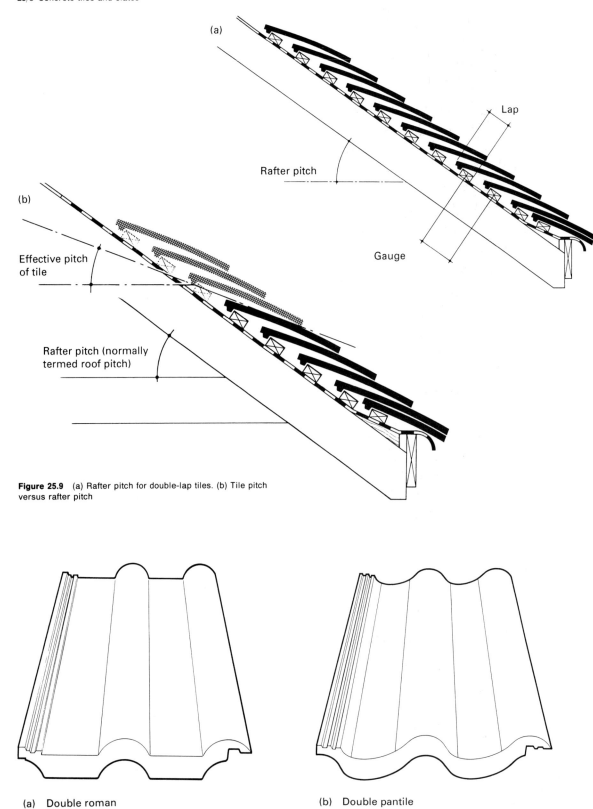

Figure 25.9 (a) Rafter pitch for double-lap tiles. (b) Tile pitch versus rafter pitch

(a)   Double roman   (b)   Double pantile

Figure 25.10 Various designs of concrete interlocking tiles

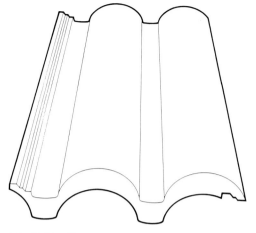

(c) Bold roll

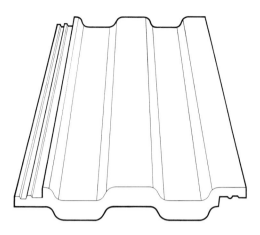

(d) Wide troughed concrete interlocking tile

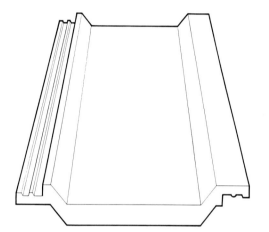

(e) Wide troughed concrete interlocking tile,
suitable for low pitches

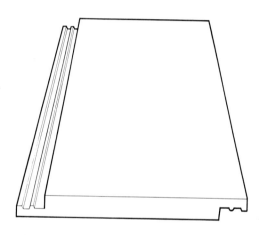

(f) Flat concrete interlocking tile

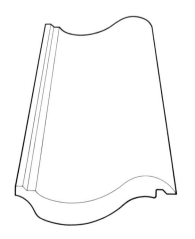

(g) Single pantile

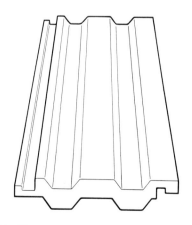

(h) Narrow troughed concrete interlocking tile

Figure 25.10 *(continued)*

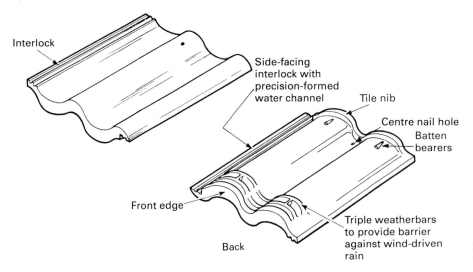

Figure 25.11 Back and face of an interlocking tile

of the tile profile can also have a significant effect on the performance of the roof with respect to resistance to driving rain and wind loads.

Maximum resistance to wind uplift can be achieved by optimizing the ratio of tile weight to tail thickness, thereby achieving a centre of gravity closer to the leading edge of the tile. Surface finish and profile can also help to improve the effects of air velocities and local pressure coefficients close to the roof surface.

Concrete interlocking tiles are suitable for a wide range of roof pitches, depending on design and surface finish. Granular or sand-faced tiles are restricted to use in steeper pitches as the water flow is somewhat slower at low pitches. In determining the minimum pitch for interlocking-tile designs due account is taken of their performance when laid to resist wind-blown rain and snow. The tile pitch for a single-lap interlocking tile is approximately 5° less than the rafter pitch. The practicable minimum for a flat concrete slate tile is 17.5°, although some manufacturers offer products which can be specified for roof pitches of 15° and 12.5°.

25.2.6 Appearance

By virtue of the material, concrete tiles can be produced in a wide range of surface textures, finishes and colours. Broadly speaking, tiles are available in either granular- or smooth-finished surfaces. The fine-silica-sand granules applied to the surface give a textured and mature appearance, especially when different colours are mixed in a 'multi-blend'. The sand facing also assists the weathering process, although in certain areas it may encourage moss growth (see Section 25.2.7.2).

Smooth-finish tiles have a fully pigmented body and most manufacturers apply an acrylic paint to the surface to improve weathering (see Section 25.2.7.1). Careful 'blending' of black pigment within the concrete mix produces a streaked effect reminiscent of weathered tiles subjected to a sooty industrial environment. These colours have become very popular in recent years. Highly glazed tiles are not in vogue at present although one manufacturer produces two colours of red and yellow blended with grey.

25.2.7 Roof-surface effects

25.2.7.1 Efflorescence

Efflorescence is a general term used in the construction industry to describe white deposits or stains on many building materials.

When found on concrete roof tiles and other cement-based products it is commonly known as lime bloom. It is particularly prevalent on through-coloured concrete tiles manufactured from Portland cement. The white deposit which appears on the surface of the tile can be concentrated in white patches or as an overall lightening in colour.

The cause of efflorescence lies in the chemical composition of the cement. When water is added to cement a series of reactions takes place which results in setting and hardening. The water also releases the free lime in the cement in the form of calcium hydroxide ions which migrate via capillaries to the surface. The calcium hydroxide reacts with carbon dioxide from the atmosphere to form a white surface deposit of calcium carbonate crystals which we know as efflorescence.

Darker and through-coloured tiles show more surface whitening, but this can be weathered away over a few years of exposure to wind and rain. The phenomenon is purely superficial and does not affect the durability or strength of concrete, the original colour or the functional properties of the tile.

In order to combat the visual detraction of efflorescence, some manufacturers apply a clear polymer acrylic film to the tile surface, which acts like a seal and inhibits the appearance of white stains on the surface. As the risk of efflorescence is greatest in the early years of curing it is applied purely as a temporary measure. The polymer acrylic film gradually weathers away leaving a matt-surface finish.

Granular or sanded surface tiles can be similarly treated, and in this case the acrylic also helps to bond the granules to the pigmented cementitious base colour.

25.2.7.2 Lichens and mosses

Lichen spores are present in the air and can start growing on most roofing materials. Concrete tiles demonstrate very little discolouration by lichens due to their alkalinity which makes them slightly fungicidal in character.

Although the tiles themselves are unaffected by the growth of lichens and mosses, these can cause problems if allowed to block valleys and gutters. Lichens and mosses can be removed by spraying with a toxic chemical wash or by trailing copper wires across the roof which creates a copper carbonate 'run-off' which kills the spores. It is unadvisable to scrape the mosses off as this can damage and scratch the surface of the tiles, thereby making them more visually unattractive than before.

25.2.8 Performance criteria

25.2.8.1 Weather resistance

Of all the performance criteria for a roofing material, weather resistance is perhaps the most important. Resistance to driving rain, permeability and wind forces must be tested. There is no British Standard wind/driving-rain test for overlapping tiles, but one manufacturer and the Building Research Establishment have developed a test for this purpose. A method of measuring wind speed and related rainfall rates at 2-min intervals has been developed. This is based on the worst-driving-rain index recorded in the UK at Plymouth in 1957. A 1-m^2 section of roof is subjected to rainfall of 38 mm h^{-1} with an associated wind speed of 13.4 m s^{-1} for a period of 1 h. In addition, a deluge test assesses the short-term high rainfall rates without wind, at a rainfall rate of 225 mm h^{-1} for a period of 2 min.

Permeability is assessed in accordance with BS 473.550: 1990 with a 2-m^2 area of roof experiencing 75 mm h^{-1} of simulated direct rainfall and 150 mm h^{-1} of simulated accumulated rainfall over 2 h. A semiquantitative visual inspection of the rear surface of the tiles is then made. No visible signs of free water in the form of droplets is permitted, although a maximum of 25% damp area on any one tile is acceptable in order to satisfy the test.

25.2.8.2 Durability

Over the design life of most roofs many materials will exhibit natural weathering and slight changes in colour. Concrete roof tiles, having a low water absorption (7% maximum of dry weight) and not being laminar in structure, will resist frost action. Evidence of satisfactory use has been achieved in Scandinavia where prolonged freeze–thaw cycles down to temperatures of −20°C have been experienced.

Concrete tiles are also resistant to extremes of high surface temperatures. Surface temperatures of +70°C have been measured on dark coloured tiles in Europe and South Africa.

Resistance to ultraviolet radiation with respect to coloured coatings and the tile body has been proven and several polymer-based products are applied to the tiles to resist these successfully.

Atmospheric pollution and the damage from sulphur and nitrogen oxides can have a dramatic effect on roofing materials in industrial areas. Concrete tiles exhibit good resistance to environmental pollution except where sulphur dioxide levels are greater than 70 μg m^{-3} of air, whence accelerated surface erosion may occur.

Impact resistance is an important criterion, particularly in areas such as South Africa, where concrete roof tiles have satisfactorily resisted an impact energy of 20 J equivalent to the terminal velocity of a 45-mm diameter hailstone.

25.2.8.3 Structural stability

All roof designs must be capable of withstanding anticipated dead and imposed loads. Concrete tiles are tested in accordance with BS 473.550: 1990 by means of a transverse strength test. Wet samples are supported with the top surface uppermost on the bottom two bearers of a flexural testing machine. The distance between the bearers being two-thirds the length of the tile (plain tiles 190 mm). The load is applied centrally through a third bearer at a uniform rate to a maximum of 6500 N min^{-1} (see *Figure 25.12*).

The average breaking load (in newtons; of six samples selected) applied along the width of the tile midway between the supports on a clear span two-thirds of the length of the tile must not be less than:

(1) double-lap tiles 305-mm wide and above—not less than 2.1 × effective width;
(2) single-lap tiles of all sizes—not less than 3.2 × effective width.

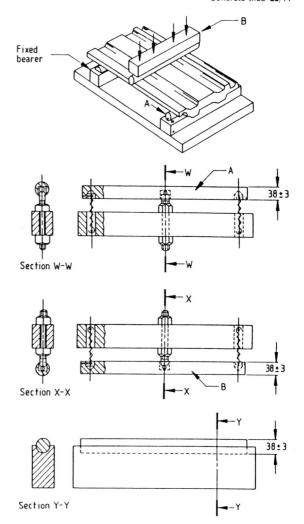

Figure 25.12 Diagram to show the apparatus used for the transverse strength test as specified in BS 473.550: 1990. Extracts from BS 473.550 are reproduced with the permission of BSI. Complete copies of the standard can be obtained by post from BSI Sales, Linford Wood, Milton Keynes, MK14 6LE.

For example, for a double Roman tile of dimensions 413 mm × 330 mm, the transverse test (wet) gives 976 N (3.2 × 305, i.e. width minus side lock). For plain tiles (267 mm × 165 mm) the average breaking load applied along the width of the tile midway between the supports on a clear span of 190 mm must not be less than 490 N.

Roof structures are required to withstand the anticipated dead and imposed loads stipulated in the Building Regulations. In addition, all parts of the roof must be designed for wind loadings determined by Code of Practice CP3 and BS 5534: Part 1: 1978 and Part 2: 1986 for the particular location and exposure conditions concerned.

It is misleading to assume that the high weight of concrete tiles (45–54 kg m^{-2}), compared with lightweight roofing materials, imposes serious design limitations or has unfavourable cost impact on building design. The weight of the roof covering is only one component of the total roof load, which must be considered when designing the roof structure of the building.

Roofs must be designed to withstand wind speeds of between 38 and 56 m s^{-1}. At a design wind speed of 44 m s^{-1} the uplift on a tiled roof of 27.5° pitch is over twice the downward weight of the roof covering and timbers. In this situation the weight of concrete tiles provides an advantageous reduction in uplift and hence reduces the amount of fixings required.

25.2.9 Sitework and installation

Tiles should be laid in accordance with the recommendations of BS 5534: Part 1: 1990. Typical roof loadings of concrete tiles are given in *Table 25.2*.

25.2.9.1 Groundwork

The common practice in England is to lay reinforced bitumen felt type BS 747: 1F: 1977 draped over the rafters. In Scotland, it is traditional to lay rigid sarking or boarding over rafters. Bitumen felt of adequate strength with a vapour permeability of not less than 36 g m^{-2} per 24 h at 25°C and a relative humidity of 75% when tested to BS 3177 should be laid directly onto the boarding.

Vertical laps should be a minimum of 100 mm with horizontal laps of 150 mm for unsupported and 100 mm for fully supported felt.

At the eaves of the roof the underlay should drain any water into the eaves gutter and should extend over the tilting piece and fascia board into the gutter. Water traps behind the fascia should be avoided. Proprietary eaves ventilation systems now incorporate felt support.

There is an increasing use of polyvinyl chloride (PVC) underlays beneath tiling and these should be of a minimum thickness to withstand wind uplift and extensibility.

25.2.9.2 Setting out

As soon as felting is completed the tiler should set out the roof along the eaves starting with the correct overhang at the right-hand verge. By closing or opening the sidelock of interlocking tiles the correct overhang at the left-hand verge can be achieved. If this is not possible, tiles can be cut using a carborundum disc cutter or, alternatively, half tiles can be employed.

Chalk or ochre lines are struck from eaves to ridge to check the vertical alignment and timber gauges are used to measure the horizontal coursing. Positioning the top and bottom battens must take place after the fascias and bargeboards are in position. For single-lap interlocking tiles the batten carrying the eaves course should be positioned so that the bottom edge of the tiles are over the centre line of the gutter; this is normally 50–65 mm for a 100-mm gutter.

When fixing the top and bottom battens the location of the nibs in relation to the top of the tile must be taken into account. For plain tiles the battens for the eaves undercourse must be positioned so that the front edges align.

The distance from the top of the eaves batten to the top course batten can be measured and divided up equally to ensure that the maximum gauge of the tiles is not exceeded. The eaves course of tiles should follow the same plane as the rest of the roof and, therefore, the fascia must be positioned at the correct height above the top edge of the rafter (normally the depth of the batten section plus the overall thickness of the tile at the bottom edge).

25.2.9.3 Interlocking tiles

Concrete interlocking tiles must be laid with a minimum headlap of 75 mm. Tiles should be mechanically fixed where required to resist wind uplift in accordance with BS 5534: 1978.

On roof pitches of 45–54° each tile should be nailed and at roof pitches of 55° and over each tile should be both nailed and clipped.

To avoid cutting tiles at the top course the gauge should be reduced by

(1) reducing equally on all courses; or
(2) reducing on the first three courses from the eave.

Under no circumstances should the gauge be increased as this would result in a decrease of the lap below the minimum.

Verges (bedded) Verges should be formed by bedding the tiles onto an undercloak of asbestos cement or fibre-reinforced cement strip (1200 mm × 150 mm). The undercloak should be laid rough-side upwards and closely butted together with a slight tilt downwards to provide a drip at the outside edge.

Any inequalities in the brickwork should be levelled off by laying the undercloak onto a buttering of mortar bringing the height up to the adjacent rafter. The roofing underlay should be carried over the cavity wall and covered by the inside edge of the undercloak. When laid on boarding each length of undercloak should be nailed at a maximum of 300-mm centres.

When forming a verge on bargeboards the tiling battens must extend to the outer edge of the bargeboard. The undercloak is then placed between the battens and bargeboard, overhanging by a maximum of 50 mm, and nailed through.

All verge tiles must be bedded and fixed either by nailing or by clipping. Verge clips should be nailed to the top of the battens with two 25 mm × 3.35 mm aluminium nails with the upstand level and the extreme edge of the undercloak (see *Figure 25.13(a)*). Under normal conditions the roof can be set out to avoid cutting, but where this is not possible care should be taken to ensure that the cut tiles are symmetrical at both verges.

Table 25.2 Typical roof loadings (kg m^{-2}) at 30° rafter pitch

Roof tile/slate	Slope load				Plan load*		
	Tile	Batten	Underlay	Dead load	Dead load	Snow load (imposed)	Total load
Reconstructed stone slates (457 mm × 457 mm)	80.0	2.56	1.20	83.76	96.72	76.50	173.22
Concrete plain tile	78.20	4.30	1.20	83.70	96.64	76.50	173.14
Concrete interlocking tile	45.50	1.49	1.20	48.19	55.64	76.50	132.14
Lightweight concrete interlocking tile	28.0	1.49	1.20	30.69	35.43	76.50	111.93
Polymer-modified-cement concrete interlocking slates	23.5	1.94	1.20	26.64	30.76	76.50	107.26
Fibre–cement slate (600 mm × 300 mm)	21.5	1.94	1.20	24.64	28.45	76.50	104.95

* Load on plan = [Load on slope (including felt and battens) × cos(roof pitch (at 30° = 0.866))].

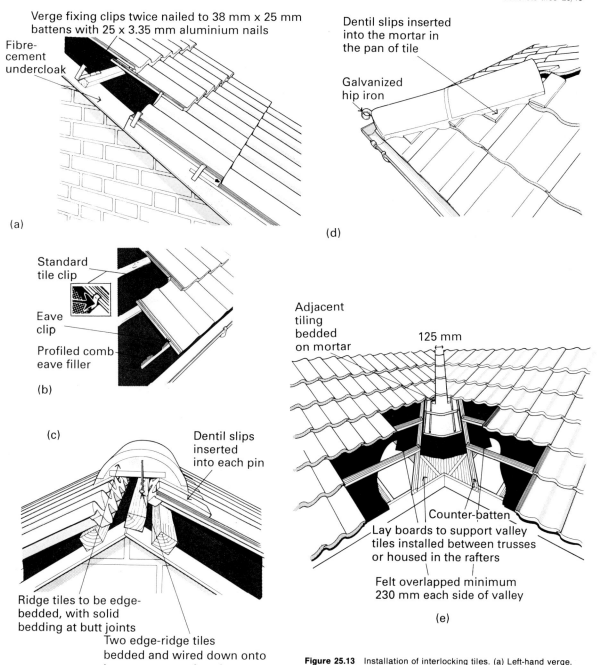

Verge fixing clips twice nailed to 38 mm x 25 mm battens with 25 x 3.35 mm aluminium nails

Fibre-cement undercloak

(a)

Standard tile clip

Eave clip

Profiled comb eave filler

(b)

(c)

Ridge tiles to be edge-bedded, with solid bedding at butt joints

Two edge-ridge tiles bedded and wired down onto batten at apex of roof

Dentil slips inserted into the mortar in the pan of tile

Galvanized hip iron

(d)

Dentil slips inserted into each pin

Adjacent tiling bedded on mortar

125 mm

Counter-batten

Lay boards to support valley tiles installed between trusses or housed in the rafters

Felt overlapped minimum 230 mm each side of valley

(e)

Figure 25.13 Installation of interlocking tiles. (a) Left-hand verge. (b) Eave. (c) Ridge. (d) Hip with segmental ridge. (e) Trough valley

All mortar bedding should be struck off flush and neatly pointed.

Eaves The eave course (*Figure 25.13(b)*) of tiling must be supported by a continuous tilting piece or fascia board in such a way that the tiles neither tilt nor droop in relation to the main body of the tiling. To achieve this the outside edge of the fascia board or tiling piece should project above the top face of the rafter by the depth of the batten plus the thickness of the tile where it rests on the fascia board.

The tiles should overhang the fascia board by an amount sufficient to ensure that water discharges into the centre of the gutter. If the gutter is not fixed at the time of tiling an overhang of 50 mm should be allowed. Where soffit boarding is not provided the overhang portion of the rafters should be covered with close boarding onto which the tilting fillet is fixed.

Each eave course tile should be fixed with a nail or a purpose-made clip (*Figure 25.14*) nailed to the top of the fascia board. A purpose-made eave filler is nailed with 25 mm × 3.35 mm aluminium nails with or without the clip, to the top of the fascia

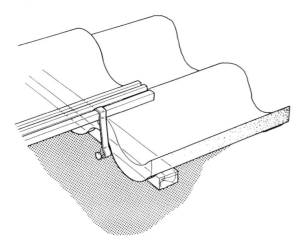

Figure 25.14 Interlocking tile with fixing clip

to prevent the ingress of birds into the roofspace. The underlay should be drawn taut over the front edge of the fascia board before fixing.

The use of a tilting eave or sprocket is not recommended with interlocking tiles as this renders the anticapillary devices ineffective (see *Figure 25.15*).

Ridge Ridge tiles of similar colour and texture to that of the main roof tiles should be edge-bedded onto the top course tiles with solid bedding at butt joints. The mortar at butt joints should be supported by pieces of tile which should be in two halves where it has to pass either side of a fixing wire.

A minimum of 75-mm cover should be provided over the top course tiles and the exposed mortar should be neatly pointed. Fair ends to ridges should be filled with mortar inset with pieces of plain tile and neatly pointed. (See *Figure 25.13(c)*.)

Hip Hips should be covered with hip tiles of similar colour and texture to that of the main roof tiles. The tiling should be cut closely to the rake of the hip and the ridge tiles edge-bedded with solid bedding at butt joints, onto the adjacent roof tiles.

A galvanized hip iron, 6-mm thick for roof pitches of 35° and above and 4-mm thick for roof pitches below 35°, should be fixed at the base of the hip tree with two 2.65-mm diameter screws or nails. (See *Figure 25.13(d)*.)

The first hip tile should be shaped at the foot to the line of tiling at the eave and the fair end filled with mortar inset with pieces of tile and neatly pointed.

The junction of hip and ridge should be mitred using a standard three-way mitre and solid bedded.

Valleys Valleys should be constructed using trough-valley tiles, or a metal sheet made of lead or other approved material laid on the boarding. Open metal valleys can be used at all pitches and are especially useful where a valley forms the junction between two roof slopes of different pitches. (See *Figure 25.13(e)*.)

25.2.9.4 Plain tiles

Main roof Plain concrete tiles must be laid broken bond with a minimum headlap of 65 mm and to a maximum gauge of 100 mm using purpose-made tile-and-a-half tiles at right- and left-hand verges. Tiles should be fixed where required to resist wind uplift in accordance with BS 5534: 1990.

All tiles at eaves, verges and top courses, and each tile in every fifth course should be nailed with two 38 mm × 2.65 mm aluminium nails. For pitches of 60° and above each tile should be nailed twice.

Battens Approved quality softwood tiling battens 38 mm × 25 mm (for rafter spacing not exceeding 600 mm) or 38 mm × 19 mm (for rafter spacing not exceeding 450 mm) should be fixed to a maximum gauge of 100 mm and secured with wire nails. It is recommended that in coastal areas steel nails should be hot-dip galvanized. Battens should be at least

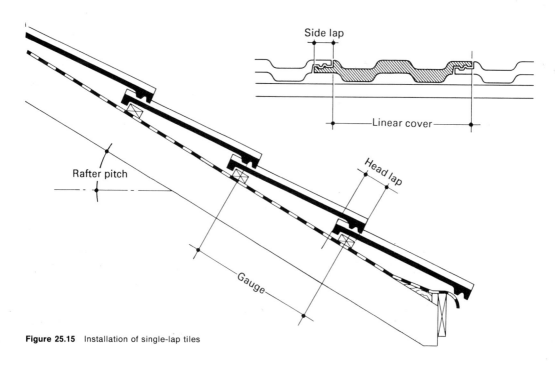

Figure 25.15 Installation of single-lap tiles

1.2 m in length, sufficient to be supported at each end and intermediately by at least three rafters, trusses or walls. Butt joints over intermediate supports should be staggered so that nor more than one batten in four is joined on any one rafter. Batten ends must be sawn.

Battening on boarded roofs with underlay should be supported on counterbattens to increase ventilation under the tiles and to allow free drainage of any water that may reach the underlay.

Verges Verges should be formed by bedding the tiles onto an undercloak of plain tiles or asbestos cement or fibre-reinforced cement strip (1200 mm × 150 mm). If a plain tile undercloak is used the tiles should be laid face down with the 165-mm edge exposed. Strip undercloak should be laid rough-side upwards and closely butted together with a slight tilt downwards to provide a drip at the outside edge.

Any inequalities in the brickwork should be levelled off by laying the undercloak onto a buttering of mortar bringing the height up to the adjacent rafter. The roofing underlay should be carried over the cavity wall and covered by the inside edge of the undercloak. When laid on boarding each length of undercloak should be nailed at a maximum of 300-mm centres.

When forming a verge on bargeboards the tiling battens must extend to the outer edge of the bargeboard. The undercloak is then placed between the battens and bargeboard, overhanging by a maximum of 50 mm, and nailed through.

All tiles at the verges should be bedded and the tiling must be finished with tile-and-a-half tiles in alternate courses. (See *Figure 25.16(a)*.)

Under normal conditions the roof can be set out to avoid cutting, but where this is not possible care should be taken to ensure that the cut tiles are not used at the verge.

All mortar bedding should be struck off flush and neatly pointed in one operation leaving the exposed edge of the tiles clean.

Eaves The eave course of tiling must be supported by a continuous tilting piece or fascia board in such a way that the tiles neither tilt nor droop in relation to the main body of tiling. To achieve this the outside edge of the fascia board or tilting piece should project above the top face of the rafter by the depth of the batten plus the thickness of the tile where it rests on the fascia board. The tiles should overhang the fascia board by an amount sufficient to ensure that water discharges into the centre of the gutter. If the gutter is not fixed at the time of tiling an overhang of 50 mm should be allowed.

To prevent the felt sagging and forming a water trap behind the fascia board a continuous wedge-shaped timber fillet or batten should be provided. The felt should slope over this support and extend into the gutter to drain away any moisture present.

Where soffit boarding is not provided the overhanging portion of the rafters should be covered with close boarding onto which the tilting fillet is fixed.

A double course of tiles must be laid at the eaves formed by laying a first course of shorter eaves (tiles 193-mm long), with a course of full tiles laid broken bond on top. Both these courses should be nailed. (See *Figure 25.16(b)*.)

Ridge Segmental ridge tiles of similar colour and texture to that of the main roof tiles should be edge-bedded onto the top course tiles with solid bedding at butt joints. The mortar at butt joints should be supported by pieces of tile.

A single course of tiles should be laid at the ridge using:

(1) the longer tops tile of length 225 mm nailed to a batten covering a course of full tiles laid broken bond beneath; and

(2) the shorter eaves or tops tile of length 193 mm mechanically fixed to the full tiles, laid broken bond beneath, with a purpose-made wire clip.

A minimum of 75-mm cover should be provided over the top-course tiles and the exposed mortar should be neatly pointed. Fair ends to ridges should be filled with mortar inset with pieces of plain tile and neatly pointed. (See *Figure 25.16(c)*.)

Valleys Valleys should be formed with purpose-made valley tiles or open construction using metal. The traditional laced or swept valleys may also be used, but involve a great deal of cutting. When valley tiles are to be used they should be laid without nailing or bedding to the main roof tiling. When trussed rafter roofs are encountered the tiling battens need support at the valley where the roof slopes intersect. Timber valleyboards should be fixed between rafters to provide support for the tiling battens and valley tiles (the position of the valley tree in traditional construction). (See *Figure 25.16(d)*.)

Hip Hips should be covered with segmental ridge tiles (*Figure 25.16(e)*) or purpose-made bonnet hip tiles (*Figure 25.16(f)*) of similar colour and texture to that of the main roof tiles. When segmental ridge tiles are used the tiling should be cut closely to the rake of the hip and the ridge tiles, edge-bedded, with solid bedding at butt joints, on the adjacent roof tiles. A galvanized 6-mm thick hip iron should be fixed at the base of the hip tree with two 2.65-mm diameter screws or nails.

The first hip tile should be shaped at the foot to the line of tiling at the eave and the fair end filled with mortar inset with pieces of tile and neatly pointed. The junction of hip and ridge should be mitred with a standard three-way mitre and solid bedded.

Bonnet hip tiles should be laid to course and bond with the tiling on each side of the hip. The roof tiles should be neatly and cleanly cut against the edges of the Bonnet hips, using tile-and-a-half where necessary to avoid the use of small pieces of tile. Bonnet hip tiles should be secured with a 70 mm × 2.65 mm aluminium nail fixed through to the hip tree and bedded and struck pointed in cement mortar, the pointing being kept slightly back from the edge of the hip tile and undercut.

The end of the first Bonnet hip tile should be filled with pieces of plain tile set in cement mortar.

Abutments At all abutments where the tiling meets wall or chimneys an adequate flashing material must be used to weather the junction. The roof tiles should be brought up close to the wall, by cutting if necessary, and the underlay returned up the wall. Tile-and-a-half tiles should be used in alternate courses to provide broken bond.

Weathering the abutment should be carried out with a cover flashing dressed well down onto the tiling and used in conjunction with lead soakers.

25.2.9.5 Vertical plain and feature tiles

Battens On timber frame construction approved quality softwood tiling battens 38 mm × 25 mm (for support spacing not exceeding 600 mm) or 38 mm × 19 mm (for support spacing not exceeding 450 mm) should be fixed to a maximum gauge of 115 mm and secured with wire nails to timber studding. It is recommended that in coastal areas steel nails should be hot-dip galvanized. Battens should be at least 1.2 m in length, sufficient to be supported at each end and intermediately by at least three studs or walls. Butt joints over intermediate supports should be staggered so that not more than one batten in four is joined on any one stud. Batten ends must be sawn.

On masonry construction, plain and feature tiles may be fixed either direct to battens or to battens and counter battens securely

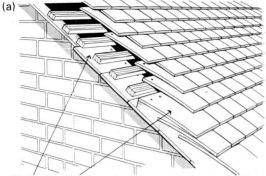

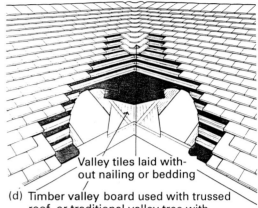

(a)

Plain tiles laid face down as an undercloak; tile-and-a-half used in alternate courses, mortar bedding struck off flush and neatly pointed

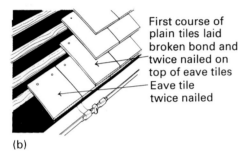

First course of plain tiles laid broken bond and twice nailed on top of eave tiles

Eave tile twice nailed

(b)

Valley tiles laid without nailing or bedding

(d) Timber valley board used with trussed roof, or traditional valley tree with rafter and purlin roof, in order to support the tiling battens and valley tiles

(c) Segmental ridge tile, two end tiles to be secured by fixing wire to nail in batten at apex of roof

Supporting tile piece

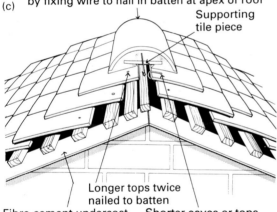

Fibre-cement undercoat laid rough side upwards

Longer tops twice nailed to batten

Shorter eaves or tops tile secured with clips

(e)

Segmental ridge, edge bedded with solid bedding at butt joints

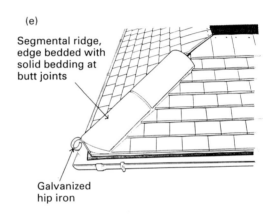

Galvanized hip iron

(f)

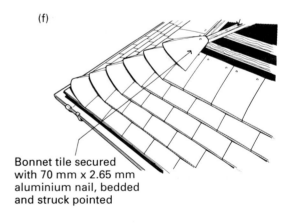

Bonnet tile secured with 70 mm x 2.65 mm aluminium nail, bedded and struck pointed

Figure 25.16 Installation of plain tiles. (a) Verge. (b) Eave. (c) Ridge. (d) Valley. (e) Hip with segmental ridge. (f) Bonnet hips

fixed to the wall face with cut nails. (If dense concrete blocks are encountered advice with regard to the type of fixing required should be obtained from the block manufacturer.) The use of counter battens reduces the amount of direct nailing to a solid wall; the battens should be securely fixed by means of plugs or timber plates embedded in the wall. The reader's attention is drawn to the National House Building Council (NHBC) Standards 1991, Vol 2, Part 7 which require timber battens to

be pretreated against decay, i.e. CCA pressure to BS 4072 or double vacuum. Batten nails should be hot-dip galvanized.

Underlay When tiles are laid over masonry construction, felt or other approved underlay should be employed, lapped 75 mm horizontally and 150 mm vertically and secured with clout nails ensuring that the edge distance of the fixings is not less than 50 mm.

When vertical tiling is used as a facing for timber framed construction, a suitable underlay should be provided in the form of a breather membrane (which permits limited transfer of moisture).

The reader is referred to NHBC Standards 1991, Vol 2, Part 7.

Fixing Vertical plain and feature tiles should be laid to a minimum lap of 35 mm and a maximum gauge of 115 mm, each tile being fixed with two 38 mm × 2.65 mm aluminium nails.

Eaves A double course of tiles must be laid at the eaves formed by laying a first course of 193 mm long eave tiles with a course of full tiles laid broken bond on top. The eave tile must be tilted a minimum of 65 mm from the face of the groundwork by using a timber fillet. This allows the lower course to fit closely. Both eave courses should be nailed twice using 38 mm × 2.65 mm aluminium nails.

Top courses The top tiles should be a course of purpose-made 225-mm long tiles, each tile to be nailed as before. Where a top course is formed under a window sill, a lead flashing supplied by the plumber should be dressed down over the top course tiles for at least 100 mm, and cut level or to an approved finish.

Angles Purpose-made internal or external angle tiles should be used at all corners. Left- and right-hand angles of 90° are available to provide a broken bond with the main tiling, which should be neatly cut to the angled tiles.

Where the use of purpose-made angle tiles is impractical, a simple but effective way to overcome the problem is to close mitre the tiling over lead soakers. This method is also useful where vertical tiling is sprocketed at the eave and it is difficult to fit angle tiles. In this case it is best to neatly mitre the tiles over soakers and use angle tiles as soon as the sprocket is finished.

Gables At raking abutments such as gable ends, the tiles should be splay-cut in a 'Winchester' cut finished with a tile-and-a-half at the end of each course to avoid the use of small triangular pieces of tile. The last tile against the main roof verge should be nailed securely.

If 'Winchester' cutting is used on gable ends where the roof pitch is 30° or less, the tiling gauge may need to be reduced to 100 mm or 90 mm in order to avoid a too greatly splayed cut. It is most likely that two tile-and-a-half tiles adjacent to one another will be needed to overcome this. 'Winchester' cutting is not practical on roof pitches below 22.5°. It is important that the vertical bond of the main tiling is maintained when using 'Winchester' cut. A full tile-and-a-half should always be used at the apex cut to the appropriate rake. Feature tiles are not recommended for use at gable ends as their shape is impractical for 'Winchester' cutting.

Abutment Where the tiling meets an abutment, tile-and-a-half tiles are to be used in alternate courses to provide broken bond.

25.2.10 Thermal insulation

Concrete tiles have low thermal resistance compared with alternative roofing materials such as thin sheet-metal profiles. However, the thermal performance of a roof system must be assessed by taking into account the groundwork specification, including battens, underlay and roof openings.

The Building Regulations 1985 require that the roof of a dwelling should have a U thermal transmittance value of not more than $0.25\ \mathrm{W\ m^{-2}\ K^{-1}}$ for dwellings and $0.45\ \mathrm{W\ m^{-2}\ K^{-1}}$ for other buildings. When calculating the thermal resistance of roofing materials, due account must be taken of the resistance of the tile–felt airspace and not just the resistance of the slates and tiles.

A 30° pitched roof of timber trussed rafters covered with slates or concrete tiles on timber battens with sarking felt underlay and plasterboard ceiling will require 100-mm mineral-fibre or glass-fibre insulation laid on the ceiling to provide a U value to meet regulations.

25.2.11 Condensation

The significance of condensation in roofs has become more important with more highly insulated buildings and changes in life-style. Higher levels of water vapour are evident in modern buildings which naturally ascends into the roof space. Roof pitch and climatic conditions also play an important role in contributing towards condensation problems.

Prevention of condensation in roof voids is best achieved by the provision of natural air ventilation. Whilst concrete tiles allow some degree of natural ventilation by their interlocking nature, additional apertures are required in the form of eaves, tile and ridge ventilators. The Building Regulations 1985 require that all roofs be ventilated at the eaves equivalent to a continuous 10-mm wide gap on opposite sides of the roof. At pitches of 15° or less this gap must be increased to 25 mm. In addition, BS 5250: 1989 also recommends ridge ventilation equivalent to a continuous 5-mm gap.

The increasing use of dry, mechanically fixed and ventilated concrete-roof-tile systems ensures that roofs are well ventilated to prevent condensation. Most manufacturers offer complete eave, ridge and tile ventilation products to satisfy this requirement.

25.2.12 Sound insulation

External noise can penetrate a building through the walls, windows and roof. In most cases the roof is the least important of these, but where buildings are close to airports or traffic from elevated roadways, sound insulation of the roof is an important consideration.

Normal road, rail and aircraft noise has a frequency of between 100 and 3000 Hz. A concrete-tiled roof has a sound reduction potential of about 30–35 dB. The addition of thermal insulation at ceiling and rafter level can increase this figure to about 45 dB (BRE Digests 128 and 129).

25.2.13 Fire resistance

Concrete tiles are non-combustible (BS 476: Part 4: 1970 (1984)) and have an external SAA fire rating (BS 476: Part 3: 1975). There is no restriction of use in the UK for either roof or wall-cladding applications.

25.3 Lightweight-aggregate tiles

Two manufacturers in the UK have recently introduced tiles made of lightweight aggregates. These products are aimed at the reroofing market where the weight of replacement roof covering is often critical in relation to roof loadings. The tiles have a laid weight of $28\ \mathrm{kg\ m^{-2}}$ at 75-mm lap which means that they can be used on roof structures previously clad with slates, usually without the need for structural reinforcement of roof timbers. It is claimed that the reduction in weight has been achieved without sacrificing flexural strength which is estimated to be about 20% greater than standard concrete tiles. One manufacturer has achieved this without a reduction in the thickness of the body of the tile in order to comply with the requirements of BS 473.550: 1990.

25.3.1 Manufacture

The tiles are manufactured using the same process as conventional concrete tiles (see Section 25.2.4), but more careful control of mixing materials and curing of tiles is necessary.

25.3.2 Installation

Tiles are installed in the same manner as conventional concrete tiles, but due to their light weight each tile must be mechanically fixed to resist wind uplift forces. Care must be exercised by installers in handling and trafficking of all roof areas in order to avoid breakage.

25.4 Slates

Man-made slates used as a roofing material fall into four basic categories:

(1) concrete reconstructed stone slates;
(2) fibre-cement slates;
(3) resin- and polymer-bonded slates; and
(4) polymer-modified-cement slates.

The physical properties of the different types of man-made slates are given in *Table 25.3*.

25.4.1 Concrete re-constructed stone slates

25.4.1.1 Description and development

There are several products on the market which are designed to resemble traditional stone slates historically from areas of the country like the Cotswolds, Yorkshire and Derbyshire. Production of concrete slates began in the 1960s as the sources of natural stone roofing materials declined and there was a demand for an alternative product, especially for conservation work.

25.4.1.2 Types

Several manufacturers offer a range of designs from simple, flat, thin rectangular slates to random-sized slates with variable thicknesses and textured surfaces. All common designs are for double-lap laying, although one manufacturer has recently developed an interlocking single-lap product in varying widths. (See *Figure 25.17*.)

25.4.1.3 Authority

There is no British Standard for concrete reconstructed stone slates or tiles, although most manufacturers apply the requirements of BS 473.550: 1990 for strength and durability standards. Sizes and thicknesses of the product are often variable, and hence are not covered by British Standard requirements.

25.4.1.4 Manufacture

The raw materials (sand, cement, oolitic limestone and water) are mixed in a similar process to that used for ordinary concrete-tile production but with an added variegated colour mix. The mixture is poured into moulds taken from natural-stone masters and then cured under controlled environmental conditions and high humidity. One manufacturer uses a concrete mix coated with colour which is then compacted by rolling under pressure to form the slate. 'Reconstituted-stone' slates incorporate fragments of the original stone which is blended into the mix. Random-sized slates are stamped with numbers to assist in laying to the correct pattern on the roof.

25.4.1.5 Appearance

The slates are textured and coloured such that they closely match the characteristics of the regional stone of the part of the country where the stone roofing slates have been traditionally used. Some manufacturers use local crushed natural stone as an aggregate to improve the representation. The textured surface of the slates encourages the growth of lichen and moss and the roof weathers to an accurate reproduction of the natural material.

25.4.1.6 Weather resistance

Slates are laid double-lap and, therefore, exhibit similar characteristics to traditional natural slate. The rough or irregular undersurface of some patterns allows natural air movement between the slates, thereby preventing capillary action in line with BS 473.550: 1990.

25.4.1.7 Strength and durability

Reconstructed slates are unaffected by frost or other natural agencies and are not prone to warping or delamination. Most products comply with the BS 473.550: 1990 strength requirements for concrete roof tiles.

Table 25.3 Types of man-made slates

Type of slate	Size (mm)	Max. gauge (100 mm lap) (mm)	No. of slates per m² (100 mm lap)	Metre run battens per m²	Weight (kg m⁻²)	Min. pitch (°)
Fibre cement (double lap)	600 × 300	250	13.3	4.0	21.0	20
	500 × 250	200	20.0	5.0	19.5	20
	400 × 200	155	31.9	6.45	21.6	20
Reconstructed stone slates						
North England	457 × 305 to 686 × 457	190–279	17.2–7.82	3.58–5.24	80–99	15–25
Cotswold	Length 300–550 Width 200–500	110–200	22 (80 mm lap)	6.25	82	30
Interlocking state						
Resin bonded	300 × 336	250	13.3 (75 mm lap)	4.0	17	25
PMC concrete*	325–330	250	13.3 (75 mm lap)	4.0	23.5	25

* PMC, polymer-modified cement.

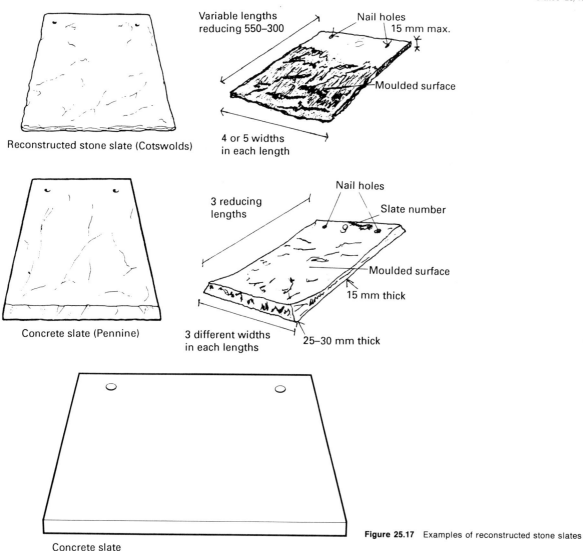

Reconstructed stone slate (Cotswolds)

Variable lengths
reducing 550–300

Nail holes
15 mm max.

Moulded surface

4 or 5 widths
in each length

Concrete slate (Pennine)

3 reducing
lengths

Nail holes

Slate number

Moulded surface

15 mm thick

3 different widths
in each lengths

25–30 mm thick

Concrete slate

Figure 25.17 Examples of reconstructed stone slates

25.4.1.8 Installation and sitework

The installation of reconstructed-stone slates is shown schematically in *Figure 25.18*.

Diminishing course slates After checking the rafter length and eave oversail the roof should be felted out and battened from eaves to ridge in accordance with the batten details. Slates are laid first on any small roof areas intersecting the main roof, e.g. dormers, using short-length slates. Slates are then laid on valleys and verges and cut to the hips as necessary. The main roof areas should be stacked out with slates of varying lengths and widths; undereave slates should be laid first and then the main roof areas covered using the full range of slate widths. Under-ridge slates should be hung on the top of the last main slate course and bed ridged in mortar.

Standard-sized slates The roof should be felted and battened in accordance with maximum-gauge recommendations. Special

under-eaves slate should be laid at the eaves and then full-length slate laid on the main roof by hanging above the batten with two flat-headed copper-wire nails or aluminium-alloy nails. (Roof pitches over 40° should be nailed to the batten using 38 mm long nails.) A special top course slate should be used at the ridge.

At verges, slate-and-a-half and slate are used in alternate courses with a maximum tilt of 12 mm. Verges should be bedded in mortar and surplus mortar struck off. All slates should be nailed.

Purpose-made hip tiles are used at hips, nailed to the hip rafter with an aluminium or alloy nail (minimum 65-mm long). When slating from hips one should start with a slate and a half slate, cut as required to maintain the correct side lap. Purpose-made valley slates are also available for valleys which are laid and coursed into the main roof. Ridge tile profiles are available in a wide range of sizes to suit both low- and steep-pitched roofs.

Slates can be laid on roofs from 25–47.5° pitch (depending on the size and coursing arrangements).

Figure 25.18 Installation of reconstructed stone slates. CC, change course

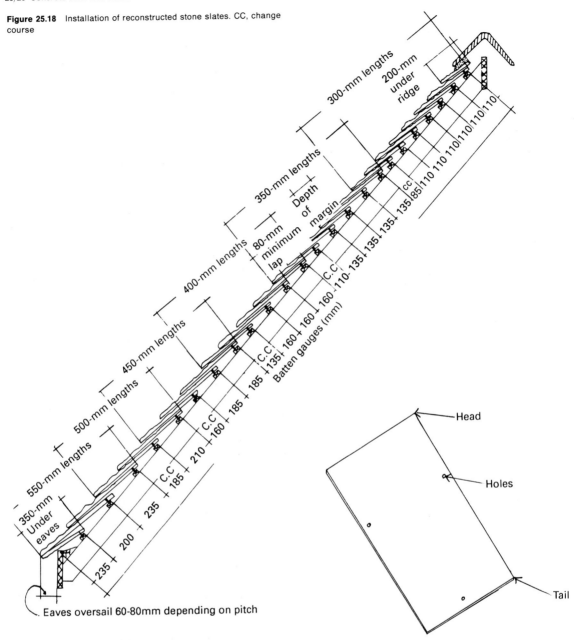

. Eaves oversail 60-80mm depending on pitch

25.4.2 Fibre-cement slates

25.4.2.1 Description and development

Until recently, all synthetic slates were produced using cement bonded with asbestos fibres, but the health scare over the use of asbestos has resulted in the introduction of synthetic fibres and filling compounds as a substitute. Around 1900, an Austrian, Ludwig Hatzchek, discovered the compatibility of chrysotile asbestos fibre and ordinary Portland cement (OPC) and produced the first asbestos–cement sheet material. Examples of the early production can still be seen on roofs in Austria where diamond-shaped slates were fixed on domestic buildings (see Section 25.2.1). These diagonal slates were more economical to use, since they are only single lap and represent an ingenious method of roofing which is both economical and lightweight.

Figure 25.19 Typical man-made fibre–cement slates

Asbestos–cement slates were first produced in England in 1908 and many diagonal pattern shapes were used on lightweight timber buildings. Straight-cover rectangular slates were also produced as were pantiles and corrugated sheets.

The aesthetic preference for straight-cover slates meant that after the Second World War the production of diagonal slates was discontinued. Standard size 'Duchess' and 'Countess' slate sizes were produced, usually with two-centre nail holes. These were fixed by nails at the centre, as in ordinary slating, and a copper disc rivet passed up through the joint of the slates under and through a hole in the tail of the slate; this disc was used to hold down the tail of the slate. (See *Figure 25.19*.)

25.4.2.2 Authority

Double-lap slates manufactured using asbestos fibres should comply with BS 690: Part 4: 1974. Asbestos-free alternatives require Agrément Board Certification and most manufacturers offer a 30-year guarantee.

25.4.2.3 Manufacture

Man-made slates are manufactured from ordinary Portland cement (to BS 12: 1978 requirements), water and either naturally occurring mineral fibres, or a white asbestos 10% by weight combination of synthetic cellulose fibres, sheet formers and fillers which are bonded together by the cement to form a tough and versatile sheet material.

The process for making fibre-cement slates is closely similar to conventional heavy-paper and board production methods. A 10% aqueous slurry of either asbestos (or formulated fibres), pigment and cement is held in a vat in which a sieve cylinder rotates. The cylinder simultaneously picks up and drains the solids. A continuous conveyor belt rides over the top surface of the sieve cylinder and deposits the solids as a thin laminated layer. The belt turns over at one end of the machine and passes over vacuum boxes which drain off excess moisture. The solid material is then passed on to a roller press or mandrel. The laminated sheet is wound on continuously until the sheet is of the required thickness.

During this process the fibres in the material align, giving strength to the final product. The slates are then fed into an autoclave chamber for final curing and to have holes drilled for fixing.

Several manufacturers apply surface coatings to prevent efflorescence and there are several processes which produce a random textured surface and dressed edges.

25.4.2.4 Types

Fibre-cement slates are available in a range of popular sizes ranging from 600 mm × 300 mm to 400 mm × 200 mm and are available in a wide range of colours, textures and shapes. There are also several decorative feature patterns available for vertical application.

25.4.2.5 Appearance

There are numerous textured and coloured finishes available from the traditional semi-matt finish resembling natural slate to the randomly textured and riven surface of dressed natural slate. One manufacturer produces a randomly mottled surface giving a variegated effect of various shades of brown and russet. Acrylic paint is applied to the surface of the slates to prevent efflorescence (see Section 25.2.7.1).

25.4.2.6 Weather resistance

Although slates are laid double lap and in staggered 'bond' to prevent the ingress of water at the joints, they are flat by design and hence are affected by capillary attraction. The 'angle of creep' underneath the slates is dependent on the pitch and exposure of the roof (see *Figure 25.20*). Increasing the lap of the slates will prevent creep water from entering nail holes or passing over the heads of lower slates. Tests to establish watertightness to BS 624 can establish that no drops of water will form and that permeability can be reduced by the acrylic surface finish. Absorption of moisture is a maximum of 18%.

25.4.2.7 Durability

Several manufacturers guarantee their product for 30 years and

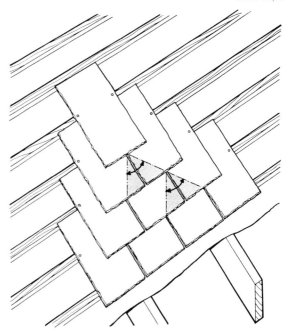

Figure 25.20 Angle of creep underneath slates where water can enter joints

may have Agrément Board Certification. Fibre–cement slates are unaffected by frost when tested to BS 4624: 1981 and are rot proof and immune from insect or vermin attack. The acrylic surface paint treatment applied to some slates also prevents the growth of moss and lichens. Over a longer period it can be expected that slates may lighten in colour as a result of exposure to ultraviolet radiation and in highly polluted atmospheres a slight surface softening of the cement may occur.

25.4.2.8 Structural stability

Fibre–cement slates have a density of between 1600 and 1800 kg m^{-3} when tested in accordance with BS 4624: 1981: Section 14.

25.4.2.9 Fire resistance

Fibre–cement slates can all achieve a class-AA rating in accordance with BS 476: Part 3: 1958 and some products have a class-0 rating as defined in the Building Regulations E15.

25.4.3 Resin- and polymer-bonded slates

Produced as a direct alternative to fibre–cement material, resin-bonded slates appeared about 8 years ago. Manufactured using natural aggregates of crushed slate and stone, the material is reinforced with glass fibre in a polyester or acrylic resin binder.

25.4.3.1 Manufacture

Slates are produced in thin flat sheets or moulded at high temperatures under pressure to form an authetic riven surface with deckled front edge. The high crushed aggregate content and somewhat translucent texture gives them a natural-slate finished appearance. One manufacturer offers an interlocking-slate design (*Figure 25.21*) which has improved flexural and impact strength and is some 15% lighter in weight than the fibre–cement slates currently in use.

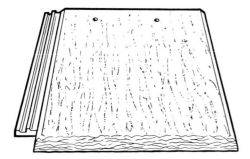

Figure 25.21   Polymer-modified-concrete interlocking slate

25.4.3.2 Appearance

One of the benefits of resin-bonded slates is the wide range of colours that can be created and great care is taken to reproduce natural colours. However, accelerated ultraviolet light exposure tests reveal a degree of colour loss over a fairly short period of time.

25.4.3.3 Durability

The product is highly resistant to air-borne pollution, and durable in the most adverse weather conditions. The material has high toughness and its impact strength helps to reduce breakages. The resinous surface also helps to prevent mosses and lichens from adhering to the slate surface.

25.4.3.4 Fire resistance

The high resin and polymer content of the slates means that they may only achieve a Class-2 fire rating for spread of flame and may, therefore, be unsuitable for cladding use in certain situations, as stipulated in the Building Regulations.

25.4.4 Polymer-modified-cement slates

The recent introduction of a thin interlocking slate by one manufacturer is a significant development in man-made roofing-materials technology. Polymer-modified cement is an adaptation of normal concrete in which part of the mixing water is replaced by an aqueous polymer emulsion. This process confers excellent workability to the concrete mix with a low water:cement ratio, greatly reducing the void content of the mortar. The final result is a concrete with a much greater flexural load-carrying capacity and improved chemical and frost resistance. The employment of crushed-slate granules as an aggregate makes this product very competitive with other fibre–cement products being both lightweight and extremely strong.

The following properties can also be attributed to this product:

(1) low water absorption (less than 1%);
(2) no tendency to curl once the material has been through the curing process;
(3) very high resistance to frost; and
(4) much lower rate of surface erosion than standard concrete.

25.4.4.1 Manufacture

Unlike fibre–cement and resin-bonded slates, polymer-modified-cement slates lend themselves to extrusion technology similar

to that of normal concrete tiles. Production rate is greatly increased due to the rapid curing of the material after manufacture and slates can be delivered for use immediately after being removed from the curing kilns.

25.4.4.2 Appearance

As slates are manufactured using extrusion technology, it is more difficult to apply surface textures and riven cut edges. However, the application of rollered and random surface patterns is achieved with great effect. Unlike the resin/polymer-bonded slates, polymer-modified-cement slates exhibit high resistance to ultraviolet light and the acrylic-paint coating provides additional protection against the formation of efflorescent salts.

25.4.4.3 Fire resistance

Because of the low polymer content of polymer-modified-cement concrete (typically 5%) a high fire performance is achievable with a class-0 rating for spread of flame. This property has obvious benefits as it means this type of slate can have unrestricted use for cladding.

25.4.5 Sitework and supply

25.4.5.1 Health and safety

Traditional asbestos-based materials are subject to the Asbestos Regulations 1969 and the Health and Safety at Work Act 1974. Certain machinery and fixing operations require basic precautions to be taken as designated by the Factory Inspectorate. In addition, it is recommended by most manufacturers that the requirements of the Construction (General Provisions) Regulations 1961, the Construction (Lifting Operations) Regulations 1961 and the Construction (Working Places) Regulations 1966 are also adhered to. BS 5534: Part 1: 1990: Section 53.3 also refers to asbestos-based roofing slates.

25.4.5.2 Handling and storage

Slates are normally packaged on pallets and shrink wrapped with a polythene hood, with approximately 1000 600 mm × 300 mm slates per pallet. It is recommended by most manufacturers that packs of slates be stored in the dry, clear of the ground and well protected from the weather. Polythene wrappers should not be regarded as sufficient protection for open storage. Exposure to the weather may encourage efflorescence, and hence for on-site storage slates must be open stacked to allow air circulation.

25.4.5.3 Site working

Although their lightness and size allows for easy handling on site, it is not recommended that the roof is loaded with more slates than can be fixed during the working day. Any necessary cutting of slates can be done by scoring with a sharp instrument and snapping over a straight edge or with a slaters zax over a horse or iron. Any additional holing can be carried out on site using a hand drill, ensuring that the hole is a minimum 20 mm from the edge of the slate. After cutting and/or drilling it is essential to clean the slates to avoid possible staining.

25.4.5.4 Installation

Man-made slates, like their natural counterparts, are a double-lap roofing material and hence must be fixed like plain tiles and laid in a broken-bond fashion. Most man-made slates are fixed with:

(1) two clout-headed copper-wire nails and a copper or alloy disc rivet; or
(2) one stainless-steel hook the tile being laid straight over.

The shank of the copper disc rivet should be loosely fitted between the two edges of the under slates and turned downslope over the top slate. Nail hooks should be driven on the centre line of battens.

Nail fixing system First and second under-eave courses of slates are laid using full-length slates cut into two unequal lengths. The second eave course starts with slate-and-a-half widths suitably holed for additional fixings. The first and second under-eave courses are secured to the first batten using copper nails with the upper course being laid 'broken-bond' over. Copper/alloy disc rivets are located with the shanks protruding between the side butt joints of the second under-eave course slates. Full-size slates are then positioned over the first and second courses of under-eave slates and secured to the second batten with two copper nails. The disc rivets are positioned so that the shanks protrude through the central hole at the lower end of the slate and so that they bend downslope to secure the tail. The main roof is slated in a diagonal fashion with cutting to roof details as necessary. (See *Figure 25.22*.)

Hook fixing system Hook fixing is a system of holding double-lap slating to battens, without nailing through holes in the slates, by attaching a hook to the batten which extends below the end-lap to secure the slate by hooking the bottom edge at the position of the vertical joint of the lower course of slates.

The hook fixing of slates is a European practice and due account must be taken of roof pitch, exposure and site windspeed when considering their use. Manufacturers should provide adequate assurance of performance.

25.5 Wind loading and fixings

British Standard Code of Practice CP3: Chapter V: Part 2: 1972 gives the basic data for the calculation of the wind loads which buildings should be capable of withstanding. By assessing the situation of a building and its shape and permeability to the wind, the lifting pressure applied to the roof in storm conditions can be calculated. It also follows that the forces acting on the tiles can be determined and, should these exceed the deadweight of the tiles, it is evident the tile will be dislodged from the roof unless restrained.

Many modern concrete tiles are laid single lap and interlock with one another, thereby being restrained by their neighbours, but, should a uniform pressure be applied over the whole roof, this effect is often insignificant and all the tiles will tend to lift together. In this situation, it is necessary to restrain the tiles by fixing them to the battens which support them. With these anomalies in mind the Code of Practice for Slating and Tiling (CP142) was reissued in 1978 as BS 5534: Part 1 (amended 1990). The new British Standard includes recent research concerning the combined action of tiles and underlay in resisting wind.

On a typical roof construction comprising several layers (boarding, felt and tiles) the pressure difference between outside and inside is divided into steps across each layer; these steps will depend on the relative permeability of the various layers and the access of air to spaces between them. Documentary

evidence recorded by the Building Research Establishment from experiments, shows that pressures are significantly reduced by felt underlay beneath the tiling. Their contribution towards shielding the underside of the tiles from the full transmission of internal pressures, have resulted in higher requirements for the strength of underlays as detailed in BS 747: 1977.

The use of sarking underlay held between the tiling battens and rafters has become standard practice in the last 20 years. The purpose of the underlay has been widely misunderstood and is, in some respects, wrongly applied. In terms of weather resistance the underlay is intended to provide a secondary line of defence against wind-driven and melting snow and not against penetration. From a wind-loading point of view, research on wind effects of tiled roofs has shown that the underlay acts, in effect, as a substantially wind-impermeable roof covering reducing wind-uplift pressures which could reach more than $3–4\,kN\,m^{-2}$ ($63/84\,lb\,ft^{-2}$) during gusts (three to four times the wind uplift).

Tensile strength fixing resistance at batten nail fixings and pull-out resistance of nails are important. With wind-resistant underlay, the slates or tiles are largely sheltered from the wind, the slates or tiles being subjected to local turbulence uplift forces. These uplift forces cannot be resisted by the deadweight of the roof covering nor by the limited number of slate or tile nails.

A standard procedure for calculating the wind loads to which tiles can be subjected is given in BS 5534: Part 1: 1978 which also acknowledges the benefits provided by the good performance of bitumen felt (BS 747: 1977, 1F quality) in resisting upward wind loads when held down by tile battens. It is now possible to design tile fixings for the effects of any remaining wind forces affecting the tile.

Slates and tiles have traditionally been fixed to battens using iron or steel nails and even wooden pegs. Eventually, these materials deteriorate under moist atmospheric conditions, allowing the slate or tile to fall from the roof. Galvanized nails are only marginally better since their zinc coating is often scratched off when fixing the tile. To guard against nail sickness BS 5534: Part 2: 1986 recommends the use of aluminium or stainless-steel nails under normal conditions of exposure. Plain or galvanized nails may be used for fixing battens to rafters, but care must be exercised when there is high humidity, where it is known that certain timber preservative treatments may corrode steel, zinc or aluminium.

During the past 30 years, the most effective method for securing interlocking tiles has been aluminium clips, which provide good tensile strength and non-corrosive qualities. Located over the side lock of the tile immediately behind the overlapped tile, and nailed to the tiling batten, the tile clip provides resistance to the applied moment more successfully than a nail fixing. The latter is closer to the pivot line where the nib touches the batten and cannot resist the uplift force at the tail. The phenomenon is also related to roof pitch and the step height of the roof covering and BS 5534: Part 1: 1990 acknowledges that at roof pitches of 45–55° all tiles should be at least nailed to battens to prevent displacement. At pitches exceeding 55° all tiles must be both head nailed and tile clipped to reduce 'chatter' in high winds.

In any assessment of wind loads on roofs it is necessary to determine specific criteria affecting the building. BS 5534: Part 2: 1986 details calculation methods which enable the designer to determine the design wind speed, dynamic wind pressure and pressure coefficient for the external surface of the roof. Finally, the wind-uplift loading on the tiles can be determined, taking into account the benefits afforded by the underlay in reducing the internal pressure transmitted to the roof underlay and tiling.

British Standard CP3: Chapter V: Part 2: 1972 describes calculations for determining wind loads based on maximum gust

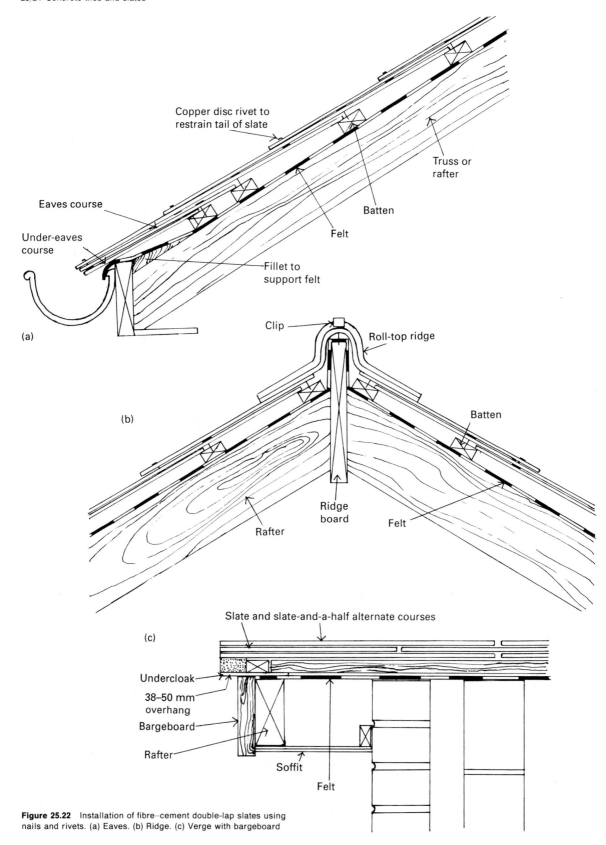

Copper disc rivet to
restrain tail of slate

Truss or
rafter

Eaves course

Batten

Under-eaves
course

Felt

Fillet to
support felt

(a)

Clip

Roll-top ridge

(b)

Batten

Ridge
board

Felt

Rafter

Slate and slate-and-a-half alternate courses

(c)

Undercloak

38–50 mm
overhang

Bargeboard

Rafter

Soffit

Felt

Figure 25.22 Installation of fibre–cement double-lap slates using
nails and rivets. (a) Eaves. (b) Ridge. (c) Verge with bargeboard

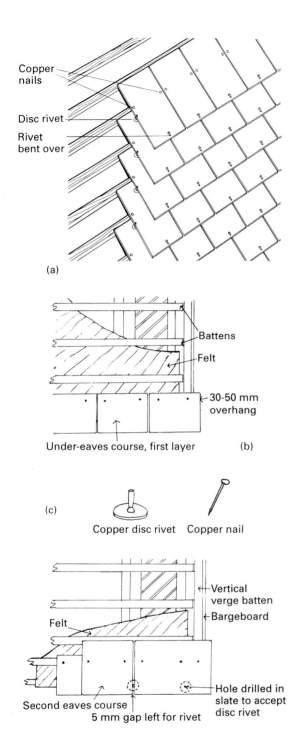

(a)

Copper nails

Disc rivet

Rivet bent over

(b)

Battens

Felt

30-50 mm overhang

Under-eaves course, first layer

(c)

Copper disc rivet   Copper nail

Felt

Vertical verge batten

Bargeboard

Hole drilled in slate to accept disc rivet

Second eaves course

5 mm gap left for rivet

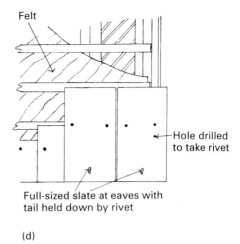

Felt

Hole drilled to take rivet

Full-sized slate at eaves with tail held down by rivet

(d)

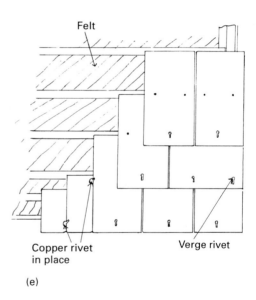

Felt

Copper rivet in place

Verge rivet

(e)

Figure 25.23 Installation of man-made slates using nails and rivets

speeds, at a height of 10 m above the ground, likely to be exceeded on average once in 50 years in open level country. Wind loads range from 38 to $56\,\mathrm{m\,s^{-1}}$ in the UK with corresponding dynamic pressures of $900\text{--}2000\,\mathrm{N\,m^{-2}}$. The design wind speed must be calculated for specific areas and is related to topographical influences, the surface roughness of the environment, gust duration appropriate to the size of the buildings and the height of the building.

Guidance on the fixing specification to meet BS 5534: Part 2: 1986 requirements is provided by the major roof-tile manufacturers and, provided that the necessary data are available concerning roof pitch, height of building to eaves and ridge, width of the building, the basic wind speed of the site, the exposure category (according to CP3: 1972), then the specifier and fixer can determine the extent of tile fixing required to resist wind uplift.

Whilst the publication of BS 5534: Part 1: 1990 has helped

to interpret CP3: 1972, it is still too complex for the use of the average contractor. BS 5534: Part 2: 1986 provides charts and tables for determining the deadweight and nail-fixing resistances against wind uplift of various types of slating and tiling in roofs of ridge height not exceeding 30 m above the ground. The charts and tables have been prepared in accordance with the recommendations of BS 5534: Part 1: 1990 with the intention that the charts may be used as design aids for quick reference in order to avoid duplication of effort by designers. They do, however, contain certain simplifying assumptions made during preparation and they should not be relied upon where high accuracy is required or in exceptional design conditions.

25.5.1 Calculation of wind loads

BS 5534, *The Code of Practice for Slating and Tiling*, is published in two parts. Part 1: 1990, *Design*, provides detailed information for calculating the wind load force on roof tiles and fittings. Part 2: 1986, *Design Charts for Fixing, Roof Slating and Tiling against Wind Uplift*, provides detailed design information for establishing nailfixing requirements.

Proprietary fixing devices, e.g. clips, tail rivets, are not covered by any British Standard, but BS 5534: Part 1: 1990 gives examples of the wind-uplift load to be resisted by a tile clip for single-lap tiles.

The basic procedure for establishing the mechanical fixing requirements is as follows. First, establish the wind-load forces acting on the roof, with a suitable underlay, using the formula

$$qt = kV^2 S_1^2, S_2^2, S_3^2, S_4^2 (1 - C_{pe})$$

Note that the dynamic pressure resulting from the design wind speed is given by $q = kV_s^2$, the value of k, according to the units of measurement used, being given in CP3: 1972. The pressure coefficient for external surfaces (C_{pe}) is also obtained from CP3: 1972.

The following information is required:

V basic wind speed of the site (maximum gust at 10 m above ground level based on 1 in 50 year probability);
H height of roof at the ridge (m);
h height of roof at the eaves (m);
w building width (m);

G ground roughness factor (according to CP3: 1972: Chapter V; determined by the Local Building Control Officer);
θ rafter pitch (degrees);
S_1 topography factor;
S_3 life-of-building factor; and
S_4 wind-direction factor (assumed to be 1 for normal locations).

Wind-load force (in N m^{-2}) is expressed for roof perimeters, local areas (a band around the perimeter equal to 0.15w of the span or height to eaves, whichever is the lesser) and the general area, the centre being the remaining area of the roof (see BS 5534: Part 1: 1990: Appendix B1).

Wind-load resistance can be calculated using

$$gtw = \frac{0.9 W_g Lw \cos \alpha}{ctb(Lo - 0.5ct)}$$

where: W_g is the deadweight of the tile at the centre of gravity; Lw is the distance of the centre of gravity of the tile from the top of tile batten; α is the tile laid angle; ctb is the step height of the tile between courses; Lo is the distance from the tail of tile from the top of tile batten; and ct is the overlap:thickness ratio. If the wind-load force exceeds the resistance of the tile by virtue of its deadweight, then mechanical fixing is considered necessary.

25.6 Costs

Comparative data on the relative installation costs of different materials (tiles and slates) are represented in *Table 25.4* as cost indices, due to the fluctuation in labour costs caused by local and market conditions. The index is based on 1 m^2 of laid roof excluding any verge or ridge details.

Accurate material costs should always be obtained from the manufacturer before calculating the installed cost. Prices are always worked out per square metre of roof slope area and not plan area, thus roof pitch has a major influence on the number of tiles/slates required. Conversely, a low-pitch roof may require more fixings to resist wind uplift. Size, complexity, structure and location also have an influence on the final installed price of the roof covering.

Table 25.4 Relative roofing costs (index 100 = £13.50): price index includes materials and labour per m² of laid roof

Slate/tile type	No.	Cost	
		Material	Labour
Man-made slates 600 mm × 300 mm laid to 100-mm lap on 38 mm × 25 mm softwood battens on BS 747: 1F underfelt	167	£17.60 78%	£4.90 22%
Concrete interlocking tiles 420 mm × 330 mm laid to 75-mm lap on 38 mm × 25 mm softwood battens on BS 747: 1F underfelt	100	£11.50 85%	£2.00 15%
Concrete plain tiles 267 mm × 165 mm laid to 65-mm lap on 38 mm × 25 mm softwood battens on BS 747: 1F underfelt	203	£22.40 82%	£4.90 18%
Reconstructed stone slates 457 mm × 457 mm laid to 76-mm lap on 38 mm × 25 mm softwood battens on BS 747: 1F underfelt	284	£28.40 80%	£7.10 20%
Lightweight concrete interlocking tiles 420 mm × 330 mm laid to 75-mm lap on 38 mm × 25 mm softwood battens on BS 747: 1F underfelt	128	£14.80 85%	£2.60 15%
Polymer-modified-cement concrete interlocking slates 325 mm × 330 mm laid to 75-mm lap on 38 mm × 25 mm softwood battens on BS 747: 1F underfelt	191	£21.40 83%	£4.40 17%
Clay plain tiles 265 mm × 165 mm laid to 65-mm lap on 38 mm × 25 mm softwood battens on BS 747: 1F underfelt	259	£30.20 86%	£4.90 14%

Single-lap interlocking tiles are one of the most cost-effective roof coverings, due to their ease of installation and large covering capacity. Synthetic slates are around 50% more expensive due to the extra quantity used in double lapping, and the additional fixings required. The higher costs of material formulation and manufacturing costs of some man-made slates and tiles also dictate higher installed prices.

Bibliography

British Standards Institution Codes and Standards

BS 473.550: 1990 Specification for concrete roof tiles and fittings
BS 476, Fire tests on building materials and structures
BS 476: Part 3: 1975, External fire exposure roof test
BS 476: Part 4: 1970 (1984) Non combustibility test for materials
BS 476: Part 8: 1972, Test methods and criteria for the fire resistance of elements of building construction
BS 680: Part 2: 1971, Specification for roofing slates (metric)
BS 690, Asbestos–cement slates and sheets
BS 690: Part 4: 1974, Slates (Fully and semi-compressed asbestos–cement slates used for roofing and walling cladding)
BS 747: 1977 (1986), Specification for roofing felts
BS 12: 1978, Specification for ordinary and rapid hardening Portland cement
BS 3177: 1959 Method of determining the permeability to water vapour of flexible sheet materials used for packaging
BS 4072 Wood preservation by means of copper/chromium/arsenic composition: Part 1: 1987, Specification for preservatives; Part 2: 1987, Wood preservation procedures
BS 4624: 1981, Methods of test for asbestos–cement building products (flat sheets, flue pipes and rainwater pipes)
BS 1014: 1975, Pigments for Portland cement and Portland cement products
BS 1199 and BS 1200, Building sands from natural sources
BS 1202: Part 3: 1974, Specification for aluminium nails
BS 5250: 1989, Code of basic data for the design of buildings. Control of condensation in dwellings
BS 5534: Part 1: 1990, Design
BS 5534: Part 2: 1986, Design charts for fixing roof slating and tiling against wind uplift
BS 6100, Glossary of building and civil engineering terms
BS 6100: Part 1: Section 1:3:2: 1985, Roofs and roofing
BS CP3: Chapter V: Part 2: 1972, Basic data for the design of buildings loading

The Building Regulations

The Building Regulations 1985
The Building Standards (Scotland)
Regulations 1981 with amendments 1982–1984
    B2, Selection and use of materials
    D16 (1), Cladding on outer face of external walls
    D19, Roofs

    D21, D22 and D23, Garages
    E17 (1), Surfaces of walls and ceilings
    G9, Resistance to moisture from rain and snow
The Building Regulations 1985, Approved Documents
    L2/3, Resistance to the passage of heat
    F1, Means of ventilation
    F2, Condensation
    B2/3/4, Fire spread
    A1, Loading
    C4, Resistance to weather and ground moisture
    Regulation 7, Materials and workmanship
The Building Regulations (Northern Ireland) 1977, as amended
    B1, Fitness of materials
    C8, Weather resistance of external walls
    C10, Weather resistance of roofs
    E7 (4), Cladding on outer face of external walls
    E15, Restruction of spread of flame over surface of walls and ceilings
    E17, Roofs

Building Research Establishment

Digest 110, Condensation
Digest 119, The assessment of wind loads
Digest 128 (1971), Insulation against external noise—1
Digest 129 (1971), Insulation against external noise—2
Digest 180, Condensation in roofs
Digest 270, Condensation in insulated domestic roofs
Defect Action Sheet 1, Slated or tiled pitched roofs. Ventilation to the outside air
Defect Action Sheet 3, Slated and tiled roofs. Restricting the entry of water vapour from the house
Defect Action Sheet 4, Pitched roofs—thermal insulation near the eaves
Defect Action Sheet 9, Pitched roofs—sarking felt underlay for roof
Defect Action Sheet 10, Pitched roofs—sarking felt underlay watertightness
Current Paper CP75/74, Roofs, roofing and the wind

Others

Architects Journal, 1041–1050 (1 Dec. 1976)
    Products in practice: tiles and slates, *Architects Journal* (6 Aug. 1980)
Roof coverings, *Architects Journal*, Suppl. (Jan. 1987)
ARCHITECTS JOURNAL LIBRARY, *Technical Study: Asbestos and Alternative Materials*
DOBSON, C., *The History of the Concrete Roofing Tile*, B. J. Batsford Ltd, London (1959)
MARLEY ROOF TILES, *Manual* (1986)
REDLAND ROOF TILES, *The Redland Roofing Manual* (1988)
ETERNIT/TAC, *Slates Compendium* (1988)
WICKERSHAM, J. H., *The David and Charles Manual of Roofing* (1987)

26

Cork

P Olley
C Olley & Sons Ltd

Contents

26.1 Introduction 26/3

26.2 Manufacture 26/3

26.3 Types 26/3
    26.3.1 Natural cork 26/3
    26.3.2 Agglomerated corkboard 26/3
    26.3.3 Composition cork 26/3
    26.3.4 Cork/rubber 26/3

26.4 Applications 26/4

26.5 Standards 26/5
    26.5.1 Dimensional stability 26/5
    26.5.2 Fire 26/5
    26.5.3 Quality 26/5

26.6 Site precautions 26/5
    26.6.1 Handling and storage 26/5
    26.6.2 Fixing 26/5
    26.6.3 Roof finishes 26/5

26.1 Introduction

Cork is a natural product obtained from the bark of the cork oak tree (*Quercus Super* L.) found primarily at the western end of the Mediterranean in Portugal, Spain and North Africa. The bark thickens and develops with age and can be harvested as a regular crop (every 9–12 years) from commercial plantations and natural forests. As a vegetable tissue, cork bark is composed of cells which are five-sided, impermeable and contain a large proportion of air. This cellular structure allows cork to be compressed and to recover its original dimensions without extrusion—a property yet to be equalled by synthetic products used in this field. Cork is, therefore, a perfect natural insulant.

Because cork is a natural material it regenerates itself without depletion of its source. It is ubiquitous and has a place in every phase of a building.

26.2 Manufacture

Corkboard is manufactured by baking (usually with superheated steam) at a temperature of 350°C and a pressure of 30 000 kg m^{-2}. There is no contact with air during this process and the cork's natural resins are released from the cells causing the granules to bond together, becoming dark brown in colour. After an appropriate period of 'cooking', a block of corkboard is produced which is cooled, rested, trimmed to size and cut into slabs.

This process causes natural cork granules with a density of approximately 200 kg m^{-2} to undergo a large expansion in volume with the release of volatile elements and a commensurate decrease in density. At the same time the expanded cork granules are compressed causing their compaction and agglomeration to form a cork block with a higher density than that of expanded granules. This density can vary from a possible minimum of 80 kg m^{-3} to over 600 kg m^{-3} depending on:

(1) degree of compression,
(2) quality of cork,
(3) granule size,
(4) purity of granulation,
(5) manufacturing process, and
(6) temperature.

The combination of these variable factors enables the manufacture of different types and densities for numerous purposes.

26.3 Types

26.3.1 Natural cork

Slabs of cork are steam treated to flatten them in order that they can be laminated to any size and thickness. As this is virtually pure cork there is no degeneration.

The reason that cork is so perfect for this application is its ability to absorb sound and vibration, to compress and then to recover, whilst essentially remaining unaltered. It will readily accept coatings which are sometimes used to protect adjacent materials from extraneous matter.

26.3.2 Agglomerated corkboard

Agglomerated corkboard is in sheet form, usually 1000 mm × 500 mm × 50 mm, or as required. Corkboard for this purpose should be of a minimum density of 11 lb ft^{-3}, or 176 kg m^{-3}. It is manufactured by the same method as insulation corkboard and looks similar. Unlike the other types, this material, being of lighter density and lower tensile strength, is usually laid inside a concrete base.

26.3.3 Composition cork

Sheets of composition cork are usually 914 mm × 610 mm (3 ft × 2 ft) × 25 mm/50 mm (1 in./2 in.), or as required. This type of material is made up of smaller granules than corkboard. A binding agent is added and the material is then subjected to heat and pressure. The grades which are suitable for this purpose should be between 15 and 30 lb ft^{-3}. There are many types and grades of composition cork which have been created for uses outside the building industry. To be assured of the correct grade, the supplier should be asked for a letter of conformity.

26.3.4 Cork/rubber

Cork/rubber sheets are usually 914 mm × 914 mm, 1000 mm × 1000 × 12 mm/25 mm, or as required. This is a mixture of cork granules and synthetic rubber binder which has been subjected to heat and pressure. There are a number of grades to suit the particular requirement of the base. Typical properties are shown in *Table 26.1* Standard thicknesses of corkboard are shown in *Table 26.3*.

Table 26.1 Variation of properties with specification

Specification reference	Cos46	Cos40	Cos70	712BNF	COR12V
Type	Synthetic	Neoprene	Synthetic	Nitrile	Neoprene
Hardness, shore A	70–80	65 ± 10	65 ± 5	70–85	65 ± 5
Tensile strength	200	250 min.	200 min.	400 min.	300
Grade	Medium	Medium	Medium	Firm	Firm
Flex	5 max.	Pass 3	3 max.	3 ×	3 max.
Specific gravity	0.71–0.75	0.63–0.72	0.56–0.72	0.80–0.88	0.85–0.95
Compression at 400 psi	25–35%	25–35%	35–45%	15–25%	—
Recovery	75% min.	80% min.	80% min.	80% min.	97.3% min.
Volume change (%)					
Oil 1	−5 to +15	0 to +5	−5 to +5	−2 to +20	—
Oil 3	0 to +20	+10 to +30	−2 to +15	+15 to +50	—
Fuel A	0 to +15	0 to +10	−2 to +10	0 to +15	—
Water absorption	—	—	—	—	—
Compression set A (ASTM)	—	—	—	—	—
Compression set B (ASTM)	—	—	—	—	—

Table 26.2 Physical characteristics of insulation corkboard

Property	Value	Standard
Density	104–128 kg m^{-3}	DIN 18–161, ISO 2189
	109 kg m^{-3} average	British Board of Agrement*
Thermal conductivity	At 0°C, 0.035–0.037 W m^{-1} K^{-1}	DIN 52–612, ISO 2502
	At 20°C, 0.42 W m^{-1} K^{-1}	British Board of Agrement*
Compressive strength	At 10%, 0.25 N mm^{-2}	DIN 18–161
Deformation under temperature	2.4% using 30 mm corkboard, 80°C	DIN 18–161
	1.4% using 50 mm corkboard, 80°C	DIN 18–161
Coefficient of thermal expansion	35 × 10^{-3} mm m^{-1} measured between 20° and 100°C	
Specific heat	1.67–2.09 kg K^{-1}	
Thermal diffusivity	0.00067 m^2 h^{-1}	
Spread of flame	Subject to coverings	
	Ext. F.A.A.	Yarsley Technical Centre (Indicative)
	Ext. F.A.B.	Warrington Test Laboratory (Indicative)
Behaviour in fire	Does not liberate toxic gases	
Working temperatures	−180°C to 110°C	
Building regulations	Deemed to satisfy material	Regulation 7. Clause 1:2
Compatability	Suitable for fully bonded bitumen specifications	
	Suitable for use under mastic asphalt	
	Suitable for single-ply fully adhered membranes	Consult Technical Dept. Literature
Wind resistance	2.5 kN m^{-3} fully bonded	
	+2.5 kN m^{-2}, additional loading layer or mechanical fastenings required	

Vermin and rot proof, does not encourage growth of fungi, mould or bacteria.
A remarkably strong, stable, resilient and safe insulant for flat-roof installations. Insulation corkboard has been proven in service for over 50 years and will give effective protection for the life-time of the waterproofing layers.

Table 26.3 Standard thicknesses of insulation corkboard

	Thickness (mm)							
	150	100	80	60	50	40	30	20
No. of square metres per pack/carton. Available standard density (104–125 kg m^{-3})	1.0	1.5	2.0	2.5	3.0	4.0	5.0	7.5
Weight (kg m^{-2}) (density 109 kg m^{-3})	16.35	10.90	8.72	6.54	5.45	4.36	3.27	2.18
U at 0°C	0.23	0.34	0.42	0.53	0.63	0.75	0.95	1.20
U at 20°C	0.26	0.38	0.47	0.60	0.69	0.84	1.05	1.34
Metal deck–maximum trough dimension. Available in heavy density (170 kg m^{-3})	150	125	125	100	100	75	75	50

Full product range includes: other sizes available to special order; prefinished boards for PVC membranes available to order; high density fillets; specific cutting to individual project requirements; and tapered roof specialists—design and production.

26.4 Applications

Pure expanded corkboard is traditionally divided into four different groups: thermal, acoustic, anti-vibration, and decorative. Experiments have shown that cork is unique in having a high performance in all these categories.

The optimum material combines an as low as possible density with the greatest mechanical and structural strength. This combines advantageous technical characteristics with a competitive price, although a material with a higher density can be perfectly acceptable. For this reason insulation corkboard cannot effectively be specified in terms of density alone.

The ideal standard of quality is achieved by careful selection of raw materials by the manufacturer, eliminating the heavier woody inner bark sometimes found in the denser grades of corkboard.

In this context it is interesting and important to note that, at the ISO TC/87 (cork) Plentay Session at Merida in March 1987, the importance of the physical properties of corkboard relative to its density was recognized and it was decided to issue a Draft Revision of the existing specification for comment and further discussion taking this factor into account. This will be circulated to member states shortly.

However, it is recommended that any material that is less than 96 and greater than 140 kN m^{-2} be given extra scrutiny to ensure that it complies with the other vital criteria.

Cork is particularly user-friendly for the following reasons:

(1) compressibility,
(2) softness,
(3) non-abrasiveness,
(4) grip on surrounding materials,
(5) ease of removal,
(6) ease of drilling, and
(7) environmentally friendly.

26.5 Standards

Whilst there are several National Standards relating to the manufacture of corkboard the International Standard ISO 2219 embraces all the major requirements as follows:

Dimensional tolerances:
   on length ± 3 mm,
   on width ± 1.5 mm,
   on thickness
      up to 25 mm thick ± 5%,
      25–50 mm thick ± 3%,
      > 50 mm thick ± 2%.
Density:
< 140 kg m^{-3}.
Modulus of rupture: > 140 kN m^{-2}.
Thermal conductivity: < 0.042 W m^{-2} °C^{-1} (at 20°C); however, at 0°C, max. 0.037 W m^{-2} °C^{-1}.
Moisture content: max. 3% by volume.
Compressive strength: at 10% compression, 120–140 kN m^{-2}.

The methods of determination of these standards are also covered by ISO specifications.

The critical properties are that density should be kept as low as is practical by using the best quality corkwood to give acceptable modulus of rupture and compressive strength figures. Poor quality material is friable and prone to disintegration and may consist of large granules with many voids or heavy woody bark.

Recovery: loading test of 4 s duration with 0–140 kN m^{-2} load. Completed 1200 times, the maximum loss of thickness is 0.12 mm of the 60 mm sample tested.

The thermal diffusivity (a measurement of heat flow calibrated against time, assessing an insulants performance in overall terms) shows that cork is both a good insulant and resistor to changes in temperature and can be used in conjunction with oil based products to improve their performance. Further, the recovery of cork after loading is significantly greater than polystyrene and many other oil based products.

26.5.1 Dimensional stability

The dimensional stability of cork is 3.4 × 10 (BOC), which means an expansion of 0.03 mm m^{-1} for a temperature rise of 1°C which would give a maximum expansion range in our climate of 0.9 mm m^{-1}. This can be compared with the value for polyurethane which is many times greater and is currently causing problems in the industry.

A high performance insulation must not only provide containment of warmth (or cold) but must not react violently to changes in internal and external conditions, especially when differing thicknesses are used on tapered insulation schemes.

Corkboard can, therefore, be described as 'benign', making it the ideal companion to the other components of a roofing structure.

26.5.2 Fire

In considering the performance of a material in a fire it is necessary to look at the roof as a whole including the deck and membrane. Therefore there is little that can be said about a material in isolation but, most importantly, cork does not emit toxic fumes and satisfies Class 2 of BS 476 (1971) as a surface with a very slow propagation of flame. Cork can therefore be considered to have good fire resistance.

From humble beginnings as ancient Eygptian fishing floats (4000 B.C.) to the Apollo Space Programme, cork has proved the ideal material for solving a range of problems.

26.5.3 Quality

In dealing with a natural material such as cork, it is particularly relevant that suppliers work to quality systems that are to the standard of BS 5750 *Quality systems*, 1982–87.

26.6 Site precautions

26.6.1 Handling and storage

Insulation corkboard is light in weight and may be cut using conventional tools. It should be handled with care to avoid damage to board edges. The slabs are shrink wrapped in polythene or corrugated export cartons which will provide short-term protection. For long-term protection they should be stored indoors or off the ground under a secure waterproof covering.

26.6.2 Fixing

Corkboard is normally bonded to the roof with hot bonding-grade bitumen, using a staggered joint arrangement. A vapour check/barrier should always be installed below the insulation and the specification carefully chosen to suit the individual project requirements. All day work joints are to be fully sealed to prevent ingress of moisture. Additional mechanical fastenings may be required for roofs in highly exposed locations. Care should be taken to follow the manufacturer's technical instructions.

26.6.3 Roof finishes

26.6.3.1 Built-up proofing

A vapour escape sheet/partial bonding layer is not recommended or required with corkboard. High performance built-up roof should be fully bonded to corkboard. The use of elastomeric membranes is recommended, although not mandatory.

26.6.3.2 Single-layer high-performance membranes

Corkboard is suitable for use with polyvinyl chloride (PVC) membranes, but it is recommended that the product is supplied with a sealed finish compatible with the adhesives to be used. The manufacturer's technical instructions should be followed carefully.

26.6.3.3 Asphalt

No thermal barrier layer is required. A loose laid standard isolating membrane should be laid over the corkboard prior to application of asphalt to MACEF (Mastic Asphalt Council Employers' Federation) recommendations.

27

Fabrics

M Malinowsky
Consulting Engineer

Contents

27.1 Sources 27/3

27.2 Manufacture 27/3
    27.2.1 The thread 27/3
    27.2.2 The woven base cloth 27/4
    27.2.3 Commonly used membrane materials 27/4

27.3 Environmental properties of fabrics 27/5
    27.3.1 Translucence 27/5
    27.3.2 Insulation 27/5

27.4 Structural properties of fabrics 27/5
    27.4.1 Tensile strength 27/5
    27.4.2 Dimensional stability 27/5
    27.4.3 Stiffness 27/5
    27.4.4 Jointing 27/6
    27.4.5 Durability 27/6

27.5 Applications 27/6

Bibliography 27/7

27.1 Sources

Woven fabrics have a long history. First dominated by natural fibres from plants, cellulose in the form of flax and cotton, and from animals, e.g. silk and wool, the initial uses of fabrics were in the manufacture of tents, sails and ropes for both domestic and military boat and shelter uses. However, these structures were restricted to a relatively small scale since their inherent fibres were highly subject to creep, rot and ultraviolet (UV) degradation. Only the well known history of sailing ships can give an obvious example of the largest applications in terms of reliable structures which, nevertheless, required a large crew to trim the sails and constantly repair and maintain the rigging.

It is only during the 20th century that fabrics have been specially designed to fit machines and structures able to bear variable loadings arising mainly from snow, wind and temperature. The development of airships provided the earliest starting point of research on fabric properties and the determination of stress–strain behaviour; but successive failures during this technological period would appear to show that fabric manufacturers were unable to provide a reliable product. At the least we should remember the Graff Zeppelin (1927), one of the most successful, despite its dreadful wreck, rigid airships combining a lightweight duralumium framework with a synthetic fabric cladding. More recently, in the late 1950s, the conjunction of artificial composites with the application of the surface-curvature principle stiffened by prestressing, made it possible to use fabric to meet the architectural requirements of reliably covering areas larger than those of conventional towing tents or circuses.

A predictable performance has been brought to fabric structures due to the fundamental change that has arisen from recent developments in coated fabrics, which resist degradation, and from improvements in structural forms and detailing which allow the full potential of these materials to be utilized and justified. The design of stressed-skin structures may utilize individual ropes or cables knotted or clamped together (net), and any of a range of fabrics, from coated fabrics to film or sheet materials. By far the largest-scale applications use coated fabrics for which a wide range of fibres and coating materials have now been studied.

Table 27.1 Fibres used as the basic components of structural cloths

---

Natural fibres
Cotton
Flax

Synthetic fibres
Polyethylene
Polyamide
Polypropylene
Viscose
Extended-chain polyethylene
Polyester tergal
Aramid, high and low modulus

Metal fibres
Steel
Copper alloys

Mineral fibres
Glass E
Glass S
Carbon
Graphite
Bore

A list of fibres used as the basic components of structural cloths is given in *Table 27.1* and a list of coating materials is given in *Table 27.2*. It is important to note that not all coatings can be applied to all base fibres. For instance, polytetrafluoroethylene (PTFE) and FEP have fairly high melting points and can, therefore, only be coated to high-temperature-resisting fibres. The main point to note, however, is that amongst the numerous compatible combinations of cloth and coating, only three are readily commercially available. These three composites are:

(1) polyvinyl chloride coated polyester (PVC/PES);
(2) PTFE-coated glass (PTFE/GS); and
(3) silicone-coated glass (VESTAR).

27.2 Manufacture

27.2.1 The thread

The initial step is to produce fibres which are spun into *yarn* and then woven into cloth. The yarn consists of an agglomeration of continuous thread called *sillionne*. The bundle process involves an appropriate series of twisting phases, the number and intensity of which depend on the type of fibre used and the mechanical properties required in the finished product. Some yarns are made by spinning two or three threads with a high twist, the exact value of which remains a manufacturer's secret.

The fineness of thread is measured by a specific unit called *Tex*, the basic principle of which is the same as that for the ancient unit *Denier* used for silk. Whereas a Denier gives the fineness of 9000 m of thread weighing 1 g, the Tex takes into account only 1000 m of thread. This ratio of 1:9 between the new and the old unit leads to a yarn of the same density having a three-fold difference in diameter. The sub-unit deciTex (or dTex, one-tenth of a Tex) is commonly used in the fabrication field. This unusual derived physical unit can be more easily grasped through the following example: a 1100-dTex titre refers to a yarn for which a 1000 m length weighs $1100/10 = 110$ g. In other words, given the *titre* (dTex) and the density δ, it is possible to calculate the fineness or, say, the diameter (μm) using the formula

$$\text{diameter} = 20 \times (\text{titre}/(\pi \times \delta))^{1/2}$$

Another significant order of magnitude is emphasized by the following two pieces of data:

(1) 150 ton day^{-1} of acrylic fibre production is equivalent to the amount of wool from 12 million sheep; and
(2) 150 ton day^{-1} of polyester fibre production is equivalent to the yield of 100 000 ha of cotton fields.

Fibres are available in a range of breaking strengths. *Table 27.3* and *Figure 27.1* give data on the breaking strength versus elongation of several different fibres.

Table 27.2 Coating materials used on structural cloths

PVC
Polyurethane
Polychloroprene
Natural rubber
Hypalon (chlorosulphonated polyethylene)
PTFE and FEP (Teflon)
Acrylic
PVF
PVDF
Silicone rubber

PVF, polyvinyl fluoride; PVDF, polyvinyl difluoride.

Table 27.3 The breaking strength versus elongation of some fibres

	Fibre	Breaking strength (hbar)	Elongation (%)
1	Carbon	210	0.3
2	Steel	350	2.0
3	Aramid	290	2.0
4	Glass S	350	3.2
5	Glass E	220	2.5
6	FCPE	270	3.8
7	FAX	90	2.0
8	Rayon	145	10.0
9	Cotton	70	6.0
10	Polyester	150	16.0
11	Nylon	115	21.0
12	Acrylic	50	24.0

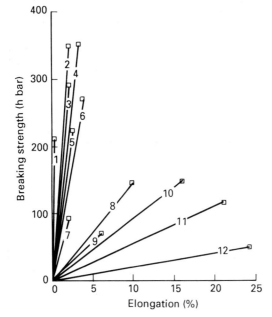

Figure 27.1 Plots of breaking strength versus elongation for the fibres listed in *Table 27.3*

27.2.2 The woven base cloth

A cloth is a woven assembly of yarns in two orthogonal directions. On a loom, the *warp* yarns are aligned lengthwise and those yarns carried transversally to and fro by the shuttle give the *weft*. Since weft yarns usually undulate, any stress imposed in that direction leads to straightening, thus compelling the initially straight warp to undulate; this process is known as crimp interchange. This problem can be partially alleviated by using a Panama weave (see *Figure 27.2*), where the yarns are woven in groups of two, three or even four, giving a flatter surface for coating.

Although Panama weave appears to be the most suitable process for coated fabrics, it is worth mentioning some others that can be used to eliminate crimp interchange:

(1) Stitch bonded fabric: the warp and weft yarns are laid over each other and held together by a knitted thread, thus eliminating crimp interchange.
(2) Triaxial weave: three sets of yarns are woven together at 60°. This weave largely improves tear strength; however, severe difficulties arise when attempting to measure practical strain in a specified direction with uneven stress loading.

27.2.3 Commonly used membrane materials

Membrane materials comprise either foils or composites, depending on the physical properties and price of the finished product.

27.2.3.1 PVC-coated polyester fabric

The most commonly used constituent, because of its low cost and the fact that it has been studied extensively over the past 25 years, is PVC-coated polyester fabric. However, this material suffers somewhat from commercial confidentiality. The PVC coating is made up of many different components blended together, but the precise amount of each one remains the manufacturer's recipe. The direct drawback for the purchaser is the great difficulty in comparing the performance of different materials.

Nevertheless, considerable improvements have been achieved in coating formulation, and a serviceability life of 15–18 years can now reasonably be expected when using a relatively thick and densely pigmented coating. Moreover, durability and self-cleansing have been improved by the addition of a weathering layer of either an acrylic compound or a PVDF coating. The use of a white-coloured coating extends the lifetime of the material since this reduces the surface temperature.

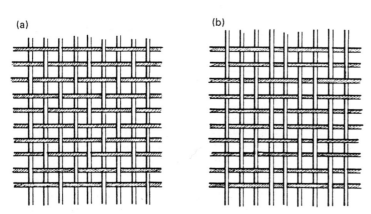
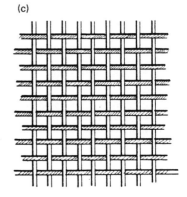

Figure 27.2 Weave types: (a) serge; (b) Panama 1 × 1; (c) Panama 2 × 2

Translucency should be kept at a low rate (6–12%) for a single membrane.

An architectural criticism of PVC coating is that it exhibits a dirt-adherence problem and, unless regular cleaning is practised, light transmission is reduced and the appearance of the outside becomes slightly dull. However, since coating problems generally show up in less than 5 years, an 8-year guarantee on the fabric given by some manufacturers (including full replacement costs) is likely to increase confidence.

To complete the description of this widely used composite, some of its significant advantages are listed below.

(1) PVC-coated polyester is easy to join by either stitching or high-frequency welding. It is also easy to handle, transport and erect.
(2) Tight fabrication tolerances are not generally required because, due to its relatively low elastic modulus, the material can absorb slight ripples arising from the welding process.
(3) The material can be produced in flameproof form (M2 in French Regulation; BS 3120 in the UK).

27.2.3.2 Teflon-coated glass-fibre cloth

Teflon-coated glass-fibre cloth was developed some 15 years ago to avoid the problems associated with PVC and mainly to produce an inherently fire-resistant fabric. PTFE coating is applied to the glass-fibre support by a dipping/sintering process. This process is repeated many times and, therefore, increases the time to delivery.

These materials give very good durability in artificial weathering tests; however, damage to the yarns by internal fretting or external abrasion mean that membranes must be fairly highly pretensioned and left undisturbed. PTFE is an inert plastic material having a very high resistance to chemical attack and is unaffected by exposure to ultraviolet radiation. There is no problem of dirt-adherence since particles are generally washed away by the rain. It is commonly accepted that this composite has a life expectancy of more than 20 years. The translucency of a single outer-skin membrane ranges from 8 to 16% and reflectivity for indirect lighting reaches 70%. The woven-glass substrate confers to the composite a zero spread of flame according to BS 476 or an equivalent French Regulation MX fire reaction.

Jointing of teflon-coated glass-fibre cloth is done by pressurized hot sealing. Compared with PVC-coated polyester, considerable care in handling, packing, and erection is required.

Teflon/glass-cloth applications are mostly concentrated in the USA and the Middle East, where the same fire regulation is followed. Very few constructions of teflon-coated glass-fibre cloth are visible in Europe because of the relatively high cost of this material (about 10 times the initial price of a PVC/polyester composite). It must be pointed out that, originally, the technology of the composite process was restricted to two US firms, but since three other sources are now available in Europe the price of this material is becoming more competitive.

27.2.3.3 Silicone-rubber-coated fibre cloth

Silicone-rubber-coated fibre cloth (VESTAR) is the most recent commercially available composite. The material is produced solely by one US firm (ODC) which combines the services of coating, fabrication and installation.

27.2.3.4 Unreinforced fluoropolymer films

Of the composites discussed here, architectural requirements are best met by using unreinforced fluoropolymer films. At present, these materials have only been designed with air-pressure prestressing. ETFE (TEFZEL) shows a useful elastic range and could possibly be used as a prestressed surface provided creep under high load does not irreversibly distort the surface.

27.3 Environmental properties of fabrics

27.3.1 Translucence

Fabric structures can be used to make uniformly translucent roofs, thus reducing artificial-light consumption. Translucence can be modulated by weaving glass fibres or by using coating pigmentation for PVC.

27.3.2 Insulation

The thermal resistance of a single-layer membrane is virtually zero and exhibits high susceptibility to condensation. The problem can be partly solved by using a double layer, but in this case translucence is minimal. In every case, it is of great importance that the designer be aware of the necessity of minimal air changes of at least three volumes per hour.

With regard to acoustic insulation, two aspects should be considered. First, acoustic insulation from outside: only sharp sounds above 500–1000 Hz are likely to be attenuated to a level close to 20 dB. Under 250 Hz, the mass law remains unavoidable and a maximum of 3-dB attenuation can be expected.

Secondly, inner acoustic correction is mostly directed by some degree of concentration of the sound achieved through the main curvature; however, it must be noted that even poorly anticlastic surfaces will not show reflection problems because of the initial acoustic permeability.

27.4 Structural properties of fabrics

27.4.1 Tensile strength

Tensile strength, a most important measure, is usually tested on a 50 mm width strip sample and the result given in Newtons per 5 cm. Some slight differences may appear due to temperature and speed of loading. As a general average, the tensile strength of fabrics ranges from 5600 to 11 000 daN m^{-1}.

27.4.2 Dimensional stability

Creep and thermal and moisture movements lead to undesirable effects on permanently stressed fabric structures since these processes involve restressing. Glass-based cloths are very stable and show very low creep. Polyester-based cloths have a more significant creep, 50% of which can be absorbed by a 200 daN m^{-1} initial prestressing. After a period of 6 months, it is necessary to restress the material unless specific absorber devices have been provided on the boundaries of the structure.

27.4.3 Stiffness

As can be seen in *Table 27.3* the breaking strain of glass fabric does not exceed 6%, while that of polyester fabric reaches more than 16%. A rule of thumb used in practical applications leads to a recommended prestressing strain level of less than 1/20 of the breaking strain. This condition ensures low stressing of fabrics during 80% of their lifespan. Though snow or wind loads may bring large deflections, they are considered as short-term effects and do not justify stiffness to be increased unless snow ponding is likely to occur.

27.4.4 Jointing

A very important step in the membrane fabrication process is seaming. The ideal seam should carry 100% of the fabric strength. This requires a high adhesion factor between cloth and coating as well as the use of a good reproducible jointing method. Stitching has often been employed, together with a seam protector to avoid ultraviolet degradation. High-frequency heating remains the quickest and simplest welding method and gives very reliable seams on PVC coatings. For PTFE, the insertion of an FEP interlayer is often necessary. For silicone-coated fabric jointing is achieved through glueing.

27.4.5 Durability

Several experimental studies and observation of the real-time behaviour over the past 20 years of polyester–PVC fabrics have shown that the main factor affecting the durability of these materials over long time exposure is the thickness and plasticity of the PVC coating used for ultraviolet-radiation insulation. However, for PTFE-coated glass, the waterproofing of the coating is the most important factor since glass fibres are weakened by water exposure.

27.5 Applications

The applications of fabrics range from temporary scaffolding sheeting to huge permanent lightweight structures covering thousands of square metres (see *Table 27.4*). The main qualities of fabrics which are widely recognized by designers when prescribing their use in the building area are:

(1) rapidity of use due to off-site manufacture;
(2) light modulation more easily regulated than with glass panes;
(3) durability of over 15 years for woven fabrics;
(4) architectural flexibility adapted to building constraints;
(5) very cheap site construction; and
(6) the environmental aspects of being able to obtain a smooth double curvature.

In terms of construction, fabric structures can be classified into three types according to the way in which pretensioning or stiffening is introduced into the membrane (see *Figure 27.3*):

(1) surface pretensioning leads to inflatable or pneumatic structures;
(2) linear pretensioning leads to arch-beam-supported structures;
(3) ponctual pretensioning corresponds to free-edge or Chinese-hat like structures.

It must be pointed out that architectural freedom as well as shape and on-site rigging grows in complexity as the construction type varies from I to III in *Figure 27.3*. Of course, variation or a combination of types are more easily found between types II and III as the drawings in *Figure 27.4* show.

Returning to architectural opportunities, it should be mentioned that fabric structures should only be applied

Table 27.4 Cost, properties and applications of fabrics

Material	Cost per m² (£)	ΔL/L* (%)	Durability (years)	Translucency (%)	Fire resistance†	Colour range	Application
Foils							
PVC	1.5		<10	90	None	All	
Polyester MYLAR	5.0		<15	95	None	All	
FEP	10	200	<25	95	M1	Clear	Green-house glazing
PETFE	10	300	>25	90	M1	Clear	
Coated fabrics							
Polyester/PVC with acrylic lacquer	2–7	16	<15	8–30	M2	All	Widely used for all types of tensile structures
Nylon/PVC	2–7	20	<12	8–30	M2	All	Poor dimensional stability
Kevlar/PVC	30–60	3	<20	Opaque	M2	All	Only used where high strength is required
Polyester/Hypalon	8–20		<20	Opaque	M0	All	Used for radar domes
Polyester/PVC with Tedlar	3–8	16	<20	7–20	M2	All	Better self-cleaning ability; little experience on welded joints
Polyester/PVDF	15–20	16	<25	35	M2	White	In development
Glass/PTFE	25–45	6	<30	5–15	M0	Ivory	Widely used in USA for permanent membrane
Kevlar/PTFE	40–65	3	<25	Opaque	M1	Ivory	Very seldom used
Glass/silicon	20	6	<25	20–50	M2	Clear	New material used for 5 years in USA
Reinforced films							
PVC/polyester	1		<10	80	M2		Widely used for clear sheeting on scaffolding
FEP or ETFE with glass, Kevlar or steel-wire mesh			<25	50–80			Not in commercial production

* Relative strain.
† M0, M1, M2, French Regulations.

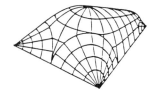

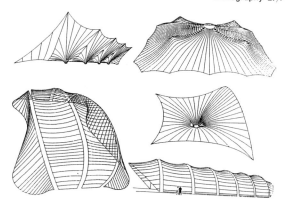

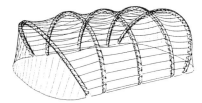

Type I: Surface pretensioning (inflatable)

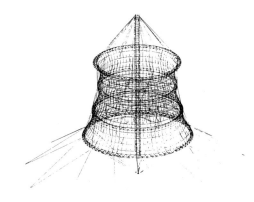

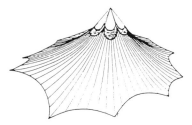

Type II: Linear pretensioning (arch supported)

Type III: Ponctual pretensioning (Chinese hat)

Figure 27.3 The three methods of pretensioning membranes

Figure 27.4 Variations and combinations of pretensioning methods II and III

whenever programmes exhibit:

(1) small, or zero, thermal or acoustic constraints; or
(2) highly important natural-lighting modulation and weather protection.

Accepting these two basic rules, it is sensible to prescribe a fabric tensile structure in the following cases:

(1) (i) Cultural, sport and exhibition hall covers; (ii) atria for hotels, warehouses and commercial centres; and (iii) industrial storage of wide span (>25 m).
(2) When the time schedule is short.
(3) When soil constraints are critical.
(4) When the owner foresees a cyclic dismantling and re-erection.
(5) When the customer requires low cost and maintenance and wishes to achieve a contemporary lightweight architecture characterized by the softness of curves.

Bibliography

BRITISH STANDARDS INSTITUTION, *BS 476*
BRITISH STANDARDS INSTITUTION, *BS 3120*
FORSTER, B., The engineered use of coated fabrics in long span roofs. *The Arup Journal* (Autumn 1985)
FRENCH REGULATION, *M0* Fire Regulation Classification
FRENCH REGULATION, *M1* Fire Regulation Classification
FRENCH REGULATION, *M2* Fire Regulation Classification
Lightweight Structures in Architecture, Vol. 2, Proceedings of the First International Conference, 24–29 August 1986, University of New South Wales, Sydney, Australia
MALINOWSKY, D., *Le Cahier des Règles de l'Art des Structures Textiles*, Groupe Arcora (1984), Les Ulis, 91945, France
MEFFERT, B., *Mechanical Properties of PVC Coated Polyester Fabrics*, University of Rheinisch-Westfälischen Techniques, Aachen, Germany (April 1978)

Geotextile Properties Related to Structure and Design

28

T S Ingold BSc, MSc, PhD, DIC, EurIng, CEng, MConsE, FICE, FIHT, FGS, FASCE, MSocIS(France)
Consulting Geotechnical Engineer

Contents

28.1 Introduction 28/3

28.2 Geotextile structure 28/3

28.3 Serviceability 28/5

28.4 Separation 28/7

28.5 Filtration 28/8

28.6 Drainage 28/11

28.7 Reinforcement 28/12

28.8 Economics 28/13

28.9 Conclusions 28/15

Acknowledgements 28/15

References 28/15

28.1 Introduction

Like any other building material, the fitness of a geotextile to serve a particular purpose is formalized in a specification of required geotextile properties. The procedure by which these required properties are evaluated is, in essence, the design process. This process may be empirical, being based on past experience, or analytical, being based on mathematical modelling, or a combination of both approaches. The empirically derived specification for a given application may be limited in as much as experience may be limited to a specific type of geotextile used in a limited range of conditions. Although a specification derived from this type of approach may be difficult to extrapolate to other conditions, it has the advantage that it incorporates the geotextile properties necessary both to perform the required function and to survive the rigours of the installation process.

In contrast, a specification derived from an analytical technique can account for a wide range of parameters which might arise in a certain application. However, with this approach care must be taken to define the required geotextile properties both to fulfill the design function and to survive the installation process. The four cardinal functions credited to geotextiles are: (i) separations, (ii) filtration, (iii) drainage and (iv) reinforcement. For a particular application one or more of these functions will be of primary importance, as illustrated in *Table 28.1*.[1]

The ranking of importance of these functions is very much conceptual because it arises from the perceived design function of the geotextile once installed. For the geotextile to perform the required design function, it must first survive the installation process without serious impairment. An example of this is the use of a geotextile filter to wrap a coarse granular drainage medium in a French drain. Here the prime design properties would be an appropriate geotextile pore size to retain soil particles in the base soil and an adequate flow capacity normal to the plane of the geotextile to transmit flow from the base soil to granular drainage medium. There is no requirement for geotextile strength at this level of assessment, however, such a requirement becomes self-evident when the construction process is considered. The geotextile would not be installed with the precision of a watchmaker and in all likelihood would be draped in the drainage trench and forced to comply with the profile of the trench by the weight of the granular drainage medium which would be placed by mechanical shovel or end-tipping. Clearly, if the geotextile did not have adequate resistance to puncture, tear and bursting, it would be unlikely to survive this process. Consequently, the ability to survive, or the 'function' of survival is of paramount importance and must be considered as part of the design.

Having defined the required geotextile properties for survival and performance of the design function, it remains to select a conforming product. This selection demands considerable thought and care because the properties of geotextiles vary widely according to geotextile structure, polymer type and the test methods employed to measure these properties. These aspects are considered in the following sections.

28.2 Geotextile structure

Geotextile fabrics generally fall into one of the two broad categories: woven or non-woven textiles. There are other fabric structures such as knitted fabrics or malimo stitch bonded fabrics. However, these are in a small minority and are, therefore, not considered further. As well as geotextile fabrics there are related non-textile products such as grids, meshes, mats and strips which may perform some of the geotextile functions. These are considered elsewhere.[2]

Woven geotextiles are manufactured using traditional weaving looms in which transverse elements (the weft) are woven between longitudinal elements (the warp). The structure of the finished fabric and, consequently, the properties of the geotextile will be governed by the particular form of the warp and weft and the polymer type used in the manufacture of these elements. By far the most common structure is formed by the weaving of flat tapes which may be extruded directly as tapes or slit from a wide sheet of film. In very heavy weight fabrics the flat tape may be twisted into a tape yarn. Most commonly, polypropylene is used in the manufacture of tape and the corresponding structure, shown in the electron microphotograph in *Figure 28.1*, is termed 'tape-on-tape'. As can be seen, this particular structure has a small open area ratio and, consequently, would be expected to have a comparatively low capacity for conducting a flow of water normal to the plane of the fabric. In contrast, if the tape elements are replaced by circular cross-section monofilaments,

Figure 28.1 Woven tape-on-tape structure

Table 28.1 Relative importance of main functions in selected applications (based on ref. 1)

Application	Separation	Filtration	Drainage-in-plane	Reinforcement
Trench drains	Secondary	Primary	Not relevant	Minor
Wall drainage	Not relevant	Primary	Primary	Not relevant
Embankments—basal drainage layer	Secondary	Primary	Not relevant to secondary	Not relevant
Subgrade stabilization	Primary	Secondary	Not relevant	Primary to secondary
Embankments—basal reinforcement	Primary to secondary	Secondary	Not relevant to minor	Primary
Walls and steep slopes—reinforcement	Not relevant to minor	Not relevant to minor	Not relevant	Primary

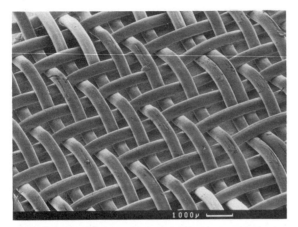

Figure 28.2 Woven monofilament-on-monofilament structure

Figure 28.3 Woven multifilament-on-multifilament structure

the resulting structure, termed 'monofilament-on-monofilament' (*Figure 28.2*) has a much larger open area ratio and an extremely high capacity to transmit water normal to the plane of the fabric. Consequently, this type of structure, usually employing polyethylene and/or polypropylene monofilaments, is appropriate in drainage applications where high flow rates are to be accommodated. Where very high tensile strength is required yet another structure is employed in which the warp and weft elements comprise low twist yarn manufactured from fine polyester (pes or pet) filaments. The resulting structure (*Figure 28.3*) is termed 'multifilament-on-multifilament'. Depending on the requirements to be met, these different structures can be combined, as shown in *Figures 28.4* and *28.5*. So, for example, the requirement for a geotextile with very high unidirectional strength and a very high water flow capacity may be met using the multifilament-on-monofilament structure shown in *Figure 28.5*. This is the essence of woven geotextiles where the fabric structure, and polymer type, may be chosen to provide the required properties defined in the design process.

The basic element in the manufacture of non-woven geotextiles is the continuous filament which is extruded from overhead 'spinnerets' onto a conveyor belt to form a loose web. The general term 'spunbonded' is used to describe this method of forming the web. An alternative method of web formation makes use of staple fibre which is essentially short lengths of filament as opposed to continuous filament. The loose web so

formed is subsequently given strength and coherence by one, or sometimes a combination of three processes:

(1) Heat bonding which involves heating and rolling the loose web of continuous filaments. This causes the filaments to melt and subsequently fuse together at their crossover points. This process is also known as thermal bonding, melt bonding or melding. A typical heat bonded structure is shown in *Figure 28.6*.

(2) Chemical or resin bonding, which involves pretreatment of the web with a chemical adhesive or synthetic resin which upon rolling causes the filaments to bond together at their points of contact. This process is used in a small minority of non-woven geotextiles.

(3) Mechanical bonding, which is achieved using a battery of thousands of fine barbed needles which reciprocate rapidly. The motion of the needles is normal to the plane of the loose web with the needles penetrating the full thickness of the web. The actual mechanism of bonding is simply entanglement of the filaments. Following 'needle punching' the entangled web is rolled to give a finish. A typical mechanically bonded structure is shown in *Figure 28.7*. Needle punching is also frequently used to bond staple fibres which are short lengths, typically 100 mm, of cut continuous filaments.

As would be expected, the structure of the geotextile and polymer type employed has a radical effect on the mechanical

Figure 28.4 Woven monofilament-on-tape structure

Figure 28.5 Woven monofilament-on-multifilament structure

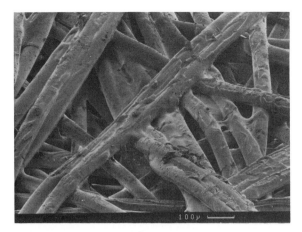

Figure 28.6 Non-woven heat-bonded structure

Figure 28.7 Non-woven mechanically bonded structure

and hydraulic properties. Some aspects of these variations are considered in the following sections which consider geotextile properties in the context of design functions.

28.3 Serviceability

Serviceability relates to the ability of the geotextile to withstand the handling and installation stresses imposed prior to and during construction. Once installed in its final position the geotextile must retain adequate properties to perform the required design function. The stresses imposed, and damage caused, during handling and installation will be a function of several factors. Prime among these will be the construction equipment employed, handling and construction techniques, the material against which the geotextile is laid and the material subsequently used to cover the geotextile. Since serviceability involves resisting the rigours of construction, it is a short-term phenomenon. For example if a geotextile filter is to fulfill its design function and service life, it must not become torn or punctured during installation; if it does there is a high probability that it will not fulfill the design function. However, in certain applications, construction-induced damage can be allowed for. A good example of this is a geotextile reinforcement where the effects of perforations or tears of an assumed size can be taken into account in assessing the design strengths. This

type of assessment will often involve the testing of geotextile samples recovered from a construction trial to compare the properties and behaviour of intact and damaged samples. Where there is any question of construction damage impairing the durability or service life of a geotextile, this aspect must be fully investigated and incorporated into the process of evaluating design parameters.

The geotextile properties required to ensure survival will vary according to the application. These have been defined for several common applications, such as drainage, erosion control and road stabilization, by 'Task Force 25' which is a committee convened by the United States Federal Highway Administration. As an example, the serviceability requirements for road stabilization are presented. The required level of geotextile serviceability related to the condition of the subgrade and the construction equipment employed is given in *Table 28.2*. As can be seen, the required level of serviceability increases from low to very high as the subgrade becomes more uneven or heavier construction plant is used. The required level of serviceability based on the type of cover material placed on the geotextile and again the bearing pressure imposed by construction plant is given in *Table 28.3*. For the particular site being considered, the required degree of serviceability is the higher of the two levels derived from *Table 28.2* or *Table 28.3*. These qualitative levels of serviceability can be quantified using the data set out in *Table 28.4*. As can be seen, any particular level of required survivability will require the specified minimum values of grab strength, puncture strength, burst strength and tear strength. Details of these tests are to be found in basic references.[4-6]

The particular properties cited in *Table 28.4* can be achieved using either woven or non-woven geotextiles, however, to achieve a required level of strength it is necessary to use a non-woven fabric of greater mass per unit area than a woven one. The variations of grab, puncture and burst strength with geotextile mass per unit area are given in *Figures 28.8* to *28.10*, respectively, for different geotextile structures and polymer types. Although woven polyester fabrics are not shown, these generally have much higher strength for weight than woven polypropylene. Trapezoidal tear strength, which is one of the required properties given in *Table 28.4*, is shown in *Figure 28.11* for various geotextile structures. Tear strength tends to increase with mass per unit area for both woven and non-woven fabrics; however, with woven fabrics tear strength is very much affected by the tensile strength of the particular warp/weft elements employed. Where extremely high tear strengths are required, woven fabrics are particularly adaptable because special high-strength warp or weft elements can be inserted at required intervals to act as 'rip-stops' which prevent tear propagation.

In western Europe, the ability of a geotextile to survive the installation process is either not quantified at all or the required performance is lumped in with properties required to fulfill the design function. For example, several countries operate systems whereby geotextiles are graded on a numerical classification scale according to their mechanical and/or hydraulic properties,[11-13] each grade being related to particular applications. As and when European or international standards are set for serviceability, they may not employ the same test methods adopted by Task Force 25, because in Europe there is a tendency to favour the wide width tensile test, California bearing ratio (CBR) plunger test and drop cone test[6] in preference to the ASTM grab test, and burst test. Consequently, the definition of properties for a given degree of serviceability may take the form shown in *Table 28.5*.

At this juncture it is appropriate to sound two notes of caution. The first relates to tests and test standards. It must be remembered that, for any particular geotextile property, there may be several different test methods and for a given fabric each test method is likely to give a different result. An illustration of

Table 28.2 Required degree of geotextile serviceability as a function of subgrade conditions and construction equipment[3]

Subgrade conditions	Construction equipment and 150–300 mm initial cover to geotextile		
	Low ground pressure equipment ($<30\,\mathrm{kN\,m^{-2}}$)	Medium ground pressure equipment ($>30\,\mathrm{kN\,m^{-2}}$ $<60\,\mathrm{kN\,m^{-2}}$)	High ground pressure equipment ($>60\,\mathrm{kN\,m^{-2}}$)
Subgrade has been cleared of all obstacles except grass, weeds, leaves and fine wood debris. Surface is smooth and level such that any shallow depressions and humps do not exceed 150 mm in depth or height. All larger depressions are filled. Alternatively, a smooth working table may be placed	Low	Moderate	High
Subgrade has been cleared of obstacles larger than small to moderate sized tree limbs and rocks. Tree trunks and stumps should be removed or covered with a partial working table. Depressions and humps should not exceed 500 m in depth or height. Larger depressions should be filled	Moderate	High	Very high
Minimal site preparation is required. Trees may be felled, delimbed and left in place. Stumps should be cut to project not more than 150 mm above subgrade. Geotextile may be draped directly over the tree trunks, stumps, large depressions and hump, holes, stream channels and large boulders. Items should be removed only if placing the geotextile and cover material over them will distort the finished road surface	High	Very high	Not recommended

Table 28.3 Required degree of geotextile serviceability as a function of cover material and construction equipment[3]

	Initial lift thickness (mm)					
	150–300		300–450		450–600	>600
	Low ground pressure equipment ($<30\,\mathrm{kN\,m^{-2}}$)	Medium ground pressure equipment (>30 $<60\,\mathrm{kN\,m^{-2}}$)	Medium ground pressure equipment (>30 $<60\,\mathrm{kN\,m^{-2}}$)	High ground pressure equipment ($>60\,\mathrm{kN\,m^{-2}}$)	High ground pressure equipment ($>60\,\mathrm{kN\,m^{-2}}$)	High ground pressure equipment ($>60\,\mathrm{kN\,m^{-2}}$)
Fine sand to 50 mm maximum size gravel, rounded to subangular	Low	Moderate	Low	Moderate	Low	Low
Coare aggregate with diameter up to one-half proposed lift thickness, may be angular	Moderate	High	Moderate	High	Moderate	Low
Some to most of aggregate with diameter greater than one-half proposed lift thickness, angular and sharp edges, few fines	High	Very high	High	Very high	High	Moderate

this is puncture resistance. The puncture strength shown in *Figure 28.9* is based on ASTM D-3787[18] in which an 8-mm diameter steel rod with a flat end advances normal to the plane of a restrained geotextile until a sufficient force is applied to cause puncture. In many western European countries, puncture resistance is measured using a similar technique except that the plunger is a 50-mm diameter CBR plunger with a flat end. Results for this type of test, to DIN 54307,[15] are given in *Figure*

28.12. Although these data show the same trends as the results in *Figure 28.9*, the measured magnitudes of puncture strength are quite different. Consequently, in comparing the properties of different geotextiles, great care must be taken to ensure that the test methods are truly comparable.

The second note of caution relates to the general issue of serviceability. The example set out in *Tables 28.2* and *28.3* are for one type of application. Other applications will have other

Table 28.4 Minimum geotextile properties[a] required for geotextile serviceability[3]

Required degree of geotextile serviceability	Grab strength (ASTM D-1682/4632)[7] (N/25 mm)	Puncture strength (modified ASTM D-751/3787)[8] (N)	Burst strength (ASTM D-751/3786)[9] (bar)	Trapezoidal tear (ASTM D-1117/4533) (N)
Very high	1200	500	30	340
High	800	340	20	225
Moderate	600	180	15	180
Low	400	135	10	135

[a] All values represent minimum average roll values (i.e. any roll in a lot should meet or exceed the minimum values given). Note: these values are normally 20% lower than manufacturers' reported typical values.

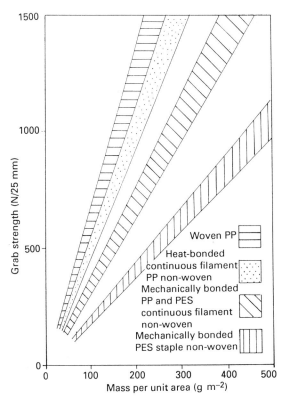

Figure 28.8 Grab strength (ASTM-D1682[7]) versus mass per unit area. PP, polypropylene; PES, polyester

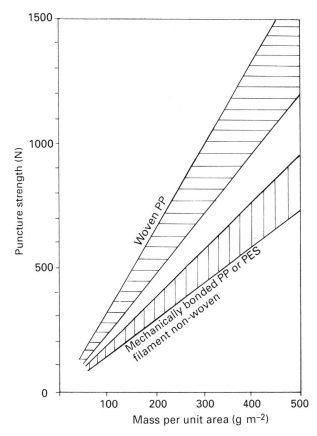

Figure 28.9 Puncture strength (ASTM D3787[18]) versus mass per unit area. PP, polypropylene; PES, polyester

serviceability criteria such as those defined by Task Force 25.[3] For example, if a geotextile is being used as a filter in a revetment to be covered by heavy armour rock, impact resistance is important if the rock is to be dumped from any appreciable height. Similarly, if a geotextile is to be used in an asphaltic overlay, care must be taken to check the melting point or reversion temperature of the polymer of the geotextile with the laying temperature of the overlay material.

28.4 Separation

Separation is perhaps the most enigmatic and ill-defined geotextile function because a geotextile seldom performs this function alone. A definition of a separator might be a geotextile placed between two different soil types to prevent intermixing.

An example of this might be a granular fill placed over a cohesive soil formation with a geotextile at the fill–formation interface. For the geotextile to act purely as a separator, the only consideration is serviceability, as described in the previous section. Clearly, this consideration is paramount because if the geotextile punctures or tears it ceases to perform the required function.

More usually the separation function is performed in parallel with one of the other prime functions. For example, if the geotextile is placed over a soft formation soil and then covered with granular fill to form an unpaved road, it may perform a reinforcing function. As the unpaved road is trafficked horizontal shear stresses will be developed on the underside of

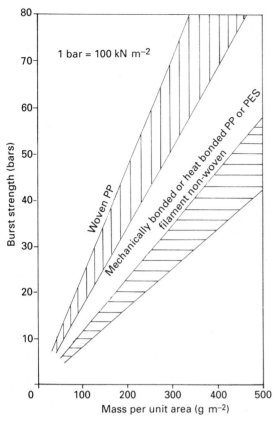

Figure 28.10 Burst strength (ASTM D3786[9]) versus mass per unit area. PP, polypropylene; PES, polyester

the granular fill. These stresses will be absorbed by the geotextile which is put into axial tension and acts as a reinforcement. Should ruts be allowed to develop in the unpaved road the geotextile will locally deform and generate in-plane tensile forces which partly support the traffic load through membrane action. To perform these functions adequately it is important that the geotextile has an appropriate axial tensile stiffness and surface roughness.

Although the demarcation between the separation and reinforcing functions is clear enough, the same is not true for separation and filtration. When a geotextile is laid and fitted over a cohesive formation it is unusual for the formation soil to be extruded through the geotextile. However, if the formation is waterlogged, then water would drain through the geotextile during construction. If the granular fill is not to be contaminated by fines from the formation soil, this introduces the need for some filtration criterion. This situation becomes more demanding for separators in paved or unpaved roads where formation pumping is to be controlled, since for the geotextile to separate the formation soil and the granular layers of the pavement it must function as a dynamic filter and drain.[19] Where a geotextile is required to act purely as a separator, then design considerations extend only to consideration of serviceability where use can be made of past experience and specifications can be drawn up using simple index test properties such as puncture, tear and burst resistance. Where the geotextile is required to perform additional functions, these must be designed for accordingly. It cannot be emphasized too strongly that it is vital to give full consideration to geotextile serviceability in this application.

28.5 Filtration

There are two broad criteria to be met for a geotextile to perform adequately as a filter. First, the pore sizes of the geotextile must be small enough to prevent significant loss of soil particles from the base soil, and secondly the geotextile must have a sufficiently high permeability to water, normal to its plane, to transmit water flowing from the base soil. These are the same basic criteria which apply to the design of a granular filter medium.

As can be seen from *Figures 28.1* to *28.7*, the size of the pores in a geotextile will vary in size and distribution with the structure of a geotextile. In woven fabrics there is a comparatively small variation in pore sizes for a given fabric structure and these pores are regularly spaced over the fabric. For non-woven fabrics there is a somewhat wider variation in pore sizes and their distribution for a given fabric. For both types of fabric the range of pore sizes is determined by sieving soil, or glass beads, of a known grading through the geotextile. The pore sizes will take up a distribution similar in form to the distribution of particle sizes for a soil. To simplify design procedures the filtration characteristics of a given geotextile are represented by a single pore size measured in microns. Common use is made of the O_{90} pore size. This means that 90% of the pores in the geotextile are this size or smaller. In comparing pore sizes of different geotextiles, care should be exercised on several accounts. Firstly the O_{90} pore size is not universally accepted as the standard pore size characterizing the geotextile. For example, filtration characteristics may be represented by some other pore size such as O_{95}. This means that 95% of the pores in the geotextile are this size or smaller and by definition $O_{95} > O_{90}$.[20] Secondly the magnitude of O_{90}, or O_{95}, will vary according to the particular test method used to measure it. Test specifications vary

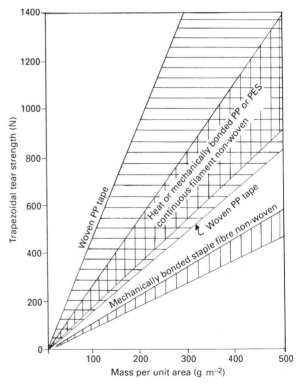

Figure 28.11 Trapezoidal tear strength (ASTM D1117[10]) versus mass per unit area. PP, polypropylene; PES, polyester

Table 28.5 Possible European format for minimum geotextile properties for serviceability

Required degree of serviceability	Tensile strength (BS 6906)[14] (kN m^{-1})	CBR (DIN 54307)[15] (N)	Trapezoidal tear (BS 4303)[16] (N)	Drop cone (SN 640550) (mm)
Very high	35	4500	500	5
High	20	2500	350	10
Medium	7	1000	175	20
Low	3	750	100	40

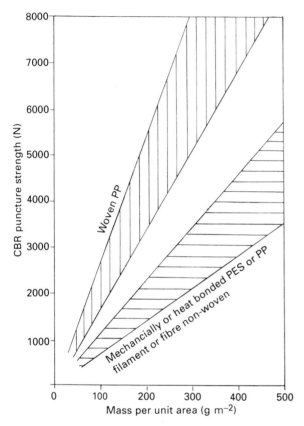

Figure 28.12 CBR puncture strength (DIN 54307[15]) versus mass per unit area. PP, polypropylene; PES, polyester

considerably;[6] however, these fall into one of the three categories of dry sieving, wet sieving or hydrodynamic sieving. Some indication of how the pore size might vary according to definition, e.g. O_{90} or O_{95}, test method and geotextile structure are indicated in *Table 28.6*. In general, the dry-sieving technique will return a larger pore size than either the wet- or hydrodynamic-sieving methods.

Pore size, say O_{90}, will vary with the structure of the geotextile and its mass per unit area. Some indication of this variation is given in *Figure 28.13*. For non-woven fabrics, pore size tends to decrease with increasing mass per unit area. This trend is more pronounced in heat-bonded than mechanically bonded fabrics as indicated by the lower bound of the envelope for non-woven fabrics in *Figure 28.13*. The O_{90} dry sieving pore size for non-woven fabrics varies from a minimum of approximately 30 μm to a maximum of some 300 μm. With woven-tape fabrics,

pore size tends to increase with mass per unit area and at heavy weights the structure may change from flat tape to tape yarn. The O_{90} pore size for such woven fabrics varies from approximately 100 to 500 μm. Much larger pore sizes are obtained for woven monofilament-on-monofilament fibres and these vary typically from 200 μm to values in excess of 1000 μm. The smallest pore size for a woven fabric is obtained using a multifilament-on-multifilament structure where O_{90} values of less than 100 μm can be obtained.

In designing geotextile filters to prevent piping under steady-state unidirectional-flow conditions, it is usual to relate the pore size to the particle size of the base soil being protected. A typical criterion would be:

$$O_{90} \leqslant \lambda d_{90}$$

where d_{90} is the 90% passing particle size of the base soil and λ is a coefficient which normally has a value between 1 and 2. There are a wide range of design rules originating from numerous workers in different countries. Very often the design rules are related to a particular definition of the characteristic pore size determined by a particular test method. Consequently, some care must be exercised not to mix a particular design method with the manufacturer's product data determined using an incompatible test method.

The other aspect of behaviour which must be taken into account in designing a filter is compatibility of permeability between geotextile and base soil. As an index test the water permeability of geotextiles is measured without the geotextile being in contact with soil. Since it is difficult to measure accurately the hydraulic gradient for flow normal to the plane of a geotextile, the permeability is defined in terms of the flow rate per unit area under a known driving head. In Europe this is commonly taken as a constant head of 100 mm. The resulting water flow, in litres per second per square metre (l s^{-1} m^{-2}), will be governed, among other things, by the structure of the geotextile as indicated in *Figure 28.14*. The lowest water permeabilities are returned by the woven-tape fabrics at typically 10–30 l s^{-1} m^{-2}. Heat-bonded non-woven fabrics return typically 30–250 l s^{-1} m^{-2}; however, with an initially dry fabric a driving head of greater than 100 mm may be required to initiate water flow. Mechanically bonded non-woven fabrics typically return to 50–300 l s^{-1} m^{-2}, whilst the highest flow rates, in some cases exceeding 1000 l s^{-1} m^{-2}, are obtained with high open ratio woven monofilament fabrics.

In translating these index test values of water permeability into the design, several aspects of behaviour must be taken into account. For example, with the thicker non-woven fabrics, water flow normal to the plane of the fabric decreases as the level of normal stress increases. This trend is indicated in *Figure 28.15* for a mechanically bonded continuous-filament fabric. In addition, when a geotextile is in contact with base soil there will be some clogging and blocking of the geotextile pores by soil fines transported from the base soil. This will result in a reduced flow rate through the geotextile. To compensate for this in non-critical applications it is common practice to select a

Table 28.6 Variation in pore size with test method

Test method	Geotextile structure				
	Woven tape (135 g m^{-2})	Non-woven heat-bonded filament (136 g m^{-2})	Non-woven mechanically bonded filament		Woven tape yarn (525 g m^{-2})
			(130 g m^{-2})	(550 g m^{-2})	
O_{90} dry sieving	145	—	228	129	360
O_{95} wet sieving	—	165	—	—	—
O_{95} dry sieving	—	160	—	—	—
O_{95} hydrodynamic sieving	105	140	130	50	125

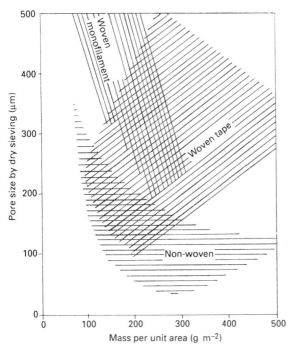

Figure 28.13 Effect of geotextile structure on pore size versus mass per unit area

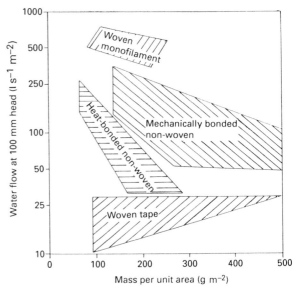

Figure 28.14 Effect of geotextile structure on water flow versus mass per unit area

geotextile with a higher permeability than that of the base soil. This, of course, is done with due regard to normal stress level in the case of thicker non-woven fabrics.

One reason why the capacity of a geotextile to transmit water normal to its plane is expressed in terms of 'water permeability' is because this parameter does not involve quantification of the hydraulic gradient operating across the geotextile. This leads to complications in matching the hydraulic properties of geotextiles to the soils which they filter in terms of the coefficient of permeability, K (m s^{-1}). Groundwater flow is generally laminar and, therefore, the flow rate is proportional to hydraulic gradient as defined by D'Arcy's law: $q = KiA$, where q is the volumetric flow rate ($\text{m}^3 \text{ s}^{-1}$), K is the coefficient of permeability (m s^{-1}), i is a dimensionless hydraulic gradient and A is the cross-sectional area of flow (m^2). Flow through most thick non-woven fabrics is close to laminar and, therefore, if the thickness of the geotextile, the driving head and the flow rate are known, it is reasonable to calculate a coefficient of

permeability for the geotextile, K_g, using D'Arcy's law. However, for thin non-woven fabrics and most woven fabrics, water flow under test conditions is non-laminar; consequently, D'Arcy's law is modified to take the form: $q^n = KiA$. The index n varies between 1 for laminar flow and 2 for purely turbulent flow. Flow conditions for a particular geotextile can only be assessed by studying a plot of flow rate against hydraulic gradient. Where this is linear, D'Arcy's law may be applied to determine K_g. Where the plot is non-linear, K_g can only be assessed using a modified version of D'Arcy's law. For non-critical applications the permeability of the geotextile, K_g, measured at an appropriate normal stress level, is generally selected to be at least 10 times greater than the permeability of the soil being filtered.[5,20] In more critical applications the time-dependent flow characteristics of the soil–geotextile system should be investigated in the laboratory.

There are no standardized test methods for quantifying the flow characteristics of soil–geotextile systems; however, two particular test methods are of interest. The first involves the long-term measurement of flow rate through the base soil in contact with the candidate geotextile filter.[5] Flow rate is found to decrease with time, due to reordering of the soil particles, until a transition at which the soil–geotextile system begins its

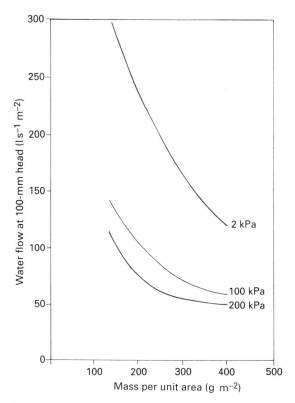

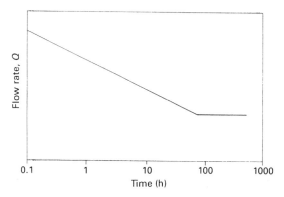

Figure 28.16 Variation of flow rate with time for a soil–geotextile system. Data from Koerner[5]

28.6 Drainage

Drainage, as a geotextile function, is taken as the ability to transmit fluid in the plane of the geotextile. Consequently, it is only the thicker non-woven fabrics, particularly mechanically bonded structures, which exhibit any useful flow capacity. This in-plane capacity, which is the product of the geotextile thickness and coefficient of permeability, is called the transmissivity and is usually measured in units of litres per second per metre width of fabric ($l\,s^{-1}\,m^{-1}$) for a given hydraulic gradient. Since the thickness of mechanically bonded non-woven fabrics reduces as the normal stress level increases, so then does the transmissivity. An indication of this, for the flow of water, is given in *Figure 28.17*. In general, geotextile fabrics are not now used for drainage of water because much higher capacity composites are available. These are laminates comprising a geotextile filter and a water-conducting core. The transmissivity of such composites can be several orders of magnitude higher than a simple fabric and flow rates of up to $10\,l\,s^{-1}\,m^{-1}$ at normal stress levels in excess of $150\,kN\,m^{-2}$ can be attained. This makes these composites particularly useful for structural drainage, for example behind retaining walls where they replace sand chimney drains or no-fines concrete drains, and for leakage detection and interception beneath geomembrane liners. The transmissivity of

Figure 28.15 Water flow versus mass per unit area. Data for normal stress levels in the range 2–2000 kPa for mechanically bonded continuous-filament polypropylene non-woven

field-simulated behaviour involving some clogging. If the slope of the flow rate versus log time plot (*Figure 28.16*) becomes zero after the transition, then the geotextile is considered compatible with the base soil under the prevailing test conditions. If the flow rate continues to decrease after the transition, increased clogging could occur. In such a case the candidate geotextile would not be suited to the base soil under test. Although laudable, this test technique has the disadvantage of long duration with the test normally being run for 1000 h. A test which can be run in 24 h and is similarly aimed at determining the hydraulic compatibility of a soil–geotextile system is the US Corps of Engineers Gradient Ratio Test.[21] This test involves measurement of the hydraulic gradients 25-mm and 50-mm upstream of the soil–geotextile interface. Due to clogging the hydraulic gradient closer to the geotextile will be higher than that further upstream. The gradient ratio is the higher hydraulic gradient, measured at 25 mm, divided by the lower hydraulic gradient measured at 50 mm. The Corps of Engineers suggest that gradient ratios greater than 3 indicate unacceptable geotextiles for the type of soil under test.[21]

All the above comments refer to unidirectional steady-state flow which is conducive to the establishment of a filter mechanism near the soil–geotextile interface. This means that the geotextile pore size may be greater than the smaller particle sizes in the base soil. However, these smaller sized particles are prevented from washing out through the geotextile by the filter cake or bridges of soil particles set up adjacent to the geotextile during the initial period of water flow. However, in situations where the water flow can reverse, for example beneath revetments, the formation of a filter cake or soil bridges cannot be relied upon and, consequently, the pore size of the geotextile may need to be reduced to retain the smaller particle sizes.[5,20]

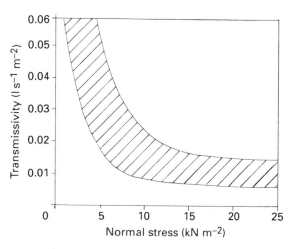

Figure 28.17 Effect of normal stress level on the transmissivity of non-woven mechanically bonded geotextiles. Data from Koerner[5]

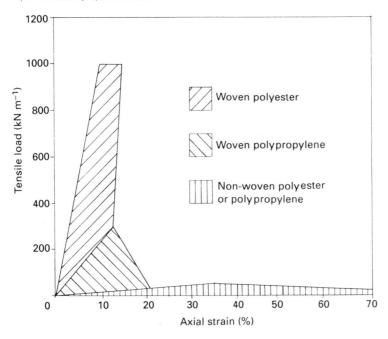

Figure 28.18 Generalized load–strain characteristics (regardless of mass per unit area); areas of overlap have been omitted for clarity

thick non-woven fabrics to gas is much higher than to water and, consequently, such fabrics are used beneath geomembrane liners to hazardous-waste containments where they function as both a gas vent and a protective cushion during construction.

28.7 Reinforcement

The most potentially exploitable and the most technically demanding application of geotextiles is soil reinforcement. The required properties for reinforcing applications vary widely depending on the precise application. In low-risk, short-term applications, such as unpaved haul roads, virtually any geotextile with adequate serviceability will perform. In remedial works such as reinforced asphaltic overlays, bitumen or asphalt impregnated non-woven fabrics have been used widely in the USA, whilst in Europe a more cautious approach includes investigation of the reinforcing properties of geogrids and leno-weave fabric grids. However, among the most demanding applications are the construction of embankments over soft ground and reinforced fill structures such as steep-sided slopes or near-vertical walls. For these applications an appropriate balance of tensile strength, axial stiffness and durability are vital.

As with other geotextile properties, tensile strength and axial stiffness are radically affected by fabric structure and polymer type. This is reflected in *Figure 28.18* which shows a generalized plot of load-strain characteristics for common structures and polymer types. By far the strongest and stiffest geotextiles are the woven polyester multifilament-on-multifilament fabrics which attain rupture strengths as high as 1000 kN m^{-1} at axial strains as low as 10% measured using constant-rate-of-strain techniques. Tensile rupture strengths for woven polypropylene rarely rise above 300 kN m^{-1}, whilst for non-woven fabrics tensile strengths would not be expected to exceed 50 kN m^{-1} using index test methods.

A more detailed presentation of the load-strain characteristics of different non-woven structures is given in *Figure 28.19*, normalized to a mass per unit area of 300 g m^{-2}, which shows tensile rupture strains typically between 40% and 100%. For

all fabric structures, tensile strength tends to increase with increasing mass per unit area, as indicated in *Figure 28.20*. As with all geotextile testing, great care must be taken in comparing tensile strengths of different fabrics to ensure that the test methods are compatible. This is particularly true of non-woven structures where the use of narrow-width samples, such as the 50-mm wide strip test, e.g. DIN 53857/1,[22] tends to underestimate tensile rupture strength and overestimate rupture strain. Using wide-width samples with width:gauge length ratios of up to 5 can increase measured tensile rupture strengths by some 30–40%. These strengths would be more representative of the plane strain conditions prevailing in most geotextile applications. The tensile load capacity of non-woven fabrics is further enhanced if the fabric is confined by a normal stress. For example, at a confining pressure of 100 kN m^{-2} and an axial strain of 40%, the tensile load capacity of a mechanically bonded fabric was found to increase by some 30%.[24]

Other than a basis for initial comparison of different geotextile products, short-term tensile strength measured using constant-rate-of-strain testing has little application in the design of embankments over soft ground or reinforced fill structures. An exception to this is in the initial stages of construction of embankments over soft ground where it is important to have an adequately high tensile strength in all directions to resist the loads imposed by any uneven filling. It has been said that woven fabrics only exhibit tensile strength in the two orthogonal directions defined by warp and weft. However, quite the reverse is true because the greatest strength, but highest elongation, will always be at some inclination to the warp and weft directions. For a fabric with equal warp and weft strengths this maximum will be along a diagonal. That an acceptable degree of tensile strength isotropy is found in most non-woven and woven structures is reflected in the measured polar tensile strength distributions presented in *Figure 28.21*.

The prime design function, namely soil reinforcement, is more sensibly based on constant load creep testing or stress relaxation tests. By applying constant loads of different magnitudes to similar samples, it is possible to assess how the tensile rupture load of the geotextile will vary with time. This will be affected

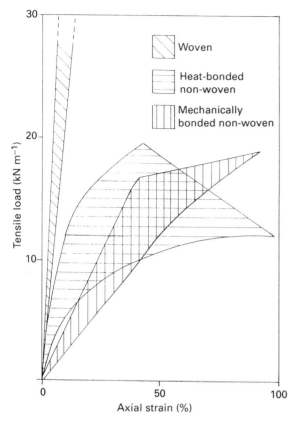

Figure 28.19 Load strain characteristics (normalized to 300 g m⁻²). Data from Andrawes and McGown[23]

by geotextile structure, polymer type, test temperature, and chemical and bacteriological environments. Factors such as preconstruction exposure to ultraviolet light and construction-induced damage will also influence the way rupture strength varies with time. Tensile rupture load will always decrease with increasing time. This decay in strength may simply vary linearly with log time or may involve a transition point beyond which there is an accelerated strength decay (*Figure 28.22*). Knowledge of the rupture strength of the reinforcement at any time is vital if the structure is to be designed against collapse by tensile failure. At all times the reinforcement must be able to provide the tensile force required by the structure to maintain stability. For an embankment constructed over soft ground, the required restoring force, provided by the basal layer of geotextile, will decrease with time and finally become zero as consolidation of the initially soft foundation nears completion. Consequently, the geotextile would be loaded for a comparatively short period rarely extending beyond a few years. In contrast, a steep-sided slope or near-vertical wall requires a restoring force for the entire design life of the structure. This may involve periods of up to 120 years, in which case the meaningful prediction of long-term rupture strengths presents a demanding technical problem.

Design against collapse is a first priority. Of parallel importance is the serviceability requirement to control deflections in the structure. For embankments on soft ground the designer would aim to limit average geotextile strain to about 5%. If this is to be achieved then the load required of the geotextile must decrease with time or be related to the load which can be carried by the geotextile, at the end of its service

life, without exceeding a predetermined strain. The decay of tensile load with time, at constant strain, can be assessed using stress relaxation tests. These involve maintaining the geotextile at a constant strain and measuring the time-dependent decay in tensile load (*Figure 28.23*). An alternative approach is to determine how the tensile axial stiffness of a geotextile decays with time at some constant strain level. Using this technique it is possible to predict, for example, what tensile load might be sustained at a given axial strain after a given time under load. These loads will be very much influenced by geotextile structure and polymer type as reflected in *Table 28.7*.

In addition to consideration of tensile failure either by rupture or movement exceeding a predetermined serviceability requirement, any design must guard against pull-out or bond failure of the geotextile. For steep-sided embankments or near-vertical walls this presents no major problem, because in relation to the tensile load to be sustained, a full-width geotextile presents a large surface area over which adequate pull-out resistance can be mobilized for modest bond lengths. In contrast, for basal reinforced embankments over soft ground the available bond strength along the base of the embankment is limited in the short term to the undrained shear strength of the foundation soil near the reinforcement interface. The bond developed at this interface controls lateral extrusion of the soft foundation soil and where this is critical it will control the entire geometry of the embankment.

28.8 Economics

The relative economics of using a geotextile-based solution will vary enormously depending on the viability, if any, of alternative

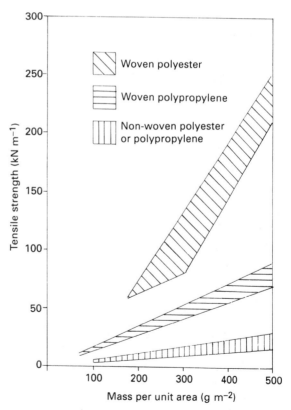

Figure 28.20 Tensile strength (DIN 53857[22]) versus mass per unit area

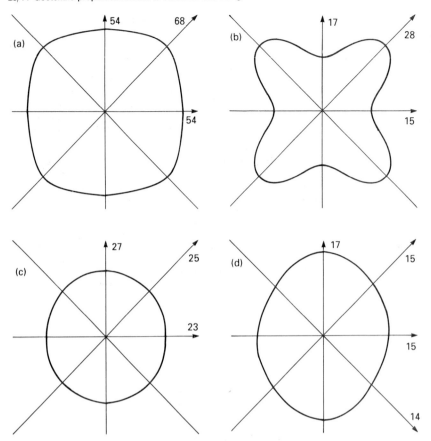

Figure 28.21 Tensile strength anisotropy. (a) Woven polyester[25]; (b) woven polypropylene[26]; (c) mechanically bonded continuous polyester filament non-woven[20]; (d) heat-bonded continuous polypropylene filament non-woven[27]. All values given are directional strengths in kN m^{-1} (not to scale)

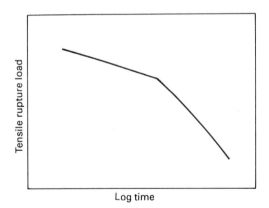

Figure 28.22 Generalized rupture load versus log time

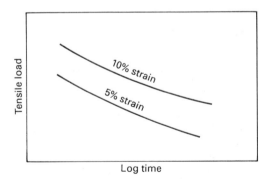

Figure 28.23 Tensile load versus time for constant strain

traditional methods. This, in turn, will be a function of specific site conditions such as price and availability of materials, plant and labour. Comparisons can be made on the relative economics of different fabric types on any number of bases. For example, *Table 28.8* shows the relative cost per unit tensile strength based on wide-width constant-rate-of-strain testing for a range of geotextile structures and polymer types. For the non-woven

structures, the mass per unit area required to give unit tensile strength, i.e. 1 kN m^{-1}, falls fairly consistently in the range 12.5–15.4 g m^{-2}. These values drop dramatically for the woven structures, being only 2.3 g m^{-2} for polyester and 3.8–5.9 g m^{-2} for polypropylene tape yarn and flat tape, respectively. The inverse of these values relates to the tensile strength obtained per kilogramme mass of geotextile. This ranges from 65 to 80 kN m^{-1} per kilogramme for non-woven fabrics up to a massive 440 kN m^{-1} for woven polyester multifilament. An

Table 28.7 Long-term load related to geotextile structure and polymer type[a]

Structure[b] and polymer	Load[c] (kN m^{-1})
Woven polyester	35
Woven polypropylene	3
Mechanically bonded polyester	2
Heat-bonded polyethylene/polypropylene	1

[a] Data from refs 28 and 29. [b] For 10% strain at 10^6 h and 20°C. [c] Normalized to 250 g m^{-2}.

approximate relative cost per unit strength given in the last column of *Table 28.8* indicates that, strength for strength, woven fabrics are 40–60% of the cost of non-woven fabrics.

Unfortunately, price proves to be the main consideration in many low-technology high-volume applications. For example, a geotextile employed with the hope of performing as an antipumping membrane at the formation–sub-base interface of a motorway pavement might be purchased at a cost of 1% of the cost of the pavement it seeks to protect, and at this price may serve no useful purpose. In contrast, a more appropriate grade of geotextile at 5% of the pavement cost might give worthwhile protection.

28.9 Conclusions

The use and specification of geotextiles should be based on empiricism founded on past experience or design based on the required functions. Having specified the required properties only then should consideration be given to the appropriate geotextile structure and polymer type. It will be found that over a wide range of applications and functions both woven and non-woven geotextiles will fill the required technical specification. Provided that the technical specification is filled, it is only then that consideration should be given to specific products and price. Value engineering should always be applied to ensure that a geotextile-based solution is indeed better value than traditional alternatives.

The perceived properties of geotextiles are very much a function of the particular test method employed and this must be borne in mind when making comparisons between different products. This problem is made particularly acute by the fact that geotextiles are truly international products which may originate from any number of different countries. Despite painstaking work by many manufacturers there will frequently be no basis for comparison between products from different origins. With few exceptions the test data provided in the manufacturer's literature will relate to simple index tests. In

some instances these data can be applied to simple empirical design methods. Even so, care should be taken to ensure that index test methods employed by different manufacturers coincide adequately with the test methods forming the basis of the empirical design.

Analytical design methods are generally limited to special applications either involving high risk or extensive ramifications in the event of malfunction. In such cases, liability is likely to rest with the design engineer rather than the supplier. For this, if no other reason, the designer should invoke appropriate design testing or systems testing to evaluate appropriate design parameters.

Geotextiles are not a panacea for all geotechnical and related problems. Rather they are a material resource which, like any other construction material, must be designed and selected to serve specific purposes. The use of geotextiles does not in itself procure the only, or most economic, solution to a construction problem. In appraising any particular problem the engineer must seek all technically viable solutions and then select the most economic of these. This solution may, or may not, involve the use of geotextiles. As with any other material there are limitations and these must be taken into account in design. For example, geotextiles are flammable and, consequently, they would not be used to construct a reinforced soil bund around a petroleum storage tank. Accepting this, the only limitations are in the mind of the designer or end-user.

Acknowledgements

The author wishes to thank the many manufacturers whose technical literature has been the source of much of the basic data presented in this chapter.

References

1 MURRAY, R. T. and McGOWN, A., 'Geotextile test procedures: background and sustained load testing', *Transport and Road Research Laboratory Application Guide No. 5*, Crowthorne (1987)
2 INGOLD, T. S. and MILLER, K. S., *Geotextiles Handbook*, Thomas Telford, London (1988)
3 CHRISTOPHER, B. R., HOLTZ, R. D. and DiMAGGIO, J. A., 'Geotextile engineering manual', *US DOT FHWA Contract No. DTFH 61-80-C-00094*, Federal Highway Administration, Washington, DC (1984)
4 VELDHUIJZEN VAN ZANTEN, R., *Geotextiles and Geomembranes in Civil Engineering*, Balkema, Rotterdam (1986)
5 KOERNER, R. M., *Designing with Geosynthetics*, Prentice-Hall, Englewood Cliffs, NJ (1985)
6 VAN DEN BERG, C. and MYLES, B., *Geotextile Testing*, International Geotextile Society, Brussels (1986)
7 AMERICAN SOCIETY FOR TESTING MATERIALS, *ASTM D-1682-64 (1975) Test methods for breaking load and elongation of*

Table 28.8 Relative cost per unit tensile strength

Geotextile structure and polymer type	Mass per unit area per unit strength (g m^{-2})(kN m^{-1})$^{-1}$	Strength per unit mass (kN m^{-2}) kg^{-1}	Relative cost per unit strength
Non-woven mechanically bonded polyester continuous filament	12.5	80	1.0
Non-woven mechanically bonded polypropylene continuous filament	15.4	65	1.0
Non-woven heat-bonded polypropylene/polyethylene continuous filament	15.4	65	1.0
Non-woven heat-bonded polypropylene continuous filament	14.3	70	0.9
Woven polyester multifilament	2.3	440	0.6
Woven polypropylene tape yarn	3.8	260	0.4
Woven polypropylene tape	5.9	170	0.4

textile fabrics; *ASTM D-4632-86 Test method for breaking load and elongation of geotextiles*, Philadelphia

8 AMERICAN SOCIETY FOR TESTING MATERIALS, *ASTM D-751-79 Method of testing coated fabrics; ASTM D-4632-86 Test method for breaking load and elongation of textiles*, Philadelphia

9 AMERICAN SOCIETY FOR TESTING MATERIALS, *ASTM D-751/3786-87 Test method for long drawn lie bursting strength of knitted goods and nonwoven fabrics*, Philadelphia

10 AMERICAN SOCIETY FOR TESTING MATERIALS, *ASTM D-1117-80 Methods of testing nonwoven fabrics; ASTM D-4533-85 Test method for trapezoid tearing strength of geotextiles*, Philadelphia

11 ALFHEIM, S. L. and SORLIE, A., 'Tests and specifications of fabrics', *Internal Report No. 776*, Statens Vegvesen Veglaoratoriet, Oslo (1977)

12 RATHMAYER, H., 'Experiences with VTT-GEO classified nonwoven geotextiles for Finnish roads', Vol. 2, *Proceedings of the 2nd International Conference on Geotextiles*, Las Vegas (1982)

13 COMITE FRANÇAISE DES GEOTEXTILES, *Géotextiles dans les Voies de Circulation*, Ministère des Transports, Paris (1981)

14 BRITISH STANDARDS INSTITUTION, *BS 6906: Part 1 Determination of tensile properties using a wide width strip*, Milton Keynes (1987)

15 DEUTSCHE INDUSTRIE NORMENANSCHLUSS, *DIN 54037*

16 BRITISH STANDARDS INSTITUTION, *BS 4303 Method for the determination of the resistance to tearing of woven fabrics by the wing-rip technique*, Milton Keynes (1968 (1986))

17 *SN 640550*

18 AMERICAN SOCIETY FOR TESTING MATERIALS, *ASTM D-3787-80 Test method for bursting strength of knitted goods*, Philadelphia

19 INGOLD, T. S. and CROWCRAFT, P., 'The notion of geotextiles as separators in roads', *Ground Engineering*, **17** (1984)

20 JOHN, N. W. M., *Geotextiles*, Blackie, Glasgow (1987)

21 HALIBURTON, T. A. and WOOD, P. D., 'Evaluation of US Army Corps of Engineers Gradient Ratio Test for geotextile performance', Vol. 1, *Proceedings of the 2nd International Conference on Geotextiles*, Las Vegas (1982)

22 DEUTSCHE INDUSTRIE NORMENANSCHLUSS, *DIN 53857/1*

23 ANDRAWES, K. Z. and McGOWN, A., 'Alteration of soil behaviour by the inclusion of materials with different properties', *TRRL Supplementary Report 457*, Crowthorne (1979)

24 ANDRAWES, K. Z. and McGOWN, A., 'Load-extension testing of geotextiles confined in soil', Vol. 3, *Proceedings of the 2nd International Conference on Geotextiles*, Las Vegas (1982)

25 VAN LEEUWEN, J. H., 'New methods of determining the stress–strain behaviour of woven and non-woven fabrics in the laboratory and in practice', Vol. II, *Proceedings of the International Conference on Fabrics in Geotechnics*, Paris (1977)

26 WARWICK, R. G., 'Woven fabrics', *Proceedings of the Geotextile Technology '84 Imperial College*, Construction Industry International, London (1984)

27 INGOLD, T. S., 'Reinforced clay', Ph.D. Thesis, Surrey University, Guildford (1980)

28 RISSEEUW, P., 'Mechanical properties of Stabilenka reinforcing fabrics subjected to long-term loads', *Report No. IEN 9427*, Enka b.v., Holland (1982)

29 ANDRAWES, K. Z., McGOWN, A. and MURRAY, R. T., 'The load–strain–time–temperature behaviour of geotextiles and geogrids', Vol. III, *Proceedings of the 3rd International Conference on Geotextiles*, Vienna (1986)

29

Glass

G K Jackson
Pilkington Glass Consultants

Contents

29.1 Introduction 29/3

29.2 Manufacture of basic flat glass 29/3
    29.2.1 Melting 29/3
    29.2.2 Forming 29/3
    29.2.3 The sheet process 29/4
    29.2.4 The rolled process 29/4
    29.2.5 Wired-glass process 29/4
    29.2.6 The float process 29/5

29.3 Types of glass 29/6
    29.3.1 Float glass 29/6
    29.3.2 Sheet glass 29/6
    29.3.3 Rolled glass 29/7
    29.3.4 Wired glass 29/7
    29.3.5 Body coloured and tinted glasses 29/8
    29.3.6 Surface-modified glass 29/8

29.4 Processed glasses 29/9
    29.4.1 Coated glass 29/9
    29.4.2 Toughened glass 29/10
    29.4.3 Laminated glass 29/13
    29.4.4 Silvered glass 29/14
    29.4.5 Other surface treatments 29/15
    29.4.6 Bent glass 29/15
    29.4.7 Insulating glass units 29/16
    29.4.8 Glass blocks 29/16
    29.4.9 Fire-resistant glasses 29/17

29.5 Structural glazing 29/18

29.6 Cutting of glass 29/18

29.7 Specification of glass 29/19

29.8 Standards 29/20

29.1 Introduction

Very little glass is found in nature, although some does occur near volcanoes where sufficient heat has been generated to cause materials to fuse together. Obsidian—natural glass—is usually impure and, therefore, lacks transparency. Primitive peoples used it to make into arrow heads, knife blades, ornaments and other tools. Such objects have been found worldwide, for example in Africa, Greece, Australia, and Mexico.

The earliest examples of man-made glass have been found in the remains of early Middle Eastern civilizations in the form of beads and small vessels, dating back some 4000 years. Glass-making techniques spread gradually from Egypt and by the 6th century BC had reached most parts of the western Mediterranean. During the last three centuries BC, glass-makers in Alexandria perfected the technique of making composite coloured glass canes and rods. These were made by drawing together a number of glasses of different colours. The rods were then cut into slices to provide repetitive designs. By the time of Christ, the Romans had spread the art of glass-making throughout the Empire and they appeared to have mastered all the technical processes involved in glass-making and decorating. The collapse of the Roman Empire caused a decline in glass-making in Europe until the Venetians revived it around 1200 AD. During the intervening period the techniques for casting stained glass and the making of stained-glass windows were developed in Lorraine and Normandy.

Whilst the Venetians rediscovered all the skills exhibited by the Romans, it is believed that these skills spread not from Rome but from the earlier industry in Syria. By the beginning of the 14th century, Venetian craftsmen had mastered, for example, the production of fine glass mirrors. By 1600 the Venetian monopoly had eroded and the techniques had spread across Europe to Bohemia, France, England and the Netherlands.

Whilst the Venetians were concentrating on mirrors and glasses for decorative purposes, the glass-makers of Lorraine and Normandy were developing methods of manufacturing flat glass. The cylinder drawn and crown processes were introduced into Britain in the 15th and 16th centuries.

The location of glass-making enterprises was usually determined by the presence of wood for fuel, and streams from which sand was obtained. Alkali was normally obtained by burning bracken or seaweed. In England most of this early activity was centred in the south of England, the Weald in Kent and Sussex being the most famous. Towards the end of the 16th century wood supplies became seriously depleted and in 1615 the use of wood for glass-making was banned by law. The ban on the use of wood encouraged the changeover to coal and with it some important changes in furnace design.

The adoption of coal was a further major influence on the location of the glass-making industry, especially as at this time the canal and railway systems had not been developed and, therefore, as well as the location of raw materials, transportation was a major factor. In the UK the four main areas of activity were Newcastle, Bristol, Birmingham and St Helens. Over the years there have been many developments in the basic manufacture of flat glass for architectural applications until at the present time the major glass-making process used is the float glass process developed by Pilkington in 1959. In the Western World over 90% of flat-glass production is by the float process.

29.2 Manufacture of basic flat glass

The manufacture of all glass products is based on four fundamental stages:

(1) melting;
(2) forming;
(3) cooling; and
(4) finishing.

29.2.1 Melting

A typical approximate composition for flat glass for architectural applications is (proportions by weight):

sand (silica) 72%;
soda ash (sodium carbonate) 13%;
limestone (calcium carbonate) 10%;
dolomite (calcium mangesium carbonate) 4%.

The raw materials are weighed and mixed in the correct proportions to produce a mixture known as *frit*. Waste broken glass (*cullet*) is recycled along with frit, usually in the proportions of 80% frit and 20% cullet.

Melting takes place in a regenerative tank furnace at 1500°C. The term regenerative is used to describe the method by which the tank/furnace exhaust gases give up much of their heat to a lattice of refractory bricks which in turn heat up the incoming combustion air. The result is a saving in fuel and a much more thermally efficient process. The fuel used is usually oil or gas.

The furnace capacity varies from about 2000 to 5000 tonne of glass melted per week. Modern float tanks work at the higher end of the output range. A typical float tank arrangement is shown in schematic form in *Figure 29.1*.

29.2.2 Forming

The molten glass leaves the furnace at about 1050°C to be formed. The forming process must take place in the temperature

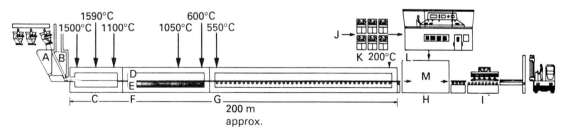

Figure 29.1 The float glass process. A, Raw material mix; B, cullet; C, oil-fired melting furnace; D, controlled atmosphere; E, molten tin; F, float bath; G, annealing lehr; H, automatic warehouse (not shown); I, automatic stacking; J, orders; K, computers; L, control point; M, computers govern the cutting processes, matching complex orders to the continuous ribbon of glass, and directing the cut glass to the appropriate part of the warehouse for stacking and despatch. The automatic warehouse stands by itself as a major advance in flat glass technology. *Illustration not to scale*

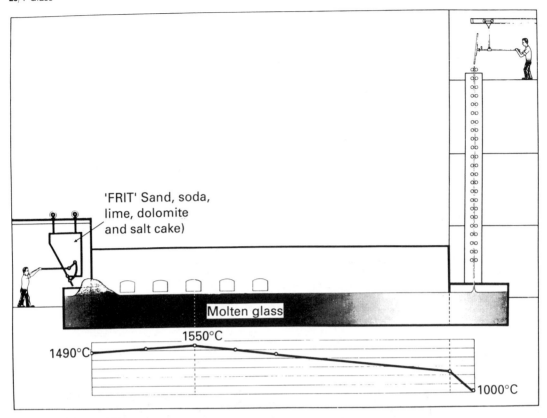

Figure 29.2 Sheet-glass manufacture: modern flat-drawn process

range 650–1050°C. Below 650°C the glass becomes too viscous to bend, stretch or shape.

There are two main forming processes in use today for flat-glass manufacture: the rolled process for the manufacture of patterned and wired glasses and the float process for producing flat transparent window glass. In less developed and Third World countries the obsolescent sheet process is still used.

29.2.3 The sheet process

In the sheet process (developed by the Pittsburgh Plate Glass Company in the 1920s) the glass at about 950°C flows from the tank and is drawn vertically as a continuous ribbon by a series of asbestos-clad rollers contained in a cast-iron tower (*Figure 29.2*).

As the ribbon is drawn, edge rollers grip the extremities of the ribbon and maintain it at a constant width. The ribbon is cooled rapidly by water boxes so that the first traction rollers do not mark the fire finish of the glass surface.

The tower which is some 10 m high functions as a vertical annealing chamber. At the top of the tower, the glass ribbon is scored and broken off into discrete plates. The thickness of the glass ribbon produced is determined by the speed at which it is drawn.

29.2.4 The rolled process

In the rolled process glass flows from the furnace to the rolling machine along a canal under carefully controlled temperature conditions. The rollers are about 25 cm in diameter, the bottom roller is engraved with the negative of the pattern to be

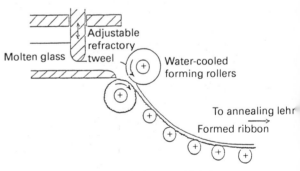

Figure 29.3 Continuous rolling of patterned flat glass

manufactured and the top roller is smooth. The final thickness of the patterned glass is controlled by the gap between the rollers which are water cooled to extract sufficient heat from the molten glass during contact to 'fix' the pattern and maintain acceptable roller-surface temperatures so as to prevent the glass sticking to the rollers. The ribbon leaves the patterning rollers at about 850°C and is transported to the annealing lehr over a series of water-cooled steel rollers.

Patterned glass is produced in 4-mm and 6-mm thickness. *Figure 29.3* shows a section through a rolling process.

29.2.5 Wired-glass process

A similar process is used for the production of wired glass. The machine in this instance consists of two independently-driven

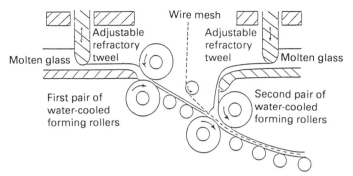

Figure 29.4 Manufacture of wired glass

Figure 29.5 Installation of polished wired glass

pairs of water-cooled rollers each fed with a ribbon of glass via separate canals from a common melting tank. The first pair of rollers produces a primary ribbon which forms the bottom portion of the final ribbon. The wire mesh is then introduced before the primary ribbon is taken through the second pair of rollers where the top portion of the final ribbon is formed.

The wire mesh is fed continuously from rolls mounted on a platform above the machine (*Figure 29.4*). The final ribbon is supported on water-cooled steel rollers as it passes into the annealing lehr.

At the end of the lehr, special cutting arrangements are needed to sever the wire and cut the glass into plates.

Because the glass comes into contact with rollers, the surface is not smooth and polished when the glass emerges from the lehr for cutting. Some production remains in this state and is

sold as wired cast, some is sent to have the surfaces ground flat and polished and is sold as polished wired glass (*Figure 29.5*).

29.2.6 The float process

The float process provides a means of combining the brilliant 'fire' finish of sheet glass with the freedom from optical distortion of plate glass without the need for the grinding and polishing of the two surfaces.

The molten glass from the melting furnace flows onto a bath of molten tin the surface of which is perfectly flat and free from irregularities. The surface of the glass in contact with the molten tin will also be perfectly flat and free from blemishes as will the upper surface of the molten glass which is in contact only with a controlled atmosphere of nitrogen and hydrogen to prevent

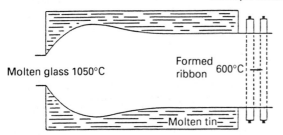

Conveyor rollers

Molten glass 1050°C

Formed ribbon 600°C

Molten tin

Figure 29.6 Plan view of simple ribbon forming process

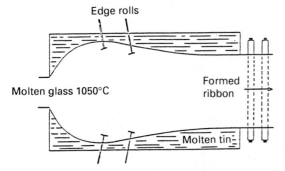

Edge rolls

Molten glass 1050°C

Formed ribbon

Molten tin

Figure 29.7 Manufacture of thin float ribbon

oxidation of the molten tin. A continuous stream of molten glass at about 1500°C is poured onto the bath of molten tin where it is held at a high enough temperature for sufficient time for any irregularities to melt out and for the surfaces to become flat and parallel.

Movement of the glass along the bath is provided by the tractive forced applied by rollers (*Figure 29.6*) which convey the continuous ribbon of glass down the length of the annealing lehr. As the ribbon moves along the tin bath it is progressively cooled until, at about 600°C, the viscosity is sufficiently high for the ribbon to come into contact with the conveyor rollers in the lehr without damage to the bottom surface. The speed at which the ribbon of glass is moved down the bath of tin determines its final thickness. In order to maintain constant ribbon width, toothed rollers (*Figure 29.7*) grip the extreme edges of the ribbon. After passage through the annealing lehr the glass is cut into appropriate sizes for delivery and storage or further processing.

29.3 Types of glass

The types of glass generally available can be usefully classified as:

(1) float glass;
(2) sheet glass;
(3) rolled glass;
(4) wired glass;
(5) body coloured/tinted glass;
(6) surface-modified glass; and
(7) processed glasses—coated glass, toughened glass, laminated glass, silvered glass, other surface treatments, bent glass, insulating glass units, glass blocks, and fire-resistant glass.

Most of these could have edge working or surface treatments incorporated for special reasons.

29.3.1 Float glass

As its name implies float glass is made using the float process. This is by far the main method of producing glass for construction purposes at the present time. Float glass is available in a wide range of thicknesses and sizes from many manufacturers. The width of float glass is limited by the width of the ribbon formed in the float bath (usually 3 m) and the maximum length of plates is limited by handling capabilities.

The approximate composition by weight of clear float glass is as follows:

Silicon	SiO_2	70–74%
Lime	CaO	5–12%
Soda	Na_2O	12–16%
Magnesium	MgO	0–5%
Aluminium	Al_2O_2	0.2–2%

Depending on the origin of the raw materials variable proportions of other trace materials will be present.

The following properties may be taken as typical of clear float glass, but it should be noted there may be minor variations between manufacturers:

Density	2560 kg m^{-3}
Hardness	6.5 Mohs
Young's modulus	$74.5 \times 10^9 \text{ Pa}$
Poisson's ratio	0.23
Specific heat	$830 \text{ J kg}^{-1} \text{ K}^{-1}$
Thermal conductivity	$1.05 \text{ W m}^{-1} \text{ K}^{-1}$
Thermal transmittance	$5.68 \text{ W m}^{-2} \text{ K}^{-1}$

Sound transmission	*Thickness* (mm)	*Sound insulation* (dB) *(mean 100–3150 kHz)*
	4	25
	6	27
	8	29
	10	30
	12	31

Coefficient of linear expansion	$7.6 \times 8.0 \times 10^{-6} \text{ K}^{-1}$
Refractive index	1.52 (380–760 mm)

The light transmission and total-solar-energy transmission of (clear) float glass is shown in *Table 29.1* for a range of common thicknesses.

29.3.2 Sheet glass

As old sheet glass plants are replaced by new float glass plants the already small proportion of sheet glass made is falling steadily. Most true sheet glass is manufactured in eastern Europe

Table 29.1 Light and total transmission of clear float glass

Thickness (mm)	*Light transmission* (%)	*Total solar energy transmission* (%)	*Normal maximum size** (mm)
3	88	83	2140 × 1220
4	87	80	2760 × 1220
5	86	77	3180 × 2100
6	85	75	4600 × 3180
8	83	70	6000 × 3300
10	84	65	6000 × 3300
12	82	61	6000 × 3300
15	76	55	3050 × 3000
19	72	48	3000 × 2900

* These sizes vary with manufacturer and for precise data individual manufactuer's literature should be consulted.

Table 29.2 Light and total solar energy transmission of clear sheet glass

Thickness (mm)	Light transmission (%)	Total solar energy transmission (%)	Normal maximum size* (mm)
3	88	83	2140 × 1220
4	87	80	2760 × 1220
5	86	77	3180 × 2100
6	85	75	4600 × 3180
8	83	70	6000 × 3300
10	84	65	6000 × 3300
12	82	61	6000 × 3300
15	76	55	3050 × 3000
19	72	48	3000 × 2900

* See footnote to *Table 29.1*.

and Third World countries. Some thin float glass is incorrectly described as sheet glass.

Because of the method of manufacture of sheet glass the surface quality is more variable than that of float glass and, therefore, sheet glass is usually graded by visual inspection into three grades designated as

O.Q. —ordinary quality;
S.Q. —selected glazing quality; and
S.S.Q.—special selected quality.

The light and total energy transmission factors for clear sheet glass are given in *Table 29.2* for a range of common thicknesses.

29.3.3 Rolled glass

This designation covers all glasses which are passed between rollers to give a specific surface finish, whether it is a definite regular pattern or a random diffusing surface. Rolled glasses are usually used where privacy or diffusion is required or where specific decorative effects are required. There is a wide range of rolled patterns to choose from, each manufacturer offering a pattern range. For details it is really necessary to consult the manufacturers' literature in order to establish what is suitable for a particular application. A selection of typical patterns is shown in *Figure 29.8*.

The depth to which the pattern is rolled into the glass and the average thickness determines the extent to which rolled patterned glasses can be laminated or toughened. Again manufacturers' literature must be consulted to establish the suitability of a particular pattern for these processes.

29.3.4 Wired glass

The production of wired glass has been described earlier. Whilst not usually classified as a true safety glass, in the event of bodily impact in the various codes of practice dealing with safety, the presence of the wires does hold the glass fragments together when breakage occurs. It is this characteristic of wired glass that has resulted in wired glass being used in large quantities in overhead glazing applications. However, the main use of wired glass has always been to create fire-resistant-glazing systems. In such installations the wire maintains the integrity of the glazed panel which, if glazed properly, can achieve fire-resistance ratings of 60–90 min.

Manufacturers' literature should be consulted for precise details of fire ratings and sizes which are acceptable. The usual thicknesses available are 7 mm for rough cast or patterned wired

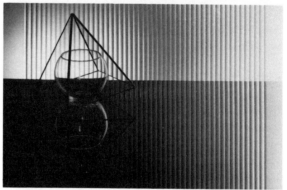

Figure 29.8 A selection of rolled patterned glasses

Figure 29.9 Wired glass in a partition providing fire protection

glass and 6 mm when in polished form. The maximum sizes are in the range 3700 mm × 3300 mm to 1840 mm × 1830 mm. On the whole polished examples tend to be the smaller sheet sizes. *Figure 29.9* shows a typical installation of wired glass in a partition providing fire protection.

29.3.5 Body coloured and tinted glasses

Body coloured and tinted glasses are produced by varying the constituents in the melting furnace. The colour is present throughout the thickness of the glass with the result that different thicknesses of the same mix will have different light and total solar energy transmissions. Thicker examples will appear more strongly coloured, which has important implications for the mixing of glass thicknesses on the same facade of a building. Body coloured and tinted glasses are used either as solar-control glasses where changes to the glass composition increase the absorption of the material and reduce the amount of light and total solar energy transmitted. So-called tinted glasses are used partly for decorative purposes.

Because the manufacture of these glasses can only be achieved by the lengthy process of changing the basic composition of the glass mix they are being superseded by other types of manufacturing processes which rely on modifying the performance and appearance of basic clear float glass. These are described in Sections 29.3.6 and 29.4.1. Body coloured and tinted glasses are normally produced in green, grey and bronze forms, although other tints are available. The individual manufacturer's literature should be consulted for details of colours, sizes and performance data. *Table 29.3* gives some typical data.

29.3.6 Surface-modified glass

Surface-modified glasses are usually produced on the float line as a continuous process and are achieved, as the name suggests, by modifying the surface of basic clear float glass. In some instances the modification occurs within the float bath whilst the

Table 29.3 Performance data for some typical body tinted glasses

Type	Thickness (mm)	Light transmission (%)	Total solar energy transmission (%)	Normal maximum sizes (mm)
Body tinted green float	6	72	62	3210 × 6000
Body tinted bronze float	4	61	70	3210 × 6000
	6	50	62	3210 × 6000
	10	33	51	3210 × 6000
	12	27	47	3210 × 6000
Body tinted bronze float	4	55	68	3210 × 6000
	6	42	60	3210 × 6000
	10	25	49	3210 × 6000
	12	19	45	3210 × 6000

glass is still in a semi-molten state. In other cases the modification occurs whilst the glass is still hot, but is at a convenient stage in the annealing cycle. Surface modification within the float bath is achieved either by bombarding the semi-molten glass with metal ions or by chemical vapour deposition. When the modification is performed during the annealing cycle the modifying process is usually referred to as a pyrolitic coating since it involves the pyrolitic decomposition of materials sprayed onto the glass surface. The modifying layer fuses with the glass surface.

Surface modified glasses are normally used for solar control or for applications where low-emissivity characteristics are required. A wide range of performance characteristics is available as a result of surface modification. The individual manufacturers' literature should be consulted to establish the range of performance, appearance and sizes available.

29.4 Processed glasses

29.4.1 Coated glass

Various processes have been developed for the application of thin coatings to large areas of flat glass. Coatings are applied to alter the performance of the basic float glass, i.e. light and radiant-heat transmission, light and radiant-heat reflection, and surface emissivity. Coatings which have been developed to have high transparency but high reflectivity of long-wave radiation (low emissivity coatings) are used to improve the thermal-insulation properties of the treated glass.

More than one coating can be applied to the glass surface to give particular properties. Coatings can be applied to glasses for incorporation in sealed-double-glazing units and for laminating. Some coatings provide distinctive colours to the glass, whilst others are neutral in appearance. Many major glass manufacturers have coating facilities, as do glass processors.

Table 29.4 Typical properties of reflective coated glasses

Coating	Light transmittance (%)	Total solar transmittance (%)	Solar reflectance (%)
Gold	42	22	40
Copper	42	25	39
Silver	42	27	47

The coatings used can be divided in two groups: metallic coatings and metallic oxide coatings. Metallic or metallic alloy coatings are applied to the glass by means of a vacuum deposition process, whilst coatings involving metallic oxide can be applied in a normal atmosphere. The application of an oxide coating requires temperatures of around 500°C which in effect 'fire' the coating to the base glass.

Metallic oxide coatings tend to be hard coatings which are sufficiently robust to withstand exposure to the normal atmosphere and weather. Metallic and metallic alloy coatings are usually softer and may not be sufficiently resistant to scratching and weathering without protection. Metallic and metallic alloy coatings are normally incorporated into double-glazing units or laminated products.

29.4.1.1 Selective coatings

In the thicknesses used, coatings of silver, copper and gold are semi-transparent, letting through varying amounts of visible radiation; however, they are much less transparent to radiation in the near-infra-red region of the solar spectrum. The optical properties of the coatings make them particularly useful as reflective treatments to create solar-control glasses.

The attenuation of radiation in the near-infra-red region occurs by reflection and, since about 50% of the total radiation from the sun occurs in this region, this makes these coatings particularly useful as solar-control coatings which reflect rather than absorb, and which, in turn, reduce admission into the room by convection and long-wave radiation. Some typical solar-control properties of double-glazing units comprising one pane of clear float glass and a pane with a metallic coating on the inner face of the outer glass are listed in *Table 29.4*.

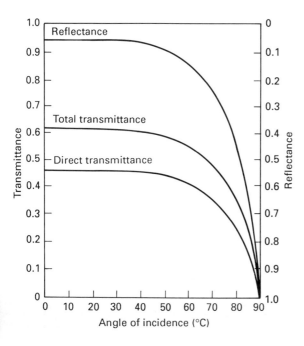

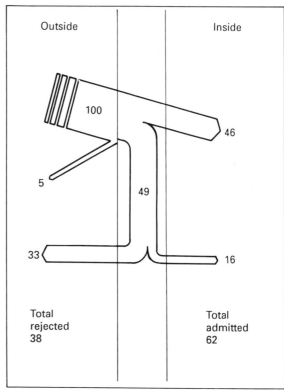

Figure 29.10 Partition of energy by a 6-mm 'Antisun' float 50/62 (bronze)

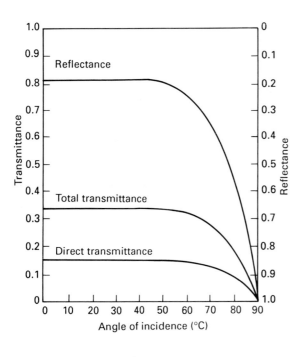

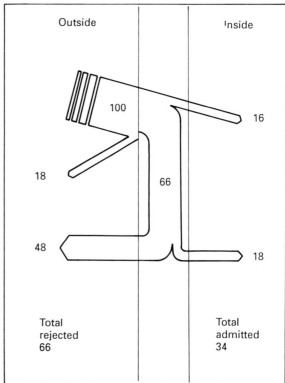

Figure 29.11 Partition of energy by a 6-mm 'SunCool' float 20/34 (silver)

The range of performance available from the use of metallic coatings is limited because of the thickness of coating which has to be applied. Glasses treated in this manner tend to have relatively low light-transmittance values. The use of additional dielectric coatings which produce interference effects allows higher light transmission and increased selectivity. In addition to allowing higher light transmission the range of colours is also increased.

There are currently products available with a wide range of colour by reflection, e.g. bronze, blue, gold, copper, and silver, with visual reflections in the range 10–50% and light transmissions in the range 10–70%. The wide range of performance available from the various types of solar-control glass, whether body tinted, surface modified, etc., is further illustrated in *Figures 29.10–29.16* which show the partition of energy as it passes through a range of glass configurations.

29.4.1.2 U-value improvements

The use of gold, copper, and silver coatings not only provides good solar protection and a range of colour effects but also allows improved thermal insulation properties. By comparison with uncoated glass, the U value of coated glass is considerably improved.

The coatings have high reflectivity in the medium and far infra-red ranges with values typically of 90–95%. This results in low emissivity from the coated surface and a reduction in the radiation exchange between the internal and external panes of a double-glazed unit. The resulting U value is significantly improved. A unit comprising two pieces of uncoated float glass and a 12 mm air-space would typically have a U value of $3.0 \text{ W m}^{-2} \text{ K}^{-1}$.

The use of two coated glasses could reduce the U value to $1.6 \text{ W m}^{-2} \text{ K}^{-1}$. If the air in the cavity is replaced by a gas such as argon or krypton the U value is reduced to $1.4 \text{ W m}^{-2} \text{ K}^{-1}$. Some typical performance possibilities are shown in *Figure 29.17*.

Coatings have also been developed to provide improved U value benefits but without significantly reducing the light and total solar radiant transmission. When incorporated in double-glazing units U values as low as $1.6 \text{ W m}^{-2} \text{ K}^{-1}$ and light transmissions of 84% are possible with these neutral coatings. These glasses are particularly useful for the glazing of dwellings. However, the coated glasses can also be used in combination with other glasses such as body tinted solar control glasses to provide not only solar-control properties but also high levels of thermal insulation.

The maximum sizes of coated-glass panes will be dependent on the facilities operated by individual manufacturers. Individual manufacturer's literature should be consulted to establish what is available. *Figure 29.18* shows a cross-section of a typical coating plant.

29.4.2 Toughened glass

Toughened glass is usually produced by reheating a piece of annealed glass to a temperature of approximately 700°C at which point it begins to soften. The surfaces of the heated glass are then cooled rapidly.

The technique creates a state of high compression in the outer surfaces of the glass and, as a result, although most other characteristics remain unchanged, the tensile strength is usually increased by a factor of four or five times that of annealed glass. When broken the toughened glass fractures into relatively small

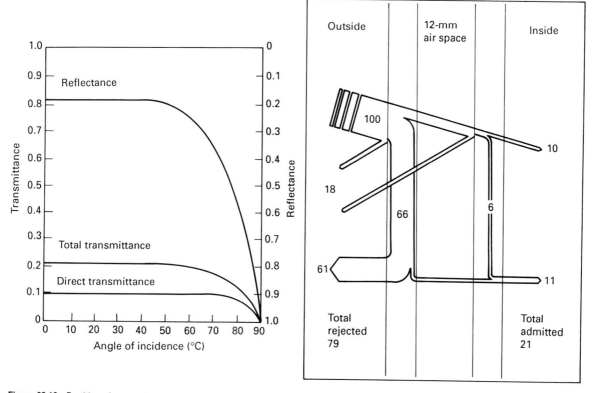

Figure 29.12 Partition of energy by a 6-mm 'SunCool' float 20/34 (silver) and a 'Kappafloat' inner pane

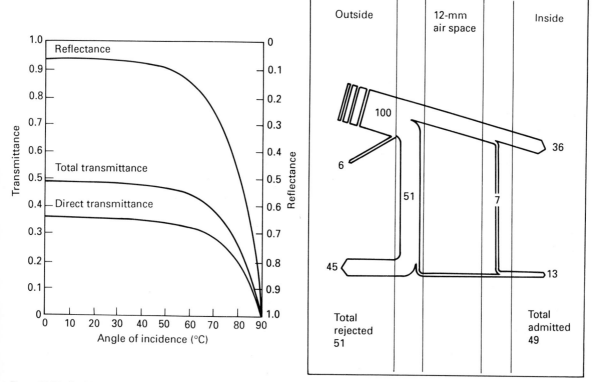

Figure 29.13 Partition of energy by a 6-mm 'Antisun' float 50/62 (bronze) and a 6-mm clear float

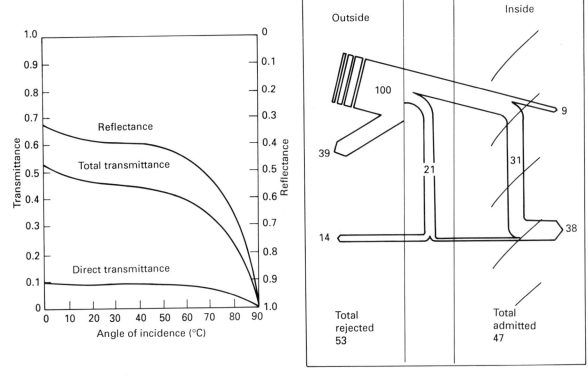

Figure 29.14 Partition of energy by a 6-mm clear float and a light coloured venetian blind

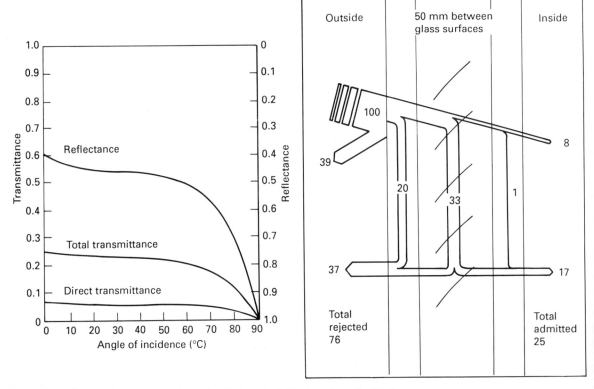

Figure 29.15 Partition of energy by two 6-mm clear floats and a light coloured venetian blind

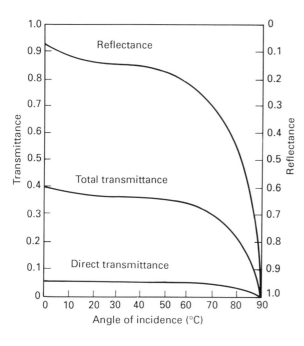

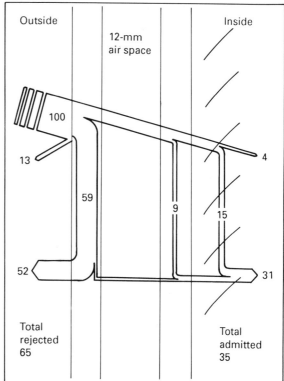

Figure 29.16 Partition of energy by a 6-mm 'Antisun' float 50/62 (bronze), a 6-mm clear float and a light coloured venetian blind

pieces usually in the form of small cubes. The lengths of the sides of the cubes are normally the same as the thickness of the glass. Because cubes of broken toughened glass do not have the sharp blade-like edges and dagger points of broken annealed glass it is regarded as a safety glazing material in the various codes of practice and standards.

Toughened glass is usually produced by one of two main methods based on heating followed by rapid cooling. In one method the glass is held vertically by tongs along the upper edge and suspended in a heating furnace to raise its temperature to about 700°C. The glass is then cooled rapidly by placing it between an array of nozzles which blast cold air onto the surfaces and cool the glass rapidly. The other process used involves supporting the glass horizontally on rollers and first passing it into the heating chamber then into the cooling area. This is known as the roller hearth process. A typical example of a roller hearth installation is shown in *Figure 29.19*. Both processes introduce some slight distortion of the glass, and the former also causes pinch marks where the tongs have gripped the glass.

All float and sheet glasses can be toughened. Many rolled patterned glasses can also be toughened depending on the profile of the patterns. Wired glasses cannot be satisfactorily toughened. The glasses which are toughened must be cut to size and have any other processing such as edge polishing and hole drilling completed before being subjected to the toughening process. Any attempt to 'work' the glass after toughening will cause the glass to shatter.

Whilst the air toughening process is being used it is possible to coat the glass with a coloured ceramic material which is then fired into the surface of the glass during the heating cycle of the toughening process. This results in a coloured opaque cladding glass which can be used in spandrel areas of buildings.

Whilst toughened glass is stronger than annealed glass of the same thickness it is more normal to use it in applications where a safe breaking pattern is required rather than in situations where additional strength is required.

The toughening process used places limits on the maximum sizes which can be handled. Typical maximum sizes are listed in *Table 29.5*.

29.4.3 Laminated glass

Laminated glass is produced by bonding two glasses together with a plastic material or a resin. The interlayer, which is usually polyvinyl butyral, can be either clear or tinted. The bonding is achieved by heating the glass/interlayer sandwich and applying pressure.

When a resin is used as the bonding medium a self-curing resin is usually poured between the two pieces of glass which are maintained at the correct separation whilst pouring and curing takes place. This process which is often referred to as 'cast in place' is more appropriate to small-scale production of special glasses.

Laminates can incorporate several thicknesses and combinations of glasses. Different thicknesses of interlayer can be specified to give a selection of products with a wide range of properties and applications. Laminated glasses can be used as safety glazing, bullet-resistant glazing, glazing for sound attenuation, solar control, vandal resistance, and for overhead applications.

When a laminated glass is broken the interlayer tends to hold the fragments of broken glass in place. The actual breakage pattern is the same as for annealed glass, although the strength of laminated glass is slightly less than that of monolithic annealed glass of the same substance.

Laminated glasses can incorporate multiple layers of inter-layer and glass plus other material such as polycarbonate to achieve specific performance characteristics. Toughened glasses can also be used as components of a laminated product.

29.4.4 Silvered glass

Silvering is a chemical process normally used to create mirrors by depositing a layer of metallic silver onto the surface of a piece of clear glass. The silver deposit is usually protected by a layer of copper which in turn is protected by a special paint coating.

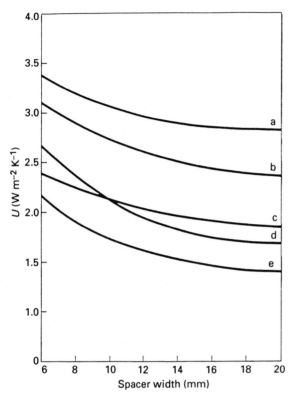

Figure 29.17 Standard U values for a variety of double-glazing systems. (a) Clear float + clear float. (b) Clear float + 'SunCool' float 20/34 (silver). (c) Triple clear float unit. (d) Clear float + Pilkington K glass. (e) Clear float + Pilkington K glass (argon filled)

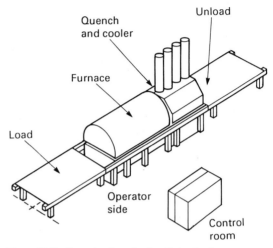

Figure 29.19 Example of a roller hearth toughening process

Table 29.5 Typical maximum sizes for toughened glass

Thickness (mm)	Size (m²)
4	2300 × 1300
5	2600 × 2000
6	4200 × 2000
10	4200 × 2000
12	4200 × 2000
15	4000 × 1800
19	4000 × 1800

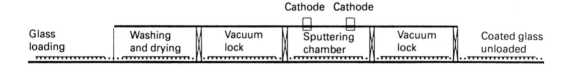

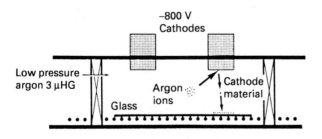

Figure 29.18 Low energy sputtering plant

The silver surface which gives the mirror its reflective properties is viewed through the glass. As an alternative to plain silver, special effects can be created by using tinted glass or by colouring the deposit of metal.

For special purposes 'front silvered' mirrors can be produced. These have the reflective material on the front surface of the glass. They are not normally used in architectural applications since the silvered surface has limited durability without additional protection.

It is also possible to create mirrors by using metals like aluminium to create the reflective surfaces.

29.4.5 Other surface treatments

In addition to those already described there are other surface treatments which can be applied to glass. These processes are used to create decorative effects or to allow the glass to perform a specialized function. Some examples of these treatments are:

(1) sand blasting;
(2) acid etching;
(3) screen printing;
(4) engraving;
(5) brilliant cutting;
(6) enamelling;
(7) staining; and
(8) painting.

These treatments are all practised by specialist glass processors who should be contacted to establish just what is available and its suitability for a specific application.

29.4.6 Bent glass

Bent glasses are produced by heating most basic glasses to the point where they soften and can either be pressed or sag bent

Figure 29.20 Bent glass in architectural applications

Table 29.6 Typical thermal transmittance (U values)*

Airspace width (mm)	U value (W m^{-2} K^{-1})
6	3.4
8	3.2
10	3.1
12	3.0
16	2.9
20	2.8

* Air in cavity; two panes of 4-mm glass.

over suitable formers. Bends can be created in one or two planes. Glass bending is a specialist operation and manufacturers' literature should be consulted to establish what is available both as standard items and as special orders. Many of the bent glasses used are in fact specially bent for a specific application.

The use of bent glass has changed significantly over the years, especially in architectural applications where plastics have become strong contenders for roof glazing in particular. Examples of bent glass in modern architectural applications are shown in *Figure 29.20*.

29.4.7 Insulating glass units

Insulating glass units incorporate two or more glasses separated by a spacer or spacers to create a cavity between each successive glass in the unit. The cavity is usually filled with dry air but sometimes an inert gas is used to modify the characteristics of the resulting units. Sealed-double-glazing units can be constructed from various combinations of glass as listed, to incorporate the following typical options:

(1) float glass;
(2) sheet glass;
(3) cast glass;
(4) polished wired glass;
(5) thermally- or chemically-toughened glass;
(6) coated glass;
(7) body tinted glass; and
(8) laminated glass.

More often than not sealed-multiple-glazing units incorporate two glasses and one spacer with dry air in the cavity, although additional panes and airspaces can be incorporated.

The spacer is attached to the glasses by a suitable adhesive and additional sealant material is then usually applied around the edges of the unit to prevent air and water penetration. The spacer is usually made of metal but can be made from plastics. Spacer widths of 5–20 mm are normal depending on the performance required from the resulting unit. The wider the airspace the higher the level of insulation provided.

Dehydrated air is normally used to fill the cavity of the unit but argon or krypton can be used to enhance the thermal-insulation properties. Heavy gases such as sulphur hexafluoride can be used in order to modify the acoustic-insulation properties of units. The spacers are often hollow and incorporate a dehydrant to ensure a low water vapour pressure in the unit and thereby reduce the likelihood of condensation forming in the unit under extreme temperature conditions.

The quality of the edge seal is of utmost importance if units are to have acceptable service lives. In addition to the use of gas filling to improve performance, triple and quadruple units can be specified. If improved thermal-insulation properties are required, low-emissivity coatings can be incorporated on one or more of the inner faces of the glasses making up the unit.

Low-emissivity coatings are produced as hard and soft coatings, as described earlier. Soft coatings are only suitable for incorporating in sealed units where the cavity protects the coating from abrasion and weathering. Hard coatings are used in sealed-unit construction but could also be used in double-window systems which are not hermetically sealed.

Sealed-double-glazing units are usually used to reduce heat transfer from the warm side to the cold side, i.e. to prevent the heat from a heated room escaping to the cooler outdoors. The width of the cavity spacer and the presence or not of a gas filling or a low-emissivity coating will influence the thermal-insulation properties of the unit. Typical thermal transmittance (U values) are given in *Table 29.6*.

The use of low-emissivity coatings on one of the glasses will further reduce the U value for a given unit constructionl *Table 29.7* indicates U values for units in which one pane is a glass with a coated surface having an emissivity of approximately 0.2. Combining a low-emissivity coating with an argon filled cavity will achieve the U values shown in *Table 29.8*.

When sealed double-glazing units are specified the method of glazing is most important if maximum service life is to be achieved. Manufacturers of units provide detailed instructions on how their units should be glazed and they should not be ignored. Typical glazing details for sealed-double-glazing units in timber or aluminium framing systems are shown in *Figures 29.21* and *29.22*, respectively.

29.4.8 Glass blocks

Glass blocks are made in a variety of patterns, sizes and colours. They are used extensively in Europe and the USA but much less so in the UK. There are many examples of their use in the external skins of buildings as well as for internal walls. A range of light-transmission, acoustic-insulation and thermal-insulation properties is possible. Glass blocks are usually laid in a manner similar to normal building bricks using a sand/lime/cement mortar.

Table 29.7 Typical thermal transmittances (U values) for a unit containing one coated pane*

Airspace width (mm)	U value (W m^{-2} K^{-1})
6	2.7
8	2.4
10	2.1
12	2.0
16	1.7
20	1.7

* Air in cavity; two panes of 4-mm glass one of which is coated (0.2 emissivity).

Table 29.8 Typical thermal transmittance (U values) for a unit containing one coated pane and an argon-filled cavity

Airspace width (mm)	U value (W m^{-2} K^{-1})
6	2.2
8	2.0
10	1.8
12	1.6
16	1.5
20	1.6

* Argon-filled cavity; two panes of 4-mm glass one which is coated (emissivity 0.2).

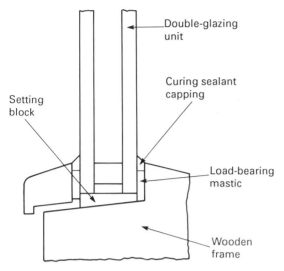

Figure 29.21 Timber frame drained glazing system

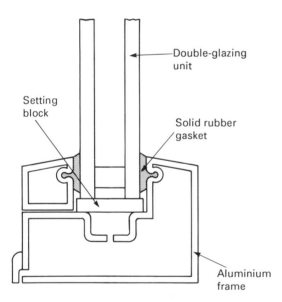

Figure 29.22 Aluminium frame drained glazing system

Blocks are usually rectangular but other shapes are manufactured. Some blocks have interlayers of diffusing materials incorporated. Manufacturers' literature should be consulted for full details of the types available.

29.4.9 Fire-resistant glasses

There are several types of fire-resistant glass available, each having its own advantages and disadvantages. Fire-resistant glasses are capable of providing 60 min of stability and integrity when correctly framed.

29.4.9.1 Wired glass

Wired glass is by far the cheapest of the fire-resistant glasses currently available. The mesh of wires embodied on the glass,

whilst presenting some slight visual obstruction but no distortion, holds the glazed panel together when the glass softens as it approaches temperatures of 650–700°C in the presence of fire. The glass may crack when exposed to a fire, but, because the wire holds the panel together, flame and smoke are contained on the fire side of the glazing. Wired glass is available in large panes and may be cut to size on site if necessary.

29.4.9.2 Laminated float glass with gel interlayers

This approach to fire resistance involves the use of multiple laminates of glass and transparent gel interlayers. When a suitably glazed panel of such glass is exposed to the heat of a fire, the gel begins to intumesce to create a rigid opaque barrier to smoke and flame. In this way containment of the fire is achieved. *Figure 29.23* shows such a glass before and after exposure to a fire. In addition to providing protection from smoke and flame the intumescent layer(s) provide protection from radiation from the heat source. These glasses must be cut to size by the manufacturer.

29.4.9.3 Prestressed borosilicate glass

This special glass must be made to size to order. It is a special glass composition which can withstand fire conditions without cracking. There are size limitations, the maximum size usually being 1.2 m × 2 m.

29.4.9.4 Toughened calcium/silica float glass

This is a toughened glass of special composition. The toughening is achieved by an abnormal heating and cooling process. The glass has to be manufactured to size. Special glazing methods are required for fire-resistant glazing if the fire-rating benefits are to be achieved (see *Figure 29.24*).

29.4.9.5 Glass blocks

Glass blocks can be used to provide fire resistance, particularly when they are incorporated in reinforced-concrete panels. For precise information on the degree of protection given by these potential solutions to fire problems the manufacturers' literature

Figure 29.23 Fire-protection glass with intumescent laminate before and after exposure to fire

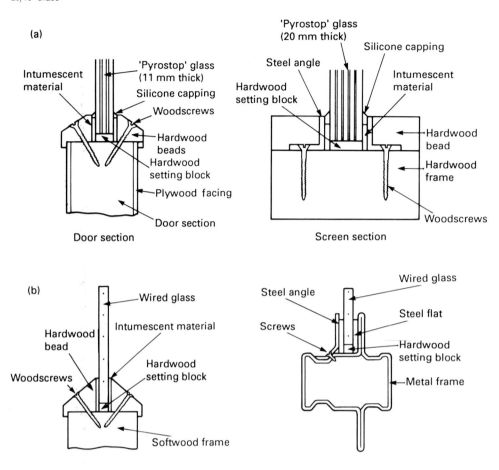

Figure 29.24 Typical fixing arrangements for fire-resistant glasses. (a) Pyrostop glass. (b) Wired glass

must be consulted since there are often limitations on the degree of protection afforded.

29.5 Structural glazing

Glass has been used successfully as a structural material for the last 25 years. Systems have been devised which allow toughened-glass plates to be assembled to create continuous glass facades without the use of mullions and transoms.

The toughened-glass plates are usually either bolted together using special metal patch fittings at their corners or by using special bolts through countersunk holes at the corners of the glass plates. In some cases the assembly is suspended from the building structure and given lateral stability and resistance to wind loading by means of glass stiffening fins attached at the junctions of plates. In other examples the glass plates are attached to a space frame or direct to the building structure. The joints between adjoining plates are sealed with a suitable silicone sealant.

Any angle of slope from vertical to horizontal can be accommodated by choosing an appropriate system. Single vertical assemblies up to 23 m (75 in.) in height have been designed. By using multiple assemblies any height is possible;

there are no limitations on length. Some typical examples of glass used as a structural material are shown in *Figures 29.25* and *29.26*.

29.6 Cutting of glass

Up to a certain thickness, about 10 mm, glass is usually cut by scoring with a diamond or tungsten carbide point or wheel, followed by snapping off along the scored line. Sometimes the cutting/scoring tool is hand held, but frequently it is automatic and an integral part of a piece of manufacturing or processing equipment. The cut edge resulting from this method of cutting is often satisfactory for the intended final use of the piece of cut glass. It may, however, be necessary to 'smooth' the cut edge by using arrising, i.e. grinding the cut edges at 45° to the glass faces to remove the sharp edges.

Where the edge of the glass is to be permanently exposed there are a variety of edge finishes based on grinding and polishing. These include

(1) flat ground edge;
(2) round edge;
(3) bevelled edge; and
(4) bull-nosed edge.

Figure 29.25   Structural glazing: Louisiana Downs Racetrack, USA

Figure 29.26   Structural glazing: Hays Wharf, London, UK

The edges can be left in a matt ground finish or they can be highly polished. Glasses thicker than 10 mm are difficult if not impossible to cut by scoring and snapping techniques. They are usually nibbled or nipped to size followed, if necessary, by grinding and polishing. Alternatively, glass may be cut by means of a diamond saw which gives a smooth matt surface which may, if necessary, be arrised, ground or polished. For complex shapes such as holes, irregularly shaped pieces, etc., a water-jet cutter can be used. Individual processors and suppliers have different ranges of equipment at their disposal and they should be consulted in order to establish the availability of products.

29.7 Specification of glass

Arriving at the correct glass specification for a specific application involves consideration of a large number of factors many of which are set out in codes of practice, standards and legislation.

For example, the size of a window may be restricted by legislation aimed at energy efficiency or the constraint could be the thickness of glass required to withstand wind loadings. If the glass is patterned it may not be made in the desired pattern in the thickness dictated by wind loading or other considerations. Each country has its own codes of practice, standards and legislation, and it is essential that the specifier ensures that all the relevant requirements are complied with.

Manufacturers and suppliers sometimes use different terminology which further adds to the confusion in the mind of the specifiers. It is most important that the specifier has a clear idea of what is required of a piece of glass, whether it is decorative, providing solar control, providing security, providing acoustic insulation or performing a structural role in the building, when a manufacturer or supplier is to be approached for advice.

29.8 Standards

There are many codes, standards, specifications, regulations, etc., which influence the use of glass in construction. The list which follows should be taken as a good indication of the type and range of documents available, but should certainly not be regarded as exhaustive.

British Standards Institution

BS 476, Fire tests on building materials and structures
BS 476: Part 3: 1975, External fire exposure roof test (Building Regulations call up 1958)
BS 476: Part 4: 1970, Non-combustibility test for materials
BS 476: Part 5: 1979, Method of test for ignitability
BS 476: Part 6: 1981, Method of test for fire propagation for products
BS 476: Part 7: 1971, Surface spread of flame tests for materials
BS 476: Part 8: 1972, Test methods and criteria for fire resistance of elements of building construction
BS 476: Part 10: 1983, Guide to the principles and application of fire testing
BS 476: Part 11: 1983, Method for assessing the heat emission from building materials
BS 476: Part 13: 1987, Method of measuring the ignitability of products subjected to thermal irradiance
BS 476: Part 20: 1987, Method of determination of the fire resistance of elements of construction (general principles)
BS 476: Part 21: 1987, Methods for determination of the fire resistance of loadbearing elements of construction
BS 476: Part 22: 1987, Methods for determination of the fire resistance of non-loadbearing elements of construction
BS 476: Part 23: 1987, Methods for determination of the contribution of components to the fire resistance of a structure
BS 476: Part 24: 1987, Method for determination of the fire resistance for ventilation ducts
BS 644
BS 644: Part 2: 1985, Wood double hung sash windows
BS 952: Glass for glazing
BS 952: Part 1: 1978, Classification
BS 952: Part 2: 1980, Terminology for work on glass
BS 1285: 1980, Specification for wood surrounds for steel windows and doors
BS 2649, Methods for analysis of glass
BS 2649: Part 1: 1955, Recommended procedure for the analysis of glasses of the soda-lime–magnesium-silica type
BS 2975: 1958, Sand for making colourless glasses
BS 3180: 1980, Specification for limestone for making colourless glasses
BS 3193: 1967, Specification for glass components for domestic appliances

BS 3447: 1962, Glossary of terms used in the glass industry
BS 4315, Methods of test for resistance to air and water penetration
BS 4315: Part 1: 1968, Windows and structural gasket-glazing systems
BS 4873: 1986, Aluminium alloy windows
BS 5051, Security glazing
BS 5051: Part 1: 1973, Bullet resistant glazing for interior use
BS 5051: Part 2: 1979, Specification for bullet resistant glazing for exterior use
BS 5286: 1978, Specification for aluminium framed sliding glass doors
BS 5357: 1976, Code of practice for the installation of security glazing
BS 5368, Methods of testing windows
BS 5368: Part 1: 1976, Air permeability windows
BS 5366: Part 2: 1980, Weathertightness test under static pressure
BS 5368: Part 3: 1978, Wind resistance tests
BS 5368: Part 4: 1978, Form of test report
BS 5516: 1977, Code of practice for patent glazing
BS 5544: 1978, Specification for anti-bandit glazing (glazing resistant to manual attack)
BS 5588, Fire precautions in the design and construction of buildings
BS 5588: Part 1: 1984, Section 1.1, Code of practice for single-family dwelling houses
BS 5588: Part 2: 1985, Code of practice for shops
BS 5588: Part 3: 1983, Code of practice for office buildings
BS 5655: Part 6: 1985, Code of practice for selection and installation (lifts and service lifts)
BS 5713: 1979, Specification for hermetically sealed flat double glazing units
BS 5750, Quality systems
BS 5750: Part 2: 1979, Specification for manufacture and installation
BS 6180: 1982, Protective barriers in and about buildings
BS 6262: 1982, Code of practice for glazing for buildings
BS 6375, Performance of windows
BS 6375: Part 1: 1983, Classsification for weathertightness
BS 6375: Part 2: 1987, Specification for operation and strength characteristics
BS 6399, Loading for buildings
BS 6399: Part 1: 1984, Code of practice for dead and imposed loads
BS 6399: Part 3: 1987, Code of practice for snow loads
BS 6510: 1984, Specification for steel windows, sills, window boards and doors
BS 8220, Guide for security of buildings against crime
BS 8220: Part 1: 1986, Dwellings
BS 8220: Part 2: 1987, Offices and shops
CP 3, Code of basic design of buildings
CP 3: Chapter 3: 1972, Sound insulation and noise reduction
CP 3: Chapter 4: Part 1: 1971, Precautions against fire: flats and maisonettes (in blocks over two storeys)
CP 3: Chapter 5: Part 2: 1972, Loading: wind loads
CP 153, Windows and rooflights
CP 153: Part 1: 1969, Cleaning and safety
CP 153: Part 2: 1970, Durability and maintenance
CP 153: Part 3: 1972, Sound insulation
PD 6512, Use of elements of structural fire protection with particular reference to the recommendations given in BS 5588
PD 6512: Part 3: 1987, Guide to the fire performance of glass

International Organization for Standardization

ISO 834: 1975, Fire resistance tests—elements of building construction

ISO 3009: 1976, Fire-resistance tests—glazed elements

ISO 6612: 1980, Windows and door height windows—wind resistance tests

ISO 6613: 1980, Windows and door height windows—air permeability test

ISO 8248: 1985, Windows and door height windows—mechanical tests

ISO 6781: 1983, Thermal insulation—qualitative detection of thermal iregularities in building envelopes—infrared method

ISO 6946-1: 1986, Thermal insulation—calculation methods. Part 1: Steady state thermal properties of building components and building elements

ISO 6946-2: 1986, Thermal insulation—calculation methods. Part 2: Thermal bridges of rectangular sections in plane structures

ISO 7345: 1987, Thermal insulation—physical quantities and definitions

ISO/TR 9165: 1988, Practical thermal properties of building materials and products

ISO 9251: 1987, Thermal insulation—heat transfer conditions and properties of materials—vocabulary

ISO 9346: 1987, Thermal insulation—mass transfer—physical quantities and definitions

American Specifications and Standards

Federal Specification DD-G-45 ID—for primary glass

Federal Specification DD-G-1403B—for tempered glass

Federal Standard 16 CFR 1201—for safety

ANSI 297.1-1975—for safety

ASTM E-6 P3, P2 and P3—for double glazing

Federal Specification DD-M-411—for mirrors

30

Mineral-Fibre Products

P M Smith
Eurosil: UK Mineral Wool Association

Contents

30.1 Introduction 30/3
    30.1.1 History 30/3
    30.1.2 Definitions and types 30/3
    30.1.3 Principal structural applications 30/3

30.2 Sources 30/3
    30.2.1 UK manufacturers 30/3
    30.2.2 Distribution of products 30/3
    30.2.3 Blown mineral wool 30/3

30.3 Manufacturing process 30/4
    30.3.1 Raw materials 30/4
    30.3.2 The manufacturing processes 30/4
    30.3.3 The finishing process 30/4
    30.3.4 Supplementary on-line processes 30/4
    30.3.5 Off-line finishing 30/5

30.4 Types 30/5
    30.4.1 Introduction to range 30/5

30.5 Roll products 30/5
    30.5.1 Unfaced lightweight rolls (general purpose) 30/5
    30.5.2 Cladding rolls 30/5
    30.5.3 Timber frame rolls (faced, flanged) 30/6
    30.5.4 Partition rolls (acoustic) 30/6
    30.5.5 Sound-deadening rolls 30/6
    30.5.6 Stitched-wire mattresses 30/6
    30.5.7 Duct wraps 30/6

30.6 Batt and slab products 30/6
    30.6.1 Timber-frame batts 30/6
    30.6.2 Cavity-wall batts (slabs): full-fill 30/6
    30.6.3 Cavity-wall batts (slabs): partial-fill 30/6
    30.6.4 Intermediate-floor slabs (acoustic) 30/7
    30.6.5 Ground-floor slabs (thermal) 30/7
    30.6.6 Flat roofing slabs 30/7
    30.6.7 Thermal/acoustic slabs (general purpose) 30/7
    30.6.8 Duct slabs 30/7
    30.6.9 Fire protection slabs 30/7
    30.6.10 Decorative lining panels 30/7

30.7 Miscellaneous products 30/7
    30.7.1 Blowing wool 30/7
    30.7.2 Laminated dry linings 30/7
    30.7.3 Ceiling tiles 30/8
    30.7.4 Sleeved cavity barriers 30/8

30.8 Chemical composition and properties 30/8
    30.8.1 Chemical composition 30/8
    30.8.2 Chemical properties 30/8

30.9 Physical properties (general) 30/8
    30.9.1 Structure and appearance 30/8
    30.9.2 Water repellancy 30/10
    30.9.3 Biological properties 30/10
    30.9.4 Permanence 30/10
    30.9.5 Handling and cutting 30/10

30.10 Thermal properties 30/10
    30.10.1 Definition of terms 30/10
    30.10.2 General principles of heat transfer 30/10
    30.10.3 Mineral-wool products as insulators 30/10
    30.10.4 Factors affecting thermal conductivity 30/11

30.11 Acoustic properties 30/11
    30.11.1 Terminology and definitions 30/11
    30.11.2 Principles of noise control 30/12
    30.11.3 Sound absorption 30/12
    30.11.4 Sound insulation 30/12

30.12 Fire properties 30/14
    30.12.1 General 30/14
    30.12.2 Fire ratings 30/14
    30.12.3 Fire performance 30/15
    30.12.4 Fire-protection requirements 30/15
    30.12.5 Applications of mineral wool 30/15

30.13 Standards and approvals 30/16
    30.13.1 British and International Standards 30/16
    30.13.2 CEN standards 30/16
    30.13.3 Building Regulations 30/17
    30.13.4 Agrément Certificates 30/17
    30.13.5 Fitness of materials 30/17

30.14 Usage and 'abusage' 30/17
    30.14.1 Introduction 30/17
    30.14.2 Roofs 30/17
    30.14.3 Walls 30/18
    30.14.4 Ground floors 30/19
    30.14.5 Acoustic applications 30/19
    30.14.6 Fire-protection applications 30/19

30.15 Proprietary brand examples 30/20

References 30/21

30.1 Introduction

30.1.1 History

Man-made mineral-fibre products have been made in the UK since the late 1880s, and in significant and increasing quantities for almost 50 years. From the early days, when relatively small quantities of crude mineral-fibre products were used almost exclusively as lagging for high temperature industrial plant, the industry has grown to a multi-billion tonne per annum, world-wide operation producing a range of different fibres to satisfy a wide variety of applications.

In addition to the insulation of all types of industrial plant and commercial equipment, man-made mineral-fibre products today include: continuous-filament glass fibres used primarily for reinforcement in a range of rubber, plastic and cement-based products; woven-glass cloths for the textile industry, small-diameter glass fibres for aircraft insulation and filtration purposes; ceramic fibres produced from refractory materials and used for very-high-temperature insulation applications; rock-fibre products used in horticulture as a growing medium and for general soil conditioning; and in their role as thermal and acoustic insulation in fridges, freezers, cookers and a whole range of 'white' goods, they are now an essential part of everyday life in almost every home in the civilized world.

It was the building and construction industry, however, that was primarily responsible for the significant increase in mineral-fibre production. The first major boost came in 1945 when, following the end of World War II, the demand for quickly erected, low cost, housing brought about a boom in lightweight prefabricated dwellings. Unlike traditional brick structures, this prefabricated construction provided no inherent thermal performance and, in order to improve living conditions, and thus protect the health and safety of the occupants, regulations were introduced requiring the inclusion of insulation in the outer skin of the dwelling.

At this stage most structural products still relied on the same bitumen bonding techniques which had been used since the turn of the century. In the mid-1950s, however, the formulation of special resin binders heralded a significant advance in manufacturing technology allowing increased production levels, more control over product characteristics, and vastly improved handling qualities.

Since the 1950s successive changes to the Building Regulations have steadily increased the levels of insulation required in buildings, initially for health and safety reasons and, with effect from the 1985 Regulations, to conserve energy. The latest technology advancements have therefore been primarily geared to increasing production to meet the ever increasing market demand.

30.1.2 Definitions and types

'Mineral fibre' is a generic term encompassing all non-metallic inorganic fibres—a fibre being a particle with a length greater than 5 μm and at least three times its diameter. Although mineral fibres occur naturally, for most modern-day applications the natural varieties have now been largely superseded by man-made alternatives.

30.1.2.1 Naturally occurring mineral fibres

Mineral fibres occur naturally as asbestos, a group of complex silicates which may contain iron, magnesium, calcium, sodium, etc., and which occur in veins as fibrous crystals. These crystals are unique in that they are capable of splitting longitudinally, when crushed, to form fibrils with diameters of much less than 1 μm (typically 0.03–0.04 μm).

30.1.2.2 Man-made mineral fibres

These are fibres manufactured primarily from glass, rock or other minerals, or from readily melted slags. These fibres cannot split longitudinally and, therefore, the diameter is fixed at the time of manufacture. Any breakage of the fibre takes place transversely, affecting length but not diameter. In the context of the construction industry, man-made mineral wool fibres are used primarily for thermal and acoustic insulation. The two most common types, which are generally referred to as 'mineral wools' because of their soft, woolly consistency, are:

(1) glass wool, a mineral wool made from glass (usually borosilicate glass) with a mean fibre diameter of 4–9 μm; and
(2) rock wool, a mineral wool made from naturally occurring igneous rock (such as basalt or diabase) with a mean fibre diameter of 4–9 μm.

30.1.3 Principal structural applications

Mineral-wool insulating products are available in a variety of forms, including rolls, batts and slabs for general use, preformed sections for pipe covering and loose wool for pouring or blowing applications. The products are used extensively in the construction industry for thermal and acoustic insulation in buildings, and for acoustic isolation of building elements (particularly floors). They provide thermal and acoustic insulation for heating, ventilating and air-conditioning systems and associated equipment, and are used in the manufacture of sound havens around noisy equipment and machinery. Mineral wools are particularly suitable for fire-stopping and general fire-protection applications, and special grades are available which meet the requirements for large and small cavity barriers.

30.2 Sources

30.2.1 UK manufacturers

Approximately 90% of all mineral-wool insulation in the UK is manufactured by the three member companies of Eurisol (the UK Mineral Wool Association): Gyproc Insulation Limited (glass wool only); Pilkington Insulation Limited (glass and rock wool); and Rockwool Limited (rock wool only). The remaining 10% or so is supplied by a number of other UK and European based manufacturers.

30.2.2 Distribution of products

Mineral-wool roll and batt (slab) products are supplied in the UK almost exclusively via specialist insulation distributors, builders merchants, and do-it-yourself (DIY) outlets. Product delivery direct from the manufacturers is generally only available to larger insulation converters and specialist end-users.

30.2.3 Blown mineral wool

Mineral-wool products for injection into external wall cavities are available only on a supply and install basis by manufacturer licensed insulation contractors. Such contractors must:

(1) be fully trained by the manufacturer to a standard approved by the Department of the Environment;
(2) operate a method of installation and maintain a standard of workmanship as approved by the British Board of Agrément; and
(3) be subject to regular checks by the manufacturer and British Board of Agrément Inspectors.

30.3 Manufacturing process

30.3.1 Raw materials

30.3.1.1 Glass wool

The principal raw material used in the manufacture of glass wool is silica or silicon dioxide—the most abundant mineral in the earth's crust—which is derived from sand or sandstone. To the sand is added an alkali, in the form usually of either sodium or potassium oxides, which improves the flow characteristics and reduces the melting temperature of the glass batch. Lime and alumina are added to stabilize the fibres and reduce the tendency to devitrification. Boric oxide and zinc oxide are added to improve the melting characteristics and viscosity of the glass.

30.3.1.2 Rock wool

Rock-wool materials are generally manufactured from naturally occurring volcanic rock (diabase), mixed with dolomite (a limestone type rock), to which coke and limestone are added to improve the characteristics and to reduce the melting temperature of the batch.

30.3.2 The manufacturing processes

The processes for producing mineral wool products from glass or rock are essentially similar, involving the conversion of molten raw materials into fibres or filaments, which are then processed to form the finished products. The melting characteristics of the basic raw materials are, however, different and require different fiberizing techniques, as follows.

30.3.2.1 Glass-wool process

After weighing and mixing, the raw materials and other ingredients pass into a furnace, where they are reduced to a molten state at temperatures of around 1350°C. From the forehearth of the furnace a stream of molten glass then flows by gravity from a bushing into a rapidly rotating steel-alloy dish which has many hundreds of fine apertures around its periphery. Glass is thrown out through these apertures by centrifugal force to form filaments which are extended further by a high-velocity blast of hot gas (*Figure 30.2*).

30.3.2.2 Rock-wool process

The raw materials are weighed and, together with coke, which acts as a fuel, pass into a special cupola furnace. Preheated air is then blasted through a series of holes near the base of the cupola, which burns the coke, driving the temperature up to a point at which the raw materials melt and combine. The molten rock flows out of the cupola at a temperature of around 1500°C into spinning wheels, which fling it off and convert it into a mass of fibres (*Figure 30.1*).

In each case the fibres are cooled and then sprayed with heat-activated bonding agents, oils and other additives, as they fall under turbulence, to be collected on a moving suction conveyor. The speed of the conveyor is controlled to adjust the weight of fibre deposited per square metre. The 'mat' then passes into a curing oven (or tempering furnace) with adjustable upper and lower pressure rollers, which set the required product thickness as the bonding agents are heat cured. By adjusting the conveyor speed and pressure-roller setting, the thickness and the density of the product are set. The mat as it leaves the curing oven is, therefore, in its final form, subject only to cutting and trimming, and the application of any facings which may be required.

30.3.3 The finishing process

After leaving the curing oven, the mat passes through a series of rotating saws which trim the edges and cut the product to the required width. Any on-line facings are then applied using either cold glue or hot-melt adhesive techniques. The products are then cut to length and finally pass into automated packaging equipment, from which the rolls or batts (slabs) emerge wrapped, labelled and ready for despatch.

30.3.4 Supplementary on-line processes

At some point in the manufacturing process, depending upon the configuration of the manufacturing line, uncured wool or cured wool mat may be diverted into a supplementary processing line for special finishing. Such operations would include:

(1) 'Blowing' wool, which is produced in 'granulated' or 'pelleted' form suitable for blowing under pressure through a hose and small-diameter nozzle. The line may be diverted

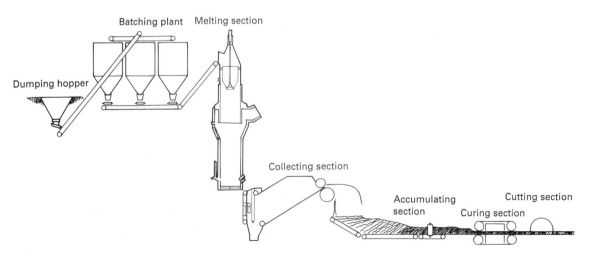

Figure 30.1 Typical rock-wool manufacturing process

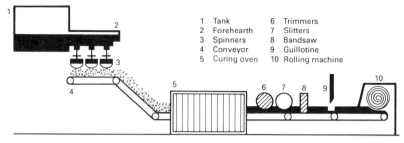

1	Tank	6	Trimmers
2	Forehearth	7	Slitters
3	Spinners	8	Bandsaw
4	Conveyor	9	Guillotine
5	Curing oven	10	Rolling machine

Figure 30.2 Typical glass-wool-manufacturing process

Figure 30.3 A selection of mineral wool insulation products

either before the mat leaves the collection chamber, or at some other point along the manufacturing line.

(2) Rigid sections, which are produced by rolling the uncured mat on a mandrel to the required thickness, and then passing through a separate curing chamber, prior to trimming and splitting. The line in this case is normally diverted immediately prior to the on-line curing oven (tempering furnace).

30.3.5 Off-line finishing

For certain specialized products, finishing is carried out off-line, as a secondary process. These products include:

(1) Mineral-wool laminates for dry-lining applications. These are mineral-wool slabs bonded to plasterboard, polyurethane or other rigid materials.

(2) Mineral-wool slabs and rolls with special facings (metallized and special plastic materials) for predominantly heating, ventilating and air conditioning (HVAC) applications.

(3) Mineral-wool lamella rolls, which are mineral-wool slabs cut into strips and rebonded on edge onto a suitable backing medium, used for HVAC applications requiring higher compression resistance.

(4) Stitched-wire mattresses, which are mineral-wool rolls 'stitched' to wire netting, and are used for high-temperature lagging and for large cavity barriers.

30.4 Types

30.4.1 Introduction to range

The versatility of the basic manufacturing process coupled with an almost endless choice of facings and secondary treatments, means that the range of product possibilities for mineral wool is very wide (*Figure 30.3*). Products are generally available in thicknesses of 13–200 mm, a choice of widths of up to 1200 mm (although in theory this can be increased to 1800 or 2400 mm depending on the width of the production line) and a wide range of densities up to 200 kg m^{-3} (10–150 kg m^{-3} is the normal range for structural applications). The product can be supplied either as loose wool, or in mat form as batts (slabs), rolls or preformed sections. If required, a wide range of standard and special facings can also be applied, using either hot or cold adhesion techniques, or by mechanical fixing (stitching). The following sections provide a guide to the main types of mineral-wool products and their applications in the construction industry. Because of the multipurpose nature of certain products, and the almost infinite variety of 'special' products the list should not be regarded as fully comprehensive.

30.5 Roll products

30.5.1 Unfaced lightweight rolls (general purpose)

Lightweight unfaced rolls of low-density mineral wool (10–12 kg m^{-3} for glass wool and 23–30 kg m^{-3} for rock wool) are typically used for domestic loft insulation but are also widely used for general thermal- and acoustic-insulation applications. Specific applications include insulation in timber frame external and internal walls, partitions and suspended ceilings, timber ventilated ground and intermediate floors, and industrial roofs and walls. Products are manufactured in accordance with BS 5803: Part 1,[1] carry BSI Kitemark certification and are non-combustible to BS 476: Part 4.[2] The rolls are available in thicknesses of 60–200 mm and in widths to suit all standard stud/joint spacings. The minimum thermal conductivity of this material is 0.04 W m^{-1} K^{-1} giving thermal resistance values of 2.0–5.0 m^2 K W^{-1}.

30.5.2 Cladding rolls

These are lightweight, flexible mineral-wool rolls for thermal and acoustic insulation and fire protection in lightweight metal-cladded industrial roof and wall systems. The density range is 10–12 kg m^{-3} for glass-wool and 23–33 kg m^{-3} for rock-wool products. The material is generally manufactured with improved tensile strength characteristics for use in long vertical drops, and available with facings of paper or foil for additional strength. Unfaced rolls are non-combustible to BS 476: Part 4.[2] The rolls are available in thicknesses of 60–100 mm and standard widths of 1000 and 1200 mm (variations are also available to suit different systems). The typical thermal conductivity of this material is 0.04 W m^{-1} K^{-1}, giving thermal resistance values of 1.5–2.5 m^2 K W^{-1} or better.

30.5.3 Timber frame rolls (faced, flanged)

These are lightweight rolls of low-density mineral wool (10.5–12 kg m^{-3} for glass wool and 23–30 kg m^{-3} for rock wool), unfaced or faced on one side with paper, polythene or aluminium foil laminate. The facing materials are wider than the rolls, and form fixing flanges of equal width along both roll edges. The material is typically used for thermal and acoustic insulation of timber frame external walls, but may be used for rafter-level insulation of pitched roofs and for insulation of cold flat-roof constructions. The basic mineral-wool mat is non-combustible to BS 476: Part 4,[2] and the aluminium-foil facing is class 1 surface spread of flame to BS 476: Part 7.[3] Polythene and aluminium-foil facings constitute vapour barriers to BS 2972.[4] The material is available in thicknesses of 60–200 mm and widths of 370 and 570 mm. The nominal thermal conductivity of this material is 0.04 W m^{-1} K^{-1}, giving thermal resistance values of 1.5–5.0 m^2 K W^{-1}.

30.5.4 Partition rolls (acoustic)

These are lightweight mineral-wool rolls designed specifically for acoustic insulation in timber and metal stud partitions and separating walls. Glass-wool rools are of 10.5–12 kg m^{-3} nominal density and unfaced. Rock-wool rolls are of 23–48 kg m^{-3} density and may be enclosed and wire stitched in fire-retardant scrim cloth. All products are non-combustible to BS 476: Part 4[2] and are class 0 as defined in the Building Regulations. The material is available in thicknesses of 25 and 50 mm and widths of 600, 900 and 1200 mm. The typical noise-reduction coefficient is 0.50–0.90 over the range 125–4000 Hz, which is comparable with the performance of acoustic ceiling tiles and other specialized acoustic products.

30.5.5 Sound-deadening rolls

These are medium density (36 kg m^{-3}) glass-wool rolls faced on one side with kraft paper or kraft paper/polythene laminate. The facing material is wider than the rolls and forms a flange along one edge only which is for joint sealing purposes. The material is specifically designed for impact sound deadening in concrete base intermediate separating floors with either timber or screed floating layers. The products provide isolation between the walking surface and supporting structure and have good compression resistance and resilience to withstand long-term cyclic floor loadings. The material satisfies resilient-layer specifications (flexible material) for 'floor type 2: concrete base' (with floating layer), as contained in Approved Document E1/2/3 to the Building Regulations 1985.[5] The thicknesses (uncompressed) available are 13 and 25 mm, and width 1200 mm.

30.5.6 Stitched-wire mattresses

These are medium- to high-density mineral-wool rolls for use as smoke and fire barriers, and as large and small cavity barriers as defined in Appendix G8 of Approved Document B to the Building Regulations 1985.[5] The rolls are faced on one side with 25-mm galvanized wire mesh, stitched through the mat with strong single-strand wire, and are generally available with an optional aluminium-foil facing below the wire mesh for additional smoke protection. Non-combustible to BS 476: Part 4,[2] these products can be used to achieve 0.5-h or 1-h fire resistance to BS 476: Part 22.[6] The material is available in a thickness of 50 mm and widths of 600, 900 and 1200 mm.

30.5.7 Duct wraps

These are low- and medium-density (16–24 kg m^{-3} for glass wool and 48 kg m^{-3} for rock wool) flexible rolls for thermal and acoustic insulation of heating, ventilating and air conditioning (HVAC) ductwork and large-diameter pipework operating at temperatures of up to 230°C. The products are available unfaced (plain) or with a bright aluminium foil facing which provides both a vapour barrier to BS 5422,[7] and a class 0 finish as defined in the Building Regulations.[5] The basic mat is non-combustible to BS 476: Part 4.[2] The basic mat and facing provide class 1 surface spread of flame rating to BS 476: Part 7.[3] The products are available in average thicknesses of 25–100 mm and standard 1000 or 1200 mm widths.

30.6 Batt and slab products

30.6.1 Timber-frame batts

These are lightweight unfaced low-density (12 kg m^{-3} for glass wool and 23 kg m^{-3} for rock wool) batts (slabs) for thermal and acoustic insulation in timber-frame buildings. They are designed primarily for thermal insulation in external-wall panels, but also suitable for roofs and ventilated timber floors, and acoustic insulation in partition and separating walls. The batts are designed to friction-fit between studs at 400/600 mm centres and sized such that two batts, end-on-end, fit standard storey height without cutting. The material is non-combustible to BS 476: Part 4.[2] Thicknesses range from 80 to 200 mm for batt dimensions 1170 mm long and 370 or 570 mm wide. The typical thermal conductivity of this material is 0.04 W m^{-1} K^{-1} giving thermal-resistance values of 2.0–5.0 m^2 K W^{-1}.

30.6.2 Cavity-wall batts (slabs): full-fill

These are semi-rigid unfaced mineral-wool batts (slabs) for use as thermal insulation and fire stopping in new external masonry cavity walls. The batts are designed to be built into the wall during construction. The products are treated during manufacture with a special water repellant which coats and seals the fibres, preventing water transmission across the product. They are generally assessed by the British Board of Agrément (BBA), and carry BBA all-exposure certificates for buildings up to 12 or 25 m in height. The material is non-combustible to BS 476: Part 4.[2] The product is available in thicknesses of 50–150 mm and in dimensions 900 × 455 mm and 1200 × 455 mm (1200 × 405 mm for modular metric brickwork). The thermal conductivity is in the range 0.034–0.037 W m^{-1} K^{-1}, giving thermal-resistance values of 1.39–4.05 m^2 K W^{-1}.

30.6.3 Cavity-wall batts (slabs): partial-fill

These are similar to full-fill cavity-wall batts (slabs), but are designed to partially fill the external wall cavity, retaining a 50 mm nominal airspace between the insulation and the outer leaf. Built into the wall cavity during construction, the batts (slabs) are retained securely against the inner masonry leaf using insulation retaining wall ties or other fixings as recommended by the manufacturer. Products are water-repellant treated (as full-fill batts). Generally assessed by the British Board of Agrément, they carry BBA all-exposure certificates for buildings up to 25 m in height. The material is non-combustible to BS

476: Part 4.[2] The product is available in thicknesses of 30–100 mm and in dimensions 1200×455 mm (1200×405 mm for modular metric brickwork). The thermal conductivity of the material is 0.33–0.34 W m^{-1} K^{-1} giving thermal resistance values of 0.91–1.32 m^2 K W^{-1}.

30.6.4 Intermediate-floor slabs (acoustic)

These are high-density (approximately 64 kg m^{-3} for glass wool and 100 kg m^{-3} for rock wool) unfaced slabs designed specifically for impact sound deadening in timber-base intermediate separating floors. The products are designed to isolate completely the walking surface from the building structure, and have high compression resistance and resilience to withstand floor loadings. The materials satisfy resilient-layer specifications for 'floor type 3A: platform floor' with absorbent blanket, as contained in Approved Document E1/2/3 to the Building Regulations 1985.[5] The slabs are available in thicknesses (uncompressed) of from 25 mm, and in slab dimensions of 600×900 mm and 600×1200 mm.

30.6.5 Ground-floor slabs (thermal)

These are high-density (75 kg m^{-3} for glass wool and 140–200 kg m^{-3} for rock wool) unfaced slabs designed specifically for the thermal insulation of concrete-base ground floors with either screed or chipboard covering. The products offer low compressibility to withstand loadings associated with ground-floor constructions. The materials are class 0 to Building Regulations[5] and class 1 surface spread of flame to BS 476: Part 7.[3] The slabs are available in thicknesses (uncompressed) of 25–100 mm, and slab dimensions of 600×900 mm and 600×1200 mm. The average thermal conductivity is 0.034 W m^{-1} K^{-1}, giving thermal resistance values of 0.74–2.94 m^2 K^{-1} W^{-1}.

30.6.6 Flat-roofing slabs

These are very high-density mineral-wool slabs (generally rock wool), specifically for thermal and acoustic insulation of metal-, concrete- or timber-deck flat roofs, for installation between the roof deck and the weathering surface. The slabs are supplied either unfaced or with a special glass tissue facing which reduces bitumen uptake and improves bonding. The slabs are also supplied in tapered form, where necessary, to provide roof falls. The slabs have high compression resistance to withstand normal roof traffic, are dimensionally stable and have good laminar strength to resist wind uplift forces. This product is designed with high thermal capacity to minimize thermal shock and prevent damage to water-proof membrane. The products offer very high levels of fire protection and easily achieve class 0 to Buildings Regulations.[5] The product is available in thicknesses of 30–100 mm, and slab sizes of 600×1200 mm and 890×1200 mm (depending on type). The material has a thermal conductivity of 0.036 W m^{-1} K^{-1}.

30.6.7 Thermal/acoustic slabs (general purpose)

These mineral-wool batts (slabs) are available in a wide range of densities (16–140 kg m^{-3} depending on type), for general building use including thermal/acoustic insulation of partitions and wall-lining systems, suspended ceilings, floors, etc. Performance and characteristics depend on density and type of batt slab. The slabs are available in thicknesses of 25–100 mm and dimensions of 1200×600 mm, 900×600 mm and 1170×570 mm.

30.6.8 Duct slabs

These are semi-rigid and rigid mineral wool batts (slabs) in the density range 16–48 kg m^{-3}. The slabs are designed for thermal and acoustic insulation of HVAC rectangular duct work and associated equipment operating generally at temperatures up to 230°C. The products are available unfaced (plain) or with a bright aluminium-foil facing which provides both a vapour barrier to BS 5422[7] and a class 0 finish as defined in Building Regulations.[5] All surfaces provide class 1 spread of flame rating to BS 476: Part 7.[3] The slabs are available in thicknesses of 25–100 mm and in dimensions of 1200×600 mm. The thermal conductivity of the material is in the range 0.031–0.038 W m^{-1} K^{-1} at 10°C.

30.6.9 Fire-protection slabs

These high density (110 kg m^{-3}) rigid rock-wool slabs are designed for the fire protection of structural steel work in buildings. The slabs are specially formulated and resin impregnated to enhance fire performance, and are suitable for continuous operation at temperatures up to 825°C. The slabs are generally supplied unfaced, but are also available with foil facing for improved water vapour resistance. The product is non-combustible to BS 476: Part 4,[2] with class 1 surface spread of flame to BS 476: Part 7.[3] The slabs will provide up to 4 h fire protection when tested in accordance with BS 476: Part 8.[8] The slabs are available in thicknesses of 25–75 mm and dimensions of 900×600 mm. The thermal conductivity of the material is 0.037 W m^{-1} K^{-1} at 50°C.

30.6.10 Decorative lining panels

These are rigid, medium-density (32 kg m^{-3}) glass-wool slabs, with a white embossed PVC facing to one surface. The panels are installed in grid systems to provide decorative thermal and acoustic internal linings to roofs, ceilings and walls in industrial buildings. The products comply with class 0 criteria of Building Regulations[5] on both faces. The panels are available in thicknesses of 50–100 mm and dimensions of 1200×600 mm and 1800×600 mm. The thermal conductivity of the material is 0.031 W m^{-1} K^{-1} and the noise-reduction coefficient is 0.82 for a 100-mm thick panel.

30.7 Miscellaneous products

30.7.1 Blowing wool

This is loose mineral wool in granular or pelleted form for the thermal insulation of existing external masonry cavity walls. The wool is injected under pressure using dry techniques. The products bond mechanically to provide a permanent insulating layer which fully and evenly fills the wall cavity. The wool is available either as white wool or with the addition of bonding resins. The products are water-repellent treated and approved by the British Board of Agrément for use in buildings up to 12 m (or 25 m for certain systems) in any exposure zone. The material is non-combustible to BS 476: Part 4,[2] and the products provide a thermal conductivity of 0.04 W m^{-1} K^{-1} when injected at nominal 24 kg m^{-3} density for glass wool and 56 kg m^{-3} for rock wool. These products are available only on a supply and fit basis, via fully trained and approved contractors.

30.7.2 Laminated dry linings

A range of laminated products is available comprising a layer of high-density mineral wool bonded to a facing of vapour-check plasterboard. The products are fixed, using either adhesive or mechanical fixing methods, to the inside of existing masonry walls to improve thermal and acoustic performance. Laminates provide class 0 surfaces as defined in Building Regulations.[5] Performance is dependent on the thickness and grade of plasterboard lining as well as on the thickness of mineral-wool backing.

30.7.3 Ceiling tiles

These are lightweight glass-wool panels with a wide choice of coloured, textured and profiled finishes, available either pressed or as flat-faced slabs. The tiles are designed as decorative lay-in thermal and acoustic insulation panels for exposed-grid suspended-ceiling systems. High-strength, low-weight panels will not warp, sag or shrink, and will retain stability even in conditions of high humidity. All types provide class 1 surface spread of flame to BS 476: Part 7[3] and achieve class 0 requirement to Building Regulations.[5] The nominal panel thickness is 5 mm for pressed tiles and 16–40 mm for flat-face tiles. Nominal panel sizes are 1200 × 600 mm and 600 × 600 mm.

30.7.4 Sleeved cavity barriers

These are flexible strips for low-density mineral wool sealed in double-flanged polythene sleeves. The product is designed to limit the sizes of cavities in the external walls of timber-frame buildings. The sleeves are fixed by stapling through one or both flanges to the timber external-wall frame and retained under compression so as to prevent fire spread via the cavity. They are acceptable as small cavity barriers as defined in Appendix G8(b)(vi) of Approved Document B to the Building Regulations 1985.[5] The product is available in thicknesses of 65 mm (for 50 mm cavities), length 1200 mm; and depshts of 65 mm upwards.

30.8 Chemical composition and properties

30.8.1 Chemical composition

The chemical composition of mineral wool will vary greatly depending on whether it is rock or glass based, and on the particular processes used for its manufacture.

Glass wools are produced from mixtures of minerals and industrial chemicals, selected to produce the final required composition and characteristics. By far the largest component by weight is silica or silicon dioxide (derived from sand), whilst other common mineral additives include limestone, dolomite, feldspar and refined borax. The industrial chemicals most commonly added are sodium carbonate (soda ash) and sodium sulphate (salt cake).

Rock wools, by contrast, are generally prepared from a single suitable mineral raw material, such as basalt or diabase, with the addition of limestone to reduce the melting temperature to an economic level.

The percentage by weight of the main chemical components for typical glass and rock-based insulating wools are shown in *Table 30.1*.

The basic mineral wool is the predominant component of the insulating material, accounting for between 90 and 99.8% of the product by weight. Other components include:

(1) phenol–formaldehyde resins (often modified with urea or lignosulphonates), 10% nominal;
(2) mineral oil, 1% nominal;
(3) silane, 0.02% nominal; and
(4) polydimethylsiloxane (or water repellants based on this), 0.1% nominal.

30.8.2 Chemical properties

30.8.2.1 Chemical resistance

Mineral-wool products are compatible with all common building materials and components, and will not cause corrosion of

Table 30.1 Chemical composition of mineral-wool fibres

Component	Content (wt%)	
	Glass wool	*Rock wool*
Silica (SiO_2)	53–65	45–54
Alumina (Al_2O_3)	2–5	8–15
Titania (TiO_2)	$\leqslant 0.2$	0.6–3
Ferric oxide (Fe_2O_3)	$\leqslant 0.35$	1.8–12.5
Ferrous oxide (FeO)		
Lime (CaO)	6.5–23.5	8–21
Magnesia (MgO)	2–5	3–14
Manganese oxide (MnO)	0.05	0.2
Sodium oxide (Na_2O)	9–18	1.6–16
Potassium oxide (K_2O)	0.8–1.7	0.4–1.6
Boric oxide (B_2O_3)	2–8	$\leqslant 0.2$

structural metals. The products are chemically inert, an aqueous extract being neutral (pH 7) or slightly alkaline. Glass-wool products are not affected by oils, corrosive vapours or most acids (except hydrofluoric and hot phosphoric acids), but may be attacked by alkaline solutions. Calciferous rock-wool products may be affected by acidic solutions and gases.

30.8.2.2 Effect of moisture

Individual mineral-wool fibres are non-cellular and non-hygroscopic. Surface moisture on the fibres is less than 0.5%, although this may increase slightly in humid atmospheres due to absorption by the coatings. Individual fibres are also free from swelling or shrinkage effects when subjected to wetting. The open nature of mineral-wool products assists diffusion, water vapour can, therefore, pass through the insulation and dissipate without condensing.

30.8.2.3 Softening point

Man-made mineral wools may be described as 'solid solutions'. As such they do not have a precise melting point, temperature merely having the effect of changing the viscosity of the 'solution'. However, for the purpose of quality control, a procedure has been adopted by which the 'softening' point of a sample can be established with reasonable accuracy.

Under this procedure, the softening point is established as the temperature in degrees centigrade at which a round fibre, nominally 0.65 mm diameter and 235 mm long, elongates under its own weight at a rate of 1 mm min^{-1} when the upper 100 mm of its length is heated in a special furnace at a rate of 5°C min^{-1}.

The softening temperatures for mineral-wool products measured by this procedure are 670°C for glass wool and 1000°C for rock wool. However, manufacturers' recommended limiting temperatures in use are 540°C for glass wool and 850°C for rock wool.

30.9 Physical properties (general)

30.9.1 Structure and appearance

Mineral-wool insulating products are composed of mineral-wool fibres of approximately 5 μm diameter, which are cemented together at the points of contact with phenolic resin binders (see *Figure 30.4*). The fibres are randomly dispersed and are oriented predominantly in the horizontal direction, giving greater strength characteristics in both directions along the plane of the mat.

Products vary in type from flexible, resilient low-density mats

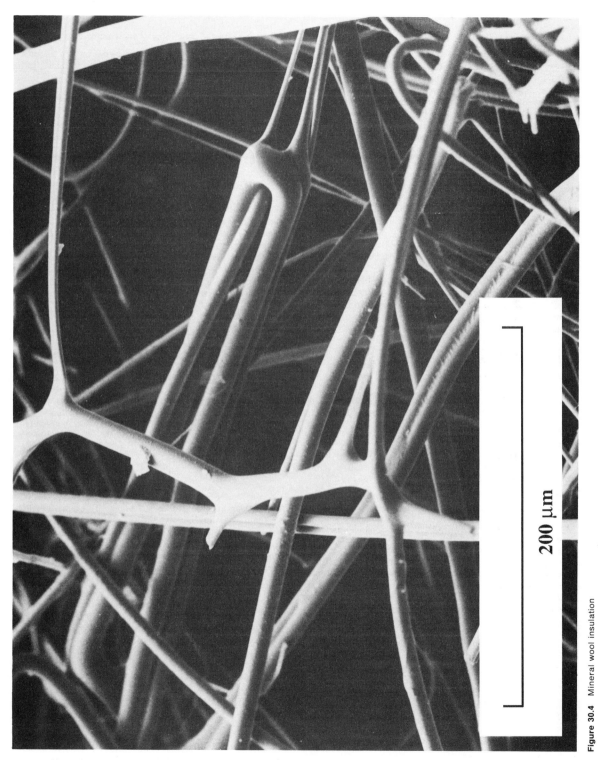

200 μm

Figure 30.4 Mineral wool insulation

which have a soft woolly texture and appearance, to rigid high-density rectangular slabs with good compression resistance and dimensional stability.

30.9.2 Water repellancy

Mineral-wool fibres are non-hygroscopic, and do not absorb water or moisture by capillary action. The addition of oils and other additives during manufacture further enhances the water repellancy of the products. The open character of mineral-wool products assists diffusion and water vapour can therefore pass freely through the insulation layer. Providing the product is not under load, any water which may enter the insulation will drain away freely without permanent impairment of the insulating properties.

30.9.3 Biological properties

Mineral-wool insulation products are completely inert and basically non-organic. They will, therefore, not provide sustenance to vermin, and will not encourage the growth of fungi, mould or bacteria.

30.9.4 Permanence

Mineral-wool products are rot-proof and have been proved in service for over 50 years. They require no maintenance and, correctly installed, will provide effective protection for the lifetime of a building.

30.9.5 Handling and cutting

Mineral-wool products are easy to handle and install, and may be simply cut where necessary with a saw or sharp-bladed knife. When handling it is advisable to wear gloves and, when working in confined areas a face mask to BS 6016[9] or BS 2091[10] should be worn in order to minimize the inhalation of dust and fibres.

30.10 Thermal properties

30.10.1 Definition of terms

In expressing the thermal performance of mineral-wool products, the following terms are generally adopted:

(1) Watt (W), the basic unit of heat flow, equalling a rate of 1 joule per second ($J\,s^{-1}$).
(2) Degrees Celcius (°C) and degrees Kelvin (K), used for the expression of temperature. Actual temperature levels are expressed in degrees Celcius (°C) and temperature differences (intervals or gradients) in Kelvin (K).
(3) Thermal conductivity (λ, $W\,m^{-1}\,K^{-1}$), which defines the ability of a material to transmit heat. It is measured in watts per square metre of surface area for a temperature gradient of 1 K per unit thickness of 1 m.
(4) Thermal resistance (R, $m^2\,K\,W^{-1}$) is a measure of the ability of a material to frustrate the flow of heat. The value is obtained by dividing thickness in metres by thermal conductivity (in $W\,m^{-1}\,K^{-1}$). Thermal resistance values are additive and, therefore, facilitate the computation of thermal transmittance (U) values.
(5) Thermal transmittance (U, $W\,m^{-2}\,K^{-1}$) defines the ability of an element of structure, consisting of given thickness of material, air spaces, etc., to transmit heat under steady-state conditions. It is a measure of the quantity of heat that will flow through unit area in unit time, per unit difference of temperature of the individual environments between which the structure intervenes. The value is calculated as the reciprocal of the sum of the resistances of each component of the structure, including the resistance contributed by inner and outer surfaces plus air spaces and cavities.

30.10.2 General principles of heat transfer

To understand why mineral-wool products are so effective in reducing heat flow through a structure, it is helpful to have a basic understanding of the general principles of heat transfer. All materials, to a greater or lesser extent, will transmit heat, and that heat will always flow from the heat source (or warmer area) towards a cooler area, in an attempt to produce temperature equilibrium. The heat transfer takes place by three basic modes: radiation, conduction and convection.

30.10.2.1 Radiation

Radiation is the process by which heat is emitted from a body and transferred through an open space as energy, by means of the emission and absorption of infra-red radiation. Unlike convection (see Section 30.10.2.3), radiation can take place in a vacuum. All materials emit radiant energy, the rate of emission being dependent on the temperature of the body and the nature of its surface. Radiant heat transfer can be significantly affected by the use of bright metallic surfaces, such as aluminium foil, which reflect the radiant energy, reducing either heat absorption on the cold face of the structure, or heat emission on the warm face.

30.10.2.2 Conduction

This is the process by which heat flows through or along a material, or from one material to another in contact with it. The rate at which the heat is conducted depends upon the thermal conductivity (λ) of the material, or materials, in question. Metals and other dense solid materials tend to have high levels of conductivity, whereas materials with a very small amount of solid matter and a large proportion of voids (gas or air bubbles, not large enough to carry heat by convection) have the lowest thermal conductivities.

30.10.2.3 Convection

Convection occurs in a liquid or a gas, through the bodily transfer of heat by fluid molecules. Generally, when a fluid (liquid or gas) comes into contact with a warmer, or colder, surface, that part of the fluid close to the surface undergoes a change in temperature. As temperature changes so does density and, consequently, the heated or cooled portions move away, causing currents to build up which carry the heat away.

In each case there is also an element of conduction across the very thin layer of fluid directly in contact with the solid surface. The speed of convection currents affects the thickness of this layer, and alters the rate of heat transfer. Consequently, heat loss by convection from a surface will be greater under conditions of forced ventilation or rapid air circulation.

Radiation is the primary mode of heat transfer. The other two modes, convection and conduction, come into play only after the molecules have absorbed the radiant energy and the initial temperature difference has been created.

30.10.3 Mineral-wool products as insulators

Mineral-wool products are extremely effective as insulators because they frustrate heat flow by all three basic modes.

(1) They place a very large number of radiation absorbers (fibres) between the two temperature boundaries. In addition,

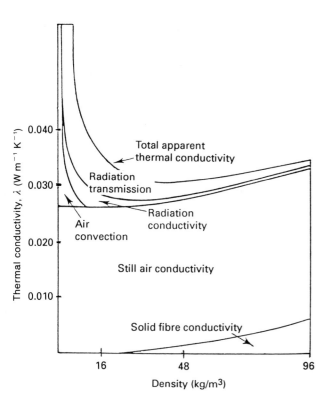

Figure 30.5 Thermal conductivity vs. density

the fibrous structure also acts to reflect and scatter the radiant energy.
(2) The size, shape and orientation of the cells (pockets) containing the liquid or gas, affect the convective heat transfer. In the case of mineral-wool products the air pockets and, consequently, the temperature gradients within the air pockets, are so small as to control or eliminate convection.
(3) Mineral-wool fibre is a poor conductor of heat. In addition, the fibrous nature of mineral-wool products with their low mass and discontinuous structure, present one of the most effective barriers to conductive heat transfer.

30.10.4 Factors affecting thermal conductivity

The relative levels of the various modes of heat transfer which work together to define the total thermal conductivity of the product, are affected by both the density and the temperature differential. The effect of density on thermal conductivity for 25 mm glass wool with a steady temperature differential of 20°C between the hot and cold faces is shown in *Figure 30.5*. This figure also shows the relative parts played by each of the heat-transfer modes under these very specific conditions.

The effect of temperature change on the thermal conductivity of a typical sample of medium density mineral wool is shown in *Figure 30.6*. For normal structural applications, however, the effect of ambient-temperature changes on thermal conductivity are relatively small and are generally disregarded for calculation purposes.

30.11 Acoustic properties

30.11.1 Terminology and definitions

Once again, in order to appreciate why mineral-wool products are so effective in controlling noise, it is necessary to have a basic

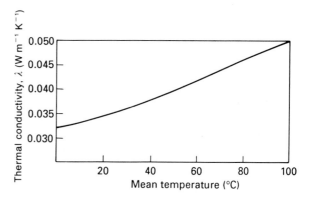

Figure 30.6 Thermal conductivity vs. temperature for medium density mineral wool

understanding of the mechanism of sound transfer, and the various standard terms associated with the science of acoustics.

30.11.1.1 Sound

Sound is a form of mechanical energy that is propagated through an elastic medium by the vibration of the molecules. Such vibrations, or sound waves, may pass through solids, liquids or gases, but in the normal process of 'hearing' the sound, it is necessary for the final transmission to be through air to activate the eardrum. Sound travels in waves in three dimensions simultaneously, and its approximate speed in air is 340 m s^{-1}, although this varies slightly according to air temperature.

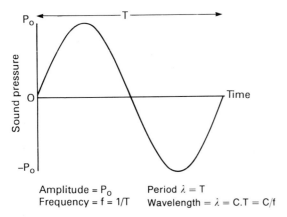

Amplitude = P_o Period λ = T
Frequency = f = 1/T   Wavelength = λ = C.T = C/f

Figure 30.7   Sound-wave formation

30.11.1.2 Acoustic pressure

The passage of sound waves through air causes a slight variation in the atmospheric pressure, this variation is called acoustic pressure. The average ear can detect pressures in the range 2×10^{-5} pascals (Pa), which is just discernible, to 20 Pa, which produces an extremely painful sensation. As the mean atmospheric pressure is 10 Pa, it can be seen that changes in acoustic pressure levels are extremely small.

30.11.1.3 Sound-pressure levels

Sound-pressure levels are expressed in units called decibels (dB). A decibel is equivalent to the smallest change in sound intensity that can be detected by the average human ear. The decibel cannot be measured directly and has no fixed value, but is a logarithmic unit that expresses the ratio between a given sound level or pressure being measured and a reference acoustic pressure. A decibel therefore indicates by what proportion a sound is greater or lesser than another. The greater the sound level the higher the decibel rating, for example, the threshold of hearing corresponds to 0 dB whilst the threshold of pain occurs at 120 dB. Under ideal conditions an increment of 1 dB is just perceptible and a 10-dB increment is clearly noticeable, the latter corresponding generally to a halving or doubling of the perceived sound level.

30.11.1.4 Wavelength, frequency and pitch

One complete movement of a vibrating body from the neutral position moving to one side and then to the other back to the neutral position is called a cycle (*Figure 30.7*). The distance that the sound travels in that cycle is called the wavelength and the number of cycles completed in 1 s is called the frequency. The unit of frequency is the hertz (Hz), if 1000 cycles occur in 1 s therefore, the wave has a frequency of 1000 Hz. The human ear responds to the range 20–20 000 Hz.

30.11.2 Principles of noise control

The control of noise (or unwanted sound) in buildings is often referred to as 'building acoustics', and includes both the reduction of noise transmission from one space to another and the control of noise levels and conditions within a space. There are two basic mechanisms by which control takes place: sound absorption, which is the reduction in sound energy on reflection at a surface, and sound insulation, the reduction in sound energy passing through a structure.

30.11.3 Sound absorption

30.11.3.1 Definition

Sound absorption is defined as the reduction in sound energy when sound is reflected from a surface. In building acoustics the property applies generally when the sound source and the recipient are in the same room.

30.11.3.2 Sound reduction by absorption

Sound absorption is achieved by converting the mechanical energy of vibration of molecules or fibres into heat. Although all materials have the ability to absorb sound, to a greater or lesser extent, those with open-textured or fibrous surfaces provide the highest degree of absorption. Hard surface materials are generally highly reflective of sound energy and, therefore, provide only a low level of absorption.

In porous materials, sound enters between fibres or through pores and is dissipated as heat. The longer the path of the sound within the materials the better is the dissipation process. In fibrous materials, the friction heat due to air-flow resistance makes the major contribution to acoustic absorption.

30.11.3.3 Performance of mineral-wool products

Glass- and rock-wool products have excellent sound-absorbing properties and are particularly effective in reducing high-frequency noise. At thicknesses up to 50 mm the products are somewhat less effective at low frequencies, but improvements can be achieved by increasing material thickness where possible or, as is often the case, by including an air gap. The effect of increasing the flow resistance of mineral-wool products is to increase sound absorption in the middle- and high-frequency range. There is, however, an optimum relationship between air-flow resistance and sound absorption. Too high a flow resistance will lead to only a low friction heat loss, and both extremes will result in reduced sound absorption.

Although mineral-wool products provide good sound absorption when the surface is exposed, this is not always practical as often some form of protection will be required. In such cases it is possible to provide a porous membrane, or a very thin plastic film material (such as 12 μm thick Melinex), which only partially reduces acoustic absorption. Generally this will have the effect of reducing performance at high frequencies, although this may be offset by improvements in low-frequency-sound absorption.

30.11.4 Sound insulation

Sound insulation is concerned with the reduction of sound which passes between two spaces separated by a dividing structural element. Sound energy may be transmitted either directly through the element, or by indirect or flanking paths through the surrounding structure. In the case of walls and partitions, sound insulation is normally only concerned with airborne sound, but in floors impact sound transmission, such as that caused by footsteps, must also be considered in addition to airborne sound.

30.11.4.1 Airborne-sound insulation

The resistance of any structural element to the passage of airborne sound is determined by measuring sound levels on either side of the element and recording the difference. This is known as the transmission loss. The level of sound insulation varies according to frequency and the results may be represented either graphically or in tabular form for frequencies at one-third octave intervals, generally over the range 100–3150 Hz. Standard test procedures defined in BS 2750[11] (ISO 140[12]) are used to

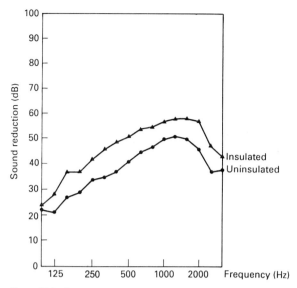

Figure 30.8 Sound-insulation performance of a typical lightweight partition

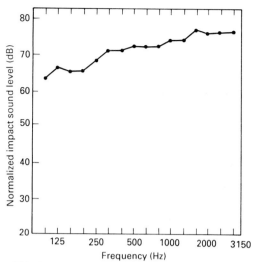

Figure 30.9 Impact-sound insulation performance of a typical concrete floor

determine the sound insulation. An example of the performance of a typical lightweight partition is shown in *Figure 30.8*.

When specifying the acoustic performance of an element it is not practical to quote the transmission loss at each individual frequency. Consequently, a method of representing the performance as single figures has been devised. The term 'sound reduction' is used to describe the resistance to airborne sound transmission.

The weighted sound-reduction index (R_w) is calculated using the method given in BS 5281[13] (ISO 717[14]) which describes a procedure for fitting a standard reference curve to the measured results plotted graphically. When the total adverse deviation of the measured results is less than 32 dB, the sound-insulation value corresponding to 500 Hz is read off and quoted as a single figure.

30.11.4.2 Impact-sound insulation

The resistance of any floor/ceiling construction to impact-sound transmission is determined by a standard 'tapping' machine used in accordance with the procedures given in BS 5821: Part 2[13] (ISO 717: Part 2[14]). In the test the noise levels in the lower room are measured in decibels at different frequencies, allowing a curve to be plotted. Using this method the lower the recorded level the better the acoustical performance of the system. *Figure 30.9* shows the performance of a typical concrete-floor construction when subjected to impact sound.

In order to compare the performance of different floor constructions, the measured results over a range of frequencies from 100 to 3150 Hz are plotted as a performance curve in accordance with BS 5821: Part 2[13] (ISO 717: Part 2[14]).

Alternatively, a single-figure method can be used in which the actual performance curve is compared with a standard performance curve. When the total adverse deviation of the measured performances is less than 32 dB, the value at 500 Hz is read off from the standard curve and a single figure is quoted as the weighted-normalized sound-pressure level (L_{nw}).

30.11.4.3 Mineral wool and sound insulation

Because of their lightweight porous nature, mineral-wool products are very efficient in absorbing sound and in reducing the intensity of sound passing through them. Their physical structure, however, means that mineral-wool products cannot generally be used in isolation, but are installed as a component of the structural element. It is, therefore, the composite performance of the structure containing mineral wool which is important, and it is this which will be considered in the following sections.

Airborne sound In single solid walls the sound-insulation performance is governed by mass—the heavier the material the greater its resistance to sound transmission. The empirical mass law makes it possible to predict the average sound insulation value of a solid structure of known mass. For example, a 100-mm thick solid block wall of average mass 100 kg m^{-2}, will have an average sound insulation of 40 dB (*Figure 30.10*).

Doubling the mass of the structure will generally provide an improvement of 5 dB (therefore doubling the wall from 100 to 200 mm thick would improve sound performance from 40 to 45 dB).

However, using lightweight-partition systems with mineral wool in the cavity it is possible to provide acoustic performance better than that predicted by the mass law. For example, a typical 100-mm metal-stud partition with 12.5-mm plasterboard on both sides, but without insulation in the cavity, has a sound-reduction index of 35 dB. By adding 40 mm mineral wool in the cavity, the performance improves to 45 dB. With a total weight of 28 kg m^{-2}, the mass law would have predicted the performance of an equivalent solid partition as 32 dB. The improvement would have been even greater had the cavity been fully filled with mineral wool.

Another method of achieving good acoustic performance with solid walls is to use lightweight wall linings, such as mineral-wool/plasterboard laminates.

Impact sound Mineral-wool products are also very effective in controlling impact noise in buildings and are widely used in floating-floor constructions for this purpose.

In concrete floors the floor finish is separated from the structural concrete base by a resilient mineral-wool layer (*Figure 30.11*).

It is important, however, that there is no connection between the floor finish and the base or the resistance to impact-sound transmission will be reduced. In addition, the insulation must not be overloaded as this will also adversely affect the performance.

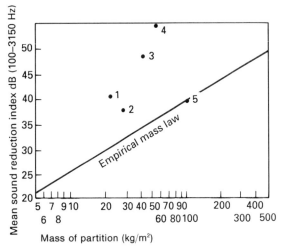

Figure 30.10 Sound insulation vs. mass

*Construction	Mass kg/m²	Mean R dB	Rw dB
1 75 mm metal stud partition with 25 mm mineral wool insulation in cavity	22	41	41
2 100 mm timber stud partition with 25 mm mineral wool insulation in cavity	27	38	40
3 100 mm metal stud partition with 25 mm mineral wool insulation in cavity	43	48	51
4 211 mm jumbo metal stud separating wall with 25 mm mineral wool insulation in cavity	55	55	59
5 100 mm solid block wall	100	40	40

The performance can be improved by increasing the mass of the floating layer and increasing the resistance of the separating layer.

In lightweight timber-platform floors it is necessary to use high-density mineral-wool batts in order to provide a higher resistance to compression loads. In this construction a lightweight quilt is generally included between the joists to reduce airborne-sound transmission (*Figure 30.12*).

30.12 Fire properties

30.12.1 General

Mineral-wool products perform well under fire conditions to frustate both the passage of heat and the spread of flames. They are, therefore, widely used in buildings for both fire-protection and fire-control situations. The products have the added advantage that they can be used for thermal- and acoustic-insulation applications in situations where fire performance is also an important criterion. The reasons for their superior performance are three-fold:

(1) the basic mineral wool is non-combustible, and does not add to the fire load of the building;
(2) the products have good thermal-insulation properties which slow and reduce heat transfer between the surfaces, giving protection to structural elements and preventing fire spread; and
(3) the surfaces of the unfaced products act to resist the spread of flame.

For general fire-stopping applications within structural elements, both glass- and rock-based products will provide a level of performance which more than satisfies the requirements of Building Regulations.[5] For certain structural fire-protection applications the higher softening temperature and higher density range of rock-wool products provides enhanced performance.

30.12.2 Fire ratings

Basic mineral wool is non-combustible. Within the product range most low- to medium-density mats, batts and slabs are also rated non-combustible when tested in accordance with BS 476: Part 4.[2] As density increases, the non-fibrous (mainly resin) content of the products also increases and this can influence combustibility. In general, the higher density products, although

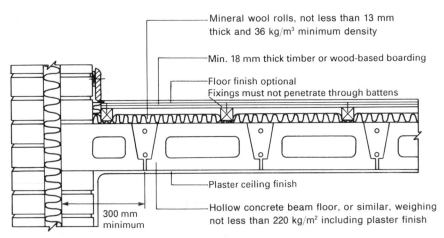

Figure 30.11 Impact-sound insulation of concrete separating floor

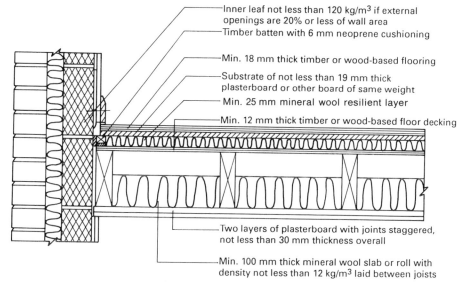

Inner leaf not less than 120 kg/m³ if external openings are 20% or less of wall area

Timber batten with 6 mm neoprene cushioning

Min. 18 mm thick timber or wood-based flooring

Substrate of not less than 19 mm thick plasterboard or other board of same weight

Min. 25 mm mineral wool resilient layer

Min. 12 mm thick timber or wood-based floor decking

Two layers of plasterboard with joints staggered, not less than 30 mm thickness overall

Min. 100 mm thick mineral wool slab or roll with density not less than 12 kg/m³ laid between joists

Figure 30.12   Impact-sound insulation of timber-base separating floor

continuing to have a very safe usage factor, do not meet the strictly defined non-combustibility standard laid down in BS 476: Part 4.[2] These higher density products do, however, meet Building Regulations[5] class 0 requirements, as they provide both a class 1 surface spread of flame rating to BS 476: Part 7,[3] and meet the fire-propagation index standards (propagation index of not more than 12 and sub-index of not more than 6) of Approved Document B2/3/4, Appendix A7/8.[15]

For applications where both high density and a non-combustibility rating are essential, special products are manufactured with a very low resin content (approximately 1%), in order to satisfy BS 476: Part 4.[2] These products are designed predominantly for the offshore and marine market, although they are used for certain structural applications where surface appearance and mechanical stability are not essential criteria.

30.12.3 Fire performance

The performance of mineral-wool products is unaffected at temperatures up to 230°C, above this temperature, however, some binder loss will be experienced. 'Evaporation' of the binder begins between 240 and 260°C and initially affects only that part of the product nearest to the heat source. Because of the natural thermal-insulating properties, a temperature gradient is established across the product and binder loss occurs progressively only as temperature increases at the hot face. Progressive binder loss may occur, but as density increases the natural cohesiveness and layering of the fibres will maintain integrity and, therefore, performance. With integrity maintained, the products will continue to provide protection until softening temperatures are reached (glass at approx. 670°C and rock at approx. 1175°C), although again the effect will be progressive across the insulation layer due to the temperature gradient. The complete process is one of softening rather than combustion, and at no stage is there any generation of significant quantities of toxic smoke or fumes.

30.12.4 Fire-protection requirements

Approved Document B2/3/4[15] to the Building Regulations 1985,[5] lays down the following requirements for the prevention of fire spread in buildings.

Internal walls; ceilings   Internal fire spread (surfaces) B2: in order to inhibit the spread of fire within the building, surfaces of materials used on walls and ceilings

(1) shall offer adequate resistance to the spread of flame over their surfaces; and
(2) shall have, if ignited, a rate of heat release which is reasonable in the circumstances.

Structure   Internal fire spread (structure) B3:

(1) the building shall be so constructed that, in the event of fire, its stability will be maintained for a reasonable period;
(2) the building or the building as extended, shall be sub-divided into compartments where this is necessary to inhibit the spread of fire within the building;
(3) concealed spaces in the structure of the fabric of the building, or the building as extended, shall be sealed and sub-divided where this is necessary to inhibit the unseen spread of fire and smoke;
(4) a wall common to two or more buildings shall offer adequate resistance to the spread of fire and smoke; and
(5) for the purposes of sub-paragraph (4) a house in a terrace and semi-detached house are each to be treated as being a separate building.

External walls; roofs   External fire spread B4:

(1) the external walls of the building shall offer adequate resistance to the spread of fire over the walls and from one building to another, having regard to the height, use and position of the building; and
(2) the roof of the building shall offer adequate resistance to the spread of fire over the roof and from one building to another, having regard to the use and position of the building.

30.12.5 Applications of mineral wool

The more common fire-protection applications for mineral-wool products in buildings include:

(1) fire protection of structural beams and columns;
(2) fire protection in separating walls;

(3) fire stopping in cavities, including external wall cavities in both timber-frame and masonry buildings;

(4) compartmentation and fire stopping in voids;

(5) fire protection of HVAC pipe work and ductwork; and

(6) flexible cavity barriers, large and small, to prevent fire spread.

Further details of selected applications are included in Section 30.14.6.

30.13 Standards and approvals

30.13.1 British and International Standards

There are a wide range of British Standards relating to aspects of the composition, manufacture, quality control and performance of mineral-wool products, and to the application of such products for thermal, acoustic and fire insulation in buildings. The standards most commonly referred to are listed below, along with their International Standards Organization (ISO) equivalent, if available.

BS 476 Fire tests for building materials and structures.
BS 476: Part 4: 1970 (1984) Non-combustibility test for materials. (ISO 1182)
BS 476: Part 7: 1987 Method of classification of the surface spread of flame of products.
BS 476: Part 8: 1972 Test methods and criteria for the fire resistance of elements of building construction. (ISO 834/ISO 6167)
BS 476: Part 11: 1982 (1988) Method for assessing the heat emission from building materials.
BS 476: Part 21: 1987 Methods for determination of the fire resistance of loadbearing elements of construction.
BS 476: Part 22: 1987 Methods for determination of the fire resistance of non-loadbearing elements of construction.

BS 874 Methods for determining thermal insulation properties.
BS 874: Part 2 Tests for thermal conductivity and related properties, Section 2.1: 1986. Guarded hot-plate method. (ISO 8302)
BS 874: Part 3 Tests for thermal transmittance and conductance, Section 3.1: 1987. Guarded hot-box method.

BS 2750 Measurement of sound insulation in buildings and of building elements.
BS 2750: Part 1: 1980 Recommendation for laboratories. (ISO 140/1)
BS 2750: Part 3: 1980 Laboratory measurements of airborne sound insulation of building elements. (ISO 140/3)
BS 2750: Part 4: 1980 Field measurements of airborne sound insulation between rooms. (ISO 140/4)
BS 2750: Part 6: 1980 Laboratory measurements of impact sound insulation of floors. (ISO 140/6)
BS 2750: Part 7: 1980 Field measurements of impact sound insulation of floors. (ISO 140/7)
BS 2750: Part 9: 1987 Method for measurement of room to room airborne sound insulation of a suspended ceiling with a plenum above it. (ISO 140/9)

BS 2972: 1975 (1984) Methods of test for inorganic thermal insulating materials.

BS 3533: 1981 Glossary of thermal insulation terms.

BS 3638: 1987 Method for measurement of sound absorption in a reverberation room. (ISO 354)

BS 3958 Thermal insulating materials.
BS 3958: Part 3: 1985 Metal mesh faced man-made mineral fibre mattresses.
BS 3958: Part 4: 1982 Bonded pre-formed man-made mineral fibre pipe sections.
BS 3958: Part 5: 1986 Specification for bonded man-made mineral fibre slabs.

BS 5250: 1975 Code of basic data for the design of buildings: the control of condensation in dwellings.

BS 5422: 1977 Specification for the use of thermal insulating materials.

BS 5502: Part 1 Buildings and structures for agriculture.
BS 5502: Section 1.4: 1986 Energy

BS 5803 Thermal insulation for use in pitched roof spaces in dwellings.
BS 5803: Part 1: 1985 Specification for man-made mineral fibre thermal insulation mats.
BS 5803: Part 2: 1985 Specification for man-made mineral fibre thermal insulation in pelleted or granular form for application by blowing.
BS 5803: Part 5: 1985 Specification for installation of man-made mineral fibre and cellulose fibre insulation.

BS 5821 Methods for rating the sound insulation in buildings and of building elements.
BS 5821: Part 1: 1984 Method for rating the airborne sound insulation in buildings and of interior building elements. (ISO 717/1)
BS 5821: Part 2: 1984 Method for rating the impact sound insulation. (ISO 717/2)
BS 5821: Part 3: 1984 Method for rating the airborne sound insulation of facade elements and facades. (ISO 717/3)

BS 6232 Thermal insulation of cavity walls by filling with blown man-made mineral fibre.
BS 6232: Part 1: 1982 Specification for the performance of installation systems.
BS 6232: Part 2: 1982 Code of practice for installation of blown man-made mineral fibre in cavity walls with masonry and/or concrete leaves.

BS 6676 Thermal insulation of cavity walls using man-made mineral fibre batts (slabs).
BS 6676: Part 1: 1986 Specification for man-made mineral fibre batts (slabs).
BS 6676: Part 2: 1986 Code of practice for installation of batts (slabs) filling the cavity

BS 8207: 1985 Code of practice for energy efficiency in buildings.

BS 8208 Guide to assessment of suitability of external cavity walls for filling with thermal insulants.
BS 8208: Part 1: 1985 Existing traditional cavity construction.

BS 8211: Part 1: 1988 Code of practice for energy efficient refurbishment of housing.

BS 8233: 1987 Code of practice for sound insulation and noise reduction in buildings.

30.13.2 CEN standards

At the time of writing, no CEN standards relating directly to insulation products are available. A number are known to be in preparation in readiness for 1992, and it is anticipated that these will, where possible, be based on existing ISO standards.

30.13.3 Building Regulations

The Approved Documents to the Building Regulations make reference to named British Standards and in some cases to Agrément Certificates. These Standards and Certificates are relevant guidance to the extent that they relate to considerations of health and safety, energy conservation and the welfare and convenience of disabled persons. Whilst not mandatory, design in accordance with these standards will be accepted as being in compliance with Regulation requirements.

30.13.4 Agrément Certificates

Certificates issued by the British Board of Agrément under arrangements agreed with the Secretary of State will assess those aspects of performance that demonstrate compliance with the Building Regulations when the product or system is properly used in accordance with terms of the Certificate. Approved Document C4[16] states that: (a) 'a rigid thermal insulating material built into the wall should be the subject of a current British Board of Agrément Certificate and the work should be carried out in accordance with the requirements of that Certificate', and (c) 'other insulating materials inserted into the cavity after the wall has been constructed . . . should be the subject of a current Certificate by the British Board of Agrément (BBA). The work should be carried out in accordance with the terms of that Certificate by operatives either directly employed by the holder of a BBA Certificate or employed by an installer approved to operate under the BBA Certificate'.

Mineral-wool products and mineral-wool-based systems in the above categories generally carry BBA Certificates. Certificates are issued to cover specific branded products, and full details can be obtained by reference to the individual manufacturers concerned.

30.13.5 Fitness of materials

The Approved Document supporting Regulation 7 of the Building Regulations[5] states that, in addition to the standards and Agrément Certificates specifically referred to in the Approved Document, alternative ways of establishing the fitness of material may be sought by reference to the following:

(1) past experience of performance capability;
(2) Agrément Certificates covering the material and its conditions of use;
(3) British Standards appropriate to the purpose and conditions of use;
(4) independent certification schemes for products, e.g. Kitemark;
(5) quality-assurance schemes complying with the relevant recommendations of BS 5750[17] 'Quality systems';
(6) test and calculations to show that the material is capable of performing the function for which it is intended; and
(7) sampling and testing by the Local Authority to establish compliance with the provisions of Schedule 1.

Many man-made mineral-wool products carry Kitemarks or have been the subject of independent test certificates for particular applications (e.g. fire performance, sound- and thermal-insulation characteristics).

30.14 Usage and 'abuse'

30.14.1 Introduction

This section deals with the principal applications for mineral-wool products in buildings. For convenience it is broken down into sections covering thermal insulation in roofs, walls and floors, followed by general acoustic and fire-protection applications. Because of the wide range of different building methods, systems and designs, it is not possible to give specific details of individual constructions, and this section is therefore intended for general guidance only. As with most structural materials, it is possible through incorrect detailing, selection and installation of mineral-wool products, to create or exacerbate problems within the building structure. The main areas of concern in insulated structures are associated with condensation and damp penetration, fire spread, cold bridging, and degradation or failure of materials in use. In many cases the problems identified may be found in identical uninsulated structures. Insulation should not be used to remedy existing building defects (e.g. dampness). Where inherent structural faults are present, however, it is possible that by adding insulation the effects of such faults may become manifest.

30.14.2 Roofs

30.14.2.1 General

Mineral-wool products are available for thermal insulation in all types of 'cold' and 'warm' (including inverted) flat-roof constructions, and in pitched roofs of both domestic and industrial design. Typical applications are shown in *Figure 30.13*.

30.14.2.2 Good practice

The main problems which may be caused by poor design and installation practices, with particular regard to the insulation, vary depending on construction, and include the following.

Pitched roof (domestic type)

(1) Condensation in roof space resulting from inadequate ventilation and/or ingress of water vapour from living areas. To avoid problems ensure adequate ventilation and seal airpaths between heated areas and unheated roof space.
(2) Frozen/burst pipes in loft. To avoid problems insulate all waterpipes and cold water tanks above the level of the insulation.
(3) Derating of electrical cables in loft. To avoid problems route cables above insulation layer, or uprate to compensate.

Pitched roof (industrial cladded) Condensation is again the biggest potential problem. Adequate ventilation coupled with measures to extract moisture at source provide the solution.

Flat roof (cold deck) The main problem here is condensation. In this construction the problem is overcome by installing a sealed vapour check on the warm side of the insulation and by providing a well ventilated airspace above the insulation.

Flat roof (warm deck sandwich)

(1) Fatigue of weatherproof membrane—selection of correct insulant will reduce stress due to thermal movement. Good detailing is also important to reduce ponding; and
(2) condensation within construction and cold bridging—provide continuous vapour barrier immediately below insulation, and ensure correct detailing at roof/wall junctions and level changes.

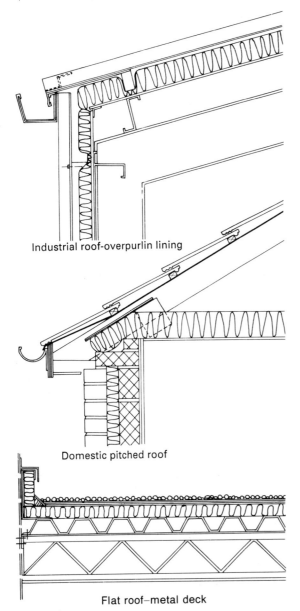

Industrial roof-overpurlin lining

Domestic pitched roof

Flat roof—metal deck

Figure 30.13 Typical applications of mineral wool for roof insulation

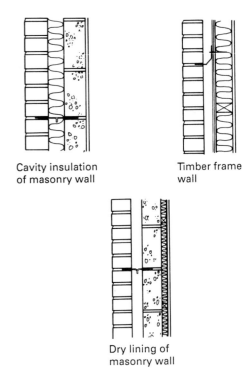

Cavity insulation
of masonry wall

Timber frame
wall

Dry lining of
masonry wall

Figure 30.14 Typical applications of mineral wool for external wall insulation

30.14.3 Walls

30.14.3.1 General

Mineral-wool products are available for insulation of all types of masonry, timber-frame and steel-frame wall constructions for internal and external applications. Typical application examples are shown in *Figure 30.14*.

30.14.3.2 Good practice

Virtually all the problems which can occur are related either to water penetration (dampness) or condensation. The causes and solutions differ depending on construction.

Masonry cavity walls (cavity insulation batts) This system had some early teething problems due to unfamiliarity with the product. Nowadays the incidence of problems is very low (around 2 in 10000 installations) and is generally related to bad design or site practice. In most cases the problems would be present whether or not the wall was filled, but the presence of insulation has caused the symptoms to manifest.

Good design should take account of prevailing exposure conditions and appropriate protective detailing should be included in exposed areas. The slabs should be installed to cover the wall area completely, with vertical and horizontal joints tightly butted, and should continue to the highest point of the wall (or top edge of batts protected with a cavity tray). Wall cavities and wall ties must at all times be kept clear of mortar, and ties must be correctly specified and installed.

In the case of batts which are installed to fill only partially the external wall cavity, it is important that these be retained securely against the inner leaf, and that a continuous cavity is retained between the insulation and the outer leaf, in accordance with manufacturers and BBA recommendations.

Timber-frame external walls The major concern in this form of construction relates to condensation caused by water vapour condensing on the element adjacent to the cold side of the insulation. The possibility of this occurring is prevented by installing a continuous vapour barrier on the warm side (room side) of the insulation, and carefully sealing all joints, junctions and gaps around services, etc.

Metal-cladded walls The major concern is condensation, which can be reduced by the provision of a ventilated cavity on the cold side of the insulation, and a vapour check on the warm side of the insulation.

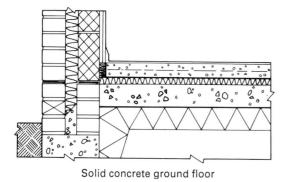

Solid concrete ground floor

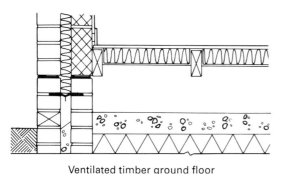

Ventilated timber ground floor

Figure 30.15 Typical applications of mineral wool in ground floors (thermal insulation)

30.14.4 Ground floors

30.14.4.1 General

Mineral-wool roll and batt (slab) products are available to meet thermal insulation requirements in all ventilated and solid ground floor constructions in all building types. Typical applications are shown in *Figure 30.15*.

30.14.4.2 Good practice

In ground-floor constructions the main problems are associated with cold bridging and condensation, although in solid concrete constructions the possibilities of loading failure or insulant damage must also be considered.

Concrete ground floors (insulation below screed) In such constructions the insulant selected must be of adequate compressive resistance to suit the floor loading, and must be protected during installation to prevent damage and moisture ingress from the screed. The screed should be reinforced and should be thick enough to counteract the bending effect under load. Cold bridging at junctions can be prevented by carrying insulation up the wall face to a level above the screed surface, and in cavity-insulated walls by starting the insulation layer below the floor level, in order to provide edge insulation to the floor slab.

Concrete ground floors (insulation below floorboarding) In this form of construction the main problems are associated with damage to the insulating layer as a result of moisture from either below or above. This can be avoided by ensuring that the floor slab is fully dry before laying insulation, and by protecting the upper surface of the insulation from liquid spillage with a continuous layer of vinyl sheeting or similar. In addition, all battens and boarding should be moisture resistant or preservative treated as an additional safeguard.

Timber suspended floors Since adequate ventilation is normally provided in the construction, condensation should not be a problem with this form of floor construction. Therefore, the major potential problem is cold bridging, either through the structure itself or at junctions. This can be avoided by sealing all gaps and junctions, and ensuring that the insulation fits tightly between joists and achieves its full design depth.

30.14.5 Acoustic applications

30.14.5.1 General

Mineral-wool products satisfy a wide range of noise-control applications in buildings, including sound insulation of suspended ceilings and partition walls, and noise control in voids. They also meet Building Regulations[5] requirements in respect of separating walls (airborne sound) and separating floors (airborne and impact sound). Typical applications of mineral wool products in acoustic control and upgrading are shown in *Figure 30.16*.

30.14.5.2 Good practice

When considering acoustic performance, individual elements can rarely be taken in isolation, as the performance is a property of the structure as a whole. In designing for acoustic standards always consider the weakest element as, regardless of the levels of insulation, the net performance of the structure will be limited to about 7 dB maximum above the performance of the weakest element.

Points for consideration in designing buildings for good sound insulation performance include the following.

Airborne sound Minimize direct air paths through the structure, seal holes and cracks and seal porous materials with plaster; use discontinuous construction techniques so as to reduce natural sound-transmission paths; identify paths for flanking transmission around elements and insulate so as to minimize this effect; avoid rigid connections in structures whenever possible; for high-performance applications consider using double independent frame walls; install sound-absorbing material in cavities and voids.

Impact sound (floors) Ensure that there is no rigid connection between the floating layer and the structure (problems may occur at floor edges, or as a result of concrete leaking through resilient layer); select isolating layer with sufficient resilience for application; use reinforced sand/cement screeds of 65 mm minimum thickness (40 mm for synthetic anhydride); build partitions off the structural slab, and confine floating floors within individual rooms.

30.14.6 Fire-protection applications

30.14.6.1 General

The excellent fire-performance properties of mineral-wool products mean that they can be used generally to provide fire-safe constructions for structural elements which must also meet required levels of thermal and/or acoustic insulation. They may also be used for the following specific applications.

(1) Fire protection in wall and floor structures used for separating and compartmentation purposes—the inclusion of certain mineral-wool products will not adversely affect system performance to BS 476: Part 8.[8]

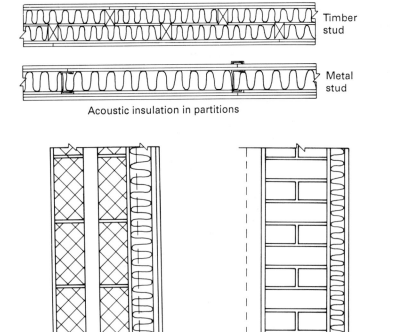

Acoustic insulation in partitions

Acoustic lining and acoustic stud framing
of existing masonry separating walls

Figure 30.16 Typical applications of mineral wool in acoustic control and upgrading

(2) Compartmentation of cavities and voids—certain wire-faced mineral-wool products are classified as suitable for 'large cavity barriers' as defined in Building Regulations.[5] These products may also be available with aluminium foil facings for enhanced smoke penetration resistance.

(3) Perimeter sealing of cavities in timber separating wall and floor constructions—'wire reinforced mineral wool blankets at least 50 mm thick' automatically qualify as 'small cavity barriers' as defined in Building Regulations.[5] In certain instances unreinforced materials may also be used.

(4) Limiting the size of cavities in the external walls of timber framed buildings—using sleeved cavity barriers (strips of mineral wool enclosed in flanged polythene tube).

(5) Sealing imperfections of fit between building elements, to restrict the penetration of smoke and flames—all mineral-wool (glass or rock) products qualify under Approved Document B, Appendix H3, to the Building Regulations[5] as 'suitable fire stopping materials'.

(6) Fire protection of structural columns and beams—using certain slabs and wired mattresses.

(7) Fire protection of HVAC ductwork and equipment.

Typical applications of mineral-wool products for fire protection are shown in *Figure 30.17*.

30.14.6.2 *Good practice*

In many cases, mineral-wool products for fire-protection applications should be installed by qualified fire-protection engineers or specialist installers. For normal domestic structural applications most problems arise from the omission or incorrect positioning of cavity barriers or fire stops. Other problems might arise from incorrect or insufficient fixing, or from failure to provide continuity in the barrier. Correct fixing information may be found in manufacturers' literature, or by reference to technical personnel.

30.15 Proprietary brand examples

The following are the more common branded products from the ranges of the three leading UK manufacturers: G, Gyproc Insulation Limited; P, Pilkington Insulation Limited; and R, Rockwool Limited.

(1) General purpose unfaced rolls:
Gypglas 1000 (G),
Crown Wool (P),
Rockwool Insulation Mat (R),
Rockwool Rollbatt (R).

(2) Cladding rolls:
Gypglas 1008 (G),
Crown Factoryclad (P),
Rockwool Cladding Roll (R).

(3) Paper faced rolls (no flanges):
Gypglas 1010 (G),
Crown Building Roll (P).

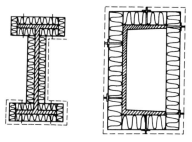

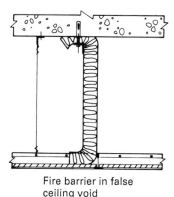

Fire protection of structural
beams and columns

Fire barrier in false
ceiling void

Figure 30.17 Typical applications of mineral wool in fire protection

(4) Timber-frame insulation products:
Gypglas 1005 (G),
Gypglas 1012 (G),
Gypglas 1022 (G),
Crown Framethern Batt (P),
Crown Frametherm Roll (P),
Crown Frametherm Roll VB (P),
Rocksil Timberfil Batt (P),
Rocksil Timberfil Roll (P),
Rockwool Timber Batt (R),
Rockwool Timber Roll (R),
Rockwool paper faced Timber Roll (R).
(5) Partition rolls:
Gypglas 1200 (G),
Rocksil Acoustic Quilt (P).
(6) Intermediate floor products (acoustic):
Gypglas 3611 (G),
Gypglas 6405 (G),
Crown Floor Slab (P),
Crown GP Quilt-sound deadening grade (P),
Rocksil Building Slab UF100 (P),
Rockwool RW5 and RW6 Rigid Slabs (R).
(7) Stitched-wire mattresses:
Frametherm Wired Cavity Barrier (P),
Rocksil Timberfil Wired Cavity Barrier (P),
Rocksil Smoke and Fire Barrier (P),
Rockwool Fire Barrier (R),
Rockwool foil-faced Fire Barrier (R).
(8) Duct insulation products:
Gypglas DR Series Rolls (G),
Gypglas GB Series Batts (G),
Crown Pipe Insulation (P),
Rocksil Pipe Insulation (P),

Crown Rigid Duct Insulation (P),
Crown Flexible Duct Insulation (P),
Rockwool Ductwrap (R),
Rockwool Duct Slab (R).
(9) Cavity wall batts/slabs:
Gypglas Cavity Wall System (G),
Crown Dritherm (P),
Crown Cavity Wall Slab (P),
Rockwool Cavity Wall Batts (R),
Rockwool Partial Fill Cavity Slab (R).
(10) Flat-roofing slabs:
Fibreglass Roof Board (P),
Rockwool Roof Decking Slab (R),
Rockwool Torch-on Roof Slab (R),
Rockwool Cut-to-falls Slab (R).
(11) Thermal/acoustic batts (medium density):
Gypglas 1605 (G),
Gypglas 2405 (G),
Crown Slabs (P),
Rocksil AT Slabs (P),
Rockwool RW2 Flexible Slab (R),
Rockwool RW3 Semi-Rigid Slab (R),
Rockwool RWA/45 Semi-Rigid Slab (R).
(12) Fire-protection slabs:
Rocksil Fire Protection Slab (P),
Firebatts 825 (R),
Conlit 100 and 150 (R).
(13) Decorative lining panels:
Crown Factoryliner (P).
(14) Blown mineral-wool cavity fill:
Walltherm (G),
Supercrown Cavity Wall Insulation (P),
Rocksil Superfil (P),
Rockwool Energy Saver Cavity Wall Insulation (R).
(15) Mineral-wool laminates:
Gyproc Tri-line (G),
Crown Dry Liner (P),
Rockwool Liner Board (R).
(16) Ceiling tiles:
Pilkington Fine Profile (P),
Accolade ceiling panel (P).
(17) Sleeved cavity barriers:
Frametherm Sleeved Cavity Barrier (P),
Rockwool TCB (R).

References

1 BRITISH STANDARDS INSTITUTION, *BS 5803 Thermal insulation for use in pitched roof spaces in dwellings, Part 1 Specification for man-made mineral fibre thermal insulation mats*, Milton Keynes (1985)
2 BRITISH STANDARDS INSTITUTION, *BS 476 Fire tests for building materials and structures, Part 4 Non-combustibility test for materials*, Milton Keynes (1970, 1984)
3 BRITISH STANDARDS INSTITUTION, *BS 476 Fire tests for building materials and structures, Part 7 Method of classification of the surface spread of flame of products*, Milton Keynes (1987)
4 BRITISH STANDARDS INSTITUTION, *BS 2972 Methods of test for inorganic thermal insulating materials*, Milton Keynes (1975, 1984)
5 *Building Regulations Approved Document E1/2/3, Airborne and impact sound*, BRE, London (1985)
6 BRITISH STANDARDS INSTITUTION, *BS 476 Fire tests for building materials and structures, Part 22 Methods for determination of the fire resistance of non-loadbearing elements of construction*, Milton Keynes (1987)
7 BRITISH STANDARDS INSTITUTION, *BS 5422 Specification for the use of thermal insulating materials*, Milton Keynes (1977)

8   BRITISH STANDARDS INSTITUTION, *BS 476 Fire tests for building materials and structures, Part 8 Test methods and criteria for the fire resistance of elements of building construction*, Milton Keynes (1972)

9   BRITISH STANDARDS INSTITUTION, *BS 6016 Filtering fireplace dust respiratators*, Milton Keynes (1980)

10 BRITISH STANDARDS INSTITUTION, *BS 2091 Respirators for protection*, Milton Keynes (1969)

11 BRITISH STANDARDS INSTITUTION, *BS 2750 Measurement of sound insulation in buildings and of building elements*, Milton Keynes (1980)

12 INTERNATIONAL STANDARDS ORGANIZATION, *ISO 140 Acoustics—measurement of sound insulation in buildings and of building elements, Parts 1–9*, Geneva (1978–1990)

13 BRITISH STANDARDS INSTITUTION, *BS 5821 Methods for rating the sound insulation in buildings and of building elements*, Milton Keynes (1984)

14 INTERNATIONAL STANDARDS ORGANIZATION, *ISO 717 Acoustics—rating of sound insulation in buildings and of building elements, Parts 1–3*, Geneva (1982)

15 *Building Regulations Approved Document B2/3/4 Fire Spread*, BRE, London (1985)

16 *Building Regulations Approved Document C4 Resistance to Moisture*, BRE, London (1985)

17 BRITISH STANDARDS INSTITUTION, *BS 5750 Quality management Parts 1–6*, Milton Keynes (1981–1987)

31

Paint: Non-absorbent Surfaces

D E J Cunningham MICorrST
Herbert Industrial Coatings

Contents

31.1 Introduction 31/3

31.2 The corrosion of steel 31/3

31.3 Surface preparation 31/3
    31.3.1 Blast cleaning 31/3
    31.3.2 Manual cleaning 31/4

31.4 Paint types 31/4
    31.4.1 Pigments 31/4
    31.4.2 Binders 31/5
    31.4.3 Solvents 31/5
    31.4.4 Volume solids 31/5

31.5 Zinc in corrosion control 31/6
    31.5.1 Calcium plumbate primer 31/6
    31.5.2 Wash primers 31/6
    31.5.3 Mordant or British Rail 'T' wash 31/6
    31.5.4 Metal sprayed zinc coatings 31/6
    31.5.5 Sherardized coatings 31/6
    31.5.6 Zinc rich primers 31/6

31.6 Specifications 31/7
    31.6.1 Small projects and rapid-construction programmes 31/7
    31.6.2 Large projects and long construction programmes 31/8

31.7 Heavy-duty coatings 31/9

References 31/9

Bibliography 31/9

31.1 Introduction

The non-absorbent materials of greatest interest to the construction industry are metals of which the most important is steel. This chapter, therefore, is concentrated on the protection and decoration of steel as a building material. Non-ferrous metals are frequently used for architectural fittings which may be coated with decorative paint and even stainless steel has occasionally required painting. Some of the high-performance paints applied to steel are also used on concrete floors and walls which are materials of low absorbency. Some reference will, therefore, be made to wall and floor treatment where there is an obvious connection with the coating types.

31.2 The corrosion of steel

Iron and steel are reactive metals which when exposed to atmospheric oxygen and moisture rapidly convert to hydrated iron oxide in the form of rust. The rusting of iron and steel is an electrochemical process which takes place on the surface when adjacent areas form cathodes and anodes, and when a film of moisture bridges these areas to act as an electrolyte. Such conditions exist on structural steel when condensation takes place and the condensate contains ions, e.g. sulphate, sulphite, chloride, nitrate and nitrite from atmospheric pollution. These ions all serve to increase the electrical conductivity of the electrolyte.

The control and prevention of corrosion may involve any process that can reduce or eliminate the electrochemical reaction. Measures may include the control of the flow of current as in cathodic protection. This measure is effective where a steel surface is continuously in contact with electrolyte, as in submerged or buried structures. Cathodic protection may consist of sacrificial anodes of metals such as zinc, or inert anodes with an impressed current. With cathodic protection, the steel may be painted but the anode is left bare. The use of corrosion inhibitors dissolved in the electrolyte is effective for closed-circuit water systems such as in water-cooling and heating plant. The control of the environment to prevent condensation will prevent corrosion as will the provision of barrier coatings to prevent electrolyte from forming on the surface.

Some or all of these mechanisms are utilized when steel is protected by a carefully specified and applied paint system. Primers contain rust inhibitors such as phosphates and chromates, or sacrificial metal particles of zinc. The paint film itself acts as a barrier of limited permeability to reduce the effect of the electrolyte. A good paint system on steel will combine the use of rust-inhibiting primers, moisture-proof-barrier coats and a surface that will satisfy other requirements, e.g. decoration, fire resistance and practicable and economic maintenance.

31.3 Surface preparation

One of the main causes of unsatisfactory coating performance is adhesion failure. The breakdown is obvious when a whole coating becomes detached from the substrate or when intercoat adhesion fails causing one coat to become detached from another in a multicoat system. The prevention of coating detachment can be avoided by careful attention to surface preparation.

New, hot-rolled steel is covered with millscale. This consists of layers of oxides of iron at thicknesses of 5–65 μm. The millscale must be removed before painting because its rate of thermal expansion differs from that of steel and this causes cracking and flaking. A paint film applied to millscale will only last as long as the scale itself adheres to the steel, which may be as little as a few weeks. Millscale is cathodic to bare steel and when covered by a film of moisture sets up corrosion cells at the junctions between scale and metal. This, in turn, causes pitting and an accumulation of soluble iron salts in the surface.

Many methods have been used to clean steel before painting, but the only effective ways of removing millscale are pickling in an inhibited acid bath or abrasive blasting. Pickling is very rarely used on steel sections used in the construction industry.

31.3.1 Blast cleaning

For new structural steel, abrasive blasting is the most favoured method of surface cleaning before painting.

Blasting may be carried out using manual equipment in which the abrasive is conveyed in a stream of compressed air through a hose to a nozzle of tungsten carbide or ceramic where it is projected on to a steel surface. The operator needs protective clothing to avoid the impact of the abrasive and the effects of breathing dust. The working area can be either in the open if dust is not environmentally objectionable or in an enclosed room with a dust-collection plant and provision for recycling and cleaning of the abrasive. Manual blasting is effective on any shape and is, therefore, suitable for blasting steel after fabrication.

Many steel fabrication works use automatic blasting plant in which prefabricated sections are passed on a conveyor through a chamber where abrasive particles are projected at the steel. The abrasive may be propelled from fixed compressed-air nozzles or, more likely, by centrifugal force using rotating wheels. Although the initial capital cost of centrifugal plant is higher than compressed-air equipment, there is a considerable improvement in efficiency due to higher blasting speeds and lower fuel costs.

Standards of blasting are covered by BS 4232: 1967,[1] Swedish Standard SIS 05 59 99: 1967[2] and the standard of the US Steel Structure Painting Council.[3]

The Swedish Standard is pictorial and is the most convenient one for use by inspectors. It includes provision for the state of steel before blasting so that the illustrations show each blast standard prefixed by a letter. Thus condition A is freshly rolled steel with a uniform layer of unbroken millscale, B is steel with adherent millscale and areas where scale has become detached and rusted, C is steel with uniform rust and no scale and D is rusty steel over a surface where corrosion has caused pitting. In practice, it is unlikely that condition C will be encountered on hot-rolled sections because pitting takes place before all the scale has been removed by weathering. Steel which has been blast cleaned and left without paint will quickly rust to state C and for many paint systems this may be cleaned by wire brushing which is also illustrated in the Swedish Standard. While wire brushing to C.Sa.3 may be satisfactory, A.Sa.3, B.Sa.3 and D.Sa.3 would be unacceptable. Since structural engineers have little choice in the condition of steel before blasting, they must assume that it can be either A, B or C and draft cleaning standards to suit all. Steel in condition D would be rejected for new fabrication, although it is encountered during refurbishment.

The British Standard is quantitative in defining the percentage of residual contaminant permitted for each quality of cleaning and the maximum roughness of the profile. It is recommended that both standards are quoted in specifications, the Swedish one for the convenience of inspectors and the British one for precise definition and to resolve possible disputes.

The three standards and their equivalent gradings are as follows:

BS 4232: 1967[1]	US SSPC[3]	SIS 05 59 00: 1967[2]
First quality	White metal	Sa.3
Second quality	Near-white	Sa.2.5
Third quality	Commercial	Sa.2

Blasting to first quality, Sa.3, is costly and difficult to achieve with automatic plant. Before metal spraying, steel is blasted to a metal spray standard BS 2569: 1964[4] which is in effect Sa.3. For most applications, Sa.3 is not necessary for painting although it may be desirable for some materials with low tolerance to inferior surface preparation or where operating conditions are exceptionally severe, e.g. off-shore structures primed with inorganic zinc silicate or surfaces subject to high operating temperatures which are coated with heat-resisting silicones.

For most paint systems, second-quality blasting, Sa.2.5, is satisfactory. Fabricators are used to working to this standard and many achieve a quality between Sa.2.5 and Sa.3.

Third-quality blasting, Sa.2, permits four times as much residual scale or rust on the surface as Sa.2.5 and because Sa.2 will not result in a significant reduction in cost, it should never be specified for new steel. It may be impossible to blast old weathered steel on site to anything better than Sa.2 and, therefore, the use of the third quality should be limited to maintenance and refurbishment.

The choice of abrasive is of significance to the effectiveness of the blast-cleaning process. The original use of blast cleaning was as a process for cleaning castings by sand blasting. The use of sand is now restricted under the foundry regulations because the dust contains silica which is hazardous.

Most automatic installations use chilled iron shot and grit which can be recycled, providing that dust and broken particles are removed. The standard for chilled iron shot and grit is BS 2451: 1963.[5]

Manual blasters use angular grit which has a faster cutting action than spherical shot. Users of centrifugal plant prefer shot which causes less wear to the machine. Shot alone tends to hammer scale into a steel surface and give a smoother profile which is inferior to the sharper pattern produced by grit. In practice, most fabricators use a mixture of shot, broken shot and grit which gives the correct blast profile and causes minimum damage to plant. The British Standard[5] sets a maximum surface profile (peak-to-trough height) of blast-cleaned steel at 100 μm.

Measurements taken of blast profiles at a number of British fabrication works show that the average is 50–60 μm. A similar profile is obtained by manual blasting using new G.24 grit while automatic blasting with new G.39 grit can give a profile as large as 250 μm; very much in excess of the maximum of 100 μm allowed in BS 4232: 1967.[1]

Where abrasive cannot be recycled and sand cannot be used under the safety regulations, a range of silica-free, disposable abrasives is available. These abrasives consist of crushed slag particles from metal-refining processes and contain silicates.

31.3.1.1 Wet blasting

Dry abrasive blasting is the most efficient method of cleaning new steel to remove scale. Weathered steel may have little or no millscale but it is likely to be pitted and the pits contaminated with soluble iron salts, rust and possibly old paint. Dry blasting followed by scrubbing with water and wetting agents, rinsing and reblasting may be necessary to remove these pollutants from the surface.

A much more efficient method of cleaning is to use wet blasting. In this process, abrasive particles are projected in a stream of water under pressure. Opinions differ as to the ideal water pressures, but the process is sufficiently flexible to allow for the removal of a single coat of paint or all the surface coating, pollutants and even a layer of the underlying steel. The value of this method of cleaning is in the removal of soluble salts from the corrosion pits and the provision of a very clean steel surface. Blasting to white metal equivalent to Sa.3 is quite possible.

Where the grit is propelled by water, the use of sand is permitted. Clean, graded, crushed-flint sand is one of the most effective and economical abrasives. The silica dust hazard is eliminated by the water.

Opinions also differ about the desirability and effectiveness of including rust inhibitors in the water. If wet-blasted steel is allowed to dry slowly, flash rusting will form on the surface. This can be avoided by quickly cleaning with pressurized water alone to remove the rust and residual abrasive particles. The wet surface should be primed with a wet steel primer as soon as the surface water has drained away. PROTECTON EP161 is a wet steel epoxy primer containing phosphate inhibitors and micaceous iron oxide that can be applied by brush or airless spray at up to 75 μm in a single coat. Surface moisture is miscible with the solvent and evaporates with it as the paint dries. Clearly, the drying time is influenced by the quantity of surface moisture when the paint is applied and the atmospheric temperature and humidity while drying.

31.3.2 Manual cleaning

The use of chipping and wire brushing is largely restricted to site maintenance work where blasting is either impracticable or uneconomic. There is no British Standard for wire brushed steel surfaces but the section in Swedish Standard SIS 05 59 00: 1967[2] shows the limitations of the process. The effect of wire brushing on scaled steel is to burnish the millscale and remove some of the rust at the cracks. On rusty steel which has previously been blast cleaned, a very good quality of surface preparation can be obtained quoted in the standard as C.Sa.3. This standard can only be obtained on steel which is free from scale and not pitted, a choice very rarely available to specifiers unless it has been blasted and allowed to rust, but not for too long.

31.4 Paint types

Paint consists of three distinct parts: the pigment, the binder and the solvent. Each of these parts may be a complex mixture of separate compounds.

31.4.1 Pigments

The pigment is the insoluble part of the paint which gives it body. It may contain rust inhibitors, materials which absorb damaging ultraviolet radiation, hard particles to impart abrasion resistance and coloured material for appearance. When considering steel coatings it is convenient to class paints in terms of pigments being either 'inhibiting', i.e. containing rust-inhibiting properties, or 'non-inhibiting', i.e. paints used as a barrier or finishes having no rust-inhibiting properties.

31.4.1.1 Inhibitive pigments

Many rust-inhibiting primers used in the past contained pigments which are now restricted. Lead containing pigments such as red lead, calcium plumbate, metallic lead, lead silico chromate and lead cyanamide are all toxic. The use of chromates is also being discouraged as hexavalent chromium compounds are known to be carcinogenic in large quantities. Most of the acceptable inhibitive primers contain either zinc metal dust or insoluble phosphate salts such as that of zinc. Zinc chromate primers are still used on non-ferrous metal surfaces.

31.4.1.2 Non-inhibitive pigments

The number of non-inhibitive pigments is almost without limit, but there are a few which feature in most barrier and finish coats for steel.

Red iron oxide, or 'red oxide', is mixed with phosphate rust inhibitors for use in many primers. The phosphates are white powders with no staining properties, while red oxide is inert, has excellent opacity and absorbs ultraviolet radiation. It is relatively inexpensive and because of its dark colour it disguises rust. This may be a disadvantage for the quality control of maintenance work.

Micaceous iron oxide (abbreviated to MIO) is a dark grey pigment in the form of flake particles which has a metallic appearance. Like red oxide it is inert and absorbs ultraviolet light, but its coarse particles give a texture to paint that not only improves its toughness and durability but provides a surface texture similar to freshly blasted steel. This enables site coatings to be applied with a minimum of surface preparation.

Carbon black is an inert coloured pigment used in most dark finishes.

Rutile titanium dioxide is the main high-quality white pigment used in barrier coats and finishes. It has very good opacity and ultraviolet radiation absorbency.

Graphite is an electrical-conducting pigment which, because it is cathodic to steel, may accelerate corrosion unless isolated from the steel surface by graphite-free primers or barrier coats. It is used in heat-resisting coatings.

Aluminium powder or flake is also used in heat-resisting paints and for light-reflecting finishes.

Organic colours are used for colour finishes. These are usually dye fixed to make them insoluble and inert.

Inorganic colours include a number of earths or ores containing coloured minerals. Some of the earth colours based on oxides or silicates of iron are safe, but many of the brightly coloured minerals are compounds of the heavy metals mercury, cadmium, arsenic and antimony which are now considered to be too toxic for use in paint.

31.4.2 Binders

The binder, vehicle or medium in a paint is the film-forming part which is usually an organic resin. For paint used on structural steel it is convenient to consider binders under three classifications: single-pack convertible paints, single-pack non-convertible paints and two-pack chemical curing paints.

31.4.2.1 Single-pack convertible paints

Single-pack convertible paints are based on drying oils or oil-modified resins. After application, the solvent evaporates to leave the film in a touch-dry or tack-free condition. The film is still soft and has little durability at this stage but hardening takes place as atmospheric oxygen reacts with the drying-oil component of the medium leading to molecular cross-linking.

Linseed and Tung oil are familiar examples of drying oils, but most modern paints of this type are based on alkyd resins. These resins are formed by the reaction of polyhydric alcohols with polybasic organic acids and condensed with drying oils. The name alkyd indicates the origin of the resin, i.e. 'alcohol acid'. Alkyds and their modifications are the most common paint media.

31.4.2.2 Single-pack non-convertible paints

Single-pack non-convertible paints dry by solvent evaporation only. Familiar examples are chlorinated rubber, vinyl copolymers and acrylics. One of the properties of these paints is that they will always dissolve in their own solvent. This can be an advantage in maintenance because an old weathered film of, say, chlorinated rubber can be overcoated after removing loose contaminants and applying fresh paint. There is no need for flatting down to obtain a key. Chlorinated rubber has very good durability in damp conditions and excellent resistance to acidic and alkaline atmospheres. It has poor solvent resistance and in sunlight tends to chalk quickly, but under polluted industrial conditions this is not objectionable.

31.4.2.3 Two-pack chemical curing paints

Two-pack chemical curing paints are those to which a curing agent is added before application. Epoxies and polyurethanes are good examples of these materials which have excellent chemical resistance and durability. One of the advantages of using two-pack epoxies is the ability to apply high film thicknesses in a single coat. This is particularly valuable for fabrication works application because the paints can be formulated with fast-drying solvents enabling work to be overcoated and handled with minimum 'down time'. As the curing agent is evenly distributed throughout the film, the coating will harden quickly and is able to withstand handling during transportation and erection. It is quite possible to apply a coat of up to 300 μm thickness at a fabrication works which will suffer little damage before the steel is erected on site.

Very smooth epoxy paints with high solvent resistance may be difficult to overcoat once they are fully cured. This is overcome by using epoxies pigmented with micaceous iron oxide at a high pigment volume concentration as the final works coat. The surface can be easily overcoated even after a delay of years.

31.4.3 Solvents

Solvents are necessary in paint to make it flow and workable. Most paints for structural steel use organic solvents, although water-thinned primers are now available. Paint specifiers are not too concerned with the composition or drying rate of solvents because their main interest is the dry film.

The paint user needs to be aware that the type of solvent used has a significant influence on the whole operation. The rate at which paint dries is a function of the solvent and some paints contain solvents which, if improperly handled, may be a health hazard. Fast-drying paints have solvents with low flash-points and these need to be contained and used in flame-free areas. Reputable manufacturers give clear health and safety information and guidance on the use of all their products so that users who follow this advice are unlikely to expose their operators or property to any risk.

31.4.4 Volume solids

The volume solids of any paint is that percentage which remains in the form of a dry film after the solvent has evaporated. This quantity is important in calculating covering rates and costs, but has no significance in evaluating the quality of a paint.

$$\text{Coverage } (\text{m}^2\,\text{l}^{-1}) = \frac{10 \times \text{volume solids}}{\text{film thickness } (\mu\text{m})}$$

Paints may have a volume solids of as little as 8% for a wash primer and up to 100% for a solventless high build floor coating or tank lining. Fast-drying prefabrication primers would have a volume solids of 20–35%. Post-fabrication primers for spraying and decorative finishes have volume solids of 40–60% and high build barrier coats 40–80%. Very high build formulations for application by airless spray or spreader have 80–100% volume solids. These figures are only a guide and values outside these ranges are possible.

Solventless paints include materials applied as dry powders. Application is by electrostatic spray after which the loosely coated article is heated. The powder first melts as a thermoplastic and flows out to form a continuous film. Further heating cures the film as in any thermosetting polymer. Powdered epoxies are applied by this method in a continuous process for coating pipes and reinforcing bars.

31.5 Zinc in corrosion control

The use of zinc metal coatings in the form of hot-dip galvanizing is very well established. In the code of practice BS 5493: 1977,[6] metal coatings, mainly zinc, are recommended for use wherever a very long time to first maintenance is required. The Zinc Development Association quotes a life of up to 50 years for galvanized steel under some conditions.

Since zinc is anodic to steel it protects by sacrificing itself, even protecting areas where the coating is damaged such as at cut edges.

Practical methods of painting galvanized surfaces are not always simple and some authorities recommend allowing the galvanizing to weather before painting is attempted. If this measure is adopted, it is essential to clean the weathered surface to remove all dirt, grease and products of corrosion which include zinc salts. The presence of zinc salts is unavoidable because the surface is highly reactive and subject to salt formation in acidic atmospheres. Most of the pollution in the atmospheres is in the form of oxides of sulphur and nitrogen which form acids with water. The acidity of rainfall in southern England has been reported as pH 4.1. Zinc metal immersed in a solution of this acidity would be penetrated at a rate of 1 mm per year. On new structures it is likely that the architect will wish to paint galvanized surface during the construction period which eliminates the option of allowing the surface to weather.

31.5.1 Calcium plumbate primer

Among the surface treatments recommended in the current literature is the use of calcium plumbate primer. This material should be avoided because the adhesion of the paint can be uncertain and calcium plumbate contains a high proportion of lead.

31.5.2 Wash primers

Wash primers are also recommended in the current literature. These are two-pack paints containing polyvinyl butyral resin, zinc chromate and phosphoric acid. They are useful for coating small areas and providing that they are not applied too heavily and the surface is clean, they give good adhesion. On large areas they may cover contamination by grease and oil and contractors have been known to use them as a substitute for cleaning. Such a practice is almost certain to lead to premature adhesion failure and is not recommended.

31.5.3 Mordant or British Rail 'T' wash

The most satisfactory treatment for pretreating galvanized surfaces for painting is the use of Mordant or British Rail 'T' wash. This is a solution of copper salts in phosphoric acid and organic solvent. It should be applied to a galvanized surface which has already been cleaned and slightly roughened. It turns a steel surface black and should be rinsed with freshwater after about 15 min to leave a permanent black stain. If the stain is removed during rinsing, it indicates that the surface is not clean and the cleaning process must be repeated. Once the surface is dry it should be coated with a non-saponifiable primer that will not react with zinc salts. Chlorinated rubber or epoxy primers are ideal for this purpose.

31.5.4 Metal sprayed zinc coatings

Metal sprayed zinc coatings have a completely different structure to those obtained by hot-dip galvanizing. They are applied by melting a zinc wire in an oxypropane flame and atomizing and projecting the metallic particles in a stream of compressed air on to a blast-cleaned steel surface. The coating is porous and the surface is rough. Porosity accounts for approximately 10% of the volume of the coating.

Freshly sprayed zinc is clean and free from grease and other contaminants. Due to its porosity and rough texture it presents a very large and reactive surface to the atmosphere. It is therefore essential to inhibit the surface as soon as possible after application and this is done with wash or etch primer. The wash primer must not be applied to excess although all of it will appear to have been absorbed into the zinc coating. The sealing of the coating should then be completed using a thinned epoxy or vinyl. If a pigmented sealer is used, the pigment should have a fine particle size and be present in low volume concentration. After sealing there are a number of primers and barrier coats that may be applied before finishing. If the sprayed metal is aluminium, the use of a wash primer is not necessary.

31.5.5 Sherardized coatings

Zinc coatings may be applied to small components such as nuts, bolts and washers by sherardizing. Sherardized coatings are applied by tumbling the cleaned parts in zinc dust at an elevated temperature, but below the melting point of zinc. As zinc coated bolts are usually painted on site, sherardizing may be preferable to galvanizing because the surface is matt and free from grease. Epoxy or chlorinated rubber primers may be applied directly without the necessity of using wash primers or mordant.

31.5.6 Zinc rich primers

Zinc rich primers are paints pigmented with zinc dust as the rust inhibitor. Their composition is covered by BS 4652: 1971.[7] There are three formulations covered by this standard but type 3 in epoxy media is the most popular for new steel. By definition in this standard, zinc rich paint must have a 62–66% pigment volume concentration and 95% by weight of the pigment must be zinc. This corresponds to over 90% by weight of zinc in the dry film.

The organic zinc rich primers give excellent corrosion resistance, particularly at low dry-film thicknesses. They are applied at up to 75 μm thickness, but due to the high pigmentation overthick coatings can exhibit mechanical weakness; excessive thicknesses have been known to delaminate. These primers are usually overcoated with epoxies or chlorinated rubber which are not adversely affected by the zinc salts which may form at the interface.

31.5.6.1 Zinc silicates

Zinc silicates are primers used mainly on offshore structures. The original inorganic silicates were based on alkali-metal silicates and zinc dust. When mixed, they could be applied to blast-cleaned steel to give a completely inorganic cement-like coating containing zinc metal. The alkali silicates have been largely replaced by organic silicates in which the zinc dust is mixed with a partially hydrolysed alkyl silicate. These cure by hydrolysis through interaction with atmospheric moisture. Once hydrolysis is complete, the coating is completely inorganic.

Zinc silicates have a very good reputation for corrosion resistance under severe conditions and they do not salt as readily as the organic zinc rich primers. They are far from user-friendly products in that they require a very good standard or blast cleaning, Sa.3 is desirable, and great care must be taken to control film thickness and the atmospheric conditions during drying and curing. Low temperatures and low humidity will retard the cure rate. Overcoating may be a problem and a tie coat may be required. Areas of low film thickness are difficult to overcoat with additional zinc silicate.

A compromise has been reached with the introduction of organic modified zinc silicates such as PROTECTON 402. These are more user-friendly than either zinc rich epoxies or the inorganic silicates. They are tolerant to imperfectly blasted surfaces and may be applied to a specified minimum dry-film thickness of 75 μm without risk of mechanical weakness on overthick areas. Furthermore, they can be overcoated with most paints after a very short time.

Surfaces which need to be protected against corrosion and also decorated may be coated with systems based on epoxy zinc silicates and epoxy micaceous iron oxide as a base for a decorative finish. This is an ideal system for a very long-life coating as an alternative to galvanizing and painting. Intercoat adhesion between the works-applied coating and the site-applied decorative finish is much better than between galvanizing and paint. It is also easy to repair transportation and erection damage.

Specifiers should understand that zinc applied by hot-dip galvanizing, metal spraying, sherardizing, electroplating or mechanical-impact plating are not paints and if left unpainted will act as sacrificial anodes with a life expectancy proportional to the weight of zinc per unit area. Technical details of metallic zinc coatings are beyond the scope of this chapter, but are available from the Zinc Development Association.[8]

Primers with zinc metal as the main pigment protect in a similar manner to metallic coatings although their integrity may be undermined if the binder is degraded.

Coating systems utilizing paint over metallic zinc coatings or zinc pigmented primers are intended to use the zinc as a last line of defence if the paint is damaged or eroded. They must be designed to avoid the risk of zinc corrosion products produced by sacrificial action destroying the paint.

31.6 Specifications

It is essential to consider the corrosion environment when drafting a paint specification for steel. The code of practice BS 5493: 1977[6] gives in the form of tables the anticipated life expectancy for a number of specifications under a variety of environmental conditions. The time quoted is to first maintenance and the coatings are the minimum to ensure protection. The specifier must take into account the requirements of the client for decorative finishes, fire protection and the scope of any maintenance that may be undertaken once the structure is in use. The code quotes metal coatings for very long life to first maintenance, i.e. in excess of 20 years. The life expectancy of some metal coatings plus paint is anticipated to give a long life, i.e. 10–20 years, and yet the application of a carefully chosen paint coating will usually increase the overall life of the metal coating.

It is clear that if a metal coating such as galvanizing is used alone it will protect steel until most of the zinc has corroded away after which it is impossible to restore the galvanizing without replacing the steel section. The paint on a painted galvanized surface can be maintained, but maintenance will be required at much shorter intervals than the life of the zinc.

BS 5493: 1977[6] classifies atmospheres as 'internal dry', 'internal wet', 'external coastal', etc. This is reasonable for the external environment, but it is more than likely that a number of different conditions exist inside a building. Exterior steel which is visible, accessible and regularly painted to maintain appearance is often less at risk than internal steel in cavities

which are outside the thermal insulation of the building and may need protection for the whole life of the structure. A recent examination of some unpainted internal columns after 60 years showed over 90% of the length to be unaffected by corrosion. The column bases which had been subjected to rising damp and the top sections which had suffered from condensation in the roof space were severely pitted by corrosion and structurally unsound. Many engineers now specify additional protection on the ends of roof beams from where they extend under the eaves to 1 m within the roof space. This section is most likely to suffer from condensation and is also the most inaccessible for maintenance.

The coating programme is significant in selecting a protective paint system.

31.6.1 Small projects and rapid-construction programmes

For small projects or a rapid-construction programme, the paint may only be required to protect the steel from the time it is fabricated until the building is in use. Shops, small factories, offices and sports halls where all the steel is internal and the temperature is maintained at a comfortable level, are good examples. Steel sections are light and the building is likely to be in use within 1 year of fabrication. Many of these structures are coated with a single coat of primer at the works and the only site painting is a coat of decorative paint on internal visible surfaces.

A typical specification for this type of project is given below in Sections 31.6.1.1 and 31.6.1.2.

31.6.1.1 At the fabrication works

The steel should be abrasive blasted to BS 4232: 1967[1] second quality (equivalent to Swedish Standard Sa.2.5[2]). If steel is blasted before fabrication, it must be maintained under conditions where condensation will not take place and cause flash rusting. If the fabricator is not satisfied that these conditions can be maintained, the use of a prefabrication blast primer is recommended. Weld damaged areas must be cleaned before priming.

One coat of high build alkyd or modified alkyd zinc phosphate primer should be applied at a minimum dry-film thickness of 75 μm. Fast-set formulations should be applied by airless spray. The architect or client may wish to specify a colour so that the primer acts as an undercoat for a decorative finish applied on site. Materials such as PROTECTON high build phosphate primer MP 273 are usually supplied in a red/brown colour, but it is manufactured in white, yellow, green, blue, grey and red either to match the finish or as a fabricator's house colour. Light-coloured primers show up damage or areas of underthickness better than the standard brown colour.

31.6.1.2 On site

All damaged areas should be cleaned and touched up with the works' primer. For internal concealed steel it is possible that no further paint treatment will be required. Where the steel is visible, it may be overcoated with the decorator's alkyd undercoat and gloss. A considerable saving in time and money will be made by using a high build decorative finish.

A survey has shown that the labour cost of applying paint on site is 3 to 4 times greater as compared with application at the fabrication works. Factory painters are specialists in a small range of products and work under good conditions, while site painters handle a very large variety of coatings and work under difficult or even hostile conditions. Works painters are more adept at applying paint to meet minimum dry-film thickness requirements, while site painters concentrate on appearance. In terms of return on cost it is sensible to have all the painting completed by the fabricator or a subcontractor off site. The site painter should touch up erection damage and preferably apply one coat of site finish.

Although the cost per litre of high build finishes is higher than that of decorators paint, the saving in labour costs and inteference with other trades from applying fewer site coats more than compensates for this. An example of comparative costings derived from a 1987 survey of site finishing yielded the following costs per square metre (DFT indicates dry-film thickness).

Decorator's undercoat @ 38 μm DFT; touch dry 2 h £0.20
Decorator's gloss finish @ 25 μm DFT; touch dry 6 h £0.20
Labour, two coats @ £1.60 per coat £3.20

Total DFT 63 μm; cost per m^2 £3.60

PROTECTON high build silicone alkyd @ 75 μm DFT
Touch dry 2 h £1.00
Labour, one coat £2.00

Total DFT 75 μm; cost per m^2 £3.00

This example shows that by using undercoat and gloss, the labour cost of the work is 89% of the whole, the dry-film thickness is reduced by 16% and the tack time is increased by a factor of 4. Even at the same thickness, the silicone alkyd is more durable with better gloss, colour retention and resistance to chalking than the decorator's alkyd. The labour cost of the silicone coating is reduced to 67% of the total.

Site painting contractors will only use high build formulations if they are clearly specified and the work needs to be checked to ensure that the correct wet-film thickness is applied to give the corresponding specified dry-film thickness. Recent formulations of high build alkyds show a further reduction in cost.

31.6.2 Large projects and long construction programmes

For larger projects where some areas will be subject to greater corrosion risk, where heavy sections are subject to more handling damage, and where construction times are longer, a much more durable painting specification is necessary. Under these conditions, epoxy coatings applied at the fabrication works more than justify the slight increase in cost. A typical specification for this type of project is given below in Sections 13.6.2.1 and 13.6.2.2.

31.6.2.1 At the fabrication works

The steel should be abrasive blasted to BS 4232: 1967[1] second quality equivalent to Swedish Specification Sa.2.5,[2] and primed within 4 h of blasting.

One coat of PROTECTON epoxy phosphate primer EP 66 should be applied at a minimum dry-film thickness of 25 μm. This may be used as a prefabrication primer, in which case weld-damaged areas must be cleaned and touched up after fabrication. A slower drying equivalent more suitable for brush application may be used for touching up weld damage. A build coat of PROTECTON high build epoxy micaceous iron oxide fast-set EP 185 should be applied at a minimum dry-film thickness of 75 μm. The total minimum dry-film thickness of works coatings should be 100 μm.

This is a basic specification which may be modified in a number of ways. To the coat of prefabrication blast primer may be added a coat of high build phosphate epoxy primer, e.g. PROTECTON EP 78, at a dry film thickness of 75 μm. In this case it is necessary to clean the weld damaged area, but it is not necessary to touch up with EP66 providing sufficient cover

of the high-build material is applied. This will increase the dry-film thickness of the works system to 150 ot 175 μm. The build coat of EP 185 may be airless sprayed in a single coat of 100 or 125 μm. This can increase the works system still more to 200 μm or even 225 μm.

It may be decided to use the rather better epoxy primers based on a zinc metal pigment. PROTECTON epoxy zinc rich primer with a volume solids of 34% is suitable as the prefabrication primer, while identical formulations with volume solids of 43 or 57% are suitable for the post-fabrication higher film thicknesses. As a high build primer, PROTECTON 402 epoxy modified zinc silicate is better than zinc rich primers. At a film thickness of 75 μm the higher film strength provides a safety factor if the applicator exceeds the minimum specified thickness. In addition to improved mechanical durability, it has a reduced rate of salting.

If the fabricator decides to blast after fabrication or use a coating subcontractor, the prefabrication primer can be eliminated if a high build primer is included in the specification. Fabricators using the submerged arc process usually prefer to blast after fabrication and the elimination of one coat can offset the higher cost of blasting with compressed-air plant.

From this example of works-applied epoxy coatings it is clear that considerable scope for variation is available to meet any number of different projects. Specifiers can take advantage of the expertise and economy of fabricators but keep the number of coats to two or two and a prefabrication primer. The use of airless spray and fast-drying formulations also reduces 'down time' at the works.

31.6.2.2 On site

The same range of single pack decorative coatings is available for application to an epoxy works system as for the single coat of alkyd primer used for light structures. The additional advantage of the epoxy micaceous iron oxide (MIO) system is that it can be overcoated with almost any paint or cementiferous coating.

High performance decorative finishes for use in a severe environment are two-pack epoxy enamels or two-pack polyurethanes with their improved resistance to chalking. Two-pack polyurethanes may be brushed over small areas but are better applied by spray. Standard materials can be applied at 40–50 μm per coat and high build formulations at 80 μm by airless spray.

For industrial finishes where there is damp or chemical pollution, a finishing system of chlorinated rubber is effective. It can be brushed or airless sprayed and is tolerant to poor weather conditions during application. Since it dries by solvent evaporation, overcoating for repair and maintenance requires little or no surface preparation. Areas which become inaccessible for a very long time, sometimes for the whole life of a structure, and may be in damp conditions can be finished in epoxy pitch.

PROTECTON coal tar epoxy can be applied at a dry film thickness of 125 μm in one coat and although the appearance is poor, this is not a disadvantage in concealed areas. Epoxy pitch is widely used under immersed conditions in foul water. Epoxy MIO can be overcoated with cement-based 'sprayed-on' fire protection on concealed steel or with intumescent paint such as UNITHERM A 60 where the steel is an architectural feature. UNITHERM is applied at a thickness of 1–2 mm and finished with a decorative coat of PROTECTON high build alkyd which also serves as a sealer. It is advisable for architects and engineers to establish fire-protection requirements before completing a structural design.

31.7 Heavy-duty coatings

The materials and specifications described in previous sections can be used for most heavy-duty applications provided that higher dry-film thicknesses are used. Bridges have been coated with epoxy systems applied at a fabrication works followed by chlorinated rubber or silicone alkyd on site. Chlorinated rubber is particularly useful for repainting weathered steel and either chlorinated rubber primers or water tolerant epoxy primers may be used for this type of site maintenance. Most of the larger bridges in the UK come under the control of government departments or British Rail who have their own specifications and systems of approval. Similarly, large chemical and oil companies have their own paint specifications which they find satisfactory for their particular conditions.

Heavy-duty specifications for severe chemical exposure present the same problems as tank linings in that there is no universal system for all environments. In an article such as this, dealing with coatings for steel in the broad sense, it is impossible to cover all the details of conditions that determine coating materials to resist the many chemicals that may be involved. Specifications for tank linings and surfaces subject to severe chemical attack include epoxies and polyurethanes, but these need to be applied at very high coating thicknesses, in some cases up to 3 mm. The use of multicoat systems of high build paints are usually acceptable up to 500 μm, but very high film builds are better applied by using solventless materials applied by spreader or hot airless spray.

The same materials can be applied to floors and walls over a suitable penetration sealer of low viscosity. The PROTECTON REAGEN range of coatings are of this type and include coating systems which can be used mixed with aggregate to give non-slip surfaces for floors. Formulations are modified to match conditions so that a full range of properties are available for resistance to chemicals, wear and impact. Water thinned materials are used where solvents are not permitted and antistatic coatings are used where sparks or static charges would be damaging. Such specialized coatings are used in chemical factories, breweries, wineries, dairies and, in fact, in any area where food, drinks or drugs are handled.

It is in the interest of all structural, chemical and plant engineers to take specialist advice when preparing paint specifications for anything but the most basic of structures. Coating technology is always advancing and, although some of the old established systems are still of value, they may have been replaced by newer products which are better, can be applied more easily or offer better return on the money invested. All new materials are now formulated with regard to health and safety in manufacture and use and also with regard to their effect on the environment.

References

1 BRITISH STANDARDS INSTITUTION, *BS 4232 Specification for the surface finish of blast-cleaned steel for painting*, Milton Keynes (1967)
2 SWEDISH STANDARDS INSTITUTION, *SIS 05 59 00 Pictorial surface preparation standards for painting steel surfaces* (1967)
3 US STEEL STRUCTURE PAINTING COUNCIL
4 BRITISH STANDARDS INSTITUTION, *BS 2569 (1964), AMD 55 (1968) Specification for sprayed metal coatings, Part 1: Protection of iron and steel by aluminium and zinc against atmospheric corrosion*, Milton Keynes
5 BRITISH STANDARDS INSTITUTION, *BS 2451 Specification for chilled iron shot and grit*, Milton Keynes (1963)
6 BRITISH STANDARDS INSTITUTION, *BS 5493 Protective coating of iron and steel structures against corrosion*, Milton Keynes (1977)
7 BRITISH STANDARDS INSTITUTION, *BS 4652 (1971), AMD 3901 (1982) Specification for metallic zinc rich priming paint (organic media)*, Milton Keynes
8 ZINC DEVELOPMENT ASSOCIATION, 34 Berkeley Square, London W1X 6AL

Bibliography

BALLARD, W. E., *Metal Spraying*, 4th edn, Griffin, London (1963)
BRITISH STANDARDS INSTITUTION, *BS 5493 Code of practice for protective coating iron and steel structures against corrosion*, Milton Keynes (1977)
BRITISH STANDARDS INSTITUTION, *BS 2015 (1965), AMD 4332 (1983) Glossary of paint terms*, Milton Keynes
BRITISH STANDARDS INSTITUTION, *DD 24 Draft for development recommendations for methods of protection against corrosion on light section steel used in building*, Milton Keynes (1973)
BRITISH STANDARDS INSTITUTION, *BS 615 Code of practice for painting of buildings*, Milton Keynes (1982)
BRITISH STANDARDS INSTITUTION, *BS 729 Specification for zinc coatings in iron and steel articles, Part 1: Hot dipped galvanised coatings*, Milton Keynes (1961)
BRITISH STANDARDS INSTITUTION, *BS 2989 Specification for hot-dip galvanised plain steel sheet and coil*, Milton Keynes (1967)
CONSTRUCTION INDUSTRY RESEARCH AND INFORMATION ASSOCIATION, *Painting Steelwork* (ed. Haigh, I. P.) *CIRIA Report 93*, Pittsburg (1971)
FANCUTT, F. and HUDSON, J. C., *Protective Painting of Structural Steel*, Chapman and Hall, London (1957)
HUDSON, J. C., *Sixth Report of the Corrosion Committee*, The Iron and Steel Institute (1959)

32

Preserving and Coating Timber

J V Crookes MSc, CChem, MRSC
Cuprinol Ltd

Contents

32.1 Introduction 32/3

32.2 Hazards to timber 32/3
    32.2.1 Fungal attack 32/3
    32.2.2 Insect attack 32/3
    32.2.3 Marine borers 32/4
    32.2.4 Weathering 32/4
    32.2.5 Chemical effects 32/4
    32.2.6 Natural durability of timber 32/4

32.3 Timber preservation 32/4
    32.3.1 Permeability of timber 32/5
    32.3.2 Types of wood preservative 32/5
    32.3.3 Preparation of timber for treatment 32/5
    32.3.4 Treatment methods—seasoned timber 32/6
    32.3.5 Treatment methods—unseasoned timber 32/7
    32.3.6 *In situ* remedial treatments 32/8
    32.3.7 Specifying preservative treatments 32/8
    32.3.8 Standard specifications 32/8
    32.3.9 Legislation and approval of wood preservatives 32/9
    32.3.10 Health, safety and environmental factors 32/9

32.4 Coatings for timber 32/9
    32.4.1 General coating types 32/9
    32.4.2 General composition 32/9
    32.4.3 Specific coating properties 32/10
    32.4.4 Water-borne versus solvent-borne coatings 32/11
    32.4.5 Factors affecting coating performance 32/11
    32.4.6 Selection of coating systems 32/11
    32.4.7 Application 32/12
    32.4.8 Standard specifications 32/12
    32.4.9 Health, safety and environmental factors 32/12

References 32/13

Bibliography 32/14

32.1 Introduction

Timber used in construction can last indefinitely under favourable conditions. However, in many situations it is subject to hazards which may cause deterioration unless the species is naturally resistant or has been adequately protected. When considering the preservation and coating of timber, it is necessary to consider where it will be used, the hazards to which it will be exposed, and the natural durability of the timber species.

32.2 Hazards to timber

The principal causes of deterioration of timber in service are: (i) fungi; (ii) insects; (iii) marine borers; and (iv) physical and chemical attack.

32.2.1 Fungal attack

Fungal attack on timber normally occurs when its moisture content exceeds about 20%. The two main groups of fungi affecting timber are 'staining fungi' and 'wood-decaying fungi'.[1]

32.2.1.1 Staining fungi

Staining fungi disfigure timber without causing any significant reduction in strength. There are two main groups of staining fungi: blue staining fungi and moulds.

Blue staining fungi, although usually associated with sap stain in green unseasoned timber, also attack timber in service. These often produce an intense blue-grey discoloration which penetrates the sapwood. Moulds, however, mainly grow on the timber surface causing only superficial staining. Both types of fungi can cause the disruption and premature failure of coatings, such as paints and exterior wood stains.[2]

32.2.1.2 Wood-decaying fungi

The most important fungi affecting timber in service are the wood-decaying fungi. There are three main categories: (i) wet rot; (ii) dry rot; and (iii) soft rot. These fungi attack the cell walls of the wood, weakening its structure and can eventually cause its total destruction. Colour changes also occur, giving rise to the terms 'brown rots' and 'white rots'. The conditions favouring decay by these types of fungi differ widely.[1, 3, 4]

(i) *Wet rot* Wet rot is caused by a variety of fungi which attack softwoods and hardwoods, inside or outside buildings. They include both 'brown' and 'white' rots. Timber most at risk has a moisture content between 30% and 50%. Wet-rot fungi are the principal cause of decay in building timbers exposed to persistent moisture or condensation, external joinery, and to timbers in ground contact. The common type of wet rot in buildings in the UK is cellar fungus (*Coniophera puteana*). The decayed wood is brown with longitudinal cracking.

(ii) *Dry rot* Dry rot only occurs inside buildings in conditions of poor ventilation and high humidity.[5] It usually attacks softwoods with a moisture content of between about 20% and 40%, but it occasionally attacks hardwoods. Dry rot, unlike wet rot, has the ability to conduct moisture to drier timber, thereby enabling it to spread beyond the area of initial attack and also to cross inert material, such as masonry. An established outbreak can cause extensive damage and is difficult to eradicate.

'True dry rot' is caused by only one fungus (*Serpula lacrymans*) which only occurs in temperate climates and is common in mainland Europe and the UK. The decayed wood is dry and brittle, usually with deep cracks across the grain. Mycelium grows over the timber and surrounding areas; this is initially white and fluffy, but can develop into a matted grey skin. The fruiting body is flat with white edges, brick-red centre, and produces masses of tiny rust coloured spores.

In other countries, e.g. North America, the term 'dry rot' is used more generally to describe certain other fungi, particularly *Poria incrassata*.[1]

(iii) *Soft rot* Soft rot is the common cause of decay in timber where conditions prevent the development of wet rot or dry rot. It is a major problem in very wet timber, such as in cooling towers and other timbers in prolonged contact with water. Soft rot also occurs in timber, including some hardwoods, in ground contact. Attack often appears to be confined to the surface of the timber, which becomes soft, and the rate of decay is relatively slow.

32.2.2 Insect attack

Most timbers are susceptible to attack by wood-destroying insects, of which there are two main groups: (i) termites (*Isoptera*); and (ii) beetles (*Coleoptera*).

32.2.2.1 Termites

Termites occur principally in the region extending 48° north and south of the equator, and are found in southern Europe, causing serious damage to timber in buildings.[6, 7] There are three main types of termite: (i) subterranean; (ii) dry wood; and (iii) damp wood.

Subterranean termites cause the most serious economic problem of all insects attacking timber in service. They live in large colonies below the ground or in 'termite hills' on the surface. Damage to timber is caused by the workers which forage long distances underground and often enter buildings through tunnels which they construct on the walls. Once attack has commenced, damage is rapid and can result in total destruction of the timbers.

Dry-wood and damp-wood termites make their nests within the wood itself. Colonies are small, as compared with subterranean termite colonies, and the rates of destruction of timber are considerably slower.

32.2.2.2 Beetles

The most common of the wood-boring beetles causing damage to timbers in service are: (i) longhorn beetle; (ii) furniture beetle; (iii) death watch beetle; and (iv) powder post (including *Lyctus*) beetles. Their occurrence varies from one region to another. Damage is caused by the insect larvae, which produce the characteristic tunnels in the timber.

(i) *Longhorn beetles* Only the house longhorn (*Hylotropes bajulus*)[8] causes significant damage to timber in service. Across the world, house longhorn is economically the most important of the wood-boring beetles, and is a major problem in mainland Europe, the USSR and the USA. The beetle occurs in the UK in a limited area south-west of London, where it is a major problem, and sporadic outbreaks have been reported in other parts of the UK.[9]

The house longhorn only attacks the sapwood of softwoods, generally in roof voids. The larvae grow up to 30 mm in length, boring tunnels 6–10 mm in diameter, and cause severe structural damage relatively quickly. In areas where house longhorn is prevalent, it is usually mandatory to preserve structural timbers.

(ii) *Furniture beetle* The common furniture beetle, or woodworm (*Anobium punctatum*),[8] occurs in temperate regions and is a major problem in parts of Continental Europe, the UK, New Zealand and elsewhere. It usually attacks the sapwood of hardwoods and softwoods and is common in roof timbers, joists, flooring and furniture. The larvae are relatively small. Flight holes are approximately 2 mm in diameter. Initially, when attack is light, the rate of damage is slow. However, over a period of years infestation can become heavy and can cause structural failure.

(*iii*) *Death watch beetle* The death watch beetle (*Xestobium rufovillosum*)[8] is a pest commonly associated with old buildings. Death watch normally attacks hardwoods which are damp and where some fungal attack is present. Occasionally it spreads to softwoods. Flight holes may be 3 mm in diameter. Severe attack causes considerable damage and the cost of repair following individual outbreaks can be high. However, its incidence is lower than that of the furniture beetle.

(*iv*) *Powder post (including Lyctus) beetles* Powder post beetles occur in the tropics and temperate regions. Infestation of the timber mostly occurs in the saw mill, and is usually restricted to the sapwood of certain hardwoods. Softwoods are not affected. Tunnels vary in diameter from 1–2 mm (*Lyctus* sp.) to 3–6 mm (*Bostrychidae* sp.). Active *Lyctus* is found in relatively new timbers with high starch content and less commonly in older dry timbers in buildings, while *Bostrychidae* sp. do not reinfest timber in climates similar to that of the UK.

(*v*) *Carpenter ants* Serious damage to structural timbers in buildings in parts of the USA and Canada is caused by carpenter ants.[1] These are true ants (*Camponotus* sp.) and live in colonies. Damage is caused when the workers excavate the timber to make nests.

32.2.3 Marine borers

Timber in the sea or brackish water is liable to damage from marine borers. Very few timber species are resistant to attack. There are two groups of marine borers: molluscs and crustaceans.[1,10–12]

Molluscs, which include shipworms, can grow to approximately 25 mm in diameter and 3 m in length, although the toredo found in temperate waters is smaller. The mollusc bores deep below the surface, producing tunnels that increase in size as it grows.

Crustaceans are small creatures, approximately 1–3 mm in diameter, and occur in intertidal waters. They tunnel close to the timber surface forming a spongy mass which becomes physically eroded. Crustaceans include *Limnoria*, commonly called the Gribble, which is found around the UK and in temperate waters.

32.2.4 Weathering

Timber exposed to the weather undergoes a number of chemical and physical changes on the surface due to the combined effects of moisture, temperature and sunlight.[13]

Sunlight causes photodegradation of the lignin, which binds together the wood fibres, causing the formation of a grey unstructured mat of fibres on the surface. On some lighter timbers this is preceded by darkening.

This is often followed by the formation of surface cracks, or 'checks', resulting from rapid changes in the surface moisture content of the timber. The effect is most pronounced where variations in atmospheric moisture are accompanied by sudden and extreme changes in surface temperature.

Whilst the effects of weathering are mainly superficial, the break-up of the surface makes the timber more susceptible to infestation by moulds and other fungi.

32.2.5 Chemical effects

Chemical attack on timber may be caused by exposure to liquids, chemical fumes or air-borne pollution. Attack is normally more rapid at higher temperatures, and hardwoods tend to be more susceptible than softwoods. The use of timber in a chemically hostile environment must be fully evaluated. In some situations specialist coatings can be used to protect the timber against chemical attack.

Whilst most timbers are resistant to weak acids, wood is degraded by strong acids, oxidizing agents and alkalis. Solutions of salts cause differing effects, depending on the salt, temperature, duration of exposure and wood species. In some cases an increase in strength has been observed, in other cases a decrease. Exposure to steam, such as in high temperature steaming processes, can cause serious reduction in the strength of the timber. Chemical effects on timber have been reviewed by Thompson.[14]

32.2.6 Natural durability of timber

The natural 'durability' of a timber species is a measure of the resistance of the heartwood to fungal decay; the sapwood is usually susceptible. Durability may also be influenced by conditions and rate of growth, position of timber in the tree and storage and processing methods.[15] The natural-durability classifications such as those used in the UK[16] and the USA,[17] based on the average life of heartwood stakes in ground contact, are given in *Table 32.1*. Whilst the majority of the world's most durable timbers are hardwoods, not all hardwoods are durable; *Shorea* species, including meranti and lauan timbers, range from non-durable to durable. The majority of commercial softwoods are fast grown, contain a large proportion of low durability sapwood, and have either non-durable or only moderately durable heartwood. Notable exceptions include pitch pine, Western red cedar and Californian redwood, which have durable heartwood.

The natural resistance of timbers to insect attack varies considerably depending on the insect species and condition of the timber. Natural durability against fungal decay should not be equated with resistance to insect attack. However, in each case the sapwood of the timber is susceptible to attack.

32.3 Timber preservation

Timber preservation is the process of impregnating wood with chemicals which are toxic to fungi or insects in order to control or eradicate these organisms. Wood preservatives differ widely in their properties, methods of application and suitability for

Table 32.1 Natural-durability classifications of some timbers[a]

Classification	Average life of stakes (years)	Examples
Very durable	>25	Teak, greenheart,
Durable	15–25	European oak, Western red cedar, Californian redwood
Moderately durable	10–15	Douglas fir, sapele, African mahogany
Non-durable	5–10	European redwood, spruce
Perishable	0–5	Beech, ramin

[a] Based on the average life of heartwood stakes in ground contact.

Table 32.2 Permeability classifications of some timbers

Classification	Examples
Permeable	Beech, ramin
Moderately resistant	European redwood
Resistant	Western red cedar, Douglas fir, sapele, spruce
Extremely resistant	Teak, greenheart, European oak, African mahogany

different situations. The effectiveness of a treatment depends on the type of preservative and on achieving an adequate penetration and retention in the timber. Timber can be preserved either when freshly felled, or after seasoning. Most construction timbers are preserved after seasoning.

32.3.1 Permeability of timber

Timbers vary in their ability to absorb fluids, and the 'permeability' of the timber species is an important factor in selecting a method of application. Permeability classifications of timbers, such as those used in the UK,[16] normally refer to the heartwood. The sapwood is usually permeable. The classifications widely used are shown in *Table 32.2.*

32.3.2 Types of wood preservative

Wood preservatives may be divided into three types: (i) tar oil; (ii) water-borne; and (iii) organic solvent. A further group includes specialist products for remedial treatment.

32.3.2.1 Tar-oil preservatives

The most common wood preservative in this category is creosote, produced by the distillation of coal tar. Different grades are obtained, varying in viscosity and volatility. All are highly toxic to fungi, insects and marine borers.

Heavy-oil creosote is used for high-hazard situations, and where a long service life (e.g. over 30 years) is required. It is normally applied hot (to reduce its viscosity) by using a high-pressure process or by the 'hot and cold tank' method. Typical uses are piling in freshwater or seawater, railway sleepers and telegraph poles.

Medium- and light-oil creosotes are used for less hazardous situations and usually where periodic retreatment can be applied. The most common methods of application are dipping/steeping, spraying and brushing. Typical uses are on fencing and farm buildings.

Creosote treatments confer a degree of water repellency to the timber, reducing its tendency to split and crack in service. Treated timber usually retains a characteristic odour for a long period and normally cannot be painted.

32.3.2.2 Water-borne preservatives

Water-borne wood preservatives are solutions of a single salt or a mixture of salts in water. They may be divided into two categories: (i) fixed-salt treatments; and (ii) water-soluble (leachable) treatments.

(i) *Fixed-salt treatments*   Fixed-salt type preservatives contain a mixture of salts which react in the timber to become insoluble and highly resistant to leaching. They are normally applied by high-pressure processes, after which the timber must be redried. The overall process may result in dimensional changes in the timber. A variety of fixed-salt preservatives are in current use.

The most common are the copper/chrome/arsenate (CCA) preservatives.

CCA treatments confer a high resistance to fungi and insects, and are suitable for internal or external structural timbers and in high hazard situations. Treated timber is pale green, odourless, clean to handle and harmless to plants. When dry, it is non-corrosive to most metals; however, under wet conditions corrosion of mild or galvanized steel or aluminium may occur. Treated timber may be painted, but is usually used externally without further treatment.

Other fixed-salt preservatives include copper/chrome/boron (CCB), acid/copper/chrome (ACC), ammoniacal copper arsenite (ACA), copper/chrome/phosphorous (CCP), and fluoride/chrome/arsenate/phenol (FCAP).

(ii) *Water-soluble (leachable) treatments*   The majority of water-soluble preservatives are solutions of boron compounds, or borates, in water. These preservatives are applied by the diffusion process to newly felled timber. Preservatives based on boron compounds are fungicidal and insecticidal, but their use is restricted to dry areas where leaching is not expected, such as in internal structural timbers.

32.3.2.3 Organic-solvent preservatives

Organic-solvent preservatives contain fungicides and/or insecticides dissolved in an organic solvent, usually a light hydrocarbon solvent similar to white spirit. Most are highly resistant to leaching. Fungicides used include: pentachlorophenol (PCP), pentachlorophenol laurate (PCPL), zinc and copper naphthenates and acypetacs zinc. Insecticides include: lindane (γ-HCH) and permethrin. Organic-solvent preservatives are normally applied by low-pressure processes or by immersion, and are suitable for low to medium hazard situations, such as structural timbers (not in ground contact) and external joinery.

Organic-solvent preservatives cause no dimensional movement in the timber. Treated timber, after solvent evaporation, is no more flammable than untreated timber. The treatments are non-corrosive to most metals.

Organic-solvent preservatives may be modified to include water repellents, tints for recognition, or other additives. However, most are formulated to be compatible with paints and glues.

PCP in heavy oil applied by a high-pressure process is the only organic-solvent preservative treatment generally approved for timber in ground contact, but is mainly used in the USA.

32.3.3 Preparation of timber for treatment

Prior to preservative treatment, timber must be debarked (occasionally the bark is retained for the sap-displacement method), be free of extraneous material, insect and fungal attack, and dried to an appropriate moisture content. Unseasoned timber may be preserved as either logs or sawn timber, and treatments require the moisture content to be as high as possible. Seasoned timber is treated either sawn or fully machined, and processes require the moisture content of the timber not to exceed 28% for water-borne preservatives, or 25% for organic-solvent-borne preservatives.

32.3.3.1 Seasoning

The two common methods of drying, or 'seasoning' timber are air drying and kiln drying.

Air drying relies on the natural evaporation of water. Logs or sawn timber are stacked outdoors. The rate and degree of drying is influenced by climatic conditions. The final moisture content of the timber can range from about 7% in dry climates to about 20–24% in temperate climates. Drying periods vary from about 3 to 12 months, depending on conditions and the timber.

Kiln drying is conducted in chambers under controlled conditions of temperature and humidity. Several types of kiln are used commercially. Timber is initially exposed to an atmosphere of high humidity which is progressively reduced and the temperature increased during the drying process. Kiln-drying is capable of drying timber to practically any moisture content, usually within one or two days depending on the timber and the type of kiln.

32.3.3.2 Conditioning

Preservative penetration can be increased by various techniques. The most commonly used, and included in standard specifications, are incising and steam conditioning.

Incising is used principally on structural timbers, poles and railway sleepers. Incisions vary in depth from about 10 to 16 mm, depending on the size of the timber, and are cut into the surface. The process is normally used for less-permeable timbers, such as spruce, Western hemlock and Douglas fir.

Steam conditioning increases the natural permeability of certain timbers, normally softwoods. The process can cause strength loss in some timbers. Certain Douglas fir, for example, should not be steam conditioned.

Other techniques used for improving permeability include compression between rollers, causing rupture of the cell membranes, and storage of timber under damp conditions allowing bacterial action, otherwise known as ponding.

Methods of seasoning and preparation of timber for preservative treatment are discussed further by Wilkinson.[18]

32.3.4 Treatment methods—seasoned timber

Wood preservatives may be applied to seasoned timber by 'pressure' or 'non-pressure' methods.[18,19]

32.3.4.1 Pressure methods

Pressure treatment methods are the most effective means of applying preservatives to seasoned timber, because of their versatility and ability to penetrate less permeable timbers. The processes are conducted in treatment vessels varying in length up to approximately 10 m for building timbers and 30 m for poles. Process schedules, or 'cycles', are varied depending on the type of preservative, permeability of the timber species and the required level of preservation.

Methods are usually classified as either 'high pressure' (approximately 700–1400 kPa) or 'low pressure' (usually

100–500 kPa). By convention, pressures quoted are gauge pressures, i.e. relative to external atmospheric pressure.

The timber is totally submerged in preservative in the treatment vessel, and pressure is applied to the preservative fluid. The quantity of preservative absorbed increases with the magnitude and duration of the pressure stage. The main pressure stage may be preceded either by a vacuum or another pressure stage, depending on the severity of the treatment. The preservative is finally drained from the treatment vessel and surplus preservative is removed in a final vacuum stage.

(i) High-pressure methods The three high-pressure methods commonly used are the Bethell, Lowry, and Rueping processes. Typical process schedules of these and other methods are given in Table 32.3.

The Bethell (full cell) process is the principal method of applying water-borne preservatives, such as copper/chrome/arsenate (CCA) preservatives, to seasoned timber for use in highly hazardous situations. The process is designed to penetrate the entire sapwood and heartwood, leaving preservative filling the cells, and a very high level of preservation is achieved. The process is also used to apply creosote. However, the heavy creosote retention often causes subsequent 'bleeding' of creosote from the timber, and its use is generally restricted to marine pilings.

The Lowry and Rueping (empty cell) processes are used for applying pentachlorophenol (PCP) in heavy oil and creosote. These processes result in lower net preservative retentions than full-cell processes and 'bleeding' of creosote is reduced. Applications include wooden foundations and transmission poles.

High-pressure treatments are often specified to a 'net preservative retention'. The required sapwood and heartwood penetration may be also included in the specification. In such cases the plant operator usually decides on the treatment schedule. Alternatively, the treatment may be specified by a 'process schedule'.

Preservative retention may be expressed in terms of either the fluid or 'dry salt' retention, and is an average value for the entire load of timber. Treatment details are given in certificates of treatment.

Mixed charges of timbers, requiring different treatment schedules, should be avoided. If this is not possible, the treatment cycle for the most resistant timber is used. However, this results in the more permeable timbers being overtreated.

Certain timbers, including Douglas fir and spruce, are liable to permanent deformation, or 'collapse' at pressures above 1000 kPa, particularly when treated with creosote.

(ii) Low-pressure methods Low-pressure processes are usually used for applying organic-solvent-type preservatives to timbers

Table 32.3 Typical pressure-treatment schedules[a]

Process type	Preliminary stage		Pressure stage		Final vacuum	
	Pressure (kPa)	Period (min)	Pressure (kPa)	Period (min)	Pressure (kPa)	Period (min)
Bethell (full cell)	−80	15–60	1000–1400	60–210	−80	15
Lowry (empty cell)			1000–1400	60–210	−80	15
Rueping (empty cell)	+400	10–60	1000–1400	60–240	−70	20
Double vacuum/pressure	−80	10	200	15	−83	20
Double vacuum	−33	3	0	3	−67	20

[a] Pressure is expressed as 'gauge' pressure.

for low- or medium-hazard situations, such as internal structural timbers, and external timbers (not in ground contact), external joinery, soffits, fascias and cladding. The two common low-pressure processes are the 'double vacuum' (DV) and the more severe 'double vacuum/pressure' (DVP) process. Typical cycles of these processes are given in *Table 32.3*.

Low-pressure processes are normally specified to an approved 'process' schedule, without reference to preservative retention. Modern treatment plants may be programmed to include standard schedules, and the processes are monitored on chart recorders. Certificates of treatment are usually issued with the treated timber.

Low-pressure treatment plants are used by major joinery manufacturers. The main advantages in production are that treatment cycles are available for the more common joinery and construction timbers. Treated joinery is dimensionally unchanged and may be painted or glued within a few days without forced drying.

(iii) Other pressure processes In addition to the more common processes described above, there are a variety of other pressure processes in commercial use. Probably the most important is the Boulton process which is used to apply creosote to unseasoned timber. The process is used extensively in North America for railway sleepers, poles, etc. The process involves preheating the timber in creosote prior to applying a full-cell or empty-cell process.

32.3.4.2 Non-pressure methods

The application of preservatives by non-pressure methods is generally less effective than that by pressure methods, and the levels of preservation against fungal decay vary considerably. However, relatively good eradication and protection against most types of insect attack can be obtained by using any of the methods.

Brushing/spraying are principally for on-site application of organic solvent preservatives and light-oil creosote, for maintenance and remedial treatments. The levels of preservation achieved are adequate for low decay hazard situations, such as internal and external timbers (not in ground contact). Two or three flood coats on all surfaces are normally sufficient. When spraying, a coarse non-atomizing spray is required.

Deluging involves passing lengths of timber through a tunnel where preservative is flooded over the surface. Excess preservative is removed before the timber leaves the tunnel. This method is equivalent to a good brush or spray treatment.

Immersion and steeping are considerably more thorough than the preceding non-pressure methods. Timber is totally submerged in the wood preservative. The duration of the treatment depends on the permeability of the timber, type of preservative, and required level of preservation. A treatment period of less than 60 min is usually referred to as an 'immersion' treatment, whereas treatments of days or weeks duration are known as 'steeping'.

Immersion treatments are approved in standards for the pretreatment of permeable timbers in low-hazard situations, such as roof timbers, cladding boards, floor joists and external softwood joinery. Steeping provides a higher level of preservation, and is usually applied to timbers for ground contact, such as posts and poles.

32.3.4.3 Plywood

Most plywoods can be satisfactorily treated using conventional methods and preservatives, including creosote.

High-pressure full cell processes using fixed-salt water-borne preservatives (e.g. copper/chrome/arsenate (CCA)) are suitable for most applications, including timbers in seawater, wood foundations, and for conditions of high humidity or severe insect attack.

High-pressure empty cell processes using fixed-salt or organic solvent (e.g. pentachlorophenol (PCP)) preservatives are suitable for situations where a lower level of preservation is required. Organic-solvent preservatives applied by certain low-pressure processes are suitable where there is only a moderate risk of decay.

32.3.5 Treatment methods—unseasoned timber

Newly felled unseasoned timber can be preserved by various methods.[18,19] The principal methods are diffusion and sap displacement, using either water-soluble or fixed-salt treatments. In some countries, oscillating pressure and alternating pressure methods are also widely used. In the UK, however, the preservation of unseasoned timber is uncommon.

The diffusion process involves immersing, or spraying, the newly sawn timber in a water-borne preservative, e.g. sodium octaborate. The timber is subsequently stacked and kept moist to allow diffusion to occur. Total penetration of the sapwood and heartwood is usually achieved. Sodium octaborate, and other water-soluble treatments, are approved in standards for internal structural timbers in dry areas where leaching is not anticipated.

Sap-displacement methods are used for applying either 'soluble' or 'fixed-salt' type water-borne preservatives to newly felled logs. The preservative is applied under pressure through a cap fixed to the butt end and penetrates the entire length of the log.

32.3.6 *In situ* remedial treatments

In situ treatments include preventive and remedial treatments against fungal/insect attack in timbers in service.

Remedial-treatment operations in buildings vary considerably in their complexity, depending on the type and extent of the infestation, which may be restricted to the timber, or extend to adjacent building materials or soil, as with dry rot or subterranean termites. Preservatives for *in situ* remedial treatment must be suitable for application by spray, brush or other on-site technique. Organic-solvent-type preservatives are widely used. Other products are used in specific situations.

Insecticidal (oil-in-water) emulsions are used in situations where high levels of organic-solvent vapour are undesirable, i.e. during and immediately after application, due to fire risk, or odour. Penetration is considerably less than with organic-solvent-type preservatives, and the treatment is less persistent. Spray emulsion treatments have little immediate eradication action, their effect is by killing emerging adult insects. Insecticidal emulsion treatments are currently only recommended in the UK for slight to moderate infestation of woodworm.[20]

Mayonnaise preservatives are insecticidal and fungicidal pastes, applied by knife. This method achieves a high level of penetration, but leaves an oily film and is normally only used on internal structural timbers.

Insecticidal smokes have been used for the fumigation of enclosed spaces. The treatment deposits a surface film of insecticide on the timber; however, it has a low persistence and annual retreatments over a period of 5–10 years may be necessary. Fumigation is less effective against some wood-boring insects, including death watch beetle, and provides no long-term protection.[21]

Preservative plugs are diffusible preservatives inserted into holes bored into the timber at intervals. The method is used as an alternative to *in situ* pressure injection. Typical uses are structural timbers and external joinery. Care is needed to avoid weakening of critical structural timbers.

Sterilizing solutions are often used in remedial work for treating other infected materials, such as brickwork, masonry and soil, including the eradication of termites. Solutions are usually water-borne and contain fungicides or insecticides, as appropriate.

32.3.7 Specifying preservative treatments

The principal considerations in determining the need for preservative treatments are:

1. risk of fungal decay or insect attack;
2. safety and economic consequences of premature failure.

In BS 5268: Part 5: 1989[22] four risk categories are distinguished.

1. Category A: negligible risk of biological degradation.
2. Category B: low risk of decay or insect attack.
3. Category C: unacceptable risk of decay.
4. Category D: high risk of decay or insect attack.

A further category M is for timbers at risk to marine borers.

If the risk of decay or insect attack is negligible, or the required life of the component is less than the expected life of the unpreserved timber, preservation is unnecessary.

If there is a significant risk of decay or insect attack, and failure would endanger life or property, the use of preservative-treated timber, or a durable timber, is necessary. Where failure would not endanger life or property the main considerations are the length of service life required and the cost of remedial work or replacement.

Design features which minimize moisture uptake by timber can significantly reduce the risks of decay. In subterranean termite areas, physical and chemical barriers should be incorporated in and around buildings.[23]

Standards, such as BS 5589: 1989,[24] provide alternative treatment specifications for components in various situations. However, compatibility of all treatments with other building materials, such as paints, glues, and metal fixtures should not be assumed. Standards may also include alternative treatments, corresponding to different levels of performance (or desired service life), and identify timber species which may be used without preservative treatment.

Guides for the specification of plywoods, including preservative treatments, have been issued by trade and other organizations.[25–27] Preservative specifications for plywoods are also included in national standards, such as American Wood Preservers' Association Commodity Standards[28] and BS 6566: Part 7.[29]

32.3.7.1 Care of treated timber

The correct storage and protection of treated timber in factory and on site is important. Neglect or mishandling can cause failure at a later stage. Timber should be stored out of ground contact in dry surroundings with good air movement. If drilled, cut or machined, a preservative treatment is required on the new surfaces.

32.3.8 Standard specifications

There is a considerable number of standards issued by national standards institutions, government departments, and other organizations relating to the preservation of timber. They take the form of preservative specifications, assay standards, preservation or commodity standards, and supplementary standards providing guidelines to specifiers.

Preparation of International (ISO) and European (EN)

Standards on wood preservation has commenced; however, it will be several years before their completion. Examples of national standards are given below.

32.3.8.1 UK

The two main bodies issuing wood-preservation standards in the UK are the British Standards Institution (BSI) and the British Wood Preserving and Damp-proofing Association (BWPDA), formerly the British Wood Preserving Association (BWPA).

(i) *British Standards* The principal British Standards relating to the treatment of building and other structural timbers are BS 1282: 1975,[30] BS 5268: Part 5: 1989[22] and BS 5589: 1989.[24]

(ii) *BWPA specifications* The BWPA Specification Manual (revised 1986) includes specifications for wood preservatives, treatment methods, commodity specifications, and related information. These are frequently referred to in British Standards.

32.3.8.2 Federal Republic of Germany

The principal standards relating to treatment of structural timbers are the Deutsches Institut für Normung (DIN) 68800 standards, in particular DIN 68800: T4.[31] In the FRG, no standards exist for wood-preservative formulations, and each preservative must first be tested and granted a 'mark of approval' (Prufzeichen) before it may be used for construction timbers.

32.3.8.3 USA

The national standards issuing body for wood preservatives in the USA is the American Wood Preservers' Association (AWPA). US Federal specifications are also issued. A number of industrial and trade organizations, with specific interests also issue standards.

32.3.8.4 Canada

Canadian Standards Association, CSA 080, wood-preservation standards follow closely the AWPA standards.

32.3.9 Legislation and approval of wood preservatives

Regulations controlling the manufacture, labelling, packaging, sale and use of wood preservatives in different countries vary considerably. Where regulations exist they are usually geared towards product registration. In some countries wood preservatives are controlled under pesticide legislation and approval is principally concerned with safety. In other countries registration also includes consideration of efficacy. Efficacy is sometimes assumed if the product conforms to a standard specification. However, in certain countries, including those where no such specification exists, the efficacy of each product must be proved. The toxicology and environmental safety of all pesticides is under increasing scrutiny.

Lists of wood-preservative products currently approved in certain countries are issued by the relevant government department and independent organizations, such as the Environmental Protection Agency (EPA) in the USA, and the Health and Safety Executive (HSE) in the UK.

32.3.10 Health, safety and environmental factors

The approval and registration schemes operating in many countries are designed to ensure that the wood preservatives in use are safe for their recommended applications, provided that precautions are followed. However, if misused, wood preservatives and the treated timber are hazardous to individuals, animals and the environment.

Safety measures depend on the type of preservative and the operation. The principal safety considerations cover the areas of:

1. transportation and storage;
2. fire;
3. operation of treatment plant;
4. handling product and freshly treated timber;
5. machining and use of treated timber;
6. pollution of soil, waterways, and atmosphere;
7. disposal of waste and treated timber.

The individuals most at risk are those who regularly use the materials. Precautions should be taken to avoid contact with skin and eyes and to avoid inhaling vapours, spray mists, or dusts from treated timber. Measures should also be taken to safeguard other personnel who could be exposed to a risk, including where remedial treatments are conducted in occupied buildings.

The disposal of waste is usually covered by separate legislation and is managed by local authorities. Caution is required in the burning of treated timber where atmospheric pollution might result, as in the case of copper/chrome/arsenate (CCA) treated timber.

Guidelines on the safe use of wood preservatives and suitable safety equipment are generally available from manufacturers and trade associations.

32.4 Coatings for timber

Coatings provide protection against the weather, moisture, dirt, surface damage, and provide a decorative finish. The majority of hidden structural timbers in buildings are not coated, although they may be treated with a wood preservative. In this section, coatings for constructional timbers and woodwork on buildings are discussed. Fire-retardent coatings and finishes principally for furnishing are not included.

32.4.1 General coating types

Coatings may be broadly classified as, paints, exterior wood stains, varnishes, and specialist coatings. Each category includes coatings of differing composition and properties for different applications. Coatings are commonly classified according to film thickness as:

1. Zero build: typically $<5\ \mu m$.
2. Low build: $5–20\ \mu m$.
3. Medium build: $20–60\ \mu m$.
4. High build: $>60\ \mu m$.

32.4.1.1 Paints

Paints are opaque 'high build' coatings with a distinct surface film. Paint systems consist of up to three components: primer, undercoat and finish. The primer reduces the porosity of absorbent surfaces and provides adhesion and a base for subsequent coats. The undercoat acts as a filler and contributes to the opacity and the uniform appearance of the paint, and the finish provides overall protection, final colour and level of gloss.

32.4.1.2 Exterior wood stains

Exterior wood stains are semitransparent, coloured 'natural' finishes. They range from penetrating 'low build' coatings to non-penetrating 'medium build' coatings with a discernible surface film. Some opaque coatings are described as 'opaque' or 'solid' wood stains.

32.4.1.3 Varnishes

Varnishes are clear or tinted 'high-build' coatings with a distinct surface film. Varnishes are most common as interior finishes, but exterior varnishes are widely available.

32.4.1.4 Specialist coatings

Coatings with a high resistance to abrasion, chemical attack, staining, etc., may be classified under the general heading of 'specialist coatings'. These are primarily for professional use.

32.4.2 General composition

Coatings contain three principal ingredients: binder, pigments, and solvent. Other ingredients include, driers (catalysts), preservatives and additives for stability or to modify coating properties.

The two main types of conventional coating are solvent-borne (oil-based) coatings, which incorporate organic solvents such as hydrocarbons (e.g. white spirit), and water-borne coatings (see also Section 32.4.4). In water-borne coatings the binder is usually dispersed as an emulsion, hence the term 'emulsion' paints, although in some countries they continue to be known as 'latex' paints.

32.4.2.1 Binders

Binders form the protective film and provide cohesion of the coating system. The level and type of binder, in combination with the pigments, largely determines the coating properties and its appearance. The four principal types of binder are: drying-oils, synthetic resins, polymer emulsions, and chemically curing resins.

Drying-oils, such as linseed, soya and tall oil, dry by reaction with atmospheric oxygen. Their main uses are in solvent-borne coatings, in combination with synthetic resins.

Synthetic resins vary in composition, flexibility, hardness, and other properties. The most common synthetic resins in conventional solvent-borne coatings are oil-modified alkyds. Normally, as the oil content is increased, the coating becomes more flexible.

Synthetic urethane-modified drying-oil/alkyd resins are used in some interior coatings for additional hardness, and resistance to abrasion and chemical stains.

Polymer emulsions are used in water-borne coatings. The most common in coatings for wood are acrylic resins, of which a wide range are produced. Polymer emulsions 'dry' by a process of coalescence (fusion) of the polymer particles as the solvent evaporates. Good drying conditions are essential for effective film formation.

Chemically curing binders usually consist of two parts: resin and catalyst. The most common types used in specialist coatings for wood, epoxy and polyurethane systems, have exceptionally good abrasion, stain and chemical resistance. Other types include moisture curing polyurethane and melamine resins.

Chlorinated rubber is sometimes used in coatings requiring a high degree of water resistance.

32.4.2.2 Pigments

Pigments provide colour and determine the transparency or opacity of the coating. They also absorb or block ultraviolet light and protect against photodegradation. The pigments most commonly used in coatings are metal oxides (e.g. titanium and iron oxides), synthetic organic pigments and low-opacity extender pigments. Laminar aluminium pigments are used in certain primer sealing paints. Lead pigments, formerly used in wood primers, and other toxic pigments, have been largely replaced by less toxic pigments.

Coating composition is discussed in detail in texts on paint technology (see Bibliography).

32.4.3 Specific coating properties

Coatings differ widely in physical and chemical characteristics. Properties especially relevant to coatings for wood, particularly outdoors, are moisture control, extensibility, adhesion and resistance to photodegradation and staining fungi and moulds.

32.4.3.1 Moisture control

The two moisture-regulating properties of coatings are water repellency and water-vapour permeability.

The water repellency of coatings is normally highest when the coating is new, and often decreases during exposure, particularly with low to medium build coatings which weather by erosion. Loss of water repellency is considered as an indication that redecoration is due.

The water-vapour permeability of coating systems varies with their composition and build,[33,34] and may be expressed as g (water vapour) m^{-2} day^{-1}. Some examples of the water-vapour permeability of coating systems are:

1. Impermeable: certain specialist coatings (typically < 5 g m^{-2} day^{-1}).
2. Low permeability: (three coat) alkyd paint systems (typically 5–35 g m^{-2} day^{-1}).
3. Medium permeability: acrylic paint systems, medium build wood stains (typically 35–100 g m^{-2} day^{-1}).
4. High permeability: low build wood stains (typically > 100 g m^{-2} day^{-1}).

The optimum permeability of a coating depends on the end use and environment. In conditions of persistently high humidity, absorption of moisture vapour is minimized by coatings of low permeability. However, where wet and dry conditions alternate, e.g. seasonal variations, more permeable coatings allow excess moisture in the wood to evaporate during dry periods.[32] If coating permeability is too high, however, rapid changes in moisture content may occur, causing surface checking and excessive dimensional movement.

For joinery, and other dimensionally critical components, studies have indicated that coating permeability should be below certain levels to avoid excessive movement or cracking. Dooper[35] concluded that, to avoid cracking, coating permeability should not exceed 50 g m^{-2} day^{-1}, whilst Burgers[36] concluded that the maximum permeability varies with timber species, viz. 60 g m^{-2} day^{-1} for European redwood, and 35 g m^{-1} day^{-1} for dark red meranti.

For components with greater dimensional freedom, and on which some surface checking is permitted, e.g. cladding and fencing, more permeable coatings, such as low build wood stains, are suitable.

32.4.3.2 Resistance to photodegradation

The ultraviolet and visible components of sunlight cause photodegradation of both wood surfaces and coatings resulting in premature coating failure. The capacity of coatings to absorb harmful radiation directly influences their durability.

High pigment levels in paints provide maximum protection, whereas lower pigment levels in semitransparent finishes provides varying degrees of protection depending on pigment level and type. Dark or highly pigmented wood stains are usually more absorbent to radiation and more durable. However, high surface temperatures, e.g. $60^{\circ}C$, can occur with dark coatings exposed to direct sunlight, affecting moisture level and the dimensional stability of the joinery.[37]

Clear coatings, such as varnishes, normally have low resistance to sunlight which largely accounts for their poor exterior durability.

32.4.3.3 Extensibility

Coatings must retain sufficient extensibility during their life to accommodate normal dimensional movement in the wood, particularly outdoors. Insufficient extensibility causes cracking of the coating, which is often followed by flaking.

Traditional solvent-borne, e.g. alkyd based, paints tend to lose their extensibility faster than water-borne acrylic paints.[34] However, solvent-borne exterior grade paints, based on 'flexible' alkyd resins and incorporating other improvements, are becoming available with improved exterior durability.

32.4.3.4 Adhesion

The term 'adhesion' with respect to coatings refers to the property of a coating to resist blistering, flaking or other types of film separation. The adhesion of coatings to wood surfaces is dependent on the surface being sound, free of contamination, and dry when coated. Coating adhesion can be also influenced by wood species, finish and quality of the timber (Section 32.4.5).

The most common causes (excluding resin exudation) of blistering on exterior woodwork are excess moisture beneath the coating and high (water) vapour pressures produced by increased surface temperatures.

Traditional solvent-borne primers generally provide better adhesion on exterior timbers than many early and low-quality water-borne primers. However, improved acrylic primers (e.g. conforming to BS 5082: 1986[38]) are now available which have comparable performance to solvent-borne primers.

32.4.3.5 Resistance to moulds and fungi

Coatings can be disfigured or disrupted by the action of staining fungi and moulds.[2] These may be present in the wood prior to application of the coating, or attack the coated surface. Fungicides effective against staining fungi and moulds are incorporated into many coatings. These chemicals do not usually have a significant wood-preserving property. Certain low build (solvent-borne) penetrating wood stains formulated with fungicides effective against wood-decaying fungi, provide a degree of wood preservation. However, penetration is less than that achieved with an unpigmented organic-solvent preservative. Water-borne coatings also contain 'in-can' preservatives to prevent action by bacteria on the liquid product.

32.4.4 Water-borne versus solvent-borne coatings

Most wood coatings (paints, exterior wood stains and varnishes) are now available as water-borne or solvent-borne products. These differ in application properties and film characteristics.

Water-borne (acrylic) coatings are relatively fast drying and, normally, may be recoated within 2–6 h. However, they are susceptible to poor drying conditions, i.e. high humidity and low temperatures can prevent full film formation and impair performance. Until dry, water-borne coatings possess poor rain resistance.

Conventional solvent-borne (e.g. alkyd) coatings dry more slowly (the recoat period is typically 12–24 h), but are more tolerant to poor weather conditions and possess better early rain resistance.

Differences in film properties are principally due to the binder systems involved. Water-borne (acrylic) coatings normally possess significantly higher initial and long-term extensibility, and exhibit higher water vapour permeability than equivalent solvent-borne alkyd based coatings.[34] However solvent-borne coatings are usually harder and more resistant to temperature and dirt pick-up.

Exterior water-borne (acrylic) paints have shown superior durability (maintenance interval 5–8 years) compared with solvent-borne paints (3–4 years).[34] However, acrylic paints have been found to be less tolerant to degraded wood surfaces, and are not ideal coatings over linseed-oil putty.[39]

32.4.5 Factors affecting coating performance

32.4.5.1 Timber species, quality and finish

The performance of coatings can vary significantly on different timbers, and may also be influenced by the method of preparation and finish of the timber.[2,39,40] Naturally durable and dimensionally stable timbers do not necessarily have good coating properties.

Softwoods commonly used for joinery (e.g. European redwood, spruce, Western hemlock), generally have good coating properties. However, high resin levels in some pines may result in resin exudation, blistering or discoloration of the coating. Surfaces with a large proportion of broad summerwood bands are also liable to early coating failure due to reduced adhesion on those areas.

Hardwoods with a high natural oil or resin content (e.g. teak, iroko and keruing) can retard drying and reduce the adhesion of coatings. Coating performance may also be reduced on hardwoods with large pores (e.g. European oak) due to weak spots where the pores are bridged by the coating.

On rough-sawn timbers the only decorative finishes generally suitable are low build wood stains.

32.4.5.2 Plywood

Most plywood used outdoors is liable to surface checking, particularly Douglas fir and Finnish birch face veneers. This often causes cracking of paint films. Exterior wood stains are usually satisfactory on plywood without overlay and on sanded surfaces; however, plywood with resin-impregnated paper overlay is generally recommended for paints.[41,42]

32.4.5.3 Design detailing

The most common cause of coating failure and decay in joinery is caused by moisture ingress due to poor design detailing, often compounded by inadequate maintenance. Design specifications for joinery should ensure close-fitting joints, efficient drainage avoiding internal voids, and the use of appropriate glazing systems.

Reduction in moisture uptake by end-grain sealing at joints and pretreatment with water-repellent wood preservatives, have also been shown significantly to improve coating performance.[43] Other measures to reduce moisture uptake include back priming (with low-permeability primer), use of moisture barriers, and good air circulation behind cladding.

Guidelines have been published on the design of cladding[44] and external joinery.[45,46]

32.4.5.4 Protection on site

Protection of timber on site prior to finishing, is crucial to the performance of the final coating. Timber components should be stored out of ground contact under dry conditions, with good air circulation. Notwithstanding these precautions, the quality of the primer is critical, especially where primed components may be exposed to the weather for extended periods.[47] Full factory finishing provides the most effective means of protection.

32.4.6 Selection of coating systems

The principal criteria in the selection of coating systems are:

1. End use (specific requirements and constraints).
2. Nature of the substrate.
3. Hazards and environment.
4. Maintenance.

Coatings for interior woodwork generally should resist abrasion, impact, soiling, heat and moisture. For most interior applications, conventional solvent-borne (alkyd or polyurethane based) coatings are satisfactory. Water-borne (acrylic) coatings are generally less resistant to moisture, but are suitable in some situations.

Internal surfaces subject to heavy wear or special hazard (e.g. chemical hazard) may require high-performance specialist coatings. Coatings for exterior woodwork should resist the effects of sunlight, moisture, atmospheric pollution, and retain sufficient extensibility to accommodate dimensional movement in the timber.

Dimensionally critical components, such as joinery, require higher build coatings with lower water-vapour permeability.

Maintenance considerations on exterior woodwork increasingly demand coating systems with improved durability and which resist blistering and flaking, for ease of maintenance, such as exterior wood stains and exterior quality wood paints.

Various guides have been published for coatings for different end uses, and the expected durability of different coating systems varies considerably.[13,48] Typical uses of exterior coatings, and maintenance periods under average conditions, are given in *Table 32.4*.

A systematic classification adopted in Germany[49] groups coatings according to their suitability for dimensionally critical components (e.g. joinery) or dimensionally free components (e.g. cladding), and also takes into consideration environmental and other factors. Minimum-performance requirements have been accepted for brush-applied coatings for wood windows.[50]

In the UK, the principal approval scheme for coatings, outside of British Standard specifications, is the British Board of Agrément Approval.

Recommendations for coating systems for different applications are given in BS 6150[51] and, more recently, BS 6952: Part 1: 1988[52] established a framework for classifying and selecting exterior wood coatings. Further parts of this standard will consider performance criteria.

32.4.7 Application

Coatings are normally applied on site by brush or spray methods. Factory application may use immersion, spray or other continuous processes, such as flow or curtain coating. The industrial application of coatings has been discussed in detail by Tatton and Drew.[53]

32.4.7.1 Surface preparation

Timber surfaces, prior to coating, should be thoroughly clean and free of mortar droppings, exuded resin, salts and other contamination. Moulds and algae should be sterilized using a proprietary fungicidal wash or household bleach solution.

Weathered surfaces should be prepared back to sound wood by using an appropriate method. The influence of alternative methods, including sanding, sand blasting and burning, on coating performance has been reported.[39]

Table 32.4 Exterior coatings—typical applications

Use/timber	Alkyd gloss paint	Solvent-borne exterior wood stains			Water-borne	
		Low build	Medium build	Opaque	Acrylic gloss paint	Acrylic matt paint low build
Joinery	*		*		*	
Cladding (smooth)	*	*	*	*	*	*
Shingles/shakes		*	*	*		*
Decking (smooth)		*	*			
Fencing (smooth)	*	*	*	*	*	*
Plywood		*		*		*
Plywood (with overlay)	*	*	*	*	*	*
Sawn/rough[a]		*		*		*
Typical maintenance (years)	3–5	2–3	3–4	3–4	⩾5	4–5

[a] Maintenance periods on rough sawn timbers may be 50% longer.

Knots and resinous areas should be coated with a suitable sealer, such as knotting, depending on the coating system. Checks and other gaps should be repaired using an oil-based stopper after application of a primer.

Oily or resinous hardwoods may be washed with a solvent, e.g. white spirit or cellulose thinner, to reduce surface oil or resin content. Hardwoods with large pores should be filled with a suitable grain filler.

Previously painted or coated surfaces should be lightly abraded and any loose material removed. The full benefits of a water-vapour permeable coating will be achieved only if any impermeable coating present is removed.

Redecoration of exterior finishes which weather by erosion, e.g. exterior wood stains, normally only require removal of surface contamination and loose material.

32.4.7.2 Application conditions

Suitable application conditions are essential to obtain good coating performance. Certain coating types (e.g. water borne) are particularly susceptible to poor conditions. In general, coatings should not be applied at temperatures below 4–5°C, or when the atmospheric humidity exceeds 75% relative humidity. The surface moisture content of the timber should be as near as possible to the in-service level, and preferably below 18%. Coatings should not be applied to surfaces on which condensation is present, or when rain or frost is expected before the coating dries. Application of coatings at higher than normal temperature can affect application properties and finish.

Application and practice are covered comprehensively in BS 6150.[51]

32.4.8 Standard specifications

Standards covering coatings include specifications for coating products (either by performance or composition), test methods, and codes of practice.

International Standards (ISO) are currently available covering terminology (ISO 4617: Parts 1–4;[54–57] ISO 4628: Parts 1–3[58–60]) and sampling and test methods. ISO Standard Specifications have not yet been issued for coating products.

European Standards on wood coatings are not currently available. Initially, standards are proposed on test methods, and classification of wood finishes.

The principal British Standards relating to coatings for timber are: BS 6150: 1982[51] (under review); BS 6952: Part 1: 1988;[52] BS 5082: 1986;[38] BS 5358: 1986;[61] and BS 4756: 1983.[62]

32.4.9 Health, safety and environmental factors

Coating products, unless classified as pesticides, are not usually approved under health-related registration schemes. However, in most countries compliance with packaging and labelling regulations, stating toxic ingredients, hazards and precautions, is required. In the EEC, individual states are required to comply with the EEC Paints Directive.[63]

Legislation or agreements exist in various countries for controlling the use of potentially hazardous ingredients in coatings, e.g. lead pigments. Certain volatile organic solvents in coatings are also controlled in some countries, such as in the USA.

The use of coatings for particular applications may also be restricted, such as toxic coatings (e.g. lead paints) on surfaces which may be licked or chewed by children or animals, or may come into direct contact with foodstuffs.

32.4.9.1 Handling and use

Potential hazards vary with product, the method of application and conditions of use. Most coatings for construction timbers are relatively low-hazard materials requiring basic safety precautions, as specified by the manufacturer and required by relevant legislation. The main considerations are: protection against inhalation of harmful vapours, mists, or dusts, skin and eye contact, fire and explosion. General safety measures include:

1. Protective clothing and eye protection.
2. Ventilation of confined spaces to maintain air-borne concentrations of vapour or mists within safe toxic and flammable limits.
3. Use of respiratory protective equipment for dust or vapours, where necessary.
4. Removal of sources of ignition where flammable or, particularly, highly flammable products are present.

Certain coatings present special hazards requiring extra precautions; in particular, two-pack or moisture-curing polyurethane coatings and two-pack epoxy coatings. Special precautions are also necessary when applying lead paints, and when preparing lead-painted surfaces.

Guidance notes on occupational exposure limits in Britain are published by HMSO.[64] A survey of legislation, standards, codes of practice and toxicology in the paint and coatings field has been published by the Paint Research Association.[65]

References

1 PANSHIN, A. J. and DE ZEEUW, C., *Textbook of Wood Technology*, 4th edn, McGraw-Hill, New York, pp. 359–404 (1980)

2 BRAVERY, A. F. and MILLER, E. R., *Rec. Annual Convention of the British Wood Preserving Association*, 14–23, London (1980)

3 CARTWRIGHT, K. St. G. and FINDLAY, W. P. K., *Decay of Timber and Its Prevention*, 2nd edn, HMSO, London (1981)

4 COGGINS, C. R., *Decay of Timber in Buildings: Dry Rot, Wet Rot and Other Fungi*, Rentokil Ltd, East Grinstead (1980)

5 HICKEN, N. E., *The Dry Rot Problem*, 2nd edn, Hutchinson and Co. Ltd, London (1972)

6 HARRIS, W. V., *Termites; Their Recognition and Control*, 2nd edn, Longman, London (1972)

7 HICKIN, N. E., *Termites a World Problem*, Hutchinson, London (1971)

8 HICKEN, N. E., *The Woodworm Problem*, 2nd edn, Hutchinson, London (1972)

9 LEA, R. G., 'House longhorn beetle survey', *BRE Information Paper 12/82*, Building Research Establishment, Watford (1982)

10 EATON, R. A., 'Preservation of marine timbers'. In *Preservation of Timber in the Tropics* (ed. Findlay, W. P. K.), Martinus Nijhoff/Dr W. Junk Publishers, Lancaster, pp. 157–191 (1985)

11 HALL, G. S. and SAUNDERS, R. G., *Marine Borer Resistance of Timber*, Timber Research and Development Association, High Wycombe (1967)

12 ANON., 'Marine borers and methods of preserving timber against their attack', *PRL Technical Note No. 59*, Building Research Establishment, Watford (1972)

13 FEIST, W. C., 'Weathering of wood in structural uses'. In *Structural Uses of Wood in Adverse Environments* (ed. Mayer, R. W. and Kellog, R. M.), Van Nostrand Reinhold, New York, pp. 156–178 (1982)

14 THOMPSON, W. S., 'Adverse environments and related design considerations'. In *Structural Uses of Wood in Adverse Environments* (ed. Mayer, R. W. and Kellog, E. M.), Van Nostrand Reinhold, New York, pp. 117–130 (1982)

15 PANSHIN, A. J. and DE ZEEUW, C., *Textbook of Wood Technology*, 4th edn, McGraw-Hill, New York, pp. 350–357 (1980)

16 ANON., 'Timbers: their natural durability and resistance to preservative treatment', *BRE Digest 296*, Building Research Establishment, Watford (1985)

17 US DEPARTMENT OF AGRICULTURE, 'Comparative resistance of heartwood of different species when used under conditions that favor decay', *FPL Technical Note 299*, Forest Products Laboratory, Madison, Wisconsin (revised 1961)

18 WILKINSON, J. G., *Industrial Timber Preservation*, Associated Business Press, London (1979)

19 PURSLOW, D. F., *Methods of Applying Wood Preservatives*, HMSO, London (1974)

20 BERRY, R. W. and ORSLER, R. J., 'Emulsion-based formulations for remedial treatments against woodworm', *BRE Information Paper 15/83*, Building Research Establishment, Watford (1983)

21 ANON., 'Insecticidal smokes for control of wood-boring insects', *PRL Technical Note No. 7*, Building Research Establishment, Watford (reprinted 1980)

22 BRITISH STANDARDS INSTITUTION, *BS 5268 Structural use of timber, Part 5: Code of practice for the preservative treatment of structural timber*, Milton Keynes (1989)

23 ANON., 'Termites and tropical building', *BRE Overseas Building Note 170*, Building Research Establishment, Watford (1976)

24 BRITISH STANDARDS INSTITUTION, *BS 5589 Code of practice for the preservation of timber*, Milton Keynes (1989)

25 ANON., *Preservative-treated Plywood*, American Plywood Association, Tacoma, Washington (1986)

26 ANON., 'Specification and treatment of exterior plywood', *TRADA Wood Information Sheet 2/3.11*, Timber Research and Development Association, High Wycombe (revised 1981)

27 ANON., 'Preservative treating veneer plywood against decay', *BRE Information Paper 24/86*, Building Research Establishment, Watford (1986)

28 AMERICAN WOOD PRESERVERS ASSOCIATION, Commodity Standards

29 BRITISH STANDARDS INSTITUTION, *BS 6566: Plywood attack Part 7 Specification for classification of resistance to fungal decay and wood borer attack*, Milton Keynes (1985)

30 BRITISH STANDARDS INSTITUTION, *BS 1282 Guide to the choice, use and application of wood preservatives*, Milton Keynes (1975)

31 DEUTSCHES INSTITUT FÜR NORMUNG, 'Holzschutz in Hochbau: bekampfungsmassnahmen gegen Pilz- und insektenbefall' ('Protection of timber used in buildings: control measures against fungal decay and insect attack'), *DIN 68800: T4*

32 MILLER, E. R., 'Evaluation of exterior wood stains at the Princes Risborough Laboratory'. In *A New Trend in Timber Protection—Exterior Wood Stains*, Building Research Establishment, Watford (1975)

33 HILDITCH, E. A. and WOODBRIDGE, R. J., 'Progress in timber finishing in Great Britain', *Oil and Colour Chemists' Association Journal*, **9**, 217–228 (1985)

34 MILLER, E. R. and BOXALL, J., 'Water-borne paints for exterior wood', *BRE Information Paper 9/84*, Building Research Establishment, Watford (1984)

35 DOOPER, R., 'Some observations in the use of exterior wood stains on softwood joinery in the Netherlands'. In *A New Trend in Timber Protection—Exterior Wood Stains*, Building Research Establishment, Watford (1975)

36 BURGERS, N., 'External finishes for joinery: stains vs. paint', *FEMIB Conference of Windows Commission*, Bad Harzburg, Germany (Feb. 1978)

37 SELL, J., *Holz als Roh- und Workstoff*, **43**, 259–267 (1985)

38 BRITISH STANDARDS INSTITUTION, *BS 5082 Water-borne priming paints for woodwork*, Milton Keynes (1986)

39 BOXALL, J. and SMITH, G. A., 'Maintaining paintwork on exterior timber', *BRE Information Paper 16/87*, Building Research Establishment, Watford (1987)

40 ANON., 'Timber for joinery', *BRE Digest 321*, Building Research Establishment, Watford (1987)

41 ANON., 'Specification for the treatment of exterior plywood', *TRADA Wood Information Sheet 2/3.11*, Timber Research and Development Association, High Wycombe (1986)

42 ANON., 'Stains and paints on plywood', *APA Pamphlet B407*, American Plywood Association, Tacoma (1977)

43 MILLER, E. R., BOXALL, J. and CAREY, J. K., 'External Joinery: end grain sealers and moisture control', *BRE Information Paper 20/87*, Building Research Establishment, Watford (1987)

44 ANON., 'External timber cladding', *TRADA Wood Information Sheet 1.2*, Timber Research and Development Association, High Wycombe (1982)

45 ANON., *Guidance Notes for Wood Windows*, British Woodworking Federation, London

46 ANON., 'Preventing decay in external joinery', *BRE Digest 304*, Building Research Establishment, Watford (1985)

47 DEARLING, T. B. and MILLER, E. R., 'Factory-applied priming paints for exterior joinery', *BRE Information Paper 17/87*, Building Research Establishment, Watford (1987)

48 ANON., 'Painting woodwork', *BRE Digest 106*, Building Research Establishment, Watford (1969)

49 ANON., *Anstrichgruppen für Holz in der Außenverwendung (Paint types for outside use on wood)*, Institut für Fenstertechnik eV, Rosenheim

50 ANON., *Anforderungen an Lasierende und deckende Beschichtungen für Holzfenster (Requirements for transparent and opaque coatings for wood windows)*, Institut für Fenstertechnik eV, Rosenheim

51 BRITISH STANDARDS INSTITUTION, *BS 6150 Code of practice for painting of buildings*, Milton Keynes (1982)

52 BRITISH STANDARDS INSTITUTION, *BS 6952 Exterior wood coating systems, Part 1: Guide to classification and selection*, Milton Keynes (1988)

53 TATTON, W. H. and DREW, E. W., *Industrial Paint Application*, 2nd edn, Newnes-Butterworths, London (1971)

54 INTERNATIONAL ORGANIZATION FOR STANDARDIZATION, *ISO 4617: Part 1*

55 INTERNATIONAL ORGANIZATION FOR STANDARDIZATION, *ISO 4617: Part 2*

56 INTERNATIONAL ORGANIZATION FOR STANDARDIZATION, *ISO 4617: Part 3*

57 INTERNATIONAL ORGANIZATION FOR STANDARDIZATION, *ISO 4617: Part 4*

58 INTERNATIONAL ORGANIZATION FOR
    STANDARDIZATION, *ISO 4628: Part 1*
59 INTERNATIONAL ORGANIZATION FOR
    STANDARDIZATION, *ISO 4628: Part 2*
60 INTERNATIONAL ORGANIZATION FOR
    STANDARDIZATION, *ISO 4628: Part 3*
61 BRITISH STANDARDS INSTITUTION, *BS 5358 Solvent-borne
    priming paints for woodwork*, Milton Keynes (1986)
62 BRITISH STANDARDS INSTITUTION, *BS 4756 Ready mixed
    aluminium priming paints for woodwork*, Milton Keynes (1983)
63 EEC, 'Paints directive', *Official Journal of the European
    Communities OJEC L 303* (7 Nov. 1977), and subsequent
    amendments
64 ANON., 'Occupational exposure limits', *Health and Safety
    Executive Guidance Note ED40*, HMSO, London
65 PAINT RESEARCH ASSOCIATION, *Health and Safety,
    Environmental Pollution and the Paint Industry*, 2nd edn, Paint
    Research Association, Teddington (1981) (supplements published
    quarterly)

Bibliography

Timber: general

BUILDING RESEARCH ESTABLISHMENT, *Handbook of
Hardwoods*, 2nd edn, HMSO, London (1975)
BUILDING RESEARCH ESTABLISHMENT, *Handbook of
Softwoods*, 2nd edn, HMSO, London (1983)
DESCH, H. E., *Timber: Its Structure, Properties and Utilization*, 6th
edn (revised by. Dinwoodie, J. R.), Macmillan Press, London (1981)
MEYER, R. W. and KELLOG, E. M. (eds), *Structural Uses of Wood
in Adverse Environments*, Van Nostrand Reinhold Co., New York
(1982)
PANSHIN, A. J. and DE ZEEUW, C., *Textbook of Wood
Technology*, 4th edn, McGraw-Hill, New York (1980)

Timber: preservation

CARTWRIGHT, K. St. G. and FINDLAY, W. P. K., *Decay of
Timber and Its Prevention*, 2nd edn, HMSO, London (1981)
FINDLAY, W. P. K., *The Preservation of Timber*, Adam & Charles
Black, London (1962)
FINDLAY, W. P. K. (ed.), *Preservation of Timber in the Tropics*,
Martinus Nijhoff/Dr W. Junk, Lancaster (1985)
HUNT, G. M. and GARRATT, G. A., *Wood Preservation*, 3rd edn,
McGraw-Hill, New York (1967)
NICHOLAS, D. D. (ed.), *Wood Deterioration and its Prevention by
Preservative Treatments: Vol. 1. Degradation and Protection of Wood;
Vol. 2. Preservative Treatment*, Syracuse University Press, New York
(1973)
RICHARDSON, B. A., *Wood Preservation*, The Construction Press,
London (1978)
TRADA, *Timber Preservation*, 3rd edn, Timber Research and
Development Association, High Wycombe (1986)
WILKINSON, J. G., *Industrial Timber Preservation*, Associated
Business Press, London (1979)

Surface coatings

HAMBURG, H. R. and MORGANS, W. M., *Hess's Paint Film
Defects. Their Causes and Cure*, 3rd edn, Chapman and Hall, London
(1979)
HURST, A. E. and GOODIER, J. H., *Painting and Decorating*, 9th
edn, Charles Griffin, High Wycombe (1980)
MORGANS, W. M., *Outlines of Paint Technology: Vol. 1. Materials;
Vol. 2. Finished Products*, Charles Griffin, High Wycombe (Vol. 1,
1982; Vol. 2, 1984)
OIL AND COLOUR CHEMISTS' ASSOCIATION, *Surface
Coatings: Vol. 1. Raw Materials and Their Usage; Vol. 2. Paints and
Their Applications*, Chapman and Hall, London (Vol. 1, 1983; Vol. 2,
1984)
SCHMID, E. V., *Exterior Durability of Organic Coatings*, FMJ
International Publications, Redhill (1988)
WELHTE, K., *The Materials and Techniques of Painting*, Van
Nostrand, New York (1975)

33

Paint: Absorbent Surfaces other than Timber

C D Lawrence
British Cement Association

Contents

33.1 Introduction 33/3

33.2 Weathering of buildings 33/3

33.3 Cleaning buildings 33/3
    33.3.1 Wet methods 33/3
    33.3.2 Dry methods 33/3

33.4 Substrate preparation 33/4

33.5 Paint application 33/4

33.6 Paints and coatings for mineral surfaces 33/5

33.7 Transport of gases and water vapour through paints 33/5

33.8 Water-borne paints 33/6
    33.8.1 Lime washes 33/6
    33.8.2 Cement paints 33/6
    33.8.3 Emulsion paints 33/6
    33.8.4 Household emulsion paints 33/7
    33.8.5 Masonry paints 33/7
    33.8.6 Textured paints 33/7
    33.8.7 Multicolour paints 33/7
    33.8.8 Bitumen emulsions 33/7

33.9 Oil-based paints 33/7
    33.9.1 Alkyd paints 33/8
    33.9.2 Urethane oil paints 33/8
    33.9.3 Epoxy ester and alkyd paints 33/8
    33.9.4 Phenolic paints 33/8

33.10 Solvent-thinned paints 33/8
    33.10.1 Acrylic paints 33/8
    33.10.2 Chlorinated rubber paints 33/9
    33.10.3 Vinyl paints 33/9
    33.10.4 Fluoro elastomer coatings 33/9
    33.10.5 Coal-tar paints 33/9
    33.10.6 Bitumen paints 33/9

33.11 Two-pack systems 33/9
    33.11.1 Epoxy resin paints 33/9
    33.11.2 Solvent-free liquid epoxy resin and hardener systems 33/10

33.11.3 Organic-solvent solution of liquid epoxy resin and hardener systems 33/10
33.11.4 Organic-solvent solution of solid epoxy resin and hardener systems 33/10
33.11.5 Water-dispersed epoxy coatings 33/10
33.11.6 Acrylic polymer coatings 33/10
33.11.7 Polyester resin coatings 33/11
33.11.8 Neoprene rubber systems 33/11
33.11.9 Chlorosulphonated polyethylene systems 33/11
33.11.10 Polysulphide rubber systems 33/11
33.11.11 Silicone rubber systems 33/11
33.11.12 Miscellaneous two-pack systems 33/11
33.11.13 Polyurethane paints 33/11

33.12 Moisture-curing polyurethane paints 33/12

33.13 Coating systems applied hot 33/12

33.14 Clear finishes, stains and sealers 33/12

33.15 Impregnants 33/12
    33.15.1 Silicones 33/13
    33.15.2 Silanes 33/13
    33.15.3 Stearates 33/13
    33.15.4 Silicates 33/13
    33.15.5 Silicofluorides 33/13

References 33/13

Bibliography 33/14

33.1 Introduction

Mineral-based floors and walls can be successfully painted provided they are in sound condition and that an appropriate paint is selected. A very wide range of paint and coating systems are available. Each product is somewhat different and its detailed formulation is usually known only to the manufacturer. The successful use of sealers and paints on external walls has been reported, but caution is necessary in the specification and execution of these treatments. The alternative of a Portland-cement render may be viable in certain situations.

There are many good quality, durable structures and buildings where unfortunate weathering patterns have resulted in a need for cleaning or painting. Dirt will not usually harm good quality concrete, so visually acceptable patterns of ageing and soiling do not need to be disturbed. There is great interest in the use of colours for whole or parts of buildings.

Waterproofing of walls and roofs is perhaps the most obvious application for paints and sealers as performance improvers. Wear-resistance properties can also be enhanced with certain floor sealers. Tough, strong paints, such as epoxy paints, should not be applied to relatively weak surfaces, otherwise fracture of the substrate may result.[1]

Painting of mineral surfaces may be recommended for added durability, but the basis for this advice needs to be assessed carefully. The microporous and generally permeable nature of natural stone, plaster, cement render, concrete, etc., will be radically changed by the application of a surface barrier and certain paint films may lead to a build-up of moisture, that could, for example, result in frost damage in outdoor exposure.[2] Partly because of this possibility, surface coatings are not generally permitted on highway structures.[3,4] The need for independent assessments of the utility and durability of individual products has been pointed out recently by Leeming and O'Brien.[5] In France, a warranty for the long-term success of a surface treatment is apparently required.[6]

Uncoated concrete should, theoretically, require little maintenance when made to recognized standards, but some blemishes and poorer quality areas are inevitably produced. Anticarbonation, antichloride and moisture-ingress-resisting coatings are now more frequently specified for structural reinforced concrete in an attempt to improve durability, either for new structures or after repair is required.[7]

33.2 Weathering of buildings

Colour and texture affect the sensitivity of building surfaces to dirt, but the appearance of concrete is also affected by its moisture content. In comparison with other common building materials, the pores in concrete are relatively fine, allowing moisture to condense at humidities significantly below saturation, thereby producing wide changes in tone or shade. The basic colour of as-cast concrete is the colour of the finest particles in the mix, normally the binder. Colour changes must be expected during the life of the concrete due to erosion by the action of rainwater and there will be a gradual change from the colour of the cement to that of the sand.

In wet climates, building surfaces often provide the right conditions for biological growth. A wide range of algae, lichen and mosses can live and grow in such climates, particularly on north-facing facades. Black and green unsightly algae seem to be associated with wetter areas and only survive on sunnier aspects where detailing produces concentrations of water flow. The first colonizers of concrete surfaces are algae, followed, when the alkalinity has dropped to near neutral, by lichens. Dirt often collects on colonized surfaces and this provides a foothold for further lichen and mosses. On horizontal surfaces, vegetation and more advanced plants may become established.

The finer particles in the atmosphere are attracted to all building surfaces and are held in position by a variety of physical and chemical bonds. If substantial amounts of moisture are present, the dirt particles can be drawn into pores by capillary forces. The sulphur dioxide in the atmosphere forms sulphuric acid which reacts with surface calcium carbonate to form gypsum. During rain, the gypsum dissolves and flows down the facade, collecting dirt. As the water is absorbed, or as it evaporates, the dirt it has been carrying is encapsulated in the gypsum which is deposited from solution and becomes bonded to the surface. These gypsum/dirt deposits can build to thicknesses of several millimetres in a relatively short time, especially if water flows long distances down the building facade.

33.3 Cleaning buildings

The choice of cleaning method will be affected by a number of factors including the type of sealer or finish that will be applied to the cleaned surface.

33.3.1 Wet methods

The simplest cleaner is water, applied in the form of a very fine spray. Working from the top of the building, only sufficient water is used to keep the deposits of dirt moist until they soften. Once the deposits have softened, they are hosed away, with the help of bristle brushes. The chief advantages of this system are its simplicity and cheapness, but the disadvantages are that there is a risk of water penetrating joints and that the work cannot be undertaken in frosty weather. Modern developments of detergents and other chemical cleansers help the dirt-softening process, and reduce the quantity of water required.

Most chemical cleaners are based on hydrochloric acid, which can permanently damage both buildings and personnel. Hydrofluoric acid is sometimes employed for cleaning sandstone, and is included in the British Standard on cleaning buildings.[8,9] The risks involved do not justify the use of either of these acids. If acids are used, window glass and metal pipework must be protected with plastic sheeting. High pressure water lances may be employed to wash down after cleaning with acids or detergents, without the need for brushing. Hot-water cleaning or even steam cleaning has certain advantages, but is usually too expensive.

33.3.2 Dry methods

A variety of grinding wheels and rotary brushes are available together with grit blasting. Grit-blasting is the preferred method for heavily soiled surfaces because it results in a surface with a satisfactory bond for the subsequent coating, but it should not be used on soft brickwork. Steel-wire brushes must not be used as the bristles can become lodged in the surface and cause rust stains. Noise and dust are problems associated with grit-blasting, and operatives must wear protective goggles and use breathing apparatus. Dry or wet grit blasting can be used on any concrete that can accept the removal of a thin layer from the surface. A wet-blasting system involves an extra operation as it is necessary to rinse down the surface, usually with a high pressure water lance.

Biological growth may be physically removed with wooden or plastic scrapers before applying a toxic wash to kill them off. The materials presently available appear to give no more than 2–3 years protection. After the toxic wash has been allowed a few days to act, the dead growths can be removed with high pressure water lances. Suitable toxic washes include solutions of household bleach and various commercial biocides and fungicides.

Rust stains can be removed using oxalic acid solution or a paste with whiting containing sodium dithionite crystals. Copper strains can be removed using ammonium chloride crystals. Spillages of oils should be tackled by physical wiping followed by absorption in a dry powder (Portland cement). Scrubbing with strong detergent may be necessary if the oil has soaked into the surface. Solvents should not be used as these are likely to take the organic material further into the concrete. Paint removers may be necessary to remove graffiti, but the preferred methods are physical scraping followed by burning off, or wet scrubbing with emulsifying agents, or steam cleaning.

33.4 Substrate preparation

Many protective barriers exert substantial stresses when they shrink during curing and a certain minimum substrate strength is therefore required. The strength of a concrete surface can be evaluated by a pull-off test, in which a 50-mm diameter core hole is drilled to a depth of 25 mm and a pipe-cap bonded to the concrete. After the bonding agent cures, the pipe-cap is attached to a hydraulic jack which pulls perpendicularly to the concrete surface. For epoxy and polyester protective barriers, a tensile strength of at least $1.5\,\text{N}\,\text{mm}^{-2}$ is required.

All paint systems need a surface free from holes or protrusions to be successful: protrusions are most easily removed by grinding; spalls and holes must be filled with Portland cement grout, or with organic polymer resin material mixed with inert fillers. Some paint systems are sensitive to small blow holes which will repeat through successive coats, whilst other coatings will bridge or fill the holes. Large surface voids can be filled with either dry-pack Portland cement mortars, polymer-modified concrete, polymer concrete, normal concrete or gunite. In indoor situations, gypsum plaster or water-mixed powder fillers may be used.

Occasionally, particularly with precast concrete products and high quality civil engineering structures, cast surfaces are too smooth and dense for good adhesion, and these may have to be lightly grit blasted. For concrete, formwork release agents and curing compounds should not be used when it is known that a coating is to be applied, unless they can be completely removed before application of the coating (or unless the system is deemed compatible by the coating supplier). Joints between building blocks need to be pointed and the surface should be as level as possible, because irregularities generally weaken the coating and lead to defects. The requirements for smooth surfaces for hospitals and the food industries has led to the development of a number of filling and regulating compounds. The compatibility of such compounds with subsequent coatings must always be investigated before use.

If a paint is applied when the ambient conditions dictate that moisture must move out of the substrate, there is a tendency to push the membrane off the surface. If these conditions occur before the paint is cured, it can seriously interfere with its adhesion. A check on the moisture level can be made by taping a sheet of polythene onto the surface and observing any visible moisture collection on the underside of the sheet during the period required for curing of the barrier. If visible moisture appears, it is likely that moisture conditions in the material will interfere with a good bond. If the moisture content is high, water-vapour permeable coatings should be considered.

Where there is a source of water continuously interfering with proper application of the coating, as in groundwater percolation situations, the water must be stopped. This may require excavation and installation of a draining or pumping system. Another option is to use chemical grout which can be pumped through holes drilled into the concrete. Cementitious quick-setting materials can be used as waterstops in order to provide temporary dry areas while a permanent repair is made.

Efflorescence will disrupt oil or alkyd paints and should therefore be removed by dry brushing and painting should be deferred until all efflorescence has ceased. The alkalinity of uncarbonated concrete will attack oil-based or alkyd resin type paints by breaking the polymer chains at the ester links, forming glycerols and fatty acid salts of the alkali metal (soap formation or saponification). These coatings should not be used without an alkali-resistant primer. Even where concrete surfaces show no signs of alkalinity, alkali metal hydroxides can still move to the concrete/paint interface and cause problems. Although some manufacturers recommend allowing concrete to weather for some months before painting, this is not always practicable. To avoid problems of dirt contamination, or to take advantage of available access, early painting is sometimes more sensible.

Surfaces that have been previously painted or treated need careful consideration. Thorough soaking, perhaps with the use of a detergent, softens many emulsion paints. Steam stripping is possible for large areas. Oil-based paints may be removed using solvent or alkali paint removers, but mechanical methods are generally preferred. Silicones and other water repellents can cause patchiness or poor adhesion for water-based paints, but some solvent-based or chemically cured finishes will be successful. If the existing paint is in good condition, it should be washed to remove dirt, grease or wax, and any glossy surfaces should be abraded. Poorly adhering or defective paint should be scraped back to a firm edge. If existing paint is flaking, blistered or generally in poor condition, it should be removed completely and the surface treated as for new work.

33.5 Paint application

To be successful, coatings should flow or spread easily on the surface. A suitable primer aids application and helps to produce a paint film without pin-holes or gaps. Low temperatures will retard the drying of water-based paints, whilst high temperatures may accelerate drying to the point at which application becomes difficult. Two-pack epoxy and polyurethane materials have reduced pot life in hot weather, whilst their curing is delayed in winter. Ventilation reduces condensation and assists drying, but must be carefully controlled as it can introduce grit and dust onto wet paint surfaces. Special situations, such as chemical works or marine environments, will require specialist advice as deposits of salts, or other pollution, can impair adhesion between coatings and substrate, or between paint coats.

Certain coating systems are applied by pouring onto the horizontal surface to be treated, notably systems that are applied hot and set during cooling, and also certain impregnation fluids.

Brushing is considered the best method of application for paint primers, as the action of the brush gives good contact between primer and substrate. Brushing is slower than other methods for larger areas and it may be more difficult to achieve a uniform coating. The need to maintain wet-edges may dictate the number of men required and the type of access to be used. Rollers are quicker than brushes but will require brushwork for cutting-in at edges and junctions. Rollers are excellent on rough surfaces but may produce an unwanted stipple effect on flat ones.

There are three types of spray equipment commonly used for spraying paint on buildings. Spraying is faster than either brush or roller methods, but introduces requirements for masking and creates safety hazards in enclosed spaces and wind-blown spray on exposed sites. Masking must be complete before operations begin and should be removed as soon as possible on completion. Air spray equipment operates at pressures of 0.2–$0.5\,\text{N}\,\text{mm}^{-2}$. All forms of air spraying give rise to 'spray mist'. 'Spray mist' is less pronounced at lower pressures; however, higher pressures give better nebulization and, therefore, better finishes, as well as being faster.

Airless sprays force the paint at pressure through a small orifice in the spray gun. The pressures used are between 0.14 and 0.22 N mm^{-2}, giving efficient nebulization and fast coverage and, because no air is used, there is almost no 'spray mist', much less paint is wasted, and masking can be greatly reduced. However, because of the high pressures used, the spray gun can be dangerous in inexperienced hands. With skill and care, airless spraying can be carried out using a hand-held shield in lieu of masking.

Air-assisted airless spray equipment is a hybrid of the two previous systems. It is claimed to give the operator the same degree of control as air spraying with the freedom from 'spray mist' and the economy of airless systems. The pressures used are normally in the range 0.06–0.12 N mm^{-2}.

33.6 Paints and coatings for mineral surfaces

BS 6150,[10] ACI 515[11] and BRE Digest 197[12] list the broad classes of paints available and their properties. Water-borne polyvinylacetate [–CH$_2$–CH(OOCCH$_3$)–] emulsion paints are the most commonly used paints, together with oil-based alkyds.

A solid film of organic polymer is the major component of conventional paints. The wet paint (in the can) may contain the final polymer in organic-solvent solution, but the viscosity of the wet paint increases rapidly with increasing polymer concentration. Alternatively, the polymer may be in the form of an emulsion in aqueous or organic liquid, or smaller intermediate organic molecules may be present in the wet paint, as pure liquid or in solution, which then polymerize during drying to form three-dimensional polymers in the cured paint film.

Another major component of paint is the pigment, which is a finely divided solid held in suspension in the liquid paint. Other finely divided solids, called extenders, may be present to aid in the physical properties of the paint film.[13] Whiteness, and opacity, can also be achieved by incorporating microvoids in the form of plastic pigments which encapsulate air voids. A gloss finish is often too harsh for external walls and a matting agent, e.g. a finely divided silica or a wax dispersion, is required in the paint formulation.

A commonly encountered parameter in paint technology is the pigment volume concentration, which is the percentage volume of pigment (and extender) in the total volume of dried paint film. During a theoretical process of adding organic polymer to a bed of pigment, the point at which the polymer just fills the voids between the pigment particles is known as the critical pigment volume concentration. Paints formulated above their critical pigment volume concentration will be porous. Consequently, films are progressively more permeable to water vapour and other gases as the pigment volume concentration is increased beyond the critical value. Typically, gloss paints have low pigment volume concentrations (15–25%), while primers, undercoats and flat paints have increasingly higher values. The pigment volume concentration of masonry paints is in the range 30–45%, while high-build textured coatings have values in the range 50–60%.

Various additives are also normally present in paints, in much smaller quantities, which modify the fluidity of the wet paint. The wet paint may be given a thixotropic character, becoming fluid when stirred and then rapidly becoming viscous after application, to reduce the likelihood of paint runs.

The liquid paint must wet the surface to be painted to ensure good adhesion; polar groups in the polymer help to form a strong bond with the substrate. Building surfaces are usually porous and this allows the paint to form a mechanical key to the surface. The dried paint film must be sufficiently flexible to allow for movement in the substrate without cracking. Linear polymers form more flexible films than do three-dimensional polymers. Flexibility is increased by introducing smaller molecules (plasticizers) into the formulation, or by spacing the cross-linking to obtain a looser structure.

The performance of a paint film is partly determined by the chemical nature of the bonds linking units in the polymer chain; these must be stable towards sunlight and moisture and also, in the case of concrete paints, towards alkali. Weathering of paint films occurs under the influence of ultraviolet radiation (absorbed by some polymers), moisture and oxygen. The surface of the paint becomes powdery as the paint polymer breaks up into smaller molecules, and the pigment present in the surface can be rubbed away. The paint film is said to have chalked.

Repair to damaged paint films can be carried out when the paint is formulated with a linear polymer, because the paint may be softened by applying solvent and allowing the surface to flow to a smooth finish; alternatively, the surface may be resprayed with the same paint. Cross-linked polymer films will not redissolve and, therefore, cannot be successfully repaired using this technique.

On the other hand, dirt encapsulation can be pronounced for simple thermoplastic linear polymers and more frequent repainting is, therefore, necessary as compared with the cross-linked polymer film. Epoxy and polyurethane paints can be restored to their original bright finish by simple washing and surfaces which require regular scrubbing with aggressive disinfectants (e.g. operating-theatre walls) are better finished with these types of paints.

Other paint properties which may be important in particular applications are resistance to high-energy radiation and behaviour in fire; certain paints are classed as fire retardant.

33.7 Transport of gases and water vapour through paints

In considering the engineering value of paint films, some importance is attached to their permeability towards oxygen, carbon dioxide and water vapour. The permeability of a gas through a polymer film depends both on its solubility and its diffusion coefficient in the film. The presence of plasticizers reduces the cohesive forces between polymer chains and increases diffusivity. An increased relative humidity also increases diffusivity, especially where there is significant dissolution of moisture in the paint polymer. The level of pigmentation also greatly affects the diffusion resistance of paint films: the resistance generally reaches a maximum near the critical pigment volume concentration, and above this figure the vapour resistance falls.

Resistivity values of most polymers towards oxygen are between 20 and 50 times the resistivities towards carbon dioxide, and the resistivities towards water vapour are at least 10 times less than those towards carbon dioxide. Increased paint thickness affects the resistance to diffusion, by providing a greater diffusion path length as thickness increases, but the quality of the barrier is usually reduced as the paint film thickness is increased. Pigments usually increase the resistivity towards carbon dioxide unless they are present in concentrations above the critical pigment volume concentration.

The underlying principle of anticarbonation coatings is to reduce the permeability of the surface to carbon dioxide (CO_2) to low values. The relevant characteristic of the paint may be expressed as the diffusion resistance μ_{CO_2}, given by

$$\mu_{CO_2} = \frac{D_L(\delta C/\delta t)}{F}$$

where D_L is the diffusion coefficient of carbon dioxide through free air and F is the diffusion flow density of carbon dioxide through the paint film, under a concentration gradient of $\delta C/\delta t$ in the paint film. The diffusion resistance indicates the number of times which a coating is more resistant to carbon dioxide than is free air, under the same conditions of temperature and humidity. The significant quantity for defining the effect of a carbonation retardant is the 'diffusion-equivalent air thickness', S_D, which is obtained by multiplying the diffusion resistance by the thickness, s, of the coating

$$S_D = \mu_{CO_2} s$$

A minimum paint thickness of 150 μm has been recommended for anticarbonation coatings on concrete. According to Klopfer,[14] a 'diffusion equivalent air thickness' of 50 m virtually prevents further carbonation.

Similar expressions have been used to characterize the movement of water (H_2O) vapour through paint films: μ_{H_2O} values of between 20 000 and 80 000 have been obtained for polyurethane paint films, leading to S_D values for complete paint systems (three coats) of between 1.77 and 3.75 m.[15] A resistivity value of less than 4 m is generally required to avoid build-up of water in concrete under the paint film.

Both Engelfried[16] and Robinson[17] have published diffusion resistance values for a wide range of paint films. From these data, it is clear that different performances can be obtained from paints of the same generic type. Few general statements can be made linking the resistivity of paints and their chemical type, except possibly that unpigmented paints and clear sealers do not usually offer as substantial a resistance to the diffusion of carbon dioxide as do pigmented films.

Waterproofing of buildings is undertaken to improve durability and to improve thermal insulation. Waterproofing requires a delicate balance between an ability to resist water penetration and an ability to allow drying out by water-vapour permeation. Kunzel[18] has developed a relationship between the water-vapour resistance, S_D, and the rate of absorption of liquid water, A, for satisfactory coating performance:

$$S_D A < 0.1 \text{ kg m}^{-1} \text{ h}^{-0.5}$$

and he proposed further restraints of $S_D < 2$ m and $A < 0.5$ kg m^{-2} h$^{-0.5}$ for satisfactory rainwater resistance.

33.8 Water-borne paints

Water-borne coatings range widely in type, appearance and composition. They have several advantages over organic-solvent paints, including reduced environmental pollution and hazard, by solvent evaporation, and lack of odour. Cleaning-up operations use water rather than expensive organic solvent. These systems are under active development for specialist applications, including anticarbonation coatings. A disadvantage is that this class of paint generally lacks the level of adhesion to the substrate shown by organic solvent and chemically cured systems. The thermoplastic nature of the cured paint polymer makes it vulnerable to soiling by absorption of dirt particles, so that simple cleaning operations do not restore the paint surface to its former brightness.

33.8.1 Lime washes

Ashurst[19] listed three variations of this traditional treatment for external walls: lime + tallow; lime + casein; and lime + pulverized-fuel ash. Roughly 10% additions of each of the modifying components are made: the first two to hot quicklime–water slurries, and the third is blended dry with slaked lime and sold ready for mixing with cold water prior to

application. Lime washes are reserved for application to traditional or historic buildings, for matching existing paint systems and after repair has been necessary. The lime washes are applied by brush, and several coats are normally required. They provide a high-quality decorative finish which is claimed to be superior to modern equivalents.

33.8.2 Cement paints

Cement paints are based on white Portland cement and are supplied as powder to be mixed with water. They set by hydration of the cement.[20] A matt cement finish with a degree of texture is obtained, which can be used for either interior or exterior exposures. The surface to be painted should be damp at the time of application and each coat should be dampened with a fine mist of plain water as soon as is practicable without disturbing the paint. Damp curing of conventional Portland-cement paint is essential. On open-textured surfaces, the paint should be applied with stiff-bristle brushes and worked well into the surface. For concrete with a smooth surface, soft whitewash brushes are best.

Cement paints are low-cost treatments, available in a small range of colours and suitable for use on porous brickwork, stonework, concrete, cement renderings, etc., with a life of 2–7 years. They are not suitable for use on gypsum plaster, metal, timber or non-porous surfaces. Deeper colours will exaggerate lime bloom and so may appear to fade or go patchy. They will erode in acidic atmospheres and support mould growth on wet areas, but they can be applied to new or damp concrete. Cement paints are prone to water marks and are not recommended for damp service. They readily show dirt and cannot be applied over other paint coatings.

Polymer-modified Portland-cement paints are variations with superior properties. The organic emulsions retard evaporation, thereby retaining the necessary water for hydration of the Portland cement so that moist curing is unnecessary.

33.8.3 Emulsion paints

In emulsion paints, the concentration of polymer in the wet paint is increased by emulsifying or dispersing polymer particles in water. Examples are dispersions of vinyl acetate copolymers, methyl methacrylate/butyl acrylate copolymers, styrene butadiene copolymers and bitumen emulsions. These paints set by evaporation of water and then rely on polymer mobility to product coherent films by coalescence of particles on the substrate. This mobility is enhanced by the incorporation of plasticizers or non-aqueous solvents, which dissolve in the polymer after water has evaporated, temporarily plasticizing the polymer before finally evaporating.

In order to produce stable water emulsions, the polymer used is generally modified to be more hydrophilic than the corresponding polymer for use in organic-solvent-solution paint. This results in the cured paint film being more readily disrupted by water.

The development of water-borne emulsion systems has proceeded rapidly and gloss paints are now available which are resistant to abrasion. Systems highly impermeable to carbon dioxide have also been described;[21] some of these paints based on vinyl acetate/ethylene/vinyl chloride copolymers are claimed to have increased flexibility and to give the highest resistances to carbon dioxide. The carbon dioxide resistances of these copolymers are comparable to those of solvent-based paints, while their water-vapour resistances are usually lower.

Emulsion paints are easy to apply, and clean up after use. The preferred method of application is by long-fibre tapered nylon brushes of 100–150 mm width. However, application can also be done by using a roller or spray gun. The paints may be applied to damp, but not wet, surfaces. If the surface is porous or extremely dry, prewetting of the surface is advisable. Thicker emulsion-based coatings may be applied by roller, spray gun or even by trowel. They can hide considerable irregularities in the substrate, but regular patterns, such as the joints of concrete blockwork, tend to remain visible. One protective system is available which utilizes acrylic emulsion coatings in conjunction with a layer of polyester fabric.

33.8.4 Household emulsion paints

The most popular household emulsion paints are based on vinyl acetate copolymerized with ethyl acetate or vinyl 'versatate' (a highly branched carboxylic acid), or plasticized with dibutyl phthalate. Acrylic latices are also available, plasticized with, e.g. butyl acrylate. Pigment is dispersed in the aqueous phase by means of suitable surfactants.

In the past the matt type of household emulsion was the most common, but 'satin', 'silk' or 'gloss' finishes are now available. Many interior grades, based on polyvinyl acetate, are not resistant to alkali and are intended for use on gypsum plaster; they are disrupted when used on uncarbonated cement products. A suitable primer should be used on porous surfaces, otherwise loss of plasticizer or coalescing solvent into the substrate can cause poor film formation.

General-purpose emulsion paints are claimed to be suitable for both interior and exterior use, but for the latter it is wiser to choose an exterior-grade product, based on polyacrylates, styrene butadiene polymers or on vinyl chloride/vinyl acetate/ethylene copolymers. These paints are suitable for easy decoration of concrete, because they are water-vapour permeable. The better exterior-quality emulsions include biocides to give some degree of resistance to mould growth and may be expected to have a life of 4–7 years.

33.8.5 Masonry paints

Masonry paints are among the most popular surface coatings applied to masonry, giving typical film thicknesses of 0.1–0.25 mm. Fine sand- and marble-textured paints generally have a slightly thicker film thickness than their smooth counterparts. Smooth textured, thick, flexible coatings have superior performance. The flexibility of the paint film is a major factor determining the long-term performance of these systems in terms of their waterproofing ability.[22]

Textured emulsion paints may be successfully employed as top-coats over acrylic or moisture curing polyurethane sealers. Alternatively, the abrasion resistance of emulsion paints may be improved by top-coating with moisture curing polyurethanes, after checking that no unfavourable interaction occurs between the emulsion and the solvent in the polyurethane. An effective fungicide may be included in the masonry paint and this will improve the durability in moist conditions.

The water-vapour permeability of masonry paints ($S_D < 4$ m for water vapour) allows long-term drying out of walls. Heavier textures appear to be prone to patchy performance, especially on rough substrates. Rougher surfaces can lead to a tendency for the paint to draw back from the surface promontories and flow into depressions where it forms thick films which are prone to cracking during cure.[23] It is recommended that where protection is required, two coats of specialist smooth emulsion are applied followed by an additional textured coating on top, as required.

33.8.6 Textured paints

For exterior applications, emulsion paints generally have a life similar to Portland-cement paints, but sand-textured and fibre-filled emulsions can give up to 10 years service. A variety of much thicker emulsion-based coatings is manufactured which contain relatively coarse graded aggregate particles (0.8–2 mm). These paints are usually applied by using a textured roller, trowel or sometimes by spray. The greater thickness of coating (1–3 mm) produces greater durability, but several hours are required for these coatings to dry out and there may be a tendency for cracking to occur. These types of rendering are not necessarily as waterproof as traditional cement renderings, but their service life should be in excess of 15 years. They are particularly useful in concealing repair work.

Powder compositions are to be mixed with water (usually based on hemihydrate plaster) to form thick pastes (bound with an emulsion polymer) are also available. These are applied manually with brushes or other tools and have decorative properties intended for interior use only. They are used extensively on concrete and other materials, but are not very water resistant and a glaze coat is required for extra protection.

33.8.7 Multicolour paints

Multicolour paints are designed to mask imperfections in surfaces and to discourage graffiti artists. In the past these paints were solvent-thinned systems applied with a special spray gun and were based on the use of two immiscible liquids. A recent departure has been the development of a water-borne paint incorporating coloured plastic solid chips, which is applied by brush or roller. An undercoat is applied which provides the background colour. A one coat top-coat is applied on top of the base coat which holds the coloured chips in suspension.

33.8.8 Bitumen emulsions

Bituminous emulsions are well-tried materials that are used for a wide range of duties, including the surface sealing of concrete.[24] These aqueous systems contain approximately 50% bitumen which coalesces and forms a continuous bitumen coating on contact with the substrate. Grades are available for safe contact with drinking water.

Bitumen-emulsion coatings are normally sufficiently water-vapour permeable to allow walls to dry out, and sufficiently resistant to prevent occasional rain from resulting in resaturation. They are available in a fairly wide range of subdued colours, but they are more frequently used in the natural black colour as a waterproofing undercoat, followed by decorative emulsion, or 'stone' paint. The thickness of coating will depend on the formulation and ranges from several millimetres built up with fibre or fabric to thin emulsion coatings. Bituminous emulsions can give up to 10 years service life depending on thickness, and are more durable when a decorative top coat is applied.

33.9 Oil-based paints

In traditional vegetable-oil paints, a solvent is not required; the drying reaction comprises interpolymer cross-linking brought about by the action of atmospheric oxygen on multiple double bonds in unsaturated fatty acids which are present as esters with glycerol (CH_2OH–$CHOH$–CH_2OH) (for example linoleic (CH_3–$(CH_2)_4$–$CH=CH$–CH_2–$CH=CH$–$(CH_2)_7$–$COOH$) and linolenic (CH_3–CH_2–$CH=CH$–CH_2–$CH=CH$–CH_2–$CH=$ CH–$(CH_2)_7$–$COOH$) acids). The oil most often used is linseed oil. There is a considerable uptake of oxygen during drying which is aided by the presence of 'dryers' in the paint formulation, e.g. cobalt, manganese or lead compounds. The drying process in the paint film may be speeded up by preoxidation of the wet paint at elevated temperature to increase the size of the polymers initially present in the wet paint. Polymer size may also be increased by reacting the oil with other natural or synthetic resins to give oleoresinous paints.

The ester linkages present are sensitive to hydrolysis in the presence of alkali. In addition, oil-based paints tend to yellow in outdoor exposure because of the sensitivity of the double bonds present to ultraviolet radiation. These paints may be filled with fine sand and film thicknesses of 700 μm have been reported. Oleoresinous paints have been shown to be effective on concrete and to withstand more than 20 years of outdoor exposure in marine environments.

33.9.1 Alkyd paints

Modern alkyd paints are improved versions of traditional oil-based paints and are produced from natural oils by displacing some of the fatty acid molecules from glycerol, followed by direct linking of the monoglycerides by means of simple dibasic acids (e.g. phthalic acid ($HOOC-C_6H_4-COOH$)). These paints contain much larger polymer molecules and are sold as solutions in organic solvents; they dry rapidly by evaporation followed by cross-linking by oxidation. They contain metal compounds as dryers, similar to oil-based paints.

Alkyd paints are available in both 'flat' and 'gloss' formulations, but the former is not very durable in external use. Gloss paints will give from 3 to 6 years life, but they tend to show up all the irregularities in the underlying surface. They are fairly impermeable to moisture and are not very suitable for use on newly completed buildings. Imitation 'stone' paints with a fine texture also have a specific decorative appearance and provide useful weather protection, with a longer outdoor life. They may contain sand, mica or coarser aggregates, and have a useful life in excess of 10 years.

Simple alkyd paints have poor alkali resistance and should not be applied to concrete without a primer or sealer. They are limited in their chemical and solvent resistance and embrittlement may occur with ageing, leading to loss of water resistance. They will rapidly deteriorate in chemical environments and are then not easily recoated with other solvent-borne coatings because of poor solvent resistance. Although widely used in exterior applications, they are subject to attack by ultraviolet radiation, and will chalk readily. The maximum solids content of alkyd wet paint is somewhat limited, and they are becoming subject to environmental limitations due to solvent-evaporation restrictions. The drying time required for simple alkyd paints is longer than that for most other coatings.

Alkyd paints can be formulated to possess varying degrees of gloss, drying time and elasticity. The colour and gloss retention of an alkyd paint can be greatly improved through modification with silicone resin. Good silicone alkyd paints are very expensive and it is often more economical to use a polyurethane or epoxy system instead. Alkali resistance can be improved by copolymerization with styrene ($C_6H_5-C=CH_2$). Mixtures of equal parts of chlorinated rubber and alkyd paints have good resistance to both water and alkali.

33.9.2 Urethane oil paints

Oil-modified urethanes are derived from natural drying oils by cross-linking partially alcoholysized oils with diisocyanates. The paints dry by solvent evaporation and oxidative cross-linking, and are quicker drying than alkyd paints. They have good abrasion resistance and resist solvents and chemicals. In general, two-pack polyurethanes give better durability than polyurethane oils. Urethane oil paints are difficult to pigment and are most commonly encountered as interior urethane type varnishes.

33.9.3 Epoxy ester and alkyd paints

Epoxy ester and alkyd paints are oil-modified epoxies which produce coatings that dry by solvent evaporation and oxidative cross-linking. They are usually made by esterifying the epoxy group and hydroxyl groups on the epoxy resin molecule with unsaturated fatty acids. They are neither as hard nor as chemically resistant as two-pack epoxies, but are easier to apply. Their value lies in their use as interior decorative barriers, especially in flooring applications. The epoxy esters have an intermediate degree of chemical resistance. Their films are hard, tough and abrasion resistant, but readily chalk and fade and, therefore, should be used only on interior surfaces.

33.9.4 Phenolic paints

These paints are made from drying-oil modified phenol–formaldehyde resins. Coatings made with these systems dry from both solvent evaporation and cross-linking by oxidation of the oil. Their properties are similar to those of chlorinated rubbers and they are of use in damp-proofing and submerged service applications. They have good chemical resistance but are generally softened by strong solvents. They discolour and embrittle with age and are difficult to recoat.

33.10 Solvent-thinned paints

Examples of solvent-thinned paints are solutions of linear polymers, such as cellulose nitrate, polyvinyl chloride, vinylidene chloride–acrylonitrile copolymers and polymethyl methacrylate. These paints dry by simple evaporation of the solvent, usually very rapidly as compared with other paint types. The incorporation of a plasticizer is often required to improve the flexibility of the film, e.g. butylbenzylphthalate for polymethyl methacrylate lacquers. The quantity of polymer present in the system is limited by the need to form wet paints which are fluid enough to be worked into the surface during application. Paints based on synthetic rubber and vinyl or acrylic resins can give up to 7 years service life.

33.10.1 Acrylic paints

Two important 'acrylic' polymers within this group of paints are polymethyl acrylate ($-CH_2-CH(COOCH_3)-$) and polymethyl methacrylate ($-CH_2-C(CH_3)(COOCH_3)-$). Linear copolymers containing roughly equal parts of methyl methacrylate and alkyl acrylate are produced for use in surface coatings, the methacrylate conferring hardness and the acrylate flexibility. Polymethyl methacrylate must be plasticized for use in paint films and the most commonly used plasticizer is butylbenzylphthalate.

Acrylic paints and stains are easily applied, have excellent wetting properties, are easily repainted and have a fair degree of chemical resistance. They also possess good colour and gloss retention on outdoor exposure and have a high water-vapour permeability while retaining a low permeability to carbon dioxide. The major advantage of the acrylate paints is their non-yellowing characteristics in natural weathering as they do not absorb ultraviolet light. They are not softened by commercial petrol, but have poor resistance to other solvents and are not as abrasion resistant as epoxy or urethane paints. It is difficult to obtain uniform colour on surfaces of varying porosity. Clear acrylics are often employed as exterior concrete sealers and primers for vinyl emulsions.

33.10.2 Chlorinated rubber paints

Chlorinated rubber paints are formed by reacting chlorine gas with natural rubber dissolved in carbon tetrachloride, until a chlorine content of 65% is achieved. The chemical structure of such paints contains aliphatic six-membered rings, linked in linear polymers $(-CHCl-CHCl-C(CH_3)Cl-)$. They are soluble in benzene, carbon tetrachloride and some other chlorinated solvents, but insoluble in petrol and alcohol. The paints are stable to acids, alkalis, water and oxidizing agents and, therefore, can be used to increase the chemical resistance of an alkyd.

Application is more difficult than for emulsion or oil-based paints. Airless spray paints are available for use on large areas, and high-build chlorinated rubber paints are preferred for the economic application of a usefully thick film in the minimum number of coats. Chlorinated rubber paints are easily recoated and weather well, although they are even more likely to chalk than alkyds and should be used only in non-critical applications in exterior decoration. Their outdoor durability is quite good but they tend to become brittle with ageing and lose their ability to resist water penetration. They have limited resistance to heat and will deteriorate if exposed above 65°C for prolonged periods.

A full range of colours is available, but some whites have shown a tendency to yellowing. The finish is usually a low gloss, but there are a number of chlorinated rubber paints containing fine or coarse particles for producing a textured surface.

Chlorinated rubber paints have a particular use in swimming pools and on concrete in water-treatment plants to reduce the growth of algae, which does not adhere strongly to them. They are too resistant to water-vapour transmission for use where moisture build-up may occur. For some of the thick, textured spray or roller-applied coatings claims of 20 years life have been made.

33.10.3 Vinyl paints

Polyvinyl chloride was developed in the 1930s in Germany and the USA. The chemical structure is one of linear polymers $(-CH_2-CHCl-CH_2-CHCl-)$. The vinyl-type polymeric paints are plasticized copolymers of vinyl chloride and vinyl acetate (2–10% acetate) dissolved in strong solvents. The copolymer can be cross-linked with suitable plasticizers. The vinyl chloride/vinyl ether copolymers are useful for coatings on concrete, but they have poor wetting and bonding characteristics. They dry very rapidly by solvent evaporation, and may be difficult to apply by hand, thus spray application is preferred.

Vinyl paints have a fair colour retention and can be used for exterior service, although they are limited in decorative finishes because of a tendency to chalk. They have excellent flexibility but loss of plasticizer may lead to embrittlement of the dried paint film. Vinyl paints have good resistance to a wide range of chemicals, including acids, alkalis, oils and fats and good water resistance: they are often used in damp-proofing applications and on submerged surfaces. They have excellent recoatability except when top-coated with other paints containing strong solvents.

33.10.4 Fluoro elastomer coatings

Very resistant fluoro elastomer coatings have been specified for lining large concrete chimneys in power stations. A coating thickness of 1.5 mm is gradually built-up by airless spraying, allowing each coat to dry for 24 h between coats. The concrete surface is grit blasted and primed before applying the necessary 20 coatings. The coating is designed to withstand temperatures of 110°C in normal service and peak temperatures of 200°C, as well as to be resistant to concentrated sulphuric acid.

33.10.5 Coal-tar paints

Coal-tar paint is a well-established material which can be used to form a waterproof coating on concrete and other building materials.[25] The paint consists of coal tar dissolved in aromatic organic solvent, derived from coal tar distillates. Adequate ventilation and protection for operatives should be provided. Coal tar may be blended with epoxy systems, either to reduce the cost of the epoxy, or to improve the performance of simple coal-tar paints.

Bituminous and coal-tar or water-tar coatings provide good waterproofing at low cost in situations where appearance is unimportant. Where cracks have to be bridged these materials are often used with glass or synthetic-fibre reinforcing fabric. They have a long history of successful use in tanking and also as waterproofers in all parts of buildings and civil engineering structures. Some tars and bitumens are not fully durable in sunlight and, accordingly, versions pigmented with aluminium powder have been developed.

33.10.6 Bitumen paints

Bitumen paints are composed of an organic solvent solution of bitumen.[26] Two types are available, one for general purposes and one for use in drinking-water tanks. The paints are intended for waterproofing and protection, and are not intended for decorative purposes. They lose their gloss rapidly if exposed to normal weathering.

These systems are protective and are not fully durable in sunlight, but can be given improved durability with a decorative emulsion paint finish. Their consistency varies according to the type of coating and method of application, thin bitumen solutions being of least value and high-build or heavy types being much better, whether solvent thinned or emulsion based. Bitumen paints are especially useful in protecting basements against the ingress of water, but coatings in these conditions must be applied to the external face.

33.11 Two-pack systems

Polyurethane and epoxy coatings are the most expensive coatings in general use on concrete. They offer longer life, freedom from biological colonization and better resistance to wear than conventional paints, but for an equivalent thickness they are normally two or three times more expensive than either water- or solvent-thinned materials.

33.11.1 Epoxy resin paints

Epoxy resins of various types have been used for many years as protective coatings for concrete. The resins were invented in Switzerland in 1943 and were initially used in adhesives, but later developed as coatings. For curing at room temperature, they are invariably two pack, one pack containing a polymer with epoxy end groups $\left(-R'-CH_0-CH_2\right)$ and one pack is the

hardener, usually a polyamine $(-R''-NH_2)$. An excess of organic amine may be reacted with an epoxy resin (to form an adduct) in order to avoid the presence of volatile amine in the wet-paint system. Fatty polyamides (long-chain amines) are also employed to cure epoxy resins and result in a more flexible product. The lower molecular weight amine hardeners show a clear tendency to induce dermatitis and are highly reactive; it is difficult to formulate them with adequate pot life.

Epoxy resins can also be cured by stoving at elevated temperatures using compounds containing hydroxyl groups, carboxylic acids, isocyanates, mercaptans, aniline formaldehydes or organic acid anhydrides. The polymerization reaction during curing occurs without elimination of water and is a simple addition reaction to form an amine link ($-R'-CH(OH)-CH_2-NH-R''-$).

The two materials must be mixed thoroughly in equivalent proportions to provide equal numbers of accessible chemical reaction sites. The pot life of the mixed paint is usually several hours and there may be some advantage in allowing some prereaction to occur before application. Depending on the selection of ingredients, the material may be cured at any convenient temperature from 10°C upwards. The chemical reaction is exothermal and the reaction rate is temperature dependent.

Hand application by brush, roller or trowel is possible as is application by machine roller. The lower molecular weight epoxy resins (the liquid resins) have dermatitic reactions and should not normally be applied by spraying; the solid, higher molecular weight resins are safe in this respect and may be applied by one or two nozzle spray guns, possibly after preheating.

Surfaces must be dry and well prepared by sand blasting or acid etching, before applying the first coat. The second coat should follow the first after not more than 24 h in order to allow polymerization to occur across coats. If this is impossible, then proper bonding may be achieved by roughening the first coat before application of the second. Weathering of the painted surface should be avoided until all the coats have been applied and cured, to avoid delamination.

The disadvantages of epoxy resins are their high cost and their relative intolerance of damp conditions; their successful employment depends on very careful surface preparation before application. They are normally glossy, but aromatic epoxy coatings strongly absorb ultraviolet radiation and chalk quickly in exterior situations. A polyurethane finish coat may be applied to avoid this problem. However, epoxy resin paints are impermeable to water vapour and should not be used on walls which are required to dry out.

33.11.2 Solvent-free liquid epoxy resin and hardener systems

Solvent-free liquid epoxy resin and hardener systems are based on liquid epoxy resins (molecular weights of approximately 380). The viscosity of the liquid resin may be reduced by incorporating reactive diluents (monofunctional or difunctional epoxides) which become bonded to the main polymer during coating, but the relatively high vapour pressure of these compounds limits the amount that can be added for reasons of toxicity. Crystallization of the liquid resin may occur, encouraged by the presence of pigments and fillers, but this can be avoided by heating the resin to above 50°C.

Hardeners are predominantly aliphatic polyamine compounds that have been partially reacted with epoxy resin. Although in general they have a slower reaction rate than pure amines, they are not as susceptible to atmospheric humidity. Polyaminoamide formulations are available that can be used for coatings on damp concrete and under water. Silicone additions to the binder (0.2–0.6%) reduce the sensitivity of the coating to moisture after hardening. The incorporation of silanes into either the hardener or the resin improves the adhesion of the paint to glazed surfaces. Certain hardeners contain phenols and are unsuitable for use in coatings in areas where drinking water or food is involved.

Single coats of these two-component systems can give coating thicknesses in excess of 300 μm and thicknesses of 2 mm have been quoted. They show negligible contraction on setting. Pigments and fillers may be incorporated during manufacture in either the resin or the hardener, except for the more reactive fillers (metal powders, zinc chromate) which may only be incorporated into the resin component.

Extenders (coal tar or hydrocarbon resins) are mainly employed with the intention of reducing cost. Formulations which incorporate tar (up to 40%) have good resistance to aqueous solutions and acids, but their resistance to organic solvents is reduced as compared with the pure epoxy coating. Tar extenders should only be added to the hardener. Where colour is important, pale hydrocarbon resins are available for incorporation (up to 25% of the total).

A system for spraying pitch epoxy coatings under seawater has been described, where an air-filled hood displaces the seawater temporarily from the concrete surface.

33.11.3 Organic-solvent solution of liquid epoxy resin and hardener systems

Organic-solvent solution of liquid epoxy resin and hardener systems are similar to the solvent-free systems described above, but are diluted to 20–30% solids with volatile solvent in order to produce low-viscosity sealers. Pigmented or filled formulations should not be used as concrete primers because filtering out of the pigment takes place at the concrete surface. Mixtures of aromatic or chlorinated hydrocarbons, alcohols, ketones and esters are employed as the organic solvent for the resin component but hardeners should not contain ketones or esters.

33.11.4 Organic-solvent solution of solid epoxy resin and hardener systems

Solutions of solid epoxy resins (molecular weights of approximately 950) and hardeners have been widely used as protective coatings for concrete for more than 30 years. Two- or three-coat systems, giving a cured film thickness of approximately 50 μm each, are used. Difficulties are experienced in releasing the solvent if thicker films are attempted. Lower solvent content formulations have been produced that contain fillers which ensure a non-sagging finish for coats up to 200 μm thick in one application by use of a spray gun. These paint systems may be pigmented or extended with coal tar in the same way as described for unsolvated epoxy systems.

33.11.5 Water-dispersed epoxy coatings

Two-pack systems based on water-borne emulsions of epoxy resins and aqueous solutions of hardeners are available. A hardener containing a high proportion of solids (80%) in aqueous solutions can be made, together with a resin in aqueous emulsion (85% solids). They can be thinned by the addition of distilled or deionized water. The hazards attached to the use of organic-solvent systems are removed. Such systems do not penetrate into the concrete significantly and are unsuitable for use as surface hardeners on finely porous substrates, but they can be applied to damp concrete and masonry surfaces. A prerequisite for film formation is evaporation of the water in the paint.

33.11.6 Acrylic polymer coatings

Acrylic polymers were invented in Germany in 1927 by Rohm and Haas, and in the UK in 1930 by ICI. Pure methylmethacrylate supplied with a dissolved polymerization inhibitor is readily polymerized during application to a glass-like polymer. The most commonly known form is Perspex. These materials can be copolymerized with a vinyl monomer (e.g. styrene or vinyl toluene) either when mixed with an activator consisting of a peroxide or when exposed to ultraviolet light, giving films of 125–250 μm thickness in one coat. A butylbenzylphthalate plasticizer is required to improve the flexibility of a polymethyl methacrylate film.

33.11.7 Polyester resin coatings

Polyester resins are linear unsaturated polyesters (molecular weight 1000–2000) which are blended with 50% reactive monomer (styrene) to form a fluid paint. The unsaturated polyesters are copolymerized with the vinyl monomer (styrene or vinyl toluene) without the elimination of water or other volatile molecules, when mixed with a hardener consisting of a peroxide and activator, giving films of 125–250 μm thickness in one coat. Polymers of this type became available in the USA in 1946. They are applied unsolvated as two- or three-component mixes.

The hardener component is generally in the form of a fine filler, but can also be a low-viscosity liquid or paste. The cure, once initiated, is a chain reaction which continues throughout the mass of the polyester resin and the mixing and proportioning of the hardener component is less critical than for epoxy resins, although the cure at the interface between the polyester resin mass and the substrate may be inhibited under certain conditions resulting in loss of adhesion. Polyester resins are considerably cheaper than epoxy resins, and have the great advantage of a rapid transition from liquid to solid during cure. The curing time for cross-linking to take place is a function of temperature.

Polyester resins are available with a usable life of approximately 20–30 min after mixing, and will develop high strength within 2–4 h. Polyester resins are also available that will cure at temperatures below 0°C. They are difficult to pigment and, therefore, are generally supplied as protective systems. These coatings have critical application requirements and must only be applied to clean, dry surfaces where alkalinity has been neutralized.

One of the disadvantages of using polyester resin coatings is that they show very much higher shrinkage on curing than epoxy resins. Polyester resins have a high degree of resistance to a wide range of aggressive chemicals. They can be used for service under water and in damp-proofing applications. They withstand temperatures up to 200°C and exhibit excellent resistance to impact.

33.11.8 Neoprene rubber systems

Polychloroprene, first synthesized in 1930, is a chloro rubber obtained by emulsion polymerization of chloroprene ($CH_2=CCl–CH=CH_2$). By comparison with natural rubber, it has outstanding resistance to oil and ageing, has high mechanical strength and abrasion resistance, and is flame retardant. Polychloroprene (neoprene) dispersions are used as coating systems for industrial service under conditions of severe chemical exposure. These materials are supplied in organic solvent with an accelerator or catalyst to be mixed in just before use.

33.11.9 Chlorosulphonated polyethylene systems

Chlorosulphonated polyethylene polymers are prepared from low-density polythene by treating it with chlorine gas in the presence of sulphur dioxide. The products contain about 30% chlorine and 1.5% sulphur, and sulphonyl chloride groups are present in the polymer. The general chemical formula of these polymers $(-[(CH_2)_6–CHCl]_{12}–CH(SO_2Cl)-)$ shows the reactive sulphonyl chloride group which may be used for cross-linking. Cross-linking is carried out with MgO or PbO. Paints based on these polymers in organic solvent, can be applied by brush, roller or spray gun, and are commonly used over neoprene sheet on roofing. They are very resistant to chemical attack and weathering.

33.11.10 Polysulphide rubber systems

Commercial production of polysulphide rubbers began in the USA in 1929. These thiokol rubbers are formed by reacting hot aqueous sodium polysulphide solution with alkyl dichlorides ($ClCH_2–CH_2Cl$). Alkyl polysulphide dispersions containing linear polymers ($-R–S–S–S-$) are used directly to produce oil, solvent and heat-resisting coatings for concrete. Various curing agents may be employed, including lead, zinc and manganese oxides.

33.11.11 Silicone rubber systems

A two-pack cold-curing silicone rubber filled with rod-shaped copolymerized styrene butyl acrylates, have been used to form surface coatings for concrete highway structures and underwater linings for canals.[27] Polydimethylsiloxanes react with alkoxy silane in the presence of a catalyst to form a flexible rubber coating which has good water-vapour permeability and is able to bridge cracks. Adhesion promoters are first applied to the concrete surface. A single-pack silicone rubber is also available, which is moisture curing. The material can be applied by brush, roller or spray gun and is particularly useful in resisting biological growth and for absorbing traffic noise.

33.11.12 Miscellaneous two-pack systems

Cold-cure urea formaldehyde two-pack varnishes are available which are catalysed by p-toluene sulphuric acid. Unsaturated polyesters and acrylics can be copolymerized with a vinyl monomer of a peroxide or when exposed to ultraviolet light, giving films of 125–250 μm thickness in one coat.

Furan mortars are supplied as two-pack systems: immediately before use the liquid furan resin (derived from partially polymerized furfural alcohol) is mixed with powder filler which contains an acid catalyst. These mortars are used in conjunction with chemical-resistant bricks and tiles for flooring and have outstanding heat and chemical resistance.

33.11.13 Polyurethane paints

Polyurethane paints are formed by the reaction of isocyanates ($-R–NCO$) with organic hydroxy groups, and contain the urethane link ($-NH–CO–O-$), or with organic amines to yield urea links ($-NH–CO–NH-$). These paints were invented by Bayer in 1937 in Germany. The reaction does not involve elimination of water or other volatile compounds. Diisocyanates are highly toxic materials which cause severe damage if inhaled, but more sophisticated versions based on a larger isocyanate molecule are available which are less toxic. Simple isocyanate (tolylene diisocyanate) is prepolymerized to form intermediates that are less volatile and, therefore, less toxic.

The systems consit of solutions of polyisocyanate and solutions of polyhydric alcohols in organic solvents, which are mixed immediately before use. Urethanes generally contain organic solvents, but water-borne formulations are now appearing on the market. The solids content is in the range 20–40%, the solvent being mineral spirit. Among the disadvantages of the isocyanate resins are the difficulties of storage and transportation due to the highly volatile nature of the solvents employed, which also have a comparatively low flash-point. Pigments and matting agents can be incorporated and all levels of gloss are available, together with systems that contain coarse particles, such as sand, to give a structured surface finish.

Aromatic polyisocyanate paints tend to form films which yellow in service, while aliphatic ones do not, but the latter are less reactive. Polyurethane paints from the aliphatic polyisocyanates have the property of absorbing virtually none of the ultraviolet range of the solar spectrum (wavelengths 300–400 nm), and the phenomena of ageing, such as yellowing and chalking, brought about by ultraviolet absorption do not occur to any great extent with this material. Aliphatic coatings may be employed in the top-coat, while aromatic ones may be present in the penetrating primer and undercoat.

Polyurethane paints have exceptional exterior durability and gloss retention. The coatings exhibit excellent abrasion and chemical resistance with toughness and flexibility. The adhesion of polyurethane coatings to concrete is extremely good and the cured coat is also fire resistant. Drying is rapid and when more than one coat is applied no more than 4 h should elapse between applications.

Polyurethane coatings may be applied to concrete and building materials to protect against moisture ingress. The water-vapour resistance to diffusion can be reduced and the flexibility of the coating increased by suitable formulation. Basically, a reduction in the number of cross-linking bonds between polymer chains is produced by choice of diisocyanate molecule and polyol: polyacrylic resin may be substituted for the polyhydric alcohol. A greater range of properties can be achieved with these two-pack polyurethane paints than can be obtained with the moisture-curing polyurethane ones described below.

Diffusion resistance to carbon dioxide is high: the influence of pigment volume is complex and follows the type of relationship with pigment content outlined previously.

The urethane reaction is not adversely affected by low temperatures and urethanes will fully cure at lower temperatures than other systems. Urethanes will not support the growth of fungi and bacteria, even when subjected to high humidity and temperature. They form tile-like surfaces which will withstand harsh detergent scrubbing and are widely used as graffiti-resistant coatings. Dirt is not absorbed by these paints, because the polymer is not thermoplastic and does not therefore tend to encapsulate the dirt particles. Simple cleaning can restore the surface to its original painted state.

Polyurethane paints are sensitive to surface moisture and must be applied to dry substrates. Coarse textured surfaces normally require the application of a fill-coat, which facilitates the formation of a continuous film, free from pin-holes. Many manufacturers have their own formulations for fill-coats to suit the requirements of their coatings. Polyurethane paints are difficult to recoat, once fully cured, unless they have been abraded or weathered.

33.12 Moisture-curing polyurethane paints

A further type of polyurethane coating is composed of a single-pack isocyanate, with chemical polymerization being achieved by reaction with the moisture in the environment. In this case, carbon dioxide gas is given off during the drying reaction. The isocyanate reacts with moisture to form an amine, with loss of carbon dioxide gas, and the amine then reacts with excess isocyanate to form a urea link. These systems can now be produced almost solvent-free, with solids contents of up to 90%.

Because such systems are sensitive to moisture, problems have arisen in the past associated with pigmentation or matt-finish formation because the adsorbed water on the pigment particles causes premature polymerization; however, these difficulties have now been overcome. Moisture-curing polyurethane paints can be used to provide a top-coat to emulsion paints, to improve their abrasion resistance and to provide graffiti-resistant coatings, after first checking that no unfavourable interacion occurs between the solvent in the polyurethane and the emulsion.

The one-pack urethane paints have excellent adhesion to concrete due to their substrate-wetting abilities and hardness. They resist a very wide variety of chemicals and are not affected by the alkalinity of cement. They have a remarkably high water-vapour permeability. They are easily applied provided that the substrate is dry. These coatings offer outstanding abrasion resistance.

Most urethane paints will yellow if used outdoors and only the aliphatic versions are suitable for decorative coatings in such exposure conditions. Some moisture-curing urethane paints embrittle with age and are difficult to recoat once fully cured, unless lightly abraded or weathered.

33.13 Coating systems applied hot

Coal tar, pitch or asphalt may be poured hot, in combination with fabrics to act as reinforcement. Combinations of asphalt, rubber and oils have sufficient strength after cooling to be satisfactory without the need for felt reinforcement. These systems are used mainly for roofing and the damp-proofing of basements and foundations.

Sulphur mortars are also applied hot in the molten state and are poured to fill joints in masonry, or as linings for sewer trenches and process vessels. In addition to elemental sulphur, these mortars also contain silica and carbon fillers and plasticizers. They may be used as protective coatings for concrete floors in chemical plant. They are ready for use as soon as they are cool, as are the other hot applied systems.

33.14 Clear finishes, stains and sealers

Clear colourless treatments are often sought to improve the water-shedding capabilities of patterned or tooled concrete surfaces, and to prevent dirt and rain streaking. Silicone water-repellents may help prevent algae growth by reducing water absorption, but they are not very resistant to dirt.

The better coatings often consist of polymethyl methacrylate, which has a high permeability to water vapour. The coatings will not fill wide cracks or blow holes, and may tend to darken the colour of the concrete and aggregates, or produce a distinct gloss. The systems used should have a high solids content in the organic-solvent solution (hence high viscosity) when used on smooth concrete. Moisture-curing polyurethane resins are also a feasible alternative, but in the past have tended to produce a more visible film, and some have not proved alkali resistant. However, these resins are permeable to water vapour and show exceptional adhesion to the substrate.

The durability of clear coatings is less than that of pigmented ones, so that a life of only a few years can be expected before further treatment is necessary unless top-coated with, for example, an emulsion paint. Any resin which produces a distinct film runs the risk of unsightly flaking failure.

33.15 Impregnants

Impregnants penetrate the surface of the concrete and are generally used as water repellents; some of them react chemically with the free lime in the concrete, or use it as a catalyst to produce other chemical changes. A number of different bases can be employed, e.g. silicones, silicates, acrylics and silanes. Linseed oil, a drying oil, has frequently been included in trials in the USA as an impregnant to protect concrete against frost damage, and good results have been obtained.[2] The depth of penetration achieved is a major factor in determining the durability of a water-repellent treatment. The depth of penetration is governed by the impregnant type, its viscosity, the solvent used, and the porosity and moisture content of the substrate.

Impregnants for concrete fall into two major groups: those which block or partially block the capillaries and those which do not block them but coat the pore walls with a hydrophobic substance. Penetration by water is resisted (up to a limited hydrostatic head) by making use of the surface tension of liquid water, by increasing the angle of contact between the water droplet and the concrete surface.

Water repellents usually do not greatly affect water-vapour transmission and, therefore, allow the concrete to 'breathe'. Such repellents have little effect on carbon dioxide diffusion and provide no protection against carbonation. It has been argued that because water repellents maintain concrete in a drier state, carbonation is aggravated.

33.15.1 Silicones

Silicone resins (polyorganosiloxanes) derived from linear polymers containing –Si–O–Si– units are dissolved in an organic solvent, usually white spirit or distillate, but are sometimes supplied in the form of water solutions of sodium methylsiliconate. They are usually applied at a concentration of up to 6%. Silicone resins are widely variable in performance. The simpler resins give excellent performance on brick and other non-alkaline silicaceous substrates. Special resins are required to perform well on concrete and other alkaline substrates.[28]

Silicones are noted for their extremely good resistance to ultraviolet radiation. They are generally inert, non-biodegradable materials, and highly resistant to oxidation and chemical attack. The effective life of silicone as a protective treatment is known to be at least 10 years. Some apparent loss of the high initial water repellency of the surface may occur in the first few months after treatment. This is a surface weathering effect, but the treatment is retained within the pores and maintains the initial low absorption values for water.

Silicones can be used to modify many other resin systems to improve gloss retention, decrease oxidation due to weathering, decrease dirt retention, and increase resistance of the surface coating to heat.

33.15.2 Silanes

Silane is silicon hydride (SiH_4), but for the purposes of the construction industry, more complex alkyl alkoxy silanes are indicated. Brethane (methyltrimethoxysilane) was developed by the Building Research Station in the 1970s for use in the preservation of stone monuments.

Most performance data now relate to iso-butyltrimethoxysilane. This silane condenses in the presence of water to form a silicone resin, with the elimination of alcohol. The Department of Transport[3,4] specify this impregnant in the pure liquid form for the protection of concrete highway structures, on surfaces that are surface dry, with the option of light grit blasting of the surface before application.

Whilst the silanes give excellent penetration and water repellency, they are applied at high concentration (40–100%) and are, therefore, much more expensive than other water repellents. Organic-solvent solutions of less volatile silanes (iso-octyltrimethoxysilane) and low molecular weight siloxane resins, incorporating cure catalysts (oligomeric silanes), are being investigated as alternatives.

Silanes have superior performance as compared with the silicones in that the latter are already polymerized before contact with the substrate, so their solutions are more viscous and penetration is difficult. Silicones are only soluble in non-polar solvents so that intimate contact with damp concrete surfaces is impossible. Furthermore, siloxanes are not as resistant towards alkali as are silanes.

Comparative studies of the performance of different surface coatings and impregnants have been reviewed,[2] and these usually place silane treatment as the most effective treatment against frost damage and chloride ingress. McCurrich et al.[29] have published data on the relative efficiency of monomeric silane in methylated spirit, oligomeric silane–siloxane in white spirit, high molecular weight silicone resin in mineral spirit and methacrylic resin in xylene. The water absorptions of coated mortar prisms after 7 days soaking under water were 2.1, 2.6, 9.3 and 9.5% respectively.

A number of manufacturers market paint systems for protecting concrete which consist of a silane impregnant coat, followed by a traditional paint, for example a pigmented solvent-based methacrylate resin or a clear acrylic sealer. McCurrich et al.[29] have published evidence for the efficiency of this combination in reducing both chloride and carbon dioxide diffusion, yet substantial water vapour permeation is allowed.

33.15.3 Stearates

Aluminium stearate is the most frequently used non-silicone water repellent. The stearate cures by reaction with moisture to form a waxy film. It is applied from solution in white spirit or similar solvent at a concentration of about 7.5%. Water repellency is variable on some siliceous substrates. At low temperatures (less than 10°C) the solution becomes viscous and the dissolved material gradually separates.

33.15.4 Silicates

Sodium silicate (Na_2SiO_3) solution (water glass) and potassium silicate (K_2SiO_3) are used to produce protective coatings on concrete surfaces. Water glass is decomposed by the lime content of the substrate and a silica rich gel is formed which seals the capillary pores. After drying, the gel forms a durable protective cover of 1–2 mm thickness, rendering the concrete surface more resistant to both mechanical wear and chemical attack.

Very long life is claimed for silicate based materials which are available in a wide range of colours. Paints based on certain potassium silicates with fillers and pigments are said to maintain the alkalinity of concrete surfaces, preventing biological colonization and inhibiting carbonation. Very many years of successful experience are claimed for these materials in Germany where they have been in use throughout this century.

Fresh concrete surface can be treated by spraying first with a diluted solution of water glass and then with a calcium chloride solution. When applied correctly, the resulting silicate enamel provides effective protection from weak acids. Water glass treatment should not be applied in places where it cannot be renewed at a later date, because the silicate layer tends to lose its protective property once it is damaged. The advantages of silicate solutions during application are that they are neither toxic nor flammable under normal conditions. A number of proprietary systems are available, probably based on similar silicate systems, which incorporate Portland cement in the coating.

33.15.5 Silicofluorides

Silicofluorides are suitable for treating concrete floors. They consist of aqueous solutions of lithium or magnesium silicofluoride. They react with the lime in the concrete to form insoluble calcium fluoride and, thereby, impart a harder more durable and dust-free surface to the concrete.

References

1 GAUL, R. W., 'Preparing concrete surfaces for coatings', *Concrete International Detroit* (17–22 Jul. 1984)

2 BEAN, D. L., 'Surface treatments to minimize concrete deterioration. Report 1, Survey of field and laboratory applications and available products', *Technical Report REMR-CS-17*, US Army Engineers Waterways Experimental Station, Vicksburg, Mississippi (1988)

3 DEPARTMENT OF TRANSPORT, 'The investigation and repair of concrete highway structures', *Highways and Traffic Departmental Advice Note BA 23/86*, HMSO, London (1986)

4 DEPARTMENT OF TRANSPORT, 'Materials for the repair of concrete highway structures', *Highways and Traffic Departmental Standard BD27/86*, HMSO, London (1986)

5 LEEMING, M. B. and O'BRIEN, T. P., 'Protection of reinforced concrete by surface treatments', *CIRIA Technical Note 130*, Construction Industry Research and Information Association, London (1987)

6 SMIT, J., 'Coating with confidence', *Construction Repair*, **2**, 14–16 (1988)

7 STROUD, C. and GARDNER, P., 'High-rise structures—current experience of investigation and repair', *Concrete Repair—Problems, Questions and Answers 24–39*, Palladian Publications, London (1988)

8 BRITISH STANDARDS INSTITUTION, *BS 6270 Cleaning and surface repair of buildings, Part 1: Natural stone, cast stone and clay and calcium silicate brick masonry*, Milton Keynes (1982)

9 BRITISH STANDARDS INSTITUTION, *BS 6270 Cleaning and surface repair of buildings, Part 2: Concrete and precast concrete masonry*, Milton Keynes (1985)

10 BRITISH STANDARDS INSTITUTION, *BS 6150 Code of practice for painting of buildings*, Milton Keynes (1982)

11 AMERICAN CONCRETE INSTITUTE (ACI), 'A guide to the use of water-proofing, damp-proofing, protective and decorative barrier system', *Manual of Concrete Practice: ACI 515*, ACI Detroit, MI (1979)

12 BUILDING RESEARCH ESTABLISHMENT, 'Painting walls. Part 1: choice of paint', *BRE Digest 197*, Building Research Station, Watford (1982)

13 LAMBOURNE, R., *Paint and Surface Coatings—Theory and Practice*, Ellis Horwood, Chichester (1987)

14 KLOPFER, H., 'The carbonation of external concrete and how to combat it', *Bautenschutz und Bausanierung*, **1**, 86 (1978)

15 KUBITZA, W., 'Polyurethane coatings on concrete and their physical properties relevant to the building sector', *Bautenschutz und Bausanierung*, **2**, 55 (1980)

16 ENGELFRIED, R., *Preventive Protection by Low-permeability Coatings. Permeability of Concrete and Its Control*, Concrete Society, London (12 Dec. 1985)

17 ROBINSON, H., 'Evaluation of coatings as carbonation barriers', *Construction Repair*, **1**, 12–18 (Feb. 1987)

18 KUNZEL, H., 'Assessment of rainproofing of exterior coatings', *IBP Communication No. 18:4*, Building Physics Institute, Stuttgart (1976)

19 ASHURST, J., *Mortars, Plasters and Renders in Conservation*, Ecclesiastical Architects' and Surveyors' Association, Diocesan Office, Canterbury (1983)

20 BRITISH STANDARDS INSTITUTION, *BS 4764 Specification for powder cement paints*, Milton Keynes (1986)

21 DESOR, U. and SELLARS, K., *Protection and Restoration of Concrete with Emulsion Paints. Coatings for Concrete*, Paint Research Association, Teddington, Middx (Mar. 1985)

22 ROTHWELL, G. W., 'Effect of external coatings on moisture contents of autoclaved aerated concrete walls'. In *Autoclaved Aerated Concrete* (ed. Wittmann, F. H.), Elsevier, Amsterdam (1983)

23 BEEDLE, H. V. A. and JONES, P. B., *Protective/Decorative Coatings for Masonry, Coatings for Concrete*, Paint Research Association, Teddington, Middx (Mar. 1985)

24 BRITISH STANDARDS INSTITUTION, *BS 434 Bitumen road emulsions*, Milton Keynes (1984)

25 BRITISH STANDARDS INSTITUTION, *BS 1070 Black paint (tar based)*, Milton Keynes (1973)

26 BRITISH STANDARDS INSTITUTION, *BS 3416 Black bitumen coating solutions for cold application*, Milton Keynes (1975)

27 WEGEHAUPT, K.-H., 'Flexible coatings for construction', *Betonwerk + Fertigteil – Technik*, **4**, 260 (1986)

28 BRITISH STANDARDS INSTITUTION, *BS 6477 Specification for water repellants for masonry surfaces*, Milton Keynes (1984)

29 McCURRICH, L. H., LAMBE, R. W. and JACKSON, J. B., 'A systematic approach to reducing chloride penetration, Bahrain Society of Engineers', *CIRIA Proceedings of the 2nd International Conference*, **1**, 533 (1987)

Bibliography

CONCRETE SOCIETY, 'Repair of concrete damaged by reinforcement corrosion', *Concrete Society Technical Report No. 26*, Wexham, Slough (1984)

CRAWFORTH, G. C., 'The role of coatings technology in alleviating the problem of condensation in buildings', *Coatings for Concrete*, Paint Research Association, Teddington, Middx (Mar. 1985)

HAWES, F., *The Maintenance and Painting of Concrete Facades*, Cement and Concrete Association, Wexham, Slough (1983)

KUBITZA, W., 'Polyurethane coatings for the protection and decoration of concrete—both indoors and out', *Bayer Technical Publication KL44357e*, Bayer, Leverkusen (1984)

PANEK, J., 'Building seals and sealants', *ASTM STP 606* (1976)

ROTHWELL, G. W., *Coatings for the Protection of Steel-reinforced Concrete. Coatings for Concrete*, Paint Research Association, Teddington, Middx (Mar. 1985)

SAUNDERS, K. J., *Organic Polymer Chemistry*, 2nd edn, Chapman and Hall, London (1988)

SCOTT, J. R. and ROFF, W. J., *Fibres, Films, Plastics and Rubbers*, Butterworths, London (1971)

SMIT, J., 'Coating with confidence', *Construction Repair* (14–16 Feb. 1988)

SPAIN AND PARTNERS (ed.), *Spon's Contractors' Handbook: Painting and Decorating*, E. and F. N. Spon, London (1988)

SPRINGLE, R., 'Biocidal coatings', *Coatings for Concrete*, Paint Research Association, Teddington, Middx (Mar. 1985)

TURNER, G. P. A., *Introduction to Paint Chemistry and Principles of Paint Technology*, 3rd edn, Chapman and Hall, London (1988)

VESIKARI, E., 'Prevention of frost-salt action on concrete by use of surface sealants', *Nordic Concrete Research*, **2**, 205 (1983)

34

Paint: Intumescent Coatings for Structural Fire Protection and Other Building Applications

D C Aslin BA
Prometheus Developments Ltd

Contents

34.1 Description 34/3

34.2 Use of intumescent coatings as fire protection 34/3

34.3 Chemistry and process 34/3
34.3.1 The intumescent coatings 34/4
34.3.2 Binder systems 34/4
34.3.3 Other components 34/4

34.4 Selection of commercial products 34/5

34.5 Performance under fire and fire-test conditions 34/6

34.6 Environmental stability 34/8

34.7 Manufacture 34/8
34.7.1 Ball milling 34/8
34.7.2 Powered ball mills (attrittors) and
bead mills 34/9
34.7.3 High shear dispersion 34/9
34.7.4 Paste mixers 34/9

34.8 Raw materials 34/10
34.8.1 Binders 34/10
34.8.2 Plasticizers 34/10
34.8.3 Spumescents 34/10
34.8.4 Carbonifics 34/10
34.8.5 Catalysts 34/11
34.8.6 Pigmentation 34/11

34.9 Forms and uses 34/11
34.9.1 Fire protection of structural steel 34/11
34.9.2 Cable tray protection 34/11
34.9.3 Flame-retardant formulations 34/12
34.9.4 Structural timber 34/12
34.9.5 Fire dampers 34/12
34.9.6 Penetration seals 34/12
34.9.7 Clear intumescent varnishes 34/12
34.9.8 Door seals and closure seals 34/12

34.10 Application 34/12

34.11 Current consumption and market levels 34/13
34.11.1 Specification and selection 34/13

34.12 Design of formulations 34/13

34.13 Certification 34/15

Bibliography 34/15

34.1 Description

Intumescence is a process in which, under the influence of heat, a solid substance transforms into an expanded, relatively rigid foam. This foam, having a lower thermal conductivity than the original substance because of the expansion, is used as a means of providing fire protection.

Commercial intumescent products are invariably applied to the surface materials of a construction as a means of imparting resistance of the material to fire, or protecting the structure from the effects of fire.

The interest in the use of intumescent coatings as a means of structural fire protection is largely derived from their apparent ease of application and other properties, when compared with other fire protection systems. The properties of various types of fire protection listed in *Table 34.1* illustrates this. Thus, it can be seen that, apart from the durability aspect, intumescent coatings have strong advantages for the architect and structural engineer. This is particularly true where the steelwork is expressed as an aspect of the design of the building.

34.2 Use of intumescent coatings as fire protection

Materials suffer from fire in two ways. Either they ignite, like wood and most polymers, or they lose their structural strength at certain temperatures. The objective of fire protection is to prevent these occurrences.

Thus coatings, including intumescent coatings, can be applied to substrates to improve their performance under fire in four ways.

(1) To improve the fire-spread characteristics of substrates that are inflammable. This would include timber and other linings, electrical cables, textiles and floor coverings.
(2) To maintain the fire-spread characteristics of materials that need to be coated for aesthetic, durability or mechanical reasons.
(3) To maintain the load-bearing characteristics of the elements of a structure under fire by improving their fire resistance.
(4) To maintain the integrity of separating fire walls.

When considering the prevention or limitation of fire spread in a structure the following factors are relevant:

(1) prevention of fire;
(2) detection of fire;
(3) restriction of fire growth;
(4) provision of means of escape;
(5) smoke-control provisions;
(6) fire resistance of the structure;
(7) compartmentation of the building;

(8) prevention of conflagration;
(9) portable extinguishing devices;
(10) fixed extinguishing systems;
(11) safety-services access; and
(12) fire-safety management.

The importance of surface coatings in fire protection arises from consideration of the requirement by design or by legislation to:

(1) prevent fire spread within the compartment of origin;
(2) prevent fire spread to neighbouring compartments;
(3) prevent fire spread across external surfaces of the building; and
(4) retain the stability of the building.

For each of these considerations intumescent products can play some part. However, some of the requirements in the above list can restrict, or run counter to the choice and use of intumescent coatings. These considerations are dealt with in Section 34.12.

The major use of fire protection coatings is in the protection of buildings or industrial structures from collapse due to loss of strength. This is particularly so in steel-framed buildings, which are a growing proportion of new commercial building, particularly in the UK.

Steel loses its structural strength at 550°C. Building regulations world-wide deem that all structures, under normal occupation, must be able to withstand the onset of the critical failure temperature, in a standard fire, for up to 4 h, depending on the use and size of the building.

Within the UK, the largest growth area in surface-coating products, both generally and in fire protection in particular, has been in thin-film intumescents. The interest is such that most paint manufacturers dealing in structural-steel protection will have considered the possibility of entering this market. However, the knowledge that a company is offering an intumescent coating with all the relevant certification, is insufficient assurance for an architect or structural engineer of an adequate fire protection installation. The final product is the installed coating, not the liquid paint as it leaves the manufacturer. All the advantages shown by the properties given in *Table 34.1* can be nullified if the installation and back-up service is inadequate.

Although the major use of intumescent products is in thin film for structural fire protection of steel, this is not an exclusive categorization and intumescent products are supplied in diverse forms, for different applications. While these other uses are discussed, the major usage clearly demands the major part of the following discussion.

34.3 Chemistry and process

Before describing how a suitable product can be selected and the installation controlled, it is necessary to outline the technical

Table 34.1 Comparative properties of various types of fire protection applied to steel structures

Protection type	Concrete encasement	Cladding panels	Cement sprays	Intumescent coatings
Installation speed	Very slow	Slow	Moderate	Fast
Interference with other trades	Great	Moderate	High	Negligible
Durability internal	Good	Good	Good	Moderate to good
Durability external	Good	Poor	Poor	Poor to good
Cost	High	Moderate to high	Low	Moderate
Appearance	Moderate	Good	Poor	Good
Conformability	Moderate	Poor	Good	Very good
Section range	Wide	Wide	Limited	Limited
Fire rating range	Wide	Wide	Moderate	Narrow

processes involved in intumescent products. In general practice the formulations currently available are almost exclusively 'phosphate catalysed intumescents'. These consist of three active components dispersed in a resinous material, usually thinned with solvents. The resin serves to 'glue' the intumescent components together and, in the dried form, to protect them from environmental degradation. Certain refractory pigments are usually added to the formulation.

34.3.1 The intumescent components

The intumescent components are listed below:

(1) A source of non-volatile acid, usually ammonium polyphosphates. These are referred to as the 'catalyst' and make up about 25% of the total formulation. Materials that are currently in use are ammonium polyphosphates, ammonium orthophosphates and melamine phosphates.
(2) An organic substance (usually a polyol) that can be decomposed by the acid liberated from the catalyst to reduce to a source of carbon. Conventionally referred to as 'carbonific' materials, those in current use are pentaerythritol, dipentaerythritol and tripentaerythritol. Starch in various forms has been used in the past.
(3) A source of inert volatile gases that assists the formation of the foam/char. These are conventionally referred to as the 'spumescent'. Normally, melamine is used. Various melamine salts such as melamine phosphate are also satisfactory. Dicyandiamide is used in cable tray protection and several water-based formulations. A variety of melamine or urea derivatives have been utilized in some patents and formulations.

34.3.2 Binder systems

The binder utilized may be of almost any polymer genera providing it can produce a low-viscosity melt as the applied temperature rises to about 150°C. In some cases this is achieved by adding plasticizer to the resin in order to adjust the melt viscosity to control the blowing action.

In general, the resins selected are non-convertible; that is, there is no chemical change between the cured and liquid state, the resins drying by evaporation of the carrier solvent only. This choice is necessitated by the selection of melting point and, by virtue of this choice, it constrains the formulation characteristics.

One exception to the generalization of the use of non-convertible resins is the epoxides group. Epoxy resins are convertible resins, there being a cross-linking of the polymer during curing. However, because of the mode of decomposition of epoxy resins, when strongly heated they reduce to a high-viscosity melt. By careful choice of the base resin, the curing agent and plasticizer, epoxy based intumescents work very well.

There exist a number of commercially available thick-film intumescents, based on epoxy resins, that are designed for use in extreme environmental conditions. The author has developed several thin-film epoxy formulations that have not yet been exploited commercially.

Few unmodified polymer types can be utilized in intumescent products. All systems in commercial use contain a plasticizer which is often a chlorinated paraffin and/or a phosphate ester. Chlorinated paraffins are useful, as in some circumstances they can assist the blowing action of the spumescent. Phosphate plasticizers have an advantage in that on decomposition they yield acid phosphates that assist the action of the catalyst.

Because the majority of intumescents are based on non-convertible resins, they are carried in a solvent pertinent to the resin in use. Thus, in summary, the resins that appear in current commercial formulations together with the relevant plasticizer

and solvent are as follows.

(1) *Solvent based:* styrene acrylics, vinyltoluene acrylics, styrene butadiene resins plasticized with chlorinated paraffins, and dispersed in aliphatic paraffinic solvents, modified with either oxygenated solvents or aromatics. Chlorinated rubbers, chlorinated polyolefins and polyvinyl/vinilidene chlorides may also be used but give very light fluffy foam/chars unless very heavily modified.
(2) *Water based:* usually polyvinyl acetate (PVA) resins, typically plasticized with phosphate plasticizers. A water-soluble coalescing solvent is added to assist film formation.
(3) *Epoxy formulations:* these are very varied, particularly with reference to the plasticizer and curing agent, but the solvent is usually a ketone or ester.

34.3.3 Other components

34.3.3.1 Pigments and fillers

In addition, except in the case of clear intumescent varnishes, the formulations include a variety of pigments and fillers. These are usually metallic oxides such as titania. Aluminium trihydrate is employed and has certain advantages, in that in addition to providing refractory residues from its decomposition, it absorbs considerable quantities of heat during decomposition. Certain other pigmentary oxides, such as molybdenum oxide and antimony trioxide, can influence the course of the decomposition reaction, causing the retention of larger proportions of the organics decomposition products into the foam char, thereby increasing its strength and resistance to ablation and, by virtue of this effect, reducing the smoke emission from the system.

34.3.3.2 Reinforcing agents

Many thick-film intumescents contain refractory fibres such as glass fibres. The object here is to strengthen and reinforce the char. The inclusion of these components makes the application procedures somewhat more difficult.

Certain systems are applied at sufficiently great thickness that it is impossible for the foam char to be self-supporting. These systems often require the application of a reinforcing mesh to be applied to steel work prior to the application of the wet intumescent coating.

34.3.3.3 Action and behaviour

The mode of action of an intumescent product under the influence of heat can be simplified into the following sequence, as the temperature increases.

(1) The binder system softens to a highly viscous melt. Generally this occurs from 70°C.
(2) Some of the plasticizer and spumescent decomposes, emitting inert gas that blankets the surface of the coating, preventing inhibition of the organic components by the fire source. This will be observed from 90°C up to and beyond the point of intumescence.
(3) The catalyst loses ammonia, releasing liquid acid and lowering the viscosity of the melt. This occurs progressively from 150°C upwards.
(4) The carbonific melts and reacts with the liquid acid, reducing to carbon and releasing water vapour.
(5) The spumescent decomposes releasing inert gas that expands the melt into a soft foam. Reactions (2)–(4) will occur simultaneously at about 210°C.
(6) The foam partially decomposes and sets into a relatively rigid char.
(7) The residual acid reacts with the pigmentary materials, if present, to form refractory phosphates.

(8) The carbonaceous char is gradually ablated by the fire source reducing the strength of the char.

This explanation is an oversimplification. Many side-effects occur and, generally, all these stages, and others, occur at the same time. In addition, the course of the reactions can be mediated and altered by the addition of a variety of functional agents.

34.4 Selection of commercial products

The foregoing description of the reactions of an intumescent product under the influence of fire conditions is not sufficient to describe the total behaviour of an intumescent product, nor is it sufficient to understand the parameters, that must be considered, when designing or selecting an intumescent coating. The state transition analysis table (*Tables 34.2–34.4*) is used to illustrate this.

An intumescent product is a product that must be designed to certain parameters which define its performance in five states linked by six transitions. The products are, therefore, unusually complex in their design requirements. *Tables 34.2–34.4* show some of the variables that must be considered in each state or transition. What is not shown is the detail of the interaction between the dependent and independent variables.

It is the understanding of these interactions and the control of the complexity that is the key to the design of intumescent products. This can allow not only the production of good fire protection, but also of a coating that is competitive to manufacture, stable in storage, easy to apply with a good finish and stable in its dried form until the onset of fire. Users are, therefore, well advised to consider all the properties of a

Table 34.2 State/transition analysis of intumescent coatings

State 1		Raw materials
	Transition 1	Manufacture
State 2		Wet product
	Transition 2	Storage
	Transition 3	Application curing, drying
State 3		Dry film
	Transition 4	Environmental degradation
	Transition 5	(a) Melt
		(b) Foam formation
		(c) Char set
State 4		Carbon char
	Transition 6	Fire degradation
State 5		Residual refractory
	Transition 7	Ablation/erosion

Table 34.3 Variables list for states

State 1 Raw materials	State 2 Wet product	State 3 Dry film	State 4 Initial foam	State 5 Residual
Target formulation	Flash point	Hardness/flexibility	Pore structure	Strength
Cost	Safety	Environmental stability	Temperature vs. strength	Insulation value
Availability	Stability—storage conditions	Dirt retention	Insulation value	Flexibility
Particle-size distribution	Packing	Gloss/finish	Flexibility	
Degradation/stability	Safety regulations	Superstrate compatibility	Strength	
Safety regulations	Rheology	Steel section		
	Surface tension	Competitive systems		
	Density	Test certification		
	Solids (%)	Cost per m^2 vs. HP/A		

Table 34.4 Variables list for transitions

Transition 1 Manufacture	Transition 2 Application	Transition 3 Foam formation	Transition 4 Degradation
Plant type	Equipment	Reaction mode	Shrinkage
Capacity	Operator skill/training	Initiation temperature	Crack formation
Utilization	Build rate	Reserve range	Ablation
Safety regulations	Solvent OEL limits	Risr rate vs. ramp rate	Secondary decomposition
Availability	Drying/curing	Fume/smoke emissions	
	Environmental limitations	Energy balance	
	Pore structure	Insulation generation	
	Application rate		
	Aeration		
	Substrate compatibility		
	Levelling/sag drain		
	Safety		
	WFT		
	Crack formation		

Table 34.5 Sample formulation

Constituent	Function	Content (%)
Pliolite VTAC-L resin 70%	Binder	10.0
Solid chlorinated paraffin	Plasticizer	8.0
Exolit 422 ammonium polyphosphate	Catalyst	25.0
Dipentaerythritol	Carbonific	7.5
Melamine	Spumescent	7.5
Tiona 535 rutile titania	Pigment	9.0
PRS	Solvent	32.6
Bentone 38	Thixotrope	0.3
Methanol	Solvent	0.1
Total		100

product and avoid the temptation to oversimplification and sub-optimization.

While many other schemes can produce intumescence, it is the relative stability of the dry solid films of modern commercial products, and the facility of their application, that is important and leads to the growing acceptance of intumescent coatings as a means of providing fire protection.

Thus, from what appears to be no more than a thick coat of paint applied to the substrate, under the influence of fire conditions the intumescent coating reacts to protect the substrate from the incident fire condition. Generally, the products once applied are not obtrusive in any design scheme, and in some circumstances may be the only acceptable solution to the design problem.

While modern products are a considerable improvement over their predecessors, it is the stability or durability of the applied film that is the major constraint or limit on the use of intumescent coatings. As fire is a chance or random effect, the fire protective coating must remain stable for the anticipated life of the structure or component until that chance incident occurs. If the user cannot be assured of this, then alternatives must be sought.

The utility of commercial intumescent products is that the foam, once formed, has sufficient durability in fire to withstand the extreme conditions present in that condition.

In order to discuss the effect of product design to meet market requirements, let us consider a particular published formulation (see *Table 34.5*).[1] The literature gives the option of grinding or high shear dispersion to manufacture the product. Such a formulation will obtain a 1-h rating on the standard 170 HP/A beam with about 1.8 mm dry film thickness under BS 476[2] conditions. This is more than twice that required by the product with the lowest dry-film-thickness requirements on the UK market. This makes the product difficult to apply and reduces the chances of being able to obtain pleasing architectural finishes. The high thicknesses also mean that good site supervision and inspection are required.

This formulation takes about 1 month to dry thoroughly. It is therefore susceptible to damage from following trades and may incur additional charges for damage rectification. In addition, it produces vast volumes of smoke under fire conditions. Smoke emanations are not currently part of UK test and certification requirements. However, one should consider whether the safety aspects of preserving the structure in one part of the building involved in a fire, will not add additional smoke load to other compartments, not involved in the fire.

This formulation probably requires the application of a top coat under all conditions, in order to preserve it from environmental degradation. It also entrains large quantities of air when put through an airless spray gun, and drags and tacks when brushed. Hence, unless the product is applied under strict control, the weight of product applied is not actually that required for fire protection. As conventional dry-film-thickness measuring apparatus is incapable of determining that a coating is porous, there is no way that the main contractor can ensure that the application is adequate. Nevertheless, such a product is still being offered on the UK market, with little modification from the above formulation.

The foregoing illustrates the care that must be used in the specification, installation and inspection of intumescent coatings. Most products offered in the market place, at first sight, do not vary a lot from this formulation published some 20 years ago, and other formulations in the public domain. However, considerable effort is put into product design by the chemists involved and very considerable improvements can be made in a formulation such as that described above with almost invisible formulation changes. That such changes and improvements can be made with minor additions of other components leads to the almost paranoic secrecy with which many manufacturers guard their formulations. It also, however, leaves the specifier with a sense of disbelief that apparently similar formulations can perform in as different a manner as is claimed by the manufacturers. These differences are very real, though there will always be some clones.

Attempts have been made to move to greater sophistication. A range of formulations based on 4,4-dinitrososulphanilide were patented in 1977 by Sawko and Riccitiello[3] working at the Ames laboratory for NASA. These formulations are available under free licence from NASA. These clever intumescent salts turn out to be quite disappointing. Under intense and rapid heat they do indeed intumesce quite spectacularly. However, under the more gentle temperature ramp such as is deemed to be typical of a cellulosic fire, they just smoke and melt in a most unimpressive manner.

All the foregoing leads to the need to develop methods that will allow these systems to be designed as integrated holistic systems. One of the advantages of the conventional phosphate catalysed formulations typified by that given above is that the optimization plateau is quite flat. This means one can alter the formulation quite considerably without substantially affecting its fire performance. It also means that considerable changes have to be made before substantial improvements can be found.

34.5 Performance under fire and fire-test conditions

Before considering how the properties of intumescent coatings vary, and the effects on their manufacture, it is worth understanding how an intumescent coating behaves under fire-test conditions, and how this behaviour is different from passive coatings, such as an insulating board.

In order to evaluate the performance of any product designed to protect elements of a structure it is universal practice under all test regimes to define a standard fire. This is done by assuming that the growth of a normal cellulosic fire follows a curve given by

$$T = T_0 + 345 \times \log_{10}(8 \times t + 1)$$

where T is the furnace temperature, T_0 is the initial temperature and t is the time (in minutes). This curve is shown in *Figure 34.1* which shows the growth of the temperature ramp vs. time.

Figure 34.2 shows the configuration of a fire-test piece installed in a column test furnace. During the test, the standard fire curve is applied to the column by means of gas- or oil-fired burners within the fire-test chamber. The temperature of the steel test piece is monitored by means of thermocouples secured to the

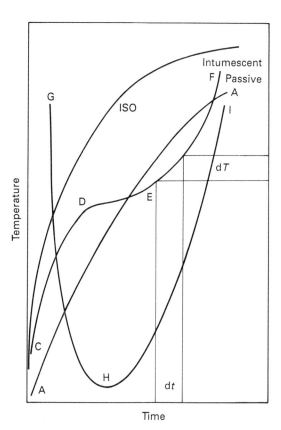

Figure 34.1 Behaviour of passive and active fire protection systems

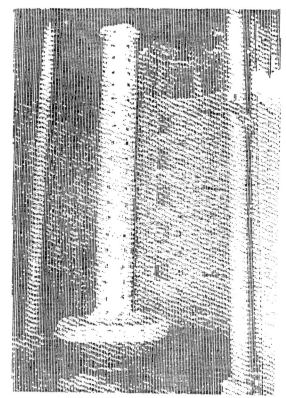

Figure 34.2 Configuration of a fire-test piece installed in a column test furnace

test piece. In some test regimes a simulated load is applied to the column until it fails to support the specified load. However, in all test regimes the thermal response is recorded. Given that the specimen is infinitely long compared to any point of measurement, that the ends of the specimen are insulated and that the specimen is fired from all sides, then the rise in temperature of the steel is proportional to the energy flowing through the insulation, under a thermal potential of the difference between the applied furnace temperature and the steel temperature. Given these assumptions, then the following derivation can be made from *Figure 34.1.*

The curve marked AA is the idealized curve of the temperature response that can be expected from a passive insulation where the insulation value, μ, is nominally constant throughout the temperature range. However, the curve CDEF is the thermal response one would expect from an intumescent coating. The section of the curve CD is the period prior to the onset of intumescence. As the foam/char develops, the thermal conductivity falls and the thermal response follows the curve DE. At some point in time, the foam char commences to decay and the thermal conductivity rises and the curve follows line EF. Eventually the steel temperature crosses the designated failure temperature.

Now, if the first derivative of the steel temperature is calculated as shown, then the resultant curve is thermal conductivity and produces a curve (if smoothed) shown (idealized) as GHI. The basic differences between various intumescent coatings can be described using this curve. Some formulations will give a rapid rise resulting in a lower minimum insulation value, followed by a rapid decay rate. Other formulations will be designed to give a slower formation of insulation and a slow decay. Clearly, the

thick-film intumescents designed to give longer fire ratings, or to withstand the more severe hydrocarbon curve required for offshore use, will be of the latter type. Low-thickness, thin-film intumescents will tend to behave more like the former type.

To illustrate this *Figure 34.3* shows the thermal response of two products, each using different design philosophies, tested under identical conditions. The slow-rise, slow-decay type gives a different steel response curve to that of the rapid-rise, rapid-decay type. However, thickness for thickness, the rapid-rise, rapid-decay type is clearly more efficient at short fire resistance ratings than the slow-rise, slow-decy one. The difference in the appearance of the foams after the test is also illustrative of this. Clearly, the former type has collapsed, whereas the slow-rise product is stable and even allows sections to be removed from the foam. If one refers to the sample formulation given above these changes could be brought about by the following changes.

(1) To increase the rate of rise the melt viscosity can be lowered, therefore the resin:plasticizer ratio will be alerted towards a greater volume of plasticizer.
(2) To give greater char durability the level of rutile titania pigmentation could be raised or lowered to give a faster rise rate. The ratio of spumescent to carbonific can be altered to give a more rapid rise by raising the melamine, or a more rigid char by lowering the ratio.
(3) The level of ammonium polyphosphate is critical, as recent studies have shown that the phosphorous level is vital for adequate intumescent and foam stability and must be about 10–12% of the total formulation.

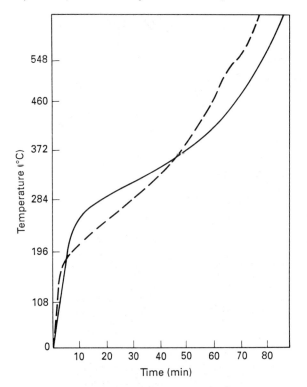

Figure 34.3 Chart-recorder plot from comparative fire test

34.6 Environmental stability

Consideration may now be given to how the requirements for environmental stability can be effected. Again the sample formulation in *Table 34.3* is used as an example.

One of the parameters used in characterizing paint-like products is the pigment volume concentration (PVC). This is given by the volume of the insoluble or pigmentary part of the formulation divided by the volume of the total solids. If an array of equally sized spheres are packed as tightly as possible with adjacent spheres in contact, then the volume occupied by the spheres is about 60% of the total. If then, the spheres are pigmentary particles and the interstitial spaces are filled with resin the model would represent a paint with a PVC of 60%. Ignoring the effect of packing fractions, and the irregularity of the pigmentary particles, a system with a PVC of greater than 60% will, therefore, have some proportion of the pigmentary particles in contact.

As the raw materials of an intumescent system are marginally water soluble, or at least hydrophobic, a resin-deficient intumescent will be very permeable to the transport of water across the film. However, lowering the PVC (raising the resin content) reduces the proportion of the functional intumescent components in the total. Thus, there is a trade-off between fire resistance efficiency for equivalent film thickness and environmental resistance. *Figure 34.4* illustrates this. The vertical axis on this figure is the performance to the Gardner straight line washability apparatus. This equipment is designed to measure the durability of coatings under normal janitorial cleaning procedures. While this test may not be ideally appropriate to intumescent coatings, in the author's experience, the durability assessment procedure can be any appropriate measure of environmental resistance, the resultant curves relating environmental stability to PVC level, nearly always approximate to the shown form.

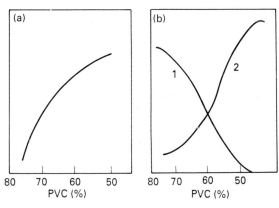

Figure 34.4 Relationship between pigment volume concentration (PVC) and durability measures. (a) Durability: paint loss on exposure. (b) Flame spread rating (curve 1) and intumescence height (curve 2)

Hence, a thick-film intumescent can easily be made relatively tolerant of environmental exposure, as there is sufficient functional material present to provide adequate fire protection. However, unless other steps are taken to modify the permeability of the binder system, thin-film intumescents will always require a top coat to give them any chance of surviving in humid conditions. It is, however, possible to make some modifications to the resin system in order that this may be done.

However, if the improvement made in permeability and water tolerance is present in the dry film, then it follows that the same condition applies to the wet film. Thus, by taking such steps, it becomes possible to apply the coating to exposed steel and tolerate a degree of inclement weather. *Figure 34.5* shows the application of such a tolerant system to exposed steelwork.

Furthermore, buildings do develop leaks and moisture pockets. High levels of humidity can build up in concealed compartments. Hence, there is not really any difference between external and internal exposure, because fire protection is supposed to work at any time, irrespective of whether a pipe or guttering has sprung a leak or ventilation has been inadvertently blocked. The point of this discussion is that the more tolerant the coating is, both during and after application, the more useful it is and the less service commitment it will require.

Thus specifiers should treat with caution any product designated as for internal use only, unless they can be sure that the application is going to be available for regular inspection.

The mode of degradation of intumescent coatings is considered in Section 34.8.

34.7 Manufacture

As all intumescent products consist of particulate material dispersed in a solution of resinous material, it follows that the manufacturing processes are all akin to those used in conventional paint manufacture. The properties and functions controlling the characteristics of the product are again the same as those used in conventional paint manufacture.

The particulate material must be thoroughly dispersed in the liquid resin solution, such that all the particles are fully wetted. This is normally achieved by using one of the shearing techniques used in paint manufacture. These techniques are described briefly in the following sections.

34.7.1 Ball milling

Large cylindrical vessels are partially filled with balls of steel or a heavy ceramic. The vessel is rotated causing the balls to roll

Figure 34.5 Application of a tolerant intumescent to exposed steel work

over each other giving a shear action. If the premix is introduced into the vessel the shearing action is applied to the paint. This causes the particles to be wetted and in-ground by the mechanical action.

34.7.2 Powered ball mills (attrittors) and bead mills

The action of these machines is the same as for a ball mill. However, instead of the balls or grinding medium rolling over each other as they fall under gravity, the grinding medium is driven by a powered agitator. An attrittor, or vibro energy mill, is a vertical ball mill with the plane of rotation or agitation being horizontal.

The particles of the grinding medium have a diameter of 6–9 mm. While batch machines of these types are common, their capacity is low. For a product required to be manufactured in such large quantities as an intumescent coating, recirculation machines are used. In these machines a large vessel holding the premix is continually circulated through the grinding chamber until the requisite measure of dispersion is obtained.

Bead mills are set horizontally with the plane of rotation being vertical. The grinding medium size is much smaller than for the attritor or ball mill, being typically of the order of 2–3 mm. The premix or millbase is then pumped across the tube, from end to end.

While multiple passes are possible with conventional paint, where the author has seen bead mills used to manufacture intumescent coatings, the growth in surface area caused by milling results in an increase in viscosity which means that only one pass is possible.

34.7.3 High shear dispersion

In this process the mill base is rotated or stirred with an immersed impeller driven at very high speed and with considerable power. The particles themselves shear against each other due to viscous drag. It is a simple process but the machines are very powerful. Obviously in this mode of manufacture, unlike those described above, no particle-size reduction takes place, and only dispersion of agglomerates occurs. The degree of wetting is as good as with the grinding techniques described above. This technique is the fastest of all shearing processes by a very considerable degree.

With thin-film intumescents designed for spray application and to achieve a reasonable aesthetic finish, it is advantageous to control the particle size of the intumescent components, which are not supplied in particle sizes normally associated with a pigmentary material (see Section 34.8). Such products can still be manufactured using high shear dispersion, taking advantage of the production speed, but the particle size of the catalyst, spumescent and carbonific can be reduced by rapid dry grinding techniques such as micronization or pinmilling.

34.7.4 Paste mixers

For products where a very high viscosity is required, such as a trowelling compound or a cable tray protection compound, the product can be manufactured on a paste mixer. The shearing action gives the same interparticular effect as with a high shear disperser, but the mill base viscosity is much higher so that a paste mixer works at low speed and high torque, whereas a high shear disperser works at high speed and a lower torque. A common dough mixer is typical of the older designs for such machines.

Typical manufacturing processes cannot be given because each sequence will be dependent on the selection of the resin type, and the machine selected or available for manufacture. However, in all cases the procedure will follow the general steps set out below.

(1) *Premix.* A dispersion base is created. This may be a solution of the resin in solvent or, in the case of water-based emulsions, the dispersion base may be merely water with dispersion aids added. The consistency of this dispersion base is entirely dependent on the requirements of the mill selected.

(2) *Mill base.* The pigmentary material is added to the mill base using a low shear dispersion technique, to produce an even mill base.

(3) *Dispersion.* The mill base is then fed to the mill or high shear disperser. The shearing or milling sequence is then applied to the mill base until some control-measure factor indicative of the success of dispersion is achieved.

(4) *Let down.* The dispersion is then let down by the addition of flow control additives. The balance of the solvent is blended in and the viscosity and rheology adjusted to whatever standards are appropriate to that product.

This sequence may seem deceptively simple. While the difficulties likely to be encountered during manufacture can be overcome by appropriate product design, a skilled paint maker can make all the difference to the ease of manufacture of a product like an intumescent coating, designed at the limit of many parameters considered normal.

34.8 Raw materials

Many of the raw materials associated with the manufacture of intumescent products are proprietary materials. As the number of components that can be considered as commodity materials are limited, once a formulation is designed and fire tested the buyer has very little possibility of dual sourcing to obtain the best competitive prices.

34.8.1 Binders

The binders have been outlined in Section 34.3.2. Except for epoxy resins, where the resins may be defined as generic types with a particular molecular structure, the supply of resins is entirely proprietary. Usually it is not possible to change one manufacturer's resin for another and expect the resultant intumescent coating to behave in the same way.

For example, suppose a product was designed and based on a resin designated by one manufacturer as a styrene acrylic with a particular solution viscosity. Because the degree of cross-linking, or branching, may be different as may be the ratio of monomers, then two apparently similar products will probably perform in entirely different ways when incorporated into an intumescent, whereas the differences may be negligible if the same substitution were made in a conventional coating product. If the melt viscosity is in any way different, then there will be a marked difference in the foam formation transition, because a higher viscosity melt will not blow to the same height, the resultant insulation value will be different and, as the density of the foam will vary from the original, then the rate of degradation will also vary.

Hence, once a formulation has been finalized and the certification completed, usually at substantial cost, then the manufacturer is tied into that particular resin type from that particular manufacturer. The manufacture of resinous materials

comprises a subject in its own right. Each generic type has a different manufacturing sequence and the detail may vary considerably from manufacturer to manufacturer. Little further information is of value within this chapter.

34.8.2 Plasticizers

Here the buyer has more freedom. Plasticizers generally are generic types and supplies can be varied.

Chlorinated paraffins are produced by the chlorination of paraffin wax. They are differentiated by the degree of chlorination (30–70%). The 70% grades are solid and provided as powders with a tendency to clump. The remainder are liquids of varying viscosities. They are generally freely soluble in many common solvents.

34.8.2.1 Phosphate plasticizers

Phosphate plasticizers are invariably phosphate esters. They may be either allyl or aryl compounds, and may be halogen substituted as well. Phosphate plasticizers have the advantage that, on pyrolysis, they yield additional phosphorous acids.

34.8.3 Spumescents

34.8.3.1 Melamine, melamine salts and 2,4,6-triaminotriazine

Melamine may be considered as a commodity material. It is manufactured primarily for use in melamine resins and is used in combustion modified, polyurethane foams. It can be obtained in particle sizes suitable for direct incorporation into fine finish intumescent products. However, it may need further reduction for some applications.

Melamine salts are obtained by precipitation from hot aqueous solutions of melamine. While they have some utility in intumescent coatings their price is up to three times that of pure melamine. Unless the application is particularly demanding the cost is generally now worth the advantage.

One particular advantage of melamine is its ability to form dimers and trimers. These polymeric forms are produced automatically under a slow heating curve. Thus, instead of the melamine decomposing to ammonia over a limited thermal range, the dimer and trimer decompose at progressively higher temperatures. This extends the range over which the blowing effect can occur.

34.8.3.2. Dicyandiamide

Dicyandiamide is obtained by the polymerization of cyanamide with subsequent purification. It is supplied as a large-particle-size crystal. It may be directly incorporated in coarse intumescent products where its higher decomposition temperature (compared to melamine) may be of value.

34.8.4 Carbonifics

34.8.4.1 Pentaerythritol

Pentaerythritol is prepared by reacting acetaldehyde with formaldehyde and is supplied as a white crystalline powder. The main consumption is in polyesters and the manufacture of pentaerythritol trinitrate which is a powerful explosive. The crystal size and form varies widely with manufacturer. It may be incorporated as supplied in coarser products but will require reduction for use in fine finish products.

Tripentaerythritol and dipentaerythritol are the dimers and trimers by ether links of pentaerythritol. These are always formed as by-products of pentaerythritol and have the advantage that they are water insoluble whereas pentaerythritol is soluble.

Tri- and di-pentaerythritol are the carbonifics of choice where durability is required from the product.

However, not all manufacturers separate the polymers from the monomer during manufacture and, therefore, supplies tend to be limited. Dipenta- and tripenta-erythritol have the highest unit price of all the components normally incorporated into an intumescent formulation. In addition, the limited supply may be a constraint on the expansion of conventional intumescent coatings as a means of fire protection.

34.8.4.2 Starches

Various starches and celluloses have been used in intumescent formulations including cheap forms such as wood flour as the carbonific. However, they do not have much utility in thin-film intumescents owing to the higher melt viscosity and decomposition temperature. The price is low in comparison with other potential carbonifics and they therefore have considerable potential for use in thick-film formulations.

34.8.5 Catalysts

34.8.5.1 Ammonium polyphosphates

It was the introduction of ammonium polyphosphates as the source of phosphorous acids under patents held by Monsanto that allowed the current growth of intumescent coatings. All previous sources of phosphorous as the decomposing acid had been derived from the very soluble orthophosphates.

The proprietary supplies of ammonium polyphosphates can be differentiated by polymer chain length and by crystal type. Each manufacturer uses a slightly different manufacturing route such that the products are characteristically different and must be considered proprietary rather than commodity, in spite of the apparent chemical similarity. Certainly, distinct differences can be detected in the performance of intumescent coatings formulated on the alternative ammonium polyphosphates. As these components make up a minimum of 25% of intumescent formulations a full discussion is required.

34.8.5.2. Crystal type

Using X-ray crystallography the products can be separated into two crystal forms: type I and type II. Type II ammonium polyphosphates are distinctly less soluble than type I products, type II having a typical solubility in distilled water of 1%, type I being in the order of 4–8%. Thus, it would be expected that the low-solubility types would have an advantage in environmentally sensitive situations. However, this difference only relates to neutral solutions. If the pH of the solute is lowered or raised, as might be the case if natural contaminating waters were incident on the product, then the situation disappears. At pH 4, or in a 1% saline solution, no distinct differences can be seen in the comparative solubilities.

However, as described above, the reaction accompanying degradation is the interaction of the ammonium polyphosphate with the melamine by loss of ammonia, this reaction being mediated by water and the pH of the reaction media. Typically, type-II ammonium polyphosphates tend to give higher pH extracts. However, this is not exclusively the case, as samples of type-I ammonium polyphosphates have been examined that indicated a greater stability by virtue of a higher solution pH and water absorption.

The other parameter affecting the performance of intumescent coatings, is the length of the phosphorous oxygen chain. Clearly, the longer the chain length the higher the viscosity of the melt. In some formulations, where the foam rise rate is sensitive and critical, changing the ammonium polyphosphate from a short-chain length type I to a long-chain length type II will alter the

fire performance considerably. This comment only applies in the author's experience to solvent- or epoxy-based formulations. Water-based formulations are insensitive to this change.

Ammonium polyphosphates are supplied in a particle reduced form, and the extra expense is very worthwhile as the lower particle size significantly improves both manufacture and application, primarily because the ammonium polyphosphate must, by necessity, comprise such a large volume of the formulation.

In recent years coated ammonium polyphosphates have been available. The products bear a significant price burden for this facility. While product stability is improved by this subterfuge, a detectable reduction in intumescent reaction rate can be observed.

34.8.6 Pigmentation

Most published formulations show an inclusion of rutile titania in the formulation. This does not only improve the performance of the product, but also acts to strengthen the residual foam/char. The titania traps the phosphorous in the foam/char as titanium pyrophosphate, thereby increasing the weight of material left in the ablating foam and extending the life of the foam/char under fire conditions. However, the grade of titania can have a strong influence on the behaviour of the system at stages other than state 5 and transformation 6.

It is not possible to cheapen intumescent products by the addition of extenders as is done with conventional coatings: firstly because there is little space in the formulation for these materials; and secondly because materials such as calcium carbonate, etc., will react with the released acid during the intumescent reaction, thereby reducing its ability to form the foam/char and increasing the melt viscosity, such that foam levels are reduced. Likewise, naive attempts to add other refractory oxides, such as magnesium oxide are doomed to failure for identical reasons. This effect is so strong that even attempts to replace the titania with other reactive pigmentary oxides will have a similar effect if the affinity of that oxide for reaction to form phosphates is greater than that of titanium oxide. In addition, further loadings of pigmentary material will sufficiently raise the melt viscosity that intumescence will be hindered.

It is believed that one of the effects of the rutile titania is to act as a nucleation point during the foam-formation phase. This is indicated by the effect of replacing the normal pigmentary titania (supplied at a particle size of $0.5\ \mu m$) with alternative grades at a larger particle size. This completely changes the foam/char structure enlarging the pore size and reducing the foam height.

34.9 Forms and uses

34.9.1 Fire protection of structural steel

This major usage has been dealt with at length throughout this discussion.

34.9.2 Cable tray protection

The insulation on electrical cables is essentially inflammable. Where many cables are gathered together in a run they are usually supported in pressed-steel trays. These cables not only form a fire hazard in themselves, but require to be protected in the event of a fire in the compartment through which they pass.

Cable tray protections are usually water-based intumescents loaded with inert fibrous and particulate fillers. Considerable thicknesses of these products, say 5–10 mm, are applied to the cable bundle. The intumescent foam rise height is low; heavy additions of flame retardants are added to prevent ignition. Additionally, there is a requirement that the intumescent char or residue must, under test, be demonstrated to have retained a degree of insulation.

34.9.3 Flame-retardant formulations

The function of these products is not primarily to prevent the passage of heat through the product but to prevent surface ignition of the substrate. For example, marine fibreglass structures require some fire protection in the vicinity of heat and fire sources such as engines and galleys.

A military application of this type is the protection of missile cases and canisters from local fire situations. The most suitable products here are the epoxy-based formulations usually applied to offshore structures. Indeed, any transportable structure of this type that requires fire protection is best treated with epoxy-based formulations, as the conventional coatings are insufficiently robust to withstand normal transportation.

34.9.4 Structural timber

Timber will produce its own form of self-insulation under fire conditions provided it can be prevented from igniting. Under an intumescent coating structural timber will form a char layer of very low thermal conductivity up to 6 mm thick. Providing that the residual timber has sufficient strength to support the structure, very good fire protection can be provided by intumescent coatings. The coatings need not be of the very robust type required for structural fire protection. Water-based products of the fast-blow, high-rise type are very efficient in this application.

34.9.5 Fire dampers

An interesting usage for intumescent products is for fire dampers. These consist of a paper honeycomb coated with a thin layer of intumescent such that in normal circumstances air is free to flow through the honeycomb. The honeycomb is supported in a steel frame such that the damper may be mounted in a ducting or other compartment penetration. Thus, under normal circumstances, the assembly acts as a ventilation grill. In the event of a fire the intumescent coating is activated. It swells to fill the spaces in the honeycomb, thus sealing the reverse side of the damper from fire occurring in the effected compartment.

34.9.6 Penetration seals

Where a service duct or cable run penetrates a fire compartment separating wall, it is necessary to seal this penetration to provide the same standard of barrier protection as was originally provided by the fire wall. This can be achieved by filling the penetration with a mineral-wool blanket. This blanket can then be overcoated with a water-based intumescent to provide the barrier with the necessary fire rating. Any gaps left in the penetration are then automatically sealed by the activating intumescent in the case of fire.

34.9.7 Clear intumescent varnishes

Where a timber element is incorporated in a structure such that the surface is a design feature of the structure, a transparent fire protection is required. This can be achieved by using clear intumescent varnishes. Unfortunately, these products, while very effective, are susceptible to moisture.

Because the more stable ammonium polyphosphates have a refractive index significantly greater than normal binders, dispersions of ammonium polyphosphates give opaque finishes.

It is therefore necessary to revert to orthophosphates to produce these products. Being water soluble and deliquescent these products have a tendency to craze. They are very effective as fire retardants, but extreme care must be taken in the application and the manufacturers' instructions for top coating must be adhered to.

34.9.8 Door seals and closure seals

This application depends on the ability of intumescent coatings to expand and fill a gap. Although the application of the products is different, they all function in the same way, whether applied as a mastic or other means. The best example is a door seal. Here a thin layer of an intumescent product is set into a rebate in the jamb of a fire door. In the event of fire occurring on one side of the structure, the intumescent will react to close and seal the gap between the jamb and the frame which would otherwise act to transmit draft and heat from one side of the barrier to the other. Such mastics can be used in a variety of situations where a small gap requires to be sealed.

34.10 Application

The application of intumescent coatings for structural fire protection is fraught with difficulties and care must be taken by both the applicator and the site supervisor. In selecting the correct product for the site under consideration, considerable aid can be provided by product design, but the major consideration is the choice of the specifier. While the application of intumescent coatings can be a quick, clean operation compared with other wet application methods such as cementacious sprays, if the product is incorrectly chosen or the application planned at the wrong stage of construction, then severe difficulties can occur.

Intumescent coatings can be applied by brush but as the coating is generally of the order of 10–50 times the thickness required by a conventional paint, the application process is necessarily slow and the finish is not good unless subsequently sanded. While this may not matter if site schedules can allow the painters and their equipment continual access to the steel work without hindering following or other trades, and the treated steelwork is to be concealed, these conditions rarely pertain to modern construction sites. Furthermore, steel-framed buildings are chosen because of their speed of erection. Slow application methods are, therefore, inappropriate. In addition, if the product is designated for internal application only, then installation can only commence at a late stage of construction.

However, a well-designed product capable of application at an early stage of construction, applied by a skilled sprayer using large airless spray equipment, can treat up to 500 m² of steel in an 8-h shift. Thus installation of the fire protection can be very rapid.

There are however a number of pitfalls to be avoided.

(1) If application is planned when the temperature is low then products will be affected in the following ways:
(a) the cure rate of epoxy-based products may be delayed indefinitely until the temperature rises;
(b) water-based products have a minimum film-forming temperature—while they may dry, the coherence of the coating will be badly affected; and
(c) solvent-based products will require additional thinning which will significantly delay the drying rate, making them susceptible to damage by following trades. In addition, the rheology system may not work well at low temperatures, affecting the finish and build rate.
(2) Solvent and epoxy based products are presented in inflammable solvents. Therefore application should not be planned

or undertaken if welding, or other similar operations, are to take place in the same location. Additionally, these solvents, while generally of low toxicity, will be released in relatively large concentrations when applied by airless spray. While this is of little concern in most situations, because application usually takes place before the building is sealed and ventilation is therefore more than adequate, some situations will occur, particularly with upgrade or alteration of use, when solvent-vapour concentrations build up beyond acceptable levels. Steps will then be required to provide additional ventilation. As a general rule these solvents are narcotic rather than toxic and exposure will result in nausea, giddiness and drowsiness. This is likely to affect adjacent trades operating in the same compartment, or in the near vicinity.

(3) Coating thicknesses are very high and site inspection should be equipped with adequate dry-film-thickness gauges to ensure that adequate installation has taken place.

(4) Many solvent-based intumescents have a tendency to entrain air and form vacuoles. The result of this is a lower weight of applied product than that indicated by the apparent dry film thickness. If the product is properly formulated, and the spray pressure is adequate to give a good even fan from the spray gun, this effect should be negligible. However, evaluation of porosity should be part of normal site-inspection routines.

(5) Unlike other fire protection systems, such as boarding and cementitious sprays, intumescent coatings are sensitive to substrate cleanliness. Situations where installation is planned in which there is a likelihood of contamination of the steel surface with cement residues, grease or moisture should be avoided. Alternatively, adequate pretreatment procedures are advisable.

(6) The top-coat recommendations of the manufacturer should be strictly adhered to. In addition, continuous over-painting for maintenance reasons should be avoided, particularly with thin-film intumescents. There will always be a point where the thickness of top coat applied will begin to affect the efficiency of the intumescent.

34.11 Current consumption and market levels

The current UK market for intumescent coatings is around 2500 tonne per annum, at an average price to the applicator of £5.00 kg^{-1}, leading to a market value of £12.5 million. This market is growing at about 5% per annum and represents only about 8% of the UK structural fire protection market (information from British Steel). Thus, the value of the total UK fire protection market is about £150 million.

Steel-framed construction is less widely used in other markets and building regulations are somewhat different. For example, the solvent-based products used in the UK are not, or only just, acceptable under the US VOC regulations. Practice in the USA is to use water-based products at thicknesses somewhat greater than is possible with solvent-based products. Epoxy-based products are used externally.

The Middle East is a growing market for steel-framed construction. One recent contract for Saudi Arabia required the use of 1000 tonne of product.

Australasia has a strong market in steel-framed structures, but a largely unexploited market for intumescent coatings.

Europe is again very diverse, with the southern states largely constructing in reinforced concrete. However, the growth in the Spanish economy is forcing the use of steel-framed structures simply for the speed of erection. Germany has a well-developed market for intumescent coatings but their use is limited by the test methods imposed. This problem may be overcome by the

harmonization procedures of 1992. France and Scandinavia have similar requirements as far as test and building regulation requirements are concerned, but neither area has been developed in terms of intumescent coatings as a means of fire protection.

Intumescent coatings also have a variety of uses other than structural fire protection, none of these has yet been fully exploited.

34.11.1 Specification and selection

The situation concerning specification is somewhat odd, from the market point of view. The final user, or end-user, is the owner or occupier of the building to which a fire protection installation has been applied. The occupier is probably unaware of the existence of the form of fire protection present on the structure, and cannot be considered as the end-user in marketing terms as he is not involved in the selection and purchase of the product. What the occupier requires is a fire-safe building. In UK practice there is no legal requirement to maintain the fire protection on a structure, it is merely required to be present at construction.

The qualitites of the product will have been selected by the specifier, who will be either an architect or a structural engineer. However, the purchaser of the product from the manufacturer is the applicator. Clearly the applicator's requirements are for efficiency of usage.

From the arguments given above it is apparent that the dry-film-thickness efficiency, which the applicator requires is counter-optimal to the environmental stability that the architect and structural engineer require. Certainly the durability of intumescents is one of the major areas of doubt in the minds of the most sophisticated of practices.

However, in marketing terms, the applicator is not really the end-user either. The nearest one can get to an end-user is the main contractor. The main contractor is interested in how quickly, efficiently and cheaply the fire protection which has been specified can be installed, and how quickly he can clear a particular trade from the site. When a trade has left a construction site the last thing the contractor wants is to call that trade back for repairs or rectification.

The requirements of the applicator are design constraints that the formulator may not take into account in the design of a product. However, although a product that is environmentally stable and has very low dry-film-thickness requirements may be the product of choice from the structural engineer's point of view, if the product causes site problems there will be resistance to the specification from the site contractor.

However, it can be argued that the present current interest in intumescent coatings in the UK is a spin-off of the success of the marketing policy of British Steel. In a construction climate largely financed by speculative construction by the financial institutions, rapid or 'fast-track' construction is greatly facilitated by steel-frame designs. This, coupled with the flexibility of the assessment system in the UK, has led to the current growth in the market in the field which is not reflected in other European markets.

34.12 Design of formulations

From the above analysis a variables list for the various stages and transitions is prepared. This list contains all the dependent and independent variables with the system boundaries taken to be as wide as possible. For example, the dry film (state 3) variables list would include hardness, flexibility, dirt retention, gloss level, substrate/superstrate comparability, dry film thickness vs. HP/A, and installed cost vs. competitive systems. Such lists are relatively easy to generate, once the analysis has been made in the form given.

What is more difficult, and this is the key to easier formulation with less blind alleys, is the elucidation of the interactions between each part of the system. The complete system analysis is in fact too involved and detailed to be described here. It is emphasized that the whole system is interactive and any attempt to make additions or alterations in a reductionist manner that concerns any one particular state or transition, will undoubtedly affect the system at some other point quite severely. Another point that should be considered is that of scatter and random error throughout the system The fire test procedures, which are the final measure upon which a specifier will select a product, are themselves subject to scatter by as much as 15%. This effect, combined with the variability inherent in the system, means that comparison of products on the basis of published fire-test results will not produce more than approximate indications.

As an example to illustrate the effects of these interactions, it is possible to incorporate molybdenum oxide into intumescent formulations, with some beneficial effect. This acts to suppress smoke emission and increases the strength of the carbon char by retaining greater quantities of carbon residues in the foam/char. Consider then the effects of the addition of molybdenum oxide using the scheme given in *Tables 34.2–34.4*. Molybdenum oxide has specific gravity of 4.69 and is sold at a particle size of about 6 μm. Given that the typical intumescent formulation shown in *Table 34.5* has a specific gravity of 1.15 and a static viscosity of 300 poise, then the standard settlement formula

$$v = \frac{2(p_s - p)r2g}{9n}$$

(where v is the velocity through the medium, p_s is the specific gravity of the particle, p is the specific gravity of the medium, r is the particle size, g is the acceleration due to gravity, and n is the static viscosity or yield point) gives the settlement rate of the molybdenum oxide as 0.14 cm day^{-1}. This means that at the end of 6 months the entire molybdenum content of a 25-l drum will be at the bottom of the can in a solid lump.

Now, while the effect of adding molybdenum oxide to the product may well give low dry film thickness for equivalent steel sizes (state 3), which might look very good on paper in comparison with competitive products, the relationship with applicators is going to be severely affected when they try to reconstitute 2 tonne of settled product on a building site (transitions 2 and 3).

Taking this example further, while the addition of molybdenum oxide may well increase the weight of foam/char produced initially (state 4), it tends to weaken the residual refractory and causes faster degradation of the char under longer exposure times at higher temperatures (transition 6). The effect of this is to reduce the dry film thickness required at shorter exposure times and with heavier sections and to limit the usefulness of the product with lighter sections and longer exposure times (state 3). Thus, before making a decision to include the effect of a product with as significant an effect of molybdenum oxide, consideration is required of the effects it would have on the application qualitites and the required marketing profile.

Alternatively, other corrective measures may have to be taken with the formulation or process sequence to overcome the detrimental effects. These alternatives will fan out to other parts of the system. Unless an understanding of these interactions has been acquired or can be predicted, then the formulator has serious problems, most easily overcome by using the approach outlined above.

A second example concerns the conditions when intumescent coatings are applied to partially completed buildings. The conditions of application are very different from the conditions inside the laboratory in which the product was developed (see

Figures 34.?? and *34.??*). The conditions of application are of contamination with cement dust, dirt from dry unscreeded floors, variable temperatures, high humidities and water and rain penetration from uncompleted walls and roofs. The formulator has two options: he can deny that anyone could work in these conditions and require that the building be near finished before his product is applied, or the product can be designed to be tolerant of the conditions that a construction worker would expect to work in, and pertains to most new construction.

Normally, applicators are under continuous pressure to finish, even in inclement weather, always have competing following trades and there are always unplanned changes to schedules. If the former approach is adopted the service team will spend a lot of time looking at coatings peeling off or running down to the floor. If at that point you attempt to tell the site agent in the presence of your applicator that the product really was not meant to be applied in those conditions, you will get a very poor reception.

Consider the two histograms shown in *Figure 34.6*. These represent the requisite dry-film-thickness requirements of two commercial thin-film intumescents, available on the UK market, for different steel sections and for different massivity factors. The top-coat requirement to the first product is added to the dry film thickness of the fire protection, and the thickness for the second product is reduced by the amount of air that is normally entrained, so that the products are compared on an approximately equivalent basis. The data for both products were collated from published data sheets. However, these data are a little difficult to interpret without sight of the original fire-test report, particularly as it is known that two different assessment systems were used to interpret the original fire-test data.

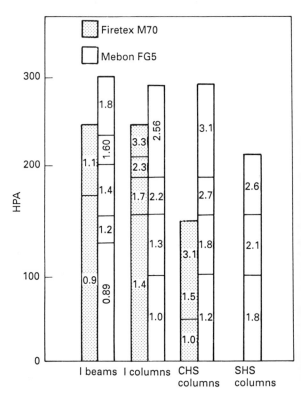

Figure 34.6 Comparative assessment histograms from Mebon FG5 and Leigh's 'Firetext M70/71'

The first formulation certainly requires more material at lower HP/A values but it has a far wider application range than the other product.

The first product, by virtue of its design, will produce a reasonable histogram for 90 min fire rating. The advantage here is that there is a reduced need to mix systems when fire protecting a building with multiple requirements on different parts of the structure. Certainly, management contractors like the concept of one product and one applicator for one project. Clearly this advantage disappears when specifiers compare products simply on a dry-film-thickness or material-required basis. It follows from this discussion that products must be selected for their overall performance.

34.13 Certification

Under any national regulatory system all fire protection products must be verified for use for the stated fire rating, or fire performance index, on some standardized assessment procedure.

The requirement for certification of intumescent products is very diverse, most systems operating not only different test regimes but different philosophies of assessment. Even where similarities can be found for the certification of passive fire protection products these frequently disappear when the special case of intumescent fire protection is considered. Indeed, at the time of writing the situation is even more uncertain, as the impending harmonization procedures required by the European construction products directive means that all test and assessment procedures are under negotiation. This even includes the requirements of the various national building regulations.

However, one can start by looking at the common aspects and where these produce different assessment regimes. What is required is a standard whereby the user can be assured that a certain thickness of the coating will provide the degree of fire protection that he is seeking to provide, either a certain resistance to structural collapse, or a resistance to penetration of a fire barrier or a degree of resistance to ignition.

Given that fire is a chance and random effect with no two fires being the same, the first commonality between all standards is the need to devise a standard fire. Generally most standards now use the ISO 834[4] curve as representing a standard fire. This is taken as being represented by the formula shown in Section 34.5 and *Figure 34.2*. Yet, even though each test regime adopts a curve representing a standard fire that appears equal, the actual temperatures inside the test furnace can in fact be somewhat different by virtue of the design of the monitoring thermocouples specified by the various standards. The ASTM specification thermocouples have much larger thermal capacity than those used in European practice. As the furnace temperature is represented by a dynamic curve, the temperature as measured by European standard thermocouples is significantly hotter than that indicated in the early part of the test curve. Hence ratings to 0.5 and 1 h in the ASTM test are more severe than the European standard.

The next difference is in the furnace design and fuel. While all floor furnaces used for testing beam elements are more or less similar, the design of column test furnaces is very different. Some designs are concentric, forming a tube around the test piece, others are fire rooms in which the loaded test piece is placed in the centre and fired from burners remote from the test piece. No specification in current existence specifies a standard furnace design. Furthermore, some specifications (German, Austrian and South Africa) require the furnace to be oil fired, whilst others require it to be gas fired. Thus, considerable differences in turbulence occur in each of the designs. As heat transfer is dependent not only on temperature difference but also on a transfer coefficient correlated with turbulence, then it follows that, given the lack of standardization, no two fire-test regimes, from furnace to furnace, can be the same.

There is even more error when considering intumescent systems. As the dimensions of a specimen protected with an intumescent coating will alter throughout a test run as the coating expands, then turbulent conditions at the surface of the foam will produce even greater variance.

The next difference is in the dimensions and form of the specimens chosen for assessment. This is guided by the philosophy of the testing regime. For example, French and Scandinavian systems take a very theoretical approach and assume that the performance of all sections can be calculated by the performance of a set standard range of specimens. The French system tests a loaded four-sided beam with short indicative columns and uses the thermal-response results to extrapolate to full-sized column sections, which are not tested.

The German and related systems require the testing of the worst-case situation, i.e. the smallest, lightest specimen and then, with the allowance of certain other indicative tests, apply those results to even the most favourable situation. The UK system allows the sponsor to choose the most favourable section and then extrapolate to the worst case, by indicative sections. However, the UK system also requires that one specimen of all considered sections, i.e. I sections, square, hollow sections and circular, hollow sections, be tested using full-scale loaded specimens in both column and beam form.

The American system requires the testing of a range of unloaded sections such as columns, but requires the use of a complex beam structure for the certification of beam systems.

If the foregoing review appears confusing, this is simply because the lack of any agreement on the detail is very real. It is hoped that there will be some progress towards harmonization in the next decade.

Bibliography

1 REAVES, R. W., *Advances in Fire Retardants*, p. 3 (1975)
2 BRITISH STANDARDS INSTITUTION, *BS 476*, Milton Keynes (1975–89)
3 SAWKO, P. M. and RICCITIELLO, S. R., *Coatings Technol.*, **624** (1977)
4 INTERNATIONAL ORGANIZATION FOR STANDARDIZATION, *ISO 834*
5 VANDERSALL, H. L., *Monsanto Technical Bulletin ic/scs 270*, p. 11 (2)

35

Plaster and Plasterboards

D O'Sullivan
Formerly of British Gypsum plc

Contents

35.1 Introduction 35/3

35.2 Plaster range 35/3
    35.2.1 Carlite premixed plasters 35/3
    35.2.2 Thistle board finish plaster 35/3
    35.2.3 Thistle universal one-coat plaster 35/3
    35.2.4 Thistle renovating plasters 35/4
    35.2.5 Thistle projection plaster 35/4
    35.2.6 Thistle X-ray plasters 35/4
    35.2.7 Thistle hardwall plaster 35/4
    35.2.8 Thistle multi-finish plaster 35/5

35.3 Plastering 35/5
    35.3.1 Preparation of internal plastering backgrounds 35/5
    35.3.2 Plastering onto plasterboard 35/5
    35.3.3 Gyproc lath 35/5
    35.3.4 Thistle baseboard 35/5
    35.3.5 Expanded polystyrene slabs 35/5
    35.3.6 Expanded metal lathing 35/5
    35.3.7 Low suction bricks 35/5
    35.3.8 Concrete backgrounds 35/5
    35.3.9 *In situ* concrete 35/5
    35.3.10 Precast concrete units 35/5
    35.3.11 Aerated concrete blocks and panels 35/6
    35.3.12 Dense aggregate concrete blocks, no fines concrete and other low-absorption backgrounds 35/6
    35.3.13 Composite wall structures 35/6

35.4 Plastering treated backgrounds 35/6

35.5 Mixing 35/6
    35.5.1 Undercoats 35/6
    35.5.2 Finish coat 35/6

35.6 Problems and remedies 35/6
    35.6.1 Cracking caused by background movement 35/6
    35.6.2 Shrinkage cracking 35/6

35.6.3 Loss of adhesion of finishing coat 35/6
35.6.4 Loss of adhesion of plaster on plasterboard 35/6
35.6.5 Quick- and slow-setting plasters 35/6
35.6.6 Dry-out 35/7

35.7 Plasterboard dry linings 35/7
    35.7.1 Gyproc wallboard 35/7
    35.7.2 Gyproc fireline board 35/7
    35.7.3 Gyproc plank 35/7
    35.7.4 Gyproc Thermal Board Plus 35/7
    35.7.5 Gyproc thermal board 35/7
    35.7.6 Paramount panels 35/7
    35.7.7 Gyproc cornice range 35/7

35.8 Composition 35/7

35.9 Performance 35/7
    35.9.1 Fire protection 35/7
    35.9.2 Sound insulation 35/8
    35.9.3 Thermal insulation 35/8
    35.9.4 Effect of high and low temperature 35/8
    35.9.5 Condensation 35/8

35.10 Design and planning considerations 35/8

35.11 Site organization 35/8
    35.11.1 Access and storage areas 35/8
    35.11.2 Off-loading 35/8
    35.11.3 Phasing of work 35/9

35.12 Site work 35/9
    35.12.1 Handling 35/9
    35.12.2 Cutting 35/9
    35.12.3 Fixing plasterboard dry linings 35/9
    35.12.4 Decoration 35/10
    35.12.5 Fixtures to plasterboard dry-lined walls 35/10
    35.12.6 Health and safety 35/10

Bibliography 35/10

Appendix 35/10

35.1 Introduction

Historically, lime and sand was the main plastering medium used in the UK, with either cement or gypsum added as a binding agent from the middle of the nineteenth century. Since the end of the last war in 1945, however, when the vast rebuilding programme demanded speedy construction methods, gypsum plasters have increasingly dominated the scene.

Gypsum plasters, which, being premixed, require only the addition of clean water on site, are light in weight, possess a controlled chemical set and offer excellent adhesion to a wide variety of backgrounds, have enabled the craft to keep pace with other major changes in the industry. The controlled set provides the plasterer with continuity of production, thereby eliminating the costly waiting time between coats necessary with sanded or cement-based plasters.

Other benefits that attract specifier and user alike include good fire resistance properties, use in low temperature conditions where plastering with sanded undercoats would not be possible, clean sites, easy estimating and ordering and a reduction in errors of mixing and proportioning. Gypsum plasters also provide a perfect base for subsequent decoration.

The use of gypsum to support decorative finishes is not a new idea. There is evidence that the mineral was used some 3000 years ago by the Egyptians who used it within the Pyramids. In the UK, the basic raw gypsum material is mined at seven sites across the length and breadth of the country from Robertsbridge in East Sussex to Kirkby Thore in Cumbria by British Gypsum Ltd, a subsidiary of BPB Industries plc. In addition to being the basic component in British Gypsum's wide range of bagged plasters, gypsum lies also at the heart of an extensive series of plasterboard products and systems available from this company in the UK and from other BPB Industries' subsidiaries throughout mainland Europe, and in Canada and India.

35.2 Plaster range

There is a type of plaster to suit every situation and the range comprises Carlite premixed plasters; Thistle board finish plaster; Thistle universal one-coat plaster; Thistle renovating plasters; Thistle projection plaster; Thistle premixed gypsum X-ray plasters; and the latest introduction, Thistle Hardwall plaster and Thistle multi-finish.

35.2.1 Carlite premixed plasters

Carlite is a range of lightweight, retarded hemihydrate premixed gypsum plasters that require only the addition of clean water to prepare them for use. The range includes four undercoat grades and a single finishing product.

Carlite Browning is an undercoat for solid backgrounds of low to moderate suction and an adequate mechanical key; Carlite Browning HSB is required for solid backgrounds of a very high suction. Carlite metal lathing is an undercoat that has been specially developed for expanded metal lathing and Carlite bonding is an undercoat for low suction backgrounds, soffits of composite floors with concrete beams, plasterboard, expanded polystyrene and surfaces treated with a polyvinyl acetate copolymer (PVAC) bonding agent. Carlite finishing is a final coat for use with all of the above listed Carlite undercoats.

Whilst dry, bagged plaster is not affected by low temperatures; plastering on frozen backgrounds must be avoided and the use of such products is negated where the temperature exceeds 43°C.

In addition, it is recommended that, where more than one layer of undercoat is applied to a background, the same product must be used throughout. The supplier also insists that Carlite Browning should not be used over Carlite bonding coat or Carlite metal lathing plasters, and it is also recommended that a PVAC bonding agent may be necessary on certain backgrounds —for instance, limestone, brick or granite aggregate concrete and normal ballast aggregate concrete with a smooth surface.

In accordance with good plastering practice, the floating coats should be ruled to an even surface and lightly scratched to form a key for Carlite finish when Carlite Browning, Browning HSB and Carlite bonding are applied.

When using Carlite metal lathing, three-coat work is required: a pricking-up coat which should be deeply scratched to form an undercut key and a floating coat which can be applied as soon as the first coat sets. Plastering to concrete demands special care and, in order to ensure good adhesion between concrete and plaster, the concrete surface should be wetted with a damp brush no more than 5–10 min before applying a floating coat of Carlite bonding coat plaster. On linings and partitions with scrimmed joints and angles the scrimming plaster should be allowed to set before the bonding coat is applied. A coat of Carlite finish should be applied, as soon as the floating coat has set, and trowelled to a smooth surface.

35.2.2 Thistle board finish plaster

Thistle board finish is a final coat for grey-faced plasterboard and normal ballast concrete suitable for plastering direct. It can be applied for plastering direct. It can be applied in two coats at a total thickness of 5 mm or in a single coat at 3 mm total thickness. When applied as a single coat the plasterboard joints must be reinforced with either Gyproc joint tape or glass fibre, self adhesive tape.

35.2.3 Thistle universal one-coat plaster

This is a gypsum-based plaster suitable for hand application to most types of internal background. It may be used in one coat at thicknesses suitable for all normal purposes on brick, block, concrete, plasterboard and expanded metal lath. Of white finish, this plaster is a hemihydrate with special additives that improve the characteristics of workability and application.

The recommended thickness of application is 13 mm for walls other than concrete, where it should not normally exceed 10 mm.

Up to 50 mm can be applied in one coat, according to the supplier, who also claims that 85–95 m^2 can be covered per tonne of Universal one-coat at a thickness of 13 mm on brick or blockwork. Metal corner beads are essential for external angles and metal depth gauge beads should be used where walls are required to be perfectly flat and level. Where the background consists of metal lathing, it should be rust protected and ribbed and, after fixing, all cut edges and damaged metal lathing, staples or nail heads should be protected with bitumen paint.

On applying Thistle Universal one-coat plaster to the grey face of plasterboards, the joints between the plasterboards must be scrimmed or treated in accordance with the manufacturer's recommendations for the particular grade of plasterboard being used.

Plaster should be applied to solid backgrounds with firm pressure, turning back to fill out the required thicknesses; use a feather edge to straighten the plaster to a reasonable plain and fill in any slacks or hollows. When the plaster has stiffened, the feather edge may be used to achieve a flat surface and a spatula can be employed for additional flattening or paring. When the plaster is sufficiently firm, it is recommended that the surface be lightly scoured with a sponge float, and subsequently trowelled to a smooth but not polished surface.

35.2.4 Thistle renovating plasters

The renovating range of plasters comprises an undercoat and a finish coat especially designed for use in older properties where moisture is still retained after successful damp-proof-course treatment. The undercoat provides early strength in damp conditions and speedy surface drying, whilst the finish has good working and setting characteristics together with high strength—although it is essential to use Thistle renovating finish over Thistle renovating plaster as soon as the undercoat has set.

It is important to note that these plasters should not be used directly on backgrounds in damp areas below ground level, or with damp-proof-course renewal systems involving either electro-osmosis or cementitious grouts.

Thistle renovating plaster is a premixed lightweight gypsum undercoat plaster containing special additives; it should be applied in thicknesses of 11 mm to cover an area of approximately 120 m^2 per 1000 kg.

Before using this plaster, the source of penetrating dampness must be identified and eliminated. Ideally, replastering should then be delayed as long as possible, especially on wet walls, to allow the backgrounds to dry out more quickly.

Any salts brought to the surface during such treatment should be removed before replastering commences, and it is recommended that existing plasterwork be hacked off to a height specified by the installer of the damp proof course. This will normally be no less than 450 mm above either the last detectable sign of dampness or the damp proof course itself.

In circumstances where time does not permit a suitable delay between the provision of a new damp proof course and replastering, and where walls are not saturated or heavily contaminated with salts, consideration should be given to the use of a water resisting bonding aid such as a Unibond universal EVA40, or an alternative based on SBR latex.

When mixed with a render coat of Thistle renovating plaster these aids will restrict the passage of moisture and offer greater resistance to efflorescence.

35.2.5 Thistle projection plaster

Thistle projection plaster has been formulated for single-coat application by machines that mix and spray in one operation. The plaster is levelled and trowelled in the conventional way and supplied in a single multipurpose grade for general internal use.

The names of machine suppliers and contractors with the necessary expertise and equipment may be obtained from any plaster manufacturer.

This plaster product consists of gypsum hemihydrate plasters combined with a number of additives to increase water retention, improve plasticity and stabilize the setting time. It should be applied in a thickness of 13 mm to walls other than concrete; on concrete soffits, the thickness should be 5–10 mm, and if the background is level and of an even suction, for instance, plasterboard, it may be possible to reduce the overall thickness to just 5 mm.

Manufacturers state that this plaster stiffens noticeably within 1 to 1.5 h of application, depending on the suction of the background. This set then progresses until the surface is hard enough to receive the final trowel at 2 to 2.5 h.

The plaster is suitable for most internal high and low suction backgrounds, including: clay bricks and blocks; engineering bricks with raked joints; clinker blocks; concrete bricks and blocks; most proprietory blocks; flint gravel aggregate concrete considered suitable for plastering directly; rust protected ribbed expanded metal lathing; Gyproc lath. Thistle baseboards and most grey faced plasterboard backgrounds.

Normal techniques for the preparation of backgrounds apply to Thistle projection plaster, although on certain types of surface a PVAC bonding agent may be used. Where Gyproc lath is the background, the projection plaster should be worked well into the joints formed by the rounded edges. The jute scrim which reinforces the joints and angles of Thistle baseboard and the ceiling and wall angles should be embedded in projection plaster; the joints do not need to be set before plastering commences. Thistle projection plaster must be used neat with only the addition of clean water. It is sprayed onto the background in the form of a ribbon by holding the nozzle of the plastering machine close to the surface. The consistency should allow the ribbons to run together, bearing in mind that the plaster is more fluid while it is being applied.

A feather edge rule should then be used to spread the plaster to a plain surface before additional material is resprayed to fill any slacks or hollows. When the plaster is sufficiently stiff, the feather edge is used again to pair down any ridges or blemishes, thus leaving a plain surface with a slightly open texture. A spatula may be used at this stage to flatten the surface completely.

After further stiffening, water should be applied with a fine spray or a brush to the surface and a hand or power float used to raise the flat and prepare the surface for finishing. At this point, internal angles should be planed to eliminate undulations.

35.2.6 Thistle X-ray plasters

Thistle X-ray plaster is a specially formulated undercoat which is applied in the traditional manner to provide standards of protection from electromagnetic radiation as required by the National Radiological Protection Board.

It is used in situations where X-ray generating equipment is installed, to achieve the required degree of radiation protection, in such areas as hospitals and medical research laboratories.

A final coat of Thistle multi-finish is required to provide a high standard of conventional, internal finish, but it is important to note that the Thistle multi-finish does not contribute to radiation protection, which is provided entirely by the specified thickness of Thistle X-ray undercoat.

35.2.7 Thistle hardwall plaster

Thistle hardwall plaster is a premixed, undercoat plaster containing a blend of special aggregates and additives which combine to provide numerous benefits to both specifier and user. In addition to gypsum plaster's well known characteristics such as controlled set, continuity of production, freedom from inherent shrinkage cracks, excellent adhesion and ease of working, Thistle hardwall also provides a quicker drying surface and stronger resistance to efflorescence compared to other types of gypsum plaster. It also provides superior impact resistance which is useful in areas of high useage. Thistle hardwall is suitable for use with a wide spectrum of brick and block substrates, expanded metal lath and application by plaster projection machine as well as by the manual method. When applied by machine the plaster is worked as an undercoat plaster in the traditional two coat plastering system. The required final coat plaster is Thistle multi-finish which is applied by hand.

35.2.8 Thistle multi-finish plaster

Thistle multi-finish is a new generation final coat plaster and has been specially formulated to perform equally well on a variety of backgrounds including grey and decorative faced Gyproc plasterboards, Thistle Hardwall, sanded undercoats and normal ballast concrete suitable to receive a thin application of plaster.

When used on undercoats of Portland cement and sand or Portland cement, lime and sand, it is important to allow the undercoat to mature before applying the finishing coat. Failure to do so could result in shrinkage cracks appearing on the surface or a complete loss of adhesion of the finishing coat from the undercoat.

35.3 Plastering

The condition of substrates can vary due to outside influences; for example, the time of year, weather conditions and degree of moisture present before or during construction. If the advice given in this chapter is followed, a satisfactory job should be ensured; however, the decision to proceed with plastering must rest with the skill and experience of the plasterer.

35.3.1 Preparation of internal plastering backgrounds

(1) All surfaces should be reasonably dry and protected from the weather.
(2) Concrete made from limestone, brick, granite, and certain lightweight aggregate and exceptionally smooth concrete, will require pretreatment with PVAC bonding agents.
(3) Grounds, doors, window frames and all wood casings should be designed to allow for the specified finished thickness of plaster. A 10 mm ground on brickwork will give an average thickness of 13 mm finished plasterboard. For two coats or more, the thickness of the grounds is always less than the finished thickness of plaster. For plastering on metal lathing, the total finished thickness will need to allow for the thickness of the metal lath.
(4) Openings, chases or other apertures should be cut before plastering.
(5) Plugging for fixtures should be completed.
(6) Piping, conduit, fixing clips or other metallic objects must be protected by galvanizing, painting or applying a thick layer of lacquer, otherwise corrosion may occur which will stain the plaster.
(7) Backgrounds should be thoroughly brushed with a hard broom to remove dust, crystallized efflorescent salts and loose mortar.
(8) Mould oil or other agents should be removed from concrete surfaces.
(9) Use Carlite browning HSB plaster for high-suction backgrounds. Where other plasters are used, suction can be controlled with water before plastering; if applying Carlite bonding coat, PVAC bonding agents can be used.
(10) Lime should not be added to plasters in contact with Gyproc plasterboards. The plasterboard must be dry.

35.3.2 Plastering onto plasterboard

Commence plastering as soon as possible after board fixing. Apply Thistle board finish plaster in two separate coats where a 5 mm thickness is required, and an undercoat of Carlite bonding coat with a final coat of Carlite finish where a 10 mm thickness is required.

35.3.3 Gyproc lath

Stagger the end joints and leave a gap not exceeding 3 mm between the rounded paper-covered edges and board ends. Before plastering, fill the recesses formed by the adjoining rounded edges and end joints flush with plaster. Reinforce all angles with jute scrim, not less than 90 mm wide, embedded in the same grade of plaster. Allow joint filling and scrimming to set, but not dry out, before applying the first coat, and straighten. Scratch the surface to provide a key for the final coat and allow to set. When the undercoat has set, apply the final coat, before the first layer dries out fully.

35.3.4 Thistle baseboard

Leave a gap not exceeding 3 mm between board edges and ends. Before plastering, fill the gaps at all joints with plaster, and reinforce the joints and angles with jute scrim, not less than 90 mm wide, embedded in the plaster. Allow joints to set, but not become dry, before applying the first coat. Scratch the surface to provide a key for the final coat and allow to set. When the first or undercoat has set but not dried out, apply the final coat.

35.3.5 Expanded polystyrene slabs

All joints and angles should be scrimmed with 90 mm jute scrim cloth embedded in the undercoat grade of plaster. Fix the slabs as instructed by the manufacturer.

35.3.6 Expanded metal lathing

Metal lathing should be protected by bituminous paint or by galvanizing. Cut ends of lath or tying wire should be bent inwards away from the plaster, and protected with bituminous paint.

35.3.7 Low suction bricks

Engineering, concrete and, in some cases, calcium silicate bricks have very little absorption so the joints must be raked well to provide a mechanical key.

35.3.8 Concrete backgrounds

Carlite bonding coat adheres to concrete surfaces of normal ballast aggregate, and should be used for all two-coat work on normal ballast *in situ*, precast and composite concrete soffits (with concrete beams and infill of material such as concrete or clinker blocks). When a wet plaster mix is applied to dry concrete, air is trapped between the two surfaces and prevents a good contact.

The concrete should, therefore, be brushed with clean water, 5–10 min before plastering.

Where the suction of the concrete is so high that the film of moisture is very quickly absorbed (for example, with certain lightweight aggregate concretes), a bonding agent may be necessary. If in doubt, a trial panel should be plastered and tested for adhesion when dry.

35.3.9 *In situ* concrete

Carlite bonding should be applied to a maximum thickness of 10 mm, made up of 8 mm floating coat and 2 mm finishing coat.

Where a greater thickness is required, each coat should be a maximum of 8 mm thick, be thoroughly cross-scratched to provide a mechanical key, and allowed to set before the next coat is applied. The floating coat should not be thicker than is necessary to bring the work to a level surface, particularly on soffits. When applying a very thin coat, do not mix the plaster to a softer consistency than normal, as this will reduce its strength. Precautions should be taken in very dry conditions to prevent the plaster from drying out before it sets.

35.3.10 Precast concrete units

Cracking between precast concrete units can be reduced by avoiding very thin coats of Carlite bonding coat. When applying a floating coat to precast concrete units, the plaster should fill all gaps between the units.

35.3.11 Aerated concrete blocks and panels

Substrates formed from this type of product, manufactured with or without lightweight aggregates, generate moderate to high suction. Either Carlite browning plaster or Carlite browing HSB may be used as a backing coat.

35.3.12 Dense aggregate concrete blocks, no fines concrete and other low-absorption backgrounds

These surfaces do not need wetting, but should be brushed down. Apply the plaster with very firm pressure, then, using the same mix, bring out to a plane surface.

35.3.13 Composite wall structures

Plastering on composite walls of concrete piers with infills of brick or block often results in cracking of the finished plasterwork due to differential movement of the background materials. To overcome this, apply a heavy building paper over the concrete piers, lapping over the brick or block by about 25 mm. Fix expanded metal lath completely over the building paper and secure to the brick at its edges.

Thus the plaster, reinforced by the metal, bridges the concrete while the building paper isolates the plaster from the concrete so that it can move freely and independently.

For widths of concrete exceeding 300 mm, or where there are concrete beams above the infill bricks, fix the metal lath to the concrete with masonry nails and, if necessary, put an expansion joint between the brick and concrete, then proceed as follows. Apply a rendering coat of Carlite metal lathing plaster to all metal lath surfaces and scratch thoroughly to form a key. Next, apply a floating coat of Carlite browning or bonding coat to the surface of the infill block. This coat should not overlap the metal lath, but should be lined on either side of it. Before the floating coat sets, use Carlite metal lathing to level the plaster on the metal lath. Scratch all surfaces for the Carlite finish plaster.

Twil-Lath, a combined metal and paper-backed lath, may be used in place of building paper and metal lathing. Full instructions are available from Tinsley Building Products Limited, P.O. Box 119, Shepcote Lane, Sheffield, S9 1TY. Alternatively, the plasterwork may be stopped at the edges by the use of Expamet casing beads, which provide expansion joints.

35.4 Plastering treated backgrounds

When plastering over glazed surfaces that are finished with oil-based paints, very smooth limestone, brick or granite aggregate or old brickwork, use Carlite bonding coat with a proprietary bonding agent applied according to the manufacturer's instructions. Use a wire brush to remove loose paint and other extraneous matter, wash with detergent, rinse and allow to dry.

35.5 Mixing

For undercoat plasters use a mixing box, or board. Mix finish plasters in a plastic bucket. Mixing equipment must be cleaned after use as portions of old mix will decrease the setting time and strength of a fresh gauging.

Once a mix has started to set, it should not be retempered. Mechanical mixers are unsuitable for Carlite plasters.

35.5.1 Undercoats

For good adhesion, apply a thin coat first with firm pressure and build up to the required thickness. Bring floating coats to a true and level surface with a straight-edge. Scratch each coat thoroughly to form a mechanical key for the next coat.

35.5.2 Finish coat

Smooth finishing coats should not be over-polished; a mat, eggshell finish should be produced.

35.6 Problems and remedies

Problems in plastering are mainly due to incorrect use of plaster. The background, undercoat and finish must be compatible.

35.6.1 Cracking caused by background movement

Cracking may be caused by structural movement of the background, the cracks taking a very definite line. These usually appear on ceilings and are caused by shrinkage and warping of timber joists, shrinkage of *in situ* concrete, or thermal and/or structural movement of precast units.

On walls, cracks generally appear round lintels and window sills, due to settlement and/or thermal movement. The cracks can be cut out and filled but, as they are likely to reappear, delay repairs for as long as possible.

35.6.2 Shrinkage cracking

Shrinkage cracking takes the form of fine hair cracks on the finished coat. Mixes based on cement or cement/lime shrink considerably on drying and, if the final coat is applied too soon, crazing or severe cracking will occur on the face of the plaster. Treatment of these fine cracks is extremely difficult and such surfaces may need to be finished with wallpaper instead of paint.

35.6.3 Loss of adhesion of finishing coat

This is caused by applying a strong finishing coat to an undercoat which is very weak because of oversanding, or the use of sand containing a large amount of loam. Loss of adhesion usually occurs with a gypsum finish applied to a cement or cement/lime-based undercoat, and is a result of applying the finish to a green (set but not dry) undercoat, possibly supplemented by poor mechanical keying. In the case of a weak undercoat, strip the plaster down to the background and replace it. If the undercoat is satisfactory, strip off the finishing coat and treat with a proprietary PVAC bonding agent, strictly in accordance with the manufacturer's instructions, before replastering.

35.6.4 Loss of adhesion of plaster on plasterboard

With Thistle board finish plaster, this is likely to be caused by adding lime to the first coat. The only remedy is to strip off the plaster coat completely. The manufacturer will advise whether the surface is suitable for replastering.

35.6.5 Quick- and slow-setting plasters

Plaster very fresh from the works and still hot could be quick-setting; the sacks should be opened to cool before use. Dirty mixing water or impurities in the mix will also speed up the set; make sure that the water and the mixing equipment are clean.

35.6.6 Dry-out

Gypsum plaster requires as much water to make it set as is driven from the gypsum in manufacture. If the plaster dries out before it has set, it will not develop its maximum strength and will remain soft and powdery. However, this is unlikely to occur if coats are thick enough and of the correct grade of plaster. For further information refer to BS 5492: 1977.

35.7 Plasterboard dry linings

In this section the use of gypsum plasterboard for dry internal linings to walls, ceilings and roofs is discussed. This is the name given to building board made of a core of aerated gypsum plaster usually enclosed between two sheets of strong paper. Plasterboard types, tools and accessories, performance, fixing systems and joint treatment are discussed.

Plasterboard dry linings continue to gain rapid popularity as an alternative to plaster finishes for a variety of important reasons. They are widely used (independently or as part of a system) in new construction and rehabilitation work to meet not only internal lining requirements but also to provide protection against the hazard of fire and condensation, or to enhance thermal or sound insulation.

In addition, the use of plasterboard dry lining systems means that little water is introduced into a building's structure at a late stage, which reduces the drying out time required. This gives greater freedom in the selection of the type of first decoration.

On site, dry lining operations are less arduous that wet plastering, a minimum of cleaning up is required and, as the services can be accommodated in the cavity between plasterboard and wall, chasing is also reduced substantially. Add to this careful consideration at the design stage, proper site organization and workmanship, and plasterboard dry lining can be favourably comparable in cost with good quality two-coat plastering.

When correctly fitted and jointed, the grades of plasterboard that are available with tapered edges will produce a surface that is as smooth as traditional plastering but with the added benefit of easier maintenance as cracking as virtually eliminated.

Over 80% of the gypsum plasterboard and plasterboard systems sold in the UK are sold under the brand names Gyproc, Thistle, and Glasroc, and these are manufactured almost exclusively from materials that are sourced by the company in its own mines or quarries. However, the plasterboard manufactured for dry lining is different from the grades produced to receive wet plasterwork, and this is identified by an ivory coloured surface onto which internal decoration may be directly applied.

In the following sections the different types of plasterboard available for dry lining purposes are described.

35.7.1 Gyproc wallboard

This board has an ivory coloured exposed surface and a grey surface on the back; its edges can be supplied tapered or square, depending on the joint treatment required. It is also available in Duplex grade which has a backing of metallized polyester film. The film acts as a reflective thermal insulator when the board is fixed facing a 20 mm minimum air space, and as a vapour control layer which reduces the passage of water vapour from inside the building into the structure and, therefore, helps to reduce the risk of interstitial condensation.

35.7.2 Gyproc fireline board

This is similar to Gyproc wallboard but is only available in a 12.5 and 15 mm thicknesses, with tapered edges. The gypsum core of this board incorporates glass fibre and additives to improve its fire protection performance.

35.7.3 Gyproc plank

Gyproc plank is also similar to gypsum wallboard, but thicker and normally supplied with tapered edges for dry lining purposes. A square edge plank with grey surface on both sides is used as a first layer in certain two-layer lining systems. Gyproc plank is also available in Duplex grade.

35.7.4 Gyproc Thermal Board Plus

This is a plasterboard thermal laminate with a backing of extruded polystyrene. It is available in six thicknesses, ranging upwards in 5-mm increments between 25 and 50 mm thicknesses. The most recent addition to the Gyproc range of thermal laminate boards, Gyproc Thermal Board Plus, has been developed to meet the April 1990 building regulations in respect of the new 0.45 W m^2 K external wall U values.

35.7.5 Gyproc thermal board

This is a laminate composed of gypsum wallboard bonded to a backing of expanded polystyrene to provide a good standard of thermal insulation and is also available in a vapour-check grade, which incorporates a vapour control layer at the interface between the wallboard and the expanded polystyrene. This membrane reduces the passage of water vapour from inside the building into the structure and, therefore, can help to reduce the risk of interstitial condensation.

35.7.6 Paramount panels

A prefabricated gypsum wallboard panel formed from two wallboards (with exposed ivory coloured faces), these panels are separated by, and bonded to, a core of cellular construction. They are available in 57 and 63 mm thicknesses, with either tapered or square edges. It is used primarily as a lightweight partition in housing.

35.7.7 Gyproc cornice range

Although the ceiling/wall angle in a room may be finished in the same way as with any other joint, plasterboard cove provides a very attractive finish. In addition to applications in new dwellings, coving is becoming increasingly popular in the do-it-yourself and general home redecoration marketplace.

35.8 Composition

Gypsum plasterboard consists of an aerated gypsum core encased in and firmly bonded to paper liners. Plasterboard products are complemented by a comprehensive range of dry-lining tools and accessories for fixing, jointing and finishing operations, e.g. foot and board lifters, dry wall hammers, wallboard trimmers, wallboard saws, utility saws, screwdriver clutch attachments, mixing tools, applicators, sponges, knives and sanders.

35.9 Performance

35.9.1 Fire protection

Due to the unique behaviour of the non-combustible gypsum core, plasterboard linings provide good fire protection when subjected to high temperatures.

Although plasterboard is combustible (when tested to BS 476: Part 4: 1970, although in the *Building Regulations 1985*, plasterboard is designated a 'material of limited combustibility'), the ivory (exposed) and grey (backing) surfaces of standard Gyproc wallboard, Fireline board, plank and Duplex grade surfaces are class 0 when tested to BS 476 Parts 6 and 7 and in accordance with the requirements of the Building Regulations. Class 0 is the highest standard required for restricting the spread of flame over wall and ceiling surfaces.

Periods of fire resistance for a few constructions that incorporate gypsum plasterboard dry linings are given in Approved Document B2/3/4.

35.9.2 Sound insulation

For maximum sound insulation to be obtained for a building element on site, all air paths such as perimeter cracks and gaps should be sealed. This can be achieved, for example, by the use of acoustical sealants around perimeters, or gypsum cove at the wall and ceiling angles. Ideally, a building element should be imperforate for optimum sound insulation.

35.9.3 Thermal insulation

Due to its aerated gypsum core, plasterboard is a low-thermal-capacity lining material. Plasterboard dry-lining systems can improve the thermal insulation of a building element and, therefore, reduce heat loss. When used in intermittently heated buildings, a plasterboard dry lining responds to heating more quickly than denser plaster finishes and allows rooms to warm up more rapidly.

Although legislation does not apply to existing housing, a large number of houses in this country have masonry walls of low thermal insulation. A most effective method of upgrading these walls to present thermal insulation standards is to apply an internal lining of plasterboard thermal laminates which can easily be fixed to pressure-impregnated timber battens or (where the background is suitable) using a special adhesive.

35.9.4 Effect of high and low temperature

Gypsum plasterboards are unsuitable for use in temperatures above 49°C. They can be subjected to freezing temperatures without risk of damage.

35.9.5 Condensation

To prevent condensation occurring, adequate heating and ventilation are necessary in addition to good thermal insulation. The absence of any of these requirements can result in condensation and mould growth on internal surfaces (surface condensation) or potentially harmful condensation within the structure (interstitial condensation).

In intermittently heated buildings, plasterboard dry linings respond quickly to heating, and surface temperatures soon rise above the dew point. Consequently, the risk of surface condensation is reduced. This risk is further reduced as the thermal insulation of the dry-lining system is increased.

However, the use of an internal thermal-insulating lining may increase the risk of interstitial condensation by making other parts of the structure colder. In this situation the use of vapour control layers, and possibly other precautions such as improved ventilation rates, should be carefully considered.

In the case of external walls, if the wall is permeable the use of Duplex plasterboard or vapour-check-grade plasterboard thermal laminates should be satisfactory. However, if the wall is impermeable, the new cavity formed by the lining should be ventilated to the outside air. It is also generally recommended that ventilation of roof spaces should be provided by means of suitable eaves ventilation.

Buildings with a similar environment to dwellings can be dealt with in a similar manner, but in more complex building types, e.g. in those with air conditioning, the need for vapour control layers should be determined by calculation. BS 5250 provides guidance.

35.10 Design and planning considerations

Plasterboard dry linings can be used in almost any type of building; however, the following design and planning factors should be taken into account.

Ideally, plasterboard dry linings should be used throughout the building and not mixed with traditional plastering. However, particular attention must be given to the choice of materials for a masonry wall which is to be dry lined to provide a satisfactory standard of sound insulation as required for dwellings by the Building Regulations.

The total thickness of a dry-lined wall system will be a combination of the thickness of plasterboard used plus the cavity formed by the fixing method. This total thickness should be considered when determining the sizes of door frames, window sills, cupboard units, etc. Dry linings usually continue into window and door reveals, and with certain types of system the thickness of door and window frames may have to be increased.

The cost of fixing and jointing is more expensive for cut boards than for uncut board. The use of cut boards should therefore be kept to a minimum.

Certain joinery work such as staircases and cupboards should be designed to be fixed to prepared grounds after completion of dry lining.

The inclusion in the design of plasterboard lightweight partitions offers planning, organizational and cost advantages.

If timber floors are specified, the flooring should be butted to the walling.

Where tapered-edge plasterboards are specified to provide smooth surfaces, jointing of the dry linings can be carried out by hand or by means of the Speed Tape mechanical jointing system, which is particularly suitable for larger contracts.

Fixing that would normally be made to a plastered wall can be made to plasterboard dry-lined walls. A dry-lined wall fixing system allows the inclusion of services behind the lining or minimizes the depth of chasing required.

35.11 Site organization

Valuable time, labour and materials can be saved by careful site organization to ensure that delivery times, quantities received and unloading points fix in with work requirements. It is very important that the dry-lining operations are carefully planned and prepared for, and that the correct type and amount of materials are ordered well in advance.

35.11.1 Access and storage areas

Ideally, gypsum materials should be kept in a dry, protected store or building. Hard access lanes and turning areas should be provided for vehicles, as gypsum materials are normally delivered on rigid or articulated flat-bed lorries when supplied direct from works.

35.11.2 Off-loading

To avoid delay and congestion, materials should be off-loaded at one central point and taken to work areas as needed. Gypsum materials should not be moved from a protected store or building to a new area during wet weather without adequate protection.

35.11.3 Phasing of work

The time between storage and use should be kept as short as possible in order to reduce the risk of damage to the materials. Plasterboards can be taken into the area where they are to be used immediately after the roof has been completed and the building made watertight.

The fixing of plasterboards can usually be carried out after internal loadbearing walls have been built, joists, structural floors and joiner's first fixings completed, and the first stage of installation of services carried out. The ceiling linings should be in position before dry lining external walls and partitions. It is desirable that glazing should be completed before dry lining commences. The operations that follow are usually joiner's second fixings, service connections and decoration. Decoration should follow as soon as possible after board fixing and joint treatment.

By adopting the above sequence of operations, the possibility of damage to the linings is reduced and, therefore, any repair work is kept to a minimum.

35.12 Site work

35.12.1 Handling

Waste can be minimized and delays avoided by careful handling and storage of materials. Plasterboards and prefabricated panels should always be carried on edge by two men. They should not be carried with their surfaces horizontal. When a board or panel is stacked, or removed from a stack, its long edge should be placed down first before being lifted, and the long edges should not be placed over each other as this may scuff the surfaces.

Boards and panels must be stacked flat on a level surface in a dry place, preferably inside a building, and protected from rising damp and inclement weather. They should be neatly aligned, and the height of the stack should not exceed 1000 mm to allow safe handling. The stacks should be situated away from areas where they are liable to impact, abuse, etc.

35.12.2 Cutting

The cutting of boards and panels should be carried out with a fine-toothed saw. Alternatively, gypsum wallboard and plank can be cut by scoring with a sharp knife, snapping the core over a straight edge and then cutting through the paper on the opposite side.

Plasterboard with an ivory-coloured surface should always be cut with the ivory side up.

35.12.3 Fixing plasterboard dry linings

The systems available for fixing plasterboard dry linings are described briefly in the following sections.

35.12.3.1 Fixing to timber frame

Trade literature gives recommendations on fixing to timber framing, including the requirements for nailing, spacing of timber supports and noggins, etc.

35.12.3.2 Dot and dab fixing (trade name: Gyproc Driwall System)

Standard tapered-edge gypsum wallboard can be applied to most dry internal brick, block or concrete walls, using dabs of the appropriate gypsum-based adhesive to secure the boards to the wall. This system cannot be used to fix Duplex grades of gypsum wallboard. Using similar techniques, backgrounds suitable for the dab fixing method can also be used with plasterboard thermal laminates to provide an internal lining and additional thermal insulation in one fixing operation. The boards are mechanically fixed into the set dabs of adhesive to maintain the fixing in the event of fire, using five nailable plugs per board. Full fixing details can be obtained from the manufacturer.

35.12.3.3 Metal channel fixing (trade name: Gyproc Driwall M/F System)

This is a method of fixing tapered-edge plasterboards to most dry, internal brick, block or concrete walls. The wall is 'straightened' by applying and aligning a series of vertical and horizontal proprietary lightweight metal channels bedded to the wall with an appropriate gypsum adhesive. When the adhesive has set, the plasterboards are screwed to all the channels using a power screwdriver. This system can be used to fix standard, Duplex grades of gypsum wallboard or plasterboard thermal laminates. Full fixing details can be obtained from the manufacturer.

35.12.3.4 Bonding to existing plastered walls

Plasterboard thermal laminates can be fixed direct to suitable, dry, plastered external walls using an appropriate adhesive.

Mechanical fixings are also required to restrain the plasterboard facing in the event of fire.

Gypsum plasterboards used for drying linings are jointed according to the type of edge detail of the boards' long edges.

35.12.3.5 Tapered edge

The abutting long edges of boards form a depression which is filled with joint filler and reinforced with joint tape. The joint is finished with joint finish and the whole surface of the board is then given a final application of a dual-purpose wallboard primer. This treatment provides smooth, seamless surfaces ready for receiving most forms of direct decoration. Approximate requirements of hand-jointing materials are as follows:

joint filler	22 kg/100 m^2;
joint tape	128–146 m/100 m^2;
joint finish	33 kg/100 m^2; and
primer	8–9 l/100 m^2.

The tools required are a 200 mm jointing applicator, a 50 mm taping knife and a jointing sponge.

The work is divided into five stages as follows:

(1) Using the applicator, apply a continuous thin band of joint filler to the taper at the board joints. Cut the required length of joint tape and press it into the band of filler using the taping knife. Make sure that the tape is firmly embedded and free from air bubbles, but with sufficient filler left under it to ensure good adhesion.

(2) Using the applicator again, follow immediately with another coat of joint filler over the tape to fill the taper level with the surface of the boards. Before the filler stiffens moisten the sponge with water and wipe off surplus material from the edges of the joint, taking care not to disturb the main joint filling. Rinse the sponge.

(3) When the filler has set but not necessarily dried (about 1 h), apply a thin layer of joint finish over the joint, using the applicator. Feather out the extreme edges with the dampened sponge.

(4) When the first coat of joint finish has dried, apply another coat in a broad band over the joint and feather out as before.

(5) When the joints are dry, even up the difference in surface texture between the board surface and the joint by applying one coat of a dual purpose primer over the entire wall or ceiling surface with the jointing sponge to leave a light, even texture.

35.12.3.6 Cut edge joints

Cut edges should ideally occur only at internal angles, but where they are unavoidable they can be taped as follows. First sandpaper the edges to remove paper burrs, then fill the gap between the boards flush with the board surface with joint filler. After the filler has set, make a thin application of joint finish over the joint and bed the tape in this as tightly as possible. Two more coats of joint finish should be applied as described in steps (3) and (4) above, the first coat being allowed to dry before the second one is applied.

35.12.3.7 Nail heads

Nail or screw heads should be 'spotted', i.e. the depression over the heads should be filled flush with the board surface. This is done in two thin coats, the first of joint filler, the second with joint finish. This can be done while the main joints are setting or drying between stages.

35.12.3.8 Internal angles (including wall/ceiling angles)

Fill any gap between the boards at angles with joint filler. Cut the tape to the required length and crease it firmly down the middle. Apply a thin band of joint finish to either side of the angle and press the tape into the angle, ensuring that air bubbles are eliminated but leaving a thin layer of finish under it to ensure good adhesion. Apply a thin layer of joint finish over the tape and feather out the edges with the damp sponge.

When this layer has dried, make a further application of joint finish to both sides of the angle, and feather the edges again.

35.12.3.9 External angles

External angles can be reinforced with corner tape to give a clean sharp edge. Dry-wall angle bead is used where maximum protection is required.

35.12.3.10 Square edges

Square edges are used to provide featured or cover-strip joints.

35.12.4 Decoration

After joint treatment and nail/screw head spotting has dried, decoration, including any decorator's preparatory work, should follow with the minimum of delay.

The manufacturers of paint or applied finishing products should be consulted regarding their recommendations for the use of their products on gypsum plasterboards for dry lining. Gyproc dry-wall top coat (a dual-purpose primer) has been especially formulated for use on the ivory coloured surface of plasterboard. A single coat seals the surface and allows greater coverage and more uniform finish to be obtained from the paint used. A top coat must be used before paperhanging to facilitate the subsequent removal of the paper. Where textured finishes are to be used, or where decoration is delayed, it is strongly recommended that a top coat is applied as soon as possible after board fixing is completed.

35.12.5 Fixtures to plasterboard dry-lined walls

The recommendations given here are principally concerned with fixtures at the time of erection. Subsequent fixtures in use are rather more awkward, particularly where heavier fixtures are required, since steps must be taken to prevent, for example, deflection of the lining.

With dry-lined walls there is normally a cavity to be bridged between the boards and the background; the fixing device should be long enough to allow for this and to penetrate well into the solid wall or background.

It is extremely important that the drilling of the board and fixing of the fixing device is carried out as carefully and accurately as possible, otherwise the performance of the fixing can be considerably affected. The manufacturer's recommendation as to the drill size for any device is particularly important, and holes should always be drilled and not punched.

Where heavy to medium weight fixtures are to be made to walls with plasterboard linings, and the loads are to be applied to the plasterboard face through narrow or small-area bearings such as wall brackets or coat hooks, then timber face plates should be used.

35.12.6 Health and safety

Precautions to be observed in the use and fixing of plasterboard dry linings, systems and accessories should be obtained from the manufacturer's relevant literature.

The installation of electrical services should be carried out in accordance with the recommendations of the Institution of Electrical Engineers. The cables should be protected by conduit, or other suitable precautions must be taken, to prevent abrasion where these pass through metal framing.

Bibliography

Approved Document B2/3/4 Fire Spread. HMSO, London
BRITISH STANDARDS INSTITUTION, *BS 476 Non-combustibility test for materials*, Part 4, Milton Keynes (1970)
BRITISH STANDARDS INSTITUTION, *BS 5250 Control of condensation in dwellings*, Milton Keynes (1975)
BRITISH STANDARDS INSTITUTION, *BS 5492, The Building Regulations 1985 (for England and Wales)* Milton Keynes (1977)

Appendix

The use of plasterboard as an internal dry lining finish is a relatively recent application. The earliest type of plasterboard was invented in the last years of the nineteenth century by an American called Augustine Sackett—and then it was an accident! It is said that Sackett originally set out to develop a lightweight packing case and one of his earlier attempts, utilizing a wooden frame covered by boards consisting of a number of layers of paper strongly fixed together by tiers of tar, appeared at first to be useful and inexpensive. But the invention was flawed and, in transit, the cases failed to stand up to the heat of the sun and, consequently, the pitch or tar melted, destroying both packaging and contents.

However, undeterred, Sackett and an associate, Fred L. Kane, conceived an idea of making a wallboard for walls and ceilings using 8 or 10 plys of paper and a thin intervening coating of pitch to produce a board approximately 3/16 in. thick; the problem there was that the pitch ran through the paper and ruined the decorations.

The pair had a bright idea—they tried plaster of Paris, applied thinly to layers of bogus manilla paper, passing this through a wheel of approximately 20 feet in diameter and leaving it to dry for several days. It is said that when the board was cut down it was very stiff and strong. A patent was granted on the product in May 1894 and a drawing for that patent application showed a board of six plys.

Since about 1898 plasterboard has hardly altered in concept; the number of plys has been reduced, of course, and the quality of plaster and paper has improved but, most importantly, technological achievements have meant that a wider variety of boards is now available to meet an ever increasing range of applications.

36

Polymers in Construction: An Overview

L J Tabor FPRI
Fosroc CCD Ltd

Contents

36.1 Introduction 36/3
36.1.1 What are polymers 36/3

36.2 Natural polymers—harnessed by man 36/3

36.3 Synthetic polymers—thermosets 36/3

36.4 Synthetic polymers—thermoplastics 36/4

36.5 Coatings, castings and laminates 36/4

36.6 Resin mortars 36/4

36.7 Polymer emulsions 36/5

36.8 Seals and sealants 36/5

36.9 Inorganic polymers 36/5

36.10 Reactive polymers 36/5

36.11 Rubbers 36/5

36.12 Engineering properties 36/6
36.12.1 Fire 36/6
36.12.2 Weathering 36/6

36.13 The future 36/6

36.1 Introduction

36.1.1 What are polymers?

The first reactions of many people to this topic might well be based upon an assumption that polymers are comparatively new materials to the construction industry. This is far from the case as, by strict definition, one of the oldest construction materials—timber—is in fact polymer based. So too are animal glue and natural rubber, but the layman tends to think of polymers as man-made materials, either modified natural polymers or chemically synthesized ones.

That strict definition recognizes that polymers are any material whose molecular construction is a chain of some hundreds or thousands of repeating sub-units. The sub-units are referred to as monomers. Thus, ethylene gas is a monomer which can be reacted to bring about a joining up of thousands of ethylene molecules into a long chain, often having many side branches; the polymer polyethylene. If more than one molecular species is involved, e.g. ethylene gas and vinyl acetate, the polymerized product is described as a copolymer, in this case ethylene vinyl acetate (EVA), a much more rubbery product than straight polyethylene. The length of the chains, the range of chain lengths occurring in a particular sample and the degree of branching all have considerable effect upon the physical properties of the polymer. The mobility of the chains (and hence the flexibility of the product) is a function of the chemical groups involved; the spacing of the atoms in each different chemical molecule governing the freedom of rotation of each chemical link. The natural 'rest' state of the polymer chains is for them to be coiled up something like a helical spring, but with thousands of these coiled chains tangled together. When they are mobile they may be stretched out by applying force, but will recoil when the stretching force is removed (elasticity). Temperature has a great effect on flexibility, as heat increases mobility in the chains. If there is sufficient mobility, and the only restraint against inter-chain movement is the friction due to their close proximity and entanglement, the chains may slide past each other (flow). When the temperature is reduced they will recoil in their new position and 'freeze' together again. Such polymers are referred to as thermoplastics and may repeatedly be softened by heating, re-shaped and cooled. Of course, the temperature at which sufficient mobility is attained will depend upon chemical make-up; some polymers do not soften or flow at moderately elevated temperatures and thermal decomposition may set in before any noticeable softening occurs. The problem is overcome by introducing a solvent, which will swell the polymer, moving the chains apart and reducing their restraint upon each other. The solvent is usually chosen to be of very low volatility and is termed a plasticizer, e.g. high boiling phthalate esters are used as plasticizers in the production of flexible PVC (polyvinyl chloride).

In some polymers there may be some restraint against inter-chain movement because of chemical connections between adjacent chains. This is termed cross-linking. If a limited amount of cross-linking prevents chains sliding over each other to adopt new positions when stressed, but is not enough to prevent uncoiling of the chains, when the stress is released the chains recoil to their original position. Polymers which exhibit this highly elastic extension and recovery are termed elastomers, as opposed to plastomers which exhibit plastic flow when stressed.

With greater density of cross-linking the elastic behaviour is lost and the polymer chains remain firmly intermeshed even when the temperature is raised, e.g. the highly vulcanized rubber, 'ebonite'. Polymers which are densely cross-linked are termed 'thermosets'. It is usually arranged that in the first stage of their production they are thermoplastic so that they can be moulded to shape, but the mixture incorporates the necessary chemicals to produce further cross-linking when they are maintained in the hot mould for a few minutes, or in some cases the reaction can be made to proceed to full cross-linking at room temperature by the use of more active catalysts.

36.2 Natural polymers—harnessed by man

The first of the man-modified materials was rubber. Coagulated natural rubber latex is of very little practical use because, although under certain conditions it is soft and elastic, it becomes very hard in cold conditions and soft and sticky in warmer weather. It was the development of vulcanization in 1844 which overcame these difficulties and gave us the rubber with which we are familiar in waterproof membranes, flexible seals, water-bars, bridge-bearings, electrical insulation, etc.

The next man-modified group of materials came with the development of cellulose-based plastics starting in 1862. Cellulose, a polysaccharide, occurs in all plant life and is the polymer content of timber, but cotton linters is the purest form of cellulose readily available. By treatment with acids, the cellulose molecule can be modified to make it soluble in common solvents. Cellulose nitrate and cellulose acetate were the basis of many lacquers used in wood finishing. By using non-volatile solvents as plasticizers, tough, mouldable compositions could be produced. These were fairly rigid at room temperature and intrinsically water-white and clear, so could be used for shatter-proof glazing, or could be pigmented to any colour or degree of opacity. Although moulded cellulose plastics were very widely used in commercial and domestic applications during the first half of this century, their use in construction was limited to hand rail coverings and a small amount of piping.

36.3 Synthetic polymers—thermosets

The first completely synthetic polymers were phenol–formaldehyde resins which were brought to commercial realization with the development of Bakelite in 1908. With its good electrical insulation properties and comparative ease of moulding and extrusion, this paved the way for the mass production of electrical components at a time when the electricity supply and distribution industry was developing and expanding rapidly. Although functionally very satisfactory, the colour range of phenolic moulding materials was limited to black, and dark shades of brown. The development of urea–formaldehyde resins in the early 1930s allowed the production of white and pastel shades. The physical properties of these materials were not as good as the phenolics, being somewhat sensitive to moisture and tending to discolour on heating, but they fulfilled a useful role until melamine–formaldehyde resins (1940) offered a superior, more stable, but more expensive product. These various products, still popularly known by the most familiar trade name 'Bakelite', are thermosetting materials. Besides electrical fittings, they were moulded into all manner of domestic and industrial artifacts, but found little application in the construction industry apart from secondary fitments such as toilet seats, door knobs etc. In the production of moulding powders, the basic resins were heavily filled with wood flour, cellulose fibre, mineral fillers, etc. The resins could also be used to impregnate absorbent fibrous substrates such as paper and fabrics. Laminates could be built up from impregnated layers of these materials and press-moulded into flat sheets with very good electrical and mechanical performance. Their dark colours limited their use to industrial functions such as gear wheels, bearings, heavy duty surfaces and electrical insulators, but the development of melamine–formaldehyde resins had a tremendous effect upon the building industry when laminates could be produced with light coloured pre-printed surfaces for work tops and hygienic wall linings.

36.4 Synthetic polymers—thermoplastics

The cellulose plastics were all thermoplastic, which made them much easier to process and fabricate into complex shapes and allowed the development of injection moulding from technology of the metal die-casting industry. The range of thermoplastic materials widened considerably during the 1930s with the development of polymers synthesized from coal or oil feed stocks; polystyrene, acrylics and vinyl polymers. Polystyrene had no direct bearing upon the construction industry until the 1960s when expanded polystyrene emerged as a very efficient and economical thermal insulation material. It has also become accepted as a useful low-cost void former in concrete construction and a floor slab underlay to accommodate clay heave. Vinyl polymers in the form of plasticized PVC gradually replaced rubber for electrical insulation and the lead sheathing widely used at one time for the protection of elastic cables. The chemistry and technology for processing PVC without plasticizers was developed in the late 1940s and when the economics became right, rigid or unplasticized PVC (UPVC) played a major contribution in the building and construction industries, largely replacing cast iron for rainwater goods, soil, drainage, and water supply pipes. Light weight, slight flexibility, ease of colouring and production in continuous lengths simplified and indeed revolutionized some aspects of the industry. Being much less brittle than the general purpose phenolic materials, but having fair rigidity and good external durability if suitably stabilized, rigid PVC opened up the possibilities of plastics forming some part of the fabric of buildings rather than just fittings and artifacts. Extruded UPVC sheeting began to compete with asbestos-cement and corrugated steel sheet for industrial roofing and wall cladding. Plasticized PVC was also used as a permanent decorative and protective coating on steel sheet cladding. Acrylic sheeting also entered this market when its scale of manufacture made it sufficiently competitive and this offered the additional advantage of transparency, indeed the light transmission of acrylic resins is far superior to that of glass. This factor coupled with lower density and better resistance to breakage than glass, made acrylics ideal for many lighting applications. Where severe physical abuse might be encountered, clear polycarbonate resins provided the answer to glazing applications in the 1960s. UPVC has also become a prominent material in fenestration, not as a light-transmitting material but as window frames. Being fabricated from multi-wall hollow extrusions, UPVC frames contribute significantly to thermal insulation and sound attenuation and, in the replacement market at least, are competitive in price.

Opaque, pigmented acrylic sheeting and mouldings have complemented the plastics pipe revolution as they provide the basis for the new generation of sanitary ware. Baths, basins and shower trays are thermoformed from acrylic sheet and tap tops moulded in acrylics. Complete taps are moulded in polycarbonate as an economical alternative to plated brassware.

The development of polythene in the 1940s also proved eventually to have a tremendous impact upon the construction industry. Initially only used as a high dielectric insulator for electronics, when its price came down it became another contender for the general purpose insulation of wiring and fittings, but its major role in building and construction came in the form of extruded tubing and pipes now widely used in the gas and water supply distribution systems. It is also universally used as a damp-proof membrane.

36.5 Coatings, castings and laminates

Natural polymers such as shellac and oleo-resins have been used for centuries in surface coatings, but synthetic resins widened the range of binders or 'vehicles' for paint manufacture and, indeed, improved their quality out of all recognition. The term 'polymers' is generally associated with the plastics industry, but the demarcation between paints and plastics is simply historical. It was fairly clear in earlier days because paints and varnishes were always based on resins in solution. The distinction has become blurred and we now talk of a surface coatings industry which bridges the gap. Some reactive resin systems (e.g. epoxies) are applied as liquids without solvents and they harden to give coatings of greater build and better resistance to aggressive chemicals and abrasion. Some thermoplastics (and even some thermosetting resins) can be applied as hot-melt coatings with high build. All of the resins mentioned so far have been used in the coating industry, but alkyd resins were developed specially for this purpose and have been the basis of many of the gloss paints used in the building industry for several decades. Chemically these materials are polyesters, being reaction products of polybasic acids and polyhydric alcohols, such as phthalic acid and glycerol. This development in the 1930s led, a decade later, to the development of polyester casting resins and then their use as low pressure laminating resins. This was the beginning of the glass-reinforced plastics industry and was to have a profound impact upon the construction world.

A very similar course of development was progressing at about the same time using epoxide resins. Both epoxy and polyester resins, when used as a binder for glass fibre fabrics (both woven and non-woven), produced sheet materials of considerable strength, chemical resistance and weather resistance. Being amenable to low pressure processes, in contrast to the very high pressures required for phenolic and melamine laminates, these newer laminates could be made without heat, by a simple hand lay-up process, in comparatively cheap and simple moulds in almost any complex shape, whereas phenolic and melamine laminates produced in multi-daylight hydraulic presses were essentially limited to flat sheet form.

The design freedom and economic production of the hand lay-up process made these GRP (glass reinforced plastics) laminates ideal for chemical plants, process vessel linings etc, but also suggested their use in structural building application. Whilst they enjoy the high tensile strength of the glass fibres, their elastic modulus is only one-tenth that of aluminium. With material costs making very thick section prohibitively expensive, the most efficient way of achieving rigidity was by stressed skin or monocoque design. The resulting structures were of folded plate or curvilinear form, which rather limited their use to industrial or leisure buildings. Economic use was made of GRP laminates as sheet claddings in conjunction with steel or timber frames and some building systems were developed along these lines.

36.6 Resin mortars

When using these resins to produce castings, it was necessary and more economical to use a high loading of mineral fillers. This soon made apparent the possibility of using them as binders for sands and aggregates, to produce resin mortars or concretes having much of the versatility of hydraulic cement concretes, with greatly enhanced chemical resistance, abrasion resistance and flexural strength. These resin mortars are widely used for the manufacture of artifacts such as chemically resistant process plant, sanitary ware, drainage gulleys, large diameter sewer pipes, etc. They also find considerable use as functional and decorative floor screeds and concrete repair materials.

36.7 Polymer emulsions

Reference has already been made to the use of polymers in solution for surface coating and impregnation. Some polymers can also be dispersed in non-solvents; for instance water-dispersed epoxy resin systems are used as floor coatings. This is analogous to the way in which oil-in-water or water-in-oil emulsions can be prepared for such diverse applications as machine cutting oils or face creams. The same technique of mixing two incompatible liquids with a trace of surface-active agent until one is broken down to fine stable droplets uniformly dispersed in the other, is also used in the preparation of some polymers from monomers. The monomers, which may be volatile oily liquids or gases under pressure, are dispersed in water and reacted with suitable initiators or catalysts, until the suspended monomer droplets become suspended particles of polymer. The end product is often referred to as a polymer emulsion (but polymer dispersion is the correct term) and is very similar in many ways to natural rubber latex. Many synthetic rubbers can be prepared in this manner and one, styrene–butadiene rubber, is particularly used in the construction industry. Many vinyl and acrylic polymers and co-polymers are also produced as water-based dispersions for construction work. Co-polymers are polymerized from blends of different monomers to combine the advantage of two or more basic products.

When spread out in a thin layer, most of these polymer dispersions lose their water by evaporation and the polymer particles coalesce together to form a coherent film. This clearly has applications for surface coating and many vinyl co-polymers are the bases of emulsion paints. Back in the 1920s it was found that natural rubber latex, if stabilized to resist coagulation in an alkaline medium, could be mixed with Portland cement to produce a tough flexible coating or for use as an adhesive. Many synthetic polymer dispersions can be similarly used and find particular application in upgrading the strength and abrasion resistance of floor screeds and as bonding agents between fresh wet concrete and existing hardened concrete. When incorporated into cementitious mortars they can substantially reduce the permeability of the mortar to liquids and gases, which accounts for their considerable use in concrete repair compositions.

36.8 Seals and sealants

Low modulus polymers have become essential to the construction industry in the formation of flexible seals at joints between structural elements. Preformed water-bars and joint seals, often of quite complex cross-section, are extruded from plasticized PVC, natural or synthetic rubbers. Other joint seals are formed *in situ* by the pouring of hot materials—originally bitumen, but much better performance and durability can be achieved with rubber–bitumen blends or pitch–PVC. Hot pouring is of course limited to horizontal joints, but thixotropic cold-curing polymers such as polysulphide rubbers, polyurethanes and silicones can be gun-applied into vertical joints.

36.9 Inorganic polymers

These materials represent an interesting contrast to the other polymers so far discussed, in that hitherto we have been considering wholly organic polymers, in which the repeating units always had carbon atoms linked together as their backbone. Silicon has certain similarities with carbon in its atomic structure (each has four electrons in its outer shell) and this is reflected in some analogous compounds. One result of this is the ability to form polymer chains in which alternate silicon and oxygen molecules form the backbone and this chemical linkage is more stable than that between carbon atoms, so that these polymers can withstand much higher temperatures and are more resistant to many aggressive chemicals. The generic term for polymers based upon a silicon–oxygen backbone, often with organic branches, is silicone. Silicone polymers come in many forms ranging from oils to rubbers, to hard resin coatings.

Silicone polymers have very good water-repelling properties and this is put to good use by reacting them inside the pores of concrete to form a hydrophobic lining, which prevents the capillary movement of water without blocking or sealing the pores. Concrete thus treated is resistant to the passage of liquid water, but water vapour passes freely allowing the concrete to dry out if necessary. This is achieved by impregnating the surface of the concrete with a silane monomer or a siloxane oligomer (a very short chain silicone–oxygen species which is less volatile than the silane monomer). These materials are of such small molecular size that they can easily penetrate the finest pores in concrete and then react with free lime or moisture to polymerize and form a silicone–resin lining.

36.10 Reactive polymers

Many of the polymers we have been considering are converted from liquid or semi-liquid materials into solids or rubbery solids after having been fashioned on site into the shape or form required. This means that part of the polymerization reaction is carried out on site and there are two types of chemical reaction employed. In 'addition' reactions, a chemically reactive polymer such as epoxy resin is mixed with another reactive chemical (such as an amine hardener or curing agent) which is then able to form chemical links between reactive sites on the polymer chains and connect them together into a fairly rigid network. By contrast, polyester resins contain the two reactive components (a long chain ester polymer and styrene monomer) but these are prevented from reacting with each other by the inclusion of an inhibitor. When the reaction is required to proceed, a very small quantity of a catalyst chemical (usually a peroxide) is added. For ease and safety of handling, the peroxide catalyst is usually supplied dispersed into a large volume of inert mineral filler. The use of reactive chemicals on site does require disciplined procedures and these are clearly stated in the health and safety data sheets issued by the material suppliers.

36.11 Rubbers

A number of elastomeric polymers have been developed since the late 1930s, initially to avoid dependence upon the Far East for rubber feedstocks and to circumvent the variability found in natural rubber in those days. Styrene–butadiene rubbers, butyls, polychloroprene, polysulphides, polyurethanes and silicones, to name the principal groups, have all been developed as engineering materials. Each has some particular characteristic, either in mechanical properties or chemical resistance. Meanwhile the production of natural rubber has been brought under control to provide totally reliable materials in a range of grades, with some performance properties which still cannot be matched by the synthetics.

The construction and building industry uses these rubbers for flexible seals and gaskets, water-bars, bridge bearings, vibration attenuating mountings, membranes for roofing and the lining of reservoirs etc. The miles of flexible hoses carrying compressed air and water around every construction site are also dependent upon rubber.

36.12 Engineering properties

The arrival of resin-based high strength materials presented a considerable challenge to mechanical and structural engineers. All their design experience had been founded upon generations of use of metals, timber, stone and concrete. Resin binders presented them with new concepts which many have still not mastered. Perhaps the greatest difficulty encountered has been coming to terms with the effect of heat.

The physical and mechanical properties of traditional materials, steel, concrete, masonry etc., are comparatively constant over the normal range of working temperatures encountered in construction work, say −10°C to +30°C. Although polyester and epoxy resins are technically thermosetting materials, their properties may vary considerably over this same temperature range. Their elastic modulus reduces with increasing temperature, but the effect of this change can be minimized by chemical tailoring of the resin to give a high degree of cross-linking and by using the maximum filler loading compatible with maintaining adequate workability in use.

Everyone is familiar with the 'first order' transition points of many materials; their freezing/melting point and their boiling point. Most polymers, including polyester and epoxy resins, exhibit a 'second order' effect; their glass transition temperature. This is the temperature at which there is a sharp inflection in the plot of many of their physical properties against temperature. Below their glass transition temperature the materials are hard and when stressed to the ultimate, fail in a brittle manner (although fibrous reinforcement may overcome any obvious brittleness), but above the glass transition temperature materials behave in a more rubbery fashion and the rate of creep under load is dramatically increased. Hence the glass transition temperature (T_g) represents the upper limit of any load bearing capacity of these materials. Even well below their T_g considerable creep can occur under load but, properly understood, this can be predicted and allowed for in design and can even be of some benefit. The measurement of creep under hydraulic pressure measured at various stress levels and temperatures allows engineers to calculate the safe working pressure for a particular design life in pipes (both thermosetting and thermoplastic) carrying gas, water, etc. under pressure. The same principles can be applied to the creep of resin mortars and grouts used under bridge bearings, heavy machine bases, crane rail tracks, etc. In these compressive situations the rate of creep is inversely proportional to log time, so its effect can usually be ignored after the first few months of loading. Similarly, when resins are used for the installation of rock-anchors, holding-down bolts, etc., long term monitoring over many years has shown that creep is not a problem.

On the other hand, resins can be deliberately designed to creep under stress and this is a salient feature of resin mortars formulated for use in composite construction with concrete, such as in the formation of road-joint arrises or when concrete members are rendered with an epoxy mortar to provide chemical resistance or high resistance to abrasive wear. Because the thermal coefficient of expansion of resin mortars is several times that of concrete, if the resin mortar has high strength and great rigidity the stresses arising from the thermal differential could cause debonding of mortar, or more likely, rupture of the concrete. This was the result when engineers at one time insisted on having resin mortars formulated to have an elastic modulus as close to concrete as possible. By using a somewhat lower modulus resin with some capacity to creep under stress, the strength and toughness of the resin mortar could be harnessed without any distress arising at the interface as a result of thermal changes.

36.12.1 Fire

All organic materials are combustible, but the ease of ignition and rate of combustion depend upon many factors. The first is the ease with which the bonds holding the atoms together may be broken. This varies considerably with molecular configuration. Thus polyethylene, which may be regarded almost as an ultra-high molecular weight paraffin wax, ignites easily and will support combustion, i.e. will continue to burn when the source of heat is removed. Phenolic resins, which also consist of carbon and hydrogen atoms, but linked together in a very different pattern and have an occasional oxygen atom included, will not support combustion and will only burn whilst held in a strong flame.

The inclusion of other atoms in the molecule can have a considerable effect upon combustion. Thus, PVC, which empirically may be considered as polythene with every fourth hydrogen atom replaced by a chlorine atom, is also very reluctant to burn. The flame retardant benefit of chlorine and other halogen atoms can also be achieved by blending a halogen-rich chemical into an otherwise flammable material. The effect can be greatly enhanced by including antimony oxide in the mix. The incorporation of large quantities of inert mineral fillers can have a substantial effect, particularly fillers which lose water of crystallization when heated. The ratio of mass to surface area also plays a part in regulating rate of combustion.

Whilst these various mechanisms may affect ease of ignition and the spread or extinction of the flame, given sufficient external fuel, all polymers can be consumed by fire. Nevertheless, polymer-based building components can be engineered to have adequate fire resistance for many applications. GRP panels may incorporate mineral aggregates as surface dressings with both aesthetic and fire resistant benefits. One major construction company developed a phenolic foam concrete in the late 1960s as the total load bearing element of a factory built housing system. When subjected to a statutory fire resistance test under BS 476, a 150 mm thick panel totally resisted fire penetration. Whilst one side was raised to over 1000°C in the gas fired furnace, there was no measurable temperature increase on the other face. The staff at the Fire Research Station were amazed at the performance of this material, which continued to carry 1.5 times working load throughout the test and 48 hours later required a load of 80 tonnes to bring about the failure of the 8 feet high × 4 feet wide panel. This demonstrated the benefit of combining the thermal insulation effect of a foam with the low combustibility of phenolic resins.

36.12.2 Weathering

The molecular bonds of polymers may also be vulnerable to rupture by the effect of ultraviolet radiation. Again, some polymers are very much more stable than others and the stability of all polymers can be greatly enhanced by compounding with suitable chemicals. Heat and oxygen can also encourage molecular breakdown, but these effects can be inhibited by the incorporation of anti-oxidants and other stabilizing chemicals. PVC, which has comparatively poor resistance in its unmodified state, when suitably compounded has been shown to give excellent durability in the form of rainwater goods, vinyl coated steel cladding, etc. Acrylic resins, which are intrinsically more stable give quite outstanding performance in the field of surface coatings, where a life of fifteen years is now the expected norm.

36.13 The future

It will be seen from the foregoing pages that many polymers which began their industrial life as exotic materials, such as polyethylene, which was used almost exclusively for electronics (particularly radar) during the war, eventually become low cost commodities having widespread use in the construction industry. From nylon, originally developed as a fibre-spinning polymer replacement for silk, has come a whole family of engineering polyamide resins. Most applications are in industrial engineering components, bearings, tubing and packaging, but some use is made of them in construction for bearings, hinges and latches with good wear resistance and low friction without oiling. There are many more polymers with exciting possibilities, such as high mechanical strength and serviceability at temperatures of several hundred degrees Celcius, which currently feature only in the most demanding engineering and aerospace applications. If the earlier trend continues, some of these may eventually find their way into the construction industry.

37

Natural and Synthetic Rubbers

V A Coveney PhD
Bristol Polytechnic (Mechanical Engineering Faculty)

Contents

37.1 Introduction 37/3

37.2 Production of base elastomers 37/3
   37.2.1 Natural rubber 37/3
   37.2.2 Synthetic *cis*-polyisoprenes 37/3
   37.2.3 Butyl rubbers (isobutene–isoprene rubbers) 37/3
   37.2.4 Styrene–butadiene rubbers 37/3
   37.2.5 Butadiene rubbers (polybutadiene) 37/5
   37.2.6 Nitrile rubbers 37/5
   37.2.7 Ethylene–propylene rubbers 37/5
   37.2.8 Chloroprene rubbers 37/5
   37.2.9 Polyurethane rubbers 37/5
   37.2.10 Silicone rubbers 37/5
   37.2.11 Chlorosulphonated polyethylene 37/5

37.3 Available forms 37/6

37.4 Vulcanization and 'compounding' 37/6
   37.4.1 Natural rubber 37/7
   37.4.2 Synthetic *cis*-polyisoprene 37/8
   37.4.3 Butyl rubbers 37/8
   37.4.4 Styrene–butadiene rubbers 37/8
   37.4.5 Butadiene rubbers 37/8
   37.4.6 Nitrile rubbers 37/8
   37.4.7 Ethylene–propylene rubbers 37/8
   37.4.8 Chloroprene rubbers 37/8
   37.4.9 Polyurethane rubbers 37/9
   37.4.10 Silicone rubbers 37/9
   37.4.11 Chlorosulphonated polyethylene 37/9

37.5 Moulding of thermoplastic elastomers 37/9
   37.5.1 Block co-polymer thermoplastic elastomers 37/9
   37.5.2 Thermoplastic polyolefin elastomers 37/9

37.6 Properties of elastomers 37/10
   37.6.1 Natural rubber 37/10
   37.6.2 Synthetic *cis*-polyisoprene 37/10
   37.6.3 Butyl rubbers 37/10
   37.6.4 Styrene–butadiene rubbers 37/10
   37.6.5 Butadiene rubbers 37/10
   37.6.6 Nitrile rubbers 37/10
   37.6.7 Ethylene–propylene rubbers 37/11
   37.6.8 Chloroprene rubbers 37/11
   37.6.9 Polyurethane rubbers 37/11
   37.6.10 Silicone rubbers 37/11
   37.6.11 Chlorosulphonated polyethylene 37/11
   37.6.12 Chlorinated polyethylene 37/11
   37.6.13 Ethylene–methylacrylate rubber 37/11
   37.6.14 Fluorinated hydrocarbon rubbers 37/11
   37.6.15 Polysulphide rubbers 37/11
   37.6.16 Epichlorohydrin rubbers 37/11
   37.6.17 Polypropylene oxide rubber 37/11
   37.6.18 Ethylene–vinyl acetate rubbers 37/12
   37.6.19 Polynorbornene rubbers 37/12
   37.6.20 Properties of thermoplastic elastomers 37/12

37.7. Example applications 37/12
   37.7.1 Buildings 37/12
   37.7.2 Fixtures, fittings and services 37/13
   37.7.3 Piping, hose, reservoirs and tanks 37/15
   37.7.4 Roads, railways and bridges 37/15
   37.7.5 Oil, gas, chemical engineering and mining 37/16
   37.7.6 Miscellaneous 37/16

37.8 Elastomers—appropriate and inappropriate use 37/16
   37.8.1 Mechanical considerations 37/16
   37.8.2 Stiffness and dimensional tolerances 37/17
   37.8.3 Environmental factors 37/18

37.9 Standards and specifications 37/18
   37.9.1 General 37/20
   37.9.2 Test methods for rubber 37/20
   37.9.3 Material specifications 37/20
   37.9.4 Product specifications 37/20

37.10 Conclusions 37/21

37.11 Research and Trade Associations 37/21

References 37/22

Bibliography 37/22

37.1 Introduction

Rubbers or elastomers are a large and growing class of materials. At one end of the spectrum, natural rubber and synthetics such as polychloroprene are soft materials which have the ability to undergo extensions of many hundreds of percent yet return rapidly to their original shape when the deforming force is removed. The compliance of rubbers in shear and extension coupled with their near incompressibilty means that particular techniques are often required in the stress analysis of these materials. Natural rubber (NR) was the first elastomer and is still the most heavily used. Its mechanical properties epitomize those of a fully rubbery material. Ethylene propylene rubber (EPM/EPDM) is a synthetic elastomer extensively used in construction because of its excellent resistance to weathering. The strength, and related properties, of NR and of EPDM are compared with those of other materials in *Table 37.1*.

In some applications full rubbery behaviour offers great advantages, dock fenders being one example. In other cases, such as window-frame seals and roofing membranes, only a limited degree of elasticity is required. In the latter category there is considerable overlap between elastomers, which are sometimes modified to make them more like thermoplastics, and thermoplastics which have been modified to make them more rubbery.

At the opposite end of the spectrum from natural rubber lie materials which are closely related chemically to rubbers but which are not physically rubbery. Examples include the ebonites, which are hard materials obtained by the vulcanization (heating) of natural or certain other rubbers containing very high levels of sulphur. The latter class of materials lies outside the scope of this chapter.

Additives make an important contribution in the performance of finished elastomers. Without the reinforcing action of fine particles of carbon (carbon black) or silica, some synthetic rubbers would be so weak as to be of little use. Without the protective action of added antioxidants and antiozonants, the surface of natural rubber and other rubbers based on unsaturated hydrocarbon chains would deteriorate within 1 year or so in many environments. Nevertheless, the base polymer of an elastomer remains of key importance.

The symbols and abbreviations used in this chapter are, as far as possible taken from the International Standard ISO 1629.[5]

37.2 Production of base elastomers

Elastomers are generally composed of long chains of repeated molecular units. The (small) chemical compounds which, when joined, make up the polymer chains are called 'monomers'. A co-polymer is a polymer formed from two types of monomer.

The elastomers covered in this section are limited to major types and those finding widespread use in civil engineering.

37.2.1 Natural rubber

Although there are other substances present in raw natural rubber which have an effect on the final properties of the final material, the key component is the long-chain polymer (chemically, cis-1,4-polyisoprene[6]) which is formed from *c.* 20 000 repeat units giving an average molecular weight of about 1 million times that of a hydrogen atom (*Figure 37.1*). Large numbers of plant species produce milky aqueous suspensions (latices) of cis-polyisoprenes, but only two species are of commercial interest. The principal rubber-producing plant is the tree *Hevea brasiliensis*, which thrives in warm climates with high rainfall. Substantial quantities of natural rubber are produced in Malaysia, Indonesia, Thailand, China, Sri Lanka, tropical America and tropical Africa.

Rubber is tapped from incisions made in the bark of the *Hevea* tree; there is, though, intermittent interest in a second rubber-producing plant which has to be crushed to yield its rubber latex: this is the guayule bush found in Mexico and Arizona.[7]

As is the case for many other agricultural products the consistency and yield of *Hevea* natural rubber have progressively increased over the past 50 years through selective breeding: yields in excess of 2000 kg per hectare per year are now obtained.

Some tapped latex is concentrated to about 60% rubber content and stabilized with ammonia and other preservatives, but most is converted directly into dry rubber. The latex from the trees is typically diluted to about 12% rubber content. Acetic or formic acid is added to coagulate the rubber which is then washed, dried and formed into solid bales. An important additional source of base rubber is 'cup lump' which comes from latex which has coagulated naturally in the tapping vessel. Although rubber from the tree is subject to natural variation, schemes for classification and guaranteed technical specifications have been available to ensure a consistent product since the mid-1960s.

A small proportion of natural rubber is modified chemically into methylmethacrylate grafted natural rubber (MG rubber) or epoxidized rubber (ENR).[8]

37.2.2 Synthetic *cis*-polyisoprenes

These polymers, the nearest synthetic equivalent to natural rubber, are manufactured from isoprene monomer which is available in substantial quantities from petroleum refinery operations. In order to achieve degrees of *cis*-1,4 content approaching the near 100% present in the natural rubber molecule, one of two catalyst systems is normally used: an alkyllithium system (giving approximately 93% *cis* content) or a Ziegler–Natta system (giving approximately 97% *cis* content). These small percentage differences in *cis* content can lead to significant differences in processing and properties of the end product.

37.2.3 Butyl rubbers (isobutene–isoprene rubbers)

The base polymers for these synthetic rubbers are produced by co-polymerizing isobutylene with a small proportion of isoprene monomer dissolved in methyl chloride or, alternatively, in the presence of catalysts such as BF_3 or $AlCl_3$. The temperature, which is kept low, controls the molecular weight of the polymer. Like isoprene, and most other 'feedstock' chemicals used in the manufacture of synthetic elastomers, isobutylene monomer is available in substantial quantities from petroleum refinery process. The nearness to saturation (of the carbon chain with hydrogen atoms) has a major effect on the mechanical properties obtained with the material. The small amount of isoprene facilitates sulphur vulcanization.[8]

37.2.4 Styrene–butadiene rubbers

As the name implies, styrene–butadiene rubbers (SBRs) are co-polymers of styrene and butadiene monomers—either as random or as block co-polymers. The proportion of styrene can vary between 20 and 40% in the rubber grades, but can be over 60% in the case of high styrene resins.

Styrene can be produced from the petroleum derivative ethylbenzene by a range of processes.

Butadiene monomer can be formed by dehydrogenation or oxidative dehydrogenation of butanes or butenes or by cracking of petroleum fractions.

Most SBR is still manufactured by polymerization in an aqueous emulsion of styrene and butadiene monomers. This produces essentially random polymers. However, since the 1960s, solution-polymerized SBRs have been produced com-

Table 37.1 Comparison of material properties (ranges are given where appropriate)

Property	Units	Natural rubber			Foam[d]	EPDM filled[e]	Polyethylene (high density)	Nylon 66	Aluminium	Mild steel	Glass (common)	Concrete	Wood[f] (oak)	Water
		Unfilled[a]	Filled[b]	Ebonite[c]										
Density	Mg m^{-3}	0.95	1.12[f]	1.08–1.10	0.1–0.6	1.2	0.94–0.97	1.14	2.70	7.75	2.4–2.7	2.1	0.74–0.77	1.00
Thermal properties														
Specific heat	J g^{-1} °C^{-1}	1.83	1.50	1.38	1.89	2.09[g]	2.3	1.7	0.95	0.48	0.84	1.89	1.37	4.19
Thermal conductivity	W m^{-1} °C^{-1}	0.15	0.28	0.16	0.045	0.39	0.45–0.52	0.25	230	46	1.1	1.2	0.38	0.65
Coefficient of linear expansion ($\times 10^5$)	°C	22	18	6	5–10	1.89	11–13	8	2.3	1.1	0.9–1.1	1.0–1.5	0.5[i]	7
Mechanical properties														
Hardness														
Brinell	kgf mm^{-2}	≪1	≪1	11–12	—	—	1	—	22	140	~340	—	—	0
International rubber scale[j]	IRHD	45	65	100	<20	65	98	100	100	100	100	100	100	0
Tensile strength	MPa	24[k]	24[k]	40–60	0.2–1.5	17	20–35	60–80	70–100	400–500	30–90	20–50	40–120	0
Elongation at break	%	700	550	3–8	200–300	450	20–600	60–100	5	40	3	—	—	0
Young's modulus, E[l]	MPa	1.9	5.9	3000	0.05–0.8	5.9[g]	~1000	1000–3000	70000	2.1×10^5	60000	25000–35000	9000	2050
Bulk modulus, K	MPa	2000	2000	4170	—	—	3300	—	70000	1.8×10^5	37000	—	—	2050
Poisson's ratio, ν		0.499	0.499	0.2	0.33	0.499	0.38	0.38	0.345	0.291	0.22	0.2	—	0.5
Acoustic properties														
Velocity of sound[m]	m s^{-1}	1600	1700[g]	—	—	—	—	—	6400	6000	5000–6000	4300–5300	4000[g]	1500
Electrical properties														
Volume resistivity	Ω m	10^{14}	$10^{10,n}$	10^{14}	10^{14}	$10^{10\,g,n}$	10^{15}	10^{12}	10^{-8}	10^{-6}	10^9–10^{11}	10^7–10^{10}	10^8–$10^{11,o}$	10^2–$10^{5,p}$
Dielectric constant (relative permittivity)		2.5–3.0	15	2.8	—	—	2.25–2.35	4.0–4.6	—	—	7	—	3–6	~80
Dissipation factor		0.002–0.04	0.006–0.14	0.004–0.009	—	—	<0.005	0.01–0.02	—	—	0.005	—	0.04–0.05	—

[a] Gum vulcanizate containing vulcanizing ingredients only.
[b] Vulcanizate containing c. 50 parts of a reinforcing carbon black per 100 parts, by weight, of natural rubber.
[c] Unfilled ebonite containing c. 40 parts of sulphur per 100 parts of industrial rubber. Ebonite, which is also known as 'hard rubber' in the USA, has a maximum glass transition temperature of c. 80°C, whereas unmodified natural rubber has a transition temperature as low as −70°C. For further information on natural rubber ebonite, see refs 1 and 2.
[d] Properties of latex foam and other cellular products from natural rubber will vary with extent of foaming or expansion. Young's modulus of open-cell foam can be estimated from Young's modulus of the solid rubber component and the density of the foam.[3]
[e] Typical formulation (120 parts of black, 95 parts of oil) for roof sheeting given by Easterbrook and Allen.[4]
[f] Wood is strongly anisotropic. Where appropriate, properties refer to tests along grain.
[g] Estimated value.
[h] Across grain, c. 0.2 W m^{-1} °C^{-1}.
[i] Across grain, c. 5×10^{-5}.
[j] Hardness scale range is 0 (e.g. liquid) to 100 (e.g. glass).
[k] Calculated on the original unstrained cross-sectional area; when calculated using on the cross-section just before break, the value can be as high as 200 MPa.
[l] For isotropic materials E is related to G and K as follows: $E = 2G(1 + \nu)$ and $E = 3K(1 − 2\nu)$.
[m] Compression varies in medium of large extent.
[n] Depends on filler type and concentration. High values are obtained by replacing carbon black with silica. Using specially conductive carbon black values under 10 Ω m can be achieved.
[o] The higher value applies to paraffinic timber.
[p] For distilled water.

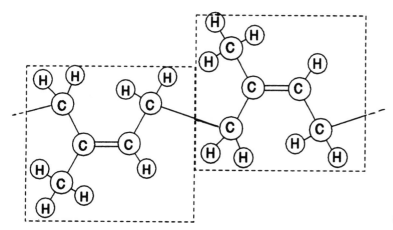

Figure 37.1 *cis*-1,4-Polyisoprene

mercially. The solution polymerization process allows more scope for control of the final polymer structure.

37.2.5 Butadiene rubbers (polybutadiene)

Polybutadiene (BR) is generally produced by polymerization of butadiene monomers in solution. The reaction can take place in a number of organic solvents in the presence of a variety of catalysts. The choice of reaction conditions including catalyst type has a major effect on the structure of the polymer.

37.2.6 Nitrile rubbers

The less specialized grades of acrylonitrile–butadiene rubbers—popularly known as nitrile rubbers (NBR)—are prepared by emulsion polymerization of acrylonitrile and butadiene monomers at low to moderate temperatures. Proportions of acrylonitrile in the final polymer are varied from below 20% to over 50% to produce materials with a wide range of properties.

There are a number of ways in which acrylonitrile monomer is produced commercially, ethylene being the usual starting point. The production of butadiene monomer is described in Section 37.2.4.

37.2.7 Ethylene–propylene rubbers

Ethylene–propylene (EPM) rubbers are the copolymers of ethylene and propylene alone; in EPDM rubbers a third monomer is also present in small quantities to introduce the unsaturation needed for sulphur vulcanization (see Section 37.4). By varying the proportions of ethylene, propylene and the type and amount of the third monomer, significant changes in properties may be achieved.

Production of ethylene–propylene rubbers involves a polymerization process using Ziegler–Natta type catalysts.[9] Polymerization is frequently performed in organic solution, but sometimes the reactions take place in suspension.

37.2.8 Chloroprene rubbers (polychlorophene)

Polychloroprene (CR) has a structure related to that of polyisoprene, the methyl group in the isoprene repeat unit being replaced by a chlorine atom. Chloroprene monomer is now predominantly produced from butadiene. Polymerization is performed in emulsion with suitable catalysts, a latex of raw chloroprene rubber being produced.

Chloroprene rubbers are available with varying chemical compositions and this can have a marked effect on the tendency to crystallize—an important parameter in categorizing these materials. Commercial chloroprene rubber consists largely of *trans*-polychloroprene—in general, the closer the proportion of this constituent is to 100% the greater the tendency of the material to crystallize rapidly. Co-polymers of chloroprene and 2,3-dichlorobutadiene are resistant to low-temperature crystallization; chloroprene–sulphur co-polymers (the DuPont G types, for example) have intermediate crystallization properties.

37.2.9 Polyurethane rubbers

The term 'polyurethene' covers a wide range of polymeric materials with urethane links. The materials are formed by the reactions of polyols with diisocyanates. Polyurethanes can be divided into polyester (AU) and polyether (EU) based materials. Polyesters are manufactured by reaction of dibasic acids with diols. (Ethylene glycol, 1,2-propylene glycol, and diethylene glycol are examples of diols used when linear polymer segments are required.) For chain branching or ultimate cross-linking, triols are used. Propylene and appropriate glycols are the common starting points or 'feedstocks' for the manufacture of polyurethanes. The two types of polyether commonly used in the production of polyurethane elastomers are polypropylene glycols and polytetramethylene glycols.

37.2.10 Silicone rubbers

These differ from other elastomers in that the main chain molecular structure consists of silicon and oxygen rather than carbon atoms—as is the case for natural and most other rubbers. As a consequence, and in marked contrast to most other synthetic elastomers, the production of silicone rubber is not heavily reliant on petroleum products. Production of silicone polymers commonly involves the reaction of elementary silicon with an alkyl halide (frequently methyl chloride). The resulting chlorosilanes subsequently react with water to give hydroxyl compounds which then condense to give a polymer structure. In the case of silicone rubbers containing vinyl groups (i.e. PVMQ and VMQ) intermediate reactions between acetylene and chlorosilanes are used. Other substituent groups are methyl (e.g. MQ), phenyl (e.g. PMQ) and fluorine (e.g. FMQ).

37.2.11 Chlorosulphonated polyethylene

Chlorosulphonated polyethylene (CSM) is produced by the random substitution of sulphonyl chloride groups and chlorine onto preformed polyethylene molecules. This is achieved by reacting a solution of polyethylene in boiling carbon tetrachloride with chlorine and with sulphur dioxide. The process converts polyethylene into a rubbery material and introduces alternative sites for cross-linking.

37.3 Available forms

Elastomers are available in solid, particulate or liquid forms prior to vulcanization (see Section 37.4). An indication of the forms available for each common elastomer type is given in *Table 37.2*.

37.4 Vulcanization and 'compounding'

Vulcanization, known also as curing, is the process whereby the polymer chains of a base elastomer are chemically cross-linked (*Figure 37.2*). The process was first applied to natural rubber in 1839 by Charles Goodyear. Previously, unvulcanized natural rubber had been used for rubber balls, erasers and macintoshes, but vulcanization resulted in an altogether stronger, more environmentally resistant material and paved the way to the use of rubber in mechanically demanding applications.

The original vulcanization process used sulphur and high temperatures (hence the name 'vulcanization'). The majority of cross-linking processes for natural and other rubbers still involve the use of sulphur and elevated temperatures. However, vulcanization conditions can vary a great deal from high-temperature (up to 200°C) cures lasting only a few seconds, through 'normal' cures typically lasting about 15 min at 150°C, to room-temperature vulcanization taking place over days or longer. The properties of the vulcanized rubber or, as it is often called, the 'vulcanizate', are influenced by the number of cross-links and their type; the properties can also be affected by other molecular modifications to the elastomer which occur during the vulcanization process.

The term 'compounding' in rubber technology refers to the mixing of various ingredients into rubber. Mixing of solid rubber is performed on open two-roll mills and in closed mixers; the high shear forces produced are used to disperse ingredients and can also be used to break down the molecular weight or 'masticate' certain rubbers. In addition to the vulcanizing chemicals, the ingredients usually include particulate fillers— these can be non-reinforcing (clay, chalk and some carbon black powders fall into this category), or reinforcing (these can be carbon black or fine silica powder). Non-reinforcing fillers, added to cheapen or harden a rubber, generally have a neutral or negative effect on strength properties. Reinforcing fillers, in contrast, tend to have a positive effect on strength properties— this is particularly true for some of the synthetics which are weak without reinforcing fillers. Silicone rubber is an example of an elastomer the strength properties of which benefit greatly from the presence of appropriate silica filler.

Frequently, rubber compounds include some oil or other plasticizer added to aid processing of the rubber prior to vulcanization and/or to influence the properties of the vulcanizate— notably stiffness or low temperature resistance. Many elastomers have antidegradants of various kinds added during compounding to improve the resistance of the final vulcanizate to, for example, attack by oxygen or ozone. Natural, butadiene and styrene–butadiene rubbers are examples of elastomers whose environmental resistance is greatly improved by the presence of appropriate antidegradants.

Vulcanized elastomeric products can be given their final shape in a number of ways. Machining of vulcanized rubber is relatively rare, except, perhaps, for trimming, but calendering of un-vulcanized sheet, coating of fabric from rubber solution, extrusion and moulding are all common.

Broadly speaking there are three types of moulding. In compression moulding a quantity of unvulcanized material is placed in a single-cavity mould (or mould area) with a closing lid or plunger which is then pressed between heated platens of a press whereupon the elastomer is shaped and vulcanized. Transfer moulding is also widely practised and here the plunger is located in the first cavity; when the moulding is under the press the rubber is forced through transfer ports into the second, shaping, cavity. Compression or transfer moulding time is normally not less than 5 min, although there is considerable

Table 37.2 Available forms of common elastomers

Elastomer	Bale/slab	Chip/pellet	Particulate	Latex	Liquid/paste	Other
Natural (NR)	**a		*	*	*	
Synthetic *cis*-polyisoprene (IR)	**a			*	*	
Butyl (IIR)	**			*	*	
Styrene–butadiene (SBR)	**b			*		
Butadiene (BR)	**a			*	*	
Nitrile (NBR)	**	*	*	*	*	
Ethylene–propylene (EPM/EPDM)	**a	*	*			*c
Chloroprene (CR)		**	*	*		
Polyurethane (AU/EU)	*				**	
Silicone (MQ, etc.)	*d				*	
Chlorosulphonated polyethylene (CSM)		*				
Ethylene acrylic (AEM)	*d					
Polyacrylic (ACM/ANM)	*	*	*	**		
Fluorinated hydrocarbon (FPM or FKM)		**			*	
Polysulphide (T)	**				*	
Epichlorohydrin (CO/ECO)	*					
Polypropylene oxide (GPO)	*					
Polynorbornene	*a		*			*d

* Available form; ** Very common form.
a Oil-extended grades are available.
b Oil-extended SBR is common. Carbon black filled master batches with and without oil are also available.
c Crumb and friable bale forms also available.
d Often partly compounded.

Figure 37.2 Elastomer chains and cross-linking. (a) Elastomer chains coiled, kinked and entangled but not chemically cross-linked. (b) Elastomer chains after vulcanization, cross-linked (●) together

variation depending on size of component, rubber formulation and temperature.

Injection moulding of a thin-walled elastomer component typically takes less than 1 min for conventional elastomers. For thermoplastic elastomers (TPE), however, chemical cross-linking does not take place during moulding; instead, within the TPE, thermoplastic areas, molten during and solid after moulding, take the place of chemical cross-links. Because there is no cure time very rapid injection moulding cycles are possible for TPEs.

With conventionally moulded elastomers it is not unusual for products to be heated in an oven after removal from a hot mould; this process, termed 'post-cure', is particularly common for certain speciality rubbers, e.g. fluorinated types. Post-cure can improve elastic recovery in the vulcanizate and reduce tendency to creep without the need for long and expensive moulding cycles.

Steam autoclaves and molten-salt baths are just two other ways in which rubber articles are cured; further methods are described by Crowther.[10]

37.4.1 Natural rubber

Vulcanization of natural rubber is normally carried out at temperatures in the range 120–180°C, although in some processes cross-linking at room temperature is used. In general the higher the temperature the more rapid is the cure. Most natural rubber (NR) is cross-linked with sulphur based vulcanizing systems. However, high levels of sulphur and long cure times would be required without additional ingredients. Accelerators speed up the cross-linking processes. Vulcanizing systems with relatively high ratios of sulphur to accelerator are called 'conventionally accelerated'; these systems give rise to cross-links most of which are formed by many sulphur atoms (polysulphidic). The lower the ratio of sulphur to accelerator the fewer sulphur atoms per cross-link. Examples of conventionally accelerated, efficient or low sulphur vulcanization (EV) and semi-EV formulations are shown in *Table 37.3*; a wide variety of natural rubber formulations may be found in the Bibliography and References. EV formulations give improved long-term high-temperature properties at the expense of strength and fatigue properties. The improved 'reversion' resistance, stability of properties at high temperature, of efficient sulphur vulcanizates also enables products with thick cross-sections to be moulded more quickly through an increase in cure temperature. Examples of sulphur-free vulcanizing systems are those based on (dicumyl) peroxide and 'Novor' (urethane), the latter giving similar results to an EV system. Normal sulphur level formulations are more resistant to low-temperature crystallization than are EV or dicumyl peroxide formulations (see Section 37.6).

Table 37.3 Natural rubber formulations

Formulation	Parts by weight	
EDS24		
Natural rubber, SMR CV	100	
Zinc oxide	5	
Stearic acid	2	
Carbon black, GPF (ASTM N-660)	20	
Process oil	2	
Antioxidant/antiozonant, HPPD	3	
Antiozonant wax	2	
CBS (accelerator)	0.6	Conventionally accelerated normal sulphur level, vulcanizing system
Sulphur	2.5	
EDS4		
Natural rubber, SMRL	100	
Zinc oxide	5	
Zinc 2-ethylhexanoate	1	
Carbon black, SRF (ASTM N-762)	30	
Antioxidant, TMQ	2	
Antiozonant, DOPD	4	
MBS (accelerator)	1.7	Semi-EV, moderately low sulphur, system
TBTD (accelerator)	0.7	
Sulphur	0.7	
EDS42		
Natural rubber, SMR CV	100	
Zinc oxide	5	
Stearic acid	2	
Carbon black, FEF (ASTM N-550)	20	
Process oil	2	
Antioxidant/antiozonant, HPPD	3	
Antiozonant wax	2	
MBS (acceletator)	2.1	EV, low sulphur system
Sulphur	0.25	
TMTD (accelerator)	1.0	

Natural rubber vulcanizates of different moduli can be obtained by varying the degree of cross-linking; however, this method is limited since too few cross-links result in a material with rather high creep, while too many cross-links limit the extensibility of the material. Oils can be added to reduce the modulus of the final vulcanizate, but more commonly are added to improve processing behaviour; high-viscosity oils are sometimes used in natural rubber to increase the damping of the final vulcanizate (similar comments apply to many other elastomers but most notably to polynorbornene rubber). The most commonly used classes of oils are naphthenic, aromatic and paraffinic; all three are products of the petrochemical industry. A principal method of adjusting the modulus, strength, fatigue and damping properties of natural and many other rubbers is by altering the quantity and type of filler.

The high shear forces produced in an internal mixer or an open mill cause a certain amount of breakdown in NR molecules. This process of 'mastication' reduces the elasticity of the unvulcanized material and facilitates shaping.

37.4.2 Synthetic *cis*-polyisoprene

Synthetic *cis*-polyisoprene, the artificial analogue of natural rubber, is generally a softer material to process and care is needed to obtain good dispersion of fillers on the open mill. The base polymer contains less, and different, non-rubber material than does natural rubber: for similar additions of vulcanizing agent this can result in the cure being somewhat slower for the synthetic material. In some cases synthetic *cis*-polyisoprene is blended with NR to 'fine-tune' the processing characteristics.

37.4.3 Butyl rubbers

There are three broad types of butyl rubber base polymer: unmodified butyl rubbers (IIR), chlorobutyl rubbers (CIIR), and bromobutyl rubbers (BIIR).

Cross-linking of IIR may be carried out with sulphur based or non-sulphur based vulcanizing systems (quinoid or phenolic resin, for example), but cure is sluggish, particularly for variants with few chemical double bonds (low unsaturation); this sluggishness necessitates the use of powerful accelerators and/or high temperatures and long cure times. Chlorobutyl and bromobutyl rubbers are less sluggish to cure and can be successfully co-vulcanized with rubbers such as NR and styrene–butadiene rubbers (SBR). Carbon black is routinely used as a reinforcing filler, and diluent oils are added to aid processing.

37.4.4 Styrene–butadiene rubbers

Styrene–butadiene rubber (SBR) is a generic term for a wide variety of rubbers. Factors affecting final properties of the vulcanizate and processing include: the relative numbers of styrene and butadiene units and their sequence distribution in the polymer chains; molecular weight (distribution) of the polymer chains; and molecular branching. In practice, however, most SBR continues to be produced by emulsion, rather than solution, processes; the range of properties for emulsion SBRs is more restricted (see Section 37.2.4); comments in this and subsequent sections are directed primarily towards this more restricted class of SBRs.

SBRs are processed in a conventional manner, but do not break down on milling (see Section 37.4.1); they are normally vulcanized with sulphur based systems. EV systems offer the same kinds of advantages over higher sulphur level vulcanizing systems for SBR as for NR (flat cure characteristic and thermal stability of vulcanizate), without the prime disadvantage of worsened fatigue properties.

SBR requires quite high (*c*. 50 pphr (parts per hundred weight of base elastomer)) quantities of reinforcing filler (usually carbon black, but sometimes silica) to achieve good strength properties. Oils are frequently included in SBR formulations—naphthenic or aromatic types are normally used.

37.4.5 Butadiene rubbers

The comments on compounding made above for SBR generally apply to butadiene rubbers (BRs) also. Although it is sometimes used alone, polybutadiene is generally used in blends with NR, SBR, IR or with (the thermoplastic) polystyrene, in this latter case to provide impact resistance.

37.4.6 Nitrile rubbers

Nitrile rubbers (NBR) vary in their acrylonitrile content; this is a key parameter affecting the properties of the final vulcanizate: the higher the acrylonitrile content the better the oil resistance and the less rubbery the material—particularly at low temperatures. NBR is frequently blended with polyvinylchloride (PVC) to improve the ability of NBR to withstand attack by ozone, etc.

Similar comments on processing, vulcanization and reinforcement apply to nitrile rubber as to SBR, except that for optimum high-temperature endurance silica fillers are sometimes favoured over carbon black. The liquid diluents used are dissimilar to those used for SBR—phthalate plasticizers and aliphatic esters being commonly used to improve the low temperature flexibility of NBR.

Carboxylated and hydrogenated nitrile rubbers are both elastomers in their own right and have their own processing requirements.

37.4.7 Ethylene–propylene rubbers

Reinforcement by carbon black, or sometimes silica, is often required for ethylene–propylene rubbers (EPDM and EPM); particular care needs to be taken with dispersion of the filler. Cross-linking of EPM rubbers is achieved with peroxide systems. For EPDM cross-linking is possible with a vulcanizing system based on sulphur and supported by powerful accelerators; however, peroxide vulcanizates are also used, especially when non-staining and improved high-temperature properties are required. Large quantities of carbon black filler and diluent oil may be incorporated into ethylene–propylene rubbers under favourable conditions. Since reactions may take place between peroxides and naphthenic or aromatic oils, paraffinic oils are the commonly used diluent for EPMs; for sulphur cured EPDMs paraffinic and naphthenic oils are used.

37.4.8 Chloroprene rubbers

The different classes of chloroprene rubber (CR) exhibit rather different processing behaviours: sulphur modified grades can be permanently softened by chemical peptizers and deliberately or inadvertently by heat before vulcanization. Vulcanization is generally carried out with sulphur free systems for all classes of polychloroprene at temperatures in the range 150–205°C. The vulcanizing system is usually based on metal oxides, typically of zinc and magnesium; red lead oxide cures can be used to give improved water resistance. CR can also be vulcanized with sulphur based systems.

Polychloroprene possesses some inherent resistance to fire but its performance, and that of many other rubbers, can be improved by avoiding the use of flammable additives and by incorporating combustion-inhibiting additives such as antimony trioxide, which acts synergistically with CR, zinc borate and hydrated alumina.

Inclusion of carbon black filler in CR formulations is standard, although the intrinsic strength of the material means that filler reinforcement is not obligatory. Naphthenic and aromatic oils are used as diluents. Ester plasticizers can also be used to soften the final vulcanizate at room and especially low temperatures; however, their incorporation can facilitate (time dependent) low-temperature crystallization and under some circumstances can, paradoxically, lead to the material being stiffer after long times at low temperature. Use of sulphur in the vulcanizing system and the presence of certain resinous plasticizers inhibits low-temperature crystallization.

37.4.9 Polyurethane rubbers

The term 'polyurethane rubber' applies to a broad class of linear block co-polymer materials: alternating molecular blocks of isocyanates, polyols and other substances.

An elastomeric product can be produced from a 'castable' polyurethane in a 'one-shot' process by reacting polyol, di-isocyanate and chain extender. More commonly, the polyol and diisocyanate are reacted together to form a prepolymer. The finished elastomer is formed by the prepolymer being 'cross-linked' by a diol or diamine chain extender. A considerable amount of cross-linking often occurs after removal of the product from the mould.

More 'conventional' (in rubber terms) processing and vulcan-ization can be applied to the 'millable' polyurethanes. In general, these are of relatively low molecular weight and are essentially linear polymers. Cross-linking is achieved by a sulphur, peroxide or diisocyanate cure system, depending on the type of millable polyurethane. Fillers are sometimes used but are not obligatory in polyurethanes which often have intrinsic strength.

Thermoplastic polyurethane rubbers (TPU) were among the first commercial thermoplastic elastomers. They include truly elastomeric materials but are processed and formed in ways more akin to plastics than to conventional rubbers. Elastic recovery tends to be poorer for TPUs than for the castable grades.

37.4.10 Silicone rubbers

Many silicone rubbers are not cured by any process resembling conventional vulcanization, and cure conditions are extremely varied for these materials.

The familiar room temperature vulcanizing (RTV) one-pack silicone rubbers (for bath sealant, etc.) are cured by atmospheric humidity. Some two-pack RTV silicone rubbers (for flexible moulds, etc.) are cured by addition $(A + B \rightarrow C)$ and others by condensation $(A + B \rightarrow C + H_2O)$ cross-linking reactions.

Neither methyl-containing (MQ) nor phenyl-containing (PMQ) rubbers can be vulcanized with sulphur: peroxide cross-linking is generally used. Vinyl containing silicone rubbers (VMQ and PVMQ) are also normally cross-linked by a peroxide. An alternative method of cross-linking is 'hydro-silation', which involves the reaction between a polymer containing vinyl groups and a material containing hydrosilane (Si–H) groups; this is the type of reaction used in the cure of liquid silicone rubbers, for example.

Silicone rubbers tend to be intrinsically weak; the use of reinforcing fillers is, therefore, of crucial importance: fine silica powder with a 'high structure' (strong tendency to agglomerate) is most commonly used.

37.4.11 Chlorosulphonated polyethylene

A significant proportion of chlorosulphonated polyethylene (CSM) rubber is used in sheet form without curing. However, a wide range of cross-linking systems are available, each giving particular advantages and disadvantages. Carbon black may be used as a filler, although other fillers such as silica enable bright colours, including brilliant white, to be achieved. Liquid diluents are sometimes used, but for high-temperature applications these need to be chosen with care.

37.5 Moulding of thermoplastic elastomers

Thermoplastic elastomers (TPEs), like other thermoplastic materials, are set into shape by cooling of the hot melt. This contrasts with conventional rubbers whose final shape is fixed by vulcanization. Moulding can, therefore, be much faster for TPEs than for traditional elastomers; furthermore, it is more practicable to reuse TPE scrap (see also Section 37.4). These two features together with the ability to cover a wide range of moduli have led to a rapid increase in the use of TPEs in recent years. The properties of moulded TPEs are, however, more sensitive to details of flow in the mould than is the case for mould-vulcanizing elastomers. This, and the fact that most TPEs show poorer elastic recovery than do high-quality cross-linking elastomers, is not a great disadvantage in a large number of applications. Whereas for conventional elastomers compounding is generally carried out by the component manufacturer, for thermoplastic elastomers precompounded grades are supplied, normally in particulate form.

Highly plasticized polyvinylchloride (PVC) can be regarded as an early TPE, perhaps because of its poor elasticity. Most present-day TPEs have been introduced over the last 30 years. There are two main classes of TPEs: the block co-polymers and the physical blends, although there are also materials with thermally labile (reformable) cross-links, e.g. ionomeric polymers, which can be classed as TPEs.

37.5.1 Block co-polymer thermoplastic elastomers

Block co-polymer TPEs are composed of alternate blocks of hard polymer (high glass transition temperature or crystalline) and soft rubbery polymer (low glass transition temperature) on a molecular scale. At high temperatures the 'hard' segments are sufficiently soft to allow flow into shape to take place. However, at moderate operating temperatures the hard segments link the soft segments together and have a similar function to chemical cross-links and reinforcing filler in a conventional vulcanized and filled rubber. Styrene–butadiene–styrene (SBS) polymers are an early example: the glassy polystyrene blocks link the rubbery polybutadiene blocks. Some ethylene–vinyl–acetate (EVA) materials can also be regarded as TPEs.

Polyether–polyester block co-polymer rubbers first became commercially available a decade after SBS, but now, together with polyurethane and polyether–polyamide materials, epito-mize the high mechanical performance TPEs. In polyether–polyester TPEs most of the polyester (hard) material is crystalline at operating temperature but some is in the amorphous phase with the polyether. This morphology makes for a strong material.

Polyurethane TPEs consist of urethane-sparse (soft) and urethane-rich (hard) segments; their morphology is broadly similar to that of polyether–polyester TPEs.

Polyether–polyamide block co-polymer TPEs consist of soft (polyether) and hard (polyamide) segments.

37.5.2 Thermoplastic polyolefin elastomers

These materials (sometimes known as TPOs) are essentially physical blends between rubbers such as ethylene–propylene rubber (EPM, EPDM), natural rubber (NR) or nitrile rubber (NBR) and polyolefin thermoplastics— typically polypropylene but sometimes polyethylene.[11] Either the rubber or the thermo-plastic may be the continuous phase, depending on the proportions present, method of preparation and other factors. More rubbery materials can be obtained by vulcanization of the rubbery phase during blending with the thermoplastic (rather than prior to blending); these materials are sometimes called 'thermoplastic elastomer alloys'. Further cross-linking is sometimes carried out after the formation of the final product, thereby blurring the demarcation between these materials and conventional elastomers. Fillers and liquid diluents are sometimes incorporated into TPEs, although such additions are not normally made by the moulder as they can adversely affect the morphology of the TPO.

37.6 Properties of elastomers

The properties of an elastomer are normally categorized into mechanical aspects such as strength, modulus or damping, and into the elastomer's tolerance to environmental factors such as high or low temperature, and exposure to oils or ozone. The balance between the importance of mechanical properties and the degree of hostility of the environment will help determine whether an elastomer is suitable for a particular function. Simplified tables and guides to the performance of different elastomers may sometimes be misleading, as environmental factors can interact with each other and with mechanical conditions. Although indications are given here of some of the complications, the primary concern in the present section is with broad indications of elastomer behaviour.

Certain elastomers, notably natural rubber (NR) and chloroprene rubber (CR), crystallize on stretching to high strains giving these materials inherent advantages in strength and resistance to fatigue. Non-strain-crystallizing elastomers such as silicone rubber and most styrene–butadiene rubbers (SBRs) require reinforcing fillers such as finely divided carbon black or silica powder to give them the strength required for many applications. Some rubbers, such as ethylene–propylene rubber and silicone rubber, have high innate resistance to degradation by ozone and diatomic oxygen in the atmosphere, whereas others, notably nitrile (NBR) and fluorinated hydrocarbon rubbers, are relatively unaffected by many mineral (petroleum-based) oils.

The design of a component can have a profound influence on the performance with regard to fatigue or environmental attack; fatigue life can be greatly improved by the avoidance of stress concentrations, while thick sections of 'non-resistant' rubber can often function adequately despite oil splashes or ozone attack.

Many elastomers capable of withstanding high temperatures for long periods without deterioration are significantly weaker at elevated temperatures. Other elastomers can sometimes be used successfully above their normal operating limit. What constitutes an acceptably long life varies according to the application from hours, or even less, to many decades.

It must also be emphasized that the properties for a given elastomer type can vary widely depending on 'compounding', ingredients, and processing details (see Section 37.4). Furthermore, elastomers are frequently blended with each other.

37.6.1 Natural rubber

Natural rubber's (NR) combination of inherent strength and high elasticity mean that, mechanically, it sets the standard for other elastomers. The damping of NR vulcanizates is generally low. It is unsuitable for heavy exposure to mineral oils; because of this and its inability to tolerate temperatures much above 100°C, NR is classified as a 'general-purpose' rubber. It is, however, resistant to a surprisingly wide range of liquids. NR's vulnerability (and that of other elastomers such as SBR) to oxidative ageing and ozone attack can be overcome in many circumstances by incorporating protective agents and avoiding high stresses at the surface of the component; in others the bulk of a component means that some surface attack is acceptable.

A typical operational temperature range is -60 to $+80°C$ (continuous). Time-dependent stiffening due to crystallization can occur at temperatures well above $-60°C$; the maximum crystallization rate occurs in the region of $-25°C$. Although such stiffening is reversed by moderate strains or warming, the use of crystallization-resistant (e.g. conventionally sulphur vulcanized) formulations may be advisable in some applications.

37.6.2 Synthetic cis-polyisoprene

Isoprene rubbers (IR) are chemically the closest of the synthetic rubbers to NR, although they contain a slightly lower percentage of cis-1,4-polyisoprene and have significantly less molecular branching. The vulcanizates are typically somewhat weaker than NR, especially at elevated temperatures.[13] A typical operational temperature range for IR is -60 to $+80°C$.

37.6.3 Butyl rubbers

The damping of butyl rubber (IIR) is typically much higher than that of NR, and this attribute is exploited in some applications.

Among the elastomers, IIR has one of the lowest permeabilities to gases, although the permeabilities of some epichlorohydrin rubbers and NBRs can be even lower. IIR has good resistance to oxidation and ozone but not to many mineral oils. Resistance to damage by flexing, abrasion and tearing can, with appropriate compounding, come close to that of NR, but IIR does have somewhat higher creep, and lower tensile strength. The typical operational temperature range is -60 to $+120°C$.

37.6.4 Styrene–butadiene rubbers

Like NR, SBRs are vulnerable to mineral oils and often require protection against oxidation and ozone attack. Strength properties can be greatly improved by appropriate fillers. Filled SBR has good abrasion resistance but is significantly weaker than NR in other respects. Mechanical damping is typically somewhat higher than for NR. A representative operational temperature range for SBRs is -40 to $+80°C$.

37.6.5 Butadiene rubbers

Butadiene rubbers (BRs) are commonly available with low, medium, high and very high ($>96\%$) contents of cis-butadiene monomeric units. (Materials such as trans-polybutadiene rubber are not dealt with here.) Very high cis content BRs strain crystallize and this somewhat improves the otherwise low strength.

BRs, like NR and SBR, frequently require protection against oxygen and are vulnerable to mineral oils. Mechanical damping can be even lower than for NR. However, other strength properties are acceptably high only for filled vulcanizates. BR is frequently used in blends with NR and SBR to enhance abrasion resistance. The normal operational temperature range is -70 to $+80°C$.

37.6.6 Nitrile rubbers

Nitrile rubbers (NBRs) were some of the first oil-resistant elastomers and continue to be popular for this reason. They have better resistance than does CR to oils and, when specially compounded, are more resistant to heat ageing, but are significantly weaker and less rubbery than CR. Oil resistance and minimum usable temperature both increase with acrylonitrile content. NBRs can be attacked by ozone and are sometimes blended with polyvinyl chloride (PVC) to increase their resistance.

Carboxylated nitrile rubber (XNBR) has significantly improved strength and abrasion properties, and hydrogenated nitrile rubber (HNBR) has excellent performance at high temperatures in chemically difficult environments.

The operational temperature range is -20 to $+110°C$.

37.6.7 Ethylene–propylene rubbers

Ethylene–propylene rubbers are a range of materials essentially immune to ozone cracking and attack by diatomic oxygen. Other useful attributes include the ability to accept high loadings of filler. These rubbers have good tolerance to water, but not to mineral oils. Inherently much weaker than NR, their strength properties can be fairly good if appropriate fillers are used. Although good bonding can be achieved it is potentially more difficult than for many other elastomers. EPM has generally better high temperature performance than does EPDM.

The operational temperature range of ethylene–propylene rubbers is -40 to $+130°C$.

376.8 Chloroprene rubbers

Chloroprene rubbers (CRs) have greater tolerance than NR to high temperatures, mineral oils and oxygen, while their strength properties approach those of NR. Chlorine compounds evolved on combustion give CR a level of fire retardancy but, in some circumstances, can pose problems themselves because of toxicity and corrosion, for example. Improved fire resistance can be obtained with appropriate additives. Special formulations may be required for prolonged contact with water.

Crystallization-resistant grades are available, but in other grades quite rapid crystallization can take place especially at temperatures around $-10°C$.

A normal operational temperature range for CR is -30 to $+100°C$.

37.6.9 Polyurethane rubbers

Urethane rubbers comprise a particularly wide range of materials and thus it is difficult to make general statements on performance. Many are strong materials, very much stiffer, less elastic and possessing higher mechanical damping than NR; several types have very good resistance to abrasion. Urethane elastomers are generally tolerant of oxygen and mineral oils, but polyester type urethane (AU) rubbers are vulnerable to degradation by moisture (hydrolysis), especially in warm conditions, and to consequent microbial attack. Polyether type urethane (EU) rubbers are very much more resistant to aqueous fluids, although these too can be attacked at high temperatures. On combustion, polyurethanes can produce highly toxic substances.

The operational temperature range of urethane rubbers is -30 to $+80°C$.

37.6.10 Silicone rubbers

Silicone rubbers are notable for their wide operational temperature range and their excellent resistance to oxygen. Their already good fire resistance can be enhanced by appropriate additives. The permeability of silicones to gases is higher than for many elastomers; they are inherently weak materials, although significant improvements in strength properties can be obtained by using appropriate fillers. Apart from fluorosilicones, the tolerance of silicone rubbers to mineral oils is not good. The performance of silicone rubbers at high temperatures can be adversely affected if they are located in a confined space.

The operational temperature range of silicone rubbers is typically -90 to $+230°C$.

37.6.11 Chlorosulphonated polyethylene

Chlorosulphonated polyethylene (CSM) rubbers are notable for their ability to produce brilliant white yet durable vulcanizates. They are resistant to water and to oxygen, and moderately so to mineral oils (depending on the chlorine content of the CSM). They are more resistant to fire than are many other elastomers. The strength properties of these generally rather stiff elastomers are moderately good.

The operational temperature range of CSM rubbers is -20 to $+120°C$.

37.6.12 Chlorinated polyethylene

Chlorinated polyethylene (CM) rubbers are resistant to oxygen and water. They have fair tolerance to mineral oils. CM rubbers are less rubbery than CSM rubbers, themselves not very rubbery elastomers.

A typical operational temperature range of CM rubbers is -20 to $+100°C$.

37.6.13 Ethylene–methylacrylate rubber

Ethylene–methylacrylate rubber (AEM) is notable for its ability to give high mechanical damping over a wide temperature range. It is also capable of accepting substantial amounts of filler (fire-retardants, for example). Vulcanizates of this rubber have generally good resistance to oxygen and to water, are moderately tolerant of mineral oils and have fair strength properties.

A representative operational temperature range of AEM is -40 to $+150°C$.

37.6.14 Fluorinated hydrocarbon rubbers

Fluorinated hydrocarbon rubbers (FPM or FKM) have excellent resistance to mineral oils, oxygen and high temperatures and are, therefore, classed as speciality elastomers. They are also tolerant of water, but the strength properties of their vulcanizates are only moderate and tend to be stiffer than for many other elastomers. The density of FKM is $c.$ 50% higher than that of natural rubber.

The operational temperature range of FKM is -20 to $+230°C$.

37.6.15 Polysulphide rubbers

Polysulphide rubbers are noted for their resistance to a wide range of fluids including mineral oils and water; they tolerate oxygen well. Polysulphides have low gas permeability but are mechanically rather weak.

A normal operational temperature range of polysulphide rubbers is -40 to $+80°C$.

37.6.16 Epichlorohydrin rubbers

Epichlorohydrin rubbers have good resistance to oxygen and many mineral oils. ECO (the co-polymer of epichlorohydrin and ethylene oxide) can give low mechanical damping. Gas permeability for CO (the homopolymer) can be significantly lower than for butyl rubber. However, epichlorohydrin rubbers can show some vulnerability to water; their strength properties are fair.

The operational temperature range is -10 to $+130°C$ for CO and -20 to $+130°C$ for ECO.

37.6.17 Polypropylene oxide rubber

Polypropylene oxide rubber (GPO) is resistant to attack by oxygen and is fairly tolerant of water and of mineral oils.

Vulcanizates of the material can give low mechanical damping but are not particularly strong.

The operational temperature range of GPO is typically -50 to $+130°$C.

37.6.18 Ethylene–vinyl acetate rubbers

The properties of these materials depend markedly on composition. Ethylene–vinyl acetate (EVA) rubbers have good resistance to oxygen and to water. They have some tolerance to petroleum based oils. Their strength properties are fair.

The operational temperature range of EVA rubbers is -40 to $+120°$C.

37.6.19 Polynorbornene rubbers

Polynorbornene rubbers (PNRs) are highly plasticized polynorbornene and the properties of the vulcanizates can depend strongly on the plasticizing oil. PNRs are notable for the fact that very soft materials can be obtained with reasonable strength properties. These rubbers are generally tolerant of water but are vulnerable to many mineral oils and to oxygen.

The operational temperature range of PNRs is -40 to $+80°$C.

37.6.20 Properties of thermoplastic elastomers

In general, thermoplastic elastomers (TPEs) show less complete immediate recovery after deformation than do many conventional elastomers and their creep rates also tend to be higher. Harder materials can be obtained with TPEs than is normal for most conventional elastomers (even polyurethanes); however, for these high modulus TPEs yield strains may be only c. 10%. Among the TPEs block co-polymer types (e.g. polyether–polyamide, polyether–polyester and polyurethane TPEs) are available which have Young's moduli of many hundreds of MPa.

37.6.20.1 Styrene–butadiene–styrene block copolymers and related materials

The resistance to the environment of styrene–butadiene– styrene (SBS) block co-polymers is similar to that of SBR, but is improved in hydrogenated grades. A typical operational temperature range is -60 to $+80°$C, although strength can be significantly reduced at temperatures below the upper limit.

37.6.20.2 Polyether–polyester block co-polymers

Polyether–polyester block co-polymers (YPBOs) are high strength materials which are resistant to ozone and also to mineral oils and many other fluids. At high temperatures, additives may be required to give protection against attack by water.

The operational temperature range of YPBOs is -40 to $+120°$C.

37.6.20.3 Polyurethane thermoplastic elastomers

Thermoplastic polyurethane (TPU) elastomers are generally strong materials which have good resistance to tearing and abrasion. TPUs, particularly polyester types, have high tolerance of ozone and of many mineral oils, but have some susceptibility to hydrolysis (attack by water). Resistance to water is better for ether based types and for harder materials (see Section 37.6.9).

The operational temperature range of TPUs is -40 to $+110°$C.

37.6.20.4 Ethylene–vinyl acetate co-polymers

Thermoplastic EVAs have good resistance to ozone but are vulnerable to mineral oils. Although not inherently flame resistant they are capable of accepting large amounts of fire retardant filler; the resulting materials are not readily flammable and give off only minimal levels of noxious gases and smoke. Thermoplastic EVAs are not normally classed as high-strength materials.

The operational temperature range of thermoplastic EVAs is -30 to $+80°$C.

37.6.20.5 Polyether–polyamide block co-polymers

These materials are resistant to ozone and a wide range of fluids, including petroleum-based oils. They have good strength and fatigue properties. They have lower densities (by c. 20%) than TPUs.

The operatational temperature range of polyether–polyamide block co-polymers is -40 to $+140°$C.

37.6.20.6 Thermoplastic polyolefin rubbers

The properties of thermoplastic polyolefin (TPO) rubbers vary very widely according to the type of rubber and thermoplastic and the method of preparation of the TPO. However, many TPOs have high resistance to ozone and general weathering. Resistance to petroleum-based oils is generally not good unless an oil-resistant rubber is used. Many TPOs cannot withstand such high stresses as the block co-polymer polyether–polyester, polyether–polyamide or the polyurethane TPEs and they are less resistant to abrasion. Some soft TPOs can, however, withstand and recover from high strains. The operational temperature range depends on the polymers used, but for EPDM/PP TPOs is -50 to $+120°$C.

37.7 Example applications

Although not used in such quantities as some other classes of materials, elastomers perform important functions in many present-day structures, especially where seals or flexible joints are required. Elastomers are used extensively to protect other materials from abrasion or corrosive fluids; they are also used to protect structures from vibration, shock or even earthquakes.

Elastomers can be: unvulcanized or partially vulcanized; unreinforced or reinforced with fabric or with steel plates; monolithic or cellular.

37.7.1 Buildings

Elastomers are used in many buildings for effective and durable weatherproofing of roofs. Elastomers with good environmental resistance such as ethylene–propylene rubber (EPM, EPDM), chlorosulphonated polyethylene (CSM), butyl rubber and plasticized polyvinylchloride (PVC), which can be regarded as a thermoplastic elastomer, are popular in single-ply roofing. Frequently, the elastomers are not vulcanized. CSM is particularly suitable where a brilliant-white surface is required for thermal or aesthetic reasons. Elastomer composites are also used for roofing: polyester reinforced EPDM or glass-fibre-reinforced chloroprene rubber (CR) coated with CSM, for example (*Figure 37.3*). Although bituminous material is commonly used for roof membranes, its temperature-dependent mechanical properties are not always adequate; these can be improved by additions of elastomeric material; styrenic block co-polymers and natural rubber are two of the elastomers employed for this purpose. EPDM, silicones, CR and now thermoplastic elastomers (thermo-

Figure 37.3 High-school building in Värnamo, Sweden: 9200 m² roof sheeting; polyester reinforced EPDM. (Photograph courtesy of Värnamo Isolerduk AB, Värnamo, Sweden)

plastic polyolefin (TPO) alloy) provide preformed joints for curtain walling and other types of exterior cladding panels (*Figure 37.4*). Gaskets are often made from expanded elastomer— frequently CR is used. For *in situ* formed expansion joints, polysulphide, silicone, acrylic and polyurethane elastomers are used—either uncured or partially cured. Seals for windows are commonly made from EPDM and sometimes CR, and now thermoplastic elastomers (TPO alloy). Again excellent environmental resistance is a key factor.

Damp-proof membranes for floors and also walls can be made by applying a coat of elastomer-based material (frequently natural rubber (NR)) before the cementatious layer.

Elastomers are widely exploited in intumescent and other fire seals and coatings, especially where flexibility is required. Depending on the application, systems such as epoxy/polysulphide elastomer or rubbers, such as ethylene–propylene, capable of accepting high loadings of appropriate fillers are used. Lattices, of styrene–butadiene rubber (SBR) or NR, for example, added to cementatious surfaces can improve crack resistance and durability in some circumstances.

Whole buildings, or parts of them, can be isolated against ground-borne vibration by supporting the structure on appropriately designed bearing pads. Good strength properties and proven durability are of paramount importance here and NR or polychloroprene rubber (CR) are the elastomers of choice (*Figure 37.5*). The bulk of the components and the low thermal conductivity of rubber gives NR a good margin of safety in the case of a fire.[13] If further fire resistance is required, the bearings may be covered in fire-retardant material.

An extension of this application has been to protect buildings and their contents against earthquakes by means of elastomeric bearings (*Figure 37.6*). Ability to withstand large strains, relatively low modulus and, above all, stability of bulk properties

over many decades are all requirements of the vulcanizate which is generally invariably based on NR.

NR or CR bearing pads can also be fitted to allow for (differential) thermal expansion in buildings or parts of buildings. Cellular elastomers are frequently used for sound deadening within buildings.

37.7.2 Fixtures, fittings and services

Elastomeric flooring in the workplace or in public places (e.g. stations and airports) performs specific functions. Ethylene–propylene rubber (EPM, EPDM), NR or combinations of elastomers provide non-slip surfaces. While NR, SBR or EPDM incorporating specialized carbon black filler produce electrically conductive and anti-static flooring. More basic impact and chemical-resistant floor coatings can be made from epoxy/polysulphide rubber. EPDM is a popular material used for draught proofing strip because of its environmental resistance.

Because of its good all-round tolerance to aqueous environments, EPDM is also widely used in pipe joint seals for potable water and waste-water pipelines; the use of NR in these applications dates back over 100 years. Seals for oil and gas pipelines are generally based on nitrile (NBR) and epichlorohydrin (CO, ECO) rubbers because these have resistance to the substances concerned (see also Section 37.7.5).

Mastics based on elastomers such as styrene–butadiene–styrene (SBS) are used for adhering wall panels and plywood subflooring. Seals for insulating, 'double', glazing require good environmental resistance: polysulphide, EPDM, urethane, butyl, silicone and thermoplastic (e.g. TPO alloy type) elastomers are used according to the balance of properties required and cost. In thermal, solar panels, EPDM, nitrile, silicone and thermoplastic elastomers are all used.

Figure 37.4 Curtain walling on the Windmill Hill site, Swindon, UK, sealed by Neoprene gaskets. (Photograph courtesy of The Leyland and Birmingham Rubber Co. Ltd)

Figure 37.5 Alexander Road Development, Camden Town, London, UK. Supported by over 1400 NR/steel ground-borne noise isolation bearings. (Photograph courtesy of the Malaysian Rubber Producers' Research Association)

Figure 37.6 Los Angeles Fire Department, Emergency Control Center. Seismic isolation by NR/steel bearings. (Photograph courtesy of the Malaysian Rubber Producers' Research Association)

Conveyor belting frequently has a composite structure, with NR or SBR normally forming the carcass in general-purpose belting. Vulcanizates based on EPDM often form the cover if heat resistance is required, while CR, NBR or NBR/PVC elastomers are used for oil resistance. CR and PVC are also employed for their superior fire resistance—in mining for example. Belting can also be made from urethane rubber. Moving walkways are composite structures, but have NR as a major component because of its strength properties.

Elastomeric seals are likely to be used whenever fluids (e.g. water or air) are piped or ducted within buildings. For example, EPDM seals are widely used in central heating systems.

A further major application of elastomers in construction is in electrical cable and flex. Plasticized PVC is used for general wiring (50 Hz, <250 V) but the polarity of the material rules it out as an insulator for high-voltage or high-frequency applications. Furthermore, the physical properties of plasticized PVC are inadequate for mechanically arduous conditions. In high-voltage and high-frequency communications cables insulation can be provided by a non-polar elastomer such as EPDM or by cross-linked polyethylene; thermoplastic elastomers (TPO type) can also be used in these areas. The choice of cable jacketing material depends on the mechanical and chemical operating environment. Thus for good mechanical properties, NR is often chosen. Where good resistance to abrasion is required, urethane rubber is an option. Chlorosulphonated polyethylene (CSM) cable jacketing has a good balance of oil, heat and general environmental resistance characteristics and can be brightly coloured. When fire resistance is a particular requirement, halogenated elastomers, e.g. CR or plasticized PVC, may be used. For cable jacketing with low toxicity/smoke emission, elastomers such as EPDM, ethylene–vinyl acetate, or ethylene–methylacrylate are heavily loaded with fire-retardant additives.

37.7.3 Piping, hose, reservoirs and tanks

Where there are abrasive particles present in a fast-flowing aqueous environment, channels and tanks are frequently lined with NR or polyurethane to protect the underlying material (e.g. steel). Where the mechanical conditions are less arduous, butyl and sometimes CSM rubbers are used.

Butyl rubber (sometimes blended with EPDM) finds frequent application as a waterproofing membrane for ponds and reservoirs, while NR or CR is often employed for waterstops. CSM rubber, with a suitable reinforcing fabric, has been used as a cover material for potable water reservoirs. Flexible piping and hose are two further areas which exploit the particular characteristics of elastomers.

37.7.4 Roads, railways and bridges

In many bridges provision for thermal expansion of the deck is made by supporting it on compliant bearings. Such bearings can be plain elastomer pads, laminated rubber/steel pads or combined elastomer and slider units ('pot bearings'). The elastomers of choice for use in bridge bearings are generally NR and CR; unconfined rubber discs in combined elastomer/slider units are the exception—these exploit the high modulus, high strength characteristics of urethane rubber.

Protective, waterproof, elastomeric coatings for bridge abutments are frequently NR or urethane rubber based. While preformed joint seals for roads, road bridges and runways are predominently made from CR in the USA, EPDM is used extensively in northern Europe and SBR in Holland. The housings for 'cats eyes' (the reflective lane markers ubiquitous in the UK) are made from NR.

Scientific investigation of the modification of bituminous road materials by elastomers dates back some 50 years.[14] Elastomers can be incorporated into the bituminous road materials for two main reasons: to facilitate road making at lower temperatures and to improve the performance of the road surface. Particular applications which benefit from elastomer modification include: overseal banding for crack repair, stress-relieving membrane to avoid surface cracking, bridge deck membranes, and surface dressing binder for improved chipping retention on 'highly stressed' sites (e.g. inclines and roundabouts). Benefits of elastomeric modification on longer stretches of road can include greatly improved durability and improved grip. Depending on the detailed requirements, climate and cost factors, the elastomer may be a thermoplastic elastomer, ethylene–vinyl acetate (EVA) or styrene–butadiene–styrene for example, natural rubber or reclaimed rubber.

Elastomers are frequently employed to improve the performance of rail systems where concrete sleepers are used. Rail pads are generally made from NR but EVA is sometimes used, while (under the) ballast mats made from NR are used in Germany to reduce vibration to the surroundings. Other systems of vibration isolation by means of elastomers have been implemented where ground-borne vibration from trains would be a particular problem—as was the case in the London–Heathrow underground link.

37.7.5 Oil, gas, chemical engineering and mining

Vibration isolation is a particular requirement on oil rigs and production platforms where accommodation modules and noisy plant can be in close proximity. NR and CR are the normal elastomers for the construction of vibration isolation bearings, although other elastomers may be used if there are special requirements; frequently the bearings double as compliant elements to allow relative thermal expansion between supported and supporting structures.

Highly stressed flexible joints for tethering systems in offshore oil platforms have been made from NR and NBR, while polyurethane is employed as a coating in many situations, e.g. mooring cable buoys in flotation units for oil-spill containment barriers. Urethane rubber has also been used to make pipeline cleaning 'pigs'.

Numerous oil-well parts are made from NBR since high acrylonitrile content NBR has very good oil resistance. Particular circumstances may require the use of other elastomers, for example carboxylated nitrile rubber (XNBR) for improved abrasion resistance. Under conditions requiring improved resistance to temperature, oil and other media, fluorinated hydrocarbon elastomers are used. Examples of elastomeric oil well/pipeline parts are seals, O-rings and blowout preventers.

In piping of gas, elastomers find widespread applications for seals, valves, etc. Typically, NBR and epichlorohydrin rubber are used.

In mining, elastomers are used in conveyor belting; fire resistance is often a requirement and the elastomers are chosen accordingly. Abrasion-resistant ball-mill linings can be made from NR; where oils are involved in the separation process XNBR can be used. NR, urethane rubber or XNBR/PVC blends form abrasion-resistant chute linings and screens.

Elastomers are employed in chemical engineering for a wide range of applications including expansion bellows and vibration dampers; the choice of elastomer type depends on the operating temperature and chemical environment.

37.7.6 Miscellaneous

One of the ways in which steep slopes of loose earth can be stabilized is by applying suitable rubber latex loaded with grass seed.

The use of impact absorbing mats to avoid injury in gymnasiums and playgrounds is extensive. The mats can be made of NR, SBR or butyl rubber. Other types of sports surfaces, e.g. high-quality running tracks, exploit the properties of elastomers to advantage (*Figure 37.7*).

Cellular rubbers can have much lower stiffness than the solid material, especially to volume changes; furthermore, they can have even lower thermal conductivities. These two characteristics lead to a wide range of applications. Latex foam (often NR or SBR) is widely used as a cushioning material for carpets, etc., while upholstery, matresses, etc., can be made from latex foam or expanded urethane rubber. Expanded urethane and polyethylene are ubiquitous domestic insulation materials and expanded CR is widely used in external gaskets in construction (see section 37.7.1).

37.8 Elastomers—appropriate and inappropriate use

Elastomers are a diverse family of materials and the distinction between them and other engineering polymers is not always a clear one. Nevertheless, designers frequently need to decide whether to use an elastomer and if so which. As illustrated by the foregoing example applications, elastomers are candidate materials wherever flexibility, a high degree of elastic energy absorption, grip/adhesion characteristics or a high Poisson ratio is called for. Elastomers, if appropriately chosen, can also protect the underlying material from abrasive or chemical attack.

37.8.1 Mechanical considerations

One of the first questions to ask in design with an elastomer is whether it can sustain the stresses and strains envisaged in the application. In this context it should be remembered that some rubbers are capable of storing considerably more energy elastically than can, for example, mild steel: natural rubber (NR) can store one order of magnitude more energy per unit volume and some two orders of magnitude more energy per unit mass.

In some situations fatigue is the most likely cause of failure. In some non-strain-crystallizing elastomers cracks can propagate in a time-dependent manner, so it can be inadvisable to subject them to steady high stresses. In strain-crystallizing elastomers such as NR and chloroprene rubber (CR), fatigue cracks generally propagate due to cyclic changes in stress; the rate of crack propagation is greater when the cyclic stress passes through zero and so, to optimize fatigue life, NR or CR components are therefore often designed to be 'preloaded'.

The weak point of a rubber component is frequently the bond between elastomer and metal or other substrate. The problem can be avoided by not using a bond at all, but often this is not possible or desirable. Where rubber–substrate bonds are necessary, strict manufacturing controls must be observed to ensure bond reliability, and particular attention needs to be paid in component design to stresses at the bond.

Other long-term considerations include age hardening/softening and creep. All elastomers have the tendency for their elastic moduli to change with time. In many cases these changes are small, and in others, sulphur vulcanized NR for example, hardening processes (cross-linking) are counterbalanced by softening processes.[15]

In general, articles should be well vulcanized at the time of moulding, or of post-cure if appropriate, to minimize the risk of further cross-linking taking place during service. This can be

Figure 37.7 Running track at Loughborough University, Loughborough, UK, based on urethane bound elastomers. (Photograph courtesy of En-tout-cas plc)

particularly important for certain combinations of elastomer and vulcanizing system which show a 'marching modulus' effect: the high temperature, modulus does not reach a plateau but continues to rise indefinitely. Prolonged vulcanization can alleviate the problem but does not necessarily stop the in-service hardening which can occur in some elastomers as a result of thermal oxidation.

All elastomers creep to some extent under constant load and relax under constant displacement. The two phenomena are related to one another and with damping.[16] Physical (reversible) creep proceeds approximately logarithmically with time and creep rates are often expressed as percentage increase in initial deflection per ten-fold increase (i.e. 'decade') of time. Physical creep rates can be kept low for unfilled elastomers: in the region of 1.5% per decade for unfilled natural rubber vulcanizates, although for filled vulcanizates creep rates are somewhat higher. Creep can also occur through chemical changes taking place in the elastomer. Chemical creep has an approximately linear dependence on time: a typical value for a natural rubber vulcanizate is 0.5% of initial deflection per annum at room temperature for anaerobic conditions.[17,18] For high-damping elastomers greater rates of physical creep can be expected, although it is possible to reduce the overall creep of a component by designing the high damping spring element to be in parallel with a low-damping low-creep element.

37.8.2 Stiffness and dimensional tolerances

Even for a given elastomer an enormous range of stiffness is possible for a component of given overall size and shape. Whereas the objective with steel springs is generally to increase the compliance by design, sometimes to the detriment of fatigue life, this is not generally the case with elastomers; here the aim is often to increase the stiffness in a particular direction by incorporating bonded 'reinforcement' layers.

The amplification of the material Young's modulus (E) to a modified compression modulus (E_c) by the shape-factor (S, *Figure 37.8*) effect is given by:

$$E_c \approx 2S^2 E$$

where $E_c \ll K$, the bulk modulus. The shape-factor effect occurs because the Young's modulus of most elastomers is c. 3 MPa, whereas the bulk modulus is c. 2000 MPa. This difference in moduli can also be exploited in design by confining the rubber (as in a pot bearing for example (see section 37.7.4)). The use of high-modulus urethane elastomers or thermoplastic elastomers provides a complementary approach.

All elastomers possess some damping but the degree varies widely between polymer types and within each polymer type depending on details of compounding as well as operational conditions such as frequency, strain amplitude and mode of

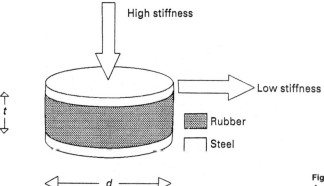

Figure 37.8 The shape factor for rubber/steel bonded units. $A_1 = (\pi d^2)/4$, $A_2 = \pi dt$, shape factor $= A_1/A_2$

deformation. In many cases of dynamic isolation the selected level of damping for a rubber component represents a compromise between off-resonance requirements (where low damping is desirable), and through-resonance/higher frequency requirements (for which higher levels of damping are desirable).[19,20] Resonant frequencies, which are a key feature in vibration isolation, depend on the ratios of relevant masses to the stiffnesses of spring elements.

Although very precise modelling of practical elastomers remains a challenging area, in many situations analytical and, increasingly, numerical methods provide predictions to a reasonable degree of accuracy;[21] accuracies in the order of 20% are normal. As far as the reproducibility of vulcanized rubber springs is concerned, tolerances of 10–15% on stiffness values are routine with much tighter tolerances being readily achievable at extra cost.

The vulcanized elastomer to be used in a component is frequently specified in terms of its indentation hardness, usually in terms of the international rubber hardness degrees (IRHD) scale. Since IRHD measurements are subject to an uncertainty of $\pm 2°$, this implicitly creates an imprecision in the specification. The relationship between hardness and elastic modulus is non-linear and complex, particularly for filled elastomers.[22] However, a change in hardness from 60 to 62 IRHD, for example, generally corresponds to a $\sim 12\%$ increase in modulus.

Virtually all elastomers undergo significant shrinkage on cooling after moulding, 3% (linear) is typical, and this is one of the factors setting normal limits to dimensional tolerances of moulded rubber items. Much finer tolerances can be achieved and several manufacturers specialize in this area of work.

37.8.3 Environmental factors

One of the most important environmental factors for elastomers is temperature: materials which are rubbery at 20°C become brittle at sufficiently low temperatures and can lose their elasticity at sufficiently high temperatures.

Design must take account of brittleness and, when appropriate, melting or pyrolysis temperatures. It is clear, for example, that care needs to be exercised over the use of high acrylonitrile content nitrile rubber (NBR) in Alaska, but there are more subtle points too. It should not be forgotten that the high temperature resistance of an elastomer is often gauged by its ability to resist time-dependent degradation at the elevated temperature rather than by its strength properties at that temperature, which may be more appropriate. Many temperature-resistant elastomers show a marked instantaneous deterioration in creep and strength properties well below the upper limit of their operating range, and this must be allowed for.

Brittleness marks the end-point of a phenomenon sometimes referred to as 'glass hardening', which results from reductions

in mobility of the elastomer molecular chains; glass hardening is essentially instantaneous on the elastomer reaching a given temperature. In contrast to glass hardening, low-temperature crystallization stiffening, in affected elastomers, notably NR and CR, can take place over very short periods or over weeks or months. The low-temperature-crystallization rate is greatest for NR near $-25°C$, whereas for CR the rate is greatest near $-10°C$. At lower temperatures crystallization rate can decrease significantly. Although the effects of this type of stiffening can be diminished or eliminated by warming or large strain cycling, it may be advisable to use crystallization-resistant 'compounds' of NR or CR for some components exposed to low temperatures for long periods.

High or low temperatures are likely to affect a large proportion of the rubber in a component and in so doing can seriously affect its performance. Other potentially harmful influences such as atmospheric gases (e.g. oxygen and ozone), ultraviolet radiation, and liquids (e.g. oils and aqueous fluids) may, in many cases, affect only the surface of a vulnerable elastomer. Factors such as intensity of exposure, the importance of aesthetic considerations, the mode of deformation, and the bulk and life expectancy of the component, need to be allowed for. An elastomer can usually be found which is extremely resistant to a particular kind of chemical attack, but this may not always be an appropriate choice when strength properties or cost considerations are taken into account. Usually a balance must be struck.

Elastomers such as NR and styrene–butadiene rubber (SBR) are not normally thought of as having good weathering resistance but, in many cases, it is more than adequate provided that the components are sufficiently thick. NR bridge bearings are an example; in many cases these can be expected to outlast the bridge itself (*Figure 37.9*). Complications can arise when there are conflicting requirements. Urethane rubber and NR have good resistance to penetrating ionizing radiation but not to high temperatures: the reverse is true of fluorinated elastomers.

It might be thought that urethane rubbers, being resistant to mineral oil, should be widely used in oil seals, but their limited high-temperature range and vulnerability to contaminant water counts against them. At the same time ethylene–propylene (EPDM) rubbers, NRs and SBRs are often loosely referred to as being non-oil-resistant; in fact, they do tolerate well many non-petroleum-based (non-mineral) oils and are used, for example, in certain types of hydraulic brake system.

37.9 Standards and specifications

Standards and specifications relating to elastomers exist to provide safeguards and some guidance; however, they cannot

Figure 37.9 Pelham bridge, Lincoln, UK, 1957 and 1990. (Photograph courtesy of Lincolnshire County Council and the Malayasian Rubber Producers' Research Association)

take the place of experience and expert advice. Given below is a list of some of the more important standards for elastomers and their uses, together with brief comments on the contents of the standard.

37.9.1 General

BS 6716 (1986) Guide to properties and types of rubber.
BS 3734 (1978) Specification for dimensional tolerances of solid moulded and extruded rubber products.
BS 3574 (1989) Specification for controlled storage and packaging of vulcanized rubber and rubber products.
BS 3558 (1980) Glossary of rubber terms.

37.9.2 Test methods for rubber

The following standards are examples of those dealing with small-scale laboratory tests for quality control, material specification, design parameters and assessment of environmental stability, e.g.

BS 903 Methods for physical testing of rubber (Parts A1–A59).

Annual Book of ASTM Standards Section 09.01 Rubber, Natural and Synthetic—General Test methods; Carbon Black.
Various International Standard test methods produced by Technical Committee ISO/TC45 (Rubber and Rubber Products), in most cases these have been adopted as National Standard methods.

37.9.3 Material specifications

37.9.3.1 General classifications

BS 5176 (1975) Specification for classification system for vulcanized rubbers.
ASTM D2000–90 Standard classification system for rubber products in automotive applications. (Although intended for the automotive industry, ASTM D2000 is used for many applications.)
ISO 4632 (1982) Rubber, vulcanized—classification—Part I Description of the classification system.

37.9.3.2 Individual rubber specifications

Note that the word 'compound' in rubber technology refers to a formulation or mixture rather than a chemical compound.

BS 1154 (1986) Natural rubber compounds.
BS 1155 (1986) Natural rubber compounds for extrusion.
BS 2751 (1990) General-purpose acrylonitrile–butadiene rubber compounds (Nitrile rubber).
BS 2752 (1990) Chloroprene rubber compounds.
BS 3227 (1990) Butyl rubber compounds (including halobutyl compounds).
BS 6014 (1990) Ethylene–propylene rubber compounds.

37.9.4 Product specifications

37.9.4.1 Bridge bearings

BS 5400 Section 9.1 (1983) Code of practice for design of bridge bearings.
BS 5400 Section 9.2 (1983) Specification for materials, manufacture and installation of bridge bearings.
ASTM D4014 –89 Specification for plain and steel-laminated elastomeric bearings for bridges.
ISO 6446 Rubber products—Bridge bearings—Specification for rubber materials (to be published).

37.9.4.2 Vibration isolation of buildings

BS 6177 (1982) Guide to selection and use of elastomeric bearings for vibration isolation of buildings.

37.9.4.3 Rail pads

International Union of Railways, UIC 864-5 Technical Specification for the supply of grooved sole plates made of rubber for placing beneath rails.

37.9.4.4 Seals and gaskets

Pipe sealing rings

BS 2494 (1990) Specification for elastomeric joint rings for pipework and pipelines.
ASTM C564–88 Specification for rubber gaskets for cast iron soil pipe and fittings.
ASTM D1869–78 Specification for rubber rings for asbestos-cement pipes.
ASTM C443–85 joints for circular concrete sewer and culvert pipe, using rubber gaskets.
ASTM C505–90 Non-reinforced concrete irrigation pipe with rubber gasket joints.
ISO 4633 (1983) Rubber seals—Joint rings for water supply, drainage and sewerage pipelines—Specification for materials.
ISO 6447 (1983) Rubber seals—Joint rings used for gas supply pipes and fittings—Specification for material.
ISO 6448 (1985) Rubber seals—Joint rings used for petroleum product supply pipes and fittings—Specification for material.

Building gaskets

BS 4255 (1986) Rubber used in preformed gaskets for weather exclusion from buildings—Part I Specification for non-cellular gaskets.
BS 6093 (1981) Code of practice for design of joints and jointing in building construction.
ASTM C509–90 Specification for cellular elastomeric preformed gasket and sealing material.
ASTM C542–90 Specification for lock-strip gaskets.
ASTM C864–90 Specification for dense elastomeric compression seal gaskets, setting blocks and spacers.
ISO 3934 (1978) Rubber building gaskets—Materials in preformed solid vulcanizates used for sealing glazing and panels—Specification.
ISO 5892 (1981) Rubber building gaskets—Materials for preformed solid vulcanized structural gaskets—Specification.

Seals for solar energy systems

ASTM D3667–90 Specification for rubber seals used in flat-plate solar collectors.
ASTM D3771–85 Specification for rubber seals used in concentrating solar collectors.
ASTM D3832–79 Specification for rubber seals containing liquid in solar energy systems.
ASTM D3903–85 Specification for rubber seals used in air-heat transport of solar energy systems.

Highway joints: paving

ASTM D1752–84 Specification for preformed sponge rubber and cork expansion joint fillers for concrete paving and structural construction.
ASTM D2628–81 Specification for preformed polychloroprene elastomeric joint seals for concrete pavements.
ASTM D3542–83 Specification for preformed polychloroprene elastomeric joint seals for bridges.
ISO 4635 (1982) Rubber, vulcanized—Preformed compression

seals for use between concrete motorway paving sections—Specification for material.

37.9.4.5 Reservoir linings

ASTM D3253–81 Specification for vulcanized rubber sheeting for pond, canal and reservoir lining.
ASTM D3254–81 Specification for fabric-reinforced vulcanized rubber sheeting for pond, canal and reservoir lining.

37.9.4.6 Chemical plant linings

BS 6374 Lining of equipment with polymeric material for the process industries—Part 5 (1985) Specification for lining with rubbers.
ASTM D3486–85 Practices for installation of vulcanizable rubber tank linings and pipe linings.

37.9.4.7 Flooring

BS 1711 (1975) Specification for solid rubber flooring.
BS 3187 (1978) Specification for electrically conducting rubber flooring.
BS 8203 (1987) Code of practice for installation of sheet and tile flooring.
BS CP204 Part 2 (1970) Code of practice for *in situ* floor finishes. (Includes cement rubber–latex systems.)

37.9.4.8 Electrical

There are many ISO and ASTM specifications as well as BS specifications in this area, e.g.

BS 6007 (1983) Specification for rubber-insulated cables for electric power and lighting.
BS 6899 (1984) Specification for rubber insulation and sheath of electric cables.

37.9.4.9 Elastomeric roofing

ASTM D3105–85 Index of methods for testing elastomeric and plastomeric roofing and waterproofing material.
ASTM D4637–87 Specification for vulcanized rubber sheet used in single-ply roof membrane. (Nearly completed.)
ASTM D5019–89 Specification for reinforced non-vulcanized polymeric sheet used in roofing membrane.
Rubber Manufacturers Association (USA), minimum requirements for non-reinforced black EPDM rubber sheets for use in roofing application, RMA Roofing Council, IRP-1, 1984.

Specifications for the use of rubbers in roofing are also being drafted by the UK based Single-Ply Membrane Association and various European (CEN) committees.

37.10 Conclusions

Little more than half a century ago elastomer selection posed few problems since there was effectively just one elastomer: natural rubber (NR). Today the situation is very different with well over 30 elastomers available. Some of these materials have opened new possibilities in architecture through their excellent resistance to weathering, others function effectively for years in aggressive fluids at temperatures that would be unthinkable for the natural material. Yet NR, closely followed by styrene–butadiene rubber (SBR), remains the world's most heavily used elastomer because of technical merit and price.

Elastomers make a special contribution to the range of construction materials available because of their elastic deformability. Nevertheless, they remain minority materials poorly understood by many of the technical people who do or could benefit from their use. These circumstances can and do result in costly mistakes being made, sometimes visibly with the failure of a component, on other occasions with the hidden costs of over-specification.

Present-day structures make extensive use of elastomers in roofing, curtain walling and in numerous other less visible sealing and jointing applications. Large numbers of bridges and flyovers are supported on long-lived reliable rubber bearings to allow for thermal expansion.

There has been a noticeable increase in the use of elastomeric pads to reduce ground-borne vibration from rail and other traffic. The reasons are clear: economic pressures for the utilization of sites near railways, coupled with demand for lower noise levels in offices and dwellings. These trends seem certain to be maintained. Noise-exclusion and energy-conservation requirements will mean that tightly fitting, multiply glazed windows will become even more commonplace; elastomers will continue to fulfill important functions in these units.

After an earthquake it is vital that emergency services remain functional and co-ordinated. Earthquake base isolation by rubber bearings of communication and co-ordination centres has recently begun. A major increase in the number of buildings and their contents protected in this way is predicted.

Modification of bituminous road materials by elastomers can result in greatly improved life and performance. However, the high initial cost has been a deterrent. Increasing levels of traffic congestion, combined with a reluctance to see ever more roads built, point to a reassessment of the overall economic costs of road damage and repair. Against this background increased use of elastomers in road materials is a distinct possibility.

Because there are already so many base elastomers available, it appears unlikely that there will be any major expansion in their number in the near future. New blends are, however, sure to appear and some existing ones will gain in popularity. Already thermoplastic elastomer (TPE) blends have begun to be used in architectural aspects of construction, a tendency which is certain to continue. Block co-polymer TPEs are already used in asphalt modification, as are other elastomers, but the newer high-performance TPEs now seem poised to take over some infrastructural roles from speciality elastomers.

Further into the future there may well be major changes in the pattern of supply of base elastomers driven by shortages in petroleum, which is the origin of most synthetic rubbers. There is likely to be a blurring of the boundaries between chemically modified NR and synthetic rubbers, since eventually the feedstocks for synthetic rubbers may be derived from materials that were living months rather than millions of years previously.

The author would like to acknowledge the help of former colleague Peter Lewis of MRPRA in producing this chapter.

37.11 Research and Trade Associations

British Rubber Manufacturers' Association Ltd. (BRMA),
90–91 Tottenham Court Road,
London W1P 0BR, UK.

Malaysian Rubber Producers' Research Association (MRPRA),
Brickendonbury,
Hertford SG13 8NL, UK.

Plastics and Rubber Institute (PRI),
11 Hobart Place,
London SW1W 0HL, UK.

RAPRA Technology Ltd.,
Shawbury,
Shrewsbury SY4 4NR, UK.

References

1 MALAYSIAN RUBBER PRODUCERS' RESEARCH ASSOCIATION, *Natural Rubber Technical Information Sheet D18*, MRPRA, Brickendonbury (1976)

2 MALAYSIAN RUBBER PRODUCERS' RESEARCH ASSOCIATION, *Natural Rubber Technical Information Sheet D19*, MRPRA, Brickendonbury (1976)

3 GENT, A. N. and THOMAS, A. G., 'Mechanics of foamed elastic materials', *Rubb. Chem. Technol.*, **36**, 597–610 (1963)

4 EASTERBROOK, E. K. and ALLEN, R. D., 'Ethylene–propylene rubber', in *Rubber Technology* (ed. Morton, M.), 3rd edn., pp. 274–275, Van Nostrand, New York (1987)

5 INTERNATIONAL ORGANIZATION FOR STANDARDIZATION, *ISO 1629*, Rubber and lattices—Nomenclature (1987)

6 CUNNEEN, J. I. and HIGGINS, G. M. C., 'Cis-trans isomerism in natural polyisoprenes', in *The Chemistry and Physics of Rubber-like Substances—Studies of Natural Rubber Producers' Research Association 2* (ed. Bateman, L.), pp. 19–40, MacLaren, London (1963)

7 MCINTYRE, D., STEPHENS, H. L. and BHOWMICK, A. K., 'Guayule rubber', in *Handbook of Elastomers—New Developments and Technology* (ed. Bhowmick, A. K. and Stephens, H. L.), pp. 1–29, Marcel Dekker, New York (1988)

8 BAKER, C. S. L., 'Modified natural rubber', in *Handbook of Elastomers—New Developments and Technology* (ed. Bhowmick, A. K. and Stephens, H. L.), pp. 31–74, Marcel Dekker, New York (1988)

9 CORBELLI, L., 'Ethylene propylene rubbers', in *Developments in Rubber Technology—2 Synthetic Rubbers* (ed. Whelan, A. and Lee, K. S.), pp. 57–129, Applied Science, London and New York (1981)

10 CROWTHER, B. G., 'Vulcanization by methods other than moulding', in *Rubber Technology and Manufacture* (ed. Blow, C. M. and Hepburn, C.), 2nd edn., pp. 351–356, Butterworths, Oxford (1987)

11 DE, S. K. and BHOWMICK, A. K. (eds), *Thermoplastic Elastomers from Rubber–Plastic Blends*, Ellis Horwood, Chichester (1990)

12 ELLIOTT, D. J., 'Comparative properties of natural rubber and synthetic isoprene rubbers', *NR Technol.*, **18**, 69–74 (1987)

13 DERHAM, C. J. and PLUNKETT, A. P., 'Fire resistance of steel laminated natural rubber bearings', *Natural Rubber Technol.*, **7**, (2), 29–37 (1976)

14 THOMPSON, P. D., 'The use of rubber in road materials', *Civil Eng.*, **57**, 1163–1166 (1962)

15 BARNARD, D. and LEWIS, P. M., 'Oxidative ageing', in *Natural Rubber Science and Technology* (ed. A. D. Roberts), pp. 621–678, Oxford University Press, Oxford (1988)

16 GENT, A. N., 'Relaxation processes in vulcanized rubber. I Relation among stress, relaxation, recovery and hysteresis', *J. Appl. Polym. Sci.*, **6**, 433–441 (1962)

17 DERHAM, C. J., 'Creep and stress relaxation and their relevance to engineering applications', *Proc. Rubber in Engineering Conference*, Imperial College, London, NRPRA (1973)

18 STEVENSON, A., 'Longevity of natural rubber in structural bearings', *Plastics Rubber Process. Appl.*, **5**, 253–258 (1985)

19 MUHR, A. H., 'Transmission of noise through rubber–metal composite springs', *Proc. Inst. Acoust.*, **11**, 627–634 (1989)

20 MUHR, A. H., 'The use of rubber noise stop pads in vibration isolation systems', *Proc. Inst. Acoust.*, **12**, 417–427 (1990)

21 FINNEY, R. H., 'Application of finite element analysis', *Elastomerics*, 18–23 (Jan. 1987)

22 MUHR, A. H., TAN, G. H. and THOMAS, A. G., 'A method of allowing for non-linearity of filled rubber in force-deformation calculations', *J. Natural Rubber Res.*, **3**, 261–276 (1988)

Bibliography

ALLEN, P. W., LINDLEY, P. B. and PAYNE, A. R., *Use of Rubber in Engineering*, Natural Rubber Producers' Research Association, MacLaren, London (1967)

BATEMAN, L., MOORE, C. G., PORTER, M. and SAVILLE, B., Chemistry of vulcanization, in *The Chemistry and Physics of Rubber-like Substances* (ed. Bateman, L.), pp. 449–561, MacLaren, London (1963)

BAYER, *Bayer Polyurethanes Handbook*, English edn, Bayer (1979)

BHOWMICK, A. K. and STEPHENS, H. L. (eds), *Handbook of Elastomers—New Developments and Technology*, Marcel Dekker, New York (1988)

BLACK, R. M., 'Recent developments in cable technology', *Proc. Rubber Plastics Technol.*, **2**, (4) 25–37 (1986)

BLACKLEY, D. C., *Synthetic Rubbers: Their Chemistry and Technology*, Applied Science, London and New York (1983)

BLOW, C. M. and HEPBURN, C. (eds), *Rubber Technology and Manufacture*, Butterworths, Guildford (1987)

Blue Book—Materials, Compounding Ingredients, Machinery and Services for the Rubber Industry, Lippincott & Peto, Akron (1990)

BROWN, R. P., *Physical Testing of Rubber*, 2nd edn, Elsevier Applied Science, London and New York (1986)

BRYDSON, J. A., *Rubbery Materials and Their Compounds*, Elsevier Applied Science, London and New York (1988)

BUCHAN, S., *Rubber in Chemical Engineering*, Federation of British Rubber and Allied Manufacturers and NRPRA (1965)

COVENEY, V. A. and THOMAS, A.G. 'The Role of Natural Rubber in Seismic Isolation—A Perspective', *Kautshuk and Gummi Kunststoffe*, **44**, number 9, 861–865 (1991)

DAMUSIS, A., (ed.) *Sealants*, Rheinhold, New York (1967)

DAVIES, B. J., *The Longevity of Natural Rubber in Engineering Application*, MRPRA, Brickendonbury (1988)

DUPONT, *Elastomer Notebook* (serial)

FELDMAN, D., *Polymeric Building Materials*, Elsevier Applied Science, London and New York (1989)

FERNANDO, M. J. and GUIRGUIS, H. R., 'Natural rubber for improved surfacing', 12th Australian Road Research Board Conference, Hobart, Tasmania, August 1984, *ARRB Proc.*, **12** (2) (1984)

FREAKLEY, P. K. and PAYNE, A. R., *Theory and Practice of Engineering with Rubber*, Applied Science, London and New York (1978)

GÖBEL, E. F., *Rubber Springs Design*, Newnes–Butterworths, Guildford (1974)

Green Book—International Standards for Quality and Packing in Natural Rubber, The International Rubber Quality and Packaging Conferences

GRUNAN, E., *Life Expectancy of Sealants in Building Construction*, Institute for Construction Research, Erstadt, Germany (1974)

HEPBURN, C., *Polyurethane Elastomers*, Applied Science, London and New York (1982)

HEPBURN, C. and REYNOLDS, R. J. W. (eds), *Elastomers: Criteria for Engineering Design*, Applied Science, London and New York (1979)

HOFMANN, W., *Rubber Technology Handbook*, Hanser/Oxford University Press, Oxford (1989)

INTERNATIONAL INSTITUTE OF SYNTHETIC RUBBER PRODUCERS, *The Synthetic Rubber Manual*, 10th edn, International Institute of Synthetic Rubber Producers Inc., Houston (1986)

INTERNATIONAL ORGANIZATION FOR STANDARDIZATION, *ISO Technical Report 7620 Rubber materials—chemical resistance* (1986)

LEGGE, N. R., HOLDEN, G. and SCHROEDER, H. E. (eds) *Thermoplastic Elastomers—a Comprehensive Review*, Hauser, Munich (1987)

LINDLEY, P. B., *Engineering Design with Natural Rubber*, MRPRA, Brickendonbury (1974) (An extensively revised version is to be published in 1991)

LOVEDAY, C. A., 'Performance with workability from modified binders', *J. Inst. Highways Transport* (June 1990)

MERNAGH, L. R. (ed.), *Rubbers Handbook*, Morgan-Grampian/Design Engineering, West Wickham (1969)

MALAYSIAN RUBBER PRODUCERS' RESEARCH ASSOCIATION, *Rubber Developments* (serial), MRPRA, Brickendonbury

MALAYSIAN RUBBER PRODUCERS' RESEARCH ASSOCIATION, *Natural Rubber Engineering Data Sheets*, MRPRA, Brickendonbury (1979–)

MALAYSIAN RUBBER PRODUCERS' RESEARCH ASSOCIATION, *Natural Rubber Formulary and Property Index*, MRPRA, Brickendonbury (1984)

MORTON, M. (ed.), *Rubber Technology*, 3rd edn, Van Nostrand, New York (1987)

MURRAY, R. M. and THOMPSON, D. C., *The Neoprenes*, international edn, E.I. DuPont de Nemours & Co., Wilmington, Delaware (1963)

PLASTICS AND RUBBER INSTITUTE, *Offshore Engineering with Elastomers*, Proc. Conference, Discussion Forum and Exhibition, Plastics and Rubber Institute, London, 5–6 June 1985

RADER, C. P. and STEMPER, J., 'Thermoplastic elastomers—a major innovation in rubber', *Progr. Rubber Plastics Technol.*, **6** (1), 50–99 (1990)

Rubber Red Book, Communication Channels Inc., Atlanta (1990)

ROBERTS, A. D. (ed.), *Natural Rubber Science and Technology*, Oxford University Press, Oxford (1988)

ROFF, W. J. and SCOTT. J. R., *Fibres, Films, Plastics and Rubbers—A Handbook of Common Polymers*, Butterworths, Guildford (1971)

RAPRA TECHNOLOGY, *Rubbicana Europe*, Shrewsbury (1990)

SMITH, D. R. (ed.), *Rubber World Magazine's Blue Book*, Lippincott and Peto, Akron (1990)

STEVENSON, A. (ed.), *Rubber in Offshore Engineering*, Adam Hilger, Bristol and London (1985)

SWEDISH INSTITUTION OF RUBBER TECHNOLOGY, *Rubber Handbook*, Swedish Institution of Rubber Technology (1990)

Thermoplastic Elastomers—An Introduction for Engineers, Mechanical Engineering Publications Ltd., London (1987)

WHELAN, A. and LEE, K. S. (eds), *Developments in Rubber Technology—1 Improving Product Performance*, Applied Science, London and New York (1979)

WHELAN, A. and LEE, K. S. (eds), *Developments in Rubber Technology—2, Synthetic Rubbers*, Applied Science, London (1981)

WHELAN, A. and LEE, K. S. (eds), *Developments in Rubber Technology—3, Thermoplastic Rubbers*, Applied Science, London and New York (1982)

38

Acrylic and Polycarbonate Plastics

M G Grantham BA, MRSC, MIQA, MIHT, CChem
Technotrade Ltd

Contents

38.1 Introduction 38/3

38.2 Acrylic plastics 38/3
    38.2.1 Properties 38/3
    38.2.2 Fabrication 38/3
    38.2.3 Serviceability 38/3
    38.2.4 Typical uses 38/3

38.3 Polycarbonates 38/3
    38.3.1 Properties 38/3
    38.3.2 Fabrication 38/5
    38.3.3 Serviceability 38/5
    38.3.4 Typical uses 38/5

38.4 Structural properties 38/5
    38.4.1 Weathering and temperature 38/5
    38.4.2 Rate and duration of loading 38/5
    38.4.3 Mechanical properties 38/5
    38.4.4 Susceptibility to crazing 38/5

38.5 Weather resistance 38/6
    38.5.1 Artificial weathering processes 38/6
    38.5.2 Outdoor exposure testing 38/7
    38.5.3 Evaluation of weathering data 38/7

38.6 Temperature effects 38/7
    38.6.1 Expansion and contraction 38/7
    38.6.2 Changes in engineering properties 38/7
    38.6.3 Impact resistance 38/7
    38.6.4 Maximum service temperature 38/7

38.7 Fire safety 38/7

Bibliography 38/7

Appendix 38/8

38.1 Introduction

This chapter is intended to provide a basic introduction to acrylic and polycarbonate plastics and some of the uses to which they can be put. Basic guidance on engineering properties is given with cautionary advice on how to use (and not to use!) the engineering data. It is by no means intended to be exhaustive and readers are referred to the bibiography at the end of the chapter for further reading. In particular, the excellent book by Ralph Montella, *Plastics in Architecture*, is essential reading. Generalized materials properties are indicated within the body of this chapter but, for an example of information that is available from a manufacturer, the reader is referred to the table given in the Appendix.

38.2 Acrylic plastics

Acrylics are normally thermoplastic substances, soluble in organic solvents. They vary from polymethylmethacrylate (Perspex), a hard, glass-clear material, to soft rubbery polymers or waxes. Certain water dispersible acrylic polymers are used to modify the workability of specialist concrete repair materials. Methacrylate polymers were first made in 1877, with polymethylmethacrylate first made in 1880. Commercial production of polyacrylates began in about 1927 by Rohm and Haas. Examples of the material in commercial use are shown in *Figures 38.1* to *38.3*.

38.2.1 Properties

38.2.1.1 Chemical properties

Acrylics tend to be soluble in most aromatic and chlorinated hydrocarbons, esters, ketones and tetrahydrofuran. When cross-linked, they can be insoluble, but will swell in chlorinated hydrocarbons.

They are plasticized by some ester type plasticizers (e.g. dibutylphthalate and tritolylphosphate), are swollen by alcohols, phenols, ether and carbon tetrachloride, but are relatively unaffected by aliphatic hydrocarbons, concentrated alkalis, most dilute acids and concentrated hydrochloric acid, aqueous solutions of salts and by oxidizing agents. They are, however, decomposed by concentrated oxidizing acids and by alkalis in alcholic solution.

38.2.1.2 Thermal properties

Specific heat: $1.47 \text{ J g}^{-1} \text{ K}^{-1}$.
Conductivity: $c.\ 0.19 \text{ W m}^{-1} \text{ °C}^{-1}$.
Coefficient of linear expansion: $0.7 \times 10^{-4} \text{ °C}^{-1}$ (20°C); $1.05 \times 10^{-4} \text{ °C}^{-1}$ (80°C).
Maximum service temperature: $c.\ 80°C$.
Decomposes at 180–190°C.

38.2.1.3 Mechanical properties

Young's modulus: $c.\ 2940 \text{ MPa}$ (decreasing to 1670 MPa at 80°C).
Tensile strength: $c.\ 70 \text{ MPa}$ (polymethylmethacrylate) falling with increasing temperature.
Elongation at break: $c.\ 4\%$ (cast sheet).
Impact strength:
　Notched Izod: 1.6 kJ m^{-2}.
　Charpy unnotched: 15 kJ m^{-2}.
　Compressive strength: 117 MPa.

38.2.2 Fabrication

Acrylic plastics may be compression moulded at about 160°C, 14 MPa, or injection moulded at 160–220°C, 140 MPa. The materials are blow mouldable and vacuum thermoformable at 100–170°C.

38.2.3 Serviceability

Acrylic plastics have excellent light fastness and resistance to exterior weathering. They are not subject to microbiological attack.

38.2.4 Typical uses

Acrylic plastics are used as sheets, mouldings, extrusions (particularly for windows), roof lights and light fittings, decorative displays, and illuminated signs. They have a variety of other uses in solvent or aqueous solution.

38.3 Polycarbonates

Polycarbonates are transparent, faintly amber coloured, thermoplastic materials showing good dimensional stability, thermal resistance and electrical properties, and also good tensile and impact strength. They are used in mouldings fibres and films.

Diphenylolalkanes, the precursors of polycarbonates were first made by A. Baeyer in 1872. A. Einhorn made the first polymers in 1898. In the 1950s, the polymers were developed commercially by Farbenfabriken Bayer AG, the General Electric Company in the USA and also by others.

38.3.1 Properties

38.3.1.1 Chemical properties

Polycarbonates are dissolved by some chlorinated hydrocarbons (e.g. chloroform and methylene chloride). They are swollen by acetone, benzene and carbon tetrachloride. Aromatic hydrocarbons, ketones and esters may cause crazing and stress cracking. Polycarbonates are resistant to aliphatic hydrocarbons, trichloroethylene, alcohols (although prolonged exposure may cause surface crazing), dilute acids and oxidizing agents. They are decomposed by hot alcoholic alkalis, organic amines and are attacked by aqueous alkalis (which may be found in some cleaning fluids).

38.3.1.2 Thermal properties

Specific heat: $1.3 \text{ J g}^{-1} \text{ K}^{-1}$.
Conductivity: $0.20 \text{ W m}^{-1} \text{ °C}^{-1}$.
Coefficient of linear expansion: $0.6–0.7 \times 10^{-4} \text{ °C}^{-1}$ (slightly higher above 60°C).
Maximum service temperature: up to 135°C, although at the higher temperature the polymers may turn brown by oxidation. (NB: there is some creep at 100°C.)
Decomposes at 310–340°C (softens above 160°C, melts at 215–230°C).

38.3.1.3 Mechanical properties

Young's modulus: $c.\ 2450 \text{ MPa}$ (significantly improved by incorporation of glass fibres).
Tensile strength: up to 70 MPa, yield at about 60 MPa (up to 140 MPa with the incorporation of glass fibres).
Elongation at break: 60–100% (yielding at 5% strain).
Impact strength:
　Notched Izod: 10 kJ m^{-2}.

(a)

(b)

Figure 38.1 Examples of the commercial use of acrylic plastics: (a) school doorways, (b) greenhouse, (c) pedestrian bridge. (Courtesy of Roehn Ltd, Milton Keynes)

(c)

Figure 38.1 *continued*

Charpy unnotched: no failure (ISO 179/1D).
Compressive strength: *c*. 80 MPa.

38.3.2 Fabrication

Polycarbonates are extrudable at 250–300°C and injection mouldable at 275–330°C and up to 140 MPa. They are vacuum thermoformable in the temperature range 160–220°C and weldable at 260°C. Polycarbonates are cementable with epoxy resins, hot melt adhesives and with solutions of the polymer in dichloromethane or dichloroethane.

38.3.3 Serviceability

Polycarbonates have good dimensional stability and are strong and tough (but may creep under load at elevated temperatures). The amber colour may increase on outdoor exposure unless lacquered with an ultraviolet absorber.

38.3.4 Typical uses

Polycarbonates are used for skylights, glazing (especially high impact security glazing), barrel vault roofs, shelves, platforms and displays.

38.4 Structural properties

Clearly, the engineer dealing with plastics is concerned with using the materials in situations where their structural and mechanical properties are important. In this respect, however, the normally published 'physical data' may have only limited usefulness because the service conditions in which the materials are to be used may place more onerous requirements on them. Furthermore, plastics are undergoing continuous development, and data taken from tables of engineering properties even a few years old may not be appropriate for the materials now available. It is up to the designer to satisfy himself that such properties as impact strength, temperature and weatherability performance are appropriate for the material he has chosen.

When attempting to use tables of basic physical data, the designer must also bear in mind the effects of a number of essential factors which will affect the structural performance. These factors are described in the following sections.

38.4.1 Weathering and temperature

Exposure of acrylic and polycarbonate plastics outdoors reduces their physical properties, the extent of reduction depending on the time of exposure and the exposure conditions. Generally the strength loss is not large and deterioration in appearance may outweigh the changes in physical and mechanical performance. When exposed to higher temperatures, both materials show a reduction in physical properties, changing from a hard engineering material to a softer or rubbery material. As such, impact strength is the only property which is not reduced. The plastics tend to behave elastically at temperatures below about 70°C; thereafter their behaviour becomes more plastic with a greater tendency to neck in the fracture region, this tendency increasing with increasing temperatures. Polycarbonates have better high-temperature properties than acrylics.

38.4.2 Rate and duration of loading

When loaded at a high rate the strength of polycarbonates and acrylics tend to increase. With a decrease in loading rate there is little change until the kind of loading associated with creep rupture comes into play. Under constant or gently increasing load over a long period, permanent deformation may occur with ultimate failure at well below the normal strength, perhaps half or less after 50 days. In design for architectural applications it is important to avoid situations where creep may occur.

38.4.3 Mechanical properties

When considering behaviour of engineering plastics with regard to strength and stiffness, the kind of behaviour noted above under long-term loading needs to be considered. The behaviour under short-term and long-term loading is quite different and the physical properties indicated elsewhere in this chapter, while a useful guide as a basis for comparing different materials, must be used with caution in real engineering design.

As mentioned previously, under short-term loading, the behaviour of plastics is elastic, showing complete recovery when stressed below the yield point even when loaded and released repeatedly (in the short term). Under prolonged loading, even below the yield point and well below the ultimate fracture load, permanent deformation will occur. The polymer chains may be considered as minute springs and under short-term loading behave elastically. Under long-term loading the 'springs' uncoil and slippage of one polymer chain against another occurs, resulting in permanent deformation.

The designer is obviously concerned, not with what will happen in the short term, but how a component will behave in the long term, under the actual service conditions to which it will be exposed. This will be dependent primarily on the length of time the component is exposed and the service temperature. However, other factors such as exposure to ultraviolet light, solvent vapours or other chemical pollutants cannot be ignored. As a basis for design, the most important properties of both acrylics and polycarbonates can be considered using a value known as the 'apparent modulus', a measure of stress/strain behaviour that depends on the temperature and time of exposure. This information is given for both acrylics and polycarbonates in *Table 38.1*. To allow for the effects of weathering, pollution, etc., it is recommended that maximum allowable stress values do not exceed those given in *Table 38.2*. If loaded in excess of these values, stress crazing will probably occur eventually, or sooner if exposed to solvent vapours.

38.4.4 Susceptibility to crazing

In common with many other plastics, both acrylics and polycarbonates can suffer from crazing: a series of fine cracks

Table 38.1 Modulus of elasticity (in MPa) vs. time and temperature

Temperature (°C)	Time of application of load (days)			
	1	10	100	1000
Acrylic*				
25	2480	2140	1875	1635
40	2240	1860	1530	1255
50	2170	1725	1380	1105
60	2000	1515	1165	880
70	1860	1380	1000	740
80	1655	1140	760	
90	1365	760	—	—
Polycarbonate†				
25	2400	2290	2185	2090
40	2055	1875	1710	1560
50	1885	1715	1565	1430

* These values can be used to calculate long-term deflection under continuously applied loads. To calculate momentary or initial deflection under long-term loads, at room temperature, use a value of 3100 MPa.
† Modulus values below 700 MPa have shown wide variation.

Table 38.2 Maximum allowable service stress (MPa)

Temperature (°C)	Loading	
	Continuous	Intermittent
Acrylic		
25	10	21
33	9	14
40	8	10
50	7.5	7.5
60	7	7
68	5.5	5.5
80	4	4
90	2	2
25 (FEL)	35	35
Polycarbonate		
−54	29	36
0	16	29
23	14	28
54	11	24
71	7	22
93	3.5	21
121	0	17
23 (FEL)	7	7

FEL, fatigue endurance limit.

appearing on the surface or within the body of the plastic, usually perpendicular to the surface. There are a variety of possible causes: excessive loading in service, residual stresses from manufacture, contact with solvent vapours, as mentioned above, and stresses induced by working the material, e.g. machining and polishing.

The cracks may often only be apparent when viewed at an angle. Random cracking more often results from solvent exposure, while orientated cracking usually results from mechanical stress. Both can occur simultaneously, if both mechanisms are present, and a synergistic effect can occur, with more severe cracking than would have resulted from either mechanism alone.

Crazing cannot be ignored, because its onset may be an early indication of component failure. With sufficient stress, the reduction in physical properties such as tensile and impact strengths, can cause premature failure.

38.5 Weather resistance

In common with all other materials, plastics undergo ageing processes. Polyacrylics and polycarbonates are no exception. In time they are liable to be subject to deterioration such as embrittlement, yellowing and soiling. It is assumed here that the effects of creep and temperature resistance were already considered at the design stage.

The effects of weathering are difficult to measure. Much of the available data is based on artificial weathering and these data need to be interpreted with caution: such data can be misleading and widely different performances can be predicted by different artificial weathering systems. In general such data are unlikely to provide much useful guidance on the long-term properties and performance of the material in an outdoor situation. Actual field test data are of much more use and both acrylics and polycarbonates have an extensive history of successful usage in a wide variety of applications.

Typically, weathering of these materials will cause:

(1) colour changes (especially yellowing, fading or darkening);
(2) hazing (becoming milky in appearance);
(3) dullness (by loss of polished finish, perhaps due to erosion of the surface); and
(4) crazing.

Exactly how a material behaves under weathering is dependent upon the exposure conditions: quite different results will be obtained if a material is employed in the tropics or in desert conditions, compared with the performances that will be obtained in a marine situation or in a heavily polluted industrial environment.

Probably the most important factor in causing permanent change in a plastic is sunlight, especially ultraviolet light. Other factors can include heat, moisture, atmospheric pollution, fungal attack and chemical attack in one form or other.

38.5.1 Artificial weathering processes

It must be appreciated that a device which will accurately predict the performance and service life of a material in a particular geographical location simply does not exist. Weather in practice is a complex combination of the elements and varies continuously from place to place and, of course, from year to year, even in the same place. For this reason, artificial weathering data can only be used as a guide to the type of deterioration that plastic may undergo, and only in the broadest sense can guidance on service life be obtained.

A typical artificial weathering device will have a central light source, usually rich in ultraviolet light with a turntable surrounding the light on which strips of the plastic may be mounted. These are generally rotated to provide alternate light and dark, and facilities to control humidity and artificial rainfall may also be provided. It must be appreciated that correlation of actual outdoor exposure with accelerated test data is always required before any accurate predictions can be made about actual service under specific conditions. This correlation will only be valid for the particular geographical location (with due regard to the variability encountered in natural weathering conditions).

38.5.2 Outdoor exposure testing

Outdoor exposure testing is generally performed by placing strips of the material on racks at an angle of 45° in a southern facing attitude. Due regard to the variability that may be experienced in practice must be made and it must be appreciated that a plastic in a cool vertical situation in a north facing application may perform quite differently.

38.5.3 Evaluation of weathering data

The simplest method of evaluating weathering is by simple visual inspection, but this needs to be performed by a specialist to yield meaningful results. Change is normally rated on a scale from 1 to 5 in half-step increments from no change to colour completely gone. The material will be rated for yellowing, fading, darkening or whitening using this simple scale.

38.6 Temperature effects

Plastics, unlike most other materials, are significantly affected by temperature. Indeed, the dictionary definition of a plastic is a material of high molecular weight, mouldable by heat or pressure or both. While extreme temperatures will affect many materials, plastics are unusual in that they undergo significant changes at temperatures likely to be encountered in the normal service environment. Temperature is likely to affect: expansion and contraction, stiffness (modulus) maximum service stress (design stress), and maximum service temperature.

38.6.1 Expansion and contraction

When designing acrylic and polycarbonate components, the coefficient of thermal expansion must be uppermost in the designer's mind. Unlike many other materials, it cannot be ignored, as significant dimensional changes can occur as a result of temperature change.

Temperature change need not only be restricted to use in service: delivery and storage temperatures need also be considered, perhaps at the height of summer or the depths of winter. The coefficients of expansion of acrylic and polycarbonate sheet are compared with those of some other common building materials in *Table 38.3*. It can be be seen from *Table 38.3* that the coefficients of thermal expansion of these plastics is some seven times that of steel or glass. For all practical purposes, a figure of 0.00007 °C^{-1} can be assumed in calculations.

It is reasonable, in the UK climate, to consider service temperature extremes of −20°C to +70°C. Translated into movement, such a temperature change could represent 6 mm of movement in a 1 m long component. In service, moisture expansion can also affect acrylics (but not polycarbonates) and this could increase in the expansion significantly. For practical purposes, over a normal temperature range, for clear (not tinted) plastic, values of 5 mm per metre length for acrylics (including

moisture expansion) and 2.5 mm per metre length for polycarbonates can be reasonably assumed.

38.6.2 Changes in engineering properties

The effects of temperature on the apparent elastic modulus and the allowable design stresses are given in *Tables 38.1* and *38.2*.

38.6.3 Impact resistance

It is normal for most plastic materials to show a drop in impact strength with temperature. Cast acrylic plastic is an exception, showing little change with falling temperature (some decrease at the very low temperatures of −40°C and below). Polycarbonates do show a loss of impact strength with falling temperature, but the impact strength is still very high at low temperatures.

38.6.4 Maximum service temperature

This information is given in the introductory data on material properties at the beginning of this chapter.

38.7 Fire safety

The disaster at Summerland on the Isle of Man in 1974 provided an object lesson in designing for fire safety to designers in plastics materials. All plastics will burn. In an actual fire they will burn at a rate depending on their chemical composition and the nature of the fire itself. It must be appreciated that small-scale fire tests will not necessarily correlate with either large-scale tests or performance in an actual fire, although large-scale tests are more likely to simulate actual behaviour.

Formulation in plastics is continually changing and earlier efforts to produce low flammability grades sometimes resulted in slower burning products which generated more smoke. For example, the first generation flame retardant polycarbonates, using halogen modified polymers, while flame retardant, produced more smoke and also had a lower impact strength. It is well known that smoke kills far more people in fires than those killed by the fire itself. The later, second generation, polymers, incorporating alkali metal salts, altered the decomposition chemistry to give different products, notably large amounts of carbon dioxide at lower temperatures, contributing to stifling of a fire.

Bibliography

ANON., 'Acrylic clads Summerland', *British Plastics*, 200–205 (1971)

BLINNE, G. and THEYSON, R., 'Engineering thermoplastics, today and tomorrow', *Modern Plastics International*, **V16** (10), 121–124 (1986)

CARTER, R. P. and REINERT, G. E., 'Second generation flame retardant polycarbonate resins', *Society of Plastics Engineering Technology Annual Technology Conference, New York, 5–8 May 1980*, SPE, Connecticut (1980)

INTERNATIONAL ORGANIZATION FOR STANDARDIZATION, *ISO 179/1D, Determination of charpy impact strength of rigid materials*, Geneva (1982)

LUTZ, Jr, J. T., 'Tough weatherable building material—acrylic modified PVC', *35th SPE Annual Technology Conference*, Montreal, Quebec, 25–28 April 1977

MONTELLA, R., *Plastics in Architecture*, M. Dekker, New York (1985)

MUELLER, R. P., 'Polycarbonate (PC), *German Plastics*, **V74**, 21–23 (1984)

ROFF, W. J. and SCOTT, R., *Fibres, Films, Plastics and Rubbers; a Handbook of Common Polymers*, Butterworths, London (1971)

Table 38.3 Some coefficients of thermal expansion

Material	Coefficient (mm mm^{-1} °C^{-1})
Cast acrylic sheet	0.000074
Polycarbonate sheet	0.000068
Aluminium	0.000023
Steel	0.000011
Plate glass	0.000009

Appendix

Typical values at 23°C and 50% relative humidity

	PLEXIGLAS GS 233, 222, 209	PLEXIGLAS XT	PLEXIDUR T	MAKROLON 281, 283, 293	Unit	Standard
Mechanical properties						
Density	1.19	1.19	1.17	1.20	g cm^{-3}	DIN 53479
Charpy impact strength	15	15	55	No failure	kJ m^{-2}	ISO 179/1D
Notched impact strength (Izod)	1.6	1.6	2.0	10	kJ m^{-2}	ISO 180/1A
Tensile strength (1/1 test specimen 3, (a) −40°C	110	100	150	80	MPa	DIN 53455
$v = 5$ mm min^{-1}) (b) 23°C	80	72	85	60	MPa	DIN 53455
(c) 70°C	40	35	20	50	MPa	
Elongational at break (1/1 test specimen 3, $v = 5$ mm min^{-1})	5.5	4.5	60	>80	%	DIN 53455
Flexural strength (standard test specimen, 80 × 10 × 4 mm)	115	105	150	90	MPa	DIN 53452
Compressive yield stress	110	103	110	80	MPa	DIN 53454
Max. safety stress (up to 40°C)	5–10	5–10	10	7.5	MPa	
Fatigue strength in alternating bending test, approx. 10^6 cycles						
(a) Unnotched test specimen	40	30	70	30	MPa	DIN 53457
(b) Notched test specimen	20	10	55	—	MPa	
Modulus of elasticity (short-term value)	3300	3300	4500	2400	MPa	DIN 53457
Dynamic shear modulus at approx. 10 Hz	1700	1700	2000	1000	MPa	DIN 53445
Indentation hardness $H_{961/30}$	200	190	220	—	MPa	DIN 53456
$H_{358/30}$	—	—	—	130	%	
Abrasion resistance with 1600 g abrasive	98	98	98	—		Similar to ASTM D 673-44
Coefficient of friction						
Plastic/plastic	0.8	0.8	—	—		
Plastic/steel	0.5	0.5	—	—		
Steel/plastic	0.45	0.45	—	—		
Poisson's ratio	0.45	0.45	0.35	0.45		
Acoustical properties						
Sound velocity (at room temp.)	2700–2800	2700–2800	—	—	m s^{-1}	
Weighted sound reduction index, R_w, at thickness:						
4 mm	26	26	—	25	dB	
6 mm	30	30	—	—		
10 mm	32	32	—	31		
Thermal properties						
Coefficient of linear thermal expansion for 0–50°C	70 × 10^{-6} (= 0.07)	70 × 10^{-6} (= 0.07)	65 × 10^{-6} (= 0.065)	65 × 10^{-6} (= 0.065)	K^{-1} (mm m^{-1} °C^{-1})	DIN 53752-A
Thermal conductivity	0.19	0.19	≈0.23	0.20	W m^{-1} K^{-1}	DIN 52612
U value for thickness						
1 mm	5.8	5.8	5.8	—	W m^{-2} K^{-1}	DIN 4701
3 mm	5.6	5.6	5.6	—		
5 mm	5.3	5.3	5.2	—		
10 mm	4.4	4.4	4.6	—		
Specific heat	1.47	1.47	1.47	1.3	J g^{-1} K^{-1}	
Forming temperature (oven temperature)	160–175	150–160	145–150	190–210	°C	

Property	Material 1	Material 2	Material 3	Material 4	Unit	Standard
Max. surface temp. (IR radiator)	200	180	160	220	°C	—
Max. permanent service temperature	80	70	60	115	°C	—
Reverse forming temperature	>80/>80/>90	>80	>70	>135	°C	—
Ignition temperature	425	430	475	570	°C	DIN 51794
Fire rating (material thickness ≥1.5 mm)	B2 normally flammable	B2 normally flammable	B2 normally flammable	B2 normally flammable (B1. flame-retarded when used for indoor applications up to 4 mm thickness)	—	DIN 4102
Vicat softening temperature, method B	115	102	80	145	°C	ISO 306
Thermal properties						
Dimensional stability under heat (Martens method)	95	85	69	115	°C	DIN 53458
Heat deflection temperature, ISO 75						DIN 53461
(a) Deflection 1.8 MPa	105/105/107	90	71	135	°C	
(b) Deflection 0.45 MPa	113/113/115	95	76	140	°C	
Electrical properties						
Volume resistivity	>10^{15}	>10^{15}	>10^{15}	>10^{15}	ohm cm	DIN VDE 0303, Part 3
Surface resistance	5×10^{13}	5×10^{13}	5×10^{13}	>10^{14}	ohm	DIN VDE 0303, Part 3
Dielectric strength (1 mm sample thickness)	≈30	≈30	≈30	35	kV mm^{-1}	DIN VDE 0303, Part 2
Dielectric constant						DIN VDE 0303, Part 4
50 Hz	3.6	3.7	4.5	3.0	—	
0.1 MHz	2.7	2.8	3.5	—	—	
Dissipation factor						
50 Hz	0.06	0.06	0.06	0.0007	—	
0.1 MHz	0.02	0.03	0.02	—	—	
Tracking resistance	KC>600	KC>600	KC>600	KA1	—	DIN VDE 0303, Part 1
Behaviour towards water						
Water absorption (from dry state) after 24 h, test specimen 50/50/4 mm	30	30	25	10	mg	DIN 53495
Max. weight gain during immersion	2.1	2.1	≈1.8	0.37	%	DIN 53495
Permeability to water vapour	2.3 × 10^{-10}	2.3 × 10^{-10}	1.5 × 10^{-10}	3.8 × 10^{-10}	g cm / cm² h Pa	
N_2	4.5 × 10^{-15}	4.5 × 10^{-10}		1.1 × 10^{-13}		
O	2.0 × 10^{-14}	2.0 × 10^{-14}		7.5 × 10^{-19}		
CO_2	1.1 × 10^{-13}	1.1 × 10^{-13}	3.2 × 10^{-12}	3.2 × 10^{-12}		
Air	8.3 × 10^{-15}	8.3 × 10^{-15}	2.6 × 10^{-13}	2.6 × 10^{-13}		
Optical properties (of clear grades)						
Light transmittance of 3 mm thick material in the visible range ($\lambda = 380$–780 nm)	≈92	≈92	≈90	≈86	%	DIN 5036 Standard illuminant D65
Reflection loss in the visible range (for each interface)	4	4	4	4	%	
Total energy transmittance	85	85	76	75	%	DIN 67507
Absorption in the visible range, at 3 mm thickness	<0.05	<0.05	≈2	≈4	%	—
Refractive index, n_D^{20}	1.491	1.491	1.508	1.586	—	DIN 53491

Reproduced courtesy of **ROEHM** Ltd, Plastics Division.

39

Polymer Dispersions

R Dennis CChem, MRSC
Doverstrand Ltd

Contents

39.1 Introduction 39/3
    39.1.1 Definitions 39/3
    39.1.2 Historical development 39/3
    39.1.3 Redispersible powder polymers 39/4

39.2 Manufacture and design variables 39/4
    39.2.1 Manufacture 39/4
    39.2.2 Design variables 39/4

39.3 Explanation of the binding ability of polymer dispersions 39/5
    39.3.1 Polymer dispersion as the only binding agent 39/5
    39.3.2 Polymer dispersion used with hydraulic cement 39/5

39.4 Selection of dispersion type 39/6
    39.4.1 Initial selection according to application 39/6
    39.4.2 Selection of dispersions for use in cementitious mixes 39/7
    39.4.3 Testing 39/7
    39.4.4 Guide notes on dispersion types 39/7

39.5 Properties and applications of mortars containing dispersions 39/9
    39.5.1 Properties of mortars containing dispersions 39/9
    39.5.2 Uses of cementitious mixes containing dispersions 39/9

39.6 Site-usage notes 39/10

References 39/11

Bibliography 39/12

39.1 Introduction

39.1.1 Definitions

A polymer is an organic compound of high molecular weight which is made by the linking (polymerization) of simple chemical units which are known as monomers. Thus if ethylene units are made to combine together, polyethylene ('polythene') is formed. Polyethylene is called a homopolymer because it is made up of only one type of unit. A polymer made up of two types of monomer is known as a copolymer, thus the monomers styrene and butadiene can combine to form the copolymer polystyrene butadiene. This is abbreviated to SBR where the R represents rubber, as SBR is a synthetic rubber. If three different monomers combine together the product is known as a terpolymer.

Polymers are available in solid, powder and liquid forms. The liquids may be solutions, dispersions or 100% polymer. In the context of this chapter a polymer dispersion is a stable suspension of solid, submicroscopic polymer particles (*Figure 39.1*) in an aqueous medium, which on drying out under the conditions of use forms a coherent film. Dispersions are often erroneously called emulsions, a term which should be reserved for two-phase suspensions where both phases are liquid. Polymer dispersions are also referred to as latices (or latexes) hence the terms latex modified concrete and latex modified mortar.

Polymer dispersions are milky white liquids which come in a wide range of viscosities and solid content. They are typically supplied at 40–70% solids, but may be supplied in a more dilute form, e.g. by diluting with water for a particular end-use such as prepack concrete-repair systems. The most common polymer dispersion product in everyday life is emulsion paint, most varieties of which should correctly be called aqueous dispersion paint.

39.1.2 Historical development

It is easy to make unmodified mortars and concretes of sufficient compressive strength, but their tensile strength, toughness, bonding properties and durability are often inadequate, particularly for thicknesses below 50 mm. Polymer dispersions can minimize these inadequacies and for this reason have been widely used with mortars and concretes since the 1920s. The first dispersion to be used for this application was natural rubber latex (NR), a product which was already being used in the construction industry for surface coatings, adhesives and bitumen modification.

The first mortars and concretes to be made containing natural rubber latex were based on high alumina cement, as this has less tendency to coagulate the latex than does Portland cement. These early products were mostly used for chemically resistant mortars, floor toppings and levelling (also sound damping) screeds on the steel decks of ships. Natural rubber latex provides good adhesive and resilience characteristics to cementitious mixes, but it has some drawbacks, i.e. poor compatibility with Portland cement unless a large proportion of stabilizer is used and poor resistance to weathering, solvents and oils. Furthermore, as it is a natural product, there is no opportunity to tailor its properties to, for example, obtain the best compromise between tensile strength and extensibility.

The Second World War stimulated research into polymerization processes for the production of synthetic rubber. This research proved to be most successful for both military and civil applications and the spin-off from this work made the production of a range of polymer dispersions economically viable.

By the 1950s polyvinyl acetate dispersion (PVA) was making inroads into some applications where natural rubber latex would previously have been used. PVA also went into new application areas such as its use as a bonding agent for gypsum plaster. PVA has excellent properties when used in dry conditions, but these properties deteriorate in the presence of water. Modified PVAs have now been developed which have better water resistance, but even these are not ideal for use in cementitious systems as there is a risk of decomposition of the polymer from the alkalis in the cement.

Further developments produced dispersions with many of the advantages of natural rubber latex/PVA, with less disadvantages. The three most useful of these new dispersions for use in cementitious systems are styrene butadiene (SBR), polyacrylic esters (PAE), also known as pure acrylics, and styrene acrylics (SA).

Many other types of dispersion are available and in this chapter, which is concerned with elastomeric and thermoplastic dispersions, reference will also be made to ethylene vinyl acetate (EVA), chloroprene (CR), acrylonitrile butadiene or nitrile butadiene rubber (NBR), polyvinyl propionate (PVP) and polyvinylidene dichloride (PVDC). Further types of dispersion are available but these will not be covered herein as they are not normally classified in the above elastomeric/thermoplastic category. These other categories are thermosetting, bituminous and mixed. Epoxy dispersions are classified as thermosetting.

In the UK there are about 15 chemical manufacturing

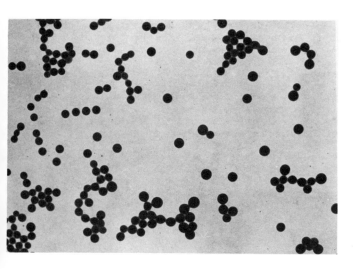

Figure 39.1 Transmission electron photomicrograph showing the spherical polymer particles in a dispersion. Each particle is typically about 0.2 micron

companies, supplying polymer dispersions for the construction industry. These companies normally sell through distributors such as chemical-admixture companies. A list of the manufacturing companies together with their addresses can be obtained from the Secretary of FeRFA, The Federation of Resin Formulators and Applicators, 1st Floor, 241 High Street, Aldershot, Herts GU11 1TJ, UK.

39.1.3 Redispersible powder polymers

Certain polymer dispersions can be spray dried to form powders which redisperse easily in water, particularly the alkaline water from cementitious systems (to remake polymer dispersions). These powders are useful in single-pack cementitious products, e.g. self-levelling floor underlayments, which the user only has to mix with water. These redispersible powders are typically based on EVAs and modified PVAs such as VA/VeoVa. This last product is a copolymer of vinyl acetate and VeoVa (registered trade name of Shell's vinyl versatate). Acrylic powders are also available but are less common.

The particles in polymer dispersions which have been remade from powder polymers are much larger than in the original dispersion, and hence the properties of the final product are not as good as they would have been if the original dispersion had been used. To some extent this loss in performance can be counteracted by increasing the proportion of powder polymer.

Dispersions such as SBRs, which dry to water-resistant films, cannot be spray dried into redispersible powders. It therefore follows that where the maximum performance is required from a polymer modified cementitious mix which will be exposed to wet conditions, a suitable polymer dispersion and not a powder product should be used.

Redispersible powder polymers may contain up to 13% filler by weight to prevent the particles from sticking together during manufacture and storage.

Further information on these materials can be obtained from: Central Chemicals (agents for Ebnöther of Switzerland), Rohm and Haas, Vinyl Products, Wacker. The addresses of these companies can be obtained from FeRFA (see Section 39.1.2).

39.2 Manufacture and design variables

39.2.1 Manufacture

Synthetic dispersions are usually made by emulsion polymerization, so-called because the monomers are in the liquid form in the reactor and are emulsified in the water phase, e.g. by using synthetic 'soaps' (surfactants) or protective colloids. The reaction between the monomers takes place in an inert atmosphere in the presence of a chemical initiator and the exothermic reaction is controlled by water cooling. Some polymer dispersions can be made at atmospheric pressure, e.g. polyvinyl acetate (PVA), styrene acrylics (SA) and polyacrylic esters (PAE), whereas others need a higher pressure, e.g. styrene butadiene (SBR) and ethylene vinylacetate (EVA). Polymer dispersions for the construction industry are made by a batch process, or semibatch process, and a batch would typically consist of about 20 wet tonnes. The reaction can take up to 10 h to achieve yields of above 95%.

Two further processes are normally needed after the polymerization to make the dispersion suitable for the end-user. The first of these extra processes is known as stripping and this reduces the free monomer content. The second extra process is compounding, i.e. blending the dispersion with water and other ingredients to produce a final product to comply with the specification. One or more of the following chemical types is commonly introduced during this compounding: water, coalescent, anti-foam, anti-oxidant, alkali, bactericide, thickener,

dispersant, freeze/thaw stabilizer, surfactant, tackifier, vulcanizing agent, etc. The actual compounding ingredients used will, of course, depend on the dispersion type and its intended end-use.

39.2.2 Design variables

One of the great advantages of synthetic polymer dispersions is that they can be tailored by the polymer chemist to match the end-use. The main variables in the polymerization process are described below.

39.2.2.1 Monomer ratio

Except in the case of homopolymers, the monomer types and proportions can be chosen to suit the end-use. Thus any ratio of styrene to butadiene can form a copolymer, but it is known that for use with cement a dispersion having a styrene:butadiene ratio of 60:40 gives a good balance of properties for many applications. A higher styrene content would give a harder film and harder mortar, but the dispersion might not film form at ambient temperatures without the use of a coalescent, and mortars containing the dispersion might not have sufficient strain capacity.

Another example concerns a PAE dispersion, made from the monomers ethyl hexyl acrylate (EHA) and methyl methacrylate (MMA). Polymerized EHA is soft, whereas polymerized MMA is hard and hence the proportions can be chosen to fit the end-use.

39.2.2.2 Electrical charge on the polymer particle and surfactant type

Polymer dispersions fall into three main classes:

1. Cationic: positive charge on the particle.
2. Anionic: negative charge on the particle.
3. Non-ionic: no charge on the particle.

Cationic dispersions are mainly of interest for improving cationic bitumen emulsions (more correctly called dispersions if the bitumen particles are in solid form), but it is also possible to use some cationic dispersions with Portland cement. Anionic and non-ionic dispersions, and mixtures of the two, are the types normally used with cement. The choice of surfactant determines whether a dispersion will be cationic, anionic or non-ionic. There are numerous chemical types in each surfactant class and this gives further opportunities for matching the product with the end-use. In general, the higher the concentration of non-ionic surfactant the greater the chemical and physical stability of the dispersion against those forces tending to promote coagulation. Some surfactants act as superplasticizers when the dispersion is used in a cementitious system.

39.2.2.3 Particle size

The particle size and particle-size distribution influence the properties of the dispersion. These parameters can be controlled, for example, by the amount of surfactant present at the start of the polymerization. Dispersions with a very small particle size, e.g. below 0.1 μm, will usually require a high proportion of surfactant or protective colloid for stability, and it may not be possible to produce them at a solids content above about 40% as their viscosity may become inconveniently high. Natural rubber latex (NR) and PVA have a mean particle size of about 1 μm, whereas the mean particle size of cement-grade SBR, SA and PAE dispersions is in the range 0.13–0.23 μm. For comparison, the mean particle size of ordinary Portland cement is about 20 μm.

39.2.2.4 Molecular weight and cross-linking

Emulsion polymerization tends to produce high molecular weight polymers with much cross-linking and this is particularly true for butadiene polymers. The degree of cross-linking is controlled by the use of chain-transfer agents. The higher the concentration of chain-transfer agent the less the cross-linking. In spite of the use of chain-transfer agents the molecular weight and degree of cross-linking is normally sufficient to prevent the dried dispersion from dissolving completely in any of the liquids which might be expected to be solvents. An indication of the degree of cross-linking can be obtained by a technique known as gel-content determination. The gel content is the percentage of the dried dispersion which will not dissolve in a specified liquid, usually toluene, under specified conditions. A low gel content facilitates good film formation and extensibility, whereas a high gel content favours high tensile strength. Gel contents of dispersions determined using the method described by Cheesman and Pollard[1] may typically vary from 5 to 85%.

39.2.2.5 Carboxylation

Carboxylation, which is particularly relevant to SBR dispersions, produces negative carboxyl groups on the polymer molecule. These polar groups improve the physical and chemical stability of the dispersion and improve its adhesion to many types of background. The carboxyl groups can produce beneficial cross links between the polymer and the calcium ions from cement. Excessive carboxylation is undesirable in dispersions for the construction industry as it increases the water sensitivity of the dried film.

39.2.2.6 Process conditions

Computer programming of temperature, pressure and dosing cycles aids batch-to-batch consistency and provides further controllable variables. Thus one possible variant from such programming concerns core-shell dispersions where the polymer composition in the core of the particle is different to that near the surface of the particle.

The six controllable variables listed above lead to an overlap in the properties obtainable from different polymer types. Thus acrylic (PAE, SA) films could be harder or softer than the film from a specified SBR. Similarly, acrylic films might be more or less water resistant than SBR films. Unfortunately, this ability to change many of the properties of a dispersion within each generic type is not recognized by some specifying authorities who often specify SBR or acrylic without any stipulations on the properties required. This problem must be resolved by means of performance specifications.

39.3 Explanation of the binding ability of polymer dispersions

39.3.1 Polymer dispersion as the only binding agent

In many adhesives, bonding agents, coatings and mastics the polymer content of the dispersion is the only binding agent in the system. The binding action results from loss of water to the background and/or evaporation into the air. As water is lost the particles of the dispersion move towards each other and when sufficient water has been lost they form a coherent binding film. *Figure 39.2* shows the particles approaching the formation of a continuous film.

39.3.2 Polymer dispersion used with hydraulic cement

When polymer dispersions are used to replace all or some of the mix water in a formulation containing a hydraulic cement, i.e. a cement which hardens by chemical reaction with water, a double binding system is established. This consists of the binding action from the polymer being synergistically reinforced by the binding action of the cement. The binding action from the dispersion is developed as described in Section 39.3.1 but, in addition, water is lost from the dispersion to hydrate the cement, and this type of water loss is not accompanied by any significant drying shrinkage.

Isenburg and Vanderhoff[2] have put forward a hypothesis supported by electron-microscope studies which may be summarized as follows. Cement products are weak in tension because they contain numerous voids. As mortar containing a polymer dispersion dries out the polymer particles coalesce together and bond strongly to the other solid components of the mix. The particles form continuous films and strands which join the opposite sides of the voids together. These films and strands partially block the internal voids in the cementitious structure thus increasing its resistance to the ingress of water and chemicals.

It can be seen from the above explanation that dispersions

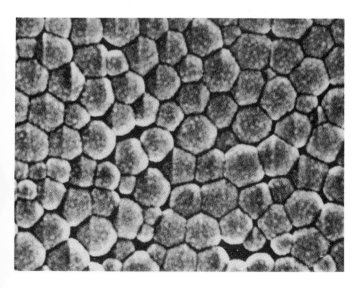

Figure 39.2 Polymer particles approaching coalescence to form a continuous film

Table 39.1 Typical physical properties of mortars modified with SBR dispersion[a]

	% Polymer dispersion by weight of cement, i.e. wet latex on cement						
	0	10	15	20	25	30	40
Water:cement	0.40	0.34	0.33	0.31	0.28	0.25	0.24
Compressive strength (N mm^{-2})	55			50			
Tensile strength (N mm^{-2})	4	5	6	7	8	8.5	9.0
Flexural strength (N mm^{-2})	10.0	11.5	14	15	16	18	19

[a] SBR was Revinex 29Y40 (47% solids). PAE (e.g. VP4001) and SA (e.g. BASF S702) gave similar results at 20% dispersion on cement, and at similar mix density. The mortar was a floor topping mix consisting of 1:3 OPC:coarse washed sand (BS 882: 1983,[4] complying with both the M and C grading) by weight. All mixes of similar dry consistency. Curing was 1 day covered in the mould and 27 days air curing. Test methods in accordance with BS 6319: Parts 2, 3 and 1.[5] The strength results on repair mortars are likely to be up to 50% lower, as a more workable mix is required. However, the proportional increases, versus the unmodified mix, will be maintained.

Table 39.2 Some examples of the selection of dispersion type according to application

Application	Conditions	Dispersion type[a]
Adhesives[b]	Dry	PVA, EVA
	Wet or dry	SBR, SA, CR
Bitumen modification		NR, SBR, CR
Bonding agents[b]	With cement, wet or dry	SBR
	Without cement, dry	PVA, EVA, PAE
	Without cement, wet or dry	SBR, PVDC
Primer paints for steel		SBR, PVC/PVDC[c]
External coatings		PAE, SA
Flexible coatings	With cement; very high flexibility	NR, PAE
Floors for animal husbandry; rubber-crumb mixes		NR, NR/SBR
Mastics		PAE
Mortar/concrete/floor screeds and toppings	Dry	PAE, SA
	Wet or dry	SBR
Oil-resistant products		CR, NBR
Ship-deck screeds		NR, SBR, PAE
Soil stabilization		SBR

[a] PVA, polyvinyl acetate; EVA, ethylene vinyl acetate; SBR, styrene butadiene; SA, styrene acrylics; CR, chloroprene; NR, natural rubber latex; PAE, polyacrylic ester; PVDC, polyvinylidene dichloride.
[b] In this context adhesives are used for joining dry solids and do not contain cement. Bonding agents are products which assist the bond of wet mixes to the background.
[c] Often modified with acrylics.

designed for use with cement reduce crack propagation and permeability. Furthermore, many of these dispersions enhance these benefits by reducing the water:cement ratio which is required for good workability. Hence the dispersions improve the tensile strength, flexural strength, toughness, crack resistance and durability of cementitious products. The data presented in *Table 39.1* show that the tensile strength of mortar can be doubled by using 25% of a proprietary polymer dispersion, based on the cement weight. Furthermore, it has been shown that most of this increase in strength is retained even after 10 years of external exposure. Perhaps this is not surprising as most of the polymer is in the body of the mortar and hence is protected from sunlight, ozone, etc.

Further mechanisms for explaining the binding ability of polymer dispersions can exist. Thus carboxylated styrene butadiene (SBR) can give chemical bonding by reaction of the carboxyl groups with the calcium ions from cement. Polymer dispersions mixed with cement can form very powerful bonding agents and one attempt at explaining their good performance is given below in respect of SBR.

SBR dispersion/cement mixtures stick well to a wide range of materials, e.g. old concrete, brick, glass, asphalt, steel, wood, stone and expanded polystyrene. The mixture of SBR and cement is a better adhesive than either the SBR, or cement/water. The reasons for the above are complex and still not fully

understood. The dispersion may improve wetting and in some cases penetration into the substrate. Probably more important is the way the polymer network interpenetrates the cement matrix. The relatively soft and deformable rubber gives good contact with the surface while the cement adds strength and stiffness to the bond. The rubber strands formed when the particles coalesce can also bridge between the mortar and the substrate.[3]

39.4 Selection of dispersion type

39.4.1 Initial selection according to application

Some examples of initial selection according to application are given in *Table 39.2*. The examples are based partly on a consideration of the properties of the dispersion and partly on typical current practice. The list may exclude some polymer types which are suitable for the given application and hence it is advisable to cross check with the manufacturers.

In all the cases listed in *Table 39.2* it is advisable to ensure that the dispersion to be used will have a minimum film forming temperature (MFFT) below the temperature at which it will be used, and that any coalescent/plasticizer which is used to achieve this does not have any undesirable side-effects. The dispersion should have good stability under the envisaged storage conditions, and in this connection it is worth noting that some dispersions deteriorate rapidly during freeze/thaw cycles and/or during storage above 35°C. The manufacturer should preferably be one which has BS 5750[5] and/or ISO 9000[6] accreditation. The manufacturer/supplier should have a good reputation for technical service.

There are few British Standards relevant to the performance of specific polymer dispersions for particular applications. BS 5270[7] regarding PVA bonding agents for gypsum plaster and BS 3544[8] and BS 4071[9] for PVA wood adhesives are, therefore, somewhat unique. There are a number of Agrément Certificates (from The British Board of Agrément) on products which contain polymer dispersions or redispersible powder polymers, e.g. repair mortars for concrete, external rendering, coatings for the corrosion protection of steel, grouted open texture Macadam, bituminous coatings, masonry paints, polymer bound plasters and adhesives.

39.4.2 Selection of dispersions for use in cementitious mixes

In addition to the points noted in Section 39.4.1, the dispersion should:

1. Not coagulate in the presence of Portland cement.
2. Not entrain excessive air in the mix. (Some dispersions contain anti-foam, whilst with others it is necessary to add anti-foam direct to the mixer.)
3. Give a suitable pot life, setting and hardening rate to the mortar and also give satisfactory placing characteristics.
4. Be resistant to alkaline hydrolysis, i.e. not decompose in the presence of alkali.
5. Not promote the corrosion of steel.
6. Make worthwhile improvements to adhesion, flexural and tensile strength, resistance to abrasion/water penetration/chemical attack. The strain capacity and crack resistance should also be improved.
7. Be economic in use. A dispersion of SBR or SA at 50% solids is about 20 times as expensive as ordinary Portland cement. Mortars modified with SBR or SA will typically be about four times as expensive per cubic metre as unmodified mixes, but this extra cost can be offset by a permissible reduction in thickness and improved performance. The relationship between the cost of the different dispersions varies with time because of fluctuations in monomer and natural rubber prices.

39.4.3 Testing

Manufacturers use up to about 20 tests to characterize a dispersion and may use a similar number of tests on the film made from the dispersion. There are, of course, specific tests for specific products such as roof coatings, modified bituminous products, and polymer modified mortars and concretes.

The comparison of dispersions for use in mortars/concretes, and the comparison of modified and unmodified mixes is not as simple as it might appear as there are many different ways of making the comparison. The conclusions of many reports would be different had the comparison been made in a different and perhaps more logical way. The sponsor of the tests must decide if the tests are to be carried out on mortars made in accordance with the supplier's instructions and the difficulty here is that different suppliers may have different instructions. Should the mixes all be tested at the same water:cement ratio, or all at the same mix consistency? Should modified and unmodified mixes be cured with the same curing regime? Should modified mixes be compared on the basis of equal polymer content or on equal cost? Should all mixes be tested at the same density? What test methods should be used?

On this last point BS 4551: 1980[10] may be recommended for the assessment of the properties of the wet mortar mixes and BS 6319: 1983/1987[11] for the assessment of the properties of hardened mixes. Tests regarding the resistance to shrinkage cracking (e.g. Coutinho ring test[12,13]) and tests for permeability[14–16] are also recommended.

Care should be taken over the terminology used by the dispersion supplier; i.e. if the word latex is used it normally refers to the wet dispersion, but it has been known for a supplier to use the word latex for the dry polymer.

39.4.4 Guide notes on dispersion types

39.4.4.1 Acrylic PAE (excluding styrene acrylics)

Full name polyacrylic ester. A copolymer of ethyl acrylate and methyl methacrylate is a typical example. Fruity odour. Ideal for use in external coatings because of their high resistance to oxidation/ultraviolet light/yellowing. As they are esters, hydrolysis is theoretically possible, but this does not seem to be a problem regarding the types sold for use with cement where they have a good track record, e.g. industrial floor toppings. High solids and very elastic varieties are available and such types can be used in mastics.

39.4.4.2 Chloroprene (CR)

Full name polychloroprene. 'Neoprene' is the product from Du Pont. The pH of the latex falls slowly during storage due to hydrolysis and release of hydrochloric acid; certain admixtures help to delay this. These dispersions are expensive, but they have some special properties, e.g. good grab for contact adhesives and good oil resistance. A cationic grade is available which can be used with cement. CR is one of the dispersions used for modifying bitumen emulsions. CR/cement mixes are also used in some proprietary car park deck renovation systems.

39.4.4.3 Ethylene vinyl acetate (EVA)

This product is an ester, i.e. a product formed from an acid and an alcohol. Esters are normally susceptible to hydrolysis, but EVA is made by a high-pressure process which gives it more stability. EVA films are more water resistant than PVA. These dispersions are slightly acidic. The dispersions became common in the UK during the early 1980s and one common use is as an interior bonding agent for plaster and render. Different properties can be obtained from EVA according to the proportion of ethylene in the polymer. EVAs are available as redispersible powders.

39.4.4.4 Natural rubber (NR)

This is a homopolymer of the elastomeric/thermoplastic type. It is available as a centrifuged product at 60% solids and as one concentrated by evaporation at up to 73% solids. Even at equal solids the centrifuged product is cheaper, but the other is easier to stabilize for use with cement. Both types normally contain some ammonia as a preservative. Very elastic but poor resistance to solvents, oils, fats, ultraviolet radiation and oxidation. Anti-oxidants help to reduce this last limitation. Softens and becomes sticky on oxidation. Used in screeds on the decks of ships, below other floor coverings. Also used in rubber-crumb flooring compositions and for the modification of hot bitumen and bitumen emulsions. NR would not be used in mortars or concretes where a high compressive strength is required. Further information can be obtained from The Malaysian Rubber Research Association of Brickendenbury, Hertfordshire SG13 8NL, UK.

39.4.4.5 Nitrile (NBR)

Full name acrylonitrile butadiene copolymer. These dispersions, and also terpolymers with styrene, have some useful properties to offer the construction industry, e.g. solvent and oil resistance, but there is little incentive for UK manufacturers to develop and market them. Further information on this type of dispersion is given in Reference 17. They are not used to any extent in the UK construction industry.

39.4.4.6 Polyvinyl acetate (PVA)

Sometimes also known as PVAc. This is a thermoplastic, homopolymer, ester. It can hydrolyse under damp alkaline conditions, i.e. revert to its original components. When this happens polyvinyl alcohol and acetic acid are formed. If cement is present the acetic acid will react with it to form calcium acetate. PVA is often compounded with an external plasticizer such as dibutyl phthalate to reduce the minimum film forming temperature (MFFT) and to make the film flexible. Typical dispersions are slightly acidic. PVA films have poor water resistance but modified PVAs are now available with better properties. PVA is one of the cheapest dispersions available and gives good all-round properties in dry conditions, particularly as an adhesive. Large quantities are used in wood adhesives and as plaster bonding agents.

39.4.4.7 Polyvinylidene dichloride (PVDC)

Also known as polyvinylidene chloride. These lattices can give exceptionally good mechanical properties to cementitious systems. Unfortunately, hydrolysis is possible, liberating hydrochloric acid. This risk has impeded the use of PVDC with cement, particularly in systems containing steel reinforcement. The dried films are resistant to water uptake/water transmission and are, therefore, used as bonding agents for floor screeds in some countries. PVDC is likely to discolour on application to alkaline backgrounds and on exposure to ultraviolet light. The dispersions often have poor freeze–thaw stability. PVDC has good external durability and is useful in fire retardant systems. The dispersions are typically supplied at a pH of about 4, i.e. slightly acidic.

39.4.4.8 Polyvinyl propionate (PVP)

This is analogous to PVA, being made from propionic acid instead of acetic acid. It is not readily available in the UK and its home country is Germany. The properties are similar to those of a PVA but it has more resistance to water and hydrolysis.

39.4.4.9 Styrene acrylics (SA)

These thermoplastic esters are made by copolymerizing styrene with one of the acrylates, e.g. ethyl acrylate or butyl acrylate. One of the most popular types for use with cement is a 50:50 styrene:butyl acrylate copolymer. SAs are often cheaper than pure acrylics and are still suitable for external coating compositions. Hydrolysis is theoretically possible, but no problems seem to occur in practice when SA is used as recommended by the leading manufacturers. Many SAs have a high minimum film forming temperature (MFFT) and need to be compounded with a coalescent. This coalescent may have some undesirable side-effects such as retardation of the hardening of cement, or migration into adjacent products. Grades are available which have a particle size below 0.1 μm and this may help penetration into the background, e.g. for sealing dusty floors. SAs are often used in ceramic-tile adhesives and one grade which is used in water resistant tile adhesives cross-links when the ammonia in the dispersion evaporates.

39.4.4.10 Styrene butadiene (SBR)

This is an elastomeric/thermoplastic copolymer. The grades commonly used with cement contain about 60% of chemically combined styrene and do not need to be compounded with a coalescent or external plasticizer. The dispersions are often carboxylated to give extra stability and improve adhesion. Carboxylated products often give a bluish colour on mixing with cement which disappears on drying. SBR is a hydrocarbon and cannot be hydrolysed; it is therefore ideal for use in cementitious systems. SBR is susceptible to oxidation and ultraviolet radiation, the product hardening on oxidation. Although oxidation and yellowing can be minimized by incorporating anti-oxidants, SBR is less suitable for use in white external coatings than say a PAE. SBR has a good track record in cementitious systems since the 1950s. Large quantities are used in floor toppings, concrete repairs and, in the USA, for making SBR-modified concrete for replacing the top 40 mm of road bridge decks which have been damaged by reinforcement corrosion (*Figure 39.3*).[18]

As far as cement grade dispersions are concerned this section may be summarized as follows: The choice for the majority of

Figure 39.3 SBR modified concrete being laid at 40 mm thickness on a North American road bridge, to provide resistance to the penetration of de-icing salts. (Courtesy of Reichhold Chemicals Inc.)

projects will be between SBR, SA and PAE, and for typical projects the technical differences between the market leaders of each polymer type will be insignificant compared with the possible variations in performance from background preparation, mix design and workmanship.

39.5 Properties and applications of mortars containing dispersions

39.5.1 Properties of mortars containing dispersions

A wide spectrum of properties can be obtained depending on the mortar/concrete mix design, dispersion type and proportion used in the mix. Styrene butadiene (SBR), styrene acrylics (SA) and polyacrylic esters (PAE) will give broadly similar properties to the mix and are usually used at a dose rate of 10–15 l per 50 kg of cement. These dispersions have a specific gravity close to 1.0 and hence the dose rate also corresponds to 10–15 kg of wet dispersion for 50 kg of cement. This dose rate is based on a dispersion solid content of about 50%. The higher dose rate may be needed if the mix is much weaker than 1:3 cement:aggregate, particularly if the aggregate is very fine. Concentrations above 15 l per 50 kg of cement are rarely used except in some grouts and flexible floor screeds. Such higher concentrations would not significantly improve the tensile strength or flexural strength and, in any case, might not be obtainable without producing an excessively wet mix if damp aggregates are used. High concentrations do give reduced permeability, increased chemical resistance and increased strain capacity.

In a 1:3 cement:sand mortar, the use of 10–12.5 l of one of the above dispersions per 50 kg of cement can double the tensile strength and increase the flexural strength by 50%. The compressive strength is not usually increased and may be decreased through air entrainment and/or the presence of soft polymer film in the mortar matrix. This is not disadvantageous as modified mortars and concretes do not require a high compressive strength in order to be tough and durable. Furthermore, it is good practice to ensure that a repair material or screed, etc., does not have a higher compressive strength or modulus of elasticity (E) value than the background. The abrasion resistance can be increased by a factor of three. The modified mixes have excellent frost resistance, enhanced chemical resistance and low permeability to gases and liquids. The modified mixes have improved toughness and impact resistance. At a dose rate of 10 l per 50 kg of cement

in the above mix the mortars may be classified as non-combustible. Modified mortars are more resistant to carbonation. Modified mortars tend to be darker in colour than unmodified ones.

Modified mortars and concretes have a similar coefficient of linear expansion to that of the unmodified material and their E value is a little lower. Because the water:cement ratio required to obtain good workability in modified mixes is low, the drying shrinkage of these mixes is also low. These properties are very desirable for concrete repairs, renders, floor screeds, etc.

A simple demonstration of the value of polymer dispersions is to paint a slurry of the dispersion mixed with cement and a slurry of water mixed with cement onto thin strips of steel. After curing it will be found that only the strip coated with the polymer dispersion can be bent without the coating flaking off. This demonstrates the improvement in adhesion and flexibility given by the polymer dispersion (*Figure 39.4*). Polymer dispersion/cement mixtures give good corrosion protection to steel and such mixtures are, therefore, used to protect reinforcing steel in vulnerable situations and also as primer/undercoats on structural steelwork.

39.5.2 Uses of cementitious mixes containing dispersions

The use of polymer dispersions should always be considered when mortars (including renders, screeds, toppings, coatings and repair mixes) and concretes below 60-mm thickness are to be used. They may also be useful in thicker sections, but cost may then be prohibitive and the drying-out process needed for the coalescence of the dispersion particles may be too slow. The dispersions are used in new site work, in maintenance work, in precast concrete factories and for many other applications. The main uses are:

1. bonding agents;
2. floor screeds, underlayments and toppings;
3. concrete repair mortars (*Figure 39.5*);
4. fixing brick slips and ceramic tiles (*Figure 39.6*);
5. bedding paviors;
6. bricklaying mortars and external renders;
7. corrosion protection of steel;
8. renders over external insulation;
9. road-bridge decks (*Figure 39.3*);
10. sprayed coatings;
11. pipe coatings (*Figures 39.7, 39.8*);
12. grouting of open-texture Macadam;

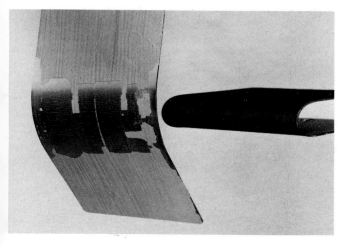

Figure 39.4 Coated steel plates. The LH plate was coated with a water/ordinary Portland cement slurry. After curing for 1 day the steel plate was slightly bent, resulting in cracking and delamination of the coating. The RH plate was coated with a SBR polymer dispersion/ordinary Portland cement slurry. After curing for 1 day it could be bent in half without any cracking or delamination of the coating. The photograph thus shows the improvement in bond and flexibility given by the polymer dispersion

13. cellar waterproofing;
14. polymer-modified roof tiles;
15. in rapid hardening mixes;
16. erosion prevention in hydraulic engineering;
17. vibration and sound deadening.

Modified cementitious mixes are often used in food-processing factories, dairies, breweries, abattoirs, animal buildings, fertilizer stores, swimming pools, sports surfaces, squash courts, ships, sea defences, cold stores, car park decks and ramps, effluent gullies and in the repair of ancient buildings. For use in food factories, for ease of cleaning epoxy or polyurethane coatings are often applied over dispersion-modified screeds. The modified

Figure 39.5 Polar bears at London Zoo proving the wet abrasion resistance of polymer modified repair mortars (Courtesy of Ronacrete Ltd and London Zoological Society)

screed provides a tough levelling base for the smooth coating and reduces the risk of osmotic blistering of the coating.

39.6 Site-usage notes

Substrates must be clean and mechanically sound. Ideally, old concrete should be scabbled or shot blasted to remove laitence, etc. A bonding agent should be used as recommended by the supplier of the dispersion, and it should be noted that some bonding agents only have an open time of about 20 min after application to the background. Epoxy bonding agents are available which combine the advantages of water resistance and long open time.

Free fall mixers should be avoided for most mix types as they do not mix low-slump modified mortars efficiently, and can entrain too much air. Forced-action mixers are strongly recommended.

The mixing time after the dispersion has been added should be minimized in order to limit air entrainment. With some dispersions it is necessary to add anti-foam direct to the mixer. The mixing sequence is not critical but it is advisable to avoid adding undiluted dispersions to dry-powder mixes. The appearance of many modified fresh mixes is deceptive as they can easily be trowelled when they seem to be too dry. The slump of the mix should be as low as possible, consistent with good compaction. A typical mix and mix sequence for a floor screed would be:

1. Pre-mix 92 kg of damp (5% moisture) washed BS 882[4] type C sand with 25 kg of ordinary Portland cement.
2. Mix in 6 l of the dispersion (approx 50% solids).
3. Mix in water in small increments until a stiff but workable mix is obtained. Very little extra water will be needed in this example as the damp sand has contributed 4.6 l and the dispersion 3 l, thus giving a water:cement ratio of 0.304 before any extra water is added.

In the above example the dispersion:cement ratio is 0.24 and the polymer:cement ratio is 0.12.

Figure 39.6 Brick slips fixed to vertical surfaces and the soffit, using SBR modified mortar with SBR/cement primer coat: Barbican Centre (Courtesy of Ronacrete Ltd)

Figures 39.7, 39.8 Use of polymer modified mortar for encasing steel sewer outfall pipes at the welded joint position, prior to dragging the pipes out to sea. The good adhesion to steel and fast build up of toughness are valuable properties for this application (Courtesy of Ronacrete Ltd)

Correct curing is important and this involves damp curing for 1–2 days followed by air dry curing. This procedure provides sufficient moisture for the cement to hydrate, followed by the drying period which is necessary for the dispersion to dry out to enable the film-forming process to take place. Polymer dispersions act to some extent as integral curing agents as far as the body of the mix is concerned. However, freshly applied polymer-modified mixes are more sensitive to surface mud cracking than unmodified mixes because they do not bleed and hence water can be lost by evaporation quicker than it can be replaced from the body of the mix. It is therefore important to apply a curing compound, or cover with polythene film, within 1 h of applying the modified mix if the drying conditions are severe, e.g. more than $200 \text{ g m}^{-2} \text{ h}^{-1}$ water loss from the surface (calculated over the first hour after placing).

Cementitious mixes containing polymer dispersions are easy to make and use. Good results will be obtained if the above recommendations are used, together with the following summary of good practice points:

1. Good background preparation is essential.
2. The suppliers recommendations regarding dampening of the background and priming must be followed.
3. Fresh, but cool, cement must be used.
4. Thoroughly washed sand must be used.
5. The mix density should be checked to ensure that the mixing method does not entrain too much air.
6. The water:cement ratio must be kept below 0.4.
7. Air-entraining agents, masonry cement or carbon black must not be used.
8. If hydrated lime is used in the mix it should not exceed 10% of the cement weight.
9. All the mix should be used within about 30 min of preparation.
10. Trowelling should proceed with the work; over-trowelling may cause blisters.
11. Tools should be cleaned with coarse wire wool and water immediately after use. White spirit helps to remove partially hardened mixes.
12. Damp cure for one or two days and then air cure.

References

1 CHEESMAN, G. C. N. and POLLARD, K. R. N., *Conference Proceedings of the Plastic and Rubber Institute*, paper 10 (1978)
2 ISENBURG, J. E. and VANDERHOFF, J. W., 'Hypothesis for reinforcement of Portland cement by polymer latex', *Journal of American Ceramic Society*, **57**, 242–245 (1974)
3 CHEESMAN, G. C. N. C., Doverstrand Ltd, private communication (1983)
4 BRITISH STANDARDS INSTITUTION, *BS 882 Specification for aggregates from natural sources for concrete*, Milton Keynes (1983)
5 BRITISH STANDARDS INSTITUTION, *BS 5750 Guide to quality management*, Milton Keynes, Parts 1–6 (1981–1987)
6 INTERNATIONAL ORGANIZATION FOR STANDARDIZATION, *ISO 9000 Quality systems—model for quality assurance*
7 BRITISH STANDARDS INSTITUTION, *BS 5270 Specification for PVAc emulsion bonding agents for indoor use with gypsum building plasters*, Milton Keynes (1989)
8 BRITISH STANDARDS INSTITUTION, *BS 3544 Methods of test for PVA adhesives for wood*, Milton Keynes (1988)
9 BRITISH STANDARDS INSTITUTION, *BS 4071 Specification for PVA adhesives for wood*, Milton Keynes (1988)
10 BRITISH STANDARDS INSTITUTION, *BS 4551 Methods of testing mortars, screeds and plasters*, Milton Keynes (1980)
11 BRITISH STANDARDS INSTITUTION, *BS 6319 Testing of resin compositions for use in construction*, Milton Keynes (1983/1987)
12 COUTINHO, A. S., 'A fissurabilidade dos cimentos, argamassas e betões por efeito da sua contraçcâo', (Cracking tendency in cements, mortars and concretes due to shrinkage), *Lab. Nac. Eng. Civil Publication No. 57* (1954) (in Portuguese with English summary)
13 McCURRICH, L. H., KEELEY, C., CHERITON, L. W. and TURNER, K. J., 'Mortar repair systems—corrosion protection for damaged reinforced concrete'. In *Corrosion of Reinforcement in Concrete Construction* (ed. A. P. Crane), Ellis Horwood, Chichester, Chap. 15, pp. 235–253 (1983)
14 BRITISH STANDARDS INSTITUTION, *BS 1881 Testing concrete, Part 5: Methods for testing hardened concrete for other than strength*, Milton Keynes, (1970)
15 BRITISH STANDARDS INSTITUTION, *BS 1881 Testing concrete*, Milton Keynes, Part 122 (1983) *Method of determination for water absorption*
16 FIGG, J., *Magazine of Concrete Research*, **25**, 213–219 (1973); **36**, 241–245 (1984)

17 OHAMA, Y., 'Polymer modified mortars and concretes'. In *Concrete Admixtures Handbook* (ed. V. S. Ramachandran), Noyes Publications, New Jersey, Chap. 7 (1984)
18 KUHLMAN, L. A., 'Latex modified concrete for the repair and rehabilitation of bridges', *FeRFA Seminar on Resins in Construction*, London (25 Oct. 1984)

Bibliography

Acrylic latex

LAVELLE, J. A., *Acrylic Latex Modified Portland Cement*, ACI Fall Convention, Baltimore, American Concrete Institute, Detroit (1986)

Bonding agents

NELSON, I., 'Vinyl acetate–ethylene copolymer emulsion building aid', *Polymers Paint Colour Journal* (20 Apr. 1983)
OHAMA, Y., 'Adhesion durability of polymer modified mortars through ten year outdoor exposure'. In *Proceedings of the 3rd International Congress on Polymers in Concrete*, Vol. 1, Nihon University, Koriyama, Japan (1981)
PERKINS, P. H., 'The use of SBR/cement slurry for bonding coats', *Concrete*, **18**, 18–19 (1984)
SASSE, H. R., *Adhesion Between Polymers and Concrete*, Chapman & Hall, London (1986)
TABOR, L. J., 'Twixt old and new: achieving a bond when casting fresh concrete against hardened concrete', ICE Conference on Structural Faults and Repair, Engineering Technics Press, Edinburgh (1985)

Carbonation

OHAMA, Y. *et al.*, 'Accelerated carbonation of polymer modified mortars by carbon dioxide pressurising method', *CAJ Review*, 288–291 (1984)

Chemical resistance

FATTUHI, N. I. and HUGHES, B. P., 'Resistance to acid attack of concrete with different admixtures or coatings', *International Journal of Cement Composites and Lightweight Concrete*, **8**, 223–230 (1986)

Concrete repair

CLEAR, K. C. and CHOLLAR, B. H., 'Styrene–butadiene latex modifiers for bridge deck overlay concrete', *National Technical Report No. FHWA RD 78-35*, Federal Highway Administration, Washington, DC (1978)
CONCRETE SOCIETY, 'Repair of concrete damaged by reinforcement corrosion', *Concrete Society Technical Report No. 26*, Wexham, Slough (1984)
KUHLMAN, L. A., 'Performance of latex modified concrete overlay', Institute for Bridge Integrity and Safety: Seminar on Bridge Rehabilitation and Modern Materials, New York (1987)
PERKINS, P. H., *Repair, Protection and Waterproofing of Concrete Structures*, Elsevier Applied Science Publishers, Amsterdam (1986)

Durability

OHAMA, Y., 'Durability performance of polymer modified mortars', Proceedings of 2nd International Conference on Durability of Building Materials and Components, Gaitherberg, USA, pp. 242–248 (1981)

Floors/paving

ALEXANDERSON, J., 'Polymer cement concrete for industrial floors', Proceedings of 3rd International Congress on Polymers in Concrete, Nihan University, Koriyama, Japan (1981)
DENNIS, R., 'The use of SBR latex in cementitious floors', Industrial Flooring Conference, London (1988)
FEDERATION OF RESIN FORMULATORS AND APPLICATORS, *Polymer Flooring Guide, Application Guide No. 6*, FRFA, Aldershot (reissued 1989)
HALL, R. E. T., 'Grouted Macadams', paper presented to Road and Buildings Materials Group of Society of Chemical Industry (21 Oct. 1982)

Freeze–thaw resistance

HIRAI, K. WATANABE, M., KAWAKAMI, K., KIKUCHI, Y. and GOTOH, K., 'Application of polymer modified mortar in renovation of concrete structure showing deterioration due to frost action', Proceedings of 3rd International Congress on Polymers in Concrete, Nihon University, Koriyama, Japan, p. 347ff. (1981)
OHAMA, Y. and SHIROISHIDA, K., *Freeze/Thaw Durability of Polymer Modified Mortars*, Nihon University, Koriyama, Japan (1983)

Manufacture

BLACKLEY, D. C., *Emulsion Polymerisation*, Applied Science Publishers, London (1975)

Redispersible powder polymers

HACKEL, E., BENG, P. and HORLER, S., 'The use of redispersible powder polymers in concrete restoration', Proceedings of 5th International Congress on Polymers in Concrete, The Concrete Society, Wexham, Slough, pp. 305–308 (1987)
SCHULZ, J., 'Dispersion powders in cement', Proceedings of 4th International Congress on Polymers in Concrete, Technisch Hochschule, Darmstadt, pp. 103–107 (1984)

General

AMERICAN CONCRETE INSTITUTE, 'Guide for the use of polymers in concrete', *ACI Journal* (Sep./Oct. 1986)
CONCRETE SOCIETY, *Concrete Society Technical Report No. 9* (1975)
CONCRETE SOCIETY, Proceedings of 1st, 2nd, 3rd, 4th and 5th International Congresses on Polymers in Concrete (1975, 1978, 1981, 1984, 1988), details from the Concrete Society
OHAMA, Y., Extensive bibliography available from Dr D. Fowler, Department of Civil Engineering, University of Texas at Austin, Ernest Cockrell Hall 5.208, Austin, Texas 78712, USA
RAMACHANDRAN, V. S., 'Polymer-modified mortars and concretes'. In *Concrete Admixtures Handbook* (ed. Y. Ohama), Noyes Publications, New Jersey, Chap. 7 (1984)

40

Polyethylene (Polyethene)

W J Allwood BSc
BP Chemicals

Contents

40.1 Structure, manufacture and properties 40/3
    40.1.1 Terminology 40/4

40.2 Fabrication and usage 40/4

40.3 Uses in building and construction 40/5
    40.3.1 Pipe and fittings systems 40/5
    40.3.2 Electrical uses 40/11
    40.3.3 Road and soil reinforcement 40/13
    40.3.4 Damp-proof membranes 40/13

40.4 European standardization 40/13

References 40/13

Bibliography 40/15

40.1 Structure, manufacture and properties

Polyethylene is a thermoplastic and is produced by polymerizing ethylene (ethene) using commercially developed processes[1]

$$nCH_2{=}CH_2 \longrightarrow [CH_2 \cdot CH_2]_n$$

ethylene   process   polyethylene

In these processes,[2-5] the single ethylene molecules with or without α-olefins are formed into molecular chains (CH_2 units) and these may be linear or branched. Branches may be short or long chain and their type may be identified by either infra-red analytical techniques or by the use of nuclear magnetic resonance (NMR). The longer the molecular chain, the higher the molecular weight and the higher the bulk melt viscosity of the polymer when it is eventually processed into a product. A convenient way of describing this property is to use the melt flow rate (MFR). The method of test is described in ISO 1133[6] and normally condition 4 (190°C, 2.16 kg load) is used. The method is based on the principle of measuring the mass of molten polyethylene flowing through a given heated die orifice under a given load in 10 min.

The way in which the molecular chains closely fit with each other in order to form crystalline regions is shown in *Figure 40.1*. Where close fitting is not possible due to the chain configuration, e.g. due to the inclusion of branches, the regions are termed amorphous. Thus polyethylene is a semicrystalline product. The theoretical density of the perfect polyethylene crystal is 1000 kg m^{-3} and that of the amorphous region is 850 kg m^{-3}.[7]

The crystallinity of polyethylene is conveniently described by measuring its density at 23°C according to ISO 1183.[8] However, it is important to specify the heat treatment given to the specimen because the crystallinity of a product will be affected by the rate of cooling from the melt. The slower the rate of cooling, the higher the density/crystallinity and vice versa. Hence, ISO 1872: Part 1[9] carefully describes the procedure for density measurement and the term 'conventional density' is defined. The values for both melt flow rate (MFR) and density have a great influence on the properties of the polyethylene. The value of these properties depends on the production conditions and process used. A list of typical polyethylene production process types is given in *Table 40.1* together with the range of melt flow rates and density now made.[10,11] The products are made on chemical plant by varying the temperature, pressure, catalyst type and polymerization medium (liquid, gas or suspension phase).

These variations lead to differences in polyethylene structure between process types and, particularly, in the spread of molecular weight. A typical normal-distribution molecular-weight spread (polydispersity) is shown in *Figure 40.2*. This distribution is normally varied by the choice of catalyst,[12,13] which greatly influences the polymerization reaction. The molecular-weight spread is normally measured by using gel permeation chromatography (GPC).

Table 40.1 Density and melt flow rate (MFR) ranges for polyethylene process types

Process type	Density (kg m^{-3})	MFR[a] (g/10 min)
High pressure, autoclave or tubular reactor	910–928	0.1–7.0
Slurry (suspension), low/medium pressure, Phillips catalysts	930–965	2[b]–4.0
Slurry (suspension), low/medium pressure, Ziegler catalysts	930–965	<1[b]–50.0
Gas phase, proprietary catalysts	910–960	<0.1–100
Solution (liquid phase), Phillips/ Zeigler	900–960	0.25–80.0

[a] 2.16 kg at 190°C (ISO 1133[6]).
[b] Load 21.6 kg.

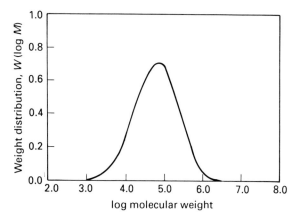

Figure 40.2 A typical normal molecular-weight distribution of polyethylene. Averages: $M(N) = 25.7$; $M(V) = 105.1$; $M(W) = 128.5$; $M(Z) = 448.9$; polydispersity $= M(W)/M(N) = 4.99$

The properties of the polyethylene are dependent on three parameters; the melt flow rate, which depends on the molecular weight; the density, which depends on the crystallinity; and the molecular-weight spread, which depends on the polydispersity. The influence of these parameters is given in a general sense in *Table 41.2*. In order to standardize these parameters, the properties are normally measured on specimens either compression moulded or injection moulded using specified conditions.[9] The values of these properties can only be a guide for comparison as the important properties are those of the manufactured product which will actually be used in service. This aspect will be explored later by application. The values of

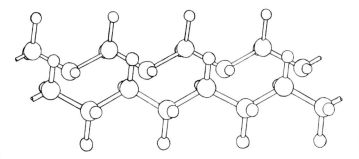

Figure 40.1 The structure of the polyethylene molecule. Large circles, carbon atoms; small circles, hydrogen atoms. ○: carbon atom; ○: hydrogen atom

Table 40.2 Typical effect of molecular weight (MW), crystallinity and molecular weight distribution[a] (MWD) on the properties of polyethylene

Property	Increase in average MW	Increase in crystallinity	Increase in breadth of a given MWD
Melt flow rate	Decrease	—	—
Density	—	Increase	—
Rate of change of bulk melt viscosity with shear rate	—	—	Increase
Tensile strength at yield	—	Increase	
Tensile strength at break	Increase	Increase	—
Elongation at break	Increase	Decrease	—
Impact strength	Increase	Increase	Decrease
Resistance to deformation	—	Increase	—
Barrier properties	—	Increase	—
Chemical resistance	Increase	Increase	—
Dielectric constant	—	Increase	—
Stiffness	—	Increase	—
Hardness	—	Increase	—
Environmental stress crack resistance	Increase	Decrease	Increase
Thermal conductivity	—	Increase	—

[a] Also known as polydispersity.

the physical properties of polyethylene measured using ISO methods of test for the density range 910–965 kg m^{-3} at a given nominal molecular weight (MFR) are given in *Table 40.3* and this shows the effect of density. The molecular-weight dependent properties are also indicated, where applicable.

40.1.1 Terminology

Polyethylenes are commonly referred to as being low density (LDPE), medium density (MDPE), high density (HDPE), linear low density (LLDPE), etc., but these labels can cause confusion to a user. For example, LLDPE is termed as such because at a density of 920 kg m^{-3} its structure is less branched (enough to be considered 'linear') than the corresponding LDPE of the

same density made by another process. It has different properties because of this difference in structure. An engineer should, therefore, consider the properties of a polyethylene material from a given 'family' of polymers made by a process. Each polyethylene 'family' should be considered for its potential performance in the product, i.e. fitness for purpose. Polyethylenes are more correctly referred to by process as in *Table 40.1*, e.g. high pressure autoclave, rather than by just using labels like, say, LDPE.

40.2 Fabrication and usage

Polyethylene is one of the easiest thermoplastics to fabricate. In order to form it into products, polyethylene is melted using heat, conveyed either by an extrusion or moulding process through a forming procedure with or without pressure, cooled, quality assured and stored for customer delivery. This is a highly simplistic view because the end fabrication process is highly sophisticated, highly instrumented and controlled. Details are better dealt with elsewhere by specific application (see Bibliography).

Typical fabrication processes are:

1. *Blow moulding*[14] to form bottles, containers, fuel tanks, large drums, etc.
2. *Film extrusion*[15,16] to make bags, sacks, breadwrap, agricultural film, etc.
3. *Injection moulding*[17] to manufacture boxes, crates, dustbins, food containers, etc.
4. *Extrusion* to make pipe[18–20] and wire/cable[21–23].

The tonnages of all types of polyethylene used in the USA, Western Europe and Japan is shown in *Table 40.4*.[24] The major constructional uses of polyethylene accounted for well over one million tonne in 1988 in the areas shown in the table. These uses are discussed below, the major ones being the manufacture of pipes and cables.

Table 40.4 The usage of polyethylene in the USA, Western Europe and Japan in 1988[24]

Application	Million tonne
Blow moulding	2.8
Film/coating	8.6
Injection moulding	2.8
Pipe/cable extrusion	1.3

Table 40.3 Physical properties of polyethylene (general)

Property	Method	Units	Polyethylene		
			Low density	Medium density	High density
Density	ISO 1183	kg m^{-1}	910–925	926–940	941–965
Tensile strength at yield	ISO 527 (type 2 speed)	MPa	8–13	13–19	19–32
Elongation at break	ISO 527 (type 2 speed)	%	50–1000, depending on molecular weight (MFR)		
Flexural modulus	ISO 178	MPa	50–200	200–700	700–1300
Impact strength (Charpy)	ISO 179	kJ m^{-2}	6 to non-break		
Vicat softening point, 1-kg load	ISO 306	°C	85–100	100–118	118–133
Environmental stress, crack resistance, F_{50} time	ISO 4599	h	<1 to >1000 h, depending on molecular weight (MFR)		
Coefficient of thermal expansion		10^{-5} °C^{-1}	10–13		

40.3 Uses in building and construction

40.3.1 Pipe and fittings systems

Extruded polyethylene pressure pipe was first used in the UK for the distribution of drinking water in the 1950s, mainly for service connections below 2-in. (50 mm) nominal bore. Both low density (LDPE) and high density polyethylenes (HDPE) were originally used as defined in BS 1972 (LDPE) and BS 3284 (HDPE) and specified black pipe which was normally jointed mechanically using metal fittings. These Standards have been, or are being, withdrawn.

Prior to 1970, DuPont (UK) introduced a gas-distribution system[25] made from medium density polyethylene (MDPE) (liquid phase process) in the USA and this was marketed as a heat fusion welded system of pipe and injection moulded fittings. The fittings were made from the same polyethylene as the pipe.

The principle of this system was taken up by British Gas and rapid development occurred in the UK culminating in the introduction of a yellow gas-distribution system conforming to rigid engineering specifications.[26] The Nationalized Joint Utilities Group (NJUG) had recommended yellow for gas pipes and blue for water pipes for the identification of buried services and these colours were introduced to reduce interference damage and accidents.

Both yellow and blue polyethylene pipe compounds were introduced into the UK market by BP Chemicals (slurry process polyethylene) in 1982 and 1987,[27] respectively, under the trade name Rigidex. In Western Europe black pipe with blue stripes is used for water and in France black pipe with yellow stripes is used for gas, whilst in Denmark, Holland, Germany mainly yellow pipe is used for gas-distribution systems.

40.3.1.1 Essential requirements[28]

(*i*) *Resistance to internal pressure* Polyethylene materials are pressure tested to failure in extruded pipe form in order to develop a log circumferential stress versus log time data relationship. The circumferential stress is as defined by Barlow's formula

$$\sigma = \frac{P \times D(D-e)}{2e} \tag{40.1}$$

where D is the outside pipe diameter, e is the wall thickness, P is the internal pressure (MPa), and σ is the circumferential stress (MPa).

The data are produced at different temperatures using established pipe-testing standard methods such as ISO 1167[29] and ASTM D2837.[30] Current thinking at the ISO Technical Committee writing Standards (TC 138) is that the data produced should be extrapolated to determine a value for long-term hydrostatic strength (LTHS) at 50 years at 20°C using the empirical formula

$$\log t = A + \frac{B}{T}\log\sigma + \frac{C}{T} \tag{40.2}$$

where A, B and C are constants, T is the temperature (K), σ is the circumferential stress (MPa) and t is time (h).

A typical plot is shown in *Figure 40.3*. The two 'slopes' in this figure have different coefficients in the equation (A_1, A_2, B_1, B_2, C_1 and C_2) because the mode of failure on the 'horizontal' line is normally ductile (by gross deformation) and where the slope is steeper (A_2, B_2 and C_2) the mode is brittle (pinhole or slit).

The LTHS, the lower 97.5% confidence level for the circumferential stress, is determined using regression analysis and validity testing according to ISO DTR 9080, which is still under preparation as a Draft Technical Report. Whilst there has

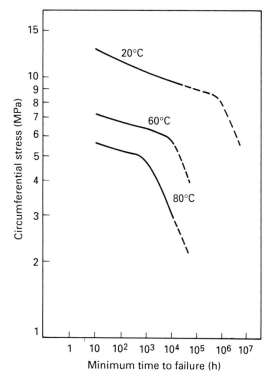

Figure 40.3 Plot of pipe stress rupture of Rigidex PC 002-50 R102. (Courtesy of BP Chemicals Ltd)

been considerable discussion and lack of experience in determining the LTHS using the empirical equation there is a great deal of merit in this approach to design and it is hoped that it will be adopted so that a universal approach is used.

The maximum allowable operating pressure (MAOP) for a pipe then relies on the use of minimum required strength (MRS) to which a design factor is applied to obtain the hydrostatic design basis (HDB).

$$\text{MAOP} = \frac{2 \times \text{MRS}}{(\text{SDR}-1) \times \text{design factor}} \tag{40.3}$$

where MRS = 3.2, 4.0, 6.3, 8 or 10 MPa for LTHS as measured by extrapolation and SDR is the standard dimension ratio (diameter divided by the wall thickness). The design factor for water is typically a minimum of 1.3 and for gas at least 2 and a minimum of 3.25 in the UK and France. The minimum required strengths (MRS) have been denoted by using the Renard series R10 and R20 and for polyethylene materials in pipe form this denotes values of 3.2, 4.0, 6.3, 8 or 10 dependent on the type of polyethylene used.

The reason for the maximum allowable pressure approach is that this is most appropriate for systems (series of pipes jointed with fittings). It is becoming more common for such assemblies to be tested to prove that the jointing used will outperform the pipe. The latest thinking in CEN indicates that a systems approach will be taken for all fluids under pressure. Pipe dimensions and pressure ratings have been standardized in order to facilitate compatibility between systems and reduce barriers to trade (see Bibliography).

(*ii*) *Deformation* Polyethylene exhibits viscoelastic behaviour, that is, it displays both viscous flow and elastic behaviour. The modulus (stress divided by strain) is, therefore, time dependent.

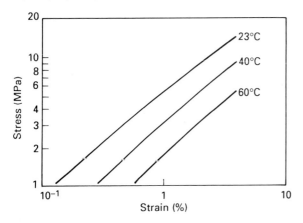

Figure 40.4 Typical 100-s isochronous stress–strain curves. (Courtesy of BP Chemicals Ltd)

The strain or deformation under a constant load increases very slowly but continuously due to flow processes in the material, and at high stresses Hooke's law is no longer obeyed.

The phenomenon, known as creep, has been studied and various mechanistic theories developed. Normally, BS 4618[32] recommendations are followed in order to produce design data. A typical set of 100-s isochronous stress/strain curves determined on pipe-grade polyethylene at 20, 60 and 80°C are shown in *Figure 40.4*. It can be seen from this figure that as the temperature increases, the degree of viscous flow increases and the importance of time in terms of the deformation properties increases.

Engineers must always consider whether a short-term modulus (100 s) or a longer term modulus (50 years) is applicable to the design of a system. Normally, the pipe in a pressure test will fail in a gross ductile or brittle manner before any failure due to slow creep occurs. In buried pipe lines, the pipe will maintain its circular cross-section under load provided that the soil is properly compacted around the pipe and it is protected against long-term collapse. Many experiments[33,34] have been carried out on buried flexible pipes to confirm this. The deformation can be calculated from Spangler's formula[35,36]

$$\frac{\Delta x}{D} = \frac{0.1P}{8EI/D + 0.061E'} \tag{40.4}$$

where Δx is the deflection, E is the creep modulus of pipe as a ring, I is the moment of inertia, P is the load, E' is the soil reaction modulus, and D is the outer diameter of the pipe.

(iii) Fracture The most common mode of failure in everyday life is fracture and the fracture behaviour of polyethylene needs to be understood even though it is regarded as a generally tough thermoplastic. Brittle fracture of polyethylene is most easily achieved in the laboratory using an impact test. Sharply notched Charpy and Izod bars are commonly used to assess resistance to fracture. These may be moulded or cut from existing pipe. Slow crack growth can also be induced by the application of stress for long periods at abnormally high temperatures or by stressing sharply notched specimens for long periods. The results of such tests are strongly dependent on the specimen geometry, but they can be rationalized by the application of fracture mechanics.

Fracture mechanics methods[37] are well established for metals and are based on the concept that flaws exist in all materials and that these flaws will propagate cracks when a critical stress condition exists at the crack tip. In a material under stress, a stress intensity factor, K, can be defined which relates the bulk

stress to the crack geometry. Cracks propagate when K reaches a critical value, K_c, the material fracture toughness.

$$K_c^2 = Y^2\sigma^2 a = EG_c \quad \text{(plane stress)} \tag{40.5}$$

$$K_c^2 = \frac{EG_c}{(1 - v^2)} \quad \text{(plane strain)} \tag{40.6}$$

where K_c is the fracture toughness; E is the material modulus, σ is the bulk stress, G_c is the strain energy release rate, a is the crack strength, v is Poisson's ratio, and Y is the geometrical function.

Plane strain conditions arise when the wall thickness of the specimen is large enough to prevent the material deforming in the through-thickness direction. In thin sections, the plane stress conditions generally apply.

The parameter K_c can be measured at slow crack speeds using single-edge-notched specimens and the fundamental flaw size has been estimated at 200 μm.[38] A typical K_c/a crack speed plot is shown in *Figure 40.5*. At high fracture speeds[37] it is easier to deduce G_c, strain energy release rate, from impact tests. This method does allow an estimation of the resistance of materials to fast crack growth which is normally measured by costly full-scale tests.[40]

Standards allow for these problems by introducing high-temperature stress rupture tests with and without notches for slow crack growth and defining a minimum G_c value or requiring a crack-propagation test for fast crack growth. Research is still being carried out, but it is certain that early problems of fracture in high density polyethylene laid in the 1960s have been overcome by the use of modern polyethylene materials (medium density polyethylene).

40.3.1.2 Gas distribution

As mentioned earlier, British Gas decided that they wanted a polyethylene gas-distribution system for up to 4-bar pressure. On the basis of rigorous performance requirements in the specification dictated by the user, the use of polyethylene in this application has been very successful. The flexibility and use of novel installation techniques (see Section 40.3.1.7) allows cost savings of up to 40% of total installation cost as compared with the cost of ductile iron pipes. The fact that a gas-tight, easily identifiable, system of joints and fittings is available has revolutionized the UK gas-distribution system. The critical aspect is the performance of the pipes and joints, i.e. the system as a whole. Performance includes resistance to internal pressure,

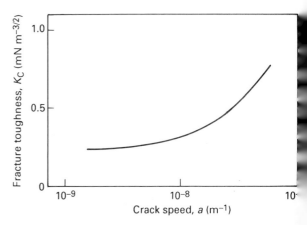

Figure 40.5 Fracture toughness of Rigidex PC 002-50 R102 as a function of crack speed: 80°C in water

Table 40.5 Physical properties of yellow gas pipe/fittings compound (medium density polyethylene)[a]

Property	Typical value	Units	Test methods
Melt flow rate 190°C, 2.16 kg	0.2	g/10 min	ISO 1133,[6] Proc. 4
Density	940	kg m^{-3}	ISO 1872[9]
Tensile stress at yield	18	MPa	ISO R527[41]
Elongation at break	>600	%	ISO R527[41]
Impact strength (Izod)	930	J m^{-1} notch	ISO 180[42]
Flexural modulus	700	MPa	ISO 178[43]
Vicat softening temperature	116	°C	ISO 306,[44] method A
Brittleness temperature	< − 70	°C	ISO 974[45]
Environmental stress crack resistance, F_{50}	>1000	h	ISO 4599[46]

[a] Courtesy of BP Chemicals Ltd.

both short term and long term. The minimum required strength (see Section 48.3.1.1(i)) required is 8.3 MPa at 20°C. The resistance of pipes to failure due to internal pressure at 80°C is required to be greater than 1000 h at a circumferential wall stress of 4 MPa.

Field failures indicate that it is secondary effects that cause leakage and a certain amount of surface damage during handling must be allowed for, especially during slip lining and narrow trenching. Thus British Gas have introduced a notched pressure test to make sure the polyethylene in pipe form has good resistance to slow crack growth. The principle of the test is to introduce four notches, to simulate damage, at 90° intervals around the pipe to a depth of 0.2 times the wall thickness. The length of the notches, the method of cutting the notch and the notch cutter are all specified. The current performance test requirement is typically 1000 h at 80°C with, for example, an internal pressure of 8 bar for a pipe of standard dimension ratio (SDR) 11 without failure.

Other performance requirements include oxidation resistance, weatherability, suitability for butt fusion and proof of compatibility between different polyethylene types. Typical physical properties of a yellow (medium density polyethylene) gas pipe compound are shown in *Table 40.5*.

A very useful property of polyethylene pipes for gas is the ability to use 'squeeze-off' techniques whereby the pipe is compressed to cut off the gas flow. This aspect is very useful in carrying out repairs on 'live' systems. The performance requirement for the pipe is to pass the basic pipe-test requirements at 80°C after squeeze-off has been performed and rerounding has taken place. Pipes up to 315 mm in diameter have been treated in this way.

Approvals for pipe/fittings manufacturers are phased[26] up to 250 mm outer diameter (OD). Phase-1 approval allows manufacture and sale and phase-2 approval allows this to be retained by running long-term tests including weathering for 1 year and subsequently testing to the specification. Above 250 mm OD, a preliminary approval stage is included before phase 1 because of the costs involved before entering into phases 1 and 2.

Process-control testing is required during pipe and fitting manufacture to demonstrate the continuing satisfactory quality

on a day-to-day basis and programmes for testing are laid out using procedures which conform to BS 5750: Part 2.[47] Also included in this standard are ongoing validation tests which may be, for example, a 10 000 h test at 20°C on jointed assemblies.

The current International Standard for gas pipes ISO 4437[48] published in 1988 is already out of date and a revision is in progress under ISO Technical Committee TC138/SC 4. In the UK, now that British Gas plc (BG plc) has been denationalized, a draft British Standard has been prepared for the use of industrial gas users as well as BG plc and manufacturers of pipe and fittings. In France also, new gas-pipe/fittings specifications have been published.[49] Standard specifications also exist in Denmark,[50] Spain, Italy, West Germany and Belgium. These National Standards vary in type and content, but all have some similarity to the ISO or the original British Gas Specifications and it is hoped that a compromise will eventually be achieved at international level to allow rigorous properly specified pipe systems to be used to ensure safety and integrity.

40.3.1.3 Water distribution

Polyethylene has been used for potable water distribution for many years. In the UK, the water industry in conjunction with the Water Research Centre and the British Plastics Federation produced *Information and Guidance Note (IGN) 4-32-02* which subsequently became BS 6572: 1985.[51] This standard covers blue pipes from 20 mm up to and including 63 mm outer diameter (OD) for operating pressures up to 12 bar at 20°C. The minimum required strength (MRS) is 8.3 MPa giving a hydrostatic design basis (HDB) of 6.3 MPa using the design factor normally used for water applications of 1.3. Although the main reason for the introduction was the blue identification of buried services, the successful use of systems for gas distribution had a profound effect. Leakage of water from broken/corroded iron pipes or poor joints could be stopped by using a heat fusion welded system with high resistance to slow crack growth coupled with pipe flexibility and facility of installation.[52,53] A black version of pipe for above-ground use (BS 6730[54]) was introduced in 1986.

The performance requirements of pipes cover both short-term and long-term resistance to internal pressure at both 20°C and 80°C. In addition, resistance to oxidation and compliance of pipe to the water-quality requirements as detailed in BS 6920[55] is required. All materials, including polyethylene compounds, are required to be submitted to the Department of the Environment New Materials Committee for approval as well as being listed by the Water Fittings Byelaws Scheme.

For sizes greater than 63 mm OD, IGN 4-32-03[56] was published in May 1987. This specification was prepared by the Water Research Centre and consists of three parts which cover different pipe sizes: Part 1, general[57]; Part 2, 90–315 mm[58]; and Part 3, 355–1000 mm.[56] The basic difference between IGN 4-32-02[59] and IGN 4-32-03[56−58] is the choice of design factor used. The HDB was chosen as 5.0 MPa but the MRS remained at 8.3 MPa, thus the design factor was 1.66. This essentially meant that the maximum operating pressure was initially 10 bar as compared with 12 bar for sizes of 63 mm and below.

Because water pipes can operate at much higher pressures than gas, a cautious attitude has been taken regarding the possibility of fast fracture, even though it has not been possible to generate a fast fracture in current pipe compounds when the pipe is full of water. The Water Research Centre/Water Authorities Association Manual for medium density polyethylene (MDPE) pipe systems for water supply has been published to offer practical advice on design, use and operation of MDPE pipelines.[60] As a result of experience and experimental work,[61] the MDPE pipes up to and including 180 mm OD have recently been rerated to 12 bar, i.e. the design factor has been reduced from 1.66 to 1.3. This typifies the dynamic nature of standards which should never be restrictive in their development and growth in the light of good experience and practice.

A separate specification, IGN 4-32-04,[62] identifies the requirements for polyethylene joints and fittings suitable for heat fusion jointing to pipes complying with IGN 4-32-03: Part 3[56] and other specifications are in preparation dealing with electrofusion jointing. A key aspect of these specifications is the requirement that the manufacturers operate an acceptable quality-assurance system in compliance with BS 5770: Part 2.[47]

40.3.1.4 Sewers/outfalls

Non-pressure sewers can be laid directly using welded strings of pipes up to 1600 mm outer diameter (OD) made from medium density (MDPE) or high density polyethylene (HDPE) or for renovation of pipelines using slip-lining techniques[63] (see Section 40.3.1.8). A further technique is to use 'Snaplock' MDPE pipe as developed by Stewarts & Lloyds Ltd. Snaplock joints are made between short lengths of pipe up to 450 mm OD and jacking or pulling lengths together in an existing manhole. This is a spigot-and-socket joint machined within the wall thickness of the pipe ends, with no interruption of internal bore or outside diameter. Each joint is supplied with an 'O' ring seal which, with the close tolerance of the machining, ensures a locktight seal when the pipes are snapped together by hydraulic force.

When slip-lining is used, the gap between the old pipeline and the new polyethylene pipe is normally filled with cementitious grout which is pumped in to support the pipe if the old pipeline collapses. The design of pipe for this purpose involves the possibility of buckling the pipe during the grouting procedure. The grout also reduces thermal expansion and contraction. A trial scheme carried out in Bolton in 1979[64] to slip line a 600 mm OD brick sewer of 140 m length with a 450 mm SDR41 showed that the contractor was on site for 5 weeks as opposed to 15 weeks for conventional open cut techniques and the capital cost per metre installed was 40–50% lower with the slip-lining technique.

The Water Research Centre, in consultation with the British Plastics Federation, prepared IGN 4-32-05[65] which defines the requirements for materials, dimensions, joint testing, marking and workmanship for black polyethylene (MDPE and HDPE) pipes intended for the renovation of gravity sewers by slip-lining where the lining is designed to act as a flexible pipeline, i.e. one in which the passive reaction of side support is required to assist resistance to deformation by vertical forces.

Polyethylene has good abrasion resistance,[66] better than ductile iron, and is not subject to build up of slime or silt because of its smooth surface and has an excellent hydraulic capacity. The fact that the nominal diameter of the sewer is reduced by slip lining rarely reduces the flow capacity of a polyethylene sewer of smaller diameter.

Larger diameter pipes (900–1600 mm) have been used for sea outfalls or sewers. Where there is a requirement for gravity-fed sewers to lie in water they must be weighted down to avoid the buoyancy effect when empty as well as the fact that polyethylene pipe floats on water. This is usually achieved by putting concrete collars at given intervals to prevent the pipe floating (*Figure 40.6*).

40.3.1.5 Hot and cold water systems

Both polyethylene and cross-linked polyethylene[67] can be used for hot and cold water systems. This application requires a combination of flexibility, resistance to internal pressure at elevated temperatures and corrosion resistance.[68]

Cross-linking of polyethylene (see Section 40.3.2.2) enhances its properties especially resistance under pressure at elevated temperatures. Cross-linking methods are discussed in Section 40.3.2.2. A current German Standard DIN 16892[69] deals with the general quality requirements and testing of cross-linked pipes designed for use with hot water. The degree of cross-linking achieved, as measured by the percentage of polyethylene insoluble in xylene after 8 h of refluxing, affects the pipe properties and minimum values are therefore specified depending on the cross-linking technique used. The cross-linking levels required are 75% for peroxide, 65% for silane and 60% for electron beam cross-linked pipe. Pressure tests at 20, 95 and 110°C are required for up to 8000 h to prove the quality of the pipes. Work is in progress to standardize (ISO TC138 in SC2/WG1) the plastic pipe systems used within buildings to carry water under pressure for:

1. The distribution of hot and cold water including potable water.
2. The hot water for heating (including under-floor heating).

Three classes of pipe system are envisaged at present:

1. Class 1: for underfloor heating, maximum service temperature 50°C.
2. Class 2: for hot-water distribution, maximum service temperature 80°C.
3. Class 3: central heating, maximum service temperature 90°C.

The draft document requires pressure testing for up to 10 000 h at temperatures up to 110°C depending on class, thermal stability, thermal and pressure cycling, pull-out testing, and leakproofness under internal pressure according to ISO 3503.[70] Quality-control testing and specific requirements, like thermal stability, will be detailed in product standards one of which will be on polyethylene.

The work is the result of international cooperation involving Sweden, Finland, France, Germany and the UK. In France, the Centre Scientifique et Technique du Batiment (CSTB) have published Technical Note No. 14 + 15/82-129[71] which qualifies pipes for such applications. Some typical general properties of polyethylene pipe are given in *Table 40.6*.

This type of cross-linked pipe, normally 8–25 mm OD, can be used for under-floor heating where the pipe is laid in loops, held by foam polystyrene, and the whole covered in a specially formulated concrete. A typical system, THERMACOME, is shown in *Figure 40.7*.

Jointing is normally mechanical as cross-linked polyethylene pipe does not melt in the normal way and normal heat fusion welding is not yet possible.

Figure 40.6 Sewage outfall ready to be installed. (Courtesy of Upnor)

Table 40.6 General hot-water pipe properties

Property	Units	Value	Method
Density	kg m^{-3}	944	NFT 54-002[72]
Thermal conductivity	W K^{-1}	0.35	DIN 56612[73]
Coefficient of expansion	mm m^{-1} K^{-1}	0.19	DIN 53752[74]
Elongation at breaking	% (100 mm min^{-1})	375	ISO R527[41]
Reversion	%	1.3	ISO 2506
Circumferential stress at 50 years	MPa (20°C)	9.87	ATEC of CSTB
	MPa (40°C)	7.05	ATEC of CSTB
	MPa (60°C)	6.45	ATEC of CSTB
	MPa (80°C)	3.90	ATEC of CSTB

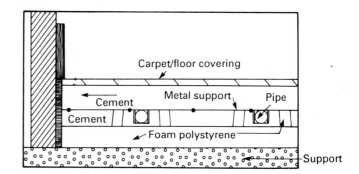

Figure 40.7 Use of a cross-linked polyethylene pipe for under-floor heating. (Courtesy of Acome, Paris)

40.3.1.6 Jointing techniques

Pipe must be joined in order to produce a usable system. Mechanical joints have been and still are used and these are normally couplers, elbows, tees, etc. Metal fittings are normally expensive and, of course, corrodable so the introduction of injection moulded fittings made from the same polymer as the pipe itself coupled with the principle of heat fusion welding[75] has increased the scope for using polyethylene systems. The major jointing techniques are the butt fusion of pipes, socket fusion of a pipe to a fitting, saddle fusion and electrofusion. Heat fusion uses a combination of temperature and pressure to cause two melted surfaces to combine so that bonding occurs and, provided the interface is cooled under pressure, the joint made is sound.

(i) Butt fusion[76] Two pipes to be joined are clamped in a butt fusion machine which is basically an alignment jig. The size of machine used will depend on the pipe to be joined, smaller machines can cope with up to 180 mm OD pipes but larger machines may have to cope with diameters of up to 1600 mm OD and hence the hydraulics are designed accordingly. Whilst the jointing is manual, sophisticated computerized recording techniques and automation are being introduced to reduce both errors and jointing times.

The procedure is as follows. The electrically heated plate is brought between the pipe ends which have been machined square to each other. The ends, when properly adjusted, are pushed against the heater plate with sufficient force to just melt the polyethylene totally around the circumferential faces of the pipes and form a bead (typically 2 mm diameter). After the bead has formed the pressure is released and a definitive heat soak time elapses. The heating plate is then removed, the plate removal time now commences and is rarely longer than 15 s at ambient temperature. The two pipes are then brought together at the correct pressure and the cooling time starts. After the elapsed

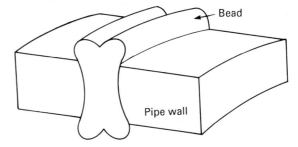

Figure 40.8 Butt fusion weld

cooling time, during which the fusion pressure is maintained, the pressure is released and the jointed pipe removed from the machine.

It is essential that this procedure is always fully defined for each material type. Temperature pressures and times must be specified to achieve a quality joint. The formation of the bead is shown in *Figure 40.8*. The procedure is open to abuse despite properly formulated training programmes and British Gas, for example, have developed an automatic butt fusion machine to minimize this problem.[77]

(ii) Socket fusion This process joins a pipe with a fitting which has a suitable socket. The heating tool consists of two faces, a male side to heat the interior of the socket surface and a female side to heat the exterior of the pipe surface. The pipe end is prepared as for butt fusion and held in a rerounding clamp to ensure an even fit into the socket. The pipe and socket fitting are positioned fully on the heated tool for a given time depending on size and thickness. They are then separated and firmly pushed together for at least 2 min. The weld is then inspected for evenness of melt pattern. This type of jointing as well as hot

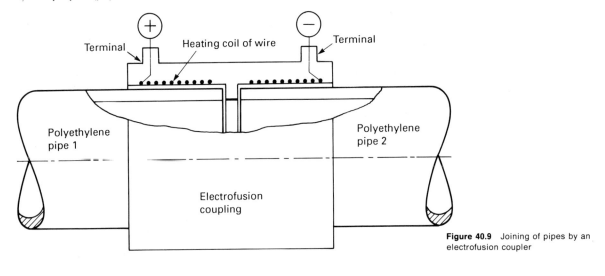

Figure 40.9 Joining of pipes by an electrofusion coupler

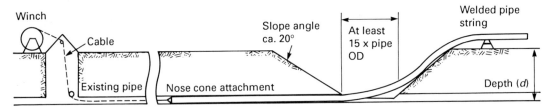

Figure 40.10 Slip lining of a polyethylene pipe

plate saddle fusion is being replaced in the UK and USA by electrofusion systems. The technique relies on the operator and, in order to reduce potential errors and abuse, electrofusion is now preferred.

(*iii*) *Saddle fusion* Tapping or branching saddles are used to 'tap-in' to an existing pipe in order to run a line to a new customer. Hot plate saddle fusion is based on a similar principle to socket fusion except that the base of the fitting is shaped to rest on the pipe, hence the term 'saddle'. The heated fusion tool is pressed onto the pipe for about 25 s to melt the surface and the saddle fitting base is then placed on the tool for a further 25 s. After this period the tool is removed and the fitting pressed firmly to the pipe to form a double weld bead. The pressure is maintained whilst cooling takes place.

In principle, saddle fusion is sound, but again there are many opportunities for error and abuse during installation and so this was the first area to be exploited in the UK by electrofusion techniques.

(*iv*) *Electrofusion*[78,79] The electrofusion technique can easily be automated and this is an attraction to the user. Fittings are heat fused to polyethylene pipes, after initially scraping the pipe, using the electrical energy supplied to a heating element which is integral to the fitting. The energy is supplied via a control box which operates for a preset time depending upon the fitting size selected. A typical injection-moulded fitting (coupler) is shown in *Figure 40.9*. Whilst the fittings themselves are complex and expensive to produce the reliability of the joint is very high. The trend towards electrofusion jointing is continuing and fittings are now available up to at least 315 mm OD. It is likely that electrofusion jointing and butt fusion will be the main elements in future systems.

40.3.1.7 Installation techniques

(*i*) *Slip lining* The flexibility of polyethylene pipe lends itself to the slip-lining of old pipes whereby a new pipe is inserted by pulling or pushing it through the old one. Butt-fusion welded 'strings' of up to 700 m in length are pulled through, using a winch, up to at least an outside diameter of 800 mm. The total installed cost is much less (up to 40% cheaper) than for relaying conventional rigid pipes and minimum disruption in heavily congested urban areas is achieved. The technique used is shown in *Figure 40.10*.

(*ii*) *Narrow trenching* The reinstatement costs for excavation are high and so being able to dig narrow trenches mechanically and to drop in butt-fusion welded strings of an outside diameter slightly less than that of the trench width is an advantage. Again the flexibility and weldability of polyethylene enables cost savings to be made.

(*iii*) *Roll down*[80] Because of the viscoelastic properties of polyethylene, the pipe is capable of being rolled down between two sets of hemispherical rollers set in line at right angles to each other. The idea is to reduce the outer diameter of the pipe, slip line an old line and then inflate the pipe using water pressure so that the inserted pipe interferes with the inner surface of the original line. This system has an advantage where non-standard old pipelines are encountered and can be done *in situ*. The process is utilized by Sub-Terra Ltd under licence from Stewarts/Lloyds Plastics.

(*iv*) *Swaging*[81] This is a British Gas process which is similar in principle to the roll-down technique, but achieves the reduction in outer diameter by a different process. The original

Figure 40.11 A coil of medium density polyethylene pipe. (Courtesy of Wavin Industrial Products)

pipe is drawn through a swaging die at ambient to 110°C and stretched to reduce the diameter. It is then inserted into the old pipeline and, if necessary, reflated using water pressure in a similar way as in the roll-down method. To date over 100 km of cast iron gas mains have been relined in this way.

(*v*) *Mole ploughing* Coils of polyethylene pipe are used as well as long welded strings. The plough excavates and the pipe is fed into the furrow which is closed afterwards as the machinery progresses forward. Long lengths can be inserted very quickly, especially in rural areas (*Figure 40.11*).

None of the above installation techniques would be successful if the particular polyethylene used did not have the viscoelasticity, flexibility, strength, ability to be fusion welded and still be capable of meeting the requirements of the application water/gas tightness. A typical coil of 180 mm OD gas pipe is shown in *Figure 40.11*. Other installation techniques such as impact moleing and directional drilling[82] could well be made more viable by the use of flexible polyethylene pipe systems.

40.3.2 Electrical uses

40.3.2.1 Telecommunications

Probably the first constructional use of polyethylene was in an insulated North Sea telephone cable in about 1939. At the outbreak of World War Two, the dielectric properties of polyethylene were needed for the development and use of RADAR. Meanwhile, during the war other applications were developed in the USA such as US Army Signal Corps assault wire and the US Navy advanced base underground telephone wire sheathing.

(*i*) *Insulation* Solid polyethylene was first used to replace paper and gutta-percha insulation because it is moisture resistant, can easily be coloured for coding and is more reliable than the old material. Polyethylene insulated systems were, however,

susceptible to water entry through faulty joints and water could penetrate under the jacket, and cause signal failure. The solution was to introduce intermittent water barriers and ultimately fillers; an illustration of such development and progress is given in *Table 40.7*. Cellular insulation[83,84] was introduced in the 1960s and many of today's networks are based on cellular insulation because the mutual capacitance of the insulated pairs can be maintained in the cable when petroleum jelly filler is introduced, without needing the larger cable dimensions which would be needed for solid insulation.

The dielectric system of an unfilled polyethylene insulated cable is partly polyethylene and partly air. Its effective permittivity (or dielectric constant) is thus greater than unity (i.e. that of air), but less than that of solid polyethylene (2.3). The required capacitance of the circuit is then obtained by the correct choice of insulation thickness.

When the air spaces are filled with petroleum jelly, the effective permittivity of the cable is increased again and the established design basis upset. The effect of filling the air spaces can be offset by making the insulation thicker. This, however, increases costs and of course the cable becomes larger, occupying more duct space. The solution was to substitute the solid polyethylene by cellular polyethylene with just sufficient expansion to restore the effective permittivity of the cable. The processing of such a cellular polyethylene compound requires very careful temperature control. The objective is to achieve a smooth outside wall with a closed cell structure with a cell size of about 15 μm diameter. If the melt temperature is too low the expansion will not occur and if too high a coarse and overexpanded structure is obtained. Thus a tolerance of ± 1°C or less is required to achieve best results especially at typical speeds of up to 2000 m min^{-1}.

A further development has been to use a solid skin compound which is coextruded with foamable product. This makes the cable more resistant to mechanical damage whilst maintaining its electrical properties. Typical compound properties are given in *Tables 40.8* and *40.9*.

Trunk network cables used to connect exchange to exchange used to be coaxial cables, but more and more are being replaced by optical fibre cables. Coaxial cables comprise two conductors one inside the other, copper in the centre and aluminium outside, but both sharing the same concentric axis. The dielectric medium that separates the two conductors can be solid polyethylene[85] or cellular polyethylene. The major advantage of the coaxial cable is that the outer conductor screens the inner one and reduces the interference caused by capacitive pick-up. Coaxial cable, however, cannot carry as many channels as optical fibres and so the use of polyethylene in trunk systems is reducing.

(*ii*) *Sheathing of telephone trunk cables*[86] The use of polyethylene as sheathing or jacketing of submarine telephone cables illustrates the basic strengths of the material, i.e. toughness, corrosion resistance, resistance to stress cracking, weatherability and ability to be processed onto cables. All types of polyethylene have been used for jacketing depending on the

Table 40.7 Development in telephone-cable construction

Date	Insulation	Jacket	Filler	Conductor
Pre-1948	Paper	—	Lead	Copper
1948	Solid PE	Black PE	—	Copper
1962–1967	Solid PE	Black PE	Intermittent barriers	Copper
1965 onwards	Cellular PE	Black PE	Petroleum jelly	Copper
1980 onwards	Cellular or solid PE	Black PE	Petroleum jelly, polyisobutylene or thixotropes	Copper or aluminium

PE, polyethylene.

Table 40.8 Some general physical properties of a foamable insulation compound[a]

Property	Units	Typical value	Method
Density	kg m^{-3}	942	Adaption of ISO 1872/1[a]
Tensile strength of cellular insulation	MPa	14	
Resistance to compression	N	175	
Resistance to thermal ageing at 105°C	h	1500	British Telecom Specification M142D
Dielectric loss angle of 1 MHz at 23°C	μR	400	
Dielectric constant of 1 MHz at 230°C		1.74	ASTM D1531: 1975

[a] All samples except for density were cellular insulation of 0.15 mm radial thickness, expanded to a specific gravity of 550–600 kg m^{-3} on a 0.5 mm diameter copper conductor.

Table 40.9 Solid skin compound properties

Property	Units	Typical value	Method
Melt flow rate	g/10 min	0.6	ISO 1133,[6] Procedure 4
Density	kg m^{-3}	945	ISO 1872: Part 1[9]
Oxidative induction time at 200°C	min	40	—
Petroleum jelly absorption at 10 days at 70°C	% gain	6	FT$_z$72 TV1
Dielectric constant		2.3	At 1 MHz ASTM D1531: 1975[97]
Dielectric loss angle	μR	200	At 1 MHz

mechanical and environmental conditions, although low density polyethylene is still the most used type.

As optical fibre cables,[87] which use digitally coded pulses of light, are capable of carrying many more channels than conventional coaxial cables, attention is being turned to protecting this more fragile system. The use of polyethylene to sheath the optical-fibre bundles and the metal support wire(s) is now a major consideration. The use of polyethylene for future trunk cables will be limited to the sheathing, thereby roughly halving the tonnage used; e.g. the use of TAT7 at 1.5 te mile^{-1} for insulation and jacketing as compared with the optical fibre TAT8 at 0.75 te mile^{-1} for jacketing only. The emphasis is thus moving away from the electrical properties of polyethylene to its protectional properties, a far cry from the situation of the early 1940s.

40.3.2.2 Power cables

After their introduction both plasticized polyvinyl chloride (PVC) and low density polyethylene (LDPE) quickly replaced oil-filled paper insulated cables in applications up to 1 kV. Polyethylene has ideal insulation characteristics and its only

disadvantage in higher voltage power cable applications was its low temperature rating (m.p. 113°C). In order to obtain enhanced properties such as heat resistance, environmental stress crack resistance and improved mechanical properties, polyethylene is cross-linked. At least three methods of cross-linking polyethylene exist:

1. A peroxide[88] is mixed with polyethylene, sometimes containing an inert filler, prior to extrusion or is added during the extrusion stage. The peroxide-containing melt is then heated up in a continuous vulcanization line to a temperature above the decomposition point of the particular peroxide. The cross-linking process takes place under pressure to avoid the creation of voids in the polyethylene melt. Either steam or inert gas is used as the pressurizing medium.
2. In the silane process[89] a vinyltrimethoxy silane is grafted onto polyethylene either by compounding or by producing an ex-reactor copolymer. The grafted polymer is extruded onto the conductor by various techniques, but the principle of the method is the cross-linking of the polyethylene in the presence of water to create Si–O–Si bonds.
3. In the irradiation process[90] the polyethylene covered cable is passed through a high energy electron beam. High filler loadings can be accommodated and the process is especially suitable for compositions with modified burning characteristics.

The manufacture of low voltage (<1 kV) cables is controlled by both national and international specifications. Whilst the electrical requirements are not onerous, cables are often used in hostile requirements and the specifications reflect this. The main requirements are in *Table 40.10*. Other aspects are important, such as ease of extrusion onto conductors at optimum production speeds coupled with good scorch resistance. In medium and high voltage power cables polyethylene is far superior to rubber or PVC insulation.

The original major advantage of extruded polyethylene insulation over the oil-filled paper cable was the absence of a dielectric fluid. Operating and maintenance activities were greatly reduced with little leakage and simple cable design. A disadvantage was the effect of the presence of foreign particles in the insulation layer in type and size. Such contamination could initiate electrical or electrochemical processes which lead to cable breakdown. Therefore procedures have been developed to manufacture high-quality insulation with extremely high standards of cleanliness and quality throughout the whole process from the manufacture of the polyethylene compound to the manufacture of the cable itself. In addition, in medium (6–60 kV) and high (60–150 kV) voltage cables it is common practice to extrude an inner core of semiconductive polyethylene

Table 40.10 National power cable specifications

Country	Specifying body	Ref. No.
Belgium	NBN	33-321
Italy	CEI	20-31
FRG	VDE	0274
France	AFNOR (NF)	33-209
USA	ICEA/NEMA	S-66-524/WC7
	UL	44

VDE	Verband Deutscher Electrotechniker
CEI	Comitato Elettrotechnico Italiano
NEMA	National Electrical Manufacturers' Association
ICEA	Insulated Cable Engineers' Association
UL	Underwriters' Laboratories
NBN	Belgian Standards Organisation
AFNOR	French Standardisation
(NF)	Norme Francaise

compound onto the metal conductor, then the insulation layer and then another outer semiconductive layer. The inner semiconductive layer homogenizes the electric field on the conductor surface and the outer semiconductive layer allows a perfectly homogenized electric field within the insulation layer. Such compounds are highly specialized and typical cable standards are: IEC 502 for 1–30 kV cable; in the FRG, VDE 0273 for 10–30 kV; and in the USA AEIC CS7-82 for 69–138 kV XLPE power cables.

As with pipes, cables need to be installed and jointed as well as repaired. This is a very specific operation and one of the most important parts consists of peeling off the outer semiconductive layer from the insulation. The delicate part of the operation lies in the fact that minor damage to the insulation surface could initiate premature cable breakdown. Therefore, special strippable semiconductive compounds have been developed for all kinds of polyethylene insulation, whilst maintaining the conductivity, processability and cross-linkage formation ability of the fully bonded components. This type of development illustrates the specialized nature of power cable polyethylene compounds and the need for continued research into optimized products.

40.3.3 Road and soil reinforcement

Polyethylene can be oriented at temperatures below its melting point and the properties enhanced depending on whether uniaxial or biaxial orientation takes place.[91] In this engineering application the most important properties are corrosion resistance and the enhanced strength achieved by orientation. An array of regularly sized, regularly spaced apertures are formed in extruded high density polyethylene sheet. The sheet is then stretched at prescribed rate and temperature conditions either to produce uniaxially oriented Tensar (characterized by elongated apertures) or stretched additionally at right angles to orient the sheet biaxially. This biaxial Tensar has rectangular apertures, the name Tensar being the trademark of Netlon Ltd who developed the idea and the process.

The oriented grids, or 'geogrids', have greatly increased tensile strength and modulus, enhancing the capability to interlock mechanically with sand/earth particles to create an efficient stress-transfer mechanism. This capability together with the corrosion resistance and resistance to creep has led to applications in embankment stabilization, land reclamation and asphalt surface reinforcement.[92] Examples include the repair of an embankment slip on the M4 near Reading as well as on parts of the M25 and M1 motorways.

40.3.4 Damp-proof membranes

Polyethylene film is used extensively on building and construction sites, especially in the less critical application of temporary protection in the UK climate. The Packaging and Industrial Films Association (PIFA) have issued a Voluntary Standard 6/83, Part 1[93] which deals with damp-proof membranes and covers the requirements for polyethylene membranes for use in concrete-floor construction. A minimum polyethylene thickness of 250 μm is specified as well as the stipulation that no rework shall be used. As expected, the impact strength, tear resistance and tensile strength are specified and it is stated that the film should be free of holes and tears.

Part 2[94] of the voluntary standard refers to temporary protective materials or general-purpose building films. Low density polyethylene film is used in this application because of its low moisture permeability, its strength and toughness. However, such a product is open to abuse either by the unscrupulous manufacturer who wishes to get rid of scrap or by the indiscriminate builder who neglects to buy the right quality or treat the film properly during installation on site.

Hence PIFA issued a voluntary standard in order to provide information, a basis for fair competition, to give the user confidence in a quality product and a means of identifying products conforming to PIFA Voluntary Standard 6.83 by labelling.

40.4 European standardization

In order to create a single European market in 1992, the following assumption has been made in the EEC. 'Harmonised standards and a common basis for their application through mutually acceptable certification and testing are the keys to removing barriers to free and fair trade'. CEN (European Committee for Non-electrotechnical Standardisation) is one of the two components of the Joint European Standards Institution (CEN/CENELEC). A construction products directive has been adopted and covers all products produced for incorporation in a permanent manner in construction works, including both buildings and civil engineering works. Products related to mechanical and electrical services are included.

Products are presumed fit for purpose if they enable the works in which they are employed to satisfy the essential requirements and those products bear the EC mark. The essential requirements are:

1. Mechanical resistance and stability.
2. Safety in case of fire.
3. Hygiene, health and environment.
4. Safety in use.
5. Protection against noise.
6. Energy economy and heat retention.

The EC mark may be achieved in various ways:

1. Compliance with a harmonized (European) standard (EN).
2. Compliance with a European Technical Approval.
3. Compliance with certain national technical specification (e.g. standard, technical approval, etc.) which has been recognized by the commission as providing a basis for a presumption of conformity with essential requirements.

Plastic pipes European Standards will be dealt with in Technical Committee TC 155. The Secretariat is held by the NNI (The Netherlands). In the UK, the Department of the Environment is the lead Ministry from whence advice can be obtained.[95] Cables, etc., are standardized separately by the other component of the Joint European Standards Institution CENELEC (European Committee for Electrotechnical Standardization).

References

1 RAUM, A. J., *Vinyl and Allied Polymers, Vol. 1: Chemistry of Polymerisation* (ed. P. D. Ritchie), pp. 43–114, Iliffe, London (1968)
2 NOWLIN, T. E., 'Low pressure manufacture of polyethylene', *Progress in Polymer Science*, **11**, 29–55 (1985)
3 STAUB, R. B., 'The Unipol process', *PRI Golden Jubilee Conference Papers*, Paper B5.4, Polyethylenes 1933–83, Plastics and Rubber Institute, London (8–10 Jun. 1983)
4 HOGAN, J. P., 'HDPE from laboratory breakthrough to a mature industry', *PRI Golden Jubilee Conference Papers*, Paper B.3, Polyethylenes 1933–83 Plastics and Rubber Institute, London (8–10 Jun. 1983)
5 BETT, K.E., CROSSLAND, B., FORD, H., and GARDNER, A.K., 'Review of the engineering developments in the high pressure polyethylene process', *PRI Golden Jubilee Conference Papers*, Paper B.1, Polyethylenes 1933–83, Plastics and Rubber Institute, London (8–10 Jun. 1983)
6 INTERNATIONAL ORGANIZATION FOR STANDARDIZATION, 'Plastics—determination of the melt flow rate of thermoplastics', *ISO 1133* (1971)

7   DOWNS, G. W., *Vinyl and Allied Polymers, Vol. 1, Molecular and Crystalline Structure* (ed. P. D. Ritchie), pp. 129–139, Iliffe, London (1968)

8   INTERNATIONAL ORGANIZATION FOR STANDARDIZATION, 'Plastics—methods for determining the density and relative density (s.g) of plastics excluding cellular plastics', *ISO 1183* (1970)

9   INTERNATIONAL ORGANIZATION FOR STANDARDIZATION, 'Plastics—polyethylene (PE) thermoplastics. Part 1: designation, *ISO 1872: Part 1* (1986)

10 MOYNIHAN, T. K., 'Evolution of a linear PE process', *PRI Golden Jubilee Papers*, Paper B.5.3, Polyethylenes 1933–83, Plastics and Rubber Institute, London (8–10 Jun. 1983)

11 WHITLEY, K. S., 'High pressure ethylene copolymers', *PRI Golden Jubilee Papers*, Paper B.2.4, Polyethylenes 1933–83, Plastics and Rubber Institute, London (8–10 Jun. 1983)

12 PARTINGTON, J. R., *General and Inorganic Chemistry*, 2nd edn, pp. 142–147, MacMillan, London (1954)

13 KAMINSKY, W., 'The development and potential of Zeigler catalysts, *PRI Golden Jubilee Conference Papers*, Paper B.5.1, Polyethylenes 1933–83, Plastics and Rubber Institute, London (8–10 Jun. 1983)

14 SCHNEIDERS, A., 'Extrusion blow moulding machines', *Kunststoffe*, **71**, 684–687 (1981)

15 ZIMMERMANN, W. J., GRÜNER, H., and WINKLER, G., 'Blown film extrusion', *Kunststoffe*, **71**, 653–659 (1981)

16 MILLER, J. C., WU, R., and CIELOWZYK, G., 'Running LLDPE blown film on your present machinery', *Plastics Engineering*, 37–41 (Jan. 1986)

17 JOHANNABER, F., 'Injection moulding machines', *Kunststoffe*, **71**, 70–715 (1981)

18 REITEMEYER, P., 'Extrusion of pipes', *Kunststoffe*, **71**, 665–667 (1981)

19 SCHIEDRUM, H. O., 'Equipment for the production of HDPE pressure pipe', *Kunststoffe*, **73**, 2–8 (1983)

20 DODROWSKY, J., 'Spiral mandrel distribution dies for pipe production', *Kunststoffe*, **78**, 302–307 (1988)

21 POTENTE, H., 'The force feed extruder must be reconsidered', *Kunststoffe*, **78**, 355–363 (1988)

22 BARTH, Hj., 'Extruders', *Kunststoffe*, **71**, 636–642 (1981)

23 KERTSCHER, E., 'Cable making equipment', *Kunststoffe*, **71**, 677–683 (1981)

24 *Modern Plastics*, Brownhill, D. (ed.) (26–32 Jan. 1989)

25 CLEREHUGH, G., 'Gas distribution services', *Polyethyl Plastics and Polymers*, 31–36 (Feb. 1970)

26 BRITISH GAS ENGINEERING, *British Gas Engineering Standard PS/PL2 polyethylene (PE) pipes for natural gas: Part 1 Pipes* (June 1986)

27 *European Plastics News*, **9**, Announcement, 40 (May 1982)

28 WALTON, D., 'Design and manufacture of buried polyethylene pipeline systems', *Pipes Pipelines International*, **28**, 21 (Nov./Dec. 1983)

29 BRITISH STANDARDS INSTITUTION, 'Determination of the resistance to constant (ISO 1167) internal pressure of thermoplastics pipe', *BS 4728* (1971)

30 AMERICAN SOCIETY FOR TESTING MATERIALS, 'Obtaining hydrostatic design basis for thermoplastic pipe materials', *ASTM D 2837* (1988)

31 INTERNATIONAL ORGANIZATION FOR STANDARDIZATION, 'Plastic pipes for the transport of fluids. Standard extrapolation method (SEM)', *ISO DTR 9080* (draft)

32 BRITISH STANDARDS INSTITUTION, 'Recommendations for the presentation of plastics design data', *BS 4618* (1970)

33 LAUER, H. J., 'Stress analysis of buried rigid PVC pipe and rigid PE pipes and sewers', *3R International*, **2** (1978)

34 GAUBE, E., 'Stress analysis calculations on rigid polyethylene and PE sewerage pipes', *Kunststoffe*, **67**, 353–356 (1977)

35 TROTT, J. T. and GAUNT, J., 'Experimental pipelines under a major road: Performance during and after road construction', *TRRL Report 692*, Transport and Road Research Laboratory, Crowthorne, UK (1976)

36 GAUNT, J., TROTT, J. J., and STEVENS, J. B., 'Static and dynamic loading tests on shallow-buried flexible pipes', Transport and Road Research Laboratory, Crowthorne, UK (1975)

37 WILLIAMS, J. G., *Philosophical Transactions of the Royal Society (London)*, Fracture behaviour of polythene pipes, **A299**, 59 (1981)

38 GRAY, A., MALLINSON, J. N., and PRICE, J. B., *Plastics and Rubber Processing and Applications*, **1**, 51 (1981)

39 PLATI, E. and WILLIAMS, J. G., 'The determination of the infrastructure parameters of polyethylene in impact', *Polymer Engineering Science*, **15**, (1975)

40 GREIG, J. M., 'Rapid crack propagation in gas pipe materials', SERC Polymer Engineering Directorate Review Meeting, Imperial College, London (Jan. 1986)

41 INTERNATIONAL ORGANIZATION FOR STANDARDIZATION, *ISO R527* Plastics: determination of tensile properties (1966) (under revision)

42 INTERNATIONAL ORGANIZATION FOR STANDARDIZATION, *ISO 180* Plastics: Determination of Izod impact strength of rigid materials (1982)

43 INTERNATIONAL ORGANIZATION FOR STANDARDIZATION, *ISO 178* Plastics: Determination of flexural properties of rigid plastics (1975)

44 INTERNATIONAL ORGANIZATION FOR STANDARDIZATION, *ISO 306* Plastics: Determination of Vicat softening temperature of thermoplastics (1987)

45 INTERNATIONAL ORGANIZATION FOR STANDARDIZATION, *ISO 974* Plastics: Determination of brittleness temperature by impact (1980)

46 INTERNATIONAL ORGANIZATION FOR STANDARDIZATION, *ISO 4599* Plastics: Determination of brittleness temperatures by impact (1980)

47 BRITISH STANDARDS INSTITUTION, 'Quality systems (EN 29002). Part 2: specification for production and installation', *BS 5750: Part 2* (1987)

48 INTERNATIONAL ORGANIZATION FOR STANDARDIZATION, 'Buried polyethylene (PE) pipes for the supply of gaseous fuels—metric series—specification', *ISO 4437* (1988)

49 'Tubes en polyethylene pour réseaux de distribution de combustibles gazeux, Norme Francaise, *NFT 54-065* (1987)

50 'Pipes, fittings and joints of polyethylene type PEM and PEH for buried gas lines', Dansk Standardiseringsrad, *DS 2131* (1980)

51 BRITISH STANDARDS INSTITUTION, 'British Standard Specification for blue polyethylene pipes up to nominal size 63 for below ground use for potable water', *BS 6472* (1985)

52 HARWOOD, J., 'The use of plastics and rubber in water and effluents', *The Plastics and Rubber Institute Conference Papers*, Paper 12 (15–17 Feb. 1982)

53 MEADOWS, A. C., 'Trials with MDPE pipe show promise and cost savings', *Pipes and Pipe Technology*, 541–542 (Dec. 1986)

54 BRITISH STANDARDS INSTITUTION, 'Specification for black polyethylene pipes up to nominal size 63 for above ground use for cold potable waters', *BS 6730*

55 BRITISH STANDARDS INSTITUTION, 'Suitability of non-metallic products for use in contact with potable water intended for human consumption with regard to their effect on the quality of the water', *BS 6920*

56 'Specification for blue polyethylene pressure pipe for cold potable water (nominal sizes 90 to 1000 for underground or protected use), *IGN 4-32-03: Issue 3* (May 1987)

57 'Specification for blue polyethylene pressure pipe for cold potable water. Part 1: general', *IGN 4-32-03: Part 1*

58 'Specification for blue polyethylene pressure pipe for cold potable water. Part 2: 90–315 mm', *IGN 4-32-03: Part 2*

59 'Specification for polyethylene pressure pipe for cold potable water (underground use),', *IGN 4-32-02: Issue 2* (Apr. 1984)

60 WATER RESEARCH CENTRE/WATER AUTHORITIES ASSOCIATION, *Manual for the Design, Installation and Operation of MDPE Pipe Systems for Water Supply Distribution*, Water Research Centre, Engineering, Swindon (Jun. 1986)

61 PLASTICS AND RUBBER INSTITUTE, *International Conference Plastics Pipes VII: Session B, Assessment for Performance*, Bath, Papers 8–12 (Sep. 1988)

62 'Specification for polyethylene socket and spigot fittings, saddles and drawn bends for fusion jointing for use with cold potable water PE pressure', *IGN 4-32-04: Issue 2* (Dec. 1988)

63 *European Plastics News*, **11**, 31 (Jan. 1984)

64 SHELDON, W. G. and COOPER, M. W., *Sliplining of a Brick Sewer*, Bolton Metropolitan Borough, Department of Engineering (May 1980)

65 'Specification for polyethylene (PE) pipes for sewer linings (non-pressure applications)', *IGN 4-32-05: Issue 1* (Apr. 1986)

66 LOWE, D. and MARSHALL, G. P., 'The abrasion resistance of polymers in slurry environments', *PRI Conference, Plastics Pipes VI*, Paper 8, University of York (Mar. 1985)

67 DENNING, J. A., 'Crosslinked polyethylene pipes', *PRI Golden Jubilee Conference Polyethylenes 1933–1983*, Paper C.1.3 (8–10 Jun. 1983)

68 HAMICH, W., 'Underfloor heating pipes protected against diffusion', *Plastics in Building*, **20**, 142–144 (1985)

69 DEUTSCHES INSTITUT FUR NORMUNG, 'Rohre aus vernetztem Polyethylene (VPE); Allgemeine Guteanforderungen und Prufung' [Crosslinked polyethylene (HPE) pipes: general quality requirements], *DIN 16892*

70 INTERNATIONAL ORGANIZATION FOR STANDARDIZATION, 'Assembled joints between fittings and polyethylene (PE) pipes test of leak proofness under pressure and bending', *ISO 3503*

71 CENTRE SCIENTIFIQUE ET TECHNIQUE DU BATIMENT, *Technical Note No. 14 + 15/82 – 129*

72 *NFT 54-002: 1981* Plastics: Thermoplastics parts for piping—Definitions: Dimensions

73 DEUTSCHES INSTITUT FUR NORMUNG, *DIN 56612*

74 DEUTSCHES INSTITUT FUR NORMUNG, *DIN 53752* (1980) [Testing of plastics—determination of the coefficient of linear thermal expansion]

75 AMERICAN SOCIETY FOR TESTING MATERIALS, 'Standard practice for heat joining polyolefins pipe and fittings', *ASTM D2657-87*

76 AMERICAN SOCIETY FOR TESTING MATERIALS, 'Butt heat fusion of polyethylene (PE) plastic fittings for polyethylene (PE) plastic pipe and tubing', *ASTM D3261-87*

77 MAINE, L. and STAFFORD, T. G., 'Infield quality control of fusion jointing methods', *International Conference on Plastics and Pipes VII*, Bath (Sep. 1988)

78 USCLAT, D., 'Characteristics of a good joint with electrofusion fittings', *PRI Conference on Plastics and Pipes VI*, Paper 31A, University of York (Mar. 1985)

79 WILLIAMS, R. G. and ANSELL, D. J., 'The development of a novel electrofusion system', *PRI Conference on Plastics and Pipes VI*, Paper 30, University of York (Mar. 1985)

80 'Roll down insertion puts the squeeze on pipe replacement costs', *Gas World*, 8–9 (Feb. 1987)

81 WILLIAMS, B. and HOLT, J., 'Swagelining—an operational overview', *No-Dig 88*, UMIST, Manchester (Jun. 1988)

82 SZCZUPAK, J. R., 'Horizontal Directional Drilling', *No-Dig 88*, Washington, DC (1988)

83 SAVOLAINEN, A., HEINO, A., and LEHTINEN, O., 'Insulation of telephone singles with cellular polythene', *WIRE Industry*, 907 (Dec. 1984)

84 VISWARIATHAN, P. S., *Journal of Electronics and Telecommunication Engineers*, **28**, 563–568 (1982)

85 NORMANTON, J. K. and ROBINSON, J. E., 'Extrusion processing of PE compounds for large-diameter communication cable insulation', *Plastics and Rubber: Processing*, 115–120 (Sep. 1979)

86 BONICEL, J. P. and BOSCD BELLET, J. J. de, 'Investigation of calbe sheath materials', *Plastics in Telecommunications Conference III*, Paper 12, The Plastics and Rubber Institute

87 ROBINSON, J. E., 'The use of polyolefin compounds in modern fibre optic cable designs', *Impact 89 Indian Petrochemicals Conference*, Vadodara, India (Feb. 1989)

88 WAGNER, H. and WARTUSCH, J., *IEEE Transactions on Electrical Insulation* **E1–12**, 395 (1977)

89 SABISTON, A. and BEVERIDGE, C., 'Crosslinking expands the scope of polyolefins', *British Plastics and Rubber*, 44–46 (Jul./Aug. 1987)

90 MUKHERJEE, A. K., GUPTA, B. D., and SHARMA, P. K., 'Radiation induced changes in polyolefins', *JMS Review: Macromolecular and Chemical Physics*, **C26**, 415–439 (1986)

91 TEMPLEMAN, J., SWEETLAND, D. B. and LANGLEY, P. A., 'The application of high strength polyolefins grids in civil engineering', *PRI Jubilee Conference on Polyethylenes 1933–83*, Paper C.7 (8–10 Jun. 1983)

92 DIXON, J. and LANGLEY, P. A., 'Geogrids for slope stabilisation', *Civil Engineering* (Jul. 1982)

93 PACKAGING AND INDUSTRIAL FILMS ASSOCIATION, 'Low density polyethylene film for building applications. Part 1: damp proof membranes', *PIFA Voluntary Standard 6/83*

94 PACKAGING AND INDUSTRIAL FILMS ASSOCIATION, 'Low density polyethylene film for building applications. Part 2: temporary protective materials', *PIFA Voluntary Standard 6/83*

95 DEPARTMENT OF THE ENVIRONMENT, (UK) Construction Industry Directorate, *Euronews Construction* (published monthly)

96 INTERNATIONAL ORGANIZATION FOR STANDARDIZATION, *ISO 1872/1* (1986) Plastics—Polyethylene (PE) Thermoplastics. Part 1 Designation

97 AMERICAN SOCIETY FOR TESTING MATERIALS, *ASTM D1531* (1990) *Test method for relative permeability (dielectric constant) and dissipation factor of the polyethylene by liquid displacement*

Bibliography

Standards catalogues

Published annually.
BS   British Standards Institute, London, UK
AFNOR   La Defense, Paris, France
DIN   Berlin, Germany
ASTM   Philadelphia, USA
IEC   Geneva, Switzerland
ISO   Geneva, Switzerland

General

RITCHIE, P. D. (ed.) *Vinyl Allied Polymers, Vol. 1, Aliphatic Polyolefins*, Iliffe, London (1968)

RAFF and DOAK (eds), *Crystalline Olefins Polymers, Part 1, Polymerisation and Structure*, Interscience, New York (1965)

RENFREW and MORGAN, *Polythene*, 2nd edn, Iliffe, London (1960)

CRAWFORD, R. J., *Plastics Engineering*, Pergamon Press, Oxford (1981)

Processing

FISHER, E. G. (ed.), *Extrusion of Plastics*, Iliffe, London (1954)

McKELVEY, J. M., *Polymer Processing*, Wiley, New York (1962)

TADMOOR and GOGAS, *Principles of Polymer Processing*, Wiley, New York (1979)

RUBIN, I. I., 'Injection moulding', Society of Plastics Engineers, *SPI Monograph*, Wiley, New York (1973)

Properties

WILLIAMS, J. G., *Stress Analysis of Polymers*, Longman, London (1973)

WILLIAMS, J. G., *Fracture Mechanics of Polymers*, Wiley, New York (1984)

WARD, I. M., *Mechanical Properties of Solid Polymers*, Wiley, New York (1983)

FERRY, J. D., *Viscoelastic Properties of Polymers*, Wiley, New York (1980)

RITCHIE, P. D. (ed.), *Physics of Plastics*, Iliffe, London (1965)

Pipe dimensions

INTERNATIONAL ORGANIZATION FOR STANDARDIZATION, 'Thermoplastic pipes—universal wall thickness table', *ISO 4065*

INTERNATIONAL ORGANIZATION FOR STANDARDIZATION, 'Specification for general requirements for (BS 5556) dimensions and pressure ratings for pipes of thermoplastics materials (metric series)', *ISO 161/1*

41

Polystyrene

J Crisfield HND(BLDG)
Vencel Resil Ltd

D A Cross BSc(Hons), DMS
Vencel Resil Ltd

D J Thompsett MA(Cantab)
Vencel Resil Ltd

Contents

41.1 History 41/3

41.2 Manufacture 41/3
    41.2.1 Manufacture of EPS 41/3
    41.2.2 Manufacture of XPS 41/3

41.3 Physical properties 41/3
    41.3.1 Compressive strength 41/4
    41.3.2 Cross-breaking strength 41/5
    41.3.3 Thermal conductivity 41/5
    41.3.4 Dimensional stability 41/5
    41.3.5 Moisture absorption 41/5
    41.3.6 Moisture-vapour transmission 41/5
    41.3.7 Tensile strength 41/5
    41.3.8 Shear strength 41/6
    41.3.9 Young's modulus of elasticity 41/6
    41.3.10 Creep 41/6
    41.3.11 Poisson's ratio 41/6

41.4 Fire properties 41/6
    41.4.1 Toxicity 41/6
    41.4.2 PS foam and BS 476 41/7

41.5 Chemical properties 41/7

41.6 Wall insulation 41/7
    41.6.1 Internal lining 41/7
    41.6.2 Cavity walls 41/7
    41.6.3 External insulation 41/8
    41.6.4 Specialist systems 41/9

41.7 Roof insulation 41/9
    41.7.1 Pitched roofs 41/9
    41.7.2 Flat roofs 41/10

41.8 Floor insulation 41/12
    41.8.1 Perimeter insulation 41/12
    41.8.2 Underslab insulation 41/12
    41.8.3 Overslab insulation 41/12
    41.8.4 Timber-floor insulation 41/13
    41.8.5 High-load-floor systems 41/14
    41.8.6 Structural floor systems 41/14
    41.8.7 Composite floor insulation panels 41/14

41.9 Civil engineering 41/14
    41.9.1 Shutters for concrete structures 41/15
    41.9.2 Flotation 41/15
    41.9.3 Road construction 41/15
    41.9.4 Foundations 41/16
    41.9.5 Clay heave 41/16

References 41/16

Bibliography 41/16

41.1 History

Synthetic polystyrene was first made over 125 years ago. However, it was not until 1936 that the first commercial production became available. In that year some 800 tonne was produced in Germany increasing to 5000 tonne by 1942.

In its solid state, polystyrene is a clear non-crystalline plastic material which is brittle. Improvements to its impact strength can be made by compounding with more rubbery polymers. These high-impact grades can be extruded or moulded into products for use inside buildings; for example in light fittings (luminaires) when adequate ultraviolet light resistance is needed to cover fluorescent tubes or as a lightweight substitute for glass in shower cubicles or screens.

It is, however, as a foamed plastic that polystyrene is mainly used in construction. Techniques for producing suitable foams were not available until 1952 when an expanded polystyrene was first exhibited at the Dusseldorf Trade Fair by BASF a German company. By the mid-1960s the benefits of the material were more widely recognized and applications began to be developed. Today, polystyrene foams are the most widely used of the plastic insulants available.

41.2 Manufacture

Two basic processes are available to produce foams from polystyrene. In order to simplify the nomenclature we will use the following abbreviations.

PS, a polystyrene foam produced by either an expansion process or an extrusion process;

EPS, a polystyrene foam manufactured by moulding blocks boards or shapes from expandable beads, sometimes referred to as a 'bead-board'; and

XPS, an extruded polystyrene foam manufactured into boards.

In many instances either EPS or XPS can be used in a given application and in this case reference will be made to PS foams. Where either one material or the other is more suitable for technical reasons this will be pointed out in the text by specific reference to EPS or XPS.

Foams are produced by mixing a volatile gas into the polymer and allowing subsequent controlled expansion by application of some type of heating which softens the polymer. As the two materials are derived from the same chemical building block shown as

$$
\begin{array}{cc}
\text{H} & \text{H} \\
| & | \\
-\text{C}- & \text{C}- \\
| & | \\
\text{H} & \bigcirc
\end{array}
$$

they share several common attributes such as similar softening points and chemical resistance. Differences which occur are due largely to the process by which the boards are manufactured.

41.2.1 Manufacture of EPS

Suspension of polymerization of the styrene building blocks is carried out in the presence of pentane in solution to produce long polymer chains incoporating pentane in solution. Granules from this process are then coated and graded by sieving. Coatings are used to improve subsequent processing. Various sizes of expandable bead are found to be suitable for different applications, many outside the building industry. For example, small beads are used to manufacture disposable cups and other grades may be preferred for moulded-packaging applications. Incorporation

of flame retardants takes place in the polymerization process. Consequently, flame-retardant and normal grades are manufactured in different production batches.

These beads are then expanded to about 50 times their volume under controlled steam pressure either through continuous or batch prefoamers. It is at this point that the final density of the product is largely controlled. The beads soften at $100°C$, allowing expansion of the pentane and the polymer. The beads are cooled, creating a vacuum within the closed cells which is corrected by migration of air into the cells over a period of hours.

To produce EPS boards the beads are usually then transferred to a mould, e.g. a box up to 24 feet long and 4 feet × 2 feet in cross-section. Once the lid is closed, steam is introduced via holes in the walls of the mould which causes the thermoplastic beads to soften once more and attempt to expand further. Now constrained by the mould, the beads fill the interstices and fuse together to form a block.

After cooling, the block is demoulded for subsequent cutting into boards using hot wires. Alternative machines are produced to allow manufacture of continuously moulded boards and semi-continuously moulded blocks. In both cases there is great flexibility in product length. Shape-moulded products can also be made for specific building applications. We are all familiar with this type of product when used as a packaging medium for electrical goods such as refrigerators or televisions.

The final products resulting are air-filled foams and usually range in density from 8 to 40 kg m^{-3} and are white in colour.

41.2.2 Manufacture of XPS

Starting from crystal polystyrene containing no blowing agents, XPS is manufactured by heating in an extruder the polymer blended with flame retardants, various additives to control nucleation of the cells, and a blowing agent the choice of which affects the thermal conductivity.

As the polymer melts the chosen blowing agent is introduced under pressure to dissolve in the polystyrene. At the end of the extruder this melt of blended polystyrene and blowing agent passes through a die into atmospheric pressure and consequently expands. Control and sizing of this expanded material determines the density and properties of the boards produced. It is normal for each manufacturer to colour code his own production, for example in the UK as blue, green or pink. Boards can be produced either singly in which case a hard skin surface results, or as blocks for subsequent cutting into boards with hot wires. Blocks up to approximately 150 mm are manufactured in widths of up to about 1.2 m. Densities of boards produced by this method range from about 28 kg m^{-3} upwards.

A variation on this process allows, by application of a vacuum to the material after it exits the die, lower densities to be produced. Values down to 20 kg m^{-3} are claimed.

Until recently, chlorofluorocarbon blowing agents (CFCs) have been used for their combination of low boiling point and non-flammability to produce XPS. This also brought benefits in thermal-conductivity performance even after allowing for some outward migration of the gas. Due to the current concern over the long-term effect of CFCs on the ozone layer and international agreement to phase out CFCs, manufacturers of XPS are moving to the use of more acceptable gases.

41.3 Physical properties

In its solid state, polystyrene has a density of 1050 kg m^{-3}. Its physical properties are well known and these are summarized in *Tables 41.1* to *41.3*. For building use the polymer is mostly used in expanded form as a cellular foam. To a very large extent the solid content of the matrix determines its physical properties, although the distribution of material and imperfections in the cellular structure also play a part. It follows that the density of the foam is the most significant factor in determining the physical properties.

The physical properties also vary according to the method of manufacture. Moulding of EPS will give slightly different properties to XPS material. This is mainly due to density differences, but also because the cellular structure of XPS is more uniform and has 100% closed cells. EPS, being made up of many discrete beads physically bonded together, has a labyrinth around the beads because total fusion of the bead surface area is not possible. The individual beads are 100% closed cell and the foam is considered 'substantially' closed cell.

Manufacturing variations will result in a normal distribution of a physical property around the mean at any given density. Each physical property described herein has a high confidence level.

41.3.1 Compressive strength

The cellular structure of expanded polystyrene gives it a complicated mechanism for resisting compression forces. On one hand there is a series of struts and ties with associated cell faces that make up the cell structure and, on the other, the gas within the cell also resists compression in the short term; long-term pressure above the elastic limit will allow creep to occur. In the totally homogeneous structure of XPS, the stress–strain curve follows the classic pattern with yield occurring at between 5% and 10% strain. EPS has a more complicated structure because of the existence of the intercellular labyrinth and, in fact, does not yield in the true sense of the form.

At levels of compression above 2% strain, both materials will exhibit long-term creep deformation caused by the pressure of the gas in the cells reducing to near atmospheric and thereby increasing the stress taken on the cell walls. As a general rule, as the density increases the compressive strength increases and the propensity to creep under a given load reduces. It should be noted that the EPS is described as carrying a compressive stress at a given strain, rather than a compressive strength. For normal purposes the strain is taken as 10%. This level of strain

Table 41.1 Physical properties of solid polystyrene

Density (kg m^{-3})	1050
Melting point (K)	510
Specific heat capacity (J kg^{-1} K^{-1})	1300
Coefficient of thermal expansion (mm^{-1} mK^{-1})	0.070
Thermal conductivity (W m^{-1} K^{-1})	0.08
Tensile strength (MPa)	50
Young's modulus (MPa)	3100

Table 41-2 The physical property requirements of EPS*

Physical property	Grade				
	SD	HD	EHD	UHD	ISD
Maximum thermal conductivity at 10°C (W m^{-1} K^{-1})	0.038	0.035	0.033	0.033	0.041
Compressive strength or compressive stress at 10% strain (kPa)					
Minimum	70	110	150	190	25
Maximum	—	—	—	—	45
Minimum cross-breaking strength (kPa)	140	170	205	275	NA
Dimension stability at 80°C					
Maximum percentage linear change	1.0	1.0	1.0	1.0	1.0
Maximum water vapour permeability at 38°C					
(ng Pa^{-1} s^{-1} m^{-1})	6.9	5.0	4.2	4.2	10.0
Burning characteristics, extent burnt (mm)					
type N			$\geqslant 125$		
type A			< 125		
Safe working load at 1% strain (kPa)	21	45	70	100	10

NA, not applicable.
* Methods of test are referred to in BS 3837: Part 1.[1]

Table 41.3 The physical property requirements of XPS*

Physical property	Skinned					Planed	
	E1	E2	E3	E4	E5	E6	E7
Compressive stress (kPa) (min.)	100	150	200	300	350	100	250
Water vapour permeability (ng Pa^{-1} s^{-1} m^{-1}) (max.)	3.2	2.7	2.4	2.1	1.9	3.8	2.4
Water absorption by immersion (max. % vol.)	1	1	1	1	1	2	2
Water absorption by diffusion (max. % vol.)	—	4	4	3	3	—	—
Thermal conductivity at 10°C (W m^{-1} K^{-1}) (max.)	0.032	0.030	0.030	0.028	0.028	0.035	0.030
Dimensional stability for 2 days at 70°C (change %) (max.)	5	5	5	5	5	5	5
Compressive creep at 40 kPa and 70°C for 7 days (change %) (max.)	—	—	5	5	5	—	5
Burning characteristics of small specimens	Maximum extent of burning 125 mm						

* Methods of test are referred to in BS 3837: Part 2.[3]

Table 41.4 BBA and WIMLAS approvals and their applications

	EPS	XPS
Partial cavity fill	*	*
Drylining laminates	*	*
External wall insulation	*	*
Floor insulation: Separate components	*	—
Laminates	*	*
Structural infill	*	—
Roof insulation: Warm flat	*	—
Inverted	—	*
Pitched sarking board	—	*
Clayheave	*	—

is chosen so that it can be measured consistently during quality-control testing.

The elastic limit for PS lies at approximately 1.5–2% strain. Values of stress quoted at a nominal 1% compression can, therefore, be used for design purposes.

41.3.2 Cross-breaking strength

Cross-breaking or flexural strength is a function of how well the polystyrene foam has been made. For XPS it shows an even distribution of correctly sized cells in the matrix and for EPS it is a measure of the fusion between the individual beads with the density having an effect if the processing conditions are held as a constant. The British Standard lays down minimum values of cross-breaking strength for each grade of material. These rise in tandem with compressive stress and are, therefore, seen to be a function of density. However, the levels are chosen to correspond to the physical requirements of material application, rather than to processing limitations.

41.3.3 Thermal conductivity

Heat transfer through foams is a complex mixture of convection, conduction and radiation, the latter being the least important. Conduction through the cell structure depends on cell size, cell distribution and cell-wall thickness, while convection is governed by cell size and and the gas entrapped in each cell. The thermal conductivity of a foam is more or less governed by the blowing agent used in processing the material and the gas filling the cell structure of the finished material. EPS is an air-filled foam and thus has a higher thermal conductivity than most XPS materials. The gas in the cells of most foam plastics is a CFC product, although there is now pressure to change the blowing agent, as mentioned earlier.

The relationship of density and thermal conductivity of commercial grades of EPS is complex. A minimum value of thermal conductivity occurs at a density of approximately 40 kg m^{-3}. For commercial densities below 40 kg m^{-3} and for densities above this value, the conductivity increases very approximately in a linear manner. This phenomenon occurs in other gas-filled foams, but the point of the minimum is shifted along the density axis.

41.3.4 Dimensional stability

The manufacture of PS foam relies on the thermoplastic nature of the material. Heat is supplied during the manufacturing processes to produce a foam. On exiting the machinery the material is substantially above room temperature and tends to 'grow' slightly. A conditioning period is, therefore, required for the material to stabilize before cutting to the finished dimensions. In the case of EPS, the post-moulding conditioning period is usually satisfied within 24–48 h of moulding. Because XPS is subjected to a higher temperature, becomes molten and strained during the extrusion process, the conditioning period is substantially longer.

Once conditioned, the materials are required to have a dimensional stability within stated limits in any direction. The test regime is for the XPS to withstand 70°C for 2 days and EPS to withstand 80°C for 7 days. These temperatures are the maximum continuous-operating temperatures of the material. Above these temperatures the materials progressively soften and shrink, eventually becoming molten at $\geqslant 150$°C.

41.3.5 Moisture absorption

PS foams are essentially hygrophobic and will not readily accept moisture into the cell structure. Where the surface is cut, rather than moulded, there is a layer of open cells and moisture may ingress into this area. Moisture may be forced into the cell structure by pressure over a given time period, the rate of absorption being roughly proportional to the pressure and logarithmically proportional to the time period.

Under identical conditions, EPS will generally have a higher moisture uptake than XPS because the labyrinth surrounding the bead structure provides an additional path of ingress. Moisture absorption is also dependent on the density and the processing conditions especially for EPS. The important point to remember is that neither material will readily absorb moisture from its surroundings and that pressure is required to force moisture into the cellular structure. Because of the inert nature of the material it will not support capillarity and can, therefore, be used in a situation where it bridges moisture barriers.

The difference in water uptake between EPS and XPS are, in most applications, unimportant. However, the better performance of XPS does mean that some applications, for example inverted roof insulation, remain the prerogative of XPS.

41.3.6 Moisture-vapour transmission

Moisture vapour acts as a gas in its mechanisms of transfer through materials. PS foams allow the transmittance of moisture vapour through the matrix, but severely retards the rate of transfer. The labyrinth around interconnecting beads of EPS allows a tortuous path through the material but does not provide free passage. In common with most properties of PS foams, the greater the density the lower the water-vapour transmission.

In some circumstances XPS is used with one or both skins intact and this markedly reduces the water-vapour transmission rate. The same is true, although to a lesser extent, with individually moulded EPS units. In the materials used commercially the water-vapour transmission rate will determine the need for a vapour-control layer. Most insulants, including EPS, will need a vapour barrier in flat-roof-insulation applications or a vapour check for internal drylining of walls. XPS, however, with a better vapour resistivity, can often be used without a vapour-control layer. It is important to treat all applications and the need for vapour barriers on their merits.

41.3.7 Tensile strength

In the context of normal insulation boards, the tensile strength is not important although it provides a natural resistance to accidental damage during transportation. Tensile strength becomes important when the PS foam is bonded to another material with adhesives to form a composite panel. The tensile strength is largely governed by the density of the foam, although the dispersion of material throughout the matrix and the cellular structure also plays a part. This is particularly true for XPS, where the method of manufacture allows the cell orientation to be adjusted. EPS can have its tensile strength adjusted within limits by the degree of fusion between the beads, which is a function of the steam pressure during moulding. However, limits are imposed by the natural tensile strength of the solid polymer.

41.3.8 Shear strength

The stress placed on PS foam is rarely of a shear nature unless the material is being used as the structural core to a sandwich panel. In these circumstances the surface area at any cross-section determines the shear strength and, consequently, the density is a limiting factor under the normal condition of uniform material dispersion. This is true for XPS, but only true for EPS if the matrix is sufficiently well fused, which is usually the case, to transfer stress without cracks starting to form. PS foams are elastic up to a maximum of 2% strain, at which point plastic deformation occurs.

To take account of this, the shear modulus is used in structural calculations, since the shear deformation contributes to the overall deflection of the panel. The shear modulus is proportional to the density of the material, within its elastic limit.

41.3.9 Young's modulus of elasticity

XPS reacts in a traditional manner when stressed and has a yield point, after which the material is subject to strain with very little increase in stress. EPS exhibits a difference stress–strain relationship to most standard building materials. To use a measurement of the stress–strain relationship with a high degree of confidence it is necessary to remain within the elastic limit of the material. The elastic limit is certainly no greater than 2% and it is usual to use a modulus of elasticity derived from the stress–strain relationship at 1% deformation. Provided that the stress limits on the material for any given property remain within the 1–2% region they can be safely used.

41.3.10 Creep

When a material is placed under load it shows two reactions to stress. The first is instantaneous and the second is time dependent. The difference between the initial strain and the strain at any future time period, under constant load, is described as the long-term-strain deformation or creep.

Creep is a phenomenon that occurs in all materials and under any conditions of stress but is more pronounced with thermoplastics. It is generally immeasurable when the stress–strain relationship remains within the elastic limits of a material. For low-density materials, such as plastic foams, where the elastic limit is quite low, i.e. typically 1–2% strain, creep can be considered not to occur at a stress which does not cause a strain greater than 1%.

41.3.11 Poisson's ratio

Poisson's ratio gives a measure of the relationship between the lateral strain and the longitudinal strain under a given load. PS foam has a Poisson's ratio of between 0.1 and 0.2. The actual value will depend more on the orientation of the cell structure than on the density of the foam.

41.4 Fire properties

Polystyrene is a combustible material. As a low-density foam the material is easily ignitable. For this reason it is recommended that PS foams should always be protected by a fire-resistant material when used in building applications. Certain decorative products, e.g. tiles and veneers, are permitted to remain uncovered, but only in conditions where they are fully adhered to a fire-resisting substrate.

BS 3837: Part 1: 1986,[1] covering EPS boards, distinguishes between two 'types' of material: type A incorporating a flame-retardant additive; and type N, normal. It is important to understand that the flame-retardant additive in PS foam, typically a brominated allyl ether, reduces the risk of ignition from small sources, but the material remains incombustible.

When a high-temperature heat source or an open flame is placed into contact with type N material it will burn fairly rapidly, whereas type A material will shrink rapidly away from the ignition source. Prolonged exposure of type A material to an ignition source may cause some combustion, but this will cease if the ignition source is removed. Tests for the presence of a flame-retardant additive have been developed for plastic foams, the usual test being BS 4735: 1974.[2] BS 3837: Part 2,[3] which covers XPS foams, allows for the manufacture of type A only.

The presence of a flame-retardant additive does not materially affect the behaviour of polystyrene once a fire has become established. Type A material will react in a similar manner to type N and is likely to contribute more smoke during combustion. Contribution to the fire load, rate of heat release and flame spread will be similar.

Once the maximum continuous-operating temperature of the foam has been exceeded, the material will soften and shrink. This becomes more evident as the temperature increases above 100°C. The material will also start to form a gaseous vapour once it is molten. If heated at a temperature of 230°C in motionless air, EPS will ignite. However, when away from a direct ignition source and under normal conditions, PS foam will require a temperature of approximately 480°C before ignition occurs.

Once the foam has commenced combustion it requires approximately 160 times its own volume of air to burn fully. Volumes of air less than this will prevent full combustion, reduce the calorific contribution of the material to a fire, and will consequently significantly increase the density of the smoke evolved. The combustion of foam is difficult to sustain in narrow cavities, such as those in brick cavity walls, for example, due to the lack of air flow through the cavity. If the cavity were to be open at the top and bottom, thus allowing cross-ventilation, combustion of the PS foam would be possible.

The calorific value of PS is 34 MJ kg^{-1}, which is nearly three times the calorific value of softwood (12 MJ kg^{-1}). However, the commercial densities of PS foam range from 10 to 50 kg m^{-3}, while softwoods have densities of 500 kg m^{-3} upwards. A comparison between the calorific value of PS at 20 kg m^{-3} and softwood would give values of 680 MJ m^{-3} and 6000 MJ m^{-3}, respectively. The maximum heat liberated with full combustion of PS foam would be around one-ninth that released by an equal volume of softwood under the same conditions.

41.4.1 Toxicity

As with any carbonaceous material, PS foam will evolve hot gases and smoke during the combustion process. The evolution process will depend on factors such as temperature, ventilation rate, available oxygen, local concentration and position of the materials involved. From these factors alone it can be seen that the determination of the toxicity of materials undergoing combustion is a complex task. PS foams will break down to carbon dioxide (CO_2), carbon monoxide (CO), water and traces of styrene. Traces of other, more complex, compounds may occur, but these can be effectively ignored. In a situation where the air flow is sufficient to allow full combustion, the two main compounds given off will be CO_2 and water. As the air flow is reduced the proportion of CO to CO_2 increases.

The toxicity of these compounds is relatively low compared with some other construction materials and the toxicity is a function of oxygen deprivation, rather than an attack on the human organism. CO has a higher affinity for the oxyhaemoglobin in the bloodstream than does oxygen and can be fatal if inhaled for 1–3 min at 10 000–15 000 parts per million (ppm). The inhalation of oxygen prior to fatality will usually reverse the effects of CO and no lasting damage will occur if the oxygen is applied sufficiently quickly. Carbon dioxide is toxic only in the sense that it prevents oxygen reaching the lungs. The temperature at which the gas is inhaled is more likely to cause damage than the gas itself.

41.4.2 PS foam and BS 476

BS 476: Part 3: 1958[4] covers the external fire exposure roof test and relates to fire testing of roofing structures when in sloping (S) or flat (F) configurations. In general, the use of PS in a roof construction will neither add to nor detract from the values obtained. Designation FAA is achieved by either roofing felts or mastic asphalt with a solar reflective layer of spa chippings. SAA will normally be achieved by the weatherproofing material, whether slate, tile or metal cladding. Inverted roof constructions with ballast or tiles achieve EXT FAA ratings.

BS 476: Part 4: 1970[5] covers the non-combustibility test for materials. In this standard PS foams are categorized as combustible.

BS 476: Part 5: 1968[6] covers the ignitability test for materials. Type A (flame retardant additive) material will achieve a class P (not easily ignitable) classification, but type N material is classified as class X (easily ignitible).

BS 476: Part 6: 1968[7] covers the fire-propagation test for materials. Test results for both i_1 and I vary according to the thickness of the material, its density and type. It is not possible to achieve results within the classifications of $i_1 = 6$ and $I = 12$ as required by the Building Regulations[8] as a constituent part of class 0 for unprotected PS.

BS 476: Part 7: 1971[9] covers the surface-spread-of-flame tests for materials. Unfaced PS foam is usually unclassifiable according to this test. Suitable facings will achieve a class 1 result. Class 1 is a necessary requirement to achieve class 0 as defined in the Building Regulations.[8]

BS 476: Part 8: 1972[10] covers the test methods and criteria for the fire resistance of elements of building construction. Tests are carried out on the full element of construction in the place of use. PS foams may be important elements in the construction but would not be tested as the sole material. This test has now been superseded by BS 476: Parts 20–23.[11]

Note that the tests listed above are as referred to in the Building Regulations,[8] though more recent versions of some tests have been published.

41.5 Chemical properties

Polystyrene is essentially an inert material. It is unaffected by the normal range of building materials that it comes into contact with, i.e. cement, plaster, concrete, etc. It is acceptable to use the material in ground that harbours sulphates. There are certain materials that PS foam should be separated from, notably silicon injected damp-proof courses, plasticized plastics (particularly polyvinyl chloride (PVC)), sealants and adhesives containing volatile solvents and coal-tar-pitch based damp-proof membranes.

PS foams should not come into contact with materials containing aromatic hydrocarbons, alcohols, industrial spirits or thinners.

41.6 Wall insulation

The insulation of walls can be carried out on three effective interfaces: the internal face, the external face, and within the wall sandwich. Each system has its own advantages and is appropriate in the right circumstances.

41.6.1 Internal lining

PS foam is placed behind a suitable fire-resistant covering to provide the required fire resistance. The exposed face may be plasterboard or mineral-based boards or, in exceptional circumstances, wet plasters. This latter method is now uncommon, except for small areas, because of the difficulty of providing a mechanical fix between the plaster and the wall behind the PS foam. Modern methods of construction emphasize the need to provide mechanical fixings to drylined systems.

Laminates of PS foam and rigid board materials are readily available with the most popular in the domestic market being plasterboard/PS foam. In industrial and commercial applications the greater rigidity and impact resistance of mineral-based boards can make them more appropriate.

The normal method of construction for laminates is to provide either a flattened surface, intermediate pads at the right line and level or to use a heavy adhesive compound as a gap-filling agent. The use of adhesive provides a method for levelling the surface of the laminate and its adhesion qualities are secondary. Mechanical fixings must be used to provide long-term support to the laminate. It is usual to provide three to four fixings per square metre of board area.

41.6.2 Cavity walls

PS foam has a large market share in cavity-wall insulation. The boards are sized to fit between wall ties at normal spacings and are fixed using a retaining clip on the wall tie. The insulation is fixed to whichever leaf of the masonry wall is constructed first. This is normally the internal leaf of blockwork but, due to the inherent moisture resistance of the foam, nothing detrimental will occur if the PS foam is fixed to the inside of the external leaf. With all current systems it is imperative that a cavity is maintained between the insulation and the leaf to which it is not fixed. This allows the cavity wall to perform its designed function, namely resistance to rain penetration, with no loss of efficacy.

The first row of wall ties is placed at 600-mm centres, usually below the DPC with the bottom edge of the boards resting on them. Because the PS foam does not support capillarity it is permitted for the boards to bridge the DPC. Insulation boards are attached to the constructed leaf after all mortar snots have been removed and the wall ties brushed clean. A lift of no more than 1350 mm should be constructed before attaching the insulation and bringing up the other leaf.

The maintained cavity should never be less than 25 mm, although some authorities recommend 50 mm designed cavities to allow for workmanship tolerances and imperfections. The wider the maintained cavity the easier it is to keep clean, using both cavity battens and post-cleaning methods. Since the purpose of the cavity is to avoid moisture penetration through the wall, it is imperative that the cavity is left clear and clean (see *Figures 41.1* and *41.2*).

Additional wall ties are used at reveals and on short sections of wall to ensure a good tight fit of the insulation. New developments incorporate edge details on the boards. A

Figure 41.1 Polystyrene insulation boards

of the PVC-sheathed cable. The embrittlement improves the electrical-insulation properties of the cable but makes it susceptible to damage if it is subsequently moved. There is no danger of an electrical fire caused by the loss of electrical insulation but, if fully surrounded by any insulation material, the cables should be derated by a factor of 75%.

41.6.3 External insulation

External insulation can be carried out by fixing or applying a weatherproof layer over the face of the insulation. Two basic methods are available—wet or dry—defined by the method of applying the weather-proofing. Dry systems use a mechanically fixed cladding material, usually fixed onto timber battens, such as tiles, slates, timber or plastic boarding. PS foam is either placed beneath or between the battens and the cladding is then attached. Great care must be taken to ensure that the efficacy of the cladding is maintained and the detailing is correct.

In common with all external-insulation methods, it is vital to ensure that if any vapour-control layer or damp-proof membranes are used they must be correctly positioned. This must be on the warm side of the insulant. Beneath slates or tiles a 'breathable' sarking felt should be used to avoid condensation damage to timbers.

Wet systems of external insulation are not widely used in the UK, but are very popular in the rest of Europe. This is largely due to the aesthetic appeal of brickwork to the majority of building owners in the UK, rather than any system deficiencies. PS foam in its expanded form (but not extruded) is the most popular material for this application throughout Europe and North America, although systems based on XPS are available. It is essential to use a rigid, low weight, stable material as the

rebated edge helps provide additional resistance to moisture penetration and cold bridging. The tongue and groove detail now available also assists in providing a positive fix to all boards, particularly small sections.

For some domestic and industrial buildings a system of EPS beads or granules may be blown into the cavity after it has been fully constructed. This does have the advantage of allowing the cavity wall to be built in a traditional manner and inspected to ensure its cleanliness before the cavity is closed and the bead pumped in under low air pressure. Problems can occur with building imperfections providing an exit for the beads and in potential post-settlement if the installation is not carried out in a careful and controlled manner. It is usual to provide an aqueous adhesive to the beads during the installation (the 'bonded' process) to prevent any settlement.

While PS foam is used extensively in masonry constructions, it is less common in timber-frame constructions. In Europe and North America, PS foam is often used as a sarking board on the outside of the structural sheathing. Common practice in the UK and Scandinavia is to use a mineral-fibre quilt between the timber studwork. There is no reason for not using PS foam, particularly as factory-finished components allow accurate placing of materials, which overcomes the potential problem of rigid boards trying to accommodate poor-tolerance setting-out.

In all circumstances of PS foam used in composite wall construction PVC electrical cables must be isolated from the insulation materials. If they are maintained in contact the plasticizer in the PVC will migrate into the PS foam. This has the effect of softening the PS foam and causing embrittlement

Figure 41.2 Wall ties in polystyrene insulation boards

North America, although systems based on XPS are available. It is essential to use a rigid, low weight, stable material as the substrate for the render or cracking of the render will result. To ensure the stability of the foam a period of ageing, usually 6–8 weeks, is required. This allows natural shrinkage of the material to take place before use.

The common method of construction is to use a thick cementitious adhesive to attach the insulation to the structure. This needs to be sound and free of loose material and dirt to ensure good adhesion. The cementitious adhesive also acts as a gap filler and allows the insulation to be laid flat and provide a level base for the finishes.

The insulation is also fixed to the wall by mechanical fixings of plastic or stainless steel. As well as providing a sound anchorage, the mechanical fixings also secure the reinforcement mesh that is used to carry the render. It should be noted that not all systems require reinforcement meshes. Once the mechanical fixing has been finished a render is applied to the surface of the boards. Each different system has its own particular render which is a proprietary mixture. This is usually applied in two coats, with the base and finish coat being of slightly different formulations. Both thick (20 mm) and thin (6 mm) render systems claim advantages, but both systems have been used successfully for many years throughout Europe and North America.

External wall insulation in the UK is primarily a refurbishment method, although the basic advantage of providing thermal storage in the wall structure would make it attractive for low-energy housing if the aesthetics were acceptable. It provides a solution to the twin problems of rain penetration and condensation in existing buildings and many of the 1960s system-built houses have benefited from a new outer skin.

Due to concern over its performance in a fire, BRE have produced a report on the performance of various proprietary external-wall-insulation systems. To overcome the potential, but minimal, risk of fire spread via the insulation material in multistorey buildings, cavity barriers of glass or rock fibre should be installed at appropriate centres, e.g. 10 m, in the insulation layer. The fixing methods of dry systems will usually ensure compartmentation of the insulant, but if not the same methodology as wet systems applies.

41.6.4 Specialist systems

Throughout Europe and North America many novel systems have been invented to use the insulation advantages of PS foam with its good mechanical strength. Most systems use the PS foam in an individually moulded unit which acts as a lost shutter to a concrete fill. The moulded units are attached together in 'Lego' fashion and supported while concrete is poured between the skins. Once the concrete has set a fully insulated structure is available for finishes to be applied.

Other systems are a variation on this theme and use a separate connector to hold two skins of PS foam apart. The mechanical separators may be in either plastic, metal or modified cast mortars. The same method of filling is adopted as with the PS foam moulded units.

Walls can be constructed of PS foam which has been machined to allow steel or timber framing to be inserted. The framing carries the structural loads and provides a sound fixing for the plasterboard or similar board material used to provide the fire resistance of the system.

All these systems have been widely accepted throughout the world but have had limited commercial success in the UK. Speed of erection and high insulation values are the main advantages of these systems, but the construction costs are rarely lower than for traditional building methods.

41.7 Roof insulation

Developments in the late 1960s on roof insulation involving PS materials have not changed significantly to date. The materials used for each element have undergone generic changes and material quality has increased considerably, but the relationship of materials has altered very little. Roofing can generally be broken into two categories: flat and pitched roof types. PS boards can be used in both types but vary in terms of position relative to the construction.

41.7.1 Pitched roofs

In pitched-roof construction the roofs are primarily designated as cold-roof constructions. This means that the void created externally to the insulation, whether it be a loft or between rafters, requires ventilation. Ventilation of the space is the prime means of preventing condensation in the timbers and subsequent rot.

One insulated pitched-roof construction type using PS boards, which is designed as a warm roof, is that where PS panels are installed at sarking level. In this case the PS panels fit between and over the rafters and are anchored by the roof finishes. In order to complete the warm-roof aspect of system, the insulation at roof level must meet the wall insulation to prevent a cold bridge. This system offers the main benefits of retaining standard roof truss timber dimensions, creating a warm roof and allowing a reasonable choice of internal finishes to the ceiling.

Installation is carried out during roof construction and, therefore, becomes part of the initial construction process rather than an extra operation from inside the building. In certain circumstances a saving in the loss of ceiling height can also be affected. PS insulation panels are designed as a top-hat section with the flanges designed in width to sit over the rafter top. Panels from either side of the rafter abut over the rafter and the subsequent joint is covered with a treated timber fixing batten running down the rafter. Across the fixing battens the traditional roof covering of sarking layer, tile battens and tiles is applied in accordance with the relevant fixing requirements of the system.

Alternative systems for producing a warm pitch roof by means of insulation at top rafter level are available on the European market and it may be that these types of system will enter the UK market in time. Variations in traditional roof-construction materials, however, will mean that these continental systems will be slow, if not limited, in their UK applicability.

The insulation of pitched roofs by means of more conventional systems is open to PS material with the incorporation of ventilated voids above the insulation, i.e. a cold-roof construction. Applications in this area can be broken down into domestic/residential and other categories for normal building procedures.

In domestic-type applications, predominantly where a plasterboard ceiling is specified, the PS insulation is positioned between and/or under the rafter and subsequently covered with an adequately fire-rated material, e.g. plasterboard. Whilst not always proven as necessary, the use of a vapour-control layer between the insulation and the plasterboard is a sound construction technique to limit interstitial condensation and associated problems in the roof structure. The vapour-control layer should be as continuous as the construction allows and any breaks should be sealed with an appropriate mastic/sealant.

Allowance of an adequate ventilation gap, normally 50 mm, above the insulation will, depending on the rafter depth, determine how positioning and fixing of the PS boards will be accomplished. Where the depth of the rafter is sufficient to allow all the required insulation thickness to be placed between the rafter, and maintain the 50 mm ventilation void above, the vapour-control layer and plasterboard are fixed directly to the rafter underside.

In circumstances where the rafter is insufficient to allow insulation and a ventilation void in its depth the insulation will need to be split into two layers and positioned between and under the rafters. Fixing of the PS insulation boards between the rafters will require backstops to maintain the ventilation void, in both the above details. Temporary tack fixing of the insulation board to the rafter side may be necessary to hold it in place prior to applying the second insulation board below. The second insulation board is applied directly beneath the rafters. Again temporary fixing may be necessary prior to fixing of the vapour-control layer and plasterboard. This second layer of insulation board is normally a minimum of 50 mm thick and at this thickness plasterboard fixing nails, of sufficient length to also hold the plasterboard, are available as a standard item.

Whilst construction requirements may be similar, materials for use in them can vary. As an alternative to the above details, variations in the vapour-control layer and the PS insulation/plasterboard are available. The plasterboard may incorporate a vapour-control membrane on its back face or an internal vapour-control layer may be applied directly to the plasterboard face. Composite insulated lining panels of plasterboard and PS insulation are available as an alternative to separate materials. Options in the method of construction are limited, however, by the use of a composite panel as they can only be fixed below or between supports.

In commercial/industrial-type applications EPS boards are available with a surface coating to achieve the required class 1 surface spread of flame rating and offer a water-vapour-control layer over the panel surface. Most often, these insulation panels are used in framed buildings where they are positioned above or below the purlin level.

Use of EPS foil-faced panels above the purlin and directly below the cladding allows rapid refurbishment or new installation of an insulated cladding system. The panels are placed into a metal T-section over the purlins to give a good aesthetic joint finish and, if necessary, a water-vapour control between the panels when combined with a mastic sealant.

Fixing of the insulation panels is carried out in conjunction with the roof cladding. Profiled metal cladding panels are placed over the insulation, positioned and fixed by either compression or spacer (stand-off) methods.

Where a compression fixing system is used, the insulation panel must have sufficient strength to withstand the initial compression load. Load-bearing characteristics of the various grades of EPS are given in Section 41.3 and should be compared to the requirements for individual systems. The purlin width in each case will play a substantial part in the determination of the resultant load requirement.

The alternative fixing, that of spacer or stand-off type, the load imposed by the fixing, through the cladding and onto the purlin, is not reliant upon the insulation panel for its support. For a spacer-type fixing system, a support of either timber or plastic replaces the EPS at the critical point of load. This method of fixing can, however, be more time consuming on site because of the need to align cladding and insulation prior to fixing in order to determine the spacer position. This is especially relevant when plastic spacer systems are used and the cladding has to be removed in order to position the plastic spacer and then replaced to fix.

A variation on the spacer fixing method is that of a stand-off fixing. In this case the essential performance criteria of load release from the insulation panel is achieved, whilst the on-site fixing time is considerably reduced as compared with that for the normal spacer system. A stand-off fixing is, in effect, a single drill fixing which encompasses the role of spacer within its depth.

In its length it has the following sections.

(1) a self-tapping bit;
(2) a reamer;
(3) a spacer section;
(4) a cladding fixing thread; and
(5) a sealing head and nut.

Fixing of foil-faced EPS or plain XPS below a roof purlin system can be carried out either at pitch of roof level or as a flat system to create a suspended-ceiling system. Generally, the flat system is restricted to flat-ceiling systems below the deck to create access areas above for services. In either case the choice of insulation board is not restricted by strength. The weight of the insulation panel is the only load imposed at bearing points.

Generally, the use of a metal or plastic support grid is considered favourably to enhance the aesthetic appearance of the finished system. In the case of the foil faced EPS panels this also removes the need for a series of punctures through the facing at fixing points. Where the insulation panels are used in standard grids of 1200×600 mm dimensions, panels of above 30 mm thick will adequately self-support.

In areas where a high degree of water-vapour sealing may be necessary, the use of a mastic sealant or tape in the grid system, prior to laying in the insulation panel, will provide protection at panel edges from the flow of water vapour around panels.

Following the continuous development of EPS production techniques, insulation panels are now available which can be profiled to suit various cladding and liner materials available. Provision of differing contours on the upper and lower faces of the EPS panel allow a virtually unlimited choice of combinations with a variation in overall panel thickness as required for thermal insulation or system design.

41.7.2 Flat roofs

Flat roofs can be designated as either cold or warm construction, related to the position of the insulation and the structural deck. In a cold-roof construction, where the insulation is below the deck, there is a requirement to ventilate the void formed, generally between timber rafters, and to ensure that no dead areas of air are created. In different orientations of the roof this total ventilation may be extremely difficult if not impossible. The warm-roof construction, where the insulation is above the structural deck, is therefore increasingly used because the need for a ventilated air space below the deck is omitted.

41.7.2.1 Cold-roof construction

PS insulation board can simply be positioned between rafters in a timber-deck construction. Generally the ventilation void will be above the insulation board. Positioning of the insulation board requires backstops along the joist to prevent lifting of the insulation boards into the ventilation gap. A vapour-control membrane should be positioned between the insulation board and the ceiling lining or alternatively a vapour-checked plasterboard used.

Where the required insulation level necessitates the use of an insulation-board thickness which, when combined with the ventilation void depth, becomes in excess of the joist depth an alternative method of fixing is required. In this instance splitting of the insulation thickness, into two boards, allows one to be positioned between the joists and the second to be fixed below both joists and previously fitted insulation board. The entire area is then covered with a vapour-control membrane and ceiling finish.

Where the cold-roof deck is of concrete or metal the

insulation boards can be fitted below, generally in a grid or timber stud system, without the need for a ventilated void above.

41.7.2.2 Warm-roof construction

Warm roofs differ in respect of the position of the insulation layer relative to the weatherproofing. Traditionally insulation is positioned below the weatherproofing. Alternatively, if the insulation layer is positioned above the weatherproofing the roof is termed an 'inverted', 'upside down' or 'inverted roof membrane' application.

The use of PS in these applications varies with each type of material taking prominence in a particular field. EPS is used in the standard type of construction where the insulation is below the weatherproofing membrane, whilst XPS is used in the inverted type of application.

The omission of a ventilated void in a warm roof construction means that an alternative method of condensation prevention has to be adopted. This generally implies a condensation-risk analysis calculation in accordance with BS 5250: 1989.[12] The calculation is designed to determine the likely risk of condensation in a roof construction, the amount of condensation over a winter and summer period and the overall net retention figure, if any. It is normally shown that with the inclusion of a vapour-control layer between the structural deck and the EPS insulation the condensation risk is low with no annual net retention of moisture.

A standard warm-roof construction will incorporate the following elements in its make up.

A structural deck This can be of almost any material construction available on the market today, timber, concrete, metal or a hybrid of these materials. Whether the deck forms an internal ceiling finish, or if this needs to be considered separately, it does not influence the insulation application requirements.

A vapour control layer This is a minimum type 1B felt to BS 747[13] or, in the case of a profiled deck, a reinforced felt type 1F to BS 747.[13] It may be necessary, where high humidity conditions prevail in the area below the roof, to provide an upgraded or double vapour-control layer to prevent interstitial condensation occurring in the roof. An upgraded vapour barrier will normally include a foil interface which gives it a superior vapour resistance.

The vapour-control layer will be bonded to the previously primed deck. All joints in the vapour-control layer must be lapped and sealed. Around the perimeter the vapour-control layer must be taken up in excess of the insulation thickness to be bonded into the weatherproofing membrane.

41.7.2.3 EPS insulation

The use of EPS insulation boards, either uniform or tapered and with a factory bonded felt or fibre board overlay, in warm-roof constructions is covered, and approved where possible, by the major roofing associations in the UK. In practice the choice between uniform or tapered EPS insulation boards depends on a variety of factors. Basically, however, these can be divided into two categories, those roofs which have drainage falls incorporated in the structure and those which require the drainage falls to be created above the structural deck. In the case of the use of tapered EPS boards, the prime objective is to create drainage falls on the roof. Due to the thickness of insulation involved, however, the overall thermal transmittance value of the roof will normally comply with, or better, the Building Regulations[8] requirements.

Where the EPS insulation board is used with a prefelted

surface the application of a minimum 13 mm thick fibre board, perlite or cork board overlay is required. The overlay board acts as a heat sink over the EPS when either BUR or mastic asphalt weatherproofing is applied.

Laminates of EPS and fibre board are available in both uniform and tapered form as an alternative to the site-applied version above.

Two EPS grades, HD and EHD, as defined in *Table 41.2* earlier, are normally used in roofing applications. Grade HD is used where normal maintenance or domestic loads are envisaged. Where there is the likelihood of higher loadings, such as commercial areas, EPS grade EHD would be used.

EPS boards are applied to the vapour control layer by mopping an area of the vapour control layer with hot bitumen and laying the EPS board onto the surface. The initial high bitumen temperature is absorbed by the vapour control layer. All EPS boards will be laid with tight butted joints and up to all perimeters.

In the case of a mastic asphalt weatherproofing system, a 50-mm wide gap must be left between the EPS boards and all upstands. This is then filled with a rigid infill material such as earth, damp sand/cement or timber to act as a support to the final mastic asphalt fillet around the perimeter of the roof.

Prefelted EPS boards have the advantage at this stage in the roof construction of being able to provide a temporary weatherproofing layer if joints and edges are sealed with felt. Where an EPS/fibre board laminate has been used, the first layer of the weatherproofing must be applied immediately. In addition, taping of the insulation boards joints may be necessary to prevent bitumen ingress where a BUR weatherproofing is applied.

Overlay board The application of an overlay board to prefelted EPS is carried out by applying a coat of hot bitumen compound to the overlay board and laying this onto the felt surface of the EPS insulation. Overlay boards should be fully butted and, in the case of a mastic asphalt weatherproofing, the overlay board should overlap the rigid infill perimeter detail by 50%.

Weatherproofing On to the overlay surface can be applied either BUR or mastic asphalt specifications in accordance with CP 144: Parts 3[14] and 4[15] and relevant trade associations.

In addition to the standard weatherproofings, a family of single-layer membranes is now widely available in the UK. These membranes do not generally involve the use of hot bitumen in their application. A felt or fibre board surface to the EPS insulation is not normally necessary.

PS boards can be used below single-layer membranes, but in some applications may require a separating layer to prevent migration of plasticizers from the membrane to the EPS foam.

41.7.2.4 XPS insulation

Where XPS is used in an inverted roof system, irrespective of the deck, the insulation is laid over the weatherproofing membrane. Protection of the weatherproofing membrane is the foremost benefit of this system. Degradation from thermal shock and solar exposure is reduced to an absolute minimum. Estimates have been put forward that the temperature fluctuation in the protected weatherproof membrane can be less than 1°C. Installation of the system can also be carried out in virtually any weather conditions as disturbance of the weatherproofing is not necessary.

In the thermal-transmittance calculation for an inverted roof construction, the thickness of the insulation is increased by 20% to compensate for intermittent heat loss. This loss is created by the flow of rainwater below the XPS board and over the weatherproofing.

An inverted roof consists of the following layers.

Waterproof membrane over structural deck This is a protection sheet or a cushioning layer, as required by some PVC membranes to prevent reaction between XPS and membrane. Alternatively, this is used as a cushioning layer over an irregular surface.

XPS insulation This is laid loose over the surface of the roof and vertically at upstands to reduce thermal bridging.

Filter fabric and ballast A filter fabric may be required, again when using plastic membranes, to prevent fines percolating through the ballast and damaging the membrane. On BUR or mastic asphalt roofs no filter fabric may be necessary if the ballast is 20–30 mm thick and clean. Ballasting of the XPS boards is necessary to prevent their movement by wind uplift pressures. Different thicknesses of XPS board require different depths of ballast to maintain their stability. On roofs subject to traffic the use of paving slabs in lieu of ballast is necessary. The paving slabs are supported on spacer pads to allow drainage below.

41.8 Floor insulation

The use of PS in insulated floor construction has been widely accepted since the early 1960s in timber, traditional solid concrete and modern pre-cast concrete or beam and block floor systems. With todays awareness of the need for energy-conservation measures and the legislative requirements of Building Regulations, the wide variety of possible floor insulation applications is of major significance. The versatility of PS allows optimum use of a material, available in a range of grades, to meet various thermal and structural requirements in the sphere of floor construction.

PS used in floor construction to provide thermal and/or structural requirements is very versatile because of the performance characteristics of the material. The same characteristics give a range of advantages in use, surpassed in all aspects by no other insulation material—it is lightweight, has good structural strength, is moisture resistant and durable, is an excellent thermal insulation and yet is easy to install and is compatible with most standard building materials. Insulation boards may be positioned vertically on either face of the foundation or horizontally either above or below the slab.

41.8.1 Perimeter insulation

In the case of ground floors it is generally considered most economical to insulate the whole floor area. This is especially true in the case of houses and other small buildings. In buildings of larger floor area, in order that the major source of heat loss from the slab, the edge, may be insulated independently of the whole floor, slab-edge or perimeter insulation can be carried out using either EPS or XPS.

The use of PS in floor construction can be grouped in the following application areas:

(1) perimeter insulation;
(2) underslab insulation;
(3) overslab insulation;
(4) timber-floor insulation;
(5) cold-store-floor insulation;
(6) high-load-floor systems;
(7) structural-floor panels; and
(8) composite-floor insulation panels.

Vertical-perimeter insulation is normally applied to a depth of at least 600 mm.

Installation of the insulation boards against the foundation is carried out prior to backfill around the foundation. The surface to receive the insulation board should be flat and even to allow first contact between the surfaces. Backfill of the trench should be carried out with care to prevent damage to the insulation board.

41.8.2 Underslab insulation

In addition to giving a solid ground-floor slab excellent thermal insulation properties, the use of PS insulation boards below it provide a rigid, robust and easy to install base on which to lay a damp-proof membrane in sheet form. Its high water-resistance characteristic makes PS insulation ideal for use above or below the damp-proof membrane under a ground-floor slab.

The range of material grades available in EPS and XPS make possible their use under differing load criteria from domestic to heavy-duty constructions.

The high compressive-strength characteristics of PS foam allows non-load-bearing walls of both masonry and stud partition construction to be built directly off the finished concrete slab without the need for slab strengthening below them.

In preparation for the laying of insulation boards or a damp-proof membrane, the hardcore base must be well compacted and suitably blinded to leave a level and even surface. The insulation boards are then laid over the prepared surface with joints closely butted. Installation of insulation vertically around the perimeter of the slab to prevent cold bridging is then carried out. Where the damp-proof membrane has been laid below the insulation all board joints should be taped to prevent grout ingress.

The concrete ground-floor slab is then laid to the specified thickness and finished as required. Protection to the insulation boards may be required if materials are to be barrowed across the surface.

41.8.3 Overslab insulation

PS insulation boards can be laid directly over a structural floor slab or system to provide a rigid and robust base for a suitable floor finish. Finishes normally applied over the polystyrene are a minimum 18 mm thick flooring-grade chipboard to BS 5669[16] or a minimum 65 mm thick sand–cement screed.

In domestic applications, the lower strength PS boards are used and will adequately support the loads associated with this type of occupancy. If the loading conditions exceed domestic equivalents then higher grades of PS foams may be necessary.

Load-bearing and other heavy partitions, must be supported by a treated-timber batten placed below the floor finish in lieu of the polystyrene. Generally this applies only where a chipboard floor finish is to be used.

The surfaces onto which the polystyrene insulation boards are to be laid must be flat and even. Minor irregularities over a tamped slab or between the elements of a pre-cast floor system may be overcome by the insulation boards. If significant irregularities occur they must be suitably removed or levelled by use of a proprietory screed, self-levelling or otherwise. A suitable damp-proof membrane may be used directly under the insulation boards if required. The insulation boards are laid over the prepared surface and tightly butted together.

41.8.3.1 Chipboard floor finish

If the damp-proof membrane has been laid below the floor slab or if a precast floor system is considered other than dry, a

Figure 41.3 Vapour-control layer above foam PS and below chipboard

Figure 41.4 PS flooring layer above foam PS and below chipboard

vapour-control layer of minimum 1000 g polythene must be laid over the PS prior to the chipboard. The vapour check must be taped at joints and taken up the perimeter walls at least 100 mm to finish behind the skirting boards. (See *Figure 41.3*.)

Flooring-grade chipboard, tongued and grooved all round,

is then laid with staggered joints over the vapour-control layer with all joints fully glued with a standard PVA woodworking adhesive. Temporary wedges are used around the floor perimeter in order to tighten the chipboard joints when the floor is complete.

A 10-mm wide expansion gap must be allowed at all chipboard perimeters. In runs in excess of 10 m, expansion gaps must be provided in the floor and treated-timber battens must be placed below expansion joints (*Figures 41.4* and *41.5*).

At positions in the floor where the tongued and grooved joint of the chipboard is lost, a treated-timber batten must be positioned below the boards, in lieu of the polystyrene, to support the butt-jointed chipboard. The batten should be firmly fixed to the structural floor. This requirement for a timber batten also applies at external doorways, but not around all room perimeters. Protection of the chipboard from water spillage should be as recommended in BS 5669.[16]

41.8.3.2. Screed-floor finish

A 65-mm thick sand–cement screed is laid directly onto the polystyrene. The recommendations of BS CP 204: Part 2[17] should be followed with the screed area not exceeding 15 m² with a length-to-width ratio not in excess of 1.5:1. If these limits are exceeded or the screed thickness reduced to at minimum 50 mm, a light-gauge galvanized-metal reinforcement should be placed centrally in the screed.

41.8.4 Timber-floor insulation

Insulation of timber ground floors can be achieved by positioning suspended EPS between the joists or XPS over or between the joists. This form of floor insulation is particularly appropriate in renovation work. The underfloor space must be ventilated.

When insulation is placed between joists a treated-timber batten or galvanized fixing is positioned on the side of the joists to give sufficient height to accommodate the insulation thickness below. An air gap of 25 mm between the insulation and timber-boarded floor finish will improve the overall thermal resistance of the floor.

Insulation boards should be cut to fit tightly between the joists and rest upon the previously positioned supports. Pinning of the top surface with galvanized nails prevents insulation-board movement.

XPS insulation boards can be laid directly over the floor joists

Figure 41.5 Expansion gap at edge of flooring

of new or existing floors. Once installed they provide the base for the required timber-board floor finish which is fixed through the insulation to the timber joists.

In refurbishment work, both types of PS can be laid over an existing timber floor prior to laying a suitable floor finish.

41.8.5 High-load-floor systems

Higher grades of PS materials make the use of PS in areas of high-load application possible. Whilst the general construction details remain similar to those previously described, the PS strength requirement has to be adjusted, by choice of grade, to suit the situation. A typical example of this area of use is that for cold-store floors.

Polystyrene insulation boards are used to reduce the amount of heat entering the cold store from the surrounding sub-base. Additionally, the ground temperature is maintained and assists in the prevention of possible ground heave.

Insulation boards in polystyrene are available in various grades, based on this strength requirement, to suit differing load criteria.

Preparation of the ground to the required level should ensure that it is firm and flat. Placing of a sub-base clean and free from contaminants should be in layers and allow adequate compaction of each.

Subsequent to blinding the sub-base, if necessary a screed is laid over the surface. Screed thickness is dependent upon its designated use, either as blinding or as a carrier for heating cables laid to prevent freezing of the soil and subsequent ground heave. The screed must be finished to at least a fine tamp or equivalent.

A suitable vapour-control layer must be laid over the screed and turned up at all abutments. Insulation boards are then laid either in two layers breaking joint or in a single layer with suitable joint detail to avoid cold bridging. The vapour-control layer is then turned down onto the insulation at perimeters and a 500 g polythene laid over the whole surface of the PS to prevent grout ingress and subsequent cold bridging. A concrete slab to the requisite design is then placed over the insulation and finished as appropriate.

41.8.6 Structural floor systems

EPS has been developed for use in a series of floor systems where it becomes part of the main structure. Used in conjunction with prestressed concrete beams, EPS infill panels replace the more traditional block or hollow pot infill.

In addition to providing the infill to the beams, the panels give the floor system an extremely high insulation value. Where the finish to the system is flooring-grade chipboard a typical U value of around 0.2 W m^{-2} K^{-1} can be achieved. Alternatively, where the finish is a reinforced structural screed a typical U value is 0.3 W m^{-2} K^{-1}.

Variation in the EPS panel design allows their use with different prestressed concrete-beam sections, which effectively designates the structural strength of the whole system.

The reinforced structural screed topping system allows a higher degree of load capacity than the chipboard system. In both systems the EPS panels are designed to prevent cold bridging of the beams by including an insulation layer above or below the beam as well as in between. EPS panels used in these systems also provide the benefits of handleability, lightweight, speed of construction and consistent quality.

Preparation of the site and substructure to receive the beams is as that for a traditional building. As with a standard beam-and-block system, the beams are set and erected in accordance with the beam manufacturer's layout drawing. Solid and spacer blocks are used to position the beams accurately.

The EPS panels are then easily fitted between the beams with closely butted joints. Additional details of the system are available from the beam manufacturers.

Finishes on the system are laid in accordance with the respective requirements for chipboard or reinforced screed. With the chipboard system a polythene vapour control layer is first positioned over the panels and turned up at perimeters. An 18-mm thick flooring-grade chipboard with tongued and grooved edges is then laid over the vapour check and the joints glued. An expansion gap of 10–12 mm must be left at all perimeter edges. Temporary wedging of the chipboard at perimeters allows the expansion gap to be maintained when the chipboard is finally tightened after glueing.

To form the structural screed system an A98 steel mesh reinforcement to BS 4482[18] is laid over the concrete-beam tops, topped and tied as necessary. A screed, generally grade 35, containing 10-mm aggregate, is then laid. Its minimum thickness over the beam head must be 40 mm. Compaction and finishing of the screed is then carried out as necessary.

41.8.7 Composite floor insulation panels

A recent development on the insulated dry-floor system has been the introduction of composte PS/timber floor finishes. In the case of EPS, the overlay is an oriented-strand board and in the case of XPS it is chipboard. The composite panels use higher grades of PS than the normal floor insulation system and are intended to cope with a greater range of end-use conditions.

Composite-panel advantages include high thermal insulation, one-operation fixing method, speedy construction and single supplier liability. A variation in board size is also available between the EPS and the XPS composites.

Laying procedures are generally as those detailed under overslab insulation, whereby the composite panels are laid onto the structural floor surface. Where a damp-proof membrane has been incorporated below a solid ground-floor slab, it is necessary to provide a vapour-control layer below the composite panel. Where the damp-proof membrane is on top of the structural slab or the structural slab is a prestressed beam and block system, no vapour-control layer is necessary.

Composite panels involve the use of tongued and grooved overlay boards. These are glued in the laying process and the whole floor system temporarily wedged at perimeters to provide a 10–12 mm expansion gap.

Services across the floor slab have to be allowed for and the PS removed from the overlay at positions corresponding with service pipe run. Total separation of the PS element from services should occur where the service entails heated pipes or electric cables. An independent duct, lagging of heated pipes, conduit or air gap are suitable methods of service isolation from PS insulation.

41.9 Civil engineering

The use of EPS in civil-engineering applications is significant. The properties which have stimulated its use include its light weight, good compressive strength, versatility of shape and the availability of the material in large blocks. It is the flexibility of sizes, combined with the relative price of EPS compared with XPS, which dictates that very little extruded product is used in civil engineering. It is true that XPS is used in colder parts of Europe for frost protection of roads and railways and has been used in one road construction as a lightweight fill in the UK, but in general the former applications are not relevant to the British climate and in the latter EPS is more competitive and convenient because of the availability of larger block sizes. The following applications, therefore, relate only to EPS except where stated.

41.9.1 Shutters for concrete structures

The versatility of shaping EPS blocks has allowed a greater freedom in the design of the external form of poured-concrete structures. Simple curves and profiles, difficult, or indeed impossible, to produce in any other way, can simply be cut from blocks and supported on timber frames to tie in with more conventional formwork. A facing of polypropylene sheet or a proprietary coating for shapes other than simple curves is used to protect the EPS and facilitate release from concrete.

Re-usable demountable shutter systems have been developed from this idea to produce formwork for steel-reinforced cast concrete floors in large buildings. On a smaller scale, a similar technique can be used to produce custom-built arch forms for brickwork or reproduce cut stone work profiles to effect repairs to existing buildings with concrete mixes (see *Figures 41.6* and *41.7*).

Figure 41.6 Placing PS demountable shuttering

EPS cylinders or profiled blocks can be used inside poured concrete to reduce the dead load of the structure, to maximize design strength and, thereby, to economize on total construction costs. Large bridge constructions use this method to reduce the mass of poured concrete. It is important that the EPS internal shutter has the correct combination of physical properties—low moisture absorption from curing concrete, good compressive resistance against concrete hydrostatic pressures and adequate cross-breaking and compressive properties—to ensure that it can be properly restrained to resist the flotation forces from wet concrete during pouring and vibration. EPS satisfactorily performs these functions using a grade (restricted duty) produced specially for the civil-engineering industry.

More recent road-building schemes have, for environmental reasons, called for sections of road to be built below ground level. A technique called 'cut and cover' is used in which a channel is excavated, the road built in the bottom and, in effect, a very wide bridge is built across the top of the channel, so that the whole construction can be recovered with soil. Poured concrete using EPS void forms lend themselves very well to this technique which has been used, for example, on the A1 to the north of London at Hatfield. The use of EPS voids in an otherwise solid-concrete construction creates a series of I-beams and optimizes the use of the materials involved.

41.9.2 Flotation

Using the same properties of light weight and water resistance, EPS is used to provide buoyancy in a variety of applications ranging from simple floats for the pens used on commercial fish farms to floating piers and walkways in marina developments. Protection is normally provided to give impact resistance where required by encasing the EPS blocks in concrete or with another suitable covering. A low-density product fulfills the requirements for this application.

41.9.3 Road construction

Scandinavian countries, particularly Norway, have pioneered the use of large EPS blocks as foundations for road embankments. Increasing interest in the UK has resulted in several projects using EPS and occasionally XPS.

Figure 41.7 Demountable shuttering before pouring

The reason for using this apparently expensive material to build up such embankments is to reduce the load of the embankment onto the subsoil. It is then possible to work over poor ground conditions without resorting to inherently expensive solutions such as piling. It is also possible to save construction time where long-term preloading might otherwise have been used to stabilize the soil.

EPS grade HD is normally found to have sufficient load-bearing capacity and, at a nominal density of 20 kg m^{-3}, can considerably reduce downward pressures of traditional fill materials with densities in the region of 2000 kg m^{-3}. For design purposes a density of 100 kg m^{-3} can be used to make allowance for long-term water absorption where continuous or frequent wetting of the base layers occurs. Proper consideration of suitable drainage needs to be taken, as does data on historic water-table levels to ensure that unwanted flotation forces cannot occur.

Vertical loads imposed on EPS blocks are transmitted downwards with very low lateral thrust. This enables design savings to be made when using this technique against structures such as bridges, or retaining walls, which do not then have to withstand the usual lateral forces from granular fills.

The Norwegian experience which is well reported extends back to the early 1970s and this is now a standard technique for road construction on poor subsoils in that country.

41.9.4 Foundations

Large quantities of EPS are used in some continental countries for construction of cellular raft foundations. This technique has also been used in the UK with the purpose of economizing on the use of reinforced concrete.

41.9.5 Clay heave

There is an application in foundations using a lightweight EPS product to accommodate forces due to clay heave. Ring beams supported on piles can be protected from the pressures generated when a previously dry clay soil expands as water is taken up. Sites cleared of trees, for example, can exhibit this phenomenon on certain clay types. Careful production of EPS boards will provide the correct balance of properties to: (i) provide adequate support to concrete ring beams during concreting with a minimum amount of compression; and (ii) to allow a significant movement to safely occur as the clay expands.

Clearly the downward forces of the building must be able to counter the upward transmitted pressure. Typically, EPS provided for this application will compress by more than 50% of its original thickness under loads of 40 kN m^{-2}. Thus building foundations can be protected from clay heave, though the technique is not suitable for normal *in situ* floor slabs which do not have adequate strength. A better solution for floors is to provide a suspended ground floor creating a void into which the soil can move.

References

1 BRITISH STANDARDS INSTITUTION, *BS 3837 Expanded polystyrene boards*, Part 1 Specification for boards manufactured from expandable beads, Milton Keynes (1986)
2 BRITISH STANDARDS INSTITUTION, *BS 4735 Horizontal burning characteristics of cellular plastics*, Milton Keynes (1974)
3 BRITISH STANDARDS INSTITUTION, *BS 3837 Expanded polystyrene boards*, Part 2 Specification for extruded boards, Milton Keynes
4 BRITISH STANDARDS INSTITUTION, *BS 476 Fire tests on building materials and structures*, Part 3 External fire exposure roof test, Milton Keynes (1958)
5 BRITISH STANDARDS INSTITUTION, *BS 476 Fire tests on building materials and structures*, Part 4 Non-combustibility test for materials, Milton Keynes (1970)
6 BRITISH STANDARDS INSTITUTION, *BS 476 Fire tests on building materials and structures*, Part 5 Method of test for ignitability, Milton Keynes (1968)
7 BRITISH STANDARDS INSTITUTION, *BS 476 Fire tests on building materials and structures*, Part 6 Method of test for fire propagation, Milton Keynes (1968)
8 *Building Regulations 1985*, HMSO, London (1985)
9 BRITISH STANDARDS INSTITUTION, *BS 476 Fire tests on building materials and structures*, Part 7 Method of classification of the surface spread of flame, Milton Keynes (1971)
10 BRITISH STANDARDS INSTITUTION, *BS 476 Fire tests on building materials and structures*, Part 8 Test methods and criteria for the fire resistance of elements of building construction, Milton Keynes (1972)
11 BRITISH STANDARDS INSTITUTION, *BS 476 Fire tests on building materials and structures*, Parts 20–23 Methods of test for fire resistance, Milton Keynes
12 BRITISH STANDARDS INSTITUTION, *BS 5250 Control of condensation in buildings*, Milton Keynes (1989)
13 BRITISH STANDARDS INSTITUTION, *BS 747 Specification of roofing felts*, Milton Keynes (1977, 1986)
14 BRITISH STANDARDS INSTITUTION, *CP 144 Roof coverings*, Part 3 Built up bitumen felt, Milton Keynes (1970)
15 BRITISH STANDARDS INSTITUTION, *CP 144 Roof coverings*, Part 4 Mastic asphalt, Milton Keynes (1970)
16 BRITISH STANDARDS INSTITUTION, *BS 5669 Specification for wood chipboard and methods of test for particle board*, Milton Keynes (1979)
17 BRITISH STANDARDS INSTITUTION, *CP 204 In-situ floor finishes*, Part 2
18 BRITISH STANDARDS INSTITUTION, *BS 4482 Specification for cold reduced steel wire for the reinforcement of concrete*, Milton Keynes (1985)

Bibliography

BRITISH STANDARDS INSTITUTION, *BS 3837 Expanded polystyrene boards*, Part 2 Specification for extruded boards, Milton Keynes (1990)
BRITISH STANDARDS INSTITUTION, *BS 6203 Guide to fire characteristics and fire performance of expanded polystyrene used in building applications*, Milton Keynes (1991)

British Board of Agrément Certificates
BRE, Thermal insulation—avoiding risks
Plastic foam in road embankments, Proceedings of the Norwegian Plastics Federation Conference, Oslo, Norway (June 1985)

42

Polytetrafluoro-ethylene

R G Bristow BSc(Eng), MICE, MIStructE
G Maunsell and Partners

Contents

42.1 Material properties 42/3
    42.1.1 General 42/3
    42.1.2 Mechanical 42/3
    42.1.3 Thermal 42/3
    42.1.4 Electrical 42/3
    42.1.5 Chemical 42/3

42.2 Manufacture 42/3

42.3 Fabrication 42/3

42.4 Applications 42/4

42.5 Bearings 42/4
    42.5.1 General 42/4
    42.5.2 PTFE 42/5
    42.5.3 Mating surface 42/5
    42.5.4 Design 42/5

42.6 Slides 42/6

42.7 Friction with PTFE surfaces 42/6

References 42/8

Bibliography 42/12

42.1 Material properties

42.1.1 General

Polytetrafluoroethylene (PTFE) is a wax-like solid having a greasy feel. It is odourless, tasteless, non-flammable and white in colour but can be pigmented. PTFE is a linear chain polymer of great molecular strength and is mainly exploited for its chemical inertness, low coefficient of friction and first class electrical properties. PTFE is not oxidized easily, it is resistant to all common solvents and remains stable at extremes of atmospheric temperatures, but it exhibits plastic deformation under load. PTFE has the largest temperature working range of all plastics and the greatest resistance to chemical attack. Within its working temperature range it is a completely inert product, but at very high temperatures, i.e. in excess of 250°C, it can give rise to decomposition products which have unpleasant effects if inhaled. The properties of PTFE are summarized in *Table 42.1*.

Table 42.1   Properties of polytetrafluorothylene

Property	Value
Physical properties	
Tensile strength	12.0–41.0 N mm^{-2}
Elongation at break	100–600%
Compressive strength	4.0–12.0 N mm^{-2}
Density (at 23°C)	2.13–2.24 g cm^{-3}
Modulus of elasticity	345–620 N mm^{-2}
Flexural strength	No break
Impact strength	0.13–0.21 J mm^{-1} of notch
Hardness (Rockwell)	D50–D65
Water absorption (24 h, 3 mm thickness)	0.01%
Thermal properties	
Coefficient of expansion (varies with temperature)	10×10^{-5}°C
Conductivity	6 cal cm cm^{-2} °C^{-1} s^{-1} $\times 10^{-4}$
Service temperature	-260–$+250$°C
Transition point	327°C
Specific heat	0.25 cal °C^{-1} g^{-1}
Flammability	Nil
Electrical properties	
Dielectric strength (short-time, 3 mm)	15 750–23 600 V mm^{-1}
Dielectric constant	2.1×10^6 cycle s^{-1}
Power factor	0.0002×10^6 cycle s^{-1}
Volume resistivity (at 23°C and 50% RH^a)	10^{19}
Arc resistance	7300 s
Chemical resistance	
Concentrated inorganic acids	Unaffected
Dilute inorganic acids	Unaffected
Organic acids	Unaffected
Strong alkalis	Unaffected
Weak alkalis	Unaffected
Petroleum products	Unaffected
Solvents	Unaffected
Sunlight	Unaffected
Weather	Excellent
Permeability	
Carbon dioxide	2.60 g m^{-2} day^{-1} mm^{-1}
Water vapour	1.38 g m^{-2} day^{-1} mm^{-1}

^{a} RH, relative humidity.

42.1.2 Mechanical

The tensile strength and modulus of elasticity of PTFE are relatively low. The stress–strain relationship is non-linear and tensile yield occurs at high deformations. Recovery after deformation does take place but is temperature dependent. For complete recovery the material must be resintered in a stress-free condition. The low temperature mechanical properties are excellent, PTFE remaining ductile down to about -200°C. It has low resistance to wear and is subject to cold flow or creep under load but these limitations can be overcome by the use of fillers and by making use of its non-stick properties. The coefficients of friction are the lowest of any solid material. Static and dynamic coefficients are similar to those of wet ice on wet ice. The specific gravity of PTFE is the highest of the plastic materials, but the surface hardness is low. It can be cut with a knife, but its water absorption is nil.

42.1.3 Thermal

PFTE remains stable over a wide temperature range. The temperature range for continuous working lies between -260°C and $+250$°C, although the upper limit can be extended to $+300$°C for intermittent use. No embrittlement takes place at low temperature. It is non-flammable but will begin to decompose if heated above $+380$°C.

42.1.4 Electrical

PTFE is one of the best solid dielectrics known because both the power factor and the dielectric constant are very low and do not vary with temperature. It is an excellent electrical insulator. It has a high break-down voltage and is non-tracking. Not being wetted by water and being non-absorbent, its surface and volume resistivities remain very high under humid conditions.

42.1.5 Chemical

PTFE is virtually immune to chemical attack throughout its whole usable range, apart from molten alkali metals and a few fluorine compounds at elevated temperatures. This, together with its low coefficient of friction produces a surface which is non-stick to all materials with the possible exception of hot sugary and resinous material. Special methods of treating the surface have been developed to make it receptive to adhesives.

42.2 Manufacture

Although PTFE is a thermal plastic polymer it cannot be formed by the conventional processes of fabrication and moulding; neither can it be plasticized. The fabrication methods which have been developed all rely to some extent on sintering, a technique borrowed from metallurgy. This consists essentially of compacting the powder polymer in the cold, and then heating the compacted form to above 327°C, subsequently cooling it to room temperature. The degree of crystallinity in the finished form depends upon the rate of cooling and can vary from about 55% to 95%. The quality requirements for PTFE manufacture are covered by BS 6564: Part 2: 1985.[1]

42.3 Fabrication

Virtually the only method of processing wrought forms of PTFE is by machining and similar methods. As PTFE is a very soft material, it is important that tools are well sharpened with very keen and polished cutting edges. Very good support of the work is essential.

PTFE has a transition point between 19°C and 25°C. It is important, therefore, that if a product is required to have good dimensional tolerances, either below or above this range, fabrication should take place at the temperature of intended use, i.e. machining should not be carried out in the transition stage. Residual stresses left in the material can cause dimensional instability as stress relief can take place at all temperatures. Annealing at a temperature higher than the eventual working temperature can cure this instability.

As stated above, at temperatures above 250°C decomposition products may be formed. Therefore, if high temperatures are likely to be reached, e.g. during machining or sintering, exhaust ventilation should be provided as near to the source of decomposition as possible. Smoking of tobacco products must not be allowed in areas where PTFE is being processed. The smoking of tobacco products contaminated by PTFE can result in a temporary 'flu-like' condition known as 'polymer fume fever'. Reference should be made to BFPA publication No. 254/1[2] for further information on health and safety.

42.4 Applications

The main uses of PTFE are in the chemical, food and pharmaceutical industries, where its chemical inertness over a large temperature range and non-stick properties are obvious advantages, and in the electrical and electronic industries where good use can be made of its excellent electrical properties. Typical uses are in pipes and linings of processing equipment, hoses, gaskets and glands, diaphragms and filters, O rings and seals. The material is applied as a release agent to machinery such as rollers, drying cylinders and conveyor belts; also to hoppers and chutes and its use for non-stick cooking utensils is well known. The low coefficient of friction is utilized in the production of bearings, sleevings and bushes. It is used for insulators and electrical components for high-temperature work such as in thermocouple leads, heating cables and insulators.

The main use of PTFE in construction is for bearings and sliding surfaces where its low coefficient of friction and chemical stability under normal conditions, as well as its resistance to water absorption and weathering make it an ideal material. Typical uses are for supporting petrochemical plant, heavy machinery, pipelines, buildings, bridge decks and the sliding elements of bridge expansion joints, where it is necessary to accommodate expansion, contraction and other reciprocating motions of a structure due to thermal, seismic or differential forces.

42.5 Bearings

42.5.1 General

A wide variety of PTFE-based bearings is available, the low-friction surfaces being used either to provide rotation by sliding over cylindrical or spherical surfaces, or to provide horizontal sliding movement, or a combination of both. Plane sliding bearings allow translation only, except for rotation about an axis perpendicular to the plane of sliding; rotation in the plane of sliding being accommodated by other means. PTFE is normally used for the lower sliding surface with the upper surface extending beyond the PTFE at extremes of movement to prevent dust and dirt settling on the lower surface where it could cause scouring of the mating surface and increase friction. For low-pressure applications the mating surface can be PTFE, but for higher pressures, such as those used in most structural applications, the surface mating with the PTFE must be harder than the PTFE and corrosion resistant. Stainless steel is usually used for plane sliding surfaces, but hard anodized aluminium

Figure 42.1 Glacier Dualign K 1200-tonne guided pot bearing. (Courtesy of the Glacier Metal Co. Ltd)

Figure 42.2 Glacier 3000-tonne guided spherical bearing being assembled. (Courtesy of the Glacier Metal Co. Ltd)

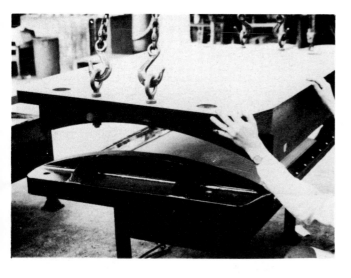

Figure 42.3 Glacier 3400-tonne anticlastic bearing being assembled. (Courtesy of the Glacier Metal Co. Ltd)

Table 42.2 Dimensions of confined PTFE

Maximum dimension of PTFE (diameter or diagonal) (mm)	Minimum thickness (mm)	Maximum projection above recess (mm)
⩽ 600	4.5	2.0
> 600 ⩽ 1200	5.0	2.5
> 1200 ⩽ 1500	6.0	3.0

Table 42.3 Thickness of bonded PTFE

Maximum dimension of PTFE (diameter or diagonal) (mm)	Minimum thickness (mm)
⩽600	1.0
>600 ⩽ 1200 (max.)	1.5

castings are used for curved sliding bearings (see *Figures 42.1–42.3*). Curved sliding bearings are classed in BS 5400: Part 9[3] as knuckle bearings. They can be either cylindrical, which allows rotation about one axis only, or spherical, which allows rotation about any axis. A special form of curved sliding bearings produced by the Glacier Metal Company and known as anticlastic consists of two cylindrical curved sliding surfaces at right angles allowing rotation about two orthogonal axes.

42.5.2 PTFE

The PTFE can either be confined in a recess or be bonded to the backing medium. In either case, it is essential that it is backed by a metal plate, the rigidity of which should be such that it retains its unloaded shape and resists shear forces under all loading conditions. The thickness of the PTFE is related to its maximum plan dimensions. The minimum thickness and maximum projection of recessed PTFE are laid down in BS 5400: Part 9[3] as given in *Table 42.2* and the thickness of bonded PTFE as given in *Table 42.3*.

Table 42.4 Thickness of stainless-steel sheet

Dimensional difference between PTFE and stainless steel[a] (mm)	Minimum thickness of stainless steel (mm)
⩽300	1.5
>300 ⩽ 500	2.0
>500 ⩽ 1500	3.0

[a] A dimensional difference in excess of 1500 mm requires special consideration.

42.5.3 Mating surface

It is very important that the surface mating with the PTFE has a highly polished finish. Tests[4] have shown that, in the long term, mechanically polished stainless steel is preferable to 'as rolled' material with the same roughness. The running surface of the mating plate should have an average peak-to-valley height, r_z, not exceeding 1 μm.[3,4]

The thickness of the mating stainless steel sheet is related to the difference in dimension between PTFE and stainless steel in the direction of travel. The minimum recommended thicknesses are given in BS 5400: Part 9[3] as shown in *Table 42.4*. It is essential that the stainless steel remains flat throughout its service life and corrosion is prevented by keeping moisture from getting between the stainless steel and its backing medium. This can be done by attaching the stainless steel to its backing plate by continuous welding along its edges or, alternatively, the stainless steel can be fixed to its backing medium with fasteners supplemented by either peripheral sealing or bonding over the full area of the stainless-steel sheet. The method of attachment should be capable of resisting the full frictional force set up in the bearing at the serviceability limit state.

42.5.4 Design

The bearing surfaces need be designed only for the serviceability limit state, but the remainder of the bearing should be designed to satisfy the requirements of both serviceability and ultimate limit states. BS 5400: Part 9[3] allows the use only of pure PTFE for normal sliding bearings, but filled PTFE is permitted to take higher stresses on guides. The maximum permitted contact

Table 42.5 Allowable sliding bearing pressures for pure PTFE

Design load effects	Maximum average contact pressure (N mm^{-2})		Maximum extreme fibre pressure (N mm^{-2})	
	Bonded PTFE	Confined PTFE	Bonded PTFE	Confined PTFE
Permanent design load effects	20	30	25	37.5
All design load effects	30	45	37.5	55

pressures in PTFE as given in BS 5400: Part 9 are shown in *Table 42.5*.

For calculation of pressures, the contact surfaces may be taken as the gross area of the PTFE without deduction of the area occupied by lubrication cavities. In the case of curved surfaces, the gross area should be taken as the projected area of the contact surface.

Horizontal forces applied to curved sliding surfaces tend to separate the contact surfaces of bearings. This could give rise to chatter, uneven wear and ingress of dirt between the sliding surfaces leading to corrosion and increased friction. Therefore, a check should be made to ensure this tendency is adequately resisted by the coincident vertical loads.

42.6 Slides

Another use for PTFE in construction is in slides used in moving heavy structures such as bridges and off-shore gas and oil rigs (see *Figures 42.4* and *42.5*). Here, again, advantage is taken of its very low coefficient of friction and absence of stick-slip characteristics. For the higher loadings, PTFE with glass-fibre filling or sintered bronze impregnated with PTFE is used.

For these situations, it is usual to have skates faced with the PTFE material running on a stainless-steel track,[5] although recently the arrangement has been reversed with the stainless-steel plates fixed to the bridge running on a continuous PTFE surface provided by Fabreeka bearing pads.[6] This latter arrangement has the following advantages:

1. There are no joints in the stainless-steel surface.
2. The PTFE sliding surface can be placed quickly and easily by leap-frogging pads on a prepared track base.
3. There is a significant reduction in the quantities of PTFE and stainless steel required.

If stainless steel is used on the track, alignment and fixing are critical. The alignment of the stainless steel must be very accurate if the thin PTFE coating on the skates is not to be scraped off as it passes over joints between the stainless-steel plates. Similarly, if the stainless steel is not adequately fixed to the base, it will buckle and prevent sliding of the skates.

It is for these reasons that some authorities are moving away from PTFE/stainless-steel slides in favour of aluminium–bronze sledges sliding on steel track. However, others consider PTFE as being the most satisfactory medium for sliding, since friction is half that of aluminium–bronze. Although the latter is cheaper than PTFE/stainless steel there is the problem of slip-stick. Guidance of the moving element is important. Since friction forces are less with PTFE, so will be the guidance forces required. Lubrication of the sliding surfaces with oil is beneficial in reducing the friction even further. Measures, such as the insertion of rubber bearings between the structure and skates, must be taken to ensure even loading on the PTFE (see *Figure 42.6*).

42.7 Friction with PTFE surfaces

Tests[7–10] have indicated that the coefficient of friction of stainless-steel plate sliding on PTFE varies with the speed of movement, contact stress between plate and PTFE, temperature, finish of mating surface and previous loading history. In general,

Figure 42.4 Sliding in Derby Inner Ring Road Bridge using PTFE skids. (Courtesy of The Glacier Metal Company Ltd)

Figure 42.5 Jacket for Murchison Platform being launched at Ardersier. (Courtesy of Conoco (UK) Ltd and Fluorocarbon Company Ltd)

the coefficient of friction between PTFE and mating surface reduces with:

1. Reducing speed of movement.
2. Increasing compressive stress.
3. Increasing temperature.
4. Increasing smoothness of mating surface.

The tests also show the initial static coefficient of friction, which relates to the force required to start movement, to be higher than the dynamic coefficient of friction which relates to the force to maintain movement, although the difference in magnitude between the two tends to reduce with increasing cycles of movement. This process is illustrated in *Figure 42.7*. During the early cycles transfer of PTFE onto the mating surface takes place leading to a reduction in friction, but after continuous running this tends to wear off giving rise to an increase in friction until a state of equilibrium is reached where loss of PTFE due to abrasion balances the PTFE being transferred. Lubrication can be used to reduce the initial friction, but in time the lubricant will be squeezed out and the coefficient of friction will tend to return to the dry run in value, as shown in *Figure 42.8*. Therefore, for purposes of design, the long-term value of the coefficient of friction is used. The use of pockets in the PTFE (*Figures 42.9 and 42.10*) to retain the lubricant is beneficial in maintaining the low coefficient of friction, as shown in *Figure 42.11*. Silicone greases have been found especially suitable for lubrication, having proved effective at temperatures below $-35°$. They do not resinify nor attack the material of the sliding surfaces. Tests on PTFE with lubrication pockets sliding on stainless steel over 5000 m of slide path show insignificant wear and virtually no increase in coefficient of friction. Attempts[4] have been made to estimate the life of the PTFE in sliding bearings, but lack of data on actual sliding speed and total sliding movement preclude detailed forecasting. The effect of temperature of the sliding surface and increasing compressive stress on the coefficient of friction is shown in *Figure 42.12*. The effect of temperature and the influence of surface finish are illustrated in *Figure 42.13* and the relationship between coefficient of friction and sliding speed shown in *Figure 42.14*.

When dealing with structural movements at low temperatures one must bear in mind that ice may form on the sliding surfaces, although bond with the PTFE is likely to be poor, and also part of the PTFE in the bearing will be moving on a little used part of the steel slider. Friction values given in BS 5400: Part 9[3] for design purposes for stainless steel sliding on pure PTFE continuously lubricated are given in *Table 42.6*. These values may be used for air temperatures down to $-24°C$. For unlubricated PTFE on stainless steel twice these values should be used, and for filled PTFE four times these values is recommended.

When large horizontal forces have to be contended with at the same time as vertical ones, the provision of PTFE rubbing surfaces may be necessary to reduce the forces generated. For example, with a vertical sliding friction value of 5% and a steel-to-steel rubbing contact for lateral loading of say 25% of

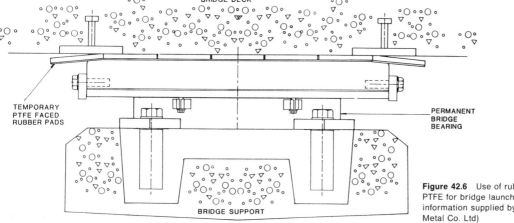

Figure 42.6 Use of rubber-backed PTFE for bridge launching. (Based on information supplied by the Glacier Metal Co. Ltd)

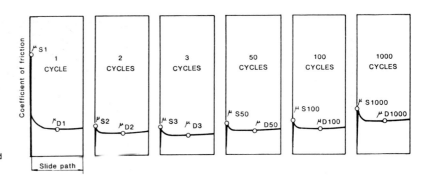

Figure 42.7 Variation of the coefficient of friction with length of travel. Based on data from Uetz and Hakenjos[7]

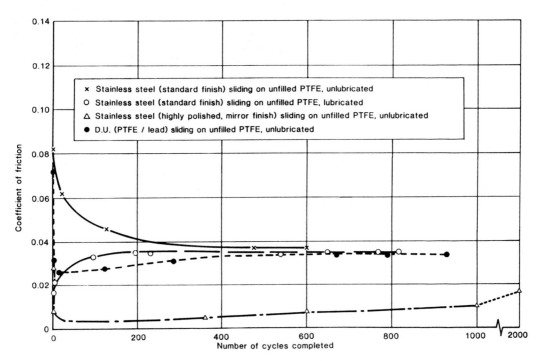

Figure 42.8 Variation of friction with type of mating surface. Sliding speed 13 mm min⁻¹; stroke 6 mm; compressive stress 35 MN m⁻²; temperature 20°C. Based on data from Taylor[10]

Table 42.6 Design parameters for stainless steel sliding on PTFE continuously lubricated

Bearing stress (N mm⁻²)	Coefficient of friction
5	0.08
10	0.06
20	0.04
≥30	0.03

the vertical, an incompatible loading situation on the superstructure can arise.

In these circumstances, to withstand higher stresses and reduce wear PTFE with glass fibre or other filling is often used. The effect of various fillings in PTFE on the coefficient of friction

is shown in *Figure 42.15*. This would seem to indicate that the use of fillers lowers the coefficient of friction. This is not borne out by other tests,[11,12] and the generally accepted view is that fillers increase the coefficient of friction as referred to above.

References

1 BRITISH STANDARDS INSTITUTION, *BS 6564 Polytetrafluorethylene (PTFE) materials and products, Part 2: Specification for fabricated unfilled polytetrafluoroethylene products,* Milton Keynes (1985)
2 BRITISH FLUOROPOLYMER PROCESSORS' ASSOCIATION, 'Industrial, health and safety for PTFE polymers', *BFPA Publication No. 254/1*
3 BRITISH STANDARDS INSTITUTION, *BS 5400 Steel, concrete and composite bridges, Part 9: Bridge bearings,* Milton Keynes (1983)
4 KAUSCHE, W. and BAIGENT, M., 'Improvements in the long term durability of bearings in bridges', *Joint Sealing and Bearing*

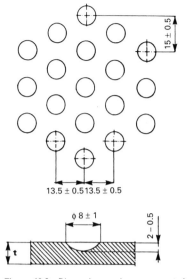

Figure 42.9 Dimensions and arrangement of grease dimples in PTFE

Figure 42.10 Glacier 3000-tonne guided spherical bearing. (Courtesy of the Glacier Metal Co. Ltd)

Systems for Concrete Structures, ACI Publication SP-94, Vol. 2, p. 581 (1986)

5 PORTER, J. A. and THOMPSON, J. O., 'The organisation and techniques for moving heavy railway bridges', *Proceedings of the Institution of Civil Engineers*, **52**, 149 (1972)

6 ATKINS, F. E. and WIGLEY, P. J. G., 'Railway underline bridges: developments within constraints of limited possession', *Proceedings of the Institution of Civil Engineers*, **84**, 989 (1988)

7 UETZ, H. and HAKENJOS, V., 'Experiments on sliding friction with PTFE in reciprocating motion', *Die Bautechnik*, **44**, 159–166 (1967)

8 HAKENJOS, V. and RICHTER, K., 'Experiments with sliding supports', *Lager im Bauwesen*, Wilhelm Ernst & Sohn, Berlin,

pp. 301–309 (1974)

9 HAKENJOS, V. and RICHTER, K., 'Long term slide friction behaviour for the material pairing pure PTFE/austenitic stainless steel for the support of bridges', *Strasse Brucke Tunnel*, **11**, 294–297 (1975)

10 TAYLOR, M. E., 'PTFE in highway bridges', *TRRL Report LR 491*, Transport and Road Research Laboratory, Crowthorne (1972)

11 JACOBSEN, F. K. and TAYLOR, R. K., 'TFE expansion bearings for highway bridges', *Report No. RDR-31*, Illinois State Division of Highways (1971)

12 UETZ, H. and BRECKEL, H., 'Friction and wear tests with PTFE', *Wear*, **10**, 185–198 (1967)

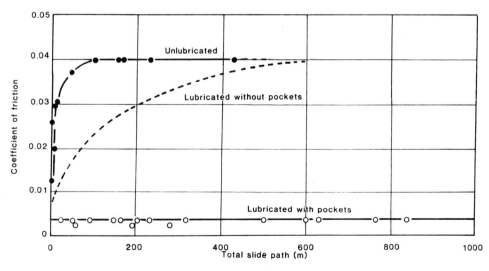

Figure 42.11 Influence of lubrication on the coefficient of friction of unfilled PTFE. Sliding speed 60 mm min^{-1}; stroke 2 mm; compressive stress 30 MN m^{-2}. Based on data from Uetz and Hakenjos[7]

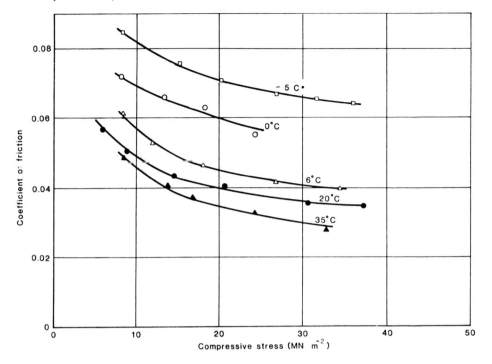

Figure 42.12 Influence of sliding plate temperature on the peak coefficient of friction on unfilled PTFE. Sliding speed 1.3 mm min^{-1}; stroke 10 mm; running-in period approximately 2000 cycles. Based on data from Taylor[10]

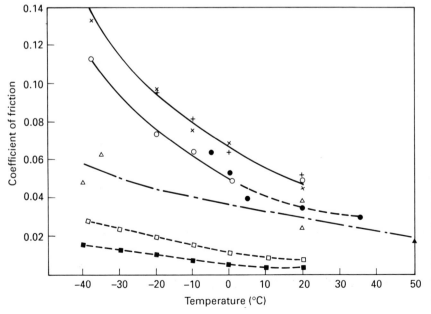

Figure 42.13 Effect of temperature coefficient of friction of unfilled PTFE. All data are run-in values for continuous rotation at compressive stress 30 MN m^{-2}. O, ×, +, Ra = 0.04 μm unlubricated, sliding speed 24 mm min^{-1}, stroke 5 mm; ●, Ra = 0.025 μm unlubricated, sliding speed 1.3 mm min^{-1}, stroke 10 mm; □, ■, Ra = 0.02 μm lubricated, sliding speed 24 mm min^{-1}, stroke 10 mm; □, static; ■, dynamic. Data from Taylor[10] (●); Hakenjos and Richter[9] (O, test I; ×, test III; +, test V); Hakenjos and Richter[8] (□, ■); Uetz and Breckel[12] (△)

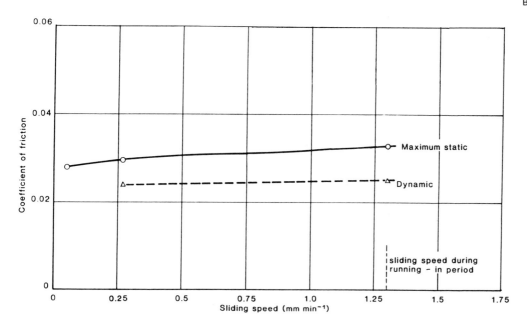

Figure 42.14 Relationship of sliding speed to coefficient of friction. Stroke 13 mm; compressive stress 35 MN m^{-2}; temperature 20°C; specimens run-in for 5000 cycles before tests. Based on data from Taylor[10]

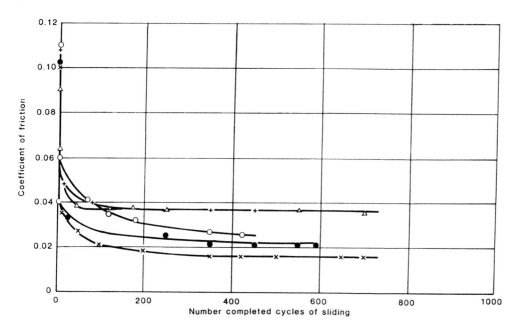

Figure 42.15 Coefficient of friction of filled PTFE materials. Sliding speed 1.3 mm min^{-1}; stroke 12 mm; compressive stress 35 MN m^{-2}; temperature 20°C. Filler: ×, 23% glass, 2% MoS$_2$; ●, 25% glass; ○, 25% carbon; △, 15% graphite; +, no filler. Based on data from Taylor[10]

Bibliography

AMERICAN SOCIETY FOR TESTING AND MATERIALS, *ASTM D1457-83a Standard specification for PTFE molding and extrusion materials* (1981)

ANDRE LTD, *Structural Bearings*, P.O. Box 4, Horninglow Road, Burton-on-Trent, Staffs DE13 0QN

ARCHARD, J. F., 'Elastic deformation and the laws of friction', *Proceedings of Royal Society of London, Series A*, **243**, 190–205 (1958)

ATKINS, F. E. and WIGLEY, P. J. G., 'Railway underline bridges: developments within constraints of limited possession', *Proceedings of the Institution of Civil Engineers*, **84**, 989–1007 (Oct. 1988)

BAIGENT, M. G., 'Practical considerations in the specification, design, manufacture, and quality control of mechanical bridge bearings', *Joint Sealing and Bearing Systems for Concrete Structures, ACI Publications SP-70*, Vol. 1, pp. 177–186 (1981)

BEST, K. H., KINGSTON, R. H. and WHATLEY, M. J., 'Incremental launching at Shepherds House Bridge', *Proceedings of the Institution of Civil Engineers*, **64**, 83–102 (Feb. 1978)

BLACK, W., 'Notes on bridge bearings', *Road Research Laboratory Report LR 382*, TRRL, Crowthorne (1971)

BOWER, G. R., *Bearing Pads of Teflon*, a report presented to the 1970 Regional Meetings of the AASHTO Committee on Bridges and Structures, E. I. du Pont de Nemours and Co. (1969)

BRITISH STANDARDS INSTITUTION, *BS 1134 Method for the assessment of surface texture, Part 1: Method and instrumentation*, Milton Keynes (1972)

BRITISH STANDARDS INSTITUTION, *BS 1134 Method for the assessment of surface texture, Part 2: General information and guidance*, Milton Keynes (1972)

BRITISH STANDARDS INSTITUTION, *BS 5400 Steel, concrete and composite bridges, Part 9: Bridge bearings; Section 9.1, Code of practice for design of bridge bearings*, Milton Keynes (1983)

BRITISH STANDARDS INSTITUTION, *BS 5400 Steel, concrete and composite bridges, Part 9: Bridge bearings; Section 9.2, Specification for materials, manufacture and installation of bridge bearings*, Milton Keynes (1983)

BRITISH STANDARDS INSTITUTION, *BS 6564 Polytetrafluoroethylene (PTFE) materials and products, Part 2: Specification for fabricated unfilled polytetrafluoroethylene products*, Milton Keynes (1985)

BURDETT, J. R. F., 'Toxicity of PTFE', *New Civil Engineer*, Letters (1989)

CCL SYSTEMS LTD, *Fabreeka—CCL Bearings*, Cabco House, Elland Road, Leeds, West Yorkshire LS11 8BH

CRAIG, W. D., Jr, 'PTFE bearings for high loads and slow oscillation', *Lubrication Engineering*, **18**, 174–181 (Apr. 1962)

DEUTSCHES INSTITUT FÜR NORMUNG, 'Structural bearings (Lager im Bauwesen), *DIN 4141* (Sep. 1984) (in German)

DEUTSCHES INSTITUT FÜR NORMUNG, 'Determination of surface roughness values of the parameter R_a, R_z, R_{max} by means of electrical instruments stylus type', *DIN 4768* (Aug. 1974) (in German)

DEUTSCHES INSTITUT FÜR NORMUNG, 'Surface roughness; terminology (Oberflachenrauheit, Begriffe)', *DIN 4762* (Sep. 1978) (in German)

EGGERT, H., *Vorlesungen über Lager im Bauwesen*, Verlag von Wilhelm Ernst & Sohn, Berlin/München (1981) (in German)

EGGERT, H., 'Standardization of bridge bearings: a report on German Standards—a proposal for international standards', *Joint Sealing and Bearing Systems for Concrete Structures, ACI Publications SP-94*, Vol. 2, pp. 543–550 (1986)

E. I. DU PONT DE NEMOURS AND CO., 'Predicting bearing wear', *The Journal of Teflon*, Reprint No. 34, Plastics Department, Wilmington, Delaware

E. I. DU PONT DE NEMOURS AND CO., *Information Bulletin for TFE–Fluorocarbon Resins Preparation and Molding of Compositions Containing Inorganic Fillers*, No. X-60d, Polychemicals Department, Wilmington, Delaware

E. I. DU PONT DE NEMOURS AND CO., 'Properties, processing and applications of TEFLON TFE—fluorocarbon fiber', *Teflon Bulletin TF-2*, Textile Fibers Department Technical Service Section, Wilmington, Delaware (May 1978)

E. I. DU PONT DE NEMOURS AND CO., *TEFLON Fluorocarbon Resin Mechanical Design Data*, Polymer Products Department, Wilmington, Delaware

E. I. DU PONT DE NEMOURS AND CO., *Bearing Pads Surfaced with TEFLON*, Polymer Products Department, Wilmington, Delaware

E. I. DU PONT DE NEMOURS AND CO., 'Big boon to building: bearing pads of TEFLON', *The Journal of Teflon* (Mar.–Apr. 1964); Reprint No. 21, Wilmington, Delaware

ELASTOMETAL LTD, *Spherical and Cylindrical Structural Bearings—Sliding & Rotational Tests Report*, Burlington, Ontario (Mar. 1983)

ELASTOMETAL LTD, *Wabo-Fyfe High Load Structural Bearing*, 4205 Fairview Street, Burlington, Ontario L7L 2A4 (1983)

FAVRE, R. and KROPF, P., 'Friction tests on sliding bearings' ('Reibungsmessungen an Gleitlagern'), *Memoires Abhandlungen*, *36-II*, International Association for Bridge and Structural Engineering, Zurich, pp. 89–104 (1976) (in German)

FLUOROCARBON CO. LTD, *PTFE Slide Bearings*, Caxton Hill, Hertford, Herts SG13 7NH

FORT, T., Jr, *Adsorption and Boundary Friction on Polymer Surfaces*, Fiber Surface Research Section, Textile Fibers Department, E. I. du Pont de Nemours and Co. (Jan. 1962)

FYFE, E. R., *Structural Disc Bearing with Bonafy Rotational Elements*, Test Report presented to 1979 Regional Meetings of AASHTO Subcommittee on Bridges and Structures

HAKENJOS, V. and GERBER, A., *Langzeit-Reibungs- und Verschleissversuche mit PTFE-Gleitlagern, Gleitpartner Austenitischer Stahl in Ausführungsart IIID*, MPA, Universität Stuttgart (Sep. 1984) (in German)

HAKENJOS, V. and RICHTER, K., *Experiments with Sliding Supports* (eds, Eggert, H., Grote, J. and Kauschke, W.), Verlag von Wilhelm Ernst & Sohn, Berlin, pp. 301–309 (1974)

HAKENJOS, V. and RICHTER, K., 'Long term slide friction behaviour for the material pairing pure PTFE/austenitic stainless steel for the support of bridges' ('Dauergleitreibungsverhalten der Gleitpaasrung PTFE weiss/Austenitischer Stahl für Auflager im Bruckenbau'), *Strasse Brucke Tunnel*, **11**, 294–297 (1975) (in German)

HAKENJOS, V., RICHTER, K., GERBER, A. and WIEDEMEYER, J., 'Studies of the movements of bridge structures as a result of temperature and traffic load, taking a steel bridge as an example' ('Untersuchung der Bewegungen von Bruckenbauwerken infolge Temperatur und Verkehrbelastung am Beispiel einer Stahlbrucke'), *Stahlbau*, **54**, 55–59 (Feb. 1985) (in German)

HEHN, K-H., 'Prufeinrichtung zur Untersuchung von Lagern', *VDI-Z 118*, **3**, 114–117 (Feb. 1976) (in German)

HOPTNER, M., *Construction of the Schmidtstedter Prestressed Concrete Bridge by Transverse Movement*, Concrete Institute of Australia (1976)

HUNTLEY-SMITH, D. R., KRATZ, R. and MARTIN, J. B., 'Slipping of PTFE bearings on long bridges', *Civil Engineer in South Africa, South African Institute of Civil Engineers*, **23**, 417–424 (Sep. 1981)

INSTITUT FÜR BAUTECHNIK, *Bedingungen für die bauliche Durchbildung und Überwachung (Guteüberwachung) von PTFE-Gleitlagern*, Berlin (1984) (in German)

JACOBSEN, F. K., 'TFE expansion bearings for highway bridges', *Report No. FHWA-IL-PR-71*, Illinois Department of Transportation, Bureau of Materials and Physical Research (Apr. 1977)

KAUSCHKE, W. and BAIGENT, M., 'Improvements in the long term durability of bearings in bridges', *Joint Sealing and Bearing Systems for Concrete Structures, ACI Publication SP-94*, Vol. 2, pp. 577–612 (1986)

KING, R. B., *Wear Properties of Dry Bearing Liners at Ambient and Elevated Temperatures—A Preliminary Survey*, Royal Aircraft Establishment, Farnborough (June 1978)

KORN, H., 'Bridge construction by extrusion sliding', *Concrete*, **9**, 16–21 (1975)

KOSTER, W., 'Design, performance and maintenance of bearings and joints', *International Association for Bridge and Structural Engineering Symposium*, Washington, DC (1982)

LEE, D. J., 'Recent experience in the specification, design installation, and maintenance of bridge bearings', *Joint Sealing and Bearing Systems for Concrete Structures, ACI Publication SP-70*, Vol. 1, pp. 161–175 (1981)

LEE, D. J., *The Theory and Practice of Bearings and Expansion Joints for Bridges*, Cement and Concrete Association, London (1971)

LEONHARDT, F., 'From past achievements to new challenges for joints and bearings', *Joint Sealing and Bearing Systems for Concrete Structures, ACI Publication SP-70*, Vol. 2, pp. 735–760 (1982)

LEWIS, R. B., 'Lubrication of teflon', *Report No. SAE690777; HS-007 682* (1969)

LONG, J. E., *Bearings in Structural Engineering*, Butterworths, London (1974)

LONG, J. E., 'Bridge bearings and joints', *Highways and Public Works*, **46**, 9–20 (Dec. 1978)

LONG, J. E., 'The performance of PTFE in bridge bearings', *Civil Engineering and Public Works Review*, **64**, 459–462 (May 1969)

MAGEBA LTD, *Robek System Pot-Type Bearings*, 21 The Causeway, Bicester, Oxon OX6 7AN

MAGEBA SA CONSULTING, *Testing Rig 100000 KN*, Switzerland (Aug. 1981)

MAHALAHA, R. S., DHODAPKAR, A. N. and DESHPANDE, V. P., 'Use of PTFE in sliding bridge bearings', *Indian Highways*, 29–34 (Mar. 1988)

MAKINSON, K. R. and TABOR, D., 'The friction and transfer of polytetrafluoroethylene', *Proceedings of Royal Society of London, Series A*, **281**, 49–61 (1964)

MANNING, D. G. and BASSI, K. G., 'Bridge bearing performance in Ontario', *Joint Sealing and Bearing Systems for Concrete Structures, ACI Publication SP-94*, Vol. 2, pp. 1017–1040 (1986)

MAURER SOHNE, *Maurer Expansion Joints*, P.O. Box 44, 18000 München 44

MAYRBAURL, R. M., 'High cycle bearing tests for the Manhattan Bridge', *Joint Sealing and Bearing Systems for Concrete Structures, ACI Publication SP-94*, Vol. 1, pp. 343–370 (1986)

MAZROI, A. and MURRAY, T. M., 'Performance of sliding bridge bearings', *Transportation Research Record N982*, pp. 12–20 (1984)

MAZROI, A., WANG, L. R. L. and MURRAY, T. M., 'Effective coefficient of friction of bridge bearings', *Research Report*, Fears Structural Engineering Laboratory, School of Civil Engineering and Environmental Science, University of Oklahoma, Norman, Oklahoma (Feb. 1982)

MILZ, W. C. and SARGENT, L. B., Jr, 'Friction characteristics of plastics', *Lubrication Engineering*, 313–317 (Sep./Oct. 1955)

NORDLIN, E. F., BOSS, J. F. and TRIMBLE, R. R., 'Tetrafluorethylene (TFE) as a bridge bearing material', *Research Report No. M&R 646142-2*, Materials and Research Department, Division of Highways, Department of Public Works, State of California (June 1970)

NORTON PERFORMANCE PLASTICS, *Slipflon Slide and Expansion Bearings*, Chesterton Works, Loomer Road, Newcastle, Staffs ST5 7HR

PAYNTER, F. R., 'Investigation of friction in PTFE bridge bearings', *Civil Engineer in South Africa*, **15**, 209–217 (Aug. 1973)

PILLSBURY, R. D., Jr, 'The hows and whys of friction for "TEFLON" resins', *The Journal of Teflon* (May 1961); Reprint No. 19, E. I. du Pont de Nemours and Co., Wilmington, Delaware

PORTER, J. A. and THOMPSON, J. O., 'The organisation and techniques for moving heavy railway bridges', *Proceedings of the Institution of Civil Engineers*, **52**, 149–167 (Aug. 1972)

PRICE, W. I. J., 'Transmission of horizontal forces and movements by bridge bearings', *Joint Sealing and Bearing Systems for Concrete Structures, ACI Publication SP-70*, Vol. 2, pp. 761–784 (1982)

PSC FREYSSINET LTD, *Tetron Disc Bearings*, The Ridgeway, Iver, Bucks SL0 9JE

PSC FREYSSINET LTD, *Tetron Spherical Bearings*, The Ridgeway, Iver, Bucks SL0 9JE

RUHRBERG, R., SCHUMANN, H. and HAGEN-DAHL, *Schaden an Brucken und anderen Ingenierbauwerken*, Dokumentation der Bundesminister für Verkehr (1982) (in German)

SHOOTER, K. V. and TABOR, D., 'The frictional properties of plastics', *Proceedings of the Physical Society, London, Section B*, **65**, 661–671 (1952)

SK BEARINGS LTD, *SK Bearings*, Pampisford, Cambridge CB2 4HG

TAYLOR, M. E., 'Low friction sliding surfaces for bridge bearings: PTFE weave', *Transport and Road Research Laboratory Report No. LR 101*, TRRL, Crowthorne (1967)

TAYLOR, M. E., 'PTFE in highway bridge bearings', TRRL, *Report No. LR-491*, Crowthorne (1972)

THE GLACIER METAL CO. LTD, *Glacier Structural Bearings*, Winterhay Lane, Ilminster, Somerset TA19 9PH

UETZ, J. and BRECKEL, H., 'Friction and wear tests with PTFE' ('Reibungs und Verschleissversuche mit PTFE'), *Wear*, **10**, 185–198 (1967) (in German)

UETZ, H. and HAKENJOS, V., 'Experiments on sliding with polytetrafluoroethylene in reciprocating motion', *Die Bautechnik*, **44**, 159–166 (May 1967)

UNIVERSITY OF TORONTO, *Load and Movement Test on 11K130 Sliding Structural Bearing*, Department of Civil Engineering (Nov. 1985)

US NATIONAL RESEARCH COUNCIL, 'Bridge bearings', *National Cooperative Highway Research Program Synthesis of Highway Practice No. 41*, Transportation Research Board, Washington, DC (1977)

WERCHOLOZ, R. J., 'The importance of design specification, manufacture and accurate installations of mechanical bridge bearings', *International Conference of Short and Medium Span Bridges*, Ottawa, Ontario (Aug. 1986)

43

Vinyl Materials

G H Arnold BSc, CEng, MIChemE
European Vinyls Corporation (UK) Ltd

Contents

43.1 Introduction 43/3

43.2 General description 43/3

43.3 Production of PVC 43/3

43.4 Compounding of PVC 43/3

43.5 Processing of PVC compositions 43/4

43.6 Properties and applications of rigid PVC (PVC-U) 43/4
43.6.1 PVC pipe 43/5
43.6.2 PVC injection-moulded fittings 43/8
43.6.3 Rigid PVC profiles 43/8
43.6.4 Rigid PVC sheet 43/10

43.7 Flexible PVC products 43/11
43.7.1 Vinyl flooring 43/11
43.7.2 Flexible tubes and profiles 43/11
43.7.3 Flexible sheeting 43/11

43.8 PVC/metal sheet laminates 43/12

43.9 Fire performance of PVC 43/12
43.9.1 Combustion properties 43/12

43.10 Future developments of PVC in the building industry 43/12

References 43/12

43.1 Introduction

The use of polyvinyl chloride (PVC) in the construction industry has become established around the world, particularly in the past 30 years. The amount of PVC used for particular applications does vary from country to country for a variety of reasons which may include the type of building methods used, the protection of vested interests, the availability of traditional materials and many others. However, if the European market for PVC in building is surveyed, it will be seen that this major thermoplastic has achieved an important status. This chapter seeks to explain some of the technical background of the product and describes the use and properties of PVC in the more important applications. By far the largest single use of PVC in the construction industry is in the pipe business which, in 1989, consumed 28% of total PVC usage. So it can be seen that the building market is a very important outlet for PVC as well as the fact that PVC provides extremely useful products for this sector. Other important applications which will be reviewed include profiles, window frames, sheet products and flooring.

43.2 General description

Polyvinyl chloride is the most widely used thermoplastic in the construction industry. The product name is often abbreviated to PVC but this needs to be more carefully qualified to enable the user to understand the nature and properties of the product he is using. Other terms which are often encountered in industry relating to PVC are 'vinyl' and 'UPVC' and, although neither of these terms is now officially sanctioned by the International Organization for Standardization (ISO) nomenclature, they are widely used, especially where the consumer is concerned and, therefore, need to be understood.

The term PVC has now come to mean a material or product made from a PVC composition, i.e. an intimate mixture of a vinyl chloride polymer or copolymer with various additives, some of which may be present (e.g. plasticizer or filler) in very substantial and, occasionally, predominant proportions.[1]

The additives which are used with PVC resins are required to enable processing to take place and include products such as heat stabilizers, lubricants, fillers and pigments, all of which are required to provide the properties required in the final product. There are other additives which are often used, such as processing aids and impact modifiers which also have a process- or property-enhancing effect. The most important group of additives are probably plasticizers, because they can impart to the PVC product a very wide range of flexible properties. Thus there are two types of PVC product used in the building industry: (i) rigid or unplasticized PVC which is based on a composition which does not contain plasticizer; and (ii) flexible or plasticized PVC. These types are defined by ISO.[2] Traditionally, the rigid forms of PVC have been called UPVC but new ISO nomenclature states that such products should be termed PVC-U and flexible PVC compositions and products should be termed PVC-P. However, it is likely that the term UPVC will be with us for some considerable time.

43.3 Production of PVC

PVC resins are manufactured by the polymerization of vinyl chloride. The monomer is nowadays commonly produced by the chlorination and oxychlorination of ethylene to dichlorethane followed by the pyrolitic dehydrochlorination to vinyl chloride.

Although other routes to vinyl chloride are possible, the above method accounts for the vast majority of PVC produced in western Europe. The polymerization process can be carried out in a number of ways to produce polymers with different processing characteristics.[3] The main types of polymers used in products made for the construction industry include suspension and emulsion polymers.

The processes used are all designed to produce a white free-flowing powder which, for suspension polymers, the most common form used for applications in the construction sector, have an average particle size of 110–170 μm. This powder can then be mixed with the additives referred to earlier to produce the required compounds. There are a number of variables associated with the detail of the manufacturing methods for producing resins, but the most important of these as far as the product is concerned is the K value which is a number related to the molecular weight of the resin and which has an important effect on the processing behaviour of the material and some of its physical properties. Most of the PVC products used in the construction industry are based on resins with K values in the range 57–70. In addition to the suspension and emulsion polymers, there are also some speciality polymers which are classified as graft copolymers which are used to impart enhanced properties, especially in impact strength, to the PVC product. These polymers are used for products such as window frames, but similar results can also be obtained by using standard suspension polymers together with the appropriate additives. A special form of emulsion polymer, called paste polymer, is also manufactured which is very fine and has a low uptake of plasticizer yet forms a stable dispersion when plasticizers are incorporated. Such dispersions are called plastisols. These polymers are used in a number of applications, but as far as the construction industry is concerned the major areas where such products are used are for coating steel and for some types of flooring.

43.4 Compounding of PVC

It was stated above that PVC resin cannot be used by itself, but has to be manufactured into compounds before it can be processed into finished articles. There are two basic forms of compound which are used in the products for the building industry and these are differentiated by their physical form. The first is called a dry blend or powder blend and is, as its name suggests, a mixture of all the required ingredients in powder form. The second form of compound is called a granulate or pellet and is produced by melt compounding the dry blend mentioned above and pelletizing the resultant product. Both forms of compound are widely used in industry, although for larger scale operations such as pipe or window-frame extrusion, there is a predominant use of dry blends. A schematic diagram of the compounding of PVC is shown in *Figure 43.1*.

The equipment in which dry blends are manufactured is called a high-speed mixer and consists of a vessel in which a blade rotates at high speed, providing an intimate mix of the ingredients. The blade also heats up the ingredients by a shearing mechanism and the blend is discharged to a cooling blender at a typical temperature of about 120°C. In the cooling blender, which is generally cold-water jacketted, the blend is cooled to a temperature of around 50°C and then discharged.

In the case of granulate, a powder blend, which in many cases has not gone through the full process described above, is fed to various forms of extruder where it is compounded before being extruded through appropriate die plates which cut the resultant melt into cylindrical pellets.

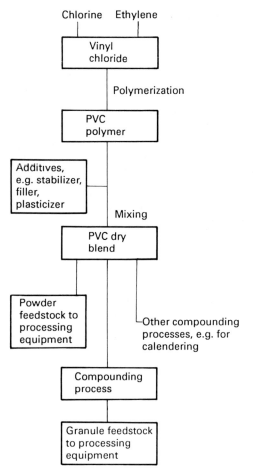

Chlorine Ethylene

Vinyl chloride

Polymerization

PVC polymer

Additives, e.g. stabilizer, filler, plasticizer

Mixing

PVC dry blend

Powder feedstock to processing equipment

Other compounding processes, e.g. for calendering

Compounding process

Granule feedstock to processing equipment

Figure 43.1 Diagrammatic scheme for preparation of PVC compound

43.5 Processing of PVC compositions

In order for any PVC product to be manufactured, appropriate processing equipment must be used. The equipment will vary according to the final product, but virtually all products for the building industry are made by either extrusion, injection moulding, or calendering. The main rigid PVC products described, such as pipes, sheet and profiles, are produced by the extrusion process and this also applies to flexible PVC profiles and sheet. A more detailed description of processing techniques is available in the literature.[1,3]

43.6 Properties and applications of rigid PVC (PVC-U)

In its final product form, PVC-U is stiff, robust and light in weight with good chemical and weathering resistance. PVC-U compares favourably with most other thermoplastics in standard flammability tests and it does not require the use of flame-retardant additives to achieve this performance. Compared with most other thermoplastics, PVC-U is relatively stiff and strong at room temperature. However, its upper continuous-service temperature is limited to about 60°C since PVC-U is essentially an amorphous material with a glass transition temperature (the temperature at which softening of the material starts to occur) of 80°C. Some important properties of PVC-U are compared with those of other common rigid thermoplastics used in the building industry in *Table 43.1*.

PVC-U is resistant to a wide range of chemicals and is only readily attacked by some ketones, aromatic and chlorinated hydrocarbons and some nitroparaffins. There are comprehensive lists published on the chemical resistance of PVC and these should be consulted when relevant.[1,4] A summary of the chemical resistance of PVC-U to some common materials is given in *Table 43.2*.

Table 43.1 A comparison of typical grades of PVC-U, polypropylene and high-density polyethylene (HDPE)

Property	Test method/ recommendation	PVC-U	Polypropylene	HDPE
Yield stress (MN m^{-2}) at 23°C	BS 2782: 1970 Method 30IG	55	25	20
Tensile modulus 100s 1% strain (GN m^{-2}) at 23°C	BS 4618	2.7–3.0	As moulded: 0.8–1.0 Annealed at 140°C: 1.2–1.4	0.7–0.95
Izod impact strength (J m^{-1})*	BS 2782: 1970 Method 306-A	110 (unmodified) 540–800 (impact modified)	110 (homopolymer) 540 (copolymer)	270–1100
Relative density		1.38–1.45	0.90–0.91	0.940–0.965
Maximum continuous service temperature (°C) from field experience		60	110	80
Coefficient of thermal expansion at 20°C (°C^{-1})	BS 4618	6×10^{-5}	12×10^{-5}	11×10^{-5}
Flammability (oxygen index) (%)	ASTM D2863-77 (Fenimore Martin test)	45	17.5	17.5

* J m^{-1} = 1.873×10^{-2} ft. lb. ft. in^{-1}.

Table 43.2 Chemical resistance of PVC-U to some common chemical products

Chemical	Temperature (°C)	
	20	60
Alcohol (40% aqueous)	+ +	+
Antifreeze	+ +	+ +
Dish-washing liquid	+ +	+ +
Detergent (diluted)	+ +	+ +
Furniture polishes	+ +	+ +
Gas oil	+ +	+ +
Lanolin	+ +	+ +
Linseed oil	+ +	+ +
Mineral oils	+ +	+ +
Moist acidic atmosphere	+ +	+
Moist alkaline atmosphere	+ +	+
Motor oils	+ +	+ +
Petrol	+ +	+ +
Sea-water	+ +	+ +
Vinegar	+ +	+ +
Vegetable oils	+ +	+ +

Key: + +, resistant; +, practically resistant.

The long term properties of PVC are important when plastics are used in engineering applications[5] and both creep and fatigue properties of PVC-U have been extensively studied with the objective of allowing good design practice. Typical creep data are given in *Figures 4.2* and *4.3*. Similarly, the influence of modulus with time and temperature has been measured since this can have a marked effect on the design of the PVC-U product (*Figure 4.4*).

The impact strength of PVC-U is often an important factor affecting its use and performance. Although PVC-U is inherently a tough material, its impact strength can be substantially enhanced by the use of special rubbery additives or by using specific copolymers which incorporate a rubbery material such as butylacrylate. Other types of modifier include methacrylate/butadiene/styrene (MBS) and chlorinated polyethylene. The effect of impact modification is shown in *Figures 43.5* and *43.6*, which show the performance of unmodified and impact-modified PVC using both unnotched and notched specimens. In addition, in *Figure 43.6* the notched impact strength of some other thermoplastics are compared with that of PVC.

43.6.1 PVC pipe

PVC-U pipe is the largest single application for PVC and typically consumes 28% of all the PVC used. This means that in western Europe nearly 1.39 million tonne of PVC are used for pipes of various types.

The general benefits of using PVC pipes in comparison with

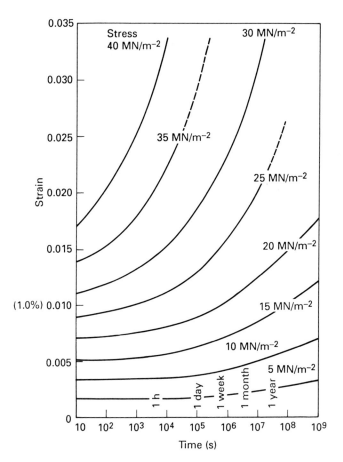

Figure 43.2 Creep in tension at 20°C for K67 PVC in a pressure pipe formulation

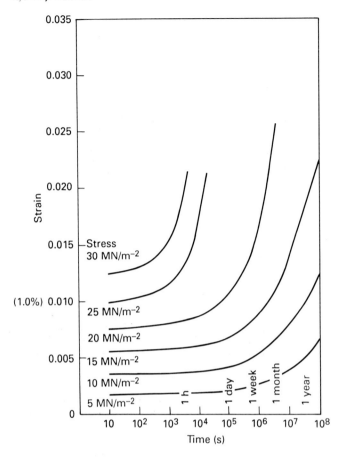

Figure 43.3 Creep in tension at 50°C for K67 PVC in a pressure pipe formulation. Samples conditioned at 50°C prior to test for 83 days

more conventional materials are:

(1) low weight;
(2) high tensile and pressure resistance;
(3) high stiffness;
(4) high durability;
(5) good creep characteristics;
(6) excellent hydraulic characteristics;
(7) good abrasion resistance;
(8) good resistance against bacterial growth;
(9) non-flammable properties; and
(10) easy to manufacture joints.

PVC-U pipes have been accepted for a wide range of applications and these are summarized together with a short description of the essential properties of PVC-U appropriate to that application in *Table 43.3*.

43.6.1.1 Major types of pipe

As can be seen in *Table 43.3* there are numerous types of pipe, each of which uses one or more properties of PVC for its effectiveness. It will also be noted that virtually all forms of pipe are subject to British Standards and there are also a wide range of equivalent continental standards. The properties and performance of these pipes are thus comprehensively characterized. Such tests include a number of standard checks such as those for tensile strength and softening point and most forms of pipe have specialized testing relevant to the application carried out, such as pressure testing for water mains pipe and deformation testing for drainage pipe. The different building properties and availability of competitive materials in each country often dictate the degree

of penetration that PVC pipe has in each main sector of the pipe industry. The comments in this section apply particularly to the situation in the UK.

(*a*) *Pressure pipe*. This product has been available in the UK for over 30 years, mainly for use as water mains but also as pipe for chemical plants and, with increasing availability of advanced processing technology, has resulted in a very-high-quality product. It is generally used in diameters of 3–12 in., but larger sizes up to 24 in. are also installed.

(*b*) *Soil pipe and rainwater goods*. These products have achieved virtually complete penetration of the market and are totally accepted by the users. A number of detailed designs of rainwater goods are available and a number of colours, e.g. black, white, grey and brown, are manufactured.

(*c*) *Drain and sewer pipe*. This has been a developing market over the past 20 years. Although competing against traditional ceramic pipe, PVC pipes have strongly established themselves in the market because of their superior properties. Drain and sewer pipes are generally installed in diameters up to 315 mm, but larger sizes can be manufactured and are used particularly in Germany.

(*d*) *Land-drainage pipe*. This product strongly established itself in the UK market for use as agricultural drainage pipe in the 1970s and 1980s, although there has been some considerable experience with its use in Europe for many years. The pipe, which is strong but lightweight, competes successfully with porous clay tiles and is made in a corrugated form so that it can be coiled, allowing for easy transportation and installation.

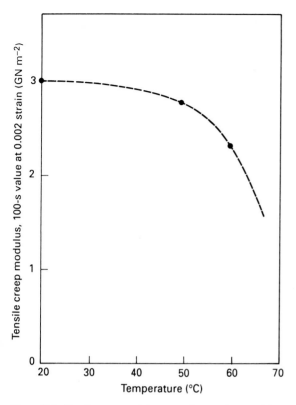

Figure 43.4 Tensile creep modulus versus temperature: modulus measured after 100 s at 0.002 strain

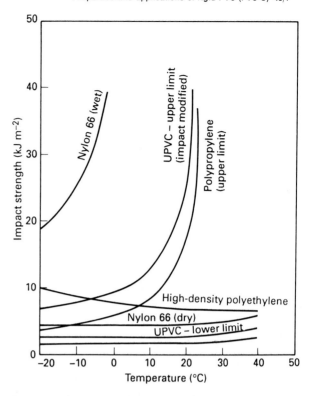

Figure 43.6 Comparison of the impact strength of PVC-U with some other thermoplastics. Charpy specimens with 250 μm notch tip radius

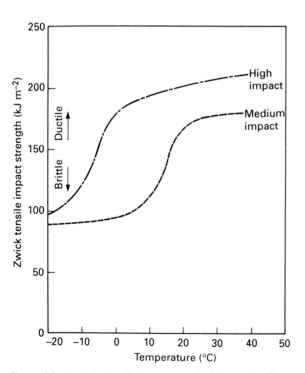

Figure 43.5 Unnotched tensile impact strength of two grades of unplasticized PVC compounds

(*e*) *Ducting.* This has been probably the fastest growing sector of the pipe market. Typically this pipe is used for the containment of telephone wiring and other cabling and British Telecom are major users of this product.

(*f*) *Electrical conduit.* Because PVC is both non-conductive and non-corrosive, electrical arcing cannot occur with PVC conduit. This product is now widely used and has shown itself to be superior to steel conduit in many sectors of the building market.

43.6.1.2 Special forms of pipe

There are a number of special pipes which have been designed for particular applications and are finding their own niche in the marketplace. Examples of these are described below.

(*a*) *Ribbed pipe.* In order to maintain cost effectiveness and competitiveness against traditional sewer-pipe products such as concrete or clay, it has been a requirement to provide a lighter weight PVC pipe which has within its design the desired properties essential for this application, the most important of which are stiffness and resistance to deformation under load. An extruded ribbed pipe where there are a series of peripheral ribs produced by a patented sizing technique fulfils this need and these products are now being manufactured in diameters above 200 mm. The process which saves about 40% by weight on a conventional pipe has been developed by Uponor who now have a number of licensees (*Figure 43.7*).

(*b*) *Hollow-walled pipe.* For the same application as ribbed pipe a form of pipe is produced by Wavin called Wavihole which consists of a pipe with closely spaced longitudinal channels in

Table 43.3 Description of types of PVC-U pipe

Type of pipe	Important properties	Relevant British Standards
Pressure pipe (water mains, chemical plants)	High tensile strength, high modulus, toughness, good creep characteristics, good flow characteristics, good chemical resistance	BS 3505 BS 3506 BS 4346 (for fittings)
Soil pipe	High modulus, toughness, good weathering	BS 4514
Rainwater goods	High modulus, toughness, good weathering, non-corrosive	BS 4576
Drain and sewer pipes	High stiffness, good creep characteristics, toughness, high tensile strength	BS 4660 BS 5481
Land-drainage pipes	High stiffness/unit weight, toughness, good weathering	BS 4962
Ducting pipe (e.g. communications ducting)	High stiffness/unit weight, toughness	British Telecom specification
Conduit	High toughness, good insulating properties	BS 6099-2-2 BS 4607

Figure 43.7 Illustration of Ultrarib sewer pipe being installed. (Courtesy of Uponor Ltd)

the wall. This also gives strength combined with a substantial weight saving.

(c) *Foamed pipe*. This is yet another form of pipe developed for the drain and sewer market, although in France such products are also used for soil pipe and ducting. The product provides a weight saving of about 30% over conventional pipe and typically consists of a foam core with co-extruded skins of solid PVC. Simpler forms are available but do not have the same degree of performance. Foamed pipes have not been widely used in Europe outside the French domestic market.

(d) *Twin-wall pipe*. In another design solution to provide a weight saving for sewer pipe, a manufacturing method has been developed using a form of co-extrusion producing a lightweight product with a smooth inside wall and a corrugated outer wall. Such pipes are now being introduced to the European market.

(e) *Spirally wound pipe*. This type of pipe consists of profile shaped to give ribs when the profile is wound round a mandrel

to manufacture a pipe. Although these pipes are used in the USA and Australia for sewer pipes and their relining, they have not yet been widely introduced to the European market.

(f) *High-strength oriented PVC pipe*. This type of product, produced by uniaxial or biaxial orientation, is designed to provide pressure resistances with lower wall thicknesses and a weight saving of up to 40%. The product also has superior impact and fatigue resistances as compared with its conventional counterpart and has been successfully used in the water-mains market.

43.6.2 PVC injection-moulded fittings

Most of the pipe applications described in the above sections require fittings to enable the pipe systems to be joined together and operate properly as a system. For example, there is a wide range of fittings associated with rainwater pipes and gutters, soil and drainage systems, to give these PVC applications a great deal of flexibility in use. Such fittings are produced from PVC by injection moulding and the products manufactured have essentially the same properties as the pipe or gutter with which they are associated.

43.6.3 Rigid PVC profiles

The generic term 'rigid PVC profile' applies to a very large number of products used in the building industry. These profiles have often been developed as substitutes for existing products made from more traditional materials such as wood, aluminium or steel. By virtue of its properties. PVC-U is relatively easy to produce in shapes of various sizes and quite high degrees of complexity and, therefore, it is impossible to cover here the full range of products which are manufactured. The main application areas where significant quantities of PVC are used are in window frames, roller shutters, curtain rail, cladding, window sills, architraves, skirting boards and electrical trunking. These products are all manufactured from unplasticized PVC in various designs and often incorporate hollow profiles to provide both light weight and strength. In addition, some applications such as cladding, window sills and skirting boards are also available in foamed PVC which has a density of between 0.5 and 0.8 compared with a density of 1.4 for its unfoamed equivalent (see Section 43.6.3.3).

43.6.3.1 Window profiles

As far as usage of PVC profiles is concerned, their use in window profiles is the largest sector for the product in western Europe and is also the fastest growing sector for PVC. Window frames made from PVC-U have been available for more than 30 years, but the pattern of usage in various countries has been very different. The countries now using significant quantities of PVC for this application are Germany and the UK where the application utilizes about 14% of the total PVC consumption. The benefits of using PVC-U for window frames are summarized in *Table 43.4*.

The materials used for PVC window frames are predominantly impact-modified PVC where the PVC polymer is copolymerized with a rubbery additive or where the formulation contains a rubbery ingredient such as butylacrylate. Some window frames are also manufactured from special formulations which do not contain impact modifier. Typical properties of an impact-modified window-frame material are given in *Table 43.5*.

One of the main benefits of PVC window frames, especially when compared with those made from aluminium, is that it has a very low thermal conductivity of 0.16 W m^{-1} °C^{-1} which is even lower than that of timber (*Figure 43.8*).

Window frames are fabricated by joining mitred profiles using hot-plate welding. By choosing the correct temperature and pressure, welds can be made which are as strong as the base material. The effect of temperature and pressure is shown in *Figure 43.9*.

A series of British Standards[6-8] relating to this application have recently been published and these cover both the performance of the window as well as the mechanical and durability characteristics of the PVC profiles.

Table 43.4 Benefits of PVC-U window frames

Property	Benefit
Low cost	Extremely competitive
High rigidity/unit cost	Lower product cost
Strong, tough, durable	Longer product life
Lightweight	Easy handling
Excellent weathering resistance	Long service life
Excellent chemical and corrosion resistance	No maintenance
Self-extinguishing	Will not cause fire or enhance its development
Low thermal conductivity	No condensation

43.6.3.2 Other rigid profiles

The remaining types of rigid PVC profiles all have essentially the same benefits as window frames. although in many cases the performance criteria are somewhat less stringent than for window frames. The major applications for these profiles in the construction industry include cladding products and roller shutters, but there is also a large variety of trim sections which find a variety of uses. The case of roller shutters is a good example of an application being very successful in one country and not in another. For example, in Germany PVC is used for 95% of roller blinds which accounts for 5% of the PVC market, whilst in the UK there is almost no use of PVC for this application.

Table 43.5 Typical properties of high-impact PVC-U window material

Property	Test method	Typical value
Tensile strength at 23°C	ISO 527 BS 2782: Method 320C	44 MPa
Tensile modulus (1% strain) at 23°C	ISO R899 BS 4618	2250 MPa
Flexural modulus	ISO 178 BS 2782: Method 335A	2400 MPa
Flexural yield stregth at 23°C	ISO 178	76 MPa
Relative density at 23°C		1.4–1.5
Charpy impact strength at 23°C	ISO 179 BS 2782: Part 3: Method 359: 1984 (0.1 mm V-notch) DIN 53453 (U-notch)	14 kJ m^{-2} 40 kJ m^{-2}
Retention of impact strength after accelerated weathering to 8 GJ m^{-2}	BS 2782: Method 359 (0.25 mm double V-notch)	>80%
Colour-fastness	BS 2782: Method 540 B ISO 4892, Xenotest BS 1006: Part A02: 1978 Colour change: 1 = most change, 5 = least change	Grey scale 4–5
Vicat softening point	ISO 306 BS 2782: Method 120 B	81°C
Flammability (oxygen index)	ASTM S2893 (Fenimore Martin)	45%
Fire resistance	BS 476: Part 7: 1971	Class 1 (most resistant)
Coefficient of linear thermal expansion		6 × 10^{-5} °C^{-1}
Coefficient of thermal conductivity at 23°C		0.16 W m^{-1} °C^{-1}
Reversion	1 h at 100°C	1.6%

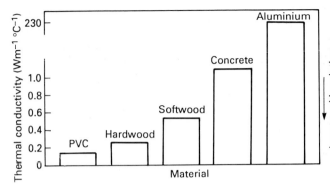

Figure 43.8 Thermal conductivity of PVC-U compared to other materials

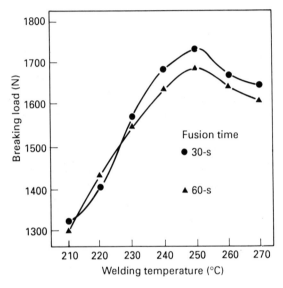

Figure 43.9 Effect of fusion time on corner strength and various welding temperatures

43.6.3.3 Cellular (foamed) PVC profiles

There are a number of special properties which make foamed PVC-U a particularly useful product for some applications, even compared with solid PVC-U. These are:

(1) low volume cost;
(2) good heat- and sound-insulation properties;
(3) low reversion and expansion;
(4) high stiffness/unit weight; and
(5) availability of easy fabrication techniques.

(Reversion is the change in dimensions measured at temperatures usually between 120 and 160°C which occurs as a result of relieving the locked-in strain produced by a sizing process such as is used for extruding pipe and profiles.)

These products are typically produced for building industry applications from rigid PVC formulations which have chemical blowing agents incorporated; examples of such materials are sodium bicarbonate and azodicarbonamide. PVC rigid foams possess all the properties of rigid PVC together with the fact that the products typically have a density of about one-half to one-third (i.e. 0.5–0.7) that of its PVC equivalent. The rigid PVC foam products used for building applications tend to have a high degree of stiffness because they are often extruded in such

a way that the outside surfaces are essentially solid PVC and in some cases foam profiles are made by co-extruding a solid skin over a foam core.

Typical applications of foamed PVC-U profiles include window boards and sills, window sub-frames, trim sections, cladding, fascia, bargeboard and soffits.

43.6.4 Rigid PVC sheet

Flat or corrugated PVC sheet is used extensively in the building sector for roofing applications and partitioning. The product is available in a range of colours, either clear or opaque, and in addition can be reinforced by the incorporation of wire lamination. These products vary in thickness from about 0.5 to 10 mm. The main service requirements are typical of those which have to be met by other PVC applications used outdoors, i.e. good weathering characteristics and adequate robustness, but in the case of transparent sheet, which is the dominant product sold in the marketplace, it is necessary to ensure a high degree of clarity which is retained over many years. The fire properties of PVC sheet are also of importance and this is particularly so where the product is used for applications such as wall lining. This aspect is dealt with in Section 43.9.

The applications of PVC sheet are numerous and include glazing, lining for tunnels and roofs, roof and dome lights, and roofing which probably consumes the majority of the PVC found in this sector of the market (*Figure 43.10*).

Rigid PVC sheet for building is produced by one of two methods. The majority of sheet, whether flat or corrugated, is produced by using a conventional extrusion process in which is fitted an appropriate die, a polishing stack and corrugating equipment, if required. The other process is carried out by calendering (a process for producing flat sheet by passing the material through flat heated rolls) and lamination of PVC and the process allows the incorporation of wire reinforcement. It is also possible to specify products with either a matt or gloss finish. There is also a special type of biaxially oriented sheet available which is claimed to impart enhanced impact resistance together with good retention of the property at temperatures down to −40°C.

Over the last few years there has been an increasing use of a double-skin box section of clear rigid PVC which is made from an impact-modified formulation. This product is used for light partitioning in buildings such as sports halls.

Foamed PVC sheet is also manufactured and its uses in the construction sector includes dry lining, cladding and ceiling boards, where it replaces traditional products such as plasterboard, hardboard and timber. Such sheet has excellent thermal and acoustic properties.

The performance, properties and dimensions of PVC corrugated sheeting are specified in BS 4203: Part 1, 1980.[9]

Figure 43.10 Darvic PVC sheet as glazing. (Courtesy of Weston Hyde Products Ltd)

43.7 Flexible PVC products

The number of flexible or plasticized PVC products used in the building industry is considerably less than in the rigid sector because, as their name implies, these products are flexible and therefore do not have the rigidity which makes unplasticized PVC such a useful material. Nevertheless, there is still significant usage of flexible PVC in the construction sector and the more important of these uses are covered in this section. Cables are not included as they are covered elsewhere under 'services'. However, it should be noted that cables insulated and /or sheathed with flexible PVC are an important application accounting for 9% of the European consumption of PVC. Furnishings such as PVC wall coverings and leather cloth are also not included in this chapter.

Because of the influence of plasticizer which can vary the softness of the product, the properties of plasticized PVC will obviously vary according to both the amount and type of plasticizer present. The typical properties which are given in *Table 43.6* show the range which is covered by plasticized PVC products.

43.7.1 Vinyl flooring

The most important application of flexible PVC in building is flooring which comes basically in two forms. The older and very well established use of PVC for floor tiles and solid flooring is produced by the calendering of PVC compositions which are filled with mineral fibre. This product is widely used in industrial buildings such as hospitals and schools as well as in domestic installations, e.g. in bathrooms and kitchens. These products

are manufactured in a wide variety of designs, have good wear characteristics, and can be easily cleaned.

The more modern types of vinyl flooring widely used in the domestic sector are much more complex products. The product is available in a number of forms of differing complexity. In its simplest form it is a two-layer product where there is a wear layer made from PVC backed by a thicker foam layer. The wear layer will generally be printed and incorporate a thin clear PVC coating to protect this. The flooring made from the multi-layer construction generally consists of a clear wear layer, a thin foam layer backed by fabric and there is also occasionally an additional layer between the foam and the fabric. Again a wide range of designs is available together with the added option of embossing which greatly adds to the types of products available. The main properties of this type of flooring are rapid recovery after compression, good wear and soiling resistance and good dimensional stability, together with a 'feel' which the solid type of PVC flooring does not possess.

43.7.2 Flexible tubes and profiles

Although flexible pipes are only used to a very minor extent compared with their rigid equivalents, some special products do find their way into building applications. In particular, heavy-duty hose, which is reinforced by a synthetic fibre braid and consists of a plasticized PVC outer layer designed to give high abrasion resistance, is found useful in association with various forms of building equipment. Other forms of this reinforced hose are where the rigid support is supplied by a continuous coil of rigid PVC over which the flexible PVC is extruded giving the product the required flexibility. The most important form of plasticized PVC profile used in the construction industry is that of water stop which is a fairly thick section used for the leak-proofing of joints in concrete structures such as dams and sewage works. There are a number of other uses, albeit important ones, for flexible PVC profiles which include an increasing use for gasketting in association with PVC window frames and increasingly as a co-extruded strip together with rigid PVC, draught excluders, the coating of wire used as chain-link fencing and a wide variety of trims and nosings for internal parts of buildings.

43.7.3 Flexible sheeting

Flexible sheeting, which can be calendered or extruded, is used in the building industry as a liner for water reservoirs, tanks and pools. In addition, it is increasingly being used for roofing membranes replacing bitumenized felt. The above applications utilize calendered sheeting and in its extruded form flexible PVC sheeting is most often seen as a clear product used for industrial doors. This product can be 5 mm thick or over and up to 1.5 m wide. Sometimes the doors are made up of strips, each 200–300 mm wide.

Table 43.6 Typical properties of flexible PVC

Property	Unit	Value
Relative density		1.19–1.68
Tensile strength	$MN\,m^{-2}$	7.5–30
Elongation at break	%	140–40
Hardness (Rockwell)		5–100
Brittleness temperature	°C	-20 to -60
Volume resistivity at 23°C	$\Omega\,cm$	10^{10}–10^{15}
Ageing resistance		Excellent
Ozone resistance		Very good

Table 43.7 Ignition properties of PVC

Property	Test method	PVC-U	Flexible PVC	Wood
Flash ignition temperature* (°C)	ASTM D1929	400	330–380	210–270
Self-ignition temperature† (°C)		450	420–430	400
Oxygen index	ISO 4589	50	23–33	21–23
ISO Radiant Core	ISO 5657			
Ignition time at 30 kW m^{-2} (s)		112	50–75	30–90
Ignition time at 50 kW m^{-2} (s)		33	17–26	4–30
Needle flame test	IEC 695-2-2	Non-ignitable	Ignition only at high levels of plasticizer	Ignitable in <20 s

* The lowest temperature of air passing around the specimen at which sufficient combustible gas is evolved to be ignited by a small external pilot flame.
† The lowest temperature of air passing around the specimen at which, in the absence of an ignition source, ignition occurs by itself.

43.8 PVC/metal sheet laminates

PVC/metal sheet laminates find an important application in the construction industry. PVC-covered steel provides excellent weather resistance whilst at the same time providing an aesthetic function, being available in a wide range of colours. The coating is made either from a flexible PVC film or by using a coating of plastisol.

43.9 Fire performance of PVC

Both rigid and flexible PVC are very widely used in the construction industry and the fire performance of the product is dependant to some extent on the formulation and, in particular, on whether the product being tested is made from rigid or flexible PVC. The chlorine content of PVC is 57% and this contributes towards efficient flame-retarding properties. In PVC-U applications the PVC element is 80% or more and, therefore, the fire behaviour of PVC determines the performance of the product. In plasticized PVC applications the presence of the plasticizer increases the flammability of the composition and product. However, for critical applications it is possible to incorporate special flame-retardant plasticizers, and another option is to incorporate special flame-retardant additives.

There are a number of sources of information on the fire behaviour of PVC which are reviewed in two PVC industry booklets[10,11] from which most of the information in this section is taken, and in which reference is made to a number of other sources which give a wide consideration of the subject, including discussion of the gases emitted when PVC is involved in fire.

43.9.1 Combustion properties

A variety of laboratory tests are available to determine the combustion properties of PVC and the results of these taken together give an overall perspective of the behaviour of PVC under actual fire conditions.

PVC is difficult to ignite using most common ignition sources and the ignitability of unplasticized PVC is one of the lowest amongst thermoplastics and even the ignitability of plasticized compositions is better than that for wood (*Table 43.7*).

A burning object will spread fire to nearby products only if it gives off enough heat to ignite them and this heat release is the most important property in terms of fire hazard. Tests[12] have shown that most materials are more prone to ignite other products than is PVC. PVC also exhibits a very good performance when tested against the various flammability tests involving spread of flame and many PVC compositions meet the best classifications for combustible building materials.

Although under burning conditions both flexible and rigid PVC will produce more smoke than wood, the smoke densities under non-flaming conditions for these materials are very similar and tests which have been carried out with PVC-U test panels to simulate real fire conditions have shown that these produce significantly less heat and smoke than plasterboard or wood.

A number of other tests have been carried out to show the excellent fire performance of unplasticized and plasticized PVC. For example, the Fire Research Station[13] carried out tests on windows made from wood and PVC and concluded that there was no difference in fire performance under the conditions used, whilst PVC flooring performed well in a radiant panel test (ASTM E648-78).[14]

The advantages of PVC in fire situations is recognized in the UK Building Regulations Approved Document B. B2/3/4.[15] Subject to satisfactory performance in a flammability test, PVC is the only plastic which is listed as being suitable for rooflights, window glazing, suspended ceilings and roof construction. Similarly, Part E12 of these regulations allows the use of PVC pipes to pass inside the building.

43.10 Future developments of PVC in the building industry

The use of PVC has been established in building applications for over 40 years so it can be regarded in many ways as having reached maturity. However, new ways of using PVC are continually being found and the development of processing technology has also contributed to a range of new forms of older products, particularly in the pipe sector. No doubt these developments will continue and, whilst it will be difficult to find completely new applications, it is probable that PVC will obtain greater penetration in existing areas. There is also the possibility of combining PVC with other materials to give products with a new range of properties, for example combining high strength with excellent insulation and durability characteristics. It is envisaged that development work will be carried out in this area and indeed some products are already on the market which combine glass fibre with PVC to give a strong, durable product with a low expansion coefficient which could provide the basis for the design of large structural profiles. There are a number of opportunities in this area and the continuing development work being carried out by the raw-material manufacturers, processors and machinery manufacturers will ensure that new products will become available for the building industry.

References

1 TITOW, W. V., *PVC Technology*, 4th edition, Elsevier Applied Science Publishers, Amsterdam (1986)

2   INTERNATIONAL ORGANIZATION FOR
    STANDARDIZATION, *ISO 1163: Part 1 Plastics—unplasticized
    compounds of homopolymers and copolymers of vinyl chloride*,
    Geneva (1985) *ISO 2898: Part 1 Plastics—plasticized compounds
    of homopolymers and copolymers of vinyl chloride*, Geneva (1986)
3   BURGESS, R. H. (Eds), *et al. Manufacture and Processing of
    PVC*, Elsevier Applied Science Publishers, Amsterdam (1982)
4   BRITISH STANDARDS INSTITUTION, *CP 314: Code of
    practice for plastics pipework*, Part 2 Thermoplastics materials,
    Milton Keynes (1973)
5   ICI VINYLS GROUP, Engineering design with unplasticised
    polyvinyl chloride, Technical Service Note W 121 (1980)
6   BRITISH STANDARDS INSTITUTION, *BS 7412 Specification
    for plastics windows made from PVC-U extruded hollow profiles*,
    Milton Keynes (1991)
7   BRITISH STANDARDS INSTITUTION, *BS 7413 Specification
    for white PVC-U extruded hollow profiles with heat welded corner
    joints for plastics windows—materials type A*, Milton Keynes (1991)
8   BRITISH STANDARDS INSTITUTION, *BS 7414 Specification
    for white PVC-U extruded hollow profiles with heat welded corner
    joints for plastic windows—materials type B*, Milton Keynes (1991)
9   BRITISH STANDARDS INSTITUTION, *BS 4203 extruded rigid
    PVC corrugated sheeting*, Milton Keynes, Parts 1 and 2 (1984)
10 BRITISH PLASTICS FEDERATION, *PVC in Fires* (1986)
11 THE VINYL INSTITUTE, USA, *Fire Properties of PVC*, (1988)
12 SMITH, E. E., Ignition, heat release and noncombustibility of
    materials, *ASTM STP 502* (A. F. Robertson, Ed.), American
    Society for Testing Materials, Philadelphia, 119 (1972)
13 FARDELL, P. J., MURRELL, J. M. and ROGOWSKI, Z. W.,
    The Performance of UPVC and Wood Double Glazed Windows, Fire
    Research Station (UK) and British Plastics Federation, London
    (1984)
14 AMERICAN SOCIETY FOR TESTING MATERIALS, *ASTM
    E648:78*
15 UK BUILDING REGULATIONS, *Approved Document B.
    B2/3/4 Fire Spread*, London (1985)

44

Aramid Fibres for Civil-Engineering Applications

C J Burgoyne PhD
Engineering Department, Cambridge University

Contents

44.1 Introduction 44/3

44.2 Development 44/3

44.3 Current production processes 44/3

44.4 Properties of aramid yarns 44/4
    44.4.1 Tensile properties 44/4
    44.4.2 Creep 44/4
    44.4.3 Stress rupture 44/5
    44.4.4 Tension–tension fatigue 44/6
    44.4.5 Impact and shock-loading resistance 44/6
    44.4.6 Compressive strength 44/7
    44.4.7 Abrasion resistance 44/7
    44.4.8 Chemical and environmental resistance 44/7
    44.4.9 Temperature effects 44/7

44.5 Applications 44/8
    44.5.1 Applications in civil and structural engineering 44/8

44.6 Conclusion 44/13

References 44/13

Appendix 44/14

44.1 Introduction

Aramid fibres are one of the high performance modern fibres[1] that are potentially of interest to civil and structural engineers, being characterized by high strength, high stiffness, low creep and resistance to corrosion. Unlike carbon and glass fibres, however, the aramid fibres are frequently used without resin impregnation, since they are much more resistant to local bending effects.

The term aramid is used to refer to aromatic polyamides containing chains of aromatic (benzene) rings, linked together with —CO— and —NH— end groups. Many forms can be produced,[2] but those based on *para* links on the aromatic ring generally give the strongest fibres.

These fibres are now available under a variety of commercial trade names, such as Kevlar (manufactured by Du Pont in America and Northern Ireland), Twaron (manufactured by Akzo in The Netherlands) and Technora (manufactured by Teijin in Japan). The fibres have a modulus greater than 40 kN mm^{-2}, and so fall within the high-performance category.[3] This category effectively excludes conventional textile fibres, nylon and polyethylene, on the basis of either strength, stiffness or creep.

The author has been involved with the testing of these materials for many years, primarily in the form of parallel-lay ropes, and much of the information presented here is based on that work. Some of the review material is taken from the Ph.D. theses of his co-workers Chambers[4] and Guimaraes,[5] and their permission to use that material is gratefully acknowledged. Valuable assistance has also been provided by various people at Du Pont, Akzo and Teijin.

44.2 Development

Du Pont produced the aramid fibre Nomex, poly(*m*-phenylene isophthalamide), in 1958, and research increased on other aramid fibres by this company and its competitors. A concentrated research effort by Du Pont led to the discovery of the precursor to Kevlar in 1965. This was known as Fibre B and was based on poly(*p*-benzamide);[6] it may be produced by either wet- or dry-spinning procedures. The development of Fibre B now appears to have been halted, however, probably owing to the high cost of the starting monomer (*p*-aminobenzoic acid) and the limited stability of the spinning dope.

The Kevlar polymer, poly(*p*-phenylene terephthalamide) or PPT, had been prepared as early as 1958, but the existing spinning techniques had failed to produce a high-strength fibre. It was known, however, that PPT polymer dissolved in concentrated sulphuric acid, and so when a technique for spinning from strong acids became available, the preparation of PPT fibres was reconsidered. When the well-known dry-jet wet-spinning process was used in conjunction with a sulphuric acid spinning dope, a PPT fibre was produced with properties that surpassed those of previous developments. Furthermore, this new breakthrough also led to increased productivity and considerable cost savings. Hence, the registered name of Kevlar was announced by Du Pont in 1973 to replace that of Fibre B.

44.3 Current production processes

Two routes are now used for the production of aramid fibres. Twaron and Kevlar are produced by a refined version of the original process, while Technora is produced by a different process which results in a fibre with slightly different properties. Twaron is virtually identical to Kevlar, and in the rest of this chapter the two materials will be treated as identical, unless otherwise stated. Technora is slightly different both chemically and physically; as far as its uses as an engineering material are concerned, however, the properties are similar to those of Kevlar. Once again, therefore, only the differences from Kevlar will be highlighted.

Kevlar and Twaron are prepared by the reaction of terephthaloyl chloride and *p*-phenylene diamine under carefully controlled conditions.[2] The polymerization takes place in a dialkyl amide solution; after drying, the polymer is dissolved in concentrated sulphuric acid, from which the fibres are spun. The fibres are washed to remove the acid, and then heat treated. By varying the degree of heat treatment given to the washed fibres, considerable variation in the Young's modulus and elongation can be produced. Du Pont produce a number of different types of the same basic Kevlar fibre, each intended for specific applications, while Akzo produce two versions of Twaron. Kevlar 29, Kevlar 49 (formerly PRD-49) and Kevlar 149 (or Kevlar 'HM') from Du Pont, and Twaron and Twaron HM from Akzo are the fibres of particular relevance to civil engineering. The chemical structure is a polymer of a single repeating unit, hence the chemical name poly(*p*-phenylene terephthalamide), and the structure:

$$\left[-NH-\bigcirc-NH-CO-\bigcirc-CO- \right]$$

Kevlar and Twaron filaments are a translucent straw colour and have a diameter of 0.012 mm, but this size is too small for practical use. The material is commercially available in the form of multifilament yarns of varying size and with a range of finishes. Woven fabric, rovings and staple fibre are also available. Most test results are quoted for 1000 filament yarns, and care is needed when comparing test results to distinguish carefully between filament and yarn results.

Technora is a co-polymer, made up of two monomer units. One is the same as the other fibres, while the other (diaminodiphenyl ether) contains an extra benzene ring, giving co-poly-(*p*-phenylene/3,4'-diphenyl ether terephthalamide) with the structure:[2]

$$\left[\left(-NH-\bigcirc-NH- \right)_m - \left(-NH-\bigcirc-O-\bigcirc-NH- \right)_n - \left(CO-\bigcirc-CO \right)_n \right]$$

The object of the change is to make possible the use of general organic solvents, rather than the concentrated sulphuric acid used in the original process. The solvent used is *N*-methyl-pyroridone (NMP), and the amorphous polymer is spun into a coagulating bath, and then drawn. Significantly, it is believed that the crystallization takes place after the spinning process, but before drawing. It is claimed that this means that, although the degree of crystallinity is similar in the two fibres, in Kevlar and Twaron the boundaries between the crystals occur in groups, giving a weaker area of amorphous material, whereas in Technora the crystal boundaries are arranged randomly throughout the fibre.[6]

Development of aramid fibres has not yet finished. Refinements of the production process will be made in an attempt to improve the quality of the product, with associated enhancements of both strength and stiffness. At the same time, different chemical structures are also being considered, with a variety of different chemical groups being placed between the aromatic rings. The best properties have been reported for aromatic heterocyclic polymers;[1,2] polybenzobisoxazole (PBO) has been produced with a strength of 3400 N mm^{-2} and a stiffness of 340 kN mm^{-2}. These particular fibres are only available in small quantities, and the costs are such that their use is restricted to very specialist applications at present.

44.4 Properties of aramid yarns

The properties possessed by aramid yarns are summarized below. Some of the descriptions are relative to the properties of other fibres, rather than to the properties of metals, but they serve as a starting point for more detailed consideration of the materials:

(1) high tensile strength;
(2) high stiffness;
(3) high specific strength;
(4) low density;
(5) low creep;
(6) finite life when subjected to high stresses;
(7) excellent longitudinal tensile fatigue performance;
(8) good shock-loading performance;
(9) poor compressive strength;
(10) moderate abrasion resistance;
(11) good chemical resistance;
(12) poor ultraviolet resistance;
(13) resistance to high temperature;
(14) relatively good thermal stability; and
(15) electrical non-conductivity.

Kevlar has been in production since 1972, and the other fibres were produced soon after, so their properties are well documented. There appears to be considerable inconsistency in the results reported in the literature, however, owing to:

(1) confusion over the particular type and grade of aramid studied;
(2) the lack of differentiation between filaments, yarns, and ropes;
(3) the adoption of a multiplicity of testing techniques; and

(4) use of a variety of measures, such as mean, minimum or characteristic values, for quantities which are variable.

For these reasons, therefore, some care needs to be taken in interpreting the published test data.

The detailed accounts of Kevlar properties given by Du Pont[7–9] and by a number of authors[10–14] have all originated from Du Pont laboratories or are based on Du Pont published data and more consistency in the results reported in these references is observed. A recent monograph[2] contains a thorough review of Kevlar and Technora properties, together with those of other aromatic high-strength fibres.

44.4.1 Tensile properties

The tensile properties of aramid yarn and alternative reinforcement materials are shown in *Table 44.1*; the specific strength of the aramids is greater than for any other commercially available fibre, apart from carbon fibres. This makes them very suitable for weight-sensitive applications, such as in the aerospace industry. Aramids also have an initial tensile strength greater than steel and a longitudinal stiffness of the same order.

Approximate stress–strain curves for the aramids are virtually linear and display negligible plastic deformation prior to failure as shown in *Figure 44.1*.

44.4.2 Creep

The creep of aramid fibres is generally considered to be a logarithmic function of time; creep rates are low when compared with other synthetic fibres such as nylon or polyester and they approach that of steel. Early work[15] indicated that the creep rates for yarns of Kevlar are fairly insensitive to loads between 20% and 50% of the ultimate load but that they decrease at lower loads. Creep rates of 0.02% and 0.052% per decade were observed at room temperature for Kevlar 49 and Kevlar 29,

Table 44.1 Comparative tensile properties*

	Ultimate tensile strength (N mm^{-2})	Strain at ultimate (%)	Initial modulus (kN mm^{-2})	Specific gravity	Specific strength†
Aramids					
Kevlar 149	2410	1.4	146	1.47	1.64
Kevlar 49	2900	1.9	120	1.44	1.92
Kevlar 29	2900	3.7	58	1.44	1.92
Twaron	2800	3.3	80	1.44	1.94
Twaron HM	2800	2.0	115	1.45	1.93
Technora	3100	4.4	71	1.39	2.23
Non-aramids					
Nylon	990	18.3	6	1.14	0.87
Polyester	1120	14.3	14	1.38	0.81
E-Glass	2500	4.0	70	2.6	0.96
S-Glass	4600	5.5	85	2.5	1.84
Carbon fibre	2200–5400	0.4–1.8	238–444	1.76–1.9	1.13–3.00
PBO	3400	1.0	340	1.5	2.27
Boron fibre	3150	0.8	379	2.49	1.27
Mild steel	300	20.0	200	7.85	0.03
Prestressing steel	1700	1.6	200	7.85	0.22

* Figures in this table should be taken as a guide only. For most fibres, even more than for bulk materials, final properties are heavily dependent on the size of the fibre and the exact details of the production process, as the wide range for carbon fibres makes clear.
† Specific strength = tensile strength/density.

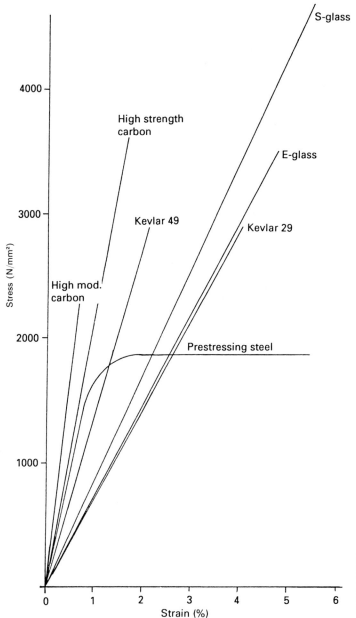

Figure 44.1 Typical stress–strain curves for aramid and some comparable alternative materials. Note that for most of these materials a wide spread of values can result from changes in details of the production process. Actual fibre tests show slight non-linearities in most cases

respectively (one decade is equivalent to one unit on a log time-scale to base 10).

Other workers have found that the rate of creep is stress dependent. Schaefgen[13] refers to work by Blades who observed a linear dependence of the creep rate with stress. Similarly, Ericksen[16,17] has found that the creep rate for Kevlar displays an increasing trend with stress. Considerable work has now been undertaken on long-term creep behaviour by Guimaraes,[5] who agreed with Blades; this is also in accordance with data published on Twaron.[18]

Work continues to extend the creep data available, but for all practical purposes it can be concluded that the creep strain over the lifetime of the structure in any application is unlikely to exceed 0.15%,[4] which is very small.

44.4.3 Stress rupture

When some materials are subjected to permanently applied loads they eventually creep to failure. This phenomenon is generally referred to as stress rupture. Considerable attention has been paid to the stress-rupture behaviour of Kevlar yarns.[19–21] In all cases it was found that Kevlar yarns would support a large proportion of their nominal short-term ultimate loadings for long periods of time, but that there was considerable variability in the stress-rupture lifetimes for any given load level.

The 'time-to-failure' under the dead-weight loading for aramids is superior to nylon and polyethylene[11] and by extrapolating the results of short-term stress-rupture tests on a logarithmic scale with time it has been suggested that yarns of

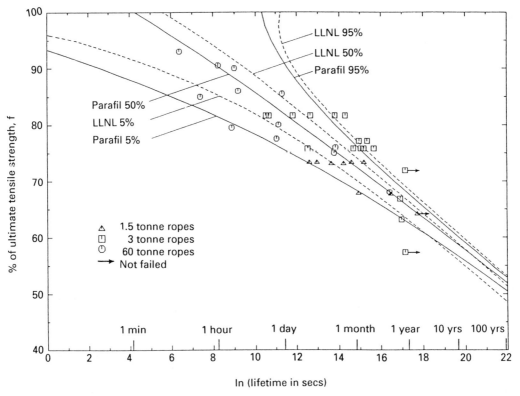

Figure 44.2 Stress-rupture data for parallel-lay aramid ropes (Parafil) made from Kevlar 49 yarn (taken from Guimaraes[5]). (——) 5%, 50% and 95% probabilities of failure based on rope tests; (– – – –) similar predictions based on Kevlar 49/epoxy composites at the Lawrence Livermore National Laboratory (LLNL)

aramid will support a load of half their breaking strength for over 100 years.

Considerable data have now been obtained for the stress-rupture behaviour of parallel-lay aramid ropes;[5,22,23] the most recent data[5] show that the mean load to give failure after 100 years is about 52% of the short-term breaking strength, and allowing for the variability of the material, it is predicted that a load of 46% of the initial breaking load will have only a 10^{-6} probability of failure after 100 years. Such figures indicate that stress rupture must be taken into account, but is unlikely to prevent the material's use in practical, long-term, applications. *Figure 44.2* shows 'time-to-break' against applied load for these ropes, and also theoretical predictions for longer term loads. The curves marked 'LLNL' refer to predictions[4] based on a large number of tests carried out at the Lawrence Livermore National Laboratory[19] on Kevlar/epoxy composite rods; the results compare well with the tests on the parallel-lay ropes.

44.4.4 Tension–tension fatigue

The fatigue performance of Kevlar has been studied,[10,11,24,25] although some of the studies were limited to the preproduction fibre PRD-49.[24] A summary of much of the research into fatigue is given in *Figure 44.3* where the fatigue performances of Kevlar and other reinforcement materials are indicated in the form of S–N curves which relate peak stress to the number of cycles which the material can withstand. The relative flatness of the S–N curves for Kevlar is an indication of the material's good fatigue performance.

The tension–tension fatigue resistance of Kevlar (when cycling

between a lower and a higher tensile force) is superior to steel. Indeed, a zero twist yarn of Kevlar 49 will run for 10 million cycles when stressed between 170 and 1700 N mm^{-2}, whereas the stresses for steel wire have to be confined to the range 100–1000 N mm^{-2} to produce failure after an equivalent number of cycles. As a result, some authors[11] have concluded that tensile fatigue is unlikely to be a limiting design criterion for typical applications of Kevlar.

There is some evidence that 'fatigue' is not a sensible measure of resistance to cyclic loads for many polymers. Tests,[26] made primarily on nylon fibres, have indicated that it was the total duration of the loading that was significant, not the number of cycles. Thus, 10 000 cycles at 10 Hz is as damaging to the fibres as 1000 cycles of the same amplitude at 1 Hz. A cumulative damage rule, based on creep-rupture data, may well prove to be the best criterion for estimating failure under cyclic loads. Some work was done in the same study on Kevlar 49, and similar results were obtained.

Tension–tension tests[27] and tension–bending tests[28] on parallel-lay aramid ropes have also shown good fatigue properties when the fibres are assembled into practical elements.

44.4.5 Impact and shock-loading resistance

The breaking strengths for Kevlar at high loading rates are comparable to, or slightly higher than, those at normal rates;[11] the energy absorption at failure in Kevlar is about half that in nylon, while the repeated shock loading of a Kevlar rope (up to 40% of its nominal breaking strength) resulted in only a 13% reduction in strength after 100 000 cycles. In addition, Kevlar 29 and Kevlar 49 have performed well in typical ballistic

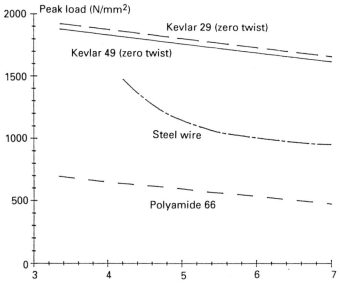

Figure 44.3 *S–N* curve for tension–tension fatigue fracture of Kevlar yarn. (Redrawn from Ferer and Swenson[11])

Logarithm of the number of cycles to failure

applications, and are widely used to manufacture bullet-proof clothing.

Kevlar may be prone to shock damage, however, if subjected to a sudden release of tension.[29,30] The rapid 'snap-back' probably produces a compressive wave and so the damage may possibly be attributed to Kevlar's weak compressive strength (q.v.).

These results and extensions to practical applications depend on the structure of the material; rope structure (parallel, braided or laid), or the presence of an epoxy matrix, will have a significant effect.

44.4.6 Compressive strength

The compressive strength of Kevlar is likely to be of importance when it is incorporated into a rigid composite, typically with epoxy resin. The ratio of tensile strength to compressive strength is about 5:1.[11,31] This poor performance is apparently due to weak lateral cohesion between the rigid longitudinal molecular chains. Kink bands (which appear to represent a shear failure across the fibre, but in fact are caused by buckling of the individual elements of the fibre) were observed using scanning electron microscopy.[31]

Practical applications of aramids will normally aim to use aramid fibres aggregated into larger elements, and to make use of the tensile strength of the fibres. Compressive stresses will only normally be developed in the terminations of such elements. Parallel-lay ropes are normally anchored by means of a termination which relies on compressive forces being developed across the fibres; these are kept at a sufficiently low and reliable anchorages have been formed in this way.[32]

44.4.7 Abrasion resistance

The moderate abrasion resistance of aramids may be a potential limitation in some applications;[25] indeed, in their raw state, it is inferior to that of nylon or polyester. However, the abrasion performance of aramid yarns can be improved considerably by the use of yarn finishes (special coatings, usually oil based) and when a combination of yarn twist, epoxy impregnation and wax

overlay is adopted. As a result, all manufacturers now produce yarns with alternative finishes. A 'standard' finish is often applied to aid yarn processing, while for rope and cable applications, where abrasion performance is especially important, a special high lubricity finish is available. For applications such as the strength element in fibre optic cables, yarns with no applied finish can be supplied.

44.4.8 Chemical and environmental resistance

The chemical resistance of aramid is outstanding except for prolonged exposure to some strong mineral acids and alkalis. Teijin claim that the resistance of their co-polymer fibre Technora is significantly better than that of the single-polymer fibres, due to the different manufacturing process, which leaves much smaller areas of amorphous material through which chemicals can penetrate.

The rate of hydrolytic degradation at 100% relative humidity at room temperature, has been estimated to be less than 1% per year,[33] and no significant loss in tensile strength is reported for both Kevlar 29 and Kevlar 49 after three years exposure to seawater.[15] All aramids are degraded substantially, however, when subjected to sources of ultraviolet radiation, (e.g. sunlight); there is some self-screening for the bulkier products but, nevertheless, external jacketing is recommended for maximum durability.

A study of the 'ageing' of Kevlar in various environments confirmed that the loss of strength is small when Kevlar is exposed to seawater and a variety of chemicals.[34]

44.4.9 Temperature effects

Only small reductions in the tensile strength of Kevlar are observed[7,8] up to a temperature of 180°C. Beyond this temperature, however, significant reductions in strength are recorded. *Figure 44.4* illustrates the thermal stability of Kevlar 49 when exposed to elevated temperatures up to 250°C for prolonged periods.[8] Despite the strength loss at high temperatures, aramids do not melt or support combustion;[35] indeed,

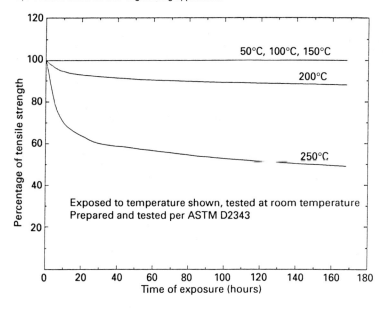

Figure 44.4 Effect of prolonged high temperature on strength of Kevlar 49 yarns. (Redrawn from Du Pont[8])

the material may be described as flame-retardant and self-extinguishing.

At cryogenic temperatures ($-170°C$) the material does not embrittle or lose its properties. In fact, under arctic conditions a slight increase in the tensile strength and modulus of Kevlar has been observed[10] and good resistance to thermal shock ($-196°C$ to $+196°C$) is reported.[34]

The thermal expansion of Kevlar 49 yarns has been studied when subjected to stress.[5] It was found that, not only did the material contract as the temperature increased, as do many polymers, but the coefficient of linear thermal expansion became more negative as the stress level increased. However, it was also found that the thermal conductivity was very low, and this may explain why tests aimed at determining the thermal expansion of ropes made from Kevlar have detected much smaller changes in length.[36]

44.5 Applications

The properties of the aramid fibres clearly makes them suitable for many applications. All the manufacturers produce a range of literature describing the uses to which the material may be put. Many of these applications are obvious ones for high-strength fibres, for example in fabrics and nets. The high stiffness and low creep of the fibres means that they are now used in high-performance yacht sails, where the shape has to be maintained under a variety of wind conditions. The good resistance to shock loads, as well as the light weight, strength and stiffness also means that the fibres are widely used in personnel protection clothing, such as bullet-proof vests.

Aramid fibres are frequently used as reinforcement for rubber, in tyres, webbing and conveyor belts. An increasing use is as a resin-based composite for the aerospace industry. Quite extensive experience has been built up with non-load-bearing panels, and now structural panels are being incorporated in modern aircraft. The fibres can be used in the form of continuous yarns, or as chopped filaments, in which form the components can be formed in injection moulding or extrusion moulding machines.

For applications where larger forces are required, the fibres have to be aggregated into larger units. Traditionally, the way this has been done, for conventional fibres, is in the form of ropes which are braided or twisted together. Such ropes have also been made from aramid yarns and are quite widely used in the marine and offshore industries, where the high strength and low creep are desirable properties.[25,37] Many forms of rope construction are used, including composite ropes in which aramid fibres provide the strength to an electrical or optical fibre conductor.

For civil and structural engineering, a number of applications can be considered. These will be considered in more detail below. A summary of proposed applications for aramids, which includes both construction and other applications, is given in *Table 44.2*.

44.5.1 Applications in civil and structural engineering

Civil and structural engineering applications differ from many of the other applications in several ways. The loads are generally higher, with forces to be resisted of the order of tens, if not hundreds, of tonnes. The loads are often of long duration (years not hours), and long-term stiffness (including both elastic stiffness and creep effects) is very often the governing criterion. To be effective, the yarns need to be aggregated together into a sufficiently large unit to apply a significant force. Several methods of achieving this will be considered in more detail below.

44.5.1.1 Pultruded sections

Pultruded sections are produced by drawing fibres through a die (of appropriate shape) in which resin is injected. A variety of fibres can be used, including glass, carbon and aramid. Many cross-sections are possible, including I-beams, box-beams and special sections for particular applications. In addition to the shape, the designer can choose the type of fibre to use, which need not be the same in different parts of the section. Thus, it is possible to have a section with aramid fibres in the tension zone and carbon fibres in the compression zone, where the aramid fibres would be unsuitable. It is also possible to use woven tapes with fibres at specified angles, to give resistance to shearing forces. Most civil engineering applications to date have used glass fibres,[38] but specialist pultrusions with aramid fibres are also likely to be used commercially soon.

These sections are relatively easy to produce, but the principal

Table 44.2 Applications of aramids and aramid composites

Ropes and cables	*Structural engineering*
Mooring lines	Pultruded beams
Guy ropes	Reinforcement for concrete
Balloon tethers	Prestressing tendons
Oil rig risers	Stay cables for bridges
Tensioner lines	
Pendant lines	
Electromechanical cables	
Aircraft/aerospace	*Automotive*
Panels, flooring	Car body panels
Escape slides	Truck chassis beams
Pressure vessels	(hybrid with carbon fibre)
Rocket motor cases	Brake linings
Propellor and helicopter blades	Clutch facings
Parachutes	Gaskets
	Hoses and belts
	Belts in tyres
Industrial	*Personnel protection*
Conveyor belts	Bullet-proof body armour
Tarpaulins	Flak-jackets
Chemical hoses	Helmets
Ventilation ducts	Work gloves
Rotor vanes	Nuclear shelters
Marine	*Sporting goods*
Boat hulls	Hockey sticks
Rigging	Tennis racquets
Canoes	Golf clubs
Coated fabrics	Fishing rods
Sails	Skis

problem for the structural applications is the difficulty of jointing such sections into structural assemblies; this is proportionally more difficult for aramids than for the weaker glass fibres. Such details are beyond the scope of this chapter, but can be found elsewhere.[39]

44.5.1.2 Reinforcing fibres for concrete

There has been considerable work carried out on the use of synthetic fibres for reinforcing concrete, and some of this work has included the use of aramid fibres.[40–42] However, for a variety of reasons, they are not suitable for this application. One of the few environments that cause degradation of aramid fibres is strongly alkaline aqueous solutions, and this is just the situation in a concrete mix. Even when the concrete has cured and most of the free water has evaporated, it is still likely that the environment will remain aggressive to the fibres. The different structure of Technora fibres, which may make them less permeable to hydroxide ions, is likely to mean that they are more resistant to this form of attack than Kevlar; indeed, floor slabs in office blocks in Japan have been built with concrete reinforced in this way.

As with all synthetic fibres, however, the benefits in using them to *reinforce* concrete are marginal, since concrete cracks at about 100 $\mu\varepsilon$, at which strain aramid fibres are carrying less than 1% of their breaking load.[43] There is some evidence that synthetic fibres assist in reducing cracking in concrete, probably as a result of the prevention of micro-cracking during hardening. It is unlikely that the strength, stiffness or resistance to creep of aramid fibres would offer significant advantages over cheaper fibres such as polypropylene, so this is unlikely to be a practical application of aramids.

44.5.1.3 Reinforcing cages for concrete

An interesting product has been tested recently in Japan, and is starting to come into experimental use in practical applications.[41,44] The aim is to make a preformed reinforcing cage for concrete, using straight longitudinal aramid fibres, with looped fibres in both the vertical and horizontal directions to resist shearing forces. The whole assembly is sprayed with epoxy resin to prevent the alkaline cement coming into contact with the fibres, and to give it some rigidity for handling purposes; the appearance of the cage is like three-dimensional knitting.

Three-dimensional grids for reinforcing beams, and two-layer grids for reinforcing slabs have been produced. The cages would only allow 10-mm aggregate to be used, and the difficulty of placing concrete in the confined spaces must be considered. However, these considerations are probably matters of site practice that can be overcome.

Test results produced for this system show that it has considerable promise as a reinforcing material, although more test data are required before it can be regarded as a suitable material for general use, particularly as regards its resistance to cracking at relatively low loads.

44.5.1.4 Pretensioning bars for concrete

Two manufacturers are producing pretensioning tendons for prestressed concrete using pultruded aramid fibres in a resin matrix. Akzo produce Arapree using the high-modulus version of Twaron, while Teijin produce AFRP (aramid fibre reinforced plastic) rod using Technora. Both systems reflect the properties of their constituent fibres.

Arapree is usually used in the form of flat strips,[45] and has been used as pretensioning tendons in the vertical posts of noise barriers on a Dutch motorway (shown in *Figure 44.5*), and in prestressed floor planks in an experimental 'house of the future' that has been constructed in Holland to demonstrate a variety of new engineering techniques. As with all pretensioning tendons, the system relies on bond between the concrete and the tendon, which must reflect the properties of the resin matrix,

Figure 44.5 Noise barrier posts pretensioned with Arapree tendons. (Courtesy of Akzo)

rather than the fibres. An external anchor, which relies on two flat wedges gripping the sides of the strip, is used to tension the tendons, and could also be used for a permanent end anchorage.

One of the problems with such pultruded systems is that the fibres, and hence the tendons, are brittle. If the tendon is fully bonded to the concrete, the tendon must undergo the same strain changes as the concrete, which in areas of high bending could produce failure of the tendon and hence brittle failure of the complete structure. Experiments are known to be underway to control the amount of bond between the tendons and the concrete by varying the texture of the surface and properties of the resin.[46]

AFRP rods are normally in the form of circular bars with diameters between 3 and 8 mm, although a flat strip version is also produced. They are designed to be used as bundles and the manufacturers have developed wedge systems to anchor the bars to a terminal, but they can also use resin mortar to bond the tendons to the end block. Experimental beams have been constructed, but it is not believed that any practical applications have been produced. These rods could also be used as pretensioning tendons in the same way that Arapree is used.

44.5.1.5 Parallel lay ropes (Parafil)

The final method for the use of aramids in civil engineering is in the parallel-lay rope; one such product (Parafil) has been developed by Linear Composites Ltd.

In conventional braided or twisted rope construction, individual fibres follow very complicated three-dimensional paths along the rope. This leads to a significant reduction in the axial stiffness of the rope; effective moduli can be as low as 30% of the fibre modulus. In structural applications, which are often stiffness governed, such reductions in properties would be unacceptable.

This problem can be overcome by the use of parallel-lay ropes, which consist of a large number of parallel yarns of the core material; since they are not twisted or braided in any way, they must be contained within a sheath of some form to maintain integrity. In the case of Parafil (*Figure 44.6*), this sheath is usually a low-modulus polyethylene. A variety of core yarns can be used in these ropes; the original ropes used polyester fibres, and were designed for mooring buoys in very deep water; they have also been used extensively for the stays on radio antennae.[32] With the advent of the aramid fibres, new versions of the ropes have been produced to exploit the higher strength and stiffness of these fibres.

The properties of the rope mirror those of the core yarns. Since every fibre in the core is effectively straight and continuous from end to end of the rope, the strength, stiffness, creep, relaxation and thermal properties of the ropes are virtually the same as those of the core yarns. The yarns are, however, slightly variable, and since any individual yarn will fail when the strain in the rope reaches the failure strain of that yarn, it is found that assemblies of variable fibres are not as strong as the mean strength of the fibres themselves. Such a result, which is adequately predicted by bundle theory,[47,48,64] leads to a quoted strength for the Parafil ropes of 1926 N mm^{-2}, as compared with about 2700 N mm^{-2} for the multi-filament yarns and about 3500 N mm^{-2} for the individual filaments themselves. Small ropes (i.e. <6 tonne breaking load) are stronger than this,[49] but the quoted strength is applicable for all large ropes that have been tested (up to 1500 tonne).

The termination system that has been developed for the ropes consists of an internal wedge (or spike) which provides a radial gripping force between the spike and the external body, so that all the fibres are anchored.[32] The length of the spike can be chosen to ensure that the transverse stresses are within the capacity of the fibres. As with the rope itself, there is no need to introduce resin anywhere in the termination. Many tests have

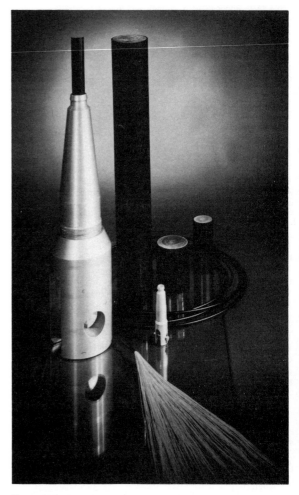

Figure 44.6 Parafil ropes and terminations. Largest rope shown is 140 mm in diameter with a breaking load at 1500 tonne. (Courtesy of Linear Composites Ltd)

been carried out on the rope fitted with this type of termination, and in virtually all cases failure occurs within the body of the rope, indicating that the termination can develop the full strength of the rope.

Once the load has been transmitted from the fibres to the terminal body, further connection to the structure can be made by fitting a variety of devices, such as clevis pins, anchorage plates, or whatever is required. *Figure 44.7* shows such a terminal modified for use as a prestressing tendon.[50] The terminal body has two threaded regions; the inner thread is used for connection to a pull rod which is attached to the jack during stressing, while the outer thread is used to provide a connection for a permanent back nut, which also allows some adjustment to take account of slack. The anchorage is capable of achieving the full strength of the rope. Reasonable care must be taken to ensure that the spike is fitted centrally within the rope (to ensure even load sharing between fibres), but otherwise no special skills are needed.[51] Anchorages for parallel-lay aramid ropes with capacities between 1 and 1500 tonne have been provided using this system. All the results quoted here have been obtained on ropes fitted with anchorages in this way.

It is normal practice, where practicable, to preload the rope to ensure that the central spike is fully drawn into the

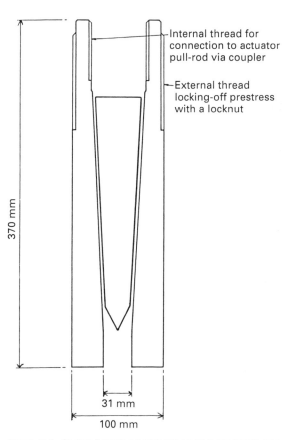

Internal thread for
connection to actuator
pull-rod via coupler

External thread
locking-off prestress
with a locknut

370 mm

31 mm

100 mm

Figure 44.7 Section through a terminal for a 60 tonne Parafil rope,
modified for connection to a jack for use in prestressing tendons

Figure 44.8 Circumferential external prestressing using Parafil
ropes at the top of a cooling tower at Thorpe Marsh Power Station.
(Courtesy of Central Electricity Generating Board)

termination. This makes sure that no subsequent movement
occurs in the termination, either on loading or unloading.

The ropes are versatile, and can be made with breaking loads
from about 1 tonne up to several thousand tonnes. Thus, a
variety of applications can be considered where it is required to
carry a concentrated tensile force by a mechanism which offers
a combination of high stiffness, low weight, high durability or
insulating and non-magnetic properties.

Clearly, prestressed concrete, particularly with external tendons, is such an application, and a variety of test beams have
been produced[4,5,65] (*Figure 44.8*). In all cases, failure occurred in
the concrete, rather than in the tendons, since the unbonded
geometry means that the tendons do not pick up significant
additional strain. Quite large cracks can open up in the concrete,
producing a composite material with an ability to absorb large
amounts of energy.

One application of Parafil that typifies its potential, both for
use as external prestressing and for repair of concrete, is the
repair of faulty cooling towers at Thorpe Marsh power station
in Yorkshire.[52] These towers were built in the early 1960s, but
were recently found to have major cracks at the top. One tower
had two vertical cracks, 12 m long and approximately 60 mm
wide, which descended from the top ring beam. The towers were
repaired by resin injection of the cracks, followed by circumferential prestressing of the towers with Parafil tendons, as
shown in *Figure 44.9*. The aramid tendons were beneficial in
several ways, since alternative steel tendons would have been
too heavy for installation by steeple-jacks, and the exposed
environment would have meant either extensive corrosion
protection, or the use of very expensive stainless-steel tendons.

Many other applications, to a variety of structural problems,
are under active consideration.[52] These typically relate to cases
where steel is unsuitable because it corrodes (such as in external
prestressing,[53] and repair of existing structures), where inspection
is impossible (such as in ground anchors and other foundation
structures), or in cases where the electromagnetic properties of
steel are unacceptable (such as in communications antennae and
certain defence applications). Although the weight of the tension
elements is rarely a governing factor in conventional prestressed
concrete structures, the low density is also important when
considering the tension members in lightweight structures,[54] and
becomes a governing factor in mooring lines for deep-water oil
exploration rigs[55] and in the suspension cables for very long
span bridges.[56]

Recent surveys of the stay cables in bridges[57,58] have shown
that steel cables are very likely to corrode, and the failure of
steel tendons in bridges[59] where they are supposedly well
protected by the alkaline environment provided by concrete
shows that existing structures may have serious problems.
Moves towards realistic 'whole-life costing' for bridge structures
are likely to mean that apparently more expensive aramid cables
become cost effective in the long term.

It is possible to envisage new forms of solution to existing
problems that become possible with the use of aramid tension
members. Many of our preconceptions of the way structures
should be designed come from the need to protect steel members
from corrosion. Thus, we embed prestressing tendons in
concrete, especially in marine environments, but open structures
in which sea- or ground-water are free to flow around the
prestressing tendons can easily be envisaged. Similarly, we can
consider prestressed brickwork, with the tendons in voids within
the structure, or, in the case of retaining walls, even in the backfill
behind the walls. Ground anchors can also be designed without
the need to make large allowances of sacrificial material to allow
for corrosion.

Very long span suspension bridges are also likely to be a
suitable use for these new materials. It has been concluded[60]
that spans of 3 km or so were possible using steel suspension
cables, but that for larger spans aramid cables of the Parafil
type would be necessary, since the high density of steel means
that for very large spans much of the strength of the steel is taken
up supporting its own weight. The current longest single span
is the Humber Bridge (1.4 km), but the Akashi bridge in Japan
on which work has just begun will have a span of 1.9 km.
However, it is reported that extreme difficulties were experienced

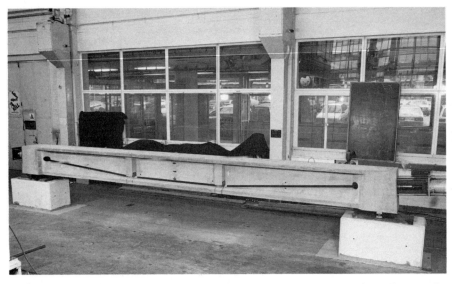

Figure 44.9 Concrete beam with a span of 8 m, prestressed with two 60 tonne Parafil ropes. (Courtesy of Imperial College)

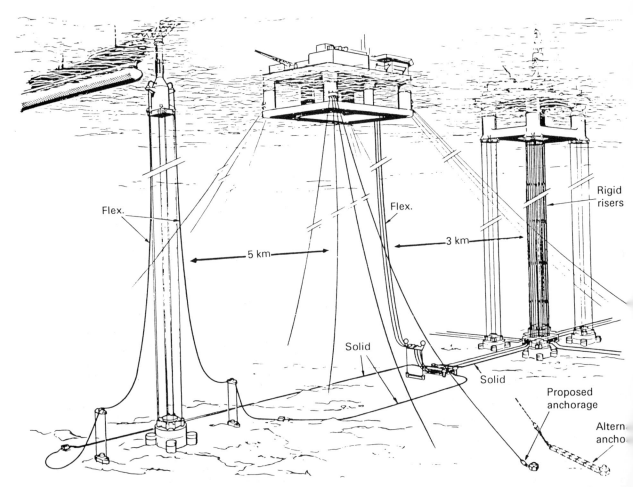

Figure 44.10 Possible configuration for offshore oil production installation in very deep water, using parallel-lay aramid ropes as tethers and anchoring ropes

in getting suitable steel for the main cables,[61] and special products had to be designed, so it is possible that the true 'break-even' point where aramid fibres will become competitive is at spans below 3 km.

A number of problems will have to be overcome for very large spans, but these relate to the aerodynamic stability of the structure, and would be a problem for any material used in long spans. It is possible that designs for large-span suspension bridges will incorporate an element of self-stressing, in which one cable is tensioned against another, or possibly the use of a number of draped cables, so that no deformation of the structure is possible without inducing direct tension in at least one of the supporting cables.[62]

In very deep water the difficulties of anchoring large platforms for exploration or production of oil have been recognized. In water depths of up to 500 m it is possible to design jacket structures which stand on the sea-bed, but in larger water depths, where exploration is now beginning, the structures will have to float. It has been concluded that steel tethers are simply too heavy for large water depths, since the platform would have to have a large amount of buoyancy simply to support the weight of the anchoring system.[55] Aramid tendons using Parafil ropes, which are almost weightless in water, provide a means of anchoring such structures in a manner which is almost independent of the water depth. A recent study has concluded that the tendons can be produced in a mobile factory on-shore, but close to the desired location. Complete anchorage assemblies can then be produced and floated into position, giving very rapid hook-up of the floating structure to the sea-bed facilities.[63] This offers considerable savings in installation costs, which is very often one of the most difficult things to control in offshore operations. *Figure 44.10* shows a number of different concepts that have been considered for the mooring of a variety of platform types in very deep water.

44.6 Conclusion

Aramid fibres have a very remarkable set of properties, which will make them suitable for many applications in a variety of fields. With strengths similar to cold drawn steel, stiffnesses of the same order and with good resistance to corrosion, we can expect to see these materials being adopted in many ways in the future, either as fibres, pultrusions or parallel-lay ropes.

References

1 REISCH, M. S., 'High performance fibres find expanding military, industrial uses', *Chem. Eng. News*, **65**, 9–14 (1987)
2 YANG, H. M., *Aromatic High-Strength Fibers*, Wiley, New York (1989)
3 JOHNSON, D. J., 'High performance organic fibres', in Happey, F. (ed.), *Applied Fibre Science*, Academic Press, London, Vol. 3, pp. 138–149 (1979)
4 CHAMBERS, J. J., 'Parallel-lay aramid ropes for use as tendons in prestressed concrete', Ph.D. Thesis, University of London (1986)
5 GUIMARAES, G. B., 'Parallel-lay aramid ropes for use in structural engineering', Ph.D. Thesis, University of London (1989)
6 TASHIRO, K., NAKATA, Y., LI, T., KOBAYASHI, M., CHATANI, Y. and TADOKORO, H., 'Structure and thermomechanical properties of high-modulus aramide copolymers. (I) An annealing effect on structure', *Sen-I Gakkaisha*, **43**, 627–636 (1987)
7 DU PONT, 'Characteristics and uses of Kevlar 29 aramid', *Bulletin No. 375*, E.I. Du Pont de Nemours and Co. (Inc.), Wilmington (1976)
8 DU PONT, 'Characteristics and uses of Kevlar 49 aramid high modulus organic fibres', *Bulletin No. K-5*, E.I. Du Pont de Nemours and Co. (Inc.), Wilmington (1981)
9 DU PONT, 'High Modulus Kevlar "HM"', *Preliminary Data Sheet*, E.I. Du Pont de Nemours and Co. (Inc.), Wilmington
10 FERER, K. M. and SWENSON, R. C., 'Aramid fibre for use as oceanographic strength members', *Report No. 8040*, Naval Research Laboratory, Washington, DC (1976)
11 WILFONG, R. E. and ZIMMERMAN, J., 'Strength and durability characteristics of Kevlar aramid fibre', *Journal of Applied Polymer Science: Applied Polymer Symposium*, **31**, 1–21 (1977)
12 SCHAEFGEN, J. R., BAIR, T. I., BALLOU, J. W., KWOLEK, S. L., MORGAN, P. J., PANAR, M. and ZIMMERMAN, J., 'Rigid chain polymers: properties of solutions and fibres', in Ciferri, A. and Ward, I. M. (eds), *Ultra-high Modulus Polymers*, Applied Science Publishers, London, pp. 173–201 (1979)
13 SCHAEFGEN, J. R., 'Aramid fibres: structure, properties and applications', in Zachariades, A. E. and Porter, R. S. (eds), *The Strength and Stiffness of Polymers*, Marcel Dekker, New York, pp. 327–355 (1983)
14 O'HEAR, N., 'Offshore applications for ropes of Kevlar aramid fibre', *Conference on Offshore Applications*, International Wire and Machinery Association, Aberdeen (1983)
15 DU PONT, 'Properties and uses of Kevlar 29 and Kevlar 49 in electromechanical cables and fibre optics', *Bulletin No. K-506A*, E.I. Du Pont de Nemours and Co. (Inc.), Wilmington (1980)
16 ERICKSEN, R. H., 'Room temperature creep of Kevlar 49/epoxy composites', *Composites*, 189–194 (July 1976)
17 ERICKSEN, R. H., 'Creep of Kevlar 49 fibres', *Proc. 2nd Symp. on Failure Modes in Composites*, Metallurgical Society of AIME, New York, p. 302 (1984)
18 NORTHOLT, M. G., 'Structuur en mechanische eigenschappen von aramidevezel', *Nederlands Tydeschrift voor Natuurhunde*, **A50** (1984)
19 CHIAO, T. T., WELLS, J. E., MOORE, R. L. and HAMSTAD, M. A., 'Stress rupture behaviour of strands of an organic fibre/epoxy matrix', *Composite Materials: Testing and Design (3rd Conference)*, ASTM STP 546, American Society of Testing and Materials, pp. 209–224 (1974)
20 GLASER, R. E., MOORE, R. L. and CHIAO, T. T., 'Life estimation of aramid/epoxy composites under sustained tension', *Composites Technology Review*, **6**, 26–35 (1984)
21 HOWARD, A. and PARRATT, N. J., 'Life prediction for aromatic polyamide reinforcements', *Proceedings of the SAMPE Conference*, San Diego (1985)
22 CHAMBERS, J. J. and BURGOYNE, C. J., 'An experimental investigation of the stress-rupture behaviour of a parallel-lay aramid rope', *J. Mat. Sci.*, **25**, 3723–3730 (1990)
23 CHAMBERS, J. J., 'Long term properties of Parafil', in Burgoyne, C. J. (ed.), *Proc. Symp. on Engineering Applications of Parafil Ropes*, pp. 21–28, London (1988)
24 BUNSELL, A. R., 'The tensile and fatigue behaviour of Kevlar-49 (PRD-49) fibre', *J. Mat. Sci.*, **10**, 1300–1308 (1975)
25 HORN, M. H., RIEWALD, P. G. and ZWEBEN, C. H., 'Strength and durability characteristics of ropes and cables from Kevlar aramid fibres', *Proc. Oceans 77 Conference*, Marine Technology Society and IEEE, pp. 24E1–24E12 (1977)
26 KENNEY, M. C., MANDELL, J. F. and McGARRY, F. J., 'Fatigue behaviour of synthetic fibres, yarns, and ropes', *J. Mat. Sci.*, **20**, 2045–2059 (1985)
27 CRAWFORD, H. and McTERNAN, L. M., '"Fatigue" properties of Parafil', in Burgoyne, C. J. (ed.), *Proc. Symp. Engineering Applications of Parafil Ropes*, pp. 29–38, London (1988)
28 HOBBS, R. E. and BURGOYNE, C. J., 'Bending fatigue in high-strength fibre ropes', *Int. J. Fatigue*, **13**, 174–180 (1991)
29 BOURGAULT, T. P., 'Design and performance of a two-stage mooring for near surface measurements', *Proc. Marine Technology Society Oceans 76 Conference*, Washington, DC, pp. 14G1–14G8 (1976)
30 BOURGAULT, T. P., 'Effects of long-term tension on Kevlar ropes', M.S. Thesis, University of Rhode Island (1980)
31 DOBB, M. G., JOHNSON, D. J. and SAVILLE, B. P., 'Compressional behaviour of Kevlar fibres', *Polymer*, **22**, 960–965 (1981)
32 KINGSTON, D., 'Development of parallel fibre tensile members', in Burgoyne, C. J. (ed.), *Proc. Symp. Engineering Applications of Parafil Ropes*, pp. 7–11, London (1988)
33 MORGAN, R. J., PRUNEDA, C. O., BUTLER, N., KONG, F. M., COLEY, L. and MOORE, R. I., 'The hydrolytic

degradation of Kevlar 49 fibres', *Proc. SAMPE Meeting*, Reno, Nevada, pp. 891–900 (1984)

34 GOURDIN, C., 'Kevlar and Kevlar reinforced composites materials ageing under various environments', in Bunsell, A. R. *et al.* (eds), *Advances in Composite Materials*, Pergamon Press, Oxford, pp. 497–505 (1980)

35 PENN, L., 'Physicochemical properties of Kevlar 49 fiber', *J. Appl. Polym. Sci.*, **23**, 59–73 (1979)

36 AMINIAN, P. K., 'Dynamic characteristics of synthetic parallel filament cables', Ph.D. Thesis, University of London (1989)

37 O'HEAR, N., 'Ropes and cables of Kevlar', *4th Int. Offshore Craft Conference*, Thomas Reed Publications, Amsterdam (1980)

38 INSTITUTION OF STRUCTURAL ENGINEERS, 'Advanced composites in structural engineering', *First Report of Informal Study Group on Advanced Composite Materials* (1989)

39 HOLLAWAY, L. and BAKER, S., 'The development of nodal joints suitable for double layer skeletal systems from fibre/matrix composites', *3rd Int. Conf. on Space Structures*, Elsevier, Amsterdam, pp. 908–914 (1984)

40 HANNANT, D. J., *Fibre Cements and Fibre Concretes*, Wiley, New York (1978)

41 NAKAGAWA, H., AKIHAMA, S. and SUENAGA, T., 'Mechanical properties of various types of fibre reinforced concretes', *Int. Conf. on Recent Developments of Fibre Reinforced Cements and Concretes*, Cardiff (1989)

42 WALTON, P. L. and MAJUMDAR, A. J., 'Creep of Kevlar 49 fibre and a Kevlar 49-cement composite', *J. Mat. Sci.*, **18**, 2939–2946 (1983)

43 HOLLAWAY, L. and BURGOYNE, C. J., 'Further applications of polymer and polymer composites', in Hollaway, L. (ed.), *Polymer and Polymer Composites in Construction*, Thomas Telford, London pp. 247–272 (1990)

44 NAKAGAWA, H. and SUENAGA, T., 'Mechanical properties of three dimensional fabric reinforced concretes and their application to buildings', *First Japan Int. SAMPE Symposium*, Makuhari, Japan (1989)

45 GERRITSE, A. and SCHURHOFF, H. J., 'Prestressing with aramid tendons', *Proc. 10th FIP Congress*, New Delhi (1986)

46 DEN UIJL, J. A. and REINHARDT, H. W., 'Bond of uncoated and epoxy coated aramide strands to cement mortar', *Symposium on Plastics in Building*, Liege, Belgium (1984)

47 DANIELS, H. E., 'The statistical theory of the strength of bundles of threads', *Proc. R. Soc., Ser. A.*, **183**, 405–435 (1945)

48 PHOENIX, S. L., 'Stochastic strength and fatigue of fibre bundles', *Int. J. Fracture*, **14**, 327–344 (1978)

49 GUIMARAES, G. B., 'Short-term profiles of Parafil', in Burgoyne, C. J. (ed.), *Proc. Symp. Engineering Applications of Parafil Ropes*, London (1988)

50 BURGOYNE, C. J. and CHAMBERS, J. J., 'Prestressing with Parafil tendons', *Concrete*, **19**, 12–16 (1985)

51 BURGOYNE, C. J., 'Laboratory testing of Parafil ropes', *Les Materiaux Nouveaux Pour la Precontrainte et le Renforcement d'Ouvrages d'Art*, LCPC, Paris (1988)

52 BURGOYNE, C. J., 'Structural applications of Type G Parafil',

Proc. Symp. on Engineering Applications of Parafil Ropes, London (1988)

53 BURGOYNE, C. J., 'Properties of polyaramid ropes and implications for their use as external prestressing tendons', in Naaman, A. E. and Breen, J. E. (eds), *External Prestressing in Bridges*, American Concrete Institute SP-120, AMI, Detroit, pp. 107–124 (1990)

54 BURGOYNE, C. J., 'Polyaramid ropes for tension structures', *1st Int. Oleg Kerensky Memorial Conference on Tension Structures*, London (1988)

55 SALAMA, M. M., 'Lightweight materials for mooring lines of deepwater tension leg platforms', *Marine Technol.*, **21**, 234–241 (1984)

56 HAMER, M., 'Across the channel by 2000', *New Sci.*, **1454**, 16–19 (1985)

57 STAFFORD, D. G. and WATSON, S. C., 'A current world-condition survey of cable elements on stayed-girder bridges', *Proc. 1st Oleg Kerensky Memorial Conference on Tension Structures*, pp. 12/2–17/2, London (1988)

58 TILLY, G. P., 'Performance of bridge cables', *Proc. 1st Oleg Kerensky Memorial Conference on Tension Structures*, pp. 22/4–28/4, London (1988)

59 WOODWARD, R. J. and WILLIAMS, F. W., 'Collapse of Ynys-y-Gwas Bridge, West Glamorgan', *Proc. Inst. Civ. Eng.*, **84**, 635–670 (1988)

60 RICHMOND, B. and HEAD, P. R., 'Alternative materials in long span bridge structures', *Proc. 1st Oleg Kerensky Memorial Conference*, London (1988)

61 FERGUSON, H., 'Longest span in the world', *New Civil Eng.*, 18–19 (4 August 1988)

62 CHESTNUTT, B. J., JENNINGS, A. and BROWN, W. C., 'Stiffness characteristics of multicable suspension bridges', *Proc. Inst. Civil Eng.*, **85**, 31–48 (1988)

63 BAXTER, C., 'Uses of Parafil ropes for mooring offshore platforms', in Burgoyne, C. J. (ed.), *Proc. Symp. Engineering Applications of Parafil Ropes*, pp. 49–62, London (1988)

64 BURGOYNE, C. J. and FLORY, J. F., 'Length effects due to yarn variability in parallel-lay ropes', *MTS-90*, Washington, DC (1990)

65 BURGOYNE, C. J., GUIMARAES, G. B. and CHAMBERS, J. J., 'Tests on beams prestressed with unbounded polyaramid tendons', *Cambridge University Engineering Department Technical Report CUED/D-Struct/TR. 132* (1991)

Appendix

The following is a list of the trade names used in this chapter.

Nomex and Kevlar are trade names of E.I. Du Pont de Nemours.
Twaron is a trade name of Aramide Maatschappij vof.
Arapree is a trade name of Akzo and Hollandsche Beton Groep.
Technora is a trade name of Teijin.
Parafil is a trade name of Linear Composites Ltd.

45

Glass Reinforced Plastics

R H Andrews
Pemtech Associates Ltd

Contents

45.1 Introduction 45/3

45.2 What are GRP materials? 45/3

45.3 GRP constituent materials 45/6
    45.3.1 Resins 45/6
    45.3.2 Glass fibre reinforcements 45/7
    45.3.3 Complementary materials used in GRP
    moulding 45/8

45.4 Methods of manufacture of GRP construction
products 45/9
    45.4.1 Contact moulding, hand laminating, or
    hand/wet lay-up 45/9
    45.4.2 Spray moulding 45/10
    45.4.3 Mechanized moulding techniques 45/10

45.5 GRP as a structural material 45/11
    45.5.1 Stress/strain behaviour 45/11
    45.5.2 Creep 45/12
    45.5.3 Fatigue 45/12
    45.5.4 Safety factors 45/12
    45.5.5 Thermal properties 45/12
    45.5.6 Structural stiffening of GRP 45/12

45.6 Using and specifying GRP for construction 45/12
    45.6.1 Dimensional stability during manufacture 45/13
    45.6.2 Gelcoats, colours and texture 45/13
    45.6.3 Fire retardancy 45/13
    45.6.4 Erection, installation and fixing 45/14

Bibliography 45/15

45.1 Introduction

Glass reinforced plastic (GRP) materials are almost uniquely adaptable for use in construction and building because of their ease of mouldability, high specific strength, lightness in weight, impermeability, non-corrosive nature and the availability of almost infinite variations of colour and finish/texture. In particular, ease of mouldability, high strength and lightness in weight makes the production and handling of physically large products, from flat panels to complex shapes, possible.

Because of these properties these materials have been used in the construction of buildings for nearly 40 years, although the more visible architectural applications have generally grown since the early 1960s. It is also probably the case that architectural and aesthetic building applications of GRP have been developed and used in the UK more than in most other countries to date.

Over the same time period, GRP materials have also become widely used in civil engineering, particularly in sewage and effluent control products, water storage and distribution, 'tanking' and a great variety of situations where corrosion resistance, impermeability and chemical/environmental resistance is important.

These materials have also become well established over many years as a concrete shuttering/forming medium, particularly where complex shapes and intricate details are required. Also commonly, GRP is used for permanent/*in situ* formwork, often facilitating the use of good decorative external GRP finishes to cement and concrete structures.

More recent materials developments in the area of GRP and 'composites' has led to rapidly increasing interest in these materials for more highly stressed and/or specialized civil engineering applications for which GRP materials may not have been considered entirely suitable in the past.

From all the above it is clear that GRP materials are of considerable importance in construction, building and civil engineering across a wide spectrum of applications from the relatively simple functional or largely decorative uses through varying combinations of structural and aesthetic importance, to entirely functional, relatively highly stressed and largely non-aesthetic situations.

Examples of well established GRP applications include:

(1) architectural forms and features, domes, arches, etc.;
(2) external cladding panels and systems;
(3) geodesic structures;
(4) translucent profiled and flat sheeting;
(5) fascias, feature mullions, transoms, etc.;
(6) gutters, downpipes and rainwater systems;
(7) dormer windows;
(8) rooflights, roof panels, mansards, etc.;
(9) feature window and door surrounds;
(10) balconies/balustrades;
(11) canopies, columns, supports, etc.;
(12) decorative and simulated features of all types including coving, cornices, etc.;
(13) plant rooms and enclosures;
(14) modular building and kiosk systems;
(15) walkways;
(16) water storage tanks and cisterns;
(17) septic tanks, sewage services, digesters, etc.;
(18) underground pipe, conduit and duct systems;
(19) concrete formwork of all types; and
(20) 'site applied' GRP linings/membranes, etc.

This list is by no means exhaustive. Examples of the use of GRP are shown in *Figures 45.1* to *45.6*.

The purpose of this chapter is to provide a broad outline of the nature and application of GRP materials and their means of application, including the key considerations of materials selection, specifications, aesthetic and structural design, and important manufacturing considerations. In addition, reference is made to site 'suitability for purpose', including handling, installation and durability considerations.

A comparison of the mechanical properties of GRP laminates and those of other structural materials is given in *Table 45.1*.

45.2 What are GRP materials?

GRP materials as normally used in the construction industry consist of 'syrupy' resins which are applied in layers to a moulding surface, together with alternating layers of glass fibre reinforcement which is usually in the form of a 'mat' of chopped strands. By means of a chemical reaction induced by a previously 'mixed in' catalyst/hardener, the resin then cures/hardens irreversibly (thus, the resin is of a 'thermosetting' nature, unlike 'thermoplastic' materials which are generally capable of being re-melted). When removed from the moulding surface, the GRP product is thus a substantially rigid glass fibre reinforced resin moulding/laminate. This simplistic description of GRP constituent materials and product manufacture will be elaborated upon in rather more detail later. However, it is important to draw attention to the fact that, in most construction industry applications, a first/external layer of resin 'gelcoat', unreinforced with glass fibres, is applied to the mould to give enhanced protection, appearance, weathering and wear properties to the moulding.

In practice in construction, the overwhelming proportion of GRP products have so far been made from glass fibre reinforced polyester resin. However, epoxide (epoxy) resins are occasionally used and phenolic resins are now being increasingly used,

Table 45.1 The mechanical properties of GRP laminates compared with those of other structural materials*

| Material | Grade | Specific gravity | Elastic modulus (GPa) | Proof strength | | Impact stength (kJ m^{-2}) | Specific strength (MPa) | Specific modulus (GPa) |
				Tensile (MPa)	Compressive (MPa)			
Mild steel	BS 15	7.8	207	240	240	50	31	27
Aluminium alloy	HE15WP	2.7	69	417	417	25	154	26
Stainless steel	316	7.92	193	241	241	1356	30	24
CSM/polyester	33†	1.47	8	80	120	75	54	5
Unidirectional GRP	82†	2.16	53	900	450	250	417	25

* Courtesy of Scott Bader Co. Ltd.
† Glass content by weight.

Figure 45.1 GRP wall cladding (Courtesy of Polystructures (Contracts) Ltd)

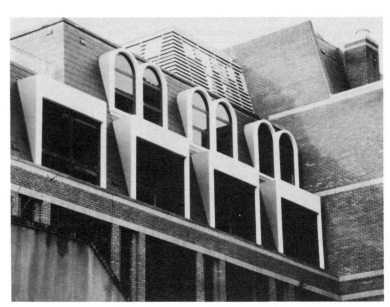

Figure 45.2 GRP feature/dormer window surrounds (Courtesy of Duroy Glassfibre Mouldings)

particularly for internal and underground area/tunnel locations. In addition, other resins and plastics, even thermoplastic matrices, may be used more in specialist construction applications in the future.

Fibres other than glass fibres are used for GRP-like applications, and this trend is now accelerating with developments in carbon fibres, aramid fibres, etc. Synthetic fibres that have been used in construction applications to date are of thermoplastic polyester, acrylic and polypropylene for pipe linings, specialist panels and rooflights, etc.

The newer carbon and aramid fibres are often used in conjunction with glass fibres and, to avoid needless confusion, it should be noted that these 'advanced composites' developments together with the use of thermoplastic matrices are currently costly and more likely to be used for 'high-tech' engineering, aerospace and specialist applications in which

finished product volume/weight are of more critical importance than is usually the case in construction.

As a result of the continuing development and evolution of materials used in GRP applications, and also partly because of the semantic fact that many names of relevant materials begin with the letter 'p', such as plastic, polymer, polyester and phenolic, there is increasing ambiguity as to the precise meaning of the term GRP.

So far as the construction industry is concerned, and also historically, the *most* correct and useful definition of GRP is that it stands for *glass* (*fibre*) *reinforced plastic(s)*, with the word *fibre* being frequently, even conventionally, omitted. Thus, the consequent subordinate convention is that a product manufactured from glass fibre reinforced *polyester* resin should be described as *polyester GRP*, and a similar product manufactured from glass fibre reinforced phenolic resin should be called

Figure 45.3 GRP refurbishment cladding
(Courtesy of Polystructures (Contracts) Ltd)

Figure 45.4 GRP canopy, cornices, etc.
(Courtesy of Brensal GRP Products Ltd)

phenolic GRP. The same convention may also be applied in the case of the use of other resins, polymers and matrices. It is also convenient to use the term *FRP* if fibres other than glass are used!

45.3 GRP constituent materials

45.3.1 Resins

45.3.1.1 Polyester resins

As has been stated, the great majority of past and present GRP construction and building applications are based on the use of polyester resins, and there is considerable diversity in the chemistry and technology of resins of this type. This diversity provides variations in the moulding characteristics and end-use performance of polyesters. The main types of polyester resin of primary interest in construction are described below.

45.3.1.2 Isophthalic polyester resins

These possess good water, weathering and chemical resistance properties, and by means of the use of additives, fillers, pigments, etc., are mainly used for gelcoats. Isophthalic resins may also be modified chemically and/or by means of fillers to improve fire retardance and to give other desired properties.

45.3.1.3 Orthophthalic polyester resins

Resins of this type are less costly and more widely used than isophthalic polyester resins; they are used for laminating most construction products, but these resins are usually specifically modified chemically and/or by means of fillers to give improved fire retardance and to give other desired properties.

Figure 45.5 GRP dome at Greenwich Observatory
(Courtesy of Anmac Ltd and Scott Bader Co. Ltd)

Figure 45.6 White GRP structural beams, on
American Express building at Brighton
(Courtesy of Brensal Plastics Ltd and Scott
Bader Co. Ltd)

45.3.1.4 Brominated polyester resins

These are polyester resins which are formulated on to brominated
compounds which is a cost-effective route for improving fire
retardancy. In particular, good durability, colour stability and
fire performance is increasingly achieved from dibromoneopentyl
glycol polyester resins in gelcoats. However, the use of such
brominated compounds *may* be affected by future legislation.

45.3.1.5 HET acid polyester resins

Resins of this type are mainly, but not exclusively, used for the
production of translucent GRP laminates with good fire
retardancy.

45.3.1.6 Phenolic resins

Resins of this type have been used for many years in high pressure moulding, e.g. Bakelite, and in pressed laminates, e.g. Formica, but it is only fairly recently that they have become relatively readily available for use in moulding processes similar to those of polyester resins, albeit rather less simply. The advantages of phenolic resins for construction applications are their improved inherent resistance to fire, and their reduced smoke-emission characteristics. However, phenolic resins cannot be self-coloured like polyester resins and they rapidly turn brown/black when exposed to sun and weather. Thus they usually require external painting/coating. Phenolic resins are also inclined to be less ductile/flexible than polyesters.

45.3.1.7 Epoxide (epoxy) resins

Resins of this type can possess better temperature, weathering and chemical resistance, and higher strength properties than polyesters or phenolics, but they are very considerably more expensive, to the extent that they are rarely used in construction applications.

The above resins and some rather more fundamental polymer chemistry background are described under the heading 'Reactive Polymers' in Chapter 36.

45.3.2 Glass fibre reinforcements

Glass fibre materials mainly consist of very thin glass filaments which are produced by drawing molten glass through very fine holes/bushings. These filaments are then further processed to produce yarns of twisted filaments for textile weaving and similar purposes. Alternatively, the filaments are bundled together in untwisted form to produce continuous glass strands. (Related processes are used to produce fibres for glass fibre insulation and alkali resistant glass fibres as used for cement reinforcement.)

It is important to be aware that, historically, it has been possible to manufacture two basic types of glass for GRP known as 'E' glass and 'A' glass. A glass has higher silica and sodium contents, thus giving good acid resistance, but lower strength, compared with E glass. In fact, A glass is now rarely used in GRP. E glass, however, is of a borosilicate nature, having a very low alkaline content. It has higher strength, better electrical performance properties, and greater moisture resistance than A glass. Accordingly, E glass is the type mainly used in GRP production.

A more recent type of glass, ECR, is also now available, being particularly durable for chemical, sewage and effluent conditions. Other more specialist types of glass are also now available, but they are not yet widely used for GRP construction applications. Normally, it is assumed that E glass is specified and used in GRP production, unless specifically identified otherwise.

The different types of glass fibre reinforcements used in GRP materials are described below.

45.3.2.1 Chopped strand mat

This form of reinforcement is the most widely used type in GRP production for all purposes, including construction. Chopped strand mat (CSM) consists of glass fibre bundles, usually but not exclusively chopped to around 50 mm in length. In CSM manufacture the fibres are deposited in random directions but at a uniform density on a 'carrier', the fibres being lightly bound together by a resin soluble 'binder', which may vary according to the resin type and product application. CSMs are produced to give a range of weights per unit area, and thus a range of corresponding thickness. The most widely used weights of chopped strand mats are 225, 300, 450, 600 and 900 g m^{-2}.

45.3.2.2 Continuous glass rovings

These consist of continuous bundles of glass strands or yarns. When used in the GRP moulding works, continuous rovings are usually passed through a resin spray head which incorporates an automatic chopping device so that resin and chopped strands may be continuously deposited on to a mould surface. Continuous rovings are also sometimes used in 'unchopped' form to fill into corners or interstices of mouldings.

45.3.2.3 Woven rovings

These are cloth-like materials made by weaving continuous, untwisted rovings, generally in a 'plain' weave. Because of the high concentration of glass fibres and the regular orientation of the fibres due to the weave, this type of reinforcement generally gives significantly higher strength moulded products than those in which chopped strand mat (CSM) is used. However, woven rovings are more costly than CSM and rather more difficult to impregnate well with resin. In addition, it is difficult, and sometimes impossible, to lay woven rovings satisfactorily onto more complex mould shapes. Accordingly, woven rovings are

Table 45.2 Typical physical properties of GRP with different types of glass fibre reinforcement*

Property	Unit	Chopped strand mat	Woven rovings	Satin weave cloth
Glass content	% wt	30	45	55
	% vol.	18	29	38
Specific gravity		1.4	1.6	1.7
Tensile strength	MPa	100	250	300
Tensile modulus	GPa	8	15	15
Compressive strength	MPa	150	150	250
Bend strength	MPa	150	250	400
Modulus in bend	GPa	7	15	15
Impact strength: izod unnotched†	kJ m^{-2}	75	125	150
Coefficient of linear expansion	× 10^{-5} °C^{-1}	30	15	12
Thermal conductivity	W m^{-1} K^{-1}	0.20	0.24	0.28

* Courtesy of Scott Bader Co. Ltd.
† Tested edgewise.

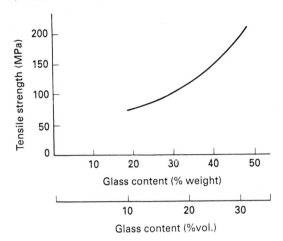

Figure 45.7 A plot of tensile strength vs. glass content for CSM (Courtesy of Scott Bader Co. Ltd)

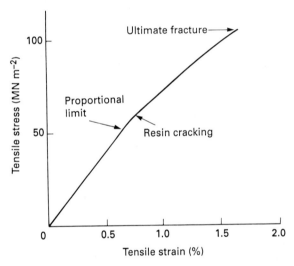

Figure 45.8 A plot of tensile strength vs. tensile strain for CSM

not frequently used in construction products, but they may be used in more highly stressed situations, including being restricted to those parts of mouldings which are subject to particular stress, deflection, fatigue or similar conditions.

45.3.2.4 Woven cloth materials

A wide range of woven glass cloth materials is produced, incorporating varying degrees of sophistication in the weaving process, and varying distributions of fibres, but inevitably these materials are quite costly and not often used in construction applications. Woven cloth materials are widely used in aerospace, automotive and 'high-tech' applications.

45.3.2.5 Continuous filament mat

This material, as its name implies, consists of a 'mat' of randomly deposited continuous strands/filaments. This form of mat is not substantially more costly than chopped strand mat, and the continuous nature of the reinforcement is particularly useful in

more mechanized methods of GRP production, helping to stabilize the location of the reinforcement when resin is added under pressure. However, this form of mat cannot be used in contact or spray moulding.

Some typical properties of GRP based upon a selection of different glass fibre reinforcements are compared in *Table 45.2*.

45.3.3 Complementary materials used in GRP moulding

For a variety of purposes a considerable range of complementary materials is used in or on GRP construction mouldings. Indeed, one of the major benefits of GRP materials and their associated moulding processes is their facility to incorporate such complementary materials and components relatively simply. Most commonly, the incorporation of complementary materials and products is directed towards augmenting the functional properties, and/or increasing the strength and stiffness of GRP products. Alternatively, or additionally, such materials are incorporated in order to reduce finished product or installed costs.

Some important complementary materials/products are described below.

45.3.3.1 Foam core materials and products

A wide variety of foam core materials and products have been and are being used in GRP construction product manufacture. In most cases the foam acts as a structural core/sandwich material to increase section modulus, but in some situations, additionally or alternatively, thermal insulation and/or other specialized characteristics are additional benefits. Some currently used foam core materials are described in the following.

Polyurethane and polyisocyanurate foams These foams have, in the past, been the most widely used foam core materials for GRP construction products. This is because of their relatively low cost, versatility and ease of working. They are also compatible with most resin types so that intermediate surface treatment of the foam is not required. Foams of this type can be used in GRP products both by means of *in situ* injection of the foaming materials between moulded 'skins' or by bonding into mouldings in the form of pre-cut slab/sheet stock. Foams of this type as used in GRP are relatively rigid and are thermosetting in nature. However, because of the inherent di-isocyanate content of these materials, due precautions are necessary in the workplace where the foam is produced, and it may sometimes be necessary for the potential combustion products of this group of foams to be taken into account in the design/specification of polyurethane/polyisocyanurate cored construction panels or products.

Phenolic foam This material is increasingly used in construction generally, as well as in GRP, because of its good fire resistance properties. However, phenolic resins are generally incompatible with polyesters and some other resins so that an intermediate surfacing/sealing material is usually necessary. Phenolic foam is most usually available in premanufactured sheet and slab form for GRP applications at present, but this is at least partly because of historical and marketing considerations.

Polyvinyl chloride foam Polyvinyl chloride (PVC) foam has been available for many years in both plasticized (i.e. more structurally flexible) and unplasticized forms. Only relatively recently has it been used in GRP applications. The use of an intermediate surfacing/sealing material is necessary when using plasticized PVC foam in GRP product manufacture. PVC foams are generally tough and durable. However, because of the thermoplastic nature of PVC foam, and its relatively high cost, it is not widely used in construction applications.

Foamed glass Obviously enough, this material is very attractive for use with GRP. However, the relatively high cost and past limited sheet size availability of this material has meant that its use in GRP construction applications has been quite limited so far.

45.3.3.2 Synthetic fibre 'mat like' materials (i.e. Coremat)

Products of this nature are relatively bulky synthetic fibre based materials, being generally specific and proprietary in nature. Because of the relatively bulky nature of such materials compared to chopped strand mat (CSM) they can be used integrally as resin impregnated cores between internal and external layers of chopped strand mat to give enhanced thickness and stiffness characteristics to laminates rather more quickly and cheaply than by using glass fibres throughout. These materials are, however, sometimes difficult to mould around corners and into more complex shapes; but they are a convenient and increasingly widely used means for substantially enhancing the strength and stiffness of flat or simply curved areas of GRP economically.

45.3.3.3 Other core materials

Other core materials used in GRP construction applications include:

(1) expanded steel,
(2) perforated steel,
(3) plywood,
(4) blockboard,
(5) balsa wood,
(6) fibre cement sheet,
(7) aluminium sheet, and
(8) profiled sheet materials of many types.

This list of materials is by no means exhaustive. (N.B. It is increasingly normal to use combinations of foam and other denser core materials, such as plywood or perforated steel sheet for example, to give enhanced stiffness, ruggedness, and fire resistance characteristics. In addition, some of these denser core materials are of particular use for specialist fire or explosion resistant panels or enclosures, and/or for sound attenuation.)

45.3.3.4 Plastic and rubber sections

Plastic and rubber sections are sometimes used in GRP products in a totally 'encapsulated', i.e. moulded/enclosed in GRP, form to create particular shapes and sections in GRP mouldings for specific design or functional purposes. GRP is also sometimes used as an external, and occasionally internal, moulded structural reinforcing medium for thermoplastic moulded sections, e.g. pipes and gutters.

45.3.3.5 Metal and timber sections

Relatively light steel and aluminium drawings, extrusions and pressings are sometimes totally encapsulated in GRP, both to give structural shape to GRP mouldings and, conversely, to protect the metal sections from corrosion, thus giving a composite GRP/metal structure. Similarly, structural steel sections, e.g. channel, T bar, angle, hollow and flat plate sections, are encapsulated in GRP, particularly for civil, structural and water/process engineering applications, e.g. tanks, tank roofs and structural cladding situations.

As before, in these heavier structural situations, whilst the steel sections may contribute in a major way to the stiffness and strength of the GRP, the moulded/composite nature of the GRP

in the composite structure may introduce flexibility into design and manufacture by reducing or eliminating jointing and fixing complexities in the steel substructure.

Whilst lighter timber sections are frequently used as a stiffening core/shape forming medium for GRP, heavier timber sections may be used in a similar structural manner to that of heavier steel sections. (Some practical and design considerations in the use of steel and timber sections in GRP are referred to later.)

45.4 Methods of manufacture of GRP construction products

45.4.1 Contact moulding, hand laminating, or hand/wet lay-up

This is the original, simplest and still the most widely used moulding technique for producing GRP construction products. Whilst the term *contact moulding* is now technically/professionally preferred, the process is still most commonly referred to in the workplace and on site as *hand laminating*, *hand lay-up* or *wet lay-up*. At its simplest, this technique requires a mould, of almost any degree of simplicity or complexity, most commonly made from GRP, which has in turn been moulded off a wood or plaster pattern. (Such 'patterns' may, however, be made from almost any product/material that is required to be reproduced. This ability to initiate the GRP mould-making and moulding process from almost any shape and material is particularly useful in the production of GRP mouldings for building refurbishment, especially embellishments, or in the manufacture of 'reproduction' products.)

A mould release agent, which may be a solid or liquid polish and/or a brush or spray applied liquid film medium is applied to the mould, followed in most cases by an initial resin gelcoat layer. This is followed by, as already mentioned, alternating layers of resin and chopped strand mat (CSM) or other reinforcements, as required. Stiff brushes, various types of rollers and other relatively simple devices are used to consolidate fully the resin/glass layers, including 'breaking down' the previously referred to binder in the case of CSM, to ensure maximum possible homogeneity and to exclude air. The moulding is then allowed to gel/cure before release from the mould.

It should be noted that whilst post-curing of finished polyester GRP mouldings in an oven or heated chamber is generally desirable, this is often not practical in the case of mouldings for construction applications, particularly physically larger products/structures. However, it is most important that the moulding process is carried on under adequately warm (i.e. not less than 15°C), dry workshop conditions, and finished mouldings should not be moved to outside storage areas in cold and/or wet weather too quickly. Post-curing of polyester GRP mouldings is, however, much more necessary in situations where maximum chemical, water and elevated temperature performance

Table 45.3 Effect of glass content on the properties of contact moulded CSM polyester laminates (typical values)*

Resin:glass ratio by weight		2:1	2.5:1	3:1
Glass content (% wt)		33	29	25
Glass content (% vol.)		20	17	14
Specific gravity	—	1.5	1.45	1.4
Tensile strength	MPa	110	100	85
Bend strength	MPa	150	130	110
Modulus in bend	GPa	7	6	5

* Courtesy of Scott Bader Co. Ltd.

is required. Phenolic and epoxide GRP mouldings almost invariably require post-curing.

Whilst the contact moulding process may seem relatively crude, and is certainly labour intensive, it in fact requires considerable 'craft skill' and has proven extremely suitable for the manufacture of single or 'short/medium run' items, from small to very large size.

Experienced personnel can achieve uniform gelcoat thickness, moulding/laminate thickness, and specified resin/glass ratio and uniformly high quality. However, good motivation and support, and a strong level of management direction and control is necessary to ensure the maintenance of these high standards.

45.4.2 Spray moulding

This technique is similar to contact moulding/hand laminating in that the quality of product is substantially dependent upon the skill of the personnel, but in this case a much more rapid rate of application of resin and glass is achieved by the use of a spray applicator incorporating a combined resin spray head and a chopping device operating on continuous glass rovings. The brush/roller consolidation techniques are generally similar to those used in normal contact moulding.

Spray moulding requires a special skill on the part of the operative to ensure that the required rate and uniformity of deposition of materials are achieved and that similar skill/performance criteria to those identified for contact moulding are met.

45.4.3 Mechanized moulding techniques

There are a number of more mechanized processes/techniques used in the manufacture of GRP products, but these techniques are in practice mainly used for construction product applications on a limited scale or, most importantly, in certain specific areas to produce specialized products on a more substantial scale. Some of these processes are described below.

45.4.3.1 Resin injection moulding

This process is useful for 'high-tech' GRP/composite products, and it is sometimes also useful for specific construction projects and applications. The process basically consists of clamping a required quantity or thickness of chopped strand mat (CSM) and/or woven rovings between matched male and female moulds, the resin then being injected into the cavity by means of a pressure or vacuum pumping system.

Although relatively low differential pressures (3/4 bar) are not often exceeded or desired, stiffness in the moulds, themselves usually made of GRP, is vital to ensure good resin flow and finished moulding thickness control.

It is sometimes possible to incorporate gelcoats in a resin injection moulding by prior coating of one or both of the moulding surfaces.

45.4.3.2 Cold press moulding

This technique consists simply, and fairly obviously, of the use of matching moulds which are closed together and sealed by means of a pressing/clamping device or press. Presses used for cold press moulding ranging from relatively simple manual clamping or screw presses to low or even quite high pressure hydraulic presses.

The glass reinforcement, which is preloaded, usually consists of CSM, continuous filament mat, or woven rovings. The resin is then usually simply poured into the reinforcement laying on the lower moulding surface before press closure.

Cold press moulding is sometimes used for construction

product manufacture when sufficient quantities of identical mouldings are required.

45.4.3.3 Hot press moulding

This process involves the use of high pressure hydraulic or similar presses. Matched metal moulds are required because of the high pressures and elevated temperatures which are necessary in the moulds to ensure flow and cure of the specialist GRP materials. GRP materials, as used in hot press moulding, sometimes include liquid resins; in the case of polyester GRP they may be liquid resin based or consist of dough-like mixes of resin, fillers and glass fibres known as DMC or, alternatively, resin preimpregnated glass mat (known as SMC) which also has a 'doughy' consistency. Phenolic GRP materials for hot press moulding consist either of preimpregnated glass mat or woven materials; or are of granular consistency, with no clear processing distinction able to be drawn from older established non-glass-reinforced phenolic compression moulding materials, e.g. Bakelite. Epoxide GRP materials as used in hot press moulding are usually in SMC or granular form.

45.4.3.4 Filament winding

This process involves drawing continuous rovings, CSM or specialist woven reinforcements through a resin 'bath', the impregnated reinforcement then being wound on to a continuously rotating mandrel or mould. Filament winding is mainly used for the production of GRP pipe, although more sophisticated control systems make it possible to make more complex closed or shaped forms/vessels.

45.4.3.5 Pultrusion and extrusion

These techniques generally consist of drawing resin impregnated continuous rovings or more specialist reinforcements through a heated die in which cure takes place. Thus it is possible to produce continuous GRP profiles/forms, which may be quite complex. To date, pultruded GRP has not been very widely applied in construction, although such applications are growing, particularly in civil and structural engineering. Pultruded products are occasionally used as reinforcing formers inserted into GRP contact or spray mouldings.

45.4.3.6 Continuous moulding

This process is mainly used for the production of corrugated/profiled and flat GRP sheet, and similar products incorporating aggregate surfaces, etc. The equipment basically consists of a continuous long 'table' which includes various stages/processes including glass supply and application, resin supply and application, shaping/profiling, elevated temperature curing, inspection and pulling/drawing equipment, followed by a sheet-cutting stage. The materials used may consist of CSM or chopped continuous rovings, and specialist polyester resins which are usually required to be of a translucent type in the case of profiled corrugated sheet manufacture.

It should be noted that it is sometimes difficult precisely to define or separate variations or combinations of the mechanized GRP production processes described. However, insofar as most established GRP construction uses are concerned, these processes are still substantially restricted to applications where fairly large quantities of products are required. It is possible that there may be a trend towards the wider use of resin injection and cold press moulding for construction applications in the future, or at least a trend away from contact moulding, but this trend may depend as much on external factors, e.g. health and safety requirements in the workplace, as on the production, technical and economic desirability of the processes themselves.

45.5 GRP as a structural material

In many, perhaps even most, applications of GRP in construction and building the materials are probably not considered initially for their relatively good structural properties. Ease of mouldability and versatility with regard to colour and texture, combined with general lightness in weight and impermeability are the most likely primary attributes of GRP for architects, engineers and specifiers. Of these properties, ease of mouldability is probably paramount, with the relatively high structural strength being implicit.

In practice, in many GRP construction applications, including some which could be deemed 'structural', there is an underlying acceptance that, if the product can be made by an experienced and competent manufacturer and is capable of 'standing up' by itself and being handled, lifted and installed on site then it is strong enough! To a very considerable extent, experience of the use of GRP in construction over a considerable number of years supports this assumption. However, the increasing demands and sophistication of Standards and Specifications, including the collective trend in UK construction towards BS 5750 procedures and certification together with evolving European Standards, etc., point toward the need for more formal design and specification approaches in the future. This is particularly the trend in the case of physically large and/or more structurally critical applications for GRP, including its use in civil engineering and for large panels and components, tanks, environmental control, and water and gas services products.

Returning to the ease of mouldability of GRP, it is clear that this feature of the material makes it possible for designers to conceive the manufacture of single large integral products which may previously have, of necessity, been fabricated/installed on site using a combination of products, materials and trades. Indeed, it is worth emphasizing that the more structurally demanding applications of GRP make desirable and uniquely achievable the manufacture of integral shapes and forms which could not have been sensibly made using other materials. In particular, complex folding or curves can be achieved with GRP and this is often structurally and aesthetically desirable. Alternatively, because of their relative lightness, impermeability, self-colour and ease of incorporation of complementary cores, components and materials, together with sometimes complex integral edge/jointing and fixing details, large relatively planar or simply curved GRP cladding and roofing panels/forms may be used as an alternative to reinforced concrete or metal fabrications.

As to structural data and performance, GRP possesses good specific tensile and compressive strengths (see *Figures 45.7* and *45.8*) but relatively lower stiffness, particularly compared to metals. Thus, the structural and aesthetic usefulness of the mouldability of GRP in enabling 'shaping for stiffness' is further emphasized. These generally high specific strength/relatively low stiffness properties of GRP are implicit in the nature of the material, particularly if one considers the normally laminar orientation of the relatively strong glass fibre reinforcement, and the relatively weak nature of the resin matrix. Thus, fairly obviously, lower resin/glass-fibre ratios for equal thickness of laminates give increased strength and stiffness properties. In addition, the stiffness of a GRP laminate can be increased if glass or other fibres can be introduced into the reinforcement transversely to the normal laminar fibre orientation.

Certain special reinforcing materials have been designed to assist in this respect, and a small proportion of the additional stiffness that is obtained from woven rovings and woven glass cloth reinforcements is derived in this manner. However, woven rovings reinforcement also contributes to increased strength and stiffness in GRP because of the greater 'dry' consolidation, orientation and effective length of the fibres, the locking effects

Table 45.4 Relative rigidity of GRP sandwich laminates in bending*

Total thickness (mm)	Single GRP skin	Two GRP skins each 1.5 mm thick with centre core	Two GRP skins each 3 mm thick with centre core
1.5	0.018		
3	0.2	0.2	
6	1.6	1.3	1.6
10	5.3	3.7	5
13	12.5	7.3	10
19	42	18	29
25	100	34	58
32	195	52	94
38	337	77	143
44	536	104	197
50	800	145	266

* Courtesy of Fibreglass Ltd and Scott Bader Co. Ltd.

of the weave and the complementary practical ease of achieving lower resin/glass ratios. Even greater strength and stiffness improvements can be achieved with woven glass cloths, for similar reasons, but at much greater cost.

It is obvious from the foregoing that GRP mouldings are not homogeneous or isotropic by most scientific criteria, although in these respects they are not dissimilar to concrete, natural stone, wood or other construction materials. However, in most normal applications of moulded GRP in construction, including those based on chopped strand mat, sprayed chopped rovings and woven rovings, the laminates may be *considered* as homogeneous and isotropic insofar as planar stresses are concerned. Thus, with due care, most of the usual theory, design formulae and conventions relating to planar stressing may be applied to GRP materials. Care is particularly necessary in the design for stiffness and in situations where the risk of buckling failure is significant.

Following the above general description of the structural nature of GRP the following notes are intended to provide some further guidance to assist with structural/engineering design using these materials.

The effect of resin/glass content on the properties of contact moulded CSM polyester is shown in *Figure 45.3*. The relationship between tensile strength and glass content is shown in *Figure 45.7*. *Figure 45.8* shows a typical stress/strain curve.

45.5.1 Stress/strain behaviour

Most commonly, uniaxial tensile stress/strain curves for GRP are obtained at constant rates of elongation. A typical curve based on a chopped strand mat (CSM) polyester laminate in a short-term tensile test to failure is shown in *Figure 45.8*. It can be seen that at relatively low strains there is a linear relationship up to a usually identifiable proportional limit. Beyond this proportional limit resin cracking occurs in an increasingly destructive manner as strain continues up to ultimate failure/rupture.

Similar stress/strain curves for short-term compression show the laminate to be linearly elastic to the point of ultimate failure, with failure usually occurring at a higher stress level than the ultimate tensile stress for the same material. In addition, there is evidence to suggest that resin cracking, debonding, etc., in compression does not occur as early or destructively as in the case of tensile testing. The strength of CSM reinforced polyester when tested in flexure is usually found to be higher than the ultimate tensile stress value, but of course such flexural strength values are usually derived using an elastic analysis.

It is important to note that, in considering the purely structural performance, testing and design of GRP, the existence, or otherwise, of gelcoats is usually ignored, although in some building applications the use of relatively thick gelcoats may, in practice, contribute significantly to the stiffness of the material.

45.5.2 Creep

GRP is prone to creep and the consequent reduced strength under long-term loading. The extent of creep is a function of the behaviour of the resin matrix. Thus, lower resin/glass ratios reduce the tendency to creep. Creep is also greater at elevated temperatures and/or in wet situations. Creep in GRP is, as with all materials, dependent upon the level of stress and/or strain to which the material is subjected. As a rule of thumb, after 25 years the tensile strength of polyester GRP reduces to approximately 40% of its short-term strength when under constant load.

45.5.3 Fatigue

Repeated loading has a significant effect on the strength of GRP. Tests typically show a reduction in strength to around 30% of the short-term tensile strength after 1 million cycles. The relationship between fatigue strength and time is quite similar for both tensile and flexural stress cycling.

45.5.4 Safety factors

The stress factors that must be considered to ensure the safety of a design are rather less easy to determine and define for GRP structures than for more homogeneous and isotropic materials. As far as the broad construction use of CSM reinforced polyester is concerned, in practice a tensile stress safety factor of 10 is most commonly used; lower factors may well be used in the case of woven rovings or even more usually in the case of woven cloth reinforcements. Lower factors of safety can sometimes be used in construction situations in which stresses are generally low and/or load cycling due to wind induced oscillation, etc., is not likely to occur. However, higher safety factors may well be required in applications where practical and/or Code/Standards deflection limits are of primary importance.

45.5.5 Thermal properties

The coefficient of thermal expansion of CSM based GRP is more than twice that of mild steel, and not dissimilar to that of aluminium and its alloys (see *Table 45.5*). The thermal conductivity is, as expected, very low. It is important to note that the relatively high coefficient of thermal expansion of GRP is

not necessarily as great a problem as it may seem, as discussed later in connection with installation and fixing (see Section 45.6.4).

The low thermal conductivity of GRP means that in bright, sunny conditions relatively high surface temperatures may be experienced. The surface temperature is very dependent on colour and, to some extent, on texture (lighter colours and higher gloss lead to higher reflectivity and thus to lower temperatures). Conversely, there is no 'heat sink' effect, as is the case with metals, and thus solar heating and cooling is rapid.

45.5.6 Structural stiffening of GRP

Reference has already been made to the practical simplicity with which metal, structural steel, timber and various sheet and board materials may be incorporated in GRP moulded construction products. From the structural designer's viewpoint, these materials and products do not present any exceptional design problems, although the compound nature of such structures may considerably increase the volume of calculations required. Of course, it is usually implicit in the structural design of such products, and is a mandatory requirement imposed upon the manufacturer, that full and effective adhesion is obtained between the GRP and the complementary structural components.

A similar philosophy may be applied to the use of foam cores in GRP, almost invariably in the form of sandwich panels. The rapidly increasing amount of sandwich panel design theory and 'ready use' formulae may usually be applied to GRP/foam sandwich panels. However, it is important to bear in mind some practical aspects of GRP materials and construction products, including curing shrinkage, relatively high thermal expansion and the low rigidity modulus compared with tensile/flexural strength. These particular facets of GRP materials require special attention to be given to facing laminate/foam core adhesion and the horizontal/transverse shear behaviour and performance of the foam core material.

In practice, techniques used by GRP manufacturers to reduce the variables in these respects include precoating foam cores with GRP materials prior to incorporating the cores into the moulded assembly. In addition, various methods are used to bond/lock outer and inner GRP faces/laminates to each other through foam cores. These techniques include the use of transverse GRP moulded strips/laminates and resin impregnated continuous rovings. However, these devices require suitable care to ensure that such discontinuities do not 'show through' unattractively on the outer surfaces of the GRP.

The relative rigidities of GRP sandwich laminates in bending are shown in *Table 45.4*.

45.6 Using and specifying GRP for construction

It is perhaps inherent in the nature of GRP materials that it is difficult, and often not helpful, to over-rigidly separate consideration of the constituent materials from the methods of manufacture and design, or from the nature and use of the finished product. This is particularly the case in construction and building because of the extent to which the 'on site' process creates demands and problems for products and materials which, whilst often transient, are critically important. Furthermore, a GRP product used in a construction or building application is implicitly competing with a considerable range of alternative and often historically older established materials whose limitations are known and accepted, even ignored—GRP products are often not so indulged. In particular, standards of initial uniformity and long-term consistency in appearance are often looked for in GRP when such standards are not quite so critically required

Table 45.5 Comparative thermal properties*

	Thermal conductivity (W m^{-1} K^{-1})	Thermal expansion coefficient ($\times 10^{-6}$ °C^{-1})	Maximum working temperature (°C)
CSM/polyester GRP	0.2	30	175†
Unidirectional GRP	0.3	10‡	250†
Mild steel	50	12	400
Light alloy	200	23	200

* Courtesy of Scott Bader Co. Ltd.
† Depending on the type of polyester resin used and the application.
‡ Measured longitudinally.

of most other materials; indeed, variations and changes in the aged appearance of many more conventional construction materials is usually regarded as acceptable, even desirable.

Nevertheless, the GRP construction product designer and manufacturer is consistently striving to maximize the functional performance and consistency in aesthetics of his products and the following notes will, hopefully, be of use to both specifiers and the recipients of specifications: in avoiding misunderstandings and in identifying particular technical, manufacturing, installation and 'suitability for use' matters.

45.6.1 Dimensional stability during manufacture

Shrinkage occurs in GRP mouldings during gelation/cure; this is entirely due to shrinkage of the resin. Thus, a lower resin/glass ratio reduces the level of curing shrinkage. Whilst it is possible to establish reasonably consistent curing shrinkage data from test pieces, it is extremely difficult to extrapolate such test data to shrinkage tolerance allowances for moulded shapes, although this is much easier for flat sheets. Accordingly, it is the responsibility of the GRP product manufacturer to make due allowance in his pattern-making, GRP mould-making and GRP product moulding processes for such shrinkage. Generally, curing shrinkage is less pronounced, or at least less of a problem in GRP products which have pronounced three-dimensional form, i.e. domes, more curvaceous products and items with relatively fewer and smaller flat areas. Because of shrinkage during cure, it is necessary and sensible to allow adequate manufacturing dimensional tolerances in GRP products, which should be the subject of informed inputs and guidance from an experienced designer or manufacturer. Considerable specific information in this respect is given in the *Design Guide for Tolerances in GRP Cladding* (published by the National GRP Construction and Engineering Federation (NGCEF).

45.6.2 Gelcoats, colours and texture

The primary functions of gelcoats in GRP construction products have already been mentioned: giving enhanced handling protection and wear and weathering resistance; and providing the desired appearance properties in the moulding/product. Most of these properties are implicit in a properly applied good quality gelcoat, but appearance is of course a function of colour, texture and durability.

It is possible to incorporate an almost infinite variety of colour pigments into polyester gelcoats, but not into phenolic gelcoats. However, polyester resins are organic materials, as indeed are most paints, and their colour will inevitably change over time to some degree. It is important that this aspect is understood by architects, designers and specifiers so that unnecessary misunderstandings and disappointments do not arise. In this respect the selection of the colour and texture of polyester GRPs is crucially important. Colour is usually incorporated into polyester GRP products by means of a pigment which is dispersed into the gelcoat resin. This process is best carried out by a specialist company prior to supply to the GRP moulder, the specialist company usually being the primary pigment paste manufacturer.

As has already been mentioned (see Section 43.3.1.1), polyester gelcoats for construction and building applications must usually be specially selected and/or modified to give enhanced fire retardancy properties and, historically, the quest for better fire performance in polyester gelcoats has acted counter to colour availability and durability. However, more recent specialist and modified gelcoat resins together with improvements in additives and pigment technology have led to more satisfactory and durable gelcoat/pigment systems being available. It is probably still the case, however, that certain

colours present greater difficulties from the durability point of view, particularly the stronger blues, reds and some browns, in which case specialist advice from resin and pigment suppliers should be sought. Polyester gelcoat colour shade selection is most conveniently made from, or at least related to, BS 4800: 1981 and BS 4904: 1978. Specialist simulated metallic flake/particle colourings for polyester gelcoats are also available and these are useful for some applications.

In selecting the colour for a GRP product it is important to ensure that as high as possible a light fastness index of pigment is used. In accordance with BS 1006: 1978, a light fastness index of 6 or better is usually necessary, an index of $\geqslant 7$ being desirable for less 'natural' colours such as reds and blues.

It is possible to reproduce almost any texture in a GRP gelcoat, textures ranging from a matt finish to very coarse finishes which may, for example, simulate riven slate or coarse 'pebbledash'. However, for most applications the preferred form of texture is roughly analogous to a medium/coarse render finish.

A consequence of this use of surface texture in GRP gelcoats is that the overall thickness of the gelcoat may be considerably greater than may usually be recommended for other applications of GRP, which is generally up to 0.5 mm. Indeed, for construction applications a thicker gelcoat layer both enhances durability and facilitates practical repairs and refurbishment to GRP mouldings, which may have been subject to damage by other trades during construction or, subsequently, during maintenance.

Specialist coating and paint materials can be used on GRP, but surface preparation and the selection of materials and their application requires special advice and care. Phenolic GRP is usually coated/painted as new for construction and building applications: epoxide primer and acrylic finish coat treatments have been found to be particularly useful and durable. Polyester GRP mouldings for buildings and construction are only occasionally painted/coated when new. The use of such treatments on new polyester GRP products is limited to situations where particularly difficult colours, multicolour or 'art' finishes are required, or where the material is to be used in a particularly difficult location. However, the painting/coating of polyester gelcoats as part of a maintenance or refurbishment programme is not difficult, special polyurethane and acrylic systems having been developed for such purposes. Such materials are usually readily available from the polyester pigment manufacturer or supplier.

45.6.3 Fire retardancy

Insofar as GRP materials are 'plastics' they may sometimes give rise to fears regarding fire behaviour, which are often, even usually, unjustified. In practice, polyester GRP presents no greater fire hazard than the use of, say, cedar wood, in certain cases being considerably less hazardous. However, polyester, phenolic and epoxide resins are all organic and, unless specially selected or modified, will burn under certain conditions. However, in a 'real fire' situation, GRP does not normally crack, splinter or explode, or shed molten droplets, in which respect the materials are superior to many conventional materials, or the finishes applied to conventional materials.

As has been stated, phenolic resins are generally superior to polyester resins in their inherent resistance to fire and reduced smoke emission characteristics. However, the inability to self-colour phenolic resin 'gelcoats' and the relative lack of versatility and adaptability of these gelcoats in terms of established GRP construction and building product specifications and moulding processes, currently inhibits the use of these resins except, most importantly, in underground and special interior locations.

Epoxide resins are rarely used in moulded GRP construction products except for special structural applications. However, these resins are incorporated in specialist resin based coatings and compounds, usually without fibrous reinforcement, for which the particular usefulness of their properties over-rides their inherently high cost. Epoxies are not too dissimilar from polyesters in terms of their fire behaviour.

As referred to already, a fundamental concern when using polyester GRP in building and construction applications is that the selection of specialist/modified gelcoats and pigment/colour systems to achieve the best possible fire retardancy *generally* acts against the best choice of appearance and colour stability. However, newer types of polyester gelcoat resins and improvements in additives and pigments have significantly reduced the degree of practical difficulty in resolving this predicament.

Separately from gelcoats, satisfactory fire retardancy can be achieved in glass fibre laminating/impregnating polyester resin systems without significant practical difficulties, although with such fire retardant laminating resins, particularly those more highly filled for lower cost, there is sometimes more difficulty in achieving lower apparent resin/glass ratios.

In the UK, the most common criterion for assessing the fire retardancy of a GRP construction product is the performance of the materials used and/or specimens from a product as tested in accordance with BS 476: Part 7: 1987. This test involves measuring the rate of spread of a controlled flame across the selected specimen. The specimen is then categorized into one of four classifications (classes 1 to 4). Class 1 includes materials having the lowest rates of spread of flame and class 4 includes materials having the highest rates of spread of flame.

Selected polyester gelcoats, and thus generally the laminates/mouldings upon which they are applied, are readily able to achieve classes 1 or 2, with the lowest category of general purpose polyester materials, not usually used in construction, normally achieving class 3.

It should be noted that translucent and self-coloured GRP products intended for roofing or external sloping surfaces are commonly tested alternatively or additionally in accordance with BS 476: Part 3: 1975. In this test specialist GRP gelcoats and/or laminating systems readily achieve the best classification (EXT.S.AA) for sloping surfaces.

For certain external locations on buildings and for many internal applications, conformity with class 0 of the requirements of the UK Building Regulations is necessary. This requires that test pieces achieve suitably low and defined indices of performance in accordance with BS 476: Part 6: 1981, together with similar test pieces achieving class 1 spread of flame performance in accordance with the spread of flame test. Mouldings made from selected polyester gelcoat and laminating systems can meet these requirements, and can thus be deemed to conform to class 0 as described in the Building Regulations.

In practice, because of the particular nature of GRP products, their application and location, waivers of the need for class 0 conformity may often be obtained from the responsible statutory authority. Thus, in practice, class 1 spread of flame performance is usually sufficient for GRP products, with a class 2 rating being acceptable for many applications/locations. Occasionally, perhaps because of the unique nature, configuration or size of a GRP building product, full-scale-product or part-product fire tests may be required, although it is sometimes difficult to define suitable criteria/'modelling' and it is questionable whether full-scale tests of this type simulate 'real fire' situations.

It is important to note that considerable effort is at present being made by the EEC to rationalize and co-ordinate fire testing and certification, and to provide specifications for materials and products with regard to fire retardancy. It is also likely that in the longer term there will be moves towards the harmonization of National Building Regulations, etc. However, at present it seems unlikely that major statutory changes in these respects will be formalized for some time.

More detailed information on fire retardancy in GRP is given in *Guidance Notes on the Specification of Fire Retardant GRP Cladding Panels* (published by the NGCEF).

Certain specialist or complementary products, materials and techniques may be used in or with GRP to modify or improve fire retardancy for particular situations, and these are described below.

45.6.3.1 Aggregate surfaces

Aggregates, ranging in size from coarse 'chippings' down to fine sands or powders may be incorporated into or bonded to the external gelcoat surface of a GRP product, thus giving exceptionally good spread of flame, fire propagation and fire penetration characteristics.

Products of this general type include proprietary aggregate faced GRP sheet which is manufactured using a continuous moulding process, or aggregate/particle finishes which may be incorporated into gelcoats or bonded to more typical GRP moulded/shaped products. When using the latter method it is particularly important that close attention be paid to aggregate/particle selection, grading and application, including care in bonding in order to ensure initial acceptability and uniformity of appearance, together with good durability.

45.6.3.2 Paint/coating systems

Reference has been made to the use of paint/coating systems on gelcoated GRP building products, and in certain situations it is possible to achieve the best possible combinations of colour, predictive durability of appearance and fire retardancy performance by using coatings, particularly coatings of a two-pack polyurethane type.

45.6.3.3 Intumescent coatings

In certain situations it may be desirable to apply an intumescent coating to the inner surfaces of a GRP building product. Such coatings are formulated to produce a carbonaceous foam when subjected to flame; this foaming process includes the propagation of inert gases which further insulate the surface against penetration of heat and flame.

45.6.3.4 Fire barriers/stops

It is usually quite simple to incorporate integrally moulded or bonded fire barriers/stops into the rear faces or interiors of GRP products/mouldings. This design approach is particularly useful when GRP is used as an external cladding to underlying conventional surfaces, e.g. brickwork, concrete block, specialist cement sheets and plasterboards.

45.6.4 Erection, installation and fixing

Because of the relatively low weight of GRP construction and building products, quite simple handling, transporting and lifting equipment can often be used. However, because GRP construction products also usually possess a high area/weight ratio, the use of steadying ropes is usually necessary on site in order to avoid damage being caused by the action of wind during lifting. Similarly, GRP products being stored on site or at the point of installation often need to be lashed or weighted down in order to avoid damage. Considerable advice regarding storage, handling and 'on site' protection of GRP products is given in the *Guidance Notes on the Storage, Handling and Protection of GRP Products* (published by the NGCEF). It is also desirable to keep works-fitted framing or battens, intended to assist in transporting, lifting or fixing GRP products in position until the time of lifting or actual fixing on site.

As has been stated, a particular advantage of GRP construction products is that they can be manufactured to incorporate an exceptional degree of complexity in shape, including at the edges of products. Thus, GRP panels and products can have almost any edge shape or profile required by the designer or specifier for reasons of aesthetics or for functional purposes (e.g. fixing, jointing, weathering and drainage). Care must be taken, however, to ensure that the designer does not become so carried away with the adaptability of GRP to complex edge details that unnecessary practical difficulties are created on site, particularly as the dimensional uniformity and tolerances of GRP products are almost always superior to that of the underlying or adjacent building structure or component.

Forms of edge detailing that have been developed for concrete, metal or timber products are generally readily reproduced in GRP products if desired, although in many cases undesirable complexities can usefully be eliminated by the use of GRP materials. The use of GRP materials also makes it possible to incorporate complex integral drainage, weathering/flashing and guttering details which may simplify the design and manufacture of adjacent products, and/or ease site installation and finishing for others.

It is also a widely used, if seldom stated, feature of GRP construction products that they can relatively simply be modified/adapted in the works or even on site to suit discrepancies arising from other trades. However, in practice it is unwise and unfair to GRP materials to carry this facility to absurd extremes, as is occasionally the case.

The relative ease with which metal brackets and rails, timber battens, etc., may be moulded or fixed to GRP products in the works, usually by using jigs, etc., in turn facilitates precise site location and fixing of GRP products at desired positions on the rear faces of products, sometimes additionally or alternatively to edge location and fixing. Most conventional and specialist forms of mechanical fixings can be adapted for GRP construction and building products use except that under no circumstances should nails, masonry pins, etc., be used. In general, the fixing of larger and heavier GRP products is done using bolts, threaded studs, steel fixing brackets, etc., usually together with 'in-works' jig drilled holes or slots, etc. Occasionally, integral bushings or specially made fixing devices may be used.

However, the majority of GRP products are likely to be site fixed by means of site drilling of GRP flanges and bolting or screwing down in a conventional manner. In these circumstances, fixing loads must be controlled and duly spread, and weather sealing achieved by the use of suitable non-metallic washers, large plastic screw or bolt heads, fixing seals, etc.

It is a commonplace that during fixing GRP flanges will often need to be pushed or pulled into position, usually to overcome site variances, and it is vital that, where this is necessary, damage is not caused to gelcoats or underlying laminates. Particular attention must be paid to incorporating adequate stiffness in fixing flange area design in order to ensure that dead loads and possible thermal, creep or wind load effects do not induce gelcoat or laminate damage. Intelligent design, proper manufacture and good fixing practice should entirely eliminate such risks.

There may appear to be a contradiction between the relatively high coefficient of thermal expansion of GRP materials and the suggestion that most GRP products are relatively simply fixed back by means of site drilled bolting, screwing, etc. The explanation for this seeming anomaly is that the higher thermal expansion of GRP is generally more than compensated for by its low modulus of rigidity, with the consequence that the strains on fixings will be much lower than may have been assumed. This mechanism of reduced thermal strains at fixings is often compounded further by the generalization that GRP products

usually incorporate a significantly greater number of fixings in practice compared with other materials, particularly for weather sealing and related reasons. A further marginal factor is the phenomenon that the modulus of rigidity of GRP reduces significantly as solar temperature increases. Much more important than these considerations, however, is the fact that most GRP products are, implicitly, of three-dimensional form and this feature coupled with low material rigidity makes it normal and generally safe for thermally induced deflections to occur transversely to the planes of the fixings. Obviously enough, in the case of the physically larger civil engineering and, thus stiffer, GRP products, it may be more necessary to provide for thermal expansion by means of more sophisticated installation/jointing and fixing systems. However, even in these situations it is probable that the major design/stress concerns at the fixings are created by *in situ* alignment, dead load and wind load considerations.

Weatherproofing of GRP product joints, including joints to other materials, can be effected by the use of most established techniques including the use of prefabricated flexible seals, impregnated foam strips and site applied mastics. Gun applied mastics are particularly suitable for weather sealing of GRP to GRP products, but such sealants should generally be of a low modulus silicone type. Occasionally, specialist low modulus polyurethane or acrylic sealants are used. When adhesive sealants are used with GRP products, it is vital that all surfaces should be dry and chemically cleaned to exclude release agents or other surface contamination. The use of recommended sealant primers is also desirable.

Bibliography

ALLEN, H. G., *Analysis and Design of Structural Sandwich Panels*, Pergamon Press, Oxford (1969)

AGREMENT BOARD, *Method of Assessment and Testing (MOAT) No. 9* Common directive for the assessment of products in glass reinforced polyester for use in building (December 1973)

ARCHITECTS JOURNAL, The art of construction. 2.1 GRP Cladding. Part 1 Production (10 June 1981)

ARCHITECTS JOURNAL, The art of construction. 2.1 GRP Cladding. Part 2 Panel design (17 June 1981)

BRITISH PLASTICS FEDERATION, *Guidance notes for the construction of GRP cladding panels* (October 1981)

BRITISH STANDARDS INSTITUTION, *BS 476 Fire tests on building materials and structures*, Milton Keynes
    Part 3 External fire exposure roof tests (1975)
    Part 4 Non-combustibility tests for materials (1970 (1984)); *AMD 2483 and 4390*
    Part 5 Method of test for ignitability (1979); *AMD 3478*
    Part 6 Method of test for fire propagation for products (1981); *AMD 4329*
    Part 7 Surface spread of flame tests for materials (1987)
    Part 8 Test methods and criteria for the fire resistance of elements of building construction (1972); *AMD 1873, 3816 and 4822*

BRITISH STANDARDS INSTITUTION, *BS 1006 Methods of test for colour fastness of textiles and leather*, Milton Keynes (1978)

BRITISH STANDARDS INSTITUTION, *BS 2782 Methods of testing plastics. Part 10 Glass reinforced plastics*, Milton Keynes (1977)

BRITISH STANDARDS INSTITUTION, *BS 3496 E glass fibre chopped strand mat for the reinforcement of polyester resin systems*, Milton Keynes (1973)

BRITISH STANDARDS INSTITUTION, *BS 3532 Unsaturated polyester resin systems for low pressure fibre reinforced plastics*, Milton Keynes (1962); *PD 5205, PD 5637, AMD 91, AMD 1001 and AMD 1672*

BRITISH STANDARDS INSTITUTION, *BS 3691 Glass fibre rovings for the reinforcement of polyester and epoxide resin systems*, Milton Keynes (1969); *AMD 746, AMD 1861 and AMD 3130*

BRITISH STANDARDS INSTITUTION, *BS 3900: Part C5 Method of test for paints: determination of film thickness*, Milton Keynes (1975)

BRITISH STANDARDS INSTITUTION, *BS 4154 Corrugated plastics translucent sheets made from thermosetting polyester resins (glass fibre reinforced)*, Milton Keynes (1985)
BRITISH STANDARDS INSTITUTION, *BS 4549 Guide to quality control requirements for reinforced plastics mouldings. Part 1 Polyester resin mouldings reinforced with chopped strand mat or randomly deposited glass fibres*, Milton Keynes (1970)
BRITISH STANDARDS INSTITUTION, *BS 4618 Recommendations for the presentation of plastics design data. Part 4 Environmental and chemical effects*, Milton Keynes
BRITISH STANDARDS INSTITUTION, *BS 4800 Colours for building purposes*, Milton Keynes (1981)
BRITISH STANDARDS INSTITUTION, *BS 4904 External cladding colours for building purposes*, Milton Keynes (1978)
BRITISH STANDARDS INSTITUTION, *BS 4994 Specification for vessels and tanks in reinforced plastics*, Milton Keynes (1973); *Supplement P.D. 6480* (1977)
BRITISH STANDARDS INSTITUTION, *BS 5606 Code of practice for accuracy in building*, Milton Keynes (1978); *AMD 4166*
BRITISH STANDARDS INSTITUTION, *BS 5750 Quality systems*
BRITISH STANDARDS INSTITUTION, *BS 6093 Code of practice for design of joints and jointing in building construction*, Milton Keynes (1981)
BRITISH STANDARDS INSTITUTION, *BS 6213 Guide to the selection of constructional sealants*, Milton Keynes (1982)
BRITISH STANDARDS INSTITUTION, *BS 6399 Loadings for buildings. Part 1 Code of practice for dead and imposed loads*, Milton Keynes (1984)
BRITISH STANDARDS INSTITUTION, *CP 3 Chapter 5. Code of basic data for the design of buildings. Part 2. Wind loads*, Milton Keynes (1972); *AMD 4952, 5152, 5343 and 6028*
BROOKES, A. J., *Cladding of buildings*, Construction Press, Harlow (1983)
BUILDING RESEARCH ESTABLISHMENT, *BRE Digest 69 Durability and application of plastics*
BUILDING RESEARCH ESTABLISHMENT, *BRE Digest 161 Reinforced plastics cladding panels* (January 1974)
BUILDING RESEARCH ESTABLISHMENT, *BRE Digest 199 Getting good fit* (March 1977)
BUILDING RESEARCH ESTABLISHMENT, *BRE Digest 217 Wall cladding defects and their diagnosis* (September 1978)
BUILDING RESEARCH ESTABLISHMENT, *BRE Digest 223 Wall cladding: design to minimise defects due to inaccuracies and movement* (March 1979)

BUILDING RESEARCH ESTABLISHMENT, *BRE Digest 227 Estimation of thermal and moisture movements and stresses:* Part 1 (July 1979)
BUILDING RESEARCH ESTABLISHMENT, *BRE Digest 228 Estimation of thermal and moisture movements and stresses:* Part 2 (August 1979)
BUILDING RESEARCH ESTABLISHMENT, *BRE Digest 229 Estimation of thermal and moisture movements and stresses:* Part 3 (September 1979)
BUILDING RESEARCH ESTABLISHMENT, *BRE Information Paper 11/79 Painting plastics* (November 1979)
HOLLAWAY, L., *Design and Specification of GRP Cladding*, Manning Rapley Publishing, Glasgow (1978)
HOLLAWAY, L., *Glass Reinforced Plastics in Construction—Engineering Aspects*, Surrey University Press, Guildford (1978)
INSTITUTE OF MECHANICAL ENGINEERS, *Designing with Fibre Reinforced Materials*, Mechanical Engineering Publishers, London (1977)
JOHNSON, A. F. (Ed.), *Engineering Design Properties of GRP*, National Physical Laboratory/British Plastics Federation, London (1978)
LEGGATT, A. J., GRP and buildings, *The Structural Engineer* (December 1976)
LEGGATT, A. J., *GRP and Buildings*, Butterworths, Guildford (1984)
NATIONAL BUILDING SPECIFICATION LTD, *NBS Section H41: GRP panel cladding/features*, Newcastle upon Tyne
NATIONAL GRP CONSTRUCTION AND ENGINEERING FEDERATION, *Guide to members and services*, NGCEF, 82 New Cavendish Street, London W1M 8AD
NATIONAL GRP CONSTRUCTION AND ENGINEERING FEDERATION, *Design guide for tolerances in GRP cladding*, NGCEF, 82 New Cavendish Street, London W1M 8AD
NATIONAL GRP CONSTRUCTION AND ENGINEERING FEDERATION, *Guidance notes on the storage, handling and protection of GRP products*, NGCEF, 82 New Cavendish Street, London W1M 8AD
NATIONAL GRP CONSTRUCTION AND ENGINEERING FEDERATION, *Guidance notes on the specification of fire retardant GRP cladding*, NGCEF, 82 New Cavendish Street, London W1M 8AD
NORRIS, J. F., CROWDER, J. R. and PROBERT, C., The weathering of glass reinforced polyesters under stress—short term behaviour, *Composites* (July 1976)
OWENS/CORNING FIBERGLAS (GB) LTD, *Design data: fibreglass composites*, Brussels
SCOTT BADER CO. LTD, *Crystic polyester handbook*, Wellingborough (1985)

46

Thermosetting Resins

S A Hurley BSc, PhD
Taywood Engineering Ltd

M L Humpage BTech, CChem, MRSC
Fosroc Technology

Contents

46.1 General description 46/3
    46.1.1 Thermosets 46/3
    46.1.2 Thermosetting resins 46/3
    46.1.3 The cure of thermosetting resins 46/4

46.2 Application 46/5
    46.2.1 Fabrication and physical forms 46/5
    46.2.2 Typical uses 46/5

46.3 The production and curing reactions of
    thermosetting resins 46/5
    46.3.1 Epoxy resins 46/6
    46.3.2 Unsaturated polyesters, acrylates and
           vinyl esters 46/7
    46.3.3 Furane resins 46/10
    46.3.4 Polyurethanes 46/10

46.4 Modification of thermosetting resins 46/11
    46.4.1 Reactive diluents, resinous modifiers
           and plasticizers 46/12
    46.4.2 Pigments, reinforcing agents and fillers 46/12
    46.4.3 Miscellaneous additives 46/13

46.5 Properties 46/13
    46.5.1 Health and safety 46/14
    46.5.2 Shelf-life 46/14
    46.5.3 Viscosity 46/14
    46.5.4 Pot life and cure rate 46/14
    46.5.5 Exotherm 46/15
    46.5.6 Cure shrinkage 46/15
    46.5.7 Mechanical properties 46/15
    46.5.8 Creep and stress relaxation 46/16
    46.5.9 Chemical resistance 46/16
    46.5.10 The effects of temperature and fire 46/16
    46.5.11 Adhesion 46/16

46.6 Responsibilities of the formulator and the
    end-user 46/16

Bibliography 46/17

46.1 General description

46.1.1 Thermosets

Polymers are large molecules composed of repeating structural units and the chemical nature of these units provides a generic description of the materials. However, the properties of polymers depend not only upon this chemical composition, but also (and very significantly) upon the spatial arrangement of the structural units in relation to one another, and the overall molecular shape, i.e. the microstructure of the polymer (*Figure 46.1*).

At the molecular level, many common polymeric materials have an extensive and continuous three-dimensional network structure (*Figure 46.1(d)*). Solid, high-molecular-weight polymers of this type which, unless degraded in the process, are essentially infusible and insoluble are known as thermosets. They are formed by irreversibly extending and cross-linking the linear or branched molecular chains of certain fusible polymeric precursors (*Figure 46.1(b)* and *46.1(c)*) via reactive groups which become network junction points. Such precursors are known as thermosetting polymers and, although the conversion to thermosets is a polymerization reaction, it is more commonly referred to as the curing or hardening process.

Once the characteristic three-dimensional network structure has been formed the external physical shape of a thermoset cannot be usefully changed by the application of heat or pressure. Although some softening may occur with increased temperature, decomposition generally takes place prior to melting.

In contrast, many non-thermosetting polymers consisting solely of discrete linear or branched molecular chains yield very viscous liquids when heated sufficiently. This purely physical process of softening and re-solidifying the polymer can be repeated indefinitely without permanently changing the molecular-chain structure (provided, of course, thermal decomposition does not occur). Such polymers, e.g. polyethylene, polystyrene and polyvinyl chloride, can be re-shaped and fabricated by the application of heat and pressure and are known conventionally as thermoplastics. The ability to melt and flow arises because the molecular chains are comparatively unrestrained and are free to move past one another. Most thermoplastics can also be dissolved in various solvents, a further demonstration of chain separation—thermosets are swollen by powerful solvents but the cross-linked structure prevents complete dissolution.

The microstructure of many elastomers (*Figure 46.1(e)*) is intermediate between that of thermosets and thermoplastics. Here, the degree of cross-linking is too low to give the characteristic molecular rigidity of thermosets. However, it is sufficient to restrain long-range movement of the molecular chains and contributes to the typical recovery of shape and dimensions on release of an applied stress.

If a cross-linked network structure is viewed in simple physical terms, then it will be readily appreciated that, even for thermosets, a property such as elastic modulus could be varied quite widely if the inherent flexibility of the chain segments and the frequency of the cross-linking junction points could also be varied. Such control of the final molecular structure, and thus many properties, can be achieved by choice of the appropriate thermosetting polymers, co-reactants, and reaction conditons.

46.1.2 Thermosetting resins

The term 'synthetic resin' is used to describe man-made thermosetting pre-polymers because, although some are low-melting-point solids, many have the viscous, sticky consistency of naturally occurring resins, e.g. those secreted from coniferous trees.

Conventional terminology can be confusing as both the cross-linked polymers and the pre-polymers are commonly described as 'resins'. Thus, one component of a two-pack epoxy adhesive is an epoxy resin which, on reaction with the second component (the hardener or curing agent), gives a cured adhesive which is also frequently referred to as an epoxy resin. Strictly, the term 'resin' should be applied only to the precursor—the cured material is simply an 'epoxy'. This dual use is widespread but, fortunately, the specific context usually conveys the exact meaning.

Thermosetting resins, whether viscous liquids or soluble, fusible solids, generally consist of low- to intermediate-molecular-weight polymers. In both physical forms, they have specific reactive, functional groups either within or at the ends of the molecular chains.

The following generic chemical types are classified as thermosetting resins:

(1) epoxies, furanes, polyurethanes and silicones;
(2) unsaturated polyesters, vinyl esters and certain acrylates; and
(3) phenol, urea, resorcinol and melamine-formaldehydes.

The thermosetting systems which incorporate formaldehyde are widely used in construction; for example, as laminates, mouldings, adhesives, surface coatings, and as binders in the manufacture of chipboard. These resins are most commonly used under factory conditions as heat is essential for the promotion of the cross-linking reactions and the fabrication process often requires the application of pressure. Similarly, heat is required to cure thermosetting silicone resins which are used as heat-resistant coatings. These systems are not dealt with in the present chapter which concentrates on the other resins noted above—materials

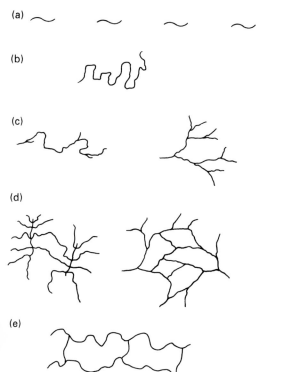

(a)

(b)

(c)

(d)

(e)

Figure 46.1 Planar representations of polymer microstructures: (a) monomers; (b) randomly coiled linear polymers (thermoplastics); (c) branched polymers; (d) cross-linked polymers (thermosets); (e) elastomeric polymer

which are widely used on site where cure takes place at the point of future service.

In general, this chapter deals with resin systems which are relatively rigid and of high strength in the cured state. Thus, cellular foamed materials and polyurethane, or silicone based elastomeric joint sealants, for example, will not be discussed.

46.1.3 The cure of thermosetting resins

In the uncured state most thermosetting resins have very limited direct application, the use of higher molecular-weight linear-chain epoxy resins as coatings being, perhaps, a notable exception to the general need for cross-linking. The essential curing or hardening process is induced via the reactive functional groups contained either within or at the ends of the resin molecules. These groups may react with each other or, more commonly, with another reactive material which thus assists the cross-linking process.

It must be appreciated that the network structure is not formed by chance, but by utilizing reactions which are designed to give a three-dimensional network (rather than simple branching or lengthening of linear polymer chains). Consequently, the number of functional groups present is important as is their chemical nature and molecular position.

For some thermosetting resins, the cure reactions take place only if heat is also applied. However, in many cases, sufficient cross-linking for excellent service properties can be obtained at normal, or even fairly low, ambient temperatures by using sufficiently reactive thermosetting resins and co-reactants.

Two common routes to the cross-linked network structures are illustrated in a simplified schematic form in *Figure 46.2*. The co-reactant may take the form of a curing agent (hardener) which becomes chemically linked within the network structure. In this case, reaction between the functional groups on the thermosetting resin and those of the curing agent commences immediately upon mixing, provided the temperature is not too low (*Figure 46.2(a)*). In other cases, the thermosetting prepolymer and a lower molecular-weight cross-linking agent may be pre-mixed, as reaction between the two does not occur unless an initiator or catalyst is added to stimulate the process (*Figure 46.2(b)*).

The importance of the number of functional groups present in the resin molecules and co-reactants was noted above. The term 'functionality' is used to define the number of groups per molecule which take part directly in polymerization or cross-linking reactions.

In the type of cross-linking scheme illustrated in *Figure 46.2(a)*, a monofunctional reactive group is situated at each end

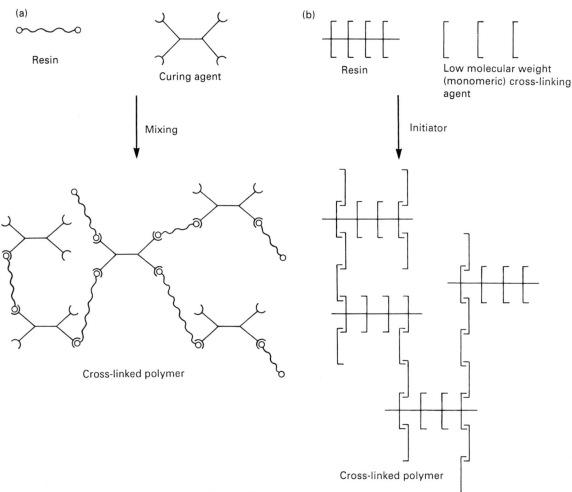

Figure 46.2 Two common routes to cross-linking of thermosetting resins

of the relatively low-molecular-weight resin molecule. Consequently, only linear polymers would be obtained if the molecular functionality of the co-reactant was also equal to 2, i.e. if both resin and curing agent were difunctional. In this type of reaction, therefore, one of the reacting materials must have a functionality of at least 3 in order to generate network junction points and, following initial branching of the chains, a cross-linked final structure.

For the type of reaction shown in *Figure 46.2(b)*, the network structure is obtained by cross-linking fairly high-molecular-weight linear polymers containing reactive groups within the molecular chain. The reactive group (denoted by the symbol ']'), may be regarded as difunctional and thus, in principle, only one of these groups on each polymer chain is sufficient for the formation of a network structure. The resin system in this case is a mixture of difunctional polymer and difunctional cross-linking agent. In practice, a greater density of cross-linking is achieved by using polymers with a number of difunctional groups within the chain.

For both of the above cases, strong covalent bonds are formed during cross-linking and, although the cure reaction may be retarded, stopped, or accelerated, once it has taken place it is irreversible.

Applied heat may be used to accelerate the rate of the reaction or, following an initial low-temperature cure, it may be used to induce further reaction, thus giving a greater degree of cross-linking (post-cure reaction); greater rigidity, or improved chemical resistance, for example, may thus be obtained.

46.2 Application

46.2.1 Fabrication and physical forms

As noted above, cured thermosetting resins cannot be shaped by heat and pressure. Consequently, fabrication for service has to be accomplished by placing the resin and co-reactant immediately after mixing, e.g. by pouring, pumping, spreading, brushing, or spraying. Conversion to the cross-linked network structure and the required rigid form then follows by irreversible chemical reaction at a pre-determined rate, possibly assisted by heat.

Rather than representing a problem, this inherent processing requirement confers versatility. It allows resins to be fabricated not just under routine factory control, but also on site under ambient conditions, an invaluable property in many civil engineering and construction applications where placing and fixing a preformed rigid shape would be impossible, or undesirable.

Thermosetting resins also give the basis for a very wide range of proprietary products which are developed by:

(1) adding modifying materials such as inert fillers and solvents to obtain a variety of physical forms; and
(2) varying the chemical nature of the resin and the co-reactant (catalyst, hardener or curing agent) to give different properties.

Thus, the physical nature prior to cross-linking can range from a low-viscosity liquid to a non-flowing mortar or concrete, with obvious benefit to specific applications. The rate of the hardening reaction can also be controlled to suit particular requirements, for example, use under different ambient conditions, or time to achieve the service properties. Furthermore, as the detailed chemical structures resulting from the cross-linking reaction are virtually unlimited, the service properties of thermosets can vary very widely.

It should be emphasized that this diversity does not give the user complete freedom to interchange generic types, or even specific formulations, as not all resin systems are suited to a given application.

46.2.2 Typical uses

Due to the great variation of chemical types and physical forms, it is not possible in a chapter of this length to discuss in detail the wide range of applications of resin based products. However, a summary of common uses in construction and civil engineering is given in *Table 46.1*.

The publications given in the bibliography at the end of this chapter should be consulted for more detailed consideration of specific applications. In addition, the extensive commercial literature which is readily available from product suppliers gives an excellent overview of the many uses of these materials.

The terms given below are commonly used in the literature—their applicability to resin systems is indicated, although they are also used for other polymer types.

Polymer–concrete (PC)	Resin binder + fillers
Polymer-impregnated concrete (PIC)	Portland cement concrete impregnated with a resin system
Polymer–Portland cement concrete (PPCC) or polymer–modified concrete (PMC)	Modification of an aqueous slurry of Portland cement concrete with a resin system

46.3 The production and curing reactions of thermosetting resins

A brief description of the more common manufacturing processes used to produce a number of thermosetting resins is given below,

Table 46.1 Uses of resin systems in construction and civil engineering

	Epoxy	Unsaturated polyester	Vinyl ester	Thermosetting acrylates	Furanes	Polyurethanes
Sealants for movement joints	(✓)*	—	—	—	—	✓†
Coatings/linings	✓	✓	✓	—	✓	✓
Chemically resistant renders	✓	✓	✓	✓	✓	✓
Impregnation	✓	✓	—	✓	—	✓
Adhesives/jointing	✓	✓	—	—	✓	✓
Floor toppings	✓	(✓)	(✓)	✓	—	✓
Repair materials	✓	✓	—	✓	—	(✓)
Gap filling/load bearing grouts	✓	✓	—	✓	—	—

* Little movement capability
† Usually in elastomeric form.

together with some examples of how these resins are cured. Due to the chemical complexities and numerous variations which are possible, this account is necessarily both simplified and illustrative. Furthermore, although space does not allow the chemical principles governing various cure reactions to be discussed in any detail, it must be emphasized that these principles determine such features as the need for thorough mixing, the rate of gelation and cure, and the ambient conditions under which a reaction will take place. Consequently, they have a significant effect on the manner in which various products must be used and the type of applications which are suitable for a given resin type.

46.3.1 Epoxy resins

Epoxy resins were first synthesized in the late 1930s, with commercial manufacture by Ciba A.G. of Switzerland (now Ciba-Geigy) and Shell Chemicals commencing in the early 1950s. Epoxies are one of the major thermosetting resins, produced in high volume and with extremely diverse applications due to their excellent adhesion to a wide variety of substrates (including wet surfaces), a high strength-to-weight ratio, outstanding toughness, high electrical resistance and excellent durability and chemical resistance.

Although many special epoxies are available, most formulations used in construction are based on a standard liquid resin which is synthesized from bisphenol-A (or bisphenol-F) and epichlorohydrin. As shown in *Figure 46.3*, the bisphenols are synthesized from phenol and either acetone (bis-A) or formaldehyde (bis-F); epichlorohydrin is produced from propylene and chlorine.

As the precursor structure shown in *Figure 46.3* contains two glycidyl ether groups per molecule, this relatively low-molecular-weight liquid epoxy resin is often referred to as a diglycidyl ether of bisphenol-A (DGEBA). Various degrees of purity are available, the 99.9% grade being virtually monomeric DGEBA, while the 95% Technical Grade, which is adequate for most applications, contains some higher molecular-weight resin.

By varying the bisphenol/epichlorohydrin ratio, as well as the reaction conditions, higher molecular-weight resins can be produced by successive addition of further reactants to the terminal epoxy groups. Thus, semi-solid to solid thermoplastic epoxy resins can be obtained which contain a range of chain lengths. It is then necessary to refer to an average molecular weight and, when this is sufficiently high, the resins can be used, for example, as solvent-based one-pack coatings which have useable properties without cross-linking.

The viscosity of DGEBA is approximately 15 Pa.s which, at 25°C and below, is rather thick for easy handling. To obtain resins with a lower viscosity, various modifiers are commonly added to DGEBA in amounts of 5–10 parts per 100 parts of resin and upwards. These viscosity reducers, or 'diluents', can be reactive materials which become fully incorporated in the final cured structure (e.g. relatively low molecular-weight glycidyl ethers) or non-reactive products which also act as conventional plasticizers in the cured resin, e.g. coal-tars, high boiling-point aromatic hydrocarbons, pine oil, dibutylphthalate, etc. Some diluents, for example benzyl and furfuryl alcohols, may also act as cure accelerators and partially react into the cured system.

The incorporation of diluents can have economic benefits due to both a unit-cost reduction and the possibility of increasing filler loadings when a lower viscosity resin binder is used. However, such use should not be viewed as giving inferior, 'cheap' formulations; when chosen appropriately and used at an optimum level, diluents can give a wide range of benefits, e.g. easier handling, more convenient reactivity and usable life, and improved surface wetting, air release, impact resistance and flexibility, etc. An optimized formulation containing such diluents can in fact out perform a typical undiluted system.

The typical epoxy resins described above cannot be cross-linked by heat alone—even heating to 200°C has little effect. In order to convert the resins into a network structure, it is necessary to add a co-reactant, or curing agent. The choice of curing agent is very important as it has a critical effect on properties such as usable life and cure-rate, temperature limits of use, viscosity, mechanical properties, chemical resistance, initial colour and colour stability, and adhesion. It has been estimated that there are well in excess of 500 curing agents for epoxies on the European market. Fortunately, selection is eased by the fact that many of these curing agents fall into reasonably well-defined groups with known characteristics.

The most commonly used epoxy curing agents in typical civil engineering and construction applications are based on aliphatic, cyclo-aliphatic and aromatic amines, and polyamides derived by reaction between vegetable oil carboxylic acids and aliphatic amines (see *Figure 46.4*). Special amine curing agents which emulsify the hydrophobic liquid epoxy resins are used for water-borne formulations.

In general, these amine curing agents are supplied as formulated proprietary materials rather than as pure chemicals; for example, as blends which may also contain catalysts and other cure modifiers. Very frequently, curing agents are supplied in the form of higher molecular-weight 'resinous amines' (adducts) derived from reaction between an epoxy resin and a simple low molecular-weight amine. While the amine functionality and the basic performance are retained, such adducts can impart more convenient mixing ratios with the resins (e.g. 50–70 parts by weight (p.b.w.)/100 p.b.w. rather than 10–20 p.b.w./100 p.b.w.), a greater range of pot-lives, less sensitivity to atmospheric conditions and easier, safer handling (less volatility and lower toxicity).

The detailed pathway of the cross-linking cure reaction varies with the particular amine used as co-reactant. However, with many amines, the mechanism can be represented by the simplified form shown in *Figure 46.5*. where a tetra-functional primary amine is used. A notable feature of the cure reaction is that low molecular-weight volatile materials are not evolved, thus avoiding the formation of voids in the solid.

It is important to note that the amine curing agent reacts by addition to the resin and becomes a permanent part of the cross-linked structure. Thus, a certain resin/curing-agent mix ratio is required to obtain an optimum degree of cross-linking and a good balance of cured resin properties. The amount of curing agent required for a particular epoxy resin type is recommended by the supplier and is often based upon experimental evaluation as well as theoretical calculations. Misproportioning of the resin/curing agent, usually beyond the $\pm 10\%$ level, is likely to lead to inferior properties; however, with some polyamide curing agents a fairly wide variation in mixing ratios may be employed to modify the flexibility of the cured resin without detriment to the other properties.

It is most important that the resin and curing agent are thoroughly mixed so that the reactive groups are brought into close proximity. Poor mixing may allow sufficient reaction for gelation, but the required service properties may not be obtained as completion of the cure reactions in the solid state becomes severely retarded.

The simplest form of an epoxy system (unfilled resin and curing agent) is used for two-pack gap- or crack-filling grouts, adhesives, clear coatings and primers. Such systems also represent the starting point for a range of formulated products which are obtained by the incorporation of pigments and fillers, etc.; for example, coatings, pastes, mortars, filled grouts and floor-toppings. Heavily filled systems (filler-to-binder ratio > 3 p.b.w./1 p.b.w. are usually supplied as three-pack products, allowing the resin and curing agent to be well mixed prior to addition of the filler.

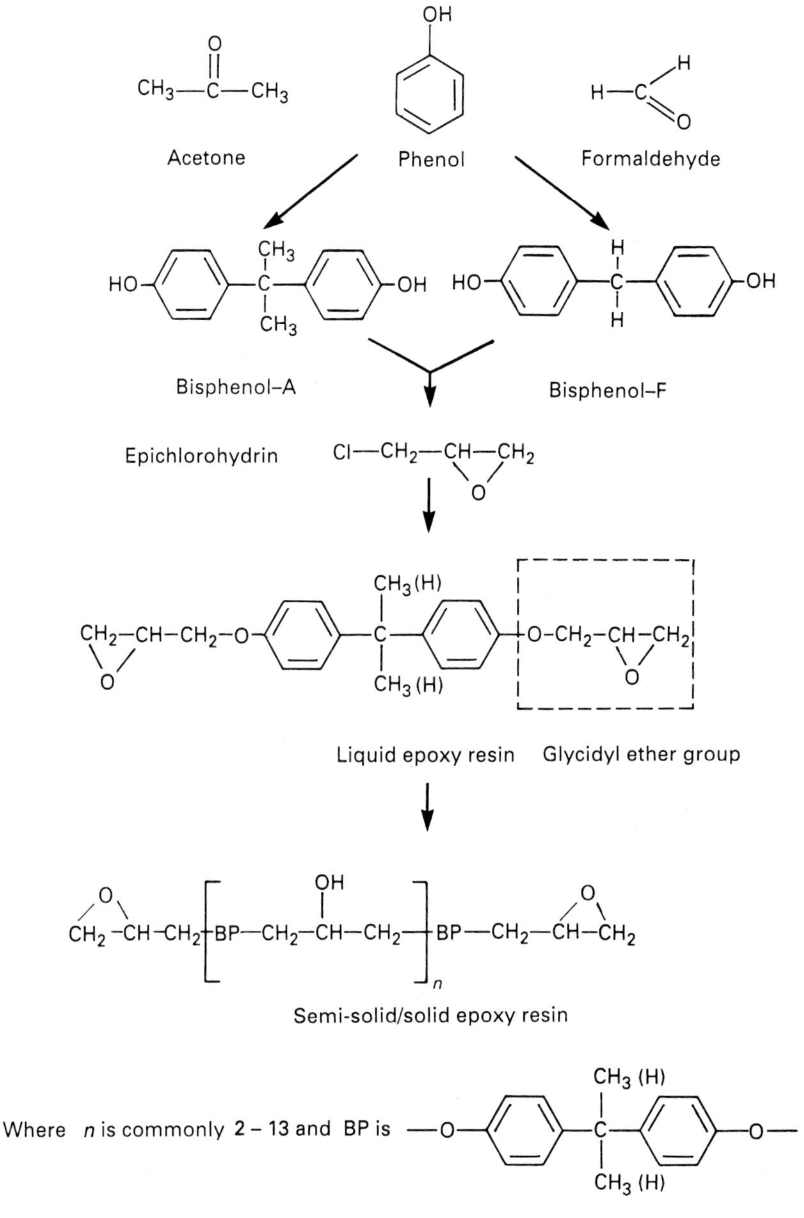

Figure 46.3 The synthesis of epoxy resins

46.3.2 Unsaturated polyesters, acrylates and vinyl esters

This group of thermosetting resins possess significantly different chemical structures. However, they are discussed under the same heading as cross-linking in all cases is achieved via the same mechanism—a chain reaction between unsaturated or double carbon–carbon bonds (C=C) initiated by free radicals.

46.3.2.1 Unsaturated polyester resins

Polyesters may be defined generally as polymers which contain

the recurring group

$$-C-O-$$
$$\parallel$$
$$O$$

in the main chain. A wide variety of polyester based materials is available commercially, ranging from surface coatings (alkyds) and plasticizers (phthalates) to fibres (Terylene). Those of interest here are linear polymers containing aliphatic unsaturation within the chain, i.e. reactive C=C bonds which provide sites for subsequent cross-linking. Polymers of this type first became available in the USA in 1946, and by about 1949 their

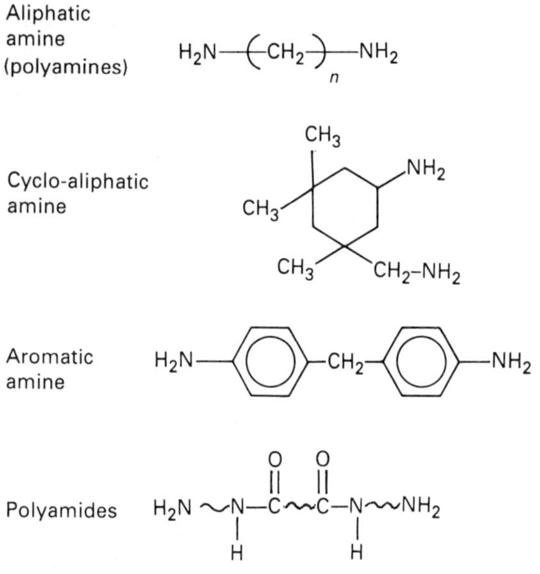

Aliphatic amine (polyamines)

H_2N—$(CH_2)_n$—NH_2

Cyclo-aliphatic amine

Aromatic amine

H_2N——CH_2——NH_2

Polyamides

Figure 46.4 Some epoxy resin curing agents

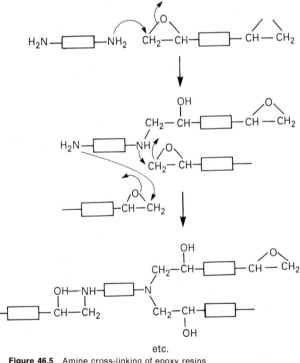

etc.

Figure 46.5 Amine cross-linking of epoxy resins

commercial use for glass-fibre-reinforced laminates was firmly established.

Linear unsaturated polyesters are prepared by an esterification reaction between a saturated diol and a mixture of polyfunctional (often dibasic) carboxylic acids. In practice, the corresponding anhydrides may be used in place of the acids. Although one of the acids must contain carbon–carbon bond unsaturation, the other (modifying) acid may be saturated, or may contain unsaturated groups of relatively low reactivity. The function of

this modifying acid is to reduce the frequency of reactive sites along the polymer chain, and hence to lower the cross-link density and brittleness of the cured resin.

Very many diols and dibasic acids may be employed in the production of unsaturated polyesters; those shown in *Figure 46.6* are among the most common. Variations may markedly influence the properties of the thermoset; for example, the flexibility and toughness, resistance to thermal degradation and chemical resistance, etc.

The unsaturated polyester itself is a thermoplastic solid at room temperature and of limited use. The molten polymer could be cross-linked directly but the reaction would be slow and the resultant structure would have poor properties. To avoid these limitations, the polyester is dissolved in an unsaturated reactive solvent as part of the manufacturing process. This additional component, invariably a vinyl monomer and most commonly styrene, thus acts as a cross-linking agent and also gives a liquid resin of usable viscosity. The unsaturated polyester resins used to formulate proprietary products are, therefore, solutions of the reactive polyester (65–70%) in a reactive monomer/solvent (30–35%). Reaction between the two components gives the cross-linked network structure.

In contrast to epoxy resins, these liquid polyesters contain all of the essential reactive groups for cross-linking; formation of the cured network structure is induced by a triggering mechanism. The reaction can be brought about solely by the action of heat, or even light. For this reason, unsaturated polyesters usually have a lower shelf-life than epoxies, even at normal ambient temperatures, although stabilizers (free-radical reaction inhibitors) are added during manufacture to avoid premature self-gelation prior to use. Stability is also enhanced by storage at low ambient temperatures in dark containers.

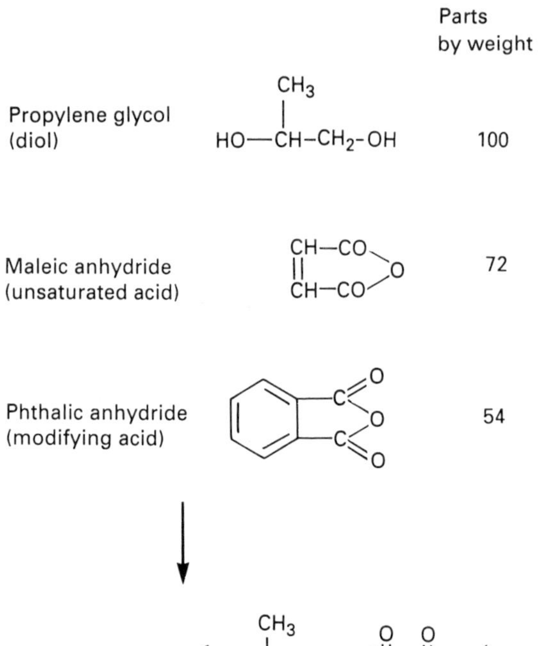

		Parts by weight
Propylene glycol (diol)	HO—CH-CH_2-OH with CH_3	100
Maleic anhydride (unsaturated acid)		72
Phthalic anhydride (modifying acid)		54

Figure 46.6 The manufacture of unsaturated polyester resin

As heat- or light-promoted cross-linking would be very difficult to control, the cure of polyesters is brought about by the addition, immediately before use, of a relatively low concentration (up to 5%) of an organic peroxide initiator, e.g. benzoyl, or cyclohexanone peroxides. Such peroxides, which are actually complex mixtures of peroxides and hydroperoxides, decompose relatively easily to give very reactive species known as free radicals. Once the low inhibitor concentration has been neutralized, these free radicals induce cross-linking via a chain reaction between the C=C bonds in the linear main chain and the solvent/monomer. This type of chain reaction leads to the formation of some full cross-links at a relatively early stage of the overall cure process. In contrast, the epoxy–amine addition reactions result in a more gradual build up of cross-linking.

When a peroxide initiator is used alone, heat is usually necessary to obtain an acceptably rapid cure (temperatures of about 70–120°C are required). To induce cure at normal and low ambient temperatures, a resin-soluble accelerator (activator or promotor) is also added, usually at a similarly low level to the peroxide. In the presence of such accelerators, commonly metal salts (e.g. cobalt octoate or cobalt naphthenate) or aromatic amines (e.g. dimethylaniline), the peroxide initiators are rapidly decomposed into the cure promoting free radicals without the application of heat.

If the complex reactions between initiator, accelerator and resin are omitted, the cure reaction of polyesters may be represented by the scheme shown in *Figure 46.7* where, as with epoxies, it may be noted that void forming volatile by-products are not evolved. The effect of the inhibitor, initiator and accelerator on the cure rate is summarized by the gel time data given in *Table 46.2*.

Although the peroxide catalyst is always mixed with the resin immediately before use, accelerators can be incorporated during the resin manufacturing process while still retaining a perfectly satisfactory shelf-life. The use of such pre-accelerated resins is

Table 46.2 Gel times for polyester resins*

Polyester resin†	Approximate gel time	
	20°C	100°C
Without inhibitor	2 weeks	30 min
With inhibitor	1 year	5 h
With inhibitor and catalyst	1 week	5 min
With inhibitor, catalyst and accelerator	15 min	2 min

* Data from British Industrial Plastics Ltd.
† Inhibitor, 0.01% hydroquinone; catalyst, 1% benzoyl peroxide; accelerator, 0.5% dimethylaniline.

obviously very convenient and they are hence readily available. It should be noted in passing that the peroxide initiators and the accelerators must always be stored and added to the resin separately as direct mixing can lead to a violent explosive reaction.

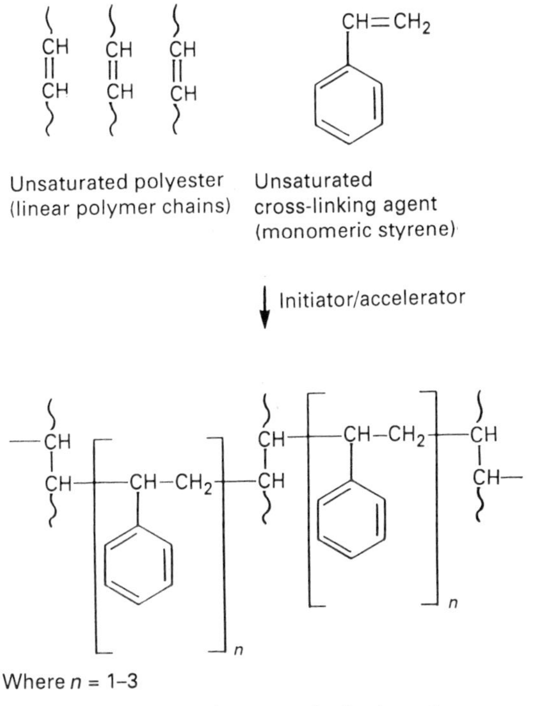

The peroxide catalysts are supplied in a diluted form, rather than as the much more hazardous neat materials; for example, as pastes (diluted with a plasticizer) or powders (dispersed onto calcium sulphate). The former are convenient when the resin-based product is a liquid or lightly filled paste. However, with the more highly filled two-pack grouts and mortars, the peroxides in powder form can be pre-blended with the fillers. Care in formulation is necessary as the peroxides are easily decomposed by many materials, e.g. carbon black pigment and iron salts present in fillers. Loss of activity during storage can lead to the delay, or complete absence, of gelation during use.

In contrast to epoxies, relatively little modification of polyester resins is carried out by the formulator. Once a pre-accelerated resin has been selected for the type of product required, formulation is concerned mainly with the appropriate level of catalyst for a given usable life and the fillers and pigments.

Polyesters, in general, are slightly more tolerant of site misuse than are epoxies. Provided they are not too extreme, variations in the catalyst level tend to affect the gelation and cure time rather than the service properties. In addition, as all the reactive sites are intimately pre-mixed in the liquid resin, cross-linking can proceed acceptably even when the catalyst and resin are mixed somewhat less than thoroughly.

46.3.2.2 Acrylate resins (acrylic esters)

By using monomers which contain both ester groups and carbon–carbon unsaturation, linear thermoplastic polymers with pendant ester side-groups can be obtained (in contrast to unsaturated polyesters where the ester groups are within the main polymer chain). This polymerization can be carried out at ambient temperatures using initiator/accelerator systems similar to those which cross-link unsaturated polyesters via a free-radical induced chain reaction.

Two very common monomers of this type are methylacrylate and methylmethacrylate (*Figure 46.8*), although many other types are available thus allowing the polymer properties to be varied widely. By incorporation of a poly- or di-functional acrylate monomer, a cross-linked network structure can be obtained as shown in *Figure 46.9*.

A wide variety of both linear and cross-linked acrylate based polymers have many uses as surface coatings, laminates and glass-fibre-reinforced plastics. However, the thermosetting acrylates of the type described above have found increasing use on site in recent years, particularly as neat resins for injection and impregnation and as filled systems which give patching mortars and floor toppings. These systems usually take the form of a viscous syrup containing the acrylate monomers, cross-linking

Unsaturated polyester (linear polymer chains)

Unsaturated cross-linking agent (monomeric styrene)

Initiator/accelerator

Where n = 1–3

Figure 46.7 The curing of unsaturated polyester resin

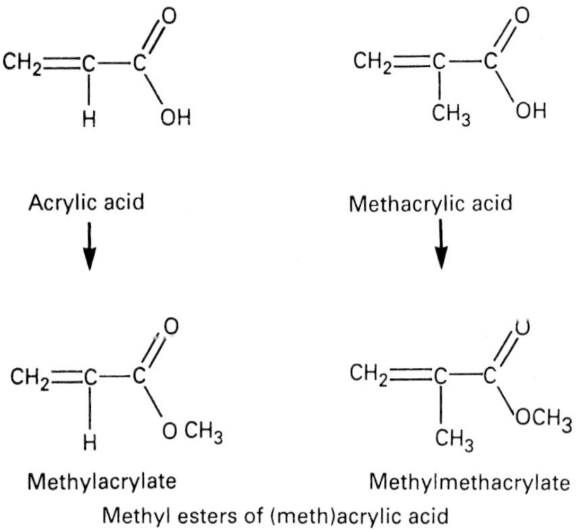

Acrylic acid

Methacrylic acid

Methylacrylate

Methylmethacrylate

Methyl esters of (meth)acrylic acid

Figure 46.8 Some acrylates

agents, and the accelerator to which the filler/peroxide blend is then added (compare with polyesters).

46.3.2.3 Vinyl ester resins

As discussed in Section 46.3.2.1, unsaturated polyester resins contain both repeating ester linkages and unsaturated carbon bonds along the backbone of the main polymer chains. After cross-linking, the ester groups remain, and the network may also contain some unreacted carbon double bonds. Both groups are potentially weak sites with regard to chemical attack such as hydrolysis and oxidation.

Improved chemical resistance can be achieved by modifying the carboxylic acid/diol chemistry, leading to a reduced number of ester groups in the main polymer chain (*Figure 46.10(b)*). With vinyl ester resins, this modification is taken a step further. Both the ester groups and the carbon double bonds are confined to the chain ends of the polymer, the main segment of which can be based on an epoxy (*Figure 46.10(c)*). Other resin variations, built upon the basic structure of unsaturated polyester and vinyl esters, are also available (*Figure 46.10(d)*) In addition to the improved chemical resistance arising from the reduced number of ester groups in the network, the longer chain segments between cross-linking points in vinyl esters usually give greater toughness compared to the more densely cross-linked conventional polyesters.

As with the polyesters, styrene is usually employed as a resin solvent/cross-linking monomer and cure is promoted at ambient temperatures using peroxide initiators and metal salt or amine accelerators—selection of the appropriate types and concentrations is again critical in obtaining the optimum overall resin performance.

Vinyl esters are more expensive than conventional polyesters. For many site applications such as bedding and anchoring grouts, mortars, and adhesives, the performance of the latter is quite satisfactory. Consequently, the use of vinyl ester tends to be confined to applications where their better performance is essential, particularly that at elevated temperatures and against aggressive chemical or ambient conditions. They are frequently used in factory processes to produce reinforced castings and laminates rather than being applied directly on-site. The full potential of the composites can then be realized by carrying out elevated-temperature post-curing in order to improve the service properties.

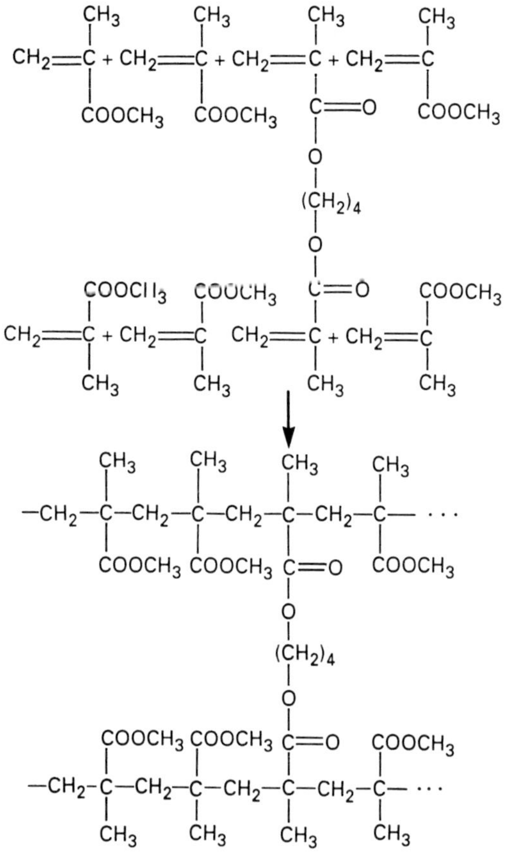

Figure 46.9 The cross-linking of acrylic resins

46.3.3 Furane resins

Although not very widely used, furane based resins are met in construction applications as filled jointing cements, grouts and mortars and, also, as surface coatings/linings and fibre-reinforced laminates. The cured resins have outstanding resistance to heat, abrasion, and many very aggressive chemicals.

The dark, free-flowing liquid resin used in these compositions is obtained by the controlled polymerization of furfuryl alcohol to a predetermined degree of conversion using an acid catalyst at a high temperature (*c.* 100°C) as shown in *Figure 46.11*. The resin obtained in this process (occasionally supplied in a ketone solvent) may then be cross-linked at room temperature using an organic acid catalyst such as *p*-toluenesulphonic acid (the mechanism of this reaction is not certain).

Unlike the resins considered earlier, which are mostly synthesized from petrochemicals, furane resins are derived from agricultural residues such as corn cobs and rice and oat hulls. These materials yield furfuraldehyde (furfural) which is then hydrogenated to furfuryl alcohol.

The furane resin systems are usually supplied as two-pack products, the liquid resin and a powder blend of the acid catalyst and fillers (silica sands, or carbon flour where resistance to hydrofluoric acid or hot concentrated alkaline solutions is required).

46.3.4 Polyurethanes

The commercial development of polyurethanes dates from the late 1930s following the pioneering work on plastics and

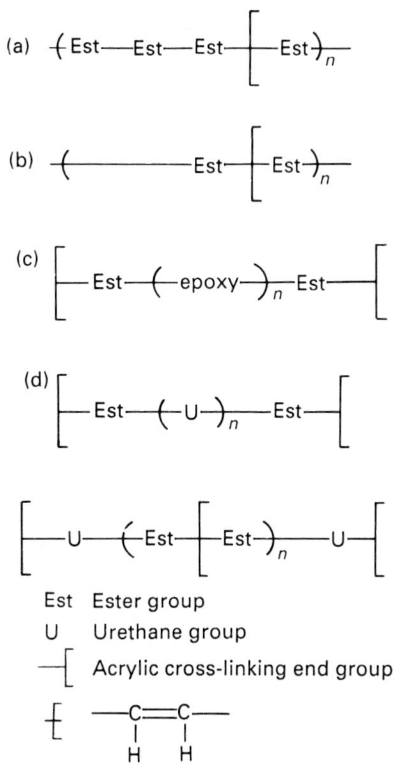

(a) $\left(Est\!-\!\!-\!Est\!-\!\!-\!Est\!-\!\!-\!\!\left[Est\right)_{n}\right.$

(b) $\left(\!-\!\!-\!\!-\!\!-\!\!-\!\!-\!\!-\!Est\!-\!\!\left[Est\right)_{n}\right.$

(c) $\left[\!-\!Est\!-\!\left(epoxy\right)_{n}\!-\!Est\!-\!\right]$

(d) $\left[\!-\!Est\!-\!\left(U\right)_{n}\!-\!Est\!-\!\right]$

$\left[\!-\!U\!-\!\left(Est\!-\!\left[Est\right)_{n}\!-\!U\!-\!\right]\right.$

Est   Ester group
U   Urethane group
⌐   Acrylic cross-linking end group
$\left\{\!\begin{array}{c}-C\!=\!C-\\ |\quad\ |\\ H\quad H\end{array}\right.$

Figure 46.10 Polyesters, vinyl esters and variations: (a) general-purpose polyester resin; (b) polyester with improved chemical resistance; (c) vinyl ester; (d) vinyl ester variations (urethane acrylates)

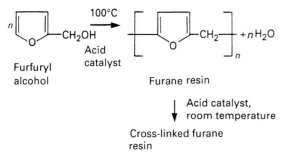

Furfuryl alcohol → Furane resin ($+nH_2O$); Acid catalyst, 100°C

| Acid catalyst, room temperature

Cross-linked furane resin

Figure 46.11 The production of furane resin

fibres by Otto Bayer in Germany. Subsequent intensive research demonstrated the versatility of polyurethanes as they became used as a basis for many adhesives, rigid foams and surface coatings and, by the 1950s, also as elastomers and flexible foams. The established mass producion of flexible foam in many countries, by the mid- to late-1950s, led to the ready availability of polyurethane raw materials and, consequently, the development of other applications followed readily.

Although they are used in mortars and, more extensively, in flooring applications, polyurethanes are perhaps most commonly encountered during construction activities as coatings and elastomeric sealants for movement joints. As such materials are not dealt with in the present chapter, the origins and formation of polyurethanes will be dealt with only briefly.

The characteristic urethane linkage ($-NH-CO-O-$) is formed by reaction between an isocyanate and a hydroxy compound as shown below:

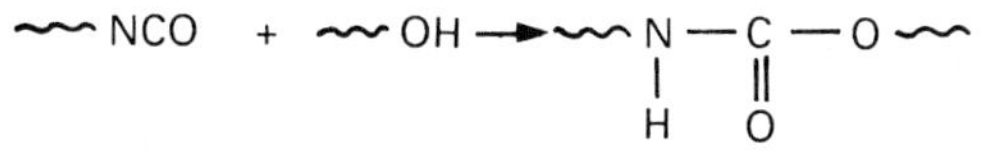

$$\sim NCO \;+\; \sim OH \longrightarrow \sim \underset{H}{N}\!-\!\underset{O}{C}\!-\!O \sim$$

It will be apparent from the earlier discussion concerning functionality (see Section 46.1.3) that a polyurethane will be obtained from the above reaction when multifunctional reactants are used. The reaction between difunctional materials will produce a linear polyurethane, while use of at least one reactant in a multifunctional form will yield a cross-linked polymer.

Cross-linked polyurethanes can be obtained from the reaction between a compound containing three or more isocyanate groups and a diol, but this approach is of limited commercial importance. A more common route to the cross-linked polymers is via reaction of a diisocyanate and a polyhydric compound (a polyol).

Schematically, this reaction is similar to the cross-linking of epoxy resins because the diisocyanate is analogous to the epoxy resin and the polyol may be equated to a multifunctional amine. In both cases, but particularly in the case of polyurethanes, side-reactions may complicate the simple cross-linking schemes outlined here. For example, isocyanates react with any chemical group containing an active hydrogen atom, including the urethane linkage itself. Such reactions may also contribute to the cross-linking process.

The most common diisocyanates used to prepare polyurethanes are toluene diisocyanate (TDI), diphenylmethane diisocyanate (MDI) and various isocyanate terminated prepolymers.

Numerous polyols are used in the production of polyurethanes. These range from low molecular-weight aliphatic diols, such as 1,4-butanediol, to polymeric hydroxy compounds (commonly based on polyethers or polyesters in the form of viscous liquids or low-melting-point solids). As in the case of the diisocyanates, blends of active materials are frequently employed in order to obtain the properties required. Individual hydroxy terminated polyester resins, for example, may have structures varying from linear to highly branched, thus giving a very wide range of polyurethane based products with different degrees of cross-link density.

The polyurethanes considered above are supplied as two-pack products. Brief mention should also be made of single-pack moisture curing polyurethanes. These are based on branched, isocyanate terminated prepolymers which cure on exposure to moisture according to the following (simplified) reaction scheme:

$$\sim NCO \;+\; H_2O \longrightarrow \sim NH_2 + CO_2$$

$$\sim NH_2 \quad \sim NCO \longrightarrow \sim NH\!-\!CO\!-\!NH \sim$$

Careful control of the formulation and avoidance of excess moisture during application is necessary in order to control the evolution of carbon dioxide and thus prevent the formation of excessive voids in the cured polymer.

46.4 Modification of thermosetting resins

As noted earlier in this chapter, a very wide range of properties can be obtained by appropriate selection of the resin and co-reactant(s) used to produce thermosets. Such variation of the basic elements may be viewed as determining the structural skeleton, or framework, for fully formulated, usable products. By analogy with building, the more specific characteristics required for given applications can then be obtained by the incorporation of additional materials. Such modifiers allow the formulator to tailor products to specific service needs, as they give scope for control of cost, physical consistency and rate of cure, in addition to final properties.

Some materials may modify the resin system merely by their physical presence. Others have a chemical effect on the cure reaction and, in some cases, they may become part of the cross-linked network. It is important that the type of modifier is carefully chosen and its level of addition optimized so that, in achieving certain requirements, other properties are not adversely affected; inevitably this may lead to some compromises in the final formulation.

The materials commonly used to modify thermosetting resin systems may be grouped in the following general categories:

(1) reactive diluents, plasticizers and resinous modifiers;
(2) fillers, pigments and reinforcing agents; and
(3) very specific additives which, at low concentrations, may be used to modify such characteristics as cure rate, bulk rheology, surface appearance and texture, air-release, adhesive capabilities, electrical conductivity and fire retardancy.

It should be noted that formulators continually seek to update their products. Care should be taken therefore in comparing the specification and performance of formulations of different vintage.

46.4.1 Reactive diluents, resinous modifiers and plasticizers

The use of reactive diluents in epoxy resin systems was discussed briefly in Section 46.3.1. In general, such diluents consist of low molecular-weight compounds containing at least one reactive epoxide group. When such diluents have a functionality of at least two, they become fully incorporated into the network in a similar manner to the resin itself. Monofunctional diluents also become part of the polymer, but they act as termination points in the growth of the cross-linked structure, thereby decreasing the final cross-link density.

A prime function of such diluents is to lower the viscosity of the resin, thus giving greater ease of handling and the potential for higher filler loadings. However, they may also have a significant effect on the prevention of resin crystallization at low temperatures, cure rate, mechanical properties, chemical resistance and surface tension—the latter property can, in turn, affect adhesive properties, the ease of wetting fillers and pigments and the ability of the system to release the air which is entrained during mixing.

In the case of polyurethane resins, the addition of low molecular-weight hydroxy (or isocyanate) compounds may fulfill a number of the functions discussed above. With unsaturated polyesters and acrylates, the level or type of cross-linking monomer may be altered, but property variations are more commonly achieved by changing the basic resin system, or by blending several resins.

A wide variety of modifiers in a resinous form is available, particularly for epoxy systems. Many of these take part in the cure reaction and they include epoxy functional polymers with very flexible linear-chain structures, isocyanates, phenolics, silicones and polysulphides.

Essentially non-reactive materials which are commonly added to resin-based systems in order to modify such properties as flexibility, toughness, thermal shock resistance and chemical resistance include coal-tar pitch, petroleum-derived bitumens, both naturally occurring and synthetic hydrocarbon resins and phthalate plasticizers.

46.4.2 Pigments, reinforcing agents and filllers

Pigments are usually added to resin systems by the formulator although, in some cases, they are made available in a dispersed, concentrated form, allowing the resin user to control colour. An inert plasticizer, or a reactive component of the system, e.g. an epoxy resin or a styrene monomer, may be used as a pigment carrier in the latter case. A specific decorative appearance given by some resin-based flooring systems is achieved by the addition of coloured thermoplastics in flake form. Micaceous iron oxide is often used as a pigment in coating systems as its lamellar structure can increase durability significantly.

The mechanical reinforcement of resin systems used in construction is most commonly achieved by the use of glass, either in mat or woven form. Glass flakes are also employed, particularly in coatings, to increase weather and chemical resistance and, hence, durability. The resilience of some resin systems may be improved by the addition of rubber in the form of crumb.

In volume terms, inert fillers represent the major method of modifying thermosetting resins. While fulfilling the two prime functions of cost reduction and control of consistency (paste, grout, mortar, etc.), such fillers also have a significant effect on many properties, for example: strength, hardness, impact and abrasion resistance; thermal coefficient of expansion; the volumetric shrinkage and the evolution of heat which occurs during the cure reaction; and long-term creep.

From the extensive range of materials which may be employed as fillers, the following are commonly and widely used: silica in the form of flour ($< 100~\mu m$), sand (up to 5 mm) and occasionally as larger aggregate; various forms of calcium carbonate (crushed limestone, and natural and precipitated chalk); barytes; and silicates, talcs, refined clays, alumina, mica and slate powder. Calcined bauxite, which is extremely resistant to polishing, is used to give surfacing materials with good skid resistance. Hollow spheres (manufactured from synthetic polymers, or glass, or obtained as a pulverized-fuel-ash by-product) are employed to give light-weight filled resin systems, as are such materials as pumice, perlite, and vermiculite.

Although fillers may affect the rate of cure by diluting the resin system, and also by reducing the heat generated by the exothermic reaction, they are not generally used to exert chemical control over the cross-linking process. Care must be taken, therefore, to avoid undesirable reactions between fillers and the components of resin systems. For example, many fillers, particularly those containing even traces of iron salts, may de-activate the peroxide catalysts used with polyester, vinyl ester and acrylate resins. Alkaline fillers may react adversely with the acidic catalysts used to cure furanes.

More obviously, the use of certain fillers would be avoided due to undesirable chemical reactions under service conditions, e.g. calcium carbonates when contact with acids is likely.

In addition to their chemical nature, the shape and particle size distribution of fillers must also be given close attention. Whereas an angular shape can give filled systems with good trowelling properties, the use of more rounded particles assists packing, thus minimizing the voids content and allowing higher filler loadings to be achieved. When silica sands are used, they are usually well graded (or occasionally gap graded) with a particle size distribution ranging from $< 100~\mu m$ up to 2–3 mm. However, the level of very fine material required for a minimum voids content in the filler must often be reduced in order to avoid a stodgy consistency and consequent handling difficulties. The gradings required by the formulator are usually obtained by blending sands with narrow particle-size distributions.

Finally, it should be noted that fillers used in resin systems must be very dry. Moisture levels of only 0.1–0.2% are sufficient to cause a marked drop in performance properties such as mechanical strength. Kiln-dried sands supplied in bags are used by the formulators of resin-based products. The further addition of sands commonly found on construction sites, even those appearing to be very dry, should not be permitted as the formulated properties are then unlikely to be achieved.

46.4.3 Miscellaneous additives

This category of modifiers, although important, will be discussed only briefly as the specific types and functions are so extensive. Virtually all the materials included under this heading are incorporated into the resin system by the formulator.

Numerous organic materials are used to accelerate the cure of epoxy resins, e.g. phenols, carboxylic acids, alcohols and tertiary amines. The cure of polyurethanes is commonly accelerated by compounds of tin.

A great variety of surface active materials, e.g. organo-silicon compounds, is used to promote adhesion by chemically coupling the cured resin to the substrate surfaces, to assist the release of entrained air, and, particularly in coatings, to control the surface appearance.

Organic compounds containing halogens (chlorine and bromine) and inorganic materials such as antimony trioxide are used to achieve fire retardancy.

The addition of electrically conducting graphite to flooring systems can prevent a build up of static and the occurrence of sparking in hazardous areas.

Waxes which float to the surface may be incorporated in polyester systems to reduce emissions of the styrene monomer and, in acrylate resins, to eliminate cure inhibition at the surface by atmospheric oxygen.

Rheological control aids known as thixotropes are also widely used in resin-based systems. These materials, which include chemically treated clays, castor-oil derivatives, fumed silica and certain polymer-based fibres, impart sag resistance, and thus allow application to inclined, vertical and overhead surfaces. Their use in poured or pumped grout systems can limit, or even eliminate, flow in the absence of applied pressure.

By virtue of molecular attractions, these thixotropes form a gel-like structure within the fluid or plastic resin system. This structure does not depend on permanent chemical bonding and, thus, it can be broken down by a mechanical action such as stirring, giving a more fluid consistency. If the system is then left in an undisturbed state, the gel-like structure is reformed at a rate which depends on the particular thixotrope employed.

46.5 Properties

The variations of the basic chemical building blocks of thermosetting resin systems outlined earlier, together with the potential for modification discussed in Section 46.4, leads to the possibility of obtaining a virtually endless number of resin-based products. As briefly shown in Section 46.2, this versatility enables resin systems to be used in a wide variety of civil engineering and construction applications. Each of these imposes certain requirements regarding ease of handling and long-term maintenance of service properties at an acceptable cost—aims which may be met in any particular case by numerous formulations. Site rather than factory use of these materials also dictates that acceptable handling and satisfactory cure are achieved under a wide range of ambient conditions.

While the relative ease with which resin formulations can be tailored to meet these demands is invaluable, it presents obvious problems in providing a summary of specific properties which is of direct value to the user or specifier of these materials. Consequently, only a brief guide to the main features of each generic resin type is given below. Some relative advantages and disadvantages of each resin type are summarized in *Table 46.3*, and *Table 46.4* provides a comparison of properties for epoxy, polyester and cementitious mortars/concretes.

For more specific data, the bibliography given at the end of this chapter should be consulted, together with suppliers' literature. The following points should be borne in mind when considering the properties of these systems.

(1) In general, the specific properties of a given product do not apply to another seemingly similar system as the formulations may differ markedly. Similarly, variations in formulation can also detract from the real value of case histories, although these always remain useful in a more general sense.

Table 46.3 Relative advantages and disadvantages of resin based systems

Resin type	Benefits	Disadvantages
Epoxies	Excellent adhesion, good chemical resistance, little cure shrinkage, relatively tolerant of cold/wet cure conditions, good mechanical properties, wide scope in formulation, wide variation in pot-life and cure time, good shelf-life	High viscosity, health and safety, chalking caused by sunlight, slow cure, limited high-temperature performance, high thermal coefficient of expansion, critical mixing
Polyurethanes	Good chemical resistance, wide range of flexibility, good mechanical properties, little cure shrinkage, good adhesion, wide formulation scope	Health and safety, water sensitivity during cure, critical mixing, high thermal coefficient of expansion
Polyesters	Fast cure, low-temperature cure, mixing tolerance, chemical resistance, good against acids, good mechanical properties, low viscosity	High cure shrinkage, adhesion limited by shrinkage, health and safety, relatively short shelf-life, chemical resistance against alkalis can be poor, exotherm
Vinyl esters	Similar to polyesters but with improved chemical resistance and elevated-temperature performance	Similar to polyesters (but with improved chemical resistance)
Acrylates	Similar to polyesters but cure shrinkage has less consequence, good intercoat adhesion	Similar to polyesters
Furanes	Outstanding acid resistance and high-temperature performance	Sensitive to alkaline conditions/surfaces during cure, brittle, high coefficient of thermal expansion

Table 46.4 A comparison of resin and ordinary Portland cement (OPC) based mortars and concretes

Property	Unit	Epoxy system	Polyester system	OPC system
Compressive strength	$N\,mm^{-2}$	55–110	55–110	15–70
Flexural strength	$N\,mm^{-2}$	20–50	25–30	2–5
Tensile strength	$N\,mm^{-2}$	10–20	10–20	1.5–4.5
Compressive modulus	$kN\,mm^{-2}$	0.5–20	2–10	20–30
Elongation at break	%	0–15	0–5	0
Linear coefficient of thermal expansion	$\times 10^{-6}°C^{-1}$	25–30	25–35	7–12
Water absorption, 7 days at 25°C	%	0–1	0.2–0.5	5–15
Maximum service temperature under load	°C	70–80	70 80	$\geqslant 300$
Rate of strength development at 20°C	hours or weeks	6–48 h	2–6 h	1–4 weeks

(2) Many measured properties of resin systems depend on the particular specimen size and test method used—due to the absence of generally accepted standards, test procedures may vary.

(3) When determining properties in the laboratory, both curing and testing are conventionally carried out at constant temperature. The time taken to achieve the same properties under laboratory and service conditions may differ significantly due to fluctuating ambient temperatures in the latter case. Thus great care regarding adequate cure must be taken when a certain level of strength, or chemical resistance, for example, is critical to service performance.

(4) Short-term properties such as mechanical strength are widely quoted, whereas information concerning longer term performance, e.g. creep, is frequently unavailable. It may be noted in passing that detailed property specifications for satisfactory long-term performance have yet to be agreed for many applications, although many demanding uses have been satisfactorily demonstrated in the field.

46.5.1 Health and safety

Many resin products contain components which in certain circumstances, can lead to both acute and chronic systemic effects via ingestion or skin absorption, respiratory problems, eye damage and dermatitis. While both raw-material suppliers and formulators expend considerable effort to eliminate such problems, few chemicals of this nature can be made completely safe. Mandatory requirements concerning product labelling and the supply of appropriate information should ensure that users of resin systems are aware both of potential risks to health and the appropriate protective requirements.

In general, epoxy resins have a low vapour pressure and low odour, although both may be increased by the presence of low molecular-weight diluents. Many epoxy curing agents tend to be more volatile, often with a marked ammoniacal pungent odour, but specially formulated low-odour curing agents are available which eliminate the risk of tainting when work has to be carried out in food-processing areas, e.g. flooring. Most epoxy resin systems present little, if any health risk once cured and some products are available which are approved for contact with potable water. Both epoxy resins and their curing agents generally possess high flash points and, consequently, present relatively low fire risks.

The cross-linking monomers present in polyester, vinyl ester, and acrylate resins are significantly volatile and possess distinctive odours. They also have relatively low flash points and, therefore, must be treated as a fire hazard. Although most organic peroxides are explosive, often on impact, this hazard is reduced by supplying the catalysts for the above resin systems in a dilute

dispersed form. Care must be taken, however, not to directly mix even these forms of the catalysts with the cure accelerators.

Following normal cure at ambient temperatures, resins of this type often contain relatively high levels of unreacted monomer. Consequently, special catalyst systems and an elevated temperature post-cure may be necessary where contact with potable water or foodstuffs is likely.

Particular attention should be given to the suppliers' instructions for handling polyurethanes, as all isocyanates are hazardous by inhalation. Often this hazard is reduced by using isocyanates which have a relatively low vapour pressure under normal ambient conditions, e.g. polyisocyanate prepolymers.

46.5.2 Shelf-life

The shelf-life of all resin systems depends on following the storage recommendations given by suppliers, particularly in the case of polyester, vinyl ester and acrylate resins.

A shelf-life of at least 1 year is normally expected to be easily attained for epoxies, two-part polyurethanes and furane resins. While an equivalent shelf-life can be obtained with the polyester and similar resins, these systems are inherently less stable as cross-linking can occur relatively easily under ambient conditions. Consequently, a shelf-life of only 6 months is frequently quoted for these materials.

46.5.3 Viscosity

The thermosetting resin systems discussed above may be used as neat liquids of relatively low viscosity or, in other applications, as highly filled systems which require heavy-duty forced action mixers and placing with firm tamping.

Due to the essential presence of very low viscosity cross-linking monomers (e.g. styrene and various acrylics), polyesters, vinyl ester and acrylate resins generally represent the lowest viscosity neat resin systems available (<1 Pa.s at 25°C). However, by using appropriate diluents and curing agents, epoxy resin systems can be obtained with sufficiently low viscosities (<5 Pa.s at 25°C) for deep injection into cracks in concrete which have a width of only 0.05–0.1 mm.

For all resin systems, the viscosity drops quite markedly over the temperature range −10 to 40°C and, consequently, when working at either climatic extreme handling difficulties can often be avoided by appropriate storage prior to mixing (in general, resins will respond very slowly to changes in ambient temperature due to their low thermal conductivity).

46.5.4 Pot life and cure rate

By appropriate formulation, the pot-life (or usable life) of thermosetting resins can be varied relatively easily from a few minutes up to at least several hours under a range of ambient conditions. To meet some special needs, for example bonding fresh concrete to old where extensive shuttering has to be fixed, the gel time of epoxy resins can be deliberately extended for many hours.

Ambient temperatures have such a marked effect on the pot-life of resin systems (10°C can change pot-life by a factor of 2) that many formulators supply specific grades of certain products for different climatic conditions.

The addition of fillers to a neat resin system may lead to either an increase or a decrease in the pot-life—a reduction in the exothermic heat of reaction (see Section 46.5.5) may slow the rate of reaction, but a non-usable consistency may be reached at a lower degree of cross-linking.

Once a thermosetting resin has set to a hard mass, it does not immediately possess the formulated service properties. Initial solidification represents a transition stage which may be attained at a relatively low degree of cross-linking. The reactions giving the network structure continue in the solid phase, although at a much reduced (and continually reducing) rate. As the extent of cross-linking continues to increase, an initial cure stage is reached where service requirements can be partly met, e.g. the ability to sustain a high proportion of full load.

The required properties are then fully developed as the final cure stage is reached. Even here, some potential for cross-linking may remain unrealized because the molecular motion required for reaction becomes so restricted. This motion can be assisted by raising the cure temperature; further reaction can then result, for example, in improved chemical resistance or increased ability to sustain loads at elevated temperatures. Use of heat in this manner is usually referred to as post-curing (a process that can occur quite naturally with a change in the ambient service conditions).

Although varying widely with the type of system, the initial cure of most resin systems is reached within 24 h (at 20°C). For some epoxy and polyurethane systems several hours may be sufficient to achieve this state. With the polyester, vinyl ester and acrylate based resins, initial cure may take only 5–10 min.

In general, epoxies and polyurethanes exhibit a gradual approach to the final cured state and full service properties may not be obtained for 7–14 days at 20°C; many polyester, vinyl ester, acrylates and furane resin systems, however, can reach the fully cured state within approximately 1 day.

At low ambient temperatures, the effective activity of the chemical groups taking part in the cure reaction can be severely reduced as the molecular mobility in the solid phase, even at a low degree of cure, can become so restricted (contrast post-curing). Consequently, cure rates at low temperatures are very much reduced and, in some cases, very little, if any, cure takes place.

The free-radical chain reactions leading to cross-linking of polyesters and similar resins can proceed relatively rapidly, even at temperatures down to about $-10°C$. However, satisfactory cure of epoxies usually requires a temperature of no less than 5°C (10°C for some systems); many polyurethane systems will cure down to about 0°C and furanes may be used at 5–10°C.

It should be noted that many systems may appear to cure well at low temperatures; for example, an acceptably high compressive strength may be obtained. However, the system may show this strength because it is, in effect, 'molecularly frozen' and in a glass-like state due to the low temperature. If the strength of a test specimen (e.g. a 40 mm cube) cured at a low temperature is determined after allowing, say, 2–3 h to warm to 20°C, then lack of cure may be shown by a much reduced strength, and by considerable deformation prior to failure (in contrast, brittle failure may be observed at the lower cure temperature despite a relatively low degree of cure). Lack of cure at a low temperature is usually a temporary phenomenon

as reaction will continue if the temperature of the resin is increased.

46.5.5 Exotherm

The reactions leading to cross-linking evolve heat and are, therefore, termed 'exothermic'. Most resin systems and many substrates are poor conductors of heat. Consequently, a considerable rise in temperature (and shortening of the pot-life) may occur, even in a resin volume of only a few litres or less, if the system is very active and lightly filled. In the extreme, with neat epoxy resins, the heat evolved may be sufficient to cause boiling and charring. The polyester type of resins tend to solidify prior to the peak temperature being attained and, in this case, an extreme exotherm can lead to expansive cracking of the solid mass. Even when these extremes are not reached, the cure exotherm can result in failures, as the contraction which occurs on cooling may give rise to stress concentrations at the resin/substrate interface and adhesive failure.

Where resins are used in very small volumes, or thin films, initial setting can be delayed as the exothermic heat of reaction is more effectively dissipated and, therefore, the temperature of the material remains close to ambient. This lengthening of the usable life can be of benefit, for example, when resins are used to repair concrete by slowly injecting fine cracks.

Due to the effect of the exotherm on pot-life, the latter should always be quoted not only at a given temperature, but also with reference to a given mass of mixed resin.

46.5.6 Cure shrinkage

In addition to the thermal contraction noted above, shrinkage of resin systems also occurs as a result of the chemical and accompanying physical changes which take place during cross-linking (both prior to and after gelation).

Epoxies and polyurethanes usually undergo very little shrinkage of this type and that which does occur is rarely of any consequence to the service performance. However, polyester, vinyl esters and acrylates undergo much higher levels of cure shrinkage (10–20% on a volumetric basis for unfilled resins, and 5–10% for typical filled systems). When a significant proportion of this shrinkage occurs in the solid state, the use of the resin for applications such as gap filling or flooring may not be possible as the shrinkage stresses may lead to debonding. This is often the case for polyester and vinyl esters, but not for the acrylate resins which are widely used as floor toppings.

46.5.7 Mechanical properties

All the resins discussed here are capable of giving very high-strength solids (compressive strengths up to 100 N mm^{-2}), although the formulated strengths may be quite low where other requirements take precedence. Similarly, modulus and ultimate strain capacity can be varied widely and thus, while some products are quite brittle (strain at failure $<1\%$), others can be rigid and tough, or soft and flexible (strain at failure of up to 100%).

Excellent impact and abrasion resistance can be achieved, leading to the extensive use of epoxies, acrylates and polyurethanes for industrial flooring where the performance requirements are very high. Some tar-extended epoxies, in combination with calcined bauxite, also have sufficient wearing resistance for use as anti-skid road surfaces.

Fatigue performance can also be very good, as demonstrated by the wide use of epoxies and polyesters to fix holding down bolts for vibrating machinery baseplates. Epoxies have also been extensively used to grout gaps under crane rails and baseplates.

46.5.8 Creep and stress relaxation

Creep of load-bearing resin systems rarely causes problems, particularly as many applications utilize filled products at normal ambient temperatures and both the stress and aspect ratio are often low. However, strain may increase unacceptably with time at more elevated temperatures.

The associated property of stress-relaxation is often beneficial and epoxies can be formulated to give this property in a controlled manner. Thus, differential stresses between a resin and substrate, due perhaps to marked differences in the thermal coefficients of expansion, or to thermal cure shrinkage, may be reduced, or alleviated.

46.5.9 Chemical resistance

Each of the resin systems discussed here has good resistance to water and dilute mineral acids and alkalis. Depending on the resin type and the specific formulation, good resistance against some strong acids and alkalis may also be obtained. Furanes, vinyl ester, and some polyesters for instance may be used in contact with fairly concentrated strong acids even at elevated temperatures. Resistance towards solvents and organic materials is more variable; for example, some epoxies are attacked easily by the organic acids contained in fruit concentrates and milk, but most are very resistant to predominantly aliphatic hydrocarbons such as petrol.

46.5.10 The effects of temperature and fire

Although the application of heat does not cause thermosets to melt and flow, it does induce some softening and possibly significant changes in such properties as modulus, creep, strength, and chemical resistance.

While many systems can be used non-structurally at temperatures up to at least 70°C, certain load-bearing applications may need to be considered more carefully if service temperatures above 40–50°C are anticipated. Any chemical changes which occur at these temperatures are more likely to be beneficial post-cure reactions than permanent degradation. Where service temperatures in excess of about 70°C have to be accommodated, particularly in non-structural applications and uses where chemical resistance is important, then furanes, vinyl esters and certain polyesters can often meet such needs.

Resin systems may also be formulated to have good resistance to thermal shock, thus allowing epoxies and polyurethanes, for example, to be used as steam-cleanable floor toppings.

The effects of fire on any material are complex and, consequently, this aspect of resin performance cannot be considered here in any detail.

Cross-linked resins are organic materials and, although they are not highly combustible, they are much more so than concrete and brick. The surface spread of flame and rate of fire penetration may be reduced by certain fillers, particularly at high filler/binder ratios, and thus many systems are self-extinguishing. However, the effects of fire, especially in structural applications, does need to be considered carefully at the selection stage. It must be kept in mind that toxic materials will be evolved from burning resins and also that a sudden loss of properties with a rapidly increasing temperature could have serious consequences.

46.5.11 Adhesion

Most thermosetting resin systems show good adhesion to a variety of substrates provided surface preparation has been carried out satisfactorily. Polyurethanes, and particularly epoxies, are perhaps outstanding in this respect, being assisted by the very low level of cure shrinkage and consequent absence of stress concentration.

Epoxy systems, if appropriately formulated, can give excellent long-term adhesion, even when applied to wet surfaces. Care must be taken, however, to distinguish between good curing and good adhesion in wet conditions, as the latter does not necessarily accompany the former. Once past the initial cure stage, epoxy resin surfaces are not particularly receptive to adhesive bonding, a property which can cause problems with multi-coat or multi-layer applications.

46.6 Responsibilities of the formulator and the end-user

Proprietary resin-based products are generated by formulators who act as a link between the end-user and the chemical companies who manufacture a very wide variety of resins, curing-agents, catalysts, and additives, etc. In general, the user has little scope to produce, or modify, resin systems to suit his particular needs and, consequently, must select a proprietary product from the range formulated, or tailor-made, for a given application. This supply chain, which also exists with other site-applied products such as surface coatings and joint sealants, is viable if all parties accept certain responsibilities.

Usually, the end-user or specifier (contractor, engineer or consultant) does not possess sufficient specialized knowledge and experience to deal with the complex chemistry and selection of components involved in the formulation of an acceptable resin product. Thus, the formulator is not merely a subdivider of bulk raw materials; he must make a balanced choice of components with appropriate judgement concerning inevitable compromises. The formulator must also provide products which:

(1) can be satisfactorily handled and cured under prevailing site conditions;
(2) have suitable properties for the service conditions envisaged; and
(3) are backed up by both short- and long-term data.

A predicament frequently confronting the user, or specifier, is that of selection from an overwhelming number of formulated products for a given application. In this case, detailed discussions should be held with the formulators, possibly backed up with advice and assistance from independent experts. However, the benefits of such contacts depend upon the end-user supplying as much information as possible regarding the intended application.

It is important to appreciate that, for some applications, the detailed property requirements have yet to be defined fully and clearly. In addition, while much short-term data may be difficult to compare, as test methods have yet to be standardized internationally, long-term information can be both difficult and expensive to obtain and, therefore, may not be available. Often, it is necessary to rely on documented case histories and, for some critical applications, special test programmes may have to be carried out. For commercial and technical reasons, formulations may be changed and this can further complicate both the selection of products based upon case histories and the usefulness of long-term data.

Once selected, a resin system must be used according to the formulator's instructions. All reputable manufacturers provide comprehensive instructions for the use of their products and these should be carefully read and understood before commencing work. The applicator must appreciate that a chemical reaction is being carried out at the point of use and that all such reactions are affected by the surrounding conditions, particularly temperature. Thus, use of a given product at unacceptably low temperatures (outside the formulator's recommendations) may lead to a very slow rate of hardening and attainment of service properties; use at unduly high temperatures may give insufficient time to place the material satisfactorily prior to hardening. Such temperature limits will vary with formulation as well as resin type. Attention must be given, therefore, to storage prior to use and likely weather conditions at the time of application and cure. Rheological characteristics at either temperature extreme may lead to poor adhesion if the material is too viscous to wet the surface thoroughly.

With most resin systems, great care must be taken to mix the components thoroughly in the correct proportion. The universal provision of pre-weighed packs ensures correct proportioning, provided the packs are used in their entirety as generally recommended. Satisfactory mixing often requires using special paddles or, for large packs of heavily filled products, forced action mixers.

Thought must be given to the pack sizes which are best suited to a specific application in order to avoid excessive exotherms and wasted or poorly applied material. The supplier's recommendations concerning surface preparation and the use of primers must always be followed as also, of course, should all requirements concerning health and safety matters.

Thus, in these areas, as well as others, both formulators and users play key roles in achieving satisfactory service properties and successful, cost-effective use. When these responsibilities are fully accepted, the great potential of resin-based systems can be realized.

Bibliography

Trade association

Information on the suppliers of formulated resin products may be obtained from: The Federation of Resin Formulators and Applicators (FeRFA), c/o Charles Allen Associates, 241 High Street, Aldershot, Hants GU11 1TJ, UK.

Testing

BRITISH STANDARDS INSTITUTION, *BS 6319 Parts 1–10 Testing of resin compositions for use in construction*, Milton Keynes (1983–90)
FEDERATION INTERNATIONALE DE LA PRECONTRAINTE *Proposal for a standard for acceptance tests and verification of epoxy bonding agents for segmental construction* (Mar. 1978)

Health and safety

CIRIA, *A guide to the safe use of chemicals in construction*, CIRIA (1981)

Bibliography

OHAMA, Y., Bibliography on polymers in concrete, *International Congress on Polymers in Concrete* (1987)

Conferences and seminars

International Congress on Polymers in Concrete: London, UK (May 1975); Austin, TX, USA (1978); Koriyama, Japan (1981); Darmstadt, Germany (1984); Brighton, UK (1987); San Francisco, CA, USA (1991)

Synthetic resins in building construction RILEM Symposium, (International Union of Testing and Research Laboratories for Materials and Structures), Paris, 4–6 September 1967
THE FEDERATION OF RESIN FORMULATORS AND APPLICATORS, *The use of resins in concrete construction and repair*, London, 18 October 1979, FeRFA, Aldershot
THE FEDERATION OF RESIN FORMULATORS AND APPLICATORS, *Resins in construction—20+ years experience*, London, 25 October 1984, FeRFA, Aldershot
THE PLASTICS INSTITUTE/INSTITUTION OF CIVIL ENGINEERS, *Resins and Concrete Symposium*, University of Newcastle-upon-Tyne, 17–18 April 1973

Books and articles

ADAMS, M., BROWNE, R. D. and FRENCH, E. L., 'Using polymer concretes', *Building Research and Practice*, 3, No. 4, 212–231 (Jul./Aug. 1975)
'Adhesives—civil engineering', *International Journal of Adhesion and Adhesives*, 2, No. 2 (Apr. 1982)
AMERICAN CONCRETE INSTITUTE *Epoxies with concrete*, Publication No. SP-21, ACI, Detroit (1968)
AMERICAN CONCRETE INSTITUTE, *Polymers in concrete*, Publication No. SP-40, ACI, Detroit (1973)
AMERICAN CONCRETE INSTITUTE, *Polymers in concrete*, Publication No. SP-58, ACI, Detroit (1978)
AMERICAN CONCRETE INSTITUTE, *Applications of polymer concrete*, Publication No. SP-69, ACI, Detroit (1981)
AMERICAN CONCRETE INSTITUTE, *Polymer concrete: uses, materials and properties*, Publication No. SP-89, ACI, Detroit (1985)
BOENIG, H. V., *Unsaturated polyesters, structure and properties*, Elsevier, Amsterdam (1964)
BRITISH PLASTICS FEDERATION/CEMENT AND CONCRETE ASSOCIATION, *A guide for the use of epoxide resins with concrete for building and civil engineering*, Advisory Note No. 12, British Plastics Federation/Cement and Concrete Association (Nov. 1968)
CONCRETE SOCIETY WORKING PARTY, *Polymer concretes–Report of a Concrete Society Working Party*. Concrete Society Technical Report No. 9, Concrete Society (Jan. 1975)
FELDMAN, D., *Polymeric building materials*, Elsevier/Applied Science, London/New York (1989)
HEWLETT, P. C. and SHAW, J. D. N., 'Structural adhesives in civil engineering', in *Developments in Adhesives—1*, Chap. 2, pp. 25–75 (ed. Wake, W. C.), Applied Science Publishers, New York (1977)
HOLLAWAY, L. (ed.), *Polymers and polymer composites in construction*, Thomas Telford, London (1990)
LEE, H. and NEVILLE, K., *Handbook of epoxy resins*, McGraw-Hill, New York (1967)
MAYS, G. C., 'Structural applications of adhesives in civil engineering', *Materials Science and Technology*, 1 (Nov. 1985)
POTTER, W. G., *Epoxide resins*, Butterworths, London (1970)
POTTER, W. G., *Uses of epoxy resins*, Newnes-Butterworths, London (1975)
SAUNDERS, J. H. and FRISCH, K. C., *Polyurethanes*, Interscience, New York (1964)
SEYMOUR, R. B. (ed.), *Plastic mortars, sealants and caulking compounds*, ACS Symposium Series 113, American Chemical Society, Washington, DC (1979)
SHAW, J. D. N., 'Adhesives in the construction industry: materials and case histories', *Construction and Building Materials*, 4, No. 2, 92–97 (Jun. 1990)
TABOR, L. J., *Effective use of epoxy and polyester resins in civil engineering*, CIRIA Report 69, CIRIA, London (Jan. 1978)

47

Silanes and Siloxanes

K Nakano Dr Eng
Osaka Cement Co. Ltd, Japan

Contents

47.1 Waterproof agents for concrete 47/3
    47.1.1 Waterproof agents 47/3

47.2 Basic structure and the reaction mechanism for impregnating waterproof agents made of silanes and siloxanes 47/3
    47.2.1 Basic structure 47/3
    47.2.2 Mechanism of reaction 47/4

47.3 Features of impregnating waterproof agents made of silanes and siloxanes 47/4
    47.3.1 Water-repellant property 47/4
    47.3.2 Water-vapour permeability 47/4
    47.3.3 Prevention of water absorption 47/4
    47.3.4 Permeability of impregnating waterproof agents 47/5

47.4 Prevention of deterioration of concrete with impregnating waterproof agents made of silanes and siloxanes 47/5
    47.4.1 Prevention of alkali–silica reaction 47/5
    47.4.2 Prevention of salt attack 47/6

47.5 Usefulness of silanes and siloxanes 47/7

References 47/7

47.1 Waterproof agents for concrete

47.1.1 Waterproof agents

Numerous factors such as water, oxygen, carbon dioxide, chloride ions, acids, ultraviolet radiation and temperature seem to be involved in the deterioration of concrete and reinforced concrete. Of these factors, water plays a major role in the alkali–aggregate reaction, frost damage and salt attack (due to chloride ions). Therefore, it seems likely that the durability of concrete structures will be greatly improved by appropriate waterproofing measures.

Waterproof agents for concrete are usually divided into two types: (1) agents which coat the entire surface of concrete; and (2) agents which penetrate into concrete and form a barrier within concrete. The former are called film-forming waterproof agents. Epoxy resins are representative of this type. The latter are called impregnating waterproof agents. *Figure 47.1* shows the commercially available impregnating waterproof agents classified by their major raw materials.

Impregnating waterproof agents are made of organic solvents or emulsions. When applied to concrete, they penetrate deeply into the material, through the capillary pores, and give concrete a waterproof property. In this way, impregnating waterproof agents can prevent the invasion of water or ions (dissolved in water) into concrete. Impregnating waterproof agents can be subdivided into silicon-containing and silicon-free agents.

47.1.2 Impregnating waterproof agents

At present, more than 40 waterproof agents of the impregnating type are commercially available. The first waterproof agent of this type was made of siliconate, which was developed in 1965. Thereafter, products made of silicon resins were developed in 1966, followed by products made of acryl resins and urethane resins (1974) and silanes (1978).

Of the silicones, methyl siliconate $[CH_3 \cdot Si(ONa)_3]$, i.e. silicone resin, is used for surface treatment of concrete, bricks and tiles. However, this substance has the following disadvantages:

(1) insufficient penetration into the material;
(2) poor durability;
(3) poor resistance to alkalis; and
(4) possibility of efflorescence if exposed to rain or sprayed water in 1–2 days after application.

Because of these properties, impregnating waterproof agents made of silicone resin have gradually been replaced by those made of silanes/siloxanes, which are now leading products amongst impregnating waterproof agents; their features are described in the following.

47.2 Basic structure and the reaction mechanism for impregnating waterproof agents made of silanes and siloxanes

47.2.1 Basic structure

Silanes/siloxanes are general terms for compounds with the chemical formula $Si_n \cdot H_{2m+2}$. The basic structure of silanes used for impregnating waterproof agents is alkylalkoxysilane in which the hydrogen has been replaced by a hydrophobic alkyl group or a reactive alkoxy group: $[R \cdot Si \cdot (OR')_3]$, where R and R' are alkyl groups such as methyl or ether groups.

If this alkylalkoxysilane monomer (shown in *Figure 47.1*) is polymerized, involving partial hydrolysis and condensation, oligomerous alkylalkoxysiloxane (shown in *Figure 47.3*) is formed.

If these silane monomers or oligomerous siloxanes are dissolved in organic solvents, impregnating waterproof agents made of silanes/siloxanes are obtained.

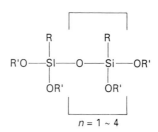

Figure 47.2 Structure of the silane monomer

Figure 47.3 Structure of oligomerous siloxane

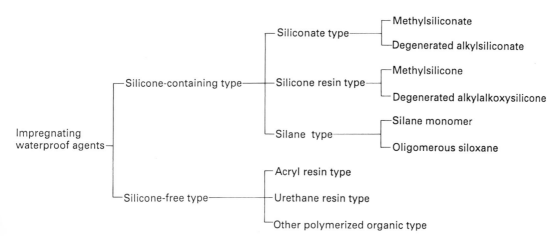

Figure 47.1 Specification of impregnating waterproof agents

There are many alkylalkoxysilanes. The permeability (a particularly important property) of impregnating waterproof agents made of silanes/siloxanes can vary according to the molecular weight of the alkyl group used. As the carbon number of the alkyl group becomes smaller (that is, the molecular weight becomes lower), the permeability becomes higher, accompanied, however, by an increase in volatility and a reduction in resistance to alkalis. As the carbon number of the alkyl group becomes larger (that is, the molecular weight becomes higher), the permeability becomes lower, although the volatility and the resistance to alkalis become lower. Other factors affecting this kind of waterproof agent include the concentration of silanes/siloxanes, the kind of solvent, the kind of surfactant, and the combination of solvent and surfactant. The effect of these factors on the features of this type of waterproof agent are considerable.

47.2.2 Mechanism of reaction

To illustrate the mechanism by which impregnating waterproof agents made of silanes/siloxanes exert their waterproofing effect, the reactions between a representative alkylalkoxysilane monomer and concrete are shown in *Figure 47.4*. As shown in this figure, the alkoxy group of the alkylalkoxysilane reacts with water to yield a silanol group (stage 1). Thus, alkylalkoxysilane becomes a reactive silane. This silane then becomes cross-linked to the hydroxyl groups on the concrete surface and pores. After the intermediate stage (stage 2), the relationship between the silane and concrete is stabilized by siloxane bonds (stage 3). At this stage, the concrete surface has been coated with hydrophobic alkyl groups and is hence highly waterproof.

47.3 Features of impregnating waterproof agents made of silanes and siloxanes

Impregnating waterproof agents made of silanes/siloxanes have

very interesting properties. Their major properties are described below.

47.3.1 Water-repellent property

When applied to concrete, a waterproof agent made of silanes/siloxanes penetrates the concrete and binds to its surface and pore surface by means of siloxane bonds. As a result, the concrete surface is covered with hydrophobic alkyl groups and becomes water-repellent.

As shown in *Figure 47.5*, the intensity of the water-repellent property is associated with the contact angle between the water and the concrete surface. As the contact angle (θ) increases, the concrete surface becomes more water-repellent. The contact angle between untreated concrete surface and water is less than 90°. When the concrete surface is treated with a waterproof agent made of silanes/siloxanes, the contact angle exceeds 90° and the concrete surface becomes highly water-repellent, as shown on the right-hand side of *Figure 47.5*. The contact angle between water and the concrete surface treated with a waterproof agent made of silanes/siloxanes is 120°.

47.3.2 Water-vapour permeability

The cavities in concrete include gel pores, capillary pores and air voids. The cavities which most profoundly affect the water-absorbing property of concrete are capillary pores which are left unfilled by hydrates in the process of hydration. The diameter of a capillary pore is about 20–5000 Å (0.002–0.5 μm). The length of a silane/siloxane molecule is about 10 Å (the length of a siloxane molecule varies according to the degree of polymerization, but the highest degree of polymerization used for this purpose is usually trimer). Therefore, capillary pores of concrete are not filled with this waterproof agent, and it is unlikely that vapour permeation into the capillary pores of concrete is suppressed by treatment of concrete with a waterproof agent made of silanes/siloxanes.

47.3.3 Prevention of water absorption

Treatment of concrete with silanes/siloxanes suppresses water absorption by concrete without obstructing the capillary pores. This effect of silane/siloxane treatment is attributable to the high water-repellent property of the wall of capillary pores after treatment with silanes/siloxanes (*Figure 47.6*).

Stage 1

$$R - \underset{\underset{OR'}{|}}{\overset{\overset{OR'}{|}}{Si}} - OR' \quad \xrightarrow{\text{Catalyst} + H_2O} \quad R - \underset{\underset{OH}{|}}{\overset{\overset{OH}{|}}{Si}} - OH$$

Alkylalkoxysilane   Reactive silanol

Stage 2   Stage 3

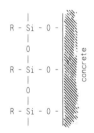

Figure 47.4 Reaction of alkylalkoxysilane and reaction between the concrete and the silane

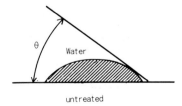

untreated

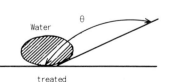

treated

Figure 47.5 Change in contact angle of water treated with silanes/siloxanes

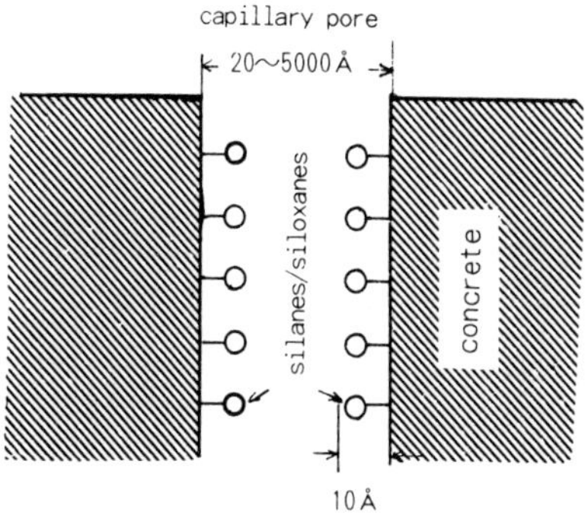

capillary pore

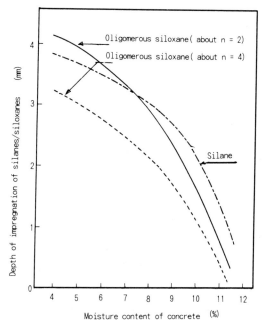

Figure 47.6 Scheme to show a capillary pore after treatment with silanes/siloxanes

Invasion of water into capillary pores (water absorption) is associated with the contact angle between the water and the wall:

$$H = \frac{2r \cdot \cos \theta}{\rho \cdot g \cdot \gamma} \tag{47.1}$$

where H is the capillary rise (in m), γ is the surface tension of rising fluid (in N m^{-1}), θ is the angle of contact, ρ is the density of water (in kg m^{-3}), g is the acceleration due to gravity (in N s^{-2}), and r is the radius of the capillary (in m).

Now, using equation (47.1) we can calculate the range of the head of water in which invasion of water into capillary pores with a diameter of 5000 Å (0.5 μm) does not occur. If we substitute 7300×10^{-5} N m^{-1} for γ, 120° for θ, 1000 kg m^{-3} for ρ, 10 m s^{-2} for g and 25×10^{-8} m (2500 Å) for r, we obtain $H = 30$ m (equivalent to 3 kgf cm^{-2}, i.e. 0.3 MPa). This means that invasion of water into capillary pores does not occur unless a very high pressure is applied.

We then calculate the range of the capillary pore diameter in which water invasion into capillary pores under an approximately 20 cm depth of water-pooled layer does not occur. If we substitute 0.2 m for H, we obtain $r = 37$ μm (370 000 Å). This means that water is not absorbed into capillary pores with a radius of less than 37 μm.

47.3.4 Permeability of impregnating waterproof agents

The permeability of impregnating waterproof agents made of silanes/siloxanes can vary according to the agent's features such as the molecular weight, the type of alkyl group and the concentration of silanes/siloxanes in the solvent. The permeability is also affected by the moisture content (particularly the surface water content) of concrete and the amount of the waterproof agent applied.

In general, the permeability of the waterproof agent of this type into concrete increases as the molecular weight of the agent decreases. Among others, the agent made of silanes or oligomerous siloxanes with a molecular weight below 500 permeates into concrete particularly well.

As the carbon number of the alkyl group constituting the waterproof agent becomes lower, the permeability of the agents into concrete becomes higher, accompanied, however, by a reduction in resistance to alkali because of elevated volatility. Considering both the permeability and the resistance to alkali, the waterproof agents with a carbon number of the alkyl group being about 8–10 seem to be most appropriate.

In the ordinary use of silanes/siloxanes in waterproof agents, silanes/siloxanes are dissolved in mineral spirit. Therefore, their concentration can affect the permeability of waterproof agents into concrete.

When a standard amount (200 g m^{-2} concrete) of a

Figure 47.7 Relationship between the moisture content of concrete and the depth of impregnation of silanes/siloxanes

waterproof agent is applied to concrete, the permeated depth of the agent increases as the concentration of silanes or siloxanes becomes higher, although it does not increase any more at concentrations over 20–30%.

Of the factors during application of waterproof agents, the moisture content (i.e. the surface moisture content) of concrete affects the depth of permeation most profoundly. *Figure 47.7* shows the relationship between the concrete surface moisture content and the depth of permeation. In this case, the depth of permeation is about 3 mm at a surface moisture content of about 8%; it increases to about 3.5 mm when the surface moisture content falls to about 6%, and it sharply decreases if the surface moisture content exceeds 10%. This means that the waterproof agent made of silanes/siloxanes cannot sufficiently permeate into concrete when the concrete surface moisture content is high, resulting in a reduction in the agent's effect of improving the durability of concrete.

47.4 Prevention of deterioration of concrete with impregnating waterproof agents made of silanes and siloxanes

47.4.1 Prevention of alkali–silica reaction

It is known that treatment with impregnating waterproof agents made of silanes/siloxanes reduces the permeability of concrete to water but hardly reduces permeability of concrete to water vapour. In order to assess the water permeation preventive effect of waterproof agents, water permeation tests were conducted at 250 mmH$_2$O head of water between untreated concrete and concrete treated with waterproof agents made of silanes/siloxanes. This experiment disclosed a water permeation of 50–150 mg cm^{-2} day^{-1} on the untreated concrete and a water permeation of 5 mg cm^{-2} day^{-1} on the treated concrete, suggesting a quite high water-shielding effect of this type of waterproof agent.[1] This water-shielding effect became higher as the amount of the waterproof agent applied was increased up to 150 g m^{-2} for concrete surface.

In the assessment of moisture permeability (vapour permeability) using 5-mm thick mortar plates, the vapour permeability was $26 \text{ mg cm}^{-2} \text{ day}^{-1}$ for the untreated mortar plate and $22 \text{ mg cm}^{-2} \text{ day}^{-1}$ (about 85% of the value for the untreated mortar plate) for the mortar plate treated with waterproof agents made of oligomerous siloxane. Thus, this type of waterproof agent was found hardly to affect the permeability of concrete to moisture.[2]

If concrete treated with silanes/siloxanes is exposed to cycles of drying and wetting, its water content will gradually decrease because of evaporation of water from it and the water-permeation preventive effect of silanes/siloxanes. This phenomenon has already been confirmed in a concrete wall[3] and through tests.[4]

An alkali–silica reaction, which damages concrete occurs when all of the following three requirements are satisfied:

(1) the presence of an alkali reactive aggregate;
(2) the presence of sufficient alkalis; and
(3) the presence of water.

If one of these three factors is removed, this reaction can be prevented.

Treatment of concrete with silanes/siloxanes is aimed at eliminating water from concrete in order to prevent the alkali–silica reaction. This is a very useful method for the repair of existing concrete structures. Although highly regarded in Japan, the method has not yet proved so successful in Europe. Perhaps there is scope here for more research.

The use of impregnating waterproof agents made of silanes/siloxanes for the prevention of concrete expansion due to alkali–silica reaction has been reported by several investigators. *Figure 47.8* shows a case where this waterproof agent was used for an outdoor concrete wall. The wall with a thickness of 20 cm and a mean height of 150 cm had cracked due to alkali–silica reaction. This wall was divided into three portions and was observed for a long period:

(1) a portion where cracks were filled with epoxy resin and the surface was treated with a waterproof agent made of oligomerous siloxane;
(2) a portion where the surface was treated with a waterproof agent and the cracks were left unfilled; and

(3) a portion which was left untreated.

This observation disclosed that treatment with a waterproof agent made of oligomerous siloxane is quite effective. This type of waterproof agent was found to effectively dry concrete with a small thickness. In the case of massive concrete in which water diffusion is very low, treatment with this type of waterproof agent will make concrete waterproof, but, because of moisture permeation, it will hardly dry the concrete.

Some silanes and siloxanes are poor in resistance to weather (resistance to ultraviolet radiation). *Figure 47.9* shows the time related effect of concrete treated with a silane monomer.[5] After about 20 weeks of exposure to the natural environment the concrete surface began to show a reduction in waterproof property. After about 50 weeks of exposure, alkali–silica reaction occurred, resulting in expansion of the concrete to a degree similar to the one observed in untreated concrete. Therefore, to preserve the effect of silanes/siloxanes for long periods, it is desirable to protect the concrete surface treated with silanes/siloxanes, with moisture-permeable elastic polymer cement or a moisture permeable coating material made of resins (epoxy resin, acryl resin, silicone resin, etc.).

47.4.2 Prevention of salt attack

As shown in *Figure 47.10*, concrete treated with a waterproof agent made of silanes/siloxanes was found to be highly resistant to invasion of chloride ions.[5] One factor responsible for this salt-shielding effect is the water-repellent effect of silanes/siloxanes which prevents the invasion of chlorides dissolved in water. The other factor is an electrical one; that is, the surface of concrete treated with silanes/siloxanes is electrically neutral, while that of untreated concrete is positively charged. The electrically neutral surface of concrete reduces the apparent diffusion of anions and improves the salt-shielding property. The quite high salt-shielding property of concrete treated silanes/siloxanes seems to be attributable to a combination of these two factors. (See *Figure 47.10*.)

The salt-shielding effect and the concrete-drying effect of silanes/siloxanes are thought effectively to prevent the corrosion of steel bars used in reinforced concrete.

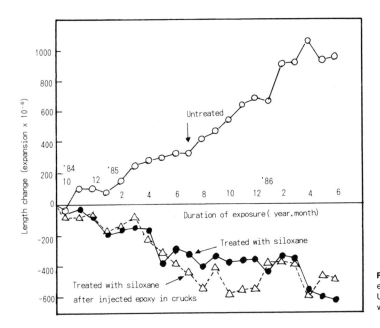

Figure 47.8 Relationship between the duration of exposure and the expansion of a concrete wall. (○) Untreated; (●) treated with siloxane; (△) treated with siloxane after injection of epoxy resin into cracks

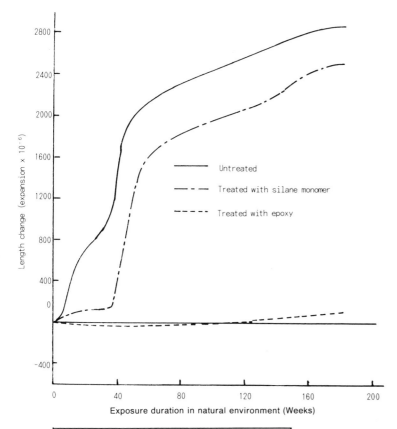

Figure 47.9 Reduction in repellant ability of a silane monomer

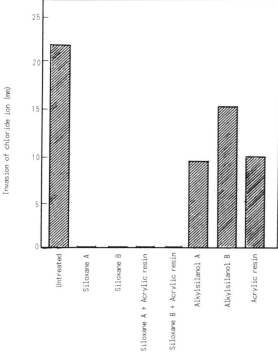

Figure 47.10 Invasion of chloride ions into concrete treated with several waterproof agents. Specimens were immersed for 28 days in saturated sodium chloride solution after treatment

47.5 Usefulness of silanes and siloxanes

Impregnating waterproof agents made of silanes/siloxanes were developed relatively recently. They are quite effective as waterproof agents for concrete and inorganic construction materials. Increasing attention will be paid to this type of waterproofing agent which may improve the durability of concrete by means of suppressing alkali–silica reaction and salt attack. This new type of waterproof agent will be further modified to meet various demands.

References

1 YAMAGUCHI, M., FUKUSHIMA, M. and YAMAGUCHI, S., 'Prevention of deterioration of concrete due to effect of impregnating material', *Bousei Kanri*, **31**, 66 (1987)
2 ÓLAFSSON, H., 'Repair of vulnerable concrete', *Proc. 6th Int. Conf. on Alkalis in Concrete*, p. 479, Danish Concrete Association, Copenhagen (1983)
3 SIMATANI, H., WAKASUGI, M., YOMODA, N. and NAKANO, K., 'Preventing effect of new inorganic extensible coating material on alkali–silica reaction', *Journal of Society of Materials (Japan)*, **36** (1987)
4 HANSHIN EXPRESSWAY PUBLIC CORPORATION, *Investigation of Alkali–Silica Reaction, the Committee Report*, Osaka, Japan (1986)
5 COMMITTEE OF RESEARCH AND INVESTIGATION ON ALKALI-AGGREGATE REACTION, Osaka, Japan, unpublished data

48

Slurries and Grouts

S A Jefferis MA, PhD, CEng, MICE, FGS
Queen Mary and Westfield College,
University of London

Contents

48.1 Introduction 48/3

48.2 Overview of applications 48/3

48.3 Materials 48/3
    48.3.1 Clays 48/4
    48.3.2 Cements 48/4
    48.3.3 Cement replacement materials 48/5
    48.3.4 Mix water and groundwater 48/5
    48.3.5 Polymer slurries 48/6
    48.3.6 Chemical grout materials 48/6

48.4 Mixing 48/7

48.5 Grout and slurry composition 48/7
    48.5.1 Drying 48/8

48.6 Excavation slurries 48/8
    48.6.1 Slurry pressure 48/8
    48.6.2 Slurry loss 48/9
    48.6.3 Slurry rheology 48/10
    48.6.4 Slurry cleaning 48/11

48.7 Bentonite–cement self-hardening slurries 48/12
    48.7.1 Properties 48/13

48.8 Structural grouts 48/13
    48.8.1 Thermal effects 48/14

48.9 Geotechnical grouts 48/14
    48.9.1 Suspension grouts 48/14
    48.9.2 Emulsion grouts 48/14

48.10 Chemical grouts 48/15
    48.10.1 Silicate ester grouts 48/15
    48.10.2 Silicate aluminate grouts 48/15

48.11 Sampling slurries and grouts 48/15
    48.11.1 Sample containers, storage and handling 48/16

48.12 Testing grouts and slurries 48/16
    48.12.1 Density 48/16
    48.12.2 Sand content 48/17
    48.12.3 Rheological measurements 48/17
    48.12.4 Flow cones 48/18
    48.12.5 The Colcrete flow trough 48/18
    48.12.6 Other rheological tests 48/18
    48.12.7 pH 48/18
    48.12.8 Filter loss 48/19

48.12.9 Bleeding 48/19
    48.12.10 Measurement of set time 48/20

48.13 Testing hardened properties 48/20
    48.13.1 Unconfined compression tests 48/20
    48.13.2 Confined drained triaxial testing 48/20
    48.13.3 Permeability tests 48/21

48.14 Specifications 48/21
    48.14.1 Materials specifications 48/21
    48.14.2 Specification of fluid properties 48/21
    48.14.3 Specification of hardened properties 48/22

48.15 Conclusions 48/23

References 48/23

Bibliography 48/24

48.1 Introduction

Grouts and slurries are examples of special materials much used in civil engineering. The diversity of uses and properties of these systems is so great that it is difficult to give a concise overview. By way of introduction it is appropriate to consider some of the fundamental similarities and differences.

Perhaps the most general common feature of grouts and slurries is that they tend to be complex non-Newtonian fluids and yet as many grouts and slurries are based on active swelling clays such as bentonite they tend to show somewhat similar fluid behaviour.

A distinction between grouts and slurries is that slurries are specifically used in slurry supported excavations such as diaphragm walling, piling and slurry tunnelling. Grouts are generally placed by injection and find a wider range of application from geotechnical engineering to structural engineering. A logical distinction between grouts and slurries would be to refer to all non-setting systems as slurries and to reserve the term grout for setting materials. However, the term self-hardening slurry has been coined for cut-off wall slurries which are setting materials. Thus grouts and slurries could be regarded as a spectrum of materials with setting grouts at one extreme and non-setting slurries at the other and self-hardening slurries as a link between the two systems. Though in practice the formulations for some self-hardening slurries may be apparently similar to those of geotechnical grouts.

An apparent similarity between grouts and slurries is that clays, Portland cements and the silicate solutions much used in grouting all involve silicon–oxygen chemistry (for example the silica layer of clays and the calcium silicate hydrates of cements). Despite this common chemistry the engineering behaviour of the materials is quite distinct. However, the common fundamental chemistry does suggest some potential for chemical compatibility of the materials and the potential for mixed systems. Indeed some of the most ancient and enduring construction materials were based on mixtures of clay and pozzolanic cements. In passing it may be noted that sodium aluminate is also used in chemical grouting and calcium aluminate hydrates are present in hydraulic cements.

For both grouts and slurries there is a wide range of special chemical systems not involving clays or hydraulic cements. In grouting these are now quite widely used though the relatively high cost tends to restrict their application to situations requiring their special properties. There are also chemical based slurries mainly developed from experience in the oil well drilling industry. These slurries are based on water soluble polymers and have been used in slurry tunnelling and to a rather more limited extent in diaphragm walling work.

Another link between slurries and grouts is that much of the equipment for testing fluid properties is common to both and is based on the equipment used for oil well drilling muds. Drilling muds have progressively developed from simple native clay systems to become complex chemical systems and it must be expected that there will be a similar trend with excavation slurries. Grouts are also used in oil well operations for cementing conductor pipes to the formation. The technology of well cementing has not significantly influenced geotechnical grouting or vice-versa but there are close parallels between oil well grouting and the filling of ducts in pre-stressed post tensioned concrete and offshore grouting for structural connections and repairs, etc.

48.2 Overview of applications

The first application of a slurry for trench excavation was to form a soil-slurry cut-off wall.[1] However, the development of structural diaphragm walling in the 1950s overshadowed the cut-off wall applications and for many years slurries were synonymous with diaphragm wall construction. In recent years much more cut-off wall work has been undertaken particularly for the control of leachate and gas from landfill sites. It is interesting to note that in the UK cement–bentonite cut-off walls are most widely used whereas in the USA soil–bentonite walls are more popular. These preferences may relate to the relative cost of materials, the availability of plant and space on site and particularly the availability of suitable backfill material.[2] Soil backfill materials are often prepared by blending the excavated material with bentonite and if required extra fines, at the side of the trench—an operation which requires more space than is necessary for a cement–bentonite wall where the slurry may be pumped from a central mixing plant.

Applications for slurries thus include slurry supported excavations for diaphragm walling, piling, slurry tunnelling and cut-off walls. The applications of slurries in piling and diaphragm walling are very similar and need not be considered separately. Slurry tunnelling involves rather different constraints; spoil conveyance and slurry cleaning become especially important. Cut-off wall slurries are again a special class of materials for which the hardened properties rather than the fluid properties are of fundamental importance.

The range of applications of grouts is much wider and includes geotechnical grouting for soil improvement and soil modification. There are also applications in piezometer and borehole sealing, etc.—operations which are often left to the discretion of site staff and for which it is difficult to obtain even typical data on mix proportions, performance, etc. Indeed specifications are often so loosely worded that neither mix proportions nor performance are adequately quantified—an unsatisfactory situation which must lead to unsatisfactory grouts. Structural grouting is much used for corrosion protection and bonding of tendons in post tensioned pre-stressed concrete. Grouts are also used in the repair of damaged concrete to replace cover, etc. Offshore, structural grouting has found considerable application for pile-sleeve and pile-socket connections and repair clamps. A relatively recent but developing application of cement grouts is the cementation of toxic or radioactive waste to reduce, risks of hazardous matter entering the biosphere.

Recently, self-hardening slurries have been used in a secant piling system to produce an economic combination of a cut-off wall and a retaining wall consisting of primary cement–bentonite piles and secondary structural concrete piles.[3]

There is of course a very wide range of other applications of slurries and grouts. It is not possible or practicable to list all uses and thus only a selection of applications has been included to show the wide diversity of uses for such materials. In the following sections a few of these applications will be discussed in more detail to bring out particular features of the systems, materials, test procedures, etc.

48.3 Materials

There is a great diversity of chemicals used to formulate grouts and slurries but the materials which are used in the greatest quantity are clays and cements. For economy or to obtain special properties cement replacement materials such as pulverized fuel ash or ground granulated blast-furnace slag may also be used. There are also applications for chemical admixtures to modify the properties of clay and cement systems as well as purely chemical systems. As many aspects of the materials used in slurries and grouts are common to both systems it is convenient to discuss them together. Furthermore the properties of both grouts and slurries are strongly influenced by the mixing equipment and procedures. Thus an understanding of grouts and slurries requires an understanding of their constituent materials and also of the effects of mixing.

48.3.1 Clays

The traditional base of slurries and many grouts is the smectite clay, bentonite. Occasionally attapulgite has been used[4] as it will disperse in salt water, though the suspension properties are often not as good as can be achieved with bentonites in fresh water. Attapulgite is much less widely available than bentonite. Local non-swelling clays may be used to form slurries but relatively high concentrations are necessary to avoid excessive settlement of the solids. This in turn makes the slurries more viscous and difficult to use. An alternative is to use a blend of swelling and non-swelling clays but the extra materials handling, batching, and quality control can make this uneconomic or impracticable.

All clay particles carry a negative charge and this is balanced by positively charged cations which are held by electrostatic forces. As these ions are held only by electrostatic forces they can be exchanged for other cations provided the overall charge balance is maintained. Factors which will influence the exchange are the relative concentrations of the ions and their valency. Generally higher valency ions will be more strongly held than lower valency ions. The size and chemical coordination number of the ions is also important, large ions tend to be held more strongly than smaller ions of equal charge. In addition to these general effects there are specific effects. For example potassium and caesium ions tend to be strongly held as they can fit into holes in the surface of many clay mineral plates and act as bridges to link particles together (it is the bridging action of potassium ions that makes illite clays non-swelling despite the fact that otherwise they are quite similar to the swelling smectite clays). The valency of the exchangeable cations modifies the clay particle–particle interaction. In particular the presence of di- and tri-valent ions (e.g. Ca^{2+} and Al^{3+}) allows closer approach of individual clay particles and so promotes edge to face flocculation and face to face aggregation. For use in slurries and grouts it is important that the clay is dispersed or loosely flocculated. Face to face aggregated clay particles (which may be likened to 'packs' of cards rather than the loose 'house of cards structure' of flocculated systems) will be coarse and of little colloidal activity. Thus they will be rapid settling and will not control bleed of grouts, etc. or develop useful suspension viscosity.

For almost all bentonite based slurries and grouts the clay is used in the sodium form. Fundamentally there are two classes of sodium bentonite: natural sodium bentonites, for example Wyoming bentonite, and ion exchanged calcium bentonites. UK bentonites are ion exchanged bentonites in which the calcium of the natural clay has been exchanged for sodium. Sodium carbonate is used for the exchange and an excess is generally used so that ion exchanged bentonites generally have a high pH of order 9.5 to 10.5. The excess sodium carbonate also tends to flocculate the clay somewhat so that ion exchanged bentonites may show relatively high gel strengths and viscosities. Natural bentonites tend to have a nearly neutral pH and to show much lower gel strengths. However, any contamination with cations (for example from salt waters or cement) may lead to a very substantial thickening.

An important role of the bentonite is to stop the slurry or grout bleeding. As bentonite is a natural material it is not surprising that bentonites from different sources can behave rather differently. For example bentonite–cement slurries may show substantial bleeding when prepared with bentonite from one source but minimal bleeding with another bentonite. Often it is difficult to identify the underlying cause of such behaviour. Excessive bleed suggests an unstable system. Bleed water is particularly significant for slurry trench cut-offs as it represents

wasted cut-off volume. Also the drop in the slurry level in the trench may lead to instability of the trench as the bleed water can escape rapidly as it does not deposit a filter cake. Furthermore slurries which show high bleed are likely to show high filtration losses (the processes are rather similar, see Section 48.12.8). It should be noted that the filter loss for bentonite–cement slurries is very substantially greater than that of pure bentonite slurries and thus some drop in trench slurry level is always to be expected for cut-off walls.

As noted for almost all applications sodium bentonites are used but more specialized mixes are being developed for cut-off walls.[5] These involve calcium bentonite and can give a much lower permeability than the equivalent cement–sodium bentonite slurries. However, if calcium bentonites are used the clay content may be much higher at up to 50% of the weight of water and a different design philosophy is necessary. Furthermore, special excavation plant may be needed because of the high density of the slurry, and chemical dispersing agents may be required to produce a sufficiently fluid mix. Though more expensive the resulting cut-off walls are potentially more resistant to aqueous leachates than conventional mixes.

48.3.2 Cements

48.3.2.1 Structural grouts

Structural grouts are almost exclusively based on hydraulic cements. Cements which may be used include ordinary Portland, sulphate resisting, high alumina and oil well cements. Oil well cements were developed for grouting the oil conductor pipes in wells to the formation, to prevent fluid migration between strata. A wide range of such cements has been developed for the special temperature and pressure conditions that can occur in oil wells.[6] Class B oil well cement has been much used for offshore structural grouting. This cement is sulphate resisting and slightly slower setting than many ordinary Portland cements. In oil well grouting the grout may have to be pumped substantial distances and thus rheology is most important. In contrast the specification for ordinary Portland cement is relatively wide and the most important parameter is perhaps the strength of concrete made from the cement with grout rheology very much a secondary parameter. Thus considerable variation in grout rheology must be expected between batches from different sources. If repeatable rheology is important the use of oil well cements should be considered. Class G cement may be particularly appropriate provided that the set time is acceptable.

Aeration of the cement (exposure to the atmosphere) also may markedly change the rheology of both geotechnical and structural grouts. For critical applications there is no substitute for trial mixes and if possible all cement should come from a single batch. The samples for the trial mix should of course come from this batch. This may cause practical difficulties if 28-day strengths are to be confirmed and aeration is to be avoided.

48.3.2.2 Geotechnical grouts

For geotechnical grouting most suspension grouts contain a hydraulic cement to provide set. In general cost will be an important parameter and this tends to limit the application of special cements (though for many such cements the extra cost may be quite small). In general if modified cements are required these are achieved by the use of cement replacement materials. A relatively recent development is the use of microfine cements for grouting.[7,8] These are cements of very fine particle size and may penetrate fine soils in a manner comparable to chemical grouts. Particle size distribution is very important for such cements, a small amount of oversize may lead to clogging and failure to penetrate. The increased fineness will give a more rapid set than ordinary Portland cement so that it may be necessary to add a retarding agent.

48.3.3 Cement replacement materials

For economy it is often appropriate to use cement replacement materials such as ground granulated blast-furnace slag or pulverized fuel ash (PFA). Whilst these materials can offer economies it is important to understand their influence on the behaviour of grouts and slurries and to realize that they cannot be used interchangeably.

For structural grouts if a replacement material is to be used the grout formulations must be specially designed. In many duct grouting situations the volume of grout to be used will be rather small so that replacement materials will offer no useful economy and indeed the extra batching and quality control measures may lead to an overall increase in cost. Also replacement systems may not offer the same chemical environment for the pre-stressing strand, etc. as is achieved with a purely Portland cement grout. Thus replacement materials should be used only if required for some special technical feature of the work.

Replacement materials may have a special role in the cementation of toxic and radioactive waste where the reduced setting exotherm can be very important in the control of thermal cracking. Also replacement materials, particularly slag, may improve the leaching behaviour of the cemented material.

PFA/cement grouts find wide application for void filling for example in old mine workings, collapsing sewers, etc. In such applications the largely spherical nature of the PFA particles may be significant in improving workability though pumping pressures for PFA/cement grouts may be greater than those of pure cement grouts.[9] PFA/cement grouts also find application in repair work.

For cut-off wall slurries PFA has rather little influence on the strength, permeability or stress–strain behaviour save that if it is used as a cement replacement material (rather than as an additional material) the permeability can increase and the strength reduce for replacement levels above about 30%. If it is used as an additional material or with only a small reduction in the cement content it serves to increase the slurry density (which may help displacement with replacement mixes, see Section 48.7) and to reduce sensitivity to drying because of the extra solids in the mix. The hydration of PFA can be improved by the use of special chemical admixtures with consequent improvement in set performance.[10]

In contrast to the sometimes rather modest influence of PFA, slag when used in bentonite-cement slurries can produce striking changes in the properties if a replacement level of over 60% is used. Below 60% slag has rather little effect. Above 60% slag replacement progressively increases strength and reduces permeability. However, at very high replacement levels the set materials tend to become rather brittle. The reduction in permeability may be be an order of magnitude or more and thus substantially improve the cut-off performance and durability of the material. The increase in strength may be less desirable particularly in weak grounds (typically cut-off materials are designed to have a strength comparable to that of the adjacent ground, see Sections 48.7.1 and 48.13.2). To control the strength and maintain the low permeability the best procedure is to reduce the total slag and cement content whilst maintaining the slag:cement ratio (this also gives a useful economy of materials). In this way mixes of permeability 10^{-9} m s^{-1} and lower can be achieved with total slag plus cement contents of 100–150 kg m^{-3}. With pure cement mixes such permeabilities may not be achieved even at 250 kg m^{-3} cement.

As both slag and PFA are by-product materials some variability between sources is to be expected—particularly for PFA. Thus trial mixes will usually be necessary to optimize a bentonite– cement–slag or PFA system.

48.3.4 Mix water and groundwater

Water will be a component of almost all grouts and slurries. As a general rule water of drinking quality is satisfactory for the preparation of grouts and slurries. If there is concern about the suitability of a water the best procedure is to prepare trial mixes with the water. Chemical analysis can provide some guidelines but it is not always possible to predict how a grout or slurry system will behave with a particular water. Both grouts and slurries are fundamentally colloid systems. Such systems are notoriously sensitive to salts and without detailed investigation it is often impossible to predict responses. Thus for commercial practice with grouts and slurries it is generally expedient to look for effects rather than to try and establish causes.

48.3.4.1 Dispersion of clays

Of the various materials used to prepare grouts and slurries the dispersion of sodium bentonites is probably most sensitive to water quality. For example problems have been encountered with magnesium ion concentrations of 50 mg l^{-1}, with calcium at above 250 mg l^{-1} and with sodium or potassium concentrations above 500 mg l^{-1}. These figures are examples and should not be taken as safe limits. The sensitivity of clays from different sources may be different and the mixing sequence may be of considerable significance. For example if the clay is added stagewise over a period of time it is possible that the clay first added may absorb and attenuate some of the damaging ions so as to allow better dispersion of the later clay. This is a rather special procedure and expensive as some clay will be wasted. Clays are relatively insensitive to anions such as chloride, sulphate, etc. Generally to obtain the most benefit from the use of bentonite it is important that it is well dispersed. However, for some clay–cement grouts the role of the clay may be more as a fine filler to reduce bleed and to make the mix more plastic. For these grouts the clay is not allowed any time to swell and hydrate prior to the addition of cement. Once cement is added to bentonite further dispersion of the clay will be inhibited by the cations from the cement.

Clay slurries may also be affected by salts in the soil or groundwater during excavation. Contamination will usually lead to an initial thickening (caused by edge to face flocculation) and ultimately, if very severe, to aggregation of the clay particles. Aggregation (face to face bonding) produces fewer thicker clay particles with a consequent thinning of the slurry (reduction in viscosity and gel) and much increased bleeding and filter loss. Contamination at this level may effectively destroy the slurry properties. In practice such contamination is rather rare in slurry supported excavations as the hydrostatic pressure of the slurry should prevent groundwater entering the excavation though some water from the excavated material may mix with the slurry (see Section 48.6.1). In oil well drilling it is sometimes necessary to drill through solid salt layers and this does cause substantial contamination. However, such a situation would be unusual in construction work. In general the effect of salt contamination in civil engineering work can be limited by careful selection of the initial slurry concentration. Occasionally it may be necessary to use a dispersing agent. Formerly ferrochrome lignosulphonate was much used as a dispersant but now a wide range of special chemicals is available including lignosulphonates without the heavy metal chromium. However, if severe salt contamination is expected polymer based slurries rather than clay based slurries should be considered.

48.3.4.2 Influence of water chemistry on cement based grouts

For grouts the presence of moderate quantities of dissolved salts in the mix water can usually be tolerated without detriment to the material, though in extreme situations[11] the results may be quite unusual (of course if pre-hydrated bentonite is to be used the rules on water quality set out above must be applied). In many offshore structural grouting operations sea water is used to prepare the grout without detriment to the set or hardened properties and indeed the use of fresh water for such grouts could be seriously questioned as in use the grout will be immersed in sea water.

The effects of salts present in the mix water may have limited effect if any induced strains, etc. can be accommodated by the material whilst in the plastic state. However, the effect of salts present in the groundwater on hardened materials must always be considered. For cement grouts any material which damages concrete (for example sulphate) must be considered as potentially damaging. For dense low water–cement ratio structural grouts the low permeability may limit the rate of attack. Despite this the effects may be more severe than for concrete as the grout may be more brittle, that is have a lower strain at failure. It is very difficult to predict how structural grouts will react to chemical attack and every situation must be examined on its own facts. Clearly as structural grouts will often be required to provide corrosion protection for steel their application in chemically contaminated environments must be very carefully considered.

In geotechnical grouting, salts in the ground which are known to affect concrete must also be expected to affect cement-based grouts. However, many grouts particularly those containing clay will have a significantly higher strain at failure than concrete and thus may not disintegrate when subjected to expansive attack, for example by sulphate, provided that there is a confining pressure comparable with the strength of the material. Thus clay–cement grouts and slurries may be slightly softened by sulphate attack but remain effectively intact provided they are subject to some confining stress as will be usual in the ground. If they are not restrained severe cracking may occur. Whilst clay–cement grouts and slurries may be much more permeable than concrete (because of their higher water to cement ratio) the actual rate of attack may still be very small.[12]

48.3.4.3 Chemical grouts

Sodium silicate may be set by the addition of electrolyte (salt) solutions, for example calcium chloride. Thus some caution must be exercised when preparing silicate grouts (and indeed any chemical grout) with waters containing significant levels of salts. Particular problems that could occur are precipitation of scale in the grout lines or early precipitation of some gel product prior to injection. Such a precipitate may clog the soil surface and substantially reduce or prevent injection.

48.3.5 Polymer slurries

Slurries based on water soluble polymers such as xanthan gum, carboxymethyl cellulose, etc. have been used quite extensively for tunnelling and to a more limited extent in diaphragm walling. In some situations there may be technical advantages favouring either polymers or clay based systems. Particular features of polymer slurries are that the polymers may be more tolerant of salt and cement contamination and they can be broken down to water viscosity by simple chemical treatment (for example with an oxidizing agent such as bleach). The chemical destruction of the polymer in a used and spoil contaminated slurry followed by settlement may produce effectively clean water and settled spoil provided the slurry does not contain a significant amount of dispersed native clay. This may much reduce slurry disposal

costs. For bentonite slurries settlement is not a practicable method for cleaning as the gel will prevent the settlement of fines.

Salt tolerance can be useful in saline soils particularly if slurries are to be repeatedly re-used. Cement tolerance also can be very useful as cement contamination can occur during concreting of diaphragm walls or grouting behind the lining in slurry tunnelling work. For bentonite slurries a small amount of cement may lead to thickening of all the contaminated slurry. Some polymers are effectively inert to cement but for others such as carboxymethyl cellulose the slurry properties are effectively destroyed by it. However, the destruction is stoichiometric so that, for example, one kilogram of cement might destroy a few hundred grams of carboxymethyl cellulose and in a slurry circuit containing perhaps hundreds of kilograms of polymer this may have no measurable effect.

Many polymers will degrade rather rapidly due to bacterial attack unless used in conjunction with a biocide. This can be used to considerable advantage in water well drilling where a filter cake of slurry solids could reduce well performance. With a polymer slurry such a cake can be left to biodegrade or be destroyed with an oxidizing agent. A similar procedure can be used to form drainage trenches. For these a trench is formed under polymer slurry and then backfilled with free draining aggregate.

Finally it should be noted that some polymers can act in synergism with clays so that the properties of a clay polymer mix can be superior to those of the clay or polymer slurry alone. In use polymer slurries may become 'contaminated' with clay from the excavation and thus when developing polymer systems it is appropriate to test all polymer slurries with a small amount of added clay, particularly if synergism is expected. The added clay need not be a swelling clay such as bentonite.

Thus as is so often the case in civil engineering there is no simple rule for selecting bentonite or polymer systems. Each system must be judged on its own merits. Cost of purchase and disposal of the slurry may be apparently important factors but it should be remembered that for most situations the slurry materials will represent only a very small part of the total cost of the works. Technical considerations therefore ought to be fundamental. However, ultimately the choice is often based on cost though convenience and/or conservatism may influence the decision.

48.3.6 Chemical grout materials

There is a very wide range of chemical grouts available[13,14] and it is not possible to provide any general guidelines. However, many chemical grout systems are based on sodium silicate and discussion of the silicate system can be used to highlight some of the parameters that must be considered when using chemical grouts.

Sodium silicate is a highly alkaline viscous liquid. It may be regarded as a mixture of sodium and silicon oxides in water. Important parameters are the solids concentration and the silicon oxide to sodium oxide ratio (the silica:soda ratio) often referred to as the n value. The n value may be expressed as a weight ratio or as a molecular ratio, that is molecules of silicon oxide (SiO_2) per molecule of sodium oxide (Na_2O). It is the silica component of the mix which polymerizes to form a solid structure. The role of the soda being to bring the silica into solution. Thus sodium silicates of high n value are to be preferred for grouting as the quantity of non-hardening sodium salt is kept to a minimum. However, for values above about 2 increasing the n value increases the viscosity of the solution and typically for grouting work n values of 3 to 3.8 (molecular ratio are used though slightly lower values may be acceptable. As the sodium hydroxide maintains the silica in solution if it is neutralized, for example by an acid, the silica will precipitate a a solid mass. This is the basis of many silicate grout systems, though silicates also may be hardened by reaction with strong electrolyte solutions such as calcium chloride or, as will be shown, by polymerization with sodium aluminate.

48.4 Mixing

Good mixing is fundamental to the preparation of all grout and slurry systems. At the most basic poor mixing may lead to systems containing regions of undispersed material, such as lumps of cement. Such lumps will not contribute to the bulk performance of the system and thus will represent wasted material. Thus at the macro level poor mixing may be manifested by large lumps of undispersed material of millimetre dimensions or greater. At the micro level the result will be poor dispersion of cement grains or clay particles, etc. At this level, dispersion may be strongly influenced by the chemistry of the suspension as well as the mixing. However, mixing may still be of sufficient influence to affect the colloidal stability of the system and thus, for example, filtration and bleeding behaviour.

With polymer slurries and chemical grouts it is important that the manufacturer's instructions regarding mixing are followed. Excessive shear during mixing may damage a polymer or modify the behaviour of a grout.

When dispersing solids such as clay or cement it is important that the mixer offers a reasonably high level of shear and that the slurry is circulated through the mixing zone. Otherwise the solids may become a sticky and intractable mass adhering to the walls, etc. of the mixer. The situation with many polymers is much worse. If they are simply poured into water they tend to lump and subsequent swelling and hydration may be very slow so that lumps persist effectively indefinitely and as a consequence much of the polymer is wasted. It is therefore essential that polymers are added to stirred water or a venturi eductor is used. If properly dispersed into the water many polymers will effectively reach full dispersion within about one hour. However, for some polymers almost instantaneous hydration can be achieved by prior dispersion in a small amount of a non-aqueous liquid which does not hydrate (swell) the polymer. In this way good dispersion of the polymer particles can be achieved so that on contact with water they do not lump together but hydrate as individual small particles and hence rapidly.

Bentonites may achieve sufficient dispersion and hydration to be usable within one to two hours though considerable further development of properties will occur after this. Testing of aged slurries suggests that the properties continue to develop on a logarithmic time scale and thus it is not possible to identify a time for full hydration. High shear mixing will break up clusters of clay particles and thus lead to more rapid development of properties (and higher gel strengths and viscosities) than low shear mixing and this effect appears to persist apparently indefinitely after mixing.[15] Thus the general rule is to use high shear mixing and to hydrate for as long as practicable, though after 24 hours the further benefit will be rather limited. Generally after mixing the clay slurry will be pumped to a storage tank to hydrate. The freshly mixed slurry will have little gel strength and thus there will be a tendency for the clay solids to settle. It is therefore good practice to homogenize the stored slurry by recirculation before it is drawn off for use.

If the slurry is likely to be contaminated by salts or cement (as it will be when preparing a cement–bentonite slurry) then at least four hours hydration should generally be allowed as the contamination may effectively stop further hydration and development of the clay slurry properties.

Sodium bentonites as natural materials vary to some extent in their compatibility with cement but if pre-hydrated clay is

used there will be initial and substantial thickening when cement is added as the clay is flocculated by the cement. After a few minutes of mixing considerable thinning will occur (due to aggregation of the clay, but note the thinning will not occur unless mixing is continued). It is therefore important that the mixers should be capable of handling the stiffening without loss of circulation, stalling, blocking, etc.

For structural grouts good mixing is fundamental. Low shear paddle type mixers will produce very different grouts from high speed, high shear mixers unless extended mixing times are used. High shear mixes will show good cohesion and reduced tendency to segregate or bleed. Low shear mixes may show substantially greater bleeding and if they come into contact with water may show insufficient cohesion to prevent the grout and water intermingling.

An apparent disadvantage of high shear mixing is that the extra energy input heats up the grout and this and the extra dispersion tends to reduce the setting time and hence the pumpable time. However, with careful design, pumpable time should not be a limiting factor and the faster setting can be an advantage as it allows less time for bleeding. High shear mixes do not necessarily show higher pumping pressures. Indeed the initial pumping pressure of low shear mixes may be higher than for high shear mixes. Actually pumping pressures seldom appear to be a problem unless high pipe flow velocities are required.[9]

High sheared mixes are also more homogeneous and thus there is less risk of blockages caused by lumps of undispersed cement. Such blockages can represent a significant problem during duct filling, etc. Blockages may also be caused by old set material dislodged from the mixer and pipework. Thus an in-line screen after the grout pump should be used to remove such material before it passes into the pipeline.

48.5 Grout and slurry composition

For polymer slurries and chemical grouts it will be necessary to follow manufacturers/suppliers guidelines when preparing the materials. For clay–cement–water systems it is more difficult to find guidelines as a very wide range of compositions may be used depending on the application, the type of mixer and, if bentonite is used, whether it is to be hydrated prior to the addition of the cement. *Figure 48.1* shows a triangular diagram indicating the main regions in the cement–water–hydrated bentonite system.

For pre-hydrated bentonite systems it is useful to consider the bentonite concentration in the mix water. Below about 2% by weight, bentonite will have rather little influence. Above

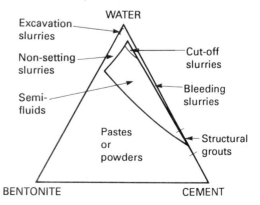

Figure 48.1 Principal regions in the bentonite–cement–water system for hydrated bentonite

about 6% bentonite the slurry is likely to become too thick to use (a useful range of 2–6% is typical for UK bentonites but the limits will depend on the source and the quality of the bentonite and may be influenced by polymer treatment).

For many grout systems, bentonite is used without pre-hydration as this means that hydration tanks are not required (in a system using hydrated bentonite tanks equal in volume to rather over one day's working will be required if 24 hours hydration is to be allowed). Also hydration requires extra time. If the bentonite is not hydrated, much higher concentrations (by weight of mix water) will be necessary to prevent bleeding though the use of bentonite will allow a higher water to solids ratio than would be possible with cement alone. The effect of the bentonite on the hardened grout will be to reduce strength and add some plasticity. For these grouts the design procedure is to select a cement to bentonite ratio and then add sufficient water to give a pumpable mix. If this leads to a mix which shows excessive bleeding then the bentonite to cement ratio must be altered or the type of mixer or mix procedure changed. Selection of an appropriate cement to bentonite ratio may have to be by trial and error. A very wide range of ratios can produce effective grouts and either bentonite or cement may be the major component. For example, the British Standard for site investigation[16] suggests that a 4:1 cement:bentonite grout may be suitable for backfilling boreholes and a 1:4 grout for sealing piezometers.

For plastic concretes (see Section 48.7) which are effectively a bentonite–cement mix plus aggregate, the cement content will usually be lower than in a mix without aggregate. Mix proportions expressed by cubic metres of plastic concrete give little indication of the proportions of the underlying bentonite–cement slurry. Thus when designing plastic concretes it is often useful to calculate the bentonite to water and cement to water ratios and to compare these with typical values for bentonite–cement slurries.

For structural grouts water to cement (w/c) ratio will be the most important parameter. Above a w/c ratio of about 0.5 bleeding will be severe and limit the applications of the grout.[17] Below w/c 0.3 the grout is unlikely to be pumpable, indeed it may be necessary to add a superplasticizer for a w/c ratio of less than about 0.35. The effects of water to cement ratio on structural grouts are discussed more fully in Section 48.8.

48.5.1 Drying

A necessary feature of all grouts and slurries is that they are initially fluids. With time, grouts or self-hardening slurries must set. However, the requirement for fluidity means that the materials must contain a significant amount of water. If this water is lost substantial shrinkage and cracking can occur and on prolonged drying many geotechnical grouts and self-hardening slurries may be reduced to coarse crumbs or even powder. Often only a small amount of water is required to maintain integrity of the solid material and thus when assessing the effects of drying it is important that tests are continued until all evaporable water is lost. Underground in the UK and similar climates there is generally sufficient moisture to prevent cracking. However, grouts and self-hardening slurries if exposed to the effects of sun and wind may crack severely. Thus cut-off walls must be capped as soon as the slurry is sufficiently set if cracking is to be avoided.

Structural grouts, although of low water to cement ratio, are not immune to cracking. Indeed they tend to show worse drying shrinkage than concretes. Large samples of structural grouts left in free air ultimately tend to crack and break up. Such effects are not seen in concrete as the aggregate limits the propagation of cracks. Thus structural grouts must be maintained in a sealed environment or submerged under water if cracking is to be avoided.

48.6 Excavation slurries

For excavation slurries the role of the slurry is to support the excavation until a permanent structural material is installed. Thus in a diaphragm wall the slurry must support the trench until the concrete is poured and in a slurry tunnelling operation the slurry must support the face of the excavation and any unlined tunnel within the slurry chamber of the machine. The fundamental parameters for excavation support and construction expediency are:

(1) slurry pressure;
(2) slurry loss: penetration, rheological blocking, bleeding and filtration;
(3) slurry rheology and slurry displacement;
(4) slurry cleaning.

These parameters are closely interlinked and generally slurry design must be a compromise.

48.6.1 Slurry pressure

In a slurry trench excavation the stabilizing pressure on the formation will be the hydrostatic pressure of the slurry less that of the groundwater. Thus the density of the slurry is a most important parameter. For slurry tunnelling the pressure in the face generally will be set by regulating the slurry supply and discharge pumps and thus slurry density is not of direct significance for excavation support.

For bentonite clay based slurries the bentonite concentration typically will be in the range 20 to 60 kg of bentonite per cubic metre of water depending on the quality of the bentonite and the application. The grain specific gravity of dry bentonites measured by water displacement generally will be of order 2800 kg m^{-3}. However, as supplied to site the clay will contain some moisture, typically of order 10% by wet weight of clay which corresponds to 11.1% by weight of dry solids (in soil mechanics the moisture content of soils is normally expressed by weight of dry solids, manufacturers' specifications for bentonite (see, for example, Reference 18), typically use wet weight). It is difficult to predict the combined density of the clay and moisture as the water may become partially bound up in the clay mineral structure. Typically the bentonite as supplied to site will have an effective density of order 2400 kg m^{-3}. Thus for a bentonite slurry concentration of 2–6% (2–6 kg bentonite, as received to 100 kg water) the corresponding densities will be in the range $1012–1034 \text{ kg m}^{-3}$. The density of clean, unused bentonite slurries is thus only very slightly greater than that of water.

For polymer based slurries the typical range of concentrations might be 0.5–2% and as the density of the polymer may be similar to that of water the slurries are effectively of water density.

During excavation, slurries will pick up spoil and it is this which makes the major contribution to slurry density. It is instructive to investigate the relationship between spoil concentration and slurry density. For a slurry of initial density ρ_s mixed with a spoil of density ρ_g the density of the mixture ρ_m is given by:

$$\rho_m = \rho_s + C(1 - \rho_s/\rho_g) \tag{48.1}$$

where C is the concentration of spoil dispersed in the contaminated slurry expressed as kilograms of spoil per cubic metre of contaminated slurry. The spoil dispersed in the slurry will be the spoil from the excavation and it should be noted that both soil grains and some or all of the water from the spoil will be dispersed in the slurry. *Table 48.1* shows the spoil content required to produce a range of contaminated slurry densities assuming that the spoil is saturated and has a density of 2000 kg m^{-3} and that all the water in the spoil is dispersed in the slurry.

Table 48.1 Effect of spoil contamination on slurry density

Bentonite slurry							
Total weight (kg)	1023	994	942	890	837	785	733
Bentonite (kg)	39	38	36	34	32	30	28
Water (kg)	984	956	906	856	805	755	705
Volume (m^3)	1.00	0.97	0.92	0.87	0.82	0.77	0.72
Spoil							
Total weight (kg)	0	56	158	260	363	465	567
Solids (kg)	0	45	127	209	291	373	456
Water (kg)	0	11	31	51	71	92	112
Volume (m^3)	0	0.03	0.08	0.13	0.18	0.23	0.28
Contaminated slurry							
Slurry density (kg m^{-3})	1023	1050	1100	1150	1200	1250	1300
Bentonite concentration (%)	4.0	3.95	3.87	3.77	3.67	3.57	3.45

All weights are per cubic metre of contaminated slurry (bentonite slurry + spoil).
Original bentonite slurry concentration 4.0%.
Spoil density assumed as 2000 kg m^{-3}.

As the slurry is contaminated its volume will increase in line with the volume of spoil dispersed into it. Thus the quantity of bentonite per cubic metre of slurry will decrease as the level of contamination increases. Because bentonite is an active swelling clay its properties will dominate the behaviour of lightly contaminated slurries. However, as can be seen from *Table 48.1* as the density rises so the volume of spoil increases substantially (at a density of 1300 kg m^{-3} the slurry contains 28% spoil by volume). Ultimately the slurry will become unacceptably thick (the contamination level at which this occurs will depend on the nature of the spoil, clearly clays will produce much greater thickening than sands but equally being more cohesive may show less tendency to disperse in the slurry during excavation and thus to contaminate it). The combination of high density and high viscosity may give poor displacement by the tremie concrete in a diaphragm wall excavation. For example the Federation of Piling Specialists[19] recommends that the slurry density should not exceed 1300 kg m^{-3} prior to concreting. If densities at or over 1300 kg m^{-3} are necessary for wall stability then high density additives such as barites (barium sulphate, density 4500 kg m^{-3}, though commercial grades may be of slightly lower density) should be used to limit the viscosity rise. Even if barites are used it may be extremely difficult to achieve full displacement of a high density slurry by concrete.

The effect of spoil contamination on the bentonite concentration is also shown by *Table 48.1*. For the example an original slurry concentration of 4% was used and for the contaminated slurries the concentration has been calculated on the total water in the system (ignoring the moisture originally present in the bentonite). For small increases in slurry density the dilution of the bentonite can be seen to be rather limited. However, the effect is quite significant at higher levels of contamination. Dilution can become very serious if the slurry is repeatedly used (contaminated) and cleaned. Whenever the slurry is used some will be lost and the volume must be made up. If fresh slurry is used for the make up the effects of dilution may be largely mitigated, though it is important to realize that the in use bentonite to water ratio will be slightly lower than the as mixed ratio. If the lost volume is made up with water in a misguided attempt to offset the thickening caused by contamination the effects may be very serious. The extra water will add to the dilution and after some uses the slurry may contain effectively no bentonite.

The slurry at the base of an excavation will normally show the highest density due to settlement of solids from higher regions. These spoil solids will settle without any associated water and thus the dilution of the bentonite in the slurry will not be as severe as suggested by the density. Hence when assessing the effects of dilution it is better to consider the density throughout the trench rather than just the maximum value.

In tunnelling operations it may be necessary to use a relatively high density slurry to prevent spoil solids settling in the slurry pipes connecting the face to the cleaning plant. Densities up to 1350 kg m^{-3} may be considered. Settlement in the pipeline will be influenced by slurry flow velocity, density and viscosity and some experimentation will be necessary to select the optimum combination for any ground type having regard to the cost of bentonite, polymers, etc., to be used in slurry preparation and the particle size distribution(s) of the soil(s) in the face. In practice for many slurry tunnelling operations the range of soil types in the face or within a reasonable length of tunnel (this will depend on the volume of slurry in the circuit) may be such that satisfactory slurry performance can be maintained without adding any bentonite or polymer and the circuit can be operated with just water.

48.6.2 Slurry loss

In any slurry excavation process slurry will be lost with the spoil. Such losses may be expensive so it is important that trench excavation slurries should drain freely from the grab and that tunnelling slurries are easily cleaned so that they are not lost with the spoil. However, this type of loss does not directly compromise the stability of the excavation as may occur with slurry losses to the ground which may raise local pore pressures and soften adjacent soils. In slurry trench excavations losses to the ground can be very serious. In slurry tunnelling it may be possible to control the face pressure to reduce the influence of losses.

Loss of slurry to the ground may occur by bulk penetration of slurry into large voids and/or filtration of slurry solids against finer soils so that only liquid is lost and the solids are deposited.

48.6.2.1 Penetration of slurry into soils

In coarse grounds the slurry will penetrate into the ground until either the voids are blocked by deposited solids or the gel strength of the slurry acting over the surface area within the void system is sufficient to resist the effective hydrostatic pressure of the slurry (the differential pressure between slurry and pore pressure in the soil), a process known as rheological blocking. For clean slurries in coarse grounds blocking by solids deposition may be rather limited. However, once excavation has progressed for some time the slurry will contain spoil of a range of sizes especially the finer sizes present in the ground (the coarse fraction may settle to the base of the excavation in slurry trenching or piling or be completely removed in the cleaning plant of a slurry tunnelling circuit). The presence of this dispersed spoil will normally ensure that deposition of solids severely limits slurry penetration.[20] It follows that in normal excavation substantial penetration should occur only in coarse strata within otherwise rather fine grounds. In this respect fissured clays may be particularly vulnerable to substantial slurry penetration. In such clays the slurry may not be able to pick up fines of a size which will block the fissures and so it may be necessary to ensure that the slurry has sufficient gel strength to limit penetration or to add polymers which promote filter cake formation, such as carboxymethyl cellulose. In certain parts of the world there is a preference for thin slurries, perhaps because of fears concerning displacement of slurry from reinforcing steel (though this seldom appears to present problems and the choice of bar type may be more important). Great care must be taken when designing thin slurries for use in soils sensitive to softening, etc., as slurry penetration or filtration can be severe. Thick slurries also must be used with care as they will be difficult to clean and the swabbing action of an excavation grab in a thick slurry may cause overbreak. Similarly, care must be taken if very thick slurries are to be used.

48.6.2.2 Rheological blocking

In coarse grounds or if high pressures are used, for example in slurry tunnelling with an entirely slurry supported face (that is if there is no mechanical support from the machine), significant slurry penetration can occur. For a slurry of yield value τ (see Section 48.6.3) penetrating a soil of effective particle diameter D and porosity n under a pressure P the distance penetrated L is given by[21]:

$$L = \frac{P}{\tau} \times \frac{n}{1-n} \times Df \qquad (48.2)$$

where f is a factor to take account of the geometry and tortuosity of the flow path (f may be of order 0.3). Thus for a slurry of yield value $10\,\mathrm{N\,m^{-2}}$ penetrating a soil of effective particle size 10 mm, the slurry may penetrate of order 2 m per metre of (water) head difference between slurry and groundwater. A problem with applying the formula is the selection of a value for D. A reasonable value could be the D_{10} of the soil (the particle diameter for which 10% of the soil is finer). Penetration into the soil is not the situation addressed in Reference 21 where the pressure to force a gelled slurry from the pores of a soil–bentonite mix was examined. For this, the gel strength (see Section 48.6.3) is a more appropriate parameter than the yield value and a different value must be used for f.

The above formula must be regarded as at best an over-simplification but for clean coarse soils it can give reasonable estimates and in particular it shows that for coarse or fissured soils penetration can be substantial.

48.6.2.3 Filtration

In fine soils or coarse soils once the slurry has ceased to penetrate due to mechanical or rheological blocking, filtration will occur. If rheological blocking has occurred the gelled slurry will behave

as a region of low permeability soil (perhaps of order $10^{-9}\,\mathrm{m\,s^{-1}}$) and thus filtration may be very slow particularly if the penetration has been extensive. Although compressed bentonite is of very low permeability, the relatively loose filter cakes deposited under slurry excavation conditions may have a permeability of order $10^{-10}\,\mathrm{m\,s^{-1}}$. The cakes may be only a few millimetres thick and thus may not represent a particularly high resistance to flow. (1 mm cake of permeability $10^{-10}\,\mathrm{m\,s^{-1}}$ will have the same resistance to flow as 1 m of soil of permeability $10^{-7}\,\mathrm{m\,s^{-1}}$.) Paradoxically the cake resistance will increase with the volume of water that has been lost through it. If there is no flow there is no cake. Thus in clay soils a minimal thickness of cake will develop as the rate of loss of water from the trench will be very small. Thus the cake will have little effect. In open gravel slurry loss may be controlled by rheological blocking (though often only after significant penetration) and because of the relatively low permeability of gelled slurry in the soil voids rather little cake may develop at the trench face. In sands a significant cake may develop so that substantially the full hydrostatic pressure of the slurry is dropped across the cake and there is little rise in the pore pressure in the sand. In silts the rather low permeability will mean that the cake will develop slowly and small rates of water loss may give rise to substantial increases in pore pressure. Therefore in silty soils filter loss control is particularly important and poor filter loss behaviour may lead to instabilities. Indeed filter loss control alone may not be sufficient, particularly if the silt is clean and cohesionless. The swabbing action of the grab during excavation may lead to liquefaction particularly if the groundwater level is high. Dewatering to lower the groundwater level to some metres below the slurry level may be necessary to ensure stability.[22]

48.6.3 Slurry rheology

For simple (Newtonian) liquids such as water there is a linear relationship between shear stress and shear rate and the fluid behaviour can be described by a single parameter, the viscosity. Slurries show more complex shear stress–shear rate behaviour. Many slurries behave as solids at low shear stresses and flow only when the shear stress exceeds a threshold value which will be

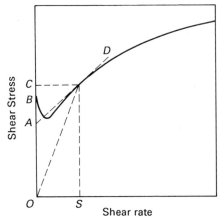

OB is the gel strength of the slurry at rest
AD is the tangent to the curve at shear rate *S*
At shear rate *S*:
Plastic viscosity = *CA/OS*
Apparent viscosity = *OC/OS*
Yield value = *OA*

Figure 48.2 Shear stress against shear rate of slurry

dependent on the shear history of the sample (as will the shear stress–shear rate relationship itself).

The simplest rheological model which may be used to describe clay slurries in the Bingham model:

$$\tau = \tau_0 + \mu\dot{\gamma} \qquad (48.3)$$

where τ is the shear stress, $\dot{\gamma}$ the shear rate, μ the plastic viscosity and τ_0 the yield value. In practice the model is a substantial over-simplification. The shear stress–shear rate plot is not a straight line as implied by equation (48.3) but a curve as shown in *Figure 48.2*. For any shear rate the tangent to the curve gives the plastic viscosity and the extrapolation of this tangent to the shear stress axis gives the yield value. The slope of the line joining any point on the curve to the origin gives the apparent viscosity—the equivalent Newtonian viscosity.

When at rest a slurry may behave as a solid and the shear stress to break this solid is known as the gel strength. The gel strength is thus the yield value at an infinitesimal shear rate. A further complication is that the rheology of clay slurries is time dependent and shear history dependent. Thus a slurry investigated after a period of high shear agitation will be found to be thinner (lower values of plastic viscosity, yield point and gel strength) than a slurry which has been left quiescent. This effect is known as thixotropy and will affect the way in which solids are held in suspension and for rheological blocking the pressure to displace a gelled slurry will be greater than that which originally caused the penetration.

As a slurry can behave as a solid, small spoil particles can be held stationary in suspension. If the particles are stationary then the shear rate will be zero and thus the gel strength is the important parameter. In theory a slurry of gel strength G (see Section 48.12.3.1 for the determination of gel strength) will hold a particle of diameter D in suspension where:

$$D = 6G/(\rho_g - \rho_s)g \qquad (48.4)$$

where ρ_g is the density of the particle, ρ_s is the density of the slurry and g is the acceleration of gravity. However, G is not a constant. During excavation the slurry will be continually disturbed and so G will be low and thus only relatively small particles will be held in suspension. Once excavation ceases G will tend to increase so that rather larger particles can be held in suspension. Thus some of the particles which were settling during excavation but which had not reached the base of the excavation will be held in the slurry once excavation ceases. Relatively large particles may move sufficiently fast to maintain a locally low value for G and thus will continue to settle. Overall the effect of the gel strength and thixotropy will be that after excavation is complete (and prior to concreting) relatively little spoil may settle from the slurry. This is advantageous as it tends to keep the base of the excavation clean. Despite this it is good practice to clean the base of an excavation prior to concreting if there has been a significant delay after the end of excavation.

Polymer slurries show rather different behaviour in that few show a true yield value, most are pseudo-plastic for which the simplest rheological model is:

$$\tau = k\dot{\gamma}^n \qquad (48.5)$$

where the k is a constant and is a measure of the consistency of the fluid and the exponent n is a function of the type of polymer and the shear rate though it may be sensibly constant over a range of shear rates. For pseudo-plastic materials n will be less than one. Materials with n greater than one show dilatant or shear thickening behaviour.

The general shape of the pseudo-plastic shear stress–shear rate curve is shown in *Figure 48.3*. Extrapolation to zero shear rate from any point on the curve will give an apparent yield value. However, the curve actually passes through the origin. Such materials therefore do not have a true yield value but show

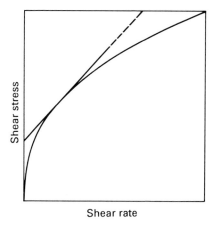

Figure 48.3 Shear stress–shear rate plot for a pseudo-plastic fluid

increasing viscosity with decreasing shear rate. Thus spoil will eventually settle from such slurries but the settlement time may be very extended for fine particles and yet rapid for coarse particles (pseudo-plastic polymers are much used in domestic products to prevent the settling of solids or the breaking of emulsions without the necessity for very viscous solutions).

Viscosity and gel strength (rather than yield value) are perhaps the most obvious and easily measured properties of slurries and therefore tend to be used for control purposes. However, there is little consensus as to what are acceptable values or even required values. The Federation of Piling Specialists offers some limited guidelines[19] but these are very broad reflecting the wide range of possible slurries. Furthermore, bentonites from different parts of the world may show quite different gel strength and viscosity values. UK bentonites are calcium bentonites which have been converted to the sodium form with sodium carbonate. Generally an excess of sodium carbonate is used which tends to flocculate the clay and thus to develop high gel strength and viscosity. In contrast Wyoming bentonites with no artifically added salts show little gel strength. The low salt concentration promotes good dispersion of the clay but a consequence of this is that if the slurry does come into contact with salts a very strong gel may develop (see Section 48.3.1).

Thus when specifying rheological parameters for slurries it is important to consider the source of the bentonite and local practice. In some parts of the world there is a preference for relatively thick slurries whereas in others the local practice is to use thin slurries. As a result severe problems may occur if specifications are lifted from one country to another without regard to the properties of the local bentonite or if the source of bentonite is changed without considering the necessary changes to the specification. Particular care must be taken with specifications which call for either very thick or very thin slurries.

48.6.4 Slurry cleaning

Bentonite is a relatively low cost material and for many years slurries were removed from site after a single use or very limited re-use. However, it is becoming progressively more difficult and expensive to dispose of liquid wastes and this has encouraged much greater re-use of slurries. As a result some form of cleaning plant is now to be found at most sites using slurries. Cleaning is of course fundamental for slurry tunnelling as the volumes of liquid waste would be enormous. Cleaning plant that may be used include:

coarse screens
fines screens

hydrocyclones
dewatering screens
centrifuges
filter belt presses
plate and frame filter presses

Coarse and fine vibrating screens are widely used and are essential to remove material which might overload, damage or block finer treatment equipment. Screens down to perhaps 2 mm opening are straightforward but for finer mesh sizes the screen area may have to be rather large if a reasonable throughput is to be achieved.

Hydrocyclones are effectively centrifuges in which the centrifugal effect is generated by the flow of the fluid itself. The hydrocyclone consists of an upper cylindrical section connected to a lower tapered section which terminates in a discharge orifice (often of adjustable diameter). The feed slurry is fed tangentially into the upper cylindrical section so that the fluid spins within the section causing the coarse solids to migrate towards the wall. The solids then flow into the tapered section and thence to the discharge (underflow) orifice. The cleaned slurry is forced towards the centre of the cylindrical section and is drawn off from a central (overflow) orifice.

Hydrocyclones are standard treatment plant for slurries. The classification or cut of a hydrocyclone improves as the cyclone diameter is reduced. Thus if fine particles are to be removed a small diameter cyclone must be used. This in turn means that the throughput per cyclone will be small and thus a number of cyclones may be required. Also small size means an increased risk of blockage by oversize material. On many sites two size ranges of hydrocyclone will be used, large 8 in. or 12 in. cyclones and smaller 3 in. or 4 in. cyclones. Typically particles over about 50 μm will be preferentially removed in a hydrocyclone system though it is possible to achieve a cut below 30 μm.

A problem with hydrocyclones is that the waste stream, the underflow, although concentrated in spoil is still a fluid and thus disposal is expensive. Some further treatment of the underflow is generally necessary. A satisfactory method of treatment is with a dewatering screen.

The dewatering screen is similar to a standard fine screen save that the screen may have wedge slots rather than square meshes and the opening may be smaller (perhaps of order 0.8 mm). The underflow from the hydrocyclone(s) is arranged to fall onto the screen which is vibrated with an eccentric motion so as to slowly convey the solids along the screen to the discharge. The passage of the solids may be slowed by dams across the screen. In operation there should be a cake of spoil along the full length of the screen so that fresh slurry falls onto the cake rather than the screen. The deposited cake acts as the filter and so removes material significantly finer than the screen opening. The underflow from the screen is the cleaned slurry and it is usually arranged that it falls directly into a holding tank. In a hydrocyclone–dewatering screen combination spoil is removed only at the dewatering screen and thus its performance controls the particle size which can be removed. The role of the hydrocyclone becomes that of a concentrator so as to limit the required screen area and to produce a slurry of sufficient solids content that a filter cake will form (without concentration the high liquid flow rate could flood the screen and/or wash all fines through it). The dewatering screen will not work unless there are sufficient solids in the hydrocyclone underflow to build a cake. Thus repeated re-cycling of a slurry through the cleaning circuit will not improve the solids removal once a filter cake has ceased to build. The overflow solids discharging from the dewatering screen should be dry enough to remove by open truck. The advantage of the dewatering screen is that a fine screening effect can be achieved without the need for a screen of fine opening which will generally be rather fragile. However, special fine screen systems (with openings down to 35 μm)

have been developed for slurries and offer a useful improvement on standard dewatering screens for fine sands, etc.

On some sites the slurry may become contaminated with clay or silt which makes it excessively thick and ultimately unsuitable for use in the excavation process. In general it will not be possible to remove clay or fine or medium silt with a hydrocyclone and dewatering screen (the screen may remove a little of this material provided there is a sufficient coarse material to build a filter cake). A more effective method for the removal of such fines is to use a centrifuge, filter belt press or plate and frame press. These are high cost items and although sometimes used on slurry tunnelling sites are seldom found on slurry trench sites unless very large volumes of spoil are to be handled, though there may be some potential for mobile plants which service a number of sites. Filter presses effectively separate the slurry into clean water and a solid cake. Centrifuges are unlikely to achieve this level of separation and normally divide the slurry into a thin cleaned slurry and a thick cream of waste solids. The solids from filter presses or centrifuges should be sufficiently dry for direct disposal by open truck. In principle the water recovered from a filter system may be returned to the slurry circuit. However, it should be used with caution as it may contain a variety of dissolved ions plus flocculants used to improve the filtration process. It is therefore unlikely to be suitable for the preparation of fresh bentonite slurry as the chemicals may inhibit the bentonite hydration.

If there is no effective plant for the removal of clay the only option is to dispose of part of the contaminated slurry and replace it with fresh slurry or water. If the slurry volume is repeatedly made up with water any bentonite or polymer in the slurry may be substantially diluted (see Section 48.6.1). This may be dangerous for slurry trench excavations but for slurry tunnelling in grounds which give clay it may not be necessary to add any bentonite or polymer and it may be possible to operate with a slurry of the native clay.

48.7 Bentonite–cement self-hardening slurries

Bentonite–cement slurries[23] are used to form cut-off walls by the slurry trench technique. For shallow walls, up to of order 10 m deep excavation will be by backhoe. For deeper walls more specialist equipment will be necessary and for very deep walls it may be necessary to excavate in panels using a cable supported or keely mounted grab as used for structural diaphragm walls. For most walls the trench will be excavated under a bentonite–cement slurry which is simply left to set and harden. However, in some circumstances, for example for very deep walls where extended excavation times will be required, the trench may be excavated under a bentonite slurry which is subsequently displaced by a bentonite–cement slurry or if a more rigid wall is required a bentonite–cement–aggregate mix, that is a plastic concrete. For bentonite–cement slurries the typical range of mix proportions will be:

Bentonite	20–60 kg
Cement	100–350 kg
Water	1000 kg

If aggregate is to be added to the mix then the bentonite and cement concentrations generally will be towards the lower end of the above ranges. Aggregates for bentonite–cement slurries should be designed as for normal concrete, that is to give good workability and avoid segregation. As aggregate will seldom be dry when used it is most important than the moisture content of the aggregate is measured and allowed for in the mix design process. A moisture content of 10% in an aggregate may reduce the effective bentonite and cement concentrations by an order of 30%. Two design philosophies are possible: for a dense mix the ratio of slurry to aggregate is arranged so that the aggregate is in grain to grain contact and the slurry just fills the voids. This will give a dense, strong mix but one which has a rather low strain at failure. Typically the slurry for such a mix will occupy perhaps 40% of the total mix volume and thus by weight the aggregate is very much the dominant component of the mix. To develop a more plastic material the bentonite–cement slurry may be designed to have a sufficiently high gel strength to hold the aggregate in suspension and limit grain to grain contact. Such a mix will require careful design of the bentonite–cement slurry and selection of the aggregate grading.

Generally it is necessry to place plastic concretes by tremie to avoid segregation. Soil–bentonite cut-off materials which are little used in the UK but have been widely used in the USA, are often placed by filling from one end of the trench by grab or tremie to create a sloping surface and then dozing material in at the top so that it slides down the slope.[2,12]

When placing a plastic concrete it is most important to ensure that the aggregate is filled up to the required top level in the trench. After placement it is very likely that some settlement of solids will occur so as to leave a surface layer of thin bentonite–cement and fines. The aggregate level should be checked after placement and prior to set and if necessary further plastic concrete added. A simpler procedure may be to accept the settlement and scrape off the thin bentonite–cement and replace it with clay as part of the trench capping process. It must, of course, be ensured that the settlement is not greater than the proposed depth of capping (capping is essential to prevent the surface region of the cut-off wall from drying out, see Section 48.5.1, and to ensure that it is subject to some effective stress, see Section 48.13.2).

48.7.1 Properties

For a cut-off wall a permeability requirement of less than 10^{-8} m s^{-1} used to be typical. More recently the recommendations of Waste Management Paper 27[24] for natural clay liners have come to be applied to cut-off walls and a permeability of 10^{-9} m s^{-1} tends to be required. It is often suggested that bentonite–cements should be designed to have a strength similar to that of the ground in which they are placed or as a variant on this to have similar elastic modulus. In practice the strength *in situ* is seldom determined, especially for non-cohesive soils where cut-offs find considerable application. Typically a minimum unconfined compressive strength of a few hundred kN m^{-2} will be specified regardless of the soil strength. In addition to the strength criterion, specifications often call for a strain of 5% without failure. However, the test conditions and the definition of failure are seldom specified. In practice what is required is that the cut-off wall can withstand some significant strain without cracking and increase in permeability. This is a difficult situation to model in the laboratory. One procedure is to carry out a confined drained triaxial test and plot the resulting stress–strain curve. Failure may be taken as the point at which the stress starts to reduce, though more correctly but impracticably as regards measurement it should be the point at which the permeability starts to increase. Under confined conditions failure should not occur below 5% strain. If unconfined tests are employed (and these are much quicker and therefore cheaper) the failure strain will typically be less than 2%. Unconfined compressive strength tests therefore do not show the strain behaviour of the material under trench conditions (see Section 48.13.2) but are useful for quality control purposes.

48.8 Structural grouts

The fundamental requirements for a structural grout are likely to be that it is of appropriate strength, is durable, completely fills the void into which it is placed and provides a suitable chemical environment to prevent the corrosion of any stressing tendons, etc. Placement generally will be by pumping and thus pumpability and the time for which the grout is pumpable become additional parameters. A substantial amount of research work on structural grouts has been carried out under the auspices of the Marine Technology Directorate Ltd.[9]

As noted in Section 48.5, typically structural grouts will have water to cement ratios in the range 0.3–0.5. Above 0.5 severe bleeding may occur (and indeed substantial bleeding can occur even at 0.3 in adverse circumstances). Below 0.3 the grouts will probably be unpumpable and it may be necessary to use a superplasticizer even to achieve a water to cement ratio of 0.35.

In practice blockages may be a greater problem than grout rheology. Blockages can occur if there are leaks in the pipework. Leaks will lead to loss of water by filtration and hence the build up of a cake of cement solids. This may lead to local blockage of the line or the cake may be dislodged and cause blockage elsewhere. Sharp bends and changes in pipe section should be avoided as blockages very often occur at such points. Blockages may even occur as a result of sudden expansions in pipe section as there is a tendency for a transition region of stiffened grout to form at such points. If any of this stiffened grout is dislodged it may cause mechanical blockage elsewhere in the pipework.

Strength is seldom a problem for duct grouts. The necessary strength can generally be achieved at a water to cement ratio of 0.4–0.5 and thus there should be no problems with pumping. Bleeding then becomes the controlling parameter. For offshore grouted connections higher strengths are often required (particularly early strengths) and thus strength may become the controlling factor for water to cement ratio. Pumping pressure and pumping time thus become more significant particularly as pumping distances may be quite considerable. Basic data on pumping pressure are outlined in Reference 9.

The complete filling of ducts, clamps or any void with grout can be a delicate operation requiring careful attention to procedure and to grout bleed and rheology. In a vertical duct or inclined duct where the grout flow is upwards the hydrostatic pressure of the grout column may ensure that the full cross-section of the duct is filled. However, in horizontal ducts or ducts where the grout flow must be downwards it may be difficult to avoid trapping air voids and very careful attention must be paid to grout vents, etc. Furthermore, for duct grouting it should be remembered that the tendon bundle is unlikely to be central and its position will vary along the length of the duct. The problem therefore is to grout an annulus of varying eccentricity which in general will not be horizontal but follow the line of tension in the structure. Ideally it would seem appropriate to grout such ducts from both ends so that voids trapped in downward sloping sections can be displaced by flow reversal to vents placed at high points. In practice the extra plant, personnel and time involved will normally preclude this. Grouting thus becomes the province of the expert and trials may be appropriate if the layout is complex or unusual. Such trials will be expensive. However, it should be remembered that the total cost of the grouting work is likely to be a fraction of the cost of the structure and yet a very limited region of corrosion could put the structure at risk.[25]

In many grouting operations it is customary to leave a reservoir of grout at the high point(s) on the assumption that the grout will flow in from the reservoir and displace any bleed water which collects. In practice this may work for a few moments but thereafter the grout stiffens sufficiently that flow is impossible (unless the pipework is of very large diameter). Almost invariably a void will be found at such points when the grout has set and thus the reservoir will have served no useful purpose (see Section 48.12.9, bleed measurement with measuring flasks). Thus the grouts must be designed to be non-bleeding and must initially fill the entire duct or void, etc.

It is common practice to pressurize ducts to reduce the volume of trapped air and to improve grout penetration. However, there are conflicts. The pressure will reduce the volume of any air voids and, for example, a void initially at atmospheric pressure may be reduced to about 1/7 of its initial volume by pressurizing to 100 p.s.i. which might be a typical lock off pressure for a duct. However, any leakage from the duct prior to set will allow the void to re-expand to a greater or lesser extent. Generally the surrounding concrete will ensure that a duct is reasonably watertight but there may be some filtration of water into the stressing strands particularly if they are not die formed. Water may then drain from the ends of the strand. It is important to keep in mind that all water loss from a duct after grouting is producing a void or voids. Furthermore, settlement of grout solids and development of bleed within the duct may lead to voids without any external loss of water. Thus in horizontal sections of duct a bleed track may form along the top surface of the duct. In inclined ducts such bleed water will migrate toward high points or in vertical ducts may collect at the top or as intermediate lenses. Particularly severe damage can occur on inclined surfaces. The bleed forms an inclined void and eventually the grout collapses to fill the void. Slumping flow of a partially stiffened grout may lead to tearing and damage which is not healed by the continuing hydration. The escaping water may also carry away some of the cement. Similar severe damage can occur if bleed lenses develop within a vertical duct and then begin to migrate upwards through the stiffening grout.

It should be recognized that all grouts have a substantial potential for bleed. In a 0.32 water to cement ratio grout the water occupies rather more than 50% of the total volume. In a typical powder the volume of voids might be 40% of the total volume (and very often substantially less than this). If a 0.32% w/c grout were to bleed so that the water occupied just 40% of the total volume rather than the initial 50% then the bleed would be 17% of the initial volume. For a 0.5 w/c grout the corresponding bleed would be 35%. It is therefore most important that duct and tendon design should be such as to minimize the rate of bleed and hence to ensure that set occurs before the full bleeding capacity of a grout has been exerted.

It is shown[9,17] that bleed can be analysed as a consolidation phenomenon similar to the self-weight consolidation of soils but limited by setting. Drainage path length is therefore fundamental. In a vertical duct the drainage path may be the height of the duct (if there are no intermediate lenses) and thus perhaps many metres. However, if there is leakage into a tendon bundle the drainage may be radial with a path length of perhaps 10–30 mm. Bleeding in a duct with such a tendon bundle will occur many orders of magnitude more rapidly and thus the amount of bleed may be very much more severe. Hence where sealed tendons may give millimetres of bleed a duct which contains tendons into which water can leak may give bleed which is of order 10% or more of the duct height (see Section 48.12.9).

48.8.1 Thermal effects

The hydration of cement is highly exothermic and in thick grout sections there may be a very substantial temperature rise just as in large concrete pours. In large grout masses, for example support bags for offshore pipelines,[9] grout temperatures may exceed 100°C unless cement replacement materials are used. Temperatures up to 140°C are not unusual. Once the temperature exceeds 100°C it is possible for the grout to be cracked by steam pressure (this will depend on the strength developed by the grout and the steam pressure and hence the grout temperature). Once the grout has cracked, loss of steam, because of its high latent heat, may become an important mechanism in limiting further temperature rise. Thus if a grout mass shows a rapid increase in temperature to over 100°C and then a plateau the presence of steam induced cracking must be suspected. The temperature rise may also cause substantial temperature differentials and thus cracking on cooling. Partial replacement of cement by PFA may reduce exotherms. Slag may also be used but caution must be exercised. At high ambient temperatures or in large masses the hydration exotherm of slag mixes can be more severe than for pure Portland cement. With high alumina cement grouts severe exotherms will occur unless the section thickness is very limited or the grout is cooled.[26] High alumina cement grouts can be very useful in the relatively low temperatures of the sub-sea offshore environment but may be difficult to control at higher ambient temperatures. High temperature rises may also need to be controlled when cement based systems are used for toxic waste encapsulation. In the relatively small sections of grout in pre-stressing ducts, temperature effects are likely to be very limited.

48.9 Geotechnical grouts

There is an enormous range of geotechnical grouts[13,27] and it is not possible to provide more than a brief introduction in a text of this nature. It is therefore proposed to give a very brief overview of some grout types and to indicate how they differ from slurries and structural grouts. Broadly grouts may be divided into three categories: suspensions, emulsions and true solutions.

48.9.1 Suspension grouts

Typically suspensions will be mixtures of cement and water or of cement, clay and water. Thus they are similar to bentonite–cement slurries. However, mix proportions, mix procedure and clay type can all be different. Suspension grouts may be used to reduce permeability and strengthen coarse soils. Typically, suspension grouts (except microfine cements, see Section 48.3.2.2) will not penetrate soils much finer than a coarse sand. Detailed information on cement grouts for soil and rock grouting is given in References 28–30.

If clay is added its role is generally to reduce segregation and improve the flow properties of the grout. Local clays may be used instead of or in addition to bentonites. Indeed if bentonite is used very often it is not allowed to hydrate for any significant time before the cement is added (or rather no hydration tanks are provided and the mixing cycle is so short as to allow no significant hydration). Thus the bentonite does not swell to produce a thixotropic gel but behaves rather as a non-swelling clay (swelling sodium bentonite will be converted to the non-swelling calcium form by the calcium ions present in cement). As a result the solids contents of these mixes and hence their strength tends to be higher than for mixes using hydrated bentonite. Thus if bentonite is not hydrated a stronger material can be obtained (though, of course, at the cost of additional materials—if the bentonite were allowed to hydrate the mix could become too thick if the same solids were used). A penalty for not hydrating the bentonite is that the bleeding of the resulting grouts is often severe unless low water to solids ratios are used.

Mixing (see Section 48.4) will be important and high shear is fundamental if a cohesive mix is to be obtained. It may be possible to obtain satisfactory grouts with low shear mixing if long mixing times are used but on site it is generally impossible to police mixing time and thus high shear mixing is much to be preferred—though with the stipulation that a minimum mix time is observed, perhaps 2 min.

48.9.2 Emulsion grouts

Emulsions such as of bitumen and water may be used for grouting. The emulsion may be designed to break naturally in the soil as the water is drawn out by capillary action so that the bitumen droplets coalesce to form a continuous system. For other grouts an emulsion breaking agent may be added to promote coalescence. Emulsions are used rather rarely, some further information can be obtained from References 13, 27 and 30.

48.10 Chemical grouts

Chemical grouts are widely used and there is a substantial range of materials available.[14] The behaviour of chemical grouts tends to be quite specific to the chemical system involved and it may take some time to develop an understanding of the special features of a new grout system. Traditionally, chemical grouts have been based on sodium silicate and two silicate systems will be discussed to highlight the wide range of behaviour that can be obtained even with one basic grout type.

If an acid or strong electrolyte solution is added to sodium silicate there is an effectively instantaneous gelation. Such a system is therefore useless for grouting work unless a two shot process of the Joosten type[31] is used (separate injection of silicate and electrolyte or acid so that the solutions interact and gel in the area to be grouted—an expensive technique which may leave some of the silicate unreacted).

48.10.1 Silicate ester grouts

To produce a delayed gelation, organic esters which slowly hydrolyse to neutralize the sodium hydroxide are used (see Section 48.3.6). Typically esters of polyhydric alcohols are used. The hydrolysis reaction is of the form:

$$\text{ester} + \text{water} \rightleftharpoons \text{alcohol} + \text{acid}$$

In the alkaline environment of a sodium silicate solution the equilibrium moves in favour of alcohol+acid as the acid is removed by reaction with the sodium hydroxide and the alcohol remains (this could leave some toxicity). The rate of hydrolysis of the ester controls the rate of neutralization and hence the set time of the grout. Set time may be varied to a limited extent by varying the ester and silicate concentrations. For major variations in set time the type of ester must be varied and manufacturers may supply a range of esters. For optimum gelation a substantial proportion of the alkali should be neutralized. However, as the esters tend to be more expensive than sodium silicate there may be a temptation to use as little ester as will give some set. Whilst this may produce a gelled product it is important to realize that this may not make optimum use of the sodium silicate and produce the most durable product. Therefore when designing silicate–ester systems it is important to consider the underlying chemistry. To make a full study of the reaction it is necessary to obtain data on the quantity of acid which is produced per unit weight of the ester (the saponification value) and also the alkali content of the silicate solution.

Sodium silicate will be shipped as a concentrated solution to avoid shipping unnecessary quantities of water. Typically the specific gravity of the concentrated solution might be of order $1300–1400 \text{ kg m}^{-3}$. Very often silicate solution densities are quoted as degrees on the Twaddell or Baume hydrometers. To convert these degree values to specific gravity use the following formulae:

Specific gravity $= 1 - (\text{degrees Twaddell}/200)$

Specific gravity $= 145/(145 - \text{degrees Baume})$

For use on site the sodium silicate solution may be diluted to perhaps 20–70% of the as supplied concentration. However, the strength of the gelled product is very sensitive to the silicate concentration and so the appropriate dilution must be carefully selected.

The ester and sodium silicate are immiscible until the ester has hydrolysed. There is therefore no problem of flash reaction, though it is important that the two phases are well homogenized and injection is rapid to avoid their re-separation (the ester will float on the silicate).

A further problem which is seen sometimes to quite substantial extent in chemical grouts is synerisis. That is a shrinkage of the grout skeleton with the exudation of fluid. Generally synerisis is quite small and may be likened to bleeding. However, with dilute formulations it can be very severe. The shrinkage may be in three dimensions and not just vertically and under gravity as in bleeding. The high surface area to volume ratio of soil pores may limit the extent of synerisis in grouted fine soils.

48.10.2 Silicate aluminate grouts

Sodium silicate may also be gelled by reaction with a small amount of sodium aluminate. The reaction is more complex than the previous neutralization reaction and it is more difficult to identify the stoichiometry.

If concentrated sodium silicate and aluminate are mixed there is a very rapid gelation. To avoid this gelation it may be necessary to dilute both the silicate and aluminate solutions from their as supplied concentrations. The system must be kept stirred as the two components are mixed, otherwise localized excess concentrations may occur so that a gel product rapidly develops as small flakes. If such flakes develop before injection they may clog the soil surface and so reduce or prevent grout injection. As the solutions have to be relatively dilute to avoid gelation on mixing, silicate–aluminate grouts may be weaker than silicate–ester hardened grouts. However, the reaction product can be non-toxic and thus particularly suitable for use near water wells, etc. The set time may be varied by altering the aluminate to silicate ratio but it is also sensitive to the silicate concentration.

Because of the differing nature of the setting reaction for aluminate and ester systems measurement of set time, etc., needs to be slightly different. This is considered in Section 48.12.10. Aluminate gelled grouts do not appear to show the rapid and substantial synerisis shown by some dilute silicate–ester grouts. However, large samples may show some slow shrinkage. This shrinkage does not appear to be solely bleeding (gravitational settlement) and it is influenced by the height and diameter of the sample. It seems that it is unlikely to occur within the pores of a soil.[39]

Chemical grouts are relatively expensive and thus injection procedures must be carefully designed. Furthermore, their low viscosity means that they may penetrate substantial distances, perhaps much greater than actually required. It is therefore common practice to use chemical grouts only after a first stage of cement or clay–cement grouting. Also chemical grouts will not be injected to rejection but rather a measured quantity injected. In principle the set time of the grout should be as short as possible permitted by the surface plant, injection rate and required penetration. Ungelled grout may tend to sink (it is likely to be denser than the groundwater) or disperse and be diluted by the groundwater or be displaced if there is a groundwater flow.

48.11 Sampling slurries and grouts

Samples for testing the properties of excavation slurries must be taken from the trench during the works. A number of sampling systems are available and the only requirements for site operation are simplicity, reliability and the ability to perform at depth in a trench (the hydrostatic pressure can jam some valve mechanisms). The sampler should be of reasonable volume as significant quantities of slurry are needed for tests (for example the Marsh funnel requires at least 1.5 l of sample). The properties of the slurry will vary with depth in the trench due to the settlement of solids. It is therefore common practice to test samples from different depths in the trench. For diaphragm wall excavations a sample should be taken from near the base of the excavation prior to concreting as this slurry will be the densest and thus the most difficult to displace with concrete. For cut-off walls it is often suggested that samples for testing the hardened properties can be cored from the wall after the slurry has set. However, experience shows that such samples are invariably so cracked or re-moulded as to be unrepresentative. Samples of the fluid slurry should be taken after the end of excavation and prior to set and poured into cylindrical moulds. Typically, samples may be taken from the top 1 m, the middle and the bottom 1 m of the trench.

For geotechnical grouts it will normally only be possible to take samples of the pure grout during the injection work. Such samples may be used for checking set time and performance of the bulk grout. They will not give an indication of the behaviour of the grouted ground. For this, samples must be cored from the grouted region, a procedure which may also yield shattered or substantially damaged specimens unless the grout is rather strong. Thus, in general, samples for testing the properties of injected soils must be prepared in the laboratory by injecting soil samples. This can be a tedious and time consuming process especially if a number of grout formulations and soil types need to be tested. It should be noted that for some chemical grouts, the strength of grouted soils can be very sensitive to the grain size. Fine sands give much higher strengths than coarser soils.

Samples for testing structural grouts may be taken from the fluid material during grouting or more rarely they may be cored after the grout has set provided that this does not damage the structure, etc. Samples may be taken for strength, bleed and rheological measurements. Generally the samples for strength testing will be taken in cube moulds. With low water to cement ratio grouts the setting exotherm can lead to substantial temperature rises in the mould (see Section 48.8.1). Therefore, it is often appropriate to cover the mould with a glass plate after filling and place it under water in a curing tank. Thus for grouts a possible application of temperature matched curing could be to demonstrate that exotherms have not been so severe as to cause damage.

High solids bentonite–cement grouts, prepared with bentonite which has not been hydrated, will be relatively strong and can sometimes be tested using samples cast in cube moulds. For strong mixes permeability should not be a problem and thus it should not be necessary to take samples to check the permeability of the material unless unusual mix designs have been adopted or there is some special reason for concern. The fluid properties of such grouts will normally be tested with a flow cone immediately after mixing.

48.11.1 Sample containers, storage and handling

When preparing any grout samples for testing of set properties care should be taken to avoid trapping air in the samples. During filling, moulds, sample tubes, etc. should be held slightly off vertical and the slurry slowly poured down the side so that air bubbles can escape. At regular intervals pouring should be stopped and the mould tapped to release bubbles. After filling the moulds should be capped and stored upright until set. Thereafter they should be stored under water in a curing tank

until required for test (unless immersed immediately after moulding to control thermal cracking).

It is most important that moulds are watertight. If there is any leakage it is very possible only water will be lost so that the solids become more concentrated. Also leakage may cause cracks to develop in the sample.

For all grouts and slurries care must be taken to ensure that the sample containers are compatible with the grout. For example, aluminium components must not be used with alkaline systems such as converted sodium bentonites, cement, sodium silicate or aluminate as they will react to liberate hydrogen gas. Plastic tubes are often satisfactory but may be unsatisfactory for some chemical grouts. If samples are cast into tubes then the tube should be wiped with mould release oil prior to casting to ease de-moulding. When preparing samples for testing in the laboratory it may be necessary to trim a significant amount of material from the ends of the samples. Thus sample tubes should be at least twice as long as the required length of test specimen.

Samples of geotechnical grouts and cut-off wall slurries will be relatively fragile and should be treated as sensitive clays. Before samples are extruded the ends of the sample tubes should be checked for burrs, etc. to ensure that the samples can be extruded cleanly. Specimens must not be sub-sampled, for example to produce three 38 mm diameter samples from a single 100 mm sample, as this will lead to unacceptable damage.

Cement–bentonite slurries and most grouts are sensitive to drying and even in a nominally sealed tube some drying may occur. Thus storage under water is the only sure procedure. Great care should be taken when transporting samples from site to the test laboratory. They must not be dropped or subjected to other impact. Ideally the tubes should be packed in wet sand during transit for protection against drying and mechanical damage. Samples should not be de-moulded until required for test.

48.12 Testing grouts and slurries

As previously explained much of the early technology for civil engineering slurries was developed from oil well drilling practice. Not surprisingly test procedures were also taken from the oil industry and details of most of the tests applied to civil engineering slurries can be found in Reference 32.

Two basic parameters for fluids are density and viscosity and for both grouts and slurries these are often regarded as the fundamental control parameters, though as explained below neither parameter may be well suited for quality control purposes.

48.12.1 Density

For grouts and slurries the most usual instrument for density measurement is the mud balance. This is an instrument rather like a steelyard save that the scale pan is replaced by a cup. The instrument thus consists of a cup rigidly fixed to a scale arm fitted with a sliding counterweight or rider (see *Figure 48.4*). In use the whole unit is mounted on a fulcrum and the rider adjusted until the instrument is balanced. Specific gravity can then be

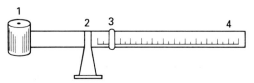

Figure 48.4 Schematic diagram of the mud balance. 1, Mud cup; 2, fulcrum; 3, rider; 4, scale

read from an engraved scale. As the balance was developed for the oil industry the range of the instrument is rather wider than is necessary for civil engineering work (typically 0.72 to 2.88 whereas construction grouts and slurries will usually have specific gravities in the range 1.0 to 2.0). The smallest scale division is 0.01 and with care the instrument can be read to 0.005 though the repeatability between readings is seldom better than 0.01. A resolution of ± 0.005 may allow the estimation of the solids content of geotechnical grouts to an accuracy of only 10% or worse. For high solids structural grouts the instrument will not allow a resolution of better than 0.01 for water to cement ratio (that is it would be difficult to distinguish water to cement ratios of 0.32 and 0.33). Thus although the mud balance can be used to identify gross errors in batching it is not suitable for accurate quality control work.

It should be noted that the instrument has three scales in addition to the specific gravity scale. These are: pounds per cubic foot, pounds per US gallon (0.833 of an Imperial gallon) and pounds per square inch per 1000 foot depth (a 1000 ft column of water exerts a pressure of 433 p.s.i.). In general none of these scales is useful for civil engineering work and the specific gravity scale should be used.

To familiarize oneself with the instrument it is a good idea to do several tests on a single batch of clean slurry. The results should agree to ± 0.01. With contaminated slurries it may be difficult to get good repeatability as the spoil may tend to settle, etc. Such slurries should be well stirred before a sample is taken for testing. The calibration of the instrument should be checked very regularly. The procedure is simply to test a sample of clean water. This should show a density in the range 0.995 to 1.005 g ml^{-1}. If the reading is outside this range set the rider to a density of 1.000 and adjust the counterweight until the beam is in balance. (The counterweight is at the far end of the beam from the cup and is usually a small recess closed by a screw plug.)

There is a pressurized version of the mud balance which is useful for thick grouts which may tend to hold air.

48.12.2 Sand content

During excavation with a slurry the density will increase due to suspension of spoil. The density of a contaminated slurry gives a measure of the total amount of spoil in the slurry but no information as to whether this is sand, silt or clay.

The sand content rig is designed to measure the bulk volume of sand (strictly material coarser than 200 mesh US, 0.075 mm, 75 μm) in a given volume of slurry. The apparatus consists of a tapered graduated tube, a small 200 mesh US sieve and a funnel. To carry out the test a fixed volume of slurry is washed on the screen and the volume of retained spoil is measured as a fraction of the original slurry volume. The result of the test is quoted as the sand content (percentage bulk volume of sand by volume of slurry).

48.12.3 Rheological measurements

The most common instrument used for measuring actual rheological parameters (rather than ranking slurries, for example, by flow time from a tunnel) is the Fann viscometer.

48.12.3.1 The Fann viscometer

The Fann viscometer (sometimes referred to as a rheometer) is a co-axial cylinders viscometer specially designed for testing slurries. Two general versions of the instrument are available: an electrically driven instrument and a hand cranked instrument. All versions of the instrument can be operated at 600 and 300 r.p.m. and have a handwheel so that the outer cylinder (the rotor sleeve) can be slowly rotated for gel strength measurements.

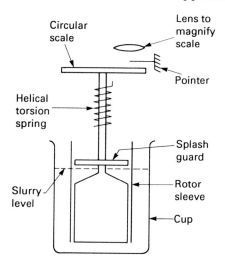

Figure 48.5 Schematic diagram of Fann viscometer

Some also have additional speeds of 200, 100, 6 and 3 r.p.m. For all versions of the instrument there is a central bob connected to a torque measuring system and outer rotating sleeve (see *Figure 48.5*). The gap between bob and sleeve is only 0.59 mm and thus it will be necessary to screen any spoil contaminated slurries before testing.

The full test procedure is given in Reference 32. Fundamentally for both types of instrument four measurements can be made:

(1) dial reading at a rotational speed of 600 r.p.m. (the 600 r.p.m. reading);
(2) dial reading at a rotational speed of 300 r.p.m. (the 300 r.p.m. reading);
(3) 10 s gel strength obtained by slowly rotating the gel strength knob until the gel breaks, after the slurry has been agitated at 600 r.p.m. and then left to rest for 10 s; and
(4) 10 min gel strength determined after a rest time of 10 min.

48.12.3.2 Calculation of results

The Fann viscometer is designed so that:

Apparent viscosity in centipoise (cP) = 600 reading/2
Plastic viscosity in cP = 600 reading − 300 reading
Gel strength, 10 s or 10 min in lb/100 ft^2 = dial reading

(lb/100 ft^2 is a unit used in the oil industry, to convert to N m^{-2} multiply the dial reading by 0.48).

For completeness note that:

Yield value in lb/100 ft^2 = (2 × 300 reading − 600 reading)

The yield value is the extrapolation of the line passing through the 600 and 300 points to the shear stress axis. Thus for the range of shear rates between 300 and 600 r.p.m. it is the yield value of that given in equation (48.3). In contrast, gel strength is the stress necessary to cause flow in a slurry which is at rest. For an ideal Bingham fluid the yield value and gel strength would be equal. Clay slurries are not ideal Bingham fluids and they show thixotropy. As a result the yield value will not be equal to the gel strength (either 10 s or 10 min). The yield value is seldom used in civil engineering.

48.12.3.3 Testing grouts with the Fann viscometer

The Fann viscometer can also be used for measurement of viscosity of chemical grouts. However, the resolution is at best

±1 cP and as many chemical grouts may have an initial viscosity of just a few centipoise it is not well suited to measuring the initial viscosity of these grouts.

The instrument is also somewhat unsatisfactory for cement based systems. Curiously many cement–bentonites have lower gel strengths than the corresponding bentonite slurry. However, the slurries may be very viscous and thus gel strength measurements may be strongly influenced by the speed at which the gel strength handwheel is turned (clay slurries tend to show a lower viscosity and higher gel which breaks sharply so that the gel strength is easily identified). For cement based grouts some semblance of gel strength repeatability can be obtained from the electrically driven instrument by regarding the 3 r.p.m. reading, measured after the appropriate rest time, as the gel strength. Strictly this is merely an apparent viscosity reading at a low shear rate. A further curious feature of cement systems is that the 10 min gel strength is often slightly lower than the 10 s value despite the fact that continuing hydration of the cement should be increasing the gel structure. This suggests the formation of a water rich layer at the bob. Overall gel strength measurements are of such poor repeatability for bentonite–cement and cement grouts that there is little point in their measurement, especially the 10 min value, measurement of which much increases the test time.

For cement based systems viscosity is rather more repeatable than gel strength though now the effect of hydration is seen and the age of the sample can strongly influence the result. Thus the Fann viscometer is not well suited for quality control of cement grouts. However, it can be useful in identifying gross variations in mix proportions, etc. but for this a much cheaper test such as the Marsh funnel flow time could be equally effective.

For low water to cement ratio structural grouts it is always doubtful whether the grout can fully penetrate the narrow annulus between rotor and bob of the instrument (the gap is only 0.59 mm). Certainly any results obtained should not be regarded as a true indication of the rheology of the grout. Slip and segregation may be dominant.

48.12.4 Flow cones

The Fann viscometer is an expensive instrument and must be used with care by a trained operator if reliable results are to be obtained. In the laboratory the detailed information that can be obtained from it can be invaluable in the investigation of different mix designs, admixtures, etc. However, there is often a need for a simple test which can be used for compliance testing at mixers, the trench side, etc. In general some form of flow cone is used. For slurries the most common cone is the Marsh funnel (see *Figure 48.6*). However, there is a wide variety of different cones and it is important that the type of cone is specified when reporting results. A cone should be specified by: the outlet diameter, the volume of grout or slurry to fill the cone, the test volume to be discharged (this may not be the full volume of the cone), and the flow time for water. Test procedures are similar for all cones and thus the procedure for just the Marsh funnel is detailed.

48.12.4.1 The Marsh funnel

The Marsh funnel is the simplest instrument for routine checking of slurry viscosity. The test procedure is simply to pour a freshly stirred sample of the slurry through the screen to fill the funnel to the under-side of the screen (a volume of 1.5 l). Then measure the time for the flow of either 946 ml (1 US quart) or 1000 ml of slurry from the funnel. The slurry viscosity is quoted as Marsh funnel seconds, the volume discharged should also be quoted.

The funnel may be checked by measuring the flow time for

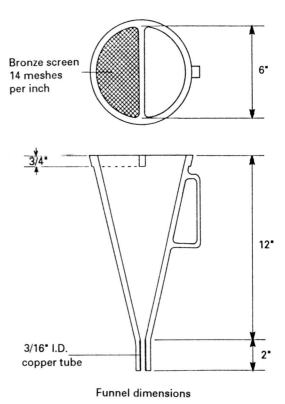

Bronze screen
14 meshes
per inch

3/4"

6"

12"

2"

3/16" I.D.
copper tube

Funnel dimensions

Figure 48.6   The Marsh funnel

water. For clean water at 21°C (70°F) the times should be as follows:

for 946 ml	25.5 to 26.5 s
for 1000 ml	27.5 to 28.5 s

No adjustment of the funnel is possible and if readings outside the above ranges are obtained it must be assumed that the funnel (or the stopwatch) is damaged.

The Marsh funnel is suitable for testing most bentonite and bentonite–cement slurries. However, for cement grouts the flow time may be very extended or the flow may stop before the required volume has been discharged. Therefore it is often necessary to use a cone of larger outlet diameter (10 mm or 12.5 mm).

48.12.5 The Colcrete flow trough

This is an empirical test used for cement based grouts. A measured quantity of grout is allowed to flow from a wide-necked funnel into a trough and the distance the grout spreads along the trough is recorded. The trough should be wetted and then allowed to stand for some moments prior to use as the reading is somewhat sensitive to the surface condition of the trough. Stiff grouts may show no flow and fluid grouts may flow over the end of the trough. However, for many grouts the instrument can give a useful guide to fluidity. The instrument is robust and very simple to use.

48.12.6 Other rheological tests

There is a very wide range of rheological test equipment available. Instruments which have been used for grouts include the Rion hand held viscometer and the atmospheric consistometer.[33] The Otto Graf viscometer[34] which consists of a torpedo shaped plunger which is allowed to fall under gravity through a tube of grout may become a standard for structural grouts.

48.12.7 pH

pH is a measure of acidity or alkalinity. pH 7 is neutral, below 7 is acid, above 7 is alkaline. pH may be measured with a glass electrode and a matched millivolt meter or with pH papers. With an electrode it should be possible to measure the pH of pure solutions to a repeatability of better than 0.05 pH units though it will be necessary to calibrate the electrode with a buffer solution prior to test and preferably to check its operation using a second buffer solution (electrodes have a rather short useful life and as they age the response becomes limited). For slurries and grouts repeatability may be rather poorer especially for cement containing or cement contaminated slurries or sodium silicate solutions all of which may have a pH of over 12.0 particularly as the response of some pH electrodes is unsatisfactory at very high or low pH.

By selecting narrow range papers it is, in theory, possible to measure pH to ± 0.1 unit. However, there can often be doubts about the indicated colour. When testing suspensions to avoid masking the colour with deposited solids apply the suspension to one side only of the paper and read the colour from the other.

48.12.7.1 Typical pH values

Most fresh slurries made with sodium bentonites converted from the calcium form will have a pH in the range 9.5 to 10.5 because of the added sodium carbonate. Used slurries (unless cement contaminated) often have a slightly lower pH than their fresh counterparts. Natural sodium bentonites such as Wyoming bentonite are of more nearly neutral pH. Cement contaminated slurries may have very high pH of order 11.5 to 12.5.

For pure cement slurries the pH will usually be about 13 and will give little information about the grout and is not of use except in rather special circumstances. For silicate and aluminate grouts the situation is similar, both are strongly alkaline. Furthermore, such solutions could damage the glass electrode of an electronic pH meter and thus tests should be carried out with caution. Concentrated silicate or aluminate solutions potentially are more damaging than the diluted solutions generally used for the actual grouting.

For other grout systems pH measurement is unlikely to be of use unless specifically recommended by the suppliers as a test procedure.

48.12.8 Filter loss

Filter loss, bleed, settlement and syneresis will all be significant for slurries and grouts as they all represent segregation processes which lead to loss of useful grout volume or function. Segregation of solid and liquid phases is a common theme and thus there may be common causes at the micro-structural level. Thus grouts and slurries which show high values for any one parameter may show high values for the others. Filter loss (sometimes known as fluid loss) is generally only measured for excavation slurries as cement and bentonite–cement grouts tend to show high losses and bleed tests are often more appropriate.

The standard apparatus used for filter loss measurement is the American Petroleum Institute fluid loss apparatus developed for testing drilling fluids. The instrument consists of a 3 in. diameter cell with a detachable base in which a filter paper supported on a wire mesh can be fitted. Details are given in Reference 32. In the test the volume of filtrate collected from a slurry sample subjected to a pressure of 100 p.s.i. for 30 min is measured.

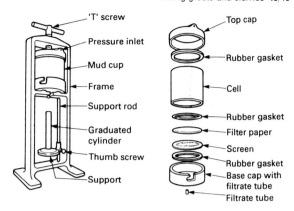

Figure 48.7 Standard filter press and mud cell assembly

48.12.9 Bleeding

Bleeding may be defined as the separation of water from the solids in a grout or slurry principally due to gravitational settlement of the solids. In clay slurries bleeding will effectively be a self-weight consolidation process and will continue until the slurry has sufficient strength to support its own weight, though there may be secondary effects which lead to continued separation of water over a very long time.

For cement grouts self-weight consolidation theory can give useful information on bleeding behaviour. However, the situation is complicated by setting and the volume changes that occur during cement hydration. (These may lead to a further small shrinkage of the grout in addition to bleeding.)

From consolidation theory it can be shown that the time for full consolidation for a depth h of grout will be a function of h^2 and it has been found that except for very shallow cement grout masses full bleed (consolidation) may be prevented by set. Thus if bleed is calculated as a function of grout depth it will be found that the percentage bleed will decrease with the grout depth. Indeed bleed is approximately independent of depth for deep grout masses[9] and thus it is misleading to quote bleed as a percentage of depth. What is a deep grout mass will depend on the rate of setting of the grout (and hence the cement type, water cement ratio, admixtures, etc.). For many low water to cement ratio grouts, bleed will be independent of depth for all grout depths greater than about 0.5 m. Thus for studies of bleed it is best to measure bleed for a series of depths from perhaps 10 cm to 1 m to see at what height it becomes independent of depth. For quality control purposes a single fixed container height and diameter may be used.

Whilst it is convenient to use the term bleeding it is actually the loss of solid volume that will be important in many grouting operations. Thus surface settlement is the important parameter as it will include not only the effects of exudation of bleed water but also any movements due to volume changes on hydration of the cement. Thus a convenient form of bleed test is to fill a container with grout and strike it off to a level surface, then after 24 h, measure the drop in surface level (the surface should be covered to prevent evaporation but the cover should not touch the grout). This is much more satisfactory than measuring bleed water which may be partially (or totally re-absorbed—many specifications require that it is fully re-absorbed though the reasoning behind this is not obvious save that it demonstrates that the bleed has been relatively limited and that there is no risk of cracking from ice formation in freezing weather). Measurement of the volume of bleed water is unsatisfactory as the peak value will occur at an unknown time after the start of the test depending on the net effect of bleeding and removal of water by hydration. Many cement grout specifications allow 2% bleed but as shown in Section 48.8 all practical grouts have a much greater potential for bleed and a specification for, say 2% bleed measured on a small sample, will not ensure satisfactory performance at full scale unless the drainage conditions are appropriate.

For clay–cement grouts it is normally satisfactory to limit bleed to 2% as measured with a 1000 ml measuring cylinder. This does not mean that problems will not occur and in particular problems of bleed and filtration may be seen when cut-off wall trenches are excavated in short lengths unless the trench is topped up after the end of excavation.

Some specifications require that the measurement of bleed is carried out in a volumetric flask with a narrow neck. The intention being to concentrate the bleed from a large volume of grout into a narrow column and so improve the accuracy of reading. Unfortunately, this procedure does not work as the bleed water will not migrate up the neck of the flask but remains on the upper surface of the bulb. Thus the procedure gives a false low reading.

48.12.10 Measurement of set time

For cement based grouts and slurries it is difficult to identify a set time as these materials have a gel strength from first mixing which increases with time until a hardened material is obtained. The setting or hardening process may be continuous with no obvious region of accelerated strength development. Set therefore tends to be defined arbitrarily as the attainment of some specified strength or penetration resistance (for example, a cone or needle penetration). Actually there may be rather little interest in the set time of many cementitious systems as they normally offer ample pumping or working time unless special cements are used or special conditions obtain.

Chemical grouts may start as effectively ideal (Newtonian) liquids with no gel strength and thus it may be possible to identify a time at which they begin to take on solid type properties such as gel strength. For single phase systems (that is grouts for which all components are miscible) the onset of gelation may be identified by drawing a wire across the surface of the grout. For pure fluids the wake closes immediately so that the wire cuts no furrow. Once the grout has begun to set a furrow will persist, though initially only momentarily. This is a very simple and highly repeatable test and perhaps the most satisfactory of all procedures as it actually identifies a change of rheological state. Sadly it will not work for a number of grouts, particularly silicate–ester systems in which the ester will float on the surface of the silicate and obscure the behaviour of the underlying material. Set time for these materials may be shown by a change of colour and quite simply that they become solid and will no longer flow, for example from a test tube—a rather less repeatable procedure but amply accurate for practical purposes.

A much less satisfactory procedure for assessing set is to specify it as the time to develop a particular viscosity, for example a specification might define set as the time to reach 100 cP on the assumption that injection will be exceedingly slow or impossible at such a viscosity. This type of definition of set is most unsatisfactory. As set occurs, bonding will develop within the grout mass, bonding which can be destroyed by small strains, in common with all solid bonding. Measurement of viscosity requires flow and therefore will destroy the developing bond structure. Depending on the geometry of the viscometer head and the shear rate, more or less structure may persist in the grout but for many systems the shear will simply break up the setting grout into independent lumps which will produce a meaningless viscosity reading. Unless very low shear rates are used the maximum recorded viscosity may be quite low. Unfortunately low shear rates are seldom suitable for the measurement of initial viscosity of chemical grouts which may be only a few centipoise and thus the corresponding shear stresses will be too low to measure.

Clearly viscosity is important for injection and therefore the procedure should be to measure the viscosity as a function of time. Readings should start as soon as the grout is mixed and may continue until after set. Set should be determined by a separate procedure, for example by wire or simply when the grout will no longer pour. The set point should then be marked on the viscosity curve. Different grout systems must be expected to show different setting behaviour and thus viscosity and set time measurements must be tailored to individual systems (not only will there be gross effects due to the nature of the setting reactions but also there may be minor influences such as the effect of the shearing action of the viscometer on set time).

48.13 Testing hardened properties

Generally for structural cement grouts the only test of hardened properties will be cube strength at a specified age or ages. Other tests on the hardened grout will not be necessary unless the application is rather special, for example, the encapsulation of wastes. For geotechnical grouts and cut-off wall slurries tests which are often specified include: unconfined compressive strength, confined drained triaxial behaviour and permeability.

48.13.1 Unconfined compression tests

For bentonite–cement and chemical grouts the samples will often be in the form of cylinders. The sample should be trimmed so that the ends are smooth, flat and parallel with a 2:1 length to diameter ratio and then mounted in a test frame such as a triaxial load frame. The sample should not be enclosed in a membrane but should be tested as soon as possible after demoulding so as to avoid drying. The loading rate is often not especially important, 5 mm min^{-1} is frequently used as it gives a rapid test. However, this gives failure within about 1 min and thus only peak load can be recorded unless automatic logging of stress and strain is available. Stress–strain plots from the test may be of interest but are seldom formally required as under unconfined conditions the strain at failure will generally be rather small. For example, for bentonite– cement slurries the strain at failure will typically be in the range 0.2–2%. It is only under confined drained conditions that these slurries show failure strains of the order of 5% or greater. The unconfined compressive strength test should be regarded as a quick and cheap test of the repeatability of the material rather like the cube strength test for concrete. It does not show the stress–strain behaviour that the grout will exhibit under confined conditions *in situ*.

48.13.2 Confined drained triaxial testing

To investigate the behaviour of the material under the confined conditions of a trench, etc. it is necessary to carry out tests under confined drained triaxial conditions. The sample is set up as for peremeability testing with top and bottom drainage and allowed to equilibrate under the applied cell pressure (which should be matched to the confining stress *in situ*) for an appropriate time which will be at least 12 h. It is then subjected to a steadily increasing strain as in a standard drained triaxial test. To ensure satisfactory drainage a slow strain rate must be used. 1–2% strain per hour is often satisfactory for bentonite–cement slurries, though this is quite fast compared with the rates used for clays. The stress–strain behaviour will be sensitive to the effective confining stress. The following behaviour is typical:

(1) Effective confining stress $< 0.5 \times$ unconfined compressive strength. Brittle type failure at strain of 0.2–2% with a stress–strain curve rather little different from that for unconfined compression save that the post-peak behaviour may be less brittle.

(2) Effective confining stress $\simeq$ unconfined compressive strength. The initial part of the loading curve is comparable to (1) above. This is followed by plastic type behaviour with the strain at peak stress increased significantly, typically to greater than 5%.

(3) Effective confining stress $>$ unconfined compressive strength. Strain hardening observed in post-peak behaviour and possibly some increase in peak strength, initial stages of loading curve similar to (1).

Thus the effective confining stress is very important. If plastic behaviour is required at low confining stresses, for example near the surface of a cut-off wall, then a low strength material is required unless it can be shown that any ground movements which require plastic behaviour will lead to increased stresses. The lack of plasticity at low confining pressures is an important reason for using a capping layer of clay on top of a cut-off wall.

48.13.3 Permeability tests

For geotechnical grouts and cut-off wall materials permeability tests must be carried out in a triaxial cell (for pure cement grouts permeabilities will be very low and quite special techniques are necessary[35]). Samples for permeability testing should not be sealed into test cells with wax, etc. Invariably this leads to false, high results. The procedure is therefore to use a standard triaxial cell fitted with top and bottom drainage. An effective confining pressure of at least 100 kPa should be used to ensure satisfactory sealing of the membrane of the sample. The sample may be back-pressured to promote saturation if there has been any drying. Generally a test gradient of order 10–20 (a head of 10–20 times the length of the sample) is satisfactory and the sample should be allowed to equilibrate for at least 12 h (or longer as appropriate) before flow measurements are taken (there should be rather little actual consolidation). Measurements then should be made over a period of at least 24 h. It should be noted that there is often a significant reduction in permeability with time if the test is continued for many days. This occurs irrespective of the age of the sample at the start of the test. For critical tests it may be appropriate to maintain permeation for days or weeks though this does make for an expensive test.

The permeant from many grouts may be markedly alkaline and thus aluminium or other alkali sensitive materials should not be used in the test equipment exposed to the permeant (see Section 48.11.1).

48.14 Specifications

Specifications for grouts should include the following components:

Specifications for materials as supplied,
Specification of fluid properties,
Specification of hardened properties.

As the properties of many grouts and slurries can develop quite slowly it is often necessary to have two further components to the specification of properties, a specification for quality control on site and a specification for confirmation of hardened properties by laboratory testing at an appropriate age. For example a 28 day strength or permeability is useless as a quality control measure for a job which may be finished before the first results become available. Very often site control specifications

will be concerned with fluid properties and those for confirmation of properties with set performance.

48.14.1 Materials specifications

48.14.1.1 Clays

The Oil Companies Materials Association Specification for Bentonite[18] is often included in specifications as a requirement for the bentonite. This is a basic specification setting limits on moisture content, wet and dry sieve analysis, apparent viscosity, and filter loss. For some bentonites the moisture content may be above the specified limit of 15% by weight of moist clay since further drying may damage or impair the properties. The dry screen analysis is not critical provided the wet screen analysis is reasonable. The viscosity specification requires that 1 tonne of clay should produce at least 16 m^3 of slurry of apparent viscosity 15 cP. The quantity of 15 cP slurry which can be produced is referred to as the yield and should not be confused with the yield value (see Section 48.6.3).

48.14.1.2 Cements

There are very many standards for cements, for example, BS 12.[36] As noted in Section 48.3.2 these standards may not address problems specific to grouting and thus for critical grouting operations it may be appropriate to add additional constraints. However, it may be difficult to obtain cements to a narrow specification unless by chance it matches the production from a particular works. Thus in general it will be necessary to carry out trial mixes on samples of cement from the proposed supplier and optimize the design for the particular cement.[37] It must be allowed that the cement from some works may be intrinsically better suited to particular grouting operations than cement from other works.

48.14.1.3 Other materials

Specifications or standards may exist for many of the other materials used in grouts and slurries. However, when using such specifications it is important to keep in mind that they may not have been written with grouting as their focus.

48.14.2 Specification of fluid properties

There is no generally agreed form of specification for cut-off wall slurries or geotechnical grouts. Because of the widely differing applications for which these materials may be used, specifications tend to be produced on an *ad hoc* basis. This can lead to confusion especially when specifications are prepared from a blend of typical clauses. For structural grouts there is more consensus. Specifications generally will include density, some measure of rheology, bleed and strength.[34]

The Federation of Piling Specialists (FPS) have produced a specification for excavation slurries for diaphragm walling work.[19] A proposal for a more general specification is given by Hodgson.[38] As only a brief discussion of specifications can be given just the FPS specification will be considered in detail. It should be noted that this specification has been developed for slurries made from UK bentonites and parts of it may be inappropriate for other bentonites or polymer based slurries.

48.14.2.1 Density

The FPS recommend that the slurry supplied to a trench for diaphragm walling work should have a density not exceeding 1100 kg m^{-3} and that the density in the trench should not exceed 1300 kg m^{-3} to ensure satisfactory displacement of slurry by concrete. The supply density of 1100 kg m^{-3} allows somewhat contaminated slurries to be re-used (a fresh bentonite slurry might have a density of order 1023 kg m^{-3} (see Section 48.6.1)).

For structural and geotechnical grout applications density will almost always be an important part of the specification even though it may not provide a good quality control parameter (see Section 48.12.1). As most grouts and slurries will be mixtures of at least two components, it is normally necessary to calculate densities by dividing the total weight of materials in the mix by the total volume assessed from the weights and densities of the individual components. If materials are to be batched on site to a particular density then great care must be taken when calculating the grout density and it is good practice to check the density of a batch of known proportions prepared under laboratory conditions (the actual and theoretical densities may differ because of the interaction of the grout components).

48.14.2.2 Rheology

The Fann viscometer can be used to test excavation slurries as it is well suited for testing clay slurries and it should be possible to obtain repeatable readings. Despite this, very few specifications actually detail what readings are required. This is because of the very wide range of results that can be obtained with different bentonites and different slurry concentrations. The normal role of the instrument is therefore to confirm repeatability of behaviour from mix to mix, day to day, etc. For this it can be very valuable. If changes are observed in slurry behaviour the cause can often be identified by consideration of the various viscosity and gel readings (a single point test such as a flow cone cannot give so much information).

The Federation of Piling Specialists[19] recommend a maximum viscosity of 20 cP for slurries supplied to a diaphragm wall excavation. It is not stated whether this is to be the apparent or plastic viscosity (see Section 48.6.3). A limit of 20 cP for apparent viscosity would be unnecessarily restrictive. However, a plastic viscosity of 20 cP is rarely achieved and thus would scarcely restrict the use of any slurry.

The specification also requires that the gel strength of the slurry is in the range 4 to 40 N m^{-2} when measured with the Fann viscometer. It is not specified whether the gel strength should be the 10 s or the 10 min value. If the 10 min value is intended the upper limit may be slightly restrictive for some bentonites.

For geotechnical grouts the rheology may be specified in terms of a flow cone time, or Colcrete flow trough reading or a Fann viscometer reading, etc. For structural grouts it seems that ultimately the preferred test will be either a flow cone or the Otto Graf viscometer.[34]

48.14.2.3 pH

The FPS specification recommends that the pH for slurries supplied to the trench pH should be in the range 9.5–12 for bentonites of UK origin (natural sodium bentonites might have a near neutral pH and polymer slurries different values again). UK bentonites typically have a pH of about 10.5. In use the pH of a slurry tends to drop and in some soils the lower limit of 9.5 may be found to be unnecessarily restrictive. If pH is low but the rheology and filter loss are acceptable, the slurry should be usable. The upper limit of pH 12 allows quite significant cement contamination. A slurry of pH 12 may show unsatisfactory rheology or fluid loss. Because of the effects of cement contamination on bentonite slurries (see Section 48.3.1) it may be preferable to dispose of a slurry of pH 12 rather than to continue to use it and possibly damage much other bentonite.

For structural and geotechnical grouts pH is unlikely to be specified or useful as a control parameter.

48.14.2.4 Filter loss

Filter loss can give interesting information on the behaviour of many grout systems. However, this information is generally of more use in grout development than grout control. As a result filter loss is rather rarely specified. For diaphragm walling slurries filter loss can influence stability in some grounds and thus there could be a case for including it in a specification. A reasonable requirement might be that the filter loss of the slurry supplied to the trench be less than 40 ml and that for the contaminated slurry from the trench to be less than 60 ml (though more stringent requirements may be appropriate for excavations in cohesionless silts, see Section 48.6.2.3). In practice these values should not be difficult to maintain unless very severe dilution (see Section 48.6.1) of the slurry has occurred or there has been contamination with cement. (These situations would almost certainly lead to unsatisfactory rheological properties anyway.)

For cement grouts and cement–bentonite slurries the filter loss will be much higher and thus it is seldom specified or measured. If values are required it will normally be appropriate to use a reduced pressure to avoid all water being drained from the slurry before the end of the test (the specified 100 p.s.i. may be appropriate for oil well drilling and some grouting operations but would be unusual in slurry trenching work). Alternatively, the filter loss may be measured over a shorter time than 30 min. If required, results may be extrapolated to 30 min by plotting the volume of filtrate collected against the square root of time.

48.14.2.5 Bleed

For bentonite slurries the bleed should be minimal when hydrated slurries are tested (though there may be a slight long term exudation of water which can be ignored for slurry excavation work). Some bleed may occur in storage tanks after mixing and before the bentonite has hydrated. If this is observed then the slurry should be homogenized by recirculation before any slurry is used (it is good practice to always do this prior to use). If severe bleed is observed in slurries which have been allowed to hydrate and recirculated then it is probable that the mix water contains dissolved salts at an unacceptable level (see Section 48.3.4.1) or the bentonite is of poor quality.

For structural and geotechnical grouts bleed tests should be carried out in a cylindrical mould of specified dimensions. Typically for cement based materials bleed may be specified to be less than 2% though this may not always ensure satisfactory performance. It may be difficult to measure bleed below 1% on site.

48.14.3 Specification of hardened properties

48.14.3.1 Compressive strength

For structural grouts a principal parameter will be the cube strength. In general this will be measured as for concrete. It should be noted that grout cubes may be much more brittle than concrete cubes and may fail near explosively.

For bentonite–cement cut-off wall materials it was the custom to specify a maximum strength to ensure plastic behaviour (see Section 48.13.2). Now it is more common to specify a minimum strength (strength has become synonymous with quality and the more subtle requirements for plasticity have been ignored). The minimum strength will depend on the application, typically it might be 100 kN m^{-2}. Lower values at perhaps 20 or 50 kN m^{-2} may be specified. However, it should be remembered that these are very low values for Portland cement containing materials and it may be difficult to maintain such strengths repeatedly. Small variations in mixing or mix proportions may cause substantial variation in strength. For some cut-off wall slurries the properties develop rather slowly so the specified age for testing may be 28 days or 90 days. It is seldom useful to measure unconfined compressive strength at ages less than 7 days unless a rather strong mix is being used. If an early indication of strength is required it is best to use a hand vane to measure shear strength.

For bentonite–cement grouts not using hydrated bentonite the water to solids ratio will be much lower than for cut-off wall slurries. Thus they will tend to be stronger. For strength measurements it may be practicable to test cubes (that is, the strength may be sufficient that the cubes will give a reasonable reading on a cube crushing machine). For softer grouts it is probably best to use the procedures set out in Section 48.13.1. It is not practicable to give typical results as the range of possible mix designs is so great.

For chemical grouts the important strength value is that of the soil *in situ* when injected with grout. The strength of the grout alone will be a poor indicator of the grouted soil strength though it may be possible to establish some guidelines.[39] Normally it will be necessary to prepare injected samples in the laboratory using either standard sands or soils from site or simulated soils. Strength values may vary enormously and again no useful data on typical results can be given.

48.14.3.2 *Permeability testing*

The water permeability of a cement–water structural grout may be of order 10^{-13} m s^{-1} or lower. Measurement of permeabilities of this order is extremely difficult and thus permeability is unlikely to be directly specified for a structural grout, rather it will be implied from the water to cement ratio.

For many years cut-off walls slurries were usually required to have a permeability of less than 10^{-8} m s^{-1} at 28 or 90 days. Waste Management Paper 27,[24] recommends a clay of permeability 10^{-9} m s^{-1} for lining landfill sites. This specification is now generally adopted for cut-off walls around such sites. This may be unnecessarily restrictive as a natural clay will be heterogeneous and a laboratory test on a prepared sample is likely to give a lower result than will be obtained in the field. Whereas cut-off wall slurries are homogeneous and laboratory results should mirror site properties.

For low water to solids ratio grouts prepared with un-hydrated bentonite permeabilities of order 10^{-7} or 10^{-8} m s^{-1} may be suitable depending on the application and the required life.

For chemical grouts fully injected soils should be effectively impermeable. It may not be possible to achieve full injection on site and thus grouted soils may show some remanent permeability. Laboratory tests may be of little help in assessing this permeability.

48.15 Conclusions

At the start of this chapter grouts and slurries were said to be generally complex non-Newtonian fluids. The reader who has reached this final section may conclude that grouts and slurries are complex in many other respects. Unfortunately this is true as the study of grouts and slurries involves many disciplines including soil mechanics, cement technology, chemistry, materials science, etc.

It is hoped that this discussion by examining the behaviour of grouts and slurries from the standpoint of a few of the disciplines involved will enable the reader to avoid some of the more common pitfalls of grout and slurry design and also to distinguish between the many different test parameters and test procedures.

References

1 SHERARD, J. L., Statistical survey of diaphragm wall applications, *Proceedings of the 7th International Conference Soil Mechanics & Foundation Engineering*, Mexico City, Specialty Session 14, 15, p. 96 (1969)

2 D'APPOLONIA, D. J. Soil–bentonite slurry trench cut-offs, *Journal Geotechnical Engineering Division, ASCE*, **106**(4), pp. 399–417 (1980), also **107**, No. GT11, pp. 1581–1583 (Nov. 1981)

3 ANON, First 'Stent Wall' installed at Kingston upon Thames, *Ground Engineering*, **18**(7) (Oct. 1985)

4 BRICE, G. J. and WOODWARD, J. C., Arab potash solar evaporation system; design and development of a novel membrane cut-off wall, *Proceedings Institution Civil Engineers Part 1*, **76**, pp. 185–205 (1984)

5 HASS, H. and HITZE, R., All round encapsulation of hazardous wastes by means of injection gels and cut-off wall materials resistant to aggressive agents, *Seminar on Hazardous Waste*, Bergamo, Italy (Oct. 1986)

6 BENSTED, J., Oilwell cements, *Chemistry and Industry*, **4**, pp. 100–105 (Feb. 1989)

7 SHIMODA, M. and OHMORI, H., Ultra fine grouting material, *ASCE Specialty Conference on Grouting in Geotechnical Engineering*, New Orleans, pp. 77–91 (1982)

8 CLARKE, W. J., Microfine cement technology, *23rd International Cement Seminar*, Atlanta, Georgia (Dec. 1987)

9 HMSO, *Grouts and grouting for construction and repair of offshore structures*, HMSO Books (1988)

10 ANON., Diaphragm walling for Sizewell B sets records, *Ground Engineering*, **22**(3), pp. 19–25 (1988)

11 JEFFERIS, S. A., The Jordan Arab Potash Project. *Proceedings Institution Civil Engineers*, **78**, pp. 641–646 (June 1985)

12 JEFFERIS, S. A., The design of cut-off walls for waste containment, in *Land disposal of hazardous wastes, Engineering and environmental issues*, Eds J. Gronow, A. Schofield, R. Jain, Ellis Horwood, Chichester, pp. 225–234 (1988)

13 HILTON, I. C., Classification of grout, in *Methods of treatment of unstable ground*, ed. F. G. Bell. Newnes-Butterworths, pp. 84–111 (1975)

14 KAROL, R. H., *Chemical grouting*, 2nd edn, Marcel Dekker, New York (1990)

15 JEFFERIS, S. A., Effects of mixing on bentonite slurries and grouts, *ASME Speciality Conference on Grouting in Geotechnical Engineering*, New Orleans, pp. 62–76 (1982)

16 BRITISH STANDARDS INSTITUTION *BS 5930 Site Investigation*, pp. 20 and 32, Milton Keynes (1981)

17 DORAN, S. M., Surface settlement and bleeding in fresh cement grouts, Ph.D. Thesis, University of London (1985)

18 OIL COMPANIES MATERIALS ASSOCIATION *Specification DFCP4 Drilling fluid materials, bentonite*, pp. 1–5 (1973)

19 FEDERATION OF PILING SPECIALISTS, Modifications (1977) to specification for cast in place concrete diaphragm walling (1973) and specification for cast in place piles formed under bentonite suspension (1975)

20 HUTCHINSON, M. T., DAW, G. P., SHOTTON, P. G., and JAMES, A. N., The properties of bentonite slurries used in diaphragm walling and their control, *Conference on Diaphragm Walls and Anchorages*, Institution of Civil Engineers, pp. 33–40 (1975)

21 XANTHAKOS, P. P., *Slurry Walls*, McGraw-Hill, New York (1979)

22 ANON., *Diaphragm walls and anchorages*, Institution of Civil Engineers, p. 105 (1975)

23 JEFFERIS, S. A., Bentonite–cement slurries for hydraulic cut-offs, *Proceedings 10th International Conference Soil Mechanics and Foundation Engineering*, Stockholm, **1**, 435–440 (June 1981)

24 HER MAJESTY'S INSPECTORATE OF POLLUTION, *Waste management paper 27, The control of landfill gas*, HMSO, London (1989)

25 WOODWARD, R. J. and WILLIAMS, F. W., Collapse of Ynys-y-Gwas Bridge, West Glamorgan, *Proceedings Institution Civil Engineers*, **84**, 635–669 (1988)

26 JEFFERIS, S. A. and MANGABHAI, R. J., Effect of temperature rise on properties of high alumina cement grout, *The Midgley Symposium on Calcium Aluminate Cements* (1990)

27 BOWEN, R., *Grouting in engineering practice*, Applied Science Publishers (1975)

28 LITTLEJOHN, G. S., Design of cement based grouts *ASCE Speciality Conference on Grouting in Geotechnical Engineering*, New Orleans, pp. 35–48 (1982)

29 HOULSBY, G., Optimum water:cement ratios for rock grouting, *Speciality Conference on Grouting in Geotechnical Engineering*, New Orleans, pp. 317–321 (1982)

30 VERFEL, J., *Rock grouting and diaphragm wall construction*, Elsevier (1989)

31 SCOTT, R. A., Fundamental considerations governing the penetrability of grouts and their ultimate resistance to displacement, in *Grouts and drilling muds in engineering practice*, Butterworths (1963)

32 ROGERS, W. F., *Composition and properties of oil well drilling fluids*, 3rd Edn, Gulf Publishing (1963)

33 AMERICAN PETROLEUM INSTITUTE, Recommended practice for testing oil well cements and cement additives, *API RP 10B* (1975)

34 BRITISH STANDARDS INSTITUTION, *Draft prEN455 Grout for prestressing tendons—Test methods*, Milton Keynes

35 JEFFERIS, S. A. and MANGABHAI, R. J., The divided flow permeameter, *Materials Research Society, Symposium Proceedings*, **137**, 209–214 (Dec. 1988)

36 BRITISH STANDARDS INSTITUTION, *BS 12 Specification for ordinary and rapid hardening Portland cement*, Milton Keynes (1978)

37 MUSZYNSKI, W. and MIERZWA, J., Possibilities of optimising the properties of prestressing grouts, *International Conference on the Rheology of Fresh Cement and Concrete*, University of Liverpool (1990)

38 HODGSON, F. T., Design and control of bentonite/clay suspensions and concrete in diaphragm wall construction, in *A review of diaphragm walls*, Institution of Civil Engineers, pp. 79–85 (1977)

39 SHEIKHBAHAI, A., Grouting with special emphasis on silicate grouts, Ph.D. Thesis, University of London (1989)

40 NATIONAL LEAD COMPANY, *Drilling mud data book*, Baroid Division (1966)

Bibliography

BOYES, R. G. H. *Structural and cut-off diaphragm walls*, Applied Science Publishers (1975)

EWERT, F-K., *Rock grouting with emphasis on dam sites*, Springer-Verlag, Berlin (1985)

HAJNAL, I., MARTON, J. and REGELE, Z., *Construction of diaphragm walls*, Wiley (1984)

ASTM, Hydraulic barriers in soil and rock, *Special Technical Publication 874* (1985)

NONWEILER, E., *Grouting theory and practice*, Elsevier (1989)

49

Stone

R N Butlin and K D Ross
Building Research Establishment, UK

Contents

49.1 Introduction 49/3

49.2 Types of building stone 49/3
49.2.1 Origins of stone 49/3
49.2.2 Sources of stone 49/3
49.2.3 Extraction of stone 49/4

49.3 The use of stone 49/4
49.3.1 Decay of stone 49/4
49.3.2 Selection of stone 49/6
49.3.3 Properties of stone 49/11

49.4 Maintenance 49/11
49.4.1 Cleaning 49/11
49.4.2 Repair of decayed stonework 49/14
49.4.3 Consolidants 49/14

References 49/15

49.1 Introduction

Stone has been used in buildings both as a structural and decorative material for a very long time. In Medieval times, the stone used for a particular building tended to be that most convenient from a nearby quarry (e.g. Wells and Lincoln Cathedrals). This meant that mainly indigenous materials were used, although there were exceptions (e.g. Canterbury and Chichester Cathedrals are built from French limestones). Today, a wide variety of stones are used in construction. This is due to a number of factors such as the supply from certain quarries being exhausted leading to less local stone being available, better methods of transport allowing stone from a wider area to be used, and the importation of foreign stones such as Italian marbles and French limestones.

This chapter is concerned only with the origin and specification of stone for the structure and cladding of buildings. It does not address the subject of the use of stone or rock as aggregates or road stone. Further, it deals mainly with stone indigenous to the British Isles, but does make reference to commonly imported stone.

49.2 Types of building stone

Natural building stones are obtained from three basic types of rock: igneous, metamorphic and sedimentary.

49.2.1 Origins of stone

49.2.1.1 Igneous rocks

Igneous rocks are those which have crystallized from molten rock or 'magma'. The grain size of the igneous rocks is determined by the rate at which the molten rock cools—a slow cooling rate producing a coarse-grained rock, and a rapid cooling rate producing fine-grained rocks. The most common igneous rock used for building in the UK is granite. Granites are coarse-grained acidic rocks (i.e. they contain at least 66% silica) and consist mainly of quartz, mica and feldspars. Their porosity is usually very low and this, together with their mineral composition, makes them very resistant to weathering. In the building industry the term 'granite' is sometimes used to describe a number of igneous rocks which are not technically true granites.

49.2.1.2 Metamorphic rocks

Metamorphic rocks were produced from sedimentary deposits which recrystallized due to the action of heat and pressure on the earth's crust. Examples of common building stones which have undergone metamorphosis are slate and marble. Slates originate from mudstones, and marbles from limestone.

49.2.1.3 Sedimentary rocks

Sedimentary rocks (i.e. sandstones and limestones) are the main source of British building stones. The formation of these rocks is a two-stage process. First a sediment is deposited; this can originate from a number of sources such as fragmentation of an earlier rock, the accumulation of animal skeletons, or by chemical deposition in lakes or seas. The second stage is cementing the sediment to form a hard rock; this is assisted by compaction and pressures generated from movements of the earth's surface.

Sandstones were formed by fragmentation of earlier rocks such as gneisses and igneous rocks. The particles of parent rock were transported mainly by the action of water and deposited in layers on the floors of seas and lakes, although transportation could also occur by other mechanisms such as wind action and glaciers. During transportation the sediments were sorted in size by the action of the water; in general, the finer particles would be carried further than coarser ones, and the longer the sediment took to be deposited the more well sorted it would be. The degree and method of sorting determined the texture of the sandstone.

The parent rock determines the mineralogy of a sandstone, but, because the sediments can be transported over large distances, one sandstone can contain sediments from many parent rocks. All sandstones contain silica along with a variety of other minerals such as mica and feldspar. Once the sediment has been laid down it can be bound together by a number of different cements:

(1) siliceous—containing silica;
(2) calcareous—containing calcium carbonate;
(3) dolomitic—containing dolomite (a double carbonate of calcium and magnesium);
(4) ferruginous—containing iron oxide; or
(5) argillaceous—containing clay.

The nature of the cementing material has a profound influence on the durability of sandstones (see Section 49.3.2.2).

Limestone sediments are usually formed from the skeletons and shells of aquatic animals or from chemically formed grains such as ooliths. Ooliths are formed by the crystallization of calcium carbonate from solution around a nucleus which could be a fragment of shell or grain of sand. Oolitic deposits are formed in seas where there is tidal action; the action of tides is essential for the formation of ooliths because unless they are constantly agitated they cannot grow as individual grains. Limestones whose sediments originate from aquatic organisms are usually formed under marine conditions but can be produced in freshwater (e.g. Doulting limestone).

Limestones are all cemented with calcium carbonate (calcite) and their durability is determined more by the structure of the rock, than by its chemical nature (see Section 49.3.1).

In some cases limestones are converted to magnesium limestones by a process called 'dolomitization'. In this process the calcite is gradually replaced by dolomite, a double carbonate of calcium and magnesium.

49.2.2 Sources of stone

Figure 49.1 shows the main areas where the various types of building stone are quarried in the UK. The production of granite for building in Britain is concentrated in two areas (Cornwall and Scotland), with other quarries in Ireland, Cumbria, Wales and Devon. A vast amount of granite and other types of igneous rocks are imported into Britain from abroad. The Natural Stone Directory[1] lists over 70 igneous rocks which are imported from countries all over the world.

There are only two true marbles quarried in the Britihs Isles, both from Ireland (some limestones which will take a polish are often referred to as marbles, the most well known being 'Purbeck Marble'). Because of the lack of indigenous marble most of that used in Britain is imported, mainly from Italy, but with substantial amounts from Portugal and other countries. Slates are quarried in Wales, Cumbria, Cornwall and Devon. A considerable amount of slate is also imported into the British Isles, mainly from Spain.

Sandstones are quarried in two main regions. The most concentrated area of quarries is the area encompassed by a circle of diameter 50 miles centred on Manchester, with another less concentrated area of quarries between the England–Scotland border and a line between Barrow in Furness and Middlesbrough.

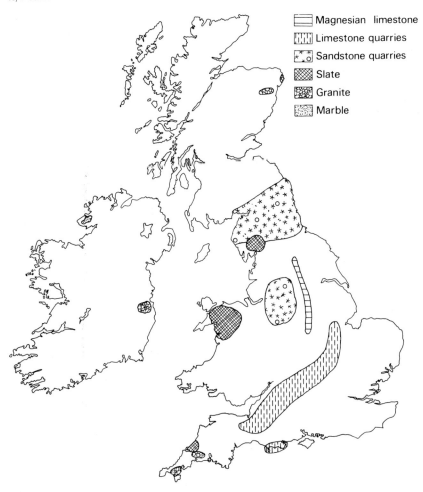

☰	Magnesian limestone
⣿	Limestone quarries
⁂	Sandstone quarries
⬚	Slate
▓	Granite
░	Marble

Figure 49.1 Map to show main quarrying areas of building stone in the UK

There are also two small groups of quarries, one near Elgin in Scotland and the other near Monmouth.

Most of the limestone quarries lie on a 25–30 mile wide belt running from Tiverton in Devon to the Wash, with other quarries as far north as Cumbria, and the Portland and Purbeck quarries to the south. There are also about four quarries in Ireland. The magnesian limestone quarries lie in a 5–10 mile wide strip to the east of the Pennines running from Nottingham in the south to Ripon in the north. A substantial amount of limestone is imported into Britain, mainly from France.

49.2.3 Extraction of stone

The traditional techniques used in the British Isles for quarrying large blocks are 'plug and feathers' and explosives (black powder). In both techniques a row of holes is drilled along the line where the fracture is required. For 'plug and feathers' two metal plates (the 'feathers') are put down each hole with a wedge (the 'plug') between them. All the wedges are driven in at the same time causing the block to split off along the line of holes. If black powder is used all the holes are charged with powder and detonated at the same time causing the block to split off. The use of dynamite is normally restricted to the quarrying of aggregates and is regarded as being too severe for block stone due to the likelihood of cracks being induced within the block.

Some of the smaller quarries which produce smaller blocks can extract the stone with nothing more than a mechanical shovel. On the continent some limestone quarries use wire saws to cut blocks of some of the softer stones.

Quarried blocks are further worked using frame saws to produce slabs or using circular saws (usually diamond tipped) to produce masonry units.

49.3 The use of stone

One of the major requirements of architects and specifiers of building stones is some measure of the performance of a given stone related to its environment, and to its position and function on the building in question. This section deals with the selection of stone and with tests for its durability. First, however, it is useful to summarize the decay mechanisms in stone so that the reasons why particular tests are used can be better understood.

49.3.1 Decay of stone

The mechanism by which a stone decays is dependent on two factors: the weathering agent, and the chemical and physical structure of the stone. There are four main weathering agents which affect stone in the UK:

(1) frost;
(2) soluble salts;

Figure 49.2 Decayed stone on St Paul's Cathedral

(3) acid deposition; and
(4) moisture and temperature cycles.

49.3.1.1 Frost

It is well known that when water freezes to form ice the process is accompanied by an increase in volume. The traditional view of frost damage is that when this occurs within the pores of a stone the structure will suffer damage if the stone is not strong enough to withstand the pressure. While the fact that water expands when it freezes will contribute to any damage, the actual mechanism of attack is more complicated. It has been demonstrated[2] that liquids such as nitrobenzene which contract on freezing can cause damage when frozen in the pore structure of stone. Whether or not a stone is resistant to frost is now thought to be related to the distribution of the size of the pores in the stone.

The pore structure affects freezing in two ways. Firstly, it is the pore structure which determines how much water is absorbed and retained under a given set of conditions; fine-pored stones tend to become more saturated than those which are coarse pored. If insufficient water is retained, damage will not occur. Thus, as a general rule, coarse-pored stones tend to be more durable than fine-pored stones. Secondly, the thermodynamics of ice nucleation (i.e. the formation of an embryonic ice crystal and its subsequent growth) are governed by the pore structure.

Put simply, once a crystal has formed it is more favourable for that crystal to continue growing than for another crystal to form. The more water that is available to allow the single crystal to continue growing, the greater is the chance of frost damage. It is this type of 'crystallization' mechanism which is now thought to be mainly responsible for frost damage.

49.3.1.2 Soluble salts

Soluble salts can contribute to stone decay in two ways. Firstly, they can cause crystallization damage by a mechanism similar to frost damage. In this case it is the evaporation of water leading to a saturated solution of salt that causes the first crystal to form, but the growth of that crystal is controlled by the same factors as is frost damage.

The second mechanism can take place in 'dry' conditions. Many salts have a number of molecules of water attached to each molecule of salt, called the 'water of crystallization'. The number of molecules can vary according to the ambient temperature and humidity. At higher temperatures and lower humidities salts tend to lose their water of crystallization; at lower temperatures and higher humidities they pick up moisture. As a salt picks up moisture its volume increases; if this expansion is restricted by the pore walls within a stone then pressures can be generated which are sufficient to cause disruption of the stone surface.

49.3.1.3 Acid deposition

Acidic gases (such as oxides of sulphur) in the atmosphere can attack stones containing carbonate minerals, e.g. calcite and dolomite. This causes damage for two reasons. Firstly, the stone is gradually eaten away with a loss of the surface, and secondly the reaction products are soluble salts which can cause crystallization damage, particularly from stones containing dolomite.

Figure 49.2 shows a picture of a statue at St Paul's Cathedral. The statue is made of limestone and is being gradually eaten away partly by acid species. The stone that remains is still quite sound, however, and will continue to give good service for many years to come. *Figure 49.3* shows an example of decay in magnesian limestone.

The worst cases of decay from acid attack occur with stones which contain small amounts of carbonate minerals such as the cementing material which holds the grains together (e.g. calcareous sandstones and some slates). These materials can

Figure 49.3 Decay in magnesian limestone

Figure 49.4 Contour scaling of stone due to wetting and drying and temperature cycles

decay very rapidly because the dissolution of a small amount of carbonate can dislodge a large number of grains.

49.3.1.4 Moisture and temperature cycles

Moisture plays an important role in the decay of stone; the mechanisms outlined above all rely on the presence of moisture. It is also possible for decay to occur when stone undergoes simple wetting and drying and thermal cycles. Attack by moisture can be chemical or physical in nature.

Physical damage can result if the cementing material of a rock contains large amounts of clay, due to the expansion of some clays when they absorb water. A combination of wetting and drying cycles and temperature cycles is also thought to contribute to contour scaling (see *Figure 49.4*). In this type of decay the wet surface region will have different physical properties (e.g. coefficient of thermal expansion) to the underlying dry region. This leads to the build up of stresses which lead to failure.

Wetting and drying cycles can cause chemical damage to occur in some pyrite-containing rocks due to the oxidation of the pyrite. Some slates are prone to this type of decay.

49.3.2 Selection of stone

49.3.2.1 Codes and standards

There are a number of British Standards and Codes of Practice which deal with the use of stone in buildings but, with the exception of slate, there is little advice on durability testing. The

standards which deal with stone are listed below, along with a brief description of the information they contain.

BS 435[3] This standard specifies finish and dimensional requirements of units made from igneous rocks (granites, basalt, gabbro and porphyry). This standard states that material should be 'good, sound, uniform in texture, free from defects and at least equal to a sample submitted by the supplier and approved by the purchaser', but does not give any practical advice on the selection of durable stone.

BS 680[4,5] The two parts to this standard cover the same information, the difference being that Part 1[4] is in imperial units whereas Part 2[5] is in metric units. The comments below relate to Part 2, which is the most appropriate today.

The standard gives advice on terminology, dimensional tolerances, marketing description and durability testing. No advice is given on fixing the slate. For assessing durability three tests are specified: acid immersion; wetting and drying; and water absorption. The standard recommends that slates intended for use under conditions of slight atmospheric pollution by acid gases should pass the water absorption and wetting and drying tests. Slates intended for use under conditions of moderate or severe atmospheric pollution should pass all three tests. No definitions are given for 'slight, moderate and severe pollution', but as a guideline rural areas can usually be regarded as areas of slight pollution and urban areas as moderate to severe.

BS 743[6] This standard includes natural slate as a material for damp-proof courses, and specifies minimum dimensions for the slates and advice on laying them (including a specification for the mortar to be used). From the point of view of durability, the standard states that the slate should be tested in accordance with BS 5642[7,8] and shall be regarded as type B slate for the purposes of testing.

BS 5390[9] This standard (formerly CP 121.201 and CP 121.202) deals with the use of natural and cast stone in ashlared, rubble and rubble-faced walls. The code deals in detail with the design and construction of walls, giving several drawings of details such as the fixing of projections, moldings and copings, the construction of parapets, and the incorporation of damp-proof courses. Consideration is also given to site practice in handling stone, scaffolding the work, as well as to maintenance and repair.

BS 5534[10,11] Part 1[10] of the standard (formerly CP 142: Part 2) deals with the use of (amongst others) natural slate as a roofing material from the design point of view. No tests are listed, but reference is made to BS 680[4,5] for testing. All aspects of design are dealt with, from specification of materials to thermal insulation and condensation. Example calculations are given for wind uplift.

Part 2[11] of this standard deals with wind uplift in more detail than Part 1.[10] The standard gives tables and graphs which are intended to save the designer of roofs time by reducing the amount of calculation that needs to be done.

BS 5642[7,8] Part 1[7] of this standard is a revision of BS 4374, and Part 2[8] is a revision of BS 3798. The standard specifies a sulphuric acid immersion test and a wetting and drying test for slate. Two grades of slate are recognized (A and B) depending on the degree of air pollution in the intended place of use. A different concentration of acid is used in the acid immersion test to distinguish between the two grades. No test is specified for natural stone—the acid immersion test specified for sandstones in BS 3798 is not included in Part 2[8] of this standard.

Table 49.1 Tests normally carried out for different types of stone

Type of stone	End use	Crystallization test	Saturation coefficient	Acid immersion	Porosity	Wet/dry	Water absorption
Limestone	General	■	*		*		
Sandstone	General	*	*	*	*		
	Severe exposure	■		■			
Slate	Roofing			*		■	■
	Copings			■		■	
	Damp course			■		■	

■. These tests should always be carried out for the stone in question. *. These tests may be required for certain applications of the stone—see text for details. Note: the test conditions may vary for different stones; details are given in the main text.

BS 6270[12] This standard covers cleaning and repair techniques for a number of materials including natural stone, but in much more detail than BS 5390.[9] Repair techniques described are replacement in natural stone, repair with mortars ('plastic repair'), and repointing (including advice on mortars for repointing). The standard does not cover structural repairs, which are discussed in BS 5390[9] and BS 5628.[13] The section on cleaning covers all the commonly used techniques, such as water-based, abrasive and chemical methods. Poultice techniques for the removal of stains on marble are also discussed.

BS 8298[14] This standard (which is a revision of CP 298) covers the use of stone as a non-load-bearing covering to buildings. Advice is given on the thicknesses of stone for various situations and fixing methods. Recommendations are given for dimensional tolerances, selection of materials (including those from which fixings are made), and design (including the calculation of movement joints). General advice is given on workmanship and maintenance.

49.3.2.2 Testing stone

Because different types of stone decay by different mechanisms, they need different tests to assess their resistance to weathering. Limestones tend to be susceptible to crystallization processes such as frost and salt attack, and some sandstones can suffer salt damage—the crystallization test (see below) simulates these two decay mechanisms. Sandstones in the UK are generally resistant to frost, but those which contain carbonate cements tend to be susceptible to acid attack from polluted environments, as are some slates for the same reason. The acid immersion test (see below) is used to detect susceptibility to acid rain. Some slates are susceptible to moisture so a wetting and drying test has been developed for this (see below).

There are other tests which are of some use in the selection of stone. If the water-retention characteristics of a stone are to be matched (for example when repairing masonry) then the porosity and saturation coefficient (see below) are useful parameters. The saturation coefficient is a measure of how much of the pore space in a stone will be full of water after soaking for a certain length of time. The amount of water absorbed is dependent on the pore structure and so is a crude measure of pore structure. Because frost resistance is dependent on pore structure the saturation coefficient can also be used to give a rapid idea of frost resistance, although the results are not as useful as those from the crystallization test.

Granites tend to be unaffected by weathering, so there is no need for a test against the weather. Similarly, all marbles will lose a polish in polluted environments so there is no test which can differentiate between different marbles. These are general rules for granite and marble which are independent of the quarry from which they come, and so there are no tests that can be usefully carried out. *Table 49.1* gives a summary of what tests are normally carried out on various types of stone. A description of the various tests is given below.

Crystallization test Since frost attack and salt damage arise basically from a process of expansive crystal formation in the surface of the stone, the most obvious test for durability is some form of crystallization test. Such tests were first developed in the first half of the nineteenth century[15] and several versions are currently in use throughout the world. Crystallization tests comprise the exposing of samples to cycles of soaking in a solution of salt (usually sodium sulphate) followed by drying in an oven. During the test the samples lose weight according to their durability; the higher the weight loss the lower the durability.

The results of the crystallization test are rather sensitive to the actual test conditions,[16] particularly the temperature of the solution during the soaking part of the cycle. Increasing the soaking temperature will decrease the weight loss, and at temperatures $> 30°C$ samples lose no weight at all. Variations in the soaking temperature do not affect the relative weight loss of different types of stone, however. The drying time is critical because if samples are not completely dried between cycles then a lower weight loss is observed than if the samples had been completely dried. Because different types of stone dry out at different rates, depending on their pore structure, incomplete drying can affect the relative weight losses.

The test most commonly used in the UK is that developed by the Building Research Establishment (BRE). The test is a comparative one in that stones of known durability are included as internal references; this is to check that the test is giving sensible and consistent results. The three internal standards currently used are: Portland, Monks Park, and Box Ground limestones. Box Ground is no longer available, but it is not particularly important which stones are used; it is more important that they cover the durability spectrum, are available over a period of years, and are of consistent quality during that period.

In the BRE test the weight loss for limestones can be used to assign a durability class which is of use when determining where in a building a particular stone can be used with confidence. The test may also be used to compare two stones of unknown quality, in which case it is less important to include internal standards, but if these are excluded the results may not be reliable for the allocation of a durability class.

The procedure for the crystallization test is as follows.

(1) Make up a stock solution of sodium sulphate by dissolving 1.4 kg of sodium sulphate decahydrate in 8.6 l of water, or by dissolving any hydrate of sodium sulphate in water until

Table 49.2 Effect of change of environment on the suitability for building zones 1–4 in *Figure 49.5*

Limestone class	Crystallization loss (%)	Inland				Exposed coastal			
		Low pollution		High pollution		Low pollution		High pollution	
		No frost	Frost	No frost	Frost	No frost	Frost	No frost	Frost
A	<1	1–4	1–4	1–4	1–4	1–4	1–4	1–4	1–4
B	1–5	2–4	2–4	2–4	2–4	2–4	2–4	2*–4	2*–4
C	>5–15	2–4	2–4	3–4	3–4	3*–4	4		
D	>15–35	3–4	4	3–4	4				
E	>35	4	4	4*					
F	Shatters early in test	4	4						

* Probably limited to a 50-year life.

the specific gravity of the solution is 1.055 at 20°C. Approximately 2 l will be needed to complete the test for each sample. The temperature of the solution should be maintained at 20±0.5°C throughout the test.

(2) Using a suitable saw, cut a representative number of 4-cm cubes of all the stones to be tested. Not less than four cubes of each stone (including the internal standards) should be tested, but unless the stone is particularly variable a maximum of six should be sufficient.

(3) Remove any loose material by washing with water, and dry the samples at 103±2°C to constant weight (overnight in a ventilated oven will usually achieve this).

(4) Remove the samples from the oven, place them in a desiccator, and allow to cool to 20±2°C. Weigh them to ±0.01 g (W_0).

(5) Label the samples and weigh them again (W_1). (The best method of labelling is to attach a heat-resistant plastic label with wire and write the sample number on the label with waterproof ink.)

(6) Place each sample in a 250-ml container and cover with fresh sodium sulphate solution to a depth of *c*. 8 mm. Leave for 2 h during which time the temperature of the sample and solution should be kept at 20±0.5°C. (Note: variations in the soaking temperature can markedly affect the results.) When the samples have been soaking for 1.5 h place a shallow tray containing 300 ml of water in the oven. (It was found empirically in the past that drying the samples in an oven which was initially humid improved the resolution of the test.)

(7) After a total of 2 h soaking, remove the samples from the solution and put them in the humid oven on wire racks. Dry the samples for 16 h at 103±2°C. If for any reason the test must be interrupted (e.g. for weekends and holidays) then the samples should be left in the hot oven.

(8) Remove the samples from the oven and allow to cool to 20±2°C. Repeat steps (6) to (8) until 15 cycles have been completed.

(9) Weigh the samples (W_f). Calculate the percentage weight loss from the expression:

$$\% \text{ wt loss} = 100(W_f - W_1)/W_0$$

(10) Calculate the mean percentage weight loss for each set of samples.

The weight loss determined in the crystallization test is used to allocate a durability class to each of the stones tested. This is done in accordance with the first two columns of *Table 49.2*. Once a durability class has been assigned, the suitability of the stone for a particular position (or 'zone') in a building (see *Figure 49.5*) under a variety of environmental conditions can be found by reference to *Table 49.2*.

Saturation coefficient and porosity The porosity of a stone is the volume of air in the stone expressed as a percentage of the total volume of the stone. Porosity is of limited use by itself and is usually used in conjunction with the saturation coefficient to match stones of similar characteristics.

The saturation coefficient, developed by Hirschwald,[17] was an attempt to devise a rapid test for frost susceptibility. The saturation coefficient is defined as the ratio of the volume of water absorbed by a sample completely immersed in cold water for 24 h to the total volume of pore space in the sample. In some countries the saturation coefficient is measured by soaking for 48 h instead of 24. In practice this makes very little difference to the result obtained since water uptake is almost complete after 24 h.

Hirschwald's reasoning behind the saturation coefficient as a measure of frost resistance was simple; because water expands by approximately 10% on freezing, a stone with less than 90% of its porosity filled with water would also contain enough air space to allow the water to expand on freezing without causing distress to the stone. In other words if the saturation coefficient was 0.9 or less then the stone should be frost resistant—his empirical observation was that stones with a saturation coefficient of more than 0.8 tended to be susceptible to frost. In general, the higher the saturation coefficient the less durable the stone tends to be.

The procedure for measuring the saturation coefficient and the porosity is as follows.

(1) Dry a representative number of samples of the stone under test at 103±2°C. The size and shape of the samples is not critical, but 4- or 5-cm cubes are normally used. Four samples of each type of stone are normally tested.

(2) Allow the samples to cool to 20°C, and then place them in a vessel connected to a rotary vacuum pump, manometer, and a tap funnel for the admission of water (see *Figure 49.6*).

(3) Evacuate the vessel to a pressure of 3 mmHg or less, and maintain the vacuum for at least 2 h.

(4) Admit air-free water into the vessel until the samples are well covered, then admit air over the water to restore atmospheric pressure. Leave the samples under water for at least 16 h.

(5) Weigh the samples suspended in water (W_1), and again in air after removing excess moisture with a damp cloth (W_2).

(6) Dry the samples in an oven at 103±2°C for 16 h. Cool the samples and weigh them dry (W_0).

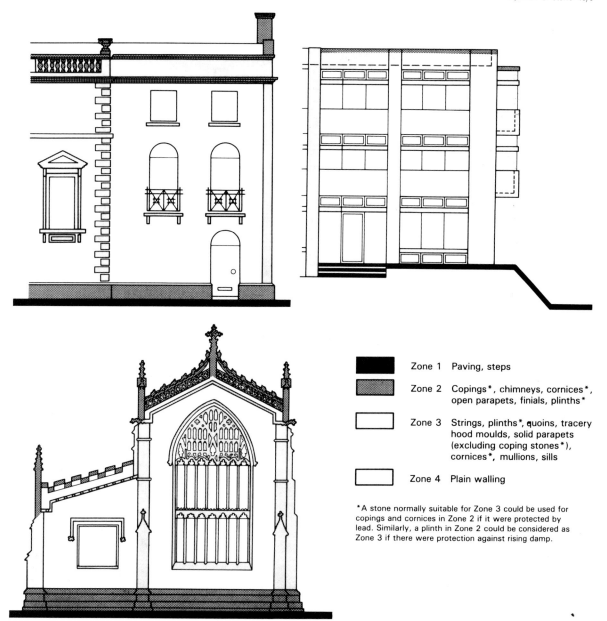

Figure 49.5 Exposure zones of buildings. *A stone normally suitable for zone 3 could be used for copings and cornices in zone 2 if it were protected by lead. Similarly, a plinth in zone 2 could be considered as zone 3 if there were protection against rising damp

(7) Immerse the dry samples in water at 15–20°C for 24 h.

(8) Remove the samples and weigh them after wiping off excess moisture with a damp cloth (W_3).

(9) Calculate the porosity (P) from the expression

$$P = 100 \frac{(W_2 - W_0)}{(W_2 - W_1)}$$

and the saturation coefficient S from

$$S = \frac{(W_3 - W_0)}{(W_2 - W_0)}$$

The usefulness of the saturation coefficient as a predictor of frost resistance depends to some extent on the porosity of the stone. For those stones with low porosities (i.e. $<10\%$) the saturation coefficient is of little value, and only really becomes useful when the porosity is 15–20%; even then it is not as good a guide as crystallization loss. A value of 0.6 or less indicates that a stone of reasonably high porosity will be resistant to frost, whereas a value of 0.85 or more indicates that it will be susceptible to frost. Between these two values it is not possible to categorize stones. It should be stressed that the values quoted above can only give an indication, and should not be relied upon to differentiate between those stones which are durable and those which are not. The saturation coefficient does have the advantage over the crystallization test in that it is much quicker to carry out.

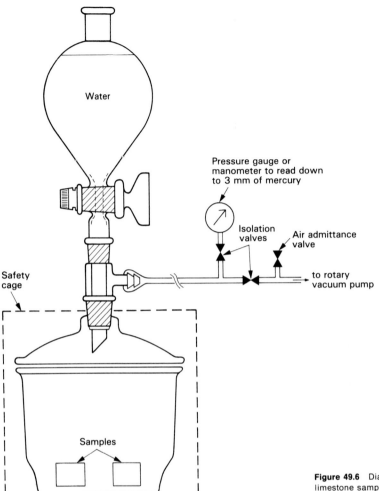

Water

Pressure gauge or
manometer to read down
to 3 mm of mercury

Isolation
valves

Air admittance
valve

to rotary
vacuum pump

Safety
cage

Samples

Figure 49.6 Diagram of apparatus used for vacuum saturation of limestone samples with water

Table 49.3 Strength of acid for acid immersion tests

Type of stone	Test or standard	Volume of 98% sulphuric acid (ml)	Volume of water (ml)
Sandstone	BRE 20%	300	2155
	BRE 40%	300	1015
Slate for roofing	BS 680	300	2100
Slate for sills and copings			
Type A	BS 5642	20	2370
Type B	BS 5642	1 vol. of acid prepared for type A slate in 4 volumes of water	

Acid immersion test This test, applicable to sandstones and slates, is used to identify those stones which are liable to decay when exposed to highly polluted atmospheres. The strength of the acid used in the test varies according to the type of stone and its end-use. For example, sandstone for general building purposes requires 20% (w/w) sulphuric acid, whereas if particularly long life is required of a stone, a stronger acid (say 40%) may be used in the test. *Table 49.3* gives the strength of acid required for various materials and end-uses.

The dilute acid is prepared in a heat-resistant glass container by slowly adding the desired amount of concentrated (98%) sulphuric acid to the relevant amount of distilled water (see *Table 49.3*), stirring constantly. Great care should be taken in preparing the solutions because a lot of heat is generated during mixing. *On no account should water be added to sulphuric acid because the heat released can cause the dilution process to become quite violent.* Protective clothing for the face, eyes and hands should be worn (for more details see Reference 18).

Table 49.4 Number of samples, sample size and volume of acid required for the acid immersion test

Type of stone	No. samples	Sample size (mm)	Volume of acid (ml)
Sandstone	6	$50 \times 50 \times 10$	200
Slate for roofing	3	$50 \times 50 \times t*$	Totally immerse
Slate for sills and copings			
Type A	6	$25 \times 25 \times 25$	250
Type B	6	$25 \times 25 \times 25$	1000

* t, Thickness of slate.

Table 49.5 Some properties of stone

Property	Units	Limestone	Sandstone	Marble	Granite	Slate
Compressive strength	MPa	14–255	34–248	69–241	96–310	138–206
Coefficient of linear thermal expansion	$°C^{-1} (\times 10^6)$	1.7–6.8	3.7–6.3	2.7–5.1	3.7–6.0	4.5–4.9
Moisture expansion	%	0.01	0.07			
Young's modulus	GPa	6.8–31.8	6.9–21	30–60	41.2–70.7	60–90
Density	$g\ cm^{-3}$	1.8–2.7	2.0–2.6	2.4–2.8	2.5–2.7	2.6–2.9
Porosity	%	$\leqslant 50$	5–31	0.6–2.3	0.4–2.3	0.1–4.3

The test procedure described below is a general one for all acid immersion tests. Acid immersion tests for slate are described in British Standards, and the procedure described in the standards should always be followed.

(1) Prepare stocks of sulphuric acid of the correct strength (see above).
(2) Prepare the relevant number of samples (see *Table 49.4* for the correct size and number of samples). Slate samples tested to British Standards should have all cut edges ground such that they are free from any visible signs of splitting or flaking. The samples should be dry.
(3) Completely immerse each sample in acid in a covered vessel, and leave for 10 days.
(4) After 10 days examine the samples for signs of splitting, swelling or softening of the surface.

The acid immersion test is a pass/fail test. If the sample shows any sign of splitting or marked softening of the surface, then it is deemed to have failed. However, loss of a few isolated grains does not constitute failure.

49.3.3 Properties of stone

Increasingly, there are requirements for engineering design calculations to accompany proposals to use certain building elements made of stone, such as cantilevered steps, lintels and balustrades. At present there is no single source of data that can provide a comprehensive range of properties of stone. Indeed, most of the data being asked for (for example tensile strength, modulus of rupture, or shear strength) have probably never been measured for most British stones. Some suppliers of building stone provide a limited amount of data for their own stones, such as density and crushing strength, but in general the data available are rather fragmented and limited to ranges for particular rock types.

Table 49.5 summarizes data from a number of sources in the literature.[19-24] The ranges quoted are all from single references, and values for individual stones may well fall outside the values given in the table. If it is important to know the exact value of

a particular property of a stone then there appears to be no alternative but to have it measured.

49.4 Maintenance

49.4.1 Cleaning

Whatever type of stone is used in a building it will at some stage need cleaning. Dirt deposits on buildings are typically soot and smoke carried by the wind onto the surface of the stonework. Sources of dirt are traffic exhausts (especially diesel engines), and local and distant combustion sources such as domestic fires and power stations. Dirt may be bound onto the surface of limestone buildings by gypsum (calcium sulphate) derived from the reaction of calcium carbonate or dolomite in the stone with sulphur dioxide in the atmosphere. In rain-washed areas it tends to be washed off, but in sheltered areas on calcareous stone a black gypsum crust develops. Water washing of limestone buildings is usually successfully in removing dirt because the gypsum that holds it there is slightly soluble in water.

Silica in sandstone binds the dirt to the surface and, being insoluble in water, tends to be unaffected by water washing. In this case more aggressive cleaning methods such as grit blasting or chemical cleaning must be used.

Staining on stone in buildings can be caused by a variety of agents such as organic growths, general urban grime, and run-off from metals. Organic growths are found on building materials in conditions where their needs of moisture, food and light are met. The acid metabolism products from organisms can etch limestone, lichens can obscure carvings and inscriptions and algae may produce disfiguring stains on masonry. The methods of removing such growths by cleaning and treatment with biocidal toxic washes such as quaternary ammonium compounds is well documented.[25]

Metal stains can be very persistent and difficult to remove. The most common metal stains are from copper and iron. Copper stains may be removed by repeated applications of an ammonia solution poultice, details of which can be found in BS 6270.[12]

Figure 49.7 A stone building after cleaning. Courtesy Glasgow District Council

Iron stains can be treated in a number of ways: on unpolished granite and sandstone by the application of hydrofluoric acid containing orthophosphoric acid; on marble, limestone, calcareous sandstone and polished granite the stain may be bleached with a poultice containing sodium dithionite, or sodium citrate for less stubborn stains. Heavy staining will require a more powerful poultice containing EDTA. The book by Ashurst and Ashurst[26] gives details on the manufacture and use of this and other poultices.

Paint and graffiti are particularly difficult to remove from porous masonry because they can be absorbed into the surface pores. If removal with water is unsuccessful then more aggressive materials will be needed. If paint removers are to be used it is preferable to use water-based ones which comply with BS 3761.[27] Paint strippers based on caustic soda can leave harmful deposits in the stone (see the section on alkaline cleaners) and so should be used with great care, and only as a last resort. Often paint can only be removed by the use of a grinding disk or grit-blasting equipment; these are likely to cause physical damage to the surface of the stone and will probably need some finishing by hand rubbing.

Recently, work has been done by the Research, Technical and Advisory Service of English Heritage[26] and Fry[28] on the use of anti-graffiti treatments for masonry. Promising results have been obtained using polyurethane resins to line the pores of stone. These treatments should not be used on decaying masonry however.

49.4.1.1 Specification of cleaning

If possible, the cleaning of a building surface should be carried out as part of a planned maintenance programme. This is more likely to be a feasible proposition for modern stone-clad buildings than for ancient monuments, principally because of the range of statuary, sheltered or unsheltered areas of older buildings in dimension stone. *Figure 49.7* is an example of the success that can be achieved with cleaning. A survey of the building and areas for cleaning are necessary prerequisites to the actual operation.

The specification for cleaning a particular building will depend on a number of factors such as stone type, the type of dirt to be cleaned off, and whether a particular cleaning method would create a hazard to the fabric of the building or people. Generally speaking, the simpler and less aggressive methods should be used first, followed by more aggressive methods only when necessary. Cleaning methods for various types of stone are given below.

It should be pointed out that a number of the techniques for cleaning stone can be hazardous to health, either because of the way the operation is carried out or because of the materials used. Under the Control of Substances Hazardous to Health (COSHH) Regulations 1988 it is the responsibility of contractors to ensure that anybody who might possibly be exposed to these hazards is adequately protected from them. Although some general advice is given in this chapter it is not possible to cover the subject in detail, and it is strongly recommended that those involved in cleaning buildings seek advice from the Health and Safety Executive.

Cleaning limestone and marble Water washing is the conventional method for cleaning calcareous stones such as marble and limestone. Water is applied to the area to be cleaned to soften the dirt which is then removed by light abrasion using a nylon brush or other non-ferrous tool. Heavily soiled areas where large sulphate 'crusts' have built up may have the bulk of the crusts removed by mechanical means, prior to final cleaning with water, and sometimes it may be necessary to use abrasive or alkaline cleaners locally for particularly difficult areas, but these should be used only as a last resort, and never for entire facades.

Cleaning sandstone and unpolished granite Although these materials can sometimes be cleaned with water it is usually necessary that they be cleaned by either abrasive methods or chemical cleaning with hydrofluoric acid. Abrasive methods can generate active silica dust which can cause silicosis, so operatives and members of the public should be protected. The problem is worse with dry grit blasting than wet grit blasting, but the water used in the latter does not remove all the active silica. After cleaning with hydrofluoric acid, some iron containing rocks can develop a brown stain due to the iron coming to the surface. For this type of stone orthophosphoric acid should be added to the hydrofluoric acid to inhibit the brown stain.

Cleaning slate and polished granite For these materials all that is required is that they are washed with clean water with a mild detergent and finished off with a chamois leather. On no account should hydrofluoric acid be used to clean polished granite, since this will remove the polish completely.

49.4.1.2 Cleaning techniques

Water washing There are many variations in the way in which water washing can be carried out including water jets, persistent wet mists, intermittent or pulse washing, water lances and steam cleaning. There are two inherent dangers associated with water washing, both of which are easily overcome with a little care. The first danger is the risk of frost damage to masonry saturated with water if cleaning takes place in cold weather, and for this reason washing should not take place if there is the likelihood of frost.

The second danger is that of water penetration of the building leading to damage to internal finishes. The likelihood of this happening can be substantially reduced by using as little water as possible. It is not necessary to have water flooding down the surface of a building during cleaning, rather it is only necessary to keep the surface moist. This will soften the dirt just as quickly enabling mild abrasion with bristle or nylon brushes to loosen the dirt allowing it to be rinsed away. Water lances, which are of limited use alone, can be used to rinse away loosened dirt, often without the need for abrasion.

On some limestones, particularly Portland stone, a brown stain can develop after cleaning with water. This is due to soluble tars being driven into the stone during cleaning, and subsequently being drawn to the surface as the stone dries out. Although this can be alarming initially, the stain normally tones down and weathers away after a year or so.

Grit blasting There are two methods of grit blasting, wet and dry. In both methods air is used to blow an abrasive grit onto the dirt which is scoured away. In the case of wet grit blasting water is introduced into the air/abrasive stream. Both the size of the gun nozzle and the grit size can be varied according to the delicacy of the work and the degree of soiling. Extreme care must be taken in all cases, however, because a great deal of damage can be done if the operatives are inexperienced.

Traditionally, the grits employed for abrasive cleaning have been sand and flint, but these are now known to be a health hazard due to their free silica content. The hazard is not eliminated with wet grit blasting, and the Health and Safety Executive advises that non-siliceous grits should be used wherever possible. Even if the non-siliceous grits are used free silica can be released from sandstone, granite and brick during abrasive cleaning and adequate safety precautions (for the protection of the operator and the public) are essential.

After dry grit blasting residual dust will remain on the building, and likewise a residual slurry will cover parts of the building after wet grit blasting. In both cases the residue should be washed off using a high-pressure water lance. Failure to do so will cause staining because the residues contain dirt that can be driven back into the pore structure of the stone by rain.

Although the only difference between the two techniques is that water is introduced into the air/abrasive mixture for wet grit cleaning, the two methods have different advantages and disadvantages. Dry grit blasting is quick and because no water is used there is no risk of frost damage or water penetrating the building. The technique is very aggressive, however, with a high risk of damage to the surface, especially arrises, and of an uneven finish (gun shading) if the operatives are unskilled. Dry grit blasting can also cause a nuisance from dust and noise, and there is a risk of drain blockage.

Wet grit blasting produces less dust than dry grit blasting, and uses less abrasive and so tends to be less aggressive. However, because water is used there is a risk of staining on limestone, and there is an increased risk of gun shading because the slurry produced can obscure the visors of the operatives.

Mechanical cleaning Mechanical methods of cleaning include brushing, scraping, rubbing with carborundum stones and the use of power tools with carborundum heads to 'spin off' the dirt. Considerable damage can be caused to soft stones and stone mouldings, and hand finishing is often required to produce an acceptable finish. The technique produces dust and if siliceous materials are being worked the dust can be dangerous to health. Again, adequate safety precautions are essential.

Chemical cleaning Chemical cleaners fall into two main classes, acids and alkalis. The main danger from chemical cleaners is contamination of the stone with soluble salts which can cuase crystallization damage (see Section 49.3.1.2). These arise either from the cleaning material itself, or from the reaction of the cleaner with the fabric of the stone. With acid cleaners soluble salts can arise from the use of neutralizing agents which are said to 'deactivate' the residual acid. If the acids are used correctly neutralizing agents are not necessary. Alkaline cleaners can react with acidic species in the atmosphere to produce salts. Once in the stone, soluble salts are extremely difficult to remove and can cause progressive damage for a long time.

Safety in the use of chemical cleaners Chemical cleaners can contain extremely hazardous substances and, therefore, require great care in their handling or use. Before a chemical cleaner is used the operative must be made aware of the potential dangers, the necessity for eye protection and protective clothing, and what to do in case of accident. Any medicines or other first-aid equipment which might be needed either by a first-aider or by professional medical persons must be purchased beforehand, and be readily available for use in an emergency. Advice on the safe storage and handling of chemical cleaners must be sought from the manufacturer and/or the Health and Safety Executive (HSE). Specific data on the hazards associated with specific chemicals, along with some information on first aid, can be found in References 29 and 30, and the HSE produce a leaflet on the safe handling of hydrofluoric acid.[31] A useful general guide to the safe use of chemicals in the construction industry is produced by CIRIA.[32]

Although it is outside the scope of this chapter to go into detail on the treatment of chemical burns, etc., it should be noted that delays in the treatment of accidents can lead to serious injury. Treatment should be immediate, even if the operative feels no initial discomfort. Delays of only a few minutes can lead to permanent disability. Chemical splashes in the eyes require immediate treatment.

Acid cleaners The most commonly used acid cleaner is based on hydrofluoric acid and is usually used as a dilute solution for sandstones and unpolished granite, and in a more dilute solution for brick and terracotta—acids attack limestones and should not be used to clean them. Cleaning some iron containing sandstones with hydrofluoric acid alone can leave brown stains on the stone. If this is a possibility then orthophosphoric acid should be added to the hydrofluoric acid to inhibit staining.

When cleaning with hydrofluoric acid the most common fault is a white bloom after cleaning. This is due to recrystallized silica and occurs when the acid has been in contact with the stone for too long and has been allowed to dry out before being washed. To avoid the problem the building should be cleaned in sections with each section being thoroughly wetted before application of the acid. The acid is brushed on carefully and systematically and left in contact with the stone for about 20 min (the contact time may have to be varied according to the building—a trial should be carried out to determine the optimum conditions). The acid is then thoroughly rinsed off with a low-volume, high-pressure water lance—it is very important that the treated area is not allowed to dry out before being rinsed off. It may be necessary to repeat the treatment if all the dirt is not removed on the first application.

Hydrochloric acid is also used for the reoval of cement and mortar deposits. The bulk of the deposit should first be removed by mechanical means, and the stone then thoroughly wetted. The residue should be treated with 5% hydrochloric acid and thoroughly washed afterwards. This acid will attack stones which contain carbonates and so should not be used on polished marbles, and should only be used with the greatest care on limestones and other calcareous stones.

Alkaline cleaners These cleaners, which are usually based on caustic soda, are used on limestones because of their speed and effectiveness. The area to be treated should be thoroughly wetted before application of the cleaner, which should be rinsed off with a high-pressure water lance. Experience has shown, however, that there is a high probability that caustic soda will remain in the fabric of the building, particularly when large areas are being treated. If the cleaner is not completely removed it will form soluble salts which will cause efflorescence and damage. Neutralization of residual caustic soda is not practical because the products of the neutralization process will be soluble salts which can themselves cause damage.

Caustic soda also forms the basis of some degreasers, which are often specified on particularly dirty areas before cleaning with acids. The same precautions should apply to the use of these materials.

49.4.2 Repair of decayed stonework

Probably the most important consideration in the durability of stone masonry is the condition of the mortar joints. If a wall is showing distress—even if nothing else is done—the pointing should be made good (see below). Often, however, more work will need to be done and this should always be carried out before repointing. The extent of any repair work is usually dictated by cost. There are four basic methods for repair, each of which will usually be accompanied by repointing:

(1) descale, i.e. remove any loose material;
(2) dress back the stonework to a sound surface;
(3) replace in new stone; or
(4) dress back the stonework and rebuild in mortar (this process is known as 'plastic repair').

Methods (1) and (2) are often quite adequate from the point of view of durability, and are particularly suited to situations where the decay is fairly uniform. Methods (3) and (4) are more labour intensive and, therefore, more expensive, but their relative cost depends on the particular job to be done. Plastic repair is sometimes regarded as a cheap option, but good plastic repair is often more expensive than replacement. For example, to repair an ashlar block in mortar will probably be more expensive than replacing in new stone when labour is taken into account, however repair of carved stone such as string courses may be more cost effective than replacement.

Plastic repairs to copings and other details which frequently become saturated is not recommended unless the repaired coping is to be further protected by lead.

49.4.2.1 Repointing

Great care should be taken when specifying repointing because much damage can be done both in the preparation of the joint before pointing, and by the use of inappropriate mortars. Removal of the old mortar can be achieved in a variety of ways, and the method chosen will depend on the condition of the joint. These joints where the existing mortar is badly decayed can easily be raked out with a bent spike, whereas those which are less decayed may need to be cut out with a hammer and plugging chisel. In extreme cases when very hard mortar must be removed it may be necessary to use power driven abrasive disks. Whatever method is used, care should always be taken to avoid injury to operatives and damage to the stones.

Joints should be cut out square and to a depth of at least 25 mm or 1.5 times the thickness of the joint, whichever is the greater. After cutting out all dust should be removed from the joint and the joint rinsed with water. When the joint is pointed the stone should be damp, but not saturated.

The durability of the pointing will depend on two factors; the mortar used and the finish given to the face of the joint. The mortar used for repointing should be no stronger than the stone that will surround it, and should be tamped into the joint such that it is well compacted and there are no air voids left. BS 6270[12] gives tables of mortar mixes for use with various types of stone. Finishes to the joint which have mortar projecting forward of the joint (e.g. 'ribbon pointing') are to be avoided, as are joints where the face of the mortar meets the stone at a shallow angle ('feather' edges). Where the arrises of the stone have been lost then the joint should be recessed to avoid feather edges, or profiled so that the mortar face meets the stone at right angles or nearly so.

49.4.2.2 Plastic repair

The term 'plastic repair' refers to the building up of decayed stonework with a mortar. The word 'plastic' refers to the consistency of the mortar mix, and does not imply that it contains any plastic (i.e. polymeric) material. When this type of repair is employed it is essential that the area to be repaired is properly prepared. Any decayed stone should be cut away and the edges of the repair should be undercut to provide a dovetail key. Feather edges to repairs should never be used. For larger areas a mechanical key in the form of ragged non-ferrous dowels, non-ferrous screws, or non-ferrous wire firmly fixed to the background should be employed.

Plastic repair should never continue across mortar joints. Rather, each block of stone should be treated independently of its neighbours and the repaired block pointed afterwards in the normal manner when the repairs have cured. Mortar should be mixed to match the colour and texture of the stone being repaired (the book by Ashurst and Ashurst[26] gives some examples on repair mixes) and should never be stronger than the stone. The repair is built up in layers up to 10 mm in thickness, each layer being allowed to cure to allow the initial shrinkage to occur. The final layer is put on proud of the finish level and worked back when green to reproduce the texture and finish of the surrounding stonework. Iron tools should not be used in the final working of the surface.

49.4.2.3 Repairs in new stone—'piecing-in'

Repairs by this method can be quite small—down to 1 in.[2] on the face. The thickness of the repair will depend on the method of fixing and the size of the repair, but will not normally be less than 1 in. Large pieces of stone can be fixed by normal masonry techniques using cramps and ties where appropriate. Smaller pieces can be grouted in, or fixed with non-ferrous dowels and resin and grouted after the resin has set.

49.4.3 Consolidants

Consolidants are materials which, when applied to friable stonework, are intended to stabilize decaying stonework and slow down or stop further decay. Although consolidants have been in use for centuries (often with disastrous results) recent heavy advertising and extravagant claims for their performance have brought them more into the public eye. To many people 'consolidant' means 'silane', but over the years several materials have been tried ranging from early work with shellac and linseed oil to the current use of (amongst others) silicon based products.

49.4.3.1 Performance requirements of a consolidant

What is required of a consolidant depends on the environment in which the stone is expected to survive. If the stone is to be exposed in a controlled environment such as a museum, the approach to consolidation will be different to that for material to be exposed outdoors. For building stone a consolidant should achieve the following:

(1) The consolidant should penetrate deeply into the stone. This is a most important feature. Treatments which penetrate only a few millimetres can produce a surface skin of consolidated material which has markedly different mechanical and physical properties to the underlying stone. This can lead to the surface of the stone blistering off causing more

rapid decay than would have occurred had nothing been done at all. In badly decayed stone the friable region can extend up to 2 cm below the surface so it is important to ensure that the treatment extends below this.

(2) The consolidant should allow the stone to breath. No matter how hard one tries it is almost impossible to prevent water getting into the fabric of a building. It is important, therefore, to take account of the possible effects of the water that will inevitably find its way behind a consolidated surface. If the water cannot dry out through the surface then it will find another route, for example via the internal wall of the building, causing damage to the internal finishes.

(3) The consolidant should encapsulate salts. Soluble salts are the most common weathering agents in the UK. Damage occurs by the repeated crystallization and dissolution of salts within the pores of stone, leading to the development of forces which disrupt the surface of the stone.

49.4.3.2 The use of consolidants

Consolidants should only be used as a last resort, i.e. when traditional methods of maintenance are unlikely to be of benefit and the stonework is decaying too rapidly to be left alone. They should only be applied by trained personnel sensitive to properties of both consolidant and stone—a great deal of harm can be done to stonework with the incorrect specification or use of consolidants.

If a consolidant is used, the work should be recorded in detail, including photographic records. The reason for detailed records is two-fold: firstly to inform future generations of the history of the treatment of the stonework; and secondly to allow objective assessment of the effectiveness of the consolidant.

References

1 STONE INDUSTRIES, *Natural Stone Directory*, 7th edition, Stone Industries, Ealing Publications Ltd. (1987)
2 HONEYBORNE, D. B. and HARRIS, P. B., 'The structure of porous building stone and its relation to weathering behaviour', *Proc. 10th Symposium of the Colston Research Society*, Bristol, 24–27 March 1958, pp. 343–359, Butterworths, London (1958)
3 BRITISH STANDARDS INSTITUTION, *BS 435 Specification for dressed natural stone kerbs, channels, quadrants and sets*, Milton Keynes (1975)
4 BRITISH STANDARDS INSTITUTION, *BS 680 Specification for roofing slates, Part 1*, Imperial units, Milton Keynes (1944)
5 BRITISH STANDARDS INSTITUTION, *BS 680 Specification for roofing slates, Part 2*, Metric units, Milton Keynes (1971)
6 BRITISH STANDARDS INSTITUTION, *BS 743 Specification for materials for damp-proof courses*, Milton Keynes (1970)
7 BRITISH STANDARDS INSTITUTION, *BS 5642 Sills and copings, Part 1 Specification for window sills of precast concrete, cast stone, clayware, slate and natural stone*, Milton Keynes (1978)
8 BRITISH STANDARDS INSTITUTION, *BS 5642 Sills and copings, Part 2 Specification for copings of precast concrete, cast stone, clayware, slate and natural stone*, Milton Keynes (1983)
9 BRITISH STANDARDS INSTITUTION, *BS 5390 Code of Practice for stone masonry*, Milton Keynes (1984)
10 BRITISH STANDARDS INSTITUTION, *BS 5534 Code of Practice for slating and tiling, Part 1 Design*, Milton Keynes (1978)
11 BRITISH STANDARDS INSTITUTION, *BS 5534 Code of Practice for slating and tiling, Part 2 Design charts for fixing roof slating and tiling against wind uplift*, Milton Keynes (1986)
12 BRITISH STANDARDS INSTITUTION, *BS 6270 Code of Practice for cleaning and surface repair of buildings, Part 1 Natural stone, cast stone and clay and calcium silicate brick masonry*, Milton Keynes (1982)
13 BRITISH STANDARDS INSTITUTION, *BS 5628, Code of practice for use of masonry Part 1 (1978 (1985)), Part 2 (1985), Part 3 (1985)* Milton Keynes
14 BRITISH STANDARDS INSTITUTION, *BS 8298 Code of Practice for the design and installation of natural stone cladding and lining*, Milton Keynes (1989)
15 DE THURY, H. *et al.*, 'On the method proposed by Mr Brard for the immediate detection of stones unable to resist the action of frost', *Ann. Chem. Phys.*, **38**, 160–192 (1828)
16 PRICE, C. A., 'The use of the sodium sulphate crystallization test for determining the weathering resistance of untreated stone', *RILEM/UNESCO Symposium*, Paris (1978)
17 HIRSCHWALD, J., *Handbuch der Bautechnischen gesteinsprüfung*, Borntraeger, Berlin (1912)
18 *Substances Hazardous to Health*, Croner Publications Ltd, New Malden (updated quarterly)
19 WINKLER, E. M., *Stone: Properties, Durability in Man's Environment*, Springer-Verlag, Berlin (1973)
20 LEARY, E., *The Building Sandstones of the British Isles*, Building Research Establishment Report, HMSO, London (1986)
21 HONEYBORNE, D. B., *The Building Limestones of France*, Building Research Establishment Report, HMSO, London (1982)
22 BEARE, T. H., 'Building-stones of Great Britain: their crushing-strength and other properties', *Minutes of Proceedings of the Institute of Civil Engineers*, Vol. cvii, Part i (1891–92)
23 ROBERTSON, E. C., 'Physical properties of building stone'. In: *Conservation of Historic Stone Buildings and Monuments*, pp. 62–86, National Academy Press, Washington, DC (1982)
24 BUILDING RESEARCH ESTABLISHMENT, *BRE Digest 228 Estimation of Thermal and Moisture Movements and Stresses*, Part 2, HMSO, London (1976)
25 BUILDING RESEARCH STATION, *BRE Digest 139 Control of Lichens, Moulds and Similar Growths*, HMSO, London (1982)
26 ASHURST, J. and ASHURST, N., *English Heritage Technical Handbook Practical Building Conservation, Vol. 1, Stone Masonry*, Gower Technical Press, London (1988)
27 BRITISH STANDARDS INSTITUTION, *BS 3761, Specification for solvent based paint remover* Milton Keynes (1986)
28 FRY, M. F., 'The problems of ornamental stonework-graffiti', *Stone Industries* (Jan./Feb. 1985)
29 SAX, N. I., *Dangerous Properties of Industrial Materials*, 3rd edition, Van Nostrand Reinhold, New York (1968)
30 STEERE, N. V. (ed.), *Handbook of Laboratory Safety*, 2nd edition, Chemical Rubber Company, Cleveland, OH (1971)
31 HEALTH AND SAFETY EXECUTIVE, *Agricultural Safety Leaflet No. AS 19 Hydrofluoric Acid*, HSE, London (1986)
32 CIRIA, *A Guide to the Safe Use of Chemicals in Construction*, Construction Industry Research and Information Association, London (1981)

50

Timber

J G Sunley MSc, FIStructE
Kewstoke Ltd

Contents

50.1 Introduction 50/3

50.2 Moisture content 50/4

50.3 Sources of timber 50/4

50.4 Timbers—their properties and their uses 50/5
    50.4.1 Species 50/5
    50.4.2 Colour 50/5
    50.4.3 Density 50/5
    50.4.4 Texture 50/5
    50.4.5 Moisture movement in service 50/5
    50.4.6 Working qualities 50/5
    50.4.7 Durability 50/5
    50.4.8 Permeability 50/13
    50.4.9 Availability 50/13
    50.4.10 Price 50/13
    50.4.11 Remarks 50/13
    50.4.12 Uses 50/13
    50.4.13 Available sizes 50/13

50.5 The structural use of timber 50/13
    50.5.1 Strength classes 50/15
    50.5.2 Stress grading 50/16
    50.5.3 Design considerations 50/16

50.6 Wood-based panel products 50/16
    50.6.1 Plywood (veneer plywood) 50/18
    50.6.2 Blockboard/laminboard (core plywoods) 50/18
    50.6.3 Wood chipboard 50/19
    50.6.4 Fibre building boards 50/19
    50.6.5 Flakeboards—waferboard and oriented-strand board (OSB) 50/20
    50.6.6 Medium-density fibreboard (MDF) 50/20
    50.6.7 Wood cement particleboard 50/20

50.7 Uses of wood-based panel products in building construction and allied applications 50/21

50.8 Timber fasteners 50/21
    50.8.1 Mechanical joints 50/21
    50.8.2 Glued joints 50/22

50.9 Structural uses of timber 50/22
    50.9.1 Glued laminated timber 50/23
    50.9.2 Trussed rafters 50/25

50.10 Joinery timber 50/27
    50.10.1 The performance of joinery products 50/28

50.11 Possible future requirements 50/32

Bibliography 50/32

50.1 Introduction

Man has always had plenty of timber available for his needs. He has ample timber available today and will always have sufficient to meet his requirements. There will be changes in the availability of particular species and developments in the manufacture of different types of product, both in the form of solid timber and wood-based sheet materials, but, from an overall point of view, there will always be sufficient timber and timber products available for constructional use.

About one-third of the World's land surface is covered by forests, representing a growing stock of around 300 000 million m³ of timber, of which nearly half are conifer trees which produce softwoods, the remainder being non-coniferous trees producing hardwoods. The pulp and paper industry takes around 40% of the value of the primary forest material with sawn wood amounting to about 38% and wood-based panel products amounting to about 22%. Set against the vast growing stock, the consumption of timber in the UK looks minute; in 1988 it was:

Sawn softwood	10 414 000 m³;
Sawn hardwood	1 410 000 m³;
Plywood	1 478 000 m³;
Chipboard	3 210 000 tonne.

Home production of timber in the UK amounts to about 21% of total timber consumption with about 16% of this being softwoods, 25% hardwoods, virtually no plywood and 45% other board materials such as chipboard.

The bulk of the timber used for building in Europe is softwood rather than hardwood (see *Figure 50.1*). The main reason for this preference is that in the past softwood has given the best combination of cost and performance and will tolerate a fair amount of abuse and yet still give an acceptable performance. Supply changes in the future mean that it will be necessary to use a wider range of species, both softwoods and hardwoods, with more variable properties than at present. Decorative hardwoods will undoubtedly achieve greater use as more leisure buildings are constructed with greater aesthetic appeal.

The large softwood-producing areas such as North America and Scandinavia now plan production against raw-material availability and are ensuring that supplies will be available as far ahead as one can see. Other developed countries are following this lead, for example New Zealand. Eventually, developing countries, with assistance, will follow and provide guaranteed supplies. Some of these may be species with which we are presently unfamiliar, but, by use of modern technology, promotion and marketing full utilization of them will be obtained.

'Softwood' and 'hardwood' are botanical terms and do not refer to the density or hardness of the wood. As it happens, most softwoods are fairly soft, though pitch pine and yew might be considered exceptions. In contrast, hardwoods can vary greatly in density and hardness; balsa is a hardwood as is obeche and so too are greenheart and *lignum vitae*.

Wood is composed of cells, which are made up of the cell wall, which varies in thickness in different timbers, and a central lumen or cavity. Most cells are long in relation to their width and are aligned axially along the tract, giving rise to the grain in wood. It is in terms of its function in the growth of the tree that some of the more important characteristics of wood can be understood. For example, one function of the stem of the tree, from which virtually all solid timber is cut, is to support the crown of leaves, the food-producing organ of the plant. The cells or individual fibres are aligned along the length of the stem

Figure 50.1 Most of the softwood constructional timber used in the UK is imported, mainly from Scandinavia, Russia and North America

Table 50.1 Comparison of structural performance of European redwood and other building materials

Material	Specific gravity (sg)	Tensile strength (T) (N mm^{-2})	T/sg	Modulus of elasticity (E) (N mm^{-2} × 10^3)	E/sg (× 10^3)	Cost (£ tonne^{-1})
Redwood	0.5	92	184	7.7	15	200
Mild steel	7.85	470	60	207	26	400
Aluminium alloy	2.7	310	115	70	26	1100
Concrete	2.3	4	2	28.6	12.5	82

so it can withstand the bending stresses induced by the movement of the crown in the wind. This gives the timber its relatively high longitudinal bending strength in relation to its weight and hence its use as, for example, floor joists in houses and other buildings.

50.2 Moisture content

When first converted wood may contain as much water as wood fibre and drying of wood is an essential process in its preparation for use. Removal of water substantially reduces the risk of fungal attack provided that the wood is kept at a moisture content below about 25%. The weight of wood is reduced by drying and most strength properties are substantially increased; although sawing wood may be more difficult in some cases, the surface finishes obtained in machine processing are greatly improved with dry wood. Any impregnation process such as preservation requires the wood to be at least partially dry and, finally, and perhaps most importantly, for wood to maintain its dimensional stability in use and give satisfactory performance in components, it should be at a moisture content close to that which it will settle down to in use. Virtually all undercover uses of timber results in a moisture content of not more than 20%.

Drying of wood requires initially the removal of water from the cell cavities and thereafter the removal of some of the water from the cell walls. It is when water is lost from the cell walls, below the so-called fibre-saturation point, that shrinkage occurs. Drying of timber from the green condition as cut to a constructional useable content of, say, 18% moisture content will result in shrinkage of the order of 3% in softwoods. However, there is some quite considerable variation between various species.

When used to its best advantage, wood is a remarkably strong material and when performance is related to weight it compares very favourably with many structural materials and particularly so when cost is considered (see *Table 50.1*).

50.3 Sources of timber

In 1983 the cost of wood and wood products, including paper and board, imported into Britain was £3.8 billion; add to this the value of the UK production and the figure exceeds £4 billion. About half this expenditure was on paper and board and about £1 billion on solid wood, that is sawn wood and logs. The volume of solid wood used in 1983 was about 9 million m^3, noticeably up on previous years but below the peak figures of the early 1970s.

About 80% by cost and rather more by volume of the solid timber used is softwood. Softwoods are the principal timbers for construction and joinery, as well as for purposes such as packaging, estate work, etc. They come, very largely, from the coniferous forests of the northern hemisphere and there are two main regions of supply, northern and central Europe, principally Sweden, Finland and Russia, and North America, mainly British Columbia. Shipments from Europe are dominated by two woods, pine or European redwood and spruce or European whitewood. The character of these two timbers varies somewhat depending on its origin—wood from more northerly latitudes is typically slowly grown with a fine texture, while that from further south is often of more vigorous growth, heavier and stronger. However, whatever their origin, pine and spruce in Europe grow to only a modest size (20–25 m in height and 30–60 cm in diameter) so that sawn timber only exceptionally exceeds a section size of 275 mm × 75 mm and most is much smaller. This is in contrast to the growth in the forests of western America where trees of 60–80 m in height and over 1 m in diameter are found, though today less frequently than formerly. Thus, for a long time, large sections of up to 300 mm^2, and clear, knot-free timber cut from the outside of large old trees could be obtained; such timber is still available, though in limited quantity, and increasing volumes of North American timber are being cut from smaller trees. There is more variety in Canadian forests with, besides the different types of pines and spruce, Douglas fir, hemlock, western red cedar, the true firs, yellow cedar and Port Orford cedar. For many years the supply was dominated by Douglas fir, but today western hemlock, usually mixed with amabilis fir (hemfir), and a mixture of spruce, pine and fir are the timbers most commonly shipped. Western red cedar, a lightweight, durable wood, is available for exterior cladding, greenhouses, summerhouses and similar purposes, but once-important woods, such as Sitka spruce, used for glider framing and racing cars, and yellow pine used for patterns and high-class joinery, are now special-purpose woods which, when available in better grades, command very high prices. Other woods obtained from elsewhere in America warrant brief mention. In California, American redwood, or sequoia, is a stable, durable, dark-red wood used for high-class joinery. Pitch pine, once an important timber of the south-eastern and Gulf states of the USA, is now obtained mainly from Central America, principally Nicaragua and Honduras, but loblolly pine (one of the woods of the pitch pine group) has been widely grown in the south-eastern states of the USA and plantation trees are being used for sawn wood and plywood.

From southern Brazil, shipments of Parana pine (not a true pine but related botanically to the monkey puzzle), provide a fine, even-textured, almost knot-free wood used for high-class interior joinery. Today, Parana pine is the only important commercial softwood from the southern hemisphere, but within a few years, radiata pine, native to California but extensively planted in Chile, New Zealand, Australia and South Africa, is expected to be available in increasing quantities on world markets, particularly from Chile and New Zealand. Finally, for the UK market, special mention must be made of sawn softwood from the UK forests. Current annual production is about 800 000 m^3, but will rise to about twice this figure by the year 2000 and could provide 20% of the national requirements. Current supply is mainly pine or spruce, but spruce, particularly

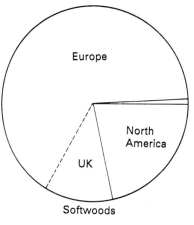 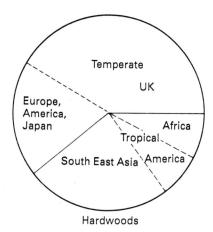

Figure 50.2 Origins of UK timber supplies 1982

Sitka spruce, will increasingly contribute to the production, providing a wood for construction as well as for more general purposes.

Hardwoods occur in most parts of the world but can generally be divided into two main types of timber: namely those from the northern temperate forests and those from tropical rain forests (*Figure 50.2*).

50.4 Timbers—their properties and uses

This section gives information on the characteristics and uses of the broad range of species which are available in the UK (see *Tables 50.2 and 50.3*). The structural properites of some species are included in BS 5268: Part 2: 1989, the timber structural design code; the following characteristics of each species are described.

50.4.1 Species

Common and botanical names and countries of origin are indicated. The species are separated into hardwoods and softwoods.

50.4.2 Colour

The colours indicated relate to the heartwood of the species. However, most species show variation in colour as well as changing colour in use and by the application of finishes. Timber exposed to light will change colour and unprotected timber exposed to the weather will eventually become silvery grey in colour.

50.4.3 Density

Timbers vary in density depending on their species and moisture content. The values quoted are average densities at 15% moisture content. The increase in weight caused by moisture can be estimated by adding 0.5% of the given weight for every 1% increase in moisture content. The symbol † indicates that the density can vary by 20% or more.

50.4.4 Texture

Surface texture is classified as fine, medium or coarse.

50.4.5 Moisture movement in service

Moisture movement in service refers to the dimensional changes that occur when dried timber is subjected to changes in atmospheric conditions (this is not directly related to the shrinkage which occurs when green timber is dried to moisture contents suitable for internal use). The movement is classed as small, medium or large. For structural purposes the movement category of a timber is not usually significant. For situations where varying humidity situations are likely to be encountered and the stability of a component is important, then a species exhibiting small movement should be specified, e.g. decorative wood flooring.

50.4.6 Working qualities

The ease of working is classified as good, medium or difficult. A difficult classification does not mean that a timber is unworkable but indicates that particular care should be taken in machining.

50.4.7 Durability

Durability relates to the resistance to fungal decay of a species. Durability is expressed by one of five classes based upon the average life of a 50 mm × 50 mm section of heartwood in ground contact. This is a particularly hazardous situation and timber used externally, but not in contact with the ground, will have a longer life than that indicated, even without treatment. These ratings refer to the heartwood only. The sapwood of all species tested has been found to be non-durable or perishable; consequently, the sapwood of all species should not be used in exposed situations without preservative treatment. The classes used are:

Very durable—>25 years;
Durable—15–25 years;
Moderately durable—10–15 years;
Non-durable—5–10 years; and
Perishable—<5 years.

Preservative treatment should be specified where the timber is not sufficiently naturally durable for the situation in which it is to be used. Guidance on the need for preservative treatment in particular situations is given in a number of British Standards including BS 5268: Part 5: 1989, BS 5589: 1989 and BS 1186: Part 1: 1986.

Table 50.2 Properties and uses of hardwoods

Species	Colour	Density (kg m⁻³)	Texture	Moisture movement	Working qualities	Durability	Permeability	Availability	Price	Remarks	Uses
Abura *Mitragyna ciliata* W. Africa	Hardwood Light brown	580*	Medium/fine	Small	Medium	Non-durable	Moderately resistant	Variable	Low	Colour variable. Resistant to acids	Interior joinery, mouldings
Afrormosia *Pericopsis elata* W. Africa	Hardwood Light brown	710	Medium/fine	Small	Medium	Very durable	Extremely resistant	Regular	Medium/high	Tends to darken on exposure, stains in contact with iron in damp conditions	Interior and exterior joinery. Furniture. Cladding
Afzelia/doussié *Afzelia spp.* W. Africa	Hardwood Reddish-brown	830*	Medium/coarse	Small	Medium/difficult	Very durable	Extremely resistant	Limited	Medium	Exudes yellow dye in damp conditions	Interior and exterior joinery. Cladding
Agba *Gossweilerodendron balsamiferum* W. Africa	Hardwood Yellowish-brown	510	Medium	Small	Good	Durable	Resistant	Regular	Low	Gum exudation may be troublesome	Interior and exterior joinery. trim. Cladding
Andiroba *Carapa guianensis* S. America	Hardwood Pink to red-brown	640	Medium/coarse	Small	Medium	Moderately durable	Extremely resistant	Limited	Low		Interior joinery
Ash, American *Fraxinus spp.* U.S.A.	Hardwood Grey, brown	670	Coarse	Medium	Medium	Non-durable	Permeable	Regular	Medium/high		Interior joinery, trim, tool handles
Ash, European *Fraxinus excelsior* Europe	Hardwood White to light brown	710*	Medium/coarse	Medium	Good	Perishable	Moderately resistant	Regular	Medium/high	Selected stock may be tough and be suitable for bending	Interior joinery, sports goods
Aspen *Populus tremuloides* Canada, U.S.A.	Hardwood Grey, white to pale brown	450	Fine	Large	Medium	Perishable/non-durable	Extremely resistant	Variable	Low		Interior joinery. Matches
Balsa *Ochroma pyramidale* S. America	Hardwood White	160*	Fine	Small	Good	Perishable	Resistant	Limited	Medium	High buoyancy value, and good insulating value	Useful for heat, sound and vibration insulation. Buoyancy aids
Balau *Shorea spp.* S.E. Asia	Hardwood Yellow-brown to red-brown	980	Medium	Medium	Medium	Very durable	Extremely resistant	Variable	Low	A hard, heavy and strong timber. Obtainable in large sizes	Heavy structural work, bridge and wharf construction
Balau, Red *Shorea spp.* S.E. Asia	Hardwood Purplish-red or dark red-brown	880	Medium	Medium	Medium	Moderately durable	Extremely resistant	Variable	Low		Heavy structural work
Basralocus *Dicorynia guianensis* Surinam. French Guiana	Hardwood Lustrous brown	720	Medium	Medium/large	Medium	Very durable	Extremely resistant	Limited	Low/medium	Acid resistant. Obtainable in large sizes	Marine and heavy construction
Basswood *Tilia americana* N. America	Hardwood Creamy white to pale brown	420	Fine	Medium	Good	Non-durable	Permeable	Limited	Low		Constructional veneer, turnery. piano keys. woodware
Beech, European *Fagus sylvatica* Europe	Hardwood Whitish to pale brown, pinkish-red when steamed	720	Fine	Large	Good	Perishable	Permeable	Regular	Low	Excellent bending properties	Furniture, interior joinery. flooring. Plywood
Birch, American *Betula spp.* N. America	Hardwood Light to dark reddish-brown	710	Fine	Large	Good	Perishable	Moderately resistant	Limited	Low		Furniture, plywood. flooring
Birch, European *Betula pubescens* Europe. Scandinavia	Hardwood White to light brown	670	Fine	Large	Good	Perishable	Permeable	Limited	Low		Plywood, furniture, turnery
Cedar, Central/South American *Cedrela spp.* Central & S. America	Hardwood Pinkish-brown to dark reddish-brown	480	Coarse	Small	Good	Durable	Extremely resistant	Limited	Low	Distinctive odour	Cabinet work, interior joinery. Racing-boat building. Cigar boxes
Cherry, American *Prunus serotina* U.S.A.	Hardwood Reddish-brown to red	580	Fine	Medium	Good	Moderately durable	No information	Limited	Medium		Cabinet making, furniture. Interior joinery
Cherry, European *Prunus avium* Europe	Hardwood Pinkish-brown	630	Fine	Medium	Good	Moderately durable	No information	Limited	Medium/high	Inclined to warp. Use in small sections	Cabinet making. furniture

Chestnut, horse *Aesculus hippocastanum* Europe	Hardwood White to pale yellow-brown	510	Fine	Small	Medium	Perishable	Permeable	Limited	Low		Brush backs, fruit trays and boxes
Chestnut, sweet *Castanea sativa* Europe	Hardwood Yellowish-brown	560	Medium	Large	Good	Durable	Extremely resistant	Limited	Medium	Stains in contact with iron in damp conditions	Interior and exterior joinery. Fencing
Danta *Nesogordonia papaverifera* W. Africa	Hardwood Reddish-brown	750	Fine	Medium	Good	Moderately durable	Resistant	Limited	Low		Flooring, joinery, turnery
Ebony *Diospyros spp.* W. Africa, India, Sri Lanka	Hardwood Black, some grey/black stripes	1030/1190	Fine	Medium	Medium	Very durable	Extremely resistant	Limited	High	Generally small sizes only available. Dust may be irritant	Used primarily for decorative work. Turnery, inlaying
Ekki/azobé† *Lophira alata* W. Africa	Hardwood Dark red to dark brown	1070	Coarse	Large	Difficult	Very durable	Extremely resistant	Limited	Medium	Moderately resistant to termite attack. Acid resistant. Obtainable in large sizes	Heavy construction, marine and freshwater construction. Bridges, sleepers, etc.
Elm, American *Ulmus americana* N. America	Hardwood Pale reddish-brown	580	Coarse	Medium	Medium	Non-durable	Moderately resistant	Limited	Medium	Good strength, toughness and bending properties	Furniture, coffins, rubbing strips
Elm, European *Ulmus spp.* Europe	Hardwood Light brown	560*	Coarse	Medium	Medium	Non-durable	Moderately resistant	Limited	Medium		Furniture, coffins, boat building
Freijo *Cordia goeldiana* S. America	Hardwood Golden brown	590	Medium	Medium/small	Medium	Durable	No information	Variable	Medium		Furniture, interior and exterior joinery
Gaboon *Aucoumea klaineana* W. Africa	Hardwood Pinkish-brown	430	Medium	Medium	Medium	Non-durable	Resistant	Limited	Medium		Used principally for plywood and blockboard
Gedu nohor/edinam *Entandrophragma angolense* W. Africa	Hardwood Reddish-brown	560	Medium	Small	Medium	Moderately durable	Extremely resistant	Limited	Low		Furniture, exterior and interior joinery
Gerongang *Cratoxylon arborescens* S.E. Asia	Hardwood Pink to red	550	Coarse	Medium	Medium	Non-durable	Permeable	Variable	Low		Interior joinery
Greenheart† *Ocotea rodiaei* Guyana	Hardwood Yellow/olive green to brown	1040	Fine	Medium	Difficult	Very durable	Extremely resistant	Variable	Medium	Available in very large sizes	Heavy construction, marine and freshwater construction. Bridges, etc.
Guarea *Guarea cedrata* W. Africa	Hardwood Pinkish-brown	590	Medium	Small	Medium	Very durable	Extremely resistant	Variable	Medium	Fine dust may be irritant. Resin exudation may occur	Furniture, interior joinery, cabinet making
Hickory *Carya spp.* N. America	Hardwood Brown to reddish-brown	830	Coarse	Large	Difficult	Non-durable	Moderately resistant	Limited	Medium	Good steam bending properties. Good shock resistance	Striking tool handles, ladder rungs, sports goods
Idigbo *Terminalia ivorensis* W. Africa	Hardwood Yellow	560*	Medium	Small	Medium	Durable	Extremely resistant	Variable	Low/medium	Stains yellow in contact with water, is acidic and may corrode ferrous metals, also stains in contact with iron when wet	Interior and exterior joinery, plywood
Iroko *Chlorophora excelsa* W. Africa	Hardwood Yellow-brown	660	Medium	Small	Medium/difficult	Very durable	Extremely resistant	Regular	Medium	Occasional deposits of stone may occur	Exterior and interior joinery, bench tops, constructional work
Jarrah† *Eucalyptus marginata* Australia	Hardwood Pink to dark red	820*	Medium	Medium	Difficult	Very durable	Extremely resistant	Limited	Low/medium		Heavy constructional work. Flooring
Jelutong *Dyera costulata* S.E. Asia	Hardwood White to yellow	470	Fine	Small	Good	Non-durable	Permeable	Regular	Low	Latex ducts may be present	Pattern making, drawing boards
Kapur† *Dryobalanops spp.* S.E. Asia	Hardwood Reddish-brown	770*	Medium	Medium	Medium	Very durable	Extremely resistant	Variable	Low	Camphor-like odour	Exterior joinery, decking, constructional use
Karri† *Eucalyptus diversicolor* Australia	Hardwood Reddish-brown	900	Medium	Large	Difficult	Durable	Extremely resistant	Limited	Medium		Heavy construction

(continued)

Table 50.2 (continued)

Species	Colour	Density (kg m⁻³)	Texture	Moisture movement	Working qualities	Durability	Permeability	Availability	Price	Remarks	Uses
Kaurula *Endospermum macrophyllum* Fiji	Hardwood Pale cream to straw-yellow	480	Medium to coarse	Small	Medium	Perishable	Permeable	Limited	Low/medium		Mouldings, interior joinery
Kempst† *Koompassia malaccensis* S.E. Asia	Hardwood Orange-red to red-brown	880	Coarse	Medium	Difficult	Durable	Resistant	Limited	Low	Slightly acidic and may encourage corrosion of ferrous metals	Heavy constructional use
Keruing, apitong, gurjun, yang† *Dipterocarpus* spp. S.E. Asia	Hardwood Pinkish-brown to dark brown	740*	Medium	Large/medium	Difficult	Moderately durable	Resistant	Regular	Low	Liable to resin exudation	Heavy and general construction. Decking, vehicle flooring
Lauan see meranti											
Lignum vitae *Guaiacum* spp. Central America	Hardwood Dark green/brown	1250	Fine	Medium	Difficult	Very durable	Extremely resistant	Limited	High	Obtainable in small sizes only	Bushes and bearings, sports goods and textile equipment
Limba/afara *Terminalia superba* W. Africa	Hardwood Pale yellow-brown/straw	560*	Medium	Small	Good	Non-durable	Moderately resistant	Limited	Low/medium		Furniture, interior joinery
Lime, European *Tilia* spp. Europe	Hardwood Yellowish-white to pale brown	560	Fine	Medium	Good	Perishable	Permeable	Limited	Low/medium		Carving, turnery, bungs, clogs
Mahogany, Africa *Khaya* spp. W. Africa	Hardwood Reddish-brown	530	Medium	Small	Medium	Moderately durable	Extremely resistant	Regular	Low/medium		Furniture, cabinet work, boat building, joinery
Mahogany, American *Swietenia macrophylla* Central and S. America, especially Brazil	Hardwood Reddish-brown	560	Medium	Small	Good	Durable	Extremely resistant	Regular	Medium		Furniture, cabinet work, interior and exterior joinery. Boat building
Makoré *Tieghemella heckelii* W. Africa	Hardwood Pinkish-brown to dark red	640	Fine	Small	Medium	Very durable	Extremely resistant	Variable	Medium	Fine dust may be irritant	Furniture, interior and exterior joinery. Boat building. Plywood
Maple, rock *Acer saccharum* N. America	Hardwood Creamy white	740	Fine	Medium	Medium	Non-durable	Resistant	Regular	Medium/high	High resistance to abrasion	Excellent flooring timber. Furniture. Sports goods
Maple, soft *Acer saccharinum* N. America	Hardwood Creamy white	650	Fine	Medium	Medium	Non-durable	Moderately resistant	Limited	Medium		Furniture. Interior joinery. Turnery
Mengkulang *Heritiera* spp. S.E. Asia	Hardwood Red, brown	720	Coarse	Small	Medium	Moderately durable	Resistant	Limited	Low		Interior joinery. Construction. Plywood
Meranti, dark red/dark red seraya/red lauan *Shorea* spp. S.E. Asia	Hardwood Medium to dark red-brown	710*	Medium	Small	Medium	Variable, generally moderately durable to durable	Resistant to extremely resistant	Regular	Low		Interior and exterior joinery. Plywood
Meranti, light red/light red seraya/white lauan *Shorea* spp. S.E. Asia	Hardwood Pale pink to mid-red	550*	Medium	Small	Medium	Variable, generally non-durable to moderately durable	Extremely resistant	Regular	Low		Interior joinery. Plywood
Meranti, yellow/yellow seraya *Shorea* spp. S.E. Asia	Hardwood Yellow-brown	660*	Medium	Small	Medium	Variable, generally non-durable to moderately durable	Extremely resistant	Limited	Low		Interior joinery. Plywood
Merbau† *Intsia* spp. S.E. Asia	Hardwood Medium to dark red-brown	830	Coarse	Small	Moderate	Durable	Extremely resistant	Variable	Low	Liable to stain when in contact with iron in damp conditions	Joinery, flooring, structural work
Nemesu *Shorea pauciflora* Malaysia	Hardwood Red-brown to dark red	710	Medium	Small	Medium	Moderately durable to durable	Resistant to extremely resistant	Regular	Low/medium		Interior and exterior joinery. Plywood

Name / Species / Origin	Type / Colour	Density	Texture	Working	Durability	Preservative treatment	Availability	Movement	Notes	Uses
Niangon *Tarrietia utilis* W. Africa	Hardwood Reddish-brown	640*	Medium	Good	Moderately durable	Extremely resistant	Variable	Medium		Interior and exterior joinery. Furniture
Nyatoh *Palaquium* spp. S.E. Asia	Hardwood Pale pink to red-brown	720	Fine	Medium	Non-durable to moderately durable	Extremely resistant	Variable	Low/medium		Interior joinery, furniture
Oak, American red *Quercus* spp. N. America	Hardwood Yellowish-brown with red tinge	790	Medium	Medium	Non-durable	Moderately resistant	Regular	Medium		Furniture. Interior joinery
Oak, American white *Quercus* spp. N. America	Hardwood Pale yellow to mid-brown	770	Medium	Medium	Durable	Extremely resistant	Regular	Medium	Due to acidic nature, may stain when in contact with iron under damp conditions. May also corrode metals	Furniture, cabinet work. Tight cooperage
Oak, European *Quercus robur* Europe	Hardwood Yellowish-brown	670/720	Medium/coarse	Medium/difficult	Durable	Extremely resistant	Variable	Medium/high	Iron staining may occur in damp conditions, similarly corrosion of metals	Furniture. Interior and exterior joinery. Flooring. Tight cooperage. Fencing
Oak, Japanese *Quercus mongolica* Japan	Hardwood Pale yellow	670	Medium	Medium	Moderately durable	Extremely resistant	Variable	High		Furniture. Interior joinery
Oak, Tasmanian *Eucalyptus delegatensis* *Eucalyptus obliqua* *Eucalyptus regnans* Australia, Tasmania	Hardwood Pale pink to brown	610/710	Coarse	Medium	Moderately durable	Resistant	Limited	Medium		Furniture, interior joinery
Obeche *Triplochiton scleroxylon* W. Africa	Hardwood White to pale yellow	390	Medium	Good	Non-durable	Resistant	Regular	Low		Interior joinery, furniture. Plywood
Opepe *Nauclea diderrichii* W. Africa	Hardwood Yellow to orange-yellow	750	Coarse	Medium	Very durable	Moderately resistant	Variable	Medium		Heavy constructional work. Marine and freshwater use. Exterior joinery. Flooring
Padauk *Pterocarpus* spp. W. Africa, Andamans, Burma	Hardwood Red to dark purple-brown	640*/850	Coarse	Medium	Very durable	Moderately resistant to resistant	Limited	High	Dust may be irritant	Interior and exterior joinery, turnery. Flooring
Pau marfim *Balfourodendron riedelianum* S. America	Hardwood Yellow	800	Medium	Good	Non-durable	No information	Limited	Medium	Dust may be irritant	Interior joinery, furniture. Flooring
Plane, European *Platanus hybrida* Europe	Hardwood Mottled red-brown	640	Fine	Medium	Perishable	No information	Limited	Medium		Decorative purposes. Inlay work
Poplar *Populus* spp. Europe	Hardwood Grey, white to pale brown	450	Fine/medium	Medium	Perishable non-durable	Extremely resistant	Variable	Low		Pallet blocks, box boards, turnery. Wood wool
Purpleheart *Peltogyne* spp. Central & S. America	Hardwood Purple to purplish-brown	880	Medium	Medium/difficult	Very durable	Extremely resistant	Limited	High		Heavy construction. Flooring. Turnery
Ramin *Gonystylus* spp. S.E. Asia	Hardwood White to pale yellow	670	Medium	Good	Non-durable	Permeable	Regular	Medium		Mouldings, furniture
Rosewood *Dalbergia* spp. S. America, India	Hardwood Medium to dark purplish-brown with black streaks	870*	Medium	Medium	Very durable	Extremely resistant	Limited	High	Sizes may be limited	Interior joinery, cabinet work, turnery
Sapele *Entandrophragma cylindricum* W. Africa	Hardwood Medium reddish-brown with marked stripe figure	640	Medium	Medium	Moderately durable	Resistant	Regular	Medium		Interior joinery, furniture, flooring
Sepetir *Sindora* spp. S.E. Asia	Hardwood Golden brown	640*/830	Medium	Difficult	Durable	Extremely resistant	Limited	Low		Joinery, furniture
Seraya—see meranti										
Sycamore *Acer pseudoplatanus* Europe	Hardwood White or yellowish-white	630	Fine	Good	Perishable	Permeable	Limited	Medium/high		Turnery, textile equipment. Joinery

(continued)

Table 50.2 (continued)

Species	Colour	Density (kg m⁻³)	Texture	Moisture movement	Working qualities	Durability	Permeability	Availability	Price	Remarks	Uses
Taun *Pometia pinnata* S.E. Asia	Hardwood Pale pinkish-brown	750	Coarse	Medium	Medium	Moderately durable	Moderately resistant	Limited	Low		Structural work, turnery, joinery, furniture
Teak† *Tectona grandis* Burma, Thailand	Hardwood Golden brown, sometimes with dark markings	660	Medium	Small	Medium	Very durable	Extremely resistant	Regular	High	Fine dust may be irritant. Good chemical resistance. Resistance to termites	Furniture, interior and exterior joinery. Boat building
Utile *Entandrophragma utile* W. Africa	Hardwood Reddish-brown	660	Medium	Medium	Medium	Durable	Extremely resistant	Regular	Medium/ high		Interior and exterior joinery. Furniture and cabinet work
Virola/baboen *Virola* spp. *Dialyanthera* spp. S. America	Hardwood Pale pinkish-brown	430/* 670	Medium	Medium	Medium	Non-durable	Permeable	Limited	Low		Carpentry, furniture, plywood, mouldings
Wallaba *Eperua falcata* *Eperua grandiflora* Guyana	Hardwood Dull reddish-brown	910	Coarse	Medium	Medium	Very durable	Extremely resistant	Limited	Medium	Gum exudation likely	Transmission poles, flooring, decking, heavy construction
Walnut, Africa *Lovoa trichilioides* W. Africa	Hardwood Yellowish-brown, sometimes with dark streaks	560	Medium	Small	Medium	Moderately durable	Extremely resistant	Variable	Medium		Furniture, cabinet work. Interior and exterior joinery
Walnut, America *Juglans nigra* N. America	Hardwood Rich dark brown	660	Coarse	Small/ medium	Good	Very durable	Resistant	Variable	High		Furniture, gun stocks
Walnut, European *Juglans regia* Europe	Hardwood Grey-brown with dark streaks	670	Coarse	Medium	Good	Moderately durable	Resistant	Limited	High	Staining likely if in contact with iron under damp conditions	Furniture, turnery, gun stocks
Wenge *Millettia laurentii* *Millettia stuhlmannii* Central & E. Africa	Hardwood Dark brown with fine black veining	880	Coarse	Small	Good	Durable	Extremely resistant	Limited	High		Interior and exterior joinery. Flooring, turnery
Willow *Salix* spp. Europe	Hardwood Pinkish-white	450	Fine	Small	Good	Perishable	Resistant	Limited	Medium/ high		Cricket bats, boxes, crates

* Density can vary by 20% or more.
† Structural properties included in BS 5268: Part 2: 1988.

Table 50.3 Properties and uses of softwoods

Species	Colour	Density (kg m⁻³)	Texture	Moisture movement	Working qualities	Durability	Permeability	Availability	Price	Remarks	Uses
Cedar of Lebanon *Cedrus libani* Europe	Softwood Light brown	580	Medium	Medium/ small	Good	Durable	Resistant	Limited	Medium	Pungent cedar odour	Joinery, garden furniture, gates
Douglas fir† *Pseudotsuga menziesii* N. America and UK	Softwood Light reddish-brown	530	Medium	Small	Good	Moderately durable	Resistant/ extremely resistant	Regular	Medium	Marked 'flame-like' growth ring figure. Long lengths and clear grades available	Plywood, interior and exterior joinery, construction. Vats and tanks
Hemlock, Western† *Tsuga heterophylla* N. America	Softwood Pale brown	500	Fine	Small	Good	Non-durable	Resistant	Regular	Low	Obtainable in large sizes	Construction, joinery
Larch, European† *Larix decidua* Europe	Softwood Pale reddish-brown	590	Fine	Small	Medium	Moderately durable	Resistant	Regular	Low/ medium		Boat planking, pit props, transmission poles
Larch, Japanese† *Larix kaempferi* Europe	Softwood Reddish-brown	560	Fine	Small	Medium	Moderately durable	Resistant	Regular	Medium		Stakes, general construction
Parana pine† *Araucaria angustifolia* S. America	Softwood Golden-brown with bright red streaks	550	Fine	Medium	Good	Non-durable	Moderately resistant	Regular	Medium/ high	Distortion may occur in drying	Interior joinery. Plywood
Pine, Corsican† *Pinus nigra* Europe	Softwood Light yellowish-brown	510	Coarse	Small	Medium	Non-durable	Moderately resistant	Regular	Low		Joinery, construction
Pine, Maritime *Pinus pinaster* Europe	Softwood Pale brown to yellow	510	Medium/ coarse	Medium	Good	Moderately durable	Resistant	Regular	Low		Pallets and packaging
Pine, pitch† *Pinus palustris Pinus elliottii* Southern, USA	Softwood Yellow-brown to red-brown	670	Medium	Medium	Medium	Moderately durable	Resistant	Regular	Low	Also known as longleaf yellow pine or longleaf pitch pine or American pitch pine	Interior and exterior joinery, heavy construction
Pine, radiata *Pinus radiata* S. Africa, Australia	Softwood Yellow to pale brown	480	Medium	Medium	Good	Non-durable	Permeable	Regular	Low		Furniture, packaging
Pine, Scots† *Pinus sylvestris* UK	Softwood Pale yellowish-brown to red-brown	510	Coarse	Medium	Medium	Non-durable	Moderately resistant	Regular	Low		Construction, joinery

(continued)

Table 50.3 *(continued)*

Species	Colour	Density (kg m⁻³)	Texture	Moisture movement	Working qualities	Durability	Permeability	Availability	Price	Remarks	Uses
Pine, Southern† A number of species including *Pinus palustris, Pinus elliottii, Pinus echinata, Pinus taeda* Southern USA	Softwood Pale yellow to light brown	560*	Medium	Medium	Medium	Non-durable	Moderately resistant	Regular	Low		Construction, joinery, Plywood
Pine, yellow *Pinus strobus* N. America	Softwood Pale yellow to light brown	420	Fine	Small	Good	Non-durable	Moderately resistant	Regular	Low/medium	Also known as Quebec yellow pine	Pattern making, drawing boards, doors
Redwood, European† *Pinus sylvestris* Scandinavia, USSR	Softwood Pale yellowish-brown to red-brown	510	Medium	Medium	Medium	Non-durable	Moderately resistant	Regular	Low		Construction, joinery, furniture
Spruce, Canadian† *Picea* spp. Canada	Softwood White to pale yellow	400/* 500	Medium	Small	Good	Non-durable	Resistant	Regular	Low		Construction, joinery
Spruce, Sitka† *Picea sitchensis* UK	Softwood Pinkish-brown	450	Coarse	Small	Good	Non-durable	Resistant	Regular	Low		Construction, packaging, pallets
Spruce, Western white† *Picea glauca* N. America	Softwood White to pale yellow/brown	400/* 500	Medium	Small	Good	Non-durable	Resistant	Regular	Low	Large sizes available	Construction, joinery
Western red cedar† *Thuja plicata* N. America	Softwood Reddish brown	390	Coarse	Small	Good	Durable	Resistant	Regular	Medium	An acidic timber which may corrode metals under damp conditions and cause iron staining	Shingles, exterior cladding, greenhouses, beehives
Whitewood, European† *Picea abies* and *Abies alba* Europe, Scandinavia, USSR	Softwood White to pale yellowish-brown	470	Medium	Medium	Good	Non-durable	Resistant	Regular	Low		Interior joinery, construction, flooring
Yew *Taxus baccata* Europe	Softwood Orange-brown to purple-brown	670	Medium	Small/medium	Difficult	Durable	Resistant	Limited	High	Sizes may be limited	Furniture, turnery, Interior joinery

* Density can vary by 20% or more.
† Structural properties included in BS 5268: Part 2: 1988.

50.4.8 Permeability

Permeability is the ease with which timbers can be penetrated with preservatives applied by a standard pressure impregnation treatment. The permeability categories are:

Extremely resistant—absorbs only a small amount;
Very resistant—difficult to penetrate more than 3–6 mm;
Moderately resistant—6–18 mm penetration in 2–3 h; and
Permeable—absorbs preservative without difficulty.

50.4.9 Availability

Sawn timbers may be in regular or limited supply depending on availability from producers and levels of demand. Availability is described as regular, limited or variable, although the availability of species will vary throughout the country.

50.4.10 Price

The following terms are used to indicate prices:

High—over £650 m^{-3};
Medium—£400–650 m^{-3}; and
Low—up to £400 m^{-3}.

These prices are for guidance only and are based on parcels of sawn timber not less than 1.5 m^3 ex-yard of a normal fair average specification at 1988 price levels. The prices relate to decorative hardwoods: structural softwoods will normally fall into the cheaper half of the 'low' category. Prices are for kiln-dried stock where appropriate.

50.4.11 Remarks

BS 5268: Part 2: 1989 contains comments, where necessary, on sizes and special features such as drying, staining, etc.

50.4.12 Uses

The list of uses given in the standard is not exhaustive, and most timbers can be used for more purposes than those listed.

50.4.13 Available sizes

The sizes and lengths of timbers available are obviously limited to the dimensions of the trees from which they have been converted. Most European softwood imported to the UK comes from Sweden, Finland and the USSR. Smaller quantities come from Yugoslavia, Czechoslovakia, Poland and France. In general, trees grown in Europe are smaller than those grown in Western Canada and the sawn timber is, therefore, generally of smaller dimensions. The main species from Europe are redwood and whitewood and these are widely used for building; the lower grades being used for carcassing and the better quality material for joinery.

Widths in excess of 225 mm (up to 300 mm) can be difficult to obtain and may command a higher price than smaller sections. Lengths of up to 5 m are available but, again, there is a cost penalty for the longer lengths and it may be difficult to obtain these in any quantity. Finger jointing does allow long lengths to be specified and well-made joints to BS 5291: 1984 are equally as strong as the timber.

Trees grown in North America are generally larger than those grown in Europe and larger sections and lengths may be available from this source. The species commonly imported include: western hemlock; Douglas fir and western larch (imported as D-fir–L); and western white spruce, Englemann spruce, red spruce, black spruce, lodgepole pine, jack pine, alpine fir and balsam fir (imported as spruce–pine–fir). Spruce–

pine–fir is available in widths up to 300 mm and lengths up to a maximum of approximately 9 m. Again, there may be a cost premium on the larger sections.

Softwood imported into Britain is normally sawn to the sizes given in BS 4471: 1987 (*Table 50.4*), although not all the sizes shown are readily available. The sizes stated in the Standard are basic sawn sizes for timber with a moisture content of 20%. In addition to the sawn sizes, the Standard also refers to timber machined in Canada to the requirement of the Canadian Lumber Standard (CLS timber). This is a construction-quality timber, stress graded to the National Lumber Grades Authority (NLGA) rules and machined on all four sides with rounded arrises of not more than 3-mm radius. Most of the CLS timber imported into the UK is kiln dried at source to approximately 19% moisture content. The available sizes are shown in *Table 50.5* BS 4771: 1987 also defines two other timber processes: regularizing and planing.

Regularizing is a process by which the width of a sawn section of constructional timber is made uniform throughout its length. It is used to produce accurately dimensioned timbers for structural purposes and is normally carried out only on the two faces of the timber section where accuracy is important. It removes 3 mm (5 mm is allowed for dimensions over 150 mm) from the relevant dimension of the timber and a working tolerance of ± 1 mm is allowed. Regularized sections should be specified by quoting the expected finished dimensions of the piece, e.g. 50 mm × 195 mm regularized, or 50 mm × 97 mm regularized.

Planing requires the timber section to be surfaced on at least two opposite faces and it is normal to machine all four faces (processed all round). The allowable reductions in size are set out in BS 4771: 1987 (*Table 50.6*). Planed sections may be specified by quoting the sawn size from which the finished section is machined, e.g. Ex 50 mm × 100 mm, or by giving the finished dimensions, e.g. 46 mm × 96 mm par, or by quoting both sawn and finished sizes, if appropriate. A working tolerance of ± 0.5 mm is allowed.

Dimensional availability of hardwoods is more complex to define since it is so closely related to the type and species required. Discussion with the specialist hardwood importer is the best way to establish the availability of any given species. Structural hardwoods such as keruing, jarrah, iroko, balau and karri are available in long lengths (6–8 m) and large sections. Joinery hardwoods are usually in smaller sections.

50.5 The structural use of timber

The structural use of timber in the UK is governed by BS 5268, the code of practice covering the major structural uses of timber, particularly in building. This standard is published in seven parts.

Part 1: Limit state design, materials and workmanship.
    To be published at a later date and will supplement or replace
    Part 2 (could be Eurocode 5).
Part 2: Permissible stress design, materials and workmanship.
    Published 1989.
Part 3: Trussed rafter roofs.
    Published 1985.
Part 4: Fire resistance of timber structures.
    Section 4.1: Method of calculating the fire resistance of timber members.
    Published 1978, to be revised.
    Section 4.2: Method of calculating the fire resistance of timber stud walls and joisted floor constructions. To be published.
Part 5: Preservation treatments for constructional timber.
    Published 1989.

Table 50.4 Basic sizes (cross-sectional sizes mm) of sawn softwood (from BS 4471: Part 1: 1978)

* This range of widths for 47 mm thickness will usually be available in constructional-timber quality only. The smaller sizes contained within the dotted lines are normally, but not exclusively, of European origin. The larger sizes outside the dotted lines are normally, but not exclusively, of North and South American origin.

Table 50.5 Sizes (mm) of surfaced Canadian timber (CLS sizes)

mm		
Thickness	Width	
38	63	
38	89	
38	140	
38	184	
38	235	
38	285	

Moisture content 19 %

Tolerances: minus, nil; plus, no limitation.

Table 50.6 Reductions from basic sizes to finished sizes by planing of two opposed faces (from BS 4471: 1987)*

	Reduction from basic size (mm)			
	15–35	*>35–100*	*>100–150*	*>150*
Construction timber	3	3	5	6
Matching inter-locking boards	4	4	6	6
Wood trim not specified in BS 584	5	7	7	9
Joinery and cabinet work	7	9	11	13

* Note: floorings and wood trim are covered by separate British Standards: flooring BS 1297: 1967, wood trim BS 584: 1987

Part 6: Timber frame walls. To be published.
Part 7: Calculation basis for span tables.
   Section 1: Domestic floor joists.
   Section 2: Joists for flat roofs.
   Section 3: Ceiling joists.
   Section 4: Ceiling binders.
   Section 5: Domestic rafters. To be published.
   Section 6: Domestic purlins. To be published.

BS 5268: Part 2: 1989 brings together design stresses, design methods and some general guidance on the structural use of timber. It covers a wide range of softwoods, hardwoods, plywood, tempered hardboard, jointing devices and provides design information for solid timber, glulam and built-up composite structures such as box- and I-beams. It is intended that a new Section 9 will be introduced in the future covering the structural use of chipboard.

Although structural codes are written primarily for designers, they are also relevant to a wide spectrum of interests within the construction chain, from timber suppliers and product manufacturers, through to designers and specifiers and those who build, inspect or maintain structures. The contents of BS 5268: Part 2: 1989 and the implications for timber supply and use are discussed below.

Section 1 (Introduction and general considerations) of the standard outlines the scope of the document and gives definitions of terms and symbols used; these are the symbols recommended by the International Organization for Standardization (ISO), supplemented by some subscripts specific to timber. The requirements for materials are detailed by reference to other British Standards and by reference to rules of grading agencies for timber and plywood graded outside the UK.

Moisture content is an important aspect of timber usage, this is reflected in a table which gives recommended average moisture contents for timber in four categories of end use, together with a moisture content which should not be exceeded at the time of erection (*Table 50.7*).

Section 1 also introduces various aspects of loading and sets out the timber sizes to which the tables in later sections refer. Modification factors for timber sizes not included are given in later sections.

Section 2 (Timber) of the standard lays down design stresses for the wide range of species and grades included. Grade stresses for individual softwood species are quoted in tables and modification factors for sizes other than those quoted for North American timber are tabulated. Grade stresses for individual tropical hardwoods to the HS grade of BS 5756: 1980 are given in a separate table. Information in this form enables specialist designers to use a particular species and grade to its maximum stress level and hence provide the most economical design solution for a particular application. However, the complexity of this approach for the non-specialist designer can be illustrated by one species group; hem–fir, which has 13 different bending stresses assigned to the various grade combinations.

Despite such examples, there is considerable simplicity built into the code. The most common structural softwoods, Baltic redwood, Baltic whitewood, British-grown Scots pine, imported Douglas fir, hem–fir and spruce–pine–fir, all have the same design values for bending stress: for SS grade 7.5 N mm^{-2} and for GS grade 5.3 N mm^{-2}. These softwoods account for over 80% of the structural timber usage in the UK.

50.5.1 Strength classes

A further simplification is provided by the use of nine strength classes, which cover the weakest, lowest grade of softwood to the densest, highest grade of hardwood. The strength-class system is defined primarily by bending strength (although other criteria are also included). A strength class, therefore, will contain both different grades and different species. A given species may appear in more than one strength class, depending upon its grade (see *Table 50.8*).

The strength classes SC3, SC4 and SC5 are being used increasingly and cover the major structural uses using the commonly available softwoods. Thus SC3, i.e. GS redwood,

Table 50.7 Moisture content of timber for categories of end use (from BS 5268: Part 2: 1988)

	Moisture content (%)	
	Average in service	*Max. at erection*
External uses, fully exposed	$\geqslant 18$	—
Covered and generally unheated	18	24
Covered and generally heated	16	21
Internal in continuously heated building	14	21

Table 50.8 Dry grade stresses and moduli of elasticity for strength classes

Strength class	Bending (N mm^{-2})	Modulus of elasticity (mean) (N mm^{-2})
SC1	2.8	6 800
SC2	4.1	8 000
SC3	5.3	8 800
SC4	7.5	9 900
SC5	10.0	10 700
SC6	12.5	14 100
SC7	15.0	16 200
SC8	17.5	18 700
SC9	20.5	21 600

whitewood, hem–fir and spruce–pine–fir, is widely used for floor joists. Strength class SC5 is mainly the same species machine graded for trussed rafter uses. British-grown softwood is available in SC3 timbers.

50.5.2 Stress grading

BS 5268: Part 2: 1989 refers to BS 4978: 1988 for softwoods graded either visually or by machine, in the UK or overseas. An amendment to BS 4978: 1988 allows timber to be machine graded directly to strength classes.

Softwood visually graded in Canada to the NLGA rules and in the USA to NGRDL rules is also included. Timber graded to these North American rules must be covered by, and bear the marks of, approved grading agencies; these are listed in an Appendix to the code. Timber graded to European (ECE) rules is also acceptable—this generally equates with the BS 4978: 1988 system.

An amendment to BS 5268: Part 2 published in 1989 allows the use of New Zealand radiata pine, machine graded under the BS system direct to strength classes. It also introduces timber machine graded in North America to the North American Export Standard for machine stress-rated lumber.

The grading systems used in Europe and North America deal with size in different ways. Timber stress graded to BS 4978: 1988 is graded and assigned grade stresses independent of the size of the piece. Size effects are then taken into account by the use of modification factors during the design procedures given in the code. The North American system, however, is based on use types which in turn are related to size. Size effects are therefore built in to the grade stresses given in North American codes. This has been taken into account in assigning stresses for North American graded timber in the UK code and means that North American timber of the same grade and species, but of different sizes, may appear in different strength classes. The code includes modification factors, which are dependent upon section size, for these North American species combinations.

Tropical hardwoods should be graded to the HS grade of BS 5756: 1980; grade stresses for individual timbers graded to this are provided in the code.

50.5.3 Design considerations

BS 5268: Part 2: 1988 gives separate tables of design stresses for timber graded to BS 4978: 1988 and for North American grades. In *Table 50.9* softwoods graded to BS 4978: 1988 are combined with those graded to NLGA or NGRDL joist and plank grades and to the North American Export Standard for machine stress-rated lumber. The table allows both designers and suppliers of timber to see the species/grades combinations which meet the requirements for a particular strength class.

Softwood graded to the NLGA or NGRDL structural light framing and light framing and stud grades are included in BS 5268: Part 2: 1989 and allocated into strength classes. However, in the UK, these tend to be used for specialized components and are not included in *Table 50.9*.

It should be noted that the requirements for SC5 can be met by appropriate grades of both softwood and hardwood species. *Table 50.8* shows the hardwood species/grades included in BS 5268 which meet the requirements for strength classes.

BS 5268: Part 2: 1989 includes recommendations on the suitability of timbers for specific purposes, such as joint requirements, suitability for preservative treatment, etc. These recommendations are given in footnotes to the tables in Part 2; they should be noted and taken into account in specifications (see *Table 50.10*).

Individual species/grades may have higher strength properties than those of the strength class to which it is assigned. Specialist designers can take advantage of this by basing their calculations on a particular species and grade, in which case the specification will call for a particular species, grade and size. For less specialized designs, the designer or specifier can base his calculations on the stresses given in the code for a particular strength class, or use published span tables based on strength classes.

The specification in this case will simply quote the strength class, noting any restrictions required. This allows the timber supplier to supply any of the species/grade combinations included in that strength class, thus alleviating problems in supply of a particular species.

In general it is more economical to specify the strength classes SC3, SC4 and SC5 when using structural softwoods, but to specify individual species when using tropical hardwoods. The availability of the particular species should be checked with suppliers.

The grade stresses given in BS 5268: Part 2: 1989 are for the dry exposure condition (18% moisture content or less). Modification factors are given by which the geometrical properties may be multiplied (K1) and by which the dry stresses and moduli should be multiplied (K2) to obtain figures for wet exposure. The stresses apply to long-term loading; modification factors are included for medium-term, short-term and very-short-term loading. The modulus of elasticity values in BS 5268: Part 2: 1989 do not include an element due to shear deflection; this should be taken into account for flexural members.

50.6 Wood-based panel products

Wood-based panel products are sheet materials which contain a significant amount of wood in the form of strips, veneers, chips, flakes or fibres. The categories usually recognized within this group of board materials are plywood (including blockboard and laminboard), particleboard (including wood chipboard and wood cement particleboard) and fibre building boards.

Plywood was developed to provide panels with dimensional stability and good strength properties both along and across the sheet. Wood chipboard, other particleboards and fibre building boards were developed, using forest thinnings and sawmill waste, to provide utility sheet materials with uniform properties. From these a whole family of panel products that cater for a wide variety of end uses have been developed. Plywood, particleboards and fibre building boards all include other general-purpose or utility boards and special-purpose products.

The following general board types are available:

Traditional established products:
(1) plywood (veneer plywood);
(2) blockboard and laminboard (core plywoods);

Table 50.9 Softwood species/grade combinations which satisfy the requirements for strength classes SC1–SC5

Species	Origin	Grading rules*	Grades to satisfy strength class				
			SC1	SC2	SC3	SC4	SC5
Corsican pine	UK	BS 4978		GS	M50	SS	M75
Douglas fir	UK	BS 4978		GS	M50, SS	M75	
Douglas fir–larch	Canada, USA	BS 4978	No. 3		GS	SS	
		J & P			No. 1, No. 2	Select	
		Machine			1450f-1.3E	1650f-1.5E	1650f-1.5E
							1800f-1.6E
							1950f-1.7E
							2100f-1.8E
European spruce	UK	BS 4978	GS	M50, SS	Machine graded to strength class		
Hem–fir	Canada, USA	BS 4978	No. 3		GS, M50	SS	M75
		J & P			No. 1, No. 2	Select	
		Machine			1450f-1.3E	1650f-1.5E	1650f-1.5E
							1800f-1.6E
							1950f-1.7E
							2100f-1.8E
Larch	UK	BS 4978			GS	SS	
Panama pine	Any	BS 4978			GS	SS	
Pitch pine	Caribbean				GS	SS	
Radiata pine	New Zealand	BS 4978	Machine graded to strength class				
Redwood	Imported	BS 4978			GS, M50	SS	M75
Scots pine	UK	BS 4978			GS, M50	SS, M75	
Sitka spruce	UK	BS 4978	GS	M50, SS	Machine graded to strength class		
	Canada	BS 4978			SS		
		J & P			Select		
Southern pine	USA	BS 4978			GS	SS	
		J & P			No. 1, No. 2, No. 3	Select	
		Machine			1450f-1.3E	1650f-1.5E	1650f-1.5E
							1800f-1.6E
							1950f-1.7E
							2100f-1.8E
Spruce–pine–fir	Canada	BS 4978			GS, M50	SS, M75	
		J & P	No. 3		No. 1, No. 2	Select	
		Machine			1450f-1.3E	1650f-1.5E	1650f-1.5E
							1800f-1.6E
							1950f-1.7E
							2100f-1.8E
Western red cedar	Any	BS 4978	GS	SS			
Western whitewoods	USA	BS 4978	GS		SS		
		J & P	No. 3	No. 1, No. 2	Select		
Whitewood	Imported	BS 4978			GS, M50	SS	M75

* Timber graded to BS 4978: 1988. Timber graded to Canadian NLGA or American joist and plank (J & P) grades. Note: timber graded to North American structural light framing and stud grades are included in BS 5268: Part 2: 1989. Timber graded to North American machine stress-rated grades.
The machine grades MGS and MSS can be substituted for GS and SS, respectively.
The S6, S8, MS6 and MS8 ECE grades may be substituted for GS, SS, MGS and MSS, respectively.
The BS 4978 grading rules apply to timber of a minimum size of 35 mm × 60 mm.
The classification of NLGA and NGRDL, grades into strength classes applies to timber of a minimum size of 38 mm × 114 mm.
Joist and plank No. 3 grade should not be used for tension members.
North American machine grades apply to a minimum size of 38 mm × 63 mm.
North American machine-graded timber is assigned into different strength classes depending upon the section size. See BS 5268: Part 2: 1988 for details.
BS 5268:1988 includes restrictions on fastener loads for: SC5 timbers (except pitch pine and Southern pine); British grown Sitka spruce and European spruce; US Western whitewoods; hem–fir and spruce–pine–fir in strength classes other than SC1 and SC2. See BS 5268: Part 2:1988 for details.

(3) wood chipboard;
(4) other particleboards (flaxboard, bagasse board); and
(5) fibre building boards (hardboard, medium board, fibre insulating board);

More recent developments:
(6) waferboard and orientated strand board (OSB);
(7) medium density fibreboard (MDF);
(8) wood cement particleboard.

Table 50.10 Tropical hardwoods which satisfy the requirements for strength classes SC5–SC9 (graded to the HS grade of BS 5756: 1980)*

Standard name	Strength class
Iroko	SC5
Jarrah	
Teak	
Merbau	SC6
Opepe	
Kari	SC7
Keruing	
Balau	SC8
Ekki	
Kapur	
Kempas	
Greenheart	SC9

* BS 5756: 1980 refers to BS 5450: 1977 (sizes for hardwoods and methods of measurement).

50.6.1 Plywood (veneer plywood)

50.6.1.1 Description

The BS 6100: Section 4.3 general definition of plywood, a term which includes core plywoods such as blockboard and laminboard, is a 'wood based panel product consisting of an assembly of plies bonded together, some or all of which are wood'. Veneer plywood, which is the correct term for what is usually called plywood is 'plywood in which all the plies are made of veneers orientated with their plane parallel to the surface of the panel'. The definition of plywood goes on to say that normally the direction of the grain in adjacent plies is at right angles to the outer and inner plies placed symmetrically on each side of a central ply or core. However, as long as veneer plywood is 'balanced about its centre line, plies may consist of two adjacent veneers bonded with their grain parallel'. The British Standard for plywood, BS 6566: 1985, does not recognize unbalanced construction as plywood, although some overseas standards do.

50.6.1.2 Manufacture

The practice of cross-laminating veneers for special end uses can be traced back to the pre-Christian Egyptian Empire. These crude forms of plywood were bonded with natural adhesives such as animal glue and blood albumen. Techniques changed little until the late 19th century with the advent of the rotary peeling machine. Standard plywood veneer is now produced using a peeling machine which peels a log section rather as a blade pencil sharpener works. Details vary depending on factors such as the size and species of the log, the type of plywood produced and the scale of operation.

50.6.1.3 Standards

Plywood is usually manufactured to the national standard of the country of origin. In certain cases, standards such as the British and West German Standards may be adopted by other countries as an aid to production, or marketing, or both. The following British Standards are the most relevant ones:

BS 1088 and 4079: 1966, Plywood for marine craft
BS 1203: 1979, Specification for synthetic resin adhesives (phenolic and amino-plastic) for plywood
BS 6566: 1985, Plywood, Parts 1–8.

50.6.1.4 General performance levels

Plywood is a versatile product that can combine attractive surface appearance with superior performance under hazardous conditions whilst retaining comparatively high strength/weight properties. Plywood is available in two main types: urea formaldehyde bonded and phenol formaldehyde bonded.

Urea formaldehyde bonded. This type of bond is used in moisture-resistant or interior-type plywood. Moisture-resistant plywoods will survive full exposure to weather for limited periods only. They will withstand cold water for a long period and hot water for a limited time but will fail when exposed to boiling water. Interior bonds are required to be strong and durable in dry conditions and to be resistant to cold water.

Phenol formaldehyde bonded. This type of adhesive predominates in plywood production. This type of bond is used in weather and boil proof and exterior-type plywoods. Such bonds are required to be highly resistant to weather, micro-organisms, cold and boiling water and wet and dry heat.

A third type of adhesive, urea-formaldehyde fortified with melamine and known as 'MUF' is used in some types of plywood manufactured in East and Far East Asia. Bonds are more resistant to moisture/weather than urea formaldehyde bonded plywood but less so than weather and boil proof plywood (usually phenolic bonded).

The following types of plywood are available in the UK.

Marine plywood (BS 1088/4079: 1966). This is manufactured using species classified as moderately durable or better (or exceptionally gaboon) and the veneers are bonded using phenol formaldehyde adhesive. The BS 4079: 1966 part of this joint standard deals with marine plywood treated with wood preservatives to achieve the necessary resistance to decay. These plywoods are commonly available from the UK, Israel, France, Singapore and Malaysia.

Structural plywoods. These are manufactured to national standards which ensure the strength properties of the finished product. These plywoods are available from the UK, Canda, USA, Finland and Sweden (details to be found in BS 5268: Part 2: 1989).

Utility plywoods. These are non-structural plywoods that are available in a surface-appearance grade suitable for joinery, furniture and limited exterior use. These plywoods are available from East and South East Asia, Brazil, France, Israel, Bulgaria, Czechoslovakia, Romania, Spain, Portugal and West Africa.

Decorative/overlaid and special end-use plywoods. These are commonly available from Finland, Canada, the USA, Malaysia, Singapore and other East and South East Asian countries.

50.6.2 Blockboard/laminboard (core plywoods)

50.6.2.1 Description

Blockboard and laminboards are composite boards having a core made up of strips of wood, each $\leqslant 30$ mm wide, laid separately or glued or otherwise joined together to form a slab, to each face of which is glued one or more veneers with the direction of the grain of the core strips running at right angles to that of the adjacent veneers.

50.6.2.2 Manufacture

The technique of manufacturing blockboard or laminboard developed alongside the modern plywood industry from the turn of the century. Blockboard cores comprise strips of wood about 25 mm wide, whilst laminboard cores are composed of strips of veneer on edge (or occasionally strips cut from plywood assembled on edge). The tendency is for an increasing proportion of ply mills to introduce blockboard/laminboard manufacturing facilities to use residues and to produce lower cost utility types of boards suitable for some interior purposes.

50.6.2.3 Standards

Blockboard and laminboard are not commonly marketed as being in accordance with any standard, but BS 3444: 1972 is frequently used by manufacturers as a production aid for quality-control purposes.

50.6.2.4 General performance levels

Almost invariably, blockboard and laminboard are manufactured using urea formaldehyde adhesive, the characteristics of which are outlined in Section 50.6.1.4.

Two types of blockboard and laminboard are generally available: three- and five-ply. Three-ply boards have core slabs sandwiched between one, usually thick, veneer on each face. The result is a relatively low-grade panel in terms of both appearance and strength. These panels are normally used for applications where they will be out of sight, where the structural requirements are low or where further lamination (e.g. with melamine laminate) is to be performed.

Five-ply boards have core slabs sandwiched between two veneers on each side. The inner veneers are usually 'core' or low-grade veneers and the outer veneers are high-quality or decorative veneer. Such panels have superior appearance and strength. They provide a smooth and even substrate for high-quality finishes and laminating.

50.6.3 Wood chipboard

50.6.3.1 Description

Wood chipboard is a particleboard made exclusively of wood from small particles and a binder (synthetic resin). Boards are available in thicknesses of 3 to 50 mm and may be of uniform construction through their thickness, of grade density or of distinct three- or five-layer constructions to give enhanced properties without excessive weight. Currently, about 60% of chipboard used in the UK is imported with the remainder produced in domestic mills.

50.6.3.2 Manufacture

Wood chipboard has been developed since World War II, with the advent of thermosetting adhesives. It has progressively superseded blockboard and laminboards and uses wood residues, including forest thinnings, planer and shavings and other joinery shop residue. The product is not as demanding in terms of raw materials and skilled labour as is plywood, and wood chipboard mills are now located in most countries of the world.

50.6.3.3 Standards

Chipboard is frequently manufactured to the national standard of the country of origin. British-manufactured chipboard and some imported chipboard is manufactured to BS 5669: 1979 (under revision).

50.6.3.4 General performance levels

Four main end-use types can be distinguished.

'Standard' (Type I to BS 5669: 1979). These boards have good surfaces suitable for veneering or coating. They tend to be lower in density than the following three types.

'Flooring' (Type II to BS 5669: 1979). Such boards have superior strength characteristics which make them suitable for flooring use, and are commonly available in 2400 mm × 600 mm or 1200 mm widths and their imperial equivalents. Being manufactured specifically for use as flooring they have high resistance to impact and are frequently machined to a tongued and grooved profile to facilitate laying.

'Moisture resistant' (Type III to BS 5669: 1979). These boards are manufactured using melamine fortified urea formaldehyde adhesives, or, in some cases, phenol formaldehyde and they typically have a density of $680–750\,kg\,m^{-3}$. They will not withstand prolonged wetting or exposure, but they do have characteristics superior to standard boards in damp situations. Type-III boards are equivalent to those designated 'V313' in the French Standard.

'Moisture resistant/flooring' (Type II/III to BS 5669: 1979). These boards combine the strength characteristics of flooring (type II) boards with the moisture resistance of type-III boards.

50.6.4 Fibre building boards

50.6.4.1 Description

Fibre building boards are wood-based-panel products, usually exceeding 1.5 mm in thickness, manufactured from fibres of ligno-cellulosic material with the primary bond usually derived from the felting of the fibres and their inherent adhesive properties.

50.6.4.2 Manufacture

The earliest fibre building boards, produced in the late 19th century, contained large amounts of repulped newsprint and were of relatively low density. Somewhat later, insulating boards were produced from ground wood pulp. During the 1920s and early 1930s, further techniques were developed to break solid wood down into fibres and reconstitute these under heat and pressure as a strong and durable panel hardboard.

50.6.4.3 Standards

The majority of the fibre building boards marketed in the UK are imported. The British Standard for fibre building boards (which generally aligns with the International Standard) is a performance standard in three parts:

BS 1142, 1989, Specification for fibre building boards

50.6.4.4 General performance levels

The main types of fibre building board covered by BS 1142 are listed below.

Standard hardboard (Type S). This is a dense panel product (usually more than $800\,kg\,m^{-3}$) with a very smooth face and a mesh pattern on the reverse. It has many uses in building and other industries, and also as a base for decorative boards. Thicknesses range from 2 to 6.4 mm.

Tempered hardboard. This is hardboard further treated during manufacture to give higher strength and higher resistance to moisture and abrasion. It has a density of above 960 kg m^{-3}. Two types are specified: TE and TN, with TE having higher performance requirements. Tempered hardboards have known structural properties and are suitable for structural components, external claddings and other demanding applications. Thicknesses range from 3.2 to 12.7 mm. Design is covered in BS 5268: Part 2: 1989.

Medium boards.   These are available in two distinct types: LM and HM. Type LM (low density) boards have densities in the range 350–356 kg m^{-3} and are 6.4 to 12.7 mm thick; they are used as pin boards, notice boards, linings, etc. Type HM (high density, 'panelboard') boards have densities in the range 560–800 kg m^{-3} and are 8–12 mm thick. They are used for wall linings, partitions, sheathing on timber frame houses, cladding farm buildings. (As with tempered hardboard, there are 'E' and 'N' performance levels for both types of medium board.)

Insulating board.   This is a low-density material (less than 240 kg m^{-3}) available in thicknesses of 10–25 mm. It is used for thermal insulation in ceilings, walls and roofs, and as a core material.

Bitumen-impregnated insulating board.   These are insulating boards with added bitumen content to reduce the rate of moisture absorption. They are used as roof sarking, sheathing on timber-frame houses, and floor underlays. Boards with high bitumen content (up to 35%) are used as expansion joint fillers in concrete. They are usually sold under trade names such as Flexcell and Huntonit.

In addition to the above, there is a very wide range of predecorated, embossed, surface-laminated and flame-retardant treated fibre building boards.

50.6.5   Flakeboards—waferboard and oriented-strand board (OSB)

50.6.5.1 Description

These more recently developed wood particleboards may be defined as follows.

Waferboard.   This is made from wood wafers or flakes at least 32 mm in length with the plane of the flakes parallel with that of the board but otherwise randomly orientated.

Oriented-strand board.   This is made from wood strands that are orientated in predetermined directions to simulate some of the characteristics of three-ply plywood.

50.6.5.2 Standards

Orientated-strand board currently has no specific published standard (a Draft BSI Standard has been produced). Canadian Standard CAN 3-0188: 2-M78 describes the basic properties and characteristics of the product, whilst CAN 3-01880: 0-M78 describes the test methods. Agrément Certificates are available covering use as wall, sheathing, flooring and roofing.

50.6.5.3 General performance levels

The basic difference between waferboard and oriented-strand board is that waferboard is manufactured using a random configuration of essentially rectangular flakes, whilst oriented-strand board is made from an orientated configuration of longer, narrower strands. Both board types can be made from various species of wood, but currently waferboard tends to be mainly

hardwood (aspen) and oriented-strand board mainly softwood (pine). In Canada and the USA these products are used as a substitute for several applications of plywood including wall sheathing, flooring underlay, roof sheathing and decking. They have similar strength characteristics to plywood but their long-term response to moisture and high humidity has yet to be fully assessed in service. They may be used as a substitute for wood chipboard in certain applications where smooth surfaces are not required. They are available in two grades: unsanded and sanded.

Unsanded boards have a rougher surface texture but they do have a slight sheen as a result of close contact with the press platen during manufacture and this is said to afford a degree of water repellancy. (A non-skid screen grid is pressed into one face on some panels.)

Sanded boards are suited to less-hazardous situations where a smoother texture and uniform thickness is required, for example in underlayment.

50.6.6   Medium-density fibreboard (MDF)

50.6.6.1 Description

Medium-density fibreboard, the latest development in 'dry process' fibre building board technology, is defined as 'a sheet material manufactured from fibres of ligno-cellulosic material felted together with the primary bond normally derived from a bonding agent. Other agents may be added during or after manufacture to modify the particular properties of the material'. This BS 6100 definition adds that the density usually exceeds 600 kg m^{-3} and thickness ranges between 6 and 50 mm.

50.6.6.2 Standards

The British Standard relating to medium-density fibreboard is BS 1142: 1989.

50.6.6.3 General performance levels

Medium-density fibreboard is a furniture-grade board with superior characteristics in terms of surface texture, smoothness and machinability. It is currently not marketed as a structural panel and is not currently suitable for exterior applications, but it finds use in areas such as joinery and pattern making. Its density is in the range 640–860 kg m^{-3}.

50.6.7   Wood cement particleboard

50.6.7.1 Description

Wood cement particleboard is made from small particles of wood, bonded with either Portland or magnesite cement, formed and cured into panels.

50.6.7.2 Standards

No Standard relates directly to the production of wood cementboard.

50.6.7.3 General performance levels

Wood cement board has a density of 1000–1200 kg m^{-3} or approximately twice that of plywood and about 1.75 times the density of standard-grade wood chipboard. This imposes considerable restrictions on the end use of such a product. Given this possible disadvantage and difficulties encountered in cutting and machining, the claimed advantages of wood cement board over other wood-based panel products are:

(1) superior dimensional stability in wet conditions and smooth surfaces;
(2) superior behaviour in fire;
(3) highly resistant to attack by fungi, insects and weathering; and
(4) good sound absorbance.

50.7 Uses of wood-based panel products in building construction and applied applications

The uses to which the major wood-based sheet materials can be applied are listed in *Table 50.11*. The table is not exhaustive in usage and the absence of a × does not necessarily imply unsuitability of the material. Specific designs will be required to meet the appropriate regulations and some applications may call for preservative treatment of the indicated material if the timber used in its construction is of limited durability. In many applications it would be normal to apply an appropriate surface finish to the material which will require maintenance from time to time. All types of panel products (plywood, chipboards and fibre building boards) are now produced with low surface-spread-of-flame properties. The treatments are applied to the veneers, particles or fibres before, during or after manufacture and boards are available with Class-1 certification to BS 476: Part 7: 1987. In addition, some boards have obtained Class-0 certification to the Building Regulations requirements.

Flame-retardant treatments for timber and board products are available either as post-manufacture treatments or as part of board manufacture which will upgrade from the inherent Class 3 spread of flame to Class 1 of BS 476: 1987 or even Class 0, as defined in the Building Regulations.

Products which have obtained Class-1 or Class-0 certification are listed in the Timber Research and Development Association (TRADA) Wood Information Sheet 2/3-23.

50.8 Timber fasteners

Timber fasteners can be divided into two main groups: mechanical fasteners and glued joints.

50.8.1 Mechanical joints

BS 5268: Part 2: 1989 divides the basic loads for fasteners into four categories related to the strength classes given in Section 50.5 (see *Table 50.12*). The most widely used softwoods, European redwood and whitewood in the GS and SS grades and the North American timbers hem–fir and spruce–pine–fir to the NLGA grades No. 1 and No. 2 joist and plank grades, all fall in category 2.

Section 6 of BS 5268: Part 2: 1988 covers the design of nailed, screwed, bolted and connected joints. It does not deal with punched metal fasteners with or without integral teeth. These are covered by the trussed-rafter code BS 5268: Part 3: 1985

Table 50.11 Popular uses of the major wood-based sheet materials* in building, construction and allied applications

Application	Plywoods			Chipboards			Fibre building boards			
	WBP bonded ply	Non-WBP bonded ply	Blockboard & laminboard	Type I	Type II	Type III & II/III	Hardboard	Medium board	Insulating board (softboard)	MDF
Building elements										
Sheathing	×					×	×	×	×†	
Flat roofing	×					×			×†	
Roof sarking	×					×			×†	
Cladding	×							×		
Floor underlay							×	×	×	
Floor surface (dry)	×				×					×
Floor surface (moisture hazard)	×					×				
Linings—interior partitions and wall panels	×	×		×			×	×	×	
Linings—ceilings and roofs	×	×		×			×	×	×	
Structural components										
Composite beams	×							×		
Truss gussets	×									
Stressed skin floor and roof panels	×				×	×	×			
Joinery, etc.										
Fascias and soffits	×							×		
Staircase construction	×		×		×	×				×
Window joinery										×
Mouldings and architraves				×	×					×
Furniture and built-in fitments		×	×	×			×			×
Door construction	×	×		×			×		×	×
Temporary works										
Concrete formwork	×					×	×			
Signs and hoardings	×					×	×		×	
Other										
Shopfitting, display and exhibition work	×	×	×	×			×	×		×

* MDF, Medium-density fibre board; WBP
† Bitumen-impregnated insulating board

Table 50.12 The four categories of the basic loads of fasteners (BS 5268: Part 2: 1989)

Joint strength classes	General application
1 SC1 and SC2	Low-strength softwoods
2 SC3 and SC4	Most commercial softwoods
3 SC5	High-strength softwoods and some hardwoods
4 SC6–SC9	Most hardwoods

Note: There are important exceptions in that softwoods (except pitch and Southern pine) machine graded to M75 should use fastener loads tabulated for SC3 and SC4.

Fast-grown conifers such as British grown spruce, radiata pine from New Zealand and certain whitewoods from North America should use fastener loads tabulated for SC1 and SC2.

and Agrément Certificates for each type of plate (see Section 50.9.2). Basic loads are given for nailed, screwed and bolted joints, tooth plate connector joints, split ring and shear plate connector joints.

50.8.1.1 Nails and screws

Basic loads for single fasteners subjected to long-term loading in dry conditions are tabulated. Modification factors are given to allow for other conditions and the code covers joints in plywood and tempered hardboard as well as solid timber. Steel-to-timber joints are also dealt with.

Design rules covering the spacing of fasteners are given for both lateral and withdrawal loading for standard and special improved nails. Similar design rules are given for screwed joints with specific advice on the necessary predrilling of holes. The recommendations are applicable to nails and screws which comply with BS 1202: 1974.

50.8.1.2 Bolted joints

The recommendations in the code are applicable to joints utilizing black bolts which comply with BS 4190: 1967 and washers which comply with BS 4320: 1968. Design information covering size of bolt, spacing of bolts which are linked with basic shear loads for timber-to-timber joints and steel-plate-to-timber joints are again linked with the strength-class system.

It is recommended that bolt holes be drilled to diameters as close as practical to the nominal bolt diameter, but in no case should they be more than 2 mm larger than the bolt diameter as this could affect the slip in joints and hence the deflection of completed components.

Rules are given on bolt spacing for solid timber and steel-to-solid-timber types of joints.

50.8.1.3 Tooth plate connector joints

The recommendations in the code cover round and square tooth plate connectors both double and single sided and must comply with BS 1579: 1966. Advice is given on the preparation of joints and design information covering connector spacing and end and edge distances. The code again covers timber to timber joints and steel plate to timber joints.

50.8.1.4 Split ring and shear plates

The recommendations in the code are applicable to joints using split-ring and shear-plate connectors which comply with BS 1579: 1960. Two sizes of both split-ring and shear-plate connectors are covered, namely 64-mm and 102-mm diameter

for split rings and 67-mm and 102-mm diameter for shear-plate connectors.

Design information covering washer sizes, connector spacing and end and edge distances for both types of connector are given. The loads are again linked with the strength-class system and cover timber to timber joints as well as steel plate to timber joints.

For all types of connectors information is given on the effective cross-section of the members after machining for the connectors. The effects of long-term loading, which are less than those for solid timber, and the effect of the number of joints acting together, with reduction for the values given for individual joints when used in multiple connections with the load acting in one line, are given.

50.8.2 Glued joints

The recommendations given in BS 5268: Part 2: 1989 are applicable to joints in structural components made from separate pieces of timber, plywood or tempered hardboard that are fastened together with glue, e.g. box beams, single-web beams, stressed skin panels, and glued gussets, and these should be manufactured in accordance with BS 6446: 1984. The provisions of the code only apply to structural joints for the softwood species listed in the code and a warning is given on excessively resinous pieces.

In general, glued joints are limited to members which are 50-mm thick in solid timber and with plywood not greater than 29 mm in thickness, for tempered hardboard the thickness is limited to 8 mm. There is also a warning that when mechanical fasteners are present in a glued joint they cannot be considered as contributing to the strength of the joint.

50.8.2.1 Adhesives

The glue used should be appropriate to the environment of the structure and should comply with BS 1204: 1979. *Table 50.13* gives two main types of exposure conditions of structures, namely high and low hazard, with examples of permitted adhesives for these applications.

50.8.2.2 Finger joints

Finger joints, which should be manufactured in accordance with BS 5291: 1984 are covered in the section on glued lamination. There is a section in the code which says that finger joints should not be used in principal members or other members acting alone where failure of a single joint could lead to collapse. However, finger joints may be used in load-sharing systems, provided that the failure of any single joint would not lead to collapse of the system.

Finger-joint efficiency should be assessed in accordance with BS 5291: 1984 and this should be not less than that required for the particular grade of timber in which they occur, unless the permissible stress is reduced accordingly. In no case should a finger joint profile with an efficiency rating of less than 50% be used. It may be assumed that the presence of finger joints in a cross-section does not affect its modulus of elasticity and the full cross-section may be used in calculations.

50.9 Structural uses of timber

Timber can be used for a wide range of structural uses. Two particular uses are described here in detail. These are glued laminated timber and trussed rafters.

Table 50.13 Permissible adhesive types

Exposure category and conditions	Examples of adhesives*
High hazard	
Full exposure to the weather, e.g. marine structures where the glue-line is exposed to the elements. (Glued structures other than glued laminated members are not recommended for use under this exposure condition)	RF
Buildings with warm and damp conditions where a moisture content of 0.18 is exceeded and where the glue-line temperature can exceed 50°C, e.g. launderies, swimming pools and unventilated roof spaces	PF PF/RF
Chemically polluted atmospheres, e.g. chemical works and dye works	
External single-leaf walls with protective cladding	
Low hazard	
Exterior structures protected from sun and rain, roofs of open sheds and porches	RF
Temporary structures such as concrete formwork	
Heated and ventilated buildings where the moisture content of the wood will not exceed 0.18 and where the temperature of the glue-line will remain below 50°C, e.g. interiors of houses, halls, churches and other buildings	PF PF/RF MF/UF UF

* RF, resorcinol-formaldehyde (BS 1204: Part 1: 1979, type WBP); PF, phenol-formaldehyde (BS 1204: Part 1: 1979, type WBP); PF/RF, phenol/resorcinol-formaldehyde (BS 1204: Part 1, 1979; type WBP); MF/UF, melamine/urea-formaldehyde (BS 1204: Part 1: 1979, type BR); UF, urea-formaldehyde and modified UF (BS 1204: Part 1: 1979, type MR).

50.9.1 Glued laminated timber

50.9.1.1 Introduction

Aesthetically attractive structural timber members of large cross-section and long length can be fabricated from small cross-section boards in commercial sizes by the process of glued lamination, often referred to as 'glulam'.

A glued-laminated member comprises small cross-section boards layered up and glued so that the grain is parallel, in contrast to the configuration in plywood where adjacent veneers usually have their face grain at right angles. Individual boards may be connected by scarf or finger joints to behave as continuous laminations.

Specialist manufacturers will produce laminated members in any size, section and profile required. Most manufacturing companies employ design engineers who will undertake any necessary detailed calculations and advise on construction detail.

A more recent development has been the introduction of standard straight beams which are available 'off the shelf' from some manufacturers and timber merchants. These are made in a fixed range of sizes; the merchant or manufacturer usually stocks only a selection from the range and should be consulted about sizes available.

50.9.1.2 Basic forms

A glued-laminated member can have a straight or curved profile. It can be constructed with a varying section such as in tapering beams, arches or portal frames (see *Figures 50.3–50.6*). Strength-to-weight ratio is high and the comparatively low weight makes for easier handling. Any size of cross-section and length of member can be produced by glued lamination; thus it is transportation and manufacturing space which are the size-limiting factors. As glulam is factory produced, high standards of quality, dimensional stability and finish can be achieved.

Figure 50.3 Straight laminated beams form the A-frame structure of a school at Chester-le-Street, Durham. The ground floor span is over 20 m providing space for an indoor bowls hall

Figure 50.4 The roof of the sports hall at Frome Sports Centre has cranked laminated beams spanning a total of 18 m

50.9.1.3 Design considerations

As a general guide, straight beams and columns can range from about 75 mm × 150 mm upwards, although such small sizes would not normally be price competitive with solid timber. Large members measuring over 500 mm × 2000 mm and spanning over 30 m have been made, but spans up to about 27.5 m are more usual.

A further consideration is that, as a result of the low moisture content dictated by the gluing and the random lay of pieces, the finished member will have better dimensional stability and suffer less from checks or deformation than solid wood sections which often have to complete their drying in service.

The low coefficient of expansion of timber compared with steel is also of advantage, in that expansion joints can be omitted or simplified even in large members. Similarly, timber has better resistance to corrosive industrial or marine atmospheres than either steel or concrete. The considerable savings in maintenance

costs on exterior structures like bridges make the use of glued-laminated wood, an attractive proposition to specifiers. The hazards of wet and exterior locations are met by using durable hardwood or preservative-treated softwood members.

Exterior wood stains provide surface protection, maintain appearance and are easy to restore. When subjected to fire, large timber members have a greater resistance to destruction than steel or prestressed concrete. This is because of the insulation provided by the charcoal that develops over the burning surface. Furthermore, the endurance of wood in a fire can be predicted from the outset due to its rate of charring.

50.9.1.4 Design data

For guidance on the design of glued-laminated beams the designer should refer to BS 5268: Part 2: 1988. Permissible working stresses are laid down in this standard together with information on the quality of materials and modification factors which will be needed by the design engineer.

50.9.1.5 Species and grades of timber

Much laminated work is fabricated from softwood which is generally Scandinavian whitewood or redwood, western hemlock or Douglas fir. Hardwood is used when justified by special strength or appearance requirements.

Three grade stresses for laminating are specified in BS 5268: Part 2: 1988. The grades are LA, LB and LC and are obtained by selection from BS 4978: 1988 grades for softwood or from HS grades to BS 5756: 1980 in the case of hardwood. The three grades can be determined according to the rules laid down in these standards. The grade stress levels for LA, LB and LC are about 95%, 75% and 50%, respectively, of the strength of clear timber.

A laminated member might comprise only one grade but, for reasons of economy, it is common practice to employ a combination of higher grades in the outer layers of the member and lower grades in the middle, where the stresses are lower. A typical combination could be LA/LB/LA or LB/LC/LB, with the lower grade centre section comprising one-third to one-half of the total depth.

50.9.1.6 Adhesives

Adhesives used in the construction of laminated members are required to have a strength sufficient to provide a joint at least as strong as the timber. They must also have low creep characteristics under load and have a durability suited to a beam's

Figure 50.5 Laminated portal arches provide the structural framework of this timber frame church at Selsey

Figure 50.6 The David Lloyd Tennis Centre at Heston, Middlesex, consists of three main halls of glulam arches each spanning 35.3 m with a rise of 8.4 m

conditions of service. Two types of adhesive that satisfy these requirements are casein and the synthetic resin formed from a reaction between formaldehyde and urea, phenol, resorcinol or melamine or a combination of these. These adhesives are fully specified in BS 1204: Part 1: 1979 which covers the synthetic resins. In use, it is essential for fabricators to comply precisely with the adhesive manufacturer's recommendations. *Table 50.13* gives general recommendations for adhesives.

Under normal conditions of temperature and where moisture content will not exceed 18%, casein or any of the synthetic resins can be used. Where temperatures above 37°C (100°F) can occur (in insulated roofs the temperature can reach 54°C (130°F) during summer), casein or any of the resin group, except urea, would be suitable. In damp and external locations where moisture content will exceed 18%, or where chemical pollution can occur, resorcinol formaldehyde or phenol formaldehyde only should be used under both high and normal ambient temperature conditions.

50.9.1.7 Manufacture

The manufacturing procedure for laminated members will depend upon the volume and nature of the work plus the fabricator's production facilities, but all stages of the procedure must comply with the recommendations of BS 4169: 1988. Glued-laminated members can be obtained using simple equipment, but the modern trend is towards large-scale production using more complex machinery.

Material preparation. Laminating stock is selected from commercial supplies by visual stress grading to the requirements of BS 4978: 1988 or BS 5756: 1980. The number of laminations in a member has a bearing on its strength; in general, the greater the number the higher its strength. However, in the interests of economy the number of laminations used should be kept to a minimum, but they should never be in excess of 50 mm thick. There is no structural reason why thicker laminations should not be used, but 50 mm is chosen as a size which minimizes drying costs, checking, splitting, distortion and problems in achieving adequate gluing pressure. This maximum thickness applies only to straight beams. The difficulty of bending laminations for curved beams will obviously dictate their thickness, which could be as thin as 12 mm.

Timber should be finished to a uniform thickness with smooth clean surfaces freshly prepared for gluing. Unevenness or surfaces burnished by blunt tools could cause reduced strength.

End jointing to obtain full-length laminations is usually achieved using finger joints and BS 5291: 1984 sets out sizes and types. BS 5291: 1984 lays down rules for quality control at the manufacturing stage. This is related to the permissible design strength of the joint. The selection of joint type is usually related to the strength of the timber employed. Plain glued scarf joints are permitted. These joints use more timber but, in straight beams, there is the advantage of gluing up with the overall assembly. Butt joints are also permitted (BS 4169: 1988), but the designer must take account of the strength effects of this when preparing the calculations for the glued-laminated members.

Finish. At the end of the conditioning period, and after all drilling or cutting has been completed a member is finished to the chosen standard, commonly by planing and sanding. Minor defects in appearance may be removed and holes plugged. Preservative or decorative treatment is applied as specified.

Quality control. Checks are required to be carried out at every stage of manufacture and all materials inspected to ensure their quality and suitability. The checks embrace accuracy of machining, glue mix and spreading, clamping pressure, curing times, conditioning time and overall time schedules. Glue strength and integrity are of primary importance and tests for these are laid down in BS 4169: 1988.

50.9.2 Trussed rafters

The design and production of trussed rafters is covered by BS 5268: Part 3, the most recent edition of which was published in 1985. It is a revision of CP 112: Part 3: 1973, the new title extending beyond uses in domestic construction. A brief synopsis of the code is given below.

50.9.2.1 Section 1—General

The code defines trussed rafters and states that three methods are equally acceptable for establishing their structural adequacy:

(1) Engineering calculations based on acceptable methods of analysis, including a simple approach given later, using data on material properties and joint strength characteristics as given in BS 5268: Part 2: 1989. These may need to be supplemented by additional data provided by a recognized testing authority.
(2) Load testing of trussed rafters in accordance with the procedures described in Section 8.
(3) Fabrication and use in accordance with Section 9, which gives span tables.

50.9.2.2 Section 2—Materials

The code gives the species which are permissible for trussed-rafter use (see *Table 50.14*). Compared with the old code, USA species in general are added with Southern pine in particular. Also added for the first time is British-grown Sitka spruce of M75 grade.

All timber must be stress graded in accordance with BS 4978: 1988 or as recommended in BS 5268: Part 2: 1989 for timber stress graded outside the UK.

Finger-jointed timber. The new code permits finger-jointed timber to be used. Where the finger joints fall in a random position, their efficiency rating in bending and tension is reduced by a factor averaging 0.8 to allow for the possibility of a finger joint occurring within the area of a fastener.

Plywood. Although most trussed rafters are jointed by punched metal plate fasteners, there is provision for the use of nailed or glued plywood gussets as an alternative.

Table 50.14 Species of timber

Standard name	Origin
Whitewood Redwood	Europe
Hem–fir Douglas fir–larch Spruce–pine–fir	Canada
Southern pine Hem–fir Douglas fir–larch	USA
Scots pine Corsican pine	UK

50.9.2.3 Section 3—Functional requirements

Since the publication of the first code of practice for trussed rafters, increases in the levels of roof insulation have made it necessary to reconsider the environmental conditions which may exist within the roof space, to avoid possible problems associated with condensation. As a result, clauses have been introduced dealing with thermal insulation and recommending minimum levels of ventilation.

Thermal insulation. To achieve the required standard of insulation, the insulating material is normally placed between the ceiling ties on top of the ceiling board. A cold roof space is thus created. Where it is intended to provide a room in the loft, the insulation is placed at rafter level, resulting in a warm roof space.

Condensation. In all occupied premises large quantities of vapour are generated by the occupants and their washing, cooking and bathing activities. Some of the moisture is removed by normal ventilation, but frequently the high cost of energy results in ventilation levels being deliberately restricted by the occupants.

The movement of hot, vapour-laden air into the cold parts of a roof will result in condensation with the associated risk of fungal attack or plate corrosion unless precautions are taken. For pitched roofs the most commonly adopted solution relies on restricting moisture migration by sealing all joints and service entry apertures and providing a simple vapour barrier. This is combined with effective ventilation above the insulation layer, to remove the water vapour.

Ventilation. Since modern roofs are relatively cold, normally incorporating 80–100 mm of insulation at ceiling level, the ventilation requirements have been considerably increased in the last few years. BS 5268: Part 3: 1988 gives minimum sizes of ventilation openings for both cold and warm roofs, with recommendations for monopitch as well as double-pitch roof.

Preservation. In discussing the need for preservative treatment, Part 3 makes reference to BS 5256: Part 5: 1989. A properly designed and constructed trussed-rafter roof is not at significant risk from rot or insect attack, except in areas where roof timbers must be preserved to prevent infestation by the house longhorn beetle. If preservative treatment is needed, the double vacuum system, based on an organic solvent, is best suited to modern fabrication methods of trussed rafters. The use of copper/chrome/arsenic (CCA) preservative involves rewetting the timber, and Part 3 of the code emphasizes the need for careful control when this method is applied. It states also that the type of preservative used should not increase the risk of corrosion of metal plate fasteners, making reference to Part 5 of the code for recommendations on this topic.

50.9.2.4 Section 4—Design of trussed rafters

A simplified design method is provided as an alternative to rigorous analysis. This is generally in accordance with the recommendations given in Part 2, but for rafter design a special formula is introduced which gives calculated spans approximating to the permissible spans given in the tables in Section 9 of Part 3.

Section 4 also details the loading to be applied for design, requiring water-tank loading to be included unless it is known that this is not needed. General principles for the design of joints are given, including allowance for limited misplacement of the plates during assembly.

50.9.2.5 Section 5—Design of trussed-rafter roofs

This section emphasizes the responsibility of the building designer, who may be the owner, or his appointed architect or engineer, or the actual builder in the case of small buildings, to ensure that the design of the roof and supporting structure will provide stability of the complete building.

Reference is made to the bracing details shown in Appendix A for domestic roofs within certain limits of pitch, span and wind speed. Bracing was mentioned only briefly in the previous code but was detailed in Technical Bulletin No. 1 of the International Truss Plate Association. The details are now given in BS 5268: Part 3: 1989, but a more stringent requirement is that every section of a long roof must be braced, with no interval between sets of bracing. In addition, gable walls must be attached to the roof at ceiling level in all cases and not only when the pitch exceeds a certain limit. A recent amendment to the code has simplified the required bracing requirements.

50.9.2.6 Section 6—Fabrication

More detail has been given in the revised code on methods of assembly which should enable a minimum level of performance to be achieved. The tolerances permitted in joints and general dimensions are given. A clause on marking states that every trussed rafter should be marked clearly to show the name of the manufacturer and the species and stress grade of the strength classes of the timber. The marking should also confirm that the trussed rafter has been designed and fabricated in accordance with the recommendations of BS 5268: Part 3: 1985.

50.9.2.7 Section 7—Handling, storage and erection

More extended information is given on these topics, and the erection details formerly shown in the ITPA Bulletin have been included as Appendix C. Although limits are given on deviation from the vertical of the trusses as erected, the text states that every effort should be made to erect them as near vertical as possible.

The clause dealing with battens advises that, in order to reduce hogging over separating walls, the walls should be finished 25 mm below the underside of the tiling battens and the remaining space filled with compressible non-combustible material where necessary.

A clause on the support of water tanks again makes reference to a diagram adapted from an ITPA Bulletin, and special provision must be made for situations outside those covered by the diagram. ITPA information is also incorporated for the clause dealing with hatch (*Figure 50.7*) and chimney openings in a more detailed manner than before.

50.9.2.8 Section 8—Load testing

The test procedure remains essentially the same and is generally in accordance with that given in BS 5268: Part 2: 1989 with the addition of a note on the measurement of deflection for cambered trussed rafters.

50.9.2.9 Section 9—Permissible spans

CP 112: Part 3 gave span tables for 'fink' and 'fan' trussed rafters, for only 'composite grade' timber, but tables for BS 4978: 1988 grades were published separately at a later stage. In the new code the 'fan' tables have been omitted and the tables for 'fink' trusses cater for the M50, SS or MSS and M75 grades. Strength-class-4 timber may also be used with the SS/MSS tables, and SC5 timber with the M75 tables. The M50 tables are also appropriate for British-grown Sitka spruce graded to

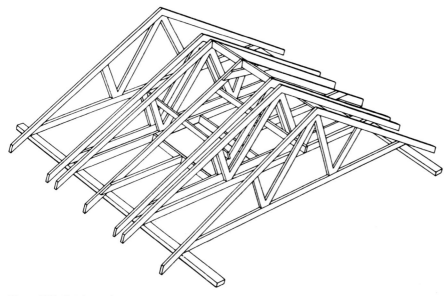

Figure 50.7 Hatch opening

the M75 stress grade. All the tables are for a standard loading which has remained unchanged in the revised code.

The maximum span tabulated in the previous code was 11 m, but in the new code it is 11 m for 35 mm thick and 12 m for 47 mm thick timbers. A change in the required bracing for the standard spans introduces diagonal bracing on the internal members, extending along the length of the roof, at spans exceeding 5 m instead of the 8 m boundary applied previously.

50.9.2.10 Section 10—Information required

The list of information required from the client has been modified and now includes the weight of the roof covering and any unusual wind conditions. A second list has been added, for information required by the client purchasing the trussed rafters. This enables a check to be made that the trusses are suitable for their intended use, and also includes the positions, fixings and sizes of any lateral supports necessary to prevent buckling of compression members. A note is added to say that details of the permanent bracing necessary to ensure the overall stability of the complete roof structure and supporting walls should be provided by the building designer.

Sources of designs. Trussed rafter designs are generally provided by the 'system owners' who supply proprietary jointing plates to their licensees undertaking the work of fabrication. Orders may be placed with any of a large number of fabricators covering the area of the UK. Most designs will be met from standard sets already computed, but special computer runs may be required for types outside the standard range.

50.10 Joinery timber

This section deals with the timber specification of joinery. Specification of timber for joinery purposes is greatly simplified by reference to BS 1186 which applies to both hardwoods and softwoods. The standard is in two parts: Part 1: 1986 deals with material quality and Part 2: 1988 with workmanship. Defining the quality required by reference to this standard is more precise

and, therefore, preferable to specifying by means of commercial shippers' marks. Most European softwood used for joinery is imported as 'unsorted' quality, that is, a mixture of the best four commercial qualities, but the actual quality of 'unsorted' timber varies according to the country of origin and the individual shipper, thus making it an unreliable specification standard. It is one of the skills of the experienced importer's buyer to know which commercial quality from the individual mill or port will meet the required end user standard.

North American softwood for joinery is graded in different ways, the best quality being termed 'clears and door stock' and being broadly equal to European 'firsts': the second quality is termed 'select merchantable' and is broadly equivalent to European 'unsorted' material. Hardwoods are usually graded as firsts or second. Firsts provide a high percentage of clear material to be achieved by cutting and will also provide long lengths of clear timber. Seconds will provide a lower percentage and shorter lengths of clear timber.

BS 1186: Part 1: 1986 describes the quality of timber required for various types of joinery and defines quality in terms of allowable or non-allowable characteristics such as knot size, type, location and frequency, sapwood, shakes and splits and rate of growth. It also defines the acceptable moisture content of the timber components at the time of their acceptance by the first purchaser (usually the building contractor).

Qualities of joinery timber for differing purposes are defined in the form of classes which must be quoted in the specification. Four classes are included in the revised version of the standard and these allow varying amounts and sizes of timber defects or characteristics on the faces of the timber component.

Class CSH: CSH stands for clear softwood and hardwood and should be specified only for joinery made from 'clear' grades of timber.

Class 1: Specified for high quality or specialized joinery. This quality of timber may require special selection and may, therefore, be more expensive compared with lower grades of the same species. The use of laminated timber is allowed and this may be necessary to achieve the standard consistently and economically. Class 1 is appropriate to both hardwoods and softwoods.

Class 2: These classes would normally be specified.

Class 3: This quality is for general-purpose joinery using species such as European redwood or European whitewood or using hardwood. They apply to both solid and laminated timber. Class 3 allows greater limits of knot size than Class 2, otherwise the classes are similar.

Within each class there are variations in the acceptability of defects and natural characteristics depending upon whether they occur on exposed, semi-concealed or concealed surfaces of the finished component. An exposed face is a surface which will be visible after the component has been installed in the buildings A semi-concealed surface is one which is not normally visible when the component is in the closed position but which becomes visible when the component is opened (for example, at a door or window jamb). A concealed surface is one which is never visible after the component has been installed (for example, the back face of a door or window frame).

It is of course possible to specify the timber quality required for purpose-made joinery by adopting the most appropriate BS 1186 class but amending the requirements with respect to any specific item; for example, by excluding finger jointing or laminating on joinery to be clear finished or by applying a more rigorous limitation on knot spacing than is accepted by the standard. However, care must be used in doing this to ensure that the specific requirement is defined. It would be helpful in such a case to reproduce the relevant clauses from the standard together with clear identification of the amendment in the written specification of the work.

In old specifications it was commonly inferred that the material to be used should always be of the very best quality available. It is rarely possible, on economic grounds, to do this today and there is, in any case, no real advantage in using a higher quality than is necessary to satisfy the end use. When deciding the quality of material required it is important to be aware of what is achievable from the timber selected. Although it would in theory be possible to achieve any species/class combination by rigorous selection it would only be economically justifiable in exceptional circumstances to require, for example, CSH (clear) grade in European redwood. It would normally be preferable to select alternative species (such as hemlock or Douglas fir) if this grade requirement were required.

The other properties which should be considered when specifying joinery timber are strength, durability, workability (especially if the component is of complex detail), dimensional stability and, of course, appearance. BS 1186: Part 1: 1986 includes in its appendix a table giving some guidance on the characteristics of the more commonly suited timber species together with an indication of their suitability for various uses. When the precise appearance of the timber is important to the finished project, the only totally reliable solution is to inspect and select the timber at the merchant's prior to its use and/or to require a sample for general approval with the manufacturer's acceptance that production will be of similar quality. Depending upon the quality and type of work, it may not be necessary to specify the species of softwood to be used but simply to define the BS 1186: Part 1: 1986 class (or classes if they vary on different parts of the finished component). When hardwood is specified it is normally necessary to name the species (using BS 881 and 589: 1974 nomenclature) in addition to defining the BS 1186 class of the timber.

The specification should also indicate whether preservative treatment is required on timber components used in external situations, and, if so, specify the type to be used. Irrespective of the durability of the timber species, sapwood is not considered durable and should either be excluded from the specifications for external components or preservative treatment specified.

50.10.1 The performance of joinery products

Architects and other specifiers of building products often need information on the performance of a particular component to aid in the preparation of an overall building design. Structural components are required to have the necessary strength to support the building and also to carry loads which may be applied either by the occupants, i.e. floor loading such as furniture, storage racks, etc., or naturally, i.e. snow or wind load. The component must be strong enough to support all these loads safely and also be sufficiently durable to have an adequate life in the environment to which it will be subjected.

In the case of non-structural elements such as doors, windows and staircases, although adequate strength is still important, other factors become significant in the selection of a product which is suitable for the particular application. If such information is required, it is generally supplied by the manufacturer as part of the specification of the product he is hoping to sell.

Many new products are, therefore, tested at the development stage to ensure that the production article will have adequate performance to meet the requirements of potential customers. Companies often prefer to use British or International Standards to assess the performance of products where these exist, but some manufacturers, and indeed some major users, write their own specifications.

British Standards for joinery products have tended to develop in recent years from being almost 'product' standards, where details of materials, design and construction are given, to mainly 'performance' standards where material selection and design are left to the manufacturers, providing that the finished article can be shown to reach the right level of performance. Product standards are useful in that they allow small manufacturers to produce items which will comply with a well-known specification and, therefore, give the customer some confidence in the adequacy of their performance. Performance standards give the customer a possibly greater guarantee of the adequacy of the product and allow the manufacturer more freedom to develop his own design. However, unless these standards cover every aspect of performance there is a danger that undue emphasis may be placed upon one particular attribute, e.g. fire resistance of doors or weathertightness of windows.

British Standards which give performance requirements for windows and stairs are now available and a new BS Draft for Development on doors has been published; thus all the main joinery products are covered even though some of the standards do not cover all important aspects of performance.

Performance standards attempt to assess the way in which a component will behave in service. These assessments are made on the basis of test results. Tests are usually developed to simulate 'in-use' conditions and may represent normal usage or, sometimes, abuse. Often a whole series of tests is necessary to cover all important aspects of a product's performance. Where a particular product can be subjected to different levels of severity of operation, different grades may be specified in a standard.

50.10.1.1 Windows

The British Standard for window performance is BS 6375: Parts 1:1989 and 2:1987. Note that Part 1 refers to BS 5368: Parts 1–3 for methods of testing. Note that these are European Standards EN 42, EN 86 and EN 77, respectively.

The development of the window-performance standard provides an example of the way in which such standards progress from a Draft for Development to the publication of a full British Standard. In this case, the original document, DD 4: 1971, dealt only with resistance to weather and suggested an exposure grading system. The standard BS 6375 deals with the weathertightness in Part 1, which contains information on grading

Table 50.15 Exposure categories for windows

Exposure (design wind pressure) (Pa)	Test pressure classes (Pa)		
	Air* permeability	Water-tightness	Wind resistance
1200†	200	100	1200
1600	300	200	1600
2000	300	200	2000
>2000 (state design wind pressure)	300	300	Design wind pressure

* Permissible air permeability levels increase with applied pressure, the levels given indicate the pressure at which leakage must not exceed 16 m³ h⁻¹ per metre length of opening joint. For full details of performance criteria refer to BS 6375: Part 1: 1989.
† A further grade is proposed in BS 6375 Part 1: 1989.

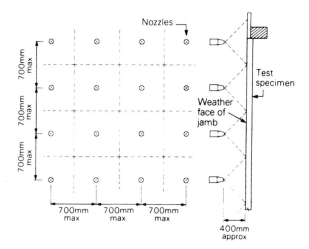

Figure 50.8 Grid system of nozzles for watertightness test, spraying method 2

windows in terms of design wind pressure from test information on air permeability, watertightness and resistance to wind loading. Part 2 deals with strength and operation and it is intended that further parts dealing with other aspects of performance will be published. BS 5368 details the methods of carrying out the three weathertightness tests, and BS 6375: Part 2 includes all the test methods needed to assess the operation and strength characteristics it specifies.

Weathertightness. It is still common within the window industry to indicate weathertightness performance levels by stating that the window types are suitable for use in severely exposed, moderately exposed or sheltered situations; this is undoubtedly a carryover from the original DD 4 gradings. The British Stndard gives a method of classification according to the pressure levels the window will resist and recommended values of performance are given for various design wind pressures.

The data given in *Table 50.15* relate to results from testing done in the following sequence:

(1) air permeability;
(2) watertightness; and
(3) wind resistance.

The last two tests are intended to show up damage that has occurred during the wind-resistance test.

BS 5368: Part 2: 1980 allows a choice of three different methods of spraying water onto the window under test, but indicates a preference for method (2) (see *Figures 50.8* and *50.9*). Three methods were included because agreement could not be reached in the European Standard Committee and, therefore, all three methods used by different countries were included.

At TRADA the tests are carried out on one of two purpose-built rigs according to the methods detailed in these British Standards, using spray method 2; which rig is used depends only on the size of window to be tested and availability of the rig.

Operation. BS 6375: Part 2 gives operating forces which the majority of people can apply for opening lights and catches of various types. Special consideration must be given to operating forces (*Table 50.16*) when selecting a window for use by the young, old or infirm.

Tests are carried out to check the forces needed to operate the fastener, both to release the sash (*Table 50.17*) and to secure it in the closed position. In addition, a check is made on the forces necessary to start and continue to move the sash in both directions.

Strength. The term strength is taken here to cover the other tests specified in BS 6375: Part 2. The performance specifications given in the standard are:

Resistance to abuse—applicable only to sliding windows, assesses the effects of excessive operating forces.
Resistance to obstructed stay track—applies only to projecting windows fitted with sliding shoe stays.
Strength of restricted opening devices, location devices and maximum opening stops—a force is applied to check the strength of the device.
Resistance to accidental loading—simulates the accidental application of body weight to an opening light.

Organizations such as the British Board of Agrément, the Property Services Agency and the Department of Health and Social Security use large numbers of windows and have laid down their own performance specifications. These agree largely with the British Standards but may have additional requirements for other characteristics, such as endurance.

The design and manufacturing standard, BS 644, Part 1: 1989 has been revised to cover currently available factory-assembled wood windows.

50.10.1.2 Wood stairs

The main standards relevant to wood stairs are: BS 585: Parts 1: 1989 and 2: 1985 and BS 5395: Part 1: 1977. In addition, consideration should be given to the requirements of stairs given in the Building Regulations.

BS 585: Part 2 specifies the performance requirements for domestic stairs constructed from certain wood based materials and the relevant test methods. The materials allowed, including timber, plywood, chipboard and various types of fibreboard, are given, together with references to the relevant British Standards. BS 1186: Part 2: 1988 is specified as giving the requirements for workmanship.

Tests and criteria for acceptance are given both for the complete stair and for the component parts such as treads, risers, nosings and balustrades. In total, nine tests are suggested, although the initial preload test is only intended to establish a datum level for subsequent deflection measurements.

Figure 50.9 Weathertightness test rig in operation

Whole-stair test. Two tests are specified on the stairs, in addition to the preload test, to check for deflection and damage sustained under load. These are a deflection test, measuring the stiffness of the stair, and a strength test.

Balustrade test. Two tests are suggested: one imposing a static horizontal load on the handrail, and the other using an impact to simulate a person falling against the balustrade. The levels set for the allowable deflection in the static horizontal load tests are under review.

Treads. There are four tests for treads, checking for deflection, strength and impact resistance of the component. These test for tread stiffness, tread impact strength, overall strength and, specifically, the resistance of the tread nosing to impact from above. The levels of performance required in this last test are under review.

Risers. Impact loads are applied to risers to ensure that the materials and methods used in construction are adequate to resist loads likely to occur in normal service.

50.10.1.3 Doors

The new Draft for Development for doors is DD 171:1987. The document was published as a Draft for Development because, although many of the test methods and performance levels have been developed for many years and are well established, some

Table 50.16 Operation of fasteners

Type of fastener	Mode of operation to secure or release sash	Maximum permitted torque (N m)	Maximum permitted force (N)
Peg stays	Push or pull	—	30
Bolts			
Fitch catches			
Over dead-centre openers			
Spring catches (release)			
Handles	Turn	10	—

Table 50.17 Operation of sash

Force	Window type		
	Hinged projecting or pivoted	Horizontal sliding	Vertical sliding
Force to initiate movement (N)	80	80	120
Force to sustain movement (N)	65	65	100

further tests have been introduced recently at the request of major users. Experience of these tests is limited and it is difficult, therefore, to set realistic performance requirements. The intention is to review DD 171 when more information is available and to publish a full British Standard.

As with most performance standards the Draft for Development deals with complete assemblies and is, therefore, only directly applicable to doorsets complete with all hardware. Provision is made, however, for the tests to be applied to door leaves by using a separate frame and fittings.

DD 171 covers most properties relevant to doors, including sound insulation, fire resistance and weathertightness, but where regulations already exist, as with fire performance, reference is simply made to the existing regulations or standards. The general concept of the document is that a door should perform satisfactorily in the situation and under its expected conditions of use.

Several properties, grouped under the headings of strength, operation and dimensional requirements are applicable to all doors and, depending upon door performance under these tests, one of four grades can be given; i.e. light duty (LD), medium duty (MD), heavy duty (HD) and severe duty (SD). The document describes these categories in more detail and gives examples of where such doors should be used (see *Table 50.18*).

For external doors, additional performance categories for weather resistance and thermal insulation may have to be considered and classifications are given in terms of W (weather) and H (thermal transmittance). The performance of a door might thus be described by means of a code for each category, e.g. MD-W1-H2.

Strength. This series of tests is intended to investigate the effects of common forms of use and abuse on the door. Nine different aspects are covered:

(1) slamming shut impact;
(2) slamming open impact—simulating the door being slammed by wind;
(3) heavy-body impact—simulating bodily impact;
(4) hard-body impact—simulating kicking or an impact by the corner of a trolley, etc.;
(5) torsion—doors may become partially jammed causing twisting when opening forces are applied;

Table 50.18 Categories of doors

Category	Description	Examples
Light duty	Low frequency of use by those with a high incentive to exercise care, e.g. private house owners—small chance of accident occurring or of misuse	Internal doors in dwellings. External doors in dwellings providing secondary access to private areas
Medium duty	Medium frequency of use primarily by those with some incentive to exercise care—some chance of accident occurring or of misuse	External doors of dwellings providing primary access. Office doors providing access to designated public areas but not for use by public or by people carrying or propelling bulky objects
Heavy duty	High frequency of use by public and others with little incentive to exercise care. Chance of accident occurring and of misuse	Doors of shops, hospitals and of other buildings which provide access to designated public areas, frequently used by people carrying or propelling bulky objects
Severe duty	Subject to frequent violent usage	Doors of stockrooms, etc., commonly opened by driving trolleys against them; doors in educational establishments, subject to frequent impact by people

Table 50.19 Operating forces for doors

Age group (years)	Levels of max. force to open and close, push or pull (N)	
	Lever handle	*Small knob*
5–7	30	20
8–11 60–75	70	35

(6) downward deformation—forces can be applied to the handle by children swinging, etc.;
(7) closure against obstruction—carpets or other objects may become caught between door and frame;
(8) resistance to jarring and vibration—a new test attempting to simulate the action of a stream of people passing through a door fitted with a closer; and
(9) abusive forces on door handles.

Some tests apply different loads according to the grade of door while others simply repeat the same cycle of loading a different number of times. The criterion for acceptance which is common to all the tests is that the door after test should continue to function normally, although there are additional criteria to be met in some cases.

Operation. In practice, a door should be easy to open, close and fasten and different age groups should be considered. Tests are carried out to measure the forces required to open, close and latch the door and these can be compared to established information for selected age groupings (*Table 50.19*). In the future, when hotel doors are being fitted with smoke seals, operating forces may become a more important factor as the seals will tend to make the doors more difficult to open and close.

Dimensional requirements. At the time of handover, a door should be free from any distortion or dimensional inaccuracy likely to affect performance and the size and shape of a door should always be measured as part of a complete series of checks. The dimensional requirements and tolerances are given in BS 4787. Part 1: 1980.

Special requirements. The Draft for Development gives criteria for acceptance and test methods for a number of special requirements, where possible by reference to other existing standards. Doors for different types of use may need to be subjected to one or more of these tests but it is likely that special door designs will also need to meet the general performance requirements. Additional tests given in the Draft for Development are for the following properties:

(1) dimensional stability—where different sides of the door are exposed to significantly different conditions;
(2) sound insulation;
(3) fire resistance;
(4) weather resistance—for external doors;
(5) thermal transmittance—normally for external doors;
(6) resistance to forced entry—different types of forced entry are recognized but no test methods are given, although reference is made to BS 8220: Part 1: 1986 for guidance on security.

There are a number of other British Standards which refer to doors detailing some of the specialist performance tests and giving design and manufacturing specifications. Of these the most relevant is BS 476: Part 22: 1987. This gives the fire-related performance tests and criteria.

50.11 Possible future requirements

Performance standards should be re-examined at intervals to determine whether the test methods and levels used need to be changed to reflect current requirements more closely. This may mean altering the load in a test, including new tests covering aspects not thought worthwhile earlier, or possibly introducing a test which was being developed when the original standard was produced. Areas which are currently being examined and which may be included in future specifications are endurance, safety and security.

Bibliography

British Standards

BS 476, Fire tests on building materials and structures
    Part 3, External fire exposure roof test (1975)
    Part 4, Non-combustibility test for materials (1970)
    Part 5, Method of test for ignitability (1979)
    Part 6, Method of test for fire propagation for products (1989)
    Part 7, Method of classification of the surface spread of flame tests of products (1987)
    Part 8, Test methods and criteria for the fire resistance of elements of building construction (1972) (Replaced by Parts 20–24)
    Part 11, Method for assessing the heat emission from building materials (1982)
    Part 20, Method for the determination of the fire resistance of elements of building construction (general principles) (1987)
    Part 21, Methods for determination of the fire resistance of loadbearing elements of construction (1987)
    Part 22, Methods for determination of the fire resistance of non-loadbearing elements of construction (1987)
    Part 23, Methods for determination of the contribution of components to the fire resistance of a structure (1987)
    Part 24, Method for the determination of the fire resistance of ventilation ducts (1987)
BS 584, Specification for wood trim (softwood) (1967)
BS 585, Wood stairs
    Part 1, Specification for stairs with closed risers for domestic use, including straight and winder flights and quarter or half landings (1989)
    Part 2, Specification for performance requirements for domestic stairs constructed of wood based materials (1985)
BS 881 and 589, Nomenclature of commercial timbers, including sources of supply (1974)
BS 8220, Guide for security of buildings against crime
    Part 1, Dwellings (1986)
BS 1088 and BS 4079, Plywood for marine craft. BS 1088: Marine plywood manufactured from selected untreated tropical hardwoods. BS 4079: Plywood made for marine uses and treated against attack by fungi or marine borers (1966, under revision)
BS 1142, Fibre building boards
    Part 1, Methods of test (1971)
    Part 2, Medium board, medium density fibreboard and hardboard (1971)
    Part 3, Insulating board (softboard) (1972)
BS 1186, Timber for and workmanship in joinery
    Part 1, Specification for timber (1986)
    Part 2, Specification for workmanship (1988)
BS 1202, Specification for nails
    Part 1, Steel nails (1974)
    Part 2, Copper nails (1974)
    Part 3, Aluminium nails (1974)
BS 1203, synthetic resin adhesives (phenolic and aminoplastic) for plywood (1979)
BS 1204, synthetic resin adhesives (phenolic and aminoplastic) for wood
    Part 1, Gap filling adhesives (1979)
    Part 2, Close contact adhesives (1979)

BS 1282, Guide to the choice, use and application of wood preservatives (1975)
BS 1297, Specification for tongued and grooved softwood flooring (1987)
BS 1579, Specification for connectors of timber (1960)
BS 3444, Specification for blockboard and laminboard (1972)
BS 4169, Specification for manufacture of glued laminated timber structural members (1988)
BS 4190, Specification for ISO metric black hexagen bolts, screws and nuts (1967)
BS 4471, Specification for sizes of sawn and processed softwood (1987)
BS 4787, Internal and external doorsets, door leaves and frames
  Part 1, Specification for dimensional requirements (1980)
BS 4978, Specification for softwood grades for structural use (1988)
BS 5268, Code of practice for the structural use of timber
  Part 1, Limit state design, materials and workmanship (to be published)
  Part 2, Permissible stress design, materials and workmanship (1989)
  Part 3, Code of practice for trussed rafter roofs (1985)
  Part 4, Fire resistance of timber structures
    Section 4.1, Method of calculating fire resistance of timber members (1978)
    Section 4.2, Methods of calculating the fire resistance of timber stud walls and joisted floor constructions (to be published in 1989)
  Part 5, Preservative treatments for constructional timber (1977; revised 1989)
  Part 6, Timber frame walls (1989)
  Part 7, Calculation basis for span tables
    Section 1, Domestic floor joists (1989)
    Section 2, Joists for flat roofs (1989)
    Section 3, Ceiling joists (1989)
    Section 4, Ceiling binders (1989)
    Section 5, Domestic rafters (to be published)
    Section 6, Domestic purlins (to be published)
BS 5291, Specification for manufacture of finger joints of structural softwood (1984)
BS 5368, Methods of testing windows
  Part 1, Air permeability test (1976)
  Part 2, Watertightness test under static pressure (1980)
  Part 3, Wind resistance tests (1978)
BS 5450, Stairs, ladders and walkways
  Part 1, Code of practice for the design of straight stairs (1977)
BS 5395, Sizes of hardwoods and methods of measurement (1977)
BS 5589, Code of practice for the preservation of timber (1989)
BS 5669, Particleboard
  Part 1, Methods of sampling, conditioning and test (1989)
  Part 2, Specification for chipboard (1989)
  Part 3, To be published
  Part 4, Specification for cement bonded particle board (1989)
  Part 5, Code of practice for the selection and application of particleboards for specific purposes (1989)
BS 5756, Specification for tropical hardwoods graded for structural use (1980)
BS 6100, Glossary of building and civil engineering terms
  Part 4, Forest products
    Section 4.3, Wood based panel products (1984)
BS 6375, Performance of windows
  Part 1, Classification for weathertightness (1989)
  Part 2, Specification for operation and strength characteristics
BS 6566, Plywood
  Part 1, Specification for the construction of panels and characteristics of plies, including markings (1985)

  Part 2, Glossary of terms (1985)
  Part 3, Specification for acceptance levels for post manufacture batch testing, including sampling (1985)
  Part 4, Specification for tolerances on the dimensions of plywood panels (1985)
  Part 5, Specification for moisture content (1985)
  Part 6, Specification for limits of defects for the classification of plywood by appearance (1985)
  Part 7, Specification for the classification of resistance to fungal decay and wood borer attack (1985)
  Part 8, Specification for bond performance of veneer plywood (1985)

CP 112, The structural use of timber (replaced by BS 5268: 1952)
  Part 2, Metric units (superseded by BS 5268: Part 2: 1971)
  Part 3, Trussed rafters for roofs of dwellings (replaced by BS 5268: Part 3)

DD 171, Guide to specifying performance requirements for hinged or pivoted doors (including test methods) (1987)

Other sources of information

BUILDING RESEARCH ESTABLISHMENT, The natural durability classification of timber, *Technical Note 40*, Princes Riseborough Laboratory, BRE, London (1979)
FIBRE BUILDING BOARD DEVELOPMENT ORGANIZATION LTD AND FURNITURE INDUSTRY RESEARCH ASSOCIATION, Medium density fibreboard (MDF), *FIDOR/FIRA Product Standard* (1983)
TIMBER RESEARCH AND DEVELOPMENT ASSOCIATION, *Timber in Construction*, BT Batsford Ltd/TRADA (1985)
Wood Information Sheets:
  1–6, Introduction to the specification of glued laminated members
  1–25, Introduction and supply of timber to BS 5268: Part 2
  1.29, Introduction to BS 5268: Part 3—trussed rafters
  1–33, The performance of joinery products
  2/3–10, Timbers—their properties and uses
  2/3–23, Introduction to wood-based panel products
  4.7, Guide to stress graded softwood
CARMICHAEL, E. N. *Timber Engineering*, E & F Spon (1984)

Overseas and International Standards

CANADIAN STANDARDS ASSOCIATION
  CAN 3-0188. 0-M78, Standard test methods for matformed wood particleboards and waferboards (1978)
  CAN 3-0188. 2-78, Waferboards (1978)
  CSA0121. Canadian Douglas fir plywood (1978)
  CSA0141, Softwood lumber (1970)
  CSA0151-M, Canadian softwood plywood (1978)
  National Lumber Grades Authority (NLGA). Standard grading rules for Canadian lumber (1980 + 1981 suppl.)

COMMISSION OF THE EUROPEAN COMMUNITIES, Common unified rules for timber structures *Eurocode No. 5* (1987)

NATIONAL BUREAU OF STANDARDS
  NBS PS1-83, Construction and industrial plywood
  NBS PS20-70, American softwood lumber standard
  National grading rules for softwood dimension lumber, NGRDL (1975)

51

Vermiculite

Edited by N C Clark
Mandoval Ltd

Contents

51.1 Introduction 51/3

51.2 Technical data 51/3

51.3 Exfoliated vermiculite 51/4

51.4 Health and safety aspects 51/4

51.5 Application of vermiculite in the building industry 51/4
    51.5.1 Applications in the UK building industry 51/4
    51.5.2 Loosefill applications 51/4
    51.5.3 Vermiculite plasters 51/5
    51.5.4 Fire protection 51/6
    51.5.5 Lightweight insulating concrete 51/7
    51.5.6 Bitumen-coated vermiculite 51/8
    51.5.7 Boards and panels 51/8

Acknowledgement 51/9

References 51/9

51.1 Introduction

Vermiculite is a member of the phyllosilicate group of minerals which embraces the chlorites, hydromicas and clay minerals. It is the geological name given to a group of hydrated laminar minerals which are magnesium aluminium iron silicates resembling mica in appearance (*Figure 51.1*). When subjected to heat, vermiculite has the unusual property of exfoliating, or expanding, due to the interlaminar generation of steam. Exfoliation produces a lightweight concertina-shaped granule (see *Figure 51.2*).

By exfoliation and/or other forms of processing, such as grinding, the bulk density, size and aspect ratio of vermiculite can be varied to suit its end-use. As it is inorganic, easy and safe to handle, sterile after exfoliation, and, chemically and thermally stable, vermiculite is increasingly used where health and safety are important. In addition, vermiculite, particularly in the exfoliated form, is odourless and mould resistant, as well as being non-combustible, insoluble in water and all organic solvents.

Vermiculite is a very versatile mineral with chemical and physical properties that can be exploited in a wide range of applications. In addition to its use in the building and construction industry, vermiculite is used in the horticultural, automotive, agricultural, refractory and foundry industries.

Vermiculite is generally mined by open-cast methods. Extraction and beneficiation methods differ according to the location of the mine and the nature of the vermiculite occurrence.

Figure 51.1 Sample of crude vermiculite

51.2 Technical data[1]

Vermiculite is found in various parts of the world, but the technical details given here relate to the Phalaborwa deposit which is the main source (about 95–100% of demand depending on country) for the European market. Palabora Mining Company vermiculite (Palabora vermiculite) as despatched from the mine consists of golden-brown flakes carefully classified into six grades, each having a specified range of particle sizes. The coarsest grade is principally between 16 and 5.6 mm, with the finest grade being between 0.710 and 0.180 mm.

Absorption capacity All grades of exfoliated vermiculite will retain liquids within the interlaminar voids of the individual particles as well as between the particles themselves. The absorption capacity varies according to grade and type of liquid: 1 l of exfoliated vermiculite has been found to absorb about 500 cm^3 of water.

Angle of repose (crude ore) This varies from 38° to 27° according to the grade and local conditions.

Aspect ratio In as-received ore this varies from 7:1 to 30:1, depending on grade. Chemical and mechanical processing can produce ratios of up to 200:1.

Cation exchange The exchangeable cation normally present in vermiculite is magnesium. The cation exchange capacity of Palabora vermiculite is up to 600 milliequivalents per kilogram. The rate of cation exchange is influenced by the specific surface. Therefore, exfoliated vermiculite has the highest rate of exchange.

Chemical analysis Vermiculite is a naturally occurring substance and its exact chemical composition varies from sample to sample and from mine to mine. When analysed chemically, crude and properly exfoliated vermiculite give the same values. The typical composition of vermiculite are given in *Table 51.1*.

Figure 51.2 Sample of exfoliated vermiculite

Table 51.1 Typical composition of vermiculite

Major constituents	Range (%)	Minor constituents	Content (%)
SiO_2	38.0–40.0	CaO	2.0
MgO	24.5–27.0	CO_2	1.5
Al_2O_3	8.0– 9.5	TiO_2	0.75
Fe_2O_3	5.0– 6.0	F	0.6
K_2	4.0– 6.0	CrO_3	0.15
H_2O	8.0–10.0	P_2O_5	0.06
		Cl	<0.05

Table 51.2 Typical loose bulk densities of exfoliated vermiculite that can be achieved with standard grades of Palabora vermiculite

Grade	Nominal particle size (crude) (mm)	Exfoliated loose bulk density (kg m^{-3})
Micron	−1.000 to +0.180	104–160
Superfine	−1.000 to +0.355	95–144
Fine	−2.800 to +0.710	88–122
Medium	−4.000 to +1.400	72–88
Large	−8.000 to +2.800	64–80
Premium	−16.000 to +5.600	56–72

Loose bulk density (crude ore) The loose bulk density of crude ore is typically between 600 and 1100 kg m^{-3} and varies according to grade and local conditions.

Melting point Collapse and coalescence of the individual flakes begins at 1330°C.

Mohs hardness The Mohs hardness factor of vermiculite is between 1 and 2.

Specific gravity The specific gravity of vermiculite is 2.5.

Specific heat The specific heat capacity of vermiculite is 1.08 kJ kg^{-1} K^{-1}.

Specific surface area The specific surface area of exfoliated vermiculite, as measured by the nitrogen absorption technique, is in the range 7.7–5.0 m^2 g^{-1} for the finest gradings.

Thermal conductivity of exfoliated vermiculite This is 0.062–0.065 W m^{-1} °C^{-1} under ambient conditions.

pH The pH of vermiculite is 8–9.5 depending on the grade and whether or not it is exfoliated.

Weight loss The weight loss of vermiculite at 105°C is 4.5–6.5% and at 950°C is 8.0–10.0%.

51.3 Exfoliated vermiculite

The majority of applications for vermiculite are in the exfoliated form. Commercial exfoliation of vermiculite is achieved by passing the crude vermiculite in a controlled manner through a furnace chamber of particular design. Exfoliation occurs at right angles to the cleavage planes, causing the flakes to expand into concertina-shaped granules.

The typical loose bulk densities and volume yields of the exfoliated product will vary depending on the origin of the vermiculite, the type of furnace used, the operating temperature, the efficiency of the vermiculite handling system and the rate of feed of the crude vermiculite into the furnace. The typical loose bulk densities that can be achieved with the standard grades of Palabora vermiculite are shown in *Table 51.2*.

51.4 Health and safety aspects[2]

Palabora vermiculite has been thoroughly tested to ensure that it does not constitute any known health hazard and a detailed dossier is available to support this point. Not all vermiculite sources can make such a categorical statement and offer to supply comprehensive data on health screening. It is advisable,

therefore, for users of vermicullte or vermiculite-containing products to specify Palabora vermiculite or obtain adequate assurance that the vermiculite employed has been properly tested for compliance with health and safety standards.

51.5 Applications of vermiculite in the building industry

The building and construction industry consumes the highest proportion of vermiculite supplies. It is estimated that over 90% of the vermiculite imported into the UK is destined for building applications.

The specific properties of vermiculite that are exploited in the building industry are:

(1) lightweight for density modification of boards, premixes and concrete;
(2) adhesion to a wide range of substrates when used in plasters and cementitious premixes. Exfoliated vermiculite gives the best possible mixture for plastering on concrete surfaces;
(3) fire resistance;
(4) thermal insulation;
(5) anti-condensation properties;
(6) resistance to cracking and stress absorption;
(7) ease of use; and
(8) acoustical modification.

51.5.1 Applications in the UK building industry

The applications of vermiculite in the UK building industry in 1989 are indicated by the following estimate of consumption

Loft insulation	6%
Fire resistant boards and panels	12%
Fire protection premixes	16%
Fire protection cladding	26%
Gypsum plaster premixes	31%
Loosefill/lightweight aggregate	4%
Gypsum boards	5%

51.5.2 Loosefill applications

Loosefill is a term applied to the use of exfoliated vermiculite in the simplest manner. This could be merely laying exfoliated vermiculite granules for a particular effect, or using it as a basic aggregate. Aspects of these uses are described in the following sections.

51.5.2.1 Loft insulation

For home insulation, loosefill vermiculite is laid between joists in lofts. The most widely used product for this application is large-grade exfoliated vermiculite under the brand 'MICAFIL' which is produced by Dupre Vermiculite of Hertford.

The free-flowing properties of exfoliated vermiculite make installation very simple. Exfoliated vermiculite granules are poured from the bag and levelled off. No cutting, shaping or folding is required and irregular shapes or variations in distances between joists are easily accommodated.

The insulating properties of vermiculite significantly reduce loss of heat in cold weather, and keep the interior of the building cool in hot weather; it also has good sound absorption characteristics. Most importantly for today's environmentally conscious markets, exfoliated vermiculite has no unpleasant side-effects, being a completely natural, fibre-free, non-irritant and non-toxic product. Installed in a loft, vermiculite is naturally fire resistant and contains no chemical additives to corrode electrical wiring or pipework. It will not sag, shrink, tear, crack or gape, nor will it affect timbers or attract vermin, and once installed, it keeps its full insulation characteristics indefinitely.

51.5.2.2 Vermiculite cavity-wall insulation

Vermiculite can be used as a cavity-wall insulation filling. However, as vermiculite tends to absorb moisture in humid conditions and then release the moisture as ambient conditions change, its use for this application in temperate latitudes is not recommended unless the exfoliated vermiculite particles have been adequately treated with a waterproofing agent.

51.5.2.3 Other loosefill uses

By virtue of its extreme versatility, exfoliated vermiculite has tended to become a dependable lightweight aggregate for many activities undertaken by builders in a wide range of applications that include lightweight insulating and fire resistant concrete, chimney insulation, insulation of domestic back boilers and flues, insulation of pipes in trenches, insulation and cushioning of plastic-lined swimming pools, farm-building insulation, and lightweight insulating roof and floor screeds, especially where there are load-bearing constraints. Some of these applications are explained in more detail below.

In this context, the extensive distribution network for MICAFIL and other exfoliated vermiculite products by Dupre Vermiculite has been a significant feature in enabling the widespread use of vermiculite as a general-purpose lightweight building aggregate.

51.5.3 Vermiculite plasters

Vermiculite plasters can be made with either gypsum or Portland cement and involve a simple mixture, usually as a factory premix, of exfoliated vermiculite and additives, as determined by the final service requirements. The advantages that all types of vermiculite plaster have over conventional types of plaster are listed below.

Light weight The dry weight of placed vermiculite plaster is less than half that of traditional sanded plaster. The lighter weight makes vermiculite plaster easier to mix, carry and apply.

Improved coverage Weight for weight a vermiculite plaster can cover a greater area when compared with plasters using denser aggregates such as sand.

Adhesion Adhesion is an exceptional feature of vermiculite plasters. Not only can they be used on all normal backgrounds but they can also be applied direct to concrete in a way that is not possible with any other type of plaster. Hacking of the

surface or the use of a special bonding agent is not necessary, provided that the concrete is clean and free of mould oil. However, certain concretes with a very high suction may require treatment with a bonding compound. Generally adhesion is improved by wetting the clean concrete prior to plastering.

Resistance to cracking Due to the ability of vermiculite to absorb local stresses, the cracking normally associated with ordinary sanded plasters is minimized. After application, vermiculite plasters are exceptionally stable within wide atmospheric limits. Vermiculite plasters will also accept nails and screws without cracking or spalling.

Workability Vermiculite plasters retain their fattiness, even on high-suction backgrounds, and can be easily worked. They accept all normal types of decoration.

Anticondensation As the surface of vermiculite plaster closely follows the temperature of the atmosphere, the risk of condensation is reduced. Sprayed applications which leave an open, textured, finish have been particularly successful in atmospheres of severe condensation such as those encountered in breweries, kitchens, swimming baths, etc.

Strength Vermiculite plasters are tough and resilient rather than hard. They will indent under impact without losing bond, rather than crack and fall away.

Thermal conductivity Vermiculite plasters have as much as two to three times the insulating capacity of traditional plasters, and this feature, combined with their low thermal capacity, reduces the rate at which heat is lost through walls and ceilings, and enables comfortable living and working temperatures to be reached quickly. This is particularly important in rooms that are only in intermittent use. In addition, pattern staining caused by heat loss through the ceiling is eliminated.

Vermiculite plasters, whether gypsum or cement based, can be applied by hand or by spraying machine. Being a non-abrasive aggregate, vermiculite is well suited to spray application. In its widest sense the term 'plasters' can refer, as on the Continent, to any coating product that is wetted up and finally prepared on site for application to surfaces such as walls, ceilings, beams or columns. In this context there are four main areas of application for 'plasters' containing vermiculite.

51.5.3.1 Internal walls

The traditionally accepted usage of the term 'plaster' implies a gypsum or Portland-cement based coating that is applied to internal walls to provide a final smooth coating before decoration. Vermiculite has been used for many years as an aggregate in British Gypsum's 'Carlite' range of plasters. 'Exfoliated vermiculite gives the best possible mixture for plastering on concrete surfaces and is, therefore, the aggregate in Carlite Bonding Coat. A percentage of Vermiculite is also present in Carlite metal lathing plaster and a fine grade has been retained in Carlite Finish' (British Gypsum, Green Book on Plastering). Apart from standard plaster products such as those in British Gypsum's Carlite range, vermiculite is employed in certain products of a number of other European plaster manufacturers, especially where difficult and porous substrates are involved.

Although the main use of vermiculite in this area of application is related to factory-made premixes, there continue to be occasions where vermiculite is used as the aggregate in a site-prepared mix. The following mixes are recommended for normal purposes, but both richer and leaner mixes may be used to meet special requirements.

Undercoat: 1–2 volumes exfoliated vermiculite (fine or superfine grade); 1 volume gypsum plaster.

Finishing coat: 1 volume exfoliated vermiculite (superfine grade); 3 volumes gypsum plaster.

51.5.3.2 Acoustical modification

Spray-applied premixed preparations of exfoliated vermiculite and mineral binders have been developed to provide a decorative acoustic plaster with a proven history of successful sound control. For ceilings such a plaster presents an unbroken soffit as an alternative to the repeated pattern of a panelled ceiling. The physical properties derived from the inclusion of vermiculite make vermiculite acoustical plasters valuable for anticondensation treatments in places such as swimming pools and kitchens.

51.5.3.3 External cladding

The use of vermiculite for external claddings has been revitalized with a comparatively new development which was pioneered in France during the 1980s. Exfoliated vermiculite is incorporated in factory premixed preparations for spray application to the outside of domestic buildings, especially where an external heat-insulation layer has been added. This application, which is a variation of 'stucco', employs about 6% by weight of vermiculite to replace sand, and provides advantages not only for the technical improvement of the product in application, but also transport economies derived from the lighter weight.

51.5.3.4 Fire protection

As fire protection is a highly specialized field it is considered in more detail in the following section.

51.5.4 Fire protection[3]

Vermiculite is recognized as a material particularly suited for fire protection. Vermiculite-based products range from factory-made boards and panels to premixed coatings which can be applied by either mechanical spray application or by hand plastering techniques.

51.5.4.1 Vermiculite fire protection for use under cellulosic fire conditions

The method by which a vermiculite fire-protection product will meet a specific fire rating is based on the approved method of calculation or listing in the country concerned. Calculations for steel protection are normally based on the concept that the thickness required varies as a function of the exposed surface area to cross-sectional area of the steel section. This function may be referred to as Hp/A, U/F, P/A and is usually expressed in units of m⁻¹. In the UK structures have been tested, coated with vermiculite cement under the fire-resistance conditions specified in BS 476: Parts 20–22: 1987[4] (an update of Part 8: 1972). Other countries have slightly different test standards. For example, ASTM E119[5] in the USA, DIN 4102: Part 2[6] in West Germany and NEN 3884[7] in Holland, but most of these standards are based on, or are broadly in accordance with, the international fire testing standard ISO R834.[8] The above-stated fire tests are sometimes referred to as cellulosic fire tests as the time/temperature curve developed during the test is considered to be approximately the same as that developed by cellulosic material, e.g. timber, under reasonable combustion conditions (see *Figure 51.3*).

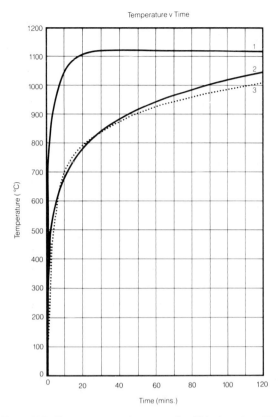

Temperature v Time

Figure 51.3 Temperature vs. time curves for: (1) hydrocarbon; (2) BS 476;[4] (3) ASTM E1192.[5]

51.5.4.2 High rise hydrocarbon fuelled fire conditions

The conditions imposed upon a structural fire-protection material within petrochemical and off-shore marine environments can be significantly more onerous than those to be found within the building industry (see *Figure 51.4*). Fire protection is typically provided to combat the heat input from one of the following three types of fire.

(1) An intense torching fire of impinging flame such as may occur from a high-pressure gas or vapour leak with turbulent premixing with air from a leaking flange. This could produce a heat flux of up to 250 kW m⁻² with flame temperatures of up to 1600°C.

(2) An enveloping fire from a flammable liquid pool fire (which typically has a heat flux of approximately 120–150 kW m⁻² with flame temperatures of 1000–1200°C).

(3) Radiant heat from an adjacent fire.

In the case of torching fires, whilst they will probably be much smaller than pool fires they are more intense and can cause rapid failure where they impinge directly on a vessel or structure. Significant radiant and convective heat will also be generated from a torching fire.

51.5.4.3 Fire protection—premixes for spray or trowelled application

Vermiculite, when combined with Portland cement in the form of a factory controlled premix, affords a number of desirable properties. Specially developed products are available for both the cellulosic and the more arduous requirements of the hydrocarbon fuelled fire.

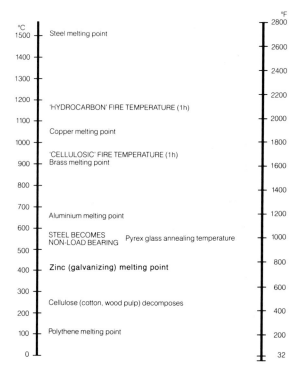

°C		°F
1500	Steel melting point	2800
1400		2600
1300		2400
1200		2200
1100	'HYDROCARBON' FIRE TEMPERATURE (1h)	2000
1000	Copper melting point	1800
900	'CELLULOSIC' FIRE TEMPERATURE (1h) Brass melting point	1600
800		1400
700	Aluminium melting point	1200
600	STEEL BECOMES NON-LOAD BEARING Pyrex glass annealing temperature	1000
500		800
400	Zinc (galvanizing) melting point	600
300	Cellulose (cotton, wood pulp) decomposes	400
200		
100	Polythene melting point	200
0		32

Figure 51.4 Conditions imposed on a structural fire-protection material within petrochemical and off-shore marine environments

Vermiculite cement is a term that has become commonly accepted as relating to the mixture of exfoliated vermiculite and Portland cement in both the dry (premix) and installed (concrete) stages. It tends to relate to dry premixes manufactured in factory-controlled conditions and which are prepared with additives for application, usually by spraying after wetting up and final mixing on site. The term 'vermiculite cement' is usually used in the context of fire-protection premixes.

Portland cement is used as a binder in vermiculite cement due to its water of hydration which, when mixed and installed, releases steam in a fire, cooling the layers between the steam generation front and the fire. Once all the water of hydration is used up, the resulting 'dry' vermiculite/cement coating acts as a thermal insulant.

51.5.4.4 Specific properties of vermiculite cement

Bonding properties of vermiculite cement The bonding properties of a vermiculite cement allow it to be applied directly to a wide variety of substrates and enable the application of considerable thicknesses without, in the majority of cases, the need for additional light-gauge-mesh retention. Application can be to unprimed or most alkali-resistant-primed steelwork and, being of a Portland cement base, vermiculite cement will not cause corrosion. In the short term a vermiculite cement will inhibit corrosion whilst its alkalinity is maintained.

Dimensional stability of vermiculite cement The properties of vermiculite enable the applied material to accommodate induced stress arising from widely varying and extreme conditions of exposure both in service, i.e. from changes in loading and moisture, and in fire conditions, i.e. the effects of hot and cold thermal shock. The ability of vermiculite to relieve stress by volume change means that the fire protection can stay in place during a fire even when subjected to impingement from fire water systems.

Since building regulations, as they apply to fire protection, are concerned only with life safety, the requirements they make upon fire resistance do not ensure that the parts of the structure will be fit for use after a fire. From the insurance point of view, however, the use of forms of construction which do not suffer irredeemable damage is relevant. Spray-applied vermiculite cement when exposed to a short-duration fire relative to the fire rating, can survive to provide a significant continuing measure of protection, despite the action of water deluge from, for example, a fireman's hose and other fire extinguishing media.

Durability of vermiculite cement Structures protected by materials which can be easily damaged by impact or abrasion may not be able to provide the protection intended in design when a fire occurs because damage makes the construction substandard in respect of fire resistance. Impact will not cause vermiculite-cement coatings applied *in situ* to become detached and will only cause local damage which will not affect the overall protection of the coating to any significant extent. This ability to indent under impact rather than crack or shatter is due to the ability of vermiculite to absorb local stresses.

51.5.4.5 Fire protection—cladding

Boards incorporating vermiculite are produced by a variety of different methods of manufacture for use as cladding to provide fire protection for (mostly) structural steelwork. The methods of manufacture are described in Section 51.5.7.

Fire-protection cladding is achieved by sawing and cutting boards of a particular thickness previously determined to provide the duration of fire protection required. A 4-h fire rating can be achieved by using vermiculite cladding. The prepared boards are fixed in place using a variety of methods that can include gluing (bonding *in situ*), screwing and/or stapling. In addition, cladding boards can be easily worked by planing and drilling.

51.5.5 Lightweight insulating concrete

Vermiculite concrete is light, insulating and fire resistant. It is simply made by mixing vermiculite, Portland cement and water, plus additives such as a plasticizer if desired. The ratio of exfoliated vermiculite to cement and the grade of vermiculite can be varied according to the properties of strength and insulation required of the concrete. There is less compaction and a higher yield when using a finer grading, and mixes made with these grades are more easily pumped. Vermiculite concrete can be cut, sawn, nailed or screwed. The lower density vermiculite concrete screeds are usually covered with a sand:cement topping mixed 4:1 or 5:1 to a minimum depth of 25 mm; screed and topping should, ideally, be laid monolithically to prevent shear fracturing between the topping and the screed. Alternatively, an unbonded topping of 50 mm or more can be used.

Vermiculite concrete can be easily mixed and placed on site, by hand and/or by mechanical equipment. The cement and water should be mixed first to form a slurry. Precise quantities of water should be used as it is important not to over-wet the vermiculite. The exfoliated vermiculite is poured into the slurry and mixed rapidly with a minimum of mechanical action to ensure complete coating of the vermiculite particles. It is important not to overmix as this can lead to undue compaction, higher density and balling up.

Site-mixed vermiculite concrete tends to be used for *in situ* floor and roof screeds, fabrication of precast products and

Table 51.3 Typical physical properties of vermiculite concrete

Vermiculite: cement (vol.)	Air dry density* (kg m^{-3})	Minimum 28-day cube strength (N mm^{-2})	Thermal conductivity† (W m^{-1} °C^{-1})	Drying shrinkage (%)
8:1	400	0.70	0.094	0.35
6:1	480	0.95	to	to
4:1	560	1.23	0.158	0.45

* Low density = 320–800 kg m^{-3}.
† Thermal insulation: $k = 0.086$ to 0.234 W m^{-1} °C^{-1}; 0.074 to 0.200 kcal m m^{-2} h^{-1} °C^{-1}. Note that thermal insulation is a function of bulk density (see text).

insulating mixes around back boilers and fire-back supports. It can also be used for swimming pool bases.

Typical physical properties of vermiculite concrete are listed in *Table 51.3*. Note that the thermal insulation value is a function of bulk density and particle size, generally the lighter the mix, the greater the thermal insulation value. When the same volume of different grades of exfoliated vermiculite are incorporated into a standard mix, the final density (and, therefore, the thermal insulation) will be influenced by the fact that the finer the grade of vermiculite the denser the product. Conversely, a mix based on Large- or Fnegrade exfoliated vermiculite and made to the same final bulk density will have the same thermal insulation value at ambient temperatures but at high temperatures the smaller particle concrete will be more insulating as there will be less thermal diffusion.

Vermiculite concrete is also non-combustible, easily laid to falls, suitable for flat roots and shell and barrel vault roofs, provides a permanent non-warping basis for surfacing materials, covers surface pipes and irregularities in the floor or roof slab, and requires no special equipment or techniques for application.

Some special considerations regarding the use of vermiculite concrete should be borne in mind. Moisture entrapped in a roof such as constructional water, rainwater or condensation, is a potential source of problems like blistering and ceiling stains and will detract from the insulating value of a screed. Consideration should therefore always be given to measures which allow the free water or moisture to escape. These include the drilling of the roof slab at low points, the installation of ventilators in the asphalt or felt roofing and the complete venting of the screed by means of ducts and ventilators.

Vermiculite concrete compresses up to 35% without disintegrating. This property has been utilized in mines where vermiculite concrete has been used to fill cavities and to build ventilation walls. These walls deform and compress without shattering when under pressure from the surrounding strata.

51.5.6 Bitumen-coated vermiculite

Vermiculite, coated and bound with a bituminous binder, is used to manufacture a dry lightweight screed mix that has low thermal conductivity, low moisture content and can be easily placed.

Bitumen vermiculite is an established product on the Continent, particularly in Switzerland, France and Germany. Its use has not, so far, developed significantly in the UK building market. It is used mainly in renovation work for the levelling, damp-proofing and sound-proofing of old floors, whether wooden or solid. The material is simply poured out and spread over the floor area, lightly compressed and finished with an appropriate floor surfacing material.

51.5.7 Boards and panels

Boards and panels are one of the most significant outlets for crude vermiculite and its potential in this area of application has been enhanced by the need to replace asbestos in a range of products. Vermiculite boards and panels are used in four main areas:

(1) fire protection cladding;
(2) ceiling tiles;
(3) partitioning; and
(4) general building uses where lightweight construction and limitation of the spread of flame are required.

The essential advantages of the presence of vermiculite in a board or panel product are that it contributes towards lighter weight and endows the product with properties of fire resistance. Moreover, vermiculite can be used in existing processes with only minimal disruption, e.g. chipboard/autoclaving.

51.5.7.1 Methods of manufacturing and product types

There are four basic methods of manufacturing boards with vermiculite.

Autoclaving[9] This method essentially involves the use of equipment of existing or former asbestos board producers. The process involves the following stages.

(1) Mixing an aqueous slurry composed mainly of:
    (a) an inorganic binder that is water settable, consisting of a calcium silicate binder, Portland cement, aluminous cement and blast-furnace-slag cement;
    (b) a fibrous reinforcing material (not asbestos) that is cellulosic (organic); and
    (c) a filler material (exfoliated vermiculite 12–50% by weight).
(2) Formation of a board from the aqueous slurry by means of any one of a variety of known processes of dewatering:
    (a) Hatschek process;
    (b) Magnani process;
    (c) use of a simple press; or
    (d) Fourdriner process.
(3) Setting-off and hardening the binder or cement by:
    (a) autoclaving (e.g. for calcium silicate);
    (b) air curing or steam heating (inorganic cement).
(4) Maturing and drying as necessary.

Compression Exfoliated vermiculite can be mixed with a binder in a process that is very similar to manufacturing chipboard. The general outline of this method is as follows.

(1) Coating granules of exfoliated vermiculite with a binder that may be organic or inorganic.
(2) Placing coated granules in a press to form a basic board shape.
(3) Placing moulded granules in a second press and compressing with heat to bond granules and binder further.
(4) Maturing the product formed in (3).

The type of board that can be produced by this basic method can be further distinguished by the type of binder employed. There are three binder types:

(1) Inorganic, e.g. sodium silicate;
(2) organic, e.g. urea formaldehyde and/or phenol formaldehyde; and
(3) other binders that may include a combination of (1) and (2) above.

The process can also involve the inclusion of fibrous reinforcing material.

The principle of adding a binder to exfoliated vermiculite in this manner can also be used for applying a thin vermiculite layer to the surface of a combustible board (e.g. chipboard) to provide improved fire resistance.

Plasterboard Vermiculite is used in its crude form in a special type of gypsym plasterboard designed to maintain its mechanical integrity during a fire. The product was originally patented by US Gypsum[10] and the consumption of vermiculite in this application has grown significantly in Europe since the patent has lapsed and market acceptability of the product has grown.

A very fine grading of vermiculite, principally the Palabora micron grade in Europe, is mixed into the gypsum slurry during the formation of the plasterboard. The crude vermiculite exfoliates during a fire to compensate for the shrinkage of gypsum at high temperature.

Simple mixture of vermiculite and a wet-mixed binder A board product can be simply made by mixing exfoliated vermiculite with a wet-mixed binder such as Portland cement or gypsum and forming and curing into a board shape. In the UK the most established use of this type of board is in fire-protection cladding of structural steel for internal service using gypsum as a binder.

Acknowledgement

The contribution of Mr W. Butcher to this chapter is gratefully acknowledged.

References

1 Technical data on Palabora vermiculite have principally been obtained by tests carried out or commissioned by Mandoval Ltd during the period 1988–90 and represents the latest information available. Whilst every effort has been made to ensure the accuracy of the data presented, Mandoval will not accept any liability that may arise from the use of this information.

2 Mandoval's dossier *Health Aspects of Vermiculite* is a collection of reports including: 'Carcinogenic screening of vermiculite (two year study in rats)', *Report No. 4238/71/396*, 'Evaluation of the tumorigenic potential of vermiculite by interpleural injection in rats', HUNTER, B. and THOMPSON, C., Huntington Research Centre; *British Journal of Industrial Medicine*, **30**, 167–173 (1973); 'Examination of vermiculite for the presence of asbestos fibres', *Report No. 22056-2*, The Ontario Research Foundation, October 1979.

3 For more information on fire protection in buildings readers are recommended to consult: *Yellow Book—Fire Protection for Structural Steel in Buildings*, The Association of Structural Fire Protection Contractors and Manufacturers Ltd. (ASTFPCM), P.O. Box 111, Aldershot, Hampshire GU11 1YW.

4 BRITISH STANDARDS INSTITUTION, *BS 476, Fire tests on building materials and structures*, Milton Keynes, Parts 20–22 (1987).

5 AMERICAN SOCIETY FOR TESTING MATERIALS, *ASTM E119, Standard methods of fire tests of building construction and materials*, Philadelphia (1979).

6 DEUTCHES INSTITUT FUR NORMUNG, *DIN 4012 Fire behaviour of building materials and building components*, Berlin (1981).

7 NEN 3884.

8 INTERNATIONAL ORGANIZATION FOR STANDARDIZATION, *ISO R834 Fire resistance tests—elements of building construction*, Geneva (1975).

9 Autoclaved boards containing vermiculite have been solely produced by the Cape Group Companies, Cape Boards Ltd and Cape Industrial Products Ltd. The process and board details are best understood from reading the *U.K. Patent No. 1498966*, published 25 January 1978 (*U.S. Patent 4132555 2.01.79*).

10 *United States Patent No. 3454456*, 8 July 1969.

Index

Abrasion resistance
  concretes, **23**/9
  polymers, **38**/8, **44**/7
Abrasive blasting (of steel), **31**/3
  dry blasting, **31**/3
  wet blasting, **31**/4
Absorbent surfaces
  painting of, **33**/1
  see also Concrete; Plaster; Timber
Accelerators
  concrete, **15**/21
    benefits of, **15**/23
    chemical types of, **15**/23
    historical background, **15**/21
    mechanism of acceleration, **15**/21
    relationship to ionic mobility of salts, **15**/22
    in sprayed concrete, **15**/23, **24**/4
    standards/specifications for, **15**/15, **15**/19, **15**/23
    types of, **15**/22
  thermosetting resin, **46**/13
Acid/alkali resistance, glass-fibre reinforced cement, **20**/11
Acid attack on stone, **49**/5
Acid cleaners (for stone), **33**/3, **49**/13
Acoustic insulation materials
  asbestos-based materials, **9**/11
  concrete blockwork, **17**/10
  mineral-fibre products, **30**/6, **30**/7, **30**/19
  vermiculite plasters, **51**/6
  see also Sound insulation...
Acoustic pressure, meaning of term, **30**/12
Acoustic properties
  definitions used, **30**/11
  elastomers, **37**/4
  mineral-fibre products, **30**/13
  polymers, **37**/4, **38**/8
Acrylic–ester resins, **46**/9
  advantages/disadvantages of, **46**/13
  applications of, **46**/9
  as concrete plasticizers, **15**/11
  cross-linking of, **46**/10
  dispersions containing, **39**/7
  production of, **46**/9, **46**/10
Acrylic paints, **33**/8
Acrylic polymer coatings, **33**/10
Acrylic polymers, **38**/3
  acoustic properties of, **38**/8
  applications of, **38**/3, **38**/4, **38**/5
  chemical properties of, **38**/3
  crazing susceptibility of, **38**/5
  dispersions containing, **39**/7, **39**/8
  effect of rate/duration of loading, **38**/5
  elastic modulus of, **38**/8
    effect of temperature/load duration, **38**/6
  electrical properties of, **38**/9
  fabrication of, **38**/3
  fire safety of, **38**/7, **38**/9

Acrylic polymers (*cont.*)
  GRC modified by, **20**/4
  historical background for, **36**/4
  impact properties of, **38**/3, **38**/7, **38**/8
  maximum allowable stress for, **38**/6
  mechanical properties of, **38**/3, **38**/5, **38**/6, **38**/8
  optical properties of, **38**/9
  serviceability of, **38**/3
  temperature effects on, **38**/5, **38**/7
  thermal expansion/contraction of, **38**/3, **38**/7, **38**/8
  thermal properties of, **38**/3, **38**/8, **38**/9
  weathering of, **38**/5, **38**/6
Acrylonitrile–butadiene rubbers *see* Nitrile rubbers
Active coatings, steels protected by, **5**/32
Adhesives, **8**/1
  applications of, **8**/5
  durability testing of, **8**/8
  in laminated-timber members, **50**/24
  limitations of site-applied adhesives, **8**/4
  performance testing of, **8**/5
  in plywood, **50**/18
  steel plates bonded to concrete using, **8**/6, **8**/12
  surface treatment for, **8**/4
  tiles fixed by, **13**/13, **13**/14
  timber joints fixed by, **50**/22
Admiralty brass, **7**/14
Admixtures
  concrete, **14**/6, **15**/1
  glass-fibre reinforced cement, **20**/4
  renders/screeds, **21**/7
  see also Accelerators; Air-entraining agents; Corrosion inhibitors; Permeability reducers; Plasticizers; Retarders; Superplasticizers; Water–reducing agents
Adverse weather conditions
  mortars used in, **21**/5
  road laying in, **10**/23
Aerated concrete blocks, **17**/4
  manufacture of, **17**/5, **17**/6
  plastering of, **35**/5
AFRP (aramid fibre reinforced plastic), **44**/9
  see also Aramid fibres
Aggregate abrasion value (AAV) test, **10**/28
  maximum values allowable, **10**/33
  typical values for, **10**/28
Aggregate crushing value (ACV) test, **10**/28
  typical values for, **10**/28
Aggregate impact (AIV) test, **10**/29
  typical values for, **10**/28
Aggregates, **14**/6, **16**/1
  alkali–aggregate reactivity of, **16**/15
    tests for, **16**/17

Aggregates (*cont.*)
  arid-zone aggregates, **16**/3
    crushed-rock aggregates, **16**/6
    natural-sand aggregates, **16**/7
  in bentonite–cement slurries, **48**/12
  in bituminous materials, **10**/3
  chalk in, **16**/8
  chloride content of, **16**/11, **16**/12
  clay in, **16**/10
  in concrete, **14**/6, **16**/1
  density of, **16**/14
  dewatering of, **16**/6
  durability of, **16**/14
  dust/fines in, **16**/10
  exposure in concrete finishes, **14**/15
  flakiness of, **10**/29
  frost resistance of, **16**/15
  in glass-fibre reinforced cement, **20**/4
  grading of, **14**/6, **16**/12
  impurities in, **16**/8
  lightweight aggregates, **14**/6, **16**/19
  mechanical properties of, **16**/14
  micas in, **16**/9
  in mortars, **21**/3
  organic impurities in, **16**/8
  particle shape of, **16**/14
  petrographic classification of, **16**/8, **16**/9, **16**/16, **16**/17
  physical properties of, **16**/12
    tests for, **10**/28
    typical values for road use, **10**/28
  processing of, **16**/4
  in renders/screeds, **21**/5, **21**/7
  requirements for use with bituminous materials, **10**/27
  salt weathering of, **16**/15
  scrubbing of, **16**/6
  sea-dredged aggregates, **16**/3
  shell content of, **16**/10
  silt in, **16**/10
  sizing of, **16**/6
  sources of, **16**/3
  in sprayed concrete, **24**/4
  sulphate content of, **16**/12
  sulphide minerals in, **16**/8
  surface texture of, **16**/14
  testing of, **10**/27
    standards for, **16**/13, **16**/17
  types of, **16**/8
  water absorption of, **16**/14
  see also Lightweight...; Middle East aggregates
Aglite (lightweight aggregate), **16**/19, **16**/21
Agrèment certificates
  glass-fibre-reinforced cement, **20**/26
  mineral-fibre products, **30**/17
  polymers, **41**/5
Agricultural products, glass-fibre reinforced cement used, **20**/16, **20**/18

Air assisted spraying (of paint), 33/4
Air drying coatings, aluminium and alloys, 2/25
Air entraining agents
  silica-fume concretes, 23/7
  standards/specifications for, 15/8, 15/9
  types of, 15/6
  use of, 15/6
Air entrainment (in concrete/mortar)
  benefits of, 15/3
  effect of cement substitutes, 15/7
  factors affecting, 15/7
  historical background, 15/3
  measurement of air for, 15/8
  mechanism of, 15/5
  recommended levels in various mix
    designs, 15/7
  spacing factor relationships, 15/4
  in sprayed concrete, 24/4
  strength of concrete affected by, 15/8
Air permeance, glass-fibre reinforced cement,
  20/12
Air void test (for bituminous materials), 10/26
Airborne-sound insulation, 30/12
  mineral-fibre products used, 30/13, 30/19
Airless spraying (of paint), 33/5
Alkali–aggregate reaction (AAR), 14/13, 16/15
  tests for, 16/17
Alkali–carbonate reaction (ACR), 16/15
Alkali–silica reaction (ASR), 16/15, 18/10
  reduction of occurence, 18/11, 47/5
Alkali–silicate reaction, 16/15
Alkaline cleaners (for stone), 33/3, 49/13
Alkyd paints, 5/33, 5/34, 33/8
  epoxy ester/alkyd paints, 33/8
  historical background for, 36/4
Alkyd-resin paints, 31/5
Aluminious cements, 18/11
  composition of, 18/11
  hydration of, 18/11
  manufacture of, 18/11
  properties of concrete, 18/11
Aluminium, 2/1
  abundance in Earth's crust, 7/3
  alloying of, 2/7
  chemical resistance of, 2/18
  electrolytic reduction of, 2/4
  extruded sections, 2/6, 2/14
  extrusion of, 2/5
  fabrication processes for, 2/4, 2/5
  food applications of, 2/18
  manufacture of, 2/3
  oxygen affinity of, 2/18
  properties of, 2/12, 2/14, 2/16, 2/17, 37/4, 38/7
  reflectivity of, 2/18
  rolling of, 2/5
  sources of, 2/3
  thermite sparking involving, 2/18
  tubes, 2/6, 2/14, 2/15
Aluminium alloy castings
  mechanical properties of, 2/16
  production of, 2/4
Aluminium alloy extruded sections, 2/6, 2/14
Aluminium alloy forgings, 2/27
  mechanical properties of, 2/7, 2/18
Aluminium alloy plate, 2/27
Aluminium alloy sheet, 2/27
Aluminium alloy structural sections, 2/26
Aluminium alloy tubes, 2/6, 2/14, 2/15, 2/27
Aluminium (and) alloys, 2/1
  acoustic properties of, 37/4
  alloying elements in, 2/8
  alloys listed, 2/21
  annealing of, 2/8
  anodizing of, 2/25
  availability of materials, 2/26
  bearing strength of, 2/16
  bending/forming of, 2/23
  blanking of, 2/23

Aluminium (and) alloys (cont.)
  casting of, 2/4
  castings, 2/27
  chemical composition of, 2/10, 2/11
  classification of, 2/7, 2/8
    alphanumerical designation, 2/8
    numerical designation, 2/8
  corrosion resistance of, 2/18
  creep properties of, 2/18
  cutting of, 2/23
  density of, 2/17, 37/4
  dielectric properties of, 2/18
  drilling of, 2/23
  ductility of, 2/18
  elastic modulus of, 2/17, 37/4
  electrical properties of, 2/17, 37/4
  elevated-temperature properties of, 2/18
  extruded sections, 2/27
  extrusion of, 2/5
  fabrication processes for, 2/4, 2/5, 2/23
  fasteners used, 2/25
  fatigue strength of, 2/18
  finishes used, 2/25
  fire resistance of, 2/18
  forging of, 2/7
  hardness of, 2/16, 37/4
  heat-treatable alloys, 2/7
    materials selection, 2/21
  impact strength of, 2/16, 45/6
  low-temperature properties of, 2/18
  magnetic properties of, 2/18
  mechanical properties of, 2/10, 2/12, 2/14,
    2/16, 2/17, 37/4
  melting point of, 2/18
  non-heat-treatable alloys, 2/7
    materials selection for, 2/22
  painting of, 2/19, 2/20, 2/21, 2/25
    pretreatment required, 2/19, 2/25
  physical properties of, 2/17
  properties of, 2/12, 2/14, 2/16, 2/17, 2/19, 37/4
  protection from
    metal-to-metal contacts, 2/20
    non-metallic contact, 2/21
  protection methods used, 2/19
  rolling of, 2/5
  shear strength of, 2/16
  standard products, 2/26
  standards for, 2/12, 2/14, 2/16, 2/27
  superplastic forming of, 2/7
  temper designations for, 2/9
  thermal conductivity of, 2/17, 37/4
  thermal expansion of, 2/17, 37/4
  types of alloys, 2/7
  welding of, 2/23
    filler metals used, 2/24
Aluminium brass, 7/14
Aluminium bronzes, 7/16
  alpha alloys, 7/17
  corrosion resistance of, 7/8
  mechanical properties of, 7/16
  phase diagram for, 7/16
  photomicrograph of, 7/18
  two-phase alloys, 7/17
Ammonium polyphosphates (in intumescent
  coatings), 34/11
  crystal types of, 34/11
Amosite (brown asbestos)
  airborne-fibre control limits, 9/14
  applications of, 9/12
  properties of, 9/14
  world production data, 9/6
Anodizing of aluminium and alloys, 2/25
Anticlasic bearings, PTFE-based, 42/5
Antisun glass, 29/9, 29/11
Aramid fibres, 44/1
  abrasion resistance of, 44/7
  applications of, 44/8
  chemical resistance of, 44/7

Aramid fibres (cont.)
  compressive strength of, 44/7
  concrete reinforced using, 44/9
  creep properties of, 44/4
  environmental resistance of, 44/7
  fatigue properties of, 44/6, 44/7
  historical background for, 44/3
  impact properties of, 44/6
  production of, 44/3
  properties of, 44/4
  pultruded sections, 44/8, 44/9
  shock-loading resistance of, 44/7
  stress–strain curves for, 44/4, 44/5
  stress-rupture properties of, 44/5
  temperature effects on, 44/7
  tensile properties of, 44/4
  thermal expansion of, 44/8
  trade names for, 44/3
Arapee (aramid fibres in resin), 44/9
Arc resistance, PTFE, 42/3
Architectural features
  concrete blockwork used, 17/4
  glass-fibre reinforced cement used, 20/16,
    20/19
Arkose (rock), 16/9
Asbestos, 9/1
  airborne-fibre control limits, 9/14
  applications of, 9/5, 9/6
  health effects of, 9/14
  historical background for, 9/4
  legislation covering, 9/13
  maintenance aspects, 9/16
  milling of, 9/4
  mining/extraction methods, 9/4
  properties of, 9/3
  removal of, 9/16
    safety procedures, 9/17
  types of, 9/3
  world production data, 9/5
Asbestos acoustic insulation materials,
  9/11
Asbestos cement products, 9/7
  British Standards for, 9/7
  encapsulation of, 9/16
  rainwater goods, 9/8
  sheeting, 9/8
  slates, 9/8, 25/20
  see also Fibre–cement slates
Asbestos fibre reinforced concrete, 14/7
Asbestos insulating board, 9/9
  encapsulation of, 9/16
  proprietary names for, 9/10
Asbestos jointing materials, 9/12
Asbestos (Licensing) Regulations (1984),
  9/13
Asbestos paper products, 9/12
Asbestos products
  British Standards for, 9/7
  encapsulation of, 9/16
Asbestos (Prohibitions) Regulations (1985),
  9/14
Asbestos Regulations (1969), 9/13
Asbestos related illnesses, 9/14, 9/15, 14/7
Asbestos (sprayed) coatings, 9/11
Asbestos textile products, 9/6
  British Standards for, 9/7
  replacement alternatives, 9/6
Asbestos thermal insulation materials, 9/10
Asbestosis, 9/14, 14/7
Asphalt base courses, 10/8
  subgrade stress affected by, 10/8
Asphalt paving machines
  insulated hopper sides used, 10/18, 10/19
  materials flow in, 10/18, 10/19
  thickness control in, 10/20
  width control in, 10/20
Asphalt regulating courses, 10/9
Asphalt road bases, 10/8

Asphalt wearing courses, **10**/3
  design-type mixes, **10**/4
  recipe mixes, **10**/3
  rock fines in, **10**/4
  sand in, **10**/3
Asphalts, **10**/3
  corkboard used with, **26**/5
  design-type mixes, **10**/4
    examples, **10**/30
  durability of, factors affecting, **10**/7
  fatigue resistance of, **10**/7
  manufacturing of, **10**/14
  medium-temperature asphalts, **10**/9, **10**/23
  mix design process for, **10**/4
  testing of, **9**/12
ASTM Standards
  concrete admixtures, **15**/8, **15**/14, **15**/18, **15**/19
  elastomers, **37**/20, **37**/21
  glass-fibre reinforced cement, **20**/26
Attapulgite (clay), **48**/4
Austenite, **5**/9
Austenitic stainless steels, **5**/8, **5**/21
Autoclaving
  calcium silicate bricks, **11**/3, **11**/5
  concrete blocks, **17**/5, **17**/6
  vermiculite boards/panels, **51**/8

Babbitt metals, **7**/32
Bainite, **5**/9
Barrier coatings, steels protected by, **5**/32
Barytite X-ray plasters, **35**/4
Base courses (in roads)
  asphalts, **10**/8
  macadams, **10**/11
Basic oxygen process (steelmaking), **5**/4
Basquin law, **5**/26
Bauxite
  deposits mapped, **2**/3
  refining of, **2**/3
Bayer process, **2**/3
Beam flexure tests, sprayed fibre concrete, **24**/12
Bearing metals, tin-containing, **7**/32
Bearing strength, aluminium and alloys, **2**/16
Bearings
  PTFE-based, **42**/4
    design of, **42**/5
    mating surface for, **42**/5
Beetles, timber attacked by, **32**/3
Bending and forming processes
  aluminium and alloys, **2**/23
  steels, **5**/6
Bending moment resistance, clay pipes, **12**/7, **12**/10
Bending strength
  cast iron, **3**/5
  glass reinforced plastics, **45**/7
Bent glass, **29**/15
  examples of use, **29**/15
Bentonite, **48**/4
  hydration of, **48**/8
  specification for, **48**/21
Bentonite–cement slurries
  aggregates in, **48**/12
  cement in, **48**/4
  clay in, **48**/4
  composition of, **48**/7
  mixing of, **48**/7
  sampling of, **48**/16
  self-hardening slurries, **48**/12
  see also Slurries
Bentonite–cement–water system, phase diagram for, **48**/7
Beryllium bronzes, **7**/17
Besab (sprayed concrete) system, **24**/7
Bessemer (steelmaking) process, **5**/4, **5**/13

Bethell (timber treatment) process, **32**/6
Bimetallic corrosion
  steels, **5**/31
  see also Galvanic corrosion
Binder courses (of road) see Base courses
Bitumen binders, **10**/29
  tests for, **10**/29
Bitumen coated vermiculite, **51**/8
Bitumen emulsion coatings, **10**/29, **33**/7
Bitumen impregnated insulating board, **50**/20
Bituminous coatings
  concrete waterproofed by, **33**/9, **33**/12
  hot application of, **33**/12
  steels protected by, **5**/33, **5**/34
Bituminous felts, **9**/12
Bituminous materials, **10**/1
  asphalts, **10**/3
  comparison of, **10**/25
  drum mixers used, **10**/16
  elastomers added, **37**/16, **37**/21
  joints in, **10**/17
  laying of
    averaging beam used, **10**/22
    by hand, **10**/17
    by machine, **10**/18
    cold-weather operations, **10**/23
    control of tolerances, **10**/21
    effect of cold lumps, **10**/20
    mat-level follower used, **10**/22
    in rainy-weather operations, **10**/24
    schedule sheet for, **10**/32
  macadams, **10**/10
  manufacture of, **10**/14
    environmental considerations, **10**/14
    problems encountered, **10**/15
  mastic asphalts, **10**/9
  precoated chippings in, **10**/22
  preparation work prior to laying, **10**/17
  recycled materials in, **10**/16
  sampling of, **10**/26
  storage of, **10**/16
  testing of, **10**/27
  types of, **10**/3
  see also Asphalts; Macadams; Mastic asphalts
Bituminous paints, **5**/33, **5**/34, **33**/9
Blanking of aluminium and alloys, **2**/23
Blast cleaning of steel, **5**/32, **31**/3
Blast-furnace slag
  in concretes, **14**/4, **14**/9, **18**/4, **18**/9, **18**/10
  see also Ground-granulated blast-furnace slag
Blister copper, **7**/9
Block copolymer thermoplastic elastomers, moulding of, **37**/9
Blockboard, **50**/18
  applications of, **50**/21
  manufacture of, **50**/18
  standards for, **50**/19
  types of, **50**/19
Blockwork
  properties of, **17**/9
  see also Concrete blockwork
Blown mineral wool (for cavity-wall filling), **30**/7
  manufacture of, **30**/4
  sources of, **30**/3
Body-centred cubic (BCC) structure, **7**/6
Bolted joints
  corrosion of, **5**/31
  timber joined by, **50**/22
Bolting methods, aluminium and alloys, **2**/25
Bolts
  steel, **5**/22
    grading system for, **5**/22
Bond strength
  silica-fume concrete, **23**/9
  sprayed concrete, **24**/10

Bonding patterns (in brickwork), **11**/10
Bonnet hip tiles, **25**/15, **25**/16
Boulton (timber treatment) process, **32**/7
Brasses
  alpha alloys, **7**/14
  beta alloys, **7**/14
  dezincification of, **7**/12
  mechanical properties of, **7**/13
  phase diagram for, **7**/13
  photomicrograph of, **7**/18
  stress-corrosion cracking of, **7**/12
  types of, **7**/14
Breccia (rock), **16**/9
Brethane, **33**/13
Bricks, **11**/1
  applications of, **11**/3, **11**/10
  clay preparation for, **11**/7
  common bricks, **11**/3
  compressive strength of, **11**/9
  damp-course bricks, **11**/4
  drying of, **11**/8
  engineering bricks, **11**/4
  facing bricks, **11**/3, **11**/5
  firing of, **11**/8
  frost resistance of, **11**/9
  hand-made bricks, **11**/6, **11**/7
  historical background for, **11**/3
  manufacture of, **11**/6
  moisture movement in, **11**/9
  plastering of, **35**/5
  pressed bricks, **11**/5, **11**/7
  properties of, **11**/8
  shaping of, **11**/7
  size of, **11**/8, **11**/9
  soft-mud bricks, **11**/5, **11**/7
  soluble-salt content of, **11**/9
  surface preparation for adhesives, **8**/4
  thermal movement of, **11**/9
  types of, **11**/3
  water absorption of, **11**/9
  wire-cut bricks, **11**/5, **11**/7
Brickwork, **11**/10
  appearance of, **11**/11
  bonding of, **11**/10
  durability of, **11**/13
  efflorescence on, **11**/9
  fire resistance of, **11**/13
  mortars for, **11**/10, **11**/13
  mortars used, **11**/10
  movement of, **11**/12
  properties of, **11**/11
  rain resistance of, **11**/12
  sound insulation of, **11**/12
  structural properties of, **11**/12
  thermal resistance of, **11**/12
Bridge bearings
  elastomers, **37**/15, **37**/20, **37**/21
  PTFE, **42**/6, **42**/7
Bridges
  adhesives used, **8**/5, **8**/6, **8**/10
  aramid cables in, **44**/11
  cast iron used, **3**/7, **3**/8
  cracks repaired by adhesives, **8**/6, **8**/10
  wrought iron used, **4**/4, **4**/8, **4**/10, **4**/11
Britannia Bridge (UK), **4**/10, **4**/11
British Board of Agrément (BBA)... see Agrément certificates
British Gas specifications, polyethylene piping, **40**/5, **40**/7
British Rail 'T' wash, **31**/6
British Standards
  aggregates, **10**/27
  aluminium and alloys, **2**/12, **2**/14, **2**/16, **2**/27
  asbestos products, **9**/7
  asphalts, **10**/3, **10**/5, **10**/10
  blast-furnace slag, **18**/7
  bricks, **11**/8, **11**/9, **11**/10, **11**/12, **11**/13
  ceramic tiles, **13**/15

British Standards (*cont.*)
  clay pipes, **12**/6
  coated macadams, **10**/10, **10**/11, **10**/12, **10**/13
  concrete admixtures, **15**/8, **15**/9, **15**/14, **15**/17, **15**/18
  concrete blocks, **17**/7
  elastomers, **37**/20, **37**/21
  galvanized steel, **7**/33
  glass, **29**/20
  glass-fibre reinforced cement, **20**/26
  joinery products, **50**/28, **50**/29, **50**/32
  mineral-fibre products, **30**/16
  polymer dispersions, **39**/7
  polystyrene foam fire tests, **41**/7
  Portland blast-furnace cements, **18**/7
  Portland cement, **14**/5, **18**/6
  pulverized-fuel ash, **18**/6
  sound-insulation testing, **30**/12, **30**/13
  steel reinforcement, **6**/3, **6**/7
  steels, **5**/13, **5**/21, **5**/36
  stone, **49**/6
  timber treatment, **32**/8
  wood-based panel products, **50**/18, **50**/19, **50**/20
Brittle fracture of steels, **5**/24
Bronze bearings, **7**/16
Bronzes *see* Aluminium...; Beryllium bronze; Gunmetal; Phosphor...; Tin bronze
Brushing (of paint), **33**/4
Building systems, glass-fibre reinforced cement used, **20**/17, **20**/19
Buildings
  cleaning of, **33**/3, **49**/11
  elastomers used, **37**/12
  weathering of, **33**/3
Butadiene rubbers (BR), **37**/5
  production of, **37**/5
  properties of, **37**/10
  vulcanizing of, **37**/8
Butt fusion welds
  polyethylene pipes, **40**/9
  steels, **5**/16
    strengths of welds, **5**/18
  wrought iron, **4**/9
Butyl rubbers, **37**/3
  applications of, **37**/12, **37**/13, **37**/15, **37**/16
  production of, **37**/3
  properties of, **37**/10
  vulcanizing of, **37**/8
Byker Viaduct (UK), adhesives used, **8**/5

Cable ducting applications
  glass-fibre reinforced cement, **20**/17
  PVC, **43**/7
Calcium chloride, as concrete accelerator, **15**/21, **15**/22, **15**/23
Calcium plumbate primer, **31**/6
Calcium silicate bricks, **11**/8
  drying shrinkage of, **11**/10
  size of, **11**/8, **11**/9
Camden Town (UK), Alexander Road Development, **37**/14
Capillary rise test (for concrete), **15**/26
Capo pull-out test (for sprayed fibre concrete), **24**/13
Carats, meaning of term, **7**/20
Carbon dioxide permeability, polymers, **42**/3
Carbon equivalent (CE) values
  calculation of, **5**/15, **6**/4
  maximum permissible, **5**/14
Carbon fibres, tensile properties of, **44**/4, **44**/5
Carbon-fibre-reinforced concrete, **14**/8
  silica fume used, **23**/9
Carbonifics (in intumescent coatings), **34**/4, **34**/10

Carboxylated nitrile rubber (XNBR)
  applications of, **37**/16
  properties of, **37**/10
Carlite range of plasters, **35**/3, **51**/5
Carpenter ants, **32**/4
Cartridge brass, **7**/14
Cast iron, **3**/1
  applications of, **3**/11, **3**/13
  appraisal of structures, **3**/7
  British Standards for, **3**/10, **3**/11
  carbon contents of, **3**/3, **3**/4, **4**/3
  compared with wrought iron, **4**/3
  ductile cast iron, **3**/11
  durability of, **3**/11
  fabrication methods for, **3**/6, **3**/7, **3**/8, **3**/12
  forms available, **3**/6
  grey cast iron, **3**/3, **3**/10
  heat resistance of, **3**/6
  history of manufacture, **3**/12
  malleable cast iron, **3**/4, **3**/11
  mechanical properties of, **3**/3, **3**/4, **3**/10, **3**/11, **3**/13
  melting point of, **3**/14
  permissible stresses for, **3**/7, **3**/8, **3**/9
  stress limits for, **3**/8, **3**/9
  types of, **3**/3, **3**/4
  welding of, **3**/10, **3**/12
  white cast iron, **3**/4
  see also Ductile...; Grey...; Malleable...; White cast iron
Casting processes
  aluminium and alloys, **2**/4
  steels, **5**/5
Catalysts (in intumescent coatings), **34**/4, **34**/10
Cathodic protection, **5**/34, **5**/35, **31**/3
Cavity walls, **11**/10, **17**/10
  mineral-fibre products in, **30**/3, **30**/6, **30**/7, **30**/18
  polystyrene foam in, **41**/7
  vermiculite in, **51**/5
Ceiling tiles, glass-wool, **30**/8
Cellular bricks, **11**/7
Cellular concrete blocks, **17**/3
Cellular rubbers, applications of, **37**/16
Cellulose-based plastics, **36**/3
Cement admixtures
  purposes of, **14**/6
  see also Admixtures
Cement paints, **33**/6
Cement paste, simplified model of, **15**/25
Cementite, **5**/9, **5**/10
Cementitious materials *see* Blast-furnace slag; Cements; Pulverized-fuel ash; Silica fume
Cements, **18**/1
  classification of, **14**/5
  factors affecting performance in concrete, **18**/8
  fineness of, **18**/7
  glass-fibre-reinforced cement, **20**/1
  handling of, **14**/5
  heat of hydration for, **18**/7
  magnesia in, **18**/7
  polymer-modified cements, **25**/22, **39**/6, **39**/9
  quality of, **14**/4
  setting time of, **14**/10, **18**/7
  soundness of, **18**/7
  special-purpose, **14**/5
  storage of, **14**/5, **20**/4
  use in glass-fibre reinforced cement, **20**/3
  see also Aluminious...; Glass-fibre-reinforced...; Polymer-modified...; Portland cement
Ceramic tiles, **13**/1
  bedding of, **13**/6, **13**/13, **13**/14
  British Standards for, **13**/15
  durability of, **13**/4
  fixing of, **13**/7
  floor tiles, **13**/14

Ceramic tiles (*cont.*)
  historical background for, **13**/3
  jointing of, **13**/6
  maintenance of, **13**/15
  manufacture of, **13**/3
  movement of, **13**/4, **13**/5
  properties of, **13**/8
  roof tiles, **13**/8
  terminology for, **13**/3
  tolerances for, **13**/8
  wall tiles, **13**/12
  see also Floor...; Roof...; Wall tiles
Certification Authority for Reinforcing Steels (CARES) scheme, **14**/16
Cetyl trimethyl ammonium bromide (CTAB), **15**/6, **15**/7
Chalk, aggregates containing, **16**/8
Challange–Cook (sprayed concrete) system, **24**/7
Chatham (Kent), cast iron structure, **3**/8
Chemical engineering applications, elastomers used, **37**/16, **37**/21
Chemical grouts, **48**/15
  materials in, **48**/6
  set-time measurement for, **48**/20
  silicate–aluminate grouts, **48**/15
  silicate–ester grouts, **48**/15
Chemical resistance
  aluminium, **2**/18, **2**/21
  clay pipes, **12**/10
  glass-fibre reinforced cement, **20**/11
  polymers, **38**/3, **42**/3, **43**/4, **43**/5, **44**/7
  thermosetting resins, **46**/16
  timber, **32**/4
Chert (rock), **16**/9
Chester-le-Street (UK), school, **50**/23
Chipboard, **50**/19
  applications of, **50**/21
  manufacture of, **50**/19
  standards for, **50**/19
  types of, **50**/19
Chip-spreading machine, **10**/23
Chloride attack (on concrete), reduction of
  silanes/siloxanes used, **47**/6, **47**/7
  silica fume used, **23**/11
Chloride permeability, silica-fume concretes, **23**/10
Chlorides in aggregates, testing for, **16**/12
Chlorinated polyethylene, properties of, **37**/11
Chlorinated rubber paints, **5**/33, **5**/34, **31**/5, **31**/9, **33**/9
Chloroprene rubbers *see* Polychloroprene rubbers
Chlorosulphonated polyethylene (CSM)
  applications of, **37**/12, **37**/15
  production of, **37**/5
  properties of, **37**/11
  vulcanizing of, **37**/9
Choisy-le-Roi Bridge (France), adhesives used, **8**/5
Chopped strand mat (CSM), **45**/7
  properties of GRP containing, **45**/7, **45**/8
Chrysotile (white asbestos)
  airborne-fibre control limits for, **9**/14
  processing of, **9**/5
  properties of, **9**/3
  world production data for, **9**/5, **9**/6
Citric acid, as concrete retarder, **15**/20
Cladding, glass-fibre reinforced cement used, **20**/17, **20**/19, **20**/20
Clay, aggregates containing, **16**/10
Clay bricks
  manufacture of, **11**/6
  properties of, **11**/9
  size of, **11**/8, **11**/9
  UK usage data for, **17**/3

Clay pipe joints
  manufacture of, **12**/5
  use of, **12**/5
Clay pipes, **12**/1
  abrasion resistance of, **12**/7
  appearance of, **12**/5
  availability of, **12**/7
  bedding for, **12**/8, **12**/10
  bending moment resistance of, **12**/7, **12**/10
  chemical resistance of, **12**/10
  cover limits for, **12**/9
  crushing strength of, **12**/7
  cutting to length, **12**/6
  flexible joints for, **12**/6
  handling and storage of, **12**/7
  heat resistance of, **12**/7
  historical background for, **12**/3
  hydraulics research for, **12**/9
  inspection of, **12**/5
  jointing of, **12**/5
    on-site, **12**/5
    repair operations, **12**/5
  manufacture of, **12**/3
    clay preparation for, **12**/3
    cooling processes, **12**/4
    drying processes, **12**/3
    energy analysis of, **12**/4
    firing processes, **12**/3
    fittings formation, **12**/3
    pipe formation, **12**/3
  research for, **12**/8
  standards for, **12**/6
  strength of, **12**/7
  structural research for, **12**/8
Clay roof tiles, **13**/8
  availability of, **13**/8
  cost comparison for, **25**/26
  fixing of, **13**/8, **13**/10
  manufacture of, **13**/3
  properties of, **13**/8
  sections available, **13**/9
  sizes of, **13**/9
  tolerances for, **13**/8
  types of, **13**/8
Clay tiles, non-roofing applications of, **13**/12
Clay-heave-protection, polystyrene foam
  used, **41**/16
Clays
  dispersion for grouts/slurries, **48**/5
  expanded clays, **16**/19, **16**/21
  permeability of, **48**/13, **48**/23
  in slurries, **48**/4, **48**/21
Cleaning of buildings, **33**/3, **49**/11
  dry methods, **33**/3, **49**/13
  specifications for, **49**/12
  wet methods, **33**/3, **49**/12, **49**/13
Clinker aggregate, **16**/20
Coal-tar paints, **33**/9
Coalbrookdale (Shrops.), Ironbridge, **3**/7, **3**/12
Coated glass, **29**/9
  coatings used, **29**/9
  manufacture of, **29**/9, **29**/14
  transmission characteristics of, **29**/9
Coated macadams, **10**/10
  see also Macadams
Coatings
  acrylic polymer coatings, **33**/10
  fluoro-elastomer coatings, **33**/9
  GRP painted with, **45**/14
  historical background for, **36**/4
  intumescent coatings, **34**/1
  for mineral surfaces, **33**/5
    impregnants, **33**/12
    oil-based paints, **33**/7
    solvent-thinned paints, **33**/8
    two-pack systems, **33**/9
    water-borne paints, **33**/6
  neoprene rubber coatings, **33**/11

Coating (*cont.*)
  polyester resin coatings, **33**/11
  polysulphide rubber coatings, **33**/11
  silicone rubber coatings, **33**/11
  for steel, **31**/4
  for timber, **32**/9
    adhesion characteristics of, **32**/10
    application considerations, **32**/12
    components of, **32**/9
    extensibility of, **32**/10
    factors affecting performance of, **32**/11
    fungi/moulds resistance of, **32**/11
    health and safety aspects, **32**/12
    moisture control by, **32**/10
    photodegradation resistance of, **32**/10
    properties of, **32**/10
    selection criteria for, **32**/11
    standards for, **32**/12
    surface preparation for, **32**/12
    types of, **32**/9
    water-borne vs solvent-borne coatings, **32**/11
    water-vapour permeability of, **32**/10
    see also Intumescent coatings; Paints; Varnishes; Zinc coatings
Coaxial cables, **40**/11
Colcrete flow trough test (for grouts), **48**/18
Cold rolling of aluminium and alloys, **2**/5
Cold weather, road laying in, **10**/23
Cold-rolled steels, **5**/6
Cold-water systems, polyethylene used, **40**/8
Cold-worked steels, **5**/12
Coloured glasses, **29**/8
Combined stresses, **1**/7
Combustion products
  expanded polystyrene, **41**/6
  PTFE, **42**/4
  PVC, **43**/13
Common (or basis) brass, **7**/14
Common bricks, **11**/3
Compaction
  bituminous materials, **10**/25
  effects of, **10**/25
  equipment used, **10**/25
  tests for, **10**/26
  concrete, **14**/14
Composite walls, plastering of, **35**/6
Composition cork, **26**/3
Compressive strength
  bricks, **11**/9
  cast iron, **3**/3, **3**/4, **3**/10
  concrete, **14**/4, **14**/11
    effect of accelerators, **15**/23
    effect of air entrainment, **15**/8
    effect of cements, **18**/8
    effect of plasticizers, **15**/12, **15**/13, **15**/14
  concrete blocks, **17**/7
  corkboard, **26**/4
  glass fibre reinforced cement, **20**/9, **20**/10
  glass reinforced plastics, **45**/7
  mortars, **17**/9, **21**/4, **46**/14
  polymer-modified mortars, **46**/14
  polymers, **38**/3, **38**/5, **41**/4, **42**/3, **44**/7
  silica-fume concretes, **23**/8
  sprayed concrete, **24**/8
  stone, **49**/11
  vermiculite concrete, **51**/8
  wrought iron, **4**/6
Concrete, **14**/1
  accelerators for, **15**/21
  acid resistance of, **14**/12
  admixtures for, **14**/6, **15**/1
  aggregates, **14**/6, **16**/1
    impurities in, **16**/8
    lightweight aggregates, **16**/19
    physical properties of, **16**/12
    processing of, **16**/4
    sources of, **16**/3

Concrete (*cont.*)
  aggregates (*cont.*)
    standards for, **16**/17
    types of, **16**/8
  air-entraining agents for, **15**/3
  alkali–aggregate reaction in, **14**/13, **18**/10
    reduction of occurence, **18**/11, **47**/5
  aluminious cements used, **18**/11
  aluminium affected by, **2**/21
  compressive strength of, **14**/4, **14**/11
    effect of accelerators, **15**/23
    effect of air entrainment, **15**/8
    effect of cements, **18**/8
    effect of plasticizers, **15**/12, **15**/13, **15**/14
  corrosion inhibitors for, **15**/24
  creep properties of, **14**/11, **14**/13
  curing of, **14**/14, **19**/3
    effect of environment, **19**/3
    effect of wind speed, **19**/3
    membranes used, **19**/3
  definition of, **14**/3
  durability of, **14**/12, **18**/9
  early-age behaviour of, **14**/10
  effect of cements on performance, **18**/8
  elastic modulus of, **14**/11
  exposed aggregate finishes, **14**/15
  fibres in, **14**/7
    advantages of, **14**/7
  flexural strength of, effect of air entrainment, **15**/8
  formwork using, **14**/14
  freeze–thaw damage in, **14**/14, **15**/4
    reduction of damage, **14**/14, **15**/4, **18**/11
  future prospects, **14**/17
  health and safety aspects, **14**/17
  high-strength (water-reduced), **15**/17
  historical background for, **14**/3
  impregnants for, **33**/12
  mix designs for, **14**/8
  permeability of, **14**/11
  permeability reducers for, **15**/24
  plastering of, **35**/5
  plasticizers for, **15**/9
  polymers added, **14**/8
  porosity of, **14**/11
  practice covering, **14**/14
  precast concrete, **14**/15
  properties of, **14**/10, **37**/4
  quality assurance for, **14**/16
  rate of strength development, **14**/4
    effect of admixtures, **15**/12, **15**/13, **15**/18, **15**/23
    effect of cement types, **18**/8
    effect of silica fume, **23**/8
    temperature effects, **14**/11, **15**/23, **18**/9
  ready-mixed concrete, **14**/6
  reinforcement of
    aramid fibres used, **44**/9
    steel used, **14**/7, **18**/10
  retarders for, **15**/18
  setting time of, **14**/10
  shrinkage of, **14**/11, **14**/12
  steel reinforcement for, **14**/7
    corrosion of, **18**/9
    protection of, **18**/10
  strength of, **14**/10, **37**/4
  sulphate attack on, **14**/12, **18**/9
  sulphate-resistant cements used, **14**/13, **18**/10, **18**/12
  surface preparation for
    adhesives, **8**/4, **8**/13
    paints, **33**/4
  temperature effect on reaction rate, **14**/11, **15**/23, **18**/9
  temperature rise in, **14**/10
    effect of accelerators, **15**/22
    effect of cement types, **18**/9
  testing of, **14**/16, **15**/26

Concrete (*cont.*)
  thermal expansion of, **14**/12
  water absorption tests for, **15**/26
  water-reducing agents for, **15**/9
  water-repellants used, **33**/12
  workability of, **14**/10
    effect of plasticizers, **15**/12, **15**/16, **15**/17
Concrete blocks, **17**/1
  architectural masonry blocks, **17**/4
  common blocks, **17**/3
  compressive strength of, **17**/7
  coursing units, **17**/4
  curing of, **17**/5
  examples of use, **17**/8
  facing blocks, **17**/4
  hollow blocks, **17**/3
  insulating blocks, **17**/4
  manufacture of, **17**/4
    autoclaved aerated block production, **17**/5, **17**/6
    egg-lay process, **17**/4
    static process, **17**/5
  moisture movement of, **17**/7
  packaging of, **17**/6
  properties of, **17**/9
  size of, **17**/6
  solid blocks, **17**/3
  thermal movement of, **17**/7
  types of, **17**/3
  UK usage data for, **17**/3
  weight of, **17**/7
Concrete blockwork, **17**/7
  appearance of, **17**/9
  durability of, **17**/11
  fire resistance of, **17**/11
  mortars used, **17**/8
  movements of, **17**/10
  plastering of, **35**/5, **35**/6
  properties of, **17**/9
  rain resistance of, **17**/9
  sound insulation using, **17**/10
  structural properties of, **17**/10
  thermal insulation using, **17**/10
Concrete bricks, **11**/8
  properties of, **11**/9
  size of, **11**/8, **11**/9
Concrete floors, insulation of, **30**/13, **30**/14, **30**/19, **41**/12
Concrete roof tiles, **25**/1
  appearance of, **25**/10
  availability of, **25**/5
  battens used, **25**/14, **25**/15
  cost comparison for, **25**/26
  double-lap plain tiles, **25**/6, **25**/8
    batten gauge for, **25**/6, **25**/8
    installation of, **25**/14
  durability of, **25**/11
  efflorescence on, **25**/10
  fire resistance of, **25**/17
  historical background, **25**/4
  installation of, **25**/12
    abutments, **25**/15
    dry-fix systems for, **25**/4, **25**/5
    eaves, **25**/13, **25**/15
    groundwork for, **25**/12
    hips, **25**/14, **25**/15
    ridge tiles, **25**/14, **25**/15
    setting out for, **25**/12
    valleys, **25**/13, **25**/14, **25**/15
    verges, **25**/12, **25**/15
  interlocking single-lap tiles, **25**/3, **25**/7, **25**/8
    installation of, **25**/12
  lichens and mosses on, **25**/10
  lightweight-aggregate roof tiles, **25**/17
  manufacture of, **25**/5
    compaction process, **25**/6
    curing processes, **25**/6
    extrusion process, **25**/6

Concrete roof tiles (*cont.*)
    materials used, **25**/5
    packaging of, **25**/6
  performance properties of, **25**/11
  roof loadings for, **25**/12
  sizes of, **25**/6
  sound insulation properties, **25**/17
  structural stability of, **25**/11
  thermal insulation properties, **25**/17
  types of, **25**/6
  weather resistance of, **25**/11
Concrete structures
  repair of, **8**/3, **8**/9
  steel plates bonded to, **8**/6
    procedure described, **8**/12
Condensation
  fabric structures, **27**/5
  plasterboard affecting, **35**/8
  roofs, **25**/19
  vermiculite plaster affecting, **51**/5
Condensed silica fume *see* Silica fume
Conduction, principles of, **30**/10
Conglomerate rock, **16**/9
Consolidants (for stone), **49**/14
  performance requirements of, **49**/14
  use of, **49**/15
Contact moulding, glass reinforced plastics, **45**/4
Continuous casting, steel made by, **5**/5
Continuous (glass) filament mat, **45**/8
Continuous glass rovings, **45**/7
Control of Asbestos at Work Regulations (1987), **9**/14
Convection, principles of, **30**/10
Conversion coatings
  aluminium and alloys, **2**/25
  steels, **5**/32
Conveyor belting, elastomers used, **37**/15
Copolymer, meaning of term, **39**/3
Copper, **7**/7
  abundance in Earth's crust, **7**/3
  applications of, **7**/11
  characteristics of, **7**/7
  corrosion of, **7**/7
  joining of, **7**/11
  production of, **7**/9
    oxide ores used, **7**/9
    sulphide ores used, **7**/9
  properties of, **7**/5, **7**/10, **7**/11, **7**/13, **7**/15, **7**/16
  sources of, **7**/9
  types of, **7**/10
Copper alloys, **7**/12
  mechanical properties of, **7**/13, **7**/15, **7**/16
  phase diagrams for, **7**/13, **7**/15, **7**/16
  see also Brasses; Bronzes; Cupro-nickel...; Gunmetal
Copper–aluminium alloys
  mechanical properties of, **7**/16
  phase diagram for, **7**/16
  see also Aluminium bronzes
Copper–beryllium alloys, **7**/17
Copper–cadmium, **7**/11
Copper chrome arsenate (CCA) wood preservatives, **32**/5
Copper–tin alloys
  mechanical properties of, **7**/15
  phase diagram for, **7**/15
  see also Tin bronzes
Copper–zinc alloys
  mechanical properties of, **7**/13
  phase diagram for, **7**/13
Cor-ten steel, corrosion of, **5**/30
Core plywood, **50**/18
  see also Blockboard
Core splitting tests (for sprayed fibre concrete), **24**/13
Coremat materials (in GRP sandwich), **45**/9

Cork, **26**/1
  dimensional stability of, **26**/5
  fire resistance of, **26**/5
  types of, **26**/3
Cork–rubber sheets, **26**/3
Corkboard
  fixing of, **26**/5
  handling and storage of, **26**/5
  manufacture of, **26**/3
  physical properties of, **26**/4
  roof finishes used, **26**/5
  standards for, **26**/5
  types of, **26**/3
Corrosion
  copper, **7**/7
  iron/steel, **5**/28, **5**/30, **31**/3
  steel reinforcement, **18**/9, **24**/11
Corrosion fatigue of steels, **5**/36
Corrosion inhibitors (for concrete), **15**/24
  benefits of, **15**/24
  chemical types of, **15**/24
  mechanism of, **15**/24
Corrosion points, **5**/31
Corrosion protection
  British Standards for, **5**/37
  steels, **5**/31, **18**/10
Corrosion resistance, aluminium alloys, **2**/18, **7**/8
Corrugated (asbestos cement) sheeting, **9**/8
Cost comparison
  fabrics, **27**/6
  geotextiles, **28**/15
  metals, **3**/12, **5**/13, **7**/3, **50**/4
  paints, **31**/8
  roof tiles/slates, **25**/26
  timber, **50**/4, **50**/6, **50**/13
Coventry Cathedral, adhesives used, **8**/5
Crack tip-opening displacement (CTOD), **5**/25
Crack-growth data, steels, **5**/27
Creep properties
  aluminium alloys, **2**/18
  concrete, **14**/11, **14**/13
  elastomers, **37**/17
  glass-fibre reinforced cement, **20**/10
  polymers, **36**/6, **40**/6, **41**/6, **43**/5, **43**/6, **44**/4
  silica-fume concretes, **23**/9
Crevice corrosion, steels, **5**/30, **5**/31
Crocidolite (blue asbestos)
  airborne-fibre control limits, **9**/14
  properties, **9**/12
  world production data, **9**/6
Cross-linking
  polyethylene, **40**/12
  rubbers, **37**/7
  thermosetting resins, **46**/4
Crushing strength, clay pipes, **12**/7, **12**/8
Cryogenic properties, Kevlar fibres, **44**/8
Crystal structures (of metals), **7**/5, **7**/6
Cupro–nickel alloys, mechanical properties, **7**/27
Curing membranes (for concrete), **19**/1
  benefits of, **19**/4
  metallic-silicate solutions, **19**/4
  resin-in-solvent solutions, **19**/4
  standards/specifications for, **19**/4
  types of, **19**/3
  wax emulsions, **19**/4
Curing processes
  concrete, **14**/14, **19**/3
  rubbers/thermosets, **37**/7, **46**/4
Cut-off wall construction, slurries used, **48**/3, **48**/12, **48**/23
Cutting processes, aluminium and alloys, **2**/23
Cylinder splitting tests, sprayed fibre concrete, **24**/13

Damp-proof course bricks, **11**/4
Damp-proof membranes, **36**/4, **40**/13
D'Arcy's Law, **28**/10
Death watch beetle, **32**/4
Decibel (unit of sound), **30**/12
Deferred-set macadams, **10**/17
Denier (unit for fibres/thread), **27**/3
DENSIT cement, **14**/17
Density
  aggregates, **16**/14, **16**/19, **16**/20
  aluminium and alloys, **2**/17, **37**/4
  asbestos, **9**/3
  corkboard, **26**/4
  elastomers, **37**/4
  glass, **29**/6, **37**/4
  glass-fibre reinforced cement, **20**/12
  mineral-fibre products, **30**/5, **30**/6, **30**/7
  non-ferrous metals, **7**/5
  polymers, **37**/4, **38**/9, **40**/3, **40**/4, **40**/9,
    40/12, **41**/4, **42**/3, **43**/4, **43**/9, **43**/11
  slurries, **48**/8, **48**/9, **48**/21
  steels, **5**/8, **37**/4
  stone, **49**/11
  timber, **50**/5, **50**/6, **50**/11
  vermiculite products, **51**/4, **51**/8
Department of Transport standard BD21/84,
  3/7, **4**/6, **4**/8, **4**/9
Derby (UK) Inner Ring Road Bridge, PTFE
  skids used, **42**/6
Development of materials, **1**/3
Diaphragm walling, slurries used, **48**/3, **48**/8,
  48/21, **48**/22
Dicyandiamide (in intumescent coatings),
  34/10
Die castings, zinc and alloys, **7**/34
Die forgings, aluminium alloys, **2**/7
Dielectric properties
  aluminium and alloys, **2**/18, **37**/4
  elastomers, **37**/4
  polymers, **37**/4, **38**/9, **40**/12, **42**/3
Differential aeration corrosion, **5**/30, **5**/31, **5**/32
Dimensional stability
  concrete, **14**/11, **14**/12
  cork, **26**/5
  expanded polystyrene, **41**/4, **41**/5
  fabrics, **27**/5
  glass reinforced plastics, **45**/13
  polymers, **41**/4, **41**/5
  vermiculite cement, **51**/7
Doors
  categories of, **50**/31
  GRC doors, **20**/21
  operating forces for, **50**/32
  timber doors, **50**/31
Double-glazing applications
  elastomers, **37**/13
  glasses, **29**/10, **29**/14, **29**/16
Drainage applications
  clay pipes, **12**/5
  geotextiles, **28**/11
  glass-fibre reinforced cement pipes, **20**/22
  PVC pipes, **43**/6, **43**/8
Draught-excluders, **43**/11
Drawn tube, aluminium and alloys, **2**/6,
  2/15
Drilling of aluminium and alloys, **2**/23
Drinking-water... see Potable-water...
Drucker's definition of plasticity, **1**/5
Dry grit blasting
  steels, **31**/4
  stone, **49**/13
Dry linings
  mineral wool bonded to, **30**/5, **30**/7
  plasterboard used, **35**/7
Dry rot (on timber), **32**/3
DSP materials, **23**/12
  concrete–fibre bond strength in, **23**/9
  water demand in, **23**/7

Ductile–brittle transition temperature
  (DBTT) of steels, **5**/11
  effect of carbon content, **5**/11
  effect of manganese content, **5**/11
Ductile cast iron
  British Standard for, **3**/11
  cost comparison for, **3**/12
  microstructure of, **3**/7
  structural use of, **3**/11
  tensile strength of, **3**/11
Ductility, aluminium and alloys, **2**/18
Duplex alloys, copper–zinc alloys, **7**/14
Durability
  aggregates, **16**/14
  aluminium and alloys, **2**/12, **2**/14, **2**/16,
    2/19
  cast iron, **3**/11
  ceramic tiles, **13**/4
  concrete, **14**/12, **18**/9
  concrete blockwork, **17**/11
  fabrics, **27**/6
  plastics, **38**/3, **38**/5
  roofing materials, **25**/11, **25**/18, **25**/21,
    25/22
  silica-fume concretes, **23**/10
  timber, **32**/4, **50**/5, **50**/6, **50**/11
  vermiculite cement, **51**/7

Earthquake-shock isolation pads, **37**/13,
  37/15, **37**/21
East Moors Viaduct (UK), adhesives used,
  8/5, **8**/6, **8**/7, **8**/8
Ebonite, properties of, **37**/4
Efflorescence
  brickwork, **11**/9
  concrete roof tiles, **25**/10
  removal before painting, **33**/4
Elastic behaviour, **1**/5
Elastic–hardening materials, one-dimensional
  loading of, **1**/6
Elastic modulus
  aluminium and alloys, **2**/17, **37**/4, **50**/4
  cast iron, **3**/6, **3**/10
  concrete, **14**/11, **37**/4, **50**/4
  elastomers, **37**/4
  glass reinforced plastics, **45**/6
  polymers, **38**/8, **42**/3
  steels, **5**/8, **37**/4, **45**/6, **50**/4
  woods, **50**/4
  see also Young's modulus
Elastic–plastic materials, one-dimensional
  loading of, **1**/6, **1**/7
Elastomers
  applications of, **37**/12
    in buildings, **37**/13
    fixtures/fittings/services, **37**/13
    oil/gas/chemical engineering/mining,
      37/16
    piping/hose/reservoirs/tanks, **37**/15
    roads/railways/bridges, **37**/15
  available forms for, **37**/6
  damping characteristics of, **37**/17
  design decisions involving, **37**/16
    mechanical properties, **37**/16
    stiffness, **37**/17
  environmental factors affecting, **37**/18
  glass hardening of, **37**/18
  meaning of term, **36**/3
  microstructure of, **37**/7, **46**/3
  production of, **37**/3
  properties of, **37**/4, **37**/10
  standards for, **37**/20
  vulcanization of, **37**/6
  weathering of, **37**/18
  see also Thermoplastic elastomers
Electric arc steelmaking, **5**/4
Electric-arc welding, wrought iron, **4**/9

Electrical cables and conduits
  elastomers used, **37**/15, **37**/20
  polymers used, **40**/12, **43**/7
Electrical conductivity
  aluminium and alloys, **2**/17
  copper, **7**/11
Electrical resistance, temperature coefficient
  for, metals, **7**/5
Electrical resistivity
  copper and alloys, **7**/5, **7**/10
  elastomers, **37**/4
  gold and silver, **7**/5
  lead and alloys, **7**/5, **7**/31
  nickel and alloys, **7**/5
  polymers, **37**/4, **38**/9, **42**/3, **43**/11
  tin and alloys, **7**/5, **7**/31
  zinc and alloys, **7**/5
Electrochemical finishes, aluminium and
  alloys, **2**/25
Electrochemical series, **5**/30, **7**/7
Electrofusion technique (for polyethylene
  pipes), **40**/10
Electrogalvanizing, **7**/34
Electroless nickel coatings, **7**/29
Electrolytic copper, **7**/11
Electropainting of aluminium and alloys, **2**/25
Electroplating
  nickel plating, **7**/28
  silver plating, **7**/30
Ellingham diagrams, **7**/4
Elongation data
  aluminium and alloys, **2**/12, **2**/14, **2**/16, **37**/4
  copper and alloys, **7**/5, **7**/10, **7**/13, **7**/15, **7**/16
  elastomers, **37**/4
  nickel and alloys, **7**/5, **7**/27
  non-ferrous metals (various), **7**/5
  polymer-modified mortars, **46**/14
  polymers, **37**/4, **38**/3, **38**/8, **40**/4, **40**/9, **42**/3,
    43/11
  steels, **5**/21, **5**/22, **5**/23, **37**/4
  wrought iron, **4**/5, **4**/6
Emulsion grouts, **48**/14
Emulsion paints, **33**/6, **39**/3
Engineering bricks, **11**/4
Environmental resistance, polymers, **44**/7
Environmental stress cracking, polymers,
  38/6, **40**/4
Epichlorohydrin rubbers
  applications of, **37**/13, **37**/16
  properties of, **37**/11
Epoxy adhesives, **8**/3
  concrete structures repaired by, **8**/9
Epoxy ester/alkyd paints, **33**/8
Epoxy paints, **5**/33, **5**/34, **31**/5, **31**/8, **33**/9
  application methods used, **33**/10
  disadvantages of, **33**/10
  extenders used, **33**/10
  hardeners used, **33**/10
  organic-solvent formulations, **33**/10
  solvent-free formulations, **33**/10
  water-dispersed formulations, **33**/10
Epoxy primers, **31**/8
Epoxy resins, **46**/6
  advantages/disadvantages of, **46**/13
  curing of, **46**/6, **46**/8
  in GRP, **45**/7, **45**/13
  historical background for, **36**/4, **46**/6
  production of, **46**/6
Equi-viscous temperature (EVT) for
  bituminous materials, **10**/29
Eternit (asbestos) boarding, **9**/9
Ethylene–methylacrylate rubber (AEM),
  properties of, **37**/11
Ethylene–propylene rubbers (EDPM/EPM)
  applications of, **37**/12, **37**/13, **37**/15, **37**/16
  production of, **37**/5
  properties of, **37**/4, **37**/11
  vulcanizing of, **37**/8

Ethylene–vinyl acetate (EVA) copolymers
  dispersions containing, **39**/7
  properties of, **37**/12
European standards
  polyethylene, **40**/13
  steels, **5**/13, **5**/21, **5**/36
Euston Station (London), wrought iron roof
  trusses, **4**/10
Excavation slurries, **48**/8
  specifications for, **48**/21, **48**/22
Exfoliated perlite, as aggregate, **16**/20
Exfoliated vermiculite
  as aggregate, **16**/20, **51**/7
  applications of, **51**/4
  fire-protection applications of, **51**/6
  loosefill applications of, **51**/4
  plastering applications, **51**/5
  properties of, **51**/4
Expanded clays and shales, **16**/19, **16**/21
Expanded metal lathing, plastering of,
  35/5
Expanded polystyrene
  chemical properties of, **41**/7
  civil-engineering applications, **41**/15
    clay-heave-protection applications,
      41/16
    flotation applications, **41**/15
    formwork applications, **41**/15
    foundation applications, **41**/16
    road-construction applications, **41**/15
  compressive strength of, **41**/4
  creep properties of, **41**/6
  cross-breaking strength of, **41**/5
  dimensional stability of, **41**/4, **41**/5
  fire properties of, **41**/6
  floor-insulation applications, **41**/12
    composite-floor insulation panels used,
      41/14
    high-load-floor systems, **41**/14
    overslab insulation, **41**/12
    perimeter insulation, **41**/12
    structural floor systems, **41**/14
    timber-floor insulation, **41**/13
  historical background for, **36**/4
  manufacture of, **41**/3
  mechanical properties of, **41**/3, **41**/5,
    41/6
  moisture absorption by, **41**/4, **41**/5
  physical properties of, **41**/3, **41**/5
  plastering of, **35**/5
  roof-insulation applications, **41**/9
    flat roofs, **41**/10
    pitched roofs, **41**/9
  shear strength of, **41**/6
  tensile strength of, **41**/5
  thermal conductivity of, **41**/4, **41**/5
  toxicity of combustion products from, **41**/6
  wall-insulation applications, **41**/7
    cavity-wall insulation, **41**/7
    external insulation, **41**/8
    internal lining method, **41**/7
    specialist systems used, **41**/9
  water-vapour transmission properties of,
    41/4, **41**/5
  Young's modulus for, **41**/6
Expanded rubbers, applications of, **37**/16
Expanded slag, **16**/19, **16**/21
Expanded vermiculite *see* Exfoliated
  vermiculite
Experiment, exploring materials by, **1**/4
Exposed aggregate finishes, **14**/15
Extruded sections and tubes, aluminium and
  alloys, **2**/6, **2**/14
Extruded wire-cut bricks, **11**/5, **11**/7
Extrusion
  aluminium and alloys, **2**/5
  glass reinforced plastics, **45**/10
  polymers, **40**/4, **43**/4

Fabrics, **27**/1
  applications of, **27**/6
  coating materials used, **27**/3
  cost comparison for, **27**/6
  dimensional stability of, **27**/5
  durability of, **27**/6
  environmental properties of, **27**/5
  fire resistance of, **27**/6
  insulation properties of, **27**/5
  joining of, **27**/6
  manufacture of, **27**/3
    cloth, **27**/4
    threads, **27**/3
  membrane materials, **27**/4
  sources of, **27**/3
  stiffness of, **27**/5
  structural properties of, **27**/5
  tensile strength of, **27**/5
  translucence of, **27**/5, **27**/6
  weave types for, **27**/4
Face-centred cubic (FCC) structure, **7**/6
Facing bricks, **11**/3, **11**/5
Fairbairn (cast iron) beams, **3**/14
Fann viscometer, **48**/17
  calculation of results, **48**/17
  grouts tested by, **48**/17
  slurries tested by, **48**/17, **48**/22
Fast fracture of steels, **5**/24
Fasteners
  steel, **5**/22
  timber joined by, **50**/21
Fatigue properties
  aluminium alloys, **2**/18
  cast iron, **3**/6, **3**/7
  glass-fibre reinforced cement, **20**/10, **20**/11
  polymers, **38**/8, **44**/6, **44**/7
  steels, **5**/26
  welded structures, **5**/28
  wrought iron, **4**/7
Fatty acid soaps, air entrainment using, **15**/5
Federation of Piling Specialists (FPS)
    specifications for slurries, **48**/9, **48**/21,
      48/22
Ferrite, **5**/9
Ferrite–pearlite steels, **5**/9
  effect of ferrite grain size, **5**/9, **5**/11
  notch-toughness of, **5**/11
  tensile properties of, **5**/10
Ferritic stainless steels, **5**/8, **5**/21
Fibre building boards, **50**/19
  applications of, **50**/21
  manufacture of, **50**/19
  standards for, **50**/19
  types of, **50**/19
Fibre–cement slates, **25**/20
  appearance of, **25**/21
  durability of, **25**/21
  fire resistance of, **25**/21
  historical background to, **25**/20
  manufacture of, **25**/21
  sizes of, **25**/18
  standards covering, **25**/21
  structural stability of, **25**/21
  types available, **25**/21
  weather resistance of, **25**/21
Fibre-filled emulsion paint, **33**/7
Fibre-reinforced concrete
  advantages of, **14**/7, **24**/3
  asbestos fibres in, **14**/7
  carbon fibres in, **14**/8
  disadvantages of, **24**/3
  glass fibres in, **14**/8, **24**/4
  mix proportions for, **24**/5
  polymer fibres in, **14**/8, **24**/5, **24**/14
  silica fume in, **23**/9, **23**/12, **24**/4
  steel fibres in, **14**/8, **24**/5, **24**/14
  see also Sprayed fibre concrete
Fibreboard, medium-density, **50**/20

Fibres
  breaking strength/elongation data for, **27**/4
  manufacture of, **27**/3
Fibrous materials, behaviour of, **1**/7
Filament winding (of GRP), **45**/10
Fillet welds (in steels), **5**/16
  strengths of welds, **5**/19, **5**/20
Filtration applications, geotextiles used, **28**/8
Fin-walled building, **11**/10
Finger-jointed timber, **50**/22, **50**/25
Finishes of aluminium and alloys, **2**/25
Finishing processes for steels, **5**/7
Fire properties
  polystyrene foam, **41**/6
  PVC, **43**/12
  thermosetting resins, **46**/16
Fire rating
  mineral-fibre products, **30**/14
  polymers, **38**/9
Fire resistance
  aluminium and alloys, **2**/18
  asbestos products, **9**/9
  cast iron, **3**/6
  concrete blockwork, **17**/11
  cork, **26**/5
  fabrics, **27**/6
  glass reinforced plastics, **45**/13
  glass-fibre reinforced cement, **20**/14
  plasterboard, **35**/7
  polymers, **36**/6, **38**/7, **42**/3, **43**/9
  roofing materials, **25**/17, **25**/21, **25**/22
  tests for, **41**/7
Fire-protection applications
  active compared with passive systems, **34**/7
  glass-fibre reinforced cement, **20**/18, **20**/21
  intumescent coatings, **34**/3
  mineral-fibre products, **30**/7, **30**/15, **30**/19
  plasterboard, **35**/7
  vermiculite, **51**/6
Fire-refined copper, **7**/11
Fire-resistant glasses, **29**/7, **29**/17
  fixing of, **29**/18
Fixing methods
  corkboard, **26**/5
  fire-resistant glass, **29**/18
  glass reinforced plastics, **45**/15
  glass-fibre reinforced cement, **20**/15
  plasterboard dry linings, **35**/9
  roof tiles, **13**/8, **25**/12
  slates, **25**/22, **25**/24
Flakeboards, **50**/20
  performance levels of, **50**/20
  standards for, **50**/20
Flammability
  polymers, **42**/3, **43**/4, **43**/9
  see also Fire resistance
Flat roofs
  cold-roof construction, **41**/10
  elastomers used, **37**/12, **37**/13
  polystyrene foams used, **41**/10
  warm-roof construction, **41**/11
    weatherproofing used, **41**/11, **41**/12
Fletton bricks, **11**/5, **11**/7
Flexible PVC sheeting, **43**/11
Flexural modulus
  cast iron, **3**/6
  polymers, **40**/4, **43**/9
Flexural strength
  mortars, **46**/14
  polymers, **38**/8, **41**/5, **42**/3, **43**/9
Flint gravels
  frost resistance of, **16**/15
  particle mineralogy of, **16**/16
  patina thickness of, **16**/16
Flint–lime bricks, **11**/3
Float glass, **29**/6
  chemical composition of, **29**/6
  as fire-resistant glass, **29**/17

Float glass (*cont.*)
  manufacture of, **29**/3, **29**/5
  properties of, **29**/6
  transmission characteristics of, **29**/6
Floor applications
  elastomers, **37**/12, **37**/21
  glass-fibre reinforced cement, **20**/19
  mineral-fibre products, **30**/7, **30**/13, **30**/14, **30**/19
  polymers, **41**/12, **43**/11
  wood-based panel products, **50**/19, **50**/21
Floor tiles
  ceramic tiles, **13**/14
   cleaning of, **13**/15
   fixing of, **13**/14
   joints for, **13**/6
   manufacture of, **13**/4
   properties of, **13**/8
   substrates for, **13**/4, **13**/6
   tolerances for, **13**/8
  thermoplastic tiles, **9**/12, **43**/11
Flotation applications, polystyrene foam used, **41**/15
Flow cones, slurries tested using, **48**/18
Flow rule, **1**/8
Flowing concrete, **15**/17
Flue piping, asbestos cement, **9**/9
Fluorinated hydrocarbon rubbers (FKM), properties of, **37**/11
Fluoro-elastomer coatings, **33**/9
Fluoropolymer films, **27**/5
Flyash *see* Pulverized-fuel ash (pfa)
Food applications, aluminium, **2**/18
Forging
  aluminium alloys, **2**/7
  steels, **5**/6
Formwork
  glass-fibre reinforced cement used, **20**/20, **20**/22
  polystyrene foam used, **41**/15
  release agents absorbed by, **22**/5
  striking of, **14**/14
  wood-based panel products used, **50**/21
Foundations, polystyrene foam used, **41**/16
Fracture toughness parameter, **5**/25
Freeze–thaw damage
  concrete, **14**/14, **15**/4
   reduction of damage, **14**/14, **15**/4, **18**/11
  stone, **49**/5
Freeze–thaw resistance
  aerated concrete, **15**/4
  aggregates, **16**/15
  bricks, **11**/9
  glass-fibre reinforced cement, **20**/12
  silica-fume concretes/mortars, **23**/10
  sprayed concrete, **24**/10
Friction properties of polymers, **38**/8, **42**/6
Frome (UK) sports hall, **50**/23
Fungal attack (on timber)
  by staining fungi, **32**/3
  by wood-decaying fungi, **32**/3
Furan mortars, **33**/11
Furane resins, **46**/9
  advantages/disadvantages of, **46**/13
  applications of, **46**/10
  production of, **46**/10, **46**/11
Furnace ash/clinker/slag, as aggregate, **16**/20
Furniture beetle, **32**/3
Fusible alloys, **7**/25

Galvanic corrosion
  comparison of metals, **7**/8
  copper, **7**/7
  steels, **5**/29
Galvanized steel, **5**/32, **5**/33, **7**/33, **31**/6
Galvanizing process, **7**/33

Gas pipes
  colour of, **40**/5
  polyethylene used, **40**/6
Gel-content determination (for polymer dispersions), **39**/5
Generalization of data, **1**/4
Geotechnical grouts, **48**/14
  cements in, **48**/4
  emulsion grouts, **48**/14
  specifications for, **48**/21, **48**/22
  suspension grouts, **48**/14
Geotextiles, **28**/1
  applications of, **28**/3
  burst strength of, **28**/7, **28**/8
  cost comparison for, **28**/15
  drainage applications, **28**/11
  economics of, **28**/13
  filtration functions of, **28**/8
  grab strength of, **28**/7
  load–strain characteristics of, **28**/12, **28**/13
  non-woven geotextiles
   heat-bonded structure, **28**/4, **28**/5
   mechanically bonded structure, **28**/4, **28**/5
  puncture strength of, **28**/7, **28**/9
  reinforcement characteristics of, **28**/12, **40**/13
  separation functions of, **28**/7
  serviceability of, **28**/5
  structure of, **28**/3
  tensile strength of, **28**/12, **28**/13
  water permeability of, **28**/9
  woven geotextiles
   monofilament-on-monofilament structure, **28**/4
   monofilament-on-multifilament structure, **28**/4
   monofilament-on-tape structure, **28**/4
   multifilament-on-multifilament structure, **28**/4
   tape-on-tape structure, **28**/3
Gilding metals, **7**/14
Gillet factors (for brasses), **7**/14
Glacier PTFE bearings, **42**/4, **42**/5, **42**/9
Glass, **29**/1
  bent glass, **29**/15
  chemical composition of, **29**/6
  coated glass, **29**/9
  coloured/tinted glasses, **29**/8
  cutting of, **29**/18
  fire-resistant glasses, **29**/17
  float glass, **29**/5, **29**/6
  historical background, **29**/3
  laminated glass, **29**/13
  manufacture of, **29**/3
   float process, **29**/3, **29**/5
   forming process, **29**/3
   melting process, **29**/3
   rolled process, **29**/4
   sheet process, **29**/4
   wired-glass process, **29**/4
  processed glasses, **29**/9
  properties of, **29**/6, **37**/4, **38**/7
  rolled glass, **29**/4, **29**/7
  sheet glass, **29**/4, **29**/6
  silvered glass, **29**/14
  sizes of, **29**/6, **29**/7, **29**/8, **29**/14
  specification of, **29**/19
  standards for, **29**/20
  structural glazing used, **29**/18
  surface preparation for adhesives, **8**/4
  surface-modified glass, **29**/8
  toughened glass, **29**/10
  types of, **29**/6
  wired glass, **29**/4, **29**/7
Glass blocks, **29**/16
  fire resistance of, **29**/17
Glass Fibre Reinforced Cement Association (GRCA), **20**/3, **20**/26

Glass fibre reinforced cement (GRC), **14**/8, **20**/1
  acid/alkali resistance of, **20**/11
  admixtures in, **20**/4
  air permeance of, **20**/12
  alkali-resistant glass fibre used, **20**/5
  apparent porosity of, **20**/12
  applications, **20**/16
   agricultural products, **20**/16, **20**/18
   architectural features, **20**/16, **20**/19
   building systems, **20**/17, **20**/19
   cable ducting, **20**/17
   cladding, **20**/17, **20**/19, **20**/20
   fire protection applications, **20**/18
   flooring/roofing applications, **20**/19, **20**/21
   formwork applications, **20**/21, **20**/22
   insulation applications, **20**/19, **20**/20, **20**/21
   irrigation/drainage applications, **20**/22
   marine applications, **20**/22
   renders, **20**/22
   sewer/shaft/tunnel lining applications, **20**/22
  bending stress–strain curves for, **20**/7
  cements in, **20**/3
  chemical resistance of, **20**/11
  compressive stress–strain curves for, **20**/6
  creep properties of, **20**/10
  density of, **20**/12
  design principles for, **20**/13
   mechanical design, **20**/13
   physical design, **20**/14
  design problems encountered, **20**/15
  design stresses encountered, **20**/13
  fatigue performance of, **20**/10, **20**/11
  fibre wash-out test for, **20**/24
  fibre-content test for, **20**/24
  fire resistance of, **20**/14
  fixing systems for, **20**/15, **20**/17
  handling of, **20**/15
  impact resistance of, **20**/8, **20**/9, **20**/10
  installation considerations, **20**/15
  joining techniques used, **20**/15
  marine environmental effects on, **20**/12
  mechanical properties of, **20**/8
   effect of ageing, **20**/8, **20**/9
   effect of fibre orientation, **20**/7
   law of mixtures applied, **20**/6
   testing of, **20**/24
  minimum thicknesses for, **20**/14
  modulus of, **20**/8, **20**/9, **20**/10
  moisture movement of, **20**/10, **20**/14
  permeability of, **20**/12
  physical properties of, **20**/10
  pigments in, **20**/5
  Poisson's ratio for, **20**/8, **20**/9, **20**/10
  polymers in, **20**/4
  potable-water applications, **20**/12
  principles of reinforcement, **20**/5
  process control for, **20**/24
  product approvals/standards for, **20**/25, **20**/26
  product testing of, **20**/24
  production of, **20**/23
   premixed GRC, **20**/23
   sprayed GRC, **20**/23
  quality control for, **20**/24
  raw materials in, **20**/3
   testing for, **20**/24
  sampling of, **20**/24
  sealing techniques used, **20**/15
  shear strength of, **20**/8, **20**/9, **20**/10
  shrinkage of, **20**/10, **20**/14
  slump test for, **20**/24
  sound insulation of, **20**/12, **20**/15
  standards for, **20**/24
   alkali-resistant glass fibre, **20**/25
   materials, **20**/25
  strain-to-failure of, **20**/7, **20**/10

Glass fibre reinforced cement (GRC) (cont.)
  stress-rupture behaviour, 20/10
  sulphate resistance of, 20/11
  tensile stress–strain curves for, 20/5
  testing of, 20/24, 20/25
    standards for, 20/26
  thermal conductivity of, 20/12, 20/14
  thermal movement of, 20/11, 20/14
  thickness control for, 20/24
  ultraviolet-light degradation of, 20/13
  water absorption by, 20/12
  water permeance of, 20/12
  water-vapour permeability of, 20/12
Glass fibres
  in GRP materials, 45/7
  health aspects of, 20/5
  tensile properties of, 44/4, 44/5
Glass foam (in GRP sandwich), 45/9
Glass hardening (of elastomers), 37/18
Glass reinforced plastics (GRP), 45/1
  aggregate surfaces used, 45/14
  applications of, 45/3
  complementary materials used, 45/8
    core materials, 45/8, 45/9
    foam core materials, 45/8
    metal sections, 45/9
    plastics/rubber sections, 45/9
    synthetic fibre materials, 45/9
    timber sections, 45/9
  constituent materials in, 45/6
  creep properties of, 45/12
  dimensional stability of, 45/13
  fatigue properties of, 45/12
  filament winding of, 45/10
  fire barriers/stops used, 45/14
  fire retardancy of, 45/13
  fixing of, 45/15
  gelcoats used, 45/4, 45/13
  hand lay-up of, 45/9
  historical background for, 36/4
  impact properties of, 45/6, 45/7
  injection moulding of, 45/10
  intumescent coatings applied to,
    45/14
  manufacture of products, 45/9
  meaning of term, 45/6
  mechanical properties of, 45/6, 45/7, 45/8,
    45/9
  moulding of, 45/9, 45/10
  on-site handling of, 45/14
  other fibres used, 45/4
  paints/coatings applied to, 45/14
  reinforcements in, 45/7
  resins in, 45/6
  safety factors for, 45/12
  specifying of, 45/12
  spray moulding of, 45/10
  stress–strain behaviour of, 45/11
  as structural material, 45/11
  structural stiffening of, 45/12
  surface preparation for adhesives, 8/4
  thermal properties of, 45/12
Glass thermal-barrier coating, 7/6, 7/22
Glass transition temperature, meaning of
  term, 36/6
Glass wool
  batt/slab products, 30/6
  chemical composition of, 30/8
  manufacture of, 30/4
  raw materials used, 30/4
  roll products, 30/5
  softening point for, 30/8
Glazing applications
  glass, 29/5, 29/15, 29/17, 29/18, 29/19
  plastics, 38/3, 38/4, 38/5, 43/10, 43/11
Gluconic acid salts (concrete plasticizers),
  15/10, 15/11
Glued joints, timber joined by, 50/22

Glued-laminated timber (glulam), 50/23
  adhesives used, 50/24
  design considerations, 50/24
  manufacture of, 50/25
Gold, 7/18
  abundance in Earth's crust, 7/3
  production of, 7/19
  properties of, 7/5
  sources of, 7/19
Gold alloys, 7/20
  colours of, 7/21
  compositions of, 7/21
Gold coatings, 7/22
Goodman diagrams, 5/26, 5/27
Graffiti, removal of, 33/4, 49/12
Granite, 49/3
  in aggregates, 16/8
  cleaning of, 49/12
  properties of, 49/11
  sources of, 49/3, 49/4
Gravity die casting of aluminium alloys,
  2/4
Greenwich Observatory (UK), GRP dome,
  45/5
Grey cast iron
  applications of, 3/4
  bending strength of, 3/5
  British Standard for, 3/10
  compressive strength of, 3/3, 3/4, 3/10
  design methods used for beams, 3/14
  elastic modulus of, 3/6, 3/10
  fatigue properties of, 3/6, 3/7
  historic materials, 3/3
  history of manufacture, 3/12
  impact resistance of, 3/5
  metallurgy of, 3/3, 3/4
  microstructure of, 3/4
  modern materials, 3/10
  proof stress data for, 3/10
  repairs to, 3/10
  shear strength of, 3/5, 3/10
  tensile strength of, 3/3, 3/4, 3/10, 3/13
Greywacke, 16/9
Grit blasting
  buildings, 33/3
  steels, 31/4
  stone, 49/13
Gritstone, 16/9
Ground-granulated blast-furnace slag
  air entrainment affected by, 15/7
  chemical composition of, 18/5
  in concretes, 14/4, 14/9, 18/4, 18/9,
    18/10
  in grouts and slurries, 48/5
  physical characteristics of, 18/5
  quality standards for, 18/6, 18/7
  sulphate resistance of concrete affected by,
    18/9, 18/10
  water-reducing agents used, 15/13
Grouting (of tiles), 13/13
Grouts, 14/10, 48/1
  applications of, 48/3
  blast-furnace slag in, 48/5
  bleed behaviour of
    measurement of, 48/19
    specification of, 48/19, 48/22
  cements in, 48/4, 48/21
  ceramic tile grouts, 13/13
  chemical grouts, 48/6, 48/15
  clays in, 48/4
  composition of, 48/7
  compressive strength of
    measurement of, 48/20
    specification of, 48/22
  density of
    determination of, 48/16
    specification of, 48/21
  effect of water chemistry on, 48/6

Grouts (cont.)
  filter loss of
    measurement of, 48/19
    specification of, 48/22
  geotechnical grouts, 48/4, 48/14
  materials in, 48/3
  meaning of term, 48/3
  mix water for, 48/5
  mixing of, 48/7
  permeability of
    measurement of, 48/21
    specification of, 48/23
  pulverized-fuel ash in, 48/5
  rheology of
    measurement of, 48/17
    specification of, 48/22
  sampling of, 48/15
  set-time measurement for, 48/20
  setting of, 48/8
    measurement of set time, 48/20
  specifications for, 48/21
  structural grouts, 48/4, 48/13
  testing of, 48/16
    hardened properties, 48/20
  triaxial testing of, 48/20
  see also Chemical...; Geotechnical...;
    Structural grouts
Gunite see Sprayed concrete
Gunmetals, 7/15
  photomicrograph of, 7/18
Gyproc cove, 35/7
Gyproc fireline board, 35/7
Gyproc lath, plastering of, 35/5
Gyproc plank, 35/7
Gyproc thermal board, 35/7
Gyproc wallboard, 35/7
Gypsum plasters see Plasters

Hall–Petch relationship, 7/9, 7/10
Hand forging of aluminium alloys, 2/7
Hand-laid bituminous materials, 10/17
Hand-made tiles, manufacture of, 13/3
Handling methods
  cement, 14/5
  glass-fibre reinforced cement, 20/15
Hardboard, 50/19
  applications of, 50/21
  manufacture of, 50/19
Hardness
  aluminium and alloys, 2/16, 37/4
  copper and alloys, 7/5, 7/13, 7/15, 7/16
  elastomers, 37/4
  glass, 29/6, 37/4
  gold and alloys, 7/5, 7/21
  lead and alloys, 7/5
  nickel and alloys, 7/5, 7/27
  nickel coatings, 7/29
  polymers, 37/4, 38/8, 42/3
  silver and alloys, 7/5
  steels, 5/15, 5/22, 37/4
  tin and alloys, 7/5
  vermiculite, 51/4
  zinc and alloys, 7/5
Hardwoods
  applications of, 50/6
  properties of, 50/6
  strength classes for, 50/18
Health and safety aspects
  asbestos products, 9/14, 25/22
  concrete, 14/17
  glass fibres, 20/5
  plasterboard, 35/10
  PTFE, 42/4
  stone cleaning, 49/13
  thermosetting resins, 46/14
  timber coatings/preservatives, 32/9, 32/12
  vermiculite, 51/4

Heat transfer, principles of, 30/10
Heptonic acid salts (concrete plasticizer), 15/10, 15/11
Heston (UK), sports building, 50/24
Hexagonal close packed (HCP) structure, 7/6
High-strength lightweight concrete, silica fume in, 23/12
High-strength low-alloy (HSLA) steels, notch toughness of, 5/12
Highway bridges
  cast iron used, 3/7, 3/8
  wrought iron used, 4/4, 4/8, 4/10, 4/11
Hodgkinson (cast iron) beams, 3/14, 3/15
Hodgkinson's empirical formula (for strength of cast iron beams), 3/15
Hollow sections
  aluminium and alloys, 2/6
  steels, 5/7, 5/22
Hook fixing systems (for slates), 25/23
Hornfels (rock), 16/9
Hot-dip zinc coatings, 7/33, 7/34
Hot-rolled steels, 5/5, 5/12
Hot-water systems, polyethylene used, 40/8
Hot-working processes (for steels), 5/6
Household emulsion paints, 33/7
Hydraulic cements, 14/3
  historical background to, 14/3
Hydrocylones, slurries cleaned by, 48/12
Hydrofluoric acid, stone cleaned using, 33/3, 49/13
Hydrogen cracking (in welds), 5/15, 5/17
β-Hydroxycarboxylate compounds, 15/18, 15/19
Hydroxycarboxylic acids (concrete plasticizers), 15/10, 15/11
Hydroxylated polymers (concrete plasticizers), 15/10, 15/11, 15/16

Ideal material behaviour, classification of, 1/5
Igneous rocks, 49/3
  see also Granites
Ignition properties see Fire...; Flammability
Impact properties
  aluminium and alloys, 2/16, 45/6
  cast iron, 3/5
  ceramic tiles, 13/4
  glass fibre reinforced cement, 20/8, 20/9, 20/10
  glass reinforced plastics, 45/6, 45/7
  polymers, 38/3, 38/8, 40/4, 42/3, 43/4, 43/5, 43/7, 43/9, 44/6
  sprayed concrete, 24/9
  steels, 5/14, 37/4, 45/6
  wrought iron, 4/7
Impact-sound insulation, 30/13
  concrete floors, 30/13, 30/14, 30/19
  timber floors, 30/14, 30/15, 30/19
Impregnants (for concrete), 33/12
  silanes, 33/13, 47/3, 47/4
  silicates, 33/13
  silicofluorides, 33/13
  silicones, 33/13
  siloxanes, 47/3, 47/4
  stearates, 33/13
  see also Permeability-reducers
Impregnating waterproofing agents, 33/13, 47/3
Inconel alloys, 7/27
Ingot casting of steels, 5/5
Initial surface absorption test (ISAT)
  concrete, 15/26
  sprayed concrete, 24/10, 24/13
Injection moulding
  glass reinforced plastics, 45/10
  polymers, 40/4, 43/8
Inorganic polymers, 36/5
Insect attack (on timber), 32/3

Insulating blocks, 17/4
Insulating board, 50/20
  applications of, 50/21
Insulation materials
  aluminium affected by, 2/21
  concrete blockwork, 17/10
  glass-fibre reinforced cement, 20/19
  renders applied to, 21/6
  wood-based panel products, 50/20
Interlocking roof tiles
  clay tiles, 13/9
  concrete tiles, 25/7, 25/8, 25/26
Intumescent coatings, 34/1
  action of, 34/4
  application methods used, 34/12
  binders in, 34/4, 34/10
  certification requirements for, 34/15
  chemistry of, 34/4
  compared with other fire protection methods, 34/3
  consumption/market data for, 34/13
  design of formulations, 34/13
  elastomers used, 37/13
  environmental stability of, 34/8
  example formulation for, 34/6
  fire protection using, 34/3
  GRP painted with, 45/14
  intumescent components of, 34/4, 34/10
  manufacture of, 34/8
    attrittors used, 34/9
    ball mills used, 34/8
    bead mills used, 34/9
    high-shear dispersion used, 34/9
    manufacturing sequence for, 34/10
    paste mixers used, 34/9
  performance of, 34/6
  pigments and fillers in, 34/4, 34/11
  plasticizers in, 34/10
  raw materials in, 34/10
  reinforcing agents in, 34/4
  selection of commercial products, 34/5
  solids volume concentration of, 34/8
  specification of, 34/13
  uses of, 34/11
    cable tray protection, 34/11
    clear varnishes, 34/10
    closure/door seals, 34/12
    fire dampers, 34/12
    flame-retardant formulations, 34/12
    penetration seals, 34/10
    timber protection, 34/12
Intumescent laminated glass, 29/17
Invar alloys, 7/28
Inverted roof membrane construction, 41/11
Iron
  abundance in Earth's crust, 7/3
  cast iron, 3/1
  corrosion of
    effect of humidity, 5/29
    effect of pollution, 5/29
  manufacture of, 5/3
  wrought iron, 4/1
  see also Cast iron; Steel; Wrought iron
Iron-carbon alloys see Steels
Irrigation applications, glass-fibre reinforced cement used, 20/22
ISO Standards
  aluminium and alloys, 2/28, 2/29
  glass, 29/20
  mineral-fibre products, 30/16
  polyethylene piping, 40/7, 40/8
  steels, 5/13, 5/36
Isobutene–isoprene rubbers see Butyl rubbers
Isoprene rubbers see cis-Polyisoprenes

Joinery products, performance of, 50/28
Joinery timber, 50/27

Kevlar fibres
  production of, 44/3
  properties of, 44/4
  see also Aramid fibres
Killed steels, 5/5

Lamellar tearing (in welds), 5/17
Laminated glass, 29/13
Laminates
  GRP
    rigidity of, 45/11
    see also Glass reinforced plastics
  historical background for, 36/4
  PVC–metal, 43/13
  see also Plywood
Laminboard, 50/18
  see also Blockboard
Land-drainage applications see Drainage applications
Landfill sites, clay lining of, 48/23
Latex foam, applications of, 37/16
Lead, 7/22
  abundance in Earth's crust, 7/3
  applications of, 7/24, 7/25
  creep of, 7/23, 7/24
  metallic lead, 7/23
  production of, 7/23
  properties, 7/5, 7/22
  sources of, 7/23
Lead–antimony alloys, creep of, 7/24
Lead pipe, 7/24
Lead sheet, 7/23
Lead–tin alloys
  phase diagram for, 7/31
  see also Solders
Lead-bismuth alloys
  compositions of, 7/25
  melting points of, 7/25
Leca (lightweight aggregate), 16/19, 16/21
Legislation, asbestos, 9/13
Lichens and mosses, 25/10, 25/21, 49/11
Light-transmission properties
  glasses, 29/6, 29/7, 29/8, 29/9
  plastics, 38/9
Lightweight aggregates, 14/6, 16/19
  density of, 16/19, 16/20
  exfoliated perlite, 16/20
  exfoliated vermiculite, 16/20, 51/7
  expanded clays/shales/slates, 16/19
  expanded polystyrene, 16/20
  expanded slag, 16/20
  furnace ash/clinker/slag, 16/20
  grading of, 16/21
  as GRC component, 20/4
  historical background for, 16/19
  manufacture of, 16/19
  properties, 16/20
  roof tiles made from, 25/17
  sintered pulverized fuel ash, 16/20
  standards for testing of, 16/20
  twentieth-century developments, 16/19
Lightweight concrete blockwork, plastering of, 35/5
Lightweight concrete roof tiles, 25/17
  cost comparison for, 25/26
  installation of, 25/18
  manufacture of, 25/18
Lightweight insulating concrete, 51/7
Lignosulphonates (concrete plasticizers), 15/10, 15/11, 15/15, 15/16, 15/17
Lime bloom see Efflorescence
Lime mortars, 11/10, 17/8
Lime washes, 33/6
Limestone, 49/3
  in aggregates, 16/8
  cleaning of, 49/12, 49/13
  properties of, 49/11

Limestone (*cont.*)
sources of, **49**/4
testing of, **49**/7, **49**/8
Limit-state approach (for wrought iron), **4**/8
Loft insulation materials
mineral-fibre products, **30**/5
polystyrene foam, **41**/9
vermiculite, **51**/4
Lok pull-out test, sprayed fibre concrete
tested by, **24**/13
Los Angeles Fire Department Emergency
Control Center, **37**/15
Loughborough University (UK), running
track, **37**/17
Low-temperature properties, aluminium and
alloys, **2**/18
Lowry (timber treatment) process, **32**/6
Lung cancer, asbestos-induced, **9**/15
Lycrete, **16**/19
Lytag, **14**/6, **16**/20

Macadams, **10**/10
base-course macadams, **10**/11
dense base course macadams, **10**/12
DoT specification for, **10**/12
open-graded base-course macadam, **10**/11
manufacturing of, **10**/14
recipe mixes for, **10**/10
road-base, **10**/11
single-course macadams, **10**/12
wearing-course macadams, **10**/12
close-graded wearing-course macadams,
10/13
dense wearing-course macadams, **10**/13
fine-graded wearing-course macadam,
10/13
medium-graded wearing-course
macadams, **10**/13
open-graded wearing-course macadams,
10/13
pervious wearing-course macadams,
10/13
Machine-laid bituminous materials, **10**/18
Magnesia in cements, **18**/7
Magnesian limestones, **49**/3
decay of, **49**/5
sources of, **49**/4
Magnetic properties, aluminium and alloys,
2/18
Maleic acid (concrete retarder), **15**/18
Malleable cast iron, **3**/4, **3**/11
microstructure of, **3**/7
Manganese brass, **7**/14
Marble, **49**/3
in aggregates, **16**/8
cleaning of, **49**/12
properties of, **49**/11
sources of, **49**/3, **49**/4
Marcasite, **16**/8
Marine applications, glass-fibre reinforced
cement used, **20**/22
Marine borers, timber attacked by, **32**/4
Marine environmental effects, glass-fibre
reinforced cement, **20**/12
Marine plywood, **50**/18
Marsh funnel, slurries tested using, **48**/18
Marshall quotient, **10**/7
Marshall test, **10**/5
asphalt mixes based on, **10**/4
typical results, **10**/5
Martensite, **5**/9
Martensitic stainless steels, **5**/8, **5**/20
Masonry, aluminium affected by, **2**/21
Masonry mortars, **21**/3
Masonry paints, **33**/7
Mastic asphalt wearing courses, **10**/9
Mazak alloys, **7**/34, **7**/35

Mechanical cleaning
steels, **31**/4
stone, **49**/13
Mechanical finishes, aluminium and alloys,
2/25
Mechanical forming processes, steels, **5**/5
Medium-density fibreboard (MDF),
50/20
applications of, **50**/21
standards of, **50**/20
Medium-temperature asphalts (MTAs), **10**/9,
10/23
specification for, **10**/31
Melamine and dimers/salts/trimers (in
intumescent coatings), **34**/10
Melamine–formaldehyde resins, historical
background for, **36**/3
Melamine–urea–formaldehyde (MUF) resins,
wood-based panel products bonded
with, **50**/18, **50**/19
Melting points, metals (various), **2**/18, **3**/4,
7/5, **7**/25
Memory alloys, **7**/17, **7**/28
Mesothelioma, **9**/14, **9**/15, **14**/7
Metal films, colour of, **7**/6, **7**/22
Metal–inert gas (MIG) process, aluminium
alloys, **2**/24
Metal sprayed zinc coatings, **31**/6
Metalock process, **3**/10
Metamorphic rocks, **49**/3
see also Marbles; Slates
Micaceous iron oxide (MIO), **31**/5, **46**/12
Micafill (exfoliated vermiculite), **51**/5
Micas, **16**/9
Microfine cements, in grouts, **48**/4
Microsilica *see* Silica fume
Middle East aggregates
alkali–aggregate reaction in, **16**/16
chloride content of, **14**/6, **16**/12, **16**/17
factors affecting, **16**/3
grading of, **16**/13
production of, **16**/6, **16**/7
salt weathering in, **16**/15
shell content of, **16**/10
sulphate content of, **16**/17
testing of, **16**/18
Mild steel
corrosion of, **5**/30
properties of, **5**/8, **37**/4, **45**/6, **45**/12
see also Steels
Millscale
paint applied to, **31**/3
removal of, **5**/31
Mineral fibre products, **30**/1
applications of, **30**/3, **30**/17
approval documentation for, **30**/17
batt/slab products, **30**/6
acoustic/thermal slabs, **30**/7, **30**/21
cavity-wall batts/slabs, **30**/6, **30**/21
decorative lining panels, **30**/7, **30**/21
duct slabs, **30**/7, **30**/21
fire-protection slabs, **30**/7, **30**/21
floor slabs, **30**/7
proprietary brand examples of, **30**/20
roofing slabs, **30**/7, **30**/21
thermal/acoustic slabs, **30**/7, **30**/21
timber-frame batts, **30**/6
biological properties of, **30**/10
blowing wool, **30**/3, **30**/7, **30**/21
cavity-wall applications of, **30**/3, **30**/6, **30**/7,
30/18
ceiling tiles, **30**/8, **30**/21
chemical composition of, **30**/8
chemical resistance of, **30**/8
density of, **30**/5, **30**/6, **30**/7
effects of moisture on, **30**/8
fire performance of, **30**/15
fire properties of, **30**/14

Mineral fibre products (*cont.*)
fire protection applications of, **30**/7, **30**/15,
30/19
fire rating of, **30**/14
fitness-of-materials established for, **30**/17
floor applications of, **30**/7, **30**/19
handling and cutting of, **30**/10
historical background for, **30**/3
as insulators, **30**/10, **30**/13
laminated dry linings, **30**/5, **30**/7, **30**/21
manufacture of, **30**/4
finishing processes, **30**/4, **30**/5
permanence of, **30**/10
physical properties of, **30**/8
proprietary brand examples, **30**/20
raw materials used, **30**/4
roll products, **30**/5
cladding rolls, **30**/5, **30**/20
duct wraps, **30**/6, **30**/21
partition rolls, **30**/6, **30**/21
proprietary brand examples of, **30**/20
sound-deadening rolls, **30**/6, **30**/21
stitched-wire mattresses, **30**/5, **30**/6, **30**/21
timber-frame rolls, **30**/6, **30**/21
unfaced lightweight rolls, **30**/5, **30**/20
roof applications of, **30**/3, **30**/7, **30**/17
slab/batt products, **30**/6
sleeved cavity barriers, **30**/8, **30**/21
softening points for, **30**/8
sound absorption by, **30**/12
sound insulation by, **30**/13
sources of, **30**/3
standards for, **30**/16
structure of, **30**/8
thermal conductivity of, **30**/5, **30**/6, **30**/7,
30/22
factors affecting, **30**/11
timber-frame applications of, **30**/6, **30**/18
types of, **30**/5
wall applications of, **30**/6, **30**/18
water repellancy of, **30**/10
Mineral fibres
definitions of, **30**/3
man-made mineral fibres, **30**/3
see also Glass wool; Rock wool
naturally occurring mineral fibres, **30**/3
types of, **30**/3
Mineral wool
cavity-wall insulation using, **30**/3, **30**/7
manufacture of, **30**/4
see also Blown mineral wool
Minerals, extraction of, **7**/4
Miner's law, **5**/26
Mining applications, elastomers used, **37**/16
Mix-design approach
bituminous materials, **10**/4
concrete, **14**/8
Models, **1**/5
Moisture-curing polyurethanes, **33**/12, **46**/11
Mole ploughing, polyethylene pipe laid by,
40/11
Monel alloys, **7**/3, **7**/26, **7**/27
Mordant wash, **31**/6
Mortars, **14**/9, **21**/3
air-entraining agents for, **15**/9
analysis of, **21**/4
brickwork mortars, **11**/10, **11**/13
compressive strength of, **17**/9, **21**/4
concrete blockwork mortars, **17**/8
materials in, **21**/3
mix proportions for, **11**/11, **17**/9, **21**/3
plasticizers in, **11**/11, **15**/9, **17**/9, **21**/3
polymer-modified mortars, **39**/6, **39**/9, **46**/14
problems with, **21**/5
properties of, **11**/11, **17**/9, **21**/3, **46**/14
purposes of, **21**/3
ready-to-use mortars, **21**/4
retarders for, **15**/20

Mortars (*cont.*)
  site batching/mixing of, **21**/3
  tile-fixing mortars, **13**/13, **13**/14
  winter working with, **21**/5
Mosaics, **13**/13
Mosses and lichens, **25**/10, **25**/21, **49**/11
Mould oils, **22**/1
  mechanisms of, **22**/3
  see also Release agents
Moulding of glass reinforced plastics, **45**/9,
  45/10
Mud balance, **48**/16
Multicolour paints, **33**/7
Muntz metal, **7**/14
Murchison (offshore) Platform, **42**/7

Nails
  slates fixed by, **25**/23
  timber joined by, **50**/22
Narrow-trenching, polyethylene pipe laid by,
  40/10
Natural rubber (NR)
  applications of, **37**/13, **37**/15, **37**/16
  dispersions containing, **39**/7
  formulations for, **37**/7
  properties of, **37**/4, **37**/10
  sources of, **37**/3
  structure of, **37**/5
  vulcanization of, **37**/7
  weatherability of, **37**/18
Naval brass, **7**/14
Needle punching (of geotextiles), **28**/4
Neoprene *see* Polychloroprene
Neoprene rubber coatings, **33**/11
Nichrome, **7**/27
Nickel, **7**/26
  abundance in Earth's crust, **7**/3
  characteristics of, **7**/26
  production of, **7**/26
  properties of, **7**/5
  sources of, **7**/26
Nickel alloys, **7**/26
  mechanical properties of, **7**/27
Nickel coatings, **7**/28
Nickel–iron alloys, **7**/28
Nickel–silver alloys, **7**/28
Nickel silvers (copper-rich alloys), **7**/28
Nickel–titanium alloys, **7**/28
Nimonic alloys, **7**/26, **7**/28
Nitrile rubbers (NBR)
  applications of, **37**/13, **37**/16
  dispersions containing, **39**/8
  production of, **37**/5
  properties of, **37**/10
  vulcanizing of, **37**/8
No-fines concrete, **14**/6
Nodular (spheroidal graphite) cast iron, **3**/11
  see also Ductile cast iron
Noise control
  mineral-fibre products used, **30**/12, **30**/13
  principles of, **30**/12
  see also Acoustic...; Sound insulation
Non-ferrous metals, **7**/1
  crystal structures of, **7**/5, **7**/6
  intersolubility of, **7**/5
  mechanical properties of, **7**/5
  physical properties of, **7**/5
  see also Aluminium; Copper; Lead; Nickel;
    Silver; Tin; Zinc
Nonylphenol 6EO (air-entraining agent),
  15/6, **15**/7
Normality (in plasticity theories), **1**/8
Normalizing (of steels), **5**/12
Notch-toughness, steels, **5**/11
Nuclear gauges, bituminous materials tested
  using, **10**/26
Nylons, properties of, **37**/4

Offshore applications
  elastomers, **37**/16
  grouts and slurries, **48**/3, **48**/4
  vermiculite, **51**/6
Offshore gas/oil platforms
  anchoring of, **44**/13
  launching of, **42**/7
Oil based paints, **5**/33, **5**/34, **31**/5, **32**/10, **33**/7
Oil well cement, **48**/4
Open-hearth (Siemens) process, **5**/4
Optical-fibre cables, **40**/11, **40**/12
Oriented-strand boards, **50**/20
Otto Graf viscometer (for grouts), **48**/18, **48**/22
Oxygen affinity of aluminium, **2**/18
Oxygen-free high-conductivity copper, **7**/10
Ozone resistance, PVC, **43**/11

Paints
  for absorbent surfaces, **33**/1
  acrylic paints, **33**/8
  alkyd paints, **33**/8
  aluminium and alloys protected by, **2**/19,
    2/20, **2**/21, **2**/25
  application methods for, **32**/12, **33**/5
  binders in, **31**/5, **32**/10
  bitumen paints, **33**/9
  bitumen-emulsion coatings, **33**/7
  cement paints, **33**/6
  chlorinated rubber paints, **33**/9
  coal-tar paints, **33**/9
  components of, **32**/9, **33**/5
  emulsion paints, **33**/6, **33**/7
  epoxy ester/alkyd paints, **33**/8
  epoxy resin paints, **33**/9
  gas/water-vapour transport through, **33**/5
  GRP painted with, **45**/14
  intumescent coatings, **34**/1
  masonry paints, **33**/7
  for mineral surfaces, **33**/5
  multicolour paints, **33**/7
  for non-absorbent surfaces, **31**/1
    components of, **31**/4
    heavy-duty coatings, **31**/9
    specifications for, **31**/7
    surface preparation methods used, **31**/3
  oil-based paints, **31**/5, **32**/10, **33**/7
  phenolic paints, **33**/8
  pigments in, **31**/4, **32**/10, **33**/5
  polyurethane paints, **33**/11
  primers used, **31**/6
  removal from stone masonry, **33**/4, **49**/12
  single-pack convertible paints, **31**/5
  single-pack non-convertible paints, **31**/5
  solids volume concentration of, **31**/5, **33**/5,
    34/9
  solvent-thinned paints, **33**/8
  solvents in, **31**/5
  steels protected by, **5**/32, **5**/34
  textured paints, **33**/7
  for timber, **32**/9
  two-pack chemical curing paints, **31**/5
  two-pack systems, **31**/5, **33**/9
  urethane oil paints, **33**/8
  vinyl paints, **33**/9
  water-borne paints, **32**/11, **33**/6
  see also Intumescent coatings; Masonry
    paints
Palabora vermiculite
  properties of, **51**/3
  see also Vermiculite
Panama-weave fabrics, **27**/4
Pantiles
  clay pantiles, **13**/9
  concrete pantiles, **25**/8, **25**/9
Parafil (parallel-lay aramid ropes), **44**/10
  applications of, **44**/11
  concrete prestressed using, **44**/11, **44**/12

Parafil (parallel-lay aramid ropes) (*cont.*)
  stress-rupture data for, **44**/6
  termination system for, **44**/10
Parana pine, **50**/4
Paris equation, **5**/27
Particleboard, **50**/20
Pearlite, **5**/9, **5**/10
Pellite (lightweight aggregate), **16**/19, **16**/20
Pentachlorophenol (PCP) wood fungicide, **32**/5
Pentaerythritol and dimers/trimers (in
  intumescent coatings), **34**/10
Peralloy, **7**/28
Percentage refusal density (PRD) test (for
  bituminous materials), **10**/26
Perforated bricks, **11**/7
Periclase (magnesia), **18**/7
Permeability
  coatings, **32**/10
  concrete, **15**/24, **47**/4
  silica-fume concrete, **23**/10
  slurries, **48**/13, **48**/23
  sprayed concrete, **24**/10
  timber, **32**/5, **50**/6, **50**/11, **50**/13
Permeability-reducers (for concrete), **15**/24
  benefits of, **15**/26
  chemical types of, **15**/26
  standards/specifications for, **15**/27
  testing of, **15**/26
  theory of, **15**/26
  see also Impregnants (for concrete)
Permeance, definition of, **20**/12
Pervious macadams, **10**/13
Petch equation, **5**/9
Petroleum bitumen, tests for, **10**/29
Pewter, **7**/32
Phase diagrams
  aluminium–zinc, **7**/36
  bentonite–cement–water, **48**/7
  copper–aluminium, **7**/16
  copper–tin, **7**/15
  copper–zinc, **7**/13
  iron–carbon, **5**/9
  tin–lead, **7**/31
Phenolic foam concrete, **36**/6
Phenolic foams, in GRP sandwich structures,
  45/8
Phenolic paints, **33**/8
Phenolic resins
  in GRP, **45**/7, **45**/13
  historical background for, **36**/3
  plywood bonded with, **50**/18
Phosphate plasticizers (in intumescent
  coatings), **34**/10
Phosphor bronzes, **7**/14
  photomicrograph of, **7**/18
Phosphorus deoxidized copper, **7**/9, **7**/11
Physical vapour deposition (PVD), **7**/22
Pickling (of steel), **5**/32
Piecing-in (of stone), **49**/14
Pig iron, **5**/3
Pigments
  in paints, **31**/4, **32**/10, **33**/5
  in thermosetting resins, **46**/12
Pipeline laying
  clay pipe, **12**/6, **12**/7
  polyethylene pipe, **40**/10
Pipeline testing, **12**/7
Piping applications
  deformation requirements for, **40**/5
  elastomers, **37**/13, **37**/15
  polymers, **40**/5, **43**/5
  pressure requirements for, **40**/5
Pitched roofs
  clay/concrete tiles used, **13**/10, **25**/23
  polystyrene foams used, **41**/9
Pittsburgh Sheet (glass) Process, **29**/4
Planned maintenance, asbestos register used,
  9/16

Plasterboard, **35**/1
  composition of, **35**/7
  cove used, **35**/7
  cutting of, **35**/9
  decoration of, **35**/10
  design/planning considerations, **35**/8
  dry lining using, **35**/7
  fire protection using, **35**/7
  fireline board, **35**/7
  fixing of, **35**/9
  fixtures to walls, **35**/10
  handling of, **35**/9
  health and safety aspects, **35**/10
  historical background for, **35**/10
  performance of, **35**/7
  plastering of, **35**/5
  site organization affecting, **35**/8
  site work involving, **35**/9
  sound insulation by, **35**/8
  temperature limits for, **35**/8
  thermal insulation by, **35**/8
  vermiculite in, **51**/9
  wallboard, **35**/7
Plastering, **35**/5
  preparation of backgrounds, **35**/5
  treated surfaces, **35**/6
  various surfaces, **35**/5
Plasters, **35**/1
  adhesion loss in, **35**/6
  aluminium affected by, **2**/21
  Carlite premixed plasters, **35**/3
  cracking caused by background movement, **35**/6
  dry-out of, **35**/6
  final-coat plasters, **35**/3
  historical background for, **35**/3
  mixing of, **35**/6
  one-coat plaster, **35**/3
  problems with, **35**/6
  projection plaster, **35**/4
  quick setting of, **35**/6
  renovating plasters, **35**/4
  shrinkage cracking of, **35**/6
  Sirapite B plaster, **35**/4
  slow-setting plaster, **35**/4, **35**/6
  Thistle range of plasters, **35**/3, **35**/4
  types of, **35**/3
  X-ray plasters, **35**/4
Plastic behaviour, **1**/5
Plastic coated steels, **5**/34, **5**/35
Plastic concrete, **48**/12
Plasticity
  combined stresses in, **1**/7
  one-dimensional loading, **1**/6
  two-dimensional loading, **1**/7
Plasticizers
  concrete, **15**/9
    acrylic acid/ester coplymers, **15**/11
    benefits of, **15**/12
    cement content affected by, **15**/12
    chemical types of, **15**/9
    historical background, **15**/9
    hydroxycarboxlic acids, **15**/10, **15**/11
    hydroxylated polymers, **15**/10, **15**/11
    lignosulphonates, **15**/10, **15**/11
    mechanism of, **15**/9, **15**/10
    set retardation using, **15**/13
    standards/specifiations for, **15**/14, **15**/15, **15**/19
    strength of concrete affected by, **15**/12
    workability of concrete affected by, **15**/12
    see also Water-reducing agents
  intumescent coating, **34**/10
  thermosetting resin, **46**/12
Plywood, **50**/18
  applications of, **50**/21
  manufacture of, **50**/18
  standards for, **50**/18

Plywood (cont.)
  treatment of, **32**/7
  types of, **50**/18
Poisson's ratio
  elastomers, **37**/4
  glass, **29**/6, **37**/4
  glass-fibre reinforced cement, **20**/8, **20**/9, **20**/10
  polymers, **37**/4, **38**/8, **41**/6
Polished Stone Value (PSV) test, **10**/27
  minimum values for road use, **10**/33
  typical values, **10**/28
Polybutadiene
  production of, **37**/5
  see also Butadiene rubbers
Polycarbonates, **38**/3
  acoustic properties of, **38**/8
  applications of, **38**/3
  chemical properties of, **38**/3
  crazing susceptibility of, **38**/5
  effect of rate/duration of loading, **38**/5
  elastic modulus of, **38**/8
    effect of temperature/load duration, **38**/6
  electrical properties of, **38**/9
  fabrication of, **38**/5
  fire safety of, **38**/7, **38**/9
  impact properties of, **38**/3, **38**/7, **38**/8
  maximum allowable stress for, **38**/6
  mechanical properties of, **38**/3, **38**/5, **38**/6, **38**/8
  optical properties of, **38**/9
  serviceability of, **38**/5
  temperature effects on, **38**/5, **38**/7
  thermal expansion/contraction of, **38**/3, **38**/7, **38**/8
  thermal properties of, **38**/3, **38**/8, **38**/9
  weathering of, **38**/5, **38**/6
Polychloroprene rubbers (CR)
  applications of, **37**/12, **37**/13, **37**/15, **37**/16
  coatings, **33**/11
  dispersions, **39**/7
  production of, **37**/5
  properties of, **37**/11
  vulcanizing of, **37**/8
Polyester resin coatings, **33**/11
  disadvantages of, **33**/11
Polyester resins, **46**/7
  advantages/disadvantages of, **46**/13
  curing of, **46**/9
  in GRP, **45**/6, **45**/13
  historical background for, **36**/4, **46**/7
  production of, **46**/8
Polyether–polyamide block copolymers, properties of, **37**/12
Polyether–polyester block copolymers, properties of, **37**/12
Polyethylene, **40**/1
  applications of, **40**/5
    damp-proof membranes, **40**/13
    electrical uses, **40**/11
    pipes, **40**/5
    road/soil-reinforcement, **40**/13
  cross-linking of, **40**/12
  European standardization for, **40**/13
  fabrication processes used, **40**/4
  fracture toughness of, **40**/6
  historical background for, **36**/4
  jointing techniques for pipes, **40**/9
  manufacture of, **40**/3
  molecular-weight distribution of, **40**/3
  piping, **40**/5
    gas-distribution pipes, **40**/6
    hot/cold-water systems, **40**/8
    installation techniques used, **40**/10
    jointing techniques used, **40**/9
    requirements for, **40**/5
    sewers, **40**/8
    water-distribution pipes, **40**/7

Polyethylene (cont.)
  properties of, **37**/4, **40**/3, **40**/4, **40**/9, **40**/12, **43**/4
    factors affecting, **40**/4
    structure of, **40**/3
    terminology for, **40**/4
    tonnage used, **40**/4
Polyglycoside-based plasticizer, **15**/11
Polyisocyanurate foams, in GRP sandwich structures, **45**/8
cis-Polyisoprenes
  production of, **37**/3
  properties of, **37**/10
  vulcanizing of, **37**/8
Polymer concretes, **14**/8, **46**/5
Polymer dispersions, **39**/1
  binding ability of, **39**/5
  as binding agents, **39**/5
  carboxylation levels in, **39**/5
  cementitious materials containing
    applications of, **39**/9
    binding mechanism for, **39**/5
    properties of, **39**/9
    selection criteria for, **39**/7
    site-usage notes for, **39**/10
  cross-linking in, **39**/5
  historical background for, **36**/5, **39**/3
  manufacture of, **39**/4
  molecular weight of, **39**/5
  monomer ratio in, **39**/4
  particle size factors in, **39**/4
  process conditions affecting, **39**/5
  redispersible powder polymers, **39**/4
  selection according to application, **39**/6
  selection for use in cementitious mixes, **39**/7
  surfactant types in, **39**/4
  testing of, **39**/7
  types of, **39**/7
  variables affecting, **39**/4
Polymer emulsions see Polymer dispersions
Polymer fibre reinforced concrete, **14**/8, **24**/5
Polymer impregnated concrete (PIC), **14**/8, **46**/5
Polymer latex bonding aids, **8**/3
Polymer modified cement (PMC) slates, **25**/22
  appearance of, **25**/22
  cost comparison for, **25**/26
  fire resistance of, **25**/22
  manufacture of, **25**/22
  sizes of, **25**/18
Polymer modified concrete, **46**/5
Polymer modified mortars
  applications of, **39**/9
  properties of, **39**/9, **46**/14
  site usage of, **39**/10
Polymer modified Portland cement paints, **33**/6
Polymer–Portland-cement concrete (PPCC), **14**/8, **46**/5
Polymer slurries, **48**/6
Polymers, **36**/1
  creep resistance of, **36**/6
  engineering properties of, **36**/6
  fire resistance of, **36**/6
  future developments in, **36**/6
  glass-transition temperatures of, **36**/6
  historical background for, **36**/3, **36**/4, **36**/5, **36**/6
  meaning of term, **36**/3, **39**/3
  thermoplastics, **36**/4
  thermosets, **36**/3
  weathering of, **36**/6
  see under individual polymer names
Polynorbornene rubbers (PNR), properties of, **37**/12
Polyolefin thermoplastic elastomers
  moulding of, **37**/9
  properties of, **37**/12

Poly(p-phenylene terephthalamide), aramid fibres made from, **44**/3
Polypropylene, properties of, **43**/4
Polypropylene fibre reinforced concrete, **24**/5, **24**/14
Poly(propylene oxide) rubber (GPO), properties of, **37**/11
Polypropylene tape geotextiles, **28**/3
Polystyrene, **41**/1
  historical background for, **41**/3
  properties of, **41**/4
  see also Expanded polystyrene
Polysulphide rubber coatings, **33**/11
Polysulphide rubbers
  applications of, **37**/13
  properties of, **37**/11
Polytetrafluoroethylene (PTFE), **42**/1
  applications of, **42**/4
    bearings, **42**/4
    slides, **42**/6
  chemical resistance of, **42**/3
  electrical properties of, **42**/3
  fabrication techniques for, **42**/3
  friction properties of, **42**/6
    effect of lubrication, **42**/7, **42**/9
    effect of mating surface, **42**/7, **42**/8
    effect of temperature, **42**/7, **42**/10
    filled PTFE materials, **42**/8, **42**/11
  glass-fibre cloth coated with, **27**/5
  manufacture of, **42**/3
  maximum sliding bearing pressures allowed, **42**/6
  mechanical properties of, **42**/3
  physical properties of, **42**/3
  thermal properties of, **42**/3
Polythene see Polyethylene
Polyurethane foams, in GRP sandwich structures, **45**/8
Polyurethane paints, **5**/33, **5**/34
  moisture-curing paints, **33**/12
  oil-modified paints, **33**/11
  two-pack systems, **33**/11
Polyurethane resins, **46**/10
  advantages/disadvantages of, **46**/13
  applications of, **46**/11
  production of, **46**/11
Polyurethane rubbers
  applications of, **37**/13, **37**/15
  production of, **37**/5
  properties of, **37**/11
  vulcanizing of, **37**/9
Polyurethane thermoplastic elastomers, properties of, **37**/12
Poly(vinyl acetate) (PVAc)
  adhesives, **8**/3
  dispersions, **39**/8
Poly(vinyl chloride) (PVC), **43**/1
  applications of, **37**/12, **37**/15, **43**/5, **43**/11
  compounding of, **43**/3
  fire performance of, **43**/12
  flexible PVC, **43**/11
    applications of, **43**/11
    properties of, **43**/11, **43**/12
  foams
    in GRP sandwich structures, **45**/8
    rigid PVC foam profiles, **43**/10
  future developments of, **43**/12
  historical background for, **36**/4
  injection-moulded fittings, **43**/8
  piping applications, **43**/5
    special forms of pipes, **43**/7
    types of pipes, **43**/6
  polyester fabric coated with, **27**/4
  processing of, **43**/4
  production of, **43**/3
  rigid PVC
    applications of, **43**/5
    creep properties of, **43**/5, **43**/6

Poly(vinyl chloride) (PVC) (cont.)
  rigid PVC (cont.)
    foamed PVC profiles, **43**/10
    ignition properties of, **43**/12
    impact properties of, **43**/5, **43**/7
    injection-moulded fittings, **43**/8
    piping, **43**/5
    profiles, **43**/8
    properties of, **43**/4, **43**/9
    sheet products, **43**/10
    thermal properties of, **43**/9, **43**/10
    weld strength of, **43**/10
Poly(vinyl propionate) (PVP) dispersions, **39**/8
Poly(vinylidene dichloride) (PVDC) dispersions, **39**/8
Porosity
  concrete, **15**/24, **47**/4
  glass-fibre reinforced cement, **20**/12
  stone, **49**/11
  welds, **5**/15
Portland blast-furnace slag, **14**/4
  British Standard requirements for, **18**/7
Portland cement, **18**/3
  British Standards for, **14**/5, **18**/6
  chemical composition of, **18**/3, **18**/5
  chemical reactions for, **18**/3
  components of, **14**/4
  in glass-fibre reinforced cement, **20**/3
  mortar/concrete properties, **46**/14
  physical characteristics of, **18**/5
  setting time of, **14**/10
  silica fume added, **18**/4, **23**/6
  surface area of, **18**/4, **23**/4
  in vermiculite cement, **51**/7
Potable-water applications
  bituminous emulsions, **33**/7
  elastomers, **37**/15
  glass-fibre reinforced cement, **20**/12
  polyethylene, **40**/7
Potential Energy Function concept, **1**/4
Powder coating (of aluminium and alloys), **2**/25
Powder post beetles, **32**/4
Power cables, polyethylene used, **40**/12
Pozzolanic reactions, **18**/4
  chemistry of, **18**/8
  silica fume, **23**/6
Precast concrete, **14**/15
  adhesives used, **8**/5
  plastering of, **35**/5
Precoated chippings, **10**/22
  spreading of, **10**/23
Premixed glass-fibre reinforced cement, **20**/23
Premixed plasters, **35**/3
Pressed bricks, **11**/5, **11**/7
Pressure die casting of aluminium alloys, **2**/4
Prestressed borosilicate glass, as fire-resistant glass, **29**/17
Prestressing steels, **6**/7
  manufacture of, **6**/7
  mechanical properties of, **6**/8
  quality assurance for, **6**/8
  site precautions for, **6**/8
  sizes and properties of, **6**/7
  terminology for, **6**/7
Projection plaster, **35**/4
Proof stress data
  aluminium and alloys, **2**/12, **2**/14, **2**/16, **45**/6
  cast iron, **3**/10
  copper and alloys, **7**/5, **7**/11, **7**/13, **7**/15, **7**/16
  glass reinforced plastics, **45**/6
  nickel and alloys, **7**/5, **7**/27
  non-ferrous metals (various), **7**/5
  steels, **5**/21, **45**/6
Protecton range of primers, **31**/4, **31**/7, **31**/8
PSA airfield runway specification, **10**/10, **16**/15
PSV see Polished Stone Value (PSV) test
Puddling furnaces, wrought iron made in, **4**/3, **4**/9

Pultruded materials, **44**/8, **44**/9, **45**/10
Pulverized-fuel ash (pfa)
  air entrainment affected by, **15**/7
  chemical composition of, **18**/5
  in concretes, **14**/4, **14**/9, **16**/20, **18**/4
  in glass-reinforced cement, **20**/4
  in grouts and slurries, **48**/5
  physical characteristics of, **18**/5
  quality standards for, **18**/5
  sulphate resistance of concrete affected by, **18**/9, **18**/10
  water-reducing agents used, **15**/13, **15**/14
Pumice, as concrete component, **16**/19
Punching of wrought iron, **4**/6
Pure metal, cost of, **7**/3
PVC-coated polyester fabric, **27**/4
Pyrite, **16**/8
Pyrostop glass, **29**/17
  fixing of, **29**/18

Quality assurance/control
  bituminous materials, **10**/4, **10**/26
  concrete, **14**/16
  sprayed concrete, **24**/12
Quarry tiles, **13**/4
Quartz, **16**/9
Quartzite, **16**/9
Quinton Bridges (UK), adhesives used, **8**/8

Radiation, principles of, **30**/10
Railway sleepers, elastomers used, **37**/16
Rain resistance, concrete blockwork, **17**/9
Rainwater goods
  asbestos cement, **9**/8
  PVC, **43**/6
Rainy weather, road laying in, **10**/24
Rapid-analysis machine (RAM) test
  concrete, **14**/16
  sprayed concrete, **24**/12
Rawcliffe Bridge (UK), adhesives used, **8**/5
Reactive polymers, **36**/5
Ready-mixed concrete, **14**/6
  quality scheme for, **14**/16
Ready-to-use mortars, **21**/4
Rebars, meaning of term, **6**/3
Reconstructed-stone (concrete) slates, **25**/18
  appearance of, **25**/18
  cost comparison for, **25**/26
  durability of, **25**/18
  installation of, **25**/19
    diminishing-course slates, **25**/19, **25**/20
    standard-sized slates, **25**/19
  manufacture of, **25**/18
  sizes of, **25**/18
  standards for, **25**/18
  types of, **25**/18
  weather resistance of, **25**/18
Red (iron) oxide, **31**/5
Redispersible powder polymers, **39**/4
Reflectivity, aluminium, **2**/18
Refractive index
  glass, **29**/6
  plastics, **38**/9
Reinforced concrete
  development of, **1**/4
  repair by resin injection, **8**/9
  steel reinforcement in, **6**/1
  strengthening by external bonding of steel plates, **8**/6
Reinforcement
  geotextiles used, **28**/12
  in sprayed concrete, **25**/5
  steel used, **6**/1
  see also Steel reinforcement
Release agents, **22**/1
  mechanisms of, **22**/3

Release agents (*cont.*)
  oil-in-water emulsions, **22**/4
  problems with, **22**/4
    absorbent shuttering, **22**/5
    overapplication of release agent, **22**/5
  types of, **22**/4
  water-in-oil emulsions, **22**/4
Renders, **14**/9, **21**/5
  application to insulation materials, **21**/6
  applications of, **21**/6
  glass-fibre reinforced cement used, **20**/22
  materials in, **21**/5
  mix proportions for, **21**/6
  problems with, **21**/7
  purpose of, **21**/5
  types of, **21**/5
Renovating plasters, **35**/4
Repairs
  adhesives used, **8**/6, **8**/9
  cast iron, **3**/10
  clay pipes, **12**/5
  concrete structures, **8**/6, **8**/9
  polymer-modified mortars used, **39**/9, **39**/10
  stonework, **49**/14
  wrought iron, **4**/9
Repave process, **10**/16
Repointing of stonework, **49**/14
Reservoir linings, elastomers used, **37**/15, **37**/20
Resin injection, concrete structures repaired
    by, **8**/9
Resin mortars, **36**/4, **36**/6
  tiles fixed by, **13**/13, **13**/14
Resin/polymer-bonded slates, **25**/21
  appearance of, **25**/22
  durability of, **25**/22
  fire resistance of, **25**/22
  manufacture of, **25**/21
  sizes of, **25**/18
Retarders (for concrete), **15**/18
  benefits of retardation, **15**/20
  chemical types of, **15**/20, **15**/21
  mechanism of retardation, **15**/18
  standards/specifiations for, **15**/15, **15**/19,
    15/20
Retford Station (Notts.), cast iron structure, **3**/9
Rheological models, **1**/5
  elasto–plastic behaviour shown, **1**/6
  relationships underlying use of, **1**/5
  two-dimensional model, **1**/7
    direct extension of results, **1**/9
Rhyolite (rock), **16**/9
Ribbed sewer pipes, **43**/7, **43**/8
Rigid–hardening plastic materials
  one-dimensional loading of, **1**/6, **1**/7
  two-dimensional loading of, **1**/8
Rigid–plastic materials, one-dimensional
    loading of, **1**/6, **1**/7
Rimming steels, **5**/5, **5**/13
Riveting methods, aluminium and alloys, **2**/25
Road bases
  asphalts, **10**/8
  macadams, **10**/11
Road construction materials
  asphalts, **10**/3
  elastomers, **37**/16
  geotextiles, **28**/12, **40**/13
  macadams, **10**/10
  mastic asphalts, **10**/9
  polystyrene foam, **41**/15
  see also Asphalts; Macadams; Mastic
    asphalts
Rock wool
  batt/slab products, **30**/6
  chemical composition of, **30**/8
  manufacture of, **30**/4
  raw materials used, **30**/4
  roll products, **30**/5
  softening point for, **30**/8

Rocks
  crushing of, **16**/5
  types of, **16**/8, **16**/9
  weathering of, **16**/4
  see also Stone
Roll-down technique, polyethylene pipe laid
    by, **40**/10
Rolled glass, **29**/7
  examples of patterns available, **29**/7
  manufacture of, **29**/4
Rolled-asphalt... *see* Asphalt...
Rollering of paint, **33**/4
Rolling processes
  aluminium and alloys, **2**/5
  steels, **5**/5
Roman concrete, **14**/3
Roman-type tiles
  clay tiles, **13**/9
  concrete tiles, **25**/8
Roof applications
  elastomers, **37**/12, **37**/21
  glass-fibre reinforced cement, **20**/19, **20**/21
  mineral-fibre products, **30**/3, **30**/7, **30**/17
  polystyrene foam, **41**/9
  vermiculite products, **51**/4, **51**/8
  wood-based panel products, **50**/20, **50**/21
Roof tiles
  appearance of, **25**/10
  availability of, **13**/8, **25**/5
  cost comparison for, **25**/26
  effect of wind loading on, **13**/10, **25**/23
  fixing of, **13**/8, **13**/10, **25**/12
  manufacture of, **13**/3, **25**/5
  properties of, **13**/8, **25**/11
  sections available, **13**/9
  sizes of, **13**/9, **25**/6, **25**/18
  tolerances for, **13**/8
  types of, **13**/8, **25**/6
  see also Clay...; Concrete roof tiles
Roofs
  condensation in, **25**/17
  effect of wind on, **13**/8
Room temperature vulcanizing (RTV)
    silicone rubbers, **37**/9
Roping steels, **5**/22
Rubbers, **37**/1
  natural rubber, **36**/3
  surface preparation for adhesives, **8**/4
  synthetic rubbers, **36**/5
  see also Butadiene...; Butyl rubbers;
      Elastomers; Ethylene–propylene...;
      Natural...; Nitrile...;
      Polychloroprene...; Polyurethane...;
      Silicone/..; Styrene––butadiene
      rubbers
Rueping (timber treatment) process, **32**/6

S–N relationships *see* Fatigue properties
Saddle fusion process (for polyethylene
    pipes), **40**/10
Salts
  concrete affected by, **23**/11, **47**/6, **47**/7
  stone affected by, **49**/5
Sand blasting of steel, **31**/4
Sand casting of aluminium alloys, **2**/4
Sand–lime bricks, **11**/3, **11**/8
  see also Calcium silicate bricks
Sand-textured paints, **33**/7
Sands
  in asphalt, **10**/3
  in glass-fibre reinforced cement, **20**/4
Sandstone
  in aggregates, **16**/9
  cleaning of, **33**/3, **49**/12
  properties of, **49**/11
  sources of, **49**/3, **49**/4
  testing of, **49**/7, **49**/8, **49**/10

Sandwich structures, foam core materials in,
    45/8
Screeds, **14**/9, **21**/7
  admixtures used, **21**/7
  curing of, **21**/8
  laying of, **21**/8
  materials in, **21**/7
  mixing of, **21**/8
  problems with, **21**/8
  purpose of, **21**/7
  types of, **21**/7
Screws, timber joined by, **50**/22
Sealants, **36**/5
  elastomers, **37**/13, **37**/15, **37**/20
Sealing techniques, glass-fibre reinforced
    cement, **20**/15
Seamless copper tubing, **7**/10
Seamless tubes, steel, **5**/6, **5**/22
Seam-welded tube, aluminium and alloys,
    2/6, **2**/15, **2**/23
Sedimentary rocks, **49**/3
  see also Limestones; Sandstones
Seismic isolation pads, **37**/13, **37**/15, **37**/21
Self-hardening slurries, **48**/12
  composition of, **48**/12
  meaning of term, **48**/3
  properties of, **48**/13
  setting of, **48**/8
    measurement of set time, **48**/20
Self-levelling concrete, **15**/17
Selsey (UK), timber-frame church, **50**/24
Semi-dry bricks, **11**/5, **11**/7
Semi-hollow sections, aluminium and alloys,
    2/6
Semi-killed steels, **5**/5
Separators, geotextiles as, **28**/7
Service temperature range
  elastomers, **37**/10, **37**/11, **37**/12
  glass reinforced plastics, **45**/12
  mortars, **46**/14
  polymers, **38**/3, **38**/7, **38**/9, **42**/3, **43**/4
Sewers
  glass-fibre reinforced cement used, **20**/22
  polymers used, **40**/8, **43**/6, **43**/7
Shaft liners, glass-fibre reinforced cement
    used, **20**/22
Shear modulus, polymers, **38**/8
Shear resistance, pipe joints, **12**/6
Shear strength
  aluminium and alloys, **2**/16
  cast iron, **3**/5, **3**/10
  glass-fibre reinforced cement, **20**/8, **20**/9,
    20/10
  wrought iron, **4**/7
Shear-plate connectors, timber joined by, **50**/22
Sheerness (Kent), cast iron structure, **3**/9
Sheet glass, **29**/6
  manufacture of, **29**/4
  transmission characteristics of, **29**/7
Sheeting
  asbestos cement, **9**/8
  polymer, **38**/3, **38**/5, **43**/10
Shelf-life of thermosetting resins, **46**/14
Shells, aggregates containing, **16**/10
Sherardized (zinc) coatings, **7**/34, **31**/6
Shock-loading resistance, Kevlar fibres,
    44/7
Shot blasting of steel, **31**/4
Shotcrete *see* Sprayed concrete
Shrinkage
  concrete, **14**/11, **14**/12
  glass-fibre reinforced cement, **20**/10,
    20/14
  silica-fume concrete, **23**/9
  sprayed concrete, **24**/10
  vermiculite concrete, **51**/8
Shuttering *see* Formwork
Siemens (steelmaking) process, **5**/4

Silanes, **47**/1
  chemical structure of, **47**/3
  concrete deterioration prevented by, **47**/5
  concrete waterproofed by, **33**/13, **47**/4
  reaction of concrete with, **47**/4
  water-repellent property of, **47**/4
  water-vapour permeability of, **47**/4
Silica fume, **23**/1
  air-entraining agents used, **15**/8
  applications of, **23**/11
  bulk density of, **23**/4
  cement content (in concrete) reduced using, **23**/11
  cement hydration affected by, **23**/5
  chemical composition of, **18**/5, **23**/3, **23**/4
  colour of, **23**/3
  as concrete component, **14**/5, **18**/4, **23**/6
  fibre-reinforced concrete affected by, **23**/9, **23**/12
  mortars affected by, **23**/6
  particle size distribution of, **23**/4
  physical characteristics of, **18**/5, **23**/3
  pore-solution composition affected by, **23**/5
  Portland cement pastes affected by, **23**/6
  production of, **14**/5, **18**/4, **23**/3
  reaction products of, **23**/5
  reactivity of, **23**/4
  sources of, **23**/3
  specific gravity of, **23**/3
  specific surface area of, **23**/4
  in sprayed concrete, **23**/12, **24**/4, **24**/7
  standards for, **23**/12
  storage of, **23**/12
  structure of, **23**/4
  transportation of, **23**/12
  types of, **23**/3
  water-reducing agents used, **15**/14
Silica-fume cement pastes
  drying shrinkage of, **23**/9
  freeze–thaw resistance of, **23**/10
  microstructure of, **23**/6
  pore structure of, **23**/6
Silica-fume concretes, **14**/5, **18**/4, **23**/6
  abrasion resistance of, **23**/9
  air entrainment used, **23**/7
  air permeability of, **23**/10
  bleeding of, **23**/7
  bond strength of, **23**/9
    aggregate–cement bond strength, **23**/9
    concrete–fibre bond strength, **23**/9
    concrete–steel bond strength, **23**/9
  chemical resistance of, **23**/11
  chloride permeability of, **23**/10
  cohesiveness of, **23**/7
  compressive strength of, **23**/8
    effects of drying, **23**/8
    rate of strength development, **23**/8
  creep properties of, **23**/9
  drying shrinkage of, **23**/10
  durability of, **23**/10
  efficiency factors for, **23**/8, **23**/9
  flexural strength of, **23**/9
  freeze–thaw resistance of, **23**/10
  high-strength lightweight concrete, **23**/12
  mechanical properties of, **23**/8
  permeability of, **23**/10
  plastic shrinkage of, **23**/7
  properties of, **23**/7
  setting time of, **23**/8
  tensile strength of, **23**/9
  ultra-high-strength concrete, **23**/12
  water demand of, **23**/7
  water permeability of, **23**/10
  Young's modulus of, **23**/9
Silica-fume grouts, **23**/12
Silica-fume mortars, **23**/6
  freeze–thaw resistance of, **23**/10
  microstructure of, **23**/6

Silica-fume mortars (*cont.*)
  pore structure of, **23**/7
Silicate–aluminate grouts, **48**/15
Silicate–ester grouts, **48**/15
Silicate grouts, **48**/6, **48**/15
Silicates, concrete treated with, **33**/13
Silicofluorides, concrete treated with, **33**/13
Silicone polymers, **36**/5
Silicone rubber coatings, **33**/11
Silicone rubbers
  applications of, **37**/12, **37**/13
  production of, **37**/5
  properties of, **37**/11
  vulcanizing of, **37**/9
Silicone-rubber-coated fibre cloth, **27**/5
Silicones, concrete treated with, **33**/13, **47**/3
Siloxanes, **47**/1
  chemical structure of, **47**/3
  concrete deterioration prevented by, **47**/5
  concrete waterproofed by, **47**/4
  water-repellent property of, **47**/4
  water-vapour permeability of, **47**/4
Silver, **7**/29
  applications of, **7**/29, **7**/30
  production of, **7**/29
  properties of, **7**/5
  sources of, **7**/29
Silver alloys, **7**/29
Silver brazes, **7**/30
Silver–copper alloys, **7**/21, **7**/29
Silver solders, **7**/30
Silvered glass, **29**/14
Single-course macadams, **10**/12
Sintag (lightweight aggregate), **16**/19, **16**/21
Sirapite B plaster, **35**/4
Skid resistance (of aggregates), test for, **10**/27
Skid-resistant road surfaces, **8**/11
Slag *see* Ground-granulated blast-furnace slag
Slate, **49**/3
  in aggregates, **16**/8
  cleaning of, **49**/12
  properties of, **49**/11
  sources of, **49**/3, **49**/4
  testing of, **49**/7, **49**/10
Slates, **25**/18
  asbestos cement slates, **9**/8, **25**/20
  cost comparison for, **25**/26
  fibre–cement slates, **25**/20
  handling and storage of, **25**/22
  installation of, **25**/22, **25**/24
  polymer-modified-cement (PMC) slates, **25**/22
  reconstructed-stone (concrete) slates, **25**/18
  resin/polymer-bonded slates, **25**/21
  site working procedures for, **25**/22
  see also Fibre–cement...;
    Polymer-modified-
    cement...;Reconstructed-stone...;
    Resin/polymer-bonded slates
SLIM (single-leaf-insulated masonry)
  method, **11**/12
Slip-lining of polyethylene pipe, **40**/10
Slump values
  glass-fibre reinforced cement, **20**/24
  silica-fume concretes, **23**/7
Slurries, **48**/1
  applications of, **48**/3
  bleed behaviour of
    determination of, **48**/19
    specification of, **48**/22
  clays in, **48**/4, **48**/21
  cleaning of, **48**/11
  composition of, **48**/7
  density of, **48**/8, **48**/9
    determination of, **48**/16
    specification of, **48**/21
  excavation slurries, **48**/8

Slurries (*cont.*)
  filter loss of, **48**/10
    determination of, **48**/19
    specification of, **48**/22
  loss into soils, **48**/9
  materials in, **48**/3
  meaning of term, **48**/3
  mixing of, **48**/7
  permeability of, **48**/13
    measurement of, **48**/21
    specification of, **48**/23
  pH of
    measurement of, **48**/18
    specification of, **48**/22
    typical values, **48**/9
  pressure exerted by, **48**/8
  rheological blocking of, **48**/10
  rheology of, **48**/10
    measurement of, **48**/17
    specification of, **48**/22
  sampling of, **48**/15
  sand content determined for, **48**/17
  self-hardening slurries, **48**/12
  testing of, **48**/16
    bleed behaviour, **48**/19
    density determination, **48**/16
    filter-loss determination, **48**/19
    hardened properties, **48**/20
    pH measurement, **48**/18
    rheological measurements, **48**/17
    sand-content determination, **48**/17
    set-time measurement, **48**/20
  see also Excavation...; Polymer...;
    Self-hardening slurries
Slurry trenching techniques, **48**/8, **48**/12
Slurry tunnelling techniques, **48**/8, **48**/9
Socket fusion process (for polyethylene
  pipes), **40**/9
Sodium abietate (air-entraining agent), **15**/6
Sodium decanoate (air-entraining agent), **15**/6
Sodium dodecyl benzene sulphonate
  (air-entraining agent), **15**/6
Soft-mud bricks, **11**/5, **11**/7
Soft-rot (on timber), **32**/3
Softwoods
  applications of, **50**/11
  properties of, **50**/11
  sizes available, **50**/13, **50**/14
  strength classes for, **50**/17
Soil
  aluminium affected by, **2**/21
  reinforcement by geotextiles, **28**/12, **40**/13
Solders, **7**/30, **7**/31
Solidification cracking (of welds), **5**/15
Solvent-thinned paints, **33**/8
Solventless paints, **31**/5
Sound, principles of, **30**/11
Sound insulation
  airborne-sound insulation, **30**/12
  impact-sound insulation, **30**/13
Sound insulation materials
  brickwork, **11**/12
  plasterboard, **35**/8
Sound insulation properties
  concrete blockwork, **17**/10
  concrete roof tiles, **25**/17
  glass, **29**/6
  glass-fibre reinforced cement, **20**/12, **20**/15
  mineral-fibre products, **30**/13
  see also Acoustic insulation...
Sound-pressure levels, meaning of term, **30**/12
Special-purpose cements, **14**/5
Specific heat
  glass, **29**/6, **37**/4
  non-ferrous metals, **7**/5, **37**/4
  polymers, **37**/4, **38**/3, **38**/9, **41**/4, **42**/3
  rubbers, **37**/4

Specific heat (*cont.*)
  steels, **5**/8, **37**/4
  vermiculite, **51**/4
Specification of
  cleaning of buildings, **49**/12
  glass reinforced plastics, **45**/12
  intumescent coatings, **34**/13
  painting of steel, **31**/7
    large/long projects, **31**/8
    small/short projects, **31**/7
  timber treatment, **32**/8
Specifications
  admixtures, **15**/8, **15**/9, **15**/11
  aggregates, **16**/15
  curing membranes, **19**/4
  glass, **29**/19
  grouts/slurries, **48**/21
  macadams, **10**/10, **10**/12
  sprayed concrete, **24**/11
  see also Standards
Splash-zones, steel corrosion in, **5**/30, **5**/32
Split-ring connectors, timber joined by, **50**/22
Sports surfaces, elastomers used, **37**/16
Spray moulding of glass reinforced plastics, **45**/10
Sprayed asbestos coating, encapsulation of, **9**/16
Sprayed asbestos coatings, **9**/11
  application to steelwork, **9**/11
Sprayed concrete, **24**/1
  accelerators in, **15**/23
  additives in, **15**/23, **24**/4, **24**/7
  aggregates in, **24**/4
  applications of, **24**/13
  bar-reinforced concrete, **24**/5
    moment capacity determination for, **24**/15
  bond strength of, **24**/10
  cement in, **24**/4
  comparison of
    dry and wet processes, **24**/3
    fibre- and mesh-reinforced sprayed
      concrete, **24**/3
  compressive strength of, **24**/8
    tests for, **24**/12, **24**/13
  construction methods affecting choice, **24**/14
  definitions used, **24**/3
  design considerations, **24**/13
  dry-mix process, **24**/5
    aggregates used, **24**/4
    compared with wet-mix process, **24**/3
    rebound losses incurred, **24**/6
    technique used, **24**/6
  flexural strength of, **24**/8
  freeze–thaw resistance of, **24**/10
  impact resistance of, **24**/9
  materials in, **24**/4
  mesh-reinforced concrete, **24**/5
    moment capacity determination for, **24**/15
  mix proportions for, **24**/5
  moment capacity determination for, **24**/15
  permeability of, **24**/10
  production of, **24**/5
    dry-mix process, **24**/5
    wet-mix process, **24**/7
  quality control for, **24**/12
    fibre-content determination, **24**/12
    panel testing, **24**/12
    preconstruction testing, **24**/12
    strength testing, **24**/12
  rebound losses for, **24**/6, **24**/8
    reduction of rebound, **23**/12, **24**/7
  reinforcement in, **24**/5
    corrosion of, **24**/11
    design considerations, **24**/14
  shrinkage of, **24**/10
  silica fume in, **23**/12, **24**/4, **24**/7
  specification of, **24**/11
  toughness of, **24**/9

Sprayed concrete (*cont.*)
  water absorption of, **24**/10
  wet-mix process
    aggregates used, **24**/4
    compared with dry-mix process, **24**/3
  see also Fibre-reinforced concrete
Sprayed fibre concrete, **24**/1
  advantages of, **24**/3
  aggregates in, **24**/4
  applications of, **24**/14
  beam flexure testing of, **24**/12
  disadvantages of, **24**/3
  fibres in, **24**/4
    corrosion of, **24**/11
    design decisions, **24**/14
    determination of content, **24**/12
  mechanical properties of, **24**/8
  moment capacity determination for, **24**/15
  physical properties of, **24**/10
  production of, **24**/5
  quality control of, **24**/12
    fibre-content determination, **24**/12
    strength testing, **24**/12, **24**/13
  silica fume in, **24**/4, **24**/7
  specification of, **24**/11
Sprayed glass-fibre reinforced cement, **20**/23, **24**/4
Sprayed zinc coatings, **31**/6
Spraying
  concrete, **24**/5
  paint, **33**/4
Spumescents (in intumescent coatings), **34**/4, **34**/10
Sputtering techniques, **7**/22
Stainless steels, **5**/20
  applications of, **5**/20
  compositions of, **5**/21
  elastic modulus, **5**/8
  elongation data for, **5**/21
  metallurgy of, **5**/20
  proof stress data for, **5**/21
  specifications of, **5**/21
  tensile strength of, **5**/21
  types of, **5**/20
  weathering of, **5**/34
Stairs, timber, **50**/29
Standards
  aggregates, **10**/27, **16**/13, **16**/17
  aluminium and alloys, **2**/12, **2**/14, **2**/16, **2**/27
  asbestos products, **9**/7
  asphalts, **10**/3, **10**/5, **10**/10
  bituminous materials, **10**/3, **10**/5, **10**/10,
    10/11, **10**/12, **10**/13
  blast-furnace slag, **18**/7
  bricks, **11**/8, **11**/9, **11**/10, **11**/12, **11**/13
  ceramic tiles, **13**/15
  clay pipes, **12**/6
  coated macadams, **10**/10, **10**/11, **10**/12, **10**/13
  concrete admixtures, **15**/8, **15**/9, **15**/14,
    15/17, **15**/19, **15**/20
  corkboard, **26**/5
  curing membranes, **19**/4
  elastomers, **37**/20
  galvanized steel, **7**/33
  glass, **29**/20
  joinery products, **50**/28, **50**/29, **50**/31, **50**/32
  mineral-fibre products, **30**/16
  polymer dispersions, **39**/7
  Portland blast-furnace cements, **18**/7
  Portland cements, **14**/5, **18**/6
  pulverized-fuel ash, **18**/6
  silica fume, **23**/12
  sound-insulation testing, **30**/12, **30**/13
  steel reinforcement, **6**/3, **6**/7
  steels, **5**/13, **5**/21, **5**/23, **5**/36
    cleaning of steels, **31**/3
  stone, **49**/6
  timber coatings/treatment, **32**/8, **32**/12

Standards (*cont.*)
  wood-based panel products, **50**/18, **50**/19,
    50/20
  see also Specifications
Stanstead Abbotts By-Pass bridge, adhesives
  used, **8**/5, **8**/9
STC code, **5**/20
Stearates, concrete treated with, **33**/13
Steel bolts, **5**/22
Steel castings, **5**/5, **5**/25
  British Standards for, **5**/37
  coding system for, **5**/25
  composition of, **5**/25
  mechanical properties of, **5**/25
Steel fibre reinforced concrete, **14**/8
  corrosion of fibres, **24**/11
  fibre types used, **24**/5, **24**/14
  silica fume used, **23**/9, **23**/12
  specification of, **24**/11
Steel reinforcement, **6**/1, **14**/7
  bars, **6**/3
    chemical composition of, **6**/4
    joining of bars, **6**/5
    methods of manufacture, **6**/3
    practical bending of, **6**/5
    product testing and certification for, **6**/5
    sizes and lengths of, **6**/4
    tensile properties of, **6**/4
    terminology for, **6**/3
    test bending of, **6**/5
    tolerances of, **6**/4
    types of, **6**/4
  British Standards for, **6**/3, **6**/7
  corrosion of, **18**/9
  protection of, **18**/10
  tensile properties of, **44**/4, **44**/5
  wire and fabric, **6**/5
    bond classification, **6**/6
    chemical composition of, **6**/6
    fabric manufacture for, **6**/5
    fabric types of, **6**/5
    practical bending for, **6**/7
    product testing and verification for, **6**/7
    rebend test of, **6**/6
    sizes of wire and bar, **6**/5
    steel manufacture for, **6**/5
    tensile properties for, **6**/6
    terminology for, **6**/5
    tolerances of, **6**/5
    wire or bar manufacture for, **6**/5
  see also Prestressing steels
Steel ropes, **5**/22
  British Standards for, **5**/37
Steels, **5**/1
  blast cleaning of, **31**/3
    wet blasting used, **31**/4
  brittle fracture of, **5**/24
  carbon contents of, **3**/3, **4**/3
  casting of, **5**/5
  cathodic protection of, **5**/34, **5**/35, **31**/3
  clean steels, **5**/9
  cold-formed section profiles, **5**/7
  composition of, **5**/3, **5**/14, **5**/21
  corrosion fatigue of, **5**/36
  corrosion of, **5**/28, **31**/3
  corrosion protection of, **5**/31
    active coatings used, **5**/32
    barrier coatings used, **5**/32
    surface treatments used, **5**/31
    cost comparison of, **5**/13
  defects in, **5**/7
    internal defects, **5**/8
    surface defects, **5**/7
  density of, **5**/8
  elastic modulus of, **5**/8, **45**/6
  elongation data for, **5**/22, **5**/23, **37**/4
  fasteners made from, **5**/22
  fatigue performance of, **5**/26

Steels (*cont.*)
  hardness of, **5**/15, **5**/22, **37**/4
  impact properties of, **5**/14, **37**/4, **45**/6
  inclusions in, **5**/8, **5**/9, **5**/15
  manual cleaning of, **31**/4
  manufacture of, **5**/3
    primary processes, **5**/3
    processes, **5**/4
    raw materials, **5**/3
    scrap used, **5**/3
    secondary processes, **5**/4
  microstructural control of, **5**/12
  microstructure of, **5**/8
    nomenclature used, **5**/9
  paints to protect, **5**/32
  physical properties of, **5**/8, **37**/4
  quality assessment of, **5**/7
  rolling of, **5**/5
  specific heat of, **5**/8
  standards for, **5**/13, **5**/36
  stress-corrosion cracking of, **5**/35
  surface preparation of
    adhesives, **8**/4, **8**/13
    paints, **31**/3
  tensile properties of, **5**/13, **5**/14, **5**/21, **5**/22,
      5/23, **37**/4
    effects of cold work on, **5**/12
  thermal conductivity of, **5**/8, **37**/4, **45**/12
  thermal expansion of, **5**/8, **37**/4, **38**/7, **45**/12
  weathering of, **5**/34
  welding of, **5**/14
    defects, **5**/15
    joint configuration and constraints, **5**/17,
        5/19
    materials suitable, **5**/15
    methods used, **5**/15
    strengths of welds, **5**/18
  see also Ferrite–pearlite...; Mild...;
      Stainless...; Weldable...steels
Steelwork, asbestos coating on, **9**/11
Sterling silver, **7**/29, **7**/30
Stiffness modulus, bituminous materials, **10**/25
Stiff-plastic bricks, **11**/7
Stitch-bonded fabrics, **27**/4, **28**/3
Stitched-wire mattresses (mineral-fibre
      products), **30**/5, **30**/6, **30**/21
Stock bricks, **11**/5
Stone, **49**/1
  cleaning of, **33**/3, **49**/11
    chemical cleaners used, **33**/3, **49**/13
    grit blasting used, **33**/3, **49**/13
    health and safety aspects, **49**/13
    mechanical methods used, **33**/3, **49**/13
    specification of, **49**/12
    techniques used, **49**/12
    water washing used, **33**/3, **49**/12
  consolidants used, **49**/14
  origins of, **49**/3
  properties of, **49**/11
  selection of, **49**/6
  sources of, **49**/3
  standards for, **49**/6
  suitability of, **49**/8
  testing of, **49**/7
    acid immersion test, **49**/10
    crystallization test, **49**/7
    saturation coefficient/porosity, **49**/8
  types of, **49**/3
  weathering of, **49**/4
  see also Granite; Limestone; Marble;
      Sandstone; Slate
Stonework
  plastic repair of, **49**/14
  repair of, **49**/14
  repointing of, **49**/14
Storage methods
  bituminous materials, **10**/16
  cement, **14**/5

Storage methods (*cont.*)
  corkboard, **26**/5
  silica fume, **23**/12
  slates, **25**/22
Stress intensity factor, **5**/24
  methods of measurement, **5**/24, **5**/25
  typical values for steels, **5**/25
Stress–strain curves
  aramid fibres, **44**/4, **44**/5
  cast iron, **3**/5
  glass reinforced plastics, **45**/8
  wrought iron, **4**/7
Stress–strain relations, classification of,
    1/4
Stress-corrosion cracking
  brasses, **7**/12
  steels, **5**/35
Stress-rupture properties of polymers,
    44/5
Structural glazing, **29**/18
Structural grouts, **48**/13
  bleeding of, **48**/14
  cements in, **48**/4
  mixing of, **48**/7
  setting of, **48**/8
    measurement of set time, **48**/20
  specifications for, **48**/21
  testing of, **48**/20
  thermal effects in, **48**/14
Structural plywood, **50**/18
Structural sections
  aluminium and alloys, **2**/6
  steels, **5**/6
Structural steels, **5**/20
  British Standards for, **5**/36
  mechanical properties of, **5**/21
Styrene acrylics (SA) dispersions, **39**/8
Styrene–butadiene rubbers (SBR)
  applications of, **37**/13, **37**/15, **37**/16
  dispersions containing, **39**/8
    mortars modified with, **39**/6
  production of, **37**/3
  properties of, **37**/10
  vulcanizing of, **37**/3
  weatherability of, **37**/18
Styrene–butadiene–styrene (SBS) block
    copolymers, properties of, **37**/12
Sucrose, as concrete retarder, **15**/20
Sulphate resistance
  concrete, **14**/12, **18**/9
  glass-fibre-reinforced cement, **20**/11
  mortars/renders, **21**/7
  silica-fume concrete, **23**/11
Sulphates in aggregates, testing for, **16**/12
Sulphonated melamine–formaldehyde
    condensates, **15**/15, **15**/16
Sulphonated naphthalene–formaldehyde
    condensates, **15**/15, **15**/16
Summerland (Isle of Man) fire, **38**/7
Suncool glass, **29**/10, **29**/11
Superalloys, nickel-based, **7**/28
Superconducting ceramics, **7**/11
Superplastic forming
  aluminium alloys, **2**/7
  process described, **7**/35
  zinc alloys, **7**/35
Superplasticizers, **15**/14
  advantages of, **15**/17
  chemical types of, **15**/15
  historical background for, **15**/14
  lignosulphonates, **15**/15, **15**/16, **15**/17
  mechanism for, **15**/14
  in silica-fume concretes, **23**/7, **23**/8
  standards/specifications for, **15**/17
  sulphonated melamine–formaldehyde
      condensates, **15**/15
  sulphonated naphthalene–formaldehyde
      condensates, **15**/15, **15**/16

Surface preparation
  absorbent surfaces, **33**/4
  brickwork, **8**/4
  concrete, **8**/4, **8**/13
  glass, **8**/4
  steels, **8**/4, **8**/13, **31**/3
  timber/wood, **8**/4, **32**/12
Surface treatment
  glass, **29**/15
  steels, **5**/31
Surface-modified glass, **29**/8
Surfactants
  as air-entraining agents, **15**/6
  in polymer dispersions, **39**/4
  in thermosetting resins, **46**/13
Suspension grouts, **48**/14
Swaging technique, polyethylene pipe laid by,
    40/10
Swinden model (for steel beams), **5**/28
Sydney Opera House (Australia), adhesives
    used, **8**/5
Synthetic rubbers, **36**/5

Tar, production of, **10**/29
Tar-coated macadams, **10**/10
  see also Macadams
Tar-oil (wood) preservatives, **32**/5
Tartaric acid, as concrete retarder, **15**/18, **15**/20
Technora *see* Aramid fibres
Teflon-coated glass-fibre cloth, **27**/5
Telecommunications applications, polymers
    used, **40**/11, **43**/7
Temper designations for aluminium and
    alloys, **2**/9
Tensar geotextile, **40**/13
Tensile strength
  aluminium and alloys, **2**/12, **2**/14, **2**/16,
      2/17, **37**/4, **50**/4
  asbestos, **9**/3
  cast iron, **3**/3, **3**/4, **3**/10, **3**/11, **3**/13
  concrete, **50**/4
  copper and alloys, **7**/5, **7**/11, **7**/13, **7**/15, **7**/16
  elastomers, **37**/4
  fabrics, **27**/5
  fibres, **44**/4
  geotextiles, **28**/12, **28**/13
  glass fibre reinforced cement, **20**/9, **20**/10
  glass reinforced plastics, **45**/7, **45**/9
  mortars, **11**/11
  nickel and alloys, **7**/5, **7**/27
  non-ferrous metals (various), **7**/5
  polymer-modified mortars, **46**/14
  polymers, **37**/4, **38**/3, **38**/8, **40**/4, **41**/4, **42**/3,
      43/9, **43**/11
  steels, **5**/13, **5**/14, **5**/21, **5**/22, **5**/23, **50**/4
  wrought iron, **4**/4, **4**/6
Termites, timber attacked by, **32**/3
Terne coatings, **7**/24
Terneplate, **7**/31
Terpolymer, meaning of term, **39**/3
Testing methods
  adhesives, **8**/5, **8**/8
  admixtures, **15**/26
  aggregates, **10**/27, **16**/12, **16**/13, **16**/17, **16**/20
  bituminous materials, **10**/5, **10**/26, **10**/27
  concrete, **14**/16, **15**/26
  geotextiles, **28**/11, **28**/12
  glass-fibre reinforced cement, **20**/24, **20**/25
  grouts and slurries, **48**/16
  polymer dispersions, **39**/7
  sprayed concrete, **24**/12, **24**/13
  steel reinforcement, **6**/5
  stone, **49**/7
Tewkesbury (Glos.), cast iron bridge, **3**/8
Tex (unit for fibres/thread), **27**/3
Textiles *see* Fabrics; Geotextiles
Textured paints, **9**/12, **33**/7

Thermal conductivity
  aluminium and alloys, **2**/17, **37**/4, **43**/10
  concrete, **43**/10
  corkboard, **26**/4
  definition of, **30**/10
  glass, **29**/6, **37**/4
  glass fibre reinforced cement, **20**/12, **20**/14
  glass reinforced plastics, **45**/7, **45**/12
  mineral-fibre products, **30**/5, **30**/6, **30**/7
  non-ferrous metals (various), **7**/5
  polymers, **37**/4, **38**/3, **38**/8, **40**/9, **41**/4, **42**/3, **43**/9, **43**/10
  rubbers, **37**/4
  steels, **5**/8, **37**/4
  timber/wood, **37**/4, **43**/10
  vermiculite products, **51**/4, **51**/8
Thermal expansion coefficient
  aluminium and alloys, **2**/17, **37**/4, **38**/7
  bricks, **11**/9
  cast iron, **3**/6
  clay roof tiles, **13**/8
  concrete blocks, **17**/7
  concretes/mortars, **14**/12, **37**/4, **46**/14
  corkboard, **26**/4
  glass, **29**/6, **37**/4, **38**/7
  glass fibre reinforced cement, **20**/11, **20**/14
  glass reinforced plastics, **45**/7, **45**/12
  non-ferrous metals (various), **7**/5
  polymer-modified mortars, **46**/14
  polymers, **37**/4, **38**/3, **38**/7, **38**/8, **40**/4, **40**/9, **41**/4, **42**/3, **43**/4, **43**/9
  rubbers, **37**/4
  steels, **5**/8, **37**/4, **38**/7
  stone, **49**/11
  wrought iron, **4**/8
Thermal insulation materials
  asbestos-based materials, **9**/10
  plasterboard, **35**/8
Thermal insulation properties
  coated glasses, **29**/10
  concrete blockwork, **17**/10
  concrete roof tiles, **25**/17
  double-glazing units, **29**/14, **29**/16
  glass-fibre reinforced cement, **20**/19
Thermal resistance, definition of, **30**/10
Thermal transmittance, definition of, **30**/10
Thermite sparking of aluminium, **2**/18
Thermoplastic elastomers
  applications of, **37**/13, **37**/15, **37**/16, **37**/21
  moulding of, **37**/9
  properties of, **37**/12
Thermoplastic polyolefin (TPO) elastomers
  moulding of, **37**/9
  properties of, **37**/12
Thermoplastic polyurethane (TPU)
    elastomers, properties of, **37**/12
Thermoplastics
  historical background for, **36**/4
  meaning of term, **36**/3
  microstructure of, **46**/3
Thermosets
  historical background for, **36**/3, **46**/6, **46**/7, **46**/10
  meaning of term, **36**/3, **46**/3
  microstructure of, **46**/3
Thermosetting resins, **46**/1
  adhesion of, **46**/16
  advantages/disadvantages of, **46**/13
  applications of, **46**/5, **46**/9, **46**/10, **46**/11
  chemical resistance of, **46**/16
  creep of, **46**/16
  cure rates for, **46**/15
  cure shrinkage of, **46**/15
  curing of, **46**/4, **46**/6, **46**/9, **46**/10, **46**/11
  diluents in, **46**/6, **46**/12
  exothermic reactions of, **46**/15
  fillers in, **46**/12
  fire properties of, **46**/16

Thermosetting resins (*cont.*)
  health and safety aspects of, **46**/14
  manufacture of, **46**/6, **46**/7, **46**/8, **46**/10, **46**/11
  meaning of term, **46**/3
  mechanical properties of, **46**/15
  modification of, **46**/11
  modifiers in, **46**/12
  pigments in, **46**/12
  plasticizers in, **46**/12
  pot life of, **46**/14
  properties of, **46**/13
  reinforcing agents in, **46**/12
  responsibilities of end-user/formulator, **46**/16
  shelf-life of, **46**/14
  stress relaxation of, **46**/16
  temperature effects, **46**/16
  viscosity of, **46**/14
  see also Acrylic/ester...; Epoxy...; Furane...; Polyester...; Polyurethane...; Vinyl ester resins
Thermosetting stoved liquid paints, **2**/25
Thiobaccillus thiooxidans, **12**/11
Thistle baseboard, plastering of, **35**/5
Thistle range of plasters
  final-coat plasters, **35**/3
  projection plaster, **35**/4
  renovating plasters, **35**/4
  universal one-coat plaster, **35**/3
Thixotropes (in thermosetting resins), **46**/13
Thomas (steelmaking) process, **5**/4
Thorpe Marsh Power Station (UK), repair of, **44**/11
Thread
  fibres used, **27**/3
  manufacture of, **27**/3
  units for, **27**/3
Tiled floors, maintenance of, **13**/15
Tiles, **13**/1
  bedding of, **13**/6, **13**/13, **13**/14
  British Standards for, **13**/15
  ceramic tiles, **13**/1
  durability of, **13**/4
  fixing of, **13**/7
  floor tiles, **9**/12, **13**/14, **43**/11
  grouting of, **13**/13
  historical background for, **13**/3
  jointing of, **13**/6
  maintenance of, **13**/15
  manufacture of, **13**/3
  movement of, **13**/4, **13**/5
  properties of, **13**/8
  roof tiles, **13**/8, **25**/1
  terminology for, **13**/3
  thermoplastic tiles, **9**/12, **43**/11
  tolerances for, **13**/8
  wall tiles, **13**/12
  see also Ceramic...; Clay...; Concrete...; Cork...; Floor...; Roof...; Wall tiles
Timber, **50**/1
  aluminium affected by, **2**/21
  applications of, **50**/6, **50**/11
  availability of, **50**/6, **50**/11, **50**/13
  chemical attack on, **32**/4
  coatings for, **32**/9
    application aspects, **32**/12
    components of, **32**/9
    factors affecting performance, **32**/11
    health and safety aspects, **32**/12
    properties of, **32**/10
    selection criteria for, **32**/11
    standards covering, **32**/12
    surface preparation for, **32**/12
    types of, **32**/9
    water-borne vs solvent-borne coatings, **32**/11
  colour of, **50**/5, **50**/6, **50**/11
  conditioning of, **32**/6

Timber (*cont.*)
  cost comparison of, **50**/4, **50**/6, **50**/11, **50**/13
  density of, **50**/5, **50**/6, **50**/11
  design considerations, **50**/16
  dimensional changes due to moisture, **50**/5, **50**/6, **50**/11
  durability of, **32**/4, **50**/6, **50**/11
  elastic modulus of, **50**/4, **50**/16
  fasteners used, **50**/21
  fungal attack on, **32**/3
    by staining fungi, **32**/3
    by wood-decaying fungi, **32**/3
  glued joints used, **50**/22
  hazards to, **32**/3
  in situ treatment of, **32**/8
  insect attack on, **32**/3
    by beetles, **32**/3
    by termites, **32**/3
  joinery specification for, **50**/27
  kiln drying of, **32**/6
  marine borers affecting, **32**/4
  mechanical fasteners used, **50**/21
  moisture content of, **50**/4, **50**/15
  permeability of, **32**/5, **50**/6, **50**/11, **50**/13
  planing of, **50**/13
  preservation of, **32**/4
    see also Wood preservatives
  properties of, **37**/4, **50**/4, **50**/5
    compared with other building materials, **50**/4
  regularizing of, **50**/13
  seasoning of, **32**/5
  sizes available, **50**/13, **50**/14, **50**/15
  sources of, **50**/4
  species of, **50**/4, **50**/6, **50**/11
  strength classes for, **50**/15
  stress grading of, **50**/16
  structural use of, **50**/13, **50**/22
  surface preparation of, **8**/4, **32**/12
  texture of, **50**/5, **50**/6, **50**/11
  treatment of, **32**/4
    high-pressure methods used, **32**/6
    in situ treatment used, **32**/8
    low-pressure methods used, **32**/6
    non-pressure methods used, **32**/7
    preparation for, **32**/5
    seasoned timber, **32**/6
    specifications for, **32**/8
    unseasoned timber, **32**/7
  UK usage data for, **50**/3
  weathering of, **32**/4, **50**/5
  workability of, **50**/5, **50**/6, **50**/11
  world (growing) stock of, **50**/3
  zinc attacked by, **7**/33
  see also Glued-laminated timber; Wood-based panel products
Timber floors, insulation of, **30**/7, **30**/14, **30**/15, **30**/19, **41**/13
Timber-frame applications
  mineral-fibre products, **30**/6, **30**/18
  polystyrene foam, **41**/8
  wood-based panel products, **50**/20
Tin, **7**/30
  abundance in Earth's crust, **7**/3
  applications of, **7**/30
  in bearings, **7**/32
  low-temperature transformation of, **7**/5, **7**/30
  production of, **7**/30
  properties of, **7**/5
  pure metal, **7**/30
  solders containing, **7**/30, **7**/31
  sources of, **7**/30
Tin–antimony solders, **7**/32
Tin bronzes, **7**/14
Tin coatings, **7**/31
Tin–lead alloys
  phase diagram for, **7**/31
  see also Solders

Tin–silver solder, 7/30, 7/32
Tin–zinc solders, 7/32
Tinted glass, 29/8
Tooth plate connector joints, timber joined by, 50/22
Top-Hat kiln, 12/4
Tough-pitch copper, 7/9, 7/11
Toughened glass, 29/10
 as fire-resistant glass, 29/17
 manufacture of, 29/13, 29/14
 sizes of, 29/14
Toughness
 fracture toughness parameter, 5/25
 polyethylene, 40/6
 sprayed concrete, 24/9
 steels, 5/11, 5/12
Translucency of fabrics, 27/5, 27/6
Tredgold (cast iron) beams, 3/14
Trenchless techniques (for pipe-laying)
 clay pipe, 12/6
 polyethylene pipe, 40/10, 40/11
Trent River Bridge (UK), adhesives used, 8/5
Triethanolamine (concrete accelerator), 15/23
Trinasco asphalts, 10/9
Trussed rafters, 50/25
 design of, 50/26
 erection of, 50/26
 fabrication of, 50/26
 functional requirements for, 50/26
 materials used, 50/25
 permissible spans for, 50/26
Tubes
 aluminium and alloys, 2/6, 2/14, 2/15
 steel, 5/22
Tungsten/inert gas (TIG) process, aluminium alloys, 2/23
Tunnels, glass-fibre reinforced cement used, 20/22
Twaron see Aramid fibres
Two-pack paints, 31/5, 33/9

Ultra-high-strength concrete, silica fume in, 23/12
Ultraviolet light, glass-fibre reinforced cement affected by, 20/13
Underfloor heating systems, polyethylene used, 40/8, 40/9
UPVC see Poly(vinyl chloride), rigid PVC
Urea–formaldehyde resins
 historical background for, 36/3
 plywood bonded with, 50/18
Urea–formaldehyde varnishes, 33/11
Urethane... see Polyurethane...
Urethane oil paints, 33/8
US Corps of Engineers Gradient Ratio Test, 28/11

Vacuum degassing (in steelmaking), 5/4
Vacuum evaporation techniques, 7/22
Värnamo (Sweden), high-school building, 37/13
Varnishes, 32/9
 intumescent varnishes, 34/12
Veneer plywood, 50/18
 see also Plywood
Vermiculite, 51/1
 applications of, 51/4
  boards and panels, 51/8
  fire-protection applications, 51/6
  insulating concrete, 51/7
  loosefill applications, 51/4
  plastering applications, 51/5
 chemical composition of, 51/4

Vermiculite (cont.)
 exfoliated/expanded vermiculite
  as aggregate, 16/20, 51/7
  applications of, 51/4
  density of, 51/4
  health and safety aspects of, 51/4
  properties of, 51/3
  sources of, 51/3
Vermiculite boards/panels, 51/8
Vermiculite cement, 51/7
 bonding properties of, 51/7
 dimensional stability of, 51/7
 durability of, 51/7
Vermiculite concrete, 51/7
 physical properties of, 51/8
Vermiculite plasters, 51/5
 adhesion of, 51/5
 anti-condensation characteristics of, 51/5
 applications of, 51/5
  acoustic plasters, 51/6
  external claddings, 51/6
  internal walls, 51/5
 coverage of, 51/5
 resilience of, 51/5
 resistance to cracking of, 51/5
 thermal conductivity of, 51/5
 weight of, 51/5
 workability of, 51/5
VESTAR cloth, 27/5
Vibrating rollers, 10/26
Vibration isolation (of buildings), 37/13, 37/16, 37/20
Vicat softening temperatures (for polymers), 38/9, 40/4, 43/9
Vinsol resin, 15/6
Vinyl compounds, 43/1
 see also Poly(vinyl...
Vinyl ester resins, 46/10
 advantages/disadvantages of, 46/13
 applications of, 46/10
 chemical structure of, 46/10, 46/11
 curing of, 46/10
Vinyl flooring, 43/11
Vinyl paints, 5/33, 5/34, 33/9
Viscous behaviour, 1/5
Vitrification processes, 12/4
Vitrified clay pipes, 12/1
 see also Clay pipes
Vulcanization, 37/6
Vulcanized rubber, 36/3
 machining of, 37/6
 production of, 37/7

Waferboard, 50/20
Walkway tiles, 9/9
Wall insulation applications
 mineral-fibre products, 30/6, 30/18
 polystyrene foam, 41/7
Wall tiles, 13/12
 availability of, 13/12
 bedding materials for, 13/12
 fixing of, 13/12
 joints for, 13/6
 manufacture of, 13/4
 properties of, 13/8
 substrates for, 13/4, 13/6
 tolerances for, 13/8
Walls see Brickwork; Concrete blockwork; Masonry
Wash primers, 31/6
Water, properties of, 37/4
Water absorption
 aggregates, 16/14
 bricks, 11/9
 concretes/mortars, 15/26, 46/14
 polymer-modified mortars, 46/14
 polymers, 38/9, 41/4, 42/3

Water absorption (cont.)
 prevention by silanes/siloxanes, 47/4
 sprayed concrete, 24/10
Water borne paints, 32/11, 33/6, 33/10
Water permeability
 geotextiles, 28/9
 glass-fibre reinforced cement, 20/12
 silica-fume concretes, 23/10
Water pipes
 colour of, 40/5
 polymers used, 40/7, 43/6
Water reducing agents (for concrete), 15/9
 benefits of, 15/12
 blast-furnace slag affected by, 15/13
 cements affected by, 15/13
 pulverized fuel-ash affected by, 15/13, 15/14
 silica fume affected by, 15/14, 23/7
 in sprayed concrete, 24/4
 standards/specifications for, 15/14
Water repellents, concrete treated with, 33/12
Water spot test (for concrete), 15/26
Water vapour permeability
 coatings, 32/10, 33/6, 33/7
 glass-fibre reinforced cement, 20/12
 polymers, 38/9, 41/4, 42/3
 silanes/siloxanes, 47/4
Water washing, stone cleaned using, 33/3, 49/12
Waterglass (sodium silicate), concrete treated with, 33/13
Waterproofing agents, types of, 47/3
Waterproofing of buildings, 33/6
Wavihole sewer pipe, 43/7
Wearing courses (in roads)
 asphalts, 10/3, 10/9
 macadams, 10/12
 mastic asphalts, 10/9
Weather conditions, effect on working
 bituminous materials, 10/23
 mortars, 21/5
Weather resistance, roofing materials, 25/11, 25/18, 25/21
Weatherability
 artificial weathering tests, 38/6
 elastomers, 37/18
 evaluation of weathering data, 38/7
 outdoor exposure tests, 38/7
 polymers, 36/6, 38/6, 42/3
 tests used, 38/6
 silanes/siloxanes, 47/6, 47/7
 timber coatings, 32/10
Weathering of buildings, 33/3
Weathering steels, 5/14, 5/29, 5/34
Weathering of stone, 49/4
Weathering of timber, 32/4
Weldable structural steels, 5/13
 grading system for, 5/13
 standards for, 5/13
 tensile strength of, 5/13, 5/14
Welded joints, corrosion of, 5/31
Welding
 aluminium alloys, 2/23
 British Standards for, 5/37
 cast iron, 3/10, 3/12
 preheat diagrams for, 5/18
 steels, 5/14
 wrought iron, 4/9
Wet grit blasting
 steels, 31/4
 stone, 49/13
Wet rot (on timber), 32/3
Wetting–drying cycles, stone affected by, 49/6
White cast iron, 3/4
White-metal bearings, 7/3, 7/32
Widmanstätten morphology, 7/16
Winchester cut (for roof tiles), 25/17
Wind action on roofs, 13/9

Wind loading
  calculation of, **25**/26
  roof tiles affected by, **13**/10, **25**/23
Window profiles
  aluminium, **29**/17
  PVC, **43**/9
  timber, **29**/17
Windows
  force needed to operate fasteners, **50**/29,
    50/31
  strength of, **50**/29
  timber-frame, **50**/28
  watertightness tests for, **50**/29, **50**/30
  see also Glazing applications
Windsor Probe test (for sprayed fibre
    concrete), **24**/13
Wire brushing
  buildings, **33**/3
  steels, **31**/4
Wire cut bricks, **11**/5, **11**/7
Wire drawing
  steels, **5**/6
  wrought iron, **4**/7
Wired glass, **29**/7
  as fire-resistant glass, **29**/7, **29**/17
  fixing of, **29**/18
  manufacture of, **29**/4
Wood
  ignition properties of, **43**/12
  properties of, **37**/4, **50**/4, **50**/5
  surface preparation of, **8**/4, **32**/12
  see also Plywood; Timber
Wood based panel products, **50**/16
  applications of, **50**/21
  see also Block...; Chip...; Fibre...; Flake...;
    Particleboard; Plywood
Wood cement particleboard, **50**/20
Wood chipboard, **50**/19

Wood decaying fungi, **32**/3
Wood preservatives
  aluminium affected by, **2**/21
  health and safety aspects of, **32**/9
  legislation and approval of, **32**/9
  organic-solvent preservatives, **32**/5
  standards for, **32**/8
  tar-oil preservatives, **32**/5
  water-borne preservatives, **32**/5
Wood stairs, **50**/29
Woodworm attack, **32**/3
Workability of concrete, **14**/10
  effect of plasticizers, **15**/12, **15**/17
Woven glass cloth materials, **45**/8
  in GRP, **45**/7
Woven (glass) rovings, **45**/7
  in GRP, **45**/7
Wrought iron, **4**/1
  anisotropy of properties, **4**/4
  appraisal of structures, **4**/8
  carbon contents of, **3**/3, **4**/3
  compared with cast iron, **4**/3
  compressive strength of, **4**/6
  durability of, **4**/9
  elongation data for, **4**/4
  fatigue properties of, **4**/7
  history of manufacture and use, **4**/9
  impact resistance of, **4**/7
  metallurgy of, **4**/3
  properties of, **4**/4, **4**/6, **4**/7, **4**/8
    effect of cold working, **4**/6
    effects of temperature, **4**/8
  repairs to, **4**/9
  riveting of, **4**/9, **4**/10, **4**/11
  shear strength of, **4**/7
  stress limits for, **4**/8
  tensile strength of, **4**/4, **4**/6
  texture of cross-section, **4**/3

Wrought iron (cont.)
  thermal expansion of, **4**/8
  types of, **4**/3
  variation of strength with size, **4**/6
  welding of, **4**/9

X-ray plasters, **35**/4

Yield surface concept, **1**/7
  example of use, **1**/8, **1**/9
Young's modulus
  elastomers, **37**/4, **37**/17
  glass, **29**/6, **37**/4
  glass-fibre reinforced cement, **20**/9
  polymers, **37**/4, **38**/3, **41**/4, **41**/6
  stone, **49**/11
  see also Elastic modulus

Zinc, **7**/32
  abundance in Earth's crust, **7**/3
  applications of, **7**/32, **7**/36
  characteristics of, **7**/32
  corrosion resistance of, **7**/32
  production of, **7**/33
  properties of, **7**/5
  sources of, **7**/33
  wrought zinc, **7**/35
Zinc coatings, **7**/33, **31**/6
Zinc–copper–titanium alloys, **7**/35
  properties, **7**/35
Zinc die castings, **7**/34
Zinc silicate primers, **31**/6
Zinc-coated steel, **5**/32, **5**/33
Zinc-rich primers, **31**/6